California Civil Procedure

California Civil Procedure

FOURTH EDITION

Walter W. Heiser
PROFESSOR OF LAW
UNIVERSITY OF SAN DIEGO SCHOOL OF LAW

CAROLINA ACADEMIC PRESS
Durham, North Carolina

ISBN 978-1-6328-4980-9
e-ISBN 978-1-63284-982-3
LCCN 2016956310

Carolina Academic Press, LLC
700 Kent Street
Durham, North Carolina 27701
Telephone (919) 489-7486
Fax (919) 493-5668
www.cap-press.com

Printed in the United States of America

Contents

Preface to Fourth Edition

There have been numerous changes in the law of civil procedure since the publication of the THIRD EDITION of the CALIFORNIA CIVIL PROCEDURE casebook in 2012. The FOURTH EDITION reflects some of the more significant developments in constitutional amendments, procedural statutes, rules of court, and case law since 2012; and preserves materials from the previous editions that remain current and relevant.

The California statutes and Rules of Court discussed and quoted in the FOURTH EDITION are current as of July 1, 2016. The judicial decisions reproduced and analyzed are based on California Supreme Court opinions published through 62 Cal. 4th 1163 (2016), and on California Court of Appeal opinions officially published through 246 Cal. App. 4th 253 (2016).

Preface to Third Edition

There have been numerous changes in the law of civil procedure since the publication of the Second Edition of the California Civil Procedure casebook in 2005. The Third Edition reflects some of the more significant developments in constitutional amendments, procedural statutes, rules of court, and case law since 2005; and preserves materials from the First and Second Editions that remain current and relevant.

The California statutes and Rules of Court discussed and quoted in the Third Edition are current as of March 1, 2012. The judicial decisions reproduced and analyzed are based on California Supreme Court opinions published through 53 Cal. 4th 735 (2012), and on California Court of Appeal opinions officially published through 192 Cal. App. 4th 1527 (2011).

Preface to Second Edition

There have been numerous changes in the law of civil procedure since the publication of the First Edition of the California Civil Procedure casebook in 1996. The Second Edition reflects some of the more significant developments in constitutional amendments, procedural statutes, rules of court, and case law, as of October 1, 2004. The Supreme Court of California has been particularly active in deciding civil procedure cases during the past eight years. The Second Edition discusses some of the more significant of these decisions, as well as numerous California Court of Appeal decisions. Likewise, the Judicial Council has been very active in revising the California Rules of Court. By comparison, the California Legislature has been somewhat less active in the area of civil procedure during this period, but what new laws it has enacted are very significant. These important procedural statutes are discussed or quoted in the Second Edition.

The judicial decisions reproduced and analyzed in the Second Edition are based on California Supreme Court opinions published through 34 Cal. 4th 366 (2004), and on California Court of Appeal opinions officially published through 111 Cal. App. 4th 1472 (2003).

Preface to First Edition

The immediate purpose of these materials is to provide a vehicle for upperclass law students to explore the complexities of civil procedure as practiced in the California state courts. The ultimate goal is to increase the competency of future California attorneys with respect to their office and courtroom practice. California Civil Procedure is an intricate series of topics, spanning the spectrum from broad theories to detailed precepts. This book attempts to achieve a balance between general principles and specific rules, with emphasis on those areas of most importance to practitioners.

The organization and methodology employed are mostly traditional. Authorities were selected for reproduction based on their coverage of essential concepts whose application to future cases will require resolution of significant analytical and policy conflicts. Extensive textual analysis places each reproduced case or statute into broader context, as do frequent questions, notes, and observations. The purpose here is two-fold: to enhance coverage of the area under consideration and, more importantly, to stimulate both individual student reflection and classroom discussion.

Although students should find these materials quite helpful in understanding topics to which they were previously exposed, this book is not intended primarily as a review of first year civil procedure. The emphasis instead is often on those areas where California procedure departs from the general or federal rules. These materials do, however, make frequent comparisons to analogous Federal Rules of Civil Procedure and federal practice.

The arrangement of the topics largely reflects the sequence of considerations likely encountered in taking a typical civil case from the stages of initial client contact to commencement of the action in court, through pretrial preparation, trial proceedings, post-trial motions, and appellate review. This sequence need not be followed. Each chapter was developed as an independent topic, and can be assigned in whatever sequence seems appropriate to the instructor.

This book contains far more material than can comfortably be covered in a typical three-credit, one-semester course. The intent is to permit each teacher to structure his or her course by choosing among the full panoply of available topics. Some schools have limited their required civil procedure course to one semester. Those schools may wish to offer more extensive upperclass California Civil Procedure courses, perhaps one focusing on pretrial procedures and another on trial and appellate procedures. This book contains sufficient material for such comprehensive courses.

Chapters 1 and 2 are short chapters designed as the initial assignment for an introductory class. After that, several sequencing options are available for a one semester course. Instructors who wish to emphasize those areas of California Civil Procedure that are unique should assign Chapters 4 (Statutes of Limitations), 5 (Conflict of Laws), 8 (Preclusive Effects of Prior Judgments), sections of Chapter 9 discussing "Doe" defendant practice, sections of Chapter 10 dealing with new party cross-complaints and equitable indemnity, sections of Chapter 12 covering default judgments and arbitration, the new trial portions of Chapter 13, and Chapters 14 and 15. Instructors who desire to add some practical professional responsibility issues may add Chapter 3 to the beginning of this list.

Instructors who wish to emphasize more basic aspects of California civil procedure may find the following sequence to their liking: Chapters 1 and 2, followed by assignments from Chapters 4 (Statutes of Limitations), 6 (The Proper Court), 8 (Preclusive Effects of Prior Judgments), 9 (Pleadings), 10 (Joinder), 11 (Discovery), and 13 (Trials). Instructors with the luxury of more than three credits or of two semesters may pick and choose among all these chapters as appropriate.

Acknowledgments

I am grateful to Professors Rex R. Perschbacher and Margaret Z. Johns, University of California at Davis School of Law, for their contributions to the first edition, many of which remain in the fourth edition. Special thanks to Katie Chifcian, Brandon Kelsey, and Robert Olsen for their research assistance on the third edition; to Mike Misa and Pancy Lin for their research assistance on the second edition; and to Elizabeth Angres, Lisa D'Errico, Tracy Frost, Beth Knisely, Amy Jackson, Byron Mousmoules, Jerry Polansy, Robin Wahl and Phebe Wang, for their research contributions to the first edition. Thanks also to Emma Catherine, Addison May, and Blake C. C. Boyer, and to Donald L. Dressler IV, for their suggestions and encouragement with respect to the fourth edition. Finally, I would like to again express my gratitude to my wife, Susan, for her continued support and patience throughout these projects.

June, 2016

California Civil Procedure

Chapter 1

Introduction to California Civil Procedure

This book is designed for those upperclass law students who intend to practice law in California and therefore wish to learn more about California civil procedure. Most upperclass law students possess considerable knowledge of civil procedure generally as a result of a required first-year civil procedure course during which they studied the Federal Rules of Civil Procedure. Some may have had exposure to the practical aspects of California civil procedure through clinical internships or clerkships. But few students—and few recent graduates for that matter—have an in-depth understanding of the important doctrines, rules, and policies which define civil litigation in California. The goal of this book, or perhaps more accurately of a course using this book, is to provide a systematic and meaningful exposition of civil procedure as practiced in the California courts.

Many students are already aware of some formal differences between civil procedure in the federal and the California courts. The California courts, for example, use different terminology. A federal court "motion to dismiss for failure to state a claim upon which relief can be granted" is called a "general demurrer" in California procedure; the federal joinder devices of "counterclaim," "cross-claim," and "impleader" are all referred to as "cross-complaints" in California; and a federal appellate court's "mandate" is a California appellate court's "remittitur." Anyone who has read a California appellate opinion published in the Official Reports (*i.e.*, California Reports and California Appellate Reports) may also know of another formal difference between federal and California practice. The California courts follow the *California Style Manual* (4th ed. 2000) instead of *The Bluebook* with respect to citation format and may prefer attorneys to do so also.

Another type of formal difference between California and federal practice may be apparent to those students with clinical or clerkship experiences: far more legal forms have been approved for use in civil litigation in the California courts. Some of these legal forms are mandatory and must be used by civil practitioners wherever applicable. Others, particularly the numerous complaint and pleading forms approved by the Judicial Council, are optional but are welcomed by the courts. And speaking of pleadings, many students are undoubtedly aware that California requires "fact" or "code" pleading and not federal "notice" pleading, although most may be hard-pressed to explain the meaning of this difference in pleading form.

The main focus of this book is not, however, on the formal differences between California and federal practice. The emphasis instead is on those aspects of California civil procedure that are not only different in form but may also make a significant difference in the preparation, presentation, and ultimate outcome of a civil case in the California as opposed to the federal system.

The methodology employed in this book includes reproduction of important California court opinions and procedural statutes, as well as extensive notes and questions, all designed to enlighten as to California procedural doctrine and practice. This book devotes particular attention to those areas of California civil procedure that are unique, both when compared to federal and to other states' procedural laws. A concomitant goal is to provide students with a brief summary of the federal or general position on each major topic as a basis of comparison and as a review of first-year civil procedure.

This book is organized into 15 chapters. Chapters 1 and 2 are introductory. Chapters 3 through 5 address some of the issues an attorney must consider before commencing civil litigation in a California court. Chapter 3 surveys important professional responsibility concerns which an attorney may need to resolve prior to undertaking client representation. Chapter 4 covers statutes of limitations and related doctrines which may time-bar an otherwise viable cause of action. Because of the importance of statutes of limitations to practitioners, and the unique treatments provided by California law, issues of accrual and tolling are explored in detail. Chapter 5 discusses the California conflict or choice-of-law doctrine, a topic not usually covered in civil procedure courses. The highly conceptual comparative impairment conflicts doctrine developed by the California courts for use in tort cases is difficult and unique, and accordingly receives considerable attention.

The next two contain materials relevant to the commencement of a civil action in the California court system. Chapter 6 surveys such issues as subject matter jurisdiction, personal jurisdiction, venue, *forum non conveniens*, forum selection agreements, and service of process. The treatment of these matters is relatively brief—a reflection of their somewhat limited importance in the California court system and of their similarities to the federal doctrines. Chapter 7 discusses provisional remedies with particular attention to California prejudgment attachment statutes.

Chapters 8 through 10 discuss the various procedural laws which determine the size of civil litigation in the California courts. Chapter 8 analyzes the preclusive effects of prior judgments. This chapter devotes considerable attention to the California primary rights doctrine which defines the res judicata (claim preclusion) effect of a prior judgment, as well as to the doctrines of collateral estoppel (issue preclusion), privity, and law of the case. Chapter 9 discusses the rules applicable to complaints, amended complaints, cross-complaints, demurrers, and motions. More importantly, this chapter includes extensive analysis of California's unique fictitious ("Doe") defendant practice which, through appropriate pleading, greatly extends most statutes of limitations. Chapter 10 provides coverage of California's permissive and compulsory joinder statutes, intervention, and other joinder devices, with emphasis on class action doctrine. Also included is an in-depth analysis of three related topics: third-party cross-complaints, comparative equitable indemnity among joint tortfeasors, and California's good faith settlement procedures.

The preparation of a civil case for trial is covered in Chapters 11 and 12. Chapter 11 surveys the California discovery statutes, with emphasis on privileges and enforcement. Chapter 12 discusses the various methods by which a case may be resolved before trial and includes extensive materials on summary judgments, involuntary dismissals for failure to prosecute, and arbitration.

The final three chapters address issues applicable to trials, judgments, and appeals in the California courts. Chapter 13 analyzes the right to jury trial as guaranteed in civil cases by the California Constitution, the conduct and supervision of jury trials, and such post-trial procedures as a motion for new trial and for judgment notwithstanding the verdict. Chapter 14 covers the procedure for obtaining and attacking judgments, and contains a useful overview of the important issues with respect to enforcement of judgments. Finally, Chapter 15 discusses appealable orders and judgments, the appellate process, and the publication of appellate opinions; and contains extensive materials on extraordinary appellate writs and administrative mandamus.

Upon completion of a course using this book, a law student or new lawyer should have a good understanding of the laws, policies, and practices that make up California civil procedure. The primary goal is to make the new attorney more competent to conduct civil litigation in the California courts. A secondary goal is to reveal the procedural advantages and disadvantages of litigating in California state courts as opposed to federal courts so that the choice between filing an action in one system or the other will be an informed one. The achievement of these goals should directly benefit not only the law student who will soon be a California attorney and that attorney's clients, but hopefully also the courts, the bar, and all others affected by California civil litigation.

Chapter 2

Sources of Procedural Law

§ 2.01 A Brief History of California Procedure

[A] Justice in Frontier California

The Spanish-Mexican settlement of California began in 1769 when an expedition set out to establish the first mission at San Diego. By 1821 when Mexico declared its independence from Spain, there were 21 missions in California. In 1781, the "Regulations for Governing the province of the Californias" were approved by the King of Spain. These regulations provided detailed rules for the organization and administration of the pueblos, the civilian settlements which began to spring up in California.

The regulations provided for each village to have a local judge, an "alcalde." In addition to serving as a judge, the alcalde functioned as the head official in the town. He mediated civil disputes between individuals through a process known as "conciliation." Each party was heard by the alcalde; then the alcalde would render judgment within eight days. The alcalde's judgment was usually final: the only form of appeal was a trip to Monterey to see the governor, and this rarely occurred. Even though the Spanish Civil Law technically governed his decisions, the alcalde had no legal training at all, so he simply used common sense and the advice of "two good men" from the town. Yet, the alcalde system was the beginning of the judiciary in California.

The Mexican period in California lasted from the time of Mexican independence in 1821 until the Mexican-American war in 1846. During this time, huge land grants were made to individuals by the governors of California, marking the rise of the ranch system. These grants were generally upheld, as was required under the treaty of Guadalupe Hildago which ended the war. In 1837, the Mexican legislature had passed an act to set up a complex judicial system in California, but this system was never actually implemented before the war. *See generally* Richard R. Powell, *Compromises of Conflicting Claims: A Century of California Law, 1760 to 1860*, 19–59 (1977).

[B] The Impact of the Fields on California Procedure

When the first California Constitution became effective on December 20, 1849, the alcalde system was still in effect. The new Constitution provided for a complex judiciary with a three-justice Supreme Court, District and County courts, and justices of the peace. However, when Stephen J. Field arrived in San Francisco on December 28, 1849, the judicial provisions of the Constitution had not been implemented. Thus in January of 1850, Field was elected First Alcade of the new town of Marysville. In

Field's words, "[I]n the anomalous condition of affairs under the American occupation, [alcaldes] exercised almost unlimited powers." He tried many cases, both civil and criminal. In May, the new District Judge Turner arrived, ending Field's tenure as alcalde. Unfortunately, the two did not get along well at all. When Field, appearing as a lawyer in Turner's court, asked permission to explain a statute, he was fined five hundred dollars and imprisoned in his own office. Turner even attempted to have Field disbarred, but the state Supreme Court reinstated him. In the ensuing public controversy, Turner threatened Field's life, and Field challenged a Turner supporter to a duel. When Field was elected to the Legislature in 1851, his first act as a member of the Judiciary Committee was to draft a new Judiciary Act which banished Turner to a new district far up in Northern California.

However, Stephen Field's greatest contribution during his term as a legislator was the Civil Practice Act of 1851. This was Stephen Field's version of the "Field Code of Civil Procedure," created in New York by his older brother David Dudley Field. California's Civil Practice Act incorporated all of the important changes in civil procedure brought about by the Field Code, including abolishing the procedural distinction between law and equity, abolishing the common law forms of pleading, and requiring pleading of "ultimate facts" instead of issue pleading. Additionally, the California Civil Practice Act included new provisions regarding exemptions for debtors in bankruptcy, and a provision allowing local usages regarding mines to govern disputes when no other law was in effect. Stephen Field also adapted New York's Code of Criminal Procedure for California. According to Stephen Field, he modified over 300 sections in the two Codes, and added over 100 new sections. The Common Law and the new procedure were accepted very quickly in a state which, at least theoretically, was governed by the Civil Law only years before. According to Powell, "Within three years after the adoption of the California Constitution, a lawyer who had practiced in an eastern state would have encountered no serious difficulties in working under the California procedures." *See* Powell, *supra* at 138–142; Stephen J. Field, *California Alcalde*, 27–57, 63–64 (1950); *see generally* Alison Reppy, *The Field Codification Concept*, in *David Dudley Field Centenary Essays*, 17 (1949).

[C] Subsequent History

In 1872, California attempted to codify its law, enacting four codes whose purpose was to "supply the defects of and give completeness to the existing legislation of the State." Cal. Stats. 1869–70, c. 516 sec. 2. The four codes were Political, Civil, Civil Procedure, and Penal. The Code of Civil Procedure retained most of the substance of Field's Civil Practice Act. From the start there was dissatisfaction about the codes, and a committee was appointed in 1873 to examine them. Stephen Field (who was then a justice of the United States Supreme Court) served on this committee, which found that the codes were "perfect in their analysis, admirable in their order and arrangement, and furnishing a complete code of laws." The enactment of the codes even brought congratulations from David Dudley Field, who was having little success getting New York to codify its own laws. In 1907 the Code of Civil Procedure was amended to eliminate overlapping and conflicting code sections. In 1929, a commission was created to produce a logical, subject-based system of codes, but this did not actually happen until 1953. The 1953 Code of Civil Procedure was substantially carried forward from the previous Code. *See* Ralph N. Kleps, *The Revision and Codification of California Statutes 1849–1953*, 42 Cal. L. Rev. 766 (1954).

In modern times, amendments to the Code of Civil Procedure have been substantially influenced by the Federal Rules of Civil Procedure. An example of this is the "transaction or occurrence" test for joinder from Federal Rules 13(a) (compulsory counterclaim) and 20(a) (permissive joinder of parties), incorporated into sections 378 (joinder of plaintiffs), 379 (joinder of defendants), and 426.10 & 426.30 (compulsory cross-complaint) of the California Code of Civil Procedure. In addition, Federal Rule 11 (representations to court upon signing pleading), Rule 19 (compulsory joinder), Rule 24(a) (intervention of right), Rule 42 (consolidation; separate trials), Rule 45 (subpoenas), and the federal discovery rules have been substantially incorporated into the California Code of Civil Procedure. *See, e.g.*, §§ 128.7 (frivolous actions), 387(b) (intervention), 389 (compulsory joinder). Despite the strong influence of the Federal Rules, California civil procedure can be quite different from federal civil procedure in many important respects. *See* Chapter 1, Introduction to California Civil Procedure, *supra*.

§ 2.02 Sources of California Procedural Laws

[A] "Written Law"

According to Section 1895 of the California Code of Civil Procedure (CCP), all laws in California are either "written" or "unwritten." The written law is contained in the California Constitution and statutes, and in the United States Constitution and statutes. CCP § 1897. Unwritten law is law "not promulgated and recorded ... but which is, nevertheless, observed and administered in the courts.... It has no certain repository, but is collected from the reports of the decisions of the courts, and the treatises of learned men." CCP § 1899.

[1] The United States Constitution and Laws

Although the origins of specific California procedural laws lie elsewhere, the United States Constitution is in one sense the ultimate source. Both as a conceptual proposition and an actual check when challenged, all state procedural laws must be consistent with the requirements of the Fourteenth Amendment. The federal Due Process Clause provides the ultimate "fairness" standard by which state procedural statutes, rules, and court actions are measured. A California procedural law which violates this federal standard is invalid and unenforceable. *See, e.g., Kulko v. Superior Court*, 436 U.S. 84, 98 S. Ct. 1690, 56 L. Ed. 2d 132 (1978) (holding California state court's exercise of personal jurisdiction over nonresident parent in child support action violated federal Due Process Clause); *Randone v. Appellate Department*, 5 Cal. 3d 536, 96 Cal. Rptr.

709, 488 P.2d 13 (1971), *cert. denied*, 407 U.S. 924 (holding then-existing California attachment statute, which authorized prejudgment attachment without notice and an opportunity for a hearing, violated Due Process Clause); *Moyal v. Lanphear*, 208 Cal. App. 3d 491, 256 Cal. Rptr. 296 (1989) (holding dismissal of plaintiff's complaint by trial court as sanction for failure to comply with local fast track deadlines violated plaintiff's due process rights).

In at least one instance the California Legislature has expressly incorporated by reference the United States Constitution into the applicable state standard. Code of Civil Procedure § 410.10, which defines the personal jurisdiction of the state courts, provides: "A court of this state may exercise jurisdiction on any basis not inconsistent with the Constitution of this state or of the United States."

Article VI of the United States Constitution makes federal statutes, as well as the federal constitution, the "supreme Law of the Land." Consequently, state courts are generally obligated to enforce substantive claims based on federal statutes. *Testa v. Katt*, 330 U.S. 386, 67 S. Ct. 810, 91 L. Ed. 967 (1947). Most federal procedural statutes, such as the jurisdiction and venue provisions in Title 28 of the United States Code, apply only to claims litigated in the federal courts. However, Congress may intend that certain federal procedural statutes apply in state court actions as well. In such cases, the federal statute will preempt contrary state law in the state court. *See, e.g., Felder v. Casey*, 487 U.S. 131, 108 S. Ct. 2302, 101 L. Ed. 2d 123 (1988) (Wisconsin Supreme Court's reliance on the state's notice-of-claim statute to bar a suit brought under federal civil rights statute held invalid); *Dice v. Akron, Canton & Youngstown Railroad Co.*, 342 U.S. 359, 72 S. Ct. 312, 96 L. Ed. 398 (1952) (Federal Employers' Liability Act required state court to follow federal practice, not contrary state practice, with respect to jury determination of fraud issues); 28 U.S.C. § 1367(d) (tolling state statute of limitations for at least 30 days as to supplemental jurisdiction claims dismissed by federal district court); the Servicemembers Civil Relief Act, 50 U.S.C. App. § 501 *et seq.* (providing comprehensive procedural protections of the rights of those in the military service in civil litigation in state and federal courts).

[2] The California Constitution

In addition to a general Due Process provision which mirrors that of the United States Constitution, the California Constitution contains a number of more specific sections which help define our civil litigation process. For example, Section 16 of Article I (as amended in 1998) provides with respect to civil jury trials:

> Trial by jury is an inviolate right and shall be secured to all, but in a civil cause three-fourths of the jury may render a verdict. * * * In a civil cause a jury may be waived by the consent of the parties expressed as prescribed by statute.

> In civil causes the jury shall consist of 12 persons or a lesser number agreed on by the parties in open court. In civil causes other than causes within the appellate jurisdiction of the court of appeal, the Legislature may provide that the jury shall consist of eight persons or a lesser number agreed on by the parties in open court.

The judicial power of the state courts, the structure of the court system, basic trial and appellate court jurisdiction, and the election and the removal of judges are all set forth in Article VI. Section 6 of Article VI establishes the Judicial Council of California; defines its membership to consist of the Chief Justice of the Supreme Court plus various other specified judges and officials; and empowers it to adopt state-wide rules for court administration, practice and procedure. Section 13 of Article VI imposes prejudicial error ("miscarriage of justice") as a prerequisite to overturning an erroneous judgment, and section 14 requires appellate decisions in writing and with reasons stated.

[3] The California Code of Civil Procedure

The Code of Civil Procedure (CCP), consisting of hundreds of statutes, is the primary source of procedural law for California state courts. This Code covers such topics as subject matter jurisdiction, statutes of limitations, joinder of parties and claims, service of process, pleadings and motions, attachment, trial and pretrial motions, extraordinary writs, appeals, judgments, and enforcement of judgments.

Unlike the relatively succinct Federal Rules of Civil Procedure which apply in federal trial courts, the California Code is lengthy, comprehensive, and quite detailed. For example, Federal Rule 56 delineates the standards and procedures for summary judgment motions on one page, but CCP § 437c takes 2 1/2 pages of similar size type; Federal Rule 30 specifies the procedures for oral depositions in 2 1/4 pages, CCP § 2025.010-.620 requires seven (7) pages to cover the same topic. The code approach employed by California usually means that most specific procedural questions can be answered by simply locating the relevant CCP sections.

Other statutory codes also contain important procedural provisions, often limited to particular types of cases. *See, e.g.,* Government Code § 900 *et seq.* (procedures for presentation of claims against public entities and officials under the California Tort Claims Act); Family Code §§ 200-291 (procedures relating to dissolution of marriage and related proceedings); Civil Code §§ 1780-1784 (remedies and procedures for actions under the Consumers Legal Remedies Act); Evidence Code §§ 450-460 (judicial notice); Business & Professions Code §§ 6146-6149 (limitations on contingent fee agreements).

[4] California Rules of Court

Pursuant to the authority contained in the California Constitution and in various code sections, the Judicial Council of California has adopted numerous state-wide rules of practice and procedure. These Rules of Court supplement statutory and constitutional provisions, and have the force of law.

The scope of the numerous and detailed California Rules of Court is difficult to characterize. Some rules govern procedures in the appellate courts, Rules 8.100-8.936, Cal. Rules of Ct.; others fine-tune civil pretrial and trial procedures in the trial courts, Rules 2.100-3.2000. Some specifically relate to family law proceedings, some to coordination of civil actions, and others to court-annexed arbitration and mediation. Rules 5.15-5.475, 3.500-3.550, 3.800-3.875, Cal. Rules of Ct. Some cover seemingly mundane topics, such as the form and size requirements of papers presented for filing specified in Rules 2.100-2.119; others provide essential information on important matters not covered elsewhere, such as the time deadlines for filing a notice of appeal in Rule 8.104. The criteria for publication of appellate opinions, for example, are found in Rules 8.1105-8.1125 and no place else:

California Rules of Court (2016)

Rule 8.1105. Publication of Appellate Opinions

(a) **Supreme Court.** All opinions of the Supreme Court are published in the Official Reports.

(b) **Courts of Appeal and appellate divisions.** Except as provided in (e), an opinion of a Court of Appeal or a superior court appellate division is published in the Official Reports if a majority of the rendering court certifies the opinion for publication before the decision is final in that court.

(c) **Standards for certification.** An opinion of a Court of Appeal or a superior court appellate division—whether it affirms or reverses a trial court order or judgment—should be certified for publication in the Official Reports if the opinion:

(1) Establishes a new rule of law;

(2) Applies an existing rule of law to a set of facts significantly different from those stated in published opinions;

(3) Modifies, explains, or criticizes with reasons given, an existing rule of law;

(4) Advances a new interpretation, clarification, criticism, or construction of a provision of a constitution, statute, ordinance, or court rule;

(5) Addresses or creates an apparent conflict in the law;

(6) Involves a legal issue of continuing public interest;

(7) Makes a significant contribution to legal literature by reviewing either the development of a common law rule or the legislative or judicial history of a provision of a constitution, statute, or other written law;

(8) Invokes a previously overlooked rule of law, or reaffirms a principle of law not applied in a recently reported decision; or

(9) Is accompanied by a separate opinion concurring or dissenting on a legal issue, and publication of the majority and separate opinions would make a significant contribution to the development of the law.

(d) **Factors not to be considered.** Factors such as the workload of the court, or the potential embarrassment of a litigant, lawyer, judge, or other person should not affect the determination of whether to publish an opinion.

(e) **Changes in publication status.**

(1) Unless otherwise ordered under (2):

(A) An opinion is no longer considered published if the rendering court grants rehearing.

(B) Grant of review by the Supreme Court of a decision by the Court of Appeal does not affect the appellate court's certification of the opinion for full or partial publication under rule 8.1105(b) or rule 8.1110, but any such Court of Appeal opinion, whether officially published in hard copy or electronically, must be accompanied by a prominent notation advising that review by the Supreme Court has been granted.

(2) The Supreme Court may order that an opinion certified for publication is not to be published or that an opinion not certified is to be published. The Supreme Court may also order depublication of part of an opinion at any time after granting review.

(f) Editing.

(1) Computer versions of all opinions of the Supreme Court and Courts of Appeal must be provided to the Reporter of Decisions on the day of filing. Opinions of superior court appellate divisions certified for publication must be provided as prescribed in rule 8.887.

(2) The Reporter of Decisions must edit opinions for publication as directed by the Supreme Court. The Reporter of Decisions must submit edited opinions to the courts for examination, correction, and approval before finalization for the Official Reports.

Rule 8.1115. Citation of Opinions

(a) **Unpublished opinion.** Except as provided in (b), an opinion of a California Court of Appeal or superior court appellate division that is not certified for publication or ordered published must not be cited or relied on by a court or a party in any other action.

(b) **Exceptions.** An unpublished opinion may be cited or relied on:

(1) When the opinion is relevant under the doctrines of law of the case, res judicata, or collateral estoppel; or

(2) When the opinion is relevant to a criminal or disciplinary action because it states reasons for a decision affecting the same defendant or respondent in another such action.

(c) **Citation procedure.** On request of the court or a party, a copy of an opinion citable under (b) must be promptly furnished to the court or the requesting party.

(d) **When a published opinion may be cited.** A published California opinion may be cited or relied on as soon as it is certified for publication or ordered published.

(e) **When review of published opinion has been granted.**

(1) *While review is pending.* Pending review and filing of the Supreme Court's opinion, unless otherwise ordered by the Supreme Court under (3), a published opinion of a Court of Appeal in the matter has no binding or prece-

dential effect, and may be cited for potentially persuasive value only. Any citation to the Court of Appeal opinion must also note the grant of review and any subsequent action by the Supreme Court.

(2) *After decision on review.* After decision on review by the Supreme Court, unless otherwise ordered by the Supreme Court under (3), a published opinion of a Court of Appeal in the matter, and any published opinion of a Court of Appeal in a mater in which the Supreme Court has ordered review and deferred action pending the decision, is citable and has binding or precedential effect, except to the extent it is inconsistent with the decision of the Supreme Court or is disapproved by that court.

(3) *Supreme Court order.* At any time after granting review or after decision on review, the Supreme Court may order that all or part of an opinion covered by (1) or (2) is not citable or has a binding or precedential effect different from that specified in (1) or (2).

Rule 8.1120. Requesting Publication of Unpublished Opinions

(a) **Request.**

(1) Any person may request that an unpublished opinion be ordered published.

(2) The request must be made by a letter to the court that rendered the opinion, concisely stating the person's interest and the reason why the opinion meets a standard for publication.

(3) The request must be delivered to the rendering court within 20 days after the opinion is filed.

(4) The request must be served on all parties.

(b) **Action by rendering court.**

(1) If the rendering court does not or cannot grant the request before the decision is final in that court, it must forward the request to the Supreme Court with a copy of its opinion, its recommendation for disposition, and a brief statement of its reasons. The rendering court must forward these materials within 15 days after the decision is final in that court.

(2) The rendering court must also send a copy of its recommendation and reasons to all parties and any person who requested publication.

(c) **Action by Supreme Court.** The Supreme Court may order the opinion published or deny the request. The court must send notice of its action to the rendering court, all parties, and any person who requested publication.

(d) **Effect of Supreme Court order to publish.** A Supreme Court order to publish is not an expression of the court's opinion of the correctness of the result of the decision or of any law stated in the opinion.

Rule 8.1125. Requesting Depublication of Published Opinions

(a) **Request.**

(1) Any person may request the Supreme Court to order that an opinion certified for publication not be published.

(2) The request must not be made as part of a petition for review, but by a separate letter to the Supreme Court not exceeding 10 pages.

(3) The request must concisely state the person's interest and the reason why the opinion should not be published.

(4) The request must be delivered to the Supreme Court within 30 days after the decision is final in the Court of Appeal.

(5) The request must be served on the rendering court and all parties.

(b) **Response.**

(1) Within 10 days after the Supreme Court receives a request under (a), the rendering court or any person may submit a response supporting or opposing the request. A response submitted by anyone other than the rendering court must state the person's interest.

(2) A response must not exceed 10 pages and must be served on the rendering court, all parties, and any person who requested depublication.

(c) **Action by Supreme Court.**

(1) The Supreme Court may order the opinion depublished or deny the request. It must send notice of its action to the rendering court, all parties, and any person who requested depublication.

(2) The Supreme Court may order an opinion depublished on its own motion, notifying the rendering court of its action.

(d) **Effect of Supreme Court order to depublish**. A Supreme Court order to depublish is not an expression of the court's opinion of the correctness of the result of the decision or of any law stated in the opinion.

The Appendix to the California Rules of Court also contains some valuable procedural information. For example, Section 3.25 of the Standards of Judicial Administration provides fairly detailed suggestions for the examination of prospective jurors in civil trials; and Section 2.2 contains case-disposition goals for implementation of the Trial Court Delay Reduction Act by the trial courts.

[5] *Local Rules of Court*

You might think a detailed Code of Civil Procedure plus hundreds of state-wide Rules of Court would provide sufficient bases for the regulation of civil procedure. Unfortunately, the California courts do not. Pursuant to the authority provided by CCP § 575.1 and Government Code § 68070(a), each county has promulgated numerous local rules applicable to civil actions in its superior courts. Typically they govern such areas of local variation as the filing requirements for papers, the procedures for scheduling hearings, telephonic rulings, and special rules for specific departments. With the advent of the Trial Court Delay Reduction Act, local rules have taken on increased importance. The following case reproduced below illustrates some of the typical concerns with local rules and their enforcement.

Tliche v. Van Quathem

Court of Appeal of California, Second Appellate District
66 Cal. App. 4th 1054, 78 Cal. Rptr. 2d 458 (1998)

ALDRICH, JUSTICE.

This appeal raises the issue of the trial court's authority and obligations regarding dismissal of a complaint for violation of local fast track rules. Plaintiff and appellant Samy Tliche doing business as Pirata Restaurant (Tliche) appeals from the order of dismissal of his complaint against defendants and respondent Carl Van Quathem, VQA Property Management, and Alca Properties (collectively Van Quathem).

Tliche contends the trial court erred in dismissing his complaint for violation of a local delay reduction rule requiring service of the summons and complaint on defendant within 60 days of filing the complaint and in denying his motion to vacate the order of dismissal. * * *

FACTUAL AND PROCEDURAL BACKGROUND

On December 21, 1995, Tliche filed a complaint against defendants for various causes of action arising from Tliche's lease of certain premises from defendants for restaurant use. Nineteen or more unsuccessful attempts were made to serve defendants through early February 1996.

On August 22, 1996, the trial court issued an order to show cause for failure to prosecute the case, citing Superior Court of Los Angeles Rules, rule 7 et seq.,[1] and Code of Civil Procedure sections 583.150, 583.360 and 583.420 and Government Code section 68608, subdivision (b). Thereafter, Tliche's counsel initiated renewed efforts to serve defendants and substituted service was eventually effected on about October 5, 1996.

---

1. Local rule 7.7 states: "(c) The failure to meet the deadline set forth in Subdivision (a) may result in the issuance of an Order to Show Cause why sanctions should not be imposed, including dismissal for failure to prosecute (Code of Civil Procedure Section 583.150 and Government Code Section 68608(b)) or, alternatively, why other action should not be taken. At the hearing on such OSC the Court may (1) impose such sanctions as authorized by law and (2) make further appropriate orders regarding the preparation of the case for trial. Failure to attend the hearing on such OSC may result in additional sanctions, including dismissal of the case (see Rule 7.13)."

Local rule 7.13 states: "The Court may impose appropriate sanctions for the failure or refusal (1) to comply with the Rules, (2) to comply with any order made hereunder or (3) to meet the time standards and/or deadlines established herein. Counsel are directed to Code of Civil Procedure sections 128, 128.5, 177.5, 575.2, 583.150, 583.430, 2016 through 2036, Government Code Section 68609(d), and Rule 227 of the California Rules of Court. Such sanctions may be imposed on a party and/or, if appropriate, on counsel for such party. While the court may impose sanctions for specified conduct, the court should do so sparingly and only when clearly warranted."

In the interim, at the September 23, 1996 hearing on the order to show cause, Tliche's counsel did not appear by 9:30 a.m., and the trial court ordered the case dismissed in its entirety. A copy of the minute order stating the case was dismissed in its entirety was sent to Tliche's counsel on that same date. The order did not specify any local rule or code section as authority for the dismissal.

On February 18, 1997, Tliche's counsel apparently believing his nonappearance was the reason for the dismissal filed a motion for an order vacating the dismissal and reinstating the complaint pursuant to Code of Civil Procedure section 473.[4] In support of the motion, Tliche's counsel submitted his declaration, corroborated by the declaration of his secretary, regarding the circumstances of his "mistake, inadvertence, surprise [and] neglect" which resulted in his nonappearance at the hearing on the order to show cause and the dismissal of the complaint. Defendants opposed the motion. In his reply to the opposition, Tliche's counsel argued defendants had avoided service for a number of months and submitted documentation of his efforts to serve defendants.

At the March 5, 1997 hearing, the trial court denied Tliche's motion to vacate the dismissal without prejudice, stating, "Although the counsel for plaintiff admits fault in his failure to appear at the hearing at which his clients' [sic.] case was dismissed, such failure to appear was not the cause of the dismissal. The case was dismissed because by the date of the hearing, 9/23/96, the case had been pending for more than 9 months and the defendant [sic.] had not been served. Local Rule 7.7 requires that the complaint be served within 60 days after it is filed. The moving papers also do not state grounds for discretionary relief for EXCUSABLE neglect because no attempt to serve the defendant after 2/11/96 is shown and no explanation is given for the unreasonable delay of almost 5 months between the date the case was dismissed and the date that the motion for relief under Code of Civil Procedure Section 473 was filed."

On March 28, 1997, Tliche filed a new motion for an order vacating the dismissal, this time supported by his declaration identical in substance to that supporting his first motion. At the April 29, 1997 hearing, the trial court took the matter off calendar on the grounds the motion had not been filed within six months of the date the case was dismissed and therefore the court lacked jurisdiction to rule on the motion. On May 5, 1997, Tliche filed a timely notice of appeal.

What are the limitations on the trial court's power to prescribe the sanction of dismissal of an action for noncompliance with local delay reduction rules? Is the sanction of dismissal for failure to serve subject to the time limits set forth in Code of

---

4. Section 473, subdivision (b) in pertinent part, states: "Notwithstanding any other requirements of this section, the court shall, whenever an application for relief is made no more than six months after entry of judgment, is in proper form, and is accompanied by an attorney's sworn affidavit attesting to his or her mistake, inadvertence, surprise, or neglect, vacate any (1) resulting default entered by the clerk against his or her client, and which will result in entry of a default judgment, or (2) resulting default judgment or dismissal entered against his or her client, unless the court finds that the default or dismissal was not in fact caused by the attorney's mistake, inadvertence, surprise, or neglect."

Civil Procedure sections 583.410 and 583.420, subdivision (a)(1), two years after the action is commenced?

DISCUSSION

1. *The Trial Court Delay Reduction Act.*

Article 5 of the Government Code, commencing with section 68600, was enacted in 1986 as a pilot project. Known as The Trial Court Delay Reduction Act (the Act), it drastically altered the management of civil cases in California. In 1990 the original act was repealed and the current, revised act, with statewide application effective July 1, 1992, was adopted.

The California Judicial Council (the Council) as the policy and rulemaking body for the courts was directed by the Legislature to promulgate "standards of timely disposition" of civil and criminal actions. (Gov. Code, § 68603, subd. (a).) In establishing these standards the Council was to be " ... guided by the principles that litigation, from commencement to resolution, should require only the time reasonably necessary for pleadings, discovery, preparation, and court events, and that any additional elapsed time is delay and should be eliminated." (*Ibid.*)

Following this mandate, the Council promulgated case disposition time standards. (Standards of Judicial Administration, § 2.1 et seq.) Under these standards, general civil cases other than a small claims or unlawful detainer case are to be resolved as follows:

"(1) 90 percent disposed of within 12 months after filing;

"(2) 98 percent disposed of within 18 months after filing;

"(3) 100 percent disposed of within 24 months after filing." (Standards of Judicial Administration, § 2.3 (b).)

Under the Act, judges are to assume responsibility " ... to eliminate delay in the progress and ultimate resolution of litigation, to assume and maintain control over the pace of litigation, to actively manage the processing of litigation from commencement to disposition, and to compel attorneys and litigants to prepare and resolve all litigation without delay, from the filing of the first document invoking court jurisdiction to final disposition of the action." (Gov. Code, § 68607.)

2. *Courts' Authority to Enact Local Rules and Impose Sanctions.*

The Legislature granted the courts' express statutory power to adopt local rules "designed to expedite and facilitate the business of the court" (Code Civ. Proc., § 575.1) in 1982. The Council is authorized to promulgate rules governing pretrial conferences in civil cases at issue. (Code Civ. Proc., § 575.)

With the legislative mandate to manage cases, the Legislature granted to the courts authority to impose sanctions for noncompliance with rules adopted to implement the Act. These include the power to dismiss actions or strike pleadings. (Gov. Code, § 68608, subd. (b).) However, in imposing the ultimate sanction of dismissal, judges are required to consider the history of the conduct of the case. Government Code section 68608, subdivision (b) provides: "Judges shall have all the powers to impose sanctions authorized by law, including the power to dismiss actions or strike pleadings, *if it appears that less severe sanctions would not be effective after taking into account the effect of previous sanctions or previous lack of compliance in the case.* Judges are encouraged to impose sanctions to achieve the purpose of this [Act]." (Italics added.)

Code of Civil Procedure section 575.2, subdivision (a) permits a court's local rules to prescribe sanctions, including dismissal of an action, for noncompliance with those rules. However, like Government Code section 68608, subdivision (b), there is an important limitation placed upon a judge's exercise of this power. This limitation is found in subsection (b) of section 575.2 which provides: "It is the intent of the Legislature that if a failure to comply with these rules is the responsibility of counsel and not of the party, any penalty shall be imposed on counsel and shall not adversely affect the party's cause of action or defense thereto."

In *Garcia v. McCutchen* (1997) 16 Cal. 4th 469, 940 P.2d 906, the California Supreme Court concluded that, under governing statutes, a court may not dismiss an action for noncompliance with local court rules implementing the Act, if the noncompliance is the responsibility of counsel, not the litigant.

In harmonizing the Act with this provision of the Code of Civil Procedure, the Supreme Court explained, "Nothing in either the statutory language or the legislative history of the Act reflects a legislative intent to override section 575.2(b)'s limits on a court's sanctioning powers or to give courts expanded dismissal powers with respect to fast track rules. Instead, the words the Legislature chose reflect a contrary intent, i.e., to give courts only those sanctioning powers 'authorized by law.' (Gov. Code, §68608(b).)" (*Id.*, at pp. 481–482.)

Therefore, there are at least two limitations or restrictions on the trial court's power to dismiss an action for noncompliance with local rules: (1) dismissal is inappropriate if the noncompliance was the responsibility of counsel alone, rather than the party (Code Civ. Proc., §575.2, subd. (b); *Garcia v. McCutchen, supra*, 16 Cal. 4th at p. 481); and (2) dismissal is appropriate only if less severe sanctions would be ineffective (Gov. Code, §68608, subd. (b)).

3. *Application of facts to the law.*

In dismissing the action on September 23, 1996, the trial court did not state its reasons. The order signed by the court stated: "ORDER TO SHOW CAUSE RE: FAILURE TO PROSECUTE THE CASE; [¶] No appearance by 9:30 a.m. [¶] Case is dismissed in its entirety. [¶] IT IS SO ORDERED." However, at the March 5, 1997 hearing on Tliche's motion for an order vacating the dismissal, the trial court explained that it dismissed the action because the case had been pending for more than nine months and the defendants had not been served, in violation of Local Rule 7.7, which requires the complaint be served within 60 days of its filing.

The act of service of the complaint when a party is represented by counsel is usually an act peculiarly within the control of counsel, and not the party. We recognize there may be cases where the party, not counsel, is the reason for non-service, for example where the party has directed the attorney not to serve the complaint. The court might, in certain cases, infer client culpability where a previous sanction order or orders have not brought about compliance with the court's local rules.

However, in this case there is no evidence of prior sanctions against either the party or counsel nor is there evidence in the record that the client was in any way responsible for the delay in service of the complaint on the defendants. Under these circumstances, the order of dismissal must be reversed. It was premature and unauthorized as the trial court failed to apply statutorily mandated principles.

4. *The Time Limitations of Code of Civil Procedure section 583.410 et seq.*

Citing *Roman v. Usary Tire & Service Center* (1994) 29 Cal. App. 4th 1422, Tliche contends the time limitations specified in the Code of Civil Procedure proscribe the trial court's authority to dismiss an action for delay in prosecution under delay reduction rules. Accordingly, Tilche argues, the case may not be dismissed unless service is delayed for more than two years.

In *Roman v. Usary Tire & Service Center, supra,* 29 Cal. App. 4th 1422, this division does not address dismissal pursuant to fast track rules. In *Roman,* the trial court dismissed the action one year and eleven months after the complaint was filed, pursuant to Code of Civil Procedure section 583.410, subdivision (a), a provision in Article 4 of Chapter 1.5 of Title 8 of the Code (Code Civ. Proc., §§ 583.410-583.430, "Discretionary Dismissal for Delay"). The court of appeal reversed the order of dismissal, holding the trial court lacked authority to dismiss this case pursuant to Code of Civil Procedure section 583.410, subdivision (a), because that provision is expressly subject to the time limitations specified in section 583.420. Section 583.420 provides, in relevant part: "(a) The court may not dismiss an action *pursuant to this article* for delay in prosecution except after one of the following conditions has occurred: [¶] (1) Service is not made within two years after the action is commenced against the defendant." (Emphasis added.) (*Roman, supra,* 29 Cal. App. 4th at pp. 1430–1431.) The decision in *Roman* has no relevance to the trial court's authority pursuant to fast track rules.

That this is so is further made clear by Code of Civil Procedure section 583.150, which provides that the entire chapter (Chapter 1.5) " … does not limit or affect the authority of a court to dismiss an action or impose other sanctions under a rule adopted by the court pursuant to Section 575.1 or by the Judicial Council pursuant to statute, or otherwise under inherent authority of the court." The fast track rules are such rules.

Therefore, there is no prohibition against a local court, by local rule, providing for dismissal of an action if the summons and complaint have not been served within 60 days provided: (1) the failure to serve is the fault of the client and not the attorney and (2) less severe sanctions have not been effective.

5. *The Motions to Vacate the Order of Dismissal.*

In light of our finding that the initial order of dismissal was invalid, the propriety of the trial court's rulings on Tliche's subsequent motions to vacate the order of dismissal is no longer pertinent. In his first motion pursuant to Code of Civil Procedure section 473, Tliche's counsel mistakenly focused on his failure to appear, not on his failure to serve, and then delayed so that his second motion to vacate the order of dismissal was untimely and beyond the jurisdiction of the court. Tliche, the client, should not lose his action through the trial court's error in ordering dismissal, which error was compounded by Tliche's own counsel's failure to challenge the order effectively.

DISPOSITION

Order of dismissal reversed. The case is remanded to the trial court with directions to vacate the order of dismissal and to reconsider the imposition of sanctions for the violation of the local delay reduction rule regarding the failure to serve the summons and complaint within 60 days.

Tliche's counsel is to bear costs of appeal.

[a] Local Rules "Not Inconsistent with State Law"

Government Code § 68070(a) expressly authorizes the adoption of local court rules "not inconsistent with law." A local court rule has the force of a procedural statute, provided it does not conflict with statutory law or with state-wide court rules. *See, e.g., Marriage of Sharples*, 223 Cal. App. 4th 160, 166 Cal. Rptr. 3d 818 (2014) (Riverside County rule requiring use of Judicial Council form held in conflict with State Rule of Court making use of such form optional); *Marriage of Woolsey*, 220 Cal. App. 4th 88, 163 Cal. Rptr. 3d 551 (2013) (Placer County rule held invalid insofar as it imposes requirements on a marital settlement agreement in addition to those required by Evidence Code § 1123 and § 250, and CCP § 664.6); *Mito v. Temple Recycling Center Corp.*, 187 Cal. App. 4th 276, 113 Cal. Rptr. 3d 445 (2010) (L.A. County Superior Court local rule which authorized clerk to reject a complaint unless accompanied by a Cover Sheet preempted by Cal. Ct. Rule 3.220(c) which required clerk to file complaint despite the absence of the Cover Sheet).

In *Elkins v. Superior Court*, 41 Cal. 4th 1337, 63 Cal. Rptr. 3d 483, 163 P. 3d 160 (2007), the California Supreme Court considered a challenge to a local superior court rule that required parties in dissolution of marriage trials to present their case by means of written declarations. The testimony of witnesses under direct examination was not allowed except in "unusual circumstances," although upon request parties were permitted to cross-examine declarants. The court held that, as applied to contested marital dissolution trials, the local rule is inconsistent with various provisions of the Evidence Code and the Code of Civil Procedure.

Although some informality and flexibility have been accepted in martial dissolution proceeding, the *Elkins* court reasoned that, pursuant to Family Code § 210, such proceedings are governed by the same statutory rules of evidence and procedure that apply in other civil trials. Written testimony in the form of a declaration constitutes hearsay and is inadmissible at trial, subject to specific statutory exceptions, unless the parties stipulate to the admission of declarations or fail to enter a hearsay objection. Although Family Code § 2336(a) requires items of proof in support of a *default* judgment be in the form of an affidavit, there is no statutory exception to the hearsay rule for contested marital dissolution *trials*. Consequently, the *Elkins* court concluded that the local rule is inconsistent with the statewide hearsay rule and therefore beyond the superior court's rule-making authority.

[b] Case Management ("Fast Track") Rules

The Trial Court Delay Reduction Act requires each county to adopt local rules of procedure, including time standards for the completion of all critical stages of the litigation process, to meet the standards for delay reduction imposed by the Act. Gov. Code §§ 68612, 68620. The Act encourages local rule experimentation to achieve its goals, subject only to the minimum statutory time periods specified in Government Code § 68616 and to the case flow management guidelines contained in Rules 3.700-3.771 and 3.1380-3.1385 of the California Rules of Court. The consequence was a proliferation of local rules which defined precisely when and how each stage of the civil litigation process must be accomplished, but with considerable variation from county to county.

Responding to the proliferation of local rules and the attendant local variations in procedure, the Judicial Council adopted new Rules of Court which set forth uniform state-wide requirements concerning motions, demurrers, discovery, case management, and the form and format of papers. Rules 2.100-2.306, 3.700-3.771 & 3.1100-3.1116, Cal. Rules of Court. Rule 3.20(a) states that, by enacting these new rules, the Judicial Council intends to preempt local rules in these fields:

> The Judicial Council has preempted all local rules relating to pleadings, demurrers, ex parte applications, motions, discovery, provisional remedies, and form and format of papers. No trial court, or any division or branch of a trial court, may enact or enforce any local rule concerning these fields. All local rules concerning these fields are null and void unless otherwise permitted or required by statute or a rule in the California Rules of Court.

However, this Judicial Council preemption does not apply to local fast track rules adopted under the Trial Court Delay Reduction Act. Rule 3.20(b)(4), Cal. Rules of Court. *See also Volkswagen of America, Inc. v. Superior Court*, 94 Cal. App. 4th 695, 114 Cal. Rptr. 2d 541 (2001) (General Order No. 55, adopted by the San Francisco Superior Court to help manage its complex asbestos litigation, not preempted by state rules).

Failure to comply with local fast track rules may lead to sanctions, usually monetary but, in appropriate circumstances, case-dispositive penalties. CCP § 575.2(a) authorizes trial courts to impose sanctions for failure to comply with any local rules, but § 575.2(b) cautions that "if the failure to comply with these rules is the responsibility of counsel and not of the party, any penalty may be imposed on counsel and shall not adversely affect the party's cause of action or defense thereto." *See Public Works Board v. Bragg*, 183 Cal. App. 3d 1018, 228 Cal. Rptr. 576 (1986) (concluding that a trial court is required on its own motion to implement CCP § 572(b), if the negligent counsel does not so move). In addition, the Trial Court Delay Reduction Act expressly addresses the imposition of sanctions for violation of local fast track rules. Gov. Code § 68608(b) states:

Judges shall have all the powers to impose sanctions authorized by law, including the power to dismiss actions or strike pleadings, if it appears that less severe sanctions would not be effective after taking into account the effect of previous sanctions or previous lack of compliance in the case.

The Courts of Appeal reached different conclusions in attempting to reconcile these two statutory provisions, disagreeing on whether the more specific authority in Government Code 68608(b) overrides the general authority in CCP § 572. The California Supreme Court subsequently resolved this issue in *Garcia v. McCutchen*, 16 Cal. 4th 469, 66 Cal. Rptr. 2d 319, 940 P.2d 906 (1997), where it held that the limitations on the power to impose case-dispositive sanctions expressed in CCP § 575.2(b) were applicable to violations of all types of local rules, including local "fast track" rules designed to implement the mandates of the Trial Reduction Delay Act. *Tliche v. Van Quathem*, reproduced *supra*, is a post-*Garcia* case.

[c] Local Departmental Rules

County-wide rules are not the only types of local rules. Often a particular branch or district of a court will adopt rules that apply solely to cases in that branch or district. In addition, an individual judge may adopt a policy which applies solely to cases in that judge's courtroom. Typically these rules were not published, but were posted outside the courtroom or announced by the judge. Pursuant to a 1993 amendment to CCP § 575.1(c), however, such individual judge and department rules must be published as part of the general publication requirements for all local rules. *See* Rule 10.613, Cal. Rules of Court (requirements for adopting, filing, distributing, and maintaining local court rules).

[B] "Unwritten" Law

[1] *Judicial Decisions*

[a] Judicial Decisions Make Procedural Law

As this casebook attests, judicial decisions are a prevalent source of procedural law. The courts not only interpret the written law, but possess the inherent power to make procedural law. For example, although CCP § 382 authorizes the class action joinder device, no California statute or court rule provides procedural criteria for its use in civil litigation generally. Nevertheless, the California Supreme Court has directed the trial courts to utilize the specific procedures prescribed by Rule 23 of the Federal Rules of Civil Procedure. *La Sala v. American Savings & Loan Assn.*, 5 Cal. 3d 864, 872, 97 Cal. Rptr. 849, 489 P.2d 1113 (1971); *see Green v. Obledo*, 29 Cal. 3d 126, 145-146, 172 Cal. Rptr. 206, 624 P.2d 256 (1981) ("It is well established that in the absence of relevant state precedents our trial courts are urged to follow the procedures prescribed in Rule 23 of the Federal Rules of Civil Procedure for conducting class actions."); *City of San Jose v. Superior Court*, 12 Cal. 3d 447, 453, 115 Cal. Rptr. 797, 525 P.2d 701 (1974) ("This court has urged trial courts to be procedurally innovative, encouraging them to incorporate procedures from outside sources in determining whether to allow the maintenance of a particular class suit. More specifically, we have directed them to rule 23 of the Federal Rules of Civil Procedure...").

[b] Retroactive Effect

The general rule is that judicial decisions in civil actions are given retroactive effect. This means that a decision of the California Supreme Court overruling a former decision or announcing a new rule of law should normally apply to all actions that already have been filed or litigated but are not yet final. *See, e.g., Newman v. Emerson Radio Corp.*, 48 Cal. 3d 973, 978, 258 Cal. Rptr. 592, 772 P.2d 1059 (1989) (observing that the California courts have consistently applied tort decisions retroactively even when those decisions declared new causes of action); *Peterson v. Superior Court*, 31 Cal. 3d 147, 151-152, 181 Cal. Rptr. 784, 642 P.2d 1305 (1982) (concluding new rule announced by Supreme Court that punitive damages are recoverable from intoxicated driver who causes personal injury should be applied retroactively).

However, the courts have recognized exceptions to the general rule when considerations of fairness and public policy precluded retrospective operation of judicial decisions. *See, e.g., Newman v. Emerson Radio Corp., supra* (collecting cases); *Moradi-Shalal v. Fireman's Fund Ins. Co.*, 46 Cal. 3d 287, 250 Cal. Rptr. 116, 758 P.2d 58 (1988) (ruling reinterpretation of a statute to preclude private third-party causes of action for unfair insurer practices not given retroactive effect; considerations of fairness and public policy required prospective application to permit those who had already embarked on litigation to receive the benefit of the court's express prior ruling on which they had relied).

The question of the retroactivity of a court decision usually arises in the context of the substantive rejection of a form of recovery, but the general rule and exceptions also apply to judicial interpretation of procedural law. *See, e.g., Howard v. Thrifty Drug & Discount Stores*, 10 Cal. 4th 424, 436, n.3, 41 Cal. Rptr. 2d 362, 895 P.2d 469 (1995) (giving decision narrowing court's former decision construing the tolling provisions of the involuntary dismissal statute for failure to prosecute retroactive effect; fairness and public policy exceptions not applicable because parties could not have justifiably relied on the previous court decision); *Isbell v. County of Sonoma*, 21 Cal. 3d 61, 74-75, 145 Cal. Rptr. 368, 577 P.2d 188 (1978) (giving decision declaring California's confession of judgment procedure unconstitutional only limited retroactive application); *Neel v. Magana, Olney, Levy, Cathart & Gelfand*, 6 Cal. 3d 176, 193, 98 Cal. Rptr. 837, 491 P.2d 421 (1971) (giving retroactive effect to holding that cause of action for legal malpractice does not accrue until client discovers, or should discover, relevant facts); *Smith v. Rae-Venter Law Group*, 29 Cal. 4th 345, 127 Cal. Rptr. 2d 516, 537-39, 58 P. 2d 367 (2002) (ruling new interpretation of a fee-shifting statute which authorizes an award of attorney fees and costs against a party "unsuccessful on appeal" from a Labor Commission wage claim decision would be applied prospectively only because the parties relied on prior interpretations of the statute in weighing the potential costs of an unsuccessful appeal).

[c] Stare Decisis

The Court of Appeal (Fourth District, Div. Three) in *Sarti v. Salt Creek, Inc.*, 167 Cal. App. 4th 1187, 85 Cal. Rptr. 3d 506 (2008), provided the following primer on the doctrine of stare decisis as applied in the California courts (*Id.* at 1193):

> All trial courts are bound by all published decisions of the Court of Appeal (*Auto Equity Sales, Inc. v. Superior Court* (1962) 57 Cal.2d 450, 455 [20 Cal. Rptr. 321, 369 P.2d 937]), the only qualifications being that the relevant point in the appellate decision must not have been disapproved by the California Supreme Court and must not be in conflict with another appellate decision. As the Supreme Court said in *Auto Equity Sales* (a case that ought to be covered in the very first weeks of every legal research and writing class in any California law school): "Under the doctrine of stare decisis, all tribunals exercising inferior jurisdiction are required to follow decisions of courts exercising superior jurisdiction. Otherwise, the doctrine of stare decisis makes no sense. The decisions of this court are binding upon and must be followed by all the state courts of California. *Decisions of every division of the District Courts of Appeal are binding upon all the justice and municipal courts and upon all the superior courts of this state,* and this is so whether or not the superior court is acting as a trial or appellate court. Courts exercising inferior jurisdiction must accept the law declared by courts of superior jurisdiction." (*Ibid.*, italics added and omitted.)[1]

> Unlike at least some federal intermediate appellate courts,[2] though, there is no horizontal stare decisis in the California Court of Appeal.[3] *This* court— this panel—is not bound by *Minder* [*v. Cielito Lindo Restaurant*, 67 Cal. App. 3d 1003, 136 Cal. Rptr. 915 (1977), an earlier decision by the Court

---

1. The passage means that a trial judge sitting in San Francisco is equally bound by decisions from divisions of the Court of Appeal sitting in Fresno, San Diego and even Orange County just as much as he or she is bound by decisions by a panel sitting in San Francisco. California doesn't work the way the federal courts do, with so-called "rules of the circuit" where a trial judge is bound to a given intermediate appellate subdivision.

2. For example, the sprawling Ninth Circuit adheres to a rule of "intracircuit stare decisis" because consistency would otherwise be impossible. (Ulrich & Sidley Austin LLP, 1 Fed. Appellate Prac. Guide 9th Cir. 2d § 8:19) ["The Ninth Circuit's 28 authorized, active judges can be combined into 3,276 different three-judge panels.... The principal way the Ninth Circuit avoids having these shifting three-judge panels issue conflicting decisions is to follow a rule of intracircuit stare decisis: panel decisions bind subsequent panels except in certain narrow situations discussed below or unless overruled by the court en banc."].)

3. (E.g., *Jessen v. Mentor Corp.* (2008) 158 Cal.App.4th 1480, 1489, fn. 10 [71 Cal. Rptr. 3d 714] ["Contrary to Jessen's contention, we are not bound by the contrary decision by Division One of this court.... 'One district or division may refuse to follow a prior decision of a different district or division, for the same reasons that influence the federal Courts of Appeals of the various circuits to make independent decisions.'" (Citation omitted.)].)

of Appeal for the Second Appellate District, Div. Five on the same issue currently under review] and we may take a more critical approach to that opinion. * * * [W]e respectfully decline to follow it.

[2] Learned Treatises (Secondary Authorities)

The California courts often rely on legal treatises and secondary authorities to illuminate gray areas of the law. The most authoritative treatise by far is the ten-volume *California Procedure* authored by Bernard E. Witkin, now in its fifth edition (2008) and supplemented annually. First published in 1954, Witkin's treatise has been cited thousands of times over the years in judicial opinions. *See* Clyde Leland, *The Ineffable Bernie Witkin*, 9 Calif. Lawyer 44 (Dec. 1989). Another influential treatise is Weil, Brown, Edmon & Karnow, *Civil Procedure Before Trial*, a loose-leaf service published by The Rutter Group and updated annually.

Precisely what qualifies as a learned treatise is unclear. Also unclear is the meaning of the reference to "treatises of learned men" in CCP § 1899 as constituting, along with court decisions, "unwritten law." Does this statutory reference mean that treatises are mandatory, as opposed to persuasive, authority? No. *See Earl W. Schott, Inc. v. Kalar*, 20 Cal. App. 4th 943, 946, n. 4, 24 Cal. Rptr. 2d 580 (1993) (noting that "secondary authority is not the law itself" and "can never be mandatory authority; it can only be persuasive"). Secondary authorities are not themselves law and do not have the binding force of statutes, court rules, or judicial precedents. Nevertheless, secondary authorities can be quite persuasive. When construing unclear procedural statutes, the California courts frequently rely on legislative histories contained in Judicial Council, California Law Revision Commission, or legislative committee reports to ascertain legislative intent.

Scholarly publications have proven very persuasive in areas not governed by statutes or court rules. For example, the conflict of law doctrine developed by the California Supreme Court for use in tort cases is based on theories expressed by influential scholars in law review articles, *see Bernhard v. Harrah's Club*, 16 Cal. 3d 313, 128 Cal. Rptr. 215, 546 P.2d 719 (1976); and specific collateral estoppel questions are often answered by reference to the Restatement (Second) of Judgments, *see, e.g., Sandoval v. Superior Court*, 140 Cal. App. 3d 932, 190 Cal. Rptr. 29 (1983). As discussed previously, the California courts often rely on legal treatises such as Witkin's *California Procedure* and Weil, Brown, Edmon & Karnow, *Civil Procedure Before Trial*.

[3] Law Revision Commission Official Comments

The California Law Revision Commission is charged by statute with the duty to examine the law and recommend legislation to make needed reforms. Government Code §§ 8280-8298. The Commission ordinarily prepares an official Comment explaining each section it recommends for enactment, amendment, or repeal. Official Comments of the California Law Revision Commission with respect to new code provisions "are declarative of the intent not only of the draftsmen of the code but also of the legislators who subsequently enacted it." *People v. Williams*, 16 Cal. 3d

663, 667-668, 128 Cal. Rptr. 888, 547 P. 2d 1000 (1976). Therefore, Official Comments "are persuasive, albeit not conclusive, evidence of that intent." *Bonanno v. Central Contra Costa Transit Auth.*, 30 Cal. 4th 139, 148, 132 Cal. Rptr. 2d 341, 65 P. 3d 807 (2003).

§ 2.03 The California Judicial System

[A] California Trial Court Unification

Prior to 1998, California's trial courts consisted of superior and municipal courts, each with its own jurisdiction and number of judges fixed by the Legislature. Subsequently, the California voters approved Proposition 220 in June, 1998, and Proposition 48 in November, 2002, that amended the California Constitution to eliminate references to the constitutional authority to vest judicial power in the municipal courts. Cal. Const. Art. VI, § 5 (repealed), § 6, § 8, § 16 & § 23. As a result of these constitutional amendments, the superior court now has jurisdiction in all matters that were previously under the jurisdiction of either the superior or municipal courts. Cal. Const., Art. VI, § 10. Even after unification, however, the jurisdictional differences between the superior courts and the former municipal courts remain relevant for purposes of certain trial court procedures, such as the size of the jury, and for purposes of the proper court for appellate review. Cal. Const., Art. I, § 16; Art. VI, § 11.

The Courts of Appeal have appellate jurisdiction as to the type of cases that were within the original jurisdiction of the superior courts on June 30, 1995, and in other cases as prescribed by statute. Cal. Const., Art. VI, § 11. As to all other cases, referred to in the legislation implementing Prop. 220 as "limited civil cases," the appellate division of the superior court has appellate jurisdiction. Cal. Const., Art. VI, § 11; CCP §§ 77-86, 904.2. Under the current statutory scheme, the definition of "limited civil cases" corresponds to the type of cases that could only be heard in municipal court prior to unification, i.e., generally speaking, civil cases in which the amount in controversy is $25,000 or less. CCP § 86. The Legislature has the authority to change appellate jurisdiction of the Courts of Appeal, and therefore necessarily of the appellate division of the superior court, by changing the jurisdictional amount in controversy. Cal. Const., Art. VI, § 11.

[B] The California Judicial System

The following profile of the California judicial system is reproduced, in part, from *California Judicial Branch* and *California Courts*, with additions and modifications taken from *2015 Court Statistics Report, Statewide Caseload Trends 2004-2005 Through 2013-2014*, published by the Judicial Council of California.

CALIFORNIA JUDICIAL BRANCH

The California court system—the largest in the nation, with more than 2,000 judicial officers, 19,000 court employees, and more than 7.5 million cases—serves over

38 million people. The state Constitution vests the judicial power of California in the Supreme Court, Courts of Appeal, and superior courts. The Constitution also provides for the formation and functions of the Judicial Council, the policymaking body for the state courts and other agencies.

CALIFORNIA SUPREME COURT

The Supreme Court of California is the state's highest court. Its decisions are binding on all other California courts. The court conducts regular sessions in San Francisco, Los Angeles, and Sacramento; it may also hold special sessions elsewhere.

Membership qualifications

One Chief Justice and six associate justices are appointed by the Governor and confirmed by the Commission on Judicial Appointments. The appointments are confirmed by the public at the next general election; justices also come before voters at the end of their 12-year terms. To be considered for appointment, a person must be an attorney admitted to practice in California or have served as a judge of a court of record in this state for 10 years immediately preceding appointment (Cal. Const., art. VI, § 10).

Jurisdiction

The Supreme Court has original jurisdiction in proceedings for extraordinary relief in the nature of mandamus, certiorari, and prohibition. The court also has original jurisdiction in habeas corpus proceedings (Cal. Const., art. VI, § 10). The state Constitution gives the Supreme Court the authority to review decisions of the state Courts of Appeal (Cal. Const., art. VI, § 12). This reviewing power enables the Supreme Court to decide important legal questions and to maintain uniformity in the law. The court selects specific issues for review, or it may decide all the issues in a case (Cal. Const., art. VI, § 12). The Constitution also directs the high court to review all cases in which a judgment of death has been pronounced by the trial court (Cal. Const., art. VI, § 11). Under state law, these cases are automatically appealed directly from the trial court to the Supreme Court (Pen. Code § 1239(b)).

In addition, the Supreme Court reviews the recommendations of the Commission on Judicial Performance and the State Bar of California concerning the discipline of judges and attorneys for misconduct. The only other matters coming directly to the Supreme Court are appeals from decisions of the Public Utilities Commission.

Business Transacted

Total filings decreased slightly from the previous year, with 7,907 (civil=1,121) filings in 2013-2014 compared with 8,027 filings in 2012-13. Dispositions fell from 8,493 in 2012-13 to 7,745 in 2013-14. Twenty-six automatic appeals (death penalty cases) were disposed of in 2013-14, compared to twenty-one in 2012-13. Filings of original proceedings in 2013-14 numbered 2,758, down from 3,015 in 2012-13. Filings in State Bar disciplinary proceedings in 2013-14 reached a total of 955.

The number of written opinions decreased, from 94 in 2012-13 to 85 in 2013-14. The Supreme Court ordered only six (6) Court of Appeal opinions depublished in

2013-14, one of the lowest numbers of opinions ordered depublished in the last 25 years. The Supreme Court continued to meet its commitment to issue decisions within 90 days of oral argument or submission of the last brief.

Petitions for Review

The total number of petitions for review of Court of Appeal decisions decreased slightly from 4,191 in 2012-13 to 4,134 in 2013-14. Petitions for review in civil appeals totaled 1,121 in 2013-14, up slightly from 1,111 in 2012-13. An additional 222 civil writ petitions were filed in 2013-14, compared to 221 in 2012-13. Petitions for review in criminal appeals were at 3013 in 2013-14, compared to 3,080 in 2012-13.

The Supreme Court granted only 59 (civil=27, criminal=32) petitions for review for expected decision in 2013-14, down from 61 the previous year. It also granted and held 47 petitions pending an expected decision in a lead case. An additional 28 petitions were granted and immediately transferred back to a Court of Appeal for further proceedings. Grants for all three reasons totaled 134, or 3 percent of petitions acted upon. As in prior years, there was a higher percentage of grants in civil matters (4%) than in criminal matters (3%).

Original Proceedings

Civil original proceedings totaled 232, and criminal totaled 2,526 in 2013-14. Habeas corpus petitions constitute the bulk of criminal writ petitions. With the exception of habeas corpus petitions, most such writ petitions seek review of interlocutory decisions of lower courts.

COURTS OF APPEAL

Established by a constitutional amendment in 1904, the Courts of Appeal are California's intermediate courts of review. California has six appellate districts, each with at least one division. The six appellate districts are composed of 19 divisions and 105 justices. District headquarters are: First District, San Francisco; Second District, Los Angeles; Third District, Sacramento; Fourth District Division One, San Diego; Fifth District, Fresno; and Sixth District, San Jose. The Legislature has constitutional authority to create new Court of Appeal districts and divisions (Cal. Const., art. VI, § 3).

Membership, qualifications

Each district (or division, in the case of the Second and Fourth Districts) has a presiding justice and two or more associate justices. The total number of justices was 105 in 2013-14. Appellate justices are appointed by the Governor and confirmed by the Commission on Judicial Appointments. The same rules that govern the selection of Supreme Court justices apply to those serving on the Courts of Appeal.

Jurisdiction

Courts of Appeal have appellate jurisdiction when superior courts have original jurisdiction, and in certain other cases prescribed by statute. Like the Supreme Court, they have original jurisdiction in habeas corpus, mandamus, certiorari, and prohibition proceedings (Cal. Const., art. VI, § 10). There were 22,515 contested matters in the Courts of Appeal during the 2013-14 fiscal year.

The Courts of Appeal also receive appeals (technically, writ proceedings) from decisions of the Workers' Compensation Appeals Board, the Agricultural Relations Appeals Board, and the Public Employment Relations Board.

Cases are decided by three-judge panels. Decisions of the panels, known as opinions, are published in the California Appellate Reports if those opinions meet certain criteria for publication. In general, the opinion is published if it establishes a new rule of law, involves a legal issue of continuing public interest, criticizes existing law, or makes a significant contribution to legal literature (Cal. Const., art. VI, § 14; Rules of Court, rule 8.1105(c)). During fiscal year 2013-14, eight (8) percent of Court of Appeal opinions were certified as meeting the criteria for publication.

Business Transacted

A total of 22,229 notices of appeal and original proceedings were filed in the Courts of Appeal in 2013-14, up slightly from 22,140 in 2012-13. Filings of records of appeal increased slightly from 13,010 in 2012-13 to 13,182 in 2013-14. A total of 5,983 notices of appeal were filed in civil cases (4,374 records of appeal).

Total filings of original writ proceedings dropped slightly to 7,016 cases in 2013-14. Likewise, civil original writ proceedings dropped slightly to 1,851, and criminal filings of original proceedings to 4,742. During the same year, 1,751 civil writ petitions were summarily denied, another 141 were dispose of by written opinion.

Total dispositions increased slightly from the previous year to 22,171 in 2013-14. Written opinions also decreased slightly to 9,780 cases (total civil=3,094) in 2013-14.

Trial Court Affirmative Rate

Among cases disposed by written opinion, there was little change from the previous year in the proportions of cases affirmed, reversed, and dismissed. As in previous fiscal years, approximately 80% of civil appeals decided by opinion, and 94 % of criminal appeals, were affirmed during 2013-14.

Opinions Certified for Publication

The publication rate of opinions remained stable at 8 percent in 2013-14. The highest publication rate was for original proceedings (22%), followed by civil appeals (16%) and, then criminal (4%) and juvenile appeals (4%).

The courts apparently interpret the standards (rule 8.1105(c)) of the California Rules of Court) for determining publishability somewhat differently. The overall publication rate ranged from a low of 5 percent (Fifth District) to a high of 10 percent (First District).

Case-Processing Time

Statewide, half of the civil appeals disposed of by opinion in 2013-14 took more than 498 days from notice of appeal to decision. The outlook was somewhat better for criminal appeals, for which the statewide median time from filing of notice of appeal to decision was 438 days.

SUPERIOR COURTS

Membership, qualifications

The superior courts have 1,706 authorized judges and 318 commissioners and referees. The California Legislature determines the number of judges in each court. Superior court judges serve six year terms and are elected by county voters on a nonpartisan ballot at a general election. Vacancies are filled through appointment by the Governor. A superior court judge (with the exception of former municipal court judges in unified courts) must have been an attorney admitted to practice law in California or have served as a judge of a court of record in this state for at least 10 years immediately preceding election or appointment.

Jurisdiction

Superior courts now have trial jurisdiction over all criminal cases including felonies, misdemeanors, and traffic matters. They also have jurisdiction over all civil cases including family law, probate, juvenile, and general civil matters. More than 7 million cases were filed in the trial courts at over 500 court locations throughout the state during 2013-2014. Appeals in limited civil cases (where $25,000 or less is at issue) and misdemeanors are heard by the appellate division of the superior court. When a small claims case is appealed, a superior court judge decides the case.

Business Transacted

Superior court filings fell slightly, from 7,726,025 in 2012-13 to 7,488,900 in 2013-14. There were 6,722,593 dispositions in 2013-14, up slightly from the number in 2012-13.

Civil case filings (excluding marital and family law petitions) decreased from 923,589 in 2012-13 to 835,215 in 2013-14. However, personal injury, property damaged, and wrongful death filings increased somewhat from 53,273 in 2012-13 to 53,924 in 2013-14. Domestic-related filings (marital and family law petitions) decreased from 389,087 in 2012-13 to 381,486 in 2013-14. Criminal case filings decreased slightly to 6,096,084 in 2013-14.

Only three (3) percent of all unlimited civil cases were disposed of by jury trials, and less than one (1) percent of limited civil cases, in 2013-14. Likewise, only two (2) percent of felony dispositions were by jury trial. The total number of all civil and criminal jury trials in 2013-14 was 9,900.

Civil Cases

Total civil filings in all case categories equaled 1,216,701 during 2013-14. Of these, only 193,190 were unlimited civil cases, 486,597 were limited civil cases, 138,968 were family law (marital) cases, and 155,428 were small claims court cases. Civil dispositions in all case categories totaled 1,184,475 including 173,420 unlimited civil cases. Only 1,226 unlimited civil cases were decided by jury trials, or 3 percent. 80 percent of all civil cases were dismissed before trial during 2013-14, including 4.5 percent for delay in prosecution.

Case-Processing Time

Civil case processing time increased compared to previous years. In 2013-14, 66% of all unlimited civil cases were disposed of within 12 months, 77% within 18 months, and 84% within 24 months. Likewise, 86% of limited civil cases were disposed of within 12 months, 93% within 18 months, and 95% within 24 months. Criminal case processing time did not change significantly, with 88 percent of all felonies being disposed of in less than 12 months.

COURT SYSTEM AGENCIES

The Constitution also provides for agencies concerned with judicial administration: Judicial Council Commission on Judicial Appointments, Commission on Judicial Performance, and Habeas Corpus Resource Center. Their duties are described below.

Judicial Council

Chaired by the Chief Justice, the Judicial Council is the governing body of the California courts. The California Constitution directs the Judicial Council to provide policy guidelines to the courts, make recommendations annually to the Governor and Legislature, and adopt and revise California Rules of Court in the areas of court administration, practice and procedure. The council performs its constitutional and other functions with the support of its staff agency, the Administrative Office of the Courts.

The 21 voting members of the Judicial Council consist of the Chief Justice, one Associate Justice of the Supreme Court, 3 justices of the Courts of Appeal, 10 judges of the superior courts, 4 attorney members appointed by the State Bar Board of Governors, and 1 member from each house of the Legislature. The Council also has approximately 11 advisory members, who include court executives or administrators. The council performs most of its work through internal committees and advisory committees and task forces.

Commission on Judicial Appointments

The Governor's appointees to the Supreme Court and the Courts of Appeal must be confirmed by the Commission on Judicial Appointments. No appellate appointment is final until the commission has filed its approval with the Secretary of State.

Commission on Judicial Performance

The California Constitution provides for a Commission on Judicial Performance, which deals with the censure, removal, retirement, or private admonishment of judges and commissioners for either misconduct or inability to perform their duties on account of permanent disability. The commission has authority to conduct proceedings against any California judge after it investigates cases of willful misconduct in office, persistent failure or inability to perform the duties of office, habitual intemperance, conduct prejudicial to the administration of justice that may be detrimental to the judicial office itself, or a disability of a permanent character that seriously interferes with performance of duties. Effective March 1, 1995, Proposition 190 authorized the commission to remove, retire, or censure a judge. Automatic Supreme Court review was eliminated, although the court is permitted discretionary review if it rules within 120 days.

Chapter 3

Considerations Before Undertaking Representation

§ 3.01 Introductory Note on Professional Responsibility Issues

In most significant civil litigation, critical decisions are made jointly by clients in consultation with their lawyers. Thus, lawyers in their role as lawyers are a worthy subject of inquiry in any civil procedure course. Lawyers in California are governed by all the laws that apply to their clients *and* by special professional obligations. These obligations are found principally in the State Bar Act that is part of the Business and Professions Code and in the California Rules of Professional Conduct. You have already or will soon study them in detail in your Professional Responsibility course that you must take during law school.

For purposes of our treatment here, we will explore some initial considerations lawyers face in undertaking the representation of a civil litigant. These considerations divide into two sets of obligations: (1) obligations lawyers owe to clients; and (2) obligations lawyers owe to the courts, to adversaries, and to third parties. We note at the outset that, absent special considerations usually involving court appointments, lawyers have no obligation to represent a client just because she walks into the lawyer's office with money to pay the lawyer's fee. Indeed, sometimes lawyers' best decisions are those *not* to represent a client.

§ 3.02 Lawyers' Duties to Their Clients

Lawyers owe their clients duties of confidentiality, of loyalty, and of competence.

[A] The Duty of Confidentiality

You will already be familiar with the attorney-client privilege that is a part of California's Evidence Code. *See* Evid. Code §§ 950–962. Although the attorney-client privilege protects clients and their lawyers from being forced to reveal confidential communications through the coercion of legal process, lawyers have an even broader obligation to protect confidential client information. This duty of confidentiality is expressed in § 6068 of the California Business and Professions Code. Prior to 2004, this statutory duty demanded absolute confidentiality.

However, pursuant to an amendment to § 6068 effective July 1, 2004, this duty is now slightly more limited in scope:

It is the duty of an attorney to do all of the following:

* * *

(e)(1) To maintain inviolate the confidence, and at every peril to himself or herself to preserve the secrets, of his or her client.

(2) Notwithstanding paragraph (1), and attorney may, but is not required to, reveal confidential information relating to the representation of a client to the extent that the attorney reasonably believes the disclosure is necessary to prevent a criminal act that the attorney reasonably believes is likely to result in death of, or substantial bodily injury to, an individual.

Fred C. Zacharias, *Privilege and Confidentiality in California*, 28 U.C. Davis L. Rev. 367, 369–71 (1995) [footnotes omitted].*

Although lawyers often use "privilege" and "confidentiality" interchangeably, courts and commentators usually have taken care to distinguish the concepts. Privilege and confidentiality have the same roots. Their shared goals include encouraging clients to rely upon attorneys, enhancing lawyers' ability to operate effectively in the adversary system, fostering client dignity and autonomy, and enabling lawyers to find out about and dissuade clients from engaging in misconduct. Traditionally, courts have administered the privilege, while lawyer organizations have determined the scope of confidentiality. Concerned with ascertaining truth and with the rights of adversaries, courts have construed privilege "narrowly." They have recognized the existence of numerous practical exceptions. In contrast, lawyers and bar organizations have been more interested in preserving attorney-client relationships. They have taken a broad and rigid view of confidentiality's scope.

California has codified these separate approaches. The California Evidence Code notes the existence of attorney-client privilege, but provides a laundry list of exceptions that courts administer. California's statutory attorney-client confidentiality rule — found in the Business and Professions Code — is interpreted by local and state bar committee opinions and enforced by a special Bar Court, rather than trial judges. [Prior to 2004,] [t]he Business and Professions Code's language demand[ed] absolute confidentiality. * * *

Notes and Questions

(1) Prior to July 1, 2004, Bus. & Prof. Code § 6068(e) contained only the language now set forth in subsection (e)(1), and therefore demanded absolute confidentiality.

---

* Reprinted with permission.

See Zacharias, *Privilege and Confidentiality in California, supra* at 371–72. What are the policy reasons for imposing such an absolute duty of confidentiality on an attorney? Do you think the current version of § 6068(e), which now permits a qualified duty in limited circumstances, reflects a better policy judgment? Why?

(2) Current § 6068(e)(2) permits, but does not require, an attorney to disclose confidential client information when a client threatens to commit a criminal act likely to result in death or substantial bodily harm. Why is this duty to disclose permissive? Under what circumstances might an attorney decide not to disclose such information? Is a bright-line, mandatory disclosure requirement preferable?

(3) If you reasonably believe that your client will commit a criminal act likely to result in the death of a third party but decide pursuant to § 6068(e)(2) not to reveal the client's secret threat, does that mean you will be immune from liability if sued for wrongful death by the family of the individual killed by your client? *See Tarasoff v. Regents of Univ. of California*, 17 Cal. 3d 425, 131 Cal. Rptr. 14, 551 P.2d 334 (1976) (holding psychiatrist liable for not disclosing patient's threat to kill third party); *but see* Zacharias, *Privilege and Confidentiality in California, supra* at 402–404 (noting that no American court has extended *Tarasoff* liability to the lawyer context).

(4) California amended its Evidence Code in 1993 to eliminate the attorney-client privilege when the lawyer reasonably believes disclosure of otherwise confidential information is necessary to prevent a criminal act that the lawyer reasonably believes is likely to result in death or substantial bodily harm to an individual. Evid. Code § 956.5. With the 2004 amendment to Business and Professions Code § 6068(e), and the subsequent adoption of Rule 3-100 of the Rules of Professional Conduct further explaining the circumstances under which disclosure of confidential information is permissible, California now joins the vast majority of American jurisdictions which have recognized a confidentiality exception to prevent serious bodily crime. *See* Fred C. Zacharias, *Lawyers As Gatekeepers*, 41 SAN DIEGO L. REV. 1387, 1398 (2004); John S. Dzienkowski, *Professional Responsibility Standards, Rules & Statutes*, pp. 97–104 (2004–2005).

[B] The Duty of Loyalty — Conflicts of Interest

California Rule of Professional Conduct 3-310(B) admonishes attorneys to avoid the representation of "adverse interests," which the Rule broadly defines to encompass a wide variety of legal, business, financial, professional, or personal relationships with a party, witness, or the subject matter of the representation. The Rule directs attorneys to disclose such real or potential conflicts, and to eliminate the conflict by refusing to represent one client or by obtaining "informed written consent" of each client after disclosure. In *Flatt v. Superior Court*, 9 Cal. 4th 275, 36 Cal. Rptr. 2d 537, 885 P.2d 950 (1994), the California Supreme Court discussed the different duties and standards applicable when the conflict of interest involves simultaneous representation of clients as opposed to successive representation of clients:

Where the potential conflict is one that arises from the *successive* representation of clients with potentially adverse interests, the courts have recognized that the chief fiduciary value jeopardized is that of client *confidentiality*. Thus, where a former client seeks to have a previous attorney disqualified from serving as counsel to a successive client in litigation adverse to the interests of the first client, the governing test requires that the client demonstrate a "*substantial relationship*" between the subjects of the antecedent and current representations.

The "substantial relationship" test mediates between two interests that are in tension in such a context — the freedom of the subsequent client to counsel of choice, on the one hand, and the interest of the former client in ensuring the permanent confidentiality of matters disclosed to the attorney in the course of the prior representation, on the other. Where the requisite substantial relationship between the subjects of the prior and the current representations can be demonstrated, access to confidential information by the attorney in the course of the first representation (relevant, by definition, to the second representation) is *presumed* and disqualification of the attorney's representation of the second client is mandatory; indeed, the disqualification extends vicariously to the entire firm. * * *

Both the interest implicated and the governing test are different, however, where an attorney's potentially conflicting representations are *simultaneous*. In such a situation — perhaps the classic case involving an attorney's interests in conflict with those of the client — the courts have discerned a distinctly separate professional value to be at risk by the attorney's adverse representations. The primary value at stake in cases of simultaneous or dual representation is the attorney's duty — and the client's legitimate expectation — of *loyalty*, rather than confidentiality. * * *

In evaluating conflict claims in dual representation cases, the courts have accordingly imposed a test that is more stringent than that of demonstrating a substantial relationship between the subject matter of successive representations. Even though the simultaneous representations may have *nothing* in common, and there is *no* risk that confidences to which counsel is a party in the one case have any relation to the other matter, disqualification may nevertheless be *required*. Indeed, in all but a few instances, the rule of disqualification in simultaneous representation cases is a *per se* or "automatic" one. * * *

The reason for such a rule is evident, even (or perhaps especially) to the nonattorney. A client who learns that his or her lawyer is also representing a litigation adversary, even with respect to a matter *wholly unrelated* to the one for which counsel was retained, cannot long be expected to sustain the level of confidence and trust in counsel that is one of the foundations of the professional relationship. All legal technicalities aside, few if any clients would be willing to suffer the prospect of their attorney continuing to represent them under such circumstances. * * * It is for that reason, and not out of concerns rooted in the obligation of client confidentiality, that courts and ethical codes alike prohibit an attorney from simultaneously representing two client adversaries, even where the substance of the representations are unrelated.[4] * * *

Flatt, supra, 9 Cal. 4th at 278–79, 282–85.

California Rule of Professional Conduct 3-310(B) directs attorneys to disclose such real or potential conflicts, and to eliminate the conflict by refusing to represent one client or by obtaining "informed written consent" of each client after disclosure. Under what circumstances might a client consent to an attorney's representation of conflicting interests? Are there some situations in which the conflicts are such that written consent may not suffice? *See Klemm v. Superior Court*, 75 Cal. App. 3d 893, 898, 142 Cal. Rptr. 509 (1977) (noting that, as a matter of law, a purported consent to dual representation of litigants with adverse interests at a contested hearing or trial was neither intelligent nor informed); *Blue Water Sunset, LLC v. Markowitz*, 192 Cal. App. 4th 477, 122 Cal. Rptr. 3d 641 (2011) (ruling disqualification was mandatory because attorney simultaneously represented clients with adverse interests when he prepared demurrer and other papers).

When a conflict of interest requires an attorney's disqualification from a matter, the disqualification normally extends vicariously to the attorney's entire law firm. *See Flatt v. Superior Court*, 9 Cal. 4th 275, 283, 36 Cal. Rptr. 2d 537, 885 P.2d 950 (1994). In *People v. Speedee Oil Change Systems, Inc.*, 20 Cal. 4th 1135, 86 Cal. Rptr. 2d 816, 980 P.2d 371 (1999), the Supreme Court applied the same disqualification rule when a party unknowingly consults an attorney "of counsel" to the law firm representing the party's adversary in the subject of the consultation. The *Speedee Oil* opinion also contains a useful general discussion of disqualification principles, and of the determination as to whether an attorney-client relationship has reached a point where the attorney can be subject to disqualification for a conflict of interest. *See Speedee Oil, supra*, 20 Cal. 4th at 1147–1152 (observing that the primary concern is whether and to what extent the attorney acquired confidential information). *See also City and County of San Francisco v. Cobra Solutions, Inc.*, 38 Cal. 4th 839, 43 Cal. Rptr. 3d 771, 135 P.3d 20 (2006) (upholding disqualification of City Attorney and his entire Office where City Attorney previously, while in private practice, represented

---

4. There are, of course, exceptions even to this rule. The principle of loyalty is for the client's benefit; most courts thus permit an attorney to continue the simultaneous representation of clients whose interests are adverse as to unrelated matters provided full disclosure is made and both agree in writing to waive the conflict. (*See, e.g.*, Steinberg & Sharpe, *Attorney Conflicts of Interest: The Need for a Coherent Framework* (1990) 66 Notre Dame L. Rev. 1, 3, fn. 7, and materials cited.) But this class of cases is a rare circumstance, typically involving corporate clients, and overcoming the presumption of "prima facie impropriety" is not easily accomplished. It is not, in any event, one that concerns us in this case, given Flatt's understandable decision not to represent Daniel in his contemplated lawsuit against Hinkle and his firm. There was thus no occasion here for disclosure and client waiver of the conflict.

a client who is not being sued by the city in a matter substantially related to the prior representation).

[C]   Taking Cases You Are Competent to Handle

Rule 3-110(A) of the California Rules of Professional Conduct makes incompetence the subject of discipline: "A member shall not intentionally, recklessly, or repeatedly fail to perform legal services with competence."

Subsection (B) defines "competence" to mean applying the "1) diligence, 2) learning and skill, and 3) mental, emotional, and physical ability reasonably necessary" to perform a legal service. Subsection (C) makes it possible for lawyers — for example, lawyers recently out of law school — to gain the necessary competence during representation:

> If a member does not have sufficient learning and skill when the legal service is undertaken, the member may nonetheless perform such services competently by 1) associating with or, where appropriate, professionally consulting another lawyer reasonably believed to be competent, or 2) by acquiring sufficient learning and skill before performance is required.

The requirement that lawyers must "intentionally, recklessly, or repeatedly" perform incompetently, limits the impact of this rule. Nevertheless, there are instances of discipline as a result of repeated failures in a single case. *See King v. State Bar*, 52 Cal. 3d 307, 276 Cal. Rptr. 176, 801 P.2d 419 (1990) (ordering attorney suspended for multiple instances of misconduct in each of two cases); *In the matter of Broderick*, 3 Cal. State Bar Ct. Rptr. 138, 154–55 (Review Dept. 1994) (multiple instances of misconduct).

There is no doubt, however, that a single instance of incompetent performance can subject a California lawyer to an action for malpractice by the injured party. *See Smith v. Lewis*, 13 Cal. 3d 349, 118 Cal. Rptr. 621, 530 P.2d 589 (1975) (affirming legal malpractice judgment against defendant attorney where defendant, due to inadequate legal research, negligently failed to assert his client's community interest in her husband's retirement benefits in prior marriage dissolution proceeding in which defendant had represented the plaintiff wife). In all aspects of his or her representation of a client, a lawyer has a duty to use the skill, prudence, and diligence commonly possessed by other lawyers in California. Failure to exercise this duty, if it injures the client, gives rise to a claim for legal malpractice.

In most instances, it is the concern over a possible malpractice claim, not discipline, that is likely to be foremost in a lawyer's mind as she makes decisions about the conduct of litigation. Although lawyers are not liable for "mere errors in judgment" or "tactical decisions" during litigation, they are liable for a failure to exercise a *well-informed* judgment or tactical decision. Lawyers must know or look up settled principles of law using standard research techniques and conduct reasonable factual investigations. In many ways, these standards parallel those required to avoid sanctions for bringing frivolous litigation. We now turn to that topic.

§ 3.03 Avoiding Meritless Litigation

Although you are possibly familiar with the tort action for malicious prosecution that is the primary subject of *Crowley v. Katleman*, reproduced below, it is probably the least efficient deterrent to frivolous litigation. In order to recover damages for malicious prosecution, the "victim" of such litigation must commence and successfully litigate another entire action, must avoid the defenses the *Crowley* court notes, and must then collect the judgment. This is expensive and time-consuming for the victim and of no real value for frivolous litigation's other victim, the courts, which must expend even more time and resources and endure not less, but more, litigation. Other alternatives, such as lawyer discipline and statutory sanctions, are more summary in character and perhaps just as effective. These alternatives are also discussed below

[A] Malicious Prosecution

Crowley v. Katleman

Supreme Court of California
8 Cal. 4th 666, 34 Cal. Rptr. 2d 386, 881 P.2d 1083 (1994)

MOSK, JUSTICE.

In *Bertero v. National General Corp.* (1974) 13 Cal. 3d 43 [118 Cal. Rptr. 184, 529 P.2d 608, 65 A.L.R.3d 878] (*Bertero*), we held that a suit for malicious prosecution lies for bringing an action charging multiple grounds of liability when some but not all of those grounds were asserted with malice and without probable cause. In the case at bar we are called on to reconsider the question. * * *

Arthur Crowley was Beldon Katleman's best friend, next-door neighbor, and attorney. In 1973 Beldon Katleman married Carole Katleman, a woman some 30 years his junior. After a brief marriage characterized by the probate court as "stormy," he divorced her in 1975. Crowley represented Beldon Katleman in the divorce proceedings, and as a result of that representation Carole Katleman became extremely hostile towards Crowley.

On January 2, 1976, Beldon Katleman executed a will, naming Crowley as executor. Crowley did not draft the will, nor did he participate in its drafting or its formal execution. The will recited that Katleman was not married; that he had an adult daughter by a prior marriage and two grandchildren by that daughter; and that he had no siblings, but that his mother was still living. In the will Katleman expressly declined to provide for his adult daughter and her issue. Instead, he made a specific bequest to his mother's longtime servant, and disposed of the residue as follows: if his mother survived him the residue would be held in trust for her benefit during her lifetime, and after her death would be distributed to Crowley; if she did not survive him, he gave the residue directly to Crowley. Crowley was named trustee. The will included a standard no contest clause disinheriting any beneficiary or heir who contested it.

In 1980 Beldon married Carole Katleman for the second time; and although, according to the probate court, "the second marriage also had its stormy moments when he threatened to again divorce Mrs. Katleman," they were still married when he died on September 28, 1988. Beldon Katleman never revoked his 1976 will, nor did he execute a subsequent will. Because Beldon Katleman's mother had died in 1982, Crowley became the principal beneficiary.

Shortly after Beldon Katleman's death, Crowley offered Carole Katleman one-half of her deceased husband's estate.[3] She refused his offer, and instead told third parties she would have Crowley disbarred and would "spend every penny or dime" to make sure he received nothing from the estate. She also told Crowley she was not aware of any will or codicil executed by Beldon Katleman other than his 1976 will. A search for such a document turned up none.

On October 4, 1988, Crowley filed a petition to probate Beldon Katleman's will. The court appointed Crowley special administrator of the estate.

On October 28, 1988, Carole Katleman, represented by the defendant attorneys, filed a will contest. As amended, the contest alleged in six separate counts six grounds for invalidating the will, to wit, that (1) Crowley exerted undue influence over Beldon Katleman; (2) Beldon Katleman revoked the will by destroying it; (3) the will was not in fact his last will; (4) he lacked testamentary capacity when he executed the will; (5) the will was not duly executed; and (6) Crowley defrauded Beldon Katleman to induce him to make the will. Carole Katleman then successfully petitioned the probate court to remove Crowley as special administrator of the estate because of the pendency of her will contest.

On December 6, 1989, the probate court granted Crowley's motion for summary adjudication of issues as to the ground of the will contest alleging lack of due execution, declaring that the will had been properly executed and witnessed. The court denied the motion as to the remaining grounds, ruling there were triable issues of material fact as to each.

Shortly before trial of the will contest Crowley again offered Carole Katleman one-half of the estate, but she again refused his offer.

After substantial discovery, the will contest was litigated in a trial lasting almost three weeks. On August 3, 1990, the probate court ruled that none of the six grounds alleged by Carole Katleman for invalidating the will was meritorious. Rather, the court adjudged that the will was not the product of either undue influence or fraud by Crowley, Beldon Katleman did not revoke the will by destroying it, the will was his last will, he had testamentary capacity when he executed the will, and the will was duly executed. The court therefore ordered the will admitted to probate and appointed Crowley its executor.

---

3. At the time of Beldon Katleman's death his estate was valued in excess of $10 million.

Carole Katleman took an appeal from the judgment. On May 22, 1991, however, she filed a voluntary dismissal of the appeal with prejudice. The judgment thereby became a final decision on the merits in Crowley's favor.

While the will contest was pending Carole Katleman also filed a claim for a share of the estate as an omitted spouse. (Prob. Code, §6560.) Crowley opposed the claim on the ground, inter alia, that by filing the will contest Carole Katleman triggered the no contest clause of the will and thus gave up her omission rights. On August 12, 1991, the probate court ruled to the contrary as a matter of law, concluded that Carole Katleman was an omitted spouse, and awarded her the share prescribed by statute, i.e., all the community property and one-half of Beldon Katleman's separate property. (*Ibid.*) In so ruling, however, the court observed that "Carole's will contest does indeed seem to be vindictive…. But even if her attack was pure vengeance, and no matter whether Mr. Crowley's righteous outrage is justified, the enforcement of the no contest clause is not a proper substitute for a malicious prosecution action for whatever damages Mr. Crowley can prove."

Some six weeks later Crowley filed the present action for malicious prosecution against Carole Katleman and the attorney defendants. The first two causes of action are against Carole Katleman. They allege that the will contest terminated in Crowley's favor and that Carole Katleman acted maliciously and without probable cause in contesting the will on the grounds that (1) it was not duly executed, (2) it was void for fraud, (3) Beldon Katleman lacked testamentary capacity, (4) it was not his last will, and (5) Beldon Katleman revoked the will by destroying it. It is further alleged that the will contest "was not premised on an honest or good faith belief by [Carole Katleman] of the merits of such claims, but was instead based upon her malicious, vindictive hatred of [Crowley], to cause [him] to suffer emotional distress, to injure his reputation, and her desire to assert as many claims as possible against him, out of spite." We observe that the first two causes of action allege that only five of the six grounds of the will contest lacked probable cause; they are silent as to the undue influence ground.

The third cause of action is against the attorney defendants. It alleges generally that they instigated and continued the will contest maliciously and without probable cause. Specifically, it alleges that the attorney defendants knew, or should have known, there was no probable cause for contesting the will on the grounds that (1) it was not duly executed, (2) it was not Beldon Katleman's last will, (3) it was void for fraud, and (4) Beldon Katleman lacked testamentary capacity; it further asserts that no reasonable attorney would have believed these grounds of the contest were legally tenable. This cause of action thus alleges that only four of the six grounds of the will contest lacked probable cause, and is silent as to the undue influence and revocation grounds.

Carole Katleman and the attorney defendants (hereafter collectively defendants) filed a general demurrer to the malicious prosecution complaint, asking the court to take judicial notice of the probate proceedings. * * *

On January 28, 1992, the court sustained defendants' demurrer without leave to amend, but failed to clearly state its reasons. Although the code requires that "the court shall include in its decision or order a statement of the specific ground or grounds upon which the decision or order is based" (Code Civ. Proc., §472d), here the court recited only that it took judicial notice of the probate proceedings and that it "bases its decision on *Sheldon Appel Co. v. Albert & Oliker*, 47 Cal. 3d 863 [254 Cal. Rptr. 336, 765 P.2d 498] (1989) and *Friedberg v. Cox*, 197 Cal. App. 3d 381 [242 Cal. Rptr. 851] (1987)." The court thereafter dismissed the malicious prosecution action in its entirety, and Crowley took this appeal.

The Court of Appeal reversed the judgment "under compulsion" of *Bertero, supra*, 13 Cal. 3d 43, 55–57. The court and defendants strongly criticized the *Bertero* rule, however, and we granted review to consider their points.

I

"To establish a cause of action for the malicious prosecution of a civil proceeding, a plaintiff must plead and prove that the prior action (1) was commenced by or at the direction of the defendant and was pursued to a legal termination in his, plaintiff's, favor [citations]; (2) was brought without probable cause [citations]; and (3) was initiated with malice [citations]." (*Bertero, supra*, 13 Cal. 3d at p. 50.)

In the case at bar it is undisputed that the will contest was initiated by defendants and that it terminated in a decision on the merits in Crowley's favor as to each ground of the contest. It is also undisputed that in charging each such ground defendants acted with malice. The dispute relates to the third element of the cause of action, i.e., lack of probable cause to bring the contest.

Because the case is before us on a demurrer, the issue is whether the complaint properly pleads the element of probable cause. Specifically, the issue is whether a malicious prosecution action for bringing a will contest on multiple grounds may be maintained when the plaintiff does not allege that *all* the grounds asserted in the contest lacked probable cause. In the case at bar, as noted above, none of the three causes of action alleges that defendants lacked probable cause for the undue influence ground.

As the Court of Appeal correctly observed, "This case is virtually identical to *Bertero*." In *Bertero, supra*, 13 Cal. 3d 43, the employee plaintiff (Bertero) sued the defendant employers for breach of an employment contract. By way of affirmative defenses the answer attacked the validity of the contract on three grounds, alleging that Bertero (1) obtained the contract by duress, (2) obtained the contract by undue influence, and (3) gave no consideration for the contract. The defendants then filed a cross-complaint against Bertero to recover salary already paid to him under the contract, alleging the same three grounds of invalidity as the answer. The matter was tried and Bertero prevailed in all respects: the judgment declared the employment contract valid, awarded Bertero damages for its breach, and dismissed the cross-complaint with prejudice.

After the judgment was affirmed on appeal, Bertero filed another action against the same defendants for malicious prosecution of their failed cross-complaint, charging that all three grounds of the cross-complaint were malicious and lacked probable cause. Again Bertero prevailed, and was awarded additional damages. On appeal from that judgment the defendants challenged, inter alia, an instruction that allowed the jury to find for Bertero even if only one of the three theories of liability in the cross-complaint lacked probable cause. Affirming the judgment with a minor modification, this court held the instruction correct. (13 Cal. 3d at pp. 55–57.)

We began by reviewing the dual harms to society and to the individual that the cause of action for malicious prosecution is designed to redress: "The malicious commencement of a civil proceeding is actionable because it harms the individual against whom the claim is made, and also because it threatens the efficient administration of justice." (*Bertero, supra*, 13 Cal. 3d at p. 50.) * * *

As noted above, defendants in the case at bar ... contend there was probable cause for the undue influence ground of the will contest because the court trying the contest found that the confidential relationship between Crowley and Beldon Katleman had given rise to a presumption of such influence. Again we rejected an identical contention in *Bertero*: "Our conclusion that an action for malicious prosecution lies when but one of alternate theories of recovery is maliciously asserted disposes of a further contention of [the defendants in *Bertero*]. * * * " (13 Cal. 3d at p. 57, fn. 5.)

Nor could defendants herein contend they were compelled to assert all the statutory grounds for a will contest under pain of being deemed to have waived them: as we said in rejecting a similar argument in *Bertero*, "A litigant is never compelled to file a malicious and fabricated action. It is not the assertion of a claim that is actionable but rather the malicious character of the assertion." (13 Cal. 3d at p. 52.)

For all these reasons the Court of Appeal was correct in concluding that "The holding in *Bertero* is controlling." Under the rule of that decision, the complaint in the case at bar states a cause of action for malicious prosecution even though it does not allege that every one of the grounds asserted in the will contest lacked probable cause. * * *

II

Unable to distinguish *Bertero*, defendants ask us to overrule it. * * * Defendants ... contend that we should abandon the rule of *Bertero, supra*, 13 Cal. 3d 43, and replace it with a new rule based on the "primary right" theory. To understand this contention it will be helpful to briefly review the main points of the primary right theory.

The primary right theory is a theory of code pleading that has long been followed in California. It provides that a "cause of action" is comprised of a "primary right" of the plaintiff, a corresponding "primary duty" of the defendant, and a wrongful act by the defendant constituting a breach of that duty. The most salient characteristic of a primary right is that it is indivisible: the violation of a single primary right gives rise to but a single cause of action. (*Slater v. Blackwood* (1975) 15 Cal. 3d 791, 795 [126 Cal. Rptr. 225, 543 P.2d 593].) A pleading that states the violation of one primary right in two causes of action contravenes the rule against "splitting" a cause of action.

As far as its content is concerned, the primary right is simply the plaintiff's right to be free from the particular injury suffered. (*Slater v. Blackwood, supra*, 15 Cal. 3d 791, 795.) It must therefore be distinguished from the *legal theory* on which liability for that injury is premised: "Even where there are multiple legal theories upon which recovery might be predicated, one injury gives rise to only one claim for relief." (*Ibid.*) The primary right must also be distinguished from the *remedy* sought: "The violation of one primary right constitutes a single cause of action, though it may entitle the injured party to many forms of relief, and the relief is not to be confounded with the cause of action, one not being determinative of the other."

* * *

[I]n their opening brief in this court defendants ... argue that (1) although the cause of action in the prior proceeding stated multiple grounds or theories of liability, it must nevertheless have been premised on the violation of a single primary right, and therefore, (2) if there was probable cause to assert the violation of that primary right on *any one* theory of liability, such probable cause is sufficient to defeat a malicious prosecution claim even if the other theories of liability lacked probable cause.

The reasoning is flawed by a non sequitur. It is true that under the primary right theory a properly pleaded cause of action must be premised on a single primary right even though it states multiple grounds of liability. But it does not follow *from the primary right theory* that probable cause to assert that cause of action on one ground of liability defeats a malicious prosecution claim when the other grounds lacked probable cause. Whether such "partial probable cause" is sufficient for this purpose, as we shall see, is a question of policy under the substantive law of malicious prosecution; the primary right theory of pleading simply does not address the matter.[11] * * *

C

Finally, defendants criticize the rule of *Bertero, supra*, 13 Cal. 3d 43, on various grounds. They make [several] arguments, adopting in large part the views of the Court of Appeal herein, but none is persuasive.

1. Defendants' main objection is that the *Bertero* rule is assertedly incompatible with "the fundamental interest which the malicious prosecution tort is designed to protect—'the interest in freedom from *unjustifiable* and *unreasonable* litigation'" (*Sheldon Appel [Co. v. Albert & Oliker* (1989) 47 Cal. 3d 863] at p. 882 [254 Cal. Rptr. 336, 765 P.2d 498]). Defendants argue that when there is probable cause for at least one of the theories of liability asserted in the prior action, the defendant has to defend against that theory in any event and hence the "litigation" is not unjustifiable and unreasonable. Of course, the defendant also has to defend against the theories of liability asserted in the prior action *without* probable cause, but defendants dismiss

---

11. In their reply brief defendants ... shift their argument. They urge that regardless of the assertion of invalid theories of liability, a malicious prosecution claim cannot be maintained if there was probable cause to assert the violation of *the primary right itself*-or, as the Court of Appeal put it, when the *cause of action* is brought with probable cause. The argument is no more persuasive than its predecessors. When a complaint alleges multiple theories of liability or "counts," the counts "are merely ways of stating the same cause of action differently." (*Bay Cities Paving & Grading, Inc. v. Lawyers' Mutual Ins. Co.* (1993) 5 Cal. 4th 854, 860, fn. 1 [21 Cal. Rptr. 2d 691, 855 P.2d 1263].) Accordingly, the only way that a litigant can show probable cause for the cause of action as a whole—or for the "primary right"—is to show probable cause for each of the counts or theories alleged. In this event the whole is indeed the sum of the parts.

that fact with the explanation that in so doing the defendant "has simply been required to respond to additional allegations and arguments directed at a single prior right."

The explanation, however, begs the question. By defining the "litigation" in issue as the prior action per se rather than each theory of liability litigated, defendants assume the point to be proved. It is true that such a defendant must in any event defend against the one valid theory of liability; but the defendant's obligation also to defend against the *invalid* theories of liability may well be so burdensome—as the complaint alleges in the case at bar—that it amounts to an impairment of the defendant's interest in freedom from unjustifiable and unreasonable litigation. Whether this is so is a question to be answered, again, not by the primary right theory but by the substantive law of malicious prosecution.

2. Next, defendants contend in effect that the *Bertero* rule is no longer necessary because the trial court now has statutory powers to deal with frivolous or delaying conduct that it lacked in 1974 when *Bertero* was decided and that provide a remedy superior to the cause of action for malicious prosecution in these circumstances. For this proposition defendants rely on a passage in *Sheldon Appel* in which we took note of legislative measures designed "to facilitate the early weeding out of patently meritless claims and to permit the imposition of sanctions in the initial lawsuit—against both litigants and attorneys—for frivolous or delaying conduct." (47 Cal. 3d at pp. 873– 874.) Among the statutes cited in *Sheldon Appel* defendants particularly stress Code of Civil Procedure section 128.5, enacted in 1981 (hereafter section 128.5). That statute authorizes trial courts to award certain expenses, including attorney fees, resulting from "bad-faith actions or tactics that are frivolous or solely intended to cause unnecessary delay." (*Id.*, subd. (a).) It is true that "actions or tactics" are defined to include, as an example, "the filing and service of a complaint" (*id.*, subd. (b)(1)), but it does not follow that the Legislature intended to substitute this remedy for the cause of action for malicious prosecution, less still to overrule *Bertero*.

The legislative history shows that the Legislature's intent was far more modest. [When the Legislature revised section 128.5 in 1988, it] added an express declaration (now section 128.5, subdivision (e)) that "The liability imposed by this section *is in addition to any other liability* imposed by law for acts or omissions within the purview of this section." (Italics added.) This declaration has been correctly cited for the proposition that "The purpose of the section was to broaden the authority of the courts to manage their calendars expeditiously; the section was not intended as a substitute for substantive causes of action arising out of the underlying facts." (*Brewster v. Southern Pacific Transportation Co.* (1991) 235 Cal. App. 3d 701, 711 [1 Cal. Rptr.2d 89], fn. omitted.) Among those substantive causes of action is, properly circumscribed, the action for malicious prosecution.

There is still another reason to conclude that the Legislature did not intend either to substitute section 128.5 for the cause of action for malicious prosecution or to overrule *Bertero*: the remedies are not coextensive. Section 128.5 allows compensation only for out-of-pocket litigation costs, including attorney fees, that directly result from the objectionable conduct; the relief cannot include consequential damages.

(*Brewster v. Southern Pacific Transportation Co.*, *supra*, 235 Cal. App. 3d at pp. 710–712.) By contrast, *Bertero* stressed that a plaintiff who pleads and proves a case of malicious prosecution may recover not only litigation costs and attorney fees but also "compensation for injury to his reputation or impairment of his social and business standing in the community [citations], and for mental or emotional distress [citation]." (13 Cal. 3d at p. 51, fn. omitted.) In appropriate cases such compensation can be well justified and significant in amount[12]

For all these reasons, section 128.5 and the cause of action for malicious prosecution provide distinct remedies that are at most alternatives to each other: as explained in the companion case of *Estate of Katleman*, *supra*, 13 Cal. App. 4th 51, 67, echoing the view of the trial court herein, "an adequate remedy for a frivolous or vindictive will contest is available in the form of an action for malicious prosecution." In a footnote at this point the Court of Appeal continued: "*Alternatively*, the trial court might have made an award of sanctions against Carole [Katleman] if it found her action to be in bad faith. (Code Civ. Proc., § 128.5; *Sheldon Appel Co. v. Albert & Oliker* (1989) 47 Cal. 3d 863, 873–874.) Additional remedies are unnecessary and inappropriate." (13 Cal. App. 4th at p. 67, fn. 8, italics added.)

3. Defendants also charge that under the *Bertero* rule the apportionment of damages between the theories of liability that are and are not supported by probable cause is difficult and "highly speculative." There is no showing, however, that juries cannot perform that task fairly and consistently if they are properly instructed—they draw more subtle distinctions every day. Moreover, any difficulty in this regard is chargeable to the tortfeasor. * * *

III

"The elements of the common law malicious-prosecution cause of action have evolved over time as an appropriate accommodation between the freedom of an individual to seek redress in the courts and the interest of a potential defendant in being free from unjustified litigation." (*Oren Royal Oaks Venture v. Greenberg, Bernhard, Weiss & Karma, Inc.* (1986) 42 Cal. 3d 1157, 1169 [232 Cal. Rptr. 567, 728 P.2d 1202].) When the prior action charged multiple grounds of liability and there was probable cause for some grounds but not for others, the question arises whether the malicious prosecution plaintiff has satisfied the requirement of showing that the prior action was brought without probable cause. We have seen that neither the statutes enacted nor the cases decided since *Bertero*, *supra*, 13 Cal. 3d 43, satisfactorily answer this question. Instead the solution lies in identifying the competing policies at work and in determining which preponderates when applied in the circumstances of the case at bar.

Defendants identify the two main policies that are served by the remedy of imposing sanctions for frivolous or delaying conduct in the original action (hereafter the sanc-

---

12. Finally, we understand that trial courts may be more reluctant to charge litigants or attorneys appearing before them with bad faith than juries to whom such persons are total strangers. The case at bar presents a striking example of this phenomenon. * * *

tions remedy): (1) it encourages free access to the courts for the settlement of disputes, and (2) it avoids burdening the judicial system by additional litigation. (*See Sheldon Appel, supra,* 47 Cal. 3d at pp. 872–873.)

* * * Defendants assert that the judicial burden caused by a subsequent malicious prosecution action is greater than the burden of defending against groundless theories of recovery in the original action. In some cases this may be true; but in other cases — and we must accept the complaint's allegations that this is such a case — to mount a defense against multiple baseless and malicious grounds may well be no less onerous than to mount a defense against separate causes of action. This is because the burden of litigating such grounds depends on such diverse factors as how many grounds are asserted, how different are the facts that must be proved to support and defeat them, how extensive is the discovery necessary to develop those facts, how many witnesses and documents are required to make that proof — even, indeed, how thoroughly the parties prepare their case and how vigorously they present and oppose it at trial. In light of these variables the most we can fairly say is that the two "judicial burden" policies tend to equalize in the balance, i.e., that the judicial cost of a subsequent malicious prosecution action is not necessarily greater than that of defending against multiple baseless and malicious grounds in the original action.

We are therefore remitted to comparing the first pair of policies stated above: we must decide which weighs more in this context — (1) the policy of encouraging free access to the courts, served by the sanctions remedy, or (2) the policy of redressing the harm suffered by individuals compelled to defend against unjustifiable litigation, served by the tort remedy.

It is true that untrammeled access to the courts promotes social peace by providing the citizenry with an alternative to potentially dangerous self-help methods of redressing private grievances. But it is not an unmixed blessing: many of our courts are burdened by overcrowded dockets and long delays, and all litigation exacts both public and private costs. We are willing as a society to incur those burdens and costs when the litigation is well founded or, even when ultimately unsuccessful, was at least initiated with probable cause and without malice. In those circumstances the balance tips in favor of the policy of encouraging judicial access. That policy becomes counterproductive, however, when it operates to promote litigation that is groundless and motivated by malice; such litigation has no place in our judicial system, and we are therefore unwilling to bear its costs.

After careful consideration, we see no reason to reach a different result when the litigation in question is the assertion of baseless and malicious grounds of liability in a single lawsuit: in both instances the balance tips in favor of the policy of making whole the individuals harmed by such abuse of our courts. * * *

For all these reasons we reaffirm the rule of *Bertero, supra,* 13 Cal. 3d 43, as the law governing the issue presented by this case.

The judgment of the Court of Appeal is affirmed.

ARABIAN, JUSTICE, dissenting.

* * *

A malicious prosecution suit imposes substantial litigation costs on both the litigants and the courts — not least because malice is such a highly factual issue that it often precludes summary disposition. It is for these reasons, among others, that we have made it clear that the policies controlling the availability of the malicious prosecution tort action transcend the interest in protecting the defendant in the prior lawsuit from having to defend against spurious claims and make it a "disfavored" cause of action that is "carefully circumscribed." In light of these concerns, I would not only reconsider the correctness of our holding in *Bertero v. National General Corp.* (1974) 13 Cal. 3d 43 [118 Cal. Rptr. 184, 529 P.2d 608, 65 A.L.R.3d 878] (*Bertero*), but would hold that where, as here, *alternative theories* of liability in support of a single *unitary right* are alleged by the plaintiff in the complaint in the first action and *one* of them is determined to have been supported by probable cause, the defendant in the first action may not pursue a derivative malicious prosecution claim. Instead, the defendant must rely on those sanctions for plaintiff's misconduct made available by statute in the original action. Such a result, of course, would require us to overrule our contrary holding in *Bertero*. * * *

[B] Lawyer Discipline

Among the duties of an attorney according to section 6068(c) of the California Business and Professions Code is "To counsel or maintain such actions, proceedings, or defenses only as appear to him or her legal or just...." Subsection (g) also counsels California lawyers: "Not to encourage either the commencement or the continuance of an action or proceeding from any corrupt motive of passion or interest." More recently, Rule 3-200 of the California Rules of Professional Conduct provides that a member of the California bar should not seek, accept or continue employment if he or she knows or should know that the client's objective is:

> (A) To bring an action, conduct a defense, assert a position in litigation, or take an appeal without probable cause and for the purpose of harassing or maliciously injuring any person; or

> (B) To present a claim or defense in litigation that is not warranted under existing law, unless it can be supported by a good faith argument for an extension, modification, or reversal of such existing law.

Violations of any one of these sections may result in discipline by the California State Bar. Disciplinary sanctions range from private reprovals (usually a private letter telling the lawyer what he did was wrong and not to do it again) through suspension and disbarment. *See* Business & Professions Code § 6078. While discipline helps the systemic interest in remedying and discouraging meritless litigation, and does so with a minimum of judicial involvement — it is handled by the State Bar unless the affected lawyer challenges the action and seeks review by the California Supreme Court — it does not provide much tangible compensation for the parties injured by the meritless litigation. The same is generally true of other sanction provisions. They are directed at the misbehaving lawyer, but are not intended to secure compensation. Examples include contempt proceedings—any monetary sanction is payable to the court—monetary sanctions payable to the county in which the court sits for violation of a lawful court order (CCP § 177.5), and sanctions for a frivolous appeal (CCP § 907).

[C] Statutory Sanctions under Code of Civil Procedure sections 128.5 and 128.7

Obviously, both traditional avenues for addressing meritless litigation have serious flaws. They are either consuming of the time of both courts and litigants (malicious prosecution) or relatively efficient, but without adequate compensatory mechanisms (discipline). In recent years, the courts and legislature have searched for a third alternative that would combine the best elements of both avenues. Currently, California has enacted statutes that copy federal practice under Rule 11 in the hope of finding the elusive golden mean.

As *Crowley* mentions, in 1981 the Legislature enacted Code of Civil Procedure section 128.5. This section authorizes trial courts to "order a party, the party's attorney, or both to pay the reasonable expenses, including attorney's fees, incurred by another party as a result of *bad faith actions or tactics* that are frivolous or solely intended to cause unnecessary delay." CCP § 128.5(a) [emphasis added]. To be considered frivolous, a bad faith action or tactic must be "totally and completely without merit or for the sole purpose of harassing an opposing party." § 128.5(b)(2). In addition, the California appellate courts have divided on the question of whether subjective bad faith is required in order to impose sanctions. Recent authority has been more supportive of a requirement that the action both lack any merit *and* have been brought for an improper purpose. *See Levy v. Blum*, 92 Cal. App. 4th 625, 112 Cal. Rptr. 2d 144 (2001); *Javor v. Dellinger*, 2 Cal. App. 4th 1258, 3 Cal. Rptr. 2d 662 (1992).

As a result of these limitations, in 1994 the Legislature added a new section 128.7 to the Code of Civil Procedure, applicable to pleadings and motions filed after January 1, 1995. Section 128.7 is patterned directly on Federal Rule of Civil Procedure 11, as amended in 1993. The section requires "[e]very pleading, petition, written notice of motion, or other similar paper shall be signed by at least one attorney of record in the attorney's individual name" or by a party not represented by an attorney. CCP § 128.7(a). The heart of the section, § 128.7(b), imposes on the attorney or party a series of "certifications" any time the attorney or party makes a "presentation" to the court:

(b) By presenting to the court, whether by signing, filing, submitting, or later advocating, a pleading, petition, written notice of motion, or other similar paper, an attorney or unrepresented party is certifying that to the best of the person's knowledge, information, and belief, formed after an inquiry reasonable under the circumstances, all of the following conditions are met:

(1) It is not being presented primarily for an improper purpose, such as to harass or to cause unnecessary delay or needless increase in the cost of litigation.

(2) The claims, defenses, and other legal contentions therein are warranted by existing law or by a nonfrivolous argument for the extension, modification, or reversal of existing law or the establishment of new law.

(3) The allegations and other factual contentions have evidentiary support or, if specifically so identified, are likely to have evidentiary support after a reasonable opportunity for further investigation or discovery.

(4) The denials of factual contentions are warranted on the evidence or, if specifically so identified, are reasonably based on a lack of information or belief.

[1] "Safe Harbor" Rule

Like the current version of federal Rule 11, sanctions are discretionary with the court, not mandatory upon finding a violation of one of the certifications. Also like Rule 11, there is a "safe harbor" provision. A party served with a motion for section 128.7 sanctions ordinarily has 21 days in which to withdraw or correct the challenged paper before the motion is filed. CCP § 128.7(c)(1); *see* § 128.7(c)(2) (21-day "safe harbor" also applies to a court's motion). Sanctions are "limited to what is sufficient to deter" repetition of the conduct. Paying the injured party's attorneys fees as a sanction is limited to specified circumstances and when "warranted for effective deterrence." § 128.7(d); *see Peake v. Underwood*, 227 Cal. App. 4th 428, 173 Cal. Rptr. 3d 634 (2014) (affirming $60,000 award to defendant for attorney fees incurred in defending plaintiff's frivolous action). Under section 128.7(d) sanctions may be made payable to the court. *See Kane v. Hurley*, 30 Cal. App. 4th 859, 35 Cal. Rptr. 2d 809 (1994), and *Levy v. Blum, supra*, 92 Cal. App. 4th at 635–638, for thorough discussions of this issue and sections 128.5 and 128.7 generally; and *Marriage of Schnabel*, 30 Cal. App. 4th 747, 36 Cal. Rptr. 2d 682 (1994), for a discussion of the imposition of sanctions, pursuant to CCP § 907, for a frivolous appeal.

[2] Voluntary Dismissal to Avoid Section 128.7 Sanctions

The "safe harbor" provision of CCP § 128.7(c)(1) requires that the party seeking sanctions follow a two-step procedure. First, the party must serve a notice of motion for sanctions on the offending party at least 21 days before filing the motion with the court, which specifically describes the sanctionable conduct. Service of the motion on the offending party begins a 21-day safe harbor period during which the sanctions motion may not be filed with the court. If the pleading is withdrawn, the motion for sanctions may not be filed with the court. If the pleading is not withdrawn, the motion for sanctions may then be filed. *See Levy v. Blum*, 92 Cal. App. 4th 625, 637, 112 Cal. Rptr. 2d 144 (2001).

If a plaintiff's complaint is dismissed during the 21-day safe harbor period, either voluntarily or involuntarily, the trial court no longer has the authority to award sanctions under § 128.7(c)(1). *See, e.g., Hart v. Avetoom*, 95 Cal. App. 4th 410, 115 Cal. Rptr. 2d 511 (2002); *Malovec v. Hamrell*, 70 Cal. App. 4th 434, 82 Cal. Rptr. 2d 712 (1999). The *Hart* court observed that allowing a party to serve and file a sanctions motion after the conclusion of the case would completely defeat the purpose of the safe harbor provision. How so? What is the purpose of the safe harbor provision? Does the trial court still have the authority to award sanctions under § 128.7(c)(1) when the offending pleading or motion is resolved by the trial court before the full 21-day safe harbor period has expired. *See Li v. Majestic Industry Hills LLC*, 177 Cal. App. 4th 585, 99 Cal. Rptr. 3d 334 (2009) (collecting cases indicating an award of sanctions in such circumstances is improper); *Banks v. Hathaway, Perrett, Webster, Powers & Chrisman*, 97 Cal. App. 4th 949, 118 Cal. Rptr. 2d 803 (2002) (ruling an order sustaining a demurrer without leave to amend does not bar a motion for § 128.7 sanctions unless the order is reduced to a judgment before the sanctions motion is served and filed).

Does a plaintiff's voluntary dismissal of his action with prejudice, after defendant's motion for § 128.7 sanctions has been filed and taken under submission, deprive the trial court of authority to grant the motion and impose sanctions on plaintiff for filing an improper complaint? *See Eichenbaum v. Alon*, 106 Cal. App. 4th 967, 131 Cal. Rptr. 2d 296 (2003) (noting the availability of § 128.7 sanctions against an offending plaintiff who has voluntarily dismissed his action depends upon whether the sanctions motion was filed before or after dismissal). Is a motion for sanctions served before, but filed after, entry of judgment moot where the service and filing complied with the safe harbor provision of CCP § 128.7(c)(1)? *See Day v. Collingwood*, 144 Cal. App. 4th 1116, 50 Cal. Rptr. 3d 903 (2006) (ruling the trial court had jurisdiction to consider postjudgment motion for sanctions).

§ 3.04 Fees and Fee Agreements

[A] Fee Agreements, Generally

High on the list of initial concerns for both lawyer and client is the matter of the lawyer's fee. Although essentially all civil litigation matters involve a negotiated fee arrangement between a client who is free to choose whether to be represented by the lawyer and a lawyer who is free to accept or reject the client matter, the amount of the lawyer's fee and the form of the fee agreement are subject to regulation by law and ethical restrictions.

California's Rules of Professional Conduct prohibit lawyers from "enter[ing] into an agreement for, charg[ing], or collect[ing] an illegal or unconscionable fee." Cal. Rules of Prof. Conduct 4-200(A). This rule provides only a series of factors for evaluating whether a fee is unconscionable "on the basis of all the facts and circumstances" at the time of the agreement. *See Shaffer v. Superior Court*, 33 Cal. App. 4th 993, 39 Cal. Rptr. 2d 506 (1995) (ruling the determination of whether client got what he paid for and therefore of whether attorney's fee was conscionable must be based on Rule 4-200 factors and not upon either the attorney's costs or profit margin).

Furthermore, virtually all California lawyers' fee agreements must be in writing. Bus. & Prof. Code section 6147 requires contingent fee agreements with plaintiffs to be in writing. Section 6148 requires a written fee agreement in all other cases, "in which it is reasonably foreseeable that the total expense to a client, including attorney fees, will exceed" $1,000.00. Other than a very minor fixed fee case, it is difficult to find a matter that does not require a written agreement under these two sections. Both sections 6147 and 6148 contain many other required provisions for fee agreements, including certain disclosures regarding the lawyer's malpractice coverage. You will be well advised to study these sections in detail. Failure to comply with these provisions renders the fee agreement voidable at the client's option, with the lawyer limited to collecting a "reasonable fee." Bus. & Prof. Code §§ 6147(b), 6148(c). The State Bar has developed a series of sample fee agreements for use in litigated matters. *See* CEB, *Fee Agreement Forms Manual* (2d ed. 2016)

Rule 2-200(A)(1) of the California Rules of Professional Conduct provides that a member of the State Bar "shall not divide a fee for legal services with a lawyer who is not a partner of, associate of, or shareholder with the member unless.... [t]he client has consented in writing thereto...." In *Chambers v. Kay*, 29 Cal. 4th 142, 126 Cal. Rptr. 2d 536, 56 P.3d 645 (2002), the Supreme Court held the plaintiff attorney's noncompliance with Rule 2-200(A)(1)'s written client consent requirement precluded plaintiff from obtaining a share of contingent fees pursuant to a fee-sharing agreement with co-counsel. *See also Fletcher v. Davis*, 33 Cal. 4th 61,14 Cal. Rptr. 3d 58, 90 P.3d 1216 (2004) (ruling an attorney who wishes to secure payment of hourly legal fees by obtaining a charging lien against the client's future recovery must obtain the client's consent in writing). Subsequently, however, in *Huskinson & Brown, LLP v. Wolf*, 32 Cal. 4th 453, 9 Cal. Rptr. 3d 693, 84 P.3d 379 (2004), the Supreme Court held that noncompliance with Rule 2-200A)(1) does not bar a plaintiff attorney from recovering a portion of those fees based on a quantum meruit award.

[B] Statutory Limits on Contingent Fees

In addition to the general prohibition against unconscionable fees, in personal injury actions against health care providers (typically medical malpractice actions), lawyers' contingent fees are limited by statute to 40% of the first $50,000; 33-1/3% of the next $50,000; 25% of the next $500,000; and 15% of the amount in excess of $600,000. Bus. & Prof. Code § 6146(a). The constitutionality of these contingent fees limits, which are part of the Medical Injury Compensation Reform Act ("MICRA"), was upheld in *Roa v. Lodi Med. Group, Inc.*, 37 Cal. 3d 920, 211 Cal. Rptr. 77, 695 P.2d 164 (1985). These MICRA limits apply "regardless of whether the recovery is by settlement, arbitration, or judgment," Bus. & Prof. Code § 6146(a); they cannot be waived by a client. *Fineberg v. Harney & Moore*, 207 Cal. App. 3d 1049, 255 Cal. Rptr. 299 (1989). MICRA prohibits an attorney from either contracting for or collecting a contingent fee in excess of the statutory limits in a medical malpractice case. Bus. & Prof. Code § 6146.

An attorney who collects fees in violation of MICRA must, of course, refund the excess fees. More significantly, an attorney's willful failure to comply with the limitations constitutes a breach of ethical duty which may result in serious disciplinary action by the State Bar. *See, e.g., In the Matter of David M. Harney*, 3 Cal. State Bar

Ct. Rptr. 226 (Rev. Dept. 1995) (State Bar Court placed prominent medical malpractice attorney on probation for two years on conditions, including six months actual suspension, for gross negligence in collecting a fee which exceeded the MICRA limits by $266,850; and observed that if it had found the attorney's violation had occurred through intentional dishonesty rather than gross neglect, disbarment would have been the appropriate discipline).

Chapter 4

Statutes of Limitations, Laches, and Related Matters

§4.01 Introductory Note

Developments in the Law—Statutes of Limitations

63 Harvard L. Rev. 1177, 1185-86 (1950)[*]

Purposes of Statutes of Limitations

When the legislature prescribes time limits on the assertion of rights, it deprives one party of the opportunity, after a time, of invoking the public power in support of an otherwise valid claim. So firmly have statues of limitations become imbedded in our law in the course of centuries that legislatures seldom reconsider them in the light of the various functions that they actually perform; the delicate process of adjustment is left to rationalization and interpretation by the courts. The primary consideration underlying such legislation is undoubtedly one of fairness to the defendant. There comes a time when he ought to be secure in his reasonable expectation that the slate has been wiped clean of ancient obligations, and he ought not to be called on to resist a claim when "evidence has been lost, memories have faded, and witnesses have disappeared." Another factor may be an estimate of the effectiveness of the courts, and a desire to relieve them of the burden of adjudicating inconsequential or tenuous claims. While these considerations run throughout the law of limitations, other collateral purposes may be important in the consideration of legislation affecting particular parties and particular types of claims.

In ordinary private civil litigation, the public policy of limitations lies in avoiding the disrupting effect that unsettled claims have on commercial intercourse. The particular period selected, however, often varies with the degree of permanence of the evidence required to prove either liability or extent of damage; sometimes it indicates the relative favor with which the legislature looks upon certain types of claims or certain classes of plaintiffs or defendants. * * *

The relative importance of statutes of limitations in implementing these various purposes will vary with the effectiveness of other legal institutions subserving the same ends. For instance, a workable Statute of Frauds, strict rules of evidence, and trained triers of fact may be more effective safeguards against the dangers of stale ev-

---

[*] Copyright 1950 by Harvard Law Review. Reprinted with permission.

idence than are arbitrarily fixed time periods. An efficient title registration system would better protect the bona fide purchaser of land than the law of adverse possession, with all its exceptions and qualifications. And a sufficiently responsible class of public officials might be enough to insure the criminal and the taxpayer against willfully delayed prosecution. Nevertheless, the certainty of the fixed time periods clearly serves the interests of everyone, for even plaintiffs benefit from a sure knowledge of the time after which a suit would be futile.

Legal Malpractice

Ronald E. Mallen & Jeffrey M. Smith

Vol. 3, § 24:3 to § 24:4 (2011 ed.)[*]

Recurring Problems — Time Limitations

The most frequently alleged error in a legal malpractice action is the failure of the attorney to comply with a time limitation. No matter the area involved, the practice of law is interwoven with requirements that acts must be performed within a specified period of time.[1] Although most of these limitations are obvious and well known, some have esoteric or uncertain meaning.

The ABA statistics show that the litigation attorney is most susceptible to missing a time limitation. Often the error is the failure to sue before the statute of limitation bars the claim. If the action is filed, the attorney must diligently prosecute the action within the statutory period or bear the risk of a discretionary dismissal or, eventually, a mandatory dismissal. If a case is tried and lost, the attorney may fail to make a timely motion for a new trial or to pursue promptly an appeal. Even if the attorney achieves a favorable judgment, time limitations may impair the right to execute upon the judgment. * * *

There is a common belief that an attorney who missed a statutory time requirement was negligent. Some courts have even treated such a showing as negligence per se. Missed time limitations usually result from the failure to find out the correct date of the loss, an inadequate or nonexistent calendaring system, or inadvertence. The error, however, may relate to a judgmental decision in interpreting facts or uncertain issues of law. * * *

Whether the attorney was negligent usually presents a question of fact to be evaluated by the standard of care. Thus, the failure to act or the rendering of erroneous advice regarding a time limitation is negligent only if the attorney failed to exercise ordinary skill and knowledge. * * *

---

* Copyright 2011 by West Publishing Company. Reprinted with permission.

1. For example, in California the complexity and awesome numbers of statutes of limitations were apparent in a compendium which abstracted statutes of limitations even three decades ago. The digests included over 1500 statutes from 27 California State Codes. The study did not include the State's Administrative Code or any county or city ordinance or regulation. *See California Statutes of Limitations*, 7 Sw. U. L. Rev. 1 (1975). [This California survey has been updated several times, most recently in 29 Sw. U. L. Rev. 679-1178 (1998)].

Recurring Problems — Time Limitations — Statistics

There is a general belief that the largest single cause of legal malpractice claims is missed time limitations. The nearly 30,000 claims collected by the National Legal Malpractice Data Center of the ABA's Standing Committee on Lawyers' Professional Liability Committee substantiates that assumption. * * *

A lawyer or law firm should know those time limitations indigenous to the practice and should learn those deadlines on matters not routinely handled. Legal work in an unfamiliar area of law should begin with the lawyer ascertaining all applicable time limitations. Underlying some missed time limitations is the failure to investigate and ascertain appropriate parties or legal theories. Unfortunately, the revelation of such remedies is often accompanied by learning that a statute of limitations expired.

Generally speaking, a civil action in California must be commenced within a statutorily prescribed period "after the cause of action shall have accrued." CCP § 312. This seemingly straightforward definition masks a welter of interrelated issues. Once a practitioner understands these issues there is little excuse for "missing" a statute of limitations.

The first of these issues is what statutory limitation period applies to a particular cause of action. Second is the question of when does a cause of action "accrue" such that the relevant statute of limitations begins to run. Third is whether any circumstances will toll or suspend the running of a limitation period after the cause of action has accrued. Fourth is when is an action considered to be "commenced" for purposes of satisfying a statute of limitations. A final issue is whether any mechanisms exist for extending the limitation period to permit joinder of new parties and causes of action after the lawsuit has commenced. Because of the importance of statutes of limitations to California practitioners, this chapter analyzes each of these issues in some detail.

The history of California statute of limitations law might be summarized as follows: The Legislature initially enacted rather short statutory time limitations for the commencement of categories of civil actions. Because these limitations often produced harsh results, the courts in effect lengthened them through a series of judicially created exceptions. More recently the Legislature has restricted these judicial exceptions with respect to certain specific causes of action. This process of judicial expansion and legislative contraction has taken place over the past few decades and continues today. *See* Stephen V. O'Neal, Note, *Accrual of Statutes of Limitations: California's Discovery Exceptions Swallow the Rule*, 68 Cal. L. Rev. 106 (1980).

§ 4.02 Ascertaining Applicable Time Limitation Periods

[A] Statutory Limitation Periods

The first step in resolving any statute of limitations problem is to ascertain the applicable statutorily prescribed limitation period. The Legislature has enacted specific statutory time limits for nearly every known cause of action. Sections 312–365 of the Code of Civil Procedure contain many of these limitations. However, numerous special limitation provisions are scattered throughout various other codes. *E.g.*, Civil Code § 1783 (action under Consumer Legal Remedies Act must be brought within 3 years); Commercial Code § 2725 (action for breach of contract for sale of goods, 4 years); Corporations Code § 25506 (action to enforce liability for prohibited practices in sales of securities); Government Code § 945.6 (action against public entity for which claim required); Insurance Code § 10350.11 (action to recover on group disability policy, 3 years); Labor Code § 5405 (worker's compensation proceedings, 1 year); Probate Code, § 9100 (creditor claims against decedent's estate); and Revenue and Taxation Code § 19371 (action by Franchise Tax Board to recover taxes due, 10 years). A brief survey indicates that nearly every California code contains at least some significant special statutes of limitations. *See California Statutes of Limitation*, 27 Sw. U. L. Rev. 679–1178 (1998), for a compendium of over 1500 of the California statutes of limitations.

[1] Statutory Classifications

The Code of Civil Procedure classifies limitation periods by several general methods. Perhaps the most common classification method is according to the substantive right involved in the action, such as libel (one year, CCP § 340(c)) or oral contract (two years, § 339). Many recent special statutes further limit this approach by also applying only to a specific category of defendants, such as actions for professional negligence against health care providers (§ 340.5) or attorneys (§ 340.6).

Another common method is classification based on the nature of the injury involved, such as personal injury (two years, CCP § 335.1) or injury to real property (three years, § 338(b)). Special statutes also may limit this approach to specific defendants, such as actions against developers for injury to real property due to latent defects (§ 337.15). A related method is classification based on the nature of the relief sought, such as actions for recovery of real property (CCP §§ 315–327).

A fairly safe assumption is that there is a statutorily prescribed limitation expressly covering every known cause of action. And if not expressly covered, the action may come under the four-year catch-all provision of CCP § 343.

[2] Categorizing Actions for Statute of Limitations Purposes

The process of finding the relevant statute of limitations usually means simply locating the specific code provision applicable to the cause of action. A lawsuit which involves several different causes of action requires that each one be analyzed separately as to the applicable limitation. The same set of facts may give rise to several distinct claims against several different defendants, some of which may be time-barred while others are not. *See, e.g., Krieger v. Nick Alexander Imports, Inc.*, 234 Cal. App. 3d 205, 285 Cal. Rptr. 717 (1991) (ruling in action for damages arising from alleged defective BMW, that causes of action based on negligence and breach of covenant of good faith were barred by applicable statutes of limitations, but those based on breach of warranty and misrepresentation were allowed to proceed as timely filed); *Romano v. Rockwell International, Inc.*, 14 Cal. 4th 479, 59 Cal. Rptr. 2d 20, 926 P.2d 1114 (1996) (applying various statutes of limitations, as relevant, to issues of accrual of plaintiff's tort, contract, and FEHA counts in a wrongful discharge action).

Consequently, precisely what claims a plaintiff decides to bring, and to some extent how a plaintiff decides to characterize them, will determine which statutes of limitations apply. Does this mean that artful pleading can be used to circumvent a statutory limitation? Regardless of the form of the pleading, a court will attempt to ascertain the substance of the action in determining the relevant statute of limitations. For example, in *Hatch v. Collins*, 225 Cal. App. 3d 1104, 275 Cal. Rptr. 476 (1990), the plaintiffs characterized their complaint as "breach of fiduciary duty" and "breach of contractual obligation" in order to come under the four-year limitation period applicable to such actions by CCP § 343 and § 337. However, the Court of Appeal viewed the complaint as essentially one for fraud and therefore governed by the three-year limitation period of CCP § 338. The court then concluded that plaintiffs' complaint, filed approximately 3-1/2 years after the action accrued, was barred. *See also Hensler v. City of Glendale*, 8 Cal. 4th 1, 22–23, 32 Cal. Rptr. 2d 244, 876 P.2d 1043 (1994) (ruling the statute of limitations applicable to inverse condemnation action is determined by the "gravaman" of the cause of action; "The nature of the right sued upon and not the form of action nor the relief demanded determines the applicability of the statute of limitations under our code").

Sometimes the substance of a claim is easy to determine, but still difficult to categorize for statute of limitations purposes. In *Beasley v. Wells Fargo Bank, N.A.*, 235 Cal. App. 3d 1383, 1 Cal. Rptr. 2d 446 (1991), for example, a class of credit cardholders sought refund of late fees collected by the defendant Bank, on the grounds that these fees were assessed pursuant to an invalid liquidated damages provision in the credit card agreement. Plaintiff's class action did not seek refund based on the written contract, but instead on an implied promise arising out of the contract. Is plaintiffs' recovery subject to the two-year statute of limitations for an action on an unwritten contract, CCP § 339(1), or the four-year statute for an action on a written contract, CCP § 337(1)?

A statute of limitations bars a cause of action commenced after the limitations period has expired. May it also bar a *defense* to a cause of action? *See Styne v. Stevens*, 26 Cal. 4th 42, 109 Cal. Rptr. 2d 14, 26 P.3d 343 (2001) ("[A] defense may be raised at any time, even if the matter alleged would be barred by a statute of limitation if asserted as the basis for affirmative relief.").

[3] Statutory Overlap

The various statutory limitations are designed to be mutually exclusive. However, the legislative classification system sometimes results in overlap in statutory coverage. One such problem arises where a cause of action is covered by a general statute and a more specific conflicting statute. For example, a damage action against a doctor for injuries caused by negligence is literally covered by CCP § 335.1, which sets forth a two-year limitation for personal injury actions, and by CCP § 340.5, which contains a more complex scheme for medical malpractice actions based on negligence. Which statute controls? Not surprisingly, the more specific medical malpractice statute applies. *See Young v. Haines*, 41 Cal. 3d 883, 894, 226 Cal. Rptr. 547, 718 P.2d 909 (1988) ("The cardinal rule of statutory construction is to ascertain and give effect to the intent of the Legislature.... Section 340.5 is part of an interrelated legislative scheme enacted to deal specifically with all medical malpractice claims. As such, it is the later, more specific statute which must be found controlling over an earlier statute, even though the earlier statute would by its terms cover the present situation.").

This problem often arises in actions covered by general limitations in the Code of Civil Procedure and in some more specialized substantive code, such as the California Uniform Commercial Code. *E.g., Collection Bureau of San Jose v. Rumsey*, 24 Cal. 4th 301, 99 Cal. Rptr. 2d 792, 6 P.3d 713 (2000) (ruling the one-year limitations period of former CCP § 353 [now CCP § 366.2], specially applicable to surviving causes of actions on the liabilities of decedents by Probate Code § 13554, and not the four-year limitations period of CCP § 377 generally applicable to open book accounts, governs an action by a collection agency against a surviving spouse for recovery of the medical expenses of a deceased spouse's last illness). *Krieger v. Nick Alexander Imports, Inc.*, 234 Cal. App. 3d 205, 285 Cal. Rptr. 717 (1991) (concluding a breach of warranty action based on Song-Beverly Consumer Warranty Act governed by limitation in Commercial Code § 2725, not by CCP § 338(a) or § 337(1)).

A similar problem arises where an action is covered by two general statutes of limitations, one addressed to the nature of the injury and the other to the substantive right involved. In *Cardoso v. American Med. Sys., Inc.*, 183 Cal. App. 3d 994, 228 Cal. Rptr. 627 (1986), plaintiffs' action was for personal injuries caused by a malfunctioning prosthesis manufactured by the defendant. Defendant demurred, based on plaintiffs' failure to commence this personal injury action within one year as required by former CCP § 340(3). Plaintiffs contended that they stated a cause of action for breach of warranty governed by the longer limitations period for contract actions. The court held that the one-year limitation of former CCP § 340(3) applied because the action was for personal injury damages, regardless of whether the action was based on tort or contract.

The cause of action in *Cardoso* also came under the plain language of Commercial Code § 2725(1), which provides a four-year limitation for an "action for breach of any contract for sale" of goods, including breach of warranty. On what basis could the court in *Cardoso* properly conclude that former CCP § 340(3) controls instead of the more recent and specific Commercial Code § 2725(1)? *See Becker v. Volkswagen of America, Inc.*, 52 Cal. App. 3d 794, 798–802, 125 Cal. Rptr. 326 (1975), for a good discussion of legislative intent behind the enactment of Commercial Code § 2725.

Occasionally a cause of action is governed by the plain language of two special statutes of limitations. Does CCP § 340.5 (medical malpractice) or Government Code § 945.6 (tort claims against governmental entities) control where the plaintiff alleges injuries due to professional negligence by a county hospital? *See Torres v. County of Los Angeles*, 209 Cal. App. 3d 325, 333, 335–37, 257 Cal. Rptr. 211 (1989); *Anson v. Merced County*, 202 Cal. App. 3d 1195, 249 Cal. Rptr. 457 (1988). Which statute of limitations—CCP § 335.1, § 340.2, § 340.5, or Gov. Code §§ 945–950—applies where a plaintiff's physical disability is caused by negligent exposure to asbestos during surgery at a state-owned medical clinic?

[4] Various Specific Statutes of Limitations in the Civil Procedure and Other Codes

As indicated above, many of the civil statutes of limitations are contained in Sections 312–365 of the Code of Civil Procedure. These are too numerous and complex to summarize here, but some of the most frequently encountered ones are: CCP § 337, written contracts generally (4 years); § 337.15, construction defects (10 years); § 338, statutory liability, trespass, fraud, and pollution (3 years); § 339, oral contracts (2 years); § 366.2, outside time limit of one year for any type of claim against a decedent; § 340.2, exposure to asbestos; § 340.5, medical malpractice; and § 340.6, attorney malpractice.

Effective January 1, 2003, the statute of limitations for assault, battery, wrongful death, and personal injury actions "caused by the wrongful act or neglect of another," has been increased to two years. CCP § 335.1 (adopted 2002). The statute of limitations for other intentional torts, such as libel, slander, and false imprisonment, remains one year. CCP § 340. The shortest statute of limitations in this Code is 30 days to contest certain local assessments, CCP § 349. Which actions have the longest statutory limitation period? *See, e.g.*, CCP § 348 (recovery of money deposited with bank) and Civil Code § 3490 (public nuisances).

Several statutes of limitation are located in other codes. Some of the most important are: Commercial Code § 2725, four years to commence action for breach of contract for sale of goods; Government Code §§ 945–945.8, actions against public entities for money damages; and Government Code §§ 950–950.6 actions against public employees for injury, discussed in § 4.04 of this Chapter, *infra*.

Various federal statutes contain statutes of limitations applicable to federal causes of action. *See Federal Statutes of Limitation*, 26 Sw. U. L. Rev. 425-891 (1997), for a compendium of over 7000 federal statutes which contain special statutes of limitations governing specific claims. The Supremacy Clause, Article VI of the United States Constitution, may require the application of a federal limitation when a federal claim is brought in state court. *See, e.g.*, *White v. Moriarty*, 15 Cal. App. 4th 1290, 19 Cal. Rptr. 2d 200 (1993) (ruling in FDIC cases, state court must follow limitation period in 12 U.S.C. § 1821, not CCP § 337(1)); *California Aviation, Inc. v. Leeds*, 233 Cal. App. 3d 724, 284 Cal. Rptr. 687 (1991) (applying two-year federal bankruptcy limitations extension statute, 11 U.S.C. § 108(a), instead of one-year state limitation statute for attorney malpractice, CCP § 340.6(a)); *Angeles Chem. Co. v. Spencer & Jones*, 44 Cal. App. 4th 112, 51 Cal. Rptr. 2d 594 (1996) (holding the federal environmental statute's limitations period and later accrual date mandated by that statute's discovery rule preempted the 10-year maximum of CCP § 337.15, where claims were based on a latent construction defect that resulted in toxic contamination of plaintiff's property).

[B] Contractual Modification of Statutory Time Period

[1] Contractual Extension of Statutory Limitation Period

Section 360.5 of the Code of Civil Procedure authorizes contractual waiver of a statutory limitation period if "the waiver is in writing and signed by the person obligated." Section 360.5 limits the duration of this waiver to four years, renewable for another four years. A written contractual waiver executed prior to the running of a statutory limitation period extends the limitation for four years from the expiration of the statutory period, renewable for another four years. *California First Bank v. Braden*, 216 Cal. App. 3d 672, 264 Cal. Rptr. 820 (1989). Does an attorney's written waiver of a statute of limitations constitute waiver "signed by the person obligated" within the meaning of § 360.5? *See Carlton Browne & Co. v. Superior Court*, 210 Cal. App. 3d 35, 258 Cal. Rptr. 118 (1989), for an analysis of this question, including an excellent discussion of the principles of statutory construction. Note that Commercial Code § 2725(1) permits parties to agree to *shorten* the period of limitations in contracts for sale of goods, but prohibits agreements to *extend* the statutory period.

[2] Contractual Abridgement of Statutory Limitation Period

Parties to a contract may also agree to a shorter limitation period for commencement of an action than is permitted by an otherwise applicable statute. Such contractual limitations are generally enforced so long as the shortened limitation period is a reasonable one which manifests no undue advantage and no unfairness. *See Lawrence v. Western Mut. Ins. Co.*, 204 Cal. App. 3d 565, 251 Cal. Rptr. 319 (1988). How should a court determine the "reasonableness" of a shorter contractual limitation period? *See Ellis v. U.S. Security Assn.*, 224 Cal. App. 4th 1213, 169 Cal. Rptr. 752 (2014) (discussing various cases); *Moreno v. Sanchez*, 106 Cal. App. 4th 1415, 1429–34, 131 Cal. Rptr. 2d 684 (2003), reproduced *infra*.

Section 2071 of the Insurance Code expressly authorizes a contractual limitation period of one year for insurance contracts. Likewise, Section 2725(1) of the Commercial Code authorizes agreements by parties to a contract for sale of goods to reduce the statutory limitation period (four years) to not less than one year. A one-year contractual limitation period has been enforced as not unreasonable in light of § 2725(1), and, when included as an additional term in the acceptance of an offer, may not even be viewed as "materially altering" a contract between merchants within the meaning of § 2207 of the Commercial Code. *Therma-Coustics Mfg., Inc. v. Borden, Inc.*, 167 Cal. App. 3d 282, 213 Cal. Rptr. 611 (1985).

[C] Legislative Modification of Statutory Time Periods

[1] Abridgement of Time to Sue

The Legislature may, from time to time, modify the length of a statutory limitations period. Such amendments raise interesting questions of retroactive application. Where the Legislature *shortens* a limitations period, retroactive application is generally permissible provided the party still has a reasonable time within which to avail itself of the remedy before the shortened statute extinguishes the right to sue. *See, e.g., Coachella Valley Mosquito & Vector Control Dist. v. Cal. Public Employment Rel. Bd.,* 35 Cal. 4th 1072, 1091–92, 29 Cal. Rptr. 3d 234, 112 P. 3d 623 (2005); *Brown v. Bleiberg,* 32 Cal. 3d 426, 437, 186 Cal. Rptr. 228, 651 P.2d 815 (1982). What constitutes a reasonable amount of time? *See Coachella Valley Mosquito, supra* (observing that when necessary to provide a reasonable time to sue, a shortened limitations period may be applied prospectively so that it commences on the effective date of the statute, rather than on the date the cause of action accrued); *Rosefield Packing Co. v. Superior Court,* 4 Cal. 2d 120, 122–24, 47 P.2d 716 (1935) (noting the question is one of constitutional law, not one committed to the discretion of the trial court; and finding one-year period found reasonable).

[2] Enlargement of Time to Sue

A more complicated question arises when the Legislature *lengthens* a limitation period. Does the new, longer period apply to causes of action that would have been time-barred under the old statute? From a constitutional due process perspective, the courts seem to agree that the Legislature is free to revive a cause of action after the statute of limitations has expired, unless the passage of the statutory period creates a prescriptive property right such as in adverse possession. *See, e.g., Liebig v. Superior Court,* 209 Cal. App. 3d 828, 831–35, 257 Cal. Rptr. 574 (1989), relying on *Chase Sec. Corp. v. Donaldson,* 325 U.S. 304, 65 S. Ct. 1137, 89 L. Ed. 1628 (1945); *Gallo v. Superior Court,* 200 Cal. App. 3d 1375, 1383, 246 Cal. Rptr. 587 (1988) ("A potential defendant has no vested right in the sense of repose conferred by his knowledge a lawsuit against him appears to be barred; [t]he issue is one of fairness and of statutory construction, rather than constitutional right").

A new statute that enlarges the statutory limitations period applies to actions that are not already barred by the original limitations period at the time the new statute goes into effect. *See Quarry v. Doe I,* 53 Cal. 4th 945, 956–57, 139 Cal. Rptr. 3d 3, 272 P. 3d 977 (2012) (discussing the prospective application of enlarged limitation periods); *Andonagui v. May Dept. Stores Co.,* 128 Cal. App. 4th 435, 27 Cal. Rptr. 3d 145 (2005) (ruling the two-year statute of limitations for personal injury action in CCP § 335.1 applies to actions not already time-barred by the one-year statute of limitations in former CCP § 340(3) when § 335.1 became effective on January 1, 2003). However, where the application of a new or amended statute of limitations would have the effect of reviving lapsed claims—claims as to which the limitations period expired before the new or amended statute became law—the general rule against retroactive application of a statute is applicable in the absence of express language to the contrary. *Quarry v. Doe I. supra,* 53 Cal. 4th at 957 ("Lapsed claims will not be considered revived without express language of revival"); see, e.g., *Liebig v. Superior Court, supra,* (concluding the 1986 amendment to CCP § 340.1, which expressly revives time-barred causes of action for childhood sexual abuse, applied retroactively); *David A. v. Superior Court,* 20 Cal. App. 4th 281, 24 Cal. Rptr. 2d 537 (1993) (construing ambiguous 1990 amendments to CCP § 340.1 as insufficient to demonstrate that the Legislature intended those amendments to revive lapsed childhood sexual abuse claims).

When the Legislature expressly provides that such an amended statute of limitations applies retroactively, can it revive an action that was previously filed by the plaintiff but dismissed pursuant to the earlier statute of limitations? *See Perez v. Roe*, 146 Cal. App. 4th 171, 52 Cal. Rptr. 3d 762 (2006) (holding the Legislature's attempt to revive plaintiffs' childhood sexual abuse actions violated the separation of powers doctrine because final judgments of dismissal had been entered in earlier actions under based on the statute of limitations previously in effect).

[D]   Calculation of Statutory Time Period

Section 12 of the Code of Civil Procedure states that "[t]he time in which any act provided by law is to be done is computed by excluding the first day, and including the last, unless the last day is a holiday, and then it is also excluded." Consequently, the day on which a cause of action accrues is excluded in computing the limitation period. *SCT, U.S.A. Inc. v. Mitsui Mfr. Bank*, 155 Cal. App. 3d 1059, 1065, 202 Cal. Rptr. 547 (1984). If the last day for commencement is a holiday, the period is extended to and including the next day not a holiday. CCP § 12a. Saturdays and Sundays are deemed holidays per CCP § 10 and § 12a; as well as any day a city, county, state or public office, other than a branch office, is closed, insofar as the business of that office is concerned. CCP §§ 12b, 135.

Certain additional holidays are specified by statute. *E.g.*, Gov. Code §§ 6700, 6701. The existence of a holiday at the end of the statutory period can mean the difference between a barred action and a viable one. *E.g.*, *Mink v. Superior Court*, 2 Cal. App. 4th 1338, 4 Cal. Rptr. 2d 195 (1992) (holding plaintiff's motion for relief from dismissal granted based on plaintiff's excusable mistake in discovering that ten-year statute of limitations had not run because period ended on a weekend, followed by a Monday holiday).

§ 4.03 Accrual of a Cause Of Action

[A]   The General California "Discovery" Rule

The first step in resolving a statute of limitations problem, as discussed above, is to ascertain the length of the statutorily prescribed period for a cause of action. Section 312 of the Code of Civil Procedure then requires that the action be commenced within that period after the cause of action has "accrued." The next question is to determine when a cause of action has "accrued" such that the statutory limitation period begins to run. This question can be quite complex in California. Surprisingly, the Code of Civil Procedure does not provide a general definition of "accrual" applicable to all statutes of limitations. Instead, the California courts have traditionally provided the general rules regarding accrual, as our principal case below illustrates. More recently, however, the Legislature has defined the accrual point for certain specific causes of action, such as medical malpractice, CCP § 340.5; legal malpractice, CCP § 340.6(a); childhood sexual abuse, CCP § 340.1(a); injury due to exposure to asbestos, CCP § 340.2; and breach of contract for sale of goods, Com. Code § 2725(2).

Jolly v. Eli Lilly & Company

Supreme Court of California
44 Cal. 3d 1103, 245 Cal. Rptr. 658, 751 P.2d 923 (1988)

PANELLI, JUSTICE.

This case presents the following questions: whether a plaintiff, in a suit for personal injury caused by a defective drug, who is unaware of any specific facts establishing wrongful conduct on the part of any drug manufacturer, may delay bringing an action until she discovers such facts; whether a claim, otherwise barred by the statute of limitations, can be revived due to our decision in *Sindell v. Abbott Laboratories* (1980) 26 Cal. 3d 588 [163 Cal. Rptr. 132, 607 P.2d 924], in which we held that a plaintiff who is unable to identify the particular manufacturer of a fungible drug that caused injury to her can state a claim by joining defendants who manufactured a substantial percentage of the market share of the allegedly defective drug; and whether the filing of the class action in *Sindell, supra,* tolled the statute of limitations for members of the putative class until the class was denied certification. We answer these questions in the negative and so conclude that the suit is time-barred.

I. *Facts*

Plaintiff Jolly was born in 1951. In 1972, she first learned that while she was in utero her mother had ingested the synthetic drug estrogen diethylstilbestrol (DES) for the prevention of miscarriage. Plaintiff was told in 1972 that DES daughters could suffer injuries. Therefore, she went to a DES clinic at the UCLA Medical Center for a checkup. She was diagnosed as having adenosis, a precancerous condition that required careful monitoring. In 1976, she had an abnormal pap smear and underwent a dilation and curettage, a surgical procedure to remove abnormal tissue. In 1978, plaintiff underwent a complete hysterectomy and a partial vaginectomy in order to remove malignancy. As of 1972, plaintiff was aware, or at least suspected, that her condition was a result of her mother's ingestion of DES during pregnancy.

Starting in 1972, plaintiff attempted to discover the manufacturer of the DES ingested by her mother. Efforts were increased in 1976 and 1978 when plaintiff's condition became acute. Unfortunately, the doctor who prescribed the drug had died, and plaintiff was unable to locate his records. Although the dispensing pharmacist did remember filling the DES prescription, he did not recall or have records pertaining to the specific brand used. This was not unusual since DES was a fungible drug, that is, hundreds of pharmaceutical companies made DES from a single agreed formula. The hospital where plaintiff was born was of no assistance because plaintiff's mother did not use DES while there.

At least as of 1978, plaintiff was aware of the pendency of one or more DES suits alleging that DES manufacturers were liable to those injured due to their failure to test or failure to warn. Although she believed that DES had caused her injuries and that those who marketed DES had wrongfully marketed a defective product, there is no conclusive evidence in the record to show that a reasonable investigation by plaintiff in 1978 would have disclosed specific proven facts that would establish any wrongful conduct on the part of a DES drug manufacturer. In fact, even today defendants allege that DES is not defective, but for purposes of summary judgment have admitted the allegation of some defectiveness.

Further, plaintiff believed that she had no cause of action if she could not identify the particular manufacturer of the drug her mother took during pregnancy. Because her efforts to identify that manufacturer were unsuccessful, plaintiff did not file suit.

In March 1980, we decided *Sindell v. Abbott Laboratories, supra*, 26 Cal. 3d 588, and held that if a plaintiff could not identify the precise drug manufacturer of the ingested DES, she could state a cause of action against the DES manufacturers of a substantial percentage of the market share of the drug. Defendants would be liable, assuming the remaining material allegations in the complaint were proven, unless they could disprove their involvement. Almost one year after *Sindell*, plaintiff Jolly brought this action.

Defendants moved for summary judgment, asserting that the action was barred by Code of Civil Procedure [former] section 340, subdivision (3),[2] setting forth a one-year statute of limitations period for an action "for injury ... caused by the wrongful act or neglect of another." Although conceding the applicability of the one-year statutory period, plaintiff denied that the suit was time-barred. She asserted that the statute did not commence until she learned of the *Sindell* decision, because only then did she realize that she would be able to successfully bring her claim.

Plaintiff maintained that *Sindell* created a new cause of action by redefining "causation." Prior to *Sindell*, she claimed, only the specific manufacturer of the pills that were ingested was deemed to have "caused" the injury. After *Sindell*, according to plaintiff, it was the generic drug DES that "caused" the harm, and therefore all DES manufacturers were tortfeasors.

The trial court granted defendants' motion and entered judgment in their favor. The Court of Appeal reversed, relying on its earlier decision in *Kensinger v. Abbott Laboratories* (1985) 171 Cal. App. 3d 376 [217 Cal. Rptr. 313]. The Court of Appeal did not address Jolly's main argument, that the statute could not begin to run until after our decision in *Sindell, supra*, except by way of a footnote declining to adopt her position. We granted defendants Eli Lilly and Company, Rexall Drug Company, and E.R. Squibb and Sons, Inc.'s subsequent petition for review.

---

2. [Effective January 1, 2003, the one-year statute of limitations for personal injury actions in former CCP § 340(3) was increased to two years by new CCP § 335.1.] All further statutory references are to the Code of Civil Procedure unless otherwise indicated.

II. *The Kensinger Decision*

As previously noted, both sides agree that the one-year limitations period of section 340, subdivision (3) applies to this case. Both sides also agree that the common law rule, that an action accrues on the date of injury (*Lambert v. McKenzie* (1901) 135 Cal. 100, 103 [67 P. 6]), applies only as modified by the "discovery rule." The discovery rule provides that the accrual date of a cause of action is delayed until the plaintiff is aware of her injury and its negligent cause.[4] (*Sanchez v. South Hoover Hospital, supra,* 18 Cal. 3d 93, 99). A plaintiff is held to her actual knowledge as well as knowledge that could reasonably be discovered through investigation of sources open to her. (*Id.* at p. 101). The parties differ as to what constitutes sufficient knowledge to start the statute running.

The Court of Appeal applied *Kensinger, supra,* 171 Cal. App. 3d 376, a factually similar case, and found that it was a question of fact as to whether the statute of limitations began to run more than one year before plaintiff Jolly filed her complaint. The *Kensinger* court acknowledged the well established rule that ignorance of the legal significance of known facts or the identity of the defendant would not delay the running of the statute—only ignorance of one or more "critical facts" could have that effect. (171 Cal. App. 3d at p. 383).

However, the key point in *Kensinger* was its determination that one "critical fact" was knowledge of some wrongful conduct. Specifically, the court held that a plaintiff may have "no knowledge of facts indicating wrongdoing by a particular defendant. In such a situation, litigation might be premature for lack of knowledge of any *factual basis* for imputing fault to a manufacturer rather than ignorance of supportive legal theories.... Knowledge of the occurrence and origin of harm cannot necessarily be equated with knowledge of the factual basis for a legal remedy...." (171 Cal. App. 3d at pp. 383–384; italics added). Accordingly, the *Kensinger* court held that the statutory clock did not begin to tick until the plaintiff knew or reasonably should have known of the facts constituting wrongful conduct, as well as the fact of her injury and its relation to DES. The Court of Appeal, applying *Kensinger,* held that it could not be said that "as a matter of law" Jolly was or should have been aware of *facts* establishing wrongdoing, e.g., "either failure to test or failure to warn," until within one year of the date she filed suit.

The rule proposed in *Kensinger* goes too far.[6] Under the discovery rule, the statute of limitations begins to run when the plaintiff suspects or should suspect that her

---

4. Defendants argue that the statute should commence when the plaintiff knows of her injury and its factual cause. Although that position has been adopted in some jurisdictions (*see e.g., United States v. Kubrick* (1979) 444 U.S. 111 (1979), it is not the rule in California [cites].

6. We recognize that some jurisdictions have adopted rules similar to that set out in *Kensinger.* (*See, e.g., Anthony v. Abbott Laboratories* (R.I. 1985) 490 A.2d 43 (relied on in *Kensinger*); *Dawson v. Eli Lilly & Co.* (D.D.C. 1982) 543 F. Supp. 1330; *Lopez v. Swyer* (1973) 62 N.J. 267 [300 A.2d 563]). However, as will be shown, the rule in California is otherwise.

injury was caused by wrongdoing, that someone has done something wrong to her.[7] As we said in *Sanchez* and reiterated in *Gutierrez*, the limitations period begins once the plaintiff " 'has notice or information of circumstances to put a reasonable person on inquiry.... ' " * * * A plaintiff need not be aware of the specific "facts" necessary to establish the claim; that is a process contemplated by pretrial discovery. Once the plaintiff has a suspicion of wrongdoing, and therefore an incentive to sue, she must decide whether to file suit or sit on her rights. So long as a suspicion exists, it is clear that the plaintiff must go find the facts; she cannot wait for the facts to find her.

For example, in *Miller v. Bechtel Corp.* (1983) 33 Cal. 3d 868 [191 Cal. Rptr. 619, 663 P.2d 177], we held that plaintiff was barred by the statute of limitations from pursuing her suit for fraud, even though she filed suit soon after she discovered facts confirming her long-held suspicion that her former husband had concealed the true worth of his assets during dissolution negotiations. We noted that the plaintiff had doubts at the time she signed the dissolution agreement as to the actual value of her husband's Bechtel stock. However, neither she nor her attorney took adequate steps then to investigate the matter. Years later, when the stock was sold for an amount well beyond that stated during the dissolution discussions, plaintiff brought suit. We held that her early suspicion put her on inquiry notice of the potential wrongdoing, which an investigation would have confirmed. Her failure timely to investigate barred the action. This conclusion was reached over a strong dissent, in which it was argued that the statute of limitations should not begin to run until plaintiff discovered the *facts* constituting the misconduct—her mere suspicion was not enough.

Another case in point is *Gray v. Reeves* (1978) 76 Cal. App. 3d 567. In *Gray*, a plaintiff suffered an allergic reaction to a drug in 1971, but delayed filing suit against the prescribing doctor and manufacturer until 1973. The Court of Appeal affirmed the trial court's award of summary judgment for defendants based on the statute of limitations. The court noted plaintiff's admission that in 1971 he knew that defendants "did something wrong." Even without specific facts as to why the drug was defective, plaintiff was on notice at that time that he had a potential cause of action. (*See also Graham v. Hansen* (1982) 128 Cal. App. 3d 965, 972–973 [180 Cal. Rptr. 604] ["If plaintiff believes because of injuries she has suffered that someone has done something wrong," the statutory period begins]).

The foregoing is fully consistent with the policy of deciding cases on the merits as well as the policies underlying the statute of limitations. In *Davies v. Krasna* (1975) 14 Cal. 3d 502, 512 [121 Cal. Rptr. 705, 535 P.2d 1161, 79 A.L.R. 3d 807], we held that the fundamental purpose of the statute is to give defendants reasonable repose, that is, to protect parties from defending stale claims. A second policy underlying the statute is to require plaintiffs to diligently pursue their claims. Because a plaintiff is under a duty to reasonably investigate and because a suspicion of wrongdoing, coupled with a knowledge of the harm and its cause, will commence the limitations

---

7. In this context, "wrong," "wrongdoing," and "wrongful" are used in their lay understanding.

period, suits are not likely to be unreasonably delayed, and those failing to act with reasonable dispatch will be barred. At the same time, plaintiffs who file suit as soon as they have reason to believe that they are entitled to recourse will not be precluded.[8]

While resolution of the statute of limitations issue is normally a question of fact, where the uncontradicted facts established through discovery are susceptible of only one legitimate inference, summary judgment is proper. In this case it is clear that application of the discovery rule supports the trial court's judgment. Plaintiff stated that as early as 1978 she was interested in "obtaining more information" about DES because she wanted to "make a claim"; she felt that someone had done something wrong to her concerning DES, that it was a defective drug and that she should be compensated.[9] She points to no evidence contradicting her candid statements. Thus, plaintiff is held to her admission; she suspected that defendants' conduct was wrongful during 1978 — well over a year before she filed suit. This suspicion would not have been allayed by any investigation. To the contrary, a timely investigation would have disclosed numerous articles concerning DES and many DES suits filed throughout the country alleging wrongdoing.

Plaintiff's contention that our decision in *Sindell* redefined "causation" and "wrongful," providing the crucial "fact" necessary for her to suspect wrongdoing, is without merit. *Sindell, supra*, 26 Cal. 3d 588, is fully discussed below. At this point it is necessary only to point out the oft-stated rule that it is the discovery of facts, not their legal significance, that starts the statute. All of the facts set out in *Sindell* that are relevant to plaintiff's case were either already known by her in 1978 or could have been discovered through a reasonable investigation.[11] Indeed, plaintiff admits that she learned of no new facts between 1978 and 1980.

---

8. To the extent that *Kensinger, supra*, 171 Cal. App. 3d 376, conflicts with the foregoing, it is disapproved. Of course, nothing stated herein affects the well-established rule that the ignorance of the legal significance of known facts or the identity of the wrongdoer will not delay the running of the statute.

9. Specifically, the following dialogue was contained in plaintiff's deposition and was part of the motion for summary judgment:

Q: "Why at that time were you interested in obtaining more information [about the DES ingested by plaintiff's mother]?
A: "To see if I had any type of recourse.
Q: "You mean in terms of making a claim or recovering from someone for your injury?
A: "Sure, yes.
Q: "In 1978 did you feel that you should have some kind of recourse?
A: "Yes.
Q: "You felt that someone had done something wrong to you?
A: "Yes.
Q: "And that you should be compensated for it?
A: "Yes.
Q: "You believed at that time, in 1978, that DES was a defective drug, is that right?
A: "Yes."

11. This case does not present us with a situation where the plaintiff conducted a prompt investigation and brought suit as soon as the results of the investigation were known, but even so filed her claim after the limitations period had expired. In such a situation, the cause of action might still be

In sum, the limitations period begins when the plaintiff suspects, or should suspect, that she has been wronged. Here, plaintiff suspected as much no later than 1978. Because she did not file suit until 1981, her suit, unless otherwise saved, is time-barred.[12]

III. *The Effect of Sindell*

Plaintiff's major argument, which was summarily rejected by the trial court and the Court of Appeal, is that our landmark decision in *Sindell v. Abbott Laboratories, supra,* constituted the "fact" that activated the statute. Plaintiff does not dispute the general rule that ignorance of the identity of the defendant does not affect the statute of limitations. However, she asserts that the rule does not apply to the facts of her case.

Plaintiff contends that prior to *Sindell*, the defective "product" was defined as the specific DES pills her mother ingested. Consequently, plaintiff could not establish a causal link between any particular manufacturer and her injury. She argues that *Sindell* redefined the defective "product" as generic DES, making all manufacturers of DES contributors to her injury. Thus, now she is able to establish a causal link between the harm suffered and defendants.

Defendants reply that this was not the intended effect of *Sindell*. They argue that *Sindell* merely shifted from plaintiff to defendants the burden of proving which manufacturer's drug caused plaintiff's injury.

There is merit in both contentions. *Sindell* is more than a mere "burden shifting" case. Although based in part on *Summers v. Tice* (1943) 33 Cal. 2d 80 [199 P.2d 1, 5 A.L.R. 2d 91], *Sindell* went beyond that precedent.[14] In *Sindell* we noted that all DES manufacturers presumptively contributed to the alleged injury in that DES was a generic drug, manufactured from an agreed formula. Hence, all DES manufacturers shared in the alleged societal wrong. We held that between an innocent plaintiff and a group of allegedly negligent defendants, one of whom probably caused the injury, the latter should bear the costs of the harm, and we were willing to fashion a new remedy to meet that goal. Therefore, we imposed liability on defendants even though there was a significant possibility that the manufacturer of the particular pills ingested by a plaintiff's mother was not a party to the suit.

At the same time, we did not create an entirely new tort, nor identify a new "product." *Sindell* merely bridged the causal gap between DES manufacturers as a group and plaintiff's injury. Where the actual manufacturer of the ingested DES is unknown, causation by joined manufacturers of a substantial share of the DES that a plaintiff's mother might have taken would be presumed, subject, of course, to each drug man-

---

timely. (*See Whitfield v. Roth* (1974) 10 Cal. 3d 874, 887–889 [112 Cal. Rptr. 540, 519 P.2d 588] [concerning the 100-day period set forth in the Government Tort Claims Act]).

12. Plaintiff's failure to file suit despite her suspicion of wrongdoing is not surprising in the context of this case. By her own admission, her real reason for delaying action was that she did not know *whom* to sue, not that she did not know *whether* to sue.

14. In *Summers*, we held that an innocent plaintiff who could not identify which of two negligent hunters shot him, but was sure that one of them was the culprit, could bring suit by joining both. The burden then shifted to each defendant to show that he did not cause the injury.

ufacturer's ability to rebut the presumption by proving that the actual pills in question were not its product.

* * *

From the foregoing, it is clear that *Sindell* did not provide plaintiff with the critical "fact" that started the limitations period. Nor did it create a new tort with an independent starting date for purposes of the statute of limitations. Rather, *Sindell* demonstrated the legal significance of facts already known to plaintiff. The statute had started to run for plaintiff well before *Sindell* was decided.

At a less legalistic but more fundamental level, plaintiff argues, with some persuasive force, that prior to *Sindell* she could not have prevailed on her suit. She notes that during the time that defendants argue her action would have been timely, *McCreery v. Eli Lilly & Co., supra,* (overruled by *Sindell, supra*) effectively barred her claim. In *McCreery*, the Court of Appeal held that a plaintiff who could not identify the precise manufacturer of the pills ingested by her mother did not allege a cause of action. Plaintiff undoubtedly fell into this group. The response to plaintiff's contention is that a change in the law, either by statute or by case law, does not revive claims otherwise barred by the statute of limitations.

The seminal case on point is *Monroe v. Trustees of the California State Colleges* (1971) 6 Cal. 3d 399 [99 Cal. Rptr. 129, 491 P.2d 1105]. Professor Monroe was fired from the California State College system for failing to take a loyalty oath. The statute requiring the oath was held constitutional in *Pockman v. Leonard* (1952) 39 Cal. 2d 676 [249 P.2d 267]. In view of that case, Professor Monroe did not seek judicial review of the state's action within the statutory period. We overruled *Pockman* in *Vogel v. County of Los Angeles* (1967) 68 Cal. 2d 18 [64 Cal. Rptr. 409, 434 P.2d 961], and declared the statute unconstitutional.

Shortly thereafter, Professor Monroe brought suit in part for back wages. We held that this portion of Professor Monroe's suit was untimely because a change in the law applied only to timely filed claims; the change could not revive claims already barred by the statute of limitations. Although prior to *Vogel*, Professor Monroe was effectively precluded from bringing his claim, it was not "impossible" for him to do so. We held that "no legal obstacle barred a judicial challenge to [his] initial discharge" and that the "mere existence of a contrary precedent has never been considered sufficient to toll the statute of limitations." Precedent is in unanimous accord with this rule.

In all of the above-cited cases, the court recognized that the rule may work a harsh result. Nonetheless, it is justified in three ways. First, the rule encourages people to bring suit to change a rule of law with which they disagree, fostering growth and preventing legal stagnation. Second, the statute of limitations is not solely a punishment for slow plaintiffs. It serves the important function of repose by allowing defendants to be free from stale litigation, especially in cases where evidence might be hard to gather due to the passage of time. Third, to hold otherwise would allow virtually unlimited litigation every time precedent changed. For example, in *Li v. Yellow Cab Co.* (1975) 13 Cal. 3d 804 [119 Cal. Rptr. 858, 532 P.2d 1226, 78 A.L.R. 3d 393], this court held that contributory negligence was not a total bar to recovery. There were undoubtedly thousands of potential plaintiffs through the years who had been reasonably advised to the contrary by competent counsel and so failed to bring suit. Nevertheless, allowing them all to sue within a year after the *Li* decision would have been untenable. Courts simply are not equipped to handle cases dating back many years, eventually brought because the law has changed. This prohibition against revival of claims can obviously create a hardship on such unfortunate plaintiffs (and a windfall to fortunate defendants). However, the hardship is no greater than that incurred by plaintiffs who received an adverse final judgment based on the "old" law and are barred from relitigating their case by res judicata. * * *

Moreover, in early 1978, plaintiff's legal situation was not as dismal as it initially appears. First, she was in no worse a position than Judith Sindell, who ultimately prevailed in changing the law. Second, there were other, more traditional theories available on which plaintiff could base her lawsuit, such as civil conspiracy or joint liability under *Summers v. Tice, supra.* While it is true that these theories were not clearly meritorious (indeed they were ultimately rejected by us in *Sindell*), they did provide plaintiff with a nonfrivolous cause of action. Although in the latter part of 1978, *McCreery, supra,* appeared to foreclose such a suit, that case was an intermediate appellate court decision. In this regard, the last word on the subject had not been spoken, and other Courts of Appeal were free to disregard that case. Therefore, plaintiff was not entirely forestalled, even as a practical matter, from bringing a timely suit.

Finally, even without using any of the above theories, plaintiff could have filed a timely complaint under section 474, which allows suit to be filed against a Doe party. From the time such a complaint is filed, the plaintiff has three years to identify and serve the defendant. Hence, in the instant case, plaintiff could have brought a timely Doe action, effectively enlarging the statute of limitations period for three years. Had she done so, her complaint would have been pending when *Sindell, supra,* was decided.

In sum, plaintiff's argument that *Sindell* created or revived her cause of action must fail. * * *

Conclusion

The judgment of the Court of Appeal is reversed. The cause is remanded with instructions to affirm the judgment of the trial court in favor of defendants.

Fox v. Ethicon Endo-surgery, Inc.

Supreme Court of California
35 Cal. 4th 797, 27 Cal. Rptr. 3d 661, 110 P. 3d 914 (2005)

MORENO, JUSTICE.

Plaintiff Brandi R. Fox filed a medical malpractice action after gastric bypass surgery performed on her resulted in severe complications. In the course of discovery, Fox received information that a medical device used during the surgery may have malfunctioned, causing her injury. Fox then amended her complaint to add a products liability cause of action against the manufacturer of the device, Ethicon Endo-Surgery, Inc. (Ethicon). Ethicon filed a demurrer raising a statute of limitations defense, to which plaintiff responded by relying upon the delayed discovery rule most recently discussed by this court in *Norgart v. Upjohn Co.* (1999) 21 Cal.4th 383 [87 Cal. Rptr. 2d 453, 981 P.2d 79] (*Norgart*).

Plaintiff alleges that she could not, with reasonable investigation, have discovered earlier that the medical device might have caused her injury. We granted review to determine whether such an allegation is sufficient to withstand demurrer, or whether we should adopt the bright-line rule announced in *Bristol-Myers Squibb Co. v. Superior Court* (1995) 32 Cal. App. 4th 959, 966 [38 Cal. Rptr. 2d 298] (*Bristol-Myers Squibb*), that "[w]hen a plaintiff has cause to sue based on knowledge or suspicion of negligence the statute [of limitations] starts to run as to *all* potential defendants."

We conclude that, under the delayed discovery rule, a cause of action accrues and the statute of limitations begins to run when the plaintiff has reason to suspect an injury and some wrongful cause, unless the plaintiff pleads and proves that a reasonable investigation at that time would not have revealed a factual basis for that particular cause of action. In that case, the statute of limitations for that cause of action will be tolled until such time as a reasonable investigation would have revealed its factual basis. We disapprove the decision in *Bristol-Myers Squibb v. Superior Court, supra*, 32 Cal.App.4th 959, to the extent that it holds to the contrary.

I. FACTS AND PROCEDURAL HISTORY

On April 10, 1999, respondent Brandi R. Fox underwent Roux-en-Y gastric bypass surgery and postsurgical treatment.[1] The operation was performed by Dr. Herbert Gladen. During the surgery, Fox was under general anesthesia and unconscious. Fox went home following the surgery, but returned soon after the surgery because she felt ill.

Fox's condition worsened, moving Dr. Gladen to perform exploratory surgery a few days after the gastric bypass operation. The exploratory surgery revealed a perforation at the stapled closure of the small intestine, which caused fluid to leak into Fox's abdominal cavity. Dr. Gladen attempted to seal the perforation. In his operative report for the exploratory surgery, Dr. Gladen failed to identify a cause for the perforation. Fox required additional medical care and remained hospitalized until March 4, 2000.

On April 6, 2000, Fox served Dr. Gladen, and the hospital and medical center in Fresno where the surgery and subsequent care took place, with a notice of intent to commence action pursuant to Code of Civil Procedure section 364. Fox filed a complaint for medical malpractice against the doctor and the treating hospitals in Fresno County

---

1. Gastric bypass surgery, used to treat morbid obesity, makes the stomach smaller and allows food to bypass part of the small intestine. In a Roux-en-Y gastric bypass, the stomach is made smaller by creating a small pouch at the top of the stomach with surgical staples or a plastic band. The smaller portion of the stomach is connected directly to the middle portion of the small intestine (jejunum), bypassing the rest of the stomach and the upper portion of the small intestine (duodenum).

Superior Court on June 28, 2000. In her complaint, Fox claimed that "[d]efendants lacked the necessary knowledge and skill to properly care for [her] condition and were negligent and unskillful in the diagnosis, treatment, and prescription procedures utilized in treating [her] condition. The negligence claimed is for negligently performing pre-surgical, surgical, and post-surgical care so as to cause injuries and damages to ... Fox."

Fox named as defendants Dr. Gladen, the hospital and medical center, and Does 1 to 100, inclusive. The complaint alleged that "the defendants named herein as DOES 1 through 100, inclusive, were the agents, servants, and employees of each of the remaining defendants, and in doing the things hereinafter alleged, were acting within the course and scope of their authority as such agents, servants, or employees, and with the permission and consent of their codefendants."

When Fox deposed Dr. Gladen on August 13, 2001, the doctor testified that he had discovered a leak at the stapled closure of Fox's small intestine during the exploratory surgery. He further noted that the bowel had been stapled with an "Ethicon GIA-type stapler," that the hospital had furnished the stapler, and that he had found on previous occasions that such a stapler had caused postsurgery leaks.

Accordingly, on November 28, 2001, Fox filed a first amended complaint adding the manufacturer of the stapler, Ethicon, as a named defendant. In the first amended complaint, Fox asserted a products liability cause of action against Ethicon, alleging that she was injured by an "Ethicon GIA-type stapler" on or about April 10, 1999. Fox used a Judicial Council form for products liability causes of action, specifying counts for strict liability relating to the design, manufacture, and assembly of the stapler, negligence, and breach of implied warranty. The first amended complaint also alleged that Fox "did not discover, nor suspect, nor was there any means through which her reasonable diligence would have revealed, or through which she would have suspected the Ethicon GIA-type stapler as a cause of her injury until the deposition of [Dr. Gladen] was taken on August 13, 2001."

Ethicon demurred to the first amended complaint, contending that the products liability claim was time-barred by the one-year statute of limitations under Code of Civil Procedure former section 340, former subdivision 3. In opposition, Fox noted that she had no knowledge that the gastric bypass surgery would involve the use of a stapler or any similar device.

Fox further stated that she never learned during the postsurgical care following the gastric bypass operation that the stapler had malfunctioned or could have caused the leakage and other problems, and that she first discovered the possibility of a stapler malfunction when her counsel notified her of Dr. Gladen's deposition testimony. Finally, Fox offered to file a second amended complaint to clarify the facts supporting her assertion that she had no reason to suspect the stapler until after Dr. Gladen's testimony, and that no reasonable person would have suspected that the Ethicon product had malfunctioned.

Fox's attorney also filed a declaration stating that neither the operative report nor the reparative operative report indicated that the stapler had malfunctioned or misfired. The declaration also stated that Dr. Gladen's testimony was taken during the normal course of discovery in a medical malpractice lawsuit, Fox was reasonably diligent in pursuing the lawsuit and discovery, and Fox could allege that Dr. Gladen never mentioned a stapler malfunction or defect during the entire course of his post-surgical care.

On June 17, 2002, the superior court sustained Ethicon's demurrer to the products liability cause of action without leave to amend, relying upon *Norgart, supra,* 21 Cal.4th 383, and *Bristol-Myers Squibb, supra,* 32 Cal.App.4th 959, to conclude that the statute of limitations barred the products liability cause of action. The superior court stated that when a plaintiff sues based on knowledge or suspicion of negligence, including medical malpractice as in Fox's case, the statute of limitations begins to run as to all defendants, including manufacturers possibly liable under products liability theories. The superior court also stated that Fox failed to demonstrate that amending the complaint could "overcome the limitations defense." Fox timely appealed from the superior court's order sustaining Ethicon's demurrer as to the products liability cause of action.

The Court of Appeal reversed the superior court's order and remanded with directions to grant Fox leave to amend to allege facts explaining why she did not have reason to discover earlier the factual basis of her products liability claim. In so ruling, the Court of Appeal held that *Bristol-Myers Squibb*'s "bright line rule of imputed simultaneous discovery of causes of action" did not apply. Ethicon petitioned this court, and we granted review.

II. DISCUSSION

This case requires us to address once again the proper application of a statute of limitations. (See *Gutierrez v. Mofid* (1985) 39 Cal.3d 892 [218 Cal. Rptr. 313, 705 P.2d 886]; *Jolly v. Eli Lilly & Co.* (1988) 44 Cal.3d 1103 [245 Cal. Rptr. 658, 751 P.2d 923] (*Jolly*); *Bernson v. Browning-Ferris Industries* (1994) 7 Cal.4th 926 [30 Cal. Rptr. 2d 440, 873 P.2d 613] (*Bernson*); *Norgart, supra,* 21 Cal.4th at p. 395.) * * *

In order to rely on the discovery rule for delayed accrual of a cause of action, "[a] plaintiff whose complaint shows on its face that his claim would be barred without the benefit of the discovery rule must specifically plead facts to show (1) the time and manner of discovery *and* (2) the inability to have made earlier discovery despite reasonable diligence." (*McKelvey v. Boeing North American, Inc.* (1999) 74 Cal.App.4th 151, 160 [86 Cal. Rptr. 2d 645].) In assessing the sufficiency of the allegations of delayed discovery, the court places the burden on the plaintiff to "show diligence"; "conclusory allegations will not withstand demurrer." (*Ibid.*)

Simply put, in order to employ the discovery rule to delay accrual of a cause of action, a potential plaintiff who suspects that an injury has been wrongfully caused must conduct a reasonable investigation of all potential causes of that injury. If such an investigation would have disclosed a factual basis for a cause of action, the statute of limitations begins to run on that cause of action when the investigation would have brought such information to light. In order to adequately allege facts supporting a theory of delayed discovery, the plaintiff must plead that, despite diligent investigation of the circumstances of the injury, he or she could not have reasonably discovered facts supporting the cause of action within the applicable statute of limitations period.

Under the statute of limitations applicable to this case, a plaintiff must bring a cause of action for products liability within one year of accrual. (Code Civ. Proc., § 340, former subd. 3.)[3] Products liability claims brought under either negligence or strict liability theories are subject to delayed accrual under the discovery rule. (See *Fireman's Fund Ins. Co. v. Sparks Const., Inc.* (2004) 114 Cal.App.4th 1135, 1150 [8 Cal. Rptr. 3d 446].) Normally, the general rule for defining the accrual of a cause of action should govern a cause of action for products liability. (See *Norgart, supra,* 21 Cal.4th at p. 404.) For both negligence and strict liability products liability claims, the last element to occur is generally, as a practical matter, the injury to the future plaintiff.

Fox alleges that she was injured by an "Ethicon GIA-type stapler" on April 10, 1999. She timely filed her medical malpractice claim on June 28, 2000.[4] Her cause of action for products liability was alleged for the first time in the first amended complaint filed on November 28, 2001, more than one year after her injury. Accordingly, Fox's products liability action would only be timely if the discovery rule acted in some fashion to delay accrual of the cause of action.[5]

The Court of Appeal below applied the discovery rule to Fox's products liability claims against Ethicon, and ordered that the trial court judgment sustaining the demurrer without leave to amend be reversed and that the case be remanded to the trial court with directions to enter an order sustaining the demurrer with leave to amend the cause of action for products liability.

"On appeal from a judgment dismissing an action after sustaining a demurrer without leave to amend, … [t]he reviewing court gives the complaint a reasonable interpretation, and treats the demurrer as admitting all material facts properly pleaded." (*Aubry v. Tri-City Hospital Dist.* (1992) 2 Cal.4th 962, 966–967 [9 Cal. Rptr.

---

3. At present, the statute of limitations for an action for injury to an individual caused by the wrongful act or neglect of another must be commenced within *two* years from the date of accrual. (Code Civ. Proc., § 335.1.) This change was effected in 2002, when the Legislature found the one-year limitations period of section 340, former subdivision 3 "unduly short" and adopted a two-year period "to ensure fairness to all parties." (Stats. 2002, ch. 448, § 1.)

4. The one-year statute of limitations period for a medical malpractice action is set forth separately in section 340.5 of the Code of Civil Procedure. The limitations period prescribed by section 340.5 may be extended by 90 days under Code of Civil Procedure section 364,….

5. Even had Fox filed her products liability claim against Ethicon simultaneously with her medical malpractice claim on June 28, 2000, the claim would likely still have been untimely absent an application of the delayed discovery rule. Fox filed her medical malpractice claim slightly more than one year after her injury on April 6, 2000, due to the above mentioned 90-day extension afforded medical malpractice claims by Code of Civil Procedure section 364, subdivision (d). However, the 90-day extension of the limitations period provided by section 364,subdivision (d) is limited to claims "based upon" professional negligence (see *Preferred Risk Mutual Ins. Co. v. Reiswig* (1999) 21 Cal.4th 208, 218 [87 Cal. Rptr. 2d 187, 980 P.2d 895]), and would therefore not extend the limitations period for a products liability claim.

2d 92, 831 P.2d 317] (*Aubry*); *Blank v. Kirwan* (1985) 39 Cal.3d 311, 318 [216 Cal. Rptr. 718, 703 P.2d 58].) * * *

Here ... we must assume to be true Fox's allegations that she "did not discover, nor suspect, nor was there any means through which her reasonable diligence would have revealed, or through which she would have suspected the Ethicon GIA-type stapler as a cause of her injury until the deposition of [Dr. Gladen] was taken on August 13, 2001." In addition, we also consider whether any defect in the first amended complaint could have been cured by Fox's proposed amendment to that complaint, in which she would have stated that she had no reason to suspect the stapler until after Dr. Gladen's testimony, and that no reasonable person would have suspected that the Ethicon product had malfunctioned.

In order to employ the discovery rule to delay accrual of a cause of action, a plaintiff must demonstrate that he or she conducted a reasonable investigation of all potential causes of his or her injury. Fox has only partially met this requirement by alleging that there was no way "through which her reasonable diligence would have revealed, or through which she would have suspected the Ethicon GIA-type stapler as a cause of her injury" until August 13, 2001. Fox's first amended complaint was, as the Court of Appeal below held, insufficient to withstand demurrer because it failed to allege specific facts supporting the allegations quoted above. The defect in Fox's first amended complaint, however, could have been cured by the proposed amendment to that complaint.

Fox's proposed second amended complaint would have properly alleged that the products liability cause of action did not accrue until after the stapler malfunction was revealed during the deposition of Dr. Gladen. The facts that Fox seeks to add to her complaint support her allegation that she did not suspect, nor did she have reason to discover, facts supporting a products liability action against Ethicon until after deposing Dr. Gladen. Accordingly, we conclude that the Court of Appeal did not err in ordering the trial court to grant Fox leave to amend her complaint.[6]

Ethicon, however, contends that we should adopt the more restrictive *Bristol-Myers Squibb* formulation of the discovery rule. Ethicon does not argue that the *Bristol-Myers Squibb* formulation is mandated by this court's decisions, or that we have expressly or impliedly adopted it, but rather asserts that the *Bristol-Myers Squibb* approach is consistent with our formulation of the discovery rule in prior cases.

In *Bristol-Myers Squibb*, the plaintiff's silicone breast implant was ruptured in an altercation in 1982. Two years later, the plaintiff learned that the implant had ruptured, that silicone was migrating down her arm, and that the silicone was a cause of physical injury in the form of ulcerations. The plaintiff argued that because she had been told that silicone was an inert and harmless substance, she did not actually suspect the

---

6. Although we hold that plaintiff has shown that the defect in the products liability claim in her first amended complaint could have been cured, we express no opinion on plaintiff's ability to prove that she should not have earlier suspected that her injuries were caused by a defective stapler.

manufacturer of the implant of wrongdoing until after reading a newspaper article in late 1990.

The Court of Appeal held that the statute of limitations on the plaintiff's products liability cause of action against the manufacturers of her silicone breast implants began to run when the statute of limitations on her medical malpractice action commenced. (*Bristol-Myers Squibb, supra,* 32 Cal.App.4th at p. 967.) As the court stated: "[w]hen a plaintiff has cause to sue based on knowledge or suspicion of negligence the statute starts to run as to *all* potential defendants," regardless of whether those defendants are alleged as wrongdoers in a separate but related cause of action. (*Id.* at p. 966.)

We have neither approved nor disapproved the *Bristol-Myers Squibb* formulation.

* * *

In our previous cases addressing the discovery rule, we affirmed that ignorance of the identity of the defendant does not delay accrual of a cause of action, but that ignorance of a generic element of the cause of action does. (*Norgart, supra,* 21 Cal.4th at p. 399.) Such a distinction certainly exists in the context of a products liability action. Although the identity of the manufacturer-wrongdoer is not an essential element of a products liability cause of action, and therefore ignorance of its identity will not delay the running of the statute of limitations (see *Bernson, supra,* 7 Cal.4th at p. 932), a plaintiff's ignorance of wrongdoing involving a product's defect will usually delay accrual because such wrongdoing is essential to that cause of action. (See, e.g., *Clark v. Baxter Healthcare Corp.* (2000) 83 Cal.App.4th 1048, 1060 [100 Cal. Rptr. 2d 223] [triable issue of fact existed as to when plaintiff knew or suspected wrongfulness component of products liability cause of action].)

It is therefore consistent with our prior applications of the discovery rule to delay accrual of a products liability cause of action even when a related medical malpractice claim has already accrued, unless the plaintiff has reason to suspect that his or her injury resulted from a defective product. More broadly stated, if a plaintiff's reasonable and diligent investigation discloses only one kind of wrongdoing when the injury was actually caused by tortious conduct of a wholly different sort, the discovery rule postpones accrual of the statute of limitations on the newly discovered claim.

In both *Jolly* and *Norgart*, the plaintiffs suspected or had reason to suspect that a product had caused their injury. In *Jolly*, the plaintiff alleged injury caused by her mother's ingestion of the synthetic drug estrogen diethylstilbestrol (DES) while Jolly was *in utero*. The undisputed evidence in that case showed that, as of 1972, Jolly at least suspected that her condition was a result of her mother's ingestion of DES. Accordingly, we held that because the plaintiff at least suspected that DES was the cause of her injuries as of 1972, the statute of limitations began to run at that time, even though Jolly was unable to establish the identity of the manufacturer of the DES ingested by her mother.

Likewise, in *Norgart*, the daughter of the plaintiffs had committed suicide in her home by intentionally taking an overdose of prescription drugs, including Halcion.

We upheld the superior court's grant of summary judgment against the plaintiffs, reversing the Court of Appeal, and finding that the plaintiffs had reason soon after their daughter's death to discover their causes of action for wrongful death against Upjohn for manufacturing and distributing Halcion. More specifically, in *Norgart* we found that there was no triable issue of material fact and that Upjohn was entitled to judgment on the statute of limitations defense because the plaintiffs had reason to discover their cause of action against Upjohn soon after their daughter's death when they learned at that time of her depression and suicide by taking an overdose of prescription drugs, including Halcion. The plaintiffs also learned of a possible connection between Halcion and the suicide, because such connection was disclosed during the plaintiffs' investigation on the drug's package insert, which warned of a possible suicide risk.

This court's decisions in *Jolly* and *Norgart* each presuppose a situation in which the factual basis for a claim was reasonably discoverable through diligent investigation. In both *Jolly* and *Norgart*, the court emphasized that the plaintiffs had ample reason to suspect the basis of their claims. Indeed, the application of the discovery rule as articulated in this opinion would not have yielded a different result had it been applied in either *Jolly* or *Norgart*.

The Court of Appeal in *Bristol-Myers Squibb* failed to distinguish between a plaintiff's ignorance of the identity of a particular defendant—a fact that is not an element of the underlying cause of action—and ignorance that a product was the cause of the injury. In *Norgart*, we made clear that a cause of action accrues when a plaintiff has reason to discover "a factual basis" for the claim. The bright-line rule announced in *Bristol-Myers Squibb*, however, applies to all defendants regardless of whether those defendants are alleged as wrongdoers in the same cause of action, or in a separate but related cause of action alleging a wholly different kind of tortious wrongdoing.

As the allegations in this case illustrate, a diligent plaintiff's investigation may only disclose an action for one type of tort (e.g., medical malpractice) and facts supporting an entirely different type of tort action (e.g., products liability) may, through no fault of the plaintiff, only come to light at a later date. Although both claims seek to redress the same physical injury to the plaintiff, they are based on two distinct types of wrongdoing and should be treated separately in that regard. Accordingly, the *Bristol-Myers Squibb* rule that all claims arising from an injury accrue simultaneously, even if based upon distinct types of wrongdoing, is inconsistent with the generic elements approach prescribed by *Norgart*. We therefore agree with the Court of Appeal below that the *Bristol-Myers Squibb* formulation is inconsistent with the iteration of the discovery rule announced in this court's earlier decisions.

Ethicon contends that the formulation of the discovery rule used by the Court of Appeal is contrary to public policy because it would encourage plaintiffs to "wait for the facts." We disagree. A plaintiff seeking to utilize the discovery rule must plead facts to show his or her inability to have discovered the necessary information earlier despite reasonable diligence. This duty to be diligent in discovering facts that would delay accrual of a cause of action ensures that plaintiffs who do "wait for the facts" will be unable to successfully avoid summary judgment against them on statute of limitations grounds.

It would be contrary to public policy to require plaintiffs to file a lawsuit "at a time when the evidence available to them failed to indicate a cause of action." (*Leaf v. City of San Mateo* (1995) 104 Cal. App. 3d 398, 408 [163 Cal. Rptr. 711].) Were plaintiffs required to file all causes of action when one cause of action accrued, as they would be under the *Bristol-Myers Squibb* rule, they would run the risk of sanctions for filing a cause of action without any factual support. (Code Civ. Proc., § 128.5; see *Finnie v. Town of Tiburon* (1988) 199 Cal. App. 3d 1, 14 [244 Cal. Rptr. 581] [holding lack of factual basis for claim to be grounds for imposing sanctions].) Indeed, it would be difficult to describe a cause of action filed by a plaintiff, before that plaintiff reasonably suspects that the cause of action is a meritorious one, as anything but frivolous. At best, the plaintiff's cause of action would be subject to demurrer for failure to specify supporting facts. In sum, the interest of the courts and of litigants against the filing of potentially meritless claims is a public policy concern that weighs heavily against the *Bristol-Myers Squibb* formulation of the discovery rule.

III. DISPOSITION

The judgment of the Court of Appeal is affirmed.

Notes and Questions Regarding Accrual and the Discovery Rule

(1) *Accrual Rule, Generally.* The California Legislature has never enacted a general statute which defines the accrual point for all categories of civil actions. The traditional judicial statement of when a statute of limitations begins to run is "upon the occurrence of the last element essential to the cause of action." *Neel v. Magana, Olney, Levy, Cathcart & Gelfand*, 6 Cal. 3d 176, 187, 98 Cal. Rptr. 837, 491 P.2d 421 (1971). This rather vague definition of "accrual" evolved into the often-stated rule that a statute of limitations begins to run on the "date of injury." A fundamental component of this traditional common law rule was that accrual will not be delayed by the plaintiff's ignorance of the fact of injury or of the identity of the wrong-doer. *See* Stephen V. O'Neal, Note, *Accrual of Statutes of Limitations: California's Discovery Exceptions Swallow the Rule*, 68 CAL. L. REV. 106, 107 (1980).

As the *Jolly* case illustrates, the discovery rule now modifies the traditional common law date-of-injury rule. In its most basic form, the discovery rule alleviates the unfairness inherent in the traditional rule where a plaintiff, despite reasonable diligence, is unable to discover the fact of injury within the applicable limitations period. This unfairness is particularly acute when the applicable statute of limitations is a short one, such as the one-year period for personal injury actions in former CCP § 340(3). Not surprisingly, many of the early cases adopting the "discovery rule" are personal injury actions. *See* O'Neal, *Accrual of Statutes of Limitations, supra*, 106–116.

(2) *The California Discovery Rule.* In *Bristol-Myers Squibb Co. v. Superior Court*, 32 Cal. App. 4th 959, 38 Cal. Rptr. 2d 298 (1995), the court applied the *Jolly* "reasonable suspicion" formula expansively to bar a negligence action against the man-

ufacturer of silicone-gel-filled breast implants. Plaintiff Jones received two breast implants performed by her doctor in 1976. In 1982, Jones was involved in an altercation with another woman which resulted in severe battery to Jones' upper torso. Jones believed one of her implants had ruptured and that the silicone had migrated to her underarm. She saw her doctor for these symptoms in 1982, and was told that it was not possible for the silicone from a ruptured implant to be in her arm.

After consulting other physicians, Jones learned by 1984 that the silicone had in fact migrated down her arm and was causing serious physical injury. She also consulted an attorney at that time about a possible malpractice claim against her doctor and a battery action against her assailant, but did not commence litigation at that time. Subsequently in December, 1990, Jones read a newspaper article about a breast implant support group, and for the first time became suspicious that the manufacturer of her implants might be responsible for her injuries. She then filed her negligence action against the defendant manufacturer in April, 1991.

Applying the *Jolly* formula to these facts, the court held that plaintiff's action against the defendant manufacturer was barred by the applicable one-year statute of limitations. The court reasoned that plaintiff Jones knew of her injury and of the facts which would create a suspicion of negligence *on the part of someone* by 1984. The court rejected plaintiff's argument that, because she initially attributed her injuries to her batterer and her doctor, she had no basis for suspicion of wrongdoing by the defendant manufacturer until 1991, stating: "As *Jolly* teaches us, however, this excuse will not suffice. When a plaintiff has cause to sue based on knowledge or suspicion of negligence, the statute starts to run as to *all* potential defendants." *Id.* at 966.

Did the Supreme Court in *Fox v. Ethicon Endo-Surgery, Inc.* approve or disapprove of the holding in *Bristol-Myers Squibb*? How so? Precisely what aspect of *Bristol-Myers Squibb* did the *Fox* court criticize?

(3) The Supreme Court in *Jolly* rejected defendant's argument that the limitations period should commence when the plaintiff knows of her injury and its factual cause. What does defendant's argument mean? How is defendant's "factual cause" discovery rule different from the discovery rule ultimately endorsed by the court in *Jolly*? Under the defendant's argument, when did the plaintiff in *Jolly* discover her injury and its *factual* cause?

(4) *The Federal Discovery Rule.* The federal courts in construing the Federal Torts Claim Act have adopted the "factual cause" version of the discovery rule. In *United States v. Kubrick*, 444 U.S. 111, 100 S. Ct. 352, 62 L. Ed. 2d 259 (1979), plaintiff suffered loss of hearing in 1968 after antibiotic treatment of an infection of the femur at a Veterans Administration hospital. In January, 1969, a specialist informed Kubrick that his hearing loss may have been caused by the antibiotic treatment. Kubrick submitted a claim for disability benefits, which was denied by the VA because there was no evidence of negligence by the VA in administering the antibiotic. Finally on June, 1971 Kubrick learned from a doctor that not only did the antibiotic cause his deafness

but that it was negligently administered. Kubrick then commenced an action in federal court in 1972, pursuant to the Federal Torts Claim Act.

The United States Supreme Court held that Kubrick's lawsuit was barred by the applicable two-year statute of limitations. The court ruled that Kubrick's claim accrued in January, 1969, when he was aware of his injury and that it was caused by the antibiotic. The court expressly rejected the view that plaintiff's claim did not accrue until June, 1971, when he first learned that his injury was negligently inflicted. The court concluded that generally a claim against the government under the Federal Torts Claim Act accrues as soon as a plaintiff is aware of his injury and its cause, even though he does not reasonably suspect his injury was the result of negligence.

Would the plaintiff's action in *Kubrick* have been barred if the federal court applied the California version of the discovery rule as set forth in *Jolly*? Why did the federal court in *Kubrick* apply federal law and not state law in determining the appropriate discovery rule?

(5) The court in *Jolly* stated that "[t]he discovery rule provides that the accrual date of a cause of action is delayed until the plaintiff is aware of her injury and its negligent cause.... A plaintiff is held to her actual knowledge as well as knowledge that could reasonably be discovered through investigation of sources open to her." *Jolly*, 44 Cal. 3d at 1109. How is this statement of the discovery rule different from the rule utilized by the Court of Appeal in *Kensinger v. Abbott Lab.*, 171 Cal. App. 3d 376, 383–84, 217 Cal. Rptr. 313 (1985), which was disapproved by the Supreme Court in *Jolly*?

(6) "*Reasonable Suspicion.*" The Supreme Court in *Jolly* restated the discovery rule as follows: "Under the discovery rule, the statute of limitations begins to run when the plaintiff suspects or should suspect that her injury was caused by wrongdoing, that someone has done something wrong to her." *Jolly*, 44 Cal. 3d at 1110. What constitutes "reasonable suspicion"? Does this have anything to do with the relationship between the plaintiff and defendant prior to litigation? *See Miller v. Brechtel Corp.*, 33 Cal. 3d 868, 191 Cal. Rptr. 619, 663 P.2d 177 (1983) (concluding limitations period commenced to run at time of marital property settlement when plaintiff suspicious of her husband's undervaluation of certain stock, and not when she learned the stock's true value when husband sold stock several years later); *Sanchez v. South Hoover Hosp.*, 18 Cal. 3d 93, 101–102, 132 Cal. Rptr. 657, 553 P.2d 1129 (1976) (ruling patient has right to rely on a lesser standard of "diminished diligence" in discovery of wrongful treatment by physician while physician-patient relationship continues, but if plaintiff does not take physician's assurances at face value, then diminished duty to discover period may be terminated or attenuated).

Does what constitutes "reasonable suspicion" depend on the nature of the injury? *See Prudential-LMI Commercial Ins. v. Superior Court*, 51 Cal. 3d 674, 687, 274 Cal. Rptr. 387, 798 P.2d 1230 (1990) (noting the more substantial or unusual the nature of the damage discovered, the greater the duty to exercise diligence in investigation). The determination of when a plaintiff became aware of facts that would lead a reasonable person to suspect wrongdoing usually is a question of fact. *See, e.g., Rosas v.*

BASF Corp., 236 Cal. App. 4th 1378, 187 Cal. Rptr. 3d 354 (2015) (reversing summary judgment with respect to whether facts know by plaintiff with respect to his lung disease would lead a reasonable person to suspect a wrongful cause for his symptoms); *Alexander v. Exxon Mobile*, 219 Cal. App. 4th 1236, 162 Cal. Rptr. 3d 617 (2013) (reversing demurrer because allegations in complaint left room for reasonable differences of opinion as when plaintiffs should have reasonably suspected that their injuries were caused by wrongdoing).

(7) *"Constructive Suspicion."* In *Nelson v. Indevus Pharm., Inc.*, 142 Cal. App. 4th 1202, 48 Cal. Rptr. 3d 668 (2006), the plaintiff, a user of the prescription diet drug Fen-phen during 1997, brought a personal injury action against the defendant drug marketer in 2003 after the plaintiff had an echocardiogram. Although it was undisputed that the plaintiff did not know about the dangers of Fen-phen before the spring of 2002, the defendant argued that plaintiff's action was barred by the statute of limitations because of the wide-spread publicity about the drug's dangers in 1997. The court rejected defendant's "constructive suspicion" argument, and held that under the discovery rule plaintiff's cause of action did not accrue in 1997. The court noted that a patient who actually learns of the dangerous side effects of a drug she has taken ignores her knowledge at her peril, but the discovery rule only requires an investigation when a plaintiff has reason to investigate. However, the plaintiff here had no obligation to read newspapers or watch television news and otherwise seek out news of dangerous side effects not disclosed by her prescribing doctor or by the drug manufacturer. *See also Unruh-Haxton v. Regents of Univ. of California*, 162 Cal. App. 4th 343, 76 Cal. Rptr. 3d 146 (2008) (Trial court improperly took judicial notice of approximately 100 newspaper articles and press releases regarding defendant's wrongdoing when it determined that plaintiffs should have suspected wrongdoing; constructive suspicion based on publicity alone was insufficient to trigger the statute of limitations).

The *Nelson* court bolstered its conclusion by referring to CCP § 340.8, which provides the statute of limitations for any civil action for injury or illness based upon exposure to a hazardous material or toxic substance. Section 340.8 provides in part: "Media reports regarding the hazardous material or toxic substance contamination do not, in and of themselves, constitute sufficient facts to put a reasonable person on injury notice that the injury or death was caused or contributed to by the wrongful act of another." The *Nelson* court ruled that under its plain meaning § 340.8 applies to cases which allege personal injury caused by harmful chemicals, and not simply to actions concerning environmental hazards.

(8) *Actual Suspicion.* The discovery rule sets forth two alternate tests for triggering the limitations period: (1) a subjective test requiring actual suspicion by the plaintiff that the injury was caused by wrongdoing; and (2) an objective test requiring a showing that a reasonable person would have suspected the injury was cause by wrongdoing. *Jolly, supra*, 44 Cal. 4th at 1110. The first to occur under these two tests begins the limitations period. *Id.* What constitutes "actual suspicion"?

The court in *Kitzig v. Nordquist*, 81 Cal. App. 4th 1384, 97 Cal. Rptr. 2d 762 (2000), considered this question in the context of a patient who obtained a second opinion during ongoing medical treatment. Between 1992 and 1995, the defendant dentist in *Kitzig* performed eight dental implant surgeries on the plaintiff. After one of these surgeries in March, 1994, an implant failed and caused a hole in plaintiff's sinus, which she discovered after experiencing food escaping from her nose when she ate. Admittedly "suspicious" that the defendant may have done something wrong because she had a hole in her sinus, plaintiff consulted a second dentist in May, 1994. That doctor reassured plaintiff that the hole was not a significant issue and that everything was fine. Plaintiff then returned to the defendant for more implant surgeries and continued her treatment with him until April, 1995, when plaintiff began treatment with an oral surgeon because the implants kept failing. Plaintiff commenced a dental malpractice action against the defendant in 1996.

Relying on *Jolly*, the defendant in *Kitzig* argued that the plaintiff's malpractice action was not commenced within one year after plaintiff was actually suspicious of wrongdoing when she consulted another doctor in May, 1994, and was therefore barred by the statute of limitations (CCP § 340.5). A majority of the court rejected this argument, finding that under the circumstances plaintiff's suspicion in May, 1994 was not "meaningful" because it had no effect on her ongoing relationship with the defendant. "Holding that a second opinion necessarily triggers a malpractice statute of limitations whenever a patient is motivated by a possible suspicion — however momentary — that her doctor was 'doing something wrong,' the majority reasoned, 'would hinder a patient's ability to obtain the best medical care.'" *Kitzig, supra*, 81 Cal. App. 4th at 1393. The dissent viewed the majority's holding as ignoring *Jolly* and as contrary to plaintiff's unequivocal admission that over one year before she filed suit she suspected that the defendant did something wrong to her, prompting her to seek another dentist's opinion. *Kitzig*, 81 Cal. App. 4th at 1402–12.

Do you agree with the majority or the dissent in *Kitzig*? Under the majority's view of the subjective test for the discovery rule, what evidence would satisfy the requirement of "actual suspicion" by the plaintiff that the injury was caused by wrongdoing? Note that the medical malpractice statute of limitations (CCP § 340.5) does not contain an express tolling exception for "continuous representation," such as the one found in the legal malpractice statute of limitations (CCP § 340.6). Was this an oversight by the Legislature when it enacted § 340.5, or are there policy reasons for tolling the limitations period during the time of "continuous representation" as to legal malpractice actions but not as to medical malpractice actions? Does the lack of such a tolling provision for medical malpractice actions undercut the majority's holding in *Kitzig*?

(9) Does the discovery rule endorsed by the Supreme Court in *Jolly* encourage or discourage unnecessary litigation? Premature litigation? In what sense might litigation be "unnecessary" or "premature"? Is the version of the discovery rule applied by the Court of Appeal in *Kensinger* preferable because it delays litigation until more specific facts are known? In rejecting the *Kensinger* rule, what policies did the Supreme Court find more important to further?

(10) Note that the Supreme Court in *Jolly* did not modify the traditional common law rule that ignorance of the legal significance of known facts will not delay the

running of a statute of limitations. What does this mean? Does this mean that the statute will run even where a party diligently investigates facts but is advised by an expert that the facts do not constitute an actionable wrong? *See, e.g., Gutierrez v. Mofid*, 39 Cal. 3d 892, 218 Cal. Rptr. 313, 705 P.2d 886 (1985) (ruling that if one has suffered appreciable harm and suspects malpractice as its cause, the fact that an attorney has given discouraging advice does not postpone commencement of the limitations period; the risk that discouraging legal advice will lead to loss of a cause of action must fall upon the plaintiff who obtains the advice, rather than upon a wholly uninvolved defendant). Does *Jolly* signify that the statute will run even where the defendant misstates the viability of the legal theory supporting plaintiff's action? *See, e.g., Neff v. New York Life Ins. Co.*, 30 Cal. 2d 165, 180 P.2d 900 (1947). Even where the defendant is an insurance company that misrepresents the legal theory of policy coverage in denying a claim? *See Love v. Fire Ins. Exchange*, 221 Cal. App. 3d 1136, 271 Cal. Rptr. 246 (1990). Or where the plaintiff relies on the defendant's representations regarding legal advice, and a fiduciary relationship existed between plaintiff and defendant? *See Eisenbaum v. Western Energy Resources, Inc.*, 218 Cal. App. 3d 314, 267 Cal. Rptr. 5 (1990).

(11) Another important limitation of the discovery rule adopted in *Jolly* is the well-established rule that the ignorance of the identity of the wrongdoer will not delay the running of a statute of limitations. In other words, the statute of limitations begins to run when a plaintiff knows of her injury, its cause, and suspects wrongdoing, even though she does not know *who* caused her injury. This was particularly a problem for the plaintiff in *Jolly*, was it not? What procedural devices are available to a plaintiff who does not know which specific defendant to sue? Should the general rule apply when, as a result of the defendant's intentional concealment, the plaintiff is not only unaware of the defendant's identity but is effectively precluded as a practical manner from ascertaining it through normal discovery procedures? *See Bernson v. Browning-Ferris Indus.*, 7 Cal. 4th 926, 30 Cal. Rptr. 2d 440, 873 P.2d 613 (1994) (holding a defendant may be equitably estopped from asserting statute of limitations when, as the result of intentional concealment, the plaintiff is unable to discover defendant's actual identity), reproduced *infra*.

(12) Do you understand the plaintiff's main argument based on *Sindell?* Are you persuaded by the court's analysis that *Sindell* did not create a new tort? Prior to *Sindell*, could plaintiff have stated a cause of action without identifying the precise manufacturer of the pills ingested by her mother? What procedural devices could the plaintiff have utilized, prior to the *Sindell* decision, to avoid the running of the statute of limitations? *See* discussion of Doe Defendants, § 9.04, *infra*.

(13) How realistic is the Supreme Court's observation that plaintiff Jolly could have initiated timely litigation despite the adverse precedent of *McCreery v. Eli Lilly & Co.*, 87 Cal. App. 3d 77, 150 Cal. Rptr. 730 (1978), which was overruled by *Sindell?* Are you persuaded by the court's justification of the rule that the existence of contrary precedent has never been considered sufficient to toll the statute of limitations? Is a less harsh rule possible, which would still satisfy the policies behind the current rule?

Is there any way to distinguish *Monroe v. Trustees of the Cal. State Colleges,* 6 Cal. 3d 399, 99 Cal. Rptr. 129, 491 P.2d 1105 (1971), relied on by the Supreme Court for this rule, from the circumstances of the *Jolly* case? Relying on *Jolly,* the Supreme Court in *Howard Jarvis Taxpayers Assn. v. City of La Habra,* 25 Cal. 4th 809, 107 Cal. Rptr. 2d 369, 23 P.3d 601 (2001), reaffirmed the principle that a change in substantive case law governing a cause of action does not revive a claim otherwise barred by the statute of limitations.

(14) In *Fox v. Ethicon Endo-Surgery, Inc.,* reproduced *supra,* the Supreme Court broadly stated that "if a plaintiff's reasonable and diligent investigation discloses only one kind of wrongdoing when the injury was actually caused by tortious conduct of a wholly different sort, the discovery rule postpones accrual of the statute of limitations on the newly discovered claim." What constitutes "tortious conduct of a wholly different sort" for purposes of the delayed discovery rule?

(15) In *Fox,* the statute of limitations defense was raised by a demurrer to the plaintiff's amended complaint in which she alleged that she could not, with reasonable investigation, have discovered earlier that the medical device might have caused her injury. Accordingly, the court assumed the truth of her allegations and held that her amended complaint was not barred by the statute of limitations. Given the nature of plaintiff's injury, do you think she will have difficulty convincing a fact-finder that she could not have discovered earlier that the stapler was the source of her injury? What facts are relevant to the question of whether she could have discovered this source of her injury earlier "with reasonable investigation"? In addition to formal discovery, what avenues of reasonable investigation are available to someone who has suffered an injury like the plaintiff's post-surgery complications?

(16) The discovery rule has now been adopted in a wide variety of tort cases. *See* Steven J. Andre, *California Personal Injury Statutes of Limitations: The Modern Tort and the Judicial Abandonment of an Archaic Doctrine,* 27 Santa Clara L. Rev. 657 (1987). Although most of these cases involve personal injuries, some involve injury to property. *E.g., Moreno v. Sanchez,* 106 Cal. App. 4th 1415, 131 Cal. Rptr. 2d 684 (2003) (collecting cases); *CAMSI IV v. Hunter Tech. Corp.,* 230 Cal. App. 3d 1525, 282 Cal. Rptr. 80 (1991). The discovery rule also applies in contract cases where the breach occurred in secret and without immediately discoverable harm. *E.g., Gryczman v. 4550 Pico Partners, Ltd.,* 107 Cal. App. 4th 1, 131 Cal. Rptr. 2d 680 (2003); *April Enterprises, Inc. v. KTTV.* 147 Cal. App. 3d 805, 827, 195 Cal. Rptr. 421 (1983).

[B]   Developing Applications of the Discovery Rule

[1]   *Judicial Evolution*

The discovery rule is still in the process of judicial evolution as new applications require. For example, in *Evans v. Eckelman,* reproduced below, the court considered whether the discovery should apply to a tort action brought by plaintiffs against their foster parent for damages resulting from alleged sexual abuse of them as children. In

Moreno v. Sanchez, also reproduced below, the court applied the rule to an action brought by plaintiff buyers against a home inspector for failure to discover certain defects in the house the plaintiffs ultimately purchased.

Evans v. Eckelman

Court of Appeal of California, First Appellate District
216 Cal. App. 3d 1609, 265 Cal. Rptr. 605 (1990)

Low, Presiding Justice.

[Plaintiffs alleged abuse occurring in 1966–68, but did not file their action until 1987. The longest then applicable limitation period for sexual molestation was three years from the wrongful act. Although the statutory limitation period was tolled during plaintiffs' minority, all plaintiffs were adults by 1977. The Court of Appeal reviewed the history of the discovery rule in California, and noted that two common themes ran through the cases applying this rule of delayed accrual.]

Two common themes run through the cases applying the discovery rule of accrual. First, the rule is applied to types of actions in which it will generally be difficult for plaintiffs to immediately detect or comprehend the breach or the resulting injuries. In some instances the cause or injuries are actually hidden, as in the case of a subterranean trespass, the erasure of video tapes held in the sole custody of the defendant (*April Enterprises, Inc. v. KTTV, supra*, 147 Cal. App. 3d at p. 832), or foreign objects left in a patient's body after surgery (*see, e.g., Ashworth v. Memorial Hospital* (1988) 206 Cal. App. 3d 1046, 1054–1062 [254 Cal. Rptr. 104]). Even when the breach and damage are not physically hidden, they may be beyond what the plaintiff could reasonably be expected to comprehend. An action for professional malpractice, for example, typically involves the professional's failure to apply his or her specialized skills and knowledge. "Corollary to this expertise is the inability of the layman to detect its misapplication; the client may not recognize the negligence of the professional when he sees it." (*Neel v. Magana, Olney, Levy, Cathcart & Gelfand*, [6 Cal. 3d 176] at p. 188 [98 Cal. Rptr. 837, 491 P.2d 421 (1971)].) The same rationale has been adopted where defendant held itself out or was required by law to be specially qualified in a trade.

Second, courts have relied on the nature of the relationship between defendant and plaintiff to explain application of the delayed accrual rule. The rule is generally applicable to confidential or fiduciary relationships. (*United States Liab. Ins. Co. v. Haidinger-Hayes, Inc.* (1970) 1 Cal. 3d 586, 598 [83 Cal. Rptr. 418, 463 P.2d 770]; ...) The fiduciary relationship carries a duty of full disclosure, and application of the discovery rule "prevents the fiduciary from obtaining immunity for an initial breach of duty by a subsequent breach of the obligation of disclosure." (*Neel v. Magana, Olney, Levy, Cathcart & Gelfand, supra*, 6 Cal. 3d at p. 189.)

The court in *April Enterprises, Inc. v. KTTV, supra*, also noted the importance of the relationship between defendant and plaintiff: "In most instances, in fact, the defendant has been in a far superior position to comprehend the act and the injury. And in many, the defendant had reason to believe the plaintiff remained ignorant he had been wronged. Thus, there is an underlying notion that plaintiffs should not suffer where circumstances prevent them from knowing they have been harmed. And often this is accompanied by the corollary notion that defendants should not be allowed to knowingly profit from their injuree's ignorance." (147 Cal. App. 3d at p. 831.)

It has been widely recognized that the shock and confusion engendered by parental molestation, together with the parent's demands for secrecy, may lead a child to deny or block the traumatic events from conscious memory, or to turn the anger and pain inward so that the child blames himself or herself for the events. (*See* Comment, *Adult Incest Survivors and the Statute of Limitations: The Delayed Discovery Rule and Long-Term Damages* (1985) 25 Santa Clara L. Rev. 191, 192–195 [hereafter Adult Incest Survivors]; *Tyson v. Tyson* (1986) 107 Wn. 2d 72 [727 P.2d 226, 234–235] (dis. opn. of Pearson, J.); cf. *People v. Bowker* (1988) 203 Cal. App. 3d 385, 393–394 [249 Cal. Rptr. 886] [expert testimony on "accommodation" patterns by molestation victims may be admitted in criminal case to dispel myths and misconceptions, for example, to explain delayed revelation or recantations]). Even where memory of the events themselves is not suppressed, it may be some time before the victim can face the full impact of the acts. (*See* Adult Incest Survivors, *supra*, at p. 194; *Tyson v. Tyson, supra*, at p. 235.) The parent-child relationship is a confidential one, placing special duties on the parent for the protection of the child's health and wellbeing, as well as special rights of custody and control. Stepparents, foster parents, and others in positions of parental authority enjoy similar rights over the child.

As a practical matter a young child has little choice but to repose his or her trust with a parent or parental figure. When such a person abuses that trust, he commits two wrongs, the first by sexually abusing the child, the second by using the child's dependency and innocence to prevent recognition or revelation of the abuse. This may be accomplished by enforcing secrecy around the acts or even by teaching the child that the sexual acts are normal or necessary to the relationship. As in the professional negligence cases, application of the delayed discovery rule would serve to prevent the molester from using the child's ignorance and trust to conceal the primary tort.

Because of the youth and ignorance of the victims, as well as the unique duties and authority held by the parent, child sexual abuse by a parent or parental figure may in some cases be as effectively concealed from the victim as an underground trespass, a foreign object left in the body after surgery, or the abstruse errors made by a hired professional. The plaintiff must plead facts showing the time and manner of the delayed discovery (*County of Alameda v. Superior Court* (1987) 195 Cal. App. 3d 1283, 1286 [241 Cal. Rptr. 312]), and if he or she can do so it would be unjust and inconsistent with previous cases to not apply the discovery rule. * * *

We conclude that the purposes of the statute of limitations and the rationale of the delayed discovery rule as it has developed in our courts require that accrual of a cause of action for child sexual abuse by a parent or similar figure of authority be delayed until the plaintiff knows or reasonably should know of the cause of action. "'[The limitations period] is intended to run against those who are neglectful of their rights and who fail to use reasonable and proper diligence in the enforcement

thereof.... It is not the policy of the law to unjustly deprive one of his remedy.... '"
(*Manguso v. Oceanside Unified School Dist., supra*, 88 Cal. App. 3d at p. 730.) * * *

Although the allegations of the complaint as it stands are insufficient to invoke
the delayed discovery rule, there is a reasonable possibility plaintiffs can amend to
allege an unawareness, lasting into adulthood, that the acts done to them were wrongful. In addition, the complaint does not preclude amendment to allege that plaintiffs
had repressed, into adulthood, memory of the events themselves; such repression
would also be sufficient to invoke the discovery rule. * * *

Moreno v. Sanchez

Court of Appeal of California, Second Appellate District
106 Cal. App. 4th 1415, 131 Cal. Rptr. 2d 684 (2003)

JOHNSON, JUSTICE.

[Plaintiffs Armando Moreno and Gloria Contreras purchased a 49-year old house
in Whittier in 1998. Under the terms of their agreement to purchase, plaintiffs had
the right to have the property inspected and to approve the inspection results as a
condition to the close of escrow. They hired a home inspector, defendant Sanchez,
to conduct the inspection.

The inspection contract, which contained a modification of the limitations periods
governing claims against the home inspector, provided: "No legal action or proceeding
of any kind, including those sounding in tort or contract, can be commenced against
Inspector/Inspection Company, or its officers, agents or employees more than one
year after the date of the subject inspection. Time is expressly of the essence herein.
This time period is shorter than otherwise provided by law."

Moreno, who is a lawyer, a Los Angeles Superior Court Commissioner and a licensed real estate broker, requested that Sanchez delete this clause. Sanchez refused.
Moreno then signed the agreement and initialed the limitations clause. Defendant
Sanchez conducted his inspection on August 18, 1998. His inspection report did not
indicate any serious problems with the heating and cooling system. After escrow
closed, the plaintiffs moved into the property in November, 1998. In December,
1998, both plaintiffs became ill. Thereafter, Contreras's illness became chronic; in
early September 1999, a culture revealed she had a bacterial infection.

In September 1999, after extensive tests by various engineers, the plaintiffs discovered
several serious defects in the house not disclosed by Sanchez's earlier inspection, including a defect in the central heating and cooling systems which permitted the unit
to draw dust, dirt and dust mites into the house. Subsequently, on October 19, 1999,
fourteen months after defendant's inspection, the plaintiffs filed this suit against
Sanchez alleging breach of contract, negligence and negligent misrepresentation. Defendant demurred on the grounds that all of the plaintiffs' claims were barred by the
one-year statute of limitations provided in the home inspection contract.

Plaintiffs filed opposition, arguing among other things, the one-year statute of
limitations was unreasonable and thus the discovery rule should apply in this instance.

Ultimately the trial court ruled the one-year statute of limitations was reasonable and thus barred each of the causes of action alleged against the defendant. Accordingly, the court sustained the defendant's demurrer without leave to amend and dismissed the complaint. Plaintiffs' appealed.]

A number of statutes specifically provide for delayed accrual of a cause of action until the discovery, or the opportunity to discover, the facts constituting the cause of action. Most notable among these are situations involving fraud or mistake. Meanwhile judicial decisions have declared the discovery rule applicable in situations where the plaintiff is unable to see or appreciate a breach has occurred. These sorts of situations typically involve underground trespass, *Oakes v. McCarthy Co.* (1968) 267 Cal. App. 2d 231, 255 [73 Cal. Rptr. 127]; negligently manufactured drugs, *Jolly v. Eli Lilly & Co.* (1988) 44 Cal.3d 1103, 1109 [245 Cal. Rptr. 658, 751 P.2d 923]; products liability, *G. D. Searle & Co. v. Superior Court* (1975) 49 Cal. App. 3d 22, 25 [122 Cal. Rptr. 218]; violations of the right of privacy, *Cain v. State Farm Mut. Auto Ins. Co.* (1976) 62 Cal. App. 3d 310, 315 [132 Cal. Rptr. 860]; latent defects in real property, *Allen v. Sundean* (1982) 137 Cal. App. 3d 216, 222 [186 Cal. Rptr. 863]; or breaches of contract committed in secret. *April Enterprises, Inc. v. KTTV* (1983) 147 Cal. App. 3d 805, 832 [195 Cal. Rptr. 421].

Delayed accrual of a cause of action is viewed as particularly appropriate where the relationship between the parties is one of special trust such as that involving a fiduciary, confidential or privileged relationship. Employing this rationale, the discovery rule has been applied, sometimes by statute and sometimes through judicial decisions, to claims against professionals such as trustees, *Cortelyou v. Imperial Land Co.* (1913) 166 Cal. 14, 20 [134 P. 981]; stockbrokers, *Twomey v. Mitchum, Jones & Templeton, Inc.* (1968) 262 Cal. App. 2d 690 [69 Cal. Rptr. 222]; escrow agents, *Amen v. Merced County Title Co.* (1962) 58 Cal.2d 528, 534, 25 Cal. Rptr. 65, 375 P.2d 33; insurance agents, *United States Liab. Ins. Co. v. Haidinger-Hayes, Inc.* (1970) 1 Cal.3d 586, 596–598 [83 Cal. Rptr. 418, 463 P.2d 770]; accountants, *Moonie v. Lynch* (1967) 256 Cal. App. 2d 361, 365–366 [64 Cal. Rptr. 55]; physicians, *Huysman v. Kirsch* (1936) 6 Cal.2d 302, 312–313 [57 P.2d 908]; attorneys, *Neel v. Magana, Olney, Levy, Cathcart & Gelfand* (1971) 6 Cal.3d 176, 187 [98 Cal. Rptr. 837, 491 P.2d 421]; and title companies, *Prudential Home Mortgage Co. v. Superior Court* (1998) 66 Cal.App.4th 1236, 1248 [78 Cal. Rptr. 2d 566].

However, justification for the discovery rule has not been restricted to regulated and licensed professions. Courts have also employed the rule of delayed accrual in cases involving trades people who have held themselves out as having a special skill, or are required by statute to possess a certain level of skill. In *Evans v. Eckelman* [(1990) 216 Cal. App. 3d 1609, 265 Cal. Rptr. 605,] the court noted the rationale behind applying the discovery rule against professionals applied with equal force to trades people who represent they have the level of skill and expertise necessary to perform a specialized service for the consuming public. The same rationale has been adopted where defendant held itself out or was required by law to be specially qualified in a trade. (*Allred v. Bekins Wide World Van Services* (1975) 45 Cal. App. 3d 984 at pp. 990–99 [120 Cal. Rptr. 312] [(packing and shipping service company)]; *Seelenfreund v. Terminix of Northern Cal., Inc.* (1978) 84 Cal. App. 3d 133 at pp. 137–138 [148 Cal. Rptr. 307](licensed termite inspection company)].)

These same considerations are present in the home inspection context as well. For many people, purchasing a residence is the single biggest investment they make in their lives. Most want as much information as possible about a property before purchasing. However, few have the knowledge or experience necessary to fully analyze the quality of a home's structure, systems or components themselves. Fewer still are also structural engineers, general contractors, electrical contractors or the like. It is precisely because most people lack the necessary skills to recognize potential defects on their own that prospective homeowners hire a home inspection company in the first instance. For a fee they entrust this responsibility to a person who represents he has sufficient knowledge, skill and expertise to discover and report on the material defects in a given property. These potential homeowners look to the professional to guide and inform their choice about a given residence, not only to learn of existing material defects, but also about other potentially serious flaws which require further investigation. However, because most people are ill equipped to know whether the home inspector in fact discovered and reported all the material defects with the home, most homeowners will not recognize a problem has been overlooked, or noticed but not reported, until something goes wrong and the damage becomes apparent. Needless to say, a faulty home inspection can have disastrous financial consequences for many homeowners.

In short, situations involving home inspectors share many characteristics with those involving other professionals in which delayed accrual has been recognized as appropriate and necessary. Although not as regulated as some fields, the Legislature has recognized the significance of the role home inspectors occupy in this state's economy, as well as the potential hazards of fraudulently or negligently performed inspections. As with other forms of professional malpractice, specialized skill is required to analyze a residence's structural and component parts. Because of the hidden nature of these systems and components a potential homeowner may not see or recognize a home inspector's negligence, and thus may not understand he has been damaged until long after the inspection date. This fact, coupled with the trust the potential homeowners must necessarily place in the professional home inspector, compel the conclusion causes of action for breach of a home inspector's duty of care should accrue in all cases, not on the date of the inspection, but when the homeowner discovers, or with the exercise of reasonable diligence should have discovered, the inspector's breach.

The delayed discovery rule is founded on important public policy considerations. In fact, these considerations are sufficient to overcome ordinary statutory time limits the Legislature has enacted. That is, the Legislature may have created a one-year statute of limitations for a certain cause of action. But if the courts determine the cause of action arises in circumstances where the delayed discovery rule applies, plaintiffs can file suit years after the expiration of the one-year statutory limitations period, assuming it takes that long to discover their cause of action. If a legislated limitations period must yield to a judicially created delayed discovery rule, how can it be argued a contractually agreed limitations period is immune from that rule and its underlying rationale?[45]

Under general California law a person has four years to bring an action on a contract. [Code Civil Pro. § 337.1.] California law also provides for a statute of limitations specifically applicable to home inspections. The Business and Professions Code similarly provides up to four years to bring suit for breach of a home inspector's duty to use the degree of care a reasonably prudent home inspector would exercise. [Business and Professions Code section 7199 provides the time to bring an action against a home inspector for "breach of duty arising from a home inspection report shall not exceed four years from the date of the inspection."] These four-year periods supply home purchasers a reasonable amount of time to discover a home inspector's breach and to file suit.

As the dissent correctly observes, the Legislature did not itself provide for a rule of delayed discovery when it enacted the four-year outside limitations period for actions against home inspectors. We can attach no special significance to this fact. Legislative adoptions of delayed discovery have often come only in response to such judicially created rules. For example, the Legislature enacted Code of Civil Procedure section 340.6 providing for delayed discovery for attorney malpractice actions in 1977, years after the Supreme Court's decision in *Neel v. Magana, Olney, Levy, Cathcart & Gelfand* [*supra*, 6 Cal.3d 176.] recognizing for the first time the propriety of the rule in the legal malpractice context. Similarly, the Legislature did not create a statutory rule of delayed discovery in the medical malpractice context until 1970 [Code Civ. Proc. section 340.5], and long after the Supreme Court judicially recognized such a rule in *Huysman v. Kirsch* [(1936) 6 Cal.2d 302, 57 P.2d 908.]. The Legislature's provision in this instance for an outside maximum limitation period is entirely consistent with other delayed discovery statutes as a mechanism to ensure the limitations period does not continue for infinity.

It is true California courts have afforded contracting parties considerable freedom to modify the length of a statute of limitations. *See, e.g., Hambrecht & Quist Venture Partners v. American Medical Internat., Inc.* (1995) 38 Cal. App. 4th 1532, 1548, 46 Cal. Rptr. 2d 33 [court enforced choice of law provision in parties' contract which provided for a shorter statute of limitations than California's]. Courts generally enforce parties' agreements for a shorter limitations period than otherwise provided by statute, provided it is reasonable. "Reasonable" in this context means the shortened period nevertheless provides sufficient time to effectively pursue a judicial remedy. * * *

However, a contractually shortened limitations period has never been recognized outside the context of straightforward transactions in which the triggering event for either a breach of a contract or for the accrual of a right is immediate and obvious.

---

45. Even assuming a homeowner could waive the benefits of the discovery rule, it would have to be a knowing waiver. The contract itself would have to apprise the homeowner of the existence of his right to the discovery rule, and what that meant, and required him to expressly waive that right. Nothing approaching such a knowing waiver occurred here. * * *

Moreover, no decision upholding the validity of a contractually shortened limitation period has done so in the context of an action against a professional or skilled expert where breach of a duty is more difficult to detect. Instead, most reported decisions upholding shortened periods involve straightforward commercial contracts plus the unambiguous breaches or accrual of rights under those contracts. [Citations and case summaries omitted.]

In short, none of these decisions upholding parties' "freedom to modify the length of the statute of limitations," is factually analogous to the case at bar. Nor do any of them involve a cause of action to which the delayed discovery rule applies. In each of the foregoing decisions the plaintiffs knew of the breaches or the accrual of rights at the moment the cause of action accrued. It was thus appropriate in those situations to permit the limitations period to run from the moment of the triggering event. In the present context, by contrast, a cause of action may not be known, or even suspected, until long after the home inspection is completed. A shortened limitations period in this context may thus foreclose an effective judicial remedy for many homeowners. For this reason, for a provision in a home inspection contract shortening the statute of limitations to be enforceable, we hold accrual of a cause of action occurs not with the inspection, but when the homeowner discovers, or through the exercise of reasonable diligence should have discovered, the breach.

* * *

It is one thing to say a contract can shorten the time period for filing a lawsuit after the lawsuit has accrued. It is quite another to say a contract can redefine when accrual occurs—especially when public policy has defined that triggering event as the plaintiff's *discovery* of his cause of action—not the date the defendant committed the acts which gave rise to that cause of action.

Indeed if courts were to enforce consumers' contractual waiver of their rights under the delayed discovery rule in contracts between home inspectors and home buyers, why not when the contracts are between lawyers and clients, physicians and patients, and in every other professional and trade relationship currently subject to that rule? In all these situations, including home inspection transactions, the supplier of services nearly always enjoys a knowledge and bargaining advantage over the consumer. So it should not prove difficult to include such provisions in most if not all such contracts. Yet, our research has not uncovered a single appellate case where a lawyer or physician or anyone else subject to the delayed discovery rule has even attempted to wiggle out of that rule by imposing a contract purporting to waive the consumer's right to the benefits of that rule.

In short, no authority exists which sanctions a contractual provision permitting parties to opt out of the benefits of the discovery rule in situations where the discovery rule would otherwise apply. This suggests there exists an implicit consensus that an effective judicial remedy against professionals or skilled crafts people requires accrual occur only upon discovery of the breach and thus the law will not tolerate contractual nullification of that policy. * * *

[W]e are unable to find a contractual provision "reasonable" where it only gives homeowners a single year to discover their causes of action against home inspectors. A four-year outside limit on the time permitted for the homeowner to discover the inspector's negligence and its adverse consequences is clearly "reasonable." A contractual provision setting a somewhat shorter outside limit conceivably might be "reasonable," too. But a *one-year* outside boundary completely vitiates the delayed discovery rule. Indeed such a provision blatantly substitutes a straight one-year statute of limitations for the delayed discovery rule.

Consistent with the policies behind this rule, we hold the buyers' causes of action did not accrue under the one-year statute of limitations provided in the home inspection contract until they discovered, or with the exercise of reasonable diligence, should have discovered the home inspector negligently failed to discover, or negligently failed to report, material defects in the home. * * * The judgment is reversed and the cause is remanded to the trial court with directions to vacate the dismissal, to overrule the demurrer, and for further proceedings consistent with this opinion. Appellants are awarded their costs on appeal.

PERLUSS, P.J., dissenting.

Under California law parties may agree to a provision shortening the statute of limitations, "qualified, however, by the requirement that the period fixed is not in itself unreasonable or is not so unreasonable as to show imposition or undue advantage. [Citations.]" (*Capehart v. Heady* (1962) 206 Cal. App. 2d 386, 388, 23 Cal. Rptr. 851; *see Hambrecht & Quist Venture Partners v. American Medical Internat., Inc.* (1995) 38 Cal. App. 4th 1532, 1548, 46 Cal. Rptr. 2d 33.) * * *

In the case at bar, the one-year limitations provision was clearly stated in the parties' contract; cautioned that it imposed a time period for filing suit that "is shorter than is otherwise provided by law"; was unambiguous in its application to both contract and tort claims; was the subject of negotiation between Moreno and the home inspector; and, after Moreno failed to obtain the inspector's agreement to delete the provision, was separately initialed by Moreno. There is no dispute the provision was reasonable in those respects. Moreover, California courts have uniformly enforced provisions shortening the four-year statutory limitations period for breach of a written contract (Code Civ. Proc., § 337, subd. 1) to one year (*e.g., Capehart v. Heady, supra,* 206 Cal. App. 2d at p. 388) and to even shorter periods, as well. (*E.g., Tebbets v. Fidelity and Casualty Co.,* [(1909)] 155 Cal. 137, at p. 138 [99 P. 501] [six months].)

The majority, however, concludes the parties' agreement is unreasonable as a matter of law because it impliedly required Moreno to waive the benefit of the nonstatutory delayed discovery rule first recognized earlier in its opinion. I respectfully disagree.

No statute prohibits the parties to a home inspection contract from agreeing to a shortened limitations period. (*Hambrecht & Quist Venture Partners, supra,* 38 Cal.App.4th at p. 1548 ["Except as restricted by statute, California courts accord contracting parties substantial freedom to modify the length of the statute of limitations."].) Indeed, permitting the parties to bargain for such a provision is fully consistent with the 1996 legislation governing practices in the home inspection industry. The parties' agreement does not otherwise offend public policy. (*See, e.g., Tebbets, supra,* 155 Cal. at p. 139 [statutes of limitations are "statutes of repose, carrying with them, not a right protected under the rule of public policy, but a mere personal right for the benefit of the individual, which may be waived"].) * * *

Moreover, while imposing a duty of reasonable care on home inspectors in [Bus. & Prof. Code] section 7196, the Legislature itself did not provide for a rule of delayed discovery, as it did, for example, when establishing the limitations period for professional malpractice actions against health care providers (Code Civ. Proc., § 340.5) and attorneys (Code Civ. Proc., § 340.6, subd. (a)) and actions for damages suffered as a result of domestic violence (Code Civ. Proc., § 340.15, subd. (a)(2)). Rather, section 7199, adopted in 1996, specifies a maximum time period within which a lawsuit must be filed *measured from the date of the inspection itself:* "The time for commencement of a legal action for breach of duty arising from a home inspection report shall not exceed four years from the date of the inspection." * * *

Whether or not the delayed discovery rule should be applied to negligence claims against a home inspector in an appropriate case, the majority advances no compelling reason to disregard the parties' express contractual agreement to limit the homebuyers' right to sue to a one-year period measured from the date of inspection. Indeed, the primary ground advanced for invalidating the parties' agreement is simply the *absence* of authority enforcing such a provision, which the majority suggests indicates "an implicit consensus" that such contractual limitations provisions are invalid. * * *

Because no statute restricts the right of the parties to a home inspection agreement to contract for a shorter limitations period, I believe the parties' "substantial freedom to modify the length of the statute of limitations" (*Hambrecht & Quist Venture Partners, supra,* 38 Cal.App.4th at p. 1548) requires that we enforce their agreement. Accordingly, I would affirm the order of the trial court sustaining [defendant's] demurrer to the second amended complaint.

Notes and Questions

(1) Is *Evans* a proper application of the discovery rule as set forth in *Jolly*? The allegations of injury due to child abuse in *Evans* present a compelling case for extension of the discovery rule. Is it a wise extension? Is the court's "unawareness" analysis limited to child abuse cases? Are there many other types of cases which would also satisfy *Evans'* "unawareness" analysis? What are they?

(2) The *Evans* reasoning was followed by the court in *Marsha V. v. Gardner*, 231 Cal. App. 3d 265, 281 Cal. Rptr. 473 (1991), a case whose facts and pleadings are nearly identical to those in *Evans*. Unlike *Evans*, however, the Court of Appeal in *Marsha V.* affirmed the trial court's sustaining of the demurrer without leave to amend because the plaintiff's attorney had indicated to the trial court that the facts as originally pleaded were the facts that occurred. *Marsha V.*, 231 Cal. App. 3d at 274. In *Curtis T. v. County of Los Angeles*, 123 Cal. App. 4th 1405, 21 Cal. Rptr. 3d 208 (2004), a

tort action against the defendant county in which the minor plaintiff alleged he was molested for several years while living in a foster home, the court followed *Evans* and held that the plaintiff "must be given leave to amend to allege, if he is able to do so truthfully—given his youth, ignorance, and inexperience, as well as his foster parents' alleged complicity in the abuse—that he lacked real awareness, until his mother's discovery of the alleged molestation, that what happened to him between the ages of five and eight was wrong." *Curtis T., supra,* 123 Cal. App. 4th at 1409.

(3) Note that the Legislature amended CCP § 340.1 in 1991, 1994, 1998, 1999, and 2002 applicable to any action commenced after January 1, 1991, to provide a comprehensive statute of limitations for child sexual abuse cases. Section 340.1(a) states:

> In an action for recovery of damages suffered as a result of childhood sexual abuse, the time for commencement of the action shall be within eight years of the date the plaintiff attains the age of majority or within three years of the date the plaintiff discovers or reasonably should have discovered that psychological injury or illness occurring after the age of majority was caused by the sexual abuse, whichever period expires later....

Is § 340.1(a) a codification of *Evans v. Eckelman, supra,* or something different? *See Lent v. Doe,* 40 Cal. App. 4th 1177, 47 Cal. Rptr. 2d 389 (1995) (ruling that under the version of § 340.1 in effect after 1994, the delayed discovery provisions of § 340.1(a) relate to injuries occurring after the age of majority, regardless of whether the plaintiff suffered actual injury at the time of abuse and never repressed his memory of the events); *Sellery v. Cressey,* 48 Cal. App. 4th 538, 55 Cal. Rptr. 2d 706 (1996) (concluding the 1991 and subsequent versions of § 340.1(a) were intended to toll the statute of limitations even for plaintiffs who recalled their childhood abuse, and therefore an action by a 37 year-old woman was not time barred because she first saw the connection between her psychological ailments and her abuse when she entered therapy in 1991 and filed her lawsuit in 1992).

(4) What combination of factors did the *Moreno* court find relevant to its determination of whether to apply the delayed discovery rule? Which factors did the court view as the most important ones? In light of *Moreno,* can you identify any professions, trades, or relationships to which the discovery rule would not apply?

(5) Do you agree with the *Moreno v. Sanchez* majority or the dissent on the question of whether the contractual modification of the four-year statute of limitations was reasonable? If parties to a contract are permitted to shorten the limitations period, why should they not also be permitted to modify the applicable accrual rule? *See Brisbane Lodging, L.P. v. Webcor Builders, Inc.,* 216 Cal. App. 4th 1249, 157 Cal. Rptr. 3d 467 (2013) (concluding that sophisticated contracting parties have the right to abrogate the delayed discovery rule). Do you think the result would have been different in *Moreno* if the contract specified the date of inspection as the accrual point but shortened the statute of limitations to two years? To four years? If the contract did not define the accrual date but simply shortened the statute of limitations to one year? *See Zamora v. Lehman,* 214 Cal. App. 4th 193, 153 Cal. Rptr. 3d 724 (2013) (enforcing

agreement that shortened four-year statute of limitations to one year but also contained language adopting the delayed discovery rule).

[2] Legislative Modification of the Discovery Rule

The discovery rule is a judicial modification of a common law rule defining "accrual." This court-made doctrine is applicable in many ordinary tort and contract cases because the Legislature has not indicated, in a general way, a contrary intent regarding "accrual." But in a number of specific areas the Legislature has now statutorily defined when certain causes of action accrue.

[a] Various Legislative Approaches

Some of these statutory provisions simply codify the basic discovery rule. *E.g.*, CCP § 338(d), action for relief based on fraud or mistake; CCP § 339(1), action upon an oral contract, except as provided in Com. Code § 2725; CCP § 359; and Civil Code § 986.

But other statutes modify, and in some instances eliminate, the discovery rule. Some of these are quite important. The most notable is contained in Section 2725 of the Commercial Code, which sets forth a four-year statute of limitations for actions for breach of any contract for sale of goods. Section 2725(2) states that a "cause of action accrues when the breach occurs, regardless of the aggrieved party's lack of knowledge of the breach." Another is CCP § 337.15 which contains a ten-year limitation for actions against real estate developers, contractors and architects for property damage arising out of a latent deficiency, which accrues upon "the substantial completion of the development or improvement." CCP § 337.15(a). *See Mills v. Forestex Co.*, 108 Cal. App. 4th 625, 134 Cal. Rptr. 2d 273 (2003) (collecting cases construing meaning of "latent defect" under § 337.15); *Creekridge Townhome Owners Assn., Inc. v. C. Scott Whitten, Inc.*, 177 Cal. App. 4th 251, 99 Cal. Rptr. 3d 258 (discussing the difference between a "patent" defect governed by CCP § 337.1 and a "latent" defect under § 337.15).

[b] Superseding Limitations

Some statutes adopt the discovery rule but include a superseding limitation period which accrues on the date of injury. The two most notable examples are CCP § 340.5, which governs actions for injury or death against health care providers based on professional negligence; and CCP § 340.6, which governs actions against attorneys for wrongful acts. Section 340.5 generally requires that a medical negligence action be commenced within three years of the date of injury or one year after discovery of the injury, "whichever occurs first." *See, e.g., McNall v. Summers*, 25 Cal. App. 4th 1300, 30 Cal. Rptr. 2d 914 (1994) (concluding plaintiff's failure to file her action within three years of the manifestation of appreciable harm overrode the one-year discovery requirement). Likewise, § 340.6 generally requires that an attorney malpractice action be commenced within four years from the date of the wrongful act or one year after discovery of the wrongful act, "whichever occurs first." *See Samuels v. Mix*, 22 Cal.

4th 1, 91 Cal. Rptr. 2d 273, 989 P.2d 701 (1999) (observing that unlike the common law discovery rule, CCP § 340.6(a) requires the *defendant* to prove when the plaintiff discovered, or should have discovered, the facts constituting the defendant's alleged attorney malpractice). Both statutes contain some exceptions, discussed *infra*, and must be examined closely. What policy considerations do these two statutory limitations schemes reflect?

Code of Civil Procedure § 340.5 has survived constitutional challenges, *see Young v. Haines*, 41 Cal. 3d 883, 226 Cal. Rptr. 547, 718 P.2d 909 (1986); *but see Torres v. County of Los Angeles*, 209 Cal. App. 3d 325, 257 Cal. Rptr. 211 (1989) (holding less advantageous accrual point determination for minors than for adults in CCP § 340.5 is arbitrary and unconstitutional); but has at times been strictly construed. *See, e.g., Brown v. Bleiberg*, 32 Cal. 3d 426, 186 Cal. Rptr. 228, 651 P.2d 815 (1982) (holding CCP § 340(3), not § 340.5, applies to medical malpractice allegations of battery and breach of warranty); *Meyer v. Carnow*, 185 Cal. App. 3d 169, 229 Cal. Rptr. 617 (1986) (ruling CCP § 340.5 does not provide limitations for action to compel arbitration of medical negligence claim; four-year limitations for actions on written contract in CCP § 337 governs).

[c] Legislative Expansion: Asbestos Exposure Litigation

In some instances the Legislature has enacted statutes which not only adopt, but actually expand, the common law discovery rule. For example, CCP § 340.2 provides that for personal injury actions based on occupational exposure to asbestos, an action must be commenced within one year after the date the plaintiff discovers that he has suffered "disability" caused by such exposure. Section 340.2(b) defines "disability" to mean loss of time from work as a result of such exposure which precludes performance of the employee's regular occupation.

When does an action accrue for an employee suffering from lung disease where the disease severely impacts her personal life, but does not preclude her from continued employment, and she actually knows it is caused by exposure to asbestos at her job? *See Uram v. Abex Corp.*, 217 Cal. App. 3d 1425, 266 Cal. Rptr. 695 (1990); *Blakey v. Superior Court*, 153 Cal. App. 3d 101, 200 Cal. Rptr. 52 (1984). Where after six months of incapacitation from lung disease, the employee returned to work with limited duties, but was diagnosed with lung cancer eight years later? *See Williamson v. Plant Insulation Co.*, 23 Cal. App. 4th 1406, 28 Cal. Rptr. 2d 751 (1994).

In *Duty v. Abex Corp.*, 214 Cal. App. 3d 742, 263 Cal. Rptr. 13 (1989), the plaintiff was exposed to asbestos while employed by defendant in 1944–45 and 1951–53. Plaintiff only worked for defendant during these wartime periods, and retired from all employment in 1968. She first began to suffer severe lung disease in 1979, and was informed that it was caused by asbestos exposure. However, plaintiff did not file a personal injury action against defendant until 1985. Is plaintiff's action barred by the statute of limitations? Does former CCP § 340(3) or § 340.2 apply? If § 340.2 applies, at what point did her cause of action accrue? The court in *Duty* noted that CCP § 340.2 was enacted because of the harsh results of applying former § 340(3) to victims of progressive disease as opposed to victims of traumatic injury, and that § 340.2 codifies the discovery rule with one significant difference: The statutory period never commences to run until plaintiff suffers a "disability" within the meaning of § 340.2(b). Did the plaintiff in *Duty* suffer such a "disability"? Can a retired person ever suffer such a "disability"? *Compare Uram v. Abex Corp., supra* (disability retirement) *with Williamson v. Plant Insulation Co., supra* (voluntary retirement).

In *Hamilton v. Asbestos Corp., Ltd.*, 22 Cal. 4th 1127, 95 Cal. Rptr. 2d 701, 998 P.2d 403 (2000), the Supreme Court resolved a progressive disease or "double-injury" issue, with respect to the statute of limitations for asbestos exposure litigation, that had divided the courts of appeal. For two decades prior to 1963, plaintiffs' decedent Arthur Mitchell was employed in various industrial workplaces where he was exposed to asbestos. Mitchell's exposure to asbestos ended in 1963 when he went into business for himself. In the 1970's, Mitchel began experiencing breathing difficulties, diagnosed in 1979 as caused by asbestosis, a noncancerous breathing problem common in workers who have suffered prolonged exposure to asbestosis. He continued to work in his business until he retired in 1989, not because of breathing difficulties but because he had reached the normal retirement age of 65.

After his retirement, Mitchell's breathing problems gradually grew worse. In 1993, he filed an action (*Mitchell I*) for damages against several parties involved in the making, selling, and using of asbestos products. Subsequently in late 1995, before the trial of *Mitchell I*, Mitchell was diagnosed with a rare form of cancer primarily triggered by exposure to asbestos. Mitchell then filed a second action for damages (*Mitchell II*) against defendant Asbestos Corporation alleging that exposure to asbestos caused his cancerous condition. The two actions were consolidated for trial. During the trial, the superior court denied defendant's motion to dismiss on the ground that *Mitchell II* was barred by the statute of limitations set forth in CCP § 340.2. The jury returned a verdict for the plaintiff, and defendant Asbestos Corporation appealed.

Giving the words of CCP § 340.2 their plain meaning, the Supreme Court held that *Mitchell II* was not time-barred. The court read § 340.2 as providing in effect that an action for injury arising from asbestos exposure must be filed within one year after the plaintiff first suffered a "disability" and noted that because this special statute defines "disability" as "loss of time from work as a result of [asbestos] exposure which preclude[d] the performance of [plaintiff's] regular occupation," Mitchell did not suffer a "disability" when he was diagnosed with asbestosis in 1979 or when he retired for reasons unrelated to his earlier asbestos exposure in 1989. *Mitchell, supra*, 22 Cal. 4th at 1140–42. Moreover, the court concluded that Mitchell did not suffer a "disability" within the meaning of § 340.2, and hence the one-year statute of limitations period had not begun to run, when he filed *Mitchell II*. *Id.* at 1142. In so ruling, the Supreme Court discussed with approval several Court of Appeal decisions to the same effect, including *Duty v. Abex Corp., supra*.

[3]   Difficult Accrual Cases

In addition to delayed discovery of injury, there are a variety of other circumstances where the accrual of a cause of action may be difficult to determine. Specific statutes and cases provide guidance in some of these circumstances. *See generally Developments In the Law—Statutes of Limitations*, 63 HARV. L. REV. 1177, 1205–1219 (1950); 3 Witkin, *California Procedure, Actions*, §§ 493–674 (5th ed. 2008). Some examples follow:

[a] Nuisance

When does a cause of action for nuisance accrue where the complained of activities occur over a long period of time? In *Baker v. Burbank-Glendale-Pasadena Airport Auth.*, 39 Cal. 3d 862, 218 Cal. Rptr. 293, 705 P.2d 866 (1985), for example, plaintiffs sued for nuisance caused by excessive noise from flights over their homes. In determining whether plaintiffs' claims were barred by the applicable three-year statute of limitations, the Supreme Court distinguished between "permanent" and "continuing" nuisance. A continuing nuisance is an ongoing disturbance which may be abated or discontinued at any time; a permanent nuisance is the type which by one act causes permanent injury. *Id.* at 868–69. A permanent nuisance action accrues upon creation of the nuisance; a continuing nuisance accrues upon every repetition of the wrongful act. *Id.* Is the plaintiffs' action in *Baker* based on continuing or permanent nuisance? What about a damage action brought by a landowner against a lessee who wrongfully contaminated the property with hazardous waste during the leasehold? *See Mangini v. Aerojet-General Corp.*, 12 Cal. 4th 1087, 51 Cal. Rptr. 2d 272, 912 P.2d 1220 (1996) (concluding the plaintiffs failed to present any substantial evidence that contamination was capable of being abated at a reasonable cost and therefore nuisance was permanent rather than continuing); *McCoy v. Gustafson*, 180 Cal. App. 4th 56, 103 Cal. 3d 37 (2009) (finding a permanent nuisance because no evidence that soil contamination by migrating oil could be abated at a reasonable cost by reasonable means).

[b] Breach of Warranty

When does the cause of action for breach of warranty accrue? *See Sweet v. Watson's Nursery*, 23 Cal. App. 2d 379, 73 P.2d 284 (1937) (distinguishing between present and prospective warranties); *Southern Cal. Enter. v. Walter & Co.*, 78 Cal. App. 2d 750, 178 P.2d 785 (1947) (collecting cases). How does the California Commercial Code deal with this problem in contracts for sale of goods? Commercial Code § 2725(2) provides: "A breach of warranty occurs when tender of delivery is made, except that where a warranty explicitly extends to future performance of the goods and discovery of the breach must await the time of such performance the cause of action accrues when the breach is or should have been discovered." What constitutes a "future performance" within the meaning of § 2725(2)? *See Krieger v. Nick Alexander Imports, Inc.*, 234 Cal. App. 3d 205, 215–19, 285 Cal. Rptr. 717 (1991) (holding a promise to repair defects that occur during a future period is the very definition of express warranty of future performance); *Carrau v. Marvin Lumber & Cedar Co.*, 93 Cal. App. 4th 281, 290–92, 112 Cal. Rptr. 2d 869 (2001) (discussing the scope of the "future performance" exception).

[c] Injury to Property

When does a cause of action for tortious injury to property accrue? When the current owner discovers the injury? Or when *any* owner—such as a prior owner—discovered the injury? For example, assume that A owns real property and negligently releases toxic waste into the soil and groundwater. A then sells the property to B, but does not reveal the toxic waste contamination. After the purchase, B discovers the damage to the property caused by A, but does nothing within the applicable one-year limitation period. B subsequently sells the property to C, but does not inform C of the toxic waste. C takes possession, and diligently discovers that the property is worthless due to A's toxic waste negligence. C files an action against A for tortious injury to the property, shortly after discovering the harm. Is C's action barred by the statute of limitations?

In *CAMSI IV v. Hunter Tech. Corp.*, 230 Cal. App. 3d 1525, 1534–35, 282 Cal. Rptr. 80 (1991), the court indicated that knowledge of injury by a prior owner is imputed to the current owner. The owner who discovers the injury must bring a claim to court within the statutory period or the claim will be barred for that and all subsequent owners. Is this rule fair to the current owner, such as C? What policies are reflected by the court's adoption of this rule? Is C without any recourse here? Should this imputation of knowledge rule apply if A and B knew of the toxic waste, and B acted as A's agent in concealing this defect when C purchased the property? *See Valenzuela v. Superior Court*, 3 Cal. App. 4th 1499, 5 Cal. Rptr. 2d 186 (1992). Are the same policy concerns controlling here? Does the cause of action accrue when an owner actually discovers such injury to property, or when a reasonably diligent inspection would have revealed the soil contamination? *See Wilshire Westwood Assn. v. Atlantic Richfield Co.*, 20 Cal. App. 4th 732, 740, 24 Cal. Rptr. 2d 562 (1993).

[d] Defamation

In *Shively v. Bozanich*, 31 Cal. 4th 1230, 7 Cal. Rptr. 3d 576, 80 P.3d 676 (2003), the Supreme Court held that although the discovery rule may apply to inherently covert defamations, a cause of action for defamation published in a book accrues on the date the book was first generally distributed to the public, regardless of the date on which the plaintiff actually learned of the existence of the book and read its contents. Likewise, the delayed discovery rule does not apply to a cause of action for unauthorized commercial appropriation of likeness, such as the unauthorized use of an image of the plaintiff on a product label that is widely distributed to the public. *Christoff v. Nestle USA, Inc.*, 47 Cal. 4th 468, 97 Cal. Rptr. 3d 798, 213 P.3d 132 (2009) (noting that although the discovery rule is inapplicable to unauthorized commercial use of likeness, repeated production of a label may begin the statute of limitations anew because the label was "republished" within the meaning of the single-publication rule). Does the discovery rule apply to delay the accrual of a cause of action for defamation contained in a publication where the publication is not widely distributed. *See Hebrew Academy of San Francisco v. Goldman*, 42 Cal. 4th 883, 70 Cal. Rptr. 3d 178, 173 P.3d 1004 (2007) (ruling the discovery rule is inapplicable not only as to books and newspapers that are published with general circulation, but also as to publications that are given only limited circulation and are not generally distributed to public).

[e] Continuous Accrual

In *Howard Jarvis Taxpayers Assn. v. City of La Habra*, 25 Cal. 4th 809, 107 Cal. Rptr. 2d 369, 23 P.3d 601 (2001), an action for declaratory and mandamus relief challenging the validity of a city ordinance and the ongoing collection of taxes pursuant to the ordinance but not seeking refunds of taxes paid, the California Supreme Court held that the defendant city's continued imposition and collection of tax is an ongoing violation upon which the limitations period begins anew with each collection.

More recently in *Aryeh v. Canon Business Solutions, Inc.*, 55 Cal. 4th 1185, 151 Cal. Rptr. 3d 827, 292 P.3d 871 (2013), the Supreme Court distinguished between two main branches of the continuing-wrong accrual principles: the "continuing violation doctrine" and the "theory of continuous accrual." The *continuing violation doctrine* aggregates a series of wrongs or injuries for purposes of the statute of limitations, treating the limitations period as accruing for all of them upon the commission or sufferance of the last of them. This doctrine applies when an injury is the product of a series of small harms, any one of which may not be actionable on its own or where the wrongful course of conduct becomes apparent only through the accumulation of a series of harms.

Under the *theory of continuous accrual*, a series of wrongs or injuries may be viewed as each triggering its own limitations period, such that suit for relief may be partially time-barred as to older events but timely as to those within the applicable limitations period. This approach applies when the complaint identifies a series of discrete, apparent, and independently actionable wrongs such that a cause of action accrues each time a wrongful action occurs, triggering a new limitations period. "[U]nlike the continuing violation doctrine, which renders an entire course of conduct actionable, the theory of continuous accrual supports recovery only for damages arising from those breaches falling within the limitations period." *Aryeh, supra*, 55 Cal. 4th at 1199. Applying *Aryeh*, the court in *Gilkyson v. Disney Enterprises, Inc.*, 244 Cal. App. 4th 1336, 198 Cal. Rptr. 3d 611 (2016), held that the continuous accrual doctrine applied to an action for breach of a contractual obligation to pay royalties in connection with use in video recordings of songs that were written for a 1967 animated movie and therefore, under CCP § 337, the plaintiffs' action was timely as to those breaches occurring within the four-year limitations period preceding the filing of the 2013 lawsuit.

[4] Special Accrual Issues in Medical Negligence Actions Governed by CCP § 340.5

[a] Section 340.5

Section 340.5 codifies the common law discovery rule for medical negligence actions. *E.g., Dolan v. Borelli*, 13 Cal. App. 4th 816, 16 Cal. Rptr. 2d 714 (1993). Difficult problems can arise in determining when a plaintiff has "discovered" the manifestation of an injury. For example, in *Dolan v. Borelli, supra,* the defendant performed surgery on plaintiff Dolan in 1985 to relieve pain in Dolan's wrist, supposedly releasing Dolan's right carpal tunnel ligament. Dolan continued to suffer pain, and consulted a second doctor. A second operation was performed on Dolan's wrist in 1986, at which time the new doctor discovered that the carpel tunnel release had not previously been performed by the defendant. When did plaintiff discover her injury within the meaning of § 340.5 and *Jolly*? In *Steingart v. White*, 198 Cal. App. 3d 406, 243 Cal. Rptr. 678 (1988), the plaintiff was aware of a lump on her breast and consulted the defendant doctor in February, 1982. Defendant advised her that the lump was benign. In April 1985 another physician diagnosed the lump as a malignancy and performed a radical mastectomy. Plaintiff commenced a negligence action against defendant in March, 1986. Is plaintiff's action barred by the one-year and/or three-year limitation in § 340.5? When did plaintiff suffer "injury" within the meaning of § 340.5?

[b] Wrongful Death Cases

When does a cause of action accrue in a medical negligence action for wrongful death? In *Larcher v. Wanless,* 18 Cal. 3d 646, 135 Cal. Rptr. 75, 557 P.2d 507 (1976), the heirs of deceased Virginia Larcher commenced a wrongful death action against the defendant doctor for negligently prescribing drugs which caused Larcher's death. Plaintiffs' decedent suffered severe paralysis beginning in 1968, and was aware of its negligent cause by 1972. Mrs. Larcher died in 1974, and her heirs filed their wrongful death action two months later. The trial court granted summary judgment for defendant on the ground that the action was barred by CCP § 340.5 because it was not filed within one year of decedent's injuries, which were discovered at latest in 1972.

The Supreme Court reversed, holding that a wrongful death cause of action does not accrue until the event of decedent's death. The court noted that wrongful death is not merely a continuation or survival of decedent's claim for personal injuries, but an entirely new cause of action created in the heirs and based on the death of the decedent as that death inflicted injury upon them. *Larcher,* 18 Cal. 3d at 656–57. Until that death, the heirs have suffered no "injury" under former CCP § 377 (now CCP §§ 377.60–377.62) and hence have no basis for filing suit. Likewise, the word "injury" in § 340.5, as that statute applies to wrongful death actions, must be read to refer to the wrongfully caused death of plaintiffs' decedent. *Id.* at 658–59.

[c] Actions by Minors

Code of Civil Procedure § 340.5 states that "[a]ctions by a minor shall be commenced within three years from the date of the alleged wrongful act," except when limited tolling provisions apply. "Wrongful act" is not synonymous with "injury," and the delayed discovery rule is not read into this accrual language for minors. *Young v. Haines, supra,* 41 Cal. 3d 883, 894–96. Consequently, § 340.5 provides different, and generally less favorable, treatment for minors than for adults with respect to accrual. What is the policy basis for this different treatment of minors? Is it a rational basis? *See Photias v. Doefler,* 45 Cal. App. 4th 1014, 53 Cal. Rptr. 2d 202 (1996) (finding no rational basis for treating minors differently from adults with respect to accrual of a cause of action for medical malpractice, and concluding CCP § 340.5 therefore violates a minor's right to equal protection of the law).

[C] Extent of Harm Required for Accrual: Appreciable and Actual Harm

Related to the issue of delayed discovery of injury is the question of how substantial must an injury be to trigger the commencement of the relevant statute of limitations. Under the traditional view, the statute of limitations begins to run as soon as the plaintiff is aware of any harm, however slight. *See Sonbergh v. MacQuarrie,* 112 Cal. App. 2d 771, 774, 247 P.2d 133 (1952). The Supreme Court modified this rule in *Davies v. Krasna,* 14 Cal. 3d 502, 121 Cal. Rptr. 705, 535 P.2d 1161 (1975), where it observed that "we generally now subscribe to the view that the period cannot run before plaintiff possesses a true cause of action, by which we mean that events have developed to a point where plaintiff is entitled to a legal remedy, not merely a symbolic judgment such as an award of nominal damages." *Davies,* 14 Cal. 3d, at p. 513. The *Davies* court formulated the following rule of general application: "[A]lthough a right to recover nominal damages will not trigger the running of the period of limitation, the infliction of appreciable and actual harm, however uncertain in amount, will commence the statutory period." *Id.* at p. 514.

The *Davies* rule presents some particularly troublesome problems where a defendant's wrongful act causes an immediate, relatively minor tangible injury—but an injury that nonetheless constitutes "appreciable and actual harm—and subsequently results in a far more substantial injury many years later. Some courts held that the earlier injury, even if less severe than the later injury, starts the statute of limitations running as to both injuries, and the expiration of the statute on the earlier injury bars a suit on the later one. *E.g., Miller v. Lakeside Vill. Condo. Assn.,* 1 Cal. App. 4th 1611, 2 Cal. Rptr. 2d 796 (1991); *DeRose v. Carswell,* 196 Cal. App. 3d 1011, 242 Cal. Rptr. 368 (1987). Other courts found that, under various theories, suit on a later manifesting injury was not time-barred even when the limitations period on the earlier injury had expired. *Zambrano v. Dorough,* 179 Cal. App. 3d 169, 224 Cal. Rptr. 323 (1986) (holding a plaintiff, who initially suffered a variety personal injuries such as pain, blood clots, and a ruptured fallopian tube caused by defendant's malpractice, was not time-barred from seeking damages for loss of reproductive capacity when three years later she developed additional injuries caused by defendants earlier malpractice that required a complete hysterectomy); *Martinez-Ferrer v. Richardson-Merrell, Inc.*, 105 Cal. App. 3d 316, 164 Cal. Rptr. 591 (1980) (finding a plaintiff who developed cataracts sixteen years after taking an anti-cholesterol drug not barred by the statute of limitations from bringing a products liability action against the manufacturer, even though the drug initially caused minor eye problems and a rash that lasted six weeks).

The longstanding rule in California is that "[a] single tort can be the foundation for but one claim for damages." *DeRose v. Carswell*, 196 Cal. App. 3d 1011, 1024, fn. 5, 242 Cal. Rptr. 368 (1987); *Miller v. Lakeside Vill. Condo. Assn.*, 1 Cal. App. 4th 1611, 1622, 2 Cal. Rptr. 2d 796 (1991). *See Grisham v. Phillip Morris U.S.A., Inc.*, 40 Cal. 4th 623, 641–46, 54 Cal. Rptr. 3d 735, 151 P.3d 1151 (2007) (discussing the rule where the plaintiff seeks alleges two types of claims: one for personal injury and another for economic injury). However, in *Pooshs v. Phillip Morris USA, Inc.*, reproduced below, the California Supreme Court recognized an exception to this rule, and resolved the troublesome "double injury problem," at least in the context of latent disease cases.

Pooshs v. Philip Morris Usa, Inc.

Supreme Court of California
51 Cal. 4th 788, 123 Cal. Rptr. 3d 578, 250 P.3d 181 (2011)

Kennard, Justice.

Plaintiff was a cigarette smoker for 35 years, from 1953 through 1987. In 1989, she was diagnosed with chronic obstructive pulmonary disease (COPD), which plaintiff knew was caused by her smoking habit. Nevertheless, she did not sue the manufacturers of the cigarettes that she had smoked, and the statutory period for doing so elapsed.

In 1990 or 1991, plaintiff was diagnosed with periodontal disease, which she knew was caused by her smoking habit. Again, she did not sue the various cigarette manufacturers, and the statutory period for doing so elapsed.

In 2003, plaintiff was diagnosed with lung cancer. This time, she sued. We must decide whether the lawsuit is barred by the statute of limitations, which requires that a suit be brought within a specified period of time after the cause of action accrues.

The matter comes to us from the United States Court of Appeals for the Ninth Circuit. (See Cal. Rules of Court, rule 8.548.) The Ninth Circuit has asked us to answer two questions: "(1) Under California law, when may two separate physical injuries arising out of the same wrongdoing be conceived of as invading two different primary rights? [¶] (2) Under California law, may two separate physical injuries—both caused by a plaintiff's use of tobacco—be considered 'qualitatively different' for the purposes of determining when the applicable statute of limitations begins to run?" (*Pooshs v. Phillip Morris USA, Inc.* (9th Cir. 2009) 561 F.3d 964, 966–967 (*Pooshs*).) In granting the Ninth Circuit's request, we restated the two questions in a single question: "When multiple distinct personal injuries allegedly arise from smoking tobacco, does the earliest injury trigger the statute of limitations for all claims, including those based on the later injury?"

We hold that two physical injuries — both caused by the same tobacco use over the same period of time — can, in some circumstances, be considered "qualitatively different" for purposes of determining when the applicable statute of limitations period begins to run. (*Grisham v. Philip Morris U.S.A., Inc.* (2007) 40 Cal.4th 623, 645 [54 Cal. Rptr. 3d 735, 151 P.3d 1151] (*Grisham*).) Specifically, when a later-discovered disease is separate and distinct from an earlier-discovered disease, the earlier disease does not trigger the statute of limitations for a lawsuit based on the later disease. This holding is consistent with the conclusions reached by courts in other jurisdictions addressing the same issue, often in the context of asbestos-related litigation.[1] We limit our holding to latent disease cases, without deciding whether the same rule should apply in other contexts.

In addressing the issue presented here, we emphasize that our role is only to answer the "question of California law" that the Ninth Circuit posed to us. (Cal. Rules of Court, rule 8.548(a).) We play no role in assessing the merits of plaintiff's factual assertions, which must be determined in the federal court. Specifically, plaintiff asserted in the federal district court that her lung cancer is a disease that is separate and distinct from her other two smoking-related diseases. Although this assertion appears plausible on its face, its resolution requires medical expertise. Here, the factual record was never developed because the federal court considered plaintiff's separate-disease assertion to be irrelevant for purposes of applying the statute of limitations, and it granted summary judgment for defendants. On plaintiff's appeal to the Ninth Circuit, that court then asked us whether plaintiff's assertion that her diseases are separate and distinct has any relevance under California statute of limitations law. The Ninth Circuit's reference order states: "For the purposes of summary judgment ... [i]t is uncontested that the etiology for lung cancer is distinct from the etiology for COPD and periodontal disease."[2] (*Pooshs, supra,* 561 F.3d at p. 967.) Therefore, in addressing the issue before us, we assume plaintiff's assertion to be true, and we focus solely on its legal implications.

---

1. The leading case is *Wilson v. Johns-Manville Sales Corp.* (D.C. Cir. 1982) 221 U.S. App. D.C. 337 [684 F.2d 111, 112] (*Wilson*), in which a federal court of appeals concluded "that time to commence litigation does not begin to run on a separate and distinct disease until that disease becomes manifest." Cases from jurisdictions throughout the United States have followed *Wilson.* (See, e.g., *Nicolo v. Philip Morris, Inc.* (1st Cir. 2000) 201 F.3d 29; *Jackson v. Johns-Manville Sales Corp.* (5th Cir. 1984) 727 F.2d 506; *Goodman v. Mead Johnson & Co.* (3d Cir. 1976) 534 F.2d 566 ... ; see also cases cited in *Grisham, supra,* 40 Cal.4th at p. 643, fn. 12.)

2. At oral argument before this court, defendants clarified that this factual point is "uncontested" *only for purposes of the summary judgment issue.* Defendants contend that even if plaintiff's diseases are separate and distinct, the point is irrelevant to the application of the statute of limitations bar, and the validity of that contention is the legal issue before us.

I

Plaintiff Nikki Pooshs filed this action in San Francisco Superior Court in January 2004, less than a year after she was diagnosed with lung cancer. The complaint named various corporate defendants, many of them cigarette manufacturers. Plaintiff alleged that she smoked cigarettes from 1953 until the end of 1987, that she was ignorant of many of the dangers associated with cigarette smoking, and that defendants misled her about those dangers, concealed from her the addictive properties of tobacco, and took other steps to induce her to smoke. She asserted 13 theories of recovery, including allegations of negligence, products liability, misrepresentation, fraud, conspiracy, failure to warn, unfair competition, and false advertising.

Defendants removed the case to federal court and then filed several motions to dismiss. After several dismissals, only four cigarette manufacturers and their public relations agent remained as defendants. These remaining defendants sought dismissal of the complaint, citing the Ninth Circuit's decision in *Soliman v. Philip Morris Inc.* (9th Cir. 2002) 311 F.3d 966 (*Soliman*). In that case, a California plaintiff alleged that he had smoked cigarettes since the late 1960's and could not quit. He claimed nicotine addiction as one of his injuries, in addition to several respiratory and emotional disorders. He further claimed that he did not learn that smoking was addictive (and that he was addicted) until late 1999. In March 2000, he sued various tobacco companies in state court. The *Soliman* defendants removed the case to federal court and then moved to dismiss the complaint on statute of limitations grounds. The defendants doubted that the plaintiff, who had smoked for 32 years, could have discovered his health problems only months before bringing suit. They argued that he had constructive knowledge much earlier, and therefore his suit was time-barred. The district court, applying California law, dismissed the complaint because of expiration of the statute of limitations period. The plaintiff appealed to the Ninth Circuit.

The Ninth Circuit affirmed the district court's judgment in *Soliman, supra,* 311 F.3d 966. The Ninth Circuit observed that the plaintiff alleged *addiction* as one of his injuries and he had constructive knowledge of that addiction long before he filed suit.[3] The court reasoned that the general public is "presumed by California law to know that smoking causes addiction" (*id.* at p. 974) and therefore a "longtime smoker" like the plaintiff may not claim delayed discovery of that injury (*id.* at p. 975). Because the plaintiff could be "charged with this knowledge" long before he filed suit, the Ninth Circuit in *Soliman* concluded that the action was time-barred. (*Ibid.*)

---

3. In *Soliman, supra,* 311 F.3d 966, the Ninth Circuit did not decide whether, under California law, addiction alone is an actionable injury. Instead, the court relied on the fact that the plaintiff had *alleged* addiction as an injury. The court said: "Soliman can't claim that his addiction is an appreciable injury and, at the same time, ask us to ignore it in determining when his claim accrued." (*Id.* at p. 973.)

Here, relying on *Soliman,* the federal district court granted defendants' motion to dismiss. The court found that "while the plaintiff in the present case may not claim addiction as an injury in quite so specific a way as did the plaintiff in *Soliman,* the allegation that the plaintiff here became addicted to nicotine and was injured by that addiction runs as a thread throughout the complaint." (*Pooshs v. Altria Group, Inc.* (N.D.Cal. 2004) 331 F. Supp. 2d 1089, 1095.) The district court found *Soliman* to be controlling and dismissed with prejudice plaintiff's claims against defendants.

Plaintiff appealed to the Ninth Circuit, which held the appeal in abeyance pending our decision in *Grisham, supra,* 40 Cal.4th 623. In *Grisham,* we considered whether the Ninth Circuit in *Soliman, supra,* had correctly construed California law. *Grisham* addressed these two questions: (1) Is there a presumption under California law that, at least since 1988, the general public has been aware of the addictive nature and health dangers of smoking (thereby barring under the statute of limitations a cause of action for addiction-based economic losses) and (2) If the cause of action for addiction-based *economic* losses is time-barred, is a claim for *physical* injuries resulting from the same tobacco use also time-barred?

With respect to the first question, we held in *Grisham, supra,* 40 Cal.4th 623, that there is no special presumption that smokers are aware of the dangers of smoking. We observed, however, that there is a general, rebuttable presumption that a plaintiff has knowledge of the wrongful causes of an injury. To rebut this general presumption a plaintiff must make certain specific allegations that the plaintiff in *Grisham* had not made and, in light of her other allegations, could not plausibly make. Accordingly, in that case the plaintiff's economic injury claim was time-barred under the applicable statute of limitations.

With respect to the second question in *Grisham,* we expressly chose not to decide whether a claim alleging smoking-related physical injury involves a different *primary right* than a claim alleging smoking-related economic injury. Instead, we decided the case solely as a matter of statute of limitations law. We noted that economic injury and physical injury are "qualitatively different" types of injury, and we concluded that an appreciable injury of the first type does not commence the statutory period for suing based on a later-discovered injury of the second type. We did not, however, address in *Grisham* whether this same distinction would apply in a case like the one now before us, where both injuries are physical.

While *Grisham* was pending before us, defendants in this case took plaintiff's deposition and learned that she had suffered from significant medical effects from smoking long before she was diagnosed with lung cancer and long before she filed her current, lung-cancer-based lawsuit. Specifically, she was diagnosed in 1989 with COPD, which is a diagnosis used to describe both emphysema and chronic bronchitis. Plaintiff also admitted knowing as early as 1989 that this pulmonary disease was caused by smoking. And later, in 1990 or 1991, she was diagnosed with periodontal disease, which her periodontist told her was caused by smoking. She did not sue defendants for either of these diseases despite knowing that they were caused by smoking.

After we decided *Grisham*, the Ninth Circuit vacated the district court's judgment in this case and remanded the matter to that court. Defendants then moved for summary judgment, this time asserting that plaintiff's physical injuries diagnosed in 1989 (COPD) and in 1990 or 1991 (periodontal disease) commenced the statutory period for bringing her present action, which is based on the third disease (lung cancer). Having suffered significant physical injuries with knowledge that smoking was the cause of those injuries, and having failed to sue defendants within the applicable statutory periods, plaintiff could not—in defendants' view—later bring suit and assert that her physical injuries turned out to be worse than previously thought. Allowing the suit under those circumstances, defendants asserted, would conflict with the well-settled rule that a statute of limitations starts to run when the plaintiff suffers "appreciable and actual harm, however uncertain in amount." (*Davies v. Krasna* (1975) 14 Cal.3d 502, 514 [121 Cal. Rptr. 705, 535 P.2d 1161] (*Davies*); see also *DeRose v. Carswell* (1987) 196 Cal. App. 3d 1011, 1022 [242 Cal. Rptr. 368] (*DeRose*).)

Plaintiff responded that her three physical injuries (COPD, periodontal disease, and lung cancer) were separate diseases, and that each was therefore the basis of a distinct primary right. Plaintiff stated "that COPD is a separate illness, which does not pre-dispose or lead to lung cancer and that it has nothing medically, biologically, or pathologically to do with lung cancer." She further argued that the primary right at issue here is not the right to be free from the wrongful exposure to tobacco smoke; rather, it is the right to be free from *lung cancer* caused by the wrongful exposure to tobacco smoke, and that this primary right is different from the right to be free from *COPD* or from *periodontal disease* caused by the wrongful exposure to tobacco smoke. The federal district court, to which the case had been remanded by the Ninth Circuit, rejected that argument.

In the view of the federal district court, plaintiff's various physical injuries were merely different ways in which she was damaged by a single alleged wrong (tobacco exposure), like suffering a broken arm and a broken leg from a single car accident. To draw distinctions among the different types of physical injury (i.e., COPD, periodontal disease, and lung cancer) that plaintiff suffered from smoking and then to allow separate suits for each injury, would—the district court said—conflict with the rule against splitting a cause of action: "The longstanding rule in California ... is that '[a] single tort can be the foundation for but one claim for damages.'" (*DeRose, supra*, 196 Cal. App. 3d at p. 1024, fn. 5.) Accordingly, the district court granted summary judgment for defendants.

Plaintiff again appealed to the Ninth Circuit, which then asked us for clarification of California law on the application of the statute of limitations when two separate diseases arise at different times from the same alleged wrongdoing. (*Pooshs, supra*, 561 F.3d at pp. 966–967.) We granted the Ninth Circuit's request.

II

A statute of limitations strikes a balance among conflicting interests. If it is unfair to bar a plaintiff from recovering on a meritorious claim, it is also unfair to require a defendant to defend against possibly false allegations concerning long-forgotten events, when important evidence may no longer be available. Thus, statutes of limitations are not mere technical defenses, allowing wrongdoers to avoid accountability. (*Norgart v. Upjohn Co.* (1999) 21 Cal.4th 383, 395–397 [87 Cal. Rptr. 2d 453, 981 P.2d 79].) Rather, they mark the point where, in the judgment of the Legislature, the equities tip in favor of the defendant (who may be innocent of wrongdoing) and against the plaintiff (who failed to take prompt action): "[T]he period allowed for instituting suit inevitably reflects a value judgment concerning the point at which the interests in favor of protecting valid claims are outweighed by the interests in prohibiting the prosecution of stale ones." (*Johnson v. Railway Express Agency* (1975) 421 U.S. 454, 463–464 [44 L. Ed. 2d 295, 95 S. Ct. 1716].)

Critical to applying a statute of limitations is determining the point when the limitations period begins to run. Generally, a plaintiff must file suit within a designated period after the cause of action *accrues*. (Code Civ. Proc., § 312.) A cause of action accrues "when [it] is complete with all of its elements" — those elements being wrongdoing, harm, and causation. (*Norgart v. Upjohn Co., supra,* 21 Cal.4th at p. 397.)

Application of the accrual rule becomes rather complex when, as here, a plaintiff is aware of both an injury and its wrongful cause but is uncertain as to how serious the resulting damages will be or whether additional injuries will later become manifest. Must the plaintiff sue even if doing so will require the jury to speculate regarding prospective damages? Or can the plaintiff delay suit until a more accurate assessment of damages becomes possible? Generally, we have answered those questions in favor of prompt litigation, even when the extent of damages remains speculative. Thus, we have held that "the infliction of appreciable and actual harm, however uncertain in amount, will commence the statutory period." (*Davies, supra,* 14 Cal.3d at p. 514.)

The most important exception to that general rule regarding accrual of a cause of action is the "discovery rule," under which accrual is postponed until the plaintiff "discovers, or has reason to discover, the cause of action." (*Norgart v. Upjohn Co., supra,* 21 Cal.4th at p. 397.) Discovery of the cause of action occurs when the plaintiff "has reason ... to suspect a factual basis" for the action. (*Id.* at p. 398; see also *Jolly v. Eli Lilly & Co.* (1988) 44 Cal.3d 1103, 1110–1111 [245 Cal. Rptr. 658, 751 P.2d 923].) "The policy reason behind the discovery rule is to ameliorate a harsh rule that would allow the limitations period for filing suit to expire before a plaintiff has or should have learned of the latent injury and its cause." (*Buttram v. Owens-Corning Fiberglas Corp.* (1997) 16 Cal.4th 520, 531 [66 Cal. Rptr. 2d 438, 941 P.2d 71].)

III

Defendants' core argument is that plaintiff's 1989-diagnosed COPD, either alone or in combination with the 1990- or 1991-diagnosed periodontal disease, constituted "appreciable and actual harm" (*Davies, supra,* 14 Cal.3d at p. 514), triggering the running of the pertinent statute of limitations on her indivisible cause of action for smoking-related injury. In 2003, plaintiff was diagnosed with lung cancer, which led her to sue defendants. As of 1991, defendants assert, plaintiff had suffered actual harm, her damages were not merely nominal,[4] and she knew that the harm she had suffered was from smoking. Therefore, in defendants' view, plaintiff should have brought her lawsuit at that time. That she might eventually develop lung cancer in 2003 was, according to defendants, merely an uncertainty as to the *amount* of harm, which did not delay the running of the statute of limitations. In short, defendants' view is that plaintiff could have sued in 1991 but failed to do so. Because defendants' argument depends heavily on the "appreciable and actual harm" rule we announced in *Davies* and then clarified in *Grisham*, we discuss those cases in detail below.

Unlike this case, *Davies, supra*, 14 Cal.3d 502, was not a personal injury case. Rather, *Davies* involved a cause of action for "breach of confidence"—that is, the breach of an obligation, imposed by law, to maintain the confidentiality of a story idea. In 1951, the plaintiff, Valentine Davies, submitted a written story in confidence to the defendant, Norman Krasna, who later incorporated the idea into a successful Broadway play. (*Davies*, at pp. 504–505, 511.) Davies knew as early as 1955 that Krasna had breached his obligation to maintain the confidentiality of the story (*id.* at p. 512), and Davies suffered actual harm at that time (because the breach " 'substantially destroyed the marketability of [the] story' " (*id.* at p. 514)). Nevertheless, Davies did not sue Krasna until 1958, when Krasna began profiting financially from the story. We held that the applicable two-year statute of limitations began to run in 1955 when Davies first learned of the breach and suffered "appreciable and actual harm." In that context, we said: "[N]either uncertainty as to the amount of damages or difficulty in proving damages tolls the period of limitations." (*Ibid.*)

Significantly, in *Davies*, we were considering only a single *type* of injury (economic injury based on the misappropriation of intellectual property), and the issue was whether uncertainty as to the extent of the damages associated with *that single injury* delayed the running of the statute of limitations. Thus, we did not consider in *Davies* whether "the infliction of appreciable and actual harm" of one type (for example, economic injury) would "commence the statutory period" with respect to harm of a *completely different type* (for example, physical injury). Nor did we consider whether "the infliction of appreciable and actual harm" in the form of a specific disease (such as COPD here) would "commence the statutory period" with respect to a *separate and distinct disease* (as the lung cancer here is alleged to be). Therefore, *Davies* does not govern this case. We have never stated what commences the running of the statutory period in a case like this one, in which a later-discovered physical injury is alleged to be separate from an earlier-discovered physical injury. Our decision in *Grisham* emphasized the limits of our holding in *Davies*.

As relevant here, the plaintiff in *Grisham, supra*, 40 Cal.4th 623, sued cigarette manufacturers for smoking-related injuries. She contended that the cigarette manufacturers had wrongfully induced her addiction to tobacco, and she alleged claims

---

4. According to the United States Department of Health & Human Services, COPD is the fourth leading cause of death in the United States. (See Centers for Disease Control and Prevention, Nat. Center for Health Statistics, Leading Causes of Death....)

for economic injury (the cost of purchasing cigarettes) and personal injury (emphysema and periodontal disease). We concluded in *Grisham* that the *economic injury* claim was barred by the applicable statute of limitations because the plaintiff knew or should have known about her injury long before she filed suit. That conclusion raised the question whether the *personal injury* claims were also barred, on the theory that the plaintiff had suffered only one indivisible harm and that the physical injuries were simply another category of damages related to that single harm. In addressing this question in *Grisham*, we did not decide whether the two injuries (economic and physical) implicated two separate primary rights. Instead, we focused exclusively on the statute of limitations, and we held that appreciable harm in the form of an *economic injury* does not begin the running of the statute of limitations on a suit to recover damages for a *physical injury*. *Grisham* interpreted the "appreciable and actual harm" rule of *Davies* to be limited to cases involving a single type of injury, and we found no case applying that rule to a later-discovered injury of a different type. (*Grisham*, at p. 644.)[6]

In *Grisham*, we also emphasized the impractical consequences of a contrary conclusion, relying on *Fox v. Ethicon Endo-Surgery, Inc.* (2005) 35 Cal.4th 797 [27 Cal. Rptr. 3d 661, 110 P.3d 914] (*Fox*). There, the plaintiff underwent gastric bypass surgery. She later sued the surgeon and the hospital for medical malpractice. During discovery, she learned that her alleged injury might have been caused by a defective stapler manufactured by a nonparty. The plaintiff then amended her complaint to add as a defendant the stapler manufacturer, which asserted the statute of limitations as a defense. We concluded in *Fox* that knowledge of the facts supporting a medical malpractice cause of action against one defendant does not necessarily commence the running of the statute of limitations with respect to a separate products liability cause of action against a *different* defendant.

---

6. As mentioned, the court in *Grisham, supra*, 40 Cal.4th 623, concluded the plaintiff's later-manifesting claim for physical injury was timely without also determining whether that claim involved the same primary right as the plaintiff's earlier-manifesting claim for economic damage. In so doing, we necessarily, albeit implicitly, assumed that, even if the plaintiff's various claims involved only a single primary right (as the defendants there asserted), we could still apply the statute of limitations separately to the plaintiff's physical injury claim. (*Id.* at pp. 643, 646.) In other words, we necessarily accepted the possibility that a plaintiff can have a single cause of action that accrues (for statute of limitations purposes) at different times with respect to different types of harm, thus permitting some damage claims to proceed although others are time-barred.

To that extent, *Grisham, supra*, 40 Cal.4th 623, logically supports the recognition of an exception to the rule that "a single tort can be the foundation for but one claim for damages." (*Miller v. Lakeside Village Condominium Assn.* (1991) 1 Cal.App.4th 1611, 1622 [2 Cal. Rptr. 2d 796]; see *DeRose, supra*, 196 Cal. App. 3d 1011, 1024.) Because the exception is inferred from *Grisham*'s holding, it is necessarily limited to cases presenting the same legal and factual situation, that is, a statute of limitations defense to a claim alleging a latent disease that is separate and distinct from, and becomes manifest long after, the initial effects of the plaintiff's injury. Of course, the need for such an exception in any particular case depends on how the relevant primary rights are defined. If two primary rights (and hence two causes of action) are alleged, those two causes of action can accrue independently for purposes of applying the statute of limitations without the need for an exception to the rule that a single tort supports only a single claim. (See Code Civ. Proc., § 312.)

Grisham, supra, 40 Cal.4th 623, involved a claim against the *same* defendants alleging *different* injuries, whereas *Fox, supra,* 35 Cal.4th 797, involved a claim against *different* defendants alleging the *same* injury. Nevertheless, we held that the policy underlying our holding in *Fox* was equally applicable in *Grisham.* In *Grisham,* we quoted the following language from *Fox:* " '[I]t would be contrary to public policy to require plaintiffs to file a lawsuit "at a time when the evidence available to them failed to indicate a cause of action." [Citations.] Were plaintiffs required to file all causes of action when one cause of action accrued, … they would run the risk of sanctions for filing a cause of action without any factual support. [Citations.] Indeed, it would be difficult to describe a cause of action filed by a plaintiff, before that plaintiff reasonably suspects that the cause of action is a meritorious one, as anything but frivolous. At best, the plaintiff's cause of action would be subject to demurrer for failure to specify supporting facts [citation].' " (*Grisham, supra,* 40 Cal.4th at pp. 644–645, quoting *Fox, supra,* 35 Cal.4th at p. 815.)

Applying that language from *Fox,* to the facts in *Grisham, supra,* 40 Cal.4th 623, we rejected a rule that "would compel cigarette smokers either to file groundless tort causes of action based on physical injury against tobacco companies as soon as they discovered they were addicted to cigarettes and had an unfair competition cause of action…, or risk losing their right to sue in tort for such physical injury." (*Id.* at p. 645.) Such a requirement, *Grisham* said, "would violate the essence of the discovery rule that a plaintiff need not file a cause of action before he or she ' "has reason at least to suspect a factual basis for its elements." [Citations.]' [Citation.]" (*Ibid.*) Furthermore, "[i]t would directly contravene 'the interest of the courts and of litigants against the filing of potentially meritless claims.' [Citation.]" (*Ibid.*)

In *Grisham,* we expressly stopped short of deciding the issue presented here, in which a single wrong gives rise to two injuries of the same general type (physical injuries), but the two injuries become manifest at different times and are alleged to be separate and distinct. Nevertheless, we see no reason not to apply to this case the logic of *Grisham.* In both cases, the injuries arose at different times and were separate from one another. In *Grisham,* the injuries were separate from one another in that one was economic and the other was physical; here, the Ninth Circuit has asked us to assume that the injuries are three separate diseases.

It is critical to consider the posture in which this matter comes to us. To defeat summary judgment in the federal district court, plaintiff needed to identify an issue of fact that, if decided in her favor, would allow her to overcome defendants' statute of limitations defense. (See generally *Anderson v. Liberty Lobby, Inc.* (1986) 477 U.S. 242, 248 [91 L. Ed. 2d 202, 106 S. Ct. 2505]; *Celotex Corp. v. Catrett* (1986) 477 U.S. 317, 322 [91 L. Ed. 2d 265, 106 S. Ct. 2548].) The issue of fact that plaintiff identified in the federal district court was that her lung cancer is a disease that is separate from her earlier-discovered COPD and periodontal disease. For example, plaintiff stated "that COPD is a separate illness, which does not pre-dispose or lead to lung cancer and that it has nothing medically, biologically, or pathologically to do with lung cancer." It is not our role to decide or even question the factual validity of that assertion.

Rather, our role is to determine, as a legal matter, whether plaintiff's assertion has any relevance under California law for purposes of applying the statute of limitations, for *that* is the question that the Ninth Circuit asked us to decide. In other words, the Ninth Circuit has asked us to assume plaintiff's assertion to be true and to decide, as a matter of California law, whether two physical injuries that constitute separate diseases and that become manifest at different times can be considered "qualitatively different" (*Grisham, supra*, 40 Cal.4th at p. 645) for purposes of applying the statute of limitations. The answer is "yes."

As already discussed, we emphasized in *Grisham* that it made little sense to require a plaintiff whose only known injury is economic to sue for personal injury damages based on the speculative possibility that a then latent physical injury might later become apparent. Likewise, here, no good reason appears to require plaintiff, who years ago suffered a smoking-related disease that is *not* lung cancer, to sue *at that time* for lung cancer damages based on the speculative possibility that lung cancer might later arise. Nothing we said in *Davies, supra*, 14 Cal.3d 502, requires such a rule, and defendants here have cited no case that supports such a rule. Moreover, although we reaffirm the application of the "appreciable and actual harm" rule to cases that do not involve latent diseases, application of that rule to bar plaintiff's lung cancer claim before her lung cancer had become manifest would violate the policy underlying the discovery rule, which, as we noted earlier, is to prevent "the limitations period ... [from] expir[ing] before a plaintiff has or should have learned of the latent injury and its cause." (*Buttram v. Owens-Corning Fiberglas Corp., supra*, 16 Cal.4th at p. 531.)

It is true that here plaintiff's COPD involved the same part of the body (the lungs) as her lung cancer. Nevertheless, as we noted earlier, the Ninth Circuit has asked that in deciding the statute of limitations issue we accept as true plaintiff's factual assertion "that COPD is a separate illness, which does not pre-dispose or lead to lung cancer and that it has nothing medically, biologically, or pathologically to do with lung cancer." Assuming that assertion to be true, it does not matter that both diseases affect the lungs. The significant point is that the later-occurring disease (lung cancer) is, according to plaintiff's offer of proof, a disease that is separate and distinct from the earlier-oc-curring disease (COPD). Therefore, under the logic of our decision in *Grisham*, the statute of limitations bar can apply to one disease without applying to the other.

IV

In response to the Ninth Circuit's inquiry, we conclude that when a later-dis-covered latent disease is separate and distinct from an earlier-discovered disease, the earlier disease does not trigger the statute of limitations for a lawsuit based on the later disease.

Notes and Questions Regarding *Pooshs* and the "Double Injury Problem"

(1) The Supreme Court in *Pooshs* held that two physical injuries in latent disease cases can be considered "qualitatively different" for purposes of determining when the applicable statute of limitations period begins to run when a later-discovered dis-

ease is "separate and distinct" from an earlier-discovered disease. What constitutes a "qualitatively different" physical injury that is "separate and distinct" from an earlier physical injury? What facts are relevant to this inquiry?

(2) The *Pooshs* decision resolves the troublesome "double injury problem" where a wrongful act first causes relatively minor actual and appreciable injury but years later results in far more substantial injury, at least in the context of latent disease cases. *See, e.g., DeRose v. Carswell*, 196 Cal. App. 3d 1011, 242 Cal. Rptr. 368 (1987) (finding one cause of action and accrual point for all tort injuries); *contra Martinez-Ferrer v. Richardson-Merrell, Inc.*, 105 Cal. App. 3d 316, 164 Cal. Rptr. 591 (1980) (ruling earlier injury and later injury constitute two cause of action and therefore two separate accrual points). Should the *Pooshs* court's reasoning also apply to double injury cases not involving latent diseases?

(3) In footnote 6 of the *Pooshs* opinion, the Supreme Court observes that "[i]f two primary rights (and hence two causes of action) are alleged, these two causes of action can accrue independently for purposes of applying the statute of limitations without the need for an exception to the rule that a single tort supports only a single claim." What does this observation mean? What is an example of when two primary rights are alleged in a case seeking damages for physical injuries?

(4) The Supreme Court in *Pooshs* specifically held that "when a later-discovered disease is separate and distinct from an earlier-discovered disease, the earlier disease does not trigger the statute of limitations for a lawsuit based on the later disease." *Pooshs*, 51 Cal. 4th at 803. What policies are furthered by this rule? Is this rule consistent with the policies underlying statutes of limitations? *See Miller v. Lakeside Vill. Condo. Assn., Inc.*, 1 Cal. App. 4th 1611 1630–34, 2 Cal. Rptr. 2d 796 (1991) (Johnson, J., concurring) (observing that independent suits for different injuries furthers judicial economy, and eliminates the risks of over or under compensating plaintiffs); Michael A. Green, *The Paradox of Statutes of Limitations in Toxic Substances Litigation*, 76 CAL. L. REV. 965, 969, 980–1014 (1988) (arguing that elimination of statutes of limitations in toxic substances litigation would improve the accuracy of litigation outcomes , enhance efficiency in the resolution of toxic substances cases, and promote the legitimacy of the litigation outcomes from society's perspective). What policies are disserved by this approach?

§ 4.04 Tolling the Statute Of Limitations

[A] Introductory Note

After a cause of action has accrued, there are a number of situations in California which will suspend the running of a statutory limitation period. Many of these general tolling provisions are set forth in Sections 351–358 of the Code of Civil Procedure. Other specific tolling provisions are included in special statutes of limitations. *E.g.*, CCP § 340.5 (statutory period for commencing medical malpractice action tolled upon proof of fraud, intentional concealment, or presence of foreign body), and CCP § 340.6 (statutory period for commencing legal malpractice action tolled during time attorney continues to represent plaintiff, etc.). But these statutory provisions do not provide the only bases for tolling. The courts have greatly expanded the application of these tolling situations through liberal interpretations of the code and, in the case of "equitable tolling," by simply creating judicial tolling doctrines based on concepts of fairness.

[B]   Specific Bases for Tolling Limitations Periods

[1]   Statutory "Disability"

If a person has a "disability" within the meaning of CCP § 352 at the time a cause of action accrues, the applicable statute of limitations is suspended during the time of such "disability." Section 352(a) defines "disability" to mean that the person is "under the age of majority" or "insane." Section 352.1 adds "imprisoned on a criminal charge." These general tolling provisions are subject to several important qualifications and exceptions.

[a]   Limitations

No person can toll a statute of limitation based on "disability" unless the disability existed when the right of action accrued. CCP § 357. Consequently, once a cause of action has accrued and the limitation period has begun to run, the period will not be suspended because of a "disability" subsequent to accrual. *Congregational Church Bldg. Society v. Osborn*, 153 Cal. 197, 94 P. 881 (1908); *but see* CCP § 354 (statute tolled by reason of state of war regardless of whether cause of action already accrued). The disability of imprisonment is further limited in two ways. First, regardless of the actual sentence, the tolling period cannot exceed two years. CCP § 352.1(a). Second, tolling provisions do not apply to most actions relating to the conditions of confinement. CCP § 352.1(c).

[b]   Exceptions

There are several important statutory exceptions to the traditional "disability" tolling provisions of CCP § 352(a). For example, these provisions do not apply to an action against a public entity or public employee on a cause of action for which a claim is required to be presented by the California Claims Act, Government Code §§ 905.2, 945.6 & 950.2, CCP § 352(b). However, the California Claims Act does contain some special tolling provisions of its own, particularly with respect to an application to present a late claim. *See, e.g.*, Gov. Code §§ 911.4 and 946.6, discussed *infra*.

Nor do they apply to medical malpractice actions, at least as to tolling during minority. CCP § 340.5 requires minors to commence actions within three years of the wrongful act, except that actions by a minor under the age of six years must be commenced within three years or prior to his eighth birthday, whichever provides a longer period. The very limited tolling period for minors in § 340.5 was upheld in *Young v. Haines*, 41 Cal. 3d 883, 226 Cal. Rptr. 547, 718 P.2d 909 (1988), although the court did also construe the other tolling provisions in the second sentence of § 340.5 as applicable to minors. Also, the one year period for filing an administrative complaint of discrimination under the Fair Employment and Housing Act (FEHA), Gov. Code § 12960, is not tolled during plaintiff's minority because FEHA is not among the statutes covered by CCP § 352. *See Balloon v. Superior Court*, 39 Cal. App. 4th 1116, 46 Cal. Rptr. 2d 161 (1995).

[2] *Absence or Nonresidence of Defendant*

One of the most controversial tolling provisions is contained in CCP § 351, which states:

> If, when the cause of action accrues against a person, he is out of the state, the action may be commenced within the term herein limited, after his return to the state, and if, after the cause of action accrues, he departs from the state, the time of his absence is not part of the time limited for the commencement of the action.

Section 351 was originally enacted in 1872, at a time when service on absent defendants in an in personam action was generally unavailable. *See* Walter W. Heiser, *Can the Tolling of Statutes of Limitations Based on the Defendants' Absence from the State Ever Be Consistent with the Commerce Clause?*, 76 Mo. L. Rev. 385, 387–89 (2011). But with the adoption of modern long-arm statutes in California, several methods of service became available to confer jurisdiction to enter a personal judgment against an absent defendant. *See, e.g.*, CCP §§ 415.20–415.50. As a result, the continued vitality of a tolling provision based on absence was subject to doubt and criticism. *See Developments in the Law — Statutes of Limitations*, 63 Harv. L. Rev. 1177, 1226–28 (1950); Samuel W. Halper, Note, *Limitation of Actions: Absence of the Defendant: Tolling the Statute of Limitations on a Foreign Cause of Action*, 1 UCLA L. Rev. 619 (1954).

However, in *Dew v. Appleberry*, 23 Cal. 3d 630, 153 Cal. Rptr. 219, 591 P.2d 509 (1979), the Supreme Court applied CCP § 351 literally despite the fact the defendant was amenable to service of process. Plaintiff was injured on defendant's premises on September 23, 1973, but did not file her action seeking personal injury damages until September 24, 1974. The court held plaintiff's action not barred by the one-year statute of limitation because the period was tolled by § 351 due to defendant's absence from California for five weeks during the year following plaintiff's injury. The court rejected defendant's argument that § 351 did not apply because defendant was always amenable to service of process. The court reasoned that repeals by implication are not favored, and therefore § 351 still applied despite the changes in the service statutes. The court noted that § 351 does not make its tolling provision depend on availability of service, but on defendant's physical presence in California.

The Court of Appeal has interpreted CCP § 351 to apply where the defendant is a nonresident of California when the cause of action accrues, despite language in § 351 suggesting a contrary construction. *See Cvecich v. Giardino*, 37 Cal. App. 2d 394, 99 P.2d 573 (1940) (ruling that although neither plaintiff nor defendant was ever a resident of California, limitation period tolled). Under this interpretation, a statute of limitations is suspended as to a non-resident defendant, and will never begin to run until the defendant actually enters the state! *Kohan v. Cohan,* 204 Cal. App. 3d 915, 251 Cal. Rptr. 570 (1988); *see also Green v. Zissis,* 5 Cal. App. 4th 1219, 7 Cal. Rptr. 2d 406 (1992) (holding statute of limitations on action to enforce judgment tolled because defendant absent from state since prior judgment). This interpretation of § 351 has particularly troubled scholars. *See Developments In the Law — Statutes of Limitations, supra,* 63 HARV. L. REV. at 1224–28; as well as judges; *see, e.g., Cardoso v. American Med. Sys., Inc., infra.* Why? What rational basis exists for the continued application of this tolling provision to nonresidents?

What if the defendant is a corporation neither incorporated in nor with its principle place of business in California, but doing business in California? Is a statute of limitations permanently suspended in California as to such nonresident corporate defendants? Is Corporations Code § 2111, which provides that a foreign corporation is amenable to process in California by service upon the Secretary of State, relevant here? *See Loope v. Greyhound Lines, Inc.,* 114 Cal. App. 2d 611, 250 P.2d 651 (1952) (holding § 351 inapplicable to nonresident defendant corporation in view of California statutory provisions relative to substituted service on foreign corporations). Should it be relevant after *Dew?*

In *Cardoso v. American Med. Sys., Inc.,* 183 Cal. App. 3d 994, 228 Cal. Rptr. 627 (1986), the Court of Appeal, relying on *Loope,* held that the availability of substituted service of process upon a nonresident corporation renders the tolling provisions of § 351 inapplicable. "To rule otherwise would result in the anomalous situation that a statute of limitation would never run in actions filed against foreign corporations. This would be contrary to the avowed purpose of such statutes to prevent stale claims." *Cardoso,* 183 Cal. App. 3d at 999. Likewise, in *Epstein v. Frank,* 125 Cal. App. 3d 111, 177 Cal. Rptr. 831 (1981), the court held that the tolling provisions of § 351 are not available to California limited partnerships where the sole general partner is absent from the state. Are *Cardoso* and *Epstein* consistent with the reasoning of *Dew?*

[a]   Constitutionality of Section 351

Until recently, constitutional challenges to the validity of CCP § 351 had been unsuccessful in state court. *See, e.g., Dew v. Appleberry, supra,* 23 Cal. 3d at 636–37; *Kohan v. Cohan, supra,* 204 Cal. App. 3d at 923–24. But in *Abramson v. Brownstein,* 897 F.2d 389 (9th Cir. 1990), the U.S. Court of Appeals concluded that CCP § 351 violates the Commerce Clause of the U.S. Constitution. Plaintiff Abramson commenced an action in federal court in California against defendant Brownstein for breach of contract. Defendant was a nonresident of California who had never been physically present in the state. The action was clearly time-barred under the relevant California statutes of limitations, unless the tolling provision of CCP § 351 applied. The federal appellate court, relying on *Bendix Autolite Corp. v. Midwesco Enter. Inc.,* 486 U.S. 888, 108 S. Ct. 2218, 100 L. Ed. 2d 896 (1988), held that § 351 did apply but is unconstitutional in violation of the Commerce Clause of the U.S. Constitution. The court ruled that § 351 forced a nonresident defendant to choose between being present in California for several years or forfeiture of the limitations defense, and, as such, was an impermissible burden on interstate commerce.

After *Abramson*, is § 351 of any further use in California? The effect of *Abramson* on CCP § 351 was considered in *Mounts v. Uyeda*, 227 Cal. App. 3d 111, 277 Cal. Rptr. 730 (1991). Plaintiff Mounts filed a tort action against defendant Uyeda for infliction of emotional distress, alleging that defendant pointed a gun at plaintiff in a threatening manner. Both parties were residents of California and both were driving cars at the time of the incident, which occurred on January 30, 1988. Plaintiff commenced her action on January 31, 1989; defendant moved for summary judgment because the action was not commenced within one year. Plaintiff sought to utilize § 351 by arguing the limitations period was tolled due to defendant's absence from the state for four days during the year.

The *Mounts* court first held that CCP § 351, and not Vehicle Code § 17463, applied to the action. Next, the court considered the effect of *Abramson v. Brownstein, supra*. The court noted that *Abramson* did not declare § 351 unconstitutional on its face. As applied to the facts before it, the court ruled that § 351 was not unconstitutional because both parties were residents of California and the alleged action did not involve interstate commerce. The court then concluded that § 351 did not violate the Commerce Clause as applied, and that the statute of limitations was tolled during defendant's absence. *Mounts, supra*, 227 Cal. App. 3d at 120–122. Subsequently, the court in *Pratali v. Gates*, 4 Cal. App. 4th 632, 5 Cal. Rptr. 2d 733 (1993), held that § 351 does not violate the Commerce Clause because the defendant, a noncommercial resident of Idaho who had defaulted on a personal note, was not engaged in interstate commerce.

The constitutional soundness of CCP § 351 was revisited in *Filet Menu, Inc. v. Cheng*, 71 Cal. App. 4th 1276, 84 Cal. Rptr. 2d 384 (1999). The *Filet Menu* court concluded that § 351 violates the Commerce Clause not only as applied to *nonresident* defendants, but also as applied to *resident* defendants who travel in the course of interstate commerce. However, the court emphasized that its conclusion was limited to travel for facilitation of interstate commerce—tolling statutory periods for the duration of out-of-state travel unrelated to interstate commerce, such as for vacation trips or to attend college, does not violate the Commerce Clause. *Id.* at 1283–84.

More recently, in *Heritage Mktg. & Ins. Services, Inc. v. Chrustawka*, 160 Cal. App. 4th 754, 73 Cal. Rptr. 3d 126 (2008), the court considered the constitutionality of CCP § 351 when applied to defendants who resided in California when the cause of action accrued but *permanently* relocated to Texas before the statute of limitations expired. The court concluded that absence-based tolling under such circumstances violated the Commerce Clause regardless of the reason for the defendants' move out of state. *Heritage Mktg., supra*, 160 Cal. App. 4th at 762–64. The court reasoned as follows (*Id.* at 764):

> By creating disincentives to travel across state lines and imposing costs on those who wish to do so, the statute prevents or limits the exercise of the right to freedom of movement. Applying section 351 under the facts of this case would impose an impermissible burden on interstate commerce as it

would force defendants to choose between remaining residents of California until the limitations periods expired or moving out of state and forfeiting the limitations defense....

Do you agree with this interpretation of the Commerce Clause? Under the reasoning employed by the *Heritage Marketing* court, under what circumstances would absence-based tolling pursuant to CCP § 351 be consistent with the Commerce Clause? For a discussion of the constitutionality of CCP § 351 and absence-based tolling statutes in effect in other states, see Walter W. Heiser, *Can the Tolling of Statutes of Limitations Based on the Defendants' Absence from the State Ever Be Consistent with the Commerce Clause?*, *supra* (arguing that CCP § 351 violates the Commerce Clause when applied to a resident defendant who is temporarily absent from California regardless of the reason for the interstate travel).

[b] Statutory Exceptions

A considerable portion of the court's opinion in *Mounts* deals with the question of whether CCP § 351 or Vehicle Code § 17463 governs with respect to tolling. *Mounts, supra*, 227 Cal. App. 3d at 114–20. Vehicle Code § 17463 contains an express exception to CCP § 351, and applies to actions arising out of the operation of a motor vehicle in California. Vehicle Code § 17463 provides that a statute of limitations shall not be tolled during a defendant's absence from the state except when defendant cannot be located through the exercise of reasonable diligence. *See Litwin v. Estate of Formela*, 186 Cal. App. 4th 607, 111 Cal. Rptr. 3d 868 (2010) (ruling Vehicle Code § 17463 excludes nonresident as well as resident motorists from § 351 absence-based tolling, and nonresident motorists may be served by serving the Director of the DMV). The court in *Mounts* concluded that Vehicle Code § 17463 did not apply to plaintiff's action, and that therefore CCP § 351 did apply. The court made no finding as to whether defendant was reasonably locatable when absent from the state, yet held Vehicle Code § 17463 inapplicable. On what basis could the court justify this holding?

Vehicle Code § 17463, in conjunction with Vehicle Code §§ 17459 and 17460, is one of the few express statutory exceptions to the operation of CCP § 351. Both CCP § 340.5 (medical malpractice) and § 340.6 (legal malpractice) contain specific special tolling provisions. Do these statutes contain an implied exception to CCP § 351? *See Laird v. Blacker*, 2 Cal. 4th 606, 618, 7 Cal. Rptr. 2d 550, 828 P.2d 691 (1992) (holding the Legislature expressly intended CCP § 340.6(a) to disallow tolling under any circumstances not enumerated in the statute); *Jocer Enter., Inc., v. Price*, 183 Cal. App. 4th 559, 569–70, 107 Cal. Rptr. 3d 539 (2010) (ruling the tolling provision of CCP § 340.6(a)(4) encompasses the circumstances set forth in § 351).

[3] *Other Statutory Tolling Provisions*

The Code of Civil Procedure contains other general tolling exceptions to the running of a statute of limitations: Section 352.5 (defendant subject to independent order of restitution for injury as a condition of probation); § 366.1 and § 366.2 (death of plaintiff or defendant extends relevant statute of limitations for certain survived actions); § 353.1 (extends relevant statute of limitations up to six months when court has assumed jurisdiction over attorney's practice); § 354 (state of war); § 355 (plaintiff has one year to file new action where prior favorable judgment for plaintiff reversed on appeal other than on the merits); and § 356 (commencement of action stayed by injunction or statutory prohibition).

[4] Professional Malpractice Statutes

Code of Civil Procedure §§ 340.5 and 340.6 contain special tolling provisions applicable only to medical and legal malpractice actions, respectively.

[a] Medical Malpractice

Section 340.5 provides:

> In an action for injury or death against a health care provider based upon such person's alleged professional negligence, the time for the commencement of action shall be three years after the date of injury or one year after the plaintiff discovers, or through the use of reasonable diligence should have discovered, the injury, whichever occurs first. *In no event shall the time for commencement of legal action exceed three years unless tolled for any of the following: (1) upon proof of fraud, (2) intentional concealment, or (3) the presence of a foreign body, which has no therapeutic or diagnostic purpose or effect, in the person of the injured person.* Actions by a minor shall be commenced within three years from the date of the alleged wrongful act except that actions by a minor under the full age of six years shall be commenced within three years or prior to his eighth birthday whichever provides a longer period. Such time limitation shall be tolled for minors for any period during which parent or guardian and defendant's insurer or health care provider have committed fraud or collusion in the failure to bring an action on behalf of the injured minor for professional negligence. (Emphasis added.)

Does § 340.5 provide the exclusive bases for tolling, such that neither § 351 nor § 352 apply? *See Belton v. Bowers Ambulance Serv.*, 20 Cal. 4th 928, 86 Cal. Rptr. 2d 107, 978 P.2d 591 (1999) (holding that although no tolling provision outside of CCP § 340.5 can extend the *three-year* maximum time period for commencement of a medical malpractice action, based on a careful reading of the plain language, § 340.5 does not provide the exclusive basis for tolling the *one-year* limitation period); *Kaplan v. Mamelak*, 162 Cal. App. 4th 637, 75 Cal. Rptr. 3d 861 (2008) (ruling CCP § 351 applies in medical malpractice cases to allow tolling of the one-year statute of limitations during any days the defendant doctor was out of state); *Alcott Rehab. Hosp. v. Superior Court*, 93 Cal. App. 4th 94, 112 Cal. Rptr. 2d 807 (2001) (ruling the insanity provision in CCP § 352 tolled the one-year statute of limitations in § 340.5 with respect to a medical malpractice action brought by a mentally incompetent women against a licensed skilled nursing facility). Such that equitable tolling doctrines, discussed *infra*, do not apply?

Does § 340.5 preclude use of extension of the limitation period by fictitious defendant practice? *See Snoke v. Bolen*, 235 Cal. App. 3d 1427, 1 Cal. Rptr. 2d 492 (1991). With respect to minors, do the tolling provisions of the fourth sentence of § 340.5 and not of the second sentence apply, or do both? In *Young v. Haines, supra*, 41 Cal. 3d at 896–901, the Supreme Court concluded that the tolling provisions of both sentences are available to minors, and that a contrary construction may be unconstitutional. Does the language of § 340.5 support this construction as to minors?

[b] Legal Malpractice

Code of Civil Procedure §§ 340.6(a)(1)–(4) provide special tolling provisions for the four-year maximum limitation period for legal malpractice actions during the time: (1) the plaintiff has not sustained "actual injury," (2) the attorney continues to represent the plaintiff regarding the specific subject matter in which the alleged negligence occurred, (3) the attorney willfully conceals facts, or (4) the plaintiff is under legal or physical disability. Does § 340.6(a) provide the exclusive basis for tolling such that CCP § 352 does not apply? § 351? Equitable tolling doctrines? Why is the limitation period tolled while the attorney continues to represent the plaintiff? Why did the Legislature include this provision for attorneys, but not for doctors in § 340.5?

[c] Legal Malpractice: "Actual Injury"

What constitutes "actual injury" within the meaning of CCP § 340.6(1)? Has a client sustained "actual injury" when an adverse administrative or trial court decision is entered against the client as a result of her attorney's negligence, but an appeal is still pending with respect to this decision? In *Laird v. Blacker*, 2 Cal. 4th 606, 7 Cal. Rptr. 2d 550, 828 P.2d 691 (1992), the Supreme Court concluded that a client suffers "actual injury" within the meaning of § 340.6 upon entry of an adverse trial court judgment due to attorney negligence, despite availability of appeal or other postjudgment relief. The court viewed accrual under § 340.6 as focusing on the discovery of malpractice—the fact and knowledge of damage—and not on the amount of that damage. *Id.* at 614–15.

In *Jordache Enter., Inc. v. Brobeck, Phleger & Harrison*, 18 Cal. 4th 739, 76 Cal. Rptr. 2d 749, 958 P.2d 1062 (1998), the Supreme Court revisited the question of what constitutes "actual injury" within the meaning of CCP § 340.6. In *Jordache*, the client (plaintiff Jordache) alleged that its attorneys (defendant Brobeck) failed to advise it about, or assert a timely claim to, liability insurance benefits covering a third party's lawsuit (the Marciano action for alleged marketing of "knockoff" apparel) against Jordache. Jordache acknowledged that it discovered Brobeck's alleged malpractice more than one year before it commenced the malpractice action. However, Jordache contended it did not sustain actual injury until it later settled its action against its insurer (National Union) for less that the full benefits Jordache claimed.

The Supreme Court ruled that "[a]ctual injury occurs when the client suffers any loss or injury cognizable as damages in a legal malpractice action based on the asserted errors or omission," *Jordache, supra*, 18 Cal. 4th at 743, and therefore injury occurred in the instant case before Jordache's settlement with its insurer [*Id.*, at 752–54]:

> Actual injury refers only to the legally cognizable damage necessary to assert the cause of action. There is no requirement that an adjudication or settlement must first confirm a causal nexus between the attorney's error and the asserted injury. The determination of actual injury requires only a factual analysis of the claimed error and its consequences. The inquiry necessarily is more qualitative than quantitative because the fact of damage, rather than the amount, is the critical factor.

> Of course, nominal damages will not end the tolling of section 340.6's limitations period. Thus, there is no basis for Jordache's expressed concern that the statutory period will run once the plaintiff sustains the "first dollar" of injury. Instead, the inquiry concerns whether "events have developed to a point where plaintiff is entitled to a legal remedy, not merely a symbolic judgment such as an award of nominal damages." However, once the plaintiff suffers actual harm, neither difficulty in proving damages nor uncertainty as to their amount tolls the limitations period.

> Here, the undisputed facts established that Jordache sustained actual injury as a result of Brobeck's alleged neglect no later than December 1987. By then, Jordache had lost millions of dollars—both in unpaid insurance benefits for defense costs in the Marciano action and in lost profits from diversion of investment funds to pay these defense costs. As Brobeck asserts, these damages were sufficiently manifest, nonspeculative, and mature that Jordache tried to recover them as damages in its insurance coverage suits. * * *

What are the practical consequences of the Supreme Court's interpretation of "actual injury"? Does the interpretation further judicial economy? Does it increase the potential for unfairness to the malpractice plaintiff? How so? What policy is furthered by the Supreme Court's interpretation? *See* Tyler T. Ochoa & Andrew J. Wistrich, *Limitation of Legal Malpractice Actions: Defining Actual Injury and the Problem of Simultaneous Litigation*, 24 Sw. U. L. Rev. 1 (1994).

When does a client sustain "actual injury" where the attorney fails to bring an action within the applicable statute of limitations? At the time the statute of limitations expired, or later when the underlying action is actually dismissed by the court as barred by the statute of limitations? In *Adams v. Paul*, 11 Cal. 4th 583, 46 Cal. Rptr. 2d 594, 904 P.2d 1205 (1995), the Supreme Court held that the determination of when a client suffers "actual injury" as a consequence of the attorney negligently missing the statute of limitations is a question of fact, and not one subject to a bright line rule. What does the *Adams* court mean by this? *See, e.g., Truong v. Glasser*, 181 Cal. App. 4th 102, 111–15, 103 Cal. Rptr. 3d 811 (2009) (finding plaintiffs first sustained actual injury when they obtained and were obligated to pay new counsel to escape the consequences of former attorney's alleged malpractice). In what factual situations does a client suffer "actual injury" at the time the statutory limitations period lapsed? Under what circumstances does a lapsed limitations period create only the potential for future harm?

[d]   Legal Malpractice: "Continuous Representation"

When does "continuous representation" cease within the meaning of § 340.6(a)(2)? *Compare Hensley v. Caietti*, 13 Cal. App. 4th 1165, 1169–73, 16 Cal. Rptr. 2d 837 (1993) (concluding the question of representation should be viewed from the perspective of the client), *with Worthington v. Rusconi*, 29 Cal. App. 4th 1488, 35 Cal. Rptr. 2d 169 (1994) (ruling CCP § 340.6(a)(2) requires an objective determination of whether the representation has ended; "continuity of representation ultimately depends, not on the client's subjective beliefs, but rather on evidence of an ongoing mutual relationship and of activities in furtherance of the relationship"), *and LaClette v. Galindo*, 184 Cal. App. 4th 919, 109 Cal. Rptr. 3d 660 (2010) (reviewing cases and concluding that continuous representation should be view objectively from the client's perspective).

The tolling provision of § 340.6(a)(2) is unaffected by the client's knowledge of the attorney's wrongful act as long as representation continues, *see O'Neill v. Tichy*, 19 Cal. App. 4th 114, 25 Cal. Rptr. 2d 162 (1993), or by the attorney's attempts to rectify the problem or to mitigate the client's damages after the malpractice manifests itself. *Fritz v. Ehrmann*, 136 Cal. App. 4th 1374, 39 Cal. Rptr. 3d 670 (2006). What if the negligent attorney abandons the client? *Gonzalez v. Kalu*, 140 Cal. App. 4th 21, 43 Cal. Rptr. 3d 866 (2006) (ruling that in the event of an attorney's unilateral withdrawal or abandonment of the client, the representation ends when the client actually has or reasonably should have no expectation that the attorney will provide further legal services).

In *Beal Bank, SSB v. Arter & Hadden, LLP*, 42 Cal. 4th 503, 66 Cal. Rptr. 3d 52, 167 P.3d 666 (2007), the Supreme Court answered a question that had divided the lower courts: When an attorney leaves a firm and takes a client with him, does the tolling in ongoing matters continue for claims against the former firm and partners? The court concluded that such tolling does not continue because when a lawyer leaves a firm and takes a client with him, the firm's representation of the client ceases.

[5]   *Servicemembers Civil Relief Act*

50 U.S.C. App. § 526 provides that "[t]he period of a servicemember's military service may not be included in computing any period limited by law ... for the bringing of any action or proceeding in any court, or in any board, bureau, commission department, or other agency ... by or against the servicemember...." This tolling provision is part of the federal Servicemembers Civil Relief Act, 50 U.S.C. App. § 501 *et seq.*

This federal tolling requirement applies to all "persons in military service," which is defined in 50 U.S.C. App. § 511. Application of § 526 is mandatory as to any person in military service; it does not require a showing of prejudice by reason of such service. *Syzemore v. County of Sacramento*, 55 Cal. App. 3d 517, 522–24, 127 Cal. Rptr. 741 (1976). Section 526 applies to all federal and California statutes of limitations, including the claim filing requirements for actions against government entities contained in the Government Code, §901 *et seq., id.*; and even to time limitations for bringing an action to trial. *Butler v. City of Los Angeles*, 153 Cal. App. 3d 520, 200 Cal. Rptr. 372 (1984).

This federally mandated tolling doctrine has considerable application in California, does it not?

[6]   The Federal "Savings" Statute

28 U.S.C. §1367, enacted by Congress in 1990, codifies the federal doctrines of pendant and ancillary jurisdiction, and renames them "supplemental jurisdiction." Section 1367(a) authorizes the federal courts to assert supplemental jurisdiction over state-based claims which are related to claims within the federal court's original jurisdiction. Section 1367(b) provides some specific restrictions on supplemental jurisdiction, and §1367(c) delineates when a federal court may decline to exercise supplemental jurisdiction. Section §1367(d) then states:

> The period of limitations for any claim asserted under subsection (a), and for any other claim in the same action that is voluntarily dismissed at the same time as or after the dismissal of the claim under subsection (a), shall be tolled while the claim is pending and for a period of 30 days after it is dismissed unless State law provides for a longer tolling period.

Section 1367(d) imposes a new tolling provision on each state. A party now has a minimum of 30 days within which to commence an action in state court on any claim previously asserted under section 1367 that was dismissed by the federal court. If a plaintiff files state and federal claims in federal court with only a few days remaining on the applicable state statute of limitations and those claims are subsequently dismissed without prejudice, how much time under 28 U.S.C. §1367(d) does the plaintiff have to file an action in state court? *See City of Los Angeles v. County of Kern*, 59 Cal. 4th 618, 174 Cal. Rptr. 3d 67, 328 P.3d 56 (2014) (interpreting §1367 to provide a afford parties a grace period allowing claims that otherwise would have become barred while pending in federal court to be pursued in state court if refiled no later than 30 days after federal court dismissal).

[7]   Equitable Tolling of Statutes of Limitations

Garabedian v. Skochko

Court of Appeal of California, Fifth Appellate District
232 Cal. App. 3d 836, 283 Cal. Rptr. 802 (1991)

STONE (W. A.), JUSTICE.

This appeal concerns whether the pendency of a federal tort claim for personal injuries against the United States government tolls the statute of limitations applicable to a state action against a defendant who was not a government employee and who was dismissed from a subsequent federal action because the federal court did not have jurisdiction over him. Under the circumstances of this case we will hold the federal tort claim did not toll the state statute of limitations.

THE CASE

The trial court sustained without leave to amend the demurrer of respondent, Steven Skochko, to the first amended complaint of appellant, Haig Garabedian, and entered a judgment of dismissal. The basis of the court's order was that the one-year statute of limitations barred appellant's action for personal injuries.

THE FACTS

In 1987 appellant was a real estate agent. He had obtained permission of the United States Department of Housing and Urban Development (HUD) to show homes owned by HUD. HUD requested him to show a particular home to potential purchasers. On June 3 he went to the HUD home to inspect the premises before showing the property. He slipped and fell into an empty swimming pool because of debris which had accumulated around the pool. He sustained serious injuries as a result of the accident.

On or about May 6, 1988, appellant filed a claim with HUD as required by the Federal Tort Claims Act. The claim did not name respondent. HUD rejected the claim by letter dated July 25, 1988, denying responsibility for appellant's injuries. The letter advised that although HUD owned the property, it was managed by respondent, an independent contractor. The letter denied HUD's responsibility for the negligent acts or omissions of the independent contractor. Until receipt of the letter rejecting the claim, appellant had no knowledge an independent contractor rather than a HUD employee managed the property.

In August 1988 appellant filed an action in federal court against respondent and the United States. One year later, pursuant to a recent United States Supreme Court decision,[2] the federal court dismissed respondent from that action without prejudice.

Appellant then filed this negligence action in state court against respondent on September 7, 1989.

DISCUSSION

Code of Civil Procedure [former] section 340, subdivision (3) required that appellant bring his state action against respondent prior to June 3, 1988—one year after the date of the accident. Instead, appellant filed his complaint more than 15 months after the expiration of the limitations period. Unless the statute of limitations was tolled for the period of time during which he pursued his federal action against HUD, his action is time-barred. Our question is whether the complaint alleges facts sufficient to establish such tolling.

---

2. *Finley v. United States* (1989) 490 U.S. 545 [104 L. Ed. 2d 593, 109 S. Ct. 2003] held the Federal Tort Claims Act does not provide a vehicle by which to invoke pendant party jurisdiction over claims which would otherwise not come within the jurisdiction of the federal court.

The complaint alleges appellant did not know, and could not have known, anyone other than a HUD employee could possibly have been responsible for the negligence that resulted in appellant's injuries. He therefore pursued his remedy under the Federal Tort Claims Act in a timely and good faith manner. He did not learn of the independent contractor status of respondent until July 27, 1988, when HUD's letter so advised him. Although appellant was unable to file an action against respondent within one year of the date of the accident, respondent nevertheless had knowledge of the claim prior to that time.

Appellant contends the statute of limitations on his state cause of action was tolled during the period between May 6, 1988, and September 7, 1989, while he was pursuing his federal remedy. He relies upon several tolling theories.

A. *Neither HUD nor Respondent "Effectively Prevented" Appellant From Proceeding in the State Court.*

As a general rule, absent some wrongdoing on the part of a defendant, a plaintiff's ignorance of his cause of action or the identity of the wrongdoer does not prevent the running of the limitations period. Although appellant implies either HUD or respondent, or both of them, are somehow responsible for his predicament, he has alleged no facts which would give rise to an estoppel or would indicate fraudulent concealment.

Thus, HUD did not effectively prevent appellant from proceeding against respondent within the limitations period. He cites no authority establishing a legal obligation by HUD to advise him of respondent's identity and status in sufficient time to investigate and initiate the appropriate proceedings.

B. *Appellant Was Not "Legally Prevented" From Proceeding in the State Court.*

Appellant claims HUD legally prevented him from proceeding in a separate state action against respondent during the time when his claim was pending against HUD. Filing a claim with the responsible federal agency is a legal prerequisite to the filing of a civil action against the United States for money damages arising out of the negligence of a government employee. (28 U.S.C. § 2675.) However, a claim is not a legal prerequisite to filing a civil action against a defendant who is not a government employee. The complaint fails to allege facts sufficient to establish appellant was somehow legally prevented from filing a state action against respondent while his claim was pending with HUD.

C. *The "Several Remedies" Rule Did Not Toll the Statute of Limitations.*

The "several remedies" rule has been recognized as a separate ground for tolling the limitations period and is based upon the principle that " ... regardless of whether the exhaustion of one remedy is a prerequisite to the pursuit of another, if the defendant is not prejudiced thereby, the running of the limitations period is tolled '[w]hen an injured person has several legal remedies and, reasonably and in good faith, pursues one.' [Citations.]" (*Elkins v. Derby* (1974) 12 Cal. 3d 410, 414 [115 Cal. Rptr. 641, 525 P.2d 81, 71 A.L.R. 3d 839].)

In addition to *Elkins*, the "several remedies" rule has been developed in three cases: *Tu-Vu Drive-In Corp. v. Davies* (1967) 66 Cal. 2d 435 [58 Cal. Rptr. 105, 426 P.2d

505]; *County of Santa Clara v. Hayes Co.* (1954) 43 Cal. 2d 615 [275 P.2d 456]; and *Myers v. County of Orange* (1970) 6 Cal. App. 3d 626 [86 Cal. Rptr. 198].

In *Myers*, a widow brought an action against the county for the wrongful discharge of her deceased husband after she failed to obtain a declaration of his reinstatement through administrative channels in order to receive death benefits. The court held the period within which she was required to file a claim with the county had been tolled while she pursued her administrative remedy.

"When an injured person has several legal remedies and, reasonably and in good faith, pursues one designed to lessen the extent of the injury or damages, the statute of limitations does not run on the other while he is thus pursuing the one...." (6 Cal. App. 3d at p. 634.)

The *Myers* court continued:

"[U]pon the death of her husband, plaintiff was faced with two alternative procedures. Being uncertain of the applicability to her situation of the doctrine of the necessary exhaustion of administrative remedies, she could either file a claim with the county for damages and thereafter institute suit, in which she would have undoubtedly been confronted with a claim by the county that the suit could not be maintained because of her failure to exhaust administrative remedies, or she could apply for a hearing by the appeal board and seek to have the order of discharge rescinded and her husband reinstated as an employee from the date of discharge until the date of his death. She chose to pursue the latter remedy, and, in our opinion, in so doing, she acted reasonably, for, if she had been successful, there would have been no damages resulting from the discharge, and no claim for damages or suit for damages would have been necessary." (*Myers v. County of Orange, supra,* 6 Cal. App. 3d at pp. 635–636.)

In *Elkins v. Derby, supra,* the court adopted the "several legal remedies" language of *Myers*. Plaintiff had timely pursued his workers' compensation remedy against the defendant but the claim was denied when the Workers' Compensation Appeals Board decided Elkins was not an "employee" within the meaning of the workers' compensation act because he had not received compensation for his services. Shortly after the board's decision became final, Elkins filed an action against the defendant for recovery for the same injuries that prompted the workers' compensation claim. The court held the statute of limitations on the personal injury action against the defendant had been tolled for the period of time during which the plaintiff had pursued the administrative remedy against the defendant. (12 Cal. 3d at p. 412.) * * *

The object of the "several remedies" rule is to excuse the plaintiff from the burden of pursuing duplicate and possibly unnecessary procedures in order to enforce the same rights or obtain the same relief. (*Elkins v. Derby, supra,* 12 Cal. 3d at pp. 412–413.)

The common thread in these cases is that the parties against whom the plaintiffs sought some kind of preliminary relief before filing suit eventually became the named defendants in the state court actions. Here, however, respondent, who became a defendant in the state court action, was not named in the federal tort claim. By the time appellant filed his federal lawsuit naming respondent as a defendant, more than one year had elapsed following the accident. * * *

We recognize that had the federal court determined respondent was a government employee rather than an independent contractor, a state action would not have been available since the Federal Tort Claims Act is the exclusive remedy for claims against a federal government employee acting within the scope of government employment. (28 U.S.C. § 2679.) Moreover, all of appellant's claims would have been resolved in the federal proceeding; the state action would not have been necessary. For purposes of tolling it is immaterial that the federal court subsequently determined respondent was not a government employee.

"[T]he question of tolling is not to be determined retrospectively depending upon the success or failure of the plaintiff in pursuing the alternative remedy. [Citation.] ... The injured person should not be required 'to predict at his peril the precise legal theory [remedy] supporting ultimate recovery. He should not be placed in the dilemma of awaiting "jurisdictional" decisions ... [of one tribunal] ... while the clock of limitations ticks in his ear.' [Citation.]" (*Myers v. County of Orange, supra,* 6 Cal. App. 3d at p. 636.)

However, as noted in *Freeman v. State Farm Mut. Auto. Ins. Co.* [(1975)] 14 Cal. 3d 473 [121 Cal. Rptr. 477, 535 P.2d 341], the underlying assumption of the "several remedies" rule is that the plaintiff is aware of alternative remedies and makes a conscious, rational and reasonable decision to pursue one remedy in order to eliminate the need to pursue the other. Those cases applying the rule do not address a situation in which the plaintiff has failed to ascertain the need to pursue an alternative remedy until after the statute of limitations has run on the alternative remedy. *Freeman* holds, albeit in a different context, that the "several remedies" rule is not available in such a situation.

Appellant has not stated facts sufficient to toll the statute of limitations on his cause of action for personal injuries against respondent for the period of time he was pursuing his remedy against HUD.

D. *"Equitable Tolling" Did Not Suspend the Period of Limitations.*

Equitable tolling of a statute of limitations was first acknowledged as a recognized doctrine with identifiable elements it *Addison v. State of California* (1978) 21 Cal. 3d 313 [146 Cal. Rptr. 224, 578 P.2d 941]. In *Addison,* state and county officers raided plaintiffs' business and seized numerous records in contemplation of criminal proceedings which were never initiated. Plaintiffs filed timely damage claims against the state and county which were denied with the warning that plaintiffs were required to file a court action on the claim within six months. Three and one-half months later, plaintiffs filed a complaint in federal court alleging violation of federal civil rights, and, on the basis of pendant jurisdiction, several state causes of action for which claims had been filed and rejected. After concluding the civil rights action would not lie against the public entities, the federal court dismissed the federal action and the remaining state causes of action, without prejudice to refiling in state court. At that point, the limitations period for bringing the state action had run. *Addison* held the filing of the federal action suspended the running of the limitations period within which a suit could be brought against the public entities. (21 Cal. 3d at p. 315.)

Addison explains:

"It is fundamental that the primary purpose of statutes of limitation is to prevent the assertion of stale claims by plaintiffs who have failed to file their action until evidence is no longer fresh and witnesses are no longer available. '[T]he right to be free of stale claims in time comes to prevail over the right to prosecute them.' (*Telegraphers v. Ry. Express Agency* (1944) 321 U.S. 342, 349 [88 L. Ed. 788, 792, 64 S. Ct. 582]; *see also Burnett v. New York Central R. Co.* (1965) 380 U.S. 424, 428 [13 L. Ed. 2d 941, 945, 85 S. Ct. 1050].) The statutes, accordingly, serve a distinct public purpose, preventing the assertion of demands which through the unexcused lapse of time, have been rendered difficult or impossible to defend. However, courts have adhered to a general policy which favors relieving plaintiff from the bar of a limitations statute when, possessing several legal remedies he, reasonably and in good faith, pursues one designed to lessen the extent of his injuries or damage. [Citations.]

" ... [A]pplication of the doctrine of equitable tolling requires timely notice, and lack of prejudice, to the defendant, and reasonable and good faith conduct on the part of the plaintiff. These elements seemingly are present here. As noted, the federal court, without prejudice, declined to assert jurisdiction over a timely filed state law cause of action and plaintiffs thereafter promptly asserted that cause in the proper state court. Unquestionably, the same set of facts may be the basis for claims under both federal and state law. We discern no reason of policy which would require plaintiffs to file simultaneously two separate actions based upon the same facts in both state and federal courts since 'duplicative proceedings are surely inefficient, awkward and laborious.' (*Elkins v. Derby, supra,* 12 Cal. 3d at p. 420; *but see Rumberg v. Weber Aircraft Corp.* (C.D.Cal. 1976) 424 F. Supp. 294.)

"Furthermore, since the federal court action was timely filed, defendants were notified of the action and had the opportunity to begin gathering their evidence and preparing their defense. No prejudice to defendants is shown, for plaintiffs' state court action was filed within one week of the dismissal of the federal suit. To apply the doctrine of equitable tolling in this case, in our view, satisfies the policy underlying the statute of limitations without ignoring the competing policy of avoiding technical and unjust forfeitures." (21 Cal. 3d at pp. 317–319.)

As stated by the *Addison* court, the three elements necessary to establish the doctrine of equitable tolling are (1) timely notice to the defendant, (2) lack of prejudice to the defendant, and (3) reasonable and good faith conduct on the part of the plaintiff. (21 Cal. 3d at p. 319.)

The central question here is whether formal notice to one defendant is sufficient notice to another defendant.

In *Thompson v. California Fair Plan Assn.* (1990) 221 Cal. App. 3d 760 [270 Cal. Rptr. 590], plaintiff filed a declaratory relief action against the defendant insurance company in order to have a policy of fire insurance reformed to reflect that she was the insured. She subsequently filed suit against the insurance company and individual agents of the insurance company alleging conspiracy to deprive her of insurance proceeds. In an effort to avoid application of the statute of limitations, she sought to invoke the doctrine of equitable tolling.

> "The timely notice requirement includes the necessity that the first claim alert the defendant in the second claim to the need to investigate the facts which form the basis for the second claim. [Citation.] Here defendant Roy W. Anderson was not named in the first suit for declaratory relief. It is difficult to imagine how he could have been alerted to the need to investigate the facts of the second claim. In addition, lack of prejudice requires that the two claims be identical or at least so similar that the defendant's investigation of the first claim will put him in a position to fairly defend the second. [Citation.]" (221 Cal. App. 3d at p. 765.) * * *

We assume, as the complaint alleges, that respondent had notice of the claim filed with HUD. We conclude, however, that the doctrine of equitable tolling does not apply merely because defendant B has obtained timely knowledge of a claim against defendant A for which defendant B knows or believes he may share liability. This point seems to have been recognized in *Collier v. City of Pasadena* (1983) 142 Cal. App. 3d 917 [191 Cal. Rptr. 681], in which the court stated, "under ordinary circumstances [a] workers' compensation claim would not equitably toll a personal injury action against a third party who might also be liable for the injury." (142 Cal. App. 3d at pp. 924–925.)

In *Dowell v. County of Contra Costa* (1985) 173 Cal. App. 3d 896 [219 Cal. Rptr. 341], plaintiff contended the statute of limitations on her cause of action against the county was tolled during the pendency of her claim against the State of California for damages arising out of the same facts. * * * The court ... addressed the arguments.

> "*The Addison court did not address the problem of whether the statute is tolled as to one defendant while awaiting action on a claim filed against another defendant.* In *Sierra Club, Inc. v. California Coastal Com., supra,* 95 Cal. App. 3d at [pages] 503–504, the court stated that the doctrine of equitable tolling applies only where the plaintiff commences a second action which is in reality a continuation of an earlier action involving the same parties, facts and cause of action. *Due to the lack of identity of the parties, the existence of continuing administrative proceedings by Dowell against the State would not toll the statute of limitation for Dowell's cause of action against the County.*
>
> "The conclusion in *Sierra Club* is consistent with the reasoning in *Addison.* The *Addison* court listed three basic requirements for application of the doctrine of equitable tolling: timely notice, lack of prejudice to the defendants and reasonable and good faith conduct on the part of the plaintiff. *(Addison v. State of California, supra* 21 Cal. 3d at p. 319.)....

"In the present case the same cannot be said. *Dowell's failure to file suit against the County until action on her claim against the state did not provide the County with notice of her intention to bring suit or prevent prejudice to the County in gathering information and preparing its defense. Since the claim proceedings against the state and County were entirely separate and the County was not put on notice of Dowell's intention to sue, the doctrine of equitable tolling was inapplicable. (Addison v. State of California, supra,* 21 Cal. 3d at pp. 319–321.)" (173 Cal. App. 3d at p. 903, italics added.)

Similarly here, although filing the claim with HUD put the agency on notice of appellant's intended suit against the government, it did not put respondent on notice of appellant's intended suit against him.

The complaint does not allege facts sufficient to toll the statute of limitations on appellant's action against respondent.

Judgment affirmed. Costs on appeal to respondent.

Prudential-LMI Commercial Insurance v. Superior Court

Supreme Court of California
51 Cal. 3d 674, 274 Cal. Rptr. 387, 798 P.2d 1230 (1990)

LUCAS, CHIEF JUSTICE.

Petitioner Prudential-LMI Commercial Insurance (Prudential) and real parties in interest (plaintiffs) each seek review of a Court of Appeal decision issuing a writ of mandate directing summary judgment in favor of Prudential. The action involves progressive property damage to an apartment house owned by plaintiffs and insured over the years by successive insurers, including Prudential. We granted review to address three issues: (i) when does the standard one-year limitation period (hereafter one-year suit provision) contained in all fire policies (pursuant to Ins. Code, § 2071)[1] begin to run in a progressive property damage case; (ii) should a rule of equitable tolling be imposed to postpone the running of the one-year suit provision from the date notice of loss is given to the insurer until formal denial of the claim; and (iii) when there are successive insurers, who is responsible for indemnifying the insured for a covered loss when the loss is not discovered until several years after it commences? The last issue can be resolved by placing responsibility on (a) the insurer insuring the risk at the time the damage began, (b) the insurer insuring the risk at the time the damage manifested itself, or (c) all insurers on the risk, under an allocation (or exposure) theory of recovery.

As explained below, we hold that the one-year suit provision begins to run on the date of inception of the loss, defined as that point in time when appreciable damage occurs and is or should be known to the insured, such that a reasonable insured would be aware that his notification duty under the policy has been triggered. We

---

1. All further statutory references are to the Insurance Code unless otherwise noted.

also hold that this limitation period should be equitably tolled from the time the insured files a timely notice, pursuant to policy notice provisions, to the time the insurer formally denies the claim in writing. In addition, we conclude that in a first party property damage case (i.e., one involving no third party liability claims), the carrier insuring the property at the time of manifestation of property damage is solely responsible for indemnification once coverage is found to exist.

As we explain further below, we emphasize that our holding is limited in application to the first party progressive property loss cases in the context of a homeowners insurance policy. As we recognized in *Garvey v. State Farm Fire & Casualty Co.* (1989) 48 Cal. 3d 395, 405–408 [257 Cal. Rptr. 292, 770 P.2d 704], there are substantial analytical differences between first party property policies and third party liability policies. Accordingly, we intimate no view as to the application of our decision in either the third party liability or commercial liability (including toxic tort) context.

BACKGROUND

1. *The Policy*

Plaintiffs, as trustees of a family trust, built an apartment house in 1970–1971 and insured it with four successive fire and extended coverage property insurers between 1971 and 1986. Prudential insured the risk between October 27, 1977, and October 27, 1980. It issued an all-risk homeowners policy which insured against "All Risks of Direct Physical Loss except as hereinafter excluded." The policy insured for both property loss and liability.

As noted above, we are concerned here only with the first party property loss portion of plaintiffs' policy. It insured against all risks of direct physical loss subject to the terms and conditions set forth in the policy, which provided definitions and general policy provisions explaining to the insured the coverages and exclusions of the policy. The specified exclusions included loss "caused by, resulting from, contributed to or aggravated by any earth movement, including but not limited to earthquake, mudflow, earth sinking, rising or shifting; unless loss by fire or explosion ensues, and this Company shall then be liable only for such ensuing loss."

The policy contained several standard provisions adopted from the "California Standard Form Fire Insurance Policy" and section 2071, entitled "Requirements in case loss occurs." The provisions in relevant part required the insured to: "give written notice … without unnecessary delay, protect the property from further damage … and within 60 days after the loss, unless such time is extended in writing by this company, the insured shall render to this company a proof of loss, signed and sworn to by the insured, stating the knowledge and belief of the insured as to the following: the time and origin of the loss, [and] the interest of the insured and all others in the property…." In the same section of the policy, the provision entitled "When loss payable" required the insurer to pay the amount of loss for which the company may be liable "60 days after proof of loss … is received by this company and ascertainment of the loss is made whether by agreement between the insured and this company expressed in writing or by the filing with this company of an award as [otherwise provided in the policy—i.e., pursuant to the policy arbitration and appraisal provisions]."

Plaintiffs' policy also contained the standard one-year suit provision first adopted by the Legislature in 1909 as part of the "California Standard Form Fire Insurance Policy." (*See* §§ 2070, 2071.) It provided: "No suit or action on this policy for the recovery of any claim shall be sustainable in any court of law or equity unless all the requirements of this policy shall have been complied with, and unless commenced within 12 months next after inception of the loss." With this background in mind, we turn to the facts underlying this claim.

2. *The Facts*

While replacing the floor covering in an apartment unit in November 1985, plaintiffs discovered an extensive crack in the foundation and floor slab of the building. In December 1985, they filed a claim with their brokers, who immediately notified Prudential and the other companies that had issued insurance policies on the property during plaintiffs' period of ownership. Prudential conducted an investigation of the claim, which included an examination under oath of plaintiffs in February 1987. Prudential concluded the crack was caused by expansive soil that caused stress, rupturing the foundation of the building. In August 1987, shortly before receiving formal written notice that their claim had been denied under the policy's earth movement exclusion, plaintiffs sued Prudential, the three other insurers that had insured the property between 1971 and 1986, and their insurance brokers or agents, alleging theories of breach of contract, bad faith, breach of fiduciary duties and negligence.

Prudential sought summary judgment and, alternatively, summary adjudication of 16 issues arising out of the complaint, contending there was no evidence any loss was suffered during its policy period and hence it could not be required to indemnify plaintiffs. Prudential observed that carpeting had been installed in 1982, covering the area later damaged, but asserted that at the time of installation (nearly two years after Prudential's coverage had ended), plaintiffs observed no damage or evidence of cracking. Prudential also claimed that because plaintiffs filed suit 20 months after filing their claim, the action was barred by the standard one-year suit provision contained in its policy, pursuant to section 2071.

The court denied the motion in its entirety, stating that triable issues existed as to whether the earth movement exclusion applied, whether the damage occurred during the policy period, and when the crack first appeared. Prudential sought a writ of mandate to review the denial of the motion, arguing only that the action was time-barred because plaintiffs failed to comply with the policy's notice-of-claim requirement and one-year suit provision.

The Court of Appeal issued a peremptory writ of mandate directing the trial court to vacate its order denying the insurer's summary judgment motion and to enter another order granting the relief requested. * * * As stated above, both plaintiffs and Prudential seek review on the one-year suit provision and successive insurer issues. We begin by discussing section 2071, the delayed discovery principle announced by the Court of Appeal, and application of the doctrine of equitable tolling to the limitations period.

DISCUSSION

1. *Section 2071: One-year Suit Provision — History of the Limitations Period*

Under California law, all fire insurance policies must be on a standard form and, except for specified exceptions, may not contain additions thereto. (§ 2070). This standard form provides that no suit or action for recovery of any claim shall be sustainable unless commenced within 12 months after the "inception of the loss." (§ 2071). * * *

When a clause in an insurance policy is authorized by statute, it is deemed consistent with public policy as established by the Legislature. In addition, the statute must be construed to implement the intent of the Legislature and should not be construed strictly against the insurer (unlike ambiguous or uncertain policy language). With this history in mind, we consider how to define the inception of a loss for purposes of triggering section 2071 when the loss occurs some time before any damage is discovered by the insured.

2. *Delayed Discovery and Inception of the Loss*

* * *

Although the concept of a standard policy was intended to provide policyholders with a clear indication of their duties under the policy, courts have not uniformly agreed when the limitation period begins to run in cases involving property damage not discovered until years after damage actually occurs. All courts recognize, however, that determination of when the statute of limitations period commences depends on the interpretation of the phrase "inception of the loss" in section 2071.

Some courts, strictly construing "inception of the loss," define it as the occurrence of the physical event causing the loss. [Citations omitted] * * * Several first party cases have acknowledged support for a delayed discovery rule that holds an insured responsible for initiating a claim based on the date on which the insured could reasonably have concluded his property suffered a loss. * * *

We agree that "inception of the loss" should be determined by reference to reasonable discovery of the loss and not necessarily turn on the occurrence of the physical event causing the loss. Accordingly, we find that California law supports the application of the following delayed discovery rule for purposes of the accrual of a cause of action under section 2071: The insured's suit on the policy will be deemed timely if it is filed within one year after "inception of the loss," defined as that point in time when appreciable damage occurs and is or should be known to the insured, such that a reasonable insured would be aware that his notification duty under the policy has been triggered. To take advantage of the benefits of a delayed discovery rule, however, the insured is required to be diligent in the face of discovered facts. The more substantial or unusual the nature of the damage discovered by the insured (e.g., the greater its deviation from what a reasonable person would consider normal wear and tear), the greater the insured's duty to notify his insurer of the loss promptly and diligently. (*See, e.g., April Enterprises, Inc. v. KTTV, supra,* 147 Cal. App. 3d 805, 833 [generally question of fact whether reasonable diligence has been exercised in discovering claim]).

Determining when appreciable damage occurs such that a reasonable insured would be on notice of a potentially insured loss is a factual matter for the trier of fact. The insured's unreasonableness in delaying notification of the loss until a particular point in time may be raised as a separate affirmative defense by an insurer in response to a complaint by the insured for recovery of benefits under the policy. The insurer has the burden of proving those allegations by a preponderance of the evidence.

In this case, plaintiffs' policy required notice of loss to be given "without unnecessary delay," and proof of loss to be filed within 60 days of the loss. A factual question remains as to the properly calculated accrual date under the delayed discovery principles announced above. Plaintiffs therefore should be allowed to amend their complaint to allege facts showing their discovery of the loss was reasonable.

3. *Doctrine of Equitable Tolling*

Our inquiry does not end with adoption of a delayed discovery rule. After filing their notice of loss, plaintiffs waited more than 18 months to file the present action. Thus, even under our delayed discovery rule, the one-year suit provision would, unless otherwise inapplicable or excused, bar plaintiffs from pursuing the present action. The seemingly anomalous conclusion — that an insured must file a lawsuit before the insurer has completed its investigation and denied the claim — has been questioned in other jurisdictions that have the identical statutory scheme as California.

Two divergent views have developed. Several state courts have strictly interpreted the standard limitation clauses. [Citations omitted.] Other state courts have devised rules to equitably toll the limitation period until an insurer's formal denial of the claim by the insured. The leading case for this view is *Peloso v. Hartford Fire Insurance Co.* [(1970)] 56 N.J. 514 [267 A.2d 498] (*Peloso*), involving an action by an insured seeking recovery for fire damage to his home. The policy contained a one-year suit provision identical to the one contained in plaintiffs' policy here. * * * Other states have followed *Peloso*'s lead. [Citations omitted.] In addition, as the parties observe, a few states have enacted statutes that expressly extend the one-year limitation provision. * * * Early California cases took inconsistent approaches to the issue. * * *

More recent cases have applied the equitable doctrines of waiver and estoppel to allow a suit filed after the limitation period expired to proceed. It is settled law that a waiver exists whenever an insurer intentionally relinquishes its right to rely on the limitations provision. * * * For example, if the insurer expressly extends the one-year suit provision during its claim investigation, the insurer waives its right to raise a timeliness defense to the insured's action. Similarly, an insurer that leads its insured to believe that an amicable adjustment of the claim will be made, thus delaying the insured's suit, will be estopped from asserting a limitation defense.

By contrast, equitable tolling has most often been applied in California when the plaintiff first files a claim before an administrative agency and then files a second proceeding after the limitation period has expired. Under these circumstances, courts have held the policy underlying the statute of limitations — prompt notice to permit complete and adequate defense — has been satisfied and that the period should be tolled in equity to preserve the plaintiff's claim. * * *

Like the *Peloso* court, we conclude the Legislature's intent to provide insureds with a full year (excluding the tolled period) in which to commence suit can be inferred from the fact that the period provided by section 2071 is considerably shorter than the usual four years for ordinary contracts (Code Civ. Proc., § 337) and ten years for an action against developers for property damage caused by latent defects. (*Id.*, § 337.15; *Peloso, supra,* 267 A.2d 498 at p. 501). We find *Peloso*'s reasoning consistent with the trend in other states toward equitable tolling of the one-year suit provision in the limited circumstances in which the insurer (or other party against whom the claim has been made) has received timely notice of the loss and thus is able to investigate the claim without suffering prejudice.

4. *Policy Considerations*

Persuasive policy considerations support equitable tolling of the limitations period: Prudential suggests that suspension of the one-year suit provision during the time the insurer investigates the loss will frustrate the provision's primary purpose of preventing the revival of stale claims. But as stated in *Bollinger* [*v. National Fire Ins. Co.* (1944) 25 Cal. 2d 399 [154 P.2d 399]], "Originally the shortened limitation periods were inserted into policies by insurers. Some courts declared such provisions void as against public policy while other courts enforced them in order to protect freedom of contract." We emphasized in *Bollinger* that the purpose of a shortened limitation period was to obtain the advantage of an early trial of the matters in dispute and to make more certain and convenient the production of evidence on which the rights of the parties depended, and not to achieve a technical forfeiture of the insured's rights by enforcing the limitation provision when the insured has given timely notice of a claim to his insurer. We do not believe that an equitable tolling of the one-year limitation period will frustrate the purpose of section 2071, or work a hardship on the insurer, whose investigation will necessarily have preceded the denial of coverage.

Moreover, the principle of equitable tolling presents several advantages in eliminating the unfair results that often occur in progressive property damage cases. First, it allows the claims process to function effectively, instead of requiring the insured to file suit *before* the claim has been investigated and determined by the insurer. Next, it protects the reasonable expectations of the insured by requiring the insurer to investigate the claim without later invoking a technical rule that often results in an unfair forfeiture of policy benefits. Although an insurer is not required to pay a claim that is not covered or to advise its insureds concerning what legal arguments to make, good faith and fair dealing require an insurer to investigate claims diligently before denying liability. Third, a doctrine of equitable tolling will further our policy of encouraging settlement between insurers and insureds, and will discourage unnecessary bad faith suits that are often the only recourse for indemnity if the insurer denies coverage after the limitation period has expired.

Equitable tolling is also consistent with the policies underlying the claim and limitation periods — e.g., the insurer is entitled to receive prompt notice of a claim and the insured is penalized for waiting too long after discovery to make a claim. For example, if an insured waits 11 months after discovering the loss to make his claim, he will have only 1 month to file his action after the claim is denied before it is timebarred under section 2071. (*See e.g., Peloso, supra,* 267 A.2d at p. 502.)

Finally, the anomaly caused by a literal application of the one-year suit provision is demonstrated by the facts of this case. Plaintiffs allege they notified Prudential of their loss in December 1985, one month after it was discovered. Assuming this delayed discovery was reasonable, they then had 60 days to file a proof of loss and Prudential had another 60 days to determine liability under the policy. During this time, any suit on the policy filed by plaintiffs would have been premature. Negotiations apparently continued until January 1987, when plaintiffs assertedly received a letter from Prudential proposing that coverage would be denied based on the earth movement exclusion unless the insureds had any additional information that would favor coverage. At this point, plaintiffs sought counsel who contacted Prudential. In February 1987, Prudential requested that plaintiffs submit to an examination under oath pursuant to policy terms. It was not until September 1987, that plaintiffs' claim was denied unequivocally. Thus, if the one-year suit provision were literally applied, plaintiff's suit would have been untimely before the insurer denied coverage.

We conclude that proper resolution of the foregoing anomaly is to allow the one-year suit provision of section 2071 to run from the date of "inception of the loss," as defined above, but to toll it from the time an insured gives notice of the damage to his insurer, pursuant to applicable policy notice provisions, until coverage is denied. As *Peloso, supra,* 267 A.2d 498, observed, "[i]n this manner, the literal language of the limitation provision is given effect; the insured is not penalized for the time consumed by the company while it pursues its contractual and statutory rights to have a proof of loss, call the insured in for examination, and consider what amount to pay; and the central idea of the limitation provision is preserved since an insured will have only 12 months to institute suit." (*Id.* at pp. 501–502.) We agree with *Peloso* that such an approach to the limitation provision is more easily applied than the concepts of waiver and estoppel in the many different fact patterns that may arise.

In the present case, plaintiffs allege that approximately one month had elapsed between the date the loss was discovered and the date notice thereof was given to Prudential. As stated above, we conclude plaintiffs should be allowed to amend their complaint to allege facts showing their action was filed within one year of their delayed discovery of the loss. If, on remand, it is determined that the delayed discovery of the loss was reasonable, the one-year suit provision would be tolled from December 1985 until September 1987, when plaintiffs were notified by Prudential that coverage was denied. Plaintiffs would then have had 11 months to institute suit against Prudential, so that any suit filed before September 1988 would be considered timely.

5. *Progressive Loss Rule*

We next examine allocation of indemnity between successive first party property insurers when the loss is continuous and progressive throughout successive policy periods, but is not discovered until it becomes appreciable, for a reasonable insured to be aware that his notification duty under the policy has been triggered. * * *

Prudential argues that even assuming the applicable one-year suit provision does not bar the suit, it should not be responsible for any covered loss because plaintiffs presented no evidence that a loss was suffered during the period of its policy term (Oct. 27, 1977, to Oct. 27, 1980). It also asserts that because its policy period ended in 1980—five years before the damage was allegedly discovered by plaintiffs—it should not be responsible for indemnification of any covered loss. Prudential asks the court to adopt a "manifestation rule" of property coverage that fixes liability for first party property losses solely on the insurer whose policy was in force at the time the progressive damage became appreciable or "manifest." In discussing both the manifestation and continuous exposure theories, we keep in mind the important distinction that must be made in a causation analysis between first party property damage cases and third party liability cases. * * *

[W]e conclude that in first party progressive property loss cases, when, as in the present case, the loss occurs over several policy periods and is not discovered until several years after it commences, the manifestation rule applies. As stated above, prior to the manifestation of damage, the loss is still a contingency under the policy and the insured has not suffered a compensable loss. Once the loss is manifested, however, the risk is no longer contingent; rather, an event has occurred that triggers indemnity unless such event is specifically excluded under the policy terms. Correspondingly, in conformity with the loss-in-progress rule, insurers whose policy terms commence after initial manifestation of the loss are not responsible for any potential claim relating to the previously discovered and manifested loss. Under this rule, the reasonable expectations of the insureds are met because they look to their present carrier for coverage. At the same time, the underwriting practices of the insurer can be made predictable because the insurer is not liable for a loss once its contract with the insured ends unless the manifestation of loss occurred during its contract term.

One final question must be addressed regarding the application of a manifestation rule of coverage in progressive loss cases: how does the rule relate to our rules of delayed discovery and equitable tolling announced above? We have previously defined the term "inception of the loss" as that point in time when appreciable damage occurs and is or should be known to the insured, such that a reasonable insured would be aware that his notification duty under the policy has been triggered. We conclude that the definition of "manifestation of the loss" must be the same. Under this standard, the date of manifestation and hence the date of inception of the loss will, in many cases, be an issue of fact for the jury to decide. When, however, the evidence supports only one conclusion, summary judgment may be appropriate. For example, when the undisputed evidence establishes that no damage had been discovered before a given date (i.e., no manifestation occurred), then insurers whose policies expired prior to that date could not be liable for the loss and would be entitled to summary judgment. The litigation can then be narrowed to include only the insurers whose policies were in effect when the damage became manifest.

CONCLUSION

Based on the principles discussed above, we conclude plaintiffs should be allowed to amend their complaint to allege that their delayed discovery of the loss at issue was reasonable, and that they timely notified Prudential of the loss without unnecessary delay following its manifestation. If it is found that plaintiffs' delayed discovery of the loss was reasonable, then the rule of equitable tolling would operate to toll the one-year suit provision from the date the insured filed a timely notice of loss to Prudential's formal denial of coverage. Whether Prudential must then indemnify plaintiffs for any covered claim under the policy necessarily depends on whether that insurer was the carrier of record on the date of manifestation of the loss. Although it appears from the present record that manifestation of loss occurred in November 1985, after Prudential's policy had expired, we note that plaintiffs have joined other insurers in the litigation. Therefore, in the absence of conclusive evidence, we decline to speculate concerning the date manifestation of loss occurred. The decision of the Court of Appeal is reversed and the cause remanded for proceedings consistent with our opinion.

Notes and Questions Regarding Equitable Tolling

(1) The Supreme Court first recognized the doctrine of "equitable tolling" in *Bollinger v. National Fire Ins. Co.*, 25 Cal. 2d 399, 154 P.2d 399 (1944), and subsequently expanded it in *Addison v. State of California, supra*, quoted extensively by the Court of Appeal in *Garabedian*. How would you define the doctrine after *Addison* and *Prudential-LMI*? What factors were important to the Supreme Court in deciding to authorize equitable tolling based on the facts of those two cases? In what other fact situations might this doctrine now apply? Could this doctrine have been of any use to the plaintiff in *Jolly v. Eli-Lilly & Co., supra*? Is this doctrine available where the plaintiff voluntarily dismisses the initial action? *See Appalachian Ins. Co. v. Mc-Donnell Douglas Corp.*, 214 Cal. App. 3d 1, 40–42, 262 Cal. Rptr. 716 (1989).

For a novel application of equitable tolling, see *Lambert v. Commonwealth Land Title Ins. Co.*, 53 Cal. 3d 1072, 282 Cal. Rptr. 445, 811 P.2d 737 (1991), where the Supreme Court held that the two-year limitation period of CCP § 339 for an action under a title insurance policy for failure to defend accrues when the insurer refuses the insured's tender of defense, but is tolled until the underlying action is terminated by final judgment. For an extended discussion, by a divided court, of the proper application of equitable tolling, *Lambert*, and *Prudential-LMI* to an action by plaintiff against the defendant title insurance company for failure to list an easement affecting property that plaintiff had purchased, see *Forman v. Chicago Title Ins. Co.*, 32 Cal. App. 4th 998, 38 Cal. Rptr. 2d 790 (1995).

In *Mitchell v. Frank R. Howard Mem. Hosp.*, 6 Cal. App. 4th 1396, 1407–08, 8 Cal. Rptr. 2d 521 (1992), the court refused to equitably toll the statute of limitations because the plaintiff had waited more than nine months after dismissal of plaintiff's identical federal court action, and already had two other virtually identical state court actions dismissed for failure to prosecute, prior to commencing the current state court action. The court, applying *Addison*, found that the plaintiff had not acted reasonably and in good faith by delaying the filing of the instant action. *See also Hull v. Central Pathology Service Med. Clinic*, 28 Cal. App. 4th 1328, 1336, 34 Cal. Rptr. 2d 175 (1994) (ruling *Bollinger* equitable tolling doctrine not satisfied because plaintiff did not diligently pursue new claims).

(2) Compare *Addison*'s equitable tolling doctrine with the federal "savings" statute, 28 U.S.C. § 1367(d). Do they operate coextensively in situations where a party seeks to refile a claim in California state court that has previously been dismissed from federal court? In *City of Los Angeles v. County of Kern*, 59 Cal. 4th 618, 174 Cal. Rptr. 3d 67, 328 P.3d 56 (2014), the Supreme Court addressed the proper interpretation of section 1367(d) which, according to the Court, "has confounded courts nationally and in California, with two near-equal camps emerging." *Id.* at 622. The Court concluded that the "statute affords parties a grace period, allowing claims that would otherwise have become barred to be pursued in state court if refiled no later than 30 days after federal court dismissal." *Id.* Under this "grace period" approach, the relevant state statute of limitations continues to run while the claims are pending in federal court. If the federal dismissal occurs after the expiration of the governing state statute limitations period, the plaintiff will have 30 days within which to refile the claims in state court. However, if the federal dismissal occurs *more* than 30 days *before* the expiration of the state limitations period, the plaintiff gets all that remaining time to refile in state court. *Id.* at 633–34. In interpreting section 1367(d), the Court rejected the "suspension approach"—the approach used in *Addison*-type equitable tolling cases, which would suspend the running of the statute of limitations during the entire time suit is pending in federal court—as inconsistent with Congressional intent. *Id.* at 632–34.

(3) The *Garabedian* court discussed the "several remedies" rule as a doctrine separate from "equitable tolling." Are these two doctrines distinguishable? Or are they simply both aspects of the equitable tolling doctrine developed in *Addison*? Do you agree with the *Garabedian* court's refusal to find equitable tolling based on *Addison*? Do you agree with the court's conclusion that the plaintiff's claim filed with HUD did not sufficiently alert defendant Skochko of the need to investigate the facts which formed the basis of plaintiff's subsequent state court action, within the meaning of *Addison*? What type of "timely notice to the defendant" does *Addison* require, anyway? Why did the plaintiff's federal court action, which did (improperly) name Skochko as a defendant based on pendant jurisdiction, not constitute the requisite "timely notice"? The plaintiff's state court complaint alleged that defendant had notice of the claim filed with HUD. Do you understand why the Court of Appeal nevertheless affirmed the trial court's sustaining of the demurrer without leave to amend? Do you agree with this affirmance?

Equitable tolling was applied in *Stalberg v. Western Title Ins. Co.*, 27 Cal. App. 4th 925, 32 Cal. Rptr. 2d 750 (1994). The plaintiffs were downstream property owners who discovered that a fictitious easement had been created across their properties in favor of upstream property owners. The plaintiffs initiated a quiet title action against the upstream owners. Western Title Insurance Co., the plaintiff's title insurer, participated in and partially financed this action. The plaintiffs learned in 1979, while the quiet title action was pending, that Western was also the title insurer for the upstream owners, and that Western had created the fictitious easement when it drafted and recorded the upstream property owners' deeds. Upon completion of the quiet title action in 1983, plaintiffs filed an action against defendant Western for slander of title. Defendant Western asserted the three-year statute of limitations for slander of title, CCP § 338(g), and plaintiff claimed the period should be equitably tolled. The court agreed with the plaintiffs, and held that the limitations period was tolled because the plaintiffs gave timely notice to the defendant and acted reasonably in pursuing first the quiet title action and then the slander of title action against defendant. Is the holding in *Stalberg* consistent with *Garabedian*? Are these cases distinguishable? How so? *See also Hopkins v. Kedzierski*, 225 Cal. App. 4th 736, 750–51, 170 Cal. Rptr. 3d 551 (2014) (discussing cases that applied equitable tolling against defendants who were not parties to a prior action but were put on timely notice by that action of the need to begin to investigate facts with respect to a second action).

(4) Recognition of the doctrine of equitable tolling may be impermissible where it is inconsistent with the legislative scheme of the relevant statute of limitations. *See, e.g., Lantzy v. Centex Homes*, 31 Cal. 4th 363, 2 Cal. Rptr. 3rd 655, 73 P.3d 517 (2003) (concluding the 10-year statutory period in CCP § 337.15 is the outside limit for an action against a developer or contractor for latent defects and is not subject to equitable tolling, but such a defendant may nonetheless be equitably estopped to assert this statute of limitations if it prevented a timely suit by its conduct upon which the plaintiff reasonably relied); *Gordon v. Law Offices of Aguirre & Meyer*, 70 Cal. App. 4th 972, 83 Cal. Rptr. 2d 119 (1999) (ruling the limitations period in CCP § 340.6 for bringing a legal malpractice action is not subject to equitable tolling because the Legislature intended the statute's explicit tolling provisions to be exclusive); *Leasequip, Inc. v. Dapeer*, 103 Cal. App. 4th 394, 126 Cal. Rptr. 2d 782 (2002) (holding the tolling provisions of CCP § 340.6 are exclusive and preclude equitable *tolling*, but do not preclude the use of equitable *estoppel*).

(5) Where exhaustion of an administrative remedy is mandatory prior to filing suit, equitable tolling is automatic. *Elkins v. Derby*, 12 Cal. 3d 410, 414, 115 Cal. Rptr. 641, 525 P. 2d 81 (1974). Is a statute of limitations also subject to equitable tolling when plaintiff *voluntarily* pursues an internal administrative remedy prior to filing a complaint? *See McDonald v. Antelope Valley Comm. Coll. Dist.*, 45 Cal. 4th 88, 84 Cal. Rptr. 3d 734, 194 P.3d 1026 (2008) (holding equitable tolling applies to the voluntary pursuit of internal administrative procedures prior to filing a FEHA claim).

[8] *Estoppel and Other Equitable Tolling Doctrines*

As the *Prudential-LMI* opinion suggests, there are other equitable tolling doctrines in addition to the one applied in *Addison* and *Prudential-LMI, supra*. One such equitable doctrine is waiver of the defense by defendant's conduct. *See, e.g., Brookview Condo. Owners' Assn. v. Heltzer Enterprises-Brookview,* 218 Cal. App. 3d 502, 512–14, 267 Cal. Rptr. 76 (1990); *Elliano v. Assurance Co. of America,* 3 Cal. App. 3d 446, 452–53, 83 Cal. Rptr. 509 (1970). A related, far-reaching doctrine is estoppel, which the *Prudential-LMI* court summarized, 51 Cal. 3d at 689–90, by reference to 3 Witkin, *California Procedure, Actions* §§ 685–700 (4th ed. 1996).

The two cases reproduced below, *Muraoka v. Budget Rent-a-Car, Inc.,* 160 Cal. App. 3d 107, 206 Cal. Rptr. 476 (1984), and *Bernson v. Browning-Ferris Indus. of California, Inc.,* 7 Cal. 4th 926, 30 Cal. Rptr. 2d 440, 873 P.2d 613 (1994), contain discussion of examples of this estoppel doctrine. In *Muraoka,* the plaintiff alleges estoppel based on defendant's unperformed promises of compensation through settlement, as well as on defendant's failure to inform plaintiff of the applicable one-year statute of limitation. In *Bernson,* the plaintiff argues estoppel based on the defendants' intentional concealment of their identity.

Muraoka v. Budget Rent-a-car, Inc.

Court of Appeal of California, Second Appellate District
160 Cal. App. 3d 107, 206 Cal. Rptr. 476 (1984)

McCLOSKY, JUSTICE.

Plaintiff John Muraoka appeals from the judgment of dismissal entered against him after the trial court sustained without leave to amend the demurrer of defendant Budget Rent-A-Car, Inc. (Budget) to plaintiff's second amended complaint.

FACTS

In substance, the material allegations of plaintiff's second amended complaint are: Plaintiff was injured on July 31, 1980, when the automobile he was driving was struck by an automobile negligently driven by John Nelson Pennington. Mr. Pennington was driving that automobile with the consent of its owner Budget. Plaintiff immediately notified Budget of the accident. On September 4, 1980, Budget sent plaintiff a letter requesting more information from him and stating that " 'upon completion of our investigation, we will immediately contact you further regarding your claim.' " In response to this request, plaintiff sent Budget copies of his medical bills and information regarding his property damage. On October 21, 1980, Budget sent plaintiff the following letter:

> "Thank you for forwarding the copies of the draft and medical bills for your property damage and bodily injury claim. We realize that Western Pioneer Insurance Company paid for your vehicle and therefore they are the party to collect for this portion of your claim.

> "The bodily injury portion however is collectable by you and in order to do so we need to have you sign the Medical Information form to obtain your doctors [sic] report on the condition while you were under his car. [sic]

> "Please sign the attached and I will forward to Dr. Sakurai for his report.

> "Then we can settle this portion of your claim."

On March 11, 1981, Dr. Sakurai, plaintiff's doctor, released plaintiff from treatment. On April 23, 1981, Budget wrote Dr. Sakurai requesting information regarding plaintiff's medical treatment. On June 15, plaintiff's insurance agent sent Budget the following correspondence at plaintiff's request:

"Mr. Muraoka called us on June 15, 1981 about 2:00 P.M. to inform us that he has not heard from you yet.

"He is quite concerned about it being almost a year since the day of the accident.

"He hopes that a settlement can be made soon without litigation since he is being pressed by his doctor for an outstanding bill.

"Mr. Muraoka requests a letter of intention at once."

On August 14, 1981, plaintiff called Ms. Albergio at Budget and was told that his medical reports had not yet been received. Plaintiff phoned Dr. Sakurai's office and was told that there had been no request for them. On August 14, Ms. Albergio requested those reports from the doctor's office and after the terms for their payment were negotiated, they were sent out on September 23. On October 13, 1981, plaintiff called Ms. Albergio but was unable to contact her. The next day, plaintiff contacted Ms. Albergio and was told that the reports had just been received and that upon their review she would contact him.

On October 22, Budget made plaintiff settlement offers of $1,400 and $1,600. On October 26, plaintiff called Budget to turn down its offer. Budget responded that its offer was final. On November 3, plaintiff told Budget that he wanted to make an equitable settlement or he would bring suit. On November 9, Budget sent plaintiff the following letter: "Following your recent telephone calls to this office a complete review of your file has been conducted. It appears that the accident in question occurred on July 31, 1980. Since the Statute of Limitations for stating a bodily injury claim is one year in California, we are respectfully closing this file at this time."

On June 30, 1982, plaintiff initiated this action by filing his original complaint. Thereafter, the trial court sustained Budget's demurrers to plaintiff's original and first amended complaints with leave to amend. Plaintiff then filed the subject second amended complaint. Budget interposed general and special demurrers to each cause of action of that complaint which the trial court sustained without leave to amend. This ruling resulted in an order (judgment) of dismissal from which plaintiff appeals.

* * *

Appellant initially contends that his "first cause of action for negligence is not barred by the statute of limitations."

The general demurrers Budget interposed to the first cause of action were that the cause of action was barred by the applicable one-year statute of limitations and that it had no duty to notify plaintiff of that statute of limitations. The trial court sustained these demurrers without leave to amend.

Where a complaint shows upon its face that the statute of limitations has run, the plaintiff may anticipate the defense of limitation of action and allege facts to establish an estoppel. (*Kunstman v. Mirizzi* (1965) 234 Cal. App. 2d 753, 755 [44 Cal. Rptr. 707].)

A defendant "cannot escape the consequences of [its] acts or conduct affirmatively engaged in to procure delay for purposes of settlement, or investigation or otherwise, upon which the [plaintiff] has relied and by which he has been induced to delay the filing of a claim until after the expiration of the statutory period. Such conduct, so relied upon, becomes the basis of an estoppel against the party responsible for the delay...." (*Benner v. Industrial Acc. Com.* (1945) 26 Cal. 2d 346, 350 [159 Cal. Rptr. 24]; ...). "Actual fraud in the technical sense, bad faith, or an intent to mislead, are not essential to create such an estoppel." (*Industrial Indem. Co. v. Ind. Acc. Com.* (1953) 115 Cal. App. 2d 684, 690 [252 P.2d 649].)

But "[before] an estoppel to assert an applicable statute of limitations may be said to exist, certain conditions must be present: '[The] party to be estopped must be apprised of the facts; the other party must be ignorant of the true state of facts, the party to be estopped must have intended that its conduct be acted upon, or so act that the other party had a right to believe that it was so intended; and the other party must rely on the conduct to its prejudice.' (*California Cigarette Concessions, Inc. v. City of Los Angeles*, 53 Cal. 2d 865, 869 [3 Cal. Rptr. 675, 350 P.2d 715]; citing *Safway Steel Products, Inc. v. Lefever*, 117 Cal. App. 2d 489, 491 [256 P.2d 32])." (*Sumrall v. City of Cypress* (1968) 258 Cal. App. 2d 565, 569 [65 Cal. Rptr. 755].)

In his second amended complaint, plaintiff pleads that as a result of Budget's above described conduct he "was lulled into a false sense of security. Plaintiff refrained from commencing a civil action for damages within the statutory time period because he was induced by defendants [sic] promises and conduct to believe that he would be fully compensated for his damages without litigation. However, these promises that plaintiff would be fully compensated for his damages were made with no intention of performing them. [¶]. Furthermore ... plaintiff was told that it would be fine with defendants to wait to settle plaintiff's claim until after defendant [sic] requested and received Dr. Sakurai's medical report. Plaintiff believed and relied upon those statements and conduct of defendants, and as a result did not consult with counsel or file a civil lawsuit within the statutory time. [¶] Furthermore ... defendant Budget affirmatively engaged in promises and conduct to procure delay for the promises of settlement and investigation (i.e., to obtain medical reports on the plaintiff), upon which plaintiff relied and by which plaintiff was induced to delay filing a civil action until after the statute of limitations expired."

Budget, in asserting that its alleged conduct is not sufficient to estop it from asserting the statute of limitations relies exclusively on *Kunstman v. Mirizzi, supra*, 234 Cal. App. 2d 753. In *Kunstman*, the plaintiff was injured on September 26, 1962. In November 1962, and several times thereafter, the defendant's insurer indicated that liability was clear and that it would settle with plaintiff, if she provided her medical reports. Plaintiff replied that her condition had not yet "bottomed out" and that medical reports would be furnished when it did. In October 1963, the insurer denied liability and informed plaintiff that it relied on the statute of limitations in doing so. Plaintiff alleged "that this conduct lulled her attorney into a sense of security which caused him to defer the filing of a complaint in the belief that the cause of action would be settled and she was thus induced to withhold such filing within the period of the proper statute of limitations, and that the defendants were estopped by this conduct from pleading the statute of limitations." (*Id.*, at p. 755.)

The trial court sustained the insurer's demurrer based upon the statute of limitations. The appellate court affirmed, holding that plaintiff failed to allege any misrepresentation, or promises on the part of the insurer sufficient in law to support plaintiff's claim that she was induced to delay, the filing of her complaint in reliance thereof. (*Kunstman v. Mirizzi, supra*, 234 Cal. App. 2d at p. 758.)

In contrast to *Kunstman*, in the case at bench plaintiff alleges that Budget was the protagonist for the delay in the settlement discussions in order to conduct an investigation and that in reliance on this conduct plaintiff "was induced to delay filing a civil action until after the statute of limitations expired." As the court in *Blake v. Wernette* (1976) 57 Cal. App. 3d 656, 660 [129 Cal. Rptr. 426] explained: "When a plaintiff relies on an estoppel against the assertion of the statute of limitations, the sufficiency of the allegations of estoppel may be tested by a general demurrer. [Citations.] Once it is determined that the elements of an estoppel have been sufficiently pleaded, however, the question whether the statute of limitations is tolled by the conduct of the defendant is one of fact which should be left for resolution by a jury and not determined upon general demurrer."

In the first cause of action of his second amended complaint, plaintiff sufficiently alleges the estoppel of Budget to plead the statute of limitations. The determination of whether the evidence provided to support those allegations will be sufficient to toll the statute of limitations is a question to be determined by the trier of fact. Accordingly, the trial court erred in sustaining the general demurrer to plaintiff's first cause of action grounded on the statute of limitations.

Plaintiff's alternative allegation in his first cause of action that the statute of limitations should be tolled because Budget "intentionally concealed from plaintiff that he must file a lawsuit within one year of his injury ..." is without merit. Plaintiff provides no discussion as to why Budget had a duty to disclose. Such a duty arises only in specified situations. Plaintiff fails to factually allege any of these.

Since plaintiff's estoppel allegations in the first cause of action were, when coupled with the other allegations therein, sufficient to state a cause of action it follows that the general demurrer to that cause of action was incorrectly sustained. We note, however, that plaintiff's allegation in that first cause of action contained insufficient facts to state a cause of action based upon defendant's supposed duty to disclose the statute of limitations. * * *

The order (judgment) of dismissal is reversed insofar as it is based upon the sustaining of demurrers to the causes of action for negligence, intentional misrepresentation, and negligent misrepresentation. In all other respects the order (judgment) of dismissal is affirmed.

Bernson v. Browning-Ferris Industries of California, Inc.

Supreme Court of California
7 Cal. 4th 926, 30 Cal. Rptr. 2d 440, 873 P.2d 613 (1994)

Arabian, Justice.

May the authors of an allegedly defamatory writing who conceal their identities be equitably estopped from pleading the statute of limitations in a libel action? * * *

I. FACTS

During the latter half of 1988, Hal Bernson, a member of the Los Angeles City Council, became aware that he was the subject of a highly critical dossier circulating among the Los Angeles media. The 36-page document, entitled "Los Angeles Councilman Hal Bernson—An Analysis of City/Campaign Financial Travel 1983–1988," stated that Bernson had used campaign funds and charged the City of Los Angeles for expenses, including "extensive personal travel" in Europe and Asia, which were "unusual" and "legally questionable." Nothing in the document identified its author, sponsor or distributor.

As explained in his opposition papers, although Bernson managed to obtain a copy of the report, he had no information as to the identity of the parties behind it until February 6, 1990. On that date, two reporters for the Los Angeles Times informed Bernson during the course of an interview that they understood the report had been prepared by defendant Browning-Ferris Industries, Inc. (BFI). Bernson immediately contacted H. Randall Stoke, legal counsel to BFI, to confirm the reporters' statements. Stoke, however, denied any knowledge of the report or its source. Several days later, Attorney Stoke sent a letter to the Los Angeles Times (copy to Bernson) in which Stoke emphatically denied that his client, BFI, had any responsibility "direct or indirect" for the preparation of the report. Further, Stoke demanded that the Times retract its attribution of authorship to BFI and "advise councilman Bernson that BFI was not ... involved in any such matter."

Accepting Attorney Stoke's representations, Bernson alleges that he remained unenlightened of the report's authorship until late May 1991. At that time, another Times reporter informed Bernson's chief deputy that an independent political consultant, defendant Mark Ryavec, had prepared the dossier on behalf of BFI. Based on this information, Bernson concluded that Stoke's previous representations of BFI's noninvolvement had been false. Less than one year later, Bernson filed the instant libel action against BFI, Mark Ryavec and Lynn Wessell (the political consultants who allegedly prepared the report) and Les Bittenson (the BFI employee who allegedly hired Ryavec and Wessell).

The trial court sustained without leave to amend defendant Ryavec's demurrer on the basis of the one-year statute of limitations applicable to Bernson's tort claims (Code Civ. Proc., [former] § 340, subd. (3)) and entered a judgment of dismissal.

The remaining defendants (BFI, Ryavec and Wessell) answered and then moved for summary judgment also on the ground that the action was time-barred. The trial court granted the motion and entered judgment in favor of BFI, Bittenson and Wessell. The Court of Appeal affirmed. We granted Bernson's petition for review.

II. DISCUSSION

Bernson contends here, as he argued below, that defendants should be estopped from asserting the statute of limitations because they affirmatively concealed the fact that they had commissioned, authored, and disseminated the allegedly defamatory dossier. The statute was equitably tolled, in Bernson's view, until he was able to discover the identity of the responsible parties in May 1991. Thus, his action—filed within one year thereof—should be deemed timely. * * *

A. *General Principles*

To evaluate and resolve this dispute requires a brief review of certain settled principles. The statute of limitations usually commences when a cause of action "accrues," and it is generally said that "an action accrues on the date of injury." (*Jolly v. Eli Lilly & Co.* (1988) 44 Cal. 3d 1103, 1109 [245 Cal. Rptr. 658, 751 P.2d 923].) Alternatively, it is often stated that the statute commences "upon the occurrence of the last element essential to the cause of action." (*Neel v. Magana, Olney, Levy, Cathcart & Gelfand* (1971) 6 Cal. 3d 176, 187 [98 Cal. Rptr. 837, 491 P.2d 421]; *Gutierrez v. Mofid* (1985) 39 Cal. 3d 892, 899 [218 Cal. Rptr. 313, 705 P.2d 886].) These general principles have been significantly modified by the common law "discovery rule," which provides that the accrual date may be "delayed until the plaintiff is aware of her injury and its negligent cause." (*Jolly v. Eli Lilly & Co., supra*, 44 Cal. 3d at p. 1109.)

A close cousin of the discovery rule is the "well accepted principle ... of fraudulent concealment." (*Sanchez v. South Hoover Hospital* (1976) 18 Cal. 3d 93, 99 [132 Cal. Rptr. 657, 553 P.2d 1129].) "It has long been established that the defendant's fraud in concealing a cause of action against him tolls the applicable statute of limitations, but only for that period during which the claim is undiscovered by plaintiff or until such time as plaintiff, by the exercise of reasonable diligence, should have discovered it." (*Ibid.*) Like the discovery rule, the rule of fraudulent concealment is an equitable principle designed to effect substantial justice between the parties; its rationale "is that the culpable defendant should be estopped from profiting by his own wrong to the extent that it hindered an 'otherwise diligent' plaintiff in discovering his cause of action." (*Id.* at p. 100, italics omitted; *see also Pashley v. Pacific Elec. Ry. Co.* (1944) 25 Cal. 2d 226, 231–232 [153 P.2d 325].)

Consistent with these principles, a cause of action for libel generally accrues when the defamatory matter is published (*Strick v. Superior Court* (1983) 143 Cal. App. 3d 916, 922 [192 Cal. Rptr. 314]); under the discovery rule, however, the date of accrual may be delayed where the defendant's actions hinder plaintiff's discovery of the defamatory matter. (*See Manguso v. Oceanside Unified School Dist.* (1979) 88 Cal. App. 3d 725 [152 Cal. Rptr. 27]; *McNair v. Worldwide Church of God* (1987) 197 Cal. App. 3d 363, 379 [242 Cal. Rptr. 823]; ...)

B. *Ignorance of Defendants Identity*

While ignorance of the existence of an injury or cause of action may delay the running of the statute of limitations until the date of discovery, the general rule in California has been that ignorance of the identity of the defendant is not essential to a claim and therefore will not toll the statute. (*See Gale v. McDaniel* (1887) 72 Cal. 334, 335 [13 P. 871]; *Jolly v. Eli Lilly & Co., supra,* 44 Cal. 3d at p. 1114.) As we have observed, "the statute of limitations begins to run when the plaintiff suspects or should suspect that her injury was caused by wrongdoing, that someone has done something wrong to her." (*Jolly v. Eli Lilly Co., supra,* 44 Cal. 3d at p. 1110.) Aggrieved parties generally need not know the exact manner in which their injuries were "effected, nor the identities of all parties who may have played a role therein." (*Teitelbaum v. Borders* (1962) 206 Cal. App. 2d 634, 639 [23 Cal. Rptr. 868].)

Although never fully articulated, the rationale for distinguishing between ignorance of the wrongdoer and ignorance of the injury itself appears to be premised on the common sense assumption that once the plaintiff is aware of the injury, the applicable limitations period (often effectively extended by the filing of a Doe complaint) normally affords sufficient opportunity to discover the identity of all the wrongdoers. As we explained in *Jolly v. Eli Lilly & Co., supra,* 44 Cal. 3d 1103 (rejecting the plaintiff's assertion that her ignorance of the particular manufacturer of the drug which caused her injuries tolled the statute): "[P]laintiff could have filed a timely complaint under [Code of Civil Procedure] section 474, which allows suit to be filed against a Doe party. From the time such a complaint is filed, the plaintiff has three years to identify and serve the defendant. [Citations.] Hence, in the instant case, plaintiff could have brought a timely Doe action, effectively enlarging the statute of limitations period for three years." (*Id.* at p. 1118.)[4] Because the plaintiff in *Jolly* was aware of some of the manufacturers, she could have utilized the normal procedure of filing suit against them, naming Doe defendants, and then taking discovery to identify the remainder. That, indeed, is the normal situation for which the fictitious name statute, Code of Civil Procedure section 474, is designed: When the plaintiff is ignorant of the name of "a defendant," the plaintiff must file suit against the known wrongdoers, and, when the Doe's true name is discovered, the complaint may be amended accordingly. (Code Civ. Proc., § 474.)

The question here, however, is whether the general rule should apply when, as a result of the defendant's intentional concealment, the plaintiff is not only unaware of the defendant's identity, but is effectively precluded as a practical matter from ascertaining it through normal discovery procedures. * * * Although we have not previously considered the issue as framed, the question has been addressed in several

---

4. Code of Civil Procedure section 583.210, subdivision (a), provides that the summons and complaint shall be served upon a defendant within three years after the complaint is filed. When the complaint is amended to substitute the true name of the defendant for the fictional name, the amended complaint "relates back" to the timely original complaint and hence is not barred by the statute of limitations. (*Barrington v. A. H. Robins Co.,* (1985) 39 Cal. 3d 146 at pp. 150–151 [216 Cal. Rptr. 405, 702 P.2d 563]; *Austin v. Massachusetts Bonding & Insurance Co.* (1961) 56 Cal. 2d 596, at p. 603 [15 Cal. Rptr. 817, 364 P.2d 68].)

other jurisdictions. * * * As these and other cases demonstrate, the equitable principle that a defendant who intentionally conceals his or her identity may be equitably estopped from asserting the statute of limitations to defeat an untimely claim, has been widely embraced. [Citations omitted.]

As many of the foregoing decisions observe, and as this court has often stated, the primary interest served by statutes of limitations is that of repose. Such statutes ensure that plaintiffs proceed diligently with their claims and mitigate the difficulties faced by defendants in defending stale claims, where factual obscurity through the loss of time, memory or supporting documentation may present unfair handicaps. (*Gutierrez v. Mofid, supra,* 39 Cal. 3d at p. 898.) Nevertheless, where the bar becomes a sword rather than a shield, wielded by a party that has intentionally cloaked its identity, factors of fairness and unjust enrichment come into play, which courts are bound to consider in equity and good conscience. As we long ago observed, "The statute of limitations was intended as a shield for [defendant's] protection against stale claims, but he may not use it to perpetrate a fraud upon otherwise diligent suitors." (*Pashley v. Pacific Elec. Ry. Co., supra,* 25 Cal. 2d at p. 231.) * * *

One should not profit from one's own wrongdoing. Accordingly, we hold that a defendant may be equitably estopped from asserting the statute of limitations when, as the result of intentional concealment, the plaintiff is unable to discover the defendant's actual identity. Although several of the out-of-state decisions cited earlier conclude that a tort claim "accrues" only when the identity of the defendant is discovered, we need not go so far here. It is sufficient to hold simply that, under the circumstances described, the statute may be equitably tolled.

The rule of equitable estoppel includes, of course, the requirement that the plaintiff exercise reasonable diligence. (*Sanchez v. South Hoover Hospital, supra,* 18 Cal. 3d at p. 99.) Thus, under our holding the statute will toll *only* until such time that the plaintiff knows, or through the exercise of reasonable diligence should have discovered, the defendant's identity. Lack of knowledge alone is not sufficient to stay the statute; a plaintiff may not disregard reasonably available avenues of inquiry which, if vigorously pursued, might yield the desired information.

One factor which must be considered pertinent to the diligence inquiry is whether the filing of a timely Doe complaint would, as a practical matter, have facilitated the discovery of the defendant's identity within the requisite three-year period for service of process. (Code Civ. Proc., § 583.210, subd. (a); *Jolly v. Eli Lilly & Co., supra,* 44 Cal. 3d at p. 1118.) Where the identity of at least one defendant is known, for example, the plaintiff must avail himself of the opportunity to file a timely complaint naming Doe defendants and take discovery. However, where the facts are such that even discovery cannot pierce a defendant's intentional efforts to conceal his identity, the plaintiff should not be penalized.

Recognition of a potential equitable estoppel under the foregoing circumstances will not unduly burden the trial courts. Indeed, our holding will have virtually *no* effect on the vast majority of civil cases. It is only in those relative few where the defendant asserts a statute of limitations defense and the plaintiff claims that he was totally ignorant of the defendant's identity as a result of the defendant's fraudulent concealment, that the issue will even arise; among those few, it will be the rare and exceptional case in which the plaintiff could genuinely claim that he was aware of no defendants, and even more rare that, given knowledge of at least one, he could not readily discover the remainder through the filing of a Doe complaint and the normal discovery processes. * * *

We conclude that a remand is appropriate. Our holding that a defendant's intentional concealment of his identity may justify an estoppel represents a new rule of law, as do our standards emphasizing the burden on the plaintiff to demonstrate reasonable diligence, including the filing of a complaint against known defendants. On remand the parties will have the opportunity in light of our decision to focus on and develop these pertinent legal and factual issues: whether, under the circumstances, defendants' anonymous commission, drafting and circulation of the allegedly defamatory dossier constituted intentional concealment; whether defendants' actions thereby deprived plaintiff, in fact, of knowledge of defendants' identity; and whether plaintiff exercised reasonable diligence in attempting to discover defendants' identity.[7] * * *

Accordingly, the judgment of the Court of Appeal is reversed, and the matter remanded for further proceedings consistent with the views expressed herein.

Notes and Questions Regarding Estoppel

(1) Under what circumstances is a defendant ever under a duty to disclose an applicable statute of limitations to a plaintiff, such that failure to disclose will provide a basis for estoppel? See *Spray, Gould & Bowers v. Associated Intl. Ins. Co.*, 71 Cal. App. 4th 1260, 84 Cal. Rptr. 2d 552 (1999) (declaring that defendant insurer's direct violation of regulations requiring the insurer to notify a claimant insured of time limits pertaining to the claim may provide a basis of estoppel against the insurer's assertion of a contract limitations defense); Insurance Code §§ 2070.1, 11580.2(k).

(2) The estoppel argument upheld by the court in *Muraoka* has been applied to a variety of circumstances in addition to misrepresentations as to the need for litigation, such as fraudulent concealment of a cause of action. See, e.g., *Griffis v. S.S. Kresge Co.*, 150 Cal. App. 3d 491, 197 Cal. Rptr. 771 (1984) (defense counsel withheld information or was overtly false regarding statutory time period); see also *Brown v. Bleiberg*, 32 Cal. 3d 426, 186 Cal. Rptr. 228, 651 P.2d 815 (1982) (estopping defendant doctor from asserting malpractice limitation because he misrepresented to plaintiff the nature and purpose of surgery performed); *Vu v. Prudential Prop. & Cas. Ins. Co.*, 26 Cal. 4th 1142, 1153–54, 113 Cal. Rptr. 2d 70, 33 P.3d 487 (2001) (ruling defendant insurer may be estopped to raise the statute of limitations defense if the plaintiff insured can

---

7. The relevant period of inquiry concerning defendants' alleged concealment and plaintiff's diligence in discovering defendants' identity is, of course, the one-year limitations period following plaintiff's discovery of the alleged defamatory writing.

show that he reasonably relied on the insurer's factual misrepresentation that his damages were less than his policy's deductible amount).

(3) This potentially far-reaching equitable estoppel doctrine does have some limitations. In *Elliott v. Contractors' State License Bd.*, 224 Cal. App. 3d 1048, 274 Cal. Rptr. 286 (1990), the court ruled that the defendant agency was not estopped to assert the statute of limitations despite plaintiff's argument that the agency never responded to plaintiff's written inquiries for clarification of the administrative law judge's order and for information about procedures and forms for appealing the order. The court found that the defendant agency did not engage in any affirmative misleading conduct, and neither owed nor assumed any duty to advise plaintiff of his rights. Other cases have reached the same conclusion on similar facts. *E.g., Barber v. Superior Court*, 234 Cal. App. 3d 1076, 285 Cal. Rptr. 668 (1991) (ruling refusal by defense expert to voluntarily cooperate with plaintiff not fraudulent concealment for purposes of estoppel of limitations); *Brookview Condo. Owners' Assn. v. Heltzer Enterprises-Brookview*, 218 Cal. App. 3d 502, 267 Cal. Rptr. 76 (1990) (Collecting cases which required misleading or deceptive act by defendant as prerequisite for estoppel to seek dismissal).

Even where the defendant does engage in affirmative misleading conduct, that conduct must have induced the plaintiff to delay filing the action for estoppel to apply. *See, e.g., Stalberg v. Western Title Ins. Co.*, 27 Cal. App. 4th 925, 931–32, 32 Cal. Rptr. 2d 750 (1994) (holding that although defendant made numerous misrepresentations regarding easement, defendant not equitably estopped from asserting statute of limitations bar because plaintiffs knew correct facts); *Lantzy v. Centrex Homes*, 31 Cal. 4th 363, 2 Cal. Rptr. 3d 655, 73 P.3d 517 (2003) (ruling defendant developer who made unfulfilled promises to repair construction defects not equitably estopped from asserting statute of limitations defense because no facts to indicate defendant's conduct induced plaintiffs homeowners to forbear suing within the 10-year limitation period of CCP § 337.15). *Snapp & Associates Ins. Services, Inc. v. Robertson*, 96 Cal App. 4th 884, 17 Cal. Rptr. 2d 331 (2002) (noting the doctrine of fraudulent concealment does not come into play, whatever the lengths to which the defendant has gone to conceal the wrongs, if a plaintiff is otherwise on notice of a potential claim).

(4) The Supreme Court in *Bernson* held that intentional concealment of the defendant's identity tolls the statute of limitations until such time as the plaintiff knows, or through the exercise of reasonable diligence should have discovered, the defendant's actual identity. The Court specifically grounded this holding in the doctrine of equitable estoppel, and expressly declined to base it on the delayed discovery rule. What difference does this make? Why was the Court reluctant to modify the California discovery rule in this manner? The *Bernson* court opined that this holding would affect only a few cases. Do you agree? Why? Would the effect be greater if the *Bernson* court had held that a cause of action does not accrue until the plaintiff discovers, or through reasonable diligence, should have discovered, the defendant's identity? How so?

(5) In *Regents of the Univ. of California v. Superior Court*, 20 Cal. 4th 509, 85 Cal. Rptr.2d 257, 976 P.2d 808 (1999), the Supreme Court discussed the judicially created doctrine of fraudulent concealment applied in *Bernson*. The purpose of the doctrine,

according to the court, is to "disarm a defendant who, by his own deception, has caused a claim to become stale and a plaintiff dilatory." *Regents of the Univ. of California,* 20 Cal. 4th at 533. The court further noted that the doctrine enters into a statute of limitations, if at all, from without by being read into it judicially. However, the language of or purpose behind a particular statute of limitations, such as the 30-day limitation set forth in the Opens Meeting Act, Gov. Code § 11130 (a), may preclude application of the doctrine of fraudulent concealment. *Id.* at 533–35.

(6) Equitable *estoppel* may be available even where the limitations statute at issue expressly precludes equitable *tolling*. *See, e.g., Lantzy v. Centrex Homes,* 31 Cal. 4th 363, 2 Cal. Rptr. 3d 655, 73 P.3d 517 (2003) (ruling ten-year limitations period to bring action for latent defect construction in CCP § 337.15 not subject to equitable tolling, but defendants may be estopped to assert this limitations defense while their promises or attempts to repair defect are pending); *Leasequip, Inc. v. Dapeer,* 103 Cal. App. 4th 394, 126 Cal. Rptr. 2d 782 (2002) (ruling that although equitable tolling not applicable to CCP § 340.6, defendant equitably estopped from raising that legal malpractice statute of limitation); *Battuello v. Battuello,* 64 Cal. App. 4th 842, 75 Cal. Rptr. 2d 548 (1998) (holding equitable estoppel prevented defendant form asserting one-year limitation in CCP § 366.2 despite that statute's express provision that precluded equitable tolling).

[9]   Tolling and Class Actions

Yet another nonstatutory grounds for tolling was recently discussed in *Jolly v. Eli Lilly & Co.,* *supra,* 44 Cal. 3d 1103, 1118–26, whose facts are set forth *supra:*

Jolly v. Eli Lilly and Company
Supreme Court of California
44 Cal. 3d 1103, 1118–1126, 245 Cal. Rptr. 658, 751 P.2d 923 (1988)

* * *

Application of American Pipe

Relying on *American Pipe & Construction Co. v. Utah* (1974) 414 U.S. 538 [38 L. Ed. 2d 713, 94 S. Ct. 756] and its progeny, plaintiff argues that the filing of the class action in *Sindell, supra,* tolled the statute of limitations with respect to individual members of the putative class until the class was denied certification in 1982. Defendants respond that the issue is not properly before us, as it was not raised below (Cal. Rules of Court, rule 29), a contention we reject in light of the issue's great public importance. Alternatively, defendants argue that the tolling principle set forth in *American Pipe, supra,* and followed by the Court of Appeal in *Bangert v. Narmco Materials, Inc.* (1984) 163 Cal. App. 3d 207 [209 Cal. Rptr. 438], has no application to the present case. We agree that *American Pipe* is inapplicable here.

We have repeatedly directed that in the absence of controlling state authority, California courts should utilize the procedures of rule 23 of the Federal Rules of Civil Procedure to ensure fairness in the resolution of class action suits. Under rule 23, the filing of a timely class action commences the action for all members of the class as subsequently determined. In *American Pipe*, the United States Supreme Court held that, under limited circumstances, if class certification is denied, the statute of limitations is tolled from the time of commencement of the suit to the time of denial of certification for all purported members of the class who either make timely motions to intervene in the surviving individual action, or who timely file their individual actions. Although we are not bound by the United States Supreme Court decisions, we nevertheless consider the applicability of *American Pipe* here.

In *American Pipe* the State of Utah commenced a civil action, claiming that defendants conspired to rig steel and concrete pipe prices in violation of the Sherman Act. The suit purported to be a class action, brought on behalf of Utah's public agencies and others who were end users of the pipe. On defendant's motion, the district court denied class action status for failure to satisfy the numerosity requirement of rule 23(a)(1) of the Federal Rules of Civil Procedure. The public agencies who were alleged as class members then filed motions to intervene. The court denied the motions on statute of limitations grounds. The Ninth Circuit reversed.

The United States Supreme Court in a unanimous decision affirmed the circuit court: "We hold that in this posture, at least where class action status has been denied solely because of failure to demonstrate that 'the class is so numerous that joinder of all members is impracticable,' the commencement of the original class suit tolls the running of the statute for all purported members of the class who make timely motions to intervene after the court has found the suit inappropriate for class action status."

In *Bangert v. Narmco Materials, Inc., supra*, the Court of Appeal extended *American Pipe* to apply to a class action suit against a plastics research plant seeking injunctive and monetary relief for property damage, economic loss and physical injuries. The asserted class consisted of persons living within a half-mile radius of the plant. The trial court denied class certification on grounds of insufficient community of interest. Thereafter the court denied as untimely plaintiffs' motion for leave to amend the complaint nunc pro tunc to add as plaintiffs 92 members of the class designated in the original complaint.

The Court of Appeal reversed. Citing *American Pipe*, the court held that the filing of the complaint tolled the running of the statute of limitations for all members of the purported class until class action certification was denied, even though, unlike *American Pipe*, denial was not for lack of numerosity, but for insufficient community of interest.

Plaintiff urges us to follow the *Bangert* court's extension of *American Pipe* so as to find that the filing of the *Sindell* class action tolled the statute of limitations applicable to her individual suit. To resolve this issue, we need to consider both the nature of the *Sindell* action and the rationale underlying *American Pipe*.

Judith Sindell filed suit in 1976. She purported to be suing on her own behalf and, "with respect to certain relief," on behalf of a class of women allegedly similarly situated. For herself, individually, Sindell claimed damages for specific personal injury suffered as a result of her mother's ingestion of DES during pregnancy. In her cause of action relating to the class claims, Sindell described the class as female residents of California "who have been exposed to DES before birth and who may or may not know that fact or danger, and as a result of which, have or may have contracted or in the future may contract adenocarcinoma or vaginal or cervical adenosis or pre-cancerous tumors of the breast or cancer of the bladder." For the class, Sindell sought only declaratory relief and an order directing defendants to publicize the dangers of DES and the necessity of medical evaluations and to fund the establishment and maintenance of clinics to provide free examinations to the DES daughters.

Six years later, in 1982, the trial court denied certification. As reason, the court cited, in relevant part, the lack of commonality among class members on issues of proximate cause, extent of injury, and appropriate medical examination or treatment. "As a general rule," the court observed, "so-called 'mass accidents' or 'common disasters' are considered not appropriate for class litigation. This inappropriateness is based upon the overwhelming uniqueness of the issues stemming from the necessity for the trier to hear and determine individually each victim's injuries, his suffering, financial loss, etc. Thus even though a common question may be involved (e.g., the defendant's tort) the matter is not suitable for a class action."

The question to be asked, then, is whether the *Sindell, supra*, mass-tort class action fits the rationale of *American Pipe, supra*. We believe the answer is no.

Underlying the tolling rule of *American Pipe* were two major policy considerations. The first was the protection of the class action device. In cases where class certification is denied for what the high court characterized as "subtle factors," unforeseeable by class members, a rule that failed to protect putative class members from the statute of limitations after denial of certification would induce potential class members to "file protective motions to intervene or to join in the event that a class was later found unsuitable," depriving class actions "of the efficiency and economy of litigation which is a principal purpose of the procedure."

The second consideration involved the effectuation of the purposes of the statute of limitations. "The policies of ensuring essential fairness to defendants and of barring a plaintiff who has 'slept on his rights,'" the high court stated, "are satisfied when, as here, a named plaintiff who is found to be representative of a class commences a suit and thereby notifies the defendants not only of the substantive claims being brought against them, but also of the number and generic identities of the potential plaintiffs who may participate in the judgment." In these circumstances, the court concluded, the purposes of the statute of limitations would not be violated by a decision to toll. (*See, generally*, Comment, *Class Actions and Statutes of Limitations* (1981) 48 U. Chi. L. Rev. 106, 108–109).

The tension between these two considerations, as at least one commentator has observed (Comment, *supra*, 48 U. Chi. L. Rev. 106, 110–111), has led lower courts in applying *American Pipe* to use different approaches. Some courts concentrate on the protection of the class action device. [Citations omitted.] Other courts focus on the policies underlying the statute of limitations and thus inquire whether the defendant received notice of a subsequent plaintiff's claim from the prior class suit. * * * [Citations omitted.] Still others apply *American Pipe* broadly to mean that the statute of limitations must always be tolled, eliminating discussion of the reason for denial of class status or the notice issue.

Considering both policy considerations—[protecting the efficiency and economy of litigation and protecting the defendant from unfair claims]—we decline to extend the tolling doctrine of *American Pipe* to the present case. Rather, for the reasons set forth below, we conclude that the *Sindell* class action complaint neither sufficiently put defendants on notice of the substance and nature of plaintiff's claims, nor served to further economy and efficiency of litigation, so as to justify affording plaintiff shelter under the protective umbrella of *American Pipe*.

This court has held that the ultimate determination of whether a class action is appropriate turns on the existence and extent of common questions of law and fact. As the trial court in the present case correctly observed, mass-tort actions for personal injury most often are not appropriate for class action certification. The major elements in tort actions for personal injury—liability, causation, and damages—may vary widely from claim to claim, creating a wide disparity in claimants' damages and issues of defendant liability, proximate cause, liability of skilled intermediaries, comparative fault, informed consent, assumption of the risk and periods of limitation. Thus, for example, in DES litigation, use of the class action device has consistently been rejected. California DES litigation has not departed from this trend; no reported California cases have approved DES litigation in class action form.

The same reasons that render certification of mass-tort claims generally inappropriate render inappropriate the application and extension of *American Pipe* to the present case. Because of the nature of the *Sindell* complaint—as indicated, Judith Sindell did not seek to certify the class as to personal injury claims, the gravamen of plaintiff's complaint—and the differences in issues of fact and law—plaintiff's action for damages puts into issue the prenatal treatment of her mother, the specific form of DES prescribed (e.g., tablet, capsule), the dosage taken, her mother's obstetrical history and many other issues necessarily involved in proving causation, damages and defenses—the *Sindell* class suit could not have apprised defendants of plaintiff's substantive claims. Therefore, plaintiff cannot now claim that Sindell's complaint put defendants on notice of allegations related to personal injury within the statutory period of limitation so that they might prepare their defense.

This deficiency in Sindell's class action suit is alone sufficient to deny plaintiff relief under *American Pipe*. As Justice Blackmun, in his concurrence in *American Pipe*, cautioned: "Our decision ... must not be regarded as encouragement to lawyers in a case of this kind to frame their pleadings as a class action, intentionally, to attract and save members of the purported class who have slept on their rights. Nor does it necessarily guarantee intervention for all members of the purported class. [¶] As the Court has indicated, the purpose of statutes of limitations is to prevent surprises 'through the revival of claims that have been allowed to slumber until evidence has been lost, memories have faded, and witnesses have disappeared.' [Citations]." (*Amer-

ican Pipe, supra, 414 U.S. 538, 561 [38 L. Ed. 2d 713, 731] (conc. opn. of Blackmun, J.).) * * *

Our position in the present case ensures that the abuse warned of by Justice Blackmun will not occur. By refusing to extend *American Pipe*'s tolling doctrine to allow the instant suit, we heed Justice Blackmun's admonishment to district judges to exercise discretion in applying the *American Pipe* rule in order to "prevent the type of abuse mentioned above and [to] preserve a defendant whole against prejudice arising from claims for which he has received no prior notice." Because the *Sindell* complaint never put defendants on notice that personal injury damages were being sought on a class basis, it would be unfair to defendants to toll the statute of limitations on such personal injury actions. And because the *Sindell* complaint did not seek personal injury damages on behalf of the class, even those absent class members who were aware of that action could not reasonably have relied on the complaint as a basis for postponing their own personal injury actions. Thus, our ruling today does not result in duplicative litigation of the sort feared by the court in *American Pipe*, nor does it deprive rule 23 of the Federal Rules of Civil Procedure of its purpose to further the efficiency and economy of litigation.

In light of our disposition, we need not address the broader question whether in any personal injury mass-tort case the filing of a class action complaint can serve to toll the statute of limitations for putative class members when the class ultimately is denied certification for lack of commonality. We observe, however, that because personal-injury mass-tort class-action claims can rarely meet the community of interest requirement in that each member's right to recover depends on facts peculiar to each particular case, such claims may be presumptively incapable of apprising defendants of "the substantive claims being brought against them" (*American Pipe, supra*, 414 U.S. 538, 555 [38 L. Ed. 2d 713, 727]), a prerequisite, in our view, to the application of *American Pipe*. This being so, putative class members would be ill advised to rely on the mere filing of a class action complaint to toll their individual statute of limitations. The presumption, rather, should be to the contrary—i.e., that lack of commonality will defeat certification and preclude application of the *American Pipe* tolling doctrine.

For the reasons previously stated, we hold that the *American Pipe* tolling rule is unavailable to plaintiff. Specifically, we find that plaintiff and other similarly situated plaintiffs seeking personal injury damages in DES cases may not rely on the *Sindell* class action suit to toll the statute of limitations pursuant to *American Pipe*.[20]

Conclusion

The judgment of the Court of Appeal is reversed. The cause is remanded with instructions to affirm the judgment of the trial court in favor of defendants.

---

20. Insofar as *Bangert v. Narmco Materials, Inc., supra*, is inconsistent with our holding, that case is disapproved.

Notes and Questions

(1) Why precisely did the Supreme Court in *Jolly* find the *American Pipe* tolling doctrine inapplicable? Although dicta, the court expressed the view that the *American Pipe* tolling doctrine does not apply when a class is ultimately denied certification for lack of commonality as opposed to numerosity. Do you understand the reasons for the court's distinction here? Do you agree with it? Is it a proper interpretation of the U.S. Supreme Court decision in *American Pipe*? Does that matter here? Note that the California Supreme Court states "we are not bound by the United States Supreme Court decisions?" Why not?

(2) Although not necessary to its decision, the court in *Jolly* forcefully indicates that the *American Pipe* tolling doctrine should never apply to personal injury mass-tort cases filed as class actions. Obviously, this is a clear message to future litigants and the lower courts.

However, in *San Francisco Unified Sch. Dist. v. W.R. Grace & Co.*, 37 Cal. App. 4th 1318, 1336–41, 44 Cal. Rptr. 2d 305 (1995), the court ruled that the three-year statute of limitations for injury to property was tolled during the period of time that plaintiff was a member of a nationwide asbestos class action certified in federal court, from the inception of the class action until plaintiff opted out of the class. The court distinguished *Jolly* by finding that, unlike the mass tort personal injury claims of the class action in *Jolly*, the property damage claims in the federal class action provided meaningful notice of plaintiff's claims against defendant Grace. *Id.* at 1338–39. *See also Becker v. McMillin Constr. Co.*, 226 Cal. App. 3d 1493, 277 Cal. Rptr. 491 (1991) (applying *American Pipe* tolling to putative class in mass tort property damage action which was decertified for lack of commonality); *Falk v. Children's Hospital Los Angeles*, 237 Cal. App. 4th 1454, 188 Cal. Rptr. 3d 686 (2015) (ruling statute of limitations tolled during prior putative class action alleging overtime and rest break violations).

[10] *Relation Back Doctrine and Cross-Complaints*

Generally, an amended complaint relates back to the date of a timely filed original complaint, and thus avoids the statute of limitations, if it (1) rests on the same general set of facts and (2) refers to the same accident and the same injuries, as the original complaint. *Barrington v. A.H. Robins Co.*, 39 Cal. 3d 146, 216 Cal. Rptr. 405, 702 P.2d 563 (1985). *See* §9.03 Amendments, *infra*. A timely filed complaint may also toll the statute of limitations as to cross-complaints filed by the defendant.

Sidney v. Superior Court

Court of Appeal of California, Second Appellate District
198 Cal. App. 3d 710, 244 Cal. Rptr. 31 (1988)

THOMPSON, JUSTICE.

In this case we hold that the statute of limitations does not bar amending a compulsory cross-complaint to state a cause of action against the plaintiff for a different injury arising from the same accident where the cause of action was not barred when the original complaint was filed. Petitioner Erik Sidney seeks a writ of mandate commanding respondent superior court to grant him leave to amend his cross-complaint to seek damages for personal injury as well as property loss. Petitioner is the defendant in a negligence action filed by plaintiff Pauline Kinoshita.

On November 7, 1985, petitioner's car collided with a vehicle driven by plaintiff Kinoshita. On February 24, 1986, plaintiff filed a complaint for personal injury and property damage against petitioner. On April 17, 1986, petitioner filed a cross-complaint for property damages against plaintiff and Al Munari Produce.[1] On April 27, 1987, petitioner filed a notice of motion for leave to amend his cross-complaint by adding a cause of action for personal injuries.[2] Petitioner alleged his failure to include the personal injury claim in his first cross-complaint was due to the "mistake" and "neglect" of prior counsel, consisting of confusion between two attorneys (one retained by petitioner and one retained by his insurer). Plaintiff opposed the motion, arguing, inter alia, that petitioner was not entitled to relief under Code of Civil Procedure section 426.50[3] because he was not acting in good faith in failing to file a cause of action for personal injuries within the statute of limitations period.

The superior court denied petitioner's motion on the express ground that the "statute of limitations appears to have run on the personal injury claim." The court explained that the "[doctrine] of relation back does not apply in this situation when the original complaint related to a claim of 'property' damage" and cited to *Barrington v. A.H. Robins Co.* (1985) 39 Cal. 3d 146 [216 Cal. Rptr. 405, 702 P.2d 563]. Petitioner sought mandamus relief and we granted an alternative writ.

DISCUSSION

Petitioner contends that the trial court erred in denying him leave to amend on the ground that the one-year statute of limitations governing personal injury claims ([former] § 340, subd. (3)) had run. Petitioner claims that the statute was tolled by the filing of plaintiff's complaint for personal injuries sustained in the same accident. We agree.

At issue is whether the rule for applying the relation back doctrine to an amended compulsory cross-complaint is the same as for an amended complaint, rather than an initial cross-complaint. In the case of a complaint, the general rule is that an "amended complaint relates back to the original complaint, and thus avoids the statute of limitations as a bar against named parties ... [only] if it: (1) rests on the same general set of facts as the original complaint; and (2) refers to the same accident and same injuries as the original complaint." (*Barrington v. A.H. Robins Co., supra*, 39 Cal. 3d 146, 151; *Smeltzley v. Nicholson Mfg. Co.* (1977) 18 Cal. 3d 932, 939–940 [136 Cal. Rptr. 269, 559 P.2d 624, 85 A.L.R.3d 121].) Thus, if the same rule applies

---

1. The original cross-complaint alleged the plaintiff was driving a vehicle owned by Al Munari Produce with Munari's consent in the course of employment and agency.

2. Although Al Munari Produce was still named as a cross-defendant in the title, the proposed first amended cross-complaint alleged that plaintiff Kinoshita was the owner as well as the driver of the vehicle and did not refer to any alleged negligence by Al Munari Produce.

3. Unless otherwise stated, all statutory references are to the Code of Civil Procedure.

to amending the cross-complaint, the trial court's ruling was proper since after the expiration of the one-year statute, a complaint alleging only property damages could not be amended to seek damages for personal injury, a different primary injury.

Although "[ordinarily] the statute of limitations will bar a cross-complaint in the same fashion as if the defendant had brought an independent action," the rule is different when "the original complaint was filed before the statute of limitations on the cross-complaint had elapsed." (*Liberty Mut. Ins. Co. v. Fales* (1973) 8 Cal. 3d 712, 715, fn. 4 [106 Cal. Rptr. 21, 505 P.2d 213]). Such a cross-complaint need only be subject-matter related to the plaintiff's complaint — i.e., arise out of the same occurrence (*see* §§ 426.10, 428.10) — to relate back to the date of filing the complaint for statute of limitation purposes.

"[The] courts have fashioned a rule that a statute of limitations is suspended or tolled as to a defendant's then unbarred causes of action against the plaintiff arising out of the same transaction by the filing of the plaintiff's complaint." (*Electronic Equipment Express, Inc. v. Donald H. Seiler & Co.* (1981) 122 Cal. App. 3d 834, 844 [176 Cal. Rptr. 239].) "The principle underlying the rule that a statute of limitations is suspended by the filing of the original complaint is that the plaintiff has thereby waived the claim and permitted the defendant to make all proper defenses to the cause of action pleaded." (*Trindade v. Superior Court* (1973) 29 Cal. App. 3d 857, 859–860 [106 Cal. Rptr. 48].)

In *Trindade*, the plaintiff timely filed a negligence action for personal injuries against defendant Trindade. More than two years after the automobile accident, Trindade filed a cross-complaint against the plaintiff for personal injuries arising from the accident. The trial court sustained a demurrer without leave to amend on statute of limitations grounds. The appellate court reversed, holding the cross-complaint was not time-barred. The *Trindade* court pointed out: "It has consistently been held that the commencement of an action tolls the statute of limitations as to a defendant's then unbarred cause of action against the plaintiff" related to the accident or occurrence upon which the action is brought.

We are satisfied that the same "relation back" standard applies for an amended cross-complaint as for an initial cross-complaint. Neither the underlying rationale of the rule nor the language of the cases proclaiming it indicates an intent to only toll the statute temporarily until an initial cross-complaint is filed. To the contrary, the waiver principle is based on plaintiff's action in commencing the action. The reason for the rule continues to exist so long as that action is pending and is unrelated to how many times it takes defendant to assert all his related defenses and claims.

Moreover, the cases make clear that the only relevant criteria for starting and ending the tolling of the statute are, respectively, the commencement of the action by the filing of the plaintiff's complaint and the end of the action by judgment. "'The statute is a bar to the defendant's affirmative claim only if the period has already run when the *complaint is filed*. The filing of the complaint suspends the statute during the pendency of the action, and the defendant may set up his [cross] claim by appropriate pleading at any time.' [Citation.]" (*Trindade v. Superior Court, supra,* 29

Cal. App. 3d at p. 860; *see also* 3 Witkin, *Cal. Procedure* (3d ed. 1985) § 322, p. 353.) Early California cases show that the principle is well established that as long as a defendant's claim existed at the commencement of the action, the statute remains suspended throughout the action. (*See, e.g., McDougald v. Hulet* (1901) 132 Cal. 154, 160–161 [64 P. 278].)

In *Whittier v. Visscher* (1922) 189 Cal. 450, 456 [209 P. 23], our Supreme Court, in rejecting a claim that a cross-complaint was barred by the statute of limitations, explained: "[The] authorities in this state seem to be agreed that if the right of action relied on was alive at the commencement of the suit the statute does not run against it, when, as in this case, the full statutory period has expired thereafter during the pendency of the action and before the claim is pleaded as a cross-complaint." * * *

Furthermore, in *McDougald v. Hulet, supra*, 132 Cal. 154, the court not only rejected the trial court's conclusion that the cross-complaint was barred but also held that the court erred in denying the defendant leave to file a second amended answer during the trial. The *McDougald* court stated that "[the] filing of the complaint suspended the running of the statute of limitations as to the matters arising out of the transaction" set forth "in the answer, whether it is called an answer, or a counterclaim, or a cross-complaint" which "existed at the commencement of the action." (*Id.* at pp. 160–161.) In holding that the refusal to permit amendment at time of trial was error, the court stressed that amendments should be liberally allowed.

We perceive no reason to fashion a rule to restart the statute of limitations running again as soon as a defendant files an initial cross-complaint. Because of the strong public policy that seeks to dispose of litigation on the merits rather than on procedural grounds, the statute of limitations is a disfavored defense which should be strictly construed so as to avoid forfeiture of rights. The objective of statutes of limitation in barring stale claims is not involved here since the amended cross-complaint arises from the same automobile collision incident as the complaint and was therefore no more stale than the complaint. Moreover, since it is well settled that the statute of limitations could not have barred defendant-petitioner from waiting to file an initial cross-complaint for personal injuries as well as property damage at any time during pendency of the action up until judgment, the amended cross-complaint filed herein before trial was no more stale than an initial cross-complaint might have been. Indeed, here the personal injury cause of action was filed a year and one-half after the accident whereas in *Trindade*, it was not filed till more than two years after.

We decline to restrict the "relation-back" rules governing amendment of a compulsory cross-complaint to those governing amendment of a complaint. Plaintiff and defendant are not in parallel positions. Plaintiff chose to initiate the lawsuit. The defendant has no choice but to defend.

Moreover, the Legislature has created a distinctive statutory scheme regulating compulsory cross-complaints. Where as here, the cause of action is related to the subject-matter of the plaintiff's complaint, defendant must raise all possible claims by cross-complaint or be forever barred from asserting any of them in any later lawsuit even as a defensive offset (§ 431.70) and even if the limitations period had not expired (§ 426.30). Furthermore, in the chapter on compulsory cross-complaints, the Legislature has not only made it clear that the court retains power to permit a defendant to amend a cross-complaint to avoid forfeiture of a related claim but has also mandated liberality in allowing such amendments at any time during the course of the lawsuit. (§ 426.50.) * * *

We, therefore, conclude that the statute of limitations does not bar amending a cross-complaint to state a cause of action against the plaintiff for a different injury arising from the same accident where the cause of action was not barred when the original complaint was filed. (See fn. 4.) Hence, the trial court erred in ruling that petitioner's cause of action for personal injury against plaintiff Kinoshita was barred by the statute of limitations since it was not barred at the time plaintiff filed his negligence action arising out of the same motor vehicle accident.[4] * * *

Notes and Questions

(1) Why did the *Sidney* court permit relation back of defendant Sidney's cross-complaint for personal injuries against plaintiff Kinoshita, when it would not have permitted relation back for a similar claim against third-party defendant Al Munari Produce Co.? *See Sidney*, fn. 4, *supra*.

(2) Assume in *Sidney* that defendant Sidney did file a timely cross-complaint against third-party defendant Al Munari Produce Co. for property damages only. Al Munari then files a cross-complaint against Sidney for negligently destroying the company vehicle. In response to Al Munari's cross-complaint, Sidney seeks to amend his cross-complaint to assert a personal injury claim against Al Munari Produce Co. Is Sidney's personal injury claim against Al Munari still barred by the statute of limitations, or does his amended cross-complaint relate back?

(3) In *Sidney*, the collision took place on November 7, 1985, and Kinoshita filed his complaint for personal injury on February 24, 1986. Assume that instead of filing an answer and cross-complaint, Sidney never entered an appearance in the action.

---

4. The proposed amended cross-complaint appears to be directed only against plaintiff Kinoshita. Petitioner apparently does not seek to state a cause of action for personal injury against cross-defendant Al Munari Produce Company. Nor could he do so. There is no tolling or "relation back" to save cross-complaints against third parties brought into the action by the defendant. No waiver can be inferred as to a third party. Since Munari did not do any act in the nature of a waiver, the reason for the rule that a statute of limitations is suspended upon the filing of the original complaint does not exist. (*Trindade v. Superior Court, supra*, 29 Cal. App. 3d 857, 859–860.) A cross-complaint against Munari must be timely on the date it is filed. In short, for purposes of the statute of limitations, such a cross-complaint against a third party is treated the same as a complaint and subject to the same "relation back" doctrine.

Here, petitioner's original cross-complaint against Munari, filed in April 1986, five months after the accident, was timely. But an amended claim for personal injury filed in April 1987 would be barred by the one-year statute of limitations. It cannot relate back to the original April 1986 cross-complaint for property damages because it does not seek recovery for the "same injuries." (*Barrington v. A.H. Robins Co., supra*, 39 Cal. 3d 146, 151....)

Two years later, the court dismissed Kinoshita's case for lack of prosecution. Sidney then files suit against Kinoshita for property and personal injury damages caused by the same collision. Defendant Kinoshita demurs on the ground that Sidney's action is barred by the statute of limitations. Plaintiff Sidney argues that Kinoshita's complaint in the first lawsuit tolled the statute of limitations as to any cause of action that could have been brought by Sidney as a cross-complaint, but was never filed, in that prior lawsuit. Does Kinoshita's complaint in the prior litigation toll the statute of limitations such that Sidney's complaint in the second lawsuit relates back to it? *See Luna Records Corp. v. Alvarado*, 232 Cal. App. 3d 1023, 283 Cal. Rptr. 865 (1991).

(4) Assume that as a result of the collision in *Sidney*, plaintiff Kinoshita suffered only property damage to his vehicle and defendant Sidney suffered only personal injuries. Kinoshita waits one and three-quarter years before filing his property damage negligence case against Sidney. Defendant Sidney is served with the complaint, and now wishes to file a cross-complaint for personal injury damages against plaintiff Kinoshita. Is Sidney's cross-complaint barred by the then-applicable one-year statute of limitations? *See* CCP § 431.70; *Constr. Protective Serv., Inc. v. TIG Specialty Ins. Co.*, 29 Cal. 4th 189, 126 Cal. Rptr. 2d 908, 57 P.3d 372 (2002) (explaining the defensive function of CCP § 431.70's set-off procedure); *Carnation Co. v. Olivet Egg Ranch*, 189 Cal. App. 3d 809, 820, 229 Cal. Rptr. 261 (1988) (noting claims must be mutual if they are to qualify as "cross-demands" under CCP § 431.70).

(5) Federal Rule of Civil Procedure 15(c)(2) permits relation back of an amended pleading when "the claim or defense asserted in the amended pleading arose out of the conduct, transaction, or occurrence set forth … in the original pleading." How is this federal relation back doctrine different from California's with respect to amended complaints? The federal standard is more liberal in allowing relation back of amended complaints, is it not? Why is the California standard, as stated in *Barrington v. A.H. Robins Co.*, limited to the "same injuries as the original complaint"? Should it be? Are the two relation back doctrines the same as to amended pleadings by the defendant? If California followed the federal doctrine, would *Sidney* have been decided differently by the Court of Appeal? By the trial court? *See* Chapter 9, Pleadings, § 9.03 Amendments, *infra*, for a more complete discussion of the federal and California relation back doctrine.

§ 4.05 Commencement of an Action

[A] Generally

The various statutes of limitations discussed above all require that an action be "commenced" within a prescribed period after the cause of action has accrued. What constitutes "commencement" of an action in California? Fortunately, the Legislature does provide a general rule here: CCP § 350 states that an action is commenced, with respect to statutes of limitations in the Code of Civil Procedure, "when the complaint is filed." Consequently, unlike some other states, California does not generally require service of the complaint and summons within the statute of limitation period.

(Beware, however, that CCP § 583.210(a) requires service of the complaint within three years of filing, and CCP § 583.420(a)(1) authorizes discretionary dismissal if not served within two years. Local "Fast Track" rules may require even shorter times for service. *See* Chapters 6 and 12, *infra*; Government Code § 68616(a).)

[B]   Choice of Law

There is one interesting exception to this general rule regarding commencement. Under certain circumstances, CCP § 361 requires a California court to apply a statute of limitations from another state. *See* Chapter 5, California Conflict of Laws Doctrine, *infra*, for a full discussion of this choice-of-law statute. Where that foreign statute incorporates the requirement that an action is commenced by service of process on the defendant, the California courts will adopt this definition of "commencement." *See, e.g. Delfosse v. C.A.C.I., Inc.-Federal*, 218 Cal. App. 3d 683, 691–92, 267 Cal. Rptr. 224 (1990).

[C]   Prerequisites to Filing Complaint

Some special statutory schemes modify the general rule of "commencement" by inserting a prerequisite to the filing of the complaint. The most important such scheme applies to actions against public entities and public employees, discussed below. Another notable modification is contained in CCP § 364 dealing with the commencement of actions based on a health care provider's professional negligence. Others are discussed *infra*.

[1]   Medical Malpractice Prelitigation Notice

CCP § 364 requires a medical malpractice plaintiff to give a defendant at least 90 days' prior notice of the intention to file the action. No particular form of notice is required, but the plaintiff must notify the defendant of the legal basis of the claim and the type of loss sustained, including with specificity the nature of the injuries suffered. CCP § 364(b). Failure to comply with this notice prerequisite does not affect the jurisdiction of the court, but will be grounds for discipline of the plaintiff's attorney. CCP § 365. *See Preferred Risk Mut. Ins. Co. v. Reiswig*, 21 Cal. 4th 208, 213–14, 87 Cal. Rptr. 2d 187, 980 P.2d 895 (1999) (ruling failure to comply with the 90-day notice provision does not invalidate court proceedings); *Edwards v. Superior Court*, 93 Cal. App. 4th 172, 112 Cal. Rptr. 2d 838 (2001) (holding failure to specify in the § 364 notice all injuries suffered cannot bar a plaintiff from including the injury unintentionally omitted from the notice in the lawsuit against the medical practitioner if it is not otherwise barred by the statute of limitations).

[a]   The 90-Day Tolling Provision

One interesting question involves the interpretation of § 364(d), which states: "If the notice is served within 90 days of the expiration of the applicable statute of limitations, the time for commencement of the action shall be extended 90 days from the service of the notice." What does this tolling provision mean? For example, if the one-year statute of limitations of § 340.5 will end on September 3, 2015, and the plaintiff serves her § 364 notice on September 2, when is the last day the complaint can be timely filed within the meaning of both § 340.5 and § 364(d)? On December 1 or December 2? Neither? Does § 364 effectively shorten the statutory limitation period from one year to nine months?

[b] Judicial Interpretations

In *Woods v. Young*, 53 Cal. 3d 315, 279 Cal. Rptr. 613, 807 P.2d 455 (1991), the Supreme Court resolved these questions concerning CCP § 364. The court interpreted § 364 as tolling the statute of limitations when the notice of intent to sue is served during, but not before, the last ninety days of the one-year limitation period. *Woods*, 53 Cal. 3d at 325. Because the statute of limitations is tolled for 90 days and not merely extended by 90 days from the date of service of the notice, this construction results in a period of one year and 90 days within which to file the lawsuit. *Id.* However, when the notice is served *before* the last 90 days of the one-year limitations period, the tolling provision of § 364(d) does not apply and the plaintiff must commence a law suit within the one-year limitations period. *Id.* at 326–27.

Why, under *Woods*, is the dilatory plaintiff who serves the § 364 notice during the last 90 days of the limitation period rewarded, but not the diligent plaintiff who serves the notice earlier? What is the purpose of the § 364 notice? Does this more favorable treatment of those who serve the § 364 during the last 90 days violate the Equal Protection Clause? *See Woods, supra*, 53 Cal. 3d at 327 ("The distinction between a plaintiff who promptly gives notice and one who gives notice in the last 90 days of the limitations period does serve the legislative objective of allowing time for negotiations without the formal initiation of legal proceedings."). What about our hypothetical plaintiff who serves the notice on the last day of the one-year limitations period, *i.e.*, September 2? After *Woods v. Young, supra*, when is the last day that plaintiff can commence a timely lawsuit? *See* 53 Cal. 3d at 326, fn. 3.

Does the 90-day tolling period of § 364(d) apply to the three-year outside limitations period in § 340.5? *See Russell v. Stanford Univ. Hosp.*, 15 Cal. 4th 783, 64 Cal. Rptr. 2d 97, 937 P.2d 640 (1997) (holding the 90-day tolling period of § 364 applies to the three-year maximum statute of limitations in the same manner that the tolling period applies to the one-year statute of limitation under CCP § 340.5).

[D] Actions Against Public Entities and Employees

[1] *Claim-Filing Requirements of California Government Claims Act*

Special prelitigation procedures and time limitations govern most civil actions against public entities and employees in California. Government Code § 900 *et seq.*; CCP § 342. These procedures require as a condition precedent to litigation that a plaintiff file a written claim in the proper form with the appropriate state or local agency. Gov. Code §§ 905, 905.2.

This claim-filing requirement applies to most claims for money or damages against the state, including claims based on tort or express contract, Gov. Code § 905.2; to most claims for money or damages against local public entities, Gov. Code § 905; and to claims against public employees for injury resulting from an act or omission in the scope of employment, Gov. Code §§ 950–950.4. There are some specific statutory exceptions to this claim presentation requirement, most notably as to actions for inverse condemnation, § 905.1; and actions against the Regents of the University of California, § 905.6. *See also* Gov. Code § 905 for a list of exceptions applicable to actions against local public entities.

The Government Code sets forth a comprehensive process for the presentation of these claims by individuals, and for the review of them by public entities. Sections 910–910.4 delineate the content requirements for these claims. But if a presented claim does not substantially comply with these content requirements, the appropriate public entity must notify the claimant of the insufficiency within 20 days to allow correction through amendment. Gov. Code §§ 910.6, 910.8. Failure to provide this notice of insufficiency constitutes a waiver of any defense based on a content defect in the claim. § 911.

A claim relating to a cause of action for death or for injury to person or to personal property must be presented not later than "six months after the accrual of the cause of action." Gov. Code § 911.2 (This section was amended in 1987. The pre-1987 time limit was only 100 days.) A claim relating to any other cause of action must be presented not later than "one year after accrual of the cause of action." § 911.2. How is the date of accrual determined for such claims? Section 901 provides that it is the date upon which the cause of action would be deemed to have accrued within the meaning of the statute of limitations which would be applicable thereto if there were no requirement that a claim be presented to the public entity. Consequently, all the accrual principles otherwise applicable to the underlying cause of action apply here, such as the "discovery rule" and the "actual and appreciable injury rule." *See, e.g.,* *Whitfield v. Roth,* 10 Cal. 3d 874, 112 Cal. Rptr. 540, 519 P.2d 588 (1974) (ruling the date of accrual for purposes of starting claim presentation in malpractice suit is when plaintiff discovers the injury and its negligent cause); *Brandon G. v. Gray,* 111 Cal. App. 4th 29, 34–36, 3 Cal. Rptr. 3d 330 (2003) (applying delayed discovery rule to determine when cause of action accrued to purposes of claims presentation process). Note, however, that pursuant to a 1981 amendment to § 901, the accrual date for a cause of action for equitable indemnity is the date upon which a defendant is served with the complaint giving rise to the defendant's claim for equitable indemnity against the public entity.

What happens if an individual fails to present a claim within the required six-month time period, but does present one later? Is the individual barred from pursuing an action in court? Not always. For unlike statutes of limitations, the claim-filing requirements are more forgiving. When a claim is presented after the six-month period, the relevant public entity must notify the claimant that the claim is being returned but that the claimant may apply for leave to present a late claim. § 911.3(a). If no such notice is given to the claimant within 45 days and the claim is proper as to content, any defense based on the untimeliness of the claim is waived. § 911.3(b).

An application for leave to present a late claim must be filed "within a reasonable time not to exceed one year after the accrual of the cause of action and shall state the reason for the delay in presenting the claim." § 911.4. This one-year period is tolled only for mental incapacity, and specifically not for minority. § 911.4. The public entity must grant this application if the failure to present a timely claim was due to (1) mistake, inadvertence, surprise or excusable neglect and the public entity was not prejudiced, § 911.6(b)(1); (2) the claimant's being a minor during all the time for the presentation of the claim, § 911.6(b)(2); (3) physical or mental incapacity caused the failure to present a timely claim, § 911.6(b)(3); or (4) death of claimant, § 911.6(b)(4).

The public entity must grant or deny the application within 45 days, although this time may be extended by agreement. § 911.6(a). Failure to act within this time period constitutes a denial of the application. § 911.6(c). This denial may be independently reviewed in court through a petition for an order relieving the claimant from presenting a § 945.4 claim. Gov. Code § 946.6. *See, e.g., Draper v. City of Los Angeles*, 52 Cal. 3d 502, 276 Cal. Rptr. 864, 802 P.2d 367 (1990) (finding the trial court improperly denied relief from claim-filing requirements where plaintiff was incapacitated and unconscious during claim-filing period, even though attorney purportedly acting on her behalf filed a claim against wrong public entity); *Munoz v. State of California*, 33 Cal. App. 4th 1767, 39 Cal. Rptr. 2d 860 (1995) (ruling the trial court properly denied plaintiff's petition for permission to file a late claim where plaintiff's application for leave to present a late claim had been misaddressed and therefore not actually received by the correct public entity within the one-year late application limitations period); *Department of Water & Power v. Superior Court*, 82 Cal. App. 4th 1288, 99 Cal. Rptr. 2d 173 (2000) (observing that the party seeking late claim relief based on mistake must establish he was diligent in investigating and pursuing the claim).

Government Code § 946.6, which authorizes judicial review of a public entity's denial of an application for leave to file a late claim, is a remedial statute that courts often construe in favor of relief whenever possible. *See, e.g., Bettencourt v. Los Rios Comm. College Dist.*, 42 Cal. 3d 270, 275–76, 228 Cal. Rptr. 190, 721 P.2d 71 (1986) (noting that a trial court decision denying relief will be scrutinized more carefully than an order granting relief); *Reneria v. Juvenile Justice, Dept. of Corrections & Rehab.*, 135 Cal. App. 4th 903, 910–11, 37 Cal. Rptr. 3d 777 (2006) (discussing cases where relief deemed proper when an attorney relies on a member of her staff to perform certain tasks, including calendaring deadlines, and the staff member errs); *Barragan v. County of Los Angeles*, 184 Cal. App. 4th 1371, 109 Cal. Rptr. 3d 501 (2010) (noting a claimant's physical disability, while not sufficient to establish incapacity, may be sufficient to render neglect in obtaining counsel during the six-month period excusable). If the court grants this order, the claimant must commence a lawsuit on the underlying cause of action within 30 days. Gov. Code § 946.6(f).

The manner of presenting a claim, or an application to present a late claim, is governed by §§ 915–915.4. Generally, a claim may be delivered or mailed to the appropriate public entity, § 915; and a mailed claim is deemed presented and received at the time of mailing, § 915.2. Beginning in 2003, each public entity subject to the Government Claims Act must provide forms specifying the information to be contained in claims against that public entity, and a person presenting a claim must use that form. Gov. Code § 910.4 (effective March 30, 2003). A claim may be returned to the person if not presented using the form. Gov. Code § 910.4.

The relevant public entity must act on a claim within 45 days after the claim has been presented, unless extended by agreement or, when the claim was presented by mail, by § 915.2. Gov. Code § 912.4. If the entity fails or refuses to act on the claim within this period, the claim shall be deemed to have been rejected on the last day of the period. § 912.4(c). Where the entity does act on a claim within this time period, the entity must notify the claimant of a total or partial rejection, with a warning that the claimant has six months to file a court action on the claim. § 913.

The claim-presenting procedure outlined above is a prerequisite to suit for money or damages against a public entity or employee. Gov. Code §§ 945.4, 950.6. The lawsuit must be commenced within six months after service of the notice of rejection; or if no such notice of rejection is given, within two years from the accrual of the cause of action. § 945.6(a)(1)&(2). These time periods may be extended due to imprisonment, § 945.6(b)&(c); but the other general statutory tolling provisions for "disability" under CCP § 352 do not apply. CCP § 352(b). Failure to allege facts demonstrating compliance or excusing compliance with the claim presentation requirement subjects a complaint against a public entity to a general demurrer for failure to state a cause of action. *State v. Superior Court*, 32 Cal. 4th 1234, 13 Cal. Rptr. 3d 534, 90 P.3d 116 (2004).

The Government Code sets forth a rather complex process for presenting claims against public entities and employees, and for commencing actions in court based on these claims. For more thorough practical analysis of this claims process, see CEB, *California Government Tort Liability Practice*, §§ 5.1–7.88 (4th ed. 2016). The legislative and judicial attitude toward this process appears to be a bit more lenient than that of other statutes of limitations, as our principal case illustrates.

Phillips v. Desert Hospital District

Supreme Court of California
49 Cal. 3d 699, 263 Cal. Rptr. 119, 780 P.2d 349 (1989)

KAUFMAN, JUSTICE.

We granted review in this case to determine whether a notice of intention to commence an action based upon a health care provider's alleged professional negligence (Code Civ. Proc., § 364, subd. (a)) may activate the notice and defense-waiver provisions (Gov. Code, §§ 910.8, 911, 911.3) of the Tort Claims Act (Gov. Code, § 900 et seq.).[1] As explained below, we conclude that a public entity must treat a notice, such as the notice at issue here, that alerts it to the existence of a claim for monetary damages and an impending lawsuit but fails to comply substantially with the claim presentation requirements of the act, as a defective "claim" that triggers the operation of sections 910.8, 911 and 911.3. These sections (1) require a public entity to notify a claimant of any insufficiencies of content or timeliness that prevent a claim as presented from satisfying the requirements of the act and (2) provide that failure to give such notice waives any defenses based on those insufficiencies.[2] * * *

On September 11, 1983, plaintiff Paula E. Phillips was admitted to Desert Hospital (hospital), a public hospital district, the defendant herein. On the advice of her doctors, she underwent a bilateral mastectomy and reconstructive surgery. Mrs. Phillips and her husband, also a plaintiff, allege that the surgery was both medically unnecessary and negligently performed and that as a result she developed complications, including gangrene. Plaintiffs further allege that, notwithstanding the unsuccessful surgery, Mrs. Phillips was released from the hospital on October 2, 1983, without being informed of the nature or extent of her condition. As a result, plaintiffs allege that Mrs. Phillips has been compelled to seek extensive additional medical treatment, including surgical intervention.

On April 6, 1984 (205 days after the surgery and 185 days after Mrs. Phillips's release from the hospital), plaintiffs' counsel mailed to the hospital a notice (hereafter 364 notice) pursuant to Code of Civil Procedure section 364, subdivision (a), which

---

1. All further statutory references are to the Government Code unless otherwise indicated.

2. Section 910.8 provides in relevant part: "If in the opinion of the board or the person designated by it a claim as presented fails to comply substantially with the requirements of Sections 910 and 910.2, ... the board or such person may, at any time within 20 days after the claim is presented, give written notice of its insufficiency, stating with particularity the defects or omissions therein.... The board may not take action on the claim for a period of 15 days after such notice is given."

Section 911 provides: "Any defense as to the sufficiency of the claim based upon a defect or omission in the claim as presented is waived by failure to give notice of insufficiency with respect to such defect or omission as provided in Section 910.8, except that no notice need be given and no waiver shall result when the claim as presented fails to state either an address to which the person presenting the claim desires notices to be sent or an address of the claimant."

At the time this dispute arose, section 911.3 provided in relevant part: "(a) When a claim that is required by Section 911.2 to be presented not later than *the 100th day* after accrual of the cause of action is presented after such time without the application provided in Section 911.4, the board or other person designated by it may, at any time within 45 days after the claim is presented, give written notice to the person presenting the claim that the claim was not filed timely and that it is being returned without further action.... [¶] (b) Any defense as to the time limit for presenting a claim described in subdivision (a) is waived by failure to give the notice set forth in subdivision (a) within 45 days after the claim is presented, except that no notice need be given and no waiver shall result when the claim as presented fails to state either an address to which the person presenting the claim desires notices to be sent or an address of the claimant." The italicized words were amended in 1987 to reflect extension of the claims presentation period to six months.

requires potential medical malpractice plaintiffs to notify health care providers of their intent to sue 90 days prior to filing a complaint.

Plaintiffs' 364 notice was typed on their law firm's stationery which bore the firm's name, address and telephone number, was signed by their attorney and stated as follows:

"Desert Hospital

1150 North Indian Avenue

Palm Springs, California 92262

"Re: *Intention to Commence Action*

Paula E. Phillips and Richard A. Phillips

Date of Incident: September 12, 1983

"To Whom It May Concern:

"This letter will serve to advise you that this office intends to commence an action against Desert Hospital on behalf of Paula E. Phillips and her husband Richard A. Phillips. This action arises out of apparent Health Care Provider Negligence (Medical Malpractice) resulting from the diagnosis, care, treatment, operation and related services rendered to Paula E. Phillips on or about September 12, 1983 at Desert Hospital, Palm Springs, California, and the subsequent complications, treatment, damages and emotional distress resulting therefrom. Mr. Phillips will claim damages for loss of consortium and for his mental and emotional suffering resulting from the damages and disfigurement to his wife." (Original italics.)

Having received no response from the hospital, plaintiffs filed a complaint on July 27, 1984, in which they alleged causes of action for negligence, willful misconduct, fraud, conspiracy to defraud, concealment, intentional and negligent infliction of emotional distress and loss of consortium. The complaint named as defendants Mrs. Phillips's treating physicians and the hospital.

The hospital demurred to the complaint on the ground that plaintiffs had failed to state a cause of action because they did not allege compliance with the claim presentation requirements of the act. * * *

The trial court sustained the demurrer without leave to amend and subsequently dismissed the amended ... complaint. Plaintiffs appealed from the order of dismissal and the Court of Appeal affirmed the judgment. Plaintiffs then petitioned for review. * * * We ... granted review and now reverse.

II

On appeal below, the court addressed the question whether plaintiffs' 364 notice complied substantially with the claim presentation requirements of the act. Finding the answer in the negative, the Court of Appeal upheld the dismissal of the plaintiffs' action. While we agree that the 364 notice does not comply substantially with the claim presentation requirements of the act (*see* fn. 7, *post*), that conclusion is not dispositive of the case. The dispositive issue is whether plaintiffs' 364 notice triggered the notice and defense-waiver provisions of the act (§§ 910.8, 911, 911.3). * * *

A. *Notice and Defense-waiver Provisions of the Tort Claims Act*

It is well settled that the purpose of the claims statutes "is to provide the public entity sufficient information to enable it to adequately investigate claims and to settle them, if appropriate, without the expense of litigation. [Citations.]" (*City of San Jose v. Superior Court* (1974) 12 Cal. 3d 447, 455 [115 Cal. Rptr. 797, 525 P.2d 701, 76 A.L.R. 3d 1223].) To achieve this purpose, section 911.2 requires a claimant to present a claim to the public entity within a specified time after accrual of the cause of action.[3] In medical malpractice cases, the action accrues on claimants' actual or constructive discovery of the malpractice. (*Martinez v. County of Los Angeles* (1978) 78 Cal. App. 3d 242, 245 [144 Cal. Rptr. 123].)

If the public entity determines a "claim as presented" fails to comply substantially with sections 910 and 910.2, and is therefore defective, the public entity may either "give written notice of [the claim's] insufficiency, stating with particularity the defects or omissions therein" within 20 days (§ 910.8; *see* fn. 2, *ante*), or waive any defense "as to the sufficiency of the claim based upon a defect or omission in the claim as presented...." (§ 911). If the public entity does send a notice of insufficiency, it may not take further action on the defective claim for a period of 15 days after such notice is given. (§ 910.8; *see* fn. 2, *ante*.) Whether or not it decides to provide a notice of insufficiency, the public entity must notify the claimant within 45 days after the claim is presented whether the claim, defective or otherwise, was timely filed. (§ 911.3, subd. (a); *see* fn. 2, *ante*.) Thus, if a section 910.8 notice of insufficiency is sent, the board must make a timeliness determination within 10 days after the last date the claimant could amend the claim to cure the insufficiency identified. Failure to provide such notice of timeliness waives a public entity's defense based on untimeliness even if the claim is otherwise insufficient, unless the claimant has failed to state in the claim an address where such notices should be sent. (§ 911.3, subd. (b); *see* fn. 2, *ante*.)

The Legislature has thus provided a comprehensive scheme which requires a claimant to notify the appropriate public entity of a claim. This notification in turn allows the public entity an opportunity to determine expeditiously the claim's timeliness and sufficiency. If the notice is untimely or lacks any of the information required by sections 910 and 910.2, the public entity may require the claimant to justify the delay or supply the missing data. If the public entity fails to require the claimant to cure such defects, then it waives certain defenses which are otherwise available to challenge a lawsuit based upon the claim. This possibility of waiver encourages public entities to investigate claims promptly, and to make and notify

---

3. Before 1987, the time specified was 100 days. In 1987, the Legislature amended sections 911.2 and 911.3, extending the period within which claims must be presented from 100 days to 6 months. The amendments do not apply to this appeal, however, nor do they affect our determination of the principal issue on appeal.

claimants of their determinations, thus enabling the claimants to perfect their claims. The overall result is an incentive to public entities to manage and control the claims made against them.

B. *Section 910 Requirements and Defective Claims*

Section 910 identifies the information a proper notice of claim should include to enable a public entity to investigate and evaluate the claim to determine whether settlement is appropriate. Prior to a 1987 amendment, section 910 provided that when a claim is presented, it "shall show:[4] [¶] (a) The name and post office address of the claimant; [¶] (b) The post office address to which the person presenting the claim desires notices to be sent; [¶] (c) The date, place and other circumstances of the occurrence or transaction which gave rise to the claim asserted; [¶] (d) A general description of the ... injury, damage or loss incurred so far as it may be known at the time of presentation of the claim; [¶] (e) The name or names of the public employee or employees causing the injury, damage, or loss, if known; and [¶] (f) The amount claimed as of the date of presentation of the claim, including the estimated amount of any prospective injury, damage, or loss, insofar as it may be known at the time of the presentation of the claim, together with the basis of computation of the amount claimed."[5]

When a public entity receives a document which contains the information required by section 910 and is signed by the claimant or her agent as required by section 910.2, the public entity has been presented with a "claim" under the act, and must act within 45 days or the claim is deemed to have been denied. (§ 912.4.) Once a claim is denied or deemed to have been denied, the claimant may then proceed to file a lawsuit. (§ 945.4.)

But it is not, as the hospital suggests, the filing of a complete and valid "claim" that triggers the notice and defense-waiver provisions of the act. Such confusion may stem from the Legislature's use of the term "claim" to describe two distinct situations. On the one hand, as previously noted, a "claim" is a notice which complies with sections 910 and 910.2. On the other hand, the notice and defense-waiver provisions, sections 910.8 and 911, use the phrase "claim as presented" to identify a "claim" which

---

4. In 1987, section 910 was amended to read in relevant part: "A claim shall be presented by the claimant ... and shall show *all of the following....*" (Amended portion italicized.) Whatever intent the Legislature may have had in adding this language is of no consequence here. The 1987 amendments apply only to actions based on acts or omissions occurring on or after January 1, 1988. Moreover, since the Legislature did not amend the notice-of-insufficiency provisions to eliminate the reference to insufficiencies due to "defects or *omissions*" (§§ 910.8, 911, italics added), our determination of what type of document triggers those provisions would not be affected even if the amendment to section 910 were applied to the instant case.

5. The 1987 amendments changed section 910, subdivision (f), to read in pertinent part: "The amount claimed *if it totals less than ten thousand dollars ($10,000).... If the amount claimed exceeds ten thousand dollars ($10,000), no dollar amount shall be included in the claim. However, it shall indicate whether jurisdiction over the claim would rest in municipal or superior court.*" ([I]talics added to reflect amendments.)

is defective due to its failure to comply substantially with sections 910 and 910.2[6] and, contrary to the hospital's position, it is *only* a "claim as presented [that] fails to comply substantially" that triggers sections 910.8, 911 and 911.3. (§ 910.8; *Foster v. McFadden* [(1973)], 30 Cal. App. 3d [943] at p. 947 [106 Cal. Rptr. 685]). Accordingly, it only remains to be determined whether the hospital was required to treat plaintiffs' 364 notice as a defective claim triggering the notice and defense-waiver provisions of sections 910.8, 911 and 911.3.

In this regard, the hospital attempts to distinguish between defective "claims" which properly trigger the act's notice and defense-waiver provisions and other notices of possible claims, such as plaintiffs' 364 notice, which, according to the hospital, it was at liberty simply to ignore without consequence. However, we perceive no principled basis for such a distinction and therefore conclude that a notice, such as plaintiffs' 364 notice, which discloses the existence of a claim that if not paid or otherwise re-solved will result in litigation, must be treated as a defective "claim" activating the notice and defense-waiver provisions of the act, sections 910.8, 911 and 911.3.

C. *Plaintiffs' Notice to the Hospital*

Plaintiffs contend that, whether or not their 364 notice was insufficient under sec-tion 910,[7] the hospital's receipt of the 364 notice activated sections 910.8, 911 and 911.3 and thus required the hospital to notify plaintiffs in writing as to (a) what ad-ditional section 910 information was necessary to allow it to initiate an investigation into the incident (§ 910.8) and (b) whether the notice of claim was timely (§ 911.3, subd. (a)). Plaintiffs further contend that the hospital, having failed to provide such notices, waived any defenses as to the sufficiency of the claim based upon omitted section 910 requirements (§ 911) or untimeliness (§ 911.3, subd. (b)).

In response, the hospital, citing *Lutz v. Tri-City Hospital* (1986) 179 Cal. App. 3d 807 [224 Cal. Rptr. 787], argues that plaintiffs' 364 notice cannot, as a matter of law, be considered a "claim" under the act. * * *

---

6. Although the notice of timeliness provision, section 911.3, subdivision (a), does not use the phrase "claim as presented," there are two reasons for concluding that section 911.3 applies both to defective claims and to claims complying substantially with sections 910 and 910.2. First, as previously noted, by providing 45 days within which a notice of timeliness must be sent to avoid waiving timeliness defenses, section 910.8 allows a public entity 10 days after expiration of the time for (1) sending a notice of insufficiency of a defective claim (20 days after the claim is presented) and (2) receiving any curing amendments (15 days thereafter) to determine whether a claim is timely. Second, the *only* ex-ception to application of the timeliness-defense waiver occurs "when the claim as presented fails to state either an address to which the person presenting the claim desires notices to be sent or an address of the claimant." (§ 911.3, subd. (b).) The insufficiency-defense waiver provision, section 911, contains the identical exclusive exception to application of the insufficiency-defense waiver.

7. Plaintiffs argue that their 364 notice complied sufficiently with the section 910 requirements to enable the hospital to investigate the incident adequately to determine if settlement negotiations were appropriate. It is indisputable, however, that the 364 notice does not state the amount plaintiffs sought in damages as required by section 910, subdivision (f), and therefore fails to comply substantially with section 910. Under the analysis adopted herein we need not address that issue further

The *Lutz* court ... distinguished a 364 notice from a section 910 claim on the ground that such a claim must be more detailed and specific than a 364 notice, which need only "set out the legal basis for the claim and the type of loss sustained, 'including with specificity the nature of the injuries suffered.'" If a claim complies substantially with sections 910 and 910.2, however, sections 910.8, 911 and 911.3 do not come into play. The latter sections become significant only when the "claim as presented" does *not* substantially comply with sections 910 and 910.2.

We conclude, therefore, that a document constitutes a "claim as presented" triggering sections 910.8, 911 and 911.3, if it discloses the existence of a "claim" which, if not satisfactorily resolved, will result in a lawsuit against the entity. A public entity's receipt of written notice that a claim for monetary damages exists and that litigation may ensue places upon the public entity the responsibility, and gives it the opportunity, to notify the potential plaintiff pursuant to sections 910.8 and 911 of the defects that render the document insufficient under sections 910 and 910.2 and thus might hamper investigation and possible settlement of the claim. Such a written notice claiming monetary damages thereby satisfies the purposes of the claims act — to facilitate investigation of disputes and their settlement without trial if appropriate.

The hospital contends that plaintiffs could never have *intended* their 364 notice to function as a claim for purposes of the act because, by plaintiffs' own admission, they were not aware of the hospital's status as a public entity. The hospital fails to explain, however, why or how a claimant's intent, even if ascertainable, is relevant to the notice and defense-waiver provisions of the act. Implementation of the purposes of the claim presentation requirements — to require public entities to manage and control claims and to encourage timely investigation and settlement to avoid needless litigation — depends not on a claimant's state of mind but rather on the information imparted to the public entity. Thus, the relevant inquiry is not into plaintiffs' subjective intent but whether their 364 notice disclosed to the hospital that they had a claim against it which, if not satisfactorily resolved, would result in their filing a lawsuit.

The Court of Appeal was concerned that if a letter captioned "Intention to Commence Action" could activate the notice and defense-waiver provisions of the act, then the hospital and other public health providers would be required to treat all such letters written by dissatisfied patients or their attorneys which threaten legal action as "claims," or else risk the loss of defenses from failing to notify the potential claimant of insufficiency or untimeliness pursuant to sections 910.8, 911 and 911.3, subdivision (b). But, provided the existence of a claim for monetary damages is definitely disclosed by the document, that burden upon the public entity is precisely the intended effect of the statutory notice and defense-waiver provisions.

Foster v. McFadden, supra, 30 Cal. App. 3d 943, is directly in point. There, the plaintiff was injured when he was struck by a bulldozer operated by a sanitation district (district) employee. The plaintiff's attorney wrote the employee a letter, and sent a copy to the district, advising the employee of the plaintiff's name, and the date and place of the accident, and asking him to forward the letter to his insurer or, if not insured, to contact the plaintiff's attorney. The district acknowledged being advised of the incident by notifying the plaintiff's attorney of the district's insurance coverage and requesting the attorney to direct further inquiries to its insurer. The plaintiff subsequently brought an action against the district. The trial court entered judgment in the district's favor based solely on its conclusion that the plaintiff had failed to comply with the claim presentation requirements of the act.

The *McFadden* court reversed, reasoning that the plaintiff's letter "accomplished the two principal purposes of a sufficient claim. It afforded the district the opportunity to make a prompt investigation of the accident occasioning the letter and it gave to the district the opportunity to settle without suit, if it so desired." Thus, the *McFadden* court concluded that the letter was sufficient to activate the notice and defense-waiver provisions of sections 910.8 and 911.[8]

The concern of the Court of Appeal below that an improperly captioned document could have an unintended legal effect is likewise misplaced. First, it is settled that the caption or title of a notice does not diminish its legal effect as a claim. More importantly, the notice and defense-waiver provisions (§§ 910.8, 911, 911.3), while falling short of placing an affirmative duty on public entities to obtain the information deemed necessary to investigate incidents and to determine whether settlement is appropriate, nevertheless furnish a strong incentive to do so by sanctioning a public entity that fails to ask the claimant for such information. Thus, if a public entity receives a document that alerts it to the existence of a claim and the possibility of a lawsuit but fails to comply substantially with sections 910 and 910.2, the purposes of the act are best served by requiring the public entity to notify the claimant of the nature of the claim's insufficiencies or lack of timeliness or else waive, by operation of sections 911 and 911.3, its defenses based on those deficiencies.

Inasmuch as the hospital failed to notify plaintiffs of the insufficiencies in their 364 notice that rendered it defective to comply substantially with sections 910 and 910.2, the hospital has waived any defenses it may have otherwise asserted based on such insufficiencies. (§ 911.) Further, as it failed to notify plaintiffs of any timeliness defects (§ 911.3, subd. (a)), the hospital has similarly waived any defenses it might have raised on the ground of plaintiffs' asserted failure to present a timely claim (§ 911.3, subd. (b)). Accordingly, there is no reason to allow plaintiffs to amend their complaint. * * *

For the foregoing reasons, we reverse the judgment of the Court of Appeal with directions to remand to the trial court with directions to vacate its order dismissing the action and to issue an order overruling the demurrer.

---

8. *McFadden* predates the enactment of section 911.3, which was added to the act in 1983 and which requires a governmental entity to respond to a claim within 45 days of receipt or waive its *timeliness* defense. The *McFadden* holding would have applied equally to that provision, had it by then been enacted.

[2] Purposes of Government Claims Act

What is the purpose of the claims statutes, Government Code § 905 *et seq.*? Of the notice required by CCP § 364? How do these purposes differ from those purposes ascribed to statutes of limitations generally? Does this explain why court decisions dealing with claim-presentation requirements have been more liberal than statute of limitations cases in permitting exceptions to the rules of timeliness? *Compare Ebersol v. Cowan*, 35 Cal. 3d 427, 197 Cal. Rptr. 601, 673 P.2d 271 (1983) (finding failure to present timely claim because plaintiffs' prior attorneys advised her she had no legal claim constitutes "excusable neglect" within meaning of Gov. Code § 946.6, justifying relief from the claim statute), *with Gutierrez v. Mofid*, 39 Cal. 3d 892, 900–903, 218 Cal. Rptr. 313, 705 P.2d 886 (1985) (ruling failure to commence lawsuit within medical malpractice statute of limitations not excused due to plaintiff's reliance on legal advice that she had no legal claim).

[3] Government Claims Act Doctrine of Substantial Compliance

[a] Substantial Compliance, Generally

Several cases following *Phillips* have found a defective claim which satisfies the purposes of the claims statute to constitute substantial compliance with Government Code §§ 910 and 910.2. *E.g., Ocean Services Corp. v. Ventura Port Dist.*, 15 Cal. App. 4th 1762, 19 Cal. Rptr. 2d 750 (1993) (concluding plaintiff's letter and amended claim substantially complied with claims statute because they enabled defendant to make early investigation of facts and assess whether to litigate or settle); *Watts v. Valley Med. Center*, 8 Cal. App. 4th 1050, 10 Cal. Rptr. 2d 794 (1992) (finding CCP § 364 notice of intention to commence medical malpractice action triggered claim presentation requirements); *Wilson v. Tri-City Hosp. Dist.*, 221 Cal. App. 3d 441, 270 Cal. Rptr. 436 (1990) (ruling letters by plaintiff's attorney to defendant hospital district demanding damages, and threatening suit, for wrongful termination constituted substantial compliance with claims statute).

Is there substantial compliance with the claim presentation requirements where the plaintiff driver seeks personal injury damages as the result of a collision with a vehicle driven by a county employee, but the plaintiff's timely claim filed with the county asserted property damages and "unspecified medical, lost income, and future medical" and did not specifically state the plaintiff was seeking personal injury damages? The court in *Connelly v. County of Fresno*, 146 Cal. App. 4th 29, 52 Cal. Rptr. 3d 720 (2006), held that the plaintiff did submit a claim that substantially complied with the Tort Claims Act because it indicated that plaintiff sought to recover damages for personal injuries suffered in the accident but that she did not yet know the extent of her injuries, and therefore enabled the defendant county to make an adequate investigation and settle the claim. Do you agree?

[b] Limits to Substantial Compliance

What are the limits of this substantial compliance doctrine? Is there substantial compliance with the claims presentation requirements when the claim is delivered to the proper public entity but to someone there other than the statute's designated recipient? *See DiCamli-Mintz v. County of Santa Clara*, 55 Cal. 4th 983, 150 Cal. Rptr. 3d 111, 289 P.3d 884 (2012) (holding that unless there is actual receipt by the proper recipient, delivery of plaintiff's claim to the wrong recipient at the defendant public entity does not satisfy the Act's claim filing requirements). When the claim is presented to the wrong, albeit a related, public entity? *Compare Life v. County of Los Angeles*, 227 Cal. App. 3d 894, 278 Cal. Rptr. 196 (1991) (finding no substantial compliance where claim sent to wrong entity and did not actually reach correct entity), *and Santee v. Santa Clara Cnty. Office of Ed.*, 220 Cal. App. 3d 702, 269 Cal. Rptr. 605 (1990) (noting substantial compliance normally raised where a timely but deficient claim has been presented to the correct public entity), *with Carlino v. Los Angeles Cnty. Flood Control Dist.*, 10 Cal. App. 4th 1526, 1532–35, 13 Cal. Rptr. 2d 437 (1992) (ruling plaintiff substantially complied with claim requirement although claim erroneously filed with Board of Supervisors instead of directly with Flood Control District because District ultimately controlled by Board).

[4]   *Minimum Requirements of a Claim*

Phillips was not a "substantial compliance" case, was it? What must a plaintiff present in order to comply with the *Phillips* court's requirement that a claim, albeit a defective one, must be filed to trigger the notice and defense-waiver provisions of Government Code §§ 910.8, 911, and 911.3? In *City of Stockton v. Superior Court*, 42 Cal. 4th 730, 68 Cal. Rptr. 3d 295, 171 P.3d 20 (2007), the plaintiff developer filed an action against the defendant city and its redevelopment agency, alleging breach of contracts that involved the rehabilitation and leasing of a hotel and the construction of a cinema. The defendants contended that the plaintiff's complaint was barred for failure to comply with the claim-filing requirements of Government Code § 905, and also cross-claimed against the plaintiff seeking damages for misrepresentation and breach of contract. In response, the plaintiff argued the defense-waiver provisions of § 910.8 and § 911 applied because the defendants did not advise plaintiff that correspondence between the parties prior to suit was insufficient to constitute a claim. In other words, the plaintiff argued that correspondence between the parties through which they attempted to restructure their plans in a mutually agreeable manner constituted a "claim as presented."

The Supreme Court rejected the plaintiff's argument because nothing in the correspondence relied on by plaintiff indicated that litigation might ensue if defendants did not comply with the terms under discussion. "This is the most essential element of a 'claim as presented,'" the court noted, "because it satisfies the primary purposes of the Government Claims Act: facilitating the investigation of disputes and their settlement without trial if appropriate." *City of Stockton, supra*, 42 Cal. 4th at 744. The court also concluded that the defendants did not waive their right to rely on the claim-filing requirements by filing a cross-complaint, but that the plaintiff may raise affirmative defenses in its answer to the cross-complaint. *Id.* at 745.

[handwritten margin note: rule from Phillips]

In *Green v. State Center Community College Dist.*, 34 Cal. App. 4th 1348, 41 Cal. Rptr. 2d 140 (1995), plaintiff Green seriously injured her ankle when she fell into a hole while walking across the grass-covered lawn of the Fresno City College. At issue was whether the following letter, mailed to the College by Green's attorney, constituted a claim sufficient to trigger the notice-waiver provisions of §§ 910.8, 911, and 911.3:

> Fresno City College
>
> 1101 E. University Avenue
>
> Fresno, CA 93741
>
> RE Our Client: Marilyn Green
>
> Date of Accident: October 7, 1991
>
> Gentlemen:
>
> Please be advised that the MAGILL LAW OFFICES has been retained as attorney for Marilyn Green relative to the personal injuries sustained from that certain accident which occurred on October 7, 1991.
>
> Accordingly, please direct all further communications and correspondence regarding this accident to this office.
>
> This is also to advise you that you do not have our authority to discuss this incident with our client without our express written approval.
>
> Thank you for your continued courtesy and cooperation in this matter.
>
> Very truly yours,
>
> MAGILL LAW OFFICES
>
> /s/T.V. Magill
>
> Timothy V. Magill

After a lengthy discussion of *Phillips*, the *Green* court concluded that the above letter was not sufficient to trigger the statutory notice-waiver provisions. Do you agree with this conclusion? Why? Based on *Phillips*, what legal standard applies in determining whether correspondence constitutes a claim that triggers the statutory notice-waiver provisions? *See Green, supra*, 34 Cal. App. 4th at 1358.

Schaefer Dixon Assn. v. Santa Ana Watershed Project Auth., 48 Cal. App. 4th 524, 55 Cal. Rptr. 2d 698 (1996), involved a contract dispute and money the plaintiff, a contractor, claimed was owed to it by the Santa Ana Water Project Authority (the agency). The contractor sent a series of letters to the agency attempting to establish its right to payment. When the agency approved payment for less than the amount claimed, the contractor's attorneys sent several letters to the agency, referring to the dispute, noting that an amount was still outstanding, and informing the agency that the contractor would file suit if the matter was not settled. The *Schaefer* court found that none of the attorneys' letters might be deemed a "claim as presented" under the Government Claims Act. The court found it significant that no letter advised the agency that litigation was imminent, and that neither the contractor nor his attorneys viewed any letter as the equivalent of a claim.

The *Schaefer* court expressed the practical concern that it may be unworkable for a public entity to determine the point at which correspondence ceases being an expression of unhappiness or the mere conveyance of information, and becomes the assertion of a compensable "claim." *Id.*, at 536. Do you agree with the conclusion reached by the *Schaefer* court?

What about the reverse of the issue decided in *Phillips*: Must a tort claim under Gov. Code § 910 also be deemed to be a notice of intent to sue for purposes of CCP § 364 if the claim contains the information required by the latter statute? The answer appears to be "no," at least where the circumstances did not establish that the claimant intended the tort claim to also function as a § 364 notice. *See Wurts v. County of Fresno*, 44 Cal. App. 4th 380, 51 Cal. Rptr. 2d 689 (1996) (ruling a claimant who has complied with the letter and spirit of both § 364 and Gov. Code § 910 is entitled to the full benefit of both statutes, including tolling for 90 days of the 6-month limitations period of Gov. Code § 945.6). Is this reasoning consistent with *Phillips*? *See Wurts, supra*, 44 Cal. App. 4th at 437–38. How would a court ascertain whether a plaintiff intended that a filed tort claim also constituted a § 364 notice of intent to sue?

[5] New Allegations in Complaint

Is there substantial compliance where a plaintiff's complaint in court contains new allegations as to the cause of plaintiff's injuries, different from those stated in the claim? In *Stockett v. Association of Cal. Water Agencies Joint Powers Ins. Auth.*, 34 Cal. 4th 441, 20 Cal. Rptr. 3d 176, 99 P.3d 500 (2004), the Supreme Court considered the question of whether a dismissed government employee is precluded under the Government Claims Act from asserting in a complaint for wrongful termination theories of illegal motivation that were not specified in the required notice of claim. Plaintiff Stockett was the general manager of the defendant Association of California Water Agencies Joint Powers Insurance Authority (JPIA), a public agency that provides insurance and risk management services to public water agencies, until his termination in 1995. Stockett presented a notice of government tort claim to JPIA, alleging he had been wrongfully terminated for supporting a female employee's sexual harassment complaints against JPIA's insurance broker, which harassment was in violation of the Fair Employment and Housing Act and the public policy of the State of California.

After JPIA denied Stockett's claim, Stockett filed a wrongful termination lawsuit against JPIA. He later moved to amend his complaint to allege he had been terminated in violation of public policy on three grounds: (1) opposing sexual harassment; (2) objecting to a conflict of interest involving a JPIA employee; and (3) exercising his First Amendment right of free speech by objecting to certain JPIA practices. Defendant JPIA unsuccessfully opposed this motion, arguing the facts in the amended complaint had not been set forth in the government tort claim. Subsequently, a jury returned a verdict for the plaintiff, awarding him $4.5 million in damages.

Defendant JPIA sought appellate review, arguing Stockett's tort claim had not provided JPIA with sufficient notice of two wrongful termination theories Stockett asserted at trial: that he was fired for opposing a conflict of interest, and that he was fired for exercising the right to free speech. The Supreme court rejected the defendant JPIA's arguments, and held that plaintiff Stockett's claim was sufficient under the Government Claims Act to give JPIA notice of all theories of wrongful termination. The court explained its holding as follows (34 Cal. 4th at 447–50):

> [Government Code] section 945.4 requires each cause of action to be presented by a claim complying with section 910, while section 910, subdivision (c) requires the claimant to state the "date, place and other circumstances of the occurrence or transaction which gave rise to the claim asserted." If the claim is rejected and the plaintiff ultimately files a complaint against the public entity, the facts underlying each cause of action in the complaint must have been fairly reflected in a timely claim. (*Nelson v. State of California* (1982) 139 Cal. App. 3d 72, 79 [188 Cal. Rptr. 479].) "[E]ven if the claim were timely, the complaint is vulnerable to a demurrer if it alleges a factual basis for recovery which is not fairly reflected in the written claim." (*Ibid.*)

> The claim, however, need not specify each particular act or omission later proven to have caused the injury. A complaint's fuller exposition of the factual basis beyond that given in the claim is not fatal, so long as the complaint is not based on an "entirely different set of facts." (*Stevenson v. San Francisco Housing Authority* (1994) 24 Cal.App.4th 269, 278 [29 Cal. Rptr. 2d 398].) Only where there has been a "complete shift in allegations, usually involving an effort to premise civil liability on acts or omissions committed at different times or by different persons than those described in the claim" have courts generally found the complaint barred. (*Blair v. Superior Court* [(1990) 218 Cal. App. 3d 221], at p. 226 [267 Cal. Rptr. 13].) Where the complaint merely elaborates or adds further detail to a claim, but is predicated on the same fundamental actions or failures to act by the defendants, courts have generally found the claim fairly reflects the facts pled in the complaint.

> Stockett's claim complied with sections 910 and 945.4. He stated the date and place of his termination, named those JPIA officers and agents he believed responsible, and generally stated the "circumstances" (§910, subd. (c)) of his termination. In addition, he stated the termination had been wrongful because it was effected in violation of California public policy. He thus notified JPIA of his wrongful termination cause of action, in compliance with section 954.4's command that each "cause of action" be presented by notice of claim. While Stockett's claim did not specifically assert his termination violated the public policies favoring free speech and opposition to public employee conflicts of interest, these theories do not represent additional causes of action and hence need not be separately presented under section 945.4.

> Unlike *Fall River v. Superior Court* (1988) 206 Cal. App. 3d 431 [253 Cal. Rptr. 587], which JPIA cites as illustrating a fatal variance between a plaintiff's claim and complaint, the additional theories pled in Stockett's amended com-

plaint did not shift liability to other parties or premise liability on acts committed at different times or places. In *Fall River*, the plaintiff was injured at school when a steel door struck his head. His notice of claim stated the injury was caused by the school's negligent maintenance of the door, but his complaint additionally alleged the school had negligently failed to supervise students engaged in horseplay. The court held the factual divergence between claim and complaint was too great; the complaint alleged liability "on an entirely different factual basis than what was set forth in the tort claim." (*Id.* at 435.) Stockett's complaint, in contrast, alleged liability on the same wrongful act, his termination, as was stated in his notice of claim.

Nor were the fundamental facts underlying Stockett's claim changed in his amended complaint. Rather, the free speech and conflict of interest theories simply elaborated and added detail to his wrongful termination claim by alleging additional motivations and reasons for JPIA's single action of wrongful termination. This case is thus similar to previous cases holding that the claim fairly reflected the theories of liability set forth in the complaint. * * *

In comparing claim and complaint, "we are mindful that '[s]o long as the policies of the claims statutes are effectuated, [the statutes] should be given a liberal construction to permit full adjudication on the merits.'" (*Smith v. County of Los Angeles* [(1989)] 214 Cal. App. 3d [266]at p. 280 [262 Cal. Rptr. 754]). If the claim gives adequate information for the public entity to investigate, additional detail and elaboration in the complaint is permitted.

By notifying JPIA of its act (wrongful termination) that caused his injury (loss of earnings, mental and physical pain and suffering) and naming those JPIA agents he believed responsible, Stockett's claim provided sufficient information for JPIA to investigate and evaluate its merits. * * *

In summary, Stockett adequately presented to JPIA his wrongful termination cause of action. His notice of claim satisfied the purposes of the claims statutes by providing sufficient information for the public entity to conduct an investigation into the merits of the wrongful termination claim, and the complaint's free speech and conflict of interest theories of termination in violation of public policy were fairly reflected in the claim because the complaint did not change the fundamental facts of the claim. Stockett was therefore not precluded from amending his complaint to include these theories or from presenting them to the jury.

In drafting a client's written claim, what should an attorney do to minimize the likelihood that the client may be barred from asserting new allegations of facts and legal theories in a subsequent court complaint?

[6] Cross-Complaints

Must a defendant comply with the claims requirements prior to filing a cross-complaint in an action initiated by a public entity plaintiff? Does the answer depend on the nature of the cross-complaint? *See Krainock v. Superior Court*, 216 Cal. App. 3d 1473, 265 Cal. Rptr. 715 (1990) (adopting rules for determining applicability of claims requirements to defensive cross-complaints).

[7]   Government Claims Act and Estoppel

The court in *Phillips* found it unnecessary to decide whether the defendants were also barred under principles of estoppel from claiming noncompliance by plaintiff with the claim presentation requirements. Do you think a public entity should ever be subject to this estoppel doctrine?

In *John R. v. Oakland Unified School District*, 48 Cal. 3d 438, 256 Cal. Rptr. 766, 769 P.2d 948 (1989), the Supreme Court noted that a public entity may be estopped from asserting the limitations of the claims statute where its agents or employees have prevented or deterred the filing of a timely claim by some affirmative act, such as misleading statements about the need for, or advisability of, a claim. *Id.* at 445. In *John R.*, the plaintiff was a junior high student who alleged sexual molestation by his teacher, and commenced litigation without presenting any timely written claim under the California Government Claims Act. The plaintiff argued that the defendant school district was estopped from raising the defense of failure to present a timely claim because the teacher had threatened to retaliate against the student if the boy reported the incidents of sexual molestation. These threats were likely motivated by the teacher's self-interest, not by an intent to prevent the student from filing a claim against the school district. Is this the type of conduct that should estop the defendant school district from raising the timeliness defense? *See John R., supra*, 48 Cal. 3d at 445–47; *J.P. v. Carlsbad Unified Sch. Dist.*, 232 Cal. App. 4th 323, 181 Cal. Rptr. 3d 286 (2014); *Doe v. Bakersfield City Sch. Dist.*, 136 Cal. App. 4th 556, 39 Cal. Rptr. 3d 79 (2006).

Does equitable estoppel also apply when a public entity's conduct prevents a plaintiff from filing a lawsuit within the time limits established by the Government Claims Act? *See, e.g., Ard v. County of Contra Costa*, 93 Cal. App. 4th 339, 112 Cal. Rptr. 2d 886 (2001) (ruling the principles of equitable estoppel apply when county's conduct prevented plaintiff from filing suit within time limit established by Gov. Code § 946.6); *Ortega v. Pajaro Valley Unified Sch. Dist.*, 64 Cal. App. 4th 1023, 1047, 75 Cal. Rptr. 2d 777, *mod.* 65 Cal. App. 4th 573 (1998) (holding a public entity may be equitably estopped from relying on the claim-presentation statutes where the public entity or one of its agents engaged in some calculated conduct or make some representation or concealed facts which induced the plaintiff not to file a claim or bring an action within the statutory time).

[8]   Government Claims Act Tolling Provisions

The statutory tolling provisions of the California Government Claims Act set forth in Government Code §§ 911.4, 911.6, and 946.6 are quite detailed and specific. These provisions preclude the use of the general statutory tolling provisions contained in the Code of Civil Procedure, pursuant to CCP § 352(b).

Does a CCP § 364 notice of intent to sue, served less than 90 days before the expiration of the six-month limitation period of Gov. Code § 945.6(a)(1) within which to commence a medical malpractice action against a public hospital, operate to toll and extend the limitations period for 90 days? *See Wurts v. County of Fresno*, 44 Cal. App. 4th 380, 51 Cal. Rptr. 2d 689 (1996) (holding a § 364 notice tolled the six-month statute of limitations for commencement of a lawsuit against a public entity, and therefore that an action commenced seven months after rejection of the tort claim by the County was not barred by Gov. Code § 945.6). For a recent decision attempting to harmonize the time limitations imposed by the Government Claims Act and by CCP § 340.5 in a medical malpractice action brought against a hospital operated by a public entity, see *Roberts v. County of Los Angeles*, 175 Cal. App. 4th 474, 96 Cal. Rptr. 3d 60 (2009) (ruling that although plaintiff met the tolled six-month statute of limitations for a claim against a public entity under Gov. Code § 945.6, the action was barred by the three-year period in CCP § 340.5).

Do the various "equitable tolling" doctrines apply to the time limitations of the California Government Claims Act, Gov. Code § 900 *et seq.*? *See Addison v. State of California*, 21 Cal. 3d 313, 146 Cal. Rptr. 224, 578 P.2d 941 (1978).

Do the claim presentation requirements of the California Government Claims Act apply when the plaintiff brings a 42 U.S.C. § 1983 federal civil rights action against a public entity or employee in state court? *See Felder v. Casey*, 487 U.S. 131, 108 S. Ct. 2302, 101 L. Ed. 2d 123 (1988). Where the plaintiff brings a state civil rights action against a public entity after exhausting the procedural requirements of the Fair Employment and Housing Act, Gov. Code § 12900 *et seq.*? *See Garcia v. Los Angeles Unified Sch. Dist.*, 173 Cal. App. 3d 701, 710, 219 Cal. Rptr. 544 (1985).

[E] Notices, Claims and Other Prerequisites

A wide variety of California statutes require the prospective plaintiff to give notice prior to filing a lawsuit, to make a preliminary claim or demand, or to take some similar procedural step prior to commencement of the litigation. *See generally* Ann Taylor Schwing, 15 *California Affirmative, Defenses, Lack of Required Certificate, Notice, Claim or Demand*, §§ 12:1–12:44 (2015). Failure to comply with these requirements may have little or no effect on the litigation, or may provide a complete defense: The severity of the penalty for noncompliance depends in part on the purpose underlying the statutory requirement. *Id.* Two of these condition precedents—notice of intention to file a medical malpractice action pursuant to CCP § 364, and the claim filing requirements for suits against government agencies and officials pursuant to Government Code § 900 *et seq.*—have already been extensively discussed above. A few additional examples warrant brief consideration.

[1] Notice to Prospective Defendant

A number of statutes simply require that a notice be given to the prospective defendant prior to or at the time of the commencement of the action. For example,

Civil Code § 3082 *et seq.* requires that certain notices be filed and served prior to enforcement of a mechanics lien. *See generally* CEB, *California Mechanics' Liens and Related Construction Remedies* (4th ed. 2015); *California Mechanics' Lien Law and Construction Industry Practice* (6th ed. 2015). Why are such preliminary notices required? Civil Code §§ 1691 and 1693 require notice of rescission be given to the party against whom relief will be sought, as a condition precedent to an action seeking to rescind a contract, "promptly upon discovering the facts which entitle him to rescind." What purpose does this notice serve? Business and Professions Code § 6201 requires written notice of the right to arbitrate a fee dispute prior to an attorney suing his client to recover unpaid attorneys' fees. The California Commercial Code requires certain notices prior to sale of personal property collateral as a prerequisite to subsequent suit for deficiency judgment, Commercial Code §§ 9610–9615; and requires that a buyer who has accepted a tender of goods must notify the seller of a breach within a reasonable time after discovery, or be barred from any remedy, § 2607. What are the purposes of these notice requirements? A variety of statutes require notice to the California Attorney General as a prerequisite to suit. *E.g.,* CCP § 388 (certain environmental pollution actions); Probate Code §§ 8111, 1209, 11701(d) & 17203 (certain probate actions involving charitable trusts).

If you are a landlord or a tenant, you may have already had experience with another notice prerequisite! *See* CCP § 1161.

Some statutes do not require notice, but instead authorize parties to a contract to require notice of injury, loss, or claim as a condition precedent to recovery. The most common examples are insurance policies. Pursuant to the Insurance Code, certain policies may include a requirement for prompt notice and proof of loss following an accident or occurrence covered by the policy. *E.g.,* Insurance Code § 6010 (fire insurance), § 10350.5 (disability coverage). There are some statutory limits here, such as notice cannot be required more promptly than 20 days after the covered incident. Ins. Code §§ 551–554. Why are such notices authorized by statute?

[2] Demand Requirements

Some statutes require not only prior notice, but also a demand for corrective action as a prerequisite to judicial relief. Most notable is Civil Code § 48a, which requires in actions for libel against newspapers and for slander by radio broadcast that a correction be demanded within 20 days after knowledge of the publication or broadcast of the statements claimed to be libelous. Failure to comply with Civil Code § 48a does not defeat the entire libel action, but limits the plaintiff's possible recovery to special damages and precludes general damages. *See Freedom Newspapers, Inc. v. Superior Court,* 4 Cal. 4th 652, 14 Cal. Rptr. 2d 839, 842 P.2d 138 (1992). Civil Code § 48.5 extends this demand requirement to television broadcasts. *See Kalpoe v. Superior Court,* 222 Cal. App. 4th 206, 166 Cal. Rptr. 3d 80 (2013) (ruling § 48a and § 48.5 apply to all types of television shows, and are not restricted to broadcasting engaged in the business of rapid and immediate dissemination of the news). Why is such notice a prerequisite to recovery of general damages but not of special damages? Why is it limited to specific categories of defendants, and not to all cases of libel and slander generally?

Some other statutes imposing a demand prerequisite to litigation include the following: Civil Code § 1782(a) (requiring a consumer to notify prospective defendant in writing and demand corrective action at least 30 days prior to bringing a class action for damages under the Consumers Legal Remedies Act, Civil Code § 1750 *et seq.*); Corporations Code § 800(b)(2) (notice and demand for remedial action on board of directors of corporation prior to commencing stockholders' derivative suit); and Civil Code § 1823 (demand for return of property from bailee).

[3] *Certificate of Merit*

Code of Civil Procedure § 411.35 requires a plaintiff's attorney to execute and file a certificate of merit before service of a complaint for damages arising out of professional negligence by an architect, engineer, or surveyor. The certificate must declare that the attorney has reviewed the facts; has consulted with an architect, engineer, or surveyor; and has concluded that there is meritorious cause for filing such action. CCP § 411.35(b). Failure to file the certificate is grounds for demurrer or motion to strike, and for an award of expenses and attorney fees. CCP § 411.35(g) and (h); *see Guinn v. Dotson*, 23 Cal. App. 4th 262, 28 Cal. Rptr. 2d 409 (1994) (dismissing negligence action against engineer for failure to file certificate of merit; defendant entitled to an award of expenses and attorney fees). Where the attorney is unable to conduct the required consultation because of a statute of limitations concern and so declares, the certificate need not be filed until within 60 days after filing the complaint. § 411.35(b)(2).

Similar rules apply to certain actions seeking damages suffered as a result of alleged childhood sexual abuse, when brought by a plaintiff 26 years of age or older. Generally, CCP § 340.1 requires such a plaintiff to file a certificates of merit, executed by the attorney for the plaintiff and by a licensed mental health practitioner, before the statute of limitations has expired. CCP § 340.1 (g) & (l); *see, e.g., Jackson v. Doe*, 192 Cal. App. 4th 742, 121 Cal. Rptr. 3d 685 (2011) (construing CCP § 340.1 (g) & (l) and affirming demurrer without leave to amend because plaintiff in childhood sexual abuse action did not file certificate of merit before the statute of limitations and 60-day grace period expired).

[4] *Notice and Claim Prerequisite*

Some statutes require not only that notice be given to the prospective defendant as a condition precedent to litigation, but also that a claim be submitted for consideration by the defendant. The claim-filing requirements for actions against public agencies and employees set forth in the California Government Claims Act, Government Code § 900 *et seq.*, discussed *supra*, are a most important example.

Other very important notice and claim requirements concern prospective plaintiffs against the estate of a decedent. Sections 9000–9399 of the Probate Code, for example, require that a claim be filed with the probate court before certain actions can be commenced or continued against a decedent's personal representative on a cause of action against the decedent. This includes demands for payment based on liability of the decedent arising in contract, tort or otherwise; for payment of taxes; and for payment of funeral expenses. Prob. Code § 9000. The time for filing such claims is governed by §§ 9100–9104. Regardless of what statute of limitations may otherwise apply, generally a creditor must commence an action within three months of the notice of rejection of the claim. Prob. Code §§ 9250, 9352, and 9353; *See Anderson v. Anderson*, 41 Cal. App. 4th 135, 138, 48 Cal. Rptr. 2d 642 (1995); *see also Dobler v. Arluk Med. Center Indus. Group, Inc.*, 89 Cal. App. 4th 530, 535–39, 107 Cal. Rptr. 2d 478 (2001) (summarizing the statutory provisions governing claims against probate and trust estates, and the various relevant statutes of limitations).

A plaintiff must also file a claim with the Department of Fair Employment and Housing (DFEH) as a condition precedent to an action for discrimination under the Fair Employment and Housing Act, Government Code § 12900 *et seq.* A plaintiff must first file a written complaint with the DFEH within one year of the alleged discriminatory practice. § 12960. The DFEH must then be given 150 days to consider the complaint, after which time a right to sue notice can be requested by the plaintiff. § 12965(b). The plaintiff then has one year after the date of the right to sue notice within which to commence an action in the appropriate court. *See* Gov. Code § 12965(b). *See Grant v. CompUSA, Inc.*, 109 Cal. App. 4th 637, 135 Cal. Rptr. 2d 177 (2003) (discussing the various FEHA preconditions to suit).

Provisions in the Civil Code require a condominium homeowners' association to complete a dispute resolution process prior to filing an action against a builder, developer, or general contractor seeking damages for construction defects. Civil Code § 6870. This elaborate process may include such events as mutual inspections and exchanges of information, settlement offers and negotiations, meet and confer sessions, and submission of the conflict to a dispute resolution facilitator. § 6870(e)–(o). Other provisions in the Civil Code also specify the rights and requirements of a homeowner with respect to a damage action for constructive defects against a builder, developer, or original seller; including applicable standards for home construction, various statutes of limitations, the burden of proof, the damages recoverable, the obligations of the homeowner, and a detailed prelitigation procedure. Civil Code §§ 895–945.5.

Several statutory schemes require a taxpayer to file a claim for a tax refund with the appropriate taxing agency as a prerequisite to an action for a tax refund in superior court. *See, e.g.*, Revenue and Taxation Code § 5141 (claim for refund of property taxes must be filed with county or city); Rev. & Tax. Code § 6932 (claim for refund of sales or use taxes must be filed before a lawsuit may be brought). *See also Geneva Towers Ltd. v. San Francisco*, 29 Cal. 4th 769, 129 Cal. Rptr. 2d 107, 60 P.3d 692 (2003) (ruling the six-month statute of limitations in Tax Code § 5141 begins to run when the county or city rejects the claim for refund in whole or in part; or, if the public entity fails to act within six months, when the claimant elects to consider the claim rejected and bring an action for a tax refund).

[5] Security for Costs

Generally, of course, a plaintiff is not required to provide security for defendant's costs as a condition precedent to an action at law. However, a number of special statutes do authorize the imposition of such undertakings, upon application of the defendant. Code of Civil Procedure § 1030(a) and (b), for example, authorizes a defendant to move for "an order requiring the plaintiff to file an undertaking to secure an award of costs and attorney's fees which may be awarded" when the plaintiff resides out of state or is a foreign corporation and "there is a reasonable possibility that the moving defendant will obtain judgment in the action." If the court grants this motion, the plaintiff must file the undertaking in the amount and within the time specified by the court. CCP § 1030(c) and (d). If the plaintiff fails to file this undertaking within the time allowed, the plaintiff's action must be dismissed as to that defendant. CCP § 1030(d).

The requirement of security of costs filed by plaintiff is also authorized in a few other special statutes, *e.g.*, CCP §§ 391–391.7 (vexatious litigants), *see Moran v. Murtaugh Miller Meyer & Nelson, LLP*, 40 Cal. 4th 780, 55 Cal. Rptr. 3d 112, 152 P.3d 416 (2007) (ruling that in assessing whether a vexatious litigant has a reasonable probability of success on his claim, the trial court may weigh the evidence presented on the motion for security); CCP § 1029.6 (personal injury actions against health care professionals); CCP § 1029.5 (negligence actions against architects, engineers, and similar professionals); Corp. Code § 800 (shareholder derivative actions).

[F] Statutes of Limitations in Federal Courts

There are no general federal statutes of limitations which govern large categories of existing federal claims for relief. There are, however, over 7000 federal statutes which contain special statutes of limitations governing specific claims. See *Federal Statutes of Limitation*, 26 Sw. U. L. Rev. 425-891 (1997), for a comprehensive survey of these specific federal statutes. Moreover, 28 U.S.C. § 1658 contains a new general statute of limitations of four years for any civil action arising under a federal statute enacted after December 1, 1990, unless a specific statute provides otherwise.

There still are many federal actions where neither a specific statute of limitation nor the new § 1658 applies. These include actions based on diversity jurisdiction, and ones based on certain federal statutes enacted before the effective date of § 1658. What statute of limitations do the federal courts apply in such circumstances? When Congress has not established a time limitation, the settled practice is to adopt the state law of limitations governing an analogous cause of action, if it is not inconsistent with federal law or policy to do so. *Wilson v. Garcia*, 471 U.S. 261, 266–67, 105 S. Ct. 1938, 85 L. Ed. 2d 254 (1985) (ruling a federal court must apply state statute of limitations for personal injury actions to 42 U.S.C. § 1983 claims); *Board of Regents v. Tomanio*, 446 U.S. 478, 483–84, 100 S. Ct. 1790, 64 L. Ed. 2d 440 (1980).

The federal courts not only must apply the appropriate state limitation period in such cases, but also the relevant state tolling statutes. *See Abramson v. Brownstein,*

897 F.2d 389 (9th Cir. 1990). Must a federal court applying a California statute of limitations also apply the California doctrine of "equitable tolling"? *See, e.g., Cervantes v. City of San Diego*, 5 F.3d 1273 (9th Cir. 1993); *Donoghue v. City of Orange*, 848 F.2d 926 (9th Cir. 1988). Why must a federal court apply state limitations law in the absence of a federal statute of limitations?

Conversely, there are situations where a federal statutory limitation must be applied in state court, despite conflicting state limitations law. This may occur when a claim based on a federal statute is brought in state court, and the federal statute contains a specific limitation period. *E.g., White v. Moriarty*, 15 Cal. App. 4th 1290, 19 Cal. Rptr. 2d 200 (1993) (ruling a state court must follow limitation period in 12 U.S.C. § 1821, not CCP § 337(1), in FDIC cases); *California Aviation, Inc. v. Leeds*, 233 Cal. App. 3d 724, 284 Cal. Rptr. 687 (1991) (Two-year federal bankruptcy limitations extension statute, 11 U.S.C. § 108(a), applies instead of one-year limitation statute for attorney malpractice, CCP § 340.6(a)). Why must a state court apply a federal statute of limitations and disregard conflicting state limitations in such circumstances? *See* Art. VI, U.S. Constitution.

[G] Procedural Aspects of Statutes of Limitations

[1] *Affirmative Defense*

Generally, a statute of limitations in California is considered to be "procedural" in the sense that it affects the remedy only, not the substantive right or obligation. 3 Witkin, *California Procedure, Actions*, §§ 432–467 (5th ed. 2008). One important consequence of this principle is that generally the statute of limitations bar is an affirmative defense which must be raised by the defendant in the trial court or the defense is waived. *E.g., Beasley v. Wells Fargo Bank*, 235 Cal. App. 3d 1383, 1401, n.9, 1 Cal. Rptr. 2d 446 (1991) (noting the statute of limitations defense is not waived where defendant failed to plead affirmative defense but raised argument in its trial brief); *Taylor v. Sanford*, 203 Cal. App. 2d 330, 345, 21 Cal. Rptr. 697 (1962). And, as we have already seen, the defense can be waived in advance by contract, CCP § 360.5; or even after the statutory period has expired, by acknowledgment, CCP § 360.

A few statutory time limitations, however, are considered "substantive" in the sense that they are regarded as conditions on the substantive right involved. *See* 3 Witkin, *California Procedure, supra*, §§ 441–445. A condition on a substantive right is generally not waivable by the parties. *Id.* As a general rule, if the Legislature creates a right or liability unknown at common law and in the same statute fixes a limitation period, the time limitation is usually considered substantive. *Williams v. Pac. Mut. Life Ins. Co.*, 186 Cal. App. 3d 941, 949–50, 231 Cal. Rptr. 234 (1986). The statute must evidence a legislative intent that the limitation is an element of the plaintiff's cause of action. *See, e.g., Walton v. City of Red Bluff*, 2 Cal. App. 4th 117, 3 Cal. Rptr. 2d 275 (1991). One consequence here is that a plaintiff must plead facts which show compliance with such a time limitation.

Traditional examples of substantive time periods are ones involving prescriptive property rights, such as adverse possession and escheat statutes. *E.g.*, CCP §§ 321–326. Modern examples often involve newly created statutory rights which include presentation of an administration claim as a prerequisite to litigation, with accompanying time limitations. In *Williams v. Pac. Mut. Life Ins. Co., supra*, for example, the court concluded that the time limitations provision of the California Fair Employment and Housing Act, Gov. Code § 12965, is a condition on a substantive right rather than a procedural limitation period for commencement of an action. As such, the plaintiff must specifically allege facts in his complaint showing compliance with this condition. *Id.*

[2] Pleading Statutes of Limitations

As discussed above, a plaintiff must plead facts showing compliance with a time limitation that is "substantive." But what about the usual situation where statutes of limitations are considered procedural? Because a defendant must raise the issue as an affirmative defense, should a plaintiff simply not worry about allegations regarding statutes of limitations in the complaint?

Even where a statute of limitations is procedural, a plaintiff may need to plead facts in anticipation of the defense. This is particularly true where a plaintiff relies on the delayed discovery rule of accrual. Failure to plead facts justifying delayed accrual will make a demurrer appropriate. *E.g.*, *CAMSI IV v. Hunter Tech. Corp.*, 230 Cal. App. 3d 1525, 282 Cal. Rptr. 80 (1991). The plaintiff must allege the time and manner of discovery, the circumstances of discovery, and why in the exercise of reasonable diligence the plaintiff could not have made discovery sooner. In *Fox v. Ethicon Endo-Surgery, Inc.*, 35 Cal. 4th 797, 27 Cal. Rptr. 3d 661, 110 P.3d 914 (2005), the Supreme Court explained these pleading requirements as follows (35 Cal. 4th at 808):

> In order to rely on the discovery rule for delayed accrual of a cause of action, "[a] plaintiff whose complaint shows on its face that his claim would be barred without the benefit of the discovery rule must specifically plead facts to show (1) the time and manner of discovery *and* (2) the inability to have made earlier discovery despite reasonable diligence." [Citation] In assessing the sufficiency of the allegations of delayed discovery, the court places the burden on the plaintiff to "show diligence"; "conclusory allegations will not withstand demurrer." [Citation]

In addition to cases involving the delayed discovery rule, can you think of other situations where the plaintiff may want to plead facts in anticipation of the defense?

Because the statute of limitations is usually an affirmative defense, it must be properly invoked by the defendant by appropriate pleading or else it may be waived. *E.g.*, *Stokes v. Henson*, 217 Cal. App. 3d 187, 193, 265 Cal. Rptr. 836 (1990). Even though a defendant raises the defense, a court may consider it waived if the defendant pleads the wrong code section and no underlying facts establishing the defense. Such was the result in *Mysel v. Gross*, 70 Cal. App. 3d at Supp. 10, 138 Cal. Rptr. 873 (1977), where the court noted there are two accepted ways to plead a statute of limitations: One method is to allege facts showing the action is barred and indicate that the lateness in commencing the action is urged as a defense; the second method is to comply with CCP § 458. *Mysel, supra*, 70 Cal. App. 3d at Supp. 14. Code of Civil Procedure section 458 states:

> In pleading the Statute of Limitations it is not necessary to state the facts showing the defense, but it may be stated generally that the cause of action is barred by the provisions of Section _____ (giving the number of the section and subdivision thereof, if it is so divided, relied upon) of the Code of Civil Procedure; and if such allegation be controverted the party pleading must establish on the trial, the facts showing that the cause of action is so barred.

[3]   *Procedural Devices for Invoking Statute of Limitations*

Resolution of a statute of limitations issue is normally a question of fact. *E.g., Jolly v. Eli Lilly & Co., supra*. What procedural devices are appropriate for raising this issue? Under what circumstances may the issue be raised by demurrer? *See* CCP § 430.30; *Roman v. County of Los Angeles*, 85 Cal. App. 4th 316, 102 Cal. Rptr. 2d 13 (2000) (A general demurrer based on statute of limitations is only permissible where dates alleged in the complaint clearly and affirmatively show that the action is barred). By motion for summary judgment? *See, e.g., Jolly v. Eli Lilly & Co., supra*. Are there any other procedural devices by which this question of fact can be resolved? *See, e.g.,* CCP § 597 and § 581c. *See also Jefferson v. County of Kern*, 98 Cal. App. 4th 606, 120 Cal. Rptr. 2d 1 (2002) (ruling the date of accrual of a cause of action is subject to a jury determination when the issue is raised in connection with a tort claim, and that right to jury trial applies when there is a bifurcated trial pursuant to CCP § 597 to separately determine a statute of limitations defense).

§ 4.06   Exhaustion of Administrative Remedies

[A]   The Exhaustion Requirement

Department of Personnel Administration v. Superior Court

Court of Appeal of California, Third Appellate District
5 Cal. App. 4th 155, 6 Cal. Rptr. 2d 714 (1992)

PUGLIA, PRESIDING JUSTICE

The State of California faced an unprecedented budgetary crisis at the outset of fiscal year 1991–1992, with expenditures projected to exceed revenues by more than $14 billion. Although the Legislature and the Governor addressed the budget shortfall in a number of ways in the Budget Act of 1991 (the Act; Stats. 1991, ch. 118), the Act does not direct a pay cut for state employees. Rather, it requires a $351 million reduction of employee compensation, and orders the Director of Finance to allocate the necessary reductions to each item of appropriation in the Act, with three exceptions. The Governor also reduced the funds provided by the Legislature for employee compensation and benefit increases. The governor gave his reasons for the reductions and approved the Act on July 16, 1991.

In this setting, negotiations continued for new collective bargaining agreements between petitioner Department of Personnel Administration (DPA) and various unions representing state employees. For purposes of this proceeding, the parties do not dispute that by autumn 1991, DPA and many of the unions had reached impasse, after negotiating and participating in mediation in good faith.

On November 5, 1991, DPA sent letters to two of the employee unions which are real parties in interest herein, California Association of Professional Scientists (CAPS) and California Association of Highway Patrolmen (CAHP), informing them of actions DPA intended to take, effective November 12, 1991, as a result of the negotiations impasse. The letter to CAPS indicated DPA would implement terms and conditions of employment as follows:

* * *

"Salaries. Effective November 12, 1991, salaries will be reduced five (5) percent as described in the State's offer of June 24, 1991. A pay letter will be issued to effectuate this change.

"Health Benefits. Effective December 1, 1991, the State employer's contribution rates will be: $157.-employee; $292.-employee plus one dependent; and, $367.-employee plus two or more dependents. These rates, as well as the rural subsidy rates, are as described in the State's last offer of August 12, 1991. [Note: Any increase in employee costs will be deducted from the November pay warrant.]"

The letter to CAHP was substantially the same.

CAPS and CAHP responded to DPA's notification of its intent to impose its final offer by filing a petition for writ of mandate and request for a stay in respondent superior court on November 8, 1991. That day, respondent court issued an alternative writ and a stay, ordering petitioners not to reduce the salaries or health care contributions for state employee members of CAPS and CAHP until respondent issued a final decision on the petition.

In addition to the two unions, the petition in the superior court named as petitioners ... a number of other unions representing state employees joined in the proceeding as real parties in interest and interveners. In addition, the Public Employment Relations Board (PERB) filed a "Statement of Jurisdiction," in the superior court proceeding asserting PERB lacks exclusive initial jurisdiction over this dispute.

After a hearing, respondent superior court indicated it would issue a writ of mandate. The court explained that Government Code section 19826, subdivision (b) expressly precludes DPA from unilaterally reducing employee wages.[6] Moreover, the court concluded ... the formula for state contributions to employee health care pre-

---

6. Further statutory references to sections of an undesignated code are to the Government Code.

miums in section 22825.1, applies so as to preclude DPA from decreasing employee health care premium contribution rates. * * *

On November 27, 1991, respondent superior court entered judgment granting a peremptory writ of mandate. The writ issued that day, commanding DPA, its director and the Controller " ... to desist and refrain from reducing the wages of State employees in recognized bargaining units, and desist and refrain from modifying the health care premium payment formula for said employees."

DPA filed the instant petition for extraordinary relief on December 13, 1991. * * * On January 14, 1992, we directed the parties to address in their briefing the question, assuming PERB had exclusive initial jurisdiction, whether any exception to the doctrine of exhaustion of administrative remedies applies so as to excuse the failure to file unfair practice charges with PERB. * * *

At the threshold is the question whether respondent superior court improperly assumed jurisdiction over a matter which is committed to PERB's exclusive initial jurisdiction. DPA contends PERB has exclusive jurisdiction because DPA's action in implementing its last, best offer arguably is either protected or prohibited as an unlawful practice under the statutes regulating state employer-employee labor relations. DPA points out that resolution of the underlying questions regarding DPA's authority after impasse to impose its last, best offer on wages and health contribution rates necessarily requires consideration and construction of the applicable labor relations statute, and contends such analysis should first be undertaken by PERB. * * *

We shall assume without deciding that DPA is correct on the jurisdictional question. Nevertheless, we shall conclude the state employee unions' failure to exhaust their administrative remedy by first filing charges of unfair practices with PERB is excused in this case because of the potential for irreparable injury and because filing with PERB would have been futile under the circumstances. * * *

In *Abelleira v. District Court of Appeal* (1941) 17 Cal. 2d 280, 293 [109 P.2d 942, 132 A.L.R. 715], the court described the purpose of the exhaustion doctrine: "The courts have repeatedly recognized the necessity of placing the numerous and complex problems arising under statutes of the type involved herein in the hands of expert bodies, familiar with the subject matter through long experience. They have pointed out that to permit the initial consideration of these matters by the courts would not only preclude the efficient operation of the acts, but would overwhelm the courts with cases of a technical, specialized character, and seriously impair their capacity to handle their normal work." (17 Cal. 2d at p. 306.)

Later cases have described additional policies served by the exhaustion doctrine. Thus, the exhaustion doctrine facilitates the development of a complete record prior to resort to the courts (*Yamaha Motor Corp. v. Superior Court* (1986) 185 Cal. App. 3d 1232, 1240–1241 [230 Cal. Rptr. 382]) and, because administrative procedure is part of the legislative process, the doctrine fulfills separation of powers concerns by requiring completion of the administrative procedure prior to court action (*County of Contra Costa v. State of California* (1986) 177 Cal. App. 3d 62, 76–77 [222 Cal. Rptr. 750]).

However, none of these policies would be served by adherence to the exhaustion doctrine in this case. When the underlying mandate proceeding was filed in the superior court, PERB took the somewhat unusual step of filing a statement disavowing jurisdiction over the dispute. Under these circumstances, the separation of powers concern articulated in *County of Contra Costa, supra,* is not implicated because the administrative body has in fact invited judicial intervention. Moreover, the facts are undisputed, so there is no need for administrative development of the record. Nor does judicial intervention interfere with the expertise of the agency or create problems of judicial economy, given that the underlying issues are within the expertise of the courts and would undoubtedly be resolved ultimately by the courts even if initial jurisdiction were found in PERB. Finally, given that this case raises questions of first impression which are bound for ultimate determination by the appellate courts, there is little concern of conflicting decisions between PERB and the courts.

Given the lack of policy support for the application of the exhaustion doctrine in this case, it behooves us to examine the exceptions to that doctrine. "*Abelleira* makes it abundantly clear that the exhaustion doctrine does *not* implicate subject matter jurisdiction but rather is a 'procedural prerequisite' 'originally devised for convenience and efficiency' and now 'followed under the doctrine of *stare decisis,* …' ([17 Cal. 2d] at pp. 288, 291.) It is 'jurisdictional' only in the sense that a court's failure to apply the rule in a situation where the issue has been properly raised can be corrected by the issuance of a writ of prohibition. [¶] Such a conclusion only makes sense when the underlying nature of the exhaustion doctrine is considered. While *Abelleira* indicates that the rule of exhaustion of administrative remedies has become 'a fundamental rule of procedure' (17 Cal. 3d [*sic*] at p. 293), courts have repeatedly recognized it is not inflexible dogma. [Citations.] There are numerous exceptions to the rule including situations where the agency indulges in unreasonable delay [citation], when the subject matter lies outside the administrative agency's jurisdiction, when pursuit of an administrative remedy would result in irreparable harm, when the agency is incapable of granting an adequate remedy, and when resort to the administrative process would be futile because it is clear what the agency's decision would be. [Citations.]" (*Green v. City of Oceanside* (1987) 194 Cal. App. 3d 212, 222 [239 Cal. Rptr. 470], original italics.)

Respondent superior court excused exhaustion of the administrative remedy in this case because the ultimate legal issues, touching upon the separation of powers between the legislative and executive branches, are better suited for determination by the courts. However, constitutional challenges are frequently raised to the application of an administrative statutory scheme, yet the courts typically require such issues be presented to the administrative agency in the first instance. (*See, e.g., Lund v. California State Employees Assn.* (1990) 222 Cal. App. 3d 174, 183 [271 Cal. Rptr. 425];….) Hence, exhaustion cannot be excused on this basis.[7]

---

7. Courts have not required exhaustion where the petitioner raises a facial challenge to the constitutionality of the administrative agency's jurisdictional statute. (*See, e.g., Lund v. California State Employees Assn., supra,* 222 Cal. App. 3d at p. 183.) But no such challenge is raised here.

However, the unique circumstances presented here suggest exhaustion should be excused under the irreparable injury and futility exceptions. The irreparable injury exception was first recognized in *Abelleira*, where the court acknowledged the exception has been applied in cases " ... dealing with rate orders of regulatory commissions, where the administrative body imposes a confiscatory rate on a public utility. Continued operation of the business at the rate imposed pending an appeal may in some instances be so unprofitable as to amount to a destruction of the business, and therefore a taking of property without due process of law." (*Abelleira v. District Court of Appeal, supra*, 17 Cal. 2d at p. 296.) The irreparable injury exception has been rarely applied. (*See, e.g., Sail'er Inn, Inc. v. Kirby* (1971) 5 Cal. 3d 1, 6–7 [95 Cal. Rptr. 329, 485 P.2d 529, 46 A.L.R.3d 351] [bar owners sought writ of mandate to prevent Alcoholic Beverages Commission from revoking their licenses because they hired women bartenders, contrary to Bus. & Prof. Code, § 25656; owners "placed in the untenable situation of having to choose whether to obey possibly conflicting federal and state laws and face a penalty under the one they choose to disobey"]; *Greenblatt v. Munro* (1958) 161 Cal. App. 2d 596, 605–607 [326 P.2d 929] [court reached question whether bar owner's conduct violated Penal Code provision so that the Department of Alcoholic Beverage Control would have benefit of that decision in reconsidering extent of penalty to impose on bar owner].)

Here, the state and its employees may suffer irreparable injury if deprived of a judicial ruling on the underlying issues prior to the expiration of the 1991–1992 fiscal year. Indeed, DPA's verified petition filed in this original proceeding acknowledges the immediate need for judicial intervention by arguing that unless the respondent court's decision is immediately reversed," ... there will be an irrevocable impact on the State's ability to balance the 1991/1992 budget which will force a reduction in the number of State employees and the layoff of an even greater number of State employees, with a corresponding greater reduction in the delivery of essential State services than would occur if Petitioners were permitted to implement the adjustments to the salary and health care premium contribution consistent with their last, best, and final offer." * * *

We take seriously the urgent need for definitive judicial review of this matter prior to the end of the 1991–1992 fiscal year. Because of the unprecedented nature of the fiscal crisis faced by the state, the urgent need for resolution of these issues prior to the end of the year, and the great potential for irreparable harm in the nature of increased layoffs of state employees, we believe the failure of the unions to exhaust their administrative remedy by filing an unfair practice charge with PERB should be excused. We recognize that had the unions filed unfair practice charges with PERB, there was at least the possibility that PERB could have ordered the same relief as that provided by respondent superior court (*see* § 3513, subd. (h), 3541.3, subd. (j)). However, it is extremely unlikely the entire process of PERB adjudication followed by judicial review (*see* § 3520) would have been completed prior to the end of this fiscal year.

Exhaustion should be excused for another, interrelated reason. Exhaustion is excused for futility " ... when the aggrieved party can positively state what the administrative agency's decision in his particular case would be." (*Ogo Associates v. City of Torrance* (1974) 37 Cal. App. 3d 830, 834 [112 Cal. Rptr. 761].) Our record does not reveal whether the unions knew PERB was declining to take jurisdiction over this matter at the time they filed their petition for extraordinary relief in the respondent superior court. However, we note PERB filed its "Statement of Jurisdiction" one week after that petition was filed. Thus, virtually at the outset of this dispute, the parties were informed what PERB's decision would be as to the underlying jurisdictional question. Assuming exhaustion of PERB's remedy was required, PERB's action in declining jurisdiction would have required the unions to seek extraordinary relief to compel PERB to consider their unfair practice charges. This process would undoubtedly have so extended the time to obtain a final judicial determination of the merits of this dispute as to render it impossible of resolution during the 1991–1992 fiscal year.[8]

For all of the reasons stated, we conclude that, assuming PERB had exclusive initial jurisdiction, the unions' failure to exhaust their administrative remedy by pursuing unfair labor practice charges with PERB is excused.

We turn now to the principal substantive issue, whether DPA may impose its last, best offer on wages after bargaining to impasse with the exclusive representatives of state employees in recognized bargaining units. The respondent court concluded section 19826, subdivision (b), in declaring DPA "shall not establish, adjust, or recommend a salary range," unambiguously precludes DPA from implementing its final wage proposal at impasse. We agree. * * *

DPA's role as salary-setter cannot be divorced from its role as the employer's negotiator. As to represented employees, the roles are one and the same. Thus, when DPA bargains to impasse without reaching agreement on salaries, the Dills Act provides that section 19826 applies. Given that subdivision (b) of section 19826 expressly precludes DPA from adjusting salaries, the sole conclusion that can be drawn is that the Legislature intended postimpasse wage disputes to be resolved through the legislative process.

Left to be decided is whether DPA had authority at impasse to impose its last, best offer regarding the rates of employer contributions to health care premiums. * * *

---

8. We express no opinion as to the propriety of PERB's filing the "Statement of Jurisdiction" in the superior court. Although DPA contends the respondent superior court erred by considering that statement in reaching its decision, DPA never objected to the statement below, and therefore waived any objection.

Nor do we intend to suggest a rule that would permit an administrative agency to control the question of its jurisdiction by filing a "Statement of Jurisdiction" in judicial proceedings. However, because PERB did so in this case, it is obvious the process of seeking a writ to compel PERB to assume jurisdiction would have greatly increased the time required to resolve this dispute, thus aggravating the potential irreparable injury. The need to resolve the legal questions in this case by an urgent deadline distinguishes *Morton v. Hollywood Park, Inc.* (1977) 73 Cal. App. 3d 248 at page 254 [139 Cal. Rptr. 584], where the court recognized the usual rule that exhaustion of administrative remedies, when necessary, includes petitioning for extraordinary relief to compel the administrative agency to take jurisdiction.

Because we conclude respondent superior court erred in its ruling with respect to the authority of DPA to impose its last, best offer as to the employer's contribution to health premium cost increases, we shall issue a peremptory writ.

Notes and Questions Regarding Exhaustion of Administrative Remedies

(1) Exhaustion of administrative remedies is a prerequisite to suit whether the administrative remedy is set forth by statute, regulation, ordinance, or rule of the agency involved. *E.g.*, *Lopez v. Civil Service Commission*, 232 Cal. App. 3d 307, 314, 283 Cal. Rptr. 447 (1991) (noting exhaustion of administrative remedies required whenever authorized by statute or by rule of the administrative agency involved); *Green v. City of Oceanside*, 194 Cal. App. 3d 212, 219–20, 239 Cal. Rptr. 470 (1987) (ruling exhaustion doctrine applies where administrative remedy is provided by statute; and applies as well when administrative procedure is provided by regulation, resolution, or ordinance).

(a) Moreover, a party who challenges the quasi-judicial determination of an entity must exhaust that entity's internal remedies whether the entity is a voluntary private or professional association, or a public agency. *Westlake Comm. Hosp. v. Superior Court*, 17 Cal. 3d 465, 131 Cal. Rptr. 90, 551 P.2d 410 (1976) (applying exhaustion doctrine to an excluded physician's failure to pursue internal remedies of private hospital before filing civil suit for damages); *see Rojo v. Kliger*, 52 Cal. 3d 65, 86, 276 Cal. Rptr. 130, 801 P.2d 373 (1990) (collecting examples of such associations, including cases involving a labor union, fraternal organizations, a university, and a veterans' association); *but see Schifando v. City of Los Angeles*, 31 Cal. 4th 1074, 6 Cal. Rptr. 3d 457, 79 P.3d 569 (2003) (holding municipal employees who claim they have suffered employment related discrimination need not exhaust city charter internal remedies in addition to those required by the California Fair Employment and Housing Act prior to filing an FEHA claim in superior court).

(b) As a general principle, the requirement of exhaustion of administrative remedies applies to defenses as well as to claims. *See Styne v. Stevens*, 26 Cal. 4th 42, 109 Cal. Rptr. 2d 14, 26 P.3d 343 (2001) (ruling that when the defendant in a court suit raises a colorable defense based on a statute which gives an administrative agency exclusive original jurisdiction over controversies arising under the statute, the merits of that defense can not be considered by the court until it has first been submitted to, and examined by, the administrative agency).

(c) For exhaustion to apply, however, there must be an administrative tribunal adjudication available which can reasonably be determined to be a condition precedent to judicial relief. *E.g.*, *Mammoth Lakes Land Acquisition, LLC v. Town of Mammoth Lakes*, 191 Cal. App. 4th 435, 120 Cal. Rptr. 3d 797 (2010) (ruling exhaustion requirement inapplicable where there is no effective administrative remedy); *City of Coachella v. Riverside County Airport Land Use Commn.*, 210 Cal. App. 3d 1277, 1287, 258 Cal. Rptr. 795 (1989) (noting that an administrative remedy is provided only in those instances where the administrative body is required to actually accept, evaluate and resolve disputes or complaints); *see Common Cause v. Bd. of Supervisors*, 49 Cal. 3d 432, 441, 261 Cal. Rptr. 574, 777 P.2d 610 (1989) (ruling a statute or regulation must clearly define machinery for the submission, evaluation, and resolution of complaints by aggrieved parties for doctrine of exhaustion to apply; mere existence of some official supervisory body not sufficient by itself to afford an administrative remedy).

(d) The overlapping authority of administrative agencies may mean that the tribunals of two separate agencies have concurrent jurisdiction to award the relief sought by a claimant. Does the doctrine of exhaustion of administrative remedies require a plaintiff to exhaust both administrative processes before commencing a lawsuit in court? *See Ruiz v. Dept. of Corrections*, 77 Cal. App. 4th 891, 92 Cal. Rptr. 2d 139 (2000) (holding a state employee may pursue her claim of employment discrimination with either the State Personnel Board or the Department of Fair Employment and Housing (FEHA), or both; but need only exhaust one of these administrative processes before initiating an action in court). *See also Murray v. Oceanside Unified Sch. Dist.*, 79 Cal. App. 4th 1338, 95 Cal. Rptr. 2d 28 (2000) (discussing the exhaustion doctrine with respect to an employment discrimination action against a public employer that was subject to administrative claims structure of both the FEHA and the Government Claims Act).

(2) Is exhaustion required where the appropriate administrative tribunal lacks jurisdiction to award all the relief sought by the plaintiff? The Supreme Court confronted this issue in *Westlake Community Hosp. v. Superior Court*, 17 Cal. 3d 465, 131 Cal. Rptr. 90, 551 P.2d 410 (1976), where the plaintiff physician commenced a civil tort suit for damages caused by the allegedly wrongful revocation of her staff privileges at the defendant hospital. The plaintiff argued that exhaustion of the hospital's internal remedies was not a prerequisite to her suit because the relief she sought in court, compensatory and exemplary damages based on various tort claims, was not available through the defendant's internal reinstatement procedures. The defendant's internal procedures could provide reinstatement of privileges but could not provide a damage remedy, and plaintiff did not seek reinstatement. Nevertheless, the Supreme Court ruled that the plaintiff was not excused from exhausting the defendant's administrative remedies, even though the absence of an internal damage remedy makes ultimate resort to the courts inevitable. *Id.* at 476–77. The Supreme Court reached the same conclusion more recently in *Campbell v. Regents of Univ. of California*, 35 Cal. 4th 311, 323, 25 Cal. Rptr. 3d 320, 106 P.3d 976 (2005) (concluding a party must exhaust administrative remedies even though the agency may not have jurisdiction to award all the relief, such as money damages, sought by the plaintiff).

What policy considerations underlying the exhaustion doctrine justify the requirement of an administrative proceeding prior to resort to the courts in such cases?

(3) Is exhaustion required when the defendant's actions give rise to a cause of action based both on statutory grounds, for which agency exhaustion is required by the statute, and on nonstatutory grounds not specifically within the agency's jurisdiction? In *Rojo v. Kliger, supra*, for example, the plaintiff asserted statutory violations of the Fair Employment and Housing Act (FEHA) and common law tort claims of wrongful discharge and emotional distress, as a result of defendant's alleged employ-

ment discrimination. Instead of submitting these claims to the administrative body established under the FEHA, the plaintiff filed a civil suit in court. The Supreme Court held exhaustion of administrative remedies under the FEHA necessary before plaintiff may proceed with her statutory FEHA claims, but held such prior resort unnecessary before plaintiff may proceed with her civil suit based on the common law claims for damages. *Id.* at 88.

The defendant in *Rojo* argued that the policy considerations underlying the exhaustion doctrine justified extending the requirement to plaintiff's related common law claims not specifically within the agency's jurisdiction, relying on *Westlake Community Hosp. v. Superior Court, supra.* The Supreme Court distinguished *Westlake* as a case dealing with exhaustion of private internal remedies, not external administrative remedies in a public context. The Court then concluded that, unlike other cases which extended *Westlake* to external public agencies, the instant case did not involve "such a paramount need for specialized agency fact-finding expertise as to require exhaustion of administrative remedies before permitting an aggrieved person to pursue … her related nonstatutory claims and remedies in court." *Id.* at 88.

What is the significance of the *Rojo* court's distinction between "private internal" and "public external" administrative remedies? Does this distinction adequately distinguish *Westlake*? Was *Edgren v. Regents of University of California, supra,* correctly decided, in light of *Rojo*? Why? After *Rojo*, what tribunal options does an employee have when pursuing employment discrimination claims?

(4) In 1943, the California Supreme Court adopted the rule that when the Legislature has provided that a petitioner before an administrative tribunal "may" seek reconsideration or rehearing of an adverse decision of that tribunal, the petitioner always must seek reconsideration in order to exhaust his or her administrative remedies prior to seeking recourse in the courts. *Alexander v. State Personnel Bd.*, 22 Cal. 2d 198, 137 P.2d 433 (1943). Subsequently, in *Sierra Club v. San Joaquin Local Agency Formation Comm.*, 21 Cal. 4th 489, 87 Cal. Rptr. 2d 702, 981 P.2d 543 (1999), the Supreme Court overruled *Alexander* and abandoned its rule, and held that the right to petition for judicial review of a final decision of an administrative agency is not necessarily affected by the party's failure to file a request for a reconsideration or rehearing before that agency. The court observed that a request for reconsideration of an agency action may be necessary, however, where appropriate to raise matters not previously brought to the agency's attention.

(5) Exhaustion of administrative remedies is not required where the administrative procedure itself is challenged for failure to comply with minimum procedural safeguards imposed by statute or by the due process clause. *See Unnamed Physician v. Bd. of Trustees of Saint Agnes Med. Center*, 93 Cal. App. 4th 607, 619–621,113 Cal. Rptr. 2d 309 (2001).

(6) *Exceptions to the Exhaustion Requirement.* The *Department of Personnel Administration v. Superior Court* opinion, reproduced *supra*, sets forth the generally recognized exceptions to the exhaustion doctrine. Their application is limited; although, as the opinion illustrates, an exception can occasionally excuse exhaustion.

(a) What factors did the court find particularly significant in applying the exceptions in *Department of Personnel Administration*? Completion of an administrative process prior to suit often means considerable delay before a definitive ruling on important legal questions. Precisely why did this delay constitute "irreparable injury" in *Department of Personnel Administration*? In *American Indian Model Schools v. Oakland Unified Sch. Dist.*, 227 Cal. App. 4th 258, 173 Cal. Rptr. 3d 544 (2014), the court applied the irreparable harm exception and upheld the trial court's issuance of a preliminary injunction to stay revocation of the plaintiff school's charters despite the plaintiff's failure to exhaust administrative remedies, because the schools would lose their faculty and student body if the injunction were not granted. Is this the same kind of irreparable injury caused by delay identified in *Department of Personnel Administration*?

(b) Why was resort to the PERB administrative process considered "futile"? The futility exception is a narrow one. *George Arakelian Farms, Inc. v. Agric. Labor Relations Bd.*, 40 Cal. 3d 654, 662–63, 221 Cal. Rptr. 488, 710 P.2d 288 (1985). It is not sufficient that a party can show what the agency's ruling would be on a particular *issue or defense*; rather exhaustion is required unless the petitioner can positively demonstrate what the agency's ruling would be on a particular *case*. *Coachella Valley Mosquito & Vector Control Dist. v. California Public Employment Relations Bd.*, 35 Cal. 4th 1072, 1081, 29 Cal. Rptr. 3d 234, 112 P.3d 623 (2005); *Jonathan Neil & Assn., Inc., v. Jones*, 33 Cal. 4th 917, 936, 16 Cal. Rptr. 3d 849, 94 P.3d 1055 (2004)

(c) Although the PERB filed a "Statement of Jurisdiction," the agency did not indicate how it would rule on the merits of plaintiff's claims. Does this mean that whenever an agency states it lacks jurisdiction over a claim, the futility exception entitles the plaintiff to judicial review of *both* the jurisdictional question *and* the merits without any further resort to the administrative process? *See Coachella Valley Mosquito, supra,* 35 Cal. 4th at 1082 ("In deciding whether to entertain a claim that an agency lacks jurisdiction before the agency proceedings have run their course, a court considers three factors: the injury or burden that exhaustion will impose, the strength of the legal argument that the agency lacks jurisdiction, and the extent to which administrative expertise may aid in resolving the jurisdictional issue"). Is *Department of Personnel Administration* really a proper application of the futility exception, as distinguished from the irreparable injury exception?

(d) The "Statement of Jurisdiction" filed by PERB in the superior court apparently was not the result of adversarial briefing by the parties. If the defendant DPA had objected to this Statement, should the courts have considered it as part of their exhaustion analyses? Although the Court of Appeal questioned the propriety of PERB's Statement, what role did this Statement play in that court's analysis?

(e) The Court of Appeal in *Department of Personnel Administration* noted that constitutional challenges to the application of an administrative agency scheme must be initially presented to the agency for determination. What are the policy reasons for requiring exhaustion of such legal issues? Should exhaustion be excused where the plaintiff presents a legal issue and the facts are undisputed? Does any recognized exception specifically excuse exhaustion on this basis alone?

[B] Waiver

The question of whether failure to exhaust administrative remedies is jurisdictional is a matter of some debate. Most courts follow the reasoning in *Green v. City of Oceanside,* 194 Cal. App. 3d 212, 222, 239 Cal. Rptr. 470 (1987), and state that the exhaustion doctrine does not implicate fundamental subject matter jurisdiction but rather is a procedural prerequisite to suit. *E.g., Kim v. Konad USA Distribution, Inc.,* 226 Cal. App.4th 1336, 1346–48, 172 Cal. Rptr. 3d 686 (2014); *Wallis v. Farmers Group, Inc.,* 220 Cal. App. 3d 718, 735–36, 269 Cal. Rptr. 299 (1990). These courts therefore hold that the exhaustion defense is waived if not raised and preserved in the trial court. *Id.* However, the Supreme Court occasionally addresses the issue of exhaustion even though not raised by the parties. *E.g., Hittle v. Santa Barbara County Employees Retirement Assn.,* 39 Cal. 3d 374, 384, 216 Cal. Rptr. 733, 703 P.2d 73 (1985). Is there any way to reconcile these two views of waiver of the exhaustion defense? Which view is better? Why?

[C] Exhaustion and Primary Jurisdiction

Although closely related to exhaustion of administrative remedies, primary jurisdiction is a distinct doctrine. The California Supreme Court recently compared the two doctrines in *Farmers Insurance Exchange v. Superior Court,* 2 Cal. 4th 377, 390–92, 6 Cal. Rptr. 2d 487, 826 P.2d 730 (1992), by quoting with approval *United States v. Western Pac. Railroad Co.,* 352 U.S. 59, 63–64, 77 S. Ct. 161, 1 L. Ed. 2d 126 (1956), as follows:

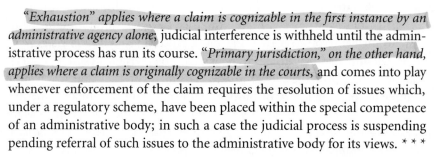

> *"Exhaustion"* applies where a claim is cognizable in the first instance by an administrative agency alone; judicial interference is withheld until the administrative process has run its course. *"Primary jurisdiction,"* on the other hand, applies where a claim is originally cognizable in the courts, and comes into play whenever enforcement of the claim requires the resolution of issues which, under a regulatory scheme, have been placed within the special competence of an administrative body; in such a case the judicial process is suspending pending referral of such issues to the administrative body for its views. * * *

The policy reasons behind the two doctrines are similar and overlapping. The exhaustion doctrine is principally grounded on concerns favoring administrative autonomy (i.e., courts should not interfere with an agency determination until the agency has reached a final decision) and judicial efficiency (i.e., overworked courts should decline to intervene in an administrative dispute unless absolutely necessary). As explained above, the primary jurisdiction doctrine advances two related policies: it enhances court decisionmaking and efficiency by allowing courts to take advantage of administrative expertise, and it helps assure uniform application of regulatory laws

No rigid formula exists for applying the primary jurisdiction doctrine. Instead, resolution generally hinges on a court's determination of the extent to which the policies noted above are implicated in a given case. This discretionary approach leaves courts with considerable flexibility to avoid application of the doctrine in appropriate situations, as required by the interests of justice.

The California Supreme Court in *Farmers Insurance* relied on several federal court cases as precedent for recognizing the primary jurisdiction doctrine. *Id.* at 388–90. Is the primary jurisdiction doctrine more appropriate for federal courts than for state courts? Why? Primary jurisdiction is analogous to what federal court abstention doctrines? *See Colorado River Water Conservation Dist. v. United States*, 424 U.S. 800, 96 S. Ct. 1236, 47 L. Ed. 2d 483 (1976); *Burford v. Sun Oil Co.*, 319 U.S. 315, 63 S. Ct. 1098, 87 L. Ed. 1424 (1943).

The plaintiff in *Farmers Insurance*, the People, filed suit against various insurers, alleging unfair business practices and seeking civil penalties and injunctive relief to enforce the Good Driver Discount policy provisions of the Insurance Code enacted pursuant to Proposition 103. The Supreme Court first determined that the People's unfair business practices claims were originally cognizable in the courts, and did not require exhaustion of administrative remedies. *Id.* at 391. The Court then proceeded to endorse and apply the primary jurisdiction doctrine, and directed the trial court to stay judicial proceedings pending administrative proceedings before the Insurance Commissioner. The Court held that the interest of judicial economy and concerns for uniformity in applying complex insurance regulations militated in favor of staying the judicial action pending completion of the administrative proceedings. *Id.* at 396–402. *See also Jonathan Neil & Assn., Inc. v. Jones*, 33 Cal. 4th 917, 16 Cal. Rptr. 3d 849, 94 P.3d 1055 (2004) (reversing judgment for defendant insured because trial court abused its discretion in not staying court proceeding and referring premium dispute issue to Insurance Commissioner under doctrine of primary jurisdiction, even though doctrine of exhaustion of administrative remedies not applicable).

The Supreme Court in *Farmers Insurance* characterized *Rojo v. Kliger, supra,* as a recent application of primary jurisdiction principles. *Farmers Insurance*, 2 Cal. 4th at 395–96. Do you understand why the Supreme Court referred to *Rojo* in this manner? The Supreme Court in *Rojo* concluded that the plaintiff there did not have to submit her common law claims for damages resulting from employment discrimination to the FEHA administrative process prior to commencing a civil suit. Why did the Supreme Court find prior resort to the administrative process unnecessary in *Rojo*, but necessary in *Farmers Insurance*? What difference in the claims and administrative processes in those two cases caused the Court to reach such different conclusions?

§ 4.07 The Doctrine of Laches

[A] Elements of Defense

[1] *In General*

Statutes of Limitations apply to all civil causes of action, whether in law or in equity. CCP § 312. In addition, the doctrine of laches applies specifically to actions seeking equitable remedies. If the defense of laches is established, the court will refuse equitable relief even though the relevant statutory period of limitations has not yet expired. *See, e.g., Conti v. Bd. of Civil Serv. Comm.,* 1 Cal. 3d 351, 82 Cal. Rptr. 337, 461 P.2d 617 (1969) (citing numerous other cases).

The basic elements of this judge-made doctrine are: "(1) The failure to assert a right, (2) for some appreciable delay, (3) which results in prejudice to the adverse party." *Marriage of Powers,* 218 Cal. App. 3d 626, 642, 267 Cal. Rptr. 350 (1990). A frequently adopted general statement of the doctrine is in *Miller v. Eisenhower Med. Center,* 27 Cal. 3d 614, 624, 166 Cal. Rptr. 826, 614 P.2d 258 (1980), quoting from *Conti v. Bd. of Civil Serv. Comm., supra,* 1 Cal. 3d at 359:

> [T]he affirmative defense of laches requires unreasonable delay in bringing suit "plus either acquiescence in the act about which plaintiff complains or prejudice to the defendant resulting from the delay...." Prejudice is never presumed; rather it must be affirmatively demonstrated by the defendant in order to sustain his burdens of proof and the production of evidence on the issue.... Generally speaking, the existence of laches is a question of fact to be determined by the trial court in light of all of the applicable circumstances, and in the absence of manifest injustice or a lack of substantial support in the evidence its determination will be sustained.

Why is there a judicially created doctrine of laches which may bar an equitable action even though the action is timely commenced according to the applicable statute of limitations? What are the policy reasons supporting this equitable defense? Are these policies any different than the policies behind statutes of limitations? What are the criticisms of this doctrine, both from a policy and an interpretive viewpoint? *See generally* Gail L. Heriot, *A Study in the Choice of Form: Statutes of Limitation and the Doctrine of Laches,* 1992 B.Y.U. L. Rev. 917 (1992). The specific requirements of the California laches doctrine are discussed below.

[2] Unreasonable Delay

The first prerequisite of the defense of laches is delay in bringing an action. But not just any delay will suffice—the delay must be considered "unreasonable." What factors do the courts consider in determining whether delay by a plaintiff is "unreasonable"? Unlike statutory time limitations, there are no hard-and-fast rules here: "The unreasonableness of delay cannot be considered in a vacuum, but must be measured against the applicable statute of limitations and the practicalities included in deciding whether to proceed with a lawsuit." *Hahn v. Bd. of Ed.,* 205 Cal. App. 3d 744, 753, 252 Cal. Rptr. 471 (1988) (concluding five-month delay in filing writ of mandate by teacher contesting reassignment not unreasonable in light of applicable three-year statute of limitations and given the concerns plaintiff must weigh before undertaking legal action, such as the potential effect of litigation on one's future career, the chances of success, the availability of alternative employment and the expenses involved).

A primary factor is the length of the plaintiff's delay in comparison to the applicable statute of limitations. *Marriage of Modnick,* 33 Cal. 3d 897, 909, 191 Cal. Rptr. 629,

663 P.2d 187 (1983) (finding two-year delay in filing motion to vacate divorce decree after discovery of fraud not unreasonable; well within three-year statute of limitations for such actions contained in CCP § 338. In determining the reasonableness of plaintiff's delay for purposes of laches, this court is "guided by the applicable statute of limitations for an action at law"). This factor is not dispositive. In many cases a delay is deemed unreasonable even though considerable time remains to commence the action under the relevant statute of limitations. *See, e.g., Conti v. Bd. of Civil Serv. Comm., supra,* 1 Cal. 3d at 357, n.3, and cases cited therein.

Another consideration in determining "unreasonableness" is whether there is some difficulty or excuse which justifies the plaintiff's delay in bringing the action. A variety of factors may be relevant here, such as plaintiff's financial inability to file suit earlier, *e.g., Forker v. Bd. of Trustees,* 160 Cal. App. 3d 13, 20, 206 Cal. Rptr. 303 (1984); *Chang v. City of Palos Verdes Estates,* 98 Cal. App. 3d 557, 562–63, 159 Cal. Rptr. 630 (1979); plaintiff's physical or mental condition, *e.g., Marriage of Modnick, supra* (ruling plaintiff not dilatory where she suffered from chronic depression and did not immediately understand significance of facts constituting fraud action); or conduct by the defendant which induces the plaintiff to delay commencement of litigation, *e.g., Williams v. Marshall,* 37 Cal. 2d 445, 456, 235 P.2d 372 (1951) ("[w]here a party protests promptly on discovering that he has been defrauded in making a contract, and enters into negotiations for a peaceful settlement, which fail, a complaint filed within a reasonable time after such failure is not barred by laches"); *Mashon v. Haddock,* 190 Cal. App. 2d 151, 174, 11 Cal. Rptr. 865 (1961) (ruling defendant by his misrepresentations about the need for an accounting was estopped from relying upon laches; "[w]here the delay in commencing action is induced by the conduct of the defendant it cannot be availed of by him as a defense."). The courts do not provide clear rules as to which of these various factors will be most significant in particular cases. What constitutes unreasonable delay necessarily varies with the circumstances of each case.

To some extent, the determination of the reasonableness of the delay is related to the element of prejudice, discussed in detail in the next section, *infra. See Marriage of Modnick, supra,* 33 Cal. 3d at 908 ("[T]he greater the prejudice, the more timely must be the relief sought."). Consequently, a relatively short delay by plaintiff may be "unreasonable" where defendant demonstrates substantial prejudice. *E.g., Finnie v. Town of Tiburon,* 199 Cal. App. 3d 1, 14, 244 Cal. Rptr. 581 (1988) (barring plaintiff's action to enjoin special town election where plaintiff did not commence action until three months after first learning of, and just two weeks before, the scheduled election; defendant town demonstrated ample prejudice resulting from this delay, such as extensive election preparations, printings, and expenses).

[3] Prejudice

The doctrine of laches requires not only unreasonable delay but also prejudice to the defendant resulting from the delay. *E.g., Conti v. Bd. of Civil Serv. Comm., supra.* Prejudice will not be presumed, but must be affirmatively proved by the defendant. *Id.; Miller v. Eisenhower Med. Center, supra.* Where the defendant fails to meet his burdens of proof and production of evidence on the issue of prejudice, laches will be denied regardless of how unreasonable the plaintiff's delay. *E.g.*, *Ragan v. City of Hawthorne*, 212 Cal. App. 3d 1361, 1368, 261 Cal. Rptr. 219 (1989) (ruling laches not established because no substantial evidence of prejudice to defendant resulting from plaintiff's three-year delay in contesting denial of retirement application); *Bono v. Clark*, 103 Cal. App. 4th 1409, 1419–20, 128 Cal. Rptr. 2d 31 (2002) (holding, despite finding of unreasonable delay, that laches not applicable because defendant presented no evidence of prejudice).

Whether a defendant's evidence establishes the requisite prejudice for laches depends on the circumstances of the case. The defendant must show that he did, or omitted to do, something due to the delay that detrimentally altered his position with respect to the plaintiff's asserted claim or right. *Conti v. Bd. of Civil Serv. Comm.*, *supra*, 1 Cal. 3d at 360 ("If the delay has caused no material change *in statu quo, ante*, i.e., no detriment suffered by the party pleading the laches, his plea is in vain."); *Johnson v. City of Loma Linda*, 24 Cal. 4th 61, 99 Cal. Rptr. 2d 316, 5 P.3d 874 (2000) (holding laches barred plaintiff from pursing FEHA claim against defendant City where plaintiff waited more than 18 months after City's personnel board rejected plaintiff's grievance before he filed his petition for administrative mandate in superior court, and then failed to pursue this petition for another 18 months; this unreasonable delay prejudiced defendant City because remedies sought by plaintiff, reinstatement and back pay, would require defendant to alter its new management structure and compel defendant to make double payments).

Typically, the courts find prejudice where defendant demonstrates it has incurred considerable expenses in reliance on plaintiff's inaction, such that enforcement of plaintiff's claimed right is inequitable, *e.g.*, *Finnie v. Town of Tiburon*, *supra*; *Holt v. Monterey County*, 128 Cal. App. 3d 797, 801, 180 Cal. Rptr. 514 (1982) (ruling challenge to approval of subdivision barred by laches where plaintiff delayed 2 1/2 years in bringing suit and developers expended over $4 million in reliance on the approval); where the defendant has already hired a permanent replacement during plaintiff's delay in bringing a reinstatement action, *e.g.*, *Vernon Fire Fighters Assn. v. City of Vernon*, 178 Cal. App. 3d 710, 723–27, 223 Cal. Rptr. 871 (1986) *but see Farmer v. City of Inglewood*, 134 Cal. App. 3d 130, 142, 185 Cal. Rptr. 9 (1982) (finding City's hiring of permanent replacement employee during 15-month delay by plaintiff in bringing action for reinstatement not to constitute sufficient prejudice for laches, following *Chang v. City of Palos Verdes Estates*, 98 Cal. App. 3d 557, 563, 159 Cal. Rptr. 630 (1979)); and where the plaintiff claims property after an unreasonable delay, and the property has significantly increased in value during the interim. *See, e.g.*, *Hamud v. Hawthorne*, 52 Cal. 2d 78, 86, 338 P.2d 387 (1959).

Prejudice may also be established where the defendant proves that the delay has resulted in loss of significant evidence. *E.g.*, *Getty v. Getty*, 187 Cal. App. 3d 1159, 1170, 232 Cal. Rptr. 603 (1986) (ruling death of important witness during time of delay constituted requisite prejudice); *City and County of San Francisco v. Pacello*, 85 Cal. App. 3d 637, 645 149 Cal. Rptr. 705 (1978) (ruling destruction of transcript of relevant administrative hearing during delay was manifest prejudice); *Vernon Fire Fighters Assn. v. City of Vernon, supra* (finding prejudice in part because witnesses and evidence no longer available due to death and retirement).

The requisite prejudice to defendant must be the result of the plaintiff's delay, and not be due to the defendant's conduct or some other cause. *See, e.g., Ateeq v. Najor,* 15 Cal. App. 4th 1351, 1359, 19 Cal. Rptr. 2d 320 (1993) (finding no laches where delay due to defendant's duress); *Marriage of Park,* 27 Cal. 3d 337, 345, n.7, 165 Cal. Rptr. 792, 612, P.2d 882 (1980) (ruling relitigation of community property rights will cause expenses, but such prejudice does not arise out of delay in bringing motion to vacate for extrinsic fraud).

[B]   Actions to Which Laches Is Applicable

The defense of laches is available in equitable actions but cannot be asserted as a bar to an action at law for money damages. *Abbott v. City of Los Angeles,* 50 Cal. 2d 438, 462, 326 P.2d 484 (1958); *Bodily v. Parkmont Village Green Homeowners Assn., Inc.,* 104 Cal. App. 3d 348, 358, 163 Cal. Rptr. 658 (1980). Laches can also be asserted in legal actions where an equitable remedy is sought, such as injunction relief. *E.g., Finnie v. Town of Tiburon,* 199 Cal. App. 3d 1, 14, 244 Cal. Rptr. 581 (1988); *see also Tustin Community Hosp., Inc. v. Santa Ana Community Hosp. Assn.,* 89 Cal. App. 3d 889, 153 Cal. Rptr. 76 (1979); constructive trust, *e.g., David Welch Co. v. Erskine & Tulley,* 203 Cal. App. 3d 884, 893–94, 250 Cal. Rptr. 339 (1988) (action for breach of fiduciary duty); or rescission of contract, *e.g., Leeper v. Beltrami,* 53 Cal. 2d 195, 211–17, 1 Cal. Rptr. 12, 347 P.2d 12 (1959) (holding action for rescission, whether legal or equitable, barred by unjustified delay regardless of whether action is for recovery of property, quiet title, or cancellation of deed); *see* Civil Code §§ 1691, 1693. The California courts have identified a number of equitable actions to which laches may be a defense. These include actions for an accounting, actions for partition of property, actions to establish or enforce a trust, actions to establish community property rights, and stockholders' derivative actions. *See* Ann Taylor Schwing, *California Affirmative, Defenses, Laches,* §§ 26:7–26:13 (2015), and authorities cited therein.

The courts also make laches available in a number of important review procedures, such as actions seeking judicial review of an administrative decision, *e.g., Miller v. Eisenhower Med. Center, supra* (suggesting that in such cases there may be substantial reasons for finding laches for delays for less than the applicable statute of limitations); *Conti v. Bd. of Civil Serv. Comm., supra* (applying laches to an administrative mandamus actions); actions to set aside judgments, *see, e.g., Marriage of Modnick, supra* (laches available in motion to set aside community property aspects of dissolution degree on grounds of extrinsic fraud); *Marriage of Park,* 27 Cal. 3d 337, 345, 165 Cal. Rptr. 792, 612 P.2d 882 (1980); and to petitions for mandamus, prohibition or certiorari seeking review of trial court rulings. *See, e.g., Peterson v. Superior Court,* 31 Cal. 3d 147, 163, 181 Cal. Rptr. 784, 642 P.2d 1305 (1982).

Although available as a defense, laches apparently is disfavored when its application would defeat a strong rule of policy adopted for public protection or benefit. *See, e.g., County of Los Angeles v. Berk*, 26 Cal. 3d 201, 222, 161 Cal. Rptr. 742, 605 P.2d 381 (1980) (observing that laches will not be asserted against the government to defeat a claim of public recreational easement in beach, when to do so would nullify a strong rule of policy adopted for the benefit of the public); *Marriage of Lugo*, 170 Cal. App. 3d 427, 435–36, 217 Cal. Rptr. 74 (1985) (ruling that despite five-year delay, county not estopped from collecting arrearages in child support payments as reimbursement for welfare payments; and observing the doctrine of laches "is rarely invoked against a public entity to defeat a policy adopted for the protection of the public, such as in the present case").

[C] Manner of Asserting Laches

Laches is an affirmative defense, and should be raised by an answer which states facts establishing the defense. *See Conti v. Bd. of Civil Serv. Comm., supra*, 1 Cal. 3d at 361. Laches may also be raised by demurrer, "but only if the complaint shows on its face unreasonable delay plus prejudice or acquiescence." *Id.* at 362; *Leeper v. Beltram, supra*. And even if a complaint alleges these elements, a demurrer will not be sustained where the complaint also alleges justification for the delay. *E.g., Barndt v. County of Los Angeles*, 211 Cal. App. 3d 397, 402–403, 259 Cal. Rptr. 372 (1989). Generally speaking, the existence of laches is a question of fact. *Conti v. Bd. of Civil Serv. Comm., supra*. After pleaded as an affirmative defense, what procedural device is appropriate for raising laches?

The party asserting laches has the burden of proof and production of evidence on the elements of this defense. *Miller v. Eisenhower Med. Center, supra*. Because laches is a question of fact, the defense must be presented in some manner at the trial court level and cannot be initially asserted on appeal. *See California Tahoe Regional Planning Agency v. Day & Night Elec., Inc.*, 163 Cal. App. 3d 898, 903, n.1, 210 Cal. Rptr. 48 (1985). The determination of laches is addressed to the discretion of the trial court, and its determination will be sustained on appeal unless there is a manifest injustice or a lack of substantial support in the evidence. *Miller v. Eisenhower Med. Center, supra*, 27 Cal. 3d at 624; *Johnson v. City of Loma Linda*, 24 Cal. 4th 61, 68, 99 Cal. Rptr. 2d 316. 5 P.3d 874 (2000) (observing that generally a trial court's laches ruling will be sustained on appeal if there is substantial evidence to support the ruling).

Chapter 5

California Conflict of Laws Doctrine

§ 5.01 Introductory Note

Whenever litigation has a connection with more than one state, the court must determine which state's legal rules should govern the various issues in the case. This determination is based on a "choice of law" or, using traditional California terminology, a "conflict of laws" analysis. This chapter will explore the choice-of-law doctrine developed and applied by the state courts in California.

A choice-of-law decision determines what law controls with respect to a variety of important litigation issues such as statute of limitations, substantive tort or contract law, and the amount and type of damages. Consequently, a choice-of-law decision may determine the very success or failure of a lawsuit.

Generally speaking, there is no choice-of-law problem where litigation has connections only with one state, and that state is also the forum state. A California court will simply apply California law to any case where the parties, events, and transactions relate only to California. But modern litigation often involves multi-state considerations. The parties may not all be residents of California, or some of the relevant transactions may have connections with another state. Such multi-state cases usually require consideration of choice-of-law questions.

Each state is free to adopt whatever choice-of-law doctrine it prefers, subject only to minimal limitations imposed by the Due Process Clause of the Fourteenth Amendment to the U.S. Constitution. *See Allstate Ins. Co. v. Hague,* 449 U.S. 302, 101 S. Ct. 633, 66 L. Ed. 2d 521 (1981) (holding that for a state's substantive law to be selected in a constitutionally permissible manner, that state must have a significant contact or aggregation of contacts with the parties and with the transaction giving rise to the litigation, creating state interests, such that choice of its law is neither arbitrary nor fundamentally unfair). Choice-of-law doctrine in most states, including California, is largely the result of court-made development and not statutory enactment. In recent years, at least six separate choice-of-law theories have found favor in one or more states. For a brief discussion of these various theories, as well as a state-by-state survey of choice-of-law doctrine, see Gregory E. Smith, *Choice of Law in the United States,* 38 Hastings L.J. 1041 (1987); Symeon C. Symeonides, *Choice of Law in the American Courts in 2014: Twenty-Eighth Annual Survey,* 63 Am. J. Comp. L. 299 (2015).

The California choice-of-law doctrine is not particularly difficult to state as a series of black letter rules. For example, the current doctrine in multi-state tort cases is succinctly stated as follows:

Analysis of a choice of law question proceeds in three steps: (1) determination of whether the potentially concerned states have different laws, (2) consideration of whether each of the states has an interest in having its law applied to the case, and (3) if the laws are different and each has an interest in having its law applied (a "true" conflict), selection of which state's law to apply by determining which state's interests would be more impaired if its policy were subordinated to the policy of the other state. *See Bernhard v. Harrah's Club*, 16 Cal. 3d 313, 320, 128 Cal. Rptr. 215, 546 P.2d 719 (1976).

Although easy to state, this doctrine is almost meaningless when stated in an historical and factual vacuum. Consequently, this chapter will begin with a brief historical account of choice-of-law doctrine, generally and in California. Next, this chapter will present several California cases and case summaries in those areas which typically involve the most difficult choice-of-law problems, *i.e.*, multi-state tort and contract cases. Finally, the chapter will survey California choice-of-law problems in a few other areas, such as statute of limitations, corporations, and family law.

A few words of caution about California choice-of-law doctrine, and these materials. Choice-of-law analysis is a complex, difficult, and fascinating topic. The doctrine is also a continually evolving one, both nationally and in California. Perhaps more than any other area of law, choice-of-law theories are influenced by scholarly thinking and writings. This undoubtedly explains why the theories are sometimes contradictory, incomprehensible, and difficult to apply in actual cases! But it also explains why the courts repeatedly rely on analysis contained in law review articles. One way to better understand California's choice-of-law doctrine is to read the articles often cited by the California courts. Accordingly, this chapter includes numerous quotations from, and citations to, these influential scholarly writings.

§ 5.02 An Overview of the Historical Evolution of Choice-of-Law Theories

[A] The First and Second Restatements

California, as well as every other state, developed a choice-of-law doctrine of some type as soon as multi-state cases began appearing in state courts. The first real attempt to unify state choice-of-law doctrines came in 1934 with the adoption by the American Law Institute (ALI) of the Restatement of Conflict of Law. A brief summary of the First Restatement, as well as of the Second Restatement adopted by the ALI in 1971, is set forth below.

William M. Richman, William L. Reynolds, and Christopher A. Whytock, Understanding Conflict of Laws

(4th ed. 2013) pp. 191–229 (footnotes omitted)[*]

THE FIRST RESTATEMENT

The traditional system for choice of law in the United States was the system embodied in the First Restatement. Based on the vested rights theory, the system consisted of a few broad, hard and fast rules coupled with an array of escape devices. Although most conflicts scholars have by now abandoned the First Restatement system, it retains surprising popularity among the courts. * * *

THE FIRST RESTATEMENT — THEORY

[a] A Bit of History

In order to understand the First Restatement system for choice of law and the vested rights theory, upon which it was based, it is important to consider a bit of the history of choice-of-law theory. Early conflicts theorists asked a question which modern writers are inclined to ignore: When an Ohio court decides a conflicts case using a principle found in Michigan law, exactly what is it doing? Is it "applying" the Michigan law, is it enforcing a Michigan "right," or is it creating an Ohio right which is modeled on a Michigan right which would have existed had the case been a wholly Michigan case?

Joseph Story, the first American writer to treat the question, thought that the forum court "applied" the foreign law based on the theory of comity — the respect which one sovereign owes another. Because comity was a discretionary doctrine, the forum court was not *required* to apply the foreign law, but did so as a matter of courtesy. Dissatisfaction with this account of the choice of law process spawned the Vested Rights Theory.

[b] Vested Rights

* * *

Under the [vested rights] theory, it was important to know when and where a particular right vested, because the law of the place where the right vested would control the content of the right. The practical result was a system of a few, broad relatively rigid choice-of-law rules. Each governed a major area of the law (e.g., torts, contracts, property) by identifying a particular contact (the tortious injury, the making of the contract, the situs of the land) as the trigger for the vesting of a right. Thus, questions in tort were decided by the law of the place of injury; questions in contract, by the law of the place of making; and questions in property, by the law of the situs of the land. * * *

THE FIRST RESTATEMENT IN PRACTICE — BROAD RULES AND ESCAPE DEVICES

In spite of ... conceptual difficulties with the vested rights theory, it was adopted by the American Law Institute and incorporated into the First Restatement. This tra-

---

ditional system of choice-of-law rules prevailed in most American courts until the work of a new generation of judges and scholars began to supplant it in the 1950s and 1960s. Even today, the First Restatement system retains a good deal of vitality. According to a recent survey of American choice-of-law decisions, 10 jurisdictions still follow the traditional method in tort cases and 12 in contract cases. Furthermore, even the states that have abandoned the First Restatement for most choice-of-law problems retain it for issues involving interests in land.

The First Restatement system for choice of law consists of a few broad, single-contact, jurisdiction-selecting rules coupled with an array of escape devices. Each of these characterizations requires a brief comment. At first glance, the rules do not appear to be few or broad; the Restatement contains over 300 sections on choice of law. Most of the sections, however, can be condensed into a few general summary rules. Nearly all questions in tort, for example, are governed by the law of the place of injury, and nearly all questions about property are governed by the law of the situs.

The rules of the First Restatement are jurisdiction-selecting rules. They pick between competing states, not between competing rules. The court does not consider the scope, content, or policy of the substantive rule of law until after the state is chosen. Thus, in making the initial choice, the First Restatement rules are not concerned with which substantive rule is "better," or which validates the parties' intentions, or which is motivated by a policy which can be advanced by its application in this case; rather, they are concerned only with identifying a particular event and the jurisdiction (state) in which that event occurred.

Another feature of the First Restatement rules is that, unlike other choice-of-law systems, they rely upon *only one* salient connection between the dispute and the state. On the issue of the validity of a contract, for example, the Center of Gravity Theory might look to several important contacts: the domicile of the parties, the place where the contract was made, the place where it was to be performed, the place where financial injury from breach might be felt. The First Restatement considers only one contact: the place of making.

The courts that applied the First Restatement were not always satisfied with the results produced by the simple, hard-and-fast rules. When faced with a rule that required choice of X's law when justice and common sense favored the law of Y, the judges found ways to avoid the rule. Typically, they did not articulate the considerations of policy, fairness, and party expectations that motivated their decisions; conflicts theory of the time was too rigidly formalistic to permit so grand a strategy. Rather, they invented escape devices — highly conceptual maneuvers which permitted them to avoid an undesirable outcome without breaking faith with the traditional system. Thus, they could recharacterize a property issue as a tort problem and escape the law of the situs in favor of the law of the place injury, or characterize a tort problem as a question of procedure and escape the law of the place of injury in favor of the law of the forum. Another possibility was renvoi; if the forum's choice-of-law rule directed the choice of X's law and the result was offensive, the court could read "X's law" to mean X's whole law — including its choice of law rules — which might refer the issue back to forum law. Finally, courts occasionally took the bull by the horns and refused for reasons of "public policy" to apply the law suggested by the First Restatement's rigid rules. * * *

Torts

[a] The Law of the Place of the Wrong

The First Restatement specifies the law of the place of the wrong for nearly all issues in torts. Thus, the law of the place of the wrong controls: the existence of a legal injury (§ 378), defendant's standard of responsibility (§ 381), causation (§ 383), contributory negligence (§ 385), the fellow-servant rule (§ 386), vicarious liability (§ 390), and the measure of damages (§ 412).

According to § 377, the place of the wrong is "in the state where the last event necessary to make an actor liable for an alleged tort takes place." In almost all circumstances, the "last event" is the injury to the plaintiff, so the "law of the place of the wrong" really means the law of the place of injury. To put the matter flippantly, "look for the blood." Typically, it does not matter that defendant's conduct may have occurred in another state. Thus, if defendant standing in state A shoots plaintiff standing in state B, the law of B will control. Similarly, if defendant negligently manufactures a product in state A which injures plaintiff in state B, the law of B will control. * * *

[b] Escaping the Law of the Place of Injury

[1] Characterization

Decisions like [*Alabama Great Southern R.R. Co. v.*] *Carroll* [97 Ala. 126, 11 So. 803 (1892) (Alabama court must apply Mississippi negligence law, which precludes recovery under fellow-servant rule, even though Alabama is location of plaintiff's residence, defendant's residence, the contract of employment, and the negligent act; solely because injury to plaintiff fortuitously occurred in Mississippi)] reveal how arbitrary and unjust the place of injury rule can be. Without abandoning the rule, courts were often able to avoid the most egregious results by employing several conceptual escape devices. The most fruitful was characterization. The ploy was to reclassify the issue for decision as a non-tort issue and thus use another First Restatement rule to generate a better result. In *Grant v. McAuliffe* [41 Cal. 2d 859, 264 P.2d 944 (1953)], the court used the substance/procedure distinction to recharacterize the issue. Plaintiffs and decedent—all residents of California—were involved in an auto accident in Arizona. Decedent died shortly after the accident, and plaintiffs sued the administrator of his estate in California. Tort actions did not survive the death of the tortfeasor under Arizona law, but they did survive according to the law of California. Justice Traynor, writing for the Supreme Court of California, avoided the application of the Arizona law and saved plaintiff's cause of action by classifying the issue of survival of actions as a procedural question to be referred to the law of the forum rather than a tort issue to be decided by the law of the place of injury.

A more typical use of characterization as an escape device involves changing the substantive law category in which the case belongs. A well-known example is *Haumschild v. Continental Casualty Co.*, [7 Wis. 2d 130, 95 N.W.2d 814 (1959)]. Plaintiff, a Wisconsin domiciliary, sued her ex-husband, also a domiciliary of Wisconsin, for injuries which she received from his negligent driving in California. California, the place of injury, had an interspousal immunity rule; Wisconsin did not. Had the Wisconsin Supreme Court followed the law of the place of injury, as dictated by Wisconsin precedent, plaintiff would have been denied a recovery—a result the court found unpalatable. Instead, the court was able to recharacterize the issue as a problem of status to be governed by the law of the marital domicile—Wisconsin. * * *

CONTRACTS

[a] The Place of Making

Before the first Restatement, American jurisdictions were divided over the proper choice-of-law rule to govern the validity of contracts. Three principles could claim some support: (1) the validation rule, which held that the validity of a contract is controlled by the law that the parties presumably intended to govern their dealings; (2) the place-of-performance rule, and (3) the place-of-making rule. * * *

[T]he First Restatement adopted the place-of-making rule. Section 332 provides that the law of the place of making controls such issues of contract validity as capacity, formalities, consideration, and defenses (illegality or fraud, for example) which might make the contract void or voidable. Determination of the place of making, therefore, is very important. * * *

There is only one major exception to the place-of-making rule. Section 358 provides that questions concerning details of performance are to be governed by the law of the place of performance. Such questions include the manner of performance, the time and place of performance, the persons by and for whom performance shall be rendered, the sufficiency of performance, and excuses for non-performance. Although §358 is the only major exception to the place-of-making rule, it is an exception so large that it threatens to swallow the rule. The Restatement was sensitive to this difficulty. Comment b to §358 hedges by suggesting that the law of the place of performance "is not applicable to the point where the substantial obligation of the parties is materially altered." Further, the Restatement acknowledges that it will not always be easy to separate issues of validity from details of performance. * * *

[b] Escaping the Place of Making

Courts developed several techniques for escaping the place-of-making rule. Two (manipulation of the place of making and use of the making/performance distinction) are specialized devices, useful only in contract actions. Three others (characterization, renvoi, and public policy) are the standard escape techniques that courts have used in all sorts of cases. * * *

PROPERTY

It has been traditional in conflicts law to distinguish between immovable and movable property. The distinction is generally comparable to that drawn between real and personal property, except that a leasehold interest is classified as an interest in immovable property in conflicts parlance, while in general property parlance, it is considered personal rather than real property. The organization of this Section follows the distinction drawn by the First Restatement between interests in land and other sorts of property.

[a] Land

The First Restatement requires application of the law of the situs (the location of the land) to nearly all questions concerning interests in land. The rule applies to conveyances of land (§§ 214–222), adverse possession (§ 224), mortgages and liens (§§ 225–231), marital property (§§ 237–238), trusts (§ 241), and succession by will or intestacy (§§ 245–254). Indeed, the situs rule is among the broadest of the First Restatement choice-of-law principles; it retains much of its authority today, even though many modern courts have abandoned the First Restatement in other areas. * * *

[b] Movables-Personal Property

[1] Inter Vivos Transactions

For nearly all inter vivos transactions of movables, the First Restatement prescribes the law of the place where the movable was located at the time of the transaction. Thus, the situs rule applies to conveyances (§§ 255–258), adverse possession (§ 259), mortgages (§ 265), conditional sales (§ 272), liens and pledges (§ 279), powers of appointment (§ 283), and trusts (§ 294). * * *

[2] Succession on Death

The First Restatement refers questions concerning testamentary disposition of movables and intestate succession of movables to the law of decedent's domicile at the time of death. * * *

THE FIRST RESTATEMENT—A CRITIQUE

The principal benefits claimed for the First Restatement system for choice of law are ease of administration, predictability, and forum neutrality. By the use of a few, simple rules, the Restatement sought to generate a system which was easy to apply, certain of outcome, and not subject to change depending upon where the suit was brought. The first goal was clearly attained; the rules are (at least on the surface) easy to understand and apply. Predictability and forum neutrality are another matter. If the rules were applied "right out of the box" perhaps these ends could be reached, but the system of escape devices substantially undermines predictability and forum neutrality. Further, the importance of ease of application, predictability, and forum neutrality can be easily overstated. A choice-of-law system which achieves those ends much more efficiently than the First Restatement is one which directs the application of the law of the state which is first (or last) in alphabetical order, yet no one has seriously argued for such a system.

A preliminary problem with the First Restatement is its very simplicity. That simplicity is bought at the price of insisting on a few broad rules which lump together cases and issues which appear quite unrelated. In tort cases, for example, the Restatement prescribes the law of the place of injury for all torts from defamation to battery to misrepresentation. It seems improbable that such diverse legal actions, restricted by widely different defenses and qualifications, could all be profitably covered by a single choice-of-law rule. On the other hand, the Restatement's categories sometimes separate problems which should be closely linked. A product liability plaintiff will typically plead a count of strict liability in tort and a count in warranty. The two theories, one descended from tort and the other from contract, seek to compensate the same injury, yet the First Restatement will apply the law of the place of injury to one theory and the law of the place of making to the other. That hardly passes an intuitive test of rationality.

A far more serious problem with the First Restatement is that it often chooses the law of a state with no interest in the resolution of the dispute. Suppose a contract is negotiated in Connecticut for the delivery of goods in Connecticut by a Connecticut seller to a Connecticut buyer. Although Connecticut is the only state with a real interest in the transaction, if the parties had concluded their negotiation at a trade convention in Florida, the Restatement would apply the law of Florida to the contract. Surely that is a triumph of form over substance.

The reason for such anomalies is that the First Restatement rules are almost entirely (and deliberately) blind to the policies behind competing internal laws. Consider an automobile accident between two Californians, plaintiff and defendant, which occurs about two miles south of the border between California and Mexico. Suppose that plaintiff is seriously injured — about $200,000 worth. Further suppose that Mexico, desiring not to impoverish tortfeasors, has established a negligence damage limitation of $6,000 but that California does not limit damages because it favors full compensation for tort victims. According to the Restatement, the law of Mexico should apply because Mexico is the place of injury. But note how applying Mexican law seriously frustrates California's policy of compensation without advancing Mexico's goal in the least. If Mexico is concerned about impoverishing tortfeasors, surely that concern does not extend to Californians. Thus, the application of the First Restatement's mechanical formula produces a foolish result here for the simple reason that the formula totally ignores the purposes behind Mexico's and California's tort rules. Such blind adherence to the letter of the law, while ignoring its spirit, would not be tolerated in a purely domestic case; why then should it be the rule for conflicts cases?

A final problem with the First Restatement is the system of escape devices. Basically the devices work to give some flexibility to the mechanical choice-of-law rules. Because the rules by and large ignore government interests, the policies behind legal rules, and justice in the individual case, the escape devices have been used to import those considerations into the choice-of-law process. In the hands of able and reflective judges, the escape devices have been potent weapons for good. * * *

But even in the hands of able judges, the escape devices can be dangerous. The danger is that First Restatement courts articulate only the technical rationales for the escape devices — not the real policy interests and considerations of justice which have, in fact, motivated them. In other words, the escape device assures that the reasons for the court's *decision* will have little to do with the reasons announced in the court's *opinion*. The result is that the court has a freedom to indulge in unprincipled decision-making, which is incompatible with the rule of law. Judges in our system have extraordinary power; the requirement that their decisions be reasoned and public is one of the only real constraints on that power. Devices which effectively hide the real reasons for decisions considerably weaken that constraint and take our judicial system far from the common law model of principled decision-making.

Despite its defects, the First Restatement has proved remarkably resilient in the courts. The most recent exhaustive survey of American choice-of-law decisions found that 10 jurisdictions still follow the traditional method in tort cases and 12 in contract cases. * * *

THE SECOND RESTATEMENT: HISTORY AND THEORY

[a] The Drafting History

Holmes' famous aphorism that a page of history is worth a volume of logic applies with special force to the Second Restatement. It is difficult to understand the document and its hybrid method without some understanding of the eighteen-year drafting history. The project began in 1953 as an attempt to respond to the withering academic criticism of the First Restatement and to accommodate the beginnings of a conflicts revolution that was occurring in the courts. It ended in 1971 as a complex, negotiated settlement among several warring factions of choice-of-law revolutionaries. As a descriptive "restatement," it was doomed to failure from the outset because it is impossible to "restate" a revolution that is in progress and whose outcome is in doubt. As a normative "pre-statement," it has proved to be a huge success among the courts, but an object of academic derision. * * *

[b] An Overview

The Restatement (Second) of Conflict of Laws is a complex approach to choice of law that borrows from the wide array of traditional and modern choice-of-law methodologies.... Like its predecessor, it is comprehensive and detailed, containing hundreds of territorial choice-of-law rules divided by subject matter (torts, contracts, property, etc.). It also incorporates, however, much modern learning from the choice-of-law revolution including grouping-of-contacts, interest analysis, validation, and party autonomy. To complicate matters further, the reception of the Second Restatement has varied widely. Excoriated by commentators, it has proved to be extremely popular among the courts. Adopted by more than half of the states and influential, as well, in the federal system, the Second Restatement is by far the most popular choice-of-law regime in the country today. The courts have added a final level of complexity with divergent interpretations of the Restatement's basic approach, some of which seems at odds with the intentions of the drafters.

Three basic elements define the choice-of-law approach of the Second Restatement: (1) §6 and the most significant relationship, (2) a few grouping-of-contacts sections, and (3) numerous sections that provide choice-of-law rules for specific legal claims and issues. These are the subjects of subsections [c]-[e].

[c] Section 6 and The Most Significant Relationship

[1] Statutory Directive

Section 6 (1) uncontroversially directs a court to follow a statutory directive of its own state on choice of law. Although the subsection is uncontroversial, its range of application is fairly narrow, as statutory directives on choice of law are quite rare. As the comments suggest, "legislatures usually legislate ... only with the local situation in mind." There are, however, a few exceptions: The Uniform Commercial Code, for example, contains choice-of-law provisions, as do many no-fault automobile accident compensation statutes.

[2] The Most Significant Relationship

A general principle that pervades the Second Restatement is the principle that an issue should be determined by the "law of the state which, with respect to that issue, has the most significant relationship to the occurrence and the parties...." Although the Restatement contains no explicit definition of the concept of "the most significant relationship," it directs courts to apply the concept according to the principles contained in § 6(2). Section 6(2) in turn sets forth "factors relevant to the choice of the applicable rule of law," including:

(a) the needs of the interstate and international systems,

(b) the relevant policies of the forum,

(c) the relevant policies of other interested states and the relative interests of those states in the determination of the particular issue,

(d) the protection of justified expectations,

(e) the basic policies underlying the particular field of law,

(f) certainty, predictability and uniformity of result, and

(g) ease in the determination and application of the law to be applied.

Section 6 (2) and the concept of the most significant relationship form the heart of the Restatement (Second). They appear in section after section, sometimes as a general residual choice-of-law directive to be used when no specific section applies (*e.g.*, § 145), sometimes as a check, such as a limit on party autonomy in contract (*e.g.*, § 187), and sometimes as an escape device used to avoid the irrational result of a presumptive reference section (*e.g.*, § 149, comment c). * * *

[e] The Specific Sections: A Wide Variety of Approaches

[1] Territorial Presumptions

The specific sections of the Second Restatement use a wide variety of choice-of-law strategies. Most, by far, are territorial references, although they differ from the single contact, jurisdiction-selecting rules of the First Restatement in one significant respect. Nearly all are presumptive references that may be overcome by use of the most significant relationship device of § 6 and the grouping of contacts sections (§§ 145 and 188)....

The strength of the presumption varies widely. In some cases, the presumption is nearly absolute. Thus nearly all issues of procedure and evidence, except for limitations, burden of proof, and privilege are referred to the law of the forum with no "most significant relationship" exception clause. Similarly, and much more controversially, the sections dealing with real property point absolutely to the law that would be applied by the courts of the situs, and most of those dealing with the succession on death of personal property refer, without an exception clause, to the law that would be applied by the courts of decedent's domicile.

The language of other sections reveals less confidence in the presumptive reference. Thus for many types of tort claims and for many types of contracts, the Second Restatement refers to a particular territorial contact, "unless, with respect to the particular issue, some other state has a more significant relationship under the principles stated in § 6" to the claim and the parties. Sections treating particular contract and tort issues are even more tentative, suggesting only that the supplied territorial reference will "usually" control.

Finally, some sections include no presumptive territorial reference at all, referring instead to the appropriate general grouping-of-contacts section, which, of course, incorporates by reference the choice-of-law principles of § 6.

[2] Non-Territorial Sections

In addition to its territorial presumptive references, the Second Restatement also uses other choice-of-law methodologies in several of its specific sections. Party autonomy figures importantly in the Restatement provisions governing consensual, planned transactions. Thus, the drafters give the parties total control over the construction of wills, trusts, and contracts, and substantial control over the validity of contracts, and inter vivos trusts of movables.

Substantivism—choosing law by the result that it produces—informs at least a few specific sections of the Restatement. The clearest examples are the validating provisions affecting usurious contracts, powers of appointment, testamentary trusts, foreign incorporations, and contract formalities. Another example is § 139, which provides for the admission into evidence of a communication if it is admissible according to the privilege law of either the forum or the state that has the most significant relationship with the communication.

Finally, a few of the specific sections of the Second Restatement are purely interest-analytic. The best examples are the sections on presumptions, as well as those on burdens of production and persuasion, which refer to the law of the forum "unless the primary purpose of the relevant rule of the state of the otherwise applicable law is to affect decision of the issue rather than to regulate the conduct of the trial."

[f] The Grouping-of-Contacts Sections

The grouping-of-contacts sections, §§ 145 (2) and 188 (2), serve a residual function; thus when an issue or a claim in tort is not treated by a specific choice-of-law directive, the forum should resort to the general rule of § 145. The early drafts of these sections are the lineal descendants of the "center of gravity" opinions that appeared early in the choice-of-law revolution, especially in New York. Later drafts, however, incorporated the insights of interest analysis and provide a greater role for policy analysis than did the center of gravity method. Thus, the final version of § 145 calls for application of the law of "the state which … has the most significant relationship to the occurrence and the parties under the principles stated in §6." Correspondingly, the role of the enumerated contacts is diminished; they are simply "to be *taken into account* [emphasis added] in applying the principles of §6."

[g] Applying the Second Restatement: The Drafters' Intent

The Restatement gives no explicit directions on how its several disparate elements should be combined into a single choice-of-law methodology. More careful scrutiny, however, reveals what the drafters probably had in mind. In the absence of a statutory choice-of-law directive, a court should determine first whether a specific section covers the issue or claim before it. Most of the specific sections will be presumptive territorial references, but some will use other choice-of-law techniques. Nearly all, however, will include some reference to §6 and perhaps to one of the grouping-of-contacts sections, as well. If no specific section covers the issue or claim, the court should refer to the general grouping-of-contacts sections, which also include a reference to §6. Thus, with either the specific sections or the general grouping-of-contacts sections, eventually the court will need to apply the factors of §6(2).

Section 6 (2)(b) and (c) clearly contemplate performing some sort of interest analysis. Presumably if that analysis indicates a false conflict, the court should apply the law of the only interested state. If the case is a non-false conflict, the court should use the factors of §6(2)(d)-(g) to resolve the true conflict or unprovided-for case. In no event, however, should the court use the grouping-of-contacts sections to justify a center-of-gravity or contact-counting approach. The contacts enumerated in the grouping-of-contacts sections have no independent significance and are relevant only insofar as they implicate the factors of §6(2).

[h] A Note on Escape Devices

The flexibility inherent in the most significant relationship test means that the escape devices so commonly employed under the vested rights theory have become more or less obsolete—at least for those who play the game by the rules of the Second Restatement. Renvoi plays but a small role in the Second Restatement, although the concept is generally available when uniformity of result is the goal, it is relegated to service in only a few areas. Substance/procedure is a game which also has a reduced role because the focus has been shifted away from mechanical labeling and toward analysis of the policies (especially the forum's interest in judicial administration) that are involved with respect to each issue in the case. Characterization, in general, still enjoys a significant status because the presumptive jurisdiction-selecting rules of the Restatement are organized by subject matter, an organization which necessarily requires characterization. At times, of course, selection of the correct label can be difficult, but the Restatement provides a partial solution to the problem by eliminating presumptive rules in some areas where the characterization might be problematic. Vicarious liability, for example, has elements of tort, contract, and status, a combination which makes it an extremely difficult problem to characterize. The Restatement finesses the issue by referring vicarious liability question to the law of the state with the most significant relationship to the issue. That reference, of course, does not eliminate the problem, but at least rids it of the characterization overtones.

Public policy is the only escape device that retains a prominent role in the 1971 Restatement. [The drafters], however, transformed it from a clumsy, post-hoc trump card into one of the general considerations of § 6. That treatment of public policy still leaves a good deal to the judge's discretion, but a stricter approach would probably do little except to drive the public policy consideration underground once again.

THE SECOND RESTATEMENT IN THE COURTS

[a] Dominance

The Second Restatement is the dominant conflict methodology in American courts today. Twenty-two jurisdictions follow the Restatement's approach in tort conflicts, and twenty-four do so in contract cases. Additionally, several other jurisdictions follow the similar "significant contacts" approach, thus yielding a majority of American jurisdictions. The next most popular American choice-of-law methodology, the traditional First Restatement approach, can claim less than half as many adherents. * * *

[c] Specific Versus General: In Practice

[An] issue that has emerged in the interpretation of the Second Restatement is the role of the specific territorial presumptions. As indicated in § 70, the drafters intended that the court's choice-of-law calculation begin with the specific territorial presumptions, where applicable, and then proceed to the "most significant relationship" analysis under § 6 and the grouping-of-contacts sections. One might expect judges familiar with the traditional territorial system to be over-deferential to the presumptive references and reluctant to engage in the more-free-form process required by § 6.

In fact, however, the opposite approach seems to prevail. There is now some evidence that many Second Restatement courts skip the initial presumptive reference and proceed directly to the "most significant relationship" analysis. The evidence for this counter-intuitive development is a citation study conducted by Professor Borchers [see Patrick J. Borchers, *Courts and the Second Conflicts Restatement: Some Observations and an Empirical Note*, 56 MD. L. Rev. 1233 (1997)]. He found in tort and contract cases that the citations to §§ 145 and 188 significantly outnumbered the total of citations to all the presumptive-reference sections combined. * * *

[B] California and the Restatements

Until the mid-1900s, California's choice-of-law doctrine generally incorporated the vested rights theory of the First Restatement. For example, California courts applied the law of the place of wrong in tort actions, regardless of the issues before the court. *See, e.g., Loranger v. Nadeau*, 215 Cal. 362, 366, 10 P.2d 63 (1932); *Ryan v. North Alaska Salmon Co.*, 153 Cal. 438, 439, 95 P. 862 (1908). In contract actions, California courts indicated that the validity of a contract was governed by the law of the place of contracting, and matters of performance were governed by the law of the place of performance. *See, e.g., Mercantile Acceptance Co. v. Frank*, 203 Cal. 483

265 P.2d 485 190 (1928); *Sullivan v. Shannon*, 25 Cal. App. 2d 422, 426, 77 P.2d 498 (1938).

The same dissatisfaction with the formalistic vested rights theory that lead to the ALI's adoption of the Second Restatement, also lead to the adoption of new conflicts doctrine by the California courts. The modern California doctrine directly relies on the Second Restatement in contract cases. And although California has not adopted the Second Restatement for tort cases, the modern California doctrine is clearly influenced by the Second Restatement's concern for government policies and interests in interstate cases.

§ 5.03   Government Interest Analysis and Tort Cases in California

[A]   An Introduction to Interest Analysis

California has not followed the Second Restatement approach in tort cases. Instead the Supreme Court adopted a competing, although not necessarily antagonistic, approach known as the "government interest analysis." The genesis of California's modern conflicts doctrine is the "interest analysis" theory developed by Professor Brainerd Currie in a series of scholarly writings. *See, e.g.*, Brainerd Currie, *Married Women's Contracts: A Study in Conflict-of-Laws Method*, 25 U. CHI. L. REV. 227 (1958); Brainerd Currie, *Notes on Methods and Objectives in the Conflict of Laws*, 1959 DUKE L.J. 171 (1959); Brainerd Currie, *The Disinterested Third State*, 28 LAW & CONTEMP. PROBS. 754 (1963). However, as this section will discuss, California's government interest analysis, although based on Currie's theory, differs from Currie's pure "interest analysis" approach in some key aspects.

In order to understand California's current conflicts doctrine, it is first necessary to master Currie's "interest analysis" terminology and methodology.

The Governmental Interest Approach to Choice of Law: an Analysis and a Reformulation, by Robert A. Sedler

25 UCLA L. REV. 181, 183–190 (1977)[*]

INTRODUCTION

The governmental interest approach formulated by the late Brainerd Currie[1] has been the catalyst of the modern "revolution" in choice of law in this country. This revolution has resulted in the widespread abandonment of the rigid, territorially

---

[*] Originally published in 25 UCLA L. Rev. 181. Copyright © 1977 by the Regents of the University of California. All rights reserved. Reprinted with permission.

1. Currie's major articles have been collected in B. CURRIE, SELECTED ESSAYS ON THE CONFLICT OF LAWS (1963) [hereinafter cited as CURRIE]. Two other articles published subsequently are Currie, *The Disinterested Third State*, 28 L. & CONTEMP. PROBS. 754 (1963); Currie, *Full Faith and Credit, Chiefly to Judgments: A Role for Congress*, 1964 SUP. CT. REV. 89 [hereinafter cited as Currie, *Full Faith*

based rules of the original Restatement in favor of a view of choice of law that emphasizes considerations of policy and fairness to the parties. Virtually all modern approaches to choice of law recognize the relevancy of the policies and interests of the involved states; the disagreement is over how much weight they are to be given in comparison with other considerations, and over whether the resolution of conflicts problems should proceed case by case, as would follow from Currie's approach, or on the basis of narrow, policy-based rules. * * *

I. CURRIE'S GOVERNMENTAL INTEREST APPROACH: UNDERLYING THEORY AND METHODOLOGY

The underlying theory of Currie's governmental interest approach is that choice of law problems should be resolved by a consideration of first, the policies behind the laws of the involved states, and second, the interest of each state, in light of those policies, in having its law applied on the particular issue as to which the laws differ. The factual contacts that the parties and the transaction have with the various states do not have independent significance, and are relevant only insofar as those contacts give rise to a governmental interest in having a particular rule of substantive law applied on a particular issue.

The methodology of interest analysis first directs scrutiny of the content of the differing laws of the forum and of the other state or states whose law is potentially applicable.[18] The content of each state's law will reflect a policy. The second determination, then, is whether, in light of the policy reflected in that law, the state has an interest in having its law applied on the point in issue.[20] Currie illustrated the application of interest analysis by a detailed consideration of the problem of married women's contract immunity involved in *Milliken v. Pratt*, and the problem of survival of actions presented by *Grant v. McAuliffe*. While fuller consideration of these cases will be left for later discussion, a review of Currie's method of determining prelim-

---

and Credit]. The basic elements of Currie's approach are summarized in R. Crampton, D. Currie & H. Kay, Conflict of Laws 221–224 (2d ed. 1975) [hereinafter cited as Crampton, Currie & Kay].

18. They will be referred to as the other involved states. We will generally use the two-state example, because this is what usually occurs in practice. A state's law is potentially applicable for conflicts purposes whenever one of the parties resides there or whenever some of the legally significant facts occurred there.

20. The methodology is summarized in *Notes on Methods and Objectives in the Conflict of Laws*, in Currie, *supra* note 1, at 183–84 (article originally published at 1959 Duke L.J. 171), and in Crampton, Currie, & Kay, *supra* note 1, at 221–24. It should be noted that the interest referred to is the interest of the state in having its law applied in the kind of situation that is before the court. Where special circumstances are present in the actual case that ordinarily are not present in that kind of situation, the interest is still deemed to exist for purposes of Currie's interest analysis.

For example, Currie sees the state where an accident occurred as having an interest in allowing a non-resident injured there to recover, because in the absence of such recovery, the non-resident might be unable to pay medical and hospital bills owed to resident creditors or might become a public charge. This interest is deemed to be present in every case where a non-resident is injured in the forum, and it would not matter in the particular case that the non-resident was immediately removed to a hospital in his home state. *The Constitution and the Choice of Law: Governmental Interests and the Judicial Function*, in Currie, *supra* note 1, at 205, 366–75 (article originally published at 26 U. Chi. L. Rev. 9 (1958)).

inarily the existence or non-existence of a governmental interest should be helpful at this juncture.

In *Milliken* [125 Mass. 374 (1878)], a Massachusetts married woman entered into a contract with a Maine creditor in Maine, by which she agreed to stand surety for the debt of her husband. The contract was valid in Maine, but would have been void in Massachusetts by reason of that state's statute protecting married women from liability on such contracts. In analyzing the policies and interests of the involved states, Currie first asked whom Massachusetts was intending to protect when it chose to subordinate its general policy of enforcing contracts to a specific policy of shielding married women from liability on surety contracts for the debts of their husbands. Since the Massachusetts legislature would not presume to decide whether married women from Maine or any other state needed such protection, the women with whose welfare it was concerned were obviously Massachusetts married women. Thus, Massachusetts had an interest in applying its law to implement its protective policy for the benefit of a Massachusetts married woman irrespective of where the creditor resided or where the contract was made. Maine's policy, on the other hand, was to promote security of transactions, and Maine had an interest in applying that policy for the benefit of the Maine creditor. Thus, in *Milliken* each involved state had an interest in applying its law in order to implement the policy reflected by that law.

In *Grant v. McAuliffe* [41 Cal. 2d 859, 264 P.2d 944 (1953)], a California victim and a California tortfeasor were involved in an Arizona accident in which the tortfeasor died. Under California law, the cause of action survived the death of the tortfeasor; under Arizona law it did not. The policy behind the California rule obviously was to protect the victim and to prefer the victim's interest over the interest of the tortfeasor's estate. As Currie put it: "California has an interest in the application of its law and policy whenever the injured person is one toward whom California has a governmental responsibility." This interest would extend to a California plaintiff injured in Arizona. In discussing the Arizona rule of non-survival of actions, Currie emphasizes the need to determine a rational policy. He deemed the legislative motivation—inertia or response to the pressures of the insurance lobby, for example—irrelevant in determining a state's policy for purposes of interest analysis: "The business of courts in conflict-of-law cases is not to judge the policies of the states, but to ascertain them and give them effect, so far as possible, when there is a legitimate basis for effectuating them." Currie found the most rational policy basis for the Arizona rule to be that the "living should not be mulcted for the wrongs of the dead." Another possible policy would be protecting the decedent's insurer from liability whenever the insured died in the accident. In any event the policy behind the Arizona law protects those interested in the estate of the decedent and, we will assume, insurers of Arizona drivers. Since the deceased was a California domiciliary, and the automobile was insured in California, the policy reflected in Arizona law would not be advanced by its application in this case. Thus, only California has an interest in applying its law.

The preliminary determination of the policies and interests of the involved states leads to a particular case's falling into one of four "interest situations": (1) the false conflict, (2) the apparent conflict, (3) the true conflict, and (4) the unprovided-for case. Each will be defined and discussed separately.

A. *The False Conflict*

When a consideration of the policies and interests of the involved states leads to the conclusion that one state has an interest in having its law applied on the point in issue while the other state does not, the false conflict is presented. In such a situation Currie advocates application of the law of the only interested state. The false conflict appears most frequently in accident cases such as *Grant v. McAuliffe*, where two parties from a recovery state are involved in an accident in a non-recovery state. In such cases, the policy of the recovery state will be advanced by the application of its law, while the non-recovery state generally will have no interest in applying its law. It is here that the place of the wrong rule of the traditional approach produces a clearly unsound result, since it requires the application of the law of the state that has no interest in having its law applied to the detriment of the interest of the state that does. And it was in such a case that the revolution in choice of law began. This breakthrough has resulted in the widespread abandonment of the traditional approach in favor of "modern solutions." Most commentators and courts agree with Currie on resolution of the false conflict: It should be resolved by applying the law of the only interested state, whether the interested state is the forum or another state.

B. *The Apparent Conflict*

When Currie looked to the interests of the involved states, his initial inquiry was directed to whether each state had a possible or hypothetical interest: Might the policy behind a state's law be advanced if it were applied on the point in issue? If each state had a possible interest, the case presented an apparent conflict. In such a situation Currie said that the court should reexamine the respective policies and interests of the involved states and ask whether a more moderate and restrained interpretation of the policy or interests of one of the states could avoid the conflict. As he put it, "There is room for restraint and enlightenment in the determination of what state policy is and where state interests lie." If the court concludes that a more moderate and restrained interpretation of the policy or interest of one state can avoid the conflict, there is, in effect, a false conflict, calling for application of the law of the only state found to have an interest.

C. *The True Conflict*

Where a reconsideration of the policies and interests of the involved states persuades the court that the conflict cannot be avoided by a more moderate and restrained interpretation of the policy or interest of one state, the case presents the true conflict. Such was the situation in *Milliken v. Pratt*. Massachusetts' policy of protecting a married women from overreaching on the part of their husbands was implicated, notwithstanding that the contract was entered into in Maine with a Maine creditor. Likewise, Maine's policy of promoting security of transactions was implicated, notwithstanding that the defendant was a resident of Massachusetts. In Curries's words, "Each state has a policy, expressed in its law, and each state has a legitimate interest, because of its relationship to one of the parties, in applying its law and policy to the determination of the case."[48]

Currie emphasizes that the traditional approach (or for that matter, any rules approach), would resolve the conflict of interests by the application of a rule which would be based, in one degree or another, on the factual contacts the transaction had with the involved states. Apart from his view that factual contacts are simply not "rational" criteria to resolve a conflict of interests, Currie objects to any resolution of the true conflict in which the forum sacrifices its own policy and interest. Whether it does so by the application of a rule or by an "assessment of the respective values of the competing legitimate interests of two sovereign states, in order to determine which is to prevail," a court performing the judicial function cannot, in Currie's view, prefer the interest of another state to its own. Therefore, in the case of the true conflict, Currie maintains that the forum must advance its own policy and interest and apply its own law.

Built into Currie's methodology, then, is the premise that the result may differ depending on where suit is brought, as it clearly will in the true conflict situation. Such differences are unavoidable, says Currie; if uniformity is to be achieved and the interest of one state is to be sacrificed in favor of another, it must be done by Congress in the exercise of its powers under the full faith and credit clause.

D. *The Unprovided-For Case*

Analysis of the policies and interests of the involved states may lead to the conclusion that neither state has an interest in having its law applied on the point in issue. Currie calls this situation the "unprovided-for case," unprovided-for because the analysis of the policies and interests of the involved states does not by itself lead to a solution. Such cases will arise because, as Currie noted, "[d]ifferent laws do not necessarily mean conflicting policies, when it is remembered that the scope of policy is limited by the legitimate interests of the respective states." He uses as an example of the unprovided-for case a *Grant v. McAuliffe* variation in which an Arizona plaintiff is injured in Arizona by a California defendant. California's policy is to protect accident victims, but it has no interest in applying this policy in favor of an Arizona plaintiff injured in Arizona by a California defendant. Arizona's policy is to protect the estates of deceased tortfeasors and their insurers; it has no interest in applying that policy in the case of a California tortfeasor. Thus neither state cares what happens, and it is necessary to go beyond the policies and interests reflected in the differing laws to decide which law should be applied.

---

48. *Married Women's Contracts: A Study in Conflict-of-Laws Method*, in CURRIE, *supra* note 1 at 107–08 (article originally published at 25 U. CHI. L. REV. 227 (1958)). The true conflict would also be presented in Currie's variation of *Grant v. McAuliffe*, where an Arizona tortfeasor injured a California plaintiff in California. *Id.* at 148–49. Whenever a recovery state plaintiff is injured by a non-recovery state defendant, a true conflict is necessarily presented. Both states are interested in applying their law on the recovery question, since the consequences of allowing or denying recovery will be felt in the parties' home states irrespective of where the accident occurred.

Currie did not fully develop solutions for the unprovided-for case. Rather, he discussed it primarily in the context of unconstitutional discrimination, *i.e.*, whether it was unconstitutional for a state to refuse to extend the benefit of its law to a nonresident party. Currie's approach [is] bereft of fully-developed solutions for this interest situation. * * *

[B] False Conflicts

Hurtado v. Superior Court

Supreme Court of California
11 Cal. 3d 574, 114 Cal. Rptr. 106, 522 P.2d 666 (1974)

SULLIVAN, JUSTICE.

In this proceeding, petitioner Manuel Cid Hurtado seeks a writ of mandate directing respondent superior court to vacate its ruling that the applicable measure of damages in the underlying action for wrongful death was that prescribed by California law without any maximum limitation, rather than that prescribed by the law of Mexico which limits the amounts of recovery. We have concluded that the trial court correctly chose the law of California. We deny the writ.

Real parties in interest, the widow and children of Antonio Hurtado (hereafter plaintiffs) commenced against Manuel Hurtado and Jack Rexius (hereafter defendants) the underlying action for damages for wrongful death, arising out of an automobile accident occurring in Sacramento County on January 19, 1969. Plaintiffs' decedent was riding in an automobile owned and operated by his cousin, defendant Manuel Hurtado. Defendant Hurtado's vehicle, while being driven along a two-lane paved road, collided with a pick-up truck, owned and operated by defendant Rexius, which was parked partially on the side of the road and partially on the pavement on which defendant Hurtado was driving. Upon impact, the truck in turn collided with an automobile parked in front of it owned by Rexius and occupied by his son. Decedent died as a result of the collision.

At all material times plaintiffs were, and now are residents and domiciliaries of the State of Zacatecas, Mexico. Decedent, at the time of the accident, was also a resident and domiciliary of the same place and was in California temporarily and only as a visitor. All three vehicles involved in the accident were registered in California; Manuel Hurtado, Jack Rexius and the latter's son were all residents of California. Both defendants denied liability.

Defendant Hurtado moved respondent court for a separate trial of the issue whether the measure of damages was to be applied according to the law of California or the law of Mexico. The motion was granted and at the ensuing trial of this issue the court took judicial notice (Evid. Code, §§ 452, 453) of the relevant Mexican law prescribing a maximum limitation of damages for wrongful death. As a result it was established that the maximum amount recoverable under Mexican law would be 24,334 pesos or $1,946.72 at the applicable exchange rate of 12.5 pesos to the dollar. After submission of the issue on briefs, the trial court announced its intended decision (Cal. Rules of Court, rule 232) and filed a memorandum opinion, ruling in substance that it would apply a measure of damages in accordance with California law and not Mexican law. Defendant Hurtado then sought a writ of mandate in the Court of Appeal to compel the trial court to vacate its ruling and to issue a ruling that Mexico's limitation of damages for wrongful death be applied. The Court of Appeal granted an alternative writ and thereafter issued a peremptory writ of mandate so directing the trial court. We granted a hearing in this court upon the petition of plaintiffs.

It is clear that mandate is an appropriate remedy to review the proceedings below. "Although it is well established that mandamus cannot be issued to control a court's discretion, in unusual circumstances the writ will lie where, under the facts, that discretion can be exercised in only one way." (*Babb v. Superior Court* (1971) 3 Cal. 3d 841, 851 [92 Cal. Rptr. 179, 479 P.2d 379]; *Mannheim v. Superior Court* (1970) 3 Cal. 3d 678, 685 [91 Cal. Rptr. 585, 478 P.2d 17]; ...) Here the facts have been stipulated to and are not in dispute. The sole issue is a question of law as to which measure of damages should be applied. The trial court is under a legal duty to apply the proper law and may be directed to perform that duty by writ of mandate. The absence of another adequate remedy was determined by the Court of Appeal when it granted the alternative writ.

In the landmark opinion authored by former Chief Justice Traynor for a unanimous court in *Reich v. Purcell* (1967) 67 Cal. 2d 551 [63 Cal. Rptr. 31, 432 P.2d 727] (*see* Symposium, *Comments on Reich v. Purcell* (1968) 15 UCLA L. Rev. 551-654), we renounced the prior rule, adhered to by courts for many years, that in tort actions the law of the place of the wrong was the applicable law in a California forum regardless of the issues before the court. We adopted in its place a rule requiring an analysis of the respective interests of the states involved (governmental interest approach) the objective of which is "to determine the law that most appropriately applies to the issue involved." (*Reich v. Purcell, supra,* at p. 554.)[2]

The issue involved in the matter before us is the measure of damages in the underlying action for wrongful death. Two states or governments are implicated: (1) California—the place of the wrong, the place of defendants' domicile and residence, and the forum; and (2) Mexico—the domicile and residence of both plaintiffs and their decedent.

The fact that two states are involved does not in itself indicate that there is a "conflict of laws" or "choice of law" problem. (Comment, *False Conflicts,* 55 Cal. L. Rev. 74, 76; Cavers, *The Choice of Law Process* (1965) pp. 89–90.) There is obviously no prob-

---

2. "The forum must search to find the proper law to apply based upon the interests of the litigants and the involved states." (*Reich v. Purcell, supra,* 67 Cal. 2d at p. 553.) The governmental interests approach is applicable not only to situations involving multistate contacts but also to those involving a state of the United States vis-a-vis a political entity of a foreign country.

lem where the laws of the two states are identical. Here, however, the laws of California and Mexico are not identical. Mexico limits recovery by the survivors of the decedent in a wrongful death action to 24,334 pesos [$1,946.72]. California provides that the heirs of the decedent are entitled to recover such sum, as under all the circumstances of the case, will be just compensation for the pecuniary loss which each heir has suffered by reason of the death of the decedent. * * *

Although the two potentially concerned states have different laws, there is still no problem in choosing the applicable rule of law where only one of the states has an interest in having its law applied. "When one of two states related to a case has a legitimate interest in the application of its law and policy and the other has none, there is no real problem; clearly the law of the interested state should be applied." (Currie, *Selected Essays on Conflicts of Laws* (1963) p. 189.)

The interest of a state in a tort rule limiting damages for wrongful death is to protect defendants from excessive financial burdens or exaggerated claims. As stated in *Reich* this interest "to avoid the imposition of excessive financial burdens on [defendants] ... is also primarily local." (*Reich v. Purcell, supra*, at p. 556; ...); that is, a state by enacting a limitation on damages is seeking to protect its residents from the imposition of these excessive financial burdens. Such a policy "does to reflect a preference that widows and orphans should be denied full recovery." (Cavers, *op. cit. supra*, at p. 151.) Since it is the plaintiffs and not the defendants who are the Mexican residents in this case, Mexico has no interest in applying its limitation of damages — Mexico has no defendant residents to protect and has no interest in denying full recovery to its residents injured by non-Mexican defendants.

As the forum, California "can only apply its own law" (*Reich v. Purcell, supra*, at p. 553). When the forum undertakes to resolve a choice-of-law problem presented to it by the litigants, it does not choose between foreign law and its own law, but selects the appropriate rule of decision for the forum to apply as its law to the case before it. (*Reich v. Purcell, supra*, at p. 553.) Therefore, when the forum state undertakes its "search to find the proper law to apply based upon the interests of the litigants and the involved states" (*Reich v. Purcell, supra*, at p. 553), it is understood that "[n]ormally, even in cases involving foreign elements, the court should be expected, as a matter of course, to apply the rule of decision found in the law of the forum." (Currie, *op. cit. supra*, at p. 183.) "Only 'when it is suggested that the law of a foreign state should furnish the rule of decision' must the forum determine the governmental policy of its own and the suggested foreign laws, preparatory to assessing whether either or both states have an interest in applying their policy to the case." (Kay, *Comments on Reich v. Purcell*, 15 UCLA L. Rev. 584, 585.) In short, generally speaking the forum will apply its own rule of decision unless a party litigant timely invokes the law of a foreign state. In such event he must demonstrate that the latter rule of decision will further the interest of the foreign state and therefore that it is an appropriate one for the forum to apply to the case before it.

In the case at bench, California as the forum should apply its own measure of damages for wrongful death, unless Mexico has an interest in having its measure of damages applied. Since, as we have previously explained, Mexico has no interest whatsoever in the application of its limitation of damages rule to the instant case, we conclude that the trial court correctly chose California law.

To recapitulate, we hold that where as here in a California action both this state as the forum and a foreign state (or country) are potentially concerned in a question of choice of law with respect to an issue in tort and it appears that the foreign state (or country) has no interest whatsoever in having its own law applied, California as the forum should apply California law. Since this was done, we deny the writ.

Nevertheless, although our holding disposes of the mandamus proceeding before us, we deem it advisable to consider the argument addressed by defendant to the interest of California in applying its measure of damages for wrongful death. We do this because the argument reflects a serious misreading of *Reich* which apparently has not been confined to the parties before us.

First, defendant contends that California has no interest in applying its measure of damages in this case because *Reich v. Purcell, supra,* determined that the interest of a state in the law governing damages in wrongful death actions is "in determining the distribution of proceeds to the beneficiaries and that interest extends only to local decedents and beneficiaries." Decedent and plaintiffs were residents of Mexico and not "local decedents and beneficiaries" in California. Therefore, so the argument runs, California has *no* interest whatever in how plaintiff survivors, residents of Mexico, should be compensated for the wrongful death of their decedent, also a resident of Mexico, and conversely Mexico *does* have an interest.

Defendant's reading of *Reich* is inaccurate. It confuses two completely independent state interests: (1) the state interest involved in *creating* a cause of action for wrongful death so as to provide *some* recovery; and (2) the state interest involved in *limiting* the *amount* of that recovery. In *Reich* this court carefully separated these two state interests, although it referred to them in the same paragraph. The state interest in creating a cause of action for wrongful death is in "determining the distribution of proceeds to the beneficiaries";[4] the state interest in limiting damage is "to avoid the imposition of excessive financial burdens on them [defendants]...."[5] (*Reich v. Purcell, supra,* at p. 556.)

In the case at bench, the entire controversy revolves about the choice of an appropriate rule of decision on the issue of the proper *measure* of damages; there is no

---

4. "Wrongful death statutes create causes of action in specified beneficiaries and distribute the proceeds to those beneficiaries. The proceeds in the hands of the beneficiaries are not distributed through the decedent's estate and, therefore, are not subject to the claims of the decedent's creditors and consequently do not provide a fund for local creditors. Accordingly, the interest of a state in a wrongful death action insofar *as plaintiffs* are concerned is in determining the distribution of proceeds to the beneficiaries and that interest extends only to local decedents and beneficiaries." (*Reich v. Purcell, supra,* at p. 556, italics added.)

5. "Missouri's limitation on damages expresses an additional concern *for defendants,* however, in that it operates to avoid the imposition of excessive financial burdens on them. That concern is also primarily local." (*Reich v. Purcell, supra,* at p. 556; italics added.)

contention that plaintiffs are not entitled under the applicable rules of decision to *some* recovery in wrongful death. The Mexican rule is a rule limiting damages. Thus, the interest of Mexico at stake is one aimed at protecting resident defendants in wrongful death actions and, as previously explained, is inapplicable to this case, because defendants are not Mexican residents. Mexico's interest in limiting damages is not concerned with providing compensation for decedent's beneficiaries. It is Mexico's interest in creating wrongful death actions which is concerned with distributing proceeds to the beneficiaries and that issue has not been raised in the case at bench.

The creation of wrongful death actions "insofar as plaintiffs are concerned" is directed toward compensating decedent's beneficiaries. California does not have this interest in applying its wrongful death statute here because plaintiffs are residents on Mexico. However, the creation of wrongful death actions is not concerned solely with plaintiffs. As to defendants the state interest in creating wrongful death actions is to deter conduct. We made this clear in *Reich*: "Missouri [as the place of wrong] is concerned with conduct within her borders and as to such conduct she has the predominant interest of the states involved." We went on to observe that the predominant interest of the state of the place of the wrong in conduct was not in rules concerning the *limitation* of damages: "Limitations of damages for wrongful death, however, have little or nothing to do with conduct. They are concerned not with how people should behave but with how survivors should be compensated." Since it was not involved in *Reich*, we left implicit in our conclusion the proposition that the predominant interest of the state of the place of the wrong in conduct is in the creation of a cause of action for wrongful death.

It is manifest that one of the primary purposes of a state in creating a cause of action in the heirs for the wrongful death of the decedent is to deter the kind of conduct within its borders which wrongfully takes life. It is also abundantly clear that a cause of action for wrongful death without any limitation as to the amount of recoverable damages strengthens the deterrent aspect of the civil sanction: "the sting of unlimited recovery ... more effectively penalize[s] the culpable defendant and deter[s] it and others similarly situated from such future conduct." (Seidelson [*The Wrongful Death Action*, 10 Duquesne L. Rev. 525 (1972)], at p. 528, fn. 12.) Therefore when the defendant is a resident of California and the tortious conduct giving rise to the wrongful death action occurs here, California's deterrent policy of full compensation is clearly advanced by application of its own law. This is precisely the situation in the case at bench. California has a decided interest in applying its own law to California defendants who allegedly caused wrongful death within its borders. On the other hand, a state which prescribes a limitation on the measure of damages modifies the sanction imposed by a countervailing concern to protect local defendants against excessive financial burdens for the conduct sought to be deterred.

It is important, therefore to recognize the three distinct aspects of a cause of action for wrongful death: (1) compensation for survivors, (2) deterrence of conduct and (3) limitation, or lack thereof, upon the damages recoverable. *Reich v. Purcell* recognizes that all three aspects are primarily local in character. The first aspect, insofar as *plaintiffs* are concerned, reflects the state's interest in providing for compensation and in determining the distribution of the proceeds, said interest extending only to local decedents and local beneficiaries (*see* fn. 4, *ante*); the second, insofar as *defendants* are concerned, reflects the state's interest in deterring conduct, said interest extending to all persons present within its borders; the third, insofar as *defendants* are concerned, reflects the state's interest in protecting resident defendants from excessive financial burdens. In making a choice of law, these three aspects of wrongful death must be carefully separated. The key step in this process is delineating the issue to be decided. * * *

Defendant's final contention is that California has no interest in extending to out-of-state residents greater rights than are afforded by the state of residence.... Defendant urges seemingly as an absolute choice of law principle that plaintiffs in wrongful death actions are not entitled to recover more than they would have recovered under the law of the state of their residence. In effect defendant argues that the state of plaintiffs' residence has an overriding interest in denying their own residents unlimited recovery.

Limitations of damages express no such state interest. A policy of limiting recovery in wrongful death actions "does not reflect a preference that widows and orphans should be denied full recovery." (Cavers, *op. cit. supra*, at p. 151.) * * *

Because Mexico has no interest in applying its limitation of damages in wrongful death actions to nonresident defendants or in denying full recovery to its resident plaintiffs, the trial court both as the forum, and as an interested state, correctly looked to its own law.

The alternative writ of mandate is discharged and the petition for a peremptory writ is denied.

Notes and Questions Regarding *Hurtado* and False Conflicts

(1) The California Supreme Court first explicitly adopted the "government interest analysis" in *Reich v. Purcell*, 67 Cal. 2d 551, 63 Cal. Rptr. 31, 432 P.2d 727 (1967), a tort case, although it implicitly applied an interest analysis in even earlier contract cases. *See, e.g., Bernkrant v. Fowler*, 55 Cal. 2d 588, 12 Cal. Rptr. 266, 360 P.2d 906 (1961).

In *Reich v. Purcell, supra*, the facts were as follows. Plaintiff Reich and his family, residents of Ohio, were involved in an automobile collision with a car driven by defendant Purcell, a resident and domiciliary of California who was on his way to a vacation in Illinois. The head-on collision took place in Missouri, and resulted in the death of plaintiff's wife and child. Plaintiff Reich then sued defendant Purcell for wrongful death in a California court. Missouri, the place of the collision, limited wrongful death recovery to $25,000. California and Ohio had no limitation on wrongful death damages. The issue before the California Supreme Court was which state's laws—Ohio, Missouri, or California-governed the limitation of damages issue.

What interest did California have in *Reich*? Missouri? Ohio? Was there a "false conflict" on this damage limitation issue, within the meaning of *Hurtado*, between the laws of Missouri on the one hand and Ohio on the other? What type of conflict was there between the laws of California and Ohio on this issue? Between the laws of California and Missouri?

(2) *Reich* and *Hurtado* are referred to as "false conflicts" cases. Isn't the California wrongful death law different from Mexico's in *Hurtado*, and isn't Ohio's different from Missouri's in *Reich*? Not only are these laws different, but aren't they in conflict on the issue of damage limitations? Then why are these cases considered examples of "false conflicts"?

(3) Over what issue was there a conflict in *Reich* and *Hurtado*? What about the underlying liability issue in each case? Should the court in *Reich* apply Ohio, Missouri, or California negligence law to the question of liability? Should the court in *Hurtado* apply California's or Mexico's negligence law on liability? Why? The court did not focus on this liability issue in *Reich* and *Hurtado*, and expressed no particular concern over the issue. Why do you suppose this was not a significant issue to the parties in *Reich* and *Hurtado*? Might it be a very significant issue today, under current negligence doctrine?

(4) Would the choice-of-law determination have been the same in *Reich* if California had a limitation on wrongful death damages, but Missouri and Ohio had no limitation? What law would the court apply to the damages issue in such a hypothetical case? Do *Reich* and *Hurtado* provide a method of resolving this hypothetical?

(5) Would the choice-of-law determination in *Hurtado* have been the same if the plaintiffs were residents of California and the defendants residents of Mexico, but the accident still occurred in California? What interest would California have in such a case? Mexico? Would this still be a "false conflict" case?

(6) By what method does the California Supreme Court in *Reich* and *Hurtado* ascertain the "interests" of the respective states with respect to the damage limitation issue? Are you confident that the court engaged in an exhaustive examination of the possible state interests? Can you think of other legitimate state interests each state may have with respect to this issue? For example, in *Hurtado* what interest does California have in *not* applying its rule of unlimited recovery against a California driver, undoubtedly insured by a California insurance company, sued in wrongful death by a Mexico (or a Missouri) plaintiff?

(7) How easy is it to ascertain a state's "interest" in a particular law when applied to a specific issue? Where does one look to find an expression of a state's interest? The legislative history of the law, if it is a statute? And what if the state's law is purely judge-made? Who determines what the state's interest is? Do you see any problems here? Consider Professor Brainerd Currie's comments on this point, which first appeared in his *Notes on Methods and Objectives in the Conflict of Laws*, 1959 DUKE L.J. 171, 178 (1959):

> This process [of determining the governmental policy and interest expressed in a law] is essentially the familiar one of construction and interpretation. Just as we determine by that process how a statute applies in time, and how

it applies to marginal domestic situations, so we may determine how it should be applied to cases involving foreign elements in order to effectuate the legislative purpose.

(a) Does Currie's comment address all the uncertainty concerns generated by this purposive approach? Does the familiar constructive process usually reveal only one policy reflected in a law, or sometimes multiple policies? A clear state interest reflected in a law, or a balance or compromise of various interests? Does this not invite a court, as Professor Reese once observed, to "decide first what rule it wishes to apply and to ascribe to that rule a purpose that makes its application appropriate while ascribing at the same time to the potentially applicable rules of other states purposes that would not be furthered by their application"? Willis L.M. Reese, *Chief Judge Fuld and Choice of Law*, 71 COLUM. L. REV. 548, 559–60 (1971) ("Another unfortunate consequence of a pure interest approach is the opportunity that it affords for judicial masquerading").

(b) Other scholars have similarly criticized this aspect of Currie's interest analysis. *See, e.g.*, Joseph William Singer, *Facing Real Conflicts*, 24 CORNELL INT'L L.J. 197, 219–20 (1991) (observing because multiple purposes can plausibly be attributed to most laws, courts have the impetus to resolve the case by finding a false conflict if they can); Lea Brilmayer, *Interest Analysis and the Myth of Legislative Intent*, 78 MICH. L. REV. 392, 405 (1980) (arguing attribution of an interest to a law is unrealistic and reflects arbitrary judicial preferences). Are these criticisms valid? Overstated? With this criticism in mind, consider the analysis in *Hernandez v. Burger*, discussed below.

(8) In *Hernandez v. Burger*, 102 Cal. App. 3d 795, 162 Cal. Rptr. 564 (1980), the plaintiff, a resident and citizen of Mexico, suffered personal injuries when he was struck by a car driven and owned by the defendants. The accident took place in Baja California, Mexico. The defendants were California residents and U.S. citizens. Plaintiff brought suit for damages against defendants in California, and argued that California's unlimited law of tort recovery applied to the issue of damages. Defendant argued that Mexico's rule of damages applied, which would limit plaintiff's recovery to a $2,000 maximum.

Plaintiff argued that Mexico's only interest in applying its limitation of damages law is to protect resident defendants against overwhelming economic burdens, citing *Reich* and *Hurtado*. And because defendants were not residents of Mexico but of California, Mexico had no legitimate interest in applying its damage limitation law to the case.

The court rejected plaintiff's arguments, and decided that Mexico's law applies. First, the court found that California's deterrent policy of full compensation did not apply because the wrongful conduct took place in Mexico, not California. Further, because plaintiff is a resident of Mexico, California has no legitimate concern in extending its unlimited damages rule to plaintiff to avoid his becoming a ward of California. Consequently, California has no interest at all in applying its law of damages to the case.

Next, the court determined that Mexico did have an interest in applying its limited damages law to the case, even though the defendants were not residents of Mexico. The court took judicial notice that a major industry in Baja California is tourism emanating from the United States, particularly California. "Fostering tourism in Baja California is, of course, a legitimate interest of Mexico and application of Mexico's limited damages law to nonresident motorists might well advance that interest." *Hernandez*, 102 Cal. App. 3d at 802.

The court then concluded that the case was one of "false conflict," with only Mexico having an interest in applying its law of damages. The court dismissed plaintiff's reliance on *Hurtado* and *Reich* as follows:

> Plaintiff relies on discussions in both *Hurtado* and *Reich* in which it was indicated that the primary interest a jurisdiction has in limiting damages in wrongful death actions is the protection of resident defendants against excessive or oppressive economic liability. (*See Hurtado v. Superior Court, supra,* 11 Cal. 3d at pp. 582–583, 586; *Reich v. Purcell, supra,* 67 Cal. 2d at p. 556.) That was, of course, true in those cases. In *Hurtado* the accident occurred in California, not in Mexico, and Mexico could have no legitimate interest in affecting the conduct of California residents in California.

> Similarly, although the accident in *Reich* occurred in Missouri, the court held that Missouri had no significant interest in applying its law limiting recovery of damages in wrongful death cases because no recovery for wrongful death in that case would have any effect whatever on Missouri. The defendant was a California resident on his way to vacation in Illinois; the decedent and the plaintiffs were residents of Ohio. The court reasoned: "That concern [avoiding the imposition of excessive financial burdens on defendants] is also primarily local and we fail to perceive any substantial interest Missouri might have in extending the benefits of its limitation of damages to travelers from states having no similar limitation. Defendant's liability should not be limited when no party to the action is from a state limiting liability and when defendant, therefore, would have secured insurance, if any, without any such limit in mind. A defendant cannot reasonably complain when compensatory damages are assessed in accordance with the law of his domicile and plaintiffs receive no more than they would had they been injured at home." (67 Cal. 2d at p. 556.)

> The reasoning of the *Reich* court points up the fundamental differences between the circumstances in that case and those in the case at bench. Here one party, plaintiff, *is* a resident of a jurisdiction limiting liability; here, plaintiff *was* injured at home; and here, plaintiff *would* recover more than he would at home if the law of Mexico were not applied. As to the consideration of insurance, even if we assume that defendants were insured for liability arising out of an accident in Mexico, it is most likely that the coverage afforded by such insurance and the premium paid therefor were fixed with the Mexican limited damages law in mind.

> We recognize that *Hurtado* and *Reich* distinguished the policies or interests involved in the creation of a cause of action (compensating resident plaintiffs)

from the policies or interests involved in the adoption of a rule limiting the amount of damages recoverable (protecting resident defendants from excessive financial burdens). (*Hurtado v. Superior Court, supra*, 11 Cal. 3d at pp. 582–583, 586; *Reich v. Purcell, supra*, 67 Cal. 2d at p. 556.) However, where a jurisdiction, here Mexico, is interested both in the fact that the accident occurred within its borders *and* in the fact that the person seeking compensation is a resident of that jurisdiction, we do not believe the interest of the state in creating a cause of action or recognizing a right to recover damages in the first instance can be totally divorced from its concurrent interest in limiting the amount of damages recoverable. It may well be that no cause of action would have been recognized had the amount of damages recoverable not been limited. Here, for example, Mexico's recognition of a right to damages and its limitation of the amount recoverable in all likelihood reflect a balancing and accommodation of competing interests based on the societal values and economic and commercial circumstances prevailing in Mexico. Thus, in this case it cannot be said that Mexico's law limiting the amount of damages recoverable is entirely unrelated to her interest in affecting conduct in Mexico.

We conclude that the interest of Mexico in the application of its law limiting damages to an accident occurring within its borders resulting in injury to one of its residents caused by a nonresident defendant is not wholly lacking; that the State of California has no interest whatever in applying its unlimited damages law to such a case; and that the trial court was correct in determining that the law of Mexico should be applied to limit plaintiff's damages in this instance.

Accordingly, the judgment is affirmed.

(a) Are you persuaded by the Court of Appeal's reasoning that *Reich* and *Hurtado* are distinguishable from the circumstances in *Hernandez*, and that this factual distinction justifies a different interest analysis outcome? What is your reaction to the *Hernandez* court's finding that Mexico's damage limitation advances the interest of tourism by Californians in Baja Mexico? Precisely how is Mexico's damage limitation law related to Mexico's interest of affecting conduct in Mexico?

(b) Assuming Missouri has an interest in encouraging tourism in the "show me" state, does this mean that *Reich* was not a false conflicts case because both Missouri (limited damages) and Ohio (unlimited damages) had an interest in applying their law? Assume the accident in *Hernandez* took place in a state of Mexico which has no interest in advancing American tourism. Would the *Hernandez* court have reached the same choice-of-law conclusion? Should it?

(c) The *Hernandez* case has been criticized as one where the court should have found that neither Mexico nor California had an interest in applying its respective damages law to the case. *See* Harold L. Korn, *The Choice-of-Law Revolution: A Critique*, 83 COLUM. L. REV. 772, 936 (1983). This would mean, using Professor Brainerd Currie's interest analysis terminology, that *Hernandez* actually represents an "unprovided-for case." Do you agree?

(9) How would Currie resolve a choice of law issue in an "unprovided-for case"? *See* Brainerd Currie, *The Disinterested Third State*, 28 L. & Contemp. Probs. 754, 775–80 (1963). How would the California Supreme Court resolve such an issue? The "unprovided-for case" (or "zero interest case") presents one of the most difficult problems for government interest analysts, and is a rich source of scholarly examination. *E.g.*, Larry Kramer, *The Myth of the Unprovided-For Case*, 75 Va. L. Rev. 1045 (1989) (concluding that there are no unprovided-for cases in the Currie sense); Brainerd Currie, *Selected Essays on Conflicts of Laws*, 545–57 (1963); Robert Sedler, *Interstate Accidents and the Unprovided for Case: Reflections on Neumeier v. Kuehner*, 1 Hofstra L. Rev. 125 (1973); Sedler, *The Governmental Interest Approach to Choice of Law*, *supra*, 25 UCLA L. Rev. at 189–90, 233–36.

(10) Would the choice-of-law determination in *Reich* and *Hurtado* be different if California still followed the First Restatement? Would it be different if California followed "the most significant relationship test" of the Second Restatement? Under § 145(2) of the Second Restatement, the state with the most significant contacts with respect to an issue in tort is determined by considering, in addition to the general factors mentioned in § 6 (reproduced *supra*), the following contacts:

(a) the place where the injury occurred,

(b) the place where the conduct causing the injury occurred,

(c) the domicile, residence, nationality, place of incorporation and place of business of the parties, and

(d) the place where the relationship, if any, between the parties is centered.

These contacts are to be evaluated according to their relative importance with respect to the particular issue.

(11) If the damage limitation issue had not been raised by the defendants in *Reich* and *Hurtado*, which state's law would govern the calculation of damages in those two cases? Why?

(12) Did the Supreme Court in *Hurtado* give any special treatment to the choice-of-law issues because the case involved the laws of another country, not simply of another state? Should the case have been treated differently? *See Wong v. Tenneco, Inc.*, 39 Cal. 3d 126, 216 Cal. Rptr. 412, 702 P.2d 570 (1985).

[C] True Conflicts

Reich and *Hurtado* both involved "false conflicts." As those cases illustrate, the California choice-of-law doctrine results in application of the law of the interested state, whether the interested state is the forum or another state. But what happens when two or more states do have an interest in having their laws applied to an issue in a case, and their laws are very different?

Bernhard v. Harrah's Club

Supreme Court of California

16 Cal. 3d 313, 128 Cal. Rptr. 215, 546 P.2d 719, *cert. denied*, 429 U.S. 859 (1976)

SULLIVAN, JUSTICE.

Plaintiff appeals from a judgment of dismissal entered upon an order sustaining without leave to amend the general demurrer of defendant Harrah's Club to plaintiff's first amended complaint.

Plaintiff's complaint, containing only one count, alleged in substance the following: Defendant Harrah's Club, a Nevada corporation, owned and operated gambling establishments in the State of Nevada in which intoxicating liquors were sold, furnished to the public and given away for consumption on the premises. Defendant advertised for and solicited in California the business of California residents at such establishments knowing and expecting that many California residents would use the public highways in going to and from defendant's drinking and gambling establishments.

On July 24, 1971, Fern and Philip Myers, in response to defendant's advertisements and solicitations, drove from their California residence to defendant's gambling and drinking club in Nevada, where they stayed until the early morning hours of July 25, 1971. During their stay, the Myers were served numerous alcoholic beverages by defendant's employees, progressively reaching a point of obvious intoxication rendering them incapable of safely driving a car. Nonetheless defendant continued to serve and furnish the Myers alcoholic beverages.

While still in this intoxicated state, the Myers drove their car back to California. Proceeding in a northeasterly direction on Highway 49, near Nevada City, California, the Myers' car, driven negligently by a still intoxicated Fern Myers, drifted across the center line into the lane of oncoming traffic and collided head-on with plaintiff Richard A. Bernhard, a resident of California, who was then driving his motorcycle along said highway. As a result of the collision plaintiff suffered severe injuries. Defendant's sale and furnishing of alcoholic beverages to the Myers, who were intoxicated to the point of being unable to drive safely, was negligent and was the proximate cause of the plaintiff's injuries in the ensuing automobile accident in California for which plaintiff prayed $100,000 in damages.

Defendant filed a general demurrer to the first amended complaint. In essence it was grounded on the following contentions: that Nevada law denies recovery against a tavern keeper by a third person for injuries proximately caused by the former by selling or furnishing alcoholic beverages to an intoxicated patron who inflicts the injuries on the latter; that Nevada law governed since the alleged tort was committed by defendant in Nevada; and that section 25602 of the California Business and Professions code which established the duty necessary for liability under our decision in *Vesely v. Sager* (1971) 5 Cal. 3d 153 [95 Cal. Rptr. 623, 486 P.2d 151], was inapplicable to a Nevada tavern. The trial court sustained the demurrer without leave to amend and entered a judgment of dismissal. This appeal followed.

We face a problem in the choice of law governing a tort action. As we have made clear on other occasions, we no longer adhere to the rule that the law of the place of the wrong is applicable in a California forum regardless of the issues before the court. (*Hurtado v. Superior Court* (1974) 11 Cal. 3d 574, 579 [114 Cal. Rptr. 106, 522 P.2d 666]; *Reich v. Purcell* (1967) 67 Cal. 2d 551, 555 [63 Cal. Rptr. 31, 432 P.2d 727].) Rather we have adopted in its place a rule requiring an analysis of the respective interests of the states involved—the objective of which is "'to determine the law that most appropriately applies to the issue involved.'" (*Hurtado, supra,* at pp. 579–580, quoting from *Reich, supra,* at p. 555.)

The issue involved in the case at bench is the civil liability of defendant tavern keeper to plaintiff, a third person, for injuries allegedly caused by the former by selling and furnishing alcoholic beverages in Nevada to intoxicated patrons who subsequently injured plaintiff in California. Two states are involved: (1) California-the place of plaintiff's residence and domicile, the place where he was injured, and the forum; and (2) Nevada-the place of defendant's residence and place of the wrong.

We observe at the start that the laws of the two states—California and Nevada— applicable to the issue involved are not identical. California imposes liability on tavern keepers in this state for conduct such as here alleged. In *Vesely v. Sager, supra,* 5 Cal. 3d 153, 166, this court rejected the contention that "civil liability for tavern keepers should be left to future legislative action.... First, liability has been denied in cases such as the one before us solely because of the judicially created rule that the furnishing of alcoholic beverages is not the proximate cause of injuries resulting from intoxication. As demonstrated, supra, this rule is patently unsound and totally inconsistent with the principles of proximate cause established in other areas of negligence law.... Second, the Legislature has expressed its intention in this area with the adoption of Evidence Code section 669, and Business and Professions Code section 25602.... It is clear that Business and Professions Code section 25602 [making it a misdemeanor to sell to an obviously intoxicated person] is a statute to which this presumption [of negligence, Evidence Code section 669] applies and that the policy expressed in the statute is to promote the safety of the people of California...." Nevada on the other hand refuses to impose such liability. In *Hamm v. Carson City Nuggett, Inc.* (1969) 85 Nev. 99 [450 P.2d 358, 359], the court held it would create neither common law liability nor liability based on the criminal statute banning sale of alcoholic beverages to a person who is drunk, because "if civil liability is to be imposed, it should be accomplished by legislative act after appropriate surveys, hearings, and investigations to ascertain the need for it and the expected consequences to follow." It is noteworthy that in *Ham* the Nevada court in relying on the common law rule denying liability cited our decision in *Cole v. Rush* (1955) 45 Cal. 2d 345 [289 P.2d 450], later overruled by us in *Vesely* to the extent that it was inconsistent with that decision.

Although California and Nevada, the two "involved states" (*Reich v. Purcell, supra,* 67 Cal. 2d 551, 553; *see also Hurtado v. Superior Court, supra,* 11 Cal. 3d 574, 579), have different laws governing the issue presented in the case at bench, we encounter a problem in selecting the applicable rule of law only if *both* states have an interest in having their respective laws applied. "[G]enerally speaking the forum will apply its own rule of decision unless a party litigant timely invokes the law of a foreign state. In such event he must demonstrate that the latter rule of decision will further the interest of the foreign state and therefore that it is an appropriate one for the forum to apply to the case before it. [Citations.]" (*Hurtado, supra*, at p. 581.)

Defendant contends that Nevada has a definite interest in having its rule of decision applied in this case in order to protect its resident tavern keepers like defendant from being subjected to a civil liability which Nevada has not imposed either by legislative enactment or decisional law. It is urged that in *Hamm v. Carson City Nuggett, supra*, the Supreme Court of Nevada clearly delineated the policy underlying denial of civil liability of tavern keepers who sell to obviously intoxicated patrons: "Those opposed to extending liability point out that to hold otherwise would subject the tavern owner to ruinous exposure every time he poured a drink and would multiply litigation endlessly in a claim-conscious society. Every liquor vendor visited by the patron who became intoxicated would be a likely defendant in subsequent litigation flowing from the patron's wrongful conduct.... Judicial restraint is a worthwhile practice when the proposed new doctrine may have implications far beyond the perception of the court asked to declare it. They urge that if civil liability is to be imposed, it should be accomplished by legislative act after appropriate surveys, hearings, and investigations.... We prefer this point of view." Accordingly defendant argues that the Nevada rule of decision is the appropriate one for the forum to apply.

Plaintiff on the other hand points out that California also has an interest in applying its own rule of decision to the case at bench. California imposes on tavern keepers civil liability to third parties injured by persons to whom the tavern keeper has sold alcoholic beverages when they are obviously intoxicated "for the purpose of protecting members of the general public from injuries to person and damage to property resulting from the excessive use of intoxicating liquor." (*Vesely v. Sager, supra*, 5 Cal. 3d 153, 165.) California, it is urged, has a special interest in affording this protection to all California residents injured in California.

Thus, since the case at bench involves a California resident (plaintiff) injured in this state by intoxicated drivers and a Nevada resident tavern keeper (defendant) which served alcoholic beverages to them in Nevada, it is clear that each state has an interest in the application of its respective law of liability and nonliability. It goes without saying that these interests conflict. Therefore, unlike *Reich v. Purcell, supra*, and *Hurtado v. Superior Court, supra*, where we were faced with "false conflicts," in the instant case for the first time since applying a governmental interest analysis as a choice of law doctrine in *Reich*, we are confronted with a "true" conflicts case. We must therefore determine the appropriate rule of decision in a controversy where each of the states involved has a legitimate but conflicting interest in applying its own law in respect to the civil liability of tavern keepers.

The search for the proper resolution of a true conflicts case, while proceeding within orthodox parameters of governmental interest analysis, has generated much scholarly examination and discussion.[1] The father of the governmental interest approach, Professor Brainerd Currie, originally took the position that in a true conflicts situation the law of the forum should always be applied. (Currie, *Selected Essays on Conflict of Laws* (1963) p. 184.) However, upon further reflection, Currie suggested that when under the governmental interest approach a preliminary analysis reveals an apparent conflict of interest upon the forum's assertion of its own rule of decision, the forum should reexamine its policy to determine if a more restrained interpretation of it is more appropriate. "[T]o assert a conflict between the interests of the forum and the foreign state is a serious matter; the mere fact that a suggested broad conception of the local interest will conflict with that of a foreign state is a sound reason why the conception should be reexamined, with a view to a more moderate and restrained interpretation both of the policy and of the circumstances in which it must be applied to effectuate the forum's legitimate purpose.... An analysis of this kind ... was brilliantly performed by Justice Traynor in *Bernkrant v. Fowler* (1961) 55 Cal. 2d 588 [12 Cal. Rptr. 266, 360 P.2d 906]." (Currie, *The Disinterested Third State* (1963) 28 Law & Contemp. Prob., pp. 754, 757; *see also* Sedler in *Symposium, Conflict of Laws Round Table, supra,* 49 Texas L. Rev. 211, at pp. 224–225.) This process of reexamination requires identification of a "real interest as opposed to a hypothetical interest" on the part of the forum (Sedler, *Value of Principled Preferences,* 49 Texas L. Rev. 224) and can be approached under principles of "comparative impairment." (Baxter, *Choice of Law and the Federal Systems, supra,* 16 Stan. L. Rev. 1–22; Horowitz, *The Law of Choice of Law in California-A Restatement, supra,* 21 UCLA L. Rev. 719, 748–758.)

Once this preliminary analysis has identified a true conflict of the governmental interests involved as applied to the parties under the particular circumstances of the case, the "comparative impairment" approach to the resolution of such conflict seeks to determine which state's interests would be more impaired if its policy were subordinated to the policy of the other state. This analysis proceeds on the principle that true conflicts should be resolved by applying the law of the state whose interest would be the more impaired if its law were not applied. Exponents of this process of analysis emphasize that it is very different from a weighing process. The court does not "'weigh' the conflicting governmental interests in the sense of determining which conflicting law manifested the 'better' or the 'worthier' social policy on the specific issue. An attempted balancing of conflicting state policies in that sense ... is difficult to justify in the context of a federal system in which, within constitutional limits, states are empowered to mold their policies as they wish.... [The process] can accurately be described as ... accommodation of conflicting state policies, as a problem of allocating

---

1. Baxter, *Choice of Law and the Federal System* (1963) 16 Stan. L. Rev. 1; Cavers, *The Choice of Law Process* (1965) pages 114–224; Horowitz, *The Law of Choice of Law in California-A Restatement* (1974) 21 UCLA L. Rev. 719, 748–758; *Conflict of Laws Round Table: A Symposium* (1972) 57 Iowa L. Rev. 1219–1270; *Symposium, Conflict of Laws Round Table* (1971) 49 Texas L. Rev. 211–245; Sedler, *Reviews-Conflicts Commentary* (1972) 50 Texas L. Rev. 1064–1083; Weintraub, *Commentary on the Conflict of Laws* (1971). We note that no case has been called to our attention, nor are we aware of one, which has discussed this problem in a context relevant to the case at bench.

domains of law-making power in multi-state contexts-limitations on the reach of state policies-as distinguished from evaluating the wisdom of those policies.... [E]mphasis is placed on the appropriate scope of conflicting state policies rather than on the 'quality' of those policies...." (Horowitz, *The Law of Choice of Law in California-A Restatement, supra,* 21 UCLA L. Rev. 719, 753; *see also* Baxter, *Choice of Law and the Federal System, supra,* 16 Stan. L. Rev. 1, 18–19.) However, the true function of this methodology can probably be appreciated only casuistically in its application to an endless variety of choice of law problems. (*See, e.g.,* the hypothetical situations set forth in *Baxter, op. cit.,* pp. 10–17). * * *

Mindful of the above principles governing our choice of law, we proceed to reexamine the California policy underlying the imposition of civil liability upon tavern keepers. At its broadest limits this policy would afford protection to all persons injured in California by intoxicated persons who have been sold or furnished alcoholic beverages while intoxicated regardless of where such beverages were sold or furnished. Such a broad policy would naturally embrace situations where the intoxicated actor had been provided with liquor by out-of-state tavern keepers. Although the State of Nevada does not impose such *civil* liability on its tavern keepers, nevertheless they are subject to *criminal* penalties under a statute making it unlawful to sell or give intoxicating liquor to any person who is drunk or known to be an habitual drunkard. (*See* Nev. Rev. Stats. 202.100; *see Hamm v. Carson City Nuggett, Inc., supra,* 450 P.2d 358.)

We need not, and accordingly do not here determine the outer limits to which California's policy should be extended, for it appears clear to us that it must encompass defendant, who as alleged in the complaint, "advertis[es] for and otherwise solicit [s] in California the business of California residents at defendant Harrah's Club Nevada drinking and gambling establishments, and knowing and expecting said California residents, in response to said advertising and solicitation, to use the public highways of the State of California in going and coming from defendant Harrah's Club Nevada drinking and gambling establishments." Defendant by the course of its chosen commercial practice has put itself at the heart of California's regulatory interest, namely to prevent tavern keepers from selling alcoholic beverages to obviously intoxicated persons who are likely to act in California in the intoxicated state. It seems clear that California cannot reasonably effectuate its policy if it does not extend its regulation to include out-of-state tavern keepers such as defendant who regularly and purposely sell intoxicating beverages to California residents in places and under conditions in which it is reasonably certain these residents will return to California and act therein while still in an intoxicated state. California's interest would be very significantly impaired if its policy were not applied to defendant.

Since the act of selling alcoholic beverages to obviously intoxicated persons is already proscribed in Nevada, the application of California's rule of civil liability would not impose an entirely new duty requiring the ability to distinguish between California residents and other patrons. Rather the imposition of such liability involves an increased economic exposure, which, at least for businesses which actively solicit extensive California patronage, is a foreseeable and coverable business expense.

Moreover, Nevada's interest in protecting its tavern keepers from civil liability of a boundless and unrestricted nature will not be significantly impaired when as in the instant case liability is imposed only on those tavern keepers who actively solicit California business.

Therefore, upon reexamining the policy underlying California's rule of decision and giving such policy a more restrained interpretation for the purpose of this case pursuant to the principles of the law of choice of law discussed above, we conclude that California has an important and abiding interest in applying its rule of decision to the case at bench, that the policy of this state would be more significantly impaired if such rule were not applied and that the trial court erred in not applying California law.

Defendant argues, however, that even if California law is applied, the demurrer was nonetheless properly sustained because the tavern keeper's duty stated in *Vesely v. Sager, supra,* 5 Cal. 3d 153, is based on Business and Professions Code section 25602, which is a criminal statute and thus without extraterritorial effect. * * *

It is also clear, as defendant's argument points out, that since, unlike the California vendor in *Vesely*, defendant was a Nevada resident which furnished the alcoholic beverage to the Myers in that state, the above California statute had no extraterritorial effect and that civil liability could not be posited on defendant's violation of a California criminal law. We recognize, therefore, that we cannot make the same determination as quoted above with respect to defendant that we made with respect to the defendant vendor in *Vesely*.

However, our decision in *Vesely* was much broader than defendant would have it. There, at the very outset of our opinion, we declared that the traditional common law rule denying recovery on the ground that the furnishing of alcoholic beverage is not the proximate cause of the injuries inflicted on a third person by an intoxicated individual "is patently unsound." (5 Cal. 3d at p. 157.) * * *

In sum, our opinion in *Vesely* struck down the old common law rule of nonliability constructed on the basis that the consumption, not the sale, of alcoholic beverages was the proximate cause of the injuries inflicted by the intoxicated person. Although we chose to impose liability on the *Vesely* defendant on the basis of his violating the applicable statute, the clear import of our decision was that there was no bar to civil liability under modern negligence law. Certainly, we said nothing in *Vesely* indicative of an intention to retain the former rule that an action at common law does not lie. The fact then, that in the case at bench, section 25602 of the Business and Professions Code is not applicable to this defendant in Nevada so as to warrant the imposition of civil liability on the basis of its violation, does not preclude recovery on the basis of negligence apart from the statute. Pertinent here is our observation in *Rowland v. Christian* (1968) 69 Cal. 2d 108, 118–119 [70 Cal. Rptr. 97, 104, 443 P.2d 561, 568]: "It bears repetition that the basic policy of this state set forth by the Legislature in section 1714 of the Civil Code is that everyone is responsible for an injury caused to another by his want of ordinary care or skill in the management of his property."

The judgment is reversed and the cause is remanded to the trial court with directions to overrule the demurrer and to allow defendant a reasonable time within which to answer.

Notes and Questions regarding *Bernhard* and True Conflicts

(1) What is California's interest in *Bernhard* in applying its third-party liability law? How does the California Supreme Court ascertain California's interest? What is Nevada's interest in applying its dram shop law? How does the court ascertain Nevada's interest?

(2) California and Nevada each had an interest in applying its third-party liability law to the liability issue in *Bernhard,* and each had different laws on this issue. *Bernhard* therefore is a case of "true conflicts," within the meaning of Professor Brainerd Currie's interest analysis. How would Professor Currie resolve a "true conflict"? What method did the Supreme Court adopt in *Bernhard*? Are they different methods? Would Currie's method result in a different outcome in *Bernhard*?

(3) Would the choice-of-law determination have been the same in *Bernhard* if the defendant had been a small tavern in Northeastern Nevada which did not advertise and did not know the plaintiffs were from California? If the accident had occurred in Nevada instead of California? If the lawsuit were filed in a Nevada Court and Nevada had a choice-of-law doctrine identical to California's?

(4) Would the choice-of-law determination have been the same in *Bernhard* if Nevada imposed no civil liability *or criminal penalties* on a tavern keeper who sells liquor to an intoxicated person? In 1973, Nevada did, in fact, repeal the criminal statute relied on by the Court in *Bernhard*. The California Supreme Court handed down its *Bernhard* decision in 1976, yet it made no reference to Nevada's elimination of criminal penalties on tavern keepers. Why did the Court ignore this change in Nevada's criminal law? Should the court have ignored this legislative repeal?

(5) In *Cable v. Sahara Tahoe Corp.*, 93 Cal. App. 3d 384, 155 Cal. Rptr. 770 (1979), a California resident was injured in Nevada in 1975 while riding as a passenger in a car driven by an Nevada resident who had become intoxicated at the defendant Nevada casino. Plaintiff sustained permanent injuries, and became a public charge in California. Plaintiff sued the defendant casino for damages in a California court, based on the liability theory relied on in *Bernhard*. Defendant demurred to the complaint, on the ground that Nevada third-party (non)liability law applied.

(a) Does *Cable* present a "true conflict"? What is California's interest in applying its liability law? What is Nevada's interest in applying its (non)liability law? The court in *Cable* concluded that a "true conflict" was "inescapable," *id.* at 392. Do you agree? The court then undertook a "comparative impairment" analysis, and decided that Nevada's interest would be more impaired if its law were not applied and therefore Nevada law should govern the liability issue. *Id.* at 393–398.

(b) What relevant factors explain the different "comparative impairment" result in *Cable* as opposed to *Bernhard*? That the accident occurred in Nevada instead of

California? That the intoxicated driver served by defendant was a resident of Nevada instead of California? Why should these factors make a difference? What would be the result in *Cable* if the tavern owner were also a resident of California?

(c) The Court in *Cable* noted that the California Legislature enacted a statute in 1978 which eliminated tavern keepers' liability in California, specifically abrogating the liability doctrine applied in *Bernhard*. Does this legislative repeal mean that *Cable* was a case of "no conflict"? Do you think this statutory repeal may have nevertheless influenced the court's "comparative impairment" analysis? How so?

(6) Does the court in *Bernhard, Reich,* and *Hurtado* set forth a clear choice-of-law rule which results in predictable choice-of-law determinations in a wide variety of tort cases? How would you characterize the California doctrine as to this predictability goal? Do these cases at least provide some general guidelines as to what factual factors are significant for choice of law analysis in tort cases? What are these factual factors? Are they different from the factors significant under the First Restatement? Are they likewise very different from the factors designated as significant under the Second Restatement's "most significant relationship" test in tort cases?

[D] Comparative Impairment

[1] Resolving True Conflicts

The most difficult question for scholars and courts who accept interest analysis is how to resolve "true conflicts." Professor Brainerd Currie's early interest analysis writings provided a simple resolution of "true conflicts," i.e., always apply the law of the forum state. Brainerd Currie, *Notes on Methods and Objectives in the Conflicts of Laws*, 1959 DUKE L.J. 171 (1959); Brainerd Currie, *Married Women's Contracts: A Study in Conflicts of Laws*, 25 U. CHI. L. REV. 227, 261–263 (1958). Later, Currie modified his method of resolving true conflicts by adding a new consideration which might avoid a true conflict. This new step applies where a court finds an "apparent conflict" between the interests of two states. At that point, the court should reconsider its interest analysis. A "more moderate and restrained interpretation" of the policy of one state or the other may reveal that only one state has a legitimate interest in applying its policy. In such cases, the "apparent conflict" is actually a "false conflict." *See* Robert Sedler, *The Government Interest Approach to Choice of Law*, *supra*, 25 UCLA L. REV. at 187–88.

[a] Professor Currie's Pure Interest Analysis Approach.

If upon reconsideration the court finds that a conflict between the legitimate interests of the two states is unavoidable, the court should apply the law of the forum. If the forum state is one of the two states with conflicting interests, the court should not sacrifice the legitimate interests of its own state. But even where the forum is disinterested but an unavoidable conflict exists between the laws of two other states, the court should apply the law of the forum. Therefore, even under Currie's modified interest analysis approach, a court must always resolve "true conflicts" by applying the law of the forum. *See* Brainerd Currie, *Comments on Babcock v. Jackson*, 63 COLUM. L. REV. 1233, 1242–1243 (1963).

[b] The California Approach

The California Supreme Court in *Bernhard* did not follow Professor Currie's method of resolving "true conflicts." Instead, the Court adopted the approach proposed by Professor William F. Baxter, as set forth in his article *Choice of Law and the Federal System*, 16 STAN. L. REV. 1 (1963), known as the "comparative impairment" approach. As the court states in *Bernhard*, Baxter's approach seeks to determine which state's interest would be more impaired if its policy were subordinated to the policy of the other state. This analysis proceeds on the principle that true conflicts should be resolved by applying the law of the state whose interests would be more impaired if its law were not applied.

[2] Professor Baxter's Comparative Impairment Analysis

The "comparative impairment" analysis, even though succinctly stated by the Court in *Bernhard*, is not so easy to comprehend. The following discussion from Baxter, *Choice of Law and the Federal Systems*, *supra*, may shed some light:

Choice of Law and the Federal System, by William F. Baxter
16 STAN. L. REV. 1, 8–22 (1964) (footnotes omitted)*

I disagree ... with [Professor] Currie's conclusion that [true] conflicts cases, cases in which each state has some interest in the application of its law, should ... be decided by applying the rule of the forum. The same analysis by which Currie distinguishes real from false conflicts cases can resolve real conflicts cases. The question "Will the social objective underlying the X rule be furthered by the application of the rule in cases like the present one?" need not necessarily be answered "Yes" or "No"; the answer will often be, "Yes, to some extent." The extent to which the purpose underlying a rule will be furthered by application or impaired by nonapplication to cases of a particular category may be regarded as the measure of the rule's pertinence and of the state's interest in the rule's application to cases within the category. Normative resolution of real conflicts cases is possible where one of the assertedly applicable rules is more pertinent to the case than the competing rule.

There will, of course, be cases in which the contending state interests appear to be in balance or nearly so. Borderline cases arise that thwart easy application of every principle of law, but they are decided nonetheless. The judge decides on the basis of some marginal factor and justifies his decision as best he can in his opinion. That some choice cases share this common fate seems preferable to subjecting them and many more to the law of the forum, a particularly undesirable mode of resolving choice questions. By eliminating doctrinal uniformity, a rule calling for application of the law of the forum impairs predictability in all primary situations unless it is

---

then possible to assert that litigation in more than one state will never be possible. Moreover, it introduces predictability at the secondary, or litigation, level where the disadvantages of predictability may equal its advantages. In these respects Currie's proposal compares unfavorably with any rule of decision, however arbitrary, that facilitates primary predictability. * * *

Differences in the degree of pertinence of a state's law to a given case may often be perceived by focusing more sharply on the character of identification that exists between the comparatively favored interest and the state. * * *

Internal rules intended to regulate conduct pose somewhat different problems from rules intended merely to distribute economic losses, but they are also susceptible to analysis in terms of governmental interests. In this context, as in the other, lawmakers often speak in universal terms but must be understood to speak with reference to their constituents. Here too the resolution of conflict-of-laws cases is essentially a process of allocating respective spheres of lawmaking influence; and if the process is to have a normative basis, the criterion must be maximum attainment of underlying purpose by all governmental entities. This necessitates identifying the focal point of concern of the contending lawmaking groups and ascertaining the comparative pertinence of that concern to the immediate case. * * *

Take, for example, a situation in which State X has a usury statute and State Y does not. State X, as well as State Y, recognized the commercial importance of performance of consensual undertakings and access to the largest possible number of customers. But in a particular class of situations X, unlike Y, has decided an exception should be made. X protects borrowers having defined characteristics from the consequences of their inadequate bargaining power or bad judgment. For internal purposes X may define the protected class broadly or narrowly and by characteristics the lender can ascertain and apply with ease or only with difficulty.

The focal point of concern of X lawmakers is the X borrower of the type protected internally. The X usury law should not be applied to a case not involving such a borrower; to do so would not further any purpose of X and would defeat not only the contrary policy of Y but also the general, though qualified, policy of X favoring commercial freedom and reliance on undertakings.

State X policy would be given maximum implementation by a choice rule that required application of X law in any case involving an X borrower of the class protected internally. Although involvement of an X borrower of the protected class is a necessary condition to the application of X law, it ought not to be a sufficient condition. A choice rule based on the state identification of the lender would give maximum scope to Y's policies but would seriously impair those of X. The protection X has afforded its borrowers probably has several consequences. Local lenders may make loans to the better risks within the class at the maximum legal rate, a rate somewhat lower than otherwise would have been afforded them, rather than forego entirely that segment of business. But another part of the protected class is denied local loans and therefore has an incentive to borrow outside the state. If the law of the state where the loan is made or is payable or of the lender's state is the choice criterion, the purpose of the X lawmakers will be substantially impaired by the emergence of a flock of lenders just across the state line.

A choice rule based on the lender's knowledge of the borrower's residence and of other characteristics of membership in the protected class affords maximum implementation of the policies of both states. Consensual expectations of the lender would be protected except when he had reason to know the transaction was forbidden by X. And the objectives of X, the borrower's state, would be shielded from wholesale evasion: the nature of the transaction assures that prior to extending credit the lender will discover in most cases the borrower's residence and in many cases other characteristics of membership in the protected class.

* * *

The preceding ... hypothetical ... illustrates several propositions. First, in choice-of-law cases there are two distinct types of governmental objectives, internal and external. The internal objectives are those underlying each state's resolution of conflicting private interests. These objectives inhere in a case even if the fact situation is wholly localized to a single state. In a usury case, for example, the competing private interests of commercial freedom and protection of economically weak borrowers are present even if the case is wholly internal to either State X or State Y. External objectives are introduced when a transaction affects persons identified with different states. They are the objectives of each state to make effective, in all situations involving persons as to whom it has responsibility for legal ordering, that resolution of contending private interests the state has made for local purposes. In each real conflicts case the external objective of one state must be subordinated. The choice problem posed is that of allocating spheres of lawmaking control.

The second proposition the hypothetical ... illustrate[s] is that one can articulate and apply a normative principle to determine which external objective to subordinate. The principle is to subordinate, in the particular case, the external objective of the state whose internal objective will be least impaired in general scope and impact by subordination in cases like the one at hand.

Implicit in the principle is an assertion that a court can and should go beyond a determination whether a state has *any* governmental interest in the application of its internal law-that a court can and should determine which state's internal objective will be least impaired by subordination in cases like the one before it. This determination is very different in kind from the weighing process often referred to by similar rubrics, but the two are often confused. Professor Freund, for example, in an early statement of a governmental interest analysis of choice-of-law problems, speaks of weighing the interests of the several states; he clearly envisions the super-value-judgment approach at several points in his article but is concerned with the comparative impairment of conflicting local objectives at other points. Professor Currie, too, in arguing that courts should not attempt to weigh the contending interests in real conflicts cases, subsumes both the super-value-judgment approach and the comparative-impairment analysis within his prohibition; he states that he sees little difference between the two. Therefore, in arguing that courts should not weigh, Professor Currie has not found it necessary to articulate separate arguments against the super-value-judgment and the comparative-impairment analysis. With respect to both he has counseled against judicial resolution on two bases: First, courts are inadequately equipped to discover the facts upon which resolution must turn; and secondly, such resolution is a highly political function not to be committed to courts in a democracy.

I agree with Currie's conclusion regarding super-value-judgments.... Neither of Currie's objections seems to me to be a compelling argument against judicial resolution of choice problems by application of the principle of comparative impairment. The inquiries that must precede application of this principle are often difficult. Judicial attempts to apply the principle often would be accompanied by inadequately artic- ulated opinions and sometimes would be demonstrably erroneous. But such failings attend judicial application of many legal criteria; and even if it is assumed that error is more common in the application of general than of precise criteria, it does not follow that all such criteria ought to be abandoned. In deciding whether real conflicts issues ought to be resolved by application of the suggested standard, the relevant question cannot be "Will such application resolve the issues infallibly?" Rather the question is, "Which is the most satisfactory of alternative modes of resolution?"

I cannot accept Professor Currie's mode of resolution as a more satisfactory alter- native. As has been noted elsewhere and conceded by Currie, it makes no provision for selection between the competing policies of other states by a forum having no in- terest of its own. A more fundamental objection is that which Currie and others have used to discredit the mechanical choice-of-law system expounded by Professor Beale and the first *Restatement*: Currie's system, like the *Restatement* system, will, in Currie's delightfully apt phraseology, "casually defeat now the one and now the other policy, depending upon a purely fortuitous circumstance." Under Currie's proposal, the for- tuitous circumstance is the act of forum selection by the plaintiff. It is fortuitous be- cause it has no greater normative content than the conceptual signposts of the *Restatement*. Indeed, with respect to real conflicts cases, the mechanical system of the *Restatement* must be preferred, for it affords the utility inherent in primary pre- dictability and avoids the costs of predictable nonuniformity.

The comparative-impairment principle is advocated because, without sacrificing primary predictability, it invokes the normative criterion of implementing state poli- cies. The principle seems to me vulnerable to attack only on the ground of uncer- tainty-that it is so vacuous in content and uncertain in application as to be inappropriate for adjudicative administration. Professor Currie seems to invoke a part of this uncertainty objection when he states that courts should not attempt to weigh the comparative external objectives because they are not equipped to discover the facts upon which resolution must turn. Neither this part of the objection..., nor the more general objection seems to me to be persuasive. * * *

The objection that courts are not equipped to discover the facts upon which res- olution must turn is equally applicable to a very large percentage of our judge-made rules of law. * * * In its briefest form the response is that the comparative-impairment principle can be applied with conviction and predictability in a substantial majority of cases and that the gains in effectuation of local policies will more than offset the costs incurred by marginal reduction of primary predictability.

Professor Currie's second reason why courts should not balance competing state interests in real conflicts cases is that to do so is to assume a "political function of a very high order ..., a function which should not be committed to courts in a democracy." Perhaps this assertion rests on his usually tacit premise that balancing interests necessarily involves making super-value judgments. A contrary view, that super-value judgments are separable from the comparative-impairment principle, is one of the cornerstones of this paper; and if Currie's second reason does depend on a premise of inseparability, I rest on my preceding argument.

Professor Currie's "political function" argument may be a corollary of his argument that courts are not equipped to ascertain necessary legislative facts; he may be saying that the legislative branch is better equipped, and therefore the matter should be left to them. This argument is irrelevant to the situation of a court required to decide cases not covered by legislative choice rules, the situation most frequent in this area. These cases must be decided, and they ought to be decided on the basis of the best assessment the court can make of comparative impairment.

More Notes and Questions regarding *Bernhard* and Comparative Impairment

(1) How different is Baxter's "comparative impairment" approach to resolving true conflicts from Currie's revised approach? Did the court in *Bernhard* treat these two approaches as synonymous? What general choice-of-law goal is furthered by "comparative impairment" that arguably is not furthered by Curries's method of resolving true conflicts? What other goal is arguably not furthered by "comparative impairment"?

(2) Both Currie and Baxter agree that a court's interest analysis must not include attempts at "super-value judgments" as to which state's law is the "better" law. Likewise, the Court in *Bernhard* emphasized that a court must "not 'weigh' the conflicting governmental interests in the sense of determining which conflicting law manifested the 'better' or the 'worthier' social policy on the specific issue." *Bernhard*, 16 Cal. 3d at 320. What are the policy reasons for this prohibition on the weighing of interests in resolving true conflicts? More importantly, what then is the nature of the proper inquiry when undertaking a comparative impairment analysis? Is this a comprehensible inquiry? Is this what the court really did in *Bernhard*?

(3) Do you agree with the court's conclusion in *Bernhard* that Nevada's interests were not substantially impaired by the imposition of civil liability on the Nevada tavern? A strong argument could be made, could it not, that if Nevada protects its taverns from liability to its own residents, Nevada has an even greater interest in preventing their liability to out-of-state residents. *See* John J. Wasilczyk, Note, *Conflict of Laws,*

65 Cal. L. Rev. 290, 296 (1977). This argument also illustrates a broader criticism of the "comparative impairment" analysis, does it not?

(4) "Comparative impairment" analysis has been criticized for imprecision, manipulability, and a propensity for interest-counting; as well as because it reflects natural law premises. Leo Kanowitz, *Comparative Impairment and Better Law: Grand Illusions in the Conflict of Laws*, 30 Hastings L.J. 255, 293 (1979). Professor Herma Hill Kay criticized "comparative impairment" on many of the same grounds, including the importation into the structure of government interest analysis of value-laden factors inconsistent with Currie's basic approach. Professor Kay recommends a return to Currie's approach whereby "true conflicts" are resolved by always applying the law of the forum. Herma Hill Kay, *The Use of Comparative Impairment to Resolve True Conflicts: An Evaluation of the California Experience*, 68 Cal. L. Rev. 577 (1980).

(5) Do you agree with these scholarly criticisms of the "comparative impairment" method? Do you agree with Professor Kay's recommendation that these criticisms can be alleviated by a return to pure Currie interest analysis?

[E] Further Development of Comparative Impairment

[1] Supreme Court Fine-Tuning

Offshore Rental Co. v. Continental Oil Co.

Supreme Court of California
22 Cal. 3d 157, 148 Cal. Rptr. 867, 583 P.2d 721 (1978)

Tobriner, Justice.

This case presents a problem of conflict of laws. Plaintiff, a California corporation, sues for the loss of services of a "key" employee, whom defendant negligently injured on defendant's premises in Louisiana. The trial court, applying Louisiana law, concluded that plaintiff could not maintain a cause of action against defendant, and accordingly dismissed the complaint. Plaintiff appeals from the judgment contending that under California law an employer has a cause of action for negligent injury to a key employee and that the trial court should therefore have applied California law. As we explain, we have concluded that the trial court correctly applied Louisiana law in this case, and thus we affirm the judgment.

Plaintiff Offshore Rental Company, a California corporation, maintains its principal place of business in California, but derives its revenues in large part from leasing oil drilling equipment in Louisiana's Gulf Coast area. Headquartered in New York, defendant Continental Oil Company, a Delaware corporation, does business in California, Louisiana, and other states.

In November 1967, plaintiff opened an office in Houston, Texas, for the purpose of establishing a base closer to the Gold Coast. In June 1968 plaintiff's vice-president, Howard C. Kaylor, went from that office to Louisiana to confer with defendant's representatives. During the course of that trip defendant negligently caused injury to Kaylor on defendant's premises in Louisiana.

At the time of his injury, Kaylor was responsible for obtaining contracts for plaintiff's increased business in Louisiana. Although defendant compensated Kaylor for his injuries, plaintiff subsequently filed the underlying action in California to recover $5 million in damages occasioned by the loss of Kaylor's services.

In a bifurcated trial on the issue of choice of law, the trial court found that "[a]ll significant contacts operative in this case [were] in the State of Louisiana with the exception of the fact that plaintiff corporation was a resident of California," and concluded as a matter of law that "[t]he question of whether or not a corporation may maintain an action for damages arising out of personal injuries to [its] employee must be determined by application of the laws of the state of Louisiana which is the state in which all significant operative contacts existed." Because the court found that Louisiana law did not permit the maintenance of such an action, the court granted judgment for defendant.

Questions of choice of law are determined in California, as plaintiff correctly contends, by the "governmental interest analysis" rather than by the trial court's "most significant contacts theory." As we announced in *Reich v. Purcell* (1967) 67 Cal. 2d 551, 553 [63 Cal. Rptr. 31, 432 P.2d 727], under the governmental interest analysis approach, the forum in a conflicts situation "must search to find the proper law to apply based upon the interests of the litigants and the involved states." As we shall explain, however, we have concluded that despite its analytic error, the trial court correctly dismissed plaintiff's cause of action.

The matter presently before us involves two states: California, the forum, a place of business for defendant, as well as plaintiff's state of incorporation and principal place of business; and Louisiana, the locus of the business of both plaintiff and defendant out of which the injury arose, and the place of the injury.[1] As we pointed out in our decision in *Hurtado v. Superior Court* (1974) 11 Cal. 3d 574 [114 Cal. Rptr. 106, 522 P.2d 666], however, the fact that two states are involved does not in itself indicate that there is a "conflict of laws" or "choice of laws" problem. As we stated in *Hurtado*, "[t]here is obviously no problem where the laws of the two states are identical." (11 Cal. 3d at p. 528.)

Here, however, the laws of Louisiana and California are not identical. In the leading case interpreting Louisiana law, *Bonfanti Industries, Inc. v. Teke, Inc.* (La. App. 1969) 224 So. 2d 15 (affd. (1969) 254 La. 779 [226 So. 2d 770]), a Louisiana corporation, relying on Louisiana Civil Code article 174, brought suit for the loss of services of one of its key officers occasioned by the Louisiana defendant's negligence. Although article 174 provides that "The master may bring an action against any man for beating or maiming his *servant*" (emphasis added), the Louisiana court held that the *corporate plaintiff* could state no cause of action in modern law for the loss of services of its officer. * * *

---

1. Neither party has urged that the law of Delaware or Texas is applicable.

On the other hand, expressions in the California cases, although chiefly dicta, support the present plaintiff's assertion that California Civil Code section 49 grants a cause of action against a third party for loss caused by an injury to a key employee due to the negligence of the third party. Section 49 provides that "The rights of personal relations forbid: … [¶](c) Any injury to a servant which affects his ability to serve his master.…" Plaintiff contends that the master-servant relation protected by section 49 encompasses plaintiff's employment relationship with its injured vice-president, and thus that section 49 grants a cause of action against defendant for damages to plaintiff caused by defendant's negligence.

If we assume, for purposes of analysis, that section 49 does provide an employer with a cause of action for negligent injury to a key employee, the laws of California and Louisiana are directly in conflict. Nonetheless, "[a]lthough the two potentially concerned states have different laws, there is still no problem in choosing the applicable rule of law where only one of the states has an interest in having its law applied.… 'When one of two states related to a case has a legitimate interest in the application of its law and policy and the other has none, there is no real problem; clearly the law of the interested state should be applied.' (Currie, *Selected Essays on the Conflict of Laws* (1963), p. 189.)" (*Hurtado v. Superior Court, supra,* 11 Cal. 3d at p. 580.)

We must therefore examine the governmental policies underlying the Louisiana and California laws, "preparatory to assessing whether either of both states have an interest in applying their policy to the case." (Kay, *Comments on Reich v. Purcell* (1968) 15 UCLA L. Rev. 584, 585.) Only if each of the states involved has a "legitimate but conflicting interest in applying its own law" will we be confronted with a "true" conflicts case. (*Bernhard v. Harrah's Club* (1976) 16 Cal. 3d 313, 319 [128 Cal. Rptr. 215, 546 P.2d 719].)

Turning first to Louisiana,[5] we note that Louisiana's refusal to permit recovery for loss of a key employee's services is predicted on the view that allowing recovery would lead to "undesirable social and legal consequences." (*Bonafanti Industries, Inc. v. Teke, Inc., supra,* 224 So. 2d at p. 17.) We interpret this conclusion as indicating Louisiana's policy to protect negligent resident tortfeasors acting within Louisiana's borders from the financial hardships caused by the assessment of excessive legal liability or exaggerated claims resulting from the loss of services of a key employee. Clearly the present defendant is a member of the class which Louisiana law seeks to protect, since defendant is a Louisiana "resident" whose negligence on its own premises has caused

---

5. Although, as plaintiff contends, defendant did not in fact "demonstrate" Louisiana's policies and interests in the application of Louisiana law, we may make our own determination of those policies and interests, without taking "evidence" as such on the matter. Plaintiff's contention rests on an unduly literal interpretation of our statement in *Hurtado v. Superior Court, supra,* 11 Cal. 3d 574, 581, that "generally speaking the forum will apply its own rule of decision unless a party litigant timely invokes the law of a foreign state. In such event he must demonstrate that the latter rule of decision will further the interest of the foreign state and therefore that it is an appropriate one for the forum to apply to the case before it." We note in this regard that Evidence Code section 452 expressly provides that "Judicial notice may be taken of … [¶](a) The decisional, constitutional, and statutory law of any state of the United States.…"

the injury in question. Thus Louisiana's interest in the application of its law to the present case is evident: negation of plaintiff's cause of action serves Louisiana's policy of avoidance of extended financial hardship to the negligent defendant.

Nevertheless, we recognize as equally clear the fact that application of California law to the present case will further California's interest. California, through section 49, expresses an interest in protecting California employers from economic harm because of negligent injury to a key employee inflicted by a third party. Moreover, California's policy of protection extends beyond such an injury inflicted within California, since California's economy and tax revenues are affected regardless of the situs of physical injury. Thus, California is interested in applying its law in the present case to plaintiff Offshore, a California corporate employer that suffered injury in Louisiana by the loss of the services of its key employee.[9]

Hence this case involves a true conflict between the law of Louisiana and the law of California. In *Bernhard v. Harrah's Club, supra,* we described the proper resolution of such a case. We rejected the notion that in a situation of true conflict the law of the forum should always be applied. Instead, as we stated, "Once [a] preliminary analysis has identified a true conflict of the governmental interests involved as applied to the parties under the particular circumstances of the case, the 'comparative impairment' approach to the resolution of such conflict seeks to determine which state's interest would be more impaired if its policy were subordinated to the policy of the other state. This analysis proceeds on the principle that true conflicts should be resolved by applying the law of the state whose interest would be the more impaired if its law were not applied." (16 Cal. 3d 313, 320.)

As Professor Horowitz has explained, this analysis does not involve the court in "weighing" the conflicting governmental interests "in the sense of determining which conflicting law manifest[s] the 'better' or the 'worthier' social policy on the specific issue. An attempted balancing of conflicting state policies in that sense ... is difficult to justify in the context of a federal system in which, within constitutional limits, states are empowered to mold their policies as they wish." (Horowitz, *The Law of Choice of Law in California-A Restatement* (1974) 21 UCLA L. Rev. 719, 753.)

---

9. While this protection of the employer is the most rational policy that can be attributed to California, it is not the only one possible. The sparse legislative history of section 49 suggests that the Legislature may have retained the statutory action for injury to a servant in the belief that this statutory cause of action was necessary in order to preserve an employer's right of subrogation under the workers' compensation law. (See Governor's Recommendation to Assem. and Sen. that Assem. Bill No. 1699 be amended (May 12, 1939) 1 Assem.J. (1939 Reg. Sess.) p. 2086. Compare Stats. 1939, ch. 1103, §5, p. 3037, with Stats. 1939, ch. 128, §1, p. 1245.) As more recent cases make clear, however, the specific subrogation statutes of the worker's compensation law are sufficient, in themselves, to establish the employer's right to subrogation (see Lab. Code, §§3850–3864; *County of San Diego v. Sanfax Corp.* (1977) 19 Cal.3d 862 [140 Cal.Rptr. 638, 568 P.2d 363]), and thus section 49 plays no substantial role in encouraging employers to meet their responsibility under the workers' compensation law. Moreover, the present defendant has compensated plaintiff's employee for his injuries; the record indicates no claim by defendant for indemnity.

Rather, the resolution of true conflict cases may be described as "essentially a process of allocating respective spheres of lawmaking influence." (Baxter, *Choice of Law and the Federal System* (1963) 16 Stan. L. Rev. 1, 11–12.) The process of allocation demands several inquiries. First, while "[i]t is not always possible to say fairly whether [the] policy [underlying a state's law] is one that was much more *strongly held* in the past than it is now, ... this ground of analysis should not be ignored." (Emphasis added.) (Von Mehren & Trautman, *The Law of Multistate Problems* (1965) p. 377.)

Professor Freund has pointed out that "Statutes [in a domestic case], by reason of their pattern or their prevalence, may evidence a legal climate of opinion which makes less oppressive the responsibility of the judge in choosing between two inferences from a statute or between two possible rules of law. A similar resort may be made in multistate cases. *If one of the competing laws is archaic and isolated in the context of the laws of the federal union, it may not unreasonably have to yield to the more prevalent and progressive law, other factors of choice being roughly equal.* A married woman's disability to make a contract, imbedded in the law of one state, may be carried away by the current if contact is made with the main stream in another state. Perhaps one of the functions of conflict-of-laws decisions is to serve as growing pains for the law of a state, at all events in a federation such as our own." (Italics added.) (Freund, *Chief Justice Stone and the Conflict of Laws* (1946) 59 Harv. L. Rev. 1210, 1216.)

Thus the current status of a statute is an important factor to be considered in a determination of comparative impairment: the policy underlying a jurisdiction's law may be deemed "attenuated and anachronistic and properly ... be limited to domestic occurrences in the event of [a multistate] clash of interests." (Freund, *Chief Justice Stone, supra,* 59 Harv. L. Rev. 1210, 1224.) Moreover, a particular statute may be an antique not only in comparison to the laws of the federal union, but also as compared with other laws of the state of its enactment. Such a statute may be infrequently enforced or interpreted even within its own jurisdiction, and, as an anachronism in that sense, should have a limited application in conflicts case.

Another chief criterion in the comparative impairment analysis is the "maximum attainment of underlying purpose by all governmental entities. This necessitates identifying the focal point of concern of the contending lawmaking groups and ascertaining the *comparative pertinence* of that concern to the immediate case." (Italics added.) (Baxter, *Choice of Law, supra,* 16 Stan. L. Rev. 1, 12.) The policy underlying a statute may be less "comparatively pertinent" if the original object of the statute is no longer of pressing importance: a statute which was once intended to remedy a matter of grave public concern may since have fallen in significance to the periphery of the state's laws. As Professor Currie observed in another context, "If the truth were known, it would probably be that [those few states which have retained the archaic law of abatement have done so] simply because of the proverbial inertial of legal institutions, and that no real policy is involved." (Selected Essays on the Conflict of Laws, *supra,* p. 143.)

Moreover, the policy underlying a statute may also be less "comparatively pertinent" if the same policy may easily be satisfied by some means other than enforcement of the statute itself. Insurance, for example, may satisfy the underlying purpose of a statute originally intended to provide compensation to tort victims. The fact the parties may reasonably be expected to plan their transactions with insurance in mind may therefore constitute a relevant element in the resolution of a true conflict.

In sum, the comparative impairment approach to the resolution of true conflicts attempts to determine the relative commitment of the respective states to the laws involved. The approach incorporates several factors for consideration: the history and current status of the states' laws; the function and purpose of those laws.

Applying the comparative impairment analysis to the present case, we first probe the history and current status of the laws before us. The majority of common law states that have considered the matter do not sanction actions for harm to business employees, recognizing that even if injury to the master-servant relationship were at one time the basis for an action at common law, the radical change in the nature of that relationship since medieval times nullifies any right by a modern corporate employer to recover for negligent injury to his employees. With the decision in *Bonfanti Industries, Inc. v. Teke, Inc., supra,* discarding the obsolete concept of recovery for loss of a servant's services, the Louisiana courts have thus joined the "main stream" of American jurisdictions: Louisiana law accords with the common law's consistent refusal generally to recognize a cause of action based on negligent, as opposed to intentional, conduct which interferes with the performance of a contract between third parties or renders its performance more expensive or burdensome.

Indeed California has itself exhibited little concern in applying section 49 to the employer-employee relationship: despite the provisions of the antique statute, no California court has heretofore squarely held that California law provides an action for harm to business employees, and no California court has recently considered the issue at all. If, as we have assumed, section 49 does provide an action for harm to key corporate employees, in Professor Freund's words the section constitutes a law "archaic and isolated in the context of the laws of the federal union." We therefore conclude that the trial judge in the present case correctly applied Louisiana, rather than California, law, since California's interest in the application of its unusual and outmoded statute is comparatively less strong than Louisiana's corollary interest, so lately expressed, in its "prevalent and progressive" law.

An examination of the function and purpose of the respective laws before us provides additional support for our limitation of the reach of California law in the present case. The accident in question occurred within Louisiana's borders; although the law of the place of the wrong is not necessarily the applicable law for all tort actions (*Reich v. Purcell, supra,* 67 Cal. 2d 551, 555), the situs of the injury remains a relevant consideration. At the heart of Louisiana's denial of liability lies the vital interest in promoting freedom of investment and enterprise *within Louisiana's borders,* among investors incorporated both in Louisiana and elsewhere. The imposition of liability on defendant, therefore, would strike at the essence of a compelling Louisiana law.

Furthermore, in connection with our search for the proper law to apply based on the "maximum attainment of underlying purpose by all governmental entities," we note the realistic fact that insurance is available to guard against the exigencies of the present case. As one commentator has remarked, "[T]he fact that the potential [tort] victim does not usually calculate his risk and plan his insurance program accordingly, hardly detracts from the consideration that he can fairly be made to bear the consequences of not doing so." (Ehrenzweig, *A Treatise on the Conflict of Laws* (1962) pp. 575–576) The present plaintiff, a business corporation, is a potential "victim" peculiarly able to calculate such risks and to plan accordingly. Plaintiff could have obtained protection against the occurrence of injury to its corporate vice-president by purchasing key employee insurance, certainly a reasonable and foreseeable business expense. By entering Louisiana, plaintiff "exposed [it]self to the risks of the territory," and should not expect to subject defendant to financial hazard that Louisiana law had not created. (Cavers, *The Choice-of-Law Process* (1965) p. 147.)[12]

Although it is equally true that defendant is a business corporation able to calculate the risks of potential tort liability and to plan accordingly, because defendant's operations in Louisiana presumably involved dealing with key employees of companies incorporated in diverse states defendant would most reasonably have anticipated a need for the protection of premises' liability insurance based on Louisiana law. Accordingly, under these circumstances, we conclude that the burden of obtaining insurance for the loss at issue here is more properly borne by the plaintiff corporation.

We have explained that Louisiana law precludes a corporate employer from stating a cause of action for losses caused by negligent injuries to a key employee. We have assumed for the purposes of the present case that California law grants a cause of action for such injuries, and thus directly conflicts with the law of Louisiana. Upon examination of the nature and purpose of the states' respective laws, however, we have determined that the California statute has historically been of minimal importance in the fabric of California law, and that the Louisiana courts have recently interpreted their analogous Louisiana statute narrowly in light of that statute's obsolescence. We do not believe that California's interests in the application of its law to the present case are so compelling as to prevent an accommodation to the stronger, more current interest of Louisiana. We conclude therefore that Louisiana's interests would be the more impaired if its law were not applied, and consequently that Louisiana law governs the present case. Since the law of Louisiana provides no cause of action for the present plaintiff, we hold that the trial court correctly dismissed plaintiff's cause of action.

The judgment is affirmed.

---

12. We emphasize that plaintiff did not expose itself to any risk that Louisiana encourages negligent conduct by resident corporations. On the contrary, as a consequence of Louisiana's general policy against negligent behavior, defendant has already been obliged to compensate plaintiff's employee for his personal injuries.

Kearney v. Salomon Smith Barney, Inc.

Supreme Court of California
39 Cal. 4th 95, 45 Cal. Rptr. 3d 730, 137 P.3d 914 (2006)

GEORGE, CHIEF JUSTICE.

The complaint in this case alleges that employees at the Atlanta-based branch of defendant Salomon Smith Barney (SSB)—a large, nationwide brokerage firm that has numerous offices and does extensive business in California—repeatedly have recorded telephone conversations with California clients without the clients' knowledge or consent. These facts give rise to a classic choice-of-law issue, because the relevant California privacy statute generally prohibits any person from recording a telephone conversation without the consent of *all* parties to the conversation, whereas the comparable Georgia statute does not prohibit the recording of a telephone conversation when the recording is made with the consent of *one* party to the conversation.

In this proceeding, several California clients of SSB filed a putative class action against SSB seeking to obtain injunctive relief against its Atlanta-based branch's continuing practice of recording telephone conversations, resulting from calls made to and from California, without knowledge or consent of the California clients, and also seeking to recover damages and/or restitution based upon recording that occurred in the past. SSB filed a demurrer to the complaint, maintaining that no relief is warranted, because the conduct of its Atlanta-based employees was and is permissible under Georgia law.

The trial court sustained SSB's demurrer and dismissed the action. The Court of Appeal affirmed the judgment rendered by the trial court, concluding that application of Georgia law is appropriate and supports the denial of all relief sought by plaintiffs. We granted review to consider the novel choice-of-law issue presented by this case. * * *

III

Beginning with Chief Justice Traynor's seminal decision for this court in *Reich v. Purcell* (1967) 67 Cal.2d 551 [63 Cal. Rptr. 31, 432 P.2d 727] (hereafter *Reich*), California has applied the so-called governmental interest analysis in resolving choice-of-law issues. In brief outline, the governmental interest approach generally involves three steps. First, the court determines whether the relevant law of each of the potentially affected jurisdictions with regard to the particular issue in question is the same or different. Second, if there is a difference, the court examines each jurisdiction's interest in the application of its own law under the circumstances of the particular case to determine whether a true conflict exists. Third, if the court finds that there is a true conflict, it carefully evaluates and compares the nature and strength of the interest of each jurisdiction in the application of its own law "to determine which state's interest would be more impaired if its policy were subordinated to the policy of the other state" (*Bernhard v. Harrah's Club* (1976) 16 Cal.3d 313, 320 [128 Cal. Rptr. 215, 546 P.2d 719], and then ultimately applies "the law of the state whose interest would be the more impaired if its law were not applied." (*Ibid.*) * * *

IV

Keeping in mind the choice-of-law principles and methodology set forth in these prior cases, we turn to the choice-of-law issue presented by the facts of this case. Here, the two potentially affected jurisdictions are California and Georgia, and the initial question is whether a conflict exists between the applicable law of each jurisdiction. In resolving that initial question, we must determine not only whether California law and Georgia law differ from one another, but also whether each state's law was intended to apply to a telephone conversation that occurs in part in California and in part in Georgia.

A

We begin with the California statutory scheme.

In 1967, the California Legislature enacted a broad, protective invasion-of-privacy statute in response to what it viewed as a serious and increasing threat to the confidentiality of private communications resulting from then recent advances in science and technology that had led to the development of new devices and techniques for eavesdropping upon and recording such private communications. One of the provisions of the 1967 legislation—section 637.2—explicitly created a new, statutory private right of action, authorizing any person who has been injured by any violation of the invasion-of-privacy legislation to bring a civil action to recover damages and to obtain injunctive relief in response to such violation.[5] * * *

GA statute does not prohibit recording of a telephone convo

The recording of telephone conversations is governed by the provisions of section 632, one of the original provisions of the 1967 legislation. Under subdivision (a) of section 632, "[e]very person who, intentionally and without the consent of *all* parties to a confidential communication, by means of any electronic amplifying or recording device, ... records the confidential communication, whether the communication is carried on among the parties in the presence of one another or by means of a telegraph, telephone, or other device" (italics added), violates the statute and is punishable as specified in the provision. * * *

As made clear by the terms of section 632 as a whole, this provision does not absolutely preclude a party to a telephone conversation from recording the conversation,

---

5. Section 637.2 currently provides in full:
   "(a) Any person who has been injured by a violation of this chapter may bring an action against the person who committed the violation for the greater of the following amounts:
      "(1) Five thousand dollars ($5,000).
      "(2) Three times the amount of actual damages, if any, sustained by the plaintiff.
   "(b) Any person may, in accordance with Chapter 3 (commencing with Section 525) of Title 7 of Part 2 of the Code of Civil Procedure, bring an action to enjoin and restrain any violation of this chapter, and may in the same action seek damages as provided by subdivision (a).
   "(c) It is not a necessary prerequisite to an action pursuant to this section that the plaintiff has suffered, or be threatened with, actual damages."

but rather simply prohibits such a party from secretly or surreptitiously recording the conversation, that is, from recording the conversation without first informing all parties to the conversation that the conversation is being recorded. If, after being so advised, another party does not wish to participate in the conversation, he or she simply may decline to continue the communication. A business that adequately advises all parties to a telephone call, at the outset of the conversation, of its intent to record the call would not violate the provision.

[Next, the Court analyzes the language and purpose of section 632, and concludes] that section 632 applies when a confidential communication takes place in part in California and in part in another state.

B

We turn next to the applicable Georgia law.

Georgia, like California, has enacted a broad statute addressing eavesdropping upon or recording of private conversations. The basic provision of the Georgia privacy statute provides in relevant part that "[i]t shall be unlawful for: (1) Any person in a clandestine manner intentionally to overhear, transmit, or record or attempt to overhear, transmit, or record the private conversation of another which shall originate in any private place...." (Ga. Code Ann. § 16-11-62.) * * *

At the same time, however, another provision of the relevant Georgia statutory scheme explicitly provides that "[n]othing in Code Section 16-11-62 [that is, the foregoing statutory provision] shall prohibit a person from intercepting a wire, oral, or electronic communication *where such person is a party to the communication or one of the parties to the communication has given prior consent to such interception.*" (Italics added.) (Ga. Code Ann. § 16-11-66.) Georgia decisions long have interpreted the relevant Georgia privacy statutes as *not* applicable to a situation in which a conversation is recorded by one of the participants in the conversation. (See, for example, *Mitchell v. State* (Ga. 1977) 239 Ga. 3 [235 S.E.2d 509, 510–511].) In this respect, of course, Georgia law differs from California law.[14]

[Next, the Court analyzes the language and purpose of the Georgia privacy statutes, and concludes that those statutes apply to a telephone call in which one of the parties is in Georgia and one of the parties is in another state.] Accordingly, we conclude that the Georgia statute, as well as the California statute, applies to the telephone

---

14. The dichotomy between the California and Georgia privacy statutes in this regard is representative of a division in analogous privacy statutes throughout the nation. Privacy statutes in a majority of states (as well as the comparable federal provision)—like the Georgia statute—prohibit the recording of private conversations except with the consent of one party to the conversation, but a sizeable minority of states (11 states, according to an apparently well-researched law review article)—including California—prohibit such recording without the consent of all parties to the conversation. (See Bast, *What's Bugging You? Inconsistencies and Irrationalities of the Law of Eavesdropping* (1998) 47 DePaul L.Rev. 837, 870.)

calls at issue in this case, and that the law of each state differs with regard to the legality of such conduct. Although it is unlawful under California law for a party to a telephone conversation to record the conversation without the knowledge of all other parties to the conversation, such conduct is not unlawful under Georgia law.

C

Plaintiffs maintain, however, that although California law and Georgia law differ, there nonetheless is no true conflict in this situation. Although it is evident that California has a legitimate interest in having its law applied in the present setting because plaintiffs are California residents whose telephone conversations in California were recorded without their knowledge or consent, plaintiffs contend that Georgia does not have an interest in having its law applied here, because the fundamental purpose of the Georgia statute is to protect the privacy of conversations that have some relationship to Georgia and in this case there is no claim that the privacy of any Georgia resident or any person or business in Georgia has been violated.

Although plaintiffs are correct that the facts of this case do not implicate the privacy interests protected by the Georgia statute, the Georgia statute also can reasonably be viewed as establishing the general ground rules under which persons in Georgia may act with regard to the recording of private conversations, including telephone calls. Because Georgia law prohibits the recording of such conversations except when the recording is made by one of the parties to the conversation or with such a party's consent, persons in Georgia reasonably may expect, at least as a general matter, that they lawfully can record their own conversations with others without obtaining the other person's consent, and Georgia has a legitimate interest in not having liability imposed on persons or businesses who have acted in Georgia in reasonable reliance on the provisions of Georgia law. Because the conduct of SSB that is at issue in this case involves activity that its employees engaged in within Georgia, we believe that Georgia possesses a legitimate interest in having its law applied in this setting.

Accordingly, we conclude that this case presents a true conflict of laws.

V

… [T]he governing authorities establish that once a court's preliminary analysis has identified a true conflict, "the 'comparative impairment' approach … seeks to determine which state's interest would be more impaired if its policy were subordinated to the policy of the other state." (*Bernhard, supra,* 16 Cal.3d 313, 320.) As our prior decisions have emphasized, in conducting this evaluation "[t]he court does not "'weigh" the conflicting governmental interests in the sense of determining which conflicting law manifest[s] the "better" or the "worthier" social policy on the specific issue'" (*ibid.*), because "'[a]n attempted balancing of conflicting state policies in that sense … [would be] difficult to justify in the context of a federal system in which, within constitutional limits, states are empowered to mold their policies as they wish.'" (*Ibid.*) Instead, the comparative impairment process can more "'accurately be described as … [an] accommodation of conflicting state policies'" (*ibid.*), attempting, to the extent practicable, to achieve "the 'maximum attainment of underlying purpose by all governmental entities.'" *Offshore Rental Co. v. Continental Oil Co.* (1978) 22 Cal.3d 157, 166 [148 Cal. Rptr. 867, 583 P.2d 721] (*Offshore Rental*).) Under the comparative impairment approach, true conflicts are resolved "by applying the law of the state whose interest would be the more impaired if its law were not applied." (*Bernhard, supra,* 16 Cal.3d at p. 320.)

We proceed to evaluate the relative impairment of each state's interests that would result were the law of the other state to be applied in this setting, beginning with California's.

A

In considering the degree of impairment of California's interest that would result if Georgia law rather than California law were applied, we note initially that the objective of protecting individuals in California from the secret recording of confidential communications by or at the behest of another party to the communication was one of the principal purposes underlying the 1967 invasion of privacy enactment. [Here the Supreme Court reviews the legislative history of the 1967 California statutes.]

In addition, it is clear that this is most certainly *not* an instance like *Offshore Rental, supra,* 22 Cal.3d 157, in which the court found that the California statute in question was "ancient" and rarely if ever utilized or relied upon and concluded that the state had little *current* interest in the application of its own law. (*Id.* at pp. 167–168.) On the contrary, California decisions repeatedly have invoked and vigorously enforced the provisions of section 632 and have looked to the policy embodied in the provision in analyzing invasion-of-privacy claims in related contexts. * * * Thus, we believe that California must be viewed as having a strong and continuing interest in the full and vigorous application of the provisions of section 632 prohibiting the recording of telephone conversations without the knowledge or consent of *all* parties to the conversation.

We also believe that the failure to apply section 632 in the present context would substantially undermine the protection afforded by the statute. Many companies who do business in California are national or international firms that have headquarters, administrative offices, or—in view of the recent trend toward outsourcing—at least telephone operators located outside of California. If businesses could maintain a regular practice of secretly recording all telephone conversations with their California clients or customers in which the business employee is located outside of California, that practice would represent a significant inroad into the privacy interest that the statute was intended to protect. As noted above, an out-of-state company that does business in another state is required, at least as a general matter, to comply with the laws of a state and locality in which it has chosen to do business. As this court determined in *Bernhard, supra,* 16 Cal.3d 313, 322–323, with regard to the need to apply California law relating to the liability of tavern owners to the out-of-state tavern owner at issue in that case, the failure to apply California law in the present context seriously would undermine the objective and purpose of the statute. * * *

In sum, we conclude that the failure to apply California law in the present context would result in a significant impairment of California's interests.

B

By contrast, we believe that, for a number of reasons, the application of California law rather than Georgia law in the context presented by the facts of this case would have a relatively less severe effect on Georgia's interests.

First, because California law, with regard to the particular matter here at issue, is more protective of privacy interests than the comparable Georgia privacy statute, the application of California law would not violate any privacy interest protected by Georgia law. In addition, there is, of course, nothing in Georgia law that *requires* any person or business to record a telephone call without providing notice to the other parties to the call, and thus persons could comply with California law without violating any provision of Georgia law.

Second, with respect to businesses in Georgia that record telephone calls, California law would apply only to those telephone calls that are made to or received from California, not to all telephone calls to and from such Georgia businesses. * * *

Furthermore, applying California law to a Georgia business's recording of telephone calls between its employees and California customers will not severely impair Georgia's interests. As discussed above, California law does not totally prohibit a party to a telephone call from recording the call, but rather prohibits only the *secret* or *undisclosed* recording of telephone conversations, that is, the recording of such calls without the knowledge of all parties to the call. Thus, if a Georgia business discloses at the outset of a call made to or received from a California customer that the call is being recorded, the parties to the call will not have a reasonable expectation that the call is not being recorded and the recording would not violate section 632. Accordingly, to the extent Georgia law is intended to protect the right of a business to record conversations when it has a legitimate business justification for doing so, the application of California law to telephone calls between a Georgia business and its California clients or customers would not defeat that interest. * * * Although the application of California law to telephone calls between Georgia and California would impair Georgia's interests to the extent Georgia law is intended to protect a business's ability *secretly* to record its customers' telephone calls, we believe that, particularly as applied to a business's blanket policy of routinely recording telephone calls to and from California customers, this consequence would represent only a relatively minor impairment of Georgia's interests.

For the foregoing reasons, we conclude that, as a realistic matter, the application of California law in this context would not result in a severe impairment of Georgia's interests.

C

Accordingly, because we have found that the interests of California would be severely impaired if its law were not applied in this context, whereas Georgia's interest would not be significantly impaired if California law rather than Georgia law were applied, we conclude that, with the one exception we discuss below, California law should apply in determining whether the alleged secret recording of telephone conversations at issue in this case constitutes an unlawful invasion of privacy.

VI

Although, for the reasons just discussed, we have concluded that, as a general matter, the comparative impairment analysis supports the application of California law in this context, we believe it is appropriate to make an exception with regard to one distinct issue — the question of SSB's potential monetary liability for its *past* conduct.

As we have noted above, prior California decisions establish that one of the objectives of the comparative impairment analysis "is the 'maximum attainment of underlying purpose by *all* governmental entities.... ' " (*Offshore Rental, supra,* 22 Cal.3d 157, 166, italics added.) In seeking to maximize each affected state's interest to the extent feasible in the present context, we believe it is appropriate, for the reasons discussed below, to restrain the application of California law with regard to the imposition of liability for acts that have occurred in the past, in order to accommodate Georgia's interest in protecting persons who acted in Georgia in reasonable reliance on Georgia law from being subjected to liability on the basis of such action.

To begin with, we recognize that Georgia has a legitimate interest in ensuring that individuals and businesses who act in Georgia with the reasonable expectation that Georgia law applies to their conduct are not thereafter unexpectedly and unforeseeably subjected to liability for such actions. The Court of Appeal in the present case relied heavily upon this interest in reaching its conclusion, and we believe that court's assessment of the substantiality of this state interest is reasonable. (Accord *People v. One 1953 Ford Victoria* (1957) 48 Cal.2d 595, 599 [311 P.2d 480] [recognizing propriety of accommodating reasonable expectations of persons who act in another state in reasonable reliance on the other state's law].)

To be sure, one legitimately might maintain that SSB reasonably should have anticipated that its recording of a telephone conversation with a California client when the client is in California would be governed by California law, regardless of where the SSB employee with whom the client is speaking happens to be located. Although SSB would have reached that conclusion had it undertaken the extended choice-of-law analysis set forth above, we recognize that at the time of SSB's past actions the few lower court decisions that had considered a legal challenge to the recording of an interstate telephone conversation had reached differing conclusions as to which state's law should apply — the law of the state where the person who recorded the conversation was situated, or instead the law of the state where the person whose words were being recorded was located. Although none of the prior cases involved the type of repeated recording of customer telephone calls by a business entity that is involved here, we nonetheless believe that prior to our resolution of the issue in this case a business entity reasonably might have been uncertain as to which state's law was applicable and reasonably might have relied upon the law of the state in which its employee was located. Under these circumstances, we believe Georgia has a legitimate interest in not having SSB subjected to liability on the basis of its employees' past actions in Georgia.

At the same time, although California law expressly authorizes the recovery of damages for violations of section 632 (§ 637.2, subd. (a)), we believe that it is appropriate to recognize that ascribing a monetary value to the invasion of privacy resulting from the secret recording of a telephone conversation is difficult in any event, and that the deterrent value of such a potential monetary recovery cannot affect conduct that already has occurred. Under these circumstances, we conclude that denying the recovery of damages for conduct that was undertaken in the past in ostensible reliance on the law of another state — and prior to our clarification of which state's law applies in this context — will not seriously impair California's interests.

Accordingly, although we conclude that in general California law is applicable in this setting and that plaintiffs may seek injunctive relief to require SSB to comply with California law in the future, we shall apply Georgia law with respect to SSB's potential monetary liability for its past conduct, thus relieving SSB of any liability for damages for its past recording of conversations. (Cf., e.g., *Ex parte Archy* (1858) 9 Cal. 147, 171 [applying clarification of choice-of-law rule prospectively].) In light of our decision, of course, out-of-state companies that do business in California now are on notice that, with regard to future conduct, they are subject to California law with regard to the recording of telephone conversations made to or received from California, and that the full range of civil sanctions afforded by California law may be imposed for future violations.

* * *

For the reasons discussed above, the judgment of the Court of Appeal is reversed insofar as it precludes plaintiffs from going forward with their action to obtain injunctive relief, and is affirmed insofar as it upholds the dismissal of the action with regard to the recovery of monetary damages and restitution. Plaintiffs shall recover their costs on appeal.

Notes and Questions

(1) Why did the court in *Offshore Rental* assume there was a true conflict between California and Louisiana law? Seven years after it decided *Offshore Rental*, the California Supreme Court finally decided whether the California statute created a cause of action on behalf of a corporation for injuries to a key employee. The Court concluded that such a doctrine has no relevance to present-day employer/employee relationships because it is "obsolete, archaic and outmoded." *I.J. Weinrot and Son, Inc. v. Jackson*, 40 Cal. 3d 327, 340, 220 Cal. Rptr. 103, 112, 708 P.2d 682, 691 (1985). Why did the court in *Offshore Rental* decline to make this determination? If it had, would there have been any need to apply "comparative impairment"?

(2) What factors did the court in *Offshore Rental* focus on as part of its comparative impairment analysis? How does this differ from *Bernhard*? Is the court's comparative impairment analysis consistent with Baxter's comparative impairment model? How would you generally describe the comparative impairment method after *Offshore*

Rental? What role did insurance play in the court's analysis? Should "the fact that parties may reasonably be expected to plan their transactions with insurance in mind" constitute a relevant element in the resolution of a true conflict? Or is this element intrinsic to a state's interest in applying its law? *See* David E. Seidelson, *Resolving Choice-of-Law Problems Through Interest Analysis in Personal Injury Actions*, 30 Duq. L. Rev. 869, 904–907 (1992).

(3) The Supreme Court's use of comparative impairment in *Offshore Rental* has been sharply criticized by scholars as an example of "better law" analysis, and therefore as an example of precisely the type of "super-value judgment" considered inappropriate by Currie and Baxter. *See* Herma Hill Kay, *The Use of Comparative Impairment to Resolve True Conflicts: An Evaluation of the California Experience*, 68 Cal. L. Rev. 577, 586–591 (1980); Leo Kanowitz, *Comparative Impairment and Better Law: Grand Illusions in the Conflict of Laws*, 30 Hastings L.J. 255, 286–300 (1978). Is this an accurate criticism of the court's analysis in *Offshore Rental*? Is it more accurate to criticize *Offshore Rental* as focusing on territorialism, and not comparative impairment, in resolving the conflict? *See* William A. Reppy, *Eclecticism in Choice of Law: Hybrid Method or Mishmash?*, 34 Mercer L. Rev. 645, 673–77 (1983).

(4) Consider again the reasons why Currie concludes that a court should not make "super-value judgments" in resolving true conflicts. Doesn't Baxter's "comparative impairment" approach inherently involve such judgments, despite the court's denial in *Bernhard*? If so, is the court in *Offshore Rental* perhaps more honest by openly determining which state's interests are more intensely held, as opposed to hiding behind objective-sounding analysis?

(5) How did the court in *Offshore Rental* determine the policies and interests of Louisiana and California with respect to the issue of recovery for loss of a key employee's services? Read closely footnote 5 of the court's opinion, *supra*. Is the court saying that it must determine a choice-of-law issue regardless of whether the issue is raised by the parties? Regardless of whether the defendant satisfactorily demonstrates that a foreign state has an interest in having its law applied to the case? How should a court determine a state's interest when that state's law may further more than one policy? Should the court attempt to ascertain the most important or most rational policy? How would a court go about doing this? *See* footnote 6, *Offshore Rental*.

(6) What do you make of the *Kearney* court's distinction between the injunctive and damages relief sought by the plaintiff, as a basis for different choice-of-law outcomes? Is this distinction consistent with government interest/comparative impairment analysis? *See Scott v. Ford Motor Co.*, 224 Cal. App. 4th 1492, 1503–1509, 169 Cal. Rptr. 3d 823 (2014) (conducting a government interest analysis to determine which state's law, California's or Michigan's, applies with respect to whether punitive damages may be awarded as a tort remedy). Does the Supreme Court's distinction reflect other choice-of-law principles? Or is the court simply making a Solomonic resolution of the parties' dispute?

(7) The unedited version of the California Supreme Court's opinion in *Kearney* contains an excellent summary of all its prior decisions — *Reich, Hurtado, Bernhard,* and *Offshore Rental* — that apply government interest analysis and the comparative impairment doctrine. See *Kearney v. Solomon Smith Barney, Inc.,* 39 Cal. 4th 95, 107–115, 45 Cal. Rptr. 3d 730, 740–46, 137 P.3d 914, 922–27 (2006).

[2]   Other States' Doctrines for Torts

Only a handful of states have adopted interest analysis as their stated choice-of-law doctrine for tort cases, and California may be the only state that has adopted the comparative impairment approach for resolution of true conflicts. *See* Peter Hay, Patrick J. Borchers, Symeon C. Symeonides, *Conflict of Laws,* §§ 2.18–2.25 (4th 2010); Symeon C. Symeonides, *Choice of Law in the American Courts in 2014: Twenty-Eighth Annual Survey,* 63 Am. J. Comp. L. 299 (2015). An empirical study of 802 reported tort cases in several states suggests, however, that in practice the Second Restatement, "interest analysis," and Professor Leflar's "better law" approach are largely indistinguishable in patterns of results. *See* Patrick J. Borchers, *The Choice-of-Law Revolution: An Empirical Study,* 49 Wash. & Lee L. Rev. 357 (1992).

The government interest analysis continues to generate an enormous amount of scholarly criticism and support. In addition to the various authorities previously referenced in this chapter, several recent writings contain useful expositions, including Harold G. Maier, *Finding the Trees in Spite of the Metaphorist: The Problem of State Interests in Choice of Law,* 56 Alb. L. Rev. 753 (1993); Douglas Laycock, *Equal Citizens of Equal and Territorial States: The Constitutional Foundations of Choice of Law,* 92 Colum. L. Rev. 249 (1992); Lea Brilmayer, *Conflict of Laws: Foundations and Future Directions,* ch. 2 (1991); Louise Weinberg, *Against Comity,* 80 Geo. L.J. 53 (1991); Joseph W. Singer, *A Pragmatic Guide to Conflicts,* 70 B.U. L. Rev. 731 (1990); Friedrich K. Juenger, *A Critique of Interest Analysis,* 32 Am. J. Comp. L. 1 (1984); Russel J. Weintraub, *A Defense of Interest Analysis in the Conflict of Laws and the Use of That Analysis in Products Liability,* 46 Ohio St. L.J. 493 (1985).

§ 5.04 California Choice-of-Law Doctrine in Contract Cases

[A]   Choice-of-Law Agreements

Nedlloyd Lines B.V. v. Superior Court

Supreme Court of California
3 Cal. 4th 459, 11 Cal. Rptr. 2d 330, 834 P.2d 1148 (1992)

Baxter, Justice.

We granted review to consider the effect of a choice-of-law clause in a contract between commercial entities to finance and operate an international shipping business. In our order granting review, we limited our consideration to the question whether and to what extent the law of Hong Kong, chosen in the parties' agreement, should be applied in ruling on defendant's demurrer to plaintiff's complaint. * * *

STATEMENT OF FACTS AND PROCEEDINGS BELOW

Plaintiff and real party in interest Seawinds Limited (Seawinds) is a shipping company, currently undergoing reorganization under chapter 11 of the United States Bankruptcy Code, whose business consists of the operation of three container ships. Seawinds was incorporated in Hong Kong in late 1982 and has its principal place of business in Redwood City, California. Defendants and petitioners Nedlloyd Lines B.V., Royal Nedlloyd Group N.V., and KNSM Lines B.V. (collectively referred to as Nedlloyd) are interrelated shipping companies incorporated in the Netherlands with their principal place of business in Rotterdam.

In March 1983, Nedlloyd and other parties (including an Oregon corporation, a Hong Kong corporation, a British corporation, three individual residents of California, and a resident of Singapore) entered into a contract with Seawinds to purchase shares of Seawinds's stock. The contract, which was entitled "Shareholders' Agreement in Respect of Seawinds Limited," stated that its purpose was "to establish [Seawinds] as a joint venture company to carry on a transportation operation." The agreement also provided that Seawinds would carry on the business of the transportation company and that the parties to the agreement would use "means reasonably available" to ensure the business was a success.

The shareholders' agreement between the parties contained the following choice-of-law and forum selection provision: "This agreement shall be governed by and construed in accordance with Hong Kong law and each party hereby irrevocably submits to the non-exclusive jurisdiction and service of process of the Hong Kong courts."

In January 1989, Seawinds sued Nedlloyd, alleging in essence that Nedlloyd breached express and implied obligations under the shareholders' agreement.... Seawinds's original and first amended complaint included causes of action for breach of contract, breach of the implied covenant of good faith and fair dealing (in both contract and tort), and breach of fiduciary duty. This matter comes before us after trial court rulings on demurrers to Seawinds's complaints.

Nedlloyd demurred to Seawinds's original complaint on the grounds that it failed to state causes of action for breach of the implied covenant of good faith and fair dealing (either in contract or in tort) and breach of fiduciary duty. In support of its demurrer, Nedlloyd contended the shareholders' agreement required the application of Hong Kong law to Seawinds's claims. In opposition to the demurrer, Seawinds argued that California law should be applied to its causes of action.

In ruling on Nedlloyd's demurrer, the trial court expressly determined that California law applied to all of Seawinds's causes of action. It sustained the demurrers with leave to amend as to all causes of action, relying on grounds not pertinent to the issues before us. Nedlloyd sought a writ of mandate from the Court of Appeal directing the application of Hong Kong law. After the Court of Appeal summarily denied Nedlloyd's initial writ petition, we granted Nedlloyd's petition for review. * * *

In the meantime, the trial court overruled Nedlloyd's demurrer to Seawinds's first amended complaint, again applying California law to Seawinds's causes of action. The Court of Appeal summarily denied Nedlloyd's second writ petition challenging the order overruling the latter demurrer; we also granted review of that order and consolidated proceedings on the two writ matters so as to preserve the choice-of-law issue for review. As noted above, we have limited review in both proceedings to the choice-of-law issue.

DISCUSSION

I. *The proper test.*

We have not previously considered the enforceability of a contractual choice-of-law provision. We have, however, addressed the closely related issue of the enforceability of a contractual choice-of-forum provision, and we have made clear that, "No satisfying reason of public policy has been suggested why enforcement should be denied a forum selection clause appearing in a contract entered into freely and voluntarily by parties who have negotiated at arm's length." (*Smith, Valentino & Smith, Inc. v. Superior Court* (1976) 17 Cal. 3d 491, 495–496 [131 Cal. Rptr. 374, 551 P.2d 1206] (*Smith*).) The forum selection provision in *Smith* was contained within a choice-of-law clause, and we observed that, "Such choice of law provisions are usually respected by California courts." (*Id.*, at p. 494.) We noted this result was consistent with the modern approach of section 187 of the Restatement Second of Conflict of Laws (Restatement). (17 Cal. 3d at p. 494.) Prior Court of Appeal decisions, although not always explicitly referring to the Restatement, also overwhelmingly reflect the modern, mainstream approach adopted in the Restatement. (*Mencor Enterprises, Inc. v. Hets Equities Corp.* (1987) 190 Cal. App. 3d 432, 435–436 [235 Cal. Rptr. 464] [explicit reference to Rest. § 187]; ...).[1]

We reaffirm this approach. In determining the enforceability of arm's-length contractual choice-of-law provisions, California courts shall apply the principles set forth in Restatement section 187, which reflects a strong policy favoring enforcement of such provisions.

More specifically, Restatement section 187, subdivision (2) sets forth the following standards: "The law of the state chosen by the parties to govern their contractual rights and duties will be applied, even if the particular issue is one which the parties could not have resolved by an explicit provision in their agreement directed to that issue, unless either (a) the chosen state has no substantial relationship to the parties or the transaction and there is no other reasonable basis for the parties' choice, or (b) application of the law of the chosen state would be contrary to a fundamental policy of a

---

1. Federal courts applying California's conflicts law have also adhered to this approach. (*Consul Ltd. v. Solide Enterprises, Inc.* (9th Cir. 1986) 802 F.2d 1143, 1146–1147; ...) The mainstream nature of this approach is further reflected by a recent study indicating that 15 states other than California follow the general approach of the Restatement Second. (Chow, *Limiting Erie in a New Age of International Law: Toward a Federal Common Law of International Choice of Law* (1988) 74 Iowa L. Rev. 165, 190–191.)

state which has a materially greater interest than the chosen state in the determination of the particular issue and which, under the rule of § 188, would be the state of the applicable law in the absence of an effective choice of law by the parties."

Briefly restated, the proper approach under Restatement section 187, subdivision (2) is for the court first to determine either: (1) whether the chosen state has a substantial relationship to the parties or their transaction, or (2) whether there is any other reasonable basis for the parties' choice of law. If neither of these tests is met, that is the end of the inquiry, and the court need not enforce the parties' choice of law. If, however, either test is met, the court must next determine whether the chosen state's law is contrary to a fundamental policy of California.[5] If there is no such conflict, the court shall enforce the parties' choice of law. If, however, there is a fundamental conflict with California law, the court must then determine whether California has a "materially greater interest than the chosen state in the determination of the particular issue...." (Rest., § 187, subd. (2).) If California has a materially greater interest than the chosen state, the choice of law shall not be enforced, for the obvious reason that in such circumstance we will decline to enforce a law contrary to this state's fundamental policy.[6] We now apply the Restatement test to the facts of this case.

II. *Application of the test in this case.*

A. *Breach of contract.*

Nedlloyd did not assert in its second demurrer that the amended complaint failed to state a cause of action under Hong Kong law for breach of contract. Rather, Nedlloyd challenged the amended complaint's breach of contract allegations only on the ground of uncertainty. (Code Civ. Proc., § 430.10, subd. (f).) In light of our order limiting review to the issue of whether Hong Kong law "should be applied in ruling on the demurrers," we need not and do not consider the correctness of the trial court's ruling on the demurrer to this cause of action. As we shall explain, however, Hong Kong law, although not asserted as a bar to Seawinds's contract cause of action at the pleading stage, does govern all causes of action pleaded in the amended complaint, including the contract cause of action.

---

5. To be more precise, we note that Restatement section 187, subdivision (2) refers not merely to the forum state-for example, California in the present case-but rather to the state " ... which, under the rule of § 188, would be the state of the applicable law in the absence of an effective choice of law by the parties." For example, there may be an occasional case in which California is the forum, and the parties have chosen the law of another state, but the law of yet a third state, rather than California's, would apply absent the parties' choice. In that situation, a California court will look to the fundamental policy of the third state in determining whether to enforce the parties' choice of law. The present case is not such a situation.

6. There may also be instances when the chosen state has a materially greater interest in the matter than does California, but enforcement of the law of the chosen state would lead to a result contrary to a fundamental policy of California. In some such cases, enforcement of the law of the chosen state may be appropriate despite California's policy to the contrary. (*S. A. Empresa, etc. v. Boeing Co., supra,* 641 F.2d 746, 749.) Careful consideration, however, of California's policy and the other state's interest would be required. No such question is present in this case, and we thus need not and do not decide how Restatement section 187 would apply in such circumstances.

B. *Implied covenant of good faith and fair dealing.*

    1. *Substantial relationship or reasonable basis.*

As to the first required determination, Hong Kong—"the chosen state"—clearly has a "substantial relationship to the parties." (Rest., § 187, subd. (2)(a).) The shareholders' agreement, which is incorporated by reference in Seawinds' first amended complaint, shows that Seawinds is incorporated under the laws of Hong Kong and has a registered office there. The same is true of one of the shareholder parties to the agreement—Red Coconut Trading Co. The incorporation of these parties in Hong Kong provides the required "substantial relationship." (*Id.*, com. f [substantial relationship present when "one of the parties is domiciled" in the chosen state]; ...)

Moreover, the presence of two Hong Kong corporations as parties also provides a "reasonable basis" for a contractual provision requiring application of Hong Kong law. "If one of the parties resides in the chosen state, the parties have a reasonable basis for their choice." (*Consul Ltd. v. Solide Enterprises, Inc., supra*, 802 F.2d 1143, 1147.) The reasonableness of choosing Hong Kong becomes manifest when the nature of the agreement before us is considered. A state of incorporation is certainly at least one government entity with a keen and intimate interest in internal corporate affairs, including the purchase and sale of its shares, as well as corporate management and operations. (*See* Corp. Code, § 102 [applying California's general corporation law to domestic corporations].)

    2. *Existence of fundamental public policy.*

We next consider whether application of the law chosen by the parties would be contrary to "a fundamental policy" of California. We perceive no fundamental policy of California requiring the application of California law to Seawinds's claims based on the implied covenant of good faith and fair dealing. The covenant is not a government regulatory policy designed to restrict freedom of contract, but an implied promise inserted in an agreement to carry out the presumed intentions of contracting parties. (*Foley v. Interactive Data Corp.* (1988) 47 Cal. 3d 654, 689–690 [254 Cal. Rptr. 211, 765 P.2d 373] (*Foley*) ["When a court enforces the implied covenant it is in essence acting to protect 'the interest in having promises performed' [citation]— the traditional realm of a contract action—rather than to protect some general duty to society which the law places on an employer without regard to the substance of its contractual obligations to its employee."].)

Seawinds directs us to no authority exalting the *implied* covenant of good faith and fair dealing over the *express* covenant of these parties that Hong Kong law shall govern their agreement. We have located none. Because Seawinds has identified no fundamental policy of our state at issue in its essentially contractual dispute with Nedlloyd, the second exception to the rule of section 187 of the Restatement does not apply.

C. *Fiduciary duty cause of action.*

    1. *Scope of the choice-of-law clause.*

Seawinds contends that, whether or not the choice-of-law clause governs Seawinds's implied covenant claim, Seawinds's fiduciary duty claim is somehow independent of the shareholders' agreement and therefore outside the intended scope of the clause. Seawinds thus concludes California law must be applied to this claim. We disagree.

When two sophisticated, commercial entities agree to a choice-of-law clause like the one in this case, the most reasonable interpretation of their actions is that they intended for the clause to apply to all causes of action arising from or related to their contract. Initially, such an interpretation is supported by the plain meaning of the language used by the parties. The choice-of-law clause in the shareholders' agreement provides: "This agreement shall be *governed by* and construed in accordance with Hong Kong law and each party hereby irrevocably submits to the nonexclusive jurisdiction and service of process of the Hong Kong courts." (Italics added.)[7]

The phrase "governed by" is a broad one signifying a relationship of absolute direction, control, and restraint. Thus, the clause reflects the parties' clear contemplation that "the agreement" is to be completely and absolutely controlled by Hong Kong law. No exceptions are provided. In the context of this case, the agreement to be controlled by Hong Kong law is a shareholders' agreement that expressly provides for the purchase of shares in Seawinds by Nedlloyd and creates the relationship between shareholder and corporation that gives rise to Seawinds's cause of action. Nedlloyd's fiduciary duties, if any, arise from—and can exist only because of—the shareholders' agreement pursuant to which Seawinds's stock was purchased by Nedlloyd.

In order to control completely the agreement of the parties, Hong Kong law must also govern the stock purchase portion of that agreement and the legal duties created by or emanating from the stock purchase, including any fiduciary duties. If Hong Kong law were not applied to these duties, it would effectively control only part of the agreement, not all of it. Such an interpretation would be inconsistent with the unrestricted character of the choice-of-law clause.

Our conclusion in this regard comports with common sense and commercial reality. When a rational business person enters into an agreement establishing a transaction or relationship and provides that disputes arising from the agreement shall be governed by the law of an identified jurisdiction, the logical conclusion is that he or she intended that law to apply to all disputes arising out of the transaction or rela-

---

7. As we have noted, the choice-of-law clause states: "This agreement shall be governed by and *construed in accordance with Hong Kong law....*" (Italics added.) The agreement, of course, includes the choice-of-law clause itself. Thus the question of whether that clause is ambiguous as to its scope (i.e., whether it includes the fiduciary duty claim) is a question of contract interpretation that in the normal course should be determined pursuant to Hong Kong law. (*S. A. Empresa, etc. v. Boeing Co.,* supra, 641 F.2d 746, 751 [interpreting choice-of-law clause pursuant to law chosen by the parties]; *McGill v. Hill* (1982) 31 Wn. App. 542 [644 P.2d 680, 683].) The parties in this case, however, did not request judicial notice of Hong Kong law on this question of interpretation (Evid. Code, §452, subd. (f)) or supply us with evidence of the relevant aspects of that law (Evid. Code, §453, subd. (b)). The question therefore becomes one of California law. (*Com'l Ins. Co. of Newark v. Pacific-Peru Const.* (9th Cir. 1977) 558 F.2d 948, 952; Rest., §136, subd. (2), com. h. p. 378.)

tionship. We seriously doubt that any rational businessperson, attempting to provide by contract for an efficient and business-like resolution of possible future disputes, would intend that the laws of multiple jurisdictions would apply to a single controversy having its origin in a single, contract-based relationship. Nor do we believe such a person would reasonably desire a protracted litigation battle concerning only the threshold question of what law was to be applied to which asserted claims or issues. Indeed, the manifest purpose of a choice-of-law clause is precisely to avoid such a battle.

Seawinds's view of the problem — which would require extensive litigation of the parties' supposed intentions regarding the choice-of-law clause to the end that the laws of multiple states might be applied to their dispute — is more likely the product of postdispute litigation strategy, not predispute contractual intent. If commercially sophisticated parties (such as those now before us) truly intend the result advocated by Seawinds, they should, in fairness to one another and in the interest of economy in dispute resolution, negotiate and obtain the assent of their fellow parties to explicit contract language specifying what jurisdiction's law applies to what issues. * * *

For the reasons stated above, we hold a valid choice-of-law clause, which provides that a specified body of law "governs" the "agreement" between the parties, encompasses all causes of action arising from or related to that agreement, regardless of how they are characterized, including tortious breaches of duties emanating from the agreement or the legal relationships it creates.

2. *Enforceability of chosen law as to fiduciary duty claim.*

Applying the test we have adopted, we find no reason not to apply the parties' choice of law to Seawinds's cause of action for breach of fiduciary duty. As we have explained, Hong Kong, the chosen state, has a "substantial relationship to the parties" because two of those parties are incorporated there. Moreover, their incorporation in that state affords a "reasonable basis" for choosing Hong Kong law.

Seawinds identifies no fundamental public policy of this state that would be offended by application of Hong Kong law to a claim by a Hong Kong corporation against its allegedly controlling shareholder. We are directed to no California statute or constitutional provision designed to preclude freedom of contract in this context. Indeed, even in the absence of a choice-of-law clause, Hong Kong's overriding interest in the internal affairs of corporations domiciled there would in most cases require application of its law. (*See* Rest., § 306 [obligations owed by majority shareholder to corporation determined by the law of the state of incorporation except in unusual circumstances not present here];....)

For strategic reasons related to its current dispute with Nedlloyd, Seawinds seeks to create a fiduciary relationship by disregarding the law Seawinds voluntarily agreed to accept as binding — the law of a state that also happens to be Seawinds's own corporate domicile. To allow Seawinds to use California law in this fashion would further no ascertainable fundamental policy of California; indeed, it would undermine California's policy of respecting the choices made by parties to voluntarily negotiated agreements.

DISPOSITION

By a choice-of-law clause in a fully negotiated commercial contract, the parties have chosen Hong Kong law to apply to their dispute in this case, including each of the causes of action asserted by Seawinds.

Seawinds's action is now proceeding based on its first amended complaint, which will be the focus of further proceedings applying Hong Kong law to resolve the parties' differences. Therefore, the judgments of the Court of Appeal in the consolidated proceedings and the matters are remanded to the Court of Appeal with instructions to issue a peremptory writ of mandate directing the trial court to reconsider its ruling on Nedlloyd's demurrer to Seawinds's first amended complaint in light of applicable Hong Kong law.

Panelli, Justice, concurring and dissenting.

I generally concur in the majority opinion's explanation of the standards controlling when a contractual choice-of-law provision will be honored by the courts of this state and with the majority's application of these standards to Seawinds's cause of action for breach of the covenant of good faith and fair dealing. I write separately to express my disagreement with the majority's conclusion, based on the record before us, that the choice-of-law clause in this case governs Seawinds's cause of action for breach of fiduciary duty. In my view, the majority's analysis of the scope of the choice-of-law clause is unsound.

The choice-of-law clause in this case reads in pertinent part: "This agreement shall be governed by and construed in accordance with Hong Kong law...." The majority determines that the scope of the choice-of-law clause, which was incorporated into the first amended complaint by attachment, extends to related, *noncontractual* causes of action, such as Seawinds's breach of fiduciary duty claim. In so doing, the majority opinion adopts the rule that "[w]hen two sophisticated, commercial entities agree to a choice-of-law clause like the one in this case, the most reasonable interpretation of their actions is that they intended for the clause to apply to all causes of action arising from or related to their contract." Without citing any authority, the majority opinion announces a binding rule of contractual interpretation, based solely upon "common sense and commercial reality." * * * In this case, the language of the incorporated contract easily can be read to apply only to contractual causes of action: "This agreement shall be governed ... by Hong Kong law."

In my view, the majority's mistaken construction of the choice-of-law clause is clear when the language used in the present contract is compared, as Nedlloyd urges us to do, with the language construed by this court in *Smith, Valentino & Smith, Inc. v. Superior Court* (1976) 17 Cal. 3d 491 [131 Cal. Rptr. 374, 551 P.2d 1206]. In that case, this court determined that claims for unfair competition and intentional interference with advantageous business relationships were governed by a choice-of-forum clause as "'actions or proceedings instituted by ... [Smith] under this Agreement with respect to any matters arising under or growing out of this agreement....'" (*id.*

at p. 497, italics in the original.) In contrast to the language used by Nedlloyd and Seawinds in their agreement, the contractual language, "arising under or growing out of this agreement," which was used in *Smith*, explicitly shows an intent to embrace related noncontractual claims, as well as contractual claims. Although similar language was readily available to them, the sophisticated parties in the present case did not draft their choice-of-law clause to clearly encompass related noncontractual causes of action. Therefore, on demurrer and in the absence of parol evidence, I cannot fairly construe the contractual language at issue here to be consistent with the interpretation proposed by Nedlloyd and adopted in the majority opinion. To do so would violate the statutory canon of contract interpretation that "[t]he language of a contract is to govern its interpretation, if the language is clear and explicit, and does not involve an absurdity." (Civ. Code, § 1638.) * * *

I am keenly aware of the need for predictability in the enforcement of commercial contracts. Nevertheless, although courts and litigants may wish the law were otherwise, not every issue can be conclusively determined at the pleading stage. On the present record, the scope of the choice-of-law clause must be construed in favor of Seawinds.

Guardian Savings & Loan Assn. v. MD Associates

Court of Appeal of California, First Appellate District
64 Cal. App. 4th 309, 75 Cal. Rptr. 2d 151 (1998)

SWAGER, JUSTICE.

MD Associates, Michael D. Barker (hereafter Barker), The Ninth and Mission Corporation and Barker-Patrinely Group, Inc., appeal from a judgment of foreclosure, entered on an order granting summary adjudication, which adjudicated two of the defendants, MD Associates and Barker, personally liable on the secured indebtedness. We affirm the judgment with respect to the principal issues on appeal....

PROCEDURAL AND FACTUAL BACKGROUND

[Plaintiff Guardian Savings, a Texas savings and loan association, brought this foreclosure action against its development partner, Michael P. Barker, and several business entities, including MD Associates, the Ninth and Mission Corporation, and the Barker-Patrinely Group, Inc. The parties had been involved in complicated multiple secured transactions concerning cross-purchases of commercial real estate located at 100 First Street and 1235 Mission Street in San Francisco, California. The parties' agreement included a choice-of-law provision that Texas law governed these transactions. Two of the promissory notes secured by the 1235 Mission Street property matured on February 28, 1995, but the defendants failed to pay the amount owing under the notes. On September 22, 1995 plaintiff Guardian Savings filed a complaint for judicial foreclosure of its security interests in 1235 Mission Street and certain pledged certificates against the various defendants. The defendants filed an answer raising a series of affirmative defenses.]

Guardian subsequently filed a motion for summary judgment or, in the alternative, for summary adjudication of each cause of action of the complaint and each of appellant's affirmative defenses. The trial court granted the motion for summary adjudication in orders filed September 3, 1996, and October 21, 1996, and entered a judgment of foreclosure. The judgment determined that MD Associates was indebted to Guardian in the amount of $14,320,911 on the first note and $2,920,878 on the second note, with additional specified interest accruing per day from September 16, 1996. It ordered the sale of the 1235 Mission Street property and the series B certificates and adjudicated MD Associates and Michael D. Barker personally liable for payment of the sums secured by the deeds of trust on the property and the pledge of the certificates. The court retained jurisdiction to determine the amount of the deficiency judgment, if any, to be entered after payment to Guardian of the proceeds of sale.

DISCUSSION

A. Choice-of-law Provision

As the principal assignment of error in this appeal, appellants contend that the trial court erred in enforcing a choice-of-law provision adopting Texas law, included in both the first and second notes secured by the 1235 Mission Street property. It is undisputed that Guardian Savings is a Texas savings and loan association. MD Associates is a joint venture between Barker and Dean Patrinely that, at the inception of this secured transaction,[1] had contacts with Texas essentially equivalent to those of a Texas domiciliary. Both notes are captioned "Houston, Texas" and give a Houston address for the joint venture; they specifically rely on Texas regulatory law and were payable at Guardian's Texas office. The joint venture agreement of MD Associates identifies Barker and Patrinely as residents of Harris County, Texas; contains a choice-of-law provision adopting Texas law; states that the joint venture is formed under the laws of the State of Texas; describes the joint venture as having a place of business at the same Houston address found in the notes; and requires notices to be given at that Houston address. In a response to answers to interrogatories, the defendants themselves describe MD Associates as a "Texas joint venture."

Appellants claim that MD Associates gave the secured notes for the purpose of acquiring the rights to 1235 Mission Street that Guardian possessed under agreements with Delta for purchase of 100 First Street and thus the notes related in substance to purchase-money security interests. While California Code of Civil Procedure section 580b bars a deficiency judgment following foreclosure of a purchase-money security interest, Texas law imposes no similar restriction. Appellants concede that, if the choice-of-law provision was enforceable, the trial court properly entered a deficiency judgment on the unpaid balance of the notes.

---

1. Though Barker declares that he moved his family to California "in 1986" and that MD Associates was headquartered in San Francisco in 1990, we find no triable issue of fact with regard to the status of the joint venture as a Texas domiciliary at the time the financing was negotiated in early 1986. In the interest of assuring the justified expectations of the parties (Rest. 2d Conf. of Laws, § 6, subd. (2)(d)), the 1990 restructuring should be governed by the same choice-of-law rule as the original financing.

In determining the enforceability of the choice-of-law provision, we are guided by the analysis in *Nedlloyd Lines B.V. v. Superior Court* (1992) 3 Cal. 4th 459 [11 Cal. Rptr. 2d 330, 834 P.2d 1148], which held a choice-of-law provision choosing Hong Kong law to be fully enforceable and applicable to the plaintiff's claims. The court rested its decision "on the choice-of-law rules derived from California decisions and the Restatement Second of Conflict of Laws[2] which reflect strong policy considerations favoring the enforcement of freely negotiated choice-of-law clauses." (*Id.* at p. 462.)

The *Nedlloyd* court adopted the "modern approach" of section 187 of the Restatement as a statement of applicable principles, stating unequivocally: "In determining the enforceability of arm's-length contractual choice-of-law provisions, California courts shall apply the principles set forth in Restatement section 187...." (*Nedlloyd Lines B.V. v. Superior Court, supra,* 3 Cal. 4th at pp. 464–465, fn. omitted.) Since the present case does not concern an issue "which the parties could have resolved by an explicit provision in their agreement" (Rest., § 187, subd. (1)) but rather the "substantial validity" of a deficiency judgment based on the provisions of secured promissory notes (Rest., § 187, com. d, p. 564), it is governed by subdivision (2) of section 187. * * *

As summarized in the *Nedlloyd* decision, the analytical approach adopted by Restatement section 187 requires "The Court first to determine either: (1) whether the chosen state has a substantial relationship to the parties or their transaction or (2) whether there is any other reasonable basis for the parties' choice of law. If neither of these tests is met, that is the end of the inquiry, and the court need not enforce the parties' choice of law. If, however, either test is met, the court must next determine whether the chosen state's law is contrary to a fundamental policy of California. If there is no such conflict, the court shall enforce the parties' choice of law. If, however, there is a fundamental conflict with California law, the court must then determine whether California has a 'materially greater interest than the chosen state in the determination of the particular issue.... ' [Citation.]" (*Nedlloyd Lines B.V. v. Superior Court, supra,* 3 Cal. 4th at p. 466, fns. omitted.)

Applying this test, it is clear that the chosen state, Texas, has a substantial relationship to the parties. "'A party's incorporation in a state is a contact sufficient to allow the parties to choose that state's law to govern their contract.'" (*Nedlloyd Lines B.V. v. Superior Court, supra,* 3 Cal. 4th at p. 467,....) Thus, the *Nedlloyd* court found a substantial relationship when two of at least nine contracting parties were incorporated in the chosen state, and, in *Hambrecht & Quist Venture Partners v. American Medical Internat., Inc.* (1995) 38 Cal. App. 4th 1532 [46 Cal. Rptr. 2d 33] at Page 1546, the court found a substantial relationship where two of the three parties to the transaction in question were incorporated in the chosen state. Here, Guardian, the payee under the promissory notes, was undisputedly a corporation formed under Texas law and doing business in that state.

We next must consider whether the application of Texas law pursuant to the choice-of-law provision is contrary to "a fundamental policy of California." We are guided

---

2. Hereafter referred to simply as Restatement.

by the purposes attributed to the antideficiency legislation, and the case law pertaining to waiver of Code of Civil Procedure section 580b[4] protections. Our analysis leads us to conclude that the bar to deficiency judgments set forth in section 580b reflects a fundamental policy that is in conflict with the choice-of-law provision contained in the agreements.

Section 580b provides in pertinent part: "No deficiency judgment shall lie in any event ... under a deed of trust ... given to the vendor to secure payment of the balance of the purchase price of that real property..., or under a deed of trust ... on a dwelling for not more than four families given to a lender to secure repayment of a loan which was in fact used to pay all or part of the purchase price of that dwelling occupied, entirely or in part, by the purchaser." It was enacted in 1933 as part of a series of statutes, including the fair-market-value limitations of sections 726 and 580a, that were intended to aid debtors who had lost real property through foreclosure in the depression. (*Cornelison v. Kornbluth* (1975) 15 Cal. 3d 590, 600–601 [125 Cal. Rptr. 557, 542 P.2d 981]; ...) The related provisions of section 580d, which bars a deficiency judgment following private sales, were enacted later in 1940. The statute assumed its present form in 1963 through an amendment, which clearly defined the rights of nonvendor purchase-money lenders. (Stats. 1963, ch. 2158, § 1, p. 4500.) The amendment distinguished between nonvendor purchase-money loans with respect to whether or not they were made for homeownership, applying the antideficiency protection only to loans for that purpose.

In *Roseleaf Corp. v. Chierighino* (1963) 59 Cal. 2d 35, 42 [27 Cal. Rptr. 873, 378 P.2d 97] (hereafter *Roseleaf*), the court ascribed the legislative purpose of section 580b to two policy objectives relating to economic stabilization-preventing overvaluation of real property and avoiding the aggravation of an economic downturn in a depression. "Section 580b places the risk of inadequate security on the purchase money mortgagee. A vendor is thus discouraged from overvaluing the security. Precarious land promotion schemes are discouraged, for the security value of the land gives purchasers a clue as to its true market value. [Citation.] If inadequacy of the security results, not from overvaluing, but from a decline in property values during a general or local depression, section 580b prevents the aggravation of the downturn that would result if defaulting purchasers were burdened with large personal liability. Section 580b thus serves as a stabilizing factor in land sales." (*Roseleaf, supra*, at p. 42.) The second of these objectives—to prevent the aggravation of a depression-induced downturn in property values—was termed the "primary purpose of section 580b" in *Cornelison v. Kornbluth, supra*, 15 Cal. 3d at p. 603, which analyzed the statutory purpose solely in terms of that objective.

A third legislative purpose—the equitable allocation of risk—finds some limited recognition in dicta and scholarly comment and is reflected in decisions limiting the scope of section 580b. In *Cornelison v. Kornbluth, supra*, 15 Cal. 3d at p. 601, the

---

4. All further references to code sections are to the Code of Civil Procedure unless otherwise indicated.

court observed that "[i]n certain situations," the Legislature regarded deficiency judgments as being "too oppressive," even when restricted by the fair-market-value limitations of sections 726 and 580a. Deficiency judgments on purchase-money security interests may sometimes be regarded as oppressive where the seller is restored to ownership of the property through the foreclosure proceedings and also retains principal payments received from the purchaser. Moreover, it has been suggested that the seller may fairly be required to assume the risk of inadequate security because the seller is better able to know the value of the land than the buyer. * * *

Finally, as it applies to homeowners, section 580b reflects a policy encouraging homeownership by limiting risks of financial loss in acquiring a home. In *Nevin v. Salk* (1975) 45 Cal. App. 3d 331, 341 [119 Cal. Rptr. 370], the court ventured the opinion that "the main goal of the Legislature in enacting and amending section 580b was to protect the ordinary buyer from personal liability when purchasing a home." While this statement may be overly broad, the importance of homeowner protection is unmistakably revealed in the 1963 amendment to section 580b. As section 580b applies to the sale of a home, the amendment extended the antideficiency protections to both vendor financing and third party financing for the purchase price; with respect to other sales, the antideficiency protection applies only to vendor financing.

Without attempting to assess the relative importance of the objectives attributed to section 580b, we are persuaded that the statute reflects a "fundamental policy" of the state within the meaning of section 187 of the Restatement. Comment g to section 187 acknowledges that "[n]o detailed statement can be made of the situations where a 'fundamental' policy of the state ... will be found to exist" and affirms only that "[t]o be 'fundamental,' a policy must in any event be a substantial one" and "need not be as strong as would be required to justify the forum in refusing to entertain suit upon a foreign cause of action...." (Rest., § 187, com. g, p. 568.)

We note that decisions in other jurisdictions have found a fundamental policy within the meaning of Restatement section 187 underlying legislation comprising a scheme of economic regulation or intended to redress "oppressive use of superior bargaining power." The policies underlying such legislation bear some analogy to the economic objectives mentioned in the *Roseleaf* decision and the equitable allocation of risk discussed above.

Our conclusion that the antideficiency legislation reflects a fundamental policy is supported by California precedents dealing with the waiver or evasion of section 580b. It is well established that "[t]he antideficiency provisions of Code of Civil Procedure section 580b may not be contractually waived as a condition of the encumbrance of real property with a purchase money mortgage or deed of trust ... so long as it continues to be secured with the original real estate." (*Palm v. Schilling, supra*, 199 Cal. App. 3d at p. 65.) Such an agreement, "if made, [is] contrary to public policy, void and ineffectual for any purpose." (*Valinda Builders, Inc. v. Bissner* (1964) 230 Cal. App. 2d 106, 112 [40 Cal. Rptr. 735].) Similarly, the courts have invalidated attempts to circumvent section 580b by looking to the substance rather than the form of a transaction. The statute has been applied even though a transaction was structured through separate escrows (*BM Property Development v. Melvin* (1988) 198 Cal. App. 3d 526, 531 [243 Cal. Rptr. 715]) or by use of a straw man (*Ziegler v. Barnes* (1988) 200 Cal. App. 3d 224, 228–230 [246 Cal. Rptr. 69]). * * *

These precedents, in our opinion, reveal a policy sufficiently strong to be characterized as fundamental within the meaning of Restatement section 187 because they elevate the statutory policy of section 580b above the consensual arrangements of the parties. If the policy underlying section 580b bars avoidance of the statute by contractual waiver or a formal structuring of a transaction, it should be fundamental enough to restrict use of a choice-of-law provision to avoid application of the statute. In many circumstances, the enforcement in California courts of a choice-of-law provision adopting out-of-state law will be the practical equivalent of enforcing a contractual waiver of section 580b. Since the threshold requirement of Restatement section 187 is met whenever the lender is a domiciliary in the chosen state,[12] creditors could often use a choice-of-law provision to accomplish a result that would be "contrary to public policy, void and ineffectual" if attempted directly by a contractual waiver.

Having concluded that section 580b reflects a fundamental policy in California, we turn to the last criterion of the Restatement test—whether California has "a materially greater interest than the chosen state in the determination of the particular issue." (Rest., § 187, subd. (2).) We construe the reference to "the particular issue" as calling for an inquiry into the specific facts of an individual case. (*Ibid.*)

The policies underlying section 580b in fact have limited application to the present case. First, the transaction does not involve the sale of a home, which would implicate the strong policies reflected in the 1963 amendment of the statute. Second, the policy of equitable risk allocation does not apply to a transaction negotiated between sophisticated Texas domiciliaries. While California may have an interest in the performance of a transaction within the state, it has a more questionable interest in the equitable nature of the transaction where the rights and duties of the parties were established by agreement of nondomiciliaries outside its jurisdiction. Such an interest is clearly absent where, as here, the bargain was negotiated between sophisticated, professional investors in a specialized field. Finally, the second objective recognized in the *Roseleaf* decision ... —to prevent the aggravation of a downturn in market prices—becomes more problematic when both parties are domiciliaries of another state. Whether or not the transaction implicates this policy will be dependent on many circumstances that cannot be as readily presumed as in the case of a transaction with more contacts within the state.

At the same time, the interest of Texas in assuring the justified expectations of the parties to an agreement has maximum force where the agreement is negotiated be-

---

12. Only five other states have purchase-money antideficiency statutes. (Comment, *Application of California's Antideficiency Statutes in Conflict of Laws Contexts, supra,* 73 Cal.L.Rev. at p. 1365, fn. 167.)

tween domiciliaries of that state. In *DeSantis v. Wackenhut Corp., supra*, 793 S.W.2d at p. 677, the Texas Supreme Court observed that "the most basic policy of contract law ... is the protection of the justified expectations of the parties. [Citations.] The parties' understanding of their respective contractual rights and obligations depends in part upon the certainty with which they may predict how the law will interpret and enforce their agreement. [Citation.] [¶] When parties to a contract ... expect to perform their respective obligations in multiple jurisdictions, they may be uncertain as to what jurisdiction's law will govern construction and enforcement of the contract. To avoid this uncertainty, they may express in their agreement their own choice that the law of a specified jurisdiction apply to their agreement. Judicial respect for their choice advances the policy of protecting their expectations."

Under the specific circumstances of the present case, we hold that California's interest in the enforcement of the policies underlying section 580 is not materially greater than Texas's policy of assuring the justified expectations of the parties. We recognize that the issue is close and limit our holding to the peculiar facts of this case: a series of complex security interests on a large commercial property, negotiated between sophisticated Texas domiciliaries. Under these narrow circumstances, we consider that Restatement section 187 calls for enforcement of the provision in the promissory note adopting Texas law. In the absence of the bar of section 580b, the trial court properly entered a judgment for the unpaid balance on the notes. * * *

Notes and Questions on California Choice-of-Law Agreements

(1) The Supreme Court in *Nedlloyd Lines* directly relied on §187(2) of the Second Restatement to formulate the test for determining enforceability of a contractual choice-of-law provision. Section 187(2) contains some ambiguities, does it not? What constitutes a "substantial relationship" between the chosen law and the parties or their transaction? What factors did the Supreme Court focus on in *Nedlloyd* to find the requisite "substantial relationship"? Would you describe this relationship between Hong Kong law and the parties as "substantial," or as "minimal"?

(a) Section 187(2) also authorizes enforcement of a choice-of-law clause where, in the absence of a "substantial relationship," there is some other "reasonable basis" for the parties' choice of law. Why would the parties choose a state's law that has no relation to the parties or their transaction? What types of contractual relationships are likely to produce such a choice? *See, e.g., 1-800-Got Junk? LLC v. Superior Court*, 189 Cal. App. 4th 500, 116 Cal. Rptr. 3d 923 (2010) (finding a reasonable basis existed for franchisor headquartered in Vancouver to specify application of Washington law in agreement with California franchisee because multistate franchisor has an interest in having all its franchise agreements governed by one body of law). What constitutes a "reasonable basis," generally? How did the *Nedlloyd* court apply this factor? Did the court apply this factor in the context anticipated by the Second Restatement?

(b) Pursuant to §187(2), a court should not enforce a choice-of-law provision when the chosen state's law is contrary to a "fundamental policy" of California. What constitutes a "fundamental policy"? Every state law expresses a policy of the state. How is a "fundamental policy" distinguishable from a run-of-the-mill policy? *See Brack v. Omni Loan Co., Ltd.*, 164 Cal. App. 4th 1312, 1323, 80 Cal. Rptr. 3d 275 (2008) ("The relative significance of a particular policy or statutory scheme can be determined by considering whether parties may, by agreement, avoid the policy or statutory requirement"); Kirt O'Neil, *Contractual Choice of Law: The Case for a New Determination of Full Faith and Credit Limitations*, 71 Tex. L. Rev. 1019 (1993). How did the *Guardian Savings* court apply this factor?

(c) In *Application Group, Inc. v. Hunter Group, Inc.*, 61 Cal. App. 4th 881, 72 Cal. Rptr. 2d 73 (1998), the court applied Restatement (Second) § 187(2)(b) and refused to enforce a contractual choice-of-law provision which specified that Maryland law governed contract related disputes because the application of Maryland law to the parties' dispute would be contrary to fundamental public policy of California. Plaintiff Application Group, a California corporation, had recruited and hired an employee from defendant Hunter Group, a competitor Maryland corporation, despite a covenant not to compete in the employee's contract with the defendant. The employee and Application Group brought an action to declare that the covenant not to compete was illegal under California law. The defendant invoked the Maryland choice-of-law clause, and argued that the covenant was valid under Maryland law. The Court of Appeal upheld the trial court's refusal to enforce the choice-of-law agreement.

Relying on *Nedlloyd Lines B.V. v. Superior Court*, the court in *Application Group* first determined that the chosen state—Maryland—had a "substantial relationship" to the parties and their transaction and that there was a "reasonable basis" for the parties' contractual choice-of-law provision, and then determined whether the clause was nevertheless unenforceable under the public policy exception of Restatement § 187(b)(2). The court found that Maryland's law was contrary to a strong public policy of the State of California expressed in § 16600 of the Business and Professions Code, which makes noncompetition covenants unenforceable.

Although both states had an interest in applying its law to this case, the court concluded that under the circumstances "California has a materially greater interest than does Maryland in the application of its law to the parties' dispute, and that California's interests would be more seriously impaired if its policy were subordinated to the policy of Maryland." *Application Group*, 61 Cal. App. 4th at 902. California's interests were to protect freedom of movement of persons whom California-based employers wish to employ in California and to ensure that California employers will be able to compete effectively for the most talented employees. Maryland's interests in enforcing noncompetition covenants was to serve Maryland employers in preventing recruitment of employees who provide "unique services," and the misuse of trade secrets.

The *Application Group* court viewed Maryland's interests as adequately protected under trade secrets laws. Moreover, the application of Maryland law would allow an out-of-state employer/competitor to limit employment and business opportunities in California. Accordingly, the court upheld the trial court's refusal to enforce the choice-of-law clause because the application of Maryland law enforcing a noncompetition covenant would be contrary to California's fundamental policy. *Application Group,* 61 Cal. App. 4th at 902. The court then concluded that California law applied, in the absence of an enforceable choice-of-law agreement, under either the government interest approach or the "relevant contacts" approach of § 188(2) of the Second Restatement. *Id.* at 903.

(d) In *American Online, Inc., v. Superior Court,* 90 Cal. App. 4th 1, 108 Cal. Rtpr. 2d 699 (2001), the court refused to enforce a choice of law clause, accompanied by a forum selection clause, in a consumer contract that designated Virginia law as governing, and Virginia as the exclusive jurisdiction for, disputes arising out of the contractual relationship. The court found these clauses unenforceable for two independent reasons. First, one of the plaintiff's causes of action sought class action relief under the California Consumers Legal Remedies Act (CLRA), Civil Code § 1750 et seq., and this Act contains a provision that voids any purported waiver of rights under the CLRA as being contrary to California public policy. "Enforcement of the contractual forum selection and choice of law clauses," the court reasoned, "would be the functional equivalent of a contractual waiver of the consumer protections under the CLRA and, thus, is prohibited under California law." *American Online,* 90 Cal. App. 4th at 5.

(e) In *ABF Capital Corp. v. Grove Properties Co.,* 126 Cal. App. 4th 204, 23 Cal. Rptr. 3d 803 (2005), the court refused to enforce a choice-of-law provision in a partnership agreement that provided the agreement would be construed under New York law. The plaintiff, a New York company, sued defendants, a California partnership and individual, for breach of contract. The superior court sustained defendants' demurrer and entered judgment for defendants. The defendants then sought an award of contractual attorney fees. The partnership agreement contained a one-sided attorney fee provision that obligated the defendants, but not the plaintiff, to pay attorney fees if plaintiff enforced the agreement through adjudication. New York law would enforce a unitary attorney fees provision. However, California law—Civil Code § 1717— would create reciprocal rights from a nonreciprocal attorney fees provision. The trial court applied New York law and denied defendants' motion for attorney fees; defendants appealed.

Applying § 187 and § 188 of the Second Restatement, the Court of Appeal concluded California law applies to the issue of attorney fees and reversed the trial court. The court first found that Civil Code § 1717 reflects a fundamental public policy of California concerning the reciprocity of attorney fees provisions in contracts. The court then decided that California has a materially greater interest than New York in the attorney fees issue because of California's strong interest in seeing its residents receive fair play with respect to attorney fees when resort is made to the California courts. "California has a materially greater interest in enforcing the equitable rules governing access to its courts—including the reciprocal attorney fees rule—than New York has in assuring the enforcement of New York law concerning attorney fees," the court reasoned, "when those attorney fees are not incurred as a result of any use of New York courts, and have no effect on the accessibility to New York courts." *ABF Capital,* 126 Cal. App. 4th at 220.

The *ABF Capital* court then addressed one final step in the analysis: Would California law apply in the absence of an effective choice-of-law agreement by the parties? The court noted that other California decisions, such as *Guardian Savings & Loan Assn. v. MD Associates*, reproduced *supra*, tend to overlook this part of the analysis. Applying the principles of government interest analysis and the factors stated in § 188 of the Second Restatement, the court concluded that California law applies. The court emphasized that under § 188, the relevant "contacts are to be evaluated according to their relative importance with respect to the particular issue," which here is the procedural issue of attorney fees and not substantive issues of the partnership or its operations. *ABF Capital*, 126 Cal. App. 4th at 220–23.

(2) Civil Code section 1646.5 authorizes an exception to the "substantial relationship" requirement for contracts relating to a transaction involving more than $250,000, including those otherwise covered by Commercial Code § 1301(a). Civil Code § 1645.5 provides that parties to such transactions may agree that the law of California may govern their rights and duties "whether or not the contract ... or transaction bears a reasonable relation to this state." What policies did the Legislature seek to further by enacting Civil Code § 1645.5? Is § 1645.5 consistent with § 187(2) of the Second Restatement? If not, does that matter? If parties rely on § 1645.5 and choose the law of a state which has no reasonable relationship to the parties, the contract, or the transaction, will a court's application of that law be unconstitutional? *See* O'Neil, *Contractual Choice of Law, supra*.

(3) In light of the *Nedlloyd* opinions, how should you state a choice-of-law provision when your client wants California law to govern only contractual disputes arising from the agreement, but wants Hong Kong law to govern any noncontractual disputes? How would you state a choice-of-law provision where your client wants California law to govern all disputes arising from the contractual relationship, and you want to draft a clause that will be enforced by all members of the Supreme Court? How would you state a provision where your client wants some aspect of California law incorporated as a term of the contract, but wants Hong Kong law to apply to any dispute arising out of the contractual relationship?

(4) Another prerequisite to enforcement of a choice-of-law clause is that the clause must be valid as a matter of contract formation principles. The court in *Nedlloyd* noted that, as with a forum selection clause, a choice-of-law clause must be entered into freely and voluntarily by the parties who have negotiated at arm's length. *Nedlloyd*, 3 Cal. 4th at 464. The clause must not be the product of fraud, undue influence, or unequal bargaining power. *See The Bremen v. Zapata Off-Shore Co.*, 407 U.S. 1, 12–13, 92 S. Ct. 1907, 32 L. Ed. 2d 513 (1972); *Cal-State Bus. Prod. & Serv., Inc. v. Ricoh*, 12 Cal. App. 4th 1666, 1678–81, 16 Cal. Rptr. 2d 417 (1993); Mark J. Kelson, *Choice-of-Law, Venue, and Consent-to-Jurisdiction Provisions in California Lending Agreements: Can Good Draftsmanship Overcome Bad Choice-of-Law Doctrine?*, 23 Loy. L.A. L. Rev. 1337, 1371–84 (1990) (discussing problems of unconscionability in choice-of-law and forum clauses in commercial lending agreements).

This means that every case which involves resistance to enforcement of a choice-of-law clause could potentially include an inquiry into whether the clause is valid under contract formation principles, does it not? *See, e.g., Furda v. Superior Court,* 161 Cal. App. 3d 418, 426, 207 Cal. Rptr. 646 (1984) (inquiring into whether forum selection clause was adhesive in nature prior to clause enforcement); Jeffry A. Liesemer, *Carnival's Got the Fun ... and the Forum: A New Look at Choice-of-Forum Clauses and the Unconscionability Doctrine After Carnival Cruise Lines, Inc. v. Shute,* 53 U. PITT. L. REV. 1025 (1992).

(a) Which state's law of contract validity governs such an inquiry—the law of the forum or the law designated in the choice-of-law clause? For example, assume in *Nedlloyd* that the plaintiff had alleged that the provision designating Hong Kong law was invalid because the provision was the product of unfair bargaining, and therefore should not be enforced. Should the California court apply Hong Kong law or California law when determining this validity issue? *See generally* Linda S. Mullenix, *Another Choice of Forum, Another Choice of Law: Consensual Adjudication Procedure in Federal Court,* 57 FORD. L. REV. 291, 346–56 (1988); Michael Gruson, *Governing-Law Clauses in International and Interstate Loan Agreements—New York Approach,* 1982 U. ILL. L. REV. 207 (1982).

(b) Another troublesome issue is whether a court should enforce a choice-of-law clause in a standard form consumer contract which, due to unequal bargaining power between buyer and seller, is not the product of free negotiation. The U.S. Supreme Court addressed this issue as to forum selection clauses in *Carnival Cruise Lines v. Shute, Inc.,* 499 U.S. 585, 111 S. Ct. 1522, 113 L. Ed. 2d 622 (1991), and concluded that such clauses in consumer contracts should generally be enforced where the consumer had notice of the clause. Because it was an admiralty jurisdiction case decided by federal common law, *Carnival Cruise* is not binding on state courts generally. *Id.* at 590. Should the California courts enforce a choice-of-law clause in a standard form consumer contract? *See Washington Mut. Bank v. Superior Court,* 24 Cal. 4th. 906, 103 Cal. Rptr. 2d 320, 15 P.3d 1071 (2001) (California has no public policy against the enforcement of choice-of-law provisions contained in contracts of adhesion where they are otherwise appropriate).

[B] Conflicts Analysis When No Choice-of-Law Agreement

Stonewall Surplus Lines Ins. Co. v. Johnson Controls, Inc.

Court of Appeal of California, Fourth Appellate District
14 Cal. App. 4th 637, 17 Cal. Rptr. 2d 713 (1993)

BENKE, ACTING PRESIDING JUSTICE.

In this case a San Diego jury returned a verdict assessing $6.5 million in exemplary damages against a Wisconsin corporation. The corporation's liability insurers, residents of Connecticut, Alabama, Texas and Illinois, filed a declaratory relief action alleging they were not required to provide the corporation with any indemnity for the exemplary damages. The corporation answered the complaint, alleging Wisconsin law governed the policies and under Wisconsin law the insurers were liable for both compensatory and punitive damages.

On cross-motions for summary judgment the trial court agreed with the insurers and entered judgment in favor of the insurers. On appeal we affirm.

The parties agree that in California an insured may not seek indemnity from an insurer for exemplary damages. Because the defective battery which gave rise to the underlying claim was manufactured in California and caused injury in California to a California resident, California has an interest which supports application of this restriction on insurance coverage.

FACTUAL AND PROCEDURAL HISTORY

A *Jones Action.*

On June 3, 1986, a resident of San Diego, Gary Jones was assisting his neighbor Fred Hill "jump-start" Hill's car. While Jones was working on Hill's battery it exploded. Jones suffered brain damage and was blinded in one eye. As a result of his injuries Jones has experienced persistent seizures.

The battery in Hill's car was manufactured in Fullerton, California, by defendant and appellant Johnson Controls, Inc. (Johnson Controls). Hill purchased the battery from a Sears store in San Diego.

Jones and his wife, Mona, filed a complaint against Hill, Sears, and Johnson Controls in superior court in San Diego. Following trial, the jury returned a verdict which found Johnson Controls and Sears had been negligent and that their negligence caused Jones's injuries. The jury found Jones had not been negligent. The jury awarded Jones $2,905,000 in compensatory damages and his wife $325,000 in damages.

In addition, the jury found Johnson Controls had acted with malice, fraud or oppression. As we have previously noted, the jury found that $6.5 million was an appropriate amount of punitive damages to impose on Johnson Controls. Judgment in the amount of $10,693,649.228 was entered against Johnson Controls.

B. *These Proceedings.*

On March 17, 1989, shortly after the verdict in the Jones action was returned, plaintiffs and respondents Stonewall Surplus Lines Insurance Company (Stonewall), Constitution State Insurance Company (Constitution) and Republic Insurance Company (Republic) filed a declaratory relief action against Johnson Controls and the Joneses in superior court in San Diego. The insurers alleged they had provided excess liability insurance to Johnson Controls at the time Jones was injured. The insurers further alleged they were not required to indemnify Johnson Controls for the exemplary damages awarded because such indemnification was contrary to public policy and because they had not been given timely notice of the Joneses' claim.

After making an unsuccessful attempt to remove the case to district court and an unsuccessful attempt to have the case dismissed on forum non conveniens grounds,

Johnson Controls filed an answer. As an affirmative defense Johnson Controls alleged the insurance policies issued by the excess insurers were governed by Wisconsin law and that, in any event, a judgment in the excess insurers' favor would be an unconstitutional impairment of Johnson Controls's contract rights and violate its right to due process of law.

The insurers moved for summary adjudication. They argued that, as alleged in their complaint, they are not liable for the punitive damages assessed against Johnson Controls. Johnson Controls filed a cross-motion for summary judgment or, in the alternative, summary adjudication. Johnson Controls, as alleged in its answer, argued the insurance contracts were governed by Wisconsin law which permits insurance companies to indemnify punitive damages awards.

The trial court agreed with the insurers and granted their motion and denied Johnson Controls's motion. Having found the insurers had no obligation to indemnify the punitive damage award and no other triable issue of material fact, the trial court entered judgment in favor of the insurers. Johnson Controls filed a timely notice of appeal.

ISSUES ON APPEAL

As it did below, Johnson Controls argues its rights under the insurance policies are governed by the law of Wisconsin, the state where its headquarters are located. Johnson Controls contends Wisconsin law is required by both conflict of laws principles and the United States Constitution. We reject these contentions and affirm the judgment.

DISCUSSION

I

We begin our analysis of Johnson Controls's conflict of laws argument by determining whether there is any conflict between the laws of California and Wisconsin. As succinctly described in *Hurtado v. Superior Court* (1974) 11 Cal. 3d 574, 580 [114 Cal. Rptr. 106, 522 P.2d 666]: "The fact that two states are involved does not in itself indicate that there is a 'conflict of laws' or 'choice of law' problem. There is obviously no problem where the laws of the two states are identical." (*Id.*, at p. 580; …)

The parties agree that in California an insurer is not liable for any portion of a judgment which awards punitive damages. (*City Products Corp. v. Globe Indemnity Co.* (1979) 88 Cal. App. 3d 31, 42 [151 Cal. Rptr. 494] (*City Products*); …) As explained in *City Products*, "the policy of this state with respect to punitive damages would be frustrated by permitting the party against whom they are awarded to pass on the liability to an insurance carrier. The objective is to impose such damages in an amount which will appropriately punish the defendant in view of 'the actual damages sustained,' the magnitude and flagrancy of the offense, the importance of the policy violated, and the wealth of the defendant." [Citation.] Consideration of the wealth of the defendant would of course be pointless if such damages could be covered by insurance. The onus of the award would depend entirely upon the amount of insurance coverage and not upon the legally relevant factors. We conclude, therefore,

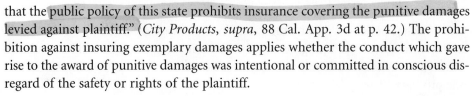

that the public policy of this state prohibits insurance covering the punitive damages levied against plaintiff." (*City Products, supra,* 88 Cal. App. 3d at p. 42.) The prohibition against insuring exemplary damages applies whether the conduct which gave rise to the award of punitive damages was intentional or committed in conscious disregard of the safety or rights of the plaintiff.

The rule in Wisconsin is different. (*See Brown v. Maxey* (1985) 124 Wis. 2d 426 [369 N.W.2d 677, 686–688].) In *Brown v. Maxey* a landlord was held liable for burns suffered by one of his tenants in a fire; in addition to compensatory damages the jury awarded $200,000 in punitive damages. The Supreme Court of Wisconsin held the jury could award punitive damages based on the landlord's reckless disregard of his tenant's safety.

The Wisconsin court also held the landlord's insurer was required under the terms of its policy to pay both the compensatory and punitive portions of the judgment. (*Brown v. Maxey, supra,* 369 N.W.2d at pp. 686–688.) The court found that as defined in the policy "[t]he term 'damages' is sufficiently broad to cover liability for both compensatory and punitive damages. Punitive damages are not specifically excluded from the policy language." (*Brown v. Maxey, supra,* 369 N.W.2d at p. 686.)

Unlike the court in *City Products,* the Wisconsin Supreme Court found that public policy did not prevent indemnity for punitive damages. "'Public policy' is no magic touchstone. This state has more than one public policy. Another and countervailing public policy favors freedom of contract, in the absence of overriding reasons for depriving the parties of that freedom. Still another public policy favors the enforcement of insurance contracts according to their terms, where the insurance company accepts the premium and reasonably represents or implies that coverage is provided. [Citation.]

" … We find no overriding reason to deprive these parties of what they have freely contracted. State Farm had the option of excluding liability for punitive damages. It failed to do so and has presumably collected premiums which it believed to be sufficient consideration for such coverage. [Citation.]

"Moreover, we are not convinced that allowing insurance coverage for punitive damages will totally alleviate the deterrent effect of such awards. For example, as a consequence of the punitive damage award, defendant Maxey's insurance premiums may rise, he may find himself unable to obtain insurance coverage, the punitive damage award may exceed coverage, and his reputation in the community may be injured.

"Finally, punitive damages are designed not only to deter and punish the wrongdoer, but also are designed to serve as a deterrent to others. Allowing insurance coverage to extend to punitive damages will not thwart this purpose." (*Brown v. Maxey, supra,* 369 N.W.2d at pp. 687–688.)

In this case we cannot avoid consideration of the conflict between the laws of California and Wisconsin. Under California law public policy prevents Johnson Controls from avoiding the deterrent effect of the punitive damages by obtaining indemnity from its insurers.

On the other hand, like the insurance policy discussed in *Brown v. Maxey*, the excess insurers' policies do not expressly exclude coverage for punitive damages. * * * Thus, under *Brown v. Maxey* the excess insurance policies would provide indemnity for the punitive damages assessed in the Jones action and Johnson Controls's contractual right to such indemnity would prevail over any public policy supporting imposition of punitive damages.

In short then, there is a true conflict of laws here because the substantive law of California leads to a different result than the substantive law of Wisconsin.

II

"California now follows a methodology characterized as the 'governmental interest' approach to choice of law problems. Applying this method, the forum must search to find the proper law to apply based upon the interests of the litigants and the involved states. (*Reich v. Purcell* [(1967)] *supra*, [67 Cal. 2d 551] at p. 553.) With the governmental interest approach, 'relevant contacts' stressed by the Restatement Second of Conflict of Laws are not disregarded, but are examined in connection with the analysis of the interest of the involved state in the issues, the character of the contract and the relevant purposes of the contract law under consideration. The forum must consider all the foreign and domestic elements and interests involved in the case to determine the applicable rule. (*Reich v. Purcell, supra,* 67 Cal. 2d at p. 555.)" (*Dixon Mobile Homes, Inc. v. Walters* (1975) 48 Cal. App. 3d 964, 972 [122 Cal. Rptr. 202], fn. omitted [overruled on other grounds by *Bullis v. Security Pacific Nat. Bank* (1978) 21 Cal. 3d 801, 815 (148 Cal. Rptr. 22, 582 P.2d 109, 7 A.L.R.4th 642)]; ...)

In considering the interests of the parties and the states involved, initially we note there is no express choice of law provision in the policies issued by the excess insurers. The absence of a choice by the parties is significant because where the parties have made a choice of law, their choice is usually enforced. (Rest. 2d Conf. of Laws, §187; ...)

Where no effective choice of law has been made by the parties, the relevant contacts to be considered in a dispute over the validity of a contract or the rights thereunder are set forth in section 188, subdivision (2) of the Restatement Second of Conflict of Laws: "(a) the place of contracting, [¶] (b) the place of negotiation of the contract, [¶] (c) the place of performance, [¶] (d) the location of the subject matter of the contract, and [¶] (e) the domicile, residence, nationality, place of incorporation and place of business of the parties. [¶] These contacts are to be evaluated according to their relative importance with respect to the particular issue." (*See also Dixon Mobile Homes, Inc. v. Walters, supra,* 48 Cal. App. 3d at p. 972; ...)

Where, as here, a casualty insurance contract is in dispute, particular importance is placed on the location of the subject matter of the contract, i.e. the location of the insured risk. (*See California Casualty Indemnity Exchange v. Pettis* (1987) 193 Cal. App. 3d 1597, 1607 [239 Cal. Rptr. 205]; Witkin, *supra*, Contracts, §71, pp. 106; Rest. 2d, Conf. of Laws, §193.) "The Restatement Second of Conflict of Laws section 193 states: "The validity of a contract of fire, surety or casualty insurance and the rights created thereby are determined by the local law of the state which the parties understood was to be the principal location of the insured risk during the term of the policy, unless with respect to the particular issue, some other state has a more significant relationship.… ' As the court explained in *Cunningham v. Equitable Life Assur. Soc. of U.S.* (2d Cir. 1981) 652 F.2d 306: 'In contracts of casualty insurance, … the principal location of the insured risk is given particular emphasis in determining the choice of the applicable law. [Citation.] This is so because location has an intimate bearing upon the nature of the risk and the parties would naturally expect the local law of the state where the risk is to be principally located to apply. [Citations.] Moreover, the state where the insured risk will be principally located during the term of the policy has an interest in the determination of issues arising under the insurance contract.' (*Id.*, at p. 308, fn. 1.)" (*California Casualty Indemnity Exchange v. Pettis, supra*, 193 Cal. App. 3d at p. 1607.)

More importantly for our purposes, "Where a multiple risk policy insures against risks located in several states, it is likely that the courts will view the transaction as if it involved separate policies, each insuring an individual risk, and apply the law of the state of principal location of the particular risk involved. (Rest. 2d, Conflict of Laws, §193, Comment f.)"[5] (Witkin, *supra*, Contracts, §71, p. 106; … *but see Vigen Const. Co. v. Millers Nat. Ins. Co.* (N.D. 1989) 436 N.W.2d 254, 257; *St. Paul Surplus Lines v. Diversified Athletic* (N.D. Ill. 1989) 707 F. Supp. 1506, 1513.[6]

We believe the multiple risk approach suggested by Witkin and the Restatement should apply here. Initially, we note that in an effort to obtain excess coverage, Johnson Controls circulated an underwriting submission prepared by its insurance broker. Attached to the underwriting submission is a list of 18 states and 5 foreign

---

5. Restatement Second, Conflict of Laws section 193, comment f, states: "A special problem is presented by multiple risk policies which insure against risks located in several states. A single policy may, for example, insure dwelling houses located in states X, Y and Z. These states may require that any fire insurance policy on buildings situated within their territory shall be in a special statutory form. If so, the single policy will usually incorporate the special statutory forms of the several states involved. Presumably, the courts would be inclined to treat such a case, at least with respect to most issues, as if it involved three policies, each insuring an individual risk. So, if the house located in state X were damaged by fire, it is thought that the court would determine the rights and obligations of the parties under the policy, at least with respect to most issues, in accordance with the local law of X. In any event, that part of a policy which incorporates the special statutory form of a state would be construed in accordance with the rules of construction of that state."

6. In *Vigen Const. Co. v. Millers Nat. Ins. Co., supra*, 436 N.W.2d at page 257 and *St. Paul Surplus Lines v. Diversified Athletic, supra*, 707 F. Supp. at page 1513, the courts relied solely on comment b to section 193 of the Restatement Second of Conflict of Laws which states in part: "The location of the insured risk will given greater weight than any other single contact in determining the state of the applicable law provided that the risk can be located, at least principally, in a single state. Situations where this cannot be done, and where the location of the risk has less significance, include (1) where the insured object will be more or less constantly on the move from state to state during the term of the policy and (2) where the policy covers a group of risks that are scattered throughout two or more states." We do not believe it is appropriate to rely solely on comment b without considering the applicability of comment f (*see* fn. 5, *ante*) and the likelihood that the parties intended to create separate policies for the risks created in separate states.

countries where Johnson Controls operates manufacturing facilities and 128 locations from Adelaide, Australia to Youngstown, Ohio where the corporation has sales and service facilities. According to the text of the underwriting submission, Johnson Controls expected to produce $2.6 billion in sales during the 1985–1986 policy period. * * *

Thus, the record here supports the conclusion Johnson Controls is a large corporation with worldwide operations and, more importantly, both Johnson Controls and its insurers carefully considered the complexity of the corporation's activities at the time the policies were issued. Under these circumstances we believe Johnson Controls and its insurers would reasonably expect not only that the corporation's liability to a third party might be governed by the law of a state with significant interests at stake, but that Johnson Controls's right to indemnity for such a claim might also be governed by that state's law. As suggested by Witkin and the Restatement, given the nature of the risks insured, this is a case where in reality Johnson Controls did not obtain a single policy which it could expect would be governed by the law of one state; rather, Johnson Controls obtained separate policies which insure separate risks located in any number of states where the corporation does business.[7]

Our adoption of the multiple risk approach is significant in measuring the competing interests of California and Wisconsin. First, there can be little doubt that from the perspective of Johnson Controls and the insurers, California is the principal location of the risk created by the defective battery. The battery was manufactured in California, sold to a retailer here and purchased by a California resident. Thus, Johnson Controls and the insurers would reasonably expect this risk to be governed by California law. (Rest. 2d, Conf. of Laws, § 193, com. f.)

As we have seen, in *Brown v. Maxey* the court found Wisconsin's interest in protecting the reasonable expectations of its insureds outweighs any additional deterrence provided by a rule which relieves insurers from responsibility for punitive damages. Because Johnson Controls would reasonably expect California law would apply to the battery it manufactured and sold here, application of the California rule would not seriously impair the expectation interest Wisconsin has sought to protect by permitting insurers to pay punitive damage awards. Rather, since we have concluded Johnson Controls obtained multiple policies, application of the California rule would give Johnson Controls the benefit of its bargain with the insurers.[8]

In contrast, failure to apply California's rule would severely impair California's interests. As we have seen California's paramount interest is in protecting its residents by deterring

---

7. We do not mean to suggest that such a multiple risk approach will be appropriate in all cases where an insured's activities expose it to liability in a number of states. In a variety of circumstances the particular risks insured or a particular policy will make it clear that the parties do not expect the insured's rights under a policy will be controlled by the location of insured event. (*See e.g.*, com. b to Rest. 2d, Conf. of Laws, § 193.)

8. We also note the court in *Brown v. Maxey* recognized Wisconsin has an interest, albeit a subsidiary one, in providing deterrence to tortfeasors. Obviously, application of the California rule would enhance that subsidiary interest.

tortfeasors. Here, the liability imposed grew out of severe injury suffered by a California resident while he was in California and caused by manufacturing and marketing activities which occurred exclusively in this state. It is difficult to imagine circumstances where California would have a greater interest in altering the future behavior of a defendant by compelling payment directly from the defendant rather than its insurers.

In sum then California's rule applies here because it is the principal location of the risk involved, because application of California's rule is entirely consistent with Wisconsin's interest in protecting the reasonable expectations of its insured and because California has a significant interest in applying its rule.

III

In addition to its choice of laws contentions, on appeal Johnson Controls argues application of California law is barred by the due process and full faith and credit clauses of the United States Constitution. (U.S. Const., 14th Amend., art. IV, §1.) We reject this argument.

Due process and full faith and credit require "that for a State's substantive law to be selected in a constitutionally permissible manner, that State must have a significant contact or significant aggregation of contacts, creating state interests, such that choice of its law is neither arbitrary nor fundamentally unfair." (*Allstate Ins. Co. v. Hague* (1981) 449 U.S. 302, 313 [66 L. Ed. 2d 521, 530–531, 101 S. Ct. 633]; *see also Phillips Petroleum Co. v. Shutts* (1985) 472 U.S. 797, 821–822 [86 L. Ed. 2d 628, 648–649, 105 S. Ct. 2965].) As we pointed out in our discussion of the choice of laws issue, California has a substantial interest in regulating Johnson Controls's manufacturing activities in this state, especially as here, where those activities have injured one of its residents.

Judgment affirmed.

Notes and Questions regarding Contracts Conflicts Analysis in the Absence of a Choice-of-Law Agreement

(1) The insurance policies in *Stonewall Surplus* did not contain choice-of-law provisions. Are there any good business reasons for not including such a clause in a contract which involves a multi-state transaction? Why do some multi-state contracts not contain a choice-of-law clause? If the insurance policies in *Stonewall Surplus* had contained clauses designating that "Wisconsin law will govern all disputes arising out of the contractual relationship," would the Court of Appeal have applied California law to the insurance coverage issue? Would such a clause be enforced under §187(2) of the Second Restatement? Under the doctrine propounded by the Supreme Court in *Nedlloyd*? What arguments might there be for not enforcing such a choice-of-law provision in a case like *Stonewall Surplus*?

(2) What was the basis of the court's choice-of-law analysis in *Stonewall Surplus*? Section 188 of the Second Restatement? The "governmental interest" doctrine? Both? The court determined that there was a true conflict of laws "because the substantive law of California leads to a different result than the substantive law of Wisconsin."

Stonewall Surplus, 14 Cal. App. 4th at 645. Does this constitute a "true conflict" within the meaning of Currie interest analysis? Did the Court of Appeal actually undertake a "governmental interest" analysis within the meaning of *Reich v. Purcell, supra*, in finding a "true conflict"; or did the court misconstrue that analysis? Is *Stonewall Surplus* more appropriately viewed as a "false conflict" case? Why?

(a) After finding a true conflict between California and Wisconsin law, how did the court in *Stonewall Surplus* resolve this conflict? By undertaking a "comparative impairment" analysis? An analysis based on the Second Restatement? Both? What factors did the court view as being determinative of the choice-of-law question? Why? Do you agree with the manner by which the court "measured" the competing interests of California and Wisconsin? Was the methodology utilized by the Court of Appeal in *Stonewall Surplus* consistent with the "comparative impairment" analysis utilized by the Supreme Court in *Bernhard v. Harrah's Club, supra*?

(b) Why did the insurers in *Stonewall Surplus* bring a declaratory judgment action in California instead of simply denying coverage and waiting for Johnson Controls, their insured, to sue them for recovery on the policies? Do you think the insurers' decision to seek declaratory relief was due, in part, to choice-of-law concerns? How so? Assume that Johnson Controls had sued the insurance companies in a Wisconsin court for breach of the insurance contract. If the Wisconsin court applied § 188 of the Second Restatement to the case, do you think that the Wisconsin court would reach the same conclusion as the California court in *Stonewall Surplus* and apply California law to the case? Should it? Wisconsin courts apparently apply Professor Robert Leflor's "better rule of law" choice-of-law doctrine to contract cases. *See* Gregory E. Smith, *Choice of Law in the United States*, 38 HASTINGS L.J. 1041, 1167–68 (1987). Even without a full understanding of that doctrine, do you think a Wisconsin court would be likely to apply California law as the "better law" in our hypothetical case? Why?

(c) What interest does Jones, the party who was injured by the Johnson Controls battery, have in the *Stonewall Surplus* case? Should the court have considered California's interest vis-a-vis Jones as part of its "governmental interest" analysis? How might this interest, if cognizable, affect the court's analysis? What if Jones were a resident of Wisconsin and had been injured by the exploding battery while vacationing in California? Should Jones' residence make any difference? What if the injury to Jones occurred in Wisconsin, not California?

(3) Since the 1967 landmark decision in *Reich v. Purcell, supra*, a tort case, and the ALI's adoption of the Second Restatement in 1971, the California Supreme Court has had only one opportunity prior to *Nedlloyd* to address choice-of-law issues in a contract case. Ironically, in that case, *Wong v. Tenneco, Inc.*, 39 Cal. 3d 126, 216 Cal. Rptr. 412, 702 P.2d 570 (1985), the Supreme Court resolved the choice-of-law issue by applying neither the government interest approach nor the Second Restatement's "most significant relationship" approach.

Plaintiff Wong, a California resident, owned and operated a produce farm in Mexico which, due to its foreign ownership, was unlawful under Mexico law. Wong entered into a series of financing and marketing agreements with Tenneco, a California corporation. Yielding to pressure from Mexican growers, Tenneco severed its relationship with Wong, eventually resulting in Wong's loss of control over his farming operations. Wong then sued Tenneco in California Superior Court for breach of contract and tort. Although a jury trial resulted in a verdict for Wong, the trial court later ruled that Wong was barred from recovery because the entire transaction was illegal under the laws of Mexico. The Supreme Court affirmed the application of Mexican law, relying on the international law doctrine of comity:

> Instead of a standard contract claim we deal with a question of the respect due the constitution and statutory laws of a sovereign nation. The parties entered into this produce marketing/financing arrangement with full knowledge that the farming operations upon which the agreement depended were being carried out in violation of Mexican Law. When one party abandoned the floundering scheme, the other sought redress in the California courts, to recover that which was unrecoverable under Mexican law. The trial court properly declined to involve our courts in this flagrant effort to circumvent Mexican law.

> The doctrine of comity is fully applicable in the present case. Under that longstanding principle of the law of nations, the forum state will generally apply the substantive law of a foreign sovereign to causes of action which arise there. (*Loranger v. Nadeau* (1932) 215 Cal. 362, 366 [10 P.2d 63, 84 A.L.R. 1264]; *Blythe v. Ayres* (1892) 96 Cal. 532, 561 [31 P. 915]. *See Stockton v. Ortiz* (1975) 47 Cal. App. 3d 183, 200 [120 Cal. Rptr. 456].) The philosophy behind the comity doctrine is easily identified: respect for the sovereignty of other states or countries, "'considerations of mutual utility and advantage'" (*Blythe, supra*, 96 Cal. at p. 561), and "business and social necessity" (*Hutchinson v. Hutchinson* (1941) 48 Cal. App. 2d 12, 22 [119 P.2d 214]). It is the first of these factors that is central to our inquiry today and compels the application of Mexican law.

(a) The dissent in *Wong* argued that the rule of comity did not apply, and that under California's government interest approach the court should find a false conflict and apply California law to the contract. The dissent quoted from *Hurtado v. Superior Court*, 11 Cal. 3d at 580, fn.2, that "[t]he government interests approach is applicable not only to situations involving multistate contacts but also to those involving a state of the United States vis-a-vis a political entity of a foreign country." The majority's only reference to the government interest analysis was in a footnote, where it observed that because Wong's "farming operation was illegal under Mexican law, the only California interest implicated is our public policy against enforcement of a contract dependent upon violation of the laws of another sovereign." *Id.* at 137, fn.13. For a discussion of *Wong* and the doctrine of comity, see Holly Sprague, Comment, *Choice of Law: A Fond Farewell to Comity and Public Policy*, 74 CAL. L. REV. 1447, 1469–77 (1986).

(b) Does *Wong*'s comity analysis mean that California courts should apply the law of a foreign country whenever the cause of action arose in that country? Or at least consider the comity doctrine in such cases? The Court of Appeal in *Corrigan v. Bjork*

Shiley Corp., 182 Cal. App. 3d 166, 277 Cal. Rptr. 247 (1986), *disapproved on other grounds, Stangvik v. Shiley, Inc.*, 54 Cal. 3d 744, 764, 1 Cal. Rptr. 2d 556, 819 P.2d 14 (1991), did not even mention the doctrine of comity in determining whether the law of Australia or California applied to a wrongful death action alleging tort and contract claims. Plaintiffs, Australian residents and relatives of the decedent, brought a products liability action against defendant, a California-based company, seeking damages for a defective heart valve prosthesis which caused the death of plaintiffs' decedent. The valve was manufactured by defendant in California, but its implantation in plaintiffs' decedent, also an Australian resident, took place in Australia. The court conducted governmental interest and comparative impairment analyses, but never mentioned comity in determining that California law—which was more favorable to plaintiffs on liability and damages—applied. How is this case different from *Wong*? From an interest analysis viewpoint, why did the court conclude that California law applied even though plaintiffs were Australian residents?

(5) As *Stonewall Surplus* illustrates, the Courts of Appeal take a hybrid approach to choice-of-law analysis in contract cases. These courts generally apply the methods set forth in the Second Restatement, but with some deference to government interest analysis. *E.g., Kracht v. Perrin, Gartland & Doyle*, 219 Cal. App. 3d 1019, 1026–27, 268 Cal. Rptr. 637 (1990) (assignment of claim); *California Cas. Indem. Exch. v. Pettis*, 193 Cal. App. 3d 1597, 239 Cal. Rptr. 205 (1987) (stacking of uninsured motorist coverage under insurance contract); *Dixon Mobile Homes, Inc. v. Walters*, 48 Cal. App. 3d 964, 122 Cal. Rptr. 202 (1975) (consumer fraud allegations regarding financing provisions in purchase order). Perhaps the most appropriate way to view the current state of California choice-of-law doctrine for contract cases is that the courts follow the Second Restatement, unless a specific application is contrary to some established use of government interest analysis. Added to this, of course, is the somewhat puzzling use of comity in international cases such as *Wong v. Tenneco, Inc., supra*.

[C]   Notes on the Restatement (Second) Conflict of Laws and Contract Issues

[1]   The Second Restatement, Generally

Restatement, Second, Conflict of Laws

American Law Institute (1971, with 1988 revisions)*

Chapter 8: CONTRACTS

Introductory Note: In the Restatement of this Subject, the term "contract" is used to refer both to legally enforceable promises and to other agreements or promises which are claimed to be enforceable but are not legally so.

---

1. *The Nature of the Subject.*

Contracts is one of the most complex and most confused areas of choice of law. This complexity results in part from the wide uses of contracts, the lawyer's universal tool in business and personal affairs. The complexity is increased by the many different kinds of contracts and of issues involving contracts and by the many relationships a single contract may have to two or more states.

The original Restatement provided (a) that issues of validity are determined by the local law of the place of contracting, which was the place where occurred the last act necessary under the forum's rules of offer and acceptance to give the contract binding effect, assuming, hypothetically, that the local law of the place where the act occurred rendered the contract binding..., and (b) that issues of performance are determined by the local law of the place of performance.... These rules were derived from the vested rights doctrine which was also responsible for the adoption by the original Restatement of the rule that rights and liabilities in tort are determined, with certain exceptions, by the local law of the "place of wrong".... The vested rights doctrine has not prevailed in the courts and is rejected in the present Chapter and throughout the present Restatement.

2. *The Changes.*

The original Contracts Chapter has been changed in four principal ways. First, the original Restatement did not acknowledge any power in the parties to choose the applicable law. The present Chapter recognizes that the parties have such power subject to certain limitations (*see* § 187). Second, the present Chapter no longer says dogmatically that, in the absence of an effective law by the parties, the validity of a contract is governed by the local law of the place of contracting. Instead, the applicable law is now said to be the local law of the state which, with respect to the particular issue, has the most significant relationship to the transaction and the parties (*see* § 188). Third, the original Restatement made a sharp distinction between matters of validity and matters of performance, stating that matters pertaining to damages, to sufficiency of performance and to excuse for nonperformance are governed by the local law of the place of performance rather than by the local law of the place of contracting. This distinction has now been abandoned, and in the present Chapter all issues involving contracts are said to be governed either by the law chosen by the parties or, in the absence of an effective choice, by the local law of the state which, with respect to the particular issue, has the most significant relationship to the transaction and the parties. Lastly, the original Restatement laid down rules applicable to the entire field of contracts and, except with respect to the location of the place of contracting, made no attempt to distinguish between particular kinds of contracts. Special rules for particular kinds of contracts are stated in Title B of this Chapter.

TOPIC 1. VALIDITY OF CONTRACTS AND RIGHTS CREATED THEREBY

TITLE A. GENERAL PRINCIPLES

Introductory Note: This Title states the general approach to be followed in determining choice-of-law questions involving contracts. Title B (§§ 189–197) deals with particular kinds of contracts, and Title C (§§ 198–207) with particular issues involving contracts.

§ 186. Applicable Law

Issues in contract are determined by the law chosen by the parties in accordance with the rule of § 187 and otherwise by the law selected in accordance with the rule of § 188.

§ 187. Law of the State Chosen by the Parties

(1) The law of the state chosen by the parties to govern their contractual rights and duties will be applied if the particular issue is one which the parties could have resolved by an explicit provision in their agreement directed to that issue.

(2) The law of the state chosen by the parties to govern their contractual rights and duties will be applied, even if the particular issue is one which the parties could not have resolved by an explicit provision in their agreement directed to that issue, unless either

(a) the chosen state has no substantial relationship to the parties or the transaction and there is no other reasonable basis for the parties choice, or (b) application of the law of the chosen state would be contrary to a fundamental policy of a state which has a materially greater interest than the chosen state in the determination of the particular issue and which, under the rule of § 188, would be the state of the applicable law in the absence of an effective choice of law by the parties.

(3) In the absence of a contrary indication of intention, the reference is to the local law of the state of the chosen law.

§ 188. Law Governing in Absence of Effective Choice by the Parties

(1) The rights and duties of the parties with respect to an issue in contract are determined by the local law of the state which, with respect to that issue, has the most significant relationship to the transaction and the parties under the principles stated in § 6.

(2) In the absence of an effective choice of law by the parties (*see* § 187), the contacts to be taken into account in applying the principles of § 6 to determine the law applicable to an issue include:

(a) the place of contracting,

(b) the place of negotiation of the contract,

(c) the place of performance,

(d) the location of the subject matter of the contract, and

(e) the domicile, residence, nationality, place of incorporation and place of business of the parties.

These contacts are to be evaluated according to their relative importance with respect to the particular issue.

(3) If the place of negotiating the contract and the place of performance are in the same state, the local law of this state will usually be applied, except as otherwise provided in §§ 189–199 and 203.

Notes and Questions regarding the Second Restatement

(1) As the quoted rules and comments indicate, the Second Restatement treatment of contract issues represents a significant departure from the vested rights theory of the First Restatement. Assuming no overriding statutory directive (*see* § 6, Second Restatement, *supra*), a court must apply the law specified by the parties in a valid choice-of-law clause. §§ 186–187. If no such contractual clause exists, or if an existing clause is invalid or unenforceable under § 187(2)(a) or (b), then generally a court must resolve a choice-of-law issue by applying the law of the state which has the "most significant relationship" to the transaction and parties. § 188.

(2) The "most significant relationship" test requires a court to consider various relevant contacts, including those specified in § 188(2). The comments to the Second Restatement emphasize that the "most significant relationship" test is not simply a matter of applying the law of the state which quantitatively has the most contacts. Instead, the existence of contacts such as those specified in § 188(2) indicate which states are most likely to be interested in having their law applied to a particular issue, as well as their relative interests in light of the relevant policies of all interested states. *See* ALI, Comment to § 188(2).

(3) The Second Restatement also provides more specific rules for particular kinds of contracts and contract issues. These specific rules apply in the absence of a valid choice of law agreement between the parties. In the hierarchy of applicability, these specific rules apply whenever a court considers the specific category of contract case or issue covered by a rule. These specific rules are intended to indicate that with certain kinds of contracts, a particular contact plays an especially important role in the determination of the state of the applicable law. ALI Introductory Note to §§ 189–197; *see, e.g., Stonewall Surplus Lines Ins. Co. v. Johnson Controls, Inc., supra.*

(a) These specific rules actually set forth presumptions as to which state's law is applicable, but these presumptions need not be followed in all circumstances. For example, Section 189 states that the validity of a contract for the transfer of an interest in land is determined by the law of the state where the land is situated unless some other state has a more significant relationship to the transaction and parties.

(b) Likewise, separate specific rules govern contracts to sell interests in chattels, § 191; life insurance contracts, § 192; contracts of fire, surety, or casualty insurance, § 193; contracts of suretyship, § 194; contracts for repayment of money lent, § 195; contracts for the rendition of services, § 196; and contracts of transportation, § 197.

(c) Sections 198–207 contain specific rules for choice-of-law questions directed at particular contract issues. For example, Section 206 states that issues relating to details of performance of a contract are determined by the local law of the place of performance. Most of these "particular issue" rules simply refer back to Sections 187–188, the general rules for choice-of-law clauses and for the "most significant contacts" test. *E.g.*, Capacity to Contract, §198(1); Formalities required for Valid Contract, §199; Effect of Misrepresentation, Duress, Undue Influence and Mistake, §201; Illegality, §202(1); Usury, §203; Measure of Recovery, §207.

[2] Statutory Directives

The Second Restatement recognizes generally that a court must follow the statutory directives of its own state on choice of law, and that the Second Restatement's principles are relevant only when there is no such statutory directive. Restatement (Second) Conflict of Laws, §6(1) and (2), *supra*. California has enacted only a few general statutory directives on choice of law, most notably in the commercial contracts area, *e.g.*, Commercial Code §1301(a), Civil Code §1646.5 (certain choice-of-law agreements); in dealing with some statute of limitation issues, CCP §361 (borrowing statute), in dealing with corporations, Corporations Code §§2115 & 2116 (shareholder derivative suits); and for some family law matters such as spousal and child support, Family Code §§4917, 4953.

One such statutory directive is §1646 of the Civil Code, which applies to contracts generally:

A contract is to be interpreted according to the law and usage of the place where it is to be performed; or, if it does not indicate a place of performance, according to the law and usage of the place where it is made.

What does §1646 mean? How does it interrelate with the Second Restatement and the governmental interest doctrine? *See Frontier Oil Corp. v. RLI Ins. Co.*, 153 Cal. App. 4th 1436, 63 Cal. Rptr. 3d 816 (2007) (ruling the choice-of-law rule in Civil Code §1646 determines the law governing the interpretation of the insurance policy, notwithstanding the application of the governmental interest test to other choice-of-law issues; and holding that although the policy was entered into in Texas between Texas parties, California law applies because California was the intended place of performance of the contract with respect to the disputed claims).

Section 10106(a) of the Commercial Code limits the law that may be chosen by parties to a consumer lease to the law of a jurisdiction which has some connection to the parties or the lease. Civil Code §755 directs that real property within this State is governed by the law of this State, except where title is in the United States. Evidence Code §311(a) provides that if the law of a foreign state or nation is applicable but cannot be determined, the court may apply California law if consistent with the Constitution, or may dismiss the action. What policy considerations are reflected in §311(a)?

§5.05 Statutes of Limitations and Choice of Law

[A] Introductory Note

One choice-of-law issue that cuts across all substantive areas of law is the question of which statute of limitations should apply to a cause of action. For many years California courts followed the traditional rule that statutes of limitations are "procedural" for choice-of-law purposes, and are therefore governed by forum law. *See, e.g., Biewend v. Biewend*, 17 Cal. 2d 108, 114, 109 P.2d 701 (1941); *Travelers Indem. Co. v. Bell*, 213 Cal. App. 2d 541, 547, 29 Cal. Rptr. 67 (1963). The California courts were influenced by the First Restatement, which embodied the general principle that forum law governed all matters of procedure, and that statutes of limitations were always "procedural." Restatement, Conflict of Laws, §§ 585, 603 & 604 (1934).

The Second Restatement rejected this rigid view of the statute of limitations, Restatement (Second) Conflict of Laws, § 142; and so have the California courts.

McCann v. Foster Wheeler LLC

Supreme Court of California
48 Cal. 4th 68, 105 Cal. Rptr. 3d 378, 225 P.3d 516 (2010)

GEORGE, CHIEF JUSTICE.

This case presents a choice-of-law issue arising in a lawsuit filed by plaintiff Terry McCann (plaintiff) to recover damages for an illness, mesothelioma, allegedly caused by his exposure to asbestos. Although the complaint seeks recovery from numerous defendants, the issue before us relates solely to the potential liability of a single defendant, Foster Wheeler LLC (Foster Wheeler), a company that specially designed, manufactured, and provided advice regarding the installation of a very large boiler at an oil refinery in Oklahoma in 1957. At the time the boiler was being installed at the Oklahoma refinery, plaintiff, then an Oklahoma resident and a newly hired engineering sales trainee employed by the construction company that was installing the boiler, allegedly was exposed to asbestos at various times over a two-week period while he observed the application of asbestos insulation to the boiler by an independent insulation contractor.

Eighteen years later, in 1975, after working at various jobs in Minnesota and Illinois, plaintiff moved to Dana Point, California, to take a position as executive director of Toastmasters International. In 2005, after having retired from his Toastmasters position in 2001 and continuing to reside in California, plaintiff was diagnosed with mesothelioma. A few months later, plaintiff filed this action in California, naming numerous defendants, including Foster Wheeler.[2]

Prior to trial, Foster Wheeler moved for summary judgment on various grounds, including that plaintiff's action against it was governed by, and barred under, an Oklahoma statute of repose that required any cause of action against a designer or constructor of an improvement to real property to be filed within 10 years of the substantial completion of the improvement. In opposing the motion, plaintiff contended, first, that his cause of action for an injury or illness caused by exposure to asbestos should be governed by the relevant California statute of limitations (under

---

2. * * * After judgment was entered in the trial court and while the case was pending on appeal, Terry McCann died. A motion was filed in the Court of Appeal to substitute his wife as successor in interest pursuant to Code of Civil Procedure section 377.32, and that court granted the motion. * * *

which the action would have been timely filed), rather than by Oklahoma law, and, second, that in any event Foster Wheeler's boiler was not an improvement to real property within the meaning of the relevant Oklahoma statute of repose.

After the trial court initially determined that Oklahoma, rather than California, law should apply to the timeliness issue…, the trial court found that Foster Wheeler was a designer of an improvement to real property within the meaning of the Oklahoma statute of repose and entered judgment dismissing Foster Wheeler as a defendant in plaintiff's underlying action.

On appeal, the Court of Appeal concluded that the trial court erred in determining that Oklahoma law rather than California law should apply in these circumstances; as a consequence, the Court of Appeal did not reach the question whether the trial court erred in finding that the action against Foster Wheeler fell within the reach of the applicable Oklahoma statute of repose. * * *

On petition by Foster Wheeler, we granted review primarily to consider whether the Court of Appeal was correct in determining (1) that Oklahoma's interest in the application of its statute of repose is substantially limited to application of the statute to companies headquartered in Oklahoma and does not equally encompass out-of-state companies who design or construct improvements to real property located in Oklahoma, and (2) that California's interests, rather than Oklahoma's interests, would be more impaired by the failure to apply the respective state's law on the facts presented here.

For the reasons discussed more fully below, we conclude that the decision of the Court of Appeal should be reversed. * * *

II

Traditionally, a state's general choice-of-law rules have been formulated by courts through judicial decisions rendered under the common law, rather than by the Legislature through statutory enactments. In California, over the past four decades this court's decisions have adopted and consistently applied the so-called "governmental interest" analysis as the appropriate general methodology for resolving choice-of-law questions in this state. (See, e.g., *Reich v. Purcell* (1967) 67 Cal.2d 551 [63 Cal. Rptr. 31, 432 P.2d 727] (*Reich*); *Bernhard v. Harrah's Club* (1976) 16 Cal.3d 313 [128 Cal. Rptr. 215, 546 P.2d 719] (*Bernhard*); *Offshore Rental Co. v. Continental Oil Co.* (1978) 22 Cal.3d 157 [148 Cal. Rptr. 867, 583 P.2d 721] (*Offshore Rental*); *Kearney v. Salomon Smith Barney, Inc.* (2006) 39 Cal.4th 95 [45 Cal. Rptr. 3d 730, 137 P.3d 914] (*Kearney*).)

With respect to the category of statutes of limitation and statutes of repose, however, many jurisdictions have enacted specific statutory provisions that address the subject of choice of law. As discussed in a leading treatise and a number of law review articles, a majority of American states have adopted so-called "borrowing statutes" that direct the courts of a state, in lawsuits filed within that state, to apply or "borrow" the relevant statute of limitations or statute of repose *of a foreign jurisdiction* under the particular circumstances specified in the statute, rather than to apply the statute of limitations of the forum jurisdiction. (See generally Leflar et al., American Conflicts Law (4th ed. 1986) §§ 127–128, pp. 348–354 (Leflar Treatise); …) * * *

California first enacted a borrowing statute very early in its history, in 1851, as part of the state's initial comprehensive legislation regulating proceedings in civil cases. (Stats. 1851, ch. 5, § 532, p. 134.) When the Code of Civil Procedure was adopted in 1872, the early 1851 statute was codified, with only a minor change in language, as section 361. The language of section 361, as enacted in 1872, remains unchanged to this day.

Section 361 provides in full: "When a cause of action has arisen in another State, or in a foreign country, and by the laws thereof an action thereon cannot there be maintained against a person by reason of the lapse of time, an action thereon shall not be maintained against him in this State, except in favor of one who has been a citizen of this State, and who has held the cause of action from the time it accrued."

Section 361 thus creates a general rule that when a cause of action has arisen in another jurisdiction but cannot be maintained against a particular defendant in that jurisdiction because of the lapse of time, the action cannot be maintained against that defendant in a California court. The statute contains an exception, however, for a plaintiff "who has been a citizen of this State, and who has held the cause of action from the time it accrued." Past cases establish that this exception applies only where the plaintiff was a California citizen at the time the cause of action accrued, and does not extend to a plaintiff who became a citizen of California after the cause of action accrued but before the lawsuit in question was filed. (See, e.g., *Biewend v. Biewend* (1941) 17 Cal.2d 108, 115 [109 P.2d 701]; *Grant v. McAuliffe* (1953) 41 Cal.2d 859, 865 [264 P.2d 944]; …)

Although application of section 361 generally is straightforward in a case involving, for example, a typical automobile accident — in which the allegedly tortious conduct, the resulting injury, and compensable damage all occur at the same time and in the same place — proper application of the statute is more problematic in a case, like the present one, in which the defendant's allegedly injury-producing conduct occurred in another state at a much earlier date but the plaintiff's resulting illness or injury does not become apparent and reasonably is not discovered until many decades later, at a time when the plaintiff has established residence in California. In the factual setting here at issue, it may be reasonably debatable whether plaintiff's cause of action against Foster Wheeler "arose" in Oklahoma or instead in California for purposes of section 361, and whether plaintiff was a citizen of California or of Oklahoma at the time the cause of action "accrued" within the meaning of the term as used in this borrowing statute.

Even if we assume either that the cause of action at issue "arose" in California for purposes of section 361 or that plaintiff was a citizen of California from the time the cause of action "accrued" within the meaning of this statute — and thus that section 361 does not *require* application of Oklahoma law rather than California law on the facts of this case — we agree with the Court of Appeal that this statute cannot properly be interpreted *to compel* application of the California statute of limitations without consideration of California's generally applicable choice-of-law principles. Although at the time section 361 was adopted, the then prevailing choice-of-law doctrine generally would have called for the application of the relevant California statute of limitations in a case in which section 361 did not mandate application of another jurisdiction's law (see, e.g., *Royal Trust Co. v. MacBean* (1914) 168 Cal. 642, 646 [144 P. 139]), nothing in section 361 indicates that this statute was intended to freeze the then prevailing general choice-of-law rules into a statutory command, so as to curtail the judiciary's long-standing authority to adopt and modify choice-of-law principles pursuant to its traditional common law role.

Accordingly, now that the earlier methodology for resolving choice-of-law issues has been replaced in this state by the governmental interest mode of analysis (see, e.g., *Reich, supra,* 67 Cal.2d 551, 553–557; *Bernhard, supra,* 16 Cal.3d 313, 316–321), in those instances in which section 361 does not mandate application of another jurisdiction's statute of limitations or statute of repose the question whether the relevant California statute of limitations (or statute of repose) or, instead, another jurisdiction's statute of limitations (or statute of repose) should be applied in a particular case must be determined through application of the governmental interest analysis that governs choice-of-law issues generally. (See, e.g., *Ashland Chemical Co. v. Provence* (1982) 129 Cal. App. 3d 790, 793–794 [181 Cal. Rptr. 340] [holding that under California law, governmental interest analysis is applicable to resolve a choice-of-law issue relating to the statute of limitations]; ...)

Thus, we now turn to the task of applying the general governmental interest analysis to the circumstances before us in the present case.

III

Recently, in *Kearney, supra,* 39 Cal.4th 95, we summarized the mode of analysis called for by the governmental interest approach. "In brief outline, the governmental interest approach generally involves three steps. First, the court determines whether the relevant law of each of the potentially affected jurisdictions with regard to the particular issue in question is the same or different. Second, if there is a difference, the court examines each jurisdiction's interest in the application of its own law under the circumstances of the particular case to determine whether a true conflict exists. Third, if the court finds that there is a true conflict, it carefully evaluates and compares the nature and strength of the interest of each jurisdiction in the application of its own law 'to determine which state's interest would be more impaired if its policy were subordinated to the policy of the other state' [citation], and then ultimately applies 'the law of the state whose interest would be more impaired if its law were not applied.'" (39 Cal.4th at pp. 107–108.)

A

With regard to the first of these steps, we agree with the Court of Appeal that "[t]he laws of Oklahoma and California clearly differ."

Under section 109 (the Oklahoma statute of repose), plaintiff's cause of action would be barred by the lapse of time, because that statute "bars any tort action which arises more than ten years after the substantial completion of the improvement to real property." (*Riley v. Brown and Root, Inc.* (1992) 1992 OK 114 [836 P.2d 1298, 1300].) Although the Oklahoma statute in question has been interpreted not to bar products liability actions against the manufacturers and sellers of mass-produced products — and thus would not preclude plaintiff from suing companies that manufactured or sold the asbestos insulation to which he was exposed — the Oklahoma Supreme Court has interpreted the statute of repose to protect a manufacturer/designer of a specially designed improvement to real property. (*Ball v. Harnischfeger Corp.* [(1994) 1994 OK 65] 877 P.2d 45, 50 ["If the manufacturer was acting as a designer, planner, construction supervisor or observer, or constructor, the statute of repose will apply. It is the specialized expertise and rendition of particularized design which separates those protected from mere manufacturers and suppliers."]; ...)

Although, as we have explained above, plaintiff argued in the Court of Appeal and continues to maintain in this court that the trial court erred in finding that the boiler in question was an improvement to real property for purposes of the Oklahoma statute of repose, the Court of Appeal never reached that issue, because it concluded that even if Foster Wheeler fell within the reach of the Oklahoma statute, under California's choice-of-law principles California law would apply. In reviewing the conclusion reached by the Court of Appeal, we similarly shall assume for purposes of determining the choice-of-law issue that Foster Wheeler's conduct brought it within the reach of the relevant Oklahoma statute of repose.[7] Under this premise, plaintiff's action against Foster Wheeler plainly would be untimely under Oklahoma law, because this action was filed more than 10 years after substantial completion of the improvement.[8]

---

7. Because the Court of Appeal did not address plaintiff's challenge to the trial court's determination that the boiler in question constituted an improvement to real property for purposes of the relevant Oklahoma statute, we conclude, in light of our determination that the appellate court erred in its resolution of the choice-of-law issue, that it is appropriate to remand this matter to the Court of Appeal to permit that court, in the first instance, to pass on plaintiff's challenge to the trial court's application of Oklahoma law to the circumstances of this case.

8. While this matter was pending before this court, the Oklahoma Legislature enacted comprehensive "lawsuit reform" legislation that includes the following provision pertaining to asbestos-related claims: "Notwithstanding any other provision of law, with respect to any asbestos or silica claim not barred as of the effective date of this act, the limitations period shall not begin to run until the exposed person or claimant discovers, or through the exercise of reasonable diligence should have discovered, that the exposed person or claimant is physically impaired as set forth in this chapter by an asbestos- or silica-related condition." (2009 Okla. House Bill No. 1603, §64, subd. A [chaptered as ch. 228].)

Although the initial clause of this provision ("Notwithstanding any other provision of law") could be interpreted to mean that the new statute creates an exception to the Oklahoma statute of repose for asbestos-related claims (permitting such claims to be brought so long as they satisfy all of the requirements and limitations embodied in the new statute), the new provision explicitly applies only "to any asbestos ... claim *not barred as of the effective date of this act*" (italics added) and thus would not affect an action, like the present one, that was barred by the Oklahoma statute of repose long before the enactment of the new legislation. Accordingly, the Oklahoma statute of repose continues to represent the relevant Oklahoma law for purposes of the present proceeding.

By contrast, plaintiff's action against Foster Wheeler clearly would be timely if California law were applied. Although this state has enacted a statute of repose applicable to causes of action arising out of a latent deficiency in the design or construction of an improvement to real property that is somewhat similar to the relevant Oklahoma statute of repose (see Code Civ. Proc., § 337.15), the California statute, unlike its Oklahoma counterpart, applies only to actions for injury to property, not to personal injury actions. (*Martinez v. Traubner* (1982) 32 Cal.3d 755, 757–761 [187 Cal. Rptr. 251, 653 P.2d 1046].) Furthermore, California has enacted a special statute of limitations explicitly governing the time for bringing an action "for injury or illness based upon exposure to asbestos," which permits such an action to be brought up to one year after the plaintiff both (1) first suffered disability *and* (2) knew or reasonably should have known that the disability was caused or contributed to by exposure to asbestos. (Code Civ. Proc., § 340.2;[10] see *Hamilton v. Asbestos Corp.* (2000) 22 Cal.4th 1127, 1138 [95 Cal. Rptr. 2d 701, 998 P.2d 403].) Here, plaintiff, who previously had retired for reasons unconnected to his asbestos-related illness, filed this action within a few months after he first was diagnosed with mesothelioma, and thus the action clearly would be timely under the provisions of section 340.2. (See *Hamilton v. Asbestos Corp., supra*, 22 Cal.4th at pp. 1138–1147.)

Accordingly, the law of Oklahoma clearly differs from the law of California with respect to the timeliness of plaintiff's cause of action.

B

The second step of the governmental interest analysis requires us to examine "each jurisdiction's interest in the application of its own law under the circumstances of the particular case to determine whether a true conflict exists." (*Kearney, supra*, 39 Cal.4th at pp. 107–108.)

Oklahoma decisions indicate that by establishing a relatively lengthy (10-year) period in which a cause of action for a deficiency in design of an improvement to real property may be brought, but at the same time terminating all liability after that deadline regardless of whether the plaintiff's injury had yet occurred or become manifest, the relevant statute of repose was intended to balance the interest of injured persons in having a remedy available for such injuries against the interest of builders, architects, and designers of real property improvements in being subject to a specified time limit during which they would remain potentially liable for their actions in connection with such improvements. (See, e.g., *St. Paul Fire & Marine Ins. Co. v. Getty Oil Co.* [(1989) 1989 OK 137] 782 P.2d 915, 920–921.) The Oklahoma high court held in *St. Paul Fire & Marine Ins. Co.* that the statute of repose, by establishing this

---

10. Code of Civil Procedure, section 340.2 provides in relevant part: "(a) In any civil action for injury or illness based upon exposure to asbestos, the time for the commencement of the action shall be the later of the following: [¶] (1) Within one year after the date the plaintiff first suffered disability. [¶] (2) Within one year after the date the plaintiff either knew, or through the exercise of reasonable diligence should have known, that such disability was caused or contributed to by such exposure. [¶] (b) 'Disability' as used in subdivision (a) means the loss of time from work as a result of such exposure which precludes the performance of the employee's regular occupation."

type of fixed time limit in which any cause of action must be brought, serves "the legitimate government objectives of providing a measure of security for building professionals whose liability could otherwise extend indefinitely." (*Id.* at p. 921.) The court further noted that the statute "also serves the legitimate objective of avoiding the difficulties in proof which arise from the passage of time." (*Ibid.*)

In discussing the interest of Oklahoma embodied in the statute, the Court of Appeal in the present case expressed the view that "Oklahoma's interest is substantially a local one, that is, an interest in protecting Oklahoma defendants from liability for conduct occurring in Oklahoma." * * *

We conclude that the Court of Appeal did not accurately assess the interest of Oklahoma embodied in the statute of repose here at issue. When a state adopts a rule of law limiting liability for commercial activity conducted within the state in order to provide what the state perceives is fair treatment to, and an appropriate incentive for, business enterprises, we believe that the state ordinarily has an interest in having that policy of limited liability applied to out-of-state companies that conduct business in the state, as well as to businesses incorporated or headquartered within the state. A state has a legitimate interest in attracting out-of-state companies to do business within the state, both to obtain tax and other revenue that such businesses may generate for the state, and to advance the opportunity of state residents to obtain employment and the products and services offered by out-of-state companies. In the absence of any explicit indication that a jurisdiction's "business friendly" statute or rule of law is intended to apply only to businesses incorporated or headquartered in that jurisdiction (or that have some other designated relationship with the state—for example, to those entities licensed by the state), as a practical and realistic matter the state's interest in having that law applied to the activities of out-of-state companies within the jurisdiction is equal to its interest in the application of the law to comparable activities engaged in by local businesses situated within the jurisdiction. * * *

Furthermore, just as the Court of Appeal erred in relying on the non-Oklahoma location of Foster Wheeler's incorporation or headquarters as a basis for determining that Oklahoma lacked an interest in having its statute of repose applied here, the appellate court similarly erred in suggesting that Oklahoma's interest in having its statute applied was negated by the circumstance that the design and manufacture of the boiler in question occurred in New York rather than in Oklahoma. The statute of repose here at issue protects not only construction-related businesses that engage in their activities at the Oklahoma site of the improvement, but also commercial entities, such as establishments performing architectural and other design-improvement work, that conduct their activities away from the location of the improvement but whose potential liability flows from a plaintiff's interaction with, or exposure to, the real property improvement in Oklahoma. Under the premise that the activities of Foster Wheeler in this case bring it within the reach of the Oklahoma statute of repose, we conclude that, for purposes of the governmental interest analysis, Oklahoma clearly possesses an interest in having the statute applied in the present case and that its interest is not diminished by the circumstance that some of Foster Wheeler's activities occurred outside of Oklahoma.

Accordingly, contrary to the view expressed by the Court of Appeal, we conclude that Oklahoma has a real and legitimate interest in having its statute of repose applied under the circumstances presented here.

At the same time, we also recognize that California has an interest in having California law applied in this case.

As discussed above, the applicable California statute — Code of Civil Procedure section 340.2 — permits an action for injury or illness based upon exposure to asbestos to be brought up to one year after the plaintiff first suffered disability (as defined by the statute) *and* knew or reasonably should have known that the disability was caused or contributed to by such exposure. This statute, enacted in 1979 to lengthen the period of time in which an asbestos-related claim may be brought, reflects a state interest in providing persons who suffer injury or illness as a result of their exposure to asbestos a fair and reasonable opportunity to seek recovery for their injury or illness, taking into account not only the typically lengthy period between exposure to asbestos and the development of disease but also the often substantial period between the initial discovery or diagnosis of a disease and the time when the disease becomes disabling. (See, e.g., *Hamilton v. Asbestos Corp., supra,* 22 Cal.4th 1127, 1138–1139; *Blakey v. Superior Court* (1984) 153 Cal. App. 3d 101, 105–106 [200 Cal. Rptr. 52]; *Nelson v. Flintkote Co.* (1985) 172 Cal. App. 3d 727, 735 [218 Cal. Rptr. 562].)

The language of section 340.2 does not specify the class of persons to whom the statute was intended to apply, but by its terms the provision is not limited only to persons who were exposed to asbestos in California. In view of the legislation's clear recognition of the unusual nature of asbestos-related injury and illness, and the statute's objective to provide injured or ill persons a fair and adequate opportunity to seek recovery for such asbestos-related harm, we conclude that California has an interest in having this statute applied to a person, like plaintiff, who is a California resident at the time the person discovers that he or she is suffering from an asbestos-related injury or illness, even when the person's exposure to asbestos occurred outside California. * * * Accordingly, California, as well as Oklahoma, has an interest in having its own law applied in this case.

Because the applicable laws of Oklahoma and California differ and each state has an interest in having its law applied under the circumstances of the present case, we are faced with a "true conflict." As explained above, in such instances we apply the so-called "comparative impairment" approach.

C

Under the comparative impairment analysis, we must "carefully evaluate[] and compare[] the nature and strength of the interest of each jurisdiction in the application of its own law 'to determine which state's interest would be more impaired if its policy were subordinated to the policy of the other state.'"(*Kearney, supra,* 39 Cal.4th 95, 108.) * * * Accordingly, our task is not to determine whether the Oklahoma rule or the California rule is the better or worthier rule, but rather to decide—in light of the legal question at issue and the relevant state interests at stake—which jurisdiction should be allocated the predominating lawmaking power under the circumstances of the present case.

In light of the relevant facts of this case, we conclude that a failure to apply Oklahoma law would significantly impair Oklahoma's interest. The conduct for which plaintiff contends Foster Wheeler should be held liable—plaintiff's alleged exposure to asbestos during the application of insulation to a boiler designed and manufactured by Foster Wheeler—occurred in Oklahoma in 1957, at a time when plaintiff was present in Oklahoma and was an Oklahoma resident. As already discussed, the circumstance that Foster Wheeler is not an Oklahoma company—the circumstance relied upon by the Court of Appeal—is not a persuasive basis for finding that the failure to apply Oklahoma law would not significantly impair Oklahoma's interest. Oklahoma's interest in the application of its statute of repose applies equally to out-of-state businesses that design improvements to real property located in Oklahoma and to Oklahoma businesses that design such improvements situated within that state.

Although California no longer follows the old choice-of-law rule that generally called for application of the law of the jurisdiction in which a defendant's allegedly tortious conduct occurred *without regard to the nature of the issue that was before the court* (see *Reich, supra,* 67 Cal.2d 551, 553), California choice-of-law cases nonetheless continue to recognize that a jurisdiction ordinarily has "the predominant interest" in regulating conduct that occurs within its borders (*Reich, supra,* 67 Cal.2d 551, 556; see *Cable v. Sahara Tahoe Corp.* (1979) 93 Cal. App. 3d 384, 394 [155 Cal. Rptr. 770]), and in being able to assure individuals and commercial entities operating within its territory that applicable limitations on liability set forth in the jurisdiction's law will be available to those individuals and businesses in the event they are faced with litigation in the future. (See, e.g., *Offshore Rental, supra,* 22 Cal.3d 157, 168; *Castro, supra,* 154 Cal.App.4th 1152, 1180; *Cable, supra,* 93 Cal. App. 3d 384, 394.)

In the present case, in the event Foster Wheeler were to be denied the protection afforded by the Oklahoma statute of repose and be subjected to the extended timeliness rule embodied in California law, the subordination of Oklahoma's interest in the application of its law would rest solely upon the circumstance that *after* defendant engaged in the allegedly tortious conduct in Oklahoma, plaintiff happened to move to a jurisdiction whose law provides more favorable treatment to plaintiff than that available under Oklahoma law.

Although here it is clear that plaintiff's move to California was not motivated by a desire to take advantage of the opportunities afforded by California law and cannot reasonably be characterized as an instance of forum shopping, the displacement of Oklahoma law limiting liability for conduct engaged in within Oklahoma, in favor of the law of a jurisdiction to which a plaintiff subsequently moved, would—notwithstanding the innocent motivation of the move—nonetheless significantly impair the interest of Oklahoma served by the statute of repose. If Oklahoma's statute were not to be applied because plaintiff had moved to a state with a different and less "business-friendly" law, Oklahoma could not provide any reasonable assurance—either to out-of-state companies or to Oklahoma businesses—that the time limitation embodied in its statute would operate to protect such businesses in the future. Because a commercial entity protected by the Oklahoma statute of repose has no way of knowing or controlling where a potential plaintiff may move in the future, subjecting such a defendant to a different rule of law based upon the law of a state to which a potential plaintiff ultimately may move would significantly undermine Oklahoma's interest in establishing a reliable rule of law governing a business's potential liability for conduct undertaken in Oklahoma.

By contrast, a failure to apply California law on the facts of the present case will effect a far less significant impairment of California's interest. Certainly, if the law of this state is not applied here, California will not be able to extend its liberal statute of limitations for asbestos-related injuries or illnesses to some potential plaintiffs whose exposure to asbestos occurred wholly outside of California. Nonetheless, our past choice-of-law decisions teach that California's interest in applying its laws providing a remedy to, or facilitating recovery by, a potential plaintiff in a case in which the defendant's allegedly tortious conduct occurred in another state is less than its interest when the defendant's conduct occurred in California. As we shall see, in a number of choice-of-law settings, California decisions have adopted a restrained view of the scope or reach of California law with regard to the imposition of liability for conduct that occurs in another jurisdiction and that would not subject the defendant to liability under the law of the other jurisdiction. Our view is that a similar restrained view of California's interest in facilitating recovery by a current California resident is warranted in evaluating the relative impairment of California's interest that would result from the failure to apply California law in the present setting.

[Here the Court discusses the comparative impairment decisions in *Offshore Rental,* *supra,* 22 Cal.3d 157, and in *Castro* [*v. Budget Rent-A-Car System, Inc.* (2007) 154 Cal.App.4th 1162 [65 Cal. Rptr. 3d 430]]. As these decisions demonstrate, in allocating the " 'respective spheres of lawmaking influence'" (*Offshore Rental, supra,* 22 Cal.3d 157, 165) in cases in which a California resident is injured by a defendant's conduct occurring in another state, past California choice-of-law decisions generally hold that when the law of the other state limits or denies liability for the conduct engaged in by the defendant in its territory, that state's interest is predominant, and California's legitimate interest in providing a remedy for, or in facilitating recovery by, a current California resident properly must be subordinated because of this state's diminished authority over activity that occurs in another state. Although under the circumstances of the present case this allocation of "lawmaking influence" results in the subordination of California's interest to the interest of Oklahoma, in other instances in which a defendant is responsible for exposing persons to the risks associated with asbestos or another toxic substance through its conduct *in California,* this general principle would allocate to *California* the predominant interest in regulating the conduct. (See, e.g., *North American Asbestos Corp. v. Superior Court* (1986) 180 Cal. App. 3d 902, 907–908 [225 Cal. Rptr. 877] [holding California law applicable when the plaintiff was exposed to asbestos in California by a company incorporated in another state, where plaintiff's action against the company would have been barred as untimely under the other state's law].)

Plaintiff contends, however, that the foregoing analysis is erroneous..* * * In arguing that Foster Wheeler should be viewed as having caused an injury that occurred in California, plaintiff relies heavily upon the circumstances that he was a resident of California when his exposure to asbestos many years earlier in Oklahoma ultimately manifested itself as an illness and caused him to incur considerable medical expenses resulting from the disease. Those circumstances, however, do not realistically distinguish the present matter from a case, such as *Castro, supra,* 154 Cal.App.4th 1162, in which a California resident is seriously injured in an automobile accident in another state and returns home to California for extensive medical treatment and long-term care. Although in such a case the plaintiff's long-term medical expenses are likely to be incurred in California and, if the plaintiff's resources are insufficient, the state ultimately may expend considerable financial resources for his or her care, past California choice-of-law decisions as we have seen have not treated that type of case as one in which a defendant's conduct has caused an injury in California. Those decisions instead have applied the choice-of-law analysis discussed above, recognizing that the state in which the alleged injury-producing conduct occurred (and in which a significant risk of harm to others is posed) generally has the predominant interest in determining the appropriate parameters of liability for conduct undertaken within its borders.

For the reasons discussed above, we conclude that Oklahoma's interest (as embodied in its statute of repose) would be more impaired if its law were not applied under the circumstances of this case than would be California's interest if its statute of limitations is not applied. Accordingly, we conclude that the Court of Appeal erred in holding that California law rather than Oklahoma law should apply to the issue before us.

IV

The judgment of the Court of Appeal is reversed and the matter is remanded to that court with directions to address plaintiff's additional contention that the trial court erred in finding that the boiler in question constituted an improvement to real property within the meaning of the relevant Oklahoma statute of repose.

Notes and Questions

(1) The California comparative impairment doctrine requires a court to resolve a true conflict by determining which state's interest would be more impaired if its policy were subordinated to the policy of the other state. How did the *McCann* court make this determination? On what factors did the *McCann* court rely in finding that Oklahoma's interest would be more impaired if its statute of repose were not applied? Do you agree with the court's assessment and comparison of the Oklahoma and the California interests? Did the *McCann* court engage in interest-weighing? Or did the court focus on territorialism, and not comparative impairment, in resolving the true conflict?

(2) *Ashland Chem. Co. v. Provence,* 129 Cal. App. 3d 790, 181 Cal. Rptr. 340 (1982), is one of the first California cases to apply governmental interest analysis to a statute of limitations issue. Plaintiff Ashland, a Kentucky corporation, sued various defendants, all residents of California, on a promissory note. The defendants promised to pay the note in Kentucky by December, 31, 1975, but did not; the note stated it was "governed and construed in accordance with the laws of the Commonwealth of Kentucky." The action would be timely if the Kentucky 15 year statute of limitations applied, but barred if California's four-year limitations statute (CCP § 337) applied. Declining to apply the "traditional" choice-of-law-theory, under which statutes of limitations are procedural and governed by forum law, the *Ashland* court instead undertook a governmental interest analysis. The court found that California was the only interested state because California is the forum and the defendants are California residents. In contrast, the court reasoned, "Kentucky has no interest in having its statute of limitations applied because here there are no Kentucky defendants and Kentucky is not the forum." *Ashland,* 129 Cal. App. 3d at 794 The *Ashland* court also refused to enforce the parties' choice-of-law agreement, in part because applying Kentucky's longer statute of limitations would violate the protective policy underlying California's shorter statute of limitations. *Id* at 794–95.

(a) Do you agree with the *Ashland* court's reasoning in refusing to enforce the promissory note's choice-of-law clause? Is the court's determination consistent with *Nedlloyd*? With § 187(2) of the Second Restatement? Does the statute of limitations in question (CCP § 337) embody a "fundamental policy" of California, within the meaning of § 187(2)?

(b) The *Ashland* court's holding raises the possibility that the court would apply Kentucky substantive contract law to the case, but the California statute of limitations. Do the Due Process and Full Faith and Credit Clauses of the U.S. Constitution permit a state court to apply another state's substantive law but its own statute of limitations to an action? *See Sun Oil Co. v. Wortman,* 486 U.S. 717, 108 S. Ct. 2117, 100 L. Ed. 2d 743 (1988) (holding the U.S. Constitution does not prohibit Kansas court from applying its own statute of limitations to all claims before it, including claims barred under other relevant state law, but applying various substantive laws of other relevant states to these same claims). What does this encourage?

(3) In *American Bank of Commerce v. Corondoni,* 169 Cal. App. 3d 368, 215 Cal. Rptr. 331 (1985), the plaintiff commenced an action in superior court to enforce a New Mexico money judgment plaintiff had obtained against defendant 7 1/2 years earlier. Defendant, a resident of California, claimed the action was barred by the 7-year New Mexico statute of limitations for enforcement of judgments. Plaintiff argued that the action was timely under the applicable California 10-year statute of limitations. The court undertook a governmental interest analysis and, relying on *Ashland Chem. Co. v. Provence, supra,* concluded that there was a "false conflict" between the New Mexico and California statutes of limitations. Do you agree? Which statute of limitations applies? Why? Whose statute of limitations would apply if the defendant were a resident of New Mexico, not California?

(4) In *Hambrecht & Quist Venture Partners v. American Med. Intl., Inc.,* 38 Cal. App. 4th 1532, 46 Cal. Rptr. 2d 33 (1996), the court addressed the question of whether a standard choice-of-law provision which stated that the contract "shall be governed by and construed in accordance with the laws of the State of Delaware" incorporated both the substantive law *and* the statutes of limitations of Delaware. The court held that the provision did require application of Delaware's three-year statute of limitations for breach of contract actions, even though it was shorter than the otherwise applicable California four-year statute of limitations (CCP § 337(1)).

The court found that because two of the three parties to the contract were incorporated in Delaware, Delaware had a "substantial relationship" to the parties and provided a "reasonable basis" for the parties' choice of Delaware law, within the meaning of § 187(2) of the Restatement (Second) of Conflict of Laws. The court also found that the application of the shorter Delaware statute of limitations to claims brought in the California courts was not contrary to a fundamental policy of California. Relying on case law and statutes which enforce reasonable agreements to shorten the four-year statute of limitations for breach of contract, the court concluded that a choice of law provision which has the effect of shortening the otherwise applicable California statute of limitations does not conflict with any fundamental policy of California and is enforceable.

Although the *Hambrecht* court cited *Ashland Chem. Co. v. Provence, supra,* as supporting its decision to enforce the shorter statute of limitations, the court questioned other aspects of the *Ashland* court's analysis, including the *Ashland* court's suggestion that a choice-of-law provision is per se unenforceable if the chosen state's statute of limitations is longer than California's. *Hambrecht, supra,* 38 Cal. App. 4th 1532, 1549, n.17. Do you agree with this criticism of the *Ashland* court's analysis? Why?

[B] The California Borrowing Statute

Because the traditional view of statute of limitations as "procedural" encouraged forum shopping, California enacted a borrowing statute in 1872, CCP § 361. *See McCann Foster Wheeler LLC,* reproduced *supra*. Section 361 states:

> When a cause of action has arisen in another State, or in a foreign country, and by the laws thereof an action thereon cannot there be maintained against a person by reason of the lapse of time, an action thereon shall not be maintained against him in this State, except in favor of one who has been a citizen of this State, and who has held the cause of action from the time it accrued.

Notes and Comments regarding California's Borrowing Statute

(1) In *McCann v. Foster Wheeler LLC,* 48 Cal. 4th 68, 84–87, 105 Cal. Rptr. 3d 378, 225 P.3d 516 (2010), reproduced *supra*, the Supreme Court discussed the general rule and exceptions contained in California's borrowing statute, CCP § 361. What are they?

What role did this borrowing statute play in the *McCann* court's decision to apply the Oklahoma statute of repose? Why did the court in *McCann* not apply § 361? Did the court determine that § 361 was inapplicable based on the facts of the case?

(2) When the manner and time of commencing an action is an integral part of the borrowed statute of limitations, the courts have construed CCP § 361 to require compliance with the borrowed state's "commencement" definition. *See, e.g., Ginise v. Zaharia,* 224 Cal. App. 2d 153, 36 Cal. Rptr. 406 (1964). Consequently, if an action is not timely commenced under a borrowed statute until the complaint and summons are served (as opposed to the general California rule that commencement for statute of limitation purposes occurs on the date of filing the complaint), the California court must follow that definition when applying § 361. *Id.* However, there is some authority for limiting this to "commencement upon service" requirements which are expressly incorporated in the borrowed state's statutory scheme, and not merely the result of judicial construction by the borrowed state's courts. *Id.* Likewise, § 361 does not mandate inclusion of a borrowed state's service requirements where those requirements do not determine when an action "commences" for statute of limitations purpose, but instead determine whether the filed action is being prosecuted with due diligence. *Delfosse v. C.A.C.I., Inc.-Federal,* 218 Cal. App. 3d 683, 691–93, 267 Cal. Rptr. 224 (1990).

(3) Section 361 may be preempted by a more specific choice-of-law statute, such as that contained in the Uniform Interstate Family Support Act, Family Code § 4953. *See Marriage of Ryan,* 22 Cal. App. 4th 841, 27 Cal. Rptr. 2d 580 (1994).

(4) Does CCP § 361 apply where the plaintiff brought the action in California to obtain complete recovery because several defendants were not amenable to service in Montana, where the cause of action arose, and not for the sole purpose of avoiding the Montana statute of limitations? *See Giest v. Sequoia Ventures, Inc.,* 83 Cal. App. 4th 300, 99 Cal. Rptr. 2d 476 (2000) (ruling section 361 does not inquire into a nonresident plaintiff's subjective intention in suing in California). Does CCP § 361 apply where the plaintiff was a citizen of California in the past but was a nonresident when his tort cause of action arose in another state? *See Cossman v. DaimlerChrysler Corp.,* 108 Cal. App. 4th 370, 133 Cal. Rptr. 2d 376 (2003) (holding a nonresident plaintiff is not exempt from the reach of section 361 unless a citizen of California at the time his claimed accrued).

§ 5.06 Miscellaneous Choice-of-Law Applications

[A] Corporations

[1] Government Interest Analysis

The California courts have applied the governmental interest and comparative impairment approaches to issues of corporation law, such as treatment of suits by or against dissolved corporations, *e.g., North American Asbestos Corp. v. Superior Court,* 180 Cal. App. 3d 902, 225 Cal. Rptr. 877 (1986) (conducting a comparative impairment analysis and concluding that California's interest in applying Corporation Code § 2010's unlimited time limit for suit by California residents against dissolved Illinois corporation for injuries arising out of its pre-dissolution asbestos activities greatly impaired if two-year Illinois limitation statute applied by California court); *Riley v. Fitzgerald*, 178 Cal. App. 3d 871, 223 Cal. Rptr. 889 (1986) (ruling Texas limitation law applied in action on behalf of dissolved Texas corporation because Texas' interest in regulatory affairs of its corporations greater than California's interest in preventing fraud by California residents against foreign residents); and in an action by directors for an order to inspect the books and records of the defendant corporation, *e.g.*, *Havlicek v. Coast-to-Coast Analytical Serv., Inc.*, 39 Cal. App. 4th 1844, 46 Cal. Rptr. 2d 696 (1995) (finding Delaware's interest in regulating the activities of its domestic corporations was less substantial where, as here, Delaware's only contact the defendant corporation was in issuing a certificate of incorporation; by contrast California has a more substantial interest because the corporation's principal place of business was in California).

In *Sullivan v. Oracle Corp.*, 51 Cal. 4th 1191, 127 Cal. Rptr. 3d 185, 254 P.3d 237 (2011), the California Supreme Court undertook a government interest analysis to determine whether the California's overtime provisions applied to non-resident employees who worked in California for a California-based employer. Two of the plaintiffs resided in Colorado and the third in Arizona, but they all worked for defendant Oracle in California as well as in several other states. Plaintiffs sought overtime compensation for their work in California pursuant to the California Labor Code's overtime provisions, which are more favorable to the plaintiffs than the overtime laws of their home states. The defendant argued that the overtime laws of Arizona and Colorado should apply because the plaintiffs resided in those states. The Supreme Court found that California has a strong interest in protecting the health and safety of its labor force, and that neither Arizona nor Colorado had any interest in regulating overtime work performed in other states. Consequently, the Court ruled, the case presented a false conflict and California law should apply. *Sullivan, supra*, 51 Cal. 4th at 1203–1206.

[2] The "Internal Affairs" Doctrine

The California courts do not apply the government interest analysis to all issues of corporation law. Where an issue concerns the internal affairs of a corporation, the courts will apply the law of the state of incorporation. *See, e.g.*, *State Farm Mut. Auto. Ins. Co. v. Superior Court*, 114 Cal. App. 4th 434, 8 Cal. Rptr. 3d 56 (2003) (reviewing authorities and concluding the law of Illinois, the place of defendant's incorporation, applies to a nationwide class action of shareholders alleging defendant's board of directors did not pay dividends as promised in the by-laws and other corporate documents); *Vaughn v. LJ Intl., Inc.*, 174 Cal. App. 4th 213, 94 Cal. Rptr. 3d 166 (2009) (ruling internal affairs doctrine in Corp. Code § 2116, not governmental interest choice-of-law test, determines which state's substantive law governs the right of a shareholder to derivatively sue corporate directors on behalf of the company); *but see Kruss v. Booth*, 185 Cal. App. 4th 699, 111 Cal. Rptr. 3d 56 (2010) (ruling that, pursuant to Corp. Code § 2115, California law governs certain internal affairs of a foreign corporation if more than half of the voting stock is held by California residents).

This traditional conflicts rule, referred to as the internal affairs doctrine, "recognizes that only one state should have the authority to regulate a corporation's internal affairs—matters peculiar to the relationships among or between the corporation and its current officers, directors, and shareholders—because otherwise a corporation could be faced with conflicting demands." *State Farm Mut., supra*, 114 Cal. App. 4th at 442.

[B] Family Law Matters

[1] Community Property

Generally, marital interests in money and property acquired during a marriage are governed by the law of the domicile of the spouses at the time of acquisition, even when such money or property is used to purchase real property in another state. *Barber v. Barber*, 51 Cal. 2d 244, 247, 331 P.2d 628 (1958); *Rozan v. Rozan*, 49 Cal. 2d 322, 326, 317 P.2d 11 (1957); *Grappo v. Coventry Fin. Corp.*, 235 Cal. App. 3d 496, 505–506, 286 Cal. Rptr. 714 (1991).

[2] Marriage

A marriage valid where contracted is valid in California, Family Code § 308; conversely, a marriage invalid where contracted is invalid in California. *E.g., Marriage of Smyklo*, 180 Cal. App. 3d 1095, 1099, 226 Cal. Rptr. 174 (1986) (ruling in action to determine validity of marriage that the California court must apply Alabama law on common law marriages); *Estate of Levie*, 50 Cal. App. 3d 572, 576, 123 Cal. Rptr. 445 (1975) (invalidating marriage in Nevada because a marriage between first cousins is invalid in California).

[3] Dissolution of Marriage

As with any other final judgment, California courts must give full faith and credit to a valid judgment of dissolution of marriage entered in another state. *See* Full Faith and Credit Clause, Art. IV, § 1, U.S. Const. However, Family Code § 2091 provides that a divorce obtained in another jurisdiction shall be of no effect in California if both parties to the marriage were domiciled in California at the time the divorce proceeding was commenced. What was the purpose of Family Code § 2091, originally enacted in 1949 as Civil Code § 5001? Is every application of § 2091 consistent with the Full Faith and Credit Clause?

[4] Child Custody and Child Support

Issues of interstate recognition, enforcement, and modification of child custody decrees are governed by the Uniform Child Custody Jurisdiction and Enforcement Act (UCCJEA), enacted in all states including California, Family Code §§ 3400–3465; the federal Parental Kidnapping Prevention Act of 1980, 28 U.S.C. § 1738A; and the federal International Child Abduction Remedies Act, 42 U.S.C. § 11601 *et seq.* For a detailed discussion of these statutory provisions, and numerous California cases applying them, see 10 Witkin, *Summary of California Law, Parent and Child*, §§ 157–193 (10th ed. 2005 & 2015 Suppl.); Anne B. Goldstein, *The Tragedy of the Interstate Child: A Critical Reexamination of the Uniform Child Custody Jurisdiction Act and the Parental Kidnapping Prevention Act*, 25 U.C. Davis L. Rev. 845 (1992). The Uniform Interstate Family Support Act (UIFSA), Family Code § 5700.101 *et seq.* (as amended effective Jan. 1, 2016), governs recognition, enforcement, and modification of sister state child and spousal support orders, including issues of jurisdiction and choice of law.

[C]   Class Actions

The California courts may deem a nationwide class action unmanageable where choice-of-law doctrine requires that numerous states' laws be applied to various class issues. *See, e.g., Washington Mut. Bank v. Superior Court*, 24 Cal. 4th. 906, 103 Cal. Rptr. 2d 320, 15 P.3d 1071 (2001) (observing that a choice-of-law determination is of central importance to issues of predominance of common legal questions and manageability where certification of a nationwide consumer class is sought by the plaintiff); *Osborne v. Subaru of Am., Inc.*, 198 Cal. App. 3d 646, 243 Cal. Rptr. 815 (1988) (denying certification of nationwide class action because various state rules on liability and damages applicable); *Clothesrigger, Inc. v. GTE Corp.*, 191 Cal. App. 3d 605, 236 Cal. Rptr. 605 (1987) (ruling that, although nationwide class action not necessarily rejected, the trial court must undertake interest analysis as to class claims); *Wershba v. Apple Computer, Inc.*, 91 Cal. App. 4th 224, 241–44, 110 Cal. Rptr. 2d 145 (2001) (finding significant contacts with California to support certification of nationwide class consisting of 2.4 million computer company customers and to support subjecting defendant to California's consumer protection laws). The same treatment is likely for nationwide class actions in federal courts, *e.g., Phillips Petroleum Co. v. Shutts*, 472 U.S. 797, 105 S. Ct. 2965, 86 L. Ed. 2d 628 (1985).

[D]   Choice-of-Law Doctrine in Federal Courts

Pursuant to *Klaxon Co. v. Stentor Elec. Mfg. Co.*, 313 U.S. 487, 61 S. Ct. 1020, 85 L. Ed. 1477 (1941), generally a federal court in a diversity action must apply the choice-of-law doctrine of the state in which it sits. *See, e.g., Paulo v. Bepex Corp.*, 792 F.2d 894, 896 (9th Cir. 1986) (applying California comparative impairment analysis in determining choice-of-law issue in products liability diversity action); *Liew v. Official Receiver and Liquidator*, 685 F.2d 1192, 1195–98 (9th Cir. 1982) (applying California governmental interest analysis).

[E]   Waiver

One way to avoid complex choice-of-law problems in multi-state cases is to simply not raise the issue. The general rule in California is that the law of the forum state applies unless a party litigant makes a timely request to invoke the law of a foreign state. *See Hurtado v. Superior Court*, 11 Cal. 3d 574, 581, 114 Cal. Rptr. 106, 522 P.2d 666 (1974). If the request is not made before the trial court, any objection to choice-of-law is deemed waived. A request made for the first time on appeal is untimely. *Danzig v. Jack Grynberg & Associates*, 161 Cal. App. 3d 1128, 1139, 208 Cal. Rptr. 336 (1984), *cert. denied*, 474 U.S. 819 (1985); *Estate of Patterson*, 108 Cal. App. 3d 197, 207, 166 Cal. Rptr. 435 (1980).

Chapter 6

The Proper Court

§ 6.01 Subject Matter Jurisdiction

[A] Introductory Note

The federal courts are courts of limited jurisdiction. The federal courts may hear only those actions which are within the constitutional grant of judicial power delineated by Article III of the U.S. Constitution, and even then only to the extent that Congress by statute authorizes the assertion of federal court jurisdiction over such actions. *See, e.g., Marbury v. Madison*, 5 U.S. (1 Cranch) 137, 2 L. Ed. 60 (1803) (holding Art. III defines outer limits of federal judicial power); *Sheldon v. Sill*, 49 U.S. (8 How.) 441, 12 L. Ed. 1147 (1850) (ruling lower federal courts have no jurisdiction except as Congress confers by statute). The statutes most often utilized for federal subject matter jurisdiction include 28 U.S.C. § 1331 (federal question), § 1332 (diversity), § 1343 (civil rights), § 1367 (supplemental jurisdiction), and § 1346 (actions against United States). When a federal court determines that it lacks statutory or constitutional authority to assert subject matter jurisdiction, the court must dismiss the claim. Resolution of such claims is left to the state courts.

The California state courts, by contrast, are courts of general jurisdiction. *See* Art. VI, § 10, California Constitution. Except for those actions within the exclusive jurisdiction of the federal courts, *e.g.,* 28 U.S.C. § 1338 (patents and copyrights), § 1346 (actions against United States), 15 U.S.C. § 78aa (federal securities claims), a California state court or tribunal has the authority to decide all causes of action presented by the parties.

[B] Superior Court Jurisdiction

[1] Trial Court Unification

Prior to 1998, California's trial courts consisted of superior and municipal courts, each with its own jurisdiction and number of judges fixed by the Legislature. Subsequently, the California voters approved Proposition 220 in June, 1998, and Proposition 48 in November, 2002, that amended the California Constitution to eliminate references to the constitutional authority to vest judicial power in the municipal courts. Cal. Const. Art. VI, § 5 (repealed), § 6, § 8, § 16 & § 23 (repealed). As a result of these constitutional amendments, the superior court now has jurisdiction in all matters that were previously under the jurisdiction of either the superior or municipal courts. Cal. Const., Art. VI, § 10. Even after unification, however, the jurisdictional differences between the superior courts and the former municipal courts remain relevant for purposes of certain trial court procedures, such as the size of the jury, and for purposes of the proper court for appellate review. Cal. Const., Art. I, § 16; Art. VI, § 11.

The Courts of Appeal have appellate jurisdiction as to the type of cases that were within the original jurisdiction of the superior courts on June 30, 1995, and in other cases as prescribed by statute. Cal. Const., Art. VI, § 11. As to all other cases — referred to in the legislation implementing Prop. 220 as "limited civil cases" — the appellate division of the superior court has appellate jurisdiction. Cal. Const., Art. VI, § 11; CCP §§ 77–86, 904.2. Under the current statutory scheme, the definition of "limited civil cases" corresponds to the type of cases that could only be heard in municipal court prior to unification, *i.e.*, generally speaking, civil cases in which the amount in controversy is $25,000 or less. CCP § 85 & § 86. The Legislature has the authority to change the appellate jurisdiction of the Courts of Appeal, and therefore necessarily of the appellate division of the superior court, by changing the jurisdictional amount in controversy. Cal. Const., Art. VI, § 11.

[2] "Limited" vs. "Unlimited" Civil Cases

[a] Limited Civil Case

Generally speaking, a "limited civil case" is an action in which the amount in controversy does not exceed $25,000. CCP §§ 85(a), 86(a) (designating various specific actions as limited civil cases). An "unlimited civil case" is an action which seeks more than $25,000, CCP § 88; or one designated as an unlimited civil case by statute regardless of the amount in controversy. *See, e.g.,* Family Code §§ 200, 4900–4976, 8500–9206 (dissolution of marriage, adoption, and support proceedings); Probate Code §§ 2200, 7050 (guardianship, conservatorship, and probate proceedings); CCP § 1250.010 (eminent domain proceedings).

Although the procedural laws applicable to civil actions generally also apply to limited civil cases, CCP § 90; there are some provisions applicable only to limited civil cases. These include limitations on pleadings, CCP § 92; simplified discovery, CCP §§ 93–96; admissibility of affidavits or declarations in lieu of direct testimony, CCP § 98; lower filing fees, Gov. Code §§ 70613, 70614; and appeal to the appellate division of the superior court instead of the court of appeal, CCP § 904.2.

[b] Reclassification

The clerk makes the initial jurisdictional classification of a civil case based on the plaintiff's classification designation in the caption of the complaint. CCP § 422.30(b); Rule 2.111(10), Cal. Rules of Ct. A party or the court on its own motion may move for reclassification of a case that is erroneously classified. CCP § 403.040; *see Stern v. Superior Court*, 105 Cal. App. 4th 223, 231–33, 129 Cal. Rptr. 2d 275 (2003) (ruling trial court abused its discretion in reclassifying the case without giving plaintiffs notice and an opportunity to contest the reclassification). If a party files an amended pleading or a cross-complaint that causes the action to exceed the maximum amount in controversy or otherwise fail to satisfy the requirements for a limited civil case, and pays a reclassification fee, the clerk must change the jurisdictional classification from limited to unlimited. CCP §§ 403.020, 403.030; *Leonard v. Superior Court*, 237 Cal. App. 4th 34, 187 Cal. Rptr. 3d 565 (2015) (directing trial court to reclassify case where defendant filed amended cross-complaint adding causes of action that increased amount in controversy to over $25,000); *see also* CCP § 403.050 (reclassification pursuant to parties' stipulation). An order reclassifying a case is not an appealable order; a party seeking appellate review of such an order must file a timely petition for a writ of mandate pursuant to CCP § 403.080. *Garau v. Torrance Unified Sch. Dist.*, 137 Cal. App. 4th 192, 40 Cal. Rptr. 3d 108 (2006).

[c]   Amount in Controversy

The "amount in controversy" means the amount of the demand, or the recovery sought, or the value of the property, that is in controversy in an action, "exclusive of attorneys' fees, interest, and costs." CCP § 85(a) The superior court must deny a motion to reclassify a civil case as "limited" (and thus keep the matter in the "unlimited" classification) unless it appears to a legal certainty that the plaintiff's damages will necessarily be less than $25,000. *See Ytuarte v. Superior Court*, 129 Cal. App. 4th 266, 276–79, 28 Cal. Rptr. 3d 474 (2005) (concluding to defeat a motion to reclassify from unlimited to limited, the party opposing reclassification must present evidence to demonstrate a possibility that the verdict will exceed $25,000); *Stern, supra*, 105 Cal. App. 4th at 233–34 (reversing trial court's reclassification from unlimited to limited action because it failed to make requisite finding that the matter would necessarily result in a verdict below the jurisdictional minimum).

The changes in court organization, procedure, and nomenclature caused by trial court unification have not altered the prior law governing the computation of that amount. *Stern, supra*, 105 Cal. App. 4th at 227, 230–31. Therefore, when a single plaintiff alleges multiple causes of action against a single defendant, the demands of all the claims are aggregated in computing the amount in controversy. *Hammell v. Superior Court*, 217 Cal. 5, 7–8, 17 P.2d 101 (1932). Aggregation is not permitted, however, when a single plaintiff has separate claims against several defendants. *Myers v. Sierra Valley Stock & Agric. Assn.*, 122 Cal. 669, 55 P. 689 (1898). When properly-joined multiple plaintiffs have joint causes of action against a single defendant, their joint claims are aggregated in computing the amount in controversy. *Frost v. Mighetto*, 22 Cal. App. 2d 612, 71 P.2d 932 (1937). However, where the joined plaintiffs' causes of action are separate, their separate claims are not aggregated. *Colla v. Carmichael U-Drive Autos*, 111 Cal. App. Supp. 784, 294 P. 378 (1930). These multiple plaintiff aggregation rules apply, for example, to class actions. *See Weaver v. Pasadena Tournament of Roses Assn.*, 32 Cal. 2d 833, 198 P.2d 514 (1948).

[d] Judgment Below Classification Minimum Amount

When a good faith demand in a complaint exceeds the amount necessary for classification as an unlimited civil case but the subsequent judgment is one that could have been rendered in a limited civil case, the court is not required to reclassify the action as a limited civil action but may refuse to award costs to the prevailing plaintiff. CCP §§ 403.040(e), 1033(a). When a plaintiff in a limited civil case recovers an amount within the jurisdictional limit of the small claims court, the court may deny costs to the prevailing plaintiff or may allow them in any amount it deems proper. CCP § 1033(b); *see, e.g., Chavez v. City of Los Angeles*, 47 Cal. 4th 970, 982–89, 104 Cal. Rptr. 3d 710, 224 P.3d 41 (2010) (holding trial court did not abuse its discretion in denying successful plaintiff statutory attorney fees as costs in an action brought as an unlimited civil case because the plaintiff recovered an amount that could have been recovered in a limited civil case).

[e] Small Claims Court

Each superior court must have a small claims division. CCP § 116.210. Generally, the small claims court has jurisdiction in actions for recovery of money if the amount of the demand does not exceed $5000, CCP § 116.220(a); and also has jurisdiction in some actions brought by a natural person if the amount of the demand does not exceed $10,000, CCP § 116.221. In such actions, CCP § 116.220(b) authorizes the court to grant equitable relief in the form of rescission, restitution, reformation, and specific performance. Is the small claims courts' jurisdiction exclusive or concurrent with the superior courts' on matters where the demand does not exceed $5000?

A plaintiff who files an action in small claims court waives any damages above the jurisdictional limit. CCP § 116.220(d). A plaintiff who litigates in small claims court has no right to appeal the judgment on the plaintiff's claim. CCP § 116.710(a). However, the defendant with respect to the plaintiff's claim, and a plaintiff with respect to a claim of the defendant, may appeal the judgment to the superior court. CCP § 116.710(b). The appeal consists of a trial *de novo* before a superior court judge. CCP § 116.770.

[f] Probate Court

The superior courts in many larger counties in California have separate departments for probate matters. Such departments have primary jurisdiction relating to certain probate matters assigned to such court by statute. *See* Probate Code § 7050 (administration of decedents' estates); *Saks v. Damon Raike & Co.*, 7 Cal. App. 4th 419, 428–30, 8 Cal. Rptr. 2d 869 (1992) (ruling that pursuant to Probate Code § 17000(a), the probate department has exclusive jurisdiction of proceedings concerning the internal affairs of trusts). The Probate Court in such proceedings is, however, a court of general jurisdiction with all the powers of the superior courts. Probate Code §§ 7050, 17001.

[C] Court vs. Administrative Tribunal Jurisdiction

[1] Exclusive Agency Jurisdiction

A statute may vest exclusive original jurisdiction in an administrative agency over controversies within its grant of power, subject to appellate judicial review, and thereby deny jurisdiction to the superior court. Such statutes and agencies include the following: The Agricultural Labor Relations Board (ALRB), with exclusive original jurisdiction over unfair labor practices, subject to judicial review by the appropriate court of appeal, pursuant to Labor Code § 1160.8 and § 1160.9; the Public Employment Relations Board (PERB), with exclusive initial jurisdiction of charges of unfair practices in public employment, subject to judicial review pursuant to Government Code § 3541.5 and § 3542; the Public Utilities Commission (PUC) with exclusive jurisdiction over broad areas to regulate the relationship between a public utility and its customers, pursuant to Public Utility Code § 1759 and § 2106; the State Bar Court with exclusive initial jurisdiction over matters involving attorney discipline subject to review and confirmation by the Supreme Court, pursuant to Business and Professions Code §§ 6078–6106.9.

Another important agency is the Workers' Compensation Appeals Board (WCAB) which, pursuant to Labor Code § 5955, has exclusive jurisdiction, not concurrent with the superior courts, over actions by employees for work-related injuries. *Scott v. Indus. Accident Comm.*, 46 Cal. 2d 76, 293 P.2d 18 (1956); *Charles J. Vacanti, M.D. Inc v. State Comp. Ins. Fund,*, 24 Cal. 4th 800, 102 Cal. Rptr. 2d 562, 14 P.3d 234 (2001) (applying two-step test for determining scope of workers compensation exclusivity); *see also Greener v. Workers Comp. Appeals Bd.*, 6 Cal. 4th 1028, 25 Cal. Rptr. 2d 539, 863 P.2d 784 (1993) (holding plaintiff's challenge to constitutionality of certain workers' compensation statutes not within subject matter jurisdiction of superior court). A decision of the WCAB may be reviewed by an appellate court. Labor Code §§ 5950, 5955; *see Greener v. Workers Comp. Appeals Bd.*, *supra*, 6 Cal. 4th at 1044–46 (ruling appellate review by writ of mandamus authorized).

[2] Jurisdiction to Determine Jurisdictional Issues

A superior court does, of course, have jurisdiction to determine questions of whether the court or an administrative agency has exclusive jurisdiction over a particular claim. *E.g.*, *Scott v. Indus. Accident Comm.*, *supra*, 46 Cal. 2d at 81–89; *Rowland v. County of Sonoma*, 220 Cal. App. 3d 331, 333, 269 Cal. Rptr. 426 (1990).

[a] Exhaustion of Administrative Remedies

Even when a statutory scheme does not divest the superior courts of initial exclusive jurisdiction, the provisions may require claimants to exhaust available administrative remedies prior to commencing an action in superior court, *e.g.*, Government Code § 11523 (judicial review of agency decision based on agency record, pursuant to California Administrative Procedure Act, Gov. Code § 11340 *et seq.*); CCP § 1094.5 (administrative mandamus for judicial review of final administrative hearing decision). *See, e.g.*, *Anton v. San Antonio Cmty. Hosp.*, 19 Cal. 3d 802, 567 P.2d 1162, 140 Cal.

Rptr. 442 (1977) (applying administrative mandamus prerequisites to decision of private community hospital); *Abelleira v. Dist. Court of Appeal*, 17 Cal. 2d 280, 293, 109 P.2d 942 (1941) (holding exhaustion of statutory administrative remedy a jurisdictional prerequisite to resort to the courts).

Although some applications of this exhaustion requirement may not implicate the superior courts' fundamental subject matter jurisdiction because the requirement may be waived or be subject to judicial exceptions, the exhaustion requirement often postpones the superior court's jurisdiction during the pendency of the administrative proceeding. *See, e.g., Abelleira, supra,* 17 Cal. 2d at 292–306; *Green v. City of Oceanside,* 194 Cal. App. 3d 212, 222, 239 Cal. Rptr. 470 (1987) (concluding exhaustion doctrine did not implicate subject matter jurisdiction but rather was a procedural prerequisite to suit); *County of Contra Costa v. State of California,* 177 Cal. App. 3d 62, 222 Cal. Rptr. 750 (1986) (observing that when no exception or waiver applied, exhaustion of an administrative remedy was a jurisdictional prerequisite to resort to the courts).

[b] Primary Jurisdiction

Even where a claim is originally cognizable in the courts and not in an administrative agency, the court, under the doctrine of primary jurisdiction, may stay judicial proceedings pending resolution of administrative proceedings on the claim. *Farmers Ins. Exch. v. Superior Court,* 2 Cal. 4th 377, 6 Cal. Rptr. 2d 487, 826 P.2d 730 (1992) (invoking primary jurisdiction doctrine to suspend court action pending resolution of administrative agency proceedings on complex insurance regulations issues). The doctrines of exhaustion of administrative remedies and primary jurisdiction are discussed in more detail in § 4.06, *supra.* The administrative mandamus provisions are discussed in § 15.03, *infra.*

[3] *No Waiver of Jurisdictional Defense*

The defense of lack of subject matter jurisdiction may be raised at any time, and by any party or by the court. CCP §§ 430.10, 430.80(a); *Unruh v. Truck Ins. Exch.,* 7 Cal. 3d 616, 622, 102 Cal. Rptr. 815, 498 P.2d 1063 (1972) (ruling lack of subject matter jurisdiction may be asserted at any time, even for the first time on appeal); *Barnick v. Longs Drug Stores, Inc.,* 203 Cal. App. 3d 377, 379–80, 250 Cal. Rptr. 10 (1988) (same). However, in the interests of judicial economy, the courts sometimes suggest that counsel may have a duty to raise this fundamental objection at an early time. *E.g., Rowland v. County of Sonoma,* 220 Cal. App. 3d 331, 335, 269 Cal. Rptr. 426 (1990). Nevertheless, subject matter jurisdiction cannot be conferred by estoppel, waiver, or consent. *Summers v. Superior Court,* 53 Cal. 2d 295, 298, 1 Cal. Rptr. 324, 347 P.2d 668 (1959); *Rowland, supra,* 220 Cal. App. 3d at 333 (noting a court must dismiss action if it lacks subject matter jurisdiction; parties cannot confer jurisdiction on civil courts by stipulation or estoppel).

§ 6.02 Personal Jurisdiction

[A] Personal Jurisdiction, Generally

Personal jurisdiction concerns the ability of a state court to enter a binding judgment against a nonresident defendant. A state court's personal jurisdiction is limited by both the Due Process Clause of the Fourteenth Amendment to the U.S. Constitution, and by that state's long-arm statute defining the court's personal jurisdiction. *Burger King Corp. v. Rudzewicz*, 471 U.S. 462, 105 S. Ct. 2174, 85 L. Ed. 2d 528 (1985); *Insurance Corp. of Ireland, Ltd. v. Compagnie des Bauxites de Guinee*, 456 U.S. 694, 702, 102 S. Ct. 2099, 72 L. Ed. 2d 492 (1982).

Unlike many states which limit the bases of their courts' personal jurisdiction by reference to specific statutory categories, the California long-arm statute, CCP § 410.10, broadly states that "[a] court of this state may exercise jurisdiction on any basis not inconsistent with the Constitution of this state or of the United States." CCP § 410.10 manifests the intent that California courts exercise the broadest possible personal jurisdiction over nonresidents, limited only by constitutional considerations. *Sibley v. Superior Court*, 16 Cal. 3d 442, 445, 128 Cal. Rptr. 34, 546 P.2d 322 (1976).

[1] *Specific Jurisdiction*

Cassiar Mining Corp. v. Superior Court

Court of Appeal of California, Fourth Appellate District
66 Cal. App. 4th 550, 78 Cal. Rptr. 2d 167 (1998)

CROSBY, JUSTICE.

For some 40 years, Cassiar Mining Corporation, a Canadian company, admittedly sold thousands of tons of raw asbestos fiber directly to California manufacturers who incorporated the asbestos into finished products. California workers allegedly were exposed to these asbestos fibers here, thereby sustaining progressive lung diseases. They claim Cassiar failed to adequately warn of the health risks.

We apply the Supreme Court's decision in *Vons Companies, Inc. v. Seabest Foods, Inc.* (1996) 14 Cal. 4th 434 [58 Cal. Rptr. 2d 899, 926 P.2d 1085] to find sufficient contacts to justify the exercise of specific jurisdiction. The instant litigation results from injuries "related to" Cassiar's forum activities of selling asbestos to certain companies located in California.

Cassiar argues there is no "evidence of record" that plaintiffs were actually exposed to the asbestos fibers it sold in California or sustained injury as a result. Following *Vons* we will not impose such a strict causation burden for jurisdictional purposes, nor will we require a mini-trial. It is manifestly "fair" to require that Cassiar account in California for the consequences of its activities within the state, and Cassiar has not presented any compelling considerations to suggest otherwise.

I

Cassiar was incorporated in Canada in 1951. It began its mining operations in British Columbia in 1953, and mined, milled, and sold raw asbestos fiber. It ceased operations in 1992, when it went bankrupt and subsequently dissolved.

Cassiar did not itself manufacture or sell any finished products. Instead it sold the raw asbestos fibers to manufacturers, including companies such as Johns-Manville, Fibreboard, and CertainTeed with plants in California. For some 38 years (from 1953 until 1991), Cassiar sold thousands of tons of raw asbestos to these California operations. It has made no sales or otherwise had any contacts with California since 1991.

Cassiar first became a target of asbestos lawsuits in the 1970s. It has appeared and defended such lawsuits in California and has not challenged California's specific jurisdiction where it admittedly supplied the raw asbestos to which the plaintiffs were exposed. (See, e.g., *Gutierrez v. Cassiar Mining Corp.* (1998) 64 Cal. App. 4th 148, 151–152 [affirming in part and reversing in part jury verdict against Cassiar for supplying asbestos to plaintiff's jobsite, a CertainTeed cement plant in Santa Clara].) As Cassiar explains, "We do not contest jurisdiction in cases where it's clearly connected to Cassiar's past contacts with the State of California. [¶] For example ... a case brought by workers who worked at the plant that Cassiar shipped fiber to, we'd answer, defend, we don't make an issue of it, but there's a difference between defending a limited number of cases where there's a clear connection with the forum and sort of an infinite number of cases where the connection is speculative at best."

The instant litigation is brought by 10 workers who allegedly sustained asbestos-related lung injuries as a result of inhaling asbestos during the course of their employment. Cassiar is one of 162 named defendants said to have manufactured, distributed, supplied, or installed asbestos products to which plaintiffs were exposed at their jobsites. Plaintiffs claim they were injured when they inhaled asbestos supplied by Cassiar to such companies as Fibreboard (in Emeryville), CertainTeed (in Santa Clara) and Johns-Manville (in Lompoc). But, unlike the worker in *Gutierrez*, none of the plaintiffs worked at the Fibreboard, CertainTeed or Johns-Manville plants where Cassiar shipped the asbestos.

Cassiar appeared specially and moved to quash service of the summons. While conceding it sold asbestos fiber to these "certain discrete locations in California between 1953 and 1991," Cassiar declared, "no sales of asbestos fiber [were made] at any time to any jobsite where any plaintiff alleges occupational exposure to asbestos...." Plaintiffs' counter declarations did not establish any causal link between their injuries and Cassiar's California sales.

The superior court denied Cassiar's motion to quash. Cassiar filed a petition for writ of mandate. We issued an order to show cause and set the matter for hearing.

II

Cassiar has a liberty interest in not being subjected to the jurisdiction of California courts if its connection with this state falls below the "minimum contacts" threshold, or if so doing will violate "traditional notions of fair play and substantial justice." (*In-*

ternational Shoe Co. v. Washington (1945) 326 U.S. 310, 316, 90 L. Ed. 95, 66 S. Ct. 154.) The minimum contacts requirement prevents nonresident defendants from being subjected to California jurisdiction " 'solely as a result of "random," "fortuitous," or "attenuated" contacts.' " (*Vons Companies, Inc. v. Seabest Foods, Inc., supra*, 14 Cal. 4th at p. 445, citing *Burger King Corp. v. Rudzewicz* (1985) 471 U.S. 462, 475, 85 Ed. 2d 528, 105 S. Ct. 2174.) This affords nonresidents some degree of predictability and certainty about when they will be subjected to the jurisdiction of the forum state. California's long-arm statute is intended to provide the broadest possible jurisdiction subject only to federal constitutional limitations. (Code Civ. Proc., § 410.10; *Sibley v. Superior Court* (1976) 16 Cal. 3d 442, 445, 128 Cal. Rptr. 34, 546 P.2d 322.)

Cassiar's contacts with California do not appear to be so continuous and systematic as to establish California's general jurisdiction over any cause of action against Cassiar, regardless of its relationship with the forum. (*As You Sow v. Crawford Laboratories, Inc.* (1996) 50 Cal. App. 4th 1859, 1868.) A Canadian company headquartered in Vancouver, Cassiar had no offices, employees, bank accounts, or real property within the state. It did not advertise in any California trade journals or publications. It had no further contacts with California once it halted ordinary business operations in 1991.

But that does not end our inquiry. Even if Cassiar had severed any California connections long before the time of suit, it still may be subject to the state's specific jurisdiction if it has (1) purposefully derived benefits from California activities, and (2) the subject lawsuit is "related to" or "arises out" of its California contacts. (See *Vons Companies, Inc. v. Seabest Foods, Inc., supra*, 14 Cal. 4th at p. 446.)

It is not true, as Cassiar has suggested, that jurisdiction is being sought merely because "we sold asbestos fiber anywhere in the world and it somehow wound up in California in some form, in some manner Cassiar had nothing to do with." Neither is jurisdiction invoked solely because of conclusory allegations in an unverified complaint. (*Goehring v. Superior Court* (1998) 62 Cal. App. 4th 894, 909.) "Merely knowing the product will enter California" does not comply with constitutional minimum contacts requirements; instead, the foreign defendant must have "some control over [the] ultimate destination" in California. (*As You Sow v. Crawford Laboratories, Inc., supra*, 50 Cal. App. 4th at p. 1869.)

Plaintiffs' declarations show—and Cassiar does not dispute—that Cassiar sold thousands of tons of raw asbestos fibers directly to California locations for some 38 years. Far from fortuitous or random connections, the record shows Cassiar purposefully directed raw asbestos fibers to these California sites. It was Cassiar, not plaintiffs, which formed a "substantial economic connection with this state." To require Cassiar to answer plaintiffs' complaint "is not to allow a third party unilaterally to draw [Cassiar] into a connection with this state; rather it was [Cassiar and the California-based manufacturers] who established the connection." (*Vons Companies, Inc. v. Seabest Foods, Inc., supra*, 14 Cal. 4th at p. 451.)[1] * * *

---

1. Other state courts have stressed this point in declining to extend jurisdiction over foreign mining companies who shipped raw asbestos ore into the national stream of commerce outside the forum

It was ... foreseeable that asbestos fiber which was directed by Cassiar to California would be used in California and could give rise to tort litigation in California. Cassiar has "knowingly availed itself of the benefits accruing from its activities within the forum...." We conclude from this history that Cassiar intended to serve the California market, thereby becoming subject to its specific jurisdiction for lawsuits having a "substantial connection" with its forum activities. (*Vons Companies, Inc. v. Seabest Foods, Inc., supra*, 14 Cal. 4th at p. 452 ["as long as the claim bears a substantial connection to the nonresident's forum contacts, the exercise of specific jurisdiction is appropriate"].)

III

Cassiar attacks plaintiffs' showing of a "substantial connection" between its California asbestos sales and plaintiffs' injuries. According to Cassiar, "you can only have specific jurisdiction if the cause of action arises out of those contacts with the state. If [it does] not, the state case has no specific jurisdiction. That's why it's critical they come up with some evidence to show that Cassiar's sales into the State of California have something to do with these plaintiffs' causes of action."

For jurisdictional purposes, we find no legal support for Cassiar's insistence upon (as counsel urged during oral argument) a "plaintiff-specific link" between its California sales of raw asbestos and the underlying litigation. Indeed, *Vons*, the leading California authority, expressly rejected similar efforts to impose such strict requirements in specific jurisdiction cases. In its place, the Supreme Court chose a "relaxed, flexible standard, rather than one requiring that the plaintiff's claim arise out of the forum contact in any narrow sense...." (*Vons Companies, Inc. v. Seabest Foods, Inc., supra*, 14 Cal. 4th at p. 455.) A unanimous court stated, "the defendant's forum activities need not be directed at the *plaintiff* in order to give rise to specific jurisdiction.... The nexus required to establish specific jurisdiction is between the defendant, the *forum*, and the litigation [citations] — not between the plaintiff and the defendant.... The relevant contacts are said to be with the *forum*, because it is the defendant's choice to take advantage of opportunities that exist in the forum that subjects it to jurisdiction." (*Id.* at pp. 457–58.)

Vons involved an E. coli outbreak at various Jack-in-the-Box restaurants in the Pacific Northwest allegedly caused by contaminated hamburger patties from a Vons meat packing plant in El Monte. Vons, which became embroiled in litigation in California, sought indemnity from WRMI, a Washington state franchisee, for mishandling the meat, which WRMI purchased and cooked in Washington. WRMI challenged

---

state. That, of course, is not our case. As discussed above, the record shows Cassiar purposely directed its activities and products toward California by selling raw asbestos to "discrete locations" within the state. Direct sales of raw asbestos to the forum satisfies specific jurisdiction even under the "stream of commerce plus" view adopted by a plurality of the United States Supreme Court in *Asahi Metal Industry Co. v. Superior Court* (1987) 480 U.S. 102, 112, 94 L. Ed. 2d 92, 107 S. Ct. 1026 (plur. opn. by O'Connor, J.).

Vons' efforts to bring it into a California forum because Vons failed to demonstrate that its tort liability had anything to do with its contacts with the California-based franchiser. According to WRMI (and the Court of Appeal), "unless the forum contact *proximately caused* the occurrence that injured the plaintiff, the connection between the contacts and the claim is insufficient to permit the exercise of specific jurisdiction." (*Id.* at p. 461.)

The Supreme Court rejected a mechanical proximate cause test for evaluating the connection between a nonresident defendant's forum activities and a plaintiff's cause of action. The court stressed that the relevant standard was painted in "relatively broad terms" (*id.* at p. 468) and formulated in the disjunctive: the cause of action either must "'arise out of' *or* be 'related to' the defendant's forum activity in order to warrant the exercise of specific jurisdiction...." (*Id.* at p. 451, italics added.)

Instead of a bright-line rule, the Supreme Court chose the amorphous "goal of fairness" (*Vons Companies, Inc. v. Seabest Foods, Inc., supra,* 14 Cal. 4th at p. 468), recognizing "few answers will be written in black and white. The greys are dominant and even among them the shades are innumerable." (*Id.* at p. 475, internal quotation marks omitted.) There is a sliding scale or continuum between the defendant's contacts and the plaintiff's claim "so that the greater the intensity of forum activity, the lesser the relationship required between the contact and the claim." (*Id.* at p. 453.)

The connection between plaintiffs' complaint and Cassiar's forum-based activities meets the *Vons* relatedness test. Plaintiffs who were exposed to asbestos fibers within California are suing Cassiar only because it purposefully sold asbestos fiber in this state. Cassiar's obligations (if any) to plaintiffs are connected to its California-based activities. The goal of fairness to defendants is met by extending the burdens of California jurisdiction over a defendant who purposefully availed itself of the benefits of selling asbestos fibers within the state. Since plaintiffs were harmed "'while engaged in activities integral to the relationship [Cassiar] sought to establish, we think the nexus between the contacts and the cause of action is sufficiently strong to survive the due process inquiry at least at the relatedness stage.'" (*Vons Companies, Inc. v. Seabest Foods, Inc., supra,* 14 Cal. 4th at p. 470.)

Our conclusion does not necessarily mean, as Cassiar contends, that it will be subject to jurisdiction in California in all asbestos cases, even those that do not involve plaintiffs exposed to fiber from Cassiar's California sales. (Cassiar gives, as an example, a plaintiff who was exposed to asbestos in Chile but who subsequently moved to California where he got sick and died.) According to the continuum described in *Vons,* "as the relationship of the defendant with the state seeking to exercise jurisdiction over him grows more tenuous, the scope of jurisdiction also retracts...." (*Vons Companies, Inc. v. Seabest Foods, Inc., supra,* 14 Cal. 4th at p. 448.) Unlike the proffered analogy of a foreign defendant, a foreign sale and a foreign exposure, the instant case involves California contacts, California plaintiffs, and a California exposure. Plaintiffs have shown the requisite connection between their causes of action and Cassiar's sales of asbestos fiber to California.

In insisting these 10 plaintiffs provide facts at the jurisdictional stage directly linking their claims with its asbestos sales, Cassiar ignores the Supreme Court's caution against mixing tort concepts with jurisdictional ones because the two are "entirely unrelated." (*Vons Companies, Inc. v. Seabest Foods, Inc., supra,* 14 Cal. 4th at p. 464.) A foreign defendant who has voluntarily chosen to affiliate itself with a forum "reasonably must anticipate exposure to litigation in the forum beyond claims that are in a narrow sense proximately caused by forum activities." (*Id.* at p. 464.) * * *

Concerns about plaintiffs' deficiencies of proof should be addressed through the substantive law of torts. If, as Cassiar contends, plaintiffs lack substantial evidence that their injuries were caused by exposure to its asbestos fibers, then Cassiar may have a way out before trial.

IV

Where, as here, plaintiffs have established sufficient minimum contacts to pass constitutional muster, the burden shifts to Cassiar to make a compelling case as to why jurisdiction is unreasonable. (*Vons Companies, Inc. v. Seabest Foods, Inc., supra,* 14 Cal. 4th at p. 449.) Cassiar has not done so. California has a strong interest in providing a forum to the 10 California residents who experienced occupational exposure to asbestos on California jobsites. Cassiar is not a stranger to California litigation (*Gutierrez v. Cassiar Mining Corp., supra,* 64 Cal. App. 4th 148) and has agreed to forum jurisdiction over asbestos-related claims arising from its California-based sales. It makes little sense to require these plaintiffs to pursue the vast bulk of this complex asbestos litigation against 161 defendants in California, but to file a separate lawsuit against Cassiar, the 162nd defendant, in British Columbia.

This is not *Asahi Metal Industry Co. v. Superior Court, supra,* 480 U.S. at p. 106, where a Taiwanese manufacturer of a motorcycle tire tube sought indemnity in California from a Japanese manufacturer of its valve assembly. Cassiar already has anticipated being called into account in California for the consequences of sales of asbestos directed to this state. In light of these factors, it is reasonable to assert specific jurisdiction here.

The petition for writ of mandate is denied. * * *

Notes and Questions

(1) *Vons Companies, Inc. v. Seabest Foods, Inc.,* 14 Cal. 4th 434, 58 Cal. Rptr. 2d 899, 926 P.2d 1085 (1996). In *Vons,* the California Supreme Court attempted to clarify the personal jurisdiction concept of "specific jurisdiction" by defining the circumstances under which a cause of action "arises out of or relates to" a defendant's contacts with the forum. This was not an easy task—the court's discussion of this due process issue covers nearly 30 Pages. *See Vons, supra,* 14 Cal. 4th at 446–75; *see also Virtual Magic Asia, Inc. v. Fil-Cartoons, Inc.,* 99 Cal. App. 4th 228, 121 Cal. Rptr. 2d 1 (2002) (discussing and applying the "substantial connection" test for specific jurisdiction in a breach of contract action). The *Cassiar* opinion, reproduced *supra,* contains a brief summary of the Court's holdings in *Vons,* but only hints at the various competing definitions considered by the Supreme Court.

The main focus of the Court's analysis in *Vons* was on the nature of the nexus between the defendant's forum activities and the plaintiff's cause of action. The defendants in *Vons* had argued for the adoption of the proximate cause test formulated by the Court of Appeal, *i.e.*, unless the defendant's forum contacts *proximately caused* the occurrence that injured the plaintiff, the connection between the contacts and the claim is insufficient to permit the exercise of specific jurisdiction. *Vons, supra*, 14 Cal. 4th at 460–62. The Supreme Court rejected the proximate cause test as too narrow and as inconsistent with fairness rationale underlying the specific jurisdiction doctrine. *Id. at* 462–64. Likewise, the Supreme Court rejected as overly restrictive a similar test proffered by the defendants, referred to as the substantive relevance test.

The plaintiff in *Vons* argued that the required relationship between the defendants' forum contacts and the plaintiff's cause of action should be determined by an expansive "but for" test, which focuses on whether the plaintiff's injury would have occurred "but for" the defendants' forum contacts. *Vons, supra*, 14 Cal. 4th at 464–66. The plaintiff pointed out that the U.S. Court of Appeals for the Ninth Circuit employed the "but for" test in its specific jurisdiction analysis in *Shute v. Carnival Cruise Lines*, 897 F.2d 377, 385 (9th Cir. 1990), and *Ballard v. Savage*, 65 F.3d 1495, 1500 (9th Cir. 1995). Despite the federal court precedent, the Court in *Vons* determined that the "but for" test was too broad and amorphous. *Vons, supra*, 14 Cal. 4th at 467–68. The *Vons* court wryly observed that "if the defendant is a lawyer who was received his or her legal education in the forum, that legal education may be said to be a 'but for' cause of any malpractice the lawyer commits anywhere in the nation, yet it hardly seems a sufficient basis for the forum to exercise jurisdiction." *Id.*, at 467.

The Supreme Court ultimately concluded in *Vons* that the appropriate inquiry for specific jurisdiction was whether the plaintiff's cause of action has a "substantial connection" with the defendants' forum activities, and defined "substantial connection" by reference to the facts of an earlier California Supreme Court decision, *Cornelison v. Chaney*, 16 Cal. 3d 143, 127 Cal. Rptr. 352, 545 P.2d 264 (1978):

> A claim need not arise directly from the defendant's forum contacts in order to be sufficiently related to the contact to warrant the exercise of specific jurisdiction. Rather, as long as the claim bears a substantial connection to the nonresident's forum contacts, the exercise of specific jurisdiction is appropriate. The due process clause is concerned with protecting nonresident defendants from being brought unfairly into court in the forum, on the basis of random contacts. That constitutional provision, however, does not provide defendants with a shield against jurisdiction when the defendant purposefully has availed himself or herself of benefits in the forum. The goal of fairness is well served by the standard we originally set out in *Cornelison, supra*, 16 Cal. 3d 143, that is, there must be a *substantial connection* between the forum contacts and the plaintiff's claim to warrant the exercise of specific jurisdiction. (*Id.* at p. 148.) * * *
>
> [I]n *Cornelison* ... we held that a California resident could sue a Nebraska defendant in California for wrongful death in connection with an accident

that occurred in Nevada. Because the defendant was engaged in the business of hauling goods by truck and made fairly frequent deliveries in California, and the accident occurred while he was en route to California for further deliveries, we found a "substantial nexus between plaintiff's cause of action and defendant's activities in California." (*Id.* at p. 149.) We explained that the appropriate inquiry is whether the plaintiff's cause of action "arises out of or has a substantial connection with a business relationship defendant has purposefully established with California." (*Ibid.*) We commented that if, as we found, the defendant's activities are not so wide ranging as to justify general jurisdiction, "then jurisdiction depends upon the quality and nature of his activity in the forum *in relation* to the particular cause of action. In such a situation, the cause of action must arise out of an act done or transaction consummated in the forum, or defendant must perform some other act by which he purposefully avails himself of the privilege of conducting activities in the forum, thereby invoking the benefits and protections of its laws. Thus, as the relationship of the defendant with the state seeking to exercise jurisdiction over him grows more tenuous, the scope of jurisdiction also retracts, and fairness is assured by limiting the circumstances under which the plaintiff can compel him to appear and defend. The crucial inquiry concerns the character of defendant's activity in the forum, whether the cause of action *arises out of or has a substantial connection* with that activity, and upon the balancing of the convenience of the parties and the interests of the state in assuming jurisdiction." (*Id.* at pp. 147–148, fn. omitted, italics added, citing *Hanson v. Denckla* (1958) 357 U.S. 235, 250–253 [2 L. Ed. 2d 1283, 1295–1298, 78 S. Ct. 1228]; ...) * * *

The Court of Appeal below focused on an asserted lack of relationship between [plaintiff] Vons, on the one hand, and [defendants] Seabest and WRMI, on the other. The court suggested this lack of relationship was critical in determining whether the claim was sufficiently related to the forum contacts to permit the exercise of specific jurisdiction in California. Contrary to the Court of Appeal's thesis, however, the defendant's forum activities need not be directed at the plaintiff in order to give rise to specific jurisdiction. (See, e.g., *Keeton v. Hustler Magazine, Inc.* (1984) 465 U.S. 770, 775 [79 L. Ed.2d 790, 798, 104 S. Ct. 1473] [publisher that distributes magazines to the public in a distant state may be held accountable in that forum for damage to victim of defamation]; *Cornelison, supra,* 16 Cal. 3d 143 [jurisdiction found although the defendant's business activities in California were not directed at the accident victim];....) The United States Supreme Court has stated more than once that the nexus required to establish specific jurisdiction is between the defendant, *the forum,* and the litigation (*Helicopteros [Nacionales de Columbia, S.A. v. Hall* (1984)] 466 U.S. [408] at p. 411 [80 L. Ed. 2d [404] at p. 409]; *Shaffer v. Heitner* (1977) 433 U.S. 186, 204 [53 L. Ed. 2d 683, 697–698, 97 S. Ct. 2569])—not between the plaintiff and the defendant. For the purpose of deciding whether a defendant has minimum contacts or purposefully has availed itself of forum benefits, the relevant contacts are said to be with the *forum*, because it is the defendant's choice to take advantage of opportunities that exist in the forum that subjects it to jurisdiction. (*Asahi Metal Industry Co. v. Superior Court* (1987) 480 U.S. 102, 112 [94 L. Ed. 2d 92, 104–105, 107 S. Ct. 1026] (plur. opn. by O'Connor, J.); *Burger King [Corp. v. Rudzewics], supra*, 471 U.S. at pp. 475, 479 [85 L. Ed. 2d at pp. 542, 545]; *Helicopteros, supra*, 466 U.S. at p. 414 [80 L. Ed. 2d at p. 409]; *Shaffer v. Heitner, supra*, 433 U.S. at p. 204 [53 L. Ed. 2d at pp. 697–698].)

Vons Companies, Inc. v. Seabest Foods, Inc., supra, 14 Cal. 4th at 457–58 (italics in original).

(2) As the Court in *Vons* acknowledged, the federal Court of Appeals for the Ninth Circuit employed the "but for" test in determining the requisite nexus between a defendant's forum contacts and a plaintiff's claim, for purposes of specific jurisdiction. The California Supreme Court in *Vons* rejected this interpretation of the Due Process Clause and instead employed the "substantial connection" test. Until this nexus issue is conclusively resolved by the U.S. Supreme Court, the difference between the California and the federal courts tests provides an interesting reason for forum shopping, does it not? How so?

(3) *Snowney v. Harrah's Entertainment, Inc.*, 35 Cal. 4th 1054, 29 Cal. Rptr. 3d 33, 112 P.3d 28 (2005). The plaintiff in *Snowney*, a California resident, filed a class action against a group of Nevada hotels for failing to provide notice of an energy surcharge imposed on hotel guests. Although these hotels conducted no business and had no bank accounts or employees in California, they did advertise heavily in California and obtained a significant percentage of their business from California residents. The advertising activities included billboards located in California, print ads in California newspapers, and ads aired on California radio and television stations. The hotels also maintained an internet web site and toll-free phone number where visitors or callers may obtain room quotes and make reservations.

The Supreme Court concluded that the superior court may properly exercise personal jurisdiction over the Nevada hotels. Based on the defendants' purposeful and successful solicitation of business from California residents, the court found they had purposefully availed themselves of the privilege of doing business in California (*Snowney*, 35 Cal. 4th at 1064–65):

> By touting the proximity of their hotels to California and providing driving directions from California to their hotels, defendants' Web site specifically targeted residents of California. Defendants also conceded that many of their patrons come from California and that some of these patrons undoubtedly made reservations using their Web site. As such, defendants have purposefully derived a benefit from their Internet activities in California, and have established a substantial connection with California through their Web site. In

doing so, defendants have "purposefully availed [themselves] of the privilege of conducting business in" California "via the Internet."

The Supreme Court also found a substantial connection between the defendants' forum activities and the plaintiff's claim sufficient for specific jurisdiction (*Snowney*, 35 Cal. 4th at 1068–69):

> [W]e find that plaintiff's claims have a substantial connection with defendants' contacts with California. Plaintiff's causes of action for unfair competition, breach of contract, unjust enrichment, and false advertising allege that defendants failed to provide notice of an energy surcharge during the reservation process and in their advertising. Thus, plaintiff's causes of action are premised on alleged omissions during defendants' consummation of transactions with California residents and in their California advertisements. Because the harm alleged by plaintiff relates directly to the content of defendants' promotional activities in California, an inherent relationship between plaintiff's claims and defendants' contacts with California exists. Given "the intensity of" defendants' activities in California, we therefore have little difficulty in finding a substantial connection between the two.

(4) General jurisdiction refers to those cases in which the plaintiff's cause of action did *not* "arise out of or relate to" the defendant's forum activities, and therefore requires "continual and systematic" forum contacts to satisfy the due process requirements for personal jurisdiction. *Vons, supra*, 14 Cal. 4th at 445–46; *Helicopteros Nacionales de Columbia, S.A. v. Hall*, 466 U.S. 408, 414, n. 9 & 416, 104 S. Ct. 1868, 80 L. Ed. 2d 404 (1984). In light of the analysis of specific jurisdiction in *Vons* and *Cassiar*, under what circumstances would a defendant be subject to personal jurisdiction in a California court under the concept of "general jurisdiction"?

[2] *General Jurisdiction*

"General jurisdiction" exists when the quantity and quality of a defendant's contacts with the forum state are sufficiently substantial that a plaintiff may litigate any dispute in the courts of the forum, even though the dispute is unrelated to those forum contacts. *See Helicopteros, supra*, 466 U.S. at 414, n. 9. Until recently, numerous courts have held that the exercise of general jurisdiction is constitutionally proper with respect to any defendant who has "continuous and systematic" business contacts, such as marketing and selling a substantial amount of its products in the forum state. *See* ROBERT C. CASAD, WILLIAM B. RICHMAN & STANLEY E. COX, JURISDICTION IN CIVIL ACTIONS § 2.05[3][a], n. 267 & n. 272 (4th ed. 2015) (citing cases). Under this concept of activities-based general jurisdiction, such a defendant could be sued in any state where it engaged in substantial business activities even though the plaintiff's cause of action was unrelated to the defendant's activities in that state.

Recently, the U.S. Supreme Court disapproved of the exercise of general (or all-purpose) jurisdiction over a corporate defendant based solely on the defendant's "substantial, continuous, and systematic course of business" in the forum state. *Daimler AG v. Bauman*, 571 U.S. ___, 134 S. Ct. 746, 760–61, 187 L. Ed. 2d 624 (2014);

Goodyear Dunlop Tires Operations, S.A. v. Brown, 564 U.S. 915, 131 S. Ct. 2846, 2856–57, 180 L. Ed. 2d 796 (2011). Instead, the Court ruled, the appropriate inquiry is whether that corporation's affiliations with the forum state render it "essentially at home" in that state. *Bauman*, 134 S. Ct. at 760–61; *Goodyear*, 131 S. Ct. at 2851 & 2853–54. For a corporation the "paradigm forum" for the exercise of general jurisdiction is where the corporation is incorporated or, if in a different state, where it has its principal place of business. *Bauman*, 134 S. Ct. at 760; *Goodyear*, 131 S. Ct. at 2851 & 2853–54. The Court also observed that a corporation may be deemed "essentially at home" in a forum other than a paradigm forum, but made it clear that only in an exceptional case would a corporation's operations in such a forum be so substantial as to render that corporation at home in that state. *Bauman*, 134 S. Ct. at 761, n. 19.

The Supreme Court's new "essentially at home" standard is designed to limit forum-shopping opportunities for plaintiffs that were previously available under the former "continuous and systematic" contacts approach to general jurisdiction. Because the Court was interpreting the Due Process Clause, the rulings in *Bauman* and *Goodyear* are binding on all state and federal courts. *E.g. Young v. Daimler AG*, 228 Cal. App. 4th 855, 175 Cal. Rptr. 3d 811 (2014) (applying *Bauman* and concluding that the defendant German corporation is not "essentially at home" in California for purposes of general jurisdiction); *Martinez v. Aero Caribbean*, 764 F.3d 1062 (9th Cir. 2014) (ruling French airplane manufacturer is not "essentially at home" in California despite defendant's extensive business activities, including sales of its airplanes, in California). For criticism of the reasoning in *Bauman* and *Goodyear* generally, and specifically of general jurisdiction in the place of incorporation, see Walter W. Heiser, *General Jurisdiction in the Place of Incorporation: An Artificial "Home" for an Artificial Person*, 53 Houston L. Rev. 631 (2016).

[B] Due Process

[1] *"Minimum Contacts"*

The "minimum contacts" analysis first developed in *International Shoe Co. v. Washington*, 326 U.S. 310, 66 S. Ct. 154, 90 L. Ed. 95 (1945), remains the central due process test for evaluating all assertions of state court personal jurisdiction over nonresident defendants. *See Daimler AG v. Bauman*, 571 U.S. ___, 134 S. Ct. 746, 754, 187 L. Ed. 2d 624 (2014) (confirming that *International Shoe* remains the "canonical opinion" in the area of personal jurisdiction); *Shaffer v. Heitner*, 433 U.S. 186, 207–12, 97 S. Ct. 2569, 53 L. Ed. 2d 683 (1977) (holding all assertions of state court personal jurisdiction must be evaluated according to the minimum contacts standards of *International Shoe* and its progeny, regardless of whether the litigation is characterized as in personam, in rem, or quasi in rem). That test is deceptively simple to state: "[D]ue process requires only that in order to subject a defendant to a judgment ... if he not be present within the territory of the forum, he have certain minimum contacts with it such that the maintenance of the suit does not offend traditional notions of fair play and substantial justice." *International Shoe Co. v. Washington, supra*, 326 U.S. at 316.

In order to exercise specific jurisdiction consistent with due process, a three-prong test must be satisfied. First, the defendant must have purposely availed itself of the forum state's benefits; second, the controversy must be related to or arise out of the defendant's contacts with the forum state; and third, the forum state exercise of personal jurisdiction must comport with fair play and substantial justice. *Vons Companies, Inc. v. Seabest Foods, Inc.*, 14 Cal. 4th 434, 446–48, 58 Cal. Rptr. 2d 899, 926 P.2d 1085 (1996).

[2] *Purposeful Availment*

The U. S. Supreme Court has described the forum contacts necessary to establish specific jurisdiction as involving variously a nonresident defendant who has "purposefully directed" his or her activities at forum residents or who has "purposefully derived benefit" from forum activities or "purposefully availed himself or herself of the privilege of conducting activities within the forum State, thus invoking the benefits and protections of its laws." *See* Burger King Corp. v. Rudzewicz, 471 U.S. 462, 471–475, 105 S. Ct. 2174, 85 L. Ed. 2d 528 (1985); *Vons, supra*, 14 Cal. 4th at 446. A particularly problematic application of the purposeful availment requirement occurs in what often is referred to as a "stream-of-commerce" case.

For example, in *Bridgestone Corp. v. Superior Court*, 99 Cal. App. 4th 767, 121 Cal. Rptr. 2d 673 (2002), the plaintiff truck driver sued his employer and Firestone, a Tennessee company that distributed Bridgestone tires in California, seeking damages for personal injuries sustained when one of the tires failed. The defendant employer then filed a cross-complaint for equitable indemnity against the Bridgestone Corporation, the manufacturer of the allegedly defective tire. Cross-defendant Bridgestone is a Japanese company that manufactures and sells its tires in only in Japan, for resale by various distributers. Bridgestone moved to quash, and arguing that merely placing goods in the stream of commerce with knowledge that they may be purchased in California does not constitute sufficient contacts to support personal jurisdiction.

The *Bridgestone* court rejected this argument, and concluded that a manufacturer's placement of goods in the stream of commerce with the expectation that they will be purchased from a distributor by consumers in California constitutes purposeful availment if the income earned by the manufacturer from the sale of its product in California is substantial. In so holding, the court declined to follow contrary dicta regarding purposeful availment in *Asahi Metal Industry Co. v. Superior Court*, 480 U.S. 102, 108–113 (1987) (O'Connor, J., plurality opinion with respect to minimum contacts). The court also found the exercise of personal jurisdiction would be fair and reasonable because, unlike *Asahi*, the cross-plaintiffs are California residents whose common interest in convenient and effective relief is best served in a California forum, and California has an interest in providing a convenient forum for its residents to redress injuries caused by out-of-state parties.

More recent decisions suggest that the *Bridgestone* court may have reach the wrong conclusion. In *Bombardier Recreational Products, Inc. v. Dow Chemical Canada ULC*, 216 Cal. App. 4th 591, 157 Cal. Rptr. 3d 66 (2013), the plaintiffs brought a products liability action against Bombardier, the manufacturer of a personal watercraft that seriously injured the plaintiff when it caught fire allegedly due to a defective fuel tank. Defendant Bombardier filed a cross-complaint for indemnity against Dow Chemical Canada, a Canadian company that manufactured the fuel tanks Bombardier installed in its watercrafts and sold them to Bombardier in Canada. Dow Chemical filed a motion to quash for lack of personal jurisdiction, which the trial court granted.

On appeal, Bombardier argued that personal jurisdiction was proper because Dow Chemical had known Bombardier would incorporate its fuel tanks in personal watercrafts it intended to sell throughout the United States, including California. After analysis of the split decision in *Asahi* and of the plurality and concurring opinions in the more recent U.S. Supreme Court decision of *J. McIntyre Machinery, Ltd. v. Nicastro*, 564 U.S. 873, 131 S. Ct. 2780, 180 L. Ed. 2d 765 (2011), the Court of Appeal concluded Dow Chemical lacks the minimum contacts with California necessary for personal jurisdiction. *Bombardier, supra*, 216 Cal. App. 4th at 596–604. The court construed the opinions in *J. McIntyre* as indicating that a majority of the Supreme Court now agrees that merely entering a product into the stream of commerce with knowledge that it might enter the forum state, without something more, is insufficient to satisfy the purposeful availment requirement. *Id.* at 598–604. In *Dow Chemical Canada ULC v. Superior Court*, 202 Cal. App. 4th 170, 134 Cal. Rptr. 3d 597 (2011), another court engaged in a similar analysis and reached the same conclusion on nearly identical facts.

[3] "Reasonableness" Factors

However, the U.S. Supreme Court has also developed some subsidiary considerations relevant to the exercise of specific jurisdiction. In rare but appropriate cases, a state court should not assert personal jurisdiction over a nonresident defendant, even one who has purposely established minimum contacts in the forum state, where the exercise of jurisdiction would not be "fair and reasonable." *Asahi Metal Industry Co. v. Superior Court*, 480 U.S. 102, 113, 107 S. Ct. 1026, 94 L. Ed. 2d 92 (1987); *but see Daimler AG v. Bauman*, 571 U.S. ___, 134 S. Ct. 746, 187 L. Ed. 2d 624 (2014) (ruling that a "reasonableness" inquiry is not relevant in general, as opposed to specific, jurisdiction cases). This so-called "reasonableness" consideration includes evaluation of several factors, such as the burden on the defendant, the interests of the forum state, and the plaintiff's interest in obtaining relief, the interstate judicial system's interest in obtaining the most efficient resolution of controversies, and the shared interest of the several states in furthering fundamental substantive social policies. *Asahi, supra*, 480 U.S. at 113; *Burger King Corp. v. Rudzewicz*, 471 U.S. 462, 475, 105 S. Ct. 2174, 85 L. Ed. 2d 528 (1985); *World-Wide Volkswagen v. Woodson*, 444 U.S. 286, 292, 100 S. Ct. 559, 62 L. Ed. 2d 490 (1980); *see Epic Communications, Inc. v. Richwave Tech., Inc.*, 179 Cal. App. 4th 314, 317–18, 336–37, 101 Cal. Rptr. 3d 572 (2009) (ruling a refusal to exercise personal jurisdiction cannot be justified by the mere fact that a claim arising from California contacts is brought by a nonresident; while the plaintiff's foreign status might reduce the state's interest in adjudicating the dispute, that is at most a subsidiary consideration which cannot by itself justify a denial of access to the California courts).

[4] The "Effects" Test

The United States Supreme Court has recognized a variant of the minimum contacts analysis for determining purposeful availment, referred to as the "effects" test. *Calder v. Jones*, 465 U.S. 783, 104 S, Ct. 1482, 79 L. Ed. 2d 804 (1984). In *Calder*, a reporter in Florida wrote an article for the National Enquirer about Shirley Jones, a well-known actress who lived and worked in California. The president and editor of the National Enquirer reviewed and approved the article, and the National Enquirer published the article. Jones sued, among others, the reporter and the editor for libel in California. The individual defendants moved to quash service of process, contending they lacked minimum contacts with California.

The U. S. Supreme Court disagreed and held that California could exercise jurisdiction over the individual defendants "based on the 'effects' of their Florida conduct in California." *Calder, supra,* 465 U.S. at 789. The court found jurisdiction proper because "California [was] the focal point both of the story and of the harm suffered." *Ibid.* "The allegedly libelous story concerned the California activities of a California resident. It impugned the professionalism of an entertainer whose television career was centered in California ... and the brunt of the harm, in terms both of [Jones's] emotional distress and the injury to her professional reputation, was suffered in California." *Id.* at 788–89. The court also noted that the individual defendants wrote or edited "an article that they knew would have a potentially devastating impact upon [Jones]. And they knew that the brunt of that injury would be felt by [Jones] in the State in which she lives and works and in which the National Enquirer has its largest circulation." *Id.* at 789–90. Subsequently, in *Walden v. Fiore*, 571 U.S. ___, 134 S. Ct. 12, 188 L. Ed. 2d 12 (2014), the U.S. Supreme Court explained that the proper question under *Calder* "is not where the plaintiff experienced a particular injury or effect, but whether the defendant's conduct connects him to the forum in a meaningful way." *Walden, supra,* 134 S. Ct. at 1125. "The crux of *Calder*," the Supreme Court further explained, "was that the reputation-based 'effects' of the alleged libel connected the defendants to California, not just to the plaintiff." *Walden,* at 1123–24.

In *Pavlovich v. Superior Court*, 29 Cal. 4th 262, 127 Cal. Rptr. 2d 329, 58 P.3d 2 (2002), the California Supreme Court applied the *Calder* "effects" test in the context of the posting of information on an internet web site. The defendant website operator, a resident of Texas, posted the source code of a computer program designed to defeat the copy protection system employed to encrypt and protect copyrighted motion pictures contained on digital versatile discs (DVD's). The plaintiff, a California trade association created by the DVD industry to control and administer licensing of encryption technology, filed an action in a California court for misappropriation of trade secrets.

In a 4–3 decision, the Supreme Court held that the trial court's exercise of personal jurisdiction was inconsistent with due process. The court ruled that the "effects" test requires intentional conduct expressly aimed at or targeting the forum state in addition to the defendant's knowledge that his intentional conduct would cause harm in the forum. *Pavlovich, supra*, 29 Cal. 4th at 270–71. But the majority concluded that the defendant's knowledge that his tortious conduct may harm certain industries centered in California — *i.e.*, the motion picture, computer, and consumer electronics industries — was insufficient to establish express aiming at California and, by itself, cannot establish purposeful availment under the effects test. *Id.* at 273–78.

The dissent agreed that the mere operation of an internet website cannot expose the operator to suit in any jurisdiction where the site's contents might be read, or where resulting injury might occur. However, the dissent viewed the defendant's internet website posting as "expressly aimed" at California because his illegal conduct intentionally targeted the movie and the computer industries, which he knew were centered in California: "[D]efendants who aim conduct at particular jurisdictions, expecting and intending that injurious effects will be felt in those specific places, cannot shield themselves from suit there simply by using the Internet, or some other generalized medium of communication, as the means of inflicting the harm." *Pavlovich, supra*, 29 Cal. 4th at 289 (Baxter, dissenting). Do you agree with the majority or the dissent in *Pavlovich*? Why? Which view is more faithful to *Calder*'s application of the "effects" test?

In *Burdick v. Superior Court*, 233 Cal. App. 4th 8, 183 Cal. Rptr. 3d 1 (2015), the court addressed whether in a lawsuit for defamation, a nonresident defendant is subject to personal jurisdiction in California on the ground that, while in his state of residence (Illinois), the defendant posted allegedly defamatory statements about the plaintiffs on the defendant's publically available Facebook page. After reviewing *Calder, Walden,* and *Pavlovich,* the court held the merely posting on the Internet defamatory comments about the plaintiffs and knowing the plaintiffs are located in the forum state are insufficient to create minimum contacts necessary to support specific personal jurisdiction in a lawsuit arising out of that posting. *Burdick, supra*, 233 Cal. App. 4th at 22–26. The court explained that "[t]hose cases require, in addition to intentional conduct causing harm to a forum resident, evidence that the nonresident defendant expressly aimed or intentionally targeted his intentional conduct at the forum state." *Id.* at 25. The *Burdick* court then concluded that the plaintiffs should be given an opportunity to request discovery limited to the issue of personal jurisdiction based on the "effects" test. *Id.* at 230–31. What facts should the plaintiffs' seek through discovery that would be relevant to the *Burdick* court jurisdictional analysis?

[5] Transient Jurisdiction

Another constitutional basis for personal jurisdiction is transient jurisdiction. *Burnham v. Superior Court*, 495 U.S. 604, 110 S. Ct. 2105, 109 L. Ed. 2d 631 (1990). Transient jurisdiction depends solely on service of the complaint and summons on the nonresident defendant while present in the forum state, regardless of whether the defendant otherwise has any minimum contacts with the forum state. *Id.*; Barbara

Surtees Goto, Comment, *International Shoe Gets the Boot: Burnham v. Superior Court Resurrects the Physical Power Theory*, 24 Loy. L.A. L. Rev. 851 (1991). The California courts endorse transient jurisdiction. *See, e.g., Silverman v. Superior Court*, 203 Cal. App. 3d 145, 150, 249 Cal. Rptr. 724 (1988) (holding personal jurisdiction proper where nonresident defendant served with process while present in California at mandatory settlement conference in a different action; California no longer recognizes immunity from service for nonresident witnesses or parties).

[6] *Nonresident Parent Corporations*

Under what circumstances is a nonresident parent corporation subject to personal jurisdiction in California based solely on the contacts of its California subsidiary? The general rule is that a parent company's ownership or control of a subsidiary corporation does not, without more, subject the parent corporation to the jurisdiction of the state where the subsidiary does business. *See, e.g., DVI, Inc. v. Superior Court*, 104 Cal. App. 4th 1080, 1092, 128 Cal. Rptr. 2d 683 (2002); *Sonora Diamond Corp. v. Superior Court*, 83 Cal. App. 4th 523, 540, 99 Cal. Rptr. 2d 824 (2000). For example, in *Sammons Enterprises, Inc. v. Superior Court*, 205 Cal. App. 3d 1427, 253 Cal. Rptr. 261 (1988), the court held that a foreign corporation is not subject to personal jurisdiction based solely on the independent activities of its wholly owned local subsidiary even where the parent exercises general executive responsibility for the operations of the subsidiary and reviews its major policy decisions.

[a] The Alter Ego and Agency Theories

However, the California courts have recognized two principles under which the contacts of the subsidiary doing business in California are attributed to the parent corporation: the alter ego doctrine and the agency theory. *See, e.g., Sonora Diamond Corp., supra*, 83 Cal. App. 4th at 537–42; *BBA Aviation PLC v. Superior Court*, 190 Cal. App. 4th 421, 429–33,117 Cal. Rptr. 3d 914 (2010); *Rollins Burdick Hunter of S. Cal., Inc. v. Alexander & Alexander Serv., Inc.*, 206 Cal. App. 3d 1, 9–11, 253 Cal. Rptr. 338 (1988). In *VirtualMagic Asia, Inc. v. Fil-Cartoons, Inc.*, 99 Cal. App. 4th 228, 121 Cal. Rptr. 2d 1 (2002), the court explained the fact-specific nature of the inquiry into whether personal jurisdiction may be asserted over a parent corporation under principles of alter ego or agency (*VirtualMagic*, 99 Cal. App. 4th at 244–45):

> The courts have recognized that if a state may exercise jurisdiction over a subsidiary corporation, it may also have jurisdiction over the parent corporation if the elements of the alter ego or principal/agent theories are present. (*Sonora Diamond Corp. v. Superior Court* [(2000)] 83 Cal. App. 4th [523] at pp. 536–537.) * * *

> The assertion of jurisdiction under either theory requires a fact-specific examination of numerous elements. The two principal questions to establish alter ego are whether there is "such a unity of interest and ownership between the corporation and its equitable owner that the separate personalities of the

corporation and the shareholder do not in reality exist" and whether there would be "an inequitable result if the acts in question are treated as those of the corporation alone." (*Sonora Diamond Corp., supra,* 83 Cal. App. 4th at p. 538.) The courts consider numerous factors, including inadequate capitalization, commingling of funds and other assets of the two entities, the holding out by one entity that it is liable for the debts of the other, identical equitable ownership in the two entities, use of the same offices and employees, use of one as a mere conduit for the affairs of the other, disregard of corporate formalities, lack of segregation of corporate records, and identical directors and officers. (*See Tomaselli v. Transamerica Ins. Co.* (1994) 25 Cal. App. 4th 1269, 1285, [31 Cal. Rptr. 2d 433].) No single factor is determinative, and instead a court must examine all the circumstances to determine whether to apply the doctrine. Moreover, even if the unity of interest and ownership element is shown, alter ego will not be applied absent evidence that an injustice would result from the recognition of separate corporate identities, and "[d]ifficulty in enforcing a judgment or collecting a debt does not satisfy this standard." (*Sonora Diamond Corp., supra,* 83 Cal. App. 4th at p. 539.)

Similarly, the principal/agent theory is a fact-driven inquiry that requires examination of whether the parent exercises a sufficient degree of control over its subsidiary to establish that the subsidiary can be described as a means through which the parent acts, or is nothing more than an incorporated department of the parent. Under those circumstances the subsidiary will be deemed to be the agent of the parent in the forum state and jurisdiction will extend to the parent. (*Sonora Diamond Corp., supra,* 83 Cal. App. 4th at p. 541.) It is the nature of the control exercised by the parent over the subsidiary that is crucial, because some degree of control is an ordinary and necessary incident of the parent's ownership of the subsidiary. Only when the degree of control exceeds this level and reflects the parent's purposeful disregard of the subsidiary's independent corporate existence that the principal/agent theory will be invoked. "As a practical matter, the parent must be shown to have moved beyond the establishment of general policy and direction for the subsidiary and in effect taken over performance of the subsidiary's *day-to-day* operations in carrying out that policy." (*Id.* at pp. 541–542, original italics.)

Some courts have questioned whether principles of "alter ego" and "agency," as applied in *VirtualMagic, supra,* can justify the exercise of specific personal jurisdiction over a nonresident parent company. For example, the court in *HealthMarkets, Inc. v. Superior Court,* 171 Cal. App. 4th 1160, 90 Cal. Rptr. 3d 527 (2009), reasoned that reliance on state substantive law of agency and alter ego to determine the constitutional limits of specific personal jurisdiction is unnecessary and is an imprecise substitute for the appropriate jurisdictional questions. The court concluded that the proper due process inquiry is as follows:

A parent company purposely avails itself of forum benefits through the activities of its subsidiary, as required to justify the exercise of specific personal

> jurisdiction, if and only if the parent deliberately directs the subsidiary's ac-
> tivities in, or having a substantial connection with, the forum state.

HealthMarkets, supra, 171 Cal. App. 4th at 1169. How does this purposeful availment inquiry differ from the alter ego and agency tests applied in *VirtualMagic*? Which approach do you think is the appropriate one? Why?

Regardless of whether the general agency theory or the more limited representative services doctrine discussed below are appropriate for personal jurisdiction analysis, they are likely irrelevant to the exercise of general or all-purpose jurisdiction. Even assuming the California contacts of a subsidiary may be attributed to a nonresident parent company, those contacts will not make the parent company "essentially at home" in California. *See Daimler AG v. Bauman,* 571 U.S. ___, 134 S. Ct. 746, 758–62, 187 L. Ed. 2d 624 (2014) (ruling that even assuming the contacts of a California subsidiary company are attributable to the defendant parent corporation, a German corporation whose principal place of business in Germany, the defendant parent is not "essentially at home" in California as required for general jurisdiction); *Young v. Daimler AG,* 228 Cal. App. 4th 855, 866–67, 175 Cal. Rptr. 3d 811 (2014) (applying *Bauman* and concluding that the representative services doctrine, a variation of the general agency theory, is irrelevant for purposes of determining whether the defendant German corporation is "essentially at home" in California for purposes of general jurisdiction).

[b] Representative Services Doctrine

The California courts also recognize the representative services doctrine, a variation of the general agency theory discussed above. *See, e.g., BBA Aviation PLC v. Superior Court,* 190 Cal. App. 4th 421, 429–33, 117 Cal. Rptr. 3d 914 (2010) (finding representative services doctrine inapplicable where foreign parent corporation is a holding company and the requisite high level of control over the subsidiary not shown); *In re Automobile Antitrust Cases I & II,* 135 Cal. App. 4th 100, 37 Cal. Rptr. 3d 258 (2005) (holding foreign parent company defendants not subject to personal jurisdiction under representative services doctrine because no evidence that defendants controlled the day-to-day activities of their local subsidiaries); *Dorel Indus., Inc. v. Superior Court,* 134 Cal. App. 4th 1267, 1269–80, 36 Cal. Rptr. 3d 742 (2005) (concluding personal jurisdiction proper with respect to defendant foreign grandparent corporation based on agency theory of representative services doctrine where defendant used local subsidiary to engage in business the defendant would otherwise have done itself). Unlike the general agency theory, the narrow representative services doctrine does not depend on whether the parent company enjoys pervasive and continuous control over the subsidiary. Instead, personal jurisdiction may be exercised over a foreign parent corporation when the local agent-subsidiary exists only to further the business of the parent, and but for the local agent's existence, the parent would be performing those functions in the forum itself. *BBA Aviation, supra,* 190 Cal. App. 4th at 430; *Automobile Antitrust Cases, supra,* 135 Cal. App. 4th at 119–121.

[7] Recent Lower Court Decisions

The California courts of appeal have decided several other interesting personal jurisdiction issues during the last few of years. *E.g.,Greenwell v. Auto-Owners Ins. Co.*, 233 Cal. App. 4th 783, 182 Cal. Rptr. 3d 873 (2015) (concluding that although defendant insurer policy covering risks in California and Arkansas satisfied the purposeful availment prong of specific jurisdiction, there was no substantial connection between the defendant's California contacts and a claim that arose out of the Arkansas risk); *Luberski, Inc. v. Oleificio F.LLI Amato S.R.L*, 171 Cal. App. 4th 409, 89 Cal. Rptr. 3d 774 (2009) (holding California court had specific jurisdiction over Italian seller because the subject of the dispute was the alleged nondelivery of $406,000 worth of olive oil to the purchaser in California); *Goldman v. Simpson,* 160 Cal. App. 4th 255, 72 Cal. Rptr. 3d 729 (2008) (ruling that once established, a court's personal jurisdiction over a defendant judgment debtor continues through subsequent proceedings in the action to enforce or renew the judgment); *Shisler v. Sanfer Sports Cars, Inc.*, 146 Cal. App. 4th 1254, 53 Cal. Rptr. 3d 335 (2006) (concluding a Florida automobile seller's maintenance of a website not sufficient to establish personal jurisdiction because it did not target California residents and there was no ongoing business relationship between the parties, despite fact that the plaintiff California buyer purchased an allegedly defective vehicle advertised on the defendant seller's web site); *Archdiocese of Milwaukee v. Superior Court*, 112 Cal. App. 4th 423, 5 Cal. Rptr. 3d 154 (2003) (upholding personal jurisdiction over Wisconsin archdiocese in an action alleging sexual molestation by a catholic priest under the "effects test" because the defendant archdiocese knew the priest was a convicted pedophile and purposely reassigned him to California).

[C] Raising the Personal Jurisdiction Defense

The Legislature amended Code of Civil Procedure § 418.10, effective January 1, 2003, for the express purpose of conforming California practice with respect to challenging personal jurisdiction to the practice under Rule 12 of the Federal Rules of Civil Procedure, by adding new § 418.10(e), reproduced below:

California Code of Civil Procedure (2016)

Section 418.10. Motion to Quash Service of Summons or to Stay or Dismiss Action; Procedure

(a) A defendant, on or before the last day of his or her time to plead or within any further time that the court may for good cause allow, may serve and file a notice of motion for one or more of the following purposes:

(1) To quash service of summons on the ground of lack of jurisdiction of the court over him or her.

(2) To stay or dismiss the action on the ground of inconvenient forum.

(3) To dismiss the action pursuant to the applicable provisions of Chapter 1.5 (commencing with Section 583.110) of Title 8 [Dismissal based on lack of diligence in service or prosecution].

(b) The notice shall designate, as the time for making the motion, a date not more than 30 days after filing of the notice. The notice shall be served in the same manner, and at the same times, prescribed by subdivision (b) of Section 1005. The service and filing of the notice shall extend the defendant's time to plead until 15 days after service upon him or her of a written notice of entry of an order denying his or her motion, except that for good cause shown the court may extend the defendant's time to plead for an additional period not exceeding 20 days.

(c) If the motion is denied by the trial court, the defendant, within 10 days after service upon him or her of a written notice of an entry of an order of the court denying his or her motion, or within any further time not exceeding 20 days that the trial court may for good cause allow, and before pleading, may petition an appropriate reviewing court for a writ of mandate to require the trial court to enter its order quashing the service of summons or staying or dismissing the action. The defendant shall file or enter his or her responsive pleading in the trial court within the time prescribed by subdivision (b) unless, on or before the last day of the defendant's time to plead, he or she serves upon the adverse party and files with the trial court a notice that he or she has petitioned for a writ of mandate. The service and filing of the notice shall extend the defendant's time to plead until 10 days after service upon him or her of a written notice of the final judgment in the mandate proceeding. The time to plead may for good cause shown be extended by the trial court for an additional period not exceeding 20 days.

(d) No default may be entered against the defendant before expiration of his or her time to plead, and no motion under this section, or under Section 473 or 473.5 when joined with a motion under this section, or application to the court or stipulation of the parties for an extension of the time to plead, shall be deemed a general appearance by the defendant.

(e) A defendant or cross-defendant may make a motion under this section and simultaneously answer, demur, or move to strike the complaint or cross-complaint.

(1) Notwithstanding Section 1014, no act by a party who makes a motion under this section, including filing an answer, demurrer, or motion to strike constitutes an appearance, unless the court denies the motion made under this section. If the court denies the motion made under this section, the defendant or cross-defendant is not deemed to have generally appeared until entry of the order denying the motion.

(2) If the motion made under this section is denied and the defendant or cross-defendant petitions for a writ of mandate pursuant to subdivision (c), the defendant or cross-defendant is not deemed to have generally appeared until the proceedings on the writ petition have finally concluded.

(3) Failure to make a motion under this section at the time of filing a demurrer or motion to strike constitutes a waiver of the issues of lack of personal jurisdiction, inadequacy of process, inadequacy of service of process, inconvenient forum, and delay in prosecution.

Section 418.11. Appearance for Ex Parte Relief or Provisional Remedy; Not General Appearance Nor Waiver of Motion Rights

An appearance at a hearing at which ex parte relief is sought, or an appearance at a hearing for which an ex parte application for a provisional remedy is made, is not a general appearance and does not constitute a waiver of the right to make a motion under Section 418.10.

Section 1014. Appearance Defined, Right to Notices Before and After Appearance

A defendant appears in an action when the defendant answers, demurs, files a notice of motion to strike, files a notice of motion to transfer pursuant to Section 396b, moves for reclassification pursuant to section 403.040, gives the plaintiff written notice of his appearance, or when an attorney gives notice of appearance for him. After appearance, a defendant or the defendant's attorney is entitled to notice of all subsequent proceedings of which notice is required to be given. Where a defendant has not appeared, service of notice or papers need not be made upon the defendant.

[1] Waivable Due Process Right

The due process personal jurisdiction requirement recognizes and protects an individual liberty interest. *Insurance Corp. of Ireland, Ltd. v. Compagnie des Bauxites de Guinea*, 456 U.S. 694, 702, 102 S. Ct. 2099, 72 L. Ed. 2d 492 (1982). Because the requirement of personal jurisdiction represents an individual right it can, like other such rights, be waived. *Id.* at 702. Such waiver may be express or implied, and traditionally occurs when a defendant does not raise this due process right in the proper procedural manner. *Id.* at 702–704.

[a] General Appearance

A defendant must raise an objection to personal jurisdiction in the manner prescribed by CCP § 418.10. Pursuant to the 2003 amendment to § 418.10, the defendant need not raise the objection by a special appearance, but may simultaneously answer, demur, or move to strike, so long as the objection is raised in defendant's first appearance. CCP § 418.10 (e) (effective Jan. 1, 2003); *see Air Machine Com SRL v. Superior Court*, 186 Cal. App. 4th 414, 112 Cal. Rptr. 3d 484 (2010) (construing § 418.10 and finding no waiver of personal jurisdiction objection where defendants filed motion to quash before they served plaintiff with an offer of judgment). If the defendant makes a general appearance, as defined in CCP § 1014, *before* filing a motion to quash objecting to personal jurisdiction, the defendant waives his right to contest the personal jurisdiction of the court. *See* CCP § 418.10(e)(3); *City of Riverside v. Horspool*, 223 Cal. App. 4th 670, 679–80, 167 Cal. Rptr. 3d 440 (2014) (ruling defendant entered a general appearance and waived any objection to personal jurisdiction or service of process by requesting a continuance to answer the complaint).

A defendant's appearance at certain *ex parte* proceedings, such as an application for a temporary restraining order or other provisional relief, does not constitute a general appearance. CCP § 418.11. However, any additional litigation conduct, such as discovery in connection with an order to show cause for a preliminary injunction, may be outside the protection of section 418.11. *Factor Health Mgmt. v. Superior Court*, 132 Cal. App. 4th 246, 33 Cal. Rptr. 3d 599 (2005). For a very thorough review of the California cases determining what activity constitutes a general appearance within the meaning of CCP § 410.50(a) even though the defendant has filed a timely motion to quash for lack of personal jurisdiction, see *Dial 800 v. Fesbinder*, 118 Cal. App. 4th 32, 50–55, 12 Cal. Rptr. 3d 711 (2004) (ruling that if a defendant seeks any affirmative relief on the merits, such as a request for an award of contractual attorney fees, the application may be deemed a general appearance).

When a defendant moves to quash service of process on jurisdictional grounds, the plaintiff has the initial burden of demonstrating facts justifying the exercise of jurisdiction. *See, e.g., Vons Companies, Inc. v. Seabest Foods, Inc.*, 14 Cal. 4th 434, 449, 58 Cal. Rptr. 2d 899, 926 P.2d 1085 (1996); *Floveyor Intl., Ltd. v. Superior Court*, 59 Cal. App. 4th 789, 69 Cal. Rptr. 2d 457 (1997) (upholding a motion to quash because the plaintiff failed to produce any evidence that the defendant had any contacts with California). Once the facts showing "minimum contacts" with the forum state have been established, however, the burden to demonstrate that the exercise of jurisdiction would be "unreasonable" shifts to the defendant. *Vons, supra*, 14 Cal. 4th at 449.

[b] Federal Procedure Compared

Under the Federal Rules of Civil Procedure, a defendant must raise an objection to personal jurisdiction in his first appearance, although he has the option of pleading it as a defense in the answer or raising it by a motion to dismiss. Rule 12(b)(2), F.R.C.P. The objection is not waived by joining it with other objections or defenses in a responsive pleading or motion. Rule 12(b)(2), (g) & (h), F.R.C.P. The defense is only waived if omitted from the first appearance, whether an answer or motions.

To what extent does the California procedure for challenging personal jurisdiction under amended CCP § 418.10 conform to federal practice? The court considered this question in *Roy v. Superior Court*, 127 Cal. App. 4th 337, 25 Cal. Rptr. 3d 488 (2005), and concluded critical differences still exist. Under federal Rule 12(b), a defendant must raise an objection to personal jurisdiction in his first appearance, although he has the option of pleading it as a defense in the answer or raising it by a motion to dismiss. A defendant may raise the objection along with any other defense without being deemed to have waived the jurisdictional objection. Rule 12(b)(2), (g) & (h), F.R.C.P. If properly plead as a defense, the objection is preserved and the defendant may challenge personal jurisdiction through the time of trial. Rule 12(b)(2), (g) & (h), F.R.C.P.; *see Roy, supra* 127 Cal. App. 4th at 343–45 (discussing the federal practice under federal Rule 12).

However, unlike federal Rule 12(b), CCP § 418.10 does not give a defendant the option to plead lack of jurisdiction as a defense and reserve determination of that issue until as late as trial. *Roy, supra*, 127 Cal. App. 4th at 345. Section 418.10 "continues to prescribe the motion to quash as the means of challenging personal jurisdiction." *Roy*, 127 Cal. App. 4th at 345. The defendant may move to quash and simultaneously file an answer containing defenses to the action, but "the latter is not a substitute for the former." *Id.* The *Roy* court held that the defendants in that case waived their objection by filing an answer that raised the personal jurisdiction defense in their first appearance and then participating in the litigation, but not filing a timely motion to quash. The court also expressed its preference for the California practice over the federal practice, noting CCP § 418.10 requires that the jurisdictional issue be raised and finally resolved at an early stage. *Id.* at 343–44. Do you agree that the California practice is preferable?

[c] Forum Selection Clauses

Can a defendant waive objections to personal jurisdiction in a particular forum in advance through a contractual consent-to-jurisdiction or forum selection clause? If an action is commenced in the contractually designated forum, can the court assert personal jurisdiction based on the clause even though the defendant lacks minimum contacts with the forum state? *See* Walter W. Heiser, *Forum Selection Clauses in State Court: Limitations on Enforcement After Stewart and Carnival Cruise*, 45 Fla. L. Rev. 361 (1993).

The California courts generally will enforce a reasonable forum selection clause. *E.g.*, *Smith, Valentino & Smith, Inc. v. Superior Court*, 17 Cal. 3d 491, 131 Cal. Rptr. 374, 551 P.2d 1206 (1976); *Cal-State Bus. Products & Serv., Inc. v. Ricoh*, 12 Cal. App. 4th 1666, 16 Cal. Rptr. 2d 417 (1993). However, the Legislature has placed some limits on forum clause enforcement in certain areas. *E.g.*, CCP § 410.42 (construction subcontracts); Commercial Code § 10106(b) (consumer leases).

What constitutes a "reasonable" forum selection clause? Is such a clause enforceable when it is a non-negotiated provision in a standard form consumer contract? When it requires a consumer to litigate a cause of action against a company in a faraway state? *See Cal-State Bus. Products and Serv., Inc., v. Ricoh*, 12 Cal. App. 4th 1666, 16 Cal. Rptr. 2d 417 (1993), reproduced and discussed *infra* in § 6.05[B]; *see also Carnival Cruise Line, Inc. v. Shute*, 499 U.S. 585, 111 S. Ct. 1522, 113 L. Ed. 2d 622 (1991).

[2] *Appellate Review*

The order of a federal district court denying a motion to dismiss for lack of personal jurisdiction is not an appealable "final decision" within the meaning of 28 U.S.C. § 1291, see *Catlin v. United States*, 324 U.S. 229, 236, 65 S. Ct. 631, 89 L. Ed. 911 (1945), although in rare cases the district court may certify the order for interlocutory appeal pursuant to 28 U.S.C. § 1292(b). *E.g.*, *Klinghoffer v. S.N.C. Achille Lauro*, 921 F.2d 21 (2d Cir. 1990). Generally a federal defendant must wait until the district court enters a final judgment on the merits to seek appellate review of the denial of a properly raised personal jurisdiction defense. *See, e.g.*, *Burger King Corp. v. Rudezewics*, 471 U.S. 462, 85 L. Ed. 2d 528, 105 S. Ct. 2174 (1985).

[a] Writ of Mandate

In contrast to the federal rules, CCP § 418.10(c) authorizes interlocutory appellate review of a trial court order denying a motion to quash, by immediate writ of mandate. Failure to timely seek such interlocutory review precludes appeal later by defendant after a decision on the merits. *See Danzig v. Jack Grynberg & Assoc.*, 161 Cal. App. 3d 1128, 1141, 208 Cal. Rptr. 336 (1984), *cert. denied*, 474 U.S. 819 (1985). An order granting a motion to quash is an appealable order. CCP § 904.1(a)(3).

[b] Federal Review Compared

How do the California rules with respect to appellate review differ from the federal rules? Which rules better promote judicial economy? Fairness? Why? *See Roy v. Superior Court*, 127 Cal. App. 4th 337, 343–44, 25 Cal. Rptr. 3d 488 (2005) (expressing preference for the California practice over the federal practice). What would be the effect in either court if a nonresident defendant specially appeared to contest personal jurisdiction and lost on this issue, but then defaulted and never further contested the action? *See Baldwin v. Iowa State Traveling Men's Assn.*, 283 U.S. 522, 51 S. Ct. 517, 75 L. Ed. 1244 (1931). Would such a defendant be in any better position to later contest personal jurisdiction by entering no appearance and permitting a default judgment? *See Baldwin, supra*, 283 U.S. at 525–26; *Marriage of Merideth*, 129 Cal. App. 3d 356, 180 Cal. Rptr. 909 (1982).

§ 6.03 Venue

[A] Statutory Venue

Brown v. Superior Court

Supreme Court of California
37 Cal. 3d 477, 208 Cal. Rptr. 724, 691 P.2d 272 (1984)

BIRD, CHIEF JUSTICE.

Do the special venue provisions of the California Fair Employment and Housing Act (FEHA) (Gov. Code, § 12965, subd. (b)) control over the general venue provisions of Code of Civil Procedure section 395, subdivision (a) where both FEHA and non-FEHA causes of action are alleged?

I.

Petitioners, Andrew Brown, Charles Jones and Sam George, were employed by real parties in interest, C.C. Myers, Inc., other corporate entities and several individuals (hereafter defendants), on a highway construction project in Alameda County. Defendants allegedly discriminated against and ultimately discharged Brown and Jones because they are black. George, who is white and was a foreman on the project, was discharged because he refused to participate in defendants' alleged discriminatory practices.

On June 22, 1981, petitioners filed a complaint against defendants in the Alameda County Superior Court, alleging (1) intentional infliction of emotional distress, (2) wrongful discharge, and (3) a violation of petitioners' federal civil rights (42 U.S.C. § 1981). Each of the three claims was based on the same factual allegations regarding liability and damages. Petitioners also filed complaints alleging employment discrimination with the California Department of Fair Employment and Housing (Department).

Sometime after petitioners filed their complaint in the superior court, the Department notified them of their right to bring a civil action under the FEHA. (Gov. Code, § 12900 et seq.)[1]

In June 1982, petitioners amended their complaint to add an FEHA cause of action and to delete the federal civil rights claim. The FEHA cause of action incorporated the same factual allegations regarding liability and damages as the emotional distress and wrongful discharge claims.[2]

Prior to filing an answer, defendants moved for a change of venue to Sacramento County on the grounds that three individual defendants resided there, the corporate defendants' principal places of business were located there, and none of the defendants resided in Alameda County. Respondent court granted the motion and ordered the case transferred to Sacramento County. No reasons were stated in support of this ruling.

Petitioners seek a writ of mandate to compel respondent court to vacate its order changing venue to Sacramento County. (Code Civ. Proc., § 400.)

II.

Venue is determined based on the complaint on file at the time the motion to change venue is made. In this case, the complaint alleged three causes of action: (1) intentional infliction of emotional distress, (2) wrongful discharge, and (3) FEHA violations.

It is undisputed that if petitioners had alleged only FEHA violations, the FEHA venue statute would govern. In that instance, venue would be in Alameda County—

---

1. All statutory references are to the Government Code unless otherwise noted.

2. The intentional infliction of emotional distress claim asserted that petitioners were entitled to compensatory damages for emotional distress, loss of earnings and punitive damages. Petitioners alleged, inter alia, that each of the defendants engaged in and/or ratified "the use of racial slurs in reference to Black people, [the] telling of jokes which degraded Black people, the discriminatory assignment of work to Black employees, the discriminatory hiring, firing and laying off of Blacks, and the provision of discriminatory terms and conditions of employment to Black persons."

The wrongful discharge cause of action incorporated all of the liability and damages allegations of the emotional distress cause of action, and additionally alleged that defendants had wrongfully discharged each petitioner.

The FEHA cause of action similarly incorporated all of the liability and damages allegations of the emotional distress cause of action and additionally alleged that (1) defendants' conduct constituted racial discrimination in employment in violation of the FEHA, (2) petitioners had satisfied the procedural conditions for the filing of an FEHA action, and (3) petitioners should be reinstated as employees.

the county in which the discriminatory practices were allegedly committed. (§ 12965, subd. (b).[3]) However, here, two non-FEHA causes of action were also alleged. These claims would normally be governed by Code of Civil Procedure section 395, subdivision (a),[4] which controls venue in "transitory" actions.[5]

This court must determine whether the special provisions of the FEHA or the general provisions of section 395 control if both FEHA and non-FEHA claims arising from the same facts are alleged in the same complaint.[6]

It is well established that a defendant is entitled to have an action tried in the county of his or her residence unless the action falls within some exception to the general venue rule. Section 395 codifies this rule and provides that the trial of the action shall be in the county of the defendant's residence, "[except] as otherwise provided by law."

Three cases have construed the "[except] as otherwise provided by law" language of section 395. In *Delgado v. Superior Court* (1977) 74 Cal. App. 3d 560 [141 Cal. Rptr. 528], the plaintiff filed an action in Sacramento County for property damage,

---

3. Section 12965, subdivision (b) provides in relevant part: "*Such an action may be brought in any county in the state in which the unlawful practice is alleged to have been committed*, in the county in which the records relevant to such practice are maintained and administered, or in the county in which the aggrieved person would have worked or would have had access to the public accommodation but for the alleged unlawful practice, but if the defendant is not found within any such county, such an action may be brought within the county of defendant's residence or principal office." (Italics added.)

4. Section 395, subdivision (a) provides in relevant part: "Except as otherwise provided by law ... the county in which the defendants or some of them reside at the commencement of the action is the proper county for the trial of the action. If the action is for injury to person or personal property ... either the county where the injury occurs ... or the county in which the defendants, or some of them reside at the commencement of the action, shall be a proper county for the trial of the action."

All further references to section 395 are to section 395, subdivision (a) of the Code of Civil Procedure.

5. For venue purposes, actions are classified as local or transitory. To determine whether an action is local or transitory, the court looks to the "main relief" sought. Where the main relief sought is personal, the action is transitory. Where the main relief relates to rights in real property, the action is local. (*See* 2 Witkin, Cal. Procedure, *supra*, Actions, § 424, at pp. 1255–1256.)

Since the main relief sought in intentional infliction of emotional distress and wrongful discharge claims is personal in nature, those actions are classified as transitory.

6. As to the corporate defendants, there is yet another relevant venue statute, Code of Civil Procedure section 395.5. That section provides in relevant part: "A corporation or association may be sued in the county where the ... liability arises...."

Petitioners argue that as to the corporate defendants, venue is proper in Alameda County because the alleged discriminatory practices occurred there.

However, it is well recognized that when a plaintiff brings an action against several defendants, both individual and corporate, in a county in which none of the defendants reside, an individual defendant has the right to change venue to the county of his or her residence. This is true even though the action was initially brought in a county where the corporate defendants may be sued under Code of Civil Procedure section 395.5. (*Carruth v. Superior Court* (1978) 80 Cal. App. 3d 215, 220–221 [145 Cal. Rptr. 344, 12 A.L.R.4th 1269]; *Mosby v. Superior Court* (1974) 43 Cal. App. 3d 219, 226 [117 Cal. Rptr. 588]; ...) Therefore, Code of Civil Procedure section 395.5 does not determine venue in this case.

personal injuries and wrongful death. The named defendants were Yolo County, a Sacramento automobile dealership and an automobile manufacturer. Yolo County moved to change venue to that county under Code of Civil Procedure section 394. That section provides that an action against a county for an injury occurring there shall be tried in that county. The superior court granted the motion.

The Court of Appeal affirmed the superior court's ruling on the ground that Code of Civil Procedure section 394 governed venue. The court reasoned that the phrase "[except] as otherwise provided by law" is a "true subordinating declaration" which permits application of section 395 only when no other venue provision applies. (*Delgado, supra,* 74 Cal. App. 3d at p. 564.) * * *

Finally, in *Tharp v. Superior Court* (1982) 32 Cal. 3d 496 [186 Cal. Rptr. 335, 651 P.2d 1141], an automobile dealership brought an action against the secretary of the New Motor Vehicles Board to dismiss certain licensing proceedings. The trial court granted the secretary's motion for change of venue to Sacramento County from Tulare County where the cause of action had arisen.

In directing the trial court to vacate its order, this court held that venue was controlled by Code of Civil Procedure section 393. Under that statute, trial had to be held in the county where the cause of action arose against the public officers for acts undertaken in their official capacity. The court concluded that that statute constituted an exception to section 395.

In each of these cases, the more specific venue provisions governed. None of these cases involved several causes of action subject to conflicting venue provisions. In each case, the prevailing venue provisions were found to be bona fide exceptions to section 395.

Here, neither party disputes that the FEHA venue statute establishes an exception to section 395. The question is whether that exception governs all the causes of action and prevails over section 395, just as the specific venue provisions did in *Delgado,* ... and *Tharp.* Thus, the issue is whether the FEHA venue statute applies to non-FEHA claims which arise from the same facts as an FEHA claim alleged in the same complaint.

In construing the FEHA venue statute, this court is guided by well-settled rules. "The fundamental rule of statutory construction is that the court should ascertain the intent of the Legislature so as to effectuate the purpose of the law. [Citations.] Moreover, 'every statute should be construed with reference to the whole system of law of which it is a part so that all may be harmonized and have effect.' [Citation.]" (*Select Base Materials v. Board of Equal.* (1959) 51 Cal. 2d 640, 645 [335 P.2d 672].) A construction rendering statutory language surplusage "'is to be avoided.'" (*Moyer v. Workmen's Comp. Appeals Bd.* (1973) 10 Cal. 3d 222, 230 [110 Cal. Rptr. 144, 514 P.2d 1224]; ...)

To determine the Legislature's intent, the court looks first to the words of the statute. However, the legislative purpose will not be "sacrificed to a literal construction of any part of the act." (*Select Base Materials v. Board of Equal., supra,* 51 Cal. 2d at

p. 645.) The language of a statute "'should not be given a literal meaning if doing so would result in absurd consequences which the Legislature did not intend.'" [Citations.] (*Younger v. Superior Court* (1978) 21 Cal. 3d 102, 113 [145 Cal. Rptr. 674, 577 P.2d 101].

With these principles in mind, this court turns to the language of the FEHA venue statute. Section 12965, subdivision (b) provides in relevant part that "the person claiming to be aggrieved may bring a *civil action under this part* [§ 12900 et seq.] against the person, employer, labor organization or employment agency named in the verified complaint.... *Such an action* may be brought in any county in the state in which the unlawful practice is alleged to have been committed...." (Italics added.)

The phrase "such an action" obviously refers to "a civil action under this part." This latter phrase is reasonably susceptible of two constructions. As defendants assert, the phrase could mean that only FEHA claims may be pursued in the county where the discriminatory practice allegedly occurred. Alternatively, as petitioners contend, the phrase could signify that *any* civil action which contains an FEHA claim may be brought in that county. Both constructions are reasonable.

It is not clear from the language of section 12965 which interpretation was intended. Therefore, this court must look at the purpose of the law to ascertain the Legislature's intent.

The FEHA establishes a comprehensive scheme for combating employment discrimination. As a matter of public policy, the FEHA recognizes the need to protect and safeguard the right and opportunity of all persons to seek and hold employment free from discrimination. (§ 12920.) This court has declared that policy to be "fundamental."

Moreover, the opportunity to be free from discriminatory practices in seeking, obtaining, and holding employment is a "civil right." (§ 12921.) Employment discrimination "foments domestic strife and unrest, deprives the state of the fullest utilization of its capacities for development and advance, and substantially and adversely affects the interest of employees, employers, and the public in general." (§ 12920.) The express purpose of the FEHA is "to provide effective remedies which will eliminate such discriminatory practices." (*Ibid.*) In addition, the Legislature has directed that the FEHA is to be construed "liberally" so as to accomplish its purposes. (§ 12993.)

Section 12965, subdivision (b) affords a wide choice of venue to persons who bring actions under the FEHA. This choice maximizes the ability of persons aggrieved by employment discrimination to seek relief from the courts, and it facilitates the enforcement of the FEHA.

In addition, venue is an important consideration for a plaintiff in an employment discrimination suit. Where the case is to be tried impacts on the cost of the litigation. Victims of employment discrimination are frequently unemployed—many times as the result of the alleged discrimination. They often lack financial resources. For such individuals, the costs of litigation pose a formidable barrier to the filing and prosecution of an FEHA action. The Legislature recognized this barrier and sought to alleviate it by providing these persons with a wide choice of venue. They should not be deprived of that choice simply because they choose to plead alternative theories of recovery. Nor should they be subject to the added burden of trying an action in a county which may be hundreds of miles away from their own choice of venue.

Venue considerations also have a substantial impact on an attorney's decision to undertake representation. An attorney is more likely to accept representation in an FEHA case if venue is available in a location that facilitates prosecution of the action and minimizes travel and other costs, including the costs of securing important witnesses for trial.

Moreover, employment discrimination cases, by their very nature, involve several causes of action arising from the same set of facts. A responsible attorney handling an employment discrimination case must plead a variety of statutory, tort and contract causes of action in order to fully protect the interests of his or her client. In these cases, an overly technical reading of section 12965 would frustrate the intent of the statute and lead to absurd results.

If the statute were construed so as to apply to cases involving only FEHA causes of action, aggrieved persons with FEHA claims would be faced with a Hobson's choice. If they wished to avail themselves of the FEHA venue rules, they would be forced to abandon their non-FEHA claims or to try those claims in a separate action in a different county than that in which the FEHA claims were tried. Such a result would fly in the face of judicial economy. On the other hand, if FEHA claimants wished to have the entire action tried in one county, they would be forced to accede to the defendant's chosen place of venue. This scenario would render the FEHA's special venue rules mere surplusage. Surely, the Legislature never intended either result.

The wide choice of venue afforded plaintiffs by the FEHA venue statute effectuates enforcement of that law by permitting venue in a county which plaintiffs deem the most appropriate and convenient. The Legislature clearly intended the FEHA venue provisions to apply not only to FEHA actions, but also to related claims pled under alternative theories but based on the same set of facts. To hold otherwise would dilute the efficacy of the injured employee's remedy by gutting the FEHA's special venue provisions. The important civil rights which the act codifies would in turn be rendered meaningless.

This court therefore holds that the special provisions of the FEHA venue statute control in cases involving FEHA claims joined with non-FEHA claims arising from the same facts.[9] Thus, the FEHA venue statute governs the entire action and section 395 does not apply. In so construing section 12965, this court adds that statute to the list of exceptions found in *Delgado* ... and *Tharp*.

---

9. In spite of this clear holding, nothing in this opinion suggests that a plaintiff may defeat a defendant's right to trial in the defendant's county of residence by simply appending an FEHA count to a complaint. In order for the FEHA venue provision to control, the non-FEHA claims must rest on similar factual allegations as the FEHA count.

Here, all the claims rest on similar facts. Also, it is clear that the FEHA claim was not added as an afterthought, but was alleged after petitioners received the requisite right-to-sue letters from the Department.

III.

This holding does not dilute what have been called "mixed action" rules. (See 6 Grossman & Van Alstyne, Cal. Practice (2d ed. 1981) Venue, §365, p. 389 et seq. [hereafter *Grossman & Van Alstyne*].) In a mixed action, a plaintiff alleges two or more causes of action each of which is governed by a different venue statute. Or, two or more defendants are named who are subject to different venue standards. "The identifying characteristic of mixed actions is that two or more inconsistent venue provisions ... appear to be concurrently applicable in the same case." (*Ibid.*)

In cases with mixed causes of action, a motion for change of venue must be granted on the entire complaint if the defendant is entitled to a change of venue on any one cause of action. (*Ah Fong v. Stearnes* (1889) 79 Cal. 30, 33 [21 P. 381]; *Morrison v. Superior Court* (1980) 100 Cal. App. 3d 852, 855–856 [161 Cal. Rptr. 169]; ... [10])

It is true that this is a mixed action. The general venue provisions of section 395 normally govern causes of action for the intentional infliction of emotional distress and wrongful discharge, while the special venue provisions of section 12965 govern FEHA causes of action. At first blush, it would appear that two different venue statutes are applicable.

However, the important public policies sought to be effectuated by the FEHA compel the conclusion that the FEHA venue provision controls here. A contrary conclusion would render the special venue provisions of the FEHA mere surplusage and frustrate the intent of the Legislature. Although the mixed action rule recognizes a preference for trial in the county of a defendant's residence, that preference is outweighed by the strong countervailing policy of the FEHA which favors a plaintiff's choice of venue.

IV.

Petitioners alleged an FEHA cause of action as well as causes of action for the intentional infliction of emotional distress and wrongful discharge. All three claims rest upon the same factual allegations, and all three are based on the same allegedly discriminatory practices. Those discriminatory practices are alleged to have been committed in Alameda County, and the action was filed in that county pursuant to the FEHA venue statute. Since that statute controls, Alameda is the proper county for the trial of this action.

Accordingly, let a peremptory writ of mandate issue directing respondent court to vacate its order changing venue to Sacramento County.[11]

---

10. The operation of the mixed action rule has also been summarized as follows: "[If] in [a mixed] action the non-residence county in which the action was commenced is improper venue with respect to one of the counts, even though good as to the rest, the entire action will be transferred on motion to the county of a defendant's residence, because the entire action, being a mixed action, is not within any statutory exception authorizing venue elsewhere than in a residence county." (*Grossman & Van Alstyne, supra*, at pp. 418–419, fn. omitted.)

11. Since petitioners' choice of venue is proper under the FEHA venue statute, this court need not address their alternative contention that injuries caused by wrongful discharge and intentional infliction of emotional distress are "injuries to person" which render venue appropriate in the "county where the injury occurs...." (§395.)

[1] General Venue Rules and Exceptions

As *Brown v. Superior Court* illustrates, various statutory provisions govern the determination of proper venue in California. These provisions often overlap in a conflicting manner, but may be reduced to one fundamental premise, as stated in CCP § 395: A defendant is entitled to have an action tried in the county of his residence unless the action falls within some statutory exception to this general venue rule. When there are multiple defendants, venue is generally proper in any county where at least one of them resides. CCP § 395. If none of the defendants resides in California, venue is generally proper in any county which plaintiff may designate in her complaint. CCP § 395; *see, e.g., Hamilton v. Superior Court*, 37 Cal. App. 3d 418, 112 Cal. Rptr. 450 (1974). As *Brown* illustrates, there are a number of statutory exceptions to these general rules of CCP § 395; these exceptions in turn may be subject to more specific exceptions. Some of the most common exceptions are discussed below. For a thorough discussion of the various venue provisions for civil actions generally, see CEB, *California Civil Procedure Before Trial, Venue* §§ 8.1–8.78 (4th ed. 2015); 3 Witkin, *California Procedure, Actions* §§ 779–904 (5th ed. 2008); Schwing, *California Affirmative Defenses, Venue* §§ 5:1–5:46 (2015).

[a] Actions Involving Real Property

The county in which real property, or some part of the property, is located is the proper venue for most actions for recovery of the property or some interest in the property. CCP § 392. The courts traditionally refer to such actions involving real property as "local actions"; and to all other actions as "transitory" actions. *E.g., Peiser v. Mettler*, 50 Cal. 2d 594, 328 P.2d 953 (1958); *Massae v. Superior Court*, 118 Cal. App. 3d 527, 173 Cal. Rptr. 527 (1981).

[b] Actions Against Public Officials and Entities

The county in which the cause of action or some part of it arose is generally the proper venue for actions against a public officer for an official act. CCP § 393(1)(b). *See, e.g., California State Parks Found. v. Superior Court*, 150 Cal. App. 4th 826, 58 Cal. Rptr. 3d 715 (2007) (examining the language of CCP § 393(b) and the public policy behind it, as well as the numerous cases interpreting the statute, and concluding that § 393 applies to cases that seek to vindicate public rights and is not limited to actions involving personal rights or property). The courts liberally construe "public officer" to include many agencies, departments, institutions, and boards. *Regents of Univ. of Cal. v. Superior Court*, 3 Cal. 3d 529, 91 Cal. Rptr. 57, 476 P.2d 457 (1970).

However, notwithstanding any other statute, where the State is named as a defendant in an action for death or injury to person or personal property, the proper venue is the county where the injury occurred. Gov. Code § 955.2. This provision is mandatory and, in multi-defendant actions, overrides otherwise applicable venue provisions. *State of California v. Superior Court*, 193 Cal. App. 3d 328, 238 Cal. Rptr. 315 (1987). Gov. Code § 955.2 expressly provides, however, that the court upon motion may change the place of trial under the same circumstances as in an action between private parties.

The proper venue for an action against the State for taking or damaging private property for public use is the county in which the property is situated. Gov. Code § 955; *see Tharp v. Superior Court*, 32 Cal. 3d 496, 186 Cal. Rptr. 335, 651 P.2d 1141 (1982) (construing exceptions stated in § 955 which authorized the Attorney General to change venue to Sacramento County).

Proper venue in actions by or against a county is governed by CCP § 394, a complicated statute which includes a removal provision, see, *e.g., Delgado v. Superior Court*, 74 Cal. App. 3d 560, 141 Cal. Rptr. 528 (1977) (ruling section 394 controls over the general provisions of § 395); *Colusa Air Pollution Control Dist. v. Superior Court*, 226 Cal. App. 3d 880, 889, 277 Cal. Rptr. 110 (1991) (comparing § 395 and the removal provisions of § 394); *Tutor-Saliba-Perini Joint Venture v. Superior Court*, 233 Cal. App. 3d 736, 285 Cal. Rptr. 1 (1991) (discussing when change of venue required under § 394 with respect to action against local agency based on negligent injury to person or property); and in actions by local public entities against the State by Gov. Code § 955.3.

[c]   Personal Injury Actions

In an action for "injury to person or personal property," or for wrongful death, the proper venue is either the county where the injury occurred or the county in which the defendants or some of them reside. CCP § 395. The courts have defined "injury to person" narrowly to include physical or bodily injury, but not injuries to character or reputation or mental or emotional distress. *E.g., Cacciaguidi v. Superior Court*, 226 Cal. App. 3d 181, 276 Cal. Rptr. 465 (1990) (holding abuse of process action not one for "injury to person"); *Carruth v. Superior Court*, 80 Cal. App. 3d 215, 145 Cal. Rptr. 344 (1978) (damage action for malicious prosecution); *Cubic Corp. v. Superior Court*, 186 Cal. App. 3d 622, 231 Cal. Rptr. 18 (1986) (action for intentional infliction of emotional distress). Why did the courts narrowly construe "injury to person" in this manner? What venue provision governs in such actions if not this one?

[d]   Dissolution of Marriage

In a dissolution of marriage proceeding, the proper venue is the county where either the petitioner or respondent has been resident for three months next preceding the commencement of proceedings. CCP § 395(a); Family Code § 2320.

[e]   Actions Against Corporations and Associations

In an action against a corporation or association, the plaintiff has several venue options: The county where the contract was made or is to be performed, or where the obligation or liability arises, or where breach occurs, or of the corporation's principal place of business. CCP § 395.5. Although § 395.5 appears to only address contract actions, the courts construe it to govern tort actions as well. *See Mission Imports, Inc.*

v. Superior Court, 31 Cal. 3d 921, 928, 184 Cal. Rptr. 296, 647 P.2d 1075 (1982); *Black Diamond Asphalt, Inc. v. Superior Court*, 109 Cal. App. 4th 166, 134 Cal. Rptr. 2d 510 (2003)(holding § 394 also applicable to statutory liability cases). The purpose of § 395.5 is to permit a wider choice of venue in suits against a corporation than is permitted in suits against an individual defendant. *Mission Imports, supra*, 31 Cal. 3d at 928. Why this purpose?

[f]   Contract Actions

In a contract action, the plaintiff has many venue options: The county where the obligation is to be performed or in which the contract was entered into, where any defendant resides; or, in certain consumer transactions for the sale of goods or services, where the buyer or lessee resided at the time of the contract or at the time of commencement of the action. CCP § 395(a) and (b).

[g]   Other Venue Exceptions

Other statutory venue exceptions include those stated in § 395.1 (actions against executors) and § 393(1)(a) (actions for recovery of statutory penalty or forfeiture); as well as several specific venue provisions stated in special statutes such as Government Code§ 12965(b) (discrimination actions under FEHA), Civil Code § 1780(c) (actions under Consumers Legal Remedies Act), Probate Code §§ 7051, 7052 (proceedings concerning administration of decedent's estate), Civil Code § 1812.10 (venue under Unruh Retail Installment Sales Act), Civil Code § 2984.4 (action under Rees-Levering Motor Vehicle Sales and Finance Act), CCP § 1250.020 (eminent domain proceedings), and Vehicle Code § 13559 (venue in action to review DMV order suspending or revoking driver's license).

[h]   "Residence" Defined

Pursuant to Government Code § 244(a), the residence of an individual is defined as the one place where a person remains and to which he or she returns in seasons of repose. The residence of a corporation is its principal place of business. *See* CCP § 395.2. What factors determine a corporation's principal place of business? *See Rosas v. Superior Court*, 25 Cal. App. 4th 671, 30 Cal. Rptr. 2d 609 (1994) (ruling for purposes of venue, corporation deemed bound by its designation of a principal place of business in corporate documents filed with the Secretary of State).

[2]   *Mixed Actions*

The general statutory venue rules and exceptions often overlap and conflict when a lawsuit involves multiple parties or causes of actions. Such "mixed actions" may occur when plaintiffs permissively join transitory and local actions or multiple transitory actions, governed by conflicting venue statutes; and when one cause of action is brought but different forms of relief, some local and others transitory, are sought. Because the venue statutes do not provide any general approach for resolving these conflicts, the courts have developed their own general rules. As you might expect with venue analysis, however, these general court-made rules may be subject to exceptions in specific cases! *See generally* Arvo Van Alstyne, *Venue of Mixed Actions in California*, 44 CAL. L. REV. 685 (1956).

[a] The "Main Relief" Rule

When a complaint alleges a single cause of action but seeks both local and transitory relief, the court will ascertain the primary object or "main relief" sought by the action to establish proper venue. *See, e.g., Peiser v. Mettler*, 50 Cal. 2d 594, 603–606, 328 P.2d 953 (1958) (In action by lessor for breach of farm lease seeking return of improvements and damages for loss of use and waste, court determined that main relief sought was transitory for venue purposes); *Massae v. Superior Court*, 118 Cal. App. 3d 527, 173 Cal. Rptr. 527 (1981) (determining in an action by trustors under deed of trust seeking declaratory relief, reformation, and damages, that the main relief is for reformation and therefore the action local and governed by CCP § 392 for venue purposes). Whether a complaint asserts a single or multiple causes of action is determined by a "primary rights" analysis. *E.g., Massae, supra*, 118 Cal. App. 3d at 533. The "primary rights" doctrine is discussed extensively in § 8.02 Res Judicata (Claim Preclusion), *infra*.

[b] Venue Follows the Transitory Cause of Action

When a complaint joins local and transitory causes of action against a defendant, the courts usually disregard the local causes of action to establish proper venue. *See, e.g., Pieser v. Mettler, supra*; *Smith v. Smith*, 88 Cal. 572, 26 P.2d 356 (1891); *Turlock Theatre Co. v. Laws*, 12 Cal. 2d 573, 86 P.2d 345 (1939). Why did the courts adopt this approach?

[c] Mixed Action Rules: Multiple Causes and Single Defendant

As the court in *Brown v. Superior Court* indicated, where there are multiple transitory causes of action subject to conflicting venue provisions, in most cases the court must grant a change of venue on the entire complaint whenever the defendant is entitled to a change of venue on any one cause of action. However, as *Brown* also illustrates, this judicial approach is subject to exceptions. What was the nature of the exception utilized by the court in *Brown*? How might this exception be stated as a general approach to determining venue in mixed actions?

[d] Mixed Action Rules: Multiple Defendants and Causes of Actions

In cases involving multiple defendants and causes of action, when venue is proper in the county in which one of the defendants resides as to one cause of action, venue is proper in that county as to all properly joined causes of action and defendants. *See, e.g., Monogram Co. v. Kingsley*, 38 Cal. 2d 28, 237 P.2d 265 (1951); *Tutor-Saliba-Perini Joint Venture v. Superior Court*, 233 Cal. App. 3d 736, 742, 285 Cal. Rptr. 1

(1991). Plaintiff's venue selection may not be defeated even if all the defendants concur in a motion to change venue to a county in which another defendant resides. *Tutor-Saliba-Perini, supra*, 233 Cal. 3d at 742. This approach applies even if some of the causes of action name only nonresidents of the county selected by plaintiff, so long as a resident defendant is named in others. *Id.*

This approach becomes more complicated when the action includes individual and corporate defendants. *See, e.g., Brown v. Superior Court, supra*, note 6; *Mosby v. Superior Court*, 43 Cal. App. 3d 219, 226, 117 Cal. Rptr. 588 (1974) (holding that when a plaintiff brings an action against several defendants, both individual and corporate, in a county which is neither the residence nor principal place of business of any defendant, an individual defendant may change venue to the county of his residence even though venue initially laid may otherwise be proper on one of the alternative grounds provided in § 395.5).

[3] *Venue Puzzles*

Based on these general statutory and judicial rules, and their exceptions, consider the following venue puzzles:

(a) In *Turlock Theatre Co. v. Laws*, 12 Cal. 2d 573, 86 P.2d 345 (1939), the plaintiff lessor brought an action against defendant lessees, residents of San Francisco County, to recover unpaid rentals under a lease of a theatre located in Stanislaus County, and to terminate the lease and recover possession of the property. The action was commenced in Stanislaus County and defendants moved to transfer venue to San Francisco County. Should the motion to transfer be granted? Why?

(b) In *Gallin v. Superior Court*, 230 Cal. App. 3d 541, 281 Cal. Rptr. 304 (1991), the plaintiff commenced a class action in San Diego County on behalf of purchasers of "Milli Vanilli" recordings against the defendant performers, manager, record producers, distributors, and others. Plaintiff claimed that the defendants committed deceptive consumer practices in violation of the Consumer Legal Remedies Act, and common law fraud and breach of contract, when they failed to disclose that the Milli Vanilli rock group did not perform its own vocals in their recordings. Defendant Gallin, the manager, moved to transfer venue to Los Angeles County on the basis that he resides there and none of the defendants reside in San Diego, relying on CCP § 395(a) and various mixed action rules. Plaintiff argued, relying on *Brown*, that venue in San Diego County was proper under the special venue provision of the Consumer Legal Remedies Act, Civil Code § 1780(c), which authorizes venue in the county where the consumer sales transaction occurred. Should the motion to transfer be granted? Why?

(c) What is the proper venue for an action based on negligent design and construction of a building? Plaintiff, owner of an office condominium project located in Merced County, commenced an action in Santa Clara County against several defendant corporations for negligence in design and construction of the project. The complaint seeks damages for diminished value of the project structures but not for the underlying real property, based on negligence, strict liability, and breach of warranty. Plaintiff and defendants are residents of Santa Clara County. Is Santa Clara a proper county for venue? Which venue statute controls here? CCP § 392 (injuries to real property)? § 395(a)? § 395.5 (corporations)? Why? *See Foundation Engineers, Inc. v. Superior Court*, 19 Cal. App. 4th 104, 23 Cal. Rptr. 2d 469 (1993).

[4] *Importance of Complaint*

Generally, as *Brown v. Superior Court* illustrates, venue must be determined based on the allegations of the complaint on file at the time the motion to transfer venue was made, *Turlock Theatre Co. v. Laws*, 12 Cal. 2d 573, 575, 86 P.2d 345 (1939); *Peiser v. Mettler, supra*, 50 Cal. 2d at 603; and not based on subsequent amendments, *see Armstrong Petroleum Corp. v. Superior Court*, 114 Cal. App. 3d 732, 738, 170 Cal. Rptr. 767 (1981). Careful drafting of the complaint is important because, although plaintiff's choice of venue is presumed correct, the complaint will be strictly construed against a plaintiff seeking to lay venue in a county other than that of the defendant's residence. *Neet v. Holmes*, 19 Cal. 2d 605, 612, 122 P.2d 557 (1942).

Is a plaintiff/cross-defendant against whom a cross-complaint has been filed entitled to seek a transfer of venue based on a claim of improper venue as determined by reference to the cross-complaint? In *K.R.L. Partnership v. Superior Court*, 120 Cal. App. 4th 490, 15 Cal. Rptr. 3d 517 (2004), the court concluded that once proper venue has been established based on the complaint, a cross-defendant is not entitled to a transfer of venue under CCP § 396b based on a compulsory cross-complaint. The court explained: "When a plaintiff commences a case, and proper venue of that case has been established in a particular county, the plaintiff may not thereafter object to that county as an improper venue for any compulsory cross-complaint the defendant must assert against the plaintiff in that case." *K.R.L. Partnership, supra*, 120 Cal. App. 4th at 498.

[a] Misjoined Defendants

A plaintiff may exercise considerable control over the proper venue determination based on the causes of action and theories plaintiff chooses to assert in the complaint, the parties named as defendants, and the relief sought. If a plaintiff *improperly* joins a defendant solely for the purpose of establishing venue in the county of that defendant's residence, however, that defendant's residence will not be considered in determining proper venue. CCP § 395(a); *Peiser v. Mettler, supra*, 50 Cal. 2d at 601–603 (ruling that in deciding a motion for transfer of venue, the trial court must determine whether the plaintiff had reasonable grounds for the belief in good faith that plaintiff had a cause of action against the resident defendant). What other legal and practical considerations also limit the plaintiff's ability to control venue by artful pleading and joinder?

[b] Declaratory Relief

Generally, venue for declaratory relief actions is determined by reference to the nature of the underlying subject matter of the action as shown by the complaint. *Mission Imports, Inc. v. Superior Court*, 31 Cal. 3d 921, 930–31, 184 Cal. Rptr. 296, 647 P.2d 1075 (1982) (holding venue in declaratory relief action determined by underlying contract claims); *Massae v. Superior Court*, 118 Cal. App. 3d 527, 533–35, 173 Cal. Rptr. 527 (1981) (concluding an action should be assessed for venue purposes in terms of its substance rather than its declaratory relief form). In what types of cases is this "inversion-of-the-parties" approach to determining venue most likely to apply? What are the problems with this rule, and its application? *See Massae v. Superior Court, supra*, 118 Cal. App. 3d at 533–36.

[5] Venue in Limited Civil Cases

The statutory provisions generally do not set forth different venue rules for limited civil cases, although they do contain specific pleading requirements regarding venue for certain smaller civil cases. *See* CCP § 396a(b).

[B] Raising Improper Venue

[1] Motion to Transfer

A defendant who wishes to contest the plaintiff's venue choice as not the proper county must "at the time he or she answers, demurs, or moves to strike, or, at his or her option, without answering, demurring, or moving to strike and within the time otherwise allowed to respond to the complaint," move to transfer the action to the proper court. CCP § 396b(a). Otherwise, the defendant's objection to the improper court is waived, and the action may be tried in the court where commenced. CCP § 396b(a).

[a] Federal Rules Compared

These California rules are similar to those of the federal courts with respect to improper venue in that generally an objection to venue is not waived in federal court by being joined with other objections or defenses, so long as the objection is raised by pleading or motion at the defendant's first appearance. Rule 12(b)(3), (g) & (h), F.R.C.P.

[b] Waiver of Wrong Venue Objection

Unlike Federal Rule 12(b) & (h), however, CCP § 396b(a) requires that the defendant make a motion to transfer venue at the time defendant files the first responsive pleading. Failure to file a separate motion to transfer at time of answer waives the objection to venue in the improper court; only raising the issue by affirmative defense in an answer is inadequate. *E.g., Northern California Dist. Council of Hod Carriers v. Pennsylvania Pipeline, Inc.*, 103 Cal. App. 3d 163, 173–74, 162 Cal. Rptr. 851 (1980); *Dugan v. Happy Tiger Records, Inc.*, 41 Cal. App. 3d 811, 819–20, note 11, 116 Cal. Rptr. 412 (1974).

[c] Jurisdictional Venue

Although venue provisions are sometimes said to be mandatory, they are not generally considered jurisdictional because an objection to venue may be waived by an untimely motion. *Barquis v. Merchants Collection Assn.*, 7 Cal. 3d 94, 101 Cal. Rptr. 745, 496 P.2d 817 (1972). However, in a few special instances where venue provisions are part of a grant of subject matter jurisdiction, they are considered jurisdictional and cannot be waived by the parties. *E.g.*, CCP § 1250.020 (venue for eminent domain proceedings), *see* Comment to CCP § 1250.020; Probate Code §§ 7051, 7052 (venue for proceedings concerning administration of decedent's estate); Art. 10A, § 6, Cal. Constitution (actions involving certain water resources legislation).

[2] Effect of Motion to Transfer

[a] Suspension of Jurisdiction

A timely filed motion to transfer venue on the ground that plaintiff commenced the action in an improper court suspends the trial court's jurisdiction to act in the case other than hearing and deciding the motion. *Mission Imports, Inc. v. Superior Court*, 31 Cal. 3d 921, 926, note 3, 184 Cal. Rptr. 296, 647 P.2d 1075 (1982); *but see* CCP § 396b(c) (ruling court in dissolution of marriage proceeding may determine motions for temporary spousal and child support prior to determination of motion to transfer venue). In what circumstances might this "suspension of jurisdiction" be significant? *See, e.g., Moore v. Powell*, 70 Cal. App. 3d 583, 138 Cal. Rptr. 914 (1977) (holding delay occasioned by change of venue determination and order does not suspend jurisdiction within meaning of CCP § 583(f) [now CCP § 583.310 and § 583.340(a)]).

[b] Appellate Review

An order of the superior court in an unlimited civil case granting or denying a motion to change the place of trial is not an appealable order, but may be reviewed by a writ of mandate. CCP § 400. Such an order in a limited civil case is appealable. CCP § 904.2(c). Why this difference in procedure for appellate review?

[c] Transfer to Proper Court

When a court determines that plaintiff's choice of venue was improper and the action transferred for that reason, the case must be transferred to any such proper court as the parties may agree upon by stipulation. CCP § 398. If the parties do not so agree, then to any proper court in the proper county as designated by the defendant. CCP § 398. Only when the parties do not so agree and the defendant does not so designate, may the court determine the proper county for transfer. CCP § 398; *Cubic Corp. v. Superior Court*, 186 Cal. App. 3d 622, 231 Cal. Rptr. 18 (1986) (ruling court may designate county of transfer only in absence of party designation). What are the policy reasons for first permitting the parties to agree on the transferee court when a transfer order is appropriate?

[3] Change of Venue for Convenience of Witnesses, Etc.

A trial court also has discretionary authority upon motion to change the place of trial for the reasons specified in § 397, including "[w]hen the convenience of witnesses and the ends of justice would be promoted by the change." CCP § 397(c). For a thorough discussion of motions to change venue, see 2 CEB, *California Civil Procedure Before Trial, Motions to Change Venue* §§ 20.1–20.42 (4th ed. 2015); 3 Witkin, *California Procedure, Actions* §§ 905–958 (5th ed. 2008).

[a] Federal Procedure Compared

Unlike the federal discretionary change of venue statute, 28 U.S.C. § 1404(a), CCP§ 397(c) does not authorize consideration of the convenience of parties or employees of parties. *See, e.g., Peiser v. Mettler*, 50 Cal. 2d 594, 612, 328 P.2d 953 (1958); *Lieberman v. Superior Court*, 194 Cal. App. 3d 396, 239 Cal. Rptr. 450 (1987). Why not? There are two limited exceptions to this general interpretation. One is when employees of one party are called as witnesses by the adverse party. *See Lieberman, supra*, 194 Cal App. 3d at 401–402. Another is when a party's physical condition makes it impossible for the party to travel to a distant county to give material evidence. *See Peiser, supra*, 50 Cal. 2d at 612. Why these two limited exceptions? Should the convenience of counsel be of any relevance? *See Lieppman v. Lieber*, 180 Cal. App. 3d 914, 920, 225 Cal. Rptr. 845 (1986).

[b] Transfer to Convenient Court

When a court orders discretionary change of venue pursuant to § 397, the action must be transferred to a court which the parties may agree upon by stipulation; or if they do not so agree, to the nearest court where the cause for making the order does not exist. CCP § 398. Does this mean that a court may order a discretionary change of venue to a county which is otherwise not a proper court under the venue statutes? If so, why? Does this mean that where a plaintiff commenced an action in an improper court and the defendant moves to transfer under CCP § 396b, the court has discretion to retain the action in the county where commenced if the convenience of witnesses will be promoted? *See* CCP § 396b(d); *Cholakian & Associates v. Superior Court*, 236 Cal. App. 4th 361, 186 Cal. Rptr. 3d 525 (holding § 396b(d) requires answers from all proper defendants be filed before an opposition to a motion to transfer to a correct court will be considered on the basis of "the convenience of witnesses and the ends of justice").

[c] Time for Motion

A § 397 motion for discretionary change of venue is not waived by failure to assert it at the time of first responsive pleading, and in fact may be considered premature if made before the defendant's answer. *See, e.g., Cooney v. Cooney*, 25 Cal. 2d 202, 208, 153 P.2d 334 (1944) (noting a motion to change venue for witness convenience should be made within a reasonable time after the case is at issue on the facts); *Thompson v. Superior Court*, 26 Cal. App. 3d 300, 306, 103 Cal. Rptr. 94 (1972) (concluding a motion for change of venue for witness convenience should be made within a reasonable time after answer is filed or after knowledge of changed circumstances). Why this difference in treatment for a § 397 motion to change venue in contrast to a § 396b motion to transfer?

[d] Payment of Fees

The venue provisions contain much statutory detail governing the procedural aspects of transfer of venue, including imposition of costs, expenses, attorney fees, and sanctions. CCP §§ 396b(b), 399. When an action is transferred because it was commenced in an improper court, the action shall not be further prosecuted in the transferee court until the specified costs and fees are paid. CCP § 399; see, e.g., *Stasz v. Eisenberg*, 190 Cal. App. 4th 1032, 120 Cal. Rptr. 3d 21 (2010) (holding trial court properly dismissed action after plaintiff failed to pay costs and attorney fees ordered when court transferred the action pursuant to CCP § 399(a)).

[4] *Removal Statute*

Code of Civil Procedure § 394, which applies to actions by or against local government entities and agencies, is a complicated removal statute designed to avoid local prejudice by permitting transfer of such actions to a neutral county for trial. *See, e.g., Garrett v. Superior Court*, 11 Cal. 3d 245, 113 Cal. Rptr. 152, 520 P.2d 968 (1974); *Colusa Air Pollution Control Dist. v. Superior Court*, 226 Cal. App. 3d 880, 889, 277 Cal. Rptr. 110 (1991). Section 394 is technically not a venue statute—a plaintiff still has the duty to bring the action initially in a proper county under the appropriate venue statute. *See, e.g., County of San Bernardino v. Superior Court*, 30 Cal. App. 4th 378, 35 Cal. Rptr. 2d 760 (1994); *Colusa, supra*, 226 Cal. App. 3d at 889–90.

When properly invoked, CCP § 394 operates as an exception to CCP § 395 even in multiple defendant actions. *Delgado v. Superior Court*, 74 Cal. App. 3d 560, 141 Cal. Rptr. 528 (1977). The court must transfer to a neutral county even though the action was properly commenced in the county of an individual defendant's residence. *Delgado*, 74 Cal. App. 3d at 563–64; *McCarthy v. Superior Court*, 191 Cal. App. 3d 1023, 1032–34, 236 Cal. Rptr. 833 (1987) (holding that because right to removal under § 394 is personal as to each defendant, venue must be changed irrespective of the existence of other defendants who are residents of the county). Section 394 requires transfer of cross-complaints asserted by or against a city or county, and may therefore result in severance of the cross-complaint from the underlying complaint. *See, e.g., Metropolitan Transit Sys. v. Superior Court*, 153 Cal. App. 4th 293, 62 Cal. Rptr. 3d 517 (2007); *Kennedy/Jenks Consultants, Inc. v. Superior Court*, 80 Cal. App. 4th 948, 95 Cal. Rptr. 2d 817 (2000); *Ohio Cas. Ins. Grp. v. Superior Court*, 30 Cal. App. 4th 444, 35 Cal. Rptr. 2d 771 (1994). The change of venue provisions of CCP § 397, however, are not subordinated to § 394. The mandatory removal language of § 394 does not prohibit a discretionary change of venue for witness convenience or impartial trial. *Paesano v. Superior Court*, 204 Cal. App. 3d 17, 250 Cal. Rptr. 842 (1988).

[5] Coordination Statutes

Code of Civil Procedure §§ 404–404.9, which authorize coordination of multiple lawsuits sharing a common question of fact or law before one judge in a selected site, may override the conventional venue statutes when utilized. *See* Rules 3.501–3.550, Cal. Rules of Ct.

[C] Contractual Venue Provisions

The California courts will not enforce a contractual provision that attempts to vest venue in a county that is not a proper county under venue statutes. *See, e.g., General Acceptance Corp. v. Robinson*, 207 Cal. 285, 277 P. 1039 (1929); *Alexander v. Superior Court*, 114 Cal. App. 4th 723, 8 Cal. Rptr. 3d 111 (2003) (concluding contractual venue selection clause that stipulates venue in a county not a proper county under CCP § 395 for a breach of contract action is invalid and unenforceable); *Arntz Builders v. Superior Court*, 122 Cal. App. 4th 1195, 19 Cal. Rptr. 3d 346 (2004) (ruling contractual venue provision purporting to waive defendant's right to transfer action brought by county to a neutral forum pursuant to CCP 394 is invalid); *see also Battaglia Enter. v. Superior Court*, 215 Cal. App. 4th 309, 154 Cal. Rptr. 3d 907 (2013) (enforcing venue selection clause where two sophisticated parties agreed to litigate an action in one of multiple statutorily permissible counties). The courts distinguish between an interstate forum selection clause, which is enforceable if reasonable, *see Smith, Valentino & Smith, Inc. v. Superior Court*, 17 Cal. 3d 491, 131 Cal. Rptr. 374, 551 P.2d 1206 (1976) (observing *General Acceptance* not controlling in interstate contracts, and holding forum selection clauses valid and enforceable unless shown to be unreasonable); and an intrastate venue selection clause, which is invalid. They also distinguish a waiver of the right to transfer venue to a proper county by failing to file a timely motion after an action has been instituted, as set forth in CCP § 396b, from a contractual provision entered into before the action has been filed designating an improper venue, which is against public policy and void. *Alexander, supra*, 114 Cal. App. 4th at 726–731; *Arntz, supra*, 122 Cal. App. 4th at 1204. Are you persuaded that these distinctions justify the refusal to enforce a venue selection agreement?

A few special statutes specifically declare such venue provisions void and unenforceable when included in certain consumer contracts. *E.g.,* CCP § 395(b) & (c) (actions arising out of most consumer transactions); Civil Code § 1804.1 (Unruh Retail Installment Sales Act); Civil Code § 2983.7(f) (Rees-Levering Motor Vehicle Sales and Finance Act); Commercial Code § 10106(b) (limitation on power of parties to consumer lease to contractually designate county for litigation). Does the existence of these explicit statutory restrictions suggest that such venue agreements may be enforceable in contracts not governed by these statutes?

§ 6.04 Service of Process

[A] Introductory Note on Manner of Service

Code of Civil Procedure Section 413.10 provides:

> Except as otherwise provided by statute, a summons shall be served on a person:
>
> (a) Within this state, as provided in this chapter.
>
> (b) Outside this state but within the United States, as provided in this chapter or as prescribed by the law of the place where the person is served.
>
> (c) Outside the United States, as provided in this chapter or as directed by the court in which the action is pending, or, if the court before or after service finds that the service is reasonably calculated to give actual notice, as prescribed by the law of the place where the person is served or as directed by the foreign authority in response to a letter rogatory. These rules are subject to the provisions of the Convention on the "Service Abroad of Judicial and Extrajudicial Documents" in Civil or Commercial Matter (Hague Service Convention).

Together with personal and subject matter jurisdiction, proper service of the complaint and summons on the defendant is a prerequisite to a valid judgment. *See, e.g., Mullane v. Central Hanover Bank & Trust Co.,* 339 U.S. 306, 70 S. Ct. 652, 94 L. Ed. 865 (1950) (holding constitutionally adequate notice is prerequisite to valid judgment); *Insurance Corp. of Ireland v. Compagnie des Bauxites de Guinea,* 456 U.S. 694, 701, 102 S. Ct. 2099, 72 L. Ed. 2d 492 (1982) (noting the validity of an order depends on the court having jurisdiction over both the subject matter and the parties); *Ault v. Dinner For Two, Inc.,* 27 Cal. App. 3d 145, 148, 103 Cal. Rptr. 572 (1972).

The Jurisdiction and Service of Process Act enacted in 1969 governs service of process in the California courts. CCP § 410.10 *et seq.* Generally speaking, the proper manner of service, and the person upon whom service must be made, depends on the place where process is to be served (*i.e.,* within California, in another state, or outside the United States) and the type of party to be served (*e.g.* an individual defendant, a corporation or association, or a public entity). CCP § 413.10–417.40.

[B] Service Within California

Bein v. Brechtel-Jochim Group, Inc.

Court of Appeal of California, Fourth Appellate District
6 Cal App. 4th 1387, 8 Cal. Rptr. 2d 351 (1992)

SONENSHINE, JUSTICE.

Brechtel-Jochim Group, Inc., Thomas W. Brechtel, Linda Brechtel, Randy Jochim and Ann Jochim appeal from a default judgment. They argue the trial court had no personal jurisdiction over them. They maintain service of summons and complaint upon a guard at the entrance of a gated community does not meet the requirements of Code of Civil Procedure section 415.20[1] because a gate guard is neither a competent member of the household nor a person apparently in charge of the business. We disagree and affirm.

I

Robert Bein and William Frost & Associates (Bein) entered into written contracts with Brechtel-Jochim Group, Inc., et al., for engineering work. Bein, claiming it had completed the job, filed the underlying action when Brechtel refused to pay. The complaint alleged breach of contract and common counts, and named Brechtel and its sole shareholders, the Brechtels and the Jochims, as defendants. Asserting the individuals were alter egos of the corporation, Bein sought to pierce the corporate veil. The complaint prayed for damages in the sum of $69,347.01 plus interest, reasonable attorney fees and costs of the suit.

Bein attempted to serve the Jochims at their home on three separate occasions. They were finally served by substitute service on a "Linda Doe" when she emerged from the residence. As she was handed the papers, she ran back into the house and turned out the lights. Two days later, Bein mailed copies of the summons and complaint to the Jochims' residence. Proofs of service and declarations verifying the attempted service were filed with the court.

Service upon the corporation and the Brechtels was equally difficult. Bein unsuccessfully attempted to serve the business and the Brechtels at the Brechtels' residence. Each time, the process server was denied access to the area by the gate guard stationed at the community's entrance. The process server finally resorted to substitute service upon the guard who, in response, threw the papers on the ground. As the process server drove away, he saw the guard retrieve the papers.

Bein mailed copies of the summons and complaint to the Brechtels' residence within a few days. Thereafter, the declaration of attempted service on the Brechtels and the corporation was timely filed, along with the proof of service of summons and complaint.

Neither the corporation nor its shareholders responded to the complaint. Bein filed requests to enter defaults as to all of the defendants and notified each defendant by mail.

At the default prove-up hearing, Douglas Frost, a Bein corporate officer, testified his counsel told him no stock was ever issued by Brechtel. Following testimony, the court entered default judgment against all named defendants in the amount prayed for in the complaint. No motions to quash service or set aside the judgment were filed by any of the defendants.

---

1. All further statutory references are to the Code of Civil Procedure unless otherwise specified.

II

Appellants challenge the court's jurisdiction, arguing service was ineffective.[2] They maintain Bein did not establish reasonable diligence in attempting to effectuate personal service. They are wrong. Section 415.20, subdivision (b) states: "If a copy of the summons and of the complaint cannot with reasonable diligence be personally delivered to the person to be served as specified in Section 416.60, 416.70, 416.80, or 416.90, a summons may be served by leaving a copy of the summons and of the complaint at such person's dwelling house, usual place of abode, usual place of business, ... in the presence of a competent member of the household or a person apparently in charge of his or her office, place of business, ... at least 18 years of age, who shall be informed of the contents thereof, and by thereafter mailing a copy of the summons and of the complaint (by first-class mail, postage prepaid) to the person to be served at the place where a copy of the summons and of the complaint were left. Service of a summons in this manner is deemed complete on the 10th day after the mailing."

" 'Ordinarily, ... two or three attempts at personal service at a proper place should fully satisfy the requirement of reasonable diligence and allow substituted service to be made.' [Citation.]" (*Espindola v. Nunez* (1988) 199 Cal. App. 3d 1389, 1392 [245 Cal. Rptr. 596].) The process server made three separate attempts to serve the Brechtels at their residence. Each time, the gate guard denied access. Substitute service was appropriate.

Appellants next maintain service on the gate guard fails to satisfy the statutory requirements.[3] Despite the great number of gated communities in the state, no California court has addressed this issue. Specifically, we must determine whether a residential

---

2. Appellants did not seek relief in the trial court; however, they attack the court's jurisdiction. Thus, they have not waived their right to appellate review of this issue.

3. The requirements for substitute service on a person are found in section 415.20, subdivision (b), set forth *ante*.

Section 415.20, subdivision (a) provides: "In lieu of personal delivery of a copy of the summons and of the complaint to the person to be served as specified in Section 416.10, ... a summons may be served by leaving a copy of the summons and of the complaint during usual office hours in his or her office with the person who is apparently in charge thereof, and by thereafter mailing a copy of the summons and of the complaint (by first-class mail, postage prepaid) to the person to be served at the place where a copy of the summons and of the complaint were left. Service of a summons in this manner is deemed complete on the 10th day after such mailing."

Section 416.10 permits service on a corporation by delivery "(a) to the person designated as agent for service of process ... ; [¶] (b) to the president or other head of the corporation, a vice president, a secretary or assistant secretary, a treasurer or assistant treasurer, a general manager, or a person authorized by the corporation to receive service of process."

Section 417.10, subdivision (a) explains the procedure for substituted service on a corporation. "If served under Section 415.10, 415.20, ... such affidavit shall recite or in other manner show the name of the person to whom a copy of the summons and of the complaint were delivered, and, if appropriate, his [or her] title or capacity in which he [or she] is served...."

gate guard is a person apparently in charge of the corporate office (§ 415.20, subd. (a)) and a competent member of the household (§ 415.20, subd. (b)).

We first note that pre-1969 service of process statutes required strict and exact compliance. However, the provisions are now to be liberally construed to effectuate service and uphold jurisdiction if actual notice has been received by the defendant, " 'and in the last analysis the question of service should be resolved by considering each situation from a practical standpoint.... ' " (*Pasadena Medi-Center Associates v. Superior Court* (1973) 9 Cal. 3d 773, 778 [108 Cal. Rptr. 828, 511 P.2d 1180].) The Supreme Court's admonition to construe the process statutes liberally extends to substituted service as well as to personal service. (*Espindola v. Nunez, supra,* 199 Cal. App. 3d 1389, 1391.) "To be constitutionally sound the form of substituted service must be 'reasonably calculated to give an interested party actual notice of the proceedings and an opportunity to be heard ... [in order that] the traditional notions of fair play and substantial justice implicit in due process are satisfied.' [Citations.]" (*Zirbes v. Stratton* (1986) 187 Cal. App. 3d 1407, 1416 [232 Cal. Rptr. 653].)

The gate guard in this case must be considered a competent member of the household[4] and the person apparently in charge. Appellants authorized the guard to control access to them and their residence. We therefore assume the relationship between appellants and the guard ensures delivery of process. *F. I. duPont, Glore Forgan & Co. v. Chen* (1977) 41 N.Y.S.2d 794 [396 N.Y.S.2d 343, 364 N.E.2d 1115] is instructive. There, the court found substitute service on an apartment building doorman was statutorily sufficient. A deputy sheriff twice attempted to serve defendants and, finding no one at home, left a card under the door. On the third try, when the doorman refused to allow him to go past the building's front entrance, the deputy served the doorman. The court reasoned "it cannot be held as a matter of law on this record that the action of the doorman in refusing permission to the Deputy Sheriff to proceed to apartment 4A was not attributable for purposes of this statute to defendants." (at p. 798 [364 N.E.2d at p. 1118].)[6] "While the defendant may control the acceptance of mail by his [or her] household, he [or she] may not thereby negate the effectiveness of service otherwise effective under the law." (*Bossuk v. Steinberg* (1982) 88 A.D.2d 358 [453 N.Y.S.2d 687, 689–690].)

Litigants have the right to choose their abodes; they do not have the right to control who may sue or serve them by denying them physical access. In *Khourie, Crew & Jaeger v. Sabek, Inc.* (1990) 220 Cal. App. 3d 1009 [269 Cal. Rptr. 687], where a corporation attempted to avoid service by refusing to unlock its door, the court determined a "defendant will not be permitted to defeat service by rendering physical service impossible." (at p. 1013.) "The evident purpose of Code of Civil Procedure section 415.20 is to

---

4. The Legislature's choice of the term household over family indicates that household is to be liberally construed. (*See* Note, *Substituted Service of Process on Individuals: Code Civ. Proc., § 415.20(b)* (1970) 21 Hastings L.J. 1257.)

6. In contrast, where the doorman did not hinder entrance, substitute service upon him was deemed unacceptable. (*Reliance Audio Visual Corp. v. Bronson* (1988) 141 Misc. 2d 671 [534 N.Y.S.2d 313].)

permit service to be completed upon a good faith attempt at physical service on a *responsible person....*" (*Ibid.*, italics added.) Service must be made upon a person whose "relationship with the person to be served makes it more likely than not that they will deliver process to the named party." (*50 Court St. Assoc. v. Mendelson et al.* (1991) 151 Misc. 2d 87 [572 N.Y.S.2d 997, 999].) Here, the gate guard's relationship with appellants made it more likely than not that he would deliver process to appellants. We note they do not claim they failed to receive notice of service.[7]

The corporation raises two other objections to its service. We are not impressed. First, they argue no good faith attempt was made to serve its designated agent. A good faith attempt to serve the agent was unnecessary because service may be made on either the corporation's agent or an officer. (*M. Lowenstein & Sons, Inc. v. Superior Court* (1978) 80 Cal. App. 3d 762 [145 Cal. Rptr. 814].) Thomas Brechtel, as president of the corporation, was an appropriate person to be served on behalf of the corporation.

Appellants further maintain the declaration of attempted service was invalid because it failed to identify the person to be served on behalf of the corporation. But minor, harmless deficiencies will not be allowed to defeat service. (*Espindola v. Nunez, supra,* 199 Cal. App. 3d 1389, 1391.)

III

Appellants argue the evidence was insufficient to find they were the alter ego of the corporation and to sustain the damage award. We note they did not seek relief from their default in the trial court. Sufficiency of the evidence is not reviewable unless relief from the default proceedings has been sought.

The judgment is affirmed. Respondents to recover costs on appeal.

Olvera v. Olvera

Court of Appeal of California, Fourth Appellate District
232 Cal. App. 3d 32, 283 Cal. Rptr. 271 (1991)

TIMLIN, JUSTICE.

Plaintiffs Elias S. Olvera, Sr., and Annie Olvera (hereinafter the Olveras) appeal from an order vacating a default judgment entered in their favor against defendant Paula Olvera (hereinafter Paula). Although the record and the briefs on appeal reflect a considerable lack of clarity with respect to the governing law, we hold that the trial court properly granted relief.

---

7. There is an additional reason to find the service here adequate. Pursuant to section 415.20, subdivision (b), the guard gate constitutes part of the dwelling. Although the parties do not address this issue, we look to *F. I. duPont.* "In our analysis if a process server is not permitted to proceed to the actual [residence by the gate guard or some other employee] the outer bounds of the actual dwelling place must be deemed to extend to the location at which the process server's progress is arrested." (*F. I. duPont, Glore Forgan & Co. v. Chen, supra,* 41 N.E.2d 794, 797 [364 N.E.2d 1115, 1117].)

STATEMENT OF FACTS

The Olveras filed this action on June 30, 1988, against Paula and Richard Olvera for breach of contract, fraud and the remedy of specific performance. Plaintiffs alleged that in 1985, they had orally agreed to lend $17,000 to defendants, and that defendants had orally agreed either to execute a second deed of trust on property located at 2840 Collingswood, in Riverside, California, as security for the loan, or to obtain a loan on the property from another source and repay plaintiffs "immediately." Plaintiffs further alleged that defendants had failed to repay the entire sum or to execute the trust deed as security, and sought the remedies of a money judgment and specific performance of the promise to execute a trust deed.

On the same date, the Olveras filed a notice of recordation of lis pendens affecting the Collingswood property. The notice included a proof of service by mail on Paula "c/o Casa Calderon, 197 Pomery, Pismo Beach, CA 93449."

On September 12, 1988, the Olveras filed an application for order for publication of summons. (Code Civ. Proc., § 415.50.)[3] The spaces in the form application which were provided for an explanation of the efforts at personal service were all filled in with the assertion that "Defendant no longer resides in Riverside, Ca., and cannot be found" or variants of this phrase. Some further explanation was given, as follows:

> "Plaintiffs have contacted Defendant Richard M. Olvera, who is their son, and who is the former husband of Defendant Paula D. Olvera; to ascertain the present whereabouts of Paula D. Olvera, but all the former husband knows is that defendant Paula D. Olvera may be somewhere in California, but her exact residence or place of employment cannot be ascertained. The plaintiffs believe that she may receive her mail by her relatives in Pismo Beach, Ca., Paula D. Olvera formerly worked as a secretary at Riverside General Hospital for about ten (10) years. She is no longer employed there or elsewhere in Riverside, Ca., to the best knowledge of Plaintiffs.

> "Plaintiffs have received a letter from Defendant Paula D. Olvera, but there was no/personal return address for said Defendant.

> "Defendant Paula D. Olvera, left no forwarding address with her former employer, to the best knowledge of the Plaintiffs."

The application was verified by plaintiff Elias Olvera; however, there was no accompanying affidavit establishing the existence of a cause of action against Paula.

The application sought publication in the Press-Enterprise, a newspaper of general circulation published in Riverside, and the order for publication so provided. There is no contention that the subsequent publication did not conform to the provisions of Government Code section 6064; a proof of publication was duly filed showing completion of publication on October 7, 1988. As publication began on September

---

3. Unless otherwise noted, all subsequent statutory references are to the Code of Civil Procedure.

16, the 28-day notice period under the Government Code expired, and service was deemed complete, on October 13.

Paula did not respond within the statutory time and her default was entered on November 17, 1988. On the same date, following testimony by Elias Olvera at a prove-up hearing, judgment was entered in favor of the Olveras and against Richard and Paula. The judgment provided that defendants were jointly liable for the principal sum of $13,997, plus attorneys' fees of $4,600, punitive damages of $6,000, and $535.60 in costs. Paula was further ordered to execute a note secured by a deed of trust on the Collingswood property in favor of the Olveras.

Notice of entry of judgment was sent to Paula on November 20, 1988, at the Collingswood address, with a request for forwarding. However, it was returned with the notation that she had left no forwarding address.

On November 3, 1989, Paula filed a "motion to set aside judgment." The stated bases were that the judgment was void due to improper service, and that it was obtained through extrinsic fraud. Paula argued both that the Olveras had failed to disclose information known to them which would have suggested to the court that they had the power to effect personal service on her, and that the use of the Press-Enterprise was not reasonably calculated to give her notice of the action.

In support of this motion, Paula filed a declaration which included the following information. On May 5, 1988, Richard had appeared at a laundry "near my residence in Pismo Beach. Richard left and returned with our son, [who was then 14 years old] in his vehicle." Three days later, Richard returned the son "to my mother's house, which was also my residence with my son...." During the summer of 1988, the son spent two months with his grandparents, the plaintiffs, and the son always knew where to reach Paula. On July 24, Paula visited her son at Richard's residence in Riverside. On September 5, she picked up her son at the Olveras' residence in Riverside.

Paula's telephone number was listed in the October 1988 telephone directory which included the Pismo Beach region; it was listed under the name "D. Olvera," as she commonly used the name "Diane." The exact date of issuance of the directory was not established.

Paula's mother had owned a restaurant in Pismo Beach called "Casa Calderon," located at 197 Pomeroy Avenue. The Olveras had visited the restaurant on several occasions and were aware that it was owned by Paula's mother; the restaurant's telephone number and address were regularly included in the telephone directories.

Finally, Paula was renting the house on Collingswood, and the tenant knew her address, as rent checks were mailed to her each month.

Paula did not submit a proposed answer or other proposed pleading with her motion.

In response, the Olveras attempted at length to rebut this showing, and also argued that Paula's facts did not prove that they knew, or could have discovered, her whereabouts. They admitted knowing about the Casa Calderon, but asserted—without factual support—that Paula was afraid of Richard and kept her residence secret. They stated that they had called Paula's mother, and that the mother had said that Paula was not there but would be given a message to call Elias Olvera. They claimed that Paula's son had never told them where she lived, and argued that their contact with the boy did not prove their knowledge of his mother's whereabouts. Similarly conceding that the Collingswood house tenant might have known Paula's address, they assert that *they* did not know it and that Paula was concealing it. They point out that the notice of entry of judgment was sent to the Collingswood address, and returned as not forwardable.

The Olveras also pointed out that on August 22, 1988, Paula wrote to them acknowledging receipt of "the letter from your attorney, which I understood to say that you put a lean [*sic*] on the house on Collingwood." The Olveras argued that this letter, which apparently refers to the notice of lis pendens, demonstrates Paula's knowledge of the lawsuit, and they also quoted her promise that she "intend [ed] to start making payments soon.... If you need to continue with the legal action, it is fine with me...."

Paula's reply regarding this letter of acknowledgement seized on the fact that plaintiffs had received a response from her to the notice sent to 197 Pomeroy in Pismo Beach; the envelope of the response displayed this as a return address as well. The Olveras' last counter-reply stressed that the telephone listing for "D. Olvera" included no address, and that they had never reached Paula at the "Casa Calderon."

At the hearing, the trial court focused on the fact that publication was requested in Riverside rather than in the Pismo Beach area, and commented that the matter appeared to fall squarely within the provisions of section 473.5. * * *

DISCUSSION

A. *Did Section 473.5 Apply to Paula?*

Section 473.5, subdivision (a), permits the court to vacate a default judgment if "service of a summons has not resulted in actual notice to a party in time to defend...." A motion for relief may be made within two years after entry of the default judgment.

Under an earlier version of this statute, the right to relief was virtually absolute in cases of constructive service. However, although that version did not mention the effect of actual notice of the lawsuit, it was established that a defendant's actual knowledge gave the court discretion to deny relief, depending on such equitable factors as diligence and laches.

The present statute has been construed by at least one commentator to preclude relief if the defendant has acquired actual knowledge of the action. (See 8 Witkin, Cal. Procedure (3d ed. 1985) Attack on Judgment in Trial Court, § 193, p. 592.) Here, Paula's August 1988 letter in response to receipt of the notice of filing lis pendens is plain proof that she was aware that the Olveras had commenced an action against her on June 30, 1988.

We note that "actual knowledge" has been strictly construed, with the aim of implementing the policy of liberally granting relief so that cases may be resolved on their merits. (*Goya v. P.E.R.U. Enterprises* (1978) 87 Cal. App. 3d 886, 891 [151 Cal. Rptr. 258].) In *Goya*, a finding of no "actual knowledge" was upheld even though the defendants concededly received actual copies of the summons and complaint; instead, the court accepted the contention that defendants' inability to understand English, and lack of business sophistication, amounted to a lack of "actual knowledge." In *Rosenthal v. Garner* (1983) 142 Cal. App. 3d 891 [191 Cal. Rptr. 300], the court allowed relief under section 473.5 where, in addition to service by publication, plaintiff had sent a copy of the summons and complaint to defendants' counsel; the court refused to find this imputed knowledge equivalent to the actual knowledge required by the statute. (Accord, *Tunis v. Barrow* (1986) 184 Cal. App. 3d 1069 [229 Cal. Rptr. 389].)

The liberal approach of these cases would arguably support a literal reading of the statute which makes actual notice irrelevant *unless acquired as a result of service of the summons*. Alternatively, it suggests that Paula's awareness that a lawsuit had been filed in June, based upon the receipt of a notice of recordation of lis pendens, did not necessarily give her "time to defend the action." Until summons is served, there is no need to respond; a defendant may believe that the action will not be pursued. Additionally, a notice of lis pendens does not necessarily disclose that any tort causes of action, such as fraud, are part of the lawsuit.

However, we do not think that this policy can be stretched too far without contravening the plain language of the statute and the practical reasons for providing a mechanism for relief. Section 415.50, authorizing service by publication, allows the court to acquire jurisdiction over a defendant who cannot be served personally or by substituted service under section 415.20 or 415.30, even after diligent effort. Jurisdiction so acquired is constitutional. (*Miller v. Superior Court* (1961) 195 Cal. App. 2d 779, 786 [16 Cal. Rptr. 36].) However, it is recognized that such service is on many occasions unlikely to result in actual notice, and to some extent the same may be true of any form of substituted or constructive service. Thus, section 473.5 reflects the understanding that if any form of service of summons does not result in actual knowledge, fundamental fairness may require that a subsequent default be set aside.

We hold that if the court has acquired jurisdiction, i.e., summons has been served, but service of summons has not resulted in actual notice to a defendant, although the defendant has acquired actual knowledge of the action from another source, this does not preclude a defendant from seeking relief under section 473.5. We note that the findings in subdivision (c) of section 473.5, which the court must make before exercising its discretion, do not include a determination by the court that defendant did not have actual notice from the summons and from no other source.

The issue remains whether under the circumstances the court abused its discretion in granting relief. A defendant who has been constructively served may have "actual knowledge" about the action from information which is fragmentary or unconfirmed. In a proper case, it may be insufficient to place upon a defendant the duty of making inquiries about the lawsuit against her or him; other circumstances—the limits of which we will not attempt to define here—may also make a strict application of the "actual knowledge" exception inequitable.

Such circumstances exist here. Paula was aware of the lawsuit after she was sent a copy of the notice of lis pendens. However, she did not know that plaintiffs had alleged a cause of action for fraud against her, or that punitive damages were sought. Her letter of August 1988, may have reflected an indifference to a lawsuit seeking only contract damages, but her reaction may well have been different had she known that she was being sued for fraud and deceit. Furthermore, at that time the court had not yet acquired jurisdiction over her by service of process. She was under no obligation to respond. Finally, she was justified in the belief that plaintiffs were aware of her whereabouts, and she could reasonably await further action by the Olveras before affirmatively making inquiries about the nature and progress of the litigation. Accordingly, we hold that the trial court did not abuse its discretion and properly vacated the judgment under section 473.5.

B. *The Service by Publication Was Invalid, and the Judgment Was Void*

As an alternative basis for affirming the judgment, we further find that the order for publication was void.

Personal service remains the method of choice under the statutes and the constitution. (See Judicial Council com., West's Ann. Code Civ. Proc. (1973 ed.) § 415.20, p. 554 [Deering's Ann. Code Civ. Proc. (1991 ed) § 415.20, p. 656]; *Evartt v. Superior Court* (1979) 89 Cal. App. 3d 795, 799 [152 Cal. Rptr. 836].) When substituted or constructive service is attempted, strict compliance with the letter and spirit of the statutes is required. (*Stern v. Judson* (1912) 163 Cal. 726, 735 [127 P. 38].) We are of the opinion that the affidavit in support of the application for permission to accomplish service by publication was both deficient on its face and materially misleading, and that the Olveras not only failed to *show* due diligence, but failed to *exercise* it. The judgment based on such service was therefore void and subject to direct or collateral attack. (*Evartt v. Superior Court, supra,* 89 Cal. App. 3d at p. 802; *Donel, Inc. v. Badalian* (1978) 87 Cal. App. 3d 327, 334 [150 Cal. Rptr. 855].)

The affidavit itself was not sufficient. It affirmatively discloses that plaintiffs had received a letter from Paula; the assertion that the letter contained no "personal" return address virtually demands some explanation of the reason why the return address which *was* given was not considered helpful. Although plaintiffs admitted knowing Paula's general whereabouts, there was no indication that they had employed any of the usual means to find her. (See *Sanford v. Smith* (1970) 11 Cal. App. 3d 991, 1001–1002 [90 Cal. Rptr. 256], approving the standards of diligence required by the local rules of Los Angeles Superior Court: recent inquiries of *all* relatives, friends, and other persons likely to know defendant's whereabouts; searches of city directories, telephone directories, tax rolls, and register of voters; and inquiries made of occupants of all real estate involved in the litigation.) Finally, plaintiffs did not allege that they had employed either a private process server or the appropriate governmental officer authorized to serve process in the Pismo Beach area to attempt personal service.

The foundational facts for the repeated allegation that Paula could not be found were so slight as to be unworthy of serious consideration. It is well established that the affidavit submitted under section 415.50 must establish reasonable diligence by "probative facts" based on personal knowledge. (*In re Behymer* (1933) 130 Cal. App. 200, 204 [19 P.2d 829]; *Sanford v. Smith, supra,* 11 Cal. App. 3d 991, 998–999.) The affidavit here was not sufficient.[9]

It is also proper to consider not only the affidavit itself, but the facts demonstrated by the applicant. (*Donel, Inc. v. Badalian, supra,* 87 Cal. App. 3d 327, 333.) In this context the Olveras' repeated claims of actual ignorance of Paula's whereabouts are not persuasive. It is not actual ignorance that permits resort to service by publication, but the inability to accomplish personal service despite the exercise of reasonable diligence. Plaintiffs argue that their grandson never told them Paula's residence—but did they ask? Paula did not return their calls—but did they, or their agent, ever personally visit Pismo Beach or the Casa Calderon? Did they ever ask Paula when she visited or picked up her son? Did they make any inquiries whatsoever through official channels?

The last factor to be considered is the choice of the Riverside Press-Enterprise for publication. Section 415.50, subdivision (b), requires the use of the "newspaper, published in this state, that is most likely to give actual notice to the party to be served...." Nothing in the affidavit, or in the more detailed facts before the trial court, supported the election of this newspaper. Plaintiffs repeatedly insisted that Paula was no longer in Riverside and admitted only that she received mail in Pismo Beach.

In short, the Olveras' entire showing below utterly fails to establish any diligence whatsoever and no concern for providing actual notice—let alone the high standard required before service by publication may be authorized. (*Sanford v. Smith, supra,* 11 Cal. App. 3d 991, 1001.) "[W]hen notice is a person's due, process which is a mere gesture is not due process. The means employed must be such as one desirous of actually informing the absentee might reasonably adopt to accomplish it." (*Mullane v. Central Hanover Tr. Co.* (1950) 339 U.S. 306, 315 [94 L. Ed. 865, 874, 70 S. Ct. 652].) The Olveras simply stuck their heads in the sand and made no reasonable effort to accomplish personal service or discover Paula's residence for substituted service. As a result, the service by publication was invalid and the judgment could not be sustained.

DISPOSITION

The requests by both sides for sanctions are denied. Plaintiffs shall pay defendant's costs on appeal.

The judgment is affirmed.

---

9. The application was not accompanied by an affidavit establishing the existence of a cause of action in favor of the Olveras, as required by section 415.50, subdivision (a)(1). The complaint, although verified, was no substitute for the required affidavit, and the existence of a cause of action was a jurisdictional prerequisite to the issuance of the order for publication. (*Harris v. Cavasso* (1977) 68 Cal. App. 3d 723, 726 [137 Cal. Rptr. 410].) Although the form application for service by publication contains a form affidavit for this purpose, it was not completed by plaintiffs.

[1] Personal Service

Personal delivery of a copy of the complaint and summons is the preferred manner of service upon defendants within California. CCP § 415.10 (individuals); CCP § 416.10–416.90 (corporations, associations, public entities, guardians).

[2] Substituted Service

[a] On Individuals

As *Bein v. Brechtel-Jochim Group, Inc.*, reproduced *supra*, illustrates, substituted service on an individual defendant is authorized only when process cannot with "reasonable diligence" be personally delivered. CCP § 415.20(b); *see also Earl W. Schott, Inc. v. Kalar*, 20 Cal. App. 4th 943, 24 Cal. Rptr. 2d 580 (1993) (holding failure to comply with due diligence requirements rendered attempted service on individual defendant and subsequent default judgment unenforceable). What constitutes "reasonable diligence" in this context? Two or three attempts at personal service at a proper place? *Compare Espindola v. Nunez*, 199 Cal. App. 3d 1389, 245 Cal. Rptr. 596 (1988) (concluding three unsuccessful attempts to personally serve defendant at home within four days constituted reasonable diligence sufficient to uphold substituted service on defendant's wife at home), *with Evartt v. Superior Court*, 89 Cal. App. 3d 795, 152 Cal. Rptr. 836 (1979) (ruling three unsuccessful attempts within two days to personally serve defendant at home while defendant on short vacation insufficient to uphold substituted service on defendant's housesitter where plaintiff made no attempt to personally serve defendant, a long-time resident, until three days before expiration of three-year period within which plaintiff must effect service).

The *Bien* court's discussion of reasonable diligence has been quoted with approval in recent decisions. *See Stafford v. Mach*, 64 Cal. App. 4th 1174, 1182–83, 75 Cal. Rptr. 2d 809 (1998) (concluding "drop service" on the actual defendant, on the sixth attempt to serve him at his home, was proper where the defendant answered the door but refused to identify himself); *Ellard v. Conway*, 94 Cal. App. 4th 540, 545–47, 114 Cal. Rptr. 2d 399 (2001) (holding substituted service on manager of private postal facility proper where process server attempted to serve defendants at their last known address, was advised by a guard at that address that defendants had moved, and subsequently contacted the U.S. Postal Service and obtained defendants' forwarding address which was a private/commercial post office box facility); *Hearn v. Howard*, 177 Cal. App. 4th 1193, 99 Cal. Rtpr. 3ed 642 (2009) (upholding substituted service on a defendant whose business address was a private post office box rental store where, after three unsuccessful attempts to personally serve the defendant, the complaint and summons were left with the mail store clerk).

Why did the plaintiff in *Bein* mail a copy of the complaint and summons to the defendant Brechtels' residence? Did this mailing, by itself, constitute a proper statutory method of service on these defendants? *See* CCP §§ 415.30, 415.40. Did it constitute valid service as a matter of due process? Was the service by plaintiff Bein on the other individual defendants, the Jochims, proper under CCP § 415.20?

Note that after the decision in *Bein, supra,* the Legislature enacted CCP § 415.21, which provides that a sheriff, marshal, or registered process server, upon proper identification, must be granted access to a gated community for purposes of performing lawful service of process.

[b] On Entities

When the defendant is a corporation, an unincorporated association, or a public entity, attempted personal service on the designated agent or officer is not a prerequisite to substitute service on someone in charge of the office during usual office hours. CCP § 415.20(a); *see Earl W. Schott, Inc. v. Kalar, supra,* 20 Cal. App. 4th at 945 (distinguishing § 415.20(a), applicable to corporations and not requiring due diligence, from § 415.20(b)). Why is a reasonable attempt at personal service a prerequisite to substitute service with respect to individual defendants, but not as to entity defendants? Why did the court in *Bein* discuss "reasonable diligence" with respect to plaintiff Bein's use of § 415.20 substitute service?

[c] Federal Rules

Rules 4(e), F.R.C.P., authorizes substitute service on someone residing at an individual defendant's place of abode as an unqualified alternative to personal service. Likewise, the vast majority of states recognize substituted "abode" service as a primary method of service; only California and a few other states relegate it to a secondary method of service. *See* Philip Craig Starti, Note, *Substituted Service of Process on Individuals: Code of Civil Procedure Section 415.20(b),* 21 HASTINGS L.J. 1257, 1278 (1970) (concluding that the requirement of reasonable diligence in CCP § 415.20(b) unnecessarily restricts use of substituted service without significantly improving the likelihood that the defendant will actually receive notice). What policy considerations support the California view of substituted "abode" service? What ones support the federal or majority rule? *See* Starti, *Substituted Service, supra* at 1274–80.

[d] Unlawful Detainer (Eviction) Actions

Unlawful detainer is a summary proceeding that calls for special procedures for service of process. Accordingly, CCP § 415.45 provides that a summons may be served on an unlawful detainer defendant by posting it on the premises, along with notice sent by certified mail to that address, if the court determines that "the party to be served cannot with reasonable diligence be served in any manner specified in [the service statutes, CCP §§ 415.10–415.95] other than publication." What does "reasonable diligence" mean in this context? *See Board of Tr. of the Leland Stanford Junior Univ. v. Ham,* 216 Cal. App. 4th 330, 156 Cal. Rptr. 3d 893 (2013) (declining to import the extraordinary measures required before publication is permitted and ruling that reasonable diligence in § 415.45 does not require a landlord to conduct an extensive investigation of all the possible whereabouts of its tenant before seeking the posting alternative); *Bank of New York Mellon v. Preciado,* 224 Cal. App. 4th Supp.

1, 8, 169 Cal. Rptr. 3d 653 (App. Div. Sup. Ct. 2013) (noting "post and mail" service under § 415.45 is not authorized as a first-resort method of service).

[3] Publication

As *Olvera v. Olvera*, reproduced *supra*, demonstrates, CCP § 415.50 permits constructive service by publication only where the court is satisfied that the party to be served cannot with "reasonable diligence" be served personally or by substitute service. How would you define this "reasonable diligence" prerequisite in light of the *Olvera* opinion? Is an exhaustive search of the relevant phone book sufficient? *See Donel, Inc. v. Badalian*, 87 Cal. App. 3d 327, 150 Cal. Rptr. 855 (1978); *In re Matthew S.*, 201 Cal. App. 3d 315, 247 Cal. Rptr. 100 (1988). How about several unsuccessful attempts to serve the defendant personally and by mail at an address obtained after an on-line search? *Giorgio v. Synergy Mgmt. Grp.*, 231 Cal. App. 4th 241, 179 Cal. Rptr. 3d 465 (2014).

[a] Reasonable Diligence

The court in *Espindola v. Nunez, supra*, 199 Cal. App. 3d at 1392–93, observed that the "reasonable diligence" showing necessary to uphold an order for service by publication under § 415.50 requires more exhaustive attempts to locate the defendant than is sufficient to uphold substituted service on an individual defendant pursuant to § 415.20(b). Why is the court's observation likely an accurate one?

[b] Proof of Diligence

A plaintiff must not only *exercise* due diligence as a prerequisite for an order of publication, but must also *show* due diligence in the application to the court. CCP § 415.50. In light of *Olvera v. Olvera, supra*, what constitutes a sufficient showing? How must the plaintiff make this showing? Is a detailed declaration by the plaintiff's attorney sufficient? *See Sanford v. Smith*, 11 Cal. App. 3d 991, 90 Cal. Rptr. 256 (1970) (ruling declaration of attorney was hearsay and not adequate to establish due diligence for publication order.).

[c] Due Process

The inability to accomplish service by other methods despite the exercise of reasonable diligence is a constitutional as well as a statutory prerequisite to resort to service by publication. *Mullane v. Central Hanover Bank & Trust Co.*, 339 U.S. 306, 70 S. Ct. 652, 94 L. Ed. 865 (1950). Due process requires "notice reasonably calculated, under all the circumstances, to apprise interested parties of the pendency of action and afford them an opportunity to present their objections." *Mullane*, 339 U. S. at 314. Resort to service by publication is constitutionally permissible in cases where it is not reasonably possible or practicable to give more adequate notice, such as where persons are missing, unknown, or whose interest or whereabouts cannot with due diligence be ascertained. *Id.* at 317–18. "Notice by mail or other means as certain to ensure actual notice is a minimum constitutional precondition to a proceeding which will adversely affect the liberty or property interest of any party ... if its name and address are reasonably ascertainable." *Mennonite Bd. of Missions v. Adams*, 462 U.S. 791, 800, 103 S. Ct. 2706, 77 L. Ed. 2d 180 (1983). Was the service by publication in *Olvera* also invalid on due process grounds?

[d] "Actual Notice"

What constitutes "actual notice" within the meaning of CCP §473.5 in a motion to vacate a default judgment entered after service by publication? Based on the discussion in *Olvera v. Olvera, supra*, does "actual notice" exist in this context only where the defendant has actual knowledge of the summons as the result of reading the published summons in the newspaper? *See Ellard v. Conway*, 94 Cal. App. 4th 540, 114 Cal. Rptr. 2d 399 (2001) (concluding that although actual knowledge from a source other than service of summons does not *preclude* a defendant from seeking relief from a default judgment under CCP §473.5, such knowledge may provide a proper basis for denying such relief where the defendants had actual knowledge of the lawsuit in time to defend the action but failed to file an answer due to inexcusable neglect).

[4] Service By Mail Within California

Code of Civil Procedure §415.30 authorizes a very limited form of service by mail within California. The plaintiff must mail copies of the complaint and summons, along with two copies of the "Notice and Acknowledgment of Receipt of Summons," and a prepaid self-addressed return envelope, to the defendant. CCP §415.30(b) specifies the required form and contents of this "Notice and Acknowledgment." *See also* Form POS-015, Judicial Council Forms. Service is not deemed complete unless the defendant executes and returns the acknowledgment. §415.30(c). Consequently, if the defendant fails to execute or return the acknowledgment form, the plaintiff must serve the defendant in some other proper method. The defendant may, however, be liable for reasonable expenses incurred by plaintiff in serving defendant by another method. §415.30(d). Rule 4(d), F.R.C.P., authorizes a similar method of service by mail within the United States, referred to as a request for waiver of service. In what category of cases is this type of service by mail likely to be effective?

[c] Service in Another State

In re the Marriage of Tusinger

Court of Appeal of California, Second Appellate District
170 Cal. App. 3d 80, 215 Cal. Rptr. 838 (1985)

GILBERT, JUSTICE.

Appellant Gary Tusinger appeals from an order of the superior court denying his motion to quash service of summons and set aside a default judgment. We affirm the order of the trial court which found that appellant had been properly served.

FACTS

Respondent Rebecca Tusinger filed a petition in California to dissolve her marriage to appellant on May 6, 1977. She mailed the summons and petition to appellant's address in Arkansas, and requested a return receipt in accordance with Code of Civil Procedure section 415.40 which provides in pertinent part: "A summons may be served on a person outside this state in any manner provided by this article or by sending a copy of the summons and of the complaint to the person to be served by first-class mail, postage prepaid, requiring a return receipt."

The summons was filed with the court on June 28, 1977, together with the return receipt, signed by appellant's mother, Margaret Tusinger. Respondent ultimately obtained a default judgment, awarding her custody of the minor children, with the issue of support reserved. On November 23, 1977, a final judgment was entered.

Meanwhile, back in Arkansas appellant filed divorce proceedings, effecting service of process by publication. In June of 1978, respondent filed an order to show cause re child and spousal support, and personally served appellant in California when he was visiting the children. Appellant did not appear, and the court granted the relief prayed for by modifying the interlocutory judgment so that respondent was awarded, among other things, child support in the amount of $200 per month per child.

When the district attorney sought to collect child support arrearages in the amount of $23,250, appellant filed his motion to quash service of summons, which was heard on February 10, 1984. The trial court found the service to be proper and denied the motion.

DISCUSSION

Appellant contends that service of the summons and petition was improper because he was not personally served. Although Code of Civil Procedure section 415.40 allows out of state service by mail, he argues, Code of Civil Procedure section 417.20 requires actual delivery to the person to be served.

Code of Civil Procedure section 417.20 provides in pertinent part: "Proof that a summons was served on a person outside this state shall be made: (a) If served in a manner specified in a statute of this state, as prescribed by Section 417.10, and if service is made by mail pursuant to Section 415.40, proof of service shall include evidence satisfactory to the court establishing actual delivery to the person to be served, by a signed return receipt or other evidence; …" Appellant's mother, not appellant, was served.

In addition, appellant argues that Code of Civil Procedure section 416.90, which allows service on an authorized agent, is not applicable because there is no evidence that appellant's mother was an authorized agent.

We agree with respondent that jurisdiction was acquired by mail under Code of Civil Procedure section 415.40 even though appellant's mother signed the return receipt, because "other evidence" demonstrated that appellant received notice. We have taken judicial notice of the superior court file (Evid. Code, § 452, subd. (d)), and in particular, exhibit A to a declaration of respondent's attorney, filed in his op-position to appellant's motion to quash. Exhibit A is a letter dated June 1, 1977, from appellant's attorney in Arkansas. The letter indicates that the attorney represents appellant and begins with the following sentence: "I am writing with reference to the divorce petition which Gary Tusinger received a few days ago and which was ini-tiated by his wife."

The trial judge, in his well-reasoned ruling on the motion, considered this letter as sufficient "other evidence" under the statute. The court came to the obvious con-clusion that sometime between May 23, 1977, and June 1, 1977, appellant took the summons and petition to his attorney who wrote to respondent's attorney. Nowhere in the record does appellant contradict this. Rather, he states in his declaration that he has "never seen the summons and petition in the California proceeding which this case is based upon." How could this be so unless appellant closed his eyes while he secreted the summons and petition in a plain paper bag, which he then delivered to his attorney? This seems unlikely, and we understand why appellant's bald assertion strained the trial judge's credulity.

"Other evidence" in Code of Civil Procedure section 417.20, means that a return receipt signed by a person being served out of state is not the only evidence to establish proof of service. The "other evidence" here was more than sufficient to satisfy the court that the summons and petition were served on appellant. * * *

The order of the trial court is affirmed.

[1] Service Options

A plaintiff has many options when required to serve a defendant located in an-other state. As *Marriage of Tusinger*, reproduced *supra*, indicates, CCP § 415.40 authorizes service of process on a defendant in another state in any manner pro-vided by in the Jurisdiction and Service of Process Act for instate service, plus service by mail. Additionally, CCP § 413.10(b) authorizes service in another state in accordance with the law of the state where the defendant is to be served. Are some of these service alternatives preferred over others, from a statutory or due process perspective? For example, must a plaintiff pursue personal service when available, as opposed to service by mail under § 415.40? *See M. Lowenstein & Sons, Inc. v. Superior Court*, 80 Cal. App. 3d 762, 145 Cal. Rptr. 814 (1978) (holding there is no constitutional requirement that personal service on out-of-state defen-dant is indispensable when practical).

Is service by publication proper where the plaintiff knew the nonresident defendant's post office box address, but could not ascertain defendant's residence or business ad-dress? *See Transamerica Title Ins. Co. v. Hendrix*, 34 Cal. App. 4th 740, 40 Cal. Rptr. 2d 614 (1995) (holding plaintiff's failure to attempt service by mail pursuant to CCP § 415.30 at a nonresident defendant's P.O. box prior to application for an order for publication made the application motion defective as a matter of law).

[2]"Other Evidence"

CCP §415.40 and §417.20(a) authorize service by mail on a person in another state when actual delivery is established by signed return receipt or by "other evidence." What are some examples of sufficient "other evidence"?

[a] *Taylor-Rush v. Multitech Corp.*, 217 Cal. App. 3d 103, 265 Cal. Rptr. 672 (1990)

The plaintiff in *Taylor-Rush* attempted service by mail pursuant to §415.40 on defendant Cohen, a resident of New York. In upholding an order quashing service, the court found the evidence of actual delivery insufficient:

> The record contains a return receipt addressed to Cohen at "425 East 58th St., *Apt. 4-D*, New York, N.Y. 10022" (italics added) and is signed by two persons other than Cohen. One signature is in the box marked "Addressee" and the other signature is in the box marked "Agent." There is no evidence who these signators are or their relationship, if any, to Cohen. Cohen's declaration states that he has never been served with the summons and complaint or the amended complaint. Although the street address reflected on the return receipt is correct, he resides in *apartment 15A*, not apartment 4-D. He has not authorized anyone, other than his wife, to accept mail on his behalf, and does not know who signed the return receipt. * * *

> The plaintiff has the burden of demonstrating by a preponderance of the evidence that all jurisdictional criteria [of CCP §415.40 and §417.20(a)] are met. (*Ziller Electronics Lab GmbH v. Superior Court* (1988) 206 Cal. App. 3d 1222, 1232–33 [254 Cal. Rptr. 410].)

> While a return receipt signed by someone authorized by a nonresident defendant to sign for his mail is sufficient, the plaintiff must provide separate evidence establishing the authority of the person who signed the return receipt on defendant's behalf. (*Neadeau v. Foster* (1982) 129 Cal. App. 3d 234, 237–38 [180 Cal. Rptr. 806].) Other evidence of actual receipt may also validate the otherwise defective service, such as where a defendant's attorney acknowledges the defendant's receipt of the summons (*In re Marriage of Tusinger* (1985) 170 Cal. App. 3d 80, 82–83 [215 Cal. Rptr. 838].) Here, however, no such evidence has been presented.

> Appellant argues that Cohen obviously received both the complaint and its amendment since he refers in his declaration to matters "alleged in the first amended complaint." She also contends other pleadings and motion papers were similarly addressed and never returned. Such contentions are without merit. A defendant is under no duty to respond to a defectively served summons. The notice requirement is not satisfied by actual knowledge of the action without service conforming to the statutory requirements, which are to be strictly construed. (*Kappel v. Bartlett* (1988) 200 Cal. App. 3d 1457,

1466–67 [246 Cal. Rptr. 815].) Due to the defective service on Cohen, no jurisdiction was acquired over him.

Why was the defendant's declaration referring to the complaint insufficient "other evidence" in *Taylor-Rush*? How was that declaration different from the attorney's declaration found sufficient "other evidence" in *Tusinger*? Why was the service by mail defective in *Taylor-Rush*, but not in *Tusinger*? Are these two cases distinguishable? How?

[b] *Dill v. Berquist Construction Co.*, 24 Cal. App. 4th 1426, 29 Cal. Rptr. 2d 746 (1994)

The plaintiff in *Dill* attempted service by mail on two nonresident defendant corporations pursuant to CCP § 415.40 and § 416.10. The plaintiff did not mail the complaint and summons to one of the corporate officers specified to receive service in CCP § 416.10, but instead mailed them directly to the corporate defendants. With respect to each mailing, a postal receipt was returned to plaintiff indicating that some employee of the corporation had signed and acknowledged delivery.

The court held that the service was invalid because the plaintiff did not mail the complaint and summons to one of the corporate individuals specified in § 416.10. *Id.* at 1436. The court recognized that substantial compliance with the statutory requirements for service of process, not strict compliance, was required, and endorsed *In re Marriage of Tusinger* as a proper application of the substantial compliance doctrine. However, the court ruled that plaintiff Dill, unlike the plaintiff in *Tusinger*, had not demonstrated that the summons was actually received by one of the persons to be served. The fact that the summons actually reached *some* employees of the defendant corporations was insufficient to establish substantial compliance; the plaintiff must demonstrate that the summons actually reached one of the corporate individuals specified in § 416.10 to accept service for the corporation. *Id.* at 1435–36.

Was compliance with the statutory service requirements in *Dill* any less substantial than in *Tusinger*? Was not the complaint and summons in *Dill* actually delivered to each corporate defendant in much the same manner as in *Tusinger*? Can these two cases be distinguished solely on the ground that the *Dill* defendants were nonresident corporations and the *Tusinger* defendant was an individual? Or are there other grounds to distinguish these two cases?

[c] *Cruz v. Fagor America, Inc.*, 146 Cal. App. 4th 488, 52 Cal. Rptr. 3d 862 (2007)

The plaintiff in *Cruz* attempted to serve the out-of-state defendant corporation by mail pursuant to CCP § 415.40 and § 416.10. The plaintiff properly addressed and mailed the complaint and summons, return receipt requested, to the defendant's president. The return receipt was signed by an individual who was not the corporation's president. The defendant's president never actually received the complaint and summons. After a default judgment was entered for the plaintiff, the defendant corporation contested the validity of the service. The plaintiff submitted a declaration of his attorney attesting that the attorney had received confirmation from a representative of the U.S. Postal Service that the individual who signed the return receipt was an employee of the defendant corporation who regularly received mail on the corporation's behalf.

The *Cruz* court found this evidence sufficient to establish that an agent authorized to receive mail on the defendant's behalf received the complaint and summons, and concluded the plaintiff had met all the statutory requirements for effective service on a nonresident corporation. The *Cruz* court distinguished *Dill v. Berquist Construction Co., supra*, because the plaintiff in *Dill* had not complied with the statutory requirements for service on a corporation under CCP § 416.10. Instead of mailing the complaint and summons to one of the corporate officers specified to receive service in § 416.10, the plaintiff in *Dill* improperly mailed them directly to the defendant corporation. The *Cruz* court also distinguished *Taylor-Rush v. Multitech Corp., supra*, as a case where the plaintiff mailed the complaint and summons to the proper defendant but at an incorrect apartment number, and there was no evidence in *Taylor-Rush* as to who the signators were or what the nature of their relationship to the defendant was, if any.

Did the *Cruz* court properly distinguish *Dill* and *Taylor-Rush*? Is *Cruz* really a case of a plaintiff submitting "other evidence" to prove actual delivery of the complaint and summons?

[3] *Service by Mail*

How is the service by mail on a person in another state authorized by § 415.40 different from the service by mail within California authorized by § 415.30? What policy considerations likely caused the Legislature to authorize more limited service by mail for in-state defendants than for out-of-state defendants? Does due process require this difference in treatment?

[4] *Due Process and Service by Mail*

Does due process require proof of actual delivery by a signed return receipt or some other evidence for valid service by mail? Does due process permit California to utilize a service-by-mail statute which only requires proof of mailing, and not proof of actual delivery? *See Mennonite Board of Missions v. Adams*, 462 U.S. 791, 103 S. Ct. 2706, 77 L. Ed. 2d 180 (1983) (ruling notice mailed to defendant's last known address is constitutional minimum in tax lien foreclosure case); *Mullane v. Central Hanover Bank & Trust Co.*, 339 U.S. 306, 70 S. Ct. 652, 94 L. Ed. 865 (1950) (holding service by mail constituted reasonable notice to large class of nonresident trust beneficiaries with identical shared interests, even though such service may not reach each individual beneficiary). If constitutionally permissible, why did the Legislature require proof of actual delivery when it enacted CCP § 415.30 and § 417.20(a)?

[5] *Substituted Service on Agent Within California*

In a wide variety of situations, California statutes authorize substituted service on a designated agent of the defendant within California.

[a] Corporations and Other Entities

Corporations, partnerships, and other entities doing business in California must designate an agent for service of process within the state. *E.g.*, Corp. Code §§ 1502–1505, 2105, 2107, 1701–1702, 2110–2111, 6210–6211, and 8210–8212 (various domestic and foreign corporations); § 15800 (partnerships); Insurance Code §§ 1600–1605 (insurance companies); CCP §§ 416.10–416.40. If no such agent for service of process is designated by the entity, substitute service may be made upon the California Secretary of State or other appropriate governmental agent. *E.g.*, Corp. Code §§ 1702, 2111, 15800(b). For a more complete list of statutes which authorize such substitute service on a governmental official, see Schwing, *California Affirmative Defenses, Lack of Proper or Effective Service* § 2.8, pp. 91–98 (2015).

[b] Contract

The parties to a contract may agree to designate an agent for service of process within the state. CCP § 416.90; *see National Equipment Rental, Ltd. v. Szukhent*, 375 U.S. 311, 84 S. Ct. 411, 11 L. Ed. 2d 354 (1964) (holding service on contractually appointed agent constitutionally adequate under due process).

[c] Implied Agent

Vehicle Code § 17451 provides that ownership or operation of a motor vehicle within California by a nonresident is the equivalent to an appointment of the Director of the Department of Motor Vehicles as agent for service of process in any action arising from an accident resulting from operation of the motor vehicle in California. If the plaintiff serves process on the Director pursuant to this section, the plaintiff must also mail a copy to the defendant. Veh. Code §§ 17454, 17455.

Does such service also confer personal jurisdiction over a nonresident defendant vehicle owner based on the concept of transient jurisdiction? A California court will be able to assert personal jurisdiction over a nonresident defendant vehicle operator consistent with due process in a damage action for injuries arising out of an accident in California, without relying on transient jurisdiction. Why? Is substitute service on an implied governmental agent constitutionally adequate notice as a matter of due process?

[d] Alternative Methods

Substituted service on a designated or implied agent is alternative to, not exclusive of, the other statutorily authorized methods of service on a defendant. *M. Lowenstein & Sons, Inc. v. Superior Court*, 80 Cal. App. 3d 762, 145 Cal. Rptr. 814 (1978) (concluding a plaintiff serving a nonresident corporation may serve designated agent pursuant to CCP § 416.10 or, alternatively, may serve by mail pursuant to CCP § 415.40); *Anderson v. Sherman*, 125 Cal. App. 3d 228, 235–37, 178 Cal. Rptr. 38 (1981) (ruling injured California resident may serve nonresident motorist pursuant to Veh. Code §§ 17454 & 17455, or CCP § 415.40).

[D] Service Outside the United States

[1] International Service Agreements

The United States has ratified two multilateral international agreements which govern service of process among signatory countries.

[a] Hague Service Convention

In 1969, the United States ratified the Hague Service Convention, which now includes such other signatories as Canada, Japan, the Peoples' Republic of China, the United Kingdom, Germany, and most of the other European countries. *See* 20 U.S.T. 361–73, T.I.A.S. No. 6638, 658 U.N.T.S. 163. For the text of this convention, and a complete list of all signatory countries, see the United States Code Annotated sections following Rule 4, F.R.C.P.

Articles 2–9 and 19 of the Hague Service Convention authorize uniform procedures for extraterritorial service of judicial documents through a Central Authority designated by each country, through diplomatic channels, or by any method permitted by the internal law of the country where the service is to be made.

Article 10 authorizes additional extraterritorial service methods, including direct service by mail; but only if the receiving country has ratified and not objected to these alternative methods. Consequently, a determination of the availability of these alternative methods requires an examination of the receiving country's accession to the Convention, as set forth in each country's "Declarations" concerning the Hague Service Convention. These Declarations are reprinted in the United States Code Annotated sections following Rule 4, F.R.C.P. The Declarations must also be consulted to determine each signatory country's requirements with respect to translation of documents to be served.

The U.S. Supreme Court in *Volkswagenwerk AG v. Schlunk*, 486 U.S. 694, 699, 108 S. Ct. 2104, 100 L. Ed. 2d 722 (1988), indicated in dicta that, by virtue of the Supremacy Clause, the Hague Service Convention preempts inconsistent methods of service prescribed by state law in all cases to which the Convention applies. CCP § 413.10(c) requires the same deference to the Convention in the California courts, as does Rule 4(f), F.R.C.P., in the federal courts. In *Yamaha Motor Co., Ltd. v. Superior Court*, 174 Cal. App. 4th 264, 94 Cal. Rptr. 3d 494 (2009), the plaintiff in a products liability action served the defendant manufacturer, a Japanese corporation, through its American subsidiary's agent for service of process. Applying the holding in *Volkswagenwerk AG v. Schlunk*, *supra*, a decision with almost identical facts, the *Yamaha* court held that the Hague Service Convention's provisions were not implicated because California law provides for service of process on a foreign corporation by serving its domestic subsidiary as agent and does not necessarily require transmittal of the relevant documents for service abroad. *See also Kott v. Superior Court*, 45 Cal. App. 4th 1126, 53 Cal. Rptr. 2d 215 (1996) (concluding service on a Canadian resident by publication in a Los Angeles newspaper did not implicate the Hague Service Convention because such service does not require the transmission of documents outside the United States); *Buchanan v. Soto*, 241 Cal. App. 4th 1353, 1366–68, 194 Cal. Rptr. 3d 663 (2015) (ruling service by publication on Mexican defendant was proper—defendant's address not known and plaintiff made reasonable, good faith, and diligent efforts to locate him; Hague Service Convention service requirements inapplicable to situations in which defendant's whereabouts cannot be ascertained despite reasonable diligence).

For an excellent discussion of the Hague Service Convention, with analysis of the disagreement among the courts over the proper construction of Article 10, see *Honda Motor Co. v. Superior Court*, 10 Cal. App. 4th 1043, 12 Cal. Rptr. 2d 861 (1992) (ruling Japan's failure to object to Article 10(a), which protects "the freedom to send judicial documents, by postal channels, directly to persons abroad," did not authorize service of process by a private litigant on a corporation in Japan by means of certified mail) and *Denlinger v. Chinadotcom Corp.*, 110 Cal. App. 4th 1396, 2 Cal. Rptr. 3d 530 (2003) (holding Article 10(a) of Hague Convention authorizes service of process by mail and therefore service by registered mail on defendants in Hong Kong was proper since China has not objected to Article 10(a) in its declarations with respect to Hong Kong).

For commentary and analysis of the Hague Service Convention, see David Epstein & Jeffrey L. Snyder, *International Litigation: A Guide to Jurisdiction, Practice and Strategy*, §§ 4.01–4.05 (4th rev. ed. 2010); Leonard A. Leo, Note, *The Interplay Between Domestic Rules Permitting Service Abroad by Mail and the Hague Convention on Service: Proposing an Amendment to the Federal Rules of Civil Procedure*, 22 CORNELL INT'L L.J. 335 (1989); Pamela R. Parmalee, Note, *International Service of Process: A Guide to Serving Process Abroad Under the Hague Convention*, 39 OKLA. L. REV. 287 (1986).

[b] Inter-American Convention

The United States ratified the Inter-American Convention on Letters Rogatory in 1986. This Convention, which includes Argentina, Guatemala, Mexico, Paraguay, Peru, the United States, and Uruguay among its signatories, authorizes international service of process by methods very similar to those of the Hague Service Convention. This Convention is reprinted in 14 INT'L LEG. MAT. 339 (1975), with additional Protocol reprinted in 18 INT'L LEG. MAT. 1238 (1979). For commentary on the Inter-American Convention, see Lucinda A. Low, *International Judicial Assistance among the American States—The Inter-American Conventions*, 18 INT'L LAW. 705 (1984); Richard D. Kearney, *Developments in Private International Law*, 81 AM. J. INT'L LAW 724 (1987) (comparing Inter-American Convention and Hague Service Convention).

[2] *Service When No Treaty Applies*

How should extraterritorial service of process be accomplished in another country when no international service treaty applies? *See* CCP § 413.10(c); Rule 4(f), F.R.C.P.

[E]   Procedures for Asserting Lack of Proper Service

[1]   Motion to Quash

A challenge to the validity of service of process must be made by filing a motion to quash on or before the last day to plead in response to the complaint. CCP § 418.10(a) & (b). Pursuant to a 2003 amendment to § 418.10, the defendant need not raise the objection by a special appearance, but may simultaneously answer, demur, or move to strike, so long as the objection is raised in defendant's first appearance. *See* CCP § 418.10 (e). If the defendant makes a general appearance, as defined in CCP § 1014, *before* filing a motion to quash objecting to lack of proper service, the defendant waives his right to contest the validity of the service. *See* CCP § 418.10(e)(3); *Fireman's Fund Ins. Co. v. Sparks Constr., Inc.*, 114 Cal. App. 4th 1135, 8 Cal. Rptr. 3d 446 (2004) (holding a defendant who makes a general appearance forfeits any objection to defective service, even when the defendant does not know at the time that such an objection is available).

When a defendant properly moves to quash service of process, the burden is on the plaintiff to prove the facts establishing valid service. *Dill v. Berquist Constr. Co.*, 24 Cal. App. 4th 1426, 1441–43, 29 Cal. Rptr. 2d 746 (1994); *Taylor-Rush v. Multitech Corp., supra*; 217 Cal. App. 3d at 110–111; *Kroopf v. Guffey*, 183 Cal. App. 3d 1351, 1356, 228 Cal. Rptr. 807 (1980). The return of a process server registered pursuant to § 22350 *et seq.* of the Business and Professions Code, however, establishes a presumption, affecting the burden of producing evidence, of the truth of the facts stated in the return. Evidence Code § 647. This presumption arises, however, only if the proof of service complies with the statutory requirements regarding such proofs. *See Dill*, supra, 24 Cal. App. 4th at 1441–42 (ruling proof of service which showed that complaint was mailed to wrong corporate officer raised no presumption of proper service).

If a motion to quash is granted, the service is quashed but the action is not dismissed. The plaintiff may attempt to perfect the court's jurisdiction by obtaining valid service, subject to applicable time limits for service such as those of CCP §§ 583.210–583.250. *Roberts v. Home Ins. Indem. Co.*, 48 Cal. App. 3d 313, 317, 121 Cal. Rptr. 862 (1975). If a motion to quash is denied, the defendant may obtain immediate appellate review by a writ of mandate. CCP § 418.10(c). If the motion is granted, the plaintiff has the right to appeal the order. CCP § 904.1(a)(3). Under what circumstances would a plaintiff appeal an order quashing service rather than simply re-serve the defendant?

The federal procedures for asserting insufficiency of process or service of process are the same as for asserting lack of personal jurisdiction. Rule 12(b), (g), and (h), F.R.C.P. Generally, the defendant must assert these defenses in the first appearance in federal court, either by motion to dismiss or in the answer, or the defenses are waived. Rule 12(h). However, a timely raised defense is not waived if combined with another motion, or if stated in the answer. Rule 12(b), (b)(4), (b)(5), & (g).

[2]   Time Limits on Service of Process

[a]   Mandatory Dismissal

The complaint and summons must be served upon a defendant within three years after the action is commenced against the defendant. CCP §§ 583.210(a), 583.110. Return of summons or other proof of service must be made within 60 days after this required time for service of the summons and complaint. CCP § 583.210(b). These time-for-service requirements do not apply if the defendant enters into a written stipulation or does some other act which constitutes a general appearance. CCP § 583.220. Other exceptions and time exclusions are set forth in CCP § 583.230 and § 583.240. Failure to serve within the prescribed time will result in mandatory dismissal of the action. CCP § 583.250; *see, e.g., Perez v. Smith*, 19 Cal. App. 4th 1595, 24 Cal. Rptr. 2d 186 (1993) (ruling action must be dismissed if complaint and summons not served within three years unless plaintiff can demonstrate defendant was not amenable to process during some portion of this period). These time-for-service rules and exceptions are discussed in more detail in § 12.03, Involuntary Dismissals, *infra*.

[b]   Discretionary Dismissal

Service not made within two years after the action is commenced against the defendant may result in discretionary dismissal for delay in prosecution pursuant to CCP §§ 583.410, 583.420(a)(1); Rule 3.1342(e), Cal. Rules of Ct. *See, e.g., Williams v. Los Angeles Unified Sch. Dist.*, 23 Cal. App. 4th 84, 28 Cal. Rptr. 2d 219 (1994) (discussing factors relevant to dismissal determination).

[c]   Court Rules

State and local fast track rules require service of the complaint on all named defendants, and proofs of service filed, within 60 days after the filing of the complaint, unless the court orders an extension of time. *E.g.*, Rule 3.110(b) & (e), Cal. Rules of Ct; San Diego Superior Court Rule 2.1.5.

[3]   Summons

The form and content requirements for a valid summons are specified in CCP § 412.20, as reflected in the Judicial Council approved summons form. Judicial Council Form SUM-100. Specific statutes may require additional or different information in the summons for particular causes of action, such as unlawful detainer, CCP § 1167, Judicial Council Form SUM-130; family law actions, Rule 5.25, Form FL-110; actions against a corporation, association, or partnership, CCP § 412.30; condemnation, CCP §§ 1250.120(b), 1250.125; and fictitious defendants, CCP § 474.

[4]   Process Servers

A summons and complaint may be served by any person who is at least 18 years of age and not a party to the action. CCP § 414.10. Consequently, although state laws also authorize a sheriff (Gov. Code § 26608), marshall (Gov. Code § 26665), or registered process server (Business and Professional Code §§ 22350–22358) to serve the complaint and summons; the plaintiff has the option to select any adult individual to serve these documents. What are the relative advantages and disadvantages of selecting the sheriff to serve process? *See* Gov. Code § 26662. A registered process server? *See* Bus. & Prof. Code §§ 22353 and 22357; CCP § 413.40; Evid. Code § 647. An attorney? *See Caldwell v. Coppola*, 219 Cal. App. 3d 859, 865, 268 Cal. Rptr. 453 (1990). Some other individual?

[5] Proof of Service

After a summons has been served, the summons must be returned together with proof of service as defined in CCP § 417.10 and § 417.20. CCP § 417.30(a); see Judicial Council Form POS-010. Actual service of process, rather than proof of service, vests a court with jurisdiction to act in a matter. *Oats v. Oats*, 148 Cal. App. 3d 416, 420, 196 Cal. Rptr. 20 (1983); *Willen v. Boggs*, 21 Cal. App. 3d 520, 523–24, 97 Cal. Rptr. 917 (1971). Proof and return of service, however, must be made within the required time limits of CCP § 583.210 to avoid mandatory dismissal. *Johnson & Johnson v. Superior Court*, 38 Cal. 3d 243, 211 Cal. Rptr. 517, 695 P.2d 1058 (1985); *Bishop v. Silva*, 234 Cal. App. 3d 1317, 285 Cal. Rptr. 910 (1991). What other purposes do return and proof of service serve? *See Johnson & Johnson, supra*, 38 Cal. 3d at 247–56; *Olvera v. Olvera*, reproduced *supra*; *Marriage of Tusinger*, reproduced *supra*.

[6] Special Service Statutes

Numerous specific statutes require or authorize service of process in a manner different from, or in addition to, that of the general service statutes for particular causes of action. Such special service statutes apply, for example, to tort actions against the State, Gov. Code §§ 955.4, 955.6–.8, or against a public agency, Gov. Code §§ 960.2–.8, CCP § 416.50; quiet title actions, CCP § 763.010–.030; condemnation actions, CCP § 1250.130 &.140; unlawful detainer actions, CCP §§ 415.45–.47; and parents' action on behalf of an injured child, CCP § 376. For a more complete list of these special manner of service statutes, see Schwing, *California Affirmative Defenses, Lack of Proper or Effective Service* § 2.2 (2015).

[7] Federal Incorporation of State Laws

Federal Rule 4, F.R.C.P., authorizes a variety of options for service of process in the federal courts. Some of the more important differences between the Federal and California service rules were already noted, *supra*. The federal service rules, however, also incorporate state law. Rule 4(e)(1) provides that, unless otherwise required by federal law, service upon an individual in a judicial district of the United States may be made by "following state law for serving a summons in an action brought in the courts of general jurisdiction in the state where the district court is located or where service is made." Rule 4(h)(1) authorizes a similar state law option for service on a corporation, partnership, or other unincorporated association.

§ 6.05 Forum Non Conveniens

[A]   Relevant Factors Under the California Doctrine

Stangvik v. Shiley Incorporated

Supreme Court of California
54 Cal. 3d 744, 1 Cal. Rptr. 2d 556, 819 P.2d 14 (1991)

MOSK, JUSTICE.

In this case we address the question of the appropriate standards to be applied in deciding whether a trial court should grant a motion based on the doctrine of forum non conveniens when the plaintiff, a resident of a foreign country, seeks to bring suit against a California corporation in the courts of this state. * * *

Plaintiffs, members of two families, one residing in Norway and the other in Sweden, are the wives and children of two men who received heart valve implants in the countries of their residence. The valves were designed and manufactured in California by defendant Shiley Incorporated (Shiley), a California corporation. In both cases, the valves allegedly failed, and the patients died. Thereafter, plaintiffs filed suit in California against Shiley and its parent company, a Delaware corporation (hereinafter defendants), alleging that the valves were defective. They sought damages based on theories of negligence, strict liability, breach of warranty, fraud, and loss of consortium. One of the complaints also sought recovery for negligent infliction of emotional distress.

Defendants moved to dismiss or stay the actions on the ground of forum non conveniens, as authorized by section 410.30 of the Code of Civil Procedure.[1] They asserted that the cases should be tried in Sweden and Norway because it was in those countries that the plaintiffs resided, the valves were sold, decedents received medical care, the alleged fraudulent representations were made, and evidence regarding the provision of health care and other matters existed. Plaintiffs countered that California was the more convenient place of trial because the valves were designed, manufactured, tested and packaged in California. The parties introduced conflicting evidence regarding plaintiffs' legal rights and remedies in Scandinavia, and each claimed that the most important and numerous documents and witnesses were located in the country which they asserted was the most appropriate place for trial. The trial court found in favor of defendants, concluding that California was an inconvenient forum and that Sweden and Norway provided adequate alternative forums for resolution of the actions. It stayed the actions, and retained jurisdiction to make such further orders as might

---

1. Section 410.30 of the Code of Civil Procedure provides in relevant part, "when a court upon motion of a party or its own motion finds that in the interest of substantial justice an action should be heard in a forum outside this state, the court shall stay or dismiss the action in whole or in part on any conditions that may be just." All further statutory references are to the Code of Civil Procedure.

become appropriate. The order was subject to seven conditions, with which defendants agreed to comply.[2]

The Court of Appeal affirmed, after discussing the various private and public interest factors relevant to a determination of the appropriate forum for the trial of an action under the doctrine of forum non conveniens. * * *

Plaintiffs claim that the convenience of the parties and public policy would be best served if the actions were tried in California, and that the Court of Appeal distorted the analysis of these factors in upholding the trial court's decision. They assert also that the appellate court failed to analyze or give weight to certain matters which prior California decisions have held are relevant to a determination of a forum non conveniens motion. We conclude that the Court of Appeal correctly decided the case and affirm its judgment.

Forum non conveniens is an equitable doctrine invoking the discretionary power of a court to decline to exercise the jurisdiction it has over a transitory cause of action when it believes that the action may be more appropriately and justly tried elsewhere. The doctrine was first applied in California in *Price v. Atchison, T. & S. F. Ry. Co.* (1954) 42 Cal. 2d 577 [268 P.2d 457, 43 A.L.R.2d 756] (hereafter *Price*). * * *

In determining whether to grant a motion based on forum non conveniens, a court must first determine whether the alternate forum is a "suitable" place for trial. If it is, the next step is to consider the private interests of the litigants and the interests of the public in retaining the action for trial in California. The private interest factors are those that make trial and the enforceability of the ensuing judgment expeditious and relatively inexpensive, such as the ease of access to sources of proof, the cost of obtaining attendance of witnesses, and the availability of compulsory process for attendance of unwilling witnesses. The public interest factors include avoidance of overburdening local courts with congested calendars, protecting the interests of potential jurors so that they are not called upon to decide cases in which the local community has little concern, and weighing the competing interests of California and the alternate jurisdiction in the litigation. (*Piper Aircraft Co. v. Reyno* (1981) 454 U.S. 235, 259–261 [70 L. Ed. 2d 419, 437–439, 102 S. Ct. 252] (hereafter *Piper*); *Gulf Oil Corp. v. Gilbert* (1947) 330 U.S. 501, 507–509 [91 L. Ed. 1055, 1061–1063, 67 S. Ct. 839].)

On a motion for forum non conveniens, the defendant, as the moving party, bears the burden of proof. The granting or denial of such a motion is within the trial court's discretion, and substantial deference is accorded its determination in this regard.

---

2. The conditions were: (1) submission to jurisdiction in Sweden and Norway; (2) compliance with discovery orders of the Scandinavian courts; (3) agreement to make past and present employees reasonably available to testify in Sweden and Norway at defendants' cost if so ordered within the discretion of Scandinavian courts; (4) tolling of the statute of limitations during the pendency of the actions in California; (5) agreement to make documents in their possession in the United States available for inspection in Sweden and Norway, as required by Scandinavian law, at defendants' expense; (6) agreement that depositions in the United States might proceed under section 2029; and (7) agreement to pay any final judgments rendered in the Scandinavian actions.

(*Piper, supra,* 454 U.S. at p. 257 [70 L. Ed. 2d at pp. 436–437]; *Credit Lyonnais Bank Nederland, N.V. v. Manatt, Phelps, Rothenberg & Tunney* (1988) 202 Cal. App. 3d 1424, 1436 [249 Cal. Rptr. 559].)

On the first of these issues, whether the case may be "suitably" tried in Norway and Sweden, the answer is clear. * * * Defendants stipulated that they would submit to jurisdiction in Sweden or Norway, respectively, as well as to the tolling of the statute of limitations during the pendency of the actions in California. Thus, the courts of Sweden and Norway present suitable forums for trial of the actions.

We proceed, then, to the second and more difficult question, whether the Court of Appeal erred in concluding that the balance of the private and public interests justified a stay of the actions. The court relied heavily on *Piper, supra,* 454 U.S. 235, in reaching its decision. *Piper,* like the present case, involved foreign plaintiffs who sought to hold an American manufacturer liable for deaths which occurred in a foreign country. There, an airplane built by the defendant in Pennsylvania, crashed in Scotland, killing several residents of that country. The representative of the decedents' estates filed a wrongful death action in federal district court, alleging negligence and strict liability. The district court in Pennsylvania granted a motion by defendants on the ground of forum non conveniens, concluding that Scotland was the appropriate forum for trial of the action. The circuit court reversed the judgment because Scottish law was less favorable to the plaintiffs than the law of Pennsylvania.

This decision was in turn reversed by the Supreme Court, in an opinion which discussed the factors to be considered in determining a forum non conveniens motion. The high court, in its analysis of the doctrine, reiterated long-standing principles, first clearly enunciated by it in *Gulf Oil Corp. v. Gilbert, supra,* 330 U.S. 501, and later applied in California in *Price, supra,* 42 Cal. 2d 577. The court warned that the private and public interest factors must be applied flexibly, without giving undue emphasis to any one element. A court should not decide that there are circumstances in which the doctrine will always apply or never apply. Otherwise, the flexibility of the doctrine would be threatened, and its application would be based on identification of a single factor rather than the balancing of several. (*Piper, supra,* 454 U.S. at pp. 249–250 [70 L. Ed. 2d at pp. 431–432].)[4] The high court recognized that there is "ordinarily a strong presumption in favor of the plaintiff's choice of forum" (*id.* at p. 255 [70 L. Ed. 2d at p. 435]), but held that a foreign plaintiff's choice deserves less deference than the choice of a resident.

The high court discussed in some detail the significance to be accorded to the fact that the law of the forum state is more favorable to the plaintiff than that of the alternate jurisdiction. In this connection, it observed that the laws of the United States in product

---

4. An undue emphasis on a single factor is especially threatening to a balanced analysis because some of the matters to be weighed will by their nature point to a grant or denial of the motion. For example, the jurisdiction's interest in deterring future wrongful conduct of the defendant will usually favor retention of the action if the defendant is a resident of the forum, whereas the court congestion factor will usually weigh in favor of trial in the alternate jurisdiction.

liability actions favor plaintiffs in several respects: the law of strict liability, which exists in almost all 50 states but only a handful of foreign countries; the existence of jury trials in such actions, resulting in sometimes generous awards, contingent attorney fee arrangements, and more liberal rules of discovery. It held that if substantial weight is given to the circumstance that the law in the forum state is more favorable to the plaintiff than the one in the alternate jurisdiction, "The American courts, which are already extremely attractive to foreign plaintiffs, would become even more attractive. The flow of litigation into the United States would increase and further congest already crowded courts. [Fn. omitted.]" (*Piper, supra*, 454 U.S. at p. 252 [70 L. Ed. 2d at p. 433].) Thus, the possibility of an unfavorable change in the law is a "relevant consideration" only if the remedy in the alternative forum "is so clearly inadequate or unsatisfactory that it is no remedy at all...." (*Id.* at p. 254 [70 L. Ed. 2d at p. 435].)[5]

After analyzing the interests of the parties and of Scotland in the litigation, the court concluded that "the incremental deterrence that would be gained if this trial were held in an American court is likely to be insignificant. The American interest in this accident is simply not sufficient to justify the enormous commitment of judicial time and resources that would inevitably be required if the case were to be tried here." (*Piper, supra*, 454 U.S. at pp. 260–261 [70 L. Ed. 2d at pp. 438–439].)[6]

In the present case, the trial court found that Sweden and Norway were adequate alternative forums. Defendants produced evidence that Norway and Sweden might permit recovery under a strict liability theory, that Norway might allow special damages (but not punitive damages) in some circumstances, and that the actions could be pursued in those countries without undue delay. Although some of this evidence was contradicted by plaintiffs, the trial court's determination of these issues is supported by substantial evidence, and we defer to its conclusion. Thus, the fact that California law would likely provide plaintiffs with certain advantages of procedural

---

5. It is not entirely clear from the language of *Piper* whether an unfavorable change of law should be given no consideration whatsoever in the forum non conveniens balance or only slight consideration. The high court states in various parts of its opinion that this factor should not be given "substantial weight" (*e.g., Piper, supra*, 454 U.S. at pp. 247, 250 [70 L. Ed. 2d at pp. 430, 432]), but in another passage it states that an unfavorable change in the law might in some circumstances be a "relevant consideration." (*Id.* at p. 254 [70 L. Ed. 2d at p. 435].) The first of these references indicates that a slight amount of weight may be accorded to an unfavorable change in the law, whereas the second implies the contrary. In our view, the fact that an alternative jurisdiction's law is less favorable to a litigant than the law of the forum should not be accorded any weight in deciding a motion for forum non conveniens provided, however, that some remedy is afforded. (*See, e.g., Lockman Found. v. Evangelical Alliance Mission* (9th Cir. 1991) 930 F.2d 764, 768–769, and cases cited.) One basis underlying the doctrine, as *Piper* and other cases hold, is to avoid burdening the trial court by requiring it to interpret the law of foreign jurisdictions, which compels it to conduct "complex exercises in comparative law." (*Piper, supra*, at p. 251 [70 L. Ed. 2d at p. 433]; *see also, e.g., Gulf Oil Corp. v. Gilbert, supra*, 330 U.S. at p. 509 [91 L. Ed. at pp. 1062–1063].) To impose such a burden on the trial court for the purpose of facilitating its consideration of a factor of only slight significance in the forum non conveniens balance would, we believe, be unwarranted.

6. The court noted that the law of California relating to forum non conveniens is "virtually identical" to federal law. (*Piper, supra*, 454 U.S. at p. 248, fn. 13 [70 L. Ed. 2d at p. 431].)

or substantive law cannot be considered as a factor in plaintiffs' favor in the forum non conveniens balance.

Next we consider the effect of the residence of the parties in deciding a motion based on forum non conveniens. Many cases hold that the plaintiff's choice of a forum should rarely be disturbed unless the balance is strongly in favor of the defendant. (E.g., *Goodwine v. Superior Court* (1965) 63 Cal. 2d 481, 485 [47 Cal. Rptr. 201, 407 P.2d 1]; *Price, supra*, 42 Cal. 2d 577, 585; ...) But the reasons advanced for this frequently reiterated rule apply only to residents of the forum state: (1) if the plaintiff is a resident of the jurisdiction in which the suit is filed, the plaintiff's choice of forum is presumed to be convenient and (2) a state has a strong interest in assuring its own residents an adequate forum for the redress of grievances (*Archibald v. Cinerama Hotels* (1976) 15 Cal. 3d 853, 859 [126 Cal. Rptr. 811, 544 P.2d 947]). [D]ismissal of an action (as opposed to a stay) was ordinarily not permitted on the basis of inconvenient forum if the plaintiff was a California resident. (15 Cal. 3d at p. 859; *Goodwine v. Superior Court, supra*, 63 Cal. 2d at p. 485.) Where, however, the plaintiff resides in a foreign country, *Piper* holds that the plaintiff's choice of forum is much less reasonable and is not entitled to the same preference as a resident of the state where the action is filed. At best, therefore, under the rule laid down in *Piper*, the fact that plaintiffs chose to file their complaint in California is not a substantial factor in favor of retaining jurisdiction here.

Defendant's residence is also a factor to be considered in the balance of convenience. If a corporation is the defendant, the state of its incorporation and the place where its principal place of business is located is presumptively a convenient forum. As noted above, Shiley is a California corporation with its principal place of business in this state. * * *

But, as *Piper, supra*, 454 U.S. 235, and other authorities make clear, this presumption is not conclusive. Even though evidence relating to the design, manufacture, and testing of the airplane involved in *Piper* was located in the United States, the plaintiffs were relegated to the Scottish courts to vindicate their claims. A resident defendant may overcome the presumption of convenience by evidence that the alternate jurisdiction is a more convenient place for trial of the action.[10]

On this issue, the parties disagree sharply. The Court of Appeal held that because virtually all witnesses and documents relating to the decedents' medical care and treatment, medical histories, loss of earnings, and all the witnesses to the familial impacts of their deaths are located in Scandinavia, it is more convenient to try the actions there. Defendants point out in addition that, although the alleged fraudulent

---

10. The effect to be given a corporate defendant's residence in the forum has two aspects: The first, discussed above, relates to the convenience of the parties. The second, examined later herein, implicates public policy considerations, such as California's interest in deciding actions against resident corporations whose conduct in this state causes injury to persons in other jurisdictions.

representations emanated from California, they were received and relied on in Scandinavia, and the Scandinavian doctors have knowledge of decedents' preexisting medical conditions, the factors relevant to a risk-benefit analysis, and the handling of the heart valves prior to implantation.

Plaintiffs counter that evidence relating to defendants' allegedly culpable conduct, such as the design, manufacture, testing and packing of the valves, is in California; that warnings and advice to doctors using the valve were issued from this state; and that investigations of the reasons for the valve failure were conducted here. Plaintiffs represented that the Scandinavian witnesses to damages and decedents' medical care have agreed that they will be available to testify in California. In addition, they assert, there are more than one million pages of documents in California that are relevant to the issue of the valve failures, and it would be extremely time consuming and costly to translate even a fraction of these into Swedish and Norwegian. Hundreds of witnesses from California and perhaps other states will be called, some of whom would not be available for trial in Scandinavia.

Defendants produced evidence that Swedish and Norwegian courts routinely receive documents into evidence that are written in English, without requiring translation. Among the conditions imposed by the trial court with which defendants agreed to comply were to make available in Norway and Sweden past and present employees of defendants and documents in their possession, as required by the Scandinavian courts.[11] They also agreed to defray the expenses for the production of these witnesses and documents.

Before deciding whether the private convenience of the parties weighs in favor of plaintiffs or defendants, we consider the interests of the California public in retaining the trial of the actions in this state. *Piper* held that the jurisdiction with the greater interest should bear the burden of entertaining the litigation. (*Piper, supra,* 454 U.S. at pp. 260–261 [70 L. Ed. 2d at pp. 438–439].)

The Court of Appeal considered four factors in holding that the public interest favored the granting of the motions: (1) California's interest in avoiding undue congestion of its courts due to the trial of foreign causes of action; (2) this state's deterrent and regulatory interests in products manufactured here; (3) appropriate deference to the laws and policy decisions of foreign governments; and (4) the competitive disadvantage to California business if resident corporations were required to defend lawsuits here based on injuries incurred in other jurisdictions.

---

11. Plaintiffs assert that the stipulation that defendants will make past and present employees available to testify in Scandinavia "if so ordered within the discretion of Swedish or Norwegian courts" does not remedy the problem because the courts in those countries have no jurisdiction to order the appearance of foreign witnesses. If the wording of this stipulation will not accomplish what was obviously its intent (to assure that defendants will attempt to the best of their ability to make employee witnesses available to testify in Scandinavian courts), plaintiffs may return to the trial court for a modification of the stipulation to accomplish that objective.

As to the first of these matters, the court concluded trial in California would unduly burden the court. It noted that foreign plaintiffs have filed 108 actions in California against Shiley relating to the heart valves, and that, according to plaintiffs, about one million pages of documents are relevant to their actions, and that the testimony of hundreds of witnesses might be required. Defendants state that the number of cases filed against Shiley involving the heart valves had increased to 235 by the time the briefs were filed. The court observed correctly that preventing court congestion resulting from the trial of foreign causes of action is an important factor in the forum non conveniens analysis.

Plaintiffs rely on authorities stating generally that if a case is "properly" before the court or if the action is "legitimately and correctly brought before it," a court will retain the case even in the face of a congested calendar. We have no argument with these propositions, and we agree with plaintiffs that dismissals or stays for forum non conveniens should not be used primarily to control a court's docket. Nevertheless, there can be no question that the already congested courts of this state would be burdened by the trial of the numerous and complex actions relating to the heart valve brought by plaintiffs who reside in foreign countries. Whether this would constitute an "undue burden," however, is another question. In order to determine that issue, we must consider other factors as well.

The appellate court next considered whether California's interest in deterring wrongful conduct justified retention of the actions. As we have already noted, in *Piper*, the high court, after observing that Scotland had the stronger interest in the litigation because the decedents who died in the airplane crash were Scottish, and all potential defendants except those before the American court were Scottish or English, held that the "incremental deterrence that would be gained if this trial were held in an American court is likely to be insignificant. The American interest in this accident is simply not sufficient to justify the enormous commitment of judicial time and resources that would inevitably be required if the case were to be tried here." (*Piper*, *supra*, 454 U.S. at pp. 260–261 [70 L. Ed. 2d at pp. 438–439].) The Court of Appeal adopted this "incremental deterrence" reasoning and concluded that California's interest in deterring wrongful conduct did not outweigh the other factors pointing to trial in Scandinavia.

Plaintiffs argue vigorously against this conclusion. They cite cases stating that California has a strong interest in regulating the conduct of manufacturers that produce products in this state which cause injury to persons in other jurisdictions. (*Hurtado v. Superior Court* (1974) 11 Cal. 3d 574, 583–584 [114 Cal. Rptr. 106, 522 P.2d 666]; *Clothesrigger, Inc. v. GTE Corp.* (1987) 191 Cal. App. 3d 605, 615 [236 Cal. Rptr. 605]; …) This interest, as the cited cases make clear, is to deter negligent conduct; the likelihood of a substantial recovery against such a manufacturer strengthens the deterrent effect.

We are persuaded that under the facts in the present case, the additional deterrence that would result if defendants were called to account for their allegedly wrongful conduct in a California court rather than in the courts of Scandinavia would be negligible. As we observe above, there are 235 lawsuits pending in California relating to the heart valve. According to defendants, some of these have been filed on behalf of persons with functioning valves who seek damages for the anxiety engendered by the apprehension that the valves may fail. At least 108 of these suits were filed by foreign residents, according to the Court of Appeal. Many valves were implanted in California, and it is safe to assume that the plaintiffs in some of the 235 actions are California residents.[13] The burden imposed on defendants in trying these cases by California residents in the California courts, and the damages that defendants might be required to pay if they are found liable, would provide sufficient deterrence to prevent wrongful conduct in the future even if the suits filed by nonresident plaintiffs were tried elsewhere. * * *

Plaintiffs place great reliance on an additional factor, which they complain the Court of Appeal failed to consider, i.e., the relationship of defendants to California. We hold above that a presumption of convenience to defendants arises from the fact that Shiley is incorporated in California and has its principal place of business here. Another aspect of defendants' connection with this state is that alleged wrongful conduct was committed here, and there is a close connection between such conduct and plaintiffs' causes of action. We agree with plaintiffs that defendants' cumulative connection with California is an appropriate matter for consideration in deciding a forum non conveniens motion. * * * While the cumulative connection of the defendant and its conduct within the state is relevant in deciding whether retention of an action would place an undue burden on the courts, we cannot look only to such circumstances; matters like the complexity of the case, whether it would consume considerable court time, and the condition of the court's docket are also relevant to the issue.

We come, then, to an assessment of the factors discussed above. We are confronted with the somewhat anomalous situation that the parties seek to try the action in a jurisdiction which would appear to violate their interest in a convenient place for trial. Both plaintiffs and defendants are willing—indeed, eager—to litigate the matter in a jurisdiction separated by an ocean and a continent from their places of residence. Although both claim that they are motivated by the convenience of the place of trial, this court, like others before it, recognizes that an additional motivating factor— and perhaps the major one—relates to the circumstance that trial in California will enhance the possibility of substantial recovery. Plaintiffs seek and defendants resist trial in the California courts substantially for this reason. In the service of this goal, they are willing to transport numerous witnesses and documents many thousand miles. * * *

... [T]here was clearly substantial evidence to sustain the trial court's determination that the balance of private and public interests favors defendants under traditional

---

13. At oral argument, it was undisputed that 30 California plaintiffs have brought suit on the same and related claims in the courts of this state.

rules laid down in prior cases. It is true that much, but not all, of the evidence concerning liability exists in California; but virtually all the evidence relating to damages is in Scandinavia. Since defendants have promised to supply documents in their possession if required by the Scandinavian courts, the fact that a large number of documents will be involved appears not to pose a significant inconvenience to plaintiffs. The Court of Appeal concluded that these documents could be admitted into evidence without translation, and although there was conflicting evidence on this score, its conclusion was supported by the record.

It is probable that both parties will suffer some disadvantage from trial in their home forums. For example, former employees of defendants may be beyond the jurisdiction of the Scandinavian courts and defendants may be unable to make good their promise to produce them for trial in Scandinavia. Conversely, defendants have no means by which to ensure that Scandinavian medical witnesses and others whose testimony might be important will attend the trial in California. But these problems are implicit in many cases in which forum non conveniens motions are made, and it is for the trial court to decide which party will be more inconvenienced.

The public interest factors clearly favor defendants' position. If we hold that the present cases may be tried in California, it will likely mean that the remaining 108 cases involving the Shiley valve will also be tried here. The burden on the California courts of trying these numerous complex actions is considerable. Moreover, California's interest in deterring future improper conduct by defendants would be amply vindicated if the actions filed by California resident plaintiffs resulted in judgments in their favor. Under all the circumstances, we hold that the Court of Appeal was correct in concluding that there was substantial evidence to support the trial court's determination that the private and public interest factors, on balance, justified the stays granted in these actions. * * *

CONCLUSION

The judgment of the Court of Appeal is affirmed.

[1] *Adequate Alternative Forum*

As *Stangvik v. Shiley, Inc.*, reproduced *supra*, indicates, a court will not dismiss an action based on forum non conveniens unless a suitable alternative forum is available to the plaintiff for trial of the action. How did the Supreme Court define this prerequisite? Because defendants can always offer to stipulate to submit to an alternative forum's jurisdiction and to waive any applicable statutes of limitations, how significant is the suitable alternative forum requirement? Is there any reason why a defendant would refuse to make these stipulations regarding an alternate place for trial? *See Delfosse v. C.A.C.I., Inc.-Federal*, 218 Cal. App. 3d 683, 688, 267 Cal. Rptr. 224 (1990).

Must a moving party show that there is an alternative forum that has personal jurisdiction over *all* the defendants in a multi-defendant action? *Compare Hansen v. Owens-Corning Fiberglass Corp.*, 51 Cal. App. 4th 753, 59 Cal. Rptr. 2d 229 (1996) (holding in an asbestos exposure case involving 200 defendants that the moving party seeking a forum non conveniens *stay* is not required show *all* defendants are subject to jurisdiction in a particular alternative forum), *and David v. Medtronic, Inc.*, 237 Cal. App. 4th 734, 188 Cal. Rptr. 3d 103 (2015) (concluding a nominal defendant not subject to personal jurisdiction in proposed alternative forum does not preclude forum non conveniens dismissal as to other defendants, but plaintiffs' action against nominal defendant must be severed and allowed to proceed in California), *with American Cemwood Corp. v. American Home Assurance Co.*, 87 Cal. App. 4th 431, 104 Cal. Rptr. 2d 670 (2001) (finding *Hansen* inapposite where the moving party seeks a *dismissal* and there are only five defendants; failure of the moving party to demonstrated that all five defendants are subject to jurisdiction in British Columbia precluded a forum non conveniens dismissal).

[a] Unfavorable Change in Law

What are the policy reasons for the Supreme Court's ruling that the possibility of an unfavorable change in law ordinarily should not be accorded *any* weight in deciding a motion for forum non conveniens? Do you agree with this ruling? Do any policy arguments support the position that such an unfavorable change should be accorded *some* weight?

[b] No Remedy Exception

The Supreme Court in *Stangvik* did suggest that an unfavorable change in law is a relevant consideration where the remedy in the alternative forum is so clearly inadequate or unsatisfactory that it is "no remedy at all." Under what circumstances does this "no remedy at all" exception apply?

In *Shiley, Inc. v. Superior Court*, 4 Cal. App. 4th 126, 6 Cal. Rptr. 2d 38 (1992), several nonresident plaintiffs commenced actions in California against defendant Shiley seeking damages for alleged emotional distress they suffered as a result of the knowledge that their implanted heart valves may be defective and malfunction, causing death. Because the valves had not yet failed, California law only recognized a viable cause of action for fraud; but none of the various states of plaintiffs' domiciles recognized any cause of action for injuries caused by a product which had not yet malfunctioned. In opposing defendant's motion to dismiss for forum non conveniens, the plaintiffs argued that their home states were not suitable places for trial because the law in those states did not recognize their causes of action. The Court of Appeal held that the "no remedy at all" exception was inapplicable and the plaintiffs' home states constituted suitable forums. The court noted that under *Stangvik* a court cannot even consider the fact that an alternative forum does not recognize a cause of action which would be available to the plaintiff under California law. The "no remedy at all" exception "applies only in 'rare circumstances,' such as where the alternative forum is a foreign country whose courts are ruled by a dictatorship, so that there is no independent judiciary or due process of law.... The exception has never been applied to a sister state, and we decline to apply it here." *Id.* at 133–34.

Is *Shiley* an accurate interpretation of *Stangvik*? Do you agree with the holding in *Shiley*? What policy considerations likely influenced the court in *Shiley*? After *Shiley*, is the "no remedy at all" exception practically meaningless in interstate, as opposed to international, litigation? *See Boaz v. Boyle & Co.* 40 Cal. App. 4th 700, 46 Cal. Rptr. 2d 888 (1995) (observing that the fact that a plaintiff will be disadvantaged by the law of the jurisdiction, or that the plaintiff will probably or even certainly lose, does not render the alternative forum "unsuitable"). How meaningful is the exception likely to be in international litigation? *See, e.g., Aghaian v. Minassian*, 234 Cal. App. 4th 427, 183 Cal. Rptr. 3d 822 (2013) (ruling a court in Iran is not a suitable alternative forum); *Chong v. Superior Court*, 58 Cal. App 4th 1032, 68 Cal. Rptr. 2d 427 (1997) (finding no evidence that the courts of Hong Kong, the alternate forum, will not continue to provide due process of law after China obtained sovereignty over the former Crown Colony in 1997).

[2] Plaintiff's Residence

As indicated in *Stangvik v. Shiley, Inc.* reproduced *supra*, Supreme Court cases have established that if the plaintiff is a California resident, the doctrine of forum non conveniens ordinarily does not permit the dismissal (as distinguished from a stay) of the action. *See Stangvik, supra*, 54 Cal. 3d at 755 and cases cited therein. The plaintiffs in *Stangvik* were not residents of California. Precisely what weight did the *Stangvik* court accord to the plaintiffs' choice of forum? *See National Football League v. Fireman's Fund Ins. Co.*, 216 Cal. App. 4th 902, 929–30, 157 Cal. Rptr. 3d 318 (2013) (concluding a nonresident plaintiff is entitled to due deference to be weighted and balanced with all the other pertinent factors). An individual resident's choice of a California court is entitle to a strong presumption of convenience in favor of the plaintiff's choice of forum. What is the residency of a multi-state unincorporated association? *See National Football League, supra*, 216 Cal. App. 4th at 920–22 (ruling the plaintiff NFL is not necessarily entitled to a strong presumption of the convenience of a California forum simply because some of its members reside in California).

The court in *Stangvik* held that a court in the state of the defendant's residence is presumptively a convenient forum. What does this mean? How strong is this presumption? What evidence did defendant Shiley show to overcome this presumption in *Stangvik*? Assume that defendant Shiley was neither incorporated nor had its principal place of business in California, but otherwise conducted extensive heart valve business activities in California? Why should a California court not be a presumptively convenient forum in such a case? What difference would this make in the nature of the evidentiary showing defendant Shiley would need to make to establish inconvenience?

[3] Dismissal vs. Stay

A court which dismisses a suit on grounds of forum non conveniens loses jurisdiction over the action. A court which stays the action retains jurisdiction over the parties and the cause, and can protect the interests of the parties pending the final decision of the foreign court. *Archibald v. Cinerama Hotels*, 15 Cal. 3d 853, 126 Cal. Rptr. 811, 544 P.2d 947 (1976). Consequently, the traditional rule is that, except in extraordinary cases, a trial court has no discretion to dismiss (as opposed to stay) an action brought by a California resident on grounds of forum non conveniens. *Archibald,* 15 Cal. 3d. at 858. The exceptional case which may justify dismissal under forum non conveniens is one in which California cannot provide an adequate forum due to lack of personal jurisdiction over an indispensable party, or has no interest in doing so, such as when no party is a California resident. *Id.* at 859.

The trial court in *Stangvik* stayed the action and retained jurisdiction to make such further orders as might become appropriate. What type of orders might become appropriate in that litigation? Could the trial court have dismissed the action, consistent with the traditional rule? Under what circumstances might a trial court which has stayed an action based on forum non conveniens decide to dissolve the stay and resume jurisdiction over the parties and the cause? *See Archibald, supra,* 15 Cal. 3d at 857–59.

Several recent decisions have relied on the distinction between a dismissal and a stay to affirm a forum non conveniens stay even though the plaintiffs are California residents. *E.g., Berg v. MTC Elec. Tech. Co.,* 61 Cal. App. 4th 349, 71 Cal. Rptr. 2d 523 (1998); *Century Indem. Co. v. Bank of America, FSB,* 58 Cal. App. 4th 408, 68 Cal. Rptr. 2d 132 (1997); *see also National Football League v. Fireman's Fund Ins. Co.,* 216 Cal. App. 4th 902, 930–33, 157 Cal. Rptr. 3d 318 (2013) (ruling defendant seeking a stay rather than a dismissal is not required prove California is a seriously inconvenient forum for nonresident plaintiff's lawsuit).

Other cases have found this distinction relevant to the threshold issue of whether there is a suitable alternative forum. *E.g., Hansen v. Owens-Corning Fiberglass Corp.,* 51 Cal. App. 4th 753, 59 Cal. Rptr. 2d 229 (1996) (holding moving party seeking a forum non conveniens *stay* not required to show all defendants are subject to personal jurisdiction in a particular alternative forum); *American Cemwood Corp. v. American Home Assurance Co.,* 87 Cal. App. 4th 431, 104 Cal. Rptr. 2d 670 (2001) (ruling the failure of the moving party to demonstrate that all defendants are subject to jurisdiction in British Columbia precluded a forum non conveniens *dismissal*); *Investors Equity Life Holding v. Schmidt,* 233 Cal. App. 4th 1363, 183 Cal. Rptr. 3d 219 (2015) (holding stay rather than dismissal is appropriate when the alternative forum's suitability depends on the defendant's stipulation to jurisdiction there and tolling of the statute of limitations).

[4] Procedures for Raising Forum Non Conveniens

[a] Before General Appearance

A defendant may move to stay or dismiss on the ground of inconvenient forum within the time available for pleading to the complaint. CCP § 418.10(a)(2). If the motion is denied, the defendant, within 10 days, may seek immediate appellate review by writ of mandate. CCP § 418.10(c); *Furda v. Superior Court,* 161 Cal App. 3d 418, 207 Cal. Rptr. 646 (1984); *see also Williamson v. Mazda Motor of America, Inc.,* 212 Cal. App. 4th 449, 150 Cal. Rptr. 3d 569 (2012) (holding defendant's unsuccessful

forum non conveniens motion brought shortly after case filed does not deprive the
court of its statutory authority to subsequently reconsider the issue once the facts of
the litigation are more fully developed).

[b]   After General Appearance

The right to raise forum non conveniens is not waived, however, by failure to make
the motion prior to a responsive pleading. CCP § 410.30; *see Marriage of Tucker*, 226
Cal. App. 3d 1249, 1257, 277 Cal. Rptr. 403 (1991) (observing that under both state
and federal law, a forum non conveniens defense need not be raised prior to filing a
responsive pleading); *Britton v. Dallas Airmotive, Inc.*, 153 Cal. App. 4th 127, 62 Cal.
Rptr. 3d 487 (2007) (concluding a defendant does not waive the forum non conveniens
issue by failing to file a preappearance forum non conveniens motion under CCP
§ 418.10). Even where the defendant has made a general appearance, either party or
the court may move for stay or dismissal based on forum non conveniens. CCP
§ 410.30(b); *see Britton, supra,* 153 Cal. App. 4th at 134–35 (ruling CCP § 418.10 applies when a defendant brings a preappearance forum non conveniens motion and
§ 410.30 applies after a defendant has appeared). A trial court order granting such a
motion, filed after a general appearance, is an appealable order. CCP § 904.1(a)(3).
What are the advantages and disadvantages of these two authorized procedures for
raising forum non conveniens? Which procedure is usually preferable? Why?

[5]   *Balance of Convenience Factors*

The court in *Stangvik* identifies several private and public interest factors that a trial
court must consider in determining a forum non conveniens motion. What other such
factors might be relevant? *See Ford Motor Co. v. Ins. Co. of N. America*, 35 Cal. App.
4th 604, 41 Cal. Rptr. 2d 342 (1995) (observing that the various factors fit roughly
into three broad categories: the relationship of the case and the parties to each forum,
concerns of judicial administration, and convenience to the parties and witnesses).
Which factors were considered most significant to the Supreme Court in *Stangvik*? Do
you think the Supreme Court would have reached the same conclusion in *Stangvik* if
none of the plaintiffs in the various other pending lawsuits were residents of California?
If only a handful of plaintiffs had commenced similar actions in California courts?

Assume that the trial court in *Stangvik* had concluded, after assessing the appropriate factors, that California was not an inconvenient forum and therefore denied
defendant Shiley's motion to dismiss. Do you think the Supreme Court would have
affirmed or reversed this decision? Why?

Assume that prior to implant, the plaintiffs had each signed agreements with defendant Shiley which specified that any litigation against Shiley that may arise as a
result of the implanted heart valve must be litigated in a court located in California.
How would such a forum selection clause affect the *Stangvik* court's analysis when
balancing the various private and public interest factors in determining defendant's
forum non conveniens motion? Would such a clause have changed the result in

Stangvik? How likely is a potential defendant to agree to a California court as the contractually designated forum?

[B]   Forum Selection Agreements

Cal-State Business Products & Services, Inc. v. Ricoh

Court of Appeal of California, Third Appellate District
12 Cal. App. 4th 1666, 16 Cal. Rptr. 2d 417 (1993)

DAVIS, JUSTICE.

INTRODUCTION

As we explain more fully in the course of this opinion, Code of Civil Procedure sections 410.30 and 418.10 (undesignated section references will be to this code) are the means by which a defendant may challenge a plaintiff's selection of California as the forum for the litigation between them. Two substantive bodies of law are affected by this procedural vehicle; the traditional (or noncontractual) doctrine of forum non conveniens and the enforceability of contractual forum-selection clauses. In light of the fact the appellant has fused aspects of these related but distinct areas, we are called upon to delineate the relevant criteria of each, to explain that this is not the proper context for application of traditional forum non conveniens principles, and to determine that a contractual forum-selection clause put in issue by the case before us is enforceable.

In response to the complaint filed by plaintiff Cal-State Business Products & Services, Inc. (Cal-State), defendant "Ricoh" moved for an order staying or dismissing this action as being brought in an inconvenient forum. (§ 410.30, 418.10.) The basis of the motion is forum-selection clauses contained in contracts between Ricoh and Cal-State which designate New York as the proper forum for any litigation connected with the contracts. The trial court ruled the action was "best decided" in New York and issued a stay pending the resolution of a suit brought by Ricoh in a New York federal court. We shall affirm.

BACKGROUND

Both parties filed declarations and exhibits in the trial court in connection with the motion. We draw our facts from these sources. [During 1990, John Fisher, the president and principal shareholder of plaintiff Cal-State, executed a series of contracts with defendant Ricoh, an office machines manufacturer headquartered in New Jersey. Under these contracts, Ricoh agreed to give Cal-State dealership rights to sell both photocopier and fax machines in the Stockton and Sacramento areas of California. These contracts contained identical integration and choice-of-law/forum clauses as follows:

> "Dealer and Ricoh agree that this Agreement, and all documents issued in connection therewith, shall be governed by and interpreted in accordance with the laws of the State of New York.... [A]ny appropriate state or federal district court located in the Borough of Manhattan, New York City, New

York shall have exclusive jurisdiction over any case of controversy arising under or in connection with this Agreement....”

A series of disputes arose between the parties during the next year. Cal-State claimed it had not received certain promised dealerships; and Ricoh claimed that Cal-State had not paid for machines it had received on credit.] ... Cal-State filed its original complaint against Ricoh in September 1991 in Sacramento County Superior Court. As amended, the complaint alleged six causes of action: restraint of trade..., unfair trade practices..., breach of contract..., two types of fraud (the representations he would receive an exclusive Stockton dealership and a copier dealership in Sacramento), and two species of negligent misrepresentation.... The motion to stay/dismiss followed in December 1991.

In his declaration in opposition to the motion, Mr. Fisher asserted he was not aware of the choice-of-forum provision, and it was never called to his attention during negotiations for either set of contracts.[7] He further claimed all witnesses familiar with the negotiation resided in California. Ricoh claimed its files were located in its New Jersey offices, close to the New York forum, as were corporate witnesses who made decisions regarding Cal-State’s territory and contracts. Ricoh also produced the first page of a complaint it filed in the Southern District of the New York federal court seeking payment on the debt owed by Cal-State on its account with Ricoh ... filed in early 1992.

[The trial court granted Ricoh’s motion to stay.] Cal-State timely sought the proper remedy of appeal. (§ 904.1, subd. (c).)

DISCUSSION

I. *Forum Non Conveniens.*

Ultimately, we must be concerned with the principles governing enforcement of a contractual choice-of-forum clause. First, however, we discuss a related matter.

A

As originated in federal case law, imported into California case law, and codified in section 410.30,[8] the doctrine of forum non conveniens allows a trial court discretion to decline to exercise jurisdiction over a cause and parties otherwise properly before it if it concludes the action may be more appropriately and justly tried elsewhere. (*Stangvik v. Shiley Inc.* (1991) 54 Cal. 3d 744, 751 [1 Cal. Rptr. 2d 556, 819 P.2d 14]; *Great Northern Ry. Co. v. Superior Court* (1970) 12 Cal. App. 3d 105, 109 [90 Cal. Rptr. 461].) The doctrine is most typically applied where the parties and the transaction underlying the litigation are foreign to the forum. The defendant bears the

---

7. Since he did not claim there was any active concealment of this clause in the arm’s-length negotiations between the parties, this assertion-which strains credulity-is immaterial, as we long ago held (*Greve v. Taft Realty Co.* (1929) 101 Cal. App. 343, 351–353 [281 P. 641]; ...) and as has been held in New York (*Generale Bank, New York Branch v. Choudhury* (S.D.N.Y. 1991) 779 F. Supp. 303, 305 [applying New York law]). Cal-State has not pressed this fact on appeal.

8. Section 410.30 and its procedural companion, section 418.10, codify the doctrine without specifying any particular factors, leaving those to be developed by case law.

burden of proof in attempting to override the plaintiff's choice of forum. There is a 25-factor analysis to guide the trial court in its resolution of the issue, which is not disturbed absent an abuse of discretion. These factors may be boiled down to three basic principles. Foremost is the availability of a suitable alternative forum for the plaintiff. (*Stangvik, supra*, 54 Cal. 3d at pp. 751–752; Judicial Council com., 14 West's Ann. Code Civ. Proc. (1973 ed. at p. 492; Rest. 2d, Conf. of Laws, § 84, com. c.) The court then balances factors relating to the private interests of the litigants and the public interests of the forum state; among these, a resident plaintiff's choice of the forum is given substantial weight. (*Stangvik, supra*, 54 Cal. 3d at pp. 751, 754–755; Rest. 2d, Conf. of Laws, § 84, com. c.) * * *

B

We have set out these principles applicable to noncontractually based forum non conveniens motions principally because of … the plaintiff's arguments. * * * Cal-State asserts that applying the principles summarized above to the evidence adduced in connection with the motion demonstrates the trial court abused its discretion in disturbing Cal-State's choice of California as a forum. * * *

Neither the conclusory language used in ruling on the motion nor the scope of the forum-selection clauses forces us to apply principles of forum non conveniens that are applicable where a plaintiff had unbridled freedom to choose the forum and the defendant was simply seeking to substitute that choice with a forum more to its liking. We instead shift our attention to principles applied in the situation where a plaintiff has contracted away its right to its forum of preference and a defendant is seeking to enforce its contractual right to its preferred forum.

II. *Enforcement of Forum-Selection Clauses.*

A

Under the modern rule, "The parties agreement as to the place of the action cannot oust a state of judicial jurisdiction, but such an agreement will be given effect unless it is unfair or unreasonable." (Rest. 2d, Conf. of Laws, § 80; …) California declared its adherence to this rule in *Smith, Valentino & Smith, Inc. v. Superior Court* (1976) 17 Cal. 3d 491 [131 Cal. Rptr. 374, 551 P.2d 1206] (*Smith*)[11] * * * In so holding, the court relied on the United States Supreme Court decision in *The Bremen v. Zapata Off-Shore Co.* (1972) 407 U.S. 1, 10 [32 L. Ed. 2d 513, 520–521, 92 S. Ct. 1907], which had enforced a forum-selection clause as a matter of federal common law in an admiralty proceeding.

"[A forum-selection provision] will be disregarded if it is the result of overreaching or of the unfair use of unequal bargaining power or if the forum chosen by the parties

---

11. There has been no discussion by the parties regarding the enforceability of the choice-of-law provision in the contract. Assuming New York law applies, Ricoh adduced authority in the trial court that New York follows the Restatement Second rule. (*DiRuocco v. Flamingo Beach Hotel & Casino Inc.* (1990) 163 A.D.2d 270 [557 N.Y.S.2d 140].) In the absence of any evidence that the courts of New York have placed nuances upon the Restatement Second rule which differ from California law, we may apply the law of our own jurisdiction. (*Nedlloyd Lines B.V., supra*, 3 Cal. 4th at p. 469, fn. 7.)

would be a seriously inconvenient one for the trial of the partic[u]lar action." (Rest. 2d, Conf. of Laws, § 80, com. a.) The *Smith* court agreed with this formulation. "No satisfying reason of public policy has been suggested why enforcement should be denied a forum selection clause appearing in a contract entered into *freely* and *voluntarily* by parties who have negotiated *at arms' length*. For the foregoing reasons, we conclude that forum selection clauses are valid and may be given effect [] in the court's discretion and in the absence of a showing that enforcement ... would be *unreasonable*." (*Smith, supra,* 17 Cal. 3d at pp. 495–496 [italics supplied].)

[T]he *Smith* court gave some content to the otherwise-empty husk of the conclusory term "unreasonable"; "the party assailing the clause [must] establish[] that its enforcement would be unreasonable, i.e. that the forum selected would be *unavailable* or *unable to accomplish substantial justice*." (17 Cal. 3d at p. 494, italics supplied; accord *The Bremen, supra,* 407 U.S. at p. 18, 32 L. Ed. 2d at p. 525].) As a further measure of reasonability, the court in *Furda v. Superior Court* (1984) 161 Cal. App. 3d 418 [207 Cal. Rptr. 646] added a requirement that the choice of forum have some rational basis in light of the facts underlying the transaction. (*Id.* at p. 426; cf. *The Bremen, supra,* 407 U.S. at p. 17 [32 L. Ed. 2d at pp. 524–525] [remarking that choice of forum reasonable because neutral and experienced in subject matter].) On the other hand, neither inconvenience nor additional expense in litigating in the selected forum is part of the test of unreasonability. (*Smith, supra,* 17 Cal. 3d at p. 496; *Furda, supra,* 161 Cal. App. 3d at pp. 426–427; *The Bremen, supra,* 407 U.S. at p. 16 [32 L. Ed. 2d at pp. 523–524]).

The fact the forum-selection clause is contained in a contract of adhesion and was not the subject of bargaining does not defeat enforcement as a matter of law, where there is no evidence of unfair use of superior power to impose the contract upon the other party and where the covenant is within the reasonable expectations of the party against whom it is being enforced. (*Bos Material Handling, Inc. v. Crown Controls Corp.* (1982) 137 Cal. App. 3d 99, 108 [186 Cal. Rptr. 740]; *Carnival Cruise Lines v. Shute* (1991) [499] U.S. [585, 594–95] [113 L. Ed. 2d 622,633, 111 S. Ct. 1522]; *Furda, supra,* 161 Cal. App. 3d at p. 426; cf. *Eads v. Woodmen of the World Life Ins.* (Okl. Ct. App. 1989) 785 P.2d 328, 329, 331 [contract invalid because plaintiff required to sign it in order to retain job].) That a business with transactions in multiple jurisdictions might insist on one forum in all its contracts is not of itself objectionable. (*Carnival Cruise Lines, supra,* [499] U.S. at p. [593–95] [113 L. Ed. 2d at pp. 632, 633].)

Although not pertinent here, we also note a court will refuse to enforce a forum-selection clause if this will bring about a result contrary to the public policy of the forum. (*Furda, supra,* 161 Cal. App. 3d at p. 427; *The Bremen, supra,* 407 U.S. at p. 15 [32 L. Ed. 2d at p. 523].)

A defendant may enforce a forum-selection clause by bringing a motion pursuant to sections 410.30 and 418.10, the statutes governing forum non conveniens motions, because they are the ones which generally authorize a trial court to decline jurisdiction when unreasonably invoked and provide a procedure for the motion. Significantly, the party opposing the enforcement of a forum-selection clause (generally the plaintiff) bears the burden of proof.

In contrast with the abuse-of-discretion standard of review applicable in a non-contractual forum non conveniens motion, a substantial-evidence standard of review applies where a forum has been selected by contract. (*Lifeco Services Corp. v. Superior Court* (1990) 222 Cal. App. 3d 331, 334 [271 Cal. Rptr. 385].)

* * *

B

Having set out the applicable legal principles, we turn to the plaintiff's pertinent arguments.

Cal-State's first argument relating to the clauses asserts the forum-selection clause should not be enforced because it was a boilerplate term over which no negotiation was possible and which was outside Cal-State's reasonable expectations. However, as the authority we have cited above makes clear, the fact that Cal-State had no power to change this term of the contract is of no import so long as it signed the contract freely and voluntarily, and possessed the power to walk away from negotiations if displeased with the provision. Nor is the provision outside the reasonable expectations of Cal-State-obviously if two parties to a contract are domiciled on opposite coasts, either one party or the other will wind up with the home-court advantage (in the more literal sense of the expression), so the plaintiff would have to recognize this would be part of the price of doing business with Ricoh (indeed, as noted, the plaintiff has abandoned on appeal his claim that he was unaware of the clause). Finally, the fact that Ricoh insists on litigating all its contractual disputes in New York is not irrational, and there is no evidence the forum was selected with the design to thwart an opponent's ability to litigate.

The plaintiff argues the lack of "nexus" of the chosen forum (New York) to the domicile of the parties or the place of execution of the contracts renders the choice of forum unenforceable. However, Cal-State takes too limited a view of the nexus requirement. The choice of forum need only have a "reasonable" basis even if it is unrelated to the domiciles or transactions involved. (Cf. Rest. 2d, Conf. of Laws, § 187, com. f [selection of law unrelated to parties].) While New York City is not (strictly speaking) Ricoh's domicile, it is a major commercial center with propinquity to Ricoh's headquarters. Without denigrating the abilities of the New Jersey courts, we find it reasonable for Ricoh to wish to make use of the New York City courts which would have (at least institutionally) a great deal of expertise in commercial litigation. (*The Bremen, supra,* 407 U.S. at p. 17 [32 L. Ed. 2d at pp. 524–525] [reasonable to choose neutral forum with expertise in subject matter].) Thus, there is nothing *irrational* about the forum selected by the contract which would defeat its enforcement.

[T]he plaintiff asserts the factors relevant to a forum non conveniens motion which is *not* contractually based also form part of the analysis where a forum has been selected pursuant to contract. We cannot accept this proposition. * * * As we noted earlier, the general factors [for forum non conveniens] are pertinent only in the *absence* of a contractual provision, since under those circumstances neither party possesses a right to any particular forum and the selection of one over the other requires the weighing of a gamut of factors of public and private convenience, not to mention the strong interest of a plaintiff's domicile in providing the plaintiff access to its courts. However, a party which has contracted away its right to choose its home forum (as well as all the concomitant conveniences of a home forum) has presumably done so because the value it receives from the negotiated deal is worth the chance the party may be required to litigate disputes elsewhere. To apply the general factors in this context would in essence be rewriting the bargain struck between the parties, which might not have been consummated in the absence of the forum selection clause. Therefore, we will not include the *Great Northern* factors into our analysis of the validity of the clauses. * * *

The plaintiff is left with its claim that New York is a forum which is unavailable or unable to accomplish substantial justice. At most, the plaintiff here has shown increased inconvenience and expense, which is insufficient. Therefore, the forum-selection clause may properly be enforced through a stay on the California action. It should be noted that the California action remains available in the event the New York forum in fact proves unavailable.

DISPOSITION

The judgment (order) is affirmed.

Notes and Questions on Forum Selection Agreements

(1) *Forum Clauses, Generally.* The California courts, like the federal courts and those of all but a handful of other states, will enforce a freely negotiated forum selection clause unless the resisting party shows that enforcement would be "unreasonable." The courts in other states have developed several different notions of whether clause enforcement is "unreasonable." How did the court in *Cal-State* define this test? What would be a clear example of when clause enforcement would be "unreasonable"? When the contractually designated forum is very inconvenient and expensive to the resisting party and its witnesses? When the witnesses to be called by the resisting party are not subject to the compulsory process of the contractually designated forum? For a discussion of these and related questions, see Walter W. Heiser, *Forum Selection Clauses in State Courts: Limitations on Enforcement after Stewart and Carnival Cruise,* 45 FLA. L. REV. 361 (1993).

(2) *Forum Clauses and Forum Non Conveniens.* The court in *Cal-State* observed that a defendant may enforce a forum selection clause by bringing a forum non conveniens motion, where a plaintiff commences the action in a court other than the contractually designated forum. When a plaintiff does commence an action in the designated forum, does the existence of the forum clause preclude an attempt by the defendant to change the forum by a motion based on forum non conveniens? Is this what the court held in *Cal-State*? When parties agree to a forum selection clause, precisely what rights do they waive as part of the bargaining process? What interests do they have the power to contractually waive? Can they waive all the private and public interests associated with a forum non conveniens motion? For a discussion

of the relationship between forum selection clauses and forum non conveniens, see Heiser, *Forum Selection Clauses in State Courts, supra,* 45 FLA. L. REV. at 393–401 (1993).

(3) *Validity of Forum Clauses in Consumer Contracts.* The first Supreme Court cases, both U.S. and California, to approve the modern rule favoring enforcement of forum selection clauses involved freely negotiated contracts between commercial entities of roughly equal bargaining power. *The Bremen v. Zapata Off-Shore Co.,* 407 U.S. 1, 92 S. Ct. 1907, 32 L. Ed. 2d 513 (1972); *Smith, Valentino & Smith, Inc. v. Superior Court,* 17 Cal. 3d 491, 131 Cal. Rptr. 374, 551 P.2d 1206 (1976). More recently, the U.S. Supreme Court extended this modern rule to enforcement of forum clauses in non-negotiated standard form consumer contracts, at least where the consumers had notice of the clause. *Carnival Cruise Lines, Inc. v. Shute,* 499 U.S. 585, 111 S. Ct. 1522, 113 L. Ed. 2d 622 (1991) (enforcing clause even though it required Washington consumers to litigate in Florida courts). The California courts seem to have taken the same approach.

(a) The California courts apparently have adopted the *Carnival Cruise Lines* approach. *See, e.g., Net2Phone, Inc. v. Superior Court,* 109 Cal. App. 4th 583, 135 Cal. Rptr. 2d 149 (2003) (enforcing forum selection clause between customers and defendant telecommunications services provider designating New Jersey courts, where clause accessed via hyperlink in defendant's internet website); *Intershop Communications AG v. Superior Court,* 104 Cal. App. 4th 191, 201–202, 127 Cal. Rptr. 2d 847 (2002) (finding enforceable a forum selection clause within an adhesion contract, which required plaintiff employee to litigate breach of stock options exchange agreement in Germany, so long as the clause provided adequate notice to the plaintiff that he was agreeing to the jurisdiction cited in the contract); *Lu v. Dryclean-U.S.A. of Cal., Inc.,* 11 Cal. App. 4th 1490, 14 Cal. Rptr. 2d 906 (1992) (enforcing forum selection clause in franchise agreement requiring plaintiffs, individual franchisees, to litigate in Florida).

(b) However, in *American Online, Inc., v. Superior Court,* 90 Cal. App. 4th 1, 108 Cal. Rtpr. 2d 699 (2001), the court refused to enforce a forum selection clause in a consumer contract that designated Virginia as the jurisdiction in which all disputes arising out of the relationship must be litigated, and included a choice of law clause requiring that Virginia law be applied to any such dispute. The court found the clauses unenforceable for two independent reasons. First, one of the plaintiff's causes of action sought class action relief under the California Consumers Legal Remedies Act (CLRA), Civil Code § 1750 *et seq.,* and this Act contains a provision that voids any purported waiver of rights under the CLRA as being contrary to California public policy. "Enforcement of the contractual forum selection and choice of law clauses," the court reasoned, "would be the functional equivalent of a contractual waiver of the consumer protections under the CLRA and, thus, is prohibited under California law." *American Online, supra,* 90 Cal. App. 4th at 5; *see also Verdugo v. Alliantgroup, LP,* 237 Cal. App. 4th 141, 187 Cal. Rtpr. 3d 613 (2015) (holding forum clause in employment contract designating Texas court violates public policy on employee compensation, protected by anti-waiver provision in California Labor Code, and is therefore unenforceable).

Second, the *American Online* court also found the clauses unenforceable because Virginia law does not allow consumer lawsuits to be brought as class actions and the available remedies are more limited than those afforded by California law. Accordingly, the rights of the plaintiff and the California consumer class members "would be substantially diminished if they are required to litigate their dispute in Virginia, thereby violating an important public policy underlying California's consumer protection law." *American Online*, 90 Cal. App. 4th at 5. Do you agree with this second, independent reason for finding the clauses unenforceable?

(c) In *Aral v. Earthlink, Inc*, 134 Cal. App. 4th 544, 36 Cal. Rptr. 3d 229 (2005), the court refused to enforce a forum selection clause designating Georgia as the forum. The plaintiffs, California consumers, brought an action under California's unfair competition law against defendant, a Georgia internet provider, alleging the plaintiffs were improperly charged for high speed service during periods between the time the service was ordered and the time the service could be accessed. The court concluded that a forum selection clause that requires a consumer to travel 2,000 miles to recover a small sum is not reasonable.

(d) The California Legislature has recently added some protection for consumers with respect to enforcement of forum selection clauses in certain actions where the amount in controversy is less than $5000. Pursuant to CCP § 116.225, an agreement entered into after January 1, 2003 establishing a forum outside California for an action arising from the provision of goods, services, property, or extensions of credit primarily for personal, family or household purposes that is otherwise within the jurisdiction of the small claims court of California is contrary to public policy and is void and unenforceable.

(4) The United States Supreme Court decision in *Carnival Cruise Lines, Inc. v. Shute, supra*, enforcing a forum selection clause in a standard consumer form contract, was an admiralty jurisdiction case based on federal common law and therefore not binding on state courts generally. Scholars have roundly criticized that decision as incorrect from the viewpoint of economic, social, political, and contract policies. *See, e.g.*, Lee Goldman, *My Way and the Highway: The Law and Economics of Choice of Forum Clauses in Consumer Form Contracts*, 86 Nw. U. L. Rev. 700 (1992); Jeffrey A. Liesener, *Carnival's Got the Fun ... and the Forum: A New Look at Choice-of-Forum Clauses and the Unconscionability Doctrine After Carnival Cruise Lines, Inc. v. Shute*, 53 U. Pitt. L. Rev. 1025 (1992); Linda S. Mullenix, *Another Easy Case, Some More Bad Law: Carnival Cruise Lines and Contractual Personal Jurisdiction*, 27 Tex. Int'l L.J. 323 (1992). Do you agree with these criticisms?

(5) *Forum Selection and Choice-of-Law Clauses*. As *Cal-State* illustrates, a choice-of-law clause often accompanies a forum selection clause in a contract. If the contractually designated law is that of a state other than the forum state, which state's law determines the enforceability of the forum selection clause? For example, in *Smith, Valentino & Smith, Inc. v. Superior Court, supra*, the plaintiff commenced a breach of agency contract action in a California superior court in contravention of a forum selection clause which designated Pennsylvania courts as the exclusive forums for

contract-related litigation. The agency contract also provided that Pennsylvania law governed disputes concerning the contract. The plaintiff argued that the clause was void and unenforceable under California law, although Pennsylvania law would enforce a reasonable forum clause. Which state's law — California or Pennsylvania — should the California court apply in determining whether or not to enforce the forum selection clause? *See Smith, Valentino & Smith, Inc. v. Superior Court, supra,* 17 Cal. 3d at 494–95; *see also Nedlloyd Lines B.V. v. Superior Court,* 3 Cal. 4th 459, 11 Cal. Rptr. 2d 330, 834 P.2d 1148 (1992); Linda S. Mullenix, *Another Choice of Forum, Another Choice of Law: Consensual Adjudicatory Procedure in Federal Court,* 57 FORDHAM L. REV. 291, 346–56 (1988); J. Zachary Courson, *Yavuz v. 61 MM, Ltd.: A New Federal Standard—Applying Contracting Parties' Choice of Law to the Analysis of Forum Selection Agreements,* 85 DENVER U. L. REV. 597 (2008) (discussing various cases).

Chapter 7

Provisional Remedies

§ 7.01 Attachment and Related Prejudgment Remedies

[A] Writ of Attachment

Attachment is a provisional remedy which permits a plaintiff creditor to seize property in advance of trial and judgment to secure the payment of any judgment eventually awarded. *See generally* 6 Witkin, *California Procedure, Provisional Remedies* §§ 46–244 (5th ed. 2008). Attachment is an ancillary remedy in California — a complaint commencing the main action must first be filed before plaintiff may apply for a writ of attachment. CCP § 484.010.

Western Steel and Ship Repair, Inc. v. RMI, Inc.
Court of Appeal of California, Fourth Appellate District
176 Cal. App. 3d 1108, 222 Cal. Rptr. 556 (1986)

KREMER, PRESIDING JUSTICE.

RMI, Inc. (RMI) appeals from the trial court order denying its motion to quash a writ of attachment and release the attached property. * * *

Respondent Western Steel and Ship Repair, Inc. (Western) was RMI's subcontractor on a vessel overhaul job for the United States Navy. Western sued RMI in contract for unpaid amounts allegedly owing under the subcontract. On the day it filed the complaint, October 16, 1985, Western obtained an ex parte attachment of RMI's funds. The ex parte writ of attachment was obtained by authority of Code of Civil Procedure section 485.010 which requires a showing that great or irreparable injury will result if issuance of the writ of attachment is delayed for a noticed hearing. The showing of great or irreparable injury which Western made in the superior court to obtain the ex parte writ consisted of (1) an attorney declaration executed by Western's attorney, Friedenberg, saying he gave no notice of the attachment procedure, based on the statements contained in an attached declaration by Winthrop (President of Western) regarding "the shaky financial condition" of RMI and "probability that RMI, INC. would take action to conceal its assets if it had any notice of this proceeding,...."; (2) the Winthrop declaration, which said RMI told Western it did not have the money presently to pay the claim against it and asked if Western would agree to settlement terms involving an 18-month payment schedule, and based on these facts and the "precarious financial condition of RMI" Winthrop believed if RMI were given notice of the attachment it would "take whatever steps were necessary to hide its assets so as to prevent attachment of these assets."

The next day, October 17, Western levied the writ against $45,510 in an RMI bank account. Later that day, unaware of the attachment, RMI issued payroll checks, which later were dishonored for insufficient funds on account of the attachment.

RMI first learned of the attachment the afternoon of October 17 when the bank refused to permit a routine withdrawal. RMI immediately attempted to attack the writ of attachment by an ex parte motion to quash. Counsel for both RMI and Western appeared before a judge the afternoon of October 17; the judge ruled that although a Judicial Council form used by the superior court (Judicial Council Form AT-170) permitted an ex parte attack on a writ of attachment, the statutes do not provide for such a procedure; accordingly, the judge treated the ex parte motion to quash as a motion to shorten time, which was granted, with a hearing set for the following day, October 18, on RMI's motion to quash the writ of attachment.

The hearing set for October 18 was that day continued to October 21, for unknown reasons. When the matter was heard on October 21, RMI contended (1) Western had not established probable validity of its claim (a requirement of prejudgment attachment) and (2) its showing of great or irreparable injury was insufficient to justify ex parte issuance of the writ. Western took the position the relevant statute governing the motion to quash, Code of Civil Procedure section 485.240, prevented reargument of the question of great or irreparable injury. However, RMI argued it could not constitutionally be precluded from arguing the sufficiency of Western's showing in support of an ex parte writ of attachment.

During the hearing, the trial judge made statements which are somewhat conflicting and which cast in doubt his reasons for the ruling. At one point he appeared to refuse to consider the constitutional challenge; then later he indicated a belief in the statute's validity; and he did permit RMI to argue the question of great or irreparable injury, which permission could indicate his belief in RMI's entitlement to a hearing despite the statute. Regardless of what his reasons were, he eventually denied RMI's motion to quash the writ.

On its appeal from that order, RMI contends the trial judge shirked his obligation to rule on the statute's constitutionality, and also argues lack of justification for the ex parte issuance of the writ. RMI does not contend here that the attachment is otherwise improper, nor does the record reveal any serious dispute as to the validity of the underlying attachment, aside from questions as to the propriety of ex parte issuance.

DISCUSSION

The specific requirements for an ex parte attachment are stated as follows in Code of Civil Procedure section 485.220: "(a) The court shall examine the application and supporting affidavit and, except as provided in Section 486.030, shall issue a right to attach order, which shall state the amount to be secured by the attachment, and order a writ of attachment to be issued upon the filing of an undertaking as provided by Sections 489.210 and 489.220, if it finds all of the following: (1) The claim upon which the attachment is based is one upon which an attachment may be issued. [¶] (2) The plaintiff has established the probable validity of the claim upon which the attachment is based. [¶] (3) The attachment is not sought for a purpose other than the recovery upon the claim.... [¶] (4) The affidavit accompanying the application shows that the property sought to be attached, or the portion thereof to be specified in the writ, is not exempt from attachment. [¶] (5) The plaintiff will suffer great or irreparable injury (within the meaning of Section 485.010) if issuance of the order is delayed until the matter can be heard on notice."

In addition to the requirement of great or irreparable injury, the statutes governing ex parte attachments also require the attachment to satisfy the general requirements for prejudgment attachments. Those requirements here relevant are that the action be a claim for money, based on a contract, where the total claim is fixed or readily ascertainable and not less than $500 (Code Civ. Proc., § 483.010, subd. (a)); that the claim be unsecured (Code Civ. Proc., § 483.010, subd. (b)); and that the application for attachment be accompanied by an affidavit "showing that the plaintiff on the facts presented would be entitled to a judgment on the claim upon which the attachment is based" (Code Civ. Proc., § 484.030).

Finally, the debtor on a motion to quash may attack either the validity of the attachment or its amount, but specifically may not argue the issue whether the writ should have been issued ex parte. The statute (quoted in full, *supra*) says, "It shall not be grounds to set aside an order that the plaintiff would not have suffered great or irreparable injury ... if issuance of the order had been delayed until the matter could have been heard on notice." (Code Civ. Proc., § 485.240, subd. (b).)

As we have said, the statute, Code of Civil Procedure section 485.240, subdivision (b), precludes review of the issue of great or irreparable injury. The reason it does so is plain. Once having occurred, the levy without notice cannot be undone, and no remedy remains to the debtor other than to challenge the validity of the attachment, if he can. A noticed procedure, namely the motion to quash, is provided for making this challenge. At the hearing on such motion, the plaintiff has the burden of proving that the attachment itself is proper (*Loeb & Loeb v. Beverly Glen Music, Inc.* (1985) 166 Cal. App. 3d 1110, 1116 [212 Cal. Rptr. 830].) If he does so, there is no practical reason to quash the writ. The damage of ex parte issuance, even if incorrect, has already been done. It would serve little purpose, and would waste time and judicial resources, to quash an otherwise properly issued writ because it should not have been issued ex parte. The issue of its validity has already been determined, and the creditor would have the immediate right to obtain another writ. * * *

Examining the facts here, we agree with RMI that insufficient justification for an ex parte writ of attachment was put before the trial court. The underlying declaration of Winthrop, President of Western, states no evidence other than RMI's immediate inability to pay to support his conclusion that "if RMI, INC. was given any notice at all of this hearing, RMI would take whatever steps were necessary to hide its assets so as to prevent attachment of these assets." Based on this declaration, Western's attorney submitted his declaration in support of the ex parte attachment saying no notice was given "based on the statements contained in the [Winthrop Declaration] ... regarding the shaky financial condition of defendant RMI, INC., and the probability that RMI, INC. would take action to conceal its assets if it had any notice of this proceeding,...." No evidence at all was presented of any past dishonesty, failure to meet obligations, or concealment of assets by RMI. These declarations are patently inadequate to meet the statutory requirement of a showing of "great or irreparable injury" based on an inference that "there is a danger that the property sought to be attached would be concealed, substantially impaired in value, or otherwise made unavailable to levy if issuance of the order were delayed...." (Code Civ. Proc., § 485.010, subds. (a), (b).) We agree with RMI that neither a precarious financial condition nor refusal to pay a disputed claim warrants an inference that a debtor will abscond with all his assets or otherwise conceal them from the creditor.

Nevertheless, as we have said, any harm resulting from the issuance of the writ without notice, about 20 days sooner than would otherwise have occurred, is now essentially moot. If we were to quash the writ and release the properties of RMI from levy, Western would be immediately entitled to another writ of attachment. Absent some compelling justification, we are reluctant to sanction such inefficient use of judicial resources and of litigants' time and money.

In the landmark case invalidating an earlier attachment statute, our Supreme Court specifically said the Legislature could draft a constitutionally valid prejudgment attachment statute, which exempted necessities and which permitted attachment before notice in "exceptional cases where, for example, the creditor can additionally demonstrate before a magistrate that an actual risk has arisen that assets will be concealed or that the debtor will abscond." (*Randone v. Appellate Department* (1971) 5 Cal. 3d 536, 563 [96 Cal. Rptr. 709, 488 P.2d 13].) The Legislature clearly had *Randone* in mind when it drafted the attachment statutes replacing the one there invalidated, and the remedy discussed here clearly comports with the decisional language, requiring the creditor to demonstrate before a magistrate the existence of risk of concealment or loss. Nothing in *Randone* requires that if the magistrate errs in appraising the risk to the creditor, an otherwise legitimate attachment must later be vacated.

The court in *Randone* was primarily concerned with two evils: the attachment of property constituting the debtor's necessities of life; and the wrongful tying up of the property of a debtor, who was likely to be ignorant of the remedies to challenge such an attachment, and was therefore apt to be deprived of much-needed assets for protracted periods of time during possibly meritless litigation. Accordingly, the court considerably narrowed the permissible scope of the prejudgment attachment remedy, and the resulting legislation reflects the considerations articulated in *Randone*: the attachment remedy is narrowly limited to liquidated, nonfrivolous claims, and as against individual debtors, must relate to a business matter (Code Civ. Proc., § 483.010); the claim must be unsecured (*id.*); the writ will only issue upon affidavit that the property sought to be attached is not exempt (Code Civ. Proc., §§ 484.510, 484.350); and necessities of life are exempted (Code Civ. Proc., §§ 487.020, 704.010 et seq.); the writ can only issue after a noticed hearing, except where, as discussed, a magistrate can be convinced great or irreparable injury will result from delay and notice; and where the writ issues ex parte, a remedy is provided, the motion to quash, which has calendar preference and can be heard promptly (Code Civ. Proc., § 485.240, subd. (e)). Regardless of whether the writ issues on notice or ex parte, the creditor has the burden of demonstrating the validity of the attachment. (*Loeb & Loeb v. Beverly Glen Music, Inc., supra.*) By these safeguards, it would appear the Legislature has done all that it can to comply with *Randone* and still provide an ex parte attachment remedy in limited circumstances.

These procedures fairly meet the concerns of *Randone*. We do not think the *Randone* court was concerned with a situation, as here, where the attachment is not wrongful—where it is a legitimate prejudgment remedy—but where it was erroneously issued too soon. Under such circumstances, no real harm is done, and to provide the sanction of quashing the writ would waste the time of all concerned. * * *

We conclude that whatever were the reasons of the trial judge, he reached the correct result. The order denying the motion to quash the writ of attachment is affirmed.

[1] The Attachment Law (CCP § 482.010 et seq.)

Attachment procedures are solely creatures of statute and, as such, must be strictly construed. *Bank of America v. Salinas Nissan*, 207 Cal. App. 3d 260, 270, 254 Cal. Rptr. 748 (1989). The current California attachment statutes, CCP §§ 481.010 *et. seq.*, are collectively referred to as "The Attachment Law." CCP § 482.010. As our principal case indicates, The Attachment Law is the legislative response to the due process concerns of *Randone v. Appellate Dept.*, 5 Cal. 3d 536, 96 Cal. Rptr. 709, 488 P.2d 13 (1971). After extensive study and recommendations by the Law Revision Commission, the Legislature comprehensively revised the entire attachment procedure, effective 1977. *See generally* 11 *Cal. L. Revision Commn. Reports* 701 (1973).

[2] Attachment Limitations

The Attachment Law contains several substantive and procedural limitations on the availability of prejudgment attachment. Some of these limitations are based on the constitutional concerns expressed in *Randone v. Appellate Dept., supra.* Other limitations reflect the Legislature's balancing of creditor and debtor interests.

[a] Attachment Limited to Certain Claims

The current statutory scheme limits the availability of attachment to certain specific claims. As to resident defendants, there are four basic restrictions on the types of actions in which prejudgment attachment is authorized. Generally, (1) the action must be on a claim for money based on express or implied contract, CCP § 483.010(a); (2) the total amount in controversy must be a fixed or readily ascertainable amount not less than $500, exclusive of costs, interest and legal fees, CCP § 483.010(a); (3) the claim must not be secured or, if originally secured, the security has become valueless or has decreased in value to less than the amount owing on the claim, CCP § 483.010(b); and (4), "[i]f the action is against a defendant who is a natural person, an attachment may be issued only on a claim which arises out of the conduct by the defendant of a trade, business, or profession." CCP § 483.010(c).

What are the likely policy reasons for these four statutory restrictions? Are any of them mandated by the Supreme Court's constitutional ruling in *Randone*? As discussed below, these general restrictions do not apply initially to attachments where the defendant debtor is a nonresident of California.

[b] Attachment Limited to Certain Property

Where the defendant is a corporation or partnership, all corporate or partnership property is, generally, subject to attachment. CCP § 487.010(a) & (b). However, where the defendant is a natural person, CCP § 487.010(c) specifies the property which is subject to attachment. Although this list is quite comprehensive, another important statutory protection further limits the availability of a natural person's property to attachment.

Pursuant to CCP § 487.020, certain property of a natural person is exempt from attachment. This includes all property exempt from enforcement of a money judgment, such as certain household furnishings, government benefits, and other personal property (up to a statutorily specified amount of equity, *see, e.g.*, CCP §§ 704.010-704.210); property necessary for the support of a defendant who is a natural person or for such defendant's family; and earnings as defined by CCP § 706.011 which includes compensation payable by an employer to an employee for personal services whether designated as wages, salary, commission, bonus or otherwise. A recorded homestead declaration does not exempt a homestead from attachment, although the attachment lien attaches only the amount of any surplus over the total of all liens, encumbrances, and the homestead exemption. CCP § 487.025. These exemptions from attachments do not apply to non-natural person defendants, such as corporations or partnerships. CCP § 487.010-.020.

The procedures and time limitations for claiming exemptions from attachment of personal property are set forth in CCP §§ 482.040-482.120, and for claiming exemptions from attachment of real property in CCP §§ 482.100.

[c] "Substantive" Limitations on Attachment

If, after a hearing on a noticed application for a writ of attachment, the court finds that the claim is one upon which an attachment may be issued and the property sought to be attached is not exempt, the court must also find the following "substantive" prerequisites: (1) "The plaintiff has established the probable validity of the claim upon which the attachment is based" and (2) "The attachment is not sought for a purpose other than the recovery on the claim upon which the attachment is based," CCP § 484.090(2) & (3). How onerous are these last two requirements? How difficult is it for a plaintiff to establish the "probable validity" of a claim? CCP § 481.190 states that a claim has "probable validity" where "it is more likely than not that the plaintiff will obtain a judgment against the defendant on that claim." What does this definition mean, as a substantive standard for attachment? From a procedural perspective, what does this standard necessitate?

[d]   Undertakings

Prior to the issuance of a writ of attachment, the plaintiff must file an undertaking (bond). The bond's purpose is to pay the defendant any amount the defendant may later recover against plaintiff in a wrongful attachment action. CCP §§ 489.010-.210. An attachment issued without the required bond is void *ab initio*. *Vershbow v. Reiner*, 231 Cal. App. 3d 879, 282 Cal. Rptr. 684 (1991).

The amount of this required undertaking is statutorily set as $10,000. CCP § 489.220(a). If the defendant objects to the amount of undertaking, and the court determines that the probable recovery for wrongful attachment exceeds the statutory amount, it will order an increased amount. § 489.220(b). Why is the amount of the required undertaking statutorily limited?

[e]   Ex Parte Writ of Attachment

If a plaintiff creditor seeks an *ex parte* writ of attachment, as our principal case illustrates, the plaintiff must also show that "great or irreparable injury" would result to the plaintiff if the attachment were delayed until after a noticed hearing. CCP § 485.010(a). What showing, according to CCP § 485.010(b), will satisfy this additional requirement? How did the plaintiff in *Western Steel* fail to satisfy this requirement of showing "great or irreparable injury"? What more should the plaintiff have shown? How would the plaintiff obtain such evidence?

The court in *Western Steel* concluded that insufficient justification for an *ex parte* writ of attachment was put before the trial court. Why did the court, nevertheless, refuse to quash the writ? Do you agree with the court's reasoning? Do you think it is fair to the defendant? Do you agree with the court that any harm resulting from the issuance of the *ex parte* writ is now moot? One consequence of the *ex parte* writ attaching defendant RMD's bank account was that payroll checks issued by RMD were later dishonored for insufficient funds. Is this harm moot? Does defendant have an adequate remedy through an action for wrongful attachment? What about injured third parties?

A plaintiff's liability to a defendant for statutory wrongful attachment, as defined by CCP § 490.010, is limited to the amount of the undertaking filed by plaintiff. CCP § 489.220 specifies the undertaking amount as $10,000, unless the court ordered an increased amount. Common law remedies for wrongful attachment are available, CCP § 490.060, but may be difficult to achieve. *See* Dean Gloster, Comment, *Abuse of Process and Attachment: Toward A Balance of Power*, 30 UCLA L. Rev. 1218-1248 (1983).

[3]   *Attachment Procedures*

A writ of attachment may be issued *ex parte*, as in *Western Steel*, or may be issued after a noticed hearing.

[a] Ex Parte Attachment Procedures

Upon filing the complaint, a plaintiff may immediately apply for a writ of attachment by filing an application and supporting affidavits, and without any notice provided to the defendant. If the court determines that plaintiff's application and supporting affidavits demonstrate satisfaction of the statutory prerequisites for an *ex parte* writ, the court will issue a right to attach order and writ of attachment, upon filing of the appropriate undertaking. CCP §§ 485.010-.230. The levying officer then levies the writ (*i.e.*, attaches the property), and serves the complaint, summons, and the notice of attachment. CCP §§ 488.010-.140.

The defendant whose property has been so attached *ex parte* may thereafter apply for an order quashing the writ of attachment or reducing the amount to be secured by the attachment. CCP § 485.240. Such application is made by notice of motion and accompanying affidavits, although additional evidence may be received at the hearing. § 485.240(d). At the hearing, the court must determine whether the plaintiff is entitled to the attachment. If the court finds plaintiff is not so entitled, it must quash the writ and order release of the levy on the property. § 485.240(c). If the court finds that plaintiff is entitled, the attachment continues and plaintiff may apply for additional writs as to other property. §§ 485.240(c); 484.310-.530.

[b] Attachment Procedure on Noticed Hearing

In the absence of exceptional circumstances (*i.e.*, "great irreparable injury"), upon filing the complaint a plaintiff must apply for a writ of attachment through a noticed hearing procedure. Plaintiff must file an application for attachment, with supporting affidavits, whose content demonstrates compliance with the prerequisite for attachment. CCP §§ 484.010-0.30. Plaintiff must then serve the complaint, summons, and notice of application and hearing, informing the defendant of the scheduled hearing on the attachment application. CCP § 484.040-.050. Plaintiff must also file an undertaking. CCP §§ 489.010-.230.

If the defendant wishes to oppose issuance of the writ of attachment, the defendant must file and serve a notice of opposition no later than five days before the hearing. CCP § 484.060. A defendant who desires to claim a personal property exemption must likewise file and serve that claim no later than five days before the hearing (see discussion below). § 484.070. At the hearing, the court must consider the showing made by the parties and determine whether the plaintiff has satisfied the prerequisites to attachment. § 484.090. If the court so finds, it must issue a right to attach order and writ of attachment. § 484.090. After the writ is issued, based on plaintiff's instructions, a levying officer will levy the writ on property in the manner prescribed by statute. CCP §§ 488.010-488.740. What type of hearing is required by CCP § 484.040 prior to issuance of a prejudgment writ of attachment? According to *Hobbs v. Weiss*, 73 Cal. App. 4th 76, 86 Cal. Rptr. 2d 146 (1999), the term "hearing" in this statutory context requires an oral hearing at which the trial court may take evidence, entertain and rule on evidentiary objections, and determine the merits based on written *and* oral presentations.

A defendant who wishes to further challenge an attachment issued by the trial court after a noticed hearing must do so by means of an immediate interlocutory appeal. CCP § 904.1(a)(5); § 703.600. Failure to do so may preclude subsequent review of the attachment. *See Peck v. Hagan*, 215 Cal. App. 3d 602, 607-609, 263 Cal. Rptr. 198 (1989) (concluding failure to appeal refusal to discharge attachment has res judicata effect).

What is the res judicata effect of the trial court's finding, in issuing a writ of attachment after a noticed hearing, that plaintiff has established the probable validity of the underlying claim upon which the attachment is based? *See* CCP § 484.100 ("The court's determinations ... shall not be given in evidence nor referred to at the trial"). What is the effect on the trial of the merits of plaintiff's underlying claim of the defendant's failure to oppose the attachment or to rebut evidence offered by the plaintiff at the hearing? *See* CCP § 484.110; *Film Packagers, Inc. v. Brandywine Film Prod., Ltd.*, 193 Cal. App. 3d 824, 238 Cal. Rptr. 623 (1987).

When a plaintiff applies for a writ of attachment through the noticed hearing procedure and the defendant desires to claim at the hearing that certain personal property specified in the application is exempt from attachment, the defendant must file the claim of exemption not less than five days prior to the hearing. CCP § 484.070(a)-(e). If the plaintiff desires to oppose defendant's claim of exemption, plaintiff must file a notice of opposition not less than two days before the hearing. CCP § 484.070(f).

If the defendant fails to timely assert a claim of exemption as to personal property, or makes the claim but fails to prove it, the defendant is precluded from claiming the exemption later. CCP § 484.070(a). The exemption as to personal property is waived, even as to postjudgment execution, unless the defendant can demonstrate a change in circumstances. CCP § 482.100. With respect to an *ex parte* attachment and levy, the defendant must claim an exemption as to personal property within 30 days after service of the notice of attachment, or such exemption is likewise waived. CCP § 485.610.

However, unlike personal property, a defendant who fails to make the claim of exemption of real property at the time of attachment is not precluded from later claiming the exemption. CCP §§ 484.070(b); 485.610. The defendant debtor is permitted to claim an exemption as to real property at any time prior to entry of judgment in the action. CCP § 487.030; *see Martin v. Aboyan*, 148 Cal. App. 3d 826, 196 Cal. Rptr. 266 (1983). What policy concerns likely influenced the Legislature to enact a more forgiving exception waiver rule for real property as opposed to personal property?

[4] Nonresident Attachment

A different set of statutory principles and prerequisites govern, initially at least, the attachment of property in California owned by a nonresident. Code of Civil Procedure § 492.010 authorizes attachment in *any* action for recovery of money against a natural person who does not reside in California, a foreign corporation not qualified to do business within California, or a foreign partnership which has not designated a California agent for service of process. Moreover, a writ of attachment issued against a nonresident may be levied on *any* California property of the defendant. CCP §492.040. The plaintiff may apply for the writ of attachment *ex parte*, but with no specific showing of great or irreparable injury necessary. CCP §§492.020-.030. If the defendant wishes to challenge the propriety of the nonresident *ex parte* attachment, the defendant may apply to quash the attachment through a noticed motion procedure. CCP §492.050.

[a] Purpose

Nonresident attachment has a dual purpose: to secure property for eventual satisfaction of a judgments and, traditionally, to operate where personal jurisdiction of a defendant cannot be obtained but *quasi in rem* jurisdiction can be obtained by seizure of the nonresident's property in the state. *See Nakasone v. Randall*, 129 Cal. App. 3d 757, 760, 181 Cal. Rptr. 324 (1982) (distinguishing between nonresident attachment and ordinary attachment). Consequently, if the nonresident defendant enters a general appearance in the action, the attachment must be set aside unless plaintiff shows the attachment satisfies the various prerequisites for ordinary attachment. CCP §492.050(c); *Nakasone v. Randall, supra.*

[b] Due Process Issues

Nonresident attachment raises some serious due process issues, does it not? First, does the *ex parte* nonresident attachment process satisfy the constitutional requirements set forth by the California Supreme Court in *Randone*? Does it comply with the recent decision in *Connecticut v. Doehr*, 501 U.S. 1, 111 S. Ct. 2105, 115 L. Ed. 2d 1 (1991), where the U.S. Supreme Court held that *ex parte* attachment of real property without a showing of "exigent circumstances" (*e.g.*, imminent transfer or encumbrance) violated the defendant's due process rights under the Fourteenth Amendment? Does it comply with the Supreme Court's ruling in *Shaffer v. Heitner*, 433 U.S. 186, 97 S. Ct. 2569, 53 L. Ed. 2d 683 (1977), that all assertions of state court personal jurisdiction over an absent defendant, including *quasi in rem* jurisdiction based on attachment of property present in the forum state, must be evaluated according to the defendant's "minimum contacts" with the forum state? Are some applications of California's *quasi in rem* jurisdiction (nonresident attachment) statute directly contrary to *Shaffer*? What are some examples?

[B] Other Provisional Remedies

[1] Temporary Protective Orders

Code of Civil Procedure §§486.010-.110 authorizes another type of provisional remedy which prohibits a defendant from transferring certain assets pending a hearing on a writ of attachment. Similar to but less comprehensive than an *ex parte* attachment, a court may be willing to issue a temporary protective order in lieu of the more drastic *ex parte* writ. *See* CCP § 486.030. A temporary protective order expires forty days after issuance, or when levy of attachment is made as to specific property described in the order, whichever occurs earlier. CCP § 486.090.

[2] Claim and Delivery

Code of Civil Procedure §§ 511.010-512.120 authorize a plaintiff creditor to bring an action to recover possession of personal property before judgment by applying for the provisional remedy of claim and delivery. Upon filing the complaint, a plaintiff may apply for a writ of possession by a noticed motion or, in appropriate circumstances, *ex parte*. CCP §§ 512.010-512.020. The plaintiff creditor must show that it is entitled to possession of the property claimed, and that the property is wrongfully detained by the defendant. *See* CCP §§ 512.010 and 512.020 for the specific statutory prerequisites. If the court issues a writ of possession, the property specified may be seized by the levying officer pending final judgment in the action. §§ 512.080-512.120.

[3] Receivership

Although perhaps more commonly utilized as a means to effectuate a final judgment, CCP § 564 authorizes the superior court to appoint a receiver to manage and preserve the business or property of others pending litigation so that relief awarded by judgment will be effective. *See, e.g.*, *Security Pac. Nat. Bank v. Geernoert*, 199 Cal. App. 3d 1425, 1431-1432, 245 Cal. Rptr. 712 (1988) (appointing receiver to manage ranch operated as general partnership, in action brought by plaintiff bank to recover money loaned to defendant partnership, and observing "[a] receiver is an officer of the court appointed to manage property that is the subject of litigation").

[4] Temporary Restraining Order

Another traditional provisional remedy is the temporary restraining order and preliminary injunction. *See* CCP §§ 513.010, 525-533. These broad equitable orders are discussed in more detail in the next section. One function of a temporary restraining order is to prohibit a defendant from transferring, removing, or impairing the value of specific property. CCP § 513.020. Such use overlaps with other provisional remedies of attachment and temporary protective order.

The Attachment Law does not preclude the granting of injunctive relief, CCP § 482.020; but a plaintiff will not be permitted to utilize temporary injunctive relief as a means of circumventing the statutory prerequisites for attachment. In *Doyka v. Superior Court*, 233 Cal. App. 3d 1134, 285 Cal. Rptr. 14 (1991), for example, the Court of Appeal vacated a preliminary injunction which enjoined defendant from using the sum of $125,000 in any bank account as an attempt to attach all of defendant's liquid assets without satisfying the statutory requirements for prejudgment attachment. The plaintiff's action sought return of monies loaned to defendant, an individual, for real estate renovations, and secured by a deed of trust. In what ways did the preliminary injunction in *Dayka* fail to satisfy the statutory prerequisites for attachment?

[5] Contractual Arbitration

A party to an arbitration agreement may file in court an application for a provisional remedy in connection with an arbitrable controversy, but only upon the ground that the arbitration award to which the applicant may be entitled "may be rendered ineffectual without provisional relief." CCP § 1281.8(b). The provisional remedies available include attachments, temporary protective orders, writs of possession, and preliminary injunctions. CCP § 1281.8(a). However, this specific statutory authority for provisional judicial remedies to protect against rendering a possible arbitration award ineffectual does not supplant the general statutory requirements applicable to the requested provisional remedy. *See, e.g., Woolley v. Embassy Suites, Inc.,* 227 Cal. App. 3d 1520, 1526-29, 278 Cal. Rptr. 719 (1991) (ruling CCP § 1281.8 sets forth the threshold requirement for obtaining a preliminary injunction during an arbitration, but the applicant must also satisfy the traditional and statutory requirements of preliminary injunctive relief).

[6] Lis Pendens

A notice of the pendency of an action, commonly referred to as a "lis pendens," is an important pretrial procedure available to any party who asserts a claim to specific real property. The California Legislature, by adopting CCP § 405 *et seq.* in 1992, substantially overhauled the traditional lis pendens law. *See generally* CEB, *California Real Property Remedies and Damages* §§ 13.1-13.120 (2d ed. 2015).

Kirkeby v. Superior Court

Supreme Court of California
33 Cal. 4th 642, 15 Cal. Rptr. 3d 805, 93 P.3d 395 (2004)

BROWN, JUSTICE.

In this case, we consider whether a fraudulent conveyance claim affects title to or the right to possession of specific real property and therefore supports the recording of a notice of pendency of action — commonly referred to as a lis pendens. We conclude that it does.

FACTS

FasTags, Inc. (FasTags) is a manufacturer and wholesale seller of identification tags for pets. Petitioner Cynthia Kirkeby and her brother Frederick W. Fascenelli developed the idea for the tags and jointly hold the patent for the manufacturing processes. Frederick and his wife Diana Fascenelli (hereafter the Fascenellis) hold 51 percent of the outstanding stock in FasTags, and Kirkeby owns 39 percent. The remaining 10 percent of FasTags' outstanding stock is held by the FasTags Stock Trust, of which Kirkeby is the trustee.

After Kirkeby resigned from the FasTags board of directors in 1998, she alleged the Fascenellis looted the company. According to Kirkeby, the Fascenellis caused

FasTags to execute improper patent licenses to increase their own salaries and bonuses, to pay their personal expenses, and to make improper loans. The Fascenellis allegedly prevented Kirkeby from seeking corporate records, canceled meetings so that Kirkeby could not elect a member to the board of directors, and appointed directors without board approval.

Kirkeby filed the instant action in late 2001. In the complaint, Kirkeby alleged 27 causes of action, including a cause of action for fraudulent conveyance, and sought declaratory and injunctive relief and damages in the aggregate amount of $4.9 million on behalf of herself and FasTags.

In her fraudulent conveyance cause of action, Kirkeby alleged that Frederick obtained a $50,000 loan from FasTags by representing that he would use the borrowed funds to construct a building to house FasTags' operations. But Frederick did not use this loan for its stated purpose. According to Kirkeby, Frederick used the loan to purchase residential income property (the Oak Street Property) for himself and Diana in June 2000. After making this purchase, the Fascenellis immediately transferred their interest in the property to Italy & Greek Holdings, a family limited partnership (the Family Partnership).

Prior to the purchase of the Oak Street Property—in May 1999—Frederick also transferred his interest in his family's residence (the Clark Street Property) to the Fascenelli Family Trust. Several months later, the Fascenellis—as trustees of that trust—transferred the trust's interest in the Clark Street Property to the Family Partnership. Kirkeby alleged that the Fascenellis made both of these transfers in order to defraud creditors in the collection of their claims, and requested that the transfers be voided to the extent necessary to satisfy the claims set forth in her complaint. These transfers formed the bases of Kirkeby's fraudulent conveyance claim as set forth in her complaint.

After filing her action, Kirkeby recorded a notice of lis pendens on the Oak Street Property and the Clark Street Property. The Fascenellis moved to expunge the lis pendens. The trial court granted the motion. During the hearing on the motion to expunge, the court held that the complaint was primarily about money damages and that the recording of a lis pendens was not appropriate where a cause of action for fraudulent conveyance—Kirkeby's only claim relating to the real property at issue—was made but no ownership interest or possessory interest had been claimed in the subject properties.

Kirkeby filed a writ petition seeking review of the expungement order. The Court of Appeal denied the petition. The Court of Appeal held that Kirkeby's complaint did not affect title to or the right to possession of real property so as to support her lis pendens, as required under Code of Civil Procedure section 405.4. The Court of Appeal determined that the basis of Kirkeby's complaint was to recover money that the Fascenellis wrongfully diverted to themselves in the running of FasTags. With respect to Kirkeby's fraudulent conveyance claim, the Court of Appeal stated, "[w]ith the exception of the cause of action for fraudulent conveyance, the complaint has nothing to do with real property. And the goal of the fraudulent conveyance cause of action is to make the property available for the collection of a judgment, not to further a claim by Kirkeby to title or possession."

We granted review.

DISCUSSION

"A lis pendens is a recorded document giving constructive notice that an action has been filed affecting title or right to possession of the real property described in the notice." (*Urez Corp. v. Superior Court* (1987) 190 Cal. App. 3d 1141, 1144 [235 Cal. Rptr. 837].) A lis pendens may be filed by any party in an action who asserts a "real property claim." (Code Civ. Proc., § 405.20.)[1] Section 405.4 defines a " 'Real property claim' " as "the cause or causes of action in a pleading which would, if meritorious, affect (a) title to, or the right to possession of, specific real property...." "If the pleading filed by the claimant does not properly plead a real property claim, the lis pendens must be expunged upon motion under CCP 405.31." (Code com., 14 West's Ann. Code Civ. Proc. (2004 supp.) foll. § 405.4, p. 239.)

Section 405.30 allows the property owner to remove an improperly recorded lis pendens by bringing a motion to expunge. There are several statutory bases for expungement of a lis pendens, including the claim at issue here: claimant's pleadings, on which the lis pendens is based, do not contain a real property claim. (See § 405.31.)[2] Unlike most other motions, when a motion to expunge is brought, the burden is on the party opposing the motion to show the existence of a real property claim. (See § 405.30.)

The Fascenellis moved to expunge pursuant to section 405.31 — lack of a real property claim. Section 405.31 provides: "In proceedings under this chapter, the court shall order the notice expunged if the court finds that the pleading on which the notice is based does not contain a real property claim." In making this determination, the court must engage in a demurrer-like analysis. "Rather than analyzing whether the pleading states any claim at all, as on a general demurrer, the court must undertake the more limited analysis of whether the pleading states a real property claim." (Code com., 14 West's Ann. Code Civ. Proc., *supra*, foll. § 405.31, at p. 249.) Review "involves only a review of the adequacy of the pleading and normally should not involve evidence from either side, other than possibly that which may be judicially noticed as on a demurrer." (Code com., 14 West's Ann. Code Civ. Proc., *supra*, foll. § 405.30, at p. 248.) Therefore, review of an expungement order under section 405.31 is limited

---

1. Unless otherwise indicated, all further statutory references are to the Code of Civil Procedure.

2. Other bases for expungement include: (1) claimant's failure to comply with the recording, service or filing requirements of section 405.22 (see § 405.23); (2) claimant's failure to establish the probable validity of a real property claim by a preponderance of the evidence (see § 405.32); (3) claimant is secured by a property owner filing an undertaking (see § 405.33); and (4) claimant's failure to file an undertaking ordered by the court as a condition to maintaining a lis pendens (see § 405.34).

to whether a real property claim has been properly pled by the claimant. (Code com., 14 West's Ann. Code Civ. Proc., *supra*, foll. §405.31, at p. 249.)

Because only Kirkeby's fraudulent conveyance claim relates to real property, we must now determine whether that claim, as pled, affects "title to, or the right to possession of, specific real property." (§405.4.) We conclude it does.

A fraudulent conveyance claim is set forth in the Uniform Fraudulent Transfer Act (UFTA), which is codified in Civil Code section 3439 et seq. "A fraudulent conveyance is a transfer by the debtor of property to a third person undertaken with the intent to prevent a creditor from reaching that interest to satisfy its claim." (*Yaesu Electronics Corp. v. Tamura* (1994) 28 Cal.App.4th 8, 13 [33 Cal. Rptr. 2d 283].) A transfer under the UFTA is defined as "every mode, direct or indirect, absolute or conditional, voluntary or involuntary, of disposing of or parting with an asset…, and includes payment of money, release, lease, and creation of a lien or other encumbrance." (Civ. Code, §3439.01, subd. (i).) * * *

Civil Code section 3439.07 sets forth the remedies in a fraudulent conveyance action. Under subdivision (a)(1) of that section, a creditor who makes a successful fraudulent conveyance claim may obtain "[a]voidance of the transfer or obligation to the extent necessary to satisfy the creditor's claim." Therefore, a fraudulent conveyance claim requesting relief pursuant to Civil Code section 3439.07, subdivision (a)(1), if successful, may result in the voiding of a transfer of title of specific real property. By definition, the voiding of a transfer of real property will affect title to or possession of real property. Therefore, a fraudulent conveyance action seeking avoidance of a transfer under subdivision (a)(1) of Civil Code section 3439.07 clearly "affects title to, or the right to possession of" (Code Civ. Proc., §405.4) real property and is therefore a real property claim for the purposes of the lis pendens statutes. * * *

Nonetheless, … the Fascenellis contend a court "must look through the pleadings to ascertain the purpose of the party seeking to maintain notice of lis pendens." (*Hunting World, Inc. v. Superior Court* (1994) 22 Cal.App.4th 67, 73 [26 Cal. Rptr. 2d 923]) In support, the Fascenellis cite *Urez Corp v. Superior Court, supra,* 190 Cal. App. 3d 1141, and several other cases. The Fascenellis' argument fails based on the plain language of the applicable statute. Nowhere in the language of section 405.31, or in its legislative history, is the court directed to conduct such an examination during its demurrer-like analysis. Indeed, the legislative history expressly requires courts to consider only the specific claim as pled and to determine whether that claim is a real property claim…. * * *

… Kirkeby adequately pled a fraudulent conveyance claim by alleging that the Fascenellis transferred title of the subject properties with the intent to defraud. Specifically, she alleged "that Defendants made these transfers with the actual intent to hinder, delay, and/or defraud all of their creditors in the collection of their claims.…" Kirkeby also asked the court to void the transfers of both properties to the extent necessary to satisfy the claims in her complaint. As such, her fraudulent conveyance claim, if successful, will affect title to specific real property. Accordingly, her lis pendens was improperly expunged based on section 405.31.

In reaching this conclusion, we recognize that the lis pendens statute may be abused. "While the lis pendens statute was designed to give notice to third parties and not to aid plaintiffs in pursuing claims, the practical effect of a recorded lis pendens is to render a defendant's property unmarketable and unsuitable as security for a loan. The financial pressure exerted on the property owner may be considerable, forcing him to settle not due to the merits of the suit but to rid himself of the cloud upon his title. The potential for abuse is obvious. [Citations.]" (*La Paglia v. Superior Court, supra*, 215 Cal. App. 3d at p. 1326, abrogated on another ground by *Lewis v. Superior Court* (1999) 19 Cal.4th 1232, 1258, fn. 17 [82 Cal. Rptr. 2d 85, 970 P.2d 872].) Because of the effect of a lis pendens, "[t]he history of the lis pendens legislation indicates a legislative intent to restrict rather than broaden the application of the remedy." (*Urez v. Superior Court, supra*, 190 Cal. App. 3d at p. 1145.) Our courts have followed suit by restricting rather than broadening the application of a lis pendens. (*Ibid.*)

Nonetheless, we cannot ignore the plain language of the statute, which clearly establishes that fraudulent conveyance claims may support a lis pendens where the plaintiff seeks to void a fraudulent transfer. If this is problematic, it is up to the Legislature — and not this court — to change the law. In any event, there are many other grounds for expunging a lis pendens. For example, under section 405.32, the court is required to expunge a lis pendens "if the court finds that the claimant has not established by a preponderance of the evidence the probable validity of the real property claim." Section 405.32 — unlike section 405.31 — "expressly concerns factual merit. Provision for a demurrer-like review of the pleading is preserved in CCP 405.31." (Code com., 14 West's Ann. Code Civ. Proc., *supra*, foll. §405.32, at p. 250.) Section 405.32 therefore requires a "judicial evaluation of the merits" of a claimant's case. (Code com., 14 West's Ann. Code Civ. Proc., *supra*, foll. §405.32, at p. 250.) Under Section 405.33, even if a claimant shows a probably valid claim, the court may still order a lis pendens expunged if adequate relief for the claimant may be secured by the giving of an undertaking. In addition, "the property owner ... may be entitled to attorney fees and costs if successful" in expunging a lis pendens, and "[t]rial courts should liberally impose these sanctions upon any who file fraudulent transfer actions and record notices of lis pendens before uncovering credible evidence of fraud." (*Hunting World, supra*, 22 Cal.App.4th at p. 74.) The availability of these statutory alternatives and the possible imposition of attorney fees and sanctions should discourage abuse of the lis pendens statute. * * *

DISPOSITION

We reverse the judgment of the Court of Appeal and remand for further proceedings consistent with this opinion.

[a] The Lis Pendens Notice

Lis pendens is a notice of the pendency of an action in which a "real property claim" is alleged. CCP §405.2. As *Kirkeby* illustrates, a "real property claim" is a pleaded cause of action which would, if victorious, affect title to, or possession of, specific real property. CCP § 405.4. A lis pendens notice is a simple document which can be prepared by a party's attorney, served on adverse parties and owners of record, and recorded in each county where the potentially affected real property is located. CCP §§ 405.20, 405.21, 405.23.; *see Carr v. Rosien*, 238 Cal. App. 4th 845, 190 Cal. Rptr. 3d 245 (2015) (holding failure to mail lis pendens to defendant landowner rendered it void as to landowner and landowner's transferees). From the time of proper recordation, a purchaser, encumbrancer, or other transferee of the real property described in the notice is deemed to have constructive notice of the pending action. § 405.24. The rights and interest of the claimant in the property, as ultimately determined in the pending action, relates back to the date of the recording of the notice. § 405.24.

[b] Effect of Lis Pendens

The effect of a lis pendens is to give notice that a lawsuit has been filed which may affect title to, or possession of, real property described in the notice. A transfer of the property after a lis pendens is recorded binds the transferee to a judgment subsequently rendered in the pending action. *See Federal Deposit Ins. Co. v. Charlton*, 17 Cal. App. 4th 1066, 1069, 21 Cal. Rptr. 2d 686 (1993). But a lis pendens does not by itself make the party who recorded the notice a secured creditor nor create any priority interest. *See Stagen v. Stewart-West Coast Title Co.*, 149 Cal. App. 3d 114, 123, 196 Cal. Rptr. 732 (1983) ("A judgment favorable to the plaintiff relates to, and receives its priority from, the date the lis pendens is recorded, and is senior and prior to any interests in the property acquired after that date"); *Mira Overseas Consulting Ltd. v. Muse Family Enter., Ltd.*, 237 Cal. App. 4th 398, 187 Cal. Rptr. 3d 858 (2015) (concluding defendants' judgment lien had priority over plaintiff's judgment with respect to real property involved in two separate fraudulent transfer actions because the judgment lien related back to the date defendants recorded their lis pendens, which was earlier than date plaintiff recorded its abstract of judgment).

[c] Motion to Expunge

A party who wishes to challenge the propriety of a lis pendens, as in *Kirkeby*, may do so by moving to expunge the notice. CCP § 405.30. The court shall order the notice expunged if the pleadings do not allege a real property claim, or if the claimant has not established by a preponderance of the evidence the probable validity of her real property claim. § 405.32. The court may also expunge the notice if it finds that adequate relief can be secured to the claimant by the giving of an undertaking. § 405.33. Likewise, the court may at any time require the claimant to give an undertaking as a condition to maintaining the notice in the record title. § 405.34.

Does a lis pendens continue during the time for appeal, even though the party who recorded the lis pendens was unsuccessful at trial? The court in *Mix v. Superior Court*, 124 Cal. App. 4th 987, 21 Cal. Rptr. 3d 826 (2004), held that the trial court erred in denying the defendant's motion to expunge a lis pendens recorded by the plaintiff, where the plaintiff lost on the merits at trial. The court ruled that CCP §405.32 required the trial court to expunge a lis pendens when the claimant was unsuccessful at trial, unless the trial court was willing to find that its own decision was likely to be reversed on appeal. The plaintiff could, however, seek a stay of the expungement order pending appeal.

[d]   Is Lis Pendens a Provisional Remedy?

Although traditionally viewed as only a method of giving notice, some courts characterize the lis pendens as a provisional remedy. *See, e.g., Urez v. Superior Court*, 190 Cal. App. 3d 1141, 235 Cal. Rptr. 837 (1987). The Code Comments which accompanied the Legislature's 1992 adoption of CCP §405 *et seq.* observed that this distinction is one of semantics, not of substance: "[T]he recordation of a lis pendens gives a claimant a de facto, if not a de jure, provisional remedy." *Code Comment*, West's Ann. Cal. CCP §405.32 (1995 Suppl.). What is meant by this comment? What is the legal benefit of lis pendens to the party recording the notice? What are the practical benefits? What is the legal effect on the adverse party? What are the practical detriments? In what ways does lis pendens differ from the provisional remedy of attachment?

[e]   Availability of Lis Pendens

Lis pendens is available to any party, based on claims alleged in a complaint or cross-complaint. CCP §405.1. Either party in a dissolution of marriage action is authorized to record a lis pendens notice where interest in real property is involved. Family Code §754. However, the pleading must allege a community interest in *specific* real property in order to state a "real property claim" within the meaning of CCP §405.4. *See Gale v. Superior Court*, 122 Cal. App. 4th 1388, 19 Cal. Rptr. 3d 554 (2004) (concluding the common practice of family lawyers of not specifying items of community or separate property does not comply with the statutory requirements for lis pendens).

Do the California lis pendens statutes apply when litigation is filed in another state but involves a claim to real property located in California? *See The Formula Inc. v. Superior Court*, 168 Cal. App. 4th 1455, 86 Cal. Rptr. 3d 341 (2008) (ruling California's lis pendens statutes do not authorize recording a notice of litigation that is pending in the courts of another state). Do they apply to an arbitration proceeding involving real property? *See Manhattan Loft LLC v. Mercury Liquor, Inc.*, 173 Cal. App. 4th 1040, 93 Cal. Rptr. 3d 457 (2009) (concluding a party to a pending arbitration cannot record a lis pendens without first filing a civil action in superior court).

[C]   Official Forms and Other Resources

[1]   California Judicial Council Forms

The Judicial Council has approved an official form for nearly every step in the provisional remedy process. *E.g.*, Judicial Council Form AT-105: Application for Right to Attach Order, Temporary Protective Order, Etc.; Judicial Council Form AT-155: Notice of Opposition to Right to Attach Order and Claim of Exemption. Use of these forms, by either a plaintiff creditor or a defendant debtor as appropriate, is an efficient way to ensure that all the statutory prerequisites or oppositions to a particular provisional remedy are considered.

[2] *California Law Revision Commission Comments*

The statutory laws governing attachment and other provisional remedies in California are comprehensive and quite complex. Nevertheless, proper interpretation of the specific statutory requirements is not always easy. Of particular assistance here are the authoritative Comments of the California Law Revision Commission, which accompanied the various major revisions of the Attachment Law. *See, e.g.,* 16 *Cal. L. Revision Comm'n Reports* 703-823, 1603-1761 (1982); 11 *Cal. L. Revision Comm'n Reports* 705-739 (1973). These comments provide guidance as to the Legislature's intent. *Van Arsdale v. Hollinger,* 68 Cal. 2d 245, 249-50, 66 Cal. Rptr. 20, 437 P.2d 508 (1968) ("Reports of commissions which have proposed statutes that are subsequently adopted are entitled to substantial weight in construing the statutes."); *Bank of America v. Salinas Nissan,* 207 Cal. App. 3d 260, 267, 254 Cal. Rptr. 748 (1989) (Relying on the Law Revision Commission Comments as guidance to the legislature's intent, court construed Attachment Law as not requiring specific description in attachment application of property sought to be attached when defendant is partnership or corporation).

§ 7.02 Preliminary Injunctive Relief

[A] Preliminary Injunctions

California Code of Civil Procedure § 527 (2016)

(a) A preliminary injunction may be granted at any time before judgment upon a verified complaint, or upon affidavits if the complaint in the one case, or the affidavits in the other, show satisfactorily that sufficient grounds exist therefor. No preliminary injunction shall be granted without notice to the opposing party. * * *

(c) No temporary restraining order shall be granted without notice to the opposing party, unless both of the following requirements are satisfied:

(1) It appears from facts shown by affidavit or by the verified complaint that great or irreparable injury will result to the applicant before the matter can be heard on notice.

(2) The applicant or the applicant's attorney certifies one of the following to the court under oath:

(A) That within a reasonable time prior to the application the applicant informed the opposing party or the opposing party's attorney at what time and where the application would be made.

(B) That the applicant in good faith attempted but was unable to inform the opposing party and the opposing party's attorney, specifying the efforts made to contact them.

(C) That for reasons specified the applicant should not be required to so inform the opposing party or the opposing party's attorney.

(d) In case a temporary restraining order is granted without notice in the contingency specified in subdivision (c):

(1) The matter shall be made returnable on an order requiring cause to be shown why a preliminary injunction should not be granted, on the earliest day that the business of the court will admit of, but not later than 15 days or, if good cause appears to the court, 22 days from the date the temporary restraining order is issued.

(2) The party who obtained the temporary restraining order shall, within five days from the date the temporary restraining order is issued or two days prior to the hearing, whichever is earlier, serve on the opposing party a copy of the complaint if not previously served, the order to show cause stating the date, time, and place of the hearing, any affidavits to be used in the application, and a copy of the points and authorities in support of the application. The court may for good cause, on motion of the applicant or on its own motion, shorten the time required by this paragraph for service on the opposing party.

(3) When the matter first comes up for hearing, if the party who obtained the temporary restraining order is not ready to proceed, or if the party has failed to effect service as required by paragraph (2), the court shall dissolve the temporary restraining order.

(4) The opposing party is entitled to one continuance for a reasonable period of not less than 15 days or any shorter period requested by the opposing party, to enable the opposing party to meet the application for a preliminary injunction. If the opposing party obtains a continuance under this paragraph, the temporary restraining order shall remain in effect until the date of the continued hearing.

(5) Upon the filing of an affidavit by the applicant that the opposing party could not be served within the time required by paragraph (2), the court may reissue any temporary restraining order previously issued. The reissued order shall be made returnable as provided by paragraph (1), with the time for hearing measured from the date of reissuance. No fee shall be charged for reissuing the order.

(e) The opposing party may, in response to an order to show cause, present affidavits relating to the granting of the preliminary injunction, and if the affidavits are served on the applicant at least two days prior to the hearing, the applicant shall not be entitled to any continuance on account thereof. On the day the order is made returnable, the hearing shall take precedence of all other matters on the calendar of the day, except older matters of the same character, and matters to which special precedence may be given by law. When the cause is at issue it shall be set for trial at the earliest possible date and shall take precedence of all other cases, except older matters of the same character, and matters to which special precedence may be given by law. * * *

Abba Rubber Company v. Seaquist

Court of Appeal of California, Fourth Appellate District
235 Cal. App. 3d 1, 286 Cal. Rptr. 518 (1991)

McKinster, Justice.

FACTUAL BACKGROUND

Roy J. Seaquist began manufacturing rubber rollers under the name of ABBA Rubber Company in 1959. He sold the business in 1980. The plaintiff bought the business in 1982.

J.T. "Jose" Uribe began working at ABBA in 1973. He remained there through the various changes of ownership, rising to vice-president and general manager in 1987. His brother, J.A. "Tony" Uribe began working for the company in 1985, and later was promoted to sales manager. In these capacities, both Uribes became very familiar with the identities of ABBA's customers.

Meanwhile, Mr. Seaquist had started a metal fabrication business known as Seaquist Company (Seaquist). In 1985, following the expiration of the noncompetition clause in the agreement by which he had sold ABBA, Seaquist also began manufacturing rubber roller products. However, it had no sales force, and did not significantly expand.

On September 11, 1989, Jose Uribe either quit or was fired from ABBA. The same day, he was hired by Seaquist, which simultaneously leased a new building from which to operate an expanded rubber roller business. Several weeks later, Seaquist hired Tony Uribe as a salesman. He had been fired by the plaintiff in early 1989, and since then had been working for yet another manufacturer of rubber rollers.

While the Uribes deny taking any records from ABBA, they admit to soliciting business from some ABBA customers. They did this in part by means of a letter which announced Jose Uribe's relocation from ABBA to Seaquist, and which invited the recipient to contact him regarding Seaquist's "ability to provide ... an advantage in price, quality and service."

PROCEDURAL BACKGROUND

The plaintiff filed a complaint on June 13, 1990, which alleged misappropriation of trade secrets, unfair competition, intentional inference with business relations, breach of contract, and other theories. It named as defendants Mr. Seaquist, Jose Uribe, and Tony Uribe, and prayed for preliminary and permanent injunctive relief and damages.

Six days later, the plaintiff made an ex parte application for a temporary restraining order (TRO) and for an order to the defendants to show cause why a preliminary injunction should not issue. Ultimately, the trial court denied the application for the TRO, but granted the application for the preliminary injunction. The preliminary injunction was signed on August 20, 1990, and issued on August 24, 1990, when the plaintiff filed the requisite $1,000 undertaking.

The injunction restrained the defendants from engaging in any of the following acts:

"1. Further solicitation of business from any of the recipients of the September 15, 1989 solicitation letter sent by defendants;

"2. Solicitation of business from any person or entity who has purchased rubber rollers from ABBA between January 1, 1989 and August 7, 1990, and who was on the ABBA customer list as of September 11, 1989 (hereafter referred to as 'ABBA customers'), or facilitating any other person or entity's solicitation of ABBA customers; and

"3. Divulging, making known or making any use whatsoever of the trade secrets of ABBA, concerning the customers subject to the restraints set forth in paragraph 2 of this Preliminary Injunction, which trade secrets consist of:

"(a) the names of ABBA customers;

"(b) the contact persons for ABBA customers, their addresses and telephone numbers;

"(c) the amounts and types of rubber rollers purchased from ABBA by ABBA customers;

"(d) the dates on which each ABBA customer last purchased rubber rollers from ABBA;

"(e) information as to when each ABBA customer opened its account with ABBA; and

"(f) any other information relating to ABBA customers' needs and anticipated needs as communicated to ABBA by these customers."

CONTENTIONS

The defendants contend that the trial court abused its discretion in issuing the injunction, because the identity of the plaintiff's customers was not a trade secret. They also attack the form of the injunction, on the grounds that it does not allow them to determine, in advance and with certainty, what conduct is permissible and what conduct is prohibited. Similarly, they contend that the injunction is impermissibly overbroad, because it proscribes the solicitation of businesses which are not customers of the plaintiff or the identities of which are otherwise not secret. Finally, they assert that the amount of the undertaking specified in the injunction is inadequate. * * *

DISCUSSION

A. IS THE UNDERTAKING TOO LOW?

* * *

1. *Did the Defendants Waive Their Objection?*

As its initial response to the defendants' attack on the amount of the undertaking, the plaintiff again contends that the objection has been waived. Specifically, the plaintiff argues, without authority, that they waived their right to make such a challenge because they failed to raise the issue prior to the issuance of the trial court's ruling on the application for the preliminary injunction. Although not specifically raised by the plaintiff, we also consider whether a waiver resulted from the defendants' failure to contest the adequacy of the undertaking by a noticed motion.

a. *No Waiver by Failing to Request Undertaking in Advance.*

The conditioning of the issuance of a preliminary injunction upon the posting of an undertaking is statutorily required: "On granting an injunction, the court or judge *must* require an undertaking on the part of the applicant. . . ." (Code Civ. Proc.,[2] § 529, subd. (a), italics added.) That duty is mandatory, not discretionary. Nothing in the statute conditions the trial court's obligation to require such an undertaking upon a request from the parties. To the contrary, an injunction does not become effective until an undertaking is required and furnished, and must be dissolved if an undertaking is not filed within the time allowed by statute (§ 529, subd. (a)). Since an undertaking is an indispensable prerequisite to the issuance of a preliminary injunction, regardless of whether the party to be restrained has reminded the court to require the applicant to post one, the restrained party does not waive its right to that statutorily mandated protection by failing to affirmatively request it. Therefore, the defendants' initial silence did not waive their right to an undertaking.

Furthermore, the defendants are entitled, not merely to any undertaking, but to an undertaking in an amount sufficient to pay the defendants "such damages . . . as [they] may sustain by reason of the injunction, if the court fin ally decides that the applicant was not entitled to the injunction." (§ 529, subd. (a).) Once again, this is an obligation imposed upon the trial court by statute, independent of any request from the party to be restrained. Therefore, the mere fact that the defendants did not expressly demand, prior to the time that the trial court took the plaintiff's application for preliminary injunction under submission, that any such injunction be conditioned upon the posting of a sufficient undertaking, did not result in a waiver of their right to challenge the amount of the subsequent undertaking.

b. *No Waiver by Failing to File a Motion.*

A closer issue is whether such a waiver occurred because the defendants failed to strictly comply with the statutory procedure governing objections to the amounts of undertakings.

The Bond and Undertaking Law, enacted in 1982, applies to all bonds[3] "given as security pursuant to any statute of this state, except to the extent the statute prescribes a different rule or is inconsistent." (§§ 995.010 and 995.020, subd. (a).) Article 9 of that law, comprised of sections 995.910 through 995.960, "governs objections to a

---

2. Unless specified otherwise, all further statutory references are to the Code of Civil Procedure.
3. The law speaks primarily in terms of bonds, because it defines that term to include undertakings. (§ 995.140, subd. (a)(2).)

bond given in an action or proceeding." (§ 995.910.) An "objection" includes a contention that "[t]he amount of the bond is insufficient." (§ 995.920, subd. (b).) Thus, that article governed the challenge being made here, concerning the amount of the undertaking to be given in this action pursuant to section 529.

Section 995.930 prescribes the manner in which such an objection is to be made[.]

* * *

[A]lthough the [defendants'] objection was not in the prescribed form, it nevertheless complied with the substance of each of the statutory requirements, and thereby met the objectives of section 995.930. While the abbreviated procedure adopted by the defendants was not and is not statutorily authorized, it is doubtful whether strict compliance with the procedural requirements of the statute would have materially added to the substance, as opposed to the length, of the objection. Instead, the trial court would have been presented with the same facts, the same argument, and the same issue.

Under these facts, we find that the defendants' ex parte objection substantially complied with the statutory procedure for contesting the sufficiency of the bond. Since neither the trial court nor the plaintiff insisted upon strict compliance with section 995.930, that substantial compliance is sufficient to prevent the waiver provided by subdivision (c) of that section. Therefore, the defendants did not waive their right to have this court review the adequacy of the amount of that bond on appeal.

2. *Is the Undertaking Insufficient?*

Section 529, subdivision (a), requires that the amount of the undertaking be sufficient to "pay to the party enjoined such damages ... as the party may sustain by reason of the injunction, if the court finally decides that the applicant was not entitled to the injunction." Thus, the trial court's function is to estimate the harmful effect which the injunction is likely to have on the restrained party, and to set the undertaking at that sum. That estimation is an exercise of the trial court's sound discretion, and will not be disturbed on appeal unless it clearly appears that the trial court abused its discretion by arriving at an estimate that is arbitrary or capricious, or is beyond the bounds of reason.

In reviewing the trial court's estimation, the first step is to identify the types of damages which the law allows a restrained party to recover in the event that the issuance of the injunction is determined to have been unjustified. The sole limit imposed by the statute is that the harm must have been proximately caused by the wrongfully issued injunction. (§ 529, subd. (a).) Case law adds only the limitation that the damages be reasonably foreseeable. (*Rice v. Cook* (1891) 92 Cal. 144, 148 [28 P. 219] [not "'remote'"]; *Handy v. Samaha* (1 931) 117 Cal. App. 286, 290 [3 P.2d 602] ["'reasonably anticipated'"].)

When an injunction restrains the operation of a business, foreseeable damages include "the profits which [the operator] would have made had he not been prevented by the injunction from carrying on his business." (*Lambert v. Haskell* (1889) 80 Cal.

611, 618 [22 P. 327].) Thus, the defendants correctly sought to have the undertaking include the losses which they will incur by reason of the prohibition against their continued solicitation of business from former customers of the plaintiff. In their objection, the defendants argued that, by the plaintiff's own analysis of the evidence, those customers accounted for 87.7 percent of Seaquist's invoices, representing $26,000 in sales per month, or $315,000 per year. The plaintiff did not dispute their interpretation of the evidence, either below or on appeal. Therefore, while those lost sales will undoubtedly be offset to some degree by savings resulting from reduced sales expenses or costs of goods sold, it is undisputed that the injunction will cause the defendants to incur very substantial lost profits.

At the final hearing on the application for the injunction, the trial court appeared to believe that it would be a simple matter for the defendants to locate new customers for their products, and that the proposed injunction, restraining them from soliciting further orders from the plaintiff's customers, would be only a "minor inconvenience...." This may have been the trial court's rationale for setting the undertaking at the nominal sum of $1,000.[7] Certainly, it is the ground upon which the plaintiff seeks to justify that action.

That reasoning, however, ignores the fact that section 529 requires that the potential damages be estimated on the assumption that the preliminary injunction was wrongfully issued, i.e., that the plaintiff did not have the right to keep the defendants from soliciting its customers. Under that hypothetical circumstance, the defendants would be entitled to solicit business from both the plaintiff's former customers and entirely new customers, and thus would be entitled to retain all profits from sales to both subsets of potential buyers. Therefore, the losses which they are likely to suffer from being precluded from soliciting business from their existing customer base cannot be offset by any profits they may make from sales to new customers. A nominal undertaking cannot be justified on the ground that the defendants' profitability could remain constant, when their sales and profitability might have risen in the absence of the injunction.

Furthermore, the plaintiff's analysis ignores another type of damage which the undertaking must take into account: attorney's fees. "It is now well settled that reasonable counsel fees and expenses incurred in successfully procuring a final decision dissolving the injunction are recoverable as 'damages' within the meaning of the language of the undertaking, to the extent that those fees are for services that relate to such dissolution [citations]." *(Russell v. United Pacific Ins. Co.* (1963) 214 Cal. App. 2d 78, 88-89 [29 Cal. Rptr. 346]; ...) * * * If the preliminary injunction is valid and regular on its face, requiring the defendant to defend against the main action in order

---

7. In the abstract, $1,000 is not an insignificant sum. It may be an appropriate undertaking in cases of harassment or trespass. However, in the context of an undertaking designed to secure a business's right to recover damages resulting from the improvident issuance of legal process, it is negligible. For instance, the statutory *minimum* for an undertaking filed in connection with a superior court's writ of attachment is $7,500. (§ 489.220.)

to demonstrate that the injunction was wrongfully issued, the prevailing defendant may recover that portion of his attorney's fees attributable to defending against those causes of action on which the issuance of the preliminary injunction had been based.

Thus, in calculating the amount of the undertaking to be required in this case, the trial court should have considered at least (1) the profits to be lost by the defendants from the elimination of the vast majority of their existing customers, and (2) the attorney's fees and expenses to be incurred in either prosecuting an appeal of the preliminary injunction, or defending at trial against those causes of action upon which the preliminary injunctive relief had been granted. By setting that undertaking at $1,000, the trial court impliedly estimated that those two classes of damages would total no more than that sum.[8]

That estimation is not within the bounds of reason. Even ignoring the lost profits, there is no reasonable possibility that the attorney's fees and expenses necessary to dissolve the injunction, either through appeal or trial, would not exceed $1,000. It is well known that litigation is extraordinarily expensive. That is especially true in commercial litigation such as this, in which two businesses are fighting over the right to sell to a particular customer base amid allegations of misappropriation of trade secrets and unfair competition. * * * When attorney's fees and lost profits are added into the equation, the utter inadequacy of the undertaking is clear.

B. WAS THE ISSUANCE OF AN INJUNCTION AN ABUSE OF DISCRETION?

The plaintiff contends that the injunction was necessary to restrain the misappropriation of trade secrets, as authorized by the Uniform Trade Secrets Act (Civ. Code, §§ 3426-3426.10)....

1. *Standard of Review*

A court may enjoin actual or threatened misappropriations of trade secrets. (Civ. Code, § 3426.2, subd. (a).) "[T]rial courts should evaluate two interrelated factors when deciding whether or not to issue a preliminary injunction. The first is the likelihood that the plaintiff will prevail on the merits at trial." (*IT Corp. v. County of Imperial* (1983) 35 Cal. 3d 63, 69 [196 Cal. Rptr. 715, 672 P.2d 121].) That is because a request for an injunction must be denied "unless there is a reasonable probability that plaintiff will be successful in the assertion of his rights." (*Continental Baking Co. v. Katz, supra*, 68 Cal. 2d at p. 528.) "The second is the interim harm that the plaintiff

---

8. Since a trial court must deny an application for a preliminary injunction "unless there is a reasonable probability that plaintiff will be successful in the assertion of his rights" (*Continental Baking Co. v. Katz* (1968) 68 Cal. 2d 512, 528 [67 Cal. Rptr. 761, 439 P.2d 889]), the trial court below, by granting the application, impliedly found that the defendants were not likely to prevail at trial. From this finding, it may have reasoned that only a nominal undertaking was necessary because it was not probable that the defendants would ever be entitled to collect any damages for the harm caused by the preliminary injunction.

If so, that reasoning is fallacious. The undertaking is designed to compensate the defendants in the event, however unlikely, that the preliminary injunction is finally determined to have been unjustified. The probability that they will actually obtain such a favorable determination, either through appeal or trial, is irrelevant in determining the likely amount of those damages.

is likely to sustain if the injunction were denied as compared to the harm that the defendant is likely to suffer if the preliminary injunction were issued." (*IT Corp.*, *supra*, at pp. 69-70.) The trial court balances these two factors to determine either "'that, pending a trial on the merits, the defendant should or that he should not be restrained from exercising the right claimed by him.'" (*Id.*, p. 70, quoting from *Continental Baking Co.*, *supra*, at p. 528.)

That determination "'rests in the sound discretion of the trial court, and ... may not be interfered with on appeal, except for an abuse of discretion.'" (*IT Corp.*, *supra*, 35 Cal. 3d at p. 69 quoting from *People v. Black's Food Store* (1940) 16 Cal. 2d 59, 61 [105 P.2d 361].) "A trial court will be found to have abused its discretion only when it has 'exceeded the bounds of reason or contravened the uncontradicted evidence.'" [Citations.] Further, the burden rests with the party challenging the injunction to make a clear showing of an abuse of discretion." (*IT Corp.*, *supra*, at p. 69.)

Therefore, our inquiry is defined as follows: Have the defendants clearly shown that the trial court either exceeded the bounds of reason or contravened uncontradicted evidence when it concluded that they should be restrained from exercising their alleged right to solicit the plaintiff's customers?

2. *Definition of Trade Secret*

While the defendants also contest the form and scope of the injunction, their sole challenge to the substance of the injunction is that the trial court abused its discretion because there was no evidence, contradicted or otherwise, to establish that the plaintiff's customer list satisfied all of the elements of the definition of a trade secret.

[Here the court determines that the plaintiff's customer list constitutes a trade secret within the meaning of Civil Code § 3426.1(d).]

DISPOSITION

An injunction cannot remain in effect without an adequate undertaking. Therefore, the preliminary injunction is reversed. No further preliminary injunction shall be issued unless its issuance is conditioned upon the furnishing of an adequate undertaking. We do not purport to determine what an adequate amount would be. Rather, we leave that determination to the trial court, taking into consideration the types of damages discussed in this opinion. If further evidence or argument would assist the trial court in that determination, it may wish to conduct a hearing in the manner of Code of Civil Procedure section 995.950.

Any preliminary or permanent injunction issued in this case in the future shall both clearly and narrowly define the scope of the proscribed activities, in accordance with the views expressed in this opinion.

Appellants shall recover their costs on appeal.

[1] *Preliminary Injunctions, Generally*

As our principal case indicates, a trial court must weigh two "interrelated" factors in deciding whether to issue a preliminary injunction: (1) the likelihood that the moving party will ultimately prevail on the merits, and (2) the relative interim harm to the parties from issuance or nonissuance of the injunction. *Butt v. State of California*, 4 Cal. 4th 668, 677-78, 15 Cal. Rptr. 2d 480, 842 P.2d 1240 (1992) ("The trial court's determination must be guided by a 'mix' of the potential merit and interim-harm factors; the greater the plaintiff's showing on one, the less must be shown on the other to support an injunction"). Precisely how do these two factors "interrelate"? May the court properly deny a preliminary injunction even though it finds that the plaintiff will ultimately prevail on the merits? *See, e.g., Posey v. Leavitt*, 229 Cal. App. 3d 1236, 280 Cal. Rptr. 568 (1991) (ruling court has discretion to deny injunction even though encroachment by defendant's condominium already established in nuisance action). May the court properly grant a preliminary injunction based on severe irreparable interim harm where there is no possibility that the plaintiff will ultimately prevail on the merits? *See Common Cause v. Bd. of Supervisors*, 49 Cal. 3d 432, 442-43, 261 Cal. Rptr. 574, 777 P.2d 610 (1989).

When a party makes a sufficient showing of likelihood of success on the merits, may a trial court properly grant a preliminary injunction without considering the relative harms that would be imposed by denying or granting the preliminary injunction? *See White v. Davis*, 30 Cal. 4th 528, 561, 133 Cal. Rptr. 2d 648, 68 P.3d 74 (2003) ("[T]he decision in Common Cause did not suggest that when a party makes a sufficient showing of likely success on the merits a trial court need not consider the relative balance of hardships at all").

[2] Preliminary Injunctions: Interim Harm

The courts' discussions of the preliminary injunction factors make generalizations regarding "interim harm" very difficult. However, precedents provide the following guidelines:

[a] Irreparable Injury

A preliminary injunction is more likely when the plaintiff demonstrates that it is necessary to prevent "great or irreparable injury." CCP § 526(a)(2). Of course, what constitutes "irreparable injury" varies with the circumstances of each case. *See, e.g., Ketchens v. Reiner*, 194 Cal. App. 3d 470, 480, 239 Cal. Rptr. 549 (1987) (ruling loss of First Amendment freedoms unquestionably constituted irreparable harm); *American Acad. of Pediatrics v. Van de Kamp*, 214 Cal. App. 3d 831, 263 Cal. Rptr. 46 (1989) (ruling implementation of parental consent statute will cause irreparable harm for minors seeking therapeutic abortions); *Butt v. State of California, supra* (concluding closing of schools six weeks early due to school district revenue shortfall would cause irreparable harm to students and parents).

If the plaintiff may be fully compensated by the payment of damages in the event she prevails on the merits, then irreparable injury does not exist. *See, e.g., Tahoe Keys Property Owners v. State Water Resources Control Bd.*, 23 Cal. App. 4th 1459, 1471, 28 Cal. Rptr. 2d 734 (1994) (citing cases). The court must also consider the potential harm to the defendant and the public if a preliminary injunction is granted. *Id.* at 1472-73 (holding preliminary injunction sought to enjoin state agencies from collecting and expending allegedly unconstitutional building permit fees properly denied where plaintiff presented little risk of irreparable injury, and defendant agencies and public would suffer significant harm in their task of protecting the environment from degradation caused by development).

Plaintiffs are not required to wait until they have suffered actual harm before they apply for an injunction, but may seek injunctive relief against the threatened infringement of their rights. *See, e.g., Maria P. v. Riles,* 43 Cal. 3d 1281, 1292, 240 Cal. Rptr. 872, 743 P.2d 932 (1987); *Southern Christian Leadership Conference of Greater Los Angeles v. Malaikah Auditorium Co.,* 230 Cal. App. 3d 207, 281 Cal. Rptr. 216 (1991) (allowing plaintiff to seek preliminary in junction to prevent threatened breach of contract).

[b] Governmental Entity Applicant

"Where a government entity seeking to enjoin an alleged violation of a statute or ordinance which specifically provides for injunctive relief establishes that it is reasonably probable it will prevail on the merits, a rebuttable presumption arises that the potential harm to the public outweighs the potential harm to the defendant. If the defendant shows that it would suffer grave or irreparable harm from the issuance of the preliminary injunction, the court must then examine the relative harms to the parties." *IT Corp. v. County of Imperial,* 35 Cal. 3d 63, 72, 196 Cal. Rptr. 715, 672 P.2d 121 (1983). How does this approach to the "interim harm" factor differ from the traditional two-prong approach taken in a typical private case? Why not view the presumption as *irrebuttable*? Should this approach also apply to such statutory injunction actions brought by non-governmental parties?

[c] Special Statutes

The Legislature has enacted a number of statutes that specifically authorize injunctive relief. *E.g.,* Bus. & Prof. Code § 17078 (violation of Unfair Practices Act); Bus. & Prof. Code § 17203 (violation of unfair competition statutes); Family Code §§ 6200-6388 (restraining order pursuant to Domestic Violence Prevention Act). Some of these special statutes authorize injunctive relief without the necessity of showing injury beyond violation of the statute. *E.g.,* Bus. & Prof. Code § 17082 (unnecessary for Unfair Practices Act plaintiff to show actual or threatened injury).

Some specific injunction statutes also authorize procedural rules different from those applicable to injunctions generally. *E.g.,* CCP § 527.6 (civil harassment); CCP § 527.8 (workplace violence); Family Code §§ 240-246 (dissolution of marriage and related family law matters, prevention of domestic violence, etc.). Why did the Legislature provide special, expedited procedures in such statutes?

[3] Preliminary Injunctions: Undertaking

As *ABBA Rubber Co. v. Seaquist,* reproduced *supra,* illustrates, the posting of adequate security is, generally, a prerequisite to the issuance of a valid preliminary injunction. CCP § 529; *see, e.g., Mangini v. J.G. Durand International,* 31 Cal. App. 4th 214, 37 Cal. Rptr. 2d 153 (1994) (observing that unless a statutory exception to bond requirement is applicable, even a plaintiff whose preliminary injunction advances the public interest must post sufficient bond); *Condor Enter., Ltd. v. Valley View State Bank,* 25 Cal. App. 4th 734, 30 Cal. Rptr. 2d 613 (1994) (ruling a court may not punish with contempt or other sanctions disobedience to a preliminary injunction which is invalid because a bond was not posted). What is the purpose of this undertaking requirement? *See* CCP § 529(a). In what circumstances is a wrongfully enjoined party entitled to recover damages, under § 529, against the bond? When an appellate court determines that the trial court abused its discretion in issuing the preliminary injunction? Or when the trial court did not abuse its discretion when issuing the preliminary injunction but later determines that the applicant is not entitled to a permanent injunction? *See ABBA Rubber Co. v. Seaquist, supra; Wallace v. Miller,* 140 Cal. App. 3d 636, 189 Cal. Rptr. 637 (1983).

[a] Sufficiency of Undertaking

Within five days after the service of a preliminary injunction, the party enjoined may object to the sufficiency of the undertaking. CCP § 529(a). How does a court determine whether the required undertaking is sufficient? What, according to *ABBA Rubber,* may the court consider in determining the probable damages to the defendant that would result from a wrongfully issued preliminary injunction? Do you agree with the *ABBA Rubber* court's reasoning in finding that the $1,000 bond was insufficient? Does CCP § 529 preclude a trial court from imposing a nominal undertaking where the plaintiff's probability of success on the merits is extremely high? Should it? In *ABBA Rubber,* the defendant appealed from both the issuance of the preliminary injunction and the adequacy of the undertaking. Can a defendant appeal only the question of the sufficiency of the amount of the undertaking? *See County of Los Angeles v. City of Los Angeles,* 76 Cal. App. 4th 1025, 90 Cal. Rptr. 2d 799 (1999) (concluding a trial court's order fixing the amount of a preliminary injunction bond is not separately appealable).

[b] Federal Rules Compared

Rule 65 of the Federal Rules of Civil Procedure sets forth the procedures and requirements for issuance of temporary restraining orders and preliminary injunctions by the federal courts. The federal rules are similar to the California provisions. Rule 65(c) requires an applicant to post security "in an amount that the court considers proper" as a prerequisite to issuance of a temporary restraining order or a preliminary injunction. Despite Rule 65(c), the federal courts have upheld nominal bonds for preliminary injunctions to preserve access to the federal courts in cases of private enforcement of environmental laws. *E.g.*, *People ex rel. Van DeKamp v. Tahoe Reg'l Planning Agency*, 766 F.2d 1319, 1325-26 (9th Cir. 1985).

Does the *ABBA Rubber* court's construction of CCP § 529 preclude nominal bonds in such cases in the California courts? Should § 529 be so construed? Why? For a discussion of the case for nominal injunction bonds in environmental litigation in California, see Alexander T. Henson & Kenneth F. Gray, *Injunction Bonding in Environmental Litigation*, 19 Santa Clara L. Rev. 541 (1979).

[c] When Undertaking Not Required

An undertaking is not a prerequisite to granting a preliminary injunction in family law actions, Family Code §§ 231-246, CCP § 529(b); or where the applicant is a public entity or official, CCP § 995.220. *See City of South San Francisco v. Cypress Lawn Cemetery Assn.*, 11 Cal. App. 4th 916, 14 Cal. Rptr. 2d 323 (1992) (noting the inherent equitable powers of trial court to require bond must yield to public policy expressed in CCP § 529(b)). Moreover, in any case the court may, in its discretion, waive the requirement of a bond where the applicant is an indigent person. CCP § 995.240. What are the policy reasons for this authority to waive the bond? If the applicant is indigent and seeks waiver of the undertaking requirement, what effect might this fact have on the court's willingness to grant a preliminary injunction? What effect should it have?

[d] Waiver of Undertaking

Can the injunction bond requirement of CCP § 529 be waived or forfeited by the party to be enjoined? Although the analysis of this question in *ABBA* suggests that the bond cannot be waived or forfeited, the court in *Smith v. Adventist Health System/West*, 182 Cal. App. 4th 729, 740-49, 106 Cal. Rptr. 3d 318 (2010), held that the defendant waived its right to require a bond by failing to respond to the plaintiff's argument that a bond was unnecessary, before or after the superior court granted the preliminary injunction. The *Smith* court viewed *ABBA* as not controlling authority on this question because the trial court in *ABBA* did not find a waiver and did require a bond. *Smith*, 182 Cal. App. 4th at 742-44.

[B] Temporary Restraining Orders (TRO)

[1] TRO Prerequisites

Upon proper application, a court may enter a temporary restraining order (TRO) to preserve the status quo when "great or irreparable injury" would result to the applicant before the matter can be determined at a preliminary injunction hearing. CCP §§ 526(a)(2); 527(a). What constitutes "great or irreparable injury"? What other prerequisites must an applicant satisfy in order to seek a TRO without notice to the opposite party? Under what types of circumstances should an applicant not be required to even attempt to inform the opposing party of the application for a TRO? What are the consequences of not attempting to inform the opposite party of an *ex parte* TRO application when circumstances do not justify this failure to notify? *See, e.g., Brewster v. Southern Pac. Transp. Co.*, 235 Cal. App. 3d 701, 714, 1 Cal. Rptr. 2d 89 (1991) (sanctioning attorney for plaintiff in amount of $22,047.93 for failure to notify defendant of application for TRO).

[2] *TRO Procedural Safeguards*

As with the provisional remedy of attachment, the temporary restraining order procedure must comply with the Due Process Clause. What procedural safeguards does CCP § 527 contain with respect to the issuance of a TRO? Do they satisfy the due process concerns expressed in *Randone v. Appellate Dept.*, 5 Cal. 3d 536, 96 Cal. Rptr. 709, 488 P.2d 13 (1971)? *See Chrysler Credit Corp. v. Waegele*, 29 Cal. App. 3d 681, 105 Cal. Rptr. 914 (1973) (holding statute authorizing use of temporary restraining order is narrowly drawn and satisfies due process of law). The posting of security is not a prerequisite to the issuance of a temporary restraining order (TRO) under CCP § 529, *see Wallace v. Miller*, 140 Cal. App. 3d 636, 189 Cal. Rptr. 637 (1983); but may be required by the court. *See, e.g., City of South San Francisco v. Cypress Lawn Cemetery Assn.*, 11 Cal. App. 4th 916, 14 Cal. Rptr. 2d 323 (1992) (noting that a trial court has the inherent authority to require a bond as a condition to issuing a TRO); *Greenly v. Cooper*, 77 Cal. App. 3d 382, 143 Cal. Rptr. 514 (1978) (ruling that bond plaintiff posted in connection with a TRO could also be posted in connection with a preliminary injunction).

[a] Duration

A TRO is an interim order of limited duration designed to preserve the status quo pending a hearing on an application for a preliminary injunction. CCP § 527. What is the maximum duration of a TRO? What is the maximum duration of a preliminary injunction? Does the court's denial of a TRO application necessarily mean it will also deny a preliminary injunction? What are the substantive and procedural differences between a TRO and a preliminary injunction? Between a TRO and a prejudgment attachment? *See Doyka v. Superior Court*, 233 Cal. App. 3d 1134, 285 Cal. Rptr. 14 (1991).

[b] Enforcement

A TRO is enforceable by contempt, but only after the court acquires personal jurisdiction over the defendant. For purposes of contempt, a court has personal jurisdiction over a defendant "from the time the summons is served on him" or as of the time of a general appearance. CCP § 410.50. Does this mean that a defendant who has actual notice of a TRO may ignore it with impunity until served with the summons? *See Chrysler Credit Corp. v. Waegele, supra*, 29 Cal. App. 3d at 687-89 (upholding defendant's contempt where defendant served with TRO and deliberately violated its terms, even though not previously or concurrently served with summons).

[3] Anti-Suit Injunctions

Civil Code § 3423 authorizes a California court to restrain a party subject to its jurisdiction from proceeding in another action involving the same subject matter or the same facts when "necessary to prevent a multiplicity of proceedings." Likewise, the "first filed rule" in California means that when two courts of the same sovereignty have concurrent jurisdiction, the first to assume jurisdiction over a particular subject matter of a particular controversy takes it exclusively, and the second court should not thereafter assert control over that subject matter. *Advanced Bionics Corp. v. Medtronic, Inc.*, 29 Cal. 4th 697, 128 Cal. Rptr. 2d 172, 179, 59 P.3d 231 (2002); *see also Franklin & Franklin v. 7-Eleven Owners for Fair Franchising*, 85 Cal. App. 4th 1168, 1175-78, 102 Cal. Rptr. 2d 770 (2000) (applying the exclusive concurrent jurisdiction rule and upholding trial court's postjudgment enjoining of subsequent trials of identical actions in another superior court, pending appeal of first action).

Do these rules authorize a California court to issue a TRO enjoining a party to a California lawsuit from taking any further action in a case pending in another state that may interfere with the California court's proceedings? In *Advanced Bionics, supra*, an action filed in California by plaintiffs, a former employee and the California new employer, to declare defendant's noncompetition agreement void and unenforceable, the Supreme Court concluded that the superior court improperly issued a TRO enjoining the defendant former employer from proceeding in a later filed, parallel breach of contract action in a Minnesota court. "[E]njoining proceedings in another state requires an exceptional circumstance that outweighs the threat to judicial restraint and comity principles," the Supreme Court reasoned, but the potentially conflicting judgments that naturally result from parallel proceedings do not provide a reason for issuing a TRO. *Advanced Bionics*, 29 Cal. 4th at 708.

For a recent decision discussing the considerations relevant to the issuance of an anti-suit injunction where the later-filed parallel action is in the courts of another country, see *TSMC North America v. Semiconductor Mfg. Intl. Corp.*, 161 Cal. App. 4th 581, 74 Cal. Rptr. 3d 328 (2008) (noting the power to issue anti-suit injunctions must be used sparingly because restraining a party from pursuing an action in a court in another country involves delicate questions of international comity and judicial restraint).

Chapter 8

Preclusive Effects of Prior Judgments

§ 8.01 Introductory Note

The doctrine of res judicata describes a set of rules which determine the preclusive effect of prior judgments. The doctrine in California is almost entirely the result of judge-made law, *e.g., Slater v. Blackwood*, 15 Cal. 3d 791, 126 Cal. Rptr. 225, 543 P.2d 593 (1975); although a few statutes help define some of the rules, *e.g.,* CCP §§ 1049, 1908–1912.

The California doctrine has two familiar components. "First, it precludes parties or their privies from relitigating *the same cause of action* that has been finally determined by a court of competent jurisdiction." *Frommagen v. Board of Supervisors*, 197 Cal. App. 3d 1292, 1299, 243 Cal. Rptr. 390 (1987). This aspect of the doctrine is known as "claim preclusion," and is commonly referred to as "res judicata." "Second, although a second suit between the same parties on a different cause of action is not precluded by a prior judgment, the first judgment operates as an estoppel or conclusive adjudication as to such issues in the second action as were actually litigazted and determined in the first action." *Id.* This second aspect is known as "issue preclusion," and is commonly referred to as "collateral estoppel." One word of caution with respect to this terminology: The California courts sometimes use the term "res judicata" to refer to both claim and issue preclusion. *See DKN Holdings LLC v. Faerber*, 61 Cal. 4th 813, 823–24, 189 Cal. Rptr. 3d 809, 352 P.3d 378 (2015) (discussing several cases).

On a very general level, the California doctrine is similar to the doctrine set forth in the Restatement (Second) of Judgments (1982), Section 17, Effects of Former Adjudication—General Rules:

> A valid and final personal judgment is conclusive between the parties, except on appeal or other direct review, to the following extent:
>
> (1) If the judgment is in favor of the plaintiff, the claim is extinguished and merged in the judgment and a new claim may arise on the judgment ... ;
>
> (2) If the judgment is in favor of the defendant, the claim is extinguished and the judgment bars a subsequent action on that claim ... ;
>
> (3) A judgment in favor of either the plaintiff or the defendant is conclusive, in a subsequent action between them on the same or a different claim, with respect to any issue actually litigated and determined if its determination was essential to that judgment....

The California claim preclusion doctrine is unique, however, where it incorporates the "primary rights" theory.

§ 8.02 Res Judicata (Claim Preclusion)

[A] The Primary Rights Doctrine

Holmes v. David H. Bricker, Inc.

Supreme Court of California
70 Cal. 2d 786, 76 Cal. Rptr. 431, 452 P.2d 647 (1969)

TRAYNOR, CHIEF JUSTICE.

Plaintiffs brought this action in the municipal court to recover damages for injury to their automobile. The court sustained defendant's demurrer to the complaint without leave to amend on the ground that the action was barred by a judgment plaintiffs had obtained for personal injuries suffered in the same accident. Plaintiffs appeal from the ensuing judgment of dismissal.

On August 24, 1962, plaintiffs purchased a used automobile from defendant. The contract of sale contained an express warranty that "The used car sold herein is hereby warranted to be in good operating condition and to remain in such condition under normal use and service for a period of 30 days or 1000 miles, (whichever comes first) after delivery." On September 15, 1962, while Mr. Holmes was driving and Mrs. Holmes was riding as a passenger, the automobile crashed into a fixed object along a downgrade on a mountain road, causing injuries to plaintiffs and damage to the automobile.

On September 6, 1963, plaintiffs filed an action against defendant in the superior court to recover damages for their personal injuries. Their complaint pleaded five causes of action, each of which alleged that the accident was caused by defective brakes. The first cause of action sought recovery for breach of the express warranty quoted above; the second alleged breach of other express warranties and of the implied warranties of merchantability and fitness for the purpose intended; the third alleged defendant's failure to test and adjust the brakes as required by Vehicle Code section 24007; the fourth alleged negligent servicing, testing, and inspecting; and the fifth sought recovery on the basis of fraudulent representation that the automobile was in good condition.

On March 9, 1967, a jury returned a verdict for plaintiffs for $49,400, and the judgment entered on the verdict has become final.

On February 23, 1966, while the personal injury action was pending, plaintiffs filed this action against defendant in the municipal court for $1,138.12, the amount of damage to the automobile in the 1962 accident. The complaint pleaded two causes of action. The first was based on the express warranty in the purchase agreement. It was identical with the first cause of action in the 1963 personal injury complaint except for the damages alleged. The second sought recovery on the basis of fraudulent misrepresentations. It was dismissed by stipulation and thereafter the court sustained defendant's demurrer to the complaint without leave to amend, on the ground that "Plaintiff could and should have urged in the Superior Court action, the claim that is now made in the first cause of action."

Plaintiff contends that the trial court's ruling is contrary to the settled rule that conduct that simultaneously causes harm both to the person and to the property of one individual gives rise to two separate and distinct causes of action, one for violation of the right to freedom from legally impermissible interference with the integrity of the person and one for violation of the right to quiet enjoyment of property. This application of the primary rights theory of causes of action in California was first reflected in the permissive joinder provisions of the practice act of 1851 based on the original Field Code. (Stats. 1851, ch. 5, §64, pp. 59–60).[2] Those provisions distinguished between causes of action arising out of injuries to person and causes of action arising out of injuries to property and did not recognize any cause of action that would include tortious injuries to both person and property. Although the Legislature has broadened the scope of permissible joinder of causes of action since 1851, it has consistently recognized, both in the joinder provisions (*See, e.g.,* Code Civ. Proc., §427); and in the applicable statutes of limitation (Code Civ. Proc., §§340.3 [injury to person] and 338.3 [injury to property]) that the causes of action for injuries to person and property are separate. The cases and the commentators are in accord. (*Todhunter v. Smith* (1934) 219 Cal. 690, 693 (dictum) [28 P.2d 916]; *Bowman v. Wohlke* (1913) 166 Cal. 121 [135 P.37, Ann. Cas. 1915B 1011]; *Lamb v. Harbaugh* (1895) 105 Cal. 680 [39 P.56]; *McCarty v. Fremont* (1863) 23 Cal. 196; …)

Kidd v. Hillman (1936) 14 Cal. App. 2d 507 [58 P.2d 662], *Commercial Standard Ins. Co. v. Winfield* (1938) 24 Cal. App. 2d 477 [75 P.2d 525], and *Pacific Idem. Group v. Dunton* (1966) 243 Cal. App. 2d 504 [52 Cal. Rptr. 332], invoked by defendant, are not to the contrary. In each of these cases a former judgment had included recovery for both personal injuries and property damage growing out of an automobile accident and the court recognized that the former judgment could be pleaded as a defense to a later action for additional property damage. Accordingly, they involved only the application of the settled rule that a separate cause of action does not arise for each

---

2. "The plaintiff may unite several causes of action in the same complaint, when they all arise out of:

"1st. Contracts, express or implied; or,

"2nd. Claims to recover specific real property … or,

"3rd. Claims to recover specific personal property … or,

"4th. Claims against a trustee, by virtue of a contract, or by operation of law; or,

"5th. Injuries to character; or,

"6th. Injuries to person; or,

"7th. Injuries to property.

But the causes of action so united shall all belong to one only of these classes, and shall affect all the parties to the action, and not require different places of trial, and shall be separately stated."

separate item of property damaged as a result of one tortious act. (*Sanderson v. Niemann* (1941) 17 Cal. 2d 563, 572 [110 P.2d 1025].)

In the present case, however, plaintiffs have not pleaded a cause of action for tortious injury to their automobile, but for breach of the express written warranty in the contract of sale. The breach alleged is the identical breach of warranty alleged in their first cause of action in the prior suit. Accordingly, the crucial question is whether a single breach of the express warranty gave rise to two causes of action when it resulted in injury to both the persons and the property of plaintiffs. We hold that it did not. The warranty pleaded in this case was essentially contractual in character. It was created by agreement of the parties; it did not arise by operation of law; and it was subject to negotiation and modification at the time the contract was entered into. Under these circumstances the applicable rule is that all damages for a single breach of contract must be recovered in one action. (*Coughlin v. Blair* (153) 41 Cal. 2d 587, 598 [262 P.2d 305]; *Abbot v. 76 Land & Water Co.* (1911) 161 Cal. 42 [118 P.425]; ...)

The judgment is affirmed.

Slater v. Blackwood

Supreme Court of California
15 Cal. 3d 791, 126 Cal. Rptr. 225, 543 P.2d 593 (1975)

RICHARDSONE, JUSTICE.

We consider, and will reject, the contention that the unconstitutionality of the guest statute enunciated by us in *Brown v. Merlo* (1973) 8 Cal. 3d 855 [106 Cal. Rptr. 388, 506 P.2d 212, 66 A.L.R.3d 505] should be given retroactive effect.

Plaintiff, a minor, was injured in an automobile accident in 1969 while riding as a guest in a car driven by defendant John Blackwood and owned by the defendant Escondido Tire Supply Co., Inc. In March 1970 she filed an action for damages, the complaint being framed in contemplation of the provisions of California's then existing "guest statute" (Veh. Code, § 17158), which limited recovery to death or injuries resulting from intoxication or willful misconduct. At trial, following plaintiff's opening statement, the court granted defendants' motion for nonsuit on the ground that plaintiff's evidence would not support recovery under section 17158. Judgment for defendant was entered pursuant to Code of Civil Procedure section 581c.

Plaintiff appealed contending that the guest statute was unconstitutional and that recovery should be permitted upon a showing of negligence alone. The Court of Appeal rejected this argument and affirmed the trial court's decision. We denied a hearing in June 1972.

In February 1973 we held the guest statute unconstitutional as applied to an injured nonowner guest. (*Brown v. Merlo, supra,* 8 Cal. 3d 855.) In May of that year plaintiff, still a minor, filed a new complaint, based on the same accident and naming the same parties as defendants. Her claim was not barred by the statute of limitations. (*See*

Code Civ. Proc., § 352.) In the second action plaintiff sought recovery on a negligence theory, arguing that our decision in *Brown* should be applied retroactively. Defendants demurred to the new complaint on the ground that the original 1970 judgment was res judicata and constituted a bar to the second suit. The trial court agreed, and demurrers to the new complaint were sustained without leave to amend.

Plaintiff appeals, contending that the doctrine of res judicata is not applicable. Specifically, she argues (1) that the first judgment is not a bar to the new complaint because the judgment is based upon separate and distinct causes of action; (2) that the trial court should have exercised its discretionary power to reject the defense of res judicata in the interest of justice and fairness; and (3) that defendants are estopped from relying on res judicata in this action because they prevented plaintiff from litigating the issue in the prior proceedings. We conclude that these arguments lack merit, and that the judgment should be affirmed.

A valid final judgment on the merits in favor of a defendant serves as a complete bar to further litigation on the same cause of action. (*Busick v. Workmen's Comp. Appeals Bd.* (1972) 7 Cal. 3d 967, 973 [104 Cal. Rptr. 42, 500 P.2d 1386]; *Panos v. Great Western Packing Co.* (1943) 21 Cal. 2d 636, 639 [134 P.2d 242]; 4 Witkin, *Cal. Procedure* (2d ed. 1971) Judgment, § 192, p. 3332; Rest., Judgments, § 48.) Plaintiff in the matter before us, however, argues that the second complaint states a new "cause of action." In doing so however, she misconstrues the meaning of that term. California has consistently applied the "primary rights" theory, under which the invasion of one primary right gives rise to a single cause of action. (*Busick*, *supra*, at p. 975; *Wulfjen v. Dolton* (1944) 24 Cal. 2d 891, 895–896 [151 P.2d 846].) The "primary right" alleged to have been violated in the instant case is plaintiff's right to be free from injury to her person. (*See Panos*, *supra*, at p. 639; Rest., Judgments, § 63, com. a.) It is clearly established that " … there is but one cause of action for one personal injury [which is incurred] by reason of one wrongful act." (*Busick*, *supra*, at p. 975; *see Panos*, *supra*, at p. 638; 3 Witkin, *Cal. Procedure* (2d ed. 1971) Pleading, § 34, p. 1717.)

Our consideration of plaintiff's argument involves a significant conceptual matter. It is true that plaintiff has asserted different legal theories in the instant case and in her 1970 complaint. However, the "cause of action" is based upon the harm suffered, as opposed to the particular theory asserted by the litigant. Even where there are multiple legal theories upon which recovery might be predicated, one injury gives rise to only one claim for relief. "Hence a judgment for the defendant is a bar to a subsequent action by the plaintiff based on the same injury to the same right, even though he presents a different legal ground for relief." (3 Witkin, *supra*, Pleading, § 24, p. 1709; and *see Panos v. Great Western Packing Co.*, *supra*, 21 Cal. 2d at pp. 638–639; …) We therefore cannot accept plaintiff's first contention.

Plaintiff, however, points to certain language in *Brown v. Merlo*, *supra*, 8 Cal. 3d 855 at pp. 860, 863, in which we refer to the "cause of action" for negligence and the "cause of action" for violation of the former guest statute. It is argued that by use of such language we have implicitly agreed that a case such as this one gives rise to multiple causes of action. However, the phrase "cause of action" is "often used indiscriminately to mean what it says and to mean *counts* which state differently the same cause of action, ..." (*Eichler Homes of San Mateo, Inc. v. Superior Court* (1961) 55 Cal. 2d 845, 847 [13 Cal. Rptr. 194, 361 P.2d 914];....) When read in context it is clear that our use of the term "cause of action" in *Brown*, noted by plaintiff, refers to the "counts" asserted by the plaintiff in her complaint.

Assuming that res judicata is available to defendants in the instant matter, plaintiff argues that the trial court, nonetheless, should have exercised its discretionary power to reject the doctrine as a defense. There is some authority for the proposition that, in particular circumstances, courts may refuse to apply res judicata when to do so would constitute a manifest injustice. (*See Greenfield v. Mather* (1948) 32 Cal. 2d 23, 35 [194 P.2d 1];....) We consider the *Greenfield* doctrine of doubtful validity and it has been severely criticized. (*See* 4 Witkin, *supra*, Judgment, § 150, p. 3295, et seq.) While we find it is unnecessary for our present purposes to reach the question of whether *Greenfield* itself should be directly overruled, we expressly hold that the rule of that case is inapplicable where, as here, the only possible basis for its implementation is founded on a change in law following the original judgment.

Previous appellate decisions of this state are in accord. For example, in *Zeppi v. State of California* (1962) 203 Cal. App. 2d 386 [21 Cal. Rptr. 534], plaintiffs sued the state for personal injuries. A demurrer on the ground of governmental immunity was sustained and judgment entered for defendant. The judgment was affirmed on appeal and we denied a petition for hearing. Subsequently, in *Muskopf v. Corning Hospital Dist.* (1961) 55 Cal. 2d 211 [11 Cal. Rptr. 89, 359 P.2d 457], we held that governmental entities were no longer immune from liability for the torts of their agents. Plaintiffs in the original *Zeppi* action thereupon made a motion in the trial court to vacate the judgment on the grounds that the previous rulings sustaining the demurrer were the result of mistakes. The trial court granted this motion. In reversing, the appellate court agreed with defendant's contention that res judicata was applicable stating: "In every instance where a rule established by case law is changed by a later case the earlier rule may be said to be 'mistaken'.... Such 'mistakes' or 'injustices' are not a ground for equity's intervention. So to hold would be to emasculate, if not wipe out, the doctrine of res judicata because *the doctrine is most frequently applied to block relitigation based upon contentions that a law has been changed. Our courts have repeatedly refused to treat the self-evident hardship occasioned by a change in the law as a reason to revive dead action....*" (*Zeppi, supra*, at pp. 388–389, italics added.) The court held that under the circumstances, where the only "mistake" made in the earlier proceedings was in assuming that the law would remain unchanged, there is no discretion to reject the defense of res judicata. (*Id.*, at p. 389.)

In *Bank of America v. Department of Mental Hygiene* (1966) 246 Cal. App. 2d 578 at page 585 [54 Cal. Rptr. 899], it was said "[the] rule appears clear in California that a judgment which was contrary to the Constitution because it was based upon a statute later held invalid, is nevertheless res judicata in a subsequent suit."

We agree with the positions taken by the Courts of Appeal in *Zeppi* and *Bank of America*. It cannot be denied that judicial or legislative action which results in the overturning of established legal principles often leads to seemingly arbitrary and unwarranted distinctions in the treatment accorded similarly situated parties. However, "[public] policy and the interest of litigants alike require that there be an end to litigation." (*Panos v. Great Western Packing Co., supra*, 21 Cal. 2d 636 at p. 637.) The result urged by plaintiff, to borrow the language of Justice Traynor's dissent in *Greenfield*, would call " ... into question the finality of any judgment and thus is bound to cause infinitely more injustice in the long run than it can conceivably avert in this case." (*Greenfield v. Mather, supra*, 32 Cal. 2d at p. 36.) The consistent application of the traditional principle that final judgments, even erroneous ones, are a bar to further proceedings based on the same cause of action is necessary to the well-ordered functioning of the judicial process. It should not be impaired for the benefit of particular plaintiffs, regardless of the sympathy their plight might arouse in an individual case.

Finally, we reject plaintiff's argument that defendants, because they moved for a nonsuit in the first action, are now estopped from asserting that judgment as a bar to the instant action. It is true that a very few cases have held that the defendant in a second action is precluded from asserting res judicata as a defense because of his conduct in prior proceedings. * * * In these cases, the courts have properly noted that defendants cannot inconsistently argue that a claim is not cognizable in the first action and then, in a subsequent proceeding, contend that the same issue should have been raised in the prior litigation. Such a rule is appropriate where "the course pursued by the trial court and by counsel in an earlier action was tantamount to an express determination on the part of the court with the consent of opposing counsel that certain issues should be reserved for future adjudication, and that the doctrine of res judicata did not apply." (*Hall v. Coyle* (1952) 38 Cal. 2d 543, 546 [241 P.2d 236].)

The foregoing principle, however, is not applicable to the case before us. Defendants have not attempted to assert inconsistent positions in successive litigations. There has been no conduct on their part which can be characterized as constituting a consent, express or implied, that the issue of their negligence was to be reserved for determination in a second lawsuit. Rather, they have consistently argued that under the substantive law in effect at the time the original complaint was filed, plaintiff had no legal theory upon which recovery for her injuries could be predicated, and that a subsequent change in the law cannot be a basis for reviving a dead claim.

The theories urged by plaintiff would cast doubt on the finality of any judgment dependent upon a then valid substantive defense later held to be unavailable. The general uncertainty induced in our judicial system by such a result cannot be justified by occasional apparent inequities.

We therefore conclude that the order of the trial court sustaining defendants' demurrer on the grounds of res judicata must be sustained. The judgment is affirmed.

Sawyer v. First City Financial Corp.

Court of Appeal of California, Fourth Appellate District
124 Cal. App. 3d 390, 177 Cal. Rptr. 398 (1981)

FROELICH, JUSTICE.

Plaintiffs appeal from adverse summary judgment rulings in favor of all defendants. An understanding of the litigation requires an analysis of two separate cases involving essentially the same parties, of which the present appeal relates specifically to the second. For reference purposes these two cases will be called Sawyer I and Sawyer II. Each case arises from the same general factual background.

Factual Background

The principal parties to both cases are the plaintiffs Sawyer, owners and sellers of land; the defendants First City Financial Corporation, Ltd. (First City) and its subsidiaries, purchasers and encumbrancers of the land who sought to develop it; and Toronto Dominion Bank of California, the development lender to First City's subsidiary. The broad brush of facts is that in May of 1974 the Sawyers sold 32 acres of land in La Jolla, California, to the subsidiary of First City — F. C. Financial Associates, Ltd. — for $1,180,000 consisting of $510,000 in cash and a note secured by deed of trust in the sum of $670,000. Concurrently with the sale, F. C. Financial Associates committed to borrow $1.8 million in the form of a development loan from Toronto Dominion Bank. This loan was guaranteed by First City and was secured by a first deed of trust on the realty, the Sawyers specifically subordinating their deed of trust to the new encumbrance. The Sawyers as part of the sales documents specifically waived any deficiency judgment with respect to their note and deed of trust, with the result that after the sales and refinancing escrows closed their sole resource for collection of their $670,000 note was foreclosure on their deed of trust, now subordinate to a $1.8 million first deed of trust to the Bank.

Early in 1975, F. C. Financial Associates discontinued payments on the note to Toronto Dominion Bank, asserting that it could not proceed further with development of the land because the construction bids it had received were excessively high. Total amounts owed on the note at that time approximated $900,000. Toronto Dominion Bank commenced nonjudicial foreclosure proceedings on April 1, 1975, and purchased the land at foreclosure sale in September 1975, for its bid of $650,000. The land was ultimately transferred in December 1976 to Lexington Properties, Inc., a corporation owned by one Richard Ehrlich, for a purchase price of some $800,000.

The Sawyers contend in pleadings and other documentation that at the time of the foreclosure sale Toronto Dominion Bank had agreed to resell the realty to First City for a price equal to the bank's total investment in it, but that this transfer was delayed until the sale to Ehrlich and his corporation could be arranged, so that neither First City nor its subsidiary again appeared as record titleholder. Ehrlich and his corporation obtained development funds for the property from a corporation called Lomitas Properties, Inc., which is a corporation owned and controlled by the majority stockholders, directors and officers of First City, and which derived its funds from First City.

Appellant's view of the facts, therefore, is that the Sawyers were induced to take a nonrecourse note for more than half the consideration involved in the sale of their land, the security for which note was made subject to a large development loan. The development borrower then defaulted on the note and arranged with the development lender to foreclose, to buy in at the foreclosure sale, and to resell to the development borrower for the amount of the foreclosure sales price plus the balance of the loan guarantee. The practical effect of this transaction, it is alleged, was to wipe out the obligation to the Sawyers and permit First City to proceed with sale or development of the land without having to pay $650,000 of the purchase price. In order to avoid airing the mechanics of the transaction, the agreement between the Toronto Dominion Bank and First City was kept secret, and the resale to First City was not recorded, the ultimate purchaser being a puppet of First City set up in an apparently independent corporation, borrowing funds from a new and anonymous lending company, but actually deriving development funds indirectly from First City. We are alert to caution that the above construction of the facts from and after the foreclosure sale is that alleged by the plaintiffs, who seek the opportunity of proving same in a full-scale evidentiary trial.

Legal Proceedings

Sawyer I

Sawyer I was commenced in July of 1975. The defendants were F. C. Financial Associates, its parent First City, and, later, another subsidiary of First City (all sometimes called herein Financial); and Toronto Dominion Bank of California (Bank). The several causes of action all were based upon contractual theories. Reference was made to the land acquisition and development loan agreement executed between Financial and Bank, which provided for the construction of a planned residential development in accordance with an existing permit. The Sawyers alleged that they were third party beneficiaries of that agreement and had been damaged by the failure of Financial to perform in accordance with it. The breach is alleged not only as a simple breach of contract, but as a breach by the defendants of "a contractual duty of good faith and fair dealing." A separate cause of action asks for declaratory relief with respect to the contractual commitments; and a final cause of action seeks judicial foreclosure of the Sawyer note. The monetary relief prayed for was the amount of the note ($674,500) plus attorney fees.

The case was tried in February of 1978. By stipulation the issues were severed for trial and dispositive issues were presented to a judge, sitting without jury. The judgment rendered in March of 1978, focused upon the issue of the validity of the waiver by Sawyers of their right to a deficiency judgment. This waiver was found to be effective and judgment was rendered in favor of all defendants on all causes of action. Following affirmance on appeal, the judgment became final in December of 1979.

Sawyer II

Sawyer II was filed in January of 1978. Entitled "Complaint for Damages Based Upon Conspiracy and Fraud," it joined as defendants all of the parties named in Sawyer I and in addition the ultimate purchaser Ehrlich and his corporation, Lexington

Properties; the new financier of the development, Lomitas Properties; and a number of officers and directors of the Financial companies and the Bank. Three of the causes of action of this new lawsuit are based upon an alleged conspiracy among the defendants to cause a default in the Bank's note and trust deed, hold a sham sale, and take other action for the purpose of eliminating the obligation to the Sawyers. The only essential difference in the three causes of action is the date of commencement of the alleged conspiracy—one alleging the evil motives from the very start of the land acquisition transaction, a second alleging commencement of the conspiracy when Financial defaulted on its note payments, and a third alleging commencement of the conspiracy at the time of the foreclosure sale. The fourth cause of action uses the same factual allegations as the basis for a claim of intentional interference with contractual relation (Financial's note obligation to the Sawyers). Damages alleged are the same as in Sawyer I except that additional punitive damages are sought.

The procedural history of Sawyer II is detailed as follows:

1. Promptly upon filing Sawyer II, counsel sought to consolidate with Sawyer I, and moved for a continuance of the trial of Sawyer I. This motion was opposed by the defendants, who objected because the issues and causes of action of Sawyer II were different from those of Sawyer I, and also because the case, then pending for two and one-half years, was scheduled for trial nine days later. The court denied a motion to continue the trial of Sawyer I, and it was tried without consolidation with Sawyer II.

2. In January of 1980, the Bank and its officers moved for summary judgment in Sawyer II upon the ground of the res judicata effect of Sawyer I, and also upon the basis of a written release which had been executed in favor of the Bank in Sawyer I—removing the Bank from the case before its trial. The Honorable Douglas Woodworth denied the motion based upon res judicata, but granted the motion as to the Bank only, upon the ground of the written waiver. The bank officers moved for reconsideration on the theory that the waiver should be construed to cover them as well as the Bank, and this motion was taken under submission by the judge in March of 1980. On July 24, 1980, Judge Woodworth denied the motions by written minute order.

3. In May of 1980, a separate motion for summary judgment was filed by the Financial corporations on the ground that Sawyer I was res judicata to the issues of Sawyer II—that the plaintiffs had split their cause of action by attempting to relitigate the same issues in a second lawsuit. The bank officers (whose motion for reconsideration was then pending before Judge Woodworth) joined in this motion, and it was set for hearing before the Honorable Franklin B. Orfield. On July 25, 1980, Judge Orfield ruled in favor of all defendants on the ground of res judicata and the enforceability of the Bank's written release in Sawyer I.

The Appeal

Appellants appeal from the summary judgments of both Judge Woodworth (dismissing the Bank) and Judge Orfield (dismissing all parties).... Many bases of appeal are urged: The central and most important issue, however, is the question of res judicata. As reviewed in 3 Witkin, *California Procedure* (2d ed. 1971) Pleading, section

32 et seq., page 1715, a single cause of action cannot be split and made the subject of several suits. If a primary right is so split, determination of the issues in the first suit will be res judicata to the attempt to relitigate them in the second suit. Where the plaintiff has several causes of action, however, even though they may arise from the same factual setting, and even though they might have been joined in one suit under permissive joinder provisions, the plaintiff is privileged to bring separate actions based upon each separate cause.

Res Judicata Issue

A valid final judgment on the merits in favor of a defendant serves as a complete bar to further litigation on the same cause of action. (*Slater v. Blackwood* (1975) 15 Cal. 3d 791, 795 [126 Cal. Rptr. 225, 543 P.2d 593].) The question in this and similar cases, of course, is whether the attempted second litigation involves the "same cause of action." A "cause of action" is conceived as the remedial right in favor of a plaintiff for the violation of one "primary right." That several remedies may be available for violation of one "primary right" does not create additional "causes of action." However, it is also true that a given set of facts may give rise to the violation of more than one "primary right," thus giving a plaintiff the potential of two separate lawsuits against a single defendant. (*See* 3 Witkin, *supra*, p. 1707 et seq.) The theoretical discussion of what constitutes a "primary right" is complicated by historical precedent in several well-litigated areas establishing the question of "primary rights" in a manner perhaps contrary to the result that might be reached by a purely logical approach. For instance, the primary right to be free from personal injury has been construed as to embrace all theories of tort which might have given rise to the injury. In *Panos v. Great Western Packing Co.* (1943) 21 Cal. 2d 636 [134 P.2d 242], the plaintiff was injured in a meat packing house. His first cause of action was based upon alleged negligence of the packing house in permitting third parties to come upon the premises and operate equipment. A defense judgment was then held to bar a second suit based upon an entirely different factual theory of negligence—that the defendant itself had negligently operated the equipment. In *Slater v. Blackwood, supra,* 15 Cal. 3d 791, a defense judgment in a suit based upon violation of the guest statute (intoxication or willful misconduct) was held to bar a second suit (after the guest statute was held unconstitutional) based upon allegations of ordinary negligence.

Other examples of torts resulting in easily conceptualized types of damages have been settled, one way or the other, by precedent. While one act of tortious conduct might well be deemed to violate only one "primary right"—the right to be free from the particular unlawful conduct—the resultant (1) injury to person and (2) damage to property have been deemed creative of separate causes of action. On the other hand, one course of wrongful conduct which damages several pieces of property traditionally gives rise to only one cause of action.

Other classes of litigation, however, with perhaps less historical or precedential background, are not so well defined in terms of deciding how many "primary rights" derive from a single factual transaction. The tort in *Agarwal v. Johnson* (1979) 25 Cal. 3d 932 [160 Cal. Rptr. 141, 603 P.2d 58], was unfair treatment of a minority race employee by an employer. Plaintiff's first action was in federal court for back wages under the authority of the federal Civil Rights Act. The state Supreme Court determined this was no bar to a second suit in superior court for general and punitive damages for defamation and intentional infliction of emotional distress. Although the same set of facts is presented in each claim, one primary right is created by the federal statute prohibiting discriminatory employment practices; and the second primary right is grounded in state common law. Also, the "harm suffered" was deemed separable—damages for lost wages in the federal action, and damages for injury to reputation and peace of mind in the state case. Compare *Mattson v. City of Costa Mesa* (1980) 106 Cal. App. 3d 441 [164 Cal. Rptr. 913], where the actionable facts consisted of an unlawful arrest of the plaintiff and his abuse in confinement. His first action in federal court under the authority of the Civil Rights Act was held to be a bar to a subsequent suit in state court for negligence, assault and battery. The court found that the "primary rights" giving rise to the state common law tort action were the same as those reflected in the Civil Rights Act, and that the civil rights action was "simply a different way of expressing an invasion of the same primary rights or the assertion of a different legal theory for recovery." (*Id.*, at pp. 447–448.) In *City of Los Angeles v. Superior Court* (1978) 85 Cal. App. 3d 143, 153 [149 Cal. Rptr. 320], a federal civil rights action followed by a superior court common law tort action, both involving wrongful seizure of personal property, the appellate court reached the same conclusion and applied the bar of res judicata on the ground that "the civil rights action was designed to vindicate precisely the same interests in ... personal property that (the plaintiff) seeks to vindicate in the matter before us."

One would assume that the question of litigation of claims arising from one transaction first on the basis of contract, and then on alleged tort theories, would have received substantial appellate attention. The authorities, however, are surprisingly sparse. The Restatement of the Law, Judgments (1942) chapter 3, section 63, page 261, provides several illustrations involving actions to cancel a deed. A failure to sustain the first action on contractual grounds (i.e., failure of execution or delivery of the deed) is held to bar a subsequent action based upon fraudulent procurement— thus suggesting that the "primary right" is the right to cancel the deed (as applied to our case, to validate the note) and that this gives rise to only one cause of action, whether it be framed in contract or tort.

Respondents rely upon two cases which purport to be illustrative of contract actions followed by separate tort actions, arising from the same transaction: *Olwell v. Hopkins* (1946) 28 Cal. 2d 147 [168 P.2d 972]; and *Steiner v. Thomas* (1949) 94 Cal. App. 2d 655 [211 P.2d 321]. [Here, the court discusses *Olwell* and concludes that the court there focused only on the question of whether the dismissal without trial of the first suit on procedural grounds would operate as a bar to a second action, "recognizing that in order to constitute a bar, the dismissal must have been following an adjudication of the merits of the controversy."]

In *Steiner*, two successive actions were brought against an administrator of a decedent's estate for the purpose of recovering a certain parcel of real property which had been transferred to the decedent by the plaintiff before the decedent's death. The first action was for rescission based upon fraud, alleging that the realty had been transferred so as to permit the decedent to collect rents and that the decedent had promised to reconvey the property at a later date. The second lawsuit was based upon an alleged breach of an agreement to devise the property to the plaintiff, as evidenced by two letters from the decedent to the plaintiff. The court resolved the question of res judicata against the plaintiff, focusing on the identity or similarity of facts litigated in the first suit as compared to those in issue at the second suit. The court stated:

> "The fact is that in the former action the merits of all the facts were determined and relief was denied.... Upon presentation of the special plea in the instant action the court had merely to decide whether the facts alleged in the first suit for rescission of the contract were substantially those alleged in the second action for breach of the same contract."

The court thus construed the situation as one in which alternative remedies in contract were successively brought — related to the same contract — rather than a case in which an action on contract was followed by an action for an intentional tort related to or as part of the transaction giving rise to the contract. Neither *Orwell* nor *Steiner* appears controlling.

The case before us is not one in which the same factual structure is characterized in one complaint as a breach of contract and in another as a tort. The first action is solely on contract and is based upon the note, deed of trust, and loan and development agreement. At the time of trial the principal issue litigated was the effectiveness of the waiver of deficiency judgment, and this issue was presented in the context of contractual theories. There was no contention and no evidence was presented relating to a possible invalidation of the waiver on grounds of fraud, misrepresentation or any other tort.

Sawyer II, of course, had as its object collection of the same promissory note which was the subject matter of Sawyer I; but the basis of the claim is completely different, and rests upon a completely separate set of facts. The complaint assumes and admits that the forms of the waiver of deficiency and the subordination are technically appropriate and enforceable. The pleading reaches beyond these documents, however, to highlight other conduct of the parties alleged to be tortious. The core of the alleged wrongful conduct is an agreement among the parties to conduct what is characterized as a sham foreclosure sale, the only substantive effect of which would be secretly to discharge the obligation to Sawyer, leaving all other parties in essentially the same position as prior to the sale. Surely one's breach of contract by failing to pay a note violates a "primary right" which is separate from the "primary right" not to have the note stolen. That the two causes of action might have been joined in one lawsuit under our permissive joinder provisions (*see* 3 Witkin, *supra*, at p. 1915) does not prevent the plaintiff from bringing them in separate suits if he elects to do so. While the monetary loss may be measurable by the same promissory note amount, and hence in a general sense the same "harm" has been done in both cases, theoretically the plaintiffs have been "harmed" differently by tortious conduct destroying the value of the note, than by the contractual breach of simply failing to pay it. We conclude, therefore, that Sawyer II is based upon a separate and severable cause of action from that litigated in Sawyer I, and that it was error to grant summary judgment on the ground of res judicata.

Estoppel

A second prong to appellant's argument about the summary judgment ruling as respects res judicata is that the moving parties were estopped to deny the separate nature of the two causes of action because they had earlier opposed a motion to consolidate the two cases. Appellants rely upon *United Bank & Trust Co. v. Hunt* (1934) 1 Cal. 2d 340 [34 P.2d 1001], where the court at page 345 stated:

> Where counsel by timely notice call to a court's attention the pendency of other proceedings covering kindred matters and strive to have the same embraced within the scope of the inquiry, and such attempt is successfully blocked by opposing counsel and the trial proceeds to the investigation of the specific issue before the court, counsel who were successful in preventing the consolidation of the issues cannot be heard later to object to a trial of the related matters upon the ground of *res judicata*. The course pursued by the court and counsel ... was tantamount to an express determination on the part of the court with the consent of opposing counsel to reserve the issues involved for future adjudication. [Citation.] Litigants cannot successfully assume such inconsistent positions.

The inconsistent position asserted to have been taken by defense counsel was at the time of the hearing of a motion to continue the trial of Sawyer I. * * *

At the hearing of the motion for continuance on February 6, counsel for the defendants did argue that the case should not be continued to permit consideration of a consolidation motion because consolidation would be improper by virtue of the different theories and causes of action in Sawyer II. However, no express argument was made about, nor consideration given, to the question of the res judicata effect of the prior trial of Sawyer I. In light of the long period of preparation for trial and the then once-continued trial date impending only nine days hence, the trial court presumably considered further continuance to be prejudicial to the rights of the defendants. A court is not required to grant a continuance of a trial when the pleadings have been completed, adequate time for discovery has been provided, the issues are joined, and one side is ready for trial, even though the moving party alleges newly discovered facts or newly found issues which suggest more discovery or an amendment to the pleadings.

The reasonable interpretation to be derived from a review of the record in Sawyer I was that the court denied the motion for continuance because Sawyer I was ready for trial, had been delayed previously and should not be delayed further. Therefore, while we have determined that the motion for summary judgment should not have been granted on the ground of res judicata, we must agree with the trial court that the moving parties were not estopped by their prior conduct from making the motion.

STANIFORTH, ACTING PRESIDING JUSTICE, concurs.

WIENER, JUSTICE, Concurring.

* * *

I conclude defendants, except for the Toronto Dominion Bank and its officers, are estopped from raising the defense of res judicata. Accordingly, I agree with the result reached by the majority. * * *

Plaintiffs filed their first case (No. 369573) in July 1975; their second (No. 409803) on January 11, 1978. On January 13, 1978, plaintiffs moved to consolidate both cases because some of the parties and certain of the issues were the same. Unable to serve all defendants, plaintiffs' motion to consolidate was reset beyond February 15, 1978, the trial date in case No. 369573. Pending hearing on that motion, plaintiffs moved to continue the trial to allow the court to consider the motion for consolidation. Counsel for First City defendants in *Sawyer I,* one of whom is appellate counsel here, opposed the motion for continuance by saying there was no basis for consolidation, arguing further that "[plaintiffs] are pursuing theories of action for conspiracy and fraud in Case No. 409803, whereas in the above-captioned action plaintiffs are pursuing theories for breach of contract, declaratory relief and judicial foreclosure. *The issues raised in the two cases are necessarily and substantially different.*" (Italics supplied.) * * *

If defendants' counsel made the tactical decision to oppose the continuance on the assumption that if successful they would then be able to prevent litigation in the second case on the basis of res judicata, it would have been simple enough for them to tell the court that res judicata was involved. If they had done so the judge considering the motion would then have been able to evaluate all relevant factors affecting his decision before exercising discretion in making his ruling. In light of the language which defendants selected to oppose the motion for the continuance the ruling on which prevented the court from ever considering the merits of plaintiffs' request for consolidation, it was reasonable for both the court and plaintiffs' counsel to conclude defendants' opposition to the continuance would not prevent a trial of the second case in which the issues were represented to be "necessarily and substantially different." Accordingly, reasonably interpreted, defendants' actions fall within the narrow rule of *United Bank & Trust Co. v. Hunt, supra.* Once having represented to the court there were two different actions with different issues, they may not now stop plaintiffs from having a full trial on those "different issues." * * *

Notes and Questions on Primary Rights Analysis

(1) As our principle cases illustrate, the central feature of California's claim preclusion doctrine is that a single cause of action cannot be split and made the subject of separate lawsuits. Where a plaintiff has more than one cause of action against a defendant, however, the plaintiff may join them in one lawsuit but is not required to do so either by rules of joinder or of res judicata. In other words, a plaintiff who has two causes of action against a defendant may proceed with two separate lawsuits. A judgment in one lawsuit will have no claim preclusive effect on the other.

This makes the definition of "cause of action" of central importance, does it not? As our cases illustrate, the California courts define a "cause of action" for purposes of claim preclusion according to the "primary rights" theory, *i.e.*, the violation of each separate "primary right" gives rise to a separate cause of action and, potentially, a separate lawsuit against the same defendant.

(2) How is "primary right" defined? More importantly, how do the courts determine whether a set of facts gives rise to only one primary right as opposed to multiple primary rights? The most frequently quoted response to these questions is from *Agarwal v. Johnson*, 25 Cal. 3d 932, 954, 160 Cal. Rptr. 141, 603, P.2d 58 (1979): "Under the 'primary rights' theory adhered to in California it is true there is only a single cause of action for the invasion of one primary right.... But the significant factor is the harm suffered; that the same facts are involved in both suits is not conclusive."

How significant was this "harm suffered" factor in *Holmes v. Bricker*? *Slater v. Blackwood*? *Sawyer v. First City Financial Corp.*? Based on these three cases, is it possible to state a definition of "primary right" that will guide litigants and courts in future cases? How would you state such a rule?

[1]   A Historical Analysis

California's Unpredictable Res Judicata (Claim Preclusion) Doctrine

Walter W. Heiser, 35 San Diego L. Rev. 559, 571–576 (1998)*

The Primary Rights Theory—Living History.

The primary rights theory was developed by Professor John Norton Pomeroy[35] in the nineteenth century, and adopted by the California Supreme Court as early as 1887.[36] Under the primary rights theory advanced by Pomeroy, a "cause of action" consists of a "primary right" possessed by the plaintiff, a corresponding "primary duty" of the defendant, and a wrongful act by the defendant constituting a breach of that duty.[37]

---

* Reprinted with permission of the San Diego Law Review.

35. John Norton Pomeroy (1828–1885) was a professor at the Hastings College of Law during the nineteenth century and a prolific legal scholar. In addition to his influential multi-volume treatise on equity jurisprudence and equitable remedies, in which he explained at length the primary rights theory of a cause of action; Professor Pomeroy also published treatises on a wide variety of topics, including the civil procedure in California and other states, code pleading and remedies, constitutional law, municipal law, wills and trusts, and western water law. *See infra* notes 37....

36. *See* Hutchinson v. Ainsworth, 73 Cal. 452, 455, 15 P. 82 (1887) (citing Pomeroy and holding that the facts upon which the plaintiff's right to sue is based, and upon which the defendant's duty has arisen, coupled with the facts that make up the defendant's wrong, constitute a cause of action);....

37. *See* Crowley v. Katleman, 881 P.2d 1083, 1090 (Cal. 1994); *see also* J. Pomeroy, Remedies and Remedial Rights § 453, at 487 (1876) [hereinafter, Pomeroy, Remedies]; J. Pomeroy, Equity Jurisprudence §§ 89–95, at 75–79 (1881) [hereinafter, Pomeroy, Equity]. Professor Pomeroy observed that although the American courts had repeatedly distinguished a "cause of action" from the relief demanded in a case before them, "they have not attempted to define the term 'cause of action' in any general and abstract manner, so that this definition might be used as a test in all other cases." Pomeroy, Remedies § 452, at 486. Pomeroy then undertook to define the correct meaning of the term "cause of action," apparently relying on natural law concepts. *Id.* at 486–487.

Although the genesis of the primary rights theory is found in Pomeroy's writings, the historical evolution of the primary rights theory is intertwined with California's nineteenth century pleading and joinder rules.[38] The primary rights theory was first reflected in the permissive joinder of claims provisions of the California Practice Act of 1851. This 1851 Act, which was later codified in former Section 427 of the California Code of Civil Procedure, divided all claims into seven specific categories.[40] Claims falling within separate categories could not be joined in the same complaint, and therefore had to be pleaded in separate actions. For example, the original version of Section 427 permitted a plaintiff to join all claims for injuries to her person against a defendant in one complaint, or certain claims for injuries to her property, but prohibited plaintiff from pursuing both her personal injury and property damage claims in one lawsuit.[41]

Professor Pomeroy also undertook the onerous task of identifying all the rules which constitute "private civil law" and assigning them to mutually exclusive classes of primary rights and duties. Pomeroy, Equity §§ 89–95, at 75–79. According to Pomeroy, all such rights fell naturally into two grand divisions: those relating to "*Persons*" and those concerned with "*Things*." *Id.* at 77. The first of these divisions comprised "only those rules the exclusive object of which is to define the status of persons." *Id.* at 77.

Pomeroy separated the grand division of "Things" into two principal classes — "Real rights" and "Personal rights." *Id.* at 77–78. Real rights embraced three distinct subclasses:

1. Rights of property of every degree and kind over land and chattels, things real and things personal; 2. The rights which every person has over and to his own life, body, limbs, and good name; 3. The rights which certain classes of persons, namely husbands, parents, and masters, have over certain other persons standing in domestic relations with themselves, namely, wives, children, and servants and slaves.

Id. at 78. The second class, "Personal rights," included two subclasses: "1. Rights arising from contract;" and 2. Quasi contract and fiduciary rights arising "from some existing relation between two persons or groups of persons, which is generally created by law." *Id.* at 79. Pomeroy viewed these general classifications as embracing "all primary rights and duties, both legal and equitable, which belong to the private civil law." *Id.* at 79.

38. *See* [Robin] James, [Comment, *Res Judicata: Should California Abandon Primary Rights?*, 23 Loy. L.A. L. Rev. 551 (1989)], at 372–385; Holmes v. David H. Brickner, Inc., 452 P.2d 647, 649 (Cal. 1969). The restrictive claim joinder statutes were in effect when Pomeroy published his treatises defining the primary rights theory. *See generally* James, *supra* at 359–360; Pomeroy, Equity, *supra* note 37; Pomeroy, Remedies, *supra* note 37. * * *

40. The original version of former Section 427 (enacted in 1872) codified, without change, the permissive joinder provisions of the 1851 Act, and provided as follows:

The plaintiff may unite several causes of action in the same complaint, when they all arise out of:

1. Contracts, express or implied; or,

2. Claims to recover specific real property, with or without damages, for the withholding thereof, or for waste committed thereon, and the rents and profits of the same; or,

3. Claims to recover specific personal property, with or without damages, for the withholding thereof; or,

4. Claims against a trustee, by virtue of contract, or by operation of law; or,

5. Injuries to character; or,

6. Injuries to person; or,

7. Injuries to property.

But the causes of action so united shall all belong to only one of these classes, and shall affect all parties to the action, and not require different places of trial, and shall be separately stated. Cal. Civ. Proc. Code § 427, *repealed by* Act of July 1, 1972, ch. 244, § 23, 1971 Cal. Stat. 378.

41. *Id.*

Viewed in this historical context, Pomeroy's primary rights theory made sense when adopted by the courts in the 19th century. If, for example, the joinder rules prohibited a plaintiff from pleading claims for tortious injury to person and to property against a defendant in one lawsuit, a personal injury judgment in the first lawsuit should not extinguish plaintiff's claims for property damages in a second action.[43] Such a claim preclusive effect would have been fundamentally unfair to the plaintiff, particularly one who had established the defendant's liability in the first action. More-over, issue preclusion was available to minimize any unfairness to a defendant who had successfully defended against liability in the first lawsuit.[44]

Over time, the California courts viewed the categories of permissibly joinable claims designated in the original version of former Section 427 as synonymous with Pomeroy's classifications of primary rights. However, through frequent amendments between 1907 and 1931, the Legislature attempted to liberalize the restrictive categories of former Section 427. Although many were poorly drafted and their meaning unclear, these revisions significantly modified the seven categories of the original Section 427. * * * Th[ese] revisions, which remained in effect until the repeal of former Section 427 in 1971, meant that the statutory categories were no longer the same as Pomeroy's primary rights classifications. Consequently, the California Supreme Court sought to identify some unifying themes to assist the lower courts in applying the primary rights theory in cases where plaintiff's claims did not fall neatly into one of former Section 427's categories. This effort proved largely unenlightening. The best the Supreme Court could do was to emphasize that a judgment in a prior action was a bar to a subsequent action based on the "same injuries," even though the second action raised new theories of recovery or requested new forms of relief.[48] Other than to continue to refer to the original version of former Section 427, the Court did little to generally define what constituted the "same" as opposed to "different" injuries. Eventually, with the repeal of former Section 427, the court's explicit reliance on this joinder statute as an aid to defining primary rights came to an end.

---

43. The court in *Schermerhorn v. Los Angeles Pac. R.R. Co.*, 123 P. 351 (Cal. 1912), one of the few appellate decisions to consider this question in the context of a res judicata determination, employed precisely this reasoning in a simple car crash case. The court held that a prior judgment for property damage did not preclude plaintiff's instant suit for personal injuries, although caused by the same negligent act of the defendant. The court reasoned that the second suit was not barred because, under former § 427, the plaintiff could not have sought recovery for injuries to person and injuries to property in one action. *Id.* at 352.

44. In *Todhunter v. Smith*, 28 P.2d 916 (Cal. 1934), for example, the court held that although res judicata did not completely bar the plaintiff's second action to recover damages for personal injuries sustained in an automobile collision with the defendant, a prior judgment whereby plaintiff unsuccessfully sought recovery for damage to his car collaterally estopped the plaintiff from relitigating the issue of negligence.

48. In *Slater v. Blackwood*, 543 P.2d 593 (Cal. 1975), the court ruled that a "cause of action" is based upon the "harm suffered," as opposed to the particular legal theory asserted by the litigant, and therefore a judgment for the defendant is a bar to a subsequent action by the plaintiff based on the "same injury" to the same right, even though plaintiff presents a different legal ground for relief. * * *

Effective 1972, the California Legislature repealed Section 427 and replaced it with a modern joinder of claims statute. Recognizing that the former permissive joinder categories were arbitrary and inefficient, the Legislature eliminated such restrictions in favor of a standard which permits a plaintiff to join together *any* causes of action which she has against a defendant.[50] This unlimited joinder of claims standard, codified at Section 427.10(a), remains in effect today.[51] With the adoption of unrestricted joinder of claims, the link between claim joinder and res judicata—the historical and philosophical justification for the primary rights theory—was now completely severed. The challenge for the California Supreme Court was whether, and if so how, to reformulate the court-made res judicata doctrine in response to this legislative change. To date, on the few occasions it has had to expound on the doctrine, the Supreme Court has taken a cautious approach. The courts of appeal have been more adventuresome, but with inconsistent and therefore less predictable results.

[2] Cause of Action

Accurate use of the term "cause of action" is particularly important in applying the "primary rights" theory. This term is used in many ways for many purposes, which makes its use for res judicata purposes even more confusing. *See, e.g., Bay Cities Paving & Grading, Inc. v. Lawyers' Mut. Ins. Co.*, 5 Cal. 4th 854, 21 Cal. Rptr. 2d 691, 855, P.2d 1263 (1993) (construing "cause of action" with respect to malpractice insurance policy coverage); *Lilienthal & Fowler v. Superior Court*, 12 Cal. App. 4th 1848, 16 Cal. Rptr. 2d 458 (1993) (distinguishing "cause of action" in summary adjudication statute, where it means theory of liability, from res judicata, where it means the invasion of a primary right).

In the vernacular of lawyers, a "cause of action" most often refers to a "different theory of recovery." Even courts use the term in that manner, as in *Holmes v. Bricker*, *supra*, 70 Cal. 2d at 787 and 788. For example, many lawyers typically say that a client's personal injuries due to a defective product give rise to several "causes of action" identified as breach of warranty, breach of contract, strict liability, negligence, fraud, etc. And when they plead such a case, lawyers typically allege each of these as a separate "cause of action" in the complaint. This common use of "cause of action" is incorrect for res judicata purposes, is it not? How many "causes of action" are there in our products liability example, for res judicata purposes?

[3] Primary Rights Determined by Precedent

Despite the general uncertainty in defining a "primary right," some applications of the theory are (relatively) settled by precedent, as our principle cases indicate. Litigants can feel reasonably comfortable in determining whether one or two lawsuits

---

50. Act of July 1, 1972, ch. 244, sec. 23, §427, 1971 Cal. Stat. 380. * * *

51. Cal. Civ. Proc. Code 427.10(a) (Deering 1995) (providing that "[a] plaintiff who in a complaint, alone or with coplaintiffs, alleges a cause of action against one or more defendants may unite with such cause any other causes which he has either alone or with any coplaintiffs against any such defendants").

are permissible in such circumstances. Perhaps the most frequently encountered application involves a tort victim who simultaneously suffers both personal injury and property damage caused by the defendant's single act. A typical example is negligence litigation arising out of the crash of two cars, where one driver sues the other. The resulting personal injury to the plaintiff driver is a separate primary right from the property damage to the plaintiff's car, and may be pursued in two separate lawsuits. *See Holmes v. Bricker, supra*, and cases cited therein. Why then did the court in *Holmes v. Bricker, supra*, conclude that plaintiff's claim for property damage resulting from that car crash was the same primary right as already litigated in the prior action for personal injuries? Could the plaintiff in *Holmes* have avoided the res judicata effect of the first judgment by *pleading* the second lawsuit differently? If so, how?

Other areas (relatively) settled by precedent are also suggested in *Sawyer* and *Holmes*. One wrongful act which results in injury to several pieces of property traditionally gives rise to only one cause of action, as does one wrongful act which results in multiple personal injuries to a plaintiff. *See Sawyer* and cases cited therein; *Swartzendruber v. City of San Diego*, 3 Cal. App. 4th 896, 904, 5 Cal. Rptr. 2d 64 (1992) (Consequential damages did not support a second cause of action); *Allstate Ins. Co. v. Mel Rapton, Inc.*, 77 Cal. App. 4th 901, 92 Cal. Rptr. 2d 151 (2000) (A separate cause of action does not arise for each separate item of personal property damaged by one tortious act). However, a wrongful act which causes injury to real property has been held to constitute a separate primary right from injury to personal property situated on the real property. *McNulty v. Copp*, 125 Cal. App. 2d 697, 271 P.2d 90 (1954).

[4] *Primary Rights Distinguished from Theories of Recovery*

[a] Importance of Harm Suffered?

Slater v. Blackwood, supra, illustrates that a cause of action is based upon the harm suffered as opposed to the particular theory of recovery asserted. Likewise, the claims alleged in *Holmes v. Bricker, supra*, are actually different theories of recovery and not separate causes of action under the primary rights theory. Is *Sawyer v. First City Financial Corp., supra*, consistent with *Slater* and *Holmes*? Isn't the second action in *Sawyer* to obtain payment of the promissory note simply the same cause of action with a different legal theory—tort as opposed to contract—as the first action? The *Sawyer* court concluded that plaintiffs were harmed differently by tortious conduct destroying the value of the note than by a contract breach of failing to pay the note. Is this really a different injury? Or is it another theory for recovering the same injury? Are you persuaded by the court's analysis? Why?

In *Boeken v. Philip Morris USA, Inc.*, 48 Cal. 4th 788, 108 Cal. Rptr. 3d 806, 230 P.3d 342 (2010), after the plaintiff's husband, a cigarette smoker, was diagnosed with lung cancer, the plaintiff filed a common law action for loss of consortium against the defendant cigarette manufacturer seeking compensation for the permanent loss of companionship and affection. That action was dismissed with prejudice. Then, after her husband's death from lung cancer, the plaintiff brought a wrongful death action under CCP § 377.60 against the same defendant, again seeking compensation for loss of her husband's companionship and affection. Is the primary right at issue in the plaintiff's statutory wrongful death action for loss of consortium action the same as the primary right at issue in the plaintiff's previous common law action for loss of consortium? The Supreme Court in *Boeken* concluded that both actions sought damages for the same harm and involved the same primary right, and therefore res judicata bars the wrongful death action insofar as it concerns loss of consortium. *Boeken, supra,* 48 Cal. 4th at 800–804.

[b] *Sawyer*: Tort vs. Contract?

The primary rights ruling in *Sawyer v. First City Financial Corp., supra,* has been questioned and distinguished, but has not been disapproved. *See, e.g., Gamble v. General Foods Corp.,* 229 Cal. App. 3d 893, 902, 280 Cal. Rptr. 457 (1991) (distinguishing instant case from *Sawyer* "in that the Sawyers' first action was based on contract rights whereas second action was grounded on fraud."); *Jenkins v. Pope,* 217 Cal. App. 3d 1292, 1299, n.3, 266 Cal. Rptr. 557 (1990) (viewing *Sawyer* as finding two separate primary rights violated by a breach of contract and acts of fraud arising from different sets of facts; unlike *Sawyer,* instant case involved one primary right for failure to pay attorneys fees because actions for fraud and negligent misrepresentation were based on same acts and misrepresentations); *Wittman v. Chrysler Corp.,* 199 Cal. App. 3d 586, 593, n.3, 245 Cal. Rptr. 20 (1988) ("Brushing aside any doubts we might have about the correctness of the *Sawyer* court's reasoning, the [instant] case is distinguishable because, here, the issue of fraud *was* tendered by the Wittmans' answer [in the prior contract action], and they had an opportunity to litigate the issue in the [prior] action.").

If *Sawyer* remains good law, precisely what "law" does *Sawyer* establish? Can we safely rely on *Sawyer* for the following proposition: An action based on breach of contract constitutes a separate primary right than one based on tort, where the relief sought is the same? *See Gamble v. General Foods Corp., supra.* Why not? What about the following proposition: An action which seeks the same remedy as a prior action constitutes a separate primary right where the facts alleged in the second action are related, but different than, those of the prior action? *See Jenkins v. Pope, supra.* Why or why not? One more possibility: A plaintiff who seeks the same remedy as in a prior action but who alleges the harm was caused in a different manner alleges a separate primary right than was involved in the prior action?

In *Brenelli Amedeo, S.P.A. v. Barkara Furniture, Inc.,* 29 Cal. App. 4th 1828, 35 Cal. Rptr. 2d 348 (1994), the court relied on *Sawyer* to find the plaintiff's action was not barred by res judicata. The plaintiff company had obtained a judgment against the defendant corporation based on contractual obligations. Subsequently, plaintiff commenced a second suit alleging that the defendant's tortious conveyance of assets prevented the plaintiff from collecting on the first judgment. The court found the situation analogous to that presented in *Sawyer,* and held that plaintiff's prior action involved a different primary right than the current suit against the same defendant. *Id.* at 1836–38. Do you agree? Does *Brenelli* really involve the same situation as the one presented in *Sawyer*? For recent decisions relying on *Brenelli*'s reasoning, see *Fujifilm Corp. v. Yang*, 223 Cal. App. 4th 326, 167 Cal. Rptr. 3d 241 (2014) (holding prior breach of settlement agreement action sought to enforce a different primary right than current fraudulent transfer action); *Wells Fargo Bank, N.A. v. Weinberg*, 227 Cal. App. 4th 1, 173 Cal. Rptr. 3d 113 (2014) (ruling defendant lawyer's alter ego conduct was a separate harm from law corporation's breach of contract).

[c] Importance of Same Injury?

One of the first Supreme Court cases to clearly delineate the difference between primary rights and theories of recovery is *Panos v. Great Western Packing Co.*, 21 Cal. 2d 636, 134 P.2d 242 (1943), whose facts are briefly summarized in *Sawyer*. The court in *Panos* held that two actions seeking recovery for the same personal injuries suffered by plaintiff constituted one primary right and the same cause of action, even though the plaintiff alleged totally different factual theories of negligence in the two actions. *See also Bay Cities Paving & Grading v. Lawyers' Mut. Ins. Co.*, 5 Cal. 4th 854, 860, 21 Cal. Rptr. 2d 691, 855 P.2d 1263 (1993) (finding plaintiff had one primary right — the right to be free from negligence by its attorney in connection with a debt collection matter — in malpractice suit against the defendant attorney, even though defendant allegedly breached that right in two factually different ways).

Compare *Panos* to the more recent decision in *Branson v. Sun-Diamond Growers*, 24 Cal. App. 4th 327, 29 Cal. Rptr. 3d 314 (1994). Branson, a former marketing manager of the Sun-Diamond Growers corporation, became an independent commodity food broker and took the Sun-Diamond Growers account away from the former exclusive broker, Plate Company. Plate sued Branson for intentional interference with contract, which resulted in a verdict of $275,968 against Branson. Branson then filed a motion to compel statutory indemnification of the verdict by Sun-Diamond Growers pursuant to Corporations Code § 317, which requires a corporation to indemnify its agent against a judgment arising from the agent's good faith acts on behalf of the corporation. The court in this prior litigation held that Sun-Diamond Growers could not be ordered to indemnify Branson under § 317 because Branson had not been sued for activity undertaken as an agent of Sun-Diamond, but for activity taken entirely independently of Sun-Diamond.

Branson then commenced an action against Sun-Diamond Growers seeking indemnification for the prior judgment based on allegations of contractual and quasi-contractual rights of indemnity as opposed to statutory indemnity. The trial court found Branson's complaint barred by res judicata, and Branson appealed. After an extensive review of the doctrine of res judicata, the Court of Appeal reversed. The court held that Branson's present complaint asserted a different primary right than that involved in the prior judgment, and therefore the contractual indemnity causes of action were not barred. *Branson*, 24 Cal. App. 4th at 340–45.

Do you agree with the holding in *Branson*? Is it consistent with *Panos*? Did *Branson* involve two different injuries, or one injury and two theories of recovery? Why?

[5] Primary Rights v. Remedies

The number of different remedies a plaintiff seeks against a defendant for wrongful conduct does not necessarily determine the number of causes of action under the primary rights theory. For example, in *Duffy v. City of Long Beach*, 201 Cal. App. 3d 1352, 247 Cal. Rptr. 715 (1988), the plaintiff sued the defendant City in federal court seeking to enjoin the City from demolishing plaintiff's house as a public nuisance, alleging several federal constitutional violations. The federal court found that the defendant City violated none of plaintiff's constitutional rights in declaring his house a public nuisance. The City subsequently demolished the house as a nuisance. Plaintiff then filed suit against the City in state court alleging various violations of his constitutional rights, but this time seeking money damages for the demolition of his house. The Superior Court sustained a demurrer by defendant on the ground of res judicata.

The Court of Appeal affirmed, holding that the prior action to enjoin the impending demolition raised the same causes of action as the present action for damages filed after the actual demolition. The court ruled that requesting a different remedy does not distinguish the two lawsuits, and that "[a] mere change in the form of relief requested does not avoid the res judicata bar." *Duffy*, 201 Cal. App. 3d at 1358. *See also Tensor Group v. City of Glendale*, 14 Cal. App. 4th 154, 17 Cal. Rptr. 2d 639 (1993) (holding plaintiff's current suit for damages for inverse condemnation of its properties barred by earlier successful mandamus action seeking declaratory and injunction relief for limitation placed on plaintiff's use of its properties); *California Coastal Comm'n v. Superior Court*, 210 Cal. App. 3d 1488, 258 Cal. Rptr. 567 (1989) (ruling same primary right involved in prior administrative proceeding which imposed easement to beach as condition of obtaining a building permit as involved in subsequent inverse condemnation action for damages, only the type of relief sought is different).

Is it possible to seek the same remedy in two separate actions, with a different primary right in each lawsuit? For example, in *Nakash v. Superior Court (Marciano)*, 196 Cal. App. 3d 59, 241 Cal. Rptr. 578 (1987), the plaintiffs sought rescission of their stock purchase agreement with defendants in a prior action, which was dismissed with prejudice. Subsequently, the plaintiffs filed a second action against defendants, again seeking rescission of the same contract. Is the second action barred by the first judgment? Is rescission a cause of action or a remedy? *See id.* at 70.

[6] Inherent Ambiguity of the Primary Rights Theory

One criticism of the primary rights theory is its inherent ambiguity. *See* Walter W. Heiser, *California's Unpredictable Res Judicata (Claim Preclusion) Doctrine*, 35 SAN DIEGO L. REV. 559, 602–603 (1998); Robin James, Note, *Res Judicata: Should California Abandon Primary Rights?*, 23 LOY. L.A. L. REV. 351, 387–402 (1989). Neither the history nor the standard definitions of the doctrine provide much guidance to a court faced with an application not governed by precedent. A broad characterization of what constitutes a primary right will most likely mean that a plaintiff has only one cause of action. A narrow characterization may mean a greater number of causes of action, and more opportunities for multiple lawsuits. In light of the current policy favoring judicial economy, how is a court likely to resolve this inherent ambiguity in applying the primary rights doctrine? Consider the recent decision in *Takahashi v. Board of Education*, 202 Cal. App. 3d 1464, 249 Cal. Rptr. 578 (1988), reproduced below.

Takahashi v. Board of Education

Court of Appeal of California, Fifth Appellate District
202 Cal. App. 3d 1464, 249 Cal. Rptr. 578 (1988), *cert. denied*, 490 U.S. 1011 (1989)

HAMLIN, ASSOCIATE JUSTICE.

Plaintiff Mitsue Takahashi appeals from a judgment dismissing her causes of action against defendants Livingston Union School District, Board of Education of Livingston Union School District, Harold Thompson, Dale Eastlee and Hamilton Brannan after the trial court granted defendants' motions for summary judgment in consolidated proceedings Nos. 70836 and 71869.

The basic issue on appeal is whether or not the judgments in the litigation previously initiated by plaintiff in both California and federal courts against one or more of the defendants in these consolidated actions operate as a bar to the present actions under res judicata principles. Decision on the issue presented requires us to determine the relationship between the procedures under the California Fair Employment Practices Act (Gov. Code, § 12900 et seq.) and the schoolteacher dismissal procedures. We will conclude that the judgments in the previous litigation are res judicata on the issues in the consolidated actions and will affirm the judgment.

PROCEDURAL BACKGROUND

* * *

Plaintiff was employed by the Livingston Union School District (district) in 1960 and continued in employment there until the fall of 1980, rendering her at the time of the hearing a permanent or tenured teacher.

On May 8, 1978, plaintiff was given an evaluation of her job performance. That evaluation isolated problems with classroom management as a specific concern. She was notified at that time, during the 1977–1978 school year, that if satisfactory improvement were not shown, formal dismissal proceedings would be initiated during the 1978–1979 school year.

In an April 1979 formal evaluation of plaintiff's performance, lack of student control and classroom management were again isolated as serious problems. * * * On November 15, 1979, a further evaluation of plaintiff's job performance was made. That evaluation noted several deficiencies and further noted that a variety of suggestions had been made to improve instruction and classroom management that had not been implemented. It included the statement: "if the deviciencies [sic] so noted are not significantly corrected, dismissal is recommended."

On May 12, 1980, plaintiff was issued a document entitled "notice of intent to dismiss," along with a statement of charges indicating that cause existed to dismiss her on the basis of incompetency and that the district intended to do so. Attached to the notice of charges was a copy of the November 15, 1979, evaluation.

On June 26, 1980, a notice of accusation was served on plaintiff, informing her that unless she requested a hearing within 15 days the board of trustees of the district would proceed upon the accusation without a hearing. The hearing referred to is one to be held as provided in Education Code section 44944. The hearing was held on October 21, 1980, before the Commission on Professional Competence (Commission) pursuant to Education Code section 44944.

At the termination hearing plaintiff challenged the Commission's jurisdiction based on the district's failure to comply with the Stull Act (Ed. Code, § 44660 et seq.). That challenge was denied. In addition to the jurisdictional challenge, plaintiff raised at the administrative hearing the following issues in her defense: (1) that her students had good test scores; (2) that certain disruptive students who should not have been in the same room had been put in her classroom; (3) that other classes were also noisy; (4) that the criteria for judging incompetency were inadequate and not uniform so that no objective, verifiable determination of plaintiff's competency or incompetency could be established; and (5) that she believed she was doing as good a job as the other teachers.

There was no mention nor suggestion in the transcript of the administrative hearing of any defense based on violation of plaintiff's civil or constitutional rights.

After the administrative hearing was completed, the Commission rendered its decision ... and ordered that plaintiff be dismissed from her position effective forthwith.

On December 4, 1980, plaintiff filed in the Superior Court of Merced County a petition for writ of mandate (first action) alleging that (1) the Commission committed a prejudicial abuse of discretion in that the findings of the Commission were not supported by the evidence and the findings did not support the decision of incompetency; (2) the Commission proceeded without or in excess of its jurisdiction because incompetency may only be proved by reference to uniform, objective standards, which the district did not have; and (3) the district lacked jurisdiction to proceed because it failed to include with the 90-day notice an Education Code section 44660 evaluation (Ed. Code, § 44938), and since the focus of a charge of teacher incompetence is whether or not the students learned the required material, the charge was rebutted by evidence that plaintiff's students accomplished their academic goals. (Code Civ. Proc., § 1094.5, subd. (b)). That petition named both the California Teachers' Association (CTA) and Mitsue Takahashi as plaintiffs.

On May 1, 1981, the petition in the first action was argued and denied. The reporter's transcript of that hearing shows that plaintiff elected to argue only the lack of jurisdiction of the Commission to dismiss plaintiff because of the failure of the district to comply with the provisions of the Stull Act. The action was dismissed and judgment entered on June 9, 1981. A notice of appeal was filed on August 5, 1981. This court affirmed the trial court's denial of the petition in the first action. * * *

On November 15, 1982, plaintiff filed a complaint in the Superior Court of Merced County for damages, case No. 70836. That complaint (hereafter the common law case) alleged causes of action for breach of employment contract and conspiracy to defraud. It specifically alleged that plaintiff's employment contract was breached by the district's "terminating the plaintiff without just cause" and cited seven specific instances of such breach. The second cause of action alleged that various district employees conspired to "set the plaintiff up" to "attempt to show justification in terminating the plaintiff." The complaint in the common law case was amended on September 22, 1983, to add causes of action for intentional and negligent infliction of emotional distress.

On March 31, 1983, a separate complaint, case No. 71869, was filed seeking "monetary, injunctive and declaratory relief." That complaint (hereafter the civil rights case) alleged causes of action for (1) wrongful discharge from employment for exercise of plaintiff's First Amendment rights of freedom of speech and association; (2) unconstitutional discharge from employment for exercise of right of liberty and property in employment in violation of the right to due process (the complaint specifically alleged that: (a) plaintiff was terminated from her employment because she held a job outside of her teaching job, and (b) her right to due process was violated since no allegations or charges relating to her outside employment were made); (3) termination of employment in violation of equal protection of the laws, specifically that she was terminated for holding outside employment and that other people holding outside employment were not similarly terminated; (4) discrimination in employment on account of race and ancestry, alleging that plaintiff was terminated from her employment because defendants were "motivated by pejorative stereotypes and biases as to Japanese persons"; (5) discrimination in employment on account of sex, alleging that defendants terminated plaintiff because they used "sex differential criteria in evaluation and criticism of Takahashi"; (6) discrimination in employment on account of age, alleging "in terminating Takahashi's employment based upon 'alleged incompetence' purportedly consisting of an inability to control student behavior, defendants employed age-differential criteria." * * *

After the common law and civil rights cases were consolidated pursuant to stipulation, defendants moved for summary judgment. The motion was heard, and about three weeks later an untitled document was filed in the consolidated action reading in its entirety as follows: "Defendants have moved for summary judgment in these consolidated actions. [¶] This court concludes that previous State … court litigation bars these actions on the basis of res judicata. [¶] There are no material facts in dispute and defendants are entitled to a judgment as a matter of law. [¶] The issues here present were litigated or could have been litigated in prior administrative and mandamus proceeding. [¶] The motion is granted in both these actions." Based on this grant of the motion for summary judgment, the trial court entered a judgment dismissing the consolidated actions.

DISCUSSION

Did the trial court err in concluding that the judgment in the first action ... operates as a bar to these consolidated actions?

To determine if either judgment operates as a bar, we will examine the doctrines of res judicata and collateral estoppel and the relationship of those principles to the administrative hearing and the petition in the first action. We then apply the elements of res judicata to these consolidated actions to determine whether the same primary right is being asserted here as in the former cases and if it is being asserted against the same parties or those in privity with such parties. Finally, we will consider the effect of issues that were not litigated and the impact of claims that plaintiff asserts could not have been raised at the time of the administrative hearing or the first action. * * *

Plaintiff seems to be saying in part that the underlying action cannot be res judicata since the original action was an administrative rather than a judicial proceeding. *People v. Sims* [(1982) 32 Cal. 3d 468 [186 Cal. Rptr. 77, 651 P.2d 321]], stands for the proposition that the final judgment of an administrative hearing may have collateral estoppel effect in a subsequent court proceeding (in that case a criminal proceeding). However, plaintiff is mistaken in believing that it is the administrative proceeding that serves as the bar in this case. The first action (in the superior court) is the state court proceeding upon which the trial court based its finding of res judicata as to the consolidated actions. As discussed, that first action was brought by plaintiff in December 1980. The trial court independently reviewed the record of the administrative hearing, held a hearing at which plaintiff had the opportunity to present any argument to the court, and determined independently that cause existed to dismiss plaintiff on the basis of incompetency. That judgment has long since become final.

A. *The primary right involved here is the same as in the first action.*

Plaintiff has argued that she is not precluded from bringing the present actions since she did not assert the violation of the same rights as defenses to termination for cause in the first action. She points out that her actions involve a different primary right and the Commission did not have the authority to award her punitive damages, thus precluding an appropriate remedy in that forum.

To determine the scope of causes of action, California courts employ the "primary rights" theory. Under this theory, the underlying right sought to be enforced determines the cause of action. In determining the primary right, "the significant factor is the harm suffered." (*Agarwal v. Johnson* (1979) 25 Cal. 3d 932, 954 [160 Cal. Rptr. 141, 603 P.2d 58]). * * *

Plaintiff has ... cited *Agarwal* as support for her position that separate primary rights are involved. *Agarwal* does appear to support plaintiff's position, but it is distinguishable. In that case, the plaintiff was terminated from private employment without notice. He was notified on September 25 that he had been terminated on September 17, 1970, for insubordination. He was not able to find work for 13 months. The plaintiff's former employer made unfavorable statements about him to prospective employers. Agarwal then sued his employer for defamation and emotional distress.

Before the state court case came to trial, a federal court action on the individual and class claims of discrimination under title VII of the Civil Rights Act of 1964 (42 U.S.C. § 2000(e) et seq.) was concluded.

The California Supreme Court concluded in *Agarwal* that the federal court's determination of the claims under title VII of the Civil Rights Act of 1964 was not res judicata as to the issues raised in the state court proceeding because the harm for which Agarwal recovered damages in the state court action was different. It pointed out: "Our review of the district court's findings of fact discloses that its attention was primarily directed to McKee's [the defendant's] employment practices and the corresponding impact on racial minorities, and to statistical analyses of the McKee employee population. Although Agarwal's state court claims for defamation and intentional infliction of emotional distress arose in conjunction with the alleged violation of title VII, the fact remains that in the present action he was awarded damages for harm distinct from employment discrimination."

All of plaintiff's alleged causes of action in this consolidated action arise in conjunction with or as a result of the alleged wrongful termination of her employment. Indeed, plaintiff specifically alleges that each act complained of caused the dismissal (wrongful discharge, conspiracy, unconstitutional discharge, discharge in violation of state civil rights) or was a consequence of the termination (emotional distress, damages), part and parcel of the violation of the single primary right, the single harm suffered. Plaintiff's allegations of consequential injuries are not based upon infringement of a separate primary right.

Plaintiff has further argued that even if the same primary right is involved, the Commission could not have awarded punitive damages and she should therefore be able to bring a separate suit for punitive damages.

We agree that the Commission did not have jurisdiction to award damages, either consequential or punitive. * * * However, we disagree that the Commission's lack of authority to award damages somehow excuses plaintiff's failure to present her defenses to the district's charges of incompetency at the termination hearing. There can hardly be justification for such a position. Government Code sections 11505 and 11506 give the plaintiff the right to interpose any defense, and the Commission is required to make findings of fact and determination of issues. Right of discovery is the same in proceedings before the Commission as in civil lawsuits and continuances may be had.

If violation of constitutional and civil rights had been alleged and proved in proceedings before the Commission to determine whether the district had cause to terminate plaintiff for incompetency, such violation would have made the termination wrongful. Plaintiff would then have been in a position to bring a lawsuit against defendants based on violation of her constitutional rights alleging the damages she suffered thereby, supported by the findings of the Commission. She would also have retained her position and mitigated any possible damages.

B. *The district's employees may assert the first action as a bar to plaintiff's causes of action in this consolidated action even though they were not parties to the first action.*

Plaintiff has additionally contended that even if the doctrine of res judicata or collateral estoppel bars her causes of action against the district in these proceedings, her causes of action against the individually named defendants who were not defendants in the first action are not similarly barred. However, since *Bernhard v. Bank of America* (1942) 19 Cal. 2d 807 [122 P.2d 892], mutuality has not been a prerequisite to asserting the defense of res judicata in California. One not a party to a prior suit may successfully assert collateral estoppel as a defense if: (1) the issue decided in the prior action is identical to the one presented in the action in which the defense is asserted; (2) a final judgment has been entered in the prior action on the merits; and (3) the party against whom the defense is asserted was a party to the prior adjudication. (*Id.* at p. 812; ...). Here, all three of the individually named defendants were employees of the district and were acting within the course and scope of their employment in terminating plaintiff from her teaching position. They are sued solely because of their involvement in the termination process. The party against whom the bar is being asserted is identical to the one in the prior lawsuit. Since all of the prerequisites to asserting the defense of res judicata or collateral estoppel as stated in *Bernhard v. Bank of America, supra,* are satisfied, the district's employees are entitled to assert the decision in the first action as a bar to these consolidated actions. * * *

Clearly what plaintiff was doing in the termination hearing and the first action was defending her dismissal only on the ground that the Commission lacked jurisdiction to proceed against her since the district had not adopted uniform standards pursuant to the Stull Act. Having chosen to "put all her eggs in one basket," she cannot come back years later and add others.

D. *The final judgment in the first action is res judicata as to all issues that were or could have been litigated in that action.*

It is axiomatic that a final judgment serves as a bar not only to the issues litigated but to those that could have been litigated at the same time. In *Sutphin v. Speik* (1940) 15 Cal. 2d 195, 202 [99 P.2d 652], the California Supreme Court stated the California rule regarding the scope of res judicata as follows: "If the matter was within the scope of the action, related to the subject matter and relevant to the issues, so that it *could* have been raised, the judgment is conclusive on it despite the fact that it was not in fact expressly pleaded or otherwise urged. [Italics in original.] The reason for this is manifest. A party cannot by negligence or design withhold issues and litigate them in consecutive actions. Hence the rule is that the prior judgment is *res judicata* on matters which were raised or could have been raised, on matters litigated or litigatable. [Citations] ... 'This principle also operates to demand of a defendant that all of its defenses to the cause of action urged by the plaintiff be asserted under the penalty of forever losing the right to thereafter so urge them.'" * * *

Plaintiff's common law case is based on breach of the employment contract, conspiracy, and negligent and intentional infliction of emotional distress based on the alleged breach of contract; the civil rights case is based on plaintiff's wrongful treatment in the terms and conditions of employment because of her age, sex or race. This is all superimposed on a final state court determination that she was terminated from her employment for incompetency. Simply put, plaintiff cannot prevail against defendants on the basis that their conduct toward her that caused her termination was wrongful in the face of a final state court determination in the first action that the district had the right to terminate her for incompetency. That plaintiff elected not to litigate at the hearing before the Commission her claims that she was discriminated against in violation of her constitutional and civil rights does not detract from the finding by the Commission, and independently by the superior court, that the district had cause to dismiss her. * * *

[We conclude] that the state court's denial of plaintiff's petition for writ of mandate in the first action does bar these consolidated actions.

The judgment is affirmed. Defendants are awarded their costs on appeal.

Notes and Questions Regarding *Takahashi v. Board of Education* and Primary Rights

(1) Do you agree with the Court of Appeal's conclusion that the prior mandamus action and the present wrongful discharge action involved the same primary right? Could the court have reasonably concluded that at least two primary rights were allegedly invaded: one primary right to permanent employment if competent (pursuant to the Education Code), and a second right to employment without discrimination (pursuant to various state and federal anti-discrimination laws)? Would such a conclusion—two primary rights instead of only one—be inconsistent with the traditional definitions of the primary rights doctrine? If either interpretation is arguably consistent with the primary rights theory, why do you think the court in *Takahashi* choose to find only one primary right instead of two?

(2) The Court of Appeal distinguished *Agarwal v. Johnson* by concluding that, unlike *Agarwal*, plaintiff Takahashi suffered a "single harm" as a result of her alleged wrongful termination. Do you agree that *Agarwal* is distinguishable? Do you agree that the "same harm" was alleged by plaintiff Takahashi in her prior and present state actions? Assume that the plaintiff had won her prior mandamus action and was reinstated as a teacher. She then files a separate action against the school board for emotional distress and punitive damages, alleging that the defendant singled her out for dismissal because of her race and sex. Under the Court of Appeal's reasoning, would the favorable mandamus judgment bar this second employment discrimination action? Should it, under the "same harm" rationale of the primary rights theory?

(3) Did the *Takahashi* court take a broad or a narrow view of what constitutes a single primary right? Did the court in reality take a "transactional," as opposed to "primary rights," view of res judicata? In *Nakash v. Superior Court*, 196 Cal. App. 3d 59, 68, 241 Cal. Rptr. 578 (1987), the court suggested that in determining what con-

stitutes the "same controversy" for purposes of res judicata, "[a]nalysis has shifted from identification of a primary right upon which only one claim is allowed to determination of the existence of a transaction involving a nucleus of facts upon which only one claim is allowed." Is this an accurate characterization of the court's analysis in *Takahashi*? Is it consistent with controlling Supreme Court authority?

(4) *Craig v. County of Los Angeles,* 221 Cal. App. 3d 1294, 271 Cal. Rptr. 82 (1990). The court in *Craig v. County of Los Angeles* relied on *Agarwal* to find two primary rights involved in a similar factual situation. Plaintiff Craig sought employment as a harbor patrol officer with the Los Angeles County Sheriff's Department, but was denied the appointment for improper reasons. Craig filed a writ of mandate to enforce a Civil Service Commission recommendation that he be appointed, which resulted in a court order that Craig be hired by defendant. Craig then filed an action in federal court against defendant, alleging his job denial constituted employment discrimination in violation of federal statutes. The federal court held that these federal claims were barred by res judicata based upon the prior state mandate proceedings.

Craig then filed a third action, in state court, this time seeking damages against defendant for intentional infliction of emotional distress and fraud. Defendant demurred based on res judicata, and the trial court dismissed the complaint. The Court of Appeal reversed, holding that this damage action involves a different primary right than was involved in the prior mandate proceeding and federal action, and was not barred by res judicata. The court, *Craig*, 221 Cal. App. 3d at 1302–03, relying on *Agarwal*, reasoned as follows:

> The mandate proceedings were instituted to enforce appellant's right to employment as a harbor patrol officer. The issue of past salary or damages was not tendered or considered in that action. Only now, when appellant seeks recovery for the harm which resulted in the respondents' wrongful conduct, are these issues raised.

> Further, the type of harm involved in the mandate proceedings are different than the type of wrong in the present case. In the mandate actions, the harm suffered was the denial of the harbor patrol position despite the Commission's order that he be hired. In this action, the harm suffered included the emotional distress which resulted from respondents' wrongful conduct. The Supreme Court explained this difference in *Agarwal v. Johnson, supra,* 25 Cal. 3d 932. * * *

> Since appellant here is seeking to recover damages for harm distinct from his action to compel enforcement of the Commission's order, there are different primary rights involved. Accordingly, the mandate actions cannot bar this action.

Is *Craig* consistent with *Takahashi*? Can these two cases be reconciled? Which case is better-reasoned? Why?

(5) Compare the reasoning of *Takahashi* and *Craig* with that of *People v. Damon,* 51 Cal. App. 4th 958, 59 Cal. Rptr. 2d 504 (1996), in which the court concluded that

the rule against splitting a cause of action was inapplicable because the plaintiff was statutorily prohibited from seeking cumulative remedies in one proceeding. In *Damon*, the first proceeding initiated by the plaintiff was an administrative proceeding to suspend the license of the defendant automotive repair business for violation of the state Automotive Repair Act. The administrative tribunal found the defendant had violated the Act and placed him on probation, but the tribunal had no authority to afford the plaintiff a damage remedy. The plaintiff then commenced a separate action in court seeking monetary civil penalties authorized by the Act. The superior court rejected defendant's res judicata defense, found defendant liable on the merits, and assessed $3000 in civil penalties. The superior court's res judicata determination was affirmed on appeal.

The Court of Appeal in *Damon* ruled that res judicata was inapplicable because the administrative proceeding was one at which the civil penalty remedy could not have been sought because of limitations on the jurisdiction of the administrative tribunal, and therefore it was not possible for plaintiff to seek all the remedies in one proceeding. *People v. Damon*, 51 Cal. App. 4th 958, 969–75. The court first stated the general rule against splitting a cause of action. It also explained at length the reasons for this rule, quoting from *Wulfjen v. Dolton*, 24 Cal. 2d 891, 894–895, 151 P.2d 846 (1944) [*People v. Damon, supra*, 51 Cal. App. 4th at 974]:

> The rule against splitting a cause of action is based upon two reasons: (1) That the defendant should be protected against vexatious litigation; and (2) that it is against public policy to permit litigants to consume the time of the courts by relitigating matters already judicially determined, or by asserting claims which properly should have been settled in some prior action.

The court then concluded that the rule against splitting a cause of action does not apply because: "Here, the two actions were neither vexatious nor time-consuming because the two remedies could not have both been sought in one action." *People v. Damon, supra*, 51 Cal. App. 4th at 975.

Do you agree with the *Damon* court's reasoning? Would this reasoning have been helpful to the plaintiff in *Takahashi*? Is the *Damon* court's reasoning preferable to the two-primary-rights reasoning employed by the court in *Craig v. County of Los Angeles*, summarized *supra*? How so?

[7]   *The Declaratory Judgment Exception to Primary Rights Doctrine*

Under the Declaratory Judgment Act, a party may ask the court for a binding declaration of rights and duties. CCP § 1060. This Act also provides an exception from the bar of res judicata (claim preclusion) for declaratory judgments, stating "no judgment under this chapter shall preclude any party from obtaining additional relief based on the same facts." CCP § 1062. In *Mycogen Co. v. Monsanto Co.*, 28 Cal. 4th 888, 123 Cal. Rptr. 2d 432, 51 P.3d 297 (2002), the Supreme Court construed the Declaratory Judgment Act's exception to claim preclusion as applicable only where the plaintiff's initial action seeks *pure* declaratory relief, and not where the action seeks both declaratory relief and additional coercive relief such as damages, specific performance, or an injunction. *Id.* at 897–902. Because plaintiff Mycogen sought and received both declaratory and coercive relief in the form of specific performance in its prior breach of contract action, res judicata precluded Mycogen from seeking additional relief in the form of damages for the same breach of contract in a subsequent action. *Id.* at 903–904.

The practical effect of the *Mycogen* holding is that a plaintiff seeking to remedy a breach of contract must either seek solely declaratory relief or must seek declaratory relief plus all possible coercive relief, no matter how speculative the damages might be at the time of the breach. Is this a good rule from the standpoint of judicial economy? Even though a plaintiff seeks solely declaratory relief, a court on its own initiative may exercise its equitable jurisdiction and grant specific performance in addition to declaratory relief. Should the Act's res judicata exception apply in such cases where the coercive relief was awarded on the court's own initiative? The Supreme Court declined to answer this question in the abstract. *See Mycogen, supra,* 28 Cal. 4th at 902–903 & n. 9.

What is the preclusive effect of a pure declaratory judgment? According to *Aerojet-General Corp. v. American Excess Ins. Co.,* 97 Cal. App. 4th 387, 117 Cal. Rptr. 2d 427 (2002), the application of the doctrine of res judicata (claim preclusion), while more narrow than for other judgments, nonetheless extends to matters expressly and unambiguously declared on the face of the judgment. A party who wishes to challenge the scope of a declaratory judgment — that its breadth encompasses matters not actually litigated in the action — must do so via appeal. The scope of an unambiguous declaratory judgment cannot be collaterally attacked for a nonjurisdictional error in a subsequent lawsuit. *Aerojet-General,* 97 Cal. App. 4th at 398–402.

[B] Conduct Which Violates Both State and Federal Laws

[1] Introductory Note

The question of whether there are two primary rights, or only one primary right with two theories of recovery, arises in cases where the defendant's conduct potentially violates both federal and state laws. If the defendant's conduct does violate both federal and state laws, does it therefore automatically violate two primary rights — one based on federal law, a second based on state law?

The Supreme Court's decision in *Agarwal v. Johnson,* 25 Cal. 3d 932, 160 Cal. Rptr. 141, 603 P.2d 58 (1979), whose opinion is summarized in *Takahashi,* is sometimes cited for the proposition that conduct which violates both federal and state laws invades two separate primary rights. *See, e.g., Sawyer v. First City Financial Corp., supra.* Is this a correct interpretation of *Agarwal*? What did the *Agarwal* court find significant in determining that the defendant invaded two primary rights?

[2] One or Two Primary Rights?

Several cases have explicitly ruled on the question of whether conduct which violates both federal and state law necessarily invades two separate primary rights.

These courts all agree that where both laws are intended to redress the same harm only one primary right is involved. *E.g.*, *Federal Home Loan Bank of San Francisco v. Countrywide Fin. Corp.*, 214 Cal. App. 4th 1520, 154 Cal. Rtpr. 3d 873 (2013) (holding federal and state control person statutes imposing liability on parent company of a securities dealer involve the same primary right); *Mattson v. City of Costa Mesa*, 106 Cal. App. 3d 441, 447–48, 164 Cal. Rptr. 913 (1980) (ruling plaintiff's state court action seeking damages for unlawful arrest based on state negligence law involves same primary right as plaintiff's claim for damages under federal civil rights statute unfavorably determined by prior federal court jury verdict); *City of Los Angeles v. Superior Court (Levy)*, 85 Cal. App. 3d 143, 153, 149 Cal. Rptr. 320 (1978) (concluding plaintiff's state court action on state law grounds against defendant officials seeking damages for unlawful seizure and loss of property involved same primary right as in earlier federal civil rights action seeking damages for same seizure of property).

In *Johnson v. American Airlines, Inc.*, 157 Cal. App. 3d 427, 203 Cal. Rptr. 638 (1984), for example, plaintiff commenced an action in state court challenging defendant's mandatory maternity leave-without-pay policy under California's Fair Employment Practices Act. The Court of Appeal held that plaintiff's state action was barred by the consent decree in a prior federal class action which also challenged defendant's maternity leave policy, but under Title VII of the Federal Civil Rights Act. Plaintiff was a member of the federal class, but was not a named party. The court concluded that the "primary right" alleged in the state lawsuit is the same as that asserted in the earlier federal class action, *i.e.*, the right to be free from employment discrimination based on sex in the specific area of involuntary maternity leave. *Johnson*, 157 Cal. App. 3d at 432–33. The court flatly rejected plaintiff's argument that the state cause of action was different from, or broader than, the federal Title VII cause of action litigated in the prior federal class action. *Id.*

Relying on *Johnson v. American Airlines, Inc., supra*, the court in *Acuna v. Regents of Univ. of California*, 56 Cal. App. 4th 639, 649–50, 65 Cal. Rptr. 2d 388 (1997), observed that plaintiff's racial discrimination claims, whether brought under the federal Title VII of the Civil Rights Act of 1964 or the state Fair Employment and Housing Act (FEHA), arose from the same primary right: the right to be free of invidious employment discrimination. The court concluded that plaintiff's favorable prior federal court judgment on the Title VII claims barred the state court action for FEHA damages, even though FEHA provided different remedies than its federal counterpart. *See also City of Simi Valley v. Superior Court*, 111 Cal. App. 4th 1077, 1083–84, 4 Cal. Rptr. 3d 468 (2003) (applying *Acuna* and holding federal civil rights claim and state wrongful death cause of action constitute one primary right).

[C]   Res Judicata and Pendent Claims

[1]   Introductory Note

One particularly troublesome application of res judicata involves the preclusive effect of a prior federal court judgment on related state law claims that were or could

have been raised in the federal court action based on pendent (supplemental) jurisdiction. If the federal court extended pendent (supplemental) jurisdiction over state
law claims and resolved these claims on the merits, then obviously the federal court
judgment will preclude relitigation of these state law claims in state court. But what
is the preclusive effect on state law claims that a plaintiff could have asserted in the
federal court action as pendent claims, but chose not to raise? And what preclusive
effect does a federal court judgment have on state law claims that were raised, but
over which the federal court declined to assert pendent jurisdiction?

Koch v. Hankins

Court of Appeal of California, First Appellate District
223 Cal. App. 3d 1599, 273 Cal. Rptr. 442 (1990)

WHITE, PRESIDING JUSTICE.

In this action we consider whether the dismissal of a federal securities fraud action,
on the basis that the investments were not securities, bars a subsequent state court
action for common law fraud and legal malpractice. We hold that the federal court's
summary adjudication did not bar the state claims.

PROCEDURAL HISTORY

On May 20, 1988, plaintiffs filed a complaint in the United States District Court,
Northern District of California. The allegations of the complaint were based on a
nucleus of facts involving the fraudulent acquisition, subdivision and resale of property
in Arizona to plaintiffs. The federal action alleged that the sales of partnership interests
to plaintiffs violated section 10(b) of the Securities and Exchange Act of 1934 and
rule 10b-5 thereunder. Plaintiffs also asked the court to exercise pendent jurisdiction
over various state law claims.

On August 22, 1988, the federal court dismissed plaintiffs' pendent claims without
prejudice to their being refiled in state court. The court retained jurisdiction over
the claim predicated on federal securities law.

Plaintiffs filed the present case in state court against some of the defendants who
were named in the federal action. The complaint alleged causes of action for fraud
and legal malpractice against defendants, all of whom had been named defendants
in the federal action.

Sometime thereafter, the United States District Court granted summary judgment
in favor of defendants on the grounds that plaintiffs had not purchased securities.
Defendants demurred to plaintiffs' first amended complaint in state court on the
grounds that all plaintiffs' causes of action were conclusively barred by the doctrine
of res judicata. The court sustained defendants' demurrer, based on the federal court's
summary judgment. * * * This appeal followed.

DISCUSSION

The basic res judicata principles pertinent to this appeal are set forth in *Merry v.
Coast Community College Dist.* (1979) 97 Cal. App. 3d 214 [158 Cal. Rptr. 603]: "The

two aspects of the res judicata effect of a final judgment on the merits are: (1) The judgment bars the parties (or those in privity with them) from litigating the same cause of action in a subsequent proceeding and (2) the parties (or those in privity with them) are collaterally estopped from litigating in a subsequent proceeding on a different cause of action any issue actually litigated and determined in the former proceeding. [Citations]. The res judicata aspect which bars relitigation of the same cause of action precludes piecemeal litigation by splitting a single cause of action. [Citations]. It also precludes relitigation of the same cause of action on a different legal theory or for different relief. [Citations]. The prior final judgment on the merits settles issues which were not only actually litigated but every issue that might have been raised and litigated in the first action. [Citations.]" (*Id.*, at pp. 221–222).

When a prior judgment is rendered by a federal court, it must be given the same effect by state courts that it would have in federal court. (*Merry, supra*, 97 Cal. App. 3d at p. 222). In addition, principles governing the federal court's power over non-federal claims come into play in determining the preclusive effect of the judgment in a subsequent state court action on the state claims. (*Ibid.*)

"A federal court has the power to exercise pendent jurisdiction over state claims where the federal claim is sufficient to confer subject matter jurisdiction and the state and federal claims 'derive from a common nucleus of operative fact.' [Citation]. If, disregarding their federal or state character, 'plaintiff's claims are such that he would ordinarily be expected to try them all in one judicial proceeding, then, assuming substantiality of the federal issues there is *power* in federal courts to hear the whole.' [Citation]. Exercise of pendent jurisdiction, however, is not a matter of plaintiff's right; it rests in the discretion of the court. [Citation]. [*Mine Workers v. Gibbs*] [(1966) 383 U.S. 715, 726–727 [16 L. Ed. 2d 218, 228, 86 S. Ct. 1130]] cautioned: 'Needless decisions of state law should be avoided both as a matter of comity and to promote justice between the parties, by procuring for them a surer-footed reading of applicable law. Certainly, if the federal claims are dismissed before trial, even though not insubstantial in a jurisdictional sense, the state claims should be dismissed as well. Similarly, if it appears that the state issues substantially predominate, whether in terms of proof, of the scope of the issues raised, or of the comprehensiveness of the remedy sought, the state claims may be dismissed without prejudice and left for resolution to state tribunals.' [Citation]." (*Merry, supra*, 97 Cal. App. 3d at pp. 222–223, italics in original, fn. omitted).

In *Merry*, the plaintiff filed an action in federal court under the Civil Rights Act, the Fifth and Fourteenth Amendments and article I, section 8, clause 8 of the United States Constitution. A summary judgment was granted in favor of the defendants, the court finding no genuine issues of material fact and concluding that the complaint did not state a federal cause of action. During the pendency of the federal action, the plaintiff had filed an action in state court, alleging substantially the same facts alleged in the federal action. The trial court sustained the defendants' demurrer on the grounds that the action was barred under the doctrine of res judicata by reason of the judgment in federal court.

The Court of Appeal reversed. The court reasoned that if the plaintiff had raised his state claims in the federal action, they would clearly have been dismissed without prejudice. Since the federal claim was insubstantial and called for a summary pretrial disposition, a subsequent trial on the state claims was not barred by the judgment. (*Merry, supra,* 97 Cal. App. 3d at pp. 225–231).

Mattson v. City of Costa Mesa (1980) 106 Cal. App. 3d 441 [164 Cal. Rptr. 913], the case on which the trial court principally relied in reaching its decision, involved a different procedural history. In *Mattson,* the plaintiff filed a complaint in federal court, averring violation of his civil rights. The complaint also requested the federal court to take pendent jurisdiction of a nonfederal claim of negligence based on the same facts. After the federal court denied the plaintiff's request to take pendent jurisdiction of the state law claim, the plaintiff filed a complaint in state court, alleging the same facts as he had alleged in the federal action. However, the state complaint was not served on the defendants for two years. Following an adverse jury verdict in the federal action, the plaintiff served the defendants in the state action. The defendants' demurrer on the ground that the state action was barred by res judicata was sustained by the trial court and a judgment of dismissal was entered.

On appeal the judgment was affirmed. The court reasoned that, "[t]he initial choice by the plaintiff to file suit in federal court will not necessarily result in splitting his cause of action, because the federal court may well exercise pendent jurisdiction over the nonfederal claim. However, when the federal court has been requested to and has declined to exercise pendent jurisdiction over the nonfederal claim, the plaintiff is presented with a new choice. He may proceed to trial on the federal claim or, usually, he may elect to dismiss the federal claim without prejudice [citation] and litigate both claims in the state court [citations]. Once it is known that the federal court will not exercise pendent jurisdiction over the state claim, plaintiff's proceeding to trial in the federal court on the federal claim alone will necessarily result in splitting the plaintiff's cause of action, and that fact should be apparent to the plaintiff.

"In such circumstances the rule that would best accommodate the rights of the plaintiff to fully litigate his claim and to invoke the jurisdiction of the federal court and the right of the defendant, the courts and the public to be free of multiple litigation of the same cause of action, is that once the federal court has declined to exercise pendent jurisdiction over the state claim, if the plaintiff then elects to proceed to trial and judgment in the federal court, his entire cause of action is either merged in or barred by the federal court judgment so that he may not thereafter maintain a second suit on the same cause of action in a state court." (*Mattson, supra,* 106 Cal. App. 3d at pp. 454–455).

Mattson differs from the instant action in two significant ways. First, the federal claim was fully adjudicated in trial. The *Mattson* court explicitly distinguished that case from *Merry* where, as here, there was merely a summary judgment in federal court. (*See Mattson, supra,* 106 Cal. App. 3d at pp. 453–454; *see also Craig v. County of Los Angeles* (1990) 221 Cal. App. 3d 1294, 1299–1301 [271 Cal. Rptr. 82] [federal court's summary adjudication plus refusal to exercise pendent jurisdiction does not bar state claims]). Second, in contrast to *Mattson*, where the federal civil rights claim could be brought in state court, plaintiffs were unable to bring a claim under section 10(b) of the Securities and Exchange Act of 1934 in state court, since federal courts have exclusive jurisdiction over that claim. (15 U.S.C. § 78aa).

In resolving the present dispute we look to the Restatement Second of Judgments section 25, comment e for guidance: "A given claim may find support in theories or grounds arising from both state and federal law. When the plaintiff brings an action on the claim in a court, either state or federal, in which there is no jurisdictional obstacle to his advancing both theories or grounds, but he presents only one of them, and judgment is entered with respect to it, he may not maintain a second action in which he tenders the other theory or ground. If however, the court in the first action would clearly not have had jurisdiction to entertain the omitted theory or ground (or, having jurisdiction, would clearly have declined to exercise it as a matter of discretion), then a second action in a competent court presenting the omitted theory or ground should be held not precluded."

Here, plaintiffs could not bring their 10b-5 action in state court, since that court lacked jurisdiction to hear the claim.[5] Thus, they filed their claim in federal court and asked the federal court to exercise pendent jurisdiction over the state law claims. After the federal court declined to exercise pendent jurisdiction, trial of the state claims in a state court was not precluded.

Had dispositive factual questions actually been litigated in the federal securities action, plaintiffs would be collaterally estopped from relitigating those questions in a subsequent state action. (*Mattson, supra*, 106 Cal. App. 3d at p. 445; *Merry, supra*, 97 Cal. App. 3d at p. 221). However, since the federal court merely determined that plaintiffs' partnership interests were not securities under the Securities and Exchange Act, the federal judgment is not res judicata of plaintiffs' state claims.

The judgment is reversed. Costs are awarded to plaintiffs.

Notes and Questions Regarding Pendent Claims

(1) *Mattson v. City of Costa Mesa*, 106 Cal. App. 3d 441, 164 Cal. Rptr. 913 (1980), quoted by the court in *Koch*, sets forth the traditional California rule on the preclusive effect of a prior federal court judgment which involved a pendent state claim. What is the impact of the *Mattson* holding on the right to utilize the federal courts to pursue federal civil rights claims? Is the *Mattson* holding consistent with the position taken by the Second Restatement? See § 25, comment e, and § 26(c), comment c, Restate-

---

5. Consequently, a state judgment would not have a preclusive effect on a federal securities claim. (*See, e.g., Marrese v. American Academy of Ortho. Surgeons* (1985) 470 U.S. 373, 382 [84 L. Ed. 2d 274, 282–283, 105 S. Ct. 1327]; *Eichman v. Fotomat Corp.* (9th Cir. 1985) 759 F.2d 1434, 1437).

ment (Second) of Judgments (1982). If *Mattson* is inconsistent with the Restatement view, is *Mattson* decided improperly? In addition to its concern over claim splitting, the court in *Mattson* noted that a contrary rule would invite manipulation by a plaintiff. What type of manipulation worried the court? *See Mattson* 106 Cal. App. 3d at 455. Is this concern well-founded?

(2) There are some practical problems with the approach suggested by *Mattson*. Assume that a plaintiff alleges both a federal and a state claim in a federal lawsuit, but the federal court declines to exercise pendant jurisdiction over the state law claim. Following the advice of *Mattson*, the plaintiff then voluntarily dismisses the remaining federal claim from federal court and refiles both claims — federal and state — in a California state court. Will the plaintiff potentially have problems with applicable statutes of limitation? *See* 28 U.S.C. § 1367(d). Once the plaintiff commences the action in state court, is there anything to prevent the defendant from removing the entire action to federal court pursuant to 28 U.S.C. § 1441(a)? If the defendant does remove, must the federal court also hear the state law claim? If the federal court again declines to assert pendant jurisdiction over the state claim, is the plaintiff right back where she started with respect to *Mattson*? Is there any way to break this infinite procedural loop? *See* 28 U.S.C. § 1441(c); *see also Walton v. UTV of San Francisco, Inc.*, 776 F. Supp. 1399 (N.D. Cal. 1991).

(3) In several recent cases, the courts have taken different positions on whether to follow *Mattson*, creating some uncertainty as to the current California rule on the preclusive effect of a prior federal court judgment which involved a pendant state claim:

(a) In *Acuna v. Regents of Univ. of California*, 56 Cal. App. 4th 639, 650–52, 65 Cal. Rptr. 2d 388 (1997), the court followed the *Mattson* doctrine and concluded that a prior federal court judgment adjudicating federal claims barred plaintiff's subsequent state court action raising state claims. In the prior federal action, plaintiff sought damages for employment discrimination under various federal anti-discrimination statutes, as well as under the state Fair Employment and Housing Act (FEHA). The federal court declined to exercise pendent jurisdiction over the state FEHA claims and, after a subsequent trial, awarded plaintiff substantial compensatory damages on the federal statutory claims. Plaintiff then commenced an action in state court seeking general and punitive damages under the state FEHA, remedies not available under the federal statutes.

The court in *Acuna* concluded that the *Mattson* principle controlled. Having adjudicated the federal statutory claims in federal court, res judicata barred plaintiff from relitigating the same claims under the state FEHA even though FEHA provided different remedies than its federal counterparts. The court also distinguished *Merry* and *Craig*, as cases in which the state and federal claims did not involve the same primary right and the plaintiff in each case abandoned the federal lawsuit after the federal court declined to hear the state law claims. *Acuna*, 56 Cal. App. 4th at 650.

(b) However, in other recent cases the courts have declined to follow the *Mattson* doctrine, and have instead applied the Restatement (Second) of Judgments, §25, comment e. *See Harris v. Grimes*, 104 Cal. App. 4th 180, 187–89, 127 Cal. Rptr. 2d 791 (2002); *Lucas v. County of Los Angeles*, 47 Cal. App. 4th 277, 286–87, 54 Cal. Rptr. 2d 655 (1996); *see also City of Simi Valley v. Superior Court*, 111 Cal. App. 4th 1077, 1084, 4 Cal. Rptr. 3d 468 (2003) (indicating *Harris* and *Lucas* state the general rule). These cases distinguish between a plaintiff's splitting of a cause of action and a federal court's doing the same thing. *Harris, supra*, 104 Cal. App. 4th at 188; *Lucas*, 47 Cal. App. 4th at 286.

For example, in *Harris v. Grimes, supra*, the plaintiff filed a wrongful death action in federal court against a police officer, alleging negligence under state law and civil rights violations under federal law. Plaintiff's federal civil rights claim went to trial, but the federal court declined to exercise pendant jurisdiction over the negligence claim because it feared that trying both claims together would confuse the jury. After a defense verdict, the federal court entered judgment for the police officer on the civil rights claim but dismissed the negligence claim without prejudice to plaintiff's refiling it in state court. Plaintiff then commenced her negligence action in superior court, which was subsequently dismissed.

The question for the *Harris* court was whether plaintiff's state court action was barred by the prior federal judgment. Relying on *Mattson*, the defendant contended that the plaintiff impermissibly split her cause of action when she proceeded solely on her federal civil rights claim after the federal court declined to exercise pendant jurisdiction over her negligence claim. However, the court viewed this contention as not reflecting the current state of the law "when, as here, a federal court, instead of a party, splits a cause of action." *Harris*, 104 Cal. App. 4th at 188. Instead, the court followed *Lucas v. County of Los Angeles, supra*, which it viewed as consistent with the Second Restatement's expression of widely held legal principles, and concluded: "A federal court's discretionary refusal to exercise pendant jurisdiction over a state claim does not bar further litigation of the state claim in state court." *Harris*, 104 Cal. App. 4th at 188 (*quoting Lucas, supra*, 47 Cal. App. 4th at 286).

The *Harris* court acknowledged that *Mattson* supported the defendant's contention, but declined to follow *Mattson* "because *Lucas* is a more recent and, as reflected by the Restatement, widely endorsed pronouncement of the law." *Id.* at 188–89. "Moreover," the court reasoned, "*Mattson*'s holding was partly based upon its concern that a different rule would invite gamesmanship by plaintiffs," such as a half-hearted request to the federal court to exercise pendent jurisdiction with the hope the court would decline and thereby reserve to the plaintiff a second chance to prevail in state court. *Id.* at 189. The court found no evidence to support such concern here. *Id.*

(c) Which rule — the *Mattson* doctrine or the Second Restatement view — is the better one? Why? Is there any way these two rules can be reconciled based on the timing of a federal court's decision to decline to exercise pendant jurisdiction? Based on evidence of a plaintiff's manipulation? Would such a case-by-case determination be preferable to either *Mattson* or the Restatement rule?

[2] *State Claim Not Raised*

In both *Koch v. Hankins* and *Mattson* the plaintiff raised the state law claim in federal court, but the court exercising its discretion declined to extend pendent jurisdiction. What is the preclusive effect of a federal judgment where a plaintiff never even raises the potentially pendent state claim in federal court, but pursues it in a state court action after an unfavorable federal judgment? This was the problem resolved in *City of Los Angeles v. Superior Court*, 85 Cal. App. 3d 143, 149 Cal. Rptr. 320 (1978). Plaintiff Levy brought a civil rights action in federal court against defendant officials for the value of property unlawfully seized from him, based solely on 42 U.S.C. §1983. A jury trial resulted in a verdict for defendants. Plaintiff then filed an action in state court seeking damages against defendants for the seizure and loss of the same property, based on state conversion law. The trial court sustained a demurrer on ground of res judicata, and plaintiff appealed. The Court of Appeal eventually held that the state complaint attempted to vindicate the same primary right — plaintiff's interest in the seized property — as the prior federal lawsuit. Before reaching this conclusion, the court considered the consequence of plaintiff's failure to raise the state claims in the prior federal proceeding [85 Cal. App. 3d at 150–51]:

> There are at least three separate reasons for ignoring the state-federal distinction. First: if the facts alleged in [Levy's two lawsuits] derived "from a common nucleus of operative fact ..." (*United Mine Workers v. Gibbs* (1966) 383 U.S. 715, 725, 86 S. Ct. 1130, 1138, 16 L. Ed. 2d 218), the conversion counts could have been tried in the United States District Court under that court's "pendent jurisdiction." The "common nucleus" requirement is obviously satisfied here. Second: no one compelled Levy to file his civil rights action in the federal court. He could have sued in the state court..., where his power to join the conversion counts with his civil rights grievances would have been unquestioned. (Code Civ. Proc., §427.10.) Third: it appears to be the law that a litigant cannot avoid the impact of the rule against splitting causes of action by choosing for his first foray a tribunal of limited jurisdiction. (Rest., Judgments, §62, comm. j; cf., *Zirker v. Hughes* (1888) 77 Cal. 235, 19 P. 423.)
>
> In any event, it is clear that the rule against splitting a cause of action and the fatal consequences for violating it are the same — other things being equal — even if one aspect of the cause of action twice pursued is based on a federal, statutory right.

The court in *City of Los Angeles v. Superior Court (Levy)*, *supra*, applied the primary rights doctrine to determine the res judicata effect of a prior federal judgment. Was this the proper doctrine to apply? Would the result have been the same if the court had applied the Second Restatement?

[D]   Primary Rights vs. Restatement Doctrine

[1]   Introductory Note

The general Restatement doctrine of claim preclusion set forth in Section 17, Restatement (Second) of Judgments (1982), *supra*, appears identical to California's primary rights doctrine. Also similar is the Second Restatement's general rule prohibiting "claim splitting," Section 25:

> The rule of claim preclusion applies to extinguish a claim by the plaintiff against the defendant even though the plaintiff is prepared in the second action
>
> (1) To present evidence or grounds or theories of the case not presented in the first action, or
>
> (2) To seek remedies or forms of relief not demanded in the first action.

California courts often quote extensively from sections and comments of the Restatement as part of their analysis. *E.g.*, *Mattson v. City of Costa Mesa*, 106 Cal. App. 3d 441, 164 Cal. Rptr. 913 (1980). However, despite these general similarities, there remains a major difference between the Restatement view and the primary rights view of claim preclusion. Both doctrines prohibit claim splitting and preclude parties from relitigating a claim or cause of action already adjudicated in a prior action between them. But the Second Restatement, § 24, defines a "claim" as follows:

> (1) When a valid and final judgment rendered in an action extinguishes the plaintiff's claim pursuant to the rules of merger or bar ..., the claim extinguished includes all rights of the plaintiff to remedies against the defendant with respect to all or any part of the transaction, or series of connected transactions, out of which the action arose.
>
> (2) What factual grouping constitutes a "transaction," and what groupings constitute a "series," are to be determined pragmatically, giving weight to such considerations as whether the facts are related in time, space, origin, or motivation, whether they form a convenient trial unit, and whether their treatment as a unit conforms to the parties' expectations or business understanding usage.

How is the Restatement's "same transaction" approach different from California's "primary rights" doctrine? If California followed the Restatement's transactional approach, would *Sawyer v. First City Financial Corp.*, *supra*, have been decided differently? *Slater*? *Holmes*? *Takahashi*? The Restatement approach is sometimes said to preclude relitigation of not only those claims actually raised by the plaintiff in a prior lawsuit, but also all claims that *could* have been raised. *See, e.g., Federated Dept. Stores, Inc. v.*

Moitie, 452 U.S. 394, 101 S. Ct. 2424, 69 L. Ed. 2d 103 (1981). Why does Section 24 of the Second Restatement lead to this result?

Which approach—"primary rights" or "same transaction"—better serves the goals of judicial economy and finality of judgments? Which approach is less ambiguous in guiding litigants and courts as to claim preclusion determinations? For thoughtful criticisms of the California primary rights doctrine, see Walter W. Heiser, *California's Unpredictable Res Judicata (Claim Preclusion) Doctrine*, 35 SAN DIEGO L. REV. 559 (1998) (arguing that California's primary rights doctrine is substantively inefficient and unpredictable in application), and Robin James, Note, *Res Judicata: Should California Abandon Primary Rights?*, 23 LOY. L.A. L. REV. 351 (1989). Both authors conclude that the California courts should abandon the primary rights doctrine and adopt the Restatement's transactional approach. Heiser, *Unpredictable Res Judicata*, *supra* at 602–617; James, *Res Judicata*, *supra* at 411–14.

California's primary rights theory is mostly judge-made doctrine which could be changed or eliminated by the Supreme Court. The Supreme Court has not recently indicated any desire to do so. *See Slater, supra*; Heiser, *Unpredictable Res Judicata* , *supra*. What reasons are there for continuing with the primary rights theory of claim preclusion in California? Note that the Restatement's transactional approach has been adopted by a majority of states, as well as by the federal court when applying federal res judicata law. *See* Heiser, *Unpredictable Res Judicata*, *supra* at 569, n. 27. The primary rights doctrine is distinctly a minority view. *Id.*

California's primary rights doctrine is clearly quite different from the Restatement's transactional approach to claim preclusion. Less clear is whether California's res judicata doctrine as a whole results in a significantly different outcome than the Restatement approach when both claim and issue preclusion are applied together. The answer to this question should be postponed until after an examination of the California doctrines of issue preclusion and compulsory cross-complaints, discussed *infra*.

[2]   *Federal-State Recognition of Judgments*

[a]   Prior State Judgment in Federal Courts

One question that had troubled federal courts for several years is which doctrine of res judicata—federal or state—must be applied by a federal court in determining the preclusive effect of a prior state court judgment?

A series of U.S. Supreme Court cases construing the Full Faith and Credit Act, 28 U.S.C. § 1738, have definitively answered this question. *E.g., Marrese v. American Acad. of Orthopedic Surgeons*, 470 U.S. 373, 105 S. Ct. 1327, 84 L. Ed. 2d 274 (1985); *Parsons Steel, Inc. v. First Alabama Bank*, 474 U.S. 518, 106 S. Ct. 768, 88 L. Ed. 2d 877 (1986); *Migra v. Warren City Sch. Dist. Bd. of Ed.*, 465 U.S. 75, 104 S. Ct. 892, 79 L. Ed. 2d 56 (1984). Section 1738 requires a federal court to give a prior state court judgment the same preclusive effect in federal court as another court of that state would give it. In other words, a federal court must apply the preclusion law of the state which rendered the prior judgment. Consequently, the federal courts must apply the primary rights doctrine when determining the preclusive effect of a prior California State Court judgment. *E.g.*, *Takahashi v. Bd. of Trustees of Livingston*, 783 F.2d 848 (9th Cir. 1986), *cert. denied*, 476 U.S. 1182 (1986); *Los Angeles Branch NAACP v. Los Angeles Unified Sch. Dist.*, 750 F.2d 731 (9th Cir. 1984) (en banc).

[b]   Prior Federal Judgment in California Courts

The converse question is what law—state or federal—determines the preclusive effect given a prior federal court judgment in a subsequent California state court proceeding. The United States Supreme Court recently answered this question where subject matter jurisdiction in the prior federal action was based on diversity of citizenship under 28 U.S.C § 1332. *See Semtek Int'l, Inc. v. Lockheed Martin Corp.*, 531 U.S. 497, 121 S. Ct. 1021, 149 L. Ed. 2d 32 (2001). The Supreme Court held that, as a matter of federal common law, the claim-preclusive effect of a judgment by a federal court sitting in diversity should be determined by the claim preclusion law of the state in which the federal diversity court sits (which, coincidentally, was California in *Semtek*). *Semtek, supra*, 531 U.S. at 507–509.

The U.S. Supreme Court in *Semtek* did not address the question of whether state or federal law determines the preclusive effect of a prior federal court judgment in state court where the prior federal action was based on federal question jurisdiction. Recent decisions suggest that the California courts remain divided on the proper resolution of this question. *See City of Simi Valley v. Superior Court*, 111 Cal. App. 4th 1077, 1082–84, 4 Cal. Rptr. 3d 468 (2003) (concluding California law will determine the res judicata effect of a prior federal court § 1983 judgment on the basis of whether the federal and state actions invoke the same primary right); *Balasubramanian v. San Diego Cmty. Coll. Dist.*, 80 Cal. App. 4th 977, 95 Cal. Rptr. 2d 837 (2000) (ruling California law will determine the preclusive effect of a prior federal court judgment based on federal question jurisdiction); *but see Butcher v. Truck Ins. Exch.*, 77 Cal. App. 4th 1442, 92 Cal. Rptr. 2d 521 (2000) (noting California follows the rule that the preclusive effect of a prior judgment of a federal court is determined by federal law where the prior judgment was on the basis of federal question jurisdiction); *Louie v. BFS Retail & Commercial Operations*, LLC, 178 Cal. App. 4th 1544, 1553–54, 101 Cal. Rptr. 3d 441 (2009) (same).

[E]   Compulsory Cross-Complaints and Res Judicata

[1]   *The Compulsory Cross-Complaint Statutes*

Code of Civil Procedure §§ 426.10 and 426.30 set forth the general preclusion rules for failure to plead a compulsory cross-complaint. Section 426.30(a) states:

> Except as otherwise provided by statute, if a party against whom a complaint has been filed and served fails to allege in a cross-complaint any related cause of action which (at the time of serving his answer to the complaint) he has against the plaintiff, such party may not thereafter in any other action assert against the plaintiff the related cause of action not pleaded.

Section 426.10(a) defines "complaint" to mean a complaint or cross-complaint; § 426.10(b) defines "plaintiff" to mean a person who files a complaint or a cross-complaint. Section 426.10(c) then provides:

> "Related cause of action" means a cause of action which arises out of the same transaction, occurrences, or series of transactions or occurrences as the cause of action which the plaintiff alleges in his complaint.

[2] Transactional Standard

Section 426.10(c) utilizes the same type of "transactional" standard in defining a compulsory cross-complaint as is utilized by Rule 13(a), F.R.C.P., in defining a compulsory counterclaim, as well as by § 24 of the Restatement (Second) of Judgments (1982) in defining the scope of the claim extinguished by res judicata.

[a] Impact on Primary Rights Doctrine?

What impact does California's compulsory cross-complaint standard have on the primary rights approach to res judicata? Consider the following hypotheticals:

Carry's car collides with Van's van on California Highway 395. Both parties suffer serious injuries, and both vehicles are destroyed. Carry, relying on established primary rights precedent, decides to first sue Van in Superior Court for her personal injuries, and to later sue him in a separate lawsuit for the property damage to her car.

(1) Carry sues Van for personal injury damages, alleging her injuries were caused by Van's negligence. Defendant Van files an answer denying liability. The jury finds that plaintiff Carry was 100% negligent, and defendant Van was not negligent, and awards no damages to Carry. Van then files an action against Carry seeking damages for both his personal injuries and for the injuries to his van. Van moves for summary judgment on the issue of liability, based on collateral estoppel. Carry also moves for summary judgment, seeking dismissal of Van's complaint based on CCP §§ 426.10 and 426.30. What are the appropriate rulings on these motions?

(2) Assume in Carry's first action against Van for her personal injury damages, that defendant Van not only filed an answer but also a cross-complaint. Van's cross-complaint seeks damages for his personal injuries, alleging that his injuries were caused by Carry's negligence. The jury finds that plaintiff Carry was 30% negligent and defendant Van was 70% negligent, and awards appropriate damages. Carry then files a second lawsuit against Van seeking damages for destruction of her car. Defendant Van cross-complains for the damage to his van. What is the preclusive effect of Carry's first judgment on this second lawsuit?

[b] Should California Abandon Primary Rights?

The typical automobile crash case usually involves two primary rights and therefore two causes of action, one for personal injury and one for property damage. Also, because there usually are injuries to both parties and to their vehicles, the typical case often involves compulsory cross-complaints. Does the net practical effect of this mean that the "transactional" approach is usually applicable and not the "primary rights" approach in determining what claims *must* be litigated in the typical automobile negligence case? If so, isn't it misleading to view California as following a "primary rights" theory which permits separate lawsuits for different causes of action in such cases? Is this practical effect a sufficient reason for the Supreme Court to overrule the primary rights precedent and adopt a transactional approach to res judicata? *See* Robin James, Note, *Res Judicata: Should California Abandon Primary Rights*, 23 Loy. L.A. L. Rev. 351, 403, 413–14 (1989). Has the Legislature in effect already accomplished this for a large category of typical cases likely to involve more than one primary right? *See* Walter W. Heiser, *California's Unpredictable Res Judicata (Claim Preclusion) Doctrine*, 35 San Diego L. Rev. 559, 601 (1998).

[F]   The Requirement of Final Judgment on the Merits

[1]   Final Judgment, California Rule

The doctrine of res judicata applies only to "final" judgments and orders. *American Enter., Inc. v. Van Winkle*, 39 Cal. 2d 210, 218, 246 P.2d 935 (1952); § 13, Restatement (Second) of Judgments (1982). What constitutes a final judgment under the California doctrine? The California rule is that a judgment is not final for purposes of res judicata if it is still open to direct attack by appeal or otherwise. *E.g.*, *Agarwal v. Johnson*, 25 Cal. 3d 932, 954, n.11, 160 Cal. Rptr. 141, 603 P.2d 58 (1979); *National Union Fire Ins. Co. v. Stites Prof'l Law Corp.*, 235 Cal. App. 3d 1718, 1726, 1 Cal. Rptr. 2d 570 (1991). Consequently, an order or judgment is not final under the California rule for res judicata purposes during the pendency of an appeal; and, even though no appeal has yet been taken, until the time for appeal has expired. *See Agarwal v. Johnson, supra*, CCP § 1049.

[2]   Final Judgment, Federal Rule

The federal courts and a majority of state courts follow a rule different than California's as to when a judgment is final for res judicata purposes: A judgment once rendered is final for claim preclusion purposes until reversed on appeal, modified or set aside. *See* Joseph Shemaria, Comment, *Res Judicata and the Bifurcated Negligence Trial*, 16 UCLA L. Rev. 203, 209–10, n.23 (1969); *Calhoun v. Franchise Tax Bd.*, 20 Cal. 3d 881, 887, 574 P.2d 763, 143 Cal. Rptr. 692 (1978). The pendency of an appeal does not suspend the operation of an otherwise final judgment as res judicata. What are the benefits of the federal rule? The California rule? Which rule best promotes the policies of res judicata? What final judgment rule—California or federal—should a California court apply in determining the res judicata effect of a prior federal court judgment pending appeal? *See Calhoun v. Franchise Tax Bd., supra.*

[3] California Interpretations of Final Judgment

[a] Claim vs. Issue Preclusion

The California rule on what constitutes a final judgment is interpreted strictly when considered for purposes of claim preclusion, but less so when applied for purposes of issue preclusion. *Sandoval v. Superior Court*, 140 Cal. App. 3d 932, 936–40, 190 Cal. Rptr. 29 (1983); *see Producers Dairy Delivery Co. v. Sentry Ins. Co.*, 41 Cal. 3d 903, 226 Cal. Rptr. 558, 718 P.2d 920 (1986); *see also* Collateral Estoppel discussion, *infra*. Why this more liberal treatment for issue preclusion than for claim preclusion? *See* § 13, Restatement (Second) of Judgments (1982), comments b and g.

[b] Successive Judgments

Where two successive actions are pending which involve the same controversy, res judicata attaches to the first judgment which becomes final. *See Busick v. Workmen's Comp. Appeals Bd.*, 7 Cal. 3d 967, 977, 104 Cal. Rptr. 42, 500 P.2d 1386 (1972); *First N.B.S. Corp. v. Gabrielsen*, 179 Cal. App. 3d 1189, 1195, 225 Cal. Rptr. 254 (1986) ("When there are two separate actions involving the same issues and same parties in different courts, it is the first final judgment, even though rendered in the second action, that renders the issue res judicata in the other action."). What procedural devices are available to assure that the first court to take jurisdiction of a controversy will also be the first one to render a final judgment? *See, e.g.*, CCP §§ 597, 526(b)(1), 430.10(c).

[c] Inconsistent Judgments

Which judgment should be conclusive for res judicata purposes where a prior final judgment is not asserted as a bar in a second action involving the same controversy and the second action results in an inconsistent judgment? In *Hanley v. Hanley*, 199 Cal. App. 3d 1109, 1117, 245 Cal. Rptr. 441 (1988), the court stated the general rule, relying on § 15 of Restatement (Second) of Judgments (1982), that when inconsistent final judgments are rendered in two actions "it is the later, not the earlier, judgment that is accorded conclusive effect in a third action under the rules of res judicata." The court repeated this general rule in *Stuart v. Lilves*, 210 Cal. App. 3d 1215, 258 Cal. Rptr. 780 (1989), but noted an exception where the first of the inconsistent judgments was rendered in the state where the third action is pending: "[W]hen one of the conflicting decisions was entered by a court of the state in which the current action is pending, that decision takes precedence over the court of a sister state." *Stuart*, 210 Cal. App. 3d at 1220. The court also held that application of this exception is consistent with the Full Faith and Credit Clause. *Id.* at 1220–21. Do you agree? *See Parsons Steel, Inc. v. First Alabama Bank*, 474 U.S. 518, 106 S. Ct. 768, 88 L. Ed. 2d 877 (1986).

[4] Decision on the Merits

In order to have a res judicata (claim preclusion) effect, a judgment must not only be final but must also be rendered "on the merits." *Wilson v. Bittick*, 63 Cal. 2d 30,

35, 45 Cal. Rptr. 31, 403 P.2d 159 (1965); § 19, Restatement (Second) of Judgments (1982). The paradigm "judgment on the merits" is one entered after a full trial of the issues of fact and law, rendered by a judge or jury. § 19, Restatement, *supra*, comment a. This includes a judgment rendered on a directed verdict and a judgment notwithstanding the verdict. *Id.*, comment h.

When a judgment is rendered without a full trial on the facts, the question of whether it is on the merits becomes a little more complicated. When not dealing with the paradigm, a particular judgment must be closely scrutinized to determine whether it is or is not an adjudication on the merits. Which of the following judgments are on the merits:

[a] Default Judgment?

Generally speaking, a judgment by default is "on the merits" and is conclusive as to all issues pleaded in the complaint. *E.g., English v. English*, 9 Cal. 2d 358, 70 P.2d 625 (1937); *see* § 19, Restatement (Second) Judgments (1982), comment c. On what grounds may a defendant challenge the res judicata effect of a prior default judgment by a collateral attack? *See, e.g., Marriage of Nosbisch*, 5 Cal. App. 4th 629, 635, 6 Cal. Rptr. 2d 817 (1992); *Pennoyer v. Neff*, 95 U.S. 714, 24 L. Ed. 565 (1877).

[b] Summary Judgment?

Compare Stuart v. Lilves, 210 Cal. App. 3d 1215, 1218, 258 Cal. Rptr. 780 (1989) ("A judgment entered upon a motion for summary judgment is a determination that there is no factual dispute and one party is entitled to judgment as a matter of law.... Such a judgment is as final and conclusive a determination of the merits as a judgment after trial.") *with Koch v. Rodlin Enter., Inc.*, 223 Cal. App. 3d 1591, 1595–97, 273 Cal. Rptr. 438 (1990) (ruling summary judgment for defendant in prior action not on the merits where former judgment based on statute of limitations, noting that broad assertion that a summary judgment is as final and conclusive a determination of the merits as a judgment after trial "is not universally true.")

[c] General Demurrer?

Is a demurrer granted for failure to state facts sufficient to constitute a cause of action, pursuant to CCP § 430.10(c), always a judgment on the merits? *Compare Goddard v. Security Title Ins. & Guar. Co.*, 14 Cal. 2d 47, 52, 92 P.2d 804 (1939) (noting that even a judgment on general demurrer may not be on the merits for the defects may be technical or formal, and plaintiff may be able to correct the pleadings to state a cause of action) *with See v. Joughin*, 18 Cal. 2d 603, 607, 116 P.2d 777 (1941) (holding general demurrer in prior action barred present action where substantially same facts plead in both cases). How about a special demurrer, granted pursuant to CCP § 430.10(a)-(d) or (f)-(h)? *See Goddard, supra*, 14 Cal. 2d at 51.

[d] Stipulated Judgments and Consent Judgments?

Compare Gates v. Superior Court, 178 Cal. App. 3d 301, 308, 311, 223 Cal. Rptr. 678 (1986) (giving a compromise settlement of a lawsuit and entry of consent judgment a res judicata effect in a subsequent action, barring not only the reopening of the original controversy but also subsequent litigation of all issues which were or could have been raised in the original suit), *with California State Auto. Assn. Inter-Ins. Bureau v. Superior Court*, 50 Cal. 3d 658, n. 2, 268 Cal. Rptr. 284, 788, P.2d 1156 (1990) (noting split of authority on extent of preclusive effect of stipulated judgments, at least as to collateral estoppel); *see also Smith v. State Farm Mut. Auto. Ins. Co.*, 5 Cal. App. 4th 1104, 1114–15, 7 Cal. Rptr. 2d 131 (1992) (ruling stipulated judgments and consent judgments have a res judicata effect on subsequent proceedings between the parties or their privies, but will not bind nonparties whose interests were not represented).

Does a judgment on an offer to compromise, pursuant to CCP § 998, have a res judicata effect? A collateral estoppel effect? What is the meaning of § 998(f), which states: "Any judgment entered pursuant to this section shall be deemed to be a compromise settlement"? *See California State Auto. Assn. Inter-Ins. Bureau, supra*, 50 Cal. 3d 658, 665, n.3 (distinguishing stipulated judgments entered pursuant to CCP § 664.6 from compromise settlements entered in accordance with CCP § 998).

[e] Voluntary Dismissal?

What is the res judicata effect of a voluntary dismissal made pursuant to CCP § 581? A voluntary dismissal *with prejudice* constitutes a determination on the merits, and bars any future action on the same cause of action. *Boeken v. Philip Morris USA, Inc.*, 48 Cal. 4th 788, 793, 108 Cal. Rptr. 3d 806, 230 P.3d 342 (2010); *Torrey Pines Bank v. Superior Court*, 216 Cal. App. 3d 813, 820–21, 265 Cal. Rptr. 217 (1989). This is referred to as a "retraxit" at common law, and is equivalent to a judgment on the merits. *Gates v. Superior Court*, 178 Cal. App. 3d 301, 311, 223 Cal. Rptr. 678 (1988). The determination of whether a voluntary dismissal with prejudice bars subsequent litigation must be analyzed under principles of res judicata and collateral estoppel. *E.g., Federal Home Loan Bank of San Francisco v. Countrywide Fin. Corp.*, 214 Cal. App. 4th 1520, 154 Cal. Rptr. 3d 873 (2013); *Le Parc Cmty. Assn. v. Workers' Comp. Appeals Bd.*, 110 Cal. App. 4th 1161, 1169, 2 Cal. Rptr. 3d 408 (2003); *Morris v. Blank*, 94 Cal. App. 4th 823, 829–30, 114 Cal. Rptr. 2d 672 (2001).

[5] *Claim Preclusive Effect of Non-Judicial Tribunal Decision*

[a] Administrative Agency Decisions

Generally speaking, the final administrative determination of an administrative agency acting in a judicial or quasi-judicial capacity will be res judicata in any subsequent court proceeding. *See, e.g., Hollywood Circle, Inc. v. Dept. of Alcoholic Beverage Control*, 55 Cal. 2d 728, 732–33, 13 Cal. Rptr. 104, 361 P.2d 712 (1961); *Johnson v. Superior Court*, 24 Cal. 4th 61, 69–76, 99 Cal. Rptr. 2d 316, 5 P.3d 874 (2000). An administrative agency acts in a judicial capacity when it resolves disputed issues of fact properly before it and provides the parties with an opportunity to present evidence and fully litigate the issues. *Rymer v. Hagler*, 211 Cal. App. 3d 1171, 1178, 260 Cal. Rptr. 76 (1989). Although the res judicata rules are generally applicable to administrative decisions, their enforcement is more flexible than when applied to judicial decisions. *E.g., George Arakelian Farms, Inc. v. A.L.R.B.*, 49 Cal. 3d 1279, 1290–91, 265 Cal. Rptr. 162, 783 P.2d 749 (1989). The collateral estoppel effect of administrative determinations is discussed *infra*.

When is an administrative adjudication final for purposes of res judicata? A decision of an administrative agency is not considered final for res judicata purposes while subject to direct review in court. *See George Arakelian Farms, supra*, 49 Cal. 3d at 1290; *Long Beach Unified Sch. Dist. v. California*, 225 Cal. App. 3d 155, 169–71, 275 Cal. Rptr. 449 (1990) (ruling an administrative decision is not final if an appeal was taken or if the time for appeal has not lapsed). The agency must also consider the order as its final administrative decision on the claim. *George Arakelian Farms, supra*, 49 Cal. 3d at 1290–91.

Even if an administrative order is final, the Legislature may intend that the decision not have a res judicata effect. *See, e.g., Mahon v. Safeco Title Ins. Co.*, 199 Cal. App. 3d 616, 245 Cal. Rptr. 103 (1988) (ruling Unemployment Insurance Code § 1960 prohibits any res judicata use of judgments of the Unemployment Insurance Appeals Board); *University of Tennessee v. Elliott*, 478 U.S. 788, 106 S. Ct. 3220, 92 L. Ed. 2d 635 (1986) (holding unreviewed decision of state administrative agency may have preclusive effect on 42 U.S.C. § 1983 claim filed in federal court, but not on Title VII employment discrimination claim because such preclusion would be contrary to Congress' intent in enacting Title VII).

[b] Contractual Arbitration

Parties may contractually agree to submit certain disputes to arbitration, and not to the judicial system, for resolution. CCP § 1280 *et seq.* A valid award by an arbitrator is res judicata as to all matters within the scope of the award. *Thibodeau v. Crum*, 4 Cal. App. 4th 749, 755, 6 Cal. Rptr. 2d 27 (1992) (concluding confirmed private arbitration award between homeowner and general contractor is res judicata barring homeowner's identical claim against subcontractor); *Sartor v. Superior Court*, 136 Cal. App. 3d 322, 327–28, 187 Cal. Rptr. 247 (1982) (ruling confirmed private arbitration award in favor of architectural firm is res judicata barring homeowner's identical cause of action against firm's employees); *see also Vandenberg v. Superior Court*, 21 Cal. 4th 815, 824, n. 2, 88 Cal. Rptr. 2d 366, 982 P.2d 229 (1999) (citing *Thibodeau* and *Sarter* with apparent approval). The collateral estoppel effect of an arbitration award is discussed *infra*.

[c] Judicial Arbitration

Code of Civil Procedure § 1141.10 *et seq.* provides a system of nonbinding "judicial arbitration" of certain at-issue civil actions. Court-ordered arbitration is mandatory in certain actions in which the amount in controversy does not exceed a specified amount. CCP § 1141.11. Such arbitration may also be elected by stipulation regardless of amount in controversy, or unilaterally by the plaintiff if the plaintiff agrees that any award shall not exceed the statutory maximum. CCP § 1141.12.

Unlike contractual or "true" arbitration (*e.g.*, commercial arbitration), judicial arbitration is not necessarily binding on the parties. Any party dissatisfied with an award may request a trial *de novo*. CCP § 1141.20. As a disincentive to trial *de novo*, if the requesting party does not obtain a more favorable judgment at trial, that party is liable for significant costs and fees. § 1141.21. If a party does not request trial *de novo* within the statutory time limit, a judicial arbitration award becomes final and is not subject to appeal. § 1141.23. Code of Civil Procedure § 1141.23 provides that such a final award "shall have the same force and effect as a judgment in any civil action or proceeding."

What is the res judicata (claim preclusive) effect of a final judicial arbitration award? "[A] final judicial arbitration award, if clear and unambiguous, is res judicata in any subsequent proceeding on the same cause of action." *Flynn v. Gorton*, 207 Cal. App. 3d 1550, 1555, 255 Cal. Rptr. 768 (1989); *see State Farm Mut. Auto. Ins. Co. v. Superior Court*, 211 Cal. App. 3d 5, 259 Cal. Rptr. 50 (1989). What is the collateral estoppel (issue preclusion) effect? *See* Collateral Estoppel discussion *infra*.

[6] Sister State Judgments

[a] Res Judicata Effect

A judgment rendered by a court of a sister state is entitled to the same res judicata effect in California courts as it would have in the courts of the rendering state. *Underwriters Nat. Assurance Co. v. North Carolina Guar. Assn.*, 455 U.S. 691, 705, 102 S. Ct. 1357, 71 L. Ed. 2d 558 (1982); *Durfee v. Duke*, 375 U.S. 106, 109–11, 84 S. Ct. 242, 11 L. Ed. 2d 186 (1963); *St. Sava Mission Corp. v. Serbian E. Orthodox Diocese*, 223 Cal. App. 3d 1354, 1364, 273 Cal. Rptr. 340 (1990). This treatment is mandated by The Full Faith and Credit Clause of the United States Constitution, Art. IV, § 1; and by the Full Faith and Credit Act, 28 U.S.C. § 1738; as well as by CCP § 1913. Any challenge to according full faith and credit to a sister state judgment is limited to a determination of whether the rendering court had fundamental jurisdiction of the case. *Durfee v. Duke, supra*; *Proctor v. Vishay Intertechnology, Inc.*, 213 Cal. App. 4th 1258, 1269–75, 152 Cal. Rptr. 3d 914 (2013); *World Wide Imports, Inc. v. Bartel*, 145 Cal. App. 3d 1006, 1010, 193 Cal. Rptr. 830 (1983); CCP § 1916.

Under the Full Faith and Credit Clause, full res judicata effect attaches to a sister state's judgment where the party sought to be bound by the judgment participated in the litigation and had a full opportunity to contest the sister state's jurisdiction . *Durfee v. Duke, supra*; *Tyus v. Tyus*, 160 Cal. App. 3d 789, 792–94, 206 Cal. Rptr. 817 (1984). Full Faith and Credit requires California courts to recognize a judgment of a sister state, according it a res judicata effect, even though the judgment is erroneously decided or is in conflict with a strong public policy of California. *Tyus, supra*; *World Wide Imports, supra*; *see Underwriters Nat. Assurance Co., supra*.

[b] Enforcement of Sister State Judgments

Full Faith and Credit requires recognition of sister state judgments for purposes of enforcement, as well as for res judicata purposes. *E.g., Medical Legal Consulting Serv., Inc. v. Covarrubias, supra.* Enforcement of sister state money judgments in California is governed by The Sister State Money-Judgments Act, CCP §§ 1710.10–1710.65, which is discussed in more detail in Chapter 14, Judgments and Enforcement of Judgments, *infra.*

[7] *Pleading, Proof, and Waiver of Res Judicata*

[a] Raising Claim Preclusion

Res judicata must be properly pleaded or proved at trial, or it is waived. *See, e.g., Wolfsen v. Hathaway*, 32 Cal. 2d 632, 638, 198 P.2d 1 (1948); *Road Sprinkler Filters Local Union No. 669 v. G & G Fire Sprinklers*, 102 Cal. App. 4th 765, 772, n.6, 125 Cal. Rptr. 2d 804 (2002); *Parker v. Walker*, 5 Cal. App. 4th 1173, 1191, 6 Cal. Rptr. 2d 908 (1992); *see also* CCP §§ 456, 1908.5. The normal and appropriate method of raising res judicata is by an affirmative defense. *See, e.g., Parker v. Walker, supra.* However, res judicata can be raised by a general demurrer where the complaint pleads the former judgment. *E.g., Weil v. Barthel*, 45 Cal. 2d 835, 837, 291 P.2d 30 (1955). And even though a complaint does not plead the prior judgment, the court may take judicial notice of the prior judgment and grant a demurrer based on res judicata. *E.g., Flores v. Arroyo*, 56 Cal. 2d 492, 496–97, 15 Cal. Rptr. 87, 364 P.2d 263 (1961); *Carroll v. Puritan Leasing Co.*, 77 Cal. App. 3d 481, 486, 143 Cal. Rptr. 772 (1978) ("In analyzing a demurrer based on res judicata the court will take judicial notice of a prior judgment, whether or not pleaded, provided only that (1) the court has been correctly apprised of the judgment, and (2) the plaintiff is given adequate notice and opportunity to be heard as to the effect of the judgment," citing *Flores* and Evid. Code §§ 452(d) and 453).

[b] Raising Issue Preclusion

Unlike res judicata (claim preclusion), no special plea is required to raise collateral estoppel because it merely involves conclusive evidence of a fact in issue as opposed to a complete defense. *Dakins v. Bd. of Pension Commissioners*, 134 Cal. App. 3d 374, 387, 184 Cal. Rptr. 576 (1982); *Solari v. Atlas-Universal Serv., Inc.*, 215 Cal. App. 2d 587, 592–93, 30 Cal. Rptr. 407 (1963). Even if not raised by pleadings or during pretrial proceedings, collateral estoppel can be raised for the first time at trial. Or, in some situations, collateral estoppel can be raised for the first time in a motion to set aside a judgment after trial. *E.g., Ponce v. Tractor Supply Co.*, 29 Cal. App. 3d 500, 507, 105 Cal. Rptr. 628 (1972) (ruling trial court should take judicial notice of earlier judgment for collateral estoppel purposes, if raised before judgment becomes final). Can collateral estoppel be raised for the first time on appeal? Can collateral estoppel ever be waived by failure to raise it during trial? *See Ponce v. Tractor Supply Co., supra.*

[c] Raising Res Judicata in Appellate Court

Although normally the res judicata effect of a prior judgment must be pleaded and proven at trial, when the prior judgment becomes final during the pendency of the appeal in the instant action, the first final judgment may be raised in the appellate court in which the appeal is pending and be relied on as res judicata. *See, e.g., Busick v. Workmen's Comp. Appeals Bd.*, 7 Cal. 3d 967, 977, 104 Cal. Rptr. 42, 500 P.2d 1386 (1972); *First N.B.S. Corp. v. Gabrielsen*, 179 Cal. App. 3d 1189, 1195, 225 Cal. Rptr. 254 (1986). The same rule applies in cases involving the doctrine of collateral estoppel. *Busick, supra.*

[d] Raising Failure to Plead Compulsory Cross-Complaint

The court in *Hulsey v. Koehler*, 218 Cal. App. 3d 1150, 1153, 1158, 267 Cal. Rptr. 523 (1990), held that CCP § 426.30, which bars a claim not asserted as a cross-complaint in a prior action, is analogous to the doctrine of res judicata and must be pleaded as an affirmative defense in the subsequent action. Failure to so plead § 426.30 constitutes a waiver of this defense. The *Hulsey* court held that the trial court did not abuse discretion when it denied as untimely defendant's attempt to amend the answer at trial and raise this defense. *Id.*

[e] Proof of Res Judicata

A former judgment may be proved by introducing a certified copy of the judgment, Evidence Code §§ 1530–1532; and by judicial notice, Evidence Code §§ 452(d), 453. Questions as to the nature of the claims involved in the prior judgment may be proved by introduction of the judgment roll, other parts of the record, and, if necessary, by extrinsic evidence. *See, e.g., McClain v. Rush*, 216 Cal. App. 3d 18, 28, 264 Cal. Rptr. 563 (1989); *Southwell v. Mallery, Stern & Warford*, 194 Cal. App. 3d 140, 144, 239 Cal. Rptr. 371 (1987).

[f] Estopped to Assert Res Judicata

A party's conduct in a prior action may estop that party from asserting res judicata in a subsequent proceeding. *See, e.g., Barragan v. Banco BCH*, 188 Cal. App. 3d 283, 296–97, 232 Cal. Rptr. 758 (1986) (holding party's conduct in successfully opposing leave to file claim as cross-complaint in prior action estopped it from then asserting same claim was barred by res judicata in present action); *Union Bank & Trust Co. v. Hunt*, 1 Cal. 2d 340, 34 P.2d 1001 (1934); *but see Sawyer v. First City Financial Corp.*, 124 Cal. App. 3d 390, 403–04, 410–12 (1981), reproduced *supra.*

[G] Another Action Pending

The doctrines of res judicata, collateral estoppel, and compulsory cross-complaint are devices which determine the preclusive effect of a prior final judgment on subsequent litigation. Are there any devices which preclude litigation of a second lawsuit between the same parties which involves the same subject matter that is still pending in the first lawsuit? There are several in California, although they are quite similar and substantially overlap.

[1]   Plea in Abatement

One such device is a "plea in abatement" which, pursuant to CCP § 430.10(c), may be made by demurrer or answer when "[t]here is another action pending between the same parties on the same cause of action." The general rule appears to be that this plea may be maintained only where a judgment in the first action would be a complete bar (res judicata) to the second action. *Lord v. Garland*, 27 Cal. 2d 840, 848, 168 P.2d 5 (1946); *Plant Insulation Co. v. Fibreboard Corp.*, 224 Cal. App. 3d 781, 788, 274 Cal. Rptr. 147 (1990). A party may not split up a single cause of action and make it the basis of separate suits; the first action may be pleaded in abatement of any subsequent suit on the same claim. *Wulfjen v. Dolton*, 24 Cal. 2d 891, 894, 151 P.2d 846 (1944). The courts narrowly construe the circumstances under which a statutory plea of abatement will apply. Usually the courts require absolute identity of parties, causes of action, and remedies sought in the initial and subsequent actions. *See Plant Insulation Co. v. Fibreboard Corp., supra.*

Where a demurrer is sustained on the ground of another action pending, the proper order is not a dismissal but an abatement of the second proceeding pending termination of the first action, pursuant to CCP § 597. *Lawyers Title Ins. Corp. v. Superior Court*, 151 Cal. App. 3d 455, 459, 199 Cal. Rptr. 1 (1984); *see Leadford v. Leadford*, 6 Cal. App. 4th 571, 574, 8 Cal. Rptr. 2d 9 (1992) (ruling abatement required only where multiple actions are pending in courts of the same state; where actions are pending in courts of different states, the determination of whether to stay is discretionary, not mandatory, and should be raised by motion, not demurrer).

[2]   Exclusive Concurrent Jurisdiction

A more liberal device, similar to a statutory plea of abatement, is a stay based on the rule of "exclusive concurrent jurisdiction." Under this rule, when two courts have concurrent jurisdiction over the subject matter and parties involved in litigation, the first to assume jurisdiction has exclusive and continuing jurisdiction until such time as all necessarily related matters are resolved. *See, e.g., Marriage of Orchard*, 224 Cal. App. 3d 155, 159–60, 273 Cal. Rptr. 499 (1990); *California Union Ins. Co. v. Trinity River Land Co.*, 105 Cal. App. 3d 104, 109, 163 Cal. Rptr. 802 (1980). Priority of jurisdiction resides in the tribunal where process is first served. The rule is based on the need (1) to prevent vexatious litigation and multiplicity of suits, and (2) to avoid conflict of jurisdiction, confusion and delay in the administration of justice.

Unlike the statutory plea of abatement, the rule of exclusive concurrent jurisdiction does not require absolute identity of parties, causes of action or remedies sought in the initial and subsequent actions. *Plant Insulation Co. v. Fibreboard Corp., supra*, 224 Cal. App. 3d at 788. The parties need not be identical so long as the court exercising original jurisdiction has the power to bring before it all necessary parties; and the remedies sought need not be the same in both actions so long as the first court has power to litigate all issues and grant all the relief sought in the second. *Id.* Recent cases applying the rule do not require that the first suit would be res judicata in the second suit. *Id.* Instead, these cases have adopted a more expansive subject matter test which considers whether the first and second actions arise from the "same transaction." *Plant Insulation Co.,* 224 Cal. App. 3d at 789 (and cases cited therein).

The proper relief under exclusive concurrent jurisdiction is a stay of the second action, not a dismissal. *Plant Insulation Co.,* 224 Cal. App. 3d at 791–92. As with a statutory plea of abatement, the second court should enter on interlocutory judgment pursuant to CCP §597 to permit that court to retain jurisdiction over the subsequent action so that the court will be empowered to determine any remaining issues after final determination is made in the prior pending action. *Id.* A writ of prohibition is an appropriate remedy when the second court refuses to recognize the exclusive jurisdiction of the first court. *Lawyers Title Ins. Corp. v. Superior Court, supra,* 151 Cal. App. 3d at 460.

[3] Anti-Suit Injunctions

Civil Code §3423 authorizes a California court to restrain a party subject to its jurisdiction from proceeding in another action involving the same subject matter or the same facts when "necessary to prevent a multiplicity of proceedings." Likewise, the "first filed rule" in California means that when two courts of the same sovereignty have concurrent jurisdiction, the first to assume jurisdiction over a particular subject matter of a particular controversy takes it exclusively, and the second court should not thereafter assert control over that subject matter. *Advanced Bionics Corp. v. Medtronic, Inc.,* 29 Cal. 4th 697, 128 Cal. Rptr. 2d 172, 179, 59 P.3d 231 (2002). *See also Franklin & Franklin v. 7-Eleven Owners for Fair Franchising,* 85 Cal. App. 4th 1168, 1175–78, 102 Cal. Rptr. 2d 770 (2000) (applying the exclusive concurrent jurisdiction rule and upholding trial court's postjudgment enjoining of subsequent trials of identical actions in another superior court, pending appeal of first action); *Rynsburger v. Dairymen's Fertilizer Coop., Inc.,* 266 Cal. App. 2d 269, 72 Cal. Rptr. 102 (1968) (issuing an injunction to prevent a multiplicity of judicial proceedings, pursuant to CCP §526(b0(1)).

§8.03 Collateral Estoppel (Issue Preclusion)

[A] Introductory Note

The collateral estoppel or issue preclusion aspect of res judicata bars a party from relitigating an issue of fact or of law if that issue was actually litigated and determined by a valid and final judgment in a previous proceeding. The prior determination of the issue is conclusive in a subsequent action between the parties or their privies, whether dealing with the same or a different cause of action. *See, e.g., George Arake-*

lian Farms, Inc. v. A. L. R. B., 49 Cal. 3d 1279, 265 Cal. Rptr. 162, 783 P.2d 749 (1989) (citing § 27, Restatement Second of Judgments (1982)). Consequently, issue preclusion may be applicable in a subsequent action even though claim preclusion is unavailable.

[B]   The California Collateral Estoppel Doctrine

Sutphin v. Speik

Supreme Court of California
15 Cal. 2d 195, 99 P.2d 652 (1940)

GIBSON, JUSTICE.

This is an action to recover royalties due under an assignment of a participating royalty interest in an oil and gas lease. As will presently appear, a judgment entered in a prior action between the same parties has determined the issues involved in this case.

In 1926 the California Petroleum Corporation leased property consisting of two small lots in Huntington Beach, California (designated as lots 12 and 14), to C. K. Cole as lessee, reserving a royalty of 17 1/2 per cent. Cole assigned the lease to his wife, who on January 7, 1927, assigned to plaintiff Sutphin a royalty interest described as: "A participating royalty interest of Five per cent (5%) of the gross total production of all oil, gas and other hydrocarbons produced, saved and sold from said well on said premises, or any substitute well therefore …" Subsequently, in June, 1928, the Coles assigned the entire lessee's interest to defendant Speik, excepting therefrom landowner's royalty, and royalties theretofore sold.

At the time the assignment to plaintiff was made, a well, designated as number 3, was being drilled, which later went into production. In October, 1932, well number 3 and its equipment were destroyed by fire, and defendant drilled another well in its place, using part of the original hole and casing. This well was numbered 3A and went into production in August, 1933. In October, 1933, well number 4, located some fifty feet from number 3A, was completed, and both wells are now producing.

Plaintiff Sutphin brought his first action against the defendant Speik on October 27, 1933, to recover royalties then due under his 5 per cent participating royalty interest. Judgment was rendered in plaintiff's favor on April 5, 1934, in the sum of $6,388.82 and interest. Appended as an exhibit to the complaint in the present suit are the findings and judgment of the court in the original action. The material findings are as follows:

> That plaintiff by written assignment for valuable consideration acquired a 5 per cent interest in the total production of oil and gas from lots 12 and 14 under the oil lease between the California Petroleum Corporation and Cole.

> That at the time defendant received his assignment of the lease he had knowledge of the 5 per cent interest previously assigned to plaintiff.

That the last well (number 4) "produces from the same zone and pool as said redrilled well number 3."

That "The plaintiff is now and ever since the 7th day of January, 1927, has been the owner of said five per cent of the total production of oil, gas and other hydrocarbons produced, saved or sold from said premises, and of the moneys derived from the sale of said five per cent of said total production."

In its conclusion of law the court declared, among other things, that "plaintiff is entitled to judgment declaring him the owner of five per cent of the total production of oil, gas and other hydrocarbons produced, saved or sold from lots 12 and 14 ... whether or not same is produced from one or more wells upon said premises".

The court adjudged plaintiff to be the owner of 5 per cent of the total production of oil and gas from said lots 12 and 14, "whether same is produced from one or more wells upon said premises, and as such owner plaintiff is entitled to receive all moneys derived from the sale of said five per cent of the total production ... from said lots 12 and 14".

Defendant Speik appealed. The judgment was affirmed by the District Court of Appeal, Second Appellate District, Division One, and a hearing was denied by this court. The judgment became final and was satisfied as to the royalties then adjudged to be due. In affirming the judgment, the opinion of the District Court of Appeal, after summarizing the facts, stated that it was the defendant Speik's contention that the evidence was insufficient to support the finding of indebtedness, the finding that plaintiff was the owner of a 5 per cent interest in the total production from the property, and the finding that well number 4 produced from the same zone and pool as well number 3. The court rejected this contention, and upheld the judgment.

The present action was filed October 29, 1936, to recover royalties accruing after the entry of the judgment, and was grounded on the rights adjudicated by that judgment. Defendant pleaded as his chief defense that well number 4 does not produce from any sand or oil deposit underlying the property but was drilled as a "whipstock well" diagonally into oil producing sand under the Pacific Ocean, more than 2,000 feet from the property, and that well number 4 therefore produces from sands and oil deposits which do not extend beneath these lots.

At the trial defendant made an offer to prove that a royalty was being paid to the State of California from the production of wells number 3A and 4 by virtue of an agreement permitting production from state land under the ocean. The court excluded the offered evidence.

Counsel for plaintiff offered in evidence, among other things, Speik's opening brief and petition for hearing in the first case, and these were admitted for the limited purpose of showing similarity of contentions raised in the two actions.

It was stipulated by defendant that it was the contention of defendant in the former trial that plaintiff Sutphin had no interest in either well number 3A or 4.

The trial court in the present action made findings which reviewed the prior proceeding, and then found as follows:

That plaintiff has not received his 5 per cent royalty on oil and gas produced from wells 3A and 4 since entry of the former judgment.

That no wells other than 3A and 4 have been drilled and that "the location of said wells both above and below the surface of the ground is the same at this time as at the time the trial was had in said action and both are producing from the same sand as at the time of said former trial".

That wells 3A and 4 produce from the same zone and pool.

That it is immaterial whether they are "whipstock wells" because of the doctrine of res judicata and that all of the defenses here urged existed at the time of the former trial.

Judgment accordingly went for the plaintiff in the sum of $31,932.54 together with interest. Defendant Speik brought this appeal. * * *

This brings us to a consideration of the issues on this appeal. The lower court decided the case on the theory that the prior judgment was res judicata. If this conclusion is correct, the judgment must be affirmed on that ground alone and it is neither necessary nor proper to reexamine on their merits the various defenses urged by appellant. The prior judgment, as will be seen from an examination of its provisions and of the foregoing excerpts from the findings and conclusions, determined that plaintiff was the owner of 5 per cent of the total production of the two wells. This determination in the prior judgment necessarily establishes plaintiff's right in this action to recover royalties based on subsequent production of wells 3A and 4, unless defendant's attack on the applicability of the doctrine of res judicata is successful.

The contentions of defendant in this connection are as follows: (a) The causes of action in the two suits are different, and the judgment in the first is not res judicata in the second. (b) The issue of ownership of oil or rights therein produced from state lands by a "whipstock well" was not raised or decided in the first action, and is not res judicata. * * *

All of these contentions merely represent different methods of expressing the single defense that the assignment to plaintiff and the prior judgment in his favor were only intended to give to plaintiff a right in oil produced from a particular well or any "substitute therefor" drawing oil from strata directly underlying the leased premises; and that neither was intended, nor could be construed to establish in plaintiff any right to oil drawn through that well or any other well where the oil itself came from strata not underlying these lots.

The argument of defendant is, in substance, an attack upon the findings and judgment in the prior action, the undoubted purpose of which is to avoid the broad determination of the issues therein made. The assignment upon which plaintiff relies covered the original well number 3 (subsequently destroyed by fire) or any "substitute therefor." It was entirely within the issues of the first action for the court to determine whether wells number 3A or 4 or any other wells then on the premises were substitutes for the original and destroyed well number 3. It is clear from an examination of the findings and judgment therein that plaintiff was adjudged in the prior action to be entitled to his percentage of the production of any wells then drilled on the particular premises regardless of where the wells were bottomed, or the source of the oil delivered by them. The suggestion made by defendant that the "judgment alone should be considered and the findings disregarded if outside the scope of the judgment" can have no force in view of the settled rule that the findings constitute the decision of the court. * * *

As already indicated, defendant's contention that the doctrine of res judicata is not applicable here is grounded upon the proposition that the causes of action involved in the prior and present suit are different, and that the defenses that title had been acquired from the state, and that the oil was being taken from lands outside the boundaries of the lots, were not raised in the prior action. A complete answer to this contention may be found in an examination of the scope of the doctrine of res judicata, which has been fully considered by this court in recent cases.

First, where the causes of action and the parties are the same, a prior judgment is a complete bar in the second action. This is fundamental and is everywhere conceded.

Second, where the causes of action are different but the parties are the same, the doctrine applies so as to render conclusive matters which were decided by the first judgment. As this court said in *Todhunter v. Smith,* 219 Cal. 690, 695 [28 Pac. (2d) 916]: "A prior judgment operates as a bar against a second action upon the same cause, but in a later action upon a different claim or cause of action, it operates as an estoppel or conclusive adjudication as to such issues in the second action as were actually litigated and determined in the first action." In the instant case, for example, the severable installments of royalties due gave rise to separate causes of action; but a determination of a particular issue in the prior action is res judicata in the second action.

Next is the question, under what circumstances is a matter to be deemed decided by the prior judgment? Obviously, if it is actually raised by proper pleadings and treated as an issue in the cause, it is conclusively determined by the first judgment. But the rule goes further. If the matter was within the scope of the action, related to the subject-matter and relevant to the issues, so that it *could* have been raised, the judgment is conclusive on it despite the fact that it was not in fact expressly pleaded or otherwise urged. The reason for this is manifest. A party cannot by negligence or design withhold issues and litigate them in consecutive actions. Hence the rule is that the prior judgment is res judicata on matters which were raised or could have been raised, on matters litigated or litigable. In *Price v. Sixth District,* 201 Cal. 502, 511 [258 Pac. 387], this court said: "But an issue may not be thus split into pieces. If it has been determined in a former action, it is binding notwithstanding the parties litigant may have omitted to urge for or against it matters which, if urged, would have produced an opposite result ... This principle also operates to demand of a defendant that all of its defenses to the cause of action urged by the plaintiff be asserted under the penalty of forever losing the right to thereafter so urge them."

Defendant relies on *English v. English*, 9 Cal. (2d) 358 [70 Pac. (2d) 625]. In that action, plaintiff sued to rescind a separation agreement in which he had promised to pay his wife $200 per month until a total of $10,000 had been paid. He alleged that the agreement was obtained by fraud and duress. The wife contended that the validity of the agreement had been established by a default judgment in her favor in a suit to recover installments due under the contract, and that the issue was therefore res judicata. The court held that although a default judgment is conclusive as to facts necessary to uphold that particular judgment, it is not conclusive in a subsequent suit on a different cause of action against any defenses which defendant has, because the issues raised by these defenses were not tried and cannot be deemed adjudicated. This case states an exception to the normal rule of res judicata, limited to default judgments, and has no bearing on the situation before us.

It remains only to see whether the defense now raised by defendant, that the wells bottomed on state land, could have been raised in the first action. If so, the defense of res judicata applies. The answer seems entirely clear. At the time of the first action, wells number 3A and 4 were drilled and producing. Defendant knew or should have known of the source of the oil therefrom. If the asserted defense has merit, it was as good and available then as now. This being so, it can make no difference whether it was actually pleaded, or whether evidence was introduced thereon or not. We are not impressed by defendant's assertion that he could not have raised the defense in the first action because it would amount to an admission of trespassing on state land. The defense might have been weak, embarrassing, or dangerous to the defendant; and he may have chosen to refrain from presenting it for reasons important to himself; but this can have no present effect upon the conclusiveness of the determination in the plaintiff's favor. When we say that the issue could have been raised, we mean that it was relevant to or within the scope of the action, and not that it was at the time a defense upon which the defendant might prevail. * * *

It follows therefore from a consideration of the former judgment, in the light of these rules, that plaintiff is entitled to his present judgment without any further consideration of the merits. Accordingly, we have made no attempt to discuss the conflicting evidence on such matters as the purpose of the assignment, the source of the oil, or other points previously determined.

The judgment is affirmed.

A petition for a rehearing was denied on March 29, 1940, and the following opinion then rendered thereon:

THE COURT. — Defendant in his petition for rehearing challenges certain portions of our opinion, which he interprets as meaning that in a second suit on a different cause of action, *any issue* which could have been raised in the first suit is res judicata in the second, even though not actually determined in the first. This is not our holding, and the opinion must be read in connection with the facts of this case, and with and understanding of the issue which was, in fact, decided in the former action.

The judgment in that action awarded plaintiff 5 percent of the total production from the lots in question whether produced from one or more wells. That judgment, correctly or incorrectly, did not limit the right of plaintiff to production from wells which bottomed under the land. After that judgment became final, plaintiff's right to a portion of the production from those wells was conclusive as between the parties, even in the present suit on a different cause of action, because the basic issue thus decided in the first case is identical with that in the present case. Defendant, in his petition, has again urged that the former judgment cannot be *res judicata* as to the *new issue* of the title to oil from wells bottomed on state land, which title was acquired after the conclusion of the first action.

The difficulty with this argument is that the asserted "new issue" is not such in fact. Defendant has simply offered another legal theory by which the *same issue* might be differently decided. If he may have a new trial of the issue of right to the production of the oil from these wells because of the new argument that the source of the oil must be considered, then it would seem that in subsequent actions he can raise a "new issue" as to the title of A, B, C, or other possible claimants in addition to the state. In short, defendant's contention is that though the prior judgment determined that plaintiff had a right to a specified percentage of the production of oil from any wells on certain land, plaintiff may be compelled to relitigate that right whenever defendant can discover a new theory upon which to attack it. This proposition is without support in principle or authority.

Frommhagen v. Board of Supervisors

Court of Appeal of California, Sixth Appellate District
197 Cal. App. 3d 1292, 243 Cal. Rptr. 390 (1987)

STONE, JUSTICE.

Appellant Laurence H. Frommhagen appeals from a judgment of dismissal entered after the trial court sustained without leave to amend the demurrer filed by respondents Santa Cruz County Board of Supervisors and the County of Santa Cruz. We conclude that the trial court properly sustained the demurrer with respect to the bulk of appellant's action, but erred in sustaining the demurrer as to two of the allegations in the complaint. Consequently, we reverse the judgment and remand to the trial court for further proceedings on those two allegations only.

I. FACTS

In June of 1984, appellant filed an in pro. per. suit against respondents to invalidate service charges levied by respondents in a number of "county service areas" for the

1984–1985 fiscal year. The county service area law gives counties an alternative method of providing services to unincorporated areas by allowing the counties to create special county service areas for the provision of services such as road maintenance, sewers, and other county services. For the types of services at issue in this case, a county may determine the charge to be levied on each parcel in the service area by apportioning the total cost of the service to each parcel therein in proportion to the estimated benefits from such service to be received by each parcel. [Government Code] Section 25210.77a, subdivisions (a), (b), and (c), also provide that *each year* a county must calculate the charges to be assessed to a parcel for the service, and, after a public hearing, the board of supervisors must confirm the charges. * * *

Appellant's 1984 complaint alleged that the 1984–1985 charges were invalid on a number of grounds: First, the complaint attacked 33 service areas established to provide road maintenance on the ground that the areas improperly provided maintenance for private roads. Second, appellant complained that respondents violated section 25210.77a and Santa Cruz County Ordinance No. 3406 in establishing the county service area rates for 1984–1985. * * * Third, appellant alleged that, for various reasons, some (particularly County Service Areas Nos. 9, 9A, and 9D) if not all county service areas are special taxing districts which require voter approval under article 13A, section 4 of the California Constitution. Fourth, the imposition of a service charge in County Service Area No. 9C for operation of county refuse disposal sites violated section 25210.77f, which (according to appellant) allows for special assessments for refuse disposal only after direct billings for that service are unpaid for one year. Finally, the complaint alleged that the respondents failed to use the appropriate method to determine the benefits conferred on a particular parcel in order to calculate the fee for service owed by that parcel.

Following a two-day trial, the superior court issued its statement of decision rejecting each of appellant's contentions. * * * Appellant's appeal in this first action was dismissed on September 5, 1985, and the judgment is now final.

Undaunted by this setback, on November 20, 1985, appellant filed a subsequent complaint attacking the county service area charges established for the 1985–1986 fiscal year pursuant to section 25210.77a. As appellant himself has admitted, the allegations in this second complaint are, with three exceptions, identical in substance to those alleged in the previous complaint attacking the 1984–1985 charges. In response to this second complaint, respondents filed a demurrer alleging that the suit was barred by res judicata and the statute of limitations, and that appellant had no standing to bring the suit since he had not alleged he owned property within any of the county service areas attacked in the suit. In addition, the demurrer alleged that an admittedly new allegation stated in paragraph X of the complaint failed to state a cause of action. Appellant filed opposition to the demurrer.

On February 19, 1986, the superior court sustained the demurrer without leave to amend on the ground that the bulk of the complaint was barred by res judicata, and paragraph X failed to state a cause of action. Appellant was not afforded an opportunity to speak at the hearing.

Thereafter, a judgment of dismissal was entered in this second action and, once again, appellant appealed.

II. DISCUSSION

A. *Res Judicata/Collateral Estoppel*

Appellant contends that his second complaint is not barred by res judicata or collateral estoppel. Although we agree with appellant with respect to certain limited issues, we nevertheless find that the bulk of his complaint is barred by collateral estoppel.

Appellant points to three differences between the 1984 and 1985 complaints which he claims defeat the defense of collateral estoppel. First, in his 1985 complaint he claims that an amendment to section 25210.4a (eff. Jan. 1, 1985) now restricts road maintenance by the county to streets and highways owned by or dedicated to the county and maintained by the general public. Second, he points out that the 1984 complaint attacked the charges assessed for the 1984–1985 fiscal year, while the second complaint attacks the 1985–1986 charges. Third, he points out that the second complaint contains an allegation (in para. X) of misappropriation of surplus road resurfacing funds which was not made in the first complaint. We discuss each argument separately below.

1. *The Legal Standards*

If all of the facts necessary to show that an action is barred by res judicata are within the complaint or subject to judicial notice, a trial court may properly sustain a general demurrer. (*Carroll v. Puritan Leasing Co.* (1978) 77 Cal. App. 3d 481, 485 [143 Cal. Rptr. 772].) In ruling on a demurrer based on res judicata, a court may take judicial notice of the official acts or records of any court in this state. (*Id.* at p. 481; *Safeco Insurance Co. v. Tholen* (1981) 117 Cal. App. 3d 685, 696 [173 Cal. Rptr. 23]; Evid. Code, § 452).

The doctrine of res judicata has a double aspect. First, it precludes parties or their privies from relitigating *the same cause of action* that has been finally determined by a court of competent jurisdiction. Second, although a second suit between the same parties on a different cause of action is not precluded by a prior judgment, the first judgment operates as an estoppel or conclusive adjudication as to such issues in the second action as were actually litigated and determined in the first action. This second aspect of res judicata is commonly referred to as collateral estoppel.

2. *Appellant's First Action Is Not A Complete Bar To His Second Action*

Respondents contend that appellant's second action is barred completely by the first aspect of res judicata; that is, respondents claim appellant is attempting to litigate the same cause of action in this second suit as he did in the first. We disagree.

California has consistently applied the "primary rights" theory in defining a cause of action. Under this theory, the invasion of one "primary right" gives rise to a single cause of action, even though several remedies may be available to protect the primary right. (*Slater v. Blackwood* (1975) 15 Cal. 3d 791, 795 [126 Cal. Rptr. 225, 543 P.2d 593]; ...) Although this theory is well developed in such areas as personal injury and injuries to property, our research has failed to uncover a California case applying the theory to suits brought to attack taxes or charges levied in different years.

Nevertheless, federal authority addressing an analogous issue convinces us that appellant's suit attacking the 1985–1986 charges is not based on the same cause of action as the suit attacking the 1984–1985 charges. In *Commissioner v. Sunnen, supra,* 333 U.S. 591, the United States Supreme Court considered whether litigation of certain issues in an income tax suit involving one tax year would act as a complete bar (under the first aspect of res judicata) to a suit brought on similar or identical issues but in a later tax year. The court held: "Income taxes are levied on an annual basis. Each year is the origin of a new liability and of a separate cause of action. Thus if a claim of liability or non-liability relating to a particular tax year is litigated, a judgment on the merits is res judicata as to any subsequent proceeding involving the same claim and the same tax year. But if the later proceeding is concerned with a similar or unlike claim relating to a different tax year, the prior judgment acts as collateral estoppel only as to those matters in the second proceeding which were actually presented and determined in the first suit." (*Id.* at p. 598 [92 L. Ed. at p. 906] ...).

Similarly, in this case the service area charges are calculated each year under the procedure outlined in section 25210.77a. Thus, each year is the origin of a new charge fixing procedure, new charge liability, and, we believe, a new cause of action. In the parlance of the "primary right theory," those paying charges have a primary right to have the charges properly calculated and imposed each year. Consequently, we believe appellant's second complaint attacking the 1985–1986 charges is not based on the same cause of action as that underlying his first complaint. It follows that appellant's first action is not a complete bar to his second action.

3. Collateral Estoppel

Although appellant's suit is not barred in its entirety by the first aspect of res judicata, we believe that much of it is barred by collateral estoppel.

"The collateral estoppel aspect of res judicata will apply as to all issues which were involved in the prior case even though some *factual* matters or *legal* arguments which could have been presented in the prior case in support of such issues were not presented. Thus, where two lawsuits are brought and they arise out of the same alleged factual situation, and although the causes of action or forms of relief may be different, the prior determination of an issue in the first lawsuit becomes conclusive in the subsequent lawsuit between the same parties with respect to that issue and also with respect to every matter which might have been urged to sustain or defeat its determination. (*Pacific Mut. Life Ins. Co. v. McConnell* (1955) 44 Cal. 2d 715, 724–725 [285 P.2d 636].) If the legal principle were otherwise, litigation would end finally only when a party could no longer find counsel whose knowledge and imagination could conceive of different theories of relief based upon the same factual background." (*Safeco Insurance Co. v. Tholen, supra,* 117 Cal. App. 3d at p. 697.)

Appellant concedes that with three exceptions, the issues and allegations in his second complaint are the same as those in his first. We have examined the complaints and believe this concession is correct. All of the issues and allegations alleged in the first complaint were actually and necessarily decided by the trial court in the first action. Consequently, if appellant is to avoid collateral estoppel, he must do so by relying on the differences he has identified between the complaints. We discuss these differences below. * * *

First, in his second complaint appellant contends that an amendment to section 25210.4a (which did not become effective until after his first suit was final) now clearly "restricts road maintainence [sic] by the County in County Service Areas to streets and highways owned by the County or dedicated to the County and maintained by the general public." He claims this amendment is relevant to his contention that 33 county service areas improperly provide maintenance for private roads. Although an intervening change in law might arguably defeat a claim of collateral estoppel, appellant has failed to delineate what language in the amendment he is relying on, or to explain how it changes previous law. * * * We have examined the cited portion of the Public Contracts Code and find nothing there to support appellant's position. Appellant has lent scant assistance to this endeavor. Consequently, we conclude he has failed to carry his burden on appeal to show that the amendment to section 25210.4a has defeated respondents' claim of res judicata.

Secondly, appellant contends that collateral estoppel does not bar the present action because his second complaint attacks charges for a year different from those attacked in his first complaint. With two narrow exceptions noted below, we disagree.

The great bulk of the allegations in appellant's two complaints are not affected by the fact that they attack charges levied in different years. For example, appellant's contention that respondents may not use service area funds to maintain "private" roads is not affected by the change in year. Similarly, we cannot see how the change in year affects appellant's contention (stated in essentially identical language in both complaints) that respondents employed an improper method to calculate or apportion benefit — at least where there is no allegation that the method changed from one year to the next. Further, appellant has not suggested how the change in year affected his earlier allegations that certain county service area charges are "special taxes" within the meaning of article XIII A, section 4 of the California Constitution, or that the service area assessments for refuse disposal are improper.

After carefully examining the two complaints and the trial court's tentative decision and statement of decision in the first action, we conclude that only two allegations in the second complaint are not barred by collateral estoppel. These allegations are: (1) "The staff of defendant Board of Supervisors did not file with the Clerk of the Board a list of each and every parcel in each of the CSA's [sic] showing the service charge based upon an apportionment of cost to benefit ... as required by Section 25210.77a ... and Santa Cruz County Ordinance No. 3406"; and (2) "Defendant Board did not hold a public hearing at which parcel owners and members of the public might protest the service charges based upon an apportionment of cost to benefit (market value Increase), as required by Section 25210.77a ... and Ordinance No. 3406...."

We find that these allegations are not barred by collateral estoppel because respondents have a duty to file a list of parcel charges and hold a hearing on those charges each year. Consequently, the trial court's finding that respondents satisfied these requirements with respect to the 1984–1985 charges does not mean that respondents met these procedural requirements for the 1985–1986 charges. We therefore reverse the order of dismissal with respect to these allegations only.[4] * * *

B. *Paragraph X In Appellant's Second Complaint Does Not State A Cause of Action*

Appellant made the following allegation in paragraph X of his second complaint: "In CSA No. 9D (resurfacing of county roads) the cost of the resurfacing fell significantly short of the cost estimated for that work at the time of the creation of CSA No. 9D, and defendant County has diverted that surplus into other projects not specified in the ordinance establishing CSA No. 9D. Furthermore, the Federal Emergency Management Agency (FEMA) and the federal government [have] rebated to defendant County a portion of that cost. [¶] Under the law of assessment in California defendant County may not divert those excess monies into other projects and must return those monies to the owners of parcels assessed in CSA No. 9D."

Respondents concede that this allegation is not barred by collateral estoppel since it was not raised in the first action. However, they argued successfully below that the allegation does not state a cause of action. We agree with this conclusion. * * *

The judgment of dismissal and order sustaining demurrer without leave to amend are reversed as to paragraphs V.3 and V.4 of the complaint only. In all other respects, the judgment and orders appealed from are affirmed. Appellant's motion to strike statements from the respondents' brief is denied. The parties shall each bear their own costs on appeal. (Cal. Rules of Court, rule 26(a)).

[1] *Collateral Estoppel Doctrine, Generally*

The California courts usually follow the Restatement (Second) of Judgments when deciding questions of issue preclusion. Court opinions often quote extensively from relevant sections of the Restatement, as well as from the explanations contained in the various section "comments." *E.g., Lucido v. Superior Court,* 51 Cal. 3d 335, 272 Cal. Rptr. 767, 795 P.2d 1223 (1990); *Perez v. City of San Bruno,* 27 Cal. 3d 875, 168 Cal. Rptr. 114, 616 P.2d 1287 (1980); *In re Nathaniel P.,* 211 Cal. App. 3d 660, 259 Cal. Rptr. 555 (1989) (quoting § 28(4)); *Barker v. Hull,* 191 Cal. App. 3d 221, 226, 236 Cal. Rptr. 285 (1987) (quoting § 27, comment d); *Sandoval v. Superior Court,* 140 Cal. App. 3d 932, 190 Cal. Rptr. 29 (1983) (relying on § 29 of Second Restatement, and comments thereunder).

Section 27 of the Restatement (Second) of Judgments states the general rule of issue preclusion as follows:

---

4. We note that the trial court found these same allegations completely groundless in appellant's suit attacking the 1984–1985 charges. Consequently, these allegations might be most expediently disposed of by a motion for summary judgment, rather than a full trial.

When an issue of fact or law is actually litigated and determined by a valid and final judgment, and the determination is essential to the judgment, the determination is conclusive in a subsequent action between the parties, whether on the same or a different claim.

Section 28 provides exceptions to this general rule, most of which have been adopted by the California courts:

Although an issue is actually litigated and determined by a valid and final judgment, and the determination is essential to the judgment, relitigation of the issue in a subsequent action between the parties is not precluded in the following circumstances:

(1) The party against whom preclusion is sought could not, as a matter of law, have obtained review of the judgment in the initial action; or

(2) The issue is one of law and (a) the two actions involve claims that are substantially unrelated, or (b) a new determination is warranted in order to take account of an intervening change in the applicable legal context or otherwise to avoid inequitable administration of the laws; or

(3) A new determination of the issue is warranted by differences in the quality or extensiveness of the procedures followed in the two courts or by factors relating to the allocation of jurisdiction between them; or

(4) The party against whom preclusion is sought had a significantly heavier burden of persuasion with respect to the issue in the initial action than in the subsequent action; the burden has shifted to his adversary; or the adversary has a significantly heavier burden than he had in the first action; or

(5) There is a clear and convincing need for a new determination of the issue (a) because of the potential adverse impact of the determination on the public interest or the interests of persons not themselves parties in the initial action, (b) because it was not sufficiently foreseeable at the time of the initial action that the issue would arise in the context of a subsequent action, or (c) because the party sought to be precluded, as a result of the conduct of his adversary or other special circumstances, did not have an adequate opportunity or incentive to obtain a full and fair adjudication in the initial action.

[a] The Basic California Prerequisites

Although California courts do generally rely on the Restatement definitions in resolving collateral estoppel questions, the most common general statement of the California doctrine is as follows:

The doctrine of collateral estoppel precludes relitigation of an issue previously adjudicated if: (1) the issue necessarily decided in the previous suit is identical to the issue sought to be relitigated; (2) there was a final judgment on the merits of the previous suit; and (3) the party against whom the plea is asserted was a party, or in privity with a party, to the previous suit. *Producers Dairy*

Delivery Co. v. Sentry Ins. Co. 41 Cal. 3d 903, 910, 226 Cal. Rptr. 558, 718 P.2d 920 (1986); *Bernhard v. Bank of America*, 19 Cal. 2d 807, 122 P.2d 892 (1942).

[b]   Public Policy Considerations

The California Supreme Court restated these basic prerequisites, and distinguished between the "threshold requirements" and the public policy considerations of collateral estoppel, in *Lucido v. Superior Court*, 51 Cal. 3d 335, 341–43, 272 Cal. Rptr. 767, 795 P.2d 1223 (1990):

> Collateral estoppel precludes relitigation of issues argued and decided in prior proceedings. * * * Traditionally, we have applied the doctrine only if several threshold requirements are fulfilled. First, the issue sought to be precluded from relitigation must be identical to that decided in a former proceeding. Second, this issue must have been actually litigated in the former proceeding. Third, it must have been necessarily decided in the former proceeding. Fourth, the decision in the former proceeding must be final and on the merits. Finally, the party against whom preclusion is sought must be the same as, or in privity with, the party to the former proceeding. * * *
>
> Even assuming all the threshold requirements are satisfied, however, our analysis is not at an end. We have repeatedly looked to the public policies underlying the doctrine before concluding that collateral estoppel should be applied in a particular setting. * * * Accordingly, the public policies underlying collateral estoppel — preservation of the integrity of the judicial system, promotion of judicial economy, and protection of litigants from harassment by vexatious litigation — strongly influence whether its application in a particular circumstance would be fair to the parties and constitutes sound judicial policy.

In *Lucido*, the Supreme Court refused to apply collateral estoppel even though the threshold requirements were satisfied, because to do so would be inconsistent with these public policies. The *Lucido* court therefore held that an issue determination favorable to the defendant in a probation revocation hearing did not collaterally estop the prosecution from relitigating the identical issue in a subsequent criminal prosecution. *Id.* at 347–61.

[c]   The "Public Interest" Exception

California courts have long recognized a "public interest" exception to the doctrine of collateral estoppel. Even if the formal prerequisites to collateral estoppel are present, an important public interest may permit relitigation of issues determined in a prior judgment. Cases applying this exception usually find the requisite overriding public interest in statutes designed to protect the public. *E.g., Chern v. Bank of America*, 15 Cal. 3d 866, 872, 127 Cal. Rptr. 110, 544 P.2d 1310 (1978) (applying exception to permit relitigation of certain banking practices issues based on strong public interest to regulate banking evidenced by applicable federal and state statutes). These cases often involve a government entity as the party in whose favor the exception is applied. *E.g., Arcadia Unified Sch. Dist. v. State Dept. of Ed.,* 2 Cal. 4th 251, 257–59, 5 Cal. Rptr. 2d 545, 825 P.2d 438 (1992) (ruling State Department of Education not collaterally estopped from relitigating constitutionality of statute authorizing school districts to charge fees for pupil transportation; *City of Sacramento v. State of California,* 50 Cal. 3d 51, 64–65, 266 Cal. Rptr. 139, 785 P.2d 522 (1990) (concluding State not collaterally estopped from relitigating issue of whether the State is required to reimburse local governments for certain unemployment insurance expenses under California Constitution, even though issue determined adversely to State in prior lawsuit).

Did the Supreme Court in *Lucido* rely on this public interest exception to collateral estoppel? Do public policies of the doctrine of collateral estoppel, as indentified in *Lucido,* address the same concerns as the "public interest" exception? How do these concerns differ? *See Dailey v. City of San Diego,* 223 Cal. App. 4th 237, 258–60, 167 Cal. Rptr. 3d 123 (2013) (applying the public interest exception and the public policies underlying collateral estoppel). Is it more accurate to view the Supreme Court's policy analysis in *Lucido* as an application of the "public interest" exception rather than of the public policies underlying collateral estoppel?

[2] What Is an "Identical Issue" for Purposes of Collateral Estoppel?

Collateral estoppel, as traditionally defined by the courts in California, bars relitigation of an issue decided at a previous proceeding if the issue is "identical" to the issue sought to be relitigated. One difficulty in applying this requirement is that issues may not be totally identical in the literal sense of same time, place, and occurrence; nor in the sense of precisely the same legal context. How would you define "identical issue" in light of the opinion in *Frommhagen v. Board of Supervisors,* reproduced *supra?*

Comment c to Section 27, Restatement (Second) of Judgments (1982), offers some guidance on this problem of "identical issue":

> c. *Dimensions of an issue.* One of the most difficult problems in the application of the rule of this Section is to delineate the issue on which litigation is, or is not, foreclosed by the prior judgment. The problem involves a balancing of important interests: on the one hand, a desire not to deprive a litigant of an adequate day in court; on the other hand, a desire to prevent repetitious litigation of what is essentially the same dispute. When there is a lack of total identity between the particular matter presented in the second action and that presented in the first, there are several factors that should be considered in deciding whether for purposes of the rule of this Section the "issue" in the two proceedings is the same, for example: Is there a substantial overlap between the evidence or argument to be advanced in the second proceeding and that advanced in the first? Does the new evidence or argument involve application of the same rule of law as that involved in the prior proceeding? Could pretrial preparation and discovery relating to the matter presented in the first action reasonably be expected to have embraced the matter

sought to be presented in the second? How closely related are the claims involved in the two proceedings?

Sometimes, there is a lack of total identity between the matters involved in the two proceedings because the events in suit took place at different times. In some such instances, the overlap is so substantial that preclusion is plainly appropriate. * * * Preclusion ordinarily is proper if the question is one of the legal effect of a document identical in all relevant respects to another document whose effect was adjudicated in a prior action. And, in the absence of a showing of changed circumstances, a determination that, for example, a person was disabled, or a nonresident of the state, in one year will be conclusive with respect to the next as well. In other instances the burden of showing changed or different circumstances should be placed on the party against whom the prior judgment is asserted. * * * In still other instances, the bearing of the first determination is so marginal because of the separation in time and other factors negating any similarity that the first judgment may properly be given no effect.

An issue on which relitigation is foreclosed may be one of evidentiary fact, of "ultimate fact" (i.e., the application of law to fact), or of law. * * * Thus, for example, if the party against whom preclusion is sought did in fact litigate an issue of ultimate fact and suffered an adverse determination, new evidentiary facts may not be brought forward to obtain a different determination of that ultimate fact. * * * And similarly if the issue was one of law, new arguments may not be presented to obtain a different determination of that issue. * * *

[a]   Identical Issues: "Issue" vs. "Legal Theory"

The word "issue" has no universally agreed upon core meaning. In a typical automobile crash case there may be "issues" of injury, causation, wrongful conduct and the like. But each of these "issues" may be comprised of several other "issues" (or "sub-issues"). The issue of wrongful conduct, for example, may include the following "sub-issues": Was the collision the result of negligent conduct by the defendant? Or, did the defendant intentionally cause the collision (following an argument which, undoubtedly, involved certain hand gestures)? And the issue of negligent conduct may, in turn, include numerous possible "sub-issues," such as: Was the defendant driving too fast for road conditions? Tail-gating? Was the defendant paying attention? Was the defendant intoxicated? Was the defendant's automobile poorly maintained? Etc. And each of these "sub-issues" may include several other "issues" (or "sub-sub-issues"). For example, the question of whether or not the defendant driver was paying attention may include the following "sub-sub-issue": Was the driver looking at a billboard? Was the driver disciplining his children? Was the driver reading a map? A magazine? Talking on a cellphone while using a laptop computer and shaving?

One of the difficulties confronting a court in applying collateral estoppel doctrine is to determine at what level of generality a prior finding on one question forecloses relitigation of another question. Assume that plaintiff driver A sues defendant driver B for property damage to A's car resulting from an automobile crash, alleging negligence by defendant B in not paying attention because B was reading a magazine while driving. After trial, the court rules for defendant B, finding he was not reading a magazine while driving. A then sues B in a second action, this time for personal injuries suffered in the crash, alleging in three alternative counts: (1) negligence by B for failure to pay attention because B was disciplining his children; (2) B was intoxicated; and, (3) battery by B for intentionally bumping into A's car after an argument. Do these two cases involve identical issues? This depends on how broadly or narrowly the concept of "issue" is defined. How broadly should "issue" be defined? What are the consequences of a broad definition vs. a narrow one?

[b] Different Historical Transaction

In *Chern v. Bank of America*, 15 Cal. 3d 866, 127 Cal. Rptr. 110, 544 P.2d 1310 (1976), the Supreme Court suggested that collateral estoppel does not apply in a subsequent action involving parallel facts but concerning a "different historical transaction." *Chern*, 15 Cal. 3d at 871. The plaintiff sued defendant Bank of America over the allegedly misleading manner by which the Bank computed loan interest rates. The defendant bank asserted that plaintiff was collaterally estopped to pursue this issue because she lost a summary judgment in a prior suit raising the same interest rate computation issue brought against a different bank. Although the court found collateral estoppel inapplicable on other grounds, it also stated that collateral estoppel does not apply in a subsequent action involving parallel facts but concerning a "different historical transaction." *Id.* at 871. Is this statement in *Chern* consistent with the Restatement view expressed in comment c to Section 27, *supra*?

More recently in *County of Los Angeles v. County of Los Angeles Assessment Appeals Board*, 13 Cal. App. 4th 102, 16 Cal. Rptr. 2d 479 (1993), the court considered the "different historical transaction" question in an action brought by the County challenging the propriety of an administrative determination by its Assessment Appeals Board as to the extent of the taxable possessory interests of several car rental companies at LAX with respect to tax years 1983–1987. The Board had rejected the County's contention that the companies' possessory interests extended to the use of the airport generally, and instead determined that the companies' possessory interests extended only to their exclusive counter spaces. The County's method of assessment had greatly multiplied the appraised value of their interests, with corresponding increases in taxes. By disapproving the County's approach, the Appeals Board reduced the appraisals for tax years 1983–1987 and awarded the car rental companies tax refunds. The County then commenced a mandamus action in superior court seeking reversal of the Board's administrative decision. The car rental companies, as the real parties in interest, invoked collateral estoppel based on a 1986 judgment in which the court had found that the same companies' possessory interest for assessment purposes at LAX included only their counter spaces and that the County's method of valuation was invalid. The County argued that collateral estoppel did not apply because the prior litigation involved different tax years (1982 vs. 1983–87) and different (although materially identical) concession agreements at LAX. The superior court denied the mandamus petition, and the County appealed.

The Court of Appeal concluded that the County was foreclosed by collateral estoppel from relitigating the assessment method issue with respect to the possessory interests of these car rental companies at LAX. The court found the issue was identical to the one resolved in the 1986 judgment. The fact that the present case involved later tax years than the prior litigation did not, according to the court, "separate the issues or render them nonidentical." *Id.* at 109. Do you agree? Can this case be distinguished from the facts in *Chern*? If not, which decision is better reasoned? Why?

[c]   Change in Factual Circumstance

Under what circumstances will a change in the facts between the first and second actions alter the legal relations between the same parties, such that collateral estoppel is inapplicable because the issues are no longer identical? In *Evans v. Celotex Corp.*, 194 Cal. App. 3d 741, 238 Cal. Rptr. 259 (1987), the plaintiffs, the widow and children of the deceased Evans, appealed from a dismissal of their wrongful death complaint against defendant Celotex. Plaintiffs' complaint alleged that Evan's death was caused by exposure to asbestos products made by defendant. The trial court dismissed the wrongful death action, finding that plaintiffs were collaterally estopped from proceeding because of an adverse judgment in a prior personal injury action.

In the prior personal injury action, Evans sued Celotex, claiming that he developed asbestosis as a result of occupational exposure to asbestos products manufactured by defendant. A jury returned a general verdict for the defendant. Evans died two days later. The plaintiffs subsequently filed their wrongful death action, which was dismissed. Plaintiffs then appealed.

The Court of Appeal found that the identical issues of causation and liability were raised in the wrongful death action as were raised in the previous personal injury action, and that the general verdict implied the existence of every fact essential to support the verdict. Next, the court found that the plaintiffs were in privity with the deceased Evans, even though the prior personal injury action was a different cause of action from the wrongful death action. The court, *Evans, supra,* 194 Cal. App. 3d at 747–48, then considered plaintiff's argument that the issues in the two actions were not identical because of a change in factual circumstances:

> Plaintiffs argue that collateral estoppel cannot be applied if new facts have occurred since the judgment on the prior hearing. They claim that a lung biopsy could not be performed while the deceased was alive and that a pathological diagnosis of lung tissue was performed only after his death. Plaintiffs contend that based on the evidence available at the trial of the personal injury action, the jury concluded that the deceased's progressive deterioration was not from asbestosis but from another disease; that as a result of the better diagnostic evaluation following the autopsy, asbestosis could be proved to

be the proximate cause of his death. Plaintiffs have not indicated what this biopsy showed and how it differed, if at all, from the evidence adduced at the personal injury trial.

In *Melendres v. City of Los Angeles* (1974) 40 Cal. App. 3d 718 [115 Cal. Rptr. 409], members of the police and fire departments sued the city council to make increased salary adjustments that reflected prevailing wages in private industry as provided by the city charter. In a prior action involving the same parties 10 years earlier, the appellate court affirmed the council's finding that the charter provision did not apply because there was no corresponding job classification in private industry. At the time of the second suit, the city had adopted a plan (the Jacobs plan) of a consultant firm which created a method to enable the city to ascertain wages for sworn personnel corresponding to the prevailing wages paid to civilian employees with private industry job counterparts. (*Id.*, at p.724) Citing the prior litigation, the city argued that plaintiffs were collaterally estopped from requesting the city to pay prevailing wages as performed by persons in private industry. The trial court and reviewing court disagreed, holding that collateral estoppel does not bar a later suit if new facts of changed circumstances have occurred since the prior decision. (*Id.*, at p.730) The presence of the Jacobs plan, which did not exist at the time of the prior litigation, was deemed a sufficient change of circumstance to bar the application of collateral estoppel.

Res judicata or collateral estoppel "was never intended to operate so as to prevent a re-examination of the same question between the same parties where, in the interval between the first and second actions, the facts have materially changed or new facts have occurred which may have altered the legal rights or relations of the litigants." (*Hurd v. Albert* (1931) 214 Cal. 15, 26 [3 P.2d 545, 76 A.L.R. 1348].) Unlike the situation in *Melendres*, here, no new facts or issues came to light since the prior litigation. The legal relationship of the deceased vis-a-vis Celotex had not changed and there were no new events or conditions which altered the respective rights of the parties or caused a different legal doctrine to be applied. (Compare *Hurd v. Albert*, *supra*, at pp. 26–27 [facts changed since the prior litigation to make the enforcement of a restrictive covenant on property unenforceable].... Here, the additional test performed during the autopsy simply goes to the weight of the evidence against Celotex; i.e., this evidence did not establish a previously undiscovered theory of liability nor did it denote a change in the parties' legal rights. An exception to collateral estoppel cannot be grounded on the alleged discovery of more persuasive evidence. Otherwise, there would be no end to litigation. Accordingly, we hold that the results from the lung biopsy do not operate to prevent the application of collateral estoppel.

The judgment of dismissal is affirmed.

Do you agree with the Court of Appeal that no new facts came to light since the personal injury judgment which altered the legal relationship between the parties?

Do you agree that the situation in *Melendres* is different from that in *Evans v. Celotex*? Is *Evans* consistent with comment c to § 27 of the Restatement? Is *Melendres*? Was *Evans* correctly decided? *See Smith v. ExxonMobil Oil Corp.*, 153 Cal. App. 4th 1407, 1419, n. 7, 64 Cal. Rptr. 3d 69 (2007) (noting the *Evans* court's conclusion can only be justified if the plaintiffs were previously able to obtain and present evidence that death was caused by asbestos, and the biopsy did not provide substantially stronger evidence). For a recent decision discussing applying various factors relevant to determining whether collateral estoppels is inapplicable due to changed circumstances), see *Union Pac. R.R. Co. v. Sante Fe Pac. Pipelines, Inc.*, 231 Cal. App. 4th 134, 178–186, 180 Cal. Rptr. 3d 173 (2014).

[d]   Scrutiny of Facts Necessary

Sometimes the determination of whether issues are identical depends on the court's willingness to engage in a detailed examination of the facts. Consider the following cases:

(1) *Oro Fino Gold Mining Corp. v. County of El Dorado*, 225 Cal. App. 3d 872, 274 Cal. Rptr. 720 (1990). The petitioner mining company appealed the county's denial of a special use permit for a mineral exploration project. The County had determined that before Oro's permit application could be reconsidered, an environmental impact report (EIR) would have to be drafted. Oro contended that the county is collaterally estopped from litigating the issue of whether an EIR is required because that issue was judicially determined adversely to the County in a prior case. The prior case involved judicial approval of a special use permit granted without the requirement of an EIR for a much larger mineral exploration project on land adjacent to the proposed Oro project.

Noting that Oro's argument had a certain appeal on the surface, the court decided to "dig a bit deeper." The court then analyzed differences in the two drilling sites in relation to residential impact, the drilling methods, and the limitations imposed on the prior project's permit. The court found significant distinctions in the two projects, and therefore that collateral estoppel did not apply because the EIR issue was not "identical" in the two lawsuits.

(2) *Amador v. Unemployment Ins. Appeals Bd.*, 35 Cal. 3d 671, 200 Cal. Rptr. 298, 677 P.2d 224 (1984). The Supreme Court refused to collaterally estop the petitioner from litigating the issue of "misconduct" in her appeal from denial of unemployment insurance compensation benefits before the Unemployment Insurance Appeals Board, despite an earlier finding by the County Civil Service Commission that she could be discharged for "insubordination." The Supreme Court concluded that the two issues were not identical because the issue of "insubordination" under the county civil service rules only requires a finding that an employee has willfully failed to perform a reasonable act, whereas the issue of "misconduct" under the Unemployment Insurance Code requires a finding of bad faith insubordination "without good cause."

(3) *Bianchi v. City of San Diego*, 214 Cal. App. 3d 563, 262 Cal. Rptr. 566 (1989). The court declined to give a collateral estoppel effect to a Workers' Compensation Appeals Board finding of a policeman's "permanent disability" in a subsequent City Retirement Board hearing determining whether the policeman was permanently incapacitated from performing his job. The court held that the issues in the two proceedings were not identical. The workers' compensation proceeding decided whether the employee suffered any job-related injury; if that injury resulted in some permanent (although partial) residual loss, the board awards a permanent disability rating. In contrast, the Retirement Board focuses on a different issue: Whether the employee has suffered an injury of such magnitude that he is incapacitated from substantially performing his job responsibilities. Does this mean that a finding of permanent disability by a Workers Compensation Board can never have a collateral estoppel effect on a subsequent Retirement Board proceeding?

[e] Different Legal Context

Collateral estoppel may not apply where the same issue arises in different legal contexts. For example, in *Ruffalo v. Patterson*, 234 Cal. App. 3d 341, 285 Cal. Rptr. 647 (1991), the plaintiff sued her former attorney for malpractice, alleging that he negligently instructed her to characterize certain property as community property in her prior dissolution of marriage action. Defendant attorney argued that plaintiff was collaterally estopped by the dissolution court's determination from raising issues with respect to the community or separate character of plaintiff's property in this malpractice action. The Court of Appeal disagreed, noting that plaintiff does not seek a redetermination as to the character of her property but seeks to recover for alleged negligence in instructing her to characterize the property as community property. Therefore, the court concluded that the doctrine of collateral estoppel does not apply.

Do you agree with the court's reasoning in *Ruffalo*? Doesn't the court necessarily have to determine that the property was plaintiff's separate property in order to find that defendant committed malpractice? Doesn't this constitute a relitigation of the identical property issue determined in the prior dissolution proceeding? The court in an earlier case thought so, and on facts almost identical to those in *Ruffalo* concluded that the malpractice action was barred by collateral estoppel. *See Wall v. Donovan*, 113 Cal. App. 3d 122, 169 Cal. Rptr. 644 (1980). What policy considerations support the holding in *Ruffalo*, and make the conclusion in *Wall v. Donovan* very unattractive?

Does the resolution of an issue by a sister state court applying that state's law preclude relitigation of that issue by a California court applying California law, under the identical facts, in a subsequent cause of action between the same parties? In *American Continental Ins. Co. v. American Cas. Co.*, 86 Cal. App. 4th 929, 103 Cal. Rptr. 2d 632 (2001), the court held that an Arizona court's resolution of an issue of equitable contribution between two insurance companies under Arizona law did not preclude relitigation of that issue by a California court under California law in a subsequent action between the same parties because the "same issue" was not actually litigated and determined in the prior litigation. Would the holding be the same if the Arizona court had applied California law to this issue? If the Arizona law was the same as the California law on this issue?

[f] Different Standards of Proof

Collateral estoppel will not bar relitigation of an issue where the adversary in the second action has a significantly heavier burden of proof that he had in the first action. *See, e.g., In re Nathanel P.*, 211 Cal. App. 3d 660, 259 Cal. Rptr. 555 (1989) (holding a finding in a dependency proceeding that a father physically and sexually abused his children under a preponderance of the evidence standard did not preclude relitigation of the same issue by the father in a subsequent action to terminate his parental rights, where the standard is clear and convincing evidence); *see also People v. Sims*, 32 Cal. 3d 468, 485, 186 Cal. Rptr. 77, 651 P.2d 321 (1982). Does prior acquittal in a criminal action bar relitigation of the same issues by the state against the defendant in a subsequent civil action? *See In re Couglin*, 16 Cal. 3d 52, 58–59, 127 Cal. Rptr. 337, 545 P.2d 249 (1976); § 28(4), Restatement (Second) of Judgments (1982). Does a finding for the state in a civil action preclude relitigation of the same issues by the defendant in a related subsequent criminal action? Does a finding for the defendant and against the plaintiff state in a civil action bar the state from prosecuting the same issue in a subsequent criminal proceeding? *See People v. Sims, supra*.

What is the collateral estoppel effect of a criminal conviction on litigation of the same issues against the defendant in a subsequent civil action? *See Teitelbaum Furs, Inc. v. Dominion Ins. Co.*, 58 Cal. 2d 601, 25 Cal. Rptr. 559, 375 P.2d 439 (1962). Where the prior criminal conviction was the result of a guilty plea? *See id.; Pease v. Pease*, 201 Cal. App. 3d 29, 246 Cal. Rptr. 762 (1988) (collecting cases).

[3] *Issues Actually Litigated and Determined*

One of the most troublesome requirements of the California collateral estoppel doctrine is that issues be "actually litigated and determined" in the prior action. This prerequisite has several problematic aspects.

[a]"Issues" vs. "Theories"

California courts often describe the collateral estoppel effect of a prior judgment as precluding relitigation of "matters which were raised or could have been raised, or matters litigated or litigable," quoting *Sutphin v. Speik, supra*, 15 Cal. 2d at 202. *See, e.g., Tensor Group v. City of Glendale*, 14 Cal. App. 4th 154, 160, 17 Cal. Rptr. 2d 639 (1993); *Interinsurance Exch. of the Auto. Club v. Superior Court*, 209 Cal. App. 3d 177, 182, 257 Cal. Rptr. 37 (1989). Does this mean that collateral estoppel precludes litigation of not only issues that were actually litigated and determined in a prior case on a different cause of action, but also issues that *could* have been litigated but were not? Is this what the Supreme Court meant in *Sutphin v. Speik*? Defendant Speik thought so, and petitioned the court for a rehearing. Does the opinion accompanying the rehearing denial clarify the Supreme Court's position?

(1) *Restatement View.* Section 27 of the Restatement (Second) of Judgments, comment c, notes: "A judgment is not conclusive in a subsequent action as to issues which might have been but were not litigated and determined in the prior action." Is *Sutphin* inconsistent with the Restatement? Is there any way to reconcile *Sutphin* and its progeny with the view expressed by the Restatement in comment c? Is this another example of inadequate terminology employed by the courts in discussing res judicata/collateral estoppel questions? Or is the difference between *Sutphin* and the Restatement view much deeper than merely sloppy use of nomenclature? Would it help if the California courts clearly distinguished the concepts of "issues" versus "theories," and then consistently used these terms in their analyses? Or do these concepts and terms simply create a new problem of classification?

(2) The lower courts continue to struggle with the distinction between "issues" and "theories" made by the California Supreme Court in the Supplemental Opinion in *Sutphin v. Speik*, 15 Cal. 2d at 204, reproduced *supra*. *See, e.g, Wimsatt v. Beverly Hills Weight Loss Clinics Int'l, Inc.*, 32 Cal. App. 4th 1511, 38 Cal. Rptr. 2d 612 (1995) (observing that the distinction between "issues" and "theories" is not always easy); *Marriage of Mason*, 46 Cal. App. 4th 1025, 54 Cal. Rptr. 2d 263 (1996).

In *Marriage of Mason, supra*, Marjorie and Raymond Mason's marriage was dissolved by a judgment entered in 1993. Prior to this judgment, Majorie had operated a residential care facility at home and closed the business due to ill health. The dissolution judgment allocated various amounts of marital property to the parties, as well as spousal support. Subsequently, Raymond commenced an attack on the prior judgment, claiming that the goodwill component of the business was an "omitted asset" and worth $157,000. The superior court rejected Raymond's claim on the ground that the business was a known asset that was divided by the prior judgment, and commented that "if [husband] ... didn't raise the goodwill issue that is his tough luck." *Marriage of Mason, supra*, 46 Cal. App. 4th at 1028. The Court of Appeal affirmed. The court observed that a "party cannot by negligence or design withhold issues and litigate them in consecutive actions." 46 Cal. App. 4th at 1028. The court continued by quoting language from *Sutphin v. Speik*: "Hence the rule is that the prior judgment is res judicata on matters which were raised or could have been raised, on matters litigated or litigable." *Marriage of Mason, supra,* 46 Cal. App. 4th at 1028.

The holding in *Marriage of Mason* seems to conflict with the holding in *Henn v. Henn*, 26 Cal. 3d 323, 161 Cal. Rptr. 502, 605 P.2d 10 (1980), in which the California Supreme Court considered the collateral estoppel effect of a prior dissolution of marriage judgment on a subsequent action to establish community property interest in a pension which was not specifically adjudicated in the final decree of dissolution. A superior court had entered a final judgment in 1971 that awarded Henry and Helen Henn specific items of marital property as their separate property. Neither the pleadings nor the judgment made any mention of Henry's retirement pension. Although both parties were fully aware of its existence at the time of the dissolution proceedings, the parties did not seek, and the court did not determine, the community property rights with respect to the pension. In 1973, Helen filed a second action to establish her community property rights in her ex-husband's pension. Defendant Henry raised the defense of res judicata. The Supreme Court ruled that the claim preclusion aspect did not completely bar Helen's action, and then considered the effect of the issue preclusion aspect.

Defendant Henry Henn argued that the issue of Helen's entitlement to the assets of the community had been "actually litigated and determined" by the prior judgment. Helen argued that the prior judgment had not adjudicated the specific issue of her community property interest in the pension. The California Supreme Court determined that the "doctrine of collateral estoppel cannot be stretched to compel" the result urged by Henry. The Court explained that "the rule prohibiting the raising of any factual or legal contentions which were not actually asserted but which were within the scope of the prior action" does not mean "that issues not litigated and determined are binding in a subsequent proceeding on a new cause of action." *Henn, supra*, 26 Cal. 3d at 331. "Rather," the court continued, "it means that once an issue is litigated and determined, it is binding in a subsequent action notwithstanding that a party may have omitted to raise matters for or against it which if asserted may have produced a different outcome." *Id*. The Court therefore concluded that the doctrine of collateral estoppel was not applicable because "Henry failed to demonstrate that Helen is relying upon some specific factual or legal contention which could have been relevant to the property distributed in the 1971 decree if it had been raised." *Id*. In other words, the specific issue of Helen's interest in the pension was not "actually litigated and determined" by the prior adjudication of the parties' community property rights generally.

The Court in *Henn v. Henn* choose to define the "issue" actually litigated and determined in the prior dissolution judgment in a narrow manner so as not to include the parties' community property rights in the pension. The court in *Marriage of Mason* choose to define the "issue" determined more broadly, and viewed the goodwill of the wife's business as merely a component or sub-issue of the property already distributed by the prior dissolution judgment. Which definition of the "issue" determined is the proper one? Which one is incompatible with the Court's reasoning in *Sutphin*? If neither definition appears clearly incompatible with the reasoning in *Sutphin*, is there a problem with *Sutphin's* definition of the "issue" foreclosed by collateral estoppel?

(3) In *Murray v. Alaska Airlines, Inc.*, 50 Cal. 4th 860, 114 Cal. Rptr. 3d 241, 237 P.3d 565 (2010), the Supreme Court considered the issue-preclusive effect of a prior federal agency's investigative findings. The plaintiff, a quality assurance auditor for the defendant airline, lost his job after he brought safety concerns to the attention of the FAA. He subsequently filed an administrative complaint with the U.S. Secretary of Labor under the federal whistleblower statute, invoking a federal administrative process that was voluntary and optional. The Secretary of Labor conducted an in-

vestigation during which the defendant airline submitted documents and testimony, but the Secretary never contacted the plaintiff.

Upon completion of this one-sided investigation, the Secretary determined that the record filed to establish any causal connection between the plaintiff's termination and his whistleblower activity. The plaintiff did not file objections to the Secretary's findings and did not request a formal adjudicatory hearing to determine the contested issues de novo, both options available to him under the federal administrative process. Consequently, pursuant to the federal whistleblower statute, the Secretary's findings became final and unappealable.

Plaintiff then commenced a court action against the defendant airline, alleging wrongful termination and retaliation for whistle-blowing in violation of the public policy of California. The trial court granted summary judgment for the defendant based on collateral estoppel. A majority of the Supreme Court concluded because the plaintiff had an *opportunity* to fully contest the Secretary's determination through a judicial-like administrative procedure but chose not to do so, the dispositive issue of causation was "actually litigated" for purposes of collateral estoppel, even though the administrative complaint procedure was voluntary and optional and not a prerequisite to filing the state court wrongful termination action. *Murray, supra*, 50 Cal. 4th 877–78. The dissent strongly disagreed, reasoning that the Secretary's findings on causation should not have an issue-preclusive effect because these findings were rendered without any prior opportunity for a hearing, the submission of evidence, the confrontation of witnesses, or the presentation of argument. *Murray*, 50 Cal. 4th 883–89 (Werdegar, J., dissenting).

Do you agree with the majority or the dissent in *Murray*? Why? Is the majority in *Murray* in effect imposing collateral estoppel as a sanction for failing to exhaust the federal administrative process even though that process was voluntary, optional, and not a prerequisite to suit?

[b] Identifying Issues "Actually Litigated and Determined"

A second troublesome problem is the identification of the issues that were actually litigated and determined by a prior judgment. This process is not difficult where the court has entered detailed findings of fact and conclusions of law, but can be problematic where there is only a general verdict or judgment. *See Harris v. Grimes*, 104 Cal. App. 4th 180, 187, 127 Cal. Rptr. 2d 791 (2002) (finding no collateral estoppel effect where jury rendered a general verdict without special findings). In such circumstances, how does a subsequent court determine which issues were "actually litigated" by the prior judgment?

The party asserting collateral estoppel has the burden of proving that the issue was "raised, actually submitted for determination and determined." *Barker v. Hull*, 191 Cal. App. 3d 221, 236 Cal. Rptr. 285 (1987). An issue is actually litigated only when it is raised by the pleadings and factually resolved either by proof or by failure of proof. *Betyar v. Pierce*, 205 Cal. App. 3d 1250, 1254, 252 Cal. Rptr. 907 (1988). "For purposes of applying collateral estoppel, evidence extrinsic to the judgment roll may be used to ascertain what issues were determined in the former action." *Southwell v. Mallery, Stern & Warford*, 194 Cal. App. 3d 140, 144, 239 Cal. Rptr. 371 (1987).

Consequently, in addition to the pleadings and the judgment in the prior proceeding, a court may examine the reporter's transcript, *Southwell v. Mallery, Stern & Warford, supra*; the minute order or opinion of the trial judge, *McClain v. Rush*, 216 Cal. App. 3d 18, 264 Cal. Rptr. 563 (1989); or even the appellate opinion in the prior proceeding, *see Rutherford v. State of California*, 188 Cal. App. 3d 1267, 233 Cal. Rptr. 781 (1987). But where it is not possible to ascertain from the record what issue was determined in a prior court's ruling, that court's decision will not have a collateral estoppel effect even though certain issues were raised and could have been the basis for the prior court's action. *Henn v. Henn, supra*, 26 Cal. 3d at 331–32.

A court may take judicial notice of the entire file in a prior action. Evidence Code §§ 452(d), 459. May a court also consider declarations submitted by the attorneys as to what was actually presented for determination in the prior case? *See Barker v. Hull, supra*. May it consider declarations of an arbitrator as to what issues were submitted for decision and determined in making an arbitration award? *See Sartor v. Superior Court*, 136 Cal. App. 3d 322, 327, 187 Cal. Rptr. 247 (1982).

The party asserting collateral estoppel must not only prove that an issue was actually determined in the prior action, but also that the resisting party had a full opportunity to present the issue during the prior proceeding. Does this mean that an exhaustive adversarial hearing with oral testimony must have been held on each such issue? Or may the court restrict the presentation of an issue to declarations when, for example, the prior case was resolved through a motion to vacate a default judgment? *See Barker v. Hull, supra* (and cases discussed therein); *Groves v. Peterson*, 100 Cal. App. 4th 659, 667–69, 123 Cal. Rptr. 2d 164 (2002) (collecting cares).

[c]   Collateral Estoppel Effect of Default Judgment

A default judgment constitutes a judgment on the merits and, as such, will have a res judicata (claim preclusion) effect on subsequent actions, so long as the default is a valid judgment. *See* discussion of Res Judicata and Default Judgments, § 8.02 [F][4][a] *supra*. However, does a default judgment also have a collateral estoppel (issue preclusion) effect?

The Restatement (Second) of Judgments, Section 27, comment e, states that in the case of a judgment entered by default, none of the issues are actually litigated. Consequently, the Restatement view is that a default judgment has no collateral estoppel effect with respect to any issue raised in a subsequent action. Do the California courts follow the Restatement view? Apparently not. *See, e.g., Mitchell v. Jones*, 172 Cal. App. 2d 580, 586, 342 P.2d 603 (1959) ("[A] default judgment conclusively establishes, between the parties so far as subsequent proceedings on a different cause of action are concerned, the truth of all material allegations contained in the complaint in the first action, and every fact necessary to uphold the default judgment; but such judgment is not conclusive as to any defense or issue which was not raised and is not necessary to uphold the judgment."). For example, in *County of San Diego v. Hotz*, 168 Cal. App. 3d 605, 214 Cal. Rptr. 658 (1985), the court held that an Iowa dissolution degree entered by default which contained express findings that Hotz was the father of a child collaterally estopped defendant Hotz from contesting the issue of paternity in a subsequent action by the County of San Diego for support and reimbursement of welfare given the child.

A default judgment will have a collateral estoppel effect only as to material issues actually raised in the pleadings. *English v. English*, 9 Cal. 2d 358, 70 P.2d 625 (1937); *Four Star Elec. Inc. v. Feh Constr.*, 7 Cal. App. 4th 1375, 10 Cal. Rptr. 2d 1 (1992); *see Murray v. Alaska Airlines, Inc.*, 50 Cal. 4th 860, 871, 114 Cal. Rptr. 3d 241, 237 P.3d 565 (2010) (indicating in dicta that a default judgment is res judicata as to all issues aptly pleaded in the complaint and the defendant is estopped from denying in a subsequent action any allegations contained in the former complaint). Collateral estoppel will not, however, preclude litigation of available defenses not raised by the defendant in the prior default judgment but sought to be raised by defendant in a later suit on a different cause of action. *English v. English, supra*, 9 Cal. 2d at 363. Is there any reason to distinguish between cases where a defense is not raised due to a default judgment, and where, as in *Sutphin v. Speik, supra*, a defense is neither raised nor litigated although the merits are contested? For a critical analysis of this distinction, *see* Arlo E. Smith, Comment, *Res Judicata in California*, 40 Cal. L. Rev. 412, 421–23 (1952).

[d] Retraxit

A voluntary dismissal *with prejudice*, referred to as a "retraxit" at common law, constitutes a determination on the merits and has a res judicata (claim preclusion) effect. *See* Res Judicata discussion, § 8.02 [F][5][e] *supra*. Does a dismissal with prejudice also have a collateral estoppel effect which precludes litigation of issues in a separate lawsuit? The court in *Torrey Pines Bank v. Superior Court*, 216 Cal. App. 3d 813, 820–24, 265 Cal. Rptr. 217 (1989), concluded that a voluntary dismissal with prejudice of a prior action barred the assertion of affirmative defenses which raised the same issues in a subsequent action. One justice dissented, reasoning that since no issues were "actually litigated" by the prior voluntary dismissal, this retraxit can have no issue preclusive effect. *Id.* at 825–29. Do you agree with the majority or dissent in *Torrey Pines Bank*? Why? Several recent decisions have adopted the dissent's view. *E.g., Le Parc Cmty. Assn. v. Workers' Comp. Appeals Bd.*, 110 Cal. App. 4th 1161, 1174–75, 2 Cal. Rptr. 3d 408 (2003) (concluding that even though a dismissal with prejudice is "on the merits," because the case was voluntarily dismissed pursuant to the parties' settlement agreement, nothing was "actually litigated" or necessarily decided in that action); *Rice v. Crow*, 81 Cal. App. 4th 725, 97 Cal. Rptr. 2d 110 (2000) (ruling a voluntary dismissal with prejudice pursuant to a settlement does not have an issue preclusion effect because no issues have been actually litigated by the settlement). However, another recent decision disagreed with the dissent in *Torrey*

Pines and followed the majority opinion. *Alpha Mech., Heating & Air Conditioning, Inc. v. Travelers Cas. & Surety Co.*, 133 Cal. App. 4th 1319, 35 Cal. Rptr. 3d 496 (2005).

[e] Stipulated Judgments

What is the issue preclusive effect of a prior stipulated judgment? Several courts have applied the "raised or could have been raised" rationale of *Sutphin v. Speik* to justify the extension of collateral estoppel to a stipulated judgment. *See, e.g., California State Auto. Assn. Interins. Bureau v. Superior Court*, 50 Cal. 3d 658, 664–65, n.2, 667, 268 Cal. Rptr. 284, 788 P.2d 1156 (1990) (collecting cases and ruling that a stipulated judgment may properly be given a collateral estoppel effect as to all issues of liability, unless the scope of such issue preclusion is restricted by the parties); *Wittman v. Chrysler Corp.*, 199 Cal. App. 3d 586, 591–593, 245 Cal. Rptr. 20 (1988) (ruling that a consent judgment had a collateral estoppel effect on issues raised in the pleadings although abandoned by a party); *Marriage of Buckley*, 133 Cal. App. 3d 927, 935, 184 Cal. Rptr. 290 (1982) (ruling that a stipulated judgment determines all matters put into issue by the pleadings, and has a collateral estoppel effect on such issues unless the parties agree otherwise); *but see Landeros v. Pankey*, 39 Cal. App. 4th 1167, 46 Cal. Rptr. 2d 165 (1995) (relying on comment (e) to § 27 of the second Restatement and holding that a stipulated judgment in a prior unlawful detainer action did not preclude litigation of a habitability issue in the instant action because the stipulated judgment contained no express language manifesting an intention of the parties to preclude litigation of this issue).

[f] Need for Clearer Collateral Estoppel Guidelines

As the cases in the preceding paragraph indicate, the California courts sometimes have taken contradictory approaches to the "actually litigated and determined" requirement, thereby introducing uncertainty and unpredictability into the issue preclusion analysis. For a thorough discussion of these and other problems associated with California's current issue preclusion doctrine, see Walter W. Heiser, *California's Confusing Collateral Estoppel (Issue Preclusion) Doctrine*, 35 San Diego L. Rev. 509 (1998). Professor Heiser argues that the "actually litigated and determined" requirement should be applied in an underinclusive manner. In other words, whenever the proper application of this requirement is in doubt, the court should err on the side of underinclusion and find issue preclusion inappropriate. Professor Heiser also recommends that the California Supreme Court should disapprove of the overly broad language in *Sutphin*, and should adhere more faithfully to the issue preclusion standards of the Restatement (Second) of Judgments.

[4] Issue "Necessarily Decided" in Prior Proceeding

[a] The "Necessary" Requirement, Generally

Collateral estoppel bars relitigation of an issue determined in a prior proceeding, but only if resolution of that issue was necessary to the prior judgment. *See, e.g.,*

Bronco Wine Co v. Frank A. Logoluso Farms, 214 Cal. App. 3d 699, 262 Cal. Rptr. 899 (1989) (ruling that a finding by a court as to amount of contract damages in upholding administrative suspension of defendant's wine producer's license did not preclude court from determining amount of contract damages in subsequent breach of contract action by growers against defendant because finding in first proceeding was unnecessary to that judgment); *Marriage of Rabkin*, 179 Cal. App. 3d 1071, 225 Cal. Rptr. 219 (1986) (finding that a statement by trial court in order granting temporary increase in spousal support because marital residence not yet sold—that such sale would constitute a change in circumstances justifying a future modification in spousal support—was unnecessary to that court's decision, so given no collateral estoppel effect). In *Lucido v. Superior Court*, 51 Cal. 3d 335, 342, 272 Cal. Rptr. 767, 795 P.2d 1223 (1990), the Supreme Court construed this requirement to mean that the issue must not have been "entirely unnecessary" to the judgment in the prior proceeding.

What are the policy reasons for this "necessary" requirement? Should it apply where the parties have thoroughly litigated, and the court has actually determined, an issue in the mistaken belief that resolution of the issue was "necessary" to the previous judgment?

[b] The Alternative Grounds Rule

An interesting application of this "necessary" requirement is where a judgment is based on two or more alternative grounds and either ground, standing alone, could support the judgment. Early California decisions, such as *Wall v. Donovan*, 113 Cal. App. 3d 122, 169 Cal. Rptr. 644 (1980), applied the First Restatement of Judgments (adopted 1946) Section 68, comment (n), which the *Wall* court considered to be the California rule: "Where the judgment is based upon the matters litigated as alternative grounds, the judgment is determinative on both grounds, although either would have been sufficient to support the judgment."

More recently, the California courts have adopted approach set forth in Section 27, comments (i) & (o), of the Restatement (Second) of Judgments (1982), and announced the following rule: Where a trial court decides a case on two alternative grounds and the reviewing court affirms based on one of those grounds, declining to consider the other, the judgment is binding for purposes of collateral estoppel only on the ground addressed by the appellate court. *E.g.*, *Newport Beach Country Club, Inc. v. Founding Members of the Newport Beach Country Club*, 140 Cal. App. 4th 1120, 45 Cal. Rptr. 3d 207 (2006); *Zevnik v. Superior Court*, 159 Cal. App. 4th 76, 70 Cal. Rptr. 3d 817 (2008); *Butcher v. Truck Ins. Exch.*, 77 Cal. App. 4th 1442, 1460, 92 Cal. Rptr. 2d 521 (2000).

[5] *Issues of Law*

Collateral estoppel precludes relitigation of issues of law actually litigated and determined between the parties in a previous action on a different cause of action, as well as issues of fact. But the doctrine is much more flexible when applied to issues of law. *See, e.g.*, *City of Sacramento v. State of California*, 50 Cal. 3d 51, 64, 266 Cal.

Rptr. 139, 785 P.2d 522 (1990) (ruling public interest exception permitted state, which lost issue of law in prior action of whether state must reimburse local agencies for certain unemployment insurance expenditure, to relitigate same issue in current class action); *Rutherford v. State of California*, 188 Cal. App. 3d 1267, 1283–84, 233 Cal. Rptr. 781 (1987) (holding Department of Fish and Game is not collaterally estopped from relitigating constitutionality of Section 1603 of Fish and Game Code, despite apparent ruling in prior criminal case involving same private parties that the section is unconstitutional, based on public interest exception).

[C] Collateral Estoppel and Mutuality

[1] *Introductory Note on Mutuality*

Assume the following facts: Mrs. Clara Sather, an elderly woman, lived with Mr. and Mrs. Charles Cook. Mr. Cook opened an account with Bank of America in the name of Mrs. Sather, and deposited monies in it from Sather's other accounts. Cook used this account to write checks to cover Sather's expenses. Sather agreed to transfer all her funds to this Bank of America account. Mr. Cook eventually withdrew the entire balance and deposited it in his own personal bank account.

Mrs. Sather died shortly thereafter, and Cook became the executor of her estate. After several years, Cook filed an accounting with the Probate Court, along with his resignation. Several beneficiaries under Sather's will objected to the accounting because Cook failed to include the funds transferred by Sather to the Bank of America account. The Probate Court rejected these objections and settled the accounting, finding that during her lifetime Mrs. Sather made a gift to Cook of the amount of the deposit in question.

After Cook's discharge, one of the beneficiaries, Helen Bernhard, was appointed administratrix. She initiated an action against Bank of America seeking to recover the deposit on the grounds that the Bank was indebted to the estate for this amount because Sather never authorized its withdrawal. Defendant Bank pleaded an affirmative defense of collateral estoppel based on the prior finding that Sather had made a gift of the money in question. Plaintiff Bernhard contended that the doctrine of collateral estoppel did not apply because the defendant Bank, which was asserting the defense, was not a party to the previous action and therefore there was no mutuality of estoppel. Does collateral estoppel apply?

For many years, California courts and those of all other states would not have collaterally estopped the plaintiff administratrix from relitigating the issue of the propriety of the deposit withdrawal because of a lack of "mutuality." *See generally* E.H. Schopler, Annotation, *Mutuality of Estoppel As Prerequisite of Availability of Doctrine of Collateral Estoppel to a Stranger to the Judgment*, 31 A.L.R.3d 1044–99 (1970) (collecting cases). The concept of "mutuality" had many complicated niceties, but in essence the doctrine required that a party *asserting* collateral estoppel in a present proceeding must have been the same party, or in privity with a party, in the previous litigation. *Id.*

[2] Mutuality Doctrine Rejected

The California Supreme Court rejected the mutuality doctrine in the landmark case of *Bernhard v. Bank of America*, 19 Cal. 2d 807, 122 P.2d 892 (1942), whose facts are summarized above. The court noted that the criteria for determining *who may assert* collateral estoppel differ fundamentally from the criteria for determining *against whom* a plea of collateral estoppel may be asserted. *Bernhard*, 19 Cal. 2d at 811, 812. "There is no compelling reason ... for requiring that a party asserting a plea of [collateral estoppel] must have been a party, or in privity with a party, to the earlier litigation." *Id.* at 812. The court then articulated the now familiar inquiries for application of collateral estoppel: "Was the issue decided in the prior adjudication identical with the one presented in the action in question? Was there a final judgment on the merits? Was the party *against whom* the plea is asserted a party or in privity with a party to the prior adjudication?" *Id.* at 813.

The *Bernhard* decision had an impact far beyond California. The federal courts and most state courts have eliminated the mutuality requirement, especially where, as in *Bernhard*, the prior judgment is invoked *defensively* in a second action against a plaintiff bringing suit on an issue that plaintiff litigated and lost as plaintiff against a different defendant in a prior action. *E.g., Blonder-Tongue Lab. v. Univ. of Illinois Foundation*, 402 U.S. 313, 91 S. Ct. 1434, 28 L. Ed. 2d 788 (1971); §29, Restatement (Second) of Judgments (1982); *see generally* Schopler, *Mutuality of Estoppel, supra*.

[3] Offensive Nonmutual Collateral Estoppel

The California courts also recognize the *offensive* use of nonmutual collateral estoppel, *i.e.*, where a plaintiff is seeking to estop a defendant from relitigating the issues which the defendant previously litigated and lost against another plaintiff. *See, e.g., Imen v. Glassford*, 201 Cal. App. 3d 898, 247 Cal. Rptr. 514 (1988); *Sandoval v. Superior Court*, 140 Cal. App. 3d 932, 190 Cal. Rptr. 29 (1983). These courts apply the doctrine adopted by the U.S. Supreme Court in *Parklane Hosiery Co. v. Shore*, 439 U.S. 322, 99 S. Ct. 645, 58 L. Ed. 2d 552 (1979), for use in the federal courts.

For example, in *Imen v. Glassford, supra*, the plaintiffs, the Imens, commenced an action for fraud against defendant Glassford, a licensed real estate salesman, for inducing plaintiffs to sell their property on terms which Glassford had no intention of performing. In a prior proceeding, the California Real Estate Commissioner, also concerned with Glassford's allegedly improper conduct, accused Glassford of violating his statutory duties. After a hearing, an administrative law judge found Glassford acted fraudulently—entering into a real estate contract with clients (the Imens) having no intention of performing his written promises. The Real Estate Commissioner adopted these findings and revoked Glassford's license as a real estate salesman and broker. The Imens relied on the Commissioner's decision in successfully moving for summary adjudication on the issue of Glassford's fraud. After an evidentiary proceeding, the trial court awarded the Imens substantial compensatory and punitive damages. Defendant Glassford appealed. In affirming the trial court's use of offensive nonmutual collateral estoppel, the court explained that doctrine as follows:

In *Parklane Hosiery Co. v. Shore, supra*, 439 U.S. 322, the United States Supreme Court emphasized that courts must go through a careful weighing process to determine the fairness of applying the doctrine of collateral estoppel. In explaining the problems associated with the offensive use of collateral estoppel contrasted with its defensive use, *Parklane* cautioned that offensive use may be both inefficient and unfair to a defendant.

"If a defendant in the first action is sued for small or nominal damages, he may have little incentive to defend vigorously, particularly if future suits are not foreseeable. [Citations]. Allowing offensive collateral estoppel may also be unfair to a defendant if the judgment relied upon as a basis for the estoppel is itself inconsistent with one or more previous judgments in favor of the defendant. Still another situation where it might be unfair to apply offensive estoppel is where the second action affords the defendant procedural opportunities unavailable in the first action that could readily cause a different result." ([*Parklane*,] at pp. 330–331.)

Parklane nonetheless held that the offensive use of collateral estoppel was permitted in the broad discretion of the trial court except in certain circumstances including the situation when its application "*would be unfair to a defendant*." (*Ibid.*; italics added.)

Imen, supra, 201 Cal. App. 3d at 906. Because offensive use of nonmutual collateral estoppels encourages a plaintiff to adopt a "wait and see" attitude in hope that the first action by another plaintiff will result in a favorable judgment, the *Imen* court summarized the doctrine by quoting again from *Parklane*, 439 U. S. at 331:

The general rule should be that in cases where a plaintiff could easily have joined in the earlier action or where, either for the reasons discussed above or for other reasons, the application of offensive estoppel would be unfair to a defendant, a trial judge should not allow the use of offensive collateral estoppel.

Imen, supra, 201 Cal. App. 3d at 910–11 (Benke, J., dissenting).

The California courts recognize the need for leeway in applying nonmutual collateral estoppel so as to accord basic fairness to the parties. For example, in *Sandoval v. Superior Court*, 140 Cal. App. 3d 932, 190 Cal. Rptr. 29 (1983), the court refused to extend offensive nonmutual collateral estoppel to a prior judgment against the defendant because that judgment was inconsistent with another determination of the same issue.

Relying on Section 29(4) of the Second Restatement and *Parklane, supra*, 439 U.S. at 324–37, the court concluded that to allow the use of collateral estoppel where there are inconsistent prior verdicts on an identical issue would be arbitrary and unfair. *Sandoval, supra*, 140 Cal. App. 3d at 941–44. Is this "inconsistent judgments" exception applicable only to the offensive use of non-mutual collateral estoppel, or is it equally applicable to the defensive use as well? *See* Section 29(4), Restatement (Second) of Judgments, comment f (1982).

California courts continue to scrutinize more closely the offensive use of nonmutual collateral estoppel than the defensive use. *See, e.g., Smith v. ExxonMobil Oil Corp.,* 153 Cal. App. 4th 1407, 64 Cal. Rptr. 3d 69 (2007) (finding the application of collateral estoppel was unfair to defendant company because, through no fault of its own, it was unable at the prior adjudication to obtain expert testimony crucial to it defense on the issue of liability); *White Motor Corp. v. Terresinski,* 214 Cal. App. 3d 754, 763–64, 263 Cal. Rptr. 26 (1989) (ruling application of offensive collateral estoppel unfair even though all basic requirements of doctrine met). This is because, as the court in *Imen* observed, the offensive use may be both inefficient and unfair. The "inefficiency" concerns identified for the offensive use of nonmutual collateral estoppel do not apply to the defensive use. Why not? Are the "unfairness" concerns identified for the offensive use also inapplicable to the defensive use? *See* §29, Restatement (Second) of Judgments (1982), comment d.

Although the California Supreme Court has discarded the doctrine of mutuality, the Legislature has prohibited nonmutual collateral estoppel in some specific instances. For example, CCP §99 directs that a judgment in a limited civil case is conclusive only between the parties and their successors in interest, but does not operate as collateral estoppel by other persons. *See also* Vehicle Code §40834 (conviction for violation of Vehicle Code shall not have res judicata or collateral estoppel effect in any subsequent civil action). Why would the Legislature retain the mutuality requirements for such judgments?

[4] Collateral Estoppel Effect of Noncourt Proceedings

[a] Administrative Agency Decisions

In *People v. Sims,* 32 Cal. 3d 468, 186 Cal. Rptr. 77, 651 P.2d 321 (1982), the Supreme Court held that collateral estoppel may be applied to decisions made by administrative agencies when the agency was acting in a "judicial capacity" and resolved disputed issues of fact properly before it which the parties have had an adequate opportunity to litigate. The court in *Sims* found that an administrative fair hearing conducted by the state welfare department was a judicial-like adversary proceeding, and its determinations should be given a collateral estoppel effect. *Sims,* 32 Cal. 3d at 481–82. *See People v. Garcia,* 39 Cal. 4th 1070, 48 Cal. Rptr. 3d 75, 141 P.3d 197 (2006) (declining to reconsider the decision in Sims and again holding that the doctrine of collateral estoppel precluded the People from prosecuting for welfare fraud a welfare recipient who had been exonerated at an administrative hearing conducted by the county).

In *Pacific Lumber Co. v. State Water Res. Control Bd.,* 37 Cal. 4th 921, 38 Cal. Rptr. 3d 220. 126 P.3d 1040 (2006), the Supreme Court again recognized that collateral estoppel may be applied to a decision made by an administrative agency, based on the following factors:

> For an administrative decision to have collateral estoppel effect, it and its prior proceedings must possess a judicial character. Indicia of proceedings undertaken in a judicial capacity include a hearing before an impartial

decision maker; testimony given under oath or affirmation; a party's ability to subpoena, call, examine, and cross-examine witnesses, to introduce documentary evidence, and to make oral and written argument; the taking of a record of the proceeding; and a written statement of reasons for the decision.

Pacific Lumber, supra, 37 Cal. 4th at 944. Another relevant, but not conclusive, factor is whether the administrative decision is subject to writ review by administrative mandamus under CCP § 1094.5. *Id.,* at n. 12. Why is this factor relevant?

Administrative hearings are often not conducted according to the rules of evidence applicable to judicial trials. Should this difference automatically preclude a finding that the agency was acting in a "judicial capacity"? If not, when should a different standard for admitting evidence preclude such a finding? *See People v. Sims, supra,* 32 Cal. 3d at 480; *Lucido, supra,* 51 Cal. 3d at 345, n.6.

Does a determination by an administrator of a dispositive issue after a one-sided investigation have a collateral estoppel effect on a plaintiff in a subsequent state court action, where the plaintiff did not file objections to the administrator's findings and did not request a formal adjudicatory hearing to determine the contested issues de novo, both options available to him under the administrative process? *See Murray v. Alaska Airlines, Inc.,* 50 Cal. 4th 860, 114 Cal. Rptr. 3d 241, 237 P.3d 565 (2010) (holding that because the plaintiff had an *opportunity* to fully contest the administrator's determination through a judicial-like administrative procedure but chose not to do so, the dispositive issue was "actually litigated" for purposes of collateral estoppel, even though the administrative complaint procedure was voluntary and optional and not a prerequisite to filing the state court action). However, an unreviewed administrative finding will not be given preclusive effect in a later judicial proceeding where the Legislature did not intend the agency's findings to have a res judicata or collateral estoppel effect in a subsequent superior court damages action. *See Runyon v. Bd. of Trustees,* 48 Cal. 4th 760, 108 Cal. Rptr. 3d 557, 229 P.3d 985 (2010) (discussing various cases).

One legislative response to *People v. Sims* is Section 1960 of the Unemployment Insurance Code, enacted in 1986, which provides that a finding by the Unemployment Insurance Appeals Board "shall not be conclusive or binding in any separate or subsequent action or proceeding." What policy is Section 1960 designed to further? *See* Thomas F. Crosby, *Administrative Collateral Estoppel in California: A Critical Evaluation of People v. Sims,* 40 Hastings L. J. 907, 947–50 1989). Another legislative response is Vehicle Code § 13353.2(e), which provides that a DMV determination with respect to the suspension of a driver's license for driving while intoxicated shall have no collateral estoppel effect on a subsequent criminal prosecution; but that the DMV must immediately reinstate a suspended driver's license if a person is acquitted of criminal charges. What policy considerations are reflected in these Vehicle Code provisions? *See Gikas v. Zolin,* 6 Cal. 4th 841, 25 Cal. Rptr. 2d 500, 863 P.2d 745 (1993) (noting that the legislature made a policy decision that administrative proceedings before the DMV will not have a preclusive effect on related criminal proceedings).

[b] Contractual Arbitration

A more difficult problem is the collateral estoppel effect, if any, to be given a contractual (*e.g.*, commercial) arbitration decision. Generally, arbitration is voluntary in the sense that it is agreed to by parties as the method of resolving anticipated disputes. Typically, such arbitration proceedings are informal, do not follow formal rules of evidence, and do not include a formal record of testimony. Moreover, although arbitration awards generally are in writing, the awards need not (and often do not) state any reasons or findings in support of the decision. *See* G. Richard Shell, *Res Judicata and Collateral Estoppel Effects of Commercial Arbitration*, 35 UCLA L. Rev. 623, 628–33 (1988). Although California courts may give arbitration decisions a res judicata (claim preclusion) effect, see discussion §8.02 [F][4][e] *supra*, should they also give them a collateral estoppel (issue preclusion) effect? *See Sartor v. Superior Court*, 136 Cal. App. 3d 322, 187 Cal. Rptr. 247 (1982); Shell, *Res Judicata and Collateral Estoppel Effects*, *supra*, pp. 647–54 and 667–69. What considerations are involved here that are not involved in judicial proceedings? Why is it more problematic to give a collateral estoppel effect to an arbitration decision than to give a res judicata effect? *See* Shell, *Res Judicata and Collateral Estoppel Effects*, *supra*.

The Supreme Court has recently adopted, for California purposes, the rule that a contractual arbitration award cannot have a nonmutual collateral estoppel effect unless the arbitral parties so agree. *See Vandenberg v. Superior Court*, 21 Cal. 4th 815, 88 Cal. Rptr. 2d 366, 982 P.2d 229 (1999). Declining to follow the predominant view of other jurisdictions, the *Vandenberg* court concluded that a private arbitration award, even if judicially confirmed, can have no collateral estoppel effect in favor of third persons unless the arbitral parties agreed, in the particular case, that such a consequence should apply. The Supreme Court rejected the predominant view because its rationales gave insufficient consideration and weight to the voluntary, contractual, and informal nature of private arbitration; and to the consequent reasonable expectations of the arbitral parties. *Vandenberg*, 21 Cal. 4th at 834–37.

The *Vandenberg* court declined to address the circumstances, if any, in which a private arbitration award may have issue preclusive effect in subsequent litigation between the *same parties* on different causes of action. *Id.* at 824, n. 2. The *Vandenberg* court noted, however, that its holding did not impose or imply any limitations on the claim preclusive effect of a California law private arbitration award. *Id.*

[5] *Final Judgment for Purposes of Collateral Estoppel*

One of the requirements for collateral estoppel is that there must be a "final" judgment on the merits in the previous suit. To be "final," a judgment must be a firm and stable one, the last word of the rendering court. *Producers Dairy Delivery Co. v. Sentry Ins. Co.*, 41 Cal. 3d 903, 911, 226 Cal. Rptr. 558, 718 P.2d 920 (1986). A tentative or interlocutory order will not be given a preclusive effect. *E.g., George Arakelian Farms, Inc. v. A. L. R. B.*, 49 Cal. 3d 1279, 1289–91, 265 Cal. Rptr. 162, 783 P.2d 749 (1989) (ruling make-whole order issued by administrative agency was an interlocutory judgment with no collateral estoppel effect, even though sufficiently final to permit appellate review).

A typical application of this final judgment requirement occurs when a party obtains a judgment which is then appealed, and the case is settled prior to final resolution of the appeal. In *Sandoval v. Superior Court*, 140 Cal. App. 3d 932, 937, 190 Cal. Rptr. 29 (1983), the court held that even though an appeal is dismissed pursuant to a settlement, the trial court judgment reemerges with sufficient finality to permit the application of collateral estoppel. The Supreme Court specifically approved of the *Sandoval* reasoning and holding in *Producers Dairy Delivery Co., supra*, 41 Cal. 3d at 911.

When is a hearing decision by an administrative agency considered "final" for purposes of collateral estoppel? When the agency decision becomes final for purposes of judicial review? When the agency decision becomes final for purposes of administrative implementation? When the time for judicial review of the agency decision has expired? *See People v. Sims, supra*, 32 Cal. 3d at 485–86; *Long Beach Unified Sch. Dist. v. State of California*, 225 Cal. App. 3d 155, 168–69, 275 Cal. Rptr. 449 (1990) ("Finality for the purpose of administrative collateral estoppel may be understood as a two-step process: (1) the decision must be final with respect to action by the administrative agency ... and (2) the decision must have conclusive effect.... In other words, the decision must be free from direct attack.... A direct attack on an administrative decision may be made by appeal to the superior court for review by petition for administrative mandamus"). *See also* Eric N. Macey, Note, *The Collateral Estoppel Effect of Administrative Agency Actions in Federal Civil Litigation*, 46 Geo. Wash. L. Rev. 65, 73–77 (1977).

§ 8.04 Privity

Dyson v. State Personnel Board

Court of Appeal of California, Third Appellate District
213 Cal. App. 3d 711, 262 Cal. Rptr. 112 (1989)

Blease, Acting Presiding Justice.

In this appeal Monroe Dyson challenges the affirmance of his dismissal as a youth counselor with the Department of Youth Authority's Preston School of Industry (Preston or the agency) by the State Personnel Board (Board). The dismissal is predicated solely upon the admission in the administrative disciplinary proceeding of evidence seized by the agency from Dyson's home, consisting of nine T-shirts and two intercoms belonging to Preston. The question we resolve is whether this evidence should have been excluded from the administrative proceedings.

The items were seized from Dyson's home and held by the agency pursuant to a search for evidence that Dyson had committed the crime of theft. The search was initiated, directed and participated in by Thomas Gold, the Preston Chief of

Security, acting under his authority as a peace officer. The evidence was turned over by the agency to police authorities for use in a criminal proceeding initiated on the complaint of the agency. The evidence was there excluded and the criminal prosecution dismissed on grounds that the search violated Dyson's constitutional rights to privacy.

We will conclude that the Board is collaterally estopped to deny the constitutional invalidity of the search, as determined in the criminal proceeding. In the circumstances of this case the unconstitutionally seized evidence should have been excluded in the succeeding administrative proceeding conducted by the Board.

Facts And Procedural Background

Dyson was afforded a hearing before an administrative law judge appointed by the Board. He made a timely objection to the introduction of the evidence seized in the search of his home. The following facts, read most favorably to the agency, are taken from the record of the administrative hearing. However, the facts presented here do not bear on the issue of consent to search Dyson's home, an issue resolved adversely to the agency in the criminal proceeding which preceded the administrative disciplinary proceeding. Rather the facts bear on the question whether the agency was so involved in the search as to justify an exclusionary remedy to deter agency invasion of its employees' constitutional rights.

Mr. Dyson was dismissed from his employment as a youth counselor with the Preston School of Industry. The principal actor in the search was Tom Gold, Preston's Chief Security Officer. Gold was present in the office of Preston Superintendent Richard Colsey on June 12, 1984, when Renate Dyson, Dyson's estranged wife, called to report that Dyson had been stealing items from Preston. Colsey testified that Renate told him that "her husband was bringing things home she thought were State property and she thought he was stealing" and that the subject matters were "video materials, clothing, a telephone, and some other electronic equipment." Colsey assigned Gold to investigate the report.

Gold is a peace officer and pursued the investigation and search acting under that authority. In his view his jurisdiction extends "beyond the Walls of Preston when ... on duty." (*See* Pen. Code, §830.5, subd. (b)). He understood his peace officer status to "include [] any activity in the service of the Youth Authority outside the walls of Preston." During the investigation and search of Dyson's house he was acting in that capacity. * * *

After calling and arranging for the sheriff's officers to meet him at the Dyson house on Craft Drive, Gold went there with Mrs. Dyson, a trip of some miles. When asked why he called in the sheriff's office, Gold said: "I just wanted an assistant in going into the house as I don't have the necessary papers for someone to go in to search a house, which they said they would have her sign the day prior. If they got the consent they would have her sign the papers to search the home,.... I don't know really how far my Peace Officer's jurisdiction really does go as to what I can do with it...."

On getting into the house Gold testified:

"Q: How did you get into the house?

"A. One of the Officers asked Renate if she had a key. She said no … and she says that the window was broke out and there was a door over the window by the doorknob. He asked if he could push it open. She said yes, he did open the door on the inside, and on entry said, 'It's a Sac SO. Is anyone home?' And upon no answer, we entered the house."

According to Gold, inside the house Renate led Gold through the house, identifying things as taken from Preston. Gold made notes of identification and seized the items. He took one of the intercoms "just sitting on the nightstand" in the master bedroom and the other was found in the second bedroom. The T-shirts were found by Gold in the closet of the master bedroom where he seized them.

Gold "gathered the material or the property belonging to Preston" and put "it in the trunk of my car" and then dropped Renate off at her house and "then came back to the institution and talked with our Superintendent Richard Colsey." Thereafter (the following day), pursuant to his superior's directions, he took it to the Ione Police Department and logged it in.

The administrative law judge rendered a decision concluding that the nine T-shirts and two intercoms seized at Dyson's house were the property of the Preston School. The judge found that it could not be established that the 11 video tapes were similarly the property of the school. He also found that although a book given Mrs. Dyson by Dyson was the property of the school that Dyson intended to return it and other Preston books to the school. The judge concluded Dyson "did steal State property," to wit, the items seized from Dyson's house.

The findings of fact and proposed decision of the administrative law judge were adopted by the Board. It is that decision which we are asked to review.

Discussion

The evidence necessary to support the discipline imposed on Dyson is that seized during the search of his house. The search was initiated and directed by the agency; the evidence was seized and held by the agency, turned over by it to a prosecutorial authority for use in a criminal action, retrieved following its suppression by the court in that proceeding, and introduced in evidence in Dyson's administrative disciplinary hearing.

The dispositive issue is the admissibility of the evidence in the administrative proceeding. That turns, first, on the applicability of an exclusionary rule to the administrative proceeding and, second, on the collateral effect to be given the exclusion of the evidence in the criminal proceeding. We consider these issues seriatim.

I

* * * We are persuaded by our reasoning previously related and by the foregoing cases that the exclusionary rule is available in the circumstances of this case. The unconstitutional search could not have a tighter nexus with the agency that seeks to profit from it. The policy that led to the exclusion of the evidence in the related crim-

inal proceeding fits foursquare with exclusion in the administrative proceedings we review. * * *

Because of the particular nature of the investigation of this case and the extent of agency involvement we conclude that the exclusionary rule applies to remedy the agency invasion of its employee's constitutional rights. The same policy of deterrence would be served by the application of an exclusionary rule in circumstances such as those present here as is served in the application of the rule in criminal proceedings. The Board erred in refusing to consider the application of the exclusionary rule to the administrative disciplinary proceedings. That leads us to consider the collateral effect of the decision in the criminal proceeding to exclude the evidence made the basis of the administrative discipline.

II

In the criminal proceeding, which was initiated on the complaint of the agency on the basis of evidence provided by the agency, the court determined that the evidence was invalidly seized and therefore should be suppressed. The determination of that issue turned on the question of the consent to search allegedly given by Dyson's wife. The prosecution had the burden of proving consent by the preponderance of the evidence. It failed to meet that burden. The criminal charges were subsequently dismissed. We conclude that the agency is bound by that determination of the invalidity of the search and seizure.

Collateral estoppel has traditionally been found to bar relitigation of an issue decided at a previous court proceeding "if (1) the issue necessarily decided at the previous [proceeding] is identical to the one which is sought to be relitigated; if (2) the previous [proceeding] resulted in a final judgment on the merits; and if (3) the party against whom collateral estoppel is asserted was a party or in privity with a party at the prior [proceeding]."[2] (*People v. Taylor* (1974) 12 Cal. 3d 686, 691 [117 Cal. Rptr. 70, 527 P.2d 622]; *see also Bernhard v. Bank of America* (1942) 19 Cal. 2d 807, 813 [122 P.2d 892]).

The first two prongs are clearly met in this case. At issue in both the criminal trial and the administrative hearing was the validity of the search and seizure. The criminal proceeding was dismissed after the issue of the validity of the search was fully litigated, and the court ruled the evidence seized was inadmissible. We turn to the third prerequisite for the application of the collateral estoppel doctrine, i.e., privity between the party to be estopped and the unsuccessful party in the prior litigation.

The privity requirement has undergone an evolution in the law. "Traditionally it has been held to refer to an interest in the subject matter of litigation acquired after rendition of the judgment through or under one of the parties, as by inheritance,

---

2. Because mutuality of estoppel is no longer a requirement for the application of the doctrine (*see Bernhard v. Bank of America, supra,* 19 Cal. 2d 807), privity is a concern with respect to the party against whom the doctrine is asserted.

succession or purchase. (*Bernhard, supra*, 19 Cal. 2d at p. 811). The concept has also been expanded to refer to a mutual or successive relationship to the same rights of property, or to such an identification in interest of one person with another as to represent the same legal rights and, more recently, to a relationship between the party to be estopped and the unsuccessful party in the prior litigation which is 'sufficiently close' so as to justify application of the doctrine of collateral estoppel" (*Clemmer v. Hartford Ins. Co.* (1978) 22 Cal. 3d 865, 875 [151 Cal. Rptr. 285, 587 P.2d 1098]). Three reasons cited in support of the application of the doctrine beyond that of the identity of the parties are protection against vexatious litigation, achievement of finality of litigation in which public interests are involved, and promotion of the stability of adjudications in prior criminal actions. * * *

As one commentator has noted, the determination whether a party is in privity with another for purposes of collateral estoppel is a policy decision. "[T]he term 'privity' in itself does not state a reason for either including or excluding a person from the binding effect of a prior judgment, but rather it represents a legal conclusion that the relationship between the one who is a party on the record and the non-party is sufficiently close to afford application of the principle of preclusion. The emphasis in the analysis is upon the policy of ending litigation where there has been a fair trial of one's interests, as it has been observed that 'the doctrine of res judicata is primarily one of public policy and only secondarily of private benefit to individual litigants.'" (Vestal, *Preclusion/Res Judicata Variables: Parties* (1964) 50 Iowa L. Rev. 27, 45, fn. Omitted....)

However, the expanded notions of privity notwithstanding, collateral estoppel may be applied only if the requirements of due process are satisfied. (*Clemmer v. Hartford Ins., supra*, 22 Cal. 3d at p. 875.) "In the context of collateral estoppel, due process requires that the party to be estopped must have had an identity or community of interest with, and adequate representation by, the losing party in the first action as well as that the circumstances must have been such that the party to be estopped should reasonably have expected to be bound by the prior adjudication. [Citation.] Thus, in deciding whether to apply collateral estoppel, the court must balance the rights of the party to be estopped against the need for applying collateral estoppel in the particular case, in order to promote judicial economy by minimizing repetitive litigation, to prevent inconsistent judgments which undermine the integrity of the judicial system, or to protect against vexatious litigation. [Citations.]" (*Ibid.*)

In *People v. Sims* (1982) 32 Cal. 3d 468 [186 Cal. Rptr. 77, 651 P.2d 321], the Supreme Court held that the administrative decision exonerating a welfare recipient of welfare fraud precluded the district attorney from pursuing a criminal action against the recipient for the same alleged misconduct. The administrative agency involved in the first action, a "fair hearing" action, was the Social Services Department of Sonoma County. The district attorney's claim that it was not bound by the previous administrative determination on the ground that the county and the district attorney are not in privity with each other was rejected by the court. The court asserted "'Privity is essentially a shorthand statement that collateral estoppel is to be applied in a given case; there is no universally applicable definition of privity.' [Citation.] The concept refers 'to a relationship between the party to be estopped and the unsuccessful party in the prior litigation which is "sufficiently close" so as to justify application of the doctrine of collateral estoppel.' [Citations.]" (*Id.*, at pp. 486–487.)

The *Sims* court went on to find that the office of the district attorney and the county were "sufficiently close" to warrant application of the doctrine. "Both entities are county agencies that represented the interests of the State of California at the respective proceedings. The district attorney's office represents the State of California in the name of the 'People' at criminal prosecutions.... At fair hearings, the county welfare department acts as the 'agent' of the State. '[T]he courts have held that the agents of the same government are in privity with each other, since they represent not their own rights but the right of the government. (Fn. omitted.) [Citations.]'" (*Sims, supra*, 32 Cal. 3d at p. 487; *see also Lerner v. Los Angeles City Board of Education* (1963) 59 Cal. 2d 382, 396–399 [29 Cal. Rptr. 657, 380 P.2d 97] [city board of education bound by waiver of State Board of Education in part because city board serves as an agency of the state].) The court further noted that the close association between the county and the district attorney's office could be seen from the fact that the agencies operate jointly in investigating and controlling welfare fraud. Information gathered by the county is also used by the district attorney; if fraud evidence is uncovered by the county, it must request issuance of criminal complaint from the district attorney. The court also noted that, upon request, the "County must provide documentary evidence to the district attorney and ensure the appearances of investigators and other county officials at hearings and trials" (32 Cal. 3d at p. 488) and that in that particular case "both the criminal complaint charging respondent with fraud and the declaration filed in support of the complaint were signed by personnel of the [County Department of Social Services]." (*Id.*, at p. 488, fn. 17.)

Relying on *Sims*, this court in *Buttimer v. Alexis* (1983) 146 Cal. App. 3d 754 [194 Cal. Rptr. 603] held that the Department of Motor Vehicles was collaterally estopped from relitigating the lawfulness of the petitioner's arrest after a criminal court in connection with a Penal Code section 1538.5 suppression motion had ruled the arrest unlawful. The judgment commanding the DMV to set aside its order of suspension of the petitioner's drivers license for refusing to submit to a chemical test was affirmed on appeal. This court asserted that although "DMV may have no control over the actions of the District Attorney, however, the district attorney represents the State of California in criminal matters, and DMV represents the interests of the State of California in its hearings." (*Id.*, at p. 760.) We thus concluded that the State of California was the real party in interest in both proceedings and that therefore the requirements of privity for the application of collateral estoppel were satisfied.

We turn to the circumstances of this case. Here, Dyson is seeking the benefit of the trial court's ruling on the search and seizure issue he litigated below and is attempting to preclude the agency from relitigating the issue. The agency was not a party in the criminal action. However, we consider whether the agency had a "sufficiently close" relationship with the district attorney to warrant application of the collateral estoppel doctrine.

We note initially that the agency (Youth Authority) is a state agency. (Welf. & Inst. Code, § 1700 et seq.). It was represented at the administrative hearing by the state Attorney General.[5] The criminal action was prosecuted by the district attorney, representing the People of the State of California. Under some of the cases cited above, the fact that the "State" was involved in both actions might be considered sufficient justification to preclude the agency from relitigating the search and seizure issue. However, we do not rely on the mere characterization of both entities as agents of the "State" to find the application of collateral estoppel justified here.

The circumstances of this case reveal a "close relationship" between the significant actors in both proceedings from the very inception of the search. The search was initiated by Gold, an agent of the Youth Authority, who called in the sheriff's department for assistance. The sheriff's department serves as the investigative arm for the district attorney. Manifestly, Gold was conscious of the criminal law overlap. From the very start, a convergence between the disciplinary interests and the penal interests was evident. Evidence seized was originally retained by Gold and then later turned over to the sheriff's department. The criminal action was initiated on the complaint of Preston (the Youth Authority). Gold presumably testified at the criminal suppression motion, presenting evidence relating to the validity of the search. As a witness, he had every incentive to accurately portray the sequence of events leading up to the search.[6] Because a criminal conviction of theft would have constituted cause for the discipline of Dyson under the civil service laws (Gov. Code, § 19572, subd. (k), the agency's disciplinary interest in the criminal proceeding was direct. The district attorney had every incentive to vigorously litigate the issue of the legality of the search. The agency (through its agents) was the chief "accuser" at the criminal proceeding. Its role at the disciplinary hearing was the same. The litigation objectives of the district attorney and the Attorney General in their respective proceedings were identical.

Given the purposes of the doctrine of collateral estoppel, i.e., to promote judicial economy by minimizing repetitive litigation and to prevent inconsistent judgments which undermine the integrity of the judicial system (*People v. Taylor, supra,* 12 Cal. 3d at p. 695), we see no reason why the doctrine should not be applied here. The agency should not be given the opportunity to relitigate the validity of the search and

---

5. We recognize that the Attorney General wears many hats and was not functioning in a criminal prosecutorial role when representing the agency in this disciplinary action.

6. We recognize that the fact that an individual appears as a witness in an action does not in and of itself support a finding of privity with a party in that action for purposes of the application of collateral estoppel in a subsequent proceeding. (*Minton v. Cavaney* (1961) 56 Cal. 2d 576, 581 [15 Cal. Rptr. 641, 364 P.2d 473].)

seizure. The relationship between the district attorney in the criminal proceeding and the agency was sufficiently close to warrant preclusion of the relitigation of the issue in the disciplinary hearing.

For these reasons we conclude that the agency is collaterally estopped to deny the invalidity of the search for and seizure of this evidence.

Disposition

The judgment is reversed. The case is remanded to the trial court with the direction to issue a peremptory writ of mandate compelling the State Personnel Board to set aside Dyson's dismissal as an employee of the Department of Youth Authority's Preston School of Industry. Appellant shall recover his costs on appeal.

Notes and Questions regarding Privity

(1) *Privity, Generally.* Generally speaking, issue and claim preclusion can only be applied against parties to a prior action. Code of Civil Procedure § 1910 provides, in defining what parties are to be deemed the same: "The parties are deemed to be the same when those between whom the evidence is offered were on opposite sides in the former case...." But as our principle cases illustrate, the requirement of a "same party" is not taken literally. Not only are actual parties bound by a prior judgment, but also nonparties who are "in privity" with the actual parties. How does a California court determine whether a person is "in privity" with a party?

(2) *Modern California Privity Doctrine.* The modern doctrine of privity is set forth in the landmark case of *Clemmer v. Hartford Ins. Co.*, 22 Cal. 3d 865, 151 Cal. Rptr. 285, 587 P.2d 1098 (1978). According to the Court in *Clemmer*, "[p]rivity is a concept not readily susceptible of uniform definition." *Id.* at 875. Although traditional applications of privity were quite limited, as the *Dyson* opinion indicates the modern California doctrine is much broader. Privity now extends to any relationship between the party to be estopped and the unsuccessful party in the prior litigation which is "sufficiently close" so as to justify application of the doctrine of res judicata or collateral estoppel. *See Clemmer, supra.* What guidance does this statement of the privity doctrine give to litigants and courts? Is "sufficiently close" a workable test, or simply a conclusion? How is "sufficiently close" defined? This is a very flexible standard which is, however, limited by the requirements of due process. What are these requirements? Do the due process requirements provide a clearer definition of "sufficiently close?"

(3) *Policy Considerations.* The *Dyson* opinion astutely observes that the determination of whether a party is in privity with another for purposes of res judicata is a policy decision. What considerations does this policy decision encompass? *See Clemmer v. Hartford Ins. Co., supra; Ceresino v. Fire Ins. Exchange,* 215 Cal. App. 3d 814, 822, 264 Cal. Rptr. 30 (1989) (identifying the policy reasons for the expanded expansive definitions of privity as "to discourage repetitive litigation, to prevent inconsistent judgments, and to discourage vexatious litigation"). Is this the type of policy decision a court should be permitted to make based on vague concepts like

"sufficiently close"? Or is this the type of policy decision more appropriate for a state legislature?

How useful is the policy consideration "to prevent inconsistent judgments" in determining whether parties are in privity? Should not the policy really be "to prevent inconsistent judgments when the parties are the same or in privity"? Otherwise, the policy would always be a reason for concluding that parties are in privity, would it not? Are these policy considerations, as identified in *Dyson*, really nothing more than privity conclusions masquerading as analytical doctrine? Or do they simply send a general message to the courts: in close cases, resolve doubts in favor of a finding of privity!

(4) *Privity Statutes.* The California Legislature has delineated some categories of nonparties who are bound by a prior judgment. Code of Civil Procedure § 1908 states:

> (a) The effect of a judgment or final order in an action or special proceeding before a court or judge of this state, or of the United States, having jurisdiction to pronounce the judgment or order, is as follows:

> (2) ... [T]he judgment or order is, in respect to the matter directly adjudged, conclusive between the parties and their successors in interest by title subsequent to the commencement of the action or special proceeding, litigating for the same thing under the same title and in the same capacity, provided they have notice, actual or constructive, of the pendency of the action or proceeding.

> (b) A person who is not a party but who controls an action, individually or in cooperation with others, is bound by the adjudications of litigated matters as if he were a party if he has a proprietary or financial interest in the judgment or in the determination of a question of fact or of a question of law with reference to the same subject matter or transaction; if the other party has notice of his participation, the other party is equally bound. * * *

(5) *Privity Examples.* California courts have found privity to exist in a variety of relationships, such as:

> (a) Successors in interest. *See, e.g., Brown v. Rahman,* 231 Cal. App. 3d 1458, 282 Cal. Rptr. 815 (1991) (holding heirs of deceased in wrongful death action in privity with deceased who, in earlier personal injury action prior to death, lost on issues of causation and liability against same defendant); *Garcia v. Rehrig Intl., Inc.,* 99 Cal. App. 4th 869, 877–79, 121 Cal. Rptr. 2d 723 (2002), *Evans v. Celotex Corp.,* 194 Cal. App. 3d 741, 745–46, 238 Cal. Rptr. 259 (1987); *contra Kaiser Found. Hosp. v. Superior Court,* 254 Cal. App. 2d 327, 62 Cal. Rptr. 330 (1967); Elizabeth A. West, Comment, *Does an Adverse Judgment in a Personal Injury Action Bar a Subsequent Wrongful Death Action?,* 20 Pac. L.J. 221 (1988).

> (b) Persons represented by a fiduciary. *E.g., Armstrong v. Armstrong,* 15 Cal. 3d 942, 951, 126 Cal. Rptr. 805, 544 P.2d 941 (1976).

(c) Persons who have a proprietary or financial interest in and control the conduct of a lawsuit may be bound by the result even though not a party. *E.g., George F. Hillenbrand, Inc. v. Ins. Co. of N. America*, 104 Cal. App. 4th 784, 824–27, 128 Cal. Rptr. 2d 586 (2002); *Aronow v. La Croix*, 219 Cal. App. 3d 1039, 1050–52, 268 Cal. Rptr. 866 (1990), *cert. denied*, 498 U.S. 1105, 111 S. Ct. 1009, 112 L. Ed. 2d 1091 (1991) (ruling plaintiff, an attorney who served as co-counsel and a witness for a physician in a prior unsuccessful malicious prosecution action, had sufficient interest in and control of prior action to be in privity with respect to plaintiff's identical malicious prosecution claim against same defendants).

(d) Individual members of a homeowner association may be in privity with the association. *Kirkpatrick v. City of Oceanside*, 232 Cal. App. 3d 267, 280–81, 283 Cal. Rptr. 191 (1991). Likewise, an individual party seeking to vindicate a public interest may be in privity with a public interest group that unsuccessfully litigated the same claim. *Robertson v. City of Rialto*, 226 Cal. App. 4th 1499, 173 Cal. Rtpr. 3d 66 (2014).

(e) A Governmental entity may be in privity with the individual claimants it represents. *See, e.g., Rynsburger v. Dairymen's Fertilizer Coop., Inc.*, 266 Cal. App. 2d 269, 72 Cal. Rptr. 102 (1968) (holding property owner residents bound by adverse judgment against city which represented their interests); *Citizens For Open Access to Sand and Tide, Inc. v. Seadrift Assn.*, 60 Cal. App. 4th 1053, 1069–74, 71 Cal. Rptr. 2d 77 (1998) (finding private public interest group concerned with the recreational access to beaches was in privity with state agencies in prior lawsuit and therefore bound by a settlement agreement reached between the state agencies and various beachfront homeowners); *but see Victa v. Merle Norman Cosmetics, Inc.*, 19 Cal. App. 4th 454, 24 Cal. Rptr. 2d 117 (1993) (finding EEOC represented public interest rather than individual's in prior age discrimination action and was not in privity with individual plaintiff; injunctive consent decree in prior EEOC action therefore did not preclude individual plaintiff's age discrimination action against same defendant).

(6) *Joint and Severally Liable Parties.* In *DKN Holdings LLC v. Faerber*, 61 Cal. 4th 813, 826, 189 Cal. Rptr. 3d 809, 352 P.3d 378 (2015), the Supreme Court ruled that although parties who are jointly and severally liable on a contractual obligation may be sued in separate actions, they are not considered in privity with each other for purposes of issue or claim preclusion.

(7) *Class Actions.* A judgment on the merits in a properly certified class action is res judicata as to the absent class members as well as to the named parties. *See, e.g., Frazier v. City of Richmond*, 184 Cal. App. 3d 1491, 228 Cal. Rptr. 376 (1986) (holding declaratory judgment in prior class action on behalf of all members of city police and firemen's pension fund barred current action by fund beneficiaries because plaintiffs were members of the prior class and raised the same issues determined adversely to them in the prior class action); *Louie v. BFS Retail & Commercial Operations, LLC*,

178 Cal. App. 4th 1544, 1555, 101 Cal. Rptr. 3d 441 (2009) (collecting cases). The absent class members are in privity with the named plaintiffs and are bound by the class judgment so long as their interests were adequately protected. *Frazier, supra; Louie, supra.*

(8) *Privity Between Government Agencies.* One of the more problematic applications of the privity doctrine concerns the relationship between different agencies or branches of a governmental entity, as is illustrated by *Dyson v. California State Personnel Bd.* and the various cases discussed therein. *See also People v. Sims, supra* (concluding county district attorney in privity with county welfare department regarding welfare fraud proceedings against defendant). What factors did the court in *Dyson* find significant in concluding that the California State Personnel Board was in privity with the District Attorney in the prior criminal proceeding? Does *Dyson* stand for the proposition that two public agencies will automatically be considered in privity where they are branches of the same governmental entity, such as the same county or the state? Must some additional relationship be shown to find that they are "sufficiently close"? Or are agents of the same government always in privity with each other because they represent not their own rights, but rights of the government? *See People v. Sims, supra,* 32 Cal. 3d at 486.

(9) *Privity Between Prosecutor and DMV.* The courts of appeal were divided on the question of whether the DMV in a license revocation administrative hearing is in privity with the prosecuting attorney in a prior criminal DUI proceeding involving the same incident. Some courts have concluded that the relationship between the DMV and the district attorney was "sufficiently close" to support a finding of privity, since both agencies represent the state and have the same interest in protecting the public; but other courts reached the opposite conclusion. The California Supreme Court addressed this question in *Gikas v. Zolin,* 6 Cal. 4th 841, 25 Cal. Rptr. 2d 500, 863 P.2d 745 (1993). The Court acknowledged the conflicting lower court conclusions, but found the privity question now governed by Vehicle Code § 13353.2(e) as amended effective 1990. "[W]hatever similarities there may or may not be between this situation and that of *People v. Sims,*" the court observed, "[t]he Legislature [has now] made the policy decision that ... administrative proceedings before the DMV will *not* have a preclusive effect on related criminal proceedings." *Id.* at 851. The Legislature also specified in § 13353.2(e) exactly what preclusive effect the criminal proceeding has on the administrative: an acquittal on the criminal charges precludes DMV proceedings to suspend a license. *Id.* at 852. The court then construed § 13353.2(e) to intend that *only* a criminal "acquittal" on the merits will affect the DMV administrative proceedings; a dismissal of the criminal charges based on unlawful arrest does not preclude relitigation of that issue in a DMV license suspension proceeding. *Id.* at 852–57.

(10) *No Privity When Distinct Government Agencies.* Where two governmental agencies have distinct identities, constituencies and interests, they may not be considered in privity even where they are branches of the same government. In *Traub v. Bd. of Retirement,* 34 Cal. 3d 793, 195 Cal. Rptr. 681, 670 P.2d 335 (1983), the

plaintiff, an injured county employee, was awarded benefits against the County of Los Angeles by a decision of the Workers' Compensation Appeals Board (WCAB). The WCAB found that plaintiff's disability was due to an employment-connected injury. Plaintiff then applied for a service-connected disability pension with the Los Angeles County Board of Retirement. The Retirement Board denied plaintiff a full pension, finding that his disability was not service-connected. Plaintiff sought judicial review, and argued that the County Retirement Board was collaterally estopped from redetermining the issue of whether his disability was employment-connected. Plaintiff argued that the decision of the WCAB was conclusive on this issue, and that the Retirement Board was in privity with the county in the WCAB proceeding.

The Supreme Court concluded that there was no privity between the County, against which the WCAB award was made, and the County Retirement Board. The court found that the County Retirement Board did not act as a mere agent of the County, but instead was an independent administrator of an entity distinct and separate from the County. The court noted that the retirement system was distinct and independent of the County, that the constituency of that system was not limited to County employees, and that funding for the system was not limited to county employees. Consequently, the distinctive identity, constituency and interests of the County Retirement Board did not support privity between it and the County of Los Angeles. *Traub*, 34 Cal. 3d at 798–99.

> (a) Is the reasoning and conclusion in *Traub* consistent with the policy considerations which comprise the doctrine of privity? In what way is the interest of the County in resisting a workers' compensation claim any different than the County Retirement Board's scrutiny of a claim for a service-connected disability allowance? Is not the relationship between the County and the County Retirement Board "sufficiently close" with respect to the issue of whether the employee's disability was employment-connected?

> (b) The *Traub* reasoning has been followed by other courts. *E.g., Bianchi v. City of San Diego*, 214 Cal. App. 3d 563, 569–72, 262 Cal. Rptr. 566 (1989) (finding City of San Diego not in privity with City Retirement Board); *City of Gilroy v. State Bd of Equalization*, 212 Cal. App. 3d 589, 605–607, 260 Cal. Rptr. 723 (1989) (ruling City not in privity with State Board of Equalization with respect to tax refund issue). However, where a retirement board does act as the agent for city or county, the requisite privity will be found. *See French v. Rishell*, 40 Cal. 2d 477, 254 P.2d 26 (1953).

(11) *Stranger Not Bound by Prior Judgment.* Generally, a person who is not a party or in privity with a party is a "stranger" to an action, and is not bound by the judgment. *See, e.g., Traub v. Bd. of Retirement, supra.* This is, of course, a due process requirement which ensures that every person is entitled to an opportunity for her own day in court prior to deprivation of property, or at least the functional equivalent when in privity. *Clemmer v. Hartford Ins. Co., supra*, 22 Cal. 3d at 875; *Courtney v. Waring*, 191 Cal. App. 3d 1434, 237 Cal. Rptr. 233 (1987).

(a) Is it consistent with due process to bind a nonparty because a party to the litigation has the same interests as the nonparty, and, although not formally representing the nonparty's interests, in fact fully (albeit unsuccessfully) defends that interest? In what sense has that nonparty had his *own* day in court? Does the nonparty have an obligation to become a party when he knows of the litigation and could easily intervene? Does the nonparty's failure to intervene mean that his due process rights have been vindicated because he had a fair *opportunity* to have his own day in court but chose to waive it? See *Lewis v. County of Sacramento*, 218 Cal. App. 3d 214, 266 Cal. Rptr. 678 (1990) (ruling nonparty bound by a prior judgment where the nonparty had interests identical to a party in the action which were adequately represented by that party, knew of the litigation, participated in discovery, and easily could have intervened and become a party).

In *Martin v. Wilks*, 490 U.S. 755, 765, 109 S. Ct. 2180, 104 L. Ed 2d 835 (1989), the U.S. Supreme Court held: "Joinder as a party, rather than knowledge of a lawsuit and an opportunity to intervene, is the method by which potential parties are subjected to the jurisdiction of the court and bound by a judgment or decree. The parties to a lawsuit presumably know better than anyone else the nature and scope of relief sought in the action, and at whose expense such relief might be granted. It makes sense, therefore, to place on them a burden of bringing in additional parties where such a step is indicated, rather than placing on potential additional parties a duty to intervene when they acquire knowledge of the lawsuit."

(b) In *Rodgers v. Sargent Controls & Aerospace*, 136 Cal. App. 4th 82, 38 Cal. Rptr. 3d 528 (2006), the plaintiff worker sued the defendant company for personal injuries caused by asbestos exposure. The plaintiff alleged that the defendant was the successor entity of the source of his exposure to asbestos. The issue of successor liability had been litigated and resolved in favor of the defendant in two prior actions, in which the other plaintiffs were represented by the same attorneys as the plaintiff in *Rodgers*. The superior court found the plaintiff was collaterally estopped from claiming that the defendant was a corporate successor, and entered summary judgment for defendant.

The Court of Appeal reversed, ruling that the plaintiff was not in privity with the other workers in the prior lawsuits and therefore collateral estoppel cannot be applied. The *Rodgers* court concluded that the application of collateral estoppel would violate due process even though imposing issue preclusion would further the cognizable interests of avoiding harassment of the defendant with repeated litigation, reduce the possibility of inconsistent judgments, and promoting judicial economy. *Rodgers*, 136 Cal. App. 4th at 91–94. Although the plaintiff had a theoretical interest in the resolution of the successor liability issue in the prior cases, he had no proprietary interest in those cases. Moreover, the plaintiff had no control over the plaintiffs in the other proceedings and did not stand in a close relationship with them, nor did those plaintiffs act as his representative. The fact that the plaintiff was represented by the same counsel did not justify a finding of privity, at least without evidence that through his attorney the plaintiff participated in or controlled the adjudication of the successor liability issue in the prior actions. *Rodgers*, 136 Cal. App. 4th at 92–94.

(12) *Adequate Representation.* In the context of collateral estoppel and the privity doctrine, due process requires that the party to be estopped must be have an identity of interests with the losing party in the prior litigation and that interest must have been adequately represented in the prior litigation. Did the losing party in a prior action "adequately represent" the interests of the plaintiff in the current action where the current plaintiff identifies additional evidence and legal arguments not presented in the prior action? In *Mooney v. Caspari*, 138 Cal. App. 4th 704, 41 Cal. Rptr. 3d 728 (2006), the court ruled that a finding of privity does not depend upon an identity of evidence or arguments presented, nor upon the result obtained. According to the court, the doctrine of privity does "not require an assessment of the quality or competence of the prior legal representation provided." *Mooney, supra*, 138 Cal. App. 4th at 721. Do you agree with the *Mooney* court's reasoning? Does *Mooney* mean a representative party's conduct that shows a lack of incentive or resources to litigate a common interest is irrelevant to a privity determination? *See Gottlieb v. Kest*, 141 Cal. App. 4th 110, 149–56, 46 Cal. Rptr. 3d 7 (2006) (concluding plaintiff's individual liability as an owner of closely-held companies was not established by prior default judgment against the companies because the plaintiff was not in privity with his companies; the companies could not afford counsel, had no assets, had no incentive to defend, and therefore did not adequately represent plaintiff interests in the prior litigation).

(13) *Federal Privity Doctrine Compared.* In *Taylor v. Sturgell*, 553 U. S. 880, 128 S. Ct. 2161, 171 L. Ed. 2d 155 (2008), the U. S. Supreme Court discussed the federal common law doctrine of privity applicable when determining the preclusive effect of a prior federal court judgment in federal question cases. The Supreme Court carefully delineated six categories of recognized exceptions to the general rule against nonparty preclusion, but specifically rejected the "virtual representation" or "close enough" exception because it is based an amorphous balancing test, has unclear standards, and does not sufficiently require adequate representation of a nonparty. *Taylor*, 553 U.S. at 898–902.

§ 8.05   Law of the Case; Judicial Estoppel

[A]   Law of the Case Doctrine

Clemente v. State of California

Supreme Court of California
40 Cal. 3d 202, 219 Cal. Rptr. 445, 707 P.2d 818 (1985)

BROUSSARD, JUSTICE.

This case presents a unique cause of action as well as a somewhat complicated procedural history. Plaintiff Jose Clemente was severely injured when he was struck by a motorcycle while attempting to cross a street. The motorcyclist was never apprehended. Clemente brought suit against the State of California and Highway Patrol Officer Arthur Loxsom, alleging that Loxsom was negligent in failing to ascertain the identity of the motorcyclist.

After the trial court sustained defendants' demurrer to the complaint, the Court of Appeal reversed and remanded, holding that plaintiff could state a cause of action against Loxsom and the state. (*Clemente v. State of California* (1980) 101 Cal. App. 3d 374, 379–380 [161 Cal. Rptr. 799], hereinafter *Clemente I*.) After amending his complaint in conformity with *Clemente I*, plaintiff proceeded to trial and obtained a $2,150,000.21 judgment. Defendants appeal.

I. FACTS

On January 27, 1975, plaintiff was struck by a motorcycle while attempting to cross at an intersection. Officer Arthur Loxsom of the California Highway Patrol was on his way to freeway patrol when he was hailed by a passing motorist and directed to the scene of the accident. When Loxsom arrived at the scene, plaintiff was attempting to crawl out of the crosswalk and onto the sidewalk. He was being assisted by a group of bystanders. A man was pushing a motorcycle out of the street. Loxsom turned on his flashers in order to indicate that an accident had occurred. Several people came up to him in order to tell him how the accident had happened. He called an ambulance and the Los Angeles Police Department (LAPD). He may have also directed traffic around the intersection.

The motorcyclist, along with a van driver who had been in the lane next to the motorcycle, also approached Loxsom. The van driver told Loxsom that he had stopped to allow plaintiff to cross but that the motorcyclist had not done so and had struck him. The motorcyclist admitted that he had hit plaintiff, explaining that he had not seen him. He asked Loxsom what he should do with the motorcycle, and Loxsom directed him to move it out of the street and place it near the curb. Loxsom told the motorcyclist not to leave the scene and to await the arrival of LAPD. Loxsom left before either the ambulance or LAPD arrived. He did not obtain the name or license of the motorcyclist or the license number of the motorcycle. He also did not get any identification from the van driver. The motorcyclist and the van driver left before LAPD arrived. Despite later efforts they were never found.

Loxsom never spoke to plaintiff or examined him to ascertain whether he was seriously injured. By the time he was taken to the hospital plaintiff had lapsed into a coma and was in critical condition. He suffered severe brain damage, and is paralyzed, unable to speak, incontinent and must depend upon others to attend to his daily needs.

II. LAW OF THE CASE

Defendants contend that *Clemente I* was erroneously decided relying upon our subsequent decision in *Williams v. State of California* (1983) 34 Cal. 3d 18 [192 Cal. Rptr. 233, 664 P.2d 137] and other decisions and that Loxsom did not owe a duty to plaintiff to exercise due care in his investigation. We have concluded that the decision in *Clemente I* is law of the case, establishing Loxsom's duty to exercise due care.

In *Clemente I*, the court concluded that plaintiff could state a cause of action for negligent breach of a duty to exercise due care in the conduct of the investigation undertaken by Loxsom. The court stated:

> "The injury plaintiff alleged in this third amended complaint was the virtual destruction of any opportunity on his part to obtain compensation for his physical injuries from the apparent tortfeasor, the motorcyclist, by reason of the officer's negligence in the conduct of his investigation of the traffic accident in failing to obtain the motorcyclist's identity. What is involved under these allegations is not the discretion of Officer Loxsom in deciding whether to investigate the traffic accident, pursuant to the discretionary authority vested in him by Vehicle Code section 2412, but instead only his negligence in his conduct of the discretionary investigation. Neither the discretionary immunity of Government Code section 820.2, nor the more specific discretionary immunity of failure to enforce a statute (Gov. Code, §§ 821, 818.2) immunizes the officer and the state from the legal consequences of this negligence. Government, through its agents, is held to the same standard of care the law requires of private citizens in the performance of duties imposed or assumed.

> "We think that possible liability of the officer and the state in this case is indicated by our reasoning in the aforementioned decision of this panel, *Mann v. State of California, supra,* [1977] 70 Cal. App. 3d 773 [139 Cal. Rptr. 82]. There, we said that the lack of police protection immunity granted by Government Code section 845, extends essentially only to protection against crime and to that resulting from budgetary neglect. It does not extend to negligence as such. There, we also said that a special relationship in tort law obtained between the California highway patrol officer there involved and the stranded motorists by reason of their dependence on his expertise. Here, the completely disabled and apparently incompetent plaintiff was likewise completely dependent on Officer Loxsom following the traffic accident." (101 Cal. App. 3d at pp. 379–380).

In *People v. Shuey* (1975) 13 Cal. 3d 835, 841 [120 Cal. Rptr. 83, 533 P.2d 211], we explained the doctrine of the law of the case in this manner: "'The doctrine of the law of the case is this: That where, upon an appeal, the supreme court, in deciding the appeal, states in its opinion a principle or rule of law necessary to the decision, that principle or rule becomes the law of the case and must be adhered to throughout its subsequent progress, both in the lower court and upon subsequent appeal, and, as here assumed, in any subsequent suit for the same cause of action, and this although in its subsequent consideration this court may be clearly of the opinion that the former decision is erroneous in that particular.'"

> "The principle applies to criminal as well as civil matters, and to decisions of intermediate appellate courts as well as courts of last resort. 'Where a decision upon appeal has been rendered by a District Court of Appeal and the case is returned upon a reversal, and a second appeal comes to this court directly or intermediately, for reasons of policy and convenience, this court

generally will not inquire into the merits of said first decision, but will regard it as the law of the case.'"

However, the doctrine of law of the case which has been recognized as being harsh is merely a rule of procedure and does not go to the power of the court. It will not be adhered to where its application will result in an unjust decision. The principal ground for making an exception to the doctrine of law of the case is an intervening or contemporaneous change in the law.

Defendants contend that the exception is applicable here claiming that an intervening change in the law has occurred. They rely on *Williams v. State of California* (1983) 34 Cal. 3d 18 [192 Cal. Rptr. 233, 664 P.2d 137].

In *Williams*, plaintiff was injured when a piece of a heated brake drum from a passing truck was propelled through her windshield. Highway patrolmen arrived within a few minutes of the accident. Plaintiff claimed that the patrolmen were negligent in failing to test for the heat of the object which struck her, to secure the names of witnesses, and to attempt investigation or pursuit of the owner or driver of the truck.

The court concluded that the complaint did not state a cause of action. It was pointed out that in the absence of a special relationship, a person who has not created a peril has no duty to come to the aid of another and that the State Highway Patrol has the right but not the duty to investigate accidents. It was also pointed out that cases had denied recovery for injuries caused by the failure of police personnel to respond to requests for assistance, to investigate properly or to investigate at all when the police had not induced reliance on a promise, express or implied, that they would provide protection. The court rejected *Clemente I* stating that the duty to obtain the motorcyclist's name as pleaded in that case was "based solely" on the fact of dependence. (34 Cal. 3d at pp. 23–27).

The court also concluded that under the good Samaritan doctrine the Highway Patrol may have a duty to members of the public to exercise due care when the patrol voluntarily assumes a protective duty toward a certain member of the public and undertakes action on behalf of that member thereby inducing reliance, when an express promise to warn of a danger has induced reliance, or when the actions of the patrol place a person in peril or increase the risk of harm. The court specifically recognized that a duty of care may arise when the conduct of a patrolman in a situation of dependency results in detrimental reliance on him for protection. (34 Cal. 3d at pp. 23–25.) The court discussed *Mann v. State of California, supra,* 70 Cal. App. 3d 773 (34 Cal. 3d at p. 25) which was, as we have seen, the case relied upon in *Clemente I*. *Mann* was characterized as a case where the officers took "affirmative steps to provide assistance, lulling the injured parties into a false sense of security and perhaps preventing other assistance from being sought." (34 Cal. 3d at p. 25.)

Although *Williams* rejected *Clemente I*, it does not establish that Officer Loxsom did not have a duty to exercise care in his investigation to protect plaintiff. To the contrary, *Williams* held that the conduct of a patrolman in a situation of dependency resulting in detrimental reliance may give rise to a duty of care and recognized that there may be a duty to refrain from conduct which prevents others from giving assistance. The record herein shows that the officer spoke to the drivers of the van and motorcycle and that there were a number of bystanders assisting plaintiff after the accident who could have obtained the drivers' names and license numbers. *Williams* does not preclude liability where the officer's conduct prevents other assistance, and thus it does not constitute a change in the law warranting rejection of the law of the case that Officer Loxsom could have a duty to exercise care.

In the circumstances of the instant case, it has not been shown that application of the doctrine of law of the case will result in an unjust decision. First, the parties went to trial prior to *Williams* and presented evidence with the understanding that the officer's liability would be governed by the standard set forth in *Clemente I*. Secondly, *Clemente I* did not misapply prior law in a way which resulted in "substantial injustice." Although *Williams* served to clarify what the duties of a highway patrol officer were under a given set of circumstances, our opinion in that case recognized the possibility that such an officer might owe a member of the public a duty of care based on conduct like that shown here. * * *

The judgment is affirmed.

BIRD, CHIEF JUSTICE, and MOSK and REYNOSO, JUSCTICES, concurred.

KAUS, JUSTICE, Concurring.

I concur in the result and in all parts of the court's opinion, except—if I read it correctly—its view of the impact of *Williams v. State of California* (1983) 34 Cal. 3d 18 [192 Cal. Rptr. 233, 664 P.2d 137], on the law of the case as laid down in *Clemente I*. The court makes a valiant effort to reconcile the two decisions but, with all respect, it does not quite work. Of course *Williams* does not preclude liability where the officer's conduct prevents other assistance, but there is no evidence here that this was the case. At most, the situation was such that had trial counsel known that such proof was essential, he might have been able to produce it. The real—and only—point is that *Clemente I* did not require such proof and *Williams* was not decided until after the trial of this case. Under such circumstances, refusal to apply the doctrine of the law of the case would be most unfair. Just as that doctrine will not be adhered to "where its application will result in an unjust decision" (*DiGenova v. State Board of Education* (1962) 57 Cal. 2d 167, 179 [18 Cal. Rptr. 369, 367 P.2d 865]), it should not be laid aside where to do so would be manifestly wrong.

GRODIN, JUSTICE, concurred.

LUCAS, JUSTICE, dissenting.

I respectfully dissent. The majority, after correctly describing the doctrine of "law of the case" and the exceptions thereto, promptly ignores its own description. When law of the case might apply, "[the] principal ground for making an exception to the doctrine … is an intervening or contemporaneous change in the law. [Citations.]" What could be a clearer intervening change in the law than a Supreme Court decision expressly disapproving the prior Court of Appeal holding in the same case on the same issue?

In *Williams v. State of California* (1983) 34 Cal. 3d 18 [192 Cal. Rptr. 233, 664 P.2d 137], we summarized the decision in *Clemente v. State of California* (1980) 101 Cal. App. 3d 274 [161 Cal. Rptr. 799] (hereinafter *Clemente I*) as one in which the Court of Appeal had found liability even in the absence of an allegation that "the officer's investigation caused plaintiff not to undertake one of his own." (*Williams*, 34 Cal. 3d at p. 26.) That holding followed the finding that the pedestrian was "*dependent* on the highway patrolman." (*Ibid.*, italics in original.)

Our analysis in *Williams* concluded that more was required before a cause of action could be stated against a police official and we, therefore, *expressly disapproved Clemente I* to the extent it was inconsistent with our reasoning. (34 Cal. 3d at p. 28, fn. 9.) We concluded instead that the general rule that "one has no duty to come to the aid of another" generally applied. (*Id.*, at p. 23.) Only when a "special relationship arises" may liability be imposed. (*Id.*, at p. 24.) Thus, "when the state, through its agents, voluntarily assumes a protective duty toward a certain member of the public and undertakes action on behalf of that member, thereby inducing reliance, it is held to the same standard of care as a private person or organization. [Citations.]" (*Ibid.*) However, where allegations amount only to nonfeasance without assertions that the officer in some manner promised to undertake the tasks left undone or otherwise induced reliance on the part of the plaintiff who was in any manner prevented from acting, no duty exists and no liability will be imposed.

In other words, dependency *alone* does not create a relationship which gives rise to a duty to assist or protect the injured person. In *Williams*, the defendant had not alleged that "the officers assured her, either expressly or impliedly that they would do any of the acts she faults them for not doing, [nor were there] allegations that they conducted themselves in such a manner as to warrant reliance upon them to do the acts which the plaintiff alleges they should have done, nor finally is there any hint that they prevented plaintiff from conducting an investigation of her own." (34 Cal. 3d at p. 27, fn. omitted.) Similarly, in this case no such assertions were made.

In his petition before this court, plaintiff stated that because this case had been tried under the authority of *Clemente I*, "there was no need to plead or prove that the officer's conduct prevented other assistance from being sought, or caused plaintiff (or someone acting on his behalf) not to undertake an investigation of his own. [¶] That *issue* was *not* present either at the trial or appellate level in this proceeding." He then went on to ask us nonetheless to match the facts adduced against the *Williams* standard and to conclude that the facts were sufficient to permit him an opportunity *to amend and retry the case* which had *not* previously addressed this aspect of the officer's conduct.

The parties proceeded in the belief that *Clemente I* stated the applicable law. Even under that approach, evidence regarding the effects of the officer's conduct as are asserted here would have been relevant and of assistance to the plaintiff. As the Court of Appeal in the instant case stated, unlike the situation in *Williams*, "plaintiff in the present case has filed four amended complaints, had a jury trial on the merits, and has still been unable to establish any of the required elements necessary to establish a duty of care owed by defendant State. Clearly, further action would be futile." Accordingly, I would reverse the judgment.

Notes and Questions regarding Law of the Case

(1) *Law of the Case, Generally.* The doctrine of law of the case is related to the doctrine of res judicata/collateral estoppel, but the two doctrines apply to different circumstances. What is their basic difference in application? The doctrine of law of the case is also recognized by the court as "being harsh" and as "merely a rule of procedure." What is meant by this recognition? What appears to be the consequence of this recognition? Is not res judicata/collateral estoppel also a "rule of procedure," and does it not also produce some "harsh" results? Which doctrine do you think is viewed less favorably by the courts, and, consequently, is applied with more flexibly? Why?

(2) *Exception: Intervening Change in Law.* As *Clemente v. State of California* indicates, the courts have fashioned a number of exceptions to the doctrine. The most common exception is when there has been an intervening change in the law since the prior appellate decision. *See, e.g., People v. Whitt*, 51 Cal. 3d 620, 638–39, 274 Cal. Rptr. 252, 798 P.2d 849 (1990); *Subsequent Injuries Fund v. Indus. Accident Comm'n*, 53 Cal. 2d 392, 395, 1 Cal. Rptr. 833, 348 P.2d 193 (1960). But, as *Clemente* illustrates, not all changes in the law will justify disregarding the established law of the case. The change must be in the *controlling* rule of law. *See George Arakelian Farms, Inc. v. A. L. R. B.*, 49 Cal. 3d 1279, 1292, n.9, 265 Cal. Rptr. 162, 783 P.2d 749 (1989). If there is an intervening change in a controlling rule of law, does this exception automatically apply? What position did Justice Kaus take in his concurring opinion? *See also George Arakelian Farms, supra*, 49 Cal. 3d at 1291 ("[J]udicial economy demands that [appellant] demonstrate that failure to apply [an intervening change in case law] would be a manifest misapplication of existing legal principles and would result in a substantial injustice"); *but see DiGenova v. State Bd. of Ed.*, 57 Cal. 2d 167, 179–80, 18 Cal. Rptr. 369, 367 P.2d 865 (1962) (ruling application of doctrine would obviously result in manifest injustice where law clarified by intervening appellate decision).

(3) *Exception: Manifest Injustice.* Another general exception to law of the case is where application of the doctrine will result in a "manifest injustice" or an "unjust decision." *Yu v. Signet Bank Virginia*, 103 Cal. App. 4th 298, 311, 126 Cal. Rptr. 2d 516 (2002). Under what circumstances would there be a "manifest injustice" to apply law of the case when there has been no intervening change in controlling law? *See Searle v. Allstate Life Ins. Co.*, 38 Cal. 3d 425, 212 Cal. Rptr. 466, 696 P.2d 1308 (1985) (refusing to follow rule of law established by Court of Appeal during prior appeal because to do so would constitute a manifest misapplication of existing principles resulting in substantial injustice).

In *Searle*, the Supreme Court also viewed itself as not bound by law of the case rule because the Court determined that there should be a reversal of the current appeal on a ground that was not considered on the prior appeal, and that therefore the "reason for the rule is inoperative." *Id.* at 435–36. What is the primary purpose served by the law of the case doctrine? Why is that reason for the doctrine inoperative in circumstances such as those in *Searle*?

(4) *Exception: Unpresented Issues.* The doctrine also does not apply to issues of law that might have been, but were not, presented and determined on a prior appeal. *DiGenova v. State Bd. of Ed.*, *supra*, 57 Cal. 2d at 179; *George Arakelian Farms, supra,* 49 Cal. 3d at 1291; *Amerigas, Inc. v. Landstar Ranger, Inc.*, 230 Cal. App. 4th 1153, 1166, 179 Cal. Rptr. 3d 330 (2014). Why not?

(5) *Issues of Law.* As the name of the doctrine implies, law of the case applies to issues of law and not to issues of fact. This distinction is not always easy to determine. *See People v. Shuey*, 13 Cal. 3d 835, 842–43, 120 Cal. Rptr. 83, 533 P.2d 211 (1975) (and cases cited therein). If a party wishes to challenge a ruling made by an appellate court during a prior appeal, is it more advantageous to argue that the ruling was on an issue of law or of fact? If the court in the subsequent appeal determines that the prior ruling was on an issue of law, the law of the case doctrine will apply. What doctrine applies if the court determines that the prior ruling was on an issue of fact?

(6) *Extraordinary Writs.* Law of the case can apply to pretrial extraordinary writ proceedings. *See Kowis v. Howard*, 3 Cal. 4th 888, 894, 12 Cal. Rptr. 2d 728, 838 P.2d 250 (1992). When an appellate court issues an alternative writ, the matter is fully briefed, there is an opportunity for oral argument, and the cause is decided by a written opinion; the resultant holding establishes law of the case upon a later appeal from the final judgment. *Id.* However, the Supreme Court recently held on policy grounds that a summary denial of an extraordinary writ petition does not establish law of the case even though the sole possible ground for the denial was that the court acted on the merits. *Kowis v. Howard, supra,* 3 Cal. 4th at 897–901. Likewise, the Court ruled, for the same policy reasons, that an appellate court's summary denial of a motion to dismiss on appeal should not preclude later consideration of the issue after full review of the entire case. *Id.* What policy reasons led the Supreme Court to these rulings?

[B] Judicial Estoppel Doctrine

Several recent decisions have invoked the doctrine of judicial estoppel, which prevents a party from asserting a position in a legal proceeding that is contrary to a position previously taken in the same or some earlier proceeding. *See, e.g., Blix Street Records, Inc. v. Cassidy*, 191 Cal. App. 4th 39, 47–51,119 Cal. Rptr. 3d 574 (2010) (holding that even if the settlement agreement was not actually enforceable, plaintiffs are judicially estopped from denying its enforceability because they represented to the trial court that the case had settled and the trial court terminated the trial and discharged the jury in reliance on plaintiffs' representation); *Levin v. Ligon*, 140 Cal. App. 4th 1456, 45 Cal. Rptr. 3d 560 (2006) (ruling ex-husband's prior legal malpractice action in England, which he settled after asserting that he lost his right to any interest in the financial assets held by his former wife and accumulated during their marriage, estopped him from claiming a community property interest in these same assets); *Jackson v. Cnty. of Los Angeles*, 60 Cal. App. 4th 171, 70 Cal. Rptr. 2d 96 (1997) (concluding judicial estoppel barred plaintiff's action alleging defendant County violated the Americans with Disability Act by refusing to reinstate plaintiff as a safety police officer, the only job plaintiff wanted and a job whose duties plaintiff admitted involved substantial stress, because plaintiff had previously received a stipulated workers' compensation award based on an agreed finding that he needed a stress-free job).

The judicial estoppel doctrine applies when:

(1) [T]he same party has taken two positions; (2) the positions were taken in judicial or quasi-judicial administrative proceedings; (3) the party was successful in asserting the first position (i.e., the tribunal adopted the position or accepted is as true; (4) the two positions are totally inconsistent; and (5) the first position was not taken as a result of ignorance, fraud, or mistake.

Aguilar v. Lerner, 32 Cal. 4th 974, 986–87, 12 Cal. Rptr. 3d 287, 88 P.3d 24 (2004) (quoting *Jackson, supra*, 60 Cal. App. 4th at 183).

Because judicial estoppel is an equitable doctrine, its application is discretionary even where all necessary elements are present. For example, a party cannot invoke judicial estoppel where its application would contravene a strong and clear statutory mandate. *MW Erectors, Inc. v. Niederhauser Ornamental & Metal Works Co.*, 36 Cal. 4th 412, 421–25, 30 Cal. Rptr. 3d 755, 115 P.3d 41 (2005) (ruling judicial estoppel does not bar defendant contractor, by virtue of allegedly inconsistent positions it took in related litigation, from asserting the defense that plaintiff subcontractor was unlicensed and therefore barred from recovery under Bus. & Prof. Code § 7031). However, because judicial estoppel is an equitable doctrine designed to protect the integrity of the judiciary, the doctrine may apply even in circumstances where the earlier position was not adopted by the tribunal. *See, e.g., Drain v. Betz Lab., Inc.*, 69 Cal. App. 4th 950, 957–60, 81 Cal. Rptr. 2d 864 (1999); *Thomas v. Gordon*, 85 Cal. App. 4th 113, 118–120, 102 Cal. Rptr. 2d 28 (2000); *Jackson, supra*, 60 Cal. App. 4th at 183–84, n. 8; *but see Jogani v. Jogani*, 141 Cal. App. 4th 158, 45 Cal. Rptr. 3d 792 (2006) (finding judicial estoppel inapplicable because court in prior proceeding did not adopt or accept the truth of the plaintiff's inconsistent position, eliminating any threat to judicial integrity); *Gottlieb v. Kest*, 141 Cal. App. 4th 110, 46 Cal. Rptr. 3d 7 (2006) (same); *Minish v. Hanuman Fellowship*, 214 Cal. App. 4th 437, 448–55, 154 Cal. Rptr. 3d 87 (2013) (noting the view that judicial estoppel may apply even when a litigant's initial position was unsuccessful is not the majority view and declining to uphold the application in the absence of success).

How does judicial estoppel differ from collateral estoppel? Equitable estoppel? *See Jackson, supra*, 60 Cal. App. 4th at 182–83 (distinguishing judicial estoppel from collateral estoppel and equitable estoppel). Law of the case?

Chapter 9

Stating Claims and Defenses: Pleadings

§ 9.01 Introductory Note

California's pleading system derives from the Field Code reforms of the mid-19th century. New York's adoption of a Code of Civil Procedure followed closely upon the 1848 Report of the Commissioners on Practice and Pleadings of New York and its head, David Dudley Field. California, which joined the Union in 1850, chose the "modern" system of the time for its pleading model. The Field Code abolished the common law forms of action, merged law and equity, limited the types of pleadings, limited the effects of technical errors, and required pleading only the "facts constituting the cause of action." *See* CCP §§ 307, 422.10, 425.10, and 475.

California remains nominally a "code pleading" state. It has declined to follow the notice pleading model of the federal rules. Section 425.10(a) still requires the complaint to contain "a statement of the facts constituting the cause of action, in ordinary and concise language." However, California has liberalized the code pleading requirements. Case law reflects a reduced concern with pleading ultimate facts in precisely the correct format. Pleading of common causes of action, such as negligence, deviates considerably from the code pleading model. The theory of the pleadings has been abandoned. Although the elements of a cause of action must be present in a pleading, if the allegations give sufficient notice of plaintiff's factual theory, this is usually sufficient. Alternative and inconsistent theories may be asserted. Joinder of claims and parties has been liberalized by adopting rules similar to (and in many cases identical to) the federal rules. Amendment is liberally allowed through trial. The Judicial Council has also adopted Official Form pleadings—complaints, cross-complaints and answers—for several basic types of claims and causes of action. *See* CCP § 425.12. Identifying California as a code pleading state is thus both misleading and an oversimplification.

Section 422.10 lists the pleadings in California courts: "The pleadings allowed in civil actions are complaints, demurrers, answers and cross-complaints."

§ 9.02 The Complaint

[A] Pleading Ultimate Facts

Semole v. Sansoucie

Court of Appeal of California, Second Appellate District
28 Cal. App. 3d 714, 104 Cal. Rptr. 897 (1972)

HERDON, ACTING PRESIDING JUSTICE.

Plaintiffs (appellants) appeal from the order dismissing this action brought against defendant to recover damages for wrongful death. The dismissal was entered after defendant's demurrer to plaintiffs' second amended complaint had been sustained without leave to amend on the ground that no cause of action had been stated.

The original complaint, filed on July 11, 1966, alleges that on May 9, 1966, plaintiffs' son, John Semole, was fatally injured while loading piggyback trailers onto railroad flatcars. It named as defendants the decedent's employer, Pacific Motor Trucking Company, and a fellow employee, Robert J. Sansoucie, and 10 Does.

On December 11, 1970, the court below granted the motion of Pacific Motor Trucking Company for summary judgment and dismissed the action as to that defendant on the ground that the action against decedent's employer was barred by Labor Code section 3601 which, with inapplicable exceptions, limits the remedy to the recovery of workmen's compensation. Appellants took no appeal from that judgment but have sought to maintain the action against Sansoucie, decedent's fellow employee, by invoking Labor Code section 3601, subdivision (a)(3) which read at that time as follows: "(a) Where the conditions of compensation exist, the right to recover such compensation, pursuant to the provisions of this division is, except as provided in Section 3706, the exclusive remedy for injury or death of an employee against the employer or against any other employee of the employer acting within the scope of his employment, except that an employee, or his dependents in the event of his death, shall, in addition to the right to compensation against the employer, have a right to bring an action at law for damages against such other employee, as if this division did not apply, in the following cases:

"(3) When the injury or death is proximately caused by an act of such other employee which evinces a reckless disregard for the safety of the employee injured, and a calculated and conscious willingness to permit injury or death to such employee."

… Sansoucie filed a general demurrer to the complaint and sought a dismissal of the action on the grounds: (1) that summons was not served upon him within the three-year period as provided in Code of Civil Procedure section 581a; and (2) that the action was barred by Labor Code section 3601.

[The trial court refused to dismiss the action on the first ground but sustained the demurrer, with leave to amend, on the ground that the complaint did not allege facts sufficient to state a cause of action under Labor Code section 3601, subdivision (a)(3).

Plaintiffs filed a first and second amended complaint. In each case, defendant demurred on the ground that a cause of action under Labor Code section 3601, subdivision (a)(3) had still not been stated. The last demurrer was sustained] without leave to amend, "pursuant to points and authorities filed." Thus, the first issue presented is whether or not the second amended complaint alleges facts sufficient to state a cause of action.

The Complaint Does Set Forth Facts Sufficient to State a Cause of Action.

The earlier versions of the complaint charged respondent with negligence and reckless disregard for the safety of others. Since this action is subject to the provisions of Labor Code section 3601, above quoted, they were manifestly insufficient to state a claim, for they failed to allege the "calculated and conscious willingness to permit injury or death" required by the statute.

In an effort to remedy the indicated deficiency, the second amended complaint, the charging allegations of which are set forth in full in the margin,[1] included an allegation cast in the words of the statute. Citing the rule that allegations of "wilful misconduct" require that the facts must be stated more fully than in ordinary negligence cases (*Snider v. Whitson*, 184 Cal. App. 2d 211 [7 Cal. Rptr. 353]), respondent contends that the complaint must be held inadequate. * * *

It is well settled that "[in] considering the sufficiency of a pleading, we are bound by the rule that on appeal from a judgment entered on demurrer, the allegations of the complaint must be liberally construed with a view to attaining substantial justice among the parties. (Code Civ. Proc., §452.)" (*Youngman v. Nevada Irrigation Dist.*, 70 Cal. 2d 240, 244-245 [74 Cal. Rptr. 398, 449 P.2d 462].) Obviously, the complaint must be read as a whole, and each part must be given the meaning it derives from the total context wherein it appears.

The Supreme Court has consistently stated the guideline that "a plaintiff is required only to set forth the essential facts of his case with reasonable precision and with particularity sufficient to acquaint a defendant with the nature, source and extent of his cause of action." (*Youngman v. Nevada Irrigation Dist.*, *supra*, 70 Cal. 2d at p. 245; *Smith v. Kern County Land Co.*, *supra*, 51 Cal. 2d at p. 209.) It has also been stated that "[t]he particularity required in pleading facts depends on the extent to which the defendant in fairness needs detailed information that can be conveniently provided

---

1. VII. That this action is brought pursuant to Section 3601(a)(3) of the Labor Code of the State of California.

"VIII. That on or about the 9th day of May, 1966, at about 4:00 P.M. the defendant Robert J. Sansoucie among other things backed the aforementioned tractor and trailer into an area without first inspecting whether the area was safe and without looking into the area he was backing into.

"IX. That said conduct is prohibited by the Vehicle Code of the State of California and the Rules and Regulations governing the operation of motor vehicles by Pacific Motor Trucking Company.

"X. That the defendants further operated the vehicle in reckless disregard for the safety and calculated and conscious willingness to permit injury or death to such fellow employees."

by the plaintiff; less particularity is required where the defendant may be assumed to have knowledge of the facts equal to that possessed by the plaintiff." (*Jackson v. Pasadena City School Dist.*, 59 Cal. 2d 876, 879 [31 Cal. Rptr. 606, 382 P.2d 878]; *Burks v. Poppy Construction Co.*, 57 Cal. 2d 463, 474 [20 Cal. Rptr. 609, 370 P.2d 313].) This seems particularly applicable to a wrongful death action where none of the plaintiff-heirs was present at the site of the fatal injury.

Finally, it must be noted that the modern discovery procedures necessarily affect the amount of detail that should be required in a pleading.

Applying these principles to the case at bar, we hold that the complaint, though hardly a model of pleading, stated a cause of action. The statutory requirement is that the death be caused by a fellow-employee's act "which evinces a reckless disregard for the safety of the employee injured, and a calculated and conscious willingness to permit injury or death to such employee." (Lab. Code, § 3601, subd. (a)(3).) In substance, the complaint alleges that respondent failed to inspect the area into which he was backing and that he acted with the state of mind required by the statute. * * *

Respondent contends that paragraph X of the complaint is only a characterization—a conclusion of law—with no additional factual support. "The distinction between conclusions of law and ultimate facts is not at all clear and involves at most a matter of degree. [Citations.] For example, the courts have permitted allegations which obviously included conclusions of law and have termed them 'ultimate facts' or 'conclusions of fact.'" (*Burks v. Poppy Construction Co.*, *supra*, 57 Cal. 2d at p. 473.)

In *Smith v. Kern County Land Co.*, *supra*, 51 Cal. 2d 205, the issue was whether an allegation that defendant "desired and wished" that plaintiff come onto his land to remove tree stumps and roots was a sufficient averment of plaintiff's status as an invitee, not a licensee. The Supreme Court ruled, at page 208: "This allegation is not, as defendant contends, a mere conclusion of law. The cases it relies on are readily distinguishable. *Wheeler v. Oppenheimer*, 140 Cal. App. 2d 497 [295 P.2d 128], held only that the technical term 'bad faith' was a conclusion of law. *Faulkner v. California Toll Bridge Authority*, 40 Cal. 2d 317 [253 P.2d 659], held to be legal conclusions the allegations that an investigation was 'insufficient' and that acts were 'arbitrary capricious, fraudulent, wrongful and unlawful.' The applicability of each of these words depends on more than, as in the case at bar, the mere presence of a state of mind."

The pleading in the case at bar is not as clearly susceptible to that distinction as the pleading in *Smith*. But we do feel that the allegation here possesses enough of a factual thrust that we cannot agree with respondent's contention that it is only a characterization that adds no additional factual support.

In *Jones v. Oxnard School Dist.*, 270 Cal. App. 2d 587, 593 [75 Cal. Rptr. 836], the court stated: "The applicable principle is that the 'conclusion of law-ultimate fact' dichotomy is not an absolute but that the fair import of language used in the pleading must be received to determine whether the adversary has been fairly apprised of the factual basis of the claim against him." That, we think, places the dichotomy in its proper perspective.

Notes and Questions on the Sufficiency of the Complaint

(1) *Semole* illustrates the two issues present in evaluating the sufficiency of a complaint, and by analogy any pleading in the code pleading system. Since the complaint must contain "a statement of the *facts* constituting the *cause of action*," it must be both formally sufficient—the "facts" must be in the appropriate style of "ultimate facts"—and these facts must present each of the elements of one or more "cause[s] of action." In *Semole*, there was no question that the elements necessary to recover under the statute were clearly present—plaintiff used the very words of the statute, "calculated and conscious willingness to permit injury or death," in the complaint. Defendant objected that the allegation required more factual content and that it should be disregarded as merely a "conclusion of law."

(2) *Federal Court Pleading Standard Compared.* For several decades, pleading a fact-based cause of action was not necessary in federal court as long as the pleading gives the defendant "fair notice of what the plaintiff's claim is and the grounds upon which it rests." *Conley v. Gibson,* 355 U.S. 41, 47, 78 S. Ct. 99, 2 L. Ed. 2d 80 (1957). However, two recent U.S. Supreme Court decisions construing federal Rule 8(a)(2), *Bell Atlantic Corp. v. Twombly,* 550 U.S. 544, 127 S. Ct. 1955, 167 L. Ed. 2d 929 (2007) and *Ashcroft v. Iqbal,* 556 U.S. 662, 129 S. Ct. 1937, 173 L. Ed. 2d 868 (2009), disapproved of this traditional "notice" pleading approach. Instead, the Supreme Court adopted the following new standard for federal courts:

> To survive a motion to dismiss, a complaint must contain sufficient factual matter, accepted as true, to "state a claim to relief that is plausible on its face." [*Bell Atlantic Corp. v. Twombly,* 550 U.S. 544, 570 (2007).] A claim has facial plausibility when the plaintiff pleads factual content that allows the court to draw the reasonable inference that the defendant is liable for the misconduct alleged. *Id.,* at 556. * * *
>
> Two working principles underlie our decision in *Twombly.* First, the tenet that a court must accept as true all of the allegations contained in a complaint is inapplicable to legal conclusions. Threadbare recitals of the elements of a cause of action, supported by mere conclusory statements, do not suffice. *Id.,* at 555 (Although for the purposes of a motion to dismiss we must take all of the factual allegations in the complaint as true, we "are not bound to accept as true a legal conclusion couched as a factual allegation"). Rule 8 marks a notable and generous departure from the hyper-technical, code-pleading regime of a prior era, but it does not unlock the doors of discovery for a plaintiff armed with nothing more than conclusions. Second, only a complaint that states a plausible claim for relief survives a motion to dismiss. *Id.,* at 556. Determining whether a complaint states a plausible claim for relief will ... be a context-specific task that requires the reviewing court to draw on its judicial experience and common sense. But where the well-pleaded facts do not permit the court to infer more than the mere possibility of misconduct, the complaint has alleged—but it has not "show[n]"—"that the pleader is entitled to relief." Fed. Rule Civ. Proc. 8(a)(2).

> In keeping with these principles a court considering a motion to dismiss can choose to begin by identifying pleadings that, because they are no more than conclusions, are not entitled to the assumption of truth. While legal conclusions can provide the framework of a complaint, they must be supported by factual allegations. When there are well-pleaded factual allegations, a court should assume their veracity and then determine whether they plausibly give rise to an entitlement to relief.

Ashcroft v. Iqbal, supra, 556 U.S. at 678-79.

How does the new federal pleading standard compare with the standard endorsed in *Semole*? Does the new federal standard require more or less fact-based pleading than the *Semole* standard? Would the complaint in *Semole* have survived a demurrer (*i.e.,* a motion to dismiss for failure to state a claim) if the California court had applied the new federal standard? In your opinion, which of these two standards represents the better approach to pleading? Why?

(3) Under code pleading, the pleader can err by being either too general—using conclusions of law—or too specific—pleading evidence. The plaintiffs' complaint in *Careau & Co. v. Sec. Pac. Bus. Credit, Inc.,* 222 Cal. App. 3d 1371, 272 Cal. Rptr. 387 (1990), contained both types of defects. In *Careau,* the court considered the sufficiency of the part of the plaintiffs' complaint which alleged breach of contractual commitment to provide loans. *Id.* at 1388-91. The court ruled that the plaintiffs failed to adequately allege due satisfaction of several conditions precedent to the formation of a binding contract. The court first found that the plaintiffs alleged only general conclusions, and not the specific allegations of performance required when the condition is an event as distinguished from an act to be performed by the plaintiff. The plaintiffs then relied on their allegations of certain oral statements of the defendant bank's loan officer to show due performance. The court rejected these statements as insufficient: "While those statements may be some evidence that one or more conditions were satisfied, they do not constitute the direct, specific allegation of performance which is required. A complaint must allege the ultimate facts necessary to the statement of an actionable claim. It is both improper and insufficient for a plaintiff to simply plead the *evidence* by which he hopes to prove such ultimate facts." *Id.* at 1387.

(4) The *Semole* case also illustrate the generous standard employed by both the trial court and a reviewing court in evaluating the allegations of a complaint to determine if plaintiff states a proper cause of action: "[U]nder settled law, we assume the truth of all properly pleaded material allegations of the complaint [citations] and give it a reasonable interpretation by reading it as a whole and its parts in their context. [Citation.]" *Phillips v. Desert Hosp. Dist.,* 49 Cal. 3d 699, 702, 263 Cal. Rptr. 119, 780 P.2d 349 (1989). The appellate court should not consider a party's possible difficulty or inability to prove allegations, as long as on their face they show the pleader would be entitled to some relief. *Rader Co. v. Stone,* 178 Cal. App. 3d 10, 223 Cal. Rptr. 806 (1986).

There are, however, limits to these rules. In *Beck v. American Health Group International, Inc.,* 211 Cal. App. 3d 1555, 260 Cal. Rptr. 237 (1989), for example, the plaintiff alleged breach of contract and incorporated by reference a document that showed on its face that it was mere preparations for a contract. The Court of Appeal found this inadequate to show there was a contract, and therefore upheld a demurrer without leave to amend. If the pleader incorporates documents by reference, the pleader must also allege the meaning to be ascribed to any ambiguous aspects of the document. Otherwise the document will be taken at face value. *Id.* at 1561.

(5) A failure to "plead around" an affirmative defense that is otherwise apparent on the face of the complaint is also a failure to state a valid cause of action. In *CAMSI IV v. Hunter Tech. Corp.*, 230 Cal. App. 3d 1525, 1536-38, 282 Cal. Rptr. 80 (1991), for example, the court upheld a demurrer without leave to amend where the complaint revealed that the statute of limitations had run, and the plaintiff had failed to anticipate this defense and plead facts establishing the elements of the delayed discovery rule. *See also County of Alameda v. Superior Court*, 195 Cal. App. 3d 1283, 1286, 241 Cal. Rptr. 312 (1987) (observing that where a complaint shows on its face that the cause of action is apparently barred, the plaintiff must plead facts showing ground for suspension, delayed accrual, or application of another theory for avoidance of the statute of limitations); *Kunstman v. Mirizzi*, 234 Cal. App. 2d 753, 44 Cal. Rptr. 707 (1965) (sustaining demurrer where plaintiff failed to anticipate statute of limitations defense and to plead estoppel due to misrepresentation by defendant).

(6) *Form of Complaint.* Rules 2.100-2.119 of the California Rules of Court set forth detailed requirements for the form and format of papers presented for filing, including complaints. Rule 2.118(a) directs the clerk of court to not accept for filing any papers which do not comply with these requirements. May a local superior court condition the filing of a complaint on local rule requirements in addition to those set forth in Rules 2.100-2.119? *See Mito v. Temple Recycling Ctr. Corp.*, 187 Cal. App. 4th 276, 113 Cal. Rptr. 3d 445 (2010) (concluding complaint was timely filed on date first transmitted because state Rule 3.220(c) mandated the court clerk to file the complaint on that date even though it lacked the cover sheet required by local rule); *Carlson v. Dept. of Fish and Game*, 68 Cal. App. 4th 1268, 80 Cal. Rptr. 2d 601 (1998) (noting so long as a complaint complies with the state requirements, the clerk has a ministerial duty to file it); *Rojas v. Cutsforth*, 67 Cal. App. 4th 774, 79 Cal. Rptr. 2d 292 (1998) (ruling clerk has no authority to reject otherwise proper complaint where plaintiff violated local rule by failing to also file signed court assignment form). Rule 3.20 provides that the state rules preempt local court rules relating to pleadings, other pretrial papers, and the form and format of papers, but excepts "local court rules adopted under the Trial Court Delay Reduction Act." Rule 3.20(b)(4).

[B] Heightened Specificity Requirements in Pleading

In addition to its generally higher standard of factual specificity, code pleading, like notice pleading, requires heightened specificity in selected types of cases.

[1] Pleading Fraud

Causes of action based on fraud must be specifically pleaded; a general pleading of the legal conclusion of fraud is insufficient. *Moncada v. West Coast Quartz Corp.*, 221 Cal. App. 4th 768, 775-801, 164 Cal. Rptr. 3d 601 (2013); *Stanfield v. Starkey*, 220 Cal. App. 3d 59, 269 Cal. Rptr. 337 (1990). Each of the elements of fraud—false representation of a material fact, knowledge of its falsity, intent to defraud, justifiable reliance, and resulting damage—must be alleged in full, factually and specifically. *See, e.g., Small v. Fritz Companies, Inc.*, 30 Cal. 4th 167, 183-85, 132 Cal. Rptr. 2d 490, 65 P.3d 1255 (2003); *Nagy v. Nagy*, 210 Cal. App. 3d 1262, 1268-69, 258 Cal. Rptr. 787 (1989) (holding complaint which lacked an allegation of a definite amount of damage did not state a cause of action for fraud); *Wilhelm v. Pray, Price, Williams & Russell*, 186 Cal. App. 3d 1324, 231 Cal. Rptr. 355 (1986) (concluding complaint which failed to specifically plead factual basis for knowledge of falsity and justifiable reliance did not state fraud cause of action). What are the reasons for the requirement of heightened specificity in pleading fraud causes of action?

What does specificity mean? The courts concentrate on factual specifics. In alleging fraud against a corporation, plaintiff must allege "the names of the persons who made the allegedly fraudulent representations, their authority to speak, to whom they spoke, what they said or wrote, and when it was said or written." *Tarmann v. State Farm Mut. Auto. Ins. Co.*, 2 Cal. App. 4th 153, 157, 2 Cal. Rptr. 2d 861 (1991). In other words, the pleading of facts which show the familiar "who, what, where, when, and how." *Lazer v. Superior Court*, 12 Cal. 4th 631, 645, 49 Cal. Rptr. 2d 377, 909 P.2d 981 (1966). Less specificity is required where the allegations show defendant must necessarily possess full information concerning the facts of the controversy. *Committee on Children's Television, Inc. v. Gen. Foods Corp.*, 35 Cal. 3d 197, 197 Cal. Rptr. 783, 673 P.2d 660 (1983); *but see Goldrich v. Natural Y Surgical Specialties, Inc.*, 25 Cal. App. 4th 772, 782-83, 31 Cal. Rptr. 2d 162 (1994) (ruling plaintiff's contention that defendant manufacturers' knowledge of their own communications of allegedly fraudulent information regarding the safety of their breast implants did not relieve plaintiff of her obligation to provide any factual averments at all).

[2] Pleading Other Disfavored Causes of Action

Although fraud is the prominent instance of heightened pleading specificity, the requirement can be found in connection with other disfavored causes of action. These include products liability for exposure to toxins, *Bockrath v. Aldrich Chem. Co., Inc.*, 21 Cal. 4th 71, 86 Cal. Rptr. 2d 846, 980 P.2d 398 (1999) (holding that in a products liability suit where the plaintiff alleges long-term exposure to multiple toxins produced by multiple defendants, the plaintiff must plead specific facts explaining how a specific illness was caused by an identified product manufactured by a named defendant); tortious breach of contract, tortious interference with business relations, and unfair business practices, *Khoury v. Maly's of California, Inc.*, 14 Cal. App. 4th 612, 17 Cal. Rptr. 2d 708 (1993); civil conspiracy, *Wise v. S. Pac. Co.*, 223 Cal. App. 2d 50, 35 Cal. Rptr. 652 (1963); and certain civil actions against public officers, Government Code § 951.

[C]   Inconsistent and Alternative Pleading

Shepard & Morgan v. Lee & Daniel, Inc.

Supreme Court of California
31 Cal. 3d 256, 182 Cal. Rptr. 351, 643 P.2d 968 (1982)

RICHARDSON, JUSTICE.

A general contractor, when named as a defendant in a personal injury action which alleged job-site injuries to a construction carpenter, filed a cross-complaint charging a subcontractor with responsibility for plaintiff's injuries. The issue is whether answers made in defendant's responses to plaintiff's request for admissions regarding the cause of the accident are binding upon defendant contractor in its cross-action against the subcontractor. We conclude that, under the circumstances in this case, defendant's admissions to plaintiff are not binding in the cross-action. We further conclude that defendant was entitled to take seemingly inconsistent positions on the cause of plaintiff's injury by (1) defending plaintiff's action on the theory that no job-site hazards existed, but (2) prosecuting its cross-complaint on an alternative theory that any such hazard was caused by the cross-defendant subcontractor.

Plaintiff Terry Cole, a carpenter, was employed by R. M. Stowall (Stowall), a framing subcontractor. While securing wooden ceiling joists on a construction project in Los Angeles, plaintiff fell 20 feet to a concrete floor and was injured. Each joist was fitted into a strap-like hanger which, at two-foot intervals, had been welded to I-beams. When he fell, plaintiff had been standing with each foot on a 2-inch by 12-inch joist while nailing a spreader block between the joists.

As a result of the accident and resulting injuries, plaintiff sued both defendant general contractor, Shepard & Morgan (Shepard) and codefendant manufacturer of the joists and hanger, Simpson Company (Simpson). Shepard in turn filed a cross-complaint for indemnity against Stowall, Simpson and the subcontractor who supplied the joists and hanger, Lee & Daniel, Inc. (Lee).

[The court first held that Shepard's admission to plaintiff of its contention regarding causation was not binding upon Shepard in its cross-complaint against Lee. It pointed to the language of the request for admissions statute, Code of Civil Procedure § 2033, and fairness considerations, and noted that "no compelling reason exists for requiring Shepard to elect at its peril, and before trial, among possible alternative theories of causation."]

The foregoing reasoning is reinforced by our own prior cases which confirm that the plaintiff in a civil action cannot be forced to choose between two or more inconsistent causes of action. Instead, the *plaintiff* is entitled to introduce evidence upon all such causes and submit to the trier of fact the question as to which, if any, counts are sustained by the proof. (*Grudt v. City of Los Angeles* (1970) 2 Cal. 3d 575, 586 [86 Cal. Rptr. 465, 468 P.2d 825]; *Tanforan v. Tanforan* (1916) 173 Cal. 270, 274 [159 P. 709]; 3 Witkin, Cal. Procedure, *supra*, § 294, at p. 1968.) By similar reasoning and on principle, the *defendant* should not be forced to select one theory of defense at the risk of losing a right of indemnity from third persons. * * *

The judgment of nonsuit is reversed.

Notes and Questions on Inconsistent Pleading Allegations

(1) As the main case implicitly acknowledges, generally any pleader may assert inconsistent allegations subject to certain good faith limitations. Where the exact nature of the facts is in doubt, or where the exact legal nature of the plaintiff's right and defendant's liability depend on facts not well known to plaintiff, the pleadings may properly set forth alternative theories in varied and inconsistent counts. *Rader Co. v. Stone*, 178 Cal. App. 3d 10, 223 Cal. Rptr. 806 (1986) (ruling plaintiff not precluded from alleging in one cause of action the breach of a contract and an inconsistent theory of recovery in another case of action). However, a party cannot both assert and deny a fact that that party must know. *See, e.g., Careau & Co. v. Sec. Pac.*, 222 Cal. App. 3d 1371, 272 Cal. Rptr. 387 (1990) (concluding breach of contract action not properly pleaded where plaintiff generally alleged satisfaction of conditions precedent but also alleged facts which demonstrated conditions not fully performed).

(2) Rule 8(d) (2) & (3) of the Federal Rules of Civil Procedure permits a party in federal court to "set forth two or more statements of a claim or defense alternately or hypothetically," and to state "as many separate claims or defenses as it has, regardless of consistency." Is the federal rule the same as the California doctrine? As extensive?

[D]   Prayer for Relief

[1]   In General

A defective prayer for relief, or even the entire lack of a prayer, does not make a complaint subject to demurrer so long as the averments in the complaint state a cause of action. *Miller v. Superior Court*, 59 Cal. App. 334, 338-39, 210 P. 832 (1922). Likewise, the averments contained in the pleading determine the maximum sum which may be awarded the plaintiff in a contested cause; the prayer of the pleading is not controlling. For example, in *Castaic Clay Mfg. Co. v. Dedes*, 195 Cal. App. 3d 444, 240 Cal. Rptr. 652 (1987), the plaintiff was awarded compensatory damages in excess of those requested in the prayer for relief, and the complaint was never amended to conform to the proof offered at trial. The parties actually tried issues of damages in amounts beyond those stated in the complaint. The Court of Appeal held that the relief granted was consistent with the issues made by the complaint and voluntarily tried by the parties. *Id.* at 449-50.

[2]   Statement of Damages

Code of Civil Procedure § 425.10(b) provides that in superior court actions to recover actual or punitive damages for personal injury or wrongful death, the amount sought is *not* to be stated in the complaint. Apparently passed to avoid publicizing inflated claims against individuals and particularly health care providers, section 425.10(b) must be read with section 425.11 that gives a defending party the right at any time to request "a statement setting forth the nature and amount of damages being sought." *See also* CCP § 425.115 (statement preserving right to seek punitive damages). Even if not demanded, the statement must be filed before a default may be taken. *See, e.g., Schwab v. Rondel Homes, Inc.*, 53 Cal. 3d 428, 280 Cal. Rptr. 83, 808 P.2d 226 (1991) (vacating default judgment for $ 200,000 because plaintiff did not serve defendant with a § 425.11 statement of damages); *Debbie S. v. Ray*, 16 Cal. App. 4th 193, 19 Cal. Rptr. 2d 814 (1993) (vacating default judgment after defendant failed to appear at trial because plaintiff failed to serve a statement of damages within 60 days of trial as required by § 425.11).

[3] Special Pleading Rules for Punitive Damages

As discussed previously, by judicial decision or statute, disfavored claims often must meet more stringent pleading rules. Frequently under attack, especially by manufacturers and business groups, are claims for punitive damages. The United States Supreme Court has endorsed procedural and substantive constitutional limitations on punitive damages awards. *E.g., BMW of N. America, Inc. v. Gore*, 517 U.S. 559, 116 S. Ct. 1589, 134 L. Ed. 2d 809 (1993) (ruling Due Process Clause prohibits the imposition of excessive or arbitrary punishments on tortfeasors); *Pacific Mut. Life Ins. Co. v. Haslip*, 499 U.S. 1, 111 S. Ct. 1032, 113 L. Ed. 2d 1 (1991) (holding Due Process Clause requires certain meaningful constraints on the discretion of fact finders in assessing punitive damages). California's courts and legislature have imposed additional restrictions, including special rules barring the pleading of certain punitive damages claims without court order. California has statutory protections for negligence actions against health care providers, CCP § 425.13; and for claims against religious corporations, CCP § 425.14. Related requirements include prior screening for probable cause or other evidence substantiating claims against officers and directors of nonprofit corporations, CCP § 425.15; and certain "SLAPP" suits, CCP §§ 425.16, 425.17; and special certification requirements for malpractice actions against architects, engineers, and surveyors, CCP § 411.35.

[a] Prepleading Requirements: "Substantial Probability that the Plaintiff will Prevail"

Code of Civil Procedure § 425.13 imposes a prepleading requirement when a plaintiff seeks to plead a punitive damages claim in a malpractice action against a health care provider. Section 425.13(a) provides:

> In any action for damages arising out of the professional negligence of a health care provider, no claim for punitive damages shall be included in a complaint or other pleading unless the court enters an order allowing an amended pleading that includes a claim for punitive damages to be filed. *The court may allow the filing of an amended pleading claiming punitive damages on a motion by the party seeking the amended pleading and on the basis of the*

supporting and opposing affidavits presented that the plaintiff has established that there is a substantial probability that the plaintiff will prevail on the [punitive damages] claim pursuant to Section 3294 of the Civil Code...." (Italics added.)

The Supreme Court construed section 425.13(a)'s "substantial probability" requirement in *College Hospital, Inc. v. Superior Court*, 8 Cal. 4th 704, 34 Cal. Rptr. 2d 898, 882 P.2d 894 (1994), where the plaintiffs' alleged a cause of action for professional negligence against the defendant hospital. Plaintiffs timely moved under CCP § 425.13(a) for an order allowing them to amend the complaint to state a punitive damages claim, supported by a declarations and depositions. The defendant opposed the motion, and also submitted various declarations. The trial granted the motion and allowed plaintiffs to amend their complaint to state a punitive damages claim against the defendant hospital. The defendant petitioned for a writ of mandate to set aside the ruling. After the Court of Appeal denied defendants' petition, the Supreme Court granted review.

The defendant hospital argued that CCP § 425.13(a) contains a rigorous "weighing" test and that the statute not only disallows punitive damage claims that obviously lack merit, but also requires the trial court to assess the relative merits of a claim and to bar any punitive damages claim that does not appear highly likely to succeed at trial. The Supreme Court rejected defendant's argument with the following explanation:

> Nothing in the [legislative history] indicates that under statutes like section 425.13(a), trial courts are authorized to weigh the merits of the claim or consider its likely outcome at trial. Although such terms as "frivolous" and "meritless" are not explicitly defined, the tone and substance of the debate strongly suggest that the motion required by such statutes operates like a demurrer or motion for summary judgment in "reverse." Rather than requiring the *defendant* to defeat the plaintiff's pleading by showing it is legally or factually meritless, the motion requires the *plaintiff* to demonstrate that he possesses a legally sufficient claim which is "substantiated," that is, supported by competent, admissible evidence. * * *

> Thus, the gravamen of section 425.13(a) is that the plaintiff may not amend the complaint to include a punitive damages claim unless he both states and substantiates a legally sufficient claim. In other words, the court must deny the section 425.13(a) motion where the facts asserted in the proposed amended complaint are legally insufficient to support a punitive damages claim. (*See* §§ 430.10, 436-437.) The court also must deny the motion where the evidence provided in the "supporting and opposing affidavits" either negates or fails to reveal the actual existence of a triable claim. (*See* § 437c, subd. (c).) The section 425.13(a) motion may be granted only where the plaintiff demonstrates that both requirements are met. * * *

> Moreover, in light of the "affidavit" requirement and by analogy to summary judgment practice, substantiation of a proposed punitive damages claim occurs only where the factual recitals are made under penalty of perjury

and set forth competent admissible evidence within the personal knowledge of the declarant. (*See* §§ 437c, subds. (b) & (d), 2015.5.) Consistent with the legislative intent to protect health care defendants from the drastic effects of unwarranted punitive damage claims, the entire package of materials submitted in support of the section 425.13(a) motion should be carefully reviewed to ensure that a genuine contestable claim is indeed proposed. * * *

The next question is whether plaintiffs have stated and demonstrated a triable punitive damages claim under section 425.13(a). The basic elements of such claims are set forth in Civil Code section 3294. [T]here must be proof of "oppression, fraud, or malice." (*Id.*, subd. (a).) Moreover, the punishable acts which fall into these categories are strictly defined. Each involves "intentional," "willful," or "conscious" wrongdoing of a "despicable" or "injur[ious]" nature. (*Id.*, subd. (c).) * * *

We will independently review the proposed amended complaint and the evidence submitted in support of and opposition to the motion under section 425.13(a) to determine whether plaintiffs have stated and substantiated a legally sufficient punitive damages claim against the Hospital. Even if we view the evidence in a light most favorable to plaintiffs, it is clear they have not met the requirements of section 425.13(a).

College Hospital, supra, 8 Cal. 4th at 715-22. After examining the facts alleged in the amended complaint and the evidence—primarily from plaintiffs' declarations and deposition testimony submitted in support of these allegations pursuant to section 425.13(a) the Supreme Court concluded that no basis appears for assessing punitive damages against the defendant hospital, and that the plaintiffs failed to satisfy the requirements of section 425.13(a) when they sought to plead a punitive damages claim against the hospital.

[b] Are Prepleading Requirements Necessary?

As the *College Hospital* court notes, prepleading hurdle statutes such as CCP § 425.13 operate much like a summary judgment in reverse, placing the burden on the plaintiff to present a "legally sufficient" claim and undergo an affidavit procedure like the one employed in the determination of a motion for summary judgment. Why is this additional procedural obstacle to punitive damages allegations by a plaintiff even necessary? Cannot the same screening goal be achieved by defendant's early use of the summary judgment procedure in CCP § 437c(f), which authorizes a party to move for summary adjudication as to a claim for damages? By requiring the plaintiff to plead the substantive elements of punitive damages with specificity and in a verified complaint? By rigorous enforcement of the duty imposed by CCP § 128.7 to only plead allegations which have evidentiary support?

Prepleading hurdle statutes like CCP § 425.13 reflect obvious legislative disfavor of punitive damages claims. Are such statutes effective vehicles for the early screening out of frivolous or unsubstantiated punitive damage claims? Is the efficacy of such screening devices sufficient to justify the increased procedural costs?

Despite the apparent limitation to actions "arising out of the professional negligence of a health care provider," the Supreme Court in the *Central Pathology Service Medical Clinic, Inc. v. Superior Court*, 3 Cal. 4th 181, 10 Cal. Rptr. 2d 208, 832 P.2d 924 (1992), construed this language in CCP § 425.13 to also apply to causes of action based on intentional tort theories. Accordingly, the *Central Pathology* court directed the trial court to conduct § 425.13 proceedings to determine whether to permit the plaintiffs to amend their medical negligence complaint and assert punitive damage claims based on fraud and intentional infliction of emotional distress.

What if a plaintiff alleges a claim for punitive damages against a health care professional in the original complaint? The plaintiffs in *College Hospital* included punitive damages allegations in their original complaint. The defendant hospital moved to strike the punitive damages allegations because plaintiffs had not complied with § 425.13. This motion was granted by the trial court. How would that case have proceeded if the defendant instead had simply answered the complaint? In *Vallbona v. Springer*, 43 Cal. App. 4th 1525, 51 Cal. Rptr. 2d 311 (1996), the court concluded that § 425.13's requirement of a court order as a condition precedent to including a claim for punitive damages arising out of the professional negligence of a health care provider is not jurisdictional, and absent timely objection to a complaint's inclusion of punitive damages without court permission, the protection conferred by § 425.13 is waived. By answering and not moving to strike the punitive damages allegations, the defendants waived any rights they might have under the statute at the time of trial.

§ 9.03 Amendments

[A] Introductory Note

Dating from its adoption of the Field Code, California has liberally allowed amendment of pleadings. Code of Civil Procedure sections 469 and 470, carried over from the original Field Code, allow pleadings to be amended "upon such terms as may be just" to avoid variance between allegations in pleadings and proof at trial. Section 472 permits any pleading to be amended once as a matter "of course, and without costs, at any time before the answer or demurrer is filed...." Section 473 permits the court, "in furtherance of justice, and on any terms as may be proper," to allow parties to amend to correct mistakes; and with notice to allow "on any terms as may be just, an amendment to any pleading or proceedings in other particulars...." Case law supports these statutory directives to the courts to allow amendment except when substantial and uncorrectable prejudice can be shown by the party opposing the amendment.

[B] Amended Complaints and the Relation Back Doctrine

Honig v. Financial Corporation of America

Court of Appeal of California, Second Appellate District
6 Cal. App. 4th 960, 7 Cal. Rptr. 2d 922 (1992)

ASHBY, JUSTICE.

Appellant and plaintiff Stephen N. Honig filed a multicount civil suit against respondent and defendant New West Federal Savings and Loan Association. Also named in the suit were five employees of respondent New West, respondents and defendants Robert Blain, Thomas Kennett, Sheila Wilson, John Hamilton and Michael Fleutsch. The trial court denied appellant's motion to amend his complaint and at the same hearing granted respondents' summary judgment motions. We reverse, finding the trial court abused its discretion in refusing to permit the amendment.

FACTS

Appellant filed his complaint on February 5, 1988. In the complaint appellant alleged he began his employment with respondent New West in June 1982 with the responsibility of developing and maintaining "Jumbo" certificates of deposits. Further, appellant stated that on numerous occasions respondent New West represented to him he would be continuously employed as long as he performed satisfactorily. Appellant alleged that in contravention of public policy appellant was forced to commit illegal acts, fraud and misrepresentation in the manner in which he was directed to offer the certificates of deposits and appellant was required to decline to reveal material facts to investors. Appellant asserted that beginning in January 1987, respondents commenced a "campaign of harassment, threats, humiliation, debasement and intimidation against" appellant. The complaint asserted causes of action for (1) attempted constructive termination/breach of public policy, (2) intentional fraud and deceit, (3) negligent fraud and deceit, (4) breach of covenant of good faith and fair dealing, (5) breach of contract, (6) conspiracy, (7) intentional infliction of emotional distress, and (8) interference with prospective economic advantage. At the time the complaint was filed, appellant had not left respondent New West's employment. A fellow employee had been discharged in August 1987, and six others discharged in October 1987. Appellant contended he filed his suit as a preventative measure fearing his discharge was imminent.

According to appellant, after the initial complaint was filed, respondent New West demanded appellant attend a meeting of its ethics committee. Appellant's request that his counsel be allowed to attend the meeting was refused. Appellant submitted to respondent New West a four-page written statement in which he explained his position that he would not discuss the pending lawsuit with them. Appellant's requests that all inquiries be directed to him in writing so he could consult counsel were also refused. Additional communications passed between the parties in which appellant contended that he was entitled to counsel, that "trumped up" charges had been created, that the ethics committee's actions were in retaliation for the filing of his lawsuit and that he was acting under advice of counsel. On April 15, 1988, respondent New West discharged appellant stating he was being fired for insubordination. At the time, appellant was earning approximately $108,000.

The matter was assigned to a fast track court, a court under the Trial Court Delay Reduction Act. (Gov. Code, § 68600 et seq.) Extensive discovery was conducted, including seven days of deposing appellant. Respondents thoroughly deposed appellant on the events which occurred subsequent to the filing of the initial complaint. Extensive inquiry was made of the events surrounding the ethics committee and appellant's discharge on April 15, 1988. Additionally, questions were asked relating to his search for employment after being fired. During the deposition, appellant explained that he thought he had difficulty finding employment because he was blackballed and because he told prospective employers he had been fired.

On September 4, 1990, approximately two months before the scheduled trial, respondents filed summary judgment motions. On October 4, 1990, appellant filed an opposition to the motions as well as a motion to amend his complaint. The proposed amendment added facts which occurred after the initial complaint. It asserted a cause of action for wrongful discharge in violation of public policy contending he could not be fired for requesting advice of counsel. Additionally, it was contended the charge of insubordination was created as a pretext for the termination. The amended complaint also pled a cause of action for defamation asserting that after the termination the false reason for the discharge (gross insubordination) was repeated to others and that appellant was forced to reveal the false reason to prospective employers.

The court granted the summary judgment motions and denied appellant's motion to amend. Finding the court abused its discretion in refusing the amendment, we reverse.

DISCUSSION

[The court first concluded that the California courts have jurisdiction to hear the matter.]

AMENDMENT

We are persuaded by appellant's contention that the trial court abused its discretion in refusing him the right to amend his complaint.

In the furtherance of justice, trial courts may allow amendments to pleadings and if necessary, postpone trial. (Code Civ. Proc. § 473.) Motions to amend are appropriately granted as late as the first day of trial (e.g., *Higgins v. Del Faro* (1981) 123 Cal. App. 3d 558 [176 Cal. Rptr. 704]) or even during trial (*Rainer v. Community Memorial Hosp.* (1971) 18 Cal. App. 3d 240, 251-56 [95 Cal. Rptr. 901]) if the defendant is alerted to the charges by the factual allegations, no matter how framed (*Hirsa v. Superior Court* (1981) 118 Cal. App. 3d 486, 489 [173 Cal. Rptr. 418]) and the defendant will not be prejudiced. "When a request to amend has been denied, an appellate court is confronted by two conflicting policies. On the one hand, the trial court's discretion should not be disturbed unless it has been clearly abused; on the other, there is a strong policy in favor of liberal allowance of amendments. This conflict 'is often resolved in favor of the privilege of amending, and reversals are common where the appellant makes a reasonable showing of prejudice from the ruling.'" (*Mesler v. Bragg Management Co.* (1985) 39 Cal. 3d 290, 296-297 [216 Cal. Rptr. 443, 702 P.2d 601].) If the original pleading has not framed the issues in an articulate and precise manner, a plaintiff should not be precluded from having a trial on the merits.

Appellant's complaint was filed in February 1988. The matter was on the fast track calendar, extensive discovery was conducted, and trial was set for November 13, 1990. Respondents filed their summary judgment motions in September 1990. When appellant filed his opposition to the motions, he also filed a motion to amend. The amended complaint contained additional paragraphs relating to the claim for wrongful termination based upon the April 8, 1988, termination and the facts leading up to that discharge. Additionally, the proposed amended complaint added a charge of defamation based upon spreading to others the reason for the discharge and for the publication occurring when appellant was forced to explain to prospective employers he had been fired.

The proposed amendments finished telling the story begun in the original complaint. The added assertions described the continuation of the events asserted in the initial pleading. The parties were fully aware of the events which occurred subsequent to the original charges, including the April 8, 1988, termination and the facts which preceded the actual discharge. Additionally, respondents were fully aware of appellant's claim that he had been blackballed and that he was unable to find new employment because he told prospective employers he had been fired. Appellant was fully deposed on these issues. Thus, no prejudice would have resulted had the amendments been permitted.[2]

Respondents also contend it was improper to allow the amendments because the statute of limitations on the two additional causes of action would have run and that the relation back doctrine would not be applicable. We are not persuaded by this analysis.

"An amended complaint relates back to the original complaint, and thus avoids the statute of limitations as a bar ... if it: (1) rests on the same general set of facts as the original complaint; and (2) refers to the same accident and same injuries as the original complaint." (*Barrington v. A. H. Robins Co.* (1985) 39 Cal. 3d 146, 151 [216 Cal. Rptr. 405, 702 P.2d 563]; *Smeltzley v. Nicholson Mfg. Co.* (1977) 18 Cal. 3d 932, 934 [136 Cal. Rptr. 269, 559 P.2d 624, 85 A.L.R.3d 121].) The same general set of facts includes the same operative facts; a change in legal theory is permissible. (*Goldman v. Wilsey Foods, Inc.* (1989) 216 Cal. App. 3d 1085, 1094-95 [265 Cal. Rptr. 294].) A claim for different damages does not indicate there are different injuries. Rather, injuries may encompass the same primary rights. (*Rowland v. Superior Court (Zappia)* (1985) 171 Cal. App. 3d 1214, 1217-1218 [217 Cal. Rptr. 786].)

Here, the facts alleged in the complaint as well as the amended complaint all related to appellant's discharge. (*Goldman v. Wilsey Foods, supra,* 216 Cal. App. 3d 1085

---

2. Respondent New West argues it was prejudiced because some of the employees who had information relevant to the later circumstances were no longer employed. This, however, does not necessarily mean these persons could not be found. Thus, New West's assertion of prejudice is speculative.
* * *

[statutory civil rights claim for emotional distress related back to common law claim, as both based upon abusive language, religious harassment and discrimination].) Thus, as shown above, the amended complaint related to the same general set of facts and the same accident. They were in the chain of events which were originally pled.

Additionally, all injuries were those which were expected from a wrongful discharge, including those asserted in the defamation cause of action. It is expected that fired employees may have difficulty in obtaining new employment and that allegations surrounding their discharge may be spread to others. When an employer discharges an employee it is not unusual for the employer to defend the termination by reasserting the stated reasons for it. The claims of wrongful termination and defamation are inextricably intertwined in these circumstances. Thus, although appellant's amended complaint asserted two additional causes of action, they related back to the original complaint. While reframing appellant's claims, the proposed amendments did not significantly add new dimensions to the suit.

In finding that the amendment should have been allowed, we are well aware of the purposes behind fast track, which we support. Matters should be promptly resolved. However, if an amendment is appropriate the trial court should continue the trial if necessary, even if the matter is on fast track.

The judgment is reversed. Costs on appeal are awarded to appellant.

[1] Liberal Amendment Policy

As our principal case illustrates, the California courts will ordinarily exercise liberality in permitting amendments to pleadings at any stage of the proceedings. *E.g.*, *Hulsely v. Koehler*, 218 Cal. App. 3d 1150, 1159, 267 Cal. Rptr. 523 (1990); *California Cas. Gen. Ins. Co. v. Superior Court*, 173 Cal. App. 3d 274, 279, 218 Cal. Rptr. 817 (1985).

[a] Amended Pleadings, Generally

Code of Civil Procedure § 473 provides that "in furtherance of justice" a trial court may allow a party to amend its pleadings. Whether an amendment should be allowed rests in the sound discretion of the trial court. *Klopstock v. Superior Court*, 17 Cal. 2d 13, 19, 108 P.2d 906 (1941); *Hulsey v. Koehler, supra*. As the *Honig* decision indicates, two primary factors are relevant to the determination of whether to permit an amended complaint: whether the plaintiff has unreasonably delayed the presentation of the motion to amend, and whether this delay has resulted in substantial prejudice to the defendant. *See Duchrow v. Forrest*, 215 Cal. App. 4th 1359, 1377-82, 156 Cal. Rptr. 3d 194 (2013);Walter W. Heiser, *Relation Back of Amended Complaints: The California Courts Should Adopt a More Pragmatic Approach*, 44 SANTA CLARA L. REV. 643, 647-60 (2004) (discussing numerous cases). Some courts, like *Honig*, apply these factors in a pragmatic manner designed to permit an amendment unless it will unfairly surprise, and thereby unduly prejudice, the defendant in preparation for trial. *See, e.g., Mesler v. Bragg Mgmt. Co.*, 39 Cal. 3d 290, 297, 216 Cal. Rptr. 443, 702 P.2d

601(1985); *Redevelopment Agency v. Herrold*, 86 Cal. App. 3d 1024, 1032, 150 Cal. Rptr. 556, 560 (1978); *see also* Heiser, *Relation Back of Amended Complaints, supra* at 650-56 (collecting cases). The most important inquiry to these courts is whether the defendant as a result of pretrial discovery is already prepared to respond to the new allegations in the proposed amendment. *See* Heiser, *Relation Back of Amended Complaints, supra*.

These same factors, unreasonable delay and prejudice to the other party, inform a trial court's discretion to allow an amended answer. *W & W El Camino Real, LLC v. Fowler*, 226 Cal. App. 4th 263, 269-71, 171 Cal. Rptr. 3d 819 (2014); *Hulsely v. Koehler, supra*. Delay is more likely to produce prejudice where the proposed amendment sets forth a new affirmative defense. *See, e.g., Hulsey v. Koehler, supra* (finding no abuse of discretion where trial court denied motion to amend answer two days before trial to assert res judicata defense; plaintiff has right to know his risks and weigh his exposure prior to trial); *California Cas. Gen. Ins. Co. v. Superior Court*, 173 Cal. App. 3d 274, 279, 218 Cal. Rtpr. 817 (1985) (affirming trial court's denial of motion to amend answer to add affirmative defense filed three years after original answer where plaintiff prejudiced in its attachment strategy by the delay).

A motion to amend a pleading before trial must now be accompanied by a separate declaration which specifies: (1) The effect of the amendment, (2) why the amendment is necessary and proper, (3) when the facts giving rise to the amended allegations were discovered, and (4) the reasons why the request for amendment was not made earlier. Rule 3.1324(b), Cal. Rules of Court.

[b] Amendments to Conform to Proof

As discussed in *Walker v. Belvedere*, 16 Cal. App. 4th 1663, 20 Cal. Rptr. 2d 773 (1993), the decisional and statutory law on the subject of variances is extremely liberal in allowing amendments to conform to proof. The objective is to avoid the use of technicalities to defeat recovery by a plaintiff who has pleaded, no matter how unskillfully, sufficient facts to warrant recovery from a defendant. *General Credit Corp. v. Pichel*, 44 Cal. App. 3d 844, 849, 118 Cal. Rptr. 913 (1975). Where recovery is sought "on the same general set of facts" as pled in the complaint, and there is no prejudice to opposing party, an amendment to conform to the evidence will be granted even though the amendment gives rise to a separate and distinct cause of action. *See id.* at 850 (citing cases); *Duchrow v. Forrest, supra*, 215 Cal. App. 4th at 1377-82 (holding, in light of the nature of the amendment and prejudice, that the trial court abused its discretion by permitting amendment to conform to the proof on fourth day of five-day trial). However, where a party alleges facts amounting to a certain cause of action and the evidence sets forth an entirely separate set of facts constituting an entirely different cause of action from the one pled, the result is not an immaterial variance but a failure of proof. *See, e.g., Fineberg v. Niekerk*, 175 Cal. App. 3d 935, 939, 221 Cal. Rptr. 106 (1985); *Johnson v. DeWaard*, 113 Cal. App. 417, 298 P. 92 (1931).

[c] Amendment After Demurrer Filed or Sustained

When a trial court sustains a (general) demurrer, the court determines that the complaint does not state facts sufficient to constitute a cause of action. Denial of leave to amend is an abuse of discretion, however, if there is any reasonable possibility that the plaintiff can amend the complaint to cure its defects. *See Blank v. Kirwan*, 39 Cal. 3d 311, 318, 216 Cal. Rptr. 718, 703 P.2d 58 (1985); *Careau Co. v. Security Pacific Business Credit, Inc.*, 222 Cal. App. 3d 1371, 1386, 272 Cal. Rptr. 387 (1990), reproduced *infra*. Pursuant to a recent amendment to CCP § 472, a party may amend its pleading once without leave of court after a demurrer is *filed* but before it is heard.

An amended pleading supersedes the original one, which ceases to perform any function as a pleading. *See Foreman & Clark Corp. v. Fallon*, 3 Cal. 3d 875, 884, 92 Cal. Rptr. 162, 479 P.2d 362 (1971). Although ordinarily an appellate court will not consider the allegations of a superseded complaint, that rule does not apply when the trial court denied the plaintiff leave to include those allegations in an amended complaint. *See Committee on Children's Television, Inc. v. General Foods Corp.*, 35 Cal. 3d 197, 209, 197 Cal. Rptr. 783, 673 P.2d 660 (1983).

[2] *The Relation Back Doctrine*

[a] New Cause of Action Permitted

The *Honig v. Financial Corp. of America*, reproduced *supra*, illustrates a typical application of the traditional relation back doctrine, which permits an amended complaint to relate back to the original complaint and thereby avoid a statute of limitations bar. "The 'relation back' doctrine focuses on factual similarity rather than rights or obligations arising from the facts, and permits added causes of action to relate back to the initial complaint so long as they arise factually from the same injury." *Goldman v. Wiley Foods, Inc.*, 216 Cal. App. 3d 1085, 1094, 265 Cal. Rptr. 294 (1989) (ruling statutory civil rights claim for emotional distress related back to common law claim as both based upon defendant's religious harassment and discrimination, and therefore not barred by statute of limitations). Consequently, the fact that a plaintiff's amended complaint rests on a different legal theory and states a different cause of action is irrelevant if the two complaints relate to the same general set of facts. *See, e.g., Austin v. Massachusetts Bonding and Ins. Co.*, 56 Cal. 2d 596, 15 Cal. Rptr. 817, 364 P.2d 681 (1961) (adopting the modern relation back rule); *Smeltzley v. Nicholson Mfg. Co.*, 18 Cal. 3d 932, 136 Cal. Rptr. 269, 559 P.2d 624 (1977) (tracing development of modern relation back doctrine).

For example, in *Grudt v. City of Los Angeles*, 2 Cal. 3d 575, 86 Cal. Rptr. 465, 468 P.2d 825 (1970), the initial complaint alleged that plaintiff's husband was wrongfully killed by the city police, and pleaded liability of the city on a theory of respondeat superior. The amended complaint alleged an additional theory of active negligence by the city in retaining employees known to be dangerous. The amended complaint was held to relate back to the filing of the original complaint because the underlying cause of death was always the conduct of the police officers in the same shooting incident. *Id.* at 583-85. By contrast, the amended complaint in *Coronet Mfg. Co. v. Superior Court,* 90 Cal. App. 3d 342, 153 Cal. Rptr. 366 (1979), a wrongful death action, did not relate back and was barred by the applicable statute of limitations. The original complaint alleged death from electrocution by a hairdryer. The amended complaint changed the cause of death to electrocution by a table lamp. The court concluded that although both pleadings related to a single death and at a single location, they alleged different accidents and involved different instrumentalities. *Id.* at 347. Do you agree with the holding in *Grudt*? With the holding in *Coronet*? Why?

[b] The "Same General Set of Facts" Requirement

For the relation back doctrine to apply, the amended complaint must allege "the same general set of facts as the original complaint." *Austin, supra,* 56 Cal. 2d at 600; *Barrington v. A.H. Robins Co.,* 39 Cal. 3d 146, 151, 216 Cal. Rptr. 405, 702 P.2d 563 (1985); *see Pointe San Diego Residential Cmty. v. Procopio, Cory, Hargreaves & Savitch, LLP,* 195 Cal. App. 4th 265, 125 Cal. Rptr. 3d 540 (2011) ("In determining whether the amended complaint alleges facts that are sufficiently similar to those alleged in the original complaint, the critical inquiry is whether the defendant had adequate notice of the claim based on the original pleading"). Do you agree with the *Honig* court's conclusion that plaintiff Honig's amended complaint alleging wrongful termination and defamation related to the same general set of facts pleaded in the original complaint, which alleged harassment and intimidation? The court in *Lee v. Bank of America,* 27 Cal. App. 4th 197, 32 Cal. Rptr. 2d 388 (1994), expressly disagreed with this relation back conclusion of *Honig*.

The plaintiff in *Lee* was a branch manager for the defendant bank. After complaining to her superior about various safety hazards at the branch, she was demoted in 1988. While still employed by defendant, plaintiff Lee filed a timely complaint in 1989 alleging wrongful demotion. The defendant bank then fired Lee in April, 1989 — more than a month after she filed suit. Plaintiff amended her complaint in 1991 to allege wrongful termination; all causes of action in her amended complaint were based on the April, 1989 termination. Defendant moved for summary judgment, which the trial court granted on statute of limitations grounds. Plaintiff appealed, and contended that her amended complaint related back to her earlier one.

The Court of Appeal first found the *Honig* facts indistinguishable, and then declined to follow *Honig*. The court reviewed the "same general set of facts" test as construed in *Barrington* and numerous other decisions, and concluded that "*Honig* did not grapple with the facts in any previous decision, nor attempt to address the problem of distinct wrongful acts. Its continuation-of-the-story rationale is contrary to *Barrington....* * * * *Honig* simply concluded that because it was not 'unusual' for an employer to restate reasons for termination in the process of defending it, the amended complaint for defamation related back to the original complaint filed prior to termination. * * * *Honig* is not persuasive and we will not follow it." *Lee,* 27 Cal. App. 4th at 212.

The court then concluded that plaintiff Lee's amended complaint was not based on substantially the same general facts as her original complaint because the two pleadings were based on different wrongful conduct—wrongful demotion versus subsequent wrongful termination. The court found that "a common motive—to retaliate against an employee for complaining about wrongdoing—is hardly sufficient to fuse the demotion to the termination." *Id.* at 214. Her amended complaint therefore did not relate back, and was barred by the applicable statute of limitations. And because plaintiff's amended complaint superseded her original complaint, any causes of action for wrongful demotion were also barred.

Which construction of the "same general set of facts" test do you find more persuasive—that applied by the court in *Honig* or in *Lee*? Which is more consistent with the various policies underlying amended complaints and statutes of limitations? Why? Which construction is more like the federal relation back standard in Rule 15(c), F.R.C.P., also reproduced *infra*. The construction of the "same general set of facts" test adopted by the court in *Lee* was employed in *McCauley v. Howard Jarvis Taxpayers Assn.*, 68 Cal. App. 4th 1255, 80 Cal. Rptr. 2d 900 (1998), where the court declined to follow the "continuation-of-the-story" or "bad egg" approach to the relation back doctrine.

[c] Fictitious Defendants

The relation back doctrine often applies to amended complaints which not only allege new causes of action, but also substitute new defendants for ones named fictitiously in the original complaint. *E.g.*, *Smeltzley v. Nicholson Mfg. Co.*, *supra*. Such use of the relation back doctrine to extend applicable statutes of limitations is discussed in detail in § 9.04, California's Fictitious Defendant ("Doe") Practice, *infra*.

[d] Should the California Court Adopt a More Pragmatic Approach?

California courts typically state the current relation back doctrine as requiring that the amended complaint not only must rest on the "same general set of facts," but also must involve the "same accident and same injuries" and refer to the "same offending instrumentality" as the original complaint. *See, e.g., Barrington v. A. H. Robins Co.*, 39 Cal. 3d 146, 151, 216 Cal. Rptr. 405, 702 P.2d 563 (1985); *Smetlzley, supra*, 18 Cal. 3d at 934; *Coronet, supra*, 90 Cal. App. 3d at 347. For criticisms of these additional restrictions on the basic "same general set of facts" standard, see Walter W. Heiser, *Relation Back of Amended Complaints: The California Courts Should Adopt a More Pragmatic Approach*, 44 Santa Clara L. Rev. 643 (2004).

The author explains why the use of the "same accident," "same injury," and "same instrumentality" tests as prerequisites to relation back is inconsistent with the modern view of civil litigation where discovery and pretrial orders, not pleadings, define the issues for trial. Heiser, *Relation Back, supra*, at 660-72, 695-97. He argues that the "same general set of facts" standard should be applied in a pragmatic manner, which would focus on whether the defendant will be unfairly surprised and therefore unduly prejudiced by the amended complaint. *Id.* at 687-695. The key inquiry is whether, during the course of pretrial discovery, the defendant was already made aware of, and already has gathered facts responding to, the new allegations in the amendment. *Id.* Do you agree with these arguments? What problems do you see with such a pragmatic approach?

[e] New Plaintiffs

Does the relation back doctrine apply when the plaintiff amends the original complaint, after the statute of limitations has expired, to add an additional plaintiff who alleges the same basic set of facts? *Compare Garnison v. Board of Dir. of the United Water Conservation Dist.*, 36 Cal. App. 4th 1670, 43 Cal. Rptr. 2d 214 (1995) (applying relation back doctrine where an individual plaintiff sought to amend a petition to allege that the plaintiff was also suing in his representative capacity on behalf of an unincorporated association), *and Haley v. Dow Lewis Motors, Inc.*, 72 Cal. App. 4th 497, 85 Cal. Rptr. 2d 352 (1999) (finding trial court abused its discretion when it denied plaintiff leave to amend to substitute in the real party in interest, the trustee in bankruptcy, and that such an amendment would relate back to the date of the original complaint), *with Bartalo v. Superior Court*, 51 Cal. App. 3d 526, 124 Cal. Rptr. 370 (1975) (concluding amended complaint adding a husband as an additional plaintiff and alleging a new cause of action for loss of consortium did not relate back to the wife's original personal injury negligence complaint), *and San Diego Gas & Elec. Co. v. Superior Court*, 146 Cal. App. 4th 1545, 53 Cal. Rptr. 3d 722 (2007) (ruling that because each wrongful death claimant must show the nature of her loss as the result of the decedent's death, the addition of an omitted heir as a new plaintiff necessarily inserts a new cause of action that seeks to enforce an independent right and, consequently, the relation back doctrine does not apply).

[3] *Amendments to Correct Naming Mistakes*

Whether an amendment to change the name of a party will be allowed and will relate back to avoid the statute of limitations depends on whether the mistake is merely a misnomer in the description of the party or "a substitution or entire change of parties." *Thompson v. Palmer Corp.*, 138 Cal. App. 2d 387, 390, 291 P.2d 995 (1956). For example, in *Dilberti v. Stage Call Corp.*, 4 Cal. App. 4th 1468, 6 Cal. Rptr. 2d 563 (1992), the court considered whether a new plaintiff may be substituted for the wrong person named as the plaintiff named in the original complaint, after the statute of limitations has expired. In *Dilberti*, Francine Dilberti and her sisters Mary Jo Dilberti were involved in an automobile collision. Francine, the driver, was not injured at all, but Mary Jo, the passenger, was and she retained an attorney to represent her. A timely personal injury complaint was filed, but it named the wrong sister (Francine) as the plaintiff and did not mention Mary Jo or even the fact that there was a passenger in the car. More than a year later, Mary Jo's attorney realized his mistake and filed a motion to amend the complaint and substitute Mary Jo for Francine as plaintiff. That motion was denied, and Mary Jo appealed.

The Court of Appeal relied on the rule stated in *Bartalo v. Superior Court*, 51 Cal. App. 3d 526, 124 Cal. Rptr. 370 (1975):

> The general rule governing the permissibility of the bringing in of additional plaintiffs after the period of the statute of limitations has elapsed … is that where the additional party plaintiff, joining in a suit brought before the statute of limitations has run against the original plaintiff, seeks *to enforce an independent right*, the amended pleading does not relate back, so as to render substitution permissible.…

Dilberti, 4 Cal. App. 4th at 1471 (quoting *Bartalo*, 51 Cal. App. 3d at 533) (italics in original). Applying this rule, the *Dilberti* court concluded that the case was not one of misnomer but was a failure to name the right party as plaintiff, and affirmed the denial of the motion to amend and substitute Mary Jo for Franchine.

In *Mayberry v. Coca Cola Bottling Co.*, 244 Cal. App. 2d 350, 53 Cal. Rptr. 317 (1966), the court allowed an amended complaint to correct a naming mistake after the statute of limitations had expired. The original complaint sought damages caused by drinking a bottle of contaminated soda, and named a corporation called "Coca Cola Bottling Company of Sacramento, Ltd." as defendant. The amended complaint sought to name the correct defendant, a partnership called "Coca Cola Bottling Company of Sacramento." The court differentiated between a misnomer or erroneous description and a change of identity, and held that the amended complaint merely corrected an excusable mistake attributable to the substantial identity of the dual identities. *Id.* at 353-54. Do you agree? Is *Mayberry* distinguishable from *Diliberti*? How so? Might the doctrine of equitable estoppel apply in circumstances like *Mayberry* where the (mistakenly) named defendant and the correct defendant have strikingly similar business names, and the named defendant conducts itself as though it were properly named as defendant? *See Cuadros v. Superior Court*, 6 Cal. App. 4th 671, 8 Cal. Rptr. 2d 18 (1992) (holding plaintiff's amended complaint not barred by statute of limitations where both the right (Budget Rent-A-Car of Westwood) and the wrong (Budget Rent-A-Car, Inc.) defendant were owned by the same persons, and the wrong defendant took willful affirmative action in the litigation to mask the error from plaintiff).

In *Plumlee v. Poag*, 150 Cal. App. 3d 541, 198 Cal. Rptr. 66 (1984), the plaintiff sued a decedent's estate for breach of contract, and named the executors and administrators as defendants individually. The trial court sustained a demurrer without leave to amend on the ground that the complaint named the defendants individually and not in their representative capacities, and therefore plaintiffs failed to bring an action against the executor or administrator within the three-month Probate Code limitation. The Court of Appeal reversed. The court found that the plaintiff was entitled to cure this technical defect by amendment correctly setting forth the representative capacities in which the defendants are being sued, and that such amendment would relate back to the original complaint: "Where full notice is given and a reasonably prudent person would realize that he is the party intended to be named as the defendant, the court should treat the mistake as harmless misnomer in order to promote substantive rights." *Pumlee*, at 150 Cal. App. 3d 547. Would the court's reasoning in *Plumlee* have helped the plaintiff in *Diliberti*? *See also Pasadena Hosp. Assn., Ltd. v. Superior Court*, 204 Cal. App. 3d 1031, 1037, 251 Cal. Rptr. 686 (1988) (holding plaintiff doctor's amended defamation complaint adding plaintiff's professional corporation of which he is sole shareholder related back because the change is one of form rather than substance).

§ 9.04 California's Fictitious ("Doe") Defendant Practice

[A] Introductory Note

Practice under the Federal Rules and in many states allows plaintiffs to designate unidentified party-defendants by the use of fictitious names. At the time plaintiff files her initial complaint, she may not be aware of the correct names, or even the identities of certain defendants. Moreover, the plaintiff may need to file suit promptly to avoid the statute of limitations bar. In these circumstances, it is common for the plaintiff to designate the unidentified defendants as "Doe One," "Doe I" or some other variant that is an obvious fiction. When the correct name or identity of the actual defendant is determined through discovery, the complaint can be amended to substitute the actual defendant for one of the "Doe" defendants.

Even when this initial fiction is used, however, the plaintiff faces a second hurdle if she wants the amendment to relate back to the date the complaint was initially filed in order to avoid the statute of limitation bar. Most states permit a cause of action alleged against a newly named defendant in the amended complaint to relate back to the date of the original complaint, but in a limited set of circumstances. Generally speaking, the relation back scheme in effect in most states is similar to the pre-1991 version of Rule 15(c) of the Federal Rules of Civil Procedure. *See generally* Joel E. Smith, Annotation, *Relation Back of Amended Pleading Substituting True Name of Defendant for Fictitious Name Used in Earlier Pleading So as to Avoid Bar of Limitations*, 85 A.L.R. 3d 130-57 (1978 & 2015 Update). As interpreted by the U.S. Supreme Court in *Schiavone v. Fortune*, 477 U.S. 21, 106 S. Ct. 2379, 91 L. Ed. 2d 18 (1986), the pre-1991 Rule 15(c) provided plaintiffs a sharply limited opportunity to add new parties after the statute of limitations has run. The new party must have received the notice required by the then-existing Rule 15(c)(1)-(2) before the end of the limitations period. Thus newly-identified parties could not be added after the limitations period, under the old rule 15(c).

[1] Federal Rule 15(c)

Federal Rule 15(c) was amended in 1991 to specifically change the result in *Schiavone v. Fortune, supra*, with respect to the problem of a misnamed defendant. *See Notes of Advisory Committee on 1991 Amendment to Rule 15(c)*. Rule 15(c), after a technical amendment in 1993 and subsequently, now provides:

(c) Relation Back of Amendments.

(1) *When an Amendment Relates Back.* An amendment to a pleading relates back to the original pleading when:

(A) the law that provides the applicable statute of limitations allows relation back;

(B) the amendment asserts a claim or defense that arose out of the conduct, transaction, or occurrence set out—or attempted to be set out—in the original pleading, or

(C) the amendment changes the party or the naming of the party against whom a claim is asserted, if Rule 15(c)(1)(B) is satisfied and if, within the period provided by Rule 4(m) for service of the summons and complaint, the party to be brought in by amendment:

(i) received such notice of the action that it will not be prejudiced in defending the merits; and

(ii) knew or should have known that the action would have been brought against it, but for a mistake concerning the proper party's identity.

Under new federal Rule 15(1)(C), an amended complaint which changes the naming of a party relates back when the notice requirement of Rule 15(c)(1)(B) is satisfied within the period provided by Rule 4(m) for service of the summons and complaint. Rule 4(m) allows 90 days for such service, plus any court-granted extensions for good cause. Rule 15(c)(1)(A) requires a federal court to apply a more liberal state relation back doctrine where that state's statute of limitations is applicable to the cause of action. For a discussion of when a state statute of limitations governs in federal court, see Chapter 4, Statutes of Limitations, Laches and Related Doctrines, *supra.*

[2] *California's Doe Defendant Practice*

California's unique "Doe defendant practice" is significantly broader than that recognized in other jurisdictions and in federal practice. *See* James E. Hogan, *California's Unique Doe Defendant Practice: A Fiction Stranger Than Truth*, 30 STAN. L. REV. 51, 88-101 (1977). California allows plaintiffs to name as Doe defendants parties whom the plaintiff has no reason to believe even exist solely as insurance against the statute of limitations bar. California practice is also far more liberal in allowing relation back than Rule 15(c)(3) and its equivalent elsewhere. Designed to mitigate the harsh effects of California's short statutes of limitations, particularly in personal injury actions, California's "Doe defendant practice" permits relation back to the date of the original pleading in a broad variety of circumstances unknown to the federal courts under old Rule 15(c) or new Rule 15(c)(1)(C). Ordinarily relation back is allowed by the simple expedient of substituting the new defendant for one of the Does.

[3] Evolution of the California Doctrine

California's "Doe defendant practice" has evolved through case law interpreting three rather innocent looking statutes: Sections 474, 350, and 583.210 of the California Code of Civil Procedure. These statutes have existed in some form or other since the original Practice Act of 1851. Section 474 is the legislative centerpiece of the fictitious defendant practice, providing in pertinent part:

> When the plaintiff is ignorant of the name of a defendant, he must state that fact in the complaint, ... and such defendant may be designated in any pleading or proceeding by any name, and when his true name is discovered, the pleading or proceeding must be amended accordingly;....

As will be discussed in *Streicher v. Tommy's Electric Co.*, reproduced *infra*, the California courts have construed § 474 to include a relation back concept.

Section 350 states that an action is "commenced" for purposes of satisfying the statute of limitations "when the complaint is filed." And Section 583.210 states:

> (a) The summons and complaint shall be served upon a defendant within three years after the action is commenced against the defendant. For the purpose of this subdivision an action is commenced at the time the complaint is filed.

> (b) Return of summons or other proof of service shall be made within 60 days after the time the summons and complaint must be served upon a defendant.

How do these three sections work together? The fictitious defendant doctrine is not obvious from the text of the statutes. But when infused with some creative common law interpretations, these sections provide the basis for a unique method of extending the statute of limitations.

Streicher v. Tommy's Electric Company

Court of Appeal of California, Sixth Appellate District
164 Cal. App. 3d 876, 211 Cal. Rptr. 22 (1985)

PANELLI, PRESIDING JUSTICE.

Plaintiff appeals from a judgment of dismissal entered after defendants' demurrer to an amended complaint was sustained without leave to amend on the ground the statute of limitations barred the action. We reverse.

Facts

On October 4, 1979, plaintiff Frank Streicher filed a complaint for personal injuries sustained on July 16, 1979, at a construction site when certain radio-controlled overhead garage doors opened causing him to fall from the scaffolding upon which he was working. The complaint named as defendants Shippers Development Company (general contractor), Salinas Steel Builders, Inc. (subcontractor), Jack's Overhead Door Company, Inc. and John Hendrix (independent contractors and installers of the electronic doors), as well as four fictitious business entities (Black, White, Blue, and Grey Companies), three fictitious individuals comprising Grey Company as a partnership (Does One, Two, and Three), and ninety-seven additional fictitious defendants (Does Four through One Hundred).

The first paragraph of the complaint alleged that the true names and capacities of the fictitious defendants were unknown to plaintiff, but stated that when these were ascertained plaintiff would move to amend the complaint accordingly. Paragraph six alleged a cause of action for negligence, charging that defendants owned, possessed and controlled the construction site, that they had provided an unsafe workplace through their failure, among other things, to "supervise and control the installation and operation of radio-controlled overhead garage doors" on the worksite, and that such negligence resulted in plaintiff's injuries.

On May 18, 1982, two years and ten months after the accident, and after settlement was obtained with the named defendants, Streicher filed a first amended complaint against respondents Tommy's Electric Company and Shima American Corporation and Does Four through One Hundred. It alleged respondents designed, manufactured, marketed and sold the radio-controlled overhead door openers involved in the accident and that these openers had been defectively designed and would malfunction without human intervention. The amended complaint stated causes of action for negligence, breach of express and implied warranty, and strict products liability.[1]

On June 17, 1982, respondents demurred to the first amended complaint on the ground that the claim was barred by the one-year statute of limitations (Code Civ. Proc., § 340, subd. (3)). Respondents also moved the court to judicially notice, pursuant to Evidence Code sections 452 and 453, all the pleadings and records in its file on this case including a cross-complaint filed by Jack's Overhead Doors (one of the named defendants) and a complaint in intervention filed by Industrial Indemnity Co. (plaintiff's employer's workers' compensation carrier), both filed in February of 1980, which included respondents among the named defendants and alleged causes of action for indemnity based on a products liability theory.

Respondents argued in their moving papers that since plaintiff's amended complaint did not substitute respondents for any of the fictitiously named defendants in his original complaint, the amended complaint was in fact adding new defendants to the action and that this was not permissible after the running of the one-year statute of limitations. Respondents further argued that even if plaintiff's defective substitution of fictitious defendants was cured, the provisions of Code of Civil Procedure section

---

1. On April 29, 1982, prior to the filing of his amended complaint, Streicher served upon Shima American Corporation (Shima) a summons and a copy of the original complaint. The proof of service indicated Shima had been served as fictitious defendant "Doe Five," but the summons accompanying the complaint did not so indicate. On May 17, 1982 plaintiff and respondents stipulated to plaintiff's filing of the amended complaint, but the stipulation also indicated it did not constitute a waiver by respondents "to answer or otherwise plead" to the amended complaint.

474,[2] allowing the amendment to relate back to the filing of the original complaint, did not apply because in February of 1980 plaintiff had notice of respondents' identity through the filing of the cross-complaint and intervention pleadings, yet he had nevertheless failed to exercise due diligence in amending his complaint before the expiration of the statute of limitations in July 1980.

Streicher opposed respondents' demurrer and moved for leave to amend his complaint in order to properly substitute respondents for specifically named fictitious defendants, arguing his failure to do so constituted a procedural error which could be easily cured. Streicher also argued the benefits afforded by section 474 should apply because he was not aware of any facts constituting the basis for a products liability cause of action against respondents until March 30, 1982, when an electronics expert indicated that the electronic door controllers involved in the accident were defective.

The court sustained respondents' demurrer without leave to amend on the ground the statute of limitations barred the action. The court's minute order also noted that plaintiff's early pleadings were consistent with his belief that "before March 30, 1982 … [he] had no basis for an action against the two defendants." This appeal followed.

Discussion

On appeal, Streicher contends the trial court erroneously sustained the demurrer and abused its discretion in denying him leave to amend the complaint to cure his failure to specifically substitute respondents for fictitious defendants named in the original complaint. We find these contentions meritorious.

Preliminarily we must determine whether Streicher's first amended complaint, absent his defective substitution of respondents for the fictitiously named defendants, relates back to the filing date of the original complaint under section 474, thus defeating the bar of the statute of limitations.

"The purpose of … section 474 is to enable a plaintiff who is ignorant of the identity of the defendant to file his complaint before his claim is barred by the statute of limitations. There is a strong policy in favor of litigating cases on their merits, and the California courts have been very liberal in permitting the amendment of pleadings to bring in a defendant previously sued by fictitious name." (*Barrows v. American Motors Corp.* (1983) 144 Cal. App. 3d 1, 7 [192 Cal. Rptr. 380], citing *Austin v. Massachusetts Bonding & Insurance Co.* (1961) 56 Cal. 2d 596, 600, 602, 603 [15 Cal. Rptr. 817, 364 P.2d 681]; …). It is also well settled that the amended pleading will relate back to the date of filing of the original complaint provided it seeks recovery on the same general set of facts as alleged in the original complaint. (*Austin v. Massachusetts Bonding & Insurance Co., supra*, 56 Cal. 2d at p. 600; *Smeltzley v. Nicholson Mfg. Co.*

---

2. Unless otherwise indicated, further statutory references are to the Code of Civil Procedure. Section 474 provides in pertinent part: "When the plaintiff is ignorant of the name of a defendant, he must state that fact in the complaint, … and such defendant may be designated in any pleading or proceeding by any name, and when his true name is discovered, the pleading or proceeding must be amended accordingly.…"

(1977) 18 Cal. 3d 932, 937 [136 Cal. Rptr. 269, 559 P.2d 624, 85 A.L.R.3d 121]; *Barrows v. American Motors Corp., supra*, 144 Cal. App. 3d at p. 7). Moreover, it is clear that where the original complaint contains standard Doe allegations alleging negligence theories, it is proper to amend the complaint to bring in other defendants on warranty and products liability; since the amendment involves the same accident and injury, the amendment relates back to satisfy the statute of limitations. (*Barrows v. American Motors Corp., supra*, 144 Cal. App. 3d at p. 7; *Garrett v. Crown Coach Corp.* (1968) 259 Cal. App. 2d 647 [66 Cal. Rptr. 590].)

However, in order to claim the benefits of section 474, plaintiff's ignorance of defendant's true name must be genuine and not feigned. We must therefore look to see whether plaintiff knew defendant's true name at the time he filed his original complaint. Plaintiff's requisite ignorance of defendant's name under section 474 has been expansively interpreted by the courts to encompass situations where " 'he knew the identity of the person but was ignorant of the facts giving him a cause of action against the person [citations], or knew the name and all the facts but was unaware that the law gave him a cause of action against the fictitiously named defendant and discovered that right by reason of decisions rendered after the commencement of the action. [Citations].' " (*Marasco v. Wadsworth* (1978) 21 Cal. 3d 82, 88 [145 Cal. Rptr. 843, 578 P.2d 90], quoting with approval *Barnes v. Wilson* [(1974)] 40 Cal. App. 3d [199] at p. 205). Moreover, section 474's ignorance requirement "is restricted to the knowledge of the plaintiff *at the time of filing of the complaint*" (*Munoz v. Purdy* (1979) 91 Cal. App. 3d 942, 947 [154 Cal. Rptr. 472], italics added;…, "and does not relate to steps that should be taken after the filing of the action." (91 Cal. App. 3d at p. 947).

Guided by the foregoing principles we turn to the case at bar. Streicher's original complaint contained standard "Doe" allegations against fictitious defendants then unknown, as required by section 474. Although the original complaint alleged a cause of action for negligence against all defendants for failing to provide a safe place to work, it was proper to amend the complaint to bring in the defectively substituted defendants on the additional warranty and products liability theories of recovery since the amendment involved the same accident and injury alleged in the original complaint. (*See Smeltzley v. Nicholson Mfg. Co., supra*, 18 Cal. 3d at p. 937). It is undisputed that at the time Streicher's original complaint was filed he was ignorant of respondents' identity or of their participation in designing, manufacturing or selling the electronic door openers involved in the accident. Likewise Streicher did not know at this time any facts which would indicate the possibility the door openers were defectively designed as such flaw in design was not externally visible.

Respondents contend, nevertheless, that Streicher did not "in good faith" avail himself of the provisions of section 474 because four months after his original complaint was filed he was alerted, through the filing of cross-complaint and intervention pleadings, of respondents' role in manufacturing and distributing the electronic door devices and of the possibility they could be sued under a products liability theory of recovery. As pointed out above, plaintiff's *actual knowledge at the time* the suit is filed is dispositive in triggering the application of section 474's fictitious defendant provisions. Further, it remains undisputed that at the time of the filing of the original complaint Streicher was ignorant of respondents' identity or of their status as manufacturers and distributors of the defective door openers. Moreover, there is no requirement under section 474 that plaintiff exercise reasonable diligence in discovering either the true identity of fictitious defendants or the facts giving him a cause of action against such persons after the filing of a complaint and up to the expiration of the applicable limitation period. (*Munoz v. Purdy, supra*, 91 Cal. App. 3d at pp. 947-948; *Barrows v. American Motors Corp., supra*, 144 Cal. App. 3d at p. 10, fn. 4). As aptly stated by the court in *Munoz, supra*, "the interjection of a discovery standard into section 474 would lead to the harmful practice in all litigation of requiring that all persons who might conceivably have some connection with the lawsuit be specifically named in order to avoid the sanctions of the failure to comply with the inquiry requirements of section 474." (91 Cal. App. 3d at pp. 947-948).

Respondent also argues that, irrespective of appellant's lack of knowledge of the true identity of the fictitiously named defendants at the time he filed the original complaint, he was nonetheless "dilatory" in filing the amended complaint once he acquired knowledge of the true identity of those defendants fictitiously named. Respondent contends that unreasonable delay in filing the *amendment* after actual discovery of the true identity of a fictitiously named defendant can bar a plaintiff's resort to the fictitious name procedure. Some authority for this proposition can be found in *Barrows v. American Motor Corp., supra*, 144 Cal. App. 3d at pages 8-9, and in *Barnes v. Wilson, supra*, 40 Cal. App. 3d 199 at page 206. Here, however the trial court was only dealing with a demurrer to the amended complaint. "Defendant's demurrer, however, tests only the sufficiency of the pleadings. Nothing in the pleadings suggests that plaintiff, after learning of his cause of action against defendant, was dilatory in amending his complaint, or that defendant suffered prejudice from such delay. [citation]." (*Smeltzley v. Nicholson Mfg. Co., supra*, 18 Cal. 3d 932, at p. 939, fns. omitted). Nothing in this record suggests appellant was dilatory in amending his complaint. In fact, the trial court's order states that before March 30, 1982, "[appellant] had no basis for an action against the two defendants." Once he learned the facts giving him a cause of action against respondents on March 30, 1982, his first amended complaint naming respondents as defendants was promptly filed on May 18, 1982, within two months of discovery.

We conclude that, absent Streicher's defective substitution of respondents for the fictitiously named defendants, his first amended complaint relates back to the filing date of the original complaint under section 474, thus defeating the bar of the statute of limitations.

The issue remains whether the court abused its discretion in denying Streicher leave to amend the complaint to cure his failure to properly allege that respondents were being substituted for some of the fictitiously named defendants in the original complaint. Streicher argues this omission constituted a procedural error which was easily curable through amendment. We agree.

"It is axiomatic that if there is a reasonable possibility that a defect in the complaint can be cured by amendment or that the pleading liberally construed can state a cause of action, a demurrer should not be sustained without leave to amend. [Citations.]" (*Minsky v. City of Los Angeles* (1974) 11 Cal. 3d 113, 118-119 [113 Cal. Rptr. 102, 520 P.2d 726]). We are satisfied the amended complaint's allegations sufficiently state a cause of action for products liability against respondents. Moreover, "[an] amendment substituting the true names of fictitious defendants is not a matter of substance because it does not change the cause of action nor affect the issues raised by the pleadings. [Citation]." (*Vincent v. Grayson* (1973) 30 Cal. App. 3d 899, 905, fn. 2 [106 Cal. Rptr. 733]). Since the defect in the complaint does not affect the substance of its allegations and it is reasonably possible the defect can be cured by amendment, we conclude the trial court abused its discretion in dismissing the action without giving Streicher the opportunity to amend.

The judgment of dismissal is reversed.

General Motors Corp. v. Superior Court

Court of Appeal of California, Fourth Appellate District
48 Cal. App. 4th 580, 55 Cal. Rptr. 2d 871 (1996)

VOGEL, (MIRIAM A.), JUSTICE.

A driver wearing her seat belt is stopped in traffic. Her car is rear-ended. Although her seat belt remains fastened and does not break, her head strikes the steering wheel and she later mentions to a doctor that "the seat belt didn't hold [her]." Within one year, she sues the driver of the other car and 20 Doe defendants. More than two years after the accident, she substitutes the manufacturer of her car for a Doe defendant and adds allegations that the seat belt was defective. The manufacturer cries foul, claiming the driver knew there was a problem with the seat belt and knew the identity of the manufacturer of her car, and thus was not "ignorant" of its identity within the meaning of section 474 of the Code of Civil Procedure.[1] The driver disagrees, claiming the mere fact that the seat belt did not secure her tightly to the seat did not make her suspect that the belt's "comfort feature" (which permits it to spool out when the driver leans forward) was defective in that it allowed "the inadvertent introduction of slack." The trial court agreed with the driver and so do we.

FACTS

On November 5, 1992, Susanna Jeffrey's 1986 Chevrolet Blazer was rear-ended by a car driven by David Katsuro Akazawa. Jeffrey's face hit the steering wheel and she suffered facial injuries, including "traumatic brain injury," a broken nose and broken teeth. Jeffrey hired a lawyer (Philip Dunn) and he sent Jeffrey to Charles Furst, Ph.D. (a clinical neuropsychologist), for an evaluation. On April 27, 1993, Dr. Furst interviewed and examined Jeffrey, who told him that she had struck her nose and abdomen on the steering wheel because "the seat belt didn't hold [her]" or because the "seat

---

1. Unless otherwise stated, all section references are to the Code of Civil Procedure. Under section 474, discussed at length below, a plaintiff who is ignorant of the name of a defendant may designate that defendant by a fictitious name and then amend when the defendant's true name is discovered.

belt failed."[2] On July 6, Dr. Furst forwarded a report to Dunn, reciting Jeffrey's history and expressing his opinion of her condition. Included in Dr. Furst's description of the accident is this statement: "She was stopped on the freeway in traffic when she was rear-ended. She experienced whiplash and she struck her nose on the steering wheel, after her seat belt failed, and additionally she struck her abdomen on the wheel also." On October 7, Jeffrey sued Akazawa and Does 1 through 20, claiming damages for personal injuries and property damage caused by Akazawa's negligent driving.

In March 1995, following a non-binding arbitration award against Akazawa for more than $500,000, Dunn associated "more experienced" counsel, John D. Rowell and his firm, Rowell & Tessier. In April, Jeffrey filed a standard-form "Amendment to Complaint" adding General Motors Corporation as Doe 1. On May 19 (two and one-half years after the accident), Jeffrey filed a first amended complaint adding a products liability claim against GM, alleging that the Blazer's seat belt restraint system was defectively designed, and that GM knew it was defective but did nothing about it. A claim for punitive damages was also added.

In August, GM (then unaware of Dr. Furst's notes) moved to quash service of Jeffrey's first amended complaint on the ground that Jeffrey must have known she had a potential claim against GM when the original complaint was filed because "a seat belt either restrains a person or it does not and this fact is known immediately after" an automobile accident. Jeffrey opposed the motion, explaining in her declaration that although she obviously knew the name of the manufacturer of her car at the time she filed her original complaint, she "had no knowledge of any defect in the vehicle or the seat belt system of the vehicle." Since that time, however, she "learned that the injury [she] suffered was an injury which was most likely suffered as a result of a defect in the design of the seat belt." She learned of this defect when Rowell (her new attorney) explained it to her and identified a "so-called 'comfort feature' in the seat belt" which allows "the belt to remain in a spooled out position whenever a driver leans forward, for example, to adjust the radio or to turn on the ignition." Once the driver leans forward the belt will not retract into a snug position when the driver "leans back." She had "never noticed this condition prior to discussing this matter" with Rowell but, since that time, had become aware of it when she drove the Blazer.

Jeffrey's opposition was also supported by a declaration from Dunn explaining that he had examined the Blazer when he was first consulted by Jeffrey and that, to him, "there did not appear to be anything wrong with the passenger restraint system. Up until the time [he] discussed this matter with Mr. Rowell[, Dunn] was unaware of GM's 'comfort feature' and was completely unaware that this particular design could cause injuries such as occurred to Mrs. Jeffrey." A declaration by Rowell explained that he was involved in an unrelated matter involving "a claim that the identical 'com-

---

2. Dr. Furst's entry in Jeffrey's file is that she struck the wheel "after seat belt failed." At his deposition, he testified that he could not remember whether those were her words or his, that the word "failed" might have been his and not hers, and that she might have said "the seat belt didn't hold [her]" or used some other words to the same effect. * * *

fort feature'" on a GM vehicle caused "head injuries in a similar manner to the allegations in this case." He had conducted substantial discovery in the other case and had learned of eight additional "comfort feature" cases pending against GM, all of which were subject to protective orders prohibiting disclosure of information about the alleged defects in GM's seat belt system. As a result, it "would be quite unusual for someone such as Mr. Dunn, who does not specialize in the products liability area, to have become aware of the problems associated with the use of the 'comfort feature' design" in Jeffrey's vehicle. Implicit in Rowell's declaration is the conclusion that the average driver would be totally unaware of this problem.[5]

GM's motion to quash was denied, the court finding that Jeffrey was "not aware of any defect, design or otherwise, in the ... occupant restraint system." GM then answered and conducted discovery, at which time it learned of Dr. Furst's examination of Jeffrey and the note in Dr. Furst's file about the seat belt "failure." GM asked Rowell to dismiss Jeffrey's case against GM in exchange for a waiver of costs and a release of GM's malicious prosecution claims. When Rowell refused, GM moved for summary judgment, contending Jeffrey's claims were barred because, at the time she filed her original complaint, Jeffrey and Dunn knew there was a problem with the seat belt and knew the identity of the car's manufacturer, and thus Jeffrey was not ignorant of GM's identity within the meaning of section 474. GM supported its motion with Dr. Furst's deposition testimony, his handwritten notes, and his report to Dunn. Jeffrey opposed the motion, relying on the declarations she had filed in opposition to GM's motion to quash and contending, again, that she was ignorant within the meaning of section 474 because she did not know the seat belt system was defective.[6]

---

5. In general terms, this is the way Rowell describes the problem with the seat belt: "The shoulder belt incorporated a load limiter, known as a 'windowshade' device, or comfort feature, which allowed intentional or inadvertent introduction of slack into the seat belt. [GM] has never publicized this design problem with this system, nor did it ever recall the vehicle or request that owners, such as [Jeffrey], modify or change the belt. However, the comfort feature was removed from the design of subsequent models." * * * It appears to us that the (alleged) problem is this: When the driver gets into the car, slack is present in the shoulder belt due to the absence of an automatic cancellation feature (the purpose of which is to automatically cancel whatever slack was in the belt before the driver entered the car). When the driver buckles herself into her seat, her movement causes the "windowshade" (comfort feature) to inadvertently set excess slack. Upon impact, the driver's upper torso is flung forward and the shoulder belt retractor fails to timely lock up, causing additional seat belt webbing to extend and cause more forward movement to the driver's head. We emphasize that these are allegations, not established facts.

6. Jeffrey did not file a supplemental declaration denying that she said anything to Dr. Furst about the seat belt. * * * For purposes of this opinion, however, we are assuming that she did say something to the effect that the shoulder strap did not hold her as tight as she would have thought it would. Otherwise, as Jeffrey pointed out in the trial court, the dispute about that foundational fact would by itself mean GM was not entitled to summary judgment. (§ 437c, subd. (c).) Given the facts of this case (a low to medium speed rear-end impact and a seat belt that did not break or come undone), we do not believe much is added by Jeffrey's alleged statement to Dr. Furst. In our view, the issue is whether a driver who is dutifully wearing a seat belt and nevertheless strikes her head against the steering wheel is to be charged with actual knowledge of the basic facts of a products liability claim based on a latent defect in the design of the restraint system. Whether she stated her subjective belief is immaterial, as is the fact that she might have been suspicious.

As Jeffrey explained to the trial court, her claims against GM are not based on an allegation of a mechanical failure but rather on the allegedly defective design of the restraint system. The trial court denied GM's motion.

GM then filed a petition for a writ of mandate, asking us to compel the trial court to grant summary judgment and framing the issues as (1) whether a plaintiff may rely upon the subsequent association of more experienced counsel to bring in a new defendant under section 474 notwithstanding that "there has been no discovery of new facts" as required by section 474; (2) whether "the inexperience and malpractice" of Jeffrey's first lawyer, "who effectively violate[d] [his] ethical obligation to not take cases [he was] unqualified to handle," is a legally justifiable excuse to avoid the requirements of section 474;[8] and (3) whether a Doe amendment can relate back to the date of the original complaint when it is "admittedly based upon the same basic facts (i.e., seat belt failure) which were admittedly known when the original complaint was filed." We issued an order to show cause, received opposition from Jeffrey, and heard argument (at which time we invited and later received further briefing). We now deny the petition.

DISCUSSION

* * *

In the trial court and here, GM talks in terms of what Jeffrey should have known at the time she filed her original complaint. As we will explain, that question is immaterial in this context and the only relevant inquiry is whether Jeffrey had actual knowledge of the basic facts giving rise to her claim against GM.

I. *The Delayed Discovery Rule*

We begin by stating the delayed discovery rule GM asks us to apply in this case. Where no one related to the same injury has been sued within the applicable period of limitations (for example, where the plaintiff knows she has a medical problem but does not know her condition was caused by a defective drug), the statute of limitations begins to run "when the plaintiff suspects or should suspect that her injury was caused by wrongdoing, that someone has done something wrong to her." (*Jolly v. Eli Lilly & Co.* (1988) 44 Cal. 3d 1103, 1110 [751 P.2d 923, 245 Cal. Rptr. 658].) Stated otherwise, the limitations period begins once the plaintiff has notice or information of circum-

---

8. This pejorative attack on Dunn is uncalled for. We find nothing in the record contradicting Rowell's assertion that the alleged defects in GM's seat belt system are known to only a few lawyers. It is one thing to state the well established rule that an attorney's mistake about the statute of limitations will not save his client's case (*Gutierrez v. Mofid* (1985) 39 Cal. 3d 892, 898 [218 Cal. Rptr. 313, 705 P.2d 886]; *Miller v. Bechtel Corp.* (1983) 33 Cal. 3d 868, 875 [191 Cal. Rptr. 619, 663 P.2d 177]), quite another to launch an ad hominem attack accusing an attorney of malpractice or unethical conduct by not knowing that which is unknowable by reason of protective orders obtained by GM. In a duty to discover case, there might be an argument that, upon receipt of Dr. Furst's report and its mention of the seat belt, Dunn should have retained an expert to examine the seat belt. Since this is not such a case, we will have no more to say about this purported issue. As we view this case, the only issue is whether, at the time she filed her original complaint, Jeffrey was ignorant of the facts giving her a cause of action against GM.

stances about her injury and its negligent cause such as would put a reasonable person on inquiry. (*Id.* at p. 1109; *Gutierrez v. Mofid, supra,* 39 Cal. 3d at pp. 896-897; *Sanchez v. South Hoover Hospital* (1976) 18 Cal. 3d 93, 101 [132 Cal. Rptr. 657, 553 P.2d 1129].)

In the delayed discovery context, a "plaintiff need not be aware of the specific 'facts' necessary to establish the claim; that is a process contemplated by pretrial discovery. *Once the plaintiff has a suspicion of wrongdoing, and therefore an incentive to sue, she must decide whether to file suit or sit on her rights. So long as a suspicion exists, it is clear that the plaintiff must go find the facts; she cannot wait for the facts to find her.*" (*Jolly v. Eli Lilly & Co., supra,* 44 Cal. 3d at p. 1111, italics added; see also *Miller v. Bechtel Corp., supra,* 33 Cal. 3d at p. 875; *Graham v. Hansen* (1982) 128 Cal. App. 3d 965, 972-973 [180 Cal. Rptr. 604] [if a plaintiff believes because of injuries she has suffered that someone has done something wrong, the statutory period begins].)

The problem with GM's reliance on these cases is that they have nothing to do with section 474.

II. *The Section 474 Rules*

A. *The Statute*

Section 474 was enacted in 1872 to replace a virtually identical provision enacted in 1851 as section 69 of the Practice Act (Hogan, *California's Unique Doe Defendant Practice: A Fiction Stranger Than Truth* (1977) 30 Stan.L.Rev. 51, 57, fn. 18, henceforth cited as Doe Defendant Practice). As enacted, section 474 provided: "'When the plaintiff is ignorant of the name of the defendant, he must state that fact in the complaint, and such defendant may be designated in any pleading or proceeding by any name, and when his true name is discovered, the pleading or proceeding must be amended accordingly.'" (*Doe Defendant Practice, supra,* at p. 57, fn. 18; ...) * * * [F]or our purposes, the statute is the same now as it was in 1851.

Today, it is generally understood that when a complaint sets forth a cause of action against a defendant designated by a fictitious name because the plaintiff is genuinely ignorant of his name or identity, and his true name thereafter is discovered and substituted by amendment, he is considered a party to the action from its commencement so that the statute of limitations stops running as of the date the original complaint was filed. (*Optical Surplus, Inc. v. Superior Court* (1991) 228 Cal. App. 3d 776, 783 [279 Cal. Rptr. 194].)[10]

---

10. Although it may appear at first blush that section 474 gives a plaintiff greater rights than she would have if, in the first instance, she had failed to sue anyone, that is not necessarily so. A plaintiff who defers suit altogether may (under certain circumstances and subject to various outside limitations imposed by statute) wait years after the causative event to initiate her litigation. (See e.g., *Rose v. Fife* (1989) 207 Cal. App. 3d 760, 768 [255 Cal. Rptr. 440].) In the section 474 context, however, once *one* defendant is sued, *all* fictitiously named defendants must be brought in within a maximum period of three years—because summons must be returned within three years of its issuance. (§ 583.210.) Moreover, as a result of various trial delay reduction programs and their enabling rules, the traditional three-year period of section 583.210 is little more than a fading memory—under current rules of practice, the plaintiff must return summons and dismiss all fictitiously served defendants within six

B. *The Supreme Court's Early Views*

[Here the court discusses early Supreme Court cases construing section 474, and notes that the view expressed in *Irving v. Carpentier* (1886) 70 Cal. 23 [11 P. 391] has been followed for over 100 years. The court in *Irving* contrasted the statutory rule of section 474 to the delayed discovery rule, and concluded]: "*But the rule prescribed by the statute in this case is entirely different. It is when he is actually ignorant of a certain fact, not when he might by the use of reasonable diligence have discovered it. Whether his ignorance is from misfortune or negligence, he is alike ignorant, and this is all the statute requires. This is the true meaning of the statute. We adopt it the more readily because the party thus brought in as a defendant loses no rights by it.*" (*Irving v. Carpentier, supra,* 70 Cal. at pp. 25-27, italics added.) * * *

C. *The Current View Is One of Liberal Construction*

Whatever the judicial attitude toward section 474 might have been in the 19th Century, the Supreme Court and the Courts of Appeal of the 20th Century are uniform in their view that section 474 is to be liberally construed. (*Austin v. Massachusetts Bonding & Insurance Co.* (1961) 56 Cal. 2d 596, 602-603 [15 Cal. Rptr. 817, 364 P.2d 681]; Motor City Sales v. Superior Court (1973) 31 Cal. App. 3d 342, 345 [107 Cal. Rptr. 280]; *Barnes v. Wilson* (1974) 40 Cal. App. 3d 199, 203 [114 Cal. Rptr. 839] [the purpose of section 474 is to enable a plaintiff to commence suit in time to avoid the bar of limitations where he is ignorant of the identity of the defendant and the statute should be liberally construed to accomplish that purpose]; *Streicher v. Tommy's Electric Co.* (1985) 164 Cal. App. 3d 876, 882 [211 Cal. Rptr. 22]; *Barrows v. American Motors Corp.* (1983) 144 Cal. App. 3d 1, 7 [192 Cal. Rptr. 380] ["the California courts have been very liberal in permitting the amendment of pleadings to bring in a defendant previously sued by fictitious name"].)

In keeping with this liberal interpretation of section 474, it is now well established that even though the plaintiff knows of the existence of the defendant sued by a fictitious name, and even though the plaintiff knows the defendant's actual identity (that is, his name), the plaintiff is "ignorant" within the meaning of the statute if he lacks knowledge of that person's connection with the case or with his injuries. (*Wallis v. Southern Pac. Transportation Co.* (1976) 61 Cal. App. 3d 782, 786 [132 Cal. Rptr. 631]; *Oakes v. McCarthy Co.* (1968) 267 Cal. App. 2d 231, 253 [73 Cal. Rptr. 127] [plaintiff knew soils engineer was involved but did not know his connection to earth compacting operation]; *Parker v. Robert E. McKee, Inc.* (1992) 3 Cal. App. 4th 512, 518 [4 Cal. Rptr. 2d 347] [even where the defendant is named in the original complaint by his true name, then dismissed because the plaintiff believed his capacity relieved

---

months to one year (or at least show good cause why a little more time ought to be allowed to locate another defendant). As a practical matter, therefore, section 474 gives the plaintiff about one extra year, not the unlimited open-ended period of time GM (and the defendants in the reported cases) seem to think is an eternity or longer. (See *Munoz v. Purdy* (1979) 91 Cal. App. 3d 942, 947 [154 Cal. Rptr. 472] [the statutory scheme involving sections 474 and 583.210 "has been a satisfactory compromise between the harsh effect on a plaintiff of the statute of limitations and the unfairness to a defendant of attempting to litigate a stale claim"].)

him of liability, he may later be added (returned to the action) as a Doe defendant based on the plaintiff's discovery that he occupied different legal capacity].) The fact that the plaintiff had the means to obtain knowledge is irrelevant.

D. *To Defeat a Claim of Ignorance, It Must Be Shown That the Plaintiff Had Actual Knowledge of the Basic Facts*

Ignorance of the *facts* giving rise to a cause of action is the "ignorance" required by section 474, and the pivotal question is, "'did plaintiff know *facts*?' not 'did plaintiff know or believe that she had a cause of action based on those facts?'" (*Scherer v. Mark* (1976) 64 Cal. App. 3d 834, 841 [135 Cal. Rptr. 90]; *Hazel v. Hewlett* (1988) 201 Cal. App. 3d 1458, 1465 [247 Cal. Rptr. 723].) Although it is true that a plaintiff's ignorance of the defendant's name must be genuine (in good faith) and not feigned (*Streicher v. Tommy's Electric Co., supra,* 164 Cal. App. 3d at p. 882; …) and that a plaintiff need not be aware of each and every detail concerning a person's involvement before the plaintiff loses his ignorance (*Dover v. Sadowinski* (1983) 147 Cal. App. 3d 113, 117-118 [194 Cal. Rptr. 866]; *Optical Surplus, Inc. v. Superior Court, supra,* 228 Cal. App. 3d at p. 784), it is equally true that the plaintiff does not relinquish her rights under section 474 simply because she has a suspicion of wrongdoing arising from one or more facts she does know. (*Garrett v. Crown Coach Corp., supra,* 259 Cal. App. 2d at p. 650; *Breceda v. Gamsby* (1968) 267 Cal. App. 2d 167, 175-176 [72 Cal. Rptr. 832] [a plaintiff is entitled to the benefits of section 474 unless substantial evidence shows she was not ignorant of the facts she needed to know].)

The distinction between "actual facts" and "mere suspicion" was addressed in *Dieckmann v. Superior Court* (1985) 175 Cal. App. 3d 345 [220 Cal. Rptr. 602]: "Section 474 allows a plaintiff in good faith to delay suing particular persons as named defendants *until he has knowledge of sufficient facts to cause a reasonable person to believe liability is probable.* The distinction between a suspicion that some cause could exist and a factual basis to believe a cause exists is critical in the operation of section 474. The former is one reason attorneys include general charging allegations against fictitiously named defendants; the latter requires substitution of the defendant's true name. [The late named defendant's] present urging that its ostensible liability was always obvious to plaintiff confuses these two standards of knowledge and is based upon hindsight." (*Dieckmann v. Superior Court, supra,* 175 Cal. App. 3d at p. 363, italics added.)[14]

---

14. We note that a plaintiff bringing in a new defendant after the statute of limitations has run must, at the same time she is required to show her ignorance, also show that her new claim is based on "the same general set of facts" as alleged in the original complaint—or risk a pyrrhic victory where she gets to bring in her new defendant but loses her right to have her claim relate back to the time the original complaint was filed. In a case before us, there is no relation back problem. (*Barrows v. American Motors Corp., supra,* 144 Cal. App. 3d at p. 7 [when standard Doe allegations are included in complaint against the driver of a vehicle, a product liability claim against the manufacturer of a vehicle involved in the same accident relates back because it is based on the same accident and the same injury]; …)

Thus, for example, in *Streicher v. Tommy's Electric Co., supra,* 164 Cal. App. 3d 876, a plaintiff sued the general contractor, a subcontractor and several fictitiously named defendants for negligently causing the injuries he sustained when a radio-controlled overhead garage door opened unexpectedly, causing him to fall from scaffolding where he was working. (*Id.* at pp. 879-880.) Two years and ten months later, the plaintiff amended his complaint to add the manufacturer of the door opener and allegations that the opener was defectively designed. Although the plaintiff knew the door had opened and knew it was radio-controlled, his amendment was proper because he "did not know at [the time he filed his original complaint] any facts which would indicate the possibility that the door openers were defectively designed as *such flaw in design was not externally visible.*" (*Id.* at p. 883, italics added.)

In short, section 474 does not impose upon the plaintiff a duty to go in search of facts she does not actually have at the time she files her original pleading.[15] (*Munoz v. Purdy, supra,* 91 Cal. App. 3d at pp. 947-948 ["the interjection of a discovery standard into section 474 would lead to the harmful practice in all litigation of requiring that all persons who might conceivably have some connection with the lawsuit be specifically named in order to avoid the sanctions of the failure to comply with the inquiry requirements of section 474"].)

III.

Construed in GM's favor, the evidence is that Jeffrey "knew" the seat belt "failed" and "knew" she hit her head on the steering wheel. Construed in Jeffrey's favor, the evidence is that she gave no thought at all to the seat belt (except for her knowledge that she was wearing it at the time of the collision and that it did not break or come undone) but she did "know" that her head hit the steering wheel. As noted above (fn. 6, *ante*), the focus on whether she knew the belt "failed" is a red herring. Given a driver wearing a seat belt when her car is rear-ended by another car traveling at low or moderate speed, given the fact that the seat belt did not break or come undone, and given the fact that the driver hit her head on the steering wheel, *the ultimate issue*

---

15. We are not the first court to refuse to impose a duty of inquiry under section 474. (See *Streicher v. Tommy's Electric Co., supra,* 164 Cal. App. 3d at p. 883; *Breceda v. Gamsby, supra,* 267 Cal. App. 2d at p. 174 [the fact that the plaintiff had the means of ascertaining the needed facts earlier is not a bar to the application of section 474]; *Mishalow v. Horwald* (1964) 231 Cal. App. 2d 517, 523-524 [41 Cal. Rptr. 895] ["whether plaintiffs could or could not have ascertained the [necessary facts] before suit was filed is immaterial"]; *Marasco v. Wadsworth* (1978) 21 Cal. 3d 82, 88 [145 Cal. Rptr. 843, 578 P.2d 90]; *Snoke v. Bolen* (1991) 235 Cal. App. 3d 1427, 1432 [1 Cal. Rptr. 2d 492] [the plaintiff is not required to exercise reasonable diligence prior to filing the complaint to discover the defendant's identity or the facts giving rise to a cause of action]; *Sobeck & Associates, Inc. v. B & R Investments No. 24* (1989) 215 Cal. App. 3d 861, 867 [264 Cal. Rptr. 156] [there is no requirement that the plaintiff exercise diligence to discover the identity of the defendant after filing the complaint]; *Joslin v. H.A.S. Ins. Brokerage* (1986) 184 Cal. App. 3d 369, 376 [228 Cal. Rptr. 878] [there is no requirement that a plaintiff exercise reasonable diligence in discovering either the true identity of fictitious defendants or the facts giving him a cause of action against such persons].)

is whether Jeffrey had actual knowledge of the basic facts giving her a claim against GM. Our resolution of this issue in favor of Jeffrey is based on the following analysis.

First, we begin by identifying the theory of Jeffrey's claim against GM as one for products liability. (*Breceda v. Gamsby, supra,* 267 Cal. App. 2d at p. 177 [for purposes of section 474, the plaintiff's knowledge must be tested in the context of the theory of her claim against the new defendant].)

Second, we consider what facts Jeffrey must show to have a viable products liability claim against GM (*Dieckmann v. Superior Court, supra,* 175 Cal. App. 3d at p. 363 [under section 474, a plaintiff is not required to sue "until [s]he has knowledge of sufficient facts to cause a reasonable person to believe liability is probable"]), and note that, to prevail, she ultimately will have to prove that (a) GM was the manufacturer, (b) the seat belt system possessed a defect in design, (c) the defective design existed at the time the car left GM's possession, and (d) the defective design was a cause of her injury or enhanced the injury caused by the collision. (BAJI No. 9.00.5; *Soule v. General Motors Corp.* (1994) 8 Cal. 4th 548, 560 [34 Cal. Rptr. 2d 607, 882 P.2d 298].)

Third, we consider the means by which Jeffrey would prove her products liability claim against GM. In this regard, the essence of GM's position is that "a seat belt either restrains a person or it does not and this fact is known immediately after" an automobile accident, an argument we understand to mean that the seat belt's alleged failure is a matter so "commonly understood" by those who use it that a jury could decide this case without benefit of expert testimony. We flatly reject GM's "commonly understood" argument. Whatever merit there might be to GM's position in a case where a passenger is not wearing a seat belt, we cannot agree that it is "commonly understood" that a driver wearing a seat belt will hit her head on the steering wheel when her car is rear-ended only if there was something wrong with the seat belt. To the contrary, we believe that where, as here, the alleged defect "was not externally visible" (*Streicher v. Tommy's Electric Co., supra,* 164 Cal. App. 3d at p. 883), it cannot be said that Jeffrey had actual knowledge of any fact or circumstance suggesting a defect in the manner in which the belt was designed. * * * Whatever merit there may be to a claim that someone who is *not wearing* a seat belt knows, as a matter of "common knowledge," that her conduct contributed to her injuries, that is not what happened here.[16]

---

16. In spite of its "commonly understood" argument, GM contends it is irrelevant that Jeffrey would need an expert to prove at least two elements of her claim (that the design is, in fact, defective, and that, if it is, the defect enhanced her injuries). This is so, according to GM, because a plaintiff in a medical malpractice action may be charged with knowledge for section 474 purposes notwithstanding the need for expert testimony to prove professional negligence. (*Dover v. Sadowinski, supra,* 147 Cal. App. 3d 113; *Hazel v. Hewlett, supra,* 201 Cal. App. 3d 1458; *Scherer v. Mark, supra,* 64 Cal. App. 3d 834.) The medical malpractice cases in which a plaintiff has been charged with knowledge of facts sufficient to defeat reliance on section 474 all involve facts akin to the no-seat-belt cases (a patent problem), not this case (a latent problem).

Fourth, GM's own expert has testified that a properly operating seat belt (one with "no slack") would *not* have prevented Jeffrey from striking her head on the steering wheel. The way we understand the evidence in the record now before us, the purpose of a seat belt is to reduce (not eliminate) the number of accidents in which a driver's or passenger's head strikes the interior of the vehicle by reducing the speed of head travel and the corresponding severity of head impact.

Based upon the testimony of GM's expert and on our conclusion that such matters are not within the average driver's "common knowledge," we hold that a driver who is injured in an automobile accident when she is wearing a seat belt which appears to the naked eye to have operated in its intended fashion does not know the basic facts she needs to plead a products liability claim against the manufacturer of the seat belt. (Evid. Code, § 452, subd. (g) [judicial notice may be taken only of those "[f]acts and propositions that are of such common knowledge within the territorial jurisdiction of the court that they cannot reasonably be the subject of dispute"]; *Dieckmann v. Superior Court, supra*, 175 Cal. App. 3d at p. 362 [plaintiff's knowledge of (a) the identity of a truck's manufacturer and (b) the fact that, for no apparent reason, the truck's driveshaft dislodged while the truck was moving does not constitute sufficient cause to require plaintiff to sue the truck's manufacturer in his original complaint].) It follows that when she subsequently learns that the seat belt may have been defectively designed, she is entitled to claim the benefits of section 474.

DISPOSITION

The orders to show cause are discharged and the petitions are denied.

A petition for a rehearing was denied September 5, 1996, and the opinion was modified to read as printed. Petitioner's application for review by the Supreme Court was denied November 13, 1996.

Notes and Questions

(1) What are the policy reasons for interpreting CCP § 474's Doe defendant practice as *not* imposing upon the plaintiff a duty to exercise reasonable diligence prior to filing the original complaint to discover the defendant's identity or the facts giving rise to a cause of action? Why would the injection of such a discovery standard into § 474 be considered a "harmful practice"?

(2) The *General Motor* court's ruling that the duty to investigate considered in determining whether an initial complaint is timely is not a relevant inquiry in determining whether a Doe amendment is timely was followed and applied in *Fuller v. Tucker*, 84 Cal. App. 4th 1163, 101 Cal. Rptr. 2d 776 (2000) (holding trial court erred in finding that a medical malpractice plaintiff, who had failed to conduct a reasonable investigation to discover an anesthesiologist's name prior to filing the original complaint, was barred by the statute of limitations from amending the complaint to substitute the anesthesiologist for a Doe defendant), and in *McOwen v. Grossman*, 153 Cal. App. 4th 937, 63 Cal. Rptr. 3d 615 (2007) (applying *General Motors* and *Fuller* in a medical malpractice action).

[B]   Requirements for the Use of California's Doe Defendant Practice

As our principal cases indicate, CCP § 474, when properly used with § 350 and § 583.210, extends the statute of limitations for three years after the original complaint is filed. To fully appreciate the parameters of California's Doe defendant practice, consider the notes and questions below.

Sections 474 and 583.210 and the cases construing them set forth five requirements for the successful use of Doe defendant practice. *See* James E. Hogan, *California's Unique Doe Defendant Practice: A Fiction Stranger Than Truth*, 30 STAN. L. REV. 51 (1977). First, the plaintiff must file the original complaint (naming at least one actual defendant) before the applicable statute of limitations has expired. Second, the plaintiff must be "ignorant of the name" of any defendant designated by a fictitious name in the original complaint. Third, the plaintiff must plead this ignorance in the original complaint. Fourth, the plaintiff must allege a cause of action against the fictitious defendants in the original complaint based on the same general set of facts as the cause of action later asserted against the actually named defendants in the amended complaint. Fifth, the plaintiff must serve the amended complaint naming the actual defendants within three years of filing of the original complaint, and make return of service within 60 days after service of the complaint and summons.

[1]   Timely Filed Original Complaint

A fundamental prerequisite to Doe defendant practice is that the plaintiff must *file* the original complaint (naming at least one actual defendant) before the relevant statute of limitations has expired. In a personal injury action, for example, the plaintiff must file the complaint within two years of the accrual of the cause of action. CCP § 335.1. *See* Chapter 4, Statutes of Limitations, Laches, and Related Doctrines, *supra*, for discussion of accrual, discovery, and other statute of limitations issues.

The complaint must not only be timely filed, but must contain appropriate references to any known and any fictitious defendants. As the *Streicher* opinion suggests, any fictitious name can be used, although "Doe" is the most common. But the complaint must designate these defendants as fictitiously named defendants. Simply alleging "Doe" defendants without clearly stating that they are being sued as fictitious defendants may preclude use of § 474. *See Kerr-McGee Chem. Corp. v. Superior Court*, 160 Cal. App. 3d 594, 206 Cal. Rptr. 654 (1984) (noting that unless the pleading requirements of § 474 are met, a plaintiff may not take advantage of the fictitious defendant practice).

[2]   Ignorance of the Defendant's "Name"

Section 474 specifies that the plaintiff must be "ignorant of the name" of any defendant designated in the complaint by a fictitious name. If the plaintiff does not possess the requisite ignorance when the original complaint is filed, the Doe defendant doctrine of § 474 does not apply. What does "ignorance" mean here? The words "ignorant of the name" in § 474 have not been construed literally. A hypothetical will help illustrate their various possible meanings.

[a] Ignorance of the Defendant's Actual Name

Assume a simple automobile accident where plaintiff, Pam Passenger, a passenger in a car driven by Dirk Driver, crashes into the rear of a minivan while on the San Diego freeway. After exchanging appropriate epithets, the driver of the minivan speeds off without leaving his name. Pam Passenger is seriously injured, and seeks to sue both Dirk Driver and the minivan driver for negligently causing her injuries.

Pam Passenger knows that the minivan driver exists and knows his general identity, but does not know his name. Pam is clearly "ignorant of the name" of the minivan driver within the meaning of section 474, and can sue him as a Doe defendant. *See Hoffman v. Keeton*, 132 Cal. 195, 64 P. 264 (1901). Likewise, CCP § 474 would be applicable even if Pam only knows that the minivan driver exists, but does not know his name or even his general identity because she never saw him before he sped off. *Gale v. McDaniel*, 72 Cal. 334, 13 P. 871 (1887). Such limited use of fictitious defendant pleading is typical of its use in many other states, as well as under Rule 15(c), F.R.C.P.

[b] Ignorance of the Facts Giving Rise to the Cause of Action

Let's add some additional facts to our hypothetical. Pam Passenger was riding in Dirk Driver's new Lexus sedan when the collision occurred. Pam knows the car is a Lexus, manufactured by Toyota, Inc., because Dirk had told her all about it before the collision. A week before the statute of limitations is to expire, Pam files her complaint naming Dirk Driver as a defendant and the driver of the minivan as a fictitious defendant. She is not sure whether anyone else may be liable for her injuries, but names several other Doe defendants in her complaint as a precaution.

After months of discovery, Pam learns facts that lead her to believe that the collision may have been partially caused by a failure in the anti-lock braking system in Dirk's car. Further investigation uncovers evidence of a design defect in the Lexus' braking system. Pam now wishes to amend her original complaint and substitute Toyota, Inc. for one of the Doe defendants. Can Pam use CCP § 474 here, or is she precluded from doing so because she knew Toyota's name and identity at the time of the original complaint was filed?

The court in *Larson v. Barnett*, 101 Cal. App. 2d 282, 225 P.2d 297 (1950), ruled that a plaintiff can still utilize CCP § 474 even when the plaintiff knew the individual's name and identity at the time the original complaint was filed. The court stated, as have numerous courts since then, that it is sufficient for purposes of § 474 that the plaintiff was ignorant of the facts giving plaintiff a cause of action against the individual at the time the original complaint was filed. In *Barrows v. American Motors Corp.*, 144 Cal. App. 3d 1, 192 Cal. Rptr. 380 (1983), the court reached the same conclusion with respect to facts very similar to our hypothetical.

Now back to our hypothetical. Pam's original complaint names Dirk Driver as defendant, and several fictitious Doe defendants as a precautionary measure. As a result of investigation and discovery, Pam learns the name of the minivan driver and that he was driving the minivan in the course of his employment by the Checkers Pizza Co. at the time of the accident. Pam now wishes to amend her complaint and substitute Checkers Pizza Co. for one of the Doe defendants. Can Pam utilize CCP §474 here? Or is this simply too much ignorance because she knew neither the name, identity, and existence of this employer nor the facts giving rise to her *respondent superior* cause of action, at the time she filed her original complaint?

In *Day v. Western Loan and Bldg. Co.*, 42 Cal. App. 2d 226, 108 P.2d 702 (1940), the court was faced with facts almost identical to our hypothetical. The court stated that CCP §474 does not require a plaintiff, when suing a fictitious defendant, to plead a description identifying the person intended to be sued. The court also rejected the theory that only names, and not defendants, may be fictitious. The court concluded that §474 was applicable even though the plaintiff admittedly did not know the employer's name, identity, or existence when the original complaint was filed. As the *Streicher* decision indicates, this broad use of "ignorance" is now established practice.

[c] Ignorance That the Law Provides a Cause of Action

Back to our hypothetical once again. Assume that the accident took place in 1971. Pam Passenger wishes to sue Dirk Driver because she thinks his negligence contributed to the accident. He was tailgating the minivan and could not stop in time. Pam's attorney did some research and found the then valid California guest statute, which prohibited negligence actions by passengers against non-commercial drivers. Pam filed a timely complaint in 1972 which included Doe defendants, but did not name Dirk Driver as a defendant because of the guest statute. In 1973, the California Supreme Court held the guest statute unconstitutional, thereby permitting a cause of action by passengers against drivers.

Can Pam amend her complaint in 1973 and substitute Dirk Driver for one of the Doe defendants? At the time she filed her original complaint she knew Driver's name and identity, and the operative facts regarding Driver's potential liability. How can she possibly be "ignorant of his name" within the meaning of §474?

In *Marasco v. Wadsworth*, 21 Cal. 3d 82, 145 Cal. Rptr. 843, 578 P.2d 90 (1978), the California Supreme Court considered whether a passenger's amended complaint naming the driver related back to the original complaint, in circumstances almost identical to our hypothetical. The court held that the amended complaint did relate back pursuant to §474. Plaintiff was deemed "ignorant of the name" of the defendant if she knew the defendant's name and all the facts but was unaware the law gave her a cause of action against the fictitiously named defendant and discovered that right by reason of decisions rendered after the commencement of the action.

[d] The Requirement of Actual Ignorance

As the above discussion indicates, CCP § 474 has been construed quite broadly with respect to the requisite ignorance. As noted in *Streicher* and *General Motors*, however, the ignorance must be genuine and not feigned. The plaintiff must actually be "ignorant" of the defendant's true name when the original complaint is filed. *See, e.g.*, *Munoz v. Purdy*, 91 Cal. App. 3d 942, 154 Cal. Rptr. 472 (1979) (ruling a plaintiff must actually be ignorant of the facts giving him a cause of action against a defendant, at the time of filing of the complaint).

Is this requirement of actual ignorance based on a subjective or objective standard? Can a plaintiff be "ignorant" when a reasonable plaintiff would have easily determined the defendant's true name? Where the plaintiff has taken no steps to determine the defendant's true identity before filing the complaint? For example, in our car crash hypothetical, assume that this message was stenciled on the back of the minivan: "For pizza delivery call 555-4691." Pam Passenger wrote down this phone number before the minivan sped away. However, neither Pam nor her attorney made any attempt to call the number and find out the name of the pizza company and the driver before filing the original complaint. Can she properly sue the minivan driver and the pizza company as Doe defendants, alleging that she is ignorant of their true names? Consider the following cases:

(1) In *Irving v. Carpentier*, 70 Cal. 23, 11 P. 391 (1886), the plaintiff filed a quiet title action against certain named defendants and several fictitious defendants who claimed an interest in disputed land. After the statute of limitations had run, plaintiff sought to amend the complaint to substitute the Pacific Improvement Company for one of the fictitious defendants. The defendant company moved to dismiss the amended complaint on the grounds that plaintiff could have easily ascertained the company's name and existence before the original complaint was filed. If the plaintiff had searched the public records at the County Recorder's Office he would have readily found that the company claimed an interest in the disputed land. The Supreme Court rejected defendant's argument and allowed the amendment to relate back, stating that Section 474 applies when the plaintiff is actually ignorant of a certain fact, noting that "whether his ignorance is from misfortune or negligence, he is alike ignorant, and that is all the statute requires." *Irving*, 70 Cal. at 26.

(2) In *Wallis v. Southern Pac. Transportation Co.*, 61 Cal. App. 3d 782, 132 Cal. Rptr. 631 (1976), plaintiff Wallis was injured while operating a door on a railroad car. His original complaint named several Doe defendants, and alleged that his injuries were caused by their negligent manufacture, operation, and maintenance of the box car. After the statute of limitations had apparently expired, plaintiff sought to amend his complaint to substitute the Transportation Company for a Doe defendant. Defendant Transportation Company moved to strike the amendment on the grounds that Wallis knew of defendant's existence when he filed the original complaint. The court rejected defendant's argument, stating that the fact that Wallis knew of the defendant's existence "at the time of the commencement of the action is not controlling. . . . The question is whether he knew or reasonably should have known that he

had a cause of action against respondent." * * * "The question as to whether the plaintiff has acted in good faith in his use of section 474 rests primarily with the trial court." *Wallis*, 61 Cal. App. 3d at 786.

(3) More recently in *Parker v. Robert McKee, Inc.*, 3 Cal. App. 4th 512, 4 Cal. Rptr. 2d 347 (1992), the court considered the issue of whether §474 is applicable where plaintiff knew the defendant's name and identity, but not the capacity in which the defendant acted. Plaintiff, a security guard, suffered personal injuries allegedly due to negligent accumulation of debris on stairs in a building being remodeled. Plaintiff timely filed a Judicial Council form complaint for general negligence and premises liability which named several contractors, including McKee, as defendants. Unable to locate McKee for service of process, plaintiff voluntarily dismissed McKee as a defendant. Two years later, plaintiff discovered that McKee was not simply one of the contractors involved in the remodeling, but was the general contractor on the project.

Plaintiff then filed an amended complaint pursuant to §474, inserting McKee as a defendant in substitution for "Doe I." McKee demurred, contending that the amended complaint was barred by the one-year statute of limitation and that §474 was inapplicable because the original complaint showed on its face that plaintiff was not ignorant of defendant McKee's name. The trial court sustained the demurrer, but the Court of Appeal reversed. The appellate court reasoned that the original complaint showed plaintiff was unaware defendant McKee was the general contractor rather than merely one of numerous subcontractors. The court then concluded that the previously unknown *fact* that defendant was the *general* contractor provides a proper new factual basis for a cause of action, and for use of §474. The court viewed plaintiff's belated discovery that defendant was the general contractor as analogous to several cases, such as *Wallis* and *Barrows*, where the plaintiff knew the defendant's identity but later learned the defendant acted in a different capacity than plaintiff knew at the time of filing the original complaint. *Parker*, 3 Cal. App 4th at 516-18.

Is the plaintiff's "ignorance" in *Parker* the same type of "ignorance" found in *Wallis*? Is *Parker* simply another application of the ignorance standard stated in *Wallis*, or something different? Is *Parker* consistent with *Wallis*? How can a plaintiff be "ignorant of the name of a defendant," where the plaintiff knows the defendant's identity and believes the defendant is *a* cause of plaintiff's injuries, and actually names that defendant in the original complaint?!? Is *Parker* an inappropriate extension of §474? If plaintiff had not voluntarily dismissed McKee from the original complaint, would his amended complaint adding a cause of action against McKee as a general contractor be barred by the statute of limitation?

(4) What if the plaintiff's ignorance is due to her own negligence? Assume in our hypothetical, for example, that the minivan driver did stop after the collision and exchanged information with Pam Passenger. The minivan driver gave Pam a piece of paper with his name and other information on it. Pam, however, felt dazed from the collision and subsequently forgot about the slip of paper and the minivan driver's identity. Pam makes no effort to obtain the identity from the police report or Dirk's insurance company prior to her subsequent lawsuit. In her complaint, Pam refers to

the minivan driver as a "Doe" defendant. Is Pam "ignorant" of the minivan driver's name within the meaning of § 474?

In *Balon v. Drost*, 20 Cal. App. 4th 483, 25 Cal. Rptr. 2d 12 (1993), a divided court considered the plaintiff's forgetting of a defendant's previously known identity with no effort to refresh memory to be negligent ignorance, and held that negligent ignorance of the defendant's identity did not preclude adding that defendant under CCP § 474 after the statute of limitations expired. However, the court in *Woo v. Superior Court*, 75 Cal. App. 4th 169, 89 Cal. Rptr. 2d 20 (1999), disagreed with *Balon's* rule because it relieves forgetful plaintiffs of any obligation to refresh their memory with readily available information. Instead, the *Woo* court set forth what it perceived to be the better rule: If the plaintiff knows the defendant's identity and then forgets it at the time the complaint is filed, to use the § 474 relation-back doctrine to avoid the bar of the statute of limitations the plaintiff must have at least reviewed readily available information likely to refresh his or her memory. *Woo, supra*, 75 Cal. App. 4th at 180. Do you agree that the *Woo* court's rule is the better rule? Why?

(5) The California courts have to date construed the requisite "ignorance" very liberally. Undoubtedly, many attorneys are comforted by the notion that at times true ignorance is actually rewarded! How far can this concept be stretched? Consider the following facts in our car crash hypothetical.

Assume the car crash took place long after the California Supreme Court overturned the California guest statute. Pam Passenger's attorney conducted extensive legal research before filing the original complaint. However, due to poor research by his law clerk, Pam's attorney found the California guest statute but not the Supreme Court decision declaring it unconstitutional. Believing there was no cause of action against Dirk Driver, Pam filed a timely complaint which did not name Dirk but did allege negligence by several Doe defendants.

Two and one-half years later Pam's attorney discovered the Supreme Court case overturning the guest statute. Pam now seeks to amend her original complaint to substitute Dirk Driver for one of the Doe defendants. Driver opposes the amended complaint, arguing it is barred by the statute of limitations. In support of the amended complaint's relation back, Pam's attorney argues that the failure to discover the cause of action against Dirk Driver was due to negligence, but that Pam and he were actually "ignorant of the name" of the defendant at the time the original complaint was filed. Pam's attorney argues that § 474 is therefore applicable, citing *Irving, Wallis, Parker*, and *Marasco, supra*. How should the trial court rule on this issue? Does Section 474 encompass this type of ignorance? *See, e.g., Von Gibson v. Estate of Lynch*, 197 Cal. App. 3d 725, 730, 243 Cal. Rptr. 50 (1988) (ruling section 474 unavailable where proclaimed ignorance is that of law, not of fact).

(6) Believe it or not, there are some limits as to how "ignorant" a plaintiff can be and still use § 474:

(a) In *Beresford v. City of San Mateo*, 207 Cal. App. 3d 1180, 255 Cal. Rptr. 434 (1989), an action to stop the development of a housing project, the plaintiff was not permitted to use Section 474 to amend a prior complaint and substitute a developer for a Doe defendant. Although the original complaint properly pled ignorance and named fictitious defendants, it also included minutes of city council meetings that disclosed the developer's identity.

(b) In *Hazel v. Hewlett*, 201 Cal. App. 3d 1458, 247 Cal. Rptr. 723 (1988), the court upheld a trial court's determination that plaintiff did not possess good faith actual ignorance of a defendant's name when he filed the original complaint. The original complaint alleged personal injuries caused by negligence during tooth extractions by two associated dentists, naming one dentist (Stasiewitz) but suing the other (Hewlett) as a Doe defendant. The court did not permit an amendment substituting in Hewlett to relate back because the defendant showed that plaintiff knew Hewlett's name and association with Stasiewitz at the time the extractions took place. The court reached the same conclusion on similar facts in *Snoke v. Bolen*, 235 Cal. App. 3d 1427, 1 Cal. Rptr. 2d 492 (1991); *see also Optical Surplus, Inc. v. Superior Court*, 228 Cal. App. 3d 776, 279 Cal. Rptr. 194 (1991) (holding plaintiff could not utilize §474 to substitute in Optical for a Doe defendant because plaintiff lacked the requisite ignorance because a formal demand letter mailed by plaintiff to Optical clearly indicated that plaintiff knew Optical's identity as well as its alleged actionable activity when plaintiff filed the original complaint).

(c) In *Miller v. Thomas*, 121 Cal. App. 3d 440, 175 Cal. Rptr. 327 (1981), the court rejected an amendment after the statute of limitations had expired. Plaintiff was injured in an automobile collision with a auto driven by one Thomas, who identified himself by name to plaintiff and informed plaintiff that he was an undercover narcotics officer for the City of Los Angeles. The parties exchanged license numbers, and talked by phone the next day.

Plaintiff Miller's subsequent negligence action named only the City of Los Angeles as defendant, and various Doe defendants. By answer and through discovery, the City denied liability, contending that Thomas was outside the scope of his employment when the accident occurred. Plaintiff's attorney then sought to amend the complaint and substitute Thomas for one of the Doe defendants. Thomas opposed the amendment because it was filed after the statute of limitations had expired. In support of the amendment, Miller herself stated that she was ignorant of Thomas' liability when the original complaint was filed because her prior attorney had advised her that the City was ultimately liable for Miller's injuries. Miller's prior attorney also stated that it was his opinion at the time the lawsuit was filed that the officer was acting in the course of his City employment at the time of the accident.

The Court held that plaintiff was not "ignorant of the name" of defendant Thomas within the meaning of §474. The plaintiff knew of Thomas' identity and his connection with the accident prior to the lawsuit. Plaintiff's decision not to name Thomas in the original complaint was simply a tactical choice to proceed only against the City, and was not due to any lack of knowledge regarding Thomas' liability.

Is the *Miller* holding consistent with *Parker*, *Irving*, *Wallis*, and *Marasco*?

(7) There is no requirement in using § 474 that a plaintiff must exercise reasonable diligence in discovering either the true identity of fictitious defendants or facts giving rise to a cause of action against such persons. *Joslin v. H.A.S. Ins. Broker*, 184 Cal. App. 3d 369, 228 Cal. Rptr. 878 (1986); *Munoz v. Purdy*, 91 Cal. App. 3d 942, 154 Cal. Rptr. 472 (1979). There is no such requirement *before* the original complaint is filed, nor *after* the original complaint is filed. *See Streicher v. Tommy's Electric Co.*, *supra*; *General Motors Corp. v. Superior Court*, *supra*.

(a) However, as recognized in the *Streicher* opinion, there is authority for the proposition that a plaintiff must not unreasonably delay the filing of the *amended* complaint after the plaintiff actually discovers the true identity of the defendant who was fictitiously named in the original complaint. The court in *Streicher* stated that this determination could not be made on defendant's demurrer. Why not? What procedural device should defendant have utilized to properly raise this unreasonable delay issue?

(b) In *Barrows v. American Motors Corp.*, 144 Cal. App. 3d 1, 192 Cal. Rptr. 380 (1983), the plaintiffs moved for leave to amend their complaint to substitute the defendant American Motors for a Doe defendant. The defendant contended that plaintiffs should be barred from invoking § 474 because the delay between acquisition of defendant's true identify and the filing of the first amended complaint was unreasonable. The court ruled that unreasonable delay in filing an amendment after acquiring such knowledge can bar a plaintiff's resort to the fictitious name procedure. But the defendant must show not only that the plaintiff was dilatory but also that defendant suffered prejudice from the delay. Moreover, defendant must show "specific prejudice" to defendant due to the delay, and not simply the prejudice generally presumed from the policy of the statute of limitations. *Id.* at 9; *see also Sobeck & Assoc., Inc. v. B&R Inv. No. 24*, 215 Cal. App. 3d 861, 264 Cal. Rptr. 156 (1989) (concluding the amendment will relate back if made within three years of filing the original complaint, unless there is evidence of unreasonable delay by the plaintiff or specific prejudice to the defendant). What might be some examples of "specific prejudice" in this context? See *A.N. v. County of Los Angeles*, 171 Cal. App. 4th 1058, 90 Cal. Rptr. 3d 293 (2009) (ruling plaintiff, who had waited two years after learning the defendant's identity to file an amended complaint, had unreasonably delayed the filing of the Doe amendment; specific prejudice found based on the fact that the new defendant was brought into the case one month before trial and would have difficulties in preparing a defense on such short order).

[3]   Pleading "Ignorance"

[a]   Ignorance Must Be Pleaded in Original Complaint

Section 474 requires not only that plaintiff be actually ignorant of the fictitious defendant's true name, but also that this ignorance be pleaded in the timely original complaint. This simple pleading requirement is essential to a later effort to utilize the fictitious defendant process in an amended complaint. The allegation need not be fancy. All that need be alleged is something like: "Plaintiff does not know the true names of defendants sued herein as Doe 1 through Doe 20." *See* CEB *California Civil Procedure Before Trial*, § 14.14 (4th ed. 2015). The Judicial Council's Form Complaint for Personal Injury, Property Damage, Wrongful Death contains a similar allegation. *See* Forms PLD-PL-001, ¶ 6, PLD-PL-OO1(1)-(6). Failure to include this essential allegation may indicate that the plaintiff did not intend to utilize § 474. *See Nissan v. Barton*, 4 Cal. App. 3d 76, 84 Cal. Rptr. 36 (1970).

[b]   Is Failure to Plead "Ignorance" Curable by Amendment?

In *Dieckmann v. Superior Court*, 175 Cal. App. 3d 345, 220 Cal. Rptr. 602 (1986), however, the Court of Appeal viewed this particular pleading requirement as merely technical, and curable by amendment after the limitation period had expired. The plaintiff's original complaint listed several fictitious defendants, and inartfully alleged that "the true names and capacities of the DOE defendants, whether individual, corporate or otherwise ... are sued as fictitious persons." The court concluded that plaintiff could still utilize § 474, and could correct this pleading omission by including the required allegations of ignorance in the same amended complaint that substitutes in the actual defendant. Recognizing that the defendant may only be served with the amended complaint, the court observed that "a defendant sued originally by a fictitious name and later sued by substitution of his true name is in no worse position if the plaintiff, who was actually ignorant of the true name when the complaint was filed, is permitted also to add an omitted allegation of such ignorance." *Id.* at 359.

Should this same reasoning used by the court in *Dieckmann* permit a plaintiff to utilize § 474 even though plaintiff makes absolutely no reference to fictitious defendants in the original complaint? Because a Doe defendant is not served with the original complaint, how is a defendant prejudiced if the amended complaint adds both previously omitted Doe allegations *and* substitutes the actual defendant for one of these Doe defendants? Are there other considerations here in addition to prejudice to the defendant?

As *Streicher v. Tommy's Electric Co.*, reproduced *supra*, illustrates, the courts also consider noncompliance with the party substitution requirements of CCP § 474 as a procedural defect that can be cured. *See Woo v. Superior Court*, 75 Cal. App 4th 169, 176-77, 89 Cal. Rptr. 2d 20 (1999) (ruling plaintiff not foreclosed from using § 474's relation-back even though plaintiff's amended complaint did not identify the newly named defendant as a substitute for a previously named fictitious defendant and the summons served did not identify the individual defendant as a defendant previously sue under a fictitious name); *but see Carol Gilbert, Inc. v. Haller*, 179 Cal. App. 4th 852, 101 Cal.

Rptr. 3d 843 (2009) (holding plaintiff must comply with the requirement of §474 that a summons notify the recipient that he is being sued as a fictitiously named defendant).

[4] The Relation Back Doctrine

Section 474 provides the legislative basis for California's fictitious defendant practice. However, CCP § 474 gives no hint of how this practice may be used to extend a statute of limitations. This essential ingredient of the practice is provided by the common law doctrine of relation back.

[a] Requirements

The California Supreme Court in *Austin v. Massachusetts Bonding & Ins. Co.*, 56 Cal. 2d 596, 364 P.2d 681, 15 Cal. Rptr. 817 (1961), succinctly stated the relation back doctrine as follows: "Where a complaint sets forth, or attempts to set forth, a cause of action against a defendant designated by fictitious name and his true name is thereafter discovered and substituted by amendment, he is considered a party to the action from its commencement so that the statute of limitations stops running as of the date of the earlier pleading." *Austin*, 56 Cal. 2d at 599.

Thus if the original complaint naming Doe defendants is filed within the applicable statute of limitations, the amended complaint substituting in an actual defendant will relate back and be considered timely filed against the actual defendant!

One rather technical but important requirement is that the original complaint must allege a cause of action against the fictitious defendants as well as against any known defendants. Such charging allegations against fictitious defendants permit the fiction that the amended pleading relates back to something already existing in the original pleading. Without such charging allegations, the amended pleading would be viewed as stating for the first time a cause of action against a newly named defendant. The amended pleading would then initiate a wholly new cause of action instead of amending an existing one, and its timeliness for limitations purpose would be computed from the date the amended pleading was filed and not from the date the original pleading was filed.

The requirement that the original pleading must contain charging allegations against the fictitious defendants is therefore an essential basic rule of the relation back doctrine. How difficult is it to comply with this rule? Not very. All a plaintiff must do is add an "s" to "defendant" in the charging allegations, and be sure that the complaint does not limit the word "defendants" to those sued by their correct names. *See, e.g.*, Judicial Council Pleading Forms PLD-PL-001(1)-(6).

[b] New Causes of Action

As the *Streicher* and *General Motors* opinions demonstrates, the amended complaint relates back to the date of filing the original complaint as to the newly substituted actual defendant. In addition, the amended complaint can include any new cause of action against the defendant not alleged in the original complaint to the extent that it seeks recovery on the same general facts as the original complaint, and refers to the same accident and same injuries as the original complaint. *Barrington v. A.H. Robbins Co.*, 39 Cal. 3d 146, 216 Cal. Rptr. 405, 702 P.2d 563 (1985). California's relation back doctrine is discussed in more detail *supra* in § 9.03 [B][2]. *See also* Walter W. Heiser, *Relation Back of Amended Complaints: The California Courts Should Adopt a More Pragmatic Approach*, 44 Santa Clara L. Rev. 643, 647-60 (2004).

[5] Service Within Three Years

Code of Civil Procedure Section 583.210, which amended former CCP § 581a, requires that the summons and complaint must be served upon a defendant within three years of filing the complaint, and return of service must be made within sixty days of such service. With respect to fictitious defendants, this means that a plaintiff must serve the amended complaint and summons on the Doe defendant within three years after the filing of the *original* complaint, in situations where the amended complaint relates back. Thus, CCP § 583.210 imposes a three-year limit on the relation back aspect of the fictitious defendant practice.

[a] Mandatory Dismissal

If not served within three years, the complaint must be dismissed for lack of jurisdiction as to the unserved defendants. CCP § 583.250. There are some exceptions to this three-year service rule such as where the defendant was not amenable to the process of the court; or, where service for any other reason was impossible, impracticable, or futile due to causes beyond plaintiff's control. CCP § 583.240. However, failure to discover relevant facts or evidence is expressly not a cause beyond the plaintiff's control. CCP § 583.240(d).

[b] Discretionary Dismissal

Even though a proper Doe defendant complaint has been filed within the applicable statute of limitations, it is not a good idea for a plaintiff to wait until the end of the three-year period to discover and serve the actual defendant. In *Clark v. Stabond Corp.*, 197 Cal. App. 3d 50, 242 Cal. Rptr. 676 (1987), for example, the Court of Appeal upheld the discretionary dismissal of a complaint naming a Doe defendant which was not served on the true defendant within two years of the filing of the original complaint. The court held that CCP § 474 and § 583.210, which allow up to three years to serve a fictitious defendant, do not preclude discretionary dismissal for failure to effect service within two years pursuant to CCP § 583.420(a)(1). Rule 3.1342(e), Cal. Rules of Ct., sets forth the relevant factors to be considered by a court in determining a § 583.420 motion.

[6] Other Limitations on Section 474

The Doe defendant practice of Sections 474 and 583.210 may be subject to a form of pre-emption when other specific statutory schemes mandate that the actual defendant be sued within a specified period of time.

[a] Torts Claim Act

Most notable of these is the California Tort Claims Act which requires that a suit against a public entity, on a cause of action for which a claim is required to be filed, must be commenced within six months of service of notice of rejection of the claim. Government Code § 945.6. This six-month period of limitations has been held to be mandatory and must be strictly followed, and ordinarily cannot be extended by use of the fictitious defendant practice. *See Chase v. State of California,* 67 Cal. App. 3d 808, 136 Cal. Rptr. 833 (1977).

However, this limitation on the use of CCP § 474 has been held to apply only to public entities, and not to public employees of the entity. *Olden v. Hatchell,* 154 Cal. App. 3d 1032, 201 Cal. Rptr. 715 (1984). Consequently, an amended complaint substituting a public employee for a Doe defendant will relate back so long as the original complaint was filed within the six-month limitation period applicable to public entities. *Id.* Why are public entities treated differently than public employees? What aspect of the claims presentation prerequisite makes it unlikely that a plaintiff could ever effectively utilize the fictitious defendant practice to substitute in a public entity defendant? Are there any narrow circumstances under which a plaintiff could appropriately utilize the Doe defendant practice to bring in a public entity, consistent with the claims presentation statutes? *See Carlino v. Los Angeles Cnty. Flood Control Dist.,* 10 Cal. App. 4th 1526, 13 Cal. Rptr. 2d 437 (1992).

[b] Fast Track and Fictitious Defendant Practice

The Trial Court Delay Reduction Act of 1986, and the various "fast track" rules adopted thereunder, did not deal directly with the fictitious defendant practice. Many state and local rules did, however, appear to impact the practice. For example, a typical fast track requirement is that the complaint must be served within 60 days of its filing, unless a certificate of progress is filed indicating why service has not been effected and what is being done to effect service. *See, e.g.,* San Diego County Superior Court Rule 2.1.5; Rule 3.110, Cal. Rules of Ct. Such requirements, as well as the various other time-limitation goals of each fast track program, frequently meant that judges would dismiss unnamed Doe defendants as early as six months after an action was filed. *See* Peter J. Hinton, *California's Trip on the Fast Track: Where Can It Take Us?,* 11 CEB Civ. Lit. Rep. 243, 246 (Sept. 1989).

The original 1986 Act was repealed in 1990, and a new set of statutory provisions enacted. Government Code 68600 *et seq.* Under the present Act, Doe defendants may not be dismissed prior to the conclusion of the introduction of evidence at trial, except on stipulation or motion of the parties. Gov. Code § 68616(h). What effect will this new provision have on the fictitious defendant practice? *See General Motors Corp. v. Superior Court, supra,* 48 Cal. App. 4th at 589, n.10.

[7] Practical Considerations

It is somewhat of a misnomer to call California's fictitious defendant practice "Doe" defendant practice. Any fictitious name can be used. However, it is probably not a good idea to use esoteric fictitious names, such as "Bambi I through X," because courts expect "Doe's" and may become confused. Most of the mystery of pleading fictitious defendants has been eliminated by various Judicial Council Summons and Complaint forms. *See* Forms PLD-PL-001, ¶ 6, PLD-PL-001 (1)-(6). Samples of these pleading forms are set forth below:

PLD-PI-001

ATTORNEY OR PARTY WITHOUT ATTORNEY *(Name, State Bar number, and address):*	FOR COURT USE ONLY

TELEPHONE NO: FAX NO. *(Optional):*

E-MAIL ADDRESS *(Optional):*

ATTORNEY FOR *(Name):*

SUPERIOR COURT OF CALIFORNIA, COUNTY OF

STREET ADDRESS:

MAILING ADDRESS:

CITY AND ZIP CODE:

BRANCH NAME:

PLAINTIFF:

DEFENDANT:

☐ DOES 1 TO _____

COMPLAINT—Personal Injury, Property Damage, Wrongful Death
☐ **AMENDED** *(Number):*

Type *(check all that apply):*
☐ **MOTOR VEHICLE**   ☐ **OTHER** *(specify):*
☐ **Property Damage**   ☐ **Wrongful Death**
☐ **Personal Injury**   ☐ **Other Damages** *(specify):*

Jurisdiction *(check all that apply):*
☐ **ACTION IS A LIMITED CIVIL CASE**
    Amount demanded ☐ **does not exceed $10,000**
                    ☐ **exceeds $10,000, but does not exceed $25,000**
☐ **ACTION IS AN UNLIMITED CIVIL CASE (exceeds $25,000)**
☐ **ACTION IS RECLASSIFIED by this amended complaint**
        ☐ **from limited to unlimited**
        ☐ **from unlimited to limited**

CASE NUMBER:

1. **Plaintiff** *(name or names):*
   alleges causes of action against **defendant** *(name or names):*

2. This pleading, including attachments and exhibits, consists of the following number of pages:

3. Each plaintiff named above is a competent adult
   a. ☐ **except plaintiff** *(name):*
      (1) ☐ a corporation qualified to do business in California
      (2) ☐ an unincorporated entity *(describe):*
      (3) ☐ a public entity *(describe):*
      (4) ☐ a minor ☐ an adult
          (a) ☐ for whom a guardian or conservator of the estate or a guardian ad litem has been appointed
          (b) ☐ other *(specify):*
      (5) ☐ other *(specify):*
   b. ☐ **except plaintiff** *(name):*
      (1) ☐ a corporation qualified to do business in California
      (2) ☐ an unincorporated entity *(describe):*
      (3) ☐ a public entity *(describe):*
      (4) ☐ a minor ☐ an adult
          (a) ☐ for whom a guardian or conservator of the estate or a guardian ad litem has been appointed
          (b) ☐ other *(specify):*
      (5) ☐ other *(specify):*

☐ Information about additional plaintiffs who are not competent adults is shown in Attachment 3.

Page 1 of 3

Form Approved for Optional Use
Judicial Council of California
PLD-PI-001 [Rev. January 1, 2007]

COMPLAINT—Personal Injury, Property Damage, Wrongful Death

Code of Civil Procedure, § 425.12
www.courtinfo.ca.gov

PLD-PI-001

SHORT TITLE:	CASE NUMBER:

4. ☐ Plaintiff *(name)*:

is doing business under the fictitious name *(specify)*:

and has complied with the fictitious business name laws.

5. Each defendant named above is a natural person

a. ☐ **except** defendant *(name)*:
  (1) ☐ a business organization, form unknown
  (2) ☐ a corporation
  (3) ☐ an unincorporated entity *(describe)*:

  (4) ☐ a public entity *(describe)*:

  (5) ☐ other *(specify)*:

c. ☐ **except** defendant *(name)*:
  (1) ☐ a business organization, form unknown
  (2) ☐ a corporation
  (3) ☐ an unincorporated entity *(describe)*:

  (4) ☐ a public entity *(describe)*:

  (5) ☐ other *(specify)*:

b. ☐ **except** defendant *(name)*:
  (1) ☐ a business organization, form unknown
  (2) ☐ a corporation
  (3) ☐ an unincorporated entity *(describe)*:

  (4) ☐ a public entity *(describe)*:

  (5) ☐ other *(specify)*:

d. ☐ **except** defendant *(name)*:
  (1) ☐ a business organization, form unknown
  (2) ☐ a corporation
  (3) ☐ an unincorporated entity *(describe)*:

  (4) ☐ a public entity *(describe)*:

  (5) ☐ other *(specify)*:

☐ Information about additional defendants who are not natural persons is contained in Attachment 5.

6. The true names of defendants sued as Does are unknown to plaintiff.

  a. ☐ Doe defendants *(specify Doe numbers)*: _____ were the agents or employees of other named defendants and acted within the scope of that agency or employment.

  b. ☐ Doe defendants *(specify Doe numbers)*:_____ are persons whose capacities are unknown to plaintiff.

7. ☐ Defendants who are joined under Code of Civil Procedure section 382 are *(names)*:

8. This court is the proper court because

  a. ☐ at least one defendant now resides in its jurisdictional area.
  b. ☐ the principal place of business of a defendant corporation or unincorporated association is in its jurisdictional area.
  c. ☐ injury to person or damage to personal property occurred in its jurisdictional area.
  d. ☐ other *(specify)*:

9. ☐ Plaintiff is required to comply with a claims statute, **and**
  a. ☐ has complied with applicable claims statutes, **or**
  b. ☐ is excused from complying because *(specify)*:

PLD-PI-001

SHORT TITLE:	CASE NUMBER:

10. The following causes of action are attached and the statements above apply to each *(each complaint must have one or more causes of action attached):*
   a. ☐ Motor Vehicle
   b. ☐ General Negligence
   c. ☐ Intentional Tort
   d. ☐ Products Liability
   e. ☐ Premises Liability
   f. ☐ Other *(specify):*

11. Plaintiff has suffered
   a. ☐ wage loss
   b. ☐ loss of use of property
   c. ☐ hospital and medical expenses
   d. ☐ general damage
   e. ☐ property damage
   f. ☐ loss of earning capacity
   g. ☐ other damage *(specify):*

12. ☐ The damages claimed for wrongful death and the relationships of plaintiff to the deceased are
   a. ☐ listed in Attachment 12.
   b. ☐ as follows:

13. The relief sought in this complaint is within the jurisdiction of this court.

14. **Plaintiff prays** for judgment for costs of suit; for such relief as is fair, just, and equitable; and for
   a. (1) ☐ compensatory damages
      (2) ☐ punitive damages
      The amount of damages is *(in cases for personal injury or wrongful death, you must check (1)):*
      (1) ☐ according to proof
      (2) ☐ in the amount of: $

15. ☐ The paragraphs of this complaint alleged on information and belief are as follows *(specify paragraph numbers):*

Date:

▶

_____
(TYPE OR PRINT NAME)

_____
(SIGNATURE OF PLAINTIFF OR ATTORNEY)

PLD-PI-001 [Rev. January 1, 2007]

COMPLAINT—Personal Injury, Property Damage, Wrongful Death

Page 3 of 3

PLD-PI-001(1)

SHORT TITLE:	CASE NUMBER:

CAUSE OF ACTION—Motor Vehicle

_____ (number)

ATTACHMENT TO ☐ Complaint ☐ Cross - Complaint

(Use a separate cause of action form for each cause of action.)

Plaintiff *(name):*

MV- 1. Plaintiff alleges the acts of defendants were negligent; the acts were the legal (proximate) cause of injuries
and damages to plaintiff; the acts occurred
on *(date):*
at *(place):*

MV- 2. DEFENDANTS
a. ☐ The defendants who operated a motor vehicle are *(names):*

☐ Does _____ to _____

b. ☐ The defendants who employed the persons who operated a motor vehicle in the course of their employment
are *(names):*

☐ Does _____ to _____

c. ☐ The defendants who owned the motor vehicle which was operated with their permission are *(names):*

☐ Does _____ to _____

d. ☐ The defendants who entrusted the motor vehicle are *(names):*

☐ Does _____ to _____

e. ☐ The defendants who were the agents and employees of the other defendants and acted within the scope
of the agency were *(names):*

☐ Does _____ to _____

f. ☐ The defendants who are liable to plaintiffs for other reasons and the reasons for the liability are
☐ listed in Attachment MV-2f ☐ as follows:

☐ Does _____ to _____   Page _____

Page 1 of 1

[C]   Federal Rule 15(c) Compared

[1]   Federal Rule 15(c)(1)(C)

As discussed in the Introductory Note, §9.04 [A], *supra*, Federal Rule 15(c) was amended in 1991 to remove the restrictive construction imposed by *Schiavone v. Fortune*, 477 U.S. 21, 106 S. Ct. 2379, 91 L. Ed. 2d 18 (1986). Was the amendment to Rule 15(c) a significant expansion of the federal relation back doctrine with respect to adding new parties? Why not? Under amended Rule 15(c)(1)(C), an amended complaint adding a new party may relate back only if the newly named defendant had timely notice of the original complaint and knows his omission form the original complaint was due to a naming mistake by the plaintiff. *See Krupski v. Costa Crociere*, 560 U. S. 538, 130 S. Ct. 2485, 177 L. Ed. 2d 48 (2010) (holding relation back under federal Rule 15(c)(1)(C) depends on whether the defendant to be added knew or should have known during the Rule 4(m) period that, absent some mistake, the action would have been brought against him or her, and not on whether the plaintiff knew or should have known that defendant's identity as the proper defendant). How does Rule 15(c)(1)(C) differ from California's fictitious defendant practice? For a discussion of these differences, see Walter W. Heiser, *Relation Back of Amended Complaints: The California Courts Should Adopt a More Pragmatic Approach*, 44 SANTA CLARA L. REV. 643, 678-83 (2004).

[2]   Federal Rule 15(c)(1)(A)

Federal Rule 15(c)(1)(A), added in 1991, is an entirely new provision which authorizes relation back of amendments when permitted by "the law that provides the applicable statute of limitations." Essentially, if state law provides the controlling statute of limitations and affords a more forgiving principle of relation back than is provided by Rule 15(c)(1)(B) and (C), the state doctrine should be available to save the cause of action. *See Notes of Advisory Committee on 1991 Amendment to Rule 15(c)(1)*. This apparently means that where California law provides the statute of limitations applicable to a cause of action in federal court, the California fictitious defendant doctrine is authorized for that action. *See* David D. Siegel, *The Recent (Dec. 1, 1991) Changes in the Federal Rules of Civil Procedure*, 142 F.R.D. 359, 362-66 (1992). For a discussion of when state statutes of limitations are applicable to claims in federal court, see Chapter 4, Statutes of Limitations, Laches, and Related Doctrines, *supra*.

Rule 15(c)(1)(A) is a revolutionary departure from the strictness and uniformity of former Rule 15(c). However, it existence is not totally unexpected. In *Lindley v. General Elec. Co.*, 780 F.2d 797 (9th Cir. 1986), *cert. denied*, 476 U.S. 1186 (1986), the Ninth Circuit Court of Appeals had already held that California's fictitious defendant practice embodied in CCP §474 applied to extend the applicable statute of limitations in diversity cases in federal court, and was not limited by the pre-1991 version of Rule 15(c). Why did the *Lindley* court reach this conclusion? Did it have anything to do with the *Erie* doctrine? Does *Lindley* apply to non-diversity cases in federal court, when California law provides the statute of limitations? *See Cabrales v. County of Los Angeles*, 864 F.2d 1454 (9th Cir. 1988) (§1983 action).

The consequence of new Rule 15(c)(1)(A) is that you may be able to utilize California's Doe defendant practice in certain federal court actions, as well as in California state court litigation! *See, e.g., Kreines v. United States*, 959 F.2d 834, 836-38 (9th Cir. 1992) (applying California Doe defendant practice of CCP § 474 to allow relation back of amended complaint substituting in named federal agents in *Bivens* claim based on Fourth Amendment); *Motley v. Parks*, 198 F.R.D. 532 (C.D. Cal. 2000) (applying California's doe defendant practice in a § 1983 action). The precise meaning of new Rule 15(c)(1), and its relationship to the remainder of Rule 15(c), will undoubtedly be clarified through case law. Reading Rule 15(c)(1) and (2) together, do you see an argument that the California fictitious defendant relation back doctrine will be even more expansive when applied in a federal court than when applied in a California court?

§ 9.05 The Demurrer

[A] Introductory Note

[1] General and Special Demurrers

A demurrer presents an objection to a complaint, cross-complaint, or answer when the ground for objection appears on the face of such pleading, and from any matter of which the court may take judicial notice. CCP § 430.30(a). When any ground for objection to a complaint or cross-complaint does not appear on the face of the pleading, the objection may be taken by answer. CCP § 430.30(b). A party objecting to a complaint or cross-complaint may demur and answer at the same time. § 430.30(c).

The grounds for objection to a complaint or cross-complaint are set forth in CCP § 430.10, which provides:

The party against whom a complaint or cross-complaint has been filed may object, by demurrer or answer as provided in Section 430.30, to the pleading on any one or more of the following grounds:

(a) The court has no jurisdiction of the subject of the cause of action alleged in the pleading.

(b) The person who filed the pleading does not have the legal capacity to sue.

(c) There is another action pending between the same parties on the same cause of action.

(d) There is a defect or misjoinder of parties.

(e) The pleading does not state facts sufficient to constitute a cause of action.

(f) The pleading is uncertain. As used in this subdivision, "uncertain" includes ambiguous and unintelligible.

(g) In an action founded upon a contract, it cannot be ascertained from the pleading whether the contract is written, is oral, or is implied by conduct.

(h) No certificate was filed as required by Section 411.35 [Malpractice action against architect or engineer].

(i) No certificate was filed as required by Section 411.36 [Association action for negligence against licensed contractor].

The grounds for objection to an answer are contained in CCP § 430.20.

The statutes do not distinguish between "general" and "special" demurrers, but courts and attorneys usually do. *See, e.g.*, 5 Witkin, *California Procedure, Pleading* §§ 951-953 (5th ed. 2008) (citing cases). A demurrer on the ground that the pleading does not state facts sufficient to constitute a cause of action, CCP § 430.10(e), is typically referred to as a "general demurrer"; one based on any other ground stated in CCP § 430.10 as a "special demurrer." Courts sometimes describe a general demurrer as attacking the substantive sufficiency of a pleading, whereas a special demurrer merely attacks the form. *See* Witkin, *California Procedure, supra*. This description of the distinction is of dubious accuracy and utility, but nevertheless persists. *Id.*

The discussion below will focus primarily on general demurrers. For discussion of the various grounds and standards for special demurrers, see 5 Witkin, *California Procedure, Pleading* §§ 968-978 (5th ed. 2008).

[2] *Procedures*

Although technically considered a pleading, the procedural rules generally treat a demurrer like a motion. *See* Rules 3.1103(c) and 3.1320, Cal. Rules of Ct. A demurrer may be taken to the whole complaint or cross-complaint, or to any causes of action stated therein. CCP § 430.50. Each ground of demurrer must be distinctly specified, and must state whether it applies to the entire pleading or specified causes of action or defenses. CCP § 430.60; Rule 3.1320. Additional procedural requirements for the notice and hearing are set forth in Rule 3.1320. Before filing a demurrer, the demurring party must meet and confer with the opposing party to determine whether an agreement can be reached that would resolve the objection raised in the demurrer. CCP § 430.41 (eff. Jan. 1, 2016). After a demurrer is filed but before it is heard, a party may amend its pleading once without leave of court. CCP § 472 (eff. January 1, 2016).

A party must demur to a complaint or cross-complaint within 30 days after service, and to an answer within 10 days. CCP § 412.20(a)(3), § 430.40. Failure to timely object to a pleading by demurrer or answer constitutes a waiver of all grounds for objection except an objection that the court lacks subject matter jurisdiction or that the pleading does not state facts sufficient to constitute a cause of action or a defense. CCP § 430.80; *see Collins v. Rocha*, 7 Cal. 3d 232, 239, 102 Cal. Rptr. 1, 497 P.2d 225 (1972) (ruling defendant's failure to raise uncertainty of complaint by a timely special demurrer deemed a waiver of such pleading defect).

When a demurrer is sustained, the court must state in the order the specific grounds upon which the decision is based. CCP § 472d. However, if such statement of grounds is not requested by the party against whom the demurrer was sustained, this requirement is waived. *See* CCP § 472d; *Krawitz v. Rusch*, 209 Cal. App. 3d 957, 962, 257 Cal. Rptr. 610 (1989).

[3] Federal Rules Compared

Federal Rule 7(c) abolished the use of demurrers in federal courts, although other federal rules authorize various motions which perform similar functions. Rules 12(b)(1), 12(b)(7), and 12(e), for example, provide grounds for dismissal nearly identical to a special demurrer for lack of subject matter jurisdiction, misjoinder of parties, and uncertain pleading, respectively. And Rule 12(b)(6), which authorizes a motion to dismiss for failure to state a claim upon which relief can be granted, corresponds to a general demurrer.

[B] Standards for General Demurrers

[1] General Demurrer Assumes Truth of Allegations

A demurrer does not test the truth of the allegations in a pleading, only the legal sufficiency of the pleading. *See Committee on Children's Television, Inc. v. Gen. Foods Corp.*, 35 Cal. 3d 197, 197 Cal. Rptr. 783, 673 P.2d 660 (1983). The court must "assume the truth of all properly pleaded material allegations of the complaint and give it a reasonable interpretation by reading it as a whole and its parts in their context." *Phillips v. Desert Hosp. Dist.*, 49 Cal. 3d 699, 702, 263 Cal. Rptr. 119, 780 P.2d 349 (1989). Consequently, a demurrer must be denied where the factual allegations state a cause of action but the defendant contests their accuracy. *See, e.g., Committee on Children's Television, supra* (concluding defendants' contention that the words and images of their television commercials were not misrepresentations, as plaintiffs had alleged in the complaint, framed a factual issue for resolution by trial, not demurrer); *Selleck v. Globe Int'l, Inc.*, 166 Cal. App. 3d 1123, 212 Cal. Rptr. 838 (1985) (holding trial court erred in sustaining demurrer where the stated the contents of the article and alleged that the article was libelous on its face because the article was reasonably susceptible of a defamatory meaning on its face and therefore is libelous per se).

In *Aragon-Haas v. Family Sec. Ins. Services, Inc.*, 231 Cal. App. 3d 232, 282 Cal. Rptr. 233 (1991), the plaintiff sued her former employer, seeking damages for wrongful discharge. Plaintiff alleged breach of a written employment contract, a copy of which she attached to her complaint. The trial court sustained defendant's demurrer on the ground that the contract gave defendant the right to fire plaintiff without cause after the first year of employment. The Court of Appeal found the contract ambiguous, and reversed (*id.* at 239):

> Where a complaint is based on a written contract which it sets out in full,
> a general demurrer to the complaint admits not only the contents of the in-

strument but also any pleaded meaning to which the instrument is reasonably susceptible. While plaintiff's interpretation of the contract ultimately may prove invalid, it was improper to resolve the issue against her solely on her own pleading. "In ruling on a demurrer, the likelihood that the pleader will be able to prove his allegations is not the question." [Citation.]

[2] Judicial Notice

Dryden v. Tri-Valley Growers

Court of Appeal of California, First Appellate District
65 Cal. App. 3d 990, 135 Cal. Rptr. 720 (1977)

KANE, JUSTICE.

Plaintiffs, James Dryden, individually, and with Paul R. Minasian and Malcolm R. Minasian acting as a partnership of Dryden, Minasian & Minasian, appeal from the trial court's judgment dismissing the action against respondent Tri-Valley Growers after the demurrer to the third, fourth, fifth and sixth causes of action of the first amended complaint (complaint) was sustained without leave to amend.

The background facts appearing in the complaint reveal that commencing in 1970 appellants entered into a series of contracts with Henry and Margaret Irving (Irvings), the owners of Villa D'Oro Olive Oil Company, an olive oil processing plant located in Butte County, California. The contracts, which by incorporation became a part of the complaint, provided for the sale of certain waste products of olive oil production, including cracked, dried and de-oiled olive pits, olive pumice (the skin and meat of the olive), and olive oil soap stock (hereinafter: by-products or materials) to appellants. For the purpose of utilizing and selling such materials, appellants installed conveyors, wooden sideboards and building supports on the premises of Villa D'Oro. While some of the materials were subject to immediate sale and delivery, others were to be produced and delivered in the future. With regard to the purchase of future products, appellants were granted a right of option extending until July 15, 1982. The contracts provided that the provisions contained therein would bind not only Irvings, the original sellers, but also the successor owners of the Villa D'Oro Olive Oil Company.

The facts further disclose that following the execution of the subject contracts a legal dispute arose between the parties. As a result, in letters dated June 16 and September 11, 1973, the Irvings advised appellants that they intended to rescind and cancel the subject contracts on grounds of material breach and fraudulent representations on the part of appellants. An action filed in Butte County followed, in which appellants sought declaratory and related relief against the Irvings.

While the Butte County action was pending, by a contract concluded on or about May 23, 1974, the Irvings transferred the ownership of the plant to respondent Tri-Valley Growers. Thereupon, appellants brought the present action against respondent and several unnamed persons. The complaint purported to state causes of action on tort theories of intentional interference with contractual and/or advantageous economic and business relationships. General damages were sought in the sum of

$1,000,000; special damages in the sum of $1,000,000; and exemplary damages in the sum of $5,000,000. Respondent filed a general demurrer to the original complaint which was sustained with leave to amend. Upon the filing of the first amended complaint, respondent again demurred, claiming that the third, fourth, fifth and sixth causes of action failed to state facts sufficient to constitute a cause of action. This time the trial court sustained the demurrer without leave to amend and dismissed the case against respondent.

Appellants insist that the facts stated in the third, fourth, fifth and sixth counts of the complaint are sufficient to support a cause of action based on the tort theory of intentional interference with contractual relations and/or on the broader concept of interference with prospective economic advantage. A review of the governing legal principles along with an examination of the factual allegations of the complaint has led us to the conclusion that the judgment of the trial court must be affirmed. * * *

In proceeding to analyze the precise issue presented for determination, we initially observe that despite the broad language of the complaint purporting to state a cause of action for interference with "advantageous relationships, procedures and business," the gist of appellants' grievance is that, by buying the Villa D'Oro Olive Oil Plant from Irvings, respondent unjustifiably interfered with and induced the breach of the existing contracts between appellants and Irvings. The vital issue awaiting adjudication, therefore, is whether the disputed counts stated sufficient facts to support a cause of action under the theory of interference with contractual relations.

The elements of a cause of action predicated on interference with contract are well defined. Accordingly, in order to plead an actionable wrong under this theory, plaintiff must allege that (1) he had a valid and existing contract; (2) *the defendant had knowledge of the contract and intended to induce its breach*; (3) the contract was in fact breached by the contracting party; (4) *the breach was caused by the defendant's unjustified or wrongful conduct*; and (5) the plaintiff has suffered damage.

When tested by the foregoing standards, the challenged causes of action display blatant deficiencies on their face, rendering them vulnerable to a general demurrer.

Thus, the third and fifth causes of action allege that respondent acquired knowledge of the contracts entered into between appellants and Irvings only on May 24, 1974, one day *after* the execution of the purchase contract with the Irvings. It is elementary that interference with contractual rights and economic advantage is an intentional tort. Accordingly, it has been held that an action for interference with contractual rights lies only if the defendant's act *induced* the breach of contract between the plaintiff and the third party or if the defendant *purposely* caused a third person not to perform the contract with another. Since the third and fifth causes of action not only fail to indicate that respondent induced or otherwise purposely caused the breach of the contract, but also fail to allege that at the time of purchasing the plant respondent was even aware of the existence of previous contracts between appellants and Irvings, such causes of action are fatally defective.

* * *

Turning to the fourth and sixth causes of action, we observe that they contain alternative allegations that the olive oil processing plant was obtained by respondent with prior knowledge of the contracts between appellants and Irvings. Furthermore, it is alleged that respondent interfered with said contracts by inducing the Irvings to sell the plant and by refusing thereafter to perform the terms and provisions of the contracts; that said acts of respondent were undertaken knowingly and intentionally for the purpose of preventing the performance of said contracts and that as a direct result of respondent's conduct appellants incurred sizeable damages. While the aforestated allegations seemingly support a cause of action based on interference with contractual rights, when read in light of the record as a whole, they too fail to withstand an attack by demurrer.

It is axiomatic that a general demurrer may consider not only the facts appearing upon the face of the complaint but also any matter of which the court is required to, or may, take judicial notice (Code Civ. Proc., § 430.30; *Hinckley v. Bechtel Corp.* (1974) 41 Cal. App. 3d 206 [116 Cal. Rptr. 33]; *Legg v. Mutual Benefit Health & Accident Assn.* (1960) 184 Cal. App. 2d 482 [7 Cal. Rptr. 595]; 3 Witkin, Cal. Procedure (2d ed. 1971) § 798, p. 2412). In the case at bench the record shows that the trial court took judicial notice of two letters incorporated in the second amended complaint filed by appellants against the Irvings in the Butte County Superior Court action. As indicated before, in said letters, dated June 16 and September 11, 1973, respectively, appellants were notified that due to a number of reasons, including material breach of contract, fraudulent inducement to enter into contracts, fraudulent representations made by appellants, the Irvings elected to cancel and rescind the contracts relative to the sale of olive oil by-products.

The purported cancellation and rescission of the contracts at issue prior to the sale of the plant to respondent bears special significance with regard to the determination of this case.

It has been repeatedly held that a plaintiff, seeking to hold one liable for unjustifiably inducing another to breach a contract, must allege that the contract would otherwise have been performed, and that it was breached and abandoned by reason of the defendant's wrongful act and that such act was the moving cause thereof. [Citations omitted.]

The allegations of the fourth and sixth causes of action in conjunction with the matters judicially noticed conclusively demonstrate that the performance of the disputed contracts had been abandoned and discontinued by the Irvings many months prior to the transfer of the plant to respondent. Under these circumstances, proximate causation, a vital element of the cause of action, was lacking as a matter of law. It goes without saying that in the absence of a showing that respondent's act was the proximate cause of the injury, appellants failed to allege a valid cause of action based on interference with contractual relations.

[Here the court discusses an additional, alternate reason why the demurrer must be upheld.]

The judgment is affirmed.

[a] Mandatory Judicial Notice

Evidence Code Section 451 requires a court to take judicial notice of certain specified California and federal laws, as well as "[f]acts and propositions of generalized knowledge that are so universally known that they cannot reasonably be the subject of dispute." What facts are "universally known"? *See* 1 Witkin, *California Evidence, Judicial Notice* §§ 32-35 (5th ed. 2012).

[b] Permissive Judicial Notice

A court may also take judicial notice of a variety of other laws such as local and federal rules, foreign state rules and acts, and federal regulations; as well as "[f]acts and propositions that are not reasonably subject to dispute and are capable of immediate and accurate determination by resort to sources of reasonably indisputable accuracy." Evidence Code § 452; *see, e.g., Arce v. Kaiser Found. Health Plan, Inc.*, 181 Cal. App. 4th 471, 482-85,104 Cal. Rptr. 3d 545 (2010) (taking judicial notice of pleadings filed in other cases and of a report of a legislative commission, but not of a transcript and videotaped recording of a television interview); *Carleton v. Tortosa*, 14 Cal. App. 4th 745, 753, n.1, 17 Cal. Rptr. 2d 734 (1993) (ruling brochures and summaries by private corporations not properly subjects of judicial notice, but official publications and bulletin of California Department of Real Estate are not reasonably subject to dispute); *Ross v. Creel Printing & Publ'g Co.*, 100 Cal. App. 4th 736, 743-44, 122 Cal. Rptr. 2d 787 (2002) (declining to take judicial notice of district attorney handbook where defendant provided no information about the handbook's source, purpose, or official ratification). For a good discussion of judicial notice of the legal effect of a legally operative document, see *Scott v. JPMorgan Chase Bank*, 214 Cal. App. 4th 743, 752-66, 154 Cal. Rptr. 3d 394 (2013) (sustaining demurrer after ruling the trial court properly took judicial notice of the fact and legal effect of a contract between the defendant bank and the federal government).

Such use of judicial notice may permit the court to consider dispositive matter not alleged in the complaint. *See, e.g., Beresford Neighborhood Assn. v. City of San Mateo*, 207 Cal. App. 3d 1180, 1191, 255 Cal. Rptr. 434 (1989) (ruling trial court properly took judicial notice of city municipal code governing bidding procedures when considering demurrer); *but see Gould v. Maryland Sound Indus., Inc.*, 31 Cal. App. 4th 1137, 37 Cal. Rptr. 2d 718 (1995) (concluding because the issue of whether plaintiff was employed under a written or oral contract was the "fact" in dispute, the trial court erred in taking judicial notice of a written employment contract between the parties submitted by the defendant as an attachment to its points and authorities at demurrer stage, and therefore improperly sustained demurrer to plaintiff's breach of oral contract claims).

[c] Judicial Notice of Court Records

In ruling on a demurrer, a court may take judicial notice of court records in the same or any other action. Evidence Code § 452(d); *Sirott v. Latts*, 6 Cal. App. 4th

923, 8 Cal. Rptr. 2d 206 (1992) (ruling superior court properly took judicial notice of court and arbitration records in sustaining demurrer on ground that legal malpractice complaint barred by statute of limitations); *Fowler v. Howell* , 42 Cal. App. 4th 1746, 50 Cal. Rptr. 2d 484 (1996) (taking judicial notice of existence of records and files of a state administrative board).

Although judicial notice is appropriate to establish the *existence* of the material in court records, judicial notice of the *content* of these records for the purpose of establishing truth of the content is improper. *See, e.g.*, *Kilroy v. State of California*, 119 Cal. App. 4th 140, 14 Cal. Rptr. 3d 109 (2004) (ruling factual finding in a prior judicial decision may not establish the truth of that fact for purposes of judicial notice; however a factual finding in a prior judicial opinion may be the proper subject of judicial notice if it has a res judicata or collateral estoppel effect in a subsequent action); *Sosinsky v. Grant*, 6 Cal. App. 4th 1548, 1560-70, 8 Cal. Rptr. 2d 552 (1992) (concluding trial court properly refused to consider facts in court documents from a prior action; the court may take judicial notice of the existence of each document in a court file, but cannot take judicial notice of the truth of the facts asserted in findings of fact); *Richtek USA Inc. v. UPI Semiconductor Corp.*, 242 Cal. App. 4th 651, 658-61, 195 Cal. Rptr. 3d 430 (2015) (same); *but see Lockley v. Law Office of Cantrell, Green, Pekich, Cruz & McCort* , 91 Cal App. 4th 875, 110 Cal. Rptr. 2d 877 (2001) (holding trial court may take judicial notice that a court of appeal has made factual findings in another case involving the same parties, but may not take judicial notice of the truth of such factual findings unless they are the product of an adversary hearing which involved the question of their existence or nonexistence and are supported by substantial evidence).

In *Columbia Casualty Co. v. Northwestern National Ins. Co.*, 231 Cal. App. 3d 457, 473, 282 Cal. Rptr. 389 (1991), the court explained the reason for this distinction:

> While judicial notice is appropriate to establish the existence of the material in court records, judicial notice of the content of these records for the purpose of establishing truth of the content is distinctly improper.

> Judicial notice of the truth of the content of court records is appropriate only when the existence of the record itself precludes contravention of that which is recited in it, for example where findings of fact, conclusions of law or judgments bind a party for purposes of res judicata or collateral estoppel. (2 Jefferson, Cal. Evidence Benchbook, *supra*, Judicial Notice, § 47.2, pp. 1757-58; *In re Tanya F.* (1980) 111 Cal. App. 3d 436, 440 [168 Cal. Rptr. 713].) Otherwise judicial notice for the truth of the content of court records is not appropriate either because the truth of the content is reasonably subject to dispute, or because the content is hearsay.

Did the court in *Dryden* honor this distinction?

[3] *Judicial Council Form Complaints*

The California Judicial Council has approved numerous form complaints and cross-complaints for many typical causes of action. *See* Rule 1.45, Cal. Rules of Ct.

Through a combination of boxes to be checked and blanks to be filled in, these forms guide the preparer through all the steps necessary to plead the essential elements of the relevant cause of action.

Is a Judicial Council form complaint immune from attack by way of demurrer? No, according to the court in *People ex rel. Dept. of Transp. v. Superior Court*, 5 Cal. App. 4th 1480, 7 Cal. Rptr. 2d 498 (1992), where the plaintiff used a form complaint for personal injury to sue Caltrans for allegedly maintaining public property in a dangerous condition. Defendant Caltrans demurred on the ground that the complaint did not adequately, nor with the requisite specificity, allege the elements of this cause of action against a government entity. The trial court stated that a Judicial Council form is nondemurrable, and overruled the demurrer. The Court of Appeal directed the trial court to sustain the demurrer with leave to amend and observed (*id.* at 1485):

> In some cases, merely checking a box on a Judicial Council form complaint will be sufficient. In other cases, such as this one, where specific allegations need to be alleged, the form complaint is like a partially completed painting. It is up to the pleader to add the details that complete the picture. The form complaint here, standing alone, is no more immune to demurrer than any other complaint that fails to meet essential pleading requirements to state a cause of action.

[4] Demurrer vs. Answer

Objections to a complaint which may be properly raised by demurrer may also be raised by answer, or by both if filed at the same time. CCP §§ 430.10, 430.30, 472a(a). However, an objection whose resolution requires consideration of new or additional information—facts not appearing on the face of the complaint or judicially noticeable—must be raised by an answer. *See, e.g., Cravens v. Coghlan*, 154 Cal. App. 2d 215, 315 P.2d 910 (1957) (ruling defendant cannot raise plaintiff's lack of capacity to sue in a demurrer because that objection required proof of facts extrinsic to the complaint; such new information must be raised in an answer). Why not by demurrer?

When a demurrer to a complaint or cross-complaint is overruled and no answer is yet filed, unless otherwise ordered an answer must then be filed within 10 days. CCP § 472a(b); Rule 3.1320(j), Cal. Rules of Ct.

[C] Amendment After Sustained Demurrer

Careau & Co. v. Security Pacific Business Credit, Inc.

Court of Appeal of California, Second Appellate District
222 Cal. App. 3d 1371, 272 Cal. Rptr. 387 (1990)

CROSKEY, JUSTICE.

* * *

Plaintiffs appeal from a judgment which was based upon an order sustaining demurrers without leave to amend and an order granting defendants' motion for judgment on the pleadings. In this appeal we are asked to decide the propriety of such orders as well as the trial court's denial of a motion for reconsideration of the order sustaining the demurrers. * * *

FACTUAL BACKGROUND

At the heart of these consolidated actions is the effort to finance the purchase of an egg production facility in Moorpark, California, known as Julius Goldman's Egg City (Egg City). Plaintiffs, or at least one of the plaintiffs, sought to purchase Egg City and sought funding of $13 million from defendants. This financing never materialized and plaintiffs were allegedly unable to make the purchase until a new lender was found. They eventually obtained the necessary funding elsewhere, but on less desirable terms. Plaintiffs filed these actions, contending, inter alia, that defendants (1) breached oral and written contracts, (2) breached the implied covenant of good faith and fair dealing, (3) denied in bad faith the contract's existence, (4) engaged in fraud and negligent misrepresentations, and (5) interfered with plaintiffs' contractual and business relationships and prospective economic advantages. * * *

DISCUSSION

* * *

On appeal, plaintiffs challenge only the fact that the trial court sustained demurrers to the first amended complaints *without leave to amend* and then, in spite of the allegations in the proposed second amended complaints, refused to reconsider that order. We therefore presume that the demurrers to their first amended complaints were properly sustained.

As we already have noted, it is an abuse of discretion to sustain demurrers without leave to amend if there is a reasonable possibility that the plaintiff can amend the complaint to cure its defects. (*Cooper v. Leslie Salt Co.* (1969) 70 Cal. 2d 627, 636 [75 Cal. Rptr. 766, 451 P.2d 406]; *Goodman v. Kennedy* (1976) 18 Cal. 3d 335, 349 [75 Cal. Rptr. 766, 451 P.2d 406]). To meet the plaintiff's burden of showing abuse of discretion, the plaintiff must show how the complaint can be amended to state a cause of action. (*Goodman v. Kennedy, supra,* 18 Cal. 3d at p. 349.) However, such a showing need not be made in the trial court so long as it is made to the reviewing court. (Code Civ. Proc. §472c; *Nestle v. City of Santa Monica* (1972) 6 Cal. 3d 920, 939 [101 Cal. Rptr. 568, 496 P.2d 480]; …). * * *

Plaintiffs argue that the second amended complaints do allege viable causes of action but, even if we also find them deficient, they have a right to the opportunity of further amendment. The general rule is that allegations of a complaint are to be liberally construed with a view to substantive justice between the parties. (*King v. Central Bank* (1977) 18 Cal. 3d 840, 843 [135 Cal. Rptr. 771, 558 P.2d 857].) An order sustaining a demurrer without leave to amend will constitute an abuse of discretion if there is any reasonable possibility that the defect can be cured by an amendment. This rule is liberally applied to permit further amendment not only where the defect is one of form but also where it is one of substance, provided the pleader did not have " 'a fair prior opportunity to correct the substantive defect.' " (*Leach v. Drum-*

mond Medical Group, Inc. (1983) 144 Cal. App. 3d 362, 368 [192 Cal. Rptr. 650], quoting *Larwin-Southern California, Inc. v. JGB Investment Co.* (1979) 101 Cal. App. 3d 626, 635 [162 Cal. Rptr. 52].)

On the other hand, there is nothing in the general rule of liberal allowance of pleading amendment which "requires an appellate court to hold that the trial judge has abused his discretion if on appeal the plaintiffs can suggest no legal theory or state of facts which they wish to add by way of amendment." (*HFH, Ltd. v. Superior Court* (1975) 15 Cal. 3d 508, 513, fn. 3 [125 Cal. Rptr. 365, 542 P.2d 237].) The burden is on the plaintiffs to demonstrate that the trial court abused its discretion and to show in what manner the pleadings can be amended and how such amendments will change the legal effect of their pleadings. (*Goodman v. Kennedy, supra,* 18 Cal. 3d 335, 349 ...).

With such general principles in mind we will examine each of the causes of action alleged by the plaintiffs.

Whether the Complaints Plead Sufficient Facts to State a Cause of Action on Any Theory

a. *Claims Based on Contract*

[The court examined the various contract causes of action alleged by the plaintiffs and concluded they did not state a cause of action. The court found the plaintiffs' allegations as to satisfaction of certain conditions precedent were insufficient to demonstrate the existence of a binding contract.]

These pleading defects are at once matters of both form and substance. However, we cannot conclude, without effectively resolving a factual issue, that there is no reasonable possibility of plaintiffs making the direct allegations necessary to demonstrate the existence of a binding contract. Therefore, it is appropriate that plaintiffs be given the opportunity to correct the specific pleading errors we have described. It was therefore error to sustain a demurrer to these contract counts without leave to amend. * * *

c. *Tort Claims Based on Alleged Bad Faith*

Plaintiffs attempt to assert two separate causes of action based upon a claim of bad faith. Each necessarily depends upon the existence of a valid and existing contractual relationship. As we have already concluded that plaintiffs have failed to plead the existence of a contract we could dispose of these counts summarily. However, there are significant additional reasons upon which we rely to support our view that plaintiffs have not alleged a basis for relief on either theory. In addition, plaintiffs will be given a further opportunity to plead the existence of a contract. We therefore deal with these two claims in some detail.

(1) *Tortious Breach of Implied Covenant of Good Faith and Fair Dealing*

Arguing that it is "settled" that there is a "special relationship" between a bank and its customers, plaintiffs contend that defendants have tortiously breached the covenant of good faith implied in their contractual relationship. Pleading in conclusory language that defendants "exercised great bargaining power" over them and that the circumstances of the transaction created "a special confidential and fiduciary duty" to them, plaintiffs allege that such breach resulted from (1) the refusal to provide the financing described in the [bank's letter of intent to loan], (2) a "deceitful and pretextual" explanation for such refusal and (3) the disclosure of confidential financial information to third parties.

Although plaintiffs have characterized this count as the *tortious* breach of the implied covenant, it is obviously possible to state a cause of action for a breach of such covenant even though no basis for a tort recovery exists. Thus, we must consider if a cause of action has been stated *on any theory*, irrespective of the label attached by the pleader. After a review of the applicable law, we will conclude that plaintiffs' allegations are not sufficient to state any cause of action for a breach of the implied covenant of good faith, irrespective of the remedy sought. * * *

A "'breach of the implied covenant of good faith and fair dealing involves something beyond breach of the contractual duty itself' and it has been held that '[b]ad faith implies unfair dealing rather than mistaken judgment.... [Citation.]' [Citation.]" (*Congleton v. National Union Fire Ins. Co.* (1987) 189 Cal. App. 3d 51, 59 [234 Cal. Rptr. 218].) * * *

In insurance cases there is a well-developed history recognizing a tort remedy for a breach of the implied covenant. (*Foley v. Interactive Data Corp.* (1988), 47 Cal. 3d 654, 684 [254 Cal. Rptr. 211, 765 P.2d 373].) A review of those cases demonstrates that the existence of this remedy has been justified by the "special relationship" existing between insurer and insured, which is characterized by elements of public interest, adhesion and fiduciary responsibility. In addition, it is essential to a recovery in tort that the insurer, in breaching the implied covenant, have acted unreasonably.

However, whether such a concept has any application in noninsurance cases appears to be increasingly problematic. Indeed, the proposition that tort damages might be allowed for a breach of the implied covenant in noninsurance cases is barely 10 years old and is based entirely on dicta from 2 earlier opinions which the Supreme Court has recently questioned. To appreciate just how difficult it is to assert such a claim, a short historical review is appropriate. [The court discusses *Tameny v. Atlantic Richfield Co.* (1980) 27 Cal. 3d 167 [164 Cal. Rptr. 839, 610 P.2d 1330] and *Seaman's Direct Buying Service, Inc. v. Standard Oil Co., supra,* which cast doubt on the extension of the "special relationship" tort concept beyond the insurer/insured relationship.]

In *Wallis v. Superior Court* (1984) 160 Cal. App. 3d 1109 [207 Cal. Rptr. 123] (*Wallis*), the court announced a five-part description of the characteristics of the "special relationship" which must be present in a noninsurance contractual dispute in order to justify tort recovery for a breach of the implied covenant. However, in its most recent discussion of this issue, the Supreme Court refused to apply this approach to employment cases.

In *Foley*, the court held that it was "not convinced that a 'special relationship' analogous to that between insurer and insured" existed in the usual employment relationship so as to justify recognition of a tort remedy for a breach of the implied covenant. (47 Cal. 3d at p. 692.) Indeed, the court even suggested that *any* extension of tort remedies to noninsurance cases is not justified.... Nonetheless, the *Foley* court did limit its holding to the employer-employee relationship and did not expressly reject the *Wallis* definitional efforts; however, it did suggest that it is still an open question as to whether "the special relationship model is an appropriate one to follow in determining whether to expand tort recovery." (*Id.*, at p. 692.)

From this history, it seems clear to us that the recognition of a tort remedy for a breach of the implied covenant in a noninsurance contract has little authoritative support. In fact, with but one arguable exception and apart from decisions disapproved by *Foley*, every case which has considered the issue has rejected the recognition of a special relationship between specific contracting parties. However, as the *Foley* court did not see fit to specifically reject the ... consideration of the noninsurance special relationship, or the *Wallis* criteria for determining its existence, we decline to do so. Indeed, the *Foley* court's discussion of why the employment relationship was dissimilar to that of insurer and insured essentially relied upon a *Wallis* analysis. (*Foley, supra,* 47 Cal. 3d at p. 692.)

More recently, in *Mitsui Manufacturers Bank v. Superior Court, supra,* 212 Cal. App. 3d 726, 733, the court discussed similar criteria in concluding that a lender and commercial borrower did not share a special relationship sufficient to justify a tort claim. The court restated the standard to be applied in terms very similar to those used by *Wallis*. "It is the nature of the contract that is critical, whether it reflects unequal bargaining strength between the parties, an inadequacy of ordinary contract damages or other remedies, adhesiveness of contract provisions adversely impacting the damaged party which are either neutral toward or benefit the other, public concerns that parties to certain types of contracts conduct themselves in a particular manner, the reasonable expectations of the parties or a fiduciary relationship in which the financial dependence or personal security by the damaged party has been entrusted to the other. There are undoubtedly other significant factors and it may be that not all must be present in every case which might give rise to tort damages." (*Id.* at p. 731.) Whatever the present efficacy of this analytical restatement, we find that plaintiffs here have failed to allege sufficient facts to demonstrate that they satisfy the requirements set forth in either *Wallis* or *Mitsui*.

This case presents a rather common commercial banking transaction. The plaintiffs, seeking to make a profit motivated investment in the form of a leveraged buyout of a going business, entered into arms length negotiations with a unit of a major lending institution. There were no indicia of unequal bargaining here, no adhesive agreements, no indication that one party had any particular advantage over the other. Indeed, it appears that the terms of the central document, the [letter of intent to loan], was the product of meaningful negotiations between the parties. Moreover, it does not appear that plaintiffs were neither in a particularly vulnerable position nor in need of any special protection. Finally, ordinary contract damages are obviously adequate to make plaintiffs whole for any compensable misconduct on the part of the defendants.

Under no reasonable perspective of the facts in this case would the *Wallis/Mitsui* standards be satisfied. Given the allegations set out in plaintiffs' second amended pleadings, the "transaction involved here is the quintessentially ordinary arms-length commercial transaction between two parties of equal bargaining strength, breaches of which are adequately remedied by ordinary contract damages." (*Mitsui Manufacturers Bank v. Superior Court, supra*, 212 Cal. App. 3d at p. 731.) Whatever may be the viability of the proposition that a bank can have a special relationship with a depositor so as to justify a tort recovery for breach of the implied covenant, there is neither authority nor reason for according such characterization to the relationship between a bank and a commercial borrower.

Therefore, since it is patently clear that no "special relationship" exists sufficient to support a tort recovery for an alleged breach of the implied covenant of good faith, plaintiffs can state no basis for recovery in tort. Moreover, as they have alleged nothing more than a duplicative claim for contract damages, the trial court was correct in sustaining a demurrer to this count without leave to amend. * * *

Notes and Questions regarding Sustained Demurrer and Leave to Amend

(1) The trial court in *Careau* sustained the demurrers without leave to amend. Why did the Court of Appeal hold that the trial court erred in sustaining the demurrers to the contract counts without leave to amend, but affirmed the sustaining of the demurrer to the bad faith tort count without leave to amend? Could the plaintiffs amend their complaint to allege facts which stated a "special relationship" under the *Wallis/Mitsui* standards? Why not?

(2) The *Careau* opinion sets forth the abuse of discretion standard generally applied by appellate courts when reviewing a demurrer sustained without leave to amend. *See Blank v. Kirwan, supra*, 39 Cal. 3d at 318. What a plaintiff must demonstrate to establish abuse of discretion will vary with the ground for the demurrer. Should an appellate court more readily find an abuse of discretion where a general demurrer is sustained without leave to amend as to an initial, as opposed to a previously amended, complaint? *See 1119 Delaware v. Continental Land Title Co.*, 16 Cal. App. 4th 992, 998, 20 Cal. Rptr. 2d 438 (1993) (sustaining demurrer without leave to amend constituted abuse of discretion where original complaint did not show on its face it was incapable of stating cause of action upon amendment).

(3) When a demurrer is sustained, CCP § 472d requires the trial court to include in its order a statement of the specific grounds upon which the decision is based. This section has been interpreted, however, to require affirmance of the trial court's order on appeal if any of the grounds raised by the defendant require the sustaining of the demurrer, whether or not the court specifies all such grounds. *See, e.g., Gonzales v. State of California*, 68 Cal. App. 3d 621, 627, 137 Cal. Rptr. 681 (1977) (noting the validity of the trial court's action in sustaining the demurrer is reviewed, not the court's statement of reasons for its action). What, then, is the purpose of the statement of reasons required by CCP § 472d?

(4) A special demurrer for uncertainty will be sustained only where the uncertainty is with respect to essential elements of the pleading, but not where the ambiguous facts

alleged are presumptively within the knowledge of the demurring party. *See, e.g., Gonzales v. State of California, supra,* 68 Cal. App. 3d at 631 (concluding a special demurrer should not be sustained if the allegations of the complaint are sufficiently clear to apprise the defendant of the issues that must be met); *Bacon v. Wahrhaftig,* 97 Cal. App. 2d 599, 218 P.2d 144 (1950) (ruling a demurrer for uncertainty not appropriate where ambiguous allegations refer to immaterial matter). Does a trial court automatically abuse its discretion when it sustains such a special demurrer without leave to amend?

(5) If a trial court sustained a demurrer with leave to amend a complaint and the plaintiff fails to do so, the court must enter a judgment of dismissal upon motion by either party. CCP § 581(f)(2). If the dismissal is appealed, the appellate court must strictly construe the complaint and presume that the plaintiff has stated as strong a case as she can. *Gonzales v. State of California, supra,* 68 Cal. App. 3d at 635. Why would a plaintiff not amend her complaint after a demurrer was sustained with leave to amend? Why would a *plaintiff* then move for dismissal?

(6) When the trial court makes an order sustaining a demurrer without leave to amend, the question of whether the court abused its discretion in making this order is open on appeal even though no request to amend the pleading was made. CCP § 472c(a). If the demurrer is sustained as to fewer than all causes of action within a complaint or cross-complaint, or as to an affirmative defense but not an entire answer, the aggrieved party may claim the trial court's order as error in an appeal from the final judgment in the action. CCP § 472c(b).

§ 9.06 Motions Related to Pleadings

[A] Motion to Strike

[1] Grounds

A trial court may, upon motion made pursuant to CCP § 435 or at any time in its discretion, strike out any irrelevant, false, or improper matter inserted in any pleading; or any part of a pleading not filed in conformity with court rules, order, or other laws. CCP § 436(a) & (b). A motion to strike is generally used to reach defects in a pleading which are not subject to demurrer. *Pierson v. Sharp Mem'l Hosp., Inc.,* 216 Cal. App. 3d 340, 342, 264 Cal. Rptr. 673 (1989). For example, a motion to strike does not lie to attack a complaint for insufficiency of allegations to justify relief; that is a ground for general demurrer. *See id.* (concluding a motion to strike may be treated as a motion for judgment on the pleadings if complaint clearly deficient); *Warren v. Atchison, Topeka & Santa Fe Ry.,* 19 Cal. App. 3d 24, 41, 96 Cal. Rptr. 317 (1971) (treating an improper motion to strike as a demurrer).

A common use of the motion is to strike punitive damage allegations from a medical malpractice complaint because the plaintiff failed to comply with the pre-pleading requirements of CCP § 425.13, *see, e.g., Looney v. Superior Court,* 16 Cal. App. 4th 521, 20 Cal. Rptr. 2d 182 (1993); *Cummings Med. Corp. v. Occupational Med. Corp.,*

10 Cal. App. 4th 1291, 1298, 13 Cal. Rptr. 2d 585 (1992); or to strike an amount of personal injury or punitive damages alleged in a complaint, *see* CCP § 425.10(b), Civil Code § 3295(e). What are some other common examples of the proper use of a motion to strike? *See* 2 CEB, *California Civil Procedure Before Trial, Motions to Strike* §§ 24.3-24.6 (4th ed. 2015).

[2] Procedures

A motion to strike must be filed "within the time allowed to respond to a pleading." CCP § 435(b)(1); *but see* CCP § 435(e) & 438(i)(1)(A) (motion to strike certain late filed amended pleadings). Pleading subject to motions to strike include demurrers, answers, complaints, and cross-complaints. CCP § 435(a). The grounds for a motion to strike must appear on the face of the challenged pleading or in matter which the court may judicially notice. CCP § 437(a). A motion to strike which is based on more than the pleadings may be treated as a motion for summary judgment. *See, e.g., City and Cnty. of San Francisco v. Strahlendorf*, 7 Cal. App. 4th 1911, 1913-14, 9 Cal. Rptr. 2d 817 (1992).

[3] Motion to Strike pursuant to "Anti-SLAPP" Statute

Code of Civil Procedure § 425.16 (the anti-SLAPP statute) authorizes a special type of motion to strike by which a defendant may obtain a dismissal of strategic lawsuit against public participation (SLAPP), *i.e.,* "a cause of action against a person arising from any act of that person in furtherance of the person's right of petition or free speech under the United States or California Constitution in connection with a public issue." CCP § 425.16(b)(1). In ruling on an anti-SLAPP motion to strike, the court must first decide whether the defendant has made a threshold showing that the challenged cause of action is one arising from protected free speech activity, as defined in the statute (CCP §§ 425.16(b)(1), 725.17). *See, e.g., Flatley v. Mauro*, 39 Cal. 4th 299, 46 Cal. Rptr. 3d 606, 139 P.3d 2 (2006) (ruling a defendant whose assertedly protected speech was illegal as a matter of law—such as communications that constituted criminal extortion—and therefore unprotected by constitutional guarantees of free speech, cannot use the anti-SLAPP statute to strike a plaintiff's complaint); *Oasis West Realty v. Goldman*, 51 Cal. 4th 811, 124 Cal. Rptr. 3d 256, 250 P.3d 1115 (2011) (denying special motion to strike in an action against client's former attorney alleging misuse of client's confidential information because such misuse is not protected free speech). If the court finds such a showing has been made, it must then determine whether the plaintiff has demonstrated a probability of prevailing on the claim. CCP § 425.16(b)(1). *See, e.g., Taus v. Loftus*, 40 Cal. 4th 683, 54 Cal. Rptr. 3d 775, 151 P.3d 1185 (2007) (striking most of plaintiff's invasion of privacy claims that alleged defendants, authors and publishers of two scholarly articles, had disclosed information about plaintiff's private life); *Jarrow Formulas, Inc. v. LaMarche*, 31 Cal. 4th 728, 3 Cal. Rptr. 3d 636, 74 P.3d 737 (2003) (applying anti-SLAPP statute to malicious prosecution actions).

In order to establish the requisite probability of prevailing and thereby defeat the anti-SLAPP motion to strike, the plaintiff "must demonstrate that the complaint is both legally sufficient and supported by a sufficient prima facie showing of facts to sustain a favorable judgment if the evidence submitted by the plaintiff is credited." *Navellier v. Sletten*, 29 Cal. 4th 82, 88-89, 124 Cal. Rptr. 2d 530, 52 P.3d 703 (2002). Under CCP § 425.16(b)(2), the trial court in making these determinations considers "the pleadings, and supporting and opposing affidavits stating the facts upon which the liability or defense is based." How does this special anti-SLAPP motion to strike differ from the ordinary motion to strike authorized by CCP 435? From a motion for summary judgment? From a motion for an order allowing a plaintiff to allege a punitive damages claim against a health care provider, pursuant to CCP § 425.13? *See College Hosp., Inc. v. Superior Court*, 8 Cal. 4th 704, 34 Cal. Rptr. 2d 898, 882 P.2d 894 (1994), discussed *supra*.

In 2005, the Legislature enacted CCP § 425.18 and thereby added another twist to anti-SLAPP law—the SLAPPback. CCP § 425.18(b)(1) defines a "SLAPPback" as any cause of action for malicious prosecution or abuse of process arising from the filing or maintenance of a prior cause of action that has been dismissed pursuant to a special motion to strike under CCP § 425.16. CCP § 425.18 treats SLAPPbacks differently from ordinary malicious prosecution actions in two ways. First, it makes certain favorable procedures available to a SLAPPback plaintiff when confronted with an anti-SLAPP motion to strike. CCP §§ 425.18(c)-(g). Second, it exempts a SLAPPback from an anti-SLAPP motion to strike when that motion is brought by a party whose filing or maintenance of the prior cause of action from which the SLAPPback arises was illegal as a matter of law. CCP § 425.18(h). For a discussion of these various statutory provisions, see *Soukup v. Law Offices of Herbert Hafif*, 39 Cal. 4th 260, 46 Cal. Rptr. 3d 638, 139 P.3d 30 (2006).

[B] Motion for Judgment on the Pleadings

[1] Grounds

The grounds for a motion for judgment on the pleadings are limited by statute to either failure of a pleading to state facts sufficient to constitute a cause of action or a defense, or lack of subject matter jurisdiction. CCP §§ 438(a)-(c). The grounds for the motion must appear on the face of the challenged pleading or from matters judicially noticed. CCP § 438(d); *see, e.g., Evans v. California Trailer Court, Inc.*, 28 Cal. App. 4th 540, 33 Cal. Rptr. 2d 646 (1994) (holding trial court properly considered facts alleged in complaint plus judicially noticed recorded deed); *Harris v. Grimes*, 104 Cal. App. 4th 180, 186, n.4, 127 Cal. Rptr. 2d 791 (2004) (ruling judgment on the pleadings may rely on evidence outside the pleadings if no objection made). In an appeal from a motion granting judgment on the pleadings, the appellate court accepts as true the facts alleged in the complaint and reviews the legal issues de novo. *Angelucci v. Century Super Club*, 41 Cal. 4th 160, 166, 59 Cal. Rptr. 3d 142, 158 P.3d 718 (2007).

A motion for judgment on the pleadings performs the function of a general demurrer. *See Evans v. California Trailer Court, Inc., supra*, 28 Cal. 4th at 548 (ruling rules governing demurrers applied); *Barker v. Hull*, 191 Cal. App. 3d 221, 224, 236

Cal. Rptr. 285 (1987) (applying the same standards); *Ludgate Ins. Co. v. Lockheed Martin Corp.*, 82 Cal. App. 4th 592, 601-10, 98 Cal. Rptr. 2d 277 (2000) (noting all facts in complaint are deemed admitted). Unlike a demurrer, a motion for judgment on the pleadings may be asserted at any time after all the pleadings are filed, although court permission is necessary to make the motion during trial. CCP § 438(e). The motion may be made even though the moving party did not demur to the complaint or answer. CCP § 438(g)(2). Unless there is a material change in applicable case law or statute, however, a moving party may not make the motion on the same grounds as was the basis for an overruled demurrer. CCP § 438(g)(1). The standard governing a trial court's determination of a motion for judgment on the pleadings is quite different from the standard governing consideration of a motion for summary judgment. See *Columbia Casualty v. Northwestern Nat. Ins.*, 231 Cal. App. 3d 457, 282 Cal. Rptr. 389 (1991) (explaining the differences in the standards for the two motions).

[2] Leave to Amend

As with a sustained demurrer, a judgment on the pleadings should be granted with leave to amend if there is any reasonable possibility that the plaintiff can amend the complaint and state a good cause of action. *See, e.g., Virginia G. v. ABC Unified Sch. Dist.*, 15 Cal. App. 4th 1848, 1852, 19 Cal. Rptr. 2d 671 (1993); *La Jolla Village Homeowners' Assn. v. Superior Court*, 212 Cal. App. 3d 1131, 1141, 261 Cal. Rptr. 146 (1989). Where a motion for judgment on the pleadings is granted as to the original complaint, denial of leave to amend constitutes an abuse of discretion unless the pleading shows on its face that it is incapable of curative amendment. *See Virginia G. v. ABC Unified Sch. Dist., supra* (concluding trial court erred in granting motion for judgment on the pleadings where complaint by student against school district alleging sexual molestation by teacher could be amended to properly allege negligent hiring and supervision of the teacher).

When the motion is granted with leave to amend, the amended complaint or answer must be filed within 30 days. CCP § 438(h)(2). If no amended pleading is filed, the moving party must move for entry of judgment in its favor. CCP § 438(i)(1)(B). If an amended pleading is filed after the time for amendment has expired, the moving party must move to strike the pleading and enter judgment in its favor. CCP § 438(h)(4) & (i)(1)(A).

§ 9.07 The Answer

[A] Introductory Note

A defendant served with a complaint has three principal choices: (1) do nothing and risk entry of default and a default judgment; (2) attack the complaint and seek a partial or complete dismissal of the action through use of the demurrer and other related motions; or (3) respond to the complaint on its own terms through the answer. This section takes up the third of the options. Conceptually, preparing and filing an answer is the normal procedural response; whether in practice it is the most common response is not at all clear. The answer is a pleading, just like the complaint, that responds to the allegations in the complaint. Except in those few instances where a defending party can file a general denial (*see* CCP § 431.40(a)), answers contain three types of responses. First, portions of the complaint may be admitted, either by express admission or by failure to deny. *See* CCP §§ 431.30(f), 431.20(a). Second, allegations in the complaint may be controverted by general or specific denials (§ 431.30(b)(1)), on the basis of information or belief (§ 431.30(d) & (f)), or on the ground of lack of information or belief (§ 431.30(d) & (e)). Third, the answer may respond by stating defenses (usually called "affirmative defenses") that provide a defense to the complaint even if its allegations are true. *See* CCP § 431.30(b)(2) & (g).

If the defending party seeks affirmative relief against the party filing the complaint, the defending party must proceed by separate cross-complaint. CCP § 431.30(c); *see* § 9.08, *infra*. The requirement of a separate cross-complaint differs from the federal practice that combines answers and counterclaims (but not third-party complaints, also called cross-complaints under California law) in the same pleading. *See* Rules 13 and 14, Federal Rules of Civil Procedure. As in the case of complaints, the California Judicial Council has provided Official Form answers. *See, e.g.*, Form PLD-PL-003 (Answer-Personal Injury); Form PLD-C-010 (Answer-Contract).

[B] Denials

[1] *Failure to Deny Constitutes an Admission*

"Every material allegation of the complaint or cross-complaint, not controverted by the answer, shall, for purposes of the action, be taken as true." CCP § 431.20(a). Failure to properly deny a material allegation therefore constitutes an admission. *Valerio v. Andrew Youngquist Constr.*, 103 Cal. App. 4th 1264, 1271-72, 127 Cal. Rptr. 2d 436 (2002) (noting an admission in a pleading is conclusive on the pleader). In *Hennefer v. Butcher*, 182 Cal. App. 3d 492, 227 Cal. Rptr. 318 (1986), for example, the plaintiff buyers sued the defendant seller for specific performance of a real property sales agreement. The seller argued that specific performance was inappropriate because the plaintiff did not prove the requisite reasonableness and adequacy of consideration. The court held that the fairness and reasonableness of the contract was not a possible issue because the defendant seller failed to deny the buyers' allegations in their complaint that the consideration named in the contract was the "fair and reasonable value" of the property. *Hennefer*, 182 Cal. App. 3d at 504.

[2] *General vs. Specific Denials*

The pleading statutes require specific and positive denials when answering a verified complaint, CCP § 431.30(b); but permit a general denial in lieu of an answer when the complaint is not verified, in a limited civil case, or when the amount sought in the complaint does not exceed $1,000, CCP §§ 431.30(d), 431.40. *See, e. g., Conley v. Lieber*, 97 Cal. App. 3d 646, 158 Cal. Rptr. 770 (1979) (holding defendant's answer, which denied "generally and specifically each and every allegation contained" in the complaint, effectively denied plaintiff's allegations regarding causation and damages). A general denial simply states: "Defendant denies each and every allegation in plaintiff's complaint." *See* California Judicial Council Form PLD-050.

What are the advantages and disadvantages of the general denial? Why might a defendant not use the general denial even when authorized to do so? What should a plaintiff do to prevent a defendant's use of the general denial?

[3]   Functions of the Answer

An answer delineates the contested issues of fact through admissions and denials, and requires the plaintiff to prove all material allegations in the complaint controverted by the answer. CCP § 590. A timely filed answer also prevents the plaintiff from obtaining a default judgment from the answering defendant. *See* CCP § 585. Generally, a defendant must file an answer within 30 days after service of a complaint or cross-complaint, unless the defendant obtains an extension or files a demurrer, motion to quash, or some other responsive motion. *See, e.g.*, CCP § 412.20(a)(3), § 418.10(a)(1) (motion to quash), § 418.10(a)(2) (motion on ground of inconvenient forum), § 396b (motion to transfer), § 435 (motion to strike), § 472b (demurrer). The answer also provides the vehicle for raising objections to pleadings that cannot be taken by demurrer because the ground does not appear on the face of the pleading, CCP §§ 430.10, 430.30(b); and for stating defenses, CCP §§ 431.30(b), 590. The filing of an answer also constitutes a general appearance. CCP § 1014. What other purposes do answers serve?

[C]   Raising "New Matter"

An answer must contain a statement of any "new matter" constituting a defense. CCP § 431.30(b)(2). Each defense must be separately stated and separately numbered. CCP § 431.30(g).

Hulsey v. Koehler

Court of Appeal of California, Third Appellate District
218 Cal. App. 3d 1150, 267 Cal. Rptr. 523 (1990)

SCOTLAND, JUSTICE.

Defendant, Dr. Judith P. Koehler (hereinafter Koehler) appeals from a judgment entered in favor of plaintiffs, John and June Hulsey (hereinafter the Hulseys) granting declaratory relief and reformation of a promissory note executed in connection with the Hulseys' sale of a mobilehome park to Koehler in 1980.

At trial, Koehler moved to amend her answer to assert Code of Civil Procedure section 426.30[1] as an affirmative defense, alleging that the cause of action for reformation was barred because the Hulseys had failed to seek reformation by cross-com-

---

1. Further statutory references are to the Code of Civil Procedure unless otherwise specified.

plaint in an earlier lawsuit Koehler had filed against the Hulseys for claims arising from the sale of the mobilehome park. Section 426.30 is California's compulsory cross-complaint statute which bars claims that could have been raised by cross-complaint in a prior action between the parties. The trial court denied the motion as untimely.

On appeal, Koehler contends that the trial court abused its discretion in denying her motion to amend. In addition, Koehler claims that she was entitled to assert section 426.30 as a defense even without amending her answer, because it need not be specially pleaded as an affirmative defense. We disagree with both contentions and shall affirm the judgment.

FACTS

On January 26, 1980, the parties executed a Commercial Purchase Agreement and Deposit Receipt (deposit receipt) in which Koehler agreed to purchase the Golden Oaks Mobile Estates in Oroville for the sum of $372,000, with the Hulseys carrying back a note secured by a deed of trust on the property. Among other things, the deposit receipt required Koehler to make a $60,000 down payment in two installments, $30,000 at close of escrow and $30,000 on September 15, 1980. The deposit receipt also stated, "Principle [sic] reductions of $30,000 (thirty-thousand) to be made 12 months and 24 months from close of escrow. Balance to be due & payable 7 years from close of escrow."

The escrow instructions prepared by the title company differed from the terms of the deposit receipt. The instructions provided for "a principal payment of $30,000.00 due on or before September 15, 1980, and … an additional principal payment of $30,000.00 due between the end of the 12th month and the end of the 24th month after close of escrow."

Upon reviewing the escrow instructions, the Hulseys did not observe this change in language, which, as the trial court noted, "in effect meant that [they were] signing away one of the $30,000.00 principal reductions previously agreed to by the parties." Koehler did recognize the discrepancy but did not point it out to either the escrow officer or the Hulseys as they sat in the title company reviewing the documents.

The parties signed the instructions without modification and, when escrow closed on June 1, 1980, the title company prepared a promissory note consistent with the escrow instructions rather than the deposit receipt. The note was executed by Koehler and mailed to the Hulseys.

The Hulseys first discovered the disparity in terms when they reviewed the promissory note upon returning from vacation in September 1980. They immediately contacted the title company and requested an amended escrow instruction together with a new promissory note. These were prepared and forwarded to Koehler, who refused to sign them.

In October 1980, Koehler filed a lawsuit against the Hulseys, alleging that she was the victim of fraud and misrepresentation in the sale of the mobilehome park. A jury returned a unanimous verdict in favor of the Hulseys.

Thereafter, when Koehler failed to pay the second $30,000 principal reduction, the Hulseys commenced this litigation. Following a trial without jury, the court found that, because of a mistake of fact, the note drafted by the title company failed to reflect the true intention of the parties. * * * The trial court ... awarded the Hulseys a judgment in the amount of $97,528.48.

DISCUSSION

The following facts and procedural background are pertinent to Koehler's contention that the trial court erred in precluding her from raising section 426.30 as a defense:

As previously indicated, this action was preceded by a lawsuit filed by Koehler alleging fraud, misrepresentation, and breach of contract in the sale of the mobilehome park. Koehler asserted that the Hulseys and their realtor misrepresented both the amount of income generated by the park and its capacity for recreational vehicles and mobilehomes. The Hulseys cross-complained for intentional interference with business relations, alleging that Koehler interfered with the sale of two mobilehome units which the Hulseys maintained at the park. Although by then they were aware of the discrepancy between the deposit receipt and the promissory note, the Hulseys did not assert by cross-complaint a request for reformation of the note. Jury verdicts were entered for the Hulseys on Koehler's complaint and for Koehler on the Hulseys' cross-complaint.

When Koehler later failed to pay the second $30,000 principal reduction, the Hulseys commenced this litigation seeking declaratory relief, reformation, specific performance of the default provisions of the deed of trust, and appointment of a receiver. In her answer, Koehler asserted two affirmative defenses: failure to state a cause of action and full performance of the terms of the promissory note.

At trial, Koehler moved to amend her answer to conform to proof by asserting section 426.30 as an affirmative defense. Koehler's counsel explained that he did not raise section 426.30 earlier, because he first discovered it as a potential defense two days before trial while reading the deposition testimony of Mrs. Hulsey. At that time, he learned the Hulseys were aware of the discrepancy in the promissory note before they answered the complaint in the prior litigation and, therefore, should be barred from seeking reformation in this case, because they could have requested it by cross-complaint in the prior action. The trial court denied the motion to amend as untimely.

Koehler contends that the trial court erred in not allowing her to raise section 426.30 as a defense because it need not be specially pleaded. Koehler likens this statutory defense to the doctrine of collateral estoppel, which requires no special pleading.

While we agree that a party is not required to specially allege collateral estoppel as a defense (*Dakins v. Board of Pension Commissioners* (1982) 134 Cal. App. 3d 374, 387 [184 Cal. Rptr. 576]; 5 Witkin, Cal. Procedure (3d ed. 1985) Pleading, § 1050, p. 466), contrary to Koehler's claim, the compulsory cross-complaint rule of section 426.30 is not an extension of this doctrine.

Collateral estoppel precludes parties from litigating an issue previously determined in another cause of action between them or their privities. As a prerequisite for asserting this doctrine, it must be shown that the issue was, in fact, litigated and decided in the prior action. * * *

Since section 426.30 bars claims which the party failed to assert by cross-complaint in a previous action arising from the same occurrence, it necessarily bars issues which were never litigated and never actually decided. Thus, the scope and effect of section 426.30 is analogous to that of res judicata rather than collateral estoppel. * * * [R]es judicata precludes parties from splitting a cause of action into a series of suits in piecemeal litigation, since it operates as a bar not only when the grounds for recovery in the second action are identical to those pleaded in the first but also where a different theory or request for relief is asserted.

Section 426.30 serves the same purpose as the doctrine of res judicata by requiring the settlement in a single action of all conflicting claims between the parties arising from the same transaction. As Koehler recognizes, the public policy served by the enactment of section 426.30 is the law's abhorrence of a multiplicity of lawsuits.

We discern no difference between the operation of section 426.30 and the doctrine of res judicata. * * * Just as a plaintiff cannot split a cause of action by failing to assert all claims against the defendant arising from a transaction, neither can a defendant split a cause of action by failing to assert by cross-complaint all the claims against the plaintiff arising from the same transaction.

Unlike collateral estoppel, an objection based on the doctrine of res judicata must be specially pleaded or it is waived. (7 Witkin, Cal. Procedure (3d ed. 1985) Judgment, § 198, pp. 636-637.) The reason for this distinction is that res judicata results in a complete defense whereas collateral estoppel "merely involves conclusive evidence of a fact in issue." (*Solari v. Atlas-Universal Service, Inc.* (1963) 215 Cal. App.2d 587, 592-593 [30 Cal. Rptr. 407].)

Likewise, as a statutory bar to splitting a cause of action, section 426.30 must be specially pleaded. It is well established that a rule against splitting of actions is for the benefit of the defendant and is waived by the failure to specifically plead the defense. (*Williams v. Krumsiek* (1952) 109 Cal. App. 2d 456, 460 [241 P.2d 40]; 4 Witkin, Cal. Procedure (3d ed. 1985) Pleading § 36, p. 78.) In this regard, we find noteworthy the statement by the court in *Datta v. Staab* (1959) 173 Cal. App. 2d 613, 619 [343 P.2d 977] that a defense based on the statutory predecessor to section 426.30 must be "seasonably and properly raised." * * *

Since we find that a defense based on section 426.30 must be specially pleaded, we reject Koehler's contention that her affirmative defense of failure to state facts sufficient to constitute a cause of action effectively incorporated the section 426.30 defense and was sufficient to raise it.

Lastly, we consider whether the trial court erred in denying Koehler's motion to amend her answer to assert section 426.30 as a defense.

Section 473 permits the trial court in its discretion to allow amendments to pleadings in the furtherance of justice. Ordinarily, courts should "exercise liberality" in permitting amendments at any stage of the proceeding. (*Permalab-Metalab Equipment*

Corp. v. Maryland Cas. Co. (1972) 25 Cal. App. 3d 465, 472 [102 Cal. Rptr. 26]; 5 Witkin, Cal. Procedure (3d. ed. 1985) Pleading, § 1121, p. 537.) In particular, liberality should be displayed in allowing amendments to answers, for a defendant denied leave to amend is permanently deprived of a defense.

"[N]evertheless, whether such an amendment shall be allowed rests in the sound discretion of the trial court. [Citations.] And courts are much more critical of proposed amendments to answers when offered after long unexplained delay or on the eve of trial [citations], or where there is a lack of diligence, or there is prejudice to the other party (citations)." (*Permalab-Metalab Equipment Corp. v. Maryland Cas. Co.,* supra, 25 Cal. App. 3d at p. 472.)

Here, Koehler moved to amend at trial to conform to proof more than three years after she answered the Hulseys' amended complaint. Defense counsel's excuse for this delay was simply that he discovered section 426.30 as a potential defense only two days before trial while reading the transcript of Mrs. Hulsey's deposition. In denying the motion as untimely, the trial court impliedly found an unreasonable lack of diligence in the belated assertion of this defense. Moreover, the trial court noted that the delay had prejudiced the Hulseys: "I think that's particularly true in this case, wherein we have an attorney's fee provision. [¶] And I think the plaintiff has a right to know his risk and weighs his exposure prior to trial. And I think very arguably prior to trial preparation. But certainly prior to the time that he puts on his evidence."

On the facts before it, the trial court did not abuse its discretion in denying the motion to amend.

The judgment is affirmed.

[1] *Affirmative Defenses*

New matter constituting an affirmative defense must be stated in the answer. As *Hulsey* illustrates, failure to plead an affirmative defense waives that defense. *See, e.g., California Acad. of Sciences v. County of Fresno,* 192 Cal. App. 3d 1436, 1442, 238 Cal. Rptr. 154 (1987) (rejecting defendant's waiver and estoppel arguments because defendant failed to raise them as affirmative defenses in its answer); *Carranza v. Noroian,* 240 Cal. App. 2d 481, 488, 49 Cal. Rptr. 629 (1966) (ruling general denial constituted waiver of defendant's right to prove setoff based on independent and different contract); *Minton v. Cavaney,* 56 Cal. 2d 576, 581, 15 Cal. Rptr. 641, 364 P.2d 473 (1961) (concluding defendant waived statute of limitations defense by failing to plead that defense in the answer or by demurrer); *see generally* 2 CEB, *California Civil Procedure Before Trial, Answers* § 25.32 (4th ed. 2015); 5 Witkin, *California Procedure, Pleading* §§ 1081-1128 (5th ed. 2008).

A plaintiff need not answer affirmative defenses raised in defendant's answer to the complaint; affirmative defenses are deemed controverted and a plaintiff may introduce evidence on the issue at trial. CCP § 431.20(b); *see, e.g., Aerojet General Corp. v. Superior Court,* 177 Cal. App. 3d 950, 953, 233 Cal. Rptr. 249 (1986).

[2] What Constitutes "New Matter"?

Under CCP § 431.30(b)(2), the answer to a complaint must include "[a] statement of any new matter constituting a defense." The phrase "new matter" refers to something relied on by a defendant which is not put in issue by the plaintiff. *State Farm Mutual Auto Ins. Co. v. Superior Court*, 228 Cal. App. 3d 721, 725, 279 Cal. Rptr. 116 (1991). Thus, where matters are not responsive to allegations of the complaint, they must be raised in the answer as "new matter." *Id.* Where, however, the answer sets forth facts showing some essential allegation of the complaint is not true, such facts are not "new matter" but only a traverse. *Id.* Accordingly, what is put in issue by a denial is limited to the allegations of the complaint. Consider the following cases.

In *State Farm Mutual Auto Ins. Co. v. Superior Court, supra,* the plaintiffs-insureds alleged the cause of action of bad faith handling of an insurance claim. The defendant State Farm filed a general denial to the complaint. Subsequently at trial, the defendant insurer sought to introduce evidence to establish the defense of reliance on advice of counsel in its claims handling. The trial court excluded the evidence on the ground that State Farm had failed to specifically plead advice of counsel as a defense in its answer. The Court of Appeal directed the trial court to permit State Farm to offer this evidence (*State Farm.* 228 Cal. App. 3d at 726):

> State Farm contends the defense of advice of counsel is not "new matter" and thus it need not be specifically pleaded in the answer. We agree. In response to a plaintiff's allegations of bad faith and malice, a defendant is entitled to show it acted reasonably and with proper cause based on the advice of its counsel. Good faith reliance on counsel's advice simply negates allegations of bad faith and malice as it tends to show the insurer had proper cause for its actions. Because advice of counsel is directed to an essential element of a plaintiff's cause of action, it does not constitute new matter and need not be specifically alleged.

In *FPI Development, Inc. v. Nakashima*, 231 Cal. App. 3d 367, 282 Cal. Rptr. 508 (1991), plaintiffs' complaint pled a cause of action on a promissory note. Defendants' answer contained a general denial. The court held that the denial put in issue all material allegations of the complaint which comprise the essential elements of plaintiffs' cause of action. This encompasses such defenses as the contract is wholly void, the note was not executed, and the defendants paid in accordance with its terms. However, the court viewed the denial as not putting in issue the defense that the note was a sham transaction (*id.* at 403):

> [T]he facts necessary to show that the transaction was a sham are matters not encompassed in the denial of the ultimate fact of execution alleged in the complaint. The defense is in the nature of "Yes—the facts alleged are true"—but they do not render us liable because of additional facts, i.e., those about the sham. Where a party participates in a sham the intention is that the note not be taken as a jural act by the one upon whom the sham is perpetrated. It will not lie in the mouth of the participant to say there was no

execution of the note. The defense, if any, is that there was an execution but that the plaintiff cannot take advantage of it. For that reason a denial of execution does not put such a theory in issue.

Do you agree with the holding in *State Farm Mutual*? In *FPI Development*? Are the two holdings consistent with each other? Distinguishable? How so?

[D] Verification of the Answer

When the complaint is verified, the answer must also be verified. CCP § 446. However, a plaintiff must raise the failure to verify the answer prior to commencement of trial. When the plaintiff proceeds to trial without objecting to the lack of verification, she waives any right to object to defendant's pleading error. *See, e.g., Zavala v. Bd. of Trustees*, 16 Cal. App. 4th 1755, 1761, 20 Cal. Rptr. 2d 768 (1993). What is the purpose of the requirement of a verified answer? Section 446 permits an attorney to verify an answer for a party absent from the county, or when the attorney is an officer of a corporate party. Does verification constitute a waiver of the attorney-client privilege as to matters admitted or denied in the answer? *See Alpha Beta Co. v. Superior Court*, 157 Cal. App. 3d 818, 829-31, 203 Cal. Rptr. 752 (1984) (ruling vague and conclusory disclosures in an answer verified by general counsel for defendant corporation did not constitute a waiver of the attorney-client privilege).

§ 9.08 Cross-Complaints

[A] Introductory Note

The California cross-complaint is a multi-purpose pleading device which permits a party defending against a cause of action to assert her own affirmative cause of action against an opposing party, a co-party, or some other person not already a party to the action. CCP §§ 428.10-428.80. The California cross-complaint serves the same functions as the familiar counterclaim, cross-claim, and third-party impleader in federal court. *See* Rules 13 and 14, Federal Rules of Civil Procedure. The California Legislature opted for the "one-term-fits-all" approach in 1971 when it eliminated technical limitations of prior methods of countersuits and replaced them with a single form of pleading. *See, e.g.,* CCP § 428.80 (counterclaims abolished and deemed cross-complaints); Jack H. Friedenthal, *Joinder of Claims, Counterclaims, and Cross-Complaints: Suggested Revisions of the California Provisions*, 23 STAN. L. REV. 1, 17-39 (1970); *1970 Law Revision Commission Report*, pp. 518-51.

The cross-complaint is one of the four types of pleadings allowed in civil actions, CCP § 422.10; and is the only pleading other than a complaint that can demand affirmative relief. 2 CEB, *Civil Procedure Before Trial, Cross-Complaints* § 26.3 (4th ed. 2015); *see* CCP § 431.30(c) (Affirmative relief cannot be claimed in an answer). A cross-complaint must be filed and served as a separate document, and must comply with the same form and content rules applicable to a complaint. *Civil Procedure Before*

Trial, supra at §§ 26.44, 26.50-26.52; *see* CCP §§ 425.10, 428.40-428.60. A cross-complaint must, within 30 days after service, be responded to in the same manner as an original complaint. CCP § 432.10. Dismissal of the underlying complaint does not constitute a dismissal of a cross-complaint. *See* CCP § 581(i).

[B] Compulsory and Permissive Cross-Complaints

Currie Medical Specialties, Inc. v. Newell Bowen

Court of Appeal of California, Fourth Appellate District
136 Cal. App. 3d 774, 186 Cal. Rptr. 543 (1982)

BROWN (GERALD), PRESIDING JUSTICE.

Currie Medical Specialties, Inc. sued Newell Bowen for breach of contract, fraud, negligent misrepresentation, intentional interference with prospective business advantage and unfair competition. Bowen's motion for summary judgment based on Currie's failure to comply with Code of Civil Procedure section 426.30 was granted. Currie appeals the judgment.

This is the second action between these parties. In 1979, Bowen sued Currie in the federal court for violating the Lanham Act (15 U.S.C. § 1051 et seq.) and unfair competition. Currie answered but made no counterclaim. Four months after Currie answered, the suit was dismissed with prejudice by stipulation of the parties.

The superior court found the claim made by Currie in the current action was a compulsory counterclaim in the earlier case and is barred by section 426.30.

Currie and Bowen sell labels to hospitals. In 1978, the parties orally contracted for Currie to stop selling its labels and become a distributor of Bowen's labels. In this action, Currie alleges Bowen breached the agreement and was guilty of fraud in its formation. In the earlier federal action Bowen alleged Currie usurped Bowen's customer lists, sales manuals and style of label while distributing for Bowen and then, after the contractual relationship was terminated, entered into unfair competition with Bowen.

The sole issue here is whether Currie's claim based on termination of the contract was a compulsory counterclaim in the earlier action under section 426.30. That section reads: "Except as otherwise provided by statute, if a party against whom a complaint has been filed and served fails to allege in a cross- complaint any related cause of action which (at the time of serving his answer to the complaint) he has against the plaintiff, such party may not thereafter in any other action assert against the plaintiff the related cause of action not pleaded." This section, however, does not apply where: "Both the court in which the action is pending and any other court to which the action is transferrable pursuant to Section 396 are prohibited by the federal or state constitution or by a statute from entertaining the cause of action not pleaded." (Code Civ. Proc., § 426.40.) The question becomes whether the federal district court had jurisdiction to hear Currie's claim.

The parties agree there was no diversity or federal question jurisdiction applicable to Currie's claim. The dispute focuses on whether the federal court could have heard the claim under its ancillary jurisdiction. If Currie's claim arose out of the same transaction or occurrence which was the basis of Bowen's complaint, it was covered by ancillary jurisdiction and was a compulsory counterclaim (Fed. Rules Civ. Proc., rule 13(a), 28 U.S.C.; *Albright v. Gates* (9th Cir. 1966) 362 F.2d 928). The transaction or occurrence test is dispositive of this entire action because it settles the ancillary jurisdiction question and defines "related cause of action" as it is used in section 426.30. (*See* Code Civ. Proc., § 426.10.)

Albright v. Gates, supra, cites *United Artists Corp. v. Masterpiece Productions* (2d Cir. 1955) 221 F.2d 213, as providing the controlling interpretation of the transaction or occurrence test. *United Artists* holds the test requires "not an absolute identity of factual backgrounds for the two claims, but only a logical relationship between them." (*Id.* at p. 216.) This logical relationship approach is the majority rule among the federal courts (Wright & Miller, Federal Practice and Procedure: Civil (1971) § 1410). At the heart of the approach is the question of duplication of time and effort; i.e., are any factual or legal issues relevant to both claims?

The claims of Bowen and Currie involve common issues of law and fact. The nature of the contractual relationship is central to Currie's claim; it is likewise relevant to Bowen's claim because of the allegation Currie usurped Bowen's business properties during the relationship. Currie's answer to Bowen's complaint in federal court argued for estoppel based on Bowen's previous actions; those actions were the same as those which are the basis of Currie's current complaint. This overlap of issues satisfies the logical relation approach to the transaction or occurrence test. This common transaction, in turn, creates ancillary jurisdiction. Therefore, the exception to section 426.30 found in section 426.40 is not applicable.

The transaction common to both claims also triggers application of section 426.30. *Saunders v. New Capital for Small Businesses, Inc.* (1964) 231 Cal. App. 2d 324 [41 Cal. Rptr. 703] holds section 426.30 is a parallel provision to federal rule 13(a); it is the presence of a common transaction which renders the counterclaim compulsory. The California courts have also adopted the expansive logical relation test of *United Artists* (*Ranchers Bank v. Pressman* (1971) 19 Cal. App. 3d 612 [97 Cal. Rptr. 78]; *Saunders v. New Capital for Small Businesses, Inc., supra,* 231 Cal. App. 2d 324). The presence of issues common to the claims of Bowen and Currie creates ancillary jurisdiction at the same time it requires section 426.30 be applied.

Currie contends the logical relation test is improperly broad when it is used to bar a claim; the policy in favor of giving each person a day in court is stressed. The case law does not support Currie. The waiver provision of section 426.30 is mandatory, the policy in favor of hearing all related claims in a single action controlling (*Sylvester v. Soulsburg* (1967) 252 Cal. App. 2d 185 [60 Cal. Rptr. 218]; *Brenner v. Mitchum, Jones & Templeton, Inc.* (9th Cir. 1974) 494 F.2d 881). The 1979 federal action was the proper time and place for Currie's claim.

Judgment affirmed.

Crocker National Bank v. Emerald

Court of Appeal of California, Third Appellate District
221 Cal. App. 3d 852, 270 Cal. Rptr. 699 (1990)

DeCristoforo, Justice.

Defendant, Robert M. Emerald, proceeding inpropria persona, appeals from a judgment granting plaintiff Crocker National Bank's motion for summary judgment. Crocker's motion for summary judgment stems from a collection action brought by Crocker against Emerald for nonpayment on a promissory note. Emerald appeals from the judgment of dismissal following the order granting summary judgment, contending triable issues of fact exist as to whether Crocker has complied with California Uniform Commercial Code section 9504 subdivision (3) which requires the sale of collateral to be conducted in a commercially reasonable manner. Emerald also ... contends the trial court abused its discretion in denying him leave to file a cross-complaint. * * * We shall reverse the order granting summary judgment ... and affirm the trial court's denial of leave to file a cross-complaint.

FACTUAL AND PROCEDURAL BACKGROUND

This dispute between Crocker and Emerald has stretched on for nine years. It began when Emerald, the owner of a logging business, signed a promissory note with Crocker in the principal sum of $430,962.30. The note was payable in 30 monthly installments of $14,365.41, with the unpaid balance due and payable on December 15, 1978. An agreement giving Crocker a security interest in 52 items of equipment owned by Emerald's logging business secured the payment obligation.

Emerald's business experienced financial difficulties caused by the 1975 recession in the logging industry. Emerald realized he would be unable to make the series of payments due on May 15, 1976, and monthly thereafter. He failed to make the installment payment due May 15, 1976. Pursuant to the terms of the promissory note, Crocker elected to declare the entire unpaid balance to be due after the May 15, 1976, default, and made demand on Emerald for payment. In April 1976, with Crocker's consent, Emerald decided to sell some of the equipment securing the promissory note and to apply the proceeds to the balance due.

With Crocker's consent, Emerald sold 18 items of equipment, and the proceeds of the sale were credited to the balance due on the promissory note, reducing the balance to $128,966.86.

Crocker filed suit against Emerald to recover the balance due on the promissory note, plus collection charges, interest and attorney's fees. Emerald answered the complaint and filed a cross-complaint against Crocker alleging breach of fiduciary duty and violation of the Unruh Act. The trial court sustained Crocker's demurrer and granted Emerald leave to amend. Emerald amended his cross-complaint four times, each time the trial court sustained Crocker's demurrer, on the final occasion without leave to amend. * * *

In December of 1987, Crocker filed a ... summary judgment motion, which forms the basis of this appeal. In its motion, Crocker attempted to comply with California Uniform Commercial Code section 9504 by adopting Emerald's own valuation of ... 13 items of collateral left in issue.... Crocker used the values Emerald had assigned to each piece of equipment in his declarations and deposition testimony, and offered to give Emerald "credit" and reduce his debt by these amounts. Therefore, according to Crocker, since Emerald had been credited with the amount he believed the equipment was worth, the question of whether the sale of the collateral was commercially reasonable became moot.

In response, Emerald filed a motion for leave to file a cross-complaint and an amended answer. The trial court granted Emerald's motion for leave to file an amended answer, but denied leave to file a cross-complaint.

Following oral argument, the court granted Crocker's motion for summary judgment. Following entry of judgment, Emerald filed a timely notice of appeal. * * *

II. *Commercially Reasonable Sale of Collateral*

At the core of this controversy is California Uniform Commercial Code section 9504. Section 9504 provides that, in the event of default by the debtor, the secured party may liquidate the security and apply the proceeds to the unpaid balance of the debt. If there remains a deficiency, the debtor is liable for the balance. Subdivision 3 of section 9504 imposes upon the secured party the duty to conduct the sale of the collateral in a commercially reasonable manner, and to provide timely notice of the sale to the debtor. * * *

We find that a secured creditor cannot by unilateral action after nine years of litigation, suddenly accept the debtor's earlier estimate of the fair market value of the collateral, and thereby deny the debtor the *opportunity* to challenge the commercial reasonableness of the sale. "Whether a sale is conducted in a commercially reasonable manner is a question of fact and the answer depends on all of the circumstances existing at the time of the sale." (*Clark Equipment Co. v. Mastelotto, Inc.* (1978) 87 Cal. App. 3d 88, 96 [150 Cal. Rptr. 797].) Therefore, we reverse the trial court's order granting summary judgment.

III. *Denial of Leave to File Cross-complaint*

Emerald claims the trial court erred in denying him leave to file a cross-complaint. He argues his proposed cross-complaint is a compulsory cross-complaint under Code of Civil Procedure section 426.30. As a compulsory cross-complaint, Emerald asserts his complaint is governed by Code of Civil Procedure section 426.50, which makes permission to assert an unpleaded cause of action mandatory.

Code of Civil Procedure section 426.30, subdivision (a), which defines compulsory cross-complaints, states: "Except as otherwise provided by statute, if a party against whom a complaint has been filed and served fails to allege in a cross-complaint any related cause of action which (at the time of serving his answer to the complaint) he has against the plaintiff, such party may not thereafter in any other action assert against the plaintiff the related cause of action not pleaded." "Related cause of action" is defined in Code of Civil Procedure section 426.10, subdivision (c) as "a cause of action which arises out of the same transaction, occurrence or series of transactions or occurrences as the cause of action which the plaintiff alleges in his complaint."

Code of Civil Procedure section 426.50 authorizes relief from excusable failure to plead: "A party who fails to plead a cause of action subject to the requirements of this article, whether through oversight, inadvertence, mistake, neglect, or other cause, may apply to the court for leave to amend his pleading, or to file a cross-complaint, to assert such cause at any time during the course of the action. The court, after notice to the adverse party, *shall grant*, upon such terms as may be just to the parties, leave to amend the pleading, or to file the cross-complaint, to assert such cause if the party who failed to plead the cause acted in good faith. This subdivision shall be liberally construed to avoid forfeiture of causes of action." (Italics added.)

Emerald's proposed cross-complaint alleges (1) gross negligence; (2) fraud, deceit, and menace; and (3) intentional infliction of emotional distress.

Emerald bases his claim of gross negligence on Crocker's alleged failure to dispose of the 13 remaining items of collateral in a commercially reasonable manner pursuant to section 9504. Emerald attempted to cross-complain based on this same alleged conduct in five previous cross-complaints, to each of which Crocker successfully demurred. Thus, Emerald has not "failed" to plead a related cause of action in the past, as required by Code of Civil Procedure section 426.50. Instead, he has attempted to plead a cause of action, based on Crocker's alleged misconduct, on five separate occasions. His final effort was met with a demurrer which the trial court sustained without leave to amend.

Moreover, Emerald's proposed second and third causes of action for fraud, deceit, menace and intentional infliction of emotional distress, are based on Crocker's actions which allegedly took place in February 1982. Emerald contends Crocker engaged in "a campaign of fraud, deceit and unfair practices against cross-complainant, calculated and conceived to usurp" his property beginning in February 1982. These actions, Emerald claims, caused him severe emotional distress.

To be considered a compulsory cross-complaint, a related cause of action must have existed at the time of the service of Emerald's answer to Crocker's complaint. (Code Civ. Proc., §426.30, subd. (a).) Emerald filed his answer in August 1980, and the second and third causes of action are based on actions which allegedly took place in February 1982. Therefore, Emerald's second and third causes of action are not compulsory cross-complaints, and are not governed by Code of Civil Procedure section 426.50.

Instead, Emerald's proposed cross-complaint is a permissive cross-complaint, governed by Code of Civil Procedure section 428.50, subdivision (c) which states: "A party shall obtain leave of court to file any cross-complaint except one filed within the time specified in subdivision (a) or (b). Leave may be granted in the interest of justice at any time during the course of the action." Permission to file a permissive cross-complaint is solely within the trial court's discretion. (*Orient Handel v. United States Fid. and Guar. Co.* (1987) 192 Cal. App. 3d 684, 701 [237 Cal. Rptr. 667].)

We find the trial court did not abuse its discretion in refusing Emerald leave to file the cross-complaint. Emerald sought leave to file his cross-complaint seven years after the onset of litigation, and five years after a demurrer was sustained to Emerald's fifth amended cross-complaint without leave to amend. Moreover, Emerald's motion for leave to file a cross-complaint was filed only five months before the trial date.

Emerald provides no explanation for his delay in seeking the court's permission to file his proposed cross-complaint. Emerald knew of the facts upon which he based his first cause of action for gross negligence since at least August 1980, when he filed his first proposed cross-complaint. In addition, the facts upon which he based his second and third causes of action were known to him since 1986. Emerald's declaration in support of his motion for reconsideration, following the trial court's order granting Crocker's motion for extension of a writ of attachment, contains the same allegations as his proposed cross-complaint.

Given Emerald's lack of explanation concerning his failure to seek leave of the court between 1986 and 1988, we find the trial court acted within its discretion in denying Emerald leave to file his cross-complaint.

* * *

We reverse the order granting summary judgment and judgment thereon, and remand for further proceedings consistent with this opinion. We affirm the trial court's denial of Emerald's motion for leave to file a cross-complaint. Emerald shall recover costs on appeal.

[1] *Compulsory Cross-complaint*

As our principal cases illustrate, a "related cause of action" is subject to forfeiture if not alleged in a cross-complaint. CCP § 426.30. There are some statutory exceptions to this compulsory cross-complaint requirement, such as those discussed in our principal cases. In addition, the compulsory cross-complaint waiver rule does not apply where the court lacked personal jurisdiction over the person who failed to plead the related cause of action, where the person who failed to plead did not file an answer, and where the cause of action not pleaded required the presence of additional parties over whom the court cannot acquire jurisdiction. CCP §§ 426.30(b); 426.40.

[a] "Related Cause of Action"

As *Currie Medical Specialties* illustrates, the courts broadly construe the statutory definition of "related cause of action" to encompass any affirmative claim for relief which evolved from a series of logically interrelated acts or occurrences. *See also Align Tech., Inc. v. Tran*, 179 Cal. App. 4th 949, 959–68, 102 Cal. Rptr. 3d 343 (2009); *Silver Org. Ltd. v. Frank*, 217 Cal. App. 3d 94, 101, 265 Cal. Rptr. 681 (1990). This transactional standard is expansive and ambiguous, but informs a party to err on the side of pleading an arguably related cause of action.

The federal courts utilize a similar logical relation test when applying the compulsory counterclaim standard of Federal Rule 13(a). *See, e.g., Burlington Northern*

R.R. Co. v. Strong, 907 F.2d 707, 711 (7th Cir. 1990); *Maddox v. Kentucky Fin. Co., Inc.*, 736 F.2d 380, 382 (6th Cir. 1984); *United States v. Heyward-Robinson Co.*, 430 F.2d 1077 (2d Cir. 1970). The federal ancillary jurisdiction issue discussed in *Currie Medical Specialties* is now governed by the federal supplemental jurisdiction statute, 28 U.S.C. § 1367, which apparently codified prior federal case law on this point. *See, e.g., Unique Concepts, Inc. v. Manuel*, 930 F.2d 573, 574–75 (7th Cir. 1991); Shay S. Scott, Comment, *Supplemental Jurisdiction Under 28 U.S.C. § 1367*, 72 Or. L. Rev. 695 (1993).

[b] Time For Filing

Normally, a party must file a cross-complaint against any party who filed a complaint or cross-complaint against her before or at the same time as the answer. CCP § 428.50(a). Other cross-complaints (third-party, etc.) may be filed at any time before the court has set a date for trial. CCP § 428.50(b). A party must obtain leave of court to file a cross-complaint at some later time. CCP § 428.50(c).

Section 426.50 authorizes relief from an excusable failure to timely plead a cross-complaint, and directs that such authority "shall be liberally construed to avoid forfeiture of causes of action." Absent a finding of bad faith, CCP § 426.50 does not permit a trial court to deny a motion to file a late compulsory cross-complaint. *See, e.g., Silver Org. Ltd. v. Frank*, 217 Cal. App. 3d 94, 265 Cal. Rptr. 681 (1990) (concluding trial court erred in denying defendant's motion to file compulsory cross-complaint on eve of trial where insufficient evidence of bad faith). If the cross-complaint in *Crocker* had been a compulsory one, would the trial court's denial of leave to file still be proper?

[c] Res Judicata Compared

Recall the discussion of res judicata (claim preclusion) in Chapter 8, Preclusive Effects of Prior Judgments, *supra*. The California courts follow the primary rights doctrine of res judicata and permit a plaintiff to bring a separate lawsuit against the same defendant for violation of each separate primary right. *See, e.g., Slater v. Blackwood*, 15 Cal. 3d 791, 126 Cal. Rptr. 225, 543 P.2d 593 (1975); *Holmes v. David H. Bricker, Inc.*, 70 Cal. 2d 786, 76 Cal. Rptr. 431, 452 P.2d 647 (1969). A valid final judgment on the merits in favor of a defendant does, however, serve as a complete bar to further litigation on the same cause of action. *Slater v. Blackwood, supra*, 15 Cal. 3d at 795. But a "cause of action" is defined as the remedial right in favor of a plaintiff for the violation of one "primary right." *Id.*

A factual transaction may give rise to the violation of more than one primary right, and therefore give a plaintiff the potential of two separate lawsuits against a single defendant. Under established primary rights precedent, for example, one tortious act may violate two primary rights and create two separate causes of action: one for injury to person and a second for damages to property. *See Slater v. Blackwood, supra; Holmes v. David H. Bricker, Inc., supra*. A typical example is negligence litigation arising out of the crash of two cars, where one driver sues the other. The resulting personal injury to the plaintiff driver is a separate cause of action from the property damage to plaintiff's car, and may be pursued in two separate lawsuits.

The cross-complaint statutes utilize a "transactional" standard—not a primary rights standard—in defining compulsory cross-complaints. CCP §§ 426.30(a), 426.10(c). What impact does this transactional cross-complaint standard have on the primary rights approach to res judicata? Consider the following typical occurrence. Sam Saguaro's car collided with Laura Lorry's truck. Both parties suffered personal injuries, and both vehicles were totaled. Plaintiff Saguaro sued defendant Lorry in superior court for personal injury damages, alleging his injuries were caused by defendant's negligence. Defendant answered and cross-complained against plaintiff. Defendant Lorry's cross-complaint sought damages for her own personal injuries, alleging they were caused by plaintiff's negligence. The jury found plaintiff Saguaro 5% negligent and defendant Lorry 95% negligent, and awarded appropriate damages.

Plaintiff Saguaro filed a subsequent lawsuit against defendant Lorry seeking damages for the destruction of his car. Because plaintiff's second suit is based on a separate primary right, his cause of action is not barred by res judicata. Is plaintiff's second action barred by CCP § 426.10(c) and § 426.30(a)? Why? If defendant Lorry had won the first lawsuit, would her subsequent suit against Sam Saguaro for property damage to her truck be barred? Why? The compulsory cross-complaint statutes effectively replace the primary rights approach with a transactional standard in such typical cases, do they not?

[2] Cross-Complaint vs. Affirmative Defense

[a] General Distinctions

A cross-complaint shares some of the attributes of an affirmative defense, but the two are quite distinct devices. An affirmative defense may provide a partial or complete bar to recovery on an opposing party's complaint or cross-complaint. In contrast, a cross-complaint permits the pleader to obtain relief regardless of the opposing party's recovery, and that relief may be different than, or in excess of, the opposing party's recovery. A cross-complaint is not limited to seeking relief from an opposing party, but may assert a cause of action against a co-party or a wholly new party. CCP § 428.10(b).

[b] Setoff

In situations where persons have cross-demands for money against each other and an action is commenced by one such person, CCP § 431.70 provides "the other person may assert in the answer the defense of payment in that the two demands are compensated so far as they equal each other." Is this setoff the same as an affirmative defense? If the defendant's demand exceeds the plaintiff's, why would the defendant utilize a setoff and not a cross-complaint? *See* CCP § 431.70. Is a setoff barred if it should have been asserted as a compulsory cross-complaint in an earlier action? *See id.*

[c] Equitable Indemnity

A typical use of the cross-complaint device is to seek equitable indemnity from a joint tortfeasor. Such a cross-complaint must be permitted unless it would operate against public policy. *See, e.g., Platt v. Coldwell Banker Residential Real Estate Serv.,* 217 Cal. App. 3d 1439, 266 Cal. Rptr. 601 (1990) (ruling new party cross-complaint for equitable indemnity must be permitted even though liability will be apportioned in the underlying comparative negligence action); *Daon Corp. v. Place Homeowners Assn.,* 207 Cal. App. 3d 1449, 1454-55, 255 Cal. Rptr. 448 (1989) (noting that a defendant may file a cross-complaint against any person from whom the defendant seeks total or partial indemnity on the basis of comparative fault).

[d] Statutes of Limitations

Ordinarily, statutes of limitations will apply to a cross-complaint in the same fashion as they apply to an independent action. *Liberty Mut. Ins. Co. v. Fales,* 8 Cal. 3d 712, 715, note 4, 106 Cal. Rptr. 21, 505 P.2d 213 (1973). However, when an original complaint was filed before the statute of limitations on a cross-complaint had elapsed, the cross-complaint will relate back to the date of the complaint for statute of limitation purposes. *See, e.g., Sidney v. Superior Court,* 198 Cal. App. 3d 710, 244 Cal. Rptr. 31 (1988). This relation-back rule applies only to a related cause of action—one which arises out of the same transaction or occurrence alleged in the complaint. *Id.* Even where a cross-complaint is barred, a defendant may be able to assert a cross-demand as a setoff. *See* CCP §431.70.

Chapter 10

Joinder of Parties and Claims

§ 10.01   Permissive Joinder of Parties and Claims

[A]   Permissive Joinder of Plaintiffs

Code of Civil Procedure Section 378 permits joinder of plaintiffs if they assert any right to relief "arising out of the same transaction, occurrence, or series of transactions or occurrences and if any question of law or fact common to all these persons will arise in the action...." The courts liberally construe this statutory standard so as to permit joinder of plaintiffs. In *Anaya v. Superior Court*, 160 Cal. App. 3d 228, 206 Cal. Rptr. 520 (1984), for example, numerous employees of the Occidental Petroleum Corporation joined in one lawsuit seeking damages for exposure to certain toxic chemicals over the course of 20-30 years. Defendant demurred, contending that each plaintiff's claim was based on facts entirely different from the transactions giving rise to the causes of action of the other plaintiffs. The trial court ruled that plaintiffs were misjoined and must file separate complaints. The Court of Appeal issued a writ of mandate directing the trial court to vacate the decision sustaining the demurrer. After analyzing various cases applying CCP § 378, the Court of Appeal found no misjoinder of the plaintiffs (*Anaya*, 160 Cal. App. 3d at 233):

> The employees are said to have been exposed to harmful chemicals at one location over a period of many years by inhalation, drinking of water, and physical contact. Thus, they were all involved in the same series of transactions of occurrences and assert rights to relief therefrom. The fact that each employee was not exposed on every occasion any other employee was exposed does not destroy the community of interest linking these petitioners.

In *State Farm Fire & Casualty Co. v. Superior Court*, 45 Cal. App. 4th 1093, 1112-14, 53 Cal. Rptr. 2d 229 (1996), the court held that a Group of insured homeowners, whose homes were destroyed by an earthquake, were properly joined as plaintiffs under CCP § 378. Plaintiffs' complaint alleged that the defendant insurer had defrauded them by reducing their earthquake coverage without adequate notice, and also alleged systematic claims handling practices which invaded the rights of plaintiffs as insureds. The court found that the allegations of inadequate notice clearly reflected a claim containing common facts central to the alleged deception. *State Farm, supra,* 45 Cal. App. 4th at 1113. As to the allegations of systematic claims handling practices, the court ruled that "[w]hile not every plaintiff ... may have been victimized by the same claims handling practice, that is a matter which can be resolved by discovery; and the trial court will always retain the right to sever the claims of particular plaintiffs in order to prevent prejudice to State Farm." *State Farm*, 45 Cal. App. 4th at 1113-14; *see also Petersen v. Bank of America*, 232 Cal. App. 4th 238, 181 Cal. Rptr. 3d 330 (2014) (holding permissive joinder of 965 plaintiff borrowers alleging fraud by defendant lender was available because common questions pertaining to the same series of loan transactions made the issue of liability amenable to mass action treatment, and because joinder would promote economies of scale and conservation of judicial resources).

[B] Permissive Joinder of Defendants

Farmers Insurance Exchange v. Adams

Court of Appeal of California, First Appellate District
170 Cal. App. 3d 712, 216 Cal. Rptr. 287 (1985)

MERRILL, JUSTICE.

The appellants in this action, Farmers Insurance Exchange, Fire Insurance Exchange, Truck Insurance Exchange and Mid-Century Insurance Company (Farmers) filed a complaint for declaratory relief in Marin County against over 300 named defendants (Insureds) and 5,000 Doe defendants. The complaint was later amended to name further defendants. Two demurrers and motions to dismiss were filed by Insureds; one by Christopher and Judith Bryant and one by Richard J. and Patricia Daly. The trial court sustained the demurrers without leave to amend and dismissed the amended complaint. Judgment was entered accordingly. This appeal followed.

I

In our review of the judgment entered pursuant to the order sustaining the general demurrer, we must accept the material facts alleged in the complaint as true. The following are the material facts set forth in Farmers' amended complaint.

Northern California experienced a heavy storm in early January of 1982. Many homeowners experienced damage to their real and/or personal property because of subsurface and ground water and earth movement conditions.

Each of the more than 300 named defendants was insured at the time of the storm by one of six types of Farmers' homeowners policies. These policies are "all risk" policies which enumerate various exclusions from coverage, including "losses caused by, resulting from, contributed to, aggravated by, or caused indirectly or directly by any earth movement, water damage, or enforcement of ordinance or law." Each of the named Insureds has reported damage to property arising out of conditions created by the January storm, and has submitted a claim under one of the policies issued by Farmers. Insureds reside in communities throughout Northern California from Yuba City to Moss Beach. Farmers denied the claims on the ground that the "efficient proximate cause" of Insureds' losses are excluded perils. The Insureds, on the other hand, contend that included risks were contributing causes of their losses giving rise to coverage under their policies.

By their amended complaint, Farmers sought the following declaration: "[That] because of the exclusions and exceptions set forth in the various property insurance policies issued by plaintiffs to defendants, that said policies do not provide coverage for damage or losses arising out of the January storm because the efficient proximate cause of the damage or loss claimed was an excluded cause, notwithstanding that one or more intermediate causes may have contributed to the loss or damage."

II

[In part II, the court concludes that the trial court correctly sustained the demurrer for failure to state a cause of action. After reviewing conflicting case law, the court held that where a loss is caused concurrently by both an included and an excluded peril, there may be insurance coverage without establishing that the included peril was the efficient proximate cause (the cause that sets other causes in motion).]

III

The trial court's second basis for sustaining the demurrer to Farmers' complaint was misjoinder of the various defendant Insureds, because of the need to individually analyze the causation question with regard to each insured. Appellants contend that joinder was appropriate in this case.

Permissive joinder of defendants in a civil action is proper where the complaint asserts against them any right to relief arising out of the same transaction, occurrence, or series of transactions or occurrences and if any question of law or fact common to all defendants will arise in the action. (Code Civ. Proc., § 379.)

In the instant case, joinder is inappropriate because Farmers' alleged right to declaratory relief against the numerous Insureds did not arise out of the same transaction or occurrence. Although it is true that the January 1982 storm played a role in the damage to Insureds' property, it cannot be said that all the claims of the Insureds arose out of the same transaction or occurrence.... While it may be possible to join certain of the Insureds upon more specific factual allegations, we find it improper to label the damage herein to innumerable types of structures, occurring at widely separated locations within the state, resulting from a myriad of causes, and under various conditions as the "same transaction or occurrence" within the meaning of Code of Civil Procedure section 379. The requirement of same transaction or occurrence has not been met and joinder may not be had. The trial court properly sustained the demurrer on this ground. (*See* Code Civ. Proc., § 430.10, subd. (d).) * * *

The order sustaining the demurrers without leave to amend, the order granting the motions to dismiss and the judgment are affirmed.

Notes and Questions regarding Permissive Joinder

(1) In *Garvey v. State Farm Fire & Casualty Co.*, 48 Cal. 3d 395, 257 Cal. Rptr. 292, 770 P.2d 704 (1989), the California Supreme Court held that in first-party insurance claims, coverage exists only if the covered concurrent cause is the efficient proximate cause, a predominant cause, of the loss. In so ruling, the Supreme Court specifically disapproved of *Farmers Insurance Exchange v. Adams*, reproduced *supra*,

on this substantive first-party property insurance coverage issue (as opposed to a third-party liability coverage issue).

Assume that the complaint in *Farmers Insurance Exchange v. Adams, supra,* had been filed after the Supreme Court's decision in *Garvey.* The Court of Appeal in *Farmers* would not have affirmed the order sustaining the demurrer on the substantive "efficient proximate cause" question. Would the court have also reached a different conclusion on the procedural misjoinder of defendants' issue? Why?

(2) Contrast the *Farmers* holding on misjoinder with that in *Colusa Air Pollution Control Dist. v. Superior Court,* 226 Cal. App. 3d 880, 277 Cal. Rptr. 110 (1991). In *Colusa,* the plaintiffs were several manufacturers, retailers, and contractors who did business throughout California; and the defendants were two statewide public agencies and six regional district air pollution control agencies. The plaintiffs sought to maintain their right to make, sell, and apply various architectural coatings which would be effectively banned under recent amendments to defendants' air pollution regulations.

The district agency defendants asserted that they were improperly joined under CCP § 379 because they are different entities which enforce regulations only within their regions, and that they each adopted local regulation amendments that were in some ways different and imposed different standards on plaintiffs' products. Therefore they argued that the adoption of the local amendments was not the same "transaction or occurrence" within the meaning of § 379.

The Court of Appeal held that joinder of the regional defendant agencies was proper under CCP § 379. The court reasoned that the adoption of local amendments by each district defendant constituted a series of occurrences, each of which was substantially the same; and that the plaintiff's claims arise from the same series of facts: the initial proposal of amendments to air pollution standards by the statewide defendants and the adoption of those proposals in substantially the same form in local amendments by the several district defendants.

Do you agree with the court's reasoning and holding in *Colusa?* Is *Colusa* consistent with *Farmers?*

(3) There are important advantages to joining all co-defendants in one lawsuit where each defendant blames another defendant for the plaintiff's injuries. A typical example is a tort case where each defendant denies negligence, but argues that the plaintiff's injuries were caused by another defendant's negligence. If the plaintiff pursues separate actions against each defendant, there is a risk that the plaintiff will recover nothing even though the jury finds that her injuries were caused by *some* defendant's negligence. How so? What are the other advantages of joining several co-defendants into one action? What are the disadvantages?

(4) Misjoinder of parties may be raised by demurrer or by answer. CCP § 430.10(d). Misjoinder is not a jurisdictional defect; so the objection is waived if not raised. CCP § 430.80. Which party is entitled to raise this objection?

(5) A few special statutes preclude joinder of certain parties even though the requirements of CCP § 378 or § 379 are satisfied. For example, Insurance Code

§ 11580(b)(2) prohibits joinder of an insurance company in an action against its insured; and under Corporations Code § 15526, generally a limited partner is not a proper party to proceedings by or against a partnership. What are the policy reasons for such limitations on joinder? Other special statutes require joinder of parties in certain circumstances. *E.g.*, Vehicle Code § 17152 (in negligence action against owner of vehicle, the driver shall be made a party defendant); Family Code §§ 2060-2065 (employee pension benefit plan shall be joined as party in dissolution of marriage proceeding in which either party claims an interest); CCP § 762.030(a) (if person required to be named as a defendant is dead, the plaintiff shall join the personal representative as a defendant). What are the policy reasons for such compulsory joinder?

(6) The broad permissive joinder test of CCP § 378 and § 379 is essentially the same as that of Rule 20(a) of the Federal Rules of Civil Procedure. *See Cal. Law Revision Comm'n Comments—1971 Amendments.*

[C] Permissive Joinder of Claims

Code of Civil Procedure § 427.10 provides that a plaintiff who alleges a cause of action against one or more defendants "may unite with such cause any other causes which he has ... against any such defendants." This provision effectively eliminates misjoinder of claims as a defense so long as joinder of parties is proper, does it not? *See Landau v. Salam*, 4 Cal. 3d 901, 905, 95 Cal. Rptr. 46, 484 P.2d 1390 (1971).

§ 10.02 Compulsory Joinder of Parties

Sierra Club, Inc. v. California Coastal Commission

Court of Appeal of California, First Appellate District
95 Cal. App. 3d 495, 157 Cal. Rptr. 190 (1979)

Rouse, Justice.

Plaintiff, Sierra Club, Inc., appeals from an adverse judgment in favor of William Moores, doing business as Moores Associates (Moores), the California Coastal Commission (Commission) and the North Coast Regional Commission (regional commission). The primary issue presented is whether the developer of a real estate project is an indispensable party to an action brought by a third party to set aside a permit authorizing the project.

The record reveals that on January 26, 1978, plaintiff, Sierra Club, Inc., commenced this action by filing a petition for a writ of mandate against the regional commission and the commission. The petition alleged that on November 13, 1977, the regional commission granted to Moores a permit authorizing a 42-lot subdivision and the construction of 16 condominium units in a scenic area of the coast; that plaintiff had objected to the granting of the permit and thereafter appealed the regional commission's decision to the commission; and that on November 29 or 30, 1977, the commission voted to decline to hear plaintiff's appeal on the ground that it raised no substantial issue. Plaintiff alleged that the regional commission's finding and declaration that the proposed development conformed to section 30250 of the Public Resources Code were unsupported by substantial evidence and contrary to law and that the commission had abused its discretion in concluding that plaintiff's appeal had raised no substantial issue. Plaintiff sought a writ of mandate setting aside the decisions by both the regional commission and the commission.

On March 7, 1978, plaintiff filed an amended petition which differed from the original petition only in that it named Moores, the developer of the project, as the real party in interest.

On March 20, 1978, Moores moved for judgment on the pleadings and for dismissal of the action. This motion was based upon the ground that any cause of action against Moores was barred by section 30801 of the Public Resources Code, since it had not been commenced within 60 days of the commission's decision. It was also alleged that Moores was an indispensable party to the action and that dismissal should therefore be granted in favor of the regional commission and the commission as well as Moores.

Following the filing of extensive points and authorities by the parties, the court granted the motion, rendered judgment on the pleadings in favor of Moores and granted a dismissal without prejudice in favor of Moores, the regional commission and the commission. Plaintiff filed a timely notice of appeal from the judgment.

Section 30801 of the Public Resources Code provides that any aggrieved person may obtain review of a decision by a regional commission or by the commission by filing a mandamus action, pursuant to section 1094.5 of the Code of Civil Procedure, within 60 days after such decision has become final.

In this instance, plaintiff commenced its action against the regional commission and the commission within the required 60-day period, but failed to include the developer, Moores, as a party to the action until well after the 60 days had expired. This raises the question whether such omission constituted a sufficient basis for dismissal of the action.

Plaintiff's first contention on appeal is that dismissal of the action was improper because Moores was not an indispensable party; further, that even if Moores was an indispensable party, the court was in error in determining that plaintiff's failure to make Moores a party within the required 60-day period deprived the court of subject matter jurisdiction.

This latter argument is somewhat misleading, since it presupposes that the trial court dismissed the action on the basis that plaintiff's failure to join Moores in a timely fashion deprived the court of subject matter jurisdiction. There is nothing in the record to support such assertion. An examination of the memorandum of points and authorities filed in the trial court demonstrates that Moores has never claimed a lack of subject matter jurisdiction, but merely asked that the trial court dismiss the action as an "exercise of discretion."

Section 389 of the Code of Civil Procedure, which sets forth the rules governing the compulsory joinder of parties, requires the joinder of "(a) A person who is subject to service of process and whose joinder will not deprive the court of jurisdiction over the subject matter of the action ... if (1) in his absence complete relief cannot be accorded among those already parties or (2) he claims an interest relating to the subject of the action and is so situated that the disposition of the action in his absence may (i) as a practical matter impair or impede his ability to protect that interest or (ii) leave any of the persons already parties subject to a substantial risk of incurring double, multiple, or otherwise inconsistent obligations by reason of his claimed interest...."

Subdivision (b) of that statute provides that "If a person as described in paragraph (1) or (2) of subdivision (a) cannot be made a party, the court shall determine whether in equity and good conscience the action should proceed among the parties before it, or should be dismissed without prejudice, the absent person being thus regarded as indispensable. The factors to be considered by the court include: (1) to what extent a judgment rendered in the person's absence might be prejudicial to him or those already parties; (2) the extent to which, by protective provisions in the judgment, by the shaping of relief, or other measures, the prejudice can be lessened or avoided; (3) whether a judgment rendered in the person's absence will be adequate; (4) whether the plaintiff or cross-complainant will have an adequate remedy if the action is dismissed for nonjoinder."

Failure to join an "indispensable" party is not "a jurisdictional defect" in the fundamental sense; even in the absence of an "indispensable" party, the court still has the power to render a decision as to the parties before it which will stand. It is for reasons of equity and convenience, and not because it is without power to proceed, that the court should not proceed with a case where it determines that an "indispensable" party is absent and cannot be joined. (*Kraus v. Willow Park Public Golf Course* (1977) 73 Cal. App. 3d 354, 364 [140 Cal. Rptr. 744].)

The *Kraus* court expressed the view that section 389 of the Code of Civil Procedure, even before it was amended to its present form in 1971, had never provided that the absence of an indispensable party deprived a court of subject matter jurisdiction. The court further observed that any possible doubts on that subject had been eliminated in 1971 when the statute was amended to conform to rule 19, Federal Rules of Civil Procedure. The court noted that the cases construing the federal rule had consistently held that it was for discretionary and equitable reasons, and not for any lack of jurisdiction, that the court may decline to proceed in the absence of an indispensable party.

We concur with the conclusion of the *Kraus* court that section 389 does not now provide, and never has provided, that the absence of an indispensable party deprives a court of subject matter jurisdiction. Rather, the decision whether to proceed with the action in the absence of a particular party is one within the court's discretion, as governed by the various factors enumerated in subdivision (b) of section 389, Code of Civil Procedure.

Where the plaintiff seeks some type of affirmative relief which, if granted, would injure or affect the interest of a third person not joined, that third person is an indispensable party. * * *

Looking to the language of section 389 of the Code of Civil Procedure, we conclude that Moores fulfilled the requirements of both paragraphs (1) and (2) of subdivision (a). Moores was a party in whose absence complete relief could not be accorded to those already parties, within the meaning of paragraph (1), since Moores would not be bound by any judgment adversely affecting his permit and would be free to collaterally attack any such judgment. Likewise, Moores met the requirements of paragraph (2), since he claimed an interest relating to the subject of the action and was so situated that the disposition of the action in his absence might impair his ability to protect that interest or leave any of the persons already parties (the regional commission and the commission) subject to a substantial risk of incurring inconsistent obligations by reason of Moores' claimed interest. The requisite factors enumerated in subdivision (b) of the statute were also present, since it is evident that a judgment in favor of plaintiff would be prejudicial to Moores and that such a judgment might well be inadequate since subject to collateral attack by Moores. Accordingly, we conclude that the trial court was correct in determining that Moores was an indispensable party within the meaning of section 389 of the Code of Civil Procedure, and that dismissal of the action was the appropriate procedure. * * *

Subdivision (b) of section 389, Code of Civil Procedure, authorizes dismissal of an action where a person determined to be indispensable "cannot be made a party." We have already concluded that Moores was properly found to be an indispensable party. Obviously, Moores could not be made a party to the action, since the statute of limitations had run and Moores was unwilling to waive that defense. * * *

We note, also, that plaintiff has not complied with the provisions of subdivision (c) of section 389, Code of Civil Procedure, which requires that "A complaint ... shall state the names, if known to the pleader, of any persons as described in paragraph (1) or (2) of subdivision (a) who are not joined, *and the reasons why they are not joined.*" (Italics supplied.) Although Moores was clearly such a party, it appears that no attempt was made to explain plaintiff's failure to join him. * * *

The judgment is affirmed.

Notes and Questions regarding Compulsory Joinder

(1) As *Sierra Club* illustrates, CCP § 389 requires joinder of any person who is subject to service of process and whose joinder will not deprive the court of subject matter jurisdiction, and who meets one of the criteria stated in § 389(a). In such circumstances, the trial court should not dismiss, but should order joinder of the missing person. *See, e.g., Conrad v. Unemployment Ins. Appeals Bd.*, 47 Cal. App. 3d 237, 241, 120 Cal. Rptr. 803 (1975); *Deltakeeper v. Oakdale Irrigation Dist.*, 94 Cal. App. 4th 1092, 1100-1105, 115 Cal. Rptr. 2d 244 (2001). If joinder is not possible, then the trial court must consider factors such as those contained in § 389(b) to determine whether, as an exercise of eq-

uitable discretion, the action should proceed with the existing parties or should be dismissed. *See, e.g., County of Imperial v. Superior Court,* 152 Cal. App. 4th 13, 25–41, 61 Cal. Rptr. 3d 145 (2007); *Tracy Press, Inc. v. Superior Court,* 164 Cal. App. 4th 1290, 1297–1302, 80 Cal. Rptr. 3d 464 (2008). Only if the trial court determines dismissal appropriate is the absent person regarded as "indispensable."

Several recent cases have extensively evaluated the CCP § 389(b) factors in determining whether to dismiss or proceed in the absence of a person who should be joined under § 389(a). *See, e.g., Deltakeeper, supra,* 94 Cal. App. 4th at 1105-1109 (concluding, in a writ proceeding challenging an environmental impact report for a project involving a joint district water purchase agreement, the trial court erred in dismissing the writ petition for failure to join all of the water purchasers as indispensable parties because the nonjoined parties' interests were adequately represented by the existing parties and there was no adequate remedy if the action is dismissed as the statute of limitations had run for joining more parties); *People ex rel. Lungren v. Community Redevelopment Agency,* 56 Cal. App. 4th 868, 65 Cal. Rptr. 2d 786 (1997) (holding trial court abused its discretion in dismissing a complaint filed by the Attorney General against a city's community redevelopment agency to set aside a contract between the agency and an American Indian tribe under which the agency would transfer real property to the tribe for development of a gaming casino, where the tribe could not be joined because of its sovereign immunity); *Save Our Bay, Inc. v. San Diego Unified Port Dist.,* 42 Cal. App. 4th 686, 49 Cal. Rptr. 2d 847 (1996) (affirming dismissal of a mandate proceeding brought by an environmental organization challenging the adequacy of an environmental impact report for a marine project where the landowner, whose land had to be acquired to complete the project, was an indispensable party who could not be joined because a statutory 30-day limitation period for joining the landowner had expired).

(2) Do you understand why the term "indispensable party" is conclusory, and is of little analytical value in applying § 389? *See, e.g., In re Marriage of Mena,* 212 Cal. App. 3d 12, 18, n.5, 260 Cal. Rptr. 314 (1989).

(3) Is it accurate for the court in *Sierra Club* to state that "even in the absence of an 'indispensable' party, the court has the power to render a decision as to the parties before it?" *See also McKeon v. Hastings College,* 185 Cal. App. 3d 877, 890, 230 Cal. Rptr. 176 (1986). Or to state that "[w]here the plaintiff seeks some type of affirmative relief which, if granted, would injure or affect the interest of a third person not joined, that third person is an indispensable party?" Or that "[a]n indispensable party is not bound by a judgment in an action in which he was not joined?" *Inland Counties Reg'l Ctr., Inc. v. Office of Admin. Hearings,* 193 Cal. App. 3d 700, 706, 238 Cal. Rptr. 422 (1987). These statements would be correct if the phrase "person who should be joined pursuant to § 389(a)" were substituted for "indispensable party." Why?

(4) Some special statutes provide for mandatory joinder of certain parties. *E.g.,* Vehicle Code § 17152 (In negligence action against owner of vehicle, the driver shall be made a party defendant); Family Code §§ 2060-2065 (Employee pension benefit plan shall be joined as party in dissolution of marriage proceeding in which either party claims an interest); CCP § 762.030(a) (If person required to be named as a defendant is dead, the

plaintiff shall join the personal representative as a defendant). Several others explicitly provide that particular persons need not be joined. *E.g.*, CCP § 369 (Executor, administrator, or trustee may sue without joining persons for whose benefit the action is prosecuted); CCP § 370 (Married person may sue or be sued without joining spouse).

(5) A number of prior court decisions provide useful precedents as to whether certain categories of persons must be joined under § 389. For example, all persons with an interest in real property at the time suit is brought to enforce a mechanic's lien on that property must be made parties. *Monterey S.P. Partnership v. W.L. Bangham, Inc.*, 49 Cal. 3d 454, 459, 261 Cal. Rptr. 587, 777 P.2d 623 (1989) (observing that if not made parties, they are in no way bound by the proceedings). All beneficiaries of a trust must be joined where their relative interests are contested, but are not indispensable parties to an action against trustees for an accounting or for breach of fiduciary duty. *See Copley v. Copley*, 126 Cal. App. 3d 248, 297-98, 178 Cal. Rptr. 842 (1981). Normally, all partners are regarded as indispensable parties in an action for dissolution of a partnership; *see Kraus v. Willow Park Public Golf Course*, 73 Cal. App. 3d 354, 369, 140 Cal. Rptr. 744 (1977); and a corporation is an indispensable party in a stockholder derivative action. *Stockton v. Ortiz*, 47 Cal. App. 3d 183, 191–92, 120 Cal. Rptr. 456 (1975).

As *Sierra Club* illustrates, where litigation challenges the propriety of government action which confers a benefit on a third person, that person has been considered an indispensable party. *Beresford Neighborhood Assn. v. City of San Mateo*, 207 Cal. App. 3d 1180, 1189, 255 Cal. Rptr. 434 (1989) (following *Sierra Club*'s reasoning, but noting that joinder not necessary when challenge is to a general plan which applies equally to all developments in the area); *see also In re Marriage of Mena*, 212 Cal. App. 3d 12, 260 Cal. Rptr. 314 (1989) (ruling county may be indispensable party in family law action determining child support payments where children receiving welfare assistance).

(6) In an action seeking either to enforce or set aside a contract, all contracting parties generally must be joined. *See, e.g., Vanoni v. County of Sonoma*, 40 Cal. App. 3d 743, 746-47, 115 Cal. Rptr. 485 (1974); *Northrop Corp. v. McDonnell Douglas Corp.*, 705 F.2d 1030, 1042–46 (9th Cir. 1983), *cert. denied*, 464 U.S. 849 (1983). If all such contracting parties cannot be joined, must the court regard them as indispensable parties and dismiss? *See, e.g.*, CCP § 410.70.

(7) May a plaintiff proceed against only one tortfeasor, or does § 389(a) require joinder of all tortfeasors in one action? *See, e.g., Country Wide Home Loans v. Superior Court*, 69 Cal. App. 4th 785, 82 Cal. Rptr. 2d 63 (1999); *Stanbaugh v. Superior Court*, 62 Cal. App. 3d 231, 132 Cal. Rptr. 843 (1976); *Temple v. Synthes Corp.*, 498 U.S. 5, 7, 111. S. Ct. 315, 316, 112 L. Ed 2d 263 (1990) (holding federal Rule 19(a) does not require joinder of all joint tortfeasors as defendants in a single lawsuit). Why would a plaintiff not want to join all tortfeasors as defendants? Why would a defendant want to force joinder of other tortfeasors?

(8) *Federal Rule 19.* Code of Civil Procedure § 389 conforms substantially to Rule 19 of the Federal Rules of Civil Procedure; and federal cases interpreting the federal rule may be relevant. *See, e.g., Dreamweaver Andalusians LLC v. Prudential Ins. Co.*,

234 Cal. App 4th 1168, 1174-76, 184 Cal. Rtpr. 3d 735 (2015); *Copley v. Copley*, 126 Cal. App. 3d 248, 296, 178 Cal. Rptr. 842 (1981). For example, in *Union Carbide Corp. v. Superior Court*, 36 Cal. 3d 15, 201 Cal. Rptr. 580, 679 P.2d 14 (1984), an anti-trust defendant argued that unless other potential claimants were joined defendant would be subject to a "substantial risk" of multiple liability within the meaning of § 389(a). The California Supreme Court, by reference to federal cases applying Rule 19(a)(1)(B)(ii), construed "substantial risk" to mean more than a theoretical possibility that an absent party might assert or claim for the same loss. "The risk must be substantial as a practical matter." *Id.* at 21.

(9) Which of the factors identified in subdivision (b) of § 389 is the most important in influencing a trial court to proceed with only the parties already before it as opposed to dismissal of the action? Why? *See, e.g., County of San Joaquin v. State Water Resources Control Bd.*, 54 Cal. App. 4th 1144, 1149, 63 Cal. Rptr. 2d 277 (1997) (noting that the subdivision (b) factors "are not arranged in a hierarchical order, and no factor is determinative or necessarily more important than another"); *Simonelli v. City of Carmel-by-the-Sea*, 240 Cal. App. 4th 480, 485, 192 Cal. Rptr. 3d 609 (2015) (indicating that potential prejudice to an absent person's interest is the critical issue in determining whether that person is an indispensable party).

(10) The defense of nonjoinder of parties is usually raised by demurrer or by answer. CCP § 430.10(d). The trial court may raise failure to join on its own motion in certain circumstances, *see Howard v. Data Storage Associates, Inc.*, 125 Cal. App. 3d 689, 697, 178 Cal. Rptr. 269 (1981); and the absent person may even apply to be made a party in actions involving real or personal property, CCP § 389.5. The issue of nonjoinder may be raised for the first time on appeal, but is properly limited to the argument that the absence of a party precluded the trial court from rendering any effective judgment between the parties before it. *See, e.g., County of Alameda v. State Board of Control, supra*, 14 Cal. App. 4th at 1105, n.5 (noting failure to join indispensable party may be raised for first time on appeal only where the trial court was unable to render effective judgment between the parties before it); *Jermstad v. McNelis*, 210 Cal. App. 3d 528, 538, 258 Cal. Rptr. 519 (1989) (ruling claim of error in failing to join absent party is not recognizable on appeal unless appropriately raised in the trial court or there is some compelling reason of equity or policy which warrants belated consideration).

(11) Pursuant to the authority of Family Code §§ 211, 2021 & 2060-2074, the Judicial Council has promulgated special rules governing the joinder of parties in proceedings under the Family Law Act. Rules 5.24 & 5.29, Cal. Rules of Ct.

§ 10.03 Interpleader

[A] California Interpleader Requirements and Procedures

Interpleader is a device which permits the stakeholder, who may be liable to several claimants but does not know which ones, to join all claimants in a single action and require them to litigate their respective claims to property or funds held by the stakeholder. *See* CCP § 386(b). Classic interpleader occurs where the stakeholder has no interest in the property or fund sought to be interpleaded, and seeks joinder of all adverse claimants to force them to litigate their claims among themselves. *See, e.g., Pacific Loan Mgmt. Corp. v. Superior Court*, 196 Cal. App. 3d 1485, 242 Cal. Rptr. 547 (1987); *Dial 800 v. Fesbinder*, 118 Cal. App. 4th 32, 12 Cal. Rptr. 3d 711 (2004). Once the court determines that interpleader is proper and the stakeholder deposits the property or funds with the clerk, the court may discharge the disinterested stakeholder from liability to any of the claimants. CCP § 386(a) & (b).

Is interpleader unavailable in California where the stakeholder claims an interest in all or a portion of the deposited property? *See* CCP § 386(b) (authorizing interpleading party to deny liability in whole or in part to any or all of the claimants).

The purpose of interpleader is "to prevent a multiplicity of suits and double vexation." *Shopoff Cavillo LLP v. Hyon*, 167 Cal. App. 4th 1489, 1513, 85 Cal. Rptr. 3d 268 (2008); *see City of Morgan Hill v. Brown*, 71 Cal. App. 4th 1114, 1122–1126, 84 Cal. Rptr. 2d 361 (1999) (discussing the purposes of interpleader and the requirement that each of the defendants assert claims to the same thing, debt, or duty); *Westamerica Bank v. City of Berkeley*, 201 Cal. App. 4th 598, 133 Cal. Rptr. 3d 883 (2011) (dismissing interpleader action because no reasonable probability that plaintiff bank will be subject to double claims that may give rise to double liability). Who is interpleader designed to protect? Why? In what typical factual situations is interpleader appropriate? *See, e.g., Farmers New World Life Ins. Co. v. Rees*, 219 Cal. App. 4th 307, 161 Cal. Rtpr. 3d 678 (2013) (ruling interpleader action brought by plaintiff insurance company was appropriate where multiple heirs claimed the mutually exclusive right to life insurance benefits under life insurance policy). Is interpleader available only to a plaintiff who files a separate interpleader action or may a defendant utilize interpleader in certain circumstances? *See, e.g., Surety Co. of the Pac. v. Piver*, 149 Cal. App. 3d Supp. 29, 197 Cal. Rptr. 531 (1983). What options does a defendant have with respect to utilization of interpleader? *See* CCP §§ 386(a) & (b); 386.6.

Does the stakeholder have an obligation to monitor the action and dismiss parties who assert no claim to the stake? What obligation does an interpleader action impose on the claimants? As between the plaintiff-stakeholder and the defendants-claimants, is a classic interpleader action adversarial? *See Cantu v. Resolution Trust Corp.*, 4 Cal. App. 4th 857, 6 Cal. Rptr. 2d 151 (1992). When the stakeholder deposits funds with the clerk in an interpleader action, any obligation for interest on the part of the stakeholder ceases to accrue. CCP § 386(c). Upon application, the court must order such deposit invested in an interest-bearing account. CCP § 386.1. The court may also award the stakeholder costs and attorney fees. CCP § 386.6.

The trial court may restrain all parties to an interpleader action from instituting or further prosecuting any other proceedings in any California court which may affect the rights or obligations of parties to the interpleader. CCP § 386(f). Does this mean that a court exercising interpleader jurisdiction may enjoin the enforcement of a prior judgment which may affect interpleaded property or funds? *See, e.g., Surety Co. of the Pac. v. Piver*, *supra*, 149 Cal. App. 3d at Supp. 31 (holding various claimants to a particular fund or property should be permitted to proceed to judgments in a proper forum of their choice, but may be restrained in the interpleader action as to enforcement of those judgments).

[B] Federal Interpleader

Interpleader is available in federal court, either by federal statute or by federal rule, in situations nearly identical to those contained in CCP. § 386, with even clearer indication that a stakeholder need not be disinterested. 28 U.S.C. § 1335; Rule 22, F.R.C.P. Federal statutory interpleader pursuant to 28 U.S.C. § 1335 provides federal court jurisdiction over interpleader actions involving $500 or more in controversy based on "minimal diversity" between claimants (*i.e.*, only one claimant must be a citizen of a state different from that of the other claimants). *State Farm Fire & Cas. Co. v. Tashire*, 386 U.S. 523, 87 S. Ct. 1199, 18 L. Ed. 2d 270 (1967). To facilitate use of federal statutory interpleader, 28 U.S.C. § 2361 authorizes nationwide service of process on all claimants, and 28 U.S.C. § 1397 allows venue in a judicial district where any claimant resides. And, arguably, the requirements for personal jurisdiction are much relaxed. *See* Wright, Miller & Kane, *Federal Practice and Procedure: Civil 3d* § 1711 (West 2001); *see also* Herbert Hovenkamp, *Personal Jurisdiction and Venue in the Federal Courts: A Policy Analysis*, 67 Iowa L. Rev. 485 (1982).

There are many advantages to proceeding under the liberal federal interpleader statutes in federal court as opposed to proceeding under CCP § 386 in California state court, are there not? What are they? Under what circumstances would you advise a stakeholder to utilize § 386 in state court? Under what circumstances must a stakeholder proceed with interpleader in state court?

§ 10.04 New Party Cross-Complaints and Equitable Indemnity

[A] Cross-Complaints Adding New Parties

American Motorcycle Association v. Superior Court

Supreme Court of California
20 Cal. 3d 578, 146 Cal. Rptr. 182, 578 P.2d 899 (1978)

TOBRINER, JUSTICE.

Three years ago, in *Li v. Yellow Cab Co.* (1975) 13 Cal. 3d 804 [119 Cal. Rptr. 858, 532 P.2d 1226], we concluded that the harsh and much criticized contributory negligence doctrine, which totally barred an injured person from recovering damages whenever his own negligence had contributed in any degree to the injury, should be replaced in this state by a rule of comparative negligence, under which an injured individual's recovery is simply proportionately diminished, rather than completely eliminated, when he is partially responsible for the injury. In reaching the conclusion to adopt comparative negligence in *Li*, we explicitly recognized that our innovation inevitably raised numerous collateral issues, "[the] most serious [of which] are those attendant upon the administration of a rule of comparative negligence in cases involving multiple parties." (13 Cal. 3d at p. 823.) * * *

For the reasons explained below, we have reached the following conclusions with respect to the multiple party issues presented by this case. First, we conclude that our adoption of comparative negligence to ameliorate the inequitable consequences of the contributory negligence rule does not warrant the abolition or contraction of the established "joint and several liability" doctrine; each tortfeasor whose negligence is a proximate cause of an indivisible injury remains individually liable for all compensable damages attributable to that injury. * * *

Second, although we have determined that *Li* does not mandate a diminution of the rights of injured persons through the elimination of the joint and several liability rule, we conclude that the general principles embodied in *Li* do warrant a reevaluation of the common law equitable indemnity doctrine, which relates to the allocation of loss *among* multiple tortfeasors. * * * Prior to *Li*, of course, the notion of apportioning liability on the basis of comparative fault was completely alien to California common law. In light of *Li*, however, we think that the long-recognized common law equitable indemnity doctrine should be modified to permit, in appropriate cases, a right of partial indemnity, under which liability among multiple tortfeasors may be apportioned on a comparative negligence basis. * * *

Third, we conclude that California's current contribution statutes do not preclude our court from evolving this common law right of comparative indemnity. * * *

Fourth, and finally, we explain that under the governing provisions of the Code of Civil Procedure, a named defendant is authorized to file a cross-complaint against any person, whether already a party to the action or not, from whom the named defendant seeks to obtain total or partial indemnity. Although the trial court retains the authority to postpone the trial of the indemnity question if it believes such action is appropriate to avoid unduly complicating the plaintiff's suit, the court may not preclude the filing of such a cross-complaint altogether.

In light of these determinations, we conclude that a writ of mandate should issue, directing the trial court to permit petitioner-defendant to file a cross-complaint for partial indemnity against previously unjoined alleged concurrent tortfeasors.

1. *The facts*

In the underlying action in this case, plaintiff Glen Gregos, a teenage boy, seeks to recover damages for serious injuries which he incurred while participating in a cross-country motorcycle race for novices. Glen's second amended complaint alleges, in relevant part, that defendants American Motorcycle Association (AMA) and the Viking Motorcycle Club (Viking)—the organizations that sponsored and collected the entry fee for the race—negligently designed, managed, supervised and administered the race, and negligently solicited the entrants for the race. The second amended complaint further alleges that as a direct and proximate cause of such negligence, Glen suffered a crushing of his spine, resulting in the permanent loss of the use of his legs and his permanent inability to perform sexual functions. Although the negligence count of the complaint does not identify the specific acts or omissions of which plaintiff complains, additional allegations in the complaint assert, inter alia, that defendants failed to give the novice participants reasonable instructions that were necessary for their safety, failed to segregate the entrants into reasonable classes of equivalently skilled participants, and failed to limit the entry of participants to prevent the racecourse from becoming overcrowded and hazardous.

AMA filed an answer to the complaint, denying the charging allegations and asserting a number of affirmative defenses, including a claim that Glen's own negligence was a proximate cause of his injuries. Thereafter, AMA sought leave of court to file a cross-complaint, which purported to state two causes of action against Glen's parents. The first cause of action alleges that at all relevant times Glen's parents (1) knew that motorcycle racing is a dangerous sport, (2) were "knowledgeable and fully cognizant" of the training and instruction which Glen had received on the handling and operation of his motorcycle, and (3) directly participated in Glen's decision to enter the race by signing a parental consent form. This initial cause of action asserts that in permitting Glen's entry into the race, his parents negligently failed to exercise their power of supervision over their minor child; moreover, the cross-complaint asserts that while AMA's negligence, if any, was "passive," that of Glen's parents was "active." On the basis of these allegations, the first cause of action seeks indemnity from Glen's parents if AMA is found liable to Glen.

In the second cause of action of its proposed cross-complaint, AMA seeks declaratory relief. It reasserts Glen's parents' negligence, declares that Glen has failed to join his parents in the action, and asks for a declaration of the "allocable negligence" of Glen's parents so that "the damages awarded [against AMA], if any, [may] be reduced by the percentage of damages allocable to cross-defendants' negligence." [T]his second cause of action is based on an implicit assumption that the *Li* decision abrogates the rule of joint and several liability of concurrent tortfeasors and establishes in its stead a new rule of "proportionate liability," under which each concurrent tortfeasor who has proximately caused an indivisible harm may be held liable only for a portion of plaintiff's recovery, determined on a comparative fault basis.

The trial court, though candidly critical of the current state of the law, concluded that existing legal doctrines did not support AMA's proposed cross-complaint, and accordingly denied AMA's motion for leave to file the cross-complaint. AMA petitioned the Court of Appeal for a writ of mandate to compel the trial court to grant its motion, and the Court of Appeal, recognizing the recurrent nature of the issues presented and the need for a speedy resolution of these multiple party questions, issued an alternative writ; ultimately, the court granted a peremptory writ of mandate. In view of the obvious statewide importance of the questions at issue, we ordered a hearing in this case on our own motion. All parties concede that the case is properly before us.

2. *The adoption of comparative negligence in Li does not warrant the abolition of joint and several liability of concurrent tortfeasors.*

* * *

In cases involving multiple tortfeasors, the principle that each tortfeasor is personally liable for any indivisible injury of which his negligence is a proximate cause has commonly been expressed in terms of "joint and several liability." * * *

In the concurrent tortfeasor context, however, the "joint and several liability" label does not express the imposition of any form of vicarious liability, but instead simply embodies the general common law principle, noted above, that a tortfeasor is liable for any injury of which his negligence is a proximate cause. Liability attaches to a concurrent tortfeasor in this situation not because he is responsible for the acts of other independent tortfeasors who may also have caused the injury, but because he is responsible for all damage of which his own negligence was a proximate cause. When independent negligent actions of a number of tortfeasors are each a proximate cause of a single injury, each tortfeasor is thus personally liable for the damage sustained, and the injured person may sue one or all of the tortfeasors to obtain a recovery for his injuries; the fact that one of the tortfeasors is impecunious or otherwise immune from suit does not relieve another tortfeasor of his liability for damage which he himself has proximately caused. * * *

In the instant case AMA argues that the *Li* decision, by repudiating the all-or-nothing contributory negligence rule and replacing it by a rule which simply diminishes an injured party's recovery on the basis of his comparative fault, in effect undermined the fundamental rationale of the entire joint and several liability doctrine as applied to concurrent tortfeasors. * * * As we explain, for a number of reasons we cannot accept AMA's argument.

First, the simple feasibility of apportioning fault on a comparative negligence basis does not render an indivisible injury "divisible" for purposes of the joint and several liability rule. As we have already explained, a concurrent tortfeasor is liable for the whole of an indivisible injury whenever his negligence is a proximate cause of that injury. * * * [T]he mere fact that it may be possible to assign some percentage figure to the relative culpability of one negligent defendant as compared to another does not in any way suggest that each defendant's negligence is not a proximate cause of the entire indivisible injury.

Second, abandonment of the joint and several liability rule is not warranted by AMA's claim that, after *Li*, a plaintiff is no longer "innocent." Initially, of course, it is by no means invariably true that after *Li* injured plaintiffs will be guilty of negligence. * * * Although we recognized in *Li* that a plaintiff's self-directed negligence would justify reducing his recovery in proportion to his degree of fault for the accident,[2] the

---

2. A question has arisen as to whether our *Li* opinion, in mandating that a plaintiff's recovery be diminished in proportion to the plaintiff's negligence, intended that the plaintiff's conduct be compared with each individual tortfeasor's negligence, with the cumulative negligence of all named defendants or with all other negligent conduct that contributed to the injury. The California BAJI Committee,

fact remains that insofar as the plaintiff's conduct creates only a risk of self-injury, such conduct, unlike that of a negligent defendant, is not tortious.

Finally, from a realistic standpoint, we think that AMA's suggested abandonment of the joint and several liability rule would work a serious and unwarranted deleterious effect on the practical ability of negligently injured persons to receive adequate compensation for their injuries. One of the principal by-products of the joint and several liability rule is that it frequently permits an injured person to obtain full recovery for his injuries even when one or more of the responsible parties do not have the financial resources to cover their liability. In such a case the rule recognizes that fairness dictates that the "wronged party should not be deprived of his right to redress," but that "[the] wrongdoers should be left to work out between themselves any apportionment." (*Summers v. Tice* (1948) 33 Cal. 2d 80, 88 [199 P.2d 1, 5 A.L.R.2d 91].) The *Li* decision does not detract in the slightest from this pragmatic policy determination.

For all of the foregoing reasons, we reject AMA's suggestion that our adoption of comparative negligence logically compels the abolition of joint and several liability of concurrent tortfeasors. * * * [W]e hold that after *Li*, a concurrent tortfeasor whose negligence is a proximate cause of an indivisible injury remains liable for the total amount of damages, diminished only "in proportion to the amount of negligence attributable to the person recovering." (13 Cal. 3d at p. 829.)

3. *Upon reexamination of the common law equitable indemnity doctrine in light of the principles underlying Li, we conclude that the doctrine should be modified to permit partial indemnity among concurrent tortfeasors on a comparative fault basis.*

Although, as discussed above, we are not persuaded that our decision in *Li* calls for a fundamental alteration of the rights of injured plaintiffs vis-a-vis concurrent tortfeasors through the abolition of joint and several liability, the question remains whether the broad principles underlying *Li* warrant any modification of this state's common law rules governing the allocation of loss among multiple tortfeasors. * * * Taking our cue from a recent decision of the highest court of one of our sister states, we conclude—in line with *Li's* objectives—that the California common law equitable indemnity doctrine should be modified to permit a concurrent tortfeasor to obtain partial indemnity from other concurrent tortfeasors on a comparative fault basis.

* * *

---

which specifically addressed this issue after *Li*, concluded that "the contributory negligence of the plaintiff must be proportioned to the combined negligence of plaintiff and of all the tort-feasors, whether or not joined as parties ... whose negligence proximately caused or contributed to plaintiff's injury." (Use note, BAJI No. 14.90 (5th ed. 1975 pocket pt.) p. 152.)

We agree with this conclusion, ... In determining to what degree the injury was due to the fault of the plaintiff, it is logically essential that the plaintiff's negligence be weighed against the combined total of all other causative negligence; moreover, inasmuch as a plaintiff's actual damages do not vary by virtue of the particular defendants who happen to be before the court, we do not think that the damages which a plaintiff may recover against defendants who are joint and severally liable should fluctuate in such a manner.

In *Li*, after concluding "that logic, practical experience, and fundamental justice counsel against the retention of the doctrine rendering contributory negligence a complete bar to recovery" (13 Cal. 3d at pp. 812-813), we made clear our conviction that the discarded doctrine "should be replaced in this state *by a system under which liability for damage will be borne by those whose negligence caused it in direct proportion to their respective fault.*" (Italics added.) (*Id.*, at p. 813.)

In order to attain such a system, in which liability for an indivisible injury caused by concurrent tortfeasors will be borne by each individual tortfeasor "in direct proportion to [his] respective fault," we conclude that the current equitable indemnity rule should be modified to permit a concurrent tortfeasor to obtain partial indemnity from other concurrent tortfeasors on a comparative fault basis. * * *

   4. *California's contribution statutes do not preclude this court from adopting comparative partial indemnity as a modification of the common law equitable indemnity doctrine.*

None of the parties to the instant proceeding, and none of the numerous amici who have filed briefs, seriously takes issue with our conclusion that a rule of comparative partial indemnity is more consistent with the principles underlying *Li* than the prior "all-or-nothing" indemnity doctrine. The principal argument raised in opposition to the recognition of a common law comparative indemnity rule is the claim that California's existing contribution statutes, section 875 *et seq.* of the Code of Civil Procedure,[3] preclude such a judicial development.... [W]e reject th[is] contention....

---

   3. Sections 875 to 879 provide in full:
      Section 875:
      "(a) Where a money judgment has been rendered jointly against two or more defendants in a tort action there shall be a right of contribution among them as hereinafter provided.
      "(b) Such right of contribution shall be administered in accordance with the principles of equity.
      "(c) Such right of contribution may be enforced only after one tortfeasor has, by payment, discharged the joint judgment or has paid more than his pro rata share thereof. It shall be limited to the excess so paid over the pro rata share of the person so paying and in no event shall any tortfeasor be compelled to make contribution beyond his own pro rata share of the entire judgment.
      "(d) There shall be no right of contribution in favor of any tortfeasor who has intentionally injured the injured person.
      "(e) A liability insurer who by payment has discharged the liability of a tortfeasor judgment debtor shall be subrogated to his right of contribution.
      "(f) This title shall not impair any right of indemnity under existing law, and where one tortfeasor judgment debtor is entitled to indemnity from another there shall be no right of contribution between them.
      "(g) This title shall not impair the right of a plaintiff to satisfy a judgment in full as against any tortfeasor judgment debtor."
      Section 876:
      "(a) The pro rata share of each tortfeasor judgment debtor shall be determined by dividing the entire judgment equally among all of them.
      "(b) Where one or more persons are held liable solely for the tort of one of them or of another, as in the case of the liability of a master for the tort of his servant, they shall con-

[I]n enacting the 1957 contribution legislation the Legislature did not intend to prevent the judiciary from expanding the common law equitable indemnity doctrine in the manner described above.... [S]ince 1957 the equitable indemnity doctrine has undergone considerable judicial development in this state, and yet it has never been thought that such growth in the common law was barred by the contribution statute.

Several amici argue alternatively that even if the contribution statute was not intended to preclude the development of a common law comparative indemnity doctrine, our court should decline to adopt such a doctrine because it would assertedly undermine the strong public policy in favor of encouraging settlement of litigation embodied in section 877 of the Code of Civil Procedure, one of the provisions of the current statutory contribution scheme. As amici point out, section 877 creates significant incentives for both tortfeasors and injured plaintiffs to settle lawsuits: the tortfeasor who enters into a good faith settlement is discharged from any liability for contribution to any other tortfeasor, and the plaintiff's ultimate award against any other tortfeasor is diminished only by the actual amount of the settlement rather than by the settling tortfeasor's pro rata share of the judgment. Amici suggest that these incentives will be lost by the recognition of a partial indemnity doctrine.

Although section 877 reflects a strong public policy in favor of settlement, this statutory policy does not in any way conflict with the recognition of a common law partial indemnity doctrine but rather can, and should, be preserved as an integral part of the partial indemnity doctrine that we adopt today. Thus, while we recognize that section 877, by its terms, releases a settling tortfeasor only from liability for contribution and not partial indemnity, we conclude that from a realistic perspective the legislative policy underlying the provision dictates that a tortfeasor who has entered into a "good faith" settlement with the plaintiff must also be discharged from any claim for partial or comparative indemnity that may be pressed by a concurrent tortfeasor. * * * Moreover, to preserve the incentive to settle which section 877 provides to injured plaintiffs, we conclude that a plaintiff's recovery from nonsettling tortfeasors should be diminished only by the amount that the plaintiff has actually recovered in a good faith settlement, rather than by an amount measured by the settling tortfeasor's proportionate responsibility for the injury.

Accordingly, we conclude that Code of Civil Procedure section 875 et seq. do not preclude the development of new common law principles in this area, and we hold

---

tribute a single pro rata share, as to which there may be indemnity between them."

Section 877:

"Where a release, dismissal with or without prejudice, or a covenant not to sue or not to enforce judgment is given in good faith before verdict or judgment to one or more of a number of tortfeasors claimed to be liable for the same tort —

"(a) It shall not discharge any other such tortfeasor from liability unless its terms so provide, but it shall reduce the claims against the others in the amount stipulated by the release, the dismissal or the covenant, or in the amount of the consideration paid for it whichever is the greater; and

"(b) It shall discharge the tortfeasor to whom it is given from all liability for any contribution to any other tortfeasors." * * *

that under the common law of this state a concurrent tortfeasor may seek partial indemnity from another concurrent tortfeasor on a comparative fault basis.

5. *Under the allegations of the cross-complaint, AMA may be entitled to obtain partial indemnification from Glen's parents, and thus the trial court, pursuant to Code of Civil Procedure section 428.10 et seq., should have granted AMA leave to file the cross-complaint.*

Having concluded that a concurrent tortfeasor enjoys a common law right to obtain partial indemnification from other concurrent tortfeasors on a comparative fault basis, we must finally determine whether, in the instant case, AMA may properly assert that right by cross-complaint against Glen's parents, who were not named as codefendants in Glen's amended complaint. As we explain, the governing provisions of the Code of Civil Procedure clearly authorize AMA to seek indemnification from a previously unnamed party through such a cross-complaint. Accordingly, we conclude that the trial court erred in denying AMA leave to file its pleading. * * *

Section 428.10 provides in relevant part: "A party against whom a cause of action has been asserted ... may file a cross-complaint setting forth ... (b) Any cause of action he has against a person alleged to be liable thereon, *whether or not such person is already a party to the action,* if the cause of action asserted in his cross-complaint (1) arises out of the same transaction [or] occurrence ... as the cause brought against him or (2) asserts a claim, right or interest in the ... controversy which is the subject of the cause brought against him." (Italics added.)

Section 428.20 reiterates the propriety of filing such a cross-complaint against a previously unnamed party, and section 428.70 explicitly confirms the fact that a cross-complaint may be founded on a claim of total or partial indemnity by defining a "third-party plaintiff" as one who files a cross-complaint claiming "the right to recover all *or part* of any amount for which he may be held liable" on the original complaint. The history of the legislation leaves no doubt but that these provisions authorize a defendant to file a cross-complaint against a person, not named in the original complaint, from whom he claims he is entitled to indemnity. (*See* Recommendation and Study Relating to Counterclaims and Cross Complaints, Joinder of Causes of Action and Related Provisions (1970) 10 Cal. Law Revision Com. Rep. pp. 551-555.)

Although real parties in interest claim that the effect of permitting a defendant to bring in parties whom the plaintiff has declined to join will have the undesirable effect of greatly complicating personal injury litigation and will deprive the plaintiff of the asserted "right" to control the size and scope of the proceeding, as our court observed in *Roylance [v. Doelger* (1962)] (57 Cal. 2d at pp. 261-262, [19 Cal. Rptr. 7, 368 P.2d 535]) to the extent that such claims are legitimate the problem may be partially obviated by the trial court's judicious use of the authority afforded by Code of Civil Procedure section 1048. Section 1048, subdivision (b) currently provides: "The court, in furtherance of convenience or to avoid prejudice, or when separate trials will be conducive to expedition and economy, may order a separate trial of any cause of action, *including a cause of action asserted in a cross-complaint,* or of any separate issue or any number of causes of action or issues, preserving the right of trial by jury required by the Constitution or a statute of this state or of the United States."

In this context, of course, a trial court, in determining whether to sever a comparative indemnity claim, will have to take into consideration the fact that when the plaintiff is alleged to have been partially at fault for the injury, each of the third party defendants will have the right to litigate the question of the plaintiff's proportionate fault for the accident; as a consequence, we recognize that in this context severance may at times not be an attractive alternative. Nonetheless, having already noted that under the comparative negligence doctrine a plaintiff's recovery should be diminished only by that proportion which the plaintiff's negligence bears to that of all tortfeasors (*see* fn. 2, *ante*), we think it only fair that a defendant who may be jointly and severally liable for all of the plaintiff's damages be permitted to bring other concurrent tortfeasors into the suit. Thus, we conclude that the interaction of the partial indemnity doctrine with California's existing cross-complaint procedures works no undue prejudice to the rights of plaintiffs.

Accordingly, we conclude that under the governing statutory provisions a defendant is generally authorized to file a cross-complaint against a concurrent tortfeasor for partial indemnity on a comparative fault basis, even when such concurrent tortfeasor has not been named a defendant in the original complaint. In the instant case, the allegations of AMA's cross-complaint are sufficient to suggest that Glen's parents' negligence may possibly have been a concurrent cause of Glen's injuries. While we, of course, intimate absolutely no opinion as to the merits of the claim, if it is established that the parents were indeed negligent in supervising their son and that such negligence was a proximate cause of injury, under the governing California common law rule Glen's parents could be held liable for the resulting damages. Thus, we believe that AMA's cross-complaint states a cause of action for comparative indemnity and that the trial court should have permitted its filing. * * *

Notes and Questions regarding New Party Cross-complaints

(1) *New Party Cross-Complaints, Generally.* CCP § 428.10 and § 428.20 authorize cross-complaints which add new parties, so long as they satisfy the "same transaction or occurrence" test of § 428.10(b). The cross-complainant may join any person as cross-complainant or cross-defendant, subject only to the liberal permissive party joinder standards of CCP § 378 and § 379. Moreover, the cross-complainant may join any other cause of action he has against any cross-defendants, except in an eminent domain proceeding. CCP § 428.30.

(2) *New Party Cross-Complaints for Indemnity.* CCP § 428.70 specifically applies to those new party cross-complaints which include claims for indemnity or contribution, such as those in *American Motorcycle.* The person asserting such claims by cross-complaint is defined as the "third-party plaintiff"; the person alleged in the cross-complaint to be liable to the third-party plaintiff is defined as the "third-party defendant."

Section 428.70(b) then authorizes the third-party defendant to file as a separate document a "special answer alleging against the person who asserted the cause of action against the third-party plaintiff any defenses which a third-party plaintiff has to such cause of action." What problem is the "special answer" designed to avoid? *See* 10 *Cal. Law Division Comm'n Report* (1971), p. 555. Consider the following scenario: Plaintiff P sues defendant D for breach of contract. Defendant answers, but fails to raise the defense that P's action is barred by the applicable statute of limitation. Defendant D also files a cross-complaint against new party NP, alleging that NP had agreed to indemnify D for any judgment in favor of P entered against D. Third-party defendant NP answers D's cross-complaint, and also files a "special answer" alleging that plaintiff P's complaint against D is barred by the applicable statute of limitation. P moves to strike NP's special answer, arguing that this defense was waived by defendant D and therefore is not available to NP. Should the court grant this motion? Why? *See Administrative Mgmt. Serv., Inc. v. Fidelity & Deposit Co.*, 129 Cal. App. 3d 484, 181 Cal. Rptr. 141 (1982).

(3) *Federal Third-Party Practice.* Rule 14(a), F.R.C.P., authorizes a third-party impleader practice virtually identical to the new party cross-complaint practice set forth in CCP §§ 428.10, .20 & .70, although Federal Rule 14(a) is limited to assertion of third-party claims where liability is in some way dependent on the outcome of the main claim and is secondary or derivative thereto, *e.g., Stewart v. American Int'l Oil & Gas Co.*, 845 F.2d 196, 199-200 (9th Cir. 1988); and Rule 13(h) authorizes joinder of new parties in circumstances analogous to that of CCP § 428.30. A federal court must, of course, have original or supplemental subject matter jurisdiction over such third-party claims in order to consider them. *See, e.g.*, 28 U.S.C. § 1332 and § 1367(b).

[B] Equitable Indemnity

[1] Introductory Note

In addition to the procedural holding on new party cross-complaints, the Supreme Court opinion in *American Motorcycle* contains several important substantive law rulings concerning comparative liability, contribution and indemnity, and "good faith" settlements. What are these rulings? Why are they significant to tortfeasor-defendants? What effect do these rulings have on plaintiffs? Is the effect beneficial or not as to plaintiffs? Why? How is equitable indemnity calculated when one of the defendant joint tortfeasors is insolvent? When the plaintiff settles with fewer than all of the joint tortfeasors? Does *American Motorcycle* state a broad or narrow definition of "joint tortfeasor?" *See Turcon Constr., Inc. v. Norton-Villiers, Ltd.*, 139 Cal. App. 3d 280, 283, 185 Cal. Rptr. 580 (1983). Do any statutes modify these *American Motorcycle* rulings?

Bracket v. State of California

Court of Appeal of California, First Appellate District
180 Cal. App. 3d 1171, 226 Cal. Rptr. 1 (1986)

NEWSOM, JUSTICE.

The instant appeal is from judgment in an action for comparative equitable indemnity. The factual background may be summarized as follows.

Larry Edward Spencer sustained serious injuries when a motor vehicle which he was driving on State Route 17 in Santa Clara County collided head-on with a truck driven by James Gardner. The accident was precipitated by an unsafe lane change made by respondent George Bracket, who at the time was driving a vehicle owned by respondent House of Lamps, which caused Gardner to swerve his truck across the center line of the highway and collide with Spencer's oncoming car.

Spencer filed suit for his personal injuries against Gardner and respondents. Gardner settled with Spencer before trial for the full amount of his insurance coverage, $350,000. The action then proceeded to trial, and the jury awarded Spencer $2.5 million. Respondents satisfied the remainder of the judgment by paying Spencer $2.15 million. Appellant was not a party to Spencer's action for personal injuries.

Respondents subsequently commenced an action against the State of California (hereafter the state or appellant) for comparative equitable indemnity, alleging that Spencer's injuries were primarily caused by the state's failure to provide a median barrier separating the northbound and southbound directions of traffic on State Route 17. The issues of liability and damages were severed for trial. The jury found that the state's failure to remedy the dangerous condition of State Route 17 was a cause of Spencer's injuries, and apportioned the comparative responsibility of the parties as follows: 85 percent to respondents; 10 percent to appellant; and 5 percent to Gardner. Thereafter, the trial court entered judgment for respondents against the state for $226,315.66, computed according to the following formula: "$2,500,000 less $350,000 credit times 10/95." In so doing, the trial court essentially determined that, after subtracting the full amount of Gardner's contribution to the judgment, respondents and appellants should share in the judgment in proportion to their fault as found by the jury.

Appellant does not challenge the allocation of fault made by the jury, but objects to the trial court's apportionment and award of damages. In appellant's view the trial court erred in crediting respondents with the payment made by James Gardner before apportioning damages in accordance with the relative fault of the parties as determined by the jury. According to appellant, the proper measure of damages to respondents in this indemnity action was $25,000: an amount representing the contribution made by respondents "in excess of their proportionate share of the $2,500,000 judgment recovered by Larry Edward Spencer." Appellant submits that such an award fairly compensates respondents for their loss, and asks us to modify the judgment accordingly.

The issue may be stated as follows: where a joint tortfeasor settles with the plaintiff before trial for an amount later determined to be an overpayment, as did Gardner, should the remainder of the plaintiff's judgment, after deduction of the overpayment, be allocated among the nonsettling joint tortfeasors in accordance with their proportionate share of fault; or, instead, is it proper to limit a nonsettling joint tortfeasor's recovery in an indemnity action to that amount paid the plaintiff by the party seeking indemnity which exceeds its comparative share of fault, without first deducting the overpayment from the total judgment for respondent? In the case before us, the difference in the two measures of damages is $201,315.66—that is, the difference between $226,315.66, which sum was arrived at by subtracting Gardner's contribution to the judgment ($350,000) then multiplying the remainder, $2.15 million, by appellant's comparative fault, 10/95ths, and $25,000, which represents the sum due respondents were we merely to award indemnification for the amount they paid Spencer in excess of their total proportionate share of the liability.

Our high court's decision in *American Motorcycle Assn. v. Superior Court* (1978) 20 Cal. 3d 578 [146 Cal. Rptr. 182, 578 P.2d 899], serves as the foundation for our inquiry. In *American* Motorcycle, the court declared that the "equitable indemnity rule should be modified to permit a concurrent tortfeasor to obtain partial indemnity from other concurrent tortfeasors on a comparative fault basis." (Id., at p. 598; ...) "This change in the law was a response to California's adoption in 1975 of the system of comparative fault where 'liability for damage [would] be borne by those whose negligence caused it in direct proportion to their respective fault.' (*Li v. Yellow Cab Co.* (1975) 13 Cal. 3d 804, 813..., fn. omitted.)" Thus, *American Motorcycle Assn.* calls for "apportionment of loss between the wrongdoers in proportion to their relative culpability" (*id.*, at p. 595), so as to "permit the equitable sharing of loss between multiple tortfeasors" (*id.*, at p. 597) rather than the imposition of the loss upon one or the other tortfeasor.

The very cornerstone of the equitable indemnity doctrine outlined in *American Motorcycle* is a fair distribution of loss among joint tortfeasors in proportion to fault. Such is the general nature of indemnity, which seeks as a matter of fairness to have one party " 'make good a loss or damage another [party] has incurred.' " (*Valley Circle Estates v. VTN Consolidated, Inc.* (1983) 33 Cal. 3d 604, 614 [189 Cal. Rptr. 871, 659 P.2d 1160].) Thus, in determining the effect of an overpayment by a settling joint tortfeasor upon the competing rights of the remaining joint tortfeasors to indemnification, we seek to further the goal of equitable indemnity in order to effectuate a fair apportionment of loss according to relative culpability. (*American Motorcycle Assn.*, *supra*, 20 Cal. 3d at p. 595.)

The formula proposed by the state, however, fails to comport with the *American Motorcycle* apportionment of loss standard. Were we to limit respondents' recovery in the instant indemnity action to the amount they paid to Spencer which was in excess of their subsequently determined comparative fault, i.e., $25,000, appellant would receive the entire benefit of Gardner's overpayment while ultimately contributing a much smaller percentage—1 percent, in fact—than the 10 percent relative culpability found attributable to them by the jury. In contrast, respondents would not share in the overpayment, but would continue to be liable for a full 85 percent share of the loss despite the "windfall" created by Gardner's excessively generous contribution to plaintiff's judgment. The inequity of such an apportionment is palpable.

Several recent cases have confronted the problem of apportionment of damages where one of several joint tortfeasors is judgment proof as a result of insolvency or settlement with a plaintiff for less than the subsequently decreed comparative responsibility of that party.[1] (*Ambriz v. Kress* (1983) 148 Cal. App. 3d 963 [196 Cal. Rptr. 417]; *Lyly & Sons Trucking Co. v. State of California* (1983) 147 Cal. App. 3d 353 [195 Cal. Rptr. 116]; *Paradise Valley Hospital v. Schlossman* (1983) 143 Cal. App. 3d 87 [191 Cal. Rptr. 531].) In each of such cases there has been an underpayment, or shortfall, and the remaining joint tortfeasors in an indemnity action have sought to avoid liability for the additional loss caused thereby.

The rule which has emerged is that solvent tortfeasors in an indemnity action must share in direct proportion to their respective degree of fault the liability of their judgment-proof co-actors, with the apportionment made as though the judgment-proof tortfeasors had not been involved in the accident. "[The] sharing must be proportional to the remaining tortfeasors' degree of comparative fault." (*Sagadin v. Ripper, supra,* 175 Cal. App. 3d 1141, 1174.) In *Ambriz, supra,* at pages 968-969, the court explained its conclusion, quoting *Paradise Valley, supra,* at page 93, as follows: "In *American Motorcycle,* joint and several liability principles are conjoined with the concept of liability governed by proportionate fault to which is added the right of equitable contribution. These premises, so constellated, give form and outline for the next logical extension and application of these rules. An insolvent defendant's shortfall should be shared proportionally by the solvent defendants as though the insolvent or absent person had originally not participated." In *Paradise Valley, supra,* the court also observed that as the plaintiff receives reimbursement for his injuries from joint tortfeasors, the rights and liabilities of the parties must continually be adjusted in accordance with the concept of proportionate fault.

Appellant's proffered readjustment of liability neither accounts for the comparative fault of the parties nor results in an equitable sharing of the overpayment in proportion to the relative culpability of the parties. It disregards the comparative equitable indemnity principles of *American Motorcycle,* arbitrarily placing the burden of additional liability upon the party picked by plaintiff to be the named defendant. As noted in *Lyly & Sons Trucking Co. v. State of California, supra,* 147 Cal. App. 3d 353, 358: "Caprice is not often justice."

We find the method of calculating damages employed by the trial court to be both equitable and faithful to the purpose of indemnity actions "to allow an equitable balancing of the books among those liable for the injury." (*Lyly & Sons Trucking Co. v. State of California, supra,* 147 Cal. App. 3d 353, 357.) By crediting both appellants and respondents with the overpayment, then apportioning the remainder of the judg-

---

1. A tortfeasor who enters into a good faith settlement with plaintiff, such as Gardner, is discharged from any claim of partial or comparative indemnity that may be pressed by a concurrent tortfeasor. (Code Civ. Proc., § 877.6, subd. (c); *American Motorcycle Assn., supra,* 20 Cal. 3d at p. 604; ...)

ment according to the comparative fault of the parties as found by the jury, the trial court followed the directive of ~~American Motorcycle~~ to achieve wherever possible an equitable sharing of the loss among joint tortfeasors on a comparative fault basis: an adjustment has been made following the overpayment by Gardner so that the remaining joint tortfeasors share the loss in direct proportion to their respective degree of fault.[2]

Finally, the state submits that by awarding respondents more than their actual loss the trial court violated section 875, subdivision (c) of the Code of Civil Procedure, which provides that the right of contribution of a joint tortfeasor who has discharged the joint judgment is limited "to the excess so paid over the pro rata share of the person so paying...."[3] But, in *American Motorcycle*, the court explained that section 875 and its companion statutes do not preclude partial indemnity from a concurrent tortfeasor on a comparative fault basis. Neither, then, does this legislation interdict the extension of this sound doctrine to direct the apportionment of loss in the event of an overpayment by a joint tortfeasor. Respondents, who paid Spencer's damages less the settlement by Gardner, are permitted to collect the excess they paid over their pro rata share of the loss. We therefore conclude that the trial court's award was proper.

The judgment is modified to award respondents the amount of $226,315.78, and as so modified is affirmed.

Abbott Ford, Inc. v. Superior Court

Supreme Court of California

43 Cal. 3d 858, 239 Cal. Rptr. 626, 741 P.2d 124 (1987)

PANELLI, JUSTICE.

The issue presented here is whether a "sliding scale recovery agreement,"[1] entered into by plaintiffs and one of several defendants in a personal injury action, represents

Sliding Scale Settlements

2. That this is so is borne out by the fact that the same indemnification figure, $226,315.78, arrived at by way of the trial court's measure of damages, is also obtained by using the more complex formula of crediting appellant and respondent with their proportionate share of Gardner's overpayment of $225,000 ($23,684.22 or 10/95ths, for appellant, and $201,315.78, or 85/95ths for respondents then subtracting this proportionate share of the overpayment of each from the amounts they should have paid had Gardner settled for his proper 5 percent share. We note, however, that the trial court's calculation using this (proper) formula was very slightly in error, the correct measure of damage being $226,315.78 rather than $226,315.66.

3. In full, subdivision (c) of section 875 reads: "Such right of contribution may be enforced only after one tortfeasor has, by payment, discharged the joint judgment or has paid more than his pro rata share thereof. *It shall be limited to the excess so paid* over the pro rata share of the person so paying and in no event shall any tortfeasor be compelled to make contribution beyond his own pro rata share of the entire judgment." (Italics added.)

1. Section 877.5, subdivision (b) of the Code of Civil Procedure defines "sliding scale recovery agreement" for purposes of that section as "an agreement or covenant between a plaintiff or plaintiffs and one or more, but not all, alleged tortfeasor defendants, where the agreement limits the liability of the agreeing tortfeasor defendants to an amount which is dependent upon the amount of recovery which the plaintiff is able to recover from the non-agreeing defendant or defendants. This includes, but is not limited to, agreements within the scope of Section 877, and agreements in the form of a

a "good faith" settlement within the meaning of sections 877 and 877.6 of the Code of Civil Procedure,[2] so as to relieve the settling defendant of any liability for contribution or equitable comparative indemnity to other defendants in the action. The trial court concluded that the agreement in question was not a good faith settlement and denied the settling defendant's motion to bar cross-complaints by the remaining defendants. The settling defendant then sought review by writ of mandate, and ultimately the Court of Appeal—after remand by this court—concluded that while the "good faith" of such a sliding scale agreement must properly be measured by the standard set forth in our recent decision in *Tech-Bilt, Inc. v. Woodward-Clyde & Associates* (1985) 38 Cal. 3d 488 [213 Cal. Rptr. 256, 698 P.2d 159], the agreement at issue here satisfied that standard as a matter of law. We granted review to consider the question of the appropriate application of the statutory "good faith" requirement in the context of sliding scale agreements.

I

To place the issue in perspective, we review the facts and the litigation background as revealed by the declarations and other materials that were presented to the trial court in connection with its hearing on the good faith settlement question.

The underlying personal injury action in this case arose out of a somewhat unusual automobile accident that occurred on September 10, 1981. At the time of the accident, Ramsey Sneed was driving a used 1979 Ford Econoline van that he had purchased from Abbott Ford, Inc. (Abbott). As Sneed was driving, the left rear wheel came off the van and crashed into the windshield of an on-coming car, a 1965 Mercury station wagon driven by Phyllis Smith. The windshield shattered and Smith suffered serious injuries, including the loss of sight in both eyes and the loss of her sense of smell.

Thereafter, Smith and her husband (hereafter plaintiffs) filed the underlying lawsuit against four defendants—(1) Sneed, (2) Abbott, (3) Ford Motor Company (Ford) and (4) Sears, Roebuck & Co. (Sears)—seeking recovery on a variety of theories. Plaintiffs' mandatory settlement conference statement—prepared after considerable discovery—summarized the case against each defendant as follows:

(1) With regard to Sneed, plaintiffs claimed that he had been negligent in the maintenance and operation of his van, and had continued to drive the vehicle after hearing sounds indicating that there might be some difficulty with the wheels.

(2) With regard to Abbott—a car dealer which had purchased the van used, had "customized" it by replacing the original wheels and tires with "deep dish mag wheels" and oversized tires, and had then resold it to Sneed—plaintiffs sought recovery on both negligence and strict liability theories. With regard to the negligence claim, dis-

---

loan from the agreeing tortfeasor defendant to the plaintiff or plaintiffs which is repayable in whole or in part from the recovery against the non agreeing tortfeasor defendant."

As noted below, in the legal literature and in other jurisdictions such agreements are commonly known as "Mary Carter" agreements. For convenience, we shall generally refer to such agreements simply as sliding scale agreements.

2. Unless otherwise noted, all section references are to the Code of Civil Procedure.

covery revealed that Ford, the manufacturer of the van, had provided a warning in its owner's manual—which Abbott received—cautioning against the installation of "aftermarket wheel assemblies," like the "deep dish mag wheels," on the van. Despite the warning, Abbott had installed the customized wheel assembly, had failed to give the owner's manual or provide any other warning to Sneed, and had failed to advise Sneed of the need to retighten the lug nuts on the wheel assembly periodically because of their tendency to become loose.

(3) With regard to Ford—which had manufactured both the van and the station wagon involved in the accident—plaintiffs claimed that liability could be posited on the basis of Ford's relationship with each vehicle. With respect to the van, plaintiffs relied on both strict liability and negligence theories, suggesting that, notwithstanding the warning provided in its owner's manual, Ford should have reasonably foreseen that potentially dangerous aftermarket wheel assemblies would be installed and should have taken further steps—such as attaching a warning against such installation to the vehicle itself—to minimize the problem. With respect to the station wagon, plaintiffs alleged that a defect in the design of the windshield led it to shatter on impact by the wheel and tire, aggravating plaintiffs' injuries.

(4) Finally, with regard to Sears—which had serviced the van three months before the accident—plaintiffs claimed that while Sears' service records indicated that Sneed had neither requested nor been charged for a brake check, Sneed had in fact requested such a check and Sears' employees had either negligently replaced the wheels on the van or had negligently failed to conduct an inspection which would have revealed the looseness of the lug nuts. * * *

With the case in this posture, a mandatory settlement conference was set for March 26, 1984. In anticipation of that conference, representatives of Abbott, Ford and Sears met on March 14, 1984. At that meeting, Abbott's counsel stated that he believed a reasonable settlement value for the case was $2.5 million and that Abbott was willing to contribute 70 percent of that sum.[5] Counsel for Ford and Sears, however, maintained that their clients had only minimal, if any, responsibility for the accident and were unwilling to bear 30 percent—$750,000—of such a settlement.

At about the same time, plaintiffs offered to settle with Ford or Sears if they would enter into a sliding scale agreement guaranteeing plaintiffs $1.5 million. Both Ford and Sears declined the offer.

On March 23, 1984, three days before the settlement conference, plaintiffs filed their "mandatory settlement conference statement" setting forth the facts of the case, their theories of liability against all parties, and their expected recovery. With respect to liability, the statement concluded: "The liability of Abbott Ford in this case is clear on either a products liability theory or on a negligence theory because Abbott Ford modified the van with unsafe, defective after-market wheels and tires notwithstanding Ford's warning to the contrary. Ford's and Sears' liability is not as clear as Abbott

---

5. Abbott's liability insurance policy provided coverage of $3.25 million.

Ford's, but it is for the jury to decide whether they should be held accountable for this accident. The liability of Sneed is also clear because he had the last opportunity to avoid the accident." With respect to damages, the statement declared that—on the basis of a detailed review of damage awards in numerous cases involving similar injuries—"[p]laintiffs expect a favorable verdict in this case in an amount not less than $3,000,000."

Three days later, at the mandatory settlement conference, Abbott's insurer announced that it had agreed in principle to enter into a sliding scale agreement with plaintiffs, guaranteeing plaintiffs a recovery of $3 million. Several months later, plaintiffs and Abbott's insurer formally entered into the sliding scale agreement that is the focus of the present proceeding.

The agreement—which took the form of two separate contracts, one with each plaintiff, twenty-two and twenty pages in length respectively—contained three key and interrelated elements:

(1) Abbott's insurer guaranteed Phyllis Smith an ultimate recovery of $2.9 million, and her husband an ultimate recovery of $100,000; if, at the conclusion of the lawsuit, plaintiffs had not collected the guaranteed amounts from the remaining defendants, Abbott's insurer would pay the balance up to the guaranteed sum. Thus, if plaintiffs recovered $3 million or more from Ford and Sears, Abbott would not bear any ultimate liability to plaintiffs; if plaintiffs recovered less than $3 million from Ford and Sears, Abbott would be obligated to pay plaintiffs the difference. In return for these guaranties, plaintiffs agreed (a) to dismiss all of their actions against Abbott and (b) to continue to prosecute their action against Ford and Sears[6] in the same way that they would have in the absence of the agreement—through appeal, if necessary—"except that [plaintiffs] shall not settle all or any portion of this litigation with defendants Ford and Sears Roebuck for less than the amount of [their] guaranty, without the express written consent of" Abbott's insurer.

(2) In addition to providing the guaranties, Abbott's insurer agreed to make substantial, periodic no-interest loans to plaintiffs and their attorneys during the course of the litigation. Under the agreement, a total of $390,000 in interest-free loans had been made to plaintiffs and their attorneys by January 1986, and Abbott's insurer was obligated to pay plaintiffs and attorneys the full $3 million—in the form of a loan—by July 1, 1987, if plaintiffs' action had not been terminated by then. The agreement provided that the loan payments would serve as credits for the insurer's obligations under the guaranty provision; if plaintiffs collected $3 million or more from Ford and Sears, plaintiffs were obligated to repay the loans in full—but without interest—to Abbott's insurer.

(3) Finally, the agreement contained an additional provision under which the insurer agreed to pay plaintiffs the full $3 million outright if the agreements were found to be invalid or not in good faith.

---

6. The settlement agreements disclose that plaintiffs had previously settled their case against Sneed for $25,000, the amount of Sneed's liability insurance.

On August 30, 1984, a few months after the sliding scale agreement was signed, Abbott moved in the trial court pursuant to section 877.6 for an order declaring the agreement to be in good faith and dismissing all claims against Abbott for contribution or comparative indemnity. Both Ford and Sears opposed the motion, arguing, inter alia, (1) that sliding scale agreements, by their nature, cannot constitute good faith settlements within the meaning of the relevant statutes, and (2) that, in any event, the settlement agreement at issue here was not a good faith settlement because "the settlement price is potentially grossly disproportionate to Abbott Ford's fair share of the damages."

On September 10, 1984, the trial court held a hearing on Abbott's section 877.6 motion. At the conclusion of the hearing, the court entered a minute order denying Abbott's request to have the agreement declared a good faith settlement so as to bar Ford's and Sears' indemnity cross-complaints against it. The court's order stated that its determination was based "on the fact that Abbott Ford has not paid any amount in settlement and that the guarantee agreement does not constitute a settlement, but rather constitutes a gambling transaction."

Abbott thereafter sought review of the trial court's order in the present writ proceeding, as authorized by section 877.6, subdivision (e). * * * ... [T]he Court of Appeal concluded that the "good faith" standard embodied in *Tech-Bilt* does apply to sliding scale agreements. Nonetheless, the court found that even under the *Tech-Bilt* standard the agreement at issue here constituted a good faith settlement as a matter of law. We again granted review to consider the important and difficult issues presented by the case.

II

As Ford and Sears point out, sliding scale — or, as they are more commonly known throughout the country, "Mary Carter"[9] — agreements have engendered a considerable body of academic commentary, much quite critical of this genre of settlement agreements. Relying on this literature, and a few out-of-state cases, Ford and Sears urge us to hold all such agreements contrary to public policy and invalid as a matter of law.

The majority of out-of-state decisions have, however, declined either to condemn or condone such agreements categorically (*see, e.g., Vermont Union School v. H.P. Cummings Const.* (1983) 143 Vt. 416 [469 A.2d 742, 749-750], and cases cited) and ... we believe such a cautious approach to the problems posed by sliding scale agreements is appropriate. * * *

---

9. The term "Mary Carter" agreement is derived from the name of one of the earliest cases involving such an agreement, *Booth v. Mary Carter Paint Company* (Fla. App. 1967) 202 So. 2d 8. * * * Such agreements are also occasionally referred to by other terms. In Arizona, this type of agreement is generally known as a "Gallagher covenant," from the case of *City of Tucson v. Gallagher* (1971) 14 Ariz. App. 385 [483 P.2d 798] which dealt with such an agreement. At least one commentator has referred to such an agreement as a "guaranteed verdict agreement." (Bodine, *The Case Against Guaranteed Verdict Agreements* (1980) 29 Def. L.J. 233.) Where the agreement takes the form of a loan, it is sometimes called a "loan receipt agreement" (McKay, *Loan Agreement: A Settlement Device that Deserves Close Scrutiny* (1976) 10 Val. U.L. Rev. 231), though the "loan receipt" terminology derives from a distinct device developed in the admiralty insurance field.

In the present case, the question before us is not the broad one of the validity of sliding scale agreements in general, but the more limited question of whether the sliding scale agreement at issue here should properly be considered a "good faith" settlement under the relevant statutory provisions so as to absolve Abbott from any liability for contribution or indemnity to the remaining codefendants, Ford and Sears. As we shall see, that issue in itself raises a number of complex questions.

III

As we explained in our recent decision in *Tech-Bilt*, the provisions of sections 877 and 877.6[14] — governing the effect that a settlement agreement has on a settling defendant's potential liability to other defendants for contribution or comparative indemnity — have two major goals: the equitable sharing of costs among the parties at fault and the encouragement of settlements. (38 Cal. 3d at pp. 494-496.) The provisions of section 877 make it quite clear that the two goals are inextricably linked. Section 877 establishes that a good faith settlement bars other defendants from seeking contribution from the settling defendant (§ 877, subd. (b)), but at the same time provides that the plaintiff's claims against the other defendants are to be reduced by "the amount of consideration paid for" the settlement (§ 877, subd. (a)). Thus, while a good faith settlement cuts off the right of other defendants to seek contribution or comparative indemnity from the settling defendant, the nonsettling defendants obtain in return a reduction in their ultimate liability to the plaintiff.

---

14. Section 877 provides in full: "Where a release, dismissal with or without prejudice, or a covenant not to sue or not to enforce judgment is given in good faith before verdict or judgment to one or more of a number of tortfeasors claimed to be liable for the same tort — [¶] (a) It shall not discharge any other such tortfeasor from liability unless its terms so provide, but it shall reduce the claims against the others in the amount stipulated by the release, the dismissal or the covenant, or in the amount of the consideration paid for it whichever is the greater; and [¶] (b) It shall discharge the tortfeasor to whom it is given from all liability for any contribution to any other tortfeasors."

Section 877.6 provides in full:

"(a) Any party to an action wherein it is alleged that two or more parties are joint tortfeasors shall be entitled to a hearing on the issue of the good faith of a settlement entered into by the plaintiff or other claimant and one or more alleged tortfeasors, upon giving notice thereof in the manner provided in Sections 1010 and 1011 at least 20 days before the hearing. * * *

"(b) The issue of the good faith of a settlement may be determined by the court on the basis of affidavits served with the notice of hearing, and any counteraffidavits filed in response thereto, or the court may, in its discretion, receive other evidence at the hearing.

"(c) A determination by the court that the settlement was made in good faith shall bar any other joint tortfeasor from any further claims against the settling tortfeasor for equitable comparative contribution, or partial or comparative indemnity, based on comparative negligence or comparative fault.

"(d) The party asserting the lack of good faith shall have the burden of proof on that issue.

"(e) When a determination of good faith or lack of good faith of a settlement is made, any party aggrieved by the determination may petition the proper court to review the determination by writ of mandate. The petition for writ of mandate shall be filed within 20 days after service of written notice of the determination, or within such additional time not exceeding 20 days as the trial court may allow. * * *

"The running of any period of time after which an action would be subject to dismissal pursuant to Section 583 shall be tolled during the period of review of a determination pursuant to this subdivision."

Tech-Bilt recognized that the "good faith" requirement of sections 877 and 877.6 is the key to the harmonization of the twin statutory objectives. "The good faith provision of section 877 mandates that the courts review agreements purportedly made under its aegis to insure that such settlements appropriately balance the contribution statute's dual objectives." (38 Cal. 3d at p. 494, fn. omitted.) At the same time, we explained that the "good faith" concept cannot be captured in a simple formula. "'Lack of good faith encompasses many kinds of behavior. It may characterize one or both sides to a settlement. When profit is involved, the ingenuity of man spawns limitless varieties of unfairness. Thus, formulation of a precise definition of good faith is neither possible nor practicable. The Legislature has here incorporated by reference the general equitable principle of contribution law which frowns on unfair settlements, *including those which are so poorly related to the value of the case as to impose a potentially disproportionate cost on the defendant ultimately selected for suit.'*" (*Id.*, at pp. 494-495, italics added in *Tech-Bilt*].)

Rejecting the line of cases — beginning with *Dompeling v. Superior Court* (1981) 117 Cal. App. 3d 798 [173 Cal. Rptr.] — which had indicated that settling parties were free "to further their respective interests without regard to the effect of their settlement upon other defendants" (*id.*, at pp. 809-810) so long as they refrained "from tortious or other wrongful conduct" (*ibid.*), we concluded in *Tech-Bilt* that "[a] more appropriate definition of 'good faith,' in keeping with the policies of *American Motorcycle Assn. v. Superior Court*, (1978) 20 Cal. 3d 578] and the statute, would enable the trial court to inquire, among other things, *whether the amount of the settlement is within the reasonable range of the settling tortfeasor's proportional share of comparative liability for the plaintiff's injuries.*" (38 Cal. 3d at p. 499, italics added.)[16]

Elaborating on the parameters of the good faith concept, we observed that "the intent and policies underlying section 877.6 require that a number of factors be taken into account including a rough approximation of plaintiffs' total recovery and the settlor's proportionate liability, the amount paid in settlement, the allocation of settlement proceeds among plaintiffs, and a recognition that a settlor should pay less in settlement than he would if he were found liable after a trial. Other relevant considerations include the financial conditions and insurance policy limits of settling defendants, as well as the existence of collusion, fraud or tortious conduct aimed to injure the interests of nonsettling defendants. [Citation.] Finally, practical considerations obviously require that the evaluation be made on the basis of information available at the time of settlement. '[A] defendant's settlement figure must not be grossly disproportionate

---

16. The dissent takes issue with our interpretation of the term "good faith" as it is used in section 877. According to the dissent, "good faith" under section 877 "simply requires noncollusive conduct" on the part of the settling parties. However, as noted above, we considered and rejected that very contention in our recent decision in *Tech-Bilt, Inc. v. Woodward-Clyde & Associates* (1985) 38 Cal. 3d 488 [213 Cal. Rptr. 256, 698 P.2d 159]. We find no compelling reason to reexamine or overturn the conclusions reached in *Tech-Bilt*.

to what a reasonable person, at the time of the settlement, would estimate the settling defendant's liability to be.' (*Torres v. Union Pacific R.R. Co.* (1984) 157 Cal. App. 3d 499, 509 [203 Cal. Rptr 825].) *The party asserting the lack of good faith, who has the burden of proof on that issue [citation], should be permitted to demonstrate, if he can, that the settlement is so far 'out of the ballpark' in relation to these factors as to be inconsistent with the equitable objectives of the statute. Such a demonstration would establish that the proposed settlement was not a 'settlement made in good faith' within the terms of section 877.6."* (*Id.*, at pp. 499-500, italics added, fn. omitted.)

By requiring a settling defendant to settle "in the ballpark" in order to gain immunity from contribution or comparative indemnity, the good faith requirement of sections 877 and 877.6 assures that—by virtue of the "set-off" embodied in section 877, subdivision (a)—the nonsettling defendants' liability to the plaintiff will be reduced by a sum that is not "grossly disproportionate" to the settling defendant's share of liability, thus providing at least some rough measure of fair apportionment of loss between the settling and nonsettling defendants.

As *Tech-Bilt* emphasizes, of course, a "good faith" settlement does not call for perfect or even nearly perfect apportionment of liability. In order to encourage settlement, it is quite proper for a settling defendant to pay less than his proportionate share of the anticipated damages. What is required is simply that the settlement not be grossly disproportionate to the settlor's fair share. As the Court of Appeal observed in *Torres v. Union Pacific R.R. Co.*, *supra*, 157 Cal. App. 3d 499, 507: "If [a settling] codefendant wishes to enjoy the section 877 bar against indemnity, he must make some attempt to place the price of his settlement within a reasonable range of his relative share of the liability."

As noted above, the Court of Appeal—after remand from this court—concluded that the "good faith" standard articulated in *Tech-Bilt* applies to sliding scale agreements. Abbott has not challenged that conclusion here and, in any event, we agree with the Court of Appeal's conclusion on this point. Neither section 877 nor section 877.6 exempts sliding scale agreements from its "good faith" requirement, and nothing in section 877.5[18]—a provision which was enacted to protect against the unfair con-

---

18. Section 877.5, subdivision (a) provides: "(a) Where an agreement or covenant is made which provides for a sliding scale recovery agreement between one or more, but not all, alleged defendant tortfeasors and the plaintiff or plaintiffs: [¶] (1) The parties entering into any such agreement or covenant shall promptly inform the court in which the action is pending of the existence of the agreement or covenant and its terms and provisions; and [¶] (2) If the action is tried before a jury, and a defendant party to the agreement is a witness, the court shall, upon motion of a party, disclose to the jury the existence and content of the agreement or covenant, unless the court finds that such disclosure will create substantial danger of undue prejudice, of confusing the issues, or of misleading the jury. [¶] The jury disclosure herein required shall be no more than necessary to be sure that the jury understands (1) the essential nature of the agreement, but not including the amount paid, or any contingency, and (2) the possibility that the agreement may bias the testimony of the alleged tortfeasor or tortfeasors who entered into the agreement." Section 877.5, subdivision (b), which defines "sliding scale recovery agreement" for purposes of the provision, is quoted in full in footnote 1, *ante*.

sequences that may flow from undisclosed sliding scale agreements—indicates that such agreements need not meet the generally applicable good faith standard. Indeed, the legislative history of section 877.5 suggests that the Legislature contemplated that a broad good faith standard ... would apply to such agreements.

The crucial question presented by this case is how *Tech-Bilt's* good faith standard should apply to sliding scale agreements. Ford and Sears claim broadly that sliding scale agreements can never satisfy the good faith standard of *Tech-Bilt*, asserting that such agreements, by their very nature, irreconcilably conflict with *both goals*—fair apportionment of loss and encouragement of settlement—sought to be advanced by the statutory scheme. In addition, they argue that even if some sliding scale agreements may properly be found to be good faith settlements, the agreements at issue here clearly cannot. We first consider the claims with respect to apportionment of loss.

A

Ford and Sears argue initially that sliding scale agreements inevitably thwart the goal of a fair apportionment of loss among responsible tortfeasors. Because, by definition, such an agreement is one in which the settling defendant's final out-of-pocket payment to the plaintiff is dependent on the amount which the plaintiff ultimately recovers from the remaining defendants, Ford and Sears insist that such an agreement always has the effect of improperly shifting the settling defendant's share of liability onto the nonsettling defendants, thus undermining equitable apportionment. To support their claim, Ford and Sears note that under the sliding scale agreement at issue here, if a jury were to assess plaintiffs' damages from the accident at $3 million or more and to find that Ford or Sears was in any degree responsible for the injury, Ford or Sears would ostensibly be required to bear *all* of the damages, and Abbott—the party who, by all appearances, is the most culpable tortfeasor[20]—would escape any ultimate out-of-pocket loss whatsoever. Ford and Sears argue that such a result cannot be squared with the statutory goal of fairly apportioning loss among the responsible tortfeasors.

* * *

In analyzing the apportionment problem, it is important to keep in mind that, under the terms of section 877, a settlement—if found to be in "good faith"—has two interrelated consequences: (1) it discharges the settling tortfeasor from all liability to other defendants for contribution or indemnity, and (2) it reduces the plaintiff's claims against the other defendants by "the amount of consideration paid for it." Although past cases have often overlooked the interrelationship of these two features in our view the ultimate analysis of the effect of the sliding scale agreement resolves itself to a consideration of fairness to the nonsettling defendants. If a court finds that

---

20. During settlement negotiations, it will be recalled, Abbott agreed to bear 70 percent of its proposed $2.5 million settlement, and plaintiffs' settlement conference memorandum clearly designated Abbott as the principal tortfeasor.

a settling defendant, by entering into a sliding scale agreement, has realistically paid a "consideration" that is within its *Tech- Bilt* "ballpark," and if the nonsettling defendants obtain a reduction in the plaintiff's claims against them in an amount equal to that consideration, the statutory fair apportionment objective should be satisfied. Accordingly, the analysis of whether a sliding scale agreement conflicts with the fair apportionment objective lies in "the amount of consideration" which is attributed to the settling defendant as the "payment" for his release from liability by entering into the sliding scale agreement. Since the sliding scale agreement is given by the settling defendant in exchange for the plaintiff's release and the immunity from contribution or indemnity from the claims of the nonsettling cotortfeasors, we should assume the exchange is of equivalents. If we focus, then, not on what the settling defendant gave up, but rather what he received, then we have a simple application of the *Tech-Bilt* rules. This is so because one of the principal difficulties in this area has been the attempt to arrive at an accurate evaluation of the "price" or "consideration" which has been paid by a settling defendant who enters into a sliding scale arrangement.

Unlike an ordinary settlement agreement in which the amount the settling defendant has paid — and correspondingly the amount to be deducted from the plaintiff's claims against the remaining defendants — is typically easy to identify, the contingent nature of a sliding scale obligation has created considerable confusion as to the proper valuation of such an agreement.

The parties are in sharp disagreement on this point. Ford and Sears argue that the "consideration paid" should be calculated solely by reference to the amount of any *noncontingent* payment which the settling defendant has made to the plaintiff under the agreement; in this case, where Abbott has made no noncontingent payment, they suggest that the "consideration" or cost paid by Abbott should be valued at zero. Abbott, on the other hand, points to the fact that it has guaranteed plaintiffs a $3 million recovery, and argues the consideration which it has paid should be fixed at its possible maximum payment, $3 million.

The economic reality, we believe, lies between these two extreme positions. Contrary to the arguments of Ford and Sears, a guaranty agreement, even if totally contingent, is not completely cost-free from the point of view of the guarantor. At the same time and contrary to the position of Abbott, however, the "cost" or "price" of such an agreement is not equal to the maximum amount that the guarantor may possibly be required to pay under the agreement. Accordingly, given the nature of sliding scale agreements, we believe the court should not be burdened with the obligation to determine the actual value of such an agreement by the use of actuarial or other valuation methods. Rather, the parties to such an agreement, since they are in the best position to place a monetary figure on its value, should have the burden of establishing the monetary value of the sliding scale agreement.

In many cases, negotiations between the parties will have included a traditional "straight" settlement as an alternative to the sliding scale agreement, and this background will give the settling parties a vantage point in declaring the agreement's value. In addition, since the plaintiff and the settling defendant are likely to have somewhat different, and somewhat conflicting interests in placing a value on the agreement—the plaintiff would prefer the value to be on the low side to reduce the amount that its claims against other defendants will be reduced; the settling defendant will want the value to be high enough to assure that the agreement is found to be within its *Tech-Bilt* "ballpark" so as to relieve it of liability for comparative indemnity or contribution—requiring a joint valuation by the plaintiff and the settling defendant should generally produce a reasonable valuation. (*See* Comment, *California Code of Civil Procedure Sections 877, 877.5, and 877.6: The Settlement Game in the Ballpark that Tech-Bilt* (1986) 13 Pepperdine L. Rev. 823, 857.)

Once the parties to the agreement have declared its value, a nonsettling defendant either (1) can accept that value and attempt to show that the settlement is not in good faith because the assigned value is not within the settling defendant's *Tech-Bilt* ballpark, or (2) can attempt to prove that the parties' assigned value is too low and that a greater reduction in plaintiff's claims against the remaining defendants is actually warranted.

* * *

B

In addition to the fair apportionment issue, Ford and Sears contend that sliding scale agreements in general, and the agreement in this case in particular, should be found not in "good faith" because such agreements improperly impede the *full* settlement of the case. We pointed out in *Tech-Bilt* that "from the standpoint of the public interest and the legal process, a prime value in encouraging settlement lies in '[removing] [the case] from the judicial system, and this occurs only when *all* claims relating to the loss are settled.'" (38 Cal. 3d at p. 500.) * * *

As Ford and Sears point out, the most obvious conflict between sliding scale agreements and a subsequent settlement of the balance of the lawsuit is posed by explicit provisions contained in most sliding scale agreements which purport to grant the settling defendant a "veto power" over any subsequent settlement which would affect the settling defendant's ultimate out-of-pocket costs under the guaranty agreement. The provision contained in the agreement in the present case is fairly typical in this regard, providing that "[plaintiffs] shall not settle all or any portion of this litigation with defendants Ford and Sears Roebuck for less than the amount of [their] [guaranteed recovery], *without the express written consent of [Abbott's insurer].*" (Italics added.)

The reason for the inclusion of some such "veto" provision in a sliding scale agreement is, of course, readily apparent. Because the settling defendant has agreed to guarantee that the plaintiff ultimately recovers some minimum amount, it "has an obvious and legitimate interest in ensuring that the plaintiff diligently prosecutes its claims against the remaining defendants." While it may be reasonable for the earlier settling defendant to reserve the right to veto subsequent settlements which are unfairly low and which would result in its bearing an ultimate out-of-pocket cost higher than its fair share of the plaintiff's damages, there is no similar compelling justification for permitting that defendant to bar the remaining defendants from settling with the plaintiff for an amount that is sufficiently high that it would not have such an unfair effect. An open-ended veto provision conflicts with the public policy which favors the full settlement of litigation and may frequently result in unnecessary trials. Accordingly, we conclude that to be valid and enforceable, such a veto provision must, by its terms, be confined only to those subsequent settlements that will require the earlier settling defendant to bear more than its fair "ballpark" share of damages. * * *

IV

As discussed above, Abbott maintains that the sliding scale agreement in this case is not disproportionate to its fair share of liability and does not improperly impair full settlement of the action. It also apparently contends, however, that even if the agreement were found to be flawed in those respects, the agreement should nonetheless be found to be a good faith settlement within the meaning of sections 877 and 877.6 because of two additional considerations. We discuss each in turn.

Abbott first emphasizes that sliding scale agreements like those at issue here— and, in particular, the no-interest loan provisions of the agreement—provide injured victims with a speedy source of revenue which enables such victims both to support themselves immediately and to litigate their claims against other defendants. It points out that a number of courts and commentators have taken note of these beneficial aspects of such agreements.

We agree that affording an injured person prompt payment of funds for his losses serves a very important state interest. But nothing we have said above is inconsistent with that purpose. We have not suggested that it is improper for a settlement agreement to take the form of a noninterest loan from the settling defendant to the plaintiff, repayable out of the proceeds of any recovery;[26] rather, we simply note that the value of such a loan will realistically be considered by the parties to the agreement in arriving at the agreement's value. Of course, if a plaintiff chooses to release his or her claims against a defendant for less than that defendant's "ballpark" figure, the plaintiff remains free to do so; if, however, the settling defendant wishes to obtain immunity from potential claims for comparative indemnity or contribution under sections 877 and 877.6, (1) the "consideration" paid by it must not be grossly disproportionate to its fair share of responsibility and (2) the remaining defendants are entitled to have the plaintiff's claims against them reduced by the amount of the consideration paid. Although plaintiffs may be less willing to enter into such agreements once they recognize that their claims against the nonsettling defendants will be reduced by the value of

---

26. Some out-of-state decisions have found such loan agreements invalid as violative of the common law doctrines of champerty and maintenance, which generally preclude a "stranger" to a lawsuit from financing the litigation in return for a portion of any recovery. California, however, has never adopted the common law doctrines of champerty and maintenance, and thus the fact that a settlement takes the form of such a loan does not in itself render the settlement invalid.

the agreement,[27] we do not believe that consequence can itself justify a contrary result. Offsets have been routinely required in normal settlement agreements since the inception of section 877, and we can find no justification for exempting the more questionable sliding scale agreements from similar treatment. * * *

V

In sum, we conclude: (1) that *Tech-Bilt's* good faith standard applies to sliding scale agreements, (2) that to satisfy the statutory objective of a fair apportionment of loss (i) the "consideration" paid by a defendant who enters into a sliding scale agreement must fall within the *Tech-Bilt* "ballpark" and (ii) the plaintiffs' claims against the remaining defendants must be reduced by the amount of the "consideration paid" by the settling defendant, (3) that any unreasonable or bad faith conduct of the nonsettling defendants which impeded the settlement process and led to the sliding scale agreement may be taken into account in determining whether the agreement satisfies the "ballpark" standard, and (4) that any provision which purports to give a settling defendant a "veto" over subsequent settlements is valid only if it is limited to settlements which would leave the earlier settling defendant to bear more than its fair share of liability for the plaintiff's damages.

* * *

[2] Effect of Good Faith Settlement

What effect does a good faith pretrial settlement have on the settling parties? On the nonsettling parties? What rights does a settling defendant have with respect to equitable indemnification from other joint tortfeasors? Calculators ready? Consider the following examples:

[a] First, an easy hypothetical

Plaintiff sued three joint tortfeasors for injuries caused by their alleged negligence. Plaintiff settles with defendant A for $50,000 prior to trial, and the settlement is determined to be in good faith within the meaning of CCP § 877.6. Defendants file cross-complaints for equitable indemnity against each other. Following a trial, the jury awards plaintiff $260,000, allocating fault as follows: Defendant A (10%), defendant B (30%), and defendant C (60%).

---

27. The rapid increase in the attractiveness of such agreements to plaintiffs in recent years may have been based, in large part, on the fact that prior decisions have permitted plaintiffs to receive the substantial benefits of sliding scale agreements without any corresponding reduction in their claims against the remaining defendants. Moreover, as a result of our resolution of the issues presented in this case, defendants may also find such agreements less attractive in the future. The result of the offset requirement will be a reduction in the amount of exposure of a nonsettling defendant to the plaintiff by the amount of the settling parties' declaration of value, thereby increasing the odds that the settling defendant will be obligated to perform under its guaranty agreement with plaintiff. Thus, after trial, the obligation of the settling defendant to the plaintiff under the sliding scale agreement will now be the difference, if any, between the amount of total damages awarded against a nonsettling defendant, reduced by the valuation of the sliding scale agreement, and the guaranteed amount.

If defendant B pays the entire judgment, how much is B entitled to recover from defendant A? From defendant C? How much is defendant A entitled to recover from defendant B? From defendant C?

[b]   Now for a real case

Plaintiff auto passenger sued defendants auto driver, Truck Company and country club for injuries suffered in an automobile collision. Defendant Truck Company filed a new party cross-complaint for equitable indemnity against the State of California, alleging negligent maintenance of the highway. All defendants settle with plaintiff for a total of $920,000, with defendant Truck Company paying $875,000 of this total amount. Defendant Truck Company proceeds against the State for equitable indemnity, and the court determines that reasonable damages for plaintiff's injuries is $875,000 and that the allocation of fault is: State (10%), Truck Company (40%), and other defendants (50%). The trial court enters judgment for Truck Company against the State for $87,500. Is this equitable indemnity judgment for the correct amount? Explain your calculations. *See Lily & Sons Trucking Co. v. State of California*, 147 Cal. App. 3d 353, 195 Cal. Rptr. 116 (1983).

[c]   A more difficult real case

Plaintiff Driver and plaintiff Passenger were seriously injured when Driver's Toyota land cruiser rolled over. Driver had purchased the land cruiser from defendant Dealer. Driver, a teenager, was intoxicated at the time of the crash, having illegally obtained alcohol first from Friend's Parents and later from Wine Store.

(1) Plaintiff Passenger sued joint tortfeasor defendants Driver, Dealer, Toyota, and Friend's Parents for negligence. Prior to trial, plaintiff Passenger settled with all defendants (except for Friend's Parents) in the amount of $1,525,173 (of which $200,000 was paid by Toyota and $955,000 by Dealer). Passenger proceeded to trial against Friend's Parents, and the jury returned a special verdict of $1,249,136 against Friend's Parents. Toyota sought equitable indemnity from the other defendants, particularly Friend's Parents. The jury apportioned fault among the defendants as follows: Driver (60%), Dealer (15%), Toyota (15%), Friend's Parents (10%). Defendants Dealer and Toyota filed cross-complaints for equitable indemnity against the other defendants. How much is Dealer entitled to recover from Friend's Parents? From the other defendants? How much is Toyota entitled to recover from Friend's Parents? From the other defendants? Explain your calculations. If you need some help, see *Sagadin v. Ripper*, 175 Cal. App. 3d 1141, 1174, 221 Cal. Rptr. 675 (1985).

(2) Plaintiff Driver also sued defendant Co-Driver, Dealer, Toyota, and Friend's Parents for personal injury damages. Before trial, plaintiff Driver settled with Co-Driver in the amount of $334,913; and proceeded to trial against defendants Dealer, Toyota, and Friend's Parents. The jury rendered a special verdict of $1,250,500 against these defendants, apportioning fault as follows: Plaintiff Driver (60%), Defendant Toyota (15%), Defendant Dealer (15%), and defendant Friend's Parents (10%). What

is the net amount of the joint and several judgment entered against these three defendants? *See Sagadin v. Ripper, supra,* 175 Cal. App. 3d at 1171. The three defendants also filed cross-complaints for equitable indemnity against each other. What is the proper amount of each defendant's share in these indemnity actions? Explain your calculations.

[d] Complications in Calculating Offset Credits

What is the proper amount of the offset credit for a good faith settlement where the settling defendant has not actually paid the settlement amount at the time judgment is entered against the nonsettling defendants? In *Garcia v. Duro Dyne Corp.,* 156 Cal. App. 4th 92, 67 Cal. Rptr. 3d 100 (2007), the plaintiffs brought a personal injury action against numerous defendants, including manufacturers, distributors, and general contractors, seeking damages for cancer allegedly caused by exposure to asbestos-containing products. The plaintiffs settled with several defendants before trial in the total amount of $925,176, and proceeded to trial against the nonsettling manufacturer. The jury found the defendant manufacturer was 3% at fault, and returned a verdict of $1.9 million in favor of the plaintiffs. The defendant then asked the court to reduce the jury's economic damages award the total amount of the good faith settlements attributable to economic damages. The trial court denied this request because, at the time of the trial, $700,000 of the settlement monies remained unpaid for over six months.

On appeal, the *Garcia* court held that a nonsettling defendant is not entitled to an offset for a settlement until the monies have been paid to the plaintiff, but that the judgment must include a reservation of jurisdiction for the trial court to calculate and award offset credits to the defendant for any future payments that are made by the settling defendants. *Garcia,* 156 Cal. App. 4th at 100–102. Do you agree with this holding? If the settling defendants *never* pay the settlement monies, does this mean the nonsettling defendant receives no offset credit but is barred from seeking equitable indemnity from the settling defendants? Is that fair?

[3] *Good Faith Settlement Determination*

[a] Relevant Factors

The Supreme Court described the factors relevant to a judicial determination of "good faith" settlement within the meaning of CCP § 877.6 in *Tech-Bilt, Inc. v. Woodward-Clyde & Associates,* 38 Cal. 3d 488, 494-99, 213 Cal. Rptr. 256, 698 P.2d 159 (1985), quoted at length in *Abbott Ford.* Which factors appear to be the most important? The amount of the settlement in light of the settling defendant's likely liability? What other factors are significant? The trial court has wide discretion, however, in deciding whether a settlement is in good faith and in arriving at an allocation of valuation of the various interests involved. *See, e.g., North County Contractors' Assn. v. Touchstone Ins. Serv.,* 27 Cal. App. 4th 1085, 1095, 33 Cal. Rptr. 2d 166 (1994) ("An educated guess is the best a judge can do when deciding whether a settlement is made in good faith"); *Erreca's v. Superior Court,* 19 Cal. App. 4th 1475, 24 Cal. Rptr. 156

(1993) (ruling the trial court must be accorded wide discretion to ensure that new forms of settlements are kept within the bounds of fairness to both settling and non-settling parties).

In applying the *Tech-Bilt* factors to make a "good faith" settlement determination, a trial court must not only consider whether the settlement amount is in the ballpark of the settling defendant's potential liability to the plaintiff but must also consider the settling defendant's proportionate share of liability to other defendants on their claims for equitable indemnity, *See, e.g., TSI Seismic Tenant Space, Inc. v. Superior Court*, 149 Cal. App. 4th 159, 56 Cal. Rptr. 3d 751 (2007) (concluding trial court erred in finding the settlement between plaintiff developer and defendant geotechnical engineering company for $50,000, the maximum payment under the limitation of liability clause in the contract between plaintiff and the settling defendant, without also considering defendant's proportionate share of culpability and its potential for liability to the nonsettling defendants for indemnity); *Long Beach Mem'l Med. Ctr. v. Superior Court*, 172 Cal. App. 4th 865, 91 Cal. Rptr. 494 (2009) (holding the good faith settlement determination in a medical negligence action against the defendant hospital, the treating physicians, and other defendants where the plaintiffs settled with the defendant hospital and the other defendants, except the physicians, for a total of $8 million and the physicians subsequently settled with the plaintiffs for $200,000 vacated because the $200,000 settlement was wholly disproportionate to the defendant physicians' share of liability to the plaintiff and also was disproportionate to the physicians' potential liability to the defendant hospital).

[b] Valuation Problems

In *County of Los Angeles v. Guerrero*, 209 Cal. App. 3d 1149, 257 Cal. Rptr. 287 (1989), the plaintiff sued defendants Guerrero (driver of other auto) and County (maintained road) seeking damages in excess of $1 million for injuries sustained in an auto accident. Prior to commencing litigation, plaintiff settled with defendant Guerrero for $30,000, the maximum amount of Guerrero's insurance coverage. The trial court found a "good faith" settlement even though Guerrero's likely fault exceeded 50% and the County's was less than 50%. The Court of Appeal, applying the *Tech-Bilt* factors, upheld the "good faith" determination. Although the settlement amount was disproportionately low, the court found it reasonable due to defendant Guerrero's limited insurance and relative insolvency. *Id.* at 1157-58. The court reached the same conclusion on similar facts in *Schmidt v. Superior Court*, 205 Cal. App. 3d 1244, 253 Cal. Rptr. 137 (1988) (upholding good faith settlement determination where defendant settles $500,000 action for $55,000, the limit of her auto insurance coverage, and has no other assets).

Is a settlement for the amount of a defendant's maximum insurance coverage always a "good faith" settlement? Why not? *See* Florrie Young Roberts, *The Financial Condition and Insurance Policy Limits of a Joint Tortfeasor Wishing to Settle in Good Faith: Problems of Discovery and Confidentiality*, 26 Santa Clara L. Rev. 63 (1986).

The Supreme Court in *Tech-Bilt* found a settlement for a waiver of costs did not constitute a good faith settlement under the circumstances of that case. *Tech-Bilt, supra,* 38 Cal. 3d at 501-502. Is a settlement for a waiver of costs always a "bad faith" settlement? *See West v. Superior Court,* 27 Cal. App. 4th 1625, 34 Cal. Rptr. 2d 409 (1994).

Valuation of noncash consideration for settlement can be particularly troublesome. For example, settling defendants may assign to the plaintiff their indemnity and contribution rights against nonsettling defendants as part of the settlement package, and these settling parties may attribute a dollar value to these assignment rights. What criteria should a trial court consider in determining whether the attributed valuation is appropriate? *See, e.g., Regan Roofing Co. v. Superior Court,* 21 Cal. App. 4th 1685, 1710-15, 27 Cal. Rptr. 2d 62 (1994) (holding information in record was inadequate to support $5,000 valuation for assignment of potential $2 million in indemnity rights); *Erreca's v. Superior Court,* 19 Cal. App. 4th 1475, 1496-99, 24 Cal. Rptr. 2d 156 (1993) (approving $300,000 valuation for assignment rights where potential recovery could be $1.5 million).

[c] Evidentiary Basis

The settling parties must present a clear and complete description of the settlement sufficient to permit the trial court to properly apply the *Tech-Bilt* factors. "At a minimum, a party seeking confirmation of a settlement must explain to the court and to all other parties: who has settled with whom, the dollar amount of each settlement, if any settlement is allocated, how it is allocated between issues and/or parties, what nonmonetary consideration has been included, and how the parties to the settlement value the nonmonetary consideration." *Alcal Roofing & Insulation v. Superior Court,* 8 Cal. App. 4th 1121, 1129, 10 Cal. Rptr. 2d 844 (1992). *See Brehm Communities v. Superior Court,* 88 Cal. App. 4th 730, 103 Cal. Rptr. 2d 918 (2001) (ordering trial court to vacate its order finding settlement to be in good faith because the settling parties did not present competent evidence of the value of the nonmonetary consideration to be transferred by them and did not reduce this value by the value of any consideration passing from the plaintiff to the settling defendants).

[d] Allocation of Settlement Amounts in Complex Litigation

The good faith settlement and subsequent offset determinations can become very complicated in complex litigation—lawsuits involving multiple plaintiffs and causes of action with different damages, and numerous defendants, many of whom may be liable on some but not all claims. A frequently encountered example is comprehensive construction defects litigation. In such cases, several homeowners in a subdivision sue a variety of potentially responsible defendants, including the developer-seller and numerous subcontractors such as the designers, the graders, soil engineers, drywallers, plumbers, and roofers, etc. The trial court must require any settling parties, as part of the good faith settlement determination process, to allocate specific settlement amounts to certain issues and claims. *See, e.g., Regan Roofing Co. v. Superior Court,*

27 Cal. App. 4th 1085, 27 Cal. Rptr. 2d 62 (1994); *Erreca's v. Superior Court*, 19 Cal. App. 4th 1475, 24 Cal. Rptr. 2d 156 (1993).

The trial court's good faith determination therefore evaluates not only the valuation of the overall settlement, but also of the allocation of settlement proceeds as to various issues and parties. *See, e.g., Regan Roofing, supra; Errica's, supra; L. C. Rudd & Son, Inc. v. Superior Court*, 52 Cal. App. 4th 742, 60 Cal. Rptr. 2d 703 (1997) (ordering trial court to vacate its good faith settlement determination where the evidence showed that the "soils and foundations" claims constituted approximately 55.1% to 61.1% of the total cost of repair, but only $15,000 of the $75,000 allocated to repair liability was allocated to the grading contractor's potential liability). Why is a good faith evaluation necessary with respect to how the overall settlement amount is divided among issues and parties? Why is this particularly important where the defendant developer-seller settled with the plaintiffs, but various defendant subcontractors do not? How should this evaluation be accomplished?

The court in *Erreca's v. Superior Court, supra*, 19 Cal. App. 4th at 1495-96, addressed the evidentiary showing required to support approval of settlement allocations in complex cases: "To the rules set forth in *Alcal* [*Roofing & Insulation v. Superior Court, supra*], ... we add the following principles: A party seeking confirmation of a settlement must explain to the court and all other parties ... the evidentiary basis for any allocations and valuations made, and must demonstrate that the allocation was reached in a sufficiently adversarial manner to justify the presumption that a reasonable valuation was reached." Why is such additional evidence essential to the good faith settlement determination when the valuations and allocations are challenged by non-settling defendants? This situation is analogous to cases in which settlement payments are contingent or where noncash consideration is paid for settlement, is it not? How so? *See Regan Roofing Co. v. Superior Court, supra*, 21 Cal. App. 4th at 1701, 1705. Is the good faith settlement evaluation process in such complex cases also analogous to that endorsed by the *Abbott Ford* court for sliding scale settlements? How so?

[e] Total Equitable Indemnity

Despite some earlier lower court decisions to the contrary, the Supreme Court in *Far West Financial Corp. v. D & S Co., Inc.*, 46 Cal. 3d 796, 800, 251 Cal. Rptr. 202, 760 P.2d 399 (1988), held that a "good faith" settlement under CCP § 877.6 bars not only claims by other joint tortfeasors for *partial* equitable indemnity, but also claims for *total* equitable indemnity.

[f] Rights of Settling Defendant

When a defendant tortfeasor enters into a "good faith" settlement with the plaintiff, what rights does that defendant have with respect to recovery from nonsettling joint tortfeasors? *See, e.g., Bolamperti v. Laurco Mfr.*, 164 Cal. App. 3d 249, 210 Cal. Rptr. 155 (1985); *Sears, Roebuck & Co. v. Int'l Harvester Co.*, 82 Cal. App. 3d 492, 497, 147 Cal. Rptr. 262 (1978). What rights does a settling defendant have with respect to recovery from other joint tortfeasor defendants who subsequently also settle with the plaintiff before trial, but several months after the first defendant's settlement? *See Mill Valley Refuse Co. v. Superior Court*, 108 Cal. App. 3d 707, 166 Cal. Rptr. 687 (1980).

[g] Which Parties Bound?

A determination of "good faith" binds only those joint tortfeasors who were parties to the action at the time of the determination and were given an opportunity to be heard on the good faith of the settlement. *Singer Co. v. Superior Court*, 179 Cal. App. 3d 875, 881, 225 Cal. Rptr. 159 (1986); *see also* CCP § 877.6(a). What constitutional principle is the source of this limitation? To what extent is an insurer of a tortfeasor bound by a good faith determination as to the terms of a settlement and stipulated judgment, where the insurer was not a party to the settled action and did not participate in the settlement? *Compare Pac. Estates, Inc. v. Superior Court*, 13 Cal. App. 4th 1561, 17 Cal. Rptr. 2d 434 (1993) (ruling nonparticipating excess insurer not bound by "good faith" determination of settlement) *with Diamond Heights Homeowners Assn. v. National American Ins. Co.*, 227 Cal. App. 3d 563, 277 Cal. Rptr. 906 (1991) (holding that although not a party to the action or settlement, excess insurer who filed objections to settlement bound by "good faith" determination).

[4] Fair Responsibility Act of 1986

The voter-approved Fair Responsibility Act of 1986 (Prop. 51), Civil Code §§ 1431-1431.5, modifies the common law rule of joint and several liability by making each defendant's liability for "non-economic" damages several and not joint in comparative fault cases. "Each defendant shall be liable only for the amount of non-economic damages allocated to that defendant in direct proportion to that defendant's percentage of fault." CC § 1431.2(a). "Non-economic damages" are defined in CC § 1431.2(b)(2); "economic damages" in CC § 1431.2(b)(1). How does this Act modify the common law principles announced in *American Motorcycle*? How does the Fair Responsibility Act affect the apportionment calculations in a "good faith" settlement situation? Consider the following facts:

(1) Plaintiff sues defendants A, B, and C for personal injuries caused by defendants' alleged joint negligence. Plaintiff settles with defendant A for $300,000 before trial. The jury renders a verdict for plaintiff against all defendants for a total amount of $1 million in economic damages and another $1 million in non-economic damages. The special verdict allocates fault as follows: defendant A (60%), defendant B (30%), and defendant C (10%). Defendant B is insolvent. How much is plaintiff entitled to recover from defendant C?

(2) Assume the same facts as above, except that defendant A had settled for $1.5 million ($750,000 designated for economic damages, and $750,000 for non-economic damages), and that defendant A had filed an action for equitable indemnity

against defendants B and C. How much is defendant A entitled to recover from defendant B? From defendant C? How much is plaintiff entitled to recover from defendant C?

(3) Plaintiffs filed a products liability action against defendants Ford Motor Company (car manufacturer) and Allied-Signal, Inc. (seat belt manufacturer) for the wrongful death of their daughter, who was killed during a single car accident. Before trial, plaintiffs reached a good faith settlement with Ford of $382,500. At trial, plaintiffs and defendant Allied-Signal stipulated that plaintiffs made no claim for economic loss and any jury award would be deemed purely non-economic. The jury found damages of $500,000, and assigned comparative fault 35% to Allied-Signal, 45% to Ford, and 20% to decedent. The trial court then gave judgment for $175,000 against defendant Allied-Signal. Allied-Signal appealed, and argued that the judgment against it should be reduced to $17,500. Did the trial court correctly compute the amount of the judgment against defendant Allied-Signal? Why? *See Hoch v. Allied-Signal, Inc.*, 24 Cal. App. 4th 48, 29 Cal. Rptr. 2d 615 (1994).

(4) Apportionment becomes more complicated where the plaintiff is partially at fault, and a settlement amount paid by a defendant does not differentiate between economic and non-economic damages.

For example, in *Espinoza v. Machonga*, 9 Cal. App. 4th 268, 11 Cal. Rptr. 2d 498 (1992), plaintiff Espinoza sued defendants Machonga and Housing Authority for eye injuries caused by shattered glass from a door. Plaintiff settled with the defendant Housing Authority for $5,000. The case proceeded to trial, and the court awarded plaintiff the sums of $6,242.94 for economic damages (medical expenses) and $15,000 for non-economic damages (general damages). The trial court apportioned fault as follows: plaintiff Espinoza (10%), defendant Housing Authority (45%), and defendant Machonga (45%). At the parties' request, the trial court ruled that the proper portion of the judgment for which defendant Machonga was liable was $10,900.88. Defendant Machonga appealed. Were the trial court's calculations correct when it ruled that Machonga was liable to Espinoza in the amount of $10,900.88? Why? Explain your calculations. If you need help, see *Espinoza, supra*, 9 Cal. App. 4th at 271-77.

(a) Several recent decisions have applied *Espinoza*'s formula for calculating offsets: The portion of the settlement which may be set off from a judgment of economic damages is determined by application of the percentage of the economic damages awarded in relationship to the total award of damages. *See, e.g., Ehret v. Congoleum Corp.*, 73 Cal. App. 4th 1308, 87 Cal. Rptr. 2d 363 (1999) (holding that in the absence of a court-approved pretrial allocation of a settlement between economic and noneconomic damages, the trial court must base the allocation on the percentage reflected in the jury verdict); *McComber v. Wells*, 72 Cal. App. 4th 512, 517-18, 85 Cal. Rptr. 2d 376 (1999) (determining the setoff to which the nonsettling defendants were entitled where the jury found the settling defendants were not negligent); *Hackett v. John Crane, Inc.*, 98 Cal. App. 4th 1233, 120 Cal. Rptr. 2d 662 (2002) (applying the *Espinoza* formula in a wrongful death action). The Supreme Court referred to *Espinoza* as providing a "widely accepted method" for making postverdict allocations in Prop.

51 cases. *Rashidi v. Moser*, 60 Cal. 4th 718, 722, 181 Cal. Rptr. 3d 59, 339 P.3d 344 (2014).

(b) What is the impact of the Fair Responsibility Act on a settling tortfeasor's right to seek comparative equitable indemnity from a nonsettling concurrent tortfeasor? In *Union Pacific Corp. v. Wengert*, 79 Cal. App. 4th 1444, 95 Cal. Rptr. 2d 68 (2000), the court concluded that comparative equitable indemnity is available only for that portion of the settlement attributable to economic damages, because that is the extent of the underlying joint obligation. According to the court, a defendant has no right to settle the plaintiff's claim against another party for noneconomic damages; each defendant is entitled to severally negotiate or litigate its own several liability. *Union Pacific*, 79 Cal. App. 4th at 1450-52. Does the Act so complicate settlement strategies that its unpredictable impact may actually discourage pretrial settlements? *See id* at 1451-52.

(c) The Medical Injury Compensation Reform Act (MICRA), Civil Code § 3333.2, limits the total amount of any award of noneconomic damages in an action against health care providers based on professional negligence to $250,000. In *Rashidi v. Moser*, 60 Cal. 4th 718, 181 Cal. Rptr. 3d 59, 339 P.3d 344 (2014), the Supreme Court considered the interplay between the MICRA cap, Proposition 51, and settlements with other tortfeasors who are subject to MICRA. In *Rashidi*, the plaintiff (who went permanently blind in one eye after catheter surgery to stop a severe nosebleed) filed a negligence action against three defendants, a physician, a hospital, and a medical supplies manufacturer. Prior to trial, the plaintiff entered into a settlement with two of the defendants, the hospital ($350,000) and the manufacturer, and proceeded to trial against the nonsettling physician alone.

The jury awarded plaintiff $1.325 million in noneconomic damages and $125,000 in economic damages, and also determined that the defendant physician failed to establish any comparative fault on the part of the two settling defendants. After the trial court reduced the noneconomic damages to $250,000—the MICRA maximum— the defendant physician argued that this $250,000 should be further reduced by the amount of the settlement with the hospital allocated to noneconomic damages (approximately $233,000), so that the plaintiff's total recovery for noneconomic damages would not exceed the MICRA cap. The Supreme Court rejected this argument and concluded that the MICRA cap applies only to *judgments* awarding noneconomic damages. Therefore, the amount the plaintiff recovered for noneconomic *losses* from the hospital by way of settlement was excluded from the cap, and the $250,000 in noneconomic damages imposed on the defendant physician should not be further reduced by a portion of the settlement.

(5) When the plaintiff settles with fewer than all defendants in a Prop. 51 case, the settlement value must be allocated between economic and non-economic damages to determine liability between the nonsettling defendants and plaintiff, as well as to determine equitable indemnity among the joint tortfeasor defendants. Why? The plaintiff would want as little as possible of the settlement amount allocated to economic damages, would she not? Why? In contrast, a nonsettling defendant would want as much

as possible allocated to economic damages, would it not? Why? And although the settling defendant's interest is less obvious, in most circumstances he would also want as much as possible of the settlement amount allocated to economic damages. Why?

For a good discussion of these competing interests in Prop. 51 case settlements, see Haning, Flahavan, Cheng & Wright, *California Practice Guide: Personal Injury* §§ 4:185.20-.29 (The Rutter Group), quoted with approval in *Espinoza v. Machonga, supra*, 9 Cal. App. 4th at 275-76. Is the settling parties' express allocation of economic and non-economic damages as part of the settlement agreement binding on the trial court? *See Jones v. John Crane, Inc.*, 132 Cal. App. 4th 990, 1006-11, 35 Cal. Rptr. 3d 144 (2005) (concluding the allocation of the proceeds that was specified in the settlement agreement but was never judicially approved must be disregarded; the post-trial allocation of the prior settlement should mirror the jury's apportionment of economic and noneconomic damages); *Greathouse v. Amcord, Inc.*, 35 Cal. App. 4th 831, 41 Cal. Rptr. 2d 561 (1995) (holding that in a post-trial motion for apportionment of settlement, the jury's apportionment of total damages between economic and non-economic damages is binding on the trial court, not the allocation designated in the pre-trial agreement between the settling parties). Why not?

(6) The Supreme Court upheld the constitutionality of the Fair Responsibility Act of 1986 in *Evangelatos v. Superior Court*, 44 Cal. 3d 1188, 246 Cal. Rptr. 629, 753 P.2d 585 (1988). In *DaFonte v. Up-Right, Inc.*, 2 Cal. 4th 593, 7 Cal. Rptr. 2d 238, 828 P.2d 140 (1992), the court construed Civil Code § 1431.2 to mean that a defendant's liability for non-economic damages cannot exceed his proportionate share of fault as compared to all fault responsible for the plaintiff's injuries, not merely that of the defendants present in the lawsuit. *DaFonte*, 2 Cal. 4th at 603.

(7) Is an intentional tortfeasor entitled to a reduction or apportionment of noneconomic damages under the Fair Responsibility Act of 1986 (Prop. 51), CCP §§ 1431-1431.5? *See Thomas v. Duggins Constr. Co.*, 139 Cal. App. 4th 1105, 44 Cal. Rptr. 3d 66 (2006) (holding Prop. 51 does not apply in favor of an intentional tortfeasor as against a plaintiff or negligent tortfeasor; an intentional tortfeasor is liable for the entirety of the plaintiff's damages). Are defendants entitled to a reduction or apportionment of noneconomic damages under Prop. 51 in a strict liability action? *Compare Bostick v. Flex Equip. Co.*, 147 Cal. App. 4th 80, 54 Cal. Rptr. 3d 28 (2007) (ruling that in a strict products liability action involving a single defective product where all of the defendants are in the same chain of distribution, Proposition 51 does not eliminate the liable defendant's joint responsibility for noneconomic damages because that defendant's liability is not based on fault but rather is imposed by a rule of law as a matter of public policy) and *Wimberly v. Derby Cycle Corp.*, 56 Cal. App. 4th 618, 65 Cal. Rptr. 2d 532 (199& (holding Prop. 51 does not apply in a strict product liability action involving a single indivisible injury) *with Arena v. Owens-Corning Fiberglas Corp.*, 63 Cal. App. 4th 1178, 74 Cal. Rptr. 2d 580 (1998) (concluding Prop 51 is applicable in a strict liability asbestos exposure case where multiple products manufactured by different defendants caused the plaintiff's injuries and the evidence provides a basis to allocate liability for noneconomic damages between defective prod-

ucts) and *Wilson v. John Crane, Inc.*, 81 Cal. App. 4th 847, 851–59, 97 Cal. Rptr. 3d 240 (2000) (same).

[5] Statute of Limitations

Generally speaking, a cause of action for equitable indemnity does not accrue for statute of limitation purposes when the original tort occurs, but instead accrues at the time the tort defendant pays a judgment or settlement as to which he is entitled to indemnity. *Department of Transp. v. Superior Court*, 26 Cal. 3d 744, 163 Cal. Rptr. 585, 608 P.2d 673 (1980). This accrual rule applies even though the tort defendant seeks partial comparative equitable indemnity, and even though the third-party defendant is a government entity covered by the claim filing requirements of the California Tort Claims Act. *Id.* at 760-62. A few special statutes, most notably CCP § 337.15(c) relating to actions against property developers for latent defects, alter these common law accrual rules for indemnity actions. *See, e.g., Time for Living, Inc. v. Guy Hatfield Homes/All American Dev. Co.*, 230 Cal. App. 3d 30, 280 Cal. Rptr. 904 (1991).

[6] Equitable Indemnity in Non-Negligence Actions

[a] Strict Liability and Intentional Torts

Comparative equitable indemnity among joint tortfeasors applies even though the defendants' liability to plaintiff is based on strict liability, *see, e.g., GEM Developers v. Hallcraft Homes of San Diego, Inc.*, 213 Cal. App. 3d 419, 261 Cal. Rptr. 626 (1989); *Gentry Constr. Co. v. Superior Court*, 212 Cal. App. 3d 177, 260 Cal. Rptr. 421 (1989); or on willful misconduct, *see, e.g., Southern Pac. Transp. Co. v. State of California*, 115 Cal. App. 3d 116, 121, 171 Cal. Rptr. 187 (1981). However, contribution pursuant to CCP § 875 is not available where the tortfeasor has intentionally injured the plaintiff. CCP § 875(d). Although the Supreme Court has not yet determined whether an intentional tortfeasor may obtain equitable indemnity from concurrent intentional tortfeasors on a comparative fault basis, *see, e.g., Molko v. Holy Spirit Assn.*, 46 Cal. 3d 1092, 1127–28, 252 Cal. Rptr. 122, 762 P.2d 46 (1988), *cert. denied*, 490 U.S. 1084 (1989); a divided Court of Appeal has concluded the doctrine of equitable indemnity applies to intentional tortfeasors. *Baird v. Jones*, 21 Cal. App. 4th 684, 27 Cal. Rptr. 2d 232 (1993).

[b] Contract Actions

The Legislature in 1987 expanded the scope of § 877.6 to include "co-obligors on a contract debt" as well as "joint tortfeasors." The purpose of this 1987 amendment was to provide a similarly efficient mechanism to determine the good faith of any settlement in a multiparty contract action. *See Pacific Estates, Inc. v. Superior Court*, 13 Cal. App. 4th 1561, 17 Cal. Rptr. 2d 434 (1993). Does § 877.6 apply when a lawsuit is brought by an insured against multiple insurers allegedly covering the same loss, one insurer settles with the insured, and the settling insurer seeks to use the good faith order approving the settlement to avoid cross-claims for contribution from the other insurers? *See Hartford Accident & Indem. Co. v. Superior Court*, 29 Cal. App.

4th 435, 34 Cal. Rptr. 2d 520 (1994) (concluding insurance companies are not "co-obligors" under §877.6; each insurer owed primary coverage responsibilities springing from its own separate contractual undertaking); *Herrick Corp. v. Canadian Ins. Co.*, 29 Cal. App. 4th 753, 34 Cal. Rptr. 2d 844 (1994) (ruling two primary insurers sharing same risk were not "co-obligors" on a single contract debt; settlement by insured tortfeasor does not preclude contribution action between the two primary insurers); *but see Diamond Heights Homeowners Assn. v. National American Ins. Co.*, 227 Cal. App. 3d 563, 277 Cal. Rptr. 906 (1991) (viewing excess insurer as co-obligor with primary insurer).

[c] Public Policy Limitations

The doctrine of equitable indemnity is not available in cases where it would operate against public policy. *Western Steamship Lines, Inc. v. San Pedro Peninsula Hosp.*, 8 Cal. 4th 100, 109-110, 32 Cal. Rptr. 2d 263, 876 P.2d 1062 (1994); *Paragon Real Estate Grp. of San Francisco, Inc. v. Hansen*, 178 Cal. App. 4th 177, 187-90, 100 Cal. Rptr. 3d 234 (2009). One such type of case is where a predecessor attorney seeks indemnification for malpractice from his successor attorney. *See Western Steamship, supra*, 8 Cal. 4th at 110 & n.7; *Musser v. Provencher*, 28 Cal. 4th 274, 121 Cal. Rptr. 2d 373, 48 P.3d 408 (2002) (observing that the policies of avoiding conflicts of interest and protecting confidentiality of attorney-client communications bars indemnification in predecessor/successor cases). However, these policies do not preclude *concurrent counsel* or *co-counsel* from suing one another for indemnification of legal malpractice damages. *Musser*, 28 Cal. 4th at 281-85. Why are these policy considerations different in these two types of legal malpractice cases?

[7] Contribution

What purpose does the contribution statutes, CCP §§875-876, now serve after *American Motorcycle*? A joint tortfeasor may want to utilize statutory contribution when it is more favorable to apportion liability among all defendants on a pro rata rather than a comparative fault basis. Why will this strategy not work when there is a pretrial settlement? However, by its terms, CCP §877 applies only to prejudgment, not postjudgment, settlements; whereas the contribution statutes expressly apply to "judgments." CCP §§875, 876. *See Jhaveri v. Teitelbaum*, 176 Cal. App. 4th 740, 750, 98 Cal. Rptr. 3d 268 (2009); *Be v. Western Truck Exch.*, 55 Cal. App. 4th 1139, 64 Cal. Rptr. 2d 527 (1997). Consequently, although antiquated as a concept, pro rata contribution does apply where a defendant seeks *post*-judgment contribution (as opposed to *pre*-judgment equitable indemnity based on comparative fault) from joint tortfeasors also subject to the judgment. *Coca-Cola Bottling Co. v. Lucky Stores, Inc.*, 11 Cal. App. 4th 1372, 14 Cal. Rptr. 2d 673 (1992) (holding joint tortfeasor entitled to seek statutory contribution even though claim for equitable indemnity had been previously denied).

Code of Civil Procedure §877 and §877.6 govern only good faith pretrial settlements. In *Leung v. Verdugo Hills Hospital*, 55 Cal. 4th 291, 145 Cal. Rptr. 3d 553, 282 P.3d

1250 (2012), the Supreme Court considered the effect on the apportionment of liability among joint tortfeasors when one tortfeasor's settlement, resulting in a release of liability, was judicially determined *not* to have been made in "good faith," thus rendering inapplicable the apportionment scheme of CCP § 877. The Court considered several different approaches before adopting the "setoff-with-contribution" approach. Under this approach, the nonsettling joint tortfeasors remain jointly and severally liable, the amount paid in settlement is credited against any damages awarded against the nonsettling tortfeasors, and the nonsettling tortfeasors are entitled to contribution from the settling tortfeasor for damages they have paid in excess of their equitable share of liability.

[8]   *Sliding Scale Agreements and Other Untraditional Settlements*

[a]   Sliding Scale Agreements

Why may parties view sliding scale (or "Mary Carter") settlements as more desirable than traditional fixed-amount settlements? What benefits did the sliding scale agreement in *Abbott Ford* confer on the plaintiffs? The Supreme Court declined to categorically condemn or condone sliding scale settlements. *Abbott Ford, Inc. v. Superior Court, supra*, 43 Cal. 3d at 870. Why? Can you think of some agreement terms which the court would consider contrary to public policy? Do the various rulings by the court in *Abbott Ford* make sliding scale agreements less attractive to plaintiffs? Less attractive to defendants? Why? *See Abbott Ford, supra*, 43 Cal. 3d at 885, fn. 27.

CCP § 877.5(a) requires parties entering into a sliding scale recovery agreement to promptly notify the court of its existence and terms. Why? What unfair consequences may flow from undisclosed sliding scale settlements? *See Alcala Co. v. Superior Court*, 49 Cal. App. 4th 1308, 57 Cal. Rptr. 2d 349 (1996) (noting mandatory disclosure of sliding scale agreements necessary so that the factfinder will understand the true alignment of the interests of the litigating parties and their witness).

Are you persuaded by the court's reasoning in adopting a joint valuation approach to sliding scale settlements? What are the alternatives? Realistically, how can a nonsettling defendant establish that the value assigned is not within the settling defendant's *Tech-Bilt* "ballpark"? Or that the assigned value is too low? *See United Serv. Auto. Assn. v. Superior Court*, 93 Cal. App. 4th 633, 113 Cal. Rptr. 2d 328 (2001) (vacating trial court's good faith settlement determination where the valuation the settling parties placed on the contingent loan was not supported by analysis, expert opinion, or substantial evidence). Do you understand why it is appropriate for a trial court to take into account the nonsettling defendants' conduct in determining whether a sliding scale agreement is in good faith for purposes of CCP § 877 and § 877.6? *Abbot, Ford, supra*, 43 Cal. 3d at 881-82.

As *Abbott Ford* illustrates, a settling defendant as part of the sliding scale agreement typically retains a "veto power" over subsequent settlements between plaintiff and other defendants. What purpose does this contractual veto power serve? An open-ended veto provision violates public policy; a settling defendant cannot veto a subsequent settlement with another defendant which is sufficiently high so as to be in the *Tech-Bilt* "ballpark." Why? This holding requires the trial court to determine not only the good faith of any settlements, but also the good faith of any "vetoes," does it not? There are considerable costs in judicial economy, are there not?

[b] Conditional Settlements

The plaintiff may settle with one of several defendant tortfeasors for a fixed amount on the condition that this defendant remain in the lawsuit and participate in the trial. *E.g., Everman v. Superior Court*, 8 Cal. App. 4th 466, 10 Cal. Rptr. 2d 176 (1992). The plaintiff may want such a condition to protect against "empty chair" arguments by nonsettling defendants at trial. What does this mean? In what types of cases should a plaintiff be most concerned about "empty chair" arguments?

Can such a conditional settlement be considered in "good faith" under § 877.6, or is it subject to disapproval because collusive and inherently unfair to nonsettling defendants? The court in *Everman* ruled that such a conditional settlement, although not a sliding scale agreement governed by § 877.5, will bar co-defendant equitable indemnity claims if it meets the *Tech-Bilt* standards. However, as a general rule the terms of such an agreement should be disclosed to the jury during trial. *Everman, supra*, 8 Cal. App. 4th at 473; see also *Diamond v. Reshko*, 239 Cal. App. 4th 828, 191 Cal. Rptr 3d 438 (2015) (holding exclusion of conditional settlement agreement from evidence required reversal of judgment). Why require this disclosure?

[c] Structured Settlements

A structured settlement usually includes an up-front lump sum payment plus installment payments over a period of several years. How should a court determine the value of a structured settlement for "good faith" purposes? How about a noncash settlement where the parties agreed to take specified actions with no amount exchanged? *See, e.g., Arbuthnot v. Relocation Realty Serv. Corp.*, 227 Cal. App. 3d 682, 278 Cal. Rptr. 135 (1991).

[9] *Good Faith Settlement Procedures*

Code of Civil Procedure § 877.6, which codifies *American Motorcycle*, sets forth the procedures for a speedy resolution by the trial court of the issue of the good faith of a settlement. CCP § 877.5 contains additional procedural requirements applicable to sliding scale settlements. Whenever a court determines that a settlement is in good faith, the settling defendant may utilize summary judgment, judgment on the pleadings, demurrer, or motion to dismiss, as appropriate to effectuate the bar of CCP § 877.6(c). *See, e.g., Shane v. Superior Court*, 160 Cal. App. 3d 1237, 207 Cal. Rptr. 210 (1984).

Any party aggrieved by a trial court's determination of the good faith or lack of good faith of a settlement may seek immediate appellate review by writ of mandate. CCP § 877.6(e); *see, e.g., Toyota Motor Sales U.S.A. v. Superior Court*, 220 Cal. App. 3d 864, 269 Cal. Rptr. 647 (1990) (holding trial court abused its discretion in finding settlement in good faith, and issuing a issued writ of mandate directing trial court to vacate good faith determination order). May an aggrieved party forgo writ review and instead seek to have the determination reviewed for the first time on appeal from the final judgment arising out of the trial of the plaintiff's claims against the nonsettling defendants? The courts are split on this issue. *See, e.g., Main Fiber Products, Inc. v. Morgan & Franz Ins. Co.*, 73 Cal. App. 4th 1130, 87 Cal. Rptr. 2d 108 (1999) (concluding failure to seek immediate writ review pursuant to § 877.6(e) precluded appellate review of a good faith determination by means of an appeal from the final judgment); *O'Hearn v. Hillcrest Gym & Fitness Ctr., Inc.*, 115 Cal. App. 4th 491, 9 Cal. Rptr. 3d 342 (2004) (ruling a party wishing to challenge the merits of a "good faith settlement" determination must do so via a petition for writ of mandate in the manner and within the time prescribed in CCP § 877.6(e)); *but see Maryland Casualty Co. v. Andreini & Co.*, 81 Cal. App. 4th 1413, 97 Cal. Rptr. 2d 752 (2000) (concluding trial court's good faith settlement determination is subject to appellate review on appeal from final judgment where the nonsettling defendant's timely petition for pretrial writ review had been summarily denied); *Cahill v. San Diego Gas & Elec. Co.*, 194 Cal. App. 4th 939, 951–56, 124 Cal. Rptr. 78 (2011) (ruling review by writ pursuant to § 877.6(e) is a permissive, not mandatory, means of challenging a good faith settlement determination and does not preclude an appeal after a final judgment).

[10] Indemnity in Federal Courts

In diversity and other cases where federal courts must apply California state law, the federal courts follow CCP § 877 and § 877.6. *E.g., Slottow v. American Cas. Co.*, 10 F.3d 1355 (9th Cir. 1993) (applying California's *Tech-Bilt* standards, federal court determined settlement allocation not made in good faith); *Commercial Union Ins. Co. v. Ford Motor Co.*, 640 F.2d 210 (9th Cir. 1981) (applying CCP § 877 in indemnity action based on diversity jurisdiction); *Owen v. United States*, 713 F.2d 1461 (9th Cir. 1983) (applying CCP §§ 877 and 877.6 to U.S. claim for partial indemnity in Federal Torts Claim Act case).

[a] Federal Common Law Doctrine of Contribution

The federal courts must apply federal contribution and indemnity law wherever such law preempts analogous state law. *E.g., Miller v. Christopher*, 887 F.2d 902, 905 (9th Cir. 1989) (applying federal common law of contribution, not California state law, to tort case based on federal admiralty law). In *Franklin v. Kaypro Corp.*, 884 F.2d 1222 (9th Cir. 1989), *cert. denied*, 498 U.S. 890 (1990), the court ruled that the right of contribution among tortfeasors in federal securities action is governed by the Federal Securities Act; and that how this contribution right applies is a matter of federal common law. The court rejected the California offset approach to calculating liability of nonsettling defendants, and disparaged the efficacy of the good faith settlement approach. *Franklin*, 884 F. 2d at 1230. Instead, the court adopted the following federal common law (*Id*. at 1231):

> Nonsettling defendants are … barred from further rights of contribution
> from the settling defendants. At trial, the jury is asked not only to determine

the total dollar damage amount, but also the percentage of culpability of each of the settling defendants. Nonsettling defendants as a whole will then be required to pay the percentage of the total amount for which they are responsible. The nonsettling defendants will be jointly and severally liable for that percentage, and will continue to have rights of contribution against one another.

This approach satisfies the statutory goal of punishing each wrongdoer. Patently collusive or inadequate settlements are prohibited. * * *

The goal of equity is also satisfied. Settling defendants pay an amount to which they voluntarily agree. The bar on further contribution extinguishes further risk on their part. Nonsettling defendants never pay more than they would if all parties had gone to trial. This comports with the equitable purpose of contribution.... Furthermore, this approach leaves the burden of proof intact, alleviating [a nonsettling defendant's] complaint that a good faith hearing under section 877.6 forces the burden of proof onto the nonsettling defendants. Obviously, there will be a certain amount of "fingerpointing" at the "empty chair".... However, settling defendants will be protected by the bar order, and the financial motives of both plaintiffs and nonsettling defendants to vigorously press their arguments at trial will be unchanged.

The United States Supreme Court in *McDermott, Inc. v. AmClyde*, 511 U.S. 202, 114 S. Ct. 1461, 128 L. Ed. 2d 148 (1994), adopted the *Franklin v. Kaypro* federal common law approach to settlement and contribution for admiralty jurisdiction cases. The Supreme Court rejected the California offset and good faith settlement approach in favor of a "proportionate share approach" which involves a credit for the settling defendants' proportionate share of responsibility for the total obligation. "Under this approach, no suits for contribution from the settling defendants are permitted, nor are they necessary, because the nonsettling defendants pay no more than their share of the judgment." *McDermott*, 511 U.S. at 209. The Supreme Court's opinion contains an enlightening comparison of the effect of these various possible approaches on judicial economy, settlement, and equitable allocation of liability. *Id*. at 210-217.

Under what circumstances would the federal common law doctrine of contribution apply in the California state courts? *See Hernandez v. Badger Constr. Equip. Co.*, 28 Cal. App. 4th 1791, 1804-10, 34 Cal. Rptr. 2d 732 (1994).

[b] Comparison of Federal and California Approaches

How is the federal common law approach to settlement and indemnity adopted by the courts in *Franklin v. Kaypro* and *McDermott, Inc. v. AmClyde* different than the California approach? In what ways are they similar? Which approach better serves the twin goals of equitable sharing of costs among the parties at fault and the encouragement of settlements? Why? For an excellent discussion of the effect of these various approaches on settlement, see Lewis A. Kornhauser & Richard L. Revesz, *Settlement Under Joint and Several Liability*, 68 N.Y.U. L. Rev. 427 (1993).

§ 10.05 Intervention

[A] The California Requirements

Simpson Redwood Co. v. State of California

Court of Appeal of California, First Appellate District
196 Cal. App. 3d 1192, 242 Cal. Rptr. 447 (1987)

NEWSOM, JUSTICE.

Respondent Simpson Lumber Company (hereafter Simpson) initiated this action by filing a complaint to quiet title and for declaratory relief against the State of California (hereafter the State), seeking title to specified parcels of real property located in Humboldt County in Township 12 North, Range 1 East, Humboldt Meridian. Promptly thereafter, appellant Save-The-Redwoods League (hereafter appellant or the League) filed a motion for leave to intervene (Code Civ. Proc., § 387, subd. (a)) in the action, asserting an interest in the old growth redwood forest sought by Simpson in its complaint. * * *

In 1923, the State began acquiring property for inclusion in the proposed Prairie Creek Redwoods State Park. Appellant contemporaneously embarked upon a program of land acquisition in the area for the purpose of eventual donation to state and federal parks, purchasing property with contributions from its members and other private donors, who were promised that their contributions would be used to preserve redwood groves within the state park system.

The land so acquired by appellant, which includes all of the parcels to which Simpson claims title in this litigation, was donated to the State in 1932 by way of grant deeds. * * * With property donated by appellant and acquired through purchases, the State established Prairie Creek Redwoods State Park (hereafter the Park) in 1933. * * *

Simpson acquired property contiguous to the Park from its predecessor in interest, Sage Land and Improvement Company (hereafter Sage). In 1944, Sage had hired A.B. Bones to determine the precise boundary between its property and the park. * * * The record shows that in conducting its logging operations, Simpson thereafter relied upon Bones's survey, as did the Park. Bones's survey also provided the "base" for subsequent surveys in the area.

Then, in 1978, the Bureau of Land Management performed a "dependent resurvey" of the east boundary of the subject township, and specified adjacent townships (hereafter the BLM survey) in anticipation of the establishment of the Redwood National Park in that area. * * * As a result of the BLM survey, the federal government claimed land for Redwood National Park—in the subject township—formerly accepted as belonging to Simpson. In response, Simpson filed a quiet title action against the federal government in 1980 in federal district court seeking to invalidate the BLM survey. This action was settled by a stipulated judgment, pursuant to which Simpson acknowledged the validity of the BLM survey in exchange for a conveyance of the land it was already occupying and using in accordance with the Gilcrest and Bones surveys.

The survey controversy resurfaced in 1984, however, when the federal government initiated condemnation proceedings against Simpson to acquire property for construction of a bypass for Highway 101 in Humboldt County. Suddenly, Simpson found the BLM survey to its liking because the south-westward shift of boundaries effectuated thereby would result in a claim of additional acreage for which it would receive compensation in the inverse condemnation case. Accordingly, Simpson filed the instant quiet title action, alleging the validity of the BLM survey and resulting entitlement to the small parcel at issue in the federal inverse condemnation proceeding, and claiming title to the remaining 160-acre strip of land along the northwest border of the park. In denying Simpson's right to the latter parcel of property, the State has asserted the priority of the ... survey—the same survey which Simpson previously embraced. The estimated current value of the land at issue is $4 million.

Appellant contends that the trial court erred in denying its motion to intervene in Simpson's quiet title action under section 387, subdivision (a) of the Code of Civil Procedure, which,[2] in pertinent part, provides: "Upon timely application, any person, who has an interest in the matter in litigation, or in the success of either of the parties, or an interest against both, may intervene in the action or proceeding." The purpose of allowing intervention is to promote fairness by involving all parties potentially affected by a judgment. The right to intervene granted by section 387, subdivision (a), is not absolute, however; intervention is properly permitted only if the requirements of the statute have been satisfied. The trial court is vested with discretion to determine whether the standards for intervention have been met.

Simpson argues that appellant's interest in the underlying action is indirect and remote, and so does not justify intervention. It is well settled that the intervener's interest in the matter in litigation must be direct, not consequential, and that it must be an interest which is proper to be determined in the action in which intervention is sought. The "interest" referred to in section 387, subdivision (a), "must be of such direct or immediate character, that the intervener will either gain or lose by the direct legal operation and effect of the judgment." (*Knight v. Alefosio* [(1984)] 158 Cal. App. 3d at p. 721 [205 Cal. Rptr. 42]; ...)

But the nature of the necessary direct interest in the litigation is undescribed by the statute. Nor is the decisional law helpful. As has been said: "[The] point at which one's interest in the success of one of the parties to the action becomes direct, and not consequential, is not easily fixed. It has been the subject of much judicial discussion." (*Fireman's Fund Ins. Co. v. Gerlach* (1976) 56 Cal. App. 3d 299, 302 [128 Cal. Rptr. 396].) Whether the intervener's interest is sufficiently direct must be decided on the facts of each case. (*People ex rel. Rominger v. County of Trinity* (1983) 147 Cal. App. 3d 655, 661 [195 Cal. Rptr. 186]; ...) But it is established that the intervener need neither claim a pecuniary interest nor a specific legal or equitable interest in the

---

2. All further statutory references are to the Code of Civil Procedure unless otherwise indicated.

subject matter of the litigation. And section 387 should be liberally construed in favor of intervention.

We find in the record ample evidence of appellant's direct, substantial interest in the case. Appellant has asserted that its members frequently use the Park for recreational purposes. We learn too from the record that the League was instrumental in the establishment of the Park; in fact, all of the parcels in dispute once belonged to the League, and were donated to the State for the sole and express purpose of inclusion in the Park. Memorial groves, named after members of the League, lie within the disputed area and would certainly not be maintained in their present pristine condition under Simpson's ownership. The League has also claimed, without contradiction, that its reputation and integrity as a conservation organization will suffer if property which it acquired through donation and targeted for preservation is transferred to private ownership for exploitation.

That appellant's members are frequent users of the Park, will not, standing alone, justify intervention. Intervention cannot be predicated *solely* on the League's contribution to the creation of the Park, and while appellant donated the land which comprised a part of the park, it no longer claims a legal or equitable interest in the property in dispute. Moreover, appellant's support for the State's claim to the property is an insufficient basis for intervention. Still, appellant's interests in the underlying litigation extend far beyond a general and historical preference for preservation of the current borders of the Park. The League was formed and continues to exist for the purpose of conserving lands such as those in dispute here in their natural state, and has so represented itself to members and donors. If property acquired by donation in an effort to create and preserve a park is privately exploited, the impact upon appellant's reputation might well translate into loss of future support and contributions.

That appellant will not suffer direct *pecuniary* harm, and has failed to establish with absolute certainty the detriment an adverse judgment might cause, does not defeat its right to intervene. It is not necessary that an intervener's interest " 'be such that he will *inevitably* be affected by the judgment. It is enough that there be a substantial *probability* that his interests will be so affected.' " (*People ex rel. Rominger v. County of Trinity, supra,* 147 Cal. App. 3d 655, 663; …) Here, we think appellant has demonstrated a cognizable interest in perpetuating its role and furthering its avowed policies.

Yet another factor which favors a finding of appellant's direct interest in the subject litigation is its present right to control development of the property, which would of course be altered by a judgment in favor of respondent. As one of the exhibits demonstrate, in donating land to the State the League placed a recital in the deed specifying that such property be used for "state park purposes." " 'It is well settled that where a grant deed is for a specified, limited and definite purpose, the subject of the grant cannot be used for another and different purpose.' [Citations.]" (*Big Sur Properties v. Mott* (1976) 62 Cal. App. 3d 99, 103 [132 Cal. Rptr. 835].) Hence, only as long as the State owns the property in dispute, can appellant rely upon the restrictive language to prevent an inconsistent use of the donated parcels. For this and the related reasons earlier described, we conclude that appellant has demonstrated the requisite specific and direct interest in the outcome of the litigation justifying intervention, and that the trial court's contrary finding was error.

We turn next to the issue of potential delay and confusion which arguably might flow from intervention. Even if otherwise proper, "intervention will not be allowed when it would retard the principal suit, or require a reopening of the case for further evidence, or delay the trial of the action, or change the position of the original parties. [Citation.]" (*Sanders v. Pacific Gas & Elec. Co.* (1975) 53 Cal. App. 3d 661, 669 [126 Cal. Rptr. 415]; …) Respondent argues that such is the case here, in that appellant will raise issues of implied dedication which have not heretofore been presented by the State as part of its claim to the disputed property, thereby impermissibly enlarging the scope of the litigation.

While appellant undeniably intends to introduce new causes of action, our analysis of the nature of such new matters convinces us it will not delay the litigation, change the position of the parties, or even require introduction of additional evidence. Thus, appellant will claim that respondent, in law or in fact, dedicated the land in dispute to the public. Resolution of that issue will center upon essentially the same facts as those involved in the State's claims of adverse possession and agreed boundaries. We perceive no danger that the dedication issue will prolong, confuse or disrupt the present lawsuit.

Nor do we find that intervention would subvert the salutary purposes of section 387, subdivision (b), to obviate delays and prevent a multiplicity of suits arising out of the same facts, while protecting the interests of those affected by the judgment. On the contrary, were intervention to be denied in the present case, appellant would be forced to bring a separate action against Simpson.

A final telling factor in our decision is the conviction that appellant's own substantial interests probably cannot be adequately served by the State's sole participation in the suit, since it here seeks merely to protect its fee interest in the property, which may turn out to be simply pecuniary in nature. The State might, for example, choose to settle the case for a monetary consideration in exchange for relinquishment of its claims of title to the land. But appellant's interest in the litigation—to preserve the property in its natural condition—is singular and indeed unique, and powerfully militates in favor of intervention.

For all of the foregoing reasons we conclude that the trial court's denial of the motion to intervene was an abuse of discretion. The judgment is reversed and the case remanded to the trial court with directions to grant appellant's motion to intervene and to conduct further proceedings in accordance with the views expressed herein. Costs are awarded to appellant Save-The-Redwoods League.

[1] *Permissive Intervention*

As *Simpson Redwood*, reproduced *supra*, indicates, the line between a "direct and immediate" interest which satisfies CCP § 387(a), and an "indirect and consequential" one which is insufficient for permissive intervention, is not always readily apparent.

In *Bustop v. Superior Court,* 69 Cal. App. 3d 66, 71, 137 Cal. Rptr. 793 (1977), the court held that a group of white parents opposed to mandatory busing of students had sufficient interest "in a sound educational system and in the operation of that system in accordance with the law" to permit intervention in an action where a school district was required to formulate a desegregation plan. Such plan would have a "direct social, educational and economic impact" on all students and parents in the district. *Bustop, supra.* Based on this broad view of "direct and immediate interest," what other political action groups could be permitted to intervene in this desegregation litigation? What limitations are there on intervention by such groups?

After the appellate ruling in *Bustop,* another organization entitled BEST (Better Education for Students Today) also sought intervention in the trial court. BEST's complaint in intervention disavowed any position toward any integration plan, but asserted that its members were well-intentioned citizens who would certainly have developed positions on the issues by the time they got to court. Should BEST be permitted to intervene? For a criticism of the reasoning in *Bustop* as an improper extension of the permissive intervention statute, see Stephen C. Yeazell, *Intervention and the Idea of Litigation: A Commentary on the Los Angeles School Case,* 25 UCLA L. Rev. 244 (1977).

In *People ex rel. Rominger v. County of Trinity,* 147 Cal. App. 3d 655, 195 Cal. Rptr. 186 (1983), the Court of Appeal found that the trial court abused its discretion in not permitting the Sierra Club to intervene in litigation between the State of California and the County of Trinity. The State sought declaratory and injunctive relief, alleging that the County's ordinance prohibiting aerial spraying of phenoxy herbicides was preempted by state law. The Sierra Club sought to intervene, alleging, among other grounds, that its members would be specifically harmed if spraying resumed in Trinity County. The Sierra Club asserted that its members use these forest lands and exposure to these chemicals would harm them. The Court of Appeal concluded that the Sierra Club, as representative of its members who use the resources of Trinity County, has a direct and immediate, rather than consequential and remote, interest in this litigation. *Rominger,* 147 Cal. App. 3d at 663.

Would the type of interest alleged by the Sierra Club in *Rominger,* by itself, be considered "direct and immediate" under the *Simpson Redwood* reasoning? What type of interest alleged by the Save-the-Redwoods League did that court consider sufficient for permissive intervention? Insufficient? Do you understand why these distinctions were made?

[a] Direct Interest

Which of the following parties assert a direct interest sufficient to permit intervention under CCP § 387(a)?

(1) A local historic preservation organization which is opposed to the construction of a proposed apartment complex to be located adjacent to a single-family residential neighborhood designated an historic district, and seeks to intervene in litigation between the developer and the city over the right to a city construction permit? An as-

sociation of homeowners who reside in the historic district? The president of the association who, as a taxpayer, seeks to complain of waste of city funds? And who also resides in the historic district? *See Highland Dev. Co. v. City of Los Angeles*, 170 Cal. App. 3d 169, 179-80, 215 Cal. Rptr. 881 (1985).

(2) A school district, the ultimate beneficiary of a city's school impact fee policy, which seeks to intervene in an action brought by subdividers against the city to declare unconstitutional the city resolution adopting the school impact fee policy? A legislatively-created Local Agency Formation Commission whose statutory purpose is to discourage urban sprawl and encourage orderly development of local governmental agencies, which seeks to intervene in the same litigation? *See Timberidge Enter., Inc. v. City of Santa Rosa*, 86 Cal. App. 3d 873, 150 Cal. Rptr. 606 (1978).

(3) An automobile insurance company that has paid property damage benefits to its insured after an auto accident and under the policy is subrogated to its insured rights, which seeks to intervene as a partial subrogee in a personal injury and property damage action brought by its insured against the other driver? *See Hausmann v. Farmers Ins. Exch.*, 213 Cal. App. 2d 611, 29 Cal. Rptr. 75 (1963). An insurer who denies coverage and refuses to defend its insured when sued by an injured plaintiff? *See Hinton v. Beck*, 176 Cal. App. 4th 1378, 98 Cal. Rptr. 3d 612 (2009). An automobile insurer who defends its insured when sued by an injured plaintiff but reserves the right to contest coverage, when the insured attempts to settle the case without the participation of the insurer? *See Gray v. Begley*, 182 Cal. App. 4th 1509, 106 Cal. Rptr. 3d 729 (2010).

(4) Individual investors who seek restitution of their investment funds and request permission to intervene in a civil action brought by the district attorney against defendants for investment fraud involving the sale of oil contracts, where the district attorney and defendants have proposed settlement which would take much of defendants' resources for statutory civil penalties. *See People v. Superior Court (Good)*, 17 Cal. 3d 732, 736-37, 131 Cal. Rptr. 800, 552 P.2d 760 (1976).

[b] Discretion

Granting or denying leave to intervene under § 387(a) is in the discretion of the trial court. *See, e.g., Lincoln National Life Ins. Co. v. State Bd. of Equalization*, 30 Cal. App. 4th 1411, 36 Cal. Rptr. 2d 397 (1994) (ruling that unless a special statute prohibits intervention, the trial court's discretion to permit intervention should be liberally construed in favor of intervention). Even if an applicant establishes the requisite interest in the litigation, a trial court may deny permissive intervention. What factors did the court in *Simpson Redwood* consider in exercising this discretion? How did it apply these factors?

In *Royal Indemnity Co. v. United Enterprises, Inc.*, 162 Cal. App. 4th 194, 75 Cal. Rptr. 3d 481 (2009), the court outlined the general guidelines for allowing permissive intervention:

> Under section 387, subdivision (a), the trial court in its discretion may allow a third party to intervene in litigation pending between other parties

if "(1) the proper procedures have been followed; (2) the nonparty has a direct and immediate interest in the action; (3) the intervention will not enlarge the issues in the litigation; and (4) the reasons for the intervention outweigh any opposition by the parties presently in the action. The permissive intervention statute balances the interests of others who will be affected by the judgment against the interests of the original parties in pursuing their litigation unburdened by others."

Royal Indemnity, supra, 162 Cal. App. at 203–204 (quoting *City and County of San Francisco v. State of California,* 128 Cal. App. 4th 1030, 1036–39, 27 Cal. Rptr. 3d 722 (2005)).

[2] Intervention of Right

In 1977, the Legislature enacted CCP § 387(b), which added intervention of right to traditional permissive intervention:

> If any provision of law confers an unconditional right to intervene or if the person seeking intervention claims an interest relating to the property or transaction which is the subject of the action and that person is so situated that the disposition of the action may as a practical matter impair or impede that person's ability to protect that interest, unless that person's interest is adequately represented by existing parties, the court shall, upon timely application, permit that person to intervene.

CCP § 387(b) is modeled after Rule 24(b), F.R.C.P. *See* Comment, *Civil Procedure; Intervention,* 9 Pac. L.J. 356-58 (1978).

[a] Statutory Prerequisites of CCP § 387(b)

In the absence of a statute which confers an unconditional right to intervene, a person seeking leave to intervene of right must demonstrate the satisfaction of three prerequisites. What are they? Did the Save-the-Redwoods League meet these criteria in *Simpson Redwood*? Although numerous federal court decisions liberally construe federal Rule 24(b), there are very few California appellate court decisions construing CCP § 387(b). *See, e.g., Hodge v. Kirkpatrick Dev., Inc.,* 130 Cal. App. 4th 540, 30 Cal. Rptr. 3d 303 (2005) (holding an insurance company has the right to intervene in a construction defect lawsuit brought by insureds against third party tortfeasors, where the insurance company obtained partial subrogation rights against the third parties by paying a portion of the insured's claims for property damages to their house); *California Physicians' Serv. v. Superior Court,* 102 Cal. App. 3d 91, 162, Cal. Rptr. 266 (1980) (construing "transaction" and "interest impairment" in § 387). What advantage is there to pursuing intervention of right as opposed to permissive intervention?

[b] Special Statutes

A number of special statutes confer an unconditional right to intervene within the meaning of § 387(b), such as CCP § 1250.230 (any person claiming interest in property subject of eminent domain proceeding), Corporations Code § 1800(c) (a shareholder or creditor of corporation authorized to intervene in involuntary dissolution proceedings against the corporation), Civil Code § 1781(e)(3) (members of consumer class action authorized to intervene through counsel), Gov. Code § 12606, Water Code § 2780, and Labor Code § 3853 (employer has unconditional right to intervene in action by an employee, injured in the course of employment, against third party). Code of Civil Procedure § 389.5 authorizes a party who has an interest in the subject of an action to recover or claim property to make application to the court to be made a party. How is this joinder statute different than CCP § 387?

[B] Intervention Procedures

[1] Status of Intervener

An intervener becomes an actual party to the action, either a plaintiff or defendant (unless adverse to both), with all of the same procedural rights and remedies of the original parties. *See Catello v. I.T.T. General Controls*, 152 Cal. App. 3d 1009, 1013, 200 Cal. Rptr. 4 (1984). Although courts often state that an intervener "must take the proceedings as it finds them at the time of intervention," *e.g.*, *Hospital Council of N. California v. Superior Court*, 30 Cal. App. 3d 331, 336, 106 Cal. Rptr. 247 (1973); *Bustop v. Superior Court, supra*, 69 Cal. App. 3d at 72; an intervener is not limited by every procedural decision made by the original parties. For example, an intervener may move to disqualify a judge, even if the parties are content to try the lawsuit in that court; may object to the jurisdiction of the court or that pleadings do not state a cause of action; and may not be deprived of its right to jury trial by the parties' waiver. *See, e.g.*, *Deutschmann v. Sears Roebuck & Co.*, 132 Cal. App. 3d 912, 916, 183 Cal. Rptr. 573 (1982), and cases cited therein. An intervener may pursue affirmative relief not sought by the plaintiff, *e.g.*, *Belt-Casualty Co. v. Furman*, 218 Cal. 359, 23 P.2d 293 (1933); and may appeal an adverse judgment even where the original party defaults, *e.g.*, *Jade K. v. Viguri*, 210 Cal. App. 3d 1459, 1468, 258 Cal. Rptr. 907 (1989).

[2] Timely Application

A party seeking intervention, whether permissive or of right, must make a "timely application" to the court. CCP § 387(a) & (b). *See Ziani Homeowners Assn. v. Brookfield Ziani*, 243 Cal. App. 4th 274, 196 Cal. Rtpr. 3d 399 (2015) (ruling timeliness of motion to intervene based upon the date movants knew or should have known their interests were not being adequately protected in the litigation, not upon the date the complaint was filed). What constitutes a timely application varies with the circumstances of each case, and ultimately depends on the court's discretion. In *Mallick v. Superior Court*, 89 Cal. App. 3d 434, 152 Cal. Rptr. 503 (1979), for example, the court permitted class members to intervene to remove the class representative, even though the action was pending on appeal. The court noted that "intervention is possible, if otherwise appropriate, at any time, even after judgment." *Mallick*, 89 Cal. App. 3d at 437.

A person who is legally aggrieved by a judgment may become a party to the record and obtain a right to appeal by moving to vacate the judgment, *County of Alameda v. Carleson*, 5 Cal. 3d 730, 736-37, 97 Cal. Rptr. 385, 488 P.2d 953 (1971); or by moving for a new trial, *Lippman v. City of Los Angeles*, 234 Cal. App. 3d 1630, 286 Cal. Rptr. 406 (1991). The intervenor must have an "immediate, pecuniary, and substantial" interest in the judgment. *County of Alameda v. Carleson, supra.*

Intervention may be denied where there is an unreasonable delay after learning of the action. *E.g., Sanders v. Pacific Gas & Elec. Co.*, 53 Cal. App. 3d 661, 668, 126 Cal. Rptr. 415 (1975). In *Northern California Psychiatric Society v. City of Berkeley*, 178 Cal. App. 3d 90, 223 Cal. Rptr. 609 (1986), for example, the court ruled that a coalition's motion to intervene was not timely where the coalition had been involved in the litigation for six months as amicus but did not seek to intervene until after a summary judgment motion was fully briefed and argued, and the trial court had already indicated its intention to grant summary judgment. But in *Jade K. v. Viguri*, 210 Cal. App. 3d 1459, 1468, 258 Cal. Rptr. 907 (1989), the court considered timely an insurance company's complaint in intervention seeking to vacate and appeal a default entered against its insured because the insurance company was never notified of the default.

[3] *Intervention Application Procedure*

An application for intervention is made by a "complaint in intervention" setting forth the grounds upon which the intervention rests, filed with the court and served on existing parties. CCP § 387(a). The intervener's pleading is entitled "Complaint in Intervention" regardless of whether the intervener seeks to be regarded as a plaintiff or a defendant, or claims adversely to both. CCP § 387(a), *see Timberidge Enter., Inc. v. City of Santa Rosa*, 86 Cal. App. 3d 873, 150 Cal. Rptr. 606 (1978). The complaint in intervention must set forth the grounds upon which intervention rests and otherwise comply with CCP § 387. *Bowles v. Superior Court*, 44 Cal. 2d 574, 589, 263 P.2d 704 (1955) (holding complaint in intervention defective because it did not allege that applicants joined with plaintiff or united with defendants, or demanded anything adverse to both); *Sutter Health Uninsured Pricing Cases*, 171 Cal. App. 4th 495, 513, 89 Cal. Rptr. 3d 615 (2009) (ruling failure to tender a proposed complaint in intervention constitutes a proper basis for denial of a motion to intervene).

There can be no actual intervention without leave of court. CCP § 387(a); *Lohnes v. Astron Computer Products*, 94 Cal. App. 4th 1150, 115 Cal. Rptr. 2d 34 (2001) (ruling that whether intervention is permissive or mandatory, a petition to seek leave to intervene is required; without the permission of the court, a party lacks any standing to the action).

An order denying leave to intervene is immediately appealable. *See Bowles, supra*, 44 Cal. 2d at 582; *County of Alameda v. Carleson*, 5 Cal. 3d 730, 736, 97 Cal. Rptr. 385, 488 P.2d 953 (1971); but an order granting leave to intervene may be reviewed only on appeal from final judgment, *see Adoption of Lenn E., supra*, 182 Cal App. 3d at 217-18. Why? *See generally* Chapter 15, Appeals and Writs, *infra*. Where the question litigated is purely one of law, a person denied leave to intervene may obtain substantially the same advantage of intervention by permission to file an amicus brief. *See, e.g., Squire v. City & County of San Francisco*, 12 Cal. App. 3d 974, 979, 91 Cal. Rptr. 347 (1970).

[C]   Federal Intervention Rules

[1]   *Intervention of Right*

Rule 24(a), F.R.C.P., governs intervention of right, and is nearly identical to CCP § 387(b). The federal courts have been quite liberal in finding the requisite interest, practical impairment, and inadequate representation. *See generally* Wright, Miller & Kane, *Federal Practice and Procedure: Civil 3d* §§ 1904, 1906-1909 (West 2007). Rule 24(a) clearly does not require that the would-be intervener will be legally bound to establish that "the disposition of the action may as a practical matter impair or impede" his ability to protect his interest. *Advisory Committee Notes to Rule 24(a)(2)*, 39 F.R.P. 69, 110 (1966). Indeed, in proper circumstances, even the stare decisis effect of the judgment in an action may supply the practical disadvantage which warrants intervention of right. *See, e.g., Atlantis Dev. Corp. v. United States*, 379 F.2d 818, 828-29 (5th Cir. 1967); *Corby Recreation, Inc. v. General Elec. Co.*, 581 F.2d 175, 177 (8th Cir. 1978); *Federal Practice and Procedure, supra*, § 1908.2.

[2]   *Permissive Intervention*

Rule 24(b), F.R.C.P., permits intervention, upon timely application and in the trial court's discretion, when an applicant's claim or defense and the existing action have "a question of law and fact in common." This federal permissive intervention standard is much broader than that of CCP § 387(a). How so? Rule 24(b) does not require that an applicant have any direct personal interest in the subject of the litigation. *See Federal Practice and Procedure, supra*, § 1911. However, the federal justiciability doctrines, particularly the doctrine of standing, may impose a similar interest requirement. *See, e.g., Warth v. Seldin*, 422 U.S. 490, 95 S. Ct. 2197, 45 L. Ed. 2d 343 (1975) (holding an intervening plaintiff must demonstrate a distinct and palpable injury to itself caused by defendant in order to satisfy standing doctrine). And, as with all federal joinder devices, a federal court must have subject matter jurisdiction of persons and claims sought to be added by Rule 24 intervention. *See* 28 U.S.C. § 1367.

§ 10.06 Capacity, Real Party in Interest, and Standing

[A]   Capacity

A party who possesses a right under substantive law must have the "capacity" to sue or be sued. Problems arise in two types of cases: (1) Incapacity of a person due to a disability; and, (2) incapacity of an organization not legally recognized as an entity for purposes of suit. *See generally California Civil Practice — Procedure* §§ 3:7-3:13 (2015); 4 Witkin, *California Procedure, Pleading*, §§ 70-119 (5th ed. 2008).

[1] Disability

[a] Minors and Incompetents

The most common form of "disability" for a natural person is infancy or incompetency. A minor or incompetent person must appear through either a guardian appointed to represent that person's interests generally, or by a guardian ad litem appointed by the court for a specific lawsuit. CCP §§ 372, 373. A guardian ad litem is not a party to the lawsuit but only a representative of the minor or incompetent, *In re Marriage of Higgason*, 10 Cal. 3d 476, 484, 110 Cal. Rptr. 897, 516 P.2d 289 (1973); and has limited power to make procedural litigation decisions, but has no power to compromise the ward's substantive rights without approval by the court. CCP §§ 372, 373.5; *see Torres v. Friedman*, 169 Cal. App. 3d 880, 887, 215 Cal. Rptr. 604 (1985) (ruling guardian ad litem is essentially an agent of the court whose duty is to protect rights of the ward; and cannot prejudice ward's substantive rights by admissions, waiver, or stipulations).

Failure to appoint a guardian ad litem for a minor is not a jurisdictional defect—judgment entered against an unrepresented minor is not void but is voidable by the minor after she attains majority. *E.g., Hughes v. Quackenbush*, 1 Cal. App. 2d 349, 362, 37 P.2d 99 (1934). The procedure for appointment of a guardian ad litem is governed by CCP § 373. The appointment may properly be made on an *ex parte* application. *Sarracino v. Superior Court*, 13 Cal. 3d 1, 118 Cal. Rptr. 21, 529 P.2d 53 (1974). A guardian ad litem who is not himself an attorney must employ one. *Torres v. Friedman, supra.* Why? *See* Business & Professions Code § 6125.

[b] Corporations

A corporation may be "disabled"—incapable of suing or defending in a particular case—when it has not complied with certain statutory requirements. *E.g.,* Corp. Code § 2203(c) (foreign corporation must comply with certain statutory conditions before transacting business); Rev. & Tax. Code §§ 23301, 23301.5 (failure to pay state franchise taxes may preclude corporation from prosecuting or defending actions). A suspended corporation may have its powers reinstated after satisfying its statutory obligations. Rev. & Tax. Code § 23305. What are the consequences of suspension and of subsequent revival of powers? *See, e.g., Palm Valley Homeowners Assn., Inc. v. Design MTC*, 85 Cal. App. 4th 553, 102 Cal. Rptr. 2d 350 (2000) (ruling corporation suspended under the Corporations Code for failure to file required statements disabled from participating in litigation activities); *Bourghis v. Lord*, 56 Cal. 4th 320, 153 Cal. Rptr. 3d 510, 295 P.3d 895 (2013) (holding that although notices of appeal filed by suspended corporation were invalid when filed, the corporation may proceed with the appeals after its corporate powers have been revived even if the revival occurs after the time for appeal has expired); *ABA Recovery Services, Inc. v. Konold*, 198 Cal. App. 3d 720, 244 Cal. Rptr. 27 (1988) (holding a corporation suspended for failure to pay taxes lacked legal capacity to bring civil action, and the action will be barred if statute of limitations runs out before revival of corporation's powers under Rev. & Tax Code § 23305).

At common law, a dissolved corporation ceased to exist and could not sue or be sued. However, under Corporations Code §§ 2010-2011 a party may sue a dissolved corporation, even though the defendant corporation had already dissolved prior to the time the action was filed. *Penasquitos, Inc. v. Superior Court*, 53 Cal. 3d 1180, 283 Cal. Rptr. 135, 812 P.2d 154 (1991) (holding § 2010 permits not only continuation of, but also the initiation of, suits against dissolved domestic corporations); *but see Greb v. Diamond Int'l Corp.*, 56 Cal. 4th 243, 153 Cal. Rptr. 3d 198, 295 P.3d 198 (2013) (holding California's survival statute, Corp. Code § 2010, does not apply to foreign corporations—those formed in states other than California—transacting business in California). What about a corporation which disappears through merger during a pending action? *See* Corp. Code § 1107. Before litigation commences?

[2] Entity Status of Organizations

Natural persons, corporations, and government bodies are generally considered entities which have the capacity to sue or be sued. Corporations Code § 207 ("[A] corporation shall have all of the powers of a natural person in carrying out its business activities."); Government Code § 945 ("A public entity may sue or be sued."). Under former California common law, and current law in some other states, an unincorporated association was not considered a legal entity which had the capacity to sue or be sued.

[a] Partnerships and Other Unincorporated Associations

However, under CCP § 369.5 [formerly § 388] entity status is now conferred on partnerships and other unincorporated associations such that they may sue or be sued in their own organizational name. *See, e.g., Clean Air Transp. Sys. v. San Mateo Cnty. Transit Dist.*, 198 Cal. App. 3d 576, 243 Cal. Rptr. 799 (1988), *cert. denied*, 488 U.S. 862 (1988) (holding unincorporated association has capacity to sue as a distinct legal entity, but must be represented by counsel in court); *Barr v. United Methodist Church*, 90 Cal. App. 3d 259, 266, 153 Cal. Rptr. 322 (1979) (ruling church may be sued as a legal entity under former CCP § 388(a); "The criteria applied to determine whether an entity is an unincorporated association are no more complicated than (1) a group whose members have a common purpose, and (2) who function under a common name under circumstances where fairness requires the group be recognized as a legal entity."). A plaintiff therefore may sue an unincorporated association, its individual members, or both. CCP § 369.5.

[b] Estates

Although an estate is generally not considered a legal entity with capacity to sue or be sued, an action to establish a decedent's liability for which the decedent was protected by insurance may be commenced or continued against the decedent's estate without the need to join as a party the decedent's personal representative or successor in interest. Probate Code §§ 550-555; *see Van Gibson v. Estate of Lynch*, 197 Cal. App. 3d 725, 243 Cal. Rptr. 50 (1988) (holding plaintiff in negligence action for personal injuries could sue decedent's personal representative pursuant to Prob. Code § 573 [now CCP § 377.42] or the decedent's estate pursuant to Prob. Code § 550, or could pursue both remedies).

[3]   Raising the Capacity Issue

Unless the governing statute states otherwise, a complaint need not allege the plaintiff's capacity to sue. *Hydrotech Sys., Ltd. v. Oasis Waterpark, supra,* 52 Cal. 3d at 994, n.4. The question of capacity may be raised by demurrer or by answer. CCP §§ 430.10(b), 430.30. If not so raised, the objection of lack of capacity is waived. CCP § 430.80; *see Tinsley v. Palo Alto Unified Sch. Dist.,* 91 Cal. App. 3d 871, 883, 154 Cal. Rptr. 591 (1979).

[4]   Capacity in Federal Court

Rule 17(b), F.R.C.P., governs the question of capacity to sue or be sued in federal court. Rule 17(b) generally requires application of state capacity law. For example, capacity of an individual shall be determined by the law of the individual's domicile, and of a corporation by the law under which it is organized. *See, e.g., Community Elec. Serv. v. National Elec. Contractors Assn., Inc.,* 869 F.2d 1235, 1239 (9th Cir. 1989) (ruling capacity of plaintiff corporation is determined by law of California, the state of incorporation, per Rule 17(b); and holding plaintiff suspended under Cal. Rev. & Tax Code § 23301 for failure to pay state franchise taxes lacked capacity to bring federal antitrust suit in federal court). In all other cases, the law of the state in which the district court is located applies, except that an unincorporated association may always sue or be sued in its common name for purposes of asserting a federal constitutional or statutory right. Rule 17(b). Why this difference for unincorporated associations asserting federal rights?

[B]   Real Party in Interest and Standing

[1]   The General California Doctrine

Code of Civil Procedure § 367 provides: "Every action must be prosecuted in the name of the real party in interest, except as otherwise provided by statute."

Hector F. v. El Centro Elementary School District

Court of Appeal of California, Fourth Appellate District
227 Cal. App. 4th 331, 173 Cal. Rptr. 3d 413 (2014)

BENKE, ACTING P. JUSTICE.

By way of its enactment of a scheme of interrelated statutes, the Legislature has imposed on public schools in California an affirmative duty to protect public school students from discrimination and harassment engendered by race, gender, sexual orientation or disability. In particular, Education Code section 32282 requires that public schools develop and implement comprehensive school safety plans which include a discrimination and harassment policy. (Ed. Code, § 32282, subd. (a)(2)(E).)

The Legislature has encouraged schools to include in their safety plans, "to the extent that resources are available, … policies and procedures aimed at the prevention of bullying." (Ed. Code, § 32282, subd. (f).)

Appellant Hector F. is the father of three children. While Hector's oldest son, Brian, was a student at King Elementary School (King) and Kennedy Middle School (Kennedy), in El Centro, Brian was diagnosed with a number of emotional disabilities. Although an individualized education plan was developed for Brian, according to Hector's petition for a writ of mandate, Brian was subjected to physical and verbal abuse by other children because of his disabilities and the fact that English is his second language. In response to complaints about the abuse Hector and his wife made, Hector alleges school officials did not intervene and provide any protection for Brian, but instead suggested Brian change classrooms.

Hector filed a complaint for damages and a petition for a writ of mandate in the trial court. Hector, as guardian ad litem, sought damages on behalf of Brian and, on his own behalf, relief in mandate and as a taxpayer requiring that respondent El Centro Elementary School District (the district), which operates King and Kennedy, comply with the requirements of the discrimination and harassment provisions of the Government Code and the Education Code. In particular Hector alleged on information and belief that the district has neither adopted nor implemented comprehensive safety plans for its schools that meet the requirements of Education Code section 32282.

Brian matriculated from Kennedy before these proceedings commenced and attends a high school operated by a separate school district. However, Hector's younger two children were enrolled at King at the time Hector filed his petition.

The district filed a demurrer to that portion of Hector's complaint and petition in which Hector sought relief on his own behalf. The district asserted that because Brian no longer attends any school operated by the district and because Hector has not alleged his other children have been subjected to discrimination or harassment, Hector does not have standing to assert, as an individual, and on his own behalf, any violation of the statutory provisions he relies upon. The trial court sustained the district's demurrer without leave to amend and entered judgment in favor of the district on Hector's individual claims. We reverse.

As a citizen and taxpayer Hector has standing to seek enforcement of laws in which there is an identified public as well as private interest. The statutory provisions asserted by Hector articulate a well identified public interest in maintaining a system of taxpayer-funded public education which is free of the destructive influence of discrimination, harassment and bullying. Because Hector has standing to bring his claims, we reverse the judgment and remand for further proceedings. * * *

PROCEDURAL HISTORY

In January 2012, Hector … filed a complaint against the district for damages on behalf of Brian. [An amended complaint, filed on behalf of Brian and Hector] alleged three causes of action, which seek relief by way of mandate, one cause of action for declaratory relief, one cause of action, which alleges the waste of taxpayer funds, and one cause of action for negligence. The mandate and declaratory relief causes of action alleged violations of the state's antidiscrimination and antiharassment statutes; the mandate causes of action asked for an order compelling the district to comply with its statutory obligations and the declaratory relief action asked for a determination the district violated those obligations.

The taxpayer cause of action alleged the district wasted funds in responding to harassment complaints because the district did so in a manner which discriminated against Hispanic students and students with disabilities. The negligence cause of action alleged that the district and individual employees of the district did not properly respond to complaints that Brian was being subjected to physical and verbal abuse.

The district filed a demurrer to the [amended complaint] in which it argued that neither Brian nor Hector had standing to seek any mandatory or declaratory relief. * * * The trial court sustained the demurrer without leave to amend and entered a judgment of dismissal against Hector. [Hector appealed.]

DISCUSSION

* * *

II

As we noted at the outset, the Legislature has enacted a scheme of interrelated statutes, which attempt to protect public school students from discrimination and harassment engendered by race, gender, sexual orientation or disability. By its terms Government Code section 11135, subdivision (a) states in pertinent part: "No person in the State of California shall, on the basis of race, national origin, ethnic group identification, religion, age, sex, sexual orientation, color, genetic information, or disability, be unlawfully denied full and equal access to the benefits of, or be unlawfully subjected to discrimination under, any program or activity that is conducted, operated, or administered by the state or by any state agency, is funded directly by the state, or receives any financial assistance from the state."

In turn, Education Code section 201 states in pertinent part:

"(a) All pupils have the right to participate fully in the educational process, free from discrimination and harassment.

"(b) California's public schools have an affirmative obligation to combat racism, sexism, and other forms of bias, and a responsibility to provide equal educational opportunity. * * *

As a means of implementing the right of students to be free of discrimination and harassment set forth in Education Code section 201, Education Code section 32281, subdivision (a) provides that each school district is responsible for the development of comprehensive school safety plans for each of its schools. Education Code section 32282, subdivision (a)(2)(E) provides that, among other matters, each comprehensive school safety plan shall include a "discrimination and harassment policy consistent with the prohibition against discrimination contained in [Education Code section

201]." Education Code section 32282, subdivision (f) further provides that: "As comprehensive school safety plans are reviewed and updated, the Legislature encourages all plans, to the extent that resources are available, to include policies and procedures aimed at the prevention of bullying."

As we explain, *post*, Hector had standing to seek enforcement of these antidiscrimination and antiharassment enactments.

III

In the seminal case of *Green v. Obledo* (1981) 29 Cal.3d 126, 144 [172 Cal. Rptr. 206, 624 P.2d 256], the court set forth the standing principles which govern Hector's mandate claims: "It is true that ordinarily the writ of mandate will be issued only to persons who are 'beneficially interested.'" (Code Civ. Proc., § 1086.) Yet, in *Bd. of Soc. Welfare v. County of L.A.* (1945) 27 Cal.2d 98 [162 P.2d 627], this court recognized an exception to the general rule "'where the question is one of public right and the object of the mandamus is to procure the enforcement of a public duty, the [plaintiff] need not show that he has any legal or special interest in the result, since it is sufficient that he is interested as a citizen in having the laws executed and the duty in question enforced'" (*id.*, at pp. 100-101). The exception promotes the policy of guaranteeing citizens the opportunity to ensure that no governmental body impairs or defeats the purpose of legislation establishing a public right. (*Id.* at p. 100.) It has often been invoked by California courts. (*Green v. Obledo*, at p. 144.)

In *Green v. Obledo*, the plaintiffs challenged a state regulation, which limited the work-related expenses welfare recipients could exclude from their household income in calculating the amount of their welfare grants. In particular the regulation provided a flat mileage rate deduction for automobile use rather than a recipient's actual automobile costs. However the regulation also imposed limitations on the amount of other work-related expenses that could be deducted from household income.

The plaintiffs alleged the regulation was in conflict with the federal law, which established and governed the welfare program, and alleged further that their actual transportation costs exceeded the amount of the mileage allowance permitted under the regulation. The plaintiffs, although they did not allege that the other work-related expense limitations had affected them, challenged the regulation in its entirety and sought relief in mandate from it.

The trial court found the plaintiffs had standing to challenge the automobile expense limitations, but had no standing with respect to the remainder of the regulation. The Supreme Court disagreed and found standing with respect to the entire statute: "There can be no question that the proper calculation of AFDC benefits is a matter of public right [citation], and plaintiffs herein are certainly citizens seeking to procure the enforcement of a public duty. [Citation.] It follows that plaintiffs have standing to seek a writ of mandate commanding defendants to cease enforcing [the regulation] in its entirety. The trial court erred in ruling otherwise, and in limiting the scope of the evidentiary hearing accordingly. Plaintiffs are therefore entitled to a new hearing on their cause of action for writ of mandate, and to a determination of the validity of the remainder of the regulation." (*Green v. Obledo, supra,* 29 Cal.3d at p. 145, fn. omitted.)

Significantly, the public interest exception to the rule requiring litigants seeking mandate have a beneficial interest in the relief they seek has been applied with respect to duties imposed by the Legislature on schools and school districts. In *Doe v. Albany Unified School Dist.* (2010) 190 Cal.App.4th 668 [118 Cal. Rptr. 3d 507] (*Doe*), the court considered relief available under the provisions of Education Code section 51210, which require that public school curriculum include not less than 200 minutes of physical education each 10 school days. In finding the public interest exception applied to permit enforcement of the physical education requirement by members of the public, the court stated: "As for plaintiff Donald D., if his interest as the parent of plaintiff Doe in the latter's education is not a sufficient beneficial interest in itself [citation], he certainly has an interest as a citizen in seeing that section 51210, subdivision (g), is properly enforced. 'The beneficial interest standard is so broad, even citizen or taxpayer standing may be sufficient to obtain relief in mandamus. "[W]here a public right is involved, and the object of the writ of mandate is to procure enforcement of a public duty," a citizen is beneficially interested within the meaning of Code of Civil Procedure section 1086 if "he is interested in having the public duty enforced." ' [Citation.] This public interest exception " 'promotes the policy of guaranteeing citizens the opportunity to ensure that no governmental body impairs or defeats the purpose of legislation establishing a public right.' "" (*Doe, supra,* 190 Cal.App.4th at p. 685.) * * *

The public interest exception is not unlimited and does not provide the public standing in all contexts. Indeed the court in *Green v. Obledo, supra,* 29 Cal.3d at p. 145 recognized the public interest exception "may be outweighed in a proper case by competing considerations of a more urgent nature." * * * In *Sacramento County Fire Protection Dist. v. Sacramento County Assessment Appeals Bd.* (1999) 75 Cal.App.4th 327, 330-335 [89 Cal. Rptr. 2d 215], a local assessment appeals board accepted a stipulation between a county assessor and a landowner substantially reducing the value of a large tract of land that had been contaminated. By virtue of the reduction, a local fire district was required to pay the landowner a substantial refund of taxes the district had collected. The court found the district had no special interest in the assessment over and above the interest of the public at large and that allowing the district to challenge the reduced assessment by mandate under the public interest exception would undermine the assessment process in which the district's interest was adequately represented by the county. (*Id.* at pp. 331-334.)

Here, there is a manifest public interest in enforcing the antidiscrimination and antiharassment statutes Hector asserts. Indeed in enacting the statutes the Legislature itself has articulated that interest: "It is the policy of the State of California to afford all persons in public schools, regardless of their disability, gender, gender identity, gender expression, nationality, race or ethnicity, religion, sexual orientation, or any other characteristic ... equal rights and opportunities in the educational institutions of the state. The purpose of this chapter is to prohibit acts that are contrary to that policy and to provide remedies therefor." (Ed. Code, § 200.) More particularly in enacting Education Code section 201, the Legislature found both that: "(c) Harassment on school grounds directed at an individual on the basis of personal characteristics or status creates a hostile environment and jeopardizes equal educational opportunity as guaranteed by the California Constitution and the United States Constitution" and "(d) There is an urgent need to prevent and respond to acts of hate violence and bias-related incidents that are occurring at an increasing rate in California's public schools." (*Id.* at subds. (c) & (d).)

Plainly the public interest in ensuring public schools are free from discrimination, harassment and bullying as articulated in Government Code section 11135, and Education Code sections 200, 201, 220, 32261, 32280, 32281 and 32282, is as great or greater than the public interest in assuring schools provide the mandated minimum number of hours of physical education the court considered in *Doe*. Thus a strong argument can be made that if the public interest exception permits members of the public to enforce the relatively narrow physical education requirements of Education Code 51210, members of the public may also enforce the broader provisions protecting students from discrimination, harassment and bullying. * * *

In sum then, Hector's attempt to enforce the antidiscrimination and antiharassment statutes adopted by the Legislature falls squarely within the public interest exception to the rule, which otherwise requires a beneficial interest in mandate actions. There is a manifest public interest in enforcing the antibullying statutes and there are no urgent competing interests which outweigh that public interest. Thus, the trial court erred in sustaining the district's demurrer on the grounds Hector lacked standing.

In particular, Hector had standing to assert his first three causes of action, which expressly seek relief in mandate. The public interest in enforcing the antidiscrimination and antiharassment statutes also provides Hector with standing to bring a taxpayer action under Code of Civil Procedure section 526a.

DISPOSITION

The judgment dismissing Hector's claim is reversed with instructions to vacate the order sustaining the district's demurrer. Hector is to recover his costs of appeal.

Notes and Questions regarding Real Party in Interest/standing Doctrine

(1) The real party in interest/standing doctrine is related to the doctrine of capacity; and in some cases, such as the right of an assignee or subrogee to sue, they are virtually indistinguishable. However, unlike lack of capacity to sue where a party has a cause of action but is unable to assert it due to "disability," lack of standing goes to the very existence of a cause of action. *See, e.g., McKinny v. Bd. of Trustees,* 31 Cal. 3d 79, 90, 181 Cal. Rptr. 549, 642 P.2d 460 (1982) ("It is elementary that a plaintiff who lacks standing cannot state a valid cause of action"). Consequently, an objection to standing is not waived by failure to raise it by demurrer or answer, and may be raised at any point in the proceedings. *Common Cause v. Bd. of Super-*

visors, 49 Cal. 3d 432, 438, 261 Cal. Rptr. 574, 777 P.2d 610 (1989); *McKinny v. Bd. of Trustees, supra.*

(2) Code of Civil Procedure Section 367 requires that every action be prosecuted in the name of the "real party in interest," but does not generally define what that phrase means. Unless a statute specifically grants standing, the real party determination is made by reference to the substantive law—the person possessing the right to sue under the applicable substantive law ordinarily is the real party in interest. *See, e.g., Wallner v. Parry Prof'l Bldg., Ltd.*, 22 Cal. App. 4th 1446, 1449, 27 Cal. Rptr. 2d 834 (1994) (concluding that when a partnership has a claim, the real party in interest is the partnership; but a limited partner held to be the real party in interest in a limited partner's derivative action to enforce a claim which the limited partnership possesses against the general partners but which the partnership refuses to enforce); *County of Alameda v. State Bd. of Control*, 14 Cal. App. 4th 1096, 18 Cal. Rptr. 2d 487 (1993) (holding county and county taxpayer lacked standing to assert claims of crime victims for reimbursement from state Crime Restitution Fund because statutory substantive right to make such a claim belongs only to crime victims under Gov. Code §§ 13959-60); *Killian v. Millard*, 228 Cal. App. 3d 1601, 1605, 279 Cal. Rptr. 877 (1991) (ruling defendant, who had no substantive right in contract between plaintiff and third parties, lacked standing to seek to void that contract); *Associated Builders & Contractors, Inc. v. San Francisco Airports Comm'n*, 21 Cal. 4th 352, 87 Cal. Rptr. 2d 654, 981 P.2d 499 (1999) (discussing the requirements for associational standing).

(3) The courts are unable to develop a useful general test because the applicable substantive law obviously varies from case to case. *Midpeninsula Citizens for Fair Housing v. Westwood Investor*, 221 Cal. App. 3d 1377, 1385, 271 Cal. Rptr. 99 (1990) ("Standing requirements will vary from statute to statute based upon the intent of the Legislature and the purpose for which the particular statute was enacted"; therefore plaintiff citizen group lacked standing to challenge defendant's rental policy under the "person aggrieved" requirement of the Unruh Act, Civil Code § 52; but had standing to sue "on behalf of the general public" under the Unfair Competition Statute, Bus. & Prof. Code § 17204); *Committee on Children's Television, Inc. v. General Foods Corp.*, 35 Cal. 3d 197, 210-11, 197 Cal. Rptr. 783, 673 P.2d 660 (1983) (holding organizations, parents, and children had standing to bring suit for deceptive advertising against cereal manufacturer under broad authority of certain consumer protection statutes, and may under fraud statute if complaint amended; but lacked standing for breach of fiduciary duty action).

(4) As *Hector F.*, reproduced *supra*, demonstrates, the policy in favor of liberal standing in public interest cases is very strong. For example, in *Common Cause v. Bd. of Supervisors*, 49 Cal. 3d 432, 261 Cal. Rptr. 574, 777 P.2d 610 (1989), plaintiff taxpayers sought an injunction to compel Los Angeles County to implement state-mandated voter outreach programs. The defendant County contended that the plaintiffs lacked standing under § 526a because their suit sought to compel, rather than halt, expenditure of county funds. The Supreme Court found it unnecessary to apply

§ 526a, but held that the plaintiffs have standing as citizens to seek enforcement of a public right. *Id.* at 439.

(5) The real party in interest/standing problems occur when the party bringing a cause of action in a civil lawsuit has filed a federal bankruptcy petition. The general rule seems to be that the trustee in bankruptcy is the real party in interest as to any causes of action that accrued to the petitioner prior to the bankruptcy filing, but the petitioner has standing to bring any cause of action that accrued subsequent to the filing of the bankruptcy petition. *See Haley v. Dow Lewis Motors, Inc.*, 72 Cal. App. 4th 497, 85 Cal. Rptr. 2d 352 (1999) (collecting cases); *see also Cloud v. Northrop Grumman Corp.*, 67 Cal. App. 4th 995, 79 Cal. Rptr. 2d 544 (1998) (holding plaintiff lacked standing because her wrongful termination cause of action was the property of her bankruptcy estate, but plaintiff simply needed to amend her complaint to substitute in the trustee as the real party in interest); *but see Bostonian v. Liberty Savings Bank*, 52 Cal. App. 4th 1075, 61 Cal. Rptr. 2d 68 (1997) (ruling trustee in bankruptcy is the real party in interest as to a cause of action that accrued after the filing of a bankruptcy petition, where that cause arose from an asset in the bankruptcy estate).

(6) *Ripeness and Mootness.* The criteria for standing are intertwined with the concepts of ripeness and mootness. A case is considered ripe when the facts present an actual dispute that permit a court to make a degree finally disposing of the controversy that require a judicial resolution, as opposed to issuing a purely advisory opinion. *See, e.g., Pacific Legal Found. v. California Coastal Comm'n*, 33 Cal. 3d 158, 170, 188 Cal. Rptr. 104, 655 P.2d 306 (1982); *Wilson & Wilson v. City Council of Redwood City*, 191 Cal. App. 4th 1559, 1573-74, 120 Cal. Rptr. 3d 665 (2011). A case is considered moot when the facts at one time presented an actual controversy but, due to a change in circumstances, cease to do so such that a court cannot grant the plaintiff any effectual relief. *See Wilson & Wilson, supra*, 191Cal. App. 4th at 677-78 (discussing several mootness cases). How are these two doctrines intertwined with the standing doctrine?

[2] Statutory Exceptions

There are several statutory exceptions to the real party in interest requirement.

[a] Personal Representatives and Trustees

One such statutory exception is CCP § 369, which authorizes such persons as a personal representative (as defined by Probate Code § 58) and a trustee of an express trust, to sue without joining as parties the persons for whose benefit the action is prosecuted. The courts interpret § 369 as authorizing the legal representative of an estate, not the heirs or legatees of the deceased, to sue for debts due the estate. *E.g., Klopstock v. Superior Court*, 17 Cal. 2d 13, 17, 108 P.2d 906 (1941).

Although the general rule is that the trustee is the real party in interest when a cause of action is prosecuted on behalf of a trust, the California courts have recognized a common law exception to this rule permitting a trust beneficiary to bring an action against third parties who actively participate in a trustee's breach of trust.

See, e.g., Harnedy v. Whitty, 110 Cal. App. 4th 1333, 2 Cal. Rptr. 2d 798 (2003) (concluding that when a claim alleges breach of trust by the trustee, a beneficiary has standing to pursue such claim against either the trustee directly, the trustee and participating third parties, or such third parties alone); *Wolf v. Mitchell, Silberberg & Knupp*, 76 Cal. App. 4th 1030, 90 Cal. Rptr. 2d 792 (1999); *City of Atascadero v. Merrill Lynch, Pierce, Fenner & Smith, Inc.*, 68 Cal. App. 4th 445, 80 Cal. Rptr. 2d 329 (1998).

[b] Homeowner Associations

CCP § 1368.3 [formerly, CCP § 374] contains another exception, which authorizes associations established to manage common interest developments to bring certain actions as the real party in interest without joining individual owners. *See, e.g., Duffey v. Superior Court*, 3 Cal. App. 4th 425, 4 Cal. Rptr. 2d 334 (1992) (ruling homeowners association had standing under former § 374(a) to seek declaratory relief action to obtain an authoritative interpretation of governing CC&Rs); *see* Matthew T. Powers, Comment, *Homeowner Association Standing in California: A Proposal to Expand the Role of the Unit Owner*, 26 Santa Clara L. Rev. 619 (1986). Of course, a homeowners association may have standing to sue as the representative of the individual homeowners. *See Market Lofts v. 9th Street Market*, 222 Cal. App. 4th 924, 932-33, 166 Cal. Rptr. 3d 469 (2014) (collecting cases).

[c] Other Statutory Exceptions

Other statutory exceptions include CCP § 377.60 [formerly § 377] (heirs or dependent parents authorized to maintain wrongful death actions), Civil Code § 798.87(c) (mobile home park resident, management, or city attorney authorized to bring civil action to remedy violation of park rules), Family Code § 4000 (either other parent or child may bring action against errant parent who willfully fails to provide child support), Unemployment Insurance Code § 409.2 (any interested person or organization may bring certain actions for declaratory relief), and CCP § 526a (taxpayers suits).

[3] *Standing vs. Real Party in Interest*

The California courts generally treat the concept of standing as synonymous with that of real party in interest. *See, e.g., Armstone v. Peninsular Fire Ins. Co.*, 226 Cal. App. 3d 1019, 1023, 277 Cal. Rptr. 260 (1991) ("Persons have standing to sue when they are real parties in interest"); *Don Rose Oil Co., Inc. v. Lindsley*, 160 Cal. App. 3d 752, 759, 206 Cal. Rptr. 670 (1984). The courts tend to refer to the doctrine as "standing" in cases involving public interest laws or an organization's right to sue on behalf of its members, and refer to it as "real party in interest" in more traditional private party litigation.

[a] Purposes

The California courts define the purposes of each doctrine in similar, but not identical, terms. The standing requirement is designed "to ensure that the courts will decide only actual controversies between parties with a sufficient interest in the subject matter of the dispute to press their case with vigor." *Common Cause v. Bd. of Supervisors*, 49 Cal. 3d 432, 439, 261 Cal. Rptr. 574, 777 P.2d 610 (1989); *Harmon v. City & County of San Francisco*, 7 Cal. 3d 150, 159, 101 Cal. Rptr. 880, 496 P.2d 1248 (1972). The real party rule is designed "to protect a defendant from a multiplicity of suits and from further annoyance and vexation, and to fix and determine the real liability which is alleged in the complaint." *Bank of Orient v. Superior Court*, 67 Cal. App. 3d 588, 594, 136 Cal. Rptr. 741 (1977). Are the differences in these two statements of purpose meaningful?

[b] More Than One Real Party

There may be more than one real party in interest under the applicable substantive law. *See Municipal Court v. Bloodgood*, 137 Cal. App. 3d 29, 44, 186 Cal. Rptr. 807 (1982). For example, in a case involving a partial assignment (or subrogation) of a claim, both the assignor and the assignee are real parties in interest with respect to the claim and both have standing to sue. *See Cain v. State Farm Mut. Auto. Ins. Co.*, 47 Cal. App. 3d 783, 795, 121 Cal. Rptr. 200 (1975); *see Bank of Orient v. Superior Court, supra; Crofton v. Young*, 48 Cal. App. 2d 452, 456, 119 P.2d 1003 (1941) (holding that where entire interest was assigned, the assignee was the only real party in interest). Such cases generally require joinder of all real parties in interest. Why? What purpose is furthered by requiring such joinder?

[4] *Taxpayer Lawsuits*

Code of Civil Procedure § 526a establishes a unique authority for taxpayer standing, providing in relevant part: "An action to obtain a judgment, restraining and preventing any illegal expenditure of, waste of … funds … of a county, town, city or city and county of the state, may be maintained against any officer thereof … by a citizen resident therein … who is … liable to pay, or, within one year before the commencement of the action, has paid, a tax therein."

[a] Liberal Construction

The California Supreme Court has consistently construed § 526a liberally to achieve its remedial purpose: "to enable a large body of the citizenry to challenge governmental action which would otherwise go unchallenged in the courts because of the standing requirement." *Blair v. Pitchess*, 5 Cal. 3d 258, 267-68, 96 Cal. Rptr. 42, 486 P.2d 1242 (1971) (concluding taxpayers had standing to challenge claim and delivery statute enforced by county officials); *Van Atta v. Scott*, 27 Cal. 3d 424, 447, 166 Cal. Rptr. 149, 613 P.2d 210 (1980) (holding taxpayers had standing to challenge constitutionality of county pre-trial release and detention program even though directly affected persons — pretrial detainees — were not parties).

The plaintiff taxpayer has standing even though she alleges no special personal injury or interest; and even though other individuals exist who were directly affected by the challenged government action. *E.g., Arrieta v. Mahon*, 31 Cal. 3d 381, 386-87, 182 Cal. Rptr. 770, 644 P.2d 1249 (1982) (ruling taxpayers had standing to challenge constitutionality of county's policy in enforcing eviction writs regardless of whether plaintiffs or defendants had a special, personal interest in the outcome); *White v. Davis*, 13 Cal. 3d 757, 764, 120 Cal. Rptr. 94, 533 P.2d 222 (1975) (holding taxpayers had standing to challenge constitutionality of police intelligence gathering in university classrooms; no showing of special injury to particular taxpayer was necessary).

The California Supreme Court has permitted taxpayer suits for declaratory relief, damages, and mandamus, in addition to ones for injunctive relief, *e.g., Van Atta v. Scott, supra*, 27 Cal. 3d at 449-50, n. 25-n. 27 (citing cases); and has permitted such suits against state, as well as local, officials. *See Blair v. Pitchess, supra*, 5 Cal. 3d at 267-68. The California Supreme Court has upheld taxpayer standing even though a federal court had previously dismissed the same case for lack of federal standing. *See White v. Davis, supra*, 13 Cal. 3d at 764 (ruling plaintiffs had standing as taxpayers to challenge constitutionality of ongoing undercover activities on UCLA campus).

[b]   Restrictions on Taxpayer Suits

The only court imposed limitation on taxpayer standing under § 526a is that the suit must seek to measure government performance against a legal standard or duty—such as violation of the Constitution, a statute or an ordinance—but must not trespass into the domain of legislative or executive discretion. *Harmon v. City & Cnty. of San Francisco*, 7 Cal. 3d 150, 159, 101 Cal. Rptr. 880, 496 P.2d 1248 (1972) (ruling taxpayer had standing to challenge city's method of appraising city property for sale as violation of city charter); *California Assn. for Safety Ed. v. Brown*, 30 Cal. App. 4th 1264, 1281-84, 36 Cal. Rptr. 2d 404 (1994) (holding taxpayer suit not appropriate to compel state agency to allocate certain state funds to reimburse cost of driver's training because state under no duty to use such funds to pay driver training expenses for high school districts).

Of course, the plaintiff must also be a taxpayer. *E.g., Torres v. City of Yorba Linda*, 13 Cal. App. 4th 1035, 1046-48, 17 Cal. Rptr. 2d 400 (1993) (ruling plaintiffs' alleged payment of city sales tax as consumers did not establish their status as taxpayers for taxpayer standing because sales tax is levied upon the retailer, not upon the consumer); *Cornelius v. Los Angeles Cnty. Metro. Trans. Auth.*, 49 Cal. App. 4th 1761, 1774-80, 57 Cal. Rptr. 2d 618 (1996) (holding plaintiff lacked standing as a taxpayer to challenge a county transportation authority's affirmative action program because the plaintiff was not a resident of the county and did not pay real estate taxes in the county); *Chiatello v. City & County of San Francisco*,189 Cal. App. 4th 472, 480-98, 117 Cal. Rptr. 3d 169 (2010) (noting a taxpayer who is not subject to the tax lacks standing to enjoin the collection of the allegedly illegal tax); *see Taxpayers for Accountable Sch. Bond Spending v. San Diego Unified Sch. Dist.*, 215 Cal. App. 4th 1013, 1031-33, 156 Cal. Rptr. 3d 449 (2013) (concluding that even though plaintiff organization itself did not pay taxes, it had standing because it members were taxpayers).

[c]   Taxpayer Suits in Federal Courts

The broad favorable treatment afforded taxpayer suits under § 526a is not fully appreciated unless contrasted to the generally hostile reception such suits receive in federal court. *E.g., Valley Forge Christian Coll. v. Americans United for Separation of Church & State, Inc.*, 454 U.S. 464, 477, 102 S. Ct. 752, 70 L. Ed. 2d 700 (1982) (holding taxpayers lacked standing to challenge constitutionality of federal land transfer to religious college because "the expenditure of public funds in an allegedly unconstitutional manner is not an injury sufficient to confer standing, even though the plaintiff contributes to the public coffers as a taxpayer"); *cf. Flast v. Cohen*, 392 U.S. 83, 88 S. Ct. 1942, 20 L. Ed. 2d 947 (1968) (approving a limited exception permitting taxpayer standing).

In light of the California courts' liberal attitude toward standing in public interest suits, does the doctrine present any real limitation on such actions against government officials? Is there any reason to pursue such suits in federal court?

[5]   *Federal Standing and Real Party Doctrines*

[a]   Real Party Rule

Rule 17(a), F.R.C.P., outlines the federal real party in interest doctrine. The federal rule has the same meaning and purposes as the California doctrine, but has additional consequences for subject matter jurisdiction. *See, e.g., Gogolin & Stelfer v. Karn's Auto Imports, Inc.*, 886 F.2d 100, 102 (5th Cir. 1989) (noting purpose of rule is to prevent multiple conflicting lawsuits by persons who would not be bound by res judicata principles); *see generally* Wright, Miller & Kane, *Federal Practice and Procedure: Civil 3d* §§ 1543-58 (2010). The citizenship of real parties, but not nominal ones, is relevant for determining diversity jurisdiction under 28 U.S.C. § 1332. *Navarro Savings Assn. v. Lee*, 446 U.S. 458, 460-61, 100 S. Ct. 1779, 64 L. Ed. 2d 425 (1980).

[b]   Article III Standing Requirements

The doctrine of standing in federal court implements Article III of the U.S. Constitution, which limits the federal judicial power to resolution of "cases" and "controversies." *See, e.g., Valley Forge Christian Coll. v. Americans United for Separation of Church & State, Inc.*, 454 U.S. 464, 470-76, 102 S. Ct. 752, 70 L. Ed. 2d 700 (1982). The federal doctrine is quite complex in its application, and has been summarized as follows (*Id.* at 472-75):

> [A]t an irreducible minimum, Art. III requires the party who invokes the court's authority to "show that he personally has suffered some actual or threatened injury as a result of the putatively illegal conduct of the defendant," and that the injury "fairly can be traced to the challenged action" and "is likely to be redressed by a favorable decision." In this manner does Art. III limit the federal judicial power "to those disputes which confine federal courts to a role consistent with a system of separated powers and which are traditionally thought to be capable of resolution through the judicial process."

* * *

Beyond the constitutional requirements, the federal judiciary has also adhered to a set of prudential principles that bear on the question of standing. Thus, this Court has held that "the plaintiff generally must assert his own legal rights and interests, and cannot rest his claim to relief on the legal rights or interests of third parties." In addition, even where the plaintiff has alleged redressable injury sufficient to meet the requirements of Art. III, the Court has refrained from adjudicating "abstract questions of wide public significance" which amount to "generalized grievances," pervasively shared and most appropriately addressed in the representative branches. Finally, the Court has required that the plaintiff's complaint fall within "the zone of interests to be protected or regulated by the statute or constitutional guarantee in question."

[c] Federal Standing Requirements in State Courts

The California courts have repeatedly held that the restrictive federal standing requirements do not determine the scope of standing provided by a California statute in state court. *E.g.*, *White v. Dan's, supra*, 13 Cal. 3d at 764; *Midpeninsula Citizens for Fair Housing v. Westwood Investors*, 221 Cal. App. 3d 1377, 1385-88, 271 Cal. Rptr. 99 (1990). Why are the California courts free to disregard U.S. Supreme Court pronouncements on standing? Is this a violation of Article III? Of the Supremacy Clause? Why not? The different effect of these standing doctrines is most pronounced in taxpayer suits. *See* discussion of California taxpayer suits, *supra*.

[C]   Survival of Actions

[1] Legislative Revision

As part of a comprehensive revision of the statutes regarding litigation which involves decedents, the Legislature in 1992 enacted CCP §§ 377.10-377.62 to govern the effect of the death on parties to civil actions. *See* 3 Witkin, *California Procedure, Actions* §§ 12-17 (5th ed. 2008) for a discussion of these revisions.

[2] Survival Statutes

As with earlier survival statutes, CCP § 377.20 provides that unless there is some specific statutory exception, "a cause of action for or against a person is not lost by reason of the person's death, but survives subject to the applicable limitation period."

[a]   Decedent's Cause of Action

An action that survives may be commenced or continued by the decedent's personal representative or, if none, by the decedent's successor in interest as defined in CCP §§ 377.10 & .11. CCP §§ 377.30 & .31. The procedure for commencement or continuation by a successor in interest is specified in CCP § 377.32. In an action by a personal representative or successor in interest on the decedent's cause of action, the damages recoverable are limited to the loss the decedent sustained before death, including punitive damages, but not including damages for pain, suffering, or disfigurement. CCP § 377.34; *see*

Sullivan v. Delta Air Lines, Inc., 15 Cal. 4th 288, 63 Cal. Rptr. 2d 74, 935 P.2d 781 (1997) (holding CCP § 377.34 does not bar recovery of pain and suffering damages awarded in a judgment if the plaintiff dies after the judgment was rendered but while an appeal is pending). What are the likely policy reasons for this limitation on recoverable damages?

[b] Cause of Action Against Decedent

Subject to compliance with the creditor claims requirements of the Probate Code, a cause of action against a decedent that survives may be asserted against the decedent's personal representative or, to the extent permitted by statute, against the decedent's successor in interest. CCP § 377.40. All damages are recoverable that might have been recoverable had the decedent lived, except punitive damages. CCP § 377.42; *see Whelan v. Rallo,* 52 Cal. App. 4th 989, 60 Cal. Rptr. 2d 876 (1997) (construing CCP § 377.42 as extinguishing the right to punitive damages only if the defendant died before judgment was entered). What are the likely policy reasons for this limitation on recoverable damages?

§ 10.07 Class Actions

[A] General California Requirements

[1] Introductory Note

The class action is the ultimate joinder device. One or more named plaintiffs may represent the interests of thousands of absentee class members, and may obtain a class judgment that will bind those absentees by res judicata. *See, e.g., Daar v. Yellow Cab Co.,* 67 Cal. 2d 695, 63 Cal. Rptr. 724, 433 P.2d 732 (1967) (holding class action by taxicab customer against taxicab company on behalf of all others similarly situated to recover excessive charges would be res judicata on thousands of class members); *Lazar v. Hertz Corp.,* 143 Cal. App. 3d 128, 191 Cal. Rptr. 849 (1983) (affirming class action on behalf of approximately 5,000,000 rental car customers); *Cartt v. Superior Court,* 50 Cal. App. 3d 960, 124 Cal. Rptr. 376 (1975) (upholding consumer class action on behalf of over 700,000 credit card holders). Recently adopted California Rules of Court now govern the management of class actions, including motions to certify or decertify a class, case conferences, notice to class members, orders in the conduct of class actions, discovery from unnamed class members, and settlement and dismissals of class actions. *See* Cal. Rules of Ct. 3.760-3.771.

[a] No Comprehensive Class Action Statute

Despite the obvious importance of the class actions and their concomitant potential for procedural problems, the California Legislature has yet to enact a comprehensive statute which specifically governs all applications of the class action device. As *Richmond v. Dart Industries,* reproduced *infra,* illustrates, the courts rely on CCP § 382 as the general authority for class actions and on Civil Code § 1781 for procedural guidelines.

In the absence of controlling California authority, the California Supreme Court has suggested that trial courts utilize the class action procedures of Rule 23 of the Federal Rules of Civil Procedure. *City of San Jose v. Superior Court*, 12 Cal. 3d 447, 453, 115 Cal. Rptr. 797, 525 P.2d 701 (1974) (ruling trial courts should be procedurally innovative and incorporate class action procedures from outside sources, specifically Rule 23, F.R.C.P.); *La Sala v. American Sav. & Loan Assn.*, 5 Cal. 3d 864, 872, 97 Cal. Rptr. 849, 489 P.2d 1113 (1971). Consequently, the California courts often cite federal court interpretations of Federal Rule 23 as authority when determining state court class action procedural issues. *See, e.g., Bell v. American Title Ins. Co.*, 226 Cal. App. 3d 1589, 277 Cal. Rptr. 583 (1991) (analyzing federal court interpretations of the notice requirements for class actions certified under federal Rules 23(b)(1),(2), and (3) to determine propriety of class settlement that precludes opt outs); *Carter v. City of Los Angeles*, 224 Cal. App. 4th 808, 169 Cal. Rptr. 3d 131 (2014) (relying on recent U.S. Supreme Court decision construing federal Rule 23(b) to determine when a trial court should afford class members a right to opt out). You might therefore expect that the California courts' treatment of the class action device would be identical to that of the federal courts. In most applications, that expectation is reality. But in a few important procedural areas, discussed below, the California courts' approach differs markedly from that of the federal courts.

[b]   Prerequisites

The general California prerequisites for maintenance of a class action are identified in *Richmond v. Dart Industries, infra,* as: The party seeking certification as a class action representative must establish the existence of an ascertainable class and a well-defined community of interest among the class members. This general test embodies several more specific factors which are analyzed in the notes following our principal case.

Richmond v. Dart Industries, Inc.

Supreme Court of California
29 Cal. 3d 462, 174 Cal. Rptr. 515, 629 P.2d 23 (1981)

Bird, Justice.

May a trial court deny a motion to certify a class if the defendants are able to show there was antagonism to the lawsuit on behalf of some absent class members? A secondary issue centers on whether the plaintiffs' prayer for rescission and punitive damages prevents the use of a class action suit.

I.

Tahoe Donner Subdivision is a recreational home site with approximately 6,000 lots near Truckee, California. Dart Industries, Inc. (Dart) developed the subdivision in 1971 and sold approximately 2,600 lots by 1976. Then, 157 past and present owners at Tahoe Donner filed suit based on claims of fraud and violations of the Subdivided Lands legislation (Bus. & Prof. Code, § 11000 et seq.). * * *

In their complaint, plaintiffs alleged that Dart or its subsidiary, Dart Resorts, failed to plan and provide for adequate water supply, sewage treatment facilities, recreational facilities, and maintenance. They prayed for compensatory and punitive damages, rescission, declaratory relief, and requested that a constructive trust be established to ensure that there was sufficient money to provide adequate facilities.

Each individual who purchased a lot at Tahoe Donner was given a copy of the Final Subdivision Public Report. That report gave assurances that there would be an adequate water supply, sewage treatment and recreational facilities for the entire development. It is the alleged violation of these assurances upon which plaintiffs base their suit.

Plaintiffs filed a class certification motion under Code of Civil Procedure section 382 which authorizes class action suits. They requested that the trial court grant them the right to represent all of the record owners of Tahoe Donner lots. A certification hearing was held on the 17th and 18th of November 1977.

Plaintiffs based their motion for class certification on the allegations of their complaint, their declarations, exhibits incorporated in the record, and points and authorities. The thrust of their argument was that a class action was proper since they had established an ascertainable class and a well-defined community of interest among the class members. (See *Daar v. Yellow Cab Co.* (1967) 67 Cal. 2d 695, 704 [63 Cal. Rptr. 724, 433 P.2d 732].) The ascertainable class, they maintained, consisted of the record owners of lots at Tahoe Donner who had received the Final Subdivision Public Report and since each member of the class was affected by the failure of Dart to meet the needs of the subdivision, the requirement of a community of interest was also met.

In order to prove that they could adequately represent the entire class, the plaintiffs filed declarations by their attorneys as to the attorneys' experience with class action suits. Individuals who were personally aware of the attorneys' prior experience, also filed declarations.

The Tahoe Donner Association (TDA), interveners in this lawsuit, opposed the motion to certify the class. This association automatically includes in its membership any purchaser of a lot at Tahoe Donner. At the time TDA decided to intervene, Dart had a controlling interest in the association since a majority of the Tahoe Donner lots were still owned by Dart. Furthermore, Dart then had three representatives on the five-member board of directors of this association and the president of TDA was Mr. Sid Karsh, president of Dart Resorts.

At the certification hearing, a "survey" conducted with Dart's assistance in the spring of 1976 was introduced to attempt to show that there was antagonism within the class to be represented. The "survey" consisted of a flyer entitled "Support Your Project!," which was sent to the property owners by Dart Resorts on the approval of its president, Mr. Karsh. The flyer was written by a homeowner, Mr. Jess Huffman, who subsequently reimbursed Dart Resorts for the cost of producing and mailing the pamphlet.

The flyer accused plaintiffs of damaging the Dart project by filing their lawsuit. It was claimed that the lawsuit was "more emotional than factual." There was no attempt to present the opposite viewpoint or even to list the factual allegations contained in the complaint that there had been problems with adequate water and sewage connections. The flyer boldly stated: "Dart has gone the distance, plus the extra mile, to meet their [sic] commitments to us, the property owners."

The pamphlet invited each property owner to return to Mr. Huffman the lower portion of the flyer after checking one of the boxes which indicated that (1) the owner felt that "Tahoe Donner is a fine project and Dart is meeting their [sic] commitments"; or (2) the owner was "not satisfied with Dart's efforts to meet their [sic] commitments"; or (3) the owner could be "counted on to contribute some funds towards the 'support Tahoe Donner' effort."

Of the 2,600 lot owners to whom it was mailed, only 325 responded. Testimony was adduced which indicated that 266 of those who responded checked the first alternative, 41 checked the second, and 18 simply returned the flyer unmarked. Some of the responses asked for more information and indicated they were unaware of the lawsuit. In comments appended to the returned flyers, some owners indicated support for the project but wished more information about the lawsuit and others endorsed Mr. Huffman's approach.

The trial court denied class certification on July 11, 1978. The order of the court rested primarily on the results of the Huffman/Dart survey and the opposition of the Tahoe Donner Association to the suit. The court concluded that plaintiffs had not "carried the burden of proving the 'representative party has interests which are compatible with, and not antagonistic to those whom he (Richmond et al.) would represent.'" This appeal followed.

II.

"Class actions serve an important function in our judicial system. By establishing a technique whereby the claims of many individuals can be resolved at the same time, the class suit both eliminates the possibility of repetitious litigation and provides small claimants with a method of obtaining redress for claims which would otherwise be too small to warrant individual litigation." (*Eisen v. Carlisle & Jacquelin* (2d Cir. 1968) 391 F.2d 555, 560.) Because of these important dual functions, courts and legislators have looked with increasing favor on the class action device. Dramatic developments in class action procedure have marked the last two decades, with the expansive amendments in 1966 of rule 23 of the Federal Rules of Civil Procedure (28 U.S.C.) and with the passage in 1970 of the Consumers Legal Remedies Act[7] in California. As a result of these

---

7. In 1970, the California Legislature passed the Consumers Legal Remedies Act (Civ. Code, § 1750 et seq.), including Civil Code section 1781, which states in relevant part:

"(a) Any consumer entitled to bring an action under Section 1780 may, if the unlawful method, act, or practice has caused damage to other consumers similarly situated, bring an action on behalf of himself and such other consumers to recover damages or obtain other relief as provided for in Section 1780.

"(b) The court shall permit the suit to be maintained on behalf of all members of the represented class if all of the following conditions exist:

"(1) It is impracticable to bring all members of the class before the court.

"(2) The questions of law or fact common to the class are substantially similar and predominate over the questions affecting the individual members.

"(3) The claims or defenses of the representative plaintiffs are typical of the claims or defenses of the class.

and other changes, the class action, which began as a child of the equity courts with limited usefulness, has matured and expanded to meet the needs of modern society.

Code of Civil Procedure section 382 authorizes class action suits in California "when the question is one of a common or general interest, of many persons, or when the parties are numerous, and it is impracticable to bring them all before the court...." The party seeking certification as a class representative must establish the existence of an ascertainable class and a well-defined community of interest among the class members. (*Daar v. Yellow Cab Co., supra,* 67 Cal. 2d at p. 704.) The community of interest requirement embodies three factors: (1) predominant common questions of law or fact; (2) class representatives with claims or defenses typical of the class; and (3) class representatives who can adequately represent the class. (*See* Civ. Code, § 1781, subds. (b)(2)-(4).)

A decision by a trial court denying certification to an entire class is an appealable order. (*Daar v. Yellow Cab Co., supra,* 67 Cal. 2d at pp. 698-699). However, trial courts have been given great discretion with regard to class certification. For example, in the absence of other error, this court will not disturb a trial court ruling on class certification which is supported by substantial evidence unless (1) improper criteria were used; or (2) erroneous legal assumptions were made.

The party seeking class certification has the burden of proving the adequacy of its representation. (*See, e.g.,* Civ. Code, § 1781, subd. (b)(4).) However, when the party opposing certification presents evidence that indicates widespread antagonism to the class suit, the adequacy of representation is called into question. "It is axiomatic that a putative representative cannot adequately protect the class if his interests are antagonistic to or in conflict with the objectives of those he purports to represent. But only a conflict that goes to the very subject matter of the litigation will defeat a party's claim of representative status. Moreover, if the court can utilize Rule 23(c)(4) to divide the class into subclasses or to separate those issues that merit class action treatment so as to remove any antagonism, then the action need not be dismissed." (7 Wright & Miller, Federal Practice and Procedure (1972) Civil, § 1768, pp. 638-639, fns. omitted [hereinafter Wright & Miller].)

When the vast majority of a class perceives its interest as diametrically opposed to that of the named representatives, a trial court cannot equitably grant the named plaintiffs the right to pursue the litigation on behalf of the entire class. The trial court can permit the plaintiffs to represent a smaller class if the minority can meet the requirements for class certification by showing an ascertainable class and a community of interest which is not coextensive with the larger class.

"(4) The representative plaintiffs will fairly and adequately protect the interests of the class."

Although section 1781 is not directly applicable to the present action because of the definition of a consumer as an "individual who seeks or acquires ... goods or services...." (Civ. Code, § 1761, subd. (d)), this court has suggested that section 1781 and rule 23 may be used as procedural guidelines to ensure fairness in class action suits. (*Vasquez v. Superior Court* (1971) 4 Cal. 3d 800, 821 [94 Cal. Rptr. 796, 484 P.2d 964, 53 A.L.R.3d 513].)

If the vast majority of the class do not oppose the suit, the minority may have its views presented either as a subclass or as interveners.

In this case, plaintiffs contend that the trial court erred when it held in effect that a showing of any antagonism within the group to be certified is sufficient to defeat a motion for certification. If the antagonism is insignificant, plaintiffs argue, it should not be sufficient to defeat class certification. Two Court of Appeal decisions of this state provide authority for this position.

In *Fanucchi v. Coberly-West Co.* (1957) 151 Cal. App. 2d 72 [311 P.2d 33], the court held that even though one-third of the proposed class signed affidavits stating that they did not wish to be a part of the class, the class action suit could not be barred. "If [the opponents of the class] do not want to be paid they need not claim their share of any recovery which may result, but they may not thus defeat the right of the remaining growers to maintain a class action...." (*Id.*, at p. 82.) Quite clearly, the *Fanucchi* court felt that class members who opposed the suit should not be able to defeat the right of the remaining members of the class to maintain a representative action.

In *Hebbard v. Colgrove* (1972) 28 Cal. App. 3d 1017 [105 Cal. Rptr. 172], the Court of Appeal cited *Fanucchi* with approval, holding that several antagonistic class members out of a total of 50 could not defeat class certification. Even though the dissident class members intervened on the defendants' side in the federal class suit that was a companion to *Hebbard*, the court held that their antagonism only went to their "desire to proceed or belief in the culpability of the defendants." Therefore, the interests of these class members could still be represented by the named plaintiffs "even though [the absent members] may ... forego their share of the recovery." (*Id.*, at p. 1030.) * * *

The essential question presented by this case is whether antagonism *per se* by members of a class should automatically preclude the certification of a class. Since this state has a public policy which encourages the use of the class action device, rules promulgated by this court should reflect that policy. One scholarly commentary suggests that "[differences] which do not raise questions as to the very legitimacy of the class action process, ... but which merely reflect variances in view as to the proper outcome of a suit, do not provide reason for a court to refuse to hear a class suit." (*Developments—Class Actions (1976)*, 89 Harv. L. Rev. 1318 at p. 1490.)

Further, "[most] differences in situation or interest among class members ... should not bar class suit. If the factual circumstances underlying class members' claims differ, or if class members disagree as to the proper theory of liability, the trial judge, through use of techniques like subclassing or intervention, may incorporate the class differences into the litigative process, and give all class members their due in deciding what is the proper outcome of the litigation. Even if differences among class members are more fundamental, having to do with the type of relief which should be sought or indeed with whether the class opponent ought to be held liable at all, judicial accommodation appears to provide a sufficient mechanism for the protection of absentee interests. So long as a dispute concerns the outcome of litigation, the trial judge is in a position to isolate the differing positions, judge their validity in light of the substantive law governing the case, and shape the outcome of the suit to give the various class interests the weight to which the law entitles them." (*Id.*, at pp. 1490-1492.)

When a class contains various viewpoints, the courts may ensure that these viewpoints are represented by allowing them to join as interveners (as TDA did in this case) or as additional representatives of subclasses within the full class. (Fed. Rules Civ. Proc., rule 23 (c)(4); 7 Wright & Miller, *supra*, at p. 639....) This would ensure that the trial court was fully aware of the differing views within the class. Additional protection is afforded to absent class members by the provisions which allow a class member to opt out of the class if he or she does not wish to be bound by the result of the suit. (Fed. Rules Civ. Proc., rule 23(c)(2).)

Since the judicial system substantially benefits by the efficient use of its resources, class certifications should not be denied so long as the absent class members' rights are adequately protected. Additionally, there is great value in including the differing viewpoints, rather than precluding the class suit. Inclusion will have the secondary effect of giving the trier of fact more information which should ultimately result in a more informed decision.

In *La Sala v. American Sav. & Loan Assn.* (1971) 5 Cal. 3d 864, 875, footnote 10 [97 Cal. Rptr. 849, 489 P.2d 1113], this court urged trial courts to define classes in such a manner as to "'permit utilization of the class action procedure.'" If this court were to adopt a rule that any antagonism (6 percent in this case) by class members to the lawsuit is sufficient to defeat class treatment, it would bar a large number of class suits. Furthermore, such a rule would encourage defendants to exploit this loophole by seeking out or attempting improperly to sow dissension within a class. Divergent viewpoints can be brought into the litigation when the trial court allows intervention and/or well-defined subclasses within the class.

This policy is in accord with the decisions of our Courts of Appeal in *Fanucchi* and *Hebbard*. Since the defendants did not establish in the trial court that there was either a conflict of interest[9] or overwhelming disapproval of the lawsuit within the class which would defeat the purpose of class adjudication, the trial court erred when it refused certification.

The results of the flyer questionnaire show no more than approximately 6 percent of the class of some 4,000 persons antagonistic to the class action suit. This small number should not be sufficient to defeat the motion for certification. Similarly, the intervention of an association which is largely under the control of Dart should not be sufficient evidence of antagonism to deny the certification. Any property owners

---

9. The trial court also based its decision on an alleged conflict of interest of Harold Berliner, lead attorney for plaintiffs. He allegedly participated in a lawsuit by another land development company seeking sewer connections which might otherwise have been allotted to the Tahoe Donner Subdivision. Defendants claim that this representation by Berliner, without the consent of plaintiffs herein, disqualifies him from representing the class even though he is no longer involved in the other case. The trial court found that there was a conflict at least at the initial stage of the current lawsuit. However, since that alleged conflict of interest had already been resolved by the time of the certification motion, the plaintiffs may not be denied class status on that basis.

whose interests differ from those of the named plaintiffs can be adequately protected by the interveners and the representatives of subclasses, if the trial court finds it appropriate to set up subclasses. A sizeable number of owners of Tahoe Donner lots have chosen to join as named plaintiffs in this suit. This large group should not be denied the opportunity to proceed as a class simply because 6 percent of the potential class members may be antagonistic to their lawsuit.[10]

Next, defendants claim that a prayer for rescission or punitive damages requires the trial court to deny class certification because the remedies prayed for create conflicting interests within the class. The defendants contend that since the property owners are dependent upon Dart for services and maintenance at Tahoe Donner, the relief prayed for creates a conflict between the named plaintiffs and the absent class members by threatening the subdivision's financial stability.

This issue appears to be one of first impression in this state. * * * In *Tober v. Charnita, Inc.* (M.D. Pa. 1973) 58 F.R.D. 74, the federal court faced a similar issue. That court's holding is instructive. "The named plaintiffs do not seek common relief for the entire class but rather seek alternative relief in the form of an option to either rescind the transaction or retain possession of the land purchased and seek damages. The defendants have suggested the possibility that the interests of those class members who seek rescission may become adverse to those who wish to retain possession of their land. It may be contended that wide-scale rescission by a number of class members may have an adverse effect upon the value of the lands of those members who wish to retain possession.... While the court recognizes the potential for a conflict of interest between certain class members, we are not prepared to deny class action status at this time upon the prospect of a conflict which may or may not arise in the future. It may later become apparent that only a small number of the class may successfully seek rescission. Rescission is not a remedy which is automatically granted but must be sought within a reasonable time after discovery of the grounds upon which the remedy is sought. And too, any adverse interest may later be avoided by establishing sub-classes rather than by a denial of class action status. Under Rule 23(c) and (d) the court may modify, alter or amend its class action order at any time before a decision on the merits is reached. Included therein is the power to create sub-classes or terminate class action status at such time as it appears that an insolvable conflict of interest has arisen." (58 F.R.D. at p. 80, fn. omitted.)

The defendants ask this court to reject the *Tober* rule and to follow *Young v. Trailwood Lakes, Inc.* (E.D.Ky. 1974) 61 F.R.D. 666. In *Young,* the plaintiff sought class certification in a controversy arising out of alleged misrepresentations in the sale of subdivision lots. The plaintiff charged a violation of the Consumer Credit Protection Act (15 U.S.C. § 1601 et seq.) and the Interstate Land Sales Full Disclosure Act (15 U.S.C. § 1701 et seq.). The court found that the claims were not proper as class actions. The *Young* court went on to cite *Tober* but then ignored its holding by stating that

---

10. It should also be noted that the trial court will be in a better position to assess the true feelings of the class after court-approved, objectively worded notice is sent to the entire class and the absent members are given an opportunity to elect nonparticipation in this lawsuit.

"conceivably antagonistic goals" of rescission and damages "preclude effective administration as a class action." (*Id.*, at p. 667.)

The *Tober* rule is the more prudent rule to adopt since the trial court has continuing jurisdiction to decertify the class. If there is evidence presented at a later date of an actual conflict, the court may act.... [I]t is preferable to defer the decision to deny class certification until after notice has gone out and such future time as the trial court has the most complete information at its disposal.

To rule otherwise would invite the kind of speculation that went on in the trial court below. To illustrate "ambivalence" by a named plaintiff, the trial court relied on the deposition of a lot owner, Mr. Warren Estes, who testified that he would be most pleased if the project could go forward without the many problems which the lawsuit sought to remedy. This testimony was used as evidence that there was an inconsistency between the position of the named plaintiffs and their attorneys regarding rescission and punitive damages.

However, this assertion of inconsistency overlooks the obvious. There is no inconsistency between the filing of a lawsuit to remedy an alleged fraud and the hope that the subdivision will be completed in conformity with the original promises made by Dart. Both the named plaintiffs and the absent class members seek the benefit of the bargain they made with the defendants. Why else would the plaintiffs have asked for the imposition of a constructive trust on any profits from the development in order to ensure that adequate facilities were provided? Nevertheless, some plaintiffs may have suffered damage not capable of remedy under that trust, e.g., those owners who faced foreclosure after the Department of Real Estate's ban on the sale of lots. Since the seeking of common relief is no longer a prerequisite to a class suit (*Daar v. Yellow Cab Co.*, supra, 67 Cal. 2d at pp. 707-713), a prayer for relief that includes rescission and a request for punitive damages should not bar certification for a class suit.

Finally, the defendants contend that the plaintiffs failed to meet their burden of proof that the class is ascertainable and has a well-defined community of interests. In *Vasquez*, this court noted that "[s]ubstantial benefits both to the litigants and to the court should be found before the imposition of a judgment binding on absent parties can be justified, and the determination of the question whether a class action is appropriate will depend upon whether the common questions are sufficiently pervasive to permit adjudication in a class action rather than in a multiplicity of suits." (4 Cal. 3d at p. 810.)

Reviewing courts consistently look to the allegations of the complaint and the declarations of attorneys representing the plaintiff class to resolve this question. (*See, e.g., Vasquez v. Superior Court*, supra, ...) The issue of ascertainability of the class is a relatively simple matter. In this case, the record owners of the lots at Tahoe Donner are easily identified and located. Joinder of all the potential plaintiffs would not be practicable in a case involving over 2,600 sales of lots.

As to whether there is a community of interest here, the court must find that predominant questions of law or fact are common to the class as a whole. (*See* Civ. Code,

§ 1781, subd. (b)(2).) Written misrepresentation claims provide an adequate basis for a finding of common questions within the class. The trial court below found that there were common questions of law and fact. The plaintiffs' claims were typical of those of the entire class. (*See* Civ. Code, § 1781, subd. (b)(3).)

The thrust of this suit is the inadequacy of the plans for necessities such as adequate water and sewage removal. If there is such a violation, it will affect every lot owner within the subdivision. The named plaintiffs may plead their additional individual claims or they may waive them. The absent class members have the option of dropping out of the lawsuit to protect their separate claims. Since individual claims of the class members are adequately protected, there is no reason to place an obstacle in the path of plaintiffs' suit.

The question that concerned the trial court was whether the plaintiffs had proved the element of adequate representation. In *Eisen v. Carlisle & Jacquelin, supra,* 391 F.2d at page 562, the federal court discussed the several factors involved in the resolution of such an issue. "To be sure, an essential concomitant of adequate representation is that the party's attorney be qualified, experienced and generally able to conduct the proposed litigation. Additionally, it is necessary to eliminate so far as possible the likelihood that the litigants are involved in a collusive suit or that plaintiff has interests antagonistic to those of the remainder of the class."

There is no issue of collusion here since none was raised. Plaintiffs established that 242 lot owners seek to represent the class and that their attorneys have substantial experience in class action litigation. Since the plaintiffs need not show that "every member of the class [is] enthusiastic about the maintenance of the lawsuit," they have met their burden in this regard. Further, no present and substantial conflict between the interests of the absent class members and the named plaintiffs was shown.

Since plaintiffs have met the legal tests set forth for class certification, it was error for the trial court to deny their motion to certify based on antagonism within the class. * * *

[2]   The "Ascertainable Class" Requirement

Whether a class is ascertainable may be determined by examining the class definition, the size of the class, and the means available for identifying class members at the remedial stage. *Reyes v. San Diego Cnty. Bd. of Supervisors,* 196 Cal. App. 3d 1263, 1274, 242 Cal. Rptr. 339 (1987); *Sevidal v. Target Corp.,* 189 Cal. App. 4th 905, 918-22, 117 Cal. Rptr. 3d 66 (2010); *Cohen v. DIRECTV, Inc.,* 178 Cal. App. 4th 966, 975-78, 101 Cal. Rptr. 3d 37 (2009). A class is ascertainable if it identifies a group of unnamed plaintiffs by describing a set of common characteristics sufficient to allow a member of that group to identify himself or herself as having a right to recover based on the description. *Aguirre v. Amscan Holdings, Inc.,* 234 Cal. App. 4th 1290, 1299-1300, 184 Cal. Rptr. 3d 415 (2015) (collecting cases). If the existence of an ascertainable class has been shown, there is no need to identify or locate its individual members in order to bind all members by the judgment. *Daar v. Yellow Cab Co.,* 67

Cal. 2d 695, 706, 63 Cal. Rptr. 724, 433 P.2d 732 (1967); *Aguirre v. Amscan Holdings, Inc., supra.*

[a] "Community of Interest" Intertwined

The "ascertainable class" requirement is intertwined with the "community of interest" requirement. *Clausing v. San Francisco Unified Sch. Dist.*, 221 Cal. App. 3d 1224, 271 Cal. Rptr. 72 (1990); *Hicks v. Kaufman & Broad Home Corp.*, 89 Cal. App. 4th 908, 107 Cal. Rptr. 2d 761 (2001) (discussing the separate purposes of these two requirements). As the Supreme Court has observed, "whether there is an ascertainable class depends in turn upon the community of interest among the class members in the questions of law and fact involved." *Daar v. Yellow Cab Co., supra,* 67 Cal. 2d at 706. What is meant by this observation? In what sense are these two requirements "intertwined"?

[b] Broad Consumer Classes

Some fairly broad class definitions have satisfied the "ascertainable class" requirements. For example, in *Lazar v. Hertz Corp., supra,* 143 Cal. App. 3d at 137, the court upheld a class defined by the plaintiff's complaint as "composed of all persons in the State of California who rented automobiles from Hertz during the period commencing November 1, 1976, and ending November 1, 1980 … and who were charged a refueling service charge for returning their rented automobiles without having refilled the fuel tank." And in *Clothesrigger, Inc. v. GTE Corp.*, 191 Cal. App. 3d 605, 236 Cal. Rptr. 605 (1987), the court found ascertainable a class defined as "all persons nationwide subscribing to Sprint since January 1, 1981, who were charged for one or more unanswered long distance calls." *Id.* at 617. *See also Daar v. Yellow Cab Co., supra* (approving class of all persons who used Yellow Cab taxicab services in Los Angeles during a four-year period and were charged more than the approved rate); *Wershba v. Apple Computer, Inc.*, 91 Cal. App. 4th 224, 110 Cal. Rptr. 2d 145 (2001) (affirming certification and settlement of a nationwide class action alleging that defendant Apple Computer, a California corporation, had rescinded its policy of free technical phone support to its approximately 2.4 million customers in violation of California's consumer protection law).

[3] *The Community of Interest Requirement*

This broadly stated pragmatic requirement embodies several related factors, whose application varies with the facts and circumstances of each individual case.

[a] Common Questions of Law or Fact Must Predominate Over Individual Issues

A class action cannot be maintained where each member's right to recovery depends on facts peculiar to his case "because the community of interest requirement is not satisfied if every member of the alleged class would be required to litigate numerous and substantial questions determining his individual right to recover." *City of San*

Jose v. Superior Court, 12 Cal. 3d 447, 459, 115 Cal. Rptr. 797, 525 P.2d 701 (1974). "Only in an extraordinary situation would a class action be justified where, subsequent to the class judgment, the members would be required to individually prove not only damages but also liability." *Id.* at 463. Why this rule?

(1) This factor does not require a common or identical recovery as a prerequisite to a class action. *Daar v. Yellow Cab Co., supra*, 67 Cal. 2d at 707-709. Nor is a class action inappropriate simply because each member of the class may at some point be required to make an individual showing as to eligibility for recovery or the amount of damages. *Sav-On Drug Stores, Inc. v. Superior Court*, 34 Cal. 4th 319, 332-35, 17 Cal. Rptr. 3d 906, 96 P.3d 194 (2004); *Employment Dev. Dept. v. Superior Court*, 30 Cal. 3d 256, 266, 178 Cal. Rptr. 612, 637 P.2d 575 (1981). The fact that each member of the class must prove his separate claim to a portion of any recovery is only one factor to be considered in determining whether a class action is proper. *Vasquez v. Superior Court, supra*, 4 Cal. 3d at 809; *Sav-On Drug Stores, supra*, 34 Cal. 4th at 334-35; *see Evans v. Lasco Bathware, Inc.*, 178 Cal. App. 4th 1417, 1427-32, 101 Cal. Rptr. 3d 354 (2009) (reviewing cases and concluding a trial court has the discretion to deny class certification when it concludes the fact and extent of each class member's injury requires individualized inquiries that defeat predominance).

(2) Where individual issues regarding *liability and damages* substantially predominate over common factual questions, however, class action treatment is rarely appropriate. *Lockheed Martin Corp. v. Superior Court*, 29 Cal. 4th 1096. 131 Cal. Rptr. 2d 1, 63 P.3d 913 (2003) (reversing certification of a medical monitoring class consisting of over 50,000 residents of Redlands, California who had consumed drinking water allegedly contaminated by the defendants' discharges of toxic chemicals over several decades because plaintiffs failed to demonstrate by substantial evidence that these common issues of causation and damages *predominate* over the individual ones); *City of San Jose v. Superior Court, supra*, 12 Cal. 3d at 458-63 (holding in a nuisance and inverse condemnation action by homeowners for diminution of market value of their property due to flight pattern of municipal airport is inappropriate for class treatment because recovery predicated on facts peculiar to each prospective plaintiff). Why? What are the policy reasons for refusing class treatment in such circumstances?

(3) This common questions factor usually precludes class certification of mass tort actions for personal injuries. *See, e.g., Clausing v. San Francisco Unified Sch. Dist., supra*; *Basurco v. 21st Century Ins. Co.*, 108 Cal. App. 4th 110, 133 Cal. Rptr. 2d 367 (2003); *see also Jolly v. Eli Lilly & Co.*, 44 Cal. 3d 1103, 1123, 245 Cal. Rptr. 658, 751 P.2d 923 (1988) (noting mass tort actions for personal injury are rarely appropriate for class certification because their major elements — liability, proximate cause, and damages — may vary widely as to each individual claimant). Mass tort actions, such as products liability or airline disaster actions, often involve questions of law and fact common to the entire class of injured claimants, do they not? Why is class action treatment inappropriate for such cases? Is there any other procedure by which some of the benefits of the class action device may be achieved in such

cases? *See* CCP § 404 *et seq.*; Rules 3.500-3.550, Cal. Rules of Court (coordination proceedings).

(4) The California courts appear more willing to find this common questions factor satisfied in consumer rights cases, even though the alleged class-wide fraud or other unfair conduct involved numerous separate and individual transactions. *See, e.g., Vasquez v. Superior Court, supra,* 4 Cal. 3d at 811-15 (holding consumers may maintain a class action seeking rescission of installment contracts to purchase merchandise based on alleged fraudulent misrepresentations; facts justified inference of class-wide misrepresentations and reliance such that individual proof unnecessary); *Massachusetts Mut. Life Ins. Co. v. Superior Court,* 97 Cal. App. 4th 1282, 119 Cal. Rptr. 2d 190 (2002) (affirming in a consumer fraud action the trial court's certification of a class consisting of 33,000 people who, over a period of 15 years, purchased a particular type of life insurance product from the defendant where the purchases by each class member gave rise to an inference of common reliance on defendant's alleged material misrepresentations); *McAdams v. Monier, Inc.,* 182 Cal. App. 4th 174, 180-87, 105 Cal. Rptr. 3d 704 (2010) (reversing denial of certification of consumer class action that alleged manufacturer had misrepresented the quality of its roof tiles; inference of common reliance was adequate to show each class member was mislead); *but see Kavruck v. Blue Cross of Cal.,* 108 Cal. App. 4th 773, 134 Cal. Rptr. 2d 152 (2003) (holding denial of class certification proper where action for fraud against health insurance company required proof of oral representations on a subscriber-by-subscriber basis); *Tucker v. Pac. Bell Mobile Serv.,* 208 Cal. App. 4th 201, 145 Cal. Rptr. 3d 340 (2012) (ruling consumers could not maintain class action because alleged misrepresentations were communicated through various means and allegedly fraudulent of practice would involve individualized inquiries).

Why are the California courts more flexible in finding common questions in consumer class actions than in mass-tort actions? Does this difference in class treatment have anything to do with the applicable substantive law? *See* The Consumers Legal Remedies Act (CLRA), Civil Code § 1750 *et seq.; Thompson v. Auto. Club of S. Cal.,* 217 Cal. App. 4th 719, 728, n. 2, 158 Cal. Rptr. 3d 694 (2013) (noting that one key difference between CCP § 382 and the CLRA is that "under the CLRA, if all the requirements are satisfied, the court must certify the class"); *Tucker, supra,* 208 Cal. App. 4th at 216, n. 9 (noting that Civil Code § 1781 "sets out four conditions that, if met, mandate certification of a class").

(5) This common questions factor may also cause a court to decline to certify a nationwide class action where California's choice-of-law rules would require the application of different states' laws to various class members based on their residency. *E.g., Washington Mut. Bank v. Superior Court,* 24 Cal. 4th 906, 926, 103 Cal. Rptr. 2d 320, 15 P.3d 1071 (2001) (ruling class action proponent "must credibly demonstrate, through a thorough analysis of the applicable state laws, that state law variations will not swamp common issues and defeat predominance"); *Osborne v. Subaru of America, Inc.,* 198 Cal. App. 3d 646, 243 Cal. Rptr. 815 (1988) (holding nationwide class of automobile owners inappropriate because conflicts rules would

require adjudication of numerous separate questions of other states' laws); *Clothes-rigger, Inc. v. GTE Corp.*, 191 Cal. App. 3d 605, 236 Cal. Rptr. 605 (1987) (ruling nationwide class of long distance telephone subscribers may be appropriate if conflicts analysis results in application of similar legal questions to all class members); *Rutledge v. Hewlett-Packard Co.*, 238 Cal. App. 4th 1164, 190 Cal. Rptr. 3d 411 (2015) (reversing trial court's order denying nationwide class certification where, under conflicts analysis, California's consumer protection laws would apply to class members).

(6) May certification of a proposed class be denied based upon the trial court's preliminary assessment that the cause of action alleged on behalf of the class lacks sufficient merit? In *Linder v. Thrifty Oil Co.*, 23 Cal. 4th 429, 439-40, 97 Cal. Rptr. 2d 179, 2 P.3d 27 (2000), the Supreme Court indicated that the question of class certification is essentially a procedural one that does not ask whether an action is legally or factually meritorious. Subsequently, in *Brinker Restaurant Corp. v. Superior Court*, 53 Cal. 4th 1004, 139 Cal. Rptr. 3d 315, 273 P.3d 513 (2012), the California Supreme Court summarized the principles governing whether trial courts should resolve threshold disputes over the merits when ruling on class certification motions:

> Presented with a class certification motion, a trial court must examine the plaintiff's theory of recovery, assess the nature of the legal and factual disputes likely to be presented, and decide whether individual or common issues predominate. To the extent the propriety of certification depends upon disputed threshold legal or factual questions, a court may, and indeed must, resolve them. Out of respect for the problems arising from one-way intervention, however, a court generally should eschew resolution of such issues unless necessary. Consequently, a trial court does not abuse its discretion if it certifies (or denies certification of) a class without deciding one or more issues affecting the nature of a given element if resolution of such issues would not affect the ultimate certification decision.

Brinker, supra, 53 Cal. 4th at 1025; *see Hendershot v Ready to Roll Transp., Inc.*, 228 Cal. App. 4th 1213, 175 Cal. Rptr. 3d 917 (2014) (applying *Brinker* and concluding trial court improperly considered the merits of defendant's affirmative defenses in its class action "numerosity" analysis); *Morgan v. Wet Seal, Inc.*, 210 Cal. App. 4th 1341, 149 Cal. Rptr. 3d 70 (2012) (applying *Brinker* and ruling trial court properly considered the merits of the class claims in order to assess whether common issues predominate); *Hall v. Rite Aid Corp.*, 226 Cal. App. 4th 278, 171 Cal. Rptr. 3d 504 (2014) (applying *Brinker* and holding the trial court erred because its decertification order was based on an assessment of the merits of the class claims rather than on whether the theory was amenable to class treatment).

(7) The California courts have long recognized that class action litigation is a superior method of resolving claims alleging violations of California's wage and hour laws. Courts in such cases have been willing to find the ascertainable class and common questions factors satisfied despite the existence of some individual issues. *E.g., Martinez v. Joe's Crab Shack Holdings*, 213 Cal. App. 4th 362, 179 Cal. Rptr. 3d 867 (2014); *Jaimez v. Daiohs USA, Inc.*, 181 Cal. App. 4th 1286, 105 Cal. Rptr. 3d 443 (2010);

Ghazaryan v. Diva Limousine, Ltd., 169 Cal. App. 4th 1524, 87 Cal. Rptr. 3d 518 (2008); *Aguiar v. Cintas Corp. No. 2*, 144 Cal. App. 4th 121, 50 Cal. Rptr. 3d 135 (2006).

In *Brinker Restaurant Corp. v. Superior Court*, 53 Cal. 4th 1004, 139 Cal. Rptr. 3d 315, 273 P.3d 513 (2012), the California Supreme Court discussed whether common questions predominated over individual issues with respect to a putative class action seeking monetary remedies on behalf of the cooks, wait staff, and other hourly employees who staffed the defendant employer's restaurants. Plaintiffs alleged that defendants failed to provide these employees meal and rest breaks, and required them to work "off-the-clock," in violation of California's wage and hour laws. In reviewing the trial court's certification of subclasses, the Supreme Court first observed that "whether common or individual questions predominate will often depend upon resolution of issues closely tied to the merits." *Brinker, supra,* 53 Cal. 4th at 1024.

As to the specific subclasses, the Court noted that "[c]laims alleging a uniform policy consistently applied to a group of employees is in violation of the wage and hour laws are the sort routinely, and properly, found suitable for class treatment." *Brinker*, 53 Cal. 4th at 1033. Because the plaintiffs pleaded and presented substantial evidence of a uniform rest break policy, the Court concluded that the trial court properly certified a rest break subclass. However, because the plaintiffs presented no substantial evidence of a uniform, companywide policy regarding off-the-clock work, proof of off-the-clock liability would have to be determined on an employee-by-employee basis, demonstrating who worked off the clock, how long they worked, and whether the defendants knew of their work. Accordingly, as to the off-the-clock subclass, the Court concluded that common questions did not predominate and class certification was therefore inappropriate.

Post-*Brinker* decisions often deny class certification where the plaintiffs are unable to prove a uniform policy, such as a companywide practice denying employees meal/rest breaks. *E.g., Dailey v. Sears, Roebuck & Co.*, 214 Cal. App. 4th 874, 154 Cal. Rptr. 3d 480 (2013); *Sotelo v. Medianews Group, Inc.*, 207 Cal. App. 4th 639, 143 Cal. Rptr. 3d 293 (2012); *Tien v. Tenet Healthcare Corp.*, 209 Cal. App. 4th 1077, 147 Cal. Rptr. 3d 620 (2012); *but see Bradley v. Networkers Int'l, LLC*, 211 Cal. App. 4th 1129, 150 Cal. Rptr. 3d 268 (2012) (reversing denial of class certification where plaintiffs alleged the defendant employer's *lack* of a meal and rest break policy violated the California wage and hour laws). However, other post-*Brinker* decisions focus on whether class treatment is nonetheless appropriate even though there are individual issues of liability or damages. *See, e.g., Duran v. U.S. Bank Nat'l Assn.*, 59 Cal. 4th 1, 172 Cal. Rptr. 3d 371, 325 P.3d 916 (2014) (ruling that it may be possible to manage individual issues through the use of surveys and statistical sampling); *Ayala v. Antelope Valley Newspapers, Inc.*, 59 Cal. 4th 522, 173 Cal. Rtpr. 3d 332, 317 P.3d 165 (2014) (cautioning trial courts to avoid focusing on inevitable variations in the actions of individual employees and to instead focus on the policies—formal or informal—in force in the workplace); *Martinez v. Joe's Crab Shack Holdings*, 213 Cal. App. 4th 362, 179 Cal. Rptr. 3d 867 (2014) (reversing denial of class certification and observing that by refocusing its analysis on the policies and practices of the employer and their effect on the putative class, the trial court may in fact find that class treatment is a more efficient and effective means of resolving the plaintiffs' overtime claims).

[b] Class Action Treatment Must Result in Substantial Benefits that are Superior to the Alternatives

As *Richmond v. Dart Industries* indicates, this flexible factor overlaps with the common questions factor, and generally requires consideration of whether common questions are sufficiently pervasive such that class treatment is more advantageous than multiple individual suits. *See Vasquez v. Superior Court, supra,* 4 Cal. 3d at 810; *City of San Jose v. Superior Court, supra,* 12 Cal. 3d at 460.

This factor is sometimes equated with the "superiority" requirement of federal Rule 23(b)(3): For a class action to be maintained, it must be "superior to other available methods for the fair and efficient adjudication of the controversy," including consideration of "the difficulties likely to be encountered in the management of a class action." *See, e.g., Dean Witter Reynolds, Inc. v. Superior Court,* 211 Cal. App. 3d 758, 773, 259 Cal. Rptr. 789 (1989) (finding class treatment of unfair competition claims not demonstrably superior to individual action where statute empowered court to grant injunctive relief, including restitution, in favor of absent persons without certifying a class, but denied compensatory damages); *Lazar v. Hertz Corp., supra,* 143 Cal. App. 3d at 143-44 (holding consumer class action superior to alternative of asserting claims against fund deposited by defendant).

[c] Manageability

The "substantial benefits" factor also includes a "manageability" requirement analogous to the one in federal Rule 23(b)(3). Even if the existence of common issues appears to warrant class treatment, a trial court "must also conclude that the litigation of individual issues, including those arising from affirmative defenses, can be managed fairly and efficiently." *Duran v. U.S. Bank Nat. Assn.,* 59 Cal. 4th 1, 29, 172 Cal. Rptr. 3d 371, 325 P.3d 916 (2014); *see Ayala v. Antelope Valley Newspapers, Inc.,* 59 Cal. 4th 522, 173 Cal. Rptr. 3d 332, 327 P.3d 165 (2014) (discussing manageability of individual liability issues in a wage and hour class action). Defenses that raise individual questions about the calculation of damages generally do not defeat class certification, but "a defense in which liability itself is predicated on factual questions specific to individual claimants poses a much greater challenge to manageability." *Duran, supra.*

If sufficient common questions exist to support class certification, it may be possible to manage individual issues regarding liability and damages through the use of representative testimony, surveys, statistical sampling, or other procedures employing statistical methodology. *Duran, supra,* 59 Cal. 4th at 29-42; *see Bell v. Farmers Ins. Exch.,* 115 Cal. App. 4th 715, 9 Cal. Rptr. 3d 544 (2004) (employing statistical sampling to prove damages in a wage and hour class action); *Alberts v. Aurora Behavioral Heath Care,* 241 Cal. App. 4th 388, 193 Cal. Rptr. 783 (2015) (ruling trial court erred in refusing to consider statistical evidence regarding common behavior toward class members); *Tyson Foods, Inc. v. Bouaphakeo*, ___ U.S. ___, 136 S. Ct. 1036, 194 L. Ed. 2d 124 (2016) (approving the use of representative and statistical evidence in class actions in federal courts). To be valid, the statistical sampling must be representative of the entire class, developed with input from the parties' experts, randomly selected and not biased in one party's favor, and have a tolerable margin of error. *Duran, supra*, 59 Cal. 4th at 31-50. Most importantly, a class action management plan based on a statistical model of proof must not deprive the defendant of the ability to litigate relevant affirmative defenses, even when proof of these defenses turn on individual questions. *Duran, supra*, 59 Cal. 4th at 33-39.

[d] The Class Representative Must Adequately Represent the Interests of the Class

This factor reflects a basic due process concern: The absentee members of a class are not bound by a class judgment unless their interests were in fact adequately represented by the named parties. *Hansberry v. Lee*, 311 U.S. 32, 61 S. Ct. 115, 85 L. Ed. 22 (1940); *City of San Jose v. Superior Court, supra*, 12 Cal. 3d at 463. The California courts have developed several related inquiries to assist in the determination of whether class certification is appropriate based on this factor.

(1) *Are the Interests of the Representative Party in Conflict with the Interests of the Class?* As *Richmond v. Dart Industries* illustrates, *some* conflict between the interests of the class representative and the class members will not necessary preclude class certification. What type of conflict of such interests will defeat a class action? Do you agree with the Supreme Court's determination in *Richmond* that the conflict there did not preclude class certification? Why? What procedural devices may be utilized to minimize such conflict and permit class treatment? *See generally* Deborah L. Rhode, *Class Conflicts in Class Actions*, 34 STAN. L. REV. 1183 (1982).

The California courts rarely deny class certification where potential conflicts of interests can be removed by modification of the class definition by an appropriate procedural device. *See, e.g., Daniels v. Centennial Grp., Inc.*, 16 Cal. App. 4th 467, 21 Cal. Rptr. 2d 1 (1993) (ruling potential conflict between class representatives and the class over claim of rescission of partnership consolidation as opposed to damages can be avoided by subclasses or by certifying a class as to damage relief only); *Aguiar v. Cintas Corp. No. 2*, 144 Cal. App. 4th 121, 50 Cal. Rptr. 3d 135 (2006) (concluding class action alleging defendant employer violated living wage ordinance applicable to employees who worked at least 20 hours per week was proper because the putative class can be divided into subclasses of those employees who worked at least 20 hours per week and those who did not); *National Solar Equip. Owners' Assn. v. Grumman Corp.*, 235 Cal. App. 3d 1273, 1 Cal. Rptr. 2d 325 (1991) (ruling conflict not irreconcilable and can be cured by the time class seeks certification through redefinition of class, subclasses, or exclusions).

However, where the conflict is unavoidable, class certification must be denied. *See, e.g., Knox v. Streatfield*, 79 Cal. App. 3d 565, 145 Cal. Rptr. 39 (1978) (holding class action on behalf of all owners of a subdivision to enforce restrictions against those owners allegedly in violation is inappropriate due to conflict of interests between violating and nonviolating members of the class); *Seastrom v. Neways, Inc.*, 149 Cal. App. 4th 1496, 57 Cal. Rptr. 903 (2007) (concluding in an action against a manufacturer of an oral spray for illegally selling the spray without a prescription, the distributors of the oral spray could not represent a class consisting of all persons who purchased the spray without a prescription because the distributors made commissions on the sale of the product to class members and are therefore potential defendants).

(2) *Is the Class Representative a Member of the Class She Purports to Represent?* Under certain circumstances, class certification may be denied when the named plaintiff does not suffer the same injury as the members of the class. *See, e.g., Stephens v. Montgomery Ward*, 193 Cal. App. 3d 411, 422, 238 Cal. Rptr. 602 (1987) (ruling plaintiff saleswoman in a department store chain, who had been promoted to department manager twice before, was not an appropriate representative for a class of female employees alleging that defendant failed to promote women to department manager positions); *Fuhrman v. California Satellite Sys.*, 179 Cal. App. 3d 408, 425, 231 Cal. Rptr. 113 (1986) (holding plaintiff, who never received defendant's satellite cable television signals, could not represent class of consumers who did receive the defendant's signals, in action for emotional distress caused by defendant's letters threatening unlawful receipt of signals).

(a) This consideration is not inflexibly applied. For example, a named plaintiff may properly represent proposed classes even though not strictly a member of each class, so long as there is a sufficient community of interests between the plaintiff and each class. *See, e.g., Daniels v. Centennial Grp., Inc.*, 16 Cal. App. 467, 473, 21 Cal. Rptr. 2d 1 (1993); *Wershba v. Apple Computer, Inc.*, 91 Cal. App. 4th 224, 238-39, 110 Cal. Rptr. 2d 145 (2001). More importantly, a defendant's grant of individual relief to the named plaintiffs in a class action does not, in itself, necessarily render the plaintiffs unfit to represent the class. *Kagan v. Gibralter Sav. & Loan Assn.*, 35 Cal. 3d 582, 200 Cal. Rptr. 38, 676 P.2d 1060 (1984); *La Sala v. American Sav. & Loan Assn.*, 5 Cal. 3d 864, 97 Cal. Rptr. 849, 489 P.2d 1113 (1971). What are the policy reasons for permitting a class action to proceed even though the defendant has provided individual relief to the representative party?

(b) A class action does not become moot simply because the representative plaintiff's individual claim is moot. *Johnson v. Hamilton*, 15 Cal. 3d 461, 465, 125 Cal. Rptr. 129, 541 P.2d 881 (1975). Even if the named plaintiff receives all the benefits she seeks in the complaint, such success does not divest her of the duty to continue the action for the benefit of others similarly situated. *See La Sala v. American Sav. & Loan Assn., supra*, 5 Cal. 3d at 871 (holding trial court must determine whether named plaintiff will continue to fairly and adequately protect interest of the class); *Wallace v. GEICO General Ins. Co.*, 183 Cal. App. 4th 1390, 108 Cal. Rptr. 3d 375 (2010) (ruling proper procedure in a "pickoff" situation is for the trial court to consider whether the named plaintiff will continue fairly to represent the class in light of the individual relief offer by the defendant); Jean Wegman Burns, *Standing and Mootness in Class Actions: A Search for Consistency*, 22 U.C. DAVIS L. REV. 1239 (1989). What is the policy reason for this continuing duty to represent the class? Is it a wise policy, in light of the named plaintiff's lack of stake in the litigation?

(c) Does a class action become moot when the named plaintiff *voluntarily* settles her individual claims after the trial court denied class certification, but settlement reserves the right to appeal the "class claim?" *See, e.g., Watkins v. Wachovia Corp.*, 172 Cal. App. 4th 1576, 92 Cal. Rptr. 3d 409 (2009) (concluding that unlike the involuntary resolution, or "pick off," of a representative plaintiff's claim, voluntary settlement of the class representative's individual claim means the plaintiff is no longer a member of the class and therefore moots her right to appeal denial of class certification); *Larner v. Los Angeles Doctors Hosp. Associates*, 168 Cal. App. 4th 1291, 86 Cal. Rptr. 3d 324 (2008) (holding representative plaintiff who voluntarily settled after denial of class certification could not proceed with an appeal of an adverse class certification ruling).

(3) May a plaintiff obtain precertification discovery in a class action for the express purpose of identifying potential substitute class action plaintiffs? *See Best Buy Stores v. Superior Court*, 137 Cal. App. 4th 772, 40 Cal. Rptr. 3d 575 (2006) (finding trial court did not abuse its discretion in permitting precertification discovery for the purpose of identifying potential class action plaintiffs after plaintiff attorney found he could not act as both class representative and as counsel for the class); *CashCall, Inc. v. Superior Court*, 159 Cal. App. 4th 273, 71 Cal. Rptr. 3d 441 (2008) (applying balancing test where named plaintiffs who have *never* been members of the class seek precertification discovery of the identities of class members; the "trial court must expressly identify any potential abuses of the class action procedure that may be created if discovery is permitted, and the danger of such abuses against the rights of the parties under the circumstances"); *but see First American Title Ins. Co. v. Superior Court*, 146 Cal. App. 4th 1564, 53 Cal. Rptr. 3d 734 (2007) (holding trial court abused its discretion in permitting precertification discovery where the plaintiff class representative was not, and never had been, a member of the class he purports to represent); *CVS Pharmacy, Inc. v. Superior Court*, 241 Cal. App. 4th 300, 193 Cal. Rptr. 3d 574 (2015) (same).

(4) *The Claims of the Class Representative Must Be Typical of the Claims of the Class.* This factor restates the various considerations embodied in the requirement that the representative party must adequately represent the interest of the class. Named plaintiffs do not adequately represent the class members when they "fail to raise claims or seek relief reasonably expected to be raised by members of the class and thus pursue a course which, even should the litigation be resolved in favor of the class, would deprive class members of many elements of damage." *City of San Jose v. Superior Court*, 12 Cal. 3d at 464; *see Evans v. Lasco Bathware, Inc.*, 178 Cal. App. 4th 1417, 1432-34, 101 Cal. Rptr. 3d 354 (2009) (holding plaintiffs, by limiting homeowners' class action to recovery of cost of replacing defective shower pans, were not adequate class representatives because that recovery would forfeit additional recoveries, such as consequential damages to other parts of the house); *Janik v. Rudy, Exelrod & Zieff*, 119 Cal. App. 4th 930, 14 Cal. Rptr. 3d 751 (2004) (ruling class action attorney has obligations that may extend beyond the claims as certified to related claims arising out of the same set of

facts that class members reasonably could expect to be asserted in conjunction with the certified claims). What is the purpose of this typicality requirement?

(5) *The Plaintiff's Attorney Must Be Qualified to Conduct the Proposed Class Action Litigation.* Adequacy of counsel may be particularly important in class actions which involve complex procedural and substantive issues, and require high levels of competency and resources. *See McGowan v. Faulkner Concrete Pipe Co.*, 659 F.2d 554, 559 (5th Cir. 1981) (concluding trial judge properly considered displayed incompetency of attorney for proposed class in denying class certification); Rule 23(g), FRCP. This consideration, however, is rarely mentioned as a significant factor by the California courts in their class action decisions. *See, e.g., Miller v. Woods*, 148 Cal. App. 3d 862, 874, 196 Cal. Rptr. 69 (1983) (ruling that in order for the representative to adequately represent the class, the representative's attorney must be qualified, experienced and generally able to conduct the proposed litigation); *McGhee v. Bank of America*, 60 Cal. App. 3d 442, 450, 131 Cal. Rptr. 482 (1976) (finding plaintiff's attorneys are qualified and able to act as attorneys for the class). For most class actions, is not the quality of the class representative's attorney far more important than the attributes of the named plaintiff? Why? Does this requirement open the door to abuse by excluding all but a small number of favored attorneys from conducting a major class action suit?

[B] Class Action Procedures

[1] Introductory Note

Because few generally applicable state statutes or rules exist to govern class action procedures, California courts usually followed the procedural provisions of Consumers Legal Remedies Act, Civil Code § 1781(c)-(g), in all civil actions. *Vasquez v. Superior Court, supra.* And in the absence of relevant state precedents, the courts often utilized the procedure prescribed in Rule 23 of the Federal Rules of Civil Procedure. *See, e.g., City of San Jose v. Superior Court, supra*, 12 Cal. 3d at 145-46; *Bangert v. Narmco Materials, Inc.*, 163 Cal. App. 3d 207, 209 Cal. Rptr. 438 (1984).

California Rules of Court now govern the management of class actions, including motions to certify or decertify a class, case conferences, notice to class members, orders in the conduct of class actions, discovery from unnamed class members, and settlement and dismissals of class actions. *See* Cal. Rules of Ct. 3.760-3.771.

[2] Raising the Class Action Issue

[a] Raising the Issue by Demurrer or by Certification Motion

The trial court may decide the issue of class certification on demurrer — sustaining a demurrer where the complaint on its face fails to allege facts sufficient to establish the requisite ascertainable class and community of interest. *See, e.g., TJX Companies, Inc. v. Superior Court*, 87 Cal. App. 4th 747, 104 Cal. Rptr. 2d 810 (2001) (collecting cases); *Brown v. Regents of Univ. of Cal.*, 151 Cal. App. 3d 982, 985-86, 108 Cal. Rptr. 916 (1984). The preferable procedure, however, is for the trial court to make the class action determination subsequent to the pleading stage, after notice and a certification hearing. *See, e.g., Gutierrez v. California Commerce Club, Inc.*, 187 Cal. App. 4th 969, 976-80, 114 Cal. Rptr. 3d 611 (2010) (noting that as a general principle, class suitability should not be determined at the pleading stage); *Prince v. CLS Transp., Inc.*, 118 Cal. App. 4th 1320, 13 Cal. Rptr. 3d 725 (2004) (reversing trial court's order sustaining a demurrer to the class action allegations in a complaint brought by employees seeking class recovery for nonpayment of overtime compensation and observing that it is only in mass tort actions, or other actions equally unsuited to class action treatment, that class suitability can and should be determined at the pleading stage). This determination may be made on motion of either plaintiff or defendant, or on the court's own motion. *City of San Jose v. Superior Court, supra*, 12 Cal. 3d at 453. Why should the trial court delay the class determination until after the pleading stages?

After certification, a trial court retains flexibility to manage the class action, including to decertify the class if the court subsequently discovers that a class action is not appropriate. *E.g., Weinstat v. Dentsply Int'l, Inc.*, 180 Cal. App. 4th 1213, 103 Cal. Rptr. 3d 614 (2010); *Williams v. Superior Court*, 221 Cal. App. 4th 1353, 1360-61, 165 Cal. Rptr. 3d 340 (2013). To prevail on a decertification motion, a party must generally show that new law or newly discovered evidence constitutes changed circumstances making continued class treatment improper. *Green v. Obledo*, 29 Cal. 3d 126, 148, 172 Cal. Rptr. 206, 624 P.2d 256 (1981); *Kight v. Cashcall, Inc.*, 231 Cal. App. 4th 112, 125-28, 179 Cal. Rptr. 3d 439 (2014); *Williams v. Superior Court, supra*.

[b] Class Action Discovery

In *Pioneer Electronics (USA), Inc. v. Superior Court*, 40 Cal. 4th 360, 53 Cal. Rptr. 3d 513, 150 P.3d 198 (2007), the Supreme Court addressed the issue of whether a named plaintiff can use discovery to identify class members prior to certification of the class. The court concluded that contact information regarding the identity of potential class members is generally discoverable, so that the named plaintiff may learn the names of other persons who might assist in prosecuting the case. *Pioneer Electronics, supra*, 40 Cal. 4th at 373. If the information sought implicates privacy concerns, the trial court should balance competing interests and provide notice so a class member may register an objection to disclosure. *Id.* at 373-375; *see Crab Addison, Inc. v. Superior Court*, 169 Cal. App. 4th 958, 87 Cal. Rptr. 3d 400 (2008) (upholding named plaintiff's discovery of class members' names, addresses, and telephone numbers in a class action alleging wage and overtime violations); *Lee v. Dynamex, Inc.*, 166 Cal. App. 4th 1325, 83 Cal. Rptr. 3d 241 (2008) (holding trial court abused its discretion in denying plaintiff's motion to compel disclosure of identity of potential class members because without this discovery, plaintiff lacked the means to develop evidence capable of supporting his motion for class certification).

[3] Class Determination Prior to Liability Decision

Although the trial court may properly delay the class certification decision until after the pleading stages of litigation, as a general rule the court must resolve class certification issues before reaching a decision on the merits. *Fireside Bank v. Superior Court*, 40 Cal. 4th 1069, 1083-84, 56 Cal. Rptr. 3d 861, 155 P.3d 268 (2007) (ruling that although trial courts generally have broad discretion to manage and order class affairs, in the absence of a defense waiver they should not resolve the merits in a putative class action case before class certification and notice issues absent a compelling justification for doing so); *Green v. Obledo*, 29 Cal. 3d 126, 172 Cal. Rptr. 206, 624 P.2d 256 (1981). From a defendant's viewpoint, it is very important and beneficial to know whether the action will be certified as a class action before final determination of the substantive issues. Why? *See Fireside Bank, supra,* 40 Cal. 4th at 1078-82; *People v. Pacific Land Research Co.,* 20 Cal. 3d 10, 16-17, 141 Cal. Rptr. 20, 569 P.2d 125 (1977); *Home Sav. & Loan Assn. v. Superior Court,* 42 Cal. App. 3d 1006, 117 Cal. Rptr. 485 (1974). From a plaintiff's viewpoint, a defendant's motion to decertify a previously certified class may be highly problematic where the trial court delays resolution of the decertification issues until the decision on the merits. Why? *See Green v. Obledo, supra,* 29 Cal. 3d at 146-49.

[4] *Appellate Review of Class Determination*

A trial court order denying class certification to an entire class is an immediately appealable order. *Daar v. Yellow Cab Co., supra,* 67 Cal. 2d at 699 (holding order held appealable because it effectively terminated the entire action as to all members of the class); *In re Baycol Cases I and II,* 51 Cal. 4th 751, 122 Cal. Rptr. 3d 153, 248 P.3d 681 (2011) (holding that if an order terminates class claims but individual claims survive, the order terminating class claims is immediately appealable under the "death knell" doctrine adopted in *Daar*). An order which denies class certification as to some causes of action but grants it as to others is not appealable as a matter of right, but may be reviewed by discretionary extraordinary writ. *See, e.g., Vasquez, supra,* 4 Cal. 3d at 806-807; *Blue Chip Stamps v. Superior Court,* 18 Cal. 3d 381, 134 Cal. Rptr. 393, 556 P.2d 755 (1976) (issuing writ of mandamus directing trial court to vacate order which certified class against defendant). However, if an order terminates class claims *and* individual claims, appeal lies from the subsequent entry of final judgment, not the order. *Baycol, supra,* 51 Cal. 4th at 760-62.

Trial courts have discretion in granting or denying motions for class certification. When denying class certification, a trial court must state its reasons, and the appellate court must review these reasons for correctness. *Linder v. Thrifty Oil Co.,* 23 Cal. 4th 429, 435-36, 97 Cal. Rptr. 2d 179, 2 P.3d 27 (2000). The appellate court may only consider the actual reasons stated by the trial court and must ignore any unexpressed reasons that may support the ruling. *Ayala v. Antelope Valley Newspapers, Inc.,* 59 Cal. 4th 522, 530, 173 Cal. Rptr. 3d 332, 327 P.3d 165 (2014); *Linder, supra.* If the stated reasons are erroneous—unsupported by substantial evidence, based on improper criteria or incorrect assumptions—the order denying class certification must be reversed. *Linder, supra,* 23 Cal. 4th at 436; *Ayala, supra,* 59 Cal. 4th at 530; *Alberts v. Aurora Behavioral Health Care,* 241 Cal. App. 4th 388, 193 Cal. Rptr. 3d 783 (2015) (reversing order denying class certification where trial court's stated reasons were without merit, and remanding for further consideration regarding predominance and manageability); *Knapp v. AT&T Wireless Serv., Inc.*, 195 Cal. App. 4th 932, 124 Cal. Rptr. 3d 565 (2011) (affirming denial of class action where substantial evidence supported trial court's stated reason of lack of commonality).

[a] Federal Approach Compared

Pursuant to Rule 23(f), F.R.C.P., a U.S. Court of Appeals "may permit an appeal from an order of a district court granting or denying class-action certification ... if a petition for permission to appeal is filed with the circuit court within 14 days after the order is entered." If the Court of Appeals declines to permit an interlocutory appeal, the district court's class certification order is reviewable only on appeal from the subsequent final judgment on the merits. *Cooper & Lybrand v. Livesey*, 437 U. S. 403, 98 S. Ct. 54, 57 L. Ed. 2d 351 (1978). How is the approach taken in new federal Rule 23(f) different than the California approach to interlocutory appellate review of class certification decisions? Is the federal approach preferable to the California approach? How so?

[b] Problems with California Rule

The California rule authorizing interlocutory appeals from class decertification orders creates some unanticipated problems. In *Stephen v. Enterprise Rent-A-Car*, 235 Cal. App. 3d 806, 1 Cal. Rptr. 2d 130 (1991), for example, plaintiff brought an action on behalf of a class of consumers seeking relief for alleged unconscionably high rates charged by defendant for collision damage waiver in car rental contracts. Plaintiff moved for class certification, which the trial court denied by order after a hearing. Plaintiff did not appeal this order, but instead filed a renewed motion for class certification a few months later. The trial court denied this renewed motion, and plaintiff sought appellate review. The Court of Appeal held that the plaintiff's failure to appeal the trial court's first order denying class certification precluded subsequent motions to certify, even if based on new evidence. Because state law grants immediate appellate review of such orders, to allow both interlocutory appeals and successive motions to certify would be impracticable. Although bringing new motions on new evidence after court has initially certified a class is appropriate, successive motions after a court has initially denied certification is not.

Do you understand the reasons for the *Stephen* court's holding? Do you agree with them? Does this holding affect your preferences with respect to the federal as opposed to the California policy on the appealability of class certification orders? How so?

[C] Notice to Class Members

[1] Notice Requirements, Generally

Code of Civil Procedure § 382 is silent on the issue of notice to class members. The California courts generally follow federal Rule 23(b) to determine whether a certified class is the type which requires mandatory notice to the absentee members of the class. *E.g., Bell v. American Title Ins. Co.*, 226 Cal. App. 3d 1589, 277 Cal. Rptr. 583 (1991), *Frazer v. City of Richmond*, 184 Cal. App. 3d 1491, 228 Cal. Rptr. 376 (1986); *Lowry v. Obledo*, 111 Cal. App. 3d 14, 23, 169 Cal. Rptr. 732 (1980). Consequently, mandatory notice to members of the class is required for those classes which satisfy only the definitions of Rule 23(b)(3); any notice is discretionary as to Rule 23(b)(1) and (b)(2) classes. Rule 23(c)(2) and (d), F.R.C.P.

[2] *Nature of Required Notice: Individual vs. Publication*

When a California court determines that *some* notice to the class as certified is required, the court does not necessarily follow federal Rule 23(c) to determine the precise nature of the class notice. *E.g., Cartt v. Superior Court*, 50 Cal. App. 3d 960, 124 Cal. Rptr. 376 (1975); *Cooper v. American Sav. & Loan Assn.*, 55 Cal. App. 3d 274, 127 Cal. Rptr. 579 (1976). Instead, the court would apply the manner of notice requirements of Civil Code § 1781(d), which authorizes notice by publication if personal notification is unreasonably expensive, and Civil Code § 1781(e), which governs the content of class notice with respect to requests for exclusion. *E.g., Cartt, supra*, 50 Cal. App. 3d at 970-75; *Cooper, supra*, 55 Cal. App. 3d at 283-85.

Rule 3.766 of the California Rule of Court now provides some guidance on the procedures and content of notice to class members in all class actions. With respect to the manner of giving notice, Rules 3.766(e) and (f) require the court to consider:

> (e)(1) The interests of the class; (2) The type of relief requested; (3) The stake of the individual class members; (4) The cost of notifying class members; (5) The resources of the parties; (6) The possible prejudice to class members who do not receive notice; and (7) The res judicata effect on class members.

> (f) If personal notification is unreasonably expensive or the stake of the individual class members is insubstantial, or if it appears that all members of the class cannot be notified personally, the court may order a means of notice reasonably calculated to apprise the class members of the pendency of the action—for example, publication in a newspaper of magazine; broadcasting on television, radio, or the Internet; or posting or distribution through a trade or professional association, union, or public interest group.

[a] Notice to Permit "Opt Out"

The California courts construe Civil Code § 1781(d) as requiring individual mailed notice to class members where members of the class have a substantial damage claim such that members may decide to "opt out" of the class and pursue their independent remedies. *Cooper v. American Sav. & Loan Assn., supra*, 55 Cal. App. 3d at 285. However, when membership in the class is huge and damages per member minimal, notice by publication may be adequate. *Cooper, supra*, 55 Cal. App. 3d at 284-86; *Cartt v. Superior Court, supra*, 50 Cal. App. 3d at 971-73. *See* Rule 3.766(f), Cal. Rules of Ct., reproduced *supra*.

With respect to the type of notice required for members of the class, the California courts view federal Rule 23 as useful, but not binding, and have declined to follow the construction of federal Rule 23(c)(2) in *Eisen v. Carlisle & Jacquelin*, 417 U.S. 156, 94 S. Ct. 2140, 40 L. Ed. 2d 732 (1974). *See, e.g., Cartt v. Superior Court, supra*, 50 Cal. App. 3d at 966-76; *Cooper v. American Sav. & Loan Assn., supra*, 55 Cal. App. 3d at 283. In *Eisen*, the U.S. Supreme Court held that federal Rule 23(c)(2) requires, for any class action maintained under Rule 23(b)(3), individual notice mailed to all class members who are identifiable through reasonable effort. *Eisen*, 417 U.S. at 173-77. The *Eisen* court ruled that publication notice would not be adequate notice even though the cost of providing individual notice to 2,250,000 class members was prohibitively high and no individual class member had a large enough damage claim to justify litigation of a separate claim. *Id.* at 174-77. *Compare* California Rule 3.766(e) & (f), reproduced *supra*.

[b] Due Process Concerns

Is the California rule, which apparently permits publication notice even where the names and addresses of the class members may be ascertained through reasonable effort, consistent with the Due Process Clause? *See Cartt v. Superior Court, supra*, 50 Cal. App. 3d at 979-76; *see also Mullane v. Central Hanover Bank & Trust Co.*, 339 U.S. 306, 70 S. Ct. 652, 94 L. Ed. 865 (1950); Linda J. Lopez, Note, *Cartt v. Superior Court: Notice and Consumer Class Actions in California*, 64 CAL. L. REV. 1222 (1976).

[3] *Who Pays the Cost of Class Notice*

The California Legislature has specifically authorized trial courts in consumer class actions to impose the cost of notice to the class upon either the plaintiff or the defendant. Civil Code § 1781(d). The Supreme Court extended this rule to all class actions in *Civil Service Employees Ins. Co. v. Superior Court*, 22 Cal. 3d 362, 374-81, 149 Cal. Rptr. 360, 584 P.2d 497 (1978), where it held that California trial courts clearly possess the authority to impose notice costs on either party in a class action. The Court also held that the imposition of class notice costs on a defendant was consistent with due process if, prior to the trial court order, the defendant had a full hearing on the issue of who should bear the cost of notifying the class during the pendency of the suit. *Id.* at 379-81. *See also* Rules 3.766(b) & (c), Cal. Rules of Ct.

[a] Cost Allocation Factors?

What factors are relevant to this allocation of class notice cost decision? The trial court's preliminary view of the strength of the plaintiff's claim? The cost of class notice in relation to the amount of the potential recovery for each individual class member? Which party is more capable of affording the financial burden of notice? *See Civil Service Employees, supra*, 22 Cal. 3d at 380-81; *Cartt, supra*, 50 Cal. App. 3d at 974-75.

[b] Federal Rule Compared

In contrast to the California rule, the federal rules do not authorize a federal court to impose the cost of class notice on the defendant. The U.S. Supreme Court in *Eisen v. Carlisle & Jacquelin*, 417 U.S. 156, 177-79, 94 S. Ct. 2140, 40 L. Ed. 2d 732 (1974), held that federal Rule 23 does not authorize departure from the usual rule that a plaintiff must initially bear the cost of notice to the class. The California Supreme Court in *Civil Service Employees* refused to follow *Eisen*, finding *Eisen* not binding on the California courts. Was this refusal proper? Why?

The issue of whether a trial court may impose the cost of class notice on the defendant is extremely important in many class actions. Why? What are the criticisms of the federal court rule? The California rule? For more discussion of these contrasting rules, see James R. McCall, *Due Process and Consumer Protection: Concepts and Realities in Procedure and Substance — Class Action Issues*, 25 HASTINGS L.J. 1351 (1974).

[4] Right to Opt Out of Class

The main purpose of providing proper notice of the pendency of a class action is to advise class members of their options: (1) To remain members of the class represented by plaintiff's counsel and become bound by a favorable or unfavorable judgment in the action, or (2) to intervene in the action through counsel of their own choosing, or (3) to "opt out" of the class action and pursue their own independent actions. *Home Sav. & Loan Assn. v. Superior Court*, 42 Cal. App. 3d 1006, 1010, 117 Cal. Rptr. 485 (1974); Civil Code § 1781(e); Rule 23(c)(2), F.R.C.P; *see* Rule 3.766(b)-(d), Cal. Rules of Ct. A class member will be bound by the class action judgment unless that member affirmatively requests exclusion. Rule 23(c)(2), F.R.C.P.; Civil Code § 1781(e).

[a] Due Process Concerns

An individual class member has no right to opt out of a class action certified under federal Rule 23(b)(1) or (b)(2). Why not? An individual class member does have the right to opt out of a Rule 23(b)(3) class action. Why?

A broader constitutional issue is whether an individual class member has a due process right to opt out of any class action which seeks money damages on behalf of the class. In *Phillips Petroleum Co. v. Shutts*, 472 U.S. 797, 105 S. Ct. 2965, 86 L. Ed. 2d 628 (1985), a class action for money damages brought in the Kansas state courts on behalf of thousands of class members many of whom were not Kansas residents, the U.S. Supreme Court held that before a court can bind an absent nonresident plaintiff to a class action judgment, "due process requires at a minimum that an absent plaintiff be provided with an opportunity to remove himself from the class by executing and returning an 'opt out' or 'request for exclusion' form to the court...." *Shutts*, 472 U.S. at 812. However, the Court expressly limited its holding "to those class actions which seek to bind known plaintiffs concerning claims wholly or predominantly for money judgments," and intimated "no view concerning other types of class actions, such as those seeking injunctive relief." *Id.* at 811-12, fn. 3; *see Bell v. American Title Ins. Co.*, 226 Cal. App. 3d 1589, 1609-11, 277 Cal. Rptr. 583 (1991) (ruling *Shutts'* due process holding does not apply to a class action seeking injunctive relief even though the class also sought restitution and price rollbacks, because the class claims are not predominantly for monetary relief); Arthur R. Miller & David Crump, *Jurisdiction and Choice of Law in Multistate Class Actions after Phillips Petroleum Co. v. Shutts*, 96 Yale L.J. 1, 38-57 (1986); Brian Wolfman & Alan B. Morrison, *What the Shutts Opt-Out Right Is and What It Ought To Be*, 74 U.M.K.C. L. Rev. 729 (2006).

[b] Determination of Opt Out Right

Most courts determine whether class members are entitled to notice and the right to opt out based on whether the appropriate relief sought by the class action is exclusively or predominantly for money damages. *E.g., Bell v. American Title Ins. Co., supra*, 226 Cal. App. 3d at 1609-11; *Frazer, supra*, 184 Cal. App. 3d at 1500-1504; *Carter v. City of Los Angeles*, 224 Cal. App. 4th 808, 169 Cal. Rptr. 3d 131 (2014). However, the U.S. Court of Appeals for the Ninth Circuit in *Brown v. Ticor Title Ins. Co.*, 982 F.2d 386 (9th Cir. 1992), *cert. dismissed*, 511 U.S. 117, 114 S. Ct. 1359 (1994), held that in order to bind an absentee class member concerning a claim for money damages, the court must provide the class member with an opportunity to opt out of the class action. The court, relying on *Shutt's* due process analysis, declined to extend res judicata to a prior class judgment for money damages where that class had been certified under federal Rule 23(b)(1) and (b)(2) and provided no right to opt out.

[5] Settlement

[a] Court Approval Required

A class action shall not be dismissed without approval of the court. CCP § 581(k); Civil Code § 1781(f); Rules 3.769 & 3,770, Cal. Rules of Ct. A trial court has broad discretion to determine whether a class action settlement is fair, but should consider the following relevant factors, identified in *Dunk v. Ford Motor Co.*, 48 Cal. App. 4th 1794, 1801, 56 Cal. Rptr. 2d 483 (1996):

> The strength of plaintiffs' case, the risk, expense, complexity and likely duration of further litigation, the risk of maintaining class action status through trial, the amount offered in settlement, the extent of discovery completed and the state of the proceedings, the experience and views of counsel, the presence of a governmental participant, and the reaction of the class members to the proposed settlement. The list of factors is not exhaustive and should be tailored to each case. Due regard should be given to what is otherwise a private consensual agreement between the parties.

The court in *Dunk, supra*, applied these factors and upheld the settlement of a nationwide class action brought against Ford Motor Company for alleged defects in the doors of certain cars, under which each class member would receive a coupon redeemable for $400 off the price of any new Ford vehicle. *See also 7-Eleven Owners For Fair Franchising v. Southland Corp.*, 85 Cal. App. 4th 1135, 102 Cal. Rptr. 2d 777 (2000) (applying the fairness factors identified in *Dunk*, and affirming the trial court's approval of the settlement of a national class); *Wershba v. Apple Computer, Inc.*, 91 Cal. App. 4th 224, 110 Cal. Rptr. 2d 145 (2001) (ruling application of the four factors identified in *Dunk* leads to presumption that settlement of national class action was fair, a presumption the objectors failed to overcome); *Clark v. American Residential Serv. LLC*, 175 Cal. App. 4th 785, 96 Cal. Rptr. 3d 441 (2009)(applying *Dunk* factors to determine whether the terms of a proposed class action settlement are fair, adequate, and reasonable).

When applying these and other relevant factors, the trial court must independently satisfy itself that the consideration being received for the release of the class members' claims is reasonable in light of the strengths and weaknesses of the claims and the risks of the particular litigation. *Kullar v. Foot Locker Retail, Inc.*, 168 Cal. App. 4th 116, 127-33, 85 Cal. Rptr. 3d 20 (2008); *Clark, supra*, 175 Cal. App. 4th at 798-804. Therefore, the trial court must receive evidence and consider enough information about the nature and magnitude of the claims being settled, as well as the impediments to recovery, to make an independent assessment of the settlement terms, *Kullar, supra*, 168 Cal. App. 4th at 131-33; *Munos v. BCI Coca-Cola Bottling Co.*, 186 Cal. App. 4th 399, 408-411, 112 Cal. Rptr. 3d 324 (2010); and may not simply accept class counsel's conclusion that as to value of the class claims, *Clark, supra*, 175 Cal. App. 4th at 801-804. Where this process is followed properly by the trial court, even the approval of a disfavored coupon settlement that includes substantial attorney fees may be considered fair, adequate, and reasonable. *Chavez v. Netflix, Inc.*, 162 Cal. App. 4th 43, 52- 55, 60-66, 75 Cal. Rptr. 3d 413 (2008).

[b] The Notice Requirement

Dismissal of class actions is one area where generally applicable state law exists to guide litigants and trial courts. Code of Civil Procedure §581(k) requires notice to the class and court approval prior to dismissal of an action determined to be a class action under CCP §§382. Rules 3.769 and 3.770 also govern settlement and dismissal of class actions, including the manner of notice to class members of a proposed class settlement or dismissal. *See, e.g., Wershba v. Apple Computer, Inc.*, 91 Cal. App. 4th 224, 110 Cal. Rptr. 2d 145 (2001) (affirming settlement of a nationwide class action alleging that defendant Apple Computer had rescinded its policy of free technical phone support to its customers in violation of California's consumer protection law, and approving methods of notice which included notice mailed e-mailed directly to more than 2.4 million class members and also published in USA Today and MacWorld, as well as the posting of notice by Apple on its internet homepage); *Cellphone Termination Fee Cases*, 186 Cal. App. 4th 1380, 1390-93, 113 Cal. Rptr. 3d 510 (2010) (upholding notice of proposed class settlement that included short-form publication and mail notice that directed class members to a settlement website to learn more information about the terms of the proposed settlement).

Notice of a proposed settlement to the putative class and subsequent court approval may be required even though the trial court has not yet certified the action as a class action. *See* Rule 3.770(c), Cal. Rules of Ct.; *La Sala v. American Sav. & Loan Assn.*, *supra*, 5 Cal. 3d at 872-73. Why is such notice and approval necessary for a precertification settlement? What are the advantages and disadvantages of this approach? What are the advantages and disadvantages of an approach which does not require notice to the putative class of a precertification settlement by the named parties? *See* J. Spencer Schuster, *Precertification Settlement of Class Actions: Will California Follow the Federal Lead?*, 40 Hastings L.J. 863 (1989); Michael A. Almond, *Settling Rule 23 Class Actions at the Precertification Stage: Is Notice Required?*, 56 N. C. L. Rev. 303 (1978).

[c] Conflicts of Interest

Settlement of class action suits produces some very troublesome problems. Every class action settlement process contains the potential for serious conflicts of interest among the various participants. For example, the attorney for the plaintiff class may favor a proposed class settlement with the defendant but the named plaintiff, who is more concerned with vindication of rights than with monetary recovery, may not. *See* Mary Kay Kane, *Of Carrots and Sticks: Evaluating the Role of the Class Action Lawyer*, 66 Tex. L. Rev. 385 (1987). Or the representative plaintiffs may favor a proposed settlement but certain members of the class may not. Under what circumstances is this latter conflict likely to occur? Does notice to class members and an opportunity to object to a proposed settlement eliminate such a conflict? For a discussion of these issues, see Sylvia R. Lazos, Note, *Abuse in Plaintiff Class Action Settlements: The Need for A Guardian During Pretrial Settlement Negotiations*, 84 Mich. L. Rev. 308 (1985); John C. Coffee, Jr., *Understanding the Plaintiff's Attorney: The Implications of Economic Theory for Private Enforcement of Law Through Class and Derivative Actions*, 86 Colum. L. Rev. 669 (1986); Jonathan R. Macey & Geoffrey P. Miller, *The Plaintiffs' Attorney's Role in Class Action and Derivative Litigation: Economic Analysis and Recommendations for Reform*, 58 U. Chi. L. Rev. 1 (1991).

[D] Class Action Remedies

A trial court in a class action has the same authority to award the full range of legal and equitable remedies as the court would have in an individual action. In addition, the California courts apparently have authority to award "fluid class" relief in appropriate cases.

[1] Fluid Class Recovery

The propriety of fluid class recovery in California has not been entirely free from doubt. The Supreme Court in *Blue Chip Stamps v. Superior Court*, 18 Cal. 3d 381, 134 Cal. Rptr. 393, 556 P.2d 755 (1976), seemed to find such relief improper because of the lack of correlation between those persons injured by a defendant and those to be compensated by the fluid class relief. The Court of Appeal in *Bruno v. Superior Court*, 127 Cal. App. 3d 120, 179 Cal. Rptr. 342 (1981), however, did not read *Blue Chip Stamps* as prohibiting fluid class recovery in California class actions.

The plaintiffs in *Bruno* sought to represent a class of over one million people who had purchased milk at defendants' supermarkets over a three-year period, alleging that the defendants unlawfully fixed milk prices at an artificially high level. Plaintiffs alleged that the average claim of each class member did not exceed $125, and sought a class-wide award of damages. They also requested that said sum to be paid on the basis of individual claims presented and to the extent class members do not present such claims, on the basis, as the Court deems appropriate, either: "(1) of a lowering of fluid milk prices in [Orange and Los Angeles Counties] by each of the defendants, or (2) of depositing said sum with the State of California, or a unit thereof, for the limited purpose of being applied to eleemosynary purposes benefiting the consuming public in [Orange and Los Angeles Counties]" *Bruno*, 127 Cal. App. 3d at 120. The trial court granted defendants' motion to strike from the complaint the two methods of distributing those damages which would not be paid out on the basis of individual class member claims.

The Court of Appeal held that the trial court erred in granting defendants' motion to strike the "fluid class" procedures to distribute damages. After analyzing *Blue Chip Stamps* and several other state and federal decisions, the court concluded that fluid class recovery was not improper in class actions in general, although the specific law under which the action was brought might preclude the use of such a damage distribution device. The court then ruled that fluid class recovery was not prohibited by the state antitrust law upon which plaintiffs based their class causes of action.

[a] Supreme Court Endorsement

More recently in *State v. Levi Strauss & Co.*, 41 Cal. 3d 460, 224 Cal. Rptr. 605, 715 P.2d 564 (1986), the Supreme Court approved a class action settlement which included fluid class relief, and referred to *Bruno v. Superior Court* as a "well-reasoned opinion." The class action in *Levi Strauss* was brought by the attorney general against the defendant manufacturer of jeans, seeking monetary relief for millions of consumers who allegedly were overcharged on jeans purchased during the early 1970's. The trial court approved a class settlement which included a cash refund distribution plan for individual claimants (over one million individual claims were subsequently received); and the Supreme Court approved the establishment of a "consumer trust fund" to further the purposes of the state consumer protection laws and provide indirect compensation to class members. *Levi Strauss*, 41 Cal 3d at 475.

The Supreme Court generally endorsed the propriety of fluid recovery in consumer class actions, and stated some guidelines for its use (*Levi Strauss*, 41 Cal. 3d at 472-76):

> The implementation of fluid recovery involves three steps. First, the defendant's total damage liability is paid over to a class fund. Second, individual

class members are afforded an opportunity to collect their individual shares by proving their particular damages, usually according to a lowered standard of proof. Third, any residue remaining after individual claims have been paid is distributed by one of several practical procedures that have been developed by the courts.

In order to assess the propriety of the fluid recovery method selected by the trial court in the present case, it is necessary to review briefly the available alternatives. The principal methods include a rollback of the defendant's prices, escheat to a governmental body for either specified or general purposes, establishment of a consumer trust fund, and claimant fund sharing. All of these methods promote the policies of disgorgement and deterrence by ensuring that the residue of the recovery does not revert to the wrongdoer. However, they differ substantially in their compensatory effect and in their suitability for particular cases.

In determining which method to employ, the courts should consider: (1) the amount of compensation provided to class members, including nonclaiming (or "silent") members; (2) the proportion of class members sharing in the recovery; (3) the extent to which benefits will "spill over" to nonclass members and the degree to which the spillover benefits will effectuate the purposes of the underlying substantive law; and (4) the costs of administration.

Under the price rollback approach, the uncollected portion of the fund is distributed through the market by lowering the price of the defendant's product for a specified period. * * * Price rollbacks are particularly effective for remedying overcharges on items which are repeatedly purchased by the same individuals. In cases involving such "repeat items," the individuals who were overcharged are likely to benefit from the reduced prices.

None of the parties have proposed a price rollback in the present action. This method is not appropriate in nonmonopoly markets like the jeans market since it compels consumers to collect their refunds by making further purchases of the defendant's products, to the detriment of the defendant's competitors. Further, the price of jeans to the consumer is fixed not by the defendant, but by independent retailers. Hence, a price rollback would pose difficult if not insuperable management problems.

A second form of fluid distribution is "earmarked escheat." Under this approach, the uncollected funds are disbursed to a reasonable governmental organization for use on projects that benefit noncollecting class members and promote the purposes of the underlying cause of action. * * *

Earmarked escheat provides indirect compensation to silent class members. The recipient governmental body may use class funds to ameliorate the effects of past harm and to reduce the risk of future harm. Administrative costs are minimized by utilizing already extant governmental bodies to administer the fund. Since earmarked escheat depends for its success upon the active cooperation of the government, it should not be employed where—as in the present case—the relevant governmental body opposes its use.

Another alternative is general escheat: payment of the recovery to the general fund of a governmental body. Of all the fluid recovery devices, general escheat provides the least focused compensation to the class. The benefits of the recovery are spread among all taxpayers, and there is no attempt to ensure that the spillover is used to effectuate the purposes of the substantive law. The only advantage of general escheat is ease of administration. Hence, it is usually regarded as a last resort for use when a more precise remedy cannot be found.

Intervener advocates a relatively new and increasingly popular form of fluid recovery—the establishment of a "consumer trust fund." Under this approach, the court appoints a board of directors to administer the recovery in the interests of the class.

Like earmarked escheat, the consumer trust fund device uses the residue to further the purposes of the substantive law and provide indirect compensation to class members. Unlike earmarked escheat, there is no danger that the recovery will be submerged in the state's general fund. However, the consumer trust fund device does entail the establishment of a new organization with its own administrative expenses. To avoid this additional cost, some courts have allocated the funds directly to responsible private organizations. * * *

Finally, the residue, or the fund itself, may be divided among the individual claimants. As initially approved, the present settlement incorporated this "claimant fund sharing" approach. * * * Unlike other methods of fluid recovery, claimant fund sharing uses the entire class recovery to provide monetary compensation to individual class members. Hence, in an appropriate case, it may yield a greater and more direct compensatory impact.

However, claimant fund sharing provides no benefits to silent class members. Further, if there is a windfall, it goes not to further the purposes of the substantive law, but to overcompensate legitimate claimants or to pay erroneous or fraudulent claims. Hence, the advantages of claimant fund sharing can only be realized where a large proportion of class members participate and submit accurate claims.

[b] Legislative Endorsement

In 1993 the Legislature enacted CCP § 384, which specifically endorses the concept of fluid class recovery. Section 384(a) states that the intent of the Legislature in enacting this section is "to ensure that the unpaid residuals in class action litigation are distributed, to the extent possible, in a manner designed to either further the purposes of the underlying causes of action, or to promote justice for all Californians." Section 383(b) provides general procedural guidelines for distribution of monetary class action judgments. *See In re Vitamin Cases*, 107 Cal. App. 4th 820, 132 Cal. Rptr.

2d 425 (2003) (concluding CCP § 384 does not require that individual class members receive a portion of the award, and therefore does not preclude a fluid recovery which distributes the entire class settlement to charitable and nonprofit organizations); *Cundiff v. Verizon California, Inc.*, 167 Cal. App. 4th 718, 84 Cal. Rptr. 3d 377 (2008) (holding CCP § 384 is not limited to fluid class recovery cases, and therefore applies to the "unpaid residue" that results from uncashed and returned settlement checks sent to individual class members). Amendments to CCP § 384(b) effective 2002 expressly authorize a court to distribute any unpaid residual derived from a class action judgment "to nonprofit organizations or foundations to support projects that will benefit the class or similarly situated persons, or that promote the law consistent with the objectives and purposes of the underlying cause of action...."

In *Kraus v. Trinity Management Services, Inc.*, 23 Cal. 4th 116, 96 Cal. Rptr. 2d 485, 999 P.2d 718 (2000), the Supreme Court ruled that although the Legislature authorized employment of the fluid recovery remedy in class actions in CCP § 384, it had not expressly authorize disgorgement into a fluid recovery fund in an unfair competition (UCL) action brought on behalf of absent persons by a private party pursuant to Business and Professions Code § 17200 *et seq.*, but not certified as a class action. In a companion case the Supreme Court concluded in light of *Krause* that disgorgement to a fluid recovery fund of all profits the defendant company may have earned by unlawfully withholding overtime wages was not permitted, although the defendant could properly be compelled to restore unpaid wages to its employees. *See Cortez v. Purolator Air Filtration Products Co.*, 23 Cal. 4th 163, 96 Cal. Rptr. 2d 518, 999 P.2d 706 (2000).

[c] Controversial Remedy

Most federal courts have disapproved of the use of fluid class recovery as a possible remedy in class actions. *E.g., Eisen v. Carlisle & Jacquelin*, 479 F.2d 1005, 1017-18 (2d Cir. 1973), *vacated on other grounds*, 417 U.S. 156 (1974). The fluid class recovery concept remains very controversial. Why? What are the objections to this type of relief? Do any of these objections have a constitutional basis? How so? Why is the potential of fluid class recovery so important to plaintiffs and plaintiffs' attorneys in consumer litigation? The fluid class recovery controversy has produced much scholarly discussion, most of which supports such relief in appropriate cases. *See, e.g.,* James R. McCall, Patricia Sturdevant, Laura Kaplan & Gail Hillebrand, *Greater Representation for California Consumers—Fluid Recovery, Consumer Trust Funds, and Representative Actions*, 46 HASTINGS L.J. 797 (1995); Gail Hillebrand & Daniel Torrence, *Claims Procedures in Large Consumer Class Actions and Equitable Distribution of Benefits*, 28 SANTA CLARA L. REV. 747 (1988); Martin H. Redish, Peter Julian & Samantha Zyontz, *Cy Pres Relief and the Pathologies of the Modern Class Action: A Normative and Empirical Analysis*, 62 FLA. L. REV. 617 (2010).

[2] Attorney Fees

The class action attorney may obtain payment of attorney fees from a portion of a class action settlement. *See Rebney v. Wells Fargo Bank*, 220 Cal. App. 3d 1117,

1142-44, 269 Cal. Rptr. 844 (1990). Any such attorney fees agreement must be disclosed to the members of the class, and approved by the court as part of the settlement process. *Id.* at 1144; *see* Rule 3.769(b), Cal. Rules of Court. If the class action is not settled but proceeds to trial, a successful class attorney may be entitled to an award of statutory attorney fees in an amount which reflects the nature of the class-wide services rendered. *See Rebney, supra,* 220 Cal. App. 3d at 1142-43; *Miller v. Woods,* 148 Cal. App. 3d 862, 875, 196 Cal. Rptr. 69 (1983); CCP § 1021.5. What are the advantages and disadvantages to a plaintiff of proceeding as a class action as opposed to an individual action? To a defendant? To the attorney for the plaintiff?

When determining a reasonable amount of attorney fees to be awarded to class counsel who has successfully negotiated a class action settlement, the lodestar multiplier methodology (under which the court calculates attorney fee amounts based on time spent and reasonable hourly compensation for each attorney) may be a preferable alternative to a fee calculated purely as a percentage of class recovery. *See Dunk v. Ford Motor Co.,* 48 Cal. App. 4th 1794, 1809-10, 56 Cal. Rptr. 2d 483 (1996) (reversing the trial court's approval of $1 million in attorney fees to class counsel because the trial court had improperly utilized the percentage-of-common-fund-method and not the preferred "lodestar" method); *Chavez v. Netflix, Inc.,* 162 Cal. App. 4th 43, 75 Cal. Rptr. 3d 413 (2008) (affirming an attorney fee award of $2,040,000, calculated by using the lodestar method enhanced by a 2.5 multiplier based on what the market would pay for comparable litigation services rendered pursuant to a fee agreement, as part of a consumer law class action settlement); *Roos v. Honeywell Int'l, Inc.,* 241 Cal. App. 4th 1472, 194 Cal. Rtpr. 3d 735 (2015) (upholding attorney fee award of $3,056,259 calculated by lodestar method up to a cap of 37.5% of the common fund recovery imposed by the trial court).

For discussion of the role of the class action counsel, see Jonathan R. Macy & Geoffrey P. Miller, *The Plaintiffs' Attorney's Role in Class Action and Derivative Litigation: Economic Analysis and Recommendations for Reform,* 58 U. CHI. L. REV. 1 (1991); Bryant Garth, Ilene H. Nagel & S. Jay Plager, *The Institution of the Private Attorney General: Perspectives from an Empirical Study of Class Action Litigation,* 61 S. CAL. L. REV. 353 (1988); John C. Coffee, Jr., *Understanding the Plaintiff's Attorney: The Implications of Economic Theory for Private Enforcement of Law Through Class Actions and Derivative Actions,* 86 COLUM. L. REV. 669 (1986).

Where a defendant prevails on the merits in a class action and is entitled to recover costs and attorney fees, the named plaintiffs are jointly and severally liable to pay the award of costs and fees. *See Van de Kamp v. Bank of America,* 204 Cal. App. 3d 819, 251 Cal. Rptr. 530 (1988). Are the absent members of the class also liable for a successful defendant's costs and attorney fees? *See Earley v. Superior Court,* 79 Cal. App. 4th 1420, 95 Cal. Rptr. 2d 57 (2000) (holding the only time absent class members who have failed to opt-out should be liable for fees and costs is when the class *prevails* and the class members accept the benefit of a common fund recovery). What are the policy reasons for holding absent class members liable for costs and fees when the class wins but not when the defendant wins?

[3] Incentive Payments to Class Representatives

Recent California decisions have approved the concept of awarding enhancement or incentive payments to named plaintiffs to compensate them for the expense and risk they have incurred in conferring a benefit on other members of the class. *E.g., Clark v. American Residential Serv. LLC*, 175 Cal. App. 4th 785, 96 Cal. Rptr. 3d 441 (2009); *Cellphone Termination Fee Cases*, 186 Cal. App. 4th 1380, 113 Cal. Rptr. 3d 510 (2010); *Munoz v. BCI Coca-Cola Bottling Co.*, 186 Cal. App. 4th 399, 412, 112 Cal. Rptr. 3d 324 (2010). Whether an enhancement award is justified, and whether the amount of the award is appropriate, depends on several factors including the amount of time and effort spent by the class representative and the risk to the class representative in commencing suit, both financial and otherwise. *See Clark, supra*, 175 Cal. App. 4th at 804-807 (approving the concept of incentive awards generally but reversing the trial court's approval of enhancements of $25,000 to each named plaintiff because no rationale was provided to show that this sum was fair and reasonable); *Cellphone Termination Fee Cases, supra*, 186 Cal. App. at 1393-95 (affirming trial court's incentive awards of $10,000 to each class representative where evidence indicated that each class representative actively participated in the litigation and worked with class counsel to assist in the prosecution of the litigation).

Chapter 11

Discovery

§ 11.01 California Discovery Principles

[A] Introductory Note

In 1986, the California Legislature adopted the Civil Discovery Act which had been proposed by the State Bar Judicial Council Joint Commission on Discovery and drafted by the Commission's Reporter, Professor James E. Hogan of the UC Davis School of Law. This landmark legislation reorganized and clarified the original Discovery Act of 1956, incorporated existing case law construing the Discovery Act of 1956, and implemented the many recommendations of the Commission. The 1986 Act serves as a convenient resource for studying the California civil discovery system.

This chapter explores the current civil discovery system in California, recognizing where the current approach is consistent with long-standing rules and highlighting departures from those rules. This chapter begins by addressing fundamental principles that govern the use of all discovery devices, including coverage of the Civil Discovery Act, the scope of discovery, and the protection of privileged information and attorney work product. It then turns to an examination of the individual discovery devices— interrogatories, inspections, physical examinations, expert disclosure, depositions, and requests for admissions. Finally, the available enforcement mechanisms are examined, including motions to compel, monetary sanctions and other sanctions.

[B] Coverage of the Civil Discovery Statutes

[1] General Coverage

The Discovery Act applies to all civil actions pending in the superior court (except the small claims division), CCP §§ 2016.010–.070, 2017.010–.020; including family court proceedings, *Schnabel v. Superior Court*, 5 Cal. 4th 704, 21 Cal. Rptr. 2d 200, 854 P.2d 1117 (1993). It does not apply to administrative proceedings, *Shively v. Stewart*, 65 Cal. 2d 475, 55 Cal. Rptr. 217, 421 P.2d 65 (1966); nor to juvenile court proceedings, *Joe Z. v. Superior Court*, 3 Cal. 3d 797, 91 Cal. Rptr. 594, 478 P.2d 26 (1970).

[2] Limited Civil Cases

In limited civil cases—generally, cases in which the amount in controversy does not exceed $25,000—numerical restrictions control the use of depositions, interrogatories, inspection demands, and requests for admissions. CCP §§ 94, 95. To promote affordable litigation in those courts where the amount in controversy is $25,000 or less, the law limits the parties to one deposition per adverse party. As to interrogatories, inspection demands and requests for admission, the combined total permitted is 35 per adverse party. Additional discovery is allowed by court order or by stipulation. CCP §95(a) and (b).

[3] Small Claims Court

In small claims court, discovery is not allowed for two reasons. First, the Legislature has adopted no statutory provisions permitting discovery in these proceedings, which are designed to be inexpensive and expeditious. Second, the courts have concluded that the Legislature did not intend formal discovery to be permitted either in the small claims action itself or the de novo review by the superior court. *Bruno v. Superior Court*, 219 Cal. App. 3d 1359, 269 Cal. Rptr. 142 (1990); CCP §§ 116.310; 116.770.

[4] Post-Judgment Discovery

The Discovery Act applies to discovery in the aid of enforcement of a money judgment only to the extent provided in Code of Civil Procedure §708.010 *et seq*. CCP §2016.070. Authorized discovery devices include written interrogatories, inspection of documents, and debtor examinations. CCP §§708.020, 708.030, 708.110.

[5] Arbitration

Outside of the California court system, the Discovery Act applies in some arbitration proceedings by statute and in others by agreement. Specifically, where arbitration is mandatory, the Discovery Act may be extended to the proceedings. For example, with limited exceptions, the Discovery Act applies to proceedings under the Uninsured Motorists Act and the Judicial Arbitration Rules for Civil cases. Insurance Code §11580.2(f); Rule 3.822, Cal. Rules of Ct. In contractual arbitrations, the Discovery Act applies to claims for personal injury or wrongful death. CCP §1283.1(a). Also, the parties may agree to adopt the Act's procedures in other arbitration proceedings. CCP §1283.1(b).

[C] Scope of Discovery under the Act, Generally

The landmark case establishing the broad scope of modern California civil discovery is *Greyhound Corp. v. Superior Court*, 56 Cal. 2d 355, 15 Cal. Rptr. 90, 364 P.2d 266 (1961). From its review of the legislative history of the discovery statutes, the Supreme Court concluded that the Legislature intended to afford discovery that was even less restrictive than the federal rules allowed in order to take the game element out of trial preparation. *Greyhound*, 56 Cal. 2d at 374–76. As the Court observed: "The Legislature has now acted. It has authorized the fishing expedition.... No longer can the time-honored cry of 'fishing expedition' serve to preclude a party from inquiring into the facts underlying his opponent's case." *Id.* at 385. The Supreme Court also found that the Legislature intended to bestow broad discretion on the trial courts which should be liberally exercised to favor discovery. *Id.* at 378–80.

California Code of Civil Procedure (2016)

§ 2017.010. Matters subject to discovery

Unless otherwise limited by order of the court in accordance with this title, any party may obtain discovery regarding any matter, not privileged, that is relevant to the subject matter involved in the pending action or to the determination of any motion made in that action, if the matter either is itself admissible in evidence or appears reasonably calculated to lead to the discovery of admissible evidence. Discovery may relate to the claim or defense of the party seeking discovery or of any other party to the action. Discovery may be obtained of the identity and location of persons having knowledge of any discoverable matter, as well as of the existence, description, nature, custody, condition, and location of any document, electronically stored information, tangible thing, or land or other property.

Notes and Questions regarding Scope of Discovery

(1) *Relevancy.* Although the language "reasonably calculated to lead to the discovery of admissible evidence" in CCP § 2017.010 gives some guidance for determining what is "relevant to the subject matter," no precise or universal test of relevancy is furnished by the discovery statutes. As explained by the California Supreme Court in *Pacific Telephone & Telegraph Co. v. Superior Court*, 2 Cal. 3d 161, 172–75, 84 Cal. Rptr. 718, 465 P.2d 854 (1970), the question of relevancy must be "determined in each case according to the teachings of reason and judicial experience:"

> Although we have not been able to articulate a single, comprehensive standard of relevancy, we have established a few guidelines. Past cases make clear that the "relevancy of the subject matter" criterion is a broader concept than "relevancy to the issues," the test which prevailed prior to the enactment of the current discovery scheme. Matters sought are properly discoverable if they will aid in a party's preparation for trial. In addition, because all issues and argument that will come to light at trial often cannot be ascertained at a time when discovery is sought, courts may appropriately give the applicant substantial leeway, especially when the precise issues of the litigation of the governing legal standards are not clearly established; a decision of relevance for purposes of discovery is in no sense a determination of relevance for purposes of trial.

> In sum, the relevance of the subject matter standard must be reasonably applied; in accordance with the liberal policies underlying the discovery procedures, doubts as to relevance should generally be resolved in favor of permitting discovery. Given this very liberal and flexible standard of relevancy, a party attempting to show that a court abused its discretion in finding material relevant for purposes of discovery bears an extremely heavy burden. An appellate court cannot reverse a trial court's grant of discovery under a "relevancy" attack unless it concludes that the answers sought by a given line of questioning cannot as a reasonable possibility lead to the discovery of admissible evidence or be helpful in preparation for trial. * * *

Although one of the purposes of discovery is to permit the parties to learn the issues on which they are in agreement and thereby simplify the trial, one party, by conceding some matters, cannot unilaterally close the door to all discovery concerning that concession. Section [2017.010], provides a test of relevancy of the subject matter, *not* relevancy of the issues and "[t]he relevancy (of the subject matter of the action) is be determined ... by the potential as well as actual issues in the case." [Citations omitted.] Even if, by concession in a pleading a party removes, perhaps temporarily, a given issue from the case, the scope of discoverable information will not necessarily be narrowed.

(2) *Inadmissible Evidence.* The scope of discovery encompasses relevant matter that "either is itself admissible in evidence or appears to be reasonably calculated to lead to the discovery of admissible evidence." CCP § 2017.010; *see Children's Hosp. Cent. California v. Blue Cross of California,* 226 Cal. App. 4th 1260, 1276, 172 Cal. Rptr, 3d 861 (2014) ("For discovery purposes, information is relevant if it might reasonably assist a party in evaluating the case, preparing for trial, or facilitating settlement. Admissibility is not the test."). For example, in *Norton v. Superior Court,* 24 Cal. App. 4th 1750, 30 Cal. Rptr. 2d 217 (1994), the defendant in a malpractice action sought discovery of documents stating the terms of plaintiffs' recovery from their insurer — evidence which was inadmissible to mitigate damages under the collateral source rule. The Court of Appeal held that the documents might lead to the discovery of admissible evidence, and ordered the trial court to inspect the documents in camera in order to make this determination. Based on *Pacific Telephone,* quoted *supra,* what standard should a trial court utilize in determining whether requested inadmissible evidence might lead to admissible evidence?

(3) *Insurance.* In addition to providing broad guidelines, CCP §§ 2017.210–.740 directly address certain controversial discovery issues. Specifically, CCP § 2017.210 expressly allows discovery of insurance coverage. A party may obtain discovery of the existence and contents of insurance policies, including the identity of the carrier, the nature and limits of the coverage, and whether the insurance carrier is disputing coverage of the claim involved in the action. § 2017.210; *see Catholic Mut. Relief Society v. Superior Court,* 42 Cal. 4th 358, 64 Cal. Rptr. 3d 434, 165 P.3d 154 (2007) (concluding although insurance coverage information is discoverable under § 2017.210, information regarding *reinsurance* is not discoverable unless reinsurance agreement is functioning in the same way as a liability policy or where the reinsurance agreement is itself the subject matter of the litigation). Discovery of this information, however, does not make it admissible at trial. § 2017.210. Why is pretrial discovery of insurance information authorized, but not its admission at trial?

(4) *Financial Worth.* The California Supreme Court has ruled that the burden is on the plaintiff to introduce evidence of the defendant's financial worth to support an award of punitive damages. *Adams v. Murakami,* 54 Cal. 3d 105, 284 Cal. Rptr. 318, 813 P.2d 1348 (1991). The Court based this ruling in part on the availability of obtaining financial information through discovery. *Adams,* 54 Cal. 3d at 121.

(a) *Punitive Damages.* To prevent the abusive discovery of financial information on a frivolously alleged claim for punitive damages, the Legislature adopted specific safeguards authorizing the trial court to grant a protective order requiring the plaintiff to establish a prima facie right to recover punitive damages before any evidence of the defendant's net worth may be discovered. Civil Code § 3295.

(b) *Substantive Claims.* Civil Code § 3295 does not apply, however, where the plaintiff needs the financial information to prove the substance of the claim. For example, where the plaintiff alleged that the defendant had failed to distribute limited partnership profits, the trial court abused its discretion in refusing to allow discovery of defendant's financial information. *Rawnsley v. Superior Court*, 183 Cal. App. 3d 86, 227 Cal. Rptr. 806 (1986).

§ 11.02 Protection of Privileged Information

[A] Privilege, Generally

As we have seen, CCP § 2017.010 limits the scope of discovery to matters which are not privileged. The laws of privilege are not set out in the Discovery Act but are provided by the California Constitution, the Evidence Code, other statutes, and decisional law. Essentially, any privilege which protects against disclosure at trial also applies to discovery. While the term "privilege" is used generally to refer to information protected from disclosure, it is more accurate to divide the subject into (1) those matters which are truly privileged and entitled to absolute protection and (2) those matters which are entitled to qualified protection and subject to compelled disclosure in the interests of justice.

With respect to the assertion of a claim of privilege in discovery proceedings, the key change in the Discovery Act of 1986 is its codification of the decisional law holding that a failure to object on the grounds of privilege will operate as a waiver of the privilege. CCP §§ 2025.460(a), 2028.050(a), and 2030.290(a); 2 Hogan & Weber, *California Civil Discovery* § 12.1 (2d ed. 2005 & Supp. 2015). Conversely, the assertion of a privilege during discovery may bar introduction at trial of the evidence withheld. *See Xebec Dev. Partners, Ltd. v. National Union Fire Ins. Co.*, 12 Cal. App. 4th 501, 15 Cal. Rptr. 2d 726 (1993) (ruling plaintiff who asserted attorney-client privilege as to certain billing materials during discovery cannot waive the privilege at trial to prove amount of recoverable attorneys' fees because too late to cure prejudice to defendant).

A thorough examination of privileges is beyond the scope of this chapter. To understand the scope and limitations of a particular privilege, one should review the applicable statutory and decisional law. For a general discussion, see 2 Hogan and Weber, *California Civil Discovery* § 12.1–13.20 *et seq* (2005 & Supp. 2015); CEB, *California Civil Discovery Practice* §§ 3.1–3.199 (4th ed. 2015); Weil, Brown, Edmon & Karnow, *Civil Procedure Before Trial* ¶ 8:109 *et seq* (The Rutter Group 2015).

[B]   Absolute Privileges

The California Evidence Code codifies the absolute privileges which include:

(a) the privilege against self incrimination (Evid. Code §940 et seq.);

(b) the attorney-client privilege (Evid. Code §952 et seq.);

(c) the spousal privilege (Evid. Code §970 et seq.);

(d) the physician-patient privilege (Evid. Code §992 et seq.);

(e) the psychotherapist-patient privilege (Evid. Code §1012 et seq.);

(f) the clergyman-penitent privilege (Evid. Code §1030);

(g) the sexual assault victim-counselor privilege (Evid. Code §1035.4);

(h) the official information privilege (Evid. Code §1040 et seq.); and

(i) the Mediation Privilege (Evid. Code §§703.5, 1119, 1121).

Information covered by these privileges is protected from disclosure regardless of its relevance to the issues and the need for disclosure. *Rittenhouse v. Superior Court*, 235 Cal. App. 3d 1584, 1 Cal. Rptr. 2d 595 (1991); *see* 2 Hogan & Weber, *California Civil Discovery* §12.1 (2005 & Supp. 2015); Weil, Brown, Edmon & Karnow, *Civil Procedure Before Trial* ¶8:110.1 (The Rutter Group 2015).

[1]   The Attorney-Client Privilege

Costco Wholesale Corp. v. Superior Court

Supreme Court of California

47 Cal. 4th 725, 101 Cal. Rptr. 3d 758, 219 P.3d 736 (2009)

WERDEGAR, JUSTICE.

In this case we consider whether the trial court erred by directing a referee to conduct an in camera review of an opinion letter sent by outside counsel to a corporate client, allowing the referee to redact the letter to conceal that portion the referee believed to be privileged, and ordering the client to disclose the remainder to the opposing party. We conclude the court's directions and order violated the attorney-client privilege, and violated as well the statutory prohibition against requiring disclosure of information claimed to be subject to the attorney-client privilege in order to rule on a claim of privilege. (Evid. Code, §915, subd. (a).)

BACKGROUND

In June 2000, Costco Wholesale Corporation (Costco), which operates warehouse-style retail establishments throughout California, retained the law firm of Sheppard, Mullin, Richter & Hampton to provide legal advice regarding whether certain Costco warehouse managers in California were exempt from California's wage and overtime laws. Attorney Kelly Hensley, an expert in wage and hour law, undertook the assignment, ultimately producing for Costco the 22-page opinion letter at issue here. The letter followed conversations held by Hensley with two warehouse managers Costco had made available to her. Costco, the managers, and Hensley understood the communications between the managers and Hensley were, and would remain, confidential. Similarly, Costco and Hensley understood that Hensley's opinion letter was, and would remain, confidential.

Several years later, real parties in interest, Costco employees (hereafter collectively referred to as plaintiffs), filed this class action against Costco, claiming that from 1999 through 2001 Costco had misclassified some of its managers as "exempt" employees and therefore had failed to pay them the overtime wages they were due as nonexempt employees. In the course of the litigation, plaintiffs sought to compel discovery of Hensley's opinion letter. Costco objected on the grounds the letter was subject to the attorney-client privilege and the attorney work product doctrine. Plaintiffs disagreed, arguing ... that the letter contained unprivileged matter....

The trial court, over Costco's objection, ordered a discovery referee to conduct an in camera review of Hensley's opinion letter to determine the merits of Costco's claims of attorney-client privilege and work product doctrine. The referee produced a heavily redacted version of the letter, stating her conclusion that although much of it "constitutes attorney client communications and/or the type of attorney observations, impressions and opinions plainly protected as work product," those portions of text involving "factual information about various employees' job responsibilities" are protected by neither the privilege nor the doctrine. The referee explained that statements obtained in attorney interviews of corporate employee witnesses generally are not protected by the corporation's attorney-client privilege and do not become cloaked with the privilege by reason of having been incorporated into a later communication between the attorney and the client. She also found that while interviewing the two Costco managers, Hensley had acted not as an attorney but as a fact finder. The trial court ... adopted the findings and conclusions of the referee and ordered Costco to produce a version of the letter in the same form as recommended and redacted by the referee.

Costco petitioned the Court of Appeal for a writ of mandate, arguing the trial court had erred by ordering the in camera review of Hensley's opinion letter and by ordering disclosure of a redacted version of the letter. The Court of Appeal denied the petition. * * *

We hold the attorney-client privilege attaches to Hensley's opinion letter in its entirety, irrespective of the letter's content. Further, Evidence Code section 915 prohibits disclosure of the information claimed to be privileged as a confidential communication between attorney and client "in order to rule on the claim of privilege." (*Id.*, subd. (a).) Finally, contrary to the Court of Appeal's holding, a party seeking extraordinary relief from a discovery order that wrongfully invades the attorney-client relationship need not also establish that its case will be harmed by disclosure of the evidence.

As we find the attorney-client privilege precludes discovery of the opinion letter, we do not consider whether the work product doctrine would also apply to prevent its discovery. And, as the trial court's ruling extended only to the opinion letter, neither do we consider the separate but related question of whether, independent of the letter, the conversations between Hensley and Costco's warehouse managers might be subject to either the attorney-client privilege or the work product doctrine.

DISCUSSION

I.

The attorney-client privilege, set forth at Evidence Code section 954, confers a privilege on the client "to refuse to disclose, and to prevent another from disclosing, a confidential communication between client and lawyer…." The privilege "has been a hallmark of Anglo-American jurisprudence for almost 400 years." (*Mitchell v. Superior Court* (1984) 37 Cal.3d 591, 599 [208 Cal. Rptr. 886, 691 P.2d 642].) Its fundamental purpose "is to safeguard the confidential relationship between clients and their attorneys so as to promote full and open discussion of the facts and tactics surrounding individual legal matters. [Citation.] … [¶] Although exercise of the privilege may occasionally result in the suppression of relevant evidence, the Legislature of this state has determined that these concerns are outweighed by the importance of preserving confidentiality in the attorney-client relationship. As this court has stated: 'The privilege is given on grounds of public policy in the belief that the benefits derived therefrom justify the risk that unjust decisions may sometimes result from the suppression of relevant evidence.' [Citations.]" (*Id.* at pp. 599–600.) "[T]he privilege is absolute and disclosure may not be ordered, without regard to relevance, necessity or any particular circumstances peculiar to the case." (*Gordon v. Superior Court* (1997) 55 Cal.App.4th 1546, 1557 [65 Cal. Rptr. 2d 53].)

* * * The party claiming the privilege has the burden of establishing the preliminary facts necessary to support its exercise, i.e., a communication made in the course of an attorney-client relationship. (*D. I. Chadbourne, Inc.* [*v. Superior Court* (1964) 60 Cal. 2d 723], at p. 729 [36 Cal. Rptr. 468, 388 P.2d 700]; *Wellpoint Health Networks, Inc. v. Superior Court* (1997) 59 Cal.App.4th 110, 123 [68 Cal. Rptr. 2d 844].) Once that party establishes facts necessary to support a prima facie claim of privilege, the communication is presumed to have been made in confidence and the opponent of the claim of privilege has the burden of proof to establish the communication was not confidential or that the privilege does not for other reasons apply. (Evid. Code, §917, subd. (a); *Wellpoint Health Networks, Inc.*, at pp. 123–124.)

That Costco engaged Hensley to provide it with legal advice and that the opinion letter was a communication between Costco's attorney (Hensley) and Costco are undisputed. The letter was "confidential," defined as "information transmitted between a client and his or her lawyer in the course of [the attorney-client] relationship and in confidence by a means which, so far as the client is aware, discloses the information to no third persons other than those who are present to further the interest of the client in the consultation or those to whom disclosure is reasonably necessary for the transmission of the information or the accomplishment of the purpose for which the lawyer is consulted…." (Evid. Code, §952.) Indeed, the referee heavily redacted the letter because she believed it was a confidential communication between attorney and client. That Hensley's opinion letter may not have been prepared in anticipation of litigation is of no consequence; the privilege attaches to any legal advice given in the course of an attorney-client relationship. (*Roberts v. City of Palmdale* (1993) 5 Cal.4th 363, 371 [20 Cal. Rptr. 2d 330, 853 P.2d 496];....) And it is settled that a corporate client such as Costco can claim the privilege. (Evid. Code, §954, final par.; *D. I. Chadbourne, Inc. v. Superior Court, supra*, 60 Cal.2d at pp. 732, 736.) The undisputed facts, therefore, make out a prima facie claim of privilege.

I.

The attorney-client privilege attaches to a confidential communication between the attorney and the client and bars discovery of the communication irrespective of whether it includes unprivileged material. As we explained in *Mitchell v. Superior Court, supra*, 37 Cal.3d at page 600: "[T]he privilege covers the transmission of documents which are available to the public, and not merely information in the sole possession of the attorney or client. In this regard, it is the actual fact of the transmission which merits protection, since discovery of the transmission of specific public documents might very well reveal the transmitter's intended strategy." We therefore held in *Mitchell* that a client could not be questioned about warnings from her attorney about the health effects of an industrial chemical even if the warnings might be described as factual matter rather than legal advice. We observed: "Neither the statutes articulating the attorney-client privilege nor the cases which have interpreted it make any differentiation between 'factual' and 'legal' information." (*Id.* at p. 601; see *In re Jordan* (1974) 12 Cal.3d 575, 580 [116 Cal. Rptr. 371, 526 P.2d 523] [finding the attorney-client privilege attached to copies of cases and law review articles transmitted by an attorney to the attorney's client].)

Focusing on the warehouse managers' statements to Attorney Hensley, plaintiffs point out that the statements of a corporate employee to the corporation's attorney are not privileged if the employee speaks as an independent witness, even if the employer requires the employee to make the statement. (*D. I. Chadbourne, Inc. v. Superior Court, supra*, 60 Cal.2d at p. 737.) They further maintain that when a corporate employer has more than one purpose for directing an employee to make a report, whether the employee's statement should be classified as that of the corporation or as that of an independent witness depends upon the employer's "dominant purpose" in requiring the employee to make the statement. (*Id.* at p. 737.) And they emphasize that the question of whether the employer's dominant purpose in requiring a report was for transmittal to an attorney in the course of professional employment, like the question of whether a particular employee's statement was that of an independent witness, is for the trial court or other finder of fact, whose conclusion is binding on the reviewing court if supported by substantial evidence. (*HLC Properties, Ltd. v. Superior Court*, [(2005)] 35 Cal.4th [54] at p. 60 [24 Cal. Rptr. 3d 199, 105 P.3d 560]; *Martin v. Workers' Comp. Appeals Bd.* (1997) 59 Cal.App.4th 333, 346–347 [69 Cal. Rptr. 2d 138].)

These points have little to do with the case before us. In *Chadbourne* we considered whether a corporate employee, reporting to the corporation's attorney, was speaking on behalf of the corporation so that his report was in effect the communication of the corporate client. (*D. I. Chadbourne, Inc. v. Superior Court, supra*, 60 Cal.2d at pp. 736–

738.) In that context, the dominant-purpose test determines whether the relationship between the attorney and the corporate employee is an attorney-client relationship; if the corporation's dominant purpose in requiring the employee to make a statement is the confidential transmittal to the corporation's attorney of information emanating from the corporation, the communication is privileged. (*Id.* at p. 737.) And as we have explained, because the privilege protects the *transmission* of information, if the communication is privileged, it does not become unprivileged simply because it contains material that could be discovered by some other means. *Chadbourne* and its progeny therefore would be relevant if we were considering whether the statements of the warehouse managers interviewed by Hensley were themselves subject to the attorney-client privilege. But these authorities are not relevant to the question before us: whether the communication between Costco's attorney and Costco was privileged. * * *

Plaintiffs next point out that the attorney-client privilege does not attach to an attorney's communications when the client's dominant purpose in retaining the attorney was something other than to provide the client with a legal opinion or legal advice. (… *Aetna Casualty & Surety Co. v. Superior Court* (1984) 153 Cal. App. 3d 467, 475 [200 Cal. Rptr. 471].) For example, the privilege is not applicable when the attorney acts merely as a negotiator for the client or is providing business advice (see *Aetna Casualty & Surety Co.*, at p. 475); in that case, the relationship between the parties to the communication is not one of attorney-client. But while plaintiffs insist Hensley's interviews of Costco's warehouse managers was simple fact gathering that could have been done by a nonattorney, they have never disputed that Costco retained Hensley, an expert in California wage and hour law, to provide it with legal advice regarding the exempt status of some of its employees, nor did the trial court base its discovery order on a finding that Costco's dominant purpose in retaining Hensley was to obtain her services as a fact gatherer. * * * Here, Hensley was presented with a question requiring legal analysis and was asked to investigate the facts she needed to render a legal opinion. As we have explained, when the communication is a confidential one between attorney and client, the entire communication, including its recitation or summary of factual material, is privileged. In sum, if, as plaintiffs contend, the factual material referred to or summarized in Hensley's opinion letter is itself unprivileged it may be discoverable by some other means, but plaintiffs may not obtain it by compelling disclosure of the letter.

III.

There is a second reason for overturning the discovery order. Evidence Code section 915 provides, with exceptions not applicable here, that "the presiding officer may not require disclosure of information claimed to be privileged under this division[3] … in order to rule on the claim of privilege…." (Evid. Code, § 915, subd. (a).) Section 915 also prohibits disclosure of information claimed to be privileged work product under

---

3. "[T]his division," division 8 of the Evidence Code, includes not just the attorney-client privilege (Evid. Code, § 954), but a variety of others arising out of confidential relationships, such as the marital privilege (*id.*, § 980), the physician-patient privilege (*id.*, § 994), the psychotherapist-patient privilege (*id.*, § 1014) and the clergy-penitent privilege (*id.*, § 1033).

Code of Civil Procedure section 2018.030, subdivision (b), but, as to the work product privilege, if the court is unable to rule on the claim of privilege "without requiring disclosure of the information claimed to be privileged, the court may require the person from whom disclosure is sought or the person authorized to claim the privilege, or both, to disclose the information in chambers out of the presence and hearing of all persons except the person authorized to claim the privilege and any other persons as the person authorized to claim the privilege is willing to have present." (Evid. Code, §915, subd. (b).) No comparable provision permits in camera disclosure of information alleged to be protected by the attorney-client privilege. (*Southern Cal. Gas Co. v. Public Utilities Com.* (1990) 50 Cal.3d 31, 45, fn. 19 [265 Cal. Rptr. 801, 784 P.2d 1373].)[4] Nonetheless, the trial court caused Hensley's opinion letter to be reviewed at the in camera hearing, and its order compelling Costco to produce the redacted version of the letter was based in large part on the referee's review of the very information Costco claimed to be privileged. * * *

... [T]he attorney-client privilege is a legislative creation, which courts have no power to limit by recognizing implied exceptions. (*Roberts v. City of Palmdale, supra,* 5 Cal.4th at p. 373.) Concern that a party may be able to prevent discovery of relevant information therefore provides no justification for inferring an exception to Evidence Code section 915. As noted earlier, it has long been understood that " '[t]he privilege is given on grounds of public policy in the belief that the benefits derived therefrom justify the risk that unjust decisions may sometimes result from the suppression of relevant evidence.' " (*Mitchell v. Superior Court, supra,* 37 Cal.3d at p. 600.) And because the privilege protects a *transmission* irrespective of its content, there should be no need to examine the content in order to rule on a claim of privilege. * * *

IV.

The remaining question is whether the Court of Appeal was justified in denying Costco relief despite the invalidity of the trial court's order. The court concluded extraordinary relief was not warranted because Costco had not demonstrated it would be irreparably harmed by the release of the opinion letter in redacted form because much of the remaining material could easily be obtained by some other means. This reasoning implies that the harm in an order compelling disclosure of privileged information is the risk the party seeking disclosure will obtain information to which it is not entitled. But, as we have said, the fundamental purpose of the attorney-client privilege is the preservation of the confidential relationship between attorney and client (*Mitchell v. Superior Court, supra,* 37 Cal.3d at p. 599), and the primary harm in the discovery of privileged material is the disruption of that relationship (*Roberts*

---

4. Because a court may order disclosure of information in order to determine whether it is protected by the work product doctrine, but may not order its disclosure to determine if it is subject to the attorney-client privilege, a court should without requiring disclosure first determine if the information is subject to the attorney-client privilege. If the court determines the privilege does not apply, it may then consider whether to order disclosure of the information at an in camera hearing for the purpose of deciding if it is protected work product.

v. Superior Court (1973) 9 Cal.3d 330, 336 [107 Cal. Rptr. 309, 508 P.2d 309]), not the risk that parties seeking discovery may obtain information to which they are not entitled. * * *

Accordingly, Costco is entitled to relief because the trial court's order threatened the confidential relationship between Costco and its attorney. Costco was not also required to demonstrate that its ability to present its case would be prejudiced by the discovery of the opinion letter.

DISPOSITION

The judgment of the Court of Appeal is reversed. The case is remanded to that court with directions to issue a writ of mandate vacating the trial court's order compelling discovery and to remand the case to the trial court for further proceedings consistent with this opinion.

Notes and Questions regarding Attorney-client Privilege

(1) The attorney-client privilege protects the communication between the attorney and the client; it does not protect the underlying facts upon which the communications are based. *See, e.g., Aerojet-General Corp. v. Transport Indem. Ins.*, 18 Cal. App. 4th 996, 1004, 22 Cal. Rptr. 2d 862 (1993). Thus in *Costco Wholesale Corp. v. Superior Court*, reproduced *supra*, the opinion letter was privileged, but facts regarding the employees' job responsibilities are discoverable. How should discovery questions be framed to obtain this factual information?

(2) The attorney-client privilege extends to experts who are retained as advisors or consultants to evaluate some aspect of the client's case. *See* 2 Hogan & Weber, *California Civil Discovery* § 12.11 (2d ed. 2005 & Supp. 2015) (collecting cases). If the expert is later designated as a trial expert, the privilege will be waived. *DeLuca v. State Fish Co., Inc.*, 217 Cal. App. 4th 671, 687–691, 158 Cal. Rptr. 3d 761 (2013) (collecting cases and holding that the attorney-client privilege applies prior to designation but not subsequent to it); *California Civil Discovery*, *supra*, at § 12.12; *but see Shooker v. Superior Court*, 111 Cal. App. 4th 923, 4 Cal. Rptr. 3d 334 (2003) (ruling designation of a party as an expert trial witness is not an implied waiver of the attorney-client privilege if the designation is withdrawn before the party discloses a significant part of a privileged communication).

(3) As the *Costco Wholesale* opinion indicates, the attorney-client privilege can be claimed by a corporate client. Evid. Code § 954. Should the privilege apply when a corporation is involved in litigation with its own shareholders? Under California law, the privilege applies even for closely-held corporations. *See Hoiles v. Superior Court*, 157 Cal. App. 3d 1192, 1198–1199, 204 Cal. Rptr. 111, 114–115 (1984); *but see Garner v. Wolfinbarger*, 430 F.2d 1093, 1101 (5th Cir. 1970).

(4) The attorney-client privilege may apply to statements made to someone who is not an attorney, such as an insurance claims representative, where the "dominant purpose" of the communication is for use by an attorney to defend against possible

litigation. *See, e.g., Soltani-Rastegar v. Superior Court*, 208 Cal. App. 3d 424, 256 Cal. Rptr. 255 (1989) (concluding statements given to insurer for purpose of defending against claims are protected from discovery by attorney-client privilege even though litigation was only a threat on the horizon and attorneys had not yet been selected to meet that threat). In a wrongful death action, does the attorney-client privilege apply to confidential occurrence reports, prepared by the defendant hospital, regarding the deceased's condition during his hospital stay? *See Scripps Health v. Superior Court*, 109 Cal. App. 4th 529, 135 Cal. Rptr. 2d 126 (2003) (finding occurrence reports are protected by attorney-client privilege because their dominant purpose was for attorney review in anticipation of litigation).

(5) *Trustees.* A trustee can claim the attorney-client privilege if the trustee, *qua* trustee, becomes the attorney's client. *See Wells Fargo Bank v. Superior Court*, 22 Cal. 4th 201, 91 Cal. Rptr. 2d 716, 990 P.2d 591 (2000) (holding a trustee may assert the attorney-client privilege against the beneficiaries with respect to confidential communications between the trustee and its attorneys, regardless of whether the communications are on the subject of the trust administration or of the trustee's own potential liability). Who is the holder of the attorney-client privilege when the trustee resigns and, in a subsequent accounting proceeding, the successor trustee seeks production of documents from the predecessor trustee which contain confidential attorney-client communications while the predecessor was acting as trustee? *See Moeller v. Superior Court*, 16 Cal. 4th 1124, 69 Cal. Rptr. 2d 317, 947 P.2d 279 (1997) (concluding the power to assert the attorney-client privilege with respect to confidential communications a predecessor trustee has had with its attorney on matters concerning trust administration passes from the predecessor trustee to its successor upon the successor's assumption of the office of trustee, unless the predecessor trustee sought legal advice in its personal capacity out of a genuine concern for possible future charges of breach of fiduciary duty).

(6) *Waiver.* Evidence Code § 912(a) recognizes that the attorney-client privilege is waived "if any holder of the privilege, without coercion, has disclosed a significant part of the communication or has consented to such disclosure made by anyone." In *Hiott v. Superior Court*, 16 Cal. App. 4th 712, 20 Cal. Rptr. 2d 157 (1993), a personal injury case, the defendant claimed the plaintiff had waived her attorney-client privilege by stating in response to defendant's discovery request that she would produce a videotape of her consultation with her attorney while she was in the hospital. Plaintiff argued that there had been no waiver because she never actually produced the videotape. Was plaintiff's consent to disclosure sufficient to constitute a waiver even though the disclosure had never occurred? *See Hiott*, 16 Cal. App. 4th at 719–20.

(7) *Waiver by Failure to Object to Discovery.* A failure to include an objection to discovery expressly based on the attorney-client privilege in the initial response to a discovery request will constitute a waiver of that privilege. *See Scottsdale Ins. Co. v. Superior Court*, 59 Cal App. 4th 263, 69 Cal. Rptr. 2d 112 (1997) (ruling insurer waived its attorney-client privilege with respect to documents sought to be produced

because the insurer failed to include an objection based on the privilege in its initial response); *but see Korea Data Sys. Co. v. Superior Court*, 51 Cal. App. 4th 1513, 59 Cal. Rptr. 2d 925 (1997) (finding no waiver of attorney-client privilege occurred where a reference to that privilege was asserted in a timely response to discovery requests, even though the objections were general and nonspecific).

(8) *Exceptions.* The Evidence Code recognizes certain statutory exceptions to the attorney-client privilege. Evidence Code § 956 provides an exception to the privilege where the client consults the attorney to obtain advice in perpetrating a crime or fraud. *See State Farm Fire & Cas. Co. v. Superior Court*, 54 Cal. App. 4th 625, 643– 649, 62 Cal. Rptr. 2d 834 (1997) (applying the crime/fraud exception to the attorney-client privilege). Evidence Code § 958 provides an exception to the privilege where the attorney is sued for malpractice. As *Costco* indicates, courts have no authority to adopt implied or judge-made exceptions to the attorney-client privilege; the only exceptions are those recognized by statute. *See Palmer v. Superior Court*, 231 Cal. App. 4th 1214, 180 Cal. Rptr. 3d 620 (2014) (collecting cases).

(9) *Joint-Client Exception.* A joint-client exception applies where an insurance company employs an attorney to represent its insured. The insured may discover communications between the insurance company and the attorney, *Glacier General Assurance Co. v. Superior Court*, 95 Cal. App. 3d 836, 842, 157 Cal. Rptr. 435, 438 (1979); but the communications are privileged as to third parties. *See Bank of America, N.A. v. Superior Court*, 212 Cal. App. 4th 1076, 151 Cal. Rptr. 3d 526 (2013) (ruling that when an insurer retains counsel to defend its insured, a tripartite attorney-client relationship arises among the insurer, insured, and counsel). What about other cases where multiple clients consult a lawyer together on a matter of common interest? Evidence Code § 962 recognizes that in such cases none of those clients may claim a privilege as to the other clients, but the consultation is privileged as to third-parties.

(10) *The Mediation Privilege.* Independent of the attorney-client privilege, all communications between participants in the course of a mediation are confidential. Evid. Code §§ 703.5, 1119, 1121; CCP § 1775.10. *See Cassel v. Superior Court*, 51 Cal. 4th 113, 119 Cal. Rptr. 3d 437, 244 P.3d 1080 (2011) (holding private mediation-related discussions between the mediating client and his attorneys are nondiscoverable and inadmissible by reason of the mediation confidentiality statute and, unlike the attorney-client privilege, there is no exception where the client seeks to use these confidential communications as evidence in a legal malpractice suit against the attorneys); *Foxgate Homeowners' Assn., Inc. v. Bramalea California, Inc.*, 26 Cal. 4th 1, 108 Cal. Rptr. 2d 642, 25 P.3d 1117 (2001) (ruling that while a party may do so, a mediator may not report to the court about the conduct of participants in a mediation session, even for the purpose of advising the court about the bad faith conduct of a party during mediation that might warrant sanctions); *Eisendrath v. Superior Court*, 109 Cal. App. 4th 351, 134 Cal. Rptr. 2d 716 (2003) (concluding parties' confidential mediation communications not admissible absent express consent of both parties).

[2] The Physician-Patient Privilege

[a] Scope of Physician-Patient Privilege

The physician-patient privilege is designed to protect "confidential communications between patient and physician." Evidence Code § 992. This phrase is defined to include "information obtained by an examination of the patient, transmitted between a patient and his physician in the course of that relationship and in confidence ... and includes a diagnosis made and the advice given by the physician in the course of that relationship." Evidence Code § 992. See *Torres v. Superior Court*, 221 Cal. App. 3d 181, 270 Cal. Rptr. 401 (1990) (holding a nonparty physician who treated a malpractice claimant may testify as an expert for the defense but not with respect to any confidential communications protected by the physician-patient privilege).

Evidence Code § 990 defines the term "physician" for purposes of the physician-patient privilege. The term covers both California doctors as well as those licensed to practice in any state or nation and those whom the patient reasonably believes to be licensed practitioners. Evidence Code § 994 provides that a physician-patient relationship may be established with a medical corporation and doctors on its staff. Evidence Code § 991 defines the term "patient" for purposes of the physician-patient privilege. The term covers those who undergo a consultation or examination to secure a diagnosis, preventive, palliative or curative treatment of a physical, mental or emotional condition.

The California courts are highly protective of medical information about nonparties, despite the clear relevance the information may have to pending litigation. For example, in a medical malpractice case where the doctor claimed he had performed the procedure at issue on numerous other patients, the plaintiff was denied discovery of those patients' names. *Marcus v. Superior Court*, 18 Cal. App. 3d 22, 95 Cal. Rptr. 545 (1971). Similarly, in a products liability action involving an adverse drug reaction, the plaintiff was denied discovery of the names of other doctors who had prescribed the drug and reported adverse reactions. *Henard v. Superior Court*, 26 Cal. App. 3d 129, 133, 102 Cal. Rptr. 721 (1972); *see also Binder v. Superior Court*, 196 Cal. App. 3d 893, 242 Cal. Rptr. 231 (1987) (denying in medical malpractice action where survivors of a patient who died from melanoma sought discovery of photographs of defendant's other patients who had melanoma, on grounds of physician-patient privilege and privacy); *Snibbe v. Superior Court*, 224 Cal. App. 4th 184, 168 Cal. Rptr. 3d 548 (2014) (ruling the physician-patient privilege not violated by limited production of redacted records which do not reveal patients' identities). Why are the courts so protective of this relevant information?

[b] Psychotherapist-Patient Privilege

The psychotherapist-patient privilege is similar in many respects to the physician-patient privilege. *See* Evidence Code §§ 1010–1028. It protects communications to psychiatrists, psychologists, clinical social workers, and licensed marriage, family and child counselors, Evidence Code § 1010; and also extends to communications during group therapy, *San Diego Trolley, Inc. v. Superior Court*, 87 Cal. App. 4th 1083, 105

Cal. Rptr. 2d 476 (2001) (discussing the scope of the privilege); *Lovett v. Superior Court*, 203 Cal. App. 3d 521, 250 Cal. Rptr. 25 (1988).

One important exception to the psychotherapist-patient privilege is the "dangerous patient" exception set out in Evidence Code § 1024. This exception has been very broadly interpreted in *People v. Wharton*, 53 Cal. 3d 522, 280 Cal. Rptr. 631, 809 P.2d 290 (1991) (concluding psychotherapist's warning to patient's intended victim was not covered by the privilege where there was reasonable cause for psychotherapist to believe that the patient was dangerous and disclosure of the communication was necessary to prevent any harm) and *Menendez v. Superior Court*, 3 Cal. 4th 435, 11 Cal. Rptr. 2d 92, 834 P.2d 786 (1992) (holding dangerous patient exception applicable to communications during a session which caused psychologist to reasonably believe that patients were dangerous to the psychologist and his wife and lover, and that disclosure was necessary to prevent any harm).

[C] Qualified Privileges

In addition to these absolute privileges, certain sensitive information may be protected from discovery unless the interests of justice compel disclosure. These qualified areas of protection include:

(a) the newsgatherer's immunity (Evid. Code § 1070);

(b) the medical staff privilege (Evid. Code § 1157);

(c) the trade secret privilege (Evid. Code § 1060);

(d) the taxpayer's privilege (Rev. and Tax. Code §§ 7056, 19282, 26451); and

(e) the constitutional protection of privacy (Cal. Const., Art I, § 1).

[1] *The Right of Privacy*

Valley Bank of Nevada v. Superior Court

Supreme Court of California
15 Cal. 3d 652, 125 Cal. Rptr. 553, 542 P.2d 977 (1975)

RICHARDSON, JUSTICE.

[The Bank sued to recover on a promissory note. The borrowers defended on the grounds that the Bank had misrepresented the availability of other financing in order to induce them to enter into the transaction. To prove these allegations, the borrowers sought to discover information about transactions between the bank and some other customers. The Bank objected on the grounds that it was entitled to protect the privacy of its customers and was not willing to disclose information about confidential transactions of its customers. The trial court ordered the information disclosed. The Bank sought a writ of mandate or prohibition to compel the trial court to issue a protective order.

The Court addressed the threshold question of relevancy and observed that according to the liberal policies underlying discovery procedures, doubts as to relevance should be resolved in favor of permitting discovery. The Court concluded that under this standard the information at issue was relevant.]

Assuming relevance, and considering Bank's contention that such information is privileged and protected from discovery, we review the statutory privilege described in the Evidence Code (§ 900 et seq.). There is revealed no bank-customer privilege akin to the lawyer-client privilege (Evid. Code, § 950 et seq.) or the physician-patient privilege (*id.*, § 990 et seq.). Indeed, the general rule appears to be that there exists no common law privilege with respect to bank customer information. Furthermore, it is clear that the privileges contained in the Evidence Code are exclusive and the courts are not free to create new privileges as a matter of judicial policy. Evid. Code § 911, subd. (d); *Pitchess v. Superior Court* (1974) 11 Cal. 3d 531, 539–540 [113 Cal. Rptr. 897, 522 P.2d 305].)

Nevertheless, despite the exclusivity of the Evidence Code on the subject of privileges and the absence of either a common law or statutory authority, overriding constitutional considerations may exist which impel us to recognize some limited form of protection for confidential information given to a bank by its customers.

A constitutional amendment adopted in 1974 elevated the right of privacy to an "inalienable right" expressly protected by force of constitutional mandate. (Cal. Const., art. I, § 1.) Although the amendment is new and its scope as yet is neither carefully defined nor analyzed by the courts, we may safely assume that the right of privacy extends to one's confidential financial affairs as well as to the details of one's personal life. Indeed, we recently discussed at length the "reasonable expectation of privacy" which a bank customer entertains with respect to financial information disclosed to his bank. Thus, in *Burrows v. Superior Court* (1974) 13 Cal. 3d 238 [118 Cal. Rptr. 166, 529 P.2d 590], we held that customer information voluntarily disclosed by a bank to law enforcement officers without the customer's knowledge or consent constituted the product of an unlawful search and seizure under article I, section 13, of the California Constitution. We stated in *Burrows* that "It cannot be gainsaid that the customer of a bank expects that the documents, such as checks, which he transmits to the bank in the course of his business operations, will remain private, and that such an expectation is reasonable.... A bank customer's reasonable expectation is that, *absent compulsion by legal process*, the matters he reveals to the bank will be utilized by the bank only for internal banking purposes." (Italics added, 13 Cal. 3d at p. 243.) Similarly, it is the general rule in other jurisdictions that a bank impliedly agrees not to divulge confidential information without the customer's consent unless compelled by court order.

As is apparent from the foregoing discussion, we indulge in a careful balancing of the right of civil litigants to discover relevant facts, on the one hand, with the right of bank customers to maintain reasonable privacy regarding their financial affairs, on the other. * * *

Striking a balance between the competing considerations, we conclude that before confidential customer information may be disclosed in the course of civil discovery proceedings, the bank must take reasonable steps to notify its customer of the pendency and nature of the proceedings and to afford the customer a fair opportunity to assert his interests by objecting to disclosure, by seeking an appropriate protective order, or by instituting other legal proceedings to limit the scope or nature of the matters sought to be discovered.

The variances of time, place, and circumstances which may invoke application of the foregoing principle cannot be anticipated, but in evaluating claims for protection of bank customers, the trial courts are vested with the same discretion which they generally exercise in passing upon other claims of confidentiality. We have previously expressed those considerations which, among others, will affect the exercise of the trial court's discretion. They include " ... the purpose of the information sought, the effect that disclosure will have on the parties and on the trial, the nature of the objections urged by the party resisting disclosure, and ability of the court to make an alternative order which may grant partial disclosure, disclosure in another form, or disclosure only in the event that the party seeking the information undertakes certain specified burdens which appear just under the circumstances." [Citation omitted.] Where it is possible to do so, " ... the courts should impose partial limitations rather than outright denial of discovery." [Citation omitted.]

With respect to bank customer information, the trial court has available certain procedural devices which may be useful in fashioning an appropriate order that will, so far as possible, accommodate considerations of both disclosure and confidentiality. These include deletion of the customer's name (evidently inappropriate in the instant case), ordering that the information be sealed, to be opened only on further order of court, and the holding of *in camera* hearings. There may well be others which ingenious courts and counsel may develop.

Let a writ of mandate issue directing the trial court to vacate its order granting discovery herein and to conduct further proceedings consistent with this opinion.

Babcock v. Superior Court

Court of Appeal of California, Second Appellate District

29 Cal. App. 4th 721, 35 Cal. Rptr. 2d 462 (1994)

GILBERT, JUSTICE.

Here we complete a trilogy of cases in which we consider discovery of financial records of people living with ex-spouses.

In *In re Marriage of Tapia* (1989) 211 Cal. App. 3d 628 [259 Cal. Rptr. 459], we held that contributions by third persons to an ex-spouse's living expenses should be considered by the trial court in determining the ex-spouse's ability to pay spousal or child support.

In *Harris v. Superior Court* (1992) 3 Cal. App. 4th 661 [4 Cal. Rptr. 2d 564], we held that *Tapia* should not be read to allow automatic discovery of the financial records of ex-spouses living with a third person. We held that when such discovery might be appropriate, the trial court should balance the third party's right of privacy against the ex-spouse's right to know.

Here we further refine and explain the duties and responsibilities of the court and of parties in those cases in which the judge makes a preliminary determination that discovery is appropriate. * * *

FACTS

Petitioner, Jamie Babcock, has resided with Dennis DiGiovanni since June of 1992 when he separated from real party, Denise DiGiovanni, his first wife. Ms. Babcock had been employed by Mr. DiGiovanni at his business, Road Tech, Inc., between the years 1987 and 1991. She had been unemployed since January of 1991.

Ms. Babcock owned a home valued at approximately $341,000, for which she made a $91,000 down payment in December 1991. She also owned a $30,000 automobile for which she made a down payment of $7,500 in June of 1992.

Ms. DiGiovanni suspected that the funds for the house and car had come from community funds. Ms. DiGiovanni found a loan application for Ms. Babcock's automobile, in which Ms. Babcock declared that she was the vice-president of sales and marketing for Road Tech, Inc., and was earning $7,900 per month.

On April 22, 1994, Ms. DiGiovanni deposed Ms. Babcock. Babcock refused to answer any questions concerning the source of the money for the down payments. Ms. Babcock did deny, however, that the money had come from Mr. DiGiovanni.

A few days later, Ms. DiGiovanni served a subpoena on two banks and on an automobile dealership to produce records of Ms. Babcock's loan applications, checks, and other related documents. Ms. Babcock moved the court to quash the subpoenas, to impose sanctions, or in the alternative, to have an in camera inspection. Included in the motion was a declaration from Dennis DiGiovanni attesting that no money from him or from the community had been used to purchase the home or the Toyota.

Ms. DiGiovanni moved to compel production of bank and other financial documents. (Code Civ. Proc., § 2020.) She also moved to join Ms. Babcock in the dissolution proceeding upon the grounds that there had been a wrongful diversion to her of community funds. (Fam. Code, § 1100, subd. (b).)

Respondent superior court denied the motion to quash, and imposed sanctions upon Ms. Babcock in the sum of $764. It also granted Ms. DiGiovanni's motions to compel production of Ms. Babcock's loan documents and of every check of more than $1,000 deposited, from whatever source, into her bank account during the period of January 1, 1991, through July 31, 1992. The court denied Ms. DiGiovanni's request to view Ms. Babcock's tax returns.

Ms. Babcock now seeks review by way of an extraordinary writ. She asserts that respondent court erred in requiring the production of records which are not directly relevant to the proceeding and in ordering disclosure without a protective order and without first conducting an in camera inspection.

Ms. Babcock lacks an adequate remedy at law. We therefore have granted an alternative writ of mandate relating to the issue of the need for an in camera inspection and for a protective order. We have also stayed the order compelling production of the documents.

Ms. Babcock also claims her joinder in this action was improper.

DISCUSSION

Joinder

Joinder is proper, where a spouse alleges that the other spouse has illegally made a gift of community funds. (*See* Fam. Code, 1100, subd. (b), 2021; Cal. Rules of Court, rule 1250 [now rule 5.150].) Accordingly, we deny the petition on the joinder issue.

In Camera Hearing

It is elemental that a party has a privacy interest in his or her personal financial records. (*Valley Bank of Nevada v. Superior Court* (1975) 15 Cal. 3d 652, 656 [125 Cal. Rptr. 553, 542 P.2d 977].) This right applies to nonmarital cohabitants. (*Harris v. Superior Court, supra*, 3 Cal. App. 4th at p. 668.) To paraphrase *Harris*, it does not follow that merely because Ms. Babcock lives in the same house with Mr. DiGiovanni she has waived her right of privacy. (*Ibid.*)

Ms. Babcock cites the *Harris* case to support her position. In *Harris*, we said that the law favors the proponent who initially seeks discovery of missing community assets from his or her former spouse, instead of seeking it from the former spouse's cohabitant. But, as the Supreme Court pointed out in *Schnabel v. Superior Court* (1993) 5 Cal. 4th 704, 713–714 [21 Cal. Rptr. 2d 200, 854 P.2d 1117], we "did not ... completely exclude the possibility of discovery [of financial records] from the third party." On the contrary, we stated that "'... some discovery of a third party's financial records may be appropriate ... [where, for example, said party] ... is suddenly living in sumptuous surroundings [or is] driving luxury cars....'" (*Harris v. Superior Court, supra*, 3 Cal. App. 4th at p. 668.)

It is true, Ms. DiGiovanni has not as yet taken her former husband's deposition. Her reluctance stems from her belief that he is not truthful. Nevertheless, she is not barred from discovery, as it is undisputed that Ms. Babcock had acquired an interest in a $341,000 home and a $30,000 automobile despite being unemployed for several years.

We conclude that the trial court acted well within its discretion in finding that Ms. DiGiovanni made a sufficient showing that Ms. Babcock may have been the beneficiary of community funds. No doubt the court disbelieved the assertions of Ms. Babcock and Mr. DiGiovanni that he was not the donor of any of the funds for the home or the automobile. Here, there was a sufficient showing to allow Ms. DiGiovanni to inquire into the source of these funds. (*See Harris v. Superior Court, supra*, 3 Cal. App. 4th at p. 668.)

We now turn to the question whether respondent superior court should have reviewed in camera the documents which Ms. DiGiovanni wishes to discover.

A party seeking the judicial prescreening of documents has the burden of showing good cause. (*Schnabel v. Superior Court, supra*, 5 Cal. 4th at p. 714.) Given the nature of the documents sought, and the showing made by Ms. DiGiovanni, Ms. Babcock is entitled to an in camera inspection of her documents. (*Schnabel v. Superior Court, supra,* 5 Cal. 4th at p. 714; *Harris v. Superior Court, supra,* 3 Cal. App. 4th at p. 668.)

Respondent court declined Ms. Babcock's request for an in camera inspection because it did not have the time to go over what it believed to be a prodigious task of sorting through a confusing array of financial records. In the return to the alternative writ, counsel for Ms. DiGiovanni characterized this task as daunting because the trial judge would not understand the importance of the documents he would be called upon to review. Nor would he be familiar with the sundry names of those persons or entities who may have deposited funds into Ms. Babcock's bank account.

It is true that reviewing a melange of loan and financial documents could be a Herculean task. Such an inspection could impose an undue burden upon a busy family law court. * * * The trial court, however, has a remedy. As the appellate court pointed out in *Tera Pharmaceuticals, Inc. v. Superior Court* (1985) 170 Cal. App. 3d. 530, 532 [215 Cal. Rptr. 923], " ... judges should shift the burden [of proof] to counsel, where it belongs...." Just as Dante had the services of the poet Virgil to guide him through the labyrinth of the Inferno, so too may the court require counsel for the deponent to act as its guide.

Counsel for a deponent wishing to protect the privacy interests of his or her client bears the burden of assisting the court to conduct an in camera hearing. The deponent knows the importance and significance of the documents, and can identify the persons or entities who have deposited funds into the deponent's bank account. In a declaration under penalty of perjury, the deponent can provide the court with a precise summary which explains the source of funds coming into the bank account, and which explains to whom checks are paid, and the purpose of such payment.

Suppose for example the deponent's parents wish to give her funds for the down payment on a house. The parents have another child whom they prefer not know about this gift. If the court has sufficient proof that the funds were supplied by the deponent's parents, the court would undoubtedly disallow discovery. So too, would the court disallow discovery, for example, if the deponent showed that the funds came from a recently acquired inheritance.

In the instant case, the trial court should order the financial records be presented in camera. If Ms. Babcock wishes to convince the court that her financial records are not discoverable, she may prepare for the court's consideration, declarations under penalty of perjury explaining the details of all of those financial transactions over $1,000. The court is in the best position to decide how helpful are the declarations. If the court in its discretion, decides that the declarations do not adequately enlighten, then the court may order the discovery of the records.

We are confident that where there are legitimate privacy concerns about records that have no relevance to the action, conscientious counsel will draft a concise summary for signature by the client, or other relevant declarant, explaining, under penalty of perjury, the source and expenditure of funds. Under these circumstances, the trial court's burden should be relatively light.

Protective Order

Finally, there is the question of the need for a protective order. "[T]he third party deponent is *presumptively* entitled to a protective order that limits disclosure of financial information. [Citation.]" (Italics added.) (*Harris v. Superior Court, supra,* 3 Cal. App. 4th at p. 668.) Thus, upon the ordering of disclosure of certain financial documents, the trial court is obliged to limit disclosure of "such information only for purposes related to the lawsuit, and only by persons having a legitimate interest in that information for such purposes. [Citations.]" (*Moskowitz v. Superior Court* (1983) 137 Cal. App. 3d 313, 319 [187 Cal. Rptr. 4].)[3]

"Simply because certain information is so important to the resolution of the issues in a lawsuit that the need for discovery of it overrides the right of privacy does not mean that all protection for it is lost. The one whose privacy is involved is presumptively entitled to a protective order limiting the use of the information to the litigation itself, and barring its dissemination for purposes not related to a fair resolution of the action." (2 Hogan, Modern Cal. Discovery 4th (1988) § 12.28, p. 185.)

Sanctions

The imposition of sanctions was not warranted here. *Harris* envisions the case in which discovery of an ex-spouse's living companion would be appropriate. Although this may be one of those cases, Ms. Babcock is entitled to a protective order. Her counsel tried to resolve the discovery dispute with opposing counsel. In a letter to Ms. DiGiovanni's counsel, he stated, "I have offered to produce names, declarations and the paper trail of the monies used by my client, Jamie Babcock, to purchase the Toyota vehicle and her home. I will produce this information in camera, for you and Judge Hadden only."

There was a legitimate difference of opinion between counsel as to the applicability of *Harris,* and Ms. Babcock offered to produce the information in camera. We conclude that she acted in good faith and under circumstances that would make the imposition of sanctions unjust. (Code Civ. Proc., § 2023, subd. (b)(1); *see Mc-Donald v. John P. Scripps Newspaper* (1989) 210 Cal. App. 3d 100, 106 [257 Cal. Rptr. 473].)

Let a writ of mandate issue ordering the respondent superior court to: (1) vacate its order of sanctions; (2) set aside its order in which it denied Ms. Babcock's request

---

3. For an example of a prototypical protective order, see *In re First Peoples Bank Shareholders Litigation* (D.N.J. 1988) 121 F.R.D. 219, 230. In that case, the trial court ordered disclosure of certain sensitive information upon condition that the materials could be discussed by counsel in consulting with their clients. Copies were not to be given to the clients, nor would any person be permitted to use such information for any purposes other than the current litigation.

for an in camera inspection and for a protective order; and (3) enter a new order that conforms with the views expressed in this opinion. The alternative writ is discharged and the stay is dissolved. The parties to bear their own costs.

[a] Consumer Records

The problem of inadequate safeguards of consumer records has been specifically addressed in the Civil Discovery Act in CCP §§ 1985.3, 2020.410(d) & .510(c), requiring notice to the consumer or the consumer's written authorization to release personal documents. For a good review of the jurisprudence of the constitutional right of privacy, as applied in the context of a consumer class action, see *Pioneer Electronics (USA), Inc. v. Superior Court*, 40 Cal. 4th 360, 53 Cal. Rptr. 3d 513, 150 P.3d 198 (2007) (applying balancing test to determine the extent the right of privacy protects purchasers from having their identifying information disclosed to the plaintiff in a consumer rights class action against the defendant seller, where the plaintiff needs the information to facilitate communication with potential class members).

[b] Tax Returns

The California Supreme Court created a privilege to protect tax returns in recognition of the sensitivity of private financial information and the policy of facilitating collection of taxes. *Schnabel v. Superior Court*, 5 Cal. 4th 704, 718–723, 21Cal. Rptr. 2d 200, 854 P.2d 1117 (1993) (collecting cases); *Webb v. Standard Oil of California*, 49 Cal. 2d 509, 319 P.2d 621 (1957); *Sav-On Drugs, Inc. v. Superior Court*, 15 Cal. 3d 1, 123 Cal. Rptr. 283, 538, P.2d 739 (1975). While this privilege has been broadly construed, by statute it does not apply in child and spousal support proceedings. Family Code § 3552.

[c] Medical Records

Numerous reported decisions have recognized that a patient has a privacy interest in a doctor's medical records pertaining to the patient's physical or mental condition. *See, e.g., Lantz v. Superior Court*, 28 Cal. App. 4th 1839, 34 Cal. Rptr. 2d 358 (collecting cases). What factors should a trial court consider in balancing one party's privacy interest against the opposing party's stated need for such records? *See Lantz*, 28 Cal. App. 4th at 1853–57. In an action for negligent screening of blood donors, how should the courts strike the balance between the plaintiff's need to discover information from the donors and the donors' right to privacy? *See Irwin Memorial Blood Bank v. Superior Court*, 229 Cal. App. 3d 151, 279 Cal. Rptr. 911 (1991) (no depositions of blood donors allowed); *see also Watson v. Lowcountry Red Cross*, 974 F.2d 482 (4th Cir. 1992) (ordering deposition of donor be by written questions rather than live testimony).

How should the balance be struck in an action by parents and their children against a sperm bank alleging the transmission of a serious kidney disease to the children by the sperm donor? *See Johnson v. Superior Court*, 80 Cal. App. 4th 1050, 95 Cal. Rptr. 2d 864 (2000) (holding donor's constitutional right of privacy in his medical history and identity outweighed by the public policy expressed in Family Code §7613, which provides for disclosure of insemination records under certain circumstances, and the state's compelling interest in the health and welfare of children).

[d] Sexual History

Information about a person's sexual history is frequently the subject of a privacy claim. CCP §2017.220 specifically protects a plaintiff in a sexual harassment case from disclosure of this information. *See, e.g., Knottgen v. Superior Court*, 224 Cal. App. 3d 11, 273 Cal. Rptr. 636 (1990). But the issue arises in other cases where §2017(d) does not apply. *See Boler v. Superior Court*, 201 Cal. App. 3d 467, 247 Cal. Rptr. 185 (1987) (holding defendant in sexual harassment case not required to disclose names of all past employees with whom he had intimate relations). Should a plaintiff seeking damages for wrongful death of a spouse be compelled to disclose extramarital affairs? *See Morales v. Superior Court*, 99 Cal. App. 3d 283, 160 Cal. Rptr. 194 (1980) (ruling plaintiff must state frequency of extramarital encounters, but not the names and addresses of the other parties).

In an action brought by one spouse against the other spouse alleging that the defendant knowingly or negligently transmitted the HIV virus to the plaintiff, does the constitutional right of privacy preclude the plaintiff from discovering information about the defendant's sexual conduct before and during the marriage? *See John B. v. Superior Court*, 38 Cal. 4th 1177, 45 Cal. Rptr. 3d 316, 137 P.3d 153 (2006) (balancing husband's right to privacy against wife's right to discovery relevant facts, and concluding that husband's medical records and sexual history were discoverable in order to confirm or refute wife's allegations that husband knowingly or negligently infected wife with HIV).

[e] Memberships

The identity of members of clubs and organizations is another difficult area. For example, should a church be forced to turn over a list of its ministers? *See Church of Hakeem, Inc. v. Superior Court*, 110 Cal. App. 3d 384, 168 Cal. Rptr. 13 (1980). Should a private club be forced to turn over a list of rejected applicants? *See Olympic Club v. Superior Court*, 229 Cal. App. 3d 358, 282 Cal. Rptr. 1 (1991). Why is this a difficult area?

In litigation concerning the scope of the anti-abortion protesters' rights to engage in activities outside Planned Parenthood's facilities, should Planned Parenthood be ordered to disclose, pursuant to a protective order, the names, residential addresses, and telephone numbers of staff and volunteers who have knowledge relevant to the litigation? *See Planned Parenthood Golden Gate v. Superior Court*, 83 Cal. App. 4th 347, 99 Cal. Rptr. 2d 627 (2000) (finding the privacy interests at stake were particularly strong because the consequences of disclosure of this private information were profound, and therefore outweighed the need for discovery). Should a public interest organization seeking an award of attorney fees under the private attorney general statute be required to disclose the identities of, and donations by, the contributors to its litigation fund? *See Save Open Space Santa Monica Mountains v. Superior Court*, 84 Cal. App. 4th 235, 100 Cal. Rptr. 2d 725 (2000) (ruling need for discovery outweighed associational privacy interests, where evidence sought was crucial to court's analysis of attorney fees request).

[f] Personnel Information

Employment and personnel information has been found to be outside the scope of discovery. For example, in a wrongful termination case the plaintiff was denied access to information in the personnel files of other employees absent a showing of compelling need. *Perez v. County of Santa Clara*, 111 Cal. App. 4th 671, 3 Cal. Rptr. 2d 867 (2003) (concluding that, in action by nurse alleging disparate disciplinary treatment based on race, trial court properly granted a protective order restricting plaintiff's access to personnel records of other nurses at correctional facility); *Harding Lawson Assoc. v. Superior Court*, 10 Cal. App. 4th 7, 12 Cal. Rptr. 2d 538 (1992). The protection of this information has also been applied to information about a party to the action. *See Kahn v. Superior Court*, 188 Cal. App. 3d 752, 233 Cal. Rptr. 662 (1987) (denying plaintiff information about the tenure discussions in a case alleging wrongful denial of tenure because to allow discovery would impede full and candid discussions of candidates' qualifications).

[g] Employment Records

The need to protect employment and personnel information has heightened significance in certain professions. For this reason, the law extends additional protection to police personnel files (Evidence Code § 1043 and Penal Code § 832.7) and to medical board proceedings (Evid. Code § 1157). *See Fox v. Kramer*, 22 Cal. 4th 531, 93 Cal. Rptr. 2d 497, 994 P.2d 343 (2000) (concluding Evid. Code § 1157(a) makes a hospital's peer review committee records immune from discovery); *County of Riverside v. Superior Court*, 27 Cal. 4th 793, 118 Cal. Rptr. 2d 167, 42 P.3d 1034 (2002) (ruling specific provisions of the Public Safety Officers Procedural Bill of Rights Act, Gov. Code §§ 3301–3306, giving peace officers a right to view adverse comments in their personnel files, take precedence over the more general statutory and common law privileges which prohibit disclosure). Why is such information protected?

[h] Private Settlement Agreements

A confidential settlement agreement reached in a related case may also be protected from disclosure by the right of privacy. *See Hinshaw, Winkler, Draa, Marsh & Still v. Superior Court*, 51 Cal. App. 4th 233, 58 Cal. Rptr. 2d 791 (1996) (holding plaintiffs in a legal malpractice action were not entitled to discovery of confidential settlement agreements reached in the original case in which they were dropped by their attorney, because of the policy favoring settlements and the speculative nature of measuring plaintiffs' damages by these settlements). For discussion of access to pretrial settlements and discovery where the settling parties agreed that the settlement will remain confidential and that any information obtained through discovery will not be disclosed to third parties, see Walter W. Heiser, *Public Access to Confidential Discovery: The California Perspective*, 35 W. St. U. L. Rev. 55 (2007).

[i] Financial Condition in Punitive Damages Claims

Pretrial discovery of a defendant's financial condition is not permitted with respect to a claim for punitive damages unless the plaintiff upon motion, on the basis of supporting and opposing affidavits presented, establishes that there is a "substantial probability" that the plaintiff will prevail on the claim for punitive damages. Civil Code § 3295(c). Need a plaintiff only present evidence of a prima facie case supporting a claim for punitive damages — that is, evidence sufficient to avoid summary judgment on the issue — to obtain an order permitting discovery of a defendant's financial condition? *See Jabro v. Superior Court*, 95 Cal. App. 4th 754, 115 Cal. Rptr. 2d 843 (2002) (concluding that before a court may enter an order permitting discovery of defendant's financial condition under § 3295(c), it must weigh the evidence submitted by both sides and make a finding that it is very likely the plaintiff will prevail on his claim for punitive damages); *Guardado v. Superior Court*, 163 Cal. App. 4th 91, 98, 77 Cal. Rptr. 3d 149 (2008) (ruling the weighing of evidence pursuant to § 3295(c) does not mean that the trial court must resolve contested issues of fact as to the merits of the claim).

[D] Protection of Attorney's Work Product

[1] Introductory Note

In addition to protecting information within the scope of traditional privilege law, the Discovery Act provides a specific scheme for protecting an attorney's work product. CCP § 2018.010–2018.080. Section 2018.020 reflects the State policy of assuring protection of the work product of attorneys, insurers, consultants, and agents both in anticipation of litigation and for trial. This protection provides incentive for thorough preparation, promotes investigation of both strengths and weaknesses of a case, and prevents one party from taking unfair advantage of another's efforts.

To further this policy, CCP § 2018.030 provides both absolute and conditional work product protection. Absolute protection is provided to "[a]ny writing that reflects an attorney's impressions, conclusions, opinions, or legal research or theories." CCP § 2018.030(a). Qualified protection is afforded to any other work product which is only discoverable where "the court determines that denial of discovery will unfairly prejudice the party seeking discovery in preparing that party's claim or defense or will result in an injustice." CCP § 2018.030(b).

[2] California's Work Product Doctrines

Coito v. Superior Court

Supreme Court of California
54 Cal. 4th 480; 278 P.3d 860; 142 Cal. Rptr. 3d 607 (2012)

LIU, JUSTICE.

In California, an attorney's work product is protected by statute. (Code Civ. Proc., § 2018.010 et seq.; all further unlabeled statutory references are to the Code of Civ. Proc.) Absolute protection is afforded to writings that reflect "an attorney's impressions, conclusions, opinions, or legal research or theories." (§ 2018.030, subd. (a).) All other work product receives qualified protection; such material "is not discoverable unless the court determines that denial of discovery will unfairly prejudice the party seeking discovery in preparing that party's claim or defense or will result in an injustice." (§ 2018.030, subd. (b).)

In this case, we decide what work product protection, if any, should be accorded two items: first, recordings of witness interviews conducted by investigators employed by defendant's counsel, and second, information concerning the identity of witnesses from whom defendant's counsel has obtained statements. Defendant objected to plaintiff's requests for discovery of these items, invoking the work product privilege. The trial court sustained the objection, concluding as a matter of law that the recorded witness interviews were entitled to absolute work product protection and that the other information sought was work product entitled to qualified protection. A divided Court of Appeal reversed, concluding that work product protection does not apply to any of the disputed items. The Court of Appeal issued a writ of mandate directing the trial court to grant the motion to compel discovery.

We conclude that the Court of Appeal erred. In light of the legislatively declared policy and the legislative history of the work product privilege, we hold that the recorded witness statements are entitled as a matter of law to at least qualified work product protection. The witness statements may be entitled to absolute protection if defendant can show that disclosure would reveal its "attorney's impressions, conclusions, opinions, or legal research or theories." (§ 2018.030, subd. (a).) If not, then the items may be subject to discovery if plaintiff can show that "denial of discovery will unfairly prejudice [her] in preparing [her] claim ... or will result in an injustice." (§ 2018.030, subd. (b).)

As to the identity of witnesses from whom defendant's counsel has obtained statements, we hold that such information is not automatically entitled as a matter of law to absolute or qualified work product protection. In order to invoke the privilege, defendant must persuade the trial court that disclosure would reveal the attorney's tactics, impressions, or evaluation of the case (absolute privilege) or would result in opposing counsel taking undue advantage of the attorney's industry or efforts (qualified privilege).

We reverse the judgment of the Court of Appeal and remand the matter for further proceedings, consistent with our opinion, to determine whether the disputed materials should be produced.

I.

On March 9, 2007, 13-year-old Jeremy Wilson drowned in the Tuolumne River in Modesto, California. His mother, Debra Coito, filed a complaint for wrongful death naming several defendants, including the State of California. The Department of Water Resources (DWR) is the agency defending the action for the state, represented by the Attorney General.

Six other juveniles witnessed what happened. There were allegations that all of the juveniles, including the decedent, were engaged in criminal conduct immediately before the drowning. On November 12, 2008, after codefendant City of Modesto had noticed the depositions of five of the six juvenile witnesses, counsel for the state sent two investigators, both special agents from the Bureau of Investigation of the Department of Justice, to interview four of the juveniles. The state's counsel provided the investigators with questions he wanted asked. Each interview was audio-recorded and saved on a separate compact disc.

On January 27, 2009, the City of Modesto began its deposition of one of the four interviewed witnesses. The state's counsel used the content of the witness's recorded interview in questioning the witness at the deposition.

On February 5, 2009, plaintiff served the state with supplemental interrogatories and document demands. The interrogatories included Judicial Council form interrogatory No. 12.3, which sought the names, addresses, and telephone numbers of individuals from whom written or recorded statements had been obtained. The document demands sought production of the audio recordings of the four witness interviews. The state objected to the requested discovery based on the work product privilege.

Plaintiff filed a motion to compel an answer to form interrogatory No. 12.3 and the production of the recorded interviews. In support of the motion, plaintiff filed declarations from two of the interviewed witnesses asserting that they had not intended their statements to be confidential. The state opposed the motion, relying primarily on *Nacht & Lewis Architects, Inc. v. Superior Court* (1996) 47 Cal.App.4th 214, 217 [54 Cal. Rptr. 2d 575] (*Nacht & Lewis*), which held that recorded witness statements are entitled to absolute work product protection and that information sought by form interrogatory No. 12.3 is entitled to qualified work product protection.

After an April 10, 2009 hearing, and without having reviewed the audio recordings, the trial court issued a written order that relied on *Nacht & Lewis* in denying plaintiff's motion except as to the recording used by the state to examine the witness during the January 27, 2009 deposition. As to that recording, the court reasoned that the state had waived the work product privilege by using the interview to examine the witness during the deposition.

Plaintiff petitioned for a writ of mandate that the Court of Appeal granted. The majority, relying on *Greyhound Corp. v. Superior Court* (1961) 56 Cal.2d 355 [15 Cal.

Rptr. 90, 364 P.2d 266] (*Greyhound*) and expressly declining to follow *Nacht & Lewis*, concluded that witness interviews and the information sought by form interrogatory No. 12.3 are not entitled as a matter of law to absolute or qualified work product protection. Because defendant's attorney made no showing of entitlement to work product protection in the specific context of this case, the Court of Appeal directed the trial court to compel discovery. Justice Kane wrote a concurring and dissenting opinion. While agreeing that the trial court's order denying discovery should be vacated, he concluded that the recorded interviews were entitled as a matter of law to at least qualified work product protection, whereas the information sought by form interrogatory No. 12.3 must be produced unless the objecting party has made an adequate showing to support a claim of qualified privilege.

We granted review. As with all matters of statutory construction, our review of the Court of Appeal's interpretation of the work product statute is de novo. (*Imperial Merchant Services, Inc. v. Hunt* (2009) 47 Cal.4th 381, 387 [97 Cal. Rptr. 3d 464, 212 P.3d 736].)

II.

California's civil work product privilege is codified in section 2018.030. Subdivision (a) provides absolute protection to any "writing that reflects an attorney's impressions, conclusions, opinions, or legal research or theories." (§ 2018.030, subd. (a).) Such a writing "is not discoverable under any circumstances." (*Ibid.*) The term "writing" includes any form of recorded information, including audio recordings. (§ 2016.020, subd. (c) [adopting the definition set forth in Evid. Code, § 250].) Section 2018.030, subdivision (b) provides qualified protection for all other work product. Such material "is not discoverable unless the court determines that denial of discovery will unfairly prejudice the party seeking discovery in preparing that party's claim or defense or will result in an injustice." (§ 2018.030, subd. (b).) Here, we address the work product privilege in the civil context only, as criminal discovery is regulated by a different statute. (Pen. Code, § 1054 et seq.)

The language of section 2018.030 does not otherwise define or describe "work product." Courts have resolved whether particular materials constitute work product on a case-by-case basis (*City of Long Beach v. Superior Court* (1976) 64 Cal. App. 3d 65, 71 [134 Cal. Rptr. 468]), although they have sometimes taken different approaches. Some courts have attempted to answer the question by distinguishing between "derivative" or "nonderivative" material, or between "interpretative" and "evidentiary" material. (E.g., *Fellows v. Superior Court* (1980) 108 Cal. App. 3d 55, 68–69 [166 Cal. Rptr. 274] (*Fellows*); *Rodriguez v. McDonnell Douglas Corp.* (1978) 87 Cal. App. 3d 626, 647 [151 Cal. Rptr. 399] (*Rodriguez*); *Mack v. Superior Court* (1968) 259 Cal. App. 2d 7, 10–11 [66 Cal. Rptr. 280] (*Mack*).) These cases have concluded that only derivative or interpretive material—material created by or derived from an attorney's work reflecting the attorney's evaluation of the law or facts—constitutes work product. Examples of such material include "diagrams prepared for trial, audit reports, appraisals, and other expert opinions, developed as a result of the initiative of counsel in preparing for trial." (*Mack*, at p. 10.) Nonderivative material—material that is only evidentiary in nature—does not constitute work product. Examples of such material include the identity and location of physical evidence or witnesses. (*Ibid.*; *City of Long Beach*, at p. 73.)

Other courts, instead of distinguishing between derivative and nonderivative material, have determined the scope of protected work product by relying primarily upon the policies underlying the work product statute and its legislative history. (E.g., *Dowden v. Superior Court* (1999) 73 Cal.App.4th 126, 130–133, 135 [86 Cal. Rptr. 2d 180] (*Dowden*).) Because those policies and the legislative history are instructive in resolving the instant case, we begin by reviewing the origins and development of California's work product privilege.

A.

The idea that an attorney's work product should receive protection from discovery was first recognized by the United States Supreme Court in *Hickman v. Taylor* (1947) 329 U.S. 495 [91 L. Ed. 451, 67 S. Ct. 385] (*Hickman*). * * *

The court [in *Hickman* explained]: "In performing his various duties, ... it is essential that a lawyer work with a certain degree of privacy, free from unnecessary intrusion by opposing parties and their counsel. Proper preparation of a client's case demands that he assemble information, sift what he considers to be the relevant from the irrelevant facts, prepare his legal theories and plan his strategy without undue and needless interference. That is the historical and the necessary way in which lawyers act within the framework of our system of jurisprudence to promote justice and to protect their clients' interests. This work is reflected, of course, in interviews, statements, memoranda, correspondence, briefs, mental impressions, personal beliefs, and countless other tangible and intangible ways—aptly though roughly termed by the Circuit Court of Appeals in this case as the 'work product of the lawyer.' Were such materials open to opposing counsel on mere demand, much of what is now put down in writing would remain unwritten. An attorney's thoughts, heretofore inviolate, would not be his own. Inefficiency, unfairness and sharp practices would inevitably develop in the giving of legal advice and in the preparation of cases for trial. The effect on the legal profession would be demoralizing. And the interests of the clients and the cause of justice would be poorly served." * * *

At the time *Hickman* was decided, California law protected work product only through the attorney-client privilege. * * * Against this statutory backdrop, this court in 1961 concluded that neither the attorney-client privilege nor the work product doctrine protected nonparty witness statements from discovery. (*Greyhound, supra,* 56 Cal.2d at pp. 399, 401.) * * * In response to *Greyhound*, the State Bar Committee proposed an amendment the following year with the purpose of codifying a work product privilege. [Here the court discusses the legislative history relevant to enactment of former section 2016 in 1963.]

Although the work product privilege was moved first from former section 2016 to former section 2018 and then from former section 2018 to its present location, the current text is virtually identical to the version first enacted in 1963. Section

2018.020 declares: "It is the policy of the state to do both of the following: [¶] (a) Preserve the rights of attorneys to prepare cases for trial with that degree of privacy necessary to encourage them to prepare their cases thoroughly and to investigate not only the favorable but the unfavorable aspects of those cases. [¶] (b) Prevent attorneys from taking undue advantage of their adversary's industry and efforts." Toward that end, section 2018.030 provides: "(a) A writing that reflects an attorney's impressions, conclusions, opinions, or legal research or theories is not discoverable under any circumstances. [¶] (b) The work product of an attorney, other than a writing described in subdivision (a), is not discoverable unless the court determines that denial of discovery will unfairly prejudice the party seeking discovery in preparing that party's claim or defense or will result in an injustice." As noted, section 2018.030, subdivision (a) provides absolute protection for certain work product, while subdivision (b) provides qualified protection for all other work product.

B.

In light of the origins and development of the work product privilege in California, we conclude that witness statements obtained as a result of interviews conducted by an attorney, or by an attorney's agent at the attorney's behest, constitute work product protected by section 2018.030.

As mentioned, the Legislature in enacting section 2018.030 did not define "work product" and instead left the term open to judicial interpretation. From the very inception of judicial recognition of the concept, attorney work product has been understood to include witness statements obtained through an interview conducted by an attorney. The high court in *Hickman* specifically referred to "statements" and "interviews" in its nonexclusive enumeration of items comprising the "'work product of [a] lawyer.'" (*Hickman, supra,* 329 U.S. at p. 511.) And *Hickman* held that the district court in that case improperly ordered the defendant's attorney "to produce *all written statements of witnesses*" and other items that the attorney had obtained through his own interviews. (*Id.* at p. 509, italics added; see *id.* at p. 508 [plaintiff sought "discovery as of right of oral and *written statements of witnesses* whose identity is well known and whose availability to [plaintiff] appears unimpaired" (italics added)].)

The closest we have come to examining the applicability of section 2018.030 to witness statements is our decision in *Rico v. Mitsubishi Motors Corp.* (2007) 42 Cal.4th 807 [68 Cal. Rptr. 3d 758, 171 P.3d 1092] (*Rico*). There, we held that work product "protection extends to an attorney's written notes about a witness's statements" and that "[w]hen a witness's statement and the attorney's impressions are inextricably intertwined," the entire document receives absolute protection. (*Id.* at p. 814.) The question in *Rico* was not whether a witness's statement is itself protected work product, and the document at issue was not "a verbatim record of the [witnesses'] statements" but rather a summary prepared at the request of the defendant's attorney. (*Id.* at p. 815.) *Rico* thus did not speak to the issue now before us.

Nevertheless, in finding the document protected, *Rico's* observation that "'its very existence is owed to the lawyer's thought process'" (*Rico, supra,* 42 Cal.4th at p. 815

[quoting trial court]) provides a useful touchstone for our present inquiry. There is no dispute that a statement independently prepared by a witness does not become protected work product simply upon its transmission to an attorney. (See *Wellpoint Health Networks, Inc. v. Superior Court* (1997) 59 Cal.App.4th 110, 119 [68 Cal. Rptr. 2d 844]; *Nacht & Lewis, supra,* 47 Cal.App.4th at p. 218.) The issue here is what protection, if any, should be afforded where the witness's statement has been obtained through an attorney-directed interview. "In such situations," the Court of Appeal correctly observed, "it can surely be said that the witness statement is in part the product of the attorney's work." The witness statement would not exist but for the attorney's initiative, decision, and effort to obtain it. This essential fact informs our analysis of whether absolute or qualified work product privilege applies to such witness statements.

Absolute privilege. It is not difficult to imagine that a recorded witness interview may, in some instances, reveal the "impressions, conclusions, opinions, or legal research or theories" of the attorney and thus be entitled to absolute protection. (§ 2018.030, subd. (a).) This may occur not only when a witness's statements are "inextricably intertwined" with explicit comments or notes by the attorney stating his or her impressions of the witness, the witness's statements, or other issues in the case. (*Rico, supra,* 42 Cal.4th at p. 814.) It also may occur when the questions that the attorney has chosen to ask (or not ask) provide a window into the attorney's theory of the case or the attorney's evaluation of what issues are most important. Lines of inquiry that an attorney chooses to pursue through followup questions may be especially revealing. In such situations, redaction of the attorney's questions may sometimes be appropriate and sufficient to protect privileged material. At other times, however, it may not do to simply redact the questions from the record, as the witness's statements will reveal what questions were asked. Moreover, in some cases, the very fact that the attorney has chosen to interview a particular witness may disclose important tactical or evaluative information, perhaps especially so in cases involving a multitude of witnesses. These are circumstances where absolute work product protection may apply.

We cannot say, however, that witness statements procured by an attorney will always reveal the attorney's thought process. The Court of Appeal below posited a scenario in which an attorney collects statements from witnesses to an accident with no particular foresight, strategy, selectivity, or planning: "What, for example, of the situation in which an attorney sends an investigator to interview all witnesses listed in a police report, and the investigator asks few if any questions while taking the witnesses' statements? Clearly, these statements would reveal nothing significant about the attorney's impressions, conclusions, or opinions about the case." For this reason (and such scenarios do not seem uncommon), we hold that witness statements procured by an attorney are not automatically entitled as a matter of law to absolute work product protection. Instead, the applicability of absolute protection must be determined case by case. An attorney resisting discovery of a witness statement based on absolute privilege must make a preliminary or foundational showing that disclosure would reveal his or her "impressions, conclusions, opinions, or legal research or theories." (§ 2018.030, subd. (a).) Upon an adequate showing, the trial court should then determine, by making an in camera inspection if necessary, whether absolute work product protection applies to some or all of the material.

Qualified privilege. Although witness statements obtained through an attorney-directed interview may or may not reveal the attorney's thought process, we believe such statements necessarily implicate two other interests that the Legislature sought to protect in enacting the work product privilege. Based on these interests, we conclude that witness statements procured by an attorney are entitled as a matter of law to at least qualified work product protection under section 2018.030, subdivision (b).

First, when an attorney obtains through discovery a witness statement obtained by opposing counsel through his or her own initiative, such discovery undermines the Legislature's policy to "[p]revent attorneys from taking undue advantage of their adversary's industry and efforts." (§ 2018.020, subd. (b).) Even when an attorney exercises no selectivity in determining which witnesses to interview, and even when the attorney simply records each witness's answer to a single question ("What happened?"), the attorney has expended time and effort in identifying and locating each witness, securing the witness's willingness to talk, listening to what the witness said, and preserving the witness's statement for possible future use. An attorney who seeks to discover what a witness knows is not without recourse. The attorney is free to interview the witness for himself or herself to find out what information the witness has that is relevant to the litigation. * * * Absent a showing that a witness is no longer available or accessible, or some other showing of unfair prejudice or injustice (§ 2018.030, subd. (b)), the Legislature's declared policy is to prevent an attorney from free riding on the industry and efforts of opposing counsel (§ 2018.020, subd. (b)).

Second, a default rule authorizing discovery of witness statements procured by an attorney would impede the Legislature's intent "to encourage [attorneys] to prepare their cases thoroughly and to investigate not only the favorable but the unfavorable aspects of those cases." (§ 2018.020, subd. (a).) If attorneys must worry about discovery whenever they take a statement from a witness, it is reasonably foreseeable that fewer witness statements will be recorded and that adverse information will not be memorialized. As Justice Kane observed below, without work product protection, "no meaningful privacy exists within which an attorney may have sufficient confidence to thoroughly investigate and record potentially *unfavorable* matters." This result would derogate not only from an attorney's duty and prerogative to investigate matters thoroughly, but also from the truth-seeking values that the rules of discovery are intended to promote. Accordingly, we hold that a witness statement obtained through an attorney-directed interview is, as a matter of law, entitled to at least qualified work product protection.

C.

The protection afforded by section 2018.030, subdivision (b) to the witness statements in this case is essentially the same protection that the high court afforded to the witness statements in *Hickman*. There, the court held the statements protected and placed the burden on the party seeking discovery "to establish adequate reasons to justify production," such as unavailability or inaccessibility of the witnesses. (*Hickman, supra,* 329 U.S. at p. 512.) Qualified protection of this sort, the court said, is necessary if a lawyer is to discharge his duty "to work for the advancement of justice while faithfully protecting the rightful interests of his clients." (*Id.* at p. 510.)

In reaching a contrary conclusion, the Court of Appeal below relied primarily on *Greyhound*'s conclusion that witness statements are not protected by the work product privilege. Such reliance on *Greyhound* is misplaced. As previously discussed, the Legislature's 1963 amendments to the Discovery Act were intended as a corrective to *Greyhound.* * * *

The Court of Appeal also cited several cases suggesting that witness statements made to an attorney do not constitute work product. (E.g., *Fellows, supra,* 108 Cal. App. 3d at p. 69; *People v. Williams* (1979) 93 Cal. App. 3d 40, 63–64 [155 Cal. Rptr. 414]; *Rodriguez, supra,* 87 Cal. App. 3d at p. 647; *Kadelbach v. Amaral* (1973) 31 Cal. App. 3d 814, 822 [107 Cal. Rptr. 720].) But those cases address the issue in a conclusory manner without discussing the legislatively declared policy or the history of the work product privilege. * * *

Underlying these assertions that witness statements do not constitute work product is the notion that such writings are nonderivative or noninterpretative material that is wholly evidentiary in nature. (*Fellows, supra,* 108 Cal. App. 3d at p. 69; *People v. Williams, supra,* 93 Cal. App. 3d at pp. 63–64; *Rodriguez, supra,* 87 Cal. App. 3d at p. 647.) However, … a witness statement taken by an attorney possesses both derivative characteristics (i.e., an attorney must put time and effort, and possibly thought and planning, into conducting the interview) and nonderivative characteristics (i.e., the statement may contain information regarding events provable at trial or the identity or location of physical evidence, or it may be useful for impeachment or refreshing the witness's recollection). * * *

In sum, we disapprove *Fellows v. Superior Court, supra,* 108 Cal. App. 3d 55, *People v. Williams, supra,* 93 Cal. App. 3d 40, *Rodriguez v. McDonnell Douglas Corp., supra,* 87 Cal. App. 3d 626, and *Kadelbach v. Amaral, supra,* 31 Cal. App. 3d 814 to the extent they suggest that a witness statement taken by an attorney does not, as a matter of law, constitute work product. In addition, *Greyhound, supra,* 56 Cal.2d 355, which was decided before the Legislature codified the work product privilege, should not be read as supporting such a conclusion. At the same time, we reject the dicta in *Nacht & Lewis, supra,* 47 Cal.App.4th at page 217 that said "recorded statements taken by defendants' counsel would be protected by the absolute work product privilege because they would reveal counsel's 'impressions, conclusions, opinions, or legal research or theories'...." Instead, we hold that a witness statement obtained through an attorney-directed interview is entitled as a matter of law to at least qualified work product protection. A party seeking disclosure has the burden of establishing that denial of disclosure will unfairly prejudice the party in preparing its claim or defense or will result in an injustice. (§ 2018.030, subd. (b).) If the party resisting discovery alleges that a witness statement, or portion thereof, is absolutely protected because it "reflects an attorney's impressions, conclusions, opinions, or legal research or theories" (§ 2018.030, subd. (a)), that party must make a preliminary or foundational showing in support of its claim. The trial court should then make an in camera inspection to determine whether absolute work product protection applies to some or all of the material.

In the present case, we remand the matter for consideration of whether absolute privilege applies to all or part of the recorded witness interviews. If any or all of the interviews are not absolutely protected, the trial court should consider whether plaintiff can make a sufficient showing of unfair prejudice or injustice under section 2018.030, subdivision (b) to permit discovery. We do not disturb the trial court's conclusion that the state waived the work product privilege as to the recording used to examine a witness during the January 27, 2009 deposition.

D.

In addition to the witness statements, plaintiff sought to compel defendant to answer form interrogatory No. 12.3, which asked: "Have YOU OR ANYONE ACTING ON YOUR BEHALF obtained a written or recorded statement from any individual concerning the INCIDENT?" For any such statement, the interrogatory requested (among other things) the name, address, and telephone number of the witness and the date the statement was obtained. * * *

The issue here is whether disclosure of a list of witnesses from whom an attorney took recorded statements at his or her own initiative implicates the work product privilege. Parties in litigation typically know the full universe of witnesses, not least because Judicial Council form interrogatory No. 12.1 requires parties to provide a list of all known witnesses. Thus, form interrogatory No. 12.3 specifically aims to reveal which witnesses an attorney for one party saw fit to ask for a recorded statement.

As discussed above, disclosing a list of witnesses from whom an attorney has taken recorded statements may, in some instances, reveal the attorney's impressions of the case. Take, for example, a bus accident involving 50 surviving passengers and an allegation that the driver fell asleep at the wheel. If an attorney for one of the passengers took recorded statements from only 10 individuals, disclosure of the list may well indicate the attorney's evaluation or conclusion as to which witnesses were in the best position to see the cause of the accident. (See *Hickman, supra*, 329 U.S. at p. 511 ["Proper preparation of a client's case demands that [the attorney] ... sift what he considers to be the relevant from the irrelevant facts...."].) Such information may be entitled to absolute privilege under section 2018.030, subdivision (a). If absolute privilege were inapplicable, such a list may still be entitled to qualified privilege under section 2018.030, subdivision (b) to the extent it reflects the attorney's industry and effort in selecting which witnesses to ask for a recorded statement. Perhaps the attorney devoted significant effort to tracking down bus tickets and passenger logs in order to determine which passengers sat in which seats, and then decided to take recorded statements from the 10 passengers closest to the driver. Even without obtaining the witness statements themselves, the bus company's lawyer would gain valuable information by free riding on the attorney's identification of the most salient witnesses.

Such undue advantage taking is precisely what the Legislature intended the work product privilege to prevent. (§ 2018.020, subd. (b).)

At the same time, however, we cannot say that it will always or even often be the case that a witness list responsive to form interrogatory No. 12.3 reflects counsel's premeditated and carefully considered selectivity as in the scenario above. As Justice Kane posited in his separate opinion below: "Take, for example, a typical automobile accident. The police report may disclose the existence of several witnesses. If the attorney for one party obtains witness statements from one or more of those individuals whom everyone in the case knows are percipient witnesses, that fact does not show anything definite about the attorney's evaluation of the strengths and weaknesses of the case, attorney strategy or tactics, or even the relative strength of any particular witness.... Indeed, a particular witness statement might be in an attorney's file for a host of reasons, including that the person happened to be available when the attorney sent out an investigator." Although the witness statements themselves reflect the attorney's time and effort in taking the statements and are therefore qualified work product, disclosing the list of such witnesses in Justice Kane's scenario does not implicate the problem of one attorney free riding on the work of another, as no significant work or selectivity went into creating the list.

The instant case presents another scenario in which the work product privilege may be inapplicable. Where it appears that an attorney has sought to take recorded statements from all or almost all of the known witnesses to the incident, compelling a response to form interrogatory No. 12.3 is unlikely to violate the work product privilege. As Justice Kane observed: "In our case, DWR's attorney sent an investigator to interview the eyewitnesses to the drowning. There were six eyewitnesses, although it appears only five were known at the time the statements were sought. DWR's investigator succeeded in interviewing four eyewitnesses and generated four recorded statements. These facts, had they been disclosed in a response to form interrogatory No. 12.3, would have revealed nothing of consequence regarding DWR's evaluation of the case, one way or the other." Nor would it have implicated any time or effort expended by DWR's attorney in selecting the witnesses to interview, as it does not appear that any meaningful selection occurred.

Because it is not evident that form interrogatory No. 12.3 implicates the policies underlying the work product privilege in all or even most cases, we hold that information responsive to form interrogatory No. 12.3 is not automatically entitled as a matter of law to absolute or qualified work product privilege. Instead, the interrogatory usually must be answered. However, an objecting party may be entitled to protection if it can make a preliminary or foundational showing that answering the interrogatory would reveal the attorney's tactics, impressions, or evaluation of the case, or would result in opposing counsel taking undue advantage of the attorney's industry or efforts. Upon such a showing, the trial court should then determine, by making an in camera inspection if necessary, whether absolute or qualified work product protection applies to the material in dispute. Of course, a trial court may also have to consider nonparty witnesses' privacy concerns.

CONCLUSION

We reverse the judgment of the Court of Appeal and remand the matter for further proceedings, consistent with our opinion, to determine whether the disputed materials should be produced.

Notes and Questions about Absolute and Qualified Work Product Privileges

(1) Since the adoption of former CCP §2018, three important amendments have been adopted which modify the absolute protection. First, in 1988 the Legislature provided that the State Bar may discover attorney work product where disciplinary charges are pending. CCP §2018(e) [now §2018.070]. This disclosure is subject to client approval and a protective order if necessary, but client approval is deemed to have been granted whenever a client has initiated a complaint against the attorney.

(2) Second, in 1990 the Legislature provided that no work product privilege exists in an action between an attorney and his or her client if the work protect is relevant to the attorney's alleged breach of duty. CCP §2018(f) [now §2018.080]. This provision was adopted after the California Supreme Court had granted review to resolve a conflict in the lower courts on this issue.

(3) Third, pursuant to CCP §2018.050 (effective July 1, 2005), when a lawyer is suspected of knowingly participating in a crime or fraud, there is no protection of work product in any official investigation by a law enforcement agency or proceeding by a public prosecutor if the services of the lawyer were sought or obtained to enable or aid anyone to commit a crime or fraud.

(4) *Crime-Fraud Exception in Civil Discovery.* Evidence Code §956 codifies the common law rule that the privilege protecting confidential attorney-client communications is lost if the client seeks legal assistance to plan or perpetrate a crime or fraud. The crime-fraud exception expressly applies to communications ordinarily shielded by the attorney-client privilege. Evid. Code §954. Is there a parallel crime-fraud exception to the absolute work-product privilege applicable in civil, as opposed to criminal, litigation? *See BP Alaska Exploration, Inc. v. Superior Court,* 199 Cal. App. 3d 1240, 245 Cal. Rptr. 682 (1988) (concluding the crime-fraud exception provided in Evid. Code §956 does not apply to writings protected by the absolute work product rule).

(5) *Attorney's Notes About Witness's Statements.* As discussed in *Coito,* the absolute work product privilege extends to an attorney's written notes about a witness's statements. When a witness's statement and the attorney's impressions are inextricably intertwined, absolute protection is afforded to all of the attorney's notes. *Rico v. Mitsubishi Motors Corp.,* 42 Cal. 4th 807, 814, 68 Cal. Rptr. 3d 758, 171 P.3d 1092 (2007).

(6) *Absolute Mediation Privilege.* An absolute privilege protects from disclosure "writings" prepared for the purpose of mediation, broadly defined to include such

derivative material as photographs, charts, diagrams, information compilations, expert opinions and reports. Evid. Code § 1119(b); *Rojas v. Superior Court*, 33 Cal. 4th 407, 15 Cal. Rptr. 3d 643, 93 P.3d 260 (2004).

(7) *Trial Witness Lists.* The discoverability of trial witness lists was carefully analyzed in *City of Long Beach v. Superior Court*, 64 Cal. App. 3d 65, 134 Cal. Rptr. 468 (1976), where the court concluded that the identity of trial witnesses is protected work product during discovery. *See also Snyder v. Superior Court*, 157 Cal. App. 4th 1530, 69 Cal. Rptr. 3d 600 (2007) (holding invalid general order of the Los Angeles Superior Court, which required identification of witnesses in asbestos-exposure cases, because it requires a plaintiff to disclose the identities of certain nonexpert witnesses without a motion or a showing of prejudice or injustice); *but see In re Jeanette H.*, 225 Cal. App. 3d 25, 275 Cal. Rptr. 9 (1990) (holding an order requiring the mutual exchange of witness lists at a trial setting conference, as opposed to during pretrial discovery, does not violate the attorney work product doctrine). Is discovery of a trial witnesses list protected by the absolute or the qualified work product privilege?

(8) *Experts.* Discovery of the opponent's experts has posed special concerns, especially where an expert is consulted but not expected to be called as a witness at trial. In those cases, the courts have held that the discovery of the expert is precluded except on a showing of exceptional circumstances. *E.g., Armenta v. Superior Court*, 101 Cal. App. 4th 525, 124 Cal Rptr. 2d 273 (2002); *Grand Lake Drive In, Inc. v. Superior Court*, 179 Cal. App. 2d 122, 3 Cal. Rptr. 621 (1960). For those experts who will be testifying at trial, see CCP §§ 2034.210–.470, discussed *infra* this chapter.

[3] Comparison to Federal Work Product Doctrine

The current California work product doctrine differs significantly from the federal work product doctrine. While the two doctrines had common origins, *Hickman v. Taylor* (1947) 329 U.S. 495, 67 S. Ct. 385, 91 L. Ed. 451 (1947), Code of Civil Procedure § 2018.030 expands the scope of protection and protects opinion documents absolutely.

[a] Expanded work product protection

The California rule protects any document prepared by an attorney in connection with his or her work as an attorney, regardless of whether litigation is contemplated. *Rumac v. Bottomley*, 143 Cal. App. 3d 810, 815, 192 Cal. Rptr. 104, (1983). In contrast, the federal work product rule covers only materials "prepared in anticipation of litigation or for trial." Rule 26(b)(3), F.R.C.P.

[b] Absolute protection of opinion documents

The California rule provides that "[a]ny writing that reflects an attorney's impressions, conclusions, opinions, or legal research or theories shall not be discoverable under any circumstances." CCP § 2018.030(a). In contrast, the federal work product rule offers, arguably, something less that absolute protection. It permits discovery of regular work product materials on a showing of substantial need where the party seeking discovery cannot obtain equivalent materials without undue hardship. Rule 26(b)(3), F.R.C.P. The Federal Rule then provides that in ordering discovery of such materials when the required showing has been made, the court "must protect against disclosure of the mental impressions, conclusions, opinions or legal theories of a party's attorney ... concerning the litigation." The strength of this added protection for opinion documents is unclear. The Supreme Court has suggested that perhaps only a stronger showing of necessity and unavailability is required. *Upjohn Co. v. United States*, 449 U.S. 383, 402, 101 S. Ct. 677, 66 L. Ed. 2d 584 (1981).

[c] Inadvertent Disclosure of Privileged Information

Document production pursuant to a discovery request may involve massive numbers of documents. What action is required of an attorney who receives privileged documents through inadvertence? According to the California Supreme Court in *Rico v. Mitsubishi Motors Corp.*, 42 Cal. 4th 807, 68 Cal. Rptr. 3d 758, 171 P.3d 1092 (2007), an attorney in these circumstances may not examine the documents any more closely than is necessary to ascertain that the documents are privileged. Once it becomes apparent that the content is privileged, the attorney must immediately notify opposing counsel and try to resolve the situation. A violation of this standard of professional conduct may be remedied by disqualification of the attorney from representation of the party in the litigation.

The approach to such inadvertent disclosures appears to be different in the federal courts. Pursuant to Rule 26(b)(5)(B) of the Federal Rules of Civil Procedure, if privileged information is inadvertently produced in discovery, the party making the claim of privilege may notify the party that received the information of the claim of privilege. After being so notified, that party must promptly return, sequester, or destroy the specified information, and take other remedial measures, until the claim of privilege is resolved. Which approach to inadvertent disclosure of privileged information do you prefer? Why?

§ 11.03 Individual Discovery Devices

[A] Interrogatories

[1] Introductory Note

Discovery by written interrogatories to a party is provided by CCP §§ 2030.010–.310. The main innovation of the 1986 Act was to impose a presumptive limit of 35 specially prepared interrogatories in addition to any number of official form interrogatories. § 2030(c) [now § 2030.030]. To ensure that the presumptive limit is not evaded by clever drafting, § 2030.060(f) prohibits subparts, compound, conjunctive or disjunctive special interrogatories. Interrogatories exceeding the statutory limit should be accompanied by a declaration showing a greater number is warranted. The essential contents of such a declaration is set forth in CCP § 2030.050. To accommodate the need to update information as trial approaches, § 2030.070 permits a limited number of supplemental interrogatories before trial which do not count against the presumptive limit. Section 2030.010 also codifies certain judicial interpretations of the prior law, including approval of contention (opinion or conclusion) interrogatories. § 2030.010(b).

[2] Types of Written Interrogatories

[a] Contention Interrogatories

In addition to expressly authorizing contention interrogatories in accordance with prior case law, the Civil Discovery Act also authorizes interrogatories calling for an opinion that relates to fact or the application of law to fact. CCP § 2030.010(b) provides: "An interrogatory is not objectionable because an answer to it involves an opinion or contention that relates to fact or the application of law to fact, or would be based on information obtained or legal theories developed in anticipation of litigation or in preparation for trial." This provision reflects earlier California Supreme Court decision holding that an interrogatory is not objectionable simply because it asks for an opinion or conclusion. *West Pico Furniture Co. v. Superior Court*, 56 Cal. 2d 407, 15 Cal. Rptr. 119, 364 P.2d 295 (1961); *Singer v. Superior Court*, 54 Cal. 2d 318, 5 Cal. Rptr. 697, 353 P.2d 305 (1960).

Although the practice of using contention interrogatories is well-established in California, asking legal contention questions during a deposition is not allowed. *E.g.*, *Pember v. Superior Court*, 66 Cal. 2d 601, 58 Cal. Rptr. 567, 427 P.2d 167 (1967) (reaffirming the propriety of contention interrogatories but disapproving the use of contention questions at a deposition of a layperson); *Rifkind v. Superior Court*, 22 Cal. App. 4th 1255, 27 Cal. Rptr. 2d 822 (1994) (ruling legal contention questions are not allowed even though deponent is an attorney). Why are legal contention questions appropriate for interrogatories but not for depositions? *See Rifkind*, 22 Cal. App. at 1262 (noting legal contention questions during a deposition are unfair because they ask the deponent to sort out the factual material in the cases according to specific legal contentions, and do this by memory and on the spot).

[b] Continuing Interrogatories

While contention interrogatories are expressly allowed, continuing interrogatories are expressly prohibited. CCP § 2030.060(g). "Continuing interrogatories" ask the responding party to update the answers with information acquired in the future. The Discovery Act prohibits placing this burden on the responding party and requires instead that the propounding party seek updated information through supplemental interrogatories. CCP § 2030.070.

(1) *Public Entity Exception*. One exception to this approach is allowed for governmental entities defending personal injury actions. Government Code § 985(c). This

provision requires plaintiffs to update information about collateral source benefits (i.e., the receipt of insurance payments).

(2) *Federal Approach.* Federal Rule 26(e) requires a party to supplement a discovery response if the party learns that the response is in some material respect incomplete or incorrect, due to new information. Rule 26(e), F.R.C.P. What are the relative advantages and disadvantages of the federal rule as compared to the California approach to continuing discovery? Which do you prefer? Why?

[3] Responses to Interrogatories

[a] Responses, Generally

The responding party's obligations and options are set out in CCP §§ 2030.210–.310. The responding party "shall respond in writing under oath separately to each interrogatory by (1) an answer containing the information sought to be discovered, (2) an exercise of the party's option to produce writings, or (3) an objection to the particular interrogatory." CCP § 2030.210(a). Each answer "shall be as complete and straightforward as the information reasonably available to the responding party permits." § 2030.210(b).

[b] Time

Unless the 30-day time limit to respond is extended by court order or stipulation, serious consequences flow from failure to serve a timely response. Specifically, the nonresponding party waives the right to exercise the option of producing writings and waives any objections, including privilege. CCP § 2030.290(a). The court may grant relief from a waiver where (1) the party has since served a proper response and (2) the failure to timely respond resulted from mistake, inadvertence, or excusable neglect." § 2030.290(a)(1)–(2).

[c] Protective Order

Within the 30-day limit, the responding party may seek a protective order by noticed motion. CCP § 2030.090. The parties must first attempt to informally resolve the issue. § 2030.090 If the dispute is not resolved informally, the moving party must show good cause for the issuance of a protective order. § 2030.090(b).

A protective order may be obtained on the grounds of "unwarranted annoyance, embarrassment, oppression, or undue burden or expense." CCP § 2030.090(b); *see, e.g., People ex rel. Harris v. Sarpas*, 225 Cal. App. 4th 1539, 172 Cal. Rptr. 3d 25 (2014) (holding a protective order was appropriate because special interrogatories containing several thousand questions were unduly burdensome and duplicative). An illustrative list of directions is included: (1) that the interrogatories need not be answered; (2) that the number of interrogatories is unwarranted; (3) that the time to respond be extended; (4) that the response be made on specified terms and conditions; (5) that the discovery be by deposition instead of interrogatories; (6) that a trade secret or other confidential information be protected; and (7) that answers be sealed. §2030.090(b)(1)–(7). If the moving party seeks a protective order because more that 35 specially prepared interrogatories have been served, the propounding party has the burden of justifying the interrogatories beyond the presumptive limit. §2030.040(b).

In ruling on a motion for a protective order, the court is required to impose mandatory monetary sanctions on the losing party unless it finds that party acted with "substantial justification" or other circumstances which make the imposition of sanctions "unjust." CCP §2020.090(d). For a further discussion of discovery sanctions, see §11.04 *infra* this chapter.

[d] Reasonable Effort

Cases decided under former CCP §2030 concluded that a party cannot always discharge the duty to respond by simply denying personal knowledge. *See* 1 Hogan & Weber, *California Civil Discovery*, §5.16 (2d ed. 2005 & Supp. 2015). Rather, the courts concluded that the responding party has an obligation to undertake a reasonable inquiry. *California Civil Discovery, supra,* at §5.16. This duty is expressly stated in current CCP §2030.220(c) which provides that if a party lacks personal knowledge, that party "shall make a reasonable and good faith effort to obtain information by inquiry to other natural persons or organizations, except where the information is equally available to the propounding party." This obligation requires the responding party to provide information which can be obtained from sources under its control. *Deyo v. Kilbourne,* 84 Cal. App. 3d 771, 149 Cal. Rptr. 499 (1979). This includes non-privileged information known to counsel, even if the party has no personal knowledge of the information. *See Smith v. Superior Court,* 189 Cal. App. 2d 6, 11 Cal. Rptr. 165 (1961).

[e] Oath

Responses must be verified under oath. CCP §2030.210(a). If the responding party is an entity, the responses must be verified by an officer or agent. CCP §2030.250(b). The party to whom the interrogatories are directed must sign the response under oath unless the response contains only objections. CCP §2030.250(a).

[f] Inaccurate Response

The purpose of the requirement of verified response is to enable opposing counsel to properly assess the merits of a claim or defense, and thereby further efficient resolution of disputes. *Deyo v. Kilbourne,* 84 Cal. App. 3d 771, 779–783, 149 Cal. Rptr. 499 (1978). Consequently, an attorney's use of a presigned verification, without first consulting with the client to assure that the assertions of fact are true, has been held to constitute a violation of the statutes and rules governing professional conduct. *Drociak v. State Bar of California,* 52 Cal. 3d 1085, 278 Cal. Rptr. 86, 804 P.2d 711

(1991) (upholding suspension of attorney from practice of law where attorney responded to interrogatories and attached client's presigned blank verification, without consulting client as to accuracy). What if a responding party subsequently learns that a response was inaccurate? Section 2030.310(a) permits a party to serve an amended answer without leave of court "to any interrogatory that contains information subsequently discovered, inadvertently omitted, or mistakenly stated in the initial interrogatory." To protect against possible unfairness to the party who relied on the prior answer, § 2030.310(b) authorizes the propounding party to "move for an order that the initial answer ... be deemed binding on the responding party for the purpose of the pending action." *See Government Employ. Ins. Co. v. Cruz*, 244 Cal. App. 4th 1184, 1194–95, 198 Cal. Rptr. 3d 566 (2016) (discussing the prerequisites the moving party must establish to prevail on a motion to bind). Also, a repudiated answer may be used at trial for impeachment as a prior inconsistent statement. CCP §§ 2030.310(a), 2030.410.

[g] Objections

The procedure for objections is set out in CCP § 2030.240. If only part of an interrogatory is objectionable, the remainder must be answered. § 2030.240(a). The specific grounds for an objection must be provided. If the objection is based on a claim of privilege or work product protection, that claim shall be clearly stated. § 2030.240(b). The attorney for the responding party shall sign any response that contains an objection. § 2030.250(c).

[4] *Compelling Further Responses*

If the propounding party is dissatisfied with the answers to interrogatories, CCP § 2030.300 sets forth the procedure for moving to compel a further response. Unless notice of this motion is given within 45 days of the service of the response, the propounding party waives the right to compel a further response. § 2030.300(c).

[B] Inspections

Discovery by inspections of documents, things and places is governed by two sets of statutes: CCP §§ 2031.010–.510, which applies to parties; and CCP §§ 2020.010–.510, which applies to nonparties. Both provisions are discussed below.

[1] *Demands for Inspections of Items Controlled by a Party*

[a] Inspection Procedures

Section 2031.010 provides that any party may obtain discovery by inspecting documents, tangible things, land and other property in the possession, custody or control of any other party. The defendant may make an inspection demand at any time while the plaintiff may make an inspection demand at any time 10 days after service of the summons or appearance by the party. CCP § 2031.020(a) & (b). An earlier inspection may be ordered by the court for good cause. § 2031.020(d).

Within 30 days after service of the inspection demand, the party to whom the demand has been directed shall respond to each item or category of item sought to be inspected. CCP §§ 2031.210, 2031.260. The responding party may respond by serving (1) a statement of compliance, (2) a representation of inability to comply, or (3) an objection. § 2031.210(a).

Alternatively, the responding party may seek a protective order which the court shell enter to protect anyone "from unwarranted annoyance, embarrassment, or oppression, or undue burden and expense." CCP § 2031.060. The protective order may direct: (1) that some of the items need not be produced; (2) that time to produce the items be extended; (3) that the place of production be changed; (4) that the inspection be made on specified terms and conditions; (5) that a trade secret or other confidential commercial information be protected; or (6) that the items be produced under seal. § 2031.060(b). This list is illustrative, not exclusive. On ruling on a motion for a protective order, the court shall order monetary sanctions be paid by the losing party unless it finds that party "acted with substantial justification or that other circumstances make the imposition of the sanction unjust." § 2031.060(h).

The consequences of a failure to serve a timely response are significant. Specifically, the responding party waives any objection to the demand, including one based on privilege or work product protection. CCP § 2031.300(a). The court may, however, relieve a party from the consequences of this waiver on a proper showing. § 2031.300(a); see *City of Fresno v. Superior Court*, 205 Cal. App. 3d 1459, 253 Cal. Rptr. 296 (1988) (ruling a trial court may relieve a party from the consequences of its failure to serve a timely response if the court finds the failure was the result of mistake, in advertence, or excusable neglect). The party making the demand may move for an order compelling a response. § 2031.300(b). If the responding party disobeys an order compelling a response, further appropriate sanctions may be ordered. § 2031.310.

If a party serves a timely response to an inspection demand that raises an objection based on a claim of privilege or protected work product, the response "shall provide sufficient factual information for other parties to evaluate the merits of that claim, including, if necessary, a privilege log." CCP § 2031.240(c)(1). Does the failure to provide an adequate privilege log constituted a waiver of a claimed privilege? *See, e.g., Catalina Island Yacht Club v. Superior Court*, 242 Cal. App. 4th 1116, 195 Cal. Rptr. 3d 694 (2015) (holding a privilege log that fails to provide sufficient information to rule on the attorney-client and work product objections does not constitute a waiver of those privileges; the only relief the trial court may grant, other than sanctions, is an order requiring an adequate privilege log); *People ex rel. Lockyer v. Superior Court*, 122 Cal. 4th 1060, 19 Cal. Rptr. 3d 324 (2004) (concluding that if a party responding to an inspection demand timely serves a response asserting an objection based on a privilege, the trial court lacks authority to order the objection waived even though the responding party fails to serve a privilege log or serves one that is inadequate).

[b]   Inspection Requirements

Section 2031.030 sets out the requirements of the inspection demand. The party demanding the inspection is required to specify a reasonable time and place for the inspection. If the action is in California but the defendant is out of state, may the plaintiff require the production of numerous documents at trial? *See Allee v. King*, 206 Cal. App. 3d 1081, 254 Cal. Rptr. 93 (1988) (ruling plaintiff could not require defendant to transport 20 file cabinets of documents from Texas to California for trial).

(1) Section 2031.010(a) explicitly authorizes a party to demand "to inspect and to photograph, test, or sample any tangible things that are in the possession, custody, or control" of another party. What sort of testing or sampling does this provision allow? The demanding party must specify in the demand whether the inspection activity will "alter or destroy" the item. Why?

(2) *Land.* Section 2031.010(d) authorizes a party to demand entry on land or property of another party. Moreover, the demanding party may be able to take samples which would be useful in environmental litigation and to observe operations which would be useful in products liability and employment cases. *See* 1 Hogan & Weber, *California Civil Discovery* §6.9 (2d ed. 2005 & Supp. 2015). Because the Discovery Act is permissive and not exclusive, property open to the public can be examined without recourse to CCP §2031.010(d) provided the examination can be conducted in a lawful fashion. *See Pullin v. Superior Court*, 81 Cal. App. 4th 1161, 97 Cal. Rptr. 2d 447 (2000) (concluding trial court in a slip and fall case erred in excluding testimony about a test performed on the defendant supermarket's floor by a forensic safety engineer on plaintiff's behalf without resort to any statutory discovery device).

(3) *Insurance Agreements.* While CCP §2017.210 provides that a party obtain discovery of the existence and contents of insurance agreements, it does not specifically authorize inspection of the actual policy itself. Section 2031 is also silent on this point. Faced with this silence, one court has ruled that given the broad scope of discovery and the provision of multiple methods of discovery under the Civil Discovery Act, a party may inspect the actual insurance policy itself under Section 2031, subject to any appropriate protective orders. *Irvington-Moore, Inc. v. Superior Court*, 14 Cal. App. 4th 733, 18 Cal. Rptr. 2d 49 (1993).

(4) "*Good Cause.*" A party who seeks to compel production of documents must show "good cause" for the request. CCP §2031.310(b). What constitutes "good cause" in this context? *See Glenfed Dev. Corp. v. Superior Court*, 53 Cal. App. 4th 1113, 1117, 62 Cal. Rptr. 2d 195 (1997) (Where there is no privilege issue or claim of attorney work product, the moving party's burden is met simply by a fact-specific showing of relevance).

[c]   Electronically Stored Information

Most information today is in digital rather than in paper form. Information created, stored, and used with computer technology may be critical to success or failure of a case. Consequently, the discovery of electronically stored information has become an important, and controversial, feature of modern litigation. Electronic discovery has created difficult problems for courts when the burden and costs of accessing the information makes such discovery unreasonable. One of the main issues is under what circumstances, and to what extent, should the requesting party pay the expense of information retrieval and production in a usable form. In response to this and other issues, the Federal Rules of Civil Procedure were revised effective December 1, 2006 to modernize the discovery process with respect to electronically stored discovery. *See, e.g.,* Rules 26(b)(1)&(2), 34(a), (b)(1)&(2), F.R.C.P.

In 2009, the Legislature adopted the Electronic Discovery Act, thereby amending the Civil Discovery Act in order to modernize California's discovery law with respect to electronically stored information. These new provisions provide comprehensive procedures for the handling of demands for the inspection, copying, testing, or sampling of electronically stored information. CCP §§ 2031.010–2031.320. With respect to the important issue of whether the requesting party should pay the expense of information retrieval and production in a usable form, the Act provides: "If the court finds good cause for the production of electronically stored information from a source that is not reasonably accessible, the court may set conditions for the discovery of the electronically stored information, including allocation of the expense of discovery." CCP §§ 2031.060(e), 2031.310(e).

Moreover, a court must limit the frequency or extent of discovery of electronically stored information, even from a source that is reasonably accessible, if the court determines that any of the following conditions exist:

(1) It is possible to obtain the information from some other source that is more convenient, less burdensome, or less expensive.

(2) The discovery sought is unreasonably cumulative or duplicative.

(3) The party seeking discovery has had ample opportunity by discovery in the action to obtain the information sought.

(4) The likely burden or expense of the proposed discovery outweighs the likely benefit, taking into account the amount in controversy, the resources of the parties, the importance of the issues in the litigation, and the importance of the requested discovery in resolving the issues.

CCP §§ 2031.060(f), 2031.310(f).

[2] *Inspections of Items Not Controlled by a Party*

[a] Deposition Subpoenas

In contrast to the original Discovery Act, the Civil Discovery Act of 1986 specifically provides for discovery from a nonparty. CCP §§ 2020.010–.510. These sections may be used to compel nonparties to permit inspection of records, documents, and tangible things. This inspection takes place in connection with an oral deposition and is initiated by a "deposition subpoena." A deposition subpoena may be opposed by seeking a protective order under Section 2025.420 on grounds of "unwarranted annoyance, embarrassment, or oppression, or undue burden and expense." One of the possible directions under this section is that certain items "need not be produced, inspected or copied." § 2025.420(b)(11).

As an alternative to a deposition subpoena, Section 2020.410 permits a party to serve a records-only deposition subpoena for business records. Special safeguards prevent the inappropriate disclosure of personal consumer business records. Personal records are defined to include those maintained by health care professionals, financial institutions, insurance and title companies, attorneys, telephone and utility companies, accountants, and educational institutions. CCP § 1985.3(a). When personal records are sought, the person who is the subject of the records must be notified and provided an opportunity to object to the production. CCP §§ 1985.3(b)–(k), 2020.410.

Both CCP §§ 2020.010–.030 (inspection subpoenas as to nonparties) and 2031.010–.060 (inspection demands on parties) require that records sought to be produced be designated either by specifically describing each individual item or by reasonably particularizing each category of items. *See Calcor Space Facility, Inc. v. Superior Court*, 53 Cal. App. 4th 216, 61 Cal. Rptr. 2d 567 (1997) (finding unreasonably burdensome the plaintiff's request to a nonparty gun mount manufacturer to produce all materials in its possession relating to gun mounts and dating back nearly 10 years).

[b] Inspections

In contrast to the right to inspect the land and property of a party, CCP § 2031.010, the Civil Discovery Act does not provide for the inspection of the land and property of a nonparty. CCP § 2020.020. In 1991, the federal discovery rules were amended to permit inspection of land and property. Rules 45(a), 34(c), Fed. R. Civ. P. Professor Hogan, Reporter for the Discovery Act, acknowledges the frequent need for such discovery, for example in cases where employees are injured on the job as a result of defective machinery or in litigation arising out of an airplane crash. 1 Hogan & Weber, *California Civil Discovery* § 7.5 (2d ed. 2005 & Supp. 2015). Professor Hogan recommends that California should follow the recent federal example and fill the statutory gap by making controlled access to nonparty premises a feature of the California discovery system. *California Civil Discovery, supra,* at § 7.5.

[C] Depositions

Sections 2025.010–.620 of the Civil Discovery Act provide for oral depositions in California. Other depositions are covered in the following sections: Section 2026.010, oral depositions in another state; § 2027.010, oral depositions in another country; and §§ 2028.010–.080, written depositions. This discussion will focus on oral depositions in California and then briefly consider out-of-state and written depositions.

[1] *Oral Depositions in California*

[a] Deponents

Sections 2025.010–.620 provides for depositions of both parties and nonparties. For party deponents and party-affiliated deponents, service of a deposition notice is sufficient to compel attendance. § 2025.280(a). For nonparty deponents, a deposition subpoena is required. § 2025.280(b), cross-referencing §§ 2020.010–.510. In cases where the name of the deponent is unknown, the notice may identify "a general description sufficient to identify the person or the particular class to which the person belongs." § 2025.220(a)(3). All deponents may be required to attend and give testimony and also to produce documents and things for inspection and copying. §§ 2025.220(a) & (b), cross-referencing § 2020.410.

(1) *Corporations.* With respect to a deponent who is not a natural person, CCP § 2025.230 provides that if a deposition notice describes matters on which examination is requested, "the deponent shall designate at the deposition those of its officers, directors, managing agents, employees, or agents who most are qualified to testify on its behalf as to those matters to the extent of any information known or reasonably available to the deponent." Under § 2025.230, the burden is on the corporate defendant to produce the right witnesses and to provide them with the knowledge of the information sought, including any necessary documentation as requested in the deposition notice. *See Maldonado v. Superior Court*, 94 Cal. App. 4th 1390, 115 Cal. Rptr. 2d 137 (2002) (ruling defendant company's selection of witnesses to represent the company at depositions who knew little about the topics specified in the deposition notices and who appeared without the necessary documentation was inexcusable and such behavior may justify monetary sanctions).

May a plaintiff depose the head of a corporation when there is no showing the corporate head had any involvement in the lawsuit against the corporation, and prior to the plaintiff's exhaustion of less intrusive means of discovery? The court in *Liberty Mutual Ins. Co. v. Superior Court*, 10 Cal. App. 4th 1282, 13 Cal. Rptr. 2d 363 (1992), held that an "apex" deposition is improper in such circumstances and that the trial court abused its discretion in denying a protective order.

(2) *Public Entities.* The general rule in both California and the federal courts is that heads of agencies and other top governmental executives are normally not subject to depositions, unless they have direct personal factual information pertaining to material issues in an action. *Nagle v. Superior Court*, 28 Cal. App. 4th 1465, 34 Cal. Rptr. 2d 281 (1994). Even then, a top governmental official may only be deposed upon a showing that the information cannot be obtained through other sources and through much less burdensome means. Nagle. 28 Cal. App. 4th at 1468. Should the courts recognize such protective rules when the proposed governmental official-deponent is a named party?

[b] Time

Sections 2025.210–.260 also provide for the time for scheduling and the place of the deposition. They provide that the defendant may serve a notice of a deposition at any time after service of process on or the appearance by that defendant in the action, whichever occurs first. CCP § 2025.210(a). The plaintiff cannot notice a deposition until 20 days after service on or the appearance by any defendant in the action. § 2025.210(b). Generally the deposition must be set at least ten days after service of the notice. § 2025.270(a). In cases where consumer or employment records will be produced, at least 20 days is required. § 2025.270(c). Section 2025.290 imposes a general time limit of seven hours for examination of a witness is certain types of depositions, with additional time allowable by the court if needed to fairly examine the deponent.

[c] Place of Deposition

The place of the deposition shall be either within 75 miles of the deponent's residence, or within the county where the action is pending and within 150 miles of the deponent's residence. CCP § 2025.250. The court may order a party (or a person who is an officer, director, managing agent, or employee of a party) to be deposed at a more distant location. Section 2025.260; *see, e.g., Glass v. Superior Court*, 204 Cal. App. 3d 1048, 251 Cal. Rptr. 690 (1988) (concluding the trial court incorrectly ruled that California law precluded defendant from deposing in California those members of the plaintiff foreign corporation's management team who are Indiana residents; § 2025.260 authorized defendants to obtain an order to depose these out-of-state residents in California). Also the court may enter any necessary protective orders. CCP 2025.420.

[d] Deposition Officer

Sections 2025.320–.340 specify the qualifications, duties, and other requirements applicable to the person under whose supervision an oral deposition is conducted. The main purpose of these provisions is to prevent the deposition officer from discriminating between parties or their attorneys attending the deposition with respect to the provision of services and products offered based on who is financing the deposition. *See* CCP § 2025.320. A violation of these requirements may result in a civil penalty of up to $5000 imposed by a court. § 2025.320(f).

[2] Procedures During Depositions

[a] Record and Transcript

Section 2025.330 provides for stenographic, audiotaped, and videotaped depositions. See also CCP § 2025.310 (authorizing deposition by telephone or other remote electronic device). However, unless the parties agree otherwise, the testimony must be recorded stenographically and that recording shall be transcribed. CCP §§ 2025.330(b) & .510(a). The party noticing the deposition may also record the deposition by audiotape or videotape. § 2025.330(c). Any other party, at that party's expense and upon three-day notice, may make a simultaneous audiotape or videotape record of the deposition. § 2025.330(c); *see, e.g., Green v. GTE California, Inc.*, 29

Cal. App. 4th 407, 34 Cal. Rptr. 2d 517 (1994) (sanctioning plaintiff's counsel for novel attempt to videotape defendant's counsel during plaintiff's deposition; not only did plaintiff's counsel fail to meet notice requirements, but videotaping of opposing counsel is of questionable propriety).

[b] Examination of Deponent

All parties who attend the deposition have the right to cross-examine the deponent. CCP § 2025.330(d). Alternatively, any party may send written questions which will be posed to the deponent by the deposition officer after the examination by the other parties. CCP § 2025.330(e). During a deposition, a deponent may be required to review documents to refresh a foggy recollection. *Filipoff v. Superior Court*, 56 Cal. 2d 443, 15 Cal. Rptr. 139, 364 P.2d 315 (1961). Moreover, if a deponent reviews a document to refresh his or her memory before a deposition, the document must be produced on request. Evidence Code § 771. *See International Ins. Co. v. Montrose Chem. Corp.*, 231 Cal. App. 3d 1367, 282 Cal. Rptr. 783 (1991).

In addition to answering questions, can a deponent be compelled to perform a reenactment of an incident during a videotape deposition? In *Emerson Electric Co. v. Superior Court*, 16 Cal. 4th 1101, 68 Cal. Rptr. 2d 883, 946 P.2d 841 (1997), the court considered whether a deponent could be required to give a nonverbal answer during a videotaped deposition. The issue arose in the context of a products liability action in which the plaintiff was seeking damages for injuries he allegedly suffered while using a circular saw manufactured by the defendants. During the plaintiff's deposition, he was asked to reenact the accident and to diagram the location of the saw and his position at the time of the accident. On advice of counsel, the plaintiff refused. The *Emerson* court held that the deponent could be required to provide these nonverbal answers, and could be sanctioned for refusing to do so.

[c] Objections and Protective Orders

Section 2025.460 limits the bases for objecting to deposition questions. In short, a party must object on the grounds of (1) privilege or work product protection, and with respect to (2) curable matters including the oath administered and the form of any question or answer. CCP § 2025.460. Failure to object on these grounds results in waiver of the objection. § 2025.460(a) & (b). On the other hand, certain other objections are statutorily unnecessary: "Objections to the competency of the deponent, or to the relevancy, materiality, or admissibility at trial of the testimony or of the materials produced are unnecessary and are not waived by failure to make them before or during the taking of the deposition." § 2025.460(c).

Where an issue of privilege arises and the deposing attorney persists with that line of questioning, a party may move to terminate or limit a deposition under CCP § 2025.470. This motion is also available in other circumstances where "the examination is being conducted in bad faith or in a manner that unreasonably annoys, embarrasses, or oppresses" the person being deposed. § 2025.470.

To protect confidential or sensitive information, the court may enter a protective order providing "that the deposition be sealed and thereafter opened only on order of the court." CCP § 2025.420(b)(15); *see* Rules 2.550 & 2.551, Cal. Rules of Ct. (sealed records). Such restrictions on the use of discovery information have withstood First Amendment challenges. *See Seattle Times Co. v. Rhinehart*, 467 U.S. 20, 104 S. Ct. 2199, 81 L. Ed. 2d 17 (1984); *NBC Subsidiary (KNBC-TV) v. Superior Court*, 28 Cal. 4th 1178, 1222, n. 46, 86 Cal. Rptr. 2d 778, 980 P.2d 337 (1999).

Section 2025 does not specify who may attend a deposition, although it implicitly recognizes that the parties and their counsel have the right to attend in stating that a protective order may exclude people "other than the parties to the action and their officers and counsel...." CCP § 2025.420(b)(12). Can a court restrict the number of corporate officers who attend a deposition? *See Lowy Dev. Corp. v. Superior Court*, 190 Cal. App. 3d 317, 235 Cal. Rptr. 401 (1987) (ruling trial court may issue a protective order to exclude some of the officers, if such an order is appropriate based on the size of the corporation and the complexity of the case).

[3] Use of Depositions at Trial

[a] Party vs. Nonparty

Section 2025.620 sets out the rules governing the use of depositions at trial. Unless another use is authorized by the Evidence Code, the deposition of a nonparty is generally only used to impeach or contradict live testimony. CCP § 2025.620(a). The deposition of a party or party-affiliated deponent, however, may be used by the opponent for any purpose—either as substantive evidence or for impeachment—regardless of whether the deponent testifies at trial. § 2025.620(b). Finally, the deposition of any deponent (party, party-affiliated, or nonparty) may be used at trial where the deponent is unavailable or other exceptional circumstances justify its use. CCP § 2025.620(c); *see also* 1 CEB *California Civil Discovery Practice* §§ 6.136–6.140 (4th ed. 2015).

[b] Videotape Depositions

A special provision permits the introduction at trial of a videotape of an expert's deposition. CCP §§ 2025.620(d). Two conditions must first be satisfied: (1) the party noticing the deposition stated in the deposition notice that the videotape would be introduced, and (2) the party offering the videotape notified the court and counsel what portions of the videotape would be offered in advance of trial to permit a ruling on objections. §§ 2025.620(d), .220, .340(m).

[4] Oral Depositions in Another State

Section 2026.010 sets out the procedure for deposing both parties and nonparties who are located in another state. For deponents who are parties or party-affiliated, a deposition is noticed under the procedures used in scheduling depositions within California. CCP § 2026.010(b). For deponents who are not parties, a deposition must be noticed in accordance with the procedures followed in the jurisdiction where the deposition is to be conducted. § 2026.010(c); *see International Ins. Co. v. Montrose Chem. Co.*, 231 Cal. App. 3d 1367, 282 Cal. Rptr. 783 (1991) (concluding that although § 2026 compelled plaintiff to follow Connecticut law in noticing nonparty's deposition in Connecticut, California law governs plaintiff's request to defendant to produce the defendant's documents used by nonparty to refresh his recollection before deposition). Both party deponents and non-party deponents may be required to produce documents and things at their depositions. § 2026.010(b) & (c).

If a deponent is an out-of-state resident, is CCP § 2026.010 mandatory? Or may counsel obtain an order to depose an out-of-state resident in California? *See California Glass v. Superior Court*, 204 Cal. App. 3d 1048, 251 Cal. Rptr. 690 (1988) (ruling counsel may depose an out-of-state resident who is a party by proceeding under either § 2025 (oral depositions within California) or alternatively § 2026 (oral depositions in another state)).

[5] *Oral Depositions in Another Country*

Section 2027.010 providing for oral depositions in another country follows the same approach as § 2026.010 providing for oral depositions in another state. Specifically, it provides that party and party-affiliated deponents may be deposed under the procedures followed in California and that nonparty deponents may be deposed under the procedures followed in the country where the deposition is to be conducted. § 2027.010.

The simplicity of the statutory provisions masks the complexity of the issues that arise when resistance is encountered. Under the previous Discovery Act, the California courts were reluctant to compel any discovery which could be viewed as an intrusion on foreign judicial sovereignty. As one court explained, international friction should be avoided by ordering discovery abroad to conform to the host nation's procedures. *Volkswagenwerk Aktiengesellschaft v. Superior Court*, 123 Cal. App. 3d 840, 176 Cal. Rptr. 874 (1981).

The U.S. Supreme Court rejected this approach for the federal system. *Societe Nationale Industrielle Aerospatiale v. District Court*, 482 U.S. 522 107 S. Ct. 2542, 96 L. Ed. 2d 461 (1987) (concluding Hague Evidence Convention does not provide exclusive or mandatory procedures for discovery of information located in foreign signatory's territory; the Convention does not preclude use of Federal Rules to seek discovery from a foreign litigant who is subject to the jurisdiction of a U.S. court). Recently, the court in *American Home Assurance Co. v. Societe Commerciale Toutelectric*, 104 Cal. App. 4th 406, 128 Cal. Rptr. 2d 430 (2002), held that the rule of first resort to the Hague Convention procedures announced in *Volkswagenwerk, supra*, has been superseded by the ruling in *Aerospatiale, supra*.

A word of caution about direct discovery of evidence located abroad. Many countries—even trading partners such as England, France, Canada, and Mexico—are very suspicious of American-style discovery. These countries view our party-initiated pretrial discovery methods with alarm, and are particularly hostile to depositions within their territory and to requests for production of documents. *See* Epstein & Baldwin, *International Litigation: A Guide to Jurisdiction, Practice and Strategy* §§ 10.02–

10.05 (Rev. 4th ed. 2010); Born & Rutledge, *International Civil Litigation in the United States Courts*, pp. 969–977 (5th ed. 2011). Some countries have enacted blocking statutes which prohibit compliance with such discovery requests; many make the gathering of evidence by a foreign attorney within that country a penal offense. *International Civil Litigation, supra*, at pp. 972–977. Use of the Hague Evidence Convention discovery mechanisms, or analogous customary international judicial assistance procedures, may therefore be advisable. *See* 2 CEB *California Civil Discovery Practice* §§ 13.14–13.58 (4th ed. 2015); *International Litigation, supra*, §§ 10.05–10.12; *International Civil Litigation, supra*, pp. 1024–32.

[6] Written Depositions

Under sections 2028.010–.080, all parties to the litigation may submit written questions to a deponent which will be propounded by a deposition officer who transcribes the answers. While this procedure lacks the personal contact and flexibility of an oral deposition, it is an economical device particularly useful in three situations: (1) for obtaining undisputed information from cooperative but distant deponents; (2) for deposing someone who is likely to claim some privilege in response to most questions; and (3) for protecting a deponent's identity. *See* 1 Hogan & Weber, *California Civil Discovery* § 3.4 (2d ed. 2005 & Supp. 2015). Depositions in other states and in other countries may be taken by written questions. CCP § 2028.010.

[D] Medical Examinations

Code of Civil Procedure Section 2032.020 provides for discovery by physical and mental examination of a party, an agent of a party, or a person in the custody or control of a party where that person's mental or physical condition is in controversy in a civil action. Subsections (b) and (c) specify the required qualifications of the examiner. The procedures for obtaining a medical examination fall into two categories: (1) those for the routine examination of a plaintiff in a personal injury action, and (2) those for other examinations by court order.

[1] Noticed Examination of Plaintiff in Personal Injury Action

[a] Examination Requirements

The major innovation of the Civil Discovery Act of 1986 with respect to medical examinations is the simplified procedure for the defendant in a personal injury action to obtain an examination of the plaintiff without obtaining a prior court order. Under Section 2032.220(a), "any defendant may demand one physical examination of the plaintiff, provided the examination does not include any diagnostic test or procedure that is painful, protracted, or intrusive, and is conducted at a location within 75 miles of the residence of the examinee."

In *Abex Corp. v. Superior Court*, 209 Cal. App. 3d 755, 257 Cal. Rptr. 498 (1989), the plaintiff filed a complaint alleging that he suffered injury from asbestos and asbestos-containing products produced by the defendants. The plaintiff was examined by his own medical expert who noted in a report that "the patient has several small asbestos 'corns' scattered over the palmar surfaces of the hands," and that the plaintiff had asbestos lung disease and asbestos skin disease. He further expressed his view that the diagnosis of asbestos lung disease was "further solidified by the findings of asbestos skin disease." Following this report, defendants sought to have the plaintiff examined by a dermatologist. Plaintiff refused to stipulate to a biopsy of the warts and the dermatologist agreed to first examine the plaintiff and then decide whether or not a biopsy was necessary.

The dermatologist examined plaintiff and concluded that the warts could have been caused by other factors, and that a biopsy was required to be certain. When plaintiff refused to permit a biopsy, defendants filed a motion to compel supported by a declaration of the dermatologist who stated the examination was necessary to determine the lesions' etiology: "This would involve scraping off several warts from locations as cosmetically insignificant as possible. There is minimal pain associated with the procedure as it is done under local anesthetic. The risks are minimal and include reaction to the local anesthetic, minimal scarring, and minor bleeding." Plaintiff opposed the motion, but did not furnish any affidavits regarding the danger or the discomfort of the proposed biopsy. The superior court denied the motion, and the defendants then sought appellate review.

The plaintiff opposed the motion for the biopsy arguing that the examination would require intrusive and potentially painful removal of his body tissues. The Court of Appeal concluded this argument did not provide a sound basis for denying the motion to compel because the uncontradicted medical evidence indicated that the procedure will involve little pain or danger: "Any procedure involving a local anesthetic arguably will produce some discomfort but given the fact that real party scrapes the warts off himself with a pocket knife, it strains credulity past the breaking point to believe this procedure qualifies as one that is 'painful, protracted, or intrusive' within the meaning of the discovery legislation." *Abex Corp., supra*, 209 Cal. App. 3d at 758. The Court of Appeal issued a writ of mandate directing the superior court to vacate its order denying defendants' motion to compel and to enter an order granting that motion.

[b]   Conduct of the Examination

Section 2032.510 provides specific rules for the conduct of a physical examination. A representative of an examinee or a party producing the examinee is entitled "to attend and observe any physical examination conducted for discovery purposes, and to record stenographically or by audiotape any words spoken to or by the examinee during any phase of the examination." CCP § 2032.510(a). This observer may monitor the examination, "but shall not participate in or disrupt it." § 2032.510(b).

If the observer believes that the examiner has become abusive or has engaged in unauthorized medical procedures, the observer may suspend the examination so that a protective order may be sought. CCP § 2032.510(d). On the other hand, if the examiner believes that the observer has begun to participate in or disrupt the examination, the examiner may suspend the examination so that a protective order may be sought. § 2032.510(e). Monetary sanctions shall be awarded to the unsuccessful party on a motion for a protective order. § 2032.510(f).

The automatic examination authorized by CCP § 2032.220 does not include a mental examination. This is true even where the plaintiff has put his or her mental state in issue by alleging mental distress and emotional suffering. *See Roberts v. Superior Court*, 9 Cal. 3d 330, 107 Cal. Rptr. 309, 508 P.2d 309 (1973); *Reuter v. Superior Court*, 93 Cal. App. 3d 332, 337–40, 155 Cal. Rptr. 525 (1979). A mental examination is subject to the requirements of CCP § 2032.310 and § 2032.320, requiring leave of court on a showing of good cause. However, allegations of mental and emotional injuries will support a court ordered examination. CCP §§ 2032.020(a), 2032.320; *see* discussion of court ordered examinations *infra*.

[c] Exchange of Examination Reports

After an examination, the party submitting to the exam or producing someone to be examined may demand in writing "(1) a copy of a detailed written report setting out the history, examinations, findings, including the results of all tests made, diagnoses, prognoses, and conclusions of the examiner" and "(2) a copy of reports of all earlier examinations of the same condition of the examinee made by that or any other examiner." CCP § 2032.610(a). The statute also provides that the report, if demanded, "shall be delivered within 30 days after service of the demand, or within 15 days of trial, whichever is earlier." § 2032.610(b). Failure to comply with these requirements will support a motion to compel and the imposition of sanctions. § 2032.620.

By obtaining a copy of a report under § 2032.610 or deposing the examiner, the party who submitted to the exam or produced another for examination waives any privilege and any work product protection that may exist for other reports and examinations about the same mental or physical condition. CCP § 2032.630. A party who delivers a copy of a report under § 2032.610 is entitled to receive in exchange a copy of any written examination reports of the same condition by any other physician, psychologist, or licensed health care provider. § 2032.640. That party is also entitled to any later reports about the same condition. § 2032.640. If these reports are not delivered, that party may seek an order to compel and monetary sanctions. § 2032.650.

Since the statute only requires the exchange of written reports, may plaintiff's counsel withhold as work product the identities and opinions of doctors who were consulted and examined the plaintiff but did not submit written reports? *See* CCP § 2032.630; *Kennedy v. Superior Court*, 64 Cal. App. 4th 674, 75 Cal. Rptr. 2d 373 (1998) (concluding a personal injury plaintiff who submitted to a medical examination is entitled to a report of that examination under CCP § 2032.610 even though the examining physician has not prepared one and the defendant has withdrawn the physician as an expert witness). May defense counsel withhold reports by consultants who reviewed the plaintiff's medical records but never actually examined the plaintiff in person? *See Queen of Angels Hosp. v. Superior Court*, 57 Cal. App. 3d 370, 129 Cal. Rptr. 282 (1976).

[2] *Court Ordered Examinations*

Except for the initial routine examination in a personal injury action, a party who desires to obtain discovery by a physical examination must obtain leave of court. CCP § 2032.310. The requirements for this motion are set forth in detail in the statute. Alternatively, the parties may agree in writing to any examination. CCP § 2016.030.

Vinson v. Superior Court

Supreme Court of California

43 Cal. 3d 833, 239 Cal. Rptr. 292, 740 P.2d 404 (1987)

MOSK, JUSTICE.

The plaintiff in a suit for sexual harassment and intentional infliction of severe emotional distress petitions for a writ of mandate and/or prohibition to direct respondent court to forbid her pending psychiatric examination, or in the alternative to protect her from any inquiry into her sexual history, habits, or practices. She also requests that her attorney be allowed to attend the examination if it is held. We conclude that the examination should be permitted but that a writ should issue to restrict its scope. We further conclude that her counsel should not be present. * * *

I. *The Appropriateness of a Mental Examination*

Plaintiff first contends the psychiatric examination should not be permitted because it infringes on her right to privacy. Before we can entertain this constitutional question, we must determine the statutory scope of the discovery laws. [Because the discovery was initiated under the old law, it is governed by the old law. However, many of the new provisions produce the same result.]

Code of Civil Procedure section 2032, subdivision (a) [now § 2032.020(a)], permits the mental examination of a party in any action in which the mental condition of that party is in controversy. Plaintiff disputes that her mental condition is in controversy. * * *

In the case at bar, plaintiff haled defendants into court and accused them of causing her various mental and emotional ailments. Defendants deny her charges. As a result, the existence and extent of her mental injuries is indubitably in dispute. In addition, by asserting a causal link between her mental distress and defendants' conduct, plaintiff implicitly claims it was not caused by a preexisting mental condition, thereby raising the question of alternative sources for the distress. We thus conclude that her mental state is in controversy.

We emphasize that our conclusion is based solely on the allegations of emotional and mental damages in this case. A simple sexual harassment claim asking compensation for having to endure an oppressive work environment or for wages lost following an unjust dismissal would not normally create a controversy regarding the plaintiff's mental state. To hold otherwise would mean that every person who brings such a suit implicitly asserts he or she is mentally unstable, obviously an untenable proposition.

Determining that the mental or physical condition of a party is in controversy is but the first step in our analysis. In contrast to more pedestrian discovery procedures, a mental or physical examination requires the discovering party to obtain a court order. The court may grant the motion only for good cause shown. (§ 2032, subd. (a).)[5]

Section 2036 defines a showing of "good cause" as requiring that the party produce specific facts justifying discovery and that the inquiry be relevant to the subject matter of the action or reasonably calculated to lead to the discovery of admissible evidence.[6] The requirement of a court order following a showing of good cause is doubtless designed to protect an examinee's privacy interest by preventing an examination from becoming an annoying fishing expedition. While a plaintiff may place his mental state in controversy by a general allegation of severe emotional distress, the opposing party may not require him to undergo psychiatric testing solely on the basis of speculation that something of interest may surface.

Plaintiff in the case at bar asserts that she continues to suffer diminished self-esteem, reduced motivation, sleeplessness, loss of appetite, fear, lessened ability to help others, loss of social contacts, anxiety, mental anguish, loss of reputation, and severe emotional distress. In their motion defendants pointed to these allegations. Because the truth of these claims is relevant to plaintiff's cause of action and justifying facts have been shown with specificity, good cause as to these assertions has been demonstrated. Subject to limitations necessitated by plaintiff's right to privacy, defendants must be allowed to investigate the continued existence and severity of plaintiff's alleged damages.

II. *Privacy Limitations on the Scope of a Mental Examination*

If we find, as we do, that an examination may be ordered, plaintiff urges us to circumscribe its scope to exclude any probing into her sexual history, habits, or practices. Such probing, she asserts, would intrude impermissibly into her protected sphere of privacy. Furthermore, it would tend to contravene the state's strong interest in eradicating sexual harassment by means of private suits for damages. An examination into a plaintiff's past and present sexual practices would inhibit the bringing of meritorious sexual harassment actions by compelling the plaintiff-whose privacy has already been invaded by the harassment-to suffer another intrusion into her private life.

A right to privacy was recognized in the seminal case of *Griswold v. Connecticut* (1965) 381 U.S. 479 [85 S. Ct. 1678, 14 L. Ed. 2d 510]. It protects both the marital relationship (*ibid.*) and the sexual lives of the unmarried (*Eisenstadt v. Baird* (1972) 405 U.S. 438 [92 S. Ct. 1029, 31 L. Ed. 2d 349]). More significantly, California accords privacy the constitutional status of an "inalienable right," on a par with defending

---

5. After July 1, 1987, this requirement is contained in section 2032, subdivision (d) [after July 1, 2005, in section 2032.320].

6. This section has been repealed and has apparently not been replaced by equivalent language. There is no indication, however, that the Legislature intended repeal of former section 2036 to change the requirements for good cause in regard to mental examinations.

life and possessing property. (Cal. Const., art. I, § 1; *White v. Davis* (1975) 13 Cal. 3d 757 [120 Cal. Rptr. 94, 533 P.2d 222].) California's privacy protection similarly embraces sexual relations.

Defendants acknowledge plaintiff's right to privacy in the abstract but maintain she has waived it for purposes of the present suit. * * *

Plaintiff's present mental and emotional condition is directly relevant to her claim and essential to a fair resolution of her suit; she has waived her right to privacy in this respect by alleging continuing mental ailments. But she has not, merely by initiating this suit for sexual harassment and emotional distress, implicitly waived her right to privacy in respect to her sexual history and practices. Defendants fail to explain why probing into this area is directly relevant to her claim and essential to its fair resolution. Plaintiff does not contend the alleged acts were detrimental to her present sexuality. Her sexual history is even less relevant to her claim. We conclude that she has not waived her right to sexual privacy.

But even though plaintiff retains certain unwaived privacy rights, these rights are not necessarily absolute. On occasion her privacy interests may have to give way to her opponent's right to a fair trial. Thus courts must balance the right of civil litigants to discover relevant facts against the privacy interests of persons subject to discovery.

Before proceeding, we note the Legislature recently enacted a measure designed to protect the privacy of plaintiffs in cases such as these. Section 2036.1 (operative until July 1, 1987; presently, substantially the same provision is contained in § 2017, subdivision (d) [renumbered § 2017.220, effective July 1, 2005]), provides that in a civil suit alleging conduct that constitutes sexual harassment, sexual assault, or sexual battery, any party seeking discovery concerning the plaintiff's sexual conduct with individuals other than the alleged perpetrator must establish specific facts showing good cause for that discovery, and that the inquiry is relevant to the subject matter and reasonably calculated to lead to the discovery of admissible evidence. We must determine whether the general balancing of interests embodied in this new legislation has obviated the need for us to engage in an individualized balancing of privacy with discovery in the case at bar.

In enacting the measure, the Legislature took pains to declare that "The discovery of sexual aspects of complainant's [sic] lives, as well as those of their past and current friends and acquaintances, has the clear potential to discourage complaints and to annoy and harass litigants ... without protection against it, individuals whose intimate lives are unjustifiably and offensively intruded upon might face the 'Catch- 22' of invoking their remedy only at the risk of enduring further intrusions into the details of their personal lives in discovery.... [¶] ... Absent extraordinary circumstances, inquiry into those areas should not be permitted, either in discovery or at trial." (Stats. 1985, ch. 1328, § 1.)

Nowhere do defendants establish specific facts justifying inquiry into plaintiff's zone of sexual privacy or show how such discovery would be relevant. Rather they make only the most sweeping assertions regarding the need for wide latitude in the examination. Because good cause has not been shown, discovery into this area of plaintiff's life must be denied.

Section 2036.1, thus amply protects plaintiff's privacy interests. We anticipate that in the majority of sexual harassment suits, a separate weighing of privacy against discovery will not be necessary. It should normally suffice for the court, in ruling on whether good cause exists for probing into the intimate life of a victim of sexual harassment, sexual battery, or sexual assault, to evaluate the showing of good cause in light of the legislative purpose in enacting this section and the plaintiff's constitutional right to privacy.

III. *Presence of Counsel*

In the event a limited psychiatric examination is proper, plaintiff urges us to authorize the attendance of her attorney. She fears that the examiner will stray beyond the permitted area of inquiry. Counsel would monitor the interview and shield her from inappropriate interrogation. And depicting the examination as an "alien and frankly hostile environment," she asserts that she needs her lawyer to provide her with aid and comfort.

Defendants, joined by amici California Psychiatric Association and Northern California Psychiatric Association, counter that a meaningful mental examination cannot be conducted with an attorney interposing objections. And if plaintiff's counsel is present, defense counsel would also seek to attend. Defendants maintain these adversaries would likely convert the examination into a chaotic deposition.

We contemplated whether counsel must be allowed to attend the psychiatric examination of a client in *Edwards v. Superior Court* (1976) 16 Cal. 3d 905 [130 Cal. Rptr. 14, 549 P.2d 846]. The plaintiff in *Edwards* alleged that because of the defendant school district's failure to properly instruct and supervise users of school equipment, she sustained physical and emotional injuries. The trial court granted a motion compelling her to undergo a psychiatric examination alone. Holding that the plaintiff could not insist on the presence of her counsel, a majority of this court denied her petition for a peremptory writ.

The plaintiff in *Edwards* raised many of the points urged upon us here. She asserted that her attorney should be present to protect her from improper inquiries. We were skeptical that a lawyer, unschooled in the ways of the mental health profession, would be able to discern the psychiatric relevance of the questions. And the examiner should have the freedom to probe deeply into the plaintiff's psyche without interference by a third party. (*Id.* at p. 911.) The plaintiff further suggested counsel should be present to lend her comfort and support in an inimical setting. We responded that an examinee could view almost any examination of this sort, even by her own expert, as somewhat hostile. Whatever comfort her attorney's handholding might afford was substantially outweighed by the distraction and potential disruption caused by the presence of a third person. (*Ibid.*) Finally, we concluded counsel's presence was not necessary to ensure accurate reporting. Verbatim transcription might inhibit the examinee, preventing an effective examination. Furthermore, other procedural devices—pretrial discovery of the examiner's notes or cross-examination, for example—were available for the plaintiff's protection. (*Id.* at pp. 911–912.)

[The Court reviews federal decisions addressing this issue.] These cases suggest that in the federal courts a mental examinee has no absolute right to the presence of an attorney; but when the circumstances warrant it, the courts may fashion some means of protecting an examinee from intrusive or offensive probing.

[W]e conclude that a reconsideration of [the *Edwards*] decision—which is barely 10 years old—is not justified.[9] We emphasize, however, that *Edwards* should be viewed as standing for the proposition that the presence of an attorney is not required during a mental examination. In light of their broad discretion in discovery matters, trial courts retain the power to permit the presence of counsel or to take other prophylactic measures when needed.

Plaintiff makes no showing that the court abused its discretion in excluding her counsel from the examination. Her fears are wholly unfounded at this point; not a shred of evidence has been produced to show that defendants' expert will not respect her legitimate rights to privacy or might disobey any court-imposed restrictions. Plaintiff's apprehension appears to derive less from the reality of the proposed analysis than from the popular image of mental examinations.

Plaintiff's interests can be adequately protected without having her attorney present. In the first place, section 2032 requires the court granting a physical or mental examination to specify its conditions and scope. We must assume, absent evidence to the contrary, that the examiner will proceed in an ethical manner, adhering to these constraints. And if plaintiff truly fears that the examiner will probe into impermissible areas, she may record the examination on audio tape. This is an unobtrusive measure that will permit evidence of abuse to be presented to the court in any motion for sanctions.

Plaintiff refers us to the history of psychiatric examinations for victims of sexual assault. Such examinations were widely viewed as inhibiting prosecutions for rape by implicitly placing the victim on trial, leading to a legislative prohibition of examinations to assess credibility. The victim of sexual harassment is analogous to the prosecutrix in a rape case, plaintiff asserts, and she points to legislative findings that

---

9. Section 2032, subdivision (g) (operative July 1, 1987) [now CCP § 2032.510(a)], now specifically provides for the attendance of an attorney at a physical examination. (*See Sharff v. Superior Court* (1955) 44 Cal. 2d 508 [282 P.2d 896].) Subdivision (g)(2) states, however, that nothing in the discovery statutes shall be construed to alter, amend, or affect existing case law with respect to the presence of counsel or other persons during a mental examination by agreement or court order. Had the Legislature felt it desirable to have counsel present at psychiatric examinations, it would certainly have provided for this in its thorough revision of the section. Indeed, in the course of that revision the Legislature considered and rejected a provision that would have annulled our decision in *Edwards* by permitting counsel to attend a mental examination.

discovery of sexual aspects of complainants' lives "has the clear potential to discourage complaints." (Stats. 1985, ch. 1328, § 1.) If we conclude on the basis of general considerations that a mental examination is appropriate and that it should occur without the presence of counsel, plaintiff urges us to adopt a special rule exempting those who bring harassment charges from either or both of these requirements.

We believe that in these circumstances such a special rule is unwarranted. In the first place, we should be guided by the maxim that *entia non sunt multiplicanda praeter necessitatem*: we should carve out exceptions from general rules only when the facts require it. The state admittedly has a strong interest in eradicating the evil of sexual harassment, and the threat of a mental examination could conceivably dampen a plaintiff's resolve to bring suit. But we have seen that those who allege harassment have substantial protection under existing procedural rules. In general it is unlikely that a simple sexual harassment suit will justify a mental examination. Such examinations may ordinarily be considered only in cases in which the alleged mental or emotional distress is said to be ongoing. When an examination is permitted, investigation by a psychiatrist into the private life of a plaintiff is severely constrained, and sanctions are available to guarantee those restrictions are respected.

Finally, the mental examination in this case largely grows out of plaintiff's emotional distress claim. We do not believe the state has a greater interest in preventing emotional distress in sexual harassment victims than it has in preventing such distress in the victims of any other tort.

The judgment of the Court of Appeal is reversed with directions to issue a peremptory writ of mandate compelling respondent court to limit the scope of the mental examination in accordance with the views expressed herein.

Notes and Questions regarding Mental Examinations

(1) A personal injury plaintiff seeking damages for mental and emotional injuries may be ordered to submit to a mental examination under CCP §§ 2032.310–.650. This examination may be avoided by (1) disclaiming extraordinary mental and emotional suffering and (2) agreeing not to introduce expert testimony on these issues at trial. § 2032.320.

(2) Is a party's mental condition "in controversy," within the meaning of CCP § 2032.020, when she seeks damages for severe emotional distress caused by sexual harassment, but alleges that the emotional distress ceased when the harassment ended before litigation? The court in *Doyle v. Superior Court*, 50 Cal. App. 4th 1878, 58 Cal. Rptr. 2d 476 (1996), concluded that allegations of past emotional distress did not place the party's current mental condition "in controversy," and therefore a motion to compel a mental examination should have been denied. The court reasoned that mental examinations are not authorized for the purpose of testing a person's credibility, and are only relevant to assess current mental condition and not emotional distress suffered in the past. *Doyle, supra,* 50 Cal. App. 4th at 1886. The court in *Doyle* distinguished *Vinson v. Superior Court,* reproduced *supra,* as a case based on allegations

that the plaintiff there was continuing to suffer mental distress. *Doyle*, 50 Cal. App. 4th at 1885–1886. Do you agree with this reading of *Vinson*?

(3) In contrast to physical examinations, neither counsel nor court reporters are generally allowed to attend mental examinations. *Edwards v. Superior Court*, 16 Cal. 3d 905, 910, 130 Cal. Rptr. 14, 549 P.2d 846 (1976); *see Toyota Motor Sales, U.S.A., Inc. v. Superior Court*, 189 Cal. App. 4th 1391, 117 Cal. Rptr. 3d 321 (2010) (holding trial court abused its discretion in permitting plaintiff's counsel to be present in an adjoining room during a psychiatric examination because evidence indicated that such contemporaneous monitoring would interfere with the examiner's ability to establish the necessary rapport with the plaintiff). However, as *Vinson* suggests, a court has discretion to permit counsel to attend if there is some showing of special need. Since neither counsel nor a court reporter may be present at a mental examination, § 2032.530 authorizes the recording of the entire examination on audiotape. Both examiner and the examinee have the right to record the entire examination. *Golfland Entertainment Centers, Inc. v. Superior Court*, 108 Cal. App. 4th 739, 133 Cal. Rptr. 2d 828 (2003).

[3]   Other Limits on Examinations

How many examinations may a defendant obtain in a personal injury action? In *Shapira v. Superior Court*, 224 Cal. App. 3d 1249, 274 Cal. Rptr. 516 (1990), the plaintiff submitted to two defense examinations: a physical examination by a neurologist and a mental examination by a neuropsychologist. She objected to a second mental examination by a psychiatrist, on the ground that a defendant is permitted only one mental examination under CCP § 2032. The trial court denied the examination. The Court of Appeal issued a writ compelling the trial court to exercise its discretion in ruling on the motion for a second mental exam. The *Shapira* court ruled that § 2032 did not expressly limit the number of examinations which could be ordered, and that § 2032(d) [now § 2032.310] permitted multiple examinations for good cause shown and subject to appropriate protective orders.

What other restrictions are imposed on examinations? Section 2032.020 describes those persons who may be required to submit to an examination: "Any party may obtain discovery, subject to the restrictions set forth in [Section 2019.010 et seq.], by means of a physical or mental examination of (1) a party to the action (2) an agent of any party, or (3) a natural person in the custody or under the legal control of a party, in any action in which the mental or physical condition (including the blood group) of that party or other person is in controversy in the action." Section 2032.020 presupposes that the parties who may be required to submit to examinations are proper parties to the action. *William M. v. Superior Court*, 225 Cal. App. 3d 447, 275 Cal. Rptr. 103 (1994); *see Roe v. Superior Court*, 243 Cal. App. 4th 138, 196 Cal. Rptr. 3d 317 (2015) (ruling that statute permitting mental examination of a party did not permit collateral interview of minor child's parents, nor did it entitle the party and his parents to written psychological test questions administered during the examination).

[E]   Exchange of Information About Trial Experts

[1]   Expert Witness Disclosures

One of the major changes of the Civil Discovery Act of 1986 is reflected in Section 2034.210 which provides for the compulsory exchange of the identity of expert witnesses who will testify at trial and the general nature of their testimony. After the initial trial date is set, this exchange may be initiated by either side. This section provides for the timely exchange of information to permit the opposing party to depose the designated expert and to designate additional experts if necessary.

Schreiber v. Estate of Kiser

Supreme Court of California
22 Cal. 4th 31, 91 Cal. Rptr. 2d 293, 989 P.2d 720 (1999)

BROWN, JUSTICE.

The issue in this case is whether under Code of Civil Procedure section 2034,[1] which provides for discovery of expert witness information, a trial court may preclude a treating physician, designated as an expert witness, from testifying at trial regarding causation if no expert witness declaration was submitted on his behalf. We conclude section 2034 does not require the submission of an expert witness declaration for a treating physician, and reverse the judgment of the Court of Appeal.

I. FACTUAL AND PROCEDURAL BACKGROUND

Plaintiff Faith Dawn Schreiber was involved in an automobile accident with Donald Wayne Kiser. Schreiber alleged she had suffered neck and back injuries as a result. Kiser subsequently died of causes unrelated to the accident, and Schreiber sued his estate and the City of Huntington Beach.

The Court of Appeal affirmed. The court stated the ordinary role of a treating physician is to give percipient testimony regarding what he observed, concluded, and did. Once a treating physician offers opinion testimony regarding causation, he exceeds this ordinary role, and becomes a retained expert within the meaning of section 2034, subdivision (a)(2). Thus, an expert witness declaration is required. The court stated, "to the degree that Schreiber's treating physicians were going to be used to show that her particular aches and pains were caused by the auto accident as distinct from some preexisting event, they ... were going to offer opinion, not percipient, testimony. None of Schreiber's experts actually observed the auto accident which ... prompted her suit. Absent the required expert witness declaration the trial judge was thus thoroughly correct to preclude [causation] testimony."

Schreiber's petition for rehearing was denied. We granted her petition for review.

---

1. [Renumbered as sections 2034.010–.730 effective July 1, 2005.] All statutory references are to the Code of Civil Procedure unless otherwise indicated.

II. DISCUSSION

Under section 2034, subdivision (a) [now §2034.210], any party may demand the exchange of expert witness information. In this exchange, a party may provide either "[a] list setting forth the name and address of any person whose expert opinion that party expects to offer in evidence at the trial" or "[a] statement that the party does not presently intend to offer the testimony of any expert witness." (*Id.*, subd. (f)(1)(A), (B).)

For an expert witness who "is a party or an employee of a party," or, as relevant here, "has been retained by a party for the purpose of forming and expressing an opinion in anticipation of the litigation or in preparation for the trial of the action" (§2034, subd. (a)(2)), "the exchange shall also include or be accompanied by an expert witness declaration...." (*Id.*, subd. (f)(2); *Bonds v. Roy* (1999) 20 Cal. 4th 140, 144 [83 Cal. Rptr. 2d 289, 973 P.2d 66] [declaration requirement applies to "*certain* expert witnesses*" (italics added)].) Failure to submit such a declaration may result in exclusion of the expert opinion. (§2034, subd. (j)(2).) The question here is whether a treating physician becomes a "retained" expert within the meaning of subdivision (a)(2), requiring the submission of an expert witness declaration, whenever the physician gives opinion testimony. (§2034, subds. (a)(2), (f)(2).) For the reasons that follow, we conclude he does not.

At the outset, we note that the treating physicians in this case were designated as *expert* witnesses. (§2034, subds. (a)(1), (f)(1)(A).) By its terms, subdivision (f)(1)(A) requires "[a] list setting forth the name and address of any person *whose expert opinion* that party expects to offer in evidence at the trial." (Italics added.) Thus, defendants were on notice at the time of the designation that plaintiff intended to offer opinion testimony by her treating physicians. Indeed, by definition, an "expert" witness is one entitled to give opinion testimony. Evidence Code section 801 provides that an expert's opinion testimony must generally be "[r]elated to a subject that is sufficiently beyond common experience that the opinion of an expert would assist the trier of fact; and [¶] [b]ased on matter (including his special knowledge, skill, experience, training, and education) perceived by or personally known to the witness or made known to him...." Thus, a treating physician does not *become* an expert only when nonpercipient opinion testimony is elicited.

As noted, the declaration requirement applies to only "certain" expert witnesses, i.e., those who are parties, employees of parties, or are "retained by a party for the purpose of forming and expressing an opinion in anticipation of the litigation or in preparation for the trial...." (§2034, subd. (a)(2); *Bonds v. Roy, supra*, 20 Cal. 4th at p. 144.) A treating physician generally falls into none of these categories. This is explained in section 2034's legislative history. Prior to the Civil Discovery Act of 1986, a party was required to describe the general substance of the expected testimony of every expert witness. (Former §2037.3, as amended by Stats. 1982, ch. 1400, §3, p. 5337.) That is no longer the case. [Here the court reviews section 2034's legislative history.]

A treating physician is a percipient expert, but that does not mean that his testimony is limited only to personal observations. Rather, like any other expert, he may provide both fact and opinion testimony. As the legislative history clarifies, what distinguishes the treating physician from a retained expert is not the content of the testimony, but the context in which he became familiar with the plaintiff's injuries that were ultimately the subject of litigation, and which form the factual basis for the medical opinion. The contextual nature of the inquiry is implicit in the language of section 2034, subdivision (a)(2), which describes a retained expert as one "retained by a party *for the purpose* of forming and expressing an opinion in anticipation of the litigation or in preparation for the trial of the action." (Italics added.) A treating physician is not consulted for litigation purposes, but rather learns of the plaintiff's injuries and medical history because of the underlying physician-patient relationship.

The conclusion that treating physicians generally are not experts "retained" within the meaning of section 2034, subdivision (a)(2) is supported by subdivision (i)(2), and similar language in Government Code section 68092.5, subdivision (a). These provisions clearly differentiate between the retained expert described in subdivision (a)(2), for whom an expert witness declaration is required, and a treating physician expert witness. Subdivision (i)(2) provides, "A party desiring to depose any expert witness, other than a party or employee of a party, who is either (A) an expert described in paragraph (2) of subdivision (a) except one who is a party or an employee of a party, (B) *a treating physician and surgeon or other treating health care practitioner who is to be asked during the deposition to express opinion testimony, including opinion or factual testimony regarding the past or present diagnosis or prognosis made by the practitioner or the reasons for a particular treatment decision made by the practitioner,* ... or (C) an architect, professional engineer, or licensed land surveyor, who was involved with the original project design or survey for which he or she is asked to express an opinion within his or her expertise and relevant to the action or proceeding, shall pay the expert's reasonable and customary hourly or daily fee for any time spent at the deposition...." (Italics added.)

The implication of these sections is that expert witness treating physicians are not included within the meaning of subdivision (a)(2). (See *Huntley v. Foster* (1995) 35 Cal. App. 4th 753, 754, 756 [41 Cal. Rptr. 2d 358] [expert witness declaration not required for treating physician to give opinion testimony]; *Hurtado v. Western Medical Center* (1990) 222 Cal. App. 3d 1198, 1202–1203 [272 Cal. Rptr. 324] [plaintiff not required to produce treating physicians designated as experts for deposition because they were not "retained" within the meaning of subdivisions (a)(2) and (i)(2)].) Indeed, it would be difficult to interpret subdivision (a)(2) in a contrary fashion without rendering subdivision (i)(2) superfluous.

Such a conclusion is also consistent with the discovery statutes as a whole. The identity and opinions of a party's retained experts are generally privileged unless they are going to testify at trial. (Kennedy & Martin, Cal. Expert Witness Guide (Cont. Ed. Bar 2d ed. 1999) § 10.6, p. 254.2.) Thus, were the physicians in this case consulted solely for the purpose of assisting counsel in, for example, assessing plaintiff's injuries, their identity and opinions would generally not have been discoverable. If an expert's opinion does not support the position of the hiring party, that party can effectively "bury" the witness by not calling the witness at trial and not otherwise disclosing his identity or opinion. (See 2 Weil & Brown, Cal. Practice Guide: Civil Procedure Before Trial (The Rutter Group 1998) ¶ 8:1616.2, p. 8I-31 rev. # 1 1996 [advising counsel to have consulting physician verbally report evaluation if opinion is negative and to instruct physician not to make written report to avoid disclosure of his identity and opinion under § 2032].)

Moreover, whether a retained expert will testify need not be revealed until shortly before trial. (§ 2034, subd. (b) ["A party shall make this demand no later than the 10th day after the initial trial date has been set, or 70 days before that trial date, whichever is closer to the trial date."].) It makes sense in this situation that the Legislature would require the person presenting the expert to submit an expert witness declaration. The information contained in this declaration[4] allows the parties to assess within a short time frame "whether to take the expert's deposition, to fully explore the relevant subject area at any such deposition, and to select an expert who can respond with a competing opinion on that subject area." (*Bonds v. Roy, supra,* 20 Cal. 4th at p. 147.)

By contrast, the identity and opinions of treating physicians are not privileged. Rather, because they acquire the information that forms the factual basis for their opinions independently of the litigation, they are subject to no special discovery restrictions. (2 Hogan & Weber, Cal. Civil Discovery, *supra,* § 13.13, pp. 221–222; *id.,* § 13.14, pp. 222–224.) They can be identified early in the litigation through interrogatories, production of the plaintiff's medical records, and completion of case questionnaires which by statute expressly ask for information regarding "treating physicians." (§ 93, subd. (c), 2030, 2031, 2032, subds. (i), (j).) Indeed, defendants have a strong incentive to depose treating physicians well prior to the exchange of expert information to ascertain whether their observations and conclusions support the plaintiff's allegations. (See Kennedy & Martin, Cal. Expert Witness Guide, *supra,* § 10.8, pp. 255–256.) Conceivably, some treating physicians may ultimately become defense witnesses.

Accordingly, the Legislature has apparently determined that by the time of the exchange of expert witness information, the information required by the expert witness declaration is unnecessary for treating physicians who remain in their traditional

---

4. Section 2034, subdivision (f)(2)(A)–(E) requires the expert witness declaration to include: "(A) A brief narrative statement of the qualifications of each expert. [¶] (B) A brief narrative statement of the general substance of the testimony that the expert is expected to give. [¶] (C) A representation that the expert has agreed to testify at the trial. [¶] (D) A representation that the expert will be sufficiently familiar with the pending action to submit to a meaningful oral deposition concerning the specific testimony, including any opinion and its basis, that the expert is expected to give at trial. [¶] (E) A statement of the expert's hourly and daily fee for providing deposition testimony and for consulting with the retaining attorney."

role.[5] * * * Indeed, at this point in the litigation, the treating physician has probably already been deposed. In addition, the Legislature was apparently concerned that requiring counsel to provide "[a] brief narrative statement of the general substance of the testimony that the expert is expected to give" for treating physicians and other percipient experts would violate the work product doctrine. (*Id.*, subd. (f)(2)(B);....) Finally, our interpretation avoids assigning trial judges the near-impossible task of determining whether an expert witness treating physician is providing percipient or opinion testimony.

Thus, rather than encouraging gamesmanship, the Civil Discovery Act of 1986 places litigants on roughly equal footing. To the extent a physician is retained "for the purpose of forming and expressing an opinion in anticipation of the litigation or in preparation for the trial of the action," his identity and opinions are generally privileged unless he testifies. (§ 2034, subd. (a)(2).) Should the physician testify, an expert witness declaration is required. On the other hand, to the extent a physician acquires personal knowledge of the relevant facts independently of the litigation, his identity and opinions based on those facts are not privileged in litigation presenting "an issue concerning the condition of the patient." (Evid. Code, § 996; 1 Hogan & Weber, Cal. Civil Discovery, *supra*, § 8.19, p. 437; 2 Hogan & Weber, Cal. Civil Discovery, *supra*, § 12:11, p. 62; *id.*, § 12.24, pp. 110–111.) For such a witness, no expert witness declaration is required, and he may testify as to any opinions formed on the basis of facts independently acquired and informed by his training, skill, and experience. This may well include opinions regarding causation and standard of care because such issues are inherent in a physician's work. An opposing party would therefore be prudent to ask a treating physician at his deposition whether he holds any opinions on these subjects, and if so, in what manner he obtained the factual underpinning of those opinions.

Defendants rely on *Plunkett v. Spaulding* (1997) 52 Cal. App. 4th 114 [60 Cal. Rptr. 2d 377], which in dicta upheld the exclusion of the treating physicians' standard of care testimony, stating, "expert witness declarations would not have been required if the treating physicians were expected to testify only as to their treatment of plaintiff, including diagnosis and prognosis. However, when in addition to this testimony they were asked to provide expert opinions on the standard of care that defendant should have used in treating plaintiff," they became "retained" experts within the meaning of section 2034, subdivision (a)(2), and declarations were required. (52 Cal. App. 4th at pp. 119–120.) To the extent *Plunkett* concluded a treating physician could

---

5. At oral argument, Schreiber's counsel stated it is conceivable a treating physician or any other percipient expert could later become an expert "retained by a party for the purpose of forming and expressing an opinion in anticipation of the litigation or in preparation for the trial of the action...." (§ 2034, subd. (a)(2).) We need not explore the parameters of such a metamorphosis in this opinion. Here, defendants do not contend the witnesses in question were not treating physicians. Rather, they contend that a causation opinion is per se outside the role of a treating physician because it requires information from the patient or other sources, and is not based solely on the physician's personal observations.

never, regardless of the manner in which he obtained the factual basis of his opinion, testify as to standard of care without an expert witness declaration, we disagree for the reasons discussed above. * * *

DISPOSITION

The judgment of the Court of Appeal is reversed, and the case remanded to that court for further proceedings consistent with this opinion.

Notes and Questions regarding Expert Witness Disclosures

(1) Sections 2034.210–.220 provide a specific time frame for demanding the expert disclosure. The demand cannot be made before the case is initially set for trial; the demand cannot be made later than 10 days after the initial trial date has been set or 70 days before that trial date, whichever is later. CCP § 2034.220. Can a party obtain relief for service of a premature or belated demand? The Discovery Act is silent on this question. Some courts have concluded that relief may be obtained under CCP § 473 on a showing of "mistake, inadvertence or excusable neglect." *Cottini v. Enloe Med. Ctr.*, 226 Cal. App. 4th 401, 172 Cal. Rptr. 3d 4 (2014); *Zellerino v. Brown*, 235 Cal. App. 3d 1097, 1107, 1 Cal. Rptr. 2d 222, 228 (1991).

(2) The date for the exchange must be specified in the demand and must be 20 days after service of the demand or 50 days before the initial trial, whichever is later. § 2034.230. A party who fails to meet this deadline may seek leave to submit a belated list. §§ 2034.710–.730. Absent exceptional circumstances, this motion must be made in time to permit the deposition of the expert before the 15-day deadline for experts' depositions. § 2034.710.

(3) As *Schreiber v. Estate of Kiser*, reproduced *supra*, makes clear, the disclosure required by Section CCP § 2034.210 is limited to experts who will be called to testify at trial. For retained experts, the disclosure must include an expert witness declaration setting out the expert's qualifications, the general substance of the expected testimony, a representation that the expert is ready to testify, and a statement of the expert's fees for deposition testimony. § 2034.260. For treating physicians who are regarded as percipient witnesses, the identity must be disclosed if they will be called to express an opinion, but an expert declaration is not required. *See* § 2034.210.

(4) Once a trial expert is designated, the other litigants have a right under § 2034.410 to depose that witness. For a specially retained expert, the one noticing the deposition must pay the expert's "reasonable and customary hourly or daily fee for any time spent at the deposition." CCP § 2034.430; *see* Hogan & Weber, *California Civil Discovery* § 10.10 (2d ed. 2005 & Supp. 2015). This has been construed to mean the amount the expert would charge for testimonial work. *Rancho Bernardo Dev. Co. v. Superior Court*, 2 Cal. App. 4th 358, 2 Cal. Rptr. 2d 878 (1992). The court may be called on to intervene if the fees are excessive. § 2034.470; *see Marsh v. Mountain Zephyr, Inc.*, 43 Cal. App. 4th 289, 50 Cal. Rptr. 2d 493 (1996) (noting expert's customary fee is merely one factor in determining what is a reasonable fee and holding the trial court

did not abuse its discretion in awarding the deposed expert witness $250 per hour instead of the $350 per hour the witness testified was his customary hourly fee).

(5) In addition to demanding the identity of the expert, a party may also demand the mutual and simultaneous exchange of all discoverable reports and writings. § 2034.210(c). Why is this exchange mutual and simultaneous?

(6) After the expert disclosure, a party may need to amend or supplement the expert information. If the additional testimony pertains to matters raised in an opponent's expert disclosure, then the party has a right to supplement the expert list within 20 days. CCP § 2034.280. If, however, the additional testimony relates to matters covered in the party's original disclosure, the party must seek leave of court to augment or amend the disclosure. § 2034.610–.630. Absent exceptional circumstances, this motion must be early enough to permit the deposition of the expert involved before the 15-day cut off on deposing experts. §§ 2034.610 and 2024.020.

(7) What if the designated expert has a change of opinion after the disclosure but before trial? One court has concluded that this justifies an order under § 2034.620 permitting the augmentation of the list of experts. *Dickison v. Howen*, 220 Cal. App. 3d 1471, 270 Cal. Rptr. 188 (1990).

(8) The identities and opinions of consulting experts who will not be called to testify at trial are protected work product under CCP 2018.030. *See* Kennedy & Martin, *California Expert Witness Guide* §§ 8.18–9.23 (2d ed. 2015) (collecting cases). However, once a witness is listed as a trial expert the work product privilege may be waived as to earlier reports by that expert, even those tendered while the witness was only a consultant. *See County of Los Angeles v. Superior Court*, 222 Cal. App. 3d 647, 271 Cal. Rptr. 698 (1990); *National Steel Products Co. v. Superior Court*, 164 Cal. App. 3d 476, 210 Cal. Rptr. 535 (1985); CEB, *California Civil Discovery Practice, Exchange of Expert Information* § 3.59, § 11.5 (4th ed. 2015); *but see DeLuca v. State Fish Co., Inc.*, 217 Cal. App. 4th 671, 687–691, 158 Cal. Rptr. 3d 761 (2013) (ruling an expert's opinion regarding the subject matter about which the expert will testify is discoverable, but the expert's advice rendered in a consulting capacity is still subject to qualified work product protection).

[2] *Withdrawal of Designated Expert*

It has long been recognized that the work of an expert-consultant is protected by the attorney's work product privilege. *Williamson v. Superior Court*, 21 Cal. 3d 829, 834,148 Cal. Rptr. 39, 582 P.2d 126 (1978). May a party withdraw its designation of an expert trial witness, who is not yet deposed and who remains as the party's consultant, and thereby preclude the deposition of that expert and also preclude the expert's retention by an adverse party? The court in *County of Los Angeles v. Superior Court*, 222 Cal. App. 3d 647, 271 Cal. Rptr. 698 (1990), confronted this question and answered it affirmatively:

> We hold that a party may, for tactical reasons, withdraw a previously designated expert witness, not yet deposed. If that expert continues his or her

relationship with the party as a consultant, the opposing party is barred from communicating with the expert and from retaining him or her as the opposing party's expert. To conclude otherwise would produce two undesirable results: a designated expert subsequently withdrawn could "sell" his or her opinions to the highest bidder and be free of concern about whether his or her previous consultation is protected by the work product privilege; and a party would never withdraw a previously designated expert for fear that the attorney's work product (i.e., the consultations with the withdrawn expert) would become available to the opposition.

When an attorney violates this rule, he or she must be recused. Having become privy to an opposing attorney's work product, there is no way the offending attorney could separate that knowledge from his or her preparation of the case.

County of Los Angeles, supra, 222 Cal. App. 3d at 657–78.

[3] Testimony of Undesignated Experts

[a] Limited Right to Call Undesignated Expert

In a limited number of circumstances, a party may call an expert who the party has not designated. First, pursuant to CCP § 2034.310(a), a party may call an expert to testify who has been designated by some other party to the case so long as the witness has been deposed. *Powell v. Superior Court,* 211 Cal. App. 3d 441, 259 Cal. Rptr. 390 (1989).

Second, an undesignated expert may be called as a rebuttal witness for the purpose of "impeachment." CCP § 2034.310(b). For purposes of this statute, the term impeachment has been narrowly construed. As the court in *Fish v. Guevara,* 12 Cal. App. 4th 142, 145, 15 Cal. Rptr. 2d 329 (1993), explained:

[T]his impeachment may include testimony pertaining to the falsity or nonexistence of any fact used as the foundation for any opinion by any other party's expert witness, but may not include testimony that contradicts the opinion. Hence, an undisclosed expert may testify to facts which contradict the factual basis for the opinions of other experts but may not give opinion testimony which contradicts the opinions of other experts.

For a good discussion of the difference between calling an undesignated expert for the permissible impeachment purpose of contradicting a foundational fact relied upon by a prior expert, as opposed to the impermissible purpose of expressing an opinion contrary to another expert witness, see *Howard Contracting, Inc. v. G.A. MacDonald Const. Co.,* 71 Cal. App. 4th 38, 52–54, 83 Cal. Rptr. 2d 590 (1998) (concluding trial court properly excluded pursuant to CCP § 2034(m) [now § 2034.310] testimony of undisclosed expert witness which contradicted an opinion expressed by defendant's expert about the accepted accounting practices); *Mizel v. City of Santa Monica,* 93 Cal. App. 4th 1059, 113 Cal. Rptr. 2d 649 (2001) (ruling trial court did not err in excluding testimony of defendant's undisclosed expert where that testimony would not have challenged the foundational facts of a prior expert's opinion regarding whether plaintiff was drunk but instead would have rendered a contrary opinion).

[b]   Failure to Comply with Expert Disclosure Requirements

If a party has unreasonably failed to comply with the requirements for expert disclosure under § 2034.210 with respect to a witness, the trial court upon objection is required to exclude from evidence the expert testimony of that witness. CCP § 2034.300; *see, e.g., Perry v. Bakewell Hawthorne, LLC,* 244 Cal. App. 4th 712, 198 Cal. Rptr. 3d 669 (2016) (upholding exclusion of plaintiff's proffered expert testimony, submitted in opposition to summary judgment motion, where plaintiff failed to participate in exchange of expert witness information); *Staub v. Riley,* 226 Cal. App. 4th 1437, 173 Cal. Rptr. 3d 104 (2014) (holding tardy expert witness disclosure was not so unreasonable as to bar expert witness evidence, particularly where the experts were immediately made available for depositions); *Cottini v. Enloe Med. Ctr.,* 226 Cal. App. 4th 401, 172 Cal. Rptr. 3d 4 (2014) (concluding that where the party objecting to expert testimony under § 2034.300 would be entitled to mandatory exclusion of such testimony for his own failure to comply with the expert exchange requirements, exclusion of expert testimony is discretionary, not mandatory). This rule applies where a party fails to list an expert, fails to submit a required declaration, fails to produce discoverable reports, or fails to make the expert available for the deposition. § 2034.300; *see, e.g., Waicis v. Superior Court,* 226 Cal. App. 3d 283, 276 Cal. Rptr. 45 (1990) (finding no abuse of discretion for trial court to disqualify properly designated expert witness from testifying at trial where the court found the expert had repeatedly been uncooperative in allowing his disposition to be taken).

Failure to submit an adequate expert declaration may also be grounds for excluding the expert's testimony. *Bonds v. Roy,* 20 Cal. 4th 140, 83 Cal. Rptr. 2d 289, 973 P.2d 66 (1999). The issue in *Bonds* was whether under CCP §§ 2034.210–.730, which provides for discovery of expert witness information, a trial court may preclude an expert witness from testifying at trial on a subject whose general substance was not previously described in the expert witness declaration. After reviewing the statutory framework relevant to the exchange of expert witness information, the Court concluded that such expert testimony may be precluded (*Bonds,* 20 Cal. 4th at 148–49):

> [T]he statutory scheme as a whole envisions timely disclosure of the general substance of an expert's expected testimony so that the parties may properly prepare for trial. Allowing new and unexpected testimony for the first time at trial so long as a party has submitted any expert witness declaration whatsoever is inconsistent with this purpose. We therefore conclude that the exclusion sanction of subdivision (i) [now § 2034.300] applies when a party unreasonably fails to submit an expert witness declaration that fully complies with the content requirements of subdivision (f)(2) [§ 2034.260], including the requirement that the declaration contain "[a] brief narrative statement of the general substance of the testimony that the expert is expected to give."

(Subd. (f)(2)(B) [§ 2034.260(c)(2)].) This encompasses situations, like the present one, in which a party has submitted an expert witness declaration, but the narrative statement fails to disclose the general substance of the testimony the party later wishes to elicit from the expert at trial. To expand the scope of an expert's testimony beyond what is stated in the declaration, a party must successfully move for leave to amend the declaration under subdivision (k) [§ 2034.610].

In *Jones v. Moore*, 80 Cal. App. 4th 557, 95 Cal. Rptr. 2d 216 (2000), the court affirmed the trial court's exclusion of certain testimony of plaintiff's expert because the testimony went beyond the opinions expressed by the expert at his deposition. Even though the plaintiff filed an expert witness declaration arguably broad enough to encompass the testimony plaintiff wished to produce at trial, in his subsequent deposition the expert testified as to certain specific opinions and stated these were his only opinions. Finding support from the Supreme Court's recognition in *Bonds v. Roy, supra,* that an important goal of CCP § 2034.210 is to enable parties to properly prepare for trial, the *Jones* court concluded it would be unfair and prejudicial to permit the expert to offer additional opinions at trial. *Jones, supra,* 80 Cal. App. 4th at 565–566.

The court in *Easterby v. Clark*, 171 Cal. App. 4th 772, 90 Cal. Rptr. 3d 81 (2009), summarized the overarching principle in *Bonds v. Roy* and *Jones v. Moore* as follows: A party's expert may not offer testimony at trial that exceeds the scope of his deposition testimony if the opposing party has no notice or expectation that the expert will offer the new testimony, or if notice of the new testimony comes at a time when deposing the expert is unreasonably difficult. *Easterby,* 171 Cal. App. 4th at 780.

[c] Augmentation of Expert List

A party who wishes to call at trial an expert who was not designated when expert witness information was exchanged and who is intended to take the place of a previously designated but now unavailable expert must make a motion under CCP § 2034.610 to augment that party's expert witness list to include the new expert. *Richaud v. Jennings,* 16 Cal. App. 4th 81, 19 Cal. Rptr. 2d 790 (1993). A replacement expert will not be permitted to testify, over objection, when the party seeking to call the replacement expert has failed to make an augmentation motion. *Richaud,* 16 Cal. App. 4th at 87–92. Why? What factors should the trial court consider when determining such an augmentation motion? *See Richaud,* 16 Cal. App. 4th at 92 (Augmentation motion would allow the opponent to explain the prejudice created, the proponent to demonstrate good cause for any delay, and the court to minimize any continuances and disruption of the litigation).

[F] Requests for Admissions

Under CCP §§ 2033.010–.420, a party may serve any other party a request to admit the genuineness of a document, or the truth of specific factual matters, or opinions relating to fact. Admissions are conclusive at trial, and unfounded denials may result in sanctions in the amount of the costs and fees incurred in proving the matter at trial. §§ 2033.410 & .420.

Sections 2033.020–.050 regulates the timing and number of requests for admissions. A defendant may serve requests at any time; a plaintiff may serve requests at any time after 10 days from the service of the summons on or appearance of a party. There is a presumptive limit of 35 requests for admissions; except for requests about the genuineness of documents, no party may request that any other party admit more than 35 matters. CCP § 2033.030. Requests which exceed this limit may be objected to under § 2033.030(b) and need not be answered. The parties may, however, stipulate to a greater or lesser number. If a party wishes to serve requests beyond this number, a declaration for additional discovery is permitted by § 2033.050. Each request for admission must be complete and self-contained with no subparts. § 2033.060.

A party who had been served a set of requests for admissions has two basic options: (1) seeking a protective order; or (2) responding. CCP § 2033.080 & .210. A protective order must be sought promptly and before the 30-day deadline for serving a response. § 2033.080(a). The court may enter a protective order to protect any party from annoyance, embarrassment, oppression, or undue burden or expense. § 2033.080(b); *see, e.g., Brigante v. Huang*, 20 Cal. App. 4th 1569, 25 Cal. Rptr. 2d 354 (1993) (holding trial court had the discretion to issue an appropriate protective order, even though defendant failed to file a separate motion for a protective order, where defendant cited oppression as a basis for objecting to plaintiff's motion to have requests for admissions deemed admitted). A protective order may also be sought in response to a declaration of necessity served with more than 35 requests. § 2033.080(b)(2). This motion requires the court to determine whether a response to the additional requests is required. § 2033.080(b)(2).

Unless the responding party moves for a protective order, a responding party must respond in writing under oath separately to each request within 30 days after service of the requests. CCP §§ 2033.210–.250. This time limit may be extended by stipulation, but the extension must be confirmed in writing. § 2033.260. The response must set out an answer or an objection to each request. § 2033.210. The effect of an admission is dramatic: any admitted matter is conclusively established against the party making the admission. § 2033.410(a). This effect is limited to only that party and only for the purpose of the pending action. § 2033.410(b). A party may only amend or withdraw an admission on leave of the court after notice to all parties. § 2033.300. Objections must be clearly stated, including objections as to the number of requests and objections based on privilege or work product protection. § 2033.230. If the responding party fails to admit a request because of incomplete information, the party must state that a reasonable inquiry has been conducted. § 2033.220(c). The response must be served on all parties. § 2033.250. If a party fails to make a timely response, objections to the requests are waived. § 2033.280(a). The requesting party may then move for an order that the requests be deemed admitted. § 2033.280(b).

The requesting party may seek an order compelling a further response where an initial response is too evasive or incomplete and where an initial objection is unfounded or too general. CCP § 2033.290. Notice of a motion to compel must be given within 45 days or the right to compel is waived. § 2033.290(c).

Grace v. Mansourian

Court of Appeal of California, Fourth Appellate District
240 Cal. App. 4th 523, 192 Cal. Rptr. 3d 551 (2015)

After plaintiff Timothy Grace (plaintiff), and his wife, Michelle Blair (Michelle) (collectively plaintiffs), prevailed on their personal injury action against defendants Levik Mansourian (defendant) and his mother, Satina Mansourian (collectively defendants), plaintiffs filed a motion seeking to recover costs of proof under Code of Civil Procedure section 2033.420 (all further statutory references are to this code unless otherwise stated) based on defendants' failure to admit certain requests for admissions. Plaintiffs appeal from the trial court's denial of the motion, arguing abuse of discretion. We conclude defendants had no reasonable basis to deny liability for plaintiff's ankle injury and certain treatment for it. Therefore we reverse and remand for the court to determine the reasonable amount to be awarded plaintiffs for their costs of proving these issues. The order is otherwise affirmed.

FACTS AND PROCEDURAL HISTORY

While driving into an intersection, defendant hit a car driven by plaintiff.[1] Defendant told the traffic collision investigator, Linda Villelli (Villelli), that when he entered the intersection the light was yellow and he believed he could make it through before the light turned red. An eyewitness, Kathryn Napoli (Napoli), told Villelli defendant ran the red light. A few weeks after the accident, defendants' insurance company recorded an interview with Napoli who said defendant ran the red light.

Plaintiffs subsequently filed a personal injury action, alleging defendant hit plaintiff after running a red light. According to the complaint, plaintiff suffered injury to his ankle, back, and neck. Plaintiffs alleged plaintiff continues to have pain and will require treatment, and sought general and property damages, medical expenses, loss of use of property and earning capacity, wage loss, and loss of consortium.

Plaintiffs served requests for admissions (requests) on defendants seeking admissions on negligence, causation, and damages. Plaintiffs asked defendants to admit defendant failed to stop at the red light and that the failure was negligent, the actual and legal cause of the accident, and a "substantial factor" causing both the accident and plaintiffs' damages, which included pain, suffering and emotional distress. Defendants were also asked to admit plaintiff was not negligent.

Further, plaintiffs asked defendants to admit that, as a result of the accident, plaintiff was injured and needed medical treatment. Plaintiffs also sought admissions that all treatment was a result of the accident, that all treatment was necessary and

---

1. Defendant Satina Mansourian owned the car defendant was driving.

within the standard of care, and that all medical bills were reasonable. Finally, plaintiffs asked defendants to admit plaintiff lost earnings as a result of the accident. Defendants denied all of these requests.[2]

Defendants retained a medical expert, Robert Baird, M.D., who examined plaintiff and his medical records. He agreed plaintiff fractured his ankle in two places as a result of the accident and the ankle surgery was necessary. In his opinion, plaintiff would have no future problems with his ankle and would not require additional surgery in the future, contrary to the diagnosis of one of plaintiff's doctors. Although Baird agreed plaintiff had suffered a strain or sprain of his neck and back, he disagreed any other neck and back pain were a result of the accident. He did not believe plaintiff's back surgery was necessitated by the accident, and further opined the charges for plaintiff's neck and back surgery were too high.

Defendants filed two supplemental responses to the requests, one on the eve of trial, which repeated all of the past denials.

To prepare for trial, plaintiffs deposed defendant, plaintiff, Villelli, and Napoli as to the issue of liability. Plaintiffs also retained and deposed an accident reconstruction expert. As to causation and damages, plaintiffs deposed three medical experts, an ankle specialist and two spine specialists. Baird's deposition was also taken.

Prior to jury selection and empanelment the parties stipulated to plaintiff's medical bills. A copy of the stipulation is not included in the record and it is not clear from the transcript who generated the bills and the amounts of the bills to which the parties agreed. The parties also stipulated to the amount of plaintiff's lost earnings for the one and a half weeks he was out of work following the accident and for the one week he was off following his ankle surgery.

At trial, plaintiffs called defendant, Napoli, and Villelli on the issue of liability, all of whom testified defendant ran the red light. Napoli testified that when she told Villelli defendant ran the red light, defendant asked, "'I ran the red light?'" She replied, "'Yes you did.'" Defendant did not say anything in reply.

The reports and exhibits prepared by the accident reconstruction expert showing defendant was at fault were used at trial.

Defendants did not offer any expert testimony as to liability nor any evidence on that issue other than defendant's testimony. Defendant testified that as he was approaching the intersection the light was green. As he got closer to the intersection the light turned yellow. Plaintiffs introduced testimony from defendant's deposition that he originally stated he was looking at the road. He later amended his testimony to say he was focused on both the road and the signal.

In the opening statement, defendants' lawyer stated the issue of liability was based on credibility. A witness "said that she saw [defendant] run the red light and, if that's it, that's it. [¶] [Defendant] believes, in his mind, that the light was yellow and he

---

2. Defendants did admit requests about the ownership and the identity of the drivers of the two vehicles involved in the accident.

went through it and that's his testimony. [¶] Now, we could sit there and say, well, there is a witness that said it was red, so just change your testimony, but he's not going to do that. His testimony is he believes he had the yellow light. [¶] If that was a mistake on his part, then that's a mistake on his part, but that's what he believes. He's not going to testify differently."

The jury found defendant was negligent, awarding plaintiff just over $410,000, including approximately $147,000 for medical expenses, not quite $9,000 for lost earnings, and $255,000 for pain and suffering. It also awarded Michelle $30,000 for loss of consortium.

Plaintiffs then filed a motion to recover expenses incurred in proving the facts defendants denied, seeking an award of almost $170,000 in attorney fees and just over $29,000 in costs. They argued defendants did not have a reasonable basis for denying the requests.

The court denied the motion, concluding defendants did have a reasonable basis to deny the requests. As to negligence, the court found denial was proper because defendant reasonably believed he could prevail based on his memory he did not run a red light.

As to causation, although defendants should have admitted plaintiff suffered injury to his ankle, based on Baird's opinion and testimony it was reasonable for them to deny the extent of plaintiff's claimed injuries and the necessity of all of his medical treatment. On that basis, it was also reasonable to deny treatment was within the standard of care. In addition, defendants "for the most part" stipulated to medical damages and lost wages.

Finally, denial of the amount of damages was based on the same rationale as denial of causation. Because defendants believed plaintiff's medical treatment other than for his ankle was not caused by the accident, amounts spent for other treatment were excessive and unreasonable. Further, since defendant did not believe he caused the accident, it was reasonable to deny the amount of damages.

DISCUSSION

1. *Applicable Law*

a. *Purpose of Requests for Admissions*

" 'Requests for admissions ... are primarily aimed at setting at rest a triable issue so that it will not have to be tried.... For this reason, the fact that the request is for the admission of a controversial matter, or one involving complex facts, or calls for an opinion, is of no moment. If the litigant is able to make the admission, the time for making it is during discovery procedures, and not at the trial.' [Citation.]" (*Bloxham v. Saldinger* (2014) 228 Cal.App.4th 729, 752 [175 Cal. Rptr. 3d 650]; see § 2033.010.) In addition, a request may ask a party for a legal conclusion. (§ 2033.010; *Garcia v. Hyster Co.* (1994) 28 Cal.App.4th 724, 733, 735 [34 Cal. Rptr. 2d 283] [request may seek admission party was negligent and negligence was legal cause of damages].)

" '[S]ince requests for admissions are not limited to matters within personal knowledge of the responding party, that party has a duty to make a reasonable investigation of the facts before answering items which do not fall within his personal knowledge. [Citations.]'" (*Wimberly v. Derby Cycle Corp.* (1997) 56 Cal.App.4th 618, 634 [65 Cal. Rptr. 2d 532].)

b. *Award for Failure to Admit Requests for Admissions*

When a party propounds requests for admission of the truth of certain facts and the responding party denies the requests, if the propounding party proves the truth of those facts at trial, he or she may seek an award of the reasonable costs and attorney fees incurred in proving those facts. (§ 2033.420, subd. (a).) The court is required to award those costs and fees unless it finds the party who denied the requests "had reasonable ground to believe [he or she] would prevail on the matter" or "[t]here was other good reason for the failure to admit." (§ 2033.420, subd. (b)(3), (4).) The court's determination of whether costs of proof should be awarded is reviewed for abuse of discretion. (*Laabs v. City of Victorville* (2008) 163 Cal.App.4th 1242, 1275–1276 [78 Cal. Rptr. 3d 372].)

"In evaluating whether a 'good reason' exists for denying a request to admit, 'a court may properly consider whether at the time the denial was made the party making the denial held a reasonably entertained good faith belief that the party would prevail on the issue at trial.' [Citation.]" (*Laabs v. City of Victorville, supra,* 163 Cal.App.4th at p. 1276.)

Plaintiffs must show they spent the amounts claimed to prove the issues defendants should have admitted. (§ 2033.420, subd. (a); *Garcia v Hyster Co., supra,* 28 Cal.App.4th at p. 737 [declaration setting out attorney's hourly fees and costs of proof required].) The requested amounts must be segregated from costs and fees expended to prove other issues. (See *Wimberly v. Derby Cycle Corp., supra,* 56 Cal.App.4th at p. 638; *Brooks v. American Broadcasting Co.* (1986) 179 Cal.App.3d 500, 512 [224 Cal. Rptr. 838].)

Costs of proof are recoverable only where the moving party actually proves the matters that are the subject of the requests. (§ 2033.420, subd. (a).) This means evidence must be introduced. (See Evid. Code, § 190 [definition of proof]; Weil & Brown, Cal. Practice Guide: Civil Procedure Before Trial (The Rutter Group 2015) ¶ 8:1405.3, p. 8G-35.) Further, those amounts cannot be awarded if the parties stipulated to facts, even if the responding party had previously denied them. (*Stull v. Sparrow* (2001) 92 Cal.App.4th 860, 867–868 [112 Cal. Rptr. 2d 239]; *Wagy v. Brown* (1994) 24 Cal.App.4th 1, 6 [29 Cal. Rptr. 2d 48] ["Expenses are recoverable only where the party requesting the admission 'proves ... the truth of that matter,' not where that party merely prepares to do so."].) The purpose of requests for admissions is to expedite trial and a stipulation achieves that goal. (*Stull v. Sparrow,* at p. 867.)

2. *Defendants' Denial of the Requests*

a. *Liability*

Defendants denied requests defendant failed to stop at the red light, that this conduct was negligent, and that it was the actual and legal cause of the accident. Defendants relied on defendant's belief he had entered the intersection on a yellow light.

In denying plaintiffs' motion the trial court ruled the denial was proper because defendants reasonably thought they could prevail based on defendant's belief about the color of the light when he entered the intersection. Defendants argue that belief was sufficient to support their denial and the court's finding. We disagree.

There was substantial contrary evidence supporting liability. This included plaintiff's testimony defendant ran the red light, the police report, which found defendant was at fault, Napoli's statement defendant ran the red light,[3] and plaintiffs' accident reconstruction expert who opined defendant was at fault. Moreover, defendants did not designate an expert nor did they depose plaintiffs' expert.

In light of all of this evidence, defendant's belief, however firmly held, was not reasonable. The question is not whether defendant reasonably believed he did not run the red light but whether he reasonably believed he would prevail on that issue at trial. In light of the substantial evidence defendant ran the red light, it was not reasonable for him to believe he would. We do not quarrel with the general proposition defendants cite that the testimony of even one credible witness can be substantial evidence. But, again, that is not the issue.

In *Wimberly v. Derby Cycle Corp., supra*, 56 Cal.App.4th 618, the trial court denied the plaintiff's motion for costs of proof. The Court of Appeal reversed, ruling that at the time the defendant denied the requests regarding a product defect and causation, it had no reasonable basis to believe it could prevail on those issues at trial. (*Id.* at p. 638.) It failed to designate its own expert and should have known it would be unable to use certain deposition testimony of the plaintiff's expert. In short, the defendant produced no evidence to support its position. This was not a sufficient basis to deny the requests.

The trial court here distinguished *Wimberly*, noting defendants did offer evidence as to liability, i.e., defendant's testimony. Thus, it held *Wimberly* did not apply. Defendants, too, take issue with *Wimberly*, arguing they should not be required to present expert testimony to substantiate defendant's version of the accident to avoid being liable for costs of proof.

But neither *Wimberly* nor any other case the parties cited absolutely require expert testimony. Nevertheless defendants did have a duty to investigate. (See *Bloxham v. Saldinger, supra*, 228 Cal.App.4th at p. 752 [cost of proof award proper when responding party who fails to investigate denies requests for lack of information and belief].) And the mere fact defendants presented evidence at trial is not an automatic justification for denial of the requests. Rather, the issue is whether, in light of that evidence, defendants could reasonably believe they would prevail. * * *

---

3. Defendants note Napoli's statement was unsworn and not admitted into evidence. That is not the point. What matters is that defendants knew of the contents of the statement at the time they denied the requests. Likewise, that the police report is hearsay is of no moment. The issue is the extent of defendants' knowledge of the substantial evidence he ran the red light, and, but for his perception, the lack of evidence supporting his position.

Defendants contend a party's "mere refusal to concede an issue" and requiring the opposing party to prove it should not be a sufficient basis for a costs of proof award. The statute states otherwise. Obviously, a defendant "cannot be forced to admit the fact prior to trial despite its obvious truth. [Citation.]" (*Smith v. Circle P Ranch Co.* (1978) 87 Cal.App.3d 267, 273 [150 Cal. Rptr. 828].) But the failure to do so comes with consequences, exposure to a costs of proof award.

The purpose of requests for admissions is to expedite trial by "setting at rest a triable issue so that it will not have to be tried." (*Cembrook v. Superior Court* (1961) 56 Cal.2d 423, 429 [15 Cal. Rptr. 127, 364 P.2d 303]; see *Bloxham v. Saldinger, supra*, 228 Cal.App.4th at p. 752.) If there was no reasonable basis to deny the requests, as was the case as to liability here, then that is exactly why an award is proper.

Nor are we persuaded by defendants' assertion they did not have to make a "'premature admission[]'" but could wait until trial and even after all the evidence had been admitted to concede liability. This may be correct in some circumstances but here, with the exception of the additional opinion of liability from the accident reconstruction expert, the evidence of liability did not change from the time of the accident until the conclusion of trial.

To justify denial of a request, a party must have a "*reasonable* ground" to believe he would prevail on the issue. (§ 2033.420, subd. (b)(3), italics added; see *Brooks v. American Broadcasting Co., supra*, 179 Cal.App.3d at p. 511 [party must have a "reasonably entertained good faith belief" it will prevail].) That means more than a hope or a roll of the dice. In light of the substantial evidence defendant was at fault, plus defendants' apparent understanding of the weakness of their position, as evidenced in their opening statement, defendants' sole reliance on defendant's perception he entered the intersection on a yellow light was not a reasonable basis to believe they would prevail.

Thus, plaintiffs were entitled to their reasonable costs and attorney fees associated with proving liability and the court erred in denying them.

b. *Causation and Damages*

Plaintiffs sought to have defendants admit the accident caused all of plaintiff's injuries. They also asked defendants to admit all treatment was necessary and all medical bills were reasonable.

The trial court found that, although defendants should have admitted plaintiff's ankle injury, defendants could rely on Baird's opinion and reasonably deny both the extent of plaintiff's injuries and the necessity of all of his medical treatment. The trial court also found defendants generally stipulated to medical damages and lost wages.

In addition the trial court ruled that, other than for plaintiff's ankle, it was reasonable for defendants to deny the reasonableness of treatment and its cost. Finally, because defendants did not believe defendant had caused the accident, they reasonably could deny the amount of damages.

When he testified, Baird agreed plaintiff injured his ankle in the accident, required initial treatment, the surgery, and resulting therapy. He considered the time plaintiff took off to recover from the surgery reasonable. On the basis of their expert's opinion, defendants should have admitted these facts.

We cannot determine from the record, however, whether plaintiffs are entitled to any costs of proof based on the pretrial stipulation to plaintiff's medical bills. If the stipulation included the bills for treatment of the ankle injury listed above, plaintiffs are not entitled to an award for those amounts. (*Stull v. Sparrow, supra*, 92 Cal.App.4th at pp. 867–868.) If not, the trial court shall determine the amount to which they are entitled.

Further, on the basis of the stipulation, plaintiffs are not entitled to recover costs of proof of plaintiff's lost earnings for the time immediately following the accident and after the ankle surgery.

In addition, based on Baird's opinions, it was reasonable for defendants to deny the necessity of future ankle surgery, back surgery, associated costs for and treatments of plaintiff's neck, and for any future lost wages that might result from those surgeries and treatment. Thus, plaintiffs are not entitled to the costs of proof of those items.

DISPOSITION

The order denying an award of costs of proof as to liability, injury to plaintiff's ankle, and the ankle surgery and associated treatment is reversed. The case is remanded for the trial court to determine the amount to which plaintiffs are entitled for proof of liability. If defendants did not stipulate to the amount of medical bills for the initial treatment of the ankle injury and the ankle surgery and follow-up treatment, the trial court shall also determine the amount to which plaintiffs are entitled to prove these issues. In all other respects the order is affirmed. The parties shall bear their own costs on appeal.

Notes and Questions regarding Requests for Admissions

(1) Under former Section 2033, requests for admissions were a dangerous trap for the unwary or slothful because a failure to serve a timely response resulted in automatic admissions. Moreover, a party who missed the response deadline had only 30 days to seek relief if the requesting party served a statutory notice that matters be deemed admitted. This unforgiving scheme was substantially transformed by the 1986 revision of Section 2033 which puts the burden on the requesting party to obtain a court order that the requests be deemed admitted. *See* 1 Hogan & Weber, *California Civil Discovery* § 9.15 (2d ed. 2005 & Supp. 2015).

(2) If a party to whom requests for admission have been directed fails to serve a timely response, the requesting party may move for an order that the matters specified in the requests be deemed admitted, as well as for a monetary sanction. CCP § 2033.280(b). If the delinquent party does not serve a proposed response to the admission requests prior to the hearing on the motion, the trial court must order that the matters be deemed admitted. § 2033.280(c). *See, e.g., St. Mary v. Superior Court*, 223 Cal. App. 4th 762, 167 Cal. Rptr. 3d 517 (2014) (holding trial court erred in granting defendant's motion to deem requests admitted because plaintiff served prior

to the motion hearing a response that substantially complied with the requirements of § 2033.280). The court *must* also impose a monetary sanction on the delinquent party or attorney, even where a proposed response is served before the motion hearing. CCP § 2033.280(c).

(3) If on receipt of a response the party requesting the admission deems an answer to a particular request evasive or incomplete, or an objection without merit or too general, that party may move within 45 days for an order compelling a further response. CCP § 2033.290; *see Cembrook v. Superior Court,* 56 Cal. 2d 423, 15 Cal. Rptr. 127, 364 P.2d 303 (1961) (ruling an objection that a request is for the admission of a controversial matter, or one involving complex facts, or calls for an opinion, is of no moment because such requests are aimed at expediting the trial; an unclear request may be answered by a sworn statement setting forth in detail the reasons why the responding party cannot truthfully admit or deny). If a party fails to obey an order compelling further response to requests for admission, the court may order that the matters involved in the requests be deemed admitted, and impose a monetary sanction. § 2033.290(d) & (e).

(4) Is there any recourse for a party when admissions are deemed admitted for failure of that party to respond? *See Wilcox v. Birtwhistle,* 21 Cal. 4th 973, 90 Cal. Rptr. 2d 260, 987 P.2d 727 (1999) (overturning long-standing interpretations of CCP § 2033(m) [now § 2033.300] and holding that subdivision (m) permits the withdrawal or amendment of admissions deemed admitted for failure to respond, if the admissions were the result of mistake or excusable neglect).

(5) Failure to serve timely responses not only exposes the responding party to a motion that matters be deemed admitted but also operates as a waiver to all objections to the requests, including privilege and work product objections. CCP § 2033.280(a). Relief from this waiver may be obtained by court order on two conditions: (1) the party has served a response in substantial compliance with the statutory requirements before a hearing on a motion to have the matters deemed admitted; and (2) the party can show "mistake, inadvertence, or excusable neglect." § 2033.280(a)(1) & (2).

(6) A party may be permitted to withdraw or amend an admission under Section 2033.300. This provision requires the party seeking relief to show: (1) mistake, inadvertence or excusable neglect; and (2) lack of prejudice to the requesting party. CCP § 2033.300(b); *see New Albertsons, Inc. v. Superior Court,* 168 Cal. App. 4th 1403, 86 Cal. Rptr. 3d 457 (2008) (concluding any doubts in ruling on a motion to withdraw or amend an admission under § 2033.300 must be resolved in favor of the moving party; a trial court's discretion to deny a motion under the statute is limited to circumstances where it is clear that the mistake, inadvertence, or neglect was inexcusable, or where it is clear that the withdrawal or amendment would substantially prejudice the party who obtained the admission in maintaining that party's action or defense on the merits). Does section 2033.300 apply to admissions deemed admitted for failing to respond, or only to admissions contained in an actual response? *See Wilcox v. Birtwhistle, supra,* 21 Cal. 4th at 977–83.

(7) If a party denies the truth of a matter specified in a request for admission and the requesting party later proves the truth of that matter at trial, the requesting party may move the court to recover the attorney fees and other expenses incurred in making that proof. CCP § 2033.420. Section 2033.420 further provides that unless the admission sought was of no substantial importance, the denial or objection had a reasonable basis, or there was some other good reason for the failure to admit, the court must grant this motion. *See, e.g., Grace v. Mansourian,* reproduced *supra; Wimberly v. Derby Cycle Corp.,* 56 Cal. App. 4th 618, 638, 65 Cal. Rptr. 2d 532 (1997) (rulings plaintiff was entitled to recover attorney fees and costs under § 2033.420 because the defendant was not reasonable in denying plaintiff's requests for admissions that the fork assembly on a bicycle was defective and that the defect was the proximate cause of plaintiff's injuries).

(8) May the plaintiff recover her expenses of proof under CCP § 2033.420 where the defendants denied liability for a traffic accident in response to a request for admission, but just before trial defendants filed a statement of the case in which they admitted fault for the accident and the jury subsequently awarded a verdict for plaintiff? *See Stull v. Sparrow,* 92 Cal. App. 4th 860, 112 Cal. Rptr. 2d 239 (2001) (concluding trial court did not abuse its discretion in denying plaintiff's request for reimbursement under § 2033.420 because defendants' stipulation that they would not contest liability obviated the need for plaintiff to produce any proof of that element of her case at trial).

§ 11.04 Enforcement of Discovery Requests

[A] Introductory Note

The sections of the Civil Discovery Act of 1986 providing for specific discovery devices also provide for protective orders, motions to compel, and sanctions. These provisions follow the same general scheme. First, the parties are required to meet and confer to attempt to informally resolve the dispute. If the parties fail to attempt an informal resolution, monetary sanctions are mandatory. CCP §§ 2023.010(i), .020. If the informal negotiation is unsuccessful, the dissatisfied party has 45 days (60 days for oral depositions) to move to compel discovery by court order, with the losing party being subject to mandatory monetary sanctions unless the court finds "substantial justification" for that party's position or other circumstances which would make the imposition of sanctions unjust. §§ 2025.450 & .480, 2030.290 & .300, 2031.300 & .310, 2032.240, 2033.290, & 2034.730; *see Sexton v. Superior Court,* 58 Cal. App. 4th 1403, 68 Cal. Rptr. 2d 708 (1997) (concluding the 45-day time period within which to make a motion to compel discovery is jurisdictional in the sense that its expiration renders the court without authority to rule on the motion other than to deny it); *Carter v. Superior Court,* 218 Cal. App. 3d 994, 267 Cal. Rptr. 290 (1990) (ruling party who missed the 45-day deadline for compelling production of documents under CCP § 2031.310 not barred from requesting that the same documents be brought to a deposition pursuant to CCP § 2025.450). Finally, disobedience of a court order compelling discovery can lead to the imposition of additional sanctions depending on the discovery device involved. §§ 2025.480, 2030.290, 2031.320, & 2032.420.

In addition to the specific statutes for each discovery device, Sections 2023.010–.040 generally addresses sanctions for discovery misuse. This section catalogues common misuses of the discovery process (§ 2023.010) and the sanctions available (§ 2023.030). In addition to monetary sanctions, sections 2023.030(b)–(d) authorizes an issue sanction establishing certain facts in the action; an evidence sanction prohibiting the introduction of certain evidence; a terminating sanction striking a pleading, dismissing an action or rendering default judgment; and a contempt sanction treating the misuse as contempt of court.

The Discovery Act requires, prior to the initiation of a motion to compel, that the moving party declare that he or she has made a serious attempt to obtain "an informal resolution of each issue." CCP §§ 2016.040, 2025.450, 2031.310. The Act requires that counsel undertake a reasonable and good faith attempt to talk the matter over, compare their views, consult, and deliberate. See Townsend v. Superior Court, 61 Cal. App. 4th 1431, 72 Cal. Rptr. 2d 333 (1998) (noting a good faith attempt at informal resolution entails something more than bickering with deponent's counsel at a deposition, and therefore directing the trial court to set aside an order compelling answers to deposition questions).

The level of effort at informal resolution depends on the circumstances. Greater effort may be warranted in a larger, more complex discovery context; more modest effort may suffice in a simpler, more narrowly focused case. See Obregon v. Superior Court, 67 Cal. App. 4th 424, 79 Cal. Rptr. 2d 62 (1998) (discussing the factors relevant to the determination of whether a party has made an adequate attempt at informal resolution, and concluding that the plaintiff should have made greater effort than a single brief letter to defendant after defendant's objections to plaintiff's grossly overbroad interrogatories); Stewart v. Colonial W. Agency, Inc., 87 Cal. App. 4th 1006, 105 Cal. Rptr. 2d 115 (2001) (applying the Obregon meet-and-confer factors and upholding motion to compel deposition answers where the objections were made during a deposition so counsel had an opportunity to discuss the matter face-to-face at the time the discovery dispute arose over a relatively simple issue).

[B] Sanctions

Collisson & Kaplan v. Hartunian

Court of Appeal of California, Second Appellate District
21 Cal. App. 4th 1611, 26 Cal. Rptr. 2d 786 (1994)

MASTERSON, JUSTICE.

Steven Hartunian and Sumitomo Tower, Ltd. ("defendants"), attempted to derail a fast track case through evasive answers to discovery. As a sanction for this conduct, the trial court ordered defendants' answer struck. Defendants appeal from the ensuing default judgment. We affirm the judgment and impose sanctions against defendants and their attorneys for having prosecuted a frivolous appeal.

BACKGROUND

On October 18, 1991, Collisson & Kaplan ("plaintiff") filed a complaint against defendants alleging various causes of action for nonpayment of legal fees. On November 18, 1991, defendants filed a general denial answer and raised 13 affirmative defenses.

On January 21, 1992, plaintiff served defendants with form and special interrogatories. On February 21, 1992, defendants filed verified responses to the form interrogatories. However, contrary to the requirements of Code of Civil Procedure[1] section 2030, subdivision (g) [now § 2030.210], the responses to the special interrogatories were not verified. As to the interrogatories concerning the facts underlying defendants' general denial and affirmative defenses, each defendant repeatedly invoked the stock phrase: "Defendant is compiling the information requested by this interrogatory. Defendant has not finished this compilation. Defendant will provide this information to plaintiff as soon as defendant has finished this compilation."

By letter dated February 21, 1992, plaintiff objected both to the stock phrase quoted above and to the lack of verification of the responses to the special interrogatories. Plaintiff cautioned that if defendants failed to provide appropriate responses by February 26, 1992, it would "make the necessary motion." On February 26, 1992, defendants requested an additional day to respond to plaintiff's letter due to the illness of counsel. Plaintiff agreed, but defendants never responded.

On January 21, 1992, plaintiff served defendants with a demand for the documents. On February 13, 1992, not having received a timely response, plaintiff sent defendants a letter demanding the requested documents. Defendants never responded.

On January 22, 1992, plaintiff served defendants with 46 requests for admissions, many of which dealt with the subject of genuineness of various documents. On February 24, 1992, defendants served their verified responses to these requests. As to all but one of the 46 requests, defendants objected on the ground that the requests were compound and therefore did not comply with section 2033, subdivision (c)(5). The response to the remaining request was left blank. On February 26, 1992, plaintiff sent defendants a letter pursuant to section 2033, subdivision (l), attempting to resolve the impasse. Defendants never responded.

On March 26, 1992, plaintiff filed separate motions to compel the production of documents and further responses to the interrogatories and requests for admissions. At the April 14, 1992 hearing thereon, plaintiff learned for the first time that defendants had filed a cross-complaint nearly five months earlier, which had not been served on plaintiff.[3] The trial court ordered defendants to produce the requested doc-

---

1. Unless otherwise stated, all statutory references are to the Code of Civil Procedure.

3. Rule 1306.1.2 of the Los Angeles Superior Court local rules requires that cross-complaints filed in fast track cases be served within 30 days of filing.

uments by April 30, to admit or deny the receipt of the documents identified in the first 22 requests for admissions by April 24, to meet and confer with regard to the objections to the other 24 were the basis of the motion by April 30. Additionally, the trial court sanctioned defendants in the amount of $1,168.

On April 17, 1992, plaintiff filed a motion to dismiss the cross-complaint due to defendants' failure to timely serve it. That motion was granted on May 6, 1992.

Despite the deadlines set by the trial court for defendants' further response to discovery, defendants did not serve further responses to the requests for admissions and interrogatories until April 28, 1992, and May 8, 1992, respectively. More importantly, defendants continued with their gamesmanship. The bulk of their responses to interrogatories were given from the perspective of Empire Western Investment Corporation, a corporation for which Hartunian served as president and sole shareholder. Empire was not a party to the action.[4] Similarly, in their further responses to the requests for admissions, defendants would admit only that the various exhibits were "genuine cop[ies] of the referenced statement[s] received by Empire Western Investment Corporation."

Upon receiving these responses, plaintiff wrote another letter to defendants. Therein it pointed out that Empire was not a party to the action, and sought an explanation "why [Empire] is the one providing all of the answers in these discovery responses." Defendants' letter reply indicated, inter alia: "The further responses to all discovery were made by [defendants] and verified by Mr. Hartunian. The further responses were not made by Empire. [¶] As you know, Mr. Hartunian contends that Empire (and not [defendants]) was the client with respect to the Sumitomo Tower building matter. Accordingly, Mr. Hartunian phrased the further responses with respect to this matter in terms of the relationship between Empire and your firm."

On July 16, 1992, plaintiff filed a motion requesting that defendants' answer be struck. The motion was made "on the grounds [sic] that Defendants have willfully failed to obey the previous order of this Court entered on or about April 14, 1992." Defendants opposed the motion by arguing that the responses had been made by them, and merely evidenced their legal defense that Empire (rather than defendants) had been plaintiff's client. Defendants also sought sanctions, arguing that plaintiff's motion was frivolous. Plaintiff's motion to strike the answer was granted on August 18, 1992, pursuant to sections 128.5 and 2023 and local rule 1310.

On August 26, 1992, defendants filed a motion for reconsideration. Therein they made the following offer: "In order to eliminate any confusion caused by defendants' further responses, defendants are also willing to serve additional further responses within any time period ordered by this Court." Noticeably absent, however, were proposed further responses. Instead, defendants submitted "samples of additional further responses." The trial court then continued the hearing on the motion to September 29, 1992, so as to provide plaintiff with an opportunity to respond to a declaration belatedly filed by Hartunian.

---

4. Most of defendants' responses began, "Empire is informed and believes...."

It was not until September 21, 1992, eight days before the hearing on the motion for reconsideration, that defendants submitted what they claimed were complete answers to the discovery propounded on them almost eight months earlier. The minute order from the September 29, 1992 hearing states in part as follows:

> "The motion to reconsider is granted. On reconsideration, after review of all declarations and pleadings submitted, the court has concluded that its order of August 18, 1992 striking defendant[s'] answer and entering defendant[s'] default is supported by the record, was correct, and should not be vacated or modified.
>
> "Obtaining discovery from defendant[s] in this case has been like pulling teeth.[5] The discovery history speaks for itself. Defendant[s] did not even try to remedy the situation by submission of proposed supplemental responses until this court so ordered as part of reconsideration of its August 18, 1992 order.
>
> "....
>
> "This court is convinced that while Mr. Hartunian is bent on getting his bills adjusted, he has repeatedly deliberately failed to promptly and fully cooperate with legitimate discovery which ultimately resulted in the court having to vacate the October 5, 1992 trial date."

On October 15, 1992, following a default prove-up, the trial court entered a judgment in favor of plaintiff in the amount of $105,525.90.

ISSUES

On appeal, defendants contend the trial court abused its discretion when it ordered their answer struck because (1) their responses to the requests for admissions were appropriate, (2) this was their "first effort" at drafting responses to discovery, (3) the sole purpose of the sanction was punishment, (4) the sanction was not based on the ground stated in plaintiff's notice of the motion for sanctions, and (5) less severe sanctions were available. * * *

DISCUSSION

1. *Propriety of Defendants' Responses*

Focusing on plaintiff's allegedly compound "and/or" requests for admissions,[7] defendants argue that their responses, couched in terms of what billing statements Empire had received, were appropriate. They say that their responses were proper since

---

5. With all due respect to the able and experienced trial judge, we note that this has to be one of the great judicial understatements of all time.

7. Defendants' objection to the requests for admissions was premised on the form of the requests which, when seeking to establish the genuineness of billing statements, as well as the receipt thereof, were phrased: "[The statement] is a true and correct copy of the statement for fees and costs dated [date of statement] received by Steven Hartunian and/or any entity in which he holds an interest, including but not limited to Sumitomo Tower, Ltd., Empire Investment Corporation and Empire Western Investment Corporation ('YOU') on or about the date it bears."

one of the choices offered by the requests was whether an entity in which Hartunian held an interest (e.g., Empire) had received the billing statements.

We find it hard to believe that defendants make this argument with a straight face. The discovery called for responses by defendants. Empire was not a defendant. Nonetheless, the bulk of the responses began with the phrase "Empire is informed and believes...." The code requirement is not only that the party (not a non-party) respond, but also that the responses be " ... complete and straightforward...." (§ 2033, subd. (f)(1) [now § 2030.220].) The responses made by defendants were the obverse of what the code required. They were evasive and quibbling. More bluntly stated, this was lawyer game playing at its worst.

Defendants' brief on appeal compounds their wrongdoing. For the most part, it engages in semantic exercises, discussing the claimed inherent ambiguity of the phrase "and/or." At worst, the brief contains only verbal games of tic-tac-toe or Ping-Pong, designed to obscure a deliberate indifference to responsibility in discovery. At best (i.e., if defendants are really serious in what they say), it displays a propensity to engage in sophistry worthy of a theologian of the middle ages. Either way, we have no time for such antics. We reject totally defendants' contention that their responses were proper.

2. *"First Effort"*

Defendants next argue that since this was their "first effort" at drafting responses, the trial court should not have resorted to the drastic sanction of striking their answer.

Defendants' characterization of their further responses as being their "first effort" to respond, while literally correct, is nonetheless misleading. The point that defendants fail to acknowledge is that, while this may have been their first effort to respond, it was not plaintiff's first effort at receiving straightforward responses. Defendants chose to ignore the many attempts, both formal and informal, made by plaintiff to secure fair responses from them. Accordingly, we find no abuse of discretion by the trial court.

3. *Punitive Sanctions*

Defendants next assert that, since "no substantial discovery objective existed and the trial court found no prejudice to plaintiff, the imposition of harsh sanctions was therefore entirely punitive and contrary to established law and the purpose and spirit of the Discovery Act."

We note first that the premise of defendants' assertion (i.e., no prejudice to plaintiff) is faulty. It is true that in determining whether to continue the hearing on defendants' motion for reconsideration, the court stated that plaintiff had not suffered prejudice, in the sense of being deprived of factual information about the case. Rather, due to the nature of defendants' responses, plaintiff did not "have a usable answer to discovery," i.e., a response that might be used as an admission of a party. The trial court then acknowledged that plaintiff had been prejudiced since the trial date had been vacated. * * *

What we have here is defendants' persistent refusal to share with plaintiff the facts underlying their denial of liability and their purported affirmative defenses. We also have an approaching trial date scheduled for less than two months after the sanction hearing. On this, we conclude that, "[i]n choosing this sanction, the court was attempting to tailor the sanction to the harm caused by the withheld discovery." [Citation omitted.] * * *

5. *Less Drastic Alternatives*

Defendants next contend that the trial court abused its discretion by "knowingly disregarding the requirement that the court utilize the least severe sanction necessary to achieve the objectives of discovery." An identical argument was rejected by this court in *Do It Urself Moving & Storage, Inc. v. Brown, Leifer, Slatkin & Berns* (1992) 7 Cal. App. 4th 27, [9 Cal. Rptr. 2d 396]. Our comments in that case apply with equal force to the case at bench: "[T]he question before this court is not whether the trial court should have imposed a lesser sanction; rather, the question is whether the trial court abused its discretion by imposing the sanction it chose. Moreover, imposition of a lesser sanction would have permitted [defendants] to benefit from their stalling tactics. The trial court did not abuse its discretion by tailoring the sanction to the particular abuse." (*Id.* at pp. 36–37.)

6. *Sanctions*

* * *

We have the interests of the public and the integrity of our system to protect. Accordingly, on November 18, 1993, we issued an order to show cause why sanctions for filing a frivolous appeal should not be imposed. As noted throughout this opinion, defendants' obstreperous conduct at the trial level has continued on this appeal. With sophistry and semantics, defendants have presented this court with convoluted briefs, containing half-truths concerning the actions of the parties and the trial court. Each of defendants' many arguments was without merit, yet each required a thorough examination of the record so as to resolve the issues presented.

Our Supreme Court has defined a frivolous appeal as one which "is prosecuted for an improper motive—to harass the respondent or delay the effect of an adverse judgment-or when it indisputably has no merit—when any reasonable attorney would agree that the appeal is totally and completely without merit." [Citation omitted.] By bringing this appeal, defendants have violated both of the alternative tests set forth by the Supreme Court. As noted by the court in *Young v. Rosenthal* (1989) 212 Cal. App. 3d 96, 136, [260 Cal. Rptr. 369], when a frivolous appeal is filed, "[o]thers with bona fide disputes, as well as the taxpayers, are prejudiced by the wasteful diversion of an appellate court's limited resources."

With regard to the appropriate amount of sanctions, one court has set forth a conservative estimate of $3,995 to process an average appeal. However, this figure was calculated using statistics from 1987. Surely the cost to process an average appeal has risen since 1987. Moreover, in addition to reimbursing the taxpayers for the cost of processing a frivolous appeal, a proper goal of sanctions is to deter future frivolous litigation. Accordingly, we impose sanctions in the amount of $10,000.

DISPOSITION

The judgment is affirmed. Sanctions in the amount of $10,000 are imposed jointly and severally against appellants Steven Hartunian and Sumitomo Tower, Ltd., as well as their attorneys, David S. Richman, Ginsburg, Stephan, Oringher & Richman, Daniel M. Sklar, Sklar, Levinson & Dornstein. These sanctions shall be payable to the clerk of this court, who is directed to deposit that sum in the state's general fund. The clerk is further directed to send a certified copy of this opinion to the chief trial counsel of the Los Angeles office of the State Bar of California. (Bus. & Prof. Code, § 6086.7, subd.(c).)

Notes and Questions regarding Sanctions

(1) In *Collison & Kaplan v. Hartunian*, reproduced *supra*, the defendants had engaged in repeated discovery obstruction and had been the target of several prior court orders before the terminating sanction was imposed. Can a terminating sanction be the first sanction ordered? *See Ruvalcaba v. Government Emp. Ins. Co.*, 222 Cal. App. 3d 1579, 272 Cal. Rptr. 541 (1990) (holding dismissal of action inappropriate where there was no prior court order directing the plaintiff to comply).

(2) As Professor Hogan explains, the Discovery Commission concluded that a drastic sanction should not be appropriate in the first instance where a party has failed to respond to a discovery demand because that would be a disproportionate punishment. "Accordingly, under the approach taken in the new Discovery Act, an initial failure to provide discovery, whether in the form of no response at all or in the form of an inadequate response, can result in the first instance only in the imposition of the relatively mild 'monetary' sanction." 2 Hogan & Weber, *California Civil Discovery* § 15.4 (2d ed. 2005 & Supp. 2015). The more drastic sanctions are available after the general obligation to participate in discovery has been transformed into a court order. *California Civil Discovery* at § 15.5.

(3) Several appellate decisions have emphasized the need for the trial court to tailor the sanction to fit the misconduct. For example, one court held that for failure to appear at a deposition an issue or evidence sanction would be appropriate, not a terminating sanction. *See McArthur v. Bockman*, 208 Cal. App. 3d 1076, 256 Cal. Rptr. 522 (1989); *see also Estate of Ivy*, 22 Cal. App. 4th 873, 879, 28 Cal. Rptr. 2d 16 (1994) (finding issue sanction appropriate where objections to production of documents were meritless).

For other examples of the imposition of an evidence and an issue sanction tailored to specific discovery misuse, see *Juarez v. Boy Scouts of America, Inc.*, 81 Cal. App. 4th 377, 97 Cal. Rptr. 2d 12 (2000) (ruling plaintiff is prohibited from producing at trial the evidence he repeatedly refused to produce during discovery); *Vallbona v. Springer*, 43 Cal. App. 4th 1525, 1541–1549, 51 Cal. Rptr. 2d 311 (1996) (prohibiting defendants from introducing certain documents into evidence, and certain admissions imposed, where the defendants willfully failed to respond to the plaintiff's request for production of documents); *Pate v. Channel Lumber Co.*, 51 Cal. App. 4th 1447, 59 Cal. Rptr. 2d 919 (1997) (ruling evidence sanction proper where the defendant repeatedly assured the plaintiff that all relevant documentation had been produced and then attempted mid-trial to introduce documents not discovered by plaintiff).

(4) Several recent cases demonstrate that the imposition of case-terminating sanctions may be appropriate where lesser sanctions would not bring about compliance with discovery orders. *See, e.g., Los Defensores, Inc. v. Gomez*, 223 Cal. App. 4th 377, 166 Cal. Rptr. 3d 899 (2014) (upholding entry of default and default judgment in the amount of $691,280 imposed as a sanction where plaintiffs willfully failed to comply with trial court's discovery orders); *Liberty Mut. Fire Ins. Co. v. LcL Administrators, Inc.*, 163 Cal. App. 4th 1093, 78 Cal. Rptr. 3d 200 (2008) (upholding trial court's order striking defendant's answer and cross-complaint where defendant filed evasive answers to interrogatories, and repeatedly ignored meet and confer letters and two orders compelling further responses to interrogatories); *Parker v. Wolters Kluwer United States, Inc.*, 149 Cal. App. 4th 285, 57 Cal. Rtpr. 3d 18 (2007) (ruling trial court did not abuse its discretion in dismissing plaintiff's complaint against defendant employer where previous orders and monetary sanctions failed to bring about compliance with the discovery process); *Lang v. Hochman*, 77 Cal. App. 4th 1225, 92 Cal. Rptr. 2d 322 (2000) (upholding default against defendants and dismissal of defendants' cross-complaint as sanctions for inexcusable failure to comply with three discovery orders, where trial court had progressively sanctioned defendants but defendants still did not produce requested documents); *R.S. Creative, Inc. v. Creative Cotton, Ltd.*, 75 Cal. App. 4th 486, 89 Cal. Rptr. 2d 353 (1999) (affirming dismissal of plaintiff's complaint as sanction for repeated efforts to thwart discovery, including the violation of two discovery orders and deliberate destruction of evidence by deletion of plaintiff's computer files); *TMS, Inc. v. Aihara*, 71 Cal. App. 4th 377, 83 Cal. Rptr. 2d 834 (1999) (concluding defendant's willful disobedience of trial court's order to answer post-judgment interrogatories, designed to secure information to aid in enforcement of a money judgment entered against defendant, justified dismissal of defendant's appeal from that judgment).

(5) Does a trial court have authority to impose sanctions *after* the rendering of a jury verdict for discovery misconduct that occurred before trial? In *Sherman v. Kinetic Concepts, Inc.*, 67 Cal. App. 4th 1152, 79 Cal. Rptr. 2d 641 (1998), following a jury verdict for the defendant in a products liability action, the plaintiffs fortuitously discovered that the defendant had withheld evidence — dozens of undisclosed incident reports showing that the defendant's product frequently malfunctioned causing injuries — requested during pretrial discovery. The trial court denied the plaintiffs' motions for sanctions and for a new trial. The Court of Appeal reversed, and ordered the trial court to grant a new trial and to impose monetary sanctions *at least* in an amount sufficient to compensate the plaintiffs for the cost, including attorney fees, of the first trial. The *Sherman* court, obviously appalled and angered by the defendant's and defense counsel's disgraceful conduct, commented on the defendant's litigation strategy (*Id.* at 1162):

> [The defendant], not the least bit abashed even on appeal, *admits* it had the evidence all the time and withheld it throughout the proceedings because,

in *its* opinion, the reports were irrelevant or cumulative or potentially privileged or otherwise inadmissible. How dare [the defendant] and its attorneys
play judge and jury in the trial court and then come before this court and
argue the propriety of that utterly indefensible conduct!

(6) As the *Collison & Kaplan* court recognized, discovery squabbles can waste
limited court resources and the taxpayers' money. Under CCP §639(e) and 645.1, a
trial court has discretion to appoint a referee to hear discovery motions and to apportion payment of the referee's fees among the parties in any manner the court considers fair and reasonable. *Solorzano v. Superior Court*, 18 Cal. App. 4th 603, 22 Cal.
Rptr. 2nd 401 (1993). In referring discovery disputes to a private referee, the trial
court must consider the financial impact on the parties. *McDonald v. Superior Court*,
22 Cal. App. 4th 364, 27 Cal. Rptr. 2d 310 (1994); *Lu v. Superior Court*, 55 Cal. App.
4th 1264, 64 Cal. Rptr. 2d 561 (1997) (ruling in a complex construction defect action
with a large number of separately represented parties, the trial court has the authority
under CCP §639 to appoint a discovery referee even in the absence of a current discovery dispute).

(7) As the *Collison & Kaplan* case illustrates, lawyer game-playing can frustrate
and anger the court. At what point does that conduct justify the contempt sanction?
In one case, the appellate court held that the trial court had abused its discretion in
ordering a party to serve a jail sentence for discovery abuse. *In re de la Parra*, 184
Cal. App. 3d 139, 228 Cal. Rptr. 864 (1986). The *In re de la Parra* court ruled that
this extreme sanction should be imposed only as a last resort where the court's dignity
has been compromised.

(8) Section 2023.030 authorizes a court to impose discovery sanctions, in appropriate circumstances of misuse, on a party or on an attorney, or on both. Unlike
monetary sanctions against a party, which are based on the party's misuse of the discovery process, monetary sanctions against a party's attorney require a finding that
the attorney advised that conduct. CCP §2023.030(a). In *Ghanooni v. Superior Court*,
20 Cal. App. 4th 256, 24 Cal. Rptr. 2d 501 (1993), for example, the court held that
imposition of monetary sanctions jointly on plaintiff and plaintiff's counsel for plaintiff's refusal to submit to certain X-rays constituted an abuse of discretion where
plaintiff's refusal was not based on advice of her attorney. However, in *Ellis v. Toshiba
America Info. Systems*, 218 Cal. App. 4th 853, 160 Cal. Rptr. 3d 557 (2013), the court
affirmed a sanction of $165,000 imposed (only) on plaintiff's attorney for disobeying
an inspection order and failing to meet and confer, where the discovery dispute arose
during the attorney's request for attorney fees after a class action settlement.

(9) *Court Control of Discovery*. The trial court may exercise control over the scope,
frequency, or extent of use of discovery methods pursuant to a motion for a protective
order when the court determines the discovery sought is unreasonably burdensome,
expensive, or intrusive. CCP §§2017.020, 2019.030. Local delay reduction ("Fast
Track") rules, however, shall not require shorter time periods for discovery than those
authorized under the Civil Discovery Act, CCP §§2016.010–2036.050. Gov. Code
§68616(f).

[C] Appellate Review of Sanctions Orders

Code of Civil Procedure sections 904.1(a)(11)(12) & (b) authorize appellate review of sanction orders in the following circumstances:

(a)(11) From an interlocutory judgment directing payment of monetary sanctions by a party or an attorney for a party if the amount exceeds five thousand dollars ($5,000).

(12) From an order directing payment of monetary sanctions by a party or an attorney for a party if the amount exceeds five thousand dollars ($5,000).

* * *

(b) Sanction orders or judgments of five thousand dollars ($5,000) or less against a party or an attorney for a party may be reviewed on an appeal by that party after entry of final judgment in the main action, or, at the discretion of the court of appeal, may be reviewed upon petition for an extraordinary writ.

These statutory provisions govern the appealability of discovery sanction orders. *See Green v. GTE California, Inc.*, 29 Cal. App. 4th 407, 34 Cal. Rptr. 2d 517 (1994); *Rail-Transport Employees Assn. v. Union Pac. Motor Freight*, 46 Cal. App. 4th 469, 474, 54 Cal. Rptr. 2d 713 (1996) (holding CCP § 904.1(a)(11), (12) and (b) were intended to resolve the controversy concerning the appealability of discovery sanctions; they apply "to all sanction orders in excess of $5,000, including discovery sanctions").

What are the advantages and disadvantages of authorizing an immediate appeal from superior court discovery sanction orders? Of permitting appellate court review of such orders only through the discretionary extraordinary writ procedure? Section 904.1 expressly addresses the appealability of sanctions imposed against a party or attorney. What about sanctions imposed against a nonparty for refusing to answer deposition questions or produce documents? *See Marriage of Lemen*, 113 Cal. App. 3d 769, 170 Cal. Rptr. 642 (1980) (concluding nonparty has an immediate right to appeal).

Chapter 12

Resolution of Cases Before Trial

§ 12.01 Summary Judgment

[A] Introductory Note

California practice employs the motion for summary judgment, which includes a motion for summary adjudication, as a potentially powerful procedural device to probe beneath the pleadings. Pleading motions have limited utility — they accept the facts, or at least the well-pleaded facts, contained in the pleadings as true in testing the sufficiency of claims. Except for novel or badly-pleaded causes of action, a technically skillful pleader will state proper causes of action. Nevertheless, the claim or defenses made to the claim in the pleadings may not be factually substantial enough to warrant a full trial. Summary judgment is the means for weeding out causes of action and defenses that lack merit because they are factually unsupportable. "The purpose of summary judgment is to penetrate evasive language and adept pleading and to ascertain ... the presence or absence of triable issues of fact." *Molko v. Holy Spirit Assn.*, 46 Cal. 3d 1092, 1107, 252 Cal. Rptr. 122, 762 P.2d 46 (1988).

As in the case of its federal rule equivalent (Rule 56, F.R.C.P.), California's motion for summary judgment is extensively regulated by statute. The awkwardly numbered section 437c of the Code of Civil Procedure now takes up almost three pages of an unannotated code book, all in fine print. The statute has been regularly, almost annually, amended, but its principal standards have remained constant:

> (a)(1) Any party may move for summary judgment in any action or proceeding if it is contended that the action has no merit or that there is no defense to the action or proceeding.... (b)(1) The motion shall be supported by affidavits, declarations, admissions, answers to interrogatories, depositions, and matters of which judicial notice shall or may be taken.... (c) The motion for summary judgment shall be granted if all the papers submitted show that there is no triable issue as to any material fact and that the moving party is entitled to a judgment as a matter of law....

The corollary motion for summary adjudication is used to test the merits of one or more specific causes of action, one or more affirmative defenses, one or more claims for damages, or one or more issues of duty. CCP § 437c(f); *see* CCP § 437c(t) (providing for summary adjudication of other issues upon stipulation of the parties). The relationship between the motion for summary judgment and the motion for summary adjudication is roughly equivalent to the relationship between the general demurrer and the motion to strike at the pleading stage.

Historically, the California court treated the motion for summary judgment as a drastic remedy to be used sparingly. This distrust of summary judgment as a means of disposing of litigation prior to trial began to crumble as a result of a trio of 1986 United States Supreme Court decisions. The three cases—*Matsushita Electrical Industrial Co. v. Zenith Radio Corp.*, 475 U.S. 574, 106 S. Ct. 1348, 89 L. Ed. 2d 538 (1986), *Celotex Corp. v. Catrett, 477 U.S. 317, 106 S. Ct. 2548, 91 L. Ed. 2d 265 (1986)*, and *Anderson v. Liberty Lobby, Inc.*, 477 U.S. 242, 106 S. Ct. 2505, 91 L. Ed. 2d 202 (1986)—evidenced a change of attitude to encourage summary judgment in complex litigation (*Matsushita*), to ease the burden on a defending party that contends the party with the burden of proof cannot meet that burden (*Celotex*), and to apply standards of proof and evidentiary review used at trial in directed verdict motions to the summary judgment evidence (*Anderson*). California statutory and case law has reflected this change in attitude.

[1] *Moving Party's Initial Burden*

Pursuant to a trio of recent California Supreme Court decisions, summary judgment practice in California now conforms, largely if not completely, to its federal counterpart under federal Rule 56. *See Saelzler v. Advanced Group 400*, 25 Cal. 4th 763, 107 Cal. Rptr. 2d 617, 23 P.3d 1143 (2001); *Aguilar v. Atlantic Richfield Co.*, 25 Cal. 4th 826, 107 Cal. Rptr. 2d 841, 24 P.3d 493 (2001); *Guz v. Bechtel Nat., Inc.*, 24 Cal. 4th 317, 100 Cal. Rptr. 2d 352, 8 P.3d 1089 (2000). In *Saelzler v. Advanced Group 400, supra*, the Supreme Court described the burden-shifting approach to summary judgment after the 1992 and 1993 amendments to CCP § 473c as follows:

> Under the current version of the summary judgment statute, a moving defendant need not support his motion with affirmative evidence negating an essential element of the responding party's case. Instead, the moving defendant may ... point to *the absence of evidence to support the plaintiff's case.* When that is done, the burden shifts to the plaintiff to present evidence showing there is a triable issue of material fact. If the plaintiff is unable to meet her burden of proof regarding an essential element of her case, all other facts are rendered immaterial.

Saelzler, supra, 25 Cal. 4th at 780–81(*quoting Leslie G. v. Perry & Associates*, 43 Cal. App. 4th 472, 482, 50 Cal. Rptr. 2d 785 (1996) (italics in original).

[2] *California's Burden-Shifting Approach*

Subsequently, in *Aguilar v. Atlantic Richfield, supra*, the Supreme Court again endorsed the burden-shifting approach to summary judgment described in *Saelzler*. *Aguilar, supra*, 25 Cal. 4th at 849–51. However, the *Aguilar* court further explained that the summary judgment law in California now conforms "largely but not completely" to its federal counterpart:

> [S]ummary judgment law in this state [no] longer require[s] a defendant moving for summary judgment to conclusively negate an element of the plaintiff's cause of action. In this particular too, it now accords with federal

law. All that the defendant need do is to "show[] that one or more elements of the cause of action ... cannot be established" by the plaintiff. (Code Civ. Proc., §437c, subd. (o)(2).) In other words, all that the defendant need do is to show that the plaintiff cannot establish at least one element of the cause of action—for example, that the plaintiff cannot prove element X. Although he remains free to do so, the defendant need not himself conclusively negate any such element—for example, himself prove *not X*. This is in line with the purpose of the 1992 and 1993 amendments, which was to liberalize the granting of motions for summary judgment. * * * The defendant has shown that the plaintiff cannot establish at least one element of the cause of action by showing that the plaintiff does not possess, and cannot reasonably obtain, needed evidence: The defendant must show that the plaintiff *does not possess* needed evidence, because otherwise the plaintiff might be able to establish the elements of the cause of action; the defendant must also show that the plaintiff *cannot reasonably obtain* needed evidence, because the plaintiff must be allowed a reasonable opportunity to oppose the motion (Code Civ. Proc., §437c, subd. (h)). * * *

Summary judgment law in this state, however, continues to require a defendant moving for summary judgment to present evidence, and not simply point out that the plaintiff does not possess, and cannot reasonably obtain, needed evidence. In this particular at least, it still diverges from federal law. For the defendant *must* "support[]" the "motion" with evidence including "affidavits, declarations, admissions, answers to interrogatories, depositions, and matters of which judicial notice" must or may "be taken." (Code Civ. Proc., §437c, subd. (b).) The defendant may, but need not, present evidence that conclusively negates an element of the plaintiff's cause of action. The defendant may also present evidence that the plaintiff does not possess, and cannot reasonably obtain, needed evidence—as through admissions by the plaintiff following extensive discovery to the effect that he has discovered nothing. But, as *Fairbank v. Wunderman Cato Johnson* (9th Cir. 2000) 212 F.3d 528 concludes, the defendant *must* indeed present evidence": Whereas, under federal law, "pointing out through argument" (*id*. at p. 532) may be sufficient, under state law, it is not.

Aguilar, supra, 25 Cal. 4th at 853–55. How significant is this difference between requiring a moving defendant to "present evidence" as opposed to "simply pointing out through argument," identified by the *Aguilar* court? For a discussion of this question, as well as a review of California summary judgment law after the Supreme Court's decisions in *Aguilar, Saelzler*, and *Guz*, see Glenn S. Koppel, *The California Supreme Court Speaks Out on Summary Judgment in Its Own "Trilogy" of Decisions: Has the Celotex Era Arrived?*, 42 Santa Clara Law Review 483 (2002); *see also Kid's Universe v. In2Labs*, 95 Cal. App. 4th 870, 116 Cal. Rptr. 2d 158 (2002) (discussing the burden of production language in *Aguilar*).

[B]   California Summary Judgment Procedure

The following cases illustrate California's summary judgment procedure in action, and reflect the trend toward liberalized use of the motion.

Gaggero v. Yura

Court of Appeal of California, Second Appellate District
108 Cal. App. 4th 884, 134 Cal. Rptr. 2d 313 (2003)

Mosk, Justice.

Defendant and respondent Anna Marie Yura (Yura) obtained a summary judgment against plaintiff and appellant Stephen M. Gaggero (Gaggero). Gaggero alleged that Yura breached the implied covenant of good faith and fair dealing by refusing to close a real property sales transaction. Gaggero requested, inter alia, specific performance of the real estate sales contract. The trial court held that as a matter of law Gaggero did not fulfill the requirement of being ready, willing and able to purchase the property. Seeking reversal of the summary judgment, Gaggero contends that he raised a triable issue of material fact and further argues that the trial court erred in denying his motion for reconsideration. We hold that Yura did not meet her threshold burden on summary judgment with respect to the issue of Gaggero's financial ability to purchase the property, and that Gaggero raised triable issues of material fact concerning his intent to purchase the property and the existence of an agreement to conditions, covenants, and restrictions to be placed on the property. We therefore reverse the summary judgment.

FACTUAL AND PROCEDURAL BACKGROUND

Frederick Harris (Harris), through a trust of which he was trustee, owned three adjacent parcels of real estate in Santa Monica, California: 938 Pacific Coast Highway (the 938 property), 940 Pacific Coast Highway (the 940 property), and 944 Pacific Coast Highway (the 944 property). Gaggero and Harris entered into negotiations for Gaggero to purchase the 938 property and to obtain a right of first refusal to purchase the 940 and 944 properties.

In August 1998, Gaggero's stepsister Stephanie Ray Boren (Boren) and Harris executed a Purchase and Sale Agreement (the Purchase Agreement) by which the parties agreed that Boren or her assignee would purchase the 938 property. Among its terms, the Purchase Agreement provided that as a condition of closing escrow, the buyer and seller would agree to identical covenants, conditions and restrictions (CC&R's) to be recorded against all three properties. The parties also entered into a Right of First Refusal Agreement with respect to the 940 and 944 properties — an agreement that provided that the rights of first refusal would not become effective until the close of escrow on the 938 property.

Over the next several years, Gaggero and Harris negotiated the CC&R's. Escrow did not close on the 938 property, and in May 2000 Harris died. Yura succeeded Harris as trustee of the Harris trust and refused to proceed with the sale of the 938 property. Gaggero, as Boren's assignee, filed suit against Yura, seeking specific performance of the Purchase Agreement and the Right of First Refusal Agreement. Gaggero also requested a declaratory judgment that he was entitled to have the CC&R's he claimed he and Harris had agreed upon recorded on the properties, to have escrow close on the 938 property, and to enforce the rights of first refusal on the 940 and 944 properties. In addition, Gaggero sought damages for breach of the implied covenant of good faith and fair dealing.

Yura moved the trial court for summary judgment on the grounds that Gaggero did not, and could not, establish that he was ready, willing, and able to perform under the Purchase Agreement and that Gaggero's claims were barred by the statute of frauds. The trial court granted summary judgment on the ground that Gaggero could not establish his readiness, willingness, and ability to perform his obligations under the Purchase Agreement. Gaggero moved for reconsideration of the ruling, but the motion was denied. Judgment was entered in Yura's favor. This appeal followed.

DISCUSSION

I. *Standard of Review*

* * *

A defendant moving for summary judgment meets its burden of showing that there is no merit to a cause of action if that party has shown that one or more elements of the cause of action cannot be established or that there is a complete defense to that cause of action. (Code Civ. Proc., § 437c, subd. (p)(2).) In order to obtain a summary judgment, "all that the defendant need do is to show that the plaintiff cannot establish at least one element of the cause of action.... Although he remains free to do so, the defendant need not himself conclusively negate any such element...." (*Aguilar, supra*, 25 Cal.4th at p. 853.) "The defendant has shown that the plaintiff cannot establish at least one element of the cause of action by showing that the plaintiff does not possess, and cannot reasonably obtain, needed evidence: the defendant must show that the plaintiff *does not possess* needed evidence, because otherwise the plaintiff might be able to establish the elements of the cause of action; the defendant must also show that the plaintiff *cannot reasonably obtain* needed evidence, because the plaintiff must be allowed a reasonable opportunity to oppose the motion. (Code Civ. Proc., § 437c, subd. (h).)" (*Id.* at p. 854, fn omitted.)

Once the defendant has made such a showing, the burden shifts to the plaintiff to show that a triable issue of one or more material facts exists as to that cause of action or as to a defense to the cause of action. (*Aguilar, supra*, 25 Cal.4th at p. 849; Code Civ. Proc., § 437c, subd. (p)(2).) If the plaintiff does not make this showing, summary judgment in favor of the defendant is appropriate. If the plaintiff makes such a showing, summary judgment should be denied.

II. *Yura failed to provide evidence that Gaggero could not establish the element of financial ability to perform under the Purchase Agreement.*

* * *

Yura, in her separate statement of undisputed facts—which, in combination with Gaggero's responsive separate statement and the supporting evidence provided by the parties, in this case constitutes the entire factual universe we review in connection with a summary judgment (*Lewis v. County of Sacramento* (2001) 93 Cal. App. 4th 107, 112, [113 Cal. Rptr. 2d 90])—attempts to establish that Gaggero cannot prove the element of financial readiness to perform under the Purchase Agreement. Past and present ability to perform under the Purchase Agreement is a requirement for specific performance and for breach of contract, the foundations of Gaggero's complaint. (*C. Robert Nattress & Associates v. CIDCO* (1986) 184 Cal. App. 3d 55, 64 [229 Cal. Rptr. 33] ["To obtain specific performance, a buyer must prove not only that he was ready, willing and able to perform at the time the contract was entered into but that he continued ready, willing and able to perform at the time suit was filed and during prosecution of the specific performance action"]; *Ersa Grae Corp. v. Fluor Corp.* (1991) 1 Cal.App.4th 613, 624–625 [2 Cal. Rptr. 2d 288] [element of contract breach is that the plaintiff was ready, willing, and able to perform under the contract].)

Yura's separate statement contains the following pertinent allegations of fact: "Gaggero has failed to proffer evidence that (1) he was ready, willing and able to perform under the Residential Purchase Agreement at the time the contract was entered into, and (2) he continued ready, willing and able to perform at the time this suit was filed and during prosecution of this action," and "At deposition, Gaggero refused to answer any questions concerning how he intends to pay for the 938 property." Under *Aguilar, supra,* 25 Cal.4th 826 and Code of Civil Procedure section 437c, this factual showing is insufficient to meet Yura's burden of production to make a prima facie showing that Gaggero cannot establish one or more elements of his causes of action.

Yura's first alleged fact, that Gaggero "has failed to proffer evidence" of his financial ability to purchase the 938 property at all relevant times, does not establish that Gaggero does not possess, and cannot reasonably obtain, such evidence. Yura's showing draws the court's attention to an absence of evidence to support Gaggero's claims, but the Supreme Court in *Aguilar* held that pointing out the absence of evidence to support a plaintiff's claim is insufficient to meet the moving defendant's initial burden of production. The defendant must also produce evidence that the plaintiff cannot reasonably obtain evidence to support his or her claim. *Aguilar, supra,* 25 Cal. 4th at p. 855, fn. 23 [disapproving case law "purportedly allowing a defendant moving for summary judgment simply to 'point[]' out 'an *absence of evidence* to support' an element of the plaintiff's cause of action"].)

Yura's second allegation of fact, that Gaggero refused to testify at his deposition about his financial ability to purchase the 938 property, is also insufficient to satisfy her burden of production. At deposition, Gaggero's attorney objected to questions about his financial condition on privacy grounds and instructed Gaggero not to answer; Gaggero did not answer. Gaggero's objection does not appear to have been well-taken, for Gaggero may not refuse to divulge this specific financial information after putting his ability to purchase the 938 property directly at issue by the allegations in his complaint. (See, e.g., *Harris v. Superior Court* (1992) 3 Cal. App. 4th 661, 665 [4

Cal. Rptr. 2d 564] ["The proponent of discovery of constitutionally protected material has the burden of making a threshold showing that the evidence sought is 'directly relevant' to the claim or defense"]; *Britt v. Superior Court of San Diego County* (1978) 20 Cal.3d 844, 859 [143 Cal. Rptr. 695, 574 P.2d 766] ["When such associational activities are *directly relevant* to the plaintiff's claim, and disclosure of the plaintiff's affiliations is essential to the fair resolution of the lawsuit, a trial court may properly compel such disclosure," but defendant is not entitled to discover private information when "plaintiffs' complaints do not relate to, nor put in issue, any aspect of their private associational conduct"].)

Yura's showing that Gaggero unjustifiably refused to respond to questions at his deposition does not satisfy the burden of production requirement established by *Aguilar.* Yura did not "present evidence that the plaintiff does not possess, and cannot reasonably obtain, needed evidence — as through admissions by the plaintiff following extensive discovery to the effect that he has discovered nothing." (*Aguilar, supra,* 25 Cal.4th at p. 855.) She presented evidence that Gaggero interposed an objection and refused to respond to a question at deposition, incorrectly asserting that financial ability to perform was not an element of his causes of action. Yura did not move to compel a further response. Her counsel stated, "There is no reason in the world that I [would] go file a motion to compel answers." Had Yura obtained an order compelling Gaggero to respond to questions regarding his financial ability to perform under the Purchase Agreement, and had Gaggero then responded to the questions by admitting he had no evidence to support this element of his claims, then Yura would have been able to satisfy her burden of submitting evidence that Gaggero could not establish this element of his claim. (*Ibid.* [moving defendant may satisfy burden by submitting "admissions by the plaintiff following extensive discovery to the effect that he has discovered nothing"]; …) If Gaggero continued to refuse to answer the questions, sanctions — including issue, evidence, or terminating sanctions — could be imposed against him. (Code Civ. Proc., § 2025, subd. (o).)

Yura argues that Gaggero's privacy objection should be treated as the equivalent of the factually devoid interrogatory response in *Union Bank v. Superior Court* (1995) 31 Cal.App.4th 573 [37 Cal. Rptr. 2d 653], thereby shifting the burden from Yura to Gaggero on this basis. In *Union Bank*, in response to an interrogatory requesting all facts that would support a particular element of a claim, the plaintiffs stated that they "believed" that a certain series of events occurred. (*Id.* at p. 578.) This court held that such a response satisfied the defendant's initial burden of establishing that the plaintiffs could not establish an element of their claim. (*Id.* at pp. 590, 592–593.) This case differs significantly from *Union Bank*. When the plaintiffs in *Union Bank* stated mere *beliefs* in response to a question requesting *all facts* supporting an element of their claims, the logical inference was that after discovery they possessed no facts to support that element. (*Id.* at pp. 592–593.) Here, however, no such logical inference of an absence of facts can be drawn from an objection on privacy grounds — even though it was not a proper objection. All we may deduce is that plaintiff erroneously believed that the information sought was protected by his right to privacy—not that he either possessed or did not possess such information.

For summary judgment purposes, a deposition objection and instruction not to answer are not the equivalent of a factually devoid response, and therefore cannot be used to shift the burden from the moving defendant to the plaintiff under Code of Civil Procedure section 437c, subdivision (p)(2).

Because Yura neither presented evidence making a prima facie case that Gaggero did not possess, and reasonably could not obtain, evidence of his financial ability to perform under the Purchase Agreement, nor evidence conclusively negating this element, Yura failed to meet her burden of production and the grant of summary judgment on this basis cannot stand.

III. *Yura is not entitled to summary judgment on her alternative grounds.*

Yura contends, alternatively, that even if the summary judgment cannot be sustained on the issue of Gaggero's failure to demonstrate his financial ability to purchase the 938 property, the two additional grounds on which she moved for summary judgment in the trial court provide an alternative basis for this court to uphold the award of summary judgment. Although Yura presented sufficient evidence to satisfy her burden of persuasion for summary judgment with respect to each issue, Gaggero, in turn, submitted sufficient admissible evidence to establish that a triable issue of material fact existed as to each issue, thereby precluding summary judgment. (Code Civ. Proc., § 437c, subd. (c).)

A. *Yura is not entitled to summary judgment on the ground that Gaggero had not yet decided whether to purchase the 938 property.*

Yura sought summary judgment on the ground that Gaggero could not establish the elements of readiness and willingness to perform under the Purchase Agreement because of evidence that he had not decided whether to purchase the 938 property. This evidence was sufficient to shift the burden to Gaggero. (Code Civ. Proc., § 437c, subd. (p)(2).) In opposition to the summary judgment motion, Gaggero submitted testimony that with respect to ownership of the 938 property, the only question he had not resolved was *how* to take title to the property—not *whether* to take such title. Gaggero declared that he was ready to perform under the Purchase Agreement but that the capacity in which he would take title to the 938 property was to be determined by his attorneys for tax reasons once the escrow closing date was set. This evidence is sufficient to establish the existence of a triable issue of material fact with respect to his readiness and willingness to perform under the Purchase Agreement by purchasing the 938 property. (Code Civ. Proc., § 437c, subd. (p)(2).) Accordingly, the summary judgment cannot be affirmed on this ground. (Code Civ. Proc., § 437c, subd. (c).) * * *

DISPOSITION

The judgment is reversed. Plaintiff shall recover his costs on appeal.

Juge v. County of Sacramento

Court of Appeal of California, Third Appellate District
12 Cal. App. 4th 59, 15 Cal. Rptr. 2d 598 (1993)

SCOTLAND, JUSTICE.

This case involves the pleading and notice requirements of a summary judgment proceeding. We are presented with the question whether the trial court may grant a motion for summary judgment upon a ground of law not explicitly tendered by the moving party, i.e., a ground of law identified by the trial court rather than by the movant, if application of that law to an undisputed material fact put in issue by the parties' separate statements of undisputed material facts is dispositive of a cause of action presented by the pleadings. * * *

FACTS AND PROCEDURAL BACKGROUND

Plaintiff lost control of his bicycle as he rounded the El Manto curve on the American River Bicycle Trail, and crashed into an oncoming bicyclist. The accident rendered plaintiff a quadriplegic.

He brought this action against defendant County of Sacramento, alleging negligence and premises liability. As to defendant's purported negligence, plaintiff alleged that, in designing and constructing the bicycle trail, defendant negligently failed to use design criteria and uniform specifications established by the California Department of Transportation (Caltrans) pursuant to the California Bikeways Act. (Sts. & Hy. Code, §§ 2374–2376.) Specifically, plaintiff alleged that defendant negligently "failed to utilize proper curve radiuses, design standards, warnings and design geometrics," thereby creating a dangerous condition of public property which proximately caused plaintiff's injury. As to premises liability, plaintiff repeated the aforesaid allegations and added that defendant owned the property, created the dangerous condition, and had notice of the danger in time to have corrected it.

Defendant moved for summary judgment on two grounds: its design of the bikeway is protected by design immunity (Gov. Code, § 830.6) and is not subject to the statutory "trap exception" (Gov. Code, § 830.8); and the California Bikeways Act was not in effect when the bicycle trail was designed and does not apply retroactively.

In support of its motion, defendant submitted a statement of material facts which defendant contended were undisputed. (Code Civ. Proc., § 437c, subd. (b).) Among other things, this statement asserted: (1) "At the time of the accident, plaintiff Juge was biking in an easterly direction at a recreational speed of 10 to 12 m.p.h[.], or slower," and (2) "The speed of 13 m.p.h. or less was a safe speed when negotiating the [El Manto] curve, in relation to its radius." Exhibits submitted by defendant included excerpts from a deposition in which plaintiff testified he had been traveling "[n]ominally, between ten and twelve miles an hour," had slowed "quite a bit" for an approaching ranger's truck at an intersection near the El Manto curve, and then increased his speed because he "was really going pretty slow." Defendant also submitted the declaration of another rider who testified that plaintiff did not enter the curve rapidly, and the declaration of traffic engineer Arnold Johnson who stated that "[a] speed of 13 m.p.h. or less is a proper and safe design speed for the [El Manto] curve in relation to its design radius."

In opposition to the motion for summary judgment, plaintiff did not deny he was traveling at a speed of 12 miles per hour or less. As to the design of the El Manto curve, plaintiff submitted the declaration of traffic engineer Allen L. Weber who stated the curve had a radius of 25 feet and a sight distance of 60 feet, whereas Caltrans standards predicated on speeds of 20 miles per hour require a radius of 60 feet and a sight distance of 125 feet.

The trial court granted summary judgment, ruling: "The defendant has negated an essential element of each theory of plaintiff's claim, namely causation. The declaration of Johnson is evidence that the design was adequate, and that no warning was needed, for a cyclist traveling at 13 miles [per hour] or under. The only evidence of the speed of plaintiff is that he was going 12 miles per hour or less. The declaration of Weber does not support the conclusion that the design was inadequate for a 13 mile per hour speed, or that a warning was needed for such a cyclist. Mr. Weber's declaration speaks of a 20 mile [per hour] speed. Any assumption that plaintiff was going faster would not be supported by any evidence."

Plaintiff appealed from the ensuing judgment of dismissal. In the published part of this opinion, we reject plaintiff's contention that, because defendant's moving papers did not explicitly seek summary judgment on the ground that defendant negated the element of causation, the trial court erred in granting summary judgment on this ground. In the unpublished portion of the opinion, we reject plaintiff's claims that the trial court erroneously determined the undisputed evidence established that plaintiff was going 12 miles per hour or less at the time of the accident, and improperly concluded the undisputed evidence established that the design of the El Manto curve was adequate and no warning was needed for a cyclist traveling 13 miles per hour or less.

DISCUSSION

The summary judgment proceeding permits a party to show that material factual claims put in issue by the pleadings are not in dispute and the moving party is entitled to judgment as a matter of law. (*FPI Development, Inc. v. Nakashima* (1991) 231 Cal. App. 3d 367, 381–382 [282 Cal. Rptr. 508].) "The complaint measures the materiality of the facts tendered in a defendant's challenge to the plaintiff's cause of action." (231 Cal. App. 3d at p. 381.) "'The function of the pleadings in a motion for summary judgment is to delimit the scope of the issues [;] the function of the affidavits or declarations is to disclose whether there is any triable issue of fact within the issues delimited by the pleadings.'" (*Ibid.*, quoting *Orange County Air Pollution Control Dist. v. Superior Court* (1972) 27 Cal. App. 3d 109, 113 [103 Cal. Rptr. 410].)

Code of Civil Procedure section 437c sets forth the procedural and substantive requirements for obtaining summary judgment. (Further section references are to the Code of Civil Procedure unless otherwise specified.)

"Any party may move for summary judgment in any action or proceeding if it is *contended* that the action has no merit or that there is no defense thereto...." (§437c, subd. (a), italics added; see also §437c, subd. (f) ["If it is contended that one or more causes of action within an action has no merit or that there is no defense thereto, ... any party may move for summary adjudication as to that cause or causes of action [set out in the pleadings]...."].)

Subdivision (b) of section 437c provides: "The motion shall be supported by affidavits, declarations, admissions, answers to interrogatories, depositions, and matters of which judicial notice shall or may be taken. The supporting papers shall include a separate statement setting forth plainly and concisely all *material* facts which the moving party contends are undisputed. Each of the *material* facts stated shall be followed by a reference to the supporting evidence.... [¶] ... The opposition, where appropriate, shall consist of affidavits, declarations, admissions, answers to interrogatories, depositions, and matters of which judicial notice shall or may be taken. The opposition papers shall include a separate statement which responds to each of the *material* facts contended by the moving party to be undisputed, indicating whether the opposing party agrees or disagrees that those facts are undisputed. The statement also shall set forth plainly and concisely any other *material* facts which the opposing party contends are disputed. Each *material* fact contended by the opposing party to be disputed shall be followed by a reference to the supporting evidence...." (Italics added.)

Next, section 437c, subdivision (c) states that the "motion for summary judgment shall be granted if *all the papers* submitted *show* that there is no triable issue as to any *material* fact and that the moving party is entitled to a judgment as a matter of law." (Italics added.) * * *

Subdivision (b) requires a separate statement of *material* facts which the moving party contends are undisputed, and evidence in support thereof. "[M]ateriality depends on the *issues in the case*; evidence which does not relate to a matter in issue is *immaterial*." (*People v. Hill* (1992) 3 Cal. App. 4th 16, 29 [4 Cal. Rptr. 2d 258], italics in original.) "Materiality, i.e., what matters are in issue, 'is determined mainly by the pleadings, the rules in pleading and the substantive law relating to the particular kind of case. [Citations.]" (*Ibid.*, quoting 1 Witkin, Cal. Evidence (3d ed. 1986) §286, pp. 255–256.) Therefore, in alleging "material facts" which the moving party contends are undisputed, it is incumbent upon the moving party to show the materiality of the facts by identifying, in the summary judgment pleadings, how the undisputed facts apply to specific issues raised by the complaint or answer and how they entitle the moving party to judgment as a matter of law. As has long been recognized, "the *initial duty to define the issues presented by the complaint* [*or answer*] and to challenge them factually *is on the* [*party*] *who seeks a summary judgment*." (*Conn v. National Can Corp.* (1981) 124 Cal. App. 3d 630, 638 [177 Cal. Rptr. 445], italics added; accord *Pultz v. Holgerson* (1986) 184 Cal. App. 3d 1110, 1114 [229 Cal. Rptr. 531].) This duty necessarily encompasses a pleading requirement compelling the moving papers to set forth with specificity (1) the issues tendered by the complaint or answer which are pertinent to the summary judgment motion and (2) each of the grounds of law upon which the moving party is relying in asserting that the action has no merit or there is no defense to the action. * * *

A contrary rule not only would run afoul of a commonsense reading of section 437c as a whole, but also would impose an undue burden on the trial court. As a general rule, a party should not be entitled to summary judgment based on an undisputed material fact dispositive of the action if the party has not identified in the moving papers how said fact is material to the complaint or answer and how it entitles the party to summary judgment as a matter of law. Otherwise, the trial court would have the onerous burden to detect all the issues presented by the complaint and answer and then to search through the allegations of undisputed material facts and identify the legal significance of each fact just in case that significance has been overlooked by the moving party. This is not the duty of a trial court. If a party has an objection to a cause of action or the defense thereto, that party has the obligation to call the matter to the court's attention so the trial judge will have an opportunity to remedy the situation. Moreover, a contrary rule would expose the trial court to having a summary judgment order overturned where the moving party belatedly recognizes the legal significance of an undisputed material fact contained in the moving papers but not brought to the attention of the trial court and raises (via writ petition or on appeal from the ensuing judgment) a claim that the undisputed material fact entitled the moving party to summary judgment as a matter of law. Such a result would be contrary to the general doctrine of waiver.

Accordingly, we conclude that section 437c requires the party seeking summary judgment to state with specificity in its moving papers each of the grounds of law upon which the moving party is relying in contending the action has no merit or there is no defense to the action. If the parties' separate statements of material facts and evidence in support thereof include an undisputed material fact which is dispositive of the action, but the moving party has overlooked the legal significance of that fact and has neglected to cite the applicable ground of law as a basis for summary judgment, the trial court need not address the issue. The court may deny the motion even if the court recognizes the legal significance of the undisputed material fact and knows it would entitle the party to summary judgment if the issue had been explicitly raised in the moving papers.

In this case, the dispositive facts (plaintiff's speed at the time of the accident and the safe design of the curve for use at that speed) were alleged as undisputed material facts in defendant's summary judgment papers and were not contested in plaintiff's opposition papers. However, the legal significance of these undisputed material facts was not set out as a specific contention in support of defendant's claim that plaintiff's cause of action had no merit, i.e., lack of causation was not explicitly tendered by defendant as a ground for granting summary judgment. Defendant referred to these facts only obliquely when stating in its memorandum of points and authorities in support of the motion for summary judgment: "The speed of 13 m.p.h [.], or slower when negotiating the [El Manto] curve, which was more than the speed of plaintiff when he was traveling along the curve, was a proper and safe speed in relation to the curve radius."

Even though defendant did not explicitly tender lack of causation as a basis for granting summary judgment, the trial court recognized the legal significance of the undisputed material facts and granted summary judgment on the ground that defendant had negated the issue of causation.

Plaintiff suggests that, because defendant's moving papers did not seek summary judgment explicitly on the ground that defendant negated the element of causation, the trial court had no power to grant summary judgment on that ground. Plaintiff cites no authority for this contention, and we are not aware of any.

While the trial court may deny a motion for summary judgment because the dispositive ground was not explicitly tendered in the moving papers as required by section 437c, nothing in the summary judgment statute expressly precludes the trial court from granting the motion simply because the operative ground was not expressly raised by the moving party.

Although the moving party's contention that the action has no merit or there is no defense thereto frames the issues for consideration in a summary judgment motion, it is the specification of an undisputed fact as material which, when coupled with the pleadings, establishes the legal significance of the undisputed material fact. (See *FPI Development, Inc., supra*, 231 Cal. App. 3d at pp. 381–382.) Thus, even though the moving party has overlooked the legal significance of a material fact, its existence is nonetheless fatal to the cause of action or defense thereto when the material fact is undisputed and entitles the moving party to judgment as a matter of law.

To require the trial court to close its eyes to an unmeritorious claim simply because the operative ground entitling the moving party to summary judgment was not specifically tendered by that party would elevate form over substance and would be inconsistent with the purpose of the summary judgment statute.

The summary judgment procedure provides the court and parties with a vehicle to weed the judicial system of an unmeritorious case which otherwise would consume scarce judicial resources and burden the parties with the economic and emotional costs of protracted litigation because the lack of merit is not apparent from the face of the complaint or answer. * * *

Consistent with the purpose of the summary judgment statute, we conclude that the trial court has the inherent power to grant summary judgment on a ground not explicitly tendered by the moving party when the parties' separate statements of material facts and the evidence in support thereof demonstrate the absence of a triable issue of material fact put in issue by the pleadings and negate the opponent's claim as a matter of law.

However, when the trial court grants a summary judgment motion on a ground of law not explicitly tendered by the moving party, due process of law requires that the party opposing the motion must be provided an opportunity to respond to the

ground of law identified by the court and must be given a chance to show there is a triable issue of fact material to said ground of law.

Otherwise, a party which could have shown a triable issue of material fact put in issue by the complaint or answer but neglected to do so because the point was not asserted by the moving party as a ground for summary judgment would be deprived unjustly of the chance to demonstrate the existence of a triable issue of material fact which requires the process of trial. Moreover, if the dispositive ground of law was not asserted in the trial court by the moving party and the record fails to establish that the opposing party could not have shown a triable issue of material fact had the ground of law been asserted by the moving party, a reviewing court ordinarily cannot determine if the trial court's decision was correct. (See *Folberg v. Clara G. R. Kinney Co.* (1980) 104 Cal. App. 3d 136, 140 [163 Cal. Rptr. 426] [appellate courts are powerless to sustain a summary judgment on a new theory where the point was not argued in the trial court *and* "the record does not establish that the opposing party could not have shown a triable fact issue had the point been raised...."].)

We imply no view on whether due process requires notification of and an opportunity to respond to the "new" ground of law *prior* to the trial court's ruling on the summary judgment motion. Even if that were the rule, there was no infringement of due process in this case because the record reveals the following: although defendant did not expressly argue summary judgment should be granted because the essential element of causation was negated, the point was advanced, albeit obliquely, in the papers submitted to the court; the trial court gave plaintiff notice that the court intended to grant the motion on the ground defendant had negated the element of causation; and plaintiff had an opportunity to identify triable issues of fact material to said ground but was unable to do so.

Plaintiff's complaint put in issue the element of causation when it pleaded that defendant's negligence in designing and constructing the El Manto curve of the American River Bicycle Trail and defendant's creation of this dangerous condition proximately caused plaintiff's injury suffered from a collision which occurred while plaintiff rode through the El Manto curve and lost control of his bicycle.

Although defendant did not cite lack of causation as a ground for its summary judgment motion, defendant in effect argued the point when it stated in its memorandum of points and authorities in support of the motion for summary judgment: "The speed of 13 m.p.h[.], or slower when negotiating the [El Manto] curve, which was more than the speed of plaintiff when he was traveling along the curve, was a proper and safe speed in relation to the curve radius." In support of this contention, defendant submitted Johnson's declaration that the curve was safe at speeds of 13 miles per hour or less; plaintiff's declaration that he had been riding at a nominal speed between 10 and 12 miles per hour, had slowed "quite a bit" for an approaching ranger's truck at an intersection near the El Manto curve, and then had increased his speed because he "was really going pretty slow"; and the declaration of another rider who testified that plaintiff did not enter the curve rapidly. The supporting papers included a separate statement setting forth plainly and concisely these material facts which defendant contended were undisputed. (§ 437c, subd. (b).)

In opposition to the motion for summary judgment, plaintiff did not deny he was traveling at a speed of 12 miles per hour or less at the time of the accident. Rather, in his response to defendant's separate statement of undisputed facts, plaintiff unsuccessfully objected to the introduction of his deposition testimony "on the grounds that [he] had no speedometer on his bike and he is not qualified as an expert to give an opinion as to speed at the time of the accident." As to safety of the El Manto curve's design, plaintiff submitted the declaration of traffic engineer Allen L. Weber who stated that the El Manto curve had a radius of 25 feet and a sight distance of 60 feet, whereas Caltrans standards predicated on speeds of *20 miles per hour* require a radius of 60 feet and a sight distance of 125 feet.

In reply to plaintiff's opposition, defendant noted that the objection to introduction of plaintiff's deposition testimony had no merit, and argued that plaintiff had not placed in controversy the fact that he was traveling at a speed of 12 miles per hour or less at the time of the accident. Defendant also asserted that plaintiff had failed to controvert defendant's evidence that the curve was designed safely for speeds less than 13 miles per hour.

The trial court informed the parties of its tentative ruling to grant the motion for summary judgment on the ground that defendant negated causation, an essential element of each theory of plaintiff's claim. Oral argument was requested, and a hearing was held.

Plaintiff was given an opportunity to identify triable issues of fact material to the ground relied upon by the trial court. During the hearing, the following colloquy occurred: "THE COURT: … [T]he status of the evidence is that the only evidence of speed is 12 miles an hour or under. And if you can through any of those papers point to me any evidence that says [plaintiff] was going faster, I'd like to hear it now. [¶] [PLAINTIFF'S COUNSEL]: We don't have any." On the issue of expert evidence concerning defective design, the court observed that plaintiff's expert offered an opinion only as to safety at a speed of 20 miles per hour; therefore, plaintiff had not contradicted the opinion of defendant's expert that the turn was not a dangerous condition for someone going 12 miles per hour or less.

Noting that it had discretion to grant plaintiff a continuance to present additional facts in opposition to the motion (§ 437c, subd. (h)), the trial court observed: "I don't see any indication that there's any evidence out there that you [plaintiff's counsel] haven't been able to get to." In response, counsel did not seek a continuance to present additional facts. He simply offered to provide a "clarification" of his expert's opinion. The trial court then affirmed its tentative ruling.

Under these circumstances, the trial court was not barred from granting the summary judgment motion on a ground of law raised by the trial court. * * *

DISPOSITION

The judgment of dismissal is affirmed.

Notes and Questions on Summary Judgment

(1) *Summary Judgment Burdens.* Our principal cases highlight the dispositional nature of summary judgment motions: An unstated prerequisite to the grant of summary judgment is that the motion will entirely dispose of the entire civil action. Since summary judgment motions are meant to be dispositive, they provide great insight into what complaining parties and defending parties must demonstrate in order to prevail. The most difficult burden on summary judgment, like the burden at trial, falls to the party with the burden of persuasion on the claims or issues in controversy. Thus the party with the burden of persuasion (usually the plaintiff), to prevail on its own summary judgment motion, must show that every critical element of a cause of action is established (that there "is no triable issue of fact") *and* that defendant cannot establish any defense to the cause of action. *See generally Montrose Chem. Corp. v. Superior Court*, 6 Cal. 4th 287, 24 Cal. Rptr. 2d 467, 861 P.2d 1153 (1993).

A party without the burden of persuasion (most often a defendant) can prevail on summary judgment by demonstrating plaintiff cannot prove an essential element of its cause of action, *Aguilar v. Atlantic Richfield Co.*, 25 Cal. 4th 826, 107 Cal. Rptr. 2d 841, 24 P.3d 493 (2001); by negating or disproving an essential element of the plaintiff's cause of action, *Aguilar, supra*, 25 Cal. 4th at 853; *Brantley v. Pisaro*, 42 Cal. App. 4th 1592, 50 Cal. Rptr. 2d 431 (1996); or by taking the more difficult route of establishing an undisputed affirmative defense, *Consumer Cause, Inc. v. SmileCare*, 91 Cal. App. 4th 454, 110 Cal. Rptr. 2d 627 (2001) (denying summary judgment because the defendant did not meet its initial burden to show that undisputed facts support each element of its affirmative defense).

(2) *Summary Adjudication.* A motion for summary adjudication will only be granted "if it completely disposes of a cause of action, an affirmative defense, a claim for damages, or an issue of duty." CCP § 437c(f)(1); *see, e.g. Paramount Petroleum Corp. v. Superior Court*, 227 Cal. App. 4th 226, 173 Cal. Rptr. 3d. 518 (2014) (holding trial court erred in granting summary adjudication in favor of plaintiff on liability alone and leaving damages to a later trial); *Linden Partners v. Wilshire Linden Assoc.*, 62 Cal. App. 4th 508, 73 Cal. Rptr. 2d 708 (1998) (ruling a normal and customary contractual performance obligation involved an "issue of duty" within the meaning of § 437c(f), and therefore qualified for summary adjudication treatment); *DeCastro West Chodorow & Burns, Inc. v. Superior Court*, 47 Cal. App. 4th 410, 54 Cal. Rptr. 2d 792 (1996) (concluding § 437c(f) does not permit summary adjudication of a single item of compensatory damage, as distinguished from punitive damages, which does not dispose of an entire cause of action). However, pursuant to a recent amendment to section 437c, a party may move for summary adjudication of a legal issue or claim of damages that does not completely dispose or a cause of action, affirmative defense, or issue of duty where the parties jointly stipulate to the issue to be adjudicated *and* the trial court decides to allow the motion to be filed. CCP § 437c(t) (effective Jan. 1, 2016).

(3) *Burden Shifting and "Factually Devoid" Discovery Responses.* As *Gaggero v. Yura*, reproduced *supra*, indicates, several cases have held that a defendant may rely on "factually devoid" discovery responses to sustain its burden as the moving party on

summary judgment. *See, e.g., Collin v. CalPortland Co.*, 228 Cal. App. 4th 582, 176 Cal. Rptr. 3d 279 (2014) (holding summary judgment appropriate where, in response to interrogatory requesting "all facts" supporting allegation that plaintiff was exposed to defendant's asbestos-containing product, plaintiff failed to provide facts showing exposure to defendant's product); *Union Bank v. Superior Court*, 31 Cal. App. 4th 573, 37 Cal. Rptr. 2d 653 (1995) (finding summary judgment for defendant appropriate where plaintiffs' answer to interrogatory requesting all facts that would support plaintiffs' fraud claim merely stated plaintiffs "believed" defendant had engaged in fraudulent conduct); *McGonnell v. Kaiser Gypsum Co.*, 98 Cal. App. 4th 1098, 120 Cal. Rptr. 2d 23 (2002) (concluding defendant met its summary judgment burden in wrongful death action for occupational exposure to asbestos based on deposition of plaintiffs' decedent showing plaintiffs could not establish causation); *Rio Linda Unified Sch. Dist. v. Superior Court*, 52 Cal. App. 4th 732, 60 Cal. Rptr. 2d 710 (1997) (holding summary judgment for defendant school district was appropriate in a personal injury action because, disregarding the inadmissible hearsay in a deposition to which the defendant objected, the plaintiff produced no evidence that minor plaintiff had in fact fallen from a slide on school property).

The extent to which a defendant may rely on "factually devoid" discovery responses to sustain its summary judgment burden was clarified in *Scheiding v. Dinwiddie Construction Co.*, 69 Cal. App. 4th 64, 81 Cal. Rptr. 2d 360 (1999), a decision quoted with approval by the Supreme Court in *Saelzler v. Advanced Group 400*, 25 Cal. 4th 763, 768, 107 Cal. Rptr. 2d 617, 23 P.3d 1143 (2001). After extensive analysis of the recent amendments to § 437c, the *Scheiding* court concluded that the defendant must "show" from the plaintiff's discovery responses that the only reasonable inference is that there is no further evidence available to oppose the motion. In other words, defendant's initial burden is not met by merely showing that, based on the discovery responses currently in the record, there are no facts to support an essential element of plaintiff's claim. Instead, the defendant must "show" that the discovery questions were directed to an essential element of plaintiff's claim and, based on the plaintiff's discovery answers, the only reasonable inference is that the plaintiff can produce no further evidence to support this essential element. *Scheiding, supra*, 69 Cal. App 4th at 75–84.

(4) *The Summary Judgment Evidence.* Section 437c(b)(1) states that a motion for summary judgment (or summary adjudication) must be supported by "affidavits, declarations, admissions, answers to interrogatories, depositions, and matters of which judicial notice shall or may be taken." According to section 437c(d) affidavits must be made "on personal knowledge, shall set forth admissible evidence, and shall show affirmatively that the affiant is competent to testify to the matters stated in the affidavits or declarations." Thus, the evidence that will be used to show there are no triable issues will come from discovery, both formal and informal, and on occasion from opponent admissions in pleadings or elsewhere.

(a) *Expert Witness Testimony.* As *Juge v. County of Sacramento*, reproduced *supra*, demonstrates, expert witness testimony may be relied on to support or oppose a summary judgment motion. *See, e.g., Zavala v. Arce*, 58 Cal. App. 4th 915, 934–36, 68

Cal. Rptr. 2d 571 (1998) (ruling defendant in a medical malpractice action met his statutory burden by submitting an affidavit of a medical expert that the defendant had acted well within the standard of care, and plaintiff met her burden of showing a triable issue of material fact by submitting a contrary declaration of another medical expert); *St. Mary Med. Ctr. v. Superior Court*, 50 Cal. App. 4th 1531, 58 Cal. Rptr. 2d 182 (1996) (concluding that under proper circumstances, the parties in a summary judgment proceeding should be allowed to depose an expert who supplies an affidavit in support of or in opposition to summary judgment when there is a legitimate question regarding the foundation of the opinion of the expert).

An expert witness' declaration may provide the evidentiary basis for summary judgment, but only where it satisfies the foundational requirements for admissible expert opinion testimony. *See, e.g., Kelly v. Trunk*, 66 Cal. App. 4th 519, 78 Cal. Rptr. 2d 122 (1998) (holding summary judgment improper where it was based on an expert witness' declaration that did not disclose the matter relied upon by the expert in forming the opinion expressed; an opinion unsupported by reasons or explanation did not establish the absence of a material fact issue for trial); *Hanson v. Grode*, 76 Cal. App. 4th 601, 90 Cal. Rptr. 2d 396 (1999) (declining to utilize the *Kelly* court's suggestion that even on summary judgment an expert's declaration must set forth in excruciating detail the factual basis for the opinions stated therein); *Salasguevara v. Wyeth Lab., Inc.*, 222 Cal. App. 3d 379, 271 Cal. Rptr. 780 (1990) (finding a failure to support motion with declarations from qualified expert showing him competent to testify).

(b) *Continuance to Complete Discovery*. Section 473c(h) provides that a motion for summary judgment shall be denied, or a continuance shall be granted, if the non-moving party has not had an opportunity to complete discovery necessary to oppose the motion. Such a continuance is virtually mandated upon a good faith showing by affidavit that a continuance is needed to obtain facts essential to justify opposition to the summary judgment motion. *See, e.g., Bahl v. Bank of America*, 89 Cal. App. 4th 389, 107 Cal. Rptr. 2d 270 (2001) (ruling affiant is not required to show that essential evidence does exist, but only that it may exist); *Frazee v. Seely*, 95 Cal. App. 4th 627, 115 Cal. Rptr. 2d 780 (2002) (holding trial court abused its discretion in denying a continuance where plaintiff was reasonably diligent but had not been able to complete discovery; "the interests at stake are too high to sanction the denial of a continuance without good reason").

However, the request for a continuance may be denied where the requesting party fails to make a good faith showing as to what facts essential to oppose summary judgment may exist and why such facts could not have been discovered sooner. *E.g., Rodriguez v. Oto*, 212 Cal. App. 4th 1020, 151 Cal. Rptr. 3d 667 (2013) (finding no abuse of discretion where plaintiff offered no cogent justification for his extreme tardiness in gathering key evidence); *Kojababian v. Genuine Home Loans, Inc.*, 174 Cal. App. 4th 408, 418–20, 94 Cal. Rptr. 3d 288 (2009) (finding trial court did not abuse its discretion in denying continuance where plaintiff failed to specify information he expected to discover if continuance granted); *Desaigoudar v. Meyercord*, 108 Cal. App. 4th 173, 133 Cal. Rptr. 2d 408 (2003) (concluding trial court properly denied continuance where plaintiffs did not provide an affidavit relating to the possibility that essential facts exist or explaining their reasons for not having the evidence).

(c) *Evidentiary Objections.* In *Reid v. Google, Inc.*, 50 Cal. 4th 512, 533–534, 113 Cal. Rptr. 3d 327, 235 P.3d 988 (2010), the California Supreme Court held that in the summary judgment context a trial court presented with timely evidentiary objections in the proper form must expressly rule on the individual objections, and if it does not the objections are presumed to have been overruled. *Reid v. Google, Inc.*, 50 Cal. 4th 512, 533–534, 113 Cal. Rptr. 3d 327, 235 P.3d 988 (2010); *see Serri v. Santa Clara Univ.*, 226 Cal. App. 4th 830, 172 Cal. Rptr. 3d 732 (2014) (finding that trial court abused its discretion by sustaining all objections in a blanket ruling, but the error was harmless because some evidence properly excluded and the admissible evidence did not create a triable issue of material fact). These objections are not deemed waived and are preserved for appeal. *Reid*, 50 Cal. 4th at 526–532. Written evidentiary objections made before the summary judgment hearing and oral objections made at the hearing are timely and proper under CCP § 437c(b)(5) and (d), so that either method of objection avoids waiver and preserves the objection on appeal. *Reid*, 50 Cal. 4th at 531–32. A recent amendment to section 473c now provides that the trial court need only rule on those objections to evidence it deems material to the disposition of the motion, and objections not ruled on for purposes of the motion are preserved for appellate review. CCP § 473c(q) (effective Jan. 1, 2016). Form and format requirements for presenting written objections are set in Rule 3.1354, Cal. Rules of Ct.

(5) *Summary Judgment Procedure.* Summary judgment motions are permissible 60 days after a general appearance of the party against whom the motion is brought. CCP § 437c(a). Notice of the motion and supporting papers must be served 75 days before the hearing date (subject to extension when service is made by mail); opposition papers must be served 14 days before the hearing; and reply papers five days before the hearing. § 437c(b).

The procedure for supporting and opposing papers is elaborately set out in section 437c(b): there must be separate statements setting forth "plainly and concisely all material facts which the moving party contends are undisputed"; each such fact must be followed by a reference to the supporting evidence. The opposing party must provide a separate statement that responds to each of the moving party's undisputed facts, agreeing or disagreeing with the characterization; it must set forth any other material facts that the opposing party contends are undisputed, along with references to the evidence. If either party has evidentiary objections to the other's summary judgment evidence, they must be made at the hearing or they are waived. CCP § 473c(b)(5). For a detailed explanation of the form and format requirements for motions for summary judgment or summary adjudication, see Rule 3.1350, Cal. Rules of Ct.

(6) What is the consequence of an opposing plaintiff's failure to comply with the statutory requirement of a separate statement? Some courts hold that the proper response in most instances, if the trial court is not prepared to address the merits of a motion in light of the deficient separate statement, is to give the opposing party an opportunity to file a proper separate statement rather than entering judgment against

that party based on its procedural error. *See, e.g., Parkview Villas Assn., Inc. v. State Farm Fire & Cas. Co.*, 133 Cal. App. 4th 1197, 1211–16, 35 Cal. Rptr. 3d 411 (2005) (holding trial court abused its discretion by granting summary judgment without first giving the plaintiff a chance to cure the deficiencies in its separate statement); *Collins v. Hertz Corp.*, 144 Cal. App. 4th 64, 50 Cal. Rptr. 3d 149 (2006) (affirming summary judgment for defendant where trial court struck portions of plaintiffs' new separate statement, effectively leaving defendant's facts undisputed, after the trial court afforded plaintiffs an opportunity to cure defects in their first separate statement but filed another defective separate statement). Other courts conclude that failure to comply with the separate statement requirement is sufficient grounds to grant a summary judgment motion. *See, e.g., Whitehead v. Habig*, 163 Cal. App. 4th 896, 77 Cal. Rptr. 3d 679 (2008); *Kulesa v. Castleberry*, 47 Cal. App. 4th 103, 54 Cal. Rptr. 2d 669 (1996) (concluding a trial court has discretion to grant a summary judgment motion based on the opposing plaintiff's failure to comply with the separate statement requirement, but not until it has considered all the evidence filed in conjunction with the motion and has determined no triable issue of fact exists); *United Community Church v. Garcin*, 231 Cal. App. 3d 327, 282 Cal. Rptr. 368 (1991) (noting that in ruling on a summary judgment motion, evidence not referenced in the separate statement does not exist). Which of these positions represents the better interpretation of CCP §§ 437c(b) & (c)? Why?

Of course, the moving party must establish a prima facie case of entitlement to summary judgment in order to shift the burden to the nonmoving party to file an opposing separate statement. CCP 437c(b)(1); *see Teselle v. McLoughlin*, 173 Cal. App. 4th 156, 168–173, 92 Cal. Rptr. 3d 696 (2009) (holding that because moving party defendant's separate statement did not address a material fact in the complaint and therefore did not shift burden to plaintiff to file an opposing separate statement, the trial court abused its discretion by granting summary judgment on ground that plaintiff filed late opposition statement); *Kojababian v. Genuine Home Loans, Inc.*, 174 Cal. App. 4th 408, 416–418, 94 Cal. Rptr. 3d 288 (2009) (ruling that although it would be an abuse of discretion for a trial court to grant summary judgment based on a failure to file a separate statement when the moving party has not set forth a prima facie showing for summary judgment, defendants here made such a showing and summary judgment was appropriate based on plaintiff's failure to file an opposing separate statement).

(7) May entry of summary judgment for failure of plaintiff to timely file opposition papers, such as a separate statement of disputed material facts, be avoided by the stratagem of filing a last minute request for dismissal without prejudice? *See Cravens v. State Bd. of Equalization*, 52 Cal. App. 4th 253, 60 Cal. Rptr. 2d 436 (1997) (ruling plaintiff cannot avoid summary judgment by requesting dismissal without prejudice the day before the motion hearing); *Mary Morgan, Inc. v. Melzark*, 49 Cal. App. 4th 765, 57 Cal. Rptr. 2d 4 (1996) (concluding plaintiff cannot dismiss case without prejudice after a tentative ruling granting defendant's summary judgment motion); *but see Zapanta v. Universal Care, Inc.*, 107 Cal. App. 4th 1167, 132 Cal. Rptr. 2d 842 (2003) (holding trial court erred in granting a defense motion for summary judgment

where plaintiffs filed a request for dismissal without prejudice one day before their opposition to the motion was due).

(8) Does a plaintiff who failed to timely file a separate statement have any recourse in setting aside the resulting summary judgment entered for defendant? The majority of courts have held that the mandatory "attorney-fault" provision of CCP § 473(b) only empowers a trial court to set aside a "default judgment" and a "dismissal," and does not empower a court to set aside a summary judgment. *See, e.g., Las Vegas Land & Dev. Co., LLC v. Wilkie Way, LLC,* 219 Cal. App. 4th 1086, 162 Cal. Rptr. 3d 391 (2013) (agreeing with the more recent line of cases and ruling that § 473(b) does not apply to summary judgments); *Henderson v. Pacific Gas & Elec. Co,* 187 Cal. App. 4th 215, 113 Cal. Rptr. 3d 692 (2010) (analyzing statutory language and reviewing cases, and concluding that mandatory provision of § 473(b) is inapplicable to summary judgments); *English v. IKON Bus. Solutions, Inc.,* 94 Cal. App. 4th 130, 114 Cal. Rptr. 2d 93 (2001) (concluding § 473 cannot be used to remedy attorney mistakes such as failure to provide sufficient evidence in opposition to a summary judgment motion); *but see Avila v. Chua,* 57 Cal. App. 4th 860, 67 Cal. Rptr. 2d 373 (1997) (ruling the mandatory relief provisions of CCP § 473 required the trial court to set aside the summary judgment entered for defendant, where the plaintiff's attorney submitted an affidavit stating that the failure to timely file the separate statement was due to attorney neglect).

(9) *Renewed Motions.* In *Francois v. Goel,* 35 Cal. 4th 1094, 29 Cal. Rptr. 3d 249, 112 P.3d 636 (2005), the Supreme Court concluded that CCP § 437c(f)(2) and § 1008 prohibit a *party* from making renewed motions for summary judgment not based on new facts or law, but do not limit a *court's* ability to reconsider its previous interim orders on its own motion, so long as it gives the parties notice that it may do so and reasonable opportunity to litigate the question. Likewise, CCP § 437c(f)(2) and § 1008 authorize a *party* to seek reconsideration only based upon new or different facts, circumstances, or law. *See New York Times Co. v. Superior Court,* 135 Cal. App. 4th 206, 37 Cal. Rptr. 3d 338 (2005) (vacating order granting motion for reconsideration of summary judgment because moving party failed to provide satisfactory explanation for failure to obtain new evidence through discovery and present the evidence earlier).

§ 12.02 Default Judgment

[A] Introductory Note

[1] *Generally*

A plaintiff may obtain a judgment by default against a defendant, properly served with a complaint and summons, who fails to timely file an appropriate responsive paper. CCP §§ 585, 586. Likewise, a defendant may obtain a default judgment against another defendant or a plaintiff, properly served with a cross-complaint, who fails to timely file an appropriate responsive paper. CCP §§ 585(e), 587.5. An appropriate responsive paper under CCP § 585 is an answer or demurrer; a notice of motion to strike, notice of motion to transfer, to dismiss for failure to serve within three years, to quash service of summons, or to stay or dismiss for inconvenient forum; a notice of filing writ of mandate as provided for in CCP § 418.10(c); or a petition to compel arbitration.

Occasionally a party may even obtain a default judgment as the result of a court-ordered sanction for willful discovery violations, where the sanction includes the granting of a motion to strike a pleading. *E.g.*, *Greenup v. Rodman*, 42 Cal. 3d 822, 231 Cal. Rptr. 220, 726 P.2d 1295 (1986); *Los Defensores, Inc. v. Gomez*, 223 Cal. App. 4th 377, 166 Cal. Rptr. 3d 899 (2014).

[2]   *Relief Limited to Demand*

Default judgments entered against defendants for failure to timely answer properly served complaints are commonplace. Most such default judgments involve routine procedural issues easily resolved by reference to the appropriate code section. Code of Civil Procedure Section 580, for example, directs that "[t]he relief granted to the plaintiff, if there is no answer, cannot exceed that which he or she shall have demanded in his or her complaint." Section 580 embodies a fundamental due process notice requirement, *Marriage of Lippel*, 51 Cal. 3d 1160, 1166, 276 Cal. Rptr. 290, 801 P.2d 1041 (1990); a default judgment greater than the amount specifically demanded is void as beyond the court's jurisdiction, *Greenup v. Rodman*, *supra*; *Becker v. S.P.V. Construction Co.*, 27 Cal. 3d 489, 165 Cal. Rptr. 825, 612 P.2d 915 (1980).

[3]   *General Procedures*

The procedures utilized to obtain such default judgments are also fairly routine in most cases. After the applicable time specified in the summons for responding to the served complaint has expired, the plaintiff must make written application to the clerk or the court for an entry of default. CCP §§ 585(a)–(c). The plaintiff must complete and file the *Request for Entry of Default* form adopted for use by the Judicial Council of California, Form CIV-100, along with the proof of service and return of the original summons. CCP §§ 585(a)–(c), 417.10–.30; *see Garcia v. Politis*, 192 Cal. App. 4th 1474, 122 Cal. Rptr. 3d 476 (2011) (ruling a party seeking entry of default judgment must apply for all relief sought, including attorney fees, when application is made for entry of default). An application for entry of default must include a declaration stating that a copy of the application has been mailed to the defendant's attorney or the defendant at his or her last known address. CCP § 587.

In an action to recover actual or punitive damages for personal injury or wrongful death, the process of obtaining an entry of default is a little more complex. As illustrated by our principal case, complications may arise in such actions because the plaintiff is statutorily precluded from stating in the complaint the dollar amount of actual and punitive damages demanded. CCP § 425.10(b); Civil Code § 3295(e). Consequently, the plaintiff must serve on the defendant a statement of damages setting forth the nature and amount of damages being sought, before a default may be taken.

CCP § 425.11 (personal injury damages), § 425.115 (punitive damages). This statement should be served a reasonable (usually 30 days) time before entry of defendant's default, and must be served in the same manner as a summons. CCP §§ 425.11(d), 425.115(g).

[B] Entry of Default

Generally speaking, under the procedural scheme set forth in CCP § 585(a)–(c), an "entry of default" is a prerequisite to a "default judgment." These two concepts are often lumped together, but are actually two different steps in the default process. *See, e.g., Rutan v. Summit Sports, Inc.*, 173 Cal. App. 3d 965, 970, 219 Cal. Rptr. 381 (1985) (noting the default and default judgment are separate procedures). When a defendant (or cross-defendant) has not filed the appropriate responsive paper within the prescribed time, the plaintiff (or cross-plaintiff) may request the court clerk to enter the default. Until the time of such entry, the defendant may ordinarily file a belated response without consequence. *See* 6 Witkin, *California Procedure, Proceedings Without Trial* § 134 (5th ed. 2008); Ryan L. Werner, Comment, *What a Difference a Day Makes: The Case for a Strict Approach to Untimely Pleadings*, 16 U.C. Davis L. Rev. 187 (1982). But the entry of default terminates the defendant's right to file an answer or take any other affirmative steps in the litigation until either the default is set aside or a default judgment entered. *See, e.g., Devlin v. Kearney Mesa AMC/Jeep/Renault, Inc.*, 155 Cal. App. 3d 381, 385, 202 Cal. Rptr. 204 (1984) (holding entry of default precluded defendant from participating in subsequent proceedings to determine amount of punitive damages); *Forbes v. Cameron Petroleums, Inc.*, 83 Cal. App. 3d 257, 263, 147 Cal. Rptr. 766 (1978) (ruling a demurrer or answer filed after entry of default was a legal nullity).

[C] Obtaining Default Judgments

After entry of default by the clerk, the plaintiff (or cross-plaintiff) may apply for entry of a default judgment. In some actions, the court clerk has statutory authority to enter the default judgment, CCP § 585(a); but, as discussed below, in most actions only the court has the power to enter this judgment, CCP §§ 585(b) & (c).

[1] Clerk's Judgment

[a] Clerk's Judgment Authorized in Certain Contract Actions

Section 585(a) authorizes the clerk to enter a default judgment only "[i]n an action arising upon contract or judgment for recovery of money or damages," and then only if a defendant has been served other than by publication. The entry of the default judgment by the clerk is purely a ministerial act; the clerk must enter the judgment where the plaintiff's request satisfies the requirements of CCP § 585(a). *Fallon & Co. v. U. S. Overseas Airlines, Inc.*, 194 Cal. App. 2d 546, 15 Cal. Rptr. 354 (1961); *W.A. Rose Co. v. Mun. Court*, 176 Cal. App. 2d 67, 1 Cal. Rptr. 49 (1959) (ruling writ of mandamus properly issued to compel clerk's entry of default judgment).

[b]   Clerk's Judgment May Include Interest and Costs

Section 585(a) empowers the clerk to include in the clerk's judgment interest and costs against the defendant, as well as attorneys' fees where authorized by the contract or by statute if the court by rule has adopted a schedule of attorneys' fees to be allowed. If the attorneys' fees sought are not fixed in amount by the contract or by the court's schedule of fees, or if the amount sought is greater than the schedule permits, the plaintiff must apply to the court for determination of the attorneys' fees. CCP § 585(a). A party seeking costs or attorneys' fees as part of the default judgment must request such costs and attorneys' fees on the *Request to Enter Default* form (CIV-100). CCP § 585(a); Rule 3.1700, Cal. Rules of Ct.

[c]   Authority to Enter Clerk's Judgment Narrowly Construed

Because clerks' judgments are processed without any judicial intervention, the courts strictly construe the statutory provisions which authorize such default judgments. The contract which forms the basis of a clerk's judgment must provide for some definite fixed amount of damages ascertainable from the contract or computable by mathematical calculation from its terms. *Lynch v. Bencini*, 17 Cal. 2d 521, 526, 110 P.2d 662 (1941); *Liberty Loan Corp. v. Petersen*, 24 Cal. App. 3d 915, 918, 101 Cal. Rptr. 395 (1972). The clerk cannot take evidence or exercise discretion to determine the amount of damages. *Lynch, supra*; 17 Cal. 2d at 525; *Liberty Loan, supra*, 24 Cal. App. 3d at 918.

Consequently, for example, the clerk can enter judgment under CCP § 585(a) in an action on an account stated, *e.g.*, *Fallon & Co. v. U. S. Overseas Airlines, Inc.*, 194 Cal. App. 2d 546, 551–52, 15 Cal. Rptr. 354 (1961), or on an open book account, *e.g.*, *Diamond Nat. Corp. v. Golden Empire Builders, Inc.*, 213 Cal. App. 2d 283, 28 Cal. Rptr. 616 (1963); but not in an action requiring any sort of an accounting, *e.g.*, *Crossman v. Vivienda Water Co.*, 136 Cal. 571, 574, 69 P. 220 (1902) (concluding the court must enter default judgment in action for accounting of net proceeds from sales contracts); *Ely v. Gray*, 224 Cal. App. 3d 1257, 274 Cal. Rptr. 536 (1990) (ruling clerk's judgment inappropriate for partnership dissolution and accounting action). Also, the clerk's authority to enter a default judgment may be limited in actions involving multiple causes of action, and in actions involving severally liable defendants where fewer than all have defaulted. *See* CCP §§ 579, 585 (a); 6 Witkin *California Procedure, Proceedings Without Trial* § 135 (5th ed. 2008).

[2]   Court Judgment

In all other cases, where a clerk's judgment is not authorized by CCP § 585(a), a plaintiff must apply to the court for a default judgment. This includes all actions not based on contract or on a judgment, § 585(b); actions based on a contract or a judgment where the damages or the attorneys' fees are not fixed, § 585(a); and all actions where service of the summons was by publication, § 585(c). Why does CCP § 585 require a court judgment, as opposed to a clerk's judgment, in these types of actions?

[3] Procedures for Court's Default Judgment

Section 585, as supplemented by local court rules, specifies the procedure by which a plaintiff may obtain a court's judgment. The plaintiff must apply for the relief demanded in the complaint; and "the court shall hear the evidence offered by the plaintiff, and shall render judgment in plaintiff's favor for that relief, not exceeding the amount stated in the complaint, in the statement required by § 425.11, or in the statement provided for by § 425.115, as appears by the evidence to be just." CCP §§ 585(b) & (c).

[a] Prove-up Hearing

To "prove-up" the default for the court, the plaintiff need only introduce evidence sufficient to establish a prima facie case. *Morehouse v. Wanzo*, 266 Cal. App. 2d 846, 853–54, 72 Cal. Rptr. 607 (1968); *Csordas v. U. S. Tile & Composition Roofers*, 177 Cal. App. 2d 184, 185–86, 2 Cal. Rptr. 133 (1960). Where the complaint states a cause of action and the evidence introduced establishes a prima facie case, the court must enter the default judgment. *Morehouse v. Wanzo, supra; see Johnson v. Stanhiser*, 72 Cal. App. 4th 357, 85 Cal. Rptr. 2d 82 (1999) (holding trial court erroneously applied a preponderance of the evidence standard in determining whether the plaintiff was entitled to an award of damages at a default prove-up hearing). Generally speaking, the defaulting defendant admits the truthfulness of the material allegations of the complaint, making proof of the defendant's liability unnecessary. *City of Los Angeles v. Los Angeles Farming & Milling Co.*, 150 Cal. 647, 649, 89 P. 615 (1907); *Csordas, supra*, 177 Cal. App. 2d at 186. If the complaint properly states a cause of action, the only evidentiary facts necessary at the prove-up hearing are those concerning the damages alleged in the complaint. *See, e.g., Carlsen v. Koivumaki*, 227 Cal. App. 4th 879, 174 Cal. Rptr. 3d 339 (2014); *Kim v. Westmoore Partners, Inc.*, 201 Cal. App. 4th 267, 133 Cal. Rptr. 3d 774 (2011).

[b] Use of Affidavits and Declarations

Although CCP § 585(b) authorizes the court to hold an evidentiary hearing and even utilize a referee or a jury to assess damages, the prove-up hearing is usually an informal proceeding. Section 585(d) authorizes the court to permit the use of affidavits or declarations in lieu of personal testimony so long as the facts stated in the affidavit are within the personal knowledge of the affiant, are stated with particularity, and affirmatively show the affiant's competency to testify. Such use of affidavits or declarations is commonplace, and may even be the preferred prove-up procedure under applicable local court rules. *E.g.*, Local Rule 3.201, Los Angeles Superior Court; Local Rule 2.1.8, San Diego County Superior Court; *see also* Local Rule 384, County of Orange Superior Court; Local Rule 2.34, Sacramento County Superior Court.

[4] Statutory Restrictions on Default Judgments

Various specific statutes impose additional procedural restrictions on the entry of certain default judgments. For example, CCP § 764.010 prohibits entry of a default judgment in a quiet title action unless the court hears evidence of the plaintiff's title and of the claims of any defendants. *See also* CCP § 585(c). CCP § 1088 prohibits the granting of a writ of mandamus or prohibition by default and requires such cases be heard by the court whether or not the adverse party appears. Family Code § 2336 prohibits a default judgment in a dissolution of marriage or legal separation proceeding, and requires proof of the grounds alleged presented to the court by affidavit or personal appearance. *See also* Rules 5.401–5.409, Cal. Rules of Ct. For a discussion of restrictions on default judgments in class actions, *see Kass v. Young*, 67 Cal. App. 3d 100, 136 Cal. Rptr. 469 (1977).

Certain persons are also statutorily protected against judgment by default, regardless of the nature of the action. The most notable such protection is the federal Servicemembers Civil Relief Act, 50 U.S.C. App. § 501 *et seq.*, which generally seeks to prevent the entry of a default judgment against a defendant whose military duty prevents an appearance. 50 U.S.C. App. § 520 (authorizing stay of not less than 90 days, application for additional stay, and appointment of counsel if additional stay refused). Other protected persons include fictitiously named defendants, CCP § 474; and an unwilling plaintiff joined as a defendant under CCP § 382, as in *Estate of Kuebler v. Superior Court*, 81 Cal. App. 3d 500, 504, 146 Cal. Rptr. 481 (1978).

[5] Time Restrictions

[a] Time to Respond

A default or default judgment cannot, of course, be properly entered prior to the expiration of the statutory time within which the defendant has to file an answer or other responsive paper. CCP § 585. In most actions, the summons directs the defendant to file a responsive pleading within 30 days after completion of service of the summons. CCP § 412.20(a)(3); *see also* CCP § 586(a)(1) (30 days within which to respond to amended complaint). Service is deemed complete at the time of delivery in the case of personal service, CCP § 415.10; but is deemed complete later in the case of substituted service or publication. *See, e.g.*, CCP § 415.20 (10th day after mailing when substituted service); § 415.40 (10th day after mailing when service by mail on out-of-state defendant); CCP § 415.50, Gov. Code § 6064 (On 28th day of publication when service by publication). The time to respond may be extended by stipulation, CCP § 1054; although "fast track" rules may restrict such extensions. *See* Rule 3.110(d), Cal. Rules of Ct. CCP § 586 governs the time within which a defendant must file an answer or take other appropriate action when a demurrer, motion to strike, motion to quash, or other responsive pleading has been denied or granted only in part.

[b] Time to Request Default

Section 585 does not impose any time restrictions as to when the plaintiff must request an entry of default and default judgment once the time for the defendant's responsive pleading has expired, although a lengthy delay may result in dismissal for lack of prosecution under CCP §§ 583.410–.420. However, case management rules may require the plaintiff to proceed expeditiously or face possible sanctions.

Pursuant to Rule 3.110, the plaintiff must request entry of default within 10 days after the time for service of a responsive pleading has elapsed, and must obtain a default judgment within 45 days after entry of default. Rule 3.110(g) & (h), Cal. Rules of Ct.

[6] *Default Judgments in Personal Injury and Wrongful Death Actions*

Code of Civil Procedure § 425.10(b) provides that in superior court actions to recover actual or punitive damages for personal injury or wrongful death, the amount sought is *not* to be stated in the complaint. Apparently passed to avoid publicizing inflated claims against individuals and particularly health care providers, section 425.10(b) must be read with section 425.11 that gives a defending party the right at any time to request "a statement setting forth the nature and amount of damages being sought." *See also* CCP § 425.115 (statement preserving right to seek punitive damages). Even if not demanded, the statement must be served on the defendant and filed before a default may be taken. *See, e.g., Schwab v. Rondel Homes, Inc.,* 53 Cal. 3d 428, 280 Cal. Rptr. 83, 808 P.2d 226 (1991) (vacating default judgment for $200,000 because plaintiff did not serve defendant with a § 425.11 statement of damages); *Debbie S. v. Ray,* 16 Cal. App. 4th 193, 19 Cal. Rptr. 2d 814 (1993) (vacating default judgment after defendant failed to appear at trial because plaintiff failed to serve a timely statement of damages before trial as required by § 425.11).

Code of Civil Procedure § 425.11 provides:

(b) When a complaint is filed in an action to recover damages for personal injury or wrongful death, the defendant may at any time request a statement setting forth the nature and amount of damages being sought. The request shall be served upon the plaintiff, who shall serve a responsive statement as to the damages within 15 days. In the event that a response is not served, the defendant, on notice to the plaintiff, may petition the court in which the action is pending to order the plaintiff to serve a responsive statement.

(c) If no request is made for the statement referred to in subdivision (b), the plaintiff shall serve the statement on the defendant before a default may be taken.

(d) The statement referred to in subdivision (b) shall be served in the following manner:

(1) If a party has not appeared in the action, the statement shall be served in the same manner as a summons.

(2) If a party has appeared in the action, the statement shall be served upon the party's attorney, or upon the party if the party has appeared without an attorney, in the manner provided for service of a summons or in the manner provided by Chapter 5 (commencing with Section 1010) of Title 14 of Part 2.

(e) The statement referred to in subdivision (b) may be combined with the statement described in Section 425.115 [Statement of Punitive Damages].

Notes and Questions regarding Statement of Damages and Adequate Notice

(1) *Punitive Damages.* Several statutes now prohibit any statement of the amount of punitive damages sought in a complaint or cross-complaint, *e.g.*, Civil Code § 3295(e), CCP § 425.10(b); and, in the case of medical malpractice actions, prohibit the statement of any claim for punitive damages, CCP § 425.13. CCP § 425.115 and § 585 specify the procedures for service of a statement of punitive damages, in cases where such damages are authorized, prior to entry of a default judgment.

(2) *Time for Service of Statement.* Sections 425.11 and 425.115 require service of a statement of damages before a default may be taken, but do not specify *when* a statement must be served prior to a default in order to satisfy due process. Most courts require service a "reasonable period of time" before a default may be entered, but disagree somewhat on what this means. *See, e.g.*, *Plotitsa v. Superior Court*, 140 Cal. App. 3d 755, 761, 189 Cal. Rptr. 769 (1983) (holding that at least 30 days notice of the damages amount was required before a default may be taken); *California Novelties, Inc. v. Sokoloff*, 6 Cal. App. 4th 936, 7 Cal. Rtpr. 3d 795 (1992) (holding an entry of default only 17 days after service of the statement of damages was reasonable and valid); *Schwab v. Southern Cal. Gas Co.*, 114 Cal. App. 4th 1308, 1323, 8 Cal. Rtpr. 3d 627 (2004) (concluding defendant had reasonable notice when served with statement of damages 15 days prior to entry of default); *Matera v. McLeod*, 145 Cal. App. 4th 44, 51 Cal. Rptr. 3d 331 (2006) (concluding default judgment for $596,305 is void because service of the statement of damages two days before the entry of default was not a reasonable period of time to apprise defendants of their substantial potential liability for purposes of due process).

(3) *Does a complaint which specifies the amount of personal injury or punitive damages in contravention of CCP § 425.10 provide the requisite notice for a default judgment?* In *Uva v. Evans*, 83 Cal. App. 3d 356, 147 Cal. Rptr. 795 (1978), the plaintiff's complaint specifically requested $30,000 general damages for personal injuries, contrary to § 425.10. When defendant failed to answer, the plaintiff obtained a default judgment for that amount without giving notice to the defendant of the amount of the damages sought as required by CCP § 425.11. The defendant sought to invalidate the default judgment on appeal, arguing that the statutory prohibition against specifying the amount of damages in the complaint rendered such specification a nullity for purposes of the notice required by CCP § 580. The Court of Appeal rejected defendant's argument, ruling that § 580 was fully complied with and that defendant suffered no prejudice. *Uva*, 83 Cal. App. 3d at 360–61.

The court reached the same conclusion in *Cummings Med. Corp. v. Occupational Med. Corp.*, 10 Cal. App. 4th 1291, 13 Cal. Rptr. 2d 585 (1992), where it upheld a default judgment entered for the amount of punitive damages alleged in a cross-complaint even though this statement of punitive damages violated Civil Code § 3295(e). The court noted that the defendant could not ignore the statement of punitive damages in the cross-complaint and had other methods available, including motions to strike or sanctions, to remedy the improper statement of punitive damages. *Cummings*, 10 Cal. 4th at 128. Do you agree with the holdings in *Uva* and *Cummings*? Why?

(4) The basic prerequisite of adequate notice of the specific amount of potential liability applies to default judgments in all proceedings and is not limited to personal injury and wrongful death actions.

(a) In *Marriage of Lippel*, 51 Cal. 3d 1160, 276 Cal. Rptr. 290, 801 P.2d 1041 (1990), for example, the Supreme Court held that a default judgment ordering the defendant husband to pay child support violated due process and CCP § 580 where the wife's petition for marital dissolution had not requested child support and no notice of such request was served on the defendant.

(b) In *Becker v. S.P.V. Construction Co.*, 27 Cal. 3d 489, 165 Cal. Rptr. 825, 612 P.2d 915 (1980), the Supreme Court held that the trial court exceeded its authority under § 580 when it entered a default judgment which awarded attorney's fees because the plaintiff's complaint did not contain a demand for such fees in the prayer. *See also Feminist Women's Health Ctr. v. Blythe*, 17 Cal. App. 4th 1543, 1570–71, 22 Cal. Rptr. 2d 184 (1993) (holding award of attorney fees in default judgment improper where such fees not demanded in complaint nor requested as costs in plaintiff's request to enter default).

(c) In *Ely v. Gray*, 224 Cal. App. 3d 1257, 274 Cal. Rptr. 536 (1990), the court voided a default judgment entered against a nonappearing defendant in an action for the dissolution and accounting of two partnerships. The plaintiff had not demanded any amount of damages in the complaint because an action for an accounting may not be maintained if a sum is so specified. The court, by analogy to personal injury actions and § 425.11, held that the defendant must receive a post-complaint and pre-default notice of the amount plaintiff will seek to prove due him if defendant defaults in the accounting action. *Id.* at 1263; *see also Warren v. Warren*, 240 Cal. App. 4th 373, 192 Cal. Rtpr. 3d 693 (2015) (holding that where plaintiff in an accounting action knew what his damages were and defendants did not have access to this information, notice of the amount sought must be given before a default judgment is entered); *but see Cassel v. Sullivan, Roche & Johnson*, 76 Cal. App. 4th 1157, 90 Cal. Rptr. 2d 899 (1999) (disagreeing with *Ely's* analogy to personal injury actions and requirement of pre-default notice because generally the defendant in an accounting action, not the plaintiff, has the information necessary to calculate its potential amount of exposure to liability).

(d) In *Levine v. Smith*, 145 Cal. App. 4th 1131, 52 Cal. Rptr. 3d 197 (2006), the plaintiff in legal malpractice served a complaint seeking damages according to proof and a timely statement of damages for $5.6 million damages. The defendant did not answer, and the superior court entered a default judgment for plaintiff in the amount of $2.5 million. The Court of Appeal held that the default judgment exceeded the demand in the complaint and was therefore void. The court reasoned that the statement of damages could not be used to satisfy the notice requirements of CCP § 580 in an action not involving personal injury or wrongful death. The court in *Electronic Funds Solutions, LLC v. Murphy*, 134 Cal. App. 4th 1161, 36 Cal. Rptr. 3d 663 (2005), reached the same conclusion, where the plaintiff served a statement of damages in an action for misappropriation of trade secrets. *See also Rodriguez v. Nam Min Cho*, 236 Cal. App. 4th 742, 187 Cal. Rptr. 3d 227 (2015) (following *Levine* in a wrongful termination action); *Kim v. Westmoore Partners, Inc.*, 201 Cal. App. 4th 267, 286, 133 Cal. Rtpr. 3d 774 (2011) (suit on promissory notes). Do you agree with the holdings in these cases?

[D]   Problems Caused by Amendments to the Complaint

[1]   Does an Amended Complaint Require Defendant to File an Amended Answer?

Amendments to complaints may involve problems for both plaintiffs and defendants with respect to defaults. For example, assume that the defendant timely files an answer in response to the plaintiff's complaint. The plaintiff then serves an amended complaint on the defendant, and the defendant fails to answer the amended complaint within 30 days as required by CCP § 586(a)(1). If the amended complaint contains a new or changed cause of action not adequately addressed by the original answer, the defendant's timely filed original answer will not preclude plaintiff from obtaining a default judgment under § 586(a)(1) based on the amended complaint. *See, e.g., Gray v. Hall*, 203 Cal. 306, 311–13, 265 P. 246(1928) (concluding trial court erred in entering default judgment where defendant's original answer put into issue the material allegations of plaintiff's amended complaint); *Carrasco v. Croft*, 164 Cal. App. 3d 796, 210 Cal. Rptr. 599 (1985) (ruling trial court erred in entering default judgment where plaintiff's amended complaint alleged no new causes of action against defendants, and defendants' original answer set forth affirmative defenses applicable to the amended complaint). As a practical matter, should you always file an amended answer to an amended complaint? Why?

[2]   Does an Amended Complaint Open the Default?

An amended complaint may also create a related problem for the plaintiff. Assume the plaintiff has properly obtained an entry of default, then files and serves an amended complaint on the defendant. What effect does the amended complaint have on the default? If the complaint is amended as to a matter of substance rather than mere form, the amendment opens the default and no judgment can be properly entered on the default. *Cole v. Roebling Constr. Co.*, 156 Cal. 443, 446–47, 105 P. 255 (1909); *Engenbretson & Co. v. Harrison*, 125Cal. App. 3d 436, 178 Cal. Rptr. 77 (1981). A substantive amendment supersedes the original complaint and must be served on the defendant, and affords the defaulting defendant a new time period within which to file a responsive pleading. *Ford v. Superior Court*, 34 Cal. App. 3d 338, 342–43, 109 Cal. Rptr. 844 (1973). What is the reason for this rule? What constitutes an amendment of substance as opposed to one of form? One which states a new cause of action or a new legal theory? *See Ford v. Superior Court, supra.* One which increases the amount of damages sought? *See Leo v. Dunlop*, 260 Cal. App. 2d 24, 27–28, 66 Cal. Rptr. 888 (1968). One which states a new cause of action but does not change the amount of damages sought? *See Jackson v. Bank of America*, 188 Cal. App. 3d 375, 387–91, 233 Cal. Rptr. 162 (1988). What is the effect of an amended complaint filed after entry of a default judgment based on the original complaint? *See Cole v. Roebling Constr. Co., supra.*

[E]   Res Judicata Effect of Default Judgment

Generally speaking, a judgment by default is res judicata as to all issues properly pleaded in the complaint. *People v. Sims*, 32 Cal. 3d 468, 481, 186 Cal. Rptr. 77, 651 P.2d 321 (1982); *English v. English*, 9 Cal. 2d 358, 70 P.2d 625 (1937). As noted by the court in *Four Star Electric, Inc. v. F&H Construction*, 7 Cal. App. 4th 1375, 1380, 10 Cal. Rptr. 2d 1 (1992), quoting *Mitchell v. Jones*, 172 Cal. App. 2d 580, 586–87, 147 P. 1168 (1959): "[A] default judgment conclusively establishes, between the parties so far as subsequent proceedings on a different cause of action are concerned, the truth of all material allegations contained in the complaint in the first action, and every fact necessary to uphold the default judgment; but such judgment is not conclusive as to any defense or issue which was not raised and is not necessary to uphold the judgment." Does this mean that a default judgment has a collateral estoppel (issue preclusive) as well as a res judicata (claim preclusive) effect? Should it, in light of the fact that no issue was actually litigated by the defendant?

What is the res judicata effect of a default judgment collaterally attacked for lack of jurisdiction? *See Becker v. S.P.V. Constr. Co., supra*, 27 Cal. 3d at 493; *Pennoyer v. Neff*, 95 U.S. 714, 24 L. Ed. 565 (1877). The res judicata effect of default judgments is discussed in more detail in Chapter 8, Preclusive Effects of Prior Judgments, *supra*.

[F]   Default Judgments in Federal Courts

Rule 55 of the Federal Rules of Civil Procedure sets forth procedures generally similar to those of CCP § 585 for entry of a default and a subsequent default judgment in a federal court action. Rule 55(b)(1) authorizes the entry of a default judgment by the clerk "[i]f the plaintiff's claim is for a sum certain or for a sum that can be made certain by computation." How does this authorization for a clerk's judgment differ from that stated in CCP § 585(a)? Rule 55(b)(2) requires application for a default judgment by the court in all other types of cases, as well as in cases where the defendant is a minor or is incompetent or where the defendant has appeared in the action. If the party against whom judgment by default is sought has appeared in the action, Rule 55(b)(2) requires that party be served with written notice of the application for judgment at least 7 days before the hearing on such application. What is the purpose of this notice requirement? How does this federal procedure differ from that set forth in CCP §§ 585(b) & (c) with respect to the court judgments? For a discussion of the differences between state and federal procedures for default judgments by the courts, see *Greenup v. Rodman, supra*, 42 Cal. 3d at 828–29.

Rule 54(c) requires that a default judgment "must not differ in kind from, or exceed in amount, what is demanded in the pleadings." Unlike the California pleading limitation for personal injury actions set forth in CCP § 425.10, the federal rules require a statement of the damages sought in the prayer for relief of all complaints. Rule 8(a), F.R.C.P.

[G]   Relief from Default Judgments

[1]   Introductory Note

A defendant (or cross-defendant), unhappy with a default judgment entered for failure to timely file a responsive paper, often has a myriad of procedural options available for requesting relief. Precisely which option the defendant should select depends on the reason for the default and on how promptly the defendant seeks relief.

[2]   Mandatory Relief Sought Within Six Months Based on Attorney Affidavit of Neglect

Martin Potts & Associates, Inc. v. Corsair, LLC

Court of Appeal of California, Second Appellate District
244 Cal. App. 4th 432, 197 Cal. Rptr. 3d 856 (2016)

Hoffstadt, Justice.

A trial court is required by statute to vacate a default, default judgment, or dismissal that is "in fact" caused by an attorney's "mistake, inadvertence, surprise, or neglect" if the attorney files a sworn affidavit "attesting" to such. (Code Civ. Proc., § 473, subd. (b.).).[1] Must the attorney's affidavit also disclose the reasons for his mistake, inadvertence, surprise, or neglect? We conclude the answer is "no." Although such a statement of reasons will be helpful, and may sometimes be relevant to prove the causal link between the attorney's conduct and the default, default judgment, or dismissal, a statement of reasons is not required. We accordingly affirm the trial court's order setting aside the default and default judgment in this case.

FACTS AND PROCEDURAL BACKGROUND

In 2011, defendant Corsair, LLC (Corsair), was developing a real estate project known as the Gran Plaza Outlets. In December 2011, Corsair hired plaintiff Martin Potts and Associates, Inc. (plaintiff), to provide management services for this project. When Corsair stopped paying plaintiff for those services in August 2013, plaintiff sued Corsair in February 2014 for the outstanding amount owed under theories of (1) account stated, (2) open book, and (3) breach of contract. Corsair never filed a responsive pleading. On March 25, 2014, the trial court entered an order of default

---

1. Unless otherwise indicated, all further statutory references are to the Code of Civil Procedure.

against Corsair. On August 15, 2014, the court entered a default judgment awarding plaintiff $101,760.

On October 1, 2014, Corsair moved to set aside the default and default judgment pursuant to section 473, subdivision (b). As support, Corsair submitted an affidavit from Corsair's managing member and two affidavits from an attorney named Nicholas Klein (Klein). These affidavits stated the following facts: Klein had provided legal representation to Corsair "for over 15 years." Corsair's managing member, who was plaintiff's primary contact at Corsair, had received plaintiff's complaint and other filings in this case. As he had done many times before, the managing member had his assistant forward those documents to Klein. Klein received these documents, but took no action with respect to the lawsuit. Klein admitted that "[i]t was these failures on my part, as counsel for [Corsair] that allowed the Default and Default Judgment to be entered in this matter," and that "my failure to protect the interest of [Corsair], as its counsel, is the sole reason the default was allowed to occur." Klein declined to "discuss the reasons for my failure to act in this matter." Plaintiff opposed Corsair's motion.

The trial court set aside the default and default judgment. The court found that "the default and default judgment ... were caused by ... Klein's mistake, inadvertence, surprise or neglect"—namely, that Klein did not "fil[e] a responsive pleading on behalf of [Corsair]" and did not "advis[e] [Corsair] to file a responsive pleading." The court also ordered Corsair to file a responsive pleading within 30 days, and directed Klein to pay $5,267.83 to plaintiff as "reasonable compensatory legal fees and costs." Plaintiff timely appeals.

DISCUSSION

Plaintiff argues that the trial court erred in setting aside the default and default judgment because (1) section 473, subdivision (b) requires an attorney to explain the reasons behind his "mistake, inadvertence, surprise, or neglect," and (2) Corsair did not provide this explanation or otherwise meet the requirements for relief from default and default judgment. The meaning of section 473, subdivision (b) is a question of statutory interpretation we review de novo. Whether section 473, subdivision (b)'s requirements have been satisfied in any given case is a question we review for substantial evidence where the evidence is disputed and de novo where it is undisputed. (*Carmel, Ltd. v. Tavoussi* (2009) 175 Cal.App.4th 393, 399 [95 Cal. Rptr. 3d 694] (*Carmel*) [disputed facts]; *SJP Limited Partnership v. City of Los Angeles* (2006) 136 Cal.App.4th 511, 516 [39 Cal. Rptr. 3d 55] (*SJP Limited*) [undisputed facts].)

I. *Requirements of Section 473, Subdivision (b)'s Mandatory Relief Provision*

Prior to 1989, section 473, subdivision (b) granted a trial court the discretion to relieve a party "from a judgment, dismissal, order, or other proceeding taken against him" if (1) that action was due to the party's or lawyer's "mistake, inadvertence, surprise, or excusable neglect" and (2) the request for relief was "made within a reasonable time [and] in no case exceeding six months." (§ 473, subd. (b).) In 1988, our Legislature added a second basis for relief under section 473, subdivision (b). As amended further in 1992, this additional provision provides that a "court shall, whenever an application for relief is made no more than six months after entry of judgment, is in proper form, and is accompanied by an attorney's sworn affidavit attesting to his or her mistake, inadvertence, surprise, or neglect, vacate any (1) resulting default entered by the clerk against his or her client, ... or (2) resulting default judgment or dismissal entered against his or her client, unless the court finds that the default or dismissal was not in fact caused by the attorney's mistake, inadvertence, surprise, or neglect." (*Ibid.*)

Thus, section 473, subdivision (b) "contains two distinct provisions for relief from default" (*Even Zohar Construction & Remodeling, Inc. v. Bellaire Townhouses, LLC* (2015) 61 Cal.4th 830, 838 [189 Cal. Rptr. 3d 824, 352 P.3d 391] (*Even Zohar*)) — one makes relief discretionary with the court; the other makes it mandatory. (*Todd v. Thrifty Corp.* (1995) 34 Cal.App.4th 986, 991 [40 Cal. Rptr. 2d 727] (*Todd*).) The two provisions differ in several other respects: (1) the mandatory relief provision is narrower in scope insofar as it is only available for defaults, default judgments, and dismissals, while discretionary relief is available for a broader array of orders (e.g., *Henderson v. Pacific Gas & Electric Co.* (2010) 187 Cal.App.4th 215, 228–229 [113 Cal. Rptr. 3d 692] (*Henderson*) [mandatory relief not available to set aside summary judgment order]; *Leader v. Health Industries of America, Inc.* (2001) 89 Cal.App.4th 603, 620 [107 Cal. Rptr. 2d 489] [listing types of dismissals falling outside the scope of the mandatory relief provision]); (2) the mandatory relief provision is broader in scope insofar as it is available for inexcusable neglect (*Rodrigues v. Superior Court* (2005) 127 Cal.App.4th 1027, 1033 [26 Cal. Rptr. 3d 194] (*Rodrigues*)), while discretionary relief is reserved for "*excusable* neglect" (§ 473, subd. (b), italics added; see *Carmel, supra,* 175 Cal.App.4th at pp. 399–400 [inexcusable attorney misconduct falling short of "total abandonment" not a basis for discretionary relief]); and (3) mandatory relief comes with a price — namely, the duty to pay "reasonable compensatory legal fees and costs to opposing counsel or parties" (§ 473, subd. (b)).

Plaintiff argues that the trial court's duty to grant relief from a default, default judgment, or dismissal under the mandatory relief provision is triggered only when the attorney's affidavit includes the *reasons* for the attorney's "mistake, inadvertence, surprise, or neglect." We reject this argument for several reasons.

To begin, the text of section 473, subdivision (b) does not require an explication of reasons as a prerequisite to mandatory relief. "Statutory analysis begins with the plain language of [a] statute, and if that language is unambiguous, the inquiry ends there" as well. (*KB Home Greater Los Angeles, Inc. v. Superior Court* (2014) 223 Cal.App.4th 1471, 1476 [168 Cal. Rptr. 3d 142].) As noted above, section 473, subdivision (b) makes relief mandatory only if the request for relief "is accompanied by an attorney's sworn affidavit attesting to his or her mistake, inadvertence, surprise, or neglect." (§ 473, subd. (b).) As this text indicates, what must be attested to is the mistake, inadvertence, surprise, or neglect — not the reasons for it. (Accord, *State*

Farm Fire & Casualty Co. v. Pietak (2001) 90 Cal.App.4th 600, 609 [109 Cal. Rptr. 2d 256] (*Pietak* [attorney affidavit must include "admission by counsel for the moving party that his error resulted in the entry of a default or dismissal" or a "real concession of error"].)

Even if we were to go beyond the text of section 473, subdivision (b) and consider its purpose (*Lorenz v. Commercial Acceptance Ins. Co.* (1995) 40 Cal.App.4th 981, 990 [47 Cal. Rptr. 2d 362] (*Lorenz*) [noting how courts may look to our Legislature's intent in construing statutes]), that purpose is served without requiring attorneys to spell out the reasons for their omission. The purpose of section 473, subdivision (b) generally is "to promote the determination of actions on their merits." (*Even Zohar, supra,* 61 Cal.4th at p. 839, citing *Zamora v. Clayborn Contracting Group, Inc.* (2002) 28 Cal.4th 249, 255–256 [121 Cal. Rptr. 2d 187, 47 P.3d 1056].) More specifically, section 473, subdivision (b)'s mandatory relief provision has three purposes: (1) "to relieve the innocent client of the consequences of the attorney's fault" (*Solv-All v. Superior Court* (2005) 131 Cal.App.4th 1003, 1009 [32 Cal. Rptr. 3d 202] (*Solv-All*); see *Generale Bank Nederland v. Eyes of the Beholder Ltd.* (1998) 61 Cal.App.4th 1384, 1397 [72 Cal. Rptr. 2d 188] [noting purpose is "to alleviate the hardship on parties who *lose their day in court* due solely to an inexcusable failure to act on the part of their attorneys"]); (2) "to place the burden on counsel" (*Solv-All,* at p. 1009); and (3) "to discourage additional litigation in the form of malpractice actions by the defaulted client against the errant attorney" (*ibid.*).

These purposes are advanced as long as mandatory relief is confined to situations in which the attorney, rather than the client, is the cause of the default, default judgment, or dismissal. (See *Metropolitan Service Corp. v. Casa de Palms, Ltd.* (1995) 31 Cal.App.4th 1481, 1487 [37 Cal. Rptr. 2d 575] (*Metropolitan Service*) [fault of attorney sufficient]; *SJP Limited, supra,* 136 Cal.App.4th at p. 517 [fault of attorney who is not attorney of record sufficient]; *Hu v. Fang* (2002) 104 Cal.App.4th 61, 64 [127 Cal. Rptr. 2d 756] (*Hu*) [fault of paralegal supervised by attorney sufficient]; cf. *Todd, supra,* 34 Cal.App.4th at pp. 991–992 [fault of client; not sufficient].) In other words, the purpose of the mandatory relief provision under section 473, subdivision (b) is achieved by focusing on *who* is to blame, not *why*.

Indeed, in many cases, the reasons for the attorney's mistake, inadvertence, surprise, or neglect will be irrelevant; that is because, as noted above, the mandatory relief provision entitles a party to relief even when his or her attorney's error is inexcusable. (*Graham v. Beers* (1994) 30 Cal.App.4th 1656, 1660 [36 Cal. Rptr. 2d 765] (*Graham*); *Solv-All, supra,* 131 Cal.App.4th at p. 1010 [attorney's conscious decision not to file an answer is grounds for mandatory relief]; cf. *Jerry's Shell v. Equilon Enterprises, LLC* (2005) 134 Cal.App.4th 1058, 1073–1074 [36 Cal. Rptr. 3d 637] [attorney's strategic decision to err with intent to have client later invoke § 473, subd. (b)'s mandatory relief provision precludes resort to mandatory relief].) We are reluctant to construe section 473, subdivision (b), to require in every case the production of information that will in many cases be of no use in deciding whether to grant relief.

The case law reinforces our reading of the text and purpose of section 473, subdivision (b), because the courts have thus far eschewed any rule making mandatory relief contingent upon a disclosure of reasons. In *Hu, supra,* 104 Cal.App.4th 61, the court disclaimed any requirement that "evidence" beyond the attorney's affidavit is necessary to substantiate the attorney's "mistake, inadvertence, surprise, or neglect." (*Hu,* at p. 65.) And the court in *Graham, supra,* 30 Cal.App.4th 1656 noted the following in dicta: "[C]ounsel need not show that his or her mistake, inadvertence, surprise or neglect was excusable. No reason need be given for the existence of one of these circumstances. Attestation that one of these reasons existed is sufficient to obtain relief, unless the trial court finds that the dismissal did not occur because of these reasons." (*Graham,* at p. 1660); see *Avila v. Chua* (1997) 57 Cal.App.4th 860, 869 [67 Cal. Rptr. 2d 373] [same]; *Yeap v. Leake* (1997) 60 Cal.App.4th 591, 601 [70 Cal. Rptr. 2d 680] (*Yeap*) [same]; see also *Pietak, supra,* 90 Cal.App.4th at p. 609 [noting that mandatory relief is triggered by an "indispensable admission by counsel ... that his error resulted in the entry of default or dismissal"].) The language in these cases is irreconcilable with plaintiff's contention that the reasons for an attorney's error must always be given as a precursor to mandatory relief.

Plaintiff proffers five reasons why the reasons for the attorney's mistake, inadvertence, surprise, or neglect must nevertheless be set forth in the attorney's affidavit before relief under section 473, subdivision (b) becomes mandatory. None is persuasive.

First, plaintiff argues that the mandatory relief provision of section 473, subdivision (b) employs language similar to that used in its discretionary relief provision; thus, plaintiff reasons, we must "presume that the Legislature intended the same construction." (*Estate of Griswold* (2001) 25 Cal.4th 904, 915–916 [108 Cal. Rptr. 2d 165, 24 P.3d 1191].) However, this maxim of statutory construction is inapplicable. By its very terms, the maxim applies when the language of two provisions is the same; as described in detail above, however, the statutory language creating the mandatory and discretionary relief provisions of section 473, subdivision (b) is significantly different. Moreover, this maxim does not apply when "a contrary intent clearly appears." (*Griswold,* at pp. 915–916.) Here, it does. The whole point of creating the mandatory relief provision was to make it easier to set aside a default, default judgment, or other dismissal due to attorney error, and the Legislature did so by supplementing the discretionary relief provision that required a showing of an attorney's "total abandonment" (*Carmel, supra,* 175 Cal.App.4th at pp. 399–400) with a provision that made relief automatic upon a showing of *any* error, excusable or not. Construing the two provisions to mean the same thing would fly in the face of this legislative intent.

Second, plaintiff argues that a requirement that an attorney state his or her reasons is more consistent with "the strong policy favoring the finality of judgments." (*Kulchar v. Kulchar* (1969) 1 Cal.3d 467, 470 [82 Cal. Rptr. 489, 462 P.2d 17].) But the Legislature enacted *both* provisions of section 473, subdivision (b) as an exception to this more general policy and as a means of "promot[ing] the determination of actions on their merits" (*Even Zohar, supra,* 61 Cal.4th at p. 839).

Third, plaintiff asserts that precedent supports its construction of section 473, subdivision (b)'s mandatory relief provision. Plaintiff cites language in *Even Zohar, supra,* 61 Cal.4th 840 stating that "[a]n attorney who candidly and fully acknowledges under oath the errors that have led a client into default will rarely have anything to add in a renewed motion" (*Even Zohar,* at p. 842), and in *Pietak, supra,* 90 Cal.App.4th 600 requiring a "straightforward admission of fault" (*Pietak,* at p. 610). These passages at most demand an attorney's candid, full, and straightforward acknowledgment of his or her error; they do not speak to the reasons for those errors. Plaintiff also cites a number of cases in which a party seeking relief under section 473, subdivision (b) has submitted an attorney affidavit that sets forth the reasons for the attorney's error. However, an attorney's decision in any particular case to offer more information than is statutorily required does not somehow cause that information to be statutorily required. Because none of the cases plaintiff cites holds or, for that matter even comments in passing, that the additional information offered in the attorney affidavit was required by section 473, subdivision (b), these cases lend little if any support to plaintiff's argument. [citations to these cases omitted]

Fourth, plaintiff contends that the reasons underlying the attorney's "mistake, inadvertence, surprise, or neglect" may be relevant to prove that the error was the attorney's fault rather than the client's. Plaintiff is right. As noted above, mandatory relief is available only if the default or dismissal "was … in fact caused by the attorney's mistake, inadvertence, surprise, or neglect." (§ 473, subd. (b).) Such relief is not available when the error is the client's alone (*Todd, supra,* 34 Cal.App.4th at pp. 991–992); the courts are still divided as to whether it is available when the error lies partly at the client's feet and partly at the attorney's (compare *Lang v. Hochman* (2000) 77 Cal.App.4th 1225, 1248 [92 Cal. Rptr. 2d 322] (*Lang*) [relief available only if client is "totally innocent of any wrongdoing"]; *In re Marriage of Hock, supra,* 80 Cal.App.4th at p. 1446 [same]; *Carmel, supra,* 175 Cal.App.4th at p. 400 [same] with *Benedict v. Danner Press* (2001) 87 Cal.App.4th 923, 932 [104 Cal. Rptr. 2d 896] [relief available as long as client did not engage in intentional misconduct]; *SJP Limited, supra,* 136 Cal.App.4th at p. 520 [same]; see generally *Gutierrez v. G & M Oil Co., Inc.* (2010) 184 Cal.App.4th 551, 557–558 [108 Cal. Rptr. 3d 864] [detailing split of authority]).

Where the cause of the default or dismissal is in dispute, the attorney's affidavit can serve as "a causation testing device" (*Milton, supra,* 53 Cal.App.4th at p. 867, quoting *Cisneros v. Vueve* (1995) 37 Cal.App.4th 906, 912 [44 Cal. Rptr. 2d 682]), and a statement of reasons may be quite probative regarding who is at fault (see, e.g., *Todd,* at pp. 991–992 [looking to attorney's affidavit]; *Johnson v. Pratt & Whitney Canada, Inc.* (1994) 28 Cal.App.4th 613, 621–623 [34 Cal. Rptr. 2d 26] [same]; *Lang,* at pp. 1248–1252 [same]). Because it is often unknown at the time a motion for mandatory relief is filed whether causation will be disputed, an attorney would be well served to include the reasons for his or her "mistake, inadvertence, surprise, or neglect" in the affidavit of fault. This is no doubt why practice guides so recommend.

(E.g., Weil & Brown, Cal. Practice Guide: Civil Procedure Before Trial (The Rutter Group 2015) ¶ 5:390.1, p. 5-109 [recommending that attorney "include *detailed* factual explanations as to how the claimed 'mistake' or 'neglect' occurred" (some italics omitted)].) But the fact that it may be a very good idea to include an explanation of attorney fault does not mean it is a requirement of section 473, subdivision (b)'s mandatory relief provision. For the reasons noted above, it is not.

Lastly, plaintiff argues that an attorney affidavit of fault lacking an explanation of the reason for that fault is nothing more than an "affidavit[] or declaration[] setting forth only conclusions, opinions or ultimate facts," which is "insufficient" as a matter of law. [citations omitted] We disagree. To be sure, it is not enough for the attorney to attest, "My client is entitled to relief under section 473, subdivision (b)"; that would be an impermissible conclusion of ultimate fact. But an attorney's admission of his mistake, inadvertence, surprise, or neglect is not an impermissible ultimate fact because it is precisely what section 473, subdivision (b) calls for — namely, a "sworn affidavit attesting to [the attorney's] mistake, inadvertence, surprise, or neglect" (§ 473, subd. (b)).

For all these reasons, we conclude that an attorney affidavit of fault under the mandatory relief provisions of section 473, subdivision (b) need not include an explanation of the reasons for the attorney's mistake, inadvertence, surprise, or neglect.

II. *Review of the Affidavit in This Case*

As explained above, a trial court is obligated to set aside a default, default judgment, or dismissal if the motion for mandatory relief (1) is filed within six months of the entry of judgment, (2) "is in proper form," (3) is accompanied by the attorney affidavit of fault, and (4) demonstrates that the default or dismissal was "in fact caused by the attorney's mistake, inadvertence, surprise, or neglect." (§ 473, subd. (b).) Plaintiff concedes that Corsair has met the first and second requirements, but disputes the last two.

Plaintiff challenges the sufficiency of Klein's affidavit. Specifically, he argues that Klein's affidavit is deficient because (1) Klein does not set forth the reasons for his neglect, (2) Klein's recitations are oblique and obtuse (that is, they contain statements attesting to what Klein did *not* do rather than to what he did), and (3) Klein's admissions that he failed to file a responsive pleading do not sufficiently attest to a mistake, inadvertence, surprise or neglect.

These arguments lack merit. We have rejected the first, statute-based argument. We also reject plaintiff's second contention. Although an affidavit more directly spelling out an attorney's actions might be more easily understood, Klein's declarations nevertheless unequivocally spell out that he was Corsair's lawyer; he received plaintiff's filings from Corsair; he did nothing with those papers; and his decision to do so was his and his alone. Lastly, Klein sufficiently admitted his neglect. "Neglect" includes an "omission" (*Barragan v. County of Los Angeles* (2010) 184 Cal.App.4th 1373, 1382–1383 [109 Cal. Rptr. 3d 501]), including the failure to give "proper attention to a person or thing, whether inadvertent, negligent, or willful" (*In re Ethan C.* (2012) 54 Cal.4th 610, 627 [143 Cal. Rptr. 3d 565, 279 P.3d 1052], quoting Black's Law Dictionary (8th ed. 2004)). Klein's acknowledgment that he received plaintiff's lawsuit filings from Corsair and did nothing with them qualifies as not giving them proper attention, and thus as neglect. Because we are dealing with the mandatory relief provision, it does not matter whether Klein's neglect was excusable or inexcusable.

Plaintiff also challenges the trial court's finding that Klein's neglect caused the default.[2] In particular, plaintiff argues that it is possible that Corsair directed Klein to stall by not responding to plaintiff's filings—thus making the default *Corsair's* fault—because (1) the affidavits from Klein and Corsair's managing member did not absolutely preclude the possibility that someone else at Corsair (other than the managing member) so directed Klein and (2) plaintiff presented evidence that a corporation with a similar name (Corsairs LLC) was formed days after plaintiff filed suit. However, as detailed above, those affidavits also detail Klein's failure to take any action and include his admission that it was "failures on [his] part ... that allowed the Default ... to be entered." As such, the affidavits constitute substantial evidence that Klein's neglect was the sole cause of the default. Because a conflict in the evidence does not render it insubstantial (e.g., *People v. Panah* (2005) 35 Cal.4th 395, 489 [25 Cal. Rptr. 3d 672, 107 P.3d 790]), we have no basis to disturb the court's factual finding regarding causation.

DISPOSITION

The order granting relief from default and default judgment is affirmed. Corsair is entitled to costs on appeal.

Notes and Questions regarding Mandatory Relief from Default

(1) *Mandatory Relief When Accompanied by Attorney's Affidavit of Neglect.* As *Martin Potts & Associates, Inc. v. Corsair, LLC*, reproduced *supra*, demonstrates, the 1988 amendments to CCP §473 broadened the grounds for relief from default to now include attorney mistake or neglect, even when the neglect is inexcusable. If the application is accompanied by the attorney's sworn affidavit attesting to his or her mistake or neglect, the court must vacate the default or default judgment. CCP §473(b). However, the court must direct the attorney to pay reasonable compensatory legal fees and costs to opposing counsel or parties; but cannot condition the relief from default on the attorney's payment of such fees, costs, or other sanctions and penalties. §473(b). What are the policy reasons for prohibiting conditional grants of relief in such attorney neglect situations? The 1992 amendments to §473, which extended this mandatory provision to relief from most involuntary dismissal orders, are discussed in §12.03, Involuntary Dismissals, *infra*.

(2) Section 473(b)'s attorney affidavit provision mandates relief "unless the court finds that the default ... as not in fact caused by the attorney's ... neglect." This provision requires the trial court to assess both credibility and causation in deter-

---

2. Corsair had a second lawyer as well, but the trial court found that this lawyer's "alleged statements and/or communications [to plaintiff] regarding his representation of [Corsair] and/or the reason(s) why the default was entered do not necessarily contradict and/or trump ... Klein's declarations regarding representation and fault." Plaintiff does not challenge this finding on appeal.

mining whether the default was due to attorney error. *See, e.g., Stafford v. Mach*, 64 Cal. App. 4th 1174, 75 Cal. Rptr. 2d 809 (1998) (concluding any mistake that may have contributed to the entry of default was the fault of the insurer and not any attorney, and therefore the mandatory provisions of § 473 were inapplicable); *Milton v. Perceptual Dev. Corp.*, 53 Cal. App. 4th 861, 62 Cal. Rptr. 2d 98 (1997) (upholding order vacating entry of defaults and default judgments where substantial evidence supported the trial court's finding that the attorney's admitted misconduct proximately caused both the defaults and default judgments); *Cisneros v. Vueve*, 37 Cal. App. 4th 906, 44 Cal. Rptr. 2d 682 (1995) (ruling because the attorney was not representing the defendants at the time the default was entered, he was not the proximate cause of the entry of default as required by the mandatory relief provision of § 473).

(3) Does the mandatory provision of CCP § 473(b) apply only if the party is totally innocent of any wrongdoing and the attorney was the *sole* cause of the default or dismissal? As indicated in *Martin Potts & Associates*, there is a division of authority on this question. *See Lang v. Hochman*, 77 Cal. App. 4th 1225, 92 Cal. Rptr. 2d 322 (2000) (affirming trial court's denial of relief from default judgment imposed as a discovery sanction where shared misconduct of by both defendant and counsel caused defendant's failure to comply with three discovery orders); *but see Marriage of Hock & Gordon-Hock*, 80 Cal. App. 4th 1438, 96 Cal. Rptr. 2d 546 (2000) (holding attorney negligence does not need to be the exclusive or sole cause of a client's loss for § 473's mandatory provisions to apply if it was, in fact, a proximate cause of the default); *Benedict v. Danner Press*, 87 Cal. App. 4th 923, 104 Cal. Rptr. 2d 896 (2001) (distinguishing *Lang* as a decision involving intentional misconduct by the client and holding that § 473's mandatory relief provision applied even though the default judgment was caused by the combined mistake or neglect of attorney and client).

(4) Does the mandatory relief provision of CCP § 473(b) apply when a default judgment is entered by the court after striking the defendant's answer as a sanction for failure to comply with a discovery order? *See Matera v. McLeod*, 145 Cal. App. 4th 44, 51 Cal. Rptr. 3d 331 (2006) (construing the language of § 473 and concluding the mandatory relief provision applies to all default judgments); *see Behm v. Clear View Tech.*, 241 Cal. App. 4th 1, 193 Cal. Rptr. 3d 486 (2015) (concluding trial court did not err in denying mandatory relief under § 473 from a default entered as a discovery sanction because the attorney's affidavit of fault was not credible); *Rodriquez v. Brill*, 234 Cal. App. 4th 715, 184 Cal. Rptr. 3d 265 (2015) (ruling mandatory relief under § 473 applies to dismissal of complaint granted as a discovery sanction).

(5) In *Even Zohar Construction & Remodeling, Inc. v. Bellaire*, 61 Cal. 4th 830, 189 Cal. Rptr. 3d 824, 352 P.3d 391 (2015), the California Supreme Court held that CCP § 1008 governs renewed applications for relief from default based on the mandatory provision of CCP § 473(b). Section 1008(b) requires that a party filing a renewed application for an order a court has previously refused must submit an affidavit showing what "new or different facts, circumstances, are claimed" to justify the renewed application, and show diligence with a satisfactory explanation for not presenting the

new or different information in the earlier application. If the attorney's affidavit of fault submitted with a renewed motion for mandatory relief does not comply with these requirements, as was the case with the affidavit in *Even Zohar Construction*, the renewed motion must be denied. *Even Zohar Construction, supra,* 61 Cal. 4th at 833.

(6) *Incentives to Attorneys?* What incentives are there for an attorney to prepare and file an affidavit of neglect in support of a §473 motion to set aside a default? If the attorney refuses to sign an affidavit of neglect, what must a defaulting party prove in order to convince the court, in its discretion, to grant relief from default under §473? What are the policy reasons behind the different treatment afforded defaulting parties under §473 in cases where the request for relief is accompanied by the attorney's affidavit of neglect, as opposed to those cases where no such affidavit is available? Is this difference in treatment wise policy? Why?

[3] Discretionary Relief for Excusable Neglect Sought Within Six Months

[a] Introductory Note

As indicated in *Martin Potts & Associates,* reproduced *supra,* prior to a 1988 amendment CCP §473(b) only authorized *discretionary* relief from default for *excusable* neglect or mistake. Seeking relief under the pre-amendment statute proved to be time-consuming for the parties and the courts, and often involved appellate review for abuse of discretion. Moreover, because the distinction between "excusable" versus "inexcusable" neglect proved difficult to apply, relief from default was uncertain and unpredictable. The significance of the 1988 amendment to CCP §473(b) is that it makes this distinction irrelevant and makes relief mandatory, so long as the defaulting party's attorney submits a proper affidavit of neglect. Consequently, where a defaulting party's request satisfies the prerequisites for mandatory relief, there simply is no reason to rely on §473's discretionary grounds for relief. The discretionary approach is only necessary in those few instances where mandatory relief is unavailable, such as where the request for relief does not satisfy the attorney causation requirement or involves an order not governed by the scope of the mandatory relief provision.

[b] Excusable vs. Inexcusable Neglect or Mistake

To determine whether a mistake or neglect is excusable, the court inquires whether "a reasonably prudent person under the same or similar circumstances might have made the same error." *Zamara v. Clayborn Contracting Grp., Inc.,* 28 Cal. 4th 249, 258, 121 Cal. Rptr. 2d 187, 47 P.3d 1056 (2002); *see Fasuyi v. Permatex, Inc.,* 167 Cal. App. 4th 681, 84 Cal. Rptr. 3d 351 (2008) (discussing the general principles applicable to the trial court's discretion to set aside a default judgment under CCP §473). "Unless inexcusable neglect is clear, the policy favoring trial on the merits prevails" and doubts should be resolved in favor of the request for relief from default. *Elston v. City of Turlock,* 38 Cal. 3d 227, 235, 211 Cal. Rptr. 416, 695 P.2d 713 (1985). Courts often note that "when the moving party promptly seeks relief and there is no prejudice to the opposing party, very slight evidence is required to justify relief" from a default judgment. *See, e.g., Rogalski v. Nabers Cadillac,* 11 Cal. App. 4th 816, 821, 14 Cal. Rptr. 2d 286 (1992); *Mink v. Superior Court,* 2 Cal. App. 4th 1338, 1343, 4 Cal. Rptr. 2d 195 (1992).

Examples of circumstances where the court has found excusable neglect sufficient to grant relief under § 473 include cases where settlement discussions lulled defendants into a false sense of security, *Beard v. Beard,* 16 Cal. 2d 645, 648, 107 P.2d 385 (1940); default was due to disability or illness of defendant or defendant's attorney, *e.g., Stone v. McWilliams,* 43 Cal. App. 490, 492, 185 P. 478 (1919); where the default was due to attorney's change in personnel and consequent misplacement and lack of knowledge of court papers, *Elston v. City of Turlock,* 38 Cal. 3d 227, 234–35, 211 Cal. Rptr. 416, 695 P.2d 713 (1985); *but see Henderson v. Pac. Gas & Elec. Co.,* 187 Cal. App. 4th 215, 229–252, 113 Cal. Rptr. 3d 692 (2010) (ruling attorney's failure to file timely opposition to summary judgment motion, the preparation of which the attorney delegated to his paralegal, was inexcusable neglect because attorney failed to supervise his employee). For more examples of excusable and inexcusable neglect under § 473, see 8 Witkin, *California Procedure, Attack on Judgment in Trial Court* §§ 160–169 (5th ed. 2008) and 2 CEB, *Civil Procedure Before Trial* § 38.82 (4th ed. 2015).

Even though the policy of the law favors trial on the merits, some showing of excusable neglect or mistake and of meritorious defense is necessary to set aside a default judgment under the discretionary grounds in CCP § 473. For example, relief from default has been denied where the party or his attorney deliberately refused to take timely and adequate steps to avoid default, *e.g., Elms v. Elms,* 72 Cal. App. 2d 508, 513, 164 P.2d 936 (1948); where the attorney's explanation for failure to respond to the complaint and to promptly seek relief from default was that his girlfriend was hospitalized for four days, *Beeman v. Burling,* 216 Cal. App. 3d 1586, 265 Cal. Rptr. 719 (1990); where the defendant's attorney mistakenly assumed that his unanswered requests to opposing counsel for an extension of time to file an answer was a grant of the extension, *Iott v. Franklin,* 206 Cal. App. 3d 521, 531, 253 Cal. Rptr. 635 (1988); and where the defendant's attorney mistakenly believed that the clerk's default was not conclusive, *Barragan v. Banco BCH,* 188 Cal. App. 3d 283, 301, 232 Cal. Rptr. 758 (1986).

[c] Inexcusable Neglect of Attorney Not Imputed to Client When Positive Misconduct

The inexcusable neglect of an attorney is imputed to the client, and is not grounds for § 473 relief in the absence of the attorney's affidavit of fault. *Carroll v. Abbott Lab., Inc.,* 32 Cal. 3d 892, 898, 187 Cal. Rptr. 592, 654 P.2d 775 (1982). However, when the attorney's neglect is of such an extreme degree that it amounts to "positive misconduct" — an abandonment by the lawyer of his client, and a de facto severance of the attorney-client relationship — courts have concluded that the client should not be charged with the attorney's negligence. *Carroll, supra; Buckert v. Briggs,* 15 Cal. App. 3d 296, 93 Cal. Rptr. 61 (1971); *Daley v. County of Butte,* 227 Cal. App. 2d 380, 38 Cal. Rptr. 693 (1964). However, as the Supreme Court observed in *Carroll, supra*, 32 Cal. 3d at 900, the "positive misconduct" or abandonment exception should be narrowly applied, "lest negligent attorneys find that the simplest way to gain the twin goals of rescuing clients from defaults and themselves from malpractice liability, is to rise to ever greater heights of incompetence and professional irresponsibility." Accordingly, the *Carroll* court reversed the trial court's grant of relief from dismissal under this exception, finding that although plaintiff's counsel grossly mishandled a routine discovery matter and failed to give effective representation, he continued to act on behalf of the plaintiff and therefore did not abandon his client. *Carroll, supra*, 32 Cal. 3d at 900–901; *see also Beeman v. Burling*, 216 Cal. App. 3d 1586, 265 Cal. Rptr. 719 (1990) (concluding the "positive misconduct" doctrine does not apply where the defendant's attorney continued to act, albeit ineffectively, as the defendant's representative).

[4] *Relief Must Be Sought Within Six Months*

An application for relief from default under CCP § 473 must be made within a reasonable time, not to exceed six months, after entry of the default whether accompanied by an attorney's affidavit of neglect or based on some other grounds. An even shorter time limitation may apply in an action which determines the ownership or right to possession of real or personal property. CCP § 473.

[a] Six Months Limitation

The six-month outside time limit of § 473 is jurisdictional; a trial court may not consider any motion made under § 473 after that period has elapsed. *See Jackson v. Bank of America*, 141 Cal. App. 3d 55, 59, 190 Cal. Rptr. 78 (1983); *Stevenson v. Turner*, 94 Cal. App. 3d 315, 318, 156 Cal. Rptr. 499 (1979). The six-month period runs from the date of the entry of the default or from the judgment taken thereafter, depending on whether the defendant seeks to set aside both events or only the subsequent default judgment. *Rutan v. Summit Sports, Inc.*, 173 Cal. App. 3d 965, 970, 219 Cal. Rptr. 381 (1985) (holding that because defendant's motion was made more than six months after the default was entered but within six months after the judgment, trial court had jurisdiction under § 473 to grant relief from the judgment but not the default). Under what circumstances would a defendant seek relief from a default judgment but not from the prior entry of default?

[b] Reasonable Time Limitation

In addition to being made within the six months' period, an application for discretionary relief under CCP § 473 must be made "within a reasonable time" after entry of default. What constitutes a "reasonable time" depends upon the circumstances of each particular case. *Benjamin v. Dalmo Mfg. Co.*, 31 Cal. 2d 523, 528, 190 P.2d 593 (1948) (concluding unexplained delay of three months was unreasonable); *Smith v. Pelton Water Wheel Co.*, 151 Cal. 394, 397, 90 P. 934 (1907) (ruling unexplained delay of four months was unreasonable); *Stafford v. Mach*, 64 Cal. App. 4th 1174, 75

Cal. Rptr. 2d 809 (1998) (reversing the trial court's order setting aside a default judgment because the defendant waited 4 1/2 months, until just before the six month deadline expired, to file the application for relief from default, and offered no excuse for the delay).

Does a trial court abuse its discretion when it refuses to excuse a defendant's lack of diligence in requesting relief from default where the reason for delay is the defendant's lack of funds necessary to obtain counsel? *Compare Carrasco v. Craft*, 164 Cal. App. 3d 796, 804–807, 210 Cal. Rptr. 599 (1985) (finding no abuse of discretion by trial court in finding defendant's five-month delay unreasonable although due to lack of funds, noting that "in exercising its discretion the trial court may properly take into consideration defendant's lack of funds to obtain counsel in determining whether a motion to set aside a default was brought within a reasonable time; however lack of funds does not, as a matter of law, require the setting aside of the default."), *with Buckert v. Briggs*, 15 Cal. App. 3d 296, 302, 93 Cal. Rptr. 61 (1971) (finding no abuse of discretion in trial court's granting of motion to vacate a default, despite a five-month delay in requesting relief, when reason for delay was inability to immediately pay attorney retainer).

With respect to the mandatory relief provisions of § 473(b), the courts are divided as to whether an otherwise timely affidavit of attorney fault must also satisfy reasonable diligence requirements. In *Caldwell v. Methodist Hospital*, 24 Cal. App. 4th 1521, 29 Cal. Rptr. 2d 894 (1994), for example, the court upheld the denial of the plaintiff's motion to set aside dismissal under § 473 because the motion, accompanied by counsel's admission of neglect but filed three months after the dismissal, was not filed within a reasonable time. By contrast, in *Metropolitan Service Corp. v. Casa De Palms, Ltd.*, 31 Cal. App. 4th 1481, 37 Cal. Rptr. 2d 575 (1995), the court construed the mandatory relief provisions of § 473, as further amended in 1991, to require only that an attorney's affidavit of fault be filed within six months and to not incorporate any additional diligence requirement. *See also Milton v. Perceptual Dev. Corp.*, 53 Cal. App. 4th 861, 62 Cal. Rptr. 2d 98 (1997) (following *Metropolitan Service* and concluding that the mandatory relief provisions of § 473 do not include a requirement of diligence, and therefore that such motions are timely where filed within six months of the default judgment). Which construction of the mandatory relief provisions is the better one? Why?

[5] Discretionary Relief for Lack of "Actual Notice" Pursuant to CCP § 473.5

Olvera v. Olvera

Court of Appeal of California, Fourth Appellate District
232 Cal. App. 3d 32, 283 Cal. Rptr. 271 (1991)

[This opinion, which discusses CCP § 473.5, is reproduced in § 6.04, Service of Process, *supra*. Section 473.5(a) permits the trial court to vacate a default judgment if "service of a summons has not resulted in actual notice to a party in time to defend the action...." A motion for relief under § 473.5 must be made within a reasonable time, but in no event exceeding the earlier of two years after entry of the default judgment or 180 days after service of notice of entry of the default judgment. If the trial court finds that the defaulting party's lack of actual notice was not caused by avoidance of service or inexcusable neglect, the trial court may, in its discretion, set aside the default judgment. § 473.5(c).]

Notes and Questions regarding Relief under CCP § 473.5

(1) *Lack of Actual Notice Under CCP § 473.5.* The *Olvera* court characterized its construction of the "actual notice" provision in CCP § 473.5 as both "strict" and "liberal." What did the court mean when it used such seemingly conflicting characterizations? After *Olvera*, under what circumstances will a defendant be deemed to have actual knowledge of an action so as to preclude use of § 473.5? Where the defendant actually read the summons when published in a newspaper? Where the defendant read the published summons and immediately obtained a copy of the complaint and summons from the clerk's office? Where the defendant, not personally served, read the complaint and summons posted on her front door? *See Boland v. All Persons*, 160 Cal. 486, 490, 117 P. 547 (1911). Where the plaintiff served the complaint and summons on an attorney representing defendant in a related prior litigation but the attorney did not inform the defendant? *See Rosenthal v. Garner*, 142 Cal. App. 3d 891, 895, 191 Cal. Rptr. 300 (1983) (ruling the phrase "actual notice" in § 473.5 "means genuine knowledge of the party litigant and does not contemplate notice imputed to a principal from an attorney's actual notice."); *Tunis v. Barrow*, 184 Cal. App. 3d 1069, 1077–80, 229 Cal. Rptr. 389 (1986).

(2) *Additional § 473.5 Restrictions.* As the *Olvera* opinion indicates, CCP § 473.5 contains some additional restrictions on a trial court's ability to set aside a default or default judgment based on lack of actual notice. Section 473.5 requires a defendant to file and serve the notice of motion within a reasonable time, not to exceed the earlier of two years after entry of the default judgment or 180 days after service of the notice that a default or default judgment has been entered. What are the reasons for these time period limitations? Section 473.5(c) requires the trial court to make certain findings as a prerequisite to the court's authority to exercise discretion with respect to the motion to set aside. These include a finding that the defendant's lack of actual notice in time to defend the action was not caused by defendant's "avoidance of service or inexcusable neglect." CCP § 473.5(c). What are the reasons for these restrictions?

(3) *Relief Under CCP § 473.5 Is Discretionary.* Even when a trial court makes the prerequisite findings specified in § 473.5(c), it is not required to grant the motion to set aside. The court may, as an exercise of discretion, set aside the default judgment; and even then "on whatever terms as may be just." CCP § 473.5(c). Under what circumstances is a trial court, as an exercise of this discretion, likely to not set aside a default judgment? When the court does set aside a default judgment under § 473.5, what kind of terms or conditions is it likely to impose? Why? Under what circum-

stances would it be unfair and improper for a court to condition relief from default on the payment by defendant of a monetary award designed to compensate the plaintiff for the expenses caused by granting defendant § 473.5 relief? *See Kodak Films, Inc. v. Jensen*, 230 Cal. App. 3d 1261, 285 Cal. Rptr. 728 (1991).

[6] *Relief Sought After Six Months*

[a] Equitable Relief

After the six-month period has passed, relief from default is no longer available based on the statutory grounds of CCP § 473. *But see* Family Code §§ 2120–2122 (providing for relief from judgment after six months in a dissolution of marriage cases on several grounds such as fraud, within one year after date of fraud discovered, and mistake, within one year after judgment). Independent of this statutory authority, however, a court has the inherent equity power to grant relief from a default judgment where there has been "extrinsic fraud or mistake." *Marriage of Park*, 27 Cal. 3d 337, 342, 165 Cal. Rptr. 792, 612 P.2d 882 (1980); *Weitz v. Yankosky*, 63 Cal. 2d 849, 855, 48 Cal. Rptr. 620, 409 P.2d 700 (1966); *Marriage of Stevenot*, 154 Cal. App. 3d 1051, 202 Cal. Rptr. 116 (1984). Is a court's equitable power to grant relief based on extrinsic fraud or mistake whenever discovered narrower than its power under CCP § 473? Consider the following case.

Rappleyea v. Campbell

Supreme Court of California
8 Cal. 4th 975, 35 Cal. Rptr. 2d 669, 884 P.2d 126 (1994)

Mosk, Justice.

Defendants, Arizona residents, were personally served with a summons and complaint on November 1, 1990. Defendants chose to proceed in propria persona and had an Arizona lawyer, apparently an old friend of theirs, telephone the Los Angeles Superior Court for information on filing procedures. The clerk's office told the lawyer's staff that the filing fee was $89, according to the lawyer's sworn statement. Defendants answered by mail from Arizona on or about November 26, enclosing $89. The clerk's office received the answer by November 29.

The clerk's office had misadvised defendants' informal counsel. The $89 fee was correct for a single defendant's answer. The correct filing fee for two defendants to answer was $159. The clerk's error led to a default judgment against defendants of $200,240.39.

The procedural alchemy that transformed a $70 error into a judgment for more than $200,000 is not particularly complicated. Defendants had 30 days to file their answer after they were served. (Code Civ. Proc., § 412.20, subd. (a)(3).) Their answer, if filed when first presented, hence would have been timely. But when the Los Angeles Superior Court Clerk's Office received defendants' answer and $89 check, it rejected and returned the answer. Defendants promptly sent back their answer with the correct fee, and the answer was filed on December 11, 1990.

Hence defendants' answer was filed eight days late. Meanwhile, on December 4, 1990, the first possible day to do so, plaintiff had applied to the clerk to enter default against defendants. Plaintiff mailed a copy of his application to defendants. The clerk entered defendants' default that day. * * *

On May 24, 1991, plaintiff's counsel diametrically misdescribed California law to these lay defendants, writing to inform them that "You may *not* claim that the default entered was taken against you through inadvertence, mistake, or excusable neglect." (Italics added.) To the contrary, Code of Civil Procedure section 473 (hereafter section 473) provides that a court has discretion to relieve a party "from a judgment, dismissal, order, or other proceeding taken against him or her through his or her mistake, inadvertence, surprise, or excusable neglect. Application for this relief ... shall be made within a reasonable time, in no case exceeding six months, after the judgment, dismissal, order, or proceeding was taken." (The quoted language of section 473 is slightly but not materially different from that in effect in 1991.) The effect of plaintiff's letter, intended or not, was to advise these self-represented Arizona defendants they had forfeited California legal rights that they in fact retained under section 473 before the statute's six-month limitation expired.

Late in October 1991 defendants learned a default judgment might soon be entered against them. The court mailed a minute order to them announcing that "[t]he Court would enter judgment for plaintiff against the Campbells (and others) if [plaintiff's] papers were sufficient." The court's communication apparently sounded an alarm that plaintiff's asserted warnings failed to do, because defendants quickly moved to set aside the clerk's entry of default, appearing in propria persona on December 9, 1991. The motion was argued and on January 15, 1992, was denied on the ground that good cause had not been shown.... Defendants then retained counsel, who filed a motion for reconsideration. That motion was denied as untimely. * * *

A default judgment was finally entered on January 29, 1992. Defendants appealed. A divided Court of Appeal affirmed.

There is little question we would have found an abuse of discretion if relief had been denied within the six-month period governed by section 473. Because the law favors disposing of cases on their merits, "any doubts in applying section 473 must be resolved in favor of the party seeking relief from default [citations]. Therefore, a trial court order denying relief is scrutinized more carefully than an order permitting trial on the merits." (*Elston v. City of Turlock* (1985) 38 Cal. 3d 227, 233 [211 Cal. Rptr. 416, 695 P.2d 713]; *see also Miller v. City of Hermosa Beach* (1993) 13 Cal. App. 4th 1118, 1136 [17 Cal. Rptr. 2d 408].) * * *

After six months from entry of default, a trial court may still vacate a default on equitable grounds even if statutory relief is unavailable. (*Olivera v. Grace* (1942) 19 Cal. 2d 570, 575–576 [122 P.2d 564, 140 A.L.R. 1328].) We review a challenge to a trial court's order denying a motion to vacate a default on equitable grounds as we would a decision under section 473: for an abuse of discretion. (*In re Marriage of Park*

(1980) 27 Cal. 3d 337, 347 [165 Cal. Rptr. 792, 612 P.2d 882]; *see Weitz v. Yankosky* (1966) 63 Cal. 2d 849, 854, 856 [48 Cal. Rptr. 620, 409 P.2d 700] [default judgment].)

One ground for equitable relief is extrinsic mistake—a term broadly applied when circumstances extrinsic to the litigation have unfairly cost a party a hearing on the merits. (*In re Marriage of Park, supra,* 27 Cal. 3d at p. 342; cf. *In re Marriage of Stevenot* (1984) 154 Cal. App. 3d 1051, 1066–1067 [202 Cal. Rptr. 116] [criticizing rule].) "Extrinsic mistake is found when [among other things] … a mistake led a court to do what it never intended…." (*Kulchar v. Kulchar* (1969) 1 Cal. 3d 467, 471–472 [82 Cal. Rptr. 489, 462 P.2d 17, 39 A.L.R.3d 1368]; *see Sullivan v. Lumsden* (1897) 118 Cal. 664, 669 [50 P 777] [referees' use of wrong map was extrinsic mistake and equitable relief was available because "'it is not a mistake of the law, or an inadvertent conclusion as to what the law is, but a mistake or inadvertence in doing something not intended to be done.'"].)

When a default *judgment* has been obtained, equitable relief may be given only in exceptional circumstances. "[W]hen relief under section 473 is available, there is a strong public policy in favor of granting relief and allowing the requesting party his or her day in court. Beyond this period there is a strong public policy in favor of the finality of judgments and only in exceptional circumstances should relief be granted." (*In re Marriage of Stevenot, supra,* 154 Cal. App. 3d at p. 1071….)

Apparently to further the foregoing policy, one appellate court has created a stringent test to qualify for equitable relief from default on the basis of extrinsic mistake. "To set aside a *judgment* based upon extrinsic mistake one must satisfy three elements. First, the defaulted party must demonstrate that it has a meritorious case. Second [], the party seeking to set aside the default must articulate a satisfactory excuse for not presenting a defense to the original action. Last [], the moving party must demonstrate diligence in seeking to set aside the default once … discovered." (*Stiles v. Wallis* (1983) 147 Cal. App. 3d 1143, 1147–1148 [195 Cal. Rptr. 377], italics added.) The stringent three-part formula of *Stiles* was followed by *In re Marriage of Stevenot, supra,* 154 Cal. App. 3d at page 1071, an extrinsic-fraud case.

But this case is unlike *Aheroni v. Maxwell, supra,* 205 Cal. App. 3d 284, *In re Marriage of Stevenot, supra,* 154 Cal. App. 3d 1051, or *Stiles v. Wallis, supra,* 147 Cal. App. 3d 1143, because the policy of leaving judgments final is not implicated here as it was in those decisions. Plaintiff did not obtain a default judgment until January 29, 1992, by which time defendants had moved for, and been denied, relief from default. In the meantime, plaintiff had shown scant interest in obtaining a judgment. Thus, to the extent the policy disfavoring equitable relief is based on an understandable distaste for the forfeiture of a judgment, which is vested personal property, the policy's basis is weaker in this case. Indeed, the record before us strongly suggests that the prejudice to plaintiff from defendants' motion, if that motion had succeeded, would have been virtually nil.

We need not decide, however, whether a test much different from that articulated in *Marriage of Stevenot, supra,* 154 Cal. App. 3d at page *1071, and Stiles v. Wallis, supra*, 147 Cal. App. 3d at pages 1147–1148, applies to requests for equitable relief when a default judgment has not been entered. Even under that stringent three-prong test this case's odd facts entitle defendants to relief.

We first examine whether defendants have a satisfactory excuse for failing to timely answer in the original action. To our minds, this is the same as asking whether an extrinsic mistake occurred — as relevant here, whether "a mistake led a court to do what it never intended…." (*Kulchar v. Kulchar, supra*, 1 Cal. 3d at pp. 471–472.) We conclude that the clerk's misunderstanding of the number of answering defendants constituted an extrinsic mistake. The court never intended to have defendants send the fee applicable to a sole defendant and thereby default, but that was the effect of the clerk's ministerial action. * * *

We next examine whether the defense has merit. Ordinarily a verified answer to a complaint's allegations suffices to show merit. (*Stiles v. Wallis, supra*, 147 Cal. App. 3d at p. 1148.) The answer here was not verified, but neither was the complaint. Moreover, the answer did deny, admit, or otherwise respond to the allegations. And the Arizona lawyer who informally aided defendants declared under oath that he believed "these Defendants have a very good (and certainly a justiciable) defense to the Plaintiff's claim." On the combined strength of these facts, we believe defendants have sufficiently shown merit.

The final prong of the stringent three-part test set forth in *Stiles v. Wallis, supra*, 147 Cal. App. 3d at page 1148, is whether defendants diligently tried to set aside the default once discovered.

"The greater the prejudice to the responding party, the more likely it is that the court will determine that equitable defenses such as laches or estoppel apply to the request to vacate a valid judgment." (*In re Marriage of Stevenot, supra*, 154 Cal. App. 3d at p. 1071.) Of the three items a defendant must show to win equitable relief from default, diligence is the most inextricably intertwined with prejudice. If heightened prejudice strengthens the burden of proving diligence, so must reduced prejudice weaken it. Under that view, and given this record, we believe defendants have sufficiently shown diligence.

Prejudice to a plaintiff is obviously less if judgment has not been entered when a defendant seeks equitable relief. Therefore, we believe the diligence prong simply cannot assume the importance here that it would in the ordinary case wherein the trial court would be reversing a judgment and divesting a plaintiff of a property right by granting equitable relief from default. Indeed, the court kept admonishing plaintiff that if he himself did not try more diligently to prove damages, he would be sanctioned, and once his counsel was sanctioned for failing to appear at a prove-up hearing. This indifference belies any claim plaintiff might make of eagerness to obtain an early judgment. And plaintiff incorrectly told defendants they had forfeited their legal right to seek statutory relief. These unusual facts greatly weaken any possible assertion of prejudice, and correspondingly lower the burden on defendants of showing diligence.

Under this reduced standard, defendants were not callously derelict in seeking to set aside the default. To be sure, they did not move for relief from default until December 9, 1991, more than a year after this litigation ensued; and plaintiff asserts, with some confirming evidence, that he warned defendants they were in default. However, the evidence that before October 1991 defendants understood the legal *consequences* to them personally of being in default, in a case with 12 other named and 20 Doe defendants, is confined to the boilerplate language on the face of the summons. When in October 1991 the court told defendants they might soon face a default judgment, they acted quickly. We believe defendants acted diligently enough to satisfy that requirement for equitable relief.

Having satisfied all three prongs of the stringent test, we conclude that the clerk's entry of default must be set aside and the default judgment reversed. We draw our conclusion narrowly. The clerk's error and plaintiff's incorrect statement of the law together persuade us that the court abused its discretion when it denied defendants' motion. These rare events should not combine to make defendants suffer a $200,240.39 judgment without a hearing on the merits.

As alluded to, however, we make clear that mere self-representation is not a ground for exceptionally lenient treatment. Except when a particular rule provides otherwise, the rules of civil procedure must apply equally to parties represented by counsel and those who forgo attorney representation. * * * A doctrine generally requiring or permitting exceptional treatment of parties who represent themselves would lead to a quagmire in the trial courts, and would be unfair to the other parties to litigation. Although in reaching our decision we have incidentally considered whether parties in defendants' position would reasonably have relied on advice from the clerk's office and whether they would have understood the meaning of a default, our focus is on the clerk's and plaintiff's incorrect advice rather than on defendants' ill-advised self-representation.

The Court of Appeal's judgment is reversed with directions to reverse the default judgment and to instruct the trial court to set aside the entry of default.

Kennard, Justice, Arabian, Justice, and George, Justice, concurred.

Baxter, Justice, Dissenting.

I respectfully dissent. * * * While reciting in detail a litany of error and omission which placed defendants in the unfortunate position of judgment debtors, the majority fail to identify the sole issue in this case. That question is whether the Court of Appeal erred in holding that the trial court did not abuse its discretion in refusing to grant equitable relief to defendants. It did not. Moreover, the Court of Appeal properly applied the rule governing appellate review of such discretionary trial court rulings, a rule which the majority fail even to acknowledge, let alone apply. * * *

As the majority acknowledge, defendants' motion was not made within six months and the sole source of authority to set aside the judgment lies in the trial court's equitable power to set aside the judgment on grounds that "extrinsic factors have prevented one party to the litigation from presenting his or her case." (*In re Marriage of Park* (1980) 27 Cal. 3d 337, 342 [165 Cal. Rptr. 792, 612 P.2d 882].) Here, however, since defendants knew immediately that their default had been taken, the question is not whether an extrinsic factor prevented them from filing their answer and litigating the merits, but whether any extrinsic factor led to their failure to file a reasonably timely section 473 motion. The majority identify no evidence which the trial court could not reasonably have disbelieved or rejected as a basis for concluding that relief from default was warranted. The record establishes beyond any question that defendants were aware the default had been taken and that if they were to avoid having judgment entered against them they would have to seek relief from default. * * * The Court of Appeal found nothing in the record to justify disturbing the implied finding of the trial court that plaintiff's actions had not lulled defendants into a false sense of security and thereby prevented them from participating in the action. The majority offers no explanation or authority for substituting its judgment for that of the trial court. * * *

The law governing relief on grounds of extrinsic fraud discussed in *Kulchar v. Kulchar* (1969) 1 Cal. 3d 467[82 Cal. Rptr. 489, 462 P.2d 17, 39 A.L.R.3d 1368], on which the majority rely, has no application here. Equitable relief on grounds of extrinsic fraud or mistake is not a substitute for section 473 relief. When fraud or mistake is discovered within the time limits established by section 473, relief is available pursuant to that section. This is not a policy question related to the importance of finality of judgment as the majority suggest. The Legislature has established the time within which relief on grounds of mistake may be sought by a party who is aware of the mistake. The failure to seek that relief on a timely basis necessarily forecloses the availability of equitable relief unless time of discovery of the mistake or fraud or other circumstances made it impossible for the party to make a timely motion under section 473. Deeming the motion one for equitable relief does not expand the time within which a motion should be made by a party who is aware of the grounds for such relief. The party must demonstrate diligence in attempting to seek relief under section 473. Concepts of inexcusable neglect and laches apply to motions seeking equitable relief. The court must consider the reasonableness of a party's failure to seek relief within the statutory time limit. (*See In re Marriage of Park, supra,* 27 Cal. 3d 337, 345.) Since plaintiffs failed to justify their failure to make a timely motion under section 473, the trial court would have abused its discretion had it treated their motion as one for equitable relief and granted it.

Nor is lack of prejudice to the opposing party determinative. This court simply has no power to create an alternative remedy which makes relief available to persons who have knowledge of the facts on which relief may be sought under section 473 but inexcusably fail to comply with the statutory time limit. Lack of prejudice to the other party does not "automatically enable one who fails to make his motion within six months of the default to set aside the judgment by appealing to the equity powers of the court. To hold otherwise would encourage litigants to wait until the six-month period elapses before moving to set a default judgment aside. To the extent that the court's equity power to grant relief differs from its power under section 473, the equity power must be considered narrower, not wider." (*Weitz v. Yankosky* (1966) 63 Cal. 2d 849, 857 [48 Cal. Rptr. 620, 409 P.2d 700], italics omitted.)

There is no basis in this record for a conclusion that the trial court abused its discretion in denying defendants' motion to set aside their default or for holding that defendants are entitled to equitable relief. The Court of Appeal did not err in affirming the judgment of the trial court. I would affirm the judgment of the Court of Appeal.

Lucas, Chief Justice and Werdegar, Justice, concurred.

[b] Extrinsic Fraud or Mistake

Extrinsic fraud is a broad concept that tends to encompass almost any set of extrinsic circumstances which deprive a party of a fair adversary hearing. *Marriage of Modnick*, 33 Cal. 3d 897, 905, 191 Cal. Rptr. 629, 663 P.2d 187 (1983). The particular circumstances need not qualify as fraudulent or mistaken in the strict legal sense. *Marriage of Park, supra*, 27 Cal. 3d at 342. The clearest examples of extrinsic fraud are in cases where the aggrieved party is kept in ignorance of the proceeding or is in some other way induced not to appear. *Estate of Sanders*, 40 Cal. 3d 607, 614, 221 Cal. Rptr. 432, 710 P.2d 232 (1985).

By contrast, intrinsic fraud or mistake exists where a party has been given notice of the action and has not been prevented from participating therein, but unreasonably neglected to do so. *Kulchar v. Kulchar*, 1 Cal. 3d 467, 471, 82 Cal. Rptr. 489, 462 P.2d 17 (1969); *Marriage of Stevenot*, 154 Cal. App. 3d 1051, 1069–70, 202 Cal. Rptr. 116 (1984) (holding trial court improperly set aside default judgment of dissolution of marriage where wife had been given notice of action and was not prevented from participating therein by husband, but wife failed to take any action to protect herself from default). The equity power to grant relief from a default based on extrinsic (as opposed to intrinsic) fraud or mistake is similar to the statutory power to vacate for excusable (as opposed to inexcusable) fraud or neglect under CCP § 473, although the equity power is usually considered narrower. *E.g., Weitz v. Yankosky, supra*, 63 Cal. 2d at 857; *Carroll v. Abbott Lab., Inc., supra*, 32 Cal. 3d at 901, fn.8.

Examples of circumstances in which the courts have granted relief from default due to extrinsic fraud or mistake include cases where the defendant reasonably relied on his employer and its insurance carrier to respond to the lawsuit but his employer misplaced summons and complaint while recuperating from an illness, *Desper v. King*, 251 Cal. App. 2d 659, 59 Cal. Rptr. 657 (1967); the plaintiff obtained entry of default and then lulled defendant into not timely filing a CCP § 473 motion, *Lieberman v. Aetna Ins. Co.*, 249 Cal. App. 2d 515, 527, 57 Cal. Rptr. 453 (1967); the husband obtained default dissolution of marriage against wife awarding custody of children and most community property to husband, but husband concealed fact from court and wife's attorney that wife had been involuntarily deported to Korea, *Marriage of Park, supra*, 27 Cal. 3d at 341–47; a defendant reasonably relied on a codefendant, insurer, or other third party, to defend, *Weitz v. Yankosky, supra*, 63 Cal. 2d at 851–58; and where the default was due to the incapacity or disability of the party or his attorney, *Humes v. Margil Ventures, Inc.*, 174 Cal. App. 3d 486, 499, 220 Cal. Rptr.

186 (1985). In what ways are the circumstances in *Rappleyea* similar to these examples? In what ways are they different?

[c] Intrinsic Fraud or Mistake

A fraud or mistake is intrinsic if a party has been given notice of the action and has not been prevented from participating therein, but unreasonably neglected to do so. *Kulcher v. Kulcher, supra,* 1 Cal. 3d at 472–73; *Marriage of Stevenot, supra,* 154 Cal. App. 3d at 1069. A party's mistake as to the law or the facts is usually an insufficient basis to set aside a default judgment if the party could have reasonably discovered the mistake. *Marriage of Stevenot,* 154 Cal. App. 3d at 1069–75; *Heyman v. Franchise Mortg. Acceptance Corp.,* 107 Cal. App. 4th 921, 132 Cal. Rptr. 2d 465 (2003) (concluding that although value of company was the very subject of the lawsuit, defendant's alleged misrepresentations about company's financial condition were intrinsic where plaintiff conducted no investigation or discovery into the financial condition); *Home Ins. Co. v. Zurich Ins. Co.,* 96 Cal. App. 4th 17, 116 Cal. Rptr. 2d 583 (2002) (holding misrepresentation by insurer's attorney that policy limits were $15,000 instead of $500,000, which induced injured party to settle underlying suit for $15,000 after conducting no discovery, intrinsic because a reasonable investigation and use of discovery would have disclosed the true extent of insurance coverage).

However, an honest mistake of law may be valid ground for relief where a problem is complex and debatable. *E.g., Miller v. City of Hermosa Beach,* 13 Cal. App. 4th 1118, 1136–38, 17 Cal. Rptr. 2d 408 (1993) (holding default due to failure to timely request one of several hearings required by complex California Environmental Quality Act an excusable mistake of law); *Brocktrup v. INTEP,* 190 Cal. App. 3d 323, 235 Cal. Rptr. 390 (1987) (concluding relief from default appropriate where verification law unsettled and defendant's attorney mistakenly believed he could verify responses to requests for admissions). But ignorance of the law coupled with negligence in ascertaining it will certainly sustain a finding denying relief. *See City of Ontario v. Superior Court,* 2 Cal. 3d 335, 346, 85 Cal. Rptr. 149, 466 P.2d 693 (1970); *Robbins v. Los Angeles Unified Sch. Dist.,* 3 Cal. App. 4th 313, 319, 4 Cal. Rptr. 2d 649 (1992). Were the defendants in *Rappleyea* negligent in ascertaining the law with respect to setting aside a default? In their failure to file a timely CCP § 473 motion?

[d] Viability of Extrinsic/Intrinsic Distinction

The courts have criticized the distinction between extrinsic and intrinsic fraud as "quite nebulous" and "hopelessly blurred." *Marriage of Stevenot, supra,* 154 Cal. App. 3d at 1060; *see Marriage of Baltins,* 212 Cal. App. 3d 66, 82, 260 Cal. Rptr. 403 (1989). Judge Smallwood has made a persuasive case for abolishing the extrinsic fraud rule. *See* Donald E. Smallwood, *Vacating Judgments in California: Time to Abolish the Extrinsic Fraud Rule,* 13 W. St. U. L. Rev. 105–127 (1985); *see also* Comment, *Seeking More Equitable Relief from Fraudulent Judgments: Abolishing the Extrinsic-Intrinsic Distinctions* 12 Pac. L.J. 1013 (1981). The Restatement Second of

Judgments (1982), Section 68, does not distinguish between extrinsic and intrinsic fraud. Nor does Rule 60(b) of the Federal Rules of Civil Procedure, which expressly abandoned the distinction.

What are the policy reasons for the California extrinsic-intrinsic fraud distinction? Is this a reasonable distinction? A workable one? Are the difficulties in applying this extrinsic-intrinsic fraud distinction less evident in cases where a party seeks relief from a default judgment as opposed to a judgment after an adversarial hearing? Why? Should the courts simply ignore this distinction when considering requests for relief from default judgments, but apply it to requests for relief from other judgments? Did the Supreme Court in *Rappleyea* ignore this extrinsic-intrinsic distinction when it held that the superior court's failure to set aside the entry of default (as opposed to the default *judgment*) constituted an abuse of discretion?

[7] Void Judgments

[a] Judgment Void on Its Face

A default judgment can be void for lack of personal or subject matter jurisdiction, *Forbes v. Hyde*, 31 Cal. 342, 355 (1866); lack of proper service of process, *Ramos v. Homeward Residential, Inc.*, 223 Cal. App. 4th 1434, 168 Cal. Rptr. 3d 114 (2014); or for the granting of relief which the trial court had no power to grant, *Becker v. S.P.V. Constr. Co.*, 27 Cal. 3d 489, 493, 165 Cal. Rptr. 825, 612 P.2d 915 (1980); *Heidary v. Yadollahi*, 99 Cal. App. 4th 857, 121 Cal. Rptr. 2d 695 (2002). A trial court has the inherent power to set aside a judgment void on its face at any time. *Reid v. Balter*, 14 Cal. App. 4th 1186, 1194, 18 Cal. Rptr. 2d 287 (1993); *Stevenson v. Turner*, 94 Cal. App. 3d 315, 318, 156 Cal. Rptr. 499 (1979). A default judgment in excess of the amount stated in the complaint or statement of damages, for example, can be collaterally attacked after the six-month period has expired, *Becker, supra*, 27 Cal. 3d at 492–94; *Dhawan v. Biring*, 241 Cal. App. 4th 963, 973–74, 194 Cal. Rptr. 3d 515 (2015) (collecting cases); and may even be challenged for the first time on appeal, *National Diversified Serv., Inc. v. Bernstein*, 168 Cal. App. 3d 410, 417, 214 Cal. Rptr. 113 (1985); *Petty v. Manpower, Inc.*, 94 Cal. App. 3d 794, 798, 156 Cal. Rptr. 622 (1979).

[b] Judgment Valid on Its Face But Otherwise Void

The final paragraph of CCP § 473 authorizes a trial court to set aside a judgment valid on its face but otherwise void. *E.g.*, *Rogers v. Silverman*, 216 Cal. App. 3d 1114, 265 Cal. Rptr. 286 (1989) (finding motion to vacate proper where default judgment is void because of improper service); *Manson, Iver & York v. Black*, 176 Cal. App. 4th 36, 43–47, 97 Cal. Rtpr. 3d 522 (2009) (concluding default judgment properly set aside as void because the pleadings stated an incorrect first name—Pamela instead of Paula—for the defendant). This provision of § 473 contains no express limitation period but has been construed, by analogy to CCP § 473.5, to require that a request for relief be filed within two years of the entry of the default judgment. *Rogers, supra*, 216 Cal. App. 3d at 1121–24; *but see Connelly v. Castillo, supra*, 190 Cal. App. 3d at

1589–90 (ruling a default judgment is not void where the alleged lack of jurisdiction is not evident on the face of the record; a §473 motion challenging reasonableness of notice must be filed within six months of default); *National Diversified Serv., supra,* 168 Cal. App. 3d at 415–418 (holding default judgment cannot be attacked under §473 based on a late return of summons where motion to vacate not brought within six months).

[c] Validity of Sister State Judgments

The validity of a default judgment of a sister state court sought to be enforced in California is governed by the laws of the state where it was rendered, *Huff v. Mendoza,* 109 Cal. App. 3d 677, 167 Cal. Rptr. 348 (1980); and such a sister state judgment may be vacated on any ground, including extrinsic fraud, available under California law. CCP §1710.40(a); *see Tsakos Shipping & Trading, S.A. v. Juniper Garden Town Homes, Ltd.,* 12 Cal. App. 4th 74, 15 Cal. Rptr. 2d 585 (1993) (finding sister state judgment properly set aside on grounds of extrinsic fraud where meritorious defense not raised by defendant's counsel due to conflict of interest); *see also1974 Addition, Law Revision Commission Comment to CCP §1710.40.* Can a sister state default judgment be set aside pursuant to CCP §473 on grounds of excusable neglect? Is such a collateral attack on a sister state judgment consistent with the Full Faith and Credit Clause of the U.S. Constitution? *See Liquidator of Integrity Ins. Co. v. Hendrix,* 54 Cal. App. 4th 971, 63 Cal. Rptr. 2d 240 (1997). Is CCP §1710.40(a), which authorizes a California court to vacate a sister state judgment on the grounds of extrinsic fraud, also constitutionally suspect?

[8] Independent Action in Equity

A party can also attack a default judgment upon the grounds of extrinsic fraud or mistake by commencing an independent action in equity to vacate the default judgment. *E.g., Engebretson & Co. v. Harrison,* 125 Cal. App. 3d 436, 440, 178 Cal. Rptr. 77 (1981); *Rose v. Fuqua,* 200 Cal. App. 2d 719, 724, 19 Cal. Rptr. 634 (1962). The court in an independent equity action has authority to grant relief respecting a default judgment where the defendant was prevented by extrinsic fraud or mistake from presenting a meritorious defense in the original proceedings, even though a motion to vacate a default had previously been denied. *Huff v. Mendoza, supra,* 109 Cal. App. 3d at 680–81; *Rose v. Fuqua, supra,* 200 Cal. App. 2d at 722–24; *see Groves v. Peterson,* 100 Cal. App. 4th 659, 123 Cal. Rptr. 2d 164 (2002) (ruling prior denial of motion to set aside the default in underlying action had no collateral estoppel on independent equity action); *O'Brien v. City of Santa Monica,* 220 Cal. App. 2d 67, 70, 33 Cal. Rptr. 770 (1963) (concluding a decision on motion to set aside default usually not res judicata, court can reconsider motion even though previously denied on the merits).

[9] Relief from Default Judgment in Federal Courts

Rule 60(b) of the Federal Rules of Civil Procedure, which governs requests for relief from default judgments in federal courts, provides as follows:

(b) Grounds for Relief from a Final Judgment, Order, or Proceeding. On motion and just terms, the court may relieve a party or its legal representative from a final judgment, order, or proceeding for the following reasons: (1) mistake, inadvertence, surprise, or excusable neglect; (2) newly discovered evidence that, with reasonable diligence, could not have been discovered in time to move for a new trial under Rule 59(b); (3) fraud (whether previously called intrinsic or extrinsic), misrepresentation, or misconduct by an opposing party; (4) the judgment is void; (5) the judgment has been satisfied, released, or discharged; it is based on an earlier judgment that has been reversed or vacated; or applying it prospectively is no longer equitable; or (6) any other reason that justifies relief.

(c) Timing and Effect of the Motion. (1) *Timing.* A motion under Rule 60(b) must be made within a reasonable time—and for reasons (1), (2), and (3) no more than a year after the entry of the judgment or order or the date of the proceeding. (2) *Effect on Finality.* The motion does not affect the judgment's finality or suspend its operation.

In what ways does a federal court's authority to set aside a default judgment under Rule 60(b) differ from a California state court's authority under CCP § 473 and related equitable doctrines? In what ways is it similar? Under what circumstances may a party utilize the "any other reason" grounds in Rule 60(b)(6) to set aside a default judgment? *See Klapprott v. United States*, 335 U.S. 601, 69 S. Ct. 384 (1949) (ruling relief from default judgment sought after one year is available under Rule 60(b)(6) where allegations show "extraordinary circumstances" and more than mere excusable neglect). For discussion of Rule 60(b)(6) in relation to the other grounds for relief under Rule 60(b), see Peter H. Bresnan & James P. Cornelio, Comment, *Relief from Default Judgments Under Rule 60(b)—A Study of Federal Case Law*, 49 Fordham L. Rev. 956 (1981); Mary Kay Kane, *Relief from Federal Judgments: A Morass Unrelieved by a Rule*, 30 Hastings L. Rev. 41 (1978); Thomas D. Clark, Comment, *Rule 60(b): Survey and Proposal for General Reform*, 60 Cal. L. Rev. 531 (1972).

§ 12.03 Involuntary Dismissals

[A] Introduction

If a plaintiff's lawyer fails to prosecute an action diligently, the action may be dismissed. Statutes provide for both mandatory and discretionary dismissal. *See* CCP §§ 583.110–583.430. The purpose of these statutes is to promote the trial of cases before evidence is lost or witnesses have forgotten the facts, and to protect defendants from the annoyance of an unmeritorious action remaining undecided for an indefinite period of time. *Moran v. Superior Court*, 35 Cal. 3d 229, 237, 197 Cal. Rptr. 546, 673 P.2d 216 (1983). A significant percentage of civil dispositions in the California superior courts are dismissals for delay in prosecution: 5.1% of unlimited civil cases in fiscal year 2013–14, and 4.9% in 2012–13. *See 2015 Court Statistics Report of the Judicial Council of California.*

The involuntary dismissal statutes apply to general civil actions, CCP § 583.120(a); and may even apply to some special proceedings. *See* CCP § 583.120(b); *Binyon v. State of California*, 17 Cal. App. 4th 952, 21 Cal. Rptr. 2d 673 (1993) (concluding the fact that petition for administrative mandamus involved a special proceeding did not place it beyond reach of dismissal for delay-in-prosecution statutes). These statutes apply to complaints, cross-complaints, and other initial pleadings. CCP § 583.110(b). A dismissal for lack of prosecution before trial is without prejudice. CCP § 581(b)(3). Because such dismissals are not on the merits, they have no res judicata effect. *Wilson v. Bittick*, 63 Cal. 2d 30, 35–36, 45 Cal. Rptr. 31, 403 P.2d 159 (1965). Consequently, if a cause of action is not barred by the applicable statute of limitations, a party may again litigate it after a dismissal by commencement of a new lawsuit. *See, e.g., Gonsalves v. Bank of America*, 16 Cal. 2d 169, 172–73, 105 P.2d 118 (1940); *Nassif v. Mun. Court*, 214 Cal. App. 3d 1294, 263 Cal. Rptr. 195 (1989).

In addition to the statewide diligence requirements, other state and local rules provide for involuntary dismissal. Several statutes provide specific grounds for dismissal, including failure to pay transfer costs and fees following a change of venue, failure to amend a complaint following a successful demurrer or motion to strike, failure to comply with discovery, failure to appear for trial, and failure to post court-ordered security for costs. *See generally* 2 CEB, *California Civil Procedure Before Trial, Dismissal* §§ 39.1–39.132 (4th ed. 2015). More importantly, local fast track rules implementing the Trial Court Delay Reduction Act frequently impose shorter time limits than the state statutes, and also authorize sanctions for failure to comply. Government Code §§ 68608 & 68616; CCP §§ 575.1 & 575.2. In addition, a court has inherent authority to dismiss an action for severe misconduct. *Lyons v. Wickhorst*, 42 Cal. 3d 911, 915, 231 Cal. Rptr. 738, 727 P.2d 1019 (1986).

This section will discuss: (1) Mandatory dismissals for lack of prosecution under state statues; (2) discretionary dismissals for lack of prosecution under state statutes; (3) involuntary dismissals under local fast track rules; and (4) involuntary dismissals under other state laws. A detailed chart which compares these various involuntary dismissal statutes is set forth in *CEB, California Civil Procedure Before Trial, supra*, § 39.7; *see also* Schwing, *California Affirmative Defenses* §§ 3:1–3:33, 28:1–28:36, 29.1–29.13 (2015).

[B] Mandatory Dismissals for Lack of Prosecution

Dismissal is mandatory if a plaintiff fails to meet any one of three statutory deadlines: (1) Failure to serve the action within three years of filing, CCP §§ 583.110, 583.210; (2) failure to bring the case to trial within five years, CCP § 583.310; and (3) failure to bring a case to a new trial within three years, CCP § 583.320.

[1] *Failure to Serve the Action within Three Years of Filing*

Under CCP § 583.210(a), dismissal is mandatory if the action is not served within three years of filing of the complaint. Because return of service is required within 60 days of actual service, the plaintiff has an additional 60 days after the three-year period to file the proof of service. CCP § 583.210(b). This provision applies both to named defendants and to fictitious defendants. *See Nelson v. A.H. Robins Co.*, 149 Cal. App. 3d 862, 197 Cal. Rptr. 179 (1983); *Lesko v. Superior Court*, 127 Cal. App. 3d 476, 179 Cal. Rptr. 595 (1982).

[a] Effect of Amended Complaint

When new parties are added by an amended complaint, the three-year period begins to run from the filing of the amended complaint. *See, e.g., American W. Banker v. Price Waterhouse*, 12 Cal. App. 4th 39, 14 Cal. Rptr. 2d 916 (1993) (adding new plaintiffs); *Hennessey's Tavern, Inc. v. American Air Filter Co.*, 204 Cal. App. 3d 1351, 251 Cal. Rptr. 859 (1988) (adding new defendants). Where a defendant named in an amended complaint was originally sued under a fictitious name, however, the three-year period begins when the original complaint was filed. *See Barrington v. A.H. Robins Co.*, 39 Cal. 3d 146, 216 Cal. Rptr. 405, 702 P.2d 563 (1985). But when a new cause of action based on different operative facts is alleged in the amended complaint, the three-year period runs from the filing of the amended complaint. *Barrington*, 39 Cal. 3d at 150–157.

[b] Statutory Tolling Provisions

Although dismissal for failure to serve within three years is mandatory, the plaintiff can avoid dismissal on a proper showing of tolling or excuse. Specifically, in computing the time in which service must be made, the time during which any of the following conditions existed is excluded: (a) The defendant was not amenable to service; (b) the prosecution of the action was stayed; (c) the parties were litigating the validity of service; or (d) service was "impossible, impracticable, or futile due to causes beyond plaintiff's control." CCP § 583.240. Under what circumstances is a defendant "not amenable to the process of the court" within the meaning of CCP § 583.240(b)? When the defendant is absent from, or concealed within, the state, and his whereabouts unknown? When the defendant is not subject to the court's jurisdiction? *See Watts v. Crawford*, 10 Cal. 4th 743, 42 Cal. Rptr. 2d 81, 896 P.2d 807 (1995) (concluding the relevant inquiry is whether the party was subject to being served under applicable constitutional and statutory provisions, not whether the defendant was reasonably available as a practical matter for service of process); *Perez v. Smith*, 19 Cal. App. 4th 1595, 24 Cal. Rptr. 2d 186 (1993) (ruling a defendant is amenable to service even though only method of service is by publication).

Under what circumstances is service "impossible, impracticable, or futile due to causes beyond the plaintiff's control" within the meaning of § 583.240(d)? Where the process server loses the original summons? *See Bishop v. Silva*, 234 Cal. App. 3d 1317,

1321, 285 Cal. Rptr. 910 (1991) (concluding excuse should be strictly construed; problems caused by plaintiff's counsel or process server were within plaintiff's own control). Failure to discover relevant facts or evidence is expressly not a cause beyond the plaintiff's control under CCP § 583.240(d), and therefore the plaintiff's reasonable diligence is not an excuse. *Bishop v. Silva, supra,* 234 Cal. App. 3d at 1321–24.

[c] Extensions of the Three-Year Limit

In addition to these tolling provisions, statutory exceptions to the three-year requirement apply when the parties extend the period by written stipulation, CCP § 583.220; when the parties extend the period by oral stipulation in open court, CCP § 583.230; and when the defendant makes a general appearance, CCP § 583.220. Finally, estoppel may bar the dismissal where a defendant has induced the plaintiff to delay service. *See* CCP § 583.140.

To prevent dismissal, any claimed general appearance must have occurred within the mandatory three-year period. An appearance made thereafter does not deprive a defendant of his right to dismissal. *See Busching v. Superior Court,* 12 Cal. 3d 44, 52, 115 Cal. Rptr. 241, 524 P.2d 369 (1974); *Blank v. Kirwan,* 39 Cal. 3d 311, 333, 216 Cal. Rptr. 718, 703 P.2d 58 (1985) ("[A] general appearance after the three years had run did not operate to deprive a defendant of his right to a dismissal"). A general appearance is an act by the defendant recognizing the court's jurisdiction and reflecting an intent to submit to it. *General Ins. Co. v. Superior Court,* 15 Cal. 3d 449, 124 Cal. Rptr. 745, 541 P.2d 289 (1975). Examples include filing a responsive pleading, filing a motion for transfer of venue, giving a notice of appearance, agreeing to accept service and requesting an extension of time to plead, and affirmatively engaging in discovery. *See id.*; CCP § 1014; *see also* 2 CEB, *California Civil Practice Before Trial Dismissal* § 39.21–39.22 (4th ed. 2015).

The doctrine of equitable estoppel is applicable to motions to dismiss for failure to effectuate service within three years. *See, e.g., Tresway Aero, Inc. v. Superior Court,* 5 Cal. 3d 431,437–39, 96 Cal. Rptr. 571, 487 P.2d 1211 (1971); *Brookview Condo. Owners' Assn. v. Heltzer Enterprises-Brookview,* 218 Cal. App. 3d 502, 267 Cal. Rptr. 76 (1990). If statements or conduct by the defendant lulls the plaintiff into a false sense of security resulting in inaction, and there is reasonable reliance, estoppel is available to prevent the defendant from profiting from his deception. *Tejada v. Blas* (1987) 196 Cal. App. 3d 1335, 1341, 242 Cal. Rptr. 538 (1987). For example, in *Tresway Aero, Inc. v. Superior Court, supra,* the defendant knew service was defective, but requested and received an extension to answer, fully aware that the extension would expire beyond the three-year period. Instead of answering, he moved to dismiss. The court found defendant's conduct to be a deliberate maneuver calculated to mislead plaintiff into believing service had been accomplished, and held that defendant was estopped to seek dismissal. *Tresway Aero, supra,* 5 Cal. 3d at 440–42.

[2] Failure to Bring the Case to Trial within Five Years

Under CCP § 583.310, dismissal is mandatory if the action is not brought to trial within five years after it is commenced. To determine whether this requirement has been satisfied, the key question is not whether there has actually been a trial but whether the action has been "brought to a stage where a final disposition is to be made of it." *Berri v. Superior Court*, 43 Cal. 2d 856, 859, 279 P.2d 8 (1955). Therefore, a defendant is not entitled to an involuntary dismissal on this ground where all the allegations of the complaint have been admitted or the parties have submitted an agreed statement of facts since the defendant has conceded that a trial is not required. *See* CEB, *California Civil Procedure Before Trial, supra*, § 39.25 (citing cases). For the same reason, any pretrial proceeding resulting in a final judgment within the five-year limit—such as a demurrer, a motion for summary judgment, binding arbitration, or a motion in limine—satisfies the requirement. *Id.* at §§ 39.30–39.34.

[a] When Action is "Brought to Trial"

If the matter is not resolved by a pretrial proceeding, the question arises as to when an action is "brought to trial." In a jury trial the statutory requirement is met when the jury is impaneled, i.e., when the entire panel of prospective jurors is sworn in, before voir dire. *See Hartman v. Santamarina* 30 Cal. 3d 762, 180 Cal. Rptr. 337, 639 P.2d 979 (1982); *Hilliard v. A.H. Robins Co.*, 148 Cal. App. 3d 374, 390, 196 Cal. Rptr. 117 (1983). In a court trial, the statutory requirement is met when the first witness is sworn. *Hartman, supra*, 30 Cal. 3d at 765–67; *Marriage of MacFarlane & Lang*, 8 Cal. App. 4th 247, 10 Cal. Rptr. 2d 157 (1992) (ruling partial trial satisfied five-year statute). Once the jury or first witness is sworn, the five-year statute is satisfied and the action may be continued to a later date. *Marriage of MacFarlane & Lang, supra*, 8 Cal. App. 4th at 253–57 (bifurcated dissolution of marriage proceedings).

[b] Plaintiff's Motion for Preference

The burden is on plaintiff to ensure that the action is brought to trial within the five-year period. *See Howard v. Thrifty Drug & Disc. Stores*, 10 Cal. 4th 424, 41 Cal. Rptr. 2d 362, 895 P.2d 469 (1995). As the deadline approaches, the plaintiff must move for preference under CCP § 36(e) or to specially set the case for trial under Rule 3.1335 of the California Rules of Court. *See Wale v. Rodriguez*, 206 Cal. App. 3d 129, 253 Cal. Rptr. 382 (1988). Failure to seek a preference may in itself show plaintiff's lack of diligence. *See Tejada v. Blas*, 196 Cal. App. 3d 1335, 242 Cal. Rptr. 538 (1987); *Westinghouse Elec. Corp. v. Superior Court*, 143 Cal. App. 3d 95, 107, 191 Cal. Rptr. 549 (1983).

Even where the plaintiff brings such a motion, the court has no mandatory duty to provide a preferential trial date and may decline to do so where the plaintiff has failed to show due diligence in prosecuting the action. *See, e.g., Howard, supra*, 10 Cal. 4th at 440–41 (ruling motion for preferential trial setting raises essentially the same issues as a motion for discretionary dismissal; court should consider factors listed in former Rule 373(e) [now Rule 3.1342(e)]); *Salas v. Sears, Roebuck & Co.*, 42 Cal. 3d 342, 228 Cal. Rptr. 504, 721 P.2d 590 (1986) (finding no mandatory duty to set a preferential trial date; trial court should consider such discretionary factors as the condition of court calendar, dilatory conduct by plaintiff, and prejudice to defendant of an accelerated trial date).

[c] Statutory Exceptions to Mandatory Dismissal

Although the dismissal for failure to bring a case to trial within five years is mandatory, a few statutory exceptions do apply. First, the time may be extended by written stipulation or oral stipulation in open court. CCP §§ 583.330(a) & (b); *see, e.g., Munoz v. City of Tracy*, 238 Cal. App. 4th 354, 189 Cal. Rptr. 3d 590 (2015) (holding trial court erred in dismissing case because parties executed stipulation extending time for trial to a date certain beyond the five-year deadline). Second, the time will be extended where the court's jurisdiction is suspended or prosecution is stayed. CCP §§ 583.340(a) & (b); *see, e.g., Bruns v. E-Commerce Exch., Inc.*, 51 Cal. 4th 717, 122 Cal. Rptr. 3d 331, 248 P.3d 1185 (2011) (concluding an action is "stayed" under § 583.340(b) only when the stay encompasses all proceedings in the action, and not when the stay only applies to specific aspects such as discovery; however, a partial stay may be a relevant factor in applying the discretionary "impossible, impracticable, or futile." exception under § 583.340(c)); *Spanair S.A. v. McDonnell Douglas Corp.*, 172 Cal. App. 4th 348, 90 Cal. Rptr. 3d 864 (2009) (holding trial court erred by dismissing for failure to prosecute because the trial court's jurisdiction was suspended during removal to federal court until remand back to state court, for all but seven months between filing the complaint and entry of the dismissal order). Third, the time will be extended where bringing the action to trial was "impossible, impracticable, or futile." CCP § 583.340(c). The burden is on the plaintiff to make this showing, which requires proof that the plaintiff has exercised reasonable diligence in prosecuting the case. *Moran, supra*, 35 Cal. 3d at 238. Finally, the time will be extended on a showing of waiver or estoppel. CCP § 583.140.

Nye v. 20th Century Insurance Co.

Court of Appeal of California, Second Appellate District
225 Cal. App. 3d 1041, 275 Cal. Rptr. 319 (1990)

Epstein, Justice.

The plaintiff and appellant, Carol A. Nye, appeals from an order granting respondent's motion to dismiss for failure to prosecute. (Code Civ. Proc., § 583.410; all further code citations are to the Code of Civil Procedure.) We conclude that the trial court acted within the proper exercise of its discretion in dismissing the action, and affirm.

FACTUAL AND PROCEDURAL SUMMARY

Appellant was involved in an automobile accident in April 1984. She brought this action against the respondent, 20th Century Insurance Company, her insurance carrier, after it refused to replace her damaged engine with a new engine.

The lawsuit was filed in Los Angeles Superior Court on September 12, 1984. Respondent demurred to the original complaint. An amended complaint was filed on December 28, 1984, and respondent filed its answer on January 17, 1985. Some two and one-half years later, on August 24, 1987, appellant filed an at issue memorandum, effectively placing the case on the court's schedule of matters ready to be set for conference and trial. The parties engaged in some discovery (two sets of requests for admissions propounded by respondent, interrogatories by respondent and two depositions), the last of which was completed by February 1986. Defendant filed a motion for summary judgment or summary adjudication of issues on October 11, 1988. The court ruled on that motion on November 9, 1988.

On August 2, 1989, appellant's attorney called the calendar clerk of the trial court to inquire about the status of the case, and to inform her of the upcoming running of the five-year statute (§ 583.310). He learned that no status conference had been set, and that it was unlikely that one would be set before September 12, 1989, the fifth anniversary of the lawsuit. Appellant's counsel then sought a stipulation to extend the statute from his opponent. When that was declined, he sought an order shortening time in aid of a motion to specially set, which he filed on August 4, 1989.

The trial court specially set the motion for hearing, and authorized respondent to file a motion to dismiss to be heard at the same time. Respondent filed a motion to dismiss, as authorized by the court. Both motions were heard on August 16, 1989, at which time the court denied the motion to specially set and granted the order of dismissal. The court granted reconsideration of its orders, and they were reargued on August 28, 1989, at which time they were reissued. A formal order denying special setting and dismissing the lawsuit was entered on September 12, 1989. It was followed by the instant appeal.

DISCUSSION

Appellant argues that the trial court abused its discretion in granting the motion to dismiss, and in refusing to set her case for trial before the expiration of the five-year period of section 583.310. Trial courts are given wide discretion in ruling on such motions, and their determinations may only be overturned on a showing that the discretion has been abused.

While there is a public policy favoring disposition of cases on their merits, that policy coexists with the policy "that a plaintiff shall proceed with reasonable diligence in the prosecution of an action." (§ 583.130) In *Salas v. Sears, Roebuck & Co.* (1986) 42 Cal. 3d 342, 347 [228 Cal. Rptr. 504, 721 P.2d 590], the Supreme Court pointed out that " ... although the interests of justice weigh heavily against disposing of litigation on procedural grounds—a policy we reaffirm—that policy will necessarily prevail *only* if a plaintiff makes some showing of excusable delay." (Emphasis added.) From this, it follows that "a plaintiff, in order to avoid dismissal for delay in prosecution, must show a reasonable excuse for such delay; once he makes that showing, the trial court must consider all pertinent actions, including prejudice to defendant from the delay, before deciding whether or not to dismiss." (*Cordova v. Vons Grocery Co.* (1987) 196 Cal. App. 3d 1526, 1533 [242 Cal. Rptr. 605].)

In the case before us, the appellant offered no excuse at all for her delays. Some two and one-half years elapsed between the time that her lawsuit became at issue and the time that her attorney placed it in line for trial by filing an at-issue memorandum. Her attorney waited until a mere 41 days before the expiration of the five-year period until inquiring of the court as to the status of the case. The response, that nothing was scheduled to be heard within the remaining time, should have come as no surprise. Only on receipt of this information did counsel take any action — by moving the court to specially set the case. That motion requires a showing of good cause. (California Rules of Court, Rule 375(b) [now, Rule 1335].) The only showing made was that the statutory period would run unless the case were set. As *Salas* and other authorities teach, this is not enough to compel a court to grant the motion. In effect, the motion to specially set for trial on minimal notice, if granted, would allow this plaintiff to take a "cut" in line, displacing other parties who had been diligently pursuing their causes.

Appellant argues that there is no showing that respondent was prejudiced by her delay in prosecuting the action. In point of fact, the trial court found that respondent would be prejudiced by an order for immediate trial. But even if this were not so, absence of prejudice would neither compel the trial court to grant a motion to specially set nor prevent it from granting a motion to dismiss. (*See Blank v. Kirwan* (1985) 39 Cal. 3d 311, 332 [216 Cal. Rptr. 718, 703 P.2d 58].)

Finally, appellant argues that she received less than the 45-day notice prescribed for discretionary dismissals by California Rules of Court, rule 373(a) [now, Rule 3.1335(a)]. She can hardly complain on that ground, having come to court with less than 45 days remaining before the end of the five-year period, having then sought an order shortening time so that her motion to specially set could be heard; and not having objected on the ground of insufficient notice when the trial court allowed respondent to file its motion on shortened time, or during the arguments on the merits on the motions or on reconsideration of the court's orders. Given that the court acted within its discretion in denying the motion to specially set, if the court had denied or not acted upon the motion to dismiss, dismissal under section 583.310 would have been required within a few weeks thereafter, since nothing operated to toll the running of the five-year period.

DISPOSITION

The order of dismissal is affirmed, and the purported appeal from the order granting summary adjudication of an issue is dismissed. Respondent is to have its costs on appeal.

Notes and Questions

(1) *When is the five-year period tolled due to the impossibility exception?* As the *Nye* court explains, plaintiffs who have failed to act diligently will not be allowed to cut in line ahead of diligent litigants. Under what circumstances will the five-year period

be tolled because bringing the case to trial was "impossible, impracticable, or futile" within the meaning of CCP § 583.340(c)? When a courtroom is unavailable for trial? *See, e.g., Coe v. City of Los Angeles*, 24 Cal. App. 4th 88, 29 Cal. Rptr. 2d 297 (1994) (holding trial court abused discretion in dismissing action; five-year statute must be tolled by aggregate of court-ordered continuances based upon courtroom unavailability); *Chin v. Meier*, 235 Cal. App. 3d 1473, 1 Cal. Rptr. 2d 499 (1991) (ruling a court-ordered continuance because of courtroom unavailability made it impossible for plaintiff to proceed to trial; five-year statute tolled for that period of impossibility regardless of whether a reasonable time remains to bring the action to trial before expiration of five-year limitation period); *but see De Santiago v. D & G Plumbing, Inc.*, 155 Cal. App. 4th 365, 65 Cal. Rptr. 3d 882 (2007) (concluding a 318-day continuance due to court congestion followed by another continuance for an unspecified reason, which caused the trial date to be set after expiration of the five-year period, did not qualify for the impracticability exception because the plaintiff was not reasonably diligent in prosecuting its case; instead of acquiescing in the setting the trial date, the plaintiff should have alerted the trial court that the selected date was beyond the five-year mark and requested an earlier trial date, or moved to advance the trial to an earlier date); *Jordan v. Superstar Sandcars*, 182 Cal. App. 4th 1416, 107 Cal. Rptr. 3d 5 (2010) (finding court congestion and two short moratoriums on civil trials did not make trial within five years impractical or impossible because plaintiffs failed to show that their case would not have been tried if they had been reasonably diligent).

When the plaintiff's counsel is seriously ill or otherwise disabled? *Compare Sanchez v. City of Los Angeles*, 109 Cal. App. 4th 1262, 135 Cal. Rptr. 2d 869 (2003) (ruling the fact that attorney for one defendant committed suicide during last six months of statutory period did not make it impracticable, impossible, or futile for plaintiffs to bring action to trial within meaning of § 583.320; and *Sierra Nevada Memorial-Miners Hosp., Inc. v. Superior Court*, 217 Cal. App. 3d 464, 266 Cal. Rptr. 50 (1990) (finding dismissal appropriate because no causal connection between counsel's physical disabilities and failure to satisfy five-year requirement) *with Him v. Superior Court*, 184 Cal. App. 3d 35, 228 Cal. Rptr. 839 (1986) (ruling five-year period tolled for several weeks due to counsel's illness, where counsel was sole practitioner and illness at end of five-year period) and *Tamburina v. Combined Ins. Co. of America*, 147 Cal. App. 4th 323, 54 Cal. Rptr. 3d 175 (2007) (holding stipulated continuances totaling 424 days, attributable to the plaintiff's and his attorney's serious health problems, qualified as a circumstance of impracticability within the meaning of CCP § 583.340(c)).

(a) Does CCP § 583.340(c) require a court to exclude the time during which the defendant was in default from the five years allowed to bring the case to trial? *Compare Howard, supra*, 10 Cal. 4th at 438–39 (noting the impossibility exception almost invariably applies when a default judgment has been entered, effectively bringing litigation to a standstill) *with Hughes v. Kimble*, 5 Cal. App. 4th 59, 6 Cal. Rptr. 2d 616 (1992) (ruling the time between entry of default and entry of default judgment should be excluded only if plaintiff used due diligence to obtain entry of the judgment).

(b) Does a settlement agreement between the parties reached during a judicially mandated settlement conference toll the mandatory dismissal statute where, due to a subsequent disagreement over specific payment terms, the settlement was not reduced to a judgment within the five-year period? *See Canal Street, Ltd. v. Sorich*, 77 Cal. App. 4th 602, 91 Cal. Rptr. 2d 811 (2000) (holding the time during which a settlement agreement is in effect tolls the five-year period because attempting to bring an action to trial when all issues have been resolved through settlement would be "futile" within the meaning of CCP § 583.340(c)).

(c) As a condition to being excused from the five-year requirement, a plaintiff must have exercised reasonable diligence in prosecuting the action. *Moran v. Superior Court*, 35 Cal. 3d 229, 237–38, 197 Cal. Rptr. 546, 673 P.2d 216 (1983); *Wilshire Bundy Corp. v. Auerbach*, 228 Cal. App. 3d 1280, 1286–87, 279 Cal. Rptr. 488 (1991). Consequently, the normal delays and mistakes in litigation do not toll the five-year statute. For example, the following delays do not usually toll the statute: discovery delays, attorney neglect in monitoring the case, transfer delays, extensions of time, attempted appeal from a nonappealable order, reference of the action to a referee, mistakes in time calculation, and errors by the clerk's office. *See California Civil Practice-Procedure* § 22.52 (Thompson Reuters 2015); 2 CEB, *California Civil Procedure Before Trial, Dismissal* §§ 39.51–39.62 (4th ed. 2015) (citing numerous cases of excuse and nonexcuse).

(2) *Does judicial arbitration toll the statute?* Submission of an action to judicial arbitration does not suspend the various statutory time periods. CCP § 1141.17(a). However, if an action is or remains submitted to judicial arbitration more than 4-1/2 years after plaintiff has filed the action, "then the time beginning on the date four years and six months after the plaintiff has filed the action and ending on the date on which a request for trial de novo is filed ... shall not be included in computing the five-year period." CCP § 1141.17(b). This tolling provision applies regardless of whether the judicial arbitration is mandatory, or is by stipulation or election. *See, e.g., Jackson v. Garmon*, 217 Cal. App. 3d 860, 266 Cal. Rptr. 201 (1990); *Porreco v. Red Top RV Ctr.*, 216 Cal. App. 3d 113, 124, 264 Cal. Rptr. 609 (1989). The five-year statute only stops running for arbitrations beginning or continuing into the last six months of the five-year period, and then only from the four-year six-month date after filing the action until the date a trial de novo is requested. *Howard v. Thrifty Drug & Discount Stores, supra*, 10 Cal. 4th at 434–35.

The five year deadline for bringing a civil action to trial is also tolled where the action is submitted to mediation during the last six months of the five year period. CCP §§ 583.310, 583.360(a), 1775.7(b); *see Gonzales v. County of Los Angeles*, 122 Cal. App. 4th 1124, 19 Cal. Rptr. 3d 381 (2004) (concluding tolling period authorized by CCP § 1775.7(b) for mediation operates in the same manner as when cases judicially ordered to arbitration). Under what circumstances, if any, is the five year deadline tolled where the action is submitted to mediation prior to the last six months of the five year period? *See Gaines v. Fidelity Nat. Title Ins. Co.*, 62 Cal. 4th 1081, 199 Cal. Rptr. 3d 137, 365 P.3d 904 (2016) (holding that a complete stay entered by the trial court while the parties engage in mediation will toll the five-year period, but a partial stay will not unless it results in a circumstance of impossibility, impracticality, or futility).

(3) *Is the five-year period tolled during the pendency of a petition for writ of mandate?* Courts have held that the pendency of a petition for writ of mandate may extend the statute on the grounds of impossibility, impracticality, or futility. *See, e.g., New West Fed. Savings & Loan Assn. v. Superior Court*, 223 Cal. App. 3d 1145, 273 Cal. Rptr. 37 (1990); *Kaye v. Mount La Jolla Homeowners Assn.*, 204 Cal. App. 3d 1476, 252 Cal. Rptr. 67 (1988) (interlocutory appeal).

(4) *How long does plaintiff have after tolling to bring the action to trial?* Under CCP § 583.350, if the end of the tolling period is less than six months before the five-year deadline, the plaintiff has a full six months to bring the action to trial after the end of the period of tolling or extension.

(5) *When is the defendant estopped to seek dismissal under the five-year statute?* Estoppel has been upheld where the defendant has lulled the plaintiff into a false sense of security by words or affirmative conduct. *See* CCP § 583.140; *Borglund v. Bombardier, Ltd.*, 121 Cal. App. 3d 276, 281, 175 Cal. Rptr. 150 (1981). Examples of such estoppel include cases where the defendant requested a trial continuance past the five-year deadline, where the defendant verbally assured the plaintiff that it would not move to dismiss under the statute, and where the defendant knowingly acquiesced in the plaintiff's miscalculation of the deadline. *California Civil Practice-Procedure* § 22.54 (Thompson Reuters 2015) (citing cases).

[3] *Failure to Bring the Case to New Trial within Three Years*

Under CCP § 583.320, dismissal is mandatory if the plaintiff fails to bring an action to trial within three years after a mistrial, hung jury, order for new trial, or appellate remand. *See, e.g., Finnie v. Dist. No. 1-Pac. Coast Dist. Assn.*, 9 Cal. App. 4th 1311, 12 Cal. Rptr. 2d 348 (1992). However, this section does not apply where the initial five-year period for bringing an action to trial has not yet expired; the plaintiff gets the benefit of the five-year statute. CCP § 583.320(d). A plaintiff is entitled to an extension of the three-year deadline on the same grounds as allowed for an extension of the initial five-year period. CCP §§ 583.310–583.360.

[C] Discretionary Dismissals for Lack of Prosecution

Discretionary dismissal is permitted under CCP § 583.410 when a plaintiff fails to meet any one of three statutory deadlines: Failure to serve defendant within two years, CCP § 583.420(a)(1); failure to bring the case to trial within two years, CCP § 583.420(a)(2) and Rule 3.1340, Cal. Rules of Ct.; and failure to bring a case to new trial within two years, CCP § 583.420(a)(3). *See Eliceche v. Federal Land Bank Assn.*, 103 Cal. App. 4th 1349, 128 Cal. Rptr. 2d 200 (2002) (affirming discretionary dismissal for failure to prosecute18 days short of the date set for trial).

Rule 3.1342(e) of the Rules of Court governs the court's exercise of discretion in ordering dismissals on these grounds and requires the court to be guided by the policies favoring the rights of parties to make stipulations and the disposition of actions on their merits. Moreover, before entering a discretionary dismissal, Rule 3.1342(e) requires a court to consider: the entire court file; the availability of parties for service of process; the plaintiff's diligence in effecting service; the extent of settlement discussions; the parties' diligence in discovery and pretrial proceedings; the nature and complexity of the case; the applicable law; the pendency of related litigation; the nature of extensions of time; the condition of the court's calendar; the availability of an earlier trial date; the interests of justice; and any other relevant facts or circumstances.

[1] Failure to Serve Defendant within Two Years

Whereas under CCP § 583.210(a) dismissal is mandatory where the plaintiff has failed to serve the defendant in three years, under CCP § 583.420(a)(1) a court has the discretionary authority to dismiss the action if the plaintiff has failed to serve within two years. This provision, like the mandatory statute, applies to both named and fictitious defendants. *Clark v. Stabond Corp.*, 197 Cal. App. 3d 50, 58, 242 Cal. Rptr. 676 (1987). The provisions for computing and extending time under the three-year mandatory statute apply to the two-year discretionary statute. CCP § 583.420(b).

[a] Excusable Delay

If a defendant demonstrates that discretionary dismissal is appropriate under the circumstances of the case, the burden shifts to the plaintiff to show a reasonable excuse for the delay. *See Roach v. Lewis*, 14 Cal. App. 4th 1179, 18 Cal. Rptr. 2d 281 (1993); *Putnam v. Clague*, 3 Cal. App. 4th 542, 549, 5 Cal. Rptr. 2d 25 (1992). Financial inability to conduct discovery or otherwise prosecute the lawsuit does not constitute a reasonable excuse for failure to serve a summons. *American W. Banker v. Price Waterhouse*, 12 Cal. App. 4th 39, 14 Cal. Rptr. 2d 916 (1993).

The courts are divided over the proper test to apply when determining whether a delay is excusable. In *Putnam v. Clague, supra,* 3 Cal. App. 4th at 557–558, the court applied a two prong test: The trial court judge should determine whether the explanation for the delay is "credible under all the circumstances" and, if it is, should consider whether a reasonably competent attorney could conclude that the decision to delay was justified under the circumstances. However, the court in *Roach v. Lewis, supra,* 14 Cal. App. 4th at 1184–85, rejected the *Putnam* test as giving too much deference to an attorney's strategy, and instead applied only the factors set forth in Rule 3.1342(e). For a discussion of this division by a divided court, see *Williams v. Los Angeles Unified Sch. Dist.*, 23 Cal. App. 4th 84, 28 Cal. Rptr. 2d 219 (1994), where the majority opinion favored the *Roach* approach, but the dissent applied the *Putnam* standard.

[b] Prejudice Not Required

There has been a conflict of views on the question of whether a showing of prejudice to the defendant is required to support a discretionary dismissal for failure to prosecute. Prior to the Supreme Court decision in *Blank v. Kirwan*, 39 Cal. 3d 311, 216 Cal. Rptr. 718, 703 P.2d 58 (1985), a number of appellate courts had held that a defendant must show actual prejudice caused by the plaintiff's delay. *See, e.g., Hurtado v. Statewide Home Loan Co.*, 167 Cal. App. 3d 1019, 213 Cal. Rptr. 712 (1985). These cases were impliedly overruled in *Blank*, in which the Supreme Court affirmed a discretionary dismissal although no prejudice had been shown, explaining that the legislative policy underlying the dismissal statutes is not solely to protect the defendant but also to "expedite the administration of justice by compelling every person who files an action to prosecute it with promptness and diligence." *Blank v. Kirwan, supra*, 39 Cal. 3d at 332.

After *Blank*, most courts follow the rule that a defendant need make no affirmative showing of actual prejudice to be entitled to discretionary dismissal when the delay is unreasonable. *See, e.g., Howard v. Thrifty Drug & Disc. Stores*, 10 Cal. 4th 424, 443–44, 41 Cal. Rptr. 2d 362, 895 P.2d 469 (1995) ("[W]hen a plaintiff fails to make a showing of excusable delay, the trial court remains within its discretion in dismissing the case despite the lack of actual prejudice"); *Terzian v. County of Ventura*, 24 Cal. App. 4th 78, 83, 28 Cal. Rptr. 2d 809 (1994) (ruling defendant did not have to show actual prejudice when unjustified delay in service of almost three years). But even after *Blank*, many courts consider lack of prejudice to the defendant as a valid consideration where the plaintiff has acted diligently from the outset and has offered a reasonable explanation for the delay. *See, e.g., Putnam v. Clague*, 3 Cal. App. 4th 542, 562–66, 5 Cal. Rptr. 2d 25 (1992); *Maggio, Inc. v. United Farm Workers*, 227 Cal. App. 3d 847, 883–84, 278 Cal. Rptr. 250 (1991); *see also Howard v. Thrifty Drug & Disc. Stores, supra*, 10 Cal. 4th at 442 (observing that a showing of actual prejudice, although not a prerequisite, can be a critical factor in granting a discretionary motion to dismiss). Which is the better view? Why? Many courts have concluded that a presumption of prejudice is appropriate where the plaintiff has delayed service of the complaint and summons. *See, e.g., County of Los Angeles v. Superior Court*, 203 Cal. App. 3d 1205, 1210–11, 250 Cal. Rptr. 481 (1988); *Schumpert v. Tishman Co.*, 198 Cal. App. 3d 598, 605–606, 243 Cal. Rptr. 810 (1988); *Luti v. Graco, Inc.*, 170 Cal. App. 3d 228, 233, 215 Cal. Rptr. 902 (1985). Why is prejudice presumed from a delay in service? *See Schumpert., supra*, 198 Cal. App. 3d at 604–607.

[2] *Failure to Bring the Case to Trial within Two Years*

[a] Discretionary Dismissal Rules

Whereas under CCP § 583.310 dismissal is mandatory when the plaintiff has failed to bring the case to trial within five years, under Rule 3.1340 of the California Rules of Court a court has the discretionary authority to dismiss the action where the action has not been brought to trial or conditionally settled within two years. *See, e.g., Howard v. Thrifty Drug & Disc. Stores*, 10 Cal. 4th 424, 441–44, 41 Cal. Rptr. 2d 362, 895

P.2d 469 (1995) (concluding that although plaintiff did conduct successful judicial arbitration and defendant made no showing of prejudice, trial court did not abuse its discretion in dismissing case based on former Rule 373(e) [now, Rule 3.1342(e)] factors). Code of Civil Procedure § 583.420(a)(2) adopted a three-year period, but authorized the Judicial Council to adopt a two-year period, which it did in Rule 3.1340. Under Rule 3.1340(c), "conditionally settled" means a settlement agreement has been reached that conditions dismissal on the satisfactory completion of specified terms which are not to be completed within two years after the case is filed. Notice of a conditional settlement must be filed with the court in compliance with Rule 3.1385.

The provisions for tolling and extensions that apply under the five-year mandatory dismissal rule also apply to discretionary dismissals for failure to bring an action to trial. CCP § 583.420(b); *see Danielson v. ITT Indus. Credit Co.*, 199 Cal. App. 3d 645, 245 Cal. Rptr. 126 (1988). And as with mandatory dismissal, estoppel may bar a defendant from seeking discretionary dismissal. *See Los Angeles v. Gleneagle Dev. Co.*, 62 Cal. App. 3d 543, 133 Cal. Rptr. 212 (1976).

In *Lopez v. State of California*, 49 Cal. App. 4th 1292, 57 Cal. Rptr. 2d 266 (1996), the court held that the routine setting of case for trial within 5 years, as opposed to a special motion for preferential treatment, did not preclude trial court from discretionary dismissal of the case where plaintiffs did nothing to seriously advance case to trial for the four-plus years between filing of the complaint and filing of motion to dismiss. However, in *Cohen v. Hughes Markets, Inc.*, 36 Cal. App. 4th 1693, 43 Cal. Rptr. 2d 66 (1995), the court held that the trial court erred in dismissing an action for lack of prosecution under § 583.420(a)(2)(B) and former Rule 372(a) (now, Rule 3.3140(a)), which authorize discretionary dismissal for lack of prosecution, because an action less than two years old is not subject to dismissal on that basis.

[b] Discretionary Dismissal for Failure to Appear

Pursuant to CCP § 581(b)(5), the trial court may also dismiss an action when either party fails to appear on the day set for trial, and the other party appears and asks for dismissal. *See Vernon v. Great W. Bank*, 51 Cal. App. 4th 1007, 59 Cal. Rptr. 2d 350 (1996) (affirming dismissal where the plaintiff, who had a history of not diligently prosecuting the case, failed to appear on the date set for retrial); *see also Link v. Carter*, 60 Cal. App. 4th 1315, 71 Cal. Rptr. 2d 130 (1998) (finding trial court abused its discretion in dismissing a case for failure of the plaintiff to appear at trial and in refusing to grant a continuance without taking into account the high degree of diligence plaintiff employed for over four years in attempting to bring the case to trial); *Cohen v. Hughes Markets, Inc., supra* (holding the fact that the plaintiff was not present in court when the matter was called for trial did not warrant dismissal inasmuch as plaintiff's counsel was present, a jury had to be selected, and the plaintiff would have arrived from overseas by the time his presence as a witness was required).

[c] Discretionary Dismissal and Attorney Negligence

The courts often confront the question of whether attorney negligence will be imputed to the client for purposes of discretionary dismissal for failure to bring the action to trial. The general rule is that an attorney's inexcusable neglect is chargeable to the client. *See, e.g., Carroll v. Abbott Lab., Inc.*, 32 Cal. 3d 892, 895, 187 Cal. Rptr. 592, 654 P.2d 775 (1982); *Baccus v. Superior Court*, 207 Cal. App. 3d 1526, 1533, 255 Cal. Rptr. 781 (1989). However, an exception arises where the attorneys "consistent and long-continued inaction" essentially destroys the existence of the attorney-client relationship. *Fleming v. Gallegos*, 23 Cal. App. 4th 68, 72, 28 Cal. Rptr. 2d 350 (1994) (quoting *Daley v. County of Butte*, 227 Cal. App. 2d 380, 391, 38 Cal. Rptr. 693 (1964)). The Supreme Court has indicated that this "positive misconduct" exception should be applied narrowly, and only where the attorney abandons the client through a total failure of representation and where the client is relatively free from negligence. *Carroll, supra*, 32 Cal. 3d at 900. The courts have recognized the availability of this "positive misconduct" doctrine as a possible excuse to delay in prosecution, but have applied it only in extreme cases where the plaintiff's attorney has, despite contrary assurances, totally failed to take any action. *Compare Fleming v. Gallegos, supra* (reversing dismissal for abuse of discretion where failure to prosecute due to attorney's total inaction) *with Freedman v. Pacific Gas & Elec. Co.*, 196 Cal. App. 3d 696, 242 Cal. Rptr. 8 (1987) (upholding discretionary dismissal based on unreasonable delay; plaintiff attorney's negligence not sufficient for positive misconduct excuse because attorney did file amended complaints and conduct discovery).

[d] Mandatory Relief From Dismissal Under CCP § 473(b)

Section 473(b) requires a court to vacate a dismissal when an application for relief is made within six months of the dismissal and is accompanied by an attorney's affidavit attesting that the dismissal was the result of the attorney's mistake or neglect. By express limitation, this provision of § 473(b) cannot lengthen the mandatory five-year period for bringing a case to trial in CCP § 583.310 and, by analogy, cannot lengthen the three-year period for service of process. *Bernasconi Commercial Real Estate v. St. Joseph's Reg. Healthcare Sys.*, 57 Cal. App. 4th 1078, 1080, 67 Cal. Rptr. 2d 475 (1997). Should this mandatory § 473(b) relief based on an attorney's affidavit of neglect apply to discretionary dismissals? *See Peltier v. McCloud River R.R. Co.*, 34 Cal. App. 4th 1809, 41 Cal. Rptr. 2d 182 (1995) (concluding mandatory relief provision in § 473(b) intended to reach only those dismissals which occur through attorney's failure to oppose a discretionary dismissal motion); *Graham v. Beers*, 30 Cal. App. 4th 1656, 36 Cal. Rptr. 2d 765 (1994) (holding mandatory relief under § 473(b) inapplicable to discretionary dismissal statutes).

The lower courts have struggled with the scope of the mandatory relief provisions of CCP § 473(b). The current consensus is these mandatory provisions were not intended to cover every situation where dismissal occurs due to attorney malfeasance. *See, e.g., Leader v. Health Indus. of Am., Inc.*, 89 Cal. App. 4th 603, 615–621, 107 Cal.

Rptr. 2d 489 (2001) (concluding CCP §473(b) does not mandate relief from dismissal after a hearing based on the failure to file an amended complaint within the time period specified by the trial court after a demurrer has been sustained with leave to amend); *but see Younessi v Woolf,* 244 Cal. App. 4th 1137, 198 Cal. Rptr. 3d 763 (2016) (ruling §473 applied to dismissal for failure to file a timely amended complaint after demurrer sustained where dismissal resulted from defendants' ex parte application for dismissal).

Some courts have construed the mandatory provisions of §473(b) to require relief from dismissals only in circumstances that are similar to a default judgment. *See, e.g., Hock v. Hock,* 80 Cal. App. 4th 1438, 96 Cal. Rptr. 2d 546 (2000) (holding mandatory provisions of §473 applicable to set aside judgment entered when plaintiff's attorney failed to appear at time set for trial); *Vaccaro v. Kaiman,* 63 Cal. App. 4th 761, 73 Cal. Rptr. 2d 829 (1998) (concluding CCP §473 requires the trial court to grant a timely motion to set aside a dismissal of plaintiff's complaint, accompanied by affidavit of neglect, where the dismissal was imposed as a sanction for failure to sign the complaint); *Yeap v. Leake,* 60 Cal. App. 4th 591, 70 Cal. Rptr. 2d 680 (1997) (ruling §473 required the trial court to vacate a dismissal entered where the plaintiff failed to file a timely request for a trial de novo following plaintiff's failure to appear at judicial arbitration).

In *Maynard v. Brandon,* 36 Cal. 4th 364, 30 Cal. Rptr. 3d 558, 114 P.3d 795 (2005), the Supreme Court offered the following limited guidance as to the scope of mandatory relief under §473(b):

> Notwithstanding the broad construction afforded section 473, subdivision (b), the statute does not offer relief from mandatory deadlines deemed jurisdictional in nature. (*Estate of Simmons* (1914) 168 Cal. 390, 396 [143 P. 697];....) Thus section 473, subdivision (b) cannot extend the time in which a party must move for a new trial, since this time limit is considered jurisdictional. (*Union Collection Co. v. Oliver* (1912) 162 Cal. 755, 756–757 [124 P. 435];....) Nor does section 473, subdivision (b) generally apply to dismissals attributable to a party's failure to comply with the applicable limitations period in which to institute an action, whether by complaint (*Castro v. Sacramento County Fire Protection Dist.* (1996) 47 Cal.App.4th 927, 933 [55 Cal. Rptr. 2d 193]; ...) or by writ petition (*Kupka v. Board of Administration* (1981) 122 Cal. App. 3d 791, 794–795 [176 Cal. Rptr. 214]).
>
> Furthermore, except as authorized by statute, section 473, subdivision (b) may not excuse the untimely filing of a notice of appeal. (*Pressler v. Donald L. Bren Co.* (1982) 32 Cal.3d 831, 834 fn. 5 [187 Cal. Rptr. 449, 654 P.2d 219].) "The requirement as to the time for taking an appeal is mandatory, and the court is without jurisdiction to consider one which has been taken subsequent to the expiration of the statutory period. In the absence of statutory authorization, neither the trial nor appellate courts may extend or shorten the time for appeal, even to relieve against mistake, inadvertence, accident, or misfortune." (*Stuart Whitman, Inc. v. Cataldo* (1986) 180 Cal. App. 3d 1109, 1113 [226 Cal. Rptr. 42].)

Maynard v. Brandon, supra, 36 Cal. 4th at 372–73.

[3] Failure to Bring the Case to New Trial within Two Years

Whereas dismissal is mandatory under CCP § 583.320 where the plaintiff has failed to bring the action to new trial within three years, under CCP § 583.420(a)(3) a court has the discretionary authority to dismiss an action where the plaintiff has failed to bring it to retrial within two years. Specifically, a court may dismiss an action where it has not been brought to retrial within two years after a court order declaring a mistrial or hung jury, an order granting a new trial, or a reversal on appeal requiring a new trial. CCP § 583.420(a)(3).

[D] Involuntary Dismissals under Fast Track Rules

[1] Introductory Note on Fast Track Rules

Under the Trial Court Delay Reduction Act (the Act), Government Code §§ 68600–68620, the Judicial Council has established the following time goals for disposition of unlimited civil cases assigned to the case management ("fast track") program: 75% should be disposed within 12 months of filing, 85% within 18 months, and 100% within 24 months. Rule 3.714(b)(1), Cal. Rules of Ct.; Standards of Judicial Administration, Cal. Rules of Ct., App., § 2.1(f)(1). Similar goals apply to limited civil cases: 90% should be disposed of within 12 months of filing, 98% within 18 months, and 100% within 24 months. Rule 3.714(b)(2); Standards, § 2.1(f)(2).

The Trial Court Delay Reduction Act was enacted in 1986 as a pilot project. *See Wagner v. Superior Court,* 12 Cal. App. 4th 1314, 1318, 16 Cal. Rptr. 2d 534 (1993) (discussing history of current Act). The Legislature intended to "grant to the project courts under the Act wide procedural latitude in developing their own rules and procedures to implement the Act in 'response to the urgent public need to reduce litigation delays that have reached, in some counties, scandalous proportions.'" *Laborers' Int'l Union of N. Am. v. El Dorado Landscape Co.,* 208 Cal. App. 3d 993, 1001, 256 Cal. Rptr. 632 (1989).

After substantial revision in 1988, the Legislature in 1990 repealed the original Act and enacted the new Trial Court Delay Reduction Act effective January 1, 1991. The new Act continued many of the basic policies and goals of the original Act, Gov. Code §§ 68603 & 68607; and applies in all superior courts to all civil actions except juvenile, probate, and domestic relations, and to all limited civil cases except small claims and unlawful detainer actions. Gov. Code §§ 68605.5, 68620. The new Act also continued the emphasis on delay reduction implementation through state and local rules, Gov. Code § 68616; but established minimum time periods for certain steps in the litigation process that cannot be shortened by local rule.

Government Code § 68616 (2016)

Delay reduction rules shall not require shorter time periods than as follows:

(a) Service of the complaint within 60 days after filing. Exceptions, for longer periods of time, (1) may be granted as authorized by local rule and (2) shall be granted on a showing that service could not reasonably be achieved within the time required with the exercise of due diligence consistent with the amount in controversy.

(b) Service of responsive pleadings within 30 days after service of the complaint. The parties may stipulate to an additional 15 days. Exceptions, for longer periods of time, may be granted as authorized by local rule.

(c) Time for service of notice or other paper under Sections 1005 and 1013 of the Code of Civil Procedure and time to plead after service of summons under Section 412.20 of the Code of Civil Procedure shall not be shortened except as provided in those sections.

(d) Within 30 days of service of the responsive pleadings, the parties may, by stipulation filed with the court, agree to a single continuance not to exceed 30 days.

It is the intent of the Legislature that these stipulations not detract from the efforts of the courts to comply with standards of timely disposition.

* * *

(e) A status conference, or similar event, other than a challenge to the jurisdiction of the court, shall not be required to be conducted sooner than 30 days after service of the first responsive pleadings, or 30 days after expiration of a stipulated continuance, if any, pursuant to subdivision (d).

(f) Article 3 (commencing with Section 2016) of Chapter 3 of Title 3 of Part 4 of the Code of Civil Procedure shall govern discovery, except in arbitration proceedings.

(g) A case shall not be referred to arbitration prior to 210 days after filing of the complaint, exclusive of the stipulated period provided for in subdivision (d). Any rule adopted pursuant to this article shall not contravene Sections 638 and 639 of the Code of Civil Procedure.

(h) Unnamed (DOE) defendants shall not be dismissed or severed prior to the conclusion of the introduction of evidence at trial, except upon stipulation or motion of the parties.

* * *

In practice, the critical rules are the state-wide case management rules adopted by the Judicial Council, Rules 2.30, 3.700–3.1385, Cal. Rules of Ct.; as well as the local delay reduction rules adopted by each superior court pursuant to Government Code § 68612 and CCP § 575.1. These rules establish time periods that are often dramatically shorter than those set out in the mandatory and discretionary dismissal statutes. For example, CCP § 583.210 provides that dismissal is mandatory if an action is not served within three years of filing; however, under Rule 3.110, a complaint must be served on all named defendants within 60 days after filing, unless extended by the court. Rule 3.110(b) & (e), Cal. Rules of Ct.

In addition to authorizing shorter time limits, the Act reflects a different policy toward stipulations extending time than the dismissal statutes. The dismissal statutes favor the right of parties to make stipulations in their own interests. *See* CCP § 583.130. In contrast, the Act discourages continuances by stipulation of the parties. Gov. Code § 68607(g); *see* Rule 3.1332 Cal. Rules of Ct. (setting forth good cause standards for continuance of trial date). To promote the efficient resolution of litigation, the Act limits the parties to a single continuance not to exceed 30 days. Gov. Code § 68616(d).

The Act also authorizes the Judicial Council to adopt rules establishing a "case differentiation classification system." Gov. Code § 68603(c). The implementing rules require a trial court to evaluate each case based on relevant factors, and assign each case to a case-management plan with a specified case-disposition time goal. Rules 3.714–3.715, Cal. Rules of Ct. These rules also authorize a court to exempt certain cases involving exceptional circumstances from case-disposition time goals, in the interests of justice. Rules 3.714(c), Cal. Rules of Ct.

[2] *Dismissal and Other Fast Track Sanctions*

The teeth in the Trial Court Delay Reduction Act are provided by its sanctions provisions. Government Code § 60608(b) authorizes a judge to impose a variety of sanctions for failure to comply with fast track rules, including the power to dismiss actions or strike pleadings if it appears that less severe sanctions would not be effective. *See also* Rule 2.30, Cal. Rules of Court. During the height of reliance on local rules to implement the Act, an issue arose as to whether Government Code § 68608(b) preempted CCP § 575.2, which only authorizes the imposition of sanctions that "adversely affect the party's cause of action or defense" if the failure to comply with local rules is the fault of the party and not the party's attorney. *Compare Intel Corp. v. U.S. Air, Inc.*, 228 Cal. App. 3d 1559, 279 Cal. Rptr. 569 (1991) (holding trial court properly imposed dismissal of plaintiff's complaint as a sanction for plaintiff counsel's repeated failure to comply with local fast track rules) *with Moyal v. Lanphear*, 208 Cal. App. 3d 491, 256 Cal. Rptr. 296 (1989) (affirming monetary sanctions, but holding dismissal sanction improper because no showing that client was the cause of counsel's failure to comply with local fast track rules).

The Supreme Court subsequently resolved this issue in *Garcia v. McCutchen*, 16 Cal. 4th 469, 66 Cal. Rptr. 2d 319, 940 P.2d 906 (1997), where it held that the limitations on the power to impose case-dispositive sanctions expressed in CCP § 575.2 were applicable to violations of all types of local rules, including local "fast track" rules designed to implement the mandates of the Trial Court Delay Reduction Act.

[E] Involuntary Dismissals on Other Statutory Grounds

In addition to mandatory and discretionary dismissals for failure to prosecute, other grounds for involuntary dismissals are scattered throughout the law. The broadest authority for dismissal is the court's inherent power. *See Lyons v. Wickhorst*, 42 Cal. 3d 911, 231 Cal. Rptr. 738, 727 P.2d 1019 (1986). This broad authority is "tightly circumscribed" by the Supreme Court's requirement that a court consider whether the plaintiff's conduct is so severe and deliberate as to constitute extreme circumstances and whether less drastic alternatives are available. *Lyons*, 42 Cal. 2d at 916–917. As the *Lyons* court explained, a judge must use lesser sanctions unless dismissal is the only possible way to vindicate the court's authority. *Id.*

In contrast to this broad discretionary authority, various provisions of the Code of Civil Procedure set out specific additional grounds for dismissal at various points in the litigation. For example, CCP § 399(a) permits the dismissal of an action without prejudice for failure to pay costs and fees within 30 days after a transfer for improper venue. This time period is extended if the plaintiff seeks a writ of mandate or files an appeal. CCP § 399(a). Second, CCP § 581 permits the dismissal of a complaint after a defendant successfully demurs to, or moves to strike, a complaint. Dismissals under this statute are proper where the demurrer is sustained or the motion is granted without leave to amend. CCP § 581(f). Dismissals are also proper where the demurrer is sustained or the motion is granted with leave to amend where the plaintiff fails to amend within the time limit set by the court for amendment. CCP § 581(f). Section 2023.030(d)(3) permits the dismissal of an action for discovery abuse. Finally, CCP § 581(b)(3) permits the dismissal of an action when no party appears for trial.

§ 12.04 Voluntary Dismissal

Zapanta v. Universal Care, Inc.

Court of Appeal of California, Second Appellate District
107 Cal. App. 4th 1167, 132 Cal. Rptr. 2d 842 (2003)

Doi Todd, Justice.

In this case, we address the question of whether the trial court erred in granting a defense motion for summary judgment where the plaintiffs filed a request for dismissal without prejudice one day before their opposition to the motion was due. Plaintiffs and appellants Christy Zapanta, by and through her guardian ad litem, Mary Jean Maloles, and Mary Jean Maloles, individually, maintain that they were entitled to voluntarily dismiss their action before commencement of trial under Code of Civil Procedure section 581, subdivision (b)(1). The trial court disagreed and granted summary judgment in favor of defendants and respondents Universal Care, Inc. and Eddie Quan, M.D. We reverse.

BACKGROUND

Appellants commenced this medical malpractice action against respondents on May 24, 2001. Appellants claimed that respondents' delay in diagnosing a pseudomonas bacterial infection resulted in the severe neurological impairment of

Zapanta. Zapanta's mother claimed negligent infliction of emotional distress as a by-stander witness.

On March 7, 2002, respondents filed a motion for summary judgment, which included the declaration of an expert witness, Andrew P. Novom, M.D., who concluded that respondents complied with the standard of care in the community. The hearing on the motion was originally set for April 11, 2002, but was advanced by the court to April 4, 2002, so that the motion could be heard more than 30 days before the May 6, 2002 trial date (Code Civ. Proc., § 437c, subd. (a)).

On March 20, 2002, one day before appellants' opposition to the motion was due, appellants filed a request for dismissal of the entire action without prejudice. The clerk entered the dismissal the same day.

Upon receiving a copy of the dismissal the following day, respondents learned that the motion had been taken off calendar. At respondents' request, the clerk placed the motion back on calendar. Thereafter, on March 25, 2002, respondents filed a supplemental memorandum of points and authorities asking the court to strike the request for dismissal and grant the summary judgment motion. On March 28, 2002, appellants filed a response, entitled "Opposition to Motion for Summary Judgment," in which their sole contention was that their dismissal of the action deprived the court of jurisdiction to rule on the motion.

Both parties appeared at the hearing on the summary judgment motion on April 4, 2002, and the court granted the motion. The court's subsequent written order, dated April 16, 2002, stated that the court had considered the parties' submissions and found that (1) the declaration of respondents' expert witness established there was no merit to the medical negligence cause of action, (2) there was therefore no merit to the negligent infliction of emotional distress claim, which was also time barred, and (3) the case of *Groth Bros. Oldsmobile, Inc. v. Gallagher* (2002) 97 Cal.App.4th 60 [118 Cal. Rptr. 2d 405] and other authority cited by respondents in their supplemental memorandum of points and authorities "compels the court to strike [appellants'] request for dismissal." Judgment was entered in favor of respondents on April 16, 2002. Notice of appeal was timely filed.

DISCUSSION

A. *Dismissal of Action*

The issue before us is whether the trial court erred in granting respondents' motion for summary judgment after appellants had filed a request for dismissal of the action without prejudice one day before their opposition to the motion was due. We conclude that the trial court erred and we reverse the judgment. In so doing, we note that in applying a statute to undisputed facts, our review is de novo. (*Groth Bros. Oldsmobile, Inc. v. Gallahger, supra*, 97 Cal. App. 4th 60.)

Code of Civil Procedure section 581, subdivision (b), provides that an action may be dismissed: "(1) With or without prejudice, upon written request of the plaintiff to the clerk, filed with papers in the case, or by oral or written request to the court at any time before the actual commencement of trial, upon payment of the costs, if any...." Similarly, subdivision (c) of the same section (not cited by the parties) provides: "A plaintiff may dismiss his or her complaint, or any cause of action asserted in it, in its entirety, or as to any defendant or defendants, with or without prejudice prior to the actual commencement of trial."

But the right of a plaintiff to voluntarily dismiss an action before commencement of trial is not absolute. (*Cravens v. State Bd. of Equalization* (1997) 52 Cal.App.4th 253, 256 [60 Cal. Rptr. 2d 436].) "Code of Civil Procedure section 581 recognizes exceptions to the right; other limitations have evolved through the courts' construction of the term 'commencement of trial.' These exceptions generally arise where the action has proceeded to a determinative adjudication, or to a decision that is tantamount to an adjudication." (*Ibid.*, quoting *Harris v. Billings* (1993) 16 Cal. App. 4th 1396, 1402 [20 Cal. Rptr. 2d 718].) "'Upon the proper exercise of that right, a trial court would thereafter lack jurisdiction to enter further orders in the dismissed action' [citation] except for matters such as attorney's fees. An order by a court lacking subject matter jurisdiction is void." (*Kyle v. Carmon* (1999) 71 Cal.App.4th 901, 909 [84 Cal. Rptr. 2d 303].)

Respondents rely on several cases to support their position that the dismissal was invalid and summary judgment was properly granted in their favor. In *Groth, supra,* 97 Cal.App.4th 60, the plaintiff failed to file opposition to the defendant's demurrer, and instead attempted to file an amended complaint that was rejected by the clerk. (*Id.* at p. 64.) The day before the hearing, the court issued a tentative ruling sustaining the demurrer without leave to amend. (*Ibid.*) On the day of the hearing, the plaintiff filed a voluntary dismissal without prejudice, and the trial court concluded that it lacked jurisdiction to rule on the demurrer. (*Ibid.*) The appellate court reversed. In doing so, the court relied on policy concerns previously discussed by the Supreme Court in *Wells v. Marina City Properties, Inc.* (1981) 29 Cal.3d 781, 785 [176 Cal. Rptr. 104, 632 P.2d 217], where the court held that once a general demurrer is sustained with leave to amend and the plaintiff fails to amend within the time allotted, the right to voluntarily dismiss the action is cut off. Following *Wells*, the *Groth* court concluded that allowing a plaintiff to file a voluntary dismissal without prejudice in the face of a tentative ruling that the court will sustain a demurrer without leave to amend "wastes the time and resources of the court and other parties and promotes annoying and continuous litigation," as well as undermines the tentative ruling system. (*Groth*, at p. 70.) Here, unlike *Groth*, there was no tentative ruling at the time appellants filed their request for dismissal. Thus, the policy concerns raised by *Wells* and *Groth* did not come into play.

Respondents also rely on *Cravens, supra,* 52 Cal. App. 4th 253, in which the plaintiff failed to file opposition to the defendants' motion for summary judgment. Instead, the day before the hearing, the plaintiff filed a voluntary request for dismissal without prejudice, which the clerk entered the same day. (*Id.* at pp. 255–256.) Having no notice of the dismissal, the defendants appeared at the hearing and the court granted the summary judgment motion, which was affirmed on appeal. (*Id.* at pp. 255–256, 258.) The appellate court noted that under Code of Civil Procedure section 437c, subdivision (b), failure to file opposition "may constitute a sufficient ground, in the court's discretion, for granting the motion." (*Cravens*, at p. 257.) The appellate court reasoned that in light of a record showing that the motion sufficed to entitle the defendants to summary judgment and in the absence of a timely opposition by the plaintiff, entry of summary judgment in favor of the defendants was "a formality which [plaintiff] could not avoid by the stratagem of filing a last minute request for dismissal without prejudice." (*Ibid.*)

By contrast, appellants here did not fail to file opposition to the summary judgment motion; they filed their request for dismissal *prior* to their deadline for filing opposition to the summary judgment motion, albeit by only one day. Under these circumstances, it cannot be said that judgment on the motion was a mere formality, thus distinguishing this case from *Cravens*.

Respondents also cite to *Mary Morgan, Inc. v. Melzark* (1996) 49 Cal. App. 4th 765 [57 Cal. Rptr. 2d 4]. There, the court had issued a tentative ruling granting the defendants' motions for summary judgment. A hearing on the motions was held, during which the court granted the plaintiff's request for a continuance to submit additional evidence. (*Id.* at p. 768.) Instead of doing so, the plaintiff filed a request for dismissal without prejudice. (*Ibid.*) The trial court ordered the request for dismissal stricken and entered summary judgment in favor of the defendants. (*Ibid.*) In affirming the judgment, the appellate court concluded that the plaintiff could not dismiss a case without prejudice after a tentative adverse ruling on defense motions and after the hearing on the motions had commenced but was continued for the exclusive purpose of allowing the plaintiff to produce evidence. (*Id.* at pp. 771–772.) Unlike *Mary Morgan*, here there was no similar manipulation by appellants of the judicial process, i.e., "delaying a court ruling on a defense motion in order to sneak in a voluntary dismissal."

Finally, respondents cite to *Miller v. Marina Mercy Hospital* (1984) 157 Cal. App. 3d 765 [204 Cal. Rptr. 62]. The plaintiffs in *Miller* failed to respond to defendants' requests for admissions on all issues in the case, which were therefore deemed admitted by operation of law. The trial court denied the plaintiffs' request for relief and the defendants filed a motion for summary judgment based on the deemed admissions. (*Id.* at p. 767.) One week before the hearing on the motion, the plaintiffs filed a request for dismissal without prejudice, which the clerk entered. (*Ibid.*) The trial court nevertheless granted summary judgment in favor of defendants, which was affirmed on appeal. The appellate court concluded that deemed admissions which effectively disposed of the entire case cut off the plaintiff's right to voluntary dismissal. (*Id.* at. p. 770.) But, here again, unlike *Miller*, respondents had no preexisting entitlement to a favorable disposition at the time appellants dismissed the action.

Accordingly, none of the cases cited by respondents is dispositive. At the time appellants filed their request for dismissal, the opposition to the summary judgment motion was not past due, no hearing on the motion had been held and no tentative ruling or other decision tantamount to an adjudication had been made in respondents' favor. In other words, the case had not yet reached a stage where a final disposition was a mere formality. We are mindful of respondents' concern that appellants may now have the right to refile their action, but that is so any time a plaintiff files a valid request for dismissal of his or her complaint without prejudice. The purpose behind the right of a plaintiff to voluntarily dismiss a case under Code of Civil Procedure section 581 "is to allow a plaintiff a certain amount of freedom of action within the limits prescribed by the code." (*Cal-Vada Aircraft, Inc. v. Superior Court* (1986) 179 Cal. App. 3d 435, 446 [224 Cal. Rptr. 809].) Where this right does not conflict with other statutory provisions, judicial procedures or public policy, the dismissal is valid.

We therefore find that appellants' request for dismissal without prejudice is valid and that the trial court exceeded its jurisdiction in granting respondents' motion for summary judgment. * * *

DISPOSITION

The judgment and the order granting summary judgment and striking appellants' request for dismissal without prejudice are reversed. Each side to bear their own costs on appeal.

Notes and Questions regarding Voluntary Dismissal

(1) Plaintiffs have the option, prior to trial, to voluntarily dismiss "with or without prejudice." CCP § 581(b)(1). A dismissal "without prejudice" is not a bar to the filing of a subsequent action, within the applicable statute of limitation period, predicated upon the same cause of action. *Kuperman v. Great Republic Life Ins. Co.*, 195 Cal. App. 3d 943, 947, 241 Cal. Rptr. 187 (1987). In contrast, a dismissal "with prejudice" bars a new action on the same subject matter. *See, e.g., Lama v. Comcast Cablevision*, 14 Cal. App. 4th 59, 64, 17 Cal. Rptr. 2d 224 (1993); *Torrey Pines Bank v. Superior Court*, 216 Cal. App. 3d 813, 820, 265 Cal. Rptr. 217 (1989). Under what circumstances would a plaintiff intentionally choose to dismiss an action with prejudice? Can a plaintiff obtain relief from a dismissal with prejudice where the plaintiff's attorney mistakenly checked the wrong box on the request for dismissal form? *See Romadka v. Hoge*, 232 Cal. App. 3d 1231, 283 Cal. Rptr. 878 (1991). Where the voluntary dismissal with prejudice was filed pursuant to a settlement agreement and the defendant subsequently breaches the agreement? *See Bassinger v. Rogers & Wells*, 220 Cal. App. 3d 16, 269 Cal. Rptr. 332 (1990).

(2) In addition to the various decisions discussed in *Zapanta v. Universal Care, Inc.*, reproduced *supra*, the courts in several other cases have construed the term "commencement of trial" in CCP § 581(c) to limit the right of voluntary dismissal without prejudice in a variety of pretrial situations. *E.g., Vanderkous v. Conley*, 188 Cal. App. 4th 111, 115 Cal. Rptr. 3d 249 (2010) (ruling plaintiff's voluntary dismissal of quiet title action after statement of decision issued was untimely and ineffective, even though hearing to value defendant's equitable interest in property was still pending); *Gray v. Superior Court*, 52 Cal. App. 4th 165, 60 Cal. Rptr. 2d 428 (1997) (concluding a plaintiff's right to dismiss is cut off by the commencement of evidentiary

proceedings before a referee appointed in a partition action, even though the referee's recommendations are not binding on the appointing court); *Hartbrodt v. Burke*, 42 Cal. App. 4th 168, 49 Cal. Rptr. 2d 562 (1996) (holding a plaintiff may not defeat a defendant's motion for a terminating discovery sanction by filing a voluntary dismissal just before the sanction hearing); *Goldtree v. Spreckels*, 135 Cal. 666, 672–73, 67 P. 1091 (1902) (concluding a plaintiff has no right to dismiss without prejudice if a general demurrer has been sustained without leave to amend).

According to the court in *Gray v. Superior Court, supra*, "[t]he thread running through all these cases seems to one of fairness: Once the parties commence putting forth the facts of their case before some sort of fact finder, such as an arbitrator, or at the pretrial stage a ruling is made on an issue of law or on admitted facts which effectively disposes of the plaintiff's case against him, it is unfair—perhaps a mockery of the system—to allow the plaintiff to dismiss his complaint and refile." *Gray*, 52 Cal. App. 4th at 173. Do you agree that "fairness" justifies such expansive constructions of CCP § 581(c)'s "commencement of trial" limitation?

In light of the reasoning in *Zapata* and *Gray*, can a plaintiff obtain a voluntary dismissal of an action after the defendant has obtained a tentative ruling dismissing the same action involuntarily for failure to prosecute but before the order of dismissal has been filed? *See M&R Prop. v. Thomson*, 11 Cal. App. 4th 899, 14 Cal. Rptr. 2d 579 (1992) (concluding defendant's right to a mandatory dismissal is stronger than plaintiff's right to seek voluntary dismissal, which is cut off as of the moment there is a ruling which effectively disposes of the case). Can the plaintiff obtain a voluntary dismissal without prejudice after the defendant has obtained summary adjudication of some, but not all, of the issues in the defendant's cross-complaint? *See Cal-Vada Aircraft, Inc. v. Superior Court*, 179 Cal. App. 3d 435, 224 Cal. Rptr. 809 (1986) (discussing various examples of what constitutes a "trial" within meaning of voluntary dismissal statute). Can a plaintiff decline to amend a complaint and instead obtain a dismissal without prejudice during the time granted for leave to amend following the sustaining of a demurrer? *See Parsons v. Umansky*, 28 Cal. App. 4th 867, 34 Cal. Rptr. 2d 144 (1994) (distinguishing dismissal without prejudice before time to amend has expired from dismissal after the time has lapsed).

(3) A class action may not be dismissed unless notice is given to the class and the dismissal is approved by the court. CCP § 581(k); Rule 3.770, Cal. Rules of Ct. Why are these limitations required for voluntary dismissals of class actions? A plaintiff is not permitted to dismiss an action when the defendant has filed a cross-complaint seeking affirmative relief. CCP § 581(i). What are the reasons for this limitation on the plaintiff's right to dismiss? Does this limitation apply where the defendant's answer seeks a declaration of rights or a set-off, but the defendant has not filed a cross-complaint? *See Aetna Cas. & Surety Co. v. Humboldt Loaders, Inc.*, 202 Cal. App. 3d 921, 249 Cal. Rptr. 175 (1988).

(4) After the "actual commencement of trial," a voluntary dismissal by plaintiff is with prejudice, unless all the affected parties consent to dismissal without prejudice or the court so orders on a showing of good cause. CCP § 581(e). Why might the af-

fected parties agree to such a dismissal without prejudice? Other subsections of CCP § 581 govern the effect of dismissals under other circumstances.

§ 12.05 Settlement

[A] Settlement Issues

[1] *Conflict of Interests Among Attorney, Court, and Client*

The vast majority of civil actions are resolved through settlement. The courts often acknowledge the importance of the public policy favoring settlements, and often promote this policy through their decisions. *See, e.g., Marriage of Assemi*, 7 Cal. 4th 896, 910, 30 Cal. Rptr. 2d 265, 872 P.2d 1190 (1994); *Neary v. Regents of the Univ. of California*, 3 Cal. 4th 273, 10 Cal. Rptr. 2d 859, 834 P.2d 119 (1992) (Court of Appeal should ordinarily grant parties' request for stipulated reversal of trial court judgment as part of their settlement during appeal); *Villa v. Cole*, 4 Cal. App. 4th 1327, 1338, 6 Cal. Rptr. 2d 644 (1992); *see also* Stephen McG. Bundy, *The Policy in Favor of Settlement in an Advocacy System*, 44 HASTINGS L.J. 1 (1992). This public policy also manifests itself in pretrial rules, such as Rule 3.1380 of the California Rules of Court, which mandate settlement conferences in most civil actions. *See* Carrie Menkel-Meadow, *For and Against Settlement: Uses and Abuses of the Mandatory Settlement Conference*, 33 U.C.L.A. L. REV. 485 (1985); *see also* CCP §§ 1775–1775.15; Rules 3.890–3.897, Cal. Rules of Ct. (pilot project for Los Angeles County and other counties authorizing mediation as an alternative to judicial arbitration).

Why is promotion of settlement a public policy of such paramount importance? What interest factors make settlement desirable to parties? To attorneys? To the courts? These interests may not always coincide. For example, there is the potential for a conflict of interest occurring between a client and an attorney when an attorney negotiates attorney fees as part of a settlement of the client's case. In *Ramirez v. Sturdevant*, 21 Cal. App. 4th 904, 26 Cal. Rptr. 2d 554 (1994), the Court of Appeal declined to find the inherent conflict in such dual negotiations necessarily invalidates any resulting settlement, but directed the trial court to conduct a further evidentiary review, explaining (*Ramirez*, 21 Cal. App. 4th at 924–25):

> The parties may, if they wish, negotiate a separate settlement of damages and attorney fees. That settlement, however, should be approved by an impartial tribunal charged with the duty of determining whether or not a fair and reasonable balancing of the interests of the plaintiff and plaintiff's attorney was reflected in the negotiations. The settlement may be reviewed by the court at a settlement conference, or by the court in which the action is filed on motion of a party.

> As with other situations involving a conflict of interest, in the absence of any evidence to the contrary it will be presumed that the conflict prejudiced the client. The order approving or disapproving the settlements may be re-

viewed for an abuse of discretion. Unlike the courts in the class action cases, where it must further be determined that the substantive terms of the settlement are fair and reasonable, the trial court in cases such as this is *not* charged with the duty of insuring that the settlement reflects the actual value of the case or ultimately is fair to the parties. Its duty simply is to ensure that the settlement was not tainted by conflict of interest between attorney and client.

Do you agree with the *Ramirez* court's resolution of the conflict of interest inherent in settlement negotiations which involve attorney fees? Although the *Ramirez* court requires approval of such settlements by an impartial tribunal, this approval does not require the court to determine whether the substantive terms of the settlement are fair and reasonable. Precisely what is the duty imposed on the approving court? The *substantive* terms of the settlement would seem to be relevant to the determination of whether the settlement negotiations were tainted by conflict of interest between attorney and client. Why did the *Ramirez* court reject such a substantive inquiry?

A class action cannot be settled without approval of the court after a hearing. CCP § 581(k); Rule 3.769, Cal. Rules of Ct. The settlement of an action brought on behalf of a minor or incompetent person must be approved by the court. CCP § 372. Why is court approval required in such actions?

[2] *Conflict of Interest Between Party and Party's Insurer*

A liability insurer negotiating on behalf of its insured has an obligation to accept a reasonable offer of settlement within the insurance policy limits. *Crisci v. Security Ins. Co.*, 66 Cal. 2d 425, 58 Cal. Rptr. 13, 426 P.2d 173 (1967). Refusal to accept such a settlement offer will subject the insurer to the risk of being held liable for a subsequent judgment in excess of those limits. The only permissible consideration in evaluating the reasonableness of the settlement offer is whether, in light of the victim's injuries and the probable liability of the insured, the ultimate judgment is likely to exceed the amount of the settlement offer. *Johansen v. California State Auto Assn. Inter-Ins. Bureau*, 15 Cal. 3d 9, 16, 123 Cal. Rptr. 288, 538 P.2d 744 (1975). Such factors as the desire to reduce the amount of future settlements or a belief that the policy does not provide coverage should not affect the decision as to whether the settlement offer in question is a reasonable one. *Johansen*, 15 Cal. 3d at 16–17. What are the policy reasons for this judge-made rule? This rule also makes knowledge of the liability insurance policy limits important to the adverse party-offeror, does it not? Why?

[3] *Authority to Settle*

An attorney cannot surrender any substantive right of a client, nor compromise the client's cause of action, without the client's consent or specific authorization. *See, e.g., Whittier Union High Sch. Dist. v. Superior Court*, 66 Cal. App. 3d 504, 508, 136 Cal. Rptr. 86 (1977); *Bice v. Stevens*, 160 Cal. App. 2d 222, 231–32, 325 P.2d 244 (1958); *see also Blanton v. Womancare, Inc.*, 38 Cal. 3d 396, 212 Cal. Rptr. 151, 696 P.2d 645 (1985) (concluding an attorney, merely by virtue of his employment as such, has no apparent authority to bind his client to arbitration agreement where client did not consent to the agreement). The attorney-client relationship is governed, however, by the general rules of principal and agent. *Blanton v. Womancare, Inc., supra* at 403; *Yanchor v. Kagan*, 22 Cal. App. 3d 544, 549, 99 Cal. Rptr. 367 (1971). Therefore, a settlement is binding on the client if the attorney had the express, implied, or ostensible authority to make the offer, or if the client subsequently ratifies the settlement. *See, e.g., Navrides v. Zurich Ins. Co.*, 5 Cal. 3d 698, 97 Cal. Rptr. 309, 488 P.2d 637 (1971); *Yanchor, supra*, 22 Cal. App. 3d at 549–550.

There is a presumption that an attorney has the authority to compromise the client's action, but this presumption is rebuttable. *See, e.g., Gagnon Co., Inc. v. Nevada Desert Inn*, 45 Cal. 2d 448, 460–61, 289 P.2d 466 (1955); *Slack v. Slack*, 241 Cal. App. 2d 530, 538, 50 Cal. Rptr. 763 (1966). Should a settlement be enforced where the client proves that the attorney acted beyond the scope of his authority in accepting an offer? *See Whittier Union High Sch. Dist., supra*, 66 Cal. App. 3d at 507–510; *Bice v. Stevens, supra*, 160 Cal. App. 2d at 231–234. Why? Business and Professions Code § 6103.5 requires an attorney to promptly communicate to her client any written offer of settlement made by an opposing party. What is the purpose of this requirement? Why is it limited only to written offers?

[4] Judgment by Stipulation

Code of Civil Procedure § 664.6 (2016) provides:

> If parties to pending litigation stipulate, in a writing signed by the parties outside the presence of the court or orally on the record before the court, for settlement of the case, or part thereof, the court, upon motion, may enter judgment pursuant to the terms of the settlement. If requested by the parties, the court may retain jurisdiction over the parties to enforce the settlement until performance in full of the terms of the settlement.

A party who wishes to invoke the summary procedure of § 664.6 must strictly comply with the signature requirements of that section. For example, § 664.6 does not authorize entry of judgment to enforce a settlement agreement which was signed by the parties' respective counsel but not by the plaintiff himself (who refused to sign it). *See Levy v. Superior Court*, 10 Cal. 4th 578, 41 Cal. Rptr. 2d 878, 896 P.2d 171 (1995) (construing the term "parties" in § 664.6 to mean the litigants themselves, and does not include their attorneys of record). Does § 664.6 authorize enforcement of a settlement agreement signed by a party's agent, rather than the party itself, when the agent had sole and exclusive authority to settle claims on the party's behalf? *See Gauss v. GAF Corp.*, 103 Cal. App. 4th 1110, 127 Cal. Rptr. 2d 370 (2002) (ruling a writing not signed by one of the parties does not satisfy § 664.6); *Fiege v. Cooke*, 125 Cal. App. 4th 1350, 23 Cal. Rptr. 3d 496 (2004) (concluding trial court properly enforced settlement agreed to only by parties' automobile insurers where the parties were all insured under policies that gave the insurers the right to settle without the parties' consent and to bind them to the settlement).

Does § 664.6 authorize enforcement of a settlement in a multi-party case even though all the parties in the action have not signed the agreement, but where all the parties bringing the § 664.4 motion to enforce the settlement and the parties to whom the motion is directed have signed. *See Harris v. Rudin, Richman, & Appel*, 74 Cal. App. 4th 299, 87 Cal. Rptr. 2d 822 (1999) (ruling settlement agreement not enforceable under § 664.6 because not signed by all parties to the purported settlement); *Sully-Miller Contracting Co. v. Gledson/Cashman Constr., Inc.*, 103 Cal. App. 4th 30, 126 Cal. Rptr. 2d 400 (2002) (concluding a written settlement agreement is not enforceable under § 664.6 unless it is signed by all the parties to the agreement, not merely the parties against whom the agreement is sought to be enforced). In the absence of a judgment pursuant to § 664.6, how does a party enforce a settlement agreement? *See Marriage of Assemi, supra*, 7 Cal. 4th at 904–905.

In ruling on a motion to enter judgment pursuant to § 664.6, a trial court has the power to determine whether the parties entered into a valid and binding settlement. *See, e.g., Marriage of Assemi*, 7 Cal. 4th 896, 30 Cal. Rptr. 2d 265, 872 P.2d 1190 (1994) (holding trial court empowered to resolve issues relating to binding nature or terms of disputed settlement; parties' oral stipulation of settlement during judicially supervised arbitration proceeding held "before the court" within the meaning of § 664.6 and therefore properly enforced by trial court); *Kohn v. Jaymar-Ruby, Inc.*, 23 Cal. App. 4th 1530, 28 Cal. Rptr. 2d 780 (1994) (determining oral agreement is valid and enforceable); *Critzer v. Enos*, 187 Cal. App. 4th 1242, 115 al. Rptr. 3d 203 (2010) (holding personal consent in open court by three of five to oral settlement insufficient, even though the three were the parties against whom the settlement was to be enforced). However, a trial court does not have the power to modify the terms of the settlement agreement. *See, e.g., Leeman v. Adams Extract & Spice, LLC*, 236 Cal. App. 4th 1367, 187 Cal. Rptr. 3d 220 (2015) (holding trial court committed reversible error in unilaterally modifying the attorney fees provision in the parties' settlement agreement); *Weddington Productions, Inc. v. Flick*, 60 Cal. App. 4th 793, 810, 71 Cal. Rptr. 2d 265 (1998) ("[N]othing in section 664.6 authorizes a judge to create the material terms of a settlement, as opposed to deciding what terms the parties themselves have previously agreed upon").

Independent of the process authorized by CCP § 664.6, Rule 3.1385 of the California Rules of Court requires the plaintiff or any party seeking affirmative relief to notify the court immediately upon settlement of the case and, if the settlement is unconditional, to request a dismissal within 45 days of settlement. If the party fails to timely file a dismissal request, the court must dismiss the case unless "good cause is shown why the case should not be dismissed." Rule 3.1385(b). Does a party's allegations that no enforceable settlement was reached constitute "good cause" under Rule 3.1385(b)? *See Irvine v. Regents of the Univ. of California*, 149 Cal. App. 4th 994, 57 Cal. Rptr. 3d 500 (2007) (holding allegations that no enforceable settlement has been reached precludes a trial court from dismissing the action).

[5] *Offer to Allow Judgment*

Code of Civil Procedure § 998 reflects California's policy of encouraging settlements by authorizing any party, not less than 10 days prior to commencement of trial, to serve an offer in writing upon any other party to an action to allow judgment to be taken in accordance with the terms and conditions stated in the offer. *See, e.g., Poster v. Southern Cal. Rapid Transit Dist.*, 52 Cal. 3d 266, 276 Cal. Rptr. 321, 801 P.2d 1072 (1990). If the offer is accepted, the offer with proof of acceptance shall be filed and the court must enter judgment accordingly. CCP § 998(b)(1). If the offer is not accepted prior to trial or within 30 days after it is made, whichever occurs first, it shall be deemed withdrawn. CCP § 998(b)(2). An unaccepted offer may also be revoked by the offeror prior to the expiration of the statutory period. *T.M. Cobb Co. v. Superior Court*, 36 Cal. 3d 273, 204 Cal. Rptr. 143, 682 P.2d 338 (1984).

If an offeree does not accept a § 998 offer and subsequently fails to obtain a more favorable judgment, the court may penalize the offeree under § 998 by the withholding or augmenting of allowable costs. CCP § 998(c)–(e). The problems associated with determining what constitutes a more favorable judgment, as well as other § 998 issues, are discussed in detail in § 14.04, Recovery of Costs by Prevailing Party, *infra*.

[6] *Effect of Good Faith Settlement in Multi-Party Litigation*

As is often the case, a plaintiff may only be able to reach a settlement with one or more, but not all, defendants in a multi-defendant tort or contract action. What is the effect of such a settlement on the nonsettling parties? Under CCP § 877 and § 877.6, a good faith settlement bars nonsettling defendants from seeking contribution or implied indemnity from a settling joint tortfeasor or co-obligor defendant, but at the same time reduces the nonsettling defendant's ultimate liability to the plaintiff by the amount of the settlement payment. To have this discharging effect, however, the settlement must be made in "good faith" within the meaning of CCP § 877.6. *See, e.g., Far West Fin. Corp. v. D. & S. Co., Inc.*, 46 Cal. 3d 796, 251 Cal. Rptr. 202, 760 P.2d 399 (1988) (ruling a "good faith" settlement determination under § 877.6 bars any other joint tortfeasor from any further claims against the settling tortfeasor for total, partial, or comparative contribution or equitable indemnity); *Tech-Bilt, Inc. v. Woodward-Clyde & Assoc.*, 38 Cal. 3d 488, 213 Cal. Rptr. 256, 698 P.2d 159 (1985) (holding a settlement amount must be within the "reasonable range" or "ballpark" of the settling tortfeasor's share of liability). What are the reasons for this "good faith" requirement?

Section 877.6 sets forth the procedure for obtaining a court determination of whether a settlement is in "good faith." Section 877.5 contains additional procedural disclosure requirements where the settlement involves a "sliding scale recovery agreement," *i.e.*, an agreement which limits the liability of the agreeing tortfeasor defendants to an amount dependent upon the amount of recovery which the plaintiff is able to recover from the nonagreeing defendants. *See Abbott Ford, Inc. v. Superior Court*, 43 Cal. 3d 858, 239 Cal. Rptr. 626, 721 P.2d 124 (1987) (applying good faith standards applied to sliding scale settlement agreement). For more detailed analysis of the effect of good faith settlements in multi-party litigation, see § 10.04, New Party Cross-Complaints and Equitable Indemnity, *supra*.

[7] Structured Settlements

A structured settlement is any settlement in which the compensated party is paid in whole or in part by periodic payments over time rather than by an immediate lump sum payment. 3 CEB, *Civil Procedure Before Trial* § 49.26 (4th ed. 2015). Structured settlements are common in personal injury settlements, *id.*; and are required, if requested, in any actions against health care providers that involve $50,000 or more in future damages. CCP § 667.7. A structured settlement may be advantageous to both parties. Why? A structured settlement may also present special ethical problems for an attorney with respect to calculation and timing of attorney fees. For a discussion of these and other issues associated with structured settlements, see 3 CEB, *Civil Procedure Before Trial* §§ 49.26–49.59 (4th ed. 2015).

[8] Negotiation Techniques

Mastery of negotiation skills is essential to the successful civil practitioner. A variety of helpful resources are available for this purpose, including Fisher, Ury & Patton, *Getting to Yes* (2nd ed. 2011); Gifford, *Legal Negotiation: Theory and Practice* (2nd ed. 2008); Williams, *Legal Negotiation and Settlement* (1987); (2001); Haydock, *Negotiation Practice* (1994); and Goodpaster, *A Guide to Negotiation and Mediation* (1997). These resources discuss negotiation planning, strategies, and styles; as well as techniques during the negotiation process.

§ 12.06 Arbitration

[A] Contractual Arbitration

Moncharsh v. Heily & Blase

Supreme Court of California
3 Cal. 4th 1, 10 Cal. Rptr. 2d 183, 832 P.2d 899 (1992)

Lucas, Chief Justice.

We granted review in this case to decide, inter alia, the extent to which a trial court may review an arbitrator's decision for errors of law. For the reasons discussed below, we conclude an arbitrator's decision is not generally reviewable for errors of fact or law, whether or not such error appears on the face of the award and causes substantial injustice to the parties. There are, however, limited exceptions to this general rule, which we also discuss below.

FACTS

On June 16, 1986, appellant Philip Moncharsh, an attorney, was hired by respondent Heily & Blase, a law firm. As a condition of employment as an associate attorney in the firm, Moncharsh signed an agreement containing a number of provisions governing various aspects of his employment. One provision (hereafter referred to as paragraph X-C) stated: "X-C. EMPLOYEE-ATTORNEY agrees not to do anything to cause, encourage, induce, entice, recommend, suggest, mention or otherwise cause or contribute to any of Firm's clients terminating the attorney-client relationship with Firm, and/or substituting Firm and retaining or associating Employee-attorney or any other attorney or firm as their legal counsel. In the event that any Firm client should terminate the attorney-client relationship with Firm and substitute EMPLOYEE-ATTORNEY or another attorney or law firm who[m] EMPLOYEE-ATTORNEY suggested, recommended or directed as client's successor ATTORNEY, then, in addition to any costs which client owes Firm up to the time of such substitution, as to all fees which EMPLOYEE-ATTORNEY may actually receive from that client or that client's successor attorney on any such cases, Blase will receive eighty percent (80%) of said fee and EMPLOYEE-ATTORNEY will receive twenty percent (20%) of said fee."

Moncharsh terminated his employment with Heily & Blase on February 29, 1988. DeWitt Blase, the senior partner at Heily & Blase, contacted 25 or 30 of Moncharsh's clients, noted that they had signed retainer agreements with his firm, and explained that he would now be handling their cases. Five clients, whose representation by Moncharsh predated his association with Heily & Blase, chose to have Moncharsh continue to represent them. A sixth client, Ringhof, retained Moncharsh less than two weeks before he left the firm. Moncharsh continued to represent all six clients after he left the firm.

When Blase learned Moncharsh had received fees at the conclusion of these six cases, he sought a quantum meruit share of the fees as well as a percentage of the fees pursuant to paragraph X-C of the employment agreement. Blase rejected Moncharsh's offer to settle the matter for only a quantum meruit share of the fees. The parties then invoked the arbitration clause of the employment agreement[1] and submitted the matter to an arbitrator. The arbitrator heard two days of testimony and the matter was submitted on the briefs and exhibits. * * *

The arbitrator ruled in Heily & Blase's favor, concluding that any oral side agreement between Moncharsh and Blase was never documented and that Moncharsh was thus bound by the written employee agreement. Further, the arbitrator ruled that, "except for client Ringhof, [paragraph X-C] is not unconscionable, and it does not violate the rules of professional conduct. At the time Mr. MONCHARSH agreed to the employment contract, he was a mature, experienced attorney, with employable skills. Had he not been willing to agree to the eighty/twenty (80/20) split on termination, he could simply have refused to sign the document, negotiated something different, or if negotiations were unsuccessful, his choice was to leave his employment.... ¶ ... The Arbitrator excludes the Ringhof client from the eighty/twenty (80/20) split because that client was obtained at the twilight of Mr. MONCHARSH's

---

1. The arbitration clause provided: "Any dispute arising out of this Agreement shall be subject to arbitration under the rules of the American Arbitration Association. No arbitrator shall have any power to alter, amend, modify or change any of the terms of this agreement. The decision of the arbitrator shall be final and binding on Firm and Employee-attorney." None of the rules of the American Arbitration Association have any bearing on the issues raised in this case.

relationship with HEILY & BLASE, and an eighty/twenty (80/20) split with respect to that client would be unconscionable."

Moncharsh petitioned the superior court to vacate and modify the arbitration award. (Code Civ. Proc., § 1286.2; all subsequent statutory references are to this code unless otherwise stated.) Heily & Blase responded by petitioning the court to confirm the award. (§ 1285.) The court ruled that, "The arbitrator's findings on questions of both law and fact are conclusive. A court cannot set aside an arbitrator's error of law no matter how egregious." The court allowed an exception to this rule, however, "where the error appears on the face of the award." Finding no such error, the trial court denied Moncharsh's petition to vacate and granted Heily & Blase's petition to confirm the arbitrator's award.

On appeal, the Court of Appeal also recognized the rule, announced in previous cases, generally prohibiting review of the merits of the arbitrator's award. It noted, however, that an exception exists when "an error of law appears on the face of the ruling and then only if the error would result in substantial injustice." Although Moncharsh claimed paragraph X-C violated law, public policy, and the State Bar Rules of Professional Conduct, the appellate court disagreed and affirmed the trial court judgment.

We granted review and directed the parties to address the limited issue of whether, and under what conditions, a trial court may review an arbitrator's decision.

DISCUSSION

1. *The General Rule of Arbitral Finality*

The parties in this case submitted their dispute to an arbitrator pursuant to their written agreement. This case thus involves private, or nonjudicial, arbitration. (*See Blanton v. Womancare, Inc.* (1985) 38 Cal. 3d 396, 401–402 & fn. 5 [212 Cal. Rptr. 151, 696 P.2d 645, 48 A.L.R. 4th 109] [discussing the differences between judicial and nonjudicial arbitration].) In cases involving private arbitration, "[t]he scope of arbitration is ... a matter of agreement between the parties" (*Ericksen, Arbuthnot, McCarthy, Kearney & Walsh, Inc. v. 100 Oak Street* (1983) 35 Cal. 3d 312, 323 [197 Cal. Rptr. 581, 673 P.2d 251] [hereafter *Ericksen*]), and "'[t]he powers of an arbitrator are limited and circumscribed by the agreement or stipulation of submission.'" (*O'Malley v. Petroleum Maintenance Co.* (1957) 48 Cal. 2d 107, 110 [308 P.2d 9] [hereafter *O'Malley*], quoting *Pacific Fire etc. Bureau v. Bookbinders' Union* (1952) 115 Cal. App. 2d 111, 114 [251 P.2d 694].)

Title 9 of the Code of Civil Procedure, as enacted and periodically amended by the Legislature, represents a comprehensive statutory scheme regulating private arbitration in this state. (§ 1280 et seq.) Through this detailed statutory scheme, the Legislature has expressed a "strong public policy in favor of arbitration as a speedy and relatively inexpensive means of dispute resolution." (*Ericksen, supra*, 35 Cal. 3d at p. 322; ...) * * *

The arbitration clause included in the employment agreement in this case specifically states that the arbitrator's decision would be both binding and final. The parties to this action thus clearly intended the arbitrator's decision would be final. Even had there been no such expression of intent, however, it is the general rule that parties to a private arbitration impliedly agree that the arbitrator's decision will be both binding and final. Indeed, "The very essence of the term 'arbitration' [in this context] connotes a binding award." (*Blanton v. Womancare, Inc., supra,* 38 Cal. 3d at p. 402, citing Domke on Commercial Arbitration (rev. ed. 1984) p. 1). * * *

This expectation of finality strongly informs the parties' choice of an arbitral forum over a judicial one. The arbitrator's decision should be the end, not the beginning, of the dispute. * * * Ensuring arbitral finality thus requires that judicial intervention in the arbitration process be minimized. Because the decision to arbitrate grievances evinces the parties' intent to bypass the judicial system and thus avoid potential delays at the trial and appellate levels, arbitral finality is a core component of the parties' agreement to submit to arbitration. Thus, an arbitration decision is final and conclusive *because the parties have agreed that it be so.* By ensuring that an arbitrator's decision is final and binding, courts simply assure that the parties receive the benefit of their bargain.

Moreover, "[a]rbitrators, unless specifically required to act in conformity with rules of law, may base their decision upon broad principles of justice and equity, and in doing so may expressly or impliedly reject a claim that a party might successfully have asserted in a judicial action." (*Sapp v. Barenfeld* (1949) 34 Cal. 2d 515, 523 [212 P.2d 233] ... As early as 1852, this court recognized that, "The arbitrators are not bound to award on principles of dry law, but may decide on principles of equity and good conscience, and make their award *ex aequo et bono* [according to what is just and good]." (*Muldrow v. Norris* (1852) 2 Cal. 74, 77.) * * *

Thus, both because it vindicates the intentions of the parties that the award be final, and because an arbitrator is not ordinarily constrained to decide according to the rule of law, it is the general rule that, "The merits of the controversy between the parties are not subject to judicial review." (*O'Malley, supra,* 48 Cal. 2d at p. 111; *Pacific Vegetable Oil Corp. v. C.S.T. Ltd.* (1946) 29 Cal. 2d 228, 233 [174 P.2d 441] [hereafter *Pacific Vegetable*].) More specifically, courts will not review the validity of the arbitrator's reasoning. Further, a court may not review the sufficiency of the evidence supporting an arbitrator's award.

Thus, it is the general rule that, with narrow exceptions, an arbitrator's decision cannot be reviewed for errors of fact or law. In reaffirming this general rule, we recognize there is a risk that the arbitrator will make a mistake. That risk, however, is acceptable for two reasons. First, by voluntarily submitting to arbitration, the parties have agreed to bear that risk in return for a quick, inexpensive, and conclusive resolution to their dispute. As one commentator explains, "the parties to an arbitral agreement knowingly take the risks of error of fact or law committed by the arbitrators and that this is a worthy 'trade-off' in order to obtain speedy decisions by experts in the field whose practical experience and worldly reasoning will be accepted as correct by other experts." (Sweeney, *Judicial Review of Arbitral Proceedings* (1981–1982) 5 Fordham Int'l L.J. 253, 254.) * * *

A second reason why we tolerate the risk of an erroneous decision is because the Legislature has reduced the risk to the parties of such a decision by providing for judicial review in circumstances involving serious problems with the award itself, or with the fairness of the arbitration process. As stated ante, private arbitration proceedings are governed by title 9 of the Code of Civil Procedure, sections 1280–1294.2. Section 1286.2 sets forth the grounds for vacation of an arbitrator's award. It states in pertinent part: "[T]he court shall vacate the award if the court determines that: [¶] (a) The award was procured by corruption, fraud or other undue means; [¶] (b) There was corruption in any of the arbitrators; [¶] (c) The rights of such party were substantially prejudiced by misconduct of a neutral arbitrator; [¶] (d) The arbitrators exceeded their powers and the award cannot be corrected without affecting the merits of the decision upon the controversy submitted; or [¶] (e) The rights of such party were substantially prejudiced by the refusal of the arbitrators to postpone the hearing upon sufficient cause being shown therefor or by the refusal of the arbitrators to hear evidence material to the controversy or by other conduct of the arbitrators contrary to the provisions of this title."

In addition, section 1286.6 provides grounds for correction of an arbitration award. That section states in pertinent part: "[T]he court, unless it vacates the award pursuant to Section 1286.2, shall correct the award and confirm it as corrected if the court determines that: [¶] (a) There was an evident miscalculation of figures or an evident mistake in the description of any person, thing or property referred to in the award; [¶] (b) The arbitrators exceeded their powers but the award may be corrected without affecting the merits of the decision upon the controversy submitted; or [¶] (c) the award is imperfect in a matter of form, not affecting the merits of the controversy."

The Legislature has thus substantially reduced the possibility of certain forms of error infecting the arbitration process itself (§ 1286.2, subds. (a), (b), (c)), of an arbitrator exceeding the scope of his or her arbitral powers (§ 1286.2, subd. (d), 1286.6, subd. (b)), of some obvious and easily correctable mistake in the award (§ 1286.6, subd. (a)), of one party being unfairly deprived of a fair opportunity to present his or her side of the dispute (§ 1286.2, subd. (e)), or of some other technical problem with the award (§ 1286.6, subd. (c)). In light of these statutory provisions, the residual risk to the parties of an arbitrator's erroneous decision represents an acceptable cost — obtaining the expedience and financial savings that the arbitration process provides — as compared to the judicial process.

Although it is thus the general rule that an arbitrator's decision is not ordinarily reviewable for error by either the trial or appellate courts, Moncharsh contends three exceptions to the general rule apply to his case. First, he claims a court may review an arbitrator's decision if an error of law is apparent on the face of the award and that error causes substantial injustice. Second, he claims the arbitrator exceeded his powers. (§ 1286.2, subd. (d).) Third, he argues courts will not enforce arbitration decisions that are illegal or violate public policy. We discuss each point seriatim.

2. *Error on the Face of the Arbitration Decision*

A review of the pertinent authorities yields no shortage of proclamations that a court may vacate an arbitrator's decision when (i) an error of law appears on the face of the decision, and (ii) the error causes substantial injustice. (*See, e.g., Abbott v. California State Auto. Assn.* (1977) 68 Cal. App. 3d 763, 771 [137 Cal. Rptr. 580].) Indeed, some cases hold the error need only appear on the face of the award, with no mention of resulting injustice. (*See, e.g., Park Plaza, Ltd. v. Pietz* (1987) 193 Cal. App. 3d 1414, 1420 [239 Cal. Rptr. 51].) As previously noted, however, the Legislature has set forth grounds for vacation (§ 1286.2) and correction (§ 1286.6) of an arbitration award and "[a]n error of law is not one of the grounds." (*Nogueiro v. Kaiser Foundation Hospitals, supra,* 203 Cal. App. 3d at p. 1195, and cases cited.) Because Moncharsh contends that an additional exception to the general rule for errors of law is authorized by both common law and statute, we next determine the genesis of that notion as well as its continuing validity.

a. *The Early Common Law Rule*

[Here, the Court first discusses several 19th century California Supreme Court cases which apparently adopted a common law rule permitting judicial review of an arbitrator's ruling if error appeared on the face of the award. The Court next discusses the 1927 legislation which expressed a clear public policy in favor of arbitration as an alternate method of dispute resolution. The Court then discusses *Pacific Vegetable Oil Corp. v. C.S.T., Ltd.* (1946) 29 Cal. 2d 228 [174 P.2d 441] and *Crofoot v. Blair HoldingsCorp.* (1953) 119 Cal. App. 2d 156 [260 P.2d 156], two cases analyzing the limits of judicial review under the 1927 legislation. The Court quotes extensively from both cases, including the following statement from *Crofoot*: "Under these cases it must be held that in the absence of some limiting clause in the arbitration agreement, the merits of the award, either on questions of fact or of law, *may not be reviewed except as provided in the statute. Crofoot, supra,* 119 Cal. App. 2d at p. 186 (italics added.)"].

c. *Development of the Law After 1927*

[Here, the Court discusses the California Law Revision Commission report (referred to as the "Arbitration Study") transmitted to the Governor in 1960, which recommended revisions to the statutory arbitration scheme. On the subject of the scope of judicial review, this Arbitration Study observed that numerous court rulings have developed the basic principle which set the limits for any court review: "Merits of an arbitration award either on questions of fact or of law may not be reviewed *except as provided for in the statute* in the absence of some limiting clause in the arbitration agreement...." (Arbitration Study, *supra,* pp. G-53 to G-54, italics added.).]

The California Legislature thereafter enacted a revision of the arbitration statutes. (Stats. 1961, ch. 461, p. 1540 et seq.) Former section 1288, which had set forth the grounds on which an award could be vacated, was slightly altered and renumbered as new section 1286.2, and this section still controls today. It is significant that there is no mention of the rule permitting judicial review for errors apparent on the face of the arbitration award causing substantial injustice. We may infer from this omission that the Legislature intended to reject that rule, and instead adopt the position taken in case law and endorsed in the Arbitration Study, that is, "that in the absence of some limiting clause in the arbitration agreement, the merits of the award, either on questions of fact or of law, may not be reviewed except as provided in the statute." (*Crofoot, supra,* 119 Cal. App. 2d at p. 186.)

The Legislature's intent is further revealed by an examination of other statutes. For example, in providing for arbitrating disputes arising from public construction contracts, section 1296 directs that "a court shall … vacate the award if after review of the award it determines either that the award is not supported by substantial evidence or that it is based on an error of law." By specifically providing in that provision for judicial review and correction of error, but not in section 1286.2, we may infer that the Legislature did not intend to confer traditional judicial review in private arbitration cases. * * * The law has thus evolved from its common law origins and moved towards a more clearly delineated scheme rooted in statute. A majority of California appellate decisions have followed the modern rule, established by *Pacific Vegetable, supra,* 29 Cal. 2d 228, and *Crofoot, supra,* 119 Cal. App. 2d 156, and generally limit judicial review of private arbitration awards to those grounds specified in sections 1286.2 and 1286.6. [Citations omitted.] * * *

Although the matter would seem to have been put to rest, several California decisions rendered since the 1961 statutory amendments have inexplicably resurrected the view … that an arbitration award may be vacated when an error appears on the face of the award and causes substantial injustice. [citations to these lower court decisions omitted]

In light of the development of decisional law embracing as exclusive the statutory grounds to vacate an arbitration award, as well as the apparent intent of the Legislature to generally exclude nonstatutory grounds to vacate an award, we adhere to the *Pacific Vegetable/Crofoot* line of cases that limit judicial review of private arbitration awards to those cases in which there exists a statutory ground to vacate or correct the award. Those decisions permitting review of an award where an error of law appears on the face of the award causing substantial injustice have perpetuated a point of view that is inconsistent with the modern view of private arbitration and are therefore disapproved.

3. *The Arbitrator Did Not Exceed His Powers*

Section 1286.2, subdivision (d) [now subdivision (a)(4)], provides for vacation of an arbitration award when "The arbitrators exceeded their powers and the award cannot be corrected without affecting the merits of the decision upon the controversy submitted." Moncharsh argues this statutory exception to the rule generally precluding judicial review of arbitration awards applies to his case. It is unclear, however, on what theory Moncharsh would have us conclude the arbitrator exceeded his powers. It is well settled that "arbitrators do not exceed their powers merely because they assign an erroneous reason for their decision." (*O'Malley, supra,* 48 Cal. 2d at p. 111; *Hacienda Hotel v. Culinary Workers Union* (1985) 175 Cal. App. 3d 1127, 1133 [223 Cal. Rptr. 305].) A contrary holding would permit the exception to swallow the rule of limited judicial review; a litigant could always contend the arbitrator erred and thus exceeded his powers. To the extent Moncharsh argues his case comes within section 1286.2, subdivision (d) merely because the arbitrator reached an erroneous decision, we reject the point.

Moreover, consistent with our arbitration statutes and subject to the limited exceptions discussed in section 4, post, it is within the "powers" of the arbitrator to resolve the entire "merits" of the "controversy submitted" by the parties. (§ 1286.2, subd. (d); § 1286.6, subd. (b), (c).) Obviously, the "merits" include all the contested issues of law and fact submitted to the arbitrator for decision. The arbitrator's resolution of these issues is what the parties bargained for in the arbitration agreement. Moncharsh does not argue that the arbitrator's award strayed beyond the scope of the parties' agreement by resolving issues the parties did not agree to arbitrate. The agreement to arbitrate encompassed "[a]ny dispute arising out of" the employment contract. The parties' dispute over the allocation of attorney's fees following termination of employment clearly arose out of the employment contract; the arbitrator's award does no more than resolve that dispute. Under these circumstances, the arbitrator was within his "powers" in resolving the questions of law presented to him. The award is not subject to vacation or correction based on any of the statutory grounds asserted by Moncharsh.

4. *Illegality of the Contract Permits Judicial Review*

Moncharsh next contends the arbitrator's award is subject to judicial review because paragraph X-C of the employment agreement is illegal and in violation of public policy. Focusing on the fee-splitting provision of the employment agreement, he contends that despite the limited scope of judicial review of arbitration awards, such review has historically been available when one party alleges the underlying contract, a portion thereof, or the resulting award, is illegal or in violation of public policy. Before addressing the merits of the claim, we first discuss whether Moncharsh adequately preserved the issue for appellate review.

a. *Waiver*

Respondent Heily & Blase suggests Moncharsh waived the issue of illegality by failing to object to arbitration on this ground. We reject the claim because, as we explain below, Moncharsh's allegation that paragraph X-C was illegal, even if true, does not render illegal either (i) the entire employment agreement, or (ii) the agreement to arbitrate itself. Accordingly, his illegality claim was an arbitrable one, and he did not waive the issue by failing to object to arbitration on this ground.

Section 1281.2 states that when a written agreement to arbitrate exists, the court shall compel the parties to arbitrate their dispute "unless it determines that: [¶] ... [¶] (b) *Grounds exist for the revocation of the agreement.*" (Italics added.) Although this statute does not expressly state whether grounds must exist to revoke the entire contract, the arbitration agreement only, or some other provision of the contract, a fair reading of the statutory scheme reveals the Legislature must have meant revocation of the arbitration agreement. * * *

If a contract includes an arbitration agreement, and grounds exist to revoke the entire contract, such grounds would also vitiate the arbitration agreement. Thus, if an otherwise enforceable arbitration agreement is contained in an illegal contract, a party may avoid arbitration altogether.

By contrast, when — as here — the alleged illegality goes to only a portion of the contract (that does not include the arbitration agreement), the entire controversy, including the issue of illegality, remains arbitrable.

We apply this rule here. Moncharsh does not contend the alleged illegality constitutes grounds to revoke the entire employment contract. Nor does he contend the alleged illegality voids the arbitration clause of that contract. Accordingly, the legality of the fee-splitting provision was a question for the arbitrator in the first instance. Thus, Moncharsh was not required to first raise the issue of illegality in the trial court in order to preserve the issue for later judicial review.

The issue would have been waived, however, had Moncharsh failed to raise it *before the arbitrator*. Any other conclusion is inconsistent with the basic purpose of private arbitration, which is to finally decide a dispute between the parties. Moreover, we cannot permit a party to sit on his rights, content in the knowledge that should he suffer an adverse decision, he could then raise the illegality issue in a motion to vacate the arbitrator's award. * * *

We thus hold that unless a party is claiming (i) the entire contract is illegal, or (ii) the arbitration agreement itself is illegal, he or she need not raise the illegality question prior to participating in the arbitration process, so long as the issue is raised before the arbitrator. Failure to raise the claim before the arbitrator, however, waives the claim for any future judicial review. Because Moncharsh raised the illegality issue before the arbitrator, the issue was thus properly preserved for our review.

b. *Judicial Review of Claims of Illegality*

Although Moncharsh acknowledges the general rule that an arbitrator's legal, as well as factual, determinations are final and not subject to judicial review, he argues that judicial review of the arbitrator's decision is warranted on the facts of this case. In support, he claims that the fee-splitting provision of the contract that was interpreted and enforced by the arbitrator was "illegal" and violative of "public policy" as reflected in several provisions of the Rules of Professional Conduct. Such illegality, he claims, has been recognized as a ground for judicial review as stated in a line of cases emanating from this court's decision in *Loving & Evans v. Blick* (1949) 33 Cal. 2d 603 [204 P.2d 23] [hereafter *Loving & Evans*]. * * * *Loving & Evans, supra,* 33 Cal. 2d 603, ... permitted judicial review of an arbitrator's ruling where a party claimed the entire contract or transaction was illegal. By contrast, Moncharsh challenges but a single provision of the overall employment contract. Accordingly, ... *Loving & Evans, supra,* [does not] authorize judicial review of his claim.

We recognize that there may be some limited and exceptional circumstances justifying judicial review of an arbitrator's decision when a party claims illegality affects only a portion of the underlying contract. Such cases would include those in which granting finality to an arbitrator's decision would be inconsistent with the protection of a party's statutory rights. (Accord *Shearson/American Express Inc. v. McMahon* (1987) 482 U.S. 220, 225–227 [96 L. Ed. 2d 185, 192–194, 107 S. Ct. 2332] [federal statutory claims are arbitrable under the Federal Arbitration Act unless party opposing arbitration demonstrates "that Congress intended to preclude a waiver of judicial remedies for the statutory rights at issue"].)

Without an explicit legislative expression of public policy, however, courts should be reluctant to invalidate an arbitrator's award on this ground. The reason is clear: the Legislature has already expressed its strong support for private arbitration and the finality of arbitral awards in title 9 of the Code of Civil Procedure. (§ 1280 et seq.) Absent a clear expression of illegality or public policy undermining this strong presumption in favor of private arbitration, an arbitral award should ordinarily stand immune from judicial scrutiny.

Moncharsh contends, as he did before the arbitrator, that paragraph X-C is illegal and violates public policy because, inter alia, it violates former rules 2-107 [prohibiting unconscionable fees], 2-108 [prohibiting certain types of fee splitting arrangements], and 2-109 [prohibiting agreements restricting an attorney's right to practice], of the Rules of Professional Conduct of State Bar. We perceive, however, nothing in the Rules of Professional Conduct at issue in this case that suggests resolution by an arbitrator of what is essentially an ordinary fee dispute would be inappropriate or would improperly protect the public interest. Accordingly, judicial review of the arbitrator's decision is unavailable.

CONCLUSION

We conclude that an award reached by an arbitrator pursuant to a contractual agreement to arbitrate is not subject to judicial review except on the grounds set forth in sections 1286.2 (to vacate) and 1286.6 (for correction). Further, the existence of an error of law apparent on the face of the award that causes substantial injustice does not provide grounds for judicial review.

Finally, the normal rule of limited judicial review may not be avoided by a claim that a provision of the contract, construed or applied by the arbitrator, is "illegal," except in rare cases when according finality to the arbitrator's decision would be incompatible with the protection of a statutory right. We conclude that Moncharsh has demonstrated no reason why the strong presumption in favor of the finality of the arbitral award should not apply here.

The judgment of the Court of Appeal is affirmed.

[1] *Scope of Judicial Review of Arbitration Award*

The general rule announced in *Moncharsh*, which prohibits judicial review of an arbitrator's decision for errors of fact or law, may be controversial but is certainly clear. However, the courts have experienced some problems in applying the exceptions to this general rule. The main source of difficulty is CCP § 1286.2(a)(4) [formerly § 1286.2 (d)], which directs a court to vacate an award where the "arbitrators exceeded their powers and the award cannot be corrected without affecting the merits of the decision." Consider the following questions:

[a] When Do Arbitrators "Exceed Their Powers" When Granting Relief?

Advanced Micro Devices, Inc. v. Intel Corp.

Supreme Court of California
9 Cal. 4th 362, 36 Cal. Rptr. 2d 581, 885 P.2d 994 (1994)

WERDEGAR, JUSTICE.

[The parties, two computer microchip manufacturers, had entered into a long-term technology transfer agreement. Under this agreement, the parties intended to establish a mechanism for exchanging technical information so that each party would acquire the capability to develop products suitable for sale as an alternative source for products developed by the other party. The agreement included a provision for binding arbitration of any disagreements, and defined the scope of any award as follows: "The Arbitrator may grant any remedy or relief which the Arbitrator deems just and equitable and within the scope of the agreement of the parties, including, but not limited to, specific performance of a contract." A dispute subsequently arose involving performance of the contract, which the parties submitted to arbitration. After 4-1/2 years of arbitration, the arbitrator found that Intel extensively breached its contractual obligations to act in good faith and deal fairly.

The arbitrator found that Intel, anxious to be the sole source for a highly successful new 32-bit computer microchip and convinced that the contract with Advanced Micro Devices (AMD) was to Intel's disadvantage, secretly decided not to accept any more AMD products while maintaining the public posture that AMD would be a second source for the new 32-bit microchip. The arbitrator found that Intel's plan succeeded: AMD continued for two years to believe, incorrectly, that AMD would be a second source for Intel's new microchip under the contract, and therefore AMD delayed seeking alternative ways to enter the lucrative 32-bit microchip market. The arbitrator also found that actual damages to AMD were indeterminable and nominal damages alone inequitable, and that specific performance of the technology exchange required by the contract would not alleviate the effects of Intel's breach. The arbitrator therefore awarded AMD a permanent, nonexclusive and royalty-free license to any Intel intellectual property embodied in a 32-bit microchip AMD developed through reverse engineering of the Intel microchip; as well as a further two-year extension of certain patent and copyright licenses relating to the AMD developed microchip.

When AMD petitioned the superior court to confirm the award, Intel petitioned for the award to be corrected on the ground that licensing relief exceeded the arbitrator's powers. The superior court confirmed the award, but the Court of Appeal reversed. The Court of Appeal could not find a "rational nexus" between the licensing relief and the contract, and therefore concluded that the arbitrator had exceeded his powers by improperly rewriting the parties' agreement. The Supreme Court granted review, and reversed the Court of Appeal. The Supreme Court first discussed the need for deference to an arbitrator's choice of remedies]:

Intel contends that even if California precedents require deference to an arbitrator's assessment of arbitrability, a different, less deferential rule applies to an arbitrator's choice of *remedies*. Intel's position is neither logically persuasive nor supported by precedent.

In providing for judicial vacation or correction of an award, our statutes (§§ 1286.2, subd. (d), 1286.6, subd. (b)) do not distinguish between arbitrators' power to decide an issue and their authority to choose an appropriate remedy; in either instance the test is whether arbitrators have "exceeded their powers." Because determination of appropriate relief also constitutes decision on an issue, these two aspects of the arbitrators' authority are not always neatly separable. * * *

Deference to the arbitrator is ... required by the character of the remedy decision itself. Fashioning remedies for a breach of contract or other injury is not always a simple matter of applying contractually specified relief to an easily measured injury. It may involve, as in the present case, providing relief for breach of implied covenants, as to which the parties have not specified contractual damages. It may require, also as in this case, finding a way of approximating the impact of a breach that cannot with any certainty be reduced to monetary terms. Passage of time and changed circumstances may have rendered any remedies suggested by the contract insufficient or excessive. * * *

The choice of remedy, then, may at times call on any decisionmaker's flexibility, creativity and sense of fairness. In private arbitrations, the parties have bargained for the relatively free exercise of those faculties. Arbitrators, unless specifically restricted by the agreement to following legal rules, "'may base their decisions upon broad principles of justice and equity.... ' [Citation.]" (*Moncharsh* [*v. Heily & Blase* (1992)] 3 Cal. 4th at pp. 10–11.) Were courts to reevaluate independently the merits of a particular remedy, the parties' contractual expectation of a decision according to the arbitrators' best judgment would be defeated. * * *

We do not, by the above, intend to suggest an arbitrator's exercise of discretion in ordering relief is unrestricted or unreviewable. The powers of an arbitrator derive from, and are limited by, the agreement to arbitrate. (*Moncharsh, supra,* 3 Cal. 4th at p. 8.) Awards in excess of those powers may, under sections 1286.2 and 1286.6, be corrected or vacated by the court. Unless the parties "have conferred upon the arbiter the unusual power of determining his own jurisdiction" (*McCarroll v. L.A. County etc. Carpenters* (1957) 49 Cal. 2d 45, 65–66 [315 P.2d 322]), the courts retain the ultimate authority to overturn awards as beyond the arbitrator's powers, whether for an unauthorized remedy or decision on an unsubmitted issue. * * *

The principle of arbitral finality, the practical demands of deciding on an appropriate remedy for breach, and the prior holdings of this court all dictate that arbitrators, unless expressly restricted by the agreement or the submission to arbitration, have substantial discretion to determine the scope of their contractual authority to fashion remedies, and that judicial review of their awards must be correspondingly narrow and deferential.

C. *Standard of Review*

... [W]e must attempt to articulate a standard capturing the middle ground of deferential yet meaningful review. We begin by surveying similar efforts in the Courts of Appeal and in other jurisdictions.

Recent decisions in the Courts of Appeal have employed two formulas to determine whether an arbitrator's award exceeded his or her powers. The courts have asked whether the award rests on a "completely irrational" construction of the contract (e.g., *Tate v. Saratoga Savings & Loan Assn.* (1989) 216 Cal. App. 3d 843, 855 [265 Cal. Rptr. 440]; ...) or whether it amounts to an "arbitrary remaking" of the contract (e.g., *Blue Cross of California v. Jones* (1993) 19 Cal. App. 4th 220, 228 [23 Cal. Rptr. 2d 359]; ...). These tests were combined in *Southern Cal. Rapid Transit Dist. v. United Transportation Union*, [(1992)] 5 Cal. App. 4th [416] [6 Cal. Rptr. 2d 804] at page 423, into a single formula: "Generally, a decision exceeds the arbitrator's powers only if it is so utterly irrational that it amounts to an arbitrary remaking of the contract between the parties."

These statements of the standard tend to focus the inquiry on the arbitrator's construction of the contract. Useful as such an examination may sometimes be, it is incomplete as a test of whether arbitrators have exceeded their powers in awarding a particular item of damages or other relief. The critical question with regard to remedies is not whether an arbitrator has rationally interpreted the parties' agreement, but whether the remedy chosen is rationally drawn from the contract as so interpreted. This case illustrates the distinction; Intel argues not that the arbitrator misconstrued the contract, but that the remedy he fashioned bore an insufficient relationship to the agreement as he interpreted it.

In contrast to the California cases, decisions from the federal courts applying the "essence" test announced in *Steelworkers v. Enterprise Corp.*, *supra*, 363 U.S. at page 597 [4 L. Ed. 2d at page 1428] (hereafter *Enterprise*) properly focus on the *source* of the arbitrator's chosen remedy. * * * Judicial review of remedies as outlined in the *Enterprise* decision thus looks not to whether the arbitrator correctly *interpreted* the agreement, but to whether the award is drawn from the agreement *as the arbitrator interpreted it* or derives from some extrinsic source. * * *

Although the *Enterprise* test emphasizes the source from which the arbitrator drew the award, it nevertheless is objective. The arbitrator cannot shield his decision from scrutiny "simply by making the right noises—noises of contract interpretation...." (*Ethyl Corp. v. United Steelworkers of America* (7th Cir. 1985) 768 F.2d at p. 187.) Rather, the question is whether the award is "so outre that we can infer that it was driven by a desire to do justice beyond the limits of the contract." (*Ibid.*) Restated, the test asks " 'whether the arbitrator's solution can be rationally derived from some plausible theory of the general framework or intent of the agreement.'" (*Id.* at p. 186.) * * *

We distill from these cases what we believe is a meaningful, workable and properly deferential framework for reviewing an arbitrator's choice of remedies. Arbitrators are not obliged to read contracts literally, and an award may not be vacated merely because the court is unable to find the relief granted was authorized by a specific term of the contract. The remedy awarded, however, must bear some rational relationship to the contract and the breach. The required link may be to the contractual terms as actually interpreted by the arbitrator (if the arbitrator has made that interpretation known), to an interpretation implied in the award itself, or to a plausible theory of the contract's general subject matter, framework or intent. The award must be related in a rational manner to the breach (as expressly or impliedly found by the arbitrator).[12] Where the damage is difficult to determine or measure, the arbitrator enjoys correspondingly broader discretion to fashion a remedy.

The award will be upheld so long as it was even arguably based on the contract; it may be vacated only if the reviewing court is *compelled* to infer the award was based on an extrinsic source. In close cases the arbitrator's decision must stand.

D. *Relationship of Relief to Rights Under Contract*

Intel maintains that, whatever the general standard, the cases establish one "bright-line" rule: "arbitrators may not award a remedy that conflicts with express terms of the arbitrated contract." To the extent this means arbitrators may not award remedies expressly forbidden by the arbitration agreement or submission, the point is well taken. How the violation of "an express and explicit restriction on the arbitrator's power" could be considered rationally related to a plausible interpretation of the agreement is difficult to see. * * *

To the extent Intel is advocating a broader rule — that arbitrators may not award a party benefits different from those the party could have acquired through performance of the contract — the cases do not support its position. No exact correspondence is required between the rights and obligations of a party had the contract been performed and the remedy an arbitrator may provide for the other party's breach. * * *

… [A]rbitrators, unless expressly restricted by the agreement of the parties, enjoy the authority to fashion relief they consider just and fair under the circumstances existing at the time of arbitration, so long as the remedy may be rationally derived from the contract and the breach. The rights and obligations of the parties under the contract as it was to be performed are not an unfailing guide to the remedies available

---

12. The award is rationally related to the breach if it is aimed at compensating for or alleviating the effects of the breach. We need not decide here under what circumstances a contractual arbitrator is authorized to award punitive damages. (See *Tate v. Saratoga Savings & Loan Assn.*, *supra*, 216 Cal. App. 3d at p. 855; *Todd Shipyards Corp. v. Cunard Line, Ltd.* (9th Cir. 1991) 943 F.2d 1056, 1062–1063.)

when the contract has been breached. It follows that parties entering into commercial contracts with arbitration clauses, if they wish the arbitrator's remedial authority to be specially restricted, would be well advised to set out such limitations explicitly and unambiguously in the arbitration clause. Because parties to arbitration agreements do have the power to limit possible remedies in this manner (as the dissent acknowledges), we do not believe our holding will, as the dissent speculates, discourage arbitration. * * *

The parties in the present case did not by agreement restrict the arbitrator to remedies available in a court of law. To the contrary, they adopted an AAA rule authorizing the arbitrator to grant "any remedy or relief which the Arbitrator deems just and equitable and within the scope of the agreement...." * * *

In light of the inherently flexible nature of equitable remedies, the principle of arbitral finality which forbids judicial inquiry into the legal correctness of the arbitrator's decisions on submitted issues, and the related principle that remedies available to a court are only the *minimum* available to an arbitrator (unless restricted by agreement), we cannot agree with the dissent the relief in this case was beyond the arbitrator's powers simply because the license awarded did not correspond in all its terms with a license that could have been earned through performance of the agreement.

We conclude the challenged portions of the arbitrator's award were within his authority to fashion remedies for a breach of contract. The superior court correctly confirmed the award under section 1286. The judgment of the Court of Appeal, reversing that of the superior court, is reversed.

KENNARD, JUSTICE, Dissenting.

Under Code of Civil Procedure section 1286.2, subdivision (d), a party may petition the court to vacate an arbitrator's award on the ground that "the arbitrator[] exceeded [his or her] powers." In my view, there are two sources of limitations on the remedial powers of an arbitrator deciding a contract dispute. First, because our arbitration statutes merely establish a different procedure for resolving disputes, and do not create new substantive claims or remedies, an arbitrator lacks the power to award a remedy outside the scope of those that a court could award for the same claim. Second, an arbitrator deciding a contract dispute lacks the power to make an award that has no rational linkage to the agreement or its breach. To guard against such arbitrary and irrational awards, courts have recognized that in contract disputes there should be a rational relationship between the arbitrator's interpretation of the contract and the relief awarded. This inquiry focuses on whether there is some connection between the award, on the one hand, and, on the other hand, the arbitrator's interpretation of the agreement and his or her findings of breach. * * *

... [O]ur arbitration statutes create a different process for deciding legal disputes, not different remedies for those disputes. For that reason, the potential remedies available to an arbitrator are limited to those that a court could award on the same claim. Thus, in reviewing an arbitration award to determine whether it exceeds the arbitrator's powers, a court must determine whether the award falls within the remedies authorized by law or by agreement for the legal claim the arbitrator has decided. * * *

In deciding what remedies are potentially available to the arbitrator in a given case, a court should first look at the nature of the claims being arbitrated. Unless the parties have by agreement otherwise expanded or restricted the scope of remedies available, the nature of the claims should ordinarily determine the nature of the

As a result of the majority's decision ... an arbitrator's deck of remedies is now full of wild cards. By refusing to limit arbitrators in a commercial contract dispute to the range of remedies that a court could award for the same dispute and by applying only the minimal scrutiny of the "essence" test to arbitration awards, the majority has made the potential outcomes of an arbitration impossible for the parties to predict. This uncertainty can only make arbitration substantially less desirable to many. In making arbitration a more uncertain and less attractive alternative, the majority's decision will ultimately, if unwittingly, discourage arbitration.

In my view, the better rule and the one that ultimately encourages arbitration is to require that arbitration awards both fall within the range of remedies that a court could award for the same claim and, in cases of contract dispute arbitration, bear a rational relationship to the contract. Accordingly, I would affirm that portion of the Court of Appeal's judgment holding that the arbitrator exceeded his powers....

Notes and Questions regarding Arbitrators' Powers

(1) What precisely are the differences in the standards for judicial review espoused by the majority and the dissent in *Advanced Micro Devices, supra*, with respect to the determination of whether the remedies awarded by an arbitrator exceed the arbitrator's powers? Which standard makes more sense? Is easier for a court to apply? Is more consistent with the policy favoring arbitrability of disputes expressed in the arbitration statutes? *See* Jessica T. Martin, *Advanced Micro Devices v. Intel Corp. and Judicial Review of Commercial Arbitration Awards: When Does a Remedy "Exceed" Arbitral Powers?*, 46 HASTINGS L.J. 1907 (1995). Do you agree with the dissent that the majority's standard will discourage businesses from utilizing arbitration as a method of resolving commercial disputes? Are you satisfied with the majority's response to this concern, *i.e.*, that the parties may contractually limit the arbitrator's discretion to fashion remedies by expressly agreeing to limit possible relief to that which a court may award, or by even more specific restrictions as to available relief? Why?

(2) In *Advanced Micro Devices, supra*, the Supreme Court observed that although § 1286.2 permits a court to vacate an award that exceeds the arbitrators' powers, courts should generally defer to the arbitrators' findings that determination of a particular question is within the scope of their contractual authority, and that "any doubts as to the meaning or extent of an arbitration agreement are for the arbitrators and not the court to resolve." *Advanced Micro Devices*, 9 Cal. 4th at 372. The court further noted that the general rule of arbitral finality affirmed in *Moncharsh* requires a court

to refrain from substituting its judgment for the arbitrators' in determining the contractual scope of the arbitrators' powers. *Id.* Do you agree with this interpretation of the standard of judicial review under CCP § 1286.2?

(3) As acknowledged in *Advanced Micro Devices*, the parties to a contract may agree to an arbitration provision which specifically limits the nature and scope of relief an arbitrator has authority to award. Would the award in *Advanced Micro Devices* have exceeded the arbitrator's powers if the agreement there had authorized the arbitrator to award only "normal contract remedies"? To award only "such relief that a court could award to resolve a dispute arising out of this contract"? To award relief limited to "either damages or specific performance"?

(4) Do arbitrators "exceed their powers" within the meaning of CCP § 1286.2 when they award an amount which is larger than the amount requested in the arbitration demand? *See Grubb & Ellis Co. v. Bello*, 19 Cal. App. 4th 231, 23 Cal. Rptr. 2d 281 (1993) (concluding arbitrator's authority not limited to amount in prayer because both parties participated in arbitration hearing where evidence and computation of correct amount of damages was presented). When they award attorney fees to a party who could not legally and factually have been the "prevailing party" in the underlying arbitration? *See Creative Plastering, Inc. v. Hedley Builders, Inc.*, 19 Cal. App. 4th 1662, 24 Cal. Rptr. 2d 216 (1993) (holding arbitrator did not to exceed powers in awarding attorney fees, despite possible error of law and fact, where parties agreed that the arbitrator could decide "all matters in question" arising out of contract).

(5) Do arbitrators exceed their powers when they award punitive damages? *See Little v. Auto Stiegler, Inc.*, 29 Cal. 4th 1064, 1081,130 Cal. Rptr. 2d 892, 63 P.3d 979 (2003) (ruling that for certain unwaivable claims designed to protect the public interest to be arbitrable, damage remedies equal to those in court, including punitive damages, must be available in arbitration); *J. Alexander Sec., Inc. v. Mendez*, 17 Cal. App. 4th 1083, 21 Cal. Rptr. 2d 826 (1993) (confirming award of punitive damages as not in excess of arbitrators' powers); *Rifkind & Sterling, Inc. v. Rifkind*, 28 Cal. App. 4th 1282, 33 Cal. Rptr. 2d 828 (1994) (holding the Due Process Clause, which applies only to state action, does not govern the size of the punitive damages award because arbitration is a private process arranged by contract); *Mave Enter. v. Travelers Idem. Co.*, 219 Cal. App. 4th 1408, 1434–44, 162 Cal. Rptr. 3d 671 (2013) (following *Rifkind* and confirming award of punitive damages, noting that "[i]f the punitive damages award was excessive, the arbitrator's error would be no different from other errors of law").

(6) Do Arbitrators "Exceed Their Powers" When They Order Injunctive Relief? See *Broughton v. Cigna Health Plans of California*, 21 Cal. 4th 1066, 90 Cal. Rptr. 2d 334, 988 P.2d 67 (1999) (concluding a claim for permanent injunctive relief under the Consumer Legal Remedies Act is inarbitrable because the Legislature did not intend this type of injunctive relief, where the plaintiff functions as a private attorney general and seeks to enjoin future deceptive practice on behalf of the general public, to be arbitrated); *Cruz v. Pacificare Health Sys., Inc.*, 30 Cal. 4th 303, 133 Cal. Rptr. 2d 58,

66 P.3d 1157 (2003) (extending the *Boughton* holding to claims to enjoin unfair competition under Bus. & Prof. Code § 17200 *et seq.*, brought by a plaintiff in the capacity as a private attorney general, and to enjoin misleading business advertising under Bus. & Prof. Code § 17500 *et seq.*).

The *Boughton* and *Cruz* courts declined to decide the broader question as to whether an arbitrator may ever issue a permanent injunction to resolve a private dispute and not to remedy a public wrong. *Boughton, supra,* 21 Cal. 4th at 1079–80; *Cruz, supra,* 30 Cal. 4th at 315. What is the proper answer to this broader question? Is an arbitrator precluded from issuing a permanent injunction because an arbitrator has no authority to vacate or modify an injunction? Does the fact that arbitrators are without authority to enforce their injunctions make such injunctions unworkable? *See Swan Magnetics, Inc. v. Superior Court,* 56 Cal. App. 4th 1504, 66 Cal. Rptr. 2d 541 (1997) (concluding that an arbitrator's injunction is inherently subject to modification or vacation, and envisioning such modification or vacation as occurring through the initiation of a new arbitration proceeding); *O'Hare v Mun. Res. Consultants,* 107 Cal. App. 4th 267, 278, 132 Cal. Rptr. 2d 116 (2003) (noting that it is well settled that arbitrators provide equitable relief, including permanent injunctive relief).

Code of Civil Procedure § 1281.8 authorizes a court to grant a provisional remedy in connection with an arbitrable controversy, but only where the arbitration award to which the applicant may be entitled may be rendered ineffectual without provisional relief. *See Davenport v. Blue Cross of Cal.,* 52 Cal. App. 4th 435, 60 Cal. Rptr. 2d 641 (1997) (reversing the trial court's grant of a preliminary injunction because the plaintiff never began the arbitration process and failed to make a showing that the arbitration would not be concluded within a meaningful time frame); *see also Baltazar v. Forever 21, Inc.,* 62 Cal. 4th 1237, 1246–48, 200 Cal. Rptr. 3d 7, 367 P.3d 6 (2016) (discussing CCP § 1281.8). An application to the court for such a provisional remedy does not constitute a waiver of any right to arbitration, as long as it is accompanied by a demand for arbitration and a request for a stay. CCP § 1281.8(b) & (d).

(7) Does a court have the power to correct an arbitration award to include attorney fees where the arbitrator erroneously failed or refused to award such fees to the prevailing party? In *Moshonov v. Walsh,* 22 Cal. 4th 771, 94 Cal. Rptr. 2d 597, 996 P.2d 699 (2000), the court concluded that where the arbitrator's denial of fees to the prevailing party rests on the arbitrator's interpretation of a contractual provision within the scope of the issues submitted to arbitration, the arbitrator has not "exceeded [his or her] powers" within the meaning of CCP § 1286.2(a)(4) and § 1286.6 (b). The court reasoned that such an interpretation of the contract could amount, at most, to an error of law on an issue submitted to arbitration and as such, pursuant to *Moncharsh* and *Advanced Micro Devices,* would be final and unreviewable. *See Cooper v. Lavely & Singer Prof. Corp.,* 230 Cal. App. 4th 1, 178 Cal. Rtpr. 3d 322 (2014) (applying *Moshonov*).

Likewise, in *Moore v. First Bank of San Luis Obispo*, 22 Cal. 4th 782, 94 Cal. Rptr. 2d 603, 996 P.2d 706 (2000), the Supreme Court held that the arbitrators' failure to make a finding as to the existence or nonexistence of a prevailing party, despite plaintiff's request attorney fees as the prevailing party under Civil Code § 1717, could not be judicially corrected. That failure to designate a prevailing party, according to the Supreme Court, amounted at most to an error of law on a submitted issue, which does not exceed the arbitrators' powers under the holding in *Moncharsh*, "even where such a denial order would be reversible legal error if made by a court in civil litigation." *Moore, supra*, 22 Cal. at 4th 784.

(8) Does an arbitrator exceed his powers, within the meaning of CCP §§ 1284, 1286.2 and 1286.6, when he amends the arbitration award to determine an issue he inadvertently neglected to decide? *See Century City Med. Plaza v. Sperling, Issacs & Eisenberg*, 86 Cal. App. 4th 865, 877–82, 103 Cal. Rptr. 2d 605 (2001) (holding an arbitrator does have the authority to modify or amend an award to supply a ruling on submitted issues where such ruling was *inadvertently omitted* from the original award, *and* provided the modification or amendment (1) is requested and done in a timely manner prior to confirmation of the original award, (2) does not alter the merits of the result set out in the original award, and (3) occasions no prejudice to the legitimate interests of any party); *A.M. Classic Constr., Inc. v. Tri-Build Dev. Co.*, 70 Cal. App. 4th 1470, 1478, 83 Cal. Rptr. 2d 449 (1999) (concluding an arbitrator is permitted to issue an amended award to resolve an issue omitted from the original award through mistake, inadvertence, or excusable neglect of the arbitrator if the amendment is made before judicial confirmation of the original award, is not inconsistent with other findings on the merits of the controversy, and does not cause demonstrable prejudice to the legitimate interests of any party).

(9) Is there any limitation on the scope of relief that parties my contractually empower an arbitrator to award? *See, e.g., Pacific Gas & Elec. Co. v. Superior Court*, 15 Cal. App. 4th 576, 610–12, 19 Cal. Rptr. 2d 295 (1993) (ruling an arbitration award will be unenforceable if it compels the performance of an illegal act); *All Points Traders, Inc. v. Barrington Assoc.*, 211 Cal. App. 3d 723, 259 Cal. Rptr. 780 (1989) (holding award of commission fees to investment banking firm must be vacated because commission agreement was invalid under statute requiring real estate license and award therefore violated public policy). What effect should a court give to an arbitration agreement whereby the parties confer on the arbitrator exclusive jurisdiction to resolve a dispute, not subject to *any* judicial review of the award as beyond the arbitrator's powers?

(10) *Discovery*. Arbitrators have broad statutory authority to order discovery in certain types of arbitration proceedings, including any arbitration arising out of a personal injury or wrongful death. CCP §§ 1283.1, 1283.05. All discovery disputes arising out of arbitration must be submitted first to the arbitral, not the judicial, forum. *Berglund v. Arthoscopic & Laser Ctr.*, 44 Cal. 4th 528, 535–536, 79 Cal. Rptr. 3d 370, 187 P.3d 86 (2008). An arbitrator's decision in a discovery dispute between *parties* to an arbitration agreement is subject to the same limited judicial review as

is an arbitration award on the merits. CCP § 1283.05; *Berglund, supra*, 44 Cal. 4th at 534–535. However, when the discovery dispute involves a *nonparty* to the arbitration proceeding, the nonparty is entitled to full judicial review of the arbitrator's discovery order. *Berglund*, 44 Cal. 4th at 536–539.

[b] Statutory Rights Exception to Rule of Arbitral Finality

In *Moncharsh v. Heily & Blase*, reproduced *supra*, the Supreme Court indicated that there may be exceptional circumstances justifying judicial review of an arbitrator's decision, including cases in which granting finality to an award would be inconsistent with a party's statutory rights. *Moncharsh*, 3 Cal. 4th at 32. An example of such an exceptional case is *Board of Education v. Round Valley Teachers Assn.*, 13 Cal. 4th 269, 52 Cal. Rptr. 2d 115, 914 P.2d 193 (1996), in which the Supreme Court held that an arbitrator exceeded his powers, within the meaning of CCP § 1286.2, by granting relief pursuant to the terms of a collective bargaining agreement that violated one party's specific statutory rights as set forth in the Education and Government Codes. Another is *Aguilar v. Lerner*, 32 Cal. 4th 974, 12 Cal. Rptr. 3d 287, 88 P.3d 24 (2004), where the court ruled enforcement of an arbitration agreement that violates a client's rights under the Mandatory Fee Arbitration Act (MFAA), Bus. & Prof. Code § 6200 *et seq.*, exceeded the arbitrator's powers and made judicial review of the arbitrator's decision appropriate. *See also Ahbout v. Hekmatjah*, 213 Cal. App. 4th 21, 152 Cal. Rptr. 3d 199 (2013) (concluding that Bus. & Prof. Code § 7031 constitutes an explicit legislative expression of public policy mandating disgorgement of compensation received by an unlicensed contractor, and therefore the general prohibition of judicial review of arbitration awards does not apply).

[c] Mandatory Employment Arbitration Agreements

A controversial application of the statutory rights exception to arbitral finality is *Armendariz v. Foundation Health Psychcare Services, Inc.*, 24 Cal. 4th 83, 99 Cal. Rptr. 2d 745, 6 P.3d 669 (2000), where the California Supreme Court held that employment discrimination claims under the California Fair Employment and Housing Act, Gov. Code § 12900 *et seq.*, are arbitrable *if* the arbitration permits an employee to vindicate his or her statutory rights. The Supreme Court then explained that, in order for such vindication to occur, the arbitration must meet certain minimum requirements, including neutrality of the arbitrator, the provision of adequate discovery, a written decision that will permit a limited form of judicial review, and limitations on the costs of arbitration]arbitration of must meet certain minimum requirements including neutrality of the arbitrator, the provision of adequate discovery, a written decision that will permit a limited form of judicial review, and limitations on the costs of arbitration.

In *Armendariz*, the Supreme Court's analysis regarding the validity of mandatory employment arbitration agreements was based solely on the California Arbitration Act, CCP § 1280 *et seq.* The court specifically declined to decide whether such agreements would also be valid under the Federal Arbitration Act (FAA), 9 U.S.C. § 1 *et seq. Armendariz, supra,* 24 Cal. 4th at 97–98. Seven months after the decision in *Armendariz,* the United States Supreme Court decided that issue in *Circuit City Stores, Inc. v. Saint Clair Adams,* 532 U.S. 105, 121 S. Ct. 1302, 149 L. Ed. 2d 234 (2001), with respect to an arbitration agreement which, if valid, would require the plaintiff to submit to arbitration an employment discrimination claim against his employer based on the California FEHA. The U.S. Supreme Court concluded that such agreements were not excepted from the FAA's coverage. The question of how the *Circuit City* holding effects the various *Armendariz* rulings will likely occupy the courts for some time to come. What possible effects do you see?

In *Little v. Auto Stiegler, Inc.,* 29 Cal. 4th 1064, 130 Cal. Rptr. 2d 892, 63 P.3d 979 (2003), the Supreme Court held that the minimum requirements for arbitration of unwaivable statutory claims set forth in *Armendariz*—no limitation on available damages, adequate discovery, written arbitration decision sufficient for judicial review, and no unreasonable costs—also apply to nonstatutory claims alleging an employee was terminated in violation of public policy. However, in *Boghos v. Certain Underwriters at Lloyd's of London,* 36 Cal. 4th 495, 30 Cal. Rptr. 3d at 787, 115 P.3d 68 (2005), the Supreme Court declined to extend the *Armendariz/Little* cost-shifting rule to an arbitration clause in a contract of disability coverage which, pursuant to CCP § 1284.2, required the parties to share arbitration costs. The Court compelled arbitration of the plaintiff's common law breach of contract and tort claims because, unlike *Armendariz* and *Little,* these claims were "not carefully tethered to statutory or constitutional provisions." *Boghos, supra,* 36 Cal. 4th at 508.

In *Pearson Dental Supplies, Inc. v. Superior Court,* 48 Cal. 4th 665, 108 Cal. Rptr. 3d 171, 229 P.3d 83 (2010), a case involving resolution of a statutory employment discrimination claim, an arbitrator decided in favor of the employer against the employee on the grounds that the claim was time-barred under the one-year contractual deadline for requesting arbitration. The trial court vacated the award, concluding that the arbitrator had plainly misapplied the relevant tolling statute. The Court of Appeal reversed, holding that such error was not a valid basis for vacation of an arbitration award. Upon review, the Supreme Court first concluded that the arbitrator clearly erred in ruling that the employee's claim was time-barred. *Pearson Dental, supra,* 48 Cal. 4th at 673–675. The court then held that under the particular circumstances of the case, in which a clear error of law by an arbitrator means that an employee subject to a mandatory arbitration agreement is deprived of a hearing on the merits of an unwaivable FEHA claim, the trial court did not err in vacating the award. *Id.* at 675–680.

[2] *Standard of Judicial Review Determined by the Agreement*

As *Moncharsh v. Heily & Blase,* reproduced *supra,* points out, the submission of a dispute to arbitration as an alternative to judicial adjudication is a matter of contract. To what extent can the parties contractually alter the standards of judicial review set forth in *Moncharsh* and *Advanced Micro Devices?*

Cable Connection, Inc. v. Directv, Inc.

Supreme Court of California
44 Cal. 4th 1334, 82 Cal. Rptr. 3d 229, 190 P.3d 586 (2008)

CORRIGAN, JUSTICE.

[This case presents a question regarding arbitration agreements:] May the parties structure their agreement to allow for judicial review of legal error in the arbitration award?

On [this] question, the United States Supreme Court has held that the Federal Arbitration Act (FAA; 9 U.S.C. § 1 et seq.) does not permit the parties to expand the scope of review by agreement. (*Hall Street Associates, L.L.C. v. Mattel, Inc.* (2008) 552 U.S. 576, 585–589 [170 L. Ed. 2d 254, 128 S. Ct. 1396, 1404–1405] (*Hall Street*).) However, the high court went on to say that federal law does not preclude "more searching review based on authority outside the [federal] statute," including "state statutory or common law." (*Id.* at p. 590.) In *Moncharsh v. Heily & Blase* (1992) 3 Cal.4th 1 [10 Cal. Rptr. 2d 183, 832 P.2d 899] (*Moncharsh*), this court reviewed the history of the California Arbitration Act (CAA; Code Civ. Proc., § 1280 et seq.). We concluded that the California Legislature "adopt[ed] the position taken in case law … that is, 'that in the absence of some limiting clause in the arbitration agreement, the merits of the award, either on questions of fact or of law, may not be reviewed except as provided in the statute.'" (*Moncharsh*, at p. 25, quoting *Crofoot v. Blair Holdings Corp.* (1953) 119 Cal.App.2d 156, 186 [260 P.2d 156] (*Crofoot*).)

We adhere to our holding in *Moncharsh*, recognizing that contractual limitations may alter the usual scope of review. The California rule is that the parties may obtain judicial review of the merits by express agreement. There is a statutory as well as a contractual basis for this rule; one of the grounds for review of an arbitration award is that "[t]he arbitrators exceeded their powers." (§§ 1286.2, subd. (a)(4), 1286.6, subd. (b).) Here, the parties agreed that "[t]he arbitrators shall not have the power to commit errors of law or legal reasoning, and the award may be vacated or corrected on appeal to a court of competent jurisdiction for any such error." This contract provision is enforceable under state law, and we reverse the contrary ruling of the Court of Appeal. * * *

II. DISCUSSION

A. *Contract Provisions for Judicial Review of Arbitration Awards*

[Here the California Supreme Court analyzes the U.S. Supreme Court's decision in *Hall Street Associates, LLC v. Mattel, Inc, supra*, and the question of preemption, and concludes that *Hall Street* did not preclude the California courts from applying a different rule with respect to arbitration agreements governed by the FAA.]

Section 2 of the FAA, declaring the enforceability of arbitration agreements, "create[s] a body of federal substantive law of arbitrability, applicable to any arbitration agreement within the coverage of the Act." (*Moses H. Cone Hospital v. Mercury Constr. Corp.* (1983) 460 U.S. 1, 24 [74 L. Ed. 2d 765, 103 S. Ct. 927].) The FAA governs agreements in contracts involving interstate commerce, like those in this case. (*Southland Corp. v. Keating, supra,* 465 U.S. at pp. 10–11; *Cronus Investments, Inc. v. Concierge Services* (2005) 35 Cal.4th 376, 383–384 [25 Cal. Rptr. 3d 540, 107 P.3d 217] (*Cronus*).) The United States Supreme Court has frequently held that state laws invalidating arbitration agreements on grounds applicable only to arbitration provisions contravene the policy of enforceability established by section 2 of the FAA, and are therefore preempted. (E.g., *Doctor's Associates, Inc. v. Casarotto* (1996) 517 U.S. 681, 686–688 [134 L. Ed. 2d 902, 116 S. Ct. 1652]; *Southland Corp. v. Keating, supra,* 465 U.S. at p. 16; see *Cronus,* at p. 385.)

However, "the United States Supreme Court does not read the FAA's procedural provisions to apply to state court proceedings." (*Cronus, supra,* 35 Cal.4th at p. 389.) Sections 3 and 4 of the FAA, governing stays of litigation and petitions to enforce arbitration agreements, do not apply in state court. (*Volt Info. Sciences v. Leland Stanford Jr. U.* (1989) 489 U.S. 468, 477, fn. 6 [103 L.Ed.2d 488, 109 S. Ct. 1248] (*Volt*); *Southland Corp. v. Keating, supra,* 465 U.S. at p. 16, fn. 10; *Cronus,* at pp. 389–390.) As we have noted, the provisions for judicial review of arbitration awards in sections 10 and 11 of the FAA are directed to "the United States court in and for the district wherein the award was made." We have held that similar language in sections 3 and 4 of the FAA reflects Congress's intent to limit the application of those provisions to federal courts. (*Cronus,* at pp. 388–389.) * * * We conclude that the *Hall Street* holding is restricted to proceedings to review arbitration awards under the FAA, and does not require state law to conform with its limitations.

3. Moncharsh *and the California Rule*

In *Moncharsh,* the parties' arbitration clause included no provision for an expanded scope of judicial review. (*Moncharsh, supra,* 3 Cal.4th at p. 7, fn. 1.) We considered and rejected the appellant's claim that the award was nevertheless reviewable for error of law on its face causing substantial injustice, a proposition which had some support in case law. (*Id.* at p. 28.) We reaffirmed "the general rule that an arbitrator's decision is not ordinarily reviewable for error by either the trial or appellate courts" (*id.* at p. 13), and held that the statutory grounds for review were intended to implement that rule (*id.* at pp. 27–28). * * *

Our reasoning in *Moncharsh* centered not on statutory restriction of the parties' contractual options, but on the parties' intent and the powers of the arbitrators as defined in the agreement. These factors support the enforcement of agreements for an expanded scope of review. If the parties constrain the arbitrators' authority by requiring a dispute to be decided according to the rule of law, *and* make plain their intention that the award is reviewable for legal error, the general rule of limited review has been displaced by the parties' agreement. Their expectation is not that the result of the arbitration will be final and conclusive, but rather that it will be reviewed on the merits at the request of either party. That expectation has a foundation in the statutes governing judicial review, which include the ground that "[t]he arbitrators exceeded their powers." (§§ 1286.2, subd. (a)(4), 1286.6, subd. (b).) * * *

In California, the policy favoring arbitration without the complications of traditional judicial review is based on the parties' expectations as embodied in their agreement, and the CAA rests on the same foundation. "Accordingly, policies favoring the efficiency of private arbitration as a means of dispute resolution must sometimes yield to its fundamentally contractual nature, and to the attendant requirement that arbitration shall proceed *as the parties themselves have agreed.*" (*Vandenberg v. Superior Court* (1999) 21 Cal.4th 815, 831 [88 Cal. Rptr. 2d 366, 982 P.2d 229].) The scope of judicial review is not invariably limited by statute; rather, "the parties, simply by agreeing to arbitrate, are deemed to accept limited judicial review *by implication....*" (*Ibid.*) It follows that they may expressly agree to accept a broader scope of review. * * *

Therefore, to take themselves out of the general rule that the merits of the award are not subject to judicial review, the parties must clearly agree that legal errors are an excess of arbitral authority that is reviewable by the courts. Here, the parties expressly so agreed, depriving the arbitrators of the power to commit legal error. They also specifically provided for judicial review of such error.[20] We do not decide here whether one or the other of these clauses alone, or some different formulation, would be sufficient to confer an expanded scope of review. However, we emphasize that parties seeking to allow judicial review of the merits, and to avoid an additional dispute over the scope of review, would be well advised to provide for that review explicitly and unambiguously. * * *

Review on the merits has been deemed incompatible with the goals of finality and informality that are served by arbitration and protected by the arbitration statutes. However, as discussed above, those policies draw their strength from the agreement of the parties. It is the parties who are best situated to weigh the advantages of traditional arbitration against the benefits of court review for the correction of legal error. * * *

Some courts have expressed concern that arbitration is so different from judicial proceedings that courts would be unable to adequately review the substance of arbitrators' decisions. This problem has not appeared in those circumstances where arbitration awards have been reviewed for legal error. Section 1296 has provided for review of the merits in public construction contract arbitrations since 1979. Arbitration awards have been reviewed to determine whether the arbitrators complied with statutes conferring unwaivable rights. (See, e.g., *Aguilar v. Lerner, supra*, 32 Cal.4th 974, 982–983.) Until recently, federal courts have reviewed arbitration awards under agreements calling for an expanded scope of review. Obstacles to effective review have not been evident in any of these settings.[21] Problems with the record are not reflected in the cases, but in the event they arise, there is a ready solution in the familiar rule that

---

20. The arbitration clause states: "The arbitrators shall not have the power to commit errors of law or legal reasoning, and the award may be vacated or corrected on appeal to a court of competent jurisdiction for any such error."

21. It is noteworthy that the Court of Appeal below, despite its holding limiting the scope of review, had no difficulty examining the merits of the arbitrators' decision on the alternative assumption that the award was reviewable for legal error.

the decision under review is presumed correct on matters where the record is silent. (*Ketchum v. Moses* (2001) 24 Cal.4th 1122, 1140–1141 [104 Cal. Rptr. 2d 377, 17 P.3d 735].) * * *

The judicial system reaps little benefit from forcing parties to choose between the risk of an erroneous arbitration award and the burden of litigating their dispute entirely in court. Enforcing contract provisions for review of awards on the merits relieves pressure on congested trial court dockets. Courts are spared not only the burden of conducting a trial, but also the complications of discovery disputes and other pretrial proceedings. Incorporating traditional judicial review by express agreement preserves the utility of arbitration as a way to obtain expert factual determinations without delay, while allowing the parties to protect themselves from perhaps the weakest aspect of the arbitral process, its handling of disputed rules of law.

There are also significant benefits to the development of the common law when arbitration awards are made subject to merits review by the parties' agreement. "[I]f courts are reduced to the function of merely enforcing or denying arbitral awards, without an opportunity to discuss the reasoning for the arbitral decision, the advancement of the law is stalled, as arbitral decisions carry no precedential value. Thus, expansion of judicial review gives the courts of first instance the opportunity to establish a record, and to include the reasoning of expert arbitrators into the body of the law in the form of written decisions. This procedure better advances the state of the law and facilitates the necessary beneficial input from experts in the field." (Hulea, *Contracting to Expand the Scope of Review of Foreign Arbitral Awards: An American Perspective* (2003) 29 Brook. J. Int'l L. 313, at pp. 354–355.)

These advantages, obtained with the consent of the parties, are substantial. As explained in *Moncharsh*, the drafters of the CAA established the statutory grounds for judicial review with the expectation that arbitration awards are ordinarily final and subject to a restricted scope of review, but that parties may limit the arbitrators' authority by providing for review of the merits in the arbitration agreement. (*Moncharsh, supra*, 3 Cal.4th at p. 25.) The Court of Appeal erred by refusing to enforce the parties' clearly expressed agreement in this case. * * *

MORENO, JUSTICE., Concurring and Dissenting.

I agree with the majority to the extent it holds that parties may define the arbitrator's powers in such a way as to broaden somewhat the scope of judicial review beyond the usual narrow grounds for such review set forth in *Moncharsh v. Heily & Blase* (1992) 3 Cal.4th 1 [10 Cal. Rptr. 2d 183, 832 P.2d 899]. But I disagree that parties may oblige courts to undertake full-scale judicial review of legal error in arbitration awards. Rather, the relevant statutes and the pertinent legislative history reveal a legislative intent to circumscribe the scope of judicial review and defer to the judgment of the arbitrator. As elaborated below, the statutes permit an arbitration agreement to be structured in such a way as to compel a court to vacate an award when the arbitrator, in addressing legal questions, has acted arbitrarily and unreasonably, such as departing from clearly defined contractual terms or from clear legal principles found in the body of law that the parties have agreed should be used to settle the dispute.

On the other hand, when an arbitrator's answer to a legal question is not clearly erroneous, for example, when he or she reasonably answers a legal question in which there is no settled precedent, the statute does not authorize a court to vacate an arbitrator's award merely because it disagrees with the arbitrator's conclusions, no matter what the arbitration agreement provides. Because the arbitrators in this case acted reasonably in addressing a question of unsettled law, I would affirm the judgment of the Court of Appeal.

Notes And Questions regarding *Cable Connection*

(1) What are some of the practical problems associated with judicial review of an arbitration award for errors of law? Did the majority opinion in *Cable Connection* gloss over these practical problems? From a practical viewpoint, is the approach taken in the concurring opinion preferable?

(2) Do you think the California Supreme Court will also uphold an arbitration clause which authorizes judicial review of an arbitration award for errors of fact, perhaps, for example, under the "substantial evidence" or the "clearly erroneous" standard of review? What practical problems result from permitting such review for errors of fact?

(3) Does the following language in an arbitration agreement satisfy Cable's requirement of an express provision for expanded scope of judicial review for errors of law: the arbitrator "shall render an award in accordance with substantive California law"? *See Christensen v. Smith*, 171 Cal. App. 4th 931, 90 Cal. Rptr. 3d 57 (2009) (concluding that, unlike arbitration agreement in *Cable Connections*, arbitration agreement here did not express deprive arbitrator of power to commit legal error); *Gravillis v. Coldwell Banker Residential Brokerage Co.*, 182 Cal. App. 4th 503, 106 Cal. Rptr. 3d 70 (2010) (ruling an arbitration provision requiring the arbitrator to render an award "in accordance with" or to "apply" California substantive law does not, by itself, mandate review of the award on the merits).

(4) Does the *Cable Connection* Court's conclusion that sections 3 and 4 of the FAA do not apply in state court create forum shopping opportunities, at least in those cases where both federal and state courts have concurrent subject matter jurisdiction? How so? *See Mave Enter. v. Travelers Indem. Co.*, 219 Cal. App. 4th 1408, 1422–30, 163 Cal. Rptr. 3d 671 (2013) (concluding superior court did not abuse its discretion by denying a stay of plaintiff's motion to confirm an arbitration award where the defendant had filed a petition to vacate the award in the federal court based on diversity of citizenship).

[3] *Scope of Arbitration Is Determined by the Agreement*

As *Moncharsh* points out, the arbitration agreement determines the scope of the issues that the parties intend to submit for resolution by an arbitrator as opposed to a court. *See, e.g., J. Alexander Sec., Inc. v. Mendez*, 17 Cal. App. 4th 1083, 1091, 21

Cal. Rptr. 2d 826 (1993); *Luster v. Collins*, 15 Cal. App. 4th 1338, 1346, 19 Cal. Rptr. 2d 215 (1993); *Citibank v. Crowell, Weedon & Co.*, 4 Cal. App. 4th 844, 848, 5 Cal. Rptr. 2d 906 (1992) (noting that it is the court's province to interpret the parties' agreement in order to determine whether the arbitrators exceeded their powers by deciding a dispute which was not arbitrable). How should a court determine the scope of the arbitrators' powers where the arbitration agreement is silent on key aspects of the arbitrators' authority? Or is ambiguous as to the precise scope? Why? *See Ericksen, Arbuthnot, McCarthy, Kearney & Walsh, Inc. v. 100 Oak Street*, 35 Cal. 3d 312, 323, 197 Cal. Rptr. 581, 673 P.2d 251 (1983) (ruling the California rule, as well as the federal rule with respect to the Federal Arbitration Act, is that doubts concerning the scope of arbitrable issues are to be resolved in favor of arbitration).

Although doubts about the scope of the agreement should be resolved in favor of arbitration, the terms of the specific arbitration clause under consideration must reasonably cover the dispute to which arbitration is requested. *See, e.g., RN Solution, Inc. v. Catholic Healthcare West*, 165 Cal. App. 4th 1511, 81 Cal. Rptr. 3d 892 (2008) (concluding that while the language of arbitration clause might be broadly construed to cover every type of business dispute that could arise between the two companies, the parties did not intend it to cover tort claims arising from an alleged violent physical assault by an employee of one company against an employee of the other in the context of an intimate domestic relationship between them); *Bono v. David*, 147 Cal. App. 4th 1055, 54 Cal. Rptr. 3d 837 (2007) (holding trial court properly denied motion to compel arbitration because plaintiff's defamation action was not covered by arbitration clause in the parties' real property agreement).

The question of whether arbitrators have jurisdiction to decide certain issues is to be judicially determined unless the arbitration agreement clearly and unmistakenly grants the arbitrators the power to determine their own jurisdiction, *Gilbert Street Developers, LLC v. La Quinta Homes, LLC*, 174 Cal. App. 4th 1185, 94 Cal. Rptr. 3d 918 (2009) (citing numerous cases); *Greenspan v. LADT, LLC*, 185 Cal. App. 4th 1413, 1436–47, 111 Cal. Rptr. 3d 468 (2010) (finding that, as provided by the rules of the arbitration services provider selected by the parties, the arbitrator, not the court, determined what issues are arbitrable); and the delegation clause is not invalid under state contract defenses such as fraud, duress, or unconscionability. *See, e.g., Malone v. Superior Court*, 226 Cal. App. 4th 1551, 173 Cal. Rptr. 241 (2014) (concluding clause delegating issues relating to the enforceability of the arbitration agreement to the arbitrator for resolution was clear, unmistakable, and not unconscionable); *Pinela v. Neiman Marcus Grp., Inc.*, 238 Cal. App. 4th 227, 190 Cal. Rptr. 3d 159 (2015) (ruling delegation clause was unconscionable and therefore unenforceable).

[4] *Forfeiture of Right to Arbitrate by Failure to Timely Demand Arbitration*

Private arbitration is a matter of agreement between the parties and is governed by contract law. When the parties agreed that a demand for arbitration must be made within a certain time, that demand is a condition precedent that must be performed before the contractual duty to submit the dispute to arbitration arises. *Platt Pac., Inc. v. Andelson*, 6 Cal. 4th 307, 24 Cal. Rptr. 2d 597, 862 P.2d 158 (1993) (ruling trial court properly denied plaintiff's petition to compel arbitration where plaintiff failed to file demand for arbitration with the American Arbitration Association within the time specified in the contract). In the absence of a legal excuse (*e.g.*, estoppel, waiver, etc.) or subsequent modification of the parties' agreement, the failure to submit the dispute to arbitration within the agreed time precludes judicial enforcement of the right to arbitrate. *Platt Pacific, supra*, 6 Cal. 4th at 321; *see also Citibank v. Crowell, Weedon & Co.*, 4 Cal. App. 4th 844, 5 Cal. Rptr. 2d 906 (1992) (holding that claim must be submitted to arbitration within six-year eligibility period specified in applicable municipal securities arbitration rules).

[5] *Waiver of Right to Compel Arbitration by Litigation Conduct*

A party to a contractual arbitration agreement may force a recalcitrant party to comply with the agreement by means of a petition for an order to compel arbitration pursuant to CCP § 1281.2, which is in essence a suit in equity to compel specific performance of the arbitration agreement. *See, e.g., Wagner Constr. Co. v. Pacific Mech. Corp.*, 41 Cal. 4th 19, 29, 58 Cal. Rtpr. 3d 434, 157 P.3d 1029 (2007); *Mansouri v. Superior Court*, 181 Cal. App. 4th 633, 642, 104 Cal. Rptr. 3d 824 (2010).

[a] **Necessity of Petition to Compel Arbitration and Request for Stay**

The right to compel arbitration is not self-executing. The existence of an agreement to arbitrate does not automatically usurp the judicial power vested in a trial court. *Brock v. Kaiser Found. Hosp.*, 10 Cal. App. 4th 1790, 1795, 13 Cal. Rptr. 2d 678 (1992). As a result, there is nothing to prevent one of the parties to a contractual arbitration agreement from resorting initially to an action at law in court. *Brock*, 10 Cal. App. 4th at 1795. The other party, if determined to pursue arbitration, must take appropriate action to compel arbitration. *Id.* at 1795–96. The party seeking to enforce the arbitration agreement must therefore file a CCP § 1281.2 petition in the action (or raise it as an affirmative defense), and request a stay, or else the right to contractual arbitration is waived. CCP § 1281.5; *Brock, supra*, 10 Cal. App. 4th at 1795–96.

A party's conduct while participating in litigation may also constitute of waiver of the right to compel arbitration. Although there is no single test for waiver, relevant factors include whether (1) the party has taken steps inconsistent with an intent to invoke arbitration, (2) the party has unreasonably delayed in seeking arbitration, and (3) the party has acted in bad faith or willful misconduct. *Christensen v. Dewar Dev.*, 33 Cal. 3d 778, 782, 191 Cal. Rptr. 8, 661 P.2d 1088 (1983); *see Saint Agnes Med. Ctr. v. Pacificare of Cal.*, 31 Cal. 4th 1187, 8 Cal. Rptr. 3d 517, 82 P.3d 727 (2003) (endorsing six factors, including whether participation in litigation results in prejudice to the opposing party, as relevant in determining whether party has waived its contractual right to arbitrate); *Doers v. Golden Gate Bridge Dist.*, 23 Cal. 3d 180, 185–88, 151 Cal. Rptr. 837, 588 P.2d 1261 (1979) (ruling a plaintiff's mere filing of a lawsuit does not constitute a waiver of its contractual arbitration rights); *Gloster v.*

Sonic Auto., Inc., 226 Cal. App. 4th 438, 171 Cal. Rptr. 3d 648 (2014) (finding no waiver where defendant answered complaint, engaged in other litigation conduct, and delayed one year in moving to compel arbitration because plaintiff did not demonstrate this delay was unreasonable and prejudicial): *Zamora v. Lehman*, 186 Cal. App. 4th 1, 111 Cal. Rptr. 3d 335 (2010) (holding defendants who conducted discovery in the trial court waived their right to arbitrate by delay in bringing their motion to compel arbitration and by engaging in discovery not available under the arbitration agreement).

As the above cases indicate, the issue of waiver by litigation conduct is ordinarily resolved by the trial court, not by an arbitrator. CCP § 1281.2; *Engalla v. Permanente Med. Grp., Inc.*, 15 Cal. 4th 951, 982, 64 Cal. Rptr. 3d 843, 938 P.2d 903 (1997). A court may properly find a party has not acted inconsistently with its right to arbitrate if that party delayed seeking to enforce an arbitration agreement during a time when that agreement would have been considered unenforceable under existing law. *Iskanian v. CLS. Transp. Los Angeles, LLC*, 59 Cal. 4th 348, 376, 173 Cal. Rptr. 3d 289, 327 P.3d 129 (2014); *see Bower v. Inter-Con Sys., Inc.*, 232 Cal. App. 4th 1035, 181 Cal. Rptr. 3d 729 (2014) (finding defendant's delay in filing a motion to compel arbitration was and not reasonable under *Iskanian* but instead was tactical, and concluding defendant waived its right to compel arbitration by engaging in litigation conduct in a class action). May a court deny a petition to compel arbitration on the ground that the statute of limitations has run on the claims the parties agreed to arbitrate? *See Wagner Constr. Co. v. Pacific Mech. Corp.*, 41 Cal. 4th 19, 58 Cal. Rptr. 3d 434, 157 P.3d 1029 (2007) (holding that where the parties have agreed to arbitrate any dispute arising out of their contract, the affirmative defense that the statute of limitations has run is for the arbitrator rather than the court to decide).

[b] Appealability of Order on Petition to Compel Arbitration

An order compelling arbitration is a nonappealable order which is reviewable only on appeal from the judgment confirming the arbitration award, or in certain exceptional situations by writ of mandate. *See, e.g., Muao v. Grosvenor Prop., Ltd.*, 99 Cal. App. 4th 1085, 122 Cal. Rptr. 2d 131 (2002); *Handy v. First Interstate Bank*, 13 Cal. App. 4th 917, 922, 16 Cal. Rptr. 2d 770 (1993). However, an order denying a petition to compel arbitration is appealable. CCP § 1294(a); *Henry v. Alcove Inv., Inc.*, 233 Cal. App. 3d 94, 284 Cal. Rptr. 255 (1991) (holding an order staying arbitration was the functional equivalent of an order refusing to compel arbitration, and was immediately appealable). Why this difference in treatment with respect to appealability?

[6] Validity of Arbitration Agreement

A written agreement to submit to arbitration is valid except "upon such grounds as exist for the revocation of any contract." CCP § 1281. Consequently, an arbitration agreement is unenforceable where determined to have been obtained through fraud or duress, or to be unconscionable or otherwise illegal as against public policy. *See* CCP § 1281.2(b); *Bayscene Resident Negotiators v. Bayscene Mobilehome Park*, 15 Cal.

App. 4th 119, 18 Cal. Rptr. 2d 626 (1993) (holding arbitration agreement obtained by threat of criminal prosecution constituted menace and is unenforceable as against public policy); *Armendariz v. Found. Health Psychcare Serv., Inc.*, 24 Cal. 4th 83, 99 Cal. Rptr. 2d 745, 6 P.3d 669 (2000) (finding agreement substantively and procedurally unconscionable and unenforceable where entire agreement tainted and cannot be cured by severance of offending provisions). As *Moncharsh* indicates, an arbitration agreement will not be enforced where the arbitration agreement is invalid on contract revocation grounds or where the entire contract which contains the arbitration agreement is invalid. *See Moncharsh v. Heily & Blase, supra*, 3 Cal. 4th at 29–31; *but see Ericksen, Arbuthnot, McCarthy, Kearney & Walsh, Inc. v. 100 Oak Street*, 35 Cal. 3d 312, 197 Cal. Rptr. 581, 673 P.2d 251 (1983) (deeming claims of fraud in the inducement of the contract subject to arbitration).

[a] Who Determines the Validity of the Arbitration Agreement

The courts frequently address the question of who determines the validity and enforceability of an arbitration agreement — the court or the arbitrator? Why is this an important question? As *Moncharsh* demonstrates, the California courts are developing some general rules. Where a party alleges that only the arbitration clause itself is invalid, the issue is reserved for judicial determination. *See, e.g., Bayscene Resident Negotiators, supra*, 15 Cal. App. 4th at 127–28 (citing cases); *Moncharsh, supra*, 3 Cal. 4th at 30; *Ericksen, supra*, 35 Cal. 3d at 323. Where a question of the validity of the entire contract which includes an arbitration provision is asserted, the rules are less straightforward.

In *Ericksen, supra*, 35 Cal. 3d at 323, the Supreme Court ruled that in the absence of any contrary intent in the agreement, "claims of fraud in the inducement of the contract (as distinguished from claims of fraud directed to the arbitration clause itself) will be deemed subject to arbitration." Subsequently, in *Rosenthal v. Great Western Financial Securities Corp.*, 14 Cal. 4th 394, 415–19, 58 Cal. Rptr. 2d 875, 926 P.2d 1061 (1996), the Supreme Court further explained that whereas claims of *fraud in the inducement* of the contract (*i.e.*, where the promisor knows what he is signing but his consent is induced by fraud) are arbitrable, allegations that an arbitration clause is invalid because of *fraud in the execution* of the entire contract (*i.e.*, where the promisor does not know what he is signing or does not intend to enter into a contract at all) are not arbitrable and are to be decided by the court.

Do these general rules mean that a party who questions the validity of an arbitration agreement may proceed with the arbitration and preserve the issue for later consideration by the court, upon a motion to vacate the award, after being unsuccessful in the arbitration? Or will that party waive her right to later judicially attack the validity of the arbitration agreement by voluntarily participating in the arbitration proceeding? *See Bayscene Resident Negotiators, supra*, 15 Cal. App. 4th at 129; *Kemper v. Schardt*, 143 Cal. App. 3d 557, 192 Cal. Rptr. 46 (1983). What if that party participates in the arbitration proceeding but raises the validity objection before the arbitrator? *See Moncharsh*, 3 Cal. 4th at 30–31; *Loving & Evans v. Blick*, 33 Cal. 2d 603, 607–609,

204 P.2d 23 (1949); *All Points Trader, Inc. v. Barrington Assoc.*, 211 Cal. App. 3d 723, 737, 259 Cal. Rptr. 780 (1989). In order to avoid any possible waiver of the validity objection, should that party refuse to participate in the arbitration process and force the other party to file a petition to compel arbitration under CCP § 1281.2? Why? *See Bayscene Resident Negotiators, supra,* 15 Cal. App. 4th at 129; *Kemper v. Schardt, supra,* 143 Cal. App. 3d at 560–61.

Several recent decisions have addressed the question of who determines whether an arbitration agreement is unconscionable and therefore unenforceable—the court or the arbitrator. *E.g., Baker v. Osborne Dev. Corp.*, 159 Cal. App. 4th 884, 71 Cal. Rptr. 3d 854 (2008) (ruling trial court properly determined the issue of unconscionability because the arbitration agreement did not clearly reserve to the arbitrator the issue of whether the arbitration agreement was enforceable); *Ontiveros v. DHL Express (USA), Inc.*, 164 Cal. App. 4th 494, 79 Cal. Rptr. 3d 471 (2008) (discussing several recent cases). This question is particularly difficult when the arbitration agreement explicitly provides that the arbitrator shall have exclusive authority to resolve any dispute relating to the validity and enforceability of the arbitration agreement. Many recent decisions have held that where the provision in the arbitration agreement giving the arbitrator exclusive authority to decide enforceability issues is contained in a contract of adhesion, the provision is unenforceable and the trial court is the proper gatekeeper to determine unconscionability. *E.g., Ontiveros, supra* 164 Cal. App. 4th at 503–508; *Bruni v. Didion,* 160 Cal. App. 4th 1272, 73 Cal. Rptr. 3d 395 (2008); *Murphy v. Check 'N Go of Cal., Inc.,* 156 Cal. App. 4th 138, 67 Cal. Rptr. 3d 120 (2007).

The U.S. Supreme Court addressed this question in *Rent-A-Center, West, Inc. v. Jackson,* 561 U.S. 63,130 S. Ct. 2772, 177 L. Ed. 2d 403 (2010), with respect to arbitration agreements governed by the Federal Arbitration Act (FAA), 9 U.S.C. § 1 *et seq.* The U.S. Supreme Court held that where an agreement to arbitrate includes an explicit provision that the arbitrator will determine the enforceability of the arbitration agreement, if a party challenges specifically the enforceability of that particular provision, the district court considers the challenge; but if a party challenges the enforceability of the arbitration agreement as a whole, the challenge is for the arbitrator to decide. To what extent does this approach under the FAA differ from the approach taken by the California courts with respect to arbitration agreements governed by the California arbitration statutes?

[b] Unconscionable Arbitration Agreements

An arbitration agreement will be unenforceable if determined to be procedurally (*e.g.,* in an adhesion contract) and substantively (*e.g.,* "overly harsh" or "one-sided") unconscionable. *Armendariz v. Foundation Health Psychcare Serv., Inc.,* 24 Cal. 4th 83, 99 Cal. Rptr. 2d 745, 6 P.3d 669 (2000); *see also Flores v. Transamerica Homefirst, Inc.,* 93 Cal. App. 4th 846, 113 Cal. Rptr. 2d 376 (2001) (concluding arbitration clauses contained in loan agreement and deed of trust constituted contract of adhesion imposed upon plaintiffs on a "take it or leave it" basis and thereby procedurally unconscionable, and did not display any bilaterality and were so one-sided as to be sub-stantively unconscionable); *Lhotka v. Geographic Expeditions, Inc.*, 181 Cal. App. 4th 816, 104 Cal. Rptr. 3d 844 (2010) (holding arbitration agreement in adhesion contract that contained nonreciprocal limitation on damages and indemnification for costs, and required arbitration in a location inconvenient to plaintiff customers, was un-conscionable); *Bolter v. Superior Court*, 87 Cal. App. 4th 900, 104 Cal. Rptr. 2d 888 (2001) (finding provision in adhesive franchise agreement drafted by large, wealthy, international franchiser mandating arbitration of claims by "mom and pop" California franchisee in Utah was unconscionable and therefore unenforceable, but was severable from remainder of agreement to arbitrate).

Saika v. Gold, 49 Cal. App. 4th 1074, 56 Cal. Rptr. 2d 922 (1996), also demonstrates that provisions of an arbitration agreement unduly advantageous to one party at the expense of another will not be judicially enforced. The court in *Saika* refused to enforce an arbitration agreement between a doctor and a patient which provided that if the arbitrator's award is greater than $25,000, either party could request a trial de novo by filing an action in superior court. Upon the filing of such an action, the ar-bitration award would be null and void; but if the absence of such an action, the award was binding and final. *Saika, supra*, 49 Cal. App. 4th at 1077. Why is this ar-bitration clause invalid? *See id*. at 1079–82.

In *Little v. Auto Stiegler, Inc.*, 29 Cal. 4th 1064, 130 Cal. Rptr. 2d 892, 63 P.3d 979 (2003), the Supreme Court considered the validity of a provision in a mandatory employment arbitration agreement that permitted either party to "appeal" an arbi-tration award of more than $50,000 to a second arbitrator for review. Relying on the reasoning in *Saika v. Gold, supra*, the *Little* court concluded that this arbitral appeal provision was unconscionable, but could be severed from the rest of the arbitration agreement. *Little*, 29 Cal. 4th at 1071–76. Why is this $50,000 threshold for arbitral appeal, applicable to both the employer and the employee, so inordinately beneficial to the employer as to be unconscionable? *See Little*, 29 Cal. 4th at 1073.

In *Sonic-Calabasas A, Inc. v. Moreno*, 57 Cal. 4th 1109 163 Cal. Rptr. 3d 269, 311 P.3d 184 (2013), the California Supreme Court discussed the limitations that the Fed-eral Arbitration Act (FAA) imposes on a state's capacity to enforce its rules of un-conscionability on parties to arbitration agreements that are subject to the FAA (*i.e.*, arbitration agreements in contracts involving interstate commerce). After a thorough analysis of the U.S. Supreme Court's clarifications of these limitations in *AT&T Mo-bility LLC v. Concepcion*, 563 U.S. 333, 131 S. Ct. 1740, 179 L. Ed. 2d 742 (2011) (*Concepcion*), the *Sonic-Calabasas* Court concluded that unconscionability remains a valid defense to a petition to compel arbitration. The Court further explained:

> After *Concepcion*, the exercise of that judicial function as applied to arbi-tration agreements remains intact, as the FAA expressly provides. What is new is that *Concepcion* clarifies the limits the FAA places on state uncon-scionability rules as they pertain to arbitration agreements. It is well estab-lished that such rules must not facially discriminate against arbitration and must be enforced evenhandedly. *Concepcion* goes further to make clear that

such rules, even when facially nondiscriminatory, must not disfavor arbitration *as applied* by imposing procedural requirements that "interfere[] with fundamental attributes of arbitration," especially its "lower costs, greater efficiency and speed, and the ability to choose expert adjudicators to resolve specialized disputes.' [Citation.]" (*Concepcion, supra,* 563 U.S. at pp. ___, ___ [131 S. Ct. at pp. 1748, 1751].) As the high court explained, if facial neutrality or evenhanded enforcement were the only principles limiting the scope of permissible state law defenses to arbitration, then a state court could — on grounds of unconscionability or public policy — compel the adoption of an arbitration procedure that would be arbitration in name only. It could impose judicially monitored discovery, evidentiary rules, jury trials, or other procedures that mimic court proceedings, and thereby undermine the FAA's purpose of encouraging arbitration as an efficient alternative to litigation. (131 S. Ct. at p. 1747.)

Importantly, state-law rules that do not "interfere[] with fundamental attributes of arbitration" (*Concepcion, supra,* 131 S. Ct. at p. 1748) do not implicate *Concepcion*'s limits on state unconscionability rules. As our cases have held, such rules may address issues that arise uniquely in the context of arbitration. In *Graham v. Scissor-Tail, Inc.* (1981) 28 Cal.3d 807, 826–827 [171 Cal. Rptr. 604, 623 P.2d 165] (*Scissor-Tail*), for example, we held unconscionable a provision in an arbitration agreement that effectively gave the party imposing an adhesive contract the right to choose a biased arbitrator. In addition, we held in *Armendariz* that because arbitrators, unlike judges, are paid by the parties, an equal division of costs between employer and employee has the potential in practice of being unreasonably one-sided or burdening an employee's exercise of statutory rights. (*Armendariz, supra,* 24 Cal.4th at pp. 107–113.) As these examples suggest, a facially neutral state-law rule is not preempted simply because its evenhanded application "would have a disproportionate impact on arbitration agreements." (*Concepcion,* 131 S. Ct. at p. 1747.) Under *Concepcion,* a state-law rule is preempted when its impact is such that it interferes with fundamental attributes of arbitration. (131 S. Ct. at p. 1748.)

Moreover, there are other ways an arbitration agreement may be unconscionable that have nothing to do with fundamental attributes of arbitration. In *Little* [*v. Auto Stiegler, Inc.* (2003)] 29 Cal.4th [1064,] 1071 [130 Cal. Rptr. 2d 892, 63 P.3d 979]), for example, we found unconscionable a $50,000 threshold for an arbitration appeal that decidedly favored defendants in employment contract disputes. (*Little, supra,* 29 Cal.4th at pp. 1071–1074.) In *Harper v. Ultimo* (2003) 113 Cal.App.4th 1402, 1407 [7 Cal. Rptr. 3d 418], the court found unconscionable an arbitration agreement with a damages limitation clause under which "the customer does not even have the theoretical *possibility* he or she can be made whole." And in *Ajamian v. CantorCO2e, L.P.* (2012) 203 Cal.App.4th 771, 799–800 [137 Cal. Rptr. 3d 773] (*Ajamian*), the court found unconscionable an arbitration agreement that, among other things, "impos[ed] upon [the employee] the obligation to pay [the employer's] attorney fees if [the employer] prevails in the proceeding, without granting her the right to recoup her own attorney fees if she prevails."

Consider also the form of unconscionability identified in *Gutierrez v. Autowest, Inc.* (2003) 114 Cal.App.4th 77 [7 Cal. Rptr. 3d 267] (*Gutierrez*). There, the plaintiff entered into an automobile lease agreement with the defendant automobile dealer. He subsequently sued the dealer over alleged fraud in the transaction. The adhesive agreement contained an inconspicuous arbitration clause. (*Id.* at pp. 83–84.) The Court of Appeal found that, based on the American Arbitration Association rules in effect at the time the defendant moved to compel arbitration, the plaintiff would have had to pay $ 8,000 in administrative fees to initiate the arbitration. (*Id.* at pp. 90–91.) It was undisputed that such fees exceeded the plaintiff's ability to pay. (*Id.* at p. 91.) In holding this aspect of the arbitration agreement unconscionable, *Gutierrez* said: "We conclude that where a consumer enters into an adhesive contract that mandates arbitration, it is unconscionable to condition that process on the consumer posting fees he or she cannot pay. It is self-evident that such a provision is unduly harsh and one-sided, defeats the expectations of the nondrafting party, and shocks the conscience. While arbitration may be within the reasonable expectations of consumers, a process that builds prohibitively expensive fees into the arbitration process is not. (See *Patterson v. ITT Consumer Financial Corp.* [(1993) 14 Cal.App.4th 1659, 1665 [18 Cal. Rptr. 2d 563]].) To state it simply: it is substantively unconscionable to require a consumer to give up the right to utilize the judicial system, while imposing arbitral forum fees that are prohibitively high. Whatever preference for arbitration might exist, it is not served by an adhesive agreement that effectively blocks every forum for the redress of disputes, including arbitration itself." (*Id.* at pp. 89–90, fns. omitted.)

Sonic-Calabasas, supra, 57 Cal. 4th at 1143–45. Next, the *Sonic-Calabasas* Court applied *Concepcion*'s unconscionability standard and held that the FAA preempts a state-law rule categorically prohibiting waiver of a "Berman hearing"—an administrative dispute resolution process established by the Legislature to assist employees in recovering wages owed—in a predispute arbitration agreement imposed on an employee as a condition of employment. Because compelling the parties to undergo a Berman hearing would impose significant delays in the commencement of arbitration, the Court concluded that its ruling in *Sonic-Calabasas A, Inc. v. Moreno,* 51 Cal. 4th 659, 121 Cal. Rptr. 3d 58, 247 P.3d 130 (2011), where the Court had previously determined a Berman hearing waiver in an arbitration agreement was unconscionable, is inconsistent with the FAA. *Sonic-Calabasas, supra,* 57 Cal. 4th at 1146–52.

More recently, the California Supreme Court in *Sanchez v. Valencia Holding Co., LLC,* 61 Cal. 4th 899, 190 Cal. Rptr. 3d 812, 353 P.3d 741 (2015), considered the unconscionability of an arbitration agreement in an automobile sales contract that provided, among other things, that arbitral awards of $0 or over $100,000 as well as grants but not denials of injunctive relief may be appealed to a second panel of arbitrators. The Court applied its *Sonic-Calabasas* analysis and ruled that the challenged provision did not implicate *Concepcion*'s limits on state unconscionability rules. After noting that the adhesive nature of the sales contract was sufficient to establish some degree of procedural unconscionability, the *Sanchez* Court concluded the provision was not substantively unconscionability because it was not, on its face, unreasonably one-sided. The Court distinguished *Little, supra,* by observing that the "appeal threshold provision does not, on its face, obviously favor the drafting party," explaining:

> Assuming, as the parties do, the likely scenario of the buyer as the plaintiff and the seller as the defendant, the unavailability of an appeal from an award that is greater than $0 but not greater than $100,000 means that the buyer may not appeal from a non-$0 award that he or she believes to be too small, nor may the seller appeal from a quite substantial award (up to $100,000) that it believes to be too big. It may be reasonable to assume that the ability to appeal a $0 award will favor the buyer, while the ability to appeal a $100,000 or greater award will favor the seller. But nothing in the record indicates that the latter provision is substantially more likely to be invoked than the former. We cannot say that the risks imposed on the parties are one-sided, much less unreasonably so.

Sanchez, supra, 61 Cal. 4th at 916–17; *see Baltazar v. Forever 21, Inc.,* 62 Cal. 4th 1237, 200 Cal. Rptr. 3d 7, 367 P.3d 6 (2016) (concluding arbitration agreement in employment contract was not unfairly one-sided and substantively unconscionable insofar as it allowed the parties to seek preliminary injunctive relief).

As the above decisions indicate, after *Concepcion* the unconscionability determination requires consideration of the FAA as well as California law. This determination becomes even more complicated when the parties' agreement contains a choice-of-law clause that designates the law of another state as applicable to the arbitration. *See, e.g., Brinkley v. Monterey Fin. Serv.,* 242 Cal. App. 4th 314, 196 Cal. Rptr. 3d 1 (2015) (concluding fee and cost shifting provision in arbitration agreement was unconscionable under Washington law); *Pinela v. Neiman Marcus Grp., Inc.,* 238 Cal. App. 4th 227, 190 Cal. Rptr. 3d 159 (2015) (ruling the parties' contractual choice of Texas law unenforceable because would preclude vindication of important California statutory right, and holding delegation clause and arbitration agreement as a whole unconscionable under California law).

[c] Class Arbitration Waivers

Class-wide arbitration is well accepted under California law. The California Supreme Court has held that, under some circumstances, class action waivers in an arbitration agreement are unconscionable and not enforceable. *Discover Bank v. Superior Court,* 36 Cal. 4th 148, 30 Cal. Rptr. 3d 76, 113 P.3d 1100 (2005); *Gentry v. Superior Court,* 42 Cal. 4th 443, 64 Cal. Rptr. 3d 773, 165 P.3d 556 (2007).

In *Discover Bank, supra*, 36 Cal. 4th at 162–63, the California Supreme Court concluded that class action waivers in consumer arbitration agreements are unconscionable if the agreement is in an adhesion contract and it is alleged the party with the superior bargaining power has carried out a scheme to deliberately defraud large numbers of consumers out of individually small sums of money. Subsequently, however, the U. S. Supreme Court in *AT&T Mobility v. Concepcion*, 563 U.S. 333, 131 S. Ct. 1740, 179 L. Ed. 2d 742 (2011), held that the *Discover Bank* rule is preempted by the Federal Arbitration Act (FAA). "Requiring the availability of class-wide arbitration interferes with the fundamental attributes of arbitration," the *Concepcion* court reasoned, "and thus creates a scheme inconsistent with the FAA." *Concepcion*, 131 S. Ct. at 1748. Therefore, the Court concluded that the FAA prohibits States from conditioning the enforceability of arbitration agreements on the availability of class-wide arbitration procedures. *Id.* at 1753. In another recent decision, the U. S. Supreme Court held that a California court must enforce an arbitration agreement which contains a class action waiver because the FAA preempts any attempt to avoid the holding in *Concepcion* by use of a choice of law clause requiring the application of California law. *DIRECTV, Inc. v. Imburgia*, ___ U.S. ___, 136 S. Ct. 463, 193 L. Ed. 2d 365 (2015); *see also Stolt-Nielsen S.A. v. AnimalFeeds Int'l Corp.*, 599 U.S. 662, 130 S. Ct. 1758, 176 L. Ed. 2d 605 (2010) (imposing class arbitration on parties who had not contractually agreed to do so is inconsistent with the FAA).

In *Gentry v. Superior Court, supra*, the California Supreme Court invalidated a class arbitration waiver in an employment arbitration agreement because such a provision would constitute a de facto waiver of statutory rights and impermissibly interfere with employees' ability to vindicate unwaivable rights to enforce overtime laws. Subsequently, however, in *Iskanian v. CLS Transportation Los Angeles, LLC*, 59 Cal. 4th 348, 173 Cal. Rptr. 3d 289, 327 P.3d 129 (2014), the Supreme Court repudiated its earlier holding in *Gentry*. The *Iskanian* Court summarized its reasoning as follows (*Iskanian*, 59 Cal. 4th at 359–360):

> In this case, we again address whether the Federal Arbitration Act (FAA; 9 U.S.C. § 1 et seq.) preempts a state law rule that restricts enforcement of terms in arbitration agreements. Here, an employee seeks to bring a class action lawsuit on behalf of himself and similarly situated employees for his employer's alleged failure to compensate its employees for, among other things, overtime and meal and rest periods. The employee had entered into an arbitration agreement that waived the right to class proceedings. The question is whether a state's refusal to enforce such a waiver on grounds of public policy or unconscionability is preempted by the FAA. We conclude that it is and that our holding to the contrary in *Gentry v. Superior Court* (2007) 42 Cal.4th 443 [64 Cal. Rptr. 3d 773, 165 P.3d 556] (*Gentry*) has been abrogated by recent United States Supreme Court precedent.

However, the *Iskanian* Court also concluded that another application of the arbitration agreement violated public policy and did not preclude litigation of the employee's representative action under the Labor Code Private Attorneys General Act of 2004 (PAGA), California Labor Code § 2698 *et seq.* (*Id.* at 360):

> The employee also sought to bring a representative action under the Labor Code Private Attorneys General Act of 2004 (PAGA) (Lab. Code, § 2698 et seq.). This statute authorizes an employee to bring an action for civil penalties on behalf of the state against his or her employer for Labor Code violations committed against the employee and fellow employees, with most of the proceeds of that litigation going to the state. As explained below, we conclude that an arbitration agreement requiring an employee as a condition of employment to give up the right to bring representative PAGA actions in any forum is contrary to public policy. In addition, we conclude that the FAA's goal of promoting arbitration as a means of private dispute resolution does not preclude our Legislature from deputizing employees to prosecute Labor Code violations on the state's behalf. Therefore, the FAA does not preempt a state law that prohibits waiver of PAGA representative actions in an employment contract.

More recently in *Sanchez v. Valencia Holding Co., LLC*, 61 Cal. 4th 899, 190 Cal. Rptr. 3d 812, 353 P.3d 741 (2015), the California Supreme Court ruled that, pursuant to the U.S. Supreme Court's holding in *AT& T Mobility LLC v. Concepcion*, 563 U.S. 333, 131 S. Ct. 1740, 179 L. Ed. 2d 742 (2011), the FAA preempts California's unconscionability rule prohibiting class waivers in consumer arbitration agreements. Accordingly, the *Sanchez* Court concluded the Consumer Legal Remedies Act's antiwaiver provision, California Civil Code §§ 1751, 1780–1781, is preempted insofar as it bars class waivers in arbitration agreements covered by the FAA. *Sanchez, supra,* 61 Cal. 4th at 923–24. As a result of these rulings, California's unconscionability rule prohibiting class waivers applies only in those few instances where the FAA is inapplicable. *See Garrido v. Air Liquide Indus. U.S. LP*, 241 Cal. App. 4th 833, 194 Cal. Rptr. 3d 297 (2015) (concluding FAA, which exempts employment contracts for certain transportation workers, is inapplicable and holding class action arbitration waiver unenforceable under California law).

[7] *Disqualification of Arbitrator*

[a] Appointment of Arbitrator

The method of appointing an arbitrator is typically specified by the parties in the arbitration agreement or by subsequent agreement. *See* CCP § 1281.6. In the absence of an agreed upon method, upon petition of a party the court must appoint a neutral arbitrator pursuant to CCP § 1281.6.

[b] Disclosures and Disqualification

The Legislature amended CCP § 1281.9 in 1997 and 2002 to add new statutory disclosure requirements for neutral arbitrators. A proposed arbitrator must not only disclose the existence of any ground specified in CCP § 170.1 for the disqualification of a judge, but also various other matters that "could cause a person aware of the facts to reasonably entertain a doubt that the proposed neutral arbitrator would be able to be impartial." CCP § 1281.9(a). In addition, pursuant to CCP § 1281.85 and § 1281.9(a)(2), the Judicial Council has adopted ethics standards which contain additional, comprehensive disclosure requirements for all neutral arbitrators appointed after July 1, 2002. *Ethics Standards for Neutral Arbitrators in Contractual Arbitration*, Cal. Rules of Ct., Appendix, standards 7 & 8 (disclosures), standard 10 (disqualification).

In *Jevne v. Superior Court*, 35 Cal. 4th 935, 28 Cal. Rptr. 3d 685, 111 P.3d 954 (2005), the Supreme Court held that the federal Securities Exchange Act, 15 U.S.C. § 78a *et seq.*, preempts CCP § 1281.85(a) and California's *Ethics Standards for Neutral Arbitrators in Contractual Arbitration* with respect to securities arbitration administered by the National Association of Security Dealers Dispute Resolution. However, as illustrated by several post-*Jevne* decisions, these California's ethical standards still apply to other types of arbitration and are not preempted by the FAA. *E.g., Advantage Med. Serv. LLC v. Hoffman*, 160 Cal. App. 4th 806, 72 Cal. Rptr. 3d 935 (2008) (ruling trial court properly vacated interim arbitration award based on arbitrator's failure to make disclosures required under CCP § 1281.9 and to comply with the ethical standards promulgated under § 1281.85, but arbitrator was not subject to disqualification because he had already heard a contested matter); *Ovitz v. Schulman*, 133 Cal. App. 4th 830, 35 Cal. Rptr. 3d 117 (2005) (holding arbitration award must be vacated where arbitrator failed in his initial disclosure statement to disclose timely a ground for disqualification under ethical Standard 12(b), and then knowingly accepted appointment in another case under circumstances that violated ethical Standard 12(c)).

[c] Effect of Arbitrator Bias on Award

An arbitration award must be vacated if the court determines that an arbitrator making the award either failed to timely disclose a ground for disqualification of which the arbitrator was then aware, or was subject to disqualification upon grounds specified in CCP § 1281.91 or in the ethical standards but failed upon timely demand to disqualify himself or herself. CCP § 1286.2(a)(6); *see, e.g., Mt. Holyoke Homes, L.P. v. Jeffer Mangels Butler & Mitchell, LLP*, 219 Cal. App. 4th 1299, 162 Cal. Rptr. 597 (2013) (vacating arbitration award in a legal malpractice action because arbitrator failed to timely disclose that his resume listed one of defendant firm's partners as a reference). An award must also be vacated if the court determines that the "award was procured by corruption, fraud or other undue means" or there was "corruption in any of the arbitrators." CCP § 1286.2(a)(1) & (2). Under these provisions, a court will vacate an award where a neutral arbitrator has failed to disclose interests or prior dealings that might create the "impression of possible bias." *See, e.g., Haworth v. Superior Court*, 50 Cal. 4th 372, 112 Cal. Rtpr. 3d 853, 235 P.3d 152 (2010) (concluding the appearance of partiality standard is no broader in the arbitration context than it is with regard to judicial recusal under CCP § 170.1 and is intended only to ensure the impartiality of the neutral arbitrator; it does not mandate disclosure of all matters that a party may wish to consider in deciding whether to oppose or accept the selection of an arbitrator); *Gray v. Chiu*, 212 Cal. App. 4th 1355, 151 Cal. Rptr. 3d 791 (2013) (vacating medical malpractice award where neutral arbitrator failed to disclose counsel for defendant doctor's affiliation with the firm providing the arbitrator); *Gebers v. State Farm Gen. Ins. Co.*, 38 Cal. App. 4th 1648, 1653–54, 45 Cal. Rptr. 2d 725 (1995) (vacating insurance arbitration award where independent arbitrator failed to disclose that he was currently retained by the insurer as an expert witness in two pending court actions).

[8] *Other Contractual Arbitration Statutes*

[a] Special California Arbitration Statutes

The Legislature in 1988 enacted comprehensive statutes which authorize and govern arbitration of international commercial disputes. CCP §§ 1297.11–1297.432. The Legislature has also enacted additional statutes which specifically authorize agreements to arbitrate disputes relating to construction contracts with public agencies, CCP § 1296; and medical malpractice claims, CCP § 1295.

The medical malpractice arbitration statute contains some interesting provisions not applicable to arbitration agreements generally. Sections 1295(a)–(c) specify certain language and type-size that medical malpractice arbitration agreements must contain in order to expressly notify patients they are contractually waiving their right to trial. Section 1295(e) declares that any agreement which complies with these language requirements "is not a contract of adhesion, nor unconscionable nor otherwise improper," and thereby exempts such an arbitration agreement from attack as a contract of adhesion. *Coon v. Nicola*, 17 Cal. App. 4th 1225, 21 Cal. Rptr. 2d 846 (1993). Why is this statutory "exemption" particularly important with respect to agreements to arbitrate medical malpractice claims? Does the inclusion of such language also shield the arbitration agreement from attack on the validity of patient's consent to arbitration? *See Coon, supra*, 17 Cal. App. 4th at 1233–34; *Ramirez v. Superior Court*, 103 Cal. App. 3d 746, 756–57, 163 Cal. Rptr. 233 (1980). Should it?

[b] The Federal Arbitration Act

The Federal Arbitration Act (FAA), 9 U.S.C. § 1 et seq., applies to arbitration agreements in contracts involving interstate commerce. 9 U.S.C. § 2; *Southland Corp. v. Keating*, 465 U.S. 1, 10–11, 104 S. Ct. 852, 79 L. Ed. 2d 1 (1984). Section 2 or the FAA creates a body of federal substantive law which governs the question of arbitrability in both state and federal courts. *Moses H. Cone Hosp. v. Mercury Constr. Corp.*, 460 U.S. 1, 24, 103 S. Ct. 927, 74 L. Ed. 2d 765 (1983). The FAA sets forth a liberal federal policy favoring arbitration agreements, and preempts any state law which interferes with the enforcement of arbitration agreements. *See, e.g., AT&T Mobility v. Concepcion*, 563 U.S. 333,131 S. Ct. 1740, 179 L. Ed. 2d 742 (2011) (holding section 2 of the FAA preempts California's rule classifying most class arbitration waivers in consumer contracts as unconscionable); *Perry v. Thomas*, 482 U.S. 483, 107 S. Ct. 2520, 96 L. Ed. 2d 426 (1987) (ruling FAA, which mandates enforcement of arbitration agreements, preempted § 229 of California Labor Code which provides that judicial actions for collection of wages may be maintained without regard to existence of arbitration agreements); *Basura v. U.S. Home Corp.*, 98 Cal. App. 4th 1205, 120 Cal. Rptr. 2d 328 (2002) (concluding CCP § 1298.7, which permits a residential real property purchaser to sue a developer for construction defects despite having signed a sales agreement containing an arbitration clause, is preempted by the FAA as to those sale agreements which involve interstate commerce). When the FAA applies, a court may invalidate an arbitration agreement based on generally applicable contract defenses, such as fraud or unconscionability, but cannot invalidate an arbitration agreement based on a state law applicable only to arbitration provisions. 9 U.S.C. § 2; *Doctor's Associates, Inc. v. Casarotto*, 517 U.S. 681, 116 S. Ct. 1652, 134 L. Ed. 2d 902 (1996); *Southland Corp. v. Keating, supra,* 465 U.S. at 13–16.

The FAA does not confer an absolute right to compel arbitration, but only the right to obtain an order directing that arbitration proceed in the manner provided for in the parties' agreement. 9 U.S.C. § 4. Consequently, the FAA does not preclude the parties to an interstate contract from agreeing to conduct their arbitration pursuant to the procedural rules of the California arbitration statutes. *Volt Information Sciences, Inc. v. Board of Tr. of Leland Stanford Junior Univ.*, 489 U.S. 468, 109 S. Ct. 1248, 103 L. Ed. 488 (1989); *Cronus Inv., Inc. v. Concierge Serv.*, 35 Cal. 4th 376, 25 Cal. Rptr. 3d 540, 107 P.3d 217 (2005).

The FAA states grounds for vacating an arbitration award nearly identical to those set forth in the California arbitration statutes. *Compare* 9 U.S.C. § 10 *with* CCP § 1286.2. Generally speaking, the cases interpreting the FAA and the California arbitration statutes are not in conflict with respect to such important issues as the scope of judicial review of an arbitration award and the determination of when arbitrators have exceeded their powers. *See, e.g., Advanced Micro Devices, Inc. v. Intel Corp., supra,* 9 Cal. 4th at 377–381; *Mount Diablo Med. Ctr. v. Health Net of California, Inc.*, 101 Cal. App. 4th 711, 124 Cal. Rptr. 2d 607 (2002); *Citibank v. Crowell, Weedon & Co.*, 4 Cal. App. 4th 844, 5 Cal. Rptr. 2d 906 (1992); *but see Cable Connection, Inc. v. DirecTV*, 44 Cal. 4th 1334, 82 Cal. Rptr. 3d 229, 190 P.3d 586 (2008), reproduced *supra.*

[B] Judicial Arbitration

[1] Introductory Note

The Judicial Arbitration Act, CCP § 1141.10 *et seq.*, was enacted by the Legislature in 1978 as a means of coping with the increasing cost and complexity of litigation in civil disputes. *Blanton v. Womancare, Inc.*, 38 Cal. 3d 396, 401, 212 Cal. Rptr. 151, 696 P.2d 645 (1985). The Act mandates submission to arbitration of certain categories of unlimited civil actions where the amount in controversy is determined not to exceed a specified amount ($50,000 as of 2016), CCP § 1141.11; authorizes each superior court by local rule to also require arbitration of certain limited civil cases, § 1141.11 (c) & (d); and permits submission to arbitration upon stipulation by the parties regardless of the amount in controversy, CCP § 1141.12; *see* Rule 3.811, Cal. Rules of Ct. (specifying cases subject to and exempt from judicial arbitration).

Unlike private contractual arbitration, judicial (or court-annexed) arbitration is compulsory but is not necessarily final or binding. *See Mercury Ins. Grp. v. Superior Court*, 19 Cal. 4th 332, 342–45, 79 Cal. Rptr. 2d 308, 965 P.2d 1178 (1998) (discussing the various differences between judicial and contractual arbitration). The Act provides that "[a]ny party may elect to have a de novo trial, by court or jury, both as to law and facts," and that an arbitration award is final only if a request for a de novo trial or a request for dismissal is not "filed within 60 days after the date the arbitrator files the award with the court." CCP § 1141.20. When a timely request for a trial is filed with the court, the case is restored to the civil active list and is tried as though no arbitration proceedings had occurred. Rule 3.826, Cal. Rules of Ct. "No reference may be made during the trial to the arbitration award, to the fact there had been arbitration proceedings, to the evidence adduced at the arbitration hearing, or to any other aspect of the arbitration proceedings, and none of the foregoing may be used as affirmative evidence, or by way of impeachment, or for any other purpose at the trial." Rule 3.826(c); *see, e.g., Weber v. Kessler*, 126 Cal. App. 3d 1033, 1036, 179 Cal. Rptr. 299 (1981) (ruling the trier of fact must reach its decision independently and without reference to the arbitration findings, and therefore must clearly show its independent decision by the record); CCP § 1141.25.

This lack of finality has led some courts to observe that "judicial arbitration is obviously an inapt term, for the system it describes is neither judicial nor arbitration ... 'extrajudicial mediation' would be closer to correct." *Nanfito v. Superior Court*, 2 Cal. App. 4th 315, 319, 2 Cal. Rptr. 2d 876 (1991). Is this an accurate observation?

[2] *Judicial Arbitration Award Becomes an Unappealable Judgment if No Trial Requested*

If there is no request for a de novo trial or for a dismissal and the arbitration award is not vacated under CCP § 1141.22, the award is entered in the judgment book in the amount of the award. CCP § 1141.23. Such award has the same force and effect as a judgment in any civil action, except that it is not subject to appeal. CCP § 1141.23. What disincentives are there to discourage a party, dissatisfied with the arbitration award, from exercising the right to request a de novo trial? A major disincentive is contained in CCP § 1141.21, which provides that "[i]f the judgment upon the trial de novo is not more favorable in either amount of damages awarded or the type of relief granted for the party electing the trial de novo than the arbitration award, the court shall order that party to pay [certain] costs and fees." Such costs and fees include the compensation paid to the arbitrator and the other party's costs including certain expert witness fees. CCP § 1141.21(a).

According to several surveys, although more than one-half of the cases resulting in a judicial arbitration award were returned to the civil active list after a request for de novo trial, less than 2% of the cases submitted to judicial arbitration were actually tried de novo. *See* John A. Toker, *California Arbitration and Mediation Practice Guide*

§ 7.2 (2003 & Suppl. 2014). Why are approximately 97% of the cases submitted to arbitration resolved without trial, even though in a much higher percentage of such cases a party requested a de novo trial? *See id.*

[3] Cases Subject to Judicial Arbitration

In each superior court with 18 or more judges, and in any smaller superior court where local rules so provide, most civil actions where the amount in controversy "in the opinion of the court" will not exceed $50,000 as to any plaintiff must be submitted to judicial arbitration. CCP § 1141.11; Rule 3.811, Cal. Rules of Ct.; see CCP § 1141.16 (stating standards and procedures for determination of the amount in controversy). Certain actions are exempt from arbitration, including class actions, unlawful detainer proceedings, Family Law Act proceedings, and actions seeking equitable relief. CCP §§ 1411.11–1411.15; Rule 3.811, Cal. Rules of Ct. The Judicial Arbitration Act, and the Judicial Council Rules promulgated thereunder, govern the assignment of cases, the selection of arbitrators, the conduct of the arbitration hearing, and the practical and procedural aspects of the judicial arbitration process. CCP § 1141.10 *et seq.*; Rules 3.810–3.830, Cal. Rules of Ct. Helpful practical resources include Toker, *California Arbitration Practice Guide, supra*; Weil, Brown, Edmon & Karnow, *Civil Procedure Before Trial, Ch. 13: Judicial Arbitration* (The Rutter Group 2015); and 2 CEB *California Civil Procedure Before Trial*, §§ 37.1–37.58 (4th ed. 2015).

[4] Sanctions for Failure to Participate in Judicial Arbitration

Unlike private contractual arbitration, judicial arbitration generates few difficult legal issues. One vexing problem, however, is how to deal with parties who simply choose not to participate in the arbitration process. This problem was addressed in *Lyons v. Wickhorst*, 42 Cal. 3d 911, 231 Cal. Rptr. 738, 727 P.2d 1019 (1986), where the Supreme Court recognized the inherent power of a trial court to dismiss actions but held its exercise improper as a sanction for refusal to participate in mandatory arbitration proceedings. In *Lyons*, the trial court ordered mandatory arbitration as the damages the plaintiff claimed were within the statutory limit. The plaintiff informed the arbitrator and counsel for the defendant he did not intend to present any evidence in support of his case. The defendant made no attempt to refute plaintiff's claims so no evidence was introduced at the arbitration hearing. An award was entered in favor of defendant, and plaintiff immediately requested a trial de novo. In granting defendant's motion for dismissal, the trial court stated "[plaintiff's] refusal to offer any evidence at the court-ordered arbitration hearings, 'border [ed] on contempt,' and was a 'continuing and willful rejection of the whole arbitration program.'" *Lyons*, 43 Cal. 3d at 914. The plaintiff then sought appellate review of this dismissal.

In reversing, the Supreme Court in *Lyons* noted that the monetary sanctions authorized by CCP § 128.5 for frivolous or delaying tactics were applicable to judicial arbitration proceedings, but that the Legislature chose not to provide for dismissal as a sanction for a party's refusal to participate in such arbitration. *Lyons*, 43 Cal. 3d at 918. Three justices left open the question of whether, in a particularly egregious case, a trial court would have the inherent power to dismiss the action. *Id.* at 911, 926 (concurring opinion of Justice Reynoso).

Subsequent decisions applying *Lyons* have upheld significant monetary sanctions for refusal to participate but have reversed trial court orders striking a motion for trial de novo. *See, e.g., Salowitz Org., Inc. v. Traditional Indus., Inc.*, 219 Cal. App. 3d 797, 268 Cal. Rptr. 493 (1990) (upholding trial court's award of $6,000 as sanction for failure to appear in arbitration proceedings, but reversing involuntary dismissal of de novo trial request); *Zatkin v. Cesare*, 199 Cal. App. 3d 756, 245 Cal. Rptr. 222 (1988) (holding involuntary dismissal of plaintiff's request for trial de novo is too severe a penalty for failure to fully participate in judicial arbitration even though plaintiff had elected arbitration). Should the Legislature make involuntary dismissal an available sanction in such cases? What are the policy arguments for and against such use of the dismissal sanction?

For a decision upholding the imposition of a monetary sanction of $2380 on plaintiffs' *attorney* for failure to participate meaningfully in judicial arbitration, see *Rietveid v. Rosebud Storage Partners*, 121 Cal. App. 4th 250, 16 Cal. Rptr. 3d 791 (2004), where based on their attorney's advice, plaintiffs did not attend the arbitration hearing and their attorney did not present any evidence in support of their claims.

[5] *Limited Authority to Challenge Arbitration Award When No Trial Requested*

If no party timely requests a trial de novo, the arbitration award becomes a judgment with the same force and effect as any civil judgment, except that the judgment is not subject to appeal and may not be attacked, modified, or set aside except as provided by CCP § 473 (relief from mistake, inadvertence, surprise, or excusable neglect; and from void judgments), § 1286.2(a) (grounds for vacating arbitration award where based on fraud, corruption, or prejudice), and Rule 3.828 of the California Rules of Court. CCP § 1141.23. Rule 3.828 authorizes no additional grounds, but requires that a motion to vacate must be made within six months from the entry of the judgment.

Consequently, in the absence of a request for a trial de novo, a court has very limited statutory authority to vacate an arbitration award and subsequent judgment; and has no jurisdiction to correct or modify an award based on grounds outside this statutory authority. *See, e.g., Schumacher v. Ayerve*, 9 Cal. App. 4th 1860, 1864–65, 12 Cal. Rptr. 2d 417 (1992) (holding trial court lacked jurisdiction to reduce judgment entered after arbitration award to reflect defendant's prior payment of plaintiff's medical expenses in personal injury action where impossible to determine whether lump sum award to plaintiff included compensation for medical expenses); *Pierson v. Honda*, 194 Cal. App. 3d 1411, 240 Cal. Rptr. 148 (1987) (concluding trial court lacked jurisdiction to modify or correct an arbitration award which may not have included a setoff claimed by the defendant, where defendant did not request a trial de novo).

[6] *Arbitrator Must Determine All Issues*

The arbitrator's award must determine "all issues properly raised by the pleadings, including a determination of any damages and an award of costs if appropriate." Rule 3.825(a), Cal. Rules of Ct. However, the arbitrator is not required to make findings of fact or conclusions of law, and typically merely states the total amount of damages awarded. Rule 3.825(a), Cal. Rules of Ct.

[7] *Effect of Request for Trial de Novo in Multi-Party Litigation*

Is a party to a judicial arbitration award automatically required to retry his or her case if a co-party requests a trial de novo? For example, if co-plaintiffs A and B obtain a judicial arbitration award against the defendant, and only Plaintiff A requests a de novo trial because B is satisfied with the award, are both A and B automatically required to try their cases in the court? In *Muega v. Menocal*, 50 Cal. App. 4th 868, 57 Cal. Rptr. 2d 697 (1996), the court followed the general rule that a request for a trial de novo filed by one party in a multi-party case will vacate the judicial arbitration award as to all parties and claims because, where the claims emanate from a single integrated set of facts, the award is treated as indivisible for purposes of subsequent trial. *See also Southern Pac. Transp. Co. v. Mendez Trucking, Inc.*, 66 Cal. App. 4th 691, 78 Cal. Rptr. 2d 236 (1998) (holding plaintiff's filing of request for a trial de novo returned the entire case, including cross-complaints for equitable indemnity between the defendants, to the civil trial calendar); *Trump v. Superior Court*, 118 Cal. App. 3d 411, 173 Cal. Rptr. 403 (1981) (concluding in an action where arbitrator awarded damages to plaintiff only as to one of several defendants, and awarded damages to another defendant on a compulsory cross-complaint, unsuccessful defendant's request for trial de novo required a trial as to all parties and issues raised by the pleadings).

But in *Demirgian v. Superior Court*, 187 Cal. App. 3d 372, 231 Cal. Rptr. 698 (1986), the court held that one plaintiff was not required to retry his claims in court where only his co-plaintiff requested a de novo trial because each plaintiff's claim against the defendant was independent and unrelated, both factually and legally, to the other's claim. Do you agree with this holding? *See Lewco Iron Metals, Inc. v. Superior Court*, 76 Cal. App. 4th 837, 90 Cal. Rptr. 2d 671 (1999) (questioning the validity of the *Demirgian* exception as inconsistent with the language of the statutes and court rules governing judicial arbitration).

Chapter 13

Trial Proceedings and Post-Trial Motions

§ 13.01 Introductory Note

[A] The Jury Trial Influence

The possibility of a jury trial—a one-time event before a factfinder comprised of ordinary people—influences our entire civil litigation process. Not only does the reality of the jury trial mandate certain trial, post-trial and appellate procedures, but the possibility largely dictates the rules of pleading, discovery, motions and other pretrial proceedings. So pervasive is this influence that even the procedures utilized in nonjury cases mirror those of jury trials.

The irony of this influence is that approximately 78% of all dispositions in unlimited civil cases occur without any trial (and 94% of limited civil cases), and more than 97% occur without a jury trial (and less than 1% of limited civil cases). *See* Judicial Council of California, *2015 Court Statistics Report*, Superior Courts (Fig. 21). But the possibility of trial exists in every case, and may be unavoidable in some. This chapter discusses some of the basic aspects of the civil trial process in California, with particular emphasis on jury trials.

[B] Pretrial Proceedings

[1] Delay Reduction and Case Management Rules

The Trial Court Delay Reduction Act, Government Code §§ 68600–68620, and the Civil Trial Court Management Rules adopted thereunder, Rules 3.700–3.750, California Rules of Court, have greatly increased the trial court's supervision of civil litigation prior to trial. These state-wide provisions, as implemented through local rules of court for each county, may require litigants to complete questionnaires and statements and attend a variety of pretrial conferences—all designed to expedite disposition of claims and issues. The manner of utilization, the terminology employed, and the timing and sequence of these pretrial events vary somewhat from county to county. The pretrial treatment may also vary depending on the classification (e.g., general civil case vs. complex case; long cause vs. short cause) and assignment (*e.g.*, assignment to master calendar judge vs. judge for all purposes) of each case pursuant to state and local rules on differential case management. *See* Rules 3.700–3.750, Cal. Rules of Ct.

[2] *Pretrial Conferences*

Each superior court must adopt local rules consistent with the state case management rules for general civil cases set forth in the California Rules of Court, and with the case disposition time goals set forth in sections 2.1 and 2.2 of the California Standards of Judicial Administration. Rules 3.711–3.735, Cal. Rules of Ct. The superior court must evaluate each case and, unless an exempt or a complex case, assign it to the local case management program. Rules 3.712, 3.715. This program must include one or more case management conferences, and may include a mandatory settlement conference. Rules 3.720–3.727, 3.1380, Cal. Rules of Ct.; *see generally* 3 CEB, *California Civil Procedure Before Trial, Case Management Conference and Disposition Time Goals* §§ 40.1–40.93 (4th ed. 2015).

In each general civil case, the court must set an initial case management conference to review the case within 180 days after the filing of the complaint. Rules 3.721, 3.722, Cal. Rules of Ct. At this conference, the court must review the case comprehensively and must decide whether to assign the case to an alternative dispute process or whether to set the case for trial. Rule 3.722(a). At this or any other case management conference, the court may also take appropriate action with respect to variety of other matters, such as whether all parties have been served, any additional parties may be added or pleadings amended, an early settlement conference should be scheduled, what discovery issues are anticipated and the date by which discovery will be completed, the estimated length of trial, and a date for trial. Rule 3.727.

Before the date set for the case management conference, the parties must meet and confer to consider the matters relevant to the conference; and each party must file and serve a Case Management Statement (Form CM-110). Rule 3.724, 3.725. After the conference, the court must enter a case management order setting a schedule for subsequent proceedings and otherwise providing for the management of the case. Rule 3.728. This order should include such provisions as may be appropriate, such as a date certain for trial, whether the trial will be a jury trial, the dismissal or severance of unserved defendants, the date for any additional case management conferences before trial, and the date for a mandatory settlement conference. Rule 3.728. The order issued after the case management conference controls the subsequent course of the action unless it is modified by a subsequent order. Rule 3.730.

Any party may request, or the court on its own motion may order, a judicially supervised settlement conference. Rule 3.1380(a). At least five days before the date set for the mandatory settlement conference, each party must submit to the court and serve on every other party a mandatory settlement conference statement containing a good faith settlement demand, an itemization of damages by each plaintiff, a good faith offer of settlement by each defendant, and a statement identifying and discussing in detail all facts and law pertinent to the issues of liability and damages involved in the case as to that party. Rule 3.1380(c). Trial counsel, parties, and persons with full authority to settle the case must personally attend the settlement conference, unless excused by the court for good cause. Rule 3.1380(b). A large percentage of cases settle as a result of this conference, in part because it is supervised by a judge who will not be the trial judge and therefore is a neutral person with experience on the jury value of asserted claims and defenses. *See* 3 CEB, *California Civil Procedure Before Trial* § 40.71 (4th ed. 2015).

Local rules may also require the parties to attend a final status conference a few days before trial to exchange witness and pre-marked exhibits lists and to present any motions in limine, jury instructions, special verdict forms, stipulations, and any unusual evidentiary or legal issues anticipated during trial. *E.g.*, San Diego Superior Court Rule 2.1.15; Orange County Superior Court Rule 317; Los Angeles Superior Court Rule 3.25(f)&(g). *See generally* CEB, *California Trial Practice: Civil Procedure During Trial, Court Conferences and Selected Pretrial Motions* §§ 6.2–6.5 (3d ed. 2016).

These various pretrial conferences and forms merit some additional words of caution. Failure to attend pretrial conferences or to timely file required statements and questionnaires, or to attend unprepared and not participate in good faith, or otherwise fail to comply with case management rules, may result in the imposition of substantial sanctions. Rule 2.30, Cal. Rules of Ct. (authorizing sanctions for failure to comply with applicable rules); CCP § 575.2 (authorizing sanctions for failure to comply with local rules); Gov. Code § 68608 (authorizing sanctions and encouraging judges to impose sanctions to achieve the purposes of the Trial Court Delay Reduction Act).

[3] *Trial Continuances Disfavored*

Government Code § 68607(g) requires judges to "[a]dopt and utilize a firm, consistent policy against continuances, to the maximum extent possible and reasonable, in all stages of the litigation." *See also* Gov. Code § 68616 (authorizing the parties, within 30 days of service of the responsive pleadings, to stipulate to a single pretrial continuance not to exceed 30 days); CCP § 595.2 (authorizing continuance not to exceed 30 days when all attorneys agree in writing). To ensure prompt disposition of civil cases, continuances of trials are particularly disfavored. Rule 3.1332(a) & (c), Cal. Rules of Ct. When a case is assigned a date for trial, parties and their counsel must regard the date as firm and certain. Rule 3.1332(a).

The trial court may grant a request for a trial continuance only on an "affirmative showing of good cause," such as unavailability of a party, essential witness, or trial counsel because of death, illness, or other excusable circumstances; the addition of a new party when there has not been a reasonable opportunity to conduct discovery; or a significant, unanticipated change in the status of the case. Rule 3.1332(c)(1)–(7); *see also* CCP § 595.4 (authorizing trial postponement on ground of absence of material evidence). In ruling on an application for a continuance, the trial court must consider all the facts and circumstances that are relevant to the determination, such as the proximity of the trial date, the length of the continuance requested, and the impact on other pending trials. Rule 3.1332(d)(1)–(11) (specifying several factors to be considered).

A motion for a trial continuance is addressed to the discretion of the trial court. Therefore, in rare cases, a judgment may be overturned on appeal if the trial court's abused its discretion in denying a party's request for a continuance. *See, e. g., Oliveros v. County of L. A.*, 120 Cal. App. 4th 1389, 16 Cal. Rptr. 3d 638 (2004) (reversing directed verdict of $12.5 million where defendant was unrepresented because trial counsel unexpectedly had to go to trial in another case); *Lerma v. County of Orange*, 120 Cal. App. 4th 709, 15 Cal. Rptr. 3d 609 (2004) (reversing summary judgment where trial counsel could not file opposition due to hospitalization).

[C] Disqualification of the Trial Judge

[1] Challenge for Cause: Disqualification for Actual or Perceived Bias

[a] Statutory Grounds for Disqualification

The Code of Civil Procedure specifies the grounds for disqualification of judges. *See* CCP §§ 170.1–170.9. Disqualification is required, for example, where the judge has personal knowledge of disputed evidentiary facts, served as a lawyer in the case, has a financial interest in the subject of the proceeding, or has some relationship with a party or a lawyer. CCP § 170.1(a). The statutes define these mandatory recusal grounds in more detail. *See* CCP §§ 170.1(a), 170.2, 170.5. A disqualified judge must not further participate in a proceeding, except for certain limited power to act as specified in CCP § 170.4 pending the assignment of another judge. CCP § 170.3(a)(1); *Geldermann, Inc. v. Bruner*, 229 Cal. App. 3d 662, 280 Cal. Rptr. 264 (1991) (holding judge who disqualified himself after trial and announcement of tentative decision is precluded from issuance of statement of decision).

A judge must also be disqualified where "a person aware of the facts might reasonably entertain a doubt that the judge would be able to be impartial." CCP § 170.1(a)(6)(A)(iii). This potentially broad ground for recusal was interpreted in *United Farm Workers of America v. Superior Court*, 170 Cal. App. 3d 97, 104–105, 216 Cal. Rptr. 4 (1985), to incorporate an objective standard:

> The standard for disqualification provided for in subdivision (a)(6)(C) of section 170.1 is fundamentally an objective one. It represents a legislative judgment that due to the sensitivity of the question and inherent difficulties of proof as well as the importance of public confidence in the judicial system, the issue is not limited to the existence of an actual bias. Rather, if a reasonable man would entertain doubts concerning the judge's impartiality, disqualification is mandated.... While this objective standard clearly indicates that the decision on disqualification not be based on the judge's personal view of his own impartiality, it also suggests that the litigants' necessarily partisan views not provide the applicable frame of reference. Rather, "a judge faced with a potential ground for disqualification ought to consider how his participation in a given case looks to the average person on the street." [Citation.]

Various factors may impact on how the "average person on the street" views a judge's participation in a case. One court has perceptively recognized that all other things being equal, the need for disqualification decreases by the extent to which the judge's rulings in the case are limited to purely legal matters. This is because a trial judge's factual findings are generally accorded considerable deference whereas legal rulings are subject to plenary appellate review.

Of course, the "average person on the street" does not determine whether a judge must be disqualified. That decision is initially made by the judge himself or herself. CCP § 170.3. A judge who determines herself to be disqualified may, after disclosing the basis for the disqualification, ask the parties whether they wish to waive the disqualification. § 170.3(b). If a judge who should disqualify himself fails to do so, any party may challenge that judge by a written verified statement of objection setting forth the facts constituting the grounds for disqualification. § 170.3(c)(1). The judge may then consent to disqualification, or may file an answer denying the allegations. § 170.3(c)(2)–(4). If a judge refuses to recuse himself, the question of disqualification must be heard and determined by another judge. § 170.3(c)(5). The determination of the question of the disqualification of a judge is not an appealable order, and may be reviewed only by a writ of mandate sought by one of the parties within 10 days of notice of the disqualification decision. § 170.3(d); *see Curle v. Superior Court*, 24 Cal. 4th 1057, 103 Cal. Rptr. 2d 751, 16 P.3d 166 (2001) (concluding no statute authorizes a disqualified trial judge to seek appellant review of a disqualification order).

A judge has a duty to decide any proceeding in which he or she is not disqualified. CCP § 170. Consequently, a determination that a trial judge is disqualified for apparent lack of impartiality may be overturned by an appellate court. *See, e.g., Flier v. Superior Court*, 23 Cal. App. 4th 165, 28 Cal. Rptr. 2d 383 (1994) (granting writ of mandate directing superior court to enter new and different order denying challenge for cause); *Leland Stanford Jr. Univ. v. Superior Court*, 173 Cal. App. 3d 403, 219 Cal. Rptr. 40 (1985) (directing trial court to vacate order disqualifying judge where no factual basis for finding of lack of impartiality).

[b] Constitutional Grounds for Disqualification

In *People v. Freeman*, 47 Ca. 4th 993, 103 Cal. Rptr. 3d 723, 222 P.2d 177 (2010), the California Supreme Court determined whether the appearance of bias by a judge requires recusal under the Due Process Clause of the U. S. Constitution, adopting and applying the due process standards announced by the U.S. Supreme Court in *Caperton v. A. T. Massey Coal Co., Inc.*, 556 U.S. 868, 129 S. Ct. 2252, 173 L. Ed. 2d 1208 (2009). The *Caperton* court concluded that an exceptional case presenting "extreme facts" would justify judicial disqualification based on the due process clause. *Caperton, supra*, 556 U.S. at 886–87. While a showing of actual bias is not required for judicial disqualification under the due process clause, neither is the mere appearance of bias sufficient. *Caperton*, 556 U.S. at 883–87; *Freeman, supra*, 47 Cal. 4th at 996, 1005. Instead, there must exist " 'the probability of actual bias on the part of the judge or decision-maker [that] is too high to be constitutionally tolerable.' " *Caperton*, 556 U.S. at 872 (quoting *Withrow v. Larkin*, 421 U.S. 35, 47 (1975)). Where only the appearance of bias is at issue, a litigant's recourse is to seek disqualification under state disqualification statutes. *Caperton*, 556 U.S. at 876–77, 888–90; *Freeman*, 47 Cal. 4th at 996, 1006.

In *Caperton*, the U.S. Supreme Court considered whether due process was violated by a West Virginia high court justice's refusal to recuse himself from a case involving a $50 million damage award against a coal company whose chairman had contributed $3 million to the justice's election campaign. The justice cast the deciding vote that overturned the damage award. The U. S. Supreme Court held that under the extreme facts of the case, "the probability of actual bias rises to an unconstitutional level." *Caperton, supra*, 556 U.S. at 886–87.

[2] Peremptory Challenge

Section 170.6(a)(1) directs that no judge shall try a civil action when it is established that the judge is prejudiced against any party or attorney. Section 170.6(a)(2) then provides that any party or attorney may establish this prejudice by an oral or written motion without notice supported by an affidavit which simply states that the judge before whom the action is pending "is prejudiced against a party or attorney, or the interest of the party or attorney, so that the party or attorney cannot, or believes that he or she cannot, have a fair and impartial trial or hearing before the judge...." If this motion is made according to the time limits and procedures contained in CCP § 170.6(a)(2), then, "without any further act or proof," some other judge must be assigned to try the proceeding. CCP § 170.6(a)(4). The recommended form and content of this peremptory challenge is set forth in CCP § 170.6(a)(6).

A party is permitted to make only one such challenge to a judge in any one action; however, in an action where there are multiple plaintiffs or defendants, only one challenge "for each side." CCP § 170.6(a)(4); *but see* CCP § 170.6(a)(2) (authorizing party who filed an appeal and obtained reversal of a trial court's decision to exercise peremptory challenge if same judge assigned to new trial, regardless of whether that party has previously exercised a peremptory challenge). The phrase "for each side" means a peremptory challenge by any party disqualifies the judge on behalf of all parties on that side. *Home Ins. Co. v. Superior Court*, 34 Cal. 4th 1025, 1032, 22 Cal. Rptr. 3d 885, 103 P.3d 283 (2005). When a party among several on the same side has disqualified a trial judgment pursuant to § 170.6 and is subsequently dismissed from the action, the remaining parties on the same side are not entitled to a new peremptory challenge. *Home Ins. Co., supra*, 34 Cal. 4th at 1033. Similarly, when a party on the same side has exercised its right to disqualify a judge, a late-appearing party has no right to challenge the then-current judge because that side has used its one challenge. *Id.*, at 1033. A party seeking a subsequent disqualification of the trial judge has the burden of demonstrating that its interests are substantially adverse to those of a co-party who previously exercised a peremptory challenge. *Id.* at 1034–37 (ruling defendant primary insurer and subsequently-joined co-defendant excess insurer are on the same side for purposes of § 170.6 because the excess insurer failed to factually demonstrated that its interests are substantially adverse to those of the primary insurer); *Orion Communications, Inc. v. Superior Court*, 226 Cal. App. 4th 152, 171 Cal.

Rptr. 3d 596 (2014) (vacating peremptory challenge by recently added successor company because its interests were not substantially adverse to defendant original company, which had already filed a peremptory challenge).

A peremptory challenge may generally be made any time prior to commencement of the trial or hearing, but must be made within the statutorily prescribed time limits or will be deemed waived. CCP § 170.6(a)(2); *Andrisani v. Saugus Colony Ltd.*, 8 Cal. App. 4th 517, 10 Cal. Rptr. 2d 444 (1992) (ruling right to assert peremptory challenge may be waived expressly or impliedly). These time limits may present problems in complex or coordinated actions. *See, e.g., Farmers Ins. Exch. v. Superior Court*, 10 Cal. App. 4th 1509, 13 Cal. Rptr. 2d 449 (1992) (finding peremptory challenge timely under court rule which modified the time limits of CCP § 170.6(a)(2) in coordinated actions); *Nissan Motor Corp. v. Superior Court*, 6 Cal. App. 4th 150, 7 Cal. Rptr. 2d 801 (1992) (ruling defendant's decision not to challenge the judge in one action did not constitute a waiver of its right to later challenge the judge when first action subsequently consolidated with two additional related actions against defendant). An immediate writ of mandate pursuant to CCP § 170.3(d) is the exclusive means of appellate review of an unsuccessful peremptory challenge motion. *People v. Hull*, 1 Cal. 4th 266, 2 Cal. Rptr. 2d 526, 820 P.2d 1036 (1991).

Although the general rule is that a peremptory challenge is permitted any time before the commencement of a trial or hearing, CCP § 170.6 contains several exceptions that impose various shorter time limits based on the nature (*e.g.*, within 15 days after notice of assignment to a "judge for all purposes" vs. no later than the time the case is assigned to trial in a "master calendar" court) and timing (when identity of non-all purpose judge is known within at least 10 days of trial, at least 5 days before that date) of the judicial assignment.

In light of these somewhat ambiguous and seemingly overlapping statutory provisions, the determination of the applicable time limit within which to assert a peremptory challenge to a trial judge can be quite complicated. *See Zilog, Inc. v. Superior Court*, 86 Cal. App. 4th 1309, 104 Cal. Rptr. 2d 173 (2001) (ruling that neither the direct calendar, the master calendar, nor the all purpose assignment rule applied to a case management judge assigned for all purposes except trial, but the "ten-day/five-day" rule did apply and the peremptory challenge was timely); *Motion Picture & Television Fund Hosp. v. Superior Court*, 88 Cal. App. 4th 488, 105 Cal. Rptr. 2d 872 (2001) (concluding that when new direct calendar judge is assigned to a case, the statutory time period for filing a peremptory challenge to the newly assigned judge commences when the parties receive notice of the assignment); *Entente Design, Inc. v. Superior Court*, 214 Cal. App. 4th 385, 154 Cal. Rptr. 3d 216 (2013) (determining whether an independent calendar court functioned as a master calendar court for purposes of timeliness of § 170.6 challenge).

A late appearing party in a case assigned to a judge for all purposes has the right to exercise a peremptory challenge within 15 days after appearing in the case, subject to two important exceptions under CCP § 170.6(a)(2): A party cannot exercise a peremptory challenge after the commencement of trial; and an otherwise timely peremptory challenge must be denied if the judge has presided at an earlier hearing which involved a determination of contested facts relating to the merits. CCP § 170.6(a)(2); *see, e.g., Swift v. Superior Court*, 172 Cal. App. 4th 878, 91 Cal. Rptr. 3d 504 (2009) (holding trial judge erred in striking peremptory challenge because the judge's only factual determination were made in connection with pretrial discovery motions and did not relate to the merits of the case); *California Fed. Sav. & Loan Assn. v. Superior Court*, 189 Cal. App. 3d 167, 234 Cal. Rptr. 414 (1987) (concluding trial judge's ruling on motion for summary adjudication of a "make or break" issue involving contract interpretation bars subsequent peremptory challenge); *School Dist. Of Okaloosa Cnty. v. Superior Court*, 58 Cal. App. 4th 1126, 68 Cal. Rptr. 2d 612 (1997) (ruling denial of a motion to quash for lack of personal jurisdiction, like most pretrial motions made in civil cases, does not involve a determination of facts related to the merits of the case).

Why would a party bother to challenge a judge for cause when a peremptory challenge is permitted? Are there circumstances where a challenge for cause is the only procedure available to disqualify a judge? What are these likely circumstances?

§ 13.02 Trial by Jury

[A] Right to Trial by Jury

C & K Engineering Contractors v. Amber Steel Co.

Supreme Court of California
23 Cal. 3d 1, 151 Cal. Rptr. 323, 587 P.2d 1136 (1978)

RICHARDSON, JUSTICE.

The issue posed by this case is whether or not defendant was improperly denied its constitutional right to a jury trial. (Cal. Const., art. I, § 16.) * * *

Plaintiff, a general contractor, solicited bids from defendant and other subcontractors for the installation of reinforcing steel in the construction of a waste water treatment plant in Fresno County. Plaintiff included defendant's bid in its master bid, which was ultimately accepted by the public sanitation district, the proposed owner of the plant. After defendant refused to perform in accordance with its bid on the subcontract, plaintiff brought the present action to recover $102,660 in damages for defendant's alleged breach of contract.

The allegations of plaintiff's first cause of action may be summarized: defendant submitted a written bid of $139,511 for the work; defendants gave a subsequent "verbal promise" that the work would be performed for the bid price; plaintiff "reasonably relied" on defendant's bid and promise in submitting its master bid; defendant knew or should have known that plaintiff would submit a master bid based upon defendant's bid; defendant refused to perform in accordance with its bid; plaintiff was required to expend $242,171 to perform the reinforcing steel work; as a result plaintiff was damaged in the amount of $102,660; and "Injustice can be avoided only by enforcement of defendant's promise to perform...."

Defendant's answer to the complaint alleged its bid was the result of an "honest mistake" in calculation; plaintiff knew of the mistake but failed to notify defendant or permit it to revise its bid as is customary in the industry; and plaintiff's conduct in this regard should bar it from recovering damages.

Defendant demanded a jury trial. The trial court, deeming the case to be essentially in equity, denied the request but empaneled an advisory jury to consider the sole issue of plaintiff's reasonable reliance on defendant's promise. The jury found that plaintiff reasonably relied to its detriment on defendant's bid. The trial court adopted this finding and entered judgment in plaintiff's favor for $102,620, the approximate amount of its prayer, together with interest and costs. Defendant appeals.

Defendant's primary contention is that it was improperly denied a jury trial of plaintiff's action for damages. In resolving this contention we first review the nature and derivation of the doctrine of promissory estoppel. Thereafter, we discuss certain authorities governing the right to jury trial in this state. * * *

1. *Promissory Estoppel*

The elements of the doctrine of promissory estoppel, as described concisely in section 90 of the Restatement of Contracts, are as follows: "A promise which the promisor should reasonably expect to induce action or forbearance of a definite and substantial character on the part of the promisee and which does induce such action or forbearance is binding if injustice can be avoided only by enforcement of the promise." The foregoing rule has been judicially adopted in California and it applies to actions, such as the present case, to enforce a subcontractor's bid. (*Drennan v. Star Paving Co.* [(1958)] 51 Cal. 2d 409, 413–415 [333 P.2d 757].) It is undisputed that plaintiff's complaint in the matter before us relies exclusively upon the doctrine to enforce defendant's alleged promise to perform its bid. In fact, the language of the complaint, summarized above, paraphrases that of section 90 in asserting that "Injustice can be avoided only by enforcement of defendant's promise to perform...."

We have recently characterized promissory estoppel as "a doctrine which employs *equitable* principles to satisfy the requirement that consideration must be given in exchange for the promise sought to be enforced. [Citations.]" (*Raedeke v. Gibraltar Sav. & Loan Assn.* (1974) 10 Cal. 3d 665, 672 [111 Cal. Rptr. 693, 517 P.2d 1157], italics added; see *Seymour v. Oelrichs* (1909) 156 Cal. 782, 794–800 [106 P. 88]; *Klein v. Farmer* (1948) 85 Cal. App. 2d 545, 552–553 [194 P.2d 106].) * * *

Treatise writers and commentators have confirmed the generally equitable nature of promissory estoppel in enforcing a promise which otherwise would be unenforceable. (See 3 Pomeroy, Equity Jurisprudence (5th ed. 1941) § 808b, at pp. 211–216; 1 Williston, Contracts (3d ed. 1957) § 140, pp. 618–619, fn. 6; Seavey, *Reliance Upon Gratuitous Promises or Other Conduct* (1951) 64 Harv. L. Rev. 913, 925; Henderson, *Promissory Estoppel and Traditional Contract Doctrine* (1969) 78 Yale L.J. 343, 379–380; Ames, The History of Assumpsit (1888) 2 Harv. L. Rev. 1, 14.) As expressed by Professor Henderson, "[Promissory] estoppel is a *peculiarly equitable doctrine* designed to deal with situations which, in total impact, necessarily call into play discretionary powers, …" (78 Yale L.J., *supra*, at pp. 379–380, italics added.) * * *

The equitable character of promissory estoppel is confirmed by a close scrutiny of the purpose of the doctrine, namely, that "*injustice* can be avoided only by enforcement of the promise." (Rest., Contracts, *supra*, § 90, italics added.) As expressed by us in a similar subcontractor bid case, once the prerequisites of the doctrine are met, " … *it is only fair* that plaintiff should have at least an opportunity to accept defendant's bid after the general contract has been awarded to him." (*Drennan v. Star Paving Co.*, *supra*, 51 Cal. 2d at p. 415, italics added; see also Seavey, *supra*, 64 Harv. L. Rev. at p. 925; Henderson, *supra*, 78 Yale L.J. at p. 379 ["The specific concern of Section 90 with 'injustice,' standing alone, contemplates broad judicial discretion to make use of equitable principles"].) * * *

We conclude, accordingly, that the doctrine of promissory estoppel is essentially equitable in nature, developed to provide a remedy (namely, enforcement of a gratuitous promise) which was not generally available in courts of law prior to 1850. We now move to an examination of the authorities on the subject of the right to a jury trial, to determine whether the equitable nature of plaintiff's action precluded a jury trial as a matter of right.

2. *Right to Jury Trial*

The right to a jury trial is guaranteed by our Constitution. (Cal. Const., art. I, § 16.) We have long acknowledged that the right so guaranteed, however, is the right as it existed at common law in 1850, when the Constitution was first adopted, "and what that right is, is a purely historical question, a fact which is to be ascertained like any other social, political or legal fact." (*People v. One 1941 Chevrolet Coupe* (1951) 37 Cal. 2d 283, 287 [231 P.2d 832]; accord *Southern Pac. Transp. Co. v. Superior Court* (1976) 58 Cal. App. 3d 433, 436 [129 Cal. Rptr. 912]; …) As a general proposition, "[The] jury trial is a matter of right in a civil action at law, but not in equity." (*Southern Pac. Transportation Co. v. Superior Court*, *supra*, 58 Cal. App. 3d at p. 436; …)

As we stated in *People v. One 1941 Chevrolet Coupe*, *supra*, 37 Cal. 2d 283, " 'If the action has to deal with ordinary common-law rights cognizable in courts of law, it is to that extent an action at law. In determining whether the action was one triable by a jury at common law, the court is not bound by the form of the action but rather by the nature of the rights involved and the facts of the particular case—the *gist* of the action. A jury trial must be granted where the *gist* of the action is legal, where the action is in reality cognizable at law.' " (P. 299, fn. omitted, italics added.) On the other hand, if the action is essentially one in equity and the relief sought "depends upon the application of equitable doctrines," the parties are not entitled to a jury trial. (*e.g.*, *Hartman v. Burford* (1966) 242 Cal. App. 2d 268, 270 [51 Cal. Rptr. 309] [enforcement of promise to make a will]; *Tibbitts v. Fife* (1958) 162 Cal. App. 2d 568, 572 [328 P.2d 212] [establishment of constructive trust].) Although we have said that "the legal or equitable nature of a cause of action ordinarily is determined by the mode of relief to be afforded" (*Raedeke v. Gibraltar Sav. & Loan Assn., supra,* 10 Cal. 3d 665, 672), the prayer for relief in a particular case is not conclusive. Thus, "The fact that damages is one of a full range of possible remedies does not guarantee ... the right to a jury...." (*Southern Pac. Transportation Co. v. Superior Court, supra,* 58 Cal. App. 3d at p. 437.)

In the present case, the complaint purports to seek recovery of damages for breach of contract, in form an action at law in which a right to jury trial ordinarily would exist. (*Raedeke, supra,* 10 Cal. 3d at p. 671; Code Civ. Proc., § 592.) As we have seen, however, the complaint seeks relief which was available only in equity, namely, the enforcement of defendant's gratuitous promise to perform its bid through application of the equitable doctrine of promissory estoppel. Although there is no direct authority on point, several cases have held that actions based upon the analogous principle of equitable estoppel may be tried by the court without a jury. (*Jaffe v. Albertson Co.* (1966) 243 Cal. App. 2d 592, 607–608 [53 Cal. Rptr. 25] [estoppel to bar reliance on statute of frauds]; *Moss v. Bluemm* (1964) 229 Cal. App. 2d 70, 72–73 [40 Cal. Rptr. 50] [estoppel to bar statute of limitations defense]; ...)

Defendant responds by relying primarily upon ... *Raedeke, supra,* which also concerned an action based on promissory estoppel. The *Raedeke* complaint alleged *dual* theories of traditional breach of contract and promissory estoppel. We stressed that the "resolution of the instant case did not depend entirely upon the application of equitable principles; the doctrine of promissory estoppel was only one of two alternative theories of recovery." (P. 674, fn. omitted.) Accordingly, we held in *Raedeke* that plaintiffs were entitled to a jury trial, and that the trial court erred in treating the jury's findings and verdict as advisory only. * * *

The foregoing general principles do not alter our conclusion that the present action is, essentially, one recognized only in courts of equity and, despite plaintiff's request for damages, is not an "action at law" involving, to use the *Raedeke* language, the "incidental adoption of equitable sounding measures." Defendant before us has argued that because plaintiff sought to recover damages rather than to compel defendant to perform its bid, plaintiff requested relief which is available at common law. Yet, as we have seen, damages at law were unavailable in actions for breach of a gratuitous promise. The only manner in which damages have been recognized in such cases of gratuitous promises is by application of the equitable doctrine of promissory estoppel which renders such promises legally binding. Without the employment of this doctrine, essentially equitable, there was no remedy at all. As illustrated by the express language of section 90 of the Restatement of Contracts, promissory estoppel is used to avoid injustice "by *enforcement* of the promise." (Italics added.)

Furthermore, the addition, in such cases, of a prayer for damages does not convert what is essentially an equitable action into a legal one for which a jury trial would be available. * * * [I]n the present case, the trier of fact is called upon to determine whether "injustice can be avoided only by enforcement of [defendant's] promise." (Rest., Contracts, § 90.) The "gist" of such an action is equitable. Both historically and functionally, the task of weighing such equitable considerations is to be performed by the trial court, not the jury. We conclude that the trial court properly treated the action as equitable in nature, to be tried by the court with or without an advisory jury as the court elected. * * *

The judgment is affirmed.

NEWMAN, JUSTICE, dissenting.

I dissent. The Chancery Court in England sometimes created rights, sometimes remedies. When California courts decide whether a jury trial should be assured, I believe that they should focus not on rights but on remedies. A plaintiff who seeks damages should be entitled to a jury. One who seeks specific performance or an injunction or quiet title, etc. (plus supplementary damages or "damages in lieu" that would have been allowed in Chancery) is not entitled to a jury.

The majority opinion here discusses "promissory estoppel," "equitable estoppel," "equitable principles," "equitable doctrine," "equitable nature," and even "injustice." To pretend that words like those enable us to isolate "ordinary common-law rights cognizable in courts of law" or that "the *gist* of the action" governs (quoting from *People v. One 1941 Chevrolet Coupe* (1951) 37 Cal. 2d 283, 299 [231 P.2d 832]) seems to me to be uninstructive fictionalizing. We are told that courts deal with "a purely historical question, a fact which is to be ascertained like any other social, political or legal fact" (*id.*, at p. 287). Yet how often, I wonder, do (or should) California judges instead decide whether the wisdom of a Corbin, in 1963, outweighs comments by Ames, Seavey, Shattuck, and Williston written during the period from 1888 to 1957?

In fact, most rights that are now enforced via a jury were created not by courts but by legislatures. We look at the remedy sought, not at the judicial or legislative history of the right, to decide whether the trial is to be "legal" or "equitable." There are troubling borderlines, but the basic rule should be that no jury is required when plaintiff seeks equitable relief rather than "legal" damages. That approach requires no complex, historical research regarding when and by whom certain rights were created. It also requires less reliance on the anomalies of England's unique juridical history. Courts thus may focus on a basic policy concern; that is, the typically more continuing and more personalized involvement of the trial judge in specific performance and injunctive decrees than in mere judgments for damages. * * *

Plaintiff in this case sought damages for an alleged breach of contract. He did not seek equitable relief. Thus defendant should have been granted the jury trial he requested.

[1] *Constitutional Right to Jury Trial in California Courts*

[a] The Legal/Equitable Dichotomy

Article I, Section 16, of the California Constitution *preserves* the right to jury trial in those actions in which there was a right to a jury at common law at the time the Constitution was first adopted. *Crouchman v. Superior Court*, 45 Cal. 3d 1167, 1175,

248 Cal. Rptr. 626, 755 P.2d 1075 (1988). Consequently, as *C&K Engineering*, reproduced *supra*, illustrates, the determination of the constitutional guarantee must turn on an historical analysis. The basic inquiry often is whether the gist of the action is "legal" (*i.e.*, triable by a jury at common law), or "equitable" and therefore to be resolved by the court sitting without a jury.

Most typical civil actions, such as those for damages based on traditional breach of contract or negligence on the one hand, or suits for injunctive relief only on the other, readily fall into one historical category or the other. Occasionally, as *C&K Engineering* illustrates, an action is not so easily classified. *See, e.g., Franchise Tax Bd. v. Superior Court*, 51 Cal. 4th 1006, 125 Cal. Rptr. 3d 158, 252 P.3d 450 (2011) (holding California Constitution does not require a jury trial in a statutory action against the Franchise Tax Board, as opposed to a common law right of action, for state income tax refund); *Shopoff & Cavallo LLP v. Hyon*, 167 Cal. App. 4th 1489, 85 Cal. Rptr. 3d 268 (2008) (ruling the gist of an interpleader action that seeks to resolve all claims to, and to distribute, interpleaded funds is equitable in nature); *Arciero Ranches v. Meza*, 17 Cal. App. 4th 114, 21 Cal. Rptr. 2d 127 (1993) (ruling defendants entitled to jury trial on cross-complaint seeking injunction to enforce prescriptive easement because gist of such action was considered legal and not equitable in 1850); *Van de Kamp v. Bank of America*, 204 Cal. App. 3d 819, 862–865, 251 Cal. Rptr. 530 (1988) (concluding gist of beneficiaries' action for damages against trustee was based on equitable principle of an accounting, and therefore no right to jury trial); *Wolford v. Thomas*, 190 Cal. App. 3d 347, 235 Cal. Rptr. 422 (1987) (finding no right to trial by jury where gist of complaint was for injunctive relief to abate a nuisance; fact that plaintiff also sought incidental damages does not convert essentially equitable action into a legal one).

Does the California Constitution entitle a party opposing a petition to compel contractual arbitration to a jury trial on the issue of the existence or validity of the arbitration agreement? *See Rosenthal v. Great Western Fin. Sec. Corp.*, 14 Cal. 4th 394, 410–413, 58 Cal. Rptr. 2d 875, 926 P.2d 1061 (1996) (holding a petition to compel arbitration is in essence a suit in equity to compel specific performance of a contract, and therefore plaintiffs were not entitled to a jury trial on the issue of whether the arbitration agreement was void on grounds of fraud). Is there a constitutional right to a jury trial in a declaratory relief action? *See Entin v. Superior Court*, 208 Cal. App. 4th 770, 146 Cal. Rptr. 3d 52 (2012) (concluding right to jury trial in declaratory relief actions depends on whether the issues raised in the complaint are legal or equitable in nature; plaintiff's declaratory relief claim raises factual questions pertaining to contractual rights, which are legal in nature).

Are you satisfied with the "gist of the action" historical approach adopted by the California courts? What is the source of this approach? Would a better analytical approach be to focus on the *remedy* sought, not on the history of the *right*, and to require no jury when a party seeks equitable relief rather than "legal" damages? Why do the California courts not utilize this simpler analytical approach?

[b] Actions Involving Both Legal and Equitable Issues

Where legal and equitable claims are joined in the same action, the parties are entitled to a jury trial on the legal issues. *See, e.g., Connell v. Bowes*, 19 Cal. 2d 870, 871, 123 P.2d 456 (1942); *Arciero Ranches v. Meza*, 17 Cal. App. 4th 114, 124, 21 Cal. Rptr. 2d 127 (1993) (citing cases). Ordinarily, the court will resolve the equitable issues first and then, if any legal issues remain, the jury will resolve them. *See Arciero Ranches*, 17 Cal. App. 4th at 124 (citing cases); *A-C Co. v. Security Pac. Nat'l Bank*, 173 Cal. App. 3d 462, 219 Cal. Rptr. 62 (1985); *but see Unilogic, Inc. v. Burroughs Corp.*, 10 Cal. App. 4th 612, 621–623, 12 Cal. Rptr. 2d 741 (1992) (holding where gist of plaintiff's action for conversion was legal, court had discretion to submit equitable defense of unclean hands to jury for resolution). Is this "equity first" rule consistent with the gist of the action approach? How so?

[c] Other Forms of Historical Analysis

The historical analysis does not always focus on the legal/equitable dichotomy. In *Crouchman v. Superior Court*, 45 Cal. 3d 1167, 1175, 248 Cal. Rptr. 626, 755 P.2d 1075 (1988), for example, the Supreme Court upheld the small claims court appeal statutes which require a superior court trial de novo be conducted without a jury in legal actions. The court found the legal/equitable distinction irrelevant, and instead sought to determine whether the common law at the time the Constitution was adopted provided for jury trials in actions involving small monetary claims. The court concluded that Article I, Section 16 of the California Constitution did not entitle the defendant to a jury trial because the English and American practice in 1850 was to resolve small claims actions without a jury. *Crouchman*, 45 Cal. 3d at 1175–1178.

[d] Constitutional Right to Jury Trial Not a Static Right

The "constitutional guarantee does not require adherence to the letter of common law practice, and new procedures better suited to the efficient administration of justice may be substituted if there is no impairment of the substantial features of a jury trial." *Hung v. Wang*, 8 Cal. App. 4th 908, 927–928, 11 Cal. Rptr. 2d 113 (1992), *quoting Jehl v. Southern Pac. Co.*, 66 Cal. 2d 821, 828–829, 59 Cal. Rptr. 276, 427 P.2d 988 (1967). The courts have upheld numerous modern procedural devices which require the judge to decide limited issues of fact in legal actions, and have rejected arguments that such devices constitute an unconstitutional infringement of the right to a jury trial. *See, e.g., Jehl, supra*, 66 Cal. 2d at 828–829 (upholding California additur procedure against a challenge that it impaired the constitutional right to jury trial); *Rowe v. Superior Court*, 15 Cal. App. 4th 1711, 19 Cal. Rptr. 2d 625 (1993) (concluding CCP § 425.14, which requires that plaintiffs demonstrate sufficient evidence to establish a prima facie case to recover punitive damages in order to obtain leave of court to so amend complaint, does not impair right to jury trial); *Hung, supra*, 8 Cal. App. 4th at 927–928, (holding Civil Code § 1714.10, which requires a judicial determination of reasonable probability of success prior to filing action against attorney based on civil conspiracy with client, does not infringe on constitutional right to jury trial).

[e] Statutory Right to Jury Trial

The Legislature may extend the right to trial by jury to civil actions even though that right is not mandated by the California Constitution. *See Crouchman, supra*, 45 Cal. 3d at 1172–80. Code of Civil Procedure § 1171, for example, authorizes a jury trial in unlawful detainer actions as to any issue of fact. The Probate Code authorizes a jury trial in certain proceedings where Article I, section 16, would not likely require one. *E.g.*, Probate Code § 1827 (authorizing trial by jury for proceedings to determine establishment of conservatorship); § 1860.5(e) (termination of limited conservatorship); § 2351.5(d) (modification of limited conservatorship powers).

Code of Civil Procedure § 592 requires that issues of fact in a wide variety of civil actions must be tried by a jury unless waived. The courts have construed this broad language, however, to simply preserve the common law right to jury trial and not to confer any new rights with respect to any action to which it did not previously exist. *See Crouchman, supra*, 45 Cal. 3d at 1174–1175; *County of Butte v. Superior Court*, 210 Cal. App. 3d 555, 559, 258 Cal. Rptr. 516 (1989) (concluding CCP § 592, like Article I, § 16, is historically based and does not confer right to jury trial in paternity actions).

[2] Waiver of Right to Jury Trial

The California Constitution permits the waiver of jury trial in a civil action "by the consent of the parties expressed as prescribed by statute." Cal. Const., Art. I, § 16. Code of Civil Procedure § 631 specifies the ways a jury trial may be waived. These include written consent or oral consent in open court; failure to appear at the trial; and failure to announce that a jury is required, at the time the cause is first set for trial. CCP § 631(f)(1)–(4). A party may also waive the right to a jury trial by operation of law by failing to deposit with the clerk certain jury fees in advance of the date set for trial, or additional jury fees as they subsequently become due. § 631(f)(5)–(6).

[a] Waiver Not Irrevocable

Waiver of jury pursuant to § 631 is not irrevocable. *Taylor v. Union Pac. R.R. Corp.*, 16 Cal. 3d 893, 898, 130 Cal. Rptr. 23, 549 P.2d 855 (1976); *Wharton v. Superior Court*, 231 Cal. App. 3d 100, 282 Cal. Rptr. 349 (1991). The court may, in its discretion, allow a trial by jury even though there was a waiver. CCP § 631(g). A trial court abuses its discretion as a matter of law in denying relief from an inadvertent waiver, such as for failure to timely post jury fees, where there has been no prejudice to the other party or to the court. *E.g.*, *Johnson-Stovall v. Superior Court*, 17 Cal. App. 4th 808, 21 Cal. Rptr. 2d 494 (1993); *Massie v. ARR Western Skyways, Inc.*, 4 Cal. App. 4th 405, 412, 5 Cal. Rptr. 2d 654 (1992); *but see Gann v. Williams Bros. Realty, Inc.*, 231 Cal. App. 3d 1698, 283 Cal. Rptr. 128 (1991) (finding no abuse of discretion for trial court to deny plaintiff relief from waiver for failure to timely deposit jury fees where defendants contended that to grant such relief within five days before trial would cause hardship in their trial preparation).

Denial of the right to a jury trial is reversible error per se. *Cohill v. Nationwide Auto Serv.*, 16 Cal. App. 4th 696, 700, 19 Cal. Rptr. 2d 924 (1993) (citing cases); *Van de Kamp v. Bank of America*, 204 Cal. App. 3d 819, 863, 251 Cal. Rptr. 530 (1988). Consequently, a party does not waive the right to jury trial by submitting to a nonjury trial after an erroneous denial of a jury, if the party makes a proper objection. *Cohill, supra*, 16 Cal. App. 4th at 700–01; *Escamilla v. Cal. Ins. Guar. Assn.*, 150 Cal. App. 3d 53, 197 Cal. Rptr. 463 (1983). However, some courts have held that a party should not be able to obtain a reversal of a trial court's denial of relief from a jury waiver where the party waits until after judgment to appeal, without a showing of prejudice occurring in the trial. *E.g.*, *McIntosh v. Bowman*, 151 Cal. App. 3d 357, 362–363, 198 Cal. Rptr. 533 (1984); *Gann v. Williams, supra*, 231 Cal. App. 3d at 1704. These courts view a writ of mandate as the appropriate vehicle to secure a jury trial, allegedly wrongfully withheld, without the usual demonstration of prejudice required to obtain a reversal after judgment. *McIntosh, supra*, 151 Cal. App. 3d at 364; *Gann, supra*, 231 Cal. App. 3d at 1704.

[b] Contractual Waiver in Advance of Litigation

Code of Civil Procedure § 631 constitutes the exclusive listing of the means by which a party may waive the right to jury trial when a civil action is pending. *See, e.g., Cohill, supra*, 16 Cal. App. 4th at 700; *Cooks v. Superior Court*, 224 Cal. App. 3d 723, 727, 274 Cal. Rptr. 113 (1990) (ruling superior court erred in denying jury trial as a sanction for failure to submit jury instructions within deadline set by local fast-track rules). Section 631 does not, however, prevent parties from avoiding jury trial by agreeing to submit their controversy to a nonjudicial forum, such as arbitration, *Madden v. Kaiser Found. Hosp.*, 17 Cal. 3d 699, 712–14, 131 Cal. Rptr. 882, 552 P.2d 1178 (1976) (enforcing arbitration agreement even though it contained no express waiver of jury trial); or a judicial reference, *O'Donoghue v. Superior Court*, 219 Cal. App. 4th 245, 161 Cal. Rptr. 3d 609 (2013) (holding agreement to send pending action to a referee for a hearing, determination, and report back to trial court waived defendant's right to jury trial).

Should a court enforce an agreement to waive the right to trial by jury entered into in advance of any civil litigation where one party subsequently requests a jury trial as opposed to a nonjury trial? In *Grafton Partners v. Superior Court*, 36 Cal. 4th 944, 32 Cal. Rptr. 3d 5, 116 P.3d 479 (2005), the Supreme Court held the governing California constitutional and statutory provisions, CCP § 631(f)(1)–(6), do not permit such a predispute waiver, and it is therefore unenforceable. The Supreme Court in *Grafton* distinguished arbitration agreements, which are recognized as valid even though they waive the entire package of trial rights, because the Legislature enacted a comprehensive statutory scheme authorizing predispute arbitration agreements, CCP § 1280 *et seq.* In addition, the court reasoned, arbitration conserves judicial resources far more than the selection of a court over a jury. "It is therefore rational for the Legislature to promote the use of arbitration ... by permitting predispute agreements, while not according the same advantage to jury trial waivers." *Grafton, supra,* 36 Cal. 4th at 964.

[3] *The Federal Constitutional Right to Jury Trial in Federal Courts*

The Seventh Amendment of the United States Constitution provides: "In suits at common law, where the value in controversy shall exceed twenty dollars, the right to trial by jury shall be preserved...." The federal constitutional provision applies only to trials in the federal courts, and not to state court trials. *Minneapolis & St. Louis R.R. Co. v. Bombolis,* 241 U.S. 211, 36 S. Ct. 595, 60 L. Ed. 961 (1916); *Jehl v. Southern Pac. Co., supra,* 66 Cal. 2d at 827; *Crouchman v. Superior Court, supra,* 45 Cal. 3d at 1173, n.5.

As the following summary of Seventh Amendment jurisprudence indicates, the analytical approach adopted by the federal courts when determining whether the right to jury trial attaches under the Seventh Amendment is similar to that utilized by the California state courts:

Understanding Civil Procedure[*]
The California Edition

Walter W. Heiser, Gene R. Shreve, Peter Raven-Hansen & Charles Gardner Geyh
Pages 588–593 (some footnotes omitted)

In one sense, the [Seventh] Amendment does not *create* a right to jury trial, or "guarantee" such a right in absolute terms. It merely states that "the right to trial by jury shall be preserved." The significance of this distinction is that to some extent the process of determining which issues entitle a litigant to claim a jury has turns on history. The reckoning point is English common law in 1791, the year the Amendment was ratified.

The right to a jury trial had been enjoyed to a greater or lesser extent in the colonies, but the right preserved in the Seventh Amendment was that which existed under English law. In a long line of decisions, the Supreme Court has read "common law" in the Seventh Amendment to refer to the jurisdiction of English common-law courts in 1791. These courts dispensed remedies "at law," including damage awards. Litigants in these courts enjoyed extensive rights to trial by jury. England administered at the same time a separate system of chancery of "equity" courts, dispensing equitable remedies, including injunctions. Juries were unavailable in equity proceedings.

The law-equity distinction has been central in determining the scope of the Seventh Amendment. The distinction was significantly blurred, however, by the merger of law and equity proceedings brought about by the adoption of the Federal Rules of Civil Procedure. The merger posed several serious questions about the right to jury

---

[*] Copyright 2013 by Carolina Academic Press. Reprinted with permission.

trial in federal court. The Court answered three of them in a series of Seventh Amendment decisions establishing the modern trend favoring jury trials.

The first question was whether there is a right to jury trial when the plaintiff brings an equitable claim, and defendant brings a legal counterclaim, or vice versa. The Court answered this question in *Beacon Theaters, Inc. v. Westover* [359 U.S. 500 (1959)]. Plaintiff in *Beacon* sued for equitable relief. Defendant counterclaimed for damages on antitrust grounds, demanding a jury trial. The Supreme Court held that, because the law and equity claims had issues in common, the trial court could not first try the equity portion without a jury. To permit this would "compel Beacon to split its antitrust case, trying part to a judge and part to a jury." The Court apparently assumed that, because common factual issues resolved in the initial equity phase of the case would not be open to relitigation in the later jury phase, a jury trial on them would be lost to the defendant altogether.

A second question was whether there was a right to jury trial in an action in which the plaintiff joins legal and equitable claims, and the equitable claims predominate. The Court addressed this question in *Dairy Queen, Inc. v. Wood* [369 U.S. 469 (1962)]. Plaintiff sued over defendant's alleged failure to make payments due under a trademark licensing contract, seeking an injunction against defendant's continued use of the trademark and an accounting for the sum defendant owed. The Court looked behind plaintiff's labels and concluded that "insofar as the complaint requests a money judgment it presents a claim which is unquestionably legal." [*Id.* at 476.] The Seventh Amendment "right to trial by jury," said the Court, "cannot be made to depend upon the choice of words used in the pleadings." [*Id.* at 477–478.] Moreover, the right applies "whether the trial judge chooses to characterize the legal issues presented as 'incidental' to the equitable issues or not."[199]

A third question posed by the merger of law and equity was whether jury trial was available for claims asserted by an historically equitable procedure, such as interpleader, a class action, or a derivative action. All these had been adopted by the Federal Rules of Civil Procedure. The Court answered this question in *Ross v. Bernhard* [396 U.S. 531 (1970)]. Plaintiffs brought a shareholder's derivative action under Rule 23.1. The Court of Appeals held that the action was equitable and that none of it could be tried before a jury. Again the Supreme Court reversed. The shareholder derivative device was a creature of equity, and equitable principles still explain why shareholders in such suits can sue on behalf of the corporation. Yet the Court held that "the right to jury trial attaches to those issues in derivative actions as to which the corporation, if it had been suing in its own right, would have been entitled to a jury." [396 U.S. at 532–533]. The Court added: "[A]s our cases indicate, the 'legal' nature of an issue

---

199. [369 U.S.] at 473. *Accord Tull v. United States*, 418 U.S. 412, 424–25 (1987). Thus, *Beacon* and *Dairy Queen* together stand for the proposition that if, disregarding the parties' labels, there is any claim or defense in the case—incidental or otherwise—that would be characterized as legal at English common law, it must be tried first to a jury upon timely demand.

is determined by considering, first, the pre-merger custom with reference to such questions; second, the remedy sought; and third, the practical abilities and limitations of juries." [*Id.* at 538, n.10.]

Congress has created many causes of action which were unknown to English jurisprudence in 1791. Nothing limits the authority of Congress to supplement the Seventh Amendment by creating a right to trial by jury in federal court whenever it wishes to. But, in determining whether a *constitutional* right to jury trial exists for a statutory cause of action in which Congress has not expressly created a right to jury trial, federal courts have been required to determine whether the issue at hand most closely resembles something adjudicated on the law side or on the equity side of the line in 1791.[205] In *Curtis v. Loether* [415 U.S. 189 (1974)], the plaintiff sought injunctive relief and damages against the defendant for violating her rights under the Civil Rights Act of 1968. The plaintiff argued that the Seventh Amendment did not afford defendant the right to a jury trial because the statutory cause of action post-dated 1791. The Court rejected the plaintiff's argument. "It has long been settled that the right extends beyond common law forms of action recognized at that time," the Court observed, and concluded that the Seventh Amendment guaranteed the defendant a jury trial because the "action involves rights and remedies of the sort typically enforced in an action at law."

Thirteen years later, in *Tull v. United States* [481 U.S. 412 (1987)], the United States brought suit in *Tull* against a developer for violation of the Clean Water Act. The district court denied defendant's demand for a jury trial. After a bench trial (trial before judge), the court found that defendant acted in violation of the Act and imposed numerous fines. The Court of Appeals affirmed. The Supreme Court reversed on Seventh Amendment grounds. "Prior to the enactment of the Seventh Amendment," it noted, "English courts had held that a civil penalty suit was a particular species of an action in debt that was within the jurisdiction of the courts of law." [481 U.S. at 418.] The case was thus "clearly analogous to the 18th-century action in debt, and federal courts have rightly assumed that the Seventh Amendment required a jury trial."[209]

Many commentators find the historical approach to defining the scope of the Seventh Amendment troublesome. Even if the content of old English law was clear,

---

205. Congress has also created many administrative enforcement schemes and specialized (Article I or legislative) courts in which it has failed to provide for jury trials. In addition to looking for historical analogies to decide the Seventh Amendment question in such cases, the Supreme Court has suggested that "public rights" can constitutionally be enforced in special non-jury proceedings. *See, e.g., Atlas Roofing Co. v. Occupational Safety & Health Review Comm'n*, 430 U.S. 442, 458 (1977). This formulation leaves the question of how one identifies such rights.

209. 481 U.S. at 418. Using a similar approach later, in *Feltner v. Columbia Pictures Television*, 523 U.S. 340 (1998), the Supreme Court saw a historic jury analog to the determination of statutory damages under the Copyright Act of 1976 and ruled that a right to jury trial existed under the Seventh Amendment.

analogizing new issues to it would at times be perplexing. Matters are worse because the lines between law and equity at that time were not terribly clear. Moreover, sorting cases by historical category obscures useful thought about policies which should shape the contemporary roles of judge and jury. In line with these concerns, the Supreme Court recently appeared reluctant to overstate the importance of specific investigations of 18th-century English practice in resolving jury questions under the Seventh Amendment. Rather, they are "only preliminary" to a more functional question whether the remedy sought was legal or equitable. * * *

To what extent is the analytical approach taken by the federal courts in applying the Seventh Amendment similar to the approach taken by the California state courts in applying Article I, Section 16, of the California Constitution? In what ways is the federal approach different? Do the federal courts follow an "equity first" rule?

[B]　Selection of the Jury

[1]　Selection of Trial Jury Panel

The Trial Jury Selection and Management Act, CCP §§ 190–237, governs the selection and formation of trial juries for both civil and criminal cases. CCP § 192. The jury commissioner for each county must create a master list of persons potentially qualified for jury service. CCP §§ 195–196. All persons selected for jury service must be selected at random, from sources inclusive of a representative cross-section of the area served by the court. CCP §§ 197 & 198. Approved sources are a combined list of registered voters and DMV licensed drivers, and may also include customer mailing lists, telephone directories, and utility company lists. §§ 197 & 198. The jury commissioner must also utilize random selection to create qualified juror lists from the master list, and to select jurors for trial jury panels to be sent to courtrooms for voir dire. CCP § 219. The clerk in each courtroom must randomly select names of jurors for voir dire from these panels, unless the jury commissioner provides the court with the trial jury panel list in random order, in which case the court must seat the prospective jurors in the same order as in the list. CCP § 222. A party may challenge the entire trial jury panel for failure to include a representative cross-section. CCP § 225(a).

[2]　Voir Dire in Civil Jury Trials

To select a fair and impartial jury, the trial judge initially examines prospective jurors in civil jury trials. CCP § 222.5; Rule 3.1540, Cal. Rules of Ct. The Standards of Judicial Administration recommended by the Judicial Council set forth the areas of inquiry the trial judge's examination should cover. Standard 3.25, Rule Appendix. Upon completion of the judge's initial examination, counsel for each party has the right to examine, by oral and direct questioning, any prospective jurors in order to enable counsel to intelligently exercise both peremptory challenges and challenges for cause. CCP § 222.5. The trial judge should permit liberal and probing examination calculated to discover bias or prejudice with regard to the circumstances of a particular case; the fact that a topic was included in the judge's examination should not preclude additional nonduplicative questioning in the same area by counsel. *See* CCP § 222.5. The judge must not impose unreasonable or arbitrary time limits on counsels' voir dire examination. § 222.5

Generally speaking, counsel in civil jury trials are given considerable freedom and latitude to directly voir dire prospective jurors, unless a particular counsel engages in improper questioning. CCP § 222.5. Section 222.5 defines an "improper question" as "any question that, as its dominant purpose, attempts to precondition the prospective jurors to a particular result, indoctrinate the jury, or question the prospective jurors concerning the pleadings or the applicable law." *See also* Standard 3.25(f).

[3] Challenges to Individual Jurors

[a] Challenges for Cause

A party may challenge an individual juror for cause for a general disqualification, for an implied bias, or for an actual bias. CCP §§ 225–230. Challenges for general disqualification are limited to two grounds: lack of an eligibility qualification to be a competent juror as defined in CCP § 203 or the existence of some incapacity, such as loss of hearing, which makes the person incapable of performing the duties of a juror. CCP § 228. A challenge for implied bias may be taken when the juror possesses some type of relationship to a party or interest in the action which makes the juror inappropriate for that particular case as a matter of law, as specified in CCP § 229. By contrast, actual bias is "the existence of a state of mind on the part of the juror in reference to the case, or to any of the parties, which will prevent the juror from acting with entire impartiality, and without prejudice to the substantial rights of any party." CCP § 225(b)(1)(C). How might actual bias be demonstrated during voir dire in a civil case?

A challenge for cause should be made as soon as the grounds for the challenge are known; the objection is waived if not raised before the jury is sworn. CCP § 226(a)&(c). To preserve a claim of error in the denial of a challenge for cause, the party must have exhausted its peremptory challenges and must object to the jury finally constituted or justify the failure to do so. *See, e.g., People v. Kirkpatrick*, 7 Cal. 4th 988, 1005, 30 Cal. Rptr. 2d 818, 874 P.2d 248 (1994); *Kimberly v. Kaiser Found. Hosp.*, 164 Cal. App. 3d 1166, 1169, 211 Cal. Rptr. 148 (1985). All challenges for cause must be exercised before any peremptory challenges may be taken. CCP § 226(c).

[b] Peremptory Challenges

In civil cases, each party is entitled to six peremptory challenges. CCP § 231(c). If there are more than two parties, each side is entitled to eight peremptory challenges; and if more than two sides, the court may allot additional challenges. § 231(c). The procedure for exercising peremptory challenges is specified by statute. CCP § 231(d) & (e). Peremptory challenges are taken or passed by the sides alternately, commencing with the plaintiff. § 231(d) & (e). Each party is entitled to have a full panel of jurors before exercising any peremptory challenge; the number of challenges remaining with a side is not diminished by any passing. § 231(d) & (e). When each side passes consecutively the jury selection process is complete, and the jury is then sworn. CCP § 231(d) & (e).

[c] Constitutional Limitations on Exercise of Peremptory Challenges

Traditionally, a peremptory challenge may be exercised for any reason and no explanation is necessary. CCP § 226(b). However, recent decisions applying the Fourteenth Amendment to the U.S. Constitution hold that a party to a civil lawsuit may not use peremptory challenges to exclude jurors on account of their race or gender. *Edmonson v. Leesville Concrete Co.*, 500 U.S. 614, 111 S. Ct. 2077, 114 L. Ed. 2d 660 (1991) (holding race-based exclusion in civil actions violates equal protection rights of challenged jurors).

In 2002, the Legislature added CCP § 231.5 which, after amendments, now provides that a party "may not use a peremptory challenge to remove a prospective juror on the basis of an assumption that the prospective juror is biased merely because of [his or her race, color, national origin, ethnic group identification, religion, age, sex, sexual orientation, color, genetic information, or disability], or similar grounds."

[d] Permissible Scope of Voir Dire

Code of Civil Procedure § 222.5 authorizes questions during jury examination in civil cases that are designed "to enable counsel to intelligently exercise both peremptory challenges and challenges for cause." In contrast, CCP § 223, revised by the Legislature after the electorate approved Proposition 115 in 1990, directs that examination of prospective jurors in criminal cases "shall be conducted only in aid of the exercise of challenges for cause."

[C] The Trial Process

[1] *The Order of Proceedings*

When the jury has been sworn, the trial usually proceeds in the following order: Plaintiff's opening statement, defendant's opening statement unless reserved until after plaintiff has produced its evidence, plaintiff's evidence, defendant's evidence, rebuttal evidence by both parties, plaintiff's main closing argument, defendant's closing argument, plaintiff's concluding argument, and finally the judge's instructions to the jury. CCP § 607. The same order applies to nonjury trials. CCP § 631.7. When an answer pleads a defense — such as statute of limitations or res judicata — which does not involve the merits but may constitute a bar to trial, the court may try such special defense before the trial of the merits. CCP § 597. If the court or jury finds in favor of the party asserting such special defense, no further trial is necessary. § 597.

[2] The California Evidence Code

The order of examination is specified in Evidence Code § 772. The Evidence Code also specifies the method and scope of witness examination, Evid. Code §§ 760–778; the grounds for attacking or supporting witness credibility, §§ 780–791; rules regarding opinion evidence by experts and nonexperts; §§ 800–870; judicial notice, §§ 450–460; and rules regarding hearsay, privileges, and other bases for admission or exclusion of evidence, §§ 900–1605. Further analyses of these evidentiary provisions are better left to your Evidence course, and to the several excellent textbooks available in California. *See, e.g.,* CEB, *Effective Introduction of Evidence in California* (2d ed. 2015); *Jefferson's California Evidence Benchbook* (CEB 4th ed. 2015); Cotchett, *California Courtroom Evidence* (2015); Kennedy & Martin, *California Expert Witness Guide* (CEB 2d ed. 2015); Imwinkelried & Leach, *California Evidentiary Foundations* (4th ed. 2011); Witkin, *California Evidence* (5th ed. 2015); and Heafey, Blitch, Wallace & Yandell, *California Trial Objections* (CEB 2015).

[3] Burden of Proof and Related Issues

The "burden of proof" means the obligation of a party to establish by evidence the requisite degree of belief concerning a fact in the mind of the trier of fact. Evid. Code § 115. As a general rule, a party who has the burden of proof in a civil action must persuade the factfinder of the existence or nonexistence of a fact by a preponderance of the evidence. Evid. Code § 115; *see* CACI No. 200 (2012) (providing in civil trials, "the party who is required to prove something need prove only that it is more likely to be true than not true"). A higher standard of proof—clear and convincing evidence—is only required for certain specific issues in civil cases such as proof of malice, fraud, or oppression in order to recover punitive damages in noncontract actions, Civil Code § 3294; and termination of parental rights, Family Code § 7821. CACI No. 201(2012).

The party asserting a claim or defense has the burden of proof as to each fact essential to that claim or defense, unless the constitution or a statute provides otherwise. Evid. Code §§ 500–522. The party with the burden of proof usually also has burden of producing or initially introducing evidence as to an issue. Evid. Code §§ 110, 550. Certain presumptions specified by statute will affect the burden of proof, such as the presumption that a person has failed to exercise due care if his violation of a statute proximately caused injury to another. Evid. Code § 669. Other presumptions, such as res ipsa loquitur, affect the burden of producing evidence. Evid. Code § 646. Most such presumptions are rebuttable, although a few are conclusive. *See, e.g.,* Evid. Code §§ 630–670 (rebuttable presumptions); §§ 620–624 (conclusive presumptions).

The burdens of proof and production, as well as the presumptions which may change them, have a variety of important consequences at all stages of civil litigation. How do these burdens and presumptions affect the pleadings? Summary judgment? Trial preparation? The presentation of evidence at trial? Motions during trial attacking the sufficiency of the evidence?

[4] Expedited Jury Trials

After a civil action is filed, the parties may consent to an "expedited jury trial" as authorized by the Expedited Jury Trials Act, CCP §§ 630.01–630.11. *See* Rules 3.1545–3.1552, Cal. Rules of Ct. (specifying pre-trial and trial procedures for expedited jury trials). An expedited jury trial consists of 8 or fewer jurors with no alternates, allows only 3 peremptory challenges for each side, and limits each side to 5 hours in which to complete voir dire and to present its case. CCP §§ 630.03(e)(2), 630.04. The parties also agree to wave all rights to appeal or to make any post-trial motions, except for the very limited grounds specified in the Act. CCP §§ 630.03(e)(2)(A); 630.08–630.09. A key element of this summary trial is the "high/low agreement," defined as a written agreement entered into by the parties that specifies a minimum amount of damages a plaintiff is guaranteed to receive from the defendant, and a maximum amount of damages that the defendant will be liable for, regardless of the ultimate verdict returned by the jury. CCP § 630.01(b). The high/low agreement is not disclosed to the jury.

[5] Trial Techniques

Effective trial advocacy skills are essential to success in litigation. Extended discussion of trial skills is beyond the scope of this book, and is better left to a trial practice course. A variety of excellent books on trial techniques are available, however, including Thomas A. Mauet, *Trial Techniques* (Wolters Kluwer 9th ed. 2013); Roger Haydock & John Sonsteng, *Trial Advocacy Before Judges, Jurors, and Arbitrators* (5th ed. 2015); Steven Lubet & J.C. Lore, *Modern Trial Advocacy* (NITA 5th ed. 2015); Perrin, Caldwell & Chase, *The Art and Science of Trial Advocacy* (LexisNexis 2011); Imwinkelreid, *Evidentiary Foundations* (LexisNexis 9th ed. 2014).

[D] Advising the Jury

[1] Comments by the Judge

A trial judge has the authority to call and interrogate witnesses, Evidence Code § 775; and to comment on the testimony and credibility of any witness, Art. VI, § 10, Cal. Constitution. *See, e.g., Orient Handel v. U.S. Fid. & Guar. Co.*, 192 Cal. App. 3d 684, 237 Cal. Rptr. 667 (1987) (observing a trial judge may analyze all or part of the testimony and express his views with respect to credibility, so as to aid the jury in reaching a verdict). However, a judge's power to comment on the evidence in civil cases is not unlimited. For example, in *Lewis v. Bill Robertson & Sons, Inc.*, 162 Cal. App. 3d 650, 208 Cal. Rptr. 699 (1984), the Court of Appeal found judicial misconduct and reversed a judgment based on a nine-to-three jury verdict for the defendant in a personal injury case. The trial judge in *Lewis* had commented extensively on crucial issues of proximate cause and damages, after closing arguments. These comments were clearly one-sided, essentially telling the jury that no evidence existed to show that defendant's negligence caused plaintiff's injuries. In addition, despite uncontroverted expert testimony that plaintiff had sustained permanent damage, the judge stated that the plaintiff's injuries had "healed perfectly." The Court of Appeal held that the judge's statements usurped the function of the jury as the exclusive trier of fact and misrepresented the evidence, and therefore went beyond the comment permitted by the state Constitution. *Lewis,* 162 Cal. App. 3d at 656.

[2] Closing Argument

Garcia v. Conmed Corp.

Court of Appeal of California, Sixth Appellate District
204 Cal. App. 4th 144, 147–149, 138 Cal. Rptr. 3d 665 (2012)

* * *

In conducting closing argument, attorneys for both sides have wide latitude to discuss the case. "The right of counsel to discuss the merits of a case, both as to the law and facts, is very wide, and he has the right to state fully his views as to what the evidence shows, and as to the conclusions to be fairly drawn therefrom. The adverse party cannot complain if the reasoning be faulty and the deductions illogical, as such matters are ultimately for the consideration of the jury." [Citations.] "Counsel may vigorously argue his case and is not limited to 'Chesterfieldian politeness.'" [Citations.] "An attorney is permitted to argue all reasonable inferences from the evidence, ..." [Citation.] "Only the most persuasive reasons justify handcuffing attorneys in the exercise of their advocacy within the bounds of propriety." [Citation.]

"An attorney who exceeds this wide latitude commits misconduct. For example, '[w]hile a counsel in summing up may indulge in all fair arguments in favor of his client's case, he may not assume facts not in evidence or invite the jury to speculate as to unsupported inferences.' [Citation.] Nor may counsel properly make personally insulting or derogatory remarks directed at opposing counsel or impugn counsel's motives or character. [Citation.] Additional examples abound; these are but a few." (*Cassim v. Allstate Ins. Co.* (2004) 33 Cal.4th 780, 795–796 [16 Cal. Rptr. 3d 374, 94 P.3d 513] (*Cassim*).)[1]

Attorney misconduct is an irregularity in the proceedings and a ground for a new trial. (*City of Los Angeles v. Decker* (1977) 18 Cal.3d 860, 870 [135 Cal. Rptr. 647, 558 P.2d 545] (*Decker*).) Although it is common practice to urge that attorney misconduct is an error of law justifying the grant of a motion for a new trial, a party is not required to move for a new trial before raising attorney misconduct as an issue on appeal. (See *Estate of Barber* (1957) 49 Cal.2d 112, 119 [315 P.2d 317] [generally, motion for a new trial not necessary to preserve an issue for appeal].) However, to

---

1. The California Supreme Court first used the term "Chesterfieldian politeness" in the context of the permissible scope of closing argument in *People v. Bandhauer* (1967) 66 Cal.2d 524, 529 [58 Cal. Rptr. 332, 426 P.2d 900].) The term itself is a reference to Philip Stanhope, the fourth Earl of Chesterfield, who wrote and published letters to his son and instructional books on manners and deportment, including Principles of Politeness, and of Knowing the World (1794), and who reportedly said, "Next to good breeding is genteel manners and carriage" and, "An able man shows his spirit by gentle words and resolute actions."

preserve for appeal an instance of misconduct of counsel in the presence of the jury, an objection must have been lodged at trial and the party must also have moved for a mistrial or sought a curative admonition unless the misconduct was so persistent that an admonition would have been inadequate to cure the resulting prejudice. (*Cassim, supra*, 33 Cal.4th at pp. 794–795.) This is so because "[o]ne of the primary purposes of admonition at the beginning of an improper course of argument is to avoid repetition of the remarks and thus obviate the necessity of a new trial." (*Sabella v. Southern Pac. Co.* (1969) 70 Cal.2d 311, 320 [74 Cal. Rptr. 534, 449 P.2d 750] (*Sabella*).)

But it is not enough for a party to show attorney misconduct. In order to justify a new trial, the party must demonstrate that the misconduct was prejudicial. (*Cassim, supra*, 33 Cal.4th at p. 800.) As to this issue, a reviewing court makes "an independent determination as to whether the error was prejudicial." (*Decker, supra*, 18 Cal.3d at p. 872.) It "must determine whether it is reasonably probable [that the appellant] would have achieved a more favorable result in the absence of that portion of [attorney conduct] now challenged." (*Cassim, supra*, at p. 802.) It must examine "the entire case, including the evidence adduced, the instructions delivered to the jury, and the entirety of [counsel's] argument," in determining whether misconduct occurred and whether it was sufficiently egregious to cause prejudice. (*Ibid.*) "Each case must ultimately rest upon a court's view of the overall record, taking into account such factors, inter alia, as the nature and seriousness of the remarks and misconduct, the general atmosphere, including the judge's control, of the trial, the likelihood of prejudicing the jury, and the efficacy of objection or admonition under all the circumstances." (*Sabella, supra*, 70 Cal.2d at pp. 320–321.) "[I]t is only the record as a whole, and not specific phrases out of context, that can reveal the nature and effect of such tactics." (*Id.* at p. 318.)

"Generally a claim of misconduct is entitled to no consideration on appeal unless the record shows a timely and proper objection and a request that the jury be admonished." (*Horn v. Atchison, T. & S.F. Ry. Co.* (1964) 61 Cal. 2d 602, 610 [39 Cal. Rptr. 721, 394 P.2d 561].) "'As the effect of misconduct can ordinarily be removed by an instruction to the jury to disregard it, it is generally essential, in order that such act be reviewed on appeal, that it shall first be called to the attention of the trial court at the time, to give the court an opportunity to so act in the premises, if possible, as to correct the error and avoid a mistrial. Where the action of the court is not thus invoked, the alleged misconduct will not be considered on appeal, if an admonition to the jury would have removed the effect.'" (*Cope v. Davison* (1947) *supra*, 30 Cal. 2d at p. 202.) "'It is only in extreme cases that the court, when acting promptly and speaking clearly and directly on the subject, cannot, by instructing the jury to disregard such matters, correct the impropriety of the act of counsel and remove any effect his conduct or remarks would otherwise have.' (*Tingley v. Times-Mirror Co.*, 151 Cal. 1, 23 [89 P. 1097].) ... [We] are aware of no California case wherein a plaintiff's verdict was reversed for misconduct during his counsel's argument in the lack of timely objections and a request that the jury be admonished where such admonition could be effective." (*Horn v. Atchison, T. & S.F. Ry. Co.* (1964) *supra*, 61 Cal. 2d at pp. 610–611.)

This case is neither precisely like *Horn, supra,* in which no objection or request for admonition was made until after conclusion of the closing argument (and relief was thus denied); nor like *Hoffman v. Brandt* (1966) 65 Cal. 2d 549 [55 Cal. Rptr. 417, 421 P.2d 425], in which an admonition, especially as there given by the trial court, could not have been effective under the circumstances; nor like *Love v. Wolf* (1964) 226 Cal. App. 2d 378 [38 Cal. Rptr. 183], in which admonition of the jury was requested several times but disregarded by the trial court. Here defendant remained silent as to all but one line of argument, and as to the latter he objected but failed at any time to request an admonition of the jury to disregard the remarks. Under the circumstances we conclude that defendant must be denied relief.

The record indicates that while plaintiff's counsel accused witnesses of perjury, made reference to defendant's wealth and plaintiff's lack of resources, and appealed, though indirectly, to the jurors to place themselves in plaintiff's position, all of which tactics are improper and to be condemned (*see, e.g., Hoffman v. Brandt* (1966) *supra,* 65 Cal. 2d 549; *Horn v. Atchison, T. & S.F. Ry. Co.* (1964) *supra,* 61 Cal. 2d 602; *Love v. Wolf* (1964) *supra,* 226 Cal. App. 2d 378), defendant did not once object to such remarks, much less request an admonition to the jury. "In the absence of a timely objection the offended party is deemed to have waived the claim of error through his participation in the atmosphere which produced the claim of prejudice." (*Horn v. Atchison, T. & S.F. Ry. Co.* (1964) *supra,* 61 Cal. 2d at p. 610.)

Certainly as to this particular line of argument an admonition would have been effective, especially if requested at the outset. One of the primary purposes of admonition at the beginning of an improper course of argument is to avoid repetition of the remarks and thus obviate the necessity of a new trial. (*Horn v. Atchison, T. & S.F. Ry. Co.* (1964) *supra,* 61 Cal. 2d at p. 610.) Except perhaps in cases of highly emotional or inflammatory language or reference to extremely prejudicial circumstances not in evidence, a jury must be deemed capable, if so instructed, of ignoring references to a litigant's personal or corporate virtues and confining itself to the merits of the case.

Gallagher v. Municipal Court

Supreme Court of California
31 Cal. 2d 784, 192 P.2d 905 (1948)

TRAYNOR, JUSTICE.

* * *

Attorneys must be given a substantial freedom of expression in representing their client. "An advocate is at liberty, when addressing the Court in regular course, to combat and contest strongly any adverse views of the Judge or Judges expressed on the case during its argument, to object to and protest against any course which the Judge may take and which the advocate thinks irregular or detrimental to the interests of his client, and to caution juries against any interference by the Judge with their functions, or with the advocate when addressing them, or against any strong view adverse to his client expressed by the presiding Judge upon the facts of a case before the verdict of the jury thereon. An advocate ought to be allowed freedom and latitude both in speech and in the conduct of his client's case." (Oswald, Contempt of Court (3d ed.), pp. 56–57). The public interest in an independent bar would be subverted if judges were allowed to punish attorneys summarily for contempt on purely subjective reactions to their conduct or statements.

An attorney has the duty to protect the interests of his client. He has a right to press legitimate argument and to protest an erroneous ruling. It is reported in Oswald on Contempt of Court that the following interchange occurred between Erskine and Buller, J.: "At length Erskine said, 'I stand here as an advocate for a brother citizen, and I desire that the word "only" be recorded;' whereupon Buller, J., said 'Sit down, sir! remember your duty or I shall be obliged to proceed in another manner,'—to which Erskine retorted, 'Your Lordship may proceed in whatever manner you think fit. I know my duty as well as your Lordship knows yours. I shall not alter my conduct.' The Judge took no notice of this reply. Lord Campbell speaks of the conduct of Erskine as 'a noble stand for the independence of the Bar.'" (Oswald, (3d ed.), pp. 51–52.) The foregoing quotation is illustrative of the rule … that an attorney may assert that which he believes to be correct in a forthright manner, if he is acting in the due course of a judicial proceeding.

[a] Scope of Proper Argument

Upon conclusion of the evidence at trial, the attorneys have the right to present closing arguments to the jury. CCP § 607(7). As *Garcia v. ConMed Corp., supra,* indicates, vigorous and forceful argument is not only expected, but is proper and desirable. The court must accord the attorneys considerable latitude in discussing the facts and the law. An attorney has the right to express opinions based upon fair deductions and reasonable inferences from the evidence given at trial. *Beagle v. Vasold,* 65 Cal. 2d 166, 177, 53 Cal. Rptr. 129, 417 P.2d 673 (1966) (ruling trial court erred in refusing to permit plaintiff's attorney to argue that his client's damages for pain and suffering be calculated on a "per diem" basis; such argument merely draws a reasonable inference from the evidence); *Brokopp v. Ford Motor Co.,* 71 Cal. App. 3d 841, 861, 139 Cal. Rptr. 888 (1977) (concluding an attorney may argue all reasonable inferences from the evidence and may comment on the demeanor of witnesses). The argument need not be absolutely logical, but must be based on facts in evidence. Compare *Miller v. Pac. Constructors, Inc.,* 68 Cal. App. 2d 529, 551, 157 P.2d 57 (1945) (finding illogical application of facts in evidence not prejudicial error) with *Dumas v. Stocker,* 213 Cal. App. 3d 1262, 1270, 262 Cal. Rptr. 311 (1989) (holding closing argument which continually referred to facts of defendant's wealth unsupported by any evidence constituted reversible error).

Counsel also has the right to state the pertinent law and to apply the law to the facts of the case, so long as the law so stated is correct. *See, e.g., Beaird v. Bryan,* 244 Cal. App. 2d 836, 842–43, 53 Cal. Rptr. 428 (1966) (holding trial court, in precluding discussion of law, went beyond reasonable control of counsel and unduly interfered with his presentation); *Hodges v. Stevens,* 201 Cal. App. 2d 99, 114, 20 Cal. Rptr. 129

(1962) (finding trial judge committed reversible error when he precluded counsel from discussing pertinent law during closing argument); *but see Neumann v. Bishop*, 59 Cal. App. 3d 451, 479–80, 130 Cal. Rptr. 786 (1976) (ruling it is improper for counsel to argue law when counsel knew the court would not instruct the jury on that legal theory).

The difference between proper and improper argument is difficult to define. Misstatement of the law or facts during argument is clearly improper, but beyond that the line is less clear. The general standards—such as the prohibition on appeals to the prejudice, passions or sympathy of the jury—provide minimal guidance at best. However, the courts do agree that certain specific types of argument constitute misconduct.

Evidence that a party is insured against loss arising from liability is inadmissible under Evidence Code § 1155, and an attempt to inject this subject by argument is considered misconduct. *See, e.g., Neumann v. Bishop*, 59 Cal. App. 3d at 469–73. Although an attorney may argue to the jury that her client's damages for pain and suffering may be measured in terms of a stated number of dollars for specific periods of time, *Beagle v. Vasold*, 65 Cal. 2d 166, 173–82, 53 Cal. Rptr. 129, 417 P.2d 673 (1966) (holding "per diem" argument proper), an attorney may not ask the jurors to place themselves in the plaintiff's shoes and to award such damages as they would "charge" to undergo equivalent pain and suffering. *Id.* at 182, fn.11 (disapproving so-called "golden rule" argument); *Neumann v. Bishop*, 59 Cal. App. 3d at 483–85 (holding that asking jurors whether they would accept $500,000 to trade places with the plaintiff, who was painfully crippled, is improper closing argument).

Addressing individual jurors by name during argument is improper, *Neumann v. Bishop*, 59 Cal. App. 3d at 473–474; as are other similar attempts to establish a special rapport with the jury. *See, e.g., Whitfield v. Roth*, 10 Cal. 3d 874, 890–893, 112 Cal. Rptr. 540, 519 P.2d 588 (1974) (holding defense attorney's distribution of candy and cigars to jurors in celebration of birth of his son was improper conduct). Personal attacks on opposing parties and their attorneys, whether outright or by insinuation, constitute misconduct. *See, e.g., Stone v. Foster*, 106 Cal. App. 3d 334, 164 Cal. Rptr. 901 (1980) (ruling counsel's argument, which portrayed the defendant as an evil doctor backed by a multimillion dollar medical industry and a conspiracy of silence, was improper); *Las Palmas Assoc. v. Las Palmas Ctr. Assoc.*, 235 Cal. App. 3d 1220, 1245–47, 1 Cal. Rptr. 2d 301 (1991) (holding improper argument attacking opposing party's attorneys as liars, cheaters, "whores," and as using political contributions to influence the judiciary). Appealing to the jury's self interest is also improper because such arguments tend to undermine the jury's impartiality. *See Cassim v. Allstate Ins. Co.*, 33 Cal. 4th 780, 795–800, 16 Cal. Rptr. 3d 374, 94 P.3d 513 (2004) (collecting cases).

The courts generally agree that the types of argument described in the preceding paragraph are prejudicial misconduct. However, in each of the cases cited above the appellate court held that the offended party's failure to object and request an admonishment constituted a waiver of the right to have the matter addressed on appeal. *See, e.g., Las Palmas Assoc., supra*, 235 Cal. App. 3d at 1247–48; *Neumann, supra*, 59 Cal. App. 3d at 475–82. Do you agree with these holdings? Would you consider some of the types of improper argument described above to be so prejudicial that an admonishment would be ineffective? Which types? Why?

[b] Ethical Considerations

As the quote in *Gallagher*, reproduced *supra*, suggests, an attorney has an ethical obligation to represent the interests of his or her client zealously within the bounds of the law. *See* ABA Model Rules of Professional Conduct, comment to Rule 1.3. The California Rules of Professional Conduct provide that an attorney "shall not intentionally, recklessly, or repeatedly fail to perform legal services with competence." Rule 3-110(A), Cal. Rules of Prof. Conduct. "Competence" in any legal service means to apply the "(1) diligence, (2) learning and skill, and (3) mental, emotional, and physical ability reasonably necessary for the performance of such service." Rule 3-110(B). Other rules require an attorney, in presenting a matter to a tribunal, to employ such means as are only consistent with the truth and not to mislead the judge or jury by an artifice or false statement of fact or law. Bus. & Prof. Code § 6068(d); Rule 5-200, Cal. Rules of Prof. Conduct.

[c] When Does Improper Argument Require Reversal?

Generally, misconduct of counsel during trial may not be urged on appeal as a ground for reversal absent both timely objection and request for admonition in the trial court. *See Whitfield v. Roth*, 10 Cal. 3d 874, 891–93, 112 Cal. Rptr. 540, 519 P.2d 588 (1974); *Sabella v. Southern Pac. Co.*, 70 Cal. 2d 311, 318, 74 Cal. Rptr. 534, 449 P.2d 750 (1969); *Horn v. Atchison, Topeka & Santa Fe Ry. Co.*, 61 Cal. 2d 602, 610, 39 Cal. Rptr. 721, 394 P.2d 561 (1964).

Do you agree with the premise of this general rule, *i.e.*, that an objection followed by an admonition to the jury will usually cure the adverse effect of improper argument? What are the other purposes of this rule? Under what circumstances will misconduct be so prejudicial that an admonishment would be ineffective and therefore excuse the failure to request such admonishment. *See, e.g., Simmons v. Southern Pac. Transp. Co.*, 62 Cal. App. 3d 341, 133 Cal. Rptr. 42 (1976) (holding multiple objections unnecessary where adversary engaged in flagrant and repeated episodes of misconduct); *Love v. Wolf*, 226 Cal. App. 2d 378, 391–94, 38 Cal. Rptr. 183 (1964) (concluding an admonishment may cure isolated and unemphasized error, but an attempt to rectify repeated and resounding misconduct by admonition is like trying to unring a bell). Is the strength of the merits of the offending attorney's case a relevant factor? Compare *Las Palmas Assoc., supra*, 235 Cal. App. 3d at 1248 (ruling that even a pervasive pattern of misconduct deemed to have an innocuous effect on jury's overall conclusion where the evidence of defendant's tortious act was substantial) with *Simmons v. Southern Pac. Transp. Co., supra*, 62 Cal. App. 3d at 351–59 (finding reversal for improper argument appropriate even though substantial evidence supported verdict and objections not timely made).

In *Seimon v. Southern Pac. Transp. Co.*, 67 Cal. App. 3d 600, 136 Cal. Rptr. 787 (1977), the trial court granted the defendant railroad a new trial based, in part, on improper conduct during closing argument on the issue of damages in a personal injury action. The plaintiff's attorney deliberately tried to convey an image of himself and his client as the "little guys" and financial underdogs in a battle against the "big guy" defendant railroad, which the trial court viewed as an improper appeal to the economic prejudices of the jury. The Court of Appeals affirmed the new trial order even though the attorney for the defendant failed to object or request an admonitory instruction during the trial. *Seimon*, 67 Cal. App. 3d at 604–606. Likewise in *Dumas v. Stocker*, 213 Cal. App. 3d 1262, 262 Cal. Rptr. 311 (1989), the Court of Appeal reversed a jury award of punitive damages in a personal injury action against the defendant landlord because of improper conduct by plaintiff's counsel, whose closing argument was laced with strident appeals to the passions and prejudice of the jury and references to "facts" unsupported by any evidence. *Dumas*, 213 Cal. App. 3d at 1270. The *Dumas* court ruled that the amount of the jury award raised a presumption of passion or prejudice, and that reversal was not precluded merely because the defendant neglected to request curative admonitions. *Id.* at 1270, n.15.

Is *Seimon* an exception to the general rule regarding waiver of claimed error of improper argument? Are the circumstances in *Seimon* different from those anticipated by the general rule? How so? What about *Dumas*?

[3] Jury Instructions

[a] Right to a Jury Instruction

A party is entitled upon request to correct, nonargumentative jury instructions as to the law on every theory of the case which is supported by substantial evidence, whether or not that evidence was considered persuasive by the trial court. *See, e.g., Soule v. General Motors Corp.*, 8 Cal. 4th 548, 572, 34 Cal. Rptr. 2d 607, 882 P.2d 298 (1994) (ruling trial court must instruct in specific terms that relate the party's theory to the particular case); *Hasson v. Ford Motor Co.*, 19 Cal. 3d 530, 543, 138 Cal. Rptr. 705, 564 P.2d 857 (1977). Viewing the evidence in the light most favorable to the proposing party, the court must give the requested instruction if the evidence so viewed could establish the elements of the theory presented. *Maxwell v. Powers*, 22 Cal. App. 4th 1596, 1607, 28 Cal. Rptr. 2d 62 (1994); *Bernal v. Richard Wolf Med. Instruments Corp.*, 221 Cal. App. 3d 1326, 1337–38, 272 Cal. Rptr. 41 (1990) (finding evidence, although slight, was sufficient to require the giving of a breach of warranty instruction).

The refusal to give a jury instruction adequately covering a party's theory, where that theory is supported by substantial evidence, may be considered prejudicial error. *See Soule, supra*, 8 Cal. 4th at 574–76 (collecting cases). However, in order to obtain appellate consideration of a trial court's failure to instruct on a particular issue, the aggrieved party must have requested the specific proper instruction. *Orient Handel v. U. S. Fid. & Guar. Co.*, 192 Cal. App. 3d 684, 699, 237 Cal. Rptr. 667 (1987) (citing cases); *Willden v. Washington Nat'l Ins. Co.*, 18 Cal. 3d 631, 636, 135 Cal. Rptr. 69, 557 P.2d 501 (1976). Where the court gives a jury instruction correct in law, but a party complains that it is too general, lacks clarity, or is incomplete, the party must request the additional or qualifying instruction in order to have the error reviewed. A party's failure to request any different jury instructions means that party may not argue on appeal that the trial court should have instructed differently. *Metcalf v. Cnty. of San Joaquin*, 42 Cal. 4th 1121, 1131, 72 Cal. Rptr. 3d 382, 176 P.3d 654 (2008).

The trial judge does have the authority and responsibility to instruct the jury on all controlling general principles of law, CCP § 608; but the court is under no duty in a civil case to instruct on a specific subject if no instruction is proposed. *See, e.g., Agarwal v. Johnson*, 25 Cal. 3d 932, 951, 160 Cal. Rptr. 141, 603 P.2d 58 (1979) (ruling trial court under no duty to instruct in absence of specific request, unless a complete failure to instruct on controlling legal principles); *Wank v. Richman & Garrett*, 165 Cal. App. 3d 1103, 1113–1114, 211 Cal. Rptr. 919 (1985) (noting trial court not required to act as a "backup" counsel and cure improperly drawn instruction proffered by attorney).

When a party seeks appellate review of an incorrect instruction given by the trial court, the aggrieved party must demonstrate that the erroneous instruction was prejudicial and not harmless error. *See, e.g., Soule v. Gen. Motors Corp., supra,* 8 Cal. 4th at 579–83 (concluding error in presenting certain design defect theory to jury not sufficiently prejudicial as to require reversal of judgment); *LeMons v. Regents of Univ. of Cal.,* 21 Cal. 3d 869, 876, 148 Cal. Rptr. 355, 582 P.2d 946 (1978) (ruling that while there is no precise formula for measuring the prejudicial effect of an erroneous instruction, the following factors may be considered: "(1) the degree of conflict in the evidence on critical issues; (2) whether respondent's argument to the jury may have contributed to the instruction's misleading effect; (3) whether the jury requested a rereading of the erroneous instruction or of related evidence; (4) the closeness of the jury's verdict; and (5) the effect of other instructions in remedying the error."). The test for determining whether an erroneous jury instruction was prejudicial or was harmless error is discussed in § 15.01 [E] The Prejudicial Error Rule, *infra.* Likewise, a trial court's erroneous refusal to give a specific jury instruction will not require reversal unless the aggrieved party demonstrates actual prejudice. In *Soule v. General Motors Corp., supra,* the California Supreme Court overturned numerous prior decisions treating such instructional error as reversible per se and held that "there is no rule of automatic reversal or inherent prejudice applicable to any category of civil instructional error, whether of commission or omission." *Soule,* 8 Cal. 4th at 548.

Does the *Soule* holding mean that reversible error is not presumed where the trial court instructs the jury on a legal theory for which there was no evidentiary support in the record? *See, e.g., Wilkinson v. Bay Shore Lumber Co.,* 182 Cal. App. 3d 594, 227 Cal. Rptr. 327 (1986) (ruling prejudice from erroneous instruction, unwarranted by evidence, not presumed; Art. VI, § 13 of Cal. Const. requires affirmative showing that error resulted in miscarriage of justice); *Harb v. City of Bakersfield,* 233 Cal. App. 4th 606, 633–37, 189 Cal. Rptr. 59 (2015) (rejecting bright-line rule and instead analyzing facts and circumstances of case to determine whether prejudice resulted from the erroneous giving of a comparative fault instruction).

May a party complain on appeal that the trial judge gave an erroneous instruction when that party had requested that the specific instruction be given? *See, e.g., Miller v. Kennedy,* 196 Cal. App. 3d 141, 146, 241 Cal. Rptr. 472 (1987) (concluding that under the doctrine of invited error, a party may not complain of the giving of a particular instruction which that party requested); *see also Mary M. v. City of L. A.,* 54 Cal. 3d 202, 212–213, 285 Cal. Rptr. 99, 814 P.2d 1341 (1991) (finding doctrine of invited error not applicable where the party, while making the appropriate objection to a proposed jury instruction, then acquiesced in the trial court's determination to give the instruction).

[b] Content of Jury Instructions

Jury instructions must accurately and completely state the applicable legal principles; and must not be slanted, unduly repetitious or argumentative. *See Wank v. Richman & Garrett, supra,* 165 Cal. App. 3d at 1112–14; *Stone v. Foster,* 106 Cal. App. 3d 334, 349, 164 Cal. Rptr. 901 (1980) (defining an argumentative instruction as one which embodies detailed recitals of fact drawn from the evidence in such a manner as to constitute an argument to the jury in the guise of a statement of law). The approved jury instructions adopted by the Judicial Council, set forth in *California Jury Civil Instructions* ("CACI), are recommended for use in civil cases. Rule 2.1050, Cal. Rules of Ct.

When CACI does not contain instruction on a point, the trial judge may modify the CACI instruction or develop a new instruction; but the instruction given "should be accurate, brief, understandable, impartial, and free from argument." Rule 2.1050(d). To what other sources should an attorney look when developing a proposed special jury instruction not based on a CACI instruction? *See, e.g., Sprague v. Equifax, Inc.,* 166 Cal. App. 3d 1012, 1049, 213 Cal. Rptr. 69 (1985) (taking jury instructions from appellate opinions); *Kostecky v. Henry,* 113 Cal. App. 3d 362, 170 Cal. Rptr. 197 (1980) (basing jury instruction on statute). A proposed special jury instruction submitted to the court by a party must contain a citation of any authorities supporting the statement of law therein. Rule 2.1055(d). What are the reasons for this rule?

[c] Jury Instructions Procedure

Generally speaking, counsel for the respective parties must deliver proposed jury instructions to the trial judge, and serve them upon opposing counsel, before the first witness is sworn. CCP § 607a; *see, e.g.,* Local Rule 3.25, Los Angeles Superior Court (requiring jury instruction be submitted by final status conference before trial). Thereafter, but before the commencement of closing arguments, counsel may deliver additional proposed instructions upon questions of law developed by the evidence and not disclosed by the pleadings. CCP § 607a.

Before the commencement of the closing arguments, the court *upon request* must determine whether to give, refuse, or modify the proposed instructions; must decide what additional instructions will be given; and must advise counsel of all instructions to be given. CCP §§ 607a, 609; *see, e.g.,* Local Rule 3.172, Los Angeles Superior Court (authorizing jury instruction conference before closing arguments to settle jury instructions). If during closing arguments issues are raised which have not been covered by instructions given or refused, however, the court upon request of counsel may give additional instructions on the subject matter. § 607a. Why is the judge required to advise counsel, *before* commencement of closing arguments, of all instructions to be given? Is there any reason for counsel not to request the court to provide such information regarding instructions?

[E] Jury Verdicts

[1] *Types of Verdicts*

[a] Nonunanimous Verdicts

The jury in a civil case must consist of twelve persons, unless the parties agree upon a lesser number; but may consist of eight persons in a limited civil case if the Legislature so provides, or a lesser number if agreed upon by the parties. Art. I, § 16, Cal. Const. The California Constitution does not require a unanimous jury in civil cases; a verdict rendered by three-fourths of the jury is permitted. Art. I, § 16, Cal. Const.; CCP § 618. When a civil case is submitted to a jury for special verdicts, the same nine jurors do not have to agree on each special verdict comprising the ultimate verdict. *Resch v. Volkswagen of America, Inc.*, 36 Cal. 3d 676, 205 Cal. Rptr. 827, 685 P.2d 1178 (1984) (repudiating the "identical-nine rule").

After the jury renders a written verdict, either party may require the jury to be polled in open court. CCP § 618. A juror may change his or her vote at the time of polling. *Keener v. Jeld-Wen, Inc.*, 46 Cal. 4th 247, 256, 92 Cal. Rptr. 3d 862, 206 P.3d 403 (2009). If more than one-fourth of the jurors disagree with the verdict upon polling, the jury must be sent out again for further deliberation, "but if no disagreement in expressed, then the verdict is complete and the jury discharged from the case." CCP § 618; *see Keener, supra*, 46 Cal. 4th at 262–70 (concluding juror's silence at polling does not constitute an expressed disagreement; a party's failure to object to incomplete polling before jury is discharged forfeits any claim of irregularity in polling procedure); *Bell v. Bayerische Motoren Werke Aktiengesellschaft*, 181 Cal. App. 4th 1108, 1129–30, 105 Cal. Rptr. 3d 485 (2010) (holding that when only eight jurors voted "yes" on key special verdict question during polling, failure to object before jury discharged forfeited any challenge to this apparent defect in the verdict).

A jury in federal district court must contain at least six and no more than twelve members and, unless the parties otherwise stipulate, must reach a unanimous verdict in civil cases. Rule 48, F.R.C.P. Do you prefer the federal or the California rule on nonunanimous jury verdicts? Why? Under what circumstances might the parties in a federal trial stipulate to a nonunanimous jury?

[b] General Verdicts vs. Special Verdicts

The verdict of a jury must be either a general or a special verdict. CCP § 624. Unlike a general verdict, which merely implies findings on all issues in favor of the plaintiff or defendant, a special verdict presents to the jury each ultimate fact in the case. *Falls v. Superior Court*, 194 Cal. App. 3d 851, 854–55, 239 Cal. Rptr. 862 (1987). The jury must resolve all of the ultimate facts presented to it in the special verdict, so that "nothing shall remain to the court but to draw from them conclusions of law." CCP § 624. Under the doctrine of invited error, a party who proposes a special verdict form cannot later complain that its use misled the jury or was otherwise erroneous. *Mesecher v. Cnty. of San Diego*, 9 Cal. App. 4th 1677, 1685–87, 12 Cal. Rptr. 2d 279 (1992) (holding defendant waived its right to assert error on grounds of inconsistent verdicts where verdict form jointly drafted by parties); *Myers Bldg. Indus., Ltd. v. Interface Tech., Inc.*, 13 Cal. App. 4th 949, 960–62, 17 Cal. Rptr. 2d 242 (1993).

A party does not, however, waive the right to move for a new trial on grounds of an erroneous special verdict form proposed by another party by failing to object to the form prior to its submission to the jury. *See, e.g., Neal v. Montgomery Elevator Co.*, 7 Cal. App. 4th 1194, 1198, 9 Cal. Rptr. 2d 497 (1992) (holding failure to object to special verdict form at trial did not preclude reliance on it as basis for a new trial motion; but if trial court denied the new trial motion the failure to object may waive appellate consideration of such error); *All-West Design, Inc. v. Boozer*, 183 Cal. App. 3d 1212, 1220, 228 Cal. Rptr. 736 (1986) (ruling issue of erroneous special verdict form preserved by raising it in motion for new trial).

[c] When Special Verdicts Are Recommended or Required

Generally, the decision whether to submit a general verdict or special verdicts to the jury is entirely in the discretion of the trial court. CCP § 625; *Hurlbut v. Sonora Cmty. Hosp.*, 207 Cal. App. 3d 388, 403, 254 Cal. Rptr. 840 (1989); *Stone v. Foster*, 106 Cal. App. 3d 334, 350, 164 Cal. Rptr. 901 (1980). Use of special verdicts is required by CCP § 625, however, in all cases in which issues of punitive damages are presented to the jury so that findings of punitive damages are separate from compensatory damages. Use of special verdicts, or of a general verdict accompanied by special findings, may be necessary in other situations.

In *Gorman v. Leftwich*, 218 Cal. App. 3d 141, 266 Cal. Rptr. 671 (1990), for example, the court found an abuse of discretion where the trial court refused to use requested special verdict forms with respect to calculation of damages by the jury in a medical malpractice case. Because the case involved the possibility of substantial future damages which under CCP § 667.7 must be paid periodically and not in a lump sum, the court held improper the use of a general verdict form which did not distinguish the amounts attributable to past and future damages. *Gorman*, 218 Cal. App. 3d at 150–53; *see also American Bank & Trust Co. v. Cmty. Hosp.*, 36 Cal. 3d 359, 377, 204 Cal. Rptr. 671, 683 P.2d 670 (1984) (advising the liberal use of special verdict procedure in medical malpractice cases so that individual components of jury's future damage award can be ascertained and a periodic payment schedule knowledgeably established). The Supreme Court also recommends the use of special verdicts when the jury is asked to apportion fault on a comparative basis. *Daly v.*

Gen. Motors Corp., 20 Cal. 3d 725, 743, 144 Cal. Rptr. 380, 575 P.2d 1162 (1978). Why are special verdicts particularly useful in comparative negligence cases?

Despite their necessity in some circumstances and their recommended use in others, the judicial attitude toward special verdict forms has been lukewarm. *See, e.g., Falls v. Superior Court, supra,* 194 Cal. App. 3d at 851 (noting that the requirement that the jury must resolve every controverted issue is one of the recognized pitfalls of special verdicts); *All-West Design, Inc. v. Boozer, supra,* 183 Cal. App. 3d at 1221 (observing that it is easier to tell after the fact, rather than before, whether a special verdict is helpful).

[d] General Verdict Accompanied by Special Findings

Code of Civil Procedure §625 authorizes the trial court to direct the jury to render a general verdict accompanied by special findings upon particular issues of fact. Where a special finding of facts is inconsistent with the general verdict, the former controls the latter and the court must give judgment accordingly. CCP §625. However, the court must indulge every reasonable intendment in favor of the general verdict; the general verdict will control unless beyond possibility of reconciliation with the special finding. *Hasson v. Ford Motor Co.,* 19 Cal. 3d 530, 540–41, 138 Cal. Rptr. 705, 564 P.2d 857 (1977). Is the use of a general verdict accompanied by special findings preferable to the use of special verdicts? Why? Compare *Falls v. Superior Court, supra,* 194 Cal. App. 3d at 855 (noting that the possibility of a defective or incomplete special verdict, or possibly no verdict at all, is much greater than with a general verdict that is tested by special findings) with *Hathaway v. Spiro,* 164 Cal. App. 3d 359, 367, 210 Cal. Rptr. 421 (1985) (advising that special findings be requested of juries only when there is a compelling need to do so; their use should otherwise be discouraged).

§ 13.03 Trial Without a Jury

[A] Order of Proceedings

Ordinarily, unless the court directs otherwise, the trial of a civil action by the court without a jury will proceed in the same order as in a jury trial. CCP §§607, 631.7. The lack of a jury obviously eliminates the need for jury voir dire, jury instructions, and other jury-related procedures; and may reduce (but not eliminate) the need for opening statements, closing arguments, sidebar conferences, and strict adherence to some of the rules of evidence. But in most other respects, a nonjury trial follows the familiar sequence of a jury trial.

The trial judge is the trier of fact in a nonjury trial and therefore may determine the credibility of witnesses, resolve conflicting evidence, and draw inferences from the evidence. *See, e.g., Hellman v. La Cumbre Gulf & Country Club,* 6 Cal. App. 4th 1224, 1229, 8 Cal. Rptr. 2d 293 (1992); *Davis v. Kahn,* 7 Cal. App. 3d 868, 874, 86 Cal. Rptr. 872 (1970). As discussed below, the trial judge must also announce a tentative decision and, if requested, render a statement of decision. CCP § 632. Other differences from a jury trial may also apply. For example, in ruling on a motion for new trial, the court may modify the statement of decision or the judgment, may reopen the case for further proceedings and introduction of additional evidence, or may grant a new trial. CCP § 662.

[B] Motion for Judgment

After a party has completed her presentation of evidence in a nonjury trial, the other party—without waiving his right to offer evidence in support of his defense or in rebuttal in the event the motion is not granted—may move for a judgment. CCP § 631.8(a). The court as the trier of facts must weigh the evidence, and may exercise its prerogatives as a fact finder by refusing to believe witnesses and by drawing conclusions at odds with expert opinion. § 631.8(a); *Kirk Corp. v. First Nat'l Title Co.*, 220 Cal. App. 3d 785, 806, 270 Cal. Rptr. 24 (1990).

If the court grants the motion and renders a judgment, the court must make a statement of decision. CCP § 631.8(a). What is the purpose of the motion for judgment? *See Heap v. Gen. Motors Corp.*, 66 Cal. App. 3d 824, 829, 136 Cal. Rptr. 304 (1977). Why is a trial court *required* to make a statement of decision when it enters judgment pursuant to such motion, but not when it enters a final judgment after hearing all the evidence?

[C] Statement of Decision

A superior court, in a nonjury trial not completed within one day, must announce a tentative decision by written or oral statement. Rule 3.1590(a), Cal. Rules of Ct. This tentative decision does not constitute the judgment and is not binding on the court. Rule 3.1590(b); *see, e.g., Marriage of Ditto*, 206 Cal. App. 3d 643, 646, 253 Cal. Rptr. 770 (1988) (holding trial court not bound by its statement of intended decision and may enter a wholly different judgment than the one tentatively announced); *Slavin v. Borinstein*, 25 Cal. App. 4th 713, 718–719, 30 Cal. Rptr. 2d 745 (1994) (ruling trial court has the option to direct that intended decision will become a statement of decision). Any party may request a statement of decision within 10 days after the court announces its tentative decision. CCP § 632, Rule 3.1590(d), Cal. Rules of Ct.

When the trial is concluded in less than one day, the request must be made prior to the submission of the matter for decision. § 632; Rule 3.1590(n); *see, e.g., Marriage of Gray*, 103 Cal. App. 4th 974, 127 Cal. Rptr. 2d 271 (2002) (finding request untimely because not made prior to submission of the matter to trial court in one-day trial); *Khan v. Med. Bd.*, 12 Cal. App. 4th 1834, 1840, 16 Cal. Rptr. 2d 385 (1993) (ruling failure to prepare statement of decision after one-day trial not error where appellant failed to make request prior to matter being submitted). If a party timely requests a statement of decision, the court must then follow the procedures for preparation of the proposed statement, objections, and judgment detailed in Rule 3.1590(c)–(m).

If a statement of decision is not requested, the court must merely prepare a proposed judgment following the procedures outlined in Rule 1590(h)–(i) and eventually file the judgment. The judgment so filed constitutes the decision upon which judgment is entered pursuant to CCP § 664. Rule 3.1590(h).

A trial judge's failure to prepare a written statement of decision upon timely request may constitute reversible error. *See, e.g., Whittington v. McKinney*, 234 Cal. App. 3d 123, 285 Cal. Rptr. 586 (1991) (concluding judge's failure to prepare written statement upon timely request is reversible error, unless parties agree to oral statement); *Marriage of Ananeh-Firempong*, 219 Cal. App. 3d 272, 282, 268 Cal. Rptr. 83 (1990) (ruling trial court committed reversible error in failing to render a statement of decision on issue of valuation of husband's medical practice). However, § 632 only requires a trial court to state ultimate rather than evidentiary facts; only when the court "fails to make findings on a material issue which would fairly disclose the trial court's determination would reversible error result." *Sperber v. Robinson*, 26 Cal. App. 4th 736, 745, 31 Cal. Rptr. 2d 659 (1994); *Hellman v. La Cumbre Golf & Country Club*, 6 Cal. App. 4th 1224, 1230, 8 Cal. Rptr. 2d 293 (1992) (citing cases). If the trial judge issues a statement of decision which does not resolve a controverted issue or is ambiguous, the defect must be brought to the attention of the trial court. CCP § 634. Failure to timely object to omissions or other defects constitutes a waiver of the error on appeal. *Marriage of Arceneaux*, 51 Cal. 3d 1130, 275 Cal. Rptr. 797, 800 P.2d 1227 (1990); *Sperber v. Robinson, supra*, 26 Cal. App. 4th at 744.

What are the purposes of a statement of decision? Why is it beneficial to the parties at the trial court level? At the appellate court level? Why would a party not want to request a statement of decision? Rule 52 of the Federal Rules of Civil Procedure directs a federal district judge to make findings of fact and conclusions of law in all nonjury trials when entering judgment. Federal Rule 52 imposes this obligation without the necessity of a request. In light of the benefits of a statement of decision, does the California prerequisite of a request by a party make sense? How so?

A statement of decision may be essential to meaningful appellate review of the judgment in a nonjury trial. In the absence of a statement of decision, the appellate court will presume that the trial court made all factual findings necessary to support the judgment for which substantial evidence exists in the record. *See, e.g., Slavin v. Borinstein, supra*, 25 Cal. App. 4th at 718; *Marriage of Ditto, supra*, 206 Cal. App. 3d at 647. What is the likely consequence of such a presumption? *See* § 15.01 [D], Appeals, Scope of Appellate Review, *infra*.

§ 13.04 Judicial Supervision of Jury Decisions

[A] Nonsuit and Directed Verdict

[1] *Nonsuit upon Completion of Plaintiff's Evidence*

A defendant may move for a judgment of nonsuit upon completion of plaintiff's opening statement or presentation of plaintiff's evidence in a jury trial. CCP § 581c(a).

If the motion is granted, the judgment of nonsuit operates as an adjudication on the merits unless the court specifies otherwise. CCP § 581c(c). The court may grant the motion as to some or all issues in the action; if granted partially the trial must proceed as to the remaining issues. § 581c(b). *See, e.g., Seimon v. Southern Pac. Transp. Co.*, 67 Cal. App. 3d 600, 606–609, 136 Cal. Rptr. 787 (1977) (concluding trial court erred in granting partial nonsuit as to one cause of action which removed punitive damages issues from jury's consideration because sufficient evidence to support inference of malice). If the motion is denied, the defendant still has the right to offer evidence. § 581c(a).

A motion for nonsuit is tantamount to a demurrer to the evidence by which a defendant contests the sufficiency of plaintiff's evidence before presenting his or her own. *Carson v. Facilities Dev. Co.*, 36 Cal. 3d 830, 831, 206 Cal. Rptr. 136, 686 P.2d 656 (1984). In making this evaluation of the plaintiff's evidence, the trial court must not weigh the evidence or judge the credibility of witnesses. *See, e.g., Campell v. Gen. Motors Corp.*, 32 Cal. 3d 112, 118, 184 Cal. Rptr. 891, 649 P.2d 224 (1982); *Stewart v. Truck Ins. Exch.*, 17 Cal. App. 4th, 468, 481, 21 Cal. Rptr. 2d 338 (1993).

Nonsuit is proper if a plaintiff presents insufficient evidence on an element of the case or if the plaintiff's evidence establishes an affirmative defense that defeats the cause of action. *See, e.g., Brimmer v. Cal. Charter Med., Inc.*, 180 Cal. App. 3d 678, 225 Cal. Rptr. 752 (1986) (upholding nonsuit as to some defendants because no substantial evidence of their participation in alleged malpractice); *Brezeal v. Henry Mayo Newhall Mem. Hosp.*, 234 Cal. App. 3d 1329, 1337, 286 Cal. Rptr. 207 (1991) (holding nonsuit properly granted on grounds that plaintiff's evidence established affirmative defense of good samaritan immunity).

The standard governing a motion for nonsuit at the close of plaintiff's evidence is typically stated as follows:

> "A defendant is entitled to a nonsuit if the trial court determines that, as a matter of law, the evidence presented by plaintiff is insufficient to permit a jury to find in his favor. [Citation.] 'In determining whether plaintiff's evidence is sufficient, the court may not weigh the evidence or consider the credibility of witnesses. Instead, the evidence most favorable to plaintiff must be accepted as true and conflicting evidence must be disregarded. The court must give "to the plaintiff['s] evidence all the value to which it is legally entitled, ... indulging every legitimate inference which may be drawn from the evidence in plaintiff['s] favor.' [Citation.] A mere 'scintilla of evidence' does not create a conflict for the jury's resolution; 'there must be *substantial evidence* to create the necessary conflict.' [Citation.] [¶] In reviewing a grant of nonsuit, [an appellate court is] 'guided by the same rule.... ' [Citation.]"

Nally v. Grace Cmty. Church, 47 Cal. 3d 278, 291, 253 Cal. Rptr. 97, 763 P.2d 948 (1988).

After a motion for nonsuit is made in a jury trial, the trial court ordinarily must, if so requested, permit the plaintiff to reopen its case and introduce further evidence to cure the defects in its case. *See, e.g., Abreu v. Svenhard's Swedish Bakery*, 208 Cal. App. 3d 1446, 257 Cal. Rptr. 26 (1989) (ruling refusal to permit plaintiff to present additional evidence after nonsuit motion must be prejudicial to warrant reversal); *Huang v. Garner*, 157 Cal. App. 3d 404, 416–418, 203 Cal. Rptr. 800 (1984) (reversing nonsuit where trial court refused to allow plaintiff to reopen his case). Denial of a request to reopen may be proper, however, if the plaintiff fails to specify what additional evidence would be presented and how the additional evidence would cure the defects in the case. *See, e.g., Consolidated World Inv., Inc. v. Lido Preferred Ltd.*, 9 Cal. App. 4th 373, 11 Cal. Rptr. 2d 524 (1992) (concluding where plaintiff made no offer of proof as to nature and relevance of additional evidence, vague request to reopen properly denied).

When a nonsuit motion is granted in an action for injury to persons or property on the basis that a defendant was without fault, CCP § 581c(d) prohibits any other defendant during trial, over plaintiff's objection, from attempting to attribute fault to, or commenting on the absence of involvement of, the defendant who was granted the nonsuit. What are the reasons for this prohibition?

[2] Nonsuit Upon Completion of Opening Statement

A trial court may properly grant a motion for nonsuit immediately after the completion of the plaintiff's opening statement "where it appears that counsel for the plaintiff has stated all the facts that he expects to prove and that these would not make a prima facie case." *Dameshghi v. Texaco Refining & Mktg.*, 3 Cal. App. 4th 1262, 1286, 6 Cal. Rptr. 2d 515 (1992) (affirming nonsuit after opening statement and quoting *John Norton Farms, Inc. v. Todagco*, 124 Cal. App. 3d 149, 160, 177 Cal. Rptr. 215 (1981). Such a nonsuit is warranted only when the trial court can conclude, from all the facts stated and inferences to be drawn, that there will be no evidence of sufficient substantiality to support a judgment in favor of the plaintiff. *Willis v. Gordon*, 20 Cal. 3d 629, 633, 143 Cal. Rptr. 723, 574 P.2d 794 (1978) (reversing nonsuit because opening statement contained facts from which jury could reasonably draw inference of negligence).

Because a motion for nonsuit after plaintiff's opening statement is designed to call attention to correctable defects, granting such a motion is proper only where it is clear that counsel has stated all of the facts she expects to prove. *Hamilton v. Gage Bowl, Inc.*, 6 Cal. App. 4th 1706, 1710, 8 Cal. Rptr. 2d 819 (1992) (affirming nonsuit after opening statement where record disclosed that plaintiff's counsel given every opportunity to state all of the facts he hoped to prove); *John Norton Farms, supra*, 124 Cal. App. 3d at 161. Judges are understandably reluctant to grant nonsuits at this stage and will usually afford counsel an opportunity for a supplemental opening statement. *See, e.g., Jensen v. Hewlett-Packard Co.*, 14 Cal. App. 4th 958, 18 Cal. Rptr. 2d 83 (1993) (affirming nonsuit where defendant moved for nonsuit again after supplemental opening statement because plaintiff still failed to state prima facie libel case); *Freeman v. Lind*, 181 Cal. App. 3d 791, 226 Cal. Rptr. 515 (1986) (observing that although a disfavored practice, nonsuit after plaintiff's opening statement affirmed as to two defendants and reversed as to another).

[3] Directed Verdict

After all parties have completed the presentation of all their evidence in a jury trial, any party may move for an order directing entry of a verdict in its favor. CCP § 630(a). Except for this difference in timing, a directed verdict is equivalent to a nonsuit. The test for directing a verdict is the same as for entering a nonsuit. *See, e.g., Newing v. Cheatham*, 15 Cal. 3d 351, 358–359, 124 Cal. Rptr. 193, 540 P.2d 33 (1975) (ruling a directed verdict may be granted against a party when there is no evidence of sufficient substantiality to support a verdict in favor of such party); *Estate of Lances*, 216 Cal. 397, 400, 14 P.2d 768 (1932) (noting the power of the court to direct a verdict is absolutely the same as the power to grant a nonsuit). As with a nonsuit, the court may grant a directed verdict as to some but not all issues, the directed verdict operates as an adjudication on the merits unless otherwise specified, other defendants are prohibited from attributing fault to, or commenting on the absence of, a defendant who was granted a directed verdict, and a motion for directed verdict does not constitute a waiver of the right to jury determination if the motion is not granted. CCP § 630(b)–(d). Despite these similarities, a trial court is far more reluctant to direct a verdict at the close of all the evidence than to grant a nonsuit at the end of a plaintiff's case. Why?

When a jury has been discharged without rendering a verdict, the court within 30 days may order judgment to be entered in favor of a party whenever a motion for directed verdict for that party should have been granted had a previous motion been made during trial. CCP § 630(f). What are the reasons for this power? For the 30-day expiration of this power?

[4] Motion for Mistrial

A motion for mistrial requests the court to terminate the trial prior to a verdict for error too prejudicial to correct by admonition to the jury. CEB, *California Trial Practice: Civil Procedure During Trial* § 18.83 (3d ed. 2016). Grounds for mistrial may be any misconduct or irregularity that prevents a party from having a fair trial. *California Trial Practice, supra,* at § 18.85 (citing examples and authorities); 7 Witkin, *California Procedure* § 167 (5th ed. 2008) (citing cases). Many motions for mistrial are based on some of the same grounds as those supporting a motion for new trial after the verdict. *California Trial Practice, supra* at §§ 18.85–18.99. Counsel should move for a mistrial immediately after the misconduct or irregularity occurs. *Id.* at § 18.90. Delay or failure to object, request an admonition to the jury, and move for mistrial may constitute a waiver of the right to a mistrial. *Id.* at § 18.90; *see Horn v. Atchison, Topeka & Santa Fe Ry. Co.,* 61 Cal. 2d 602, 610, 39 Cal. Rptr. 721, 394 P.2d 561 (1964) (holding defendant's failure to make timely objections and request jury admonitions during trial waived right to request mistrial after plaintiff's closing argument).

Some statutes require a judge to grant a mistrial in certain specified circumstances, such as where the jury is discharged without rendering a verdict, CCP § 616; or where a juror is discharged and no alternate juror is available and the parties do not consent to proceed with only the remaining jurors, CCP § 233. In the absence of such a statutory directive, the trial judge has broad discretion to grant or deny the motion. *Warner v. O'Connor*, 199 Cal. App. 2d 770, 18 Cal. Rptr. 902 (1962). Is a judge likely to grant a motion for mistrial? Why not?

[B] Judgment Notwithstanding the Verdict (JNOV)
Code of Civil Procedure § 629 (2016)

(a) The court, before the expiration of its power to rule on a motion for a new trial, either of its own motion, after five days' notice, or on motion of a party against whom a verdict has been rendered, shall render judgment in favor of the aggrieved party notwithstanding the verdict whenever a motion for a directed verdict for the aggrieved party should have been granted had a previous motion been made.

(b) A motion for judgment notwithstanding the verdict shall be made within the period specified by Section 659 of this code in respect of the filing and serving of notice of intention to move for a new trial. * * * The making of a motion for judgment notwithstanding the verdict shall not extend the time within which a party may file and serve notice of intention to move for a new trial. The court shall not rule upon the motion for judgment notwithstanding the verdict until the expiration of the time within which a motion for a new trial must be served and filed, and if a motion for a new trial has been filed with the court by the aggrieved party, the court shall rule upon both motions at the same time. The power of the court to rule on a motion for judgment notwithstanding the verdict shall not extend beyond the last date upon which it has the power to rule on a motion for a new trial. If a motion for judgment notwithstanding the verdict is not determined before such date, the effect shall be a denial of such motion without further order of the court. * * *

Clemmer v. Hartford Insurance Co.
Supreme Court of California
22 Cal. 3d 865, 151 Cal. Rptr. 285, 587 P.2d 1098 (1978)

[Plaintiff Clemmer, the widow of murder victim Dr. Clemmer, filed an action against the slayer's insurer based on a policy of indemnity insurance, following the insured's conviction of murder and a judgment in plaintiffs' favor in a wrongful death action against the insured. The defendant insurer, Hartford Insurance Company, defended on the ground that the loss arose from a wilful act for which the insurer was not liable under the exclusion contained in its policy and Insurance Code § 533. The jury returned a special verdict that the insured, Dr. Lovelace, lacked the mental capacity to govern his own conduct and therefore that Dr. Clemmer's death was not caused by a wilful act of the insured. Judgment was entered accordingly in favor of the plaintiff in the sum of $1,953,480. Defendant Hartford moved for a judgment notwithstanding the verdict, and for a new trial, asserting the insufficiency of the evidence to support the jury's verdict. The trial court denied the motion for a judgment notwithstanding the verdict, but vacated the jury's verdict and judgment and granted the motion for a new trial on the sole issue of whether the death was caused by a wilful act. Plaintiff appealed from the order granting a limited new trial, and defendant appealed from the order denying its motion for judgment notwithstanding the verdict.]

SUFFICIENCY OF THE EVIDENCE TO SUPPORT VERDICT AND JUDGMENT THAT THE KILLING OF DR. CLEMMER WAS NOT WILFUL-DENIAL OF MOTION FOR JUDGMENT NOTWITHSTANDING THE VERDICT

Hartford contends that the evidence as a matter of law compels the conclusions that Dr. Lovelace was possessed of his mental faculties when he killed Dr. Clemmer, and that therefore the trial court should have granted a judgment for Hartford notwithstanding the verdict.

In *Hauter v. Zogarts* (1975) 14 Cal. 3d 104, 110–111 [120 Cal. Rptr. 681, 534 P.2d 377] we said: "The trial judge's power to grant a judgment notwithstanding the verdict is identical to his power to grant a directed verdict [citations]. The trial judge cannot reweigh the evidence [citation], or judge the credibility of witnesses. [Citation.] If the evidence is conflicting or if several reasonable inferences may be drawn, the motion for judgment notwithstanding the verdict should be denied. [Citations.] 'A motion for judgment notwithstanding the verdict of a jury may properly be granted only if it appears from the evidence, viewed in the light most favorable to the party securing the verdict, that there is no substantial evidence to support the verdict. If there is any substantial evidence, or reasonable inferences to be drawn therefrom, in support of the verdict, the motion should be denied.' (*Bradenburg v. Pac. Gas & Elec. Co.* (1946) 28 Cal. 2d 282, 284 [169 P.2d 909].)"

Hartford's claim that there is no substantial evidence to support the verdict rests upon its contention that the testimony of Dr. Anselen, plaintiffs' psychiatric expert, was rendered absurd by certain internal inconsistencies, and that therefore that testimony must be disregarded. The record reflects that Dr. Anselen testified, on the one hand, that Dr. Lovelace had the mental capacity to know what he was doing and to know the nature and quality of his acts, but he also testified that Dr. Lovelace was a paranoid personality throughout his professional life, that he suffered an acute paranoid episode when Dr. Clemmer sought to terminate their professional relationship, and that Dr. Lovelace, at the time he shot Dr. Clemmer, did not have the mental capacity to deliberate and premeditate or to form the specific intent to shoot and harm the victim and did not understand the consequences of his act, being then directed by paranoid delusions.

Even if it be assumed that there are logical inconsistencies in the foregoing testimony—a matter which we need not here reach—the fact that inconsistencies may occur in the testimony of a given witness does not require that such testimony be disregarded in its entirety for the purposes of a motion for judgment notwithstanding the verdict, nor does it mean that such testimony is necessarily insufficient to support the verdict. It is for the trier of fact to consider internal inconsistencies in testimony, to resolve them if this is possible, and to determine what weight should be given to such testimony. The motion for judgment notwithstanding the verdict was properly denied. * * *

CONTENTIONS OF PLAINTIFFS REGARDING THE PROPRIETY OF GRANTING HARTFORD'S MOTION FOR NEW TRIAL

Plaintiffs contend that the specifications given by the trial court in support of its order granting a new trial were insufficient. Code of Civil Procedure section 657 provides: "When a new trial is granted, on all or part of the issues, the court shall specify the ground or grounds upon which it is granted and the court's reason or reasons for granting the new trial upon each ground stated." Here the trial judge filed a five-page memorandum setting forth his reasons for the new trial. Specifically he dealt with Dr. Lovelace's state of mind and raised substantial questions concerning the testimony of the experts relating thereto, particularly that of Dr. Anselen compared with that of Dr. DiNolfo, stating that he "rejec[ted] the opinions of Dr. Anselen, which would exonerate Dr. Lovelace from the ability to know and recognize the nature of his act and to control his conduct, as being absurd. Aside from these ill-founded opinions, there is no support for the jury's finding. I am satisfied that if the action had been between two individuals, rather than a widow and fatherless child against an insurance company, a different result would have been reached by the jury."

Specifications for new trial are sufficient if they make a record sufficiently precise to permit meaningful review. Specifications are insufficient if simply couched in the form of conclusions or statement of ultimate fact.

Here plaintiffs' attack is basically one of factual disagreement with the court's reasons for disbelieving evidence of Dr. Lovelace's lack of wilfulness. Such a factual disagreement is not adequate to show that the specifications for new trial were insufficient. The record reflects that detailed reasons were given for the trial court's decision and that the specifications reflected deliberation on the part of the trial judge such as to give this court a meaningful picture of what prompted the new trial order. The statutory purposes have thus been served.

It is next contended that a trial court's power to grant a new trial on the ground of insufficiency of the evidence (Code Civ. Proc., § 657, subd. 6) deprives plaintiffs of their right to jury trial guaranteed by article I, section 16 of the California Constitution. This attack, however, comes too late in the jurisprudential day. It has long been held that the right to jury trial is not violated by the power in question. More recently we again passed upon this point in *Dorsey v. Barba* (1952) 38 Cal. 2d 350, 358 [240 P.2d 604].

We also find wanting plaintiffs' claim that Code of Civil Procedure section 657 violates due process (Cal. Const., art. I, § 7; U.S. Const., Amend. XIV, § 1). It is but another statement of their jury trial argument discussed above, and for that reason we discuss it no further. * * *

We conclude on the basis of the foregoing that ... the orders granting a limited new trial and denying judgment notwithstanding the verdict must be affirmed....

[1] JNOV vs. New Trial Order

The trial judge's power to grant a judgment notwithstanding the verdict is the same as its power to grant a nonsuit or to direct a verdict; these powers are merely different aspects of the same judicial function and are governed by the same rules. *Reynolds v. Wilson*, 51 Cal. 2d 94, 99, 331 P.2d 48 (1958); *Beavers v. Allstate Ins. Co.*, 225 Cal. App. 3d 310, 327, 274 Cal. Rptr. 766 (1990) (citing cases). *Clemmer v. Hartford Ins. Co.*, reproduced *supra*, illustrates that, as with nonsuits and directed verdicts, the trial judge in granting JNOV must not weigh the evidence nor judge the credibility of witnesses. *See, e.g., Saari v. Jongordon Corp.*, 5 Cal. App. 4th 797, 7 Cal. Rptr. 2d 82 (1992) (ruling JNOV motion properly denied where substantial evidence to support jury verdict); *Osborn v. Irwin Mem. Blood Bank*, 5 Cal. App. 4th 234, 7 Cal. Rptr. 2d 101 (1992) (advising that in granting a JNOV motion, the court must not weigh conflicting expert opinions); *Czubinsky v. Doctors Hosp.*, 139 Cal. App. 3d 361, 188 Cal. Rptr. 685 (1983) (holding trial court erred in granting JNOV for defendant in medical malpractice action even though essential facts not in dispute; whether hospital failed to meet standard of care is decision for jury).

Clemmer also illustrates that a trial judge may, however, make such "reweighing" determinations when granting a motion for new trial on the ground of insufficiency of the evidence. Why is a trial judge permitted to reweigh the evidence in granting certain types of new trial motions but not JNOV motions?

[2] Partial JNOV

May a trial judge enter a partial JNOV to reduce excessive damages? *See, e.g., Dell'Oca v. Bank of New York Trust Co.*, 159 Cal. App. 4th 531, 553–54, 71 Cal. Rptr. 3d 737 (2008) (noting a trial court has the power, in appropriate circumstances, to grant partial JNOV); *Beavers v. Allstate Ins. Co.*, 225 Cal. App. 3d 310, 274, Cal. Rptr. 766 (1990) (ruling a trial judge's power on a motion for JNOV is not an "all-or-nothing proposition," and the judge may grant a JNOV motion on some but not all damages issues or causes of action in a case); *but see Teitel v. First L. A. Bank*, 231 Cal. App. 3d 1593, 282 Cal. Rptr. 916 (1991) (concluding the remittitur procedure of CCP § 662.5(b) is the exclusive remedy for a trial judge to employ where some damages are properly awarded, but the amount is excessive).

[3] Time Limits for JNOV Motion

Section 629 requires that a JNOV motion be filed within the time periods specified in CCP § 659 governing new trial motions. Section 659 prescribes that, after the decision is rendered, a party must file a notice of motion "[w]ithin 15 days of the date of mailing notice of entry of judgment by the clerk of the court pursuant to Section 664.5, or service upon him or her by any party of written notice of entry of judgment, or within 180 days after the entry of judgment, whichever is earliest." A trial court lacks jurisdiction to consider an untimely JNOV motion. *See, e.g., Younesi v. Lane*, 228 Cal. App. 3d 967, 279 Cal. Rptr. 89 (1991) (holding trial court lacked jurisdiction to hear plaintiff's JNOV motion filed more than 15 days after the clerk mailed copies of the minute order and judgment to plaintiff). The 15-day time limit has been held inapplicable to a JNOV motion initiated by the court as opposed to a party. *Sturgeon v. Levitt*, 94 Cal. App. 3d 957, 156 Cal. Rptr. 687 (1979). Is this a proper reading of CCP § 659?

[4] JNOV Motions Integrally Related to New Trial Motions

Section 629 expresses the legislative policy that a motion for judgment NOV be made within the same time frame allotted for a motion for new trial, and that these two motions be considered and decided together. Moreover, the power the court to rule on a JNOV motion does not extend past the same 60-day time limit within which it has the power to rule on a new trial motion, as specified in sections 629, 659, and 660. *See, e.g., Pratt v. Vencor, Inc.*, 105 Cal. App. 4th 905, 129 Cal. Rptr. 2d 741 (2003). Why did the Legislature make these two types of post-trial motions so integrally related? *See Foggy v. Ralph F. Clark & Assoc., Inc.*, 192 Cal. App. 3d 1204, 1212, 238 Cal. Rptr. 130 (1987).

Because these post-trial motions are integrally related substantively as well as procedurally, parties typically file both motions when challenging an unfavorable jury verdict. Appeals from the trial court's determinations of these motions present some interesting problems. If the trial court denies both motions and the appellate court subsequently rules that the JNOV motion should have been granted, the appellate court must order that judgment be so entered. CCP § 629 (c); *see Bank of America v. Superior Court*, 220 Cal. App. 3d 613, 269 Cal. Rptr. 596 (1990), *cert. denied*, 498 U.S. 1087 (1990) (ruling the effect of CCP § 629 is that reversal on appeal concludes the litigation just as it would have if the trial court had correctly entered the judgment NOV). If the trial court grants both motions made by the same party, what is the effect of a reversal of the NOV but not the new trial order by an appellate court? *See* CCP § 629 (d).

[5] Judgment as a Matter of Law (JNOV) in Federal Court

A federal trial court has authority to grant a motion for judgment notwithstanding the verdict where the court finds that "a reasonable jury would not have a legally sufficient evidentiary basis to find for the party." Rule 50, F.R.C.P. By a 1991 revision of Rule 50, the familiar terminology has been replaced by the term "judgment as a matter of law." A motion for directed verdict is now a pre-verdict motion for "judgment as a matter of law," and a JNOV motion is a post-verdict "renewed" motion for "judgment as a matter of law."

Federal Rule 50 also provides, as a prerequisite to a post-verdict "renewed motion" (i.e., a JNOV motion), that the party made the motion for judgment as a matter of law (*i.e.*, a motion for directed verdict) before submission of the case to the jury. What are the reasons for this requirement? *See* Notes of Advisory Committee on 1991 Amendment to Rule 50, F.R.C.P. A motion for directed verdict is not a prerequisite for a motion for a judgment notwithstanding the verdict in the California courts. *See* CCP § 629.

[C] Impeachment of Verdict for Juror Misconduct

Smoketree-Lake Murray, Ltd. v. Mills Concrete Construction Co.

Court of Appeal of California, Fourth Appellate District
234 Cal. App. 3d 1724, 286 Cal. Rptr. 435 (1991)

KREMER, JUSTICE.

Smoketree-Lake Murray, Ltd., Brehm Construction Company and Forrest W. Brehm (hereafter Developer) appeal a judgment on a cross-claim for indemnification. On appeal, Developer contends the judgment must be reversed because the trial court erred in ruling a fraud finding barred indemnification and failing to find the jury committed misconduct. We reverse.

FACTS

In 1985, the Smoketree-Lake Murray Owners' Association, Inc., sued Developer and others for damage to their condominium complex. These damages manifested themselves as cracks in walls and slabs, doors which would not close properly, patios which pulled away from buildings and cracks causing leaks in the complex's swimming pool. Developer eventually settled with the Association for over $3 million.

Developer cross-complained for indemnification against various subcontractors including Calego Excavating Company (Calego), which performed the grading work, and Mills Concrete Construction Company, Inc. (Mills), which did the concrete work. In defense, Mills and Calego contended Developer's fraud, in making misrepresentations and concealing information from the condominium purchasers, barred Developer from obtaining indemnity. Developer also raised a fraud issue, contending the subcontractors had fraudulently induced Developer to enter into narrower indemnity agreements.

The trial court, ruling a finding of fraud would preclude indemnification, bifurcated the trial.

At trial, there was evidence presented that the damage to the condominiums and pool was caused, in part, by soil movement. The soil may not have been properly compacted by Calego or properly tested by Southern California Testing Laboratory (SOCAL), the soils expert hired by Developer. There was also evidence that the concrete slabs were improperly constructed. Among other things, there was evidence that the concrete used was of inadequate quality, contained too much water and that the slabs were poured too thin. * * *

DISCUSSION

INDEMNIFICATION

As we explain below, we hold a jury's finding Developer made misrepresentations to or concealed information from third parties does not negate the express indemnity agreements entered into between Developer and the subcontractors. * * *

JUROR MISCONDUCT

Developer contends the trial court erred in denying its motion for a new trial based on juror misconduct. Developer contends: (1) one of the jurors committed prejudicial misconduct by performing an experiment on pouring concrete and (2) the jurors improperly modified one of the fraud instructions. * * *

Code of Civil Procedure section 657 provides "a new trial may be granted where the substantial rights of a party are materially affected by misconduct or irregularity in the proceedings of the jury." (*Tapia v. Barker* (1984) 160 Cal. App. 3d 761, 765 [206 Cal. Rptr. 803].)

Under Evidence Code section 1150, subdivision (a),

> "Upon an inquiry as to the validity of a verdict, any otherwise admissible evidence may be received as to statements made, or conduct, conditions, or events occurring, either within or without the jury room, of such a character as is likely to have influenced the verdict improperly. No evidence is admissible to show the effect of such statement, conduct, condition, or event upon a juror either in influencing him to assent to or dissent from the verdict or concerning the mental processes by which it was determined."

The Supreme Court has explained, "[t]he only improper influences that may be proved under [Evidence Code] section 1150 to impeach a verdict ... are those open to sight, hearing, and the other senses and thus subject to corroboration. [Citations.]" (*People v. Hutchinson* (1969) 71 Cal. 2d 342, 350 [78 Cal. Rptr. 196, 455 P.2d 132], *cert. den.* 396 U.S. 994, 24 L. Ed. 2d 457, 90 S. Ct. 491.) The "distinction between proof of overt acts, objectively ascertainable, and proof of the subjective reasoning processes of the individual juror, which can be neither corroborated nor disproved, ... has been the basic limitation on proof set by the leading decisions allowing jurors to impeach their verdicts. [Citations.]" (*Id.* at p. 349.)

As we explained in *Ford v. Bennacka* (1990) 226 Cal. App. 3d 330, 333–334 [276 Cal. Rptr. 513]:

> "[Evidence Code s]ection 1150 'does not envision a procedure whereby a trial judge, as a result of a claim of jury misconduct, reviews a "replay" of the particular language used by various jurors as they deliberated and makes a subjective determination of its propriety. Such a procedure would be too great an extension of the court's limited authority to invade the traditionally inviolate nature of the jury proceedings.' [Citation.] 'If there is one thing which is clear from the language of Evidence Code section 1150 and the case law dealing with the subject, it is that the mental processes of the jurors are beyond the hindsight probing of the trial court.' (*Maple v. Cincinnati, Inc.* (1985) 163 Cal. App. 3d 387, 394....)"

Jury misconduct raises a presumption of prejudice, and unless the presumption is rebutted, a new trial should be granted. (*In re Stankewitz* (1985) 40 Cal. 3d 391, 402 [220 Cal. Rptr. 382, 708 P.2d 1260].) "In reviewing the denial of a motion for new trial based on jury misconduct, the appellate court 'has a constitutional obligation [citation] to review the entire record, including the evidence, and to determine independently whether the act of misconduct, if it occurred, prevented the complaining party from having a fair trial.' [Citations.]" (*Tapia v. Barker, supra,* 160 Cal. App. 3d 761, 765.)

A. *Experiment by Juror Rizzo*

Juror Rizzo used a small box, filled with "kitty litter," and some crayons to demonstrate how concrete was poured.[16] In conducting the demonstration, Rizzo explained she knew about concrete construction practice from discussions with her family. In the course of the demonstration, Rizzo told the jury "how the inconsistencies in the sand—on top of which the concrete is placed—can be caused by the footprints of people walking back and forth across the building pad before the concrete is poured."

It is well established it is misconduct for a juror to conduct an independent investigation of the facts, to bring outside evidence into the jury room, to inject his or her own expertise into the jury's deliberation or to engage in an experiment which produces new evidence. (See *People v. Pierce* (1979) 24 Cal. 3d 199, 207 [155 Cal. Rptr. 657, 595 P.2d 91]; *People v. Cooper* (1979) 95 Cal. App. 3d 844, 853–854 [157 Cal. Rptr. 348].)

Our Supreme Court has explained:

> "[The jury] may carry out experiments within the lines of offered evidence, but if their experiments shall invade new fields and they shall be influenced in their verdict by discoveries from such experiments which will not fall fairly within the scope of purview of the evidence, then, manifestly, the jury has been itself taking evidence without the knowledge of either party, evidence which it is not possible for the party injured to meet, answer, or explain." (*Higgins v. L. A. Gas & Electric Co.* (1911) 159 Cal. 651, 657 [115 P. 313].)

Cases which have held jury experiments did not require reversal include People v. Cooper, *supra*, 95 Cal. App. 3d 844, and *Locksley v. Ungureanu* (1986) 178 Cal. App. 3d 457 [223 Cal. Rptr. 737]. [17]

---

16. In her declaration, Rizzo stated: "On the first day of deliberations, October 13, 1988, the jurors talked about how the slabs were built. One of the jurors, Diane, drew a picture of the forms for a slab, and looking around there were quite a few of the jurors who said and showed that they did not understand. So, three o'clock the next morning, I woke up and it came to me in my sleep I guess, how the forms look for a slab. So I got a small cardboard box, which my checks come in, and filled it partially with kitty litter and some broken crayolas. That morning I brought in with me a newspaper and my box of kitty litter and a box of crayolas. When we started to deliberate again, I asked for the floor. I asked if I may show them, like a show and tell, as to the picture that Diane had drawn. There were no objections.

"I then stated several times that this was in no way evidence for or against any one person, and there was no objections. So then I spread the paper on the table (didn't want to spill cat litter on table) and opened the box and took out the crayolas and I smoothed out the cat litter and the difference from the top of the box to where the cat litter was, I said that we would assume that this was the forms for the slab, and that the outside of the box we would say, that that was the trenches for the foundation. Then I said that the plumbers and/or other people that had to do anything to the ground before the slabs were poured, the plumbers would dig a trench for their pipes. So then I laid the crayolas down as the plumber's pipes and I had a couple of them sticking up above the forms and after this was done, they had to wait for the city inspector. And when the inspector passed the plumbing and the forms, then either the plumbers or someone else would come in and fill up the plumbing trenches and then they would come in and pour the slabs."

17. See also *Wagner v. Doulton* (1980) 112 Cal. App. 3d 945 [169 Cal. Rptr. 550], involving the drawing of a diagram of an accident scene by a juror who was also an engineer. The court found no misconduct because the diagram was based solely on the information presented during the trial and

In *Cooper*, the jury conducted an experiment on the way the defendant had thrown some contraband drugs. The court found no misconduct, explaining:

> "The experiment in the present case did not result in the generation of new evidence. [Citation.] During the trial, Officer Rowe had demonstrated the manner in which defendant had thrown the contraband. The jurors simply repeated the officer's reenactment. Nothing requires that the jury's deliberations be entirely verbal, and we would expect a conscientious jury to closely examine the testimony of the witnesses, no less so when that testimony takes the form of a physical act. There was no error in denying the motion for new trial on this ground." (*People v. Cooper, supra*, 95 Cal. App. 3d 844, 854.)

In *Locksley*, the defendant driver in an automobile accident case was blind in one eye. Two of the jurors conducted an experiment by driving with one eye closed. The court assumed the experiment constituted misconduct and concluded the trial court acted within its discretion in finding the misconduct (if any) was not prejudicial.

Cases where the courts have found jury experiments to be prejudicial misconduct include *People v. Conkling* (1896) 111 Cal. 616 [44 P. 314] and *People v. Castro* (1986) 184 Cal. App. 3d 849 [229 Cal. Rptr. 280].

In *Conkling*, a murder case, two jurors, to satisfy themselves at what distance a rifle discharge would leave powder marks on cloth, took a rifle from the courtroom and experimented with it. The court reversed because the jury had obtained evidence "by unauthorized experiments made without the presence and knowledge of the defendant." (*Higgins v. L. A. Gas & Electric Co., supra*, 159 Cal. at p. 659.) The court explained:

> "The distance between the deceased and defendant at the time of the fatal shot was fired was a vital issue in the case. The clothing worn by the deceased was in evidence, and when exhibited to the jury showed no powder marks.... [The defendant's] affidavits [showed] that during the progress of the [trial] two of the jurors borrowed a rifle similar to that with which the deceased was killed, bought some cotton drilling, retired to the outskirts of the city, and there made experiments by firing the rifle, for the purpose of determining at what distance powder marks would be carried by the fire.... [The jurors] were evidently honest, and desirous of getting at the truth of the matter; but they were too zealous, and their misconduct in this particular demands a retrial of the case. Jurors cannot be permitted to investigate the case outside the courtroom. They must decide the guilt or the innocence of the defendant upon the evidence introduced at the trial. It is impossible for this court to say that this outside investigation did not affect the result as to the character of the verdict rendered. For, when misconduct of jurors is shown, it is presumed to be injurious to defendant, unless the contrary appears. [Citations.]" (*People v. Conkling, supra*, 111 Cal. at pp. 627–628.)

---

no new evidence based on special expertise had been brought in by virtue of the fact the juror, as an engineer, may have been more skillful in drawing than the average person.

In *People v. Castro, supra,* 184 Cal. App. 3d 849, a juror, at home, used a pair of binoculars to see if a prison guard who testified at trial could have seen what he claimed through a pair of binoculars. The court concluded this constituted prejudicial misconduct.... [T]he *Castro* court found the question of whether jury misconduct in receiving evidence outside of court injured a defendant depended on: "(1) whether the jury's impartiality has been adversely affected; (2) whether the [plaintiff's] burden of proof has been lightened, and (3) whether any asserted defense has been contradicted. 'If the answer to any of these questions is in the affirmative, the defendant has been prejudiced and the [judgment] must be reversed.' [Citation.]" (*People v. Castro, supra,* 184 Cal. App. 3d at p. 856, italics omitted.)

The *Castro* court explained why it concluded the binocular experiment constituted prejudicial misconduct:

> "Applying [this] standard of review, it becomes obvious that [the juror's] experiment affected his own impartiality, it lessened the prosecution's burden of proof, and it contradicted appellant's defense that he was not the inmate who threw the burning mop into the maintenance building.

> "The very integrity of the jury deliberative process is at stake here. A juror conducted his own experiment at home which inferentially affected his verdict thereby creating a rebuttable presumption of prejudice. Because the prosecution failed to rebut the presumption and because the record does not permit a finding of harmless error, the judgment of conviction must be reversed." (*People v. Castro, supra,* 184 Cal. App. 3d at p. 857.)

Here, unlike the *Cooper* case where the jurors merely duplicated a demonstration presented at trial, Rizzo presented a new demonstration (i.e., there was no kitty litter and crayola demonstration conducted by any of the experts in the case). Further, when Rizzo conducted the demonstration, she represented she had special knowledge about concrete practices from family members, a situation very different from the *Locksley* and *Wagner* cases.[18] Rizzo additionally presented new evidence that inconsistencies in the sand on top of which the concrete is placed can be caused by the footprints of people walking back and forth across the building pad before the concrete is poured. Developer had no opportunity to challenge the accuracy of Rizzo's demonstration nor her representations of special knowledge about concrete practices.

---

18. Mills contends Developer waived any objections to Rizzo's special knowledge because she "explained in voir dire that she had knowledge of concrete work or 'cement,'" describing her father's knowledge in general terms and "[m]ost importantly, she was not asked about other family members," particularly nothing about her brother-in-law who had worked for one of the subcontractors on the Smoketree project. First, Developer's claim of juror misconduct is not based on Rizzo concealing special knowledge or bias but on her conducting a demonstration and bringing in new evidence. Further, the record indicates during voir dire, Rizzo, an accountant, when asked if she had "[a]ny knowledge of concrete work," answered: "Just cement. My father was like a handyman. He plastered outside of houses and did repair work on cabinets and stuff, and when we were children, we used to help him." This statement did not hint at Rizzo's knowledge about concrete work in construction projects nor her brother-in-law's employment by one of the Smoketree subcontractors. This record does not support Mills's waiver theory.

The trial judge here found the experiment did not require reversal, concluding: "Seems to me that the demonstration, if it were misconduct, in light of the findings of fraud, no fraud to the subs prior to that time, just is misconduct out in the air, doesn't mean anything." This statement reflects the court's belief the demonstration was relevant only to the issue of whether the subcontractors had committed fraud, an issue which the juror declarations uniformly indicated had been resolved the previous day by a vote finding neither Calego nor Mills had committed fraud. But the demonstration was also relevant to whether Developer had committed fraud, i.e., whether the deficiencies in the concrete, including the fact that the slabs were poured too thin, were due to Developer's fault rather than the fault of the subcontractors.[19]

We conclude Rizzo's demonstration constituted misconduct because it brought new evidence into the deliberations. The presumption of misconduct was not rebutted. Therefore, the finding of fraud against the Developer must be reversed.

B. *Alteration of Instructions*

Developer contends the jurors committed misconduct by modifying and misapplying an instruction on fraud in the inducement and as a result erroneously concluded Developer had committed fraud.

Since we have concluded the Rizzo experiment was prejudicial misconduct, we need not decide whether jurors committed additional misconduct by modifying an instruction. We further note the claimed jury "misconduct" here does not involve matters extrinsic to the deliberative process; rather it is intrinsic to the deliberative process. The situation here is similar to that we recently considered in *Ford v. Bennacka, supra*, 226 Cal. App. 3d 330, 336. In *Ford*, we found declarations that the jurors had confused the instructions on the plaintiff's burden of proof and on comparative negligence were not admissible.[20] We stated:

> "The declarations do not suggest any juror violated the court's instruction to follow the law by recounting his or her own outside experience on a question of law. [Citations.] The declarations do not describe overt acts, statements, or conduct showing the jury intentionally agreed to disregard applicable law and apply inapplicable law. [Citation.] Instead, *the declarations at most suggest 'deliberative error'* in the jury's collective mental process — confusion, misunderstanding, and misinterpretation of the law. On this record the court correctly declined to admit the proffered juror declarations to impeach the verdict. [Citations.]" (*Id.* at p. 336, italics added.)

Similarly, here we have, at most, a "deliberative error." (Contrast *Tapia v. Barker, supra*, 160 Cal. App. 3d 761, where juror discussions showed jurors considered reducing the judgment based on outside evidence of a collateral source of income as

---

19. Note that one of the jurors in her declaration stated Rizzo told the jurors "that the concrete subcontractors would normally not know how the dirt was placed inside their forms before the concrete was later poured — and that it was [Developer's] fault that the concrete turned out the way it did."

20. The juror declarations indicated the jury reached a consensus that each side was 50 percent negligent and believed they thus had to return a verdict in the defendant's favor.

well as the fact a juror had an improper, unrevealed bias against the plaintiff's Mexican background.) On this issue, the declarations do not reveal the use of any outside evidence or resort to outside legal authority. The declarations indicate, at most, confusion or misunderstanding by the jury in the process of deliberating, in determining how to reach a verdict using the instructions given to them by the court. This error is not the type that can be used to impeach a verdict.

DISPOSITION

The judgment is reversed. Developer to recover its costs.

Notes and Questions regarding Impeachment of Verdict

(1) *The Basic Objective/Subjective Distinction.* As our principal case illustrate, the distinction in Evidence Code § 1150 between proof of objectively ascertainable facts and proof of the subjective mental processes of jurors is the basic starting point with respect to impeachment of verdicts for juror misconduct. Juror declarations which describe objectively verifiable acts of misconduct are admissible to impeach a verdict; but declarations which describe individual or collective juror subjective mental process, purporting to show how the verdict was reached, are inadmissible.

(a) How clear is this distinction? Does the distinction permit prejudicial error to go unremedied, even where the jurors have admitted to serious misconduct? What are the policy reasons for this distinction?

(b) Is a declaration of the foreperson admissible which evidenced a discussion among the jurors to inflate their verdict to compensate for attorney fees and income taxes? *See Tramell v. McDonnell Douglas Corp.*, 163 Cal. App. 3d 157, 172–73, 209 Cal. Rptr. 427 (1984). Are affidavits from several jurors admissible which establish that the jury foreman advised the jury not to worry about the size of the verdict they might return because the trial judge had the power to reduce any excessive award? *See DiRosario v. Havens*, 196 Cal. App. 3d 1224, 1235–1238, 242 Cal. Rptr. 423 (1987). Is a jury's note, attached to and incorporated by reference on the verdict form, which reveals that the jury misconstrued its duty in apportioning damages, admissible under Evidence Code § 1150? Can multiple juror affidavits be admitted to explain the note and how the jury arrived at the damage figures recorded on the verdict? *See Maxwell v. Powers*, 22 Cal. App. 4th 1596, 28 Cal. Rptr. 2d 62 (1994).

(c) Are declarations from multiple jurors admissible where they state that two jurors, who had relatives with an injury similar to that suffered by the plaintiff, discussed their relatives' injuries and rehabilitation? *See Maple v. Cincinnati, Inc.*, 163 Cal. App. 3d 387, 209 Cal. Rptr. 451 (1985). Where three of these jurors also stated that they had made up their minds about the case before deliberations? *See Maple, supra*, 163 Cal. App. 3d at 391–94 ("[A]ttempts by judges to straight jacket a jury in its deliberations by an after-the-fact critiquing and criticizing of the language and reasoning used in those deliberations runs directly contrary to our fundamental concept of the jury function"); *but see Grobeson v. City of L. A.*, 190 Cal. App. 4th 778, 118 Cal. Rptr. 3d 798 (2010) (holding statement by juror that she had made up her mind during the second week of a five-week trial revealed her mental state but was nevertheless admissible because it also showed she had prejudged the case and thus committed misconduct).

(d) The evidence offered to impeach a verdict must not only refer to objectively ascertainable facts, but must also be "otherwise admissible evidence." Evidence Code § 1150(a). Declarations which contain inadmissible hearsay are not competent evidence. *See, e.g., People v. Williams*, 45 Cal. 3d 1268, 1318, 248 Cal. Rptr. 834, 756 P.2d 221 (ruling a jury verdict may not be impeached by hearsay affidavits); *Burns v. 20th Century Ins. Co.*, 9 Cal. App. 4th 1666, 12 Cal. Rptr. 462 (1992) (holding declarations of investigator recounting purported statements of two jurors during their deliberations are inadmissible hearsay).

(2) *The Objective/Subjective Distinction and "Deliberative Error."* Juror declarations are inadmissible where they describe juror misunderstanding and misinterpretation of the law—"deliberative error" in the jury's subjective reasoning process. *See, e.g., Bell v. Bayerische Motoren Werke Aktiengesellschaft*, 181 Cal. App. 4th 1108, 1124–26, 105 Cal. Rptr. 3d 485 (2010); *Mesecher v. County of San Diego*, 9 Cal. App. 4th 1677, 1683, 12 Cal. Rptr. 2d 279 (1992); *Ford v. Bennacka*, 226 Cal. App. 3d 330, 276 Cal. Rptr. 513 (1990). In *Ford v. Bennacka*, for example, the trial court refused to admit proffered juror declarations which disclosed obvious misapplication of basic legal principles by the jury. The jury had returned a verdict for defendant in *Ford*, a personal injury action for negligence involving a motorcycle accident. The plaintiff sought a new trial on grounds of jury misconduct, and submitted declarations from five jurors asserting that the jury had confused the concepts of comparative negligence and preponderance of the evidence. The declarations stated that the jury reached a consensus that both sides were equally negligent, and therefore believed (incorrectly) they must return a verdict for defendant because defendant's negligence did not preponderate over plaintiff's negligence. The trial court denied the motion and plaintiff appealed. The Court of Appeal held that the proffered declarations constituted improper probing of the jurors' subjective mental processes, and that the trial court properly excluded them under Evidence Code § 1150.

Likewise, in *Mesecher v. County of San Diego, supra*, the court held inadmissible several juror declarations which essentially stated that the jurors used a definition of battery in their deliberations which was more favorable to the plaintiff than the trial court's instructions. Even thought the jurors communicated their misunderstanding of the instructions to each other during deliberations, the court viewed these proffered declarations as reflecting the jurors' subjective mental processes and therefore inadmissible. *Mesecher,supra*, 9 Cal. App. 4th at 1683–84. Do you agree?

(3) The courts in both *Ford* and *Mesecher* found inapposite the Supreme Court's ruling in *Krouse v. Graham*, 19 Cal. 3d 59, 137 Cal. Rptr. 863, 562 P.2d 1022 (1977). *Krouse* stated that juror declarations are admissible to impeach a verdict where the declarations establish "an express agreement" to violate the court's instructions "or extensive discussion evidencing an implied agreement to that effect." *Krouse*, 19 Cal. 3d at 81. Do you agree that *Krouse* is distinguishable from *Ford* and *Mesecher*? Even

if the jurors in *Ford* and *Mesecher* reached no express or implied agreement to disregard the court's instructions, is not the resulting prejudice the same in all three cases? Does the objective/subjective distinction function arbitrarily and unjustly in such "deliberative error" cases? Does the objective/subjective distinction prohibit impeachment of verdicts when serious jury misconduct has occurred, such as misapplication of the jury instructions, but permit impeachment based on relatively less serious misconduct? Would you characterize the *Smoketree-Lake Murray* decision, reproduced *supra*, as an example of such a result? In light of the policy reasons for the objective/subjective distinction of Evidence Code § 1150, can you formulate a fairer standard for determining the permissible basis for impeachment of a jury verdict?

(4) In *Cove, Inc. v. Mora*, 172 Cal. App. 3d 97, 218 Cal. Rptr. 7 (1985), the trial court granted a new trial after a jury verdict for the plaintiff based on jury misconduct. Relying on *Krouse*, the trial court admitted declarations from five jurors which each said "that the jury specifically found that the plaintiff did not prove by a preponderance of the evidence that the conduct of [defendant] Mora proximately caused" plaintiff's injuries, but nevertheless awarded plaintiff damages for pain and suffering on a nonexistent legal theory. *Cove*, 172 Cal. App. 3d at 100. Did the trial curt err in admitting these five declarations? *See id.; see also Sanchez-Corea v. Bank of America*, 38 Cal. 3d 892, 910, 215 Cal. Rptr. 679, 701 P.2d 826 (1985) (holding inadmissible juror declaration asserting that the jury did not vote on the issue of defendant's liability); *Bly-Magee v. Budget Rent-a-Car Corp.*, 24 Cal. App. 4th 318, 29 Cal. Rptr. 2d 330 (1994) (holding inadmissible four juror affidavits stating that jurors did not understand special verdict form which asked them to apportion damages among all tortfeasors).

(5) *Jury Experiments.* A surprising number of verdict impeachment decisions involve jurors performing an experiment. As the cases discussed in *Smoketree-Lake Murray* indicate, not all juror experiments constitute juror misconduct. Improper experiments are those that allow the jury to discover new evidence by delving into areas not examined during trial. *People v. Collins*, 49 Cal. 4th 175, 249, 110 Cal. Rptr. 3d 384, 232 P.3d 32 (2010). Do you agree with the court in *Smoketree-Lake Murray* that the juror experiment there was misconduct? What attributes distinguish impermissible juror experiments from permissible ones? The trial court may permit the jury to take papers and other exhibits received as evidence into the jury room during deliberations. CCP § 612. Could a juror's experiment with such an exhibit constitute misconduct?

[1] Impeachment for Reliance on Juror Expertise or Other Outside Evidence

Another ground frequently asserted to impeach a verdict is that the jury was improperly influenced by outside information or by jurors' recounting their own outside experiences or expertise. The recurrent nature of such alleged juror misconduct has produced a few predictable rules. For example, a juror's reference to a dictionary for the definition of a term used in an instruction usually constitutes misconduct. *See, e.g., Glage v. Hawes Firearms Co.*, 226 Cal. App. 3d 314, 276 Cal. Rptr. 430 (1990) (holding trial court erred in denying a new trial where two jurors committed misconduct by looking up the definition of "preponderance" and discussing it with all the jurors); *Jones v. Sieve*, 203 Cal. App. 3d 359, 366, 249 Cal. Rptr. 821 (1988) (ruling juror' reference to outside sources for definition of term relevant to the subject of deliberation constituted misconduct).

[a] Exposure to Outside Information

However, because jurors do not live in a cocoon, the courts must tolerate some outside information or every verdict would be impeachable. For example, in *Elsworth v. Beech Aircraft Corp.*, 37 Cal. 3d 540, 208 Cal. Rptr. 874, 691 P.2d 630 (1984), jurors were exposed to that most persistent source of outside (mis)information: the television investigative report. The plaintiffs in *Elsworth* sought wrongful death damages against the defendant for the deaths of several persons killed in the crash of a light airplane. The plaintiffs introduced evidence that the airplane manufactured by defendant failed to comply with FAA safety regulations. After the jury returned a sizeable verdict for plaintiffs, the defendant moved for a new trial on the ground of jury misconduct. The defendant submitted a juror declaration stating that two jurors had remarked that they had watched, shortly before commencement of deliberations, a television broadcast of a program ("60 Minutes") criticizing the safety record of light aircraft. The trial court denied the motion, and the defendant appealed.

The Supreme Court affirmed, holding that even if the jurors committed misconduct, no prejudice resulted from their viewing of the program. The court doubted that simply watching a popular television program that happened to discuss the subject matter of the trial in a general way amounted to misconduct, particularly considering the jurors in question did not deliberately set out to discover information regarding the issues at trial. *Elsworth*, 37 Cal. 3d at 557–58; *see Hasson v. Ford Motor Co.*, 32 Cal. 3d 388, 185 Cal. Rptr. 654, 650 P.2d 1171 (1982) (finding no misconduct where a juror in a products liability trial inadvertently attended a lecture discussing a successful action against the same defendant for a different defect, in part because the juror did not deliberately solicit the lecturer's opinion). Do you agree with the holding in *Elsworth*? Should the fact that jurors are exposed to outside information accidentally, as opposed to deliberately, make a difference in determining whether the conduct was improper? Was prejudiced? Why?

The television program watched by the jurors in *Elsworth* mentioned defendant Beech Aircraft by name, and discussed the relationship between airplane manufacturers and the FAA. The broadcast made no reference to the specific type of aircraft, nor to the specific accident, in issue in *Elsworth*. *Elsworth*, 37 Cal. 3d at 558. Do you think the *Elsworth* court would have ruled differently if the watched program had discussed safety problems with the specific type of defendant's airplane involved in the crash? If the program had discussed the likely causes of the specific accident in issue?

[b] Jurors' Personal Experiences

The courts often struggle with another vexing problem—the extent to which a verdict should be impeachable when jurors related their personal experiences during deliberations. For example, in *Moore v. Preventive Medicine Med. Grp., Inc.*, 178 Cal. App. 3d 728, 223 Cal. Rptr. 859 (1986), a medical malpractice action where the plaintiff sought damages for pain and suffering, the court considered whether a foreperson's emotional discussion of her own experience with pain and suffering during deliberations required reversal of the jury's verdict. The *Moore* court concluded that the juror's discussion was not improper, explaining:

> Jurors do not enter deliberations with their personal histories erased, in essence retaining only the experience of the trial itself. Jurors are expected to be fully functioning human beings, bringing diverse backgrounds and experiences to the matter before them. Indeed, the purpose of voir dire is to provide counsel the opportunity to learn about a prospective juror's background, experiences, and philosophy as it relates to the matter to be heard. * * * It is inappropriate after-the-fact to complain about the particular background and experiences which a given juror brought to the deliberation process.

Moore, supra, 178 Cal. App. 3d at 741–42. The view expressed in *Moore* is not shared by all courts. For example, in *Smith v. Covell*, 100 Cal. App. 3d 947, 161 Cal. Rptr. 377 (1987); the plaintiff sought damages for personal injuries resulting from a traffic accident, including damages for back pain which first occurred six months after the accident. During deliberations, the foreman revealed to his fellow jurors that he had a back condition and that when his back "went out" it "went out right away" and "hurt right" away. *Smith*, 100 Cal. App. 3d at 952. The jury returned a verdict for the defendant. The Court of Appeal reversed, finding the foreman's comments interjected improper "evidence" in the case on the crucial issue of causation. *Id.* at 954.

In *Enyart v. City of L.A.*, 76 Cal. App. 4th 499, 90 Cal. Rptr. 2d 502 (1999), the trial court denied the defendant City of Los Angeles motion for a new trial of a negligence action based on juror misconduct where the declarations of several jurors indicated that three jurors during deliberations had expressed negative *generalizations* about the conduct and veracity of the defendants City and Los Angeles Police Department. The Court of Appeal reversed the denial, holding that the declarations demonstrated that the jurors' negative attitudes were not based solely on the evidence, were the product of bias, and were prejudicial. Do you agree with this holding? Why? Compare *Iwekaogwu v. City of L.A.*, 75 Cal. App. 4th 803, 89 Cal. Rptr. 2d 505 (1999), where the court upheld the denial of defendant City's new trial motion in an employment discrimination action, where juror declarations revealed that during deliberations one juror gave emotional descriptions of instances of discrimination he had seen as a reserve police officer. Is the evidence of juror misconduct in *Iwekaogwu* distinguishable from that in *Enyart*? How so?

In *McDonald v. Southern Pac. Transp. Co.*, 71 Cal. App. 4th 256, 83 Cal. Rptr. 2d 734 (1999), an action by a train brakeman for injuries suffered in a train yard, the trial court denied plaintiff's motion for a new trial where a juror declaration stated that another juror, a professional transportation consultant, commented at length during deliberations as to why the plaintiff's theory of how due care could have made this workplace safer was unrealistic and impractical. The Court of Appeal reversed, holding that the juror's opinions were derived from sources outside the evidence, rebutted a significant element of plaintiff's proof which was otherwise undisputed, and constituted prejudicial juror misconduct. *McDonald, supra*, 71 Cal. App. 4th at 263–67. Do you agree with this holding? Why? *See also Lankster v. Alpha Beta Co.*, 15 Cal. App. 4th 678, 18 Cal. Rptr. 923 (1993) (finding juror misconduct where a juror conducted an independent factual investigation during the trial and told the other jurors the result).

[c] Improper Chance Verdicts

Subdivision 2 of CCP § 657 specifically authorizes a new trial where jurors resort to determination by chance. Verdicts reached by tossing a coin, drawing lots, or any other form of gambling are examples of improper chance verdicts. *Chronakis v. Windsor*, 14 Cal. App. 4th 1058, 18 Cal. Rptr. 2d 106 (1993). A more sophisticated variant is the quotient verdict: Where jurors agree in advance to be bound by the average of their views as to the amount of damages, without further deliberation as to the propriety of the resulting amount. Such quotient verdicts are likewise improper. *Chronakis, supra*, 14 Cal. App. 4th at 1064–65 (citing cases). Why is a quotient verdict impermissible? Is it because the jurors utilize an average of their individual views to determine the amount of damages? Would a verdict be improper where the sum of jurors' stated views of the amount of damages was divided by twelve, and the resulting average amount was subsequently adopted by the jury after further deliberations? *See Lara v. Nevitt*, 123 Cal. App. 4th 454, 462, 19 Cal. Rptr. 3d 865 (2004) (concluding there was not an improper quotient verdict where, in order to break a deadlock after deliberations, jury agreed that each juror would submit a high and low figure for damages and, after adjustments, to calculate the average). Where the jurors agreed in advance to be bound by the average of their views, and each juror subsequently affirmed the verdict as his or her own when polled in open court? *See Chronakis, supra*, 14 Cal. App. 4th at 1067–68.

[d] Juror Inattentiveness

Courts are reluctant to overturn jury verdicts on the ground of inattentiveness during trial. The Supreme Court in *Hasson v. Ford Motor Co.*, 32 Cal. 3d 388, 185 Cal. Rptr. 634, 650 P.2d 1171 (1982), surveyed numerous cases of such alleged jury misconduct—jurors falling asleep during trial, reading newspapers during trial, consuming alcoholic beverages prior to hearing evidence—and observed that not one reported case granted a new trial on that ground. *Hasson, supra*, 32 Cal. 3d at 411–12. The *Hasson* court itself concluded that misconduct of three jurors consisting of reading a novel and working crossword puzzles during trial proceedings was not sufficiently prejudicial so as to overturn the verdict of $11.5 million awarded plaintiffs. *Id.* at 417–18. Why are the courts so reluctant to overturn a jury verdict on the ground of juror inattentiveness, even where proven by objectively ascertainable evidence of misconduct?

[2] *Presumption of Prejudice When Jury Misconduct Proven*

Proof of jury misconduct does not automatically require a new trial. The complaining party must also establish prejudice as a result of the misconduct. *Hasson v. Ford Motor Co.*, 32 Cal. 3d 388, 185 Cal. Rptr. 654, 650 P.2d 1171 (1982). "Prejudice exists if it is reasonably probable that a result more favorable to the complaining party would have been achieved in the absence of the misconduct." *Hasson*, 32 Cal. 3d at 415. Proof of juror misconduct does, however, give rise to a presumption of prejudice. This presumption "may be rebutted by an affirmative evidentiary showing that prejudice does not exist or by a reviewing court's examination of the entire record to determine whether there is a reasonable probability of actual harm to the complaining party resulting from the misconduct." *Id.* at 417 (citing cases). Some of the factors to be considered "are the strength of the evidence that the misconduct occurred, the nature and seriousness of the misconduct, and the probability that actual prejudice may have ensued." *Id.* at 417

Rebuttal evidence is often in the form of counterdeclarations from jurors stating facts to demonstrate that no prejudice actually resulted. *See, e.g.*, *Hasson, supra*, 32 Cal. 3d at 412–15 (holding counterdeclarations denying any adverse effect from improper conduct inadmissible proof of subjective mental processes of jurors; counterdeclarations denying any juror discussion of newspaper article are admissible and sufficient rebuttal); *Weathers v. Kaiser Found. Hosp.*, 5 Cal. 3d 98, 95 Cal. Rptr. 516, 485 P.2d 1132 (1971) (finding trial court did not abuse discretion in ordering new trial based on declarations of three dissenting jurors despite contradictory counterdeclarations submitted by six of the nine majority jurors). The absence of counterdeclarations does not preclude an appellate court, when reviewing an order *denying* a new trial, from conducting an independent review of the record to determine whether the presumption of prejudice was rebutted. *Hasson, supra*, 32 Cal. 3d at 416–17. When reviewing an order *granting* a new trial for jury misconduct, however, the appellate court may be unwilling to independently review the record if no counterdeclarations were filed. *See, e.g.*, *Jones v. Sieve*, 203 Cal. App. 3d 359, 368, 249 Cal. Rptr. 821 (1988). Why this difference in the standard of review? *See* Art. VI, § 13, Cal. Const.

[3] *Juror Misconduct During Voir Dire*

The intentional concealment during voir dire of bias, belief or state of mind which prevents a juror from following the court's instructions and acting in an impartial manner constitutes misconduct. *See, e.g.*, *Weathers v. Kaiser Found. Hosp.*, 5 Cal. 3d 98, 95 Cal. Rptr. 516, 485 P.2d 1132 (1971) (holding intentional concealment of racial prejudice against plaintiffs and bias in favor of defendant hospital constitutes misconduct); *Wiley v. Southern Pac. Transp. Co.*, 220 Cal. App. 3d 177, 269 Cal. Rptr.

240 (1990) (ruling intentional concealment of juror's status as the defendant in similar lawsuit is misconduct); *Tapia v. Barker*, 160 Cal. App. 3d 761, 206 Cal. Rptr. 803 (1984) (concluding concealed prejudice against plaintiff's Mexican background and against awarding damages for pain and suffering, both of which were biases the jurors had denied on voir dire, constituted misconduct); *Smith v. Covell*, 100 Cal. App. 3d 947, 954–955, 161 Cal. Rptr. 377 (1980) (finding juror's silence concealed his bias against high verdicts).

Inadvertent concealment such as an honest but mistaken answer, and incomplete disclosures because the questions propounded to the juror were ambiguous or there was inadequate follow-up questioning, may not be grounds for misconduct. *See, e.g., Wiley v. Southern Pac. Transp. Co., supra*, 220 Cal. App. 3d at 189; *Jutzi v. County of L. A.*, 196 Cal. App. 3d 637, 655, 242 Cal. Rptr. 74 (1990); *Donovan v. Poway Unified Sch. Dist.*, 167 Cal. App. 4th 567, 625–27, 84 Cal. Rptr. 3d 285 (2008). Why do the courts require a showing of *intentional* concealment of bias?

A juror's false answers or intentional concealment of relevant facts during voir dire examination not only constitutes misconduct, but also raises a presumption of prejudice. *Wiley, supra*, 220 Cal. App. 3d at 189; *Tapia, supra*, 160 Cal. App. 3d at 765–67. Is this presumption sufficient to destroy the integrity of a unanimous verdict where only one juror concealed bias? *See Weathers, supra*, 5 Cal. 3d at 109–111.

[4] *Impeachment of Verdicts in Federal Court*

Rule 606(b) of the Federal Rules of Evidence states the standards for impeachment of jury verdicts in federal courts. Rule 606(b) provides:

> Upon an inquiry into the validity of a verdict … a juror may not testify as to any matter or statement occurring during the course of the jury's deliberations or to the effect of anything upon that or any other juror's mind or emotions as influencing the juror to assent or to dissent from the verdict … or concerning the juror's mental processes in connection therewith. But a juror may testify about (1) whether extraneous prejudicial information was improperly brought to the jury's attention, (2) whether any outside influence was improperly brought to bear upon any juror, or whether there was a mistake in entering the verdict onto the verdict form. A juror's affidavit or evidence of any statement by the juror may not be received on a matter about which the juror would be precluded from testifying.

To what extent is the standard for admissibility of juror testimony in Rule 606(b) analogous to that of California Evidence Code § 1150(a)? Does your answer depend on the proper interpretation of the terms "extraneous prejudicial information" and "outside influence" in Rule 606(b)?

The U.S. Supreme Court construed Rule 606(b) in *Tanner v. United States*, 483 U.S. 107, 107 S. Ct. 2739, 97 L. Ed. 2d 90 (1987), to preclude admission of juror testimony describing juror conduct or statements during deliberations. The Supreme Court in *Tanner* considered whether the trial court properly excluded affidavits from two jurors which stated that several other jurors were often intoxicated during the trial, repeatedly smoked marijuana and ingested cocaine during the trial, and often fell asleep during the trial. The Supreme Court ruled these juror affidavits inadmissible because they revealed no "outside influence" on the jury, and found the nonjuror evidence of misconduct insufficient to impeach the verdict. *Tanner*, 483 U.S at 122–27.

Do you prefer the federal "internal/external" standard of admissibility in Rule 606(b) or the California "subjective/objective" standard in Evidence Code § 1150(a)? Why? Which promotes the goal of a competent and impartial jury? Better insulates the jury's deliberative process? If California had adopted the federal standard of Rule 606(b), would *Smoketree-Lake Murray* and the various other cases which found jury misconduct have been decided differently? Which ones?

[D] Motion for New Trial

[1] Introductory Note

The most frequently employed post-trial motion is the motion for a new trial. If granted, a new trial order authorizes a de novo trial as if the first trial never occurred, *Guzman v. Superior Court*, 19 Cal. App. 4th 705, 707, 23 Cal. Rptr. 2d 585 (1993); and permits a reexamination of an issue of fact in the same court after a trial and decision by a jury, court, or referee. CCP § 656. The grounds and procedures for new trial motions are set forth in CCP §§ 657–663.2. Because the right to move for a new trial is a creature of statute, the procedural steps prescribed by these statutes are mandatory and must be strictly followed. *Linhart v. Nelson*, 18 Cal. 3d 641, 644, 134 Cal. Rptr. 813, 557 P.2d 104 (1976); *Neal v. Montgomery Elevator Co.*, 7 Cal. App. 4th 1194, 1198, 9 Cal. Rptr. 2d 497 (1992). As the authorities reproduced below illustrate, these statutes have created a procedural minefield for attorneys and judges.

Code of Civil Procedure § 657 (2016)

The verdict may be vacated and any other decision may be modified or vacated, in whole or in part, and a new or further trial granted on all or part of the issues, on the application of the party aggrieved, for any of the following causes, materially affecting the substantial rights of such party:

1. Irregularity in the proceedings of the court, jury or adverse party, or any order of the court or abuse of discretion by which either party was prevented from having a fair trial.

2. Misconduct of the jury; and whenever any one or more of the jurors have been induced to assent to any general or special verdict, or to a finding on any question submitted to them by the court, by a resort to the determination of chance, such misconduct may be proved by the affidavit of any one of the jurors.

3. Accident or surprise, which ordinary prudence could not have guarded against.

4. Newly discovered evidence, material for the party making the application, which he could not, with reasonable diligence, have discovered and produced at the trial.

5. Excessive or inadequate damages.

6. Insufficiency of the evidence to justify the verdict or other decision, or the verdict or other decision is against law.

7. Error in law, occurring at the trial and excepted to by the party making the application.

When a new trial is granted, on all or part of the issues, the court shall specify the ground or grounds upon which it is granted and the court's reason or reasons for granting the new trial upon each ground stated.

A new trial shall not be granted upon the ground of insufficiency of the evidence to justify the verdict or other decision, nor upon the ground of excessive or inadequate damages, unless after weighing the evidence the court is convinced from the entire record, including reasonable inferences therefrom, that the court or jury clearly should have reached a different verdict or decision.

The order passing upon and determining the motion must be made and entered as provided in Section 660 and if the motion is granted must state the ground or grounds relied upon by the court, and may contain the specification of reasons. If an order granting such motion does not contain such specification of reasons, the court must, within 10 days after filing such order, prepare, sign and file such specification of reasons in writing with the clerk. The court shall not direct the attorney for a party to prepare either or both said order and said specification of reasons.

On appeal from an order granting a new trial the order shall be affirmed if it should have been granted upon any ground stated in the motion, whether or not specified in the order or specification of reasons, except that (a) the order shall not be affirmed upon the ground of the insufficiency of the evidence to justify the verdict or other decision, or upon the ground of excessive or inadequate damages, unless such ground is stated in the order granting the motion and (b) on appeal from an order granting a new trial upon the ground of the insufficiency of the evidence to justify the verdict or other decision, or upon the ground of excessive or inadequate damages, it shall be conclusively presumed that said order as to such ground was made only for the reasons specified in said order or said specification of reasons, and such order shall be reversed as to such ground only if there is no substantial basis in the record for any of such reasons.

Sanchez-Corea v. Bank of America

Supreme Court of California
38 Cal. 3d 892, 215 Cal. Rptr. 679, 701 P.2d 826 (1985)

REYNOSO, JUSTICE.

I

This case arises from a dispute over a commercial bank account maintained by the Sanchez-Coreas with the defendant Bank of America (Bank). In 1964, Antonio Sanchez-Corea formed Cormac in partnership with a third person, not a party here, who sold his interest in Cormac to Mr. Sanchez-Corea in 1971. Cormac was engaged in designing and installing electronic communications systems. From its inception, Cormac banked with defendant Bank. Between 1965 and 1973 defendant Virgil McGowen, a Bank vice president and branch manager, handled Cormac's commercial account. He arranged, without the knowledge of the Bank, for Bank funds to be used to cover overdrafts on the Cormac account. At the heart of this controversy is a disagreement over the amount of money owed by Cormac to the Bank as a result of these "loans."

An embezzlement scheme was discovered by the Bank and suspicion later focused on McGowen. The Bank audited McGowen's records and discovered that he had embezzled funds from the Bank, including $246,000 which the Bank alleges was credited to Cormac's account. Prior to discovering the McGowen embezzlement scheme, the Bank had loaned Cormac $70,000. However, upon discovery of the alleged $246,000 debt, the Bank demanded payment and refused to extend further commercial credit to Cormac.

In 1972, Cormac had begun to move into the new and growing life safety systems field and in 1974, Cormac made loan arrangements for further development and growth in this area. Equity Financing of Chicago agreed to invest $150,000 in Cormac in exchange for a 20 percent stock interest. The plan was contingent upon the reduction of the Bank's claim to $180,000 payable over 10 years and upon a $100,000 loan from the Small Business Administration. The Bank would not agree to the reduction and informed the Small Business Administration that the Sanchez-Coreas might be charged with receiving stolen property. The deal with Equity Financing of Chicago was never completed.

In April 1974, Cormac filed for proceedings under chapter 11 of the Bankruptcy Act. The company went out of business in October 1974.

The Sanchez-Coreas and the trustee in bankruptcy (hereinafter the Sanchez-Coreas) sued the Bank and McGowen for breach of contract, fraud, breach of the implied covenant of good faith and fair dealing, disparagement of credit, interference with prospective economic advantage, promissory estoppel, negligence, and intentional infliction of emotional distress. The Sanchez-Coreas requested both general and punitive damages. * * *

After a three-week trial the jury returned a verdict awarding the Sanchez-Coreas $2,100,015.50 on the complaint, consisting (as explained in answers to special interrogatories (Code Civ. Proc., §625)) of $1 million for general damages, $100,000 for emotional distress, $1 million for punitive damages against the Bank and $15.50 in punitive damages against McGowen. * * * Judgment was entered on September 25, 1979. On September 28 notice of entry of judgment was mailed to the parties.

The Bank timely moved for a new trial, asserting the following six grounds: (1) irregularity in the proceedings of the jury which prevented the defendant from having a fair trial; (2) misconduct of the jury; (3) excessive damages; (4) insufficiency of the evidence; (5) that the verdict was against law and (6) error in law to which defendant excepted during trial.

On November 27, 1979-exactly 60 days after notice of entry of judgment was mailed-the trial court granted the Bank's motion for new trial. The minute order entered by the clerk stated: "Defendants [sic] motion for new trial is granted. Specifications to follow." No grounds for the new trial order were specified at that time. Neither party asserts that this omission was the result of clerical error. On December 4, 1979, the trial court filed an "Order Granting New Trial" vacating the judgment and granting the Bank's motion. This second order explained that the sole ground for granting the motion was insufficiency of the evidence.

The Sanchez-Coreas appeal. They contend that (1) the November 27 order was defective (but not void) for failure to state the ground (insufficiency of the evidence) on which the motion was granted (Code Civ. Proc., §657) and (2) that the December 4 order was invalid because it was made after expiration of the 60-day period in which the court had jurisdiction to rule on the motion (Code Civ. Proc., §660).[1] Because, they argue, the new trial order cannot be affirmed on any ground, the order should be reversed and the judgment should be reinstated. * * * The Bank has not filed a cross-appeal as provided in California Rules of Court, rule 3(c) [now Rule 8.108(g)].

As will appear below, we agree with plaintiffs.

I

This case is governed by sections 657 and 660, which impose limitations and requirements on consideration of motions for new trials. The power of the trial court to grant a new trial may be exercised only by following the statutory procedure and is conditioned upon the timely filing of a motion for new trial, the court being without power to order a new trial *sua sponte*.

After the court is presented with a motion for a new trial, its power to rule on the motion expires at the end of the 60-day period provided by section 660. The period runs from the mailing of notice of entry of judgment by the clerk or the service of notice of entry of judgment, whichever is earlier, or if no such notice is given, from initial notice of intent to move for new trial. (§660.) If no determination is made within the 60-day period, the motion is deemed to have been denied. (*Id.*)

If the motion for new trial is granted, additional requirements are imposed by statute. In pertinent part, section 657 provides that whenever the motion is granted

---

1. All statutory references are to the Code of Civil Procedure unless otherwise indicated.

"the court shall specify the ground or grounds upon which it is granted and the court's reason or reasons for granting the new trial...." The section goes on, however, to distinguish between grounds and reasons. While the order passing upon and determining the motion "*must* state the ground or grounds relied upon by the court," the order "*may* contain the specification of reasons." (Italics added.) If the order stating the grounds does not also specify the reasons for the new trial, then "the court must, within 10 days after filing such order, prepare, sign and file such specification of reasons in writing with the clerk." Thus, under section 657, the grounds for the new trial must be stated in the order. The reasons may also be stated in the order, but the trial court has the option of filing a statement of the reasons at a later time.

Section 657 also specifies guidelines for appellate review. It provides that an order granting a new trial "shall be affirmed if it should have been granted upon any ground stated in the motion, whether or not specified in the order or specification of reasons...." One qualification to this rule is that the appellate court cannot affirm on the grounds of insufficiency of the evidence or of excessive or inadequate damages unless such ground was specified in the trial court's order. (§ 657.)

In the case at bench, the trial court stated both the grounds and the reasons only in its second order. The Sanchez-Coreas contend that the trial court's attempt to grant the Bank's motion for a new trial was defective for failure to comply with section 657, in that the initial order did not state any grounds relied upon by the court. They concede that this order, signed by the judge and filed on the 60th day after notice of entry of the judgment, complied with the jurisdictional time limit imposed by section 660. They argue, however, that the second order, filed seven days later, which for the first time stated that insufficiency of the evidence was the ground for granting the motion, was an act in excess of jurisdiction and cannot be considered by this court. Finally, they contend that this court is precluded by section 657 from affirming the new trial order on grounds of insufficient evidence or excessive damages and that on review this court can only affirm if the record supports any of the other four grounds stated in the Bank's motion for new trial. We agree.

The absence of any specification of grounds in the first order made it defective but not void under section 657.... [I]n *In re Marriage of Beilock* (1978) 81 Cal. App. 3d 713 [146 Cal. Rptr. 675] the husband argued that an order granting the wife's motion for new trial without specification of either grounds or reasons was void for failure to comply with section 657. The Court of Appeal acknowledged that "the trial judge is admonished to state his grounds and reasons, whatever they are, and this is not limited to the [insufficient] evidence and [excessive or inadequate] damages grounds. But if the text of the order made does not fulfill the statutory requirements, then the reviewing court, according to other provisions of [section 657], *must affirm the order* if it should have been granted on some *other* ground stated in the motion." (*Id.*, at p. 727, second italics added.) * * *

We conclude that the initial order of November 27, 1979, was defective, but not void and turn to the trial court's second order, which was filed on December 4, 67 days after notice of entry of judgment, and specified both the ground (insufficient evidence) and reasons for the new trial. The Bank contends that the initial order's failure to state the grounds for the new trial, was cured by the second timely filed order, because the latter order was [timely] and stated the ground and reasons relied upon by the trial court. For timeliness, the Bank relies on language in section 657 which states that where "an order granting [a new trial] motion does not contain such specification of reasons, the court must, within 10 days after filing such order, prepare, sign and file such specification of reasons in writing with the clerk." (Code Civ. Proc., § 657.) Additionally, it argues that the trial court's orders in this case are permitted by section 660, which provides: "The entry of a new trial order in the permanent minutes of the court shall constitute a determination of the motion even though such minute order as entered expressly directs that a written order be prepared, signed and filed."[3]

Section 657 clearly distinguishes between grounds and reasons. If the motion for new trial is granted the order "must state the ground or grounds relied upon by the court" and "may contain the specification of reasons." If the initial order does not contain the specification of reasons, then the court must prepare, sign and file such specification within 10 days. There is no indication in section 657 that any grounds for ordering a new trial may be initially set forth by the trial court during that 10-day period.

The Bank's position ignores "the separate and distinct meaning of the word 'reason'" as used in section 657. The statute clearly allows only grounds to be stated in the initial order, and only reasons to be stated within 10 days thereafter. We reject the construction proposed by the Bank because it vitiates the distinction between grounds and reasons and is contrary to the duty of this court "not to insert what has been omitted, or to omit what has been inserted" in a statute. (§ 1858.)[4]

The Bank relies on *La Manna v. Stewart* (1975) 13 Cal. 3d 413 [118 Cal. Rptr. 761, 530 P.2d 1073]. There, the trial court granted plaintiff's motion for new trial but did not state the ground for the motion and failed to file a timely specification

---

3. The Bank's reliance on this language is misplaced. The Law Revision Commission recommendation that advocated the addition of this language to section 660 indicates that the purpose was to clarify what must be done by the end of the 60th day in order to prevent denial of the motion by operation of law. Nothing in that report indicates that the quoted language was added to permit the trial court to state grounds for the new trial at a later date. (Recommendation Relating to the Effective Date of an Order Ruling on a Motion for New Trial (Feb. 1957) 1 Cal. Law Revision Com. Rep. (1957) pp. K9–K27.)

4. The dissent's position, that a court which orders a new trial has 10 days to state both grounds and reasons, conflicts with the wording of the statute as written by the Legislature. In the face of that wording we are compelled to disagree with the suggestion that the ground or grounds can be stated 10 days after the trial court has granted the motion. As quoted by the dissent, Witkin states that after the 1965 amendment "the 10-day limit would seem to be still applicable to the ground as well as the reasons." (5 Witkin, Cal. Procedure (2d ed. 1971) Attack on Judgment in Trial Court, § 71, p. 3646.) This suggestion, as well as the position taken in the dissenting opinion, is inconsistent with section 657's mandate that the order granting the new trial "must state the ground or grounds relied upon by the court."

of reasons. Writing for the court, Justice Mosk stated that "We reluctantly hold the [error in failing to state the ground] to be cured by the fact that the motion for new trial was predicated solely on alleged insufficiency of the evidence; inasmuch as a new trial can be granted only on a ground specified in the motion, the order in the case at bar must be deemed to have been based on a finding of such insufficiency." (*Id.*, at p. 418.)

The limited cure for failure to state grounds recognized in *La Manna* is inapplicable here. In *La Manna* the motion for new trial was made solely on one ground—insufficiency of the evidence. Here, the Bank alleged six grounds for a new trial and there is no way for this court to infer which ground or grounds were relied on in the initial order granting the new trial. Reliance on the second order stating the ground of insufficient evidence would conflict with the statutory requirement that the initial order state the ground or grounds, subject only to the trial court's power to make a specification of reasons—but not a statement of ground or grounds—at a later date. * * *

To the extent the second order, entitled by the trial court "Order Granting New Trial," purports to rule on the motion and state insufficient evidence as the ground therefor, it is defective as in excess of the 60-day jurisdictional period. (*Siegal v. Superior Court* (1968) 68 Cal. 2d 97, 101 [65 Cal. Rptr. 311, 436 P.2d 311].) The order ruling on the motion must be entered within the 60-day period (§ 660) and must itself state the ground for granting a new trial. (§ 657.) The trial court's second order, stating the ground of insufficiency of evidence was not filed until the 67th day. As Justice Mosk noted in *Siegal*, "'If a statutory period in which a court might act is jurisdictional, it is manifest that the statute should not be defeated by the simple device of a *nunc pro tunc* order.'" (68 Cal. 2d at p. 102) * * *

Accordingly, we conclude that in the case at bench the trial court's attempt, after expiration of the 60-day period allowed by section 660, to state insufficiency of the evidence as the ground for ordering a new trial was ineffective as an act in excess of jurisdiction. Having concluded that the first order was defective in that respect, we turn to the question of appellate review.

As noted previously, section 657 requires an appellate court to affirm a new trial order if it should have been granted on any ground stated in the motion. However, an appellate court cannot affirm on grounds of insufficiency of the evidence or of inadequate or excessive damages unless such ground is stated in the new trial order. Accordingly, this court cannot affirm the present order on grounds of insufficiency of the evidence or excessive damages, and must consider whether the order should be affirmed on any of the four additional grounds advanced in the Bank's motion.[9]

---

9. We recognize that an element of unfairness to the successful movant is involved when an appellate court's review is circumscribed due to the error of the trial court. (*See* Comment, *Written Specification of Reasons for New Trial Orders* (1976) 64 Cal. L. Rev. 286.) However, as recognized by Justice Mosk in *Mercer v. Perez*, "'The power of the legislature [in] specifying procedural steps for new trials is exclusive and unlimited. [Citations.] The wisdom of or necessity for certain requirements are matters for legislative and not judicial consideration and the judiciary, in its interpretation of leg-

If an order granting a new trial does not effectively state the ground or the reasons, the order has been reversed on appeal where there are no grounds stated in the motion other than insufficient evidence or excessive or inadequate damages. (*See, e.g., La Manna v. Stewart, supra*, 13 Cal. 3d 413, 425; ...) If, however, the motion states any *other* ground for a new trial, an order granting the motion will be affirmed if any such other ground legally requires a new trial. (§ 657; ...)

Where, as here, the trial court has failed to make a timely specification of any ground for the new trial order, the burden is on the movant to advance any grounds stated in the motion upon which the order should be affirmed, and a record and argument to support it. As we shall explain, the Bank has not met this burden.

One ground stated in the Bank's motion for new trial was error in law excepted to at trial. No attempt has been made to show that the order should be affirmed on this ground.

Nor may the new trial order be affirmed on the ground that the verdict "is against law." The ground is separate and distinct from the other grounds listed in section 657 and does not include any, or all, of those other separate and distinct grounds for new trial. In contrast to the grounds of insufficient evidence and excessive or inadequate damages, "the phrase 'against law' does not import a situation in which the court weighs the evidence and finds a balance against the verdict, as it does in considering the ground of insufficiency of the evidence." (*Musgrove v. Ambrose Properties* (1978) 87 Cal. App. 3d 44, 56 [150 Cal. Rptr. 722].) Because the "against law" ground is distinct from the ground of insufficiency of the evidence, a new trial order must be affirmed as against law even though that ground is not stated in the order or supported by a specification of reasons.

The jury's verdict was "against law" only if it was "unsupported by any substantial evidence, i.e., [if] the entire evidence [was] such as would justify a directed verdict against the [parties] in whose favor the verdict [was] returned." (*Kralyevich v. Magrini* (1959) 172 Cal. App. 2d 784, 789 [342 P.2d 903]; ...) "[The] function of the trial court on a motion for a directed verdict is analogous to and practically the same as that of a reviewing court in determining, on appeal, whether there is evidence in the record of sufficient substance to support a verdict." (*Estate of Lances* (1932) 216 Cal. 397, 401 [14 P.2d 768]; ...) Accordingly, we examine the record to determine whether the verdict for plaintiffs was, as a matter of law, unsupported by substantial evidence. In our examination we apply the well established rule of appellate review by considering the evidence in the light most favorable to the prevailing party, here the Sanchez-Coreas, and indulging in all legitimate and reasonable inferences indulged in to uphold the jury verdict if possible.

So examining the record, we conclude that the judgment entered upon the jury verdict is supported by substantial evidence. * * * The following evidence supported the $1 million compensatory damages award: Mr. Sanchez-Corea's testimony estab-

---

islative enactments may not usurp the legislative function by substituting its own ideas for those expressed by the legislature.'" (68 Cal. 2d at pp. 117–118) lished that Cormac was not a new or unestablished business, but had been in operation for 10 years. Although the life safety systems market was a newly developing one, Mr. Sanchez-Corea and Deputy Chief Condon of the San Francisco Fire Department testified that Cormac had been involved in that business from the very beginning. The value of Cormac's early start in the business was shown not only by the evidence of their established reputation and the high regard that others had for their work but also by the tenfold growth in contracts (sales) from $180,000 in 1970 to $1.5 million in 1973. The testimony of a Small Business Administration loan officer and loan documents prepared by the Bank and the SBA all indicated that the business community viewed Cormac as a growing company with a bright future. * * *

We conclude that the compensatory damages award was supported by substantial evidence. * * *

We turn to the award of damages for emotional distress and conclude that there is substantial evidence to support the jury's determination that defendant Bank engaged in intentional or reckless conduct which it should have known would cause such distress. There is evidence from which the jury could have determined that the Bank acted outrageously in reaction to the plight in which the Sanchez-Coreas found themselves as a result of vice president McGowen's conduct. * * *

Turning to the punitive damages award, we similarly conclude that the jury's determination is supported by substantial evidence. The jury could have determined that the Bank acted fraudulently in forcing the Sanchez-Coreas to assign all accounts receivable in return for financing at a time when the Bank knew Cormac was in critical need of further loans. * * *

Thus, we conclude that the verdict is supported by substantial evidence and that the Bank has failed to demonstrate that the verdict is against law.

The final two grounds for new trial asserted by the Bank, irregularity in the jury proceedings and misconduct of the jury, also fail to provide this court with a basis for affirming the new trial order. The Bank claims irregularity in that the same nine jurors who voted for compensatory damages did not also vote for punitive damages. This argument is without merit. Counsel has waived any defect in inconsistency in the verdict by failing to request that the jury be returned for further deliberation.

The Bank's remaining jury contentions center around a declaration claimed to invalidate the vote of one juror, Ms. Bonnell. Though when polled in open court, she voted for the general verdict for the Sanchez-Coreas, and specifically for compensatory damages, she subsequently declared that no jury vote was taken on the Bank's liability and she did not agree to liability, but that she voted for damages as a compromise because she thought that liability had been decided and she felt pressured by her employer to return to work. The applicable rule is explained in *People v. Hutchinson* (1969) 71 Cal. 2d 342 [78 Cal. Rptr. 196, 455 P.2d 132], holding that Evidence Code section 1150 "prevents one juror from upsetting a verdict of the whole jury by impugning his own or his fellow jurors' mental processes or reasons for assent or dissent. The only improper influences that may be proved under section 1150 to impeach a verdict, therefore, are those open to sight, hearing, and the other senses and thus subject to corroboration." (*Id.*, at p. 350.) Ms. Bonnell's declaration dealt only with jurors' mental processes and reasons for assent or dissent and was inadmissible for purposes of undermining the verdict.

The Bank asserted no other grounds for the motion for new trial. We conclude that there is no basis for this court to affirm the new trial order.

III

In summary, we hold that the first order granting the new trial is defective but not void. We further hold that this court is precluded from affirming the order on grounds of either insufficiency of the evidence or excessive damages. Although the second order of the trial court specifies the ground of insufficiency of evidence, that order is invalid because it was filed after the 60-day jurisdictional period prescribed by section 660. Looking to the remaining grounds for the new trial stated in defendant's motion, we conclude that they do not warrant affirming the trial court's order. Accordingly, the order vacating the judgment for plaintiffs and granting a new trial is reversed. Because defendant has failed to file a protective cross-appeal, reinstatement of the judgment will automatically be final. (*Stevens v. Parke, Davis & Co.* (1973) 9 Cal. 3d 51, 63 [107 Cal. Rptr. 45, 507 P.2d 653, 94 A.L.R.3d 1059].)

Kaus, Justice, dissenting.

I respectfully dissent. Just when the bench and bar of this state thought that all the dangers in the procedural minefield created by section 657 of the Code of Civil Procedure had been identified and charted, the court unnecessarily adds a new one. * * *

In the leading decisions in this area, *Treber v. Superior Court, supra,* 68 Cal. 2d at pages 131–134, and *Mercer v. Perez, supra,* 68 Cal. 2d at pages 112–116, this court explained carefully and persuasively why, on the one hand, the new trial order must be affirmed—in spite of a total failure to specify grounds or reasons—if justified on any ground stated in the motion except insufficiency of the evidence or excessive or inadequate damages, while, on the other hand, the statute insists that an order based on insufficiency of the evidence or excessive or inadequate damages be supported by an adequate, timely specification of reasons.[1] I respectfully challenge the majority to advance an equally principled reason explaining why a new trial order, made within the time limit of section 660 and supported by a timely, adequate statement of reasons should be of no effect.

---

1. In *In re Marriage of Beilock* (1978) 81 Cal. App. 3d 713, 725–726 [146 Cal. Rptr. 675] the court explained that this apparent seesawing between super-liberality and super-strictness "requires a realization that the Legislature in drafting section 657 had at least two different objectives in mind. Generally, one objective is to facilitate a meaningful appellate review of orders granting new trials primarily where the ground is either that the evidence is insufficient to justify the verdict or that the damages are excessive or inadequate. The second objective, assuming the given order is defective with reference to the first objective, is to prevent injustice by extending the scope of appellate review to any ground listed in the motion and not relied upon by the trial court." (Italics omitted.)

Dominguez v. Pantalone

Court Of Appeal Of California, Second Appellate District
212 Cal. App. 3d 201, 260 Cal. Rptr. 431 (1989)

LILLIE, PRESIDING JUSTICE.

Plaintiff sustained hearing loss and significant permanent brain injuries when his motorcycle collided with defendant's car, which made a left turn in front of him. After a trial which lasted about two weeks, the jury rendered its … verdict.… * * *

By special verdict, the jury found, 11 to 1, that defendant was negligent, that such negligence was a proximate cause of the accident, that plaintiff was not negligent, and that the total amount of damages suffered by plaintiff as a result of the accident was $1,557,400. Judgment was entered against defendant and in favor of plaintiff. Defendant thereafter moved for new trial on the ground, inter alia, of insufficiency of the evidence to support the verdict, and on the ground that prejudicial misconduct of plaintiff's attorney in seeking to introduce [certain opinion evidence] deprived her of a fair trial. The court denied the motion for new trial.

Defendant filed timely notice of appeal from the judgment. On appeal, she makes two primary arguments: (1) She was deprived of a fair trial as a result of "blatant and persistent misconduct by plaintiff's counsel," and (2) the trial court "improperly denied a new trial after concluding the jury had wrongly decided this case."

I. NO MISCONDUCT OF COUNSEL

Appellant contends that plaintiff's counsel, Mr. Hindin, was guilty of prejudicial misconduct in attempting, at several opportunities, to bring the investigating officer's opinion of fault before the jury after the trial court expressed its doubts that such opinion was admissible. * * *

Appellant contends that Mr. Hindin's repeated asking of the questions was a deliberate attempt to suggest to the jury a matter of an evidentiary nature after the court had ruled that the officer's opinion was not admissible, and such conduct was prejudicial because the content of the opinion was clearly suggested to the jury and defense counsel did not have an opportunity to cross-examine the officer on that subject. She also claims that the admonition was insufficient to cure the alleged prejudice and, because of the conflicting evidence at trial, such alleged misconduct caused the jury to bring in a large verdict and a finding that the plaintiff was not at fault. * * *

In assessing that prejudice, each case ultimately must rest upon this court's view of the overall record, taking into account such factors, inter alia, as the nature and seriousness of the remarks and misconduct, the general atmosphere, including the judge's control of the trial, the likelihood of prejudicing the jury, and the efficacy of objection or admonition under all the circumstances.

To the extent that appellant also claims that the trial court erred in failing to grant her a new trial on the ground of misconduct of counsel, we apply the standard of review set out in *City of Los Angeles v. Decker* (1977) 18 Cal. 3d 860 [135 Cal. Rptr. 647, 558 P.2d 545]: "In our review of such order denying a new trial, as distinguished from an order granting a new trial, we must fulfill our obligation of reviewing the entire record, including the evidence, so as to make an independent determination as to whether the [attorney misconduct] was prejudicial." (*Id.*, at p. 872, original italics.) * * *

Upon our review of the instant record, bearing in mind the trial was an adversary proceeding, we conclude that while Mr. Hindin may have been aggressive and persistent, approaching close to the line between proper and improper conduct, he did not overstep that line and did not violate the duty "to respectfully yield to the rulings of the court, *whether right or wrong*...." (*Hawk v. Superior Court* (1974) 42 Cal. App. 3d 108, 126 [116 Cal. Rptr. 713], original italics.) * * *

Without addressing the issue of the correctness of the trial court's evidentiary rulings, which are not before us on this appeal, we conclude that Mr. Hindin's attempts to find other theories of relevancy or admissibility of Officer Gilliam's opinion did not overstep "the permissible line of proper lawyering conduct." (*Hilliard v. A. H. Robins Co.* (1983) 148 Cal. App. 3d 374, 407 [196 Cal. Rptr. 117].) The trial court itself did not consider Mr. Hindin to have committed acts of misconduct because he refused defense counsel's request for an instruction on the conduct of plaintiff's attorney.

Even were the acts such as to constitute misconduct, we cannot find them to be prejudicial. This was a lengthy trial, aggressively litigated on both sides, with many witnesses and with frequent objections being made on both sides. The trial judge exercised a firm and fair control over the proceedings. Contrary to appellant's claim, the issue of Officer Gilliam's opinion was not a major theme of the trial. Moreover, before the final "admonition" to the jury, the court, in sustaining defense objections to Mr. Hindin's questions, had explained his rulings to Mr. Hindin, which explanations also further informed the jury as to its function as the trier of fact. Given the firm control of the proceedings by the trial court, which maintained an impartial and dignified atmosphere at trial, we also conclude that the admonitions given to the jury were sufficient to remove any impropriety and prejudice which could have resulted from Mr. Hindin's conduct. Because we conclude that the admonitions were sufficient, we find without merit appellant's claim that prejudice resulted from her inability to cross-examine Officer Gilliam on the subject of his opinion. * * *

We conclude that Mr. Hindin was not guilty of misconduct. Even were we to characterize his acts as misconduct, they clearly were not prejudicial. To the extent that appellant seeks review of the order denying her motion for new trial on the ground of attorney misconduct, which order is not directly appealable but may be reviewed on appeal from the judgment, we conclude that the trial court also properly denied the motion for new trial on the ground of attorney misconduct.

II. DENIAL OF MOTION FOR NEW TRIAL

Appellant claims that the trial court misconceived its duty and erroneously denied her motion for new trial on the ground of insufficiency of the evidence because it felt bound by the jury's verdict even though "the trial court independently weighed the evidence and concluded the jury clearly should have reached a different result...."

"When a trial court rules upon a motion for a new trial made upon the ground of insufficiency of the evidence, the judge is required to weigh the evidence and judge the credibility of witnesses." (*Locksley v. Ungureanu* (1986) 178 Cal. App. 3d 457, 463 [223 Cal. Rptr. 737].) "While it is the exclusive province of the jury to find the facts, it is the duty of the trial court to see that this function is intelligently and justly performed, and in the exercise of its supervisory power over the verdict, the court, on motion for a new trial, should consider the probative force of the evidence and satisfy itself that the evidence as a whole is sufficient to sustain the verdict." (*People v. Robarge* (1953) 41 Cal. 2d 628, 633 [262 P.2d 14].) Insufficiency of the evidence in this context means an absence of evidence or that the evidence received, in the individual judgment of the trial judge, is lacking in probative force to establish the proposition of fact to which it is addressed.

The court does not disregard the verdict, or decide what result it should have reached if the case had been tried without a jury, but instead "it should consider the proper weight to be accorded to the evidence and then decide whether or not, in its opinion, there is sufficient credible evidence to support the verdict." (*People v. Robarge, supra,* 41 Cal. 2d at p. 633.)

Some courts state the rule to be that "a new trial cannot be granted '... unless after weighing the evidence the court is convinced from the entire record, including reasonable inferences therefrom, *that the court or jury clearly should have reached a different verdict or decision.*'" (*Locksley v. Ungureanu, supra,* 178 Cal. App. 3d at p. 463, original italics.) Appellant interprets language similar to the foregoing in *Lippold v. Hart* (1969) 274 Cal. App. 2d 24, 25–26 [78 Cal. Rptr. 833], as suggesting essentially that the trial court must grant a new trial whenever it disagrees with the verdict. Because the language of the court in *Lippold* stating the rule appears to be incomplete and may be misleading, we prefer the better reasoned and more complete explanation of the trial court's function by the court in *People v. Robarge, supra,* 41 Cal. 2d 628, 633.

Applying the proper standard, it is clear that the trial court here correctly performed its duty. The following colloquy occurred at the hearing on the motion for new trial: "The Court: I will tell you frankly, if the court were hearing the case, I would have found at least substantial comparative negligence, but I have looked over the case. The jury did not come in with the verdict I would have come in with, but when I look at it and the matter of credibility of the witnesses, witnesses that I would have disbelieved, they believed. And witnesses I would have believed, they would have disbelieved.... [¶] Mr. Rhames [Defense counsel]: Well, your Honor, there is the law which requires the court to make an independent determination and weigh the facts.... [¶] The Court: I have, but when you talk about the one witness you had who—sure, albeit, [was] dyslexic, the jury could very well have disregarded her, with the other witness's testimony by deposition [Mr. Raven]. [¶] Deposition testimony is as good as other testimony, but with that in juxtaposition [with] the people in the ... van, I wouldn't give her—it nearly as much credence. But still, it is strictly a matter of weighing the evidence, and reasonable people can differ, and I cannot upset the verdict."

The experienced and able trial judge in the instant case impliedly found that there was sufficient credible evidence to support the verdict, and that the jury was reasonable in believing the witnesses it apparently had believed in reaching its verdict. The court recognized that it could not grant the motion for new trial simply because it would have found differently than the jury. Thus, we find without merit appellant's contention that the trial court erred in denying the motion for new trial. * * *

The judgment is affirmed.

Notes and Questions regarding New Trial Orders

(1) Was the *Sanchez-Corea* court hypertechnical when it construed CCP § 657 to require a trial court to state grounds at the time it grants a new trial order? What is the purpose of this requirement in CCP § 657? Why was this purpose not satisfied when the trial court stated the grounds seven days later in its second order? Was the Supreme Court's distinction between "grounds" and "reasons" also hypertechnical? Why not permit the trial court's subsequent statement of grounds to relate back to the date of the first new trial order? Would such relation back satisfy the objectives behind § 657?

(2) The defendant Bank relied on *LaManna v. Stewart*, 13 Cal. 3d 413, 118 Cal. Rptr. 761, 530 P.2d 1073 (1975), where the Supreme Court upheld a new trial order based on insufficiency of the evidence even though the trial court never stated any grounds nor specified reasons. Are you persuaded by the analysis in *Sanchez-Corea* which distinguished *LaManna*? If the Supreme Court was willing to deem the trial court's total failure to ever state grounds or reasons cured in *LaManna*, why not deem the trial court's failure in *Sanchez-Corea* cured by the second new trial order which stated the grounds and reasons? Are you persuaded by the Supreme Court's explanation for refusing to treat the second order as curative of the defective first order?

(3) The trial court's failure to comply with the strict requirements of CCP § 657 in *Sanchez-Corea* precluded the defendant Bank from relying on its strongest ground— insufficiency of the evidence—in arguing for affirmance of the new trial order on appeal. This seems unfair generally, but particularly because CCP § 657 prohibits a trial court from directing a party to prepare either the order or the specification of reasons. Are you satisfied with the Supreme Court's response to the obvious unfairness to the successful movant on appeal due to an error by the trial court? Was there any way by which the Supreme Court could have mitigated this unfairness, consistent with the purposes of CCP § 657? Why does § 657 prohibit a trial court from delegating to counsel the preparation of a new trial order statement of grounds or specification of reasons?

[2] *Motion for New Trial: Procedures*

[a] Aggrieved Party Must File Motion

The aggrieved party must file a written notice of intention to move for a new trial, along with a memorandum of points and authorities, with the trial court. CCP § 659, Rule 3.1600, Cal. Rules of Ct. *See Ataide v. Hamilton Copper & Steel Corp.*, 229 Cal. App. 3d 624, 630, 280 Cal. Rptr. 259 (1991) (concluding oral motion insufficient because new trial statute requires written motion). This notice must designate the grounds upon which the motion is made. CCP §659(a). The motion for new trial can only be granted on a ground specified in the notice of intention to move for a new trial. *Malkasian v. Irwin*, 61 Cal. 2d 738, 745, 40 Cal. Rptr. 78, 394 P.2d 822 (1964); *Wagner v. Singleton*, 133 Cal. App. 3d 69, 183 Cal. Rptr. 631 (1982) (holding an order granting new trial on ground of misconduct of counsel is void when motion only specified ground of insufficiency of the evidence); *Neal v. Montgomery Elevator Co.*, 7 Cal. App. 4th 1194, 1198, 9 Cal. Rptr. 2d 497 (1992) (finding new trial granted due to material error of law ruled procedurally proper where error of law listed as one of the grounds in plaintiff's notice of motion, although not urged by plaintiff in moving papers or at oral argument). What are the reasons for this limitation?

[b] New Trial Motion and Declarations Must Be Timely Filed

The notice of intention to move for a new trial must be filed within 15 days of the date of mailing notice of entry of judgment by the clerk or by a party, or within 180 days after entry of judgment, whichever is earliest. CCP §659(a). Compliance with these statutory time limits is jurisdictional; a court has no power to entertain an untimely motion nor to order a new trial on its own motion. *See, e.g., Palmer v. GTE Cal., Inc.*, 30 Cal. 4th 1265, 135 Cal. Rptr. 2d 654, 70 P.3d 1067 (2003) (discussing the statutory time limits and concluding that written notice of entry of judgment is satisfied by serving a copy of a file-stamped judgment); *Ramirez v. Moran*, 201 Cal. App. 3d 431, 437, 247 Cal. Rptr. 117 (1988) (holding a new trial motion filed after 15-day limit was invalid and therefore did not extend time to appeal the judgment); *Tri-County Elevator Co. v. Superior Court*, 135 Cal. App. 3d 271, 277, 185 Cal. Rptr. 208 (1982) (ruling trial court lacked power to consider new trial motion filed 18 days after entry of judgment mailed). Likewise, the statutory time limit for another party to file a cross-motion for new trial — 15 days from service of the first notice of intention to move per §659 — is jurisdictional. *See, e.g., Pelletier v. Eisenberg*, 177 Cal. App. 3d 558, 563, 223 Cal. Rptr. 84 (1986).

Within 10 days of filing the notice, the moving party must also file and serve any supporting affidavits. CCP §659a. Unless extended for good cause shown, this 10-day limitation precludes consideration of untimely affidavits. *See Maple v. Cincinnati, Inc.*, 163 Cal. App. 3d 387, 391–392, 209 Cal. Rptr. 451 (1985) (holding trial court erred in considering new trial affidavits filed late). The other parties have 10 days thereafter within which to file and serve counter-affidavits. CCP §659a. Failure to timely file supporting affidavits may be fatal to some new trial motions. Pursuant to CCP §658, a motion for new trial on the grounds enumerated in the first four subdivisions of CCP §657 must be presented solely by affidavit. *Linhart v. Nelson*, 18 Cal. 3d 641, 134 Cal. Rptr. 813, 557 P.2d 104 (1976) (ruling trial court properly rejected testimony of subpoenaed witnesses offered in support of new trial motion based on juror misconduct). What are the policy reasons behind CCP §658's preclusion of witnesses testimony in certain new trial motions? *See Linhart*, 18 Cal. 3d at 644–45.

A party who moves for a new trial on the ground of juror improprieties must file a "no-knowledge" declaration which states that neither the attorney nor the client was aware of the alleged misconduct prior to the verdict. *Weathers v. Kaiser Found. Hosp.*, 5 Cal. 3d 98, 103, 95 Cal. Rptr. 516, 485 P.2d 1132 (1971); *Wiley v. Southern Pac. Transp. Co.*, 220 Cal. App. 3d 177, 186–87, 269 Cal. Rptr. 240 (1989) (citing cases). What is the purpose of this "no-knowledge" declaration?

[c] The New Trial Order Must State Grounds and Specify Reasons

Section 657 requires the trial judge to state the grounds upon which the motion was granted in the new trial order, and to specify the reasons within 10 days after the order. As *Sanchez-Corea* illustrates, a trial court must strictly adhere to these mandatory procedures. *See, e.g., Hand Elec., Inc. v. Snowline Joint Unified Sch. Dist.*, 21 Cal. App. 4th 862, 867–868, 26 Cal. Rptr. 2d 446 (1994) (holding trial court's statement of reasons filed 15 days after new trial order untimely and void); *Stewart v. Truck Ins. Exch.*, 17 Cal. App. 4th 468, 484–85, 21 Cal. Rptr. 2d 338 (1993) (ruling oral statement of grounds by the judge not sufficient); *Smith v. Moffat*, 73 Cal. App. 3d 86, 140 Cal. Rptr. 566 (1977) (finding specification of reasons filed 24 days after entry of minute order untimely, and holding new trial order based on insufficiency of evidence and inadequacy of damages invalid). A new trial order which does not state grounds or specify reasons is defective but not void under § 657. *Sanchez-Corea* also demonstrates that under such circumstances an appellate court is precluded by § 657 from affirming the order on the grounds of insufficiency of the evidence or excessive damages. *See, e.g., Hand Elec., Inc., supra,* 21 Cal. App. 4th at 867–68 (ruling appellate court limited to whether new trial order should be affirmed because of error of law in jury instructions).

As discussed previously, the appellate court is further precluded from considering any other ground not designated in the motion for new trial. *See Neal v. Montgomery Elevator Co., supra,* 7 Cal. App. 4th at 1198. What are the policy reasons for imposing these statutory requirements for new trial orders on the trial courts? For imposing these statutory limitations on appellate courts when reviewing defective new trial orders? *See Stewart v. Truck Ins. Exch., supra,* 17 Cal. App. 4th at 484 (observing that these statutory requirements were "designed to serve the dual purposes of (1) promoting some deliberation on the part of the trial court in the exercise of its broad discretionary power to grant a new trial and (2) making the right of appeal more meaningful by focusing the reviewing court's attention on the portion of the record which justifies the new trial order").

(1) What constitutes an adequate specification of reasons? Section 657 provides little guidance: "When a new trial is granted, on all or part of the issues, the court shall specify the ground or grounds upon which it is granted and the court's reason or reasons for granting the new trial upon each ground stated." Must the statement of grounds and reasons be in writing? *See LaManna v. Stewart*, 13 Cal. 3d 413, 423, 118 Cal. Rptr. 761, 530 P.2d 1073 (1975) (ruling both the order and the statement of reasons must be in writing; an oral recital does not comply with the statutory di-

rective); *Thompson v. Friendly Hills Reg'l Med. Ctr.*, 71 Cal. App. 4th 544, 549–50, 84 Cal. Rptr. 2d 51 (1999) (concluding neither the transcript of the new trial hearing nor the defense counsel's notice of ruling satisfied the requirement of a written specification of reasons); *but see Twedt v. Franklin*, 109 Cal. App. 4th 413, 134 Cal. Rptr. 2d 740 (2003) (ruling the requirement of a written statement of reasons satisfied by a written order that attaches and incorporates a hearing transcript where the trial judge explains why the evidence did not support the jury's verdict).

(2) Must the specification of reasons state more than ultimate facts? *See Stevens v. Parke, Davis & Co.*, 9 Cal. 3d 51, 62, 107 Cal. Rptr. 45, 507 P.2d 653 (1973) (holding trial court's statement of ultimate fact that "the verdict is excessive, that it is not sustained by the evidence" and was "based upon prejudice and passion on the part of the jury" is an inadequate specification of reasons); *Miller v. L. A. Cnty. Flood Control Dist.*, 8 Cal. 3d 689, 698, 106 Cal. Rptr. 1, 505 P.2d 193 (1973) (finding trial court's statement of reasons that "the District completely and adequately discharged any obligation it had in the maintenance of the basin and dam" inadequate to support insufficiency of the evidence ground for new trial); *Lane v. Hughes Aircraft Co.*, 22 Cal. 4th 405, 413–15, 93 Cal. Rptr. 2d 60, 993 P.2d 388 (2000) (noting the specification must not be a mere statement of ultimate facts, and must be supported by the record; § 657, which bars a trial court from imposing upon counsel the preparation of new trial orders, does not prohibit a court from adopting material in a party's brief).

In *Romero v. Riggs*, 24 Cal. App. 4th 117, 29 Cal. Rptr. 2d 219 (1994), the trial judge granted plaintiff's new trial motion on the stated grounds of "insufficiency of the evidence to justify the [defense] verdict" on the issue of causation in a medical malpractice action. The new trial order specified the following reasons for the stated ground: "The medical evidence was overwhelming that the early onset and the severity of the effect upon the plaintiff and his early deterioration of eyesight was a direct and proximate result of the negligent failure of the defendant doctor to diagnose and treat the plaintiff's condition." The defendant argued that this specification of reasons was inadequate because the trial court did not declare which witnesses it believed or disbelieved. The Court of Appeal rejected this argument and found the statement of reasons "fully adequate both to guide appellate review and as to supply a substantial basis for the order." *Romero*, 24 Cal. App. 4th at 124. The *Romero* court relied on *Bigboy v. County of San Diego*, 154 Cal. App. 3d 397, 201 Cal. Rptr. 226 (1984), where, after a survey of several cases in which new trial orders were affirmed, the court noted "[e]ach of these cases specifically directs the appellate court's attention to some aspect of the record which convinces the trial judge the jury clearly should have reached a different decision." *Bigboy*, 154 Cal. App. 3d at 405. Is this a useful standard? A sensible interpretation of CCP § 657? Do you agree with the *Romero* court's conclusion that the trial judge's statement, quoted above, satisfied § 657? Why?

(3) In *Oakland Raiders v. National Football League*, 41 Cal. 4th 624, 61 Cal. Rptr. 3d 634, 161 P.3d 151 (2007), the Supreme Court addressed the issue of which standard of appellate review—abuse of discretion or independent review—applies when a trial court grants a new trial on the ground of jury misconduct and properly specifies

the ground for granting the motion but does not provide a statement of the reasons for granting the new trial on that ground. The Court concluded that the absence of a statement of reasons calls for "independent review" of the trial court's order, meaning a form of review that does not defer to the trial court's inferred resolution of conflicts in the evidence. *Oakland Raiders*, 41 Cal. 4th at 640.

[d] 60-Day Limit on Trial Court's Power to Decide Motion

Section 660 provides in pertinent part: " ... the power of the court to rule on a motion for a new trial shall expire 60 days from and after the mailing of notice of entry of judgment by the clerk ... or 60 days from and after service on the moving party by any party of written notice of the entry of the judgment, whichever is earlier, or if such notice has not theretofore been given, then 60 days after filing of the first notice of intention to move for a new trial. If such motion is not determined within said period of 60 days, ... the effect shall be a denial of the motion without further order of the court." A trial court lacks jurisdiction to decide a new trial motion after the 60-day limitation imposed by CCP § 660. *Siegal v. Superior Court*, 68 Cal. 2d 97, 101, 65 Cal. Rptr. 311, 736 P.2d 311 (1968); *Green v. Laibco, LLC*, 192 Cal. App. 4th 441, 446–49, 121 Cal. Rptr. 3d 415 (2011) (vacating new trial order and thereby reinstating $2.4 million judgment, because trial court ruling was on the 61st day after defendant filed the new trial motion). *Sanchez-Corea* held that a trial court also lacks jurisdiction to file the statement of grounds after the 60-day period, even though the trial court decided the motion within the 60-day limitation.

Does a trial court also lack jurisdiction to file the required specification of reasons after the 60-day period, even though 5 days earlier the trial court filed a timely new trial order and statement of grounds? *See Jordy v. County of Humboldt*, 11 Cal. App. 4th 735, 741, 14 Cal. Rptr. 2d 553 (1992). What about where the trial court granted the new trial motion by minute order within the 60-day period accompanied by a detailed oral statement of grounds and reasons dictated into the record, and then subsequently confirmed the grant by a formal written order filed after the 60-day period with a reference to the transcript of the prior oral statement? *See Steinhart v. South Coast Area Transit*, 183 Cal. App. 3d 770, 773–74, 228 Cal. Rptr. 283 (1986).

Does the mailing by the clerk of the court of a file-stamped copy of the judgment commence the 60-day period of the § 660? *See Van Beurden Ins. Serv., Inc. v. Customized Worldwide Weather Ins. Agency, Inc.*, 15 Cal. 4th 51, 61 Cal. Rptr. 2d 166, 931 P.2d 344 (1997) (construing CCP § 660 and § 664.5 to determine under what circumstances the mailing of a file-stamped copy of the judgment by the clerk of the court constitutes "notice of entry of judgment" for purposes of determining the time for a party to file and the trial court to rule on a motion for new trial); *Maroney v. Jacobsohn*, 237 Cal. App. 4th 473, 187 Cal. Rptr. 3d 720 (2015) (holding that absent notice mailed by the clerk, a party must serve notice of entry of judgment *on the moving party* to shorten the 180-day deadline under § 659 and to start the 60-day jurisdictional clock under § 660). To what extent may the merits of a new trial motion be reviewed upon appeal where the motion was denied by operation of law (i.e., by expiration of the 60-day time period)? *See Sanchez-Corea*, reproduced *supra*; *Marriage of Liu*, *supra*, 197 Cal. App. 3d at 152. Does a trial court have jurisdiction to rule, after the 60-day period has expired, on a timely-filed motion for reconsideration of a new trial order pursuant to CCP § 1008? *See Jones v. Sieve*, 203 Cal. App. 3d 359, 249 Cal. Rptr. 821 (1988).

[3] Motion for New Trial: Grounds

[a] Statutory Grounds Exclusive

Section 657 sets forth the exclusive grounds upon which a trial court may grant a new trial. *See Linhart v. Nelson*, 18 Cal. 3d 641, 134 Cal. Rptr. 813, 557 P.2d 104 (1976); *Smith v. Moffat*, 73 Cal. App. 3d 86, 93, 140 Cal. Rptr. 566 (1977). These enumerated grounds encompass both procedural errors (*e.g.*, jury misconduct and other irregularities in the proceedings) and substantive errors (*e.g.*, insufficiency of the evidence, excessive damages, and error in law) occurring during trial. A new trial may not be granted, of course, unless the error materially affects the substantial rights of the moving party—in other words, unless the error is prejudicial and not harmless. Art. VI, § 13, Cal. Const. ("No judgment shall be set aside, or new trial granted ... unless, after an examination of the entire cause, including the evidence, the court shall be of the opinion that the error complained of has resulted in a miscarriage of justice."); *see Hasson v. Ford Motor Co.*, 32 Cal. 3d 388, 185 Cal. Rptr. 654, 650 P.2d 1171 (1982) (holding new trial not required where no substantial prejudice resulted from jury misconduct); *Mosesian v. Pennwalt Corp.*, 191 Cal. App. 3d 851, 859, 236 Cal. Rptr. 778 (1987) (granting a new trial where the error was harmless violated the California Constitution).

[b] Motion an Exercise of Discretion

Regardless of whether the grounds asserted in support of a new trial motion would constitute procedural or substantive error, the determination of the motion is addressed to the trial court's discretion. *See, e.g., Romero v. Riggs*, *supra*, 24 Cal. App. 4th at 121 (applying abuse of discretion standard to new trial granted because of insufficiency of the evidence); *Hand Elec., Inc. v. Snowline Joint Unified Sch. Dist.*, *supra*, 21 Cal. App. 4th at 871 (noting that on appeal from an order granting a new trial because of misleading jury instruction, sole question is whether trial court abused its discretion). A new trial order will not be disturbed on appeal "unless a manifest and unmistakable abuse of discretion clearly appears." *See, e.g., Jiminez v. Sears, Roebuck & Co.*, 4 Cal. 3d 379, 387, 93 Cal. Rptr. 769, 482 P.2d 681 (1971) (observing that so long as a reasonable or even fairly debatable justification under law is shown for an order granting a new trial, the order will not be set aside). Why is the determination of a new trial motion asserting grounds of substantive error a matter for the trial court's discretion? Should it be? In what sense is such a motion not a matter of trial court discretion?

[c] Insufficiency of the Evidence

As *Dominguez v. Pantalone*, reproduced *supra*, illustrates, when a trial court determines a motion for new trial made upon the ground of insufficiency of the evidence, CCP § 657 requires the judge to weigh the evidence and judge the credibility of witnesses. In so doing, the court may disbelieve witnesses and draw inferences contrary to those supporting the verdict. *Locksley v. Ungureanu*, 178 Cal. App. 3d 457, 463, 223 Cal. Rptr. 737 (1986); *Widener v. Pac. Gas & Elec. Co.*, 75 Cal. App. 3d 415, 440, 142 Cal. Rptr. 304 (1977). The court may grant a new trial even though there is sufficient evidence to sustain the jury's verdict on appeal. *Candido v. Huitt*, 151 Cal. App. 3d 918, 923, 199 Cal. Rptr. 41 (1984). Nonetheless, a new trial cannot be granted "unless after weighing the evidence the court is convinced from the entire record, including reasonable inferences therefrom, that the court or jury clearly should have reached a different verdict or decision." CCP § 657. Is the standard adopted by the court in *Dominguez*, and subsequently utilized again in *Kelly-Zurian v. Wohl Shoe Co.*, 22 Cal. App. 4th 397, 413–14, 27 Cal. Rptr. 2d 457 (1994), consistent with this quoted portion of CCP § 657? Does the *Dominguez* court's standard require the trial judge to give more deference to the jury verdict than § 657 requires, or less deference? Or are the two standards really the same? If the trial court in *Dominguez* had *granted* the defendant's new trial motion and the plaintiff appealed, would the order be affirmed on appeal? Why?

How is the standard a trial judge must employ when determining a new trial motion for insufficiency of the evidence under CCP § 657 different from the standard applicable to a motion for judgment notwithstanding the verdict under CCP § 629? *See Fountain Valley Chateau Blanc Homeowners' Assn. v. Dept. of Veteran Affairs*, 67 Cal. App. 4th 743, 79 Cal. Rptr. 2d 248 (1998); *Dell'Oca v. Bank of N.Y. Trust Co.*, 159 Cal. App. 4th 531, 547–48, 71 Cal. Rptr. 3d 737 (2008). Why are these two standards different? If a trial court grants a new trial motion for insufficiency of the evidence, must it also grant an accompanying JNOV motion? If the court denies a party's new trial motion on the ground of insufficiency of the evidence, must it also deny that party's JNOV motion?

What is the standard applicable to appellate review of a trial court order granting a new trial on the basis of insufficient evidence to support the jury verdict? The Supreme Court answered this question, and several others with respect to new trial orders under CCP § 657, in *Lane v. Hughes Aircraft Co.*, 22 Cal. 4th 405, 93 Cal. Rptr. 2d 60, 993 P.2d 388 (2000). An order granting a new trial based on insufficiency of the evidence "must be sustained on appeal unless the opposing party demonstrates that no reasonable finder of fact could have found for the movant on [the trial court's] theory." *Lane, supra*, 22 Cal. 4th at 409. The reason for this deference is that the trial court, in ruling on the new trial motion, sits as an independent trier of fact. *Id.* at 412. "Therefore, the trial court's factual determinations, reflected in its decision to grant a new trial, are entitled to the same deference that an appellate court would ordinarily accord a jury's factual determinations." *Id.* The court emphasized that "so long as the outcome is uncertain at the close of trial—that is, so long as the evidence can support a verdict if favor of *either* party—a properly constructed new trial order is not subject to reversal on appeal." *Lane*, 22 Cal. 4th at 414.

[d] Excessive Damages and Conditional New Trial Orders (Remittitur)

Section 657 also requires a trial judge to weigh the evidence and judge the credibility of witnesses when determining a motion for new trial based upon the ground of excessive or inadequate damages. In ruling on a motion for a new trial for excessive damages, the trial court does not sit in an appellate capacity "but as an independent trier of fact." *Neal v. Farmers Ins. Exch.*, 21 Cal. 3d 910, 933, 148 Cal. Rptr. 389, 582 P.2d 980 (1978) (holding trial court did not abuse discretion in granting new trial motion for excessive damages where the evidence bearing on damages issue was in substantial conflict).

The trial court may, in its discretion, order a new trial limited to the issue of damages and may condition its order so that the motion is denied if the party in whose favor the verdict has been rendered consents to such reduction of damages "as the court in its independent judgment determines from the evidence to be fair and reasonable." CCP § 662.5(a)(2). Such a conditional new trial procedure, commonly referred to as "remittitur," is expressly authorized by CCP § 662.5(a)(2). Section 662.5(a)(1) authorizes the corresponding process of "additur" for inadequate damages. *See, e.g., Marshall v. Dept. of Water & Power*, 219 Cal. App. 3d 1124, 1137, 268 Cal. Rptr. 559 (1990) (increasing jury award of $1 to $100,001 by means of additur after plaintiff moved for new trial); *Pacific Corp. Grp. Holdings v. Keck*, 232 Cal. App. 4th 294, 314–21, 181 Cal. Rptr. 3d 399 (2014) (discussing the law governing a motion for new trial based on inadequate damages and a court's power to issue a conditional additur order).

Trial courts often utilize remittitur when damages are properly awarded but the amount is excessive, and a new trial can be avoided if the nonmoving party consents to a reduction. *See, e.g., Hasson v. Ford Motor Co.*, 32 Cal. 3d 388, 418–21, 185 Cal. Rptr. 654, 650 P.2d 1171 (1982) (requiring plaintiff to consent to a $1,650,000 reduction in damage award in order to avoid a new trial); *Neal, supra*, 21 Cal. 3d at 920 (Jury verdict of $1.5 million remitted to $750,000); *Grimshaw v. Ford Motor Co.*, 119 Cal. App. 3d 757, 174 Cal. Rptr. 348 (1981) (requiring plaintiff to remit all but $3.5 million of $125 million punitive damage verdict as a condition of denial of defendant's new trial motion). A trial court may not use a remittitur, however, to condition a new trial order if the damage award is excessive only because it reflects an improper apportionment of liability. *Schelbauer v. Butler Mfg. Co.*, 35 Cal. 3d 442, 198 Cal. Rptr. 155, 673 P.2d 743 (1984) (holding use of remittitur to reduce product liability award by 15% to reflect trial court's determination that plaintiff was 5% negligent and employer 10% negligent is an abuse of discretion). Why is such use of remittitur improper? What should the trial court do in such circumstances?

Must an order conditionally granting a new trial on the ground of excessive damages comply with the procedural requirements of CCP § 657, even when the plaintiff subsequently consents to the reduction and thereby negates the effect of the new trial order? The Supreme Court in *Neal v. Farmers Ins. Exch., supra*, 21 Cal. 3d at 931, held that a conditional new trial order entered pursuant to CCP § 662.5 is no less of an order granting a new trial than an unconditional one. Consequently, a conditional new trial order must comply with all the statutory requirements of

CCP § 657, including a timely and adequate specification of reasons which should "indicate the respects in which the evidence dictated a less sizeable verdict." *Neal*, 21 Cal. 3d at 932. Although the specification need not be as detailed relative to claims of excessive punitive damages as for allegations concerning compensatory damages, a proper written specification of reasons is nevertheless required in all instances. *Neal*, 21 Cal. 3d at 932–33; *see Greenfield v. Spectrum Inv. Corp.*, 174 Cal. App. 3d 111, 219 Cal. Rptr. 805 (1985) (ruling oral statement of reasons inadequate); *Ballou v. Master Properties No. 6*, 189 Cal. App. 3d 65, 234 Cal. Rptr. 264 (1987) (holding statement of reasons filed when option to accept reduction of damages expired but more than 10 days after new trial conditionally granted was untimely and inadequate).

Where a trial court grants a new trial on the grounds of excessive damages but fails to make an adequate and timely specification of reasons, the courts have held that the new trial order must be reversed and the verdict automatically reinstated. *See, e.g., Stevens v. Parke, Davis & Co., supra*, 9 Cal. 3d at 63; *Ballou, supra*, 189 Cal. App. 3d at 72; *see also LaManna v. Stewart, supra*, 13 Cal. 3d at 425 (applying the same rule where new trial order on ground of insufficiency of the evidence held invalid). Is reversal and automatic reinstatement of the verdict required by CCP § 657 under such circumstances? Is such reversal consistent with *Sanchez-Corea*?

An appellate court will not reverse a proper order granting a new trial on the ground of excessive damages, or requiring a reduction of the amount as a condition of denying one, unless the trial court plainly abused its discretion. *Neal v. Farmers Ins. Exch., supra*, 21 Cal. 3d at 933. Wholly independent of any new trial order, an appellate court also has the power to reverse a damage award that is excessive as a matter of law. *Neal*, 21 Cal. 3d at 928–29; *Las Palmas Assoc. v. La Palmas Ctr. Assoc.*, 235 Cal. App. 3d 1220, 1252–59, 1 Cal. Rptr. 2d 301 (1991) (holding a jury award of $1.27 million for fraud and $10 million as punitive damages excessive as a matter of law, and reducing the award to $232,393 and $2 million). Although a trial court may weigh the evidence and grant a new trial or order a remittitur if it finds the jury's award to be against the weight of the evidence, an appellate court is not so empowered. Why not? What standard must an appellate court apply when determining whether a jury verdict is excessive as a matter of law? *See Hasson v. Ford Motor Co., supra*, 32 Cal. 3d at 419 (ruling an appellate court may overturn an award of damages only if after reviewing the record favorably to the judgment, without weighing the evidence, the court concludes that the award is so grossly disproportionate to the harm suffered as to raise the presumption that it resulted from passion or prejudice).

The Due Process Clause of the Fourteenth Amendment to the U. S. Constitution places constraints on the amount of state court awards of punitive damages. *See State Farm Mut. Auto Ins. Co. v. Campbell*, 538 U.S. 408, 123 S. Ct. 1513, 155 Le. Ed. 2d 585 (2003); *BMW of North America v. Gore*, 517 U.S. 559, 116 S. Ct. 1589, 134 L. Ed. 2d 809 (1996). A trial or appellate court may direct the reduction of a jury's award of punitive damages under the due process standards, without ordering a new trial on the question of punitive damages. *See Roby v. McKesson Corp.*, 47 Cal. 4th 686, 101 Cal. Rptr. 3d 773, 219 P.3d 749 (2009) (concluding $1,905,000 is the maximum amount of punitive damages consistent with due process clause and directs trial court to reduce jury award of $15 million to that amount); *Amerigraphics, Inc. v. Mercury Cas. Co.*, 182 Cal. App. 4th 1538, 1557–67, 107 Cal. Rptr. 3d 307 (2010) (reversing $1.7 million award for punitive damages as excessive, and directing trial court to reduce the award to $500,000); *Pfeifer v. John Crane, Inc.*, 220 Cal. App. 4th 1270, 1298–1315, 164 Cal. Rptr. 3d 112 (2013) (applying the due process standards and affirming $14.5 million punitive damages award).

[e] Newly Discovered Evidence

In *Marriage of Liu, supra*, 197 Cal. App. 3d at 153–154, the court expressed the narrow construction typically given this ground: "In making a motion for new trial on this ground, the party seeking relief has the burden to prove that he exercised reasonable diligence to discover and produce the evidence at trial. If the party does not make this showing, the motion must be denied. Moreover, a general averment of diligence is insufficient. The moving party must state the particular acts or circumstances which establish diligence." In *Marriage of Liu*, the appellant contended that a new trial should be granted because she only discovered after trial that a previously uncooperative key expert witness was now willing to testify. The court found appellant's newly discovered evidence argument meritless because she failed to explain why she could not have discovered this prior to or during trial. *Liu*, 197 Cal. App. 3d at 154.

Even where the moving party successfully proves the requisite exercise of diligence, the party must also show that the newly discovered evidence is "material in the sense that it is likely to produce a different result" at the trial. *National Elevator Serv., Inc. v. Dept. of Indus. Relations*, 136 Cal. App. 3d 131, 138–39, 186 Cal. Rptr. 165 (1982); *Horowitz v. Noble*, 79 Cal. App. 3d 120, 138, 144 Cal. Rptr. 710 (1978). How might a party demonstrate the requisite "materiality" of newly discovered evidence?

In *Sherman v. Kinetic Concepts, Inc.*, 67 Cal. App. 4th 1152, 79 Cal. Rptr. 2d 641 (1998), following a jury verdict for the defendant in a products liability action, the plaintiffs fortuitously discovered that the defendant had withheld evidence — dozens of undisclosed incident reports showing that the defendant's product frequently malfunctioned causing injuries — requested during pretrial discovery. The trial court denied the plaintiffs' motion for a new trial on the grounds of newly discovered evidence. The Court of Appeal reversed, and ordered the trial court to grant a new trial. On the issue of whether these incident reports were material, the court concluded that the new evidence was not merely cumulative, but went to the very essence of all of the plaintiffs' defendant's claims. Defendant's non production prevented the plaintiffs not only from obtaining the information contained in the reports, but from following up; and thereby depriving the plaintiffs of the chance to tell the jury the whole story. *Sherman*, 67 Cal. App. 4th at 1161–62.

[f] Accident or Surprise

The courts apply this ground quite narrowly to preclude a new trial based on mistake, inadvertence, or neglect by a party or her attorney. *See, e.g., Marriage of Liu, supra,* 197 Cal. App. 3d at 155 (citing cases); *see also* § 14.05, Relief from Final Judgment, *infra.* A new trial may be appropriate based on this ground where a party called a last-minute expert witness, not previously identified during pretrial discovery, and a continuance is not afforded the opposing party. *See, e.g., Whitehill v. U. S. Lines, Inc.,* 177 Cal. App. 3d 1201, 1210, 223 Cal. Rptr. 452 (1986) (finding no prejudice where trial court offered to recess trial to permit deposition of surprise expert, but party refused the offer); *City of Fresno v. Harrison,* 154 Cal. App. 3d 296, 201 Cal. Rptr. 219 (1984) (concluding new trial properly granted where recently retained expert permitted to testify and continuance would be unfair).

[g] Jury Misconduct and Other Irregularities

As *Sanchez-Corea* and *Dominguez* illustrate, misconduct during trial—either by the jury, judge, or the opposing counsel—is often asserted as a ground when moving for a new trial. These grounds are discussed in considerable detail in § 13.04[C] Impeachment of Verdict for Juror Misconduct, *supra,* of this Chapter. Any irregularities which deprive a party of a fair and impartial trial may constitute grounds for a new trial under CCP § 657(1). *See, e.g., Martinez v. State of Cal.,* 238 Cal. App. 4th 559, 189 Cal. Rptr. 3d 325 (2015) (reversing judgment for defendant based on cumulative effect of egregious misconduct by defendant's attorney); *Haluck v. Ricoh Elec., Inc.,* 151 Cal. App. 4th 994, 60 Cal. Rptr. 3d 542 (2007) (finding trial judge's conduct, such as allowing only defendant's lawyer to be present when judge previewed video tape to which plaintiff objected, giving defendant's lawyer free rein to deride plaintiffs and their lawyer, using "overruled" signs to respond to objections, and using a soccer-style red card to stop plaintiffs' lawyer from talking, was sufficiently egregious and pervasive that a reasonable person could doubt whether the trial was fair and impartial); *Marriage of Carlsson,* 163 Cal. App. 4th 281, 77 Cal. Rptr. 3d 305 (2008) (ruling that by arbitrarily cutting off the presentation of evidence, the trial judge render the trial fundamentally unfair); *but see California Crane Sch., Inc. v. Nat. Comm'n for Certification of Crane Operators,* 226 Cal. App. 4th 12, 171 Cal. Rptr. 3d 752 (2014) (holding trial court did not deprive plaintiffs of a fair trial by imposing a 12-day limit on the time for trial, even though plaintiffs were unable to present rebuttable evidence).

[4] *Federal Court New Trial Motions Compared*

[a] Federal Grounds

The federal rules authorize a federal trial judge to grant a new trial "for any reason for which a new trial has heretofore been granted in an action at law in federal court." Rule 59(a)(1), F.R.C.P. This broad authority permits a federal district court to order a new trial on grounds such as insufficiency of the evidence to support the verdict, excessive damages, newly discovered evidence, misconduct of jury or opposing counsel, and other prejudicial irregularities in the proceedings. *See generally* Wright, Miller, & Kane *Federal Practice and Procedure* §§ 2805–2810 (3d ed. 2012 & Supp. 2015). The district court must apply federal standards developed under Rule 59 when considering such grounds, even in a diversity jurisdiction case applying state substantive law; except where a new trial standard is part of the state's substantive law. *Gasperini v. Center for Humanities, Inc.*, 518 U.S. 415, 116 S. Ct. 2211, 135 L. Ed. 2d 659 (1996); *see Browning-Ferris Indus. of Vermont, Inc. v. Kelco Disposal, Inc.*, 492 U.S. 257, 279, 109 S. Ct. 2909, 106 L. Ed. 2d 219 (1989). Such review of a jury verdict by a federal district court is always subject to the Seventh Amendment constraints guaranteeing the right to a jury trial; constraints which are not imposed on any state-prescribed post-trial review. *See Gasperini, supra*, 518 U.S. at 432–36.

The federal district courts commonly employ some variant of the "verdict-against-the-great-weight-of-the-evidence" standard when determining the insufficiency of the evidence to support a verdict. *See, e.g., Roebuck v. Drexel Univ.*, 852 F.2d 715, 736 (3d Cir. 1988) ("The verdict is contrary to the great weight of the evidence, thus making a new trial necessary to prevent a miscarriage of justice"); *Eyre v. McDonough Power Equip., Inc.*, 755 F.2d 416, 420 (5th Cir. 1985) (noting the district court empowered to grant motion for new trial when "verdict is against the great—but not merely the greater—weight of the evidence"); *Brown v. McGraw-Edison Co.*, 736 F.2d 609, 616–617 (10th Cir. 1984) (ruling the new trial standard is whether the verdict is "clearly, decidedly, or overwhelmingly against the weight of the evidence").

The federal courts disagree somewhat on the extent to which a federal trial judge may weigh the evidence and consider the credibility of the witnesses in determining whether a jury verdict is against the weight of the evidence. *Compare Fineman v. Armstrong World Indus., Inc.*, 980 F.2d 171, 211 (3d Cir. 1992) (observing a trial court should not usurp the prime function of the jury as the trier of facts by substituting its judgment of the facts and the credibility of the witnesses for that of the jury) *with Poynter v. Ratcliff*, 874 F.2d 219, 223 (4th Cir. 1989) (ruling a trial judge may weigh the credibility of witnesses, and may grant a new trial even if the verdict is supported by substantial evidence).

The courts all agree, however, that the federal "against the great weight" standard governing new trial motions under Rule 59 is less deferential to jury verdicts than is the standard for granting post-verdict motions for judgment as a matter of law (JNOV) under Rule 50(a). *See, e.g., Roebuck, supra*, 852 F. 2d at 735–37; *Eyre, supra*, 755 F. 2d at 420–21. Accordingly, a district judge may grant a new trial under Rule 59 upon a determination that the verdict is against the great weight of the evidence, but deny a motion for judgment as a matter of law under Rule 50(a). *See* Rule 50(c), F.R.C.P. Contrary to a Rule 50 motion, Rule 59 does not make a motion for judgment as a matter of law (directed verdict) during trial a prerequisite to a new trial order. *See, e.g., Metromedia Co. v. Fugazy*, 983 F.2d 350, 363 (2d Cir. 1992), *cert. denied*, 508 U.S. 952 (1993) (ruling if evidence was insufficient but no motion for directed verdict was made, trial court could grant a Rule 59 new trial but not a Rule 50 judgment as a matter of law).

To what extent is the federal standard for a new trial on the ground of insufficiency of the evidence under Rule 59 different than the California standard under CCP § 657? Which standard is more deferential to jury verdicts? Why? Which standard do you prefer? Why? The federal courts may also grant a new trial on the ground of excessive damages, and may condition this new trial upon a remittitur. *See, e.g., Gumbs v. Pueblo Intl., Inc.,* 823 F.2d 768 (3d Cir. 1987); *United States v. 47.14 Acres of Land,* 674 F.2d 722 (8th Cir. 1982); *see also* Irene Sann, Note, *Remittitur Practice in the Federal Courts,* 76 Colum. L. Rev. 299 (1976). Federal judges lack the authority to grant a new trial for inadequate damages conditioned upon the defendant's consent to an increase in damages, however, because such an additur is viewed as an impermissible invasion of the province of the jury and therefore precluded by the Seventh Amendment. *See Dimick v. Schiedt,* 293 U.S. 474, 55 S. Ct. 296, 79 L. Ed. 603 (1935). Why does the additur process authorized for California trial courts by CCP § 662.5(a) not violate the federal constitution? *See Jehl v. Southern Pac. Co.,* 66 Cal. 2d 821, 59 Cal. Rptr. 276, 427 P.2d 988 (1967).

[b] Federal Procedures

There are some significant differences in the procedures governing new trial motions in the federal courts as opposed to in the California state courts. A party has 28 days after entry of judgment to serve a motion for new trial in federal court under Rule 59(b), as opposed to 15 days under CCP § 659. More importantly, a federal district judge has power to order a new trial of its own initiative within this 28-day period. Rule 59(d), F.R.C.P. When a party has made a timely motion, the court may order a new trial for a reason not raised in the motion. Rule 59(d). In such circumstances, Rule 59(d) requires the district judge to specify the reasons upon which the new trial is granted, although apparently with less particularity than CCP § 657 requires of a state court judge for new trial orders generally. *See, e.g.,* 12 *Moore's Federal Practice* § 59.18 (3d ed. 2016) (observing there is no express requirement that court specify grounds upon which it granted new trial motion, except when court acts on its own initiative); *Grilliland v. Lyons,* 278 F.2d 56, 59 (9th Cir. 1960) (concluding that as a general rule, no reasons need be stated by the trial court in an order granting a party's motion for new trial). Unlike the 60-day period in CCP § 660, Rule 59 does not impose any time limit on the district court's power to rule on a party's new trial motion.

Federal Rule 59 has far fewer procedural requirements for new trial motions and orders than do the California statutes. Which approach do you prefer? Why?

Chapter 14

Judgments and Enforcement of Judgments

§ 14.01 Introductory Note on Judgments and Enforcement of Judgments

[A] Introduction to Securing and Enforcing Judgments

This Chapter examines some of the issues involved in securing and enforcing judgments. However, the materials that follow only briefly discuss the issues related to the determination of a basic judgment for money damages or for injunctive relief. Those areas are largely beyond the scope of this book, and are better left to a comprehensive course in Remedies.

This Chapter will instead focus on areas which are often neglected in courses and materials on Remedies: Recovery of prejudgment interest, costs, and attorney fees; and relief from final judgments. The California laws in these areas contain some unique aspects which make them of particular importance to parties and attorneys litigating in the California courts. This Chapter also briefly surveys the California procedures for enforcement of judgments. More complete analyses of the issues in this important area are available in courses on Creditor Rights and Debtor Remedies, Bankruptcy, and Secured Transactions.

[B] General Statutory Guidance on Judgments and Remedies

A judgment is the final determination of the rights of the parties in an action or proceeding. CCP § 577 (definition of judgment in general); § 1064 (judgment in special proceeding); §§ 1235.120 & 1235.130 (eminent domain judgment). A judgment in a legal action is typically one for money damages, and in an equitable action is typically one for permanent injunctive relief.

Several statutes provide general guidance on compensatory, preventive, and other forms of relief. These include Civil Code §§ 3294–3295 (punitive damages); §§ 3300–3318 (measure of damages for breach of contract); §§ 3333–3343.7 (measure of damages and damage limitations for tort actions); §§ 3384–3402 (specific performance); and §§ 3420–3423 (preventive relief by injunction). Moreover, many excellent resources are available which analyze the problems associated with the determination of money damages and injunctive relief in California. These include CEB, *California*

Tort Damages (2d ed. 2011); Leland M. Johns, *California Damages: Law and Proof* (5th ed. 1996); Robert L. Simmons, *Handbook of California Remedies* (1993).

§ 14.02 Interest

[A] Introductory Note on Postjudgment and Prejudgment Interest

By authority of the California Constitution, Article XV, Section 1, interest automatically accrues upon a money judgment rendered in any court. The Constitution authorizes the Legislature to set the rate of interest, not to exceed 10 percent per annum. In the absence of a legislatively established rate, the rate shall be 7 percent per annum. Art. XV, § 1, Cal. Const. The Legislature has currently set the interest rate on unsatisfied money judgments at 10%, subject to legislative change at any time. CCP § 685.010; *see Westbrook v. Fairchild*, 7 Cal. App. 4th 889, 9 Cal. Rptr. 2d 277 (1992) (ruling a judgment bears simple, not compound, interest of 10% from date of entry until satisfied or renewed).

Postjudgment interest commences to accrue on a money judgment on the date of entry of the judgment. CCP § 685.020; *Ehret v. Congoleum Corp.*, 87 Cal. App. 4th 202, 104 Cal. Rptr. 2d 370 (2001) (holding postjudgment interest runs from the date of entry of the original judgment on the jury's verdict, not from the judgment entered following a remittitur on appeal reversing a judgment notwithstanding the verdict); *Lucky United Properties Invest., Inc. v. Lee*, 213 Cal. App. 4th 635, 152 Cal. Rtpr. 3d 641 (2013) (ruling awards of prejudgment costs and attorney fees accrue interest retroactive to the date of entry of judgment, but awards of fees and costs incurred in postjudgment enforcement accrue interest from the date the amount of the costs and fees is fixed).

The Legislature has not established an interest rate for judgments against public entities generally, so the constitutional rate of 7% applies. *California Sav. & Loan Assn. v. City of L.A.*, 11 Cal. 4th 342, 45 Cal. Rptr. 2d 279, 902 P.2d 297 (1995); *but see* Civil Code § 3287(c), Gov. Code §§ 965.5, 970.1 (limiting interest on a tax or fee judgment against a public entity to an annual rate equal to the weekly average one year constant maturity U.S. Treasury yield at the time of the judgment plus 2%, not to exceed 7% per annum).

Unlike postjudgment interest, the right to recover interest as damages—commonly referred to as prejudgment interest—is based on several statutory sources. The extent of this right varies with the nature of the cause of action and whether the damages sought are liquidated or unliquidated. This patchwork of prejudgment interest authorities can be quite confusing at times, as our principal case illustrates.

Stein v. Southern California Edison Co.

Court of Appeal of California, Second Appellate District
7 Cal. App. 4th 565, 8 Cal. Rptr. 2d 907 (1992)

STONE (S.J.), PRESIDING JUSTICE.

Southern California Edison Company (hereinafter Edison) appeals from a judgment after jury trial imposing damages of $390,290.72 in favor of Richard Stein, Ellen Stein, and California Fair Plan Association (hereinafter the Steins) and prejudgment interest of $43,645.24 awarded by the trial court. Edison contends that the trial court should not have allowed the jury to decide the issue of strict liability and should not have awarded prejudgment interest. The Steins cross-appeal from the court's order awarding prejudgment interest.

The Steins claim they were entitled to prejudgment interest from a date earlier from the date Edison received notice of the damages.[1] We affirm the judgment and order after judgment.

FACTS

On September 28, 1988, the Steins' house at 2252 Las Canoas Road in the Mission Canyon area of Santa Barbara, was heavily damaged by fire. One of Edison's crews, who were in the area due to a power outage, initially reported the fire. The fire department investigator found that the flames concentrated in the electric service meter area and that the fire originated at the meter panel. He opined that the fire was of electrical origin and was caused by an electrical fault from outside the house.

The electrical power to the house was supplied by a pole-mounted transformer located near the house. The transformer changed the voltage of electricity from 16,000 volts from the high voltage lines to normal household 120/240 voltage. The transformer was connected to the house by service drop lines which attach at a weatherhead and service meter. The service meter plugs into a socket in the main service/meter panel from where the electricity is conducted to feeder connectors which carry the electricity to a circuit breaker panel inside the house.

The transformer had been modified by Edison by disabling the circuit breakers so that it could carry up to 200 to 220 percent of its normal capacity which caused a degradation and breakdown of the insulation on the transformer windings. This breakdown resulted in an electrical arc sending high voltage into the meter attached to the Steins' house. The meter exploded causing the fire. At trial, Edison's experts testified that there was no over-voltage and that the cause of the fire was an electrical fault in the house wiring. The Steins' expert testified that the transformer on the pole failed and that the high voltage surge of electricity never entered the house but went into the meter, exploding it and starting the fire.

Edison moved for nonsuit on the strict liability cause of action alleging that the electricity was a service and not a product. The court denied the motion. Steins dis-

---

1. All statutory references hereinafter are to the Civil Code unless otherwise specified.

missed other causes of action and only the cause of action for strict liability in tort went to the jury. After the jury's verdict in their favor, the Steins moved for prejudgment interest which the court awarded from date of notice of the claimed damages to Edison. These cross-appeals followed.

DISCUSSION

1. *The Judge Properly Instructed the Jury on Strict Liability.*

Edison asserts that the issue of strict liability in tort should not have been presented to the jury. It acknowledges that under California law, electricity can be a product subject to the principles of strict liability. * * * The trial court did not err in allowing the issue of strict liability to go to the jury.

2. *Trial Court Correctly Awarded Prejudgment Interest.*

Edison asserts that the trial court erred in awarding prejudgment interest because the damages were not made certain prior to trial. Furthermore, Edison asserts, there is no way to tell from the court's order whether it awarded interest under section 3287, subdivision (a), or upon section 3288, which the Steins raised as a basis for an award in a posttrial and posthearing written argument.[2]

Damages are deemed certain or capable of being made certain within section 3287, subdivision (a), where there is essentially no dispute between the parties concerning the basis of imposition of damages that are recoverable but where the dispute centers on the issue of liability giving rise to the damage. (*Fireman's Fund Ins. Co. v. Allstate Ins. Co.* (1991) 234 Cal. App. 3d 1154, 1172–1173 [286 Cal. Rptr. 146].) Two tests apply in deciding the certainty required by section 3287, subdivision (a): (1) whether the debtor knows the amount owed or (2) whether the debtor would be able to compute the damages, i.e., whether they are reasonably calculable. Denial of liability on the main theory does not make the damage uncertain within the meaning of section 3287. (*Credit Managers' Assn. v. Brubaker* (1991) 233 Cal. App. 3d 1587, 1595 [285 Cal. Rptr. 417].)

Section 3288, on the contrary, allows interest from date of monetary loss at the discretion of the trier of fact even if the damages are unliquidated. (*Greater Westchester Homeowners Assn. v. City of Los Angeles* (1979) 26 Cal. 3d 86, 102 [160 Cal. Rptr. 733, 603 P.2d 1329]; *Bullis v. Security Pac. Nat. Bank* (1978) 21 Cal. 3d 801, 814 [148 Cal. Rptr. 22, 582 P.2d 109, 7 A.L.R.4th 642].)

The Steins contend that they are entitled to prejudgment interest under either section, that Edison waived any objection to an award under section 3288, and that the court erred in not allowing interest from date of loss. The trial court's award of prejudgment interest from the date of the complaint is supported by both the record and the law.

---

2. Section 3287, subdivision (a), provides that "Every person who is entitled to recover damages certain, or capable of being made certain by calculation, and the right to recover which is vested in him upon a particular day, is entitled also to recover interest thereon from that day,...." Section 3288 provides that "In an action for the breach of an obligation not arising from contract, and in every case of oppression, fraud, or malice, interest may be given, in the discretion of the jury."

Edison did not waive any objection to an award under section 3288. The Steins specifically requested prejudgment interest under only section 3287 until after the hearing on the motion to tax costs. The court indicated its tentative decision to award interest and asked for supplemental declarations concerning the time when Edison had knowledge of their claimed damages. *After* Edison had filed its notices of appeal from the judgment and the court's order awarding prejudgment interest, the Steins asked for the first time for prejudgment interest under section 3288. Nonetheless, the court's order clearly indicates that it was relying on section 3287 and not 3288. It broke the prejudgment interest into two distinct time periods, neither running from the Steins' alleged date of loss.

We reject the Steins' argument that the court should have granted prejudgment interest under section 3288. The Steins did not request interest under that section in a timely manner. Edison was entitled to have a jury determine prejudgment interest under section 3288 since it is an issue for the trier of fact. (*Bullis v. Security Pac. Nat. Bank, supra*, 21 Cal. 3d 801, 815.) Edison did not waive that right by stipulating that the trial court could consider the matter of prejudgment interest when it considered costs. The record reveals that the parties never contemplated section 3288 at the time of the stipulation.

Did the court find the correct dates that Edison had notice of the amounts claimed? Edison did not dispute the amount of damages at any point in the litigation. It merely asked for proof of claims. Although lack of dispute is merely a factor to be considered, the court could consider it. In *Credit Managers' Assn. v. Brubaker, supra*, 233 Cal. App. 3d 1587, the reviewing court rejected an argument similar to Edison's that damages were not certain simply from the notice in the complaint and a demand letter for the exact amount requested in the complaint and awarded in the judgment. (*Id.,* at p. 1595.)

Where the amount of damages cannot be resolved except by account, verdict or judgment, interest prior to judgment is not allowable. (*Chesapeake Indus., Inc. v. Togova Enter., Inc.* (1983) 149 Cal. App. 3d 901, 907 [197 Cal. Rptr. 348].) Here, as in *Credit Managers' Assn., supra*, the amount claimed in the complaint was the amount awarded by the jury. Ascertainment of the amount did not require an accounting from conflicting evidence. The Steins provided documentation for costs of the structure, personal property and insured rents as alleged in the complaint and in their answers to interrogatories. They asserted the claimed losses for uninsured rents and labor at that time and substantiated them at trial.

Since there was no dispute in the amount claimed and no disparity in the amount claimed and the final judgment, the trial court did not err in allowing prejudgment interest from date of notice to Edison of the various losses.

We also reject Edison's claim that interest could not be awarded in a "piecemeal" fashion. *Bullis v. Security Pac. Nat. Bank, supra*, 21 Cal. 3d 801, at page 815, specifically upheld an award of interest on each of several unauthorized withdrawals from a bank account of over a four-year period, from the date of each individual withdrawal. Although *Bullis* was discussing interest under section 3288, we see no reason why its reasoning would not apply to section 3287, subdivision (a).

We similarly reject the Steins' contention that *Bullis* and *Greater Westchester* allow prejudgment interest from date of loss under section 3287. Both *Bullis* and *Greater Westchester* discussed application of section 3288. Moreover, cases such as *Leff v. Gunter* (1983) 33 Cal. 3d 508 [189 Cal. Rptr. 377, 658 P.2d 740] which have allowed prejudgment interest under 3287 from date of loss generally concern misappropriation of or wrongful withholding of funds where damages are readily ascertainable at the time plaintiff suffered the damage. Although the Steins suffered a loss on the date of the fire, the extent of the monetary loss and the amount of repair was not known on that date. Moreover, unlike the defendants in *Leff v. Gunter*, Edison did challenge the date on which damages vested.

The judgment and order appealed from are affirmed. Each party is to bear its own costs on appeal.

[B] Prejudgment Interest

[1] *Civil Code § 3287(a)*

Civil Code § 3287(a) provides the general authority for the right to recover prejudgment interest in any action, including actions in tort and in contract, for money damages. When are damages "certain or capable of being made certain by calculation" within the meaning of § 3287(a)? A "liquidated claim" is usually defined as one where the "amount of which has been agreed on by the parties to the action or is fixed by operation of law." *See Black's Law Dictionary* (9th ed. 2009). Is that how the California courts interpret the "certainty" of damages required by § 3287(a)? Consider the following cases:

[a] *Levy-Zentner Co. v. Southern Pacific Transp. Co.,* 74 Cal. App. 3d 762, 142 Cal. Rptr. 1 (1977)

Tenants of defendant Southern Pacific's warehouse, along with owners of property near the warehouse, brought a negligence action for property damages sustained when defendant's warehouse was destroyed by fire on June 29, 1969. Plaintiff Levy-Zentner owned a building adjacent to the warehouse; the northern portion of plaintiff's building was completely destroyed. In September, 1969, plaintiff Levy-Zentner, on the basis of two expert estimates, furnished defendant with information indicating the cost of repairs was $99,051.66. Plaintiff's complaint filed on November 5, 1970, alleged the identical amount. Thereafter on April 4, 1974, plaintiff filed a request for admission, with two estimates made by general adjustors for reconstruction work: $107,420 and $99,051.66. The amount of the damages due plaintiff was never put into issue by defendant. The jury subsequently returned a verdict for plaintiff Levy-Zentner in the amount of $99,051.66, and judgment was entered for this amount. Is plaintiff entitled to prejudgment interest with respect to this money judgment pursuant to § 3287(a)? If so, then from what date does the prejudgment interest accrue?

Several tenants in defendant's warehouse also sued defendant Southern Pacific for loss of equipment destroyed in the fire. During August, 1971, in responses to defendant's interrogatories, these plaintiffs listed the items damaged and the corresponding value of each damaged item. The plaintiffs' interrogatory answers provided no documentation of these values. No further inquiries were made as to the nature and amount of the damages claimed. At a pretrial conference in April, 1974, defendant Southern Pacific admitted the damages and stipulated to the amounts. The jury entered verdicts in favor of the plaintiff tenants in these amounts, and judgments were duly entered. Are these plaintiff tenants entitled to prejudgment interest pursuant to § 3287(a)? If so, then from what date does the prejudgment interest accrue?

[b] *Polster, Inc. v. Swing,* 164 Cal. App. 3d 427, 210 Cal. Rptr. 567 (1985)

The plaintiff landlord brought an action to recover damages from former tenant for failure to leave the rented premises in as good a condition as when leased. Although there was substantial damage to the premises when the defendant vacated in March, 1979, the plaintiff did not supply the defendant with accurate repair estimates within a reasonable time after the loss. Plaintiff did, however, file a complaint in April, 1979 against defendant seeking $55,000 plus interest for the cost of repairs.

The trial took place in 1983. The trial court entered judgment for plaintiff in the amount of $7,838, but denied plaintiff any prejudgment interest under § 3287(a). The Court of Appeal affirmed the denial of prejudgment interest. The Court of Appeal ruled that the plaintiff's damages were not certain within the meaning of § 3287(a) because the defendant did not know and could not readily compute the damages. Moreover, the appellate court noted that "where there is a large discrepancy between the amount of damages demanded in the complaint and the size of the eventual award, that fact militates against a finding of certainty mandated by ... section 3287(a)." Why is this discrepancy in the amounts relevant to a § 3287(a) determination? Should prejudgment interest under § 3287(a) be denied whenever the amount awarded in the judgment is smaller than the amount sought in the complaint? Why? *See Marine Terminals Corp. v. Paceco, Inc.,* 145 Cal. App. 3d 991, 193 Cal. Rptr. 687 (1983) (reviewing several cases and concluding plaintiff entitled to prejudgment interest even though statement of damages erroneously included inapplicable amounts).

[c] *Cassinos v. Union Oil Co.,* 14 Cal. App. 4th 1770, 18 Cal. Rptr 2d 574 (1993)

The plaintiff mineral rights owner filed an action against defendant oil company, an adjacent property owner, seeking damages arising from defendant's injection without permission of off-site wastewater through an oil well into plaintiff's reserve mineral estate. The trial court entered judgment for plaintiff in the amount of $3.6 million for damage to its mineral interests, calculated by determining the fair market value of the cost of disposal of this wastewater. The trial court also awarded plaintiff pre-judgment interest of $1.7 million pursuant to §3287(a), accruing from the date of the wrongful injection. Defendant appealed.

The Court of Appeal ruled that plaintiff's damage claim was "capable of being made certain by calculation" within the meaning of §3287(a) because the relevant market values were reasonably ascertainable by the defendant: "The mere fact that proof is required to determine the market value of property on a designated date will not prevent the allowance of interest under §3287." *Cassinos,* 14 Cal. App. 4th at 1789. In affirming plaintiff's right to prejudgment interest, the court noted that defendant actually knew that the fair market value of disposal of off-site wastewater was $1.75 per barrel, and also knew the number of barrels it disposed of at the time of the injection in 1984.

The plaintiff stated the approximate number of barrels of injected wastewater and the reasonable disposal rate in its 1985 complaint. The Court of Appeal found that plaintiff was entitled to prejudgment interest, but only as of the date of the complaint, not from the earlier date of injection. Is the court's conclusion as to when the pre-judgment interest begins to accrue consistent with its reasoning in finding §3287(a)'s "reasonably capable of calculation" test satisfied? *See Uzyel v. Kadisha,* 188 Cal. App. 4th 866, 919–20, 116 Cal. Rptr. 3d 244 (2010) (holding in breach of trust action against trustee, that prejudgment interest under §3287(a) properly awarded from date trusts terminated by improper sale of stock because market value of stock readily ascertainable by defendant at time of sale).

[d] Policy Conflict

Civil Code §3287(a) reflects legislative consideration of two countervailing policies with respect to an award of prejudgment interest. One is that interest traditionally has been denied on unliquidated claims because of the general equitable principle that a person who does not know what sum is owed cannot be in default for failure to pay. Thus, no prejudgment interest is assessed against a litigant for failing to pay a sum which is unascertainable prior to judgment. *See* Comment, *Interest as Damages in California,* 5 UCLA L. Rev. 262, 263, n.6 (1958). The other is that injured parties should be compensated for the loss of the use of their money during the period between the assertion of a claim and the rendition of judgment. This latter policy, according to the court in *Chesapeake Industries, Inc. v. Togara Enter., Inc.,* 149 Cal. App. 3d 901, 907, 197 Cal. Rptr. 348 (1983), has been implemented through a generally liberal construction of "certainty" under section 3287(a). Do you agree with this observation?

These competing policy considerations have lead the courts to focus on the *defendant's* knowledge about the amount of the plaintiff's claim. The fact the plaintiff or some omniscient third party knew or could calculate the amount is not sufficient. The test is: Did the defendant actually know the amount owed or from reasonably available information could the defendant have computed the award. *Chesapeake Industries, supra,* 149 Cal. App. 3d at 907 (and cases cited therein). Only if one of these two conditions is met should the court award prejudgment interest. *Id.* at 907.

[e] Effect of Unliquidated Cross-Complaint

The court in *Chesapeake Industries*, *supra*, 149 Cal. App. 3d at 907, also noted that an injured party's right to prejudgment interest is further protected by the rule that the legal interest allowable under § 3287(a) cannot be defeated by setting up an unliquidated cross-complaint as an offset, citing *California Lettuce Growers, Inc. v. Union Sugar Co.*, 45 Cal. 2d 474, 487, 289 P.2d 785 (1955). What are the policy reasons for this rule? One effect of this rule is to encourage mitigation of damages. How so? *See Coleman Eng'g Co. v. North American Aviation, Inc.*, 65 Cal. 2d 396, 409, 55 Cal. Rptr. 1, 420 P.2d 713 (1966).

Assume that Lessor L leased real property to Tenant T by written lease of 10 years term. Tenant T vacates with 3-1/2 years remaining, and stops paying the monthly rent of $4000. Lessor L repairs the premises, and subsequently relets the premises to a new substitute tenant. L sues T for repairs and rent deficiency in the amount of $115,000. Defendant T cross-complains for an accounting, seeking an offset for rents L received from the substitute tenant; which amount is unknown to defendant T. The trial court, after hearing the evidence, concluded that defendant T owes plaintiff L the sum of $35,000 as the net rental deficit. Is plaintiff L also entitled to prejudgment interest on this money judgment pursuant to Civil Code § 3287(a)? Why? On facts similar to the above hypothetical, the Court of Appeal in *Chesapeake Industries*, *supra*, overturned the trial court's award of prejudgment interest to the Lessor. In light of the various policies embodied in § 3287(a), do you agree with the Court of Appeal's conclusion? Why?

Are damages "certain" or "capable of being made certain by calculation" within the meaning of Civil Code § 3287(a), where the amount of the total loss is undisputed but the extent of plaintiff's and defendant's comparative liability for that loss is hotly disputed? The court in *Wisper Corp. v. Cal. Commerce Bank*, 49 Cal. App. 4th 948, 57 Cal. Rptr. 2d 141 (1996), concluded that § 3287(a) does not apply in a comparative negligence case. Do you agree with this conclusion? If a defendant's unliquidated cross-complaint or setoff cannot defeat a plaintiff's claim for § 3287 prejudgment interest, why should a defendant's comparative negligence defense make § 3287 inapplicable? A dissenting opinion in *Wisper* found the unliquidated offset cases persuasive, and argued that prejudgment interest should be available under § 3287(a), calculated on the appropriate percentage of the total amount of damages.

[f] Public Entities

By its terms, Civil Code § 3287(a) applies to all debtors including public entities. Other prejudgment interest provisions expressly exclude public entities and employees. *See, e.g.*, Civil Code § 3291; Government Code § 970.1.

[g] Suspension

Accrual of interest on a liquidated claim is suspended during such time as the debtor is prevented by law or by act of the creditor from paying the debt, Civil Code § 3287(a); or by an offer of payment, Civil Code § 1504.

[h] Administrative Agency Awards

Civil Code § 3287(a) has been applied to administrative agencies' retroactive awards of wages, government assistance, or retirement benefits, whether the awards were made initially by the agency or ordered by writ of mandate by a court. *See Currie v. Workers' Comp. Appeals Bd.*, 24 Cal. 4th 1109, 104 Cal. Rptr. 2d 392, 17 P.3d 749 (2001) (collecting cases and holding that § 3287(a) requires the WCAB to add prejudgment interest to an award of backpay to an employee wrongfully denied reinstatement because of an industrial injury, calculated from the date such wages would have become due).

[2] *Civil Code § 3288: Prejudgment Interest in Non-Contract Actions*

As discussed above, Civil Code § 3287(a) confers the right to prejudgment interest in non-contract as well as contract actions, so long as the damages sought are "certain." As *Stein v. Southern California Edison Co.*, reproduced *supra*, indicates, Civil Code § 3288 also authorizes prejudgment interest in non-contract actions where damages are unliquidated (*i.e.*, not "certain"). *See Michelson v. Hamada,* 29 Cal. App. 4th 1566, 36 Cal. Rptr. 2d 343 (1994) (noting jury vested with discretion to award prejudgment interest under § 3288, including compound interest, in fraud action); *Altavion, Inc. v. Konica Minolta Sys. Lab., Inc.*, 226 Cal. App. 4th 26, 171 Cal. Rptr. 3d 714 (2014) (affirming award of prejudgment interest under § 3288 in action for trade secret misappropriation). In what other ways does the operation of Civil Code § 3288 differ from § 3287(a)? When does prejudgment interest begin to accrue under § 3288? *See Michelson, supra*, 29 Cal. App. 4th at 1588–89 (concluding award of prejudgment interest should run from the date money was paid or loss occurred because duty to compensate plaintiff for loss accrued then, and no demand was necessary); *Altavion, supra*, 226 Cal. App. 4th at 70 (approving an award from the time of misappropriation of trade secret to compensate plaintiff for loss of use of royalty funds).

Prudent practice would dictate that a plaintiff request prejudgment interest pursuant to § 3288 as well as § 3287(a) prior to the trial of a tort action, would it not? Why? Why did the plaintiff fail to do so in *Stein*? Although § 3288 only grants the "jury" authority to award prejudgment interest, a trial court, when acting as a trier of fact, may award such interest under this section. *See Bullis v. Security Pac. Nat. Bank*, 21 Cal. 3d 801, 814, n.16, 148 Cal. Rptr. 22, 582 P.2d 109 (1978).

Although § 3288 appears to place no restrictions on discretionary prejudgment interest for unliquidated tort claims, the Supreme Court has held that prejudgment interest in such cases is not appropriate for the intangible noneconomic aspects of mental and emotional injury claims. *Greater Westchester Homeowners Assn. v. City of L. A.*, 26 Cal. 3d 86, 103, 160 Cal. Rptr. 733, 603 P.2d 1329 (1979). Consequently, for example, although a jury may award prejudgment interest on the amount of loss of earning capacity pursuant to § 3288 in a wrongful death action, it cannot award prejudgment interest on the amount awarded for loss of comfort, society, care and protection. *See Canavin v. Pac. Southwest Airlines*, 148 Cal. App. 3d 512, 527, 196 Cal. Rptr. 82 (1983). Is this distinction supported by the language of § 3288?

The Supreme Court in *Greater Westchester, supra,* justified its holding, in part, by observing that because general damages are inherently unliquidated and not readily subject to precise calculation, adding interest on such damages adds uncertain conjecture to speculation. *Greater Westchester,* 26 Cal. 3d at 103. Do you agree with the court's observation? What policies likely influenced the Supreme Court to give § 3288 such a narrowing construction? For a criticism of the Supreme Court's reasoning and conclusion in *Greater Westchester,* see Michael K. Brown, Comment, *The Availability of Prejudgment Interest in Personal Injury and Wrongful Death Cases,* 16 U.S.F. L. Rev. 325–56 (1982).

[3] Civil Code § 3291

Civil Code § 3291 provides that in any tort action to recover damages for personal injury, the plaintiff in the complaint may claim interest on the damages alleged. If the plaintiff makes an offer to compromise pursuant to CCP § 998 which the defendant does not timely accept, and the plaintiff obtains a more favorable judgment, the judgment *shall* bear interest at the legal rate of 10% calculated from the date of the § 998 offer until satisfaction of the judgment. *See, e.g., Johnson v. Pratt & Whitney Canada, Inc.,* 28 Cal. App. 4th 613, 34 Cal. Rptr. 2d 26 (1994) (holding trial court properly awarded prejudgment interest to plaintiffs in wrongful death action where defendant rejected plaintiffs' joint § 998 offer of $1 million and subsequently suffered adverse verdict of $2.1 million).

Section 3291 does not apply to public employees or entities; nor to actions where the personal injury damages sought are incidental to the primary claim to recover property damages for economic loss. *See, e.g., Pilimai v. Farmers Ins. Exch. Co.,* 39 Cal. 4th 133, 45 Cal. Rptr. 3d 760, 137 P.3d 939 (2006) (holding an action against an insurance company to recover policy benefits for compensation of personal injury was not eligible for an award of prejudgment interest because Civil Code § 3291 requires a personal injury action sounding in tort and does not include an action for breach of an insurance contract); *Gourley v. State Farm Mut. Auto. Ins. Co.,* 53 Cal. 3d 121, 279 Cal. Rptr. 307, 806 P.2d 1342 (1991) (ruling prejudgment interest under § 3291 not available in insurance bad faith actions because such actions are primarily brought to recover economic loss caused by tortious interference with a property right, and any damages recovered for actual personal injury such as emotional distress are incidental to the award of economic damages); *McKinney v. Cal. Portland Cement Co.,* 96 Cal. App. 4th 1214, 117 Cal. Rptr. 2d 849 (2002) (ruling an award of damages to a spouse as a result of wrongful death of her husband is a personal injury for purposes of § 3291).

Does § 3291 authorize prejudgment interest on an award of punitive damages? *See Lakin v. Watkins Assoc. Indus.,* 6 Cal. 4th 644, 662–664, 25 Cal. Rptr. 2d 109, 863 P.2d 179 (1993) (holding § 3291 authorized courts to award prejudgment interest only on damages attributable to personal injury). Is a plaintiff who obtains a judgment more favorable that his CCP § 998 offer entitled to interest on the prejudgment portion of the interest accrued under Civil Code § 3291, *i.e.,* compound interest or interest on interest? *See Hess v. Ford Motor Co.,* 27 Cal. 4th 516, 117 Cal. Rptr. 2d 220, 41 P.3d 46 (2002) (holding prejudgment interest accrued under § 3291 is not part of the judgment and a plaintiff may not obtain interest on this prejudgment interest).

[4] *Effect of Good Faith Settlement*

In *Newby v. Vroman,* 11 Cal. App. 4th 283, 14 Cal. Rptr. 2d 44 (1992), the court considered the question of how prejudgment interest under § 3288 should be calculated and imposed when, prior to judgment against a nonsettling tortfeasor, a joint tort-feasor settles with plaintiff in good faith thereby mandatorily reducing pro tanto the amount of that judgment. The court held that "(1) The prejudgment interest due plaintiff when a court applies section 3288 is first computed on the judgment without deduction or off-set for amounts paid by a settling joint tortfeasor; and (2) a plaintiff, who in good faith settles with a joint tortfeasor before judgment against a nonsettling joint tortfeasor, may thereafter recover from the nonsettling defendants: (a) prejudgment interest up to the date of settlement on the *total* judgment; and (b) prejudgment interest after the date of settlement only on the *balance* of the total judgment remaining after its reduction by the settlement sum paid." *Newby,* 11 Cal. App. 4th at 288; *see Deocampo v. Ahn,* 101 Cal. App. 4th 758, 125 Cal. Rptr. 2d 79 (2002) (applying the *Newby* formula to calculate prejudgment interest due plaintiff under Civil Code § 3291). What policy reasons dictate this rule?

[5] *Prejudgment Interest in a Breach of Contract Action*

[a] Liquidated Damages

A person entitled to recover damages for breach of obligation to pay a liquidated sum is also entitled to recover prejudgment interest from the date the claim arose. Civil Code §§ 3287(a), 3302. How does a court determine whether the contract breach involves a "liquidated" sum? Under what circumstances will the right to prejudgment interest accrue *after* a contract breach but *before* judgment?

[b] Unliquidated Damages

Civil Code § 3287(b) provides that a person who obtains a money judgment based upon a cause of action in contract where the claim was unliquidated may also recover prejudgment interest from a date prior to entry of the judgment as the court may in its discretion fix, but in no event earlier than the date the action was filed. Does § 3287(b) overlap with, and consequently limit, § 3287(a)? How should these two subsections be interpreted so as to prevent inconsistent overlap?

[c] Rate of Prejudgment Interest

What is the rate of prejudgment interest charged in contract actions? Pursuant to Civil Code § 3289(a), any legal (nonusurious) rate of interest stipulated by a contract remains chargeable after a breach, until the contract is superseded by a verdict or other new obligation. *See Roodenburg v. Pavestone Co.,* 171 Cal. App. 4th 185, 89 Cal. Rptr. 3d 558 (2009) (affirming prejudgment interest award of $489,550 calculated by using the 18 % interest rate provided in the contract). If the contract does not stipulate a legal rate of interest, the obligation shall bear interest of 10% per annum after a breach. Civil Code § 3289(b).

Special rules apply to notes secured by a deed of trust on real property, Civil Code § 3289; to retail installment contracts, Civil Code § 3289.5; and to computation of interest on condemnation awards, CCP §§ 1268.310–1268.350. *See Redevelopment Agency v. Gilmore,* 38 Cal. 3d 790, 796–807, 214 Cal. Rptr. 904, 700 P.2d 794 (1985) (concluding the determination of rate of interest in condemnation cases was a judicial, not legislative, function based on appropriate prevailing market rate); *People v. Diversified Properties Co. III,* 14 Cal. App. 4th 429, 17 Cal. Rptr. 2d 676 (1993) (holding trial court in condemnation cases must determine postjudgment rate by applying higher of market rate of interest or legislatively created apportionment rate set for in CCP § 1268.350). And, pursuant to Government Code § 926.10, prejudgment interest on a liquidated claim against a public entity is limited to 6%.

§ 14.03 Recovery of Attorney Fees

[A] Introductory Note on the American Rule and Exceptions

California follows the so-called "American Rule" with respect to the recovery of attorney fees which, in the absence of an established exception, requires each party to bear its own attorney fees. *See, e.g., Serrano v. Unruh,* 32 Cal. 3d 621, 627, 186 Cal. Rptr. 754, 652 P.2d 985 (1982); *Alyeska Pipeline Co. v. Wilderness Society,* 421 U.S. 240, 247–257, 95 S. Ct. 1612, 44 L. Ed. 2d 141 (1975). California does recognize many exceptions based on fee-shifting statutes, judge-made equitable doctrines, and contractual provisions. Not only does the Legislature authorize parties to allocate attorney fees by agreement, CCP § 1021; it also makes an otherwise unilateral contractual right to recover attorney fees reciprocally binding upon all parties in an action to enforce the contract, Civil Code § 1717.

The Legislature has enacted numerous fee-shifting statutes which authorize courts to award reasonable attorney fees to the prevailing party. *E.g.,* CCP § 1021.5 (Private Attorney General Statute); Government Code § 6259(d) (Public Records Act); Government Code § 12965(b) (Fair Employment and Housing Act); Civil Code § 1811.1 (Retail Installment Sales Act); and CCP § 425.16 (Anti-SLAPP statute). The U.S. Congress has also enacted numerous fee-shifting statutes which may apply when a party seeks enforcement of a federal statute in state court. *See, e.g., Sokolow v. Cnty. of San Mateo,* 213 Cal. App. 3d 231, 261 Cal. Rptr. 520 (1989) (directing superior court to award attorney fees under both 42 U.S.C. § 1988 and CCP § 1021.5 in civil rights action); *Green v. Obledo,* 161 Cal. App. 3d 678, 207 Cal. Rptr. 830 (1984) (requiring superior court to apply federal fee-shifting statute when federal claim brought in state court); *see also Ruckelshaus v. Sierra Club,* 463 U.S. 680, 684, 103 S. Ct. 3274, 77 L. Ed. 2d 938 (1983) (noting that Congress has enacted over 150 federal fee-shifting statutes which authorize an award to the prevailing party).

These statutory and contractual bases for recovery of attorney fees constitute very significant departures from the American Rule. In addition, although perhaps less significant in overall impact, the California courts have created several exceptions to the American Rule based on equitable theories. These include the "common fund," "substantial benefit," "private attorney general," and "third-party tort" doctrines. *See, e.g., Serrano v. Priest,* 20 Cal. 3d 25, 141 Cal. Rptr. 315, 569 P.2d 1303 (1977); *Prentice v. North American Title Guar. Corp.,* 59 Cal. 2d 618, 30 Cal. Rptr. 821, 381 P.2d 645 (1963).

Consideration of these judge-made exceptions still does not provide a complete picture of attorney fee recovery in California. In appropriate situations, a court may award attorney fees as a sanction for bad faith litigation, CCP § 128.7; for misuse of the discovery process, CCP § 2023; and for frivolous appeals, CCP § 907, Rule 8.276, Cal. Rules of Ct. And in some limited circumstances, a party may recover attorney fees as an element of damages wrongfully caused by a defendant's improper prior actions and not as compensation for legal representation in the current litigation. *Brandt v. Superior Court,* 37 Cal. 3d 813, 210 Cal. Rptr. 211, 693 P.2d 796 (1985).

A thorough understanding of these various contractual, statutory, and judge-made exceptions to the American Rule is of obvious importance to attorneys and clients alike. Several publications provide excellent in-depth analyses of the concepts and issues regarding the recovery of attorney fees in the California courts. *See, e.g.,* CEB, *California Attorney Fee Awards* (3d ed. 2016); 7 Witkin, *California Procedure,* Judgment §§ 149–323 (5th ed. 2008); *see also* Alba Conte, *Attorney Fee Awards* (3d ed. 2016). The authorities and notes reproduced below introduce some of these basic concepts and issues.

[B] Attorney Fee Awards Based on Contract

Moallem v. Coldwell Banker Commercial Group, Inc.

Court of Appeal of California, Second Appellate District
25 Cal. App. 4th 1827, 31 Cal. Rptr. 2d 253 (1994)

FUKUTO, JUSTICE.

INTRODUCTION

[This case involves an appeal] from a $1,430,937 judgment for negligence and breach of fiduciary duty, awarded to Steve Moallem, as assignee of his corporations Midland Warehouse and Distribution, Inc., and Transmotor Express, Inc. (collectively Midland), against their real estate agents, Coldwell Banker Commercial Group, Inc., and Kent Williams (collectively Coldwell). The judgment stemmed from Midland's forfeiture of a warehouse property (the property), on which it had held a lease and option to buy, after Coldwell sublet the property for Midland in violation of the lease.

The issues on appeal concern additions or offsets to the judgment that the parties contend the trial court should have made. * * *

DISCUSSION

* * *

3. Attorney Fees.

The brokerage agreement between Midland and Coldwell included a commission schedule which provided in part: "If broker [i.e., Coldwell] is required to institute legal action against Owner [i.e., Midland] relating to this Schedule or any agreement of which it is a part, Broker shall be entitled to reasonable attorneys' fees and costs."

After the jury rendered its verdict in favor of Moallem for negligence and breach of fiduciary duty but for Coldwell on Moallem's claim for breach of contract, both sides moved for an award of attorney fees by virtue of the quoted contractual provision and Civil Code section 1717 (hereafter § 1717).[1] The trial court ruled that there had been "no party prevailing on the contract" (§ 1717, subd. (b)), and therefore denied both requests for fees. Moallem, but not Coldwell, has appealed from that disposition.

In claiming entitlement to attorney fees, Moallem no longer seeks directly to invoke section 1717, which in terms allows fees only to "the party prevailing on the contract," in an "action on a contract, where the contract specifically provides that attorney's fees and costs, which are incurred to enforce that contract, shall be awarded...." (§ 1717, subd. (a).)[2] In light of this plain language, the statute has consistently been held not to afford recovery of fees for tort claims arising out of or related to such a contract. (*E.g.*, *Reynolds Metals Co. v. Alperson* (1979) 25 Cal. 3d 124, 129 [158 Cal. Rptr. 1, 599 P.2d 83]; *Stout v. Turney* (1978) 22 Cal. 3d 718, 730 [150 Cal. Rptr. 637, 586 P.2d 1228].)

Moallem instead relies primarily on a recent series of cases allowing attorney fees for tort claims where a contractual attorney fees provision was phrased broadly enough to cover such noncontractual claims. (*Xuereb v. Marcus & Millichap, Inc.* (1992) 3 Cal. App. 4th 1338 [5 Cal. Rptr. 2d 154] (*Xuereb*); accord, *Palmer v. Shawback, supra,* 17 Cal. App. 4th 296; *Lerner v. Ward* (1993) 13 Cal. App. 4th 155 [16 Cal. Rptr. 2d 486]; *3250 Wilshire Blvd. Bldg. v. W.R. Grace & Co.* (9th Cir. 1993) 990 F.2d 487.) In

---

1. Section 1717 provides in pertinent part: "(a) In any action on a contract, where the contract specifically provides that attorney's fees and costs, which are incurred to enforce that contract, shall be awarded either to one of the parties or to the prevailing party, then the party who is determined to be the party prevailing on the contract, whether he or she is the party specified in the contract or not, shall be entitled to reasonable attorney's fees in addition to other costs. [¶] Where a contract provides for attorney's fees, as set forth above, that provision shall be construed as applying to the entire contract, unless each party was represented by counsel in the negotiation and execution of the contract, and the fact of that representation is specified in the contract. [¶] Reasonable attorney's fees shall be fixed by the court, and shall be an element of the costs of suit. [¶] Attorney's fees provided for by this section shall not be subject to waiver by the parties to any contract which is entered into after the effective date of this section. Any provision in any such contract which provides for a waiver of attorney's fees is void. [¶] (b) (1) The court, upon notice and motion by a party, shall determine who is the party prevailing on the contract for purposes of this section, whether or not the suit proceeds to final judgment. Except as provided in paragraph (2), the party prevailing on the contract shall be the party who recovered a greater relief in the action on the contract. The court may also determine that there is no party prevailing on the contract for purposes of this section. [¶]...."

2. In the court below, Moallem contended that its tort causes of action were "on the contract," because they involved breaches of duties arising out of the contract. Moallem does not renew that particular argument here; he permissibly adduces a different legal rationale to be applied to the same facts. (Cf. *Palmer v. Shawback* (1993) 17 Cal. App. 4th 296, 300 [21 Cal. Rptr. 2d 575].)

all of those cases, however, the contract provisions that the courts enforced also provided for attorney fees to whichever party prevailed, whereas here the provision in question runs only in favor of Coldwell. Moallem thus occupies the difficult position of arguing that the "public policy" of reciprocity of contractual attorney fee provisions, which section 1717 appears to implement, should control a noncontractual case that is specifically beyond section 1717's ambit. Although we sympathize with Moallem's position, we conclude that, just as its reach exceeds the statute's grasp, to adopt it would overreach our judicial function.

Like the present case, the *Xuereb* line of cases all involved tort claims arising out of real estate sales transactions, in which the contract provided that attorney fees would be allowed to the prevailing party in any action "arising out of" the contract (or similar language). In each case, the court held that although the prevailing party could not claim attorney fees under section 1717 — because the action in which it had prevailed had been in tort, rather than "on the contract" — the contract's "arising out of" or equivalent language extended beyond simply actions "on the contract," and embraced the tort claims that had been decided. Therefore, under authority of Code of Civil Procedure section 1021, which permits parties to contract for attorney fees, the prevailing party was entitled to an award of fees by dint of the contract itself.[3]

The attorney fees provision in Coldwell's contract with Midland extends to any "legal action ... relating to" the contract. This language is broad enough to include tort claims of the type brought and won by Moallem here, just as in *Xuereb* and its progeny. Coldwell does not contend to the contrary. However, the critical difference between this case and the *Xuereb* cases is that in those cases the attorney fees provision specifically covered and benefited all parties to the contract, while in this case the provision specifically limits entitlement to attorney fees to Coldwell.

This difference is dispositive. In the *Xuereb* cases, the contracts did provide for attorney fees for the party that sought them, and therefore such an award of fees was sanctioned by Code of Civil Procedure section 1021, which, again, leaves the recoverability vel non of attorney fees "to the agreement, express or implied, of the parties." But in this case, for better or worse, the agreement of the parties was that only Coldwell could obtain attorney fees for an action "relating to" the contract. Thus, in contrast to *Xuereb*, Moallem's present prayer for fees lacks support in the terms of the contract and, consequently, in Code of Civil Procedure section 1021.

Moallem contends, however, that the unilateral right to attorney fees in Coldwell's contract should be available to him too, by dint of what he perceives as "[t]he public

---

3. Code of Civil Procedure section 1021 provides: "Except as attorney's fees are specifically provided for by statute, the measure and mode of compensation of attorneys and counselors at law is left to the agreement, express or implied, of the parties; but parties to actions or proceedings are entitled to their costs, as hereinafter provided."

policy of mutuality of remedy established by [section] 1717 ... the public policy that unilateral attorneys' fees provisions should be bilaterally enforced." The existence of such a public policy cannot be denied. As noted by cases decided early in section 1717's existence, the purpose of the section was to advance "the policy of the state to protect the unequal bargaining power of the 'little man' in contracts of adhesion." (*System Inv. Corp. v. Union Bank* (1971) 21 Cal. App. 3d 137, 163 [98 Cal. Rptr. 735]; *see also Coast Bank v. Holmes* (1971) 19 Cal. App. 3d 581, 596–597 [97 Cal. Rptr. 30].) Indeed, given the ability of contracting parties to provide for attorney fees under Code of Civil Procedure section 1021, section 1717's "only effect is to make an otherwise unilateral right to attorney fees reciprocally binding upon all parties to actions to enforce the contract." (*Xuereb, supra,* 3 Cal. App. 4th at p. 1342.)

Moallem's position sounds a strong call of fairness. The same policy considerations that underlie section 1717's provision for attorney fees for the prevailing party in a contract action, "whether he or she is the party specified [as entitled to recover fees] in the contract or not" (§ 1717, subd. (a)), would appear to warrant such a reciprocal allowance when the contract provides for fees not only "incurred to enforce that contract" (*ibid.*) but also on account of litigation, as here, "relating to" it.

But this is a judgment that is not ours to implement. In section 1717, the Legislature has prescribed with clarity that the public policy Moallem seeks to invoke presently applies only to attorney fees for contract actions, not tort claims. As *Xuereb* itself summarized, "By its terms ... section 1717 has a limited application. It covers only contract actions, where the theory of the case is breach of contract, and where the contract sued upon itself specifically provides for an award of attorney fees incurred to enforce that contract." (*Xuereb, supra,* 3 Cal. App. 4th at p. 1342.) Fairly or not, this restriction has for 25 years denied tort litigants the benefits of section 1717.

And so it must here. In this case the asymmetry of statutory rights between contract and tort litigants painfully appears, because Moallem could have invoked section 1717 had he prevailed on his contract claim instead of his tort claims. But that situation is a consequence only of the Legislature's enactment as it now stands. Although we can suggest that the statute be rewritten to take into account *Xuereb* and its progeny, we cannot perform that revision. The public policy underlying section 1717 may be clear. But a court is not free to advance the public policy that underlies a statute by extending the statute beyond its plain terms and established reach.

We therefore conclude that because the present contract provided for recovery of attorney fees for tort actions "relating to" the contract by Coldwell only, Moallem's request for fees under that contract was properly denied.

DISPOSITION

The judgment is affirmed in part and reversed in part, with respect to the amount awarded. The superior court shall reduce that amount in conformity with this decision. The parties shall bear their own costs on appeal.

[1] Code of Civil Procedure § 1021

Code of Civil Procedure § 1021 authorizes the parties to a contract to include an agreement as to who will recover attorney fees in the event of subsequent litigation. Section 1021 is not limited to contract actions; the parties may also agree to recovery of attorney fees in any tort actions which may arise from their underlying transactional relationship. *See, e.g., Maynard v. BTI Group, Inc.,* 216 Cal. App. 4th 984, 157 Cal. Rptr. 3d 148 (2013); *Lerner v. Ward,* 13 Cal. App. 4th 155, 16 Cal. Rptr. 2d 486 (1993); *Xuereb v. Marcus & Millichap, Inc.,* 3 Cal. App. 4th 1338, 5 Cal. Rptr. 2d 154 (1992).

[2] Civil Code § 1717

[a] Civil Code § 1717 Limited to Actions "On a Contract"

Civil Code § 1717 was enacted to establish mutuality of remedy where a contractual provision makes recovery of attorney's fees available for only one party, and to prevent oppressive use of one-sided attorney's fees provisions. *Reynolds Metals Co. v. Alperson,* 25 Cal. 3d 124, 128, 158 Cal. Rptr. 1, 599 P.2d 83 (1979). Civil Code § 1717 expressly limits this reciprocal remedy only to an action "on a contract" or "to enforce that contract." The courts construe these terms liberally to include not only a traditional action for breach of contract but also any other cause of action that involves contractual rights, such as an action to declare a contract invalid. *See Eden TP Healthcare Dist. v. Eden Med. Cntr.,* 220 Cal. App. 4th 418, 426–28, 162 Cal. Rptr. 3d 932 (2013) (discussing several cases construing "on a contract"); *Kachlon v. Markowitz,* 168 Cal. App. 4th 316, 347, 85 Cal. Rptr. 3d 532 (2008) ("In determining whether an action is 'on the contract' under section 1717, the proper focus is not on the nature of the remedy, but on the basis of the cause of action").

As *Moallem v. Coldwell Banker,* reproduced *supra,* indicates, the courts have construed this language to preclude application of § 1717 to a tort cause of action unless intertwined with a contract cause of action. *See, e.g., Reynolds Metals, supra,* 25 Cal. 3d at 129 ("Where a cause of action based on the contract providing for attorney's fees is joined with other causes of action beyond the contract, the prevailing party may recover attorney's fees under section 1717 only as they relate to the contract action"); *Xuereb v. Marcus & Millichap, Inc., supra,* 3 Cal. App. 4th at 1341–42 (holding § 1717 not applicable to action arising out of real estate transaction because plaintiffs submitted their case to jury on negligence and other tort theories but not on the pleaded breach of contract cause of action); *Loube v. Loube,* 64 Cal. App. 4th 421, 74 Cal. Rptr. 2d 906 (1998) (concluding that where the parties' retainer agreement contains an attorney fee provision, § 1717 did not apply to plaintiffs' legal malpractice claim of negligence because that claim sounded in tort, but did apply to plaintiffs' claim of excessive fees).

[b] Apportionment of Award in Combined Actions

Where a contract cause of action is combined with a noncontractual one, attorney fees awarded under § 1717 must be apportioned such that the award reflects only work performed on the contractual action. *See Reynolds Metals, supra*, 25 Cal. 3d at 129–30; *Las Palmas Assoc. v. Las Palmas Ctr. Assoc.*, 235 Cal. App. 3d 1220, 1259–1260, 1 Cal. Rptr. 2d 301 (1991); *Shadoan v. World Sav. & Loan Assn.*, 219 Cal. App. 3d 97, 107–108, 268 Cal. Rptr. 207 (1990). However, no apportionment is required when the claims are intertwined, *Brusso v. Running Springs Country Club, Inc.*, 228 Cal. App. 3d 92, 107, 278 Cal. Rptr. 758 (1991) (applying § 1717 to shareholder derivative action where contractual breach alleged in first cause of action was incorporated into remaining causes of action so that breach of contract was an element of each of the several causes of action); or where an issue is common both to a cause of action in which § 1717 fees are proper and one in which they are not allowed. *Reynolds Metals, supra*, 25 Cal. 3d at 129–30; *Erickson v. R.E.M. Concepts, Inc.*, 126 Cal. App. 4th 1073, 1082–86, 25 Cal. Rptr. 3d 39 (2005).

(1) Do you agree with this construction of Civil Code § 1717? Do you think that the plaintiff in *Moallem* should have pursued on appeal his § 1717 argument that his tort causes of action were "on the contract" because they involved breaches of duties arising out of the contract? Why?

(2) In *Siligo v. Castelluci*, 21 Cal. App. 4th 873, 26 Cal. Rptr. 2d 439 (1994), the plaintiff seller sued the defendant buyer for breach of contract for failure to perform obligations under agreements involving the sale of a gas station. The defendant filed a cross-complaint for damages, alleging that at the time of the sale plaintiff fraudulently concealed the existence of contamination caused by a gas storage tank leak. The plaintiff prevailed on both the breach of contract action and the cross-complaint, and sought attorney fees pursuant to § 1717 based on clauses in the agreements. The trial court awarded plaintiff attorney fees only for services rendered for prosecution of the breach of contract action, but not for services rendered for the defense of the fraud cross-complaint.

The Court of Appeal held that the trial court improperly limited plaintiff's attorney fee award, and that § 1717 did not preclude plaintiff from recovering all his requested attorney fees even though the language of the agreement did not encompass noncontractual claims. The court reasoned that whether a prevailing plaintiff was entitled to recover contractual attorney fees for defending against defendant's competing noncontractual claim should be determined by whether plaintiff's defense against the defendant's noncontractual claim was necessary to succeed on the contractual claim and not whether the fees can be apportioned between the two theories. *Siligo*, 21 Cal. App. 4th at 879.

(3) If an attorney fee provision is broad enough to encompass both contract and noncontract claims, it is unnecessary to apportion fees between these claims in awarding fees to the prevailing party. *See, e.g., Maynard v. BTI Group, Inc.*, 216 Cal. App. 4th 984, 157 Cal. Rptr. 3d 148 (2013); *Cruz v. Ayromloo*, 155 Cal. App. 4th 1270, 1277, 66 Cal. Rptr. 3d 725 (2007). Why is apportionment unnecessary? In such cases, the prevailing party entitled to recover fees will normally be the party whose net recovery is greater, whether or not that party prevailed on a contract cause of action. *Maynard, supra*, 216 Cal. App. 4th at 992–96. Why?

[c] Civil Code § 1717 May Apply Although Contract Unenforceable

The courts have awarded attorney fees to prevailing parties under § 1717 in situations where the contract containing the attorney fees provision was found unenforceable, rescinded, nonexistent, or invalid. *See, e.g., Torrey Pines Bank v. Hoffman,* 231 Cal. App. 3d 308, 282 Cal. Rptr. 354 (1991) (concluding defendant entitled to attorney fees under reciprocal rights of § 1717 despite successful defense that contract containing attorney fee clause was unenforceable); *Jones v. Drain,* 149 Cal. App. 3d 484, 486–490, 196 Cal. Rptr. 827 (1983) (holding prevailing defendant sued for breach of a contract containing an attorney's fees provision entitled to recover its own attorney's fees, even though the court found no contract existed); *see also Hsu v. Abbara,* 9 Cal. 4th 863, 870, 39 Cal. Rptr. 2d 824, 891 P.2d 804 (1995) ("It is now settled that a party is entitled to attorney fees under Section 1717 even when the party prevails on grounds the contract is inapplicable, invalid, unenforceable or nonexistent, if the other party would have been entitled to attorney's fees had it prevailed"); *M. Perez Co. Inc. v. Base Camp Condo. Assn. No. One,* 111 Cal. App. 4th 456, 3 Cal. Rptr. 3d 563 (2003) (collecting cases).

In *Milman v. Shukhat,* 22 Cal. App. 4th 538, 27 Cal. Rptr. 2d 526 (1994), the plaintiffs sued defendants for breach of contract and fraud as the result of a failed real estate investment project. Plaintiffs brought a declaratory relief action to determine the rights of the parties under two promissory notes containing attorney fee provisions which, on their face, appeared to have been signed by the defendants. Upon proof that defendants' signatures had been forged, the trial court entered summary judgment for defendants but denied defendants' motion for attorney fees pursuant to Civil Code § 1717.

The Court of Appeal reversed the order denying attorney fees, and held that § 1717 applied even though the relief sought by plaintiff was of a declaratory nature and even though the defendants prevailed by successfully arguing the nonexistence of the notes containing the attorney fee provisions. The court reasoned that the action "involved" a contract; and because plaintiffs would have been entitled to recover attorney fees under the contract if they had prevailed, the defendants should likewise be entitled to recover attorney fees even though it prevailed by establishing the nonexistence of the same contract. *Milman,* 22 Cal. App. 4th. at 543.

Would the *Milman* court's reasoning have been of any assistance to the plaintiff in *Moallem v. Coldwell Banker,* reproduced *supra,* in arguing that his tort causes of action were "on the contract" within the meaning of Civil Code § 1717?

[3] *Recovery of Attorney Fees by Nonsignatory*

A party who has not signed a contract containing an attorney fee provision but is the prevailing party in litigation on that contract is entitled to recover attorney fees pursuant to Civil Code § 1717. *See Reynolds Metals Co. v. Alperson,* 25 Cal. 3d 124, 128–129, 158 Cal. Rptr. 1, 599 P.2d 83 (1979). The Supreme Court has interpreted § 1717 to provide a reciprocal remedy for a nonsignatory defendant, sued on a contract as if he were a party to it, when a signatory plaintiff would clearly be entitled to attorney's fees if the plaintiff had prevailed in enforcing the contractual obligation against the defendant. *Reynolds Metals*, 25 Cal. 3d at 128. The lower courts have applied this interpretation in a variety of circumstances and awarded attorney fees to a prevailing nonsignatory plaintiff or defendant. *See, e.g., Brown Bark III, L.P. v. Haver*, 219 Cal. App. 4th 809, 162 Cal. Rptr. 3d 9 (2013) (holding nonsignatory defendant who defeated claims for breach of line of credit contracts entitled to recover attorney fees under § 1717 because defendant would have been exposed to attorney fee liability if it lost); *Loduca v. Polyzos*, 153 Cal. App. 4th 334, 62 Cal. Rptr. 3d 780 (2007) (holding property owner who successfully litigated a third-party beneficiary action for breach of contract between a subcontractor and the general contractor entitled to an award of attorney fees under the contract pursuant to § 1717).

[4] Liability of Nonsignatory for Attorney Fees

Some courts have held that a nonsignatory plaintiff who unsuccessfully pursues a breach of contract action against a defendant signatory is liable for payment of attorney fees to the prevailing defendant under Civil Code § 1717 where the contract contains an attorney fee provision. *See, e.g., Mepco Serv., Inc. v. Saddleback Valley Unified Sch. Dist.*, 189 Cal. App. 4th 1027, 117 Cal. Rptr. 3d. 494 (2010) (imposing attorney fee award under § 1717 on nonsignatory defendant school district who unsuccessfully claimed breach of performance bond in a cross-complaint); *Exarhos v. Exarhos*, 159 Cal. App. 4th 898, 72 Cal. Rptr. 3d 409 (2008) (reviewing several cases and holding that a beneficiary, and alleged successor in interest to a decedent signatory, who unsuccessfully brought a breach of contract action against a signatory defendant may be liable for contractual attorney fees pursuant to § 1717).

Other courts have declined to allow a prevailing defendant-signatory to recover attorney fees from an unsuccessful plaintiff-nonsignatory under § 1717 unless the plaintiff-nonsignatory actually would have been entitled to an award of attorney fees if plaintiff had been the prevailing party. *See, e.g., California Wholesale Material Supply, Inc. v. Norm Wilson & Sons, Inc.*, 96 Cal. App. 4th 598, 117 Cal. Rptr. 2d 390 (2002); *Sessions Payroll Mgmt., Inc. v. Noble Constr. Co.*, 84 Cal. App. 4th 671, 101 Cal. Rptr. 2d 127 (2000).

[5] "Prevailing Party" under Civil Code § 1717

Civil Code § 1717(a) provides that the party prevailing on the contract shall be entitled to reasonable attorney's fees in addition to other costs. Section 1717(b)(1) states: "The party prevailing on the contract shall be the party who recovered a greater relief in the action on the contract. The court may determine that there is no party prevailing on the contract for the purposes of this section." Determining which party has recovered greater relief is not always easy.

[a] Problems in Determining "Prevailing Party" Status

Who is the "prevailing party" as defined by § 1717(b)(1) where the plaintiff prevails on liability against a defendant, but obtains no net monetary recovery from the defendant after offset of settlement amounts plaintiff previously received from other defendants? *See Goodman v. Lozano,* 47 Cal. 4th 1327, 104 Cal. Rtpr. 3d 219, 223 P.3d 77 (2010) (construing "prevailing party" under CCP § 1032(a)(4)). Who is the "prevailing party" under § 1717(b)(1) where the trial court denies relief to plaintiff on plaintiff's complaint and to defendant on defendant's cross-complaint? *See McLarand, Vasquez & Partners, Inc. v. Downey Sav. & Loan Assn.,* 231 Cal. App. 3d 1450, 282 Cal. Rptr. 828 (1991). In *McLarand, supra,* the court held that the defendant was the "prevailing party" entitled to recover court costs under CCP § 1032. Does this mean that the defendant must also be the prevailing party for purposes of an award of attorney fees under Civil Code § 1717? *See McLarand,* 231 Cal. App. 3d at 1456. Who is the prevailing party for purposes of § 1717 where the plaintiff seeks, but is denied, injunctive relief to enforce a contract? *See Deane Gardenhome Assn. v. Denktas,* 13 Cal. App. 4th 1394, 1398, 16 Cal. Rptr. 2d 816 (1993).

[b] When No "Prevailing Party"

Civil Code §§ 1717(b)(1) expressly gives the trial court the discretion to determine that there is no prevailing party. *McLarand, supra,* 231 Cal. App. 3d at 1456 ("The trial court's determination that there was no prevailing party on the contract is an exercise of discretion. We will disturb it only if there has been a clear showing of an abuse of that discretion"). Under what circumstances may a trial court properly determine that there is no prevailing party? When the ostensibly prevailing party receives only part of the relief sought? *See Nasser v. Superior Court,* 156 Cal. App. 3d 52, 60, 202 Cal. Rptr. 552 (1984). When the plaintiff fails to recover on its complaint, and the defendant fails to recover on its cross-complaint? *See Cussler v. Crusader Entm't, LLC,* 212 Cal. App. 4th 356, 365–369, 150 Cal. Rptr. 3d 895 (2012) (affirming determination of no prevailing party under § 1717 where after years of litigation both sides recovered nothing from each other on their contract claims); *McLarand, supra,* 231 Cal. App. 3d at 1455–56. May a trial court reach the same result by declaring one party to be the prevailing party for purpose of § 1717 but awarding that party zero attorney fees? *See Deane Gardenhome Assn. v. Denktas,* 13 Cal. App. 4th 1394, 1399, 16 Cal. Rptr. 2d 816 (1993).

[c] Determining the "Prevailing Party"

In *Hsu v. Abbara,* 9 Cal. 4th 863, 39 Cal. Rptr. 2d 824, 891 P.2d 804 (1995), the Supreme Court clarified the nature of the trial court's discretion in making the prevailing party determination under § 1717 (*id.* at 875–877):

> As one Court of Appeal has explained, "[t]ypically, a determination of no prevailing party results when both parties seek relief, but neither prevails, or when the ostensibly prevailing party receives only a part of the relief sought." (*Deane Gardenhome Assn. v. Denktas* (1993) 13 Cal. App. 4th 1394, 1398 [16 Cal. Rptr. 2d 816].) By contrast, when the results of the litigation on the contract claims are not mixed—that is, when the decision on the litigated contract claims is purely good news for one party and bad news for the other—the Courts of Appeal have recognized that a trial court has no

discretion to deny attorney fees to the successful litigant. Thus, when a defendant defeats recovery by the plaintiff on the only contract claim in the action, the defendant is the party prevailing on the contract under section 1717 as a matter of law. (*See, e.g., Melamed v. City of Long Beach* (1993) 15 Cal. App. 4th 70, 84 [18 Cal. Rptr. 2d 729]; *Deane Gardenhome Assn. v. Denktas, supra,* 13 Cal. App. 4th 1394, 1398.) Similarly, a plaintiff who obtains all relief requested on the only contract claim in the action must be regarded as the party prevailing on the contract for purposes of attorney fees under section 1717. (*E.g., Texas Commerce Bank v. Garamendi* (1994) 28 Cal. App. 4th 1234, 1247 [34 Cal. Rptr. 2d 155].)

We are persuaded that this construction of section 1717 properly reflects and effectuates legislative intent. It is consistent with the underlying purposes of the statute—to achieve mutuality of remedy—and it harmonizes section 1717 internally by allowing those parties whose litigation success is not fairly disputable to claim attorney fees as a matter of right, while reserving for the trial court a measure of discretion to find no prevailing party when the results of the litigation are mixed.

Accordingly, we hold that in deciding whether there is a "party prevailing on the contract," the trial court is to compare the relief awarded on the contract claim or claims with the parties' demands on those same claims and their litigation objectives as disclosed by the pleadings, trial briefs, opening statements, and similar sources. The prevailing party determination is to be made only upon final resolution of the contract claims and only by "a comparison of the extent to which each party ha [s] succeeded and failed to succeed in its contentions." (*Bank of Idaho v. Pine Avenue Associates* (1982) 137 Cal. App. 3d 5, 15 [186 Cal. Rptr. 695].)

Here, the judgment was a "simple, unqualified win" for the Abbaras on the only contract claim between them and the Hsus. In this situation, the trial court had no discretion to deny the Abbaras their attorney fees under section 1717 by finding, expressly or impliedly, that there was no party prevailing on the contract. The record contains no substantial evidence to support such a finding. * * * When a defendant obtains a simple, unqualified victory by defeating the only contract claim in the action, section 1717 entitles the successful defendant to recover reasonable attorney fees incurred in defense of that claim if the contract contained a provision for attorney fees. The trial court has no discretion to deny attorney fees to the defendant in this situation by finding that there was no party prevailing on the contract.

(1) Based on the Supreme Court's analysis in *Hsu v. Abbara, supra,* when does § 1717 permit a trial court to exercise its discretion and find "no prevailing party"?

(2) If neither party achieves a complete victory on the contract claims, the trial court has discretion to determine which party prevailed on the contract or whether, on balance, neither party prevailed sufficiently to justify an award of attorney fees.

Scott Co. v. Bount, Inc., 20 Cal. 4th 1103, 1109, 86 Cal. Rptr. 2d 614, 979 P.2d 974 (1999) (finding no abuse of discretion when trial court determined plaintiff was the prevailing party under § 1717 where plaintiff sought to prove $2 million in damages but only succeeded in establishing about $440,000 in damages); *In re Tobacco Cases I*, 216 Cal. App. 4th 570, 577–81, 156 Cal. Rtpr. 3d 755 (2013) (holding trial court did not abuse its discretion in determining plaintiff was the prevailing party because plaintiff obtained its main litigation objective even though it failed to obtain injunctive relief or sanctions); *De La Questa v. Benham*, 193 Cal. App. 4th 1287, 123 Cal. Rptr. 3d 453 (2011) (holding trial court abused its discretion in not awarding landlord attorney fees where landlord recovered possession from tenant and 70% of claimed unpaid rent).

(3) In *Silver Creek, LLC v. BlackRock Realty Advisors, Inc.*, 173 Cal. App. 4th 1533, 93 Cal. Rptr. 3d 1533 (2009), the plaintiff seller filed an action seeking a declaration that they had validly terminated real estate sales agreements and were entitled to retain the buyer's deposit. The defendant cross-complained for specific performance or return of the deposit. The trial court ruled that the plaintiffs had properly terminated the sales agreements, but must return the buyer's deposit. The trial court also ruled that there was no prevailing party for purposes of § 1717, and the plaintiffs appealed. The *Silver Creek* court held that the trial court had abused its discretion because the plaintiffs had recovered the greater relief in the contract action. The court reasoned that the plaintiffs prevailed on the most important issue in the litigation, obtaining a declaration that they validly terminated a $29.75 million real estate sale; whereas the defendant prevailed only on the comparatively less important issue, return of the $1.13 million deposit. *Silver Creek*, 173 Cal. App. 4th at 1540–1541. Do you agree with this reasoning?

(4) Who is the prevailing party under § 1717 when an action involves multiple contracts, each one of which contains a separate attorney fee provision, and the defendant prevails on some contracts but the plaintiff on others? *See Hunt v. Fahnestock*, 220 Cal. App. 3d 628, 630, 269 Cal. Rptr. 614 (1990) (concluding when an action involves multiple independent contracts, each of which provides for attorney fees, the prevailing party for purposes of § 1717 must be determined as to each contract regardless of who prevails in the overall action). Does the answer depend on which party obtained the greater relief overall? *See Arntz Contracting Co. v. St. Paul Fire & Marine Ins. Co.*, 47 Cal. App. 4th 464, 490–92, 54 Cal. Rptr. 2d 888 (1996) (holding in an action between a general contractor and its surety for breach of various separate indemnity agreements, that the trial court erred in awarding attorney fees to the contractor as the "net" prevailing party); *Hunt, supra*, 220 Cal. App. 3d at 630–33.

[d] Prevailing Party for Costs

Does the trial court's determination that one party is the prevailing party for purposes of an award of costs under CCP § 1032 automatically mean that party is the prevailing party for purposes of an award of attorney fees under Civil Code § 1717? *See Cussler v. Crusader Entm't, LLC*, 212 Cal. App. 4th 356, 150 Cal. Rtpr. 3d 895

(2012) (concluding plaintiff is the prevailing party under § 1032, but finding no prevailing party under § 1717); *McLarand, Vasquez & Partners, Inc. v. Downey Sav. & Loan Assn., supra,* 231 Cal. App. 3d at 1456 (same). Does a finding that one party is the prevailing party under § 1717 automatically entitle that party to an award of court costs under CCP § 1032?). *See* Civil Code § 1717(a); *David S. Karton, A Law Corp. v. Dougherty,* 231 Cal. App. 4th 600, 607, 180 Cal. Rptr. 3d 55 (2014) (observing that the prevailing party under § 1717 is not necessarily the prevailing party under § 1032, and therefore attorney fees and cost issues should be analyzed separately).

[6] *Effect of Dismissal of Action on Recovery of Attorney Fees Under § 1717*

Civil Code § 1717(b)(2) provides that there shall be no prevailing party where an action has been voluntarily dismissed or dismissed pursuant to a settlement of the case. This statutory limitation on attorney fee awards under § 1717 codified the Supreme Court's holding in *International Industries v. Olen,* 21 Cal. 3d 218, 145 Cal. Rptr. 691, 577 P.2d 1031 (1978). What are the policy reasons for this limitation?

In *Santisas v. Goodin,* 17 Cal. 4th 599, 71 Cal. Rptr. 2d 830, 951 P.2d 399 (1998), the California Supreme Court concluded that in voluntary pretrial dismissal cases, Civil Code § 1717 bars recovery of attorney fees incurred in defending contract claims, but that neither § 1717 nor *International Industries, Inc. v. Olen,* 21 Cal. 3d 218, 145 Cal Rptr. 691, 577 P.2d 1031 (1978), bars recovery of attorney fees incurred in defending tort or other noncontract claims. Whether attorney fees incurred in defending tort or other noncontract claims are recoverable after a pretrial dismissal depends upon the terms of the contractual attorney fee provision. *See, e.g., Khavarian Enter. v. Commline,* 216 Cal. App. 4th 310, 156 Cal. Rptr. 3d 657 (2013) (concluding parties in an action for alleged misappropriation of trade secrets may specify in their settlement agreement that the plaintiff is the prevailing party and may apply for attorney fees after voluntary dismissal).

The *Santisas* court construed subdivision (b)(2) of § 1717, which provides that "where an action has been voluntarily dismissed or dismissed pursuant to a settlement of the case, there shall be no prevailing party for purposes of this section," as overriding or nullifying conflicting contractual provisions, such as provisions expressly allowing recovery of attorney fees in the event of voluntary dismissal or defining "prevailing party" as including parties in whose favor a dismissal has been entered. *Santisas, supra,* 17 Cal. 4th at 617. The Court continued (*Id.* at 617–18):

> When a plaintiff files a complaint containing causes of action within the scope of section 1717 (that is, causes of action sounding in contract and based on a contract containing an attorney fee provision), and the plaintiff thereafter voluntarily dismisses the action, section 1717 bars the defendant from recovering attorney fees incurred in defending those causes of action, even though the contract on its own terms authorizes recovery of those fees.
>
> This bar, however, applies only to causes of action that are based on the contract and are therefore within the scope of section 1717. If the voluntarily dismissed action also asserts causes of action that do not sound in contract,

those causes of action are not covered by section 1717, and the attorney fee provision, depending upon its wording, may afford the defendant a contractual right, not affected by section 1717, to recover attorney fees incurred in litigating those causes of action. Similarly, if a plaintiff voluntarily dismisses an action asserting only tort claims (which are beyond the scope of section 1717), and the defendant, relying on the terms of a contractual attorney fee provision, seeks recovery of all attorney fees incurred in defending the action, the plaintiff could not successfully invoke section 1717 as a bar to such recovery.

In this regard, we reject plaintiffs' argument, based on their reading of subdivision (c)(5) of Code of Civil Procedure section 1033.5, that attorney fees due under a contractual attorney fee provision may be recovered as costs only when expressly allowed under the terms of section 1717, and thus that attorney fees incurred to litigate tort or other noncontract claims, which are outside the scope of section 1717, may never be recovered as costs under a contractual attorney fee provision.

The Court then concluded that (*Id.* at 622–23):

[C]ontractual attorney fee provisions are generally enforceable in voluntary pretrial dismissal cases except as barred by section 1717. Applying this rule to the facts presented here, we further conclude that the seller defendants are entitled under the attorney fee provision of the purchase agreement to recover as costs the amount they incurred in attorney fees to defend the tort claims asserted against them in this action, and that section 1717 does not bar recovery of these fees. But we also conclude that section 1717 does bar the recovery of attorney fees incurred in the defense of the breach of contract claim.

(1) For recent cases applying the rules from *Santisas* in the context of settlement and dismissal of complicated actions involving both contract and tort claims, see *Exxess Electronixx v. Heger Realty Corp.*, 64 Cal. App. 4th 698, 75 Cal. Rptr. 2d 376 (1998) (ruling § 1717(b)(2) precluded an award of attorney fees on the contract claims, and the contractual attorney fees provision in a commercial lease did not authorize an award of fees on the tort claims); *Silver v. Boatwright Home Inspection, Inc.*, 97 Cal. App. 4th 443, 118 Cal. Rptr. 2d 475 (2002) (holding that although § 1717(b)(2) precluded an award of attorney fees on the contract claim, the plaintiffs were properly awarded attorney fees under a contractual attorney fees provision as to their tort claims because plaintiffs had attained their litigation objective through settlements).

(2) Even though a dismissal after settlement of a contract action precludes an award of attorney fees under Civil Code § 1717(b)(2), that statute does not bar a fee award where the prevailing party's right to recover attorney fees arises under some other fee-shifting statute. *See, e.g., Kim v. Euromotors West/The Auto Gallery*, 149 Cal. App. 4th 170, 56 Cal. Rptr. 3d 780 (2007); *Del Cerro Mobile Estates v. Proffer*, 87 Cal. App. 4th 943, 105 Cal. Rtpr. 2d 5 (2001).

(3) Does Civil Code § 1717(b)(2) preclude any award of attorney fees to the prevailing party on a contract claim when the parties signed a settlement agreement

which provided that the action will not be dismissed until after the trial court has determined who the "prevailing party" is and has awarded attorney fees to that party? In *Jackson v. Homeowners Assn. Monte Vista Estates-East*, 93 Cal. App. 4th 773, 113 Cal. Rptr. 2d 363 (2001), the court ruled the parties waived § 1717(b)(2) in their settlement agreement and held that, because the settlement did not evince a clear win for either side, the trial court did not abuse its discretion in awarding attorney fees to the plaintiffs. Do you agree with the *Jackson* court's ruling that § 1717(b)(2) can be waived by the parties? Is there perhaps a better way to explain the holding reached by the *Jackson* court?

[7] *Must a Fee Award Await Final Disposition of Substantive Rights?*

Although a trial court generally must wait until the final disposition of the parties' substantive rights to determine the prevailing party, *Lachkar v. Lachkar*, 182 Cal. App. 3d 641, 648–649, 227 Cal. Rptr. 501 (1986) (concluding plaintiff who successfully petitioned court to compel arbitration of a pending action is not a prevailing party under § 1717 because not a final disposition of substantive rights of parties under the contract); *Bank of Idaho v. Pine Ave. Assoc.*, 137 Cal. App. 3d 5, 15–16, 186 Cal. Rptr. 695 (1982) (ruling plaintiff who succeeded in reversing a judgment dismissing an action after demurrer sustained without leave to amend not a prevailing party under § 1717 because no reckoning of the net success of the parties); the trial court need not wait until all possible appeals have been decided to make the determination. *See, e.g., Bankes v. Lucas*, 9 Cal. App. 4th 365, 368, 11 Cal. Rptr. 2d 723 (1992); *Walsh v. New West Federal Sav. & Loan Assn.*, 234 Cal. App. 3d 1539, 1547–1548, 1 Cal. Rptr. 2d 35 (1991). If an appellate court reverses the judgment, however, it must also reverse the order granting attorney fees and costs because such an order "falls with a reversal of the judgment on which it is based." *California Grocers Assn. v. Bank of America*, 22 Cal. App. 4th 205, 220, 27 Cal. Rptr. 2d 396 (1994); *Merced Cnty. Taxpayers' Assn. v. Cardella*, 218 Cal. App. 3d 396, 402, 267 Cal. Rptr. 62 (1990).

Is a party who successfully petitioned a court to compel arbitration a prevailing party under Civil Code § 1717, or must that determination wait until the underlying substantive contract claims are resolved by the arbitrator? The court in *Otay River Constr. v. San Diego Expressway*, 158 Cal. App. 4th 796, 70 Cal. Rptr. 3d 434 (2008), held that an independent proceeding to compel arbitration is an "action on the contract" for purposes of § 1717 and that the petitioner, who obtained an unqualified win on the only contract claim at issue in the action, is the prevailing party entitled to recover attorney fees. The court viewed *Lachkar v. Lachkar, supra*, as inapposite because *Lachker* did not involve the final resolution of a discrete legal proceeding. *Otay River*, 158 Cal. App. 4th at 807; see also *Turner v. Schultz*, 175 Cal. App. 4th 974, 96 Cal. Rptr. 3d 659 (2009) (reaching the same result in similar circumstances). Likewise, when a party defeats an independent petition to compel arbitration, the action is terminated and the prevailing party is entitled to fees under § 1717. *See Frog Creek Partners, LLC v. Vance Brown, Inc.*, 206 Cal. App. 4th 515, 533, 141 Cal. Rptr. 3d 834 (2012) (collecting cases).

However, the courts are conflicted as to whether a party who prevails on a petition to compel arbitration in a pending lawsuit is entitled to attorney fees. *See, e.g., Roberts v. Packard, Packard & Johnson*, 217 Cal. App. 4th 822, 159 Cal. Rptr. 3d 180 (2013) (concluding fee award inappropriate); *Lachkar, supra* (same); *but see Benjamin, Weill & Mazer v. Kors*, 195 Cal. App. 4th 40, 125 Cal. Rptr. 3d 469 (2011) (holding such a party is routinely entitled to attorney fees even though the underlying contract claims have not yet been resolved by an arbitrator).

Is there a prevailing party under Civil Code § 1717 when the court grants a motion to quash for lack of personal jurisdiction, and therefore may never reach the merits of the plaintiff's contract claim? *See Profit Concepts Mgmt., Inc. v. Griffith*, 162 Cal. App. 4th 950, 76 Cal. Rptr. 3d 396 (2008) (ruling defendant entitled to attorney fees under § 1717 because the contract claim was finally resolved in his favor; the determination of prevailing party must be made without consideration of whether the plaintiff may refile the action later). When the court grants the defendant's motion to dismiss a contract action for forum non conveniens? *See PNEC Corp. v. Meyer*, 190 Cal. App. 4th 66, 118 Cal. Rptr. 3d 730 (2010) (holding defendant is the prevailing party entitled to an award of attorney fees; nothing in the current version of § 1717 indicates a final judgment is necessary). When the court dismisses a breach of contract action pursuant to a forum selection clause? *See Disputesuite.com, LLC v. Scorein.com*, 235 Cal. App. 4th 1261, 186 Cal. Rptr. 3d 75 (2015) (declining to follow *Profit* and *PNEC*, and holding defendants who obtained dismissal pursuant to forum clause were not entitled to fees because there was no final resolution of the contract claims).

[8] *Relationship Between Civil Code § 1717 and CCP § 998*

What is the effect on an award of attorney fees to a prevailing party under Civil Code § 1717 where the plaintiff recovers a judgment less favorable than a CCP § 998 pretrial offer made by the defendant but unaccepted by the plaintiff? May the plaintiff recover its *preoffer* attorney fees and other costs under the contractual attorney fees provision and § 1717 as the prevailing party, or does CCP § 998 cut off plaintiff's right to fees and other costs to which it would otherwise be entitled? *See Scott Co. of Cal. v. Blount, Inc.*, 20 Cal. 4th 1103, 86 Cal. Rptr. 2d 614, 979 P.2d 974 (1999) (concluding a plaintiff who rejects a settlement offer that is greater than the recovery it ultimately obtains may nonetheless recover its preoffer costs to which it would otherwise be entitled, including preoffer attorney fees in cases where attorney fees are an authorized category of recoverable costs under CCP§ 1032 and § 1033.5).

May the defendant recover its *postoffer* attorney fees in such cases? The *Scott* court concluded that under CCP § 998 a defendant whose pretrial offer is greater than the judgment received by the plaintiff is entitled to those costs, including attorney fees pursuant to Civil Code § 1717, incurred after the settlement offer to which a prevailing party would be entitled under CCP § 1032 and § 1033.5. *Scott*, 20 Cal. 4th at 1112–16. By operation of the current version of CCP § 998 (c)(1), therefore, the plaintiff is entitled to its *preoffer* § 1717 attorney fees and other costs, and the defendant is entitled to its *postoffer* § 1717 attorney fees and other costs. *Id*. at 1110–1116.

[9] Procedure for Claiming Attorney Fees Based on a Contract

[a] Noticed Motion Procedure

Civil Code § 1717(a) provides that "reasonable attorney fees shall be fixed by the court, and shall be an element of the costs of suit." A party seeking attorney fees based on a contract, where the entitlement to an award of fees is contested, must file a notice of motion to claim attorney fees within the time limit applicable for filing a notice of appeal. Rule 3.1702(a)&(b); CCP § 1033.5(c)(5); *see Kaufman v. Diskeeper Corp.*, 229 Cal. App. 4th 1, 176 Cal. Rptr. 3d 757 (2014) (holding a party seeking fees under § 1717 need not file a memorandum of costs regarding the fees, in addition to filing a fee motion in compliance with Rule 3.1702); *Russell v. Trans Pac. Group*, 19 Cal. App. 4th 1717, 24 Cal. Rptr. 2d 274 (holding noticed motion procedure for claiming attorney fees under § 1717 is mandatory; failure to file timely noticed motion precludes award of contractual attorney fees); *Dameshghi v. Texaco Refining & Mktg., Inc.*, 3 Cal. App. 4th 1262, 1288–1290, 6 Cal. Rptr. 2d 515 (1992) (concluding notice of appeal of judgment filed by plaintiff did not deprive trial court of power to proceed to determine matter of contractual attorney fees as part of the costs due prevailing party). The noticed motion procedure is also utilized for claiming attorney fees on appeal. Rules 3.1702(c) & 8.278, Cal. Rules of Ct.

[b] Calculation of Fee Amount

Generally, the court will utilize the "lodestar method" of calculating the proper amount of the fee award, unless the contract specifies some other method. *See, e.g., Syers Properties III, Inc. v. Rankin*, 226 Cal. App. 4th 691, 172 Cal. Rptr. 3d 456 (2014) (applying lodestar method to calculate attorney fees awarded under to § 1717); *Sternwest Corp. v. Ash*, 183 Cal. App. 3d 74, 76, 227 Cal. Rptr. 804 (1986) (applying lodestar enhancement); *but see Reynolds Metals Co. v. Alperson, supra*, 25 Cal. 3d at 129–30 (ruling attorney fee recovery under § 1717 limited to 15% of promissory notes as specified in attorney's fees provision of note). The "lodestar method" is discussed in more detail *infra* in § 14.03 [E].

[C] Attorney Fee Awards Based on Judge-Made Equitable Theories

The California courts have developed several nonstatutory exceptions to the general rule of CCP § 1021, each of which is based upon the inherent equity powers of the court. These equitable theories include the "common fund," "substantial benefit," "private attorney general," and "third party tort" doctrines. *Serrano v. Priest*, 20 Cal. 3d 25, 141 Cal. Rptr. 315, 569 P.2d 1303 (1977); *Prentice v. North American Title Guar. Corp.*, 59 Cal. 2d 618, 30 Cal. Rptr. 821, 381 P.2d 645 (1963). These doctrines are sometimes difficult to distinguish, and often overlap with each other as well as with the statutory private attorney general provisions of CCP § 1021.5. For a detailed comparison of these various theories, *see* CEB, *California Attorney Fee Awards, Attorney Fees Based on Equitable Theories* §§ 5.1–5.60 (3d ed. 2016).

[1] The Common Fund Theory

[a] General Doctrine

The Supreme Court in *Serrano v. Priest, supra,* 20 Cal. 3d at 35, described the common fund doctrine as follows:

> "Although American courts, in contrast to those of England, have never awarded counsels' fees as a routine component of costs, at least one exception to this rule has become as well established as the rule itself: that one who expends attorneys' fees in winning a suit which creates a fund from which others derive benefits, may require those passive beneficiaries to bear a fair share of the litigation costs." (*Quinn v. State of California* (1975) 15 Cal. 3d 162, 167 [124 Cal. Rptr. 1, 539 P.2d 761]; fns. omitted.) This, the so-called "common fund" exception to the American rule regarding the award of attorneys fees (i.e., the rule set forth in section 1021 of our Code of Civil Procedure), is grounded in "the historic power of equity to permit the trustee of a fund or property, or a party preserving or recovering a fund for the benefit of others in addition to himself, to recover his costs, including his attorneys' fees, from the fund or property itself or directly from the other parties enjoying the benefit." (*Alyeska Pipeline Co. v. Wilderness Society* (1975) 421 U.S. 240, 257 [44 L. Ed. 2d 141, 153, 95 S. Ct. 1612].)
>
> First approved by this court in the early case of *Fox v. Hale & Norcross S.M. Co.* (1895) 108 Cal. 475 [41 P. 328], the "common fund" exception has since been applied by the courts of this state in numerous cases. In all of these cases, however, the activities of the party awarded fees have resulted in the preservation or recovery of a certain or easily calculable sum of money—out of which sum or "fund" the fees are to be paid.

The considerations underlying this "common fund" doctrine are: (1) fairness to the successful litigant, whose recovery might otherwise be consumed by expenses; (2) prevention of unfair advantage by requiring passive beneficiaries to bear their fair share of the burden of recovery; and (3) encouragement of attorneys, who will be more willing to take cases if assured of prompt compensation when successfully recovering a judgment. *Quinn v. State of Cal., supra,* 15 Cal. 3d at 168; *see Crampton v. Takegoshi,* 17 Cal. App. 4th 308, 21 Cal. Rptr. 2d 284 (1993) (discussing common fund and equitable apportionment doctrines as codified in Labor Code § 3856 and § 3860).

[b] Common Fund Theory Distinguished from Other Judge-Made Exceptions

The common fund theory overlaps with, but is distinct from, the other judge-made exceptions to the American Rule of attorney fees. In *Serrano v. Priest, supra,* the Supreme Court emphasized that the common fund theory applies only where the plaintiffs' efforts have affected the creation or preservation of an identifiable fund of money out of which they seek to recover attorney fees. *Serrano*, 20 Cal.3d at 37–38. The plaintiffs in *Serrano* had successfully challenged the constitutionality of the California public school financing system, and thereby obtained injunctive relief which required the state to equalize expenditures among school systems. The Supreme Court denied attorney fees to plaintiffs under the common fund theory because the judgment did not create a fund or require any particular level of expenditure: "Whatever additional monies are made available for public education as a result of the *Serrano* judgment will flow from legislative implementation of the judgment, not from the judgment itself." *Id.* at 36. The court ultimately concluded, however, that the plaintiffs were entitled to an attorney fee award under the equitable private attorney general theory. *Id.* at 44–48.

The courts in other cases—often class actions—have awarded attorney fees under the common fund theory when the judgment does result in an identifiable fund of money from which attorney fees may be paid. *See, e.g., Consumers Lobby Against Monopolies v. Public Util. Comm'n*, 25 Cal. 3d 891, 907, 160 Cal. Rptr. 124, 603 P.2d 41 (1979) (authorizing PUC to award attorney fees under common fund theory in circumstances where quasi-judicial reparation proceedings benefited large class of ratepayers); *Bank of America v. Cory*, 164 Cal. App. 3d 66, 89–92, 210 Cal. Rptr. 351 (1985) (observing that common fund attorney fee awards usually arose out of class actions, estate, or stockholders' derivative suits; but also applied to taxpayers action which compelled state controller to recover dormant funds from banks); *Jutkowitz v. Bourne, Inc.*, 118 Cal. App. 3d 102, 173 Cal. Rptr. 248 (1981) (affirming award of attorney fees under common fund theory in minority shareholder class action against corporation which resulted in settlement that increased value of minority stock by fixed amount). Because attorney fees are paid out of a fund created by the plaintiffs for passive beneficiaries, a defendant has no standing to appeal a fee award based on the common fund theory. *Sanders v. City of L. A.*, 3 Cal. 3d 252, 263, 90 Cal. Rptr. 169 (1970).

[c] Common Fund Theory Distinguished from Private Attorney General Statute

As illustrated by *Beasley v. Wells Fargo Bank*, 235 Cal. App. 3d 1407, 1 Cal. Rptr. 2d 459 (1991), reproduced *infra*, the common fund theory also overlaps with the private attorney general doctrine codified in CCP § 1021.5. *See, e.g., Rider v. County of San Diego*, 11 Cal. App. 4th 1410, 14 Cal. Rptr. 2d 885 (1992) (concluding in a taxpayer action against county successfully challenging constitutionality of sales tax approved by bare majority of electorate, that attorney fee award should be paid pursuant to common fund theory and not CCP § 1021.5 because both sides acted in good faith to uphold public interest).

[2] *The Substantial Benefit Theory*

The "substantial benefit" theory is an outgrowth of the "common fund" doctrine, and permits an award of fees when the litigant proceeding in a representative capacity obtains a decision resulting in the conferral of a substantial benefit of a pecuniary or nonpecuniary nature on members of an ascertainable class of plaintiffs or defendants. *Serrano v. Priest, supra*, 20 Cal. 3d at 38–40. Unlike the private attorney general concept which is intended to promote the vindication of important rights affecting the public interest, the substantial benefits doctrine—like the common fund doctrine from which it emerged—rests on the principle that those who have been unjustly enriched at another's expense should under some circumstances bear their fair share of the costs entailed in producing the benefits they have obtained. *Woodland Hills Residents Assn., Inc. v. City Council*, 23 Cal. 3d 917, 943, 154 Cal. Rptr. 503, 593 P.2d 200 (1979); *Cziraki v. Thunder Cats, Inc.*, 111 Cal. App. 4th 552, 3 Cal. Rptr. 3d 419 (2003) (collecting cases that have applied the common fund and substantial benefit doctrines).

An award of attorney fees under the substantial benefit theory is available from those benefited only where the judgment bestows actual and concrete benefits and not merely conceptual or doctrinal benefits. *Serrano v. Priest, supra*, 20 Cal. 3d at 38–42; *Woodland Hills, supra*, 23 Cal. 3d at 943–47. In *Serrano*, for example, the Supreme Court found the substantial benefit doctrine inapplicable because the judgment itself conferred no concrete benefits on anyone; only in the event of legislative implementation of higher level public school expenditures would concrete benefits accrue to school children. *Serrano*, 20 Cal. 3d at 41. And in *Woodland Hills*, the Supreme Court again found the substantial benefit doctrine inapplicable because the plaintiffs' successful challenge to the defendant city's approval of a proposed subdivision conferred only intangible benefits on the general public. *Woodland Hills*, 23 Cal. 3d at 942–948. The *Woodland Hills* court also suggested that although the substantial benefit and private attorney general theories may seemingly both apply in some circumstances, the statutory private attorney doctrine of CCP § 1021.5 should govern such cases. *Id.* at 948. What are the reasons for this suggestion? For an extensive discussion of the differences between these two doctrines, see *Braude v. Auto. Club*, 178 Cal. App. 3d 994, 223 Cal. Rptr. 914 (1986).

[3] *The Equitable Private Attorney General Theory*

As previously mentioned, the Supreme Court in *Serrano v. Priest, supra*, adopted the equitable private attorney general theory which authorized an award of attorney fees to a successful party where the trial court "determines that the litigation has resulted in the vindication of a strong or societally important public policy, that the necessary costs of securing this result transcend the individual plaintiff's pecuniary interest to an extent requiring subsidization, and that a substantial number of persons stand to benefit from the decision." *Serrano*, 20 Cal. 3d at 45. The Legislature codified this doctrine when it enacted CCP § 1021.5 in 1977. *Maria P. v. Riles*, 43 Cal. 3d 1281, 1294, 240 Cal. Rptr. 872, 743 P.2d 932 (1987).

[4] The Tort of Another Doctrine

Another equitable theory of recovery of attorney fees, sometimes referred to as a fourth judge-made exception to the American Rule embodied in CCP § 1021, is the "tort of another" or "third-party tort" doctrine. *See Gray v. Don Miller & Assoc., Inc.,* 35 Cal. 3d 498, 198 Cal. Rptr. 551, 674 P.2d 253 (1984). This doctrine authorizes a party to recover compensation including attorney's fees when that party, because of the tort of another, has been required to act in the protection of his interests by bringing or defending an action against a third person. *Prentice v. North American Title Guar. Corp.,* 59 Cal. 2d 618, 620, 30 Cal. Rptr. 821, 381 P.2d 645 (1963). Many courts characterize the "tort of another" doctrine as authorizing recovery of attorney fees as an element of damages, and not as an exception to CCP § 1021. *E.g., Brandt v. Superior Court,* 37 Cal. 3d 813, 817, 210 Cal. Rptr. 211, 693 P.2d 796 (1985); *Sooy v. Peter,* 220 Cal. App. 3d 1305, 1310, 270 Cal. Rptr. 151 (1990) (collecting cases). Do you understand why these courts make this distinction? Do you agree with this characterization? Why?

[5] Exceptions Based on Equitable Theories in the Federal Courts

[a] Federal "Common Fund" Doctrine

The federal courts recognize the "common fund" exception to the American Rule, but apparently treat the "substantial benefit" rule as a part of the "common fund" exception. *See Alyeska Pipeline Co. v. Wilderness Society,* 421 U.S. 240, 257–260, 95 S. Ct. 1612, 44 L. Ed. 2d 141 (1975). The U.S. Supreme Court has specifically held, however, that in the absence of statutory authorization, federal courts under federal law could not properly award attorney fees on a private attorney general theory. *Alyeska,* 421 U.S. at 260–269.

[b] Federal "Bad Faith" Doctrine

The federal courts do recognize another equitable exception and will award fees for bad faith or "vexatious and oppressive conduct" in the conducting of a lawsuit. *Alyeska,* 421 U.S. at 258–259; *Hall v. Cole,* 412 U.S. 1, 5, 93 S. Ct. 1943, 36 L. Ed. 2d 702 (1973) (holding a federal court may award counsel fees to a successful party when the opponent has acted in bad faith, wantonly, or for oppressive reasons); *Chambers v. Nasco, Inc.,* 501 U.S. 32, 111 S. Ct. 2123, 115 L. Ed. 2d 27 (1991) (concluding a federal court has the inherent power to impose attorney's fees as a sanction for bad faith conduct).

The California courts have declined to adopt this judge-made "bad faith" exception, *see D'Amico v. Bd. of Med. Examiners,* 11 Cal. 3d 1, 26–27, 112 Cal. Rptr. 786, 520 P.2d 10 (1974), although the same result may be achieved under CCP § 128.7 which authorizes a trial court to order a party or party's attorney to pay any reasonable expenses including attorney fees "incurred by another party as a result of bad-faith actions or tactics that are frivolous or solely intended to cause unnecessary delay." *See, e.g., Brewster v. So. Pac. Transp. Co.,* 235 Cal. App. 3d 701, 1 Cal. Rptr. 2d 89 (1989) (upholding $22,000 award of attorney fees to defendant based on bad faith tactics of plaintiff's attorney); *Southern Christian Leadership Conference v. Al Malaikah Audi-*

torium Co., 230 Cal. App. 3d 207, 225–227, 281 Cal. Rptr. 216 (1991) (affirming $27,900 award of attorney fees to plaintiff based on defendant's imposition of frivolous defense); *see also* CEB, *California Attorney Fee Awards, Attorney Fees Awarded as Sanctions,* §§ 6.1–6.73 (3d ed. 2016).

[D] Attorney Fees Awarded as an Element of Damages

A trial court may award attorney fees as an element of damages under circumstances where the attorney's fees are an economic loss proximately caused by prior wrongful conduct of the defendant. *See, e.g., Brandt v. Superior Court,* 37 Cal. 3d 813, 817, 210 Cal. Rptr. 211, 693 P.2d 796 (1985) ("What we consider here is attorney's fees that are recoverable as damages resulting from a tort in the same way that medical fees would be part of the damages in a personal injury action"); *Cassim v. Allstate Ins. Co.,* 33 Cal. 4th 780, 805–813, 16 Cal. Rptr. 3d 374, 94 P.3d 513 (2004) (noting that the rule permitting recovery of attorney fees as damages in insurance bad faith cases is now well settled); *Essex Ins. Co. v. Five Star Dye House, Inc.,* 38 Cal. 4th 1252, 45 Cal. Rptr. 3d 362, 137 P.3d 192 (2006) (holding an insured's assignment of a cause of action for bad faith against an insurance company for wrongfully denying benefits due under an insurance policy carries with it the right to recover *Brandt* attorney fees that the assignee incurs to recover the policy benefits in the lawsuit against the insurance company).

In *Brandt v. Superior Court, supra,* the defendant-insurer tortiously withheld insurance benefits from the plaintiff-insured under a disability insurance policy. The plaintiff then sued to compel payment of the policy benefits, and sought attorney fees as part of the damages resulting from defendant's breach of its duty of good faith and fair dealing. The Supreme Court held that CCP § 1021 did not preclude plaintiff's recovery of attorney fees where the award was not "the measure and mode of compensation of attorneys" but was an element of damages wrongfully caused by defendant's improper actions. *Brandt,* 37 Cal. 3d at 817. The court observed that "[i]n such cases there is no recovery of attorney's fees *qua* attorney's fees. This is also true in actions for false arrest and malicious prosecution, where damages may include attorney's fees incurred to obtain release from confinement or dismissal of unjustified charges ... or to defend the prior suit." *Id.* at 818. What did the court mean by this observation? Do you agree with the court's distinction between attorney fees *qua* attorney fees and attorney fees as damages?

The *Brandt* court also noted that attorney fees sought as an element of damages must be pleaded and proved as such, and the determination of the recoverable fees must be made by the trier of fact unless the parties stipulate otherwise. *Brandt,* 37 Cal. 3d at 819; *see Vacco Indus., Inc. v. Van Den Berg,* 5 Cal. App. 4th 34, 56, 6 Cal. Rptr. 2d 602 (1992) (holding issue of attorney fees as damages must be submitted to jury; procedure followed by trial court improperly treated award of such fees as though they were costs). Why these procedural requirements, as opposed to use of the post-judgment noticed motion procedure of Rule 3.1702?

[E] Attorney Fee Awards Based on Statutory Authority

[1] *Code of Civil Procedure Section 1021.5*

Beasley v. Wells Fargo Bank

Court Of Appeal Of California, First Appellate District
235 Cal. App. 3d 1407, 1 Cal. Rptr. 2d 459 (1991)

REARDON, JUSTICE.

I. INTRODUCTION

This case is a companion to *Beasley v. Wells Fargo Bank,* A048490 [1 Cal. Rptr. 2d 446], in which we affirm a $5,227,617 judgment in a class action which challenged Wells Fargo Bank's assessment of fees against credit card customers who failed to make timely payments or exceeded their credit limits. In the present action we affirm a subsequent judgment requiring the bank to pay the plaintiffs their attorney fees, costs and expenses in the total sum of $1,958,509, based on California's "private attorney general" statute. (Code Civ. Proc., § 1021.5.)

We hold as follows: (1) the award was not precluded by the fact the litigation resulted in a common fund recovery from which attorney fees could have been paid; (2) this consumer protection action was in the public interest for purposes of a private attorney general award; (3) the trial judge did not abuse his discretion in applying a lodestar multiplier to the fee award;....

II. BACKGROUND

After judgment on the merits, the plaintiffs moved for an award of $1,133,570 in "lodestar" attorney fees with a 2.0 multiplier, $11,157 in recoverable costs (Code Civ. Proc., § 1033.5), ... and $51,433 in additional attorney fees for preparing the fee request. The judge granted the motion, citing as alternative grounds for recovery the private attorney general statute (*id.*, § 1021.5) and the reciprocal contractual attorney fees statute (Civ. Code, § 1717). The judge's order on the motion deviated from the plaintiffs' request in three respects: it applied a multiplier of 1.5 rather than 2.0 to the lodestar attorney fees (for an increased attorney fee award of $1,700,355) due to the plaintiffs' partial lack of success on the merits, ... and it awarded $50,000 rather than $51,433 for preparation of the fee request. The court rendered a judgment incorporating the order, and Wells Fargo filed a timely notice of appeal.

III. DISCUSSION

A. *Code of Civil Procedure Section 1021.5*

Wells Fargo first challenges the award of attorney fees to the extent it was based on Code of Civil Procedure section 1021.5.[1] The private attorney general statute permits a fee award when the following criteria are met: (1) the action "has resulted in the enforcement of an important right affecting the public interest," (2) "a significant benefit" has been "conferred on the general public or a large class of persons," (3)

---

1. All further statutory references are to the Code of Civil Procedure unless otherwise indicated.

"the necessity and financial burden of private enforcement are such as to make the award appropriate," and (4) the fees "should not in the interest of justice be paid out of the recovery, if any." (§ 1021.5; *see Los Angeles Police Protective League v. City of L.A.* (1986) 188 Cal. App. 3d 1, 6 [232 Cal. Rptr. 697].) Wells Fargo contends the "financial burden," "interest of justice" and "public interest" criteria are absent here.

1. *The financial burden and interest of justice criteria.*

Wells Fargo argues that in class action litigation that yields a common fund recovery, attorney fees should not be awarded under section 1021.5 because they may be paid from the common fund,[2] so that there is no financial burden from private enforcement beyond the usual American practice of requiring litigants to bear their own attorney fees, and hence the interests of justice do not preclude payment from the fund.

This is essentially an issue of first impression. * * *

It is generally said that the financial burden criterion of section 1021.5 is satisfied when the cost of litigation is disproportionate to the plaintiff's "individual" stake in the matter. (E.g., *Baggett v. Gates* (1982) 32 Cal. 3d 128, 142 [185 Cal. Rptr. 232, 649 P.2d 874]; *Woodland Hills Residents Assn., Inc. v. City Council* (1979) 23 Cal. 3d 917, 941 [154 Cal. Rptr. 503, 593 P.2d 200]). Wells Fargo argues that in common fund class actions the cost of litigation should be compared to the entire common fund that is recovered, not merely to each plaintiff's individual stake, because the common fund doctrine makes the entire fund available to pay attorney fees.

The problem with this argument is that although it is persuasive to the extent we should not limit our inquiry to each plaintiff's individual stake, it is based on a fundamental misconception that the focal point is the common fund that is actually recovered. As amici curiae point out, in comparing the cost of litigation to the plaintiffs' stake in the matter, we do not look at the plaintiffs' *actual* recovery after trial, but instead we consider "the *estimated value* of the case at the time the vital litigation decisions were being made...." (*Los Angeles Police Protective League v. City of Los Angeles, supra*, 188 Cal. App. 3d at pp. 9–10, italics added.) In other words, the inquiry looks forward from the outset of counsel's vital litigation decisions, rather than backward after judgment. This is because the purpose of section 1021.5 is to encourage public interest litigation by offering the "bounty" of a court-ordered fee, and the focus of that incentive is on the point in time when vital litigation decisions are being considered.

The opinion in *Los Angeles Police Protective League* prescribes a two-step process for determining the "estimated value" of the case. First, the court must determine the monetary value of the "gains actually attained" by the successful litigants. Second, the court "must discount these total benefits by some estimate of the probability of success at the time the vital litigation decisions were made...." (188 Cal. App. 3d at

---

2. Under the common fund theory, "when a number of persons are entitled in common to a specific fund, and an action brought by a plaintiff or plaintiffs for the benefit of all results in the creation or preservation of that fund, such plaintiff or plaintiffs may be awarded attorney's fees out of the fund." (*Serrano v. Priest* (1977) 20 Cal. 3d 25, 34 [141 Cal. Rptr. 315, 569 P.2d 1303].)

p. 9.) This "discount" is essential because of the purpose of encouraging public interest litigation as of the time vital litigation decisions are being considered. Thus, for example, if the plaintiffs had only a one-third probability of ultimate victory, the estimated value of the case was only one-third the actual recovery. (*Ibid.*)

Once estimated value is determined, it is compared to actual litigation costs. In general, a fee award will be appropriate unless estimated value "exceeds by a substantial margin the actual litigation costs." (188 Cal. App. 3d at p. 10.) In other words, unless the estimated value of the case was sufficient to absorb actual litigation costs and still provide an incentive to litigate, fees may be awarded under section 1021.5.

Also, the financial burden criterion is interrelated with the other pertinent criteria under section 1021.5. If public benefits are very significant, it is more important to encourage litigation, and thus it may be appropriate to award fees under section 1021.5 "even in situations where the litigant's own expected benefits exceed its actual costs by a substantial margin." (188 Cal. App. 3d at p. 10.) In contrast, if public benefits are modest, "the courts should award fees only where the litigant's own expected benefits do not exceed its costs by very much (or possibly are even less than the costs of the litigation)." (*Ibid.*)

Thus, the following rule may be extrapolated from the *Los Angeles Police Protective League* opinion: If the estimated value of a class action common fund recovery, determined as of the time the vital litigation decisions were being made, does not exceed actual litigation costs by a substantial margin, the financial burden of private enforcement is such as to make it appropriate to award attorney fees under section 1021.5. In contrast, if estimated value is substantially more than actual litigation costs, there should be no award under section 1021.5 unless public benefits are very significant. * * *

We must first determine the estimated value of this case, i.e., actual recovery discounted by probability of success at the time of the vital litigation decisions. We view the amount of the actual recovery as being the full $5,227,617 in the common fund — not merely each plaintiff's individual stake — since the entire fund is available to pay attorney fees under the common fund doctrine.

Wells Fargo claims that any calculation of estimated value should be made by reference to the full amount sought by the plaintiffs at the outset of the litigation (purportedly more than $23 million) rather than the actual recovery. The opinion in *Los Angeles Police Protective League* leaves some room for this sort of argument. Although the court said "gains actually attained" must be discounted by probability of success, the court also said "the litigants must discount any monetary benefits *they hope to achieve* by the probability of success." (188 Cal. App. 3d at p. 9, italics added.) This point would normally be important when there is substantial disparity between actual recovery and the amount the plaintiffs had "hoped" to recover. In the present case, however, the point is inconsequential. The amount initially "sought" from Wells Fargo could hardly be the touchstone, as it is not necessarily the same as what the plaintiffs reasonably hoped to achieve. Indeed, few plaintiffs ever expect to recover the amount they first demand. Several expert witness declarations stated that the jury verdict for

$5,227,617 was an "excellent result." This being the case, that amount would logically be within the range of what the plaintiffs had realistically hoped to achieve. In any event, under the present circumstances the only fair approach is to calculate estimated value by reference to the lesser actual recovery, since the other side of the equation—actual litigation costs—was similarly reduced by the court's use of a lesser multiplier due to the plaintiffs' partial lack of success.

Quantifying the probability of success is more difficult. However, in view of the complexity of the case (which in large measure turned on arcane accounting disputes), and the limited litigation resources available to the plaintiffs as compared with the virtually unlimited resources available to Wells Fargo, it is safe to say that the plaintiffs' likelihood of success was no greater than 50 percent, and probably much less.

Thus, the estimated value of the case was no greater, and probably much less, than half the amount of the recovery, or $2,613,808. It remains for us to compare this sum with actual litigation costs. We view those costs as being the full amount awarded, less the 1.5 lodestar multiplier, or $1,391,724. We do not include the multiplier for purposes of the financial burden criterion because the risk in pursuing the case, for which a multiplier is utilized, has been considered as a factor in quantifying the probability of success.

Comparing estimated value of $2,613,808 or less with actual litigation costs of $1,391,724, we find it a close issue whether estimated value "exceeds by a *substantial margin* the actual litigation costs." (*Los Angeles Police Protective League v. City of Los Angeles, supra,* 188 Cal. App. 3d at p. 10, italics added.) But, as further discussed below, we view this litigation as providing a very significant public benefit. This consumer protection action has directly benefitted hundreds of thousands of Wells Fargo customers. Moreover, it has undoubtedly been closely watched by lending institutions nationwide that do business in California, consequently providing an indirect benefit to non-Wells Fargo California customers who could easily number in the millions.

We therefore conclude that even if the estimated value of this case is viewed as exceeding actual litigation costs by a substantial margin, the public benefits from the litigation are so significant that an award of fees under section 1021.5 is appropriate. (188 Cal. App. 3d at p. 10.) Thus, Wells Fargo's interest of justice argument fails along with the financial burden argument on which the former is dependent.[3]

2. *The public interest criterion.*

Wells Fargo also contends this litigation did not result "in the enforcement of an important right affecting the public interest" (§ 1021.5) because it vindicated only the private rights of Wells Fargo cardholders, rather than benefitting the public as a whole, and thus there was no public interest at stake.

---

3. Wells Fargo also advances a policy argument that section 1021.5 should never be applied in common fund cases because deduction of fees from the fund would provide an incentive for the plaintiffs to litigate more "efficiently." Whatever merit there might be in this argument is eclipsed by section 1021.5's purpose of encouraging public interest litigation.

This argument confuses the question whether there was an important public interest at stake with the question whether a "significant benefit" has been "conferred on the general public or a large class of persons...." (§ 1021.5, subd. (a).) The significant benefit criterion calls for an examination whether the litigation has had a beneficial impact on the public as a whole or on a group of private parties which is sufficiently large to justify a fee award. This criterion thereby implements the general requirement that the benefit provided by the litigation inures primarily to the public. (*Marini v. Municipal Court* (1979) 99 Cal. App. 3d 829, 836 [160 Cal. Rptr. 465].) In contrast, the question whether there was an important public interest at stake merely calls for an examination of the subject matter of the action—i.e., whether the right involved was of sufficient societal importance. (*Ibid.*)

For example, in *Angelheart v. City of Burbank* (1991) 232 Cal. App. 3d 460 [285 Cal. Rptr. 463], the plaintiffs successfully challenged the application of a city ordinance to a large family day care home. The court held that although the public interest criterion of section 1021.5 was satisfied in light of the Legislature's policies underlying its preemptive regulation of such day care homes, the significant benefit element was absent because there was no evidence that the litigation had affected more than the one day care home at issue in the case. The number of persons benefitted, and hence whether the benefit was "public" or "private," was crucial to the significant benefit criterion but had nothing to do with whether there was an important public interest at stake. What mattered in the latter inquiry was whether the subject matter of the action implicated the public interest.

The present action to recover excessive fee assessments on behalf of hundreds of thousands of Wells Fargo customers, on the ground the fees were not valid as liquidated damages (Civ. Code, § 1671, subd. (d)), is appropriately characterized as a consumer protection action. (*See* Cal. Law Revision Com. com., 9 West's Ann. Civ. Code, § 1671 (1985) p. 497.) Such actions have long been judicially recognized to be vital to the public interest. (E.g., *Vasquez v. Superior Court* (1971) 4 Cal. 3d 800, 808 [94 Cal. Rptr. 796, 484 P.2d 964, 53 A.L.R.3d 513].) Accordingly, there was an important public interest at stake in this action. The question whether a significantly large number of "private" persons was benefitted so as to justify a fee award is pertinent only to the significant benefit criterion, which Wells Fargo expressly concedes is satisfied by virtue of the huge size of the class.

We conclude the financial burden, interest of justice and public interest criteria were satisfied in this case, and thus the plaintiffs were properly awarded their attorney fees under section 1021.5.[4]

B. *The Lodestar Multiplier*

Next, Wells Fargo challenges the court's decision to apply the 1.5 lodestar multiplier to the award of attorney fees. The standard of review is abuse of discretion: the trial

---

4. We therefore need not address Wells Fargo's arguments challenging the propriety of the award under Civil Code section 1717, which the trial court asserted as an alternative ground.

judge was in the best position to determine the value of the professional services rendered by plaintiffs' counsel, and we may not disturb the judge's decision on this point unless we are convinced it was clearly wrong. (*Serrano v. Priest, supra,* 20 Cal. 3d 25, 49.)

Wells Fargo contends the multiplier was inappropriate because the plaintiffs' success was "limited" and "not exceptional," in that four of their causes of action were unsuccessful and they achieved only a partial recovery on the liquidated damages theory. (*See Sokolow v. County of San Mateo* (1989) 213 Cal. App. 3d 231, 248–249 [261 Cal. Rptr. 520] [trial judge must consider degree of success in determining amount of award under section 1021.5].) But the trial judge expressly considered the lack of success on the four causes of action. The order awarding attorney fees cited the "plaintiffs' failure to prevail on many issues" as a reason for applying only a 1.5 multiplier instead of the 2.0 multiplier requested by the plaintiffs. Admittedly, the plaintiffs recovered only half the damages they requested from the jury on the liquidated damages theory, but a 50 percent recovery of $5,227,617 can hardly be called insubstantial by any standard. The jury verdict was an "excellent result" given the complexity of the case and the disparity in resources available to the opposing parties. The plaintiffs' lack of success on four causes of action but achievement of a monetary recovery which expert witnesses characterized as excellent supported the judge's decision to apply a multiplier of 1.5 instead of 2.0. We are in no position to second-guess that decision.

Wells Fargo also challenges the trial judge's reliance on the "contingency risk factor" as a basis for the multiplier. The judge said this factor, as evidenced in part by the expert witness declarations, demonstrated "that this kind of consumer class action litigation would not be pursued by counsel but for the expectation of receiving enhanced fee awards in successful cases." The bank argues that plaintiffs' counsel did not establish they had failed to recover full compensation in other consumer class actions, and thus failed to show justification for an enhancement in this case as compensation for such losses. This argument betrays an unduly narrow construction of the contingency risk factor. A multiplier might benefit counsel by making up for specific past losses, but that is not the primary purpose of the enhancement. The purpose is to compensate for the *risk* of loss generally in contingency cases *as a class.* (*Fadhl v. City and Cnty. of San Francisco* (9th Cir. 1988) 859 F.2d 649, 650.) A contingency fee is not intended to pay for previous contingency cases that the lawyer has lost. (Newberg, Attorney Fee Awards (1986) § 1.08, p. 13.) Consequently, the purpose of the multiplier does not require proof of such losses. * * *

D. *Attorney Fees on Appeal*

The plaintiffs request an award of their attorney fees for successfully defending both appeals. We conclude that, as at the trial level, they are entitled to such an award under section 1021.5. (*Laurel Heights Improvement Assn. v. Regents of University of California* (1988) 47 Cal. 3d 376, 425–427 [253 Cal. Rptr. 426, 764 P.2d 278]; *Serrano v. Unruh* (1982) 32 Cal. 3d 621, 637–639 [186 Cal. Rptr. 754, 652 P.2d 985].) The appropriate amount of the award is to be determined by the trial court.

IV. DISPOSITION

The judgment is affirmed.

Notes and Questions regarding CCP § 1021.5

(1) The Legislature adopted CCP § 1021.5 in 1977 as a codification of the private attorney general doctrine developed in prior judicial decisions such as *Serrano v. Priest,* 20 Cal. 3d 25, 141 Cal. Rptr. 315, 569 P.2d 1303 (1977). *See Maria P. v. Riles,* 43 Cal. 3d 1281, 1294, 240 Cal. Rptr. 872, 743 P.2d 932 (1987). The right to attorney fees under CCP § 1021.5 is similar to, but independent from, the right under the federal Civil Rights Attorneys' Fees Awards Act, 42 U.S.C. § 1988. *See, e.g., Sokolow v. County of San Mateo,* 213 Cal. App. 3d 231, 243–250, 261 Cal. Rptr. 520 (1989) (comparing "prevailing party" requirements under the state and federal statutes).

(2) The California courts view the federal cases applying the federal act as persuasive authority when construing § 1021.5. *See Maria P. v. Riles, supra,* 43 Cal. 3d at 1290. When a successful party vindicates an important federal constitutional or statutory right in state court, that party is entitled to attorney fees not only under CCP § 1021.5 but also under 42 U.S.C. § 1988. *See, e.g., Kerkelos v. City of San Jose,* 243 Cal. App. 4th 88, 196 Cal. Rptr. 3d 252 (2015); *Green v. Obledo,* 161 Cal. App. 3d 678, 207 Cal. Rptr. 830 (1984). Which statute controls when there is a conflict between the two as to entitlement to or calculation of an attorney fee award? *See Green,* 161 Cal. App. 3d at 682–83; *Sokolow, supra,* 213 Cal. App. at 243–46.

(3) Precisely why did the court in *Beasley v. Wells Fargo Bank,* reproduced *supra,* uphold the attorney fee award under the private attorney general statute, CCP § 1021.5, as opposed to the equitable common fund theory? Do you agree with the *Beasley* court's analysis? What is the practical reason behind the defendant's vigorous argument that the attorney fee award to the plaintiffs should be based on the common fund theory and not on § 1021.5? In circumstances where both the equitable common fund doctrine and § 1021.5 apply, under which doctrine should a court order an award of attorney fees? Why?

(4) *Expert Witness Fees.* In *Olson v. Auto. Club of So. Cal.,* 42 Cal. 4th 1142, 74 Cal. Rptr. 3d 81, 179 P.3d 882 (2008), the California Supreme Court held that a prevailing plaintiff is not entitled to an award of expert witness fees in addition to attorney fees under CCP § 1021.5. After extensive analysis, the court concluded that neither the plain language nor the legislative history of § 1021.5 authorized an award of expert witness fees, and disapproved of lower court decisions ruling otherwise. *Olson, supra,* 42 Cal. 4th at 1153, n. 6.

[2] *Other State Statutory Authority for an Award of Attorney Fees*

Although CCP § 1021.5 is the most utilized fee-shifting statute, the California Legislature has enacted over 300 other statutes which authorize an award of attorney fees to the prevailing party. *See* CEB, *California Attorney Fee Awards, Fee-Shifting Statutes* §§ 3.80–3.129 (3d ed. 2016) for a discussion of these various statutes by subject. Some of the more important of these fee-shifting statutes include Government Code § 12965(b) (authorizing an award of attorney fees to prevailing party in actions brought under the Fair Employment and Housing Act); Government Code § 6259(d) (requiring an award of reasonable attorney fees to plaintiffs who prevail under the California Public Records Act); Labor Code § 218.5 (prevailing party shall be awarded attorney fees in action for nonpayment of wages or fringe benefits); CCP § 1036 (inverse condemnation actions); Civil Code §§ 1811.1, 1794 2983.4 (actions under consumer protection statutes); Civil Code §§ 1942.4(b), 1942.5(g) (tenant actions for breach of habitability or retaliatory eviction); and Family Code §§ 2030–2034 (attorney fee award in family law cases based on relative circumstances of parties).

The courts often utilize decisions applying CCP § 1021.5 when interpreting these various other statutes authorizing an award of attorney fees to a prevailing party. *See, e.g.*, *Graciano v. Robinson Ford Sales, Inc.*, 144 Cal. App. 4th 140, 50 Cal. Rptr. 3d 273 (2006) (analyzing CCP § 1021.5 cases to determine proper amount of attorney fees award under the Consumers Legal Remedies Act, Civil Code § 1780); *Belth v. Garamendi*, 232 Cal. App. 3d 896, 283 Cal. Rptr. 829 (1991) (relying on decisions interpreting § 1021.5 in defining "prevailing party" under fee provisions of Public Records Act).

[3] Criteria For an Award Under CCP § 1021.5

The private attorney general statute, CCP § 1021.5, contains several broad criteria which must be established by a successful party to qualify for an award of attorney fees. *Press v. Lucky Stores, Inc.*, *supra*, 34 Cal. 3d at 318. These statutory criteria are summarized in *Beasley v. Wells Fargo Bank*, reproduced *supra*. The California courts liberally construe these criteria so as to effectuate the compensatory purposes of the statute, *i.e.*, to encourage lawsuits which effectuate a strong public policy by awarding substantial attorney's fees to those who successfully bring such suits and thus benefit a broad class of citizens. *Woodland Hills*, *supra*, 23 Cal. 3d at 933.

[a] "Important Right"

Section 1021.5 provides no concrete standard or test against which a court may determine whether the right indicated in a particular case is sufficiently "important" to justify a fee award, but directs the courts to exercise judgment in attempting to ascertain the strength or social importance of the right involved. *Woodland Hills*, *supra*, 23 Cal. 3d at 935. The courts have construed an "important right affecting the public interest" to include not only constitutional but also statutory rights in a variety of fields; the "importance" of a particular vindicated right is determined by a realistic assessment of that right "in terms of its relationship to the achievement of fundamental legislative goals." *Woodland Hills*, 23 Cal. 3d at 936. Important statutory rights have not been confined to any one subject; and have been found in private litigation involving racial discrimination, rights of mental patients, environmental protection, consumer protection, and unlawful government conduct. *Id.* at 935–36 (citing examples); *see Monterey/Santa Cruz Trades Council v. Cypress Marina Heights LP*, 191 Cal. App. 4th 1500, 120 Cal. Rptr. 3d 830 (2011) (finding attorney fees award under § 1021.5 appropriate where enforcement of prevailing wage requirement covenant in deed benefitted many workers and the local economy); *Indio Police Command Unit Assn. v. City of Indio*, 230 Cal. App. 4th 521, 541–43, 178 Cal. Rptr. 3d 530 (2014) (discussing numerous cases and awarding attorney fees under § 1021.5 for enforcing police officers' statutory procedural and labor rights). Litigation need not establish any new right or be a landmark case; litigation which enforces well-defined existing rights may also satisfy the importance criterion. *Press v. Lucky Stores, Inc., supra*, 34 Cal. 3d at 318; *Indio Police Command, supra*.

In *Adoption of Joshua S.*, 42 Cal. 4th 945, 70 Cal. Rptr. 3d 372, 174 P.3d 192 (2008), a former same-sex domestic partner petitioned for independent "second parent" adoption of a child conceived by artificial insemination of the mother during partnership. The birth mother challenged the petition for adoption, contending that second parent adoption is not valid. This litigation reached the California Supreme Court: In *Sharon S. v. Superior Court*, 31 Cal.4th 417, 2 Cal. Rptr. 3d 699, 73 P.3d 554 (2003), the Court validated second parent adoption, in which the same-sex partner of a birth mother adopted the mother's child, while the mother remained a co-parent. As the prevailing party, the petitioner then sought attorney fees under CCP § 1021.5. The trial court awarded such fees but the Court of Appeal reversed. The Supreme Court affirmed the Court of Appeal's judgment.

The Supreme Court in *Joshua S.* concluded CCP § 1021.5 does not authorize an award of attorney fees against an individual who has done nothing to adversely affect the rights of the public other than raise an issue in the course of private litigation that results in important legal precedent adverse to that litigant and to a portion of the public. Subsequently, in *Serrano v. Stefan Merli Plastering Co., Inc.*, 52 Cal. 4th 1018, 132 Cal. Rptr. 3d 358, 262 P.3d 568 (2011), the Supreme Court explained that *Joshua S.* recognizes an *exception* to be applied in cases where all three factors of CCP § 1021.5 are satisfied, but the party from whom fees are sought is not the party who is at least partly responsible for the policy or practice that gave rise to the litigation. *Serrano v. Stefan, supra*, 52 Cal. 4th at 1027–1028. However, the Court emphasized that "[w]hile most private attorney general fee cases involve public or quasi-public agencies whose actions have impaired the public interest, private business practices that damage important public rights may also justify a fee award under section 1021.5," citing as an example *Beasley v. Wells Fargo Bank*, reproduced *supra*. *Id.* at 1028. Do you understand when the *Joshua S.* exception applies, and why CCP § 1021.5 authorized an award of attorney fees in *Beasley* but not in *Joshua S.*?

[b] "Significant Benefit"

Section 1021.5 also requires that the litigation confer a "significant benefit, whether pecuniary or nonpecuniary, … on the general public or a large class of persons." This benefit need not be a tangible asset or a concrete gain, but may be recognized simply from the effectuation of a fundamental constitutional or statutory policy. *Woodland Hills, supra*, 23 Cal. 3d at 939. Where an action vindicates a fundamental principle, such as free speech or equal protection, the courts usually presume that the general public benefits. *Press v. Lucky Stores, Inc., supra*, 34 Cal. 3d at 319 ("While these rights are by nature individual rights, their enforcement benefits society as a whole"); *Sokolow v. County of San Mateo*, 213 Cal. App. 3d 231, 246, 261 Cal. Rptr. 520 (1989) (concluding litigation enforcing plaintiffs' fundamental right to equal protection and to be free from sex discrimination necessarily confers a significant benefit on society as a whole as well as on the individual victims of discrimination).

Likewise, substantial benefit will usually be presumed when a lawsuit results in vindication or implementation of a fundamental legislative policy. *See, e.g., Folsom v. Butte Cnty. Assn. of Governments*, 32 Cal. 3d 668, 684, 186 Cal. Rptr. 589, 652 P.2d 437 (1982) (holding attorney fee award under § 1021.5 appropriate where settlement agreement resulted in implementation of state Transportation Development Act); *Baggett v. Gates*, 32 Cal. 3d 128, 142–143, 185 Cal. Rptr. 232, 649 P.2d 874 (1982) (concluding plaintiffs, whose individual mandamus action compelled city to comply with state Public Safety Officers' Procedural Bill of Rights Act, entitled to attorney fee award under § 1021.5); *Keep Our Mountains Quiet v. County of Santa Clara*, 236 Cal. App. 4th 714, 737–34, 187 Cal. Rptr. 3d 96 (2015) (collecting cases and ruling that actions requiring a government agency to analyze or reassess environmental impacts associated with a proposed project confer a significant benefit).

The Supreme Court discussed CCP § 1021.5's "significant benefit" requirement in *Graham v. DaimlerChrysler Corp.*, 34 Cal. 4th 553, 21 Cal. Rptr. 3d 331, 101 P.3d 140 (2004). Citing and quoting from *Beasley v. Wells Fargo Bank*, reproduced *supra*, with approval, the court ruled that § 1021.5 requires both a finding of a significant benefit conferred on a substantial number of people and a determination that the subject matter of the action implicated the public interest. *Graham*, 34 Cal. 4th at 578. In other words, the enforcement of an important right must confer a substantial benefit not only on the litigants but also "on the general public or a large class of persons." CCP 1021.5; *see, e.g., Pacific Legal Found. v. California Coastal Comm'n*, 33 Cal. 3d 158, 188 Cal. Rptr. 104, 655 P.2d 306 (1982) (holding beach front property co-owner's lawsuit invaliding certain building permit conditions imposed on them by Coastal Commission did confer a significant benefit on a large class of persons); *Keep Our Mountains Quiet, supra*, 236 Cal. App. 4th at 739 (ruling that requiring the defendant county to further assess important environmental considerations regarding proposed use of park for weddings conferred a significant benefit not only on the neighbors but also on the general public); *Indio Police Command Unit Assn. v. City of Indio*, 230 Cal. App. 4th 521, 543–43, 178 Cal. Rptr. 3d 530 (2014) (concluding litigation to enforce police officers' statutory labor rights benefited not only the nine officers but a large class of other public employees as well as the general public).

[c] "Financial Burden of Private Enforcement"

This requirement of § 1021.5 is satisfied when the cost of a claimant's legal victory transcends his personal interest in the litigation. *Woodland Hills, supra*, 23 Cal. 3d at 941. When the plaintiff has no pecuniary interest in the outcome of the litigation, this requirement is obviously satisfied. *Press v. Lucky Stores, Inc., supra*, 34 Cal. 3d at 321. However, when, as in *Beasley*, the claimant does have a personal financial stake in the litigation, the application of this requirement is more difficult. The court must then determine whether the necessity for pursuing the lawsuit placed a burden on the plaintiff "out of proportion to his individual stake in the matter." *Woodland Hills, supra,* 34 Cal. 3d at 321.

(1) The *Beasley* opinion demonstrates one method of analysis for making this financial burden determination. *See also California Licensed Foresters Assn. v. State Bd. of Forestry,* 30 Cal. App. 4th 562, 35 Cal. Rptr. 2d 396 (1994) (reversing award of attorney fees because the wrong test applied in determining whether the financial burden requirement of § 1021.5 had been met; entitlement to such an award does not turn on a balance of the litigant's private interests against those of the public but on a comparison of the litigant's private interests with the anticipated costs of suit.) The court in *Beasley* also ruled that the financial burden criterion is interrelated with the other pertinent criteria under § 1021.5. This ruling was important to the *Beasley* court's financial burden determination, was it not? Should the other statutory criteria be relevant to this financial burden determination? Why?

(2) Section 1021.5 was not designed to reward litigants motivated by their own pecuniary interests who only coincidentally protect the public interest. Compare *Beach Colony II v. Cal. Coastal Com.,* 166 Cal. App. 3d 106, 112–115, 212 Cal. Rptr. 485 (1985) (ruling financial burden criterion not met where plaintiff property owner's motivation for lawsuit establishing right to reclaim lands eroded through avulsion was to make it commercially feasible for plaintiff to complete or sell a property development) with *Feminist Women's Health Ctr. v. Blythe,* 32 Cal. App. 4th 1641, 1666–69, 39 Cal. Rptr. 2d 189 (1995) (concluding that despite some financial benefit to plaintiff health center from the medical services it provides, the trial court properly awarded attorney fees to plaintiff under § 1021.5 when it granted a permanent injunction imposing restrictions on anti-abortion demonstrators at plaintiff's clinic; the record established that plaintiff's primary motive in pursuing this action was not to protect its personal financial interest, but was to ensure its ability to continue providing medical services to women).

The absence of a monetary award, or of precise amounts attached to financial incentives, does not prevent a court from determining whether the plaintiff's financial burden in pursuing a lawsuit is out of proportion to his individual stake in the matter. *See, e.g., Summit Media LLC v. City of Los Angeles,* 240 Cal. App. 4th 171, 192 Cal. Rptr. 3d 662 (2015) (affirming denial of $3 million fee award to plaintiff outdoor advertising company, who successfully challenged legality of defendant city's settlement with competitors permitting digital displays, because plaintiff financial stake was "enormous"); *Children & Families Comm'n of Fresno Cnty. v. Brown,* 228 Cal. App. 4th 45, 174 Cal. Rptr. 3d 874 (2014) (upholding denial of fee award to county children and family commissions whose lawsuit invalidated state statute authorizing transfer of their funding from state and county trust funds to state treasury because the amount saved was 80 times the amount of attorney fees expended); *California Redevelopment Assn. v. Matosantos,* 212 Cal. App. 4th 1457, 152 Cal. Rptr. 3d 269 (2013) (reversing award of attorney fees to a nonprofit association of redevelopment agencies whose lawsuit invalidated state statute transferring tax funds from redevelopment agencies because the association had a financial stake to the same extent as its members).

However, the fact that the plaintiff's personal pecuniary interest and the public interest coincide does not necessarily defeat this statutory requirement; the issue is whether the plaintiff's individual stake would have been sufficient in its own right to have motivated his participation in the litigation. *See, e.g., Keep Our Mountains Quiet v. County of Santa Clara*, 236 Cal. App. 4th 714, 739–40, 187 Cal. Rptr. 3d 96 (2015); *Otto v. City of L. A. Unified Sch. Dist.*, 106 Cal. App. 4th 328, 130 Cal. Rptr. 2d 512 (2003); *Citizens Against Rent Control v. City of Berkeley*, 181 Cal. App. 3d 213, 230, 226 Cal. Rptr. 265 (1986).

(3) The Supreme Court has suggested that a plaintiff's personal financial gain in a case may warrant placing on the prevailing plaintiff that portion of her attorney fee burden devoted to securing personal rights and on the defendant that portion devoted to protecting the public interest. *Woodland Hills, supra*, 23 Cal. 3d at 516. The Court has also held, however, that an award under § 1021.5 is proper even though the successful plaintiff has no personal liability for attorney fees because he or she was represented by attorneys employed by publicly funded legal services organizations. *Folsom v. Butte County, supra*, 32 Cal. 3d at 684. What are the policy reasons for this holding? Should the fact that the successful party has no obligation to pay attorney fees be relevant to the "financial burden" determination? Should this fact substantially reduce the amount of any attorney fee award?

(4) In *Conservatorship of Whitley,* 50 Cal. 4th 1206, 117 Cal. Rptr. 3d 342, 241 P. 3d 840 (2010), the Supreme Court held that a litigant's personal nonpecuniary motives for bringing litigation, such as environmental or aesthetic interests or the best interests of a child, may not be used to disqualify that litigant from obtaining an award of attorney fees under CCP § 1021.5. "[T]he purpose of section 1025.5 is not to compensate with attorney fees only those litigants who have altruistic or lofty motives," the Court reasoned, "but rather all litigants and attorneys who step forward to engage in public interest litigation when there are insufficient financial incentives to justify litigation in economic terms." *Whitley, supra*, 50 Cal. 4th at 1211. The Court disapproved of several cases, such as *Williams v. San Francisco Bd. of Permit Appeals*, 74 Cal. App. 4th 961, 88 Cal. Rptr. 2d 565 (1999) and *Families Unafraid to Uphold Rural El Dorado County v. Bd. of Supervisors*, 79 Cal. App. 4th 505, 94 Cal. Rptr. 2d 205 (2000), to the extent that they concluded that a litigant's nonpecuniary interests can render a litigant ineligible for CCP § 1021.5 fees.

The *Whitley* court also noted that the "financial burden of private enforcement" requires courts to focus not only on the costs of litigation but also on any offsetting financial benefits that the litigation yields or reasonably could expect to yield:

> The method for weighing costs and benefits is illustrated in *Los Angeles Police Protective League v. City of L.A.* (1986) 188 Cal. App. 3d 1[, 9–10] [232 Cal. Rptr. 697]. "The trial court must first fix—or at least estimate—the monetary value of the benefits obtained by the successful litigants them-

selves.... Once the court is able to put some kind of number on the gains actually attained it must discount these total benefits by some estimate of the probability of success at the time the vital litigation decisions were made which eventually produced the successful outcome.... Thus, if success would yield ... the litigant group ... an aggregate of $ 10,000 but there is only a one-third chance of ultimate victory they won't proceed—as a rational matter—unless their litigation costs are substantially less than $ 3,000.

Whitley, supra, 50 Cal. 4th at 1215. This is the same approach to the "financial burden of private enforcement" requirement adopted by the court in *Beasley v. Wells Fargo Bank*, reproduced *supra*.

[d] "Necessity of Private Enforcement"

Code of Civil Procedure § 1021.5 requires the court to determine that "the necessity and financial burden of private enforcement ... are such as to make the award appropriate." CCP § 1021.5(b). In making this determination—one that implicates the court's equitable discretion concerning attorney fees—the court properly considers all circumstances bearing on the question of whether private enforcement was necessary, including whether the party seeking fees attempted to settle the dispute before resorting to litigation, *Vasquez v. California*, 45 Cal. 4th 243, 245–46, 257–59, 85 Cal. Rptr. 3d 466, 195 P.3d 1049 (2008); *Environmental Protection Info. Ctr. v. Dept. of Forestry & Fire Protection*, 190 Cal. App. 4th 217, 236–38, 118 Cal. Rptr. 3d 352 (2010) (reversing § 1021.5 attorney fee awards of over $6 million and directing the trial court to consider the question of settlement efforts in determining whether private enforcement was sufficiently necessary to justify award of fees since those efforts are relevant to, though not determinative of, the necessity decision in every case); and whether private participation in enforcement is necessary when a public entity engages in parallel advocacy, *see San Diego Mun. Emp. Assn. v. City of San Diego*, 244 Cal. App. 4th 906, 198 Cal. Rptr. 3d 355 (2016) (ruling that where a private party litigates a case on the same side as a public entity, the private party must show its participation was material to the ultimate success and not merely duplicative of or cumulative to what was advanced by the public entity).

[4] *Determining the Successful Party Under CCP § 1021.5*

[a] Necessity of Causal Connection Between Lawsuit and Result Achieved

Code of Civil Procedure § 1021.5 provides that when its three statutory criteria are met, a court "may award attorney fees to a successful party in an action resulting in the enforcement of an important right affecting the public interest."

(1) *Pragmatic Approach.* The California courts take a pragmatic approach in defining who is a "successful party" within the meaning of § 1021.5. *See, e.g., Californians for Responsible Toxic Mgmt. v. Kizer*, 211 Cal. App. 3d 961, 259 Cal. Rptr. 599 (1989) (ruling plaintiff environmental group may recover attorney fees under § 1021.5 where

its lawsuit served as a catalyst for defendant's corrective behavior); *Cates v. Chiang*, 213 Cal. App. 4th 791, 806–817, 153 Cal. Rptr. 3d 285 (2013) (affirming award of attorney fees where taxpayer's lawsuit, voluntarily dismissed after a successful appeal, caused state agency to conduct audit and collect delinquent gambling fees of over $11.5 million owed to the state by several Indian tribes). For example, a § 1021.5 award is not barred because the case was settled before trial, *Folsom v. Butte County, supra*, 32 Cal. 3d at, 685 (concluding claimant settling a lawsuit may be a successful party under § 1021.5 where the underlying action contributed substantially to remedying conditions at which the action was directed); *Sagaser v. McCarthy*, 176 Cal. App. 3d 288, 314, 221 Cal. Rptr. 746 (1986) (observing case law takes a pragmatic approach in defining successful party-impact might include legislative changes, settlements, or amendments in policy).

Although the "successful party" determination must usually await final judgment in a contested action, see *Folsom, supra*, 32 Cal. 3d at 679; *Citizens Against Rent Control v. City of Berkeley*, 181 Cal. App. 3d 213, 226–227, 226 Cal. Rptr. 265 (1986), an attorney fee award may be justified even when plaintiff's legal action does not result in a favorable final judgment. *See Maria P. v. Riles, supra*, 43 Cal. 3d at 1290–1291; *Stevens v. Geduldig*, 42 Cal. 3d 24, 38, 227 Cal. Rptr. 405, 719 P.2d 1001 (1986) (remanding to trial court for determination of whether unsuccessful plaintiff entitled to § 1021.5 fee award on theory that lawsuit caused Governor's Office to reimburse other state departments and take other action).

(2) *Catalyst Theory.* In *Maria P. v. Riles, supra*, the Supreme Court noted that there must be a causal connection between the plaintiff's lawsuit and the relief obtained to justify a fee award under § 1021.5 to a successful party, and that such an award is appropriate when a plaintiff's lawsuit "was a catalyst motivating defendants to provide the primary relief sought" or when a plaintiff vindicates an important right by activating defendants to modify their behavior." *Maria P., supra*, 43 Cal. 3d at 1291–1292. "The appropriate benchmarks in determining which party prevailed are (a) the situation immediately prior to the commencement of suit, and (b) the situation today, and the role, if any, played by the litigation in effecting any changes between the two." *Id.* at 1291 (quoting *Folsom, supra*, 32 Cal. 3d at 685, fn. 31).

In *Graham v. DaimlerChrysler Corp.*, 34 Cal. 4th 553, 21 Cal. Rptr. 3d 331, 101 P.3d 140 (2004), the Supreme Court again upheld the "catalyst theory," under which attorney fees may be awarded even when the litigation does not result in a judicial resolution if the defendant changes its behavior substantially because of, and in a manner sought by, the litigation. The defendant had argued that the Court should reevaluate its endorsement of this doctrine in light of the *Buckhanon Bd. & Care Home, Inc. v. West Virginia Dept. of Health & Human Res.*, 532 U.S. 598, 121 S. Ct. 1835, 149 L. Ed. 2d 855 (2001), where the United States Supreme Court rejected the catalyst theory as a basis for attorney fee awards under various federal statutes. The *Graham* court concluded the catalyst theory should not be abolished as a basis for awards under CCP § 1021.5, but should be clarified (34 Cal. 4th at 560–61):

In order to be eligible for attorney fees under section 1021.5, a plaintiff must
not only be a catalyst to the defendant's changed behavior, but the lawsuit
must have some merit…, and the plaintiff must have engaged in a reasonable
attempt to settle its dispute with the defendant prior to litigation.

In a companion case, *Tipton-Whittingham v. City of L.A.*, 34 Cal. 4th 604, 21
Cal. Rptr. 3d 371, 101 P.3d 174 (2004), the Supreme Court held that the catalyst
theory, as articulated in *Graham*, fully applies to attorney fees awarded to the prevailing party under the Fair Employment and Housing Act, Government Code
§ 12965(b).

One of the specific limitations on the catalyst theory adopted in *Graham* is the
rule that the plaintiff in a catalyst case must have engaged in a reasonable attempt to
settle its dispute with the defendant prior to filing the lawsuit. *Graham, supra,* 34
Cal. 4th at 561. In *Vasquez v. California*, 45 Cal. 4th 243, 85 Cal. Rptr. 3d 466, 195
P.3d 1049 (2008), the California Supreme Court considered the question of whether
this rule should apply whenever fees are sought under § 1021.5. The court held that
no such categorical rule applies in noncatalyst cases. *Vasquez, supra,* 45 Cal. 4th at
251–259. However, the *Vasquez* court noted that in all cases § 1021.5(b) requires a
court to determine that "the necessity and financial burden of private enforcement"
are such as to make an attorney fee award appropriate. In making this determination,
a court properly considers all circumstances bearing on the question of whether
private enforcement was necessary, including whether the party seeking fees attempted
to resolve the matter before resorting to litigation. *Id.* at 245–246, 257–259.

In numerous other cases the courts considered the plaintiff a "successful party" under
§ 1021.5 even though the plaintiff never obtained a favorable final judgment, where
the plaintiff's lawsuit resulted in vindication of an important right. *See* CEB, *California
Attorney Fee Awards,* §§ 2.111–2.114 (3d ed. 2016). Such awards present few problems
where the plaintiff is deemed "successful" based on a settlement or a stipulated judgment.
See, e.g., Folsom, supra, 32 Cal. 3d at 677–87 (deeming plaintiffs successful party where
settlement agreement, silent as to costs and attorney fees, required defendants to establish
four public transit systems); *Planned Parenthood v. Aakhus,* 14 Cal. App. 4th 162, 173–
75, 17 Cal. Rptr. 2d 510 (1993) (concluding plaintiff successful party even though stipulated judgment enjoining defendants admitted no liability or acts of wrongdoing).

Where there is no causal connection between the plaintiff's action and the relief
obtained, an attorney fee award is not proper. *See, e.g., Westside Cmty. for Indep.
Living, Inc. v. Obledo,* 33 Cal. 3d 348, 353, 188 Cal. Rptr. 873, 657 P.2d 365 (1983)
(observing an award of attorney fees is improper if the court finds that the plaintiff's
lawsuit was "completely superfluous" in changing the defendant's behavior); *Suter v.
City of Lafayette,* 57 Cal. App. 4th 1109, 1136–1138, 67 Cal. Rptr. 2d 420 (1997)
(finding fee award not justified under the catalyst theory because there was no showing
of a causal connection between plaintiffs' lawsuit and defendant city's amendment
of a firearm ordinance); *Coalition for A Sustainable Future In Yucaipa v. City of Yucaipa,*
238 Cal. App. 4th 513, 189 Cal. Rptr. 3d 306 (2015) (affirming denial of attorney
fees because interest group's appeal of an unsuccessful action was not a substantial

factor contributing to defendant city's revocation of approval of proposed shopping center on city-owned land).

[b] Successful Party Need Not Prevail on Every Claim

A party need not prevail on every claim presented in an action, nor obtain all the results sought, in order to be considered a "successful party" within the meaning of § 1021.5. *Sokolow v. Cnty. of San Mateo*, 170 Cal. App. 3d at 231, 249–50, 261 Cal. Rptr. 520 (1989). The courts have awarded fees to partially successful plaintiffs in numerous cases. *See, e.g., Lyons v. Chinese Hosp. Assn.*, 136 Cal. App. 4th 1331, 39 Cal. Rptr. 3d 550 (2006) (holding plaintiff, although he obtained no damages on five of six claims, entitled to attorney fees because he prevailed on a significant issue by obtaining a stipulated judgment that enjoined the defendant property owner from releasing asbestos in an area open to the public); *California Common Cause v. Duffy*, 200 Cal. App. 3d 730, 246 Cal. Rptr. 285 (1987) (finding plaintiffs were "successful parties" even though they obtained only declaratory relief and not injunctive relief sought).

The fact of partial as opposed to total success, however, may affect the amount of the fees awarded. *See, e.g., Chavez v. City of L.A.*, 47 Cal. 4th 970, 989–990, 104 Cal. Rptr. 3d 710, 224 P.3d 41 (2010) (observing that although fees are not reduced when a plaintiff prevails on only one of several factually related and closely intertwined claims, a reduced fee award is appropriate when a claim achieves only limited success); *Sokolow, supra*, 170 Cal. App. 3d at 247–50 (ruling plaintiffs are "successful parties" entitled to fee award even though they did not obtain all the injunctive relief they sought, but trial court has discretion to reduce the award on basis of their partial success); *Hensley v. Eckerhart*, 461 U.S. 424, 103 S. Ct. 1933, 76 L. Ed. 2d 40 (1983).

[5] *Limited Discretion to Deny Fee Award When Statutory Criteria Satisfied*

[a] Limited Discretion to Deny Fees to Prevailing Plaintiff

Section 1021.5 states, as do most other fee-shifting statutes, that the court "may" award reasonable attorney fees to the prevailing party. Although the statutory language appears to authorize the trial court to exercise broad discretion in awarding fees, the courts have greatly limited this discretion. The controlling standard, derived from federal court construction of similar discretionary language in federal statutes, is that a prevailing plaintiff should ordinarily recover attorney fees unless special circumstances would render such an award unjust. *See Sokolow v. Cnty. of San Mateo, supra*, 213 Cal. App. 3d at 245; *City of Sacramento v. Drew*, 207 Cal. App. 3d 1287, 1296–1298, 255 Cal. Rptr. 704 (1984); *see also Hensley v. Eckerhart*, 461 U.S. 424, 429, 103 S. Ct. 1933, 76 L. Ed. 2d 40 (1983) (construing 42 U.S.C. § 1988).

Accordingly, the general rule is that a prevailing plaintiff should normally be granted an award of attorney fees. The exception for "special circumstances" is very limited. *See, e.g., Stephens v. Coldwell Banker Commercial Grp., Inc.*, 199 Cal. App. 3d 1394, 1405, 245 Cal. Rptr. 606 (1988) (noting the discretion to deny fee to prevailing plaintiff is narrow); *Schmid v. Lovette*, 154 Cal. App. 3d 466, 475, 201 Cal. Rptr. 424 (1984) (finding no "good faith" exception to either state or federal private attorney general statutes); *but see Kreutzer v. County of San Diego*, 153 Cal. App. 3d 62, 77, 200 Cal. Rptr. 322 (1984) (upholding denial of attorney fees to prevailing plaintiff under 42 U.S.C. § 1988 based on trial court's finding of special circumstance, including defendant's good faith, as justified).

[b] Limited Discretion to Award Fees to Prevailing Defendant

In contrast, the courts have construed this same discretionary statutory language as authorizing an award of attorney fees to a prevailing defendant only if the defendant can demonstrate that the plaintiff's private attorney general action was "unreasonable, frivolous, meritless, or groundless." *See, e.g., Williams v Chino Valley Indep. Fire Dist.*, 61 Cal. 4th 97, 186 Cal. Rtpr. 3d 826, 347 P.3d 976 (2015) (construing the FEHA); *People v. Roger Hedgecock for Mayor Com.*, 183 Cal. App. 3d 810, 228 Cal. Rptr. 424 (1986) (construing state Political Reform Act); *Christianberg Garment Co. v. EEOC*, 434 U.S. 412, 98 S. Ct. 694, 54 L. Ed. 2d 648 (1978) (construing federal fee-shifting statute).

[c] Policy Reasons for Limited Discretion

What are the policy reasons for these constructions of this discretionary statutory language so as to practically eliminate the trial court's discretion to deny fees to a prevailing plaintiff or to award fees to a prevailing defendant? Which construction applies when the defendant acts as a private attorney general in prevailing on a defense or a cross-complaint? *See, e.g., Hull v. Rossi*, 13 Cal. App. 4th 1763, 1768, 17 Cal. Rptr. 2d 457 (1993) (observing that § 1021.5 draws no distinctions between plaintiffs and defendants as a "successful party"); *City of Sacramento v. Drew*, 207 Cal. App. 3d 1287, 1301–1302, 255 Cal. Rptr. 704 (1989) (noting that when a party joined as a defendant successfully pursued a defense or cross-complaint that meets the requirements of § 1021.5, the initial appellation of defendant does not stand in the way of an award).

[d] Suits Involving Public Entities

Section 1021.5 expressly authorizes a fee award on behalf of a successful private party against an opposing public entity, but prohibits an award to a successful public entity unless the opposing party is also a public entity. A successful private party is not required to comply with the claim-filing requirements of the Government Code as a precondition to an award of attorney fees against a public entity. CCP § 1021.5.

[F] Calculating the Amount of the Attorney Fee Award

[1] *The Lodestar Method*

Code of Civil Procedure § 1021.5 and other fee-shifting statutes authorize an award of "reasonable" attorney fees to a prevailing party. Determining the proper amount of the fee award is often more difficult than determining who is entitled to the award. As *Beasley v. Wells Fargo Bank*, reproduced *supra*, illustrates, the California and federal courts usually follow the "lodestar" method when calculating the award amount. *See, e.g., Press v. Lucky Stores, Inc.*, 34 Cal. 3d 311, 193 Cal. Rptr. 900, 667 P.2d 704 (1983); *Serrano v. Priest*, 20 Cal. 3d 25, 141 Cal. Rptr. 315, 569 P.2d 1303 (1977).

The lodestar method, as defined by the Supreme Court in *Serrano v. Priest, supra*, requires the trial court to first determine a lodestar figure by multiplying the time spent on the case by the reasonable hourly rate for each attorney. *Serrano v. Priest*, 20 Cal. 3d at 48. Once the lodestar figure is determined, the court must consider a variety of other factors which may justify either the augmentation or the diminution of the lodestar amount. *Id.* at 49. As *Beasley* indicates, the factors identified by the *Serrano* court are not an exclusive list. Most importantly, the lodestar amount may be reduced to reflect the relative degree of success achieved by the prevailing party as the result of the litigation. *Id.* at 48–49. After consideration of these various factors, the trial court then establishes a "lodestar multiplier" which, when applied to the lodestar figure, determines the appropriate amount of the attorney fee award. *Serrano, supra*, 20 Cal. 3d at 48–49; *Press, supra*, 34 Cal. 3d at 322.

[2] Calculating the Lodestar Amount

The prevailing party is entitled to recover fees for all hours reasonably spent on prelitigation and litigation activities, including time devoted to preparing and litigating the application for the attorney fee award. *Serrano v. Unruh*, 32 Cal. 3d 621, 637–39, 186 Cal. Rptr. 754, 652 P.2d 985 (1982). This may include time spent in a related administrative proceeding where such time was useful and necessary to, and directly contributed to, the successful resolution of the litigation, *see, e.g., Californians for Responsible Toxics Mgmt. v. Kizer*, 211 Cal. App. 3d 961, 259 Cal. Rptr. 599 (1989); *Wallace v. Consumers Coop. of Berkeley, Inc.*, 170 Cal. App. 3d 836, 216 Cal. Rptr. 649 (1985); or where a quasi-judicial proceeding was a necessary prerequisite to litigation. *See, e.g., Best v. Cal. Apprenticeship Council*, 193 Cal. App. 3d 1448, 240 Cal. Rptr. 1 (1987); *see also Consumers Lobby Against Monopolies v. Public Util. Com.*, 25 Cal. 3d 891, 910, 160 Cal. Rptr. 124, 603 P.2d 41 (1979) (holding § 1021.5 did not authorize an administrative agency, as opposed to a court, to award attorney fees for work performed before the agency).

Time spent by paralegals, law clerks, and other necessary support services may be included. *See, e.g., Sundance v. Municipal Ct.*, 192 Cal. App. 3d 268, 274, 237 Cal. Rptr. 269 (1987); *Salton Bay Marina, Inc. v. Imperial Irrigation Dist.*, 172 Cal. App. 3d 914, 951, 218 Cal. Rptr. 839 (1985). The variety of components relevant to calculating the total hours worked on a matter makes accurate recordkeeping very important. Contemporaneous time records are preferred, but are not required, for proof of the number of hours worked. *See, e.g., Syers Properties III v. Rankin*, 226 Cal. App. 4th 691, 698–700, 172 Cal. Rptr. 3d 456 (2014) (collecting cases and ruling detailed billing records not required, and declarations of counsel describing work done may be sufficient); *Cates v. Chiang*, 213 Cal. App. 4th 791, 817–22, 153 Cal. Rptr. 3d 285

(2013) (collecting cases and ruling that reconstruction of time records may be permissible if there is adequate information to reach reasonable estimates of the work performed); *Sommers v. Erb*, 2 Cal. App. 4th 1644, 1651, 4 Cal. Rptr. 2d 52 (1992) (affirming trial court fee award based on counsel's estimate of hours spent on case where counsel kept no exact time sheets because of contingency fee arrangement with client).

Where documentation is inadequate, the trial court may reduce the award accordingly. *See, e.g., Mountjoy v. Bank of America*, 245 Cal. App. 4th 266, 199 Cal. Rptr. 3d 495 (2016) (finding several time entries flawed and unreasonable); *Source v. County of San Bernardino*, 235 Cal. App. 4th 1179, 185 Cal. Rptr. 3d 860 (2015) (upholding reduction of fee award because amounts of hours devoted to certain tasks were unexplained and unreasonable); *Ellis v. Toshiba American Info. Sys., Inc.*, 218 Cal. App. 4th 853, 881–86, 160 Cal. Rptr. 3d 557 (2013) (affirming denial of fee award because time records were inconsistent, contained omissions, inaccurate, contradictory, and not credible; and therefore were not usable to calculate the lodestar amount).

[a] Reasonable Hourly Rate

After the amount of reasonable time devoted to the claims for which fees may be awarded is calculated, that amount must be multiplied by a reasonable hourly rate to determine the lodestar figure. The fee claimant has the burden of establishing a reasonable hourly rate, which is usually computed by the reasonable market value of the attorneys' services. *See, e.g., Serrano v. Unruh, supra*, 32 Cal. 3d at 643; *City of Oakland v. Oakland Raiders*, 203 Cal. App. 3d at 78, 82, 249 Cal. Rptr. 608 (1988) (affirming trial court's use of "hourly rates similar to those charged by top law firms in the Bay Area" in computing fee award); *Bihun v. AT&T Info. Systems, Inc.*, 13 Cal. App. 4th 976, 997–98, 16 Cal. Rptr. 2d 787 (1993) (affirming trial court determination that $450 per hour was reasonable market rate). The market value approach applies even though the prevailing party's counsel actually charged below-market or discounted rates, *Syers Properties III, Inc. v. Rankin*, 226 Cal. App. 4th 691, 700–703, 172 Cal. Rptr. 3d 456 (2014) (collecting cases); or is publicly funded or employed by a nonprofit legal services organization, *Serrano v. Unruh, supra*, 32 Cal. 3d at 640–643; *Blum v. Stenson*, 465 U.S. 886, 104 S. Ct. 1541, 79 L. Ed. 2d 891 (1984).

[b] Proof of Market Rate

The determination of the market rate is generally based on the rates prevailing in the community for similar work; the relevant community is usually where the court is located, from which a trial court may deviate where justified by the circumstances. *See, e.g., Altavion, Inc. v. Konica Minolta Sys. Lab., Inc.*, 226 Cal. App. 4th 26, 171 Cal. Rptr. 3d 714 (2014) (ruling that the default rule is the relevant community for hourly rates is where the court is located); *In re Tobacco Cases I*, 216 Cal. App. 4th 570, 581–

89, 156 Cal. Rptr. 3d 755 (2013) (holding trial court did not abuse its discretion in using San Francisco rates rather than local San Diego rates because prevailing party showed it was impractical to use local counsel); *Center for Biological Diversity v. County. of San Bernardino*, 188 Cal. App. 4th 603, 615–620, 115 Cal. Rptr. 3d 762 (2010) (ruling fees for out-of-area attorneys should not be limited to local market rates because qualified local counsel were unavailable); *see also* CEB, *California Attorney Fee Awards, Determining the Lodestar* §§ 9.105–9.115 (3d ed. 2016) (discussing various ways by which the fee claimant may prove the appropriate market rate for attorney services).

What effect should a contingent fee agreement have on the calculation of the lodestar amount? Compare *Salton Bay Marina, Inc. v. Imperial Irrigation Dist.*, 172 Cal. App. 3d 914, 950–54, 218 Cal. Rptr. 839 (1985) (noting the intent of fee shifting statutes was to award reasonable attorney fee based on reasonable hourly rate and on number of hours actually expended and reasonably necessary; contingent fee agreement largely irrelevant but contingent nature of the award is one factor to be considered) with *Glendora Cmty. Redevelopment Agency v. Demeter*, 155 Cal. App. 3d 465, 202 Cal. Rptr. 389 (1984) (ruling attorney fee award may be made on basis of contingent fee agreement where trial court considered other factors to determine that such an award was reasonable) and *Sommers v. Erb*, 2 Cal. App. 4th 1644, 1651, 4 Cal. Rptr. 2d 52 (1992) (finding contingent fee contract a proper factor to consider in awarding attorney fees).

[3] The Lodestar Multiplier

The most controversial aspect of the lodestar method of determining attorney fee awards is the so-called lodestar "multiplier." Once a trial court has calculated the lodestar figure, the court has the discretion to increase or reduce that figure by applying a positive or negative "multiplier" based upon numerous factors or circumstances. *Serrano v. Priest, supra*, 20 Cal. 3d at 48–49; *Press v. Lucky Stores, Inc., supra*, 34 Cal. 3d at 322. Among the factors properly considered by the trial court in *Serrano* were: "(1) the novelty and difficulty of the questions involved, and the skill displayed in presenting them; (2) the extent to which the nature of the litigation precluded other employment by the attorneys; (3) the contingent nature of the fee award, both from the point of view of eventual victory on the merits and the point of view of establishing eligibility for an award; (4) the fact that an award against the state would ultimately fall upon the taxpayers; (5) the fact that the attorneys in question received public and charitable funding for the purpose of bringing law suits of the character here involved [and] (6) the fact that the monies awarded would inure not to the individual benefit of the attorneys involved but the organizations by which they are employed." *Serrano v. Priest*, 20 Cal. 3d at 49.

When deciding to enhance the lodestar amount by a positive multiplier, the trial court must not rely on the same factors on which it relied to calculate the reasonable hourly rate component of the lodestar. *See Ketchum v. Moses*, 24 Cal. 4th 1122, 104 Cal. Rptr. 2d 377, 17 P.3d 735 (2001) (observing that the factor of extraordinary skill, in particular, appears susceptible to improper double counting and that, for the most part, the difficulty of a legal question and the quality of representation are already encompassed in the lodestar).

A prevailing party may be awarded attorney fees under CCP § 1021.5 not only for the litigation of the merits of an action, but also for the litigation of matters related to the recovery of those fees. *Serrano v. Unruh*, 32 Cal. 3d 621, 632–33, 186 Cal. Rptr. 754, 652 P.2d 985 (1982). Can the amount of attorney fees for fee litigation be enhanced by a lodestar multiplier? In *Graham v. DaimlerChrysler Corp.*, 34 Cal. 4th 533, 578–84, 21 Cal. Rptr. 3d 331, 101 P.3d 140 (2004), the Supreme Court concluded that fees for fee-related litigation may be enhanced under some circumstances, but in light of the relevant multiplier factors, in most cases the enhancement for the fee litigation should be lower that the enhancement for the underlying litigation, if they are enhanced at all.

[a] Examples of Positive Lodestar Multiplier

Under the guidelines laid down by the Supreme Court in *Serrano* and its progeny, courts have endorsed multipliers which substantially enhance the amount of the ultimate fee award. *See, e.g., Cates v. Chiang*, 213 Cal. App. 4th 791, 822–25, 153 Cal. Rptr. 3d 285 (2013) (affirming positive multiplier of 1.85 of attorney fees incurred during litigation of the merits but reversing multiplier applied to fees incurred to prove the amount of the fee award); *Pellegrino v. Robert Half Intl., Inc.*, 182 Cal. App. 4th 278, 106 Cal. Rptr. 3d 265 (2010) (approving 1.75 multiplier in unfair competition action); *Chavez v. Netflix, Inc.*, 162 Cal. App. 4th 43, 75 Cal. Rptr. 3d 413 (2008) (upholding a 2.5 multiplier); *Downey Cares v. Downey Cmty. Dev. Com.*, 196 Cal. App. 3d 983, 242 Cal. Rptr. 272 (1987) (upholding trial court's multiplier of 1.5 in action invalidating city's redevelopment plan); *City of Oakland v. Oakland Raiders*, 203 Cal. App. 3d 78, 249 Cal. Rptr. 606 (1988) (raising lodestar figure of $853,756 to $2 million to account for the extraordinary novelty and complexity of the issues presented).

Although the California courts routinely use a lodestar multiplier to enhance an attorney fee award, a court is not required to do so. *Ketchum v. Moses*, 24 Cal. 4th 1122, 1138, 104 Cal. Rptr. 2d 377, 17 P.3d 735 (2001). In several cases, the courts have applied the relevant factors and declined to approve a positive multiplier. *E.g., Keep Our Mountains Quiet v. County of Santa Clara*, 236 Cal. App. 4th 714, 740–41, 187 Cal. Rptr. 3d 96 (2015); *Hogar Dulce Hogar v. Cmty. Dev. Com.*, 157 Cal. App. 4th 1358, 69 Cal. Rptr. 3d 250 (2007); *Northwest Energetic Serv., LLC v. Cal. Franchise Tax Bd.*, 159 Cal. App. 4th 841, 71 Cal. Rptr. 3d 642 (2008).

[b] Federal Approach to Lodestar Multiplier

In *Perdue v. Kenny A.*, 559 U.S. 542, 130 S. Ct. 1662, 176 L. Ed. 2d 494 (2010), the U. S. Supreme Court held that the calculation of an attorney fee award under 42 U.S.C. § 1988 based on the lodestar may be increased due to superior performance, but only in exceptional cases. The Court noted that an enhancement may not be based on a factor that is subsumed in the lodestar calculation, such as the case's novelty or complexity, or the quality of the attorney's performance. *Perdue, supra*, 559 U.S. at 553. The court then identified the rare circumstances, which require specific evidence that the lodestar fee would be inadequate to attract competent counsel, where such enhancement may be appropriate: (1) Where the method used in determining the hourly rate employed in the lodestar calculation does not adequately measure the attorney's true market value, (2) where the attorney's performance includes an extraordinary outlay of expenses and the litigation in exceptionally protracted, and (3) where there are extraordinary circumstances in which an attorney's performance involves delay in the payment of fees. *Id*. at 554–57.

To what extent do the enhancement factors endorsed by the U. S. Supreme Court in *Perdue* differ from those applied by the California courts?

[c] Independent California Rule

As *Beasley, supra*, demonstrates, the California courts have clearly adopted an independent lodestar multiplier rule, different from the federal approach, when determining an attorney fee award under CCP § 1021.5 and other state fee-shifting statutes. A California court's authority to enhance a lodestar amount by a positive multiplier is well-established. *See, e.g., Ketchum v. Moses*, 24 Cal. 4th 1122, 104 Cal. Rptr. 2d 377, 17 P.3d 735 (2001) (endorsing the use of a lodestar multiplier in determining the amount of a statutory fee award, and declining to adopt the federal rule which bars use of fee enhancements in federal court); *Serrano v. Priest, supra*, 20 Cal. 3d at 49–50.

[d] Policy Considerations

What are the policy arguments in favor of utilizing a lodestar multiplier to enhance the lodestar amount? Against its use? Is it fair to require the losing party to pay more than the successful party's actual attorney expenses? Why?

When determining a reasonable amount of attorney fees to be awarded to class counsel who has successfully negotiated a class action settlement, the lodestar multiplier methodology may be a preferable alternative to a fee calculated purely as a percentage of class recovery, which often results in exorbitant fee awards unjustified by contributions of counsel and thereby undermines confidence in bench and bar. *See Lealao v. Beneficial Cal., Inc.*, 82 Cal. App. 4th 19, 97 Cal. Rptr. 2d 797 (2001) (holding refusal to award class counsel a fee calculated *purely* as a percentage of the class recovery was not an abuse of discretion, but that the trial court has the discretion to adjust the basic lodestar through the application of a positive or negative multiplier where necessary to ensure that the fee awarded is within the range of fees freely negotiated in the legal marketplace in comparable litigation): *Thayer v. Wells Fargo Bank*, 92 Cal. App. 4th 819, 112 Cal. Rptr. 2d 284 (2002) (concluding a trial court may, but is not required to, increase the basic lodestar with a positive multiplier to ensure that the fee awarded in a class action settlement is within the range of fees freely negotiated in comparable litigation).

[e] Use of Negative Multiplier to Reflect Partial Success

The most common use of a negative multiplier is to *reduce* a lodestar amount to reflect the prevailing party's degree of success. *See, e.g., Californians for Responsible Toxics Mgmt. v. Kizer*, 211 Cal. App. 3d 961, 259 Cal. Rptr. 599 (1989) (holding 35% fractional multiplier proper where plaintiff achieved limited success through lawsuit); *Sokolow v. Cnty. of San Mateo*, 213 Cal. App. 3d 231, 261 Cal. Rptr. 520 (1989) (ruling that under state law as well as federal law, a reduced fee award is appropriate when a claimant achieves only limited success). Such negative use of a multiplier in limited success cases is not only less controversial than the positive use, but may also be required. Why? As with enhancement, a trial court's reduction through negative multiplier must bear some reasonable relationship to the lodestar figure and to the purpose of the private attorney general doctrine. *Press v. Lucky Stores, Inc., supra*, 34 Cal. 3d at 322–324 (reversing trial court's reduction of fee award because award based on arbitrary formula).

[G] Appellate Attorney Fee Awards

As a general principle, the California courts construe statutes or contracts which authorize attorney fee awards by a trial court for services at trial to also authorize recovery of fees for services on appeal, *Morcos v. Bd. of Retirement*, 51 Cal. 3d 924, 275 Cal. Rptr. 187, 800 P.2d 543 (1990) (ruling attorney fees incurred on appeal are recoverable under fee-shifting statute even though statute simply provides that "the superior court" may award fees to successful party); *Serrano v. Unruh*, 32 Cal. 3d 621, 637, 186 Cal. Rptr. 754, 652 P.2d 985 (1982) (noting that if fees are recoverable at all, pursuant to a statute or the parties' agreement, they are available for services at trial and on appeal); and to authorize recovery of fees incurred in enforcing a judgment, *see Conservatorship of McQueen*, 59 Cal. 4th 602, 174 Cal. Rptr. 3d 55, 328 P.3d 46 (2014) (discussing and distinguishing the right to recover attorney fees incurred during an appeal from right to recover attorney fees incurred in enforcing a judgment).

[H] Attorney Fee Awards for Enforcement of Judgment

Under CCP § 685.040, a judgment creditor is entitled to the reasonable and necessary costs of enforcing a judgment, including attorney fees where the underlying judgment includes an award of attorney fees to the judgment creditor pursuant to CCP § 1033.5(a)(10)(A). Section 685.040 does not create an independent authority for awarding attorney fees; a judgment creditor cannot seek fees under the substantive authority of § 685.040 itself. *Conservatorship of McQueen*, 59 Cal. 4th 602, 612–14, 174 Cal. Rptr. 3d 55, 328 P.3d 46 (2014). In other words, when a contract, fee-shifting statute, or common law doctrine provides the authority for an award of attorney fees, any such fees incurred in the enforcement of a judgment are within the scope of CCP § 685.040. *Conservatorship of McQueen, supra* (fee-shifting statute); *Gray1 CPB, LLC v. SCC Acquisitions, Inc.*, 233 Cal. App. 4th 882, 182, Cal. Rtpr. 3d 654 (2015) (contract).

[I] Procedure for Obtaining Attorney Fees Based on Statute

[1] *Pleading and Procedure*

[a] Pleading of Fee Request Not Required

Generally, a party is not required to plead a request for an attorney fee award in the complaint or answer, although prudent practice may make inclusion of the request in the prayer for relief advisable. *See, e.g., Washburn v. City of Berkeley*, 195 Cal. App. 3d 578, 583, 240 Cal. Rptr. 784 (1987) (holding plaintiff entitled to award of attorney fees despite absence of request in writ petition, because no requirement that the intent to seek attorney fees under § 1021.5 must be pleaded in the underlying action); *Green v. Obledo*, 161 Cal. App. 3d 678, 683, 207 Cal. Rptr. 830 (1984) (finding attorney fees properly awarded under § 1988 even though not explicitly tendered as a ground for the award); *Citizens Against Rent Control v. City of Berkeley*, 181 Cal. App. 3d 213, 226–27, 226 Cal. Rptr. 265 (1986) (holding trial court has jurisdiction to entertain request for fee award even when first made after judgment becomes final).

[b] Collateral Matter

An attorney fee motion is a collateral matter, ancillary to the main cause. *Serrano v. Unruh, supra*, 32 Cal. 3d at 637. Consequently, a trial court retains jurisdiction to hear a fee application even after the judgment in the underlying action has become final. *Maria P. v. Riles, supra*, 43 Cal. 3d at 1289. An order awarding or denying attorney fees made after a judgment is separately appealable pursuant to CCP § 904.1(a)(2). *Lakin v. Watkins Associated Indus.*, 6 Cal. 4th 644, 650–56, 25 Cal. Rtpr. 2d 109, 863 P.2d 179 (1993).

[2] *Noticed Motion Procedure*

Rule 3.1702 of the California Rules of Court sets forth the procedure generally applicable to claims for statutory attorney fees, and requires that a notice of motion to claim attorney fees for services in the trial court be served and filed within the time limit for filing a notice of appeal. Rule 3.1702 (a) & (b), Cal. Rules of Ct.; CCP § 1033.5(c)(5). Failure of the prevailing party to file a timely noticed motion may preclude an award of statutory attorney fees. *See Lee v. Wells Fargo Bank*, 88 Cal. App. 4th 1187, 106 Cal. Rptr. 2d 726 (2001) (collecting cases). Rules 3.1702(c) and 3.278(c)(1) govern the procedure for claiming attorney fees on appeal. *See Conservatorship of McQueen*, 59 Cal. 4th 602, 608–12, 174 Cal. Rptr. 3d 55, 328 P.3d 46 (2014) (distinguishing the procedures for claiming attorney fees incurred during appeal from the procedures for claiming attorney fees incurred in enforcing a judgment).

§ 14.04 Recovery of Costs by Prevailing Party

[A] Introductory Note

The right of a party to recover costs is purely statutory. *Perko's Enter., Inc. v. RRNS Enter.*, 4 Cal. App. 4th 238, 241, 5 Cal. Rptr. 2d 470 (1992); *McIntosh v. Crandall*, 47 Cal. App. 2d 126, 127–28, 117 P.2d 380 (1941). The Legislature in 1986 substantially revised the law governing the recovery of costs to create a more detailed and specific statutory framework and to codify existing case law. *See* CCP §§ 1032 & 1033.5. The Legislature also authorized the Judicial Council to adopt rules specifying the procedures for claiming and contesting prejudgment costs and costs on appeal. CCP § 1034. Set forth below are the relevant statutory provisions governing recovery of costs in general civil actions as amended in 1986 and subsequently, as well as portions of Rule 3.1700 of the California Rules of Court.

California Code of Civil Procedure (2016)

Section 1032. Recovery of costs by prevailing party as matter of right.

(a) As used in this section, unless the context clearly requires otherwise:

(1) "Complaint" includes a cross-complaint.

(2) "Defendant" includes a cross-defendant or a person against whom a complaint is filed.

(3) "Plaintiff" includes a cross-complainant or a party who files a complaint in intervention.

(4) "Prevailing party" includes the party with a net monetary recovery, a defendant in whose favor a dismissal is entered, a defendant where neither plaintiff nor defendant obtains any relief, and a defendant as against those plaintiffs who do not recover any relief against that defendant. When any party recovers other than monetary relief and in situations other than as specified, the "prevailing party" shall be as determined by the court, and under those circumstances, the court, in its discretion, may allow costs or not and, if allowed may apportion costs between the parties on the same or adverse sides pursuant to rules adopted under Section 1034.

(b) Except as otherwise expressly provided by statute, a prevailing party is entitled as a matter of right to recover costs in any action or proceeding.

(c) Nothing in this section shall prohibit parties from stipulating to alternative procedures for awarding costs in the litigation pursuant to rules adopted under Section 1034.

Section 1033.5. Items allowable as costs.

(a) The following items are allowable as costs under Section 1032:

(1) Filing, motion, and Jury fees.

(2) Juror food and lodging while they are kept together during trial and after the jury retires for deliberation.

(3) (A) Taking, video recording, and transcribing necessary depositions, including an original and one copy of those taken by the claimant and one copy of depositions taken by the party against whom costs are allowed.

   (B) Fees of a certified or registered interpreter for the deposition of a party or witness who does not proficiently speak or understand the English language.

   (C) Travel expenses to attend depositions.

(4) Service of process by a public officer, registered process server, or other means, as follows:

   (A) When service is by a public officer, the recoverable cost is the fee authorized by law at the time of service.

   (B) If service is by a process server registered pursuant to Chapter 16 (commencing with Section 22350) of Division 8 of the Business and Professions Code, the recoverable cost is the amount actually incurred in effecting service, including, but not limited to, a stakeout or other means employed in locating the person to be served, unless such charges are successfully challenged by a party to the action.

   (C) When service is by publication, the recoverable cost is the sum actually incurred in effecting service.

   (D) When service is by a means other than that set forth in subparagraph (A), (B) or (C), the recoverable cost is the lesser of the sum actually incurred, or the amount allowed to a public officer in this state for such service, except that the court may allow the sum actually incurred in effecting service upon application pursuant to paragraph (4) of subdivision (c).

(5) Expenses of attachment including keeper's fees.

(6) Premiums on necessary surety bonds.

(7) Ordinary witness fees pursuant to Section 68093 of the Government Code.

(8) Fees of expert witnesses ordered by the court.

(9) Transcripts of court proceedings ordered by the court.

(10) Attorney's fees, when authorized by any of the following:

   (A) Contract.

   (B) Statute.

   (C) Law.

(11) Court reporters fees as established by statute.

(12) Court interpreter fees for a qualified court interpreter appointed by the court for an indigent person represented by a qualified legal services project, as defined in Section 6213 of the Business and Professions Code.

(13) Models and enlargements of exhibits and photocopies of exhibits may be allowed if they were reasonably helpful to aid the trier of fact.

(14) Any other item that is required to be awarded to the prevailing party pursuant to statute as an incident to prevailing in the action at trial or on appeal.

(b) The following items are not allowable as costs, except when expressly authorized by law:

(1) Fees of experts not ordered by the court.

(2) Investigation expenses in preparing the case for trial.

(3) Postage, telephone, and photocopying charges, except for exhibits.

(4) Costs in investigation of jurors or in preparation for voir dire.

(5) Transcripts of court proceedings not ordered by the court.

(c) Any award of costs shall be subject to the following:

(1) Costs are allowable if incurred, whether or not paid.

(2) Allowable costs shall be reasonably necessary to the conduct of the litigation rather than merely convenient or beneficial to its preparation.

(3) Allowable costs shall be reasonable in amount.

(4) Items not mentioned in this section and items assessed upon application may be allowed or denied in the court's discretion.

(5) When any statute of this state refers to the award of "costs and attorney's fees," attorney's fees are an item and component of the costs to be awarded and are allowable as costs pursuant to subparagraph (B) of paragraph (10) of subdivision (a). Any claim not based upon the court's established schedule of attorney's fees for actions on a contract shall bear the burden of proof. Attorney's fees allowable as costs pursuant to subparagraph (B) of paragraph (10) of subdivision (a) may be fixed as follows: (A) upon a noticed motion, (B) at the time a statement of decision is rendered, (C) upon application supported by affidavit made concurrently with a claim for other costs, or (D) upon entry of default judgment. Attorney's fees allowable as costs pursuant to subparagraph (A) or (C) of paragraph (10) of subdivision (a) shall be fixed either upon a noticed motion or upon entry of a default judgment, unless otherwise provided by stipulation of the parties.

Attorney's fees awarded pursuant to Section 1717 of the Civil Code are allowable costs under Section 1032 of this code as authorized by subparagraph (A) of paragraph (10) of subdivision (a).

California Rules of Court (2016)

Rule 3.1700. Prejudgment costs.

(a) Claiming costs

(1) *Trial costs.* A prevailing party who claims costs shall serve and file a memorandum of costs within 15 days after the date of service of the notice of entry of judgment or dismissal by the clerk under Code of Civil Procedure section 664.5 or the date of service of written notice of entry of judgment or dismissal, or within 180 days after entry of judgment, whichever is first. The memorandum of costs shall be verified by

a statement of the party, attorney, or agent that to the best of his or her knowledge the items of cost are correct and were necessarily incurred in the case.

(2) *Costs on default.* A party seeking a default judgment who claims costs must request costs on the Request to Enter Default (Application to Enter Default) (form CIV-100) at the time of applying for the judgment.

(b) Contesting costs

(1) *Striking and taxing costs.* Any notice of motion to strike or to tax costs must be served and filed 15 days after service of the cost memorandum. If the cost memorandum was served by mail, the period is extended as provided in Code of Civil Procedure section 1013. If the cost memorandum was served electronically, the period is extended as provided in Code of Civil Procedure section 1010.6(a)(4).

(2) *Form of motion.* Unless objection is made to the entire cost memorandum, the motion to strike or tax costs must refer to each item objected to by the same number and appear in the same order as the corresponding cost item claimed on the memorandum of costs and must state why the item is objectionable.

(3) *Extensions of time.* The party claiming costs and the party contesting costs may agree to extend the time for serving and filing the cost memorandum and a motion to strike or tax costs. This agreement must be confirmed in writing, specify the extended date for service, and be filed with the clerk. In the absence of an agreement, the court may extend the times for serving and filing the cost memorandum or the notice of motion to strike or tax costs for a period not to exceed 30 days.

(4) *Entry of costs.* After the time has passed for a motion to strike or tax costs or for determination of that motion, the clerk must immediately enter the costs on the judgment.

[B] Prevailing Party Under CCP § 1032

Section 1032(a) clearly defines who is the "prevailing party" in a variety of typical situations. The proper interpretation of these statutory definitions is not so clear, however, in less typical applications. Consider the following questions:

[1] *Who is the Prevailing Party When Both Plaintiff and Defendant Denied Relief?*

In *McLarand, Vasquez & Partners, Inc. v. Downey Sav. & Loan Assn.*, 231 Cal. App. 3d 1450, 282 Cal. Rptr. 828 (1991), the court addressed the question of who is the "prevailing party" when the trial court denies relief to both the plaintiff on the complaint and the defendant on a cross-complaint. The plaintiff in *McLarand* filed a complaint seeking damages against the defendant for breach of contract and tortious denial of contract. The defendant cross-complained against the plaintiff, seeking damages for breach of contract, negligence, and related claims. Following a jury trial, general verdicts denying relief to both parties were entered. Is the defendant the only "prevailing party" pursuant to § 1032(a)(4)? Or are both parties "prevailing parties" under §§ 1032(a)(1)–(4), and both entitled to an award of costs, because the defendant filed a cross-complaint against the plaintiff and neither party was successful on its action? Is § 1032(a)(2), which defines a "defendant" to include a cross-defendant, of any relevance to this issue?

The court in *McLarand* held that where both parties are denied relief on their respective claims, the defendant is entitled to an award of costs but the plaintiff is not. *See also Cussler v. Crusader Entm't, LLC*, 212 Cal. App. 4th 356, 370–72, 150 Cal. Rptr. 3d 895 (2012) (ruling defendant was the prevailing party under § 1032(a)(4) where after years of litigation both sides recovered nothing from each other on their respective claims). The court rejected an interpretation of § 1032 which would make both parties "prevailing parties" and therefore both entitled to an award of costs, commenting that the "practical effect of such a result would be to conclude the prevailing party is the one who spends the most." *McLarand*, 231 Cal. App. 3d at 1453. What did the court mean by this comment? Do you agree with the *McLarand* court's interpretation of § 1032? Why?

The *McLarand* court also held that the prevailing party for purposes of an award of costs under § 1032 is not necessarily the prevailing party for purposes of an award of statutory attorney fees. *McLarand*, 231 Cal. App. 3d at 1456. Do you agree? *See Cussler, supra* (holding defendant was the prevailing party entitled to an award of costs under § 1032(a)(4), but neither party was the prevailing party for purposes of an award of attorney fees under Civil Code § 1717); *David S. Karton, A Law Corp. v. Dougherty*, 231 Cal. App. 4th 600, 607, 180 Cal. Rptr. 3d 55 (2014) (observing that the prevailing party under § 1717 is not necessarily the prevailing party under § 1032, and therefore attorney fees and cost issues should be analyzed separately).

[2] Who is the Prevailing Party When Plaintiff Recovers Nothing After Settlement Offsets?

In *Goodman v. Lozano*, 47 Cal. 4th 1327, 104 Cal. Rptr. 3d 219, 223 P.3d 77 (2010), the Supreme Court decided whether the plaintiff is the "prevailing party" when the damages awarded are reduced to zero after offsets for good faith settlements. The plaintiffs in *Goodman* sought money damages in the amount of $550,000 against numerous defendants for construction defects in their new house, alleging negligence and fraud. Plaintiffs settled with all but two of the defendants prior to trial. The plaintiffs prevailed on the issue of liability at the trial, but obtained no net monetary recovery from the remaining defendants after offset of the previous settlements with the other defendants. The trial court awarded plaintiffs $146,000, well below the $230,000 received through the settlements. Exercising its discretion under CCP § 1032(a)(4), the trial court determined the defendants were the prevailing parties because they paid nothing under the judgment. The plaintiffs appealed, arguing that they are the "prevailing parties" entitled to an award of costs and, alternatively, that the trial court abused its discretion.

The Supreme Court in *Goodman* concluded that the plaintiffs, who recovered nothing from the nonsettling defendants due to the settlement offset, did not obtain a "net monetary recovery" within the meaning of § 1032(a)(4). The Supreme Court also ruled that the trial court did not abuse its discretion in awarding costs to defendants. The trial court properly assessed the parties' litigation objectives going into trial against the results actually achieved when it determined that the defendants are the prevailing parties. *Goodman, supra,* 47 Cal. 4th at 1338–1339.

The *Goodman* court held that a plaintiff whose damage award is offset to zero by a prior settlement does not categorically qualify as a prevailing party ("the party with the net monetary recovery") as a matter of law. The court also noted that unless a party otherwise fits into one of the remaining three categories of "prevailing party" under CCP § 1032(a)(4), a trial court will have the *discretion* to make the determination as to a "prevailing party" under § 1032(a)(4). *Goodman,* 47 Cal. 4th at 1338, n. 4. Does this mean that the trial court in *Goodman* could have properly determined, as a matter of discretion, that the plaintiffs were the "prevailing parties"? Or were the defendants actually the "prevailing parties" as a matter of law under § 1032(a)(4)?

[3] Who is the Prevailing Party When Action Voluntary Dismissed After a Settlement?

In *DeSaulles v. Community Hosp. of Monterey Peninsula,* 62 Cal. 4th 1140, 202 Cal. Rtpr. 3d 429, 370 P.3d 996 (2016), the Supreme Court answered the question of who is the "prevailing party" for purposes of an award of costs where the plaintiff voluntarily dismisses the action pursuant to a settlement agreement. The Supreme Court first concluded that the definition of "prevailing party" as "a defendant in whose favor a dismissal is entered" was not intended to encompass defendants that entered into a monetary settlement in exchange for dismissal. *DeSaulles, supra,* 62 Cal. 4th at 1152–53. Next, the Court ruled that the term "recovery" in section 1032(a)(4) encompasses situations in which a defendant settles with a plaintiff for some or all of the money the plaintiff sought through litigation. *Id.* at 1154. Finally, the Court held that a plaintiff who enters into a settlement or stipulated judgment to be paid money in exchange for dismissal has obtained a "net monetary recovery" within the meaning of section 1032(a)(4), whether or not the judgment mentions the settlement. *Id.* at 1158. The Court also emphasized that these holdings establish a default rule that applies only when the parties have not resolved the matter of costs in their settlement agreement or have not stipulated "to alternative procedures for awarding costs" as authorized by section 1032(c). *Id.*

[C] Multiple Parties

Is the defendant a prevailing party entitled to immediately recover necessary deposition costs pursuant to CCP § 1032(b) and § 1033.5(a)(3) when the trial court grants dismissal as to one plaintiff, but other plaintiffs remain and may ultimately prevail against defendant at trial? *See Anderson v. Pac. Bell,* 204 Cal. App. 3d 277, 251 Cal. Rptr. 66 (1988) (concluding the right of defendant to recover costs from dismissed plaintiff not dependent on any hypothetical future right the remaining plaintiffs might have to recover their different costs if they prevail against defendant).

Where the plaintiff sued multiple defendants and one defendant was granted summary judgment, the prevailing defendant may only recover costs actually incurred by himself in defending his case and not costs jointly incurred by the remaining defendants. *See Fennessy v. DeLeuw-Cather Corp.*, 218 Cal. App. 3d 1192, 267 Cal. Rptr. 772 (1990). Is a plaintiff who prevails against only one of several defendants after a lengthy trial entitled to an award of 100% of its costs? *See Heppler v. J.M. Peters Co.*, 73 Cal. app. 4th 1265, 87 Cal. Rptr. 2d 497 (1999) (ruling plaintiff should recover only a pro rata share of these costs from the unsuccessful defendant where not all the issues in the trial were integrally associated with each defendant); *Nelson v. Anderson*, 72 Cal. App. 4th 111, 84 Cal. Rptr. 2d 753 (1999) (holding by a divided court that where the defendant settled with two other plaintiffs before trial and prevailed at trial as to the nonsettling plaintiff, an across-the-board reduction of the prevailing defendant's award of costs based upon the number of plaintiffs, without regard to the reason the costs were incurred, was not a proper determination of the necessity or reasonableness of the costs).

[D] Certain Costs Recoverable as a Matter of Right; Others as a Matter of Discretion

[1] Costs Allowable of Right

A prevailing party is entitled to recover costs as a matter of right. CCP §§ 1021, 1032(b). Section 1033.5(a) specifies those items generally recoverable as costs of right. Section 1033.5(b) specifies those costs not recoverable, "unless expressly authorized by law." *See, e.g., Desplancke v. Wilson*, 14 Cal. App. 4th 631, 635–36, 17 Cal. Rptr. 2d 586 (1993); *see also Carwash of America-PO v. Windswept Ventures No. 1*, 97 Cal. App. 4th 540, 118 Cal. Rptr. 2d 536 (2002 (holding that where judgment is entered for the plaintiff on a claim of breach of contract, and the contract contains a provision permitting the prevailing party to recover expert witness fees, such fees may not be awarded as an item of costs but must be pleaded and proven separately).

[2] Discretionary Costs

An item not specifically allowable under § 1033.5(a) nor prohibited under § 1033.5(b) may nevertheless be recoverable in the discretion of the court if "reasonably necessary to the conduct of the litigation rather than merely convenient or beneficial to its preparation." CCP § 1033.5(c)(2); *Science Applications Int'l Corp. v. Superior Court*, 39 Cal. App. 4th 1095, 46 Cal. Rptr. 2d 332 (1995).

Which of the following cost items satisfy the standard for discretionary costs in § 1033.5(c)(2)? The cost of attorney lunches during depositions? The cost of faxes? Parking, cab fares, and other local travel expenses? Courier and messenger expenses incurred in filing documents and transporting exhibits? Computer legal research? Fees paid to a state agency to obtain documents for review by an expert witness? For a discussion of these proffered discretionary costs, see *Ladas v. Cal. State Auto. Assn.*, 19 Cal. App. 4th 761, 773–76, 23 Cal. Rptr. 810 (1993).

The cost of models and enlargements of exhibits are allowable of right under CCP § 1033.5(a)(13) "if they were reasonably helpful to aid the trier of fact." However, § 1033.5(a)(13) does not authorize recovery for the costs of preparing exhibits that are not used at trial. *Ladas v. Cal. State Auto. Assn., supra*, 19 Cal. App. 4th at 773–76 (disallowing trial exhibit items because the case was dismissed before trial and therefore such exhibit expenses could not meet the requirement of § 1033.5(a)(13)). Nor are such costs expressly prohibited by § 1033.5(b). Are the costs of preparing unused trial exhibits therefore recoverable as a matter of discretion under CCP § 1033.5(c)(4)? The courts of appeal are divided on this question. *See Applegate v. St. Francis Lutheran Church*, 23 Cal. App. 4th 362, 363–64, 28 Cal. Rptr. 2d 436 (1994) (ruling only those costs items expressly prohibited by § 1033.5(b) are outside the scope of the court's discretionary authority under § 1033.5(c)(4)); *Benach v. County of L.A.*, 149 Cal. App. 4th 836, 57 Cal. Rptr. 3d 363 (2007) (finding no an abuse of discretion to award defendant costs under § 1033.5(c)(4) for photocopies of exhibits that were not used at trial where nothing indicated that the defendant could have anticipated that the exhibits would not be used); *but see Seever v. Copley Press, Inc.*, 141 Cal. App. 4th 1550, 47 Cal. Rptr. 3d 206 (2006) (CCP § 1033.5(a)(13) contains a specific limitation on recovery of exhibit costs that circumscribes the court's discretionary authority under § 1033.3(c)(4)).

[3] Costs Must Be Reasonably Necessary

Section 1033.5(c) provides that allowable costs must be reasonable in amount, and must be "reasonably necessary" to the conduct of the litigation. CCP §§ 1033.5(c)(2) & (3). The "reasonably necessary" condition applies to both items of costs recoverable as a matter of right and to items allowable at the discretion of the court. *See Perko's Enter., Inc. v. RRNS Enter.*, 4 Cal. App. 4th 238, 5 Cal. Rptr. 2d 470 (1992) (observing that the intent and effect of § 1033.5(c)(2) was to authorize a trial court to disallow recovery of costs, including filing fees, when it determines the costs were incurred unnecessarily). What does "reasonably necessary" mean in this context? A memorandum of costs is prima facie evidence the items were necessary, but when a cost bill is properly challenged, the burden shifts to the party claiming costs to prove their necessity. *Perko's Enter., supra*, 4 Cal. App. 4th at 243 (collecting cases). The determination of the necessity and reasonableness of a particular expense is "within the broad discretion of the court." *Id.*

Technological advances in the conduct of litigation have complicated the "reasonably necessary" determination. For example, in *Science Applications Int'l Corp. v. Superior Court*, 39 Cal. App. 4th 1095, 46 Cal. Rptr. 2d 332 (1995), the court struggled with whether several then-innovative cost items where reasonably necessary, observing that "[t]hese expenses are the kind the Legislature probably never contemplated if for no other reason than the technology did not exist until recently." *Id.* at 1104. The court approved some of these items but disapprove several others including the cost of editing videotape depositions for presentation of testimony to the jury because "the existence of the alternative but mundane method of reading aloud strongly suggests the editing 'was not reasonably necessary to the conduct of the litigation,' however 'convenient or beneficial' it may have been. *Id.* at 1105. Other decisions have concluded that cost items similar to those items disallowed in *Science Applications* were "reasonably necessary" and properly awarded under § 1033.5(c)(4), such as *El Dorado Meat Co. v. Yosemite Meat & Locker Serv., Inc.*, 150 Cal. App. 4th 612, 58 Cal. Rptr. 3d 590 (2007) (finding no abuse of discretion in awarding recovery of costs of $111,063 for hourly billings of personnel to process the raw business data that went into an exhibit, $3,495 for photocopying of business documents admitted into evidence as exhibits, and $2,250 for equipment to project documents on a screen during trial), and *Bender v. County of Los Angeles*, reproduced below:

Bender v. County of Los Angeles

Court of Appeal of California, Second Appellate District
217 Cal. App. 4th 968, 159 Cal. Rptr. 3d 204 (2013)

GRIMES, JUSTICE.

The Bane Act (Civ. Code, § 52.1) authorizes a civil action "against anyone who interferes, or tries to do so, by threats, intimidation, or coercion, with an individual's exercise or enjoyment of rights secured by federal or state law." (*Jones v. Kmart Corp.* (1998) 17 Cal.4th 329, 331 [70 Cal. Rptr. 2d 844, 949 P.2d 941]) Plaintiff Noel Bender brought such a lawsuit based on his unlawful arrest and the beating administered by sheriff's deputies during that arrest, while he was in handcuffs and not resisting arrest. The jury found a Bane Act violation.

Defendants, the County of Los Angeles and Sheriff's Department Deputy Scott Sorrow, contend the Bane Act does not apply when a Fourth Amendment search and seizure violation is accompanied by the use of excessive force, because "coercion is inherent" in any unlawful seizure. In an excessive force case, they say, the Bane Act requires a showing that the "threats, intimidation, or coercion" caused a violation of a separate and distinct constitutional right in addition to the Fourth Amendment violation. We disagree.

Defendants also contend a new trial should have been granted based on errors in evidentiary rulings and excessive damages, and they challenge the amount of the attorney fee award [$989,258], the award of expert witness fees [26,953.72] under Code of Civil Procedure section 998, and the costs awarded for trial technology and presentation [in the amount of $24,103.75]. We find no error and affirm the judgment.

* * *

Defendants challenge the denial of their motion to tax costs for … trial technology.

Under Code of Civil Procedure section 1032, the prevailing party is entitled as a matter of right to recover costs. Section 1033.5 identifies cost items that are allowable under section 1032 (§ 1033.5, subd. (a)); identifies items that are not allowable (*id.*, subd. (b)); and further provides that "[i]tems not mentioned in this section … may be allowed or denied in the court's discretion" (*id.*, subd. (c)(4)). Any allowable costs must be "reasonably necessary to the conduct of the litigation rather than merely convenient or beneficial to its preparation," and reasonable in amount. (*Id.*, subd. (c)(2), (3).) We review a costs award for abuse of discretion.

Plaintiff's memorandum of costs included a claim for $24,103.75 for courtroom presentations. These costs consisted of "Trial Video Computer, PowerPoint Presentation and Videotaped Deposition Synchronizing" and the cost of a trial technician for nine days of trial. Plaintiff used a PowerPoint presentation in closing argument that consisted of a detailed summary of trial testimony, documents and other evidence as well as a "comprehensive evaluation of such evidence *vis á vis* jury instructions." The costs included charges for creating designated excerpts from deposition transcripts and video, converting exhibits to computer formats (TIFF's & JPEG's), and design and production of electronic presentations. Defendants' motion to tax costs challenged this item, contending case law establishes these costs are not recoverable and that similar costs were "specifically disallowed" in *Science Applications Internat. Corp. v. Superior Court* (1995) 39 Cal.App.4th 1095, 1103 [46 Cal. Rptr. 2d 332] (*Science Applications*).

The trial court carefully considered all of defendants' contentions but ultimately declined to tax any part of these costs, explaining its reasoning in considerable detail. In essence, the court thought the costs should be allowed—in a case like this where attorney fees are recoverable costs—if the services in question "enhanced counsel's advocacy during the trial," so long as the costs were "reasonably necessary to the conduct of the litigation." The court found both points to be so: the synchronizing of the videotaped depositions, for example, including the cost of employing a projectionist to recover and retrieve the excerpts selected by counsel, both enhanced counsel's advocacy during trial and was reasonably necessary to the conduct of the litigation.

Defendants contend, based on *Science Applications*, the costs at issue are "explicitly nonrecoverable" and the trial court "had no discretion to award them." In *Science Applications*, the appellate court approved some technology costs and disapproved others. It approved costs of over $57,000 for graphic exhibit boards and over $101,000 for a video "to help the jury appreciate the difference" between manual and computer-assisted dispatch systems that were an issue in the case. (*Science Applications, supra,* 39 Cal.App.4th at p. 1104.) It disallowed costs of $200,000 for "document control and database for internal case management"; more than $47,000 for "the production of laser disks 'containing' trial exhibits"; a "graphics communication system" with costs of more than $9,000 for equipment rental and $11,000 for an onsite technician; and more than $35,000 "to have videotape depositions edited for effective presentation of the testimony to the jury." (*Id.* at pp. 1104–1105.) The *Science Applications* court was concerned with technology costs in "staggering proportions," observing if costs "are routinely awarded for high-powered technology, most parties will be unable to litigate." (*Id.* at p. 1105.)

Almost 20 years have passed since *Science Applications* was decided, during which time the use of technology in the courtroom has become commonplace (including a technician to monitor the equipment and quickly resolve any glitches), and technology costs have dramatically declined. In a witness credibility case such as this, it would be inconceivable for plaintiff's counsel to forego the use of technology to display the videotapes of plaintiff's interviews after his beating, in the patrol car and at the sheriff's station, and key parts of other witnesses' depositions. The court in *Science Applications* was "troubled by review of a case in which a party incurred over $2 million in expenses to engage in high-tech litigation resulting in recovery of only $1 million in damages." (*Science Applications, supra,* 39 Cal.App.4th at p. 1105.) This is not such a case. The costs at issue total just over $24,000, and the trial court specifically found the trial technology enhanced counsel's advocacy and was reasonably necessary to the conduct of the litigation. The court acted well within its discretion in allowing recovery of these costs. * * *

[4] Special Cost Statutes

There are a number of special statutes which expressly provide for recovery of costs in specific actions. *E.g.*, Family Code §§ 2010(f), 2030–2034 (expressly authorizing court to award costs and attorney's fees in family law cases); CCP § 1174.2 (prevailing party when tenant raises habitability defense); § 1036 (inverse condemnation proceeding costs); § 1026 (action prosecuted or defended by personal representative or trustee); § 128.7 (award of expenses when frivolous action); § 1141.21 (imposition of costs when judgment in de novo trial not more favorable than judicial arbitration award); §§ 1094.5 & 1095 (award of costs in administrative mandamus action); and Probate Code § 6544 (family allowance), § 11624 (distribution of estate), and § 9653 (fraudulent conveyance). Many of these special cost statutes authorize recovery of costs in a manner different than CCP § 1032 and § 1033.5. *E.g.*, Family Code §§ 2030–2034 (costs may be awarded during pendency of family law proceeding based on financial resources and conduct); CCP § 1036 (plaintiff in inverse condemnation proceeding may recover costs, expenses, and disbursements).

In *Williams v Chino Valley Indep. Fire Dist.*, 61 Cal. 4th 97, 186 Cal. Rtpr. 3d 826, 347 P.3d 976 (2015), the Supreme Court ruled that Government Code § 12965(a), which governs costs awards in cases under the Fair Employment and Housing Act (FEHA), is an express exception to CCP § 1032(b) and that costs that would be awarded as a matter of right under § 1032 are instead awarded in the discretion of the trial court. The Court then concluded that under Government Code § 12965(a), a prevailing party plaintiff should ordinarily receive costs and attorney fees unless special circumstances would render such an award unjust. In contrast, the Court further concluded, a prevailing defendant should not be awarded fees and costs unless the court finds the plaintiff brought or continued litigating the action without an objective basis for believing it had potential merit. *Williams, supra*, 61 Cal. 4th at 109–114.

[E] Procedures for Claiming and Contesting Costs

The procedures for claiming and for contesting costs are set forth in Rule 3.1700, reproduced *supra*. The Judicial Council has approved a form entitled "Memorandum of Costs (Summary)" (Form MC-010), as well as a "Memorandum of Costs (Worksheet)" (Form MC-011), which may be used when claiming costs. If a prevailing party fails to serve and file a memorandum of costs within the time limits of Rule 3.1700, that party waives her right to recover costs. *See, e.g., Hyrdratec, Inc. v. Sun Valley 260 Orchard & Vineyard Co.*, 223 Cal. App. 3d 924, 272 Cal. Rptr. 899 (1990); *Sanabria v. Embrey*, 92 Cal. App. 4th 422, 111 Cal. Rptr. 2d 837 (2001). Likewise, if the losing party fails to file a timely motion to tax costs (*i.e.*, a challenge to the entire cost memorandum or to individual cost items) after the prevailing party files a timely memorandum of costs, the losing party waives his right to object to costs. *Santos v. Civil Serv. Bd.*, 193 Cal. App. 3d 1442, 1447, 239 Cal. Rptr. 14 (1987).

[F] Recovery of Costs of Enforcing Judgment

Sections 1032–1038 authorize recovery of prejudgment costs, but these sections do not authorize recovery of costs incurred by a prevailing party in enforcing a judgment. Instead, Code of Civil Procedure §§ 685.040–685.100 govern the right to recover the costs of enforcing a judgment, and generally authorize a judgment creditor to recover reasonable and necessary enforcement costs. CCP § 658.040. What costs may be claimed are specified in § 685.050 and § 685.070(a); the procedures for claiming costs of enforcing judgment are set forth in § 685.070(b)–(e) and §§ 685.080–685.100. Generally, attorney fees incurred in enforcing a judgment are not allowed as recoverable costs. *See, e.g., Hambrose Reserve, Ltd. v. Faitz*, 9 Cal. App. 4th 129, 11 Cal. Rptr. 638 (1992); *Chelios v. Kaye*, 219 Cal. App. 3d 75, 268 Cal. Rptr. 38 (1990). However, attorney's fees incurred in enforcing a judgment are recoverable as costs if the underlying judgment included an award of attorney fees to the judgment creditor pursuant to a contract. CCP §§ 685.040, 1033.5(a)(10)(A); Civil Code § 1717.

[G] Effect of Statutory Offers to Compromise on Recovery of Costs

As the statute and cases reproduced below indicate, the purpose of statutory offers to compromise authorized by CCP § 998 is to encourage the settlement of lawsuits before trial by penalizing a party who fails to accept a reasonable offer from another party. *T.M. Cobb Co. v. Superior Court*, 36 Cal. 3d 273, 280, 204 Cal. Rptr. 143, 682 P.2d 338 (1984).

California Code of Civil Procedure (2016)

Section 998. Withholding or augmenting costs following rejection or acceptance of offer to allow judgment.

(a) The costs allowed under Sections 1031 and 1032 shall be withheld or augmented as provided in this section.

(b) Not less than 10 days prior to commencement of trial or arbitration (as provided in Section 1281 or 1295) of a dispute to be resolved by arbitration, any party may serve an offer in writing upon any other party to the action to allow judgment to be taken or an award to be entered in accordance with the terms and conditions stated at that time. The written offer shall include a statement of the offer, containing the terms and conditions of the judgment or award, and a provision that allows the accepting party to indicate acceptance of the offer by signing a statement that the offer is accepted. Any acceptance of the offer, whether made on the document containing the offer or on a separate document of acceptance, shall be in writing and shall be signed by counsel for the accepting party or, if not represented by counsel, by the accepting party.

(1) If the offer is accepted, the offer with proof of acceptance shall be filed and the clerk or the judge shall enter judgment accordingly. In the case of an arbitration, the offer with proof of acceptance shall be filed with the arbitrator or arbitrators who shall promptly render an award accordingly.

(2) If the offer is not accepted prior to trial or arbitration or within 30 days after it is made, whichever occurs first, it shall be deemed withdrawn, and cannot be given in evidence upon the trial or arbitration.

(3) For purposes of this subdivision, a trial or arbitration shall be deemed to be actually commenced at the beginning of the opening statement of the plaintiff or counsel, or if there is no opening statement, at the time of the administering of the oath or affirmation to the first witness, or the introduction of any evidence.

(c) (1) If an offer made by a defendant is not accepted and the plaintiff fails to obtain a more favorable judgment or award, the plaintiff shall not recover his or her postoffer costs and shall pay the defendant's costs from the time of the offer. In addition, in any action or proceeding other than an eminent domain action, the court or arbitrator, in its discretion, may require the plaintiff to pay a reasonable sum to cover postoffer costs of the services of expert witnesses, who are not regular employees of any party, actually incurred and reasonably necessary in either, or both, preparation for trial or arbitration, or during trial or arbitration, of the case by the defendant.

(2) (A) In determining whether the plaintiff obtains a more favorable judgment, the court or arbitrator shall exclude the postoffer costs.

(B) It is the intent of the Legislature in enacting subparagraph (A) to supersede the holding in *Encinitas Plaza Real v. Knight*, 209 Cal.App.3d 996, that attorney's fees awarded to the prevailing party were not costs for purposes of this section but were part of the judgment.

(d) If an offer made by a plaintiff is not accepted and the defendant fails to obtain a more favorable judgment or award in any action or proceeding other than an eminent domain action, the court or arbitrator, in its discretion, may require the defendant to pay a reasonable sum to cover postoffer costs of the services of expert witnesses, who are not regular employees of any party, actually incurred and reasonably necessary in either, or both, preparation for trial or arbitration, or during trial or arbitration, of the case by the plaintiff, in addition to plaintiff's costs.

(e) If an offer made by a defendant is not accepted and the plaintiff fails to obtain a more favorable judgment or award, the costs under this section, from the time of the offer, shall be deducted from any damages awarded in favor of the plaintiff. If the costs awarded under this section exceed the amount of the damages awarded to the plaintiff the net amount shall be awarded to the defendant and judgment or award shall be entered accordingly.

(f) Police officers shall be deemed to be expert witnesses for the purposes of this section. For purposes of this section, "plaintiff" includes a cross-complainant and "defendant" includes a cross-defendant. Any judgment or award entered pursuant to this section shall be deemed to be a compromise settlement.

(g) This chapter does not apply to either of the following:

    (1) An offer that is made by a plaintiff in an eminent domain action.

    (2) Any enforcement action brought in the name of the people of the State of California by the Attorney General, a district attorney, or a city attorney, acting as a public prosecutor.

(h) The costs for services of expert witnesses for trial under subdivisions (c) and (d) shall not exceed those specified in Section 68092.5 of the Government Code.

(i) This section shall not apply to labor arbitrations filed pursuant to memoranda of understanding under the Ralph C. Dills Act (Chapter 10.3 (commencing with Section 3512) of Division 4 of Title 1 of the Government Code).

Stallman v. Bell

Court of Appeal of California, Second Appellate District
235 Cal. App. 3d 740, 286 Cal. Rptr. 755 (1991)

Woods, Presiding Justice.

This is an appeal from an order to tax costs, and a cross-appeal from an order awarding costs. These orders followed entry of judgment in a wrongful death and personal injury action brought by Ann L. Stallman and William Stallman as the administrator of the estate of Frank Stallman against Petal Pusher Flowers, Nelda Brennan and Elissa Bell. The main appeal is brought by the Stallmans and the cross-appeal is brought by Elissa Bell. We refer to the Stallmans as appellants and to the defendants below as respondents.[1]

This cause of action arises from an automobile accident in which Frank Stallman sustained fatal injuries. Appellants filed their complaint on November 13, 1985. An amended complaint was filed on December 26, 1985, for personal injury, property damage and wrongful death. Named as defendants in various capacities were Petal Pusher Flowers, Nelda Brennan, Elissa Bell, Walter and Lynn Bell and Pilar Aldapa, Jr.

On January 8, 1988, appellants made an offer to compromise the action pursuant to Code of Civil Procedure section 998 in the amount of $225,000 "each side to bear its own costs." The offer was not accepted.[2]

The matter was tried, resulting in a verdict in appellants' favor of $224,500. Appellants then submitted a cost bill. Among other costs, appellants sought $5,854.10 in expert witness fees and $43,391.09 in prejudgment interest pursuant to Code of Civil Procedure section 998, subdivision (d) and Civil Code section 3291.

---

1. Appellants' notice of appeal is from the entire judgment, but no other issue is addressed except the order granting respondents' motion to tax costs. Such order is appealable, as is the order awarding costs from which the cross-appeal is taken. (*Hilliger v. Golden* (1980) 107 Cal. App. 3d 394, 395, fn. 1 [166 Cal. Rptr. 33]; Code Civ. Proc., § 904.1.)

2. Respondents' Brennan and Petal Pusher Flowers offered to settle for policy limits of $25,000, but this was not a statutory offer, nor was it accepted by appellants.

Code of Civil Procedure section 998, subdivision (d) provides that if "an offer made by a plaintiff is not accepted and the defendant fails to obtain a more favorable judgment, the court in its discretion may require the defendant to pay a reasonable sum to cover costs of the services of expert witnesses ... in addition to plaintiff's costs."[3] (Code Civ. Proc., § 998, subd. (d).) Additionally, Civil Code section 3291 provides that when a defendant refuses a plaintiff's offer under Code of Civil Procedure section 998, "and the plaintiff obtains a more favorable judgment, the judgment shall bear interest at the legal rate of 10 percent per annum calculated from the date of the plaintiff's first offer ... which is exceeded by the judgment, and interest shall accrue until the satisfaction of judgment."

Respondents filed motions to tax costs challenging appellants' entitlement to expert witness fees and prejudgment interest. Respondents claimed that the verdict did not exceed the statutory offer. Appellants' opposition to the motion contended that the ordinary costs due them as prevailing parties must be added to the verdict for the purposes of determining whether or not they had obtained a more favorable judgment entitling them to expert witness fees and prejudgment interest. Appellants claimed ordinary costs of at least $2,564.84 which, when added to the verdict, yielded a sum of $227,064.84, and exceeded their statutory offer.

Respondents replied that, because appellants' statutory offer had contained the provision that each side was to bear its own costs, appellants were foreclosed from adding costs to the verdict for the purpose of determining whether they had obtained a more favorable judgment. At the hearing on the motion, the trial court agreed with respondents, stating that because of the costs provision in the offer, "it is necessary to exclude costs from either side as a consideration in whether the verdict exceeded the offer, which it fell short by five hundred dollars."

Despite the fact that the trial court found that appellants had not shown they received a more favorable judgment and disallowed prejudgment interest, it nonetheless allowed appellants expert witness fees. Both parties appealed. After review, we reverse in part and affirm in part.

I

Respondents first contend that appellants' statutory offer was void from its inception because it was made jointly by both the individual plaintiff and decedent's estate. Respondents rely on *Hurlbut v. Sonora Cmty. Hospital* (1989) 207 Cal. App. 3d 388 [254 Cal. Rptr. 840], which, in turn, relies on *Randles v. Lowry* (1970) 4 Cal. App. 3d 68 [84 Cal. Rptr. 321].

Code of Civil Procedure section 998, subdivision (a) provides: "The costs allowed under Sections 1031 and 1032 shall be withheld or augmented as provided in this section." Subdivision (b) of that section provides: "Not less than 10 days prior to commencement of trial, any party may serve an offer in writing upon any other party

---

3. The costs referred to in Code of Civil Procedure section 998 are set forth in Code of Civil Procedure sections 1031 and 1032. Under the latter section "a prevailing party is entitled as a matter of right to recover costs in any action or proceeding." (Code Civ. Proc., § 1032, subd. (b).)

to the action to allow judgment to be taken in accordance with the terms and conditions stated at that time." (Code Civ. Proc., § 998, subd. (b).)

Under section 997, the predecessor statute to section 998, the court in *Randles v. Lowry, supra*, held that a single offer made by a defendant to three separate plaintiffs in a personal injury action was invalid because it could not be determined whether any one plaintiff received a less favorable result than under the offer. The defendant made a settlement offer of $2,300 to the three plaintiffs without specifying the amount offered to each. Two of the plaintiffs prevailed at trial but were awarded less than the statutory offer. On that ground, the trial court denied the plaintiffs' motion for costs.

The reviewing court reversed, characterizing the offer by defendant as a "nullity." The court explained: "The offer was made jointly to all plaintiffs, without designating how it should be divided between them. It is therefore impossible to say that any one plaintiff received a less favorable result than he would have under the offer of compromise." (*Randles v. Lowry, supra*, 4 Cal. App. 3d at p. 74.)

Randles was followed in *Hurlbut v. Sonora Cmty. Hospital, supra*, in which three plaintiffs made a joint offer to a single defendant without designating how much each plaintiff would receive. At trial, each of the plaintiffs received a verdict for less than the offer, although the aggregate was greater. The appellate court, applying *Randles*, reversed an order granting plaintiffs' expert witness costs, stating: "To consider plaintiffs' joint settlement offer as valid would deprive the defendant of the opportunity to evaluate the likelihood of each party receiving a more favorable verdict at trial. Such an offer makes it impossible to make such a determination after verdict." (*Hurlbut v. Sonora Community Hospital, supra*, at p. 410.)

More recent cases have declined to mechanically apply a rule that renders void any joint offers without first examining whether it can be determined that the party claiming costs has in fact obtained a more favorable judgment.

We took this approach in *Fortman v. Hemco, Inc.* (1989) 211 Cal. App. 3d 241 [259 Cal. Rpt. 311], a personal injury action in which the minor plaintiff and her mother, who had a separate cause of action, served a joint $1 million offer on the defendant. The mother dismissed her cause of action, and only the minor's action was tried, resulting in a verdict of $26 million plus. On appeal from the judgment, defendant, citing *Randles* and *Hurlbut*, challenged the trial court's award of prejudgment interest on the grounds that the joint offer was a nullity.

We rejected the challenge, observing that "in [the cited] cases it could not be determined after trial whether the individual plaintiffs received more than they would have received had the offer to compromise been accepted. In our case, however, it is absolutely clear that Nichole received a greater amount in damages after trial than she would have received had Hemco accepted the joint offer even if the entire amount of the offer, $1 million, is attributed to her.... [para.] Under these facts, therefore, we decline to mechanically apply *Randles*." (*Fortman v. Hemco, Inc., supra*, 211 Cal. App. 3d at p. 263.)

Similarly, in *Winston Square Homeowner's Assn. v. Centex West, Inc.* (1989) 213 Cal. App. 3d 282 [261 Cal. Rptr. 605], the defendants made a joint offer to plaintiff in an action alleging construction defects in a townhouse development. One of the defendants, Wilsey & Ham, was dismissed from the action on grounds of the statute of limitations and recovered expert witness fees under section 998. The plaintiff's challenge to the award of such costs was rejected on appeal. The court said: "[A]pplication of section 998 appears appropriate in this case. Though the joint offer did not break down the offer as to particular areas of damage or defendants, Wilsey & Ham received a judgment in its favor. Wilsey & Ham was an absolute prevailing party— it was completely absolved of any liability." (*Winston Square Homeowner's Assn. v. Centex West, Inc., supra,* at p. 294.) Thus, as in *Fortman,* the court in *Centex West* looked beyond the simple fact of the joint offer to see if it could be determined whether the party awarded costs had actually received the more favorable judgment.

In the case before us, Ann Stallman and the Estate of Frank Stallman made a joint offer to respondents in the amount of $225,000 without designating what amount of the offer was applicable to each. After trial, the jury made a unitary award of damages to both appellants in the amount of $224,500. This circumstance differs from either *Randles* or *Hurlbut* in which the individual plaintiffs received separate verdicts. Here, there is but a single verdict to be compared to a single offer, and from this comparison it can be clearly determined whether or not the appellants received a more favorable judgment.

Moreover, as appellants point out, any damages awarded to the Estate of Frank Stallman would ultimately pass to Ann Stallman who is the sole intestate heir of Frank Stallman. Accordingly, under the facts of this case, because the joint offer does not prevent a determination of whether appellants received a more favorable judgment the rule of *Randles* and *Hurlbut* is inapplicable.

II

In denying appellants' claim for costs under section 998, the court found that appellants had failed to obtain a more favorable judgment than the statutory offer. The court refused to add ordinary costs to the verdict for the purpose of making this determination. This was error.

Initially, we must distinguish between plaintiffs' and defendants' offers under section 998. Under subdivision (c) of [the pre-1997 version of] section 998, if "an offer made by a defendant is not accepted and the plaintiff fails to obtain a more favorable judgment, the plaintiff shall not recover his or her costs and shall pay the defendant's costs from the time of the offer." (§ 998, subd. (c).) Under subdivision (d) of section 998, if "an offer made by a plaintiff is not accepted and the defendant fails to obtain a more favorable judgment," the defendant may incur both expert witness fees and, under Civil Code section 3291, prejudgment interest from the time of the plaintiff's first statutory offer.

The question presented by this appeal is: When a plaintiff makes a section 998 offer that the defendant rejects, and the plaintiff obtains a verdict which, standing alone, is less than the offer, what additional costs, if any, are added to the verdict for purposes of determining whether the plaintiff received a more favorable judgment than the statutory offer. Neither the parties nor our own research has revealed a case on point.

Instead, we begin with those cases which address this issue in the context of a section 998 offer made by a defendant and rejected by a plaintiff who then obtains a verdict less than the offer. In such a case, to determine whether the plaintiff obtained a judgment more favorable than defendant's offer, preoffer costs are added to the award of damages. (*Kelly v. Yee* (1989) 213 Cal. App. 3d 336, 342 [261 Cal. Rptr. 568] ["we first add to the judgment of damages those recoverable costs and attorney's fees authorized by statute and incurred before the settlement offer. [Citations.]"]; *Shain v. City of Albany* (1980) 106 Cal. App. 3d 294, 299 [165 Cal. Rptr. 69].) Post offer costs are, however, excluded. (*Encinitas Plaza Real v. Knight* (1989) 209 Cal. App. 3d 996, 1000–1001 [257 Cal. Rptr. 646]; *Kelly v. Yee, supra*; *Bennett v. Brown* (1963) 212 Cal. App. 2d 685, 688 [28 Cal. Rptr. 485].)

The rationale for limiting the prevailing plaintiff to preoffer costs to determine favorability where the defendant has made the section 998 offer, was explained in the *Bennett* decision. In *Bennett*, the defendant made a statutory offer of $600, which the plaintiff refused. Under the then-existing statute (as under current § 998, subd. (c)), a plaintiff who failed to obtain a judgment more favorable than the defendant's offer became liable for defendant's costs from the time of the offer.

The jury returned a verdict in plaintiff's favor for $500. The trial court awarded plaintiff his costs and denied those of defendant. The appellate court reversed the order. It noted that plaintiff's preoffer costs were $99.45 which, when added to the verdict, still fell short of the $600 statutory offer. The court observed that the purpose of the statute was "to encourag[e] the settlement of litigation without trial," by penalizing a plaintiff who rejects a reasonable offer. In order to effectuate this purpose, the court concluded that "costs incurred [by the plaintiff] after the offer has been received must be excluded," when determining whether plaintiff received a more favorable judgment than the defendant's offer. To hold otherwise would enable plaintiff to dramatically increase its postoffer cost for the sole purpose of increasing the likelihood that its final judgment would exceed defendant's offer. (*Bennett v. Brown, supra*, 212 Cal. App. 2d at p. 688.)

Where, as here, it is the plaintiff who makes the section 998 offer, and the defendant who rejects it, the *Bennett* rationale does not apply. There is, then, no reason to limit the plaintiff to damages plus preoffer costs for purposes of determining whether the judgment exceeds the offer. Rather, both pre-and postoffer costs should be added to the verdict to determine the amount of the judgment. In this case it is the defendant who has impeded the statutory purpose by rejecting the offer, thus allowing the plaintiff to incur postoffer costs.

In the matter before us, however, the trial court declined to add any costs to the verdict, because appellants' statutory offer contained a provision that, if accepted, each side was to bear its own costs. Based on this language, the trial court apparently concluded that appellants had somehow waived the right to add costs to the verdict for purposes of section 998. This conclusion does not survive scrutiny.

Appellants contend that the language in the offer, "each side to bear its own costs," was included as "incentive" to respondents to settle and should have no effect on the determination of whether they ultimately received a more favorable judgment. Respondents, on the other hand, argue that in view of that language, no costs should be added to plaintiffs' verdict to determine the ultimate judgment. We reject respondents' positions.[5]

Appellants herein claimed ordinary costs in the amount of $5,208.72 as prevailing parties. (§ 1032, subd. (b).) They contend that respondents have conceded ordinary costs in the amount of $2,427.84. Either sum when added to the $224,500 verdict exceeds appellants' statutory offer of $225,998. By refusing to add ordinary costs to the verdict for the purpose of determining whether that judgment exceeded the statutory offer, the trial court erred. * * *

Apparently, the [trial] court ... focused on the language in section 998 permitting either party to submit offers to take judgment "in accordance with the terms and conditions stated at that time" (§ 998, subd. (b)), and decided that the terms and conditions of the offer control whether costs will be added to the award of damages to determine whether or not a plaintiff has received a more favorable judgment than the offer. Nothing in the language of the statute nor in any case interpreting it supports this conclusion. Nor can the result be defended on logical grounds. We agree that, under section 998, the costs provision in an offer should be taken into account to determine the amount of the offer for purposes of comparing that amount to the amount of the judgment. It does not follow, however, that the costs provision in the offer should determine what costs are added to the award of damages in order to arrive at the amount of the judgment for purposes of section 998.

* * * While it is true that section 998 offers are governed by contract law, such principles apply only when they "neither conflict with the statute nor defeat its purpose." (*T.M. Cobb Co. v. Superior Court* (1984) 36 Cal. 3d 273, 280 [204 Cal. Rptr. 143, 682 P.2d 338].)

As we have noted, the chief purpose of section 998 is to encourage settlement of litigation without trial by penalizing a party who rejects a reasonable offer and forces the action to proceed to trial. Where, as here, a plaintiff's offer includes waiver of costs and the defendant rejects the offer, thereby forcing the matter to a trial, allowing the plaintiff to add costs to the award of damages to determine whether the judgment exceeds the offer is consistent with the statutory purpose. By contrast, precluding plaintiff from doing so, and limiting plaintiff to the damages award for purposes of comparison with the offer, might, as in the case before us, reward the nonsettling defendants. Such a result is not consistent with the intent of the statute.

---

5. Appellants also sought an alternate position that the court could include the costs that they were willing to forego as part of their offer; i.e., $225,000 plus preoffer costs of $998 equals an offer to settle the case for $225,998 and that the judgment, including costs, would still exceed the offer.

Accordingly, we reverse the order of the trial court insofar as it denied interest.[6]

Turning to the cross-appeal, respondent Bell maintains that the trial court erred when it awarded expert witness fees to appellants because it had failed to determine that appellants had received a more favorable judgment under section 998, entitling them to such fees. Inasmuch as we have determined that appellants did obtain such a judgment, we affirm the order awarding them expert witness fees. The matter is remanded, however, for the trial court to determine the amount of prejudgment interest due appellants.

The judgment is affirmed in part, reversed in part and remanded. Appellants to have no costs on appeal.

Poster v. Southern California Rapid Transit Dist.

Supreme Court of California
52 Cal. 3d 266, 276 Cal. Rptr. 321, 801 P.2d 1072 (1990)

Broussard, Justice.

In this case we must determine whether a counteroffer precludes acceptance of a statutory settlement offer under Code of Civil Procedure section 998[1] and whether when a section 998 offer is served by mail, section 1013, subdivision (a) applies to extend the time to respond by five days.

FACTS

The facts underlying this settlement controversy are not disputed. On March 17, 1984, plaintiff, Gregory Poster, was a passenger on a Southern California Rapid Transit District (SCRTD) bus when he was attacked by other passengers. He sustained serious injuries when he was thrown from and run over by the bus. On May 1, 1984, plaintiff filed a personal injury action against defendants, SCRTD and the bus driver.

On December 11, 1987, acting pursuant to section 998 and Civil Code section 3291, plaintiff served defendants with an offer to compromise the action for $150,000. The offer was served by mail with proof of service, and provided that if it was accepted and notice of acceptance was given within 30 days or prior to the commencement of trial, the offer could be filed with proof of acceptance and the clerk of the court would be authorized to enter judgment in accordance therewith.

---

6. We find no merit in the additional "policy" argument raised by respondents Brennan and Petal Pusher Flowers that because they made a nonstatutory settlement offer to appellants, they should not have to bear any portion of appellants' costs under section 998. Although these respondents made a settlement offer, it was vastly less than either appellants' statutory offer or the jury's verdict. The purpose of section 998 is to induce acceptance of reasonable settlement offers, and this purpose is not satisfied simply because some offer is made.

1. All further statutory references are to the Code of Civil Procedure unless otherwise indicated.

Defendants received the offer on December 14, 1987, and engaged in further settlement negotiations with plaintiff. On December 16, 1987, defendants made a counteroffer to plaintiff in the amount of $75,000, which plaintiff refused to accept. On January 6, 1988, defendants offered $120,000 in settlement to plaintiff, to which plaintiff made no response.

On January 12, 1988, defendants advised plaintiff's attorney that they would accept the offer to compromise in the full amount of $150,000 and sent a letter formally accepting the offer. Plaintiff acknowledged the acceptance and agreed that the matter would be removed from the calendar since a settlement had been reached. Notice of acceptance, in the form of a pleading instructing the clerk of the court to enter judgment pursuant to the terms of the offer, was mailed to plaintiff on January 14, 1988.

Plaintiff's attorney, however, subsequently informed defendants that plaintiff refused to honor the settlement agreement; thereafter, defendants noticed a motion to enforce the agreement and the matter was set for hearing. The motion to enforce settlement contained a declaration from defendants' counsel that plaintiff had never revoked the offer to compromise and that plaintiff had continually led defendants to believe that the offer to compromise was open for acceptance through the time that it was accepted. * * *

The trial court found that the offer was properly accepted as required by statute and by the offer itself. It found the discussions between the parties during the time that the offer was open were simply settlement negotiations. To hold otherwise, the court determined, would serve to undermine the policy underlying section 998. The trial court ordered judgment in plaintiff's favor in the amount of $150,000.

Plaintiff appealed the judgment. The Court of Appeal concluded that section 998 offers to compromise, while revocable by the offeror, are not automatically revoked by a counteroffer since such a consequence would undermine the legislative intent of that section.

The Court of Appeal, however, went on to find that the acceptance of the statutory offer in this case was not timely, and accordingly reversed the judgment. In reaching this conclusion, the Court of Appeal held that section 1013, subdivision (a), which generally extends the time to respond by five days when service is made by mail, does not apply to section 998 offers, and therefore did not serve to extend the time for acceptance.

DISCUSSION

1. *Does a counteroffer preclude acceptance of a statutory settlement offer under section 998?*

* * *

Section 998, subdivision (b) provides in part: "Not less than 10 days prior to commencement of trial, any party may serve an offer in writing upon any other party to the action to allow judgment to be taken in accordance with the terms and conditions stated at that time. [¶] (1) If the offer is accepted, the offer with proof of acceptance shall be filed and the clerk or the judge shall enter judgment accordingly. [¶] (2) If the offer is not accepted prior to trial or within 30 days after it is made, whichever occurs first, it shall be deemed withdrawn...."

Section 998 clearly reflects this state's policy of encouraging settlements. (*See, e.g., T.M. Cobb Co. v. Superior Court* (1984) 36 Cal. 3d 273, 280 [204 Cal. Rptr. 143, 682 P.2d 338];....) In order to encourage parties to accept reasonable settlement offers made pursuant to the section, subdivisions (c) and (d) of section 998 afford the offeror a remedy against a party who has failed to accept a statutory settlement offer that proves to be reasonable. * * *

Although the procedure established by section 998 is clearly intended to encourage settlements, the statutory language is silent on a number of issues relevant to the application of the provision, including what conduct constitutes an acceptance, whether a statutory offer may be revoked by the offeror prior to the expiration of the statutorily designated period, and the effect of counteroffers on the viability of outstanding statutory settlement offers.

In *T.M. Cobb Co. v. Superior Court, supra,* 36 Cal. 3d 273 (hereafter *T.M. Cobb*), our court, in concluding that an unaccepted offer made pursuant to section 998 could be revoked by the offeror prior to expiration of the statutory period, reasoned that general principles of contract law could properly be referred to in interpreting section 998. The *T.M. Cobb* decision was careful to emphasize, however, that general contract principles should be invoked in applying section 998 "only where such principles neither conflict with the statute nor defeat its purpose.... [citations]" (36 Cal. 3d at p. 280), and the court in that case determined that the general principle that offers are revocable should be applied in the section 998 context only after concluding that the statutory policy of encouraging settlements would be best promoted by such a rule.

In asserting that defendants' counteroffer in the present case operated to revoke the section 998 offer, plaintiff relies on *Glende Motor Co. v. Superior Court* [(1984)] 159 Cal. App. 3d 389, 396–398 [205 Cal. Rptr. 622] (hereafter *Glende Motor*). In *Glende Motor*, the Court of Appeal, relying on the reference to general contract law principles in *T.M. Cobb, supra,* held that because under general common law contract principles a counteroffer which deviates from the terms of an offer generally operates to revoke the offer, a nonstatutory counteroffer which deviates from the terms of a section 998 offer similarly operates to revoke the section 998 offer.

The Court of Appeal in this case, however, declined to follow *Glende Motor, supra,* reasoning that negotiation during the 30-day period provided for in section 998 is a normal occurrence and ought not to affect the right of the offeree to ultimately accept the statutory offer in a timely fashion. The court noted that to adopt the position stated in *Glende Motor* would affect every personal injury case where negotiations followed a statutory offer—negotiations which routinely involve the making of counteroffers— and expressed the view that such a ruling would have a negative effect on encouraging settlement. We agree with the Court of Appeal's conclusion in this regard.

In our view, the rule adopted in *Glende Motor, supra,* is more likely to discourage settlements and to confuse the determination regarding the imposition of costs than the conclusion reached by the Court of Appeal in this case. The *Glende Motor* court itself recognized that section 998 was not intended to insulate the offeror from settlement negotiations for the 30-day period in which the section 998 offer was operative, and attempted to prevent its holding from stifling such negotiations by observing that "[a] mere inquiry regarding the possibility of different terms, a request for a better offer, or a comment upon the terms of the offer, is ordinarily not a counteroffer. [Citation.]" (*Glende Motor, supra*, 159 Cal. App. 3d 389, 398, fn. 12.) This aspect of the *Glende Motor* decision, however, introduces a significant and undesirable uncertainty into the section 998 procedure, and will inevitably spawn numerous disputes over whether a communication from an offeree is a counteroffer which operates to revoke the statutory offer or merely an "inquiry regarding the possibility of different terms" which leaves the offeree free to accept the outstanding section 998 offer.

The legislative purpose of section 998 is better served by the bright line rule adopted by the Court of Appeal in this case, under which a section 998 offer is not revoked by a counteroffer and may be accepted by the offeree during the statutory period unless the offer has been revoked by the offeror.[2] Accordingly, we now adopt that rule and disapprove the Court of Appeal decision in *Glende Motor, supra*, to the extent that it is contrary to our conclusion.

2. *Is the time for acceptance extended under section 1013?*

The record discloses that plaintiff mailed the statutory offer to compromise on December 11, 1987. In computing the time permitted by the statute, and not counting December 11 (*see* § 12), the offer was open for 20 days in December, but was not accepted by defendants until January 12, 1988, the 32d day. As noted, the Court of Appeal held that on these facts defendants' acceptance of the offer was not timely, concluding that the provisions of section 1013 affording a five-day extension for statutory deadlines when service is made by mail do not apply in the section 998 context. Defendants challenge the Court of Appeal's conclusion on the timeliness issue, and . . .

---

2. The *Glende Motor* court expressed its apprehension that a rule preserving the viability of a section 998 offer in the face of numerous counteroffers might deter a potential offeror from making a section 998 offer in the first place because the offer could expose him to a "bombardment" of counteroffers from the opposing party shortly before trial. Even if no section 998 offer is outstanding, however, as opposing party may make numerous settlement offers prior to trial which may have to be communicated to the client. Because an offeror remains free to revoke a section 998 offer prior to its acceptance, we do not believe that an offeror is likely to be deterred from making a section 998 offer by the fact that the offer will not be automatically revoked by the first counteroffer proffered by the offeree.

Indeed, the *Glende Motor* court itself recognized that "[s]ection 998 clearly contemplates that both plaintiffs and defendants may make statutory offers to each other, often simultaneously . . . ," and expressly disclaimed any intent to suggest "that a 998 offer terminates or loses its capacity for acceptance when another party to the action makes another 998 offer." (*Glende Motor, supra*, 159 Cal. App. 3d 389, 396, fn. 9.) Since section 998 assumes that a party will not be deterred from making a statutory settlement offer even though a statutory counteroffer will not automatically revoke the offer, we see no reason for drawing a different conclusion with regard to a nonstatutory counteroffer.

we agree with defendants that the Court of Appeal erred in finding their acceptance untimely. * * *

[W]e conclude that when a statutory settlement offer pursuant to section 998 is served by mail, the provisions of section 1013 apply and extend the 30-day period for acceptance of the offer by 5 days.

DISPOSITION

The Court of Appeal decision is affirmed insofar as it concludes that defendants' counteroffer did not operate to revoke plaintiff's section 998 offer, but the decision is reversed insofar as it concludes that section 1013 is inapplicable to statutory settlement offers made pursuant to section 998. The matter is remanded to the Court of Appeal with directions to affirm the trial court's order enforcing the settlement agreement.

Defendants shall recover their costs on appeal.

Notes and Questions regarding Recovery of Costs under CCP § 998

(1) *Revocability of Offer.* As noted in *Poster*, the Supreme Court in *T.M. Cobb Co. v. Superior Court*, 36 Cal. 3d 273, 204 Cal. Rptr. 143, 682 P.2d 338 (1984), held that an unaccepted offer of compromise made pursuant to CCP § 998 could be revoked by the offeror prior to expiration of the statutory period. The Court opined that the policy of encouraging settlements reflected in § 998 is best promoted by making § 998 offers revocable. *T.M. Cobb Co*, 36 Cal. 3d at 281. Do you agree? What arguments can be made that settlement is best encouraged by requiring the offer to remain open for the entire statutory period? *See T.M. Cobb Co.*, 36 Cal. 3d at 284–290 (Broussard, J., dissenting).

(2) *Multiple Offers by the Same Party.* When the same party makes more than one § 998 offer to an opponent, does a later offer extinguish a previous offer for purposes of § 998's cost-shifting provisions? In *Martinez v. Brownco Constr. Co.*, 56 Cal. 4th 1014, 157 Cal. Rptr. 3d 558, 301 P.3d 1167 (2013), the Supreme Court concluded that where a plaintiff makes two successive statutory offers and the defendant fails to obtain a judgment more favorable than *either* offer, allowing recovery of expert witness fees incurred from the date of the first offer is consistent with section 998's language and best promotes the statutory purpose to encourage settlements. In reaching this conclusion, the Court declined to find the "first offer rule" or the "last offer rule" controlling in all circumstances. Indeed, the *Martinez* Court suggested that the last offer rule may be appropriate where an offeree obtains a judgment less favorable than a first section 998 offer but more favorable than the later offer.

What is the status of a first offer where the defendant makes two successive § 998 offers and the first one is not accepted by the plaintiff during the statutory period, but the second offer is withdrawn by the defendant? *See One Star, Inc. v. STAAR Surgical Co.*, 179 Cal. App. 4th 1082, 102 Cal. Rtpr. 3d 195 (2009) (concluding a party's last § 998 offer is effective unless expressly revoked; if the last offer is revoked, the prior offer is the relevant offer for purposes of § 998's cost shifting rules).

(3) *Offer Must Be Reasonable and in Good Faith.* A number of courts have concluded that only reasonable settlement offers made in good faith qualify as valid offers under CCP § 998. *E.g., Elrod v. Oregon Cummins Diesel, Inc.,* 195 Cal. App. 3d 692, 241 Cal. Rptr. 108 (1987); *Wear v. Calderon,* 121 Cal. App. 3d 818, 175 Cal. Rptr. 566 (1981). Whether an offer was reasonable depends on the circumstances of the particular case, including the information available to the offeree when the offer was made. *Elrod, supra,* 195 Cal. App. 3d at 699–700. Whether a § 998 offer was reasonable is left to the discretion of the trial court. *Elrod,* 195 Cal. App. 3d at 700–702. Consider whether an abuse of discretion is shown in the following cases:

(a) The trial court found defendant's § 998 offer of $2500 unreasonable in a wrongful death action, where the plaintiff sought damages of $10 million but the defendant's liability was tenuous. *See Pineda v. Los Angeles Turf Club, Inc.,* 112 Cal. App. 3d 53, 169 Cal. Rptr. 66 (1980) (affirming because in light of "the enormous exposure" defendant faced, the trial court "could find that the defendant had no expectation its offer would be accepted"). In another case, the trial court found the defendant's § 998 offer of $10,000 and a mutual waiver of costs reasonable where plaintiffs sought $2 million in damages. *See Adams v. Ford Motor Co.,* 199 Cal. App. 4th 1475, 1484–86, 132 Cal. Rptr. 3d 424 (2011) (affirming because the reasonableness of the offer could not be evaluated simply in comparison to the damages plaintiffs sought, but should also in light of the likelihood plaintiffs would prevail at trial).

(b) In *Carver v. Chevron U.S.A., Inc.,* 97 Cal. App. 4th 132, 118 Cal. Rptr. 2d 569 (2002), a breach of contract and antitrust action brought by several gas station franchisees against their franchiser, defendant Chevron U.S.A., the defendant made a § 998 offer of $100 per plaintiff plus a waiver of attorney fees and costs. The plaintiffs rejected these offers, and subsequently lost on the merits after an appeal. The trial court awarded the defendant expert witness fees of $1,966,586 pursuant to § 998(c), and the plaintiffs appealed contending that the § 998 offers were not made in good faith. The *Carver* court found the defendant's offers to be reasonable and in good faith, in light of the circumstances as evaluated from the prospective of the defendant, and upheld the trial court's award. *Carver,* 97 Cal. App. 4th at 152–55. The value of the proposed waiver of costs and attorney fees was considerable, the *Carver* court reasoned, and defendant's success on the merits was reasonably foreseeable at the time the offer was made. *Id.* at 154; *see also Melendrez v. Ameron Int'l Corp.,* 240 Cal. App. 4th 632, 647–51, 193 Cal. Rptr. 3d 23 (2015) (upholding the reasonableness of defendant's § 998 offer of mutual waiver of costs and fees in exchange for dismissal of plaintiff's wrongful death action, in light of their likelihood of prevailing at trial).

(c) The trial court awarded expert witness fees to a defendant after jury verdict for that defendant, the manufacturer of a ladder which plaintiff claimed was defective and caused plaintiff serious back injuries. Plaintiff demanded $1.5 million in settlement, but defendant's § 998 offer was for only $5,000. Plaintiff rejected this offer, in part because a workers' compensation lien of over $35,000 would give him no net recovery if he settled for less than the amount of the lien. Defendant's § 998 offer was made after discovery proceedings in which defendant found that the ladder had been modified after it was sold, that plaintiff engaged in activities inconsistent with his claimed injuries, and that plaintiff had a previous back injury. *See Culbertson v. R.D. Werner Co.*, 190 Cal. App. 3d 704, 235 Cal. Rptr. 510 (1987). Would your answer be any different if the defendant's §998 offer were made prior to any discovery proceedings? How so?

(d) The trial court found the defendants' §998 offer of $100 reasonable in an action to recover a real estate commission of $69,000 allegedly due the plaintiffs-brokers. At the time the offer was pending, the defendants had communicated to the plaintiffs that there was no written commission agreement between the parties, and advised plaintiffs that discovery up to that time had not established any basis for liability. At the close of the plaintiffs' evidence at trial, the trial court granted the defendants' motion for nonsuit. Did the trial court abuse its discretion when it determined that the §998 offer was reasonable? *See Colbaugh v. Hartline*, 29 Cal. App. 4th 1516, 35 Cal. Rptr. 2d 213 (1994).

(f) In *Regency Outdoor Advertising, Inc. v. City of L. A.*, 39 Cal. 4th 507, 531–34, 46 Cal. Rptr. 3d 742, 139 P.3d 119 (2006), the plaintiff company sought compensation from the defendant city in an inverse condemnation action, alleging the City's planting of mature trees made several of the plaintiff's billboards less visible thereby lessening the value of plaintiff's billboards and property. The plaintiff rejected the defendant's CCP §998 offer, which was to pay plaintiff $1,000 and to remove one of the offending trees. The superior court ruled in the defendant City's on the merits, and awarded the City costs and expert witness fees pursuant to §998.

On appeal, the plaintiff argued that the City's §988 offer was unreasonably low when compared to the millions in damages asserted by the plaintiff, and therefore was not made in "good faith." "Assuming without deciding that Code of Civil Procedure section 998 entails such a requirement," the Supreme Court found that the City's offer possessed genuine value, that the City had maintained throughout the litigation that the plaintiff had no compensable right, and that the lawsuit was not a mere dispute over the extent of damages. *Regency Outdoor Advertising*, 39 Cal. 4th at 531. The Supreme Court therefore concluded the City's offer "satisfied whatever good faith requirement may apply to a settlement offer under ... section 998." *Id.*

(4) *Fair Opportunity to Evaluate Offer.* Although CCP §998(b) sets a deadline beyond which an offer cannot be served, it does not impose any minimum period following commencement of suit for service of a valid offer. Is a §998 offer reasonable when served along with the complaint and summons in a personal injury action, before formal discovery on the issue of damages? The majority in *Barba v. Perez*, 166 Cal. App. 4th 444, 82 Cal. Rptr. 3d 715 (2008), observed that in general an award of costs under §998 is discretionary and a trial court may consider whether an offer was reasonable under the circumstances, but concluded the plaintiff's offer here was reasonable because the defendant could have requested plaintiff provide informal discovery on the damage issue and/or requested an extension of time to respond to the offer. *Barba*, 166 Cal. App. 4th at 450–452. The dissent disagreed, concluding that service of a §998 offer with the complaint and summons did not give defendant

a reasonable opportunity to evaluate the plaintiff's offer. *Id.* at 452–454; *see also Najera v. Huerta*, 191 Cal. App. 4th 872, 878–79, 119 Cal. Rptr. 3d 714 (2011) (holding § 998 offer served concurrently with summons and complaint was not reasonable where no special circumstances present to show that defendant's attorney had early and access to information necessary to evaluate plaintiff's offer). Which view is the better reasoned, in light of the purposes of CCP § 998?

(5) *An Offer Must Be Recognizable as a Statutory Settlement Offer.* Because the party to whom a § 998 offer is made stands to bear additional costs at the conclusion of the case if the offer is not accepted, the offeree must have the opportunity to recognize that the offer is being made formally and pursuant to the statute. *Stell v. Jay Hales Dev. Co.*, 11 Cal. App. 4th 1214, 1230–32, 15 Cal. Rptr. 2d 220 (1992). What statements should a § 998 offer include to distinguish it from a nonstatutory offer? *See Stell*, 11 Cal. App. 4th at 1230–32.

A statutory offer to compromise must be in writing, CCP § 998(b); an oral offer is not valid. *See Saba v. Crater*, 62 Cal. App. 4th 150, 72 Cal. Rptr. 2d 401 (1998); *see also* Judicial Council Form CIV-090 (Offer to Compromise and Acceptance). CCP § 998(b), as amended in 2006, also states that the offer "shall include … a provision that allows the accepting party to indicate acceptance by signing a statement that the offer is accepted." Several decisions have concluded that an offer that fails to follow § 998's acceptance provision requirement is invalid. *See, e.g., Rouland v. Pacific Specialty Ins. Co.*, 220 Cal. App. 4th 280, 162 Cal. Rptr. 3d 887 (2013) (discussing cases); *Boeken v. Philip Morris USA Inc.*, 217 Cal. App. 4th 992, 159 Cal. Rptr. 3d 195 (2013) (invalidating offer).

(6) *Validity of Joint Offer Made to or By Multiple Parties.* As illustrated by *Stallman v. Bell*, reproduced *supra*, and the cases discussed therein, the question of the validity of a joint § 998 offer made to or by multiple parties can be quite troublesome. Do you understand why such offers may be void? *See Taing v. Johnson Scaffolding Co.*, 9 Cal. App. 4th 579, 585, 11 Cal. Rptr. 2d 820 (1992) (observing that from the perspective of the offeree, the offer must be sufficiently specific to permit the individual offeree to evaluate it and make a reasoned decision of whether to accept).

The court in *Stallman* declined to mechanically apply a rule that renders all joint offers void, but looked at the facts to determine whether a party had actually received a more favorable judgment. Can you formulate a general guideline as to when such joint offers will be considered valid or void? *See Steinfeld v. Foote-Goldman Proctologic Med. Group, Inc.*, 50 Cal. App. 4th 1542, 1550, 58 Cal. Rptr. 2d 371 (1996) ("Where … there is a singular theory of liability alleged against two defendants for a single injury, and where as joint tortfeasors they would be jointly and severally liable, an unapportioned section 998 offer made to both is valid"); *Burch v. Children's Hosp. of Orange Cnty. Thrift Stores, Inc.*, 109 Cal. App. 4th 537, 135 Cal. Rptr. 2d 404 (2003) (concluding unapportioned § 998 offer make to multiple tortfeasors not valid where defendants could be found liable, but not jointly and severally liable, for full amount of judgment which included economic and noneconomic damages); *Barnett v. First Nat. Ins. Co. of America*, 184 Cal. App. 4th 1454, 110 Cal. Rptr. 3d 99 (2010) (holding defendant's joint § 998 offer to plaintiff husband and wife is valid, regardless of whether the injuries claimed are indivisible or separate, because a cause of action for damages is community property).

The court in *Gilman v. Beverly California Corp.*, 231 Cal. App. 3d 121, 283 Cal. Rptr. 17 (1989), reached the opposite conclusion from that reached in *Stallman*. Reversing an award of prejudgment interest and expert fees, the *Gilman* court decided the joint offer of four wrongful death plaintiffs was invalid. The court rejected plaintiffs' argument that because a wrongful death action is characterized as joint, single, and indivisible, they had suffered a single, indivisible injury. Accordingly, the *Gilman* court decided:

> [T]he joint offer to compromise did not afford [defendant] the opportunity to evaluate the separate and distinct loss suffered by each plaintiff as a result of the death of [decedent]. Without an apportionment of the damages among the four plaintiffs, it is impossible to say that any one of them received a judgment more favorable than she would have received under the offer. (*Id.* at 126)

Can the results reached in *Gilman* and *Stallman* be reconciled? Which decision is better reasoned? Why? The court in *Johnson v. Pratt & Whitney Canada, Inc.*, 28 Cal. App. 4th 613, 34 Cal. Rptr. 2d 26 (1994), followed *Stallman* and rejected *Gilman* (*id.* at 630):

> The results reached in *Stallman* and *Gilman* cannot be reconciled. We find *Stallman* the better reasoned. Where a single joint cause of action is given to all heirs, who must bring *one* action and where the judgment must be for a single lump sum even though the heirs share the damages in proportion to their loss there would appear to be little, if any, justification for invalidating a joint offer. As aptly stated in *Stallman*, it is easy to compare a unitary verdict in favor of all heirs to the joint offer of all heirs to determine whether plaintiffs have achieved a more favorable judgment. (*Stallman v. Bell, supra*, 235 Cal. App. 3d 740, 747). Common sense endorses this proposition.

Johnson, supra, 28 Cal. App. 4th at 630; *see also McDaniel v. Asuncion*, 214 Cal. App. 4th 1201, 155 Cal. Rptr. 3d 71 (2013) (following *Stallman* and *Johnson* where joint offer in wrongful death action made to, not by, multiple plaintiffs). Do you agree that common sense endorses the *Stallman* result? Do any practical, common sense considerations support the *Gilman* result?

(7) When a § 998 offer is silent as to costs and fees, costs and contractual or statutory attorney fees are recoverable in addition to the amount of the accepted offer. *Calvo Fisher & Jack LLP v. Lujan*, 234 Cal. App. 4th 608, 184 Cal. Rptr. 3d 225 (2015) (collecting cases); *see DeSaulles v. Community Hosp. of Monterey Peninsula*, 62 Cal. 4th 1140, 1154, 202 Cal. Rptr. 3d 429, 370 P.3d 996 (2016) ("The cases make clear that if a settlement agreement, compromise offer pursuant to section 998, or stipulated judgment is silent on the matter of costs, the plaintiff is not barred from seeking costs"). In *Stallman v. Bell*, reproduced *supra*, the offer stated "each side to bear its own costs." Do you agree with the *Stallman* court's explanation of the effect of this cost provision on the "more favorable judgment" determination? *See Whatley-Miller*

v. Cooper, 212 Cal. App. 4th 1103, 1111, 151 Cal. Rptr. 3d 517 (2013) (ruling the significance of "each side to bear its own costs" is clear: the defendant would not be liable to the plaintiffs for costs if the § 998 offer is accepted).

[2] What Constitutes a More Favorable Judgment?

[a] Is an Award of Costs or Attorney Fees Included?

One of the more difficult issues faced by courts applying CCP § 998 is the determination of whether a party has failed to obtain a "more favorable judgment." As *Stallman v. Bell*, reproduced *supra*, illustrates, what should be included or deleted from the amount of a verdict in making this determination can be quite complicated. Several courts have reached the same conclusion as the court in *Stallman*, and have added court costs awarded to the prevailing party pursuant to CCP § 1032(b) and § 1033.5(a). *See, e.g., Hoch v. Allied-Signal, Inc.*, 24 Cal. App. 4th 48, 29 Cal. Rptr. 2d 615 (1994); *Kelly v. Yee*, 213 Cal. App. 3d 336, 342, 261 Cal. Rptr. 568 (1989); *Encinitas Plaza Real v. Knight*, 209 Cal. App. 3d 996, 257 Cal. Rptr. 646 (1989). Do you understand why the *Stallman* court added both pre-offer and post-offer costs to the plaintiffs' verdict in making the favorability determination? In a 1997 amendment to § 998(c)(2), the Legislature codified the *Stallman* court's observation that only pre-offer costs should be included to determine favorability when the defendant has made the offer. CCP § 998(c)(2)(A).

The courts were in less agreement with respect to the addition of awarded attorney fees to a verdict in determining § 998 favorability. In *Encinitas Plaza Real v. Knight*, *supra*, for example, the court held that an award of attorney fees pursuant to a contract was not an item of costs within the meaning of then-existing CCP § 1032 and § 1033.5(a)(10), and consequently could not be included in determining "more favorable judgment" under § 998. The soundness of the *Encinitas Plaza* holding became doubtful after a 1990 amendment to CCP § 1033.5(a)(10) which specifically made attorney fees authorized by contract, statute, or law an item of costs recoverable by a prevailing party. Subsequently, a 1997 amendment to CCP § 998(c) superseded the holding in *Encinitas Plaza Real v. Knight*. CCP § 998(c)(2)(B), reproduced *supra*. Section 998(c)(2)(A) now provides: "In determining whether the plaintiff obtains a more favorable judgment, the court or arbitrator shall exclude the postoffer costs."

[b] Other Additions and Subtractions

In *Goodman v. Lozano*, 47 Cal. 4th 1327, 104 Cal. Rptr. 3d 219, 223 P.3d 77 (2010), the Supreme Court held that a plaintiff who recovered nothing from the nonsettling defendants due to the offset credits for pretrial good faith settlements with other defendants did not obtain a "net monetary recovery" for purposes of determining the "prevailing party" for recovery of costs within the meaning of CCP § 1032(a)(4). Should this same reasoning apply to the determination of whether a plaintiff who rejected a CCP § 998 offer subsequently obtained a "more favorable judgment"? *See Guerrero v. Rodan Termite Control, Inc.*, 163 Cal. App. 4th 1435, 78 Cal. Rtpr. 3d 344

(2008) (holding that regardless of the proper interpretation of CCP § 1032, the determination of whether the plaintiff recovered more or less than the amount of a defendant's § 998 offer is to be made taking into account any other settlements entered as of the time the § 998 offer was outstanding). Does a plaintiff whose § 998 offer is rejected by defendant obtain a "more favorable judgment" than her offer when the jury verdict awards plaintiff more than the offer, but deduction for a workers' compensation benefits lien reduces plaintiff's judgment to an amount less than the § 998 offer? *See Manthey v. San Luis Rey Downs Enter., Inc.*, 16 Cal. App. 4th 782, 20 Cal. Rptr. 2d 265 (1993).

What about where the plaintiff rejects defendant's § 998 offer and obtains a jury verdict of compensatory damages for less than the offered amount, but the statute plaintiff sued under mandates treble damages which when totaled will exceed the defendant's § 998 offer? *See Kelly v. Yee*, 213 Cal. App. 3d 336, 261 Cal. Rptr. 568 (1989). For problems associated with determining whether plaintiffs obtained a "more favorable judgment" when defendant's § 998 offer was a structured settlement, see *Hurlbut v. Sonora Cmty. Hosp.*, 207 Cal. App. 3d 388, 407–10, 254 Cal. Rptr. 840 (1989). How are costs augmented or reduced when both plaintiff and defendant make § 998 offers, neither offer is accepted, and both parties subsequently obtained judgments more favorable than their opponents § 998 offer because the verdict was between the two offers? *See Rose v. Hertz Corp.*, 168 Cal. App. 3d Supp. 6, 214 Cal. Rptr. 795 (App. Dept. Super. Ct. 1985).

Should any prejudgment interest the plaintiff is entitled to recover under Civil Code § 3287 be included in determining whether the plaintiff obtained a "more favorable judgment" within the meaning of CCP § 998(c)? *See Bodell Constr. Co. v. Trustees of Cal. State Univ.*, 62 Cal. App. 4th 1508, 73 Cal. Rptr. 2d 450 (1998) (holding prejudgment interest awarded under § 3287 is an element of compensatory damages and is not a court cost).

[3] *Consequences of Failure to Obtain a More Favorable Judgment*

[a] Effect on Award of Costs and Expert Witness Expenses

The penalty for failing to obtain a judgment more favorable than the unaccepted offer is the withholding or augmenting of allowable costs, as specified in §§ 998(c)–(e). Costs affected by § 998 include those items recoverable pursuant to CCP § 1032 and allowable under § 1033.5; and therefore include attorney fees when authorized by contract, statute, or law. CCP § 1033.5(a)(10). *See, e.g., Duale v. Mercedes-Benz USA, LLC*, 148 Cal. App. 4th 718, 56 Cal. Rptr. 3d 19 (2007) (concluding that unless the Legislature intended to exempt a specific attorney fee-shifting statute from the operation of § 998, a plaintiff who rejected a defendant's § 998 offer and subsequently recovers a judgment less favorable than the § 998 offer can recover only his *preoffer* costs and attorney fees, and must pay the defendant's *postoffer* costs and fees). Section 998 also authorizes the trial court in its discretion to require the offeree who fails to obtain a more favorable judgment to pay the expenses for certain expert witnesses of the offeror. CCP § 998(b) & (c); *Brake v. Beech Aircraft Corp.*, 184 Cal. App. 3d

930, 939–41, 229 Cal. Rptr. 336 (1986); *see Stiles v. Estate of Ryan*, 173 (
1057, 219 Cal. Rptr. 647 (1985).

[b] Prejudgment Interest

A defendant's rejection of a § 998 offer in a personal injury tort action has an
consequence if the plaintiff subsequently obtains a more favorable judgment. Purs
to Civil Code § 3291, the judgment *shall* bear interest of 10% calculated from
date of the plaintiff's first § 998 offer and accrue until satisfaction of judgment. *St*
e.g., *Lakin v. Watkins Assoc. Indus.*, 6 Cal. 4th 644, 656–64, 25 Cal. Rptr. 2d 109, 863
P.2d 179 (1993) (concluding CC § 3291 authorizes courts to award prejudgment interest only on damages attributable to personal injury); *Pilimai v. Farmers Ins. Exch.*
Co., 39 Cal. 4th 133, 45 Cal. Rptr. 3d 760, 137 P.3d 939 (2006) (ruling an action
against an insurance company to recover policy benefits for compensation of personal
injury is an action for breach of contract and not an "action brought to recover damages for personal injury" within the meaning of CC § 3291); *Gourley v. State Farm*
Mut. Auto. Ins. Co., 53 Cal. 3d 121, 279 Cal. Rptr. 307, 806 P.2d 1342 (1991) (holding
prejudgment interest award under CCP § 3291 improper where § 998 offer rejected
by defendant in insurance bad faith action because action was for interference with
property rights, not for personal injury damages).

When there are two successive unaccepted CCP § 998 offers tendered by a successful
plaintiff in personal injury litigation, and that plaintiff subsequently recovers a judgment in excess of either offer, from the date of which offer does the prejudgment interest awarded pursuant to Civil Code § 3291 begin to run? *See Ray v. Goodman*, 142
Cal. App. 4th 83, 47 Cal. Rptr. 3d 659 (2006) (concluding that where the judgment
received by the plaintiff exceeds *both* offers, the clear language of § 3291 directs that
interest be computed from the date of the "plaintiff's first offer"); *see also Martinez*
v. Brownco Constr. Co., 56 Cal. 4th 1014, 157 Cal. Rptr. 3d 558, 301 P.3d 1167 (2013)
(holding where a plaintiff makes two successive statutory offers and the defendant
fails to obtain a judgment more favorable than *either* offer, allowing recovery of expert
witness fees incurred from the date of the first offer is consistent with § 998's language
and best promotes the statutory purpose to encourage settlements).

Is a plaintiff who obtains a judgment more favorable than his § 998 offer entitled
to interest on the prejudgment portion of the interest accrued under Civil Code
§ 3291, *i.e.*, compound interest or interest on interest? *See Hess v. Ford Motor Co.*, 27
Cal. 4th 516, 117 Cal. Rptr. 2d 220, 41 P.3d 46 (2002) (holding prejudgment interest
accrued under § 3291 is not part of the judgment and a plaintiff may not obtain
interest on this prejudgment interest).

[4] *Section 998 Applicable to Contractual Arbitration*

Pursuant to a 1997 amendment, the cost-shifting provisions of CCP § 998 are now
also applicable to contractual arbitration proceedings. In *Pilimai v. Farmers Ins. Exch.*
Co., 39 Cal. 4th 133, 45 Cal. Rptr. 3d 760, 137 P.3d 939 (2006), the Supreme Court

interpreted sections 998(a) & (d) to mean that the types of costs available to an arbitration plaintiff who obtained an arbitration award more favorable that his § 998 offer are those costs available under CCP § 1032 and CCP § 1033.5, and therefore include deposition and exhibit preparation costs.

[5] Section 998 Inapplicable to Certain Proceedings

By its terms, § 998 does not apply in an eminent domain action, CCP § 998(c) & (g); and has been construed as inapplicable to dissolution of marriage cases. *Marriage of Green*, 213 Cal. App. 3d 14, 23–24, 261 Cal. Rptr. 294 (1989). The courts have concluded that the cost-shifting provisions of § 998 are applicable to inverse condemnation actions, *Regency Outdoor Advertising, Inc. v. City of L. A.*, 39 Cal. 4th 507, 531–34, 46 Cal. Rptr. 3d 742, 139 P.3d 119 (2006); suits under the Song-Beverly-Consumer Warranty Act, Civil Code § 1790 *et seq., Murillo v. Fleetwood Enter., Inc.*, 17 Cal. 4th 985, 73 Cal. Rptr. 2d 682, 953 P.2d 858 (1998) (observing that unlike the Family Law Act, which contains specific cost-recovery provisions that constitute express exceptions to the general cost-recovery provisions of CCP §§ 1032(b) and 998, the cost-shifting provisions of Song-Beverly-Consumer Warranty Act do not expressly preclude a prevailing party from recovering § 998 costs and fees); and to judicial arbitration proceedings under CCP § 1141-10-1141.30, *Wagy v. Brown*, 24 Cal. App. 4th 1, 9, 29 Cal. Rptr. 2d 48 (1994); *Joyce v. Black*, 217 Cal. App. 3d 318, 266 Cal. Rptr. 8 (1990).

[H] Recovery of Costs in Federal Court

[1] Costs

Rule 54(d)(1) of the Federal Rules of Civil Procedure provides that unless a federal statute, the federal rules, or a court order provides otherwise, "costs—other than attorney's fees—should be to the prevailing party." Does a federal judge under Rule 54(d)(1) have more discretionary power to deny costs than does a state judge under CCP § 1032 and § 1033.5? *See generally* Wright, Miller & Kane, *Federal Practice and Procedure* § 2668 (4th ed. 2014) (surveying cases which hold that except when matter controlled by federal statute or rule, trial court is vested with sound discretion by Rule 54(d) in allowing costs to prevailing party); *see also Delta Airlines, Inc. v. August*, 450 U.S. 346, 353–56, 101 S. Ct. 1146, 67 L. Ed. 2d 287 (1981); Laura B. Bartell, *Taxation of Costs and Awards of Expenses in Federal Court*, 101 F.R.D. 553, 559–65 (1984) (collecting cases which illustrate that an award of costs is within the sound discretion of the district court). Rule 54(d)(2) governs claims for attorneys' fees in actions where the prevailing party may be entitled to an award of fees pursuant to a statute or from a common fund.

[2] Offers of Judgment

Rule 68 of the Federal Rules of Civil Procedure authorizes an offer of judgment process for federal courts analogous to that of CCP § 998. Under Federal Rule 68, however, only "a party defending against a claim" may serve an offer of judgment on the adverse party, and the other remains operative for 14 days. The consequence of rejecting an offer is also more limited than under CCP § 998. Rule 68 provides that "[i]f the judgment that the offeree finally obtains is not more favorable than the un-accepted offer, the offeree must pay the costs incurred after the offer was made." The U.S. Supreme Court construed this language to encompass only judgment in favor of an offeree and not a judgment against the offeree. *Delta Air Lines, Inc. v. August,* 450 U.S. 346, 101 S. Ct. 1146, 67 L. Ed. 2d 287 (1981). Rule 68 is simply inapplicable in a case where the plaintiff offeree lost at trial because the defendant-offeror obtained the judgment. *Delta Air Lines,* 450 U.S. at 351–52. Also, this construction makes it unnecessary to read a reasonableness requirement into Rule 68 offers. *Id.* at 355. Why? What are the policy reasons for the *Delta Air Lines* court's construction of Rule 68? What are the policy arguments for a contrary construction, *i.e.,* Rule 68 requires that a plaintiff-offeree who ultimately takes nothing *must* pay the costs incurred by the defendant-offeror after making the offer? *See id.* at 366–380 (dissenting opinion of Justice Rehnquist).

§ 14.05 Relief from Final Judgment

[A] Introductory Note

Two procedural options are available to a party who was unsuccessful in posttrial motions and chose not to appeal, but still desires relief from an otherwise valid and final judgment. One is a motion to vacate or set aside the judgment pursuant to CCP § 473, the other is a similar motion addressed to the trial court's inherent equity power. The statutory motion must be filed within six months of the judgment, and requires proof of "mistake, inadvertence, surprise, or excusable neglect." CCP § 473. (Section 473 also mandates relief from a default judgment or a dismissal when accompanied by an attorney's affidavit of fault. *See* § 12.02[G][2], Relief from Default Judgments, *supra.*) The equitable motion is appropriate when § 473 relief is no longer available, and requires proof that the judgment was obtained through extrinsic, as opposed to intrinsic, fraud or mistake. *Estate of Sanders,* 40 Cal. 3d 607, 221 Cal. Rptr. 432, 710 P.2d 232 (1985); *Kulchar v. Kulchar,* 1 Cal. 3d 467, 82 Cal. Rptr. 489, 462 P.2d 17 (1969).

The courts often comment that a party who seeks to set aside a judgment pursuant to the court's equity power must make a substantially stronger showing of the excusable nature of his or her neglect than is necessary to obtain relief under CCP § 473. *See, e.g., Carroll v. Abbott Labs, Inc.,* 32 Cal. 3d 892, 901, fn.8, 187 Cal. Rptr. 592, 654 P.2d 775 (1982); *Weitz v. Yankosky,* 63 Cal. 2d 849, 857, 48 Cal. Rptr. 620, 409 P.2d 700 (1966). The disposition of a motion seeking relief on either basis lies within the sound discretion of the trial court, and the trial court's decision will not be overturned on appeal unless there has been a clear abuse of discretion. *Elston v. City of Turlock,* 38 Cal. 3d 227, 233, 211 Cal. Rptr. 416, 695 P.2d 713 (1985); *Marriage of Connolly,* 23

Cal. 3d 590, 598, 153 Cal. Rptr. 423, 591 P.2d 911 (1979); *Weitz v. Yankosky, supra,* 63 Cal. 2d at 854.

The courts apply these same standards whether relief is sought from a default judgment or from a final judgment entered after a full adversarial trial. However, as discussed in detail in § 12.02 [G][3], Relief from Default Judgments, *supra,* unless inexcusable neglect is clear the policy favoring trial and disposition on the merits requires very slight evidence to justify a trial court setting aside a default judgment. *Elston v. City of Turlock, supra,* 38 Cal. 3d at 233; *Rogalsky v. Nabers Cadillac,* 11 Cal. App. 4th 816, 821, 14 Cal. Rptr. 2d 286 (1992). The opposite is true with respect to requests for relief from otherwise valid and final judgments entered after an adversarial hearing. As our principal case illustrates, a trial court can only exercise the power to set aside or modify a valid final judgment when the circumstances are sufficient to overcome the strong policy favoring the finality of judgments; the consequences of res judicata should be denied only in "exceptional circumstances."

Kulchar v. Kulchar

Supreme Court of California
1 Cal. 3d 467, 82 Cal. Rptr. 489, 462 P.2d 17 (1969)

TRAYNOR, CHIEF JUSTICE.

Plaintiff appeals from an order of the Superior Court of San Mateo County modifying an interlocutory decree of divorce to relieve defendant of liability to pay federal income taxes assessed against the parties on income accruing to plaintiff in New Zealand.

Plaintiff secured an interlocutory decree of divorce from defendant on July 3, 1964. The decree included the disposition of the community and separate property of the parties.[1] The decree provided, in part: "Defendant shall indemnify and hold plaintiff free and harmless in the matter of any monies due any taxing agency, whether Federal, State or County, for the calendar years prior to 1964."

In 1966, following the divorce proceedings, defendant received a tax assessment of approximately $22,000 for federal income taxes based on theretofore undisclosed income accumulated during the marriage by a New Zealand corporation in plaintiff's name. Defendant moved to modify the divorce decree to relieve him of any liability for taxes on the New Zealand income on the grounds of extrinsic fraud and extrinsic mistake. After a hearing on defendant's motion, the trial court concluded that the tax provision in the decree "was included and approved by the parties as a result of the mutual mistake of the parties and further, that there was no intent of the parties that defendant should pay United States Federal income tax resulting from income

---

1. There was no formal property settlement agreement. All provisions of the decree relating to the distribution of property were submitted to the court on the stipulation of the parties.

to plaintiff in New Zealand." The court struck the tax provision from the decree "because of the mutual mistake of the parties."

Under certain circumstances a court, sitting in equity, can set aside or modify a valid final judgment. (*Olivera v. Grace* (1942) 19 Cal. 2d 570, 575–576 [122 P.2d 564, 140 A.L.R. 1328]; *Caldwell v. Taylor* (1933) 218 Cal. 471, 475 [23 P.2d 758, 88 A.L.R. 1194].) This power, however, can only be exercised when the circumstances of the case are sufficient to overcome the strong policy favoring the finality of judgments. "A basic requirement of an action which can lead to a valid judgment is that a procedure should be adopted which in the normal case will give to the parties an opportunity for a fair trial which is reasonable in view of the requirements of public policy in the particular type of case. If this requirement is met, a judgment awarded in an action is not void merely because the particular individual against whom it was rendered did not in fact have an opportunity to present his claim or defense before an impartial tribunal.... [Public] policy requires that only in exceptional circumstances should the consequences of res judicata be denied to a valid judgment." (Rest., Judgments, § 118, com. a.)

Interlocutory divorce decrees are res judicata as to all questions determined therein, including the property rights of the parties. (*In re Williams' Estate* (1950) 36 Cal. 2d 289, 292 [233 P.2d 248, 22 A.L.R.2d 716]; *Adamson v. Adamson* (1962) 209 Cal. App. 2d 492, 501 [26 Cal. Rptr. 236].) If a property settlement is incorporated in the divorce decree, the settlement is merged with the decree and becomes the final judicial determination of the property rights of the parties. (*Broome v. Broome* (1951) 104 Cal. App. 2d 148, 154–155 [231 P.2d 171].) Thus, the rules governing extrinsic fraud and mistake apply to alimony awards and property settlements incorporated in divorce decrees. (*Jorgensen v. Jorgensen* (1948) 32 Cal. 2d 13, 18–23 [193 P.2d 728]; *Hendricks v. Hendricks* (1932) 216 Cal. 321, 323–324 [14 P.2d 83]....)

Extrinsic fraud usually arises when a party is denied a fair adversary hearing because he has been "deliberately kept in ignorance of the action or proceeding, or in some other way fraudulently prevented from presenting his claim or defense." (3 Witkin, Cal. Procedure, p. 2124.) "Where the unsuccessful party has been prevented from exhibiting fully his case, by fraud or deception practiced on him by his opponent, as by keeping him away from court, a false promise of a compromise; or where the defendant never had knowledge of the suit, being kept in ignorance by the acts of the plaintiff; or where an attorney fraudulently or without authority assumes to represent a party and connives at his defeat; or where the attorney regularly employed corruptly sells out his client's interest to the other side,—these, and similar cases which show that there has never been a real contest in the trial or hearing of the case, are reasons for which a new suit may be sustained to set aside and annul the former judgment or decree, and open the case for a new and a fair hearing." (*United States v. Throckmorton* (1878) 98 U.S. 61, 65–66 [25 L. Ed. 93, 95].)

The right to relief has also been extended to cases involving extrinsic mistake. (*Bacon v. Bacon* (1907) 150 Cal. 477, 491–492 [89 P. 317]; *Olivera v. Grace, supra,* at p. 577.) "In some cases ... the ground of relief is not so much the fraud or other misconduct of the defendant as it is the excusable neglect of the plaintiff to appear and present his claim or defense. If such neglect results in an unjust judgment, *without a fair adversary* hearing, the basis for equitable relief is present, and is often called 'extrinsic mistake.'" (3 Witkin, Cal. Procedure, p. 2128.)

Extrinsic mistake is found when a party becomes incompetent but no guardian ad litem is appointed (*Olivera v. Grace, supra,* at p. 577; *Dei Tos v. Dei Tos* (1951) 105 Cal. App. 2d 81, 84–85 [232 P.2d 873];....); when one party relies on another to defend (*Weitz v. Yankosky* (1966) 63 Cal. 2d 849, 855–856 [48 Cal. Rptr. 620, 409 P.2d 700];....); when there is reliance on an attorney who becomes incapacitated to act (*Jeffords v. Young* (1929) 98 Cal. App. 400, 405–406 [277 P. 163]; *Smith v. Busniewski* (1952) 115 Cal. App. 2d 124, 127–128 [251 P.2d 697];....); when a mistake led a court to do what it never intended (*Sullivan v. Lumsden* (1897) 118 Cal. 664, 669 [50 P. 777]; *Bacon v. Bacon, supra,* at pp. 492–493); when a mistaken belief of one party prevented proper notice of the action (*Aldabe v. Aldabe* (1962) 209 Cal. App. 2d 453, 475 [26 Cal. Rptr. 208]; *Boyle v. Boyle* (1929) 97 Cal. App. 703, 706 [276 P. 118]); or when the complaining party was disabled at the time the judgment was entered (*Watson v. Watson* (1958) 161 Cal. App. 2d 35, 39–40 [325 P.2d 1011]; *Saunders v. Saunders* (1958) 157 Cal. App. 2d 67, 72–73 [320 P.2d 131];....). Relief has also been extended to cases involving negligence of a party's attorney in not properly filing an answer (*Hallett v. Slaughter* (1943) 22 Cal. 2d 552, 556–557 [140 P.2d 3]; *Turner v. Allen* (1961) 189 Cal. App. 2d 753, 757–760 [11 Cal. Rptr. 630]); and mistaken belief as to immunity from suit (*Bartell v. Johnson* (1943) 60 Cal. App. 2d 432, 436–437 [140 P.2d 878]).[2]

Relief is denied, however, if a party has been given notice of an action and has not been prevented from participating therein. He has had an opportunity to present his case to the court and to protect himself from mistake or from any fraud attempted by his adversary. (*Jorgenson v. Jorgenson, supra,* 32 Cal. 2d 13 at p. 18; *Westphal v. Westphal* (1942) 20 Cal. 2d 393, 397 [126 P.2d 105]; *Gale v. Witt* (1948) 31 Cal. 2d 362, 367 [188 P.2d 755].) Moreover, a mutual mistake that might be sufficient to set aside a contract is not sufficient to set aside a final judgment. The principles of res judicata demand that the parties present their entire case in one proceeding. "Public policy requires that pressure be brought upon litigants to use great care in preparing cases for trial and in ascertaining all the facts. A rule which would permit the reopening of cases previously decided because of error or ignorance during the progress

---

2. The decisions in both *Hallett* and *Bartell* have been criticized. (*See* Comment (1943) 31 Cal. L. Rev. 600.) "The cases on *intrinsic fraud*, involving perjury, false documents and other reprehensible conduct by the adverse party, are far more compelling, yet relief is uniformly denied for good reason.... The *Hallett* and *Bartell* cases involve no true extrinsic factors in the accepted sense, and they raise serious questions as to the practical finality of any default judgment." (3 Witkin, Cal. Procedure, p. 2130.)

of the trial would in a large measure vitiate the effects of the rules of res judicata." (Rest., Judgments, § 126, com. a.) Courts deny relief, therefore, when the fraud or mistake is "intrinsic"; that is, when it "goes to the merits of the prior proceedings, which should have been guarded against by the plaintiff at that time." (Comment, *Equitable Relief From Judgments, Orders and Decrees Obtained by Fraud* (1934) 23 Cal. L. Rev. 79, 83–84; *see Pico v. Cohn* (1891) 91 Cal. 129, 134 [27 P. 537, 25 Am. St. Rep. 159, 13 L.R.A. 336]; *Hendricks v. Hendricks, supra*, at pp. 323–324.)

Relief is also denied when the complaining party has contributed to the fraud or mistake giving rise to the judgment thus obtained. (*Hammell v. Britton* (1941) 19 Cal. 2d 72, 80 [119 P.2d 333]; *Rudy v. Slotwinsky* (1925) 73 Cal. App. 459, 465 [238 P. 783]; Rest., Judgments, § 129.) "If the complainant was guilty of negligence in permitting the fraud to be practiced or the mistake to occur equity will deny relief." (*Wilson v. Wilson* (1942) 55 Cal. App. 2d 421, 427 [130 P.2d 782].)

Whether the case involves intrinsic or extrinsic fraud or mistake is not determined abstractly. "It is necessary to examine the facts in the light of the policy that a party who failed to assemble all his evidence at the trial should not be privileged to relitigate a case, as well as the policy permitting a party to seek relief from a judgment entered in a proceeding in which he was deprived of a fair opportunity fully to present his case." (*Jorgensen v. Jorgensen, supra*, 32 Cal. 2d 13 at p. 19.)

The evidence in the present case establishes that it is a case in which a party "failed to assemble all his evidence at the trial." Defendant testified that he knew of the New Zealand holdings prior to the divorce and that plaintiff was receiving $640 every four months from New Zealand. In defendant's divorce questionnaire, circulated to determine the extent of marital property holdings, expenses and income, he listed as plaintiff's separate property "50% stock interest in David Lloyd Co., Ltd.,—a New Zealand holding corporation for many subsidiary companies (cement, coal, paper)—exact worth unknown to defendant—estimated to run into millions of dollars." In a letter sent by defendant's attorney to plaintiff's attorney in which the principal points of the property settlement were summarized, defendant proposed to transfer to plaintiff "any interest he may have in her holdings in New Zealand." Plaintiff also knew of the holdings but did not know of their value or their tax consequences. In 1957 when preparing income tax returns, an attorney, who later represented defendant in the divorce action, made some inquiry into the nature of the New Zealand income at the request of defendant. The attorney abandoned further investigation after plaintiff stated that a law firm known to defendant's attorney had advised her that the New Zealand income was not taxable. The attorney knew that the New Zealand holdings were "sizable." Both parties testified that the tax provision was included in the decree because of an audit being conducted by the Internal Revenue Service with respect to an unrelated transaction by defendant.

Clearly the present case does not involve the failure of one spouse to disclose fully the assets to be divided upon separation. (*See Taylor v. Taylor* (1923) 192 Cal. 71 [218 P. 756, 51 A.L.R. 1074]; *Milekovich v. Quinn* (1919) 40 Cal. App. 537 [181 P. 256].) The duty to disclose arises out of the fiduciary relationship between the husband and wife. (*Vai v. Bank of America* (1961) 56 Cal. 2d 329, 337–340 [15 Cal. Rptr. 71, 364 P.2d 247]; *Jorgensen v. Jorgensen, supra*, 32 Cal. 2d 13 at pp. 19–21.) There is no evidence that the wife withheld any information relevant to the nature of her New Zealand income.

The factual situation in the present case is analogous to that in *Jorgensen v. Jorgensen, supra*. In *Jorgensen* the husband disclosed all known assets of the parties. The husband claimed certain assets as his separate property. The wife and her attorney accepted the husband's statements at face value without any independent investigation. Subsequent to the divorce decree, however, they learned that some of the assets the husband claimed as separate property were actually community property, in which the wife was entitled to a one-half interest. The wife was denied the right to set aside the property settlement agreement. "If the wife and her attorney are satisfied with the husband's classification of the property as separate or community, the wife cannot reasonably contend that fraud was committed or that there was such mistake as to allow her to overcome the finality of a judgment. Plaintiff is barred from obtaining equitable relief by her admission that she and her attorney did not investigate the facts, choosing instead to rely on the statements of the husband as to what part of the disclosed property was community property." (*Jorgensen v. Jorgensen, supra*, 32 Cal. 2d 13 at pp. 22–23;....)

In the present case both parties knew of the New Zealand assets, but the husband and his attorney chose not to investigate their taxability. The property settlement agreement expressly covered unknown tax liability. Having had full opportunity to consider all income of the wife and its concurrent tax consequences, the husband cannot now complain of the added tax burden.

The order is reversed.

Notes and Questions regarding Relief from Final Judgment

(1) *Relief Pursuant to CCP § 473*. Because the defendant husband filed his motion to modify more than six months after entry of the dissolution decree, the Supreme Court in *Kulchar* applied the equitable "extrinsic vs. intrinsic" fraud distinction in determining the propriety of the trial court's relief. Would the Supreme Court have reached a different conclusion if the defendant had filed his motion to modify within six months of the decree, thereby utilizing the "mistake or excusable neglect" standard of CCP § 473?

In *Marriage of Connolly*, 23 Cal. 3d 590, 153 Cal. Rptr. 423, 591 P.2d 911 (1979), the wife filed a timely motion to vacate a judgment dissolving her marriage and dividing community property, pursuant to CCP § 473. At issue was the value of 10,000 shares of private corporate stock the couple had owned, which was admittedly community property. The trial court awarded the stock to the husband, a director of the corporation, and awarded one-half the total value of the stock to the wife. Based on testimony by the husband that recent private sales of the stock had been in the $5–$10 range per share, the trial court found that $7.50 was a reasonable price for the stock and entered judgment accordingly. Within one month after this judgment, there was a public offering of the corporation's stock at which time the stock sold publicly for $27.50 per share. The wife then sought to reopen the dissolution judgment, contending that the husband's failure to inform the wife of the impending public offer at a higher price constituted fraud which resulted in her excusable neglect or mistake. The trial court denied wife's motion for relief under § 473 because the information regarding the proposed public offering was not confidential, and was readily available to the public and to the wife prior to trial.

The Supreme Court affirmed, finding that the wife had every opportunity to ascertain the complete status of the stock but made a tactical decision not to make her own independent investigation of the value of the stock prior to judgment. The husband was in an adversarial relationship with his wife, and had no responsibility to reveal information regarding the upcoming public stock offering or other information regarding the stock value, where such information was readily available to the wife through reasonable investigation. *Marriage of Connolly*, 23 Cal. 3d at 598–602. Does the Supreme Court's reasoning in *Marriage of Connolly* when applying § 473 appear any different than its reasoning in *Kulchar* when applying the equitable doctrine of extrinsic fraud? How so?

(2) A clear example of extrinsic fraud was reviewed in *Marriage of Park*, 27 Cal. 3d 337, 165 Cal. Rptr. 792, 612 P.2d 882 (1980), where the Supreme Court held that the failure of the husband and his attorney to disclose to the trial court that his wife's failure to appear at trial was because she had been involuntarily deported during the course of the litigation required the judgment awarding child custody and dividing community property be set aside. What makes the spouse's fraud in *Park* extrinsic, but the fraud in *Kulchar* and *Connolly* intrinsic?

(3) Many of the cases dealing with motions for relief from final judgments after trial are dissolution of marriage cases. Why? As the court commented in *Marriage of Stevenot*, 154 Cal. App. 3d 1051, 202 Cal. Rptr. 116 (1984), such cases are not only numerous but also unclear in their analyses (*Id.* at 1060):

> For the past 40 years, no family law issue has so regularly captured the attention of the California Supreme Court as has the issue of what constitutes extrinsic and intrinsic fraud. The Courts of Appeal have regularly wrestled with this problem during the same period, and it is likely that hundreds, if not thousands, of such cases have been decided by trial courts during the same period with no appeals having been filed. In 1933, our Supreme Court noted, "The distinction between intrinsic and extrinsic fraud is quite nebulous...." (*Caldwell v. Taylor* (1933) 218 Cal. 471, 479 [23 P.2d 758, 88 A.L.R. 1194].) More recently, one court correctly commented that, "the distinctions between extrinsic and intrinsic fraud are hopelessly blurred. Nonetheless, the California courts have remained married to the importance of the distinction whether or not and in fact it exists." (*In re Marriage of Guardino* (1979) 95 Cal. App. 3d 77, 89 [156 Cal. Rptr. 883].)

Why do the California courts persist in utilizing the extrinsic-intrinsic fraud distinction?

(4) Despite the vagueness of the standards applied to motions for relief in family law cases, certain patterns have developed. Courts have uniformly held, for example, that a deliberate concealment by one spouse of community assets constitutes extrinsic fraud justifying relief. *E.g.*, *Marriage of Modnick*, 33 Cal. 3d 897, 191 Cal. Rptr. 629, 663 P.2d 187 (1983) (ruling nondisclosure and active concealment of community bank account was clearly extrinsic fraud); *Marriage of Umphrey*, 218 Cal. App. 3d 647, 655, 267 Cal. Rptr. 218 (1990); *see Marriage of Stevenot, supra*, 154 Cal. App. 3d at 1068–69. Why does such concealment constitute extrinsic fraud? *See Estate of Sanders*, 40 Cal. 3d 607, 616, 221 Cal. Rptr. 432, 710 P.2d 232 (1985) ("Where there exists a relationship of trust and confidence it is the duty of one in whom the confidence is reposed to make full disclosure of all material facts within his knowledge relating to the transaction in question and any concealment of material facts is fraud").

Is it also extrinsic fraud justifying relief from judgment where one spouse disclosed the existence of an asset but misrepresented its character as separate and not community property? *See Marriage of Jacobs*, 128 Cal. App. 3d 273, 180 Cal. Rptr. 234 (1982) (finding that the wife acquiesced in the stipulation because she relied on her husband's expertise as an accountant and felt compelled to follow his lead regarding characterization of the funds); *Marriage of Umphrey, supra*, 218 Cal. App. 3d at 655–56; *Jorgensen v. Jorgensen*, 32 Cal. 2d 13, 19–21, 193 P.2d 728 (1948). Where one spouse disclosed the existence of a community asset but misrepresented the value of the asset? *See Miller v. Bechtel Corp.*, 33 Cal. 3d 868, 191 Cal. Rptr. 619, 663 P.2d 177 (1983) (ruling that when the existence of an asset is disclosed, the other party has a duty to investigate to ascertain its true character and value and any failure to do so would obviate a finding of extrinsic fraud); *Marriage of Stevenot, supra*, 154 Cal. App. 3d at 1069–76; *Marriage of Connolly, supra*, 23 Cal. 3d at 598–604.

(5) *Difficulty of Defining Extrinsic-Intrinsic Distinction.* Does the *Kulchar* opinion provide a clear definition of the extrinsic-intrinsic fraud distinction? Do the various precedents discussed in *Kulchar* produce a clear picture of when fraud or mistake will be considered extrinsic or intrinsic? For an excellent review of the numerous Supreme Court opinions applying the extrinsic-intrinsic distinction in family law cases, see *Marriage of Stevenot*, 154 Cal. App. 3d 1051, 1068–70, 202 Cal. Rptr. 116 (1984), relied on by the Supreme Court in *Rappleyea v. Campbell*, 8 Cal. 4th 975, 981–84, 35 Cal. Rptr. 2d 669, 884 P.2d 126 (1994).

(6) *Viability of the Extrinsic-Intrinsic Distinction.* Is the extrinsic-intrinsic fraud or mistake distinction a viable one? The courts have criticized the distinction as a nearly impossible one to apply. *See Marriage of Stevenot, supra*, 154 Cal. App. 3d at 1060; *Marriage of Baltins*, 212 Cal. App. 3d 66, 82, 260 Cal. Rptr. 403 (1989). Judge Smallwood has made a persuasive case for abolishing the extrinsic fraud rule. *See* Donald E. Smallwood, *Vacating Judgments in California: Time to Abolish the Extrinsic Fraud Rule*, 13 W. St. U. L. Rev. 105–127 (1985). Another commentator, in *Seeking More*

Equitable Relief from Fraudulent Judgments: Abolishing the Extrinsic-Intrinsic Distinctions, 12 PAC. L.J. 1013 (1981), after reviewing numerous California decisions, remarked (*id.* at 1014):

> The viability of the extrinsic-intrinsic distinction has been undermined further by its inconsistent application. While the courts purport to rely on the extrinsic-intrinsic distinction, an examination of California decisions indicates a strong emphasis on the presence or absence of equitable considerations in granting relief. When a party's entitlement to equitable relief depends upon the court's classification of the fraud involved, such inconsistency provides little indication of the likelihood of success under the particular factual circumstances.

The Restatement Second of Judgments (1982), Section 68, does not distinguish between extrinsic and intrinsic fraud. Nor does Rule 60(b) of the Federal Rules of Civil Procedure, which expressly abandoned this distinction.

(7) What are the policy reasons for the California extrinsic-intrinsic fraud distinction? Is this a reasonable distinction? A workable one? What would be the likely consequence of the elimination of this distinction? If this distinction were eliminated, what would a court focus on in determining whether to exercise its discretion to grant relief from judgment? For one proposed alternative test, see Smallwood, *Vacating Judgments in California, supra*, 13 W. ST. U. L. REV. at 124–25.

§ 14.06 Enforcement of Judgments

[A] Introductory Note

A party who successfully obtains a judgment often has won only the easiest part of the litigation battle. A successful decision on liability may be of very little benefit to the judgment creditor unless the judgment can be effectively enforced. California statutes and rules provide a judgment creditor with a variety of procedural mechanisms for enforcement of a judgment. Enforcement of a money judgment entered by a California court is governed by the Enforcement of Judgments Law, CCP §§ 680.010–724.260; of a judgment entered by a court in another state by the Sister State Money-Judgments Recognition Act, CCP §§ 1710.10–1710.65; and of a judgment entered by a court in another country by the Uniform Foreign-Country Money Judgments Act, CCP §§ 1713–1724. These statutory procedures can be quite complex, and contain many technicalities and exceptions. The materials in this section introduce some of the basic concepts and issues concerning enforcement of judgments. For more in-depth analyses, see CEB, *Debt Collection Practice in California*, Vol. I & II (2d ed. 2015); 8 Witkin, *California Procedure, Enforcement of Judgment* (5th ed. 2008); Ahart & Paris, *California Practice Guide, Enforcing Judgments and Debts* (The Rutter Group 2015).

[B]   Procedures for Enforcement of California Judgments

[1]   Entry of Judgment

Generally, a judgment after a jury trial must be entered by the clerk in conformity with a jury verdict within 24 hours of the rendition of the verdict, and after nonjury trial immediately upon the filing of the court's decision. CCP § 664. A judgment is not effectual for any purpose until so entered in the judgment book or analogous official record. CCP §§ 664, 668, 668.5. Although written notice of the entry of judgment must be mailed to all parties, CCP § 664.5, this notice requirement does not postpone the effectiveness of a judgment entered by the clerk. CCP § 664.

A money judgment is enforceable upon entry, CCP § 683.010; and remains enforceable for a period of 10 years after date of entry. CCP § 683.020. Upon expiration of this initial 10-year period of enforceability, and upon proper application, a money judgment may be renewed for another 10-year period. CCP §§ 683.110–683.220. These renewal provisions do not apply to a judgment or order made pursuant to the Family Code, CCP § 683.310; a judgment for child, family, or spousal support is enforceable until paid in full and is exempt from the renewal requirements. Family Code §§ 291(b), 4502. Nor do they apply to money judgments against a public entity that is subject to Government Code § 965.5 or § 970.1. CCP § 683.320.

[2]   Abstract of Judgment

An abstract of judgment contains a summary of the rendition, terms, and amount of a money judgment as well as basic information about the judgment creditor and judgment debtor. CCP § 674; Family Code § 4506. Code of Civil Procedure § 674 specifies the required contents of an abstract of judgment, as well as the effect of amendments. The Judicial Council has adopted mandatory forms for abstracts of judgments. *See* Form No. EJ-001: Abstract of Judgment (Civil and Small Claims); Form FL-480: Abstract of Support Judgment.

[3]   Judgment Lien

After obtaining a money judgment, the judgment creditor creates a judgment lien by recording an abstract of judgment or certified copy of the judgment with the county recorder. CCP §§ 697.310–697.330; § 697.060 (recording of federal court judgment). Subject to specified exceptions, a judgment lien attaches to all interests in real property owned by the judgment debtor in the county in which the abstract is recorded, and the judgment lien continues until it expires 10 years later or is satisfied or released. CCP §§ 697.310(b), 697.320(b), 697.340. The lien so created is "for the amount required to satisfy the money judgment." CCP § 697.010. A judgment creditor may also create a judgment lien on certain personal property by filing a notice of judgment lien with the Secretary of State's office in accordance with CCP § 697.510–697.670, and may create a wage garnishment lien in accordance with CCP § 706.029.

[a] Effect of Judgment Lien

The main purpose of a judgment lien is to create a security interest in the judgment creditor with respect to the judgment debtor's property. Consequently, for example, when real property encumbered by a duly recorded abstract of judgment is transferred, the transferees are charged with constructive knowledge of the encumbrance and they take title to the property subject to the judgment lien created by the abstract and not as bona fide purchasers. CCP § 697.390; Gov. Code § 27326; *see, e.g., Casey v. Gray*, 13 Cal. App. 4th 611, 16 Cal. Rptr. 2d 538 (1993) (holding abstract did not attach until recorded and therefore cannot affect previously transferred property).

[b] Priorities

The date when the judgment lien attaches, and therefore when the security interest is perfected, may be very important in determining priorities among competing liens of other judgment creditors as well as asserted interests of transferees and other claimants. CCP §§ 697.370–697.390; 697.590–697.650; *see, e.g., Waltrip v. Kimberlin*, 164 Cal. App. 4th 517, 79 Cal. Rptr. 3d 460 (2008) (discussing priority given a judgment lien versus an attorney lien for unpaid legal fees and holding, under the circumstances of the case, that the attorney lien had priority over a judgment lien); *Casey v. Gray, supra*, 13 Cal. App. 4th at 614 (holding executed and delivered quitclaim deed, although unrecorded, conveyed title free and clear of subsequently recorded abstract of judgment); *Bratcher v. Buckner*, 90 Cal. App. 4th 1177, 109 Cal. Rptr. 2d 534 (2001) (determining priorities among a judgment lien obtained by the plaintiff and several prior deeds of trusts with respect to execution and levy against certain real property owned by the defendant, and complicated by defendant's subordination agreement that placed the deeds of trust behind an SBA loan in terms of priority and by defendant's assertion of his homestead exemption). A judgment lien created on property will relate back to an earlier lien created by a prejudgment attachment on the property based on the same claim, or to an earlier enforcement lien on the same property. CCP § 697.020.

For more complete analyses of priorities of liens and security interests, consult 4 Witkin, *Summary of California Law, Security Transactions in Personal Property*, §§ 105–145 and *Secured Transactions in Real Property*, §§ 48–75 (10th ed. 2005); and 13 Witkin, *Summary of California Law, Personal Property*, §§ 216–245 (10th ed. 2005).

Nothing in the Enforcement of Judgments Law requires a judgment creditor to create a judgment lien. *See Diamond Heights Vill. Assn., Inc. v. Financial Freedom Senior Funding Corp.*, 196 Cal. App. 4th 290, 302, 126 Cal. Rptr. 3d 673 (2011); *Kahn v. Berman*, 198 Cal. App. 3d 1499, 1507, n. 7, 244 Cal. Rptr. 575 (1988). The creditor may simply choose to levy execution and thereby create an execution lien. CCP § 697.710. The general procedure for execution and levy is discussed below.

[4] Execution and Levy

Even where a judgment creditor chooses to obtain a judgment lien, the judgment creditor must take additional steps to collect on the judgment, and the usual method is to levy on specific property by writ of execution. *See Grothe v. Cortlandt Corp.*, 11 Cal. App. 4th 1313, 1320–21, 15 Cal. Rptr. 2d 38 (1992) (distinguishing between levy and the subsequent sale in the California judgment enforcement process). For a summary of the procedure for a levy on real property by writ of execution, see *Kahn v. Berman*, 198 Cal. App. 3d 1499, 1508–09, 244 Cal. Rptr. 575 (1988); *see also Grothe, supra*, 11 Cal. App. 4th at 1320–21.

[a] Writ of Execution

The judgment creditor must first obtain from the county clerk a writ of execution, directing the sheriff or other levying officer to enforce the judgment. CCP §§ 699.510, 699.520. The creditor delivers the writ to the levying officer with instructions including a description of the property to be levied upon. § 687.010. The officer levies on real property by recording a copy of the writ and a notice of levy with the county recorder. § 700.015(a). The levy creates an execution lien on the property which remains in effect for two years unless the judgment is satisfied sooner. § 697.710. Service of a copy of the writ and notice of levy on the judgment debtor triggers a 120-day grace period during which the debtor may redeem the property from the levy. § 701.545. Only after this period expires may the levying officer then proceed to notice the property for sale. CCP § 701.540 *et seq.* The judgment creditor must apply to the court for an order of sale of a dwelling within 20 days after service of the notice of levy, however, or the levying officer will release the dwelling. § 704.750. The requirements for the actual execution sale of a dwelling are set forth in CCP §§ 704.740–704.850; and for the sale of other real property in CCP §§ 701.540–701.680.

[b] Execution Lien

An execution lien remains in effect for two years after the date of issuance, unless the judgment is satisfied sooner. CCP § 697.710. Except for a sale by a superior lien-holder, "if an interest in real property subject to an execution lien is transferred or encumbered, the interest transferred or encumbered remains subject to the lien." § 697.720; *Oliver v. Bledsoe*, 5 Cal. App. 4th 998, 7 Cal. Rptr. 2d 382 (1992) (holding that unless a transfer of liened property comes within one of the enumerated exceptions of § 697.740, the execution lienholder's rights against the property remained as they were before the transfer). Likewise, if personal property subject to an execution lien is transferred or encumbered, the property remains subject to the lien, except for certain purchasers for value without knowledge of the lien and for certain holders in due course as specified in CCP §§ 697.730–697.750. An execution lien created on the same property subject to a prejudgment attachment lien under CCP §§ 481.010–493.060 on the same claim relates back to the date of the earlier lien for purposes of priorities. CCP § 697.020.

[c] Execution and Levy on Personal Property

The procedures for execution on personal property are similar to those for real property, except that, in the absence of some other method specified in CCP

§§ 700.010–700.200, levy upon tangible personal property in the possession or under the control of the judgment debtor is made by the levying officer taking the property into custody. CCP § 700.030. Levy on a deposit account prevents the financial institution from honoring checks or paying other withdrawals from the account. § 700.140.

The procedures for sale of tangible personal property are set forth in CCP §§ 701.510, 701.530–701.680; and for collection of intangible property and accounts receivable in § 701.520. The court may also appoint a receiver to preserve the value of property levied upon "if the court determines that the property is perishable or will greatly deteriorate or greatly depreciate in value or that for some other reason the interests of the parties will be best served." CCP § 699.070.

[5] Exemptions

[a] Property Subject to Enforcement

All property of the judgment debtor is subject to enforcement of a money judgment, except for that property specifically exempted by statute. CCP §§ 695.010, 699.080(a) (specifying categories of real and personal property subject to enforcement). A few statutes do designate certain property as not subject to execution. *E.g.*, CCP § 699.720 (listing specific property including an alcoholic beverage license, a debt other than earnings owing and unpaid by a public entity, the interest of a trust beneficiary, etc.); §§ 695.020–695.060; Labor Code § 4901 (workers' compensation awards); 42 U.S.C. § 407 (Social Security benefits). An even greater variety of property is exempt from execution, but only if the judgment debtor files a written claim of exemption with the levying officer within 10 days after the date of service of the notice of levy. CCP § 703.520. If the exemption is not properly and timely claimed, the exemption is waived and the property is subject to enforcement of a money judgment. CCP § 703.030.

[b] Personal Property Exemptions

Personal property exempt from enforcement if properly claimed include household furnishings, appliances, and personal effects; motor vehicles not to exceed $3,050; jewelry, heirlooms and works of art not to exceed $8,000; personal property used in a trade, business, or profession not to exceed certain statutory maximums; life insurance policies not to exceed $12,800; most private and public retirement benefits; unemployment, disability, and welfare benefits under most circumstances; personal injury, wrongful death, and workers' compensation awards or settlements under some circumstances; as well as numerous other items specified in CCP §§ 704.010–704.210 and several other state and federal statutes. Many of these personal property items are exempt by statute without making a claim; but the claim procedure must be followed, if such property is levied upon, to obtain its release. CCP § 703.510(b). The exemption amounts state above became effective April 1, 2016; these amounts are adjusted every three years. CCP§ 703.150.

The procedure for claiming an exemption is set forth in CCP §§ 703.510–703.610. When the judgment debtor files a timely claim of exemption, the creditor must be notified and has 10 days within which to file a notice of opposition with the court. §§ 703.540–703.570. The claim and opposition constitute pleadings, and will be resolved after noticed-motion hearing by an order of the court. §§ 703.580–503.610. Judicial Council forms may be utilized for making and opposing a claim of exemption. *See, e.g.*, Form EJ-160: Claim of Exemption (Enforcement of Judgment) and EJ-170: Notice of Opposition to Claim of Exemption (Enforcement of Judgment).

Given the short time a judgment debtor has to file a claim of exemption, how does the judgment debtor know which property may be exempt and the procedure for claiming an exemption? Section 700.010 requires the levying officer to serve on the judgment creditor the writ of execution and a notice of levy at the time of levy, as well as Judicial Council Form EJ-155: Exemption from Enforcement of Judgments, which lists the types of property exempt from enforcement as well as the applicable federal or state exemption statute.

[c]   Homestead Exemptions, Generally

Two types of statutory homestead exemptions are available in California to protect a dwelling from enforcement of a judgment. One type is the "declared homestead" authorized by CCP §§ 704.910–704.990, the other is the "automatic homestead" authorized by CCP §§ 704.710–704.850. Regardless of which type is utilized, the total amount of the homestead exemption is the same (the Legislature increases the amount of the homestead exemption from time to time, as it did most recently on January 1, 2013): $75,000 if the judgment debtor is a single person; $100,000 if the judgment debtor or spouse is a member of a family unit, as defined by CCP §§ 704.710(b); or $175,000 if the judgment debtor or spouse is over 65 years of age, is disabled, or of low income. CCP § 704.730. Both types apply to a "dwelling" broadly defined to include a house with outbuildings and land, a mobile home and land, a boat, or a condominium. CCP §§ 704.710(a), 704.910(c).

[d]   Homestead Exemptions: Two Types Overlap

The two types of homestead exemptions substantially overlap in application, but they are distinct and somewhat different statutory rights. *See, e.g., Fidelity Nat. Title Ins. Co. v. Schroeder*, 179 Cal. App. 4th 834, 843–45, 101 Cal. Rptr. 3d 854 (2009) (explaining the differences between the protections afforded by a declared homestead and an automatic homestead exemption); *Title Trust Deed Serv. Co. v. Pearson*, 132 Cal. App. 4th 168, 33 Cal. Rptr. 3d 311 (2005) (same). One obvious difference is that the declared homestead exemption requires that a party file a declaration of homestead in the county recorder's office which identifies the declared homestead owner, describes the declared homestead, and states that the declared homestead is the principal dwelling of the declared homestead owner or spouse. CCP §§ 704.920, 704.930. From the time of recording, the dwelling is a declared homestead for purposes of the exemption. § 704.920.

By contrast, an automatic homestead exemption applies when a party has continuously resided in a dwelling from and after the time that a judgment creditor's lien attached to the dwelling until a court's determination that the exemption applies. CCP § 704.710(c). The judgment debtor must claim this homestead exemption by filing a timely and proper claim pursuant to CCP §§ 703.510–703.610. The automatic homestead statute, does not allow an exemption on property acquired by the debtor after the judgment has been recorded unless that property was purchased with exempt proceeds for the sale, damage or destruction of a homestead within a six-month period. *See SBAM Partners, LLC v. Wang*, 164 Cal. App. 4th 903, 79 Cal. Rptr. 3d 752 (2008).

[e] Homestead Exemptions: Two Types Distinguished

Although continuous residence in the dwelling is a requirement for a successful claim of automatic homestead exemption, the declared homestead provisions do not mandate actual or continuous residence so long as the recorded declaration of homestead states the dwelling is the "principal dwelling," unless abandonment is proven by the judgment creditor. *Webb v. Trippet*, 235 Cal. App. 3d 647, 651, 286 Cal. Rptr. 742 (1991); *see In re Morse*, 11 Cal. 4th 184, 203, 44 Cal. Rptr. 2d 620, 900 P.2d 1170 (1995) (observing that *Webb* shows a declared homestead may, depending on the circumstances, offer an advantage over the automatic homestead exemption). A judgment lien does not attach to a declared homestead which names the judgment debtor as a declared homestead owner and was recorded prior to the time the abstract of judgment was recorded, unless the judgment lien is based on a judgment for child or spousal support. CCP § 704.950. However, as with an automatic homestead exemption, a declared homestead will not prevent the judgment creditor's levy by writ of execution and sale of the dwelling if the judgment debtor's equity exceeds the amount of homestead exemption plus all other existing liens and encumbrances. CCP §§ 704.800, 704.970.

[f] Homestead Exemptions: Procedures

The procedure for the forced sale of a dwelling subject to an automatic homestead exemption pursuant to an order of sale is the same as for the sale of a dwelling subject to a declared homestead exemption, CCP § 704.970(b); 704.740–704.850; as is the distribution of proceeds if the homestead is sold, CCP § 704.850. With either type of homestead, the actual forced sale of the homestead pursuant to a court order for sale is prohibited unless a bid exceeds the amount of the homestead exemption plus other liens and encumbrances on the property. CCP § 704.800.

If a bid is sufficiently high such that the forced sale of a homestead is not precluded by CCP § 704.800, how are the proceeds of the sale distributed? *See* CCP § 704.850. When a homestead is sold pursuant to a forced sale, an amount equal to the applicable homestead exemption must be distributed to the judgment debtor. § 704.850. Is this distributed amount of the sale proceeds then subject to a subsequent execution and levy? *See* CCP § 704.720. Is the homestead amount of the sale proceeds subject to execution and levy if the homestead dwelling is voluntarily sold by the judgment debtor? *See* CCP § 704.960.

Does a statutory homestead exemption apply when the forced sale of a dwelling is pursuant to a power of sale in a deed of trust and not the result of an execution on a money judgment? *See Title Trust Deed Serv. Co. v. Pearson*, 132 Cal. App. 4th 168, 33 Cal. Rptr. 3d 311 (2005) (explaining the different treatment afforded an automatic homestead and a declared homestead in the context of whether the exemption applies to the proceeds of a trustee's sale under a power of sale in a deed of trust); *Spencer v. Lowery*, 235 Cal. App. 3d 1636, 1 Cal. Rptr. 2d 795 (1991). Are judgment debtors who continuously reside in their dwellings but have conveyed title to another eligible for the statutory homestead exemption? *See, e.g., Broadway Foreclosure Inv., LLC v. Tarlesson*, 184 Cal. App. 4th 931, 109 Cal. Rptr. 3d 319 (2010) (holding judgment debtors who continuously reside in their dwellings retain a sufficient equity interest in the property to claim a homestead exemption even when they have conveyed title to another).

[6] Wage Garnishment

One of the most effective and efficient means of enforcing a money judgment is by a wage garnishment pursuant to the Wage Garnishment Law, CCP §§ 706.010–706.154. The Wage Garnishment Law authorizes a process by which the judgment creditor can compel the judgment debtor's employer to withhold a portion of the judgment debtor's earnings for subsequent collection to satisfy the money judgment. "Earnings" is broadly defined to include all compensation payable by an employer to an employee for personal services performed, "whether denominated as wages, salary, commission, bonus, or otherwise." CCP § 706.011(a).

[a] Wage Garnishment Procedures

To accomplish a wage garnishment, the judgment creditor must first obtain a writ of execution and apply for issuance of an earnings withholding order with the appropriate levying officer, and cause the levying officer to serve the earnings withholding order upon the employer of the judgment debtor. CCP §§ 706.021–706.029, 706.101–706.103. The Judicial Council has approved mandatory forms for use in applying for an earnings withholding order, as well as for the Earnings Withholding Order and for most other aspects of the wage garnishment process. *See* CCP § 706.120; Forms WG-001-WG-035. Upon proper service of an earnings withholding order, the employer has a duty to notify the employee-judgment debtor of the order, CCP §§ 706.104, 706.122; and, ultimately, to withhold the amounts required by the order and pay them over to the levying officer, § 706.022.

[b] Exemptions

Garnishment of wages is subject to several important restrictions, including earnings exemptions and various time limitations. CCP §§ 706.050–706.052; 15 USC § 1673.

Generally speaking, under these exemptions the maximum amount of an employee's earnings subject to garnishment cannot exceed 25% of the employee's take-home pay for that week, 15 U.S.C. §1673; and may even be less or zero in certain circumstances where the judgment debtor proves the earnings are necessary to support the judgment debtor or the judgment debtor's family. CCP §706.051. The maximum amount subject to wage garnishment may be as high as 50% of earnings, however, where the wage garnishment is based on a withholding order or earnings assignment order for child or spousal support. §§706.052, 706.030. A judgment debtor must apply for a wage garnishment exemption by filing a timely and proper claim of exemption and a financial statement. §706.105. If the judgment creditor contests the claimed exemption by filing a timely notice of opposition, the judgment creditor is entitled to a hearing on the claim of exemption. §706.105. An appeal lies from any court order denying a claim of exemption, or modifying or terminating an earnings withholding order. §706.105(j).

[c] Restrictions on Employer

An employer, when required by a wage withholding order to withhold and account for a portion of an employee's earnings, usually views its wage garnishment duties as an administrative nuisance. Can an employer eliminate this nuisance by simply refusing to comply with the wage withholding order? *See* CCP §706.022, 706.154. By postponing or advancing the payment of the employee's earnings to prevent the order from taking effect? *See* CCP §§706.152, 706.153. By firing the employee because of the earnings withholding order and garnishment? *See* Labor Code §2929; 15 U.S.C. §1674. Do the earnings exemptions of CCP §706.050 apply to the earnings of a self-employed person? *See Moses v. DeVersecy*, 157 Cal. App. 3d 1071, 203 Cal. Rptr. 906 (1984). How are priorities determined when multiple earnings withholding orders are served on an employer, each seeking to garnish the wages of the same employee? *See* CCP §§706.023, 706.031, 706.077.

[7] *Enforcement of Judgments Against Public Entities*

[a] Duty of Local Public Entity to Pay Judgments

The Enforcement of Judgments Law, CCP §§680.010–724.260, does not apply to enforcement of a money judgment against a public entity; instead, the enforcement provisions of Government Code §§965–965.9 or §§970–971.2 control. CCP §695.050; Gov. Code §§970.1(b) (local public entity), 965.5(b) (state). Government Code §970.2 imposes a duty on a local public entity to pay a judgment entered against it, and authorizes use of a writ of mandate to compel performance of this duty. *See, e.g., Barkley v. City of Blue Lake*, 18 Cal. App. 4th 1745, 23 Cal. Rptr. 2d 315 (1993). Debt limitations and restrictions on tax rates do not apply to tort judgments against local public entities. Gov. Code §971. Upon proper showing of unreasonable hardship, however, a court may order payment of a judgment in installments. Gov. Code §§970.6(a), 984 (Up to ten annual installments of equal amount). What are the policy reasons for excepting public entities from the execution and levy provisions of the Enforcement of Judgments Law?

[b] Duty of State with Respect to Payment of Judgments

The State is also under a duty to pay judgments against it, and acts toward payment may be compelled by a writ of mandate. Gov. Code § 965.7(a). However, a court cannot require the State, or an officer or employee of the State, to pay a tort liability claim, settlement, or judgment unless the payment is authorized by the Legislature, or other appropriate state official or department has certified that sufficient appropriation for such payment exists. Gov. Code § 965.6. What happens when the requisite authorization or certification does not exist? How can a judgment against the State be enforced if the Legislature refuses to appropriate funds for that purpose? *See* Gov. Code § 965.6. Can a state agency be compelled to pay an award of attorney fees to a successful party even though the Legislature expressly refused to appropriate funds to pay the fee award? *See Mandel v. Myers*, 29 Cal. 3d 531, 174 Cal. Rptr. 841, 629 P.2d 935 (1981) (holding that where Legislature has already appropriated funds sufficient to pay judgment, it was under a constitutional obligation to pay attorney fee award despite Legislature's intent to deny payment of a specific fee award).

[c] Judgment Against Public Employee

If the judgment is against a public employee for tort injuries arising out of an act which occurred within the scope of employment, the judgment can be enforced under the general Enforcement of Judgments Law. *See* CCP § 695.050. In most cases, however, if the employee requests the public entity employer to defend and reasonably cooperates in good faith in the defense of the action, the public entity employer must pay the judgment or settlement, including payment of punitive damages in certain circumstances. Gov. Code § 825.

[8] *Debtor Examinations and Other Discovery Devices*

The various procedures for the enforcement of a money judgment mean very little unless the judgment creditor can ascertain the existence and location of the judgment debtor's assets. The Enforcement of Judgments Law makes some useful discovery devices available for use by the judgment creditor at any time a money judgment is enforceable, unless stayed during appeal. CCP § 708.010. Section 708.020 authorizes the judgment creditor to propound written interrogatories to the judgment creditor as provided by CCP §§ 2030.030–2030.410; and § 708.030 authorizes demands for production and inspection of documents in accordance with CCP §§ 2031.010–2031.510. Section 708.120 authorizes similar discovery options with respect to third parties who possess or control property in which the judgment debtor has an interest. *See, e.g., SCC Acquisitions, Inc. v. Superior Court*, 243 Cal. App. 4th 741, 196 Cal. Rptr. 3d 533 (2015) (holding trial court properly granted motion to compel postjudgment requests for production of documents relating to third parties); *Fox Johns Lazar Pekin & Wexler, APC v. Superior Court*, 219 Cal. App. 4th 1216, 162 Cal. Rptr. 3d 571 (2013) (discussing the limited scope of third-party discovery under §708.120).

[a] Debtor's Examination

Another extremely useful discovery tool is the debtor's examination authorized by CCP §§708.110–708.205; *see Lee v. Swansboro Country Property Owners Assn.*, 151 Cal. App. 4th 575, 580–582, 59 Cal. Rptr. 3d 924 (2007) (summarizing discovery options available to a judgment creditor and discussing the advantages and disadvantages of debtor's examinations versus other discovery devices). Upon proper application by the judgment creditor, the court may order the judgment debtor to appear before the court or a referee at a specific time and place "to furnish information to aid in enforcement of the money judgment." CCP §708.110. If the judgment debtor fails to appear, the court may punish the judgment debtor for contempt. §§708.110(e), 708.170.

The proper court for the debtor's examination is the court in which the money judgment is entered, although another court may be appropriate if the judgment debtor does not reside or work in the county where the court of entry is located. §708.160. In appropriate circumstances the judgment creditor may also utilize these proceedings to examine third parties indebted to the judgment debtor or in possession of or in control of property in which the judgment debtor has an interest. §708.120; *see, e.g., Evans v. Paye*, 32 Cal. App. 4th 265, 37 Cal. Rptr. 2d 915 (1995) (ruling that upon third party's denial of an obligation owed to the judgment debtor, trial court properly conducted a hearing pursuant to §708.180 to determine whether the third party in fact owed money to the judgment debtor).

These examination proceedings function not only as a broad discovery device, but may also result in an order by the court or referee which resolves contested exemption claims, punishes for contempt, forbids transfer or other disposition of property interests, and creates a lien on property or debt. CCP §§708.140–708.205. In light of these multiple purposes, what should the attorney for the judgment creditor do in preparation for such an examination proceeding? *See* CEB, *Debt Collection in California*, §8.15–8.36 (2d ed. 2015).

[9] *Creditors' Suits and Other Miscellaneous Creditors' Remedies*

[a] Creditors' Suits

If a third person has possession and control of property in which the judgment debtor has an interest, or is indebted to the judgment debtor, a judgment creditor may bring an action against the third person to have the interest or debt applied to the satisfaction of the money judgment. CCP §708.210. The judgment debtor must be joined as a party to the action, but is not an indispensable party. §708.220. Service of the summons on the third person creates a lien on the property interest of, or debt owed to, the judgment debtor. §708.250. The judgment debtor may assert any claim of exemption applicable to the property or debt, which will then be determined by the court as part of the action. §§ 708.260, 708.280. If the judgment creditor establishes that the third person has property or a debt in which the judgment debtor has an interest, the court may order that the property or debt be applied to the satisfaction of the judgment. CCP § 708.280.

[b] Other Creditors' Remedies

Other remedies available to a judgment creditor to enforce a money judgment in appropriate circumstances include a charging order, CCP § 708.310–708.320; a lien in a pending action or special proceeding, §§ 708.410–708.480; an assignment order, §§ 708.510–708.560; and appointment of a receiver, §§ 708.620–708.630. Special procedures govern collection of a judgment where the judgment debtor is a creditor of a public entity, CCP §§ 708.710–708.795; enforcement against a franchise, §§ 708.910–708.930; and enforcement against a judgment debtor beneficial interest in certain trusts, § 709.010.

[C] Third-Party Claims

Many of the methods of levy available under the Enforcement of Judgments Law, when utilized by the judgment creditor, will adversely affect the rights and interests of persons not parties to the action. A third person claiming ownership or right to possession of real property levied upon, or a security interest or lien superior to a judgment creditor's lien on personal property, may file a third-party claim with the levying officer. CCP §§ 720.110–720.290. A proper and timely third-party claim may result in release of the property or in the filing of an undertaking by the judgment creditor, CCP §§ 720.150–720.290, 720.610–720.800; and in a court hearing to determine the validity of the third-party claim and the proper disposition of the property subject to the claim, §§ 720.310–720.430.

[D] Effect of Appeal on Enforcement of Money Judgment

The perfecting of an appeal by filing a timely notice of appeal does not automatically stay trial court proceedings to enforce a money judgment, unless a sufficient undertaking (bond) is given as specified in CCP § 917.1. The bond must be filed with the court and served on the beneficiary judgment creditor. CCP §§ 995.340(a), 995.370. The bond is effective when given; court approval is not a prerequisite. §§ 995.410(a), 995.420(a). For additional discussion of this and other methods of obtaining a stay on appeal, see § 15.01[F], Stays Pending Appeal, *infra*.

If enforcement of a judgment is stayed on appeal by the giving of a sufficient undertaking, existing enforcement liens are extinguished and new ones cannot be created during the period of the stay. CCP § 697.040(a). What happens to property and funds held in levy and subject to an execution lien when the judgment debtor subsequently perfects an appeal and meets the requirements of a stay by giving a sufficient bond? If the filing of the bond extinguishes the execution lien, must the property held subject to the lien be released and the funds returned? *Adir Int'l. LLC v. Superior Court*, 216 Cal. App. 4th 996, 157 Cal. Rptr. 3d 362 (2013) (ruling a trial court has no statutory authority to order a judgment creditor to return to a judgment debtor funds already disbursed to the creditor by the levying officer); *California Commerce Bank v. Superior Court*, 8 Cal. App. 4th 582, 10 Cal. Rptr. 2d 418 (1992) (holding where debtor obtains stay of execution pending appeal, funds held by levying officer but not yet disbursed to judgment creditor must be released and returned to the debtor).

Where one party collects money by executing on a judgment that is later overturned on appeal, the other party may seek restitution of the collected funds upon remand. CCP § 908. The court may award interest on the amount of restitution, unless to do so would be inequitable under the circumstances. *Cussler v. Crusader Enter., LLC*, 212 Cal. App. 4th 356, 369–70, 150 Cal. Rptr. 3d 895 (2012) (collecting cases).

[E]   Independent Action on Judgment

The Enforcement of Judgments Law authorizes a variety of methods of execution on an existing money judgment, as well as several supplementary or ancillary proceedings. This law expressly authorizes a judgment creditor to bring an independent action on a domestic judgment. CCP § 683.050. In other words, a judgment creditor retains the traditional option of filing a new separate action against the judgment debtor to enforce an existing money judgment. *See, e.g., Barkley v. City of Blue Lake*, 18 Cal. App. 4th 1745, 1751, 23 Cal. Rptr. 2d 315 (1993) (action against public entity); *Pratali v. Gates*, 4 Cal. App. 4th 632, 637, 5 Cal. Rptr. 2d 733 (1992) (action involving private parties).

[1]   Alternative Method to Extend Enforceable Life of Judgment

As discussed previously, a money judgment is enforceable for a 10-year period after entry and may be extended by renewal of the judgment prior to expiration of this 10-year period of enforceability. CCP §§ 683.130, 683.020. A separate action on the judgment is an alternative method to extend the enforceable life of a judgment. *Pratali, supra*, 4 Cal. App. 4th 637–38; *Green v. Zissis*, 5 Cal. App. 4th 1219, 1222, 7 Cal. Rptr. 2d 406 (1992). The statute of limitations for an action on a judgment is 10 years. CCP § 337.5.

[2]   Ten-Year Limitation Period

The 10-year period for *renewal* provided by CCP § 683.030 and the 10-year statute of limitations for a separate action provided by CCP § 337.5 are not coterminous. *Pratali, supra*, 4 Cal. App. 4th at 638. The period for renewal prescribed in § 683.020 commences on the date of entry and is not tolled for any reason; the statute of limitations for an independent action commences to run when the judgment is final and may be tolled, such as by the debtor's absence from the state under CCP § 351. *Pratali,*

4 Cal. App. 4th at 638–39. Consequently, an action on a judgment may be commenced after the period for obtaining execution of the original judgment has expired if the statute of limitations provided by § 337.5 has not yet expired. *See, e.g.*, *Green v. Zissis*, 5 Cal. App. 4th 1219, 1222–23, 7 Cal. Rptr. 2d 406 (1992); *Pratali*, 4 Cal. App. 4th at 636–39. Apart from such circumstances where an independent action is the only means of enforcement available because the time for renewal has expired, are there any other reasons for a judgment creditor to commence a new separate action on a judgment rather than use the execution methods of the Enforcement of Judgments Act? What are they?

[F]   Satisfaction of Judgment

Upon satisfaction of a money judgment as the result of levy or of the judgment debtor's payment, the judgment creditor must immediately file an acknowledgment of satisfaction of judgment with the court. CCP §§ 724.010, 724.030, 724.060 (specifying contents of acknowledgment). The judgment debtor, or other affected property owner or lienholder, may demand in writing that the judgment creditor file and deliver such an acknowledgment. § 724.050(a) & (b). If the judgment creditor does not comply with this demand within 15 days, the person making the demand may compel such filing or delivery by noticed motion and court order. § 724.050(c),(d) & (e). When an acknowledgment is filed or a writ is returned satisfied for the full amount of the judgment, the court clerk must enter satisfaction of the money judgment in the register of actions. § 724.020. Upon such entry, the clerk when requested must issue a certificate of satisfaction of judgment. § 724.100. Similar procedures apply to acknowledgment of partial satisfaction of judgment under CCP §§ 724.110– 724.120, and for acknowledgment of satisfaction of matured installments under CCP § 724.210–726.260.

What are the purposes of the acknowledgment of satisfaction of judgment? If an abstract of a money judgment has been recorded and the judgment is subsequently satisfied, CCP § 724.040 requires the judgment creditor to not only file an acknowledgment of satisfaction of judgment with the court but also to serve a copy on the judgment debtor. What are the purposes of this service requirement? Why is this satisfaction of judgment process, including the ability to compel compliance by court order, important to judgment debtors and interested third parties? A court cannot compel entry of satisfaction of judgment, of course, unless it first determines whether the judgment has in fact been satisfied.

[G]   Recovery of Enforcement Costs and Attorney Fees

Under CCP § 685.040, a judgment creditor is entitled to the reasonable and necessary costs of enforcing a judgment, including attorney fees where the underlying judgment includes an award of attorney fees to the judgment creditor pursuant to CCP § 1033.5(a)(10)(A). Section 685.040 does not create an independent authority for awarding attorney fees; a judgment creditor cannot seek fees under the substantive authority of §685.040 itself. *Conservatorship of McQueen*, 59 Cal. 4th 602, 612–14, 174 Cal. Rptr. 3d 55, 328 P.3d 46 (2014). In other words, when a contract, fee-shifting statute, or common law doctrine provides the authority for an award of attorney fees, any such fees incurred in the enforcement of the judgment are within the scope of CCP §685.040. *Conservatorship of McQueen, supra* (fee-shifting statute); *Gray1 CPB, LLC v. SCC Acquisitions, Inc.*, 233 Cal. App. 4th 882, 182, Cal. Rtpr. 3d 654 (2015) (contract).

A motion to claim enforcement costs and attorney fees must be made "before the judgment is satisfied in full," but not later than two years after the costs and fees have been incurred. CCP §685.080(a). For example, if the judgment debtor tenders full payment of the judgment by check which the judgment creditor accepts before claiming costs and fees, a subsequent memorandum of costs or costs motion will be untimely. *Conservatorship of McQueen, supra*, 59 Cal. 4th at 614–16 (holding plaintiff's motion to collect enforcement costs filed 10 days after plaintiff accepted and cashed defendant's check in full satisfaction of judgment was untimely); *Gray1 CPB, supra*, 233 Cal. App. 4th at 893–99 (holding judgment creditor's motion for enforcement attorney fees was untimely where motion filed 12 days after judgment creditor accepted a cashier's check which fully satisfied the judgment). What options are available to a judgment creditor who has not yet filed a cost memorandum or cost motion when the judgment debtor tenders an uncertified check which constitutes full satisfaction of the outstanding judgment? What about a certified check? Cash? *See Conservatorship of McQueen, supra*, 59 Cal. 4th at 614–16.

[H]   Enforcement of Injunctions and Other Nonmoney Judgments

In re Feiock

Court of Appeal of California, Fourth Appellate District
215 Cal. App. 3d 141, 263 Cal. Rptr. 437 (1989)

WALLIN, JUSTICE.

We originally granted the petition for a writ in this case. It returns to us by way of writ of certiorari from the United States Supreme Court vacating the judgment and remanding for further proceedings. Based upon new arguments, we deny the writ of habeas corpus.

I

The underlying facts remain the same. We reproduce them here with the necessary procedural update:

"Phillip Feiock seeks relief from a judgment of contempt for failure to pay child support. His primary contention concerns the constitutionality of Code of Civil Procedure section 1209.5, which requires the court presume prima facie evidence of contempt after proof of noncompliance with a valid court order.

"Feiock was ordered to pay child support for his three children as part of a dissolution action. Thereafter, in 1983 the district attorney filed an action under the Uniform Reciprocal Enforcement of Support Act, which resulted in a temporary support order of $150 per month. Feiock's failure to pay anything between September of 1984 and February of 1985 resulted in a contempt action brought by the district attorney.

"At the adjudicated contempt hearing, the parties stipulated there was a valid court order requiring Feiock to pay $150 per month directly to the district attorney's office. They also agreed Feiock was present in court when the order was made. The prosecution then offered documentary evidence from its own internal records showing Feiock's poor payment history.... [A]n employee familiar with the record-keeping procedures testified ... [about those documents]. Feiock's motion for [nonsuit] was denied after the judge ruled the presumption mandated by Code of Civil Procedure section 1209.5 applied. Feiock then testified, essentially trying to prove his inability to pay the court-ordered support. Regardless, the trial judge sustained the majority of the contempt allegations." (*In re Feiock* [(1986)] 180 Cal. App. 3d [640] at pp. 651–652 [225 Cal. Rptr. 748].)

In the prior proceedings in this court, Feiock argued that section [Code of Civil Procedure] 1209.5 created the type of mandatory presumption found violative of the due process clause in *Sandstrom v. Montana* (1979) 442 U.S. 510 [61 L. Ed. 2d 39, 99 S. Ct. 2450] and *People v. Roder* (1983) 33 Cal. 3d 491 [189 Cal. Rptr. 501, 658 P.2d 1302].... [W]e agreed with Feiock....

After hearing the case, the United States Supreme Court remanded the cause to this court to determine whether the contempt here was civil or criminal, opining that the former does not trigger application of the due process clause to presumptions. In reaching this conclusion, the high court deferred to state law on two points subsumed within our holding: ability to pay is an element of the contempt rather than a defense, and the "presumption" shifts the burden of proof rather than the burden of producing evidence.

Upon this remand, we are presented with the issue whether ability to pay is an affirmative defense. Before deciding it, we discuss the threshold question whether the proceeding here was a civil or criminal contempt.

II

In a nutshell, the Supreme Court opined that a contempt is civil for federal constitutional purposes if the order of contempt ultimately entered allows the contemner to purge the contempt by performing an act completely within the contemner's control. In such circumstances the due process considerations discussed in *People v. Roder, supra*, are inapplicable. If the contemner does not have the power to purge the contempt, the proceedings are deemed criminal.

Using that standard, the proceedings here were unmistakably criminal in nature. It is true, as noted by the Supreme Court, that Feiock had a chance to pay off the arrearage of $1,650 within the 36-month probationary period at the ordered rate of

$50 per month. However, there is not a hint in the order that the probation — considered a penalty by the Supreme Court — would terminate when the arrearage was paid off.

The judgment suspends 25 days of jail time over Feiock's head and requires that he pay $150 per month in current child support. By the plain terms of the judgment, that obligation continues for the entire term of the probation. The section of the preprinted judgment form providing for further hearing for modification is not checked. Feiock's penalty for disobedience of the original child support order was a 36-month certain probationary period with the prospect of 25 days in jail if he violated its terms. There was nothing Feiock could do, per the terms of the judgment, to alter this fact. He was subjected to criminal contempt proceedings.

III

Nevertheless, the trial court correctly denied the motion for nonsuit. For many years in California ability to pay has been considered, without much analysis, to be a matter of defense in contempt proceedings. (*In re McCarty* (1908), 154 Cal. 534, 537 [98 P. 540]; [citations omitted]....) This approach is consistent with legislative intent, constitutional law, and common sense. When this case was first before this court, the parties and the court all assumed that section 1209.5 dealt with an evidentiary presumption. It does not. [The language and purpose of section 1209.5 indicate that once] the contempt is proved any excuse or justification, such as failure to pay, is a matter of defense.

Court decisions have long upheld the constitutionality of legislation making issues such as inability to pay matters of defense. (*See Martin v. Ohio* (1987) 480 U.S. 228 [94 L. Ed. 2d 267, 107 S. Ct. 1098]; * * * Thus, there is no constitutional impediment to making inability to pay an affirmative defense, at least if there is some rational basis for doing so.

Common sense dictates that the contemner raise inability to pay. The contemner is the person in the best position to know whether inability to pay is even a consideration in the proceeding and also has the best access to evidence on the issue, particularly in cases of self-employment. Considerations of policy and convenience have led courts to sanction placement of the burden of establishing a defense on defendants under similar circumstances.

IV

* * *

Lastly, Feiock argues that at the time the original order issued, there was no finding of ability to pay. This is simply not true. Although Feiock was self-employed and any income projection was somewhat tenuous, he estimated at the hearing that he would be netting approximately $1,200 per month above housing expenses. The court, while recognizing his income could change, reasonably found Feiock had the ability to pay $150 per month.

The order to show cause is discharged and the petition for writ is denied.

Notes and Questions on the Use of Contempt Proceedings to Enforce Nonmoney Judgments

(1) In *Moss v. Superior Court*, 17 Cal. 4th 396, 71 Cal. Rptr. 2d 215, 950 P.2d 59 (1998), the California Supreme Court held there is no constitutional impediment to use of the contempt power to punish a parent for violation of a judicial child support order when the parent's financial inability to comply with the order is the result of the parent's wilful failure to seek and accept available employment that is commensurate with his or her skills and ability. The Court also addressed the allocation of the burden of proof in such contempt proceedings. Quoting extensively from *In re Feiock*, the *Moss* court concluded that the ability to comply with a support order is not an element of the contempt offense. Rather, agreeing with the opinion in *Feiock*, the Supreme Court ruled that inability to pay is an affirmative defense which must be raised by the alleged contemner.

(2) *Contempt for Disobedience of Judgment.* As *Feiock* indicates, CCP § 1209(a)(5) provides that disobedience of any lawful judgment, order, or process of a court constitutes contempt of that court. Also, CCP § 717.010 provides that a judgment not otherwise enforceable pursuant to the Enforcement of Judgments Law may be enforced by personally serving a certified copy of the judgment on the person required to obey the judgment and invoking the power of the court to punish for contempt. Does CCP § 717.010 mean that a person cannot be held in contempt for violation of an injunction unless the judgment of injunction was personally served on that person? *See, e.g., Ross v. Superior Court*, 19 Cal. 3d 899, 905–909, 141 Cal. Rptr. 133, 569 P.2d 727 (1977) (ruling an injunction binds all those with actual notice of its terms, including defendants and their agents, and need not be personally served on them to subject them to contempt for disobedience). If not, to what types of judgments does CCP § 717.010 apply?

(3) *Injunction Must Be Certain and Valid.* A court may grant an injunction under the circumstances described in CCP § 526 or Civil Code § 3422. If a defendant fails to obey the injunction, the plaintiff may seek an order of contempt to compel compliance. *See, e.g., City of Vernon v. Superior Court*, 38 Cal. 2d 509, 241 P.2d 243 (1952). A defendant cannot be found guilty of contempt, however, if the injunction violated is so uncertain that the defendant could not determine what the injunction required him to do or not to do. *Id.* at 513; *Reliable Enter., Inc. v. Superior Court*, 158 Cal. App. 3d 604, 615, 204 Cal. Rptr. 786 (1984). What is the constitutional basis for this certainty requirement? To be enforceable against a defendant, an injunction order must be directed against that defendant, either by naming the defendant as an individual or by designating a class of persons to which the defendant belongs. *See Planned Parenthood Golden Gate v. Garibaldi*, 107 Cal. App. 4th 345, 132 Cal. Rptr. 2d 46 (2003) (holding an injunction order that applies to "all persons with actual notice of this judgment" does not bind a nonparty who has actual notice of the order).

(4) *Justifications for Noncompliance with Injunction.* If a defendant has knowledge of the terms of an injunction and the ability to comply with them but takes actions which do not comply, such actions create an inference that the disobedience was in-

tentional. *City of Vernon v. Superior Court*, *supra*, 38 Cal. 2d at 518. Can the defendant justify this disobedience to a court and avoid a contempt conviction on the grounds of advice of counsel, mistake of law, or good faith? *See id.* Can the defendant challenge the validity of the injunction as a defense to a contempt proceeding? *See, e.g., Welton v. City of L. A.*, 18 Cal. 3d 497, 507–508, 134 Cal. Rptr. 668, 556 P.2d 1119 (1976) (vacating contempt order because an injunction based on an unconstitutional ordinance exceeded the issuing court's jurisdiction); *In re Berry*, 68 Cal. 2d 137, 65 Cal. Rptr. 273, 436 P.2d 273 (1968) (holding disobedience of an unconstitutional order cannot validly be punished by contempt).

(5) *Contempt Procedures.* The procedure for initiating a contempt proceeding is outlined in CCP § 1211: "When the contempt is not committed in the immediate view and presence of the court, or of the judge at chambers, an affidavit shall be presented to the court or judge of the facts constituting the contempt." The affidavit functions like a pleading in that it frames the issues and must charge facts which show a contempt has been committed. *Reliable Enter., Inc. v. Superior Court*, 158 Cal. App. 3d 604, 616, 204 Cal. Rptr. 786 (1984). Although the affidavit provides notice of the contempt charges, it may be amended to conform to the facts proved at the contempt hearing. CCP § 1211.5. A judgment of contempt will not be set aside because of defects or insufficiencies in the affidavit, unless the court concludes based on the evidence that the error complained of resulted in a miscarriage of justice. CCP § 1211.5(c).

When an affidavit showing contempt is filed, an order to show cause for contempt is issued and must be served on the alleged contemnor. CCP § 1212. The alleged contemnor may also be brought before the court by a warrant of attachment or arrest; and is entitled to answer the charges and present evidence at a hearing. CCP §§ 1212–1217. Although California defines civil and criminal contempt in separate statutes, CCP § 1218 and § 1219, the same procedural rules apply to both types of proceedings. CCP §§ 1209–1222; *Hicks v. Feiock*, 485 U.S. 624, 631, n.4, 108 S. Ct. 1423, 99 L. Ed. 2d 721 (1988).

(6) *Punishment for Contempt.* If, after answer and an evidentiary hearing, the court determines that a person is guilty of the contempt charged, the court may impose a fine not exceeding $1,000 or imprisonment not exceeding five days, or both. CCP § 1218(a) (criminal contempt). As *In re Feiock* indicates, different punishments are authorized for violations of certain family law orders. CCP § 1218(c). When the contempt consists of failure to perform an act which is yet in the power of the person to perform, he or she may be imprisoned until he or she has performed the act. CCP § 1219 (civil contempt). The punishment for civil coercive contempt may therefore be greater than for criminal punitive contempt. Why? What are the policy reasons for making the consequences of civil contempt potentially harsher than for criminal contempt?

(7) *Rights of Persons in Criminal Contempt Proceedings.* Criminal penalties may not be imposed on a contemnor who has not been afforded the protections that the U.S. Constitution requires of such criminal proceedings, including the requirement that the offense be proved beyond a reasonable doubt, *Hicks v. Feiock*, 485 U.S. 624, 632, 108 S. Ct. 1423, 99 L. Ed. 2d 721 (1988); *Mitchell v. Superior Court*, 49 Cal. 3d

1230, 265 Cal. Rptr. 144, 783 P.2d 731 (1989); *Ross v. Superior Court, supra,* 19 Cal. 3d at 913–916; and the protection against self-incrimination, *Hotaling v. Superior Court,* 191 Cal. 501, 217 P. 73 (1923) (ruling because contempt proceeding is quasi-criminal, the accused cannot be compelled to testify); *In re Witherspoon,* 162 Cal. App. 3d 1000, 209 Cal. Rptr. 67 (1984) (observing an alleged contemnor has an absolute right to refuse to appear as a witness in criminal contempt proceedings).

Because the basic statutory procedure for initiating and hearing a contempt charge is the same in California for both criminal and civil contempt, the court should make an early determination of whether the proceedings are criminal or civil. Should the court *assume* in all cases that the alleged contemnor is charged with criminal contempt and proceed accordingly? Why might this be a prudent assumption? Under what circumstances may a court safely determine that the proceedings are for civil contempt?

(8) *Constitutional Test for Determining Whether Contempt is Civil or Criminal.* The U.S. Supreme Court in *Hicks v. Feiock, supra,* 485 U.S. at 631–641, delineated the federal constitutional test for determining whether a contempt is civil or criminal. The central focus of this test is on the character of the relief imposed, and not on the purpose for which the relief was sought. *Hicks, supra,* 485 U.S. at 635–637. The Court observed that an unconditional remedy is criminal in nature because it is solely and exclusively punitive in character, whereas a conditional penalty is civil because it is specifically designed to compel the doing of some act. *Id.* at 633. The Court also noted that in contempt cases, both civil and criminal relief has aspects that can be seen as either remedial or punitive, or both, in purpose. *Id.* at 635. Consequently, conclusions about the purposes for which relief is imposed are properly drawn from an examination of the character of the relief itself. *Id.* at 636.

(9) *Contempt of Family Law Orders.* Whether a contempt proceeding is civil or criminal comes up most often in family law cases such as *Feiock* where one former spouse has violated a court's support or visitation order. *See, e.g., People v. Batey,* 183 Cal. App. 3d 1281, 228 Cal. Rptr. 787 (1986); *People v. Derner,* 182 Cal. App. 3d 588, 227 Cal. Rptr. 344 (1986). The determination of whether the contempt proceeding is civil or criminal not only affects the nature of the due process rights afforded the contemnor, but also whether a subsequent criminal prosecution will place the contemptor twice in jeopardy for the same offense. *See, e.g., People v. Derner, supra; People v. Batey, supra.*

(10) *Other Nonmoney Judgments.* A variety of other nonmoney remedies are available through litigation in California, such as a judgment for possession of real or personal property, CCP §§ 740–749.5; judicial foreclosure of mortgages, §§ 725a–730.5; a judgment quieting title to real property, §§ 760.010–764.080; and a judgment of partition or sale of real property, §§ 872.010–874.240. The appropriate corresponding code sections should be consulted for any special enforcement procedures which may apply for each such type of nonmoney judgment. In the absence of any special statutory enforcement procedures, how are these nonmoney judgments enforced? *See* CCP § 717.010.

[I]   Enforcement of Sister State Judgments

Silbrico Corp. v. Raanan

Court of Appeal of California, Second Appellate District
170 Cal. App. 3d 202, 216 Cal. Rptr. 201 (1985)

ARABIAN, JUSTICE.

INTRODUCTION

Defendant and appellant Perry Raanan (appellant) appeals a California judgment which gave full faith and credit to a Wisconsin money judgment rendered in favor of plaintiff (judgment creditor) and respondent Silbrico Corporation (Silbrico). Affirmed.

FACTS

The original litigation in this action arose out of a roofing project at a Wisconsin shopping center. That litigation was settled and a "Stipulation and Order for Dismissal" was filed in the Wisconsin Circuit Court on October 21, 1982. The stipulation was signed by, inter alia, appellant's attorney on September 30, 1982, in Milwaukee, Wisconsin. The stipulation provided that appellant would pay $12,500 to Silbrico's attorneys, but in the event that sum was not paid, written notice of default was to be given to the defaulting party and, if the default was not cured within seven days of such notice, judgment could be entered in the amount of $16,000.

On February 24, 1983, the $12,500 not having been paid, Silbrico moved the Wisconsin court for judgment in the amount of $16,000. Silbrico's motion was supported by the affidavit of Silbrico's attorney, who averred that on October 25, 1982, he notified appellant's attorney of the default pursuant to the provisions of the stipulation. He further averred that the default was not cured and that no sums whatever had been paid by appellant to Silbrico or to its attorneys. On March 3, 1983, judgment was entered in the Wisconsin Circuit Court in the amount of $16,000.

On July 28, 1983, pursuant to Code of Civil Procedure section 1710.25,[1] a California judgment was entered in the Los Angeles Superior Court based on this sister state money judgment.

On November 17, 1983, appellant moved to vacate the July 28, 1983, California judgment pursuant to Code of Civil Procedure section 1710.40 on the grounds that the Wisconsin judgment violated his due process rights to trial, notice and hearing

---

1. Code of Civil Procedure section 1710.25 provides:
   "(a) Upon the filing of the application, the clerk shall enter a judgment based upon the application for the total of the following amounts as shown therein:
   "(1) The amount remaining unpaid under the sister state judgment.
   "(2) The amount of interest accrued on the sister state judgment (computed at the rate of interest applicable to the judgment under the law of the sister state).
   "(3) The amount of the fee for filing the application for entry of the sister state judgment."(b) Entry shall be made in the same manner as entry of an original judgment of the court. From the time of entry, interest shall accrue on the judgment so entered at the rate of interest applicable to a judgment entered in this state."

and that he was not personally given notice of the default as required by the terms of the stipulation.

Thereafter, the parties stipulated to take appellant's motion to vacate the California judgment off calendar. Then, in order to cure appellant's claim of inadequate notice, Silbrico caused the March 3, 1983, Wisconsin judgment to be vacated and on February 20, 1984, caused a new Wisconsin judgment to be entered in the Wisconsin Circuit Court.

In support of its motion for entry of a new Wisconsin judgment, Silbrico had submitted the affidavit of its attorney, who averred that on December 2, 1983, appellant and his attorney were again officially notified of the default pursuant to the terms of the stipulation for dismissal, that the letter was received by appellant on December 6, 1983, and that the default had still not been cured nor any sums paid to Silbrico.

Silbrico then moved in the Los Angeles Superior Court to vacate the California judgment entered on July 28, 1983, and further moved the court to enter a new California judgment based on the new February 20, 1984, sister state judgment. Appellant opposed the motion on the grounds that (1) the Wisconsin stipulated judgment failed to meet the requirements of California Code of Civil Procedure section 1133 pertaining to "judgment by confession" and (2) that the $3,500 increase in the judgment, from $12,500 to $16,000 in the event of default, was an unenforceable "penalty" under California law. On May 11, 1984, the court granted Silbrico's motions and entered a new California judgment based on the second Wisconsin judgment. Appellant's appeal is from that May 11, 1984, California judgment.

CONTENTIONS

The Wisconsin stipulated judgment may not be given full faith and credit in a California court:

1. Because it does not meet the requirements of California Code of Civil Procedure section 1133 which pertains to "judgments by confession."

2. Because it contains "penal liquidated damages" which are unenforceable under California law.

DISCUSSION

Appellant purports to challenge the California judgment based on the Wisconsin judgment under the authority of Code of Civil Procedure section 1710.40, subdivision (a), which provides: "A judgment entered pursuant to this chapter may be vacated on any ground which would be a defense to an *action*[3] in this state on the sister state judg-

---

3. "The Sister State and Foreign Money Judgments Act (Code Civ. Proc., §§ 1710.10–1710.65) provides a simpler and more efficient method of enforcing such judgments than the *traditional action* on the judgment. The registration procedure established by the act is designed to allow parties to avoid the normal trappings of an original action, e.g., the necessity for pleadings. The optional procedure was intended to offer savings in time and money to both courts and judgment creditors, yet, at the same time, remain fair to the judgment debtor by affording him the opportunity to assert any defense that he could assert under the traditional procedure. [Citations.]" (*Tom Thumb Glove Co.*,

ment, including the ground that the amount of interest accrued on the sister state judgment and included in the judgment entered pursuant to this chapter is incorrect."

Inasmuch as the California judgment was entered pursuant to Code of Civil Procedure section 1710.25, upon an application supported by a sister state judgment which was regular on its face, the entry of the California judgment was proper and the appeal from it is unavailing. In order to preserve his grounds for appeal, appellant should have moved the superior court to vacate the second California judgment pursuant to Code of Civil Procedure section 1710.40 and then taken an appeal from the superior court's order of denial. Instead, appellant merely opposed Silbrico's motions to vacate the first California judgment and to enter the second California judgment in its place.

However, even had appellant properly raised the issues presented by this appeal, he still could not prevail. That is so because appellant has misconstrued the meaning of Code of Civil Procedure section 1710.40.

"[A] sister state money judgment entered pursuant to the provisions of the Uniform Act may be vacated in California *only* when the statutory ground or grounds therefore have been established. Section 1710.40 provides in relevant part that 'A judgment entered pursuant to this chapter may be vacated on any ground which would be a defense to an *action* in this state on a sister state judgment.' In elaborating on the defenses available under section 1710.40, the Law Revision Commission makes the following comment: 'Common defenses to enforcement of a sister state judgment include the following: the judgment is not final and unconditional (where finality means that no further action by the court rendering the judgment is necessary to resolve the matter litigated); the judgment was obtained by extrinsic fraud; the judgment was rendered in excess of jurisdiction; the judgment is not enforceable in the state of rendition; the plaintiff is guilty of misconduct; the judgment has already been paid; suit on the judgment is barred by the statute of limitations in the state where enforcement is sought.' (19A West's Ann. Codes (1982) p. 694; ... italics added.)" (*World Wide Imports, Inc. v. Bartel* (1983) 145 Cal. App. 3d 1006, 1009–1010 [193 Cal. Rptr. 830].) None of the defenses raised by appellant fall into these categories.

In *World Wide Imports, Inc. v. Bartel, supra,* the defendants conceded that none of the above enumerated defenses were available to them and that under traditional legal principles they were entitled to no relief. They insisted, however, that *Thomas v. Washington Gas Light Co.* (1980) 448 U.S. 261 [65 L. Ed. 2d 757, 100 S. Ct. 2647], had changed the existing law and that under *Thomas,* denial of the enforcement of a foreign judgment is permissible if the latter violates a fundamental public policy of the enforcing state.

The *World Wide Imports* court rejected this argument, pointing out that *Thomas* did not change the basic rule that "California must, regardless of policy objections, recognize the judgment of another state as res judicata, and this is so even though the action or proceeding which resulted in the judgment could not have been brought

---

Inc. v. Han (1978) 78 Cal. App. 3d 1, 7 [144 Cal. Rptr. 30], italics added; see *Liebow v. Superior Court* (1981) 120 Cal. App. 3d 573, 575 [175 Cal. Rptr. 26].)

under the law or policy of California." (*World Wide Imports, Inc. v. Bartel, supra,* 145 Cal. App. 3d at p. 1011.)

The court noted that California's rule is in harmony with Restatement Second of Conflict of Laws, section 117, which states: "A valid judgment rendered in one State of the United States will be recognized and enforced in a sister State *even though the strong public policy of the latter State would have precluded recovery in its courts on the original claim.*" (Italics added; *see also Tyus v. Tyus* (1984) 160 Cal. App. 3d 789, 793 [206 Cal. Rptr. 817].)

In *Thomas v. Washington Gas Light Co., supra,* 448 U.S. 261, 270 the Supreme Court set forth the governing principles as follows: "It has long been the law that 'the judgment of a state court should have the same credit, validity, and effect in every other court in the United States, which it had in the state where it was pronounced.' [Citations.] This rule, if not compelled by the Full Faith and Credit Clause itself ... is surely required by 28 U.S.C. § 1738.... [Thus], in effect, ... a State is permitted to determine the extraterritorial effect of its judgments; but it may only do so indirectly, by prescribing the effect of its judgments within the State." "The rare exceptions to the application of the full faith and credit clause arise only when there is a violation of some fundamental state public policy.... [There] is no precedent for an exception in the case of a money judgment in a civil suit." (*Id.,* at p. 222.)

"[The] law is well established that upon a claim that a foreign judgment is not entitled to full faith and credit, the permissible scope of inquiry is limited to a determination of whether the court of forum had fundamental jurisdiction in the case." (*World Wide Imports, Inc. v. Bartel, supra,* 145 Cal. App. 3d at p. 1010; *see also Tyus v. Tyus, supra,* 160 Cal. App. 3d at p. 794.) Therefore, the judgment of a sister state must be recognized in a California court if that sister state had jurisdiction over the parties and the subject matter and all interested parties were given reasonable notice and opportunity to be heard. (*World Wide Imports, Inc., supra,* 145 Cal. App. 3d at p. 1010.)

Here, appellant has never challenged the jurisdiction of the Wisconsin Circuit Court to render judgment. Further, the record shows that all interested parties were given notice and reasonable opportunity to be heard with regard to the second Wisconsin judgment on which the new California judgment was based. That being so, and since, as discussed *supra,* appellant's so-called "defenses" cannot be asserted to prevent enforcement of a sister state judgment, the trial court correctly concluded that full faith and credit must be accorded the Wisconsin judgment in issue here.

DISPOSITION

The judgment is affirmed.

Notes and Questions regarding Enforcement of Sister State Judgments

(1) The opinion in *Silbrico v. Raanan,* reproduced *supra,* discuss the procedures available to a judgment creditor who wishes to enforce a sister state judgment in California. *See also Kahn v. Berman,* 198 Cal. App. 3d 1499, 244 Cal. Rptr. 575 (1988)

(discussing the interplay of the procedures in a case involving the Enforcement of Sister State Money Judgments Act and the Enforcement of Judgments Law). Why would a judgment creditor choose the traditional method of enforcement by instituting an independent action in California as opposed to the simpler alternative method of registering the judgment in California?

(2) As the analysis in *Silbrico* suggests, the Full Faith and Credit Clause the United States Constitution is not violated by requiring that a sister-state judgment first be reduced to a California judgment before it may be enforced in California. *See M'El-moyle v. Cohen*, 38 U.S. (13 Pet.) 312, 325,10 L. Ed. 177 (1839) ("To give [a South Carolina judgment] the force of a judgment in another state, it must be made a judgment there, and can only be executed in the latter as its laws may permit); *Kahn v. Berman*, 198 Cal. App. 3d 1499, 244 Cal. Rptr. 575 (1988) (ruling that requiring a judgment creditor to follow California rather than Nevada procedures for enforcement of a Nevada judgment in California does not violate the Full Faith and Credit Clause).

(3) Code of Civil Procedure § 1710.40, as well as the Full Faith and Credit Clause, govern the grounds on which a sister state judgment may be vacated in California. Based on *Silbrico* and the authorities discussed therein, under what circumstances can a California court vacate a sister state judgment on the ground that enforcement would violate a fundamental public policy of California? *See Medical Legal Consulting Serv., Inc. v. Covarrubias*, 234 Cal. App. 3d 80, 89–93, 285 Cal. Rptr. 559 (1991) (observing that the fundamental policy exception to full faith and credit has been applied to custody and support orders, but not to money judgments; California must enforce Maryland money judgment for contractual attorney fees even though the contractual fee would violate California MICRA limitations and even though contract could be disaffirmed by minor under California policy); *Smith v. Superior Court*, 41 Cal. App. 4th 1014, 49 Cal. Rptr. 2d 20 (1996) (holding injunction issued by Michigan court enjoining engineer from testifying in any products liability litigation involving defendant automobile manufacturer not entitled to full faith and credit because irreconcilably conflicted with California policy against suppression of evidence).

(4) In *Traci & Marx Co. v. Legal Options, Inc.*, 126 Cal. App. 4th 155, 23 Cal. Rptr. 3d 685 (2005), the plaintiff sought to enforce a default judgment entered by an Ohio court entered against the defendants in the amount of $25,890 as compensatory damages and $130,000 as punitive damages. Although the plaintiff's complaint sought "compensatory damages in excess of $25,000" and "punitive damages in excess of $25,000," the Ohio court, after a default prove-up hearing, awarded plaintiff $25,890 in compensatory damages and $130,000 in punitive damages. Relying on California cases, such as *Becker v. S.P.V. Constr. Co.*, 27 Cal. 3d 489, 165 Cal. Rptr. 825, 612 P.2d 915 (1980), the superior court vacated the Ohio default judgment as void because the damages awarded exceeded the prayer for relief in the complaint. Plaintiff appealed and the Court of Appeal reversed.

The *Traci & Marx* court observed that the issue is not whether, under California law, a prayer for relief of an amount "in excess of" a specified dollar amount must result in an award of "no more than" that dollar amount, but whether the same result would obtain in Ohio. Because the defendants failed to establish that under Ohio law the "in excess of" language in the prayer for relief constitutes a ceiling rather than a floor for recoverable damages, the superior court must recognize the Ohio judgment regardless of policy objections under California law. *Traci & Marx, supra,* 126 Cal. App. 4th at 160.

(5) As *Silbrico* indicates, a sister state judgment should not be enforced where the sister state court lacked fundamental jurisdiction in the case. For example, the Full Faith and Credit Clause does not require one state to enforce a default judgment entered in another state if that judgment is invalid for lack of subject matter jurisdiction, personal jurisdiction, or proper notice. *See, e.g., Hanson v. Denckla,* 357 U.S. 235, 78 S. Ct. 1228, 2 L. Ed. 2d 1283 (1958) (lack of personal jurisdiction); *State of Arizona v. Yuen,* 179 Cal. App. 4th 169, 101 Cal. Rptr. 3d 525 (2009) (holding Arizona judgment not entitled to full faith and credit because defendant never received notice of proceedings against her); *Commercial Nat. Bank of Peoria v. Kermeen,* 225 Cal. App. 3d 396, 275 Cal. Rptr. 122 (1990) (refusing to extend full faith and credit to Illinois judgment because Illinois court's exercise of personal jurisdiction violated debtor's due process rights).

(6) As mentioned in *Silbrico,* another permissible defense under CCP § 1710.40 to enforcement of a sister state judgment is that the judgment was obtained by extrinsic fraud or mistake. *See,* § 14.05, Relief from Final Judgment, *supra.* In *Tsakos Shipping & Trading v. Juniper Garden Town Homes, Ltd.,* 12 Cal. App. 4th 74, 15 Cal. Rptr. 2d (1993); the court vacated a New York judgment entered against a limited partnership and one of its general partners for extrinsic fraud because a conflict of interest in representation by counsel in the New York action deprived the other general partners of a fair trial. The court based its conclusion on prior California cases which held that dual representation by counsel of the partnership and one partner under such circumstances constituted a conflict of interest and consequently extrinsic fraud sufficient to vacate a judgment. *Tsakos,* 12 Cal. App. 4th at 94–97. Is the *Tsakos* court's reasoning, particularly its reliance on California extrinsic fraud and conflict of interest precedent, consistent with the analysis and holdings in *Silbrico*? Did the *Tsakos* court refuse to enforce the New York judgment because it violated some fundamental public policy of California? Because the New York court lacked fundamental jurisdiction in the New York action? Assuming the *Tsakos* holding is permissible under CCP § 1710.40, is it consistent with the Full Faith and Credit Clause?

More recently, in *Liquidator of Integrity Ins. Co. v. Hendrix,* 54 Cal. App. 4th 971, 63 Cal. Rptr. 2d 240 (1997), the defendant sought to set aside a New Jersey judgment pursuant to § 473 on the grounds of excusable neglect in that hospitalization prevented the defendant from attending the trial. The court concluded that the use of § 473 to collaterally attack a sister state judgment would render the Full Faith and Credit Clause meaningless. *Hendrix,* 54 Cal. App. 4th at 978. In reaching this conclusion, the court disagreed with the in *Tsakos* court's analysis and use of § 473. *Id.* Do you agree with the holding in *Liquidator* or in *Tsakos*? Why?

(7) *Enforcement of Sister State Support Orders.* The Uniform Interstate Family Support Act (UIFSA), Family Code § 5700.101–§ 5700.905, governs recognition, enforcement, and modification of sister state child and spousal support orders. Upon registration in California, a support order issued by another state is enforceable in the same manner and is subject to the same procedures as a support order issued by a California court, although it remains an order of the issuing state. Family Code § 5700.603. A party who wishes to contest the validity or enforcement of a registered support order is limited to the defenses specified in Family Code § 5700.607. Family Code § 5700.606, § 5700.607. These defenses include "payment" or "the order has been vacated, suspended, or modified by a later order," as well as the constitutionally-based attack that the issuing tribunal lacked personal jurisdiction. § 5700.607. The requirements for modification of a child support order are set forth in Family Code § 5700.611.

[J] Enforcement of Foreign Country Judgments

The Uniform Foreign-Country Money Judgments Recognition Act, CCP §§ 1713–1724, governs the recognition and enforcement of money judgments entered by a court in a foreign country. Generally speaking, under this Act a California court must recognize a foreign civil money judgment (other than one for taxes, a fine, or support) regardless of whether that country would recognize a California judgment, so long as the foreign judgment is "final, conclusive, and enforceable" under the law of the foreign county where rendered. CCP §§ 1714–1716; *see Manco Contracting Co. v. Bezdikian*, 45 Cal. 4th 192, 85 Cal. Rptr. 3d 233, 195 P.3d 604 (2008) (ruling the law of the nation where the judgment was rendered determines whether the judgment is sufficiently final, conclusive, and enforceable to be subject to recognition in California); *Hyundai Securities Co., Ltd. v. Lee*, 215 Cal. App. 4th 682, 155 Cal. Rptr. 3d 678 (2013) (discussing the procedures for raising an issue regarding recognition of a foreign judgment). Section 1716(b) lists a variety of circumstances under which a California court shall not recognize a foreign judgment, including where the foreign court lacked subject matter or personal jurisdiction, or where the judgment "was rendered under a judicial system that does not provide impartial tribunals or procedures compatible with the requirements of due process of law."

Also, under the Act, a California court is not required to, but may as a matter of discretion, recognize a foreign judgment in specified circumstances, such as where the defendant did not receive adequate notice, the judgment was obtained by extrinsic fraud or was rendered in circumstances that substantial doubt about the integrity of the rendering court, the specific proceeding leading to the judgment was not compatible with due process, or where the judgment or cause of action on which the judgment is based "is repugnant to the public policy" of California or the United States. CCP § 1716(c)(1)–(8); *see Hyundai Securities Co., Ltd. v. Lee*, 232 Cal. App. 4th 1379, 182 Cal. Rptr. 3d 264 (2015) (discussing the stringent test for finding a public policy violation). Why is a judgment debtor permitted to challenge enforcement of a foreign country money judgment on grounds of repugnancy to the public policy of California, but prohibited from doing so with respect to enforcement of a sister state money judgment?

The troublesome problems of timing and valuation when converting foreign money judgments into domestic currency are governed by the Uniform Foreign-Money Claims Act, CCP §§ 676–676.16, which became effective in California in 1992. Under this Act, in the absence of some other agreement by the parties, a judgment or arbitration award must usually be entered in foreign money rather than U.S. dollars, and the judgment debtor must pay the judgment on the basis of the rate of exchange prevailing at the time of payment. CCP §§ 676.1–676.12.

Chapter 15

Appeals and Writs

§ 15.01 Appeals

[A] Appealable Judgments and Orders

California Code of Civil Procedure (2016)

Section 904.1. Appealable judgments and orders.

(a) An appeal, other than in a limited civil case, is to the court of appeal. An appeal, other than in a limited civil case, may be taken from any of the following:

    (1) From a judgment, except (A) an interlocutory judgment, other than as provided in paragraphs (8), (9), and (11), or (B) a judgment of contempt that is made final and conclusive by Section 1222.

    (2) From an order made after a judgment made appealable by paragraph (1).

    (3) From an order granting a motion to quash service of summons or granting a motion to stay the action on the ground of inconvenient forum, or from a written order of dismissal under Section 581d following an order granting a motion to dismiss the action on the ground of inconvenient forum.

    (4) From an order granting a new trial or denying a motion for judgment notwithstanding the verdict.

    (5) From an order discharging or refusing to discharge an attachment or granting a right to attach order.

    (6) From an order granting or dissolving an injunction, or refusing to grant or dissolve an injunction.

    (7) From an order appointing a receiver.

    (8) From an interlocutory judgment, order, or decree, hereafter made or entered in an action to redeem real or personal property from a mortgage thereof, or a lien thereon, determining the right to redeem and directing an accounting.

    (9) From an interlocutory judgment in an action for partition determining the rights and interests of the respective parties and directing partition to be made.

    (10) From an order made appealable by the provisions of the Probate Code or the Family Code.

    (11) From an interlocutory judgment directing payment of monetary sanctions by a party or an attorney for a party if the amount exceeds five thousand dollars ($5,000).

(12) From an order directing payment of monetary sanctions by a party or an attorney for a party if the amount exceeds five thousand dollars ($5,000).

(13) From an order granting or denying a special motion to strike under Section 425.16.

(b) Sanction orders or judgments of five thousand dollars ($5,000) or less against a party or an attorney for a party may be reviewed on an appeal by that party after entry of final judgment in the main action, or, at the discretion of the court of appeal, may be reviewed upon petition for an extraordinary writ.

UAP-Columbus JV 3261 32 v. Nesbitt

Court of Appeal of California, Second Appellate District
234 Cal. App. 3d 1028, 285 Cal. Rptr. 856 (1991)

DANIELSON, JUSTICE.

This matter is before us on a motion by defendant and respondent Wibbelsman to dismiss the appeal in this action for lack of jurisdiction in this court because of failure timely to file a notice of appeal. Pursuant to the request of defendant and appellant Nesbitt (rule 41(b) [now Rule 8.54], Cal. Rules of Court)[1] we placed the motion to dismiss on calendar for hearing because (a) the motion was potentially dispositive of the appeal, and (b) resolving the different interpretations of precedent by the parties might be aided by oral argument. * * *

FACTUAL AND PROCEDURAL BACKGROUND

This controversy arises from an action in interpleader and for declaratory relief brought by UAP-Columbus JV 326132, a partnership, (UAP) and The Continent, JV 326128, a partnership, (The Continent) (hereafter collectively plaintiffs), on August 5, 1987, against defendant Patrick M. Nesbitt, appellant herein, and defendant Nancy Wibbelsman, respondent herein, sometimes collectively "defendants."

Plaintiff UAP, for itself alone, asserted the first cause of action, in interpleader, seeking to compel both defendants to interplead and to litigate between themselves their conflicting claims to money, $292,400.03, which UAP had deposited with the clerk of the court. UAP alleged that each of defendants claimed some right, title or interest in the deposited money, that those claims were adverse and conflicting, and that UAP was indifferent as to which of defendants' conflicting claims was correct.

In its interpleader cause of action plaintiff UAP inserted a request for allowance of its costs and reasonable attorney fees incurred in that action from the funds UAP had deposited with the court, as authorized by Code of Civil Procedure section 386.6, subdivision (a).[2] * * *

---

1. All further references to rules are to the California Rules of Court. [The California Rules of Court were renumbered in 2007.]

2. All further statutory references are to the Code of Civil Procedure.

After intensive and protracted litigation and trial the court signed and filed its statement of decision and its judgment on March 19, 1990. In its statement of decision the court made its rulings on the issues raised by the pleadings and determined at trial, including both the interpleader and declaratory relief causes of action, but did not dispose of UAP's request for attorney fees and costs. As to those fees and costs, the trial court stated:

"H. *Plaintiffs' Costs and Fees*

"UAP's entitlement to costs and fees, and the allocation of such costs and fees as between Nesbitt and Wibbelsman, shall be determined by cost bill procedure after entry of this Judgment. Until the court makes its determination regarding the amount and allocation of such costs and fees, the clerk of the court shall not distribute any of the interpleaded funds and UAP shall not distribute the 1989 Distribution unless otherwise ordered to do so by the court."

On March 28, 1990, defendant Wibbelsman served notice of entry of judgment on defendant Nesbitt.

Fourteen days later, on April 11, 1990, the attorneys for the parties signed, and there was filed, a stipulation extending time to file a memorandum of costs to May 3, 1990.[3] On May 3, 1990, plaintiffs filed their memorandum of costs, and on May 14, 1990, they filed an amended summary of costs, both with supporting documents. Each of the defendants filed one or more motions to tax costs, together with extensive supporting papers.

The motions of defendants to tax costs were heard by the trial judge on July 23, 1990. The court disallowed certain claimed costs and, in its minute order entered July 23, 1990, ordered, inter alia: "Costs are taxed at $71,127.36 and are to be paid as follows: $47,418.24 by Wibbelsman and $23,709.12 by Nesbitt."

As we have noted, judgment was signed by the trial judge and filed ("entered," rule 2(b) [now Rule 8.104]) on March 19, 1990. On March 28, 1990, counsel for defendant Wibbelsman, now respondent, served by mail, and on March 29, 1990 filed, a notice of entry of judgment with a file-stamped copy of that judgment attached.

On July 23, 1990, defendant and appellant Nesbitt filed his notice of appeal "from ... the judgment entered on March 19, 1990 ... as modified by the Orders of this Court entered on July 23, 1990." On August 13, 1990, defendant and respondent Wibbelsman filed her notice of cross-appeal from "the Judgment entered on March 19, 1990, and from the post-judgment Order ... entered July 23, 1990."

---

3. Rule 870(a)(1) [now Rule 3.1700]requires that a party claiming costs shall serve and file a verified memorandum of costs within 15 days after date of mailing notice of entry of judgment; rule 870(b)(1) requires that any notice of motion to tax or strike costs shall be served and filed 15 days after service of the cost memorandum; and Rule 870(b)(3) provides that the parties claiming and contesting costs may agree in writing, filed with the clerk, to extend to a date certain the time for serving and filing the cost memorandum and motions to strike or tax costs.

CONTENTIONS

1. Respondent Wibbelsman moves to dismiss the appeal and contends that this court has no jurisdiction over the appeal because notice of appeal from the judgment of March 19, 1990, was not timely filed.

2. Appellant Nesbitt contends that his notice of appeal filed July 23, 1990, was timely filed because the judgment entered March 19, 1990, was interlocutory, and therefore not appealable until modified by the court's order of July 23, 1990. In support of his contention he argues that further judicial action was essential to the final determination of the rights of the parties as to 1) the amount of costs and attorney fees to be awarded to plaintiffs, and 2) the allocation of those costs and fees against and between Nesbitt and Wibbelsman.

DISCUSSION

Jurisdiction

"Jurisdiction is the threshold issue in all judicial proceedings.... Absent jurisdiction over the case or controversy, a court is without power to act.... The right of appeal of a judicial decision is wholly statutory and no judgment or order is appealable unless expressly made so by statute. [Citations.]" (*Supple v. City of Los Angeles* (1988) 201 Cal. App. 3d 1004, 1009 [247 Cal. Rptr. 554]; and *see*, §904.1.)

"[T]he requirement as to the time for taking an appeal is mandatory, and the court is without jurisdiction to consider [an appeal] which has been taken subsequent to the expiration of the statutory period." (*Estate of Hanley* (1943) 23 Cal. 2d 120, 122 [142 P.2d 423, 149 A.L.R. 1250]; *Vibert v. Berger* (1966) 64 Cal. 2d 65, 67 [48 Cal. Rptr. 886, 410 P.2d 390]; ...)

The time for filing notice of appeal is governed, under the facts of this case, by rule 2(a) [now Rule 8.104(a)], which provides that "a notice of appeal shall be filed on or before ... (2) 60 days after the date of service of a document entitled 'notice of entry' of judgment ... by any party upon the party filing the notice of appeal...."

In this case the judgment was entered on March 19, 1990; notice of entry of judgment was served by mail on March 28, 1990, and was filed on March 29, 1990; appellant's notice of appeal was filed 117 days after service, on July 23, 1990. If the judgment entered March 19, 1990, was appealable when entered, and absent some legal basis to establish that the mandates of rule 2(a) do not apply in this case, the notice of appeal from the judgment entered March 19, 1990, was not timely filed and we do not have jurisdiction to review that judgment on appeal.

A Judgment Is Appealable When No Further Judicial Action Is Essential to the Final Determination of the Rights of the Parties to the Action

Whether a judgment is, or is not, appealable is determined by its substance and legal effect. It is often said that only a "final" judgment is appealable. Section 904.1 lists the appealable judgments and orders of a superior court. It does not employ the term "final judgment"; however, it implies that only "final" judgments are appealable by excepting interlocutory judgments from appealability, with certain specified exceptions not relevant here. Essentially, a judgment is "final," so as to be appealable, when no further judicial action by the court is essential to the final determination of the rights of the parties to the action.

As our Supreme Court has stated: "It is not the form of the decree but the substance and effect of the adjudication which is determinative. As a general test, which must be adapted to the particular circumstances of the individual case, it may be said that where no issue is left for future consideration except the fact of compliance or non-compliance with the terms of the first decree, that decree is final, but where anything further in the nature of judicial action on the part of the court is essential to a final determination of the rights of the parties, the decree is interlocutory." (*Lyon v. Goss* (1942) 19 Cal. 2d 659, 670 [123 P.2d 11]; *see also*, authorities collected at 9 Witkin (3d ed. 1985) Cal. Procedure, Appeal, § 67, p. 91.)

In support of his contention that the judgment of March 19, 1990, was interlocutory, because further judicial action was essential to a final determination of the rights of the parties to the action, appellant cites to *Kinoshita v. Horio* (1986) 186 Cal. App. 3d 959 [231 Cal. Rptr. 241]. That decision is not authority for his contention.

Kinoshita was an appeal from a judgment in a proceeding for dissolution of a partnership. The reviewing court held that the judgment appealed from was interlocutory, and that the appeal must be dismissed because it was from a nonappealable order. The challenged judgment in *Kinoshita* ordered the receiver, subject to the court's approval, to sell the partnership property, pay its debts, distribute the remaining assets, and dissolve the partnership. The judgment did not specify the percentage interest held by some of the partners, nor did it provide a formula for allocating among the defendant partners the costs and expenses assessed against them. The judgment also provided that the trial court retained jurisdiction for all purposes to insure compliance with the judgment and dissolution and the distribution of the partnership assets. (*Kinoshita v. Horio, supra,* 186 Cal. App. 3d at p. 962.) Clearly, in *Kinoshita*, further judicial action was essential to the final determination of the rights of the parties to the action. To the same effect, see: Raff v. Raff (1964) 61 Cal. 2d 514 [39 Cal. Rptr. 366, 393 P.2d 678], in which our Supreme Court ruled that where an order approving the account of a receiver showed that the receiver was to continue to hold the assets and act as a receiver under orders of the court, the order was not appealable....

That was not the situation in the case at bench where, after the judgment was entered on March 19, 1990 no further judicial action by the court was essential to the final determination of the rights of the parties to the action. The issues raised by the parties in their pleadings, which were their causes of action in interpleader and for declaratory relief, had been tried and decided, and a judgment disposing of them had been signed by the court and entered. All that remained to be done was for the parties to tabulate and prove the costs which had been incurred in the process of litigation, plus attorney fees authorized by statute and incurred in litigating the interpleader causes of action, and to have the amounts of allowable costs and fees determined by the trial court, allocated between the defendants, and entered on the judgment. Nothing that took place following entry of the judgment on March 19,

1990, was judicial action essential to the final determination of the rights of the parties to the action. * * *

Attorney's Fees Are Allowable in Interpleader Actions

* * *

Section 386.6 subdivision (a) provides that "A party to an [interpleader] action ... may insert in his ... complaint ... a request for allowance of his costs and reasonable attorney fees incurred in such action. In ordering the discharge of such party, the court may, in its discretion, award such party his costs and reasonable attorney fees from the amount in dispute which has been deposited with the court. At the time of final judgment in the action the court may make such further provision for assumption of such costs and attorney fees by one or more of the adverse claimants as may appear proper."

As noted above, plaintiff UAP did insert a request for the allowance of its costs and reasonable attorney fees in its ... interpleader ... action.

Attorney Fees Awarded in Interpleader Actions Are an Item and Component of Costs

Chapter 6 of title 14, part 2, Code of Civil Procedure (§§ 1021–1038), provides for costs in civil actions. Section 1033.5, subdivision (c), paragraph (5) provides in part: "When any statute of this state refers to the award of 'costs and attorney's fees,' attorney's fees are an item and component of the costs to be awarded and are allowable as costs pursuant to subparagraph (B) of paragraph (10) of subdivision (a)."

As we have seen, section 386.6 refers to the award of costs and reasonable attorney fees in interpleader proceedings; it is one of the statutes included in the ambit of section 1033.5, subdivision (c), paragraph (5).

The Determination and Allocation of Allowable Attorney Fees and Costs by Cost Bill Procedure After Entry of Judgment Does Not Render That Judgment Interlocutory

Appellant Nesbitt urges that the judgment of March 19, 1990, was interlocutory and therefore nonappealable because the court reserved the determination and allocation of costs and attorney fees for another time. He argues that the allocation of such costs and attorney fees was a principal argument between the two defendants, and therefore further judicial action was essential to the final determination of the rights of the parties.

In support of that argument Nesbitt points to section 386.6, subdivision (a), relating to costs and attorney fees in interpleader actions, which provides, in part: "At the time of final judgment in the action the court may make such further provision for assumption of such costs and attorney fees by one or more of the adverse claimants as may appear proper." The sense of Nesbitt's argument is that the making of *such further provision* means that the judgment is not final until the costs and attorney fees have been determined, allocated and ordered. That is contrary to the naked language of the statute which requires that the further provision for costs and fees be made "[a]t the time of final judgment...." Thus the statute contemplates that a judgment which makes such a further provision is itself a final judgment.

In a further effort to support his argument that the judgment of March 19, 1990, was interlocutory, and not appealable, appellant Nesbitt points out that neither the amount nor the allocation between defendants of attorney fees and other costs was provided for in the judgment as entered. He then argues that "[u]ntil there is an actual provision for costs and attorney's fees in a court order granting a judgment of interpleader, the order is nonappealable." He argues that plaintiffs' costs and fees were not actually determined and allocated until July 23, 1990, and, therefore, the judgment entered on March 19, 1990, was not final or appealable. This argument is entirely without merit. "Costs," a term which includes allowable attorney fees that by statute are an item and component of costs, are only incidental to the main action, and are not essential to the final determination of the rights of the parties to the action.

The right to receive costs following litigation of a civil action can be waived by the party entitled to them, or can be forfeited by failure of that party properly to claim them in a timely manner. Neither such waiver nor such forfeiture renders the judgment interlocutory and not appealable.

Appellant Nesbitt further argues that the judgment of March 19 was not final and appealable because even though the award of attorney fees as costs in interpleader actions is authorized by statute the apportioning, or allocation, of the burden of paying such costs, between two defendants, requires further judicial action and renders the judgment interlocutory. There is no merit in that argument. An order apportioning attorney fees is an appealable order after final judgment under section 904.1, subdivision (b) [now, subdivision (a)(2)]. Also, section 1032, subdivision (a)(4), relating to costs provides that "the court, in its discretion, ... may apportion costs between the parties on the same or adverse sides...."

Here, the two defendants, though antagonistic to each other, were "parties on the same side" of the main action. The court had authority to apportion the costs between them.

The Procedure for Determining and Awarding Costs

The procedure to be followed in claiming and contesting prejudgment costs is prescribed by section 1034 and by rule 870 [now Rule 3.1700]. Section 1034 is the statutory authority and provides in part: "(a) Prejudgment costs allowable under this chapter shall be claimed and contested in accordance with rules adopted by the Judicial Council."

Rule 870(a)(1), as it applies to the facts of this case, provides: "A prevailing party who claims costs shall serve and file a memorandum of costs within 15 days after the date ... of service of written notice of entry of judgment...." Rule 870(b) prescribes the procedure for striking and taxing costs, and rule 870(b)(4) provides for the entry of costs *on* the judgment; it reads: "[*Entry of costs*] After the time has passed for a motion to strike or tax costs or for determination of that motion, the clerk shall enter the costs *on* the judgment forthwith." (Italics added.)

The copy of the judgment in the record on appeal reflects that, in the judgment, the court ordered and decreed that "UAP is entitled to an award of $71,127.36 ... in costs and ... in fees," to be allocated "$23,709.12 ... out of that portion of the funds which is awarded herein to Nesbitt," and "$47,418.24 ... out of that portion of the funds which is awarded herein to Wibbelsman."

In the judgment, it appears that blanks (single underscores) were originally provided for each of the three dollar amounts set forth above. The dollar amounts inscribed above each of the underscores have been inserted by handwriting, each of which is followed by a small illegible manuscription, which we assume to be the initials of the writer, followed by "7-23-90," the date on which the motions to tax costs were determined.

In any event, as we have noted above, the right to appeal a judicial decision is wholly statutory. It follows that in order to exercise that right an appellant must take his appeal from an appealable order and must comply with the procedures prescribed by statute and rules of court which govern appeals. A threshold requirement for the taking of an appeal is the filing of a timely notice of appeal.

Further, just as the right of appeal is governed by statute and by rule, so the procedure for claiming, contesting and allowing costs is governed by statute and by rule. Here the trial court properly followed the procedure prescribed by statute and by rule for determining and allocating costs, and the clerk, pursuant to rule, properly inserted the costs, as determined by the court, *on* the judgment previously entered. * * *

DECISION

The motion to dismiss the appeal in this action is denied. The purported appeal and cross-appeal from the judgment entered March 19, 1990, are dismissed because notice thereof was not timely filed. The motion to dismiss appeal is denied as to the order relating to costs filed July 23, 1990. The scope of this appeal is limited to the order of July 23, 1990. Each party shall bear its own costs on this motion.

Morehart v. County of Santa Barbara

Supreme Court of California
7 Cal. 4th 725, 29 Cal. Rptr. 2d 804, 872 P.2d 143 (1994)

LUCAS, CHIEF JUSTICE.

The Subdivision Map Act (Gov. Code, § 66410 et seq.) provides that contiguous parcels of land are not automatically merged by virtue of being held by the same owner. Such parcels "may be merged by local agencies only in accordance with the authority and procedures prescribed by this article" (*id.*, §§ 66451.10–66451.21]), which "provide[s] the sole and exclusive authority for local agency initiated merger of contiguous parcels." (*Id.*, § 66451.10, subd. (b); all section references are to the Government Code unless otherwise indicated.)

Without following those statutory procedures, defendants County of Santa Barbara and its board of supervisors (county) amended the county's zoning ordinance to require that certain parcels be of a specified minimum lot size before being developed, *unless* the parcel was "held in separate ownership" on the date the rezoning was initiated. The amendments further require that the undersized parcels be combined (i.e., merged) in order to comply to the maximum extent possible with current density standards.

Plaintiffs applied for a coastal development permit to build a residence on their undersized parcel. The county denied the application on the ground that plaintiffs could recombine their parcel with adjoining parcels. In plaintiffs' action against the county, seeking multiple kinds of relief, the trial court granted judgment for plaintiffs declaring that the county's recombination requirement was preempted by section 66451.10 and related provisions of the Subdivision Map Act, and ordering issuance of a writ of mandate directing the county to set the denial of plaintiffs' application aside. The Court of Appeal reversed, holding that even though the act provides the exclusive means by which a county may impose a merger of parcels to control their sale, lease, or financing, the act does not prevent the county's zoning law from requiring merger as a condition to permitting development. We granted review to consider that holding.

Initially we are faced with a question of appealability. The judgment appealed from resolved fewer than all of plaintiffs' causes of action, but the Court of Appeal treated it as appealable under authority of a line of Court of Appeal decisions holding that an appeal can be taken from a judgment on causes of action that have been severed from other remaining, separate and independent causes of action. We shall conclude that the judgment was not appealable but that because of unusual circumstances, including the statewide importance of the issues, we should determine the correctness of the judgment as a basis for determining whether to direct the Court of Appeal to issue a peremptory writ to the trial court. * * *

II. THRESHOLD ISSUES

A. *Appealability*

In the trial court, plaintiffs objected to a proposed statement of decision on the ground that it called for the entry of a judgment in their favor on their causes of action for a writ of mandate and declaratory relief, rather than simply ruling on the merits of those causes of action and deferring entry of a judgment until after determination of the remaining causes of action for damages for inverse condemnation and violation of civil rights. The trial court overruled the objection, stating that "[i]t makes no sense to get involved in a protracted trial on various damage claims without obtaining a final resolution on the issue of the validity of the County's ordinance."

Rule 13 [renumbered as Rule 8.204 effective 2007] of the California Rules of Court requires that an appellant's opening brief either "[state] that the appeal is from a judgment that finally disposes of all issues between the parties" or else "[explain] why the order or nonfinal judgment is appealable." The county's opening brief explained that the judgment was appealable because it resolved issues that had been severed from separate and independent issues remaining to be tried. The Court of Appeal disposed of the appealability question in a one-sentence footnote as follows: "The judgment is separately appealable on a severed issue. (Code Civ. Proc., § 1048; *Day v. Papadakis* (1991) 231 Cal. App. 3d 503, 508 [282 Cal. Rptr. 548]; *Garat v. City of Riverside* (1991) 2 Cal. App. 4th 259, 276, fn. 8 [3 Cal. Rptr. 2d 504].)"

The theory of appealability relied on by the Court of Appeal was introduced into California jurisprudence by *Schonfeld v. City of Vallejo* (1976) 50 Cal. App. 3d 401, 416–419 [123 Cal. Rptr. 669] (*Schonfeld*), and has since been developed, applied, and distinguished, but never disapproved, in a number of Court of Appeal decisions, including those cited by the present Court of Appeal. The theory has not, however, been addressed by this court. * * *

In *Schonfeld, supra,* 50 Cal. App. 3d 401, plaintiff asserted claims arising out of the defendant city's lease of a marina to Vallejo Marina, Inc. (VMI). The first cause of action alleged fraudulent representations inducing plaintiff to acquire interests in, and pay rent under, the VMI lease. The second cause of action claimed rights to enforce the lease as third party beneficiary and partial assignee. The fourth cause of action sought a declaratory adjudication that the purported partial assignment was a valid mortgage. Judgment was entered for the city on the first and second causes of action, leaving the fourth cause of action still pending.

On appeal, plaintiff Schonfeld contended that because the fourth cause of action remained pending, entry of the judgment was premature. The appellate court rejected that contention on the ground that because of certain orders of the trial court deemed to constitute a severance of the fourth cause of action (50 Cal. App. 3d at p. 416, fn. 14),[3] the dismissal of the first two causes of action resulted in a final judgment. (*Id.* at p. 419.) The court reached that conclusion even though it properly recognized the general rule that " 'there can be but one judgment in an action no matter how many counts the complaint contains' " (*Id.* at p. 417, quoting *Bank of America v. Superior Court* (1942) 20 Cal. 2d 697, 701 [128 P.2d 357]). The court further recognized that none of the established exceptions to the general rule were applicable to the case before it, but went on to explain … why it felt called upon to "augment the number of existing exceptions" * * *

The court then proceeded to announce its new exception: "[N]o reported case has dealt with the application of the one final judgment rule to a cause of action severed pursuant to Code of Civil Procedure section 1048. Under that statute, a trial court

---

3. In fact, the fourth cause of action in *Schonfeld* was not "severed"; instead the trial court ordered it be tried separately. The Court of Appeal in *Schonfeld* failed to recognize that Code of Civil Procedure section 1048 no longer authorizes severance of a civil action. A former version of the statute stated, in pertinent part: "An action may be severed and actions may be consolidated, in the discretion of the court…." (Stats. 1927, ch. 320, § 1, p.531.) In 1971, however, the statute was rewritten to its present form and no longer contains the term "severed," but instead grants trial courts the authority to "order a *separate trial* on any cause of action … or any separate issue…." (Italics added.) Unfortunately, the title given the Code of Civil Procedure section 1048 by at least one publisher still contains the word "severance" (18A West's Ann. Code Civil Procedure (1980 ed.) § 1048, p. 175), and the Legislative Committee comment to … section 1948, and many appellate courts, use the term "sever" to describe orders for separate trials within a single action. * * *

has broad discretion to consolidate or sever causes of action.... [5] Clearly, the declaratory relief [fourth] cause of action here was properly severed as it raises issues separate and independent from those of the first two causes of action. [¶] We hold, therefore, that in the instant case, since the first two causes of action were properly severed, a final judgment resulted even though the independent fourth cause of action is still pending between the same parties." (50 Cal. App. 3d at pp. 418–419.)

The majority of the appellate opinions that accept and apply this *Schonfeld* holding treat it as requiring, for appealability of a judgment on fewer than all issues, that the decided issues not only were ordered to be tried separately[7] by the trial court but also are perceived by the appellate court itself to be separate and independent from the issues remaining to be decided. (*James Talcott, Inc. v. Short* (1979) 100 Cal. App. 3d 504, 506, fn. 1 [161 Cal. Rptr. 63] [deciding appeal from partial summary judgment on causes of action to enforce debt guaranties because they were "totally 'independent'" from other causes of action alleging fraudulent conveyances of guarantors' assets]; ... *Korean United Presbyterian Church v. Presbytery of the Pacific* (1991) 230 Cal. App. 3d 480, 485, fn. 1 [281 Cal. Rptr. 396] [hearing appeal from judgment on "severed" issues because they were "reasonably separate and independent from the remaining untried issues"]; *Garat v. City of Riverside* (1991) 2 Cal. App. 4th 259, 275–279 [3 Cal. Rptr.2d 504] [hearing appeal on issues that were actually "severed" and were "separate and independent" from undecided issues].) *Day v. Papadakis, supra,* 231 Cal. App. 3d 503, adds to the requirements that the issues be tried separately and be independent from the remaining issues, a further requirement, based on *Schonfeld's* above quoted language, that "the circumstances of this case are 'so unusual' as to warrant abandonment of the [one final judgment] rule in this instance" (*Id.* at p. 513).

Other decisions, however, disregard any inquiry into whether the decided issues were separate and independent from the undecided issues. Instead, they cite *Schonfeld* as a basis for appellate jurisdiction over a judgment determinative of fewer than all the issues simply on the ground that those issues were in fact severed by the trial court. (*Highland Development Co. v. City of Los Angeles* (1985) 170 Cal. App. 3d 169, 179 [215 Cal. Rptr. 881] [basing appealability on "de facto severance" of the cause of action underlying the appealed judgment]; *Bank of the Orient v. Town of Tiburon*

---

5. Code of Civil Procedure section 1048, subdivision (b), as amended in 1971, provides: "The court, in furtherance of convenience or to avoid prejudice, or when separate trials will be conducive to expedition and economy, may order a separate trial of any cause of action, ... or of any separate issue or of any number of causes of action or issues...." The Assembly Committee comment to the section states: "Section 1048 does not deal with the authority of a court to enter a separate final judgment on fewer than all the causes of action or issues involved in an action or trial. [Citations.] This question is determined primarily by case law, and Section 1048 leaves the question to case law development." (Legis. committee com., 18A West's Ann. Code Civ. Proc., *supra,* § 1048, at p. 176.)

7. In the cases discussed, *post,* it is unclear whether issues which were purportedly "severed" from other issues were in fact *formally* severed (such that two separate cases with separate docket numbers and separate judgments would be rendered), or were merely bifurcated, that is, certain issues or causes of action were ordered tried separately.

(1990) 220 Cal. App. 3d 992, 998 and fn. 8 [269 Cal. Rptr. 690] [reciting severance of the appealed judgment and treating "[t]his procedure" as "appropriate in these unusual circumstances"].

In announcing its new exception to the one final judgment rule, the *Schonfeld* opinion purports to follow the examples of other judicially created exceptions. The examples cited apply one of two principles: (1) Judgment in a multiparty case determining all issues as to one or more parties may be treated as final even though issues remain to be resolved between other parties; and (2) the order appealed from may be amended so as to convert it into a judgment encompassing actual determinations of all remaining issues by the trial court or, if determinable as a matter of law, by the appellate court, and the notice of appeal may then be treated as a premature but valid appeal from that judgment.

Those examples, however, are consistent with the codification of the one final judgment rule in Code of Civil Procedure section 904.1, subdivision (a). Subject to exceptions not applicable here, that subdivision authorizes appeal "[f]rom a judgment, except ... an interlocutory judgment," i.e., from a judgment that is not intermediate or nonfinal but is the one final judgment. (*Knodel v. Knodel* (1975), 14 Cal. 3d 752, 760, 122 Cal. Rptr. 521, 537 P.2d 353.) Judgments that leave nothing to be decided between one or more parties and their adversaries, or that can be amended to encompass all controverted issues, have the finality required by section 904.1, subdivision (a). A judgment that disposes of fewer than all of the causes of action framed by the pleadings, however, is necessarily "interlocutory" (Code Civ. Proc., § 904.1, subd. (a)), and not yet final, as to any parties between whom another cause of action remains pending.[9] * * *

Schonfeld also notes that under rule 54(b) of the Federal Rules of Civil Procedure (hereafter rule 54(b)), "separate appealable judgments may be rendered on counts that present separate claims for relief" (50 Cal. App. 3d at p. 418).... The federal experience with rule 54(b), however, demonstrates the drawbacks of a rule that simply declares judgments on separate claims (however defined) to be appealable.

As originally promulgated in 1939, rule 54(b) merely authorized the entry of judgment on one of several claims. The entered judgment was appealable if it qualified as a "final decision" under 28 United States Code section 1291. "However, it was soon found to be inherently difficult to determine by any automatic standard of unity

---

9. There are sound reasons for the one final judgment rule. As explained in *Kinoshita v. Horio,* [1986] 186 Cal. App. 3d 959, [231 Cal. Rptr. 241] "[t]hese include the obvious fact that piecemeal disposition and multiple appeals tend to be oppressive and costly. [Citing, inter alia, *Knodel v. Knodel, supra,* 14 Cal. 3d 752, 766.] Interlocutory appeals burden the courts and impede the judicial process in a number of ways: (1) They tend to clog the appellate courts with a multiplicity of appeals.... (2) Early resort to the appellate courts tends to produce uncertainty and delay in the trial court.... (3) Until a final judgment is rendered the trial court may completely obviate an appeal by altering the rulings from which an appeal would otherwise have been taken. [Citations.] (4) Later actions by the trial court may provide a more complete record which dispels the appearance of error or establishes that it was harmless. (5) Having the benefit of a complete adjudication ... will assist the reviewing court to remedy error (if any) by giving specific directions rather than remanding for another round of open-ended proceedings." (186 Cal. App. 3d at pp. 966–967.)

which of several multiple claims were sufficiently separable from others to qualify for the relaxation of the unitary principle in favor of their appealability. The result was that the jurisdictional time for taking an appeal ... in some instances expired earlier than was foreseen by the losing party. It thus became prudent to take immediate appeals in all cases of doubtful appealability and the volume of appellate proceedings was undesirably increased.

"Largely to overcome this difficulty, Rule 54(b) was amended [effective] 1948 [to provide that]: [¶] '... the court may direct the entry of a final judgment upon one or more but less than all of the claims only upon an express determination that there is no just reason for delay.... ' [¶] To meet the demonstrated need for flexibility, the District Court is used as a 'dispatcher.' It is permitted to determine, in the first instance, the appropriate time when each 'final decision' upon 'one or more but less than all' of the claims ... is ready for appeal.... A party adversely affected by a final decision thus knows that his time for appeal will not run against him until this certification has been made." (*Sears, Roebuck & Co. v. Mackey* (1956) 351 U.S. 427, 434–436 [100 L. Ed. 1297, 105-1306, 76 S. Ct. 895]....)

The court in *Schonfeld, supra,* 50 Cal. App. 3d 401, 418, explained that it was attributing appealability to a cause of action ordered to be tried separately only because of "circumstances ... so unusual that postponement of the appeal until the final judgment on Schonfeld's fourth cause of action would cause so serious a hardship and inconvenience as to require us to augment the number of existing exceptions [to the one final judgment rule]. But like the original rule 54(b), the *Schonfeld* holding leaves it "inherently difficult to determine *by any automatic standard* ... which of several multiple claims were sufficiently separable from others to qualify for ... appealability" (*Sears, Roebuck & Co. v. Mackey, supra,* 351 U.S. 427, 434 [100 L. Ed. 2d 1297, 1305], italics added), or to determine whether the "hardship and inconvenience" that would result from postponing appeal until final disposition of the entire action are sufficient to warrant immediate appealability. If appealability under the *Schonfeld* holding is in doubt, the losing party must appeal immediately to avoid waiving rights to appellate review and may receive no authoritative ruling on the appealability issue until the case has been briefed, argued, and decided. (An earlier determination of appealability may or may not result from proceedings to dismiss the appeal initiated by the respondent or the appellate court itself.)

The California judicial system provides another, more efficient avenue for obtaining a preliminary determination whether unusual circumstances make appellate review of an interlocutory judgment appropriate and, if the determination is affirmative, obtaining the review itself. The *Schonfeld* court's reference to "circumstances ... so unusual that postponement of the appeal ... would cause ... serious ... hardship and inconvenience" seemingly describes circumstances that would make an appeal from the final judgment an inadequate remedy and thereby call upon the appellate court to issue an alternative writ of mandate as a means of reviewing the correctness of the trial court's interlocutory judgment. (Code Civ. Proc., § 1086; see 8 Witkin, Cal. Procedure, *supra,* Extraordinary Writs, § 113, p. 748.) Petitioning for the writ enables the party against whom an interlocutory judgment has been entered to obtain a summary determination of the appropriateness of immediate review. If, on the other hand, the party chooses not to file the petition, the final judgment rule of Code of Civil Procedure section 904.1, subdivision (a), together with Code of Civil Procedure section 906 protects the party's right to have the interlocutory judgment reviewed on appeal from the final judgment.

Accordingly, we hold that an appeal cannot be taken from a judgment that fails to complete the disposition of all the causes of action between the parties even if the causes of action disposed of by the judgment have been ordered to be tried separately, or may be characterized as "separate and independent" from those remaining. Statements to the contrary in *Schonfeld, supra,* 50 Cal. App. 3d 401, and its progeny are disapproved. A petition for a writ, not an appeal, is the authorized means for obtaining review of judgments and orders that lack the finality required by Code of Civil Procedure section 904.1, subdivision (a). Because the trial court's judgment in favor of plaintiffs did not complete the disposition of all of plaintiffs' causes of action against defendant county, the judgment was not appealable.

B. *Treating Appeal as Petition for Writ*

In response to our inquiry about appealability, both plaintiffs and the county strongly urge that we decide the merits of the appeal. * * *

In *Olson v. Cory* (1984) 35 Cal. 3d 390 [197 Cal. Rptr. 843, 673 P.2d 720], we granted a petition for hearing and thereby brought the case here for decision as if the appeal had originally been taken to this court. After briefing and argument, we concluded that the order from which the appeal had been taken was not appealable, but that the records and briefs included in substance the elements necessary to a proceeding for writ of mandate, and that we had power to treat the purported appeal as a petition for that writ. We also decided to exercise that power because of the unusual circumstances that the case presented. (*Olson v. Cory, supra,* 35 Cal. 3d at p. 401.) Examining the merits, we held that the trial court's order purportedly appealed from was incorrect in several respects. Accordingly, we ordered the issuance by this court of a peremptory writ of mandate, directing the trial court to vacate its order and to make a new order consistent with this court's opinion. (*Id.* at p. 408.) * * *

The briefs and record before us contain all the elements prescribed by rule 56 [now Rule 8.486] of the California Rules of Court for an original mandate proceeding. The functional equivalents of any necessary verifications (*see* Code Civ. Proc., §§ 1086, 1089) are supplied not only by the verified pleadings but also by the certifications of the clerk's transcript by the clerk of the trial court and of the reporter's transcript by the clerk and the reporter. There is no indication that the trial court as respondent would wish to appear separately or become more than a nominal party to a writ proceeding.

Furthermore, the case in its present posture presents unusual circumstances making it appropriate to ascertain from the record whether there are substantive errors that the Court of Appeal should, by writ, order the trial court to correct. One circumstance is the considerable prior case law indicating that the present appeal was proper. Although we have now disapproved that line of authority, it made counsel's perceptions of appealability not unreasonable when the appeal was taken.

Judicial economy would not be served in this case by deferring resolution of the issues decided by the Court of Appeal until final judgment on all of plaintiffs' causes of action. The merits of those issues not only have been briefed by the parties and decided by the Court of Appeal, but also have been thoughtfully addressed by a diverse group of amici curiae ... who seek clarification of the potential effect of local parcel merger requirements upon vast areas of California land, much of which was subdivided many decades ago. Further proceedings in the trial court would be unlikely to improve upon the record or briefing now presented to us for resolving the question. * * *

Accordingly, in order to determine whether we should direct the Court of Appeal to issue a peremptory writ of mandate to the trial court for the purpose of correcting that court's judgment, we turn to the merits of plaintiffs' contention that the county ordinances are preempted by the merger provisions of the Subdivision Map Act. * * *

V. CONCLUSION

* * *

The judgment from which this appeal is taken is not appealable because it does not complete the disposition of all of the causes of action against the county alleged in the complaint and therefore is not final. We have reached the merits, however, as a basis for determining whether the notice of appeal should be treated as a petition for a writ of mandate. We conclude that the trial court's judgment declaring the county ordinances to be preempted by, and therefore invalid under, sections 66451.10 to 66451.21 of the Subdivision Map Act is correct, because the purpose for which the ordinances require merger, i.e., "to comply with current density standards," is not a permissible ground for compelling merger under section 66451.11 (*see* § 66451.11, subd. (b)(7)). Accordingly, there appears no need for issuance of a writ of mandate to the trial court.

The judgment of the Court of Appeal is reversed with directions to dismiss the appeal.

[1] *The One-Final-Judgment-Rule*

As our principal cases indicate, California supposedly follows the "one-final-judgment-rule," the essence of which is that an appeal lies only from a final judgment which terminates the proceeding in the lower court by completely disposing of the matter in controversy. *E.g.*, *Kinoshita v. Horio*, 186 Cal. App. 3d 959, 963, 231 Cal. Rptr. 241 (1986); *Bank of America Nat. Trust & Sav. Assn. v. Superior Court*, 20 Cal. 2d 697, 701, 128 P.2d 357 (1942). The court in *UAP-Columbus JV 326132 v. Nesbitt*, reproduced *supra*, quoting from *Lyon v. Goss, supra*, 19 Cal. 2d at 670, sets forth the most frequently stated test for determining whether a particular decree is final. What, according to *Morehart v. County of Santa Barbara*, reproduced *supra*, are the policy reasons behind the one-final-judgment-rule?

[a] Certain Nonfinal Decisions Appealable

As a general test of whether a trial court's decree is appealable or not, the one-final-judgment-rule is obviously inaccurate. Code of Civil Procedure § 904.1 authorizes appeals from several non-final (or "interlocutory") orders, such as orders granting or refusing to grant a preliminary injunction and certain sanction orders. CCP § 904.1(a)(6), (8)–(12). Moreover, as discussed below, the California courts have developed significant nonstatutory exceptions to the rule. Why did the courts develop these judge-made exceptions?

[b] The Problem of Bifurcated Trials

CCP § 598 authorizes a trial court to complete the trial of some issues in a case before others. Is a decision against a defendant rendered in a bifurcated trial on liability a final appealable judgment even though issues of damages remain to be tried? *See, e.g., Baker v. Castaldi*, 235 Cal. App. 4th 218, 185 Cal. Rptr. 3d 17 (2015) (holding purported "judgment" that found defendants liable and plaintiffs entitled to punitive damages to be assessed at a separate trial was not appealable because it left unresolved the essential issue of the amount of punitive damages): *Plaza Tulare v. Tradewell Stores, Inc.*, 207 Cal. App. 3d 522, 524, 254 Cal. Rptr. 792 (1989) (ruling appeal from adverse decision on liability by defendant in bifurcated trial is premature); *Horton v. Jones*, 26 Cal. App. 3d 952, 103 Cal. Rptr. 399 (1972) (concluding order denying defendant's motion for judgment notwithstanding the verdict is not appealable where motion addressed to jury verdict on liability only as first part of bifurcated trial).

In dissolution of marriage actions, the court is authorized to try separately some issues, such as validity of a marital agreement, date to use for valuation of assets, or whether property separate or community, before trial of the other issues. Rule 5.390, Cal. Rules of Ct. An interlocutory appeal from such a bifurcated trial may be permitted, in the discretion of the trial and appellate courts. Family Code § 2025; Rule 5.180. *See, e.g., Marriage of Griffin*, 15 Cal. App. 4th 685, 19 Cal. Rptr. 2d 94 (1993) (holding the determination of some but not all property and support issues is not appealable until all such issues finally determined); *Marriage of Loya*, 189 Cal. App. 3d 1636, 235 Cal. Rptr. 198 (1987) (concluding a ruling on validity of antenuptial agreement bifurcated from other trial issues not appealable as final judgment); *Marriage of Noghrey*, 169 Cal. App. 3d 326, 215 Cal. Rptr. 153 (1985) (holding interim ruling on bifurcated issue of enforcement of premarital agreement is appealable).

[c] Finality Determined by Substance of Decree

As *UAP-Columbus* illustrates, the substance and effect of a decree, not its label or form, determine whether it is appealable as a final judgment. *See also Furtado v. Schriefer*, 228 Cal. App. 3d 1608, 1613–1614, 280 Cal. Rptr. 16 (1991); *Joyce v. Black*, 217 Cal. App. 3d 318, 321, 266 Cal. Rptr. 8 (1990). Would the final judgment determination in *UAP-Columbus* have been different if the trial court's March 19, 1990 decision had also included the following statement: "This interpleader decision shall not be a final judgment until this court makes its determination regarding costs and attorney fees, and this court shall retain jurisdiction of this action until such time for that purpose"? *See Furtado v. Schriefer, supra,* 228 Cal. App. 3d at 1613–1614.

(1) In *Laraway v. Pasadena Unified School Dist.,* 98 Cal. App. 4th 579, 120 Cal. Rptr. 2d 213 (2002), the plaintiff petitioned the superior court for mandamus, declaratory, and injunctive relief seeking certain public records from the defendant school district. The superior court denied the relief requested in the petition in an "order" dated August 23, 2000. This order did not award any attorney fees or costs. Subsequently, on January 29, 2001, the superior court filed a "judgment" which reiterated that the court had "ruled by Order dated August 23, 2000" on the petition, set forth the same rulings as contained in the order denying the petition, added a provision that judgment was entered in favor of respondent and against petitioner, and awarded respondent $0 in costs against petitioner. With respect to the 180-day time period within which to file a notice of appeal from the denial the plaintiff's petition, when did the time to appeal begin to run? On August 23, 2000 or on January 29, 2001? Why? *See Laraway, supra,* 98 Cal. App. 4th at 583.

(2) In *Griset v. Fair Political Practices Com.,* 25 Cal. 4th 688, 107 Cal. Rptr. 2d 149, 23 P.3d 43 (2001), the Supreme Court applied the "substance and effect not form of the decree" standard to determine whether a superior court adjudication was final and appealable. The plaintiffs had alleged four related causes of action, including a petition for writ of administrative mandate, challenging the constitutionality of a statute that required candidates for public office, and individuals or groups supporting or opposing a candidate or ballot measure, must identify themselves on any mass mailings to prospective voters. Central to all four causes of action was plaintiffs' allegation that this statute violated the right to free speech under the First Amendment. The superior court denied plaintiffs' administrative mandamus cause of action on the ground that the statute was constitutional in prohibiting anonymous mass mailings by candidates and candidate-controlled committees, as in plaintiffs' case. The superior court did not, however, formally rule on the other three causes of action. Plaintiffs appealed, and the Court of Appeal affirmed.

When the *Griset* case subsequently reached the California Supreme Court, the main issue was whether the Court of Appeal had jurisdiction to hear plaintiffs' appeal from superior court. First, the Supreme Court concluded that the superior court's decision denying plaintiffs' petition for a writ of administrative mandate was not an appealable *order* under CCP § 904.1 when the petition has been joined with other causes of action that remain unresolved. "When an order denying a petition for writ of administrative mandate does not dispose of all causes of action between the parties," the Griset court reasoned, "allowing an appeal from the denial order would defeat the purpose of the one final judgment rule by permitting the very piecemeal dispositions and multiple appeals the rule is designed to prevent." *Griset,* 25 Cal. 4th at 697.

Next, relying on *Morehart v. County of Santa Barbara*, reproduced *supra*, the *Griset* court observed that the superior court's ruling was not an appealable *judgment* if it disposed of only one of the causes of action pending between the parties. The *Griset* court then concluded, however, that superior court's ruling was indeed a final judgment because it disposed of all four causes of action between the parties, even though there was no formal entry of judgment by the superior court. Regardless of its form, the substance of the superior court's denial of plaintiffs' petition for a writ of mandate disposed of all issues in the action between plaintiffs and defendant "because it completely resolved plaintiffs' allegation — essential to all of plaintiffs' causes of action — that [the statute] was unconstitutional." *Griset*, 25 Cal. 4th at 699.

[2]   *Statutory Bases for Appeals*

Generally speaking, the right to appeal is governed by statute. Code of Civil Procedure Section 904.1, reproduced above, sets forth the statutory authority for appeals from a superior court in unlimited civil cases. Section 904.2 delineates when an appeal may be taken to the appellate division of the superior court in a limited civil case; §904.5, by reference to CCP §§116.710–116.795, indicates when an appeal may be taken from a small claims court; and CCP §§1294 and 1294.2 specify appealable orders in arbitration; and a few other statutes contain special appeal provisions, *e.g.*, Family Code §2025; CCP §597 (authorizing appeals from separate trials of special defenses). The statement often repeated by the courts — that "the right to appeal is wholly statutory," *e.g.*, *UAP-Columbus JV 3261 32 v. Nesbitt*, *supra*; *Kinoshita v. Horio*, *supra*, 186 Cal. App. 3d at 962 — is misleading. As *Morehart v. County of Santa Barbara* acknowledges, the courts permit appeals in certain circumstances despite the lack of statutory authority. These nonstatutory bases for appeal are discussed in more detail in §15.01[A][3], *infra*.

[3]   *Judge-Made Exceptions to Statutory One-Final-Judgment-Rule*

As *Morehart v. County of Santa Barbara*, reproduced *supra*, recognizes, there are at least two judicially-created exceptions to the one-final-judgment-rule as codified in CCP §904.1.

[a]   Ruling on Collateral Matter

Perhaps the most frequently utilized exception is a ruling on a collateral matter, which has been defined by the Supreme Court as follows: "When a court renders an interlocutory order collateral to the main issue, dispositive of the rights of the parties in relation to the collateral matter, and directing payment of money or performance of an act, direct appeal may be taken.... This constitutes a necessary exception to the one final judgment rule. Such a determination is substantially the same as a final judgment in an independent proceeding." *Marriage of Skelly*, 18 Cal. 3d 365, 368, 134 Cal. Rptr. 197, 556 P.2d 297 (1976).

The courts have applied this exception to permit immediate appeal of interlocutory orders in a variety of circumstances, including certain orders for payment of money sanctions, *I. J. Weinrot & Son, Inc. v. Jackson*, 40 Cal. 3d 327, 331, 220 Cal. Rptr. 103, 708 P.2d 682 (1985); orders reducing temporary spousal support, *Marriage of Skelly, supra,* 18 Cal. 3d at 367–70; and orders denying statutory award of attorney fees, *Henneberque v. City of Culver City,* 172 Cal. App. 3d 837, 842, 218 Cal. Rptr. 704 (1985). For more examples, *see* CEB, *California Civil Appellate Practice* § 3.57 (3d ed. 2015); *see also* William M. Lukens, *The Collateral Order Doctrine in California,* 15 HASTINGS L.J. 105 (1963).

Some courts do not always require, for this exception to apply, that the collateral order direct the payment of money or the performance of an act. *See, e.g., Meehan v. Hopps,* 45 Cal. 2d 213, 216–217, 288 P.2d 267 (1955) (ruling order disqualifying attorney is immediately appealable as collateral matter); *Reed v. Superior Court,* 92 Cal. App. 4th 448, 454, n. 2, 111 Cal. Rptr. 2d 842 (2001) (following *Meehan's* premise that an appeal from an order denying disqualification of counsel involves a collateral matter); *but see Samuel v. Stevedoring Serv.,* 24 Cal. App. 4th 414, 418, 29 Cal. Rptr. 2d 420 (1994) (surveying prior Supreme Court decisions and holding collateral order doctrine limited to situations where trial court orders either payment of money or performance of some act).

But most courts conclude that judicially compelled payment of money or performance of an act is an essential prerequisite. *See, e.g., Conservatorship of Rich,* 46 Cal. App. 4th 1233, 54 Cal. Rptr. 2d 459 (1996) (holding order refusing to allow substitution of attorneys was not appealable under the collateral matter doctrine); *Ponce-Bran v. Trustees of the Cal. State Univ.,* 48 Cal. App. 4th 1656, 56 Cal. Rptr. 2d 358 (1996) (concluding order denying a motion to appoint counsel was not appealable under the collateral order doctrine because the order did not direct the payment of money or the performance of an act); *Mercury Interactive Corp. v. Klein,* 158 Cal. App. 4th 60, 70 Cal. Rptr. 3d 88 (2007) (ruling order directing the unsealing of exhibits previously designated as confidential is appealable because it is a final determination of a collateral matter that directs the performance of an act—unsealing—against the party who filed the exhibits under seal). Should they? What purpose does this requirement serve?

For a good discussion of the collateral order doctrine generally, and the disagreement in the cases over whether the order must direct the payment of money or the performance of an act, see *Muller v. Fresno Cmty. Hosp. & Med. Ctr.,* 172 Cal. App. 4th 887, 91 Cal. Rptr. 3d 617 (2009). After reviewing conflicting authorities, the *Muller* court observed that "[w]hen the order does not require a payment of money or the performance of an act, the Supreme Court will find the order appealable without reference to these limitations, *as long as the court is satisfied that the order is truly collateral." Muller, supra,* 172 Cal. App. 4th at 902 (italics in original).

The fact that an interlocutory order directs payment of money or performance of an act does not, by itself, mean that the order is within the collateral matter exception. *See, e.g., Steen v. Fremont Cemetery Corp.,* 9 Cal. App. 4th 1221, 11 Cal. Rptr. 2d 780 (1992) (holding order directing service of class action notice and allocating cost of such notice not collateral matter and therefore not immediately appealable). The interlocutory order must also be "collateral," *i.e.*, distinct and severable from the general subject of the litigation and therefore not a necessary step to the correct determination of the main issue of the action. *Steen*, 9 Cal. App. 4th at 1227–28. What are the policy reasons for this exception and its limitations?

[b] Judgment Final as to One Party

When litigation involves multiple parties and a judgment is entered which leaves no issue to be determined as to one party, that party may immediately appeal that judgment even though the litigation is not final as to other parties. *E.g., Justus v. Atchison*, 19 Cal. 3d 564, 568, 139 Cal. Rptr. 97, 565 P.2d 122 (1977) (holding dismissal of all causes of action pleaded by one of two plaintiffs constitutes appealable judgment even though remaining plaintiff had joined in some of these causes of action), *disapproved on another point, Ochoa v. Superior Court*, 39 Cal. 3d 159, 171, 216 Cal. Rptr. 661, 703 P.2d 1 (1985); *Hydrotech Sys., Ltd. v. Oasis Water Park*, 52 Cal. 3d 988, 993, n.3, 277 Cal. Rptr. 517, 803 P.2d 370 (1991) (ruling order dismissing fewer than all defendants from an action is a final judgment as to them, and thus is appealable).

(1) This exception to the one-final-judgment-rule apparently is the rationale for numerous holdings that an order denying a motion to certify a class action is appealable. *E.g., Richmond v. Dart Indus., Inc.*, 29 Cal. 3d 462, 470, 174 Cal. Rptr. 515, 629 P.2d 23 (1981); *Daar v. Yellow Cab Co.*, 67 Cal. 2d 695, 699, 63 Cal. Rptr. 724, 433 P.2d 732 (1967) (ruling demurrer sustained as to class action allegations "is tantamount to a dismissal of the action as to all members of the class other than plaintiff"). In *In re Baycol Cases I and II*, 51 Cal. 4th 751, 122 Cal. Rptr. 3d 153, 248 P.3d 681 (2011), the Supreme Court clarified the rules regarding appellate review of a class action determination. If an order terminates class claims but individual claims survive, the order terminating class claims is immediately appealable under the "death knell" doctrine adopted in *Daar v, Yellow Cab Co, supra*. However, if an order terminates class claims and individual claims, appeal lies from the subsequent entry of final judgment, not the order. *Baycol, supra*, 51 Cal. 4th at 760–762.

(2) Is an order which certifies a class, but not one as extensive as plaintiff sought, an appealable order under this exception? See *Baycol, supra*, 51 Cal. 4th at 757–758 (concluding the "death knell" doctrine applies to orders that entirely terminate class claims, but not orders that only limit the scope or the number of claims available to the class). Is there any other method by which a defendant may obtain immediate appellate review of a trial court order certifying a class action? *See Blue Chip Stamps v. Superior Court*, 18 Cal. 3d 381, 134 Cal. Rptr. 393, 556 P.2d 755 (1976).

[c] Order Determining Separate and Independent Issues

Prior to the Supreme Court's 1994 decision in *Morehart v. County of Santa Barbara*, reproduced *supra*, the courts of appeal applied a third exception to the one-final-judgment-rule: an immediate appeal from a judgment on issues separate and independent from other issues still pending in the trial court. *See, e.g., Garat v. City of*

Riverside, 2 Cal. App. 4th 259, 275–280, 3 Cal. Rptr. 2d 504 (1991); *Day v. Papadakis,* 231 Cal. App. 3d 503, 282 Cal. Rptr. 548 (1991) (citing cases). The *Morehart* court clearly repudiated this exception. Do you agree with the *Morehart* court's criticisms of this developing exception? With the court's holding? Does the holding eliminate the uncertainty as to appealability inherent in the "separate and independent" exception? How so? Are you persuaded by the court's treatment of those cases in which "hardship and inconvenience" would result from postponement of appellate review until final disposition of the entire action? Does the Supreme Court provide meaningful guidance as to when a Court of Appeal should permit appellate review by extraordinary writ in such circumstances? Is the uncertainty inherent in use of an extraordinary writ to seek immediate appellate review of an interlocutory judgment any different than the uncertainty inherent in the "separate and independent" exception? How so? Which type of uncertainty is better? Why?

(1) Even before the Supreme Court ruling in *Morehart,* the general rule was that, absent one of the exceptions to the one-final-judgment-rule, dismissal of a complaint does not constitute a final appealable judgment with respect to parties as to whom a cross-complaint remains pending, even though the complaint has been fully adjudicated. *See, e.g., California Dental Assn. v. Cal. Dental Hygienists' Assn.,* 222 Cal. App. 3d 49, 59, 271 Cal. Rptr. 410 (1990); *Daon Corp. v. Place Homeowners Assn.,* 207 Cal. App. 3d 1449, 1456, 255 Cal. Rptr. 448 (1989); *Sjoberg v. Hastorf,* 33 Cal. 2d 116, 118, 199 P.2d 668 (1948) (applying same general rule when defendant's cross-complaint against plaintiff dismissed, but complaint still pending). How likely is it that the "collateral matter" exception will apply in such a cross-complaint situation? Why?

(2) The courts have readily found an appealable final judgment, however, where the dismissal of a cross-complaint adjudicates all issues as to a specific third-party cross-defendant. *E.g., County of Los Angeles v. Guerrero,* 209 Cal. App. 3d 1149, 1152, n.2, 257 Cal. Rptr. 787 (1989) (concluding that where defendant cross-complains against a third party, the dismissal of the cross-complaint is a final adverse adjudication of cross-complainant's rights against a distinct party and the order is appealable); *Miller v. Silver,* 181 Cal. App. 3d 652, 658, 226 Cal. Rptr. 479 (1986) (ruling dismissal of cross-complaint against a third party, not a defendant or plaintiff, is appealable). Is final judgment treatment in such circumstances consistent with *Morehart?* Why?

[4] Untimely Appeals

An appeal from a trial court judgment is commenced by filing a notice of appeal within the relevant time limitation specified by the California Rules of Court. *See, e.g.,* Rules 8.104 & 8.108, Cal. Rules of Ct. The timely filing of a notice of appeal is jurisdictional; failure to appeal from an appealable judgment or order within the prescribed time limit generally bars appellate review of the issues determined by the trial court's ruling. *Hollister Convalescent Hosp., Inc. v. Rico,* 15 Cal 3d 660, 666, 674, 125 Cal. Rptr. 757, 542 P.2d 1349 (1975) (appeal dismissed because notice of appeal filed one day late); *UAP-Columbus JV 3261 32 v. Nesbitt,* reproduced *supra.*

[a] Late Appeals

As our principal cases illustrate, the time for taking an appeal is mandatory. An appellate court has no jurisdiction to consider an appeal taken after the applicable limitation period. *See* Rule 8.104(b), Cal. Rules of Ct. ("If a notice of appeal is filed late, the reviewing court must dismiss the appeal"); *see also Sharp v. Union Pac. R.R. Co.,* 8 Cal. App. 4th 357, 361, 9 Cal. Rptr. 2d 925 (1992) ("[N]either mistake, inadvertence, accident, misfortune, estoppel nor waiver can afford relief from the jurisdictional necessity of filing a timely notice of appeal"); *Delmonico v. Laidlaw Waste Sys., Inc.,* 5 Cal. App. 4th 81, 6 Cal. Rptr. 2d 599 (1992) (holding appeal untimely when not filed within 60 days after service of notice of entry of judgment, pursuant to Rule 2(a)(2) [now 8.104(a)(1)], despite fact that notice stated incorrect date of entry of judgment). This strict jurisdictional requirement makes the consequences of a late appeal far more drastic than those of a premature appeal, does it not? This requirement places a premium on a thorough understanding of what constitutes an appealable judgment or order under the relevant statute, such as CCP § 904.1, as well as under the judge-made exceptions to the one-final-judgment-rule.

(1) Failure to commence a timely appeal of an interlocutory order made appealable by one of these exceptions will bar later review of the order by appeal taken after final judgment is entered by the trial court. *E.g., Stephen v. Enterprise Rent-A-Car,* 235 Cal. App. 3d 806, 1 Cal. Rptr. 2d 130 (1991) (holding failure to file timely notice of appeal from order denying class action certification bars later appeal of class issues as part of appeal from final judgment in the individual action; review of this order by later appeal not permitted because an immediate appeal of this order might have been taken); *California Dental Assn. v. California Dental Hygienists' Assn.,* 222 Cal. App. 3d 49, 60, 271 Cal. Rptr. 410 (1990) (ruling dismissal as to some parties, but not all, in multi-party lawsuit, obligates them to appeal immediately); *United Pac. Ins. Co. v. Hanover Ins. Co.,* 217 Cal. App. 3d 925, 940–43, 266 Cal. Rptr. 231 (1990) (concluding that by failing to immediately appeal interim collateral order, defendant acquiesced in the trial court's determination); *see In re Baycol Cases I and II, supra,* 51 Cal. 4th at 762, n. 8 (noting that California follows a "one shot" rule under which, if a class action order is appealable, appeal must be taken or the right to appeal is forfeited).

(2) Reconsider the judge-made exceptions to the one-final-judgment-rule. When a trial court enters an order adverse to your client which *arguably* (but not clearly) comes within one of these exceptions, what should you advise your client in order to protect her right of appellate review?

(3) Does an appellate court have any authority to permit use of an extraordinary writ to review an appealable judgment after the time for appeal has passed? Generally no, although there is some very limited authority for such review by writ in narrow, special circumstances. *E.g., Phelan v. Superior Court,* 35 Cal. 2d 363, 370–371, 217 P.2d 951 (1950) (permitting writ to be heard where uncertainty had previously existed respecting the appealability of order in question, and several earlier decisions, overruled in *Phelan,* had held that appeal was not an adequate remedy in that type of case); *see Mauro B. v. Superior Court,* 230 Cal. App. 3d 949, 953–954, 281 Cal. Rptr.

507 (1991) (reviewing the few cases permitting such writ review in narrow situations, but finding no special circumstances justifying failure to appeal and therefore writ review inappropriate).

[b] Premature Appeals

What is the consequence of filing a notice of appeal from a trial court order which turns out to be a nonappealable order? Mandatory dismissal by the appellate court for lack of jurisdiction? *See, e.g., Committee for Responsible Planning v. City of Indian Wells,* 225 Cal. App. 3d 191, 195, 275 Cal. Rptr. 57 (1990) (ruling lack of final judgment is a jurisdictional defect which court has duty to raise on own motion even if parties do not).

(1) In 2002, the Judicial Council amended the California Rules of Court governing the appellate process to expressly address the appropriate treatment of a premature notice of appeal. Rule 8.104(d)(1) now proclaims that a notice of appeal filed after judgment is rendered but before it is entered "is valid and is treated as filed immediately after entry of judgment." Less definitive is a related provision dealing with a notice of appeal filed after the superior court has announced its intended ruling but before it has rendered judgment, which simply provides that the reviewing court may treat such a premature notice of appeal as filed immediately after entry of judgment. Rule 8.104(d)(2), Cal. Rules of Ct.; *see Good v. Miller,* 214 Cal. App. 4th 472, 475–77, 153 Cal. Rptr. 3d 848 (2013) (discussing cases and declining to exercise its discretion to salvage premature appeal). A notice of appeal is filed *before* announcement of the trial court's intended ruling is untimely and cannot be treated as a premature but timely notice. *See, e.g., Silver v. Pac. Am. Fish Co., Inc.,* 190 Cal. App. 4th 688, 118 Cal. Rptr. 3d 581 (2010); *First Am. Title Co. v. Mirzaian,* 108 Cal. App. 4th 956, 134 Cal. Rptr. 2d 206 (2003).

(2) Under what circumstances, according to *Morehart,* may an appellate court treat the appeal as a petition for an extraordinary writ, and, in its discretion, consider the issues raised by the premature appeal? *See, e.g., Olson v. Cory,* 35 Cal. 3d 390, 197 Cal. Rptr. 843, 673 P.2d 720 (1983) (observing that although appellate court has power to treat purported appeal as petition for writ of mandate, it should not exercise that power except under unusual circumstances); *Doran v. Magan,* 76 Cal. App. 4th 1287, 91 Cal. Rptr. 2d 60 (1999) (holding denial of defendant's motion for entry of judgment pursuant to terms of a challenged settlement did not constitute a final appealable judgment, and deciding not to treat purported appeal as an extraordinary writ petition because defendant could not show unusual or compelling circumstances); *Stonewall Ins. Co. v. City of Palos Verdes Estates,* 46 Cal. App. 4th 1810, 1831–1832, 54 Cal. Rptr. 2d 176 (1996) (concluding a premature appeal was properly treated as a petition for writ of mandate where the appealability question was very confusing, the merits of the issues were fully briefed, and judicial economy would not be served by deferring a ruling on the merits). *See* § 15.02, Extraordinary Writs, *infra,* for discussion of the relationship between review by appeal and by extraordinary writ.

(3) In *Sullivan v. Delta Air Lines, Inc.*, 15 Cal. 4th 288, 63 Cal. Rptr. 2d 74, 935 P.2d 781 (1997), the California Supreme Court ruled that an appeal from a judgment that is not final violates the one-final-judgment-rule and must therefore be dismissed, unless the violation can be cured by amending the judgment. Where the trial court's failure to dispose of all causes of action results from mistake or inadvertence, an appellate court has the discretion to preserve the appeal by amending the judgment to reflect the manifest intent of the trial court. *Sullivan, supra*, 15 Cal. 4th at 308. Even where a cause of action remained intentionally unresolved by the trial court, the appellant may remove this impasse by voluntarily dismissing the remaining cause of action with prejudice. *Id.* at 308.

Moreover, the Court ruled that "[w]hen a party expressly waives on appeal the right to litigate an unresolved cause of action that deprived the judgment as entered of finality, the appellate court may give effect to the waiver by amending the judgment to reflect a dismissal of the cause of action with prejudice." *Sullivan*, 15 Cal. 4th at 308–309. *See also Swain v. California Cas. Ins. Co.*, 99 Cal. App. 4th 1, 5–6, 12o Cal. Rptr. 2d 808 (2002) (amending trial court's summary judgment order to make in an effective judgment); *Parker v. Robert E. McKee, Inc.*, 3 Cal. App. 4th 512, 514, 4 Cal. Rptr. 2d 347 (1992) (ruling appeal from order sustaining demurrer without leave to amend not premature despite the lack of formal judgment where appellate court exercised its power to modify the order to make it a judgment).

(4) In *Kurwa v. Kislinger*, 57 Cal. 4th 1097, 162 Cal. Rptr. 3d 516, 309 P.3d 838 (2013), the California Supreme Court considered the question of whether an appeal may be taken when a judgment disposes of fewer than all the pled causes of action and the parties agree to dismiss the remaining causes of action *without prejudice* and waive operation of the statute of limitations on those remaining causes of action. The Court concluded that such a judgment is not appealable, because the parties' agreement holding some causes of action in abeyance for possible litigation after an appeal from the trial court's judgment on others renders the judgment interlocutory and precludes appeal under the one final judgment rule.

The Supreme Court observed that a plaintiff has the right to voluntarily dismiss a cause of action *without prejudice* prior to trial and that such a dismissal, unaccompanied by an agreement for future litigation, does create sufficient finality as to that cause of action so as to allow appeal from a judgment disposing of the other causes of action. *Kurwa, supra*, 57 Cal. 4th at 1005. However, the Court explained, "when the parties agree to waive or toll the statute [of limitations] on a dismissed cause of action pending an appeal, they establish an assurance the claim *can* be revived for litigation at the appeal's conclusion. It is that assurance—the agreement keeping the dismissed count legally alive—that prevents the judgment disposing of the other causes of action from achieving finality." *Kurwa*, 57 Cal. 4th at 1105–06.

[5] Appealability of Orders

An order is a written ruling of a trial court which is not included in a judgment. CCP § 1003; *see Shpiller v. Harry C's Redlands*, 13 Cal. App. 4th 1177, 1179, 16 Cal.

Rptr. 814 (1993) ("An order is a document which contains a direction by the court that a party take or refrain from action, or that certain relief is granted or not granted.") An order is not appealable unless made so by a specific statutory provision, such as CCP §904.1(a)(2)–(12), or by one of the judge-made exceptions to the one-final-judgment-rule.

[a]   Appealability of Postjudgment Orders Under CCP §904.1(a)(2)

One of the broadest and most troublesome statutory exceptions to the general rule of nonappealability of orders is contained in CCP §904.1(a)(2), which authorizes an appeal from "an order made after a judgment made appealable" by §904.1(a)(1). In other words, this subsection authorizes an appeal from an order of the superior court entered after an appealable final judgment. CCP §904.1(a)(2) may apply to a wide variety of postjudgment orders such as ones determining motions for reconsideration pursuant to CCP §1008, motions to vacate judgment pursuant to CCP §473 or §473.5, and motions to tax costs. For a comprehensive listing of the appropriate methods of appellate review for numerous common superior court orders, with authorities listed, see CEB, *California Civil Appellate Practice* §§3.67–3.99 (3d ed. 2015).

[b]   Judicial Interpretations of CCP §904.1(a)(2)

CCP §904.1(a)(2), in essence, seems to authorize a second opportunity to appeal from a final judgment! What are the policy reasons for §904.1(a)(2)? Does this authority to appeal postjudgment orders mean that a dilatory party who failed to file a timely notice of appeal from an adverse final judgment can obtain a new order from which to appeal by simply filing a post-judgment motion attacking the prior final judgment? Not quite. Several court interpretations have imposed three limitations on what orders are appealable under §904.1(a)(2).

First, the antecedent judgment or order must itself be an appealable one. *See, e.g., I.J. Weinrot & Son, Inc. v. Jackson,* 40 Cal. 3d 327, 331, 220 Cal. Rptr. 103, 708 P.2d 682 (1985); *Joyce v. Black,* 217 Cal. App. 3d 318, 321, 266 Cal. Rptr. 8 (1990).

Second, the appeal from the order must not present the same issues as could have been presented on appeal from the antecedent judgment itself. *E.g., Rooney v. Vermont Inv. Corp.,* 10 Cal. 3d 351, 358, 110 Cal. Rptr. 353, 515 P.2d 297 (1973) (concluding an order denying a motion to vacate an appealable judgment is generally not appealable if such appeal raises only matters that could be reviewed on appeal from the judgment itself); *Blue Mountain Dev. Co. v. Carville,* 132 Cal. App. 3d 1005, 1010–1012, 183 Cal. Rptr. 594 (1982) (ruling an order denying reconsideration of judgment is appealable if supported by new evidence, but not if the reconsideration motion was based on the same showing offered in support of the original judgment).

Third, the order must either affect the antecedent judgment or relate to it either by enforcing it or staying its execution. *E.g., Olson v. Cory,* 35 Cal. 3d 390, 400, 197 Cal. Rptr. 843, 673 P.2d 720 (1983); *Williams v. Thomas,* 108 Cal. App. 3d 81, 84, 166 Cal. Rptr. 141 (1980).

[c] Order Must "Neither Add nor Subtract" from Judgment

The courts sometimes define the third prerequisite to mean that where an order after an appealable judgment simply leaves the judgment intact and "neither adds nor subtracts from it," the order is not appealable. *E.g.*, *City of Carmel-By-the-Sea v. Bd. of Supervisors*, 137 Cal. App. 3d 964, 971, 187 Cal. Rptr. 379 (1982).

The Supreme Court clarified some of the judicial interpretations of § 904.1(a)(2) in *Lakin v. Watkins Associated Industries*, 6 Cal. 4th 644, 25 Cal. Rptr. 2d 109, 863 P.2d 179 (1993). The *Lakin* court held that a postjudgment order denying an award of attorney fees, requested by the plaintiff under former CCP § 2033(o) for proving facts the defendant refused to admit during discovery, was an appealable order under § 904.1(a)(2). Referring to the "neither adds nor subtracts" standard, the court observed that "postjudgment orders that neither literally add nor subtract from the judgment can nevertheless be appealable, as long as they affect the judgment or relate to its enforcement." *Lakin*, 6 Cal. 4th at 654. The court then concluded that a postjudgment order denying attorney fees is an "order that affects the judgment or relates to its enforcement because it determines the rights and liabilities of the parties arising from the judgment, is not preliminary to later proceedings, and will not become subject to appeal after some future judgment." *Id.* at 656.

Does the *Lakin* reinterpretation of the § 904.1(a)(2) standards provide clear guidance to the lower courts? Based on *Lakin*'s reasoning, is an order denying sanctions for defendant's allegedly bad faith postjudgment and preappeal activities appealable under § 904.1(a)(2)? *See Shelton v. Rancho Mortg. & Inv. Corp.*, 94 Cal. App. 4th 1337, 1343– 45, 115 Cal. Rptr. 2d 82 (2002) (collecting cases). How about an order compelling responses to postjudgment discovery in connection with enforcement of a judgment? *See Macaluso v. Superior Court*, 219 Cal. App. 4th 1042, 162 Cal. Rptr. 3d 318 (2013) (discussing cases).

An order awarding attorney fees, if made after judgment, is separately appealable pursuant to CCP § 904.1(a)(2). *See Lakin, supra*, 6 Cal. 4th at 650–56; *First Sec. Bank of Cal. v. Paquet*, 98 Cal. App. 4th 468, 119 Cal. Rptr. 2d 787 (2002) (ruling appeal from a postjudgment fee award is authorized by § 904.1(a)(2) so long as the underlying judgment is appealable); Failure to appeal from such an order precludes appellate review, even though the appellant has appealed from the prior judgment on the merits. *See Pfeifer v. John Crane, Inc.*, 220 Cal. App. 4th 1270, 1316–18, 164 Cal. Rptr. 3d 112 (2013) (observing that when a party intends both to challenge the judgment and a postjudgment order related to costs, the normal procedure is to file appeals from the judgment and the postjudgment order); *DeZerega v. Meggs*, 83 Cal. App. 4th 28, 99 Cal. Rptr. 2d 366 (2000).

[d] New Trial and JNOV Orders

An order granting a new trial or denying a motion for judgment notwithstanding the verdict (J.N.O.V.) is expressly made appealable by § 904.1(a)(4). *See Aguilar v. Atlantic Richfield Co.*, 25 Cal. 4th 826, 858–859, 107 Cal. Rptr. 2d 841, 24 P.3d 493

(2001) (ruling any order granting a new trial is appealable pursuant to CCP § 904.1(a)(4), even one granting a new trial following an order granting summary judgment). Is an order *denying* a new trial appealable under § 904.1(a)(2)? *See Rodriguez v. Barnett*, 52 Cal. 2d 154, 156, 338 P.2d 907 (1959) (concluding an order denying a motion for new trial is nonappealable, but may be reviewed on appeal from the underlying judgment under CCP § 906); *Walker v. Los Angeles Cnty. Metro. Transp. Auth.*, 35 Cal. 4th 15, 19, 23 Cal. Rptr. 3d 490, 104 P.3d 844 (2005). An order granting a partial new trial on some parts of the judgment but not others? *See, e.g., Pacific Corporate Grp. Holdings, LLC v. Keck*, 232 Cal. App. 4th 294, 301–307, 181 Cal. Rtpr. 3d 399 (2014); *Beavers v. Allstate Ins. Co.*, 225 Cal. App. 3d 310, 329, 274 Cal. Rptr. 766 (1990). An order granting both a new trial and a judgment N.O.V.? *See* CCP § 629. An order granting a partial judgment N.O.V. on some issues and a new trial as to all other issues? *See, e.g., Beavers v. Allstate Ins. Co., supra*, 225 Cal. App. 3d at 330–31.

[6] Appealable Judgments in Federal Courts

[a] Federal Final Judgment Rule

The appellate jurisdiction of the U.S. Courts of Appeals is generally limited to review of "final decisions" of the U.S. District Courts. 28 U.S.C. § 1291. A "final decision" is typically defined as one which "ends the litigation on the merits and leaves nothing for the court to do but execute the judgment." *Coopers & Lybrand v. Livesay*, 437 U.S. 463, 467, 98 S. Ct. 2454, 57 L. Ed. 2d 351 (1978); *Catlin v. United States*, 324 U.S. 229, 233, 65 S. Ct. 631, 89 L. Ed. 911 (1945). For a detailed analysis of the "final judgment" rule in federal court, see Wright, Miller & Cooper, 15 *Federal Practice and Procedure: Jurisdiction 2d*, §§ 3905–3919.10 (West 1992 & 2015 Supp.). In 1990 Congress authorized the U.S. Supreme Court to define, through the Federal Rules of Civil Procedure, when a ruling of a district court is final for purposes of appeal under § 1291. 28 U.S.C. § 2072(c), *see* Rule 54(b), F.R.C.P., reproduced *infra*.

A few statutory exceptions to the federal "final judgment" rule authorize appellate review of a limited number of interlocutory orders. 28 U.S.C. § 1292(a). These include district court orders granting or refusing preliminary injunctions, § 1292(a)(1); appointing receivers or refusing to wind up receivership, § 1291(a)(2); and certain interlocutory decrees determining the rights and liabilities of persons in admiralty cases, § 1292(a)(3). In addition, seldom used § 1292(b) authorizes an appeal from an interlocutory order involving a controlling question of law where the district court certifies such appeal and the court of appeals, in its discretion, agrees to permit such interlocutory appeal.

Are the federal statutes delineating the right to appeal in federal courts more or less liberal in allowing interlocutory appeals than the California statutes? How so?

[b] Federal Collateral Order Doctrine

The federal courts also recognize two general non-statutory exceptions to the final judgment rule. One is the court-made "collateral order" exception, first articulated in *Cohen v. Beneficial Indus. Loan Corp.,* 337 U.S. 541, 546, 69 S. Ct. 1221, 93 L. Ed. 1528 (1949) (permitting immediate appellate review of question of whether state statute requiring security for costs in stockholder derivative suits applied to derivative suits in federal court). The U.S. Supreme Court has defined the collateral order doctrine as follows: "To come within the 'small class' of decisions excepted from the final judgment rule by *Cohen,* the order must conclusively determine the disputed question, resolve an important issue completely separate from the merits of the action, and be effectively unreviewable on appeal from a final judgment." *Coopers & Lybrand, supra,* 437 U.S. at 468 (ruling collateral order exception does not apply to interlocutory order denying class certification; and "death knell" doctrine not recognized as exception to final judgment rule); *see also Eisen v. Carlisle & Jacquelin,* 417 U.S. 156, 94 S. Ct. 2140, 40 L. Ed. 2d 732 (1974) (permitting collateral order appeal from pre-trial order imposing 90% of class action notice costs on defendant).

Recent U.S. Supreme Court cases have construed the collateral order doctrine quite narrowly, and have repeatedly held that this exception will not apply where appeal from a later final judgment will adequately, even if not perfectly, vindicate the disputed right. *E.g., Mohawk Indus., Inc. v. Carpenter,* 588 U. S. 100, 130 S. Ct. 599, 175 L. Ed. 2d 458 (2009) (holding disclosure order adverse to the attorney-client privilege does not qualify for immediate appeal under the collateral order doctrine); *Cunningham v. Hamilton County,* 527 U. S. 198, 119 S. Ct. 1915, 144 L. Ed. 2d 184 (1999) (concluding an order imposing discovery sanctions on an attorney does not meet the requirements of the collateral order doctrine); *Firestone Tire & Rubber Co. v. Risjord,* 449 U. S. 368, 375, 101 S. Ct. 669, 66 L. Ed. 2d 571 (1981) (ruling collateral order appeal improper to review denial of motion to disqualify opposing counsel in civil case). For a detailed discussion of the federal collateral order doctrine, see 15A Wright, Miller & Cooper, *Federal Practice and Procedure: Jurisdiction 2d,* §§ 3911–3911.5 (West 1992 & 2015 Supp.).

Is the collateral order doctrine developed by the federal courts more liberal in permitting immediate appeals from interlocutory orders than the similar doctrine developed by the California courts? How so?

[c] Federal Rule 54(b)

The other general exception to the federal final judgment rule is set forth in Rule 54(b), F.R.C.P., which deals with cases including multiple claims or multiple parties:

> When an action presents more than one claim for relief—whether as a claim, counterclaim, cross-claim, or third-party claim—or when multiple parties are involved, the court may direct the entry of a final judgment as to one or more, but fewer than all, claims or parties only if the court expressly determines that there is no just reason for delay. Otherwise, any order or other decision, however designated, that adjudicates fewer than all the claims

or the rights and liabilities of fewer than all the parties does not end the action as to any of the claims or parties and may be revised at any time before the entry of a judgment adjudicating all the claims and the parties' rights and liabilities.

What are the purposes of Rule 54(b)? *See Sears, Roebuck & Co. v. Mackey,* 351 U.S. 427, 435–438, 76 S. Ct. 895, 100 L. Ed. 1297 (1956). Rule 54(b) corresponds to which California court-made doctrines? Is the procedure set forth in Rule 54(b) superior to that of the California doctrines in providing certainty in determining when an appealable judgment has been made? Why? In reducing the number of premature appeals? Why? In reducing the risk of losing the right to appeal due to the late filing of a notice of appeal? Why? Should California adopt such a rule? For a comparison of Rule 54(b) and analogous California court-made doctrines, *see* Thomas Kallay, *A Study in Rule-Making by Decision: California Courts Adopt Federal Rule of Civil Procedure 54(b),* 13 Sw. U. L. Rev. 87–127 (1982). For a detailed discussion of Rule 54(b), see 10 Wright, Miller & Kane, *Federal Practice and Procedure: Civil 4th,* §§ 2653–2661 (West 2014).

[B] Standing to Appeal

"Any aggrieved party" may appeal from an adverse judgment. CCP § 902. This standing requirement is jurisdictional and cannot be waived. *E.g., Rebney v. Wells Fargo Bank,* 220 Cal. App. 3d 1117, 1132, 269 Cal. Rptr. 844 (1990); *Life v. County of L. A.,* 218 Cal. App. 3d 1287, 1292, n.3, 267 Cal. Rptr. 557 (1990).

An aggrieved party is one who has an "immediate, pecuniary, and substantial interest" that is "injuriously affected by the judgment." *E.g., California Assn. of Psychology Providers v. Rank,* 51 Cal 3d 1, 9–10, 270 Cal. Rptr. 796, 793 P.2d 2 (1990) (concluding trial court judgment against hospital which diminishes sphere of responsibility of psychiatrists vis-a-vis clinical psychologists, and thus will affect psychiatrists' income and authority at hospital, confers standing to appeal on psychiatrists' associations); *City of Riverside v. Horspool,* 223 Cal. App. 4th 670, 678–79, 167 Cal. Rptr. 3d 440 (2014) (observing that where only one of several parties appeals, the appeal includes only that portion of the judgment adverse to the appealing party's interest unless the part of the judgment appealed from is interwoven and connected with the remainder); *Rebney, supra,* 220 Cal. App. 3d at 1129–32 (ruling a party lacks standing to appeal judgment which only injuriously affects other, non-appealing, co-party's interests).

A nonparty who has an interest in the subject matter of a trial court's judgment and whose interest is adversely affected by the judgment is an "aggrieved party" within the meaning of CCP § 902, and therefore may have standing to appeal the judgment. *See Howard Contracting, Inc. v. G.A. MacDonald Constr. Co.,* 71 Cal. App. 4th 38, 83 Cal. Rptr. 2d 590 (1998). A nonparty who is legally "aggrieved" by a judgment may become a party of record and secure the right to appeal by moving to vacate the judgment under CCP § 663, *see, e.g., County of Alameda v. Carleson,* 5 Cal. 3d 730, 736–37, 97 Cal. Rptr. 385, 488 P.2d 953 (1971); *Howard Contracting,* 71 Cal. App. 4th at 58 (collecting cases); *Marriage of Burwell,* 221 Cal. App. 4th 1, 12–15, 164 Cal. Rptr.

3d 702 (2013) (applying same rule to motion to set aside under CCP § 657); or by moving for judgment notwithstanding the verdict or a new trial, *Shaw v. Hughes Aircraft Co.*, 83 Cal. App. 4th 1336, 1342–44, 100 Cal. Rptr. 2d 446 (2000). Does class counsel have standing, in his or her own right, to appeal the amount of attorney fees awarded by the trial court? *See Ruiz v. Cal. State Auto. Assn. Inter-Ins. Bureau*, 222 Cal. App. 4th 596, 606–610, 165 Cal. Rptr. 3d 896 (2013).

[1] Voluntary Dismissal?

Can a plaintiff who voluntarily dismisses an action ever be an aggrieved party? *See In re Tomi C.*, 218 Cal. App. 3d 694, 698, 267 Cal. Rptr. 210 (1990) (observing a voluntary dismissal by plaintiff is not appealable unless defendant has requested affirmative relief); *Ashland Chem. Co. v. Provence*, 129 Cal. App. 3d 790, 793, 181 Cal. Rptr. 340 (1982) (ruling plaintiff may appeal voluntary dismissal of complaint after adverse ruling by trial court, because dismissal not really voluntary but to expedite the appeal).

Can a party who consents to a stipulated judgment still be an aggrieved party? In *Norgart v. UpJohn Co.*, 21 Cal. 4th 383, 399–403, 87 Cal. Rptr. 2d 453, 981 P.2d 79 (1999), the Supreme Court affirmed the general rule that a party may not appeal a consent judgment, as well as the following recognized exception: "if the consent was merely given to facilitate an appeal following an adverse determination of a critical issue, the party will not lose his right to be heard on appeal." *Norgart*, 21 Cal. 4th at 400. Applying this general rule and exception, the *Norgart* court found that the parties' stipulation permitting the trial court's order granting defendant's motion for summary judgment was not a nonappealable consent judgment because that consent was given only pro forma to facilitate as appeal, and with the understanding on the part of both parties that the plaintiffs did not intend to abandon their right to be heard on appeal. *Id.* at 402; *see Villano v. Waterman Convalescent Hosp., Inc.*, 181 Cal. App. 4th 1189, 105 Cal. Rptr. 3d 276 (2010) (ruling judgment appealable where plaintiff, after unfavorable motion in limine rulings, stipulated to entry of judgment against her on all causes of action).

[2] Remittitur?

Can a plaintiff who has consented to a remittitur (*i.e.*, a reduction of damages awarded in lieu of a new trial, under CCP § 662.5(b)) appeal the reduced judgment entered pursuant to the remittitur? *See, e.g., Neal v. Farmers Ins. Exch.*, 21 Cal. 3d 910, 930–933, 148 Cal. Rptr. 389, 582 P.2d 980 (1978). If the defendant appeals the remitted judgment, does the plaintiff have standing to file a cross-appeal even though she consented to the remittitur? Why? *See, e.g., Rosenau v. Heimann*, 218 Cal. App. 3d 74, 77, 267 Cal. Rptr. 20 (1990); *Baker v. Pratt*, 176 Cal. App. 3d 370, 385, 222 Cal. Rptr. 253 (1986).

[3] Prevailing Party?

Under what circumstances may a prevailing party be considered "aggrieved" and have standing to appeal a favorable judgment? *See, e.g., Zarrahy v. Zarrahy*, 205 Cal.

App. 3d 1, 4, 252 Cal. Rptr. 20 (1988) (holding prevailing party has standing to appeal portions of community property judgment unfavorable to her); *Liodas v. Sahadi*, 19 Cal. 3d 278, 285, 137 Cal. Rptr. 635, 562 P.2d 316 (1977) (ruling a party seeking new trial on all issues is an aggrieved party when only a partial new trial is granted as to issue of damages, and may appeal therefrom); *Sturgeon v. Leavitt*, 94 Cal. App. 3d 957, 959, n.1, 156 Cal. Rptr. 687 (1979) (concluding a party is aggrieved and has standing to appeal when awarded less than originally demanded).

[4] Moot Appeal?

An appeal should be dismissed as moot when the occurrence of events renders it impossible for the appellate court to grant appellant any effective relief. *Eye Dog Found. v. State Bd. of Guide Dogs for the Blind*, 67 Cal. 2d 536, 541, 63 Cal. Rptr. 21, 432 P.2d 717 (1967). However, there are three discretionary exceptions to the rules regarding mootness: (1) when the case presents an issue of broad public interest likely to recur, *Edelstein v. City of San Francisco*, 29 Cal. 4th 164, 172, 126 Cal. Rptr. 2d 727, 56 P.3d 1029 (2002); *Lundquist v. Reusser*, 7 Cal. 4th 1193, 1202, n. 8, 31 Cal. Rptr. 2d 776, 875 P.2d 1279 (1994); (2) when there may be a recurrence of the controversy between the parties, *Diamond v. Bland*, 3 Cal. 3d 653, 657, 91 Cal. Rptr. 501, 477 P.2d 733 (1070); *Grier v. Alameda-Contra Costa Transit Dist.*, 55 Cal. App. 3d 325, 330, 127 Cal Rptr. 525 (1976); and (3) when a material question remains for the court's determination, *Eye Dog Foundation, supra*, 67 Cal. 2d at 541.

[C]   Timeliness of Appeals

[1]   Time Limitations for Appeals

[a]   General Time Limits

Rule 8.104, California Rules of Court, sets forth the general time limitations for civil appeals from superior court:

> (a) **Normal time**
>
> > (1) Unless a statute, rule 8.108, or rule 8.702 provides otherwise, a notice of appeal must be filed on or before the earliest of:
> >
> > > (A) 60 days after the superior court clerk serves the party filing the notice of appeal with a document entitled "Notice of Entry" of judgment or a filed-endorsed copy of the judgment, showing the date either was served;
> > >
> > > (B) 60 days after the party filing the notice of appeal serves or is served by a party with a document entitled "Notice of Entry" of judgment or a filed-endorsed copy of the judgment, accompanied by proof of service; or
> > >
> > > (C) 180 days after entry of judgment.
> >
> > (2) Service under (1)(A) and (B) may be by any method permitted by the Code of Civil Procedure, including electronic service when permitted under Code of Civil Procedure section 1010.6 and rules 2.250–2.261.

(3) If the parties stipulated in the trial court under Code of Civil Procedure section 1019.5 to waive notice of the court order being appealed, the time to appeal under (1)(C) applies unless the court or a party serves notice of entry of judgment or a filed-endorsed copy of the judgment to start the time period under (1)(A) or (B).

(b) **No extension of time; late notice of appeal**

* * * If a notice of appeal is filed late, the reviewing court must dismiss the appeal.

* * *

(d) **Premature notice of appeal**

(1) A notice of appeal filed after judgment is rendered but before it is entered is valid and is treated as filed immediately after entry of judgment.

(2) The reviewing court may treat a notice of appeal filed after the superior court has announced its intended ruling, but before it has rendered judgment, as filed immediately after entry of judgment.

(e) **Appealable order**

As used in subdivision (a) and (d), "judgment" includes an appealable order if appeal is from an appealable order.

In the usual civil case where a party serves the notice of entry of judgment, Rule 8.104(a)(1)(B) provides the relevant time limitation. Rule 8.104(a)(1)(A) is more likely to apply in dissolution of marriage cases, where superior court clerks are required to mail the notice of entry. *See* CCP § 664.5; Rule 5.413, Cal. Rules of Ct.; *but see Alan v. American Honda Motor Co.*, 40 Cal. 4th 894, 55 Cal. Rptr. 3d 534, 152 P.3d 1109 (2007) (construing Rule 8.104(a)(1) for the purpose of determining what constitutes "a document entitled 'Notice of Entry' of judgment or a filed copy of the judgment sufficient to start the 60-day period for filing a notice of appeal with respect to an order denying class certification). Rule 8.104(c) contains specific definitions of what constitutes entry of judgment or an appealable order based on the procedure followed by the trial court, and should be read closely. Rule 8.104(b) makes explicit what was implicit under older rules: If a notice of appeal is filed late, the reviewing court must dismiss the appeal. *See Hollister Convalescent Hosp., Inc. v. Rico*, 15 Cal. 3d 660, 666–674, 125 Cal. Rptr. 757, 542 P.2d 1349 (1975) (holding a reviewing court lacks jurisdiction to excuse a late-filed notice of appeal).

Code of Civil Procedure § 1010.6 authorizes a trial court to adopt local rules permitting electronic filing and service of documents in certain actions, including complex litigation, subject to certain conditions. CCP § 1010.6(c); Rule 2.251, Cal. Rule of Ct. In such circumstances, Rule 8.104(a)(2) authorizes electronic service of the "Notice of Entry" of judgment or a filed-endorsed copy of the judgment by the superior court clerk or a party. Electronic service does not extend the 60-day time limit for filing a notice of appeal. CCP § 1010.6(a)(4)(C); Rule 2.251(h)(3)(C), Cal. Rules of Ct.

[b] Extensions for Postjudgment Motions

Rule 8.108(a)–(e) provides extensions of time in which to file a notice of appeal when a party challenges a judgment by filing a notice of intention to move for a new trial or to vacate a judgment, moves for a judgment notwithstanding the verdict, or moves to reconsider an appealable order.

(1) Rule 8.108 must be read closely to determine the various circumstances in which the time to appeal is increased due to the filing of certain postjudgment motions.

(2) For these extensions to apply, the motions themselves must be timely filed and be valid within the meaning of their respective statutory authority. *E.g.*, *Payne v. Rader*, 167 Cal. App. 4th 1569, 85 Cal. Rptr. 3d 174 (2008) (concluding plaintiff's §663 motion to vacate demurrer was procedurally infirm and stated no valid grounds for relief, and therefore was invalid and did not extend the time to appeal from the judgment under Rule 8.108(c)); *Conservatorship of Townsend*, 231 Cal. App. 4th 691, 180 Cal. Rptr. 3d 117 (2014) (holding motion to vacate judgment pursuant to CCP §663a was untimely and therefore invalid, and did not extend the time within which to appeal); *Ramirez v. Moran*, 201 Cal. App. 3d 431, 436–437, 247 Cal. Rptr. 117 (1988) (ruling notice of motion, whether considered as one for new trial or to vacate judgment, untimely and therefore invalid; Rule 8.108 extension inapplicable and appeal untimely). For an example of the difficulties encountered in determining whether Rule 8.108(b)'s time extension applied such that an appeal was timely, where that determination depended on whether a motion for new trial was timely filed in and ruled on by the trial court, see *Van Beurden Ins. Serv., Inc. v. Customized World-wide Weather Ins. Agency, Inc.*, 15 Cal. 4th 51, 61 Cal. Rptr. 2d 166, 931 P.2d 344 (1997).

(3) In order to extend the jurisdictional time for filing a notice of appeal, a motion to vacate or set aside itself must be timely, *i.e.*, such a motion must be served and filed within either the *normal* time period for filing a notice of appeal under Rule 8.104, or any *shorter* time period prescribed by applicable statute. Rule 8.108(c), *see Marriage of Eben-King & King*, 80 Cal. App. 4th 92, 108–109, 95 Cal. Rptr. 2d 113 (2000) (ruling that although CCP §473 provides that a motion to set aside a judgment must be made within six months after judgment, in order to *also* extend the time for filing a notice of appeal such a §473 motion must be filed within the more limited parameters of Rule 8.104).

(4) An amended or revised judgment supersedes an otherwise-final original judgment for purposes of computing the time within which to file a notice of appeal, but only where amendment or revision constitutes a substantial modification materially affecting the rights of the parties. *See, e.g., Ellis v. Ellis*, 235 Cal. App. 4th 837, 185 Cal. Rptr. 3d 587 (2015) (discussing cases and concluding revised judgment did not extend time for appeal); *Lister v. Bowen*, 215 Cal. App. 4th 319, 329–31, 155 Cal. Rptr. 3d 50 (2013) (finding amended judgment effected a substantial modification and therefore appeal timely).

[c] Cross-Appeals

The first appeal filed in a case is the "appeal"; any subsequent appeals by any party are "cross-appeals." Rule 8.108(g), dealing with cross-appeals, provides:

(g) Cross-appeal

(1) If an appellant timely appeals from a judgment or appealable order, the time for any other party to appeal from the same judgment or order is extended until 20 days after the superior court clerk serves notification of the first appeal.

(2) If an appellant timely appeals from an order granting a motion for new trial, an order granting—within 150 days after entry of judgment—a motion to vacate the judgment, or a judgment notwithstanding the verdict, the time for any other party to appeal from the original judgment or from an order denying a motion for judgment notwithstanding the verdict is extended until 20 days after the clerk serves notification of the first appeal.

[d] Cross-Appeal When Both Sides Aggrieved

If a party is dissatisfied with part of a judgment, that party must appeal the adverse aspects of the judgment in order to raise the issues before the appellate court. Absent a cross-appeal, a respondent is limited to defending and preserving the trial court's judgment before the appellate court. *See, e.g.,* *Puritan Leasing Co. v. August,* 16 Cal. 3d 451, 463, 128 Cal. Rptr. 175, 546 P.2d 679 (1976); *Berge v. Int'l Harvester Co.,* 142 Cal. App. 3d 152, 158, 190 Cal. Rptr. 815 (1983). If, for example, a plaintiff obtains a verdict but not for as much as the law provides, what should she do (whether or not the defendant appeals)? Why?

[e] Protective Cross-Appeals

Rule 8.108(g) authorizes the filing of a protective cross-appeal by a party who has obtained an order granting a motion for new trial or to vacate the judgment. Why is such a cross-appeal from the judgment by the *successful* movant appropriate?

(1) Consider the case of *Sanchez-Corea v. Bank of America,* 38 Cal. 3d 892, 215 Cal. Rptr. 679, 701 P.2d 826 (1985). Plaintiff Sanchez-Corea obtained a $2 million jury verdict against defendant Bank of America for fraud and breach of contract. Defendant Bank moved for a new trial on a variety of grounds, including insufficiency of the evidence. The superior court granted the new trial and vacated the $2 million judgment. Plaintiff appealed from the order granting the new trial pursuant to CCP § 904.1(a)(4), but defendant filed no cross-appeal. The Supreme Court reversed the order granting a new trial because the trial court did not state its grounds for the new trial order in a timely fashion, as required by CCP § 660, and because no other grounds warranted affirming the trial court's order.

What is the status of the $2 million judgment after the Supreme Court's reversal? Can defendant now raise in the appellate court its previously successful arguments attacking the propriety of the $2 million judgment? Why not? What should the defendant have done to protect its right to raise those arguments before an appellate court?

(2) Rule 8.108(g) also authorizes a protective cross-appeal by a party whose motion for judgment notwithstanding the verdict was denied but motion for new trial was granted. Why is a protective cross-appeal necessary in such a situation? *See Berge v. Intl. Harvester Co., supra,* 142 Cal. App. 3d 152, 158–159 (observing CCP § 629 makes denial of motion for judgment notwithstanding verdict appealable by aggrieved party even though motion for new trial granted; failure to file cross-appeal when new trial order appealed precludes appellate review of the denial).

[2] *Time Limitations for Federal Appeals*

Rule 4 of the Federal Rules of Appellate Procedure sets forth the time limitations for appeals from the U. S. District Court in civil cases. Generally, the notice of appeal must be filed with the district court within 30 days after entry of the judgment or order to be appealed from. Rule 4(a)(1)(A), F.R.A.P. If the United States or an office or agency thereof is a party, the notice of appeal may be filed within 60 days after such entry. Rule 4(a)(1)(B). Cross-appeals must be filed within 14 days of the date a timely initial notice of appeal was filed, or within the time otherwise prescribed by Rule 4(a), whatever period last expires Rule 4(a)(3). As do the California rules, federal Rule 4(a)(4) authorizes time extensions when certain post-trial motions are filed. Unlike California, however, Federal Rules 4(a)(5) and (6) authorize extensions by the trial court upon a showing of excusable neglect or good cause.

[D] Scope of Appellate Review

In re Marriage of Ananeh-Firempong

Court of Appeal of California, Second Appellate District
219 Cal. App. 3d 272, 268 Cal. Rptr. 83 (1990)

WOODS (FRED), JUSTICE.

Husband appeals from a further judgment on reserved issues. He raises several issues regarding the orders and findings of the trial court. The crucial issue that we are called upon to decide is whether a request for a statement of decision pursuant to Code of Civil Procedure[1] section 632 can be oral. We conclude that it can and reverse and remand with directions to issue a statement of decision regarding the method of valuation of Husband's medical practice. Other than the finding regarding the valuation of the Husband's medical practice, the rest of the judgment is affirmed in all respects.

FACTUAL AND PROCEDURAL SYNOPSIS

Husband and Wife were married on June 7, 1978, and separated on June 13, 1984. Following a judgment of dissolution, a trial on reserved issues was held in January 1988.

---

1. Unless otherwise noted, all statutory references are to the Code of Civil Procedure.

1. The Mercedes Benz

The court found that the 1979 Mercedes Benz automobile was community property and awarded it to Husband at the value of $13,000. The court stated that it weighed heavily Husband's deposition testimony of October 1984, at which time, he had stated that the vehicle had been purchased in 1983.

Husband testified during trial that he had purchased this vehicle in November 1984, for around $10,000, that he had initially leased the vehicle for 48 months, from July 1979 through July 1983, and that in July 1983, he had extended the lease for an additional year. Husband further testified that he had confused this extension with the date of purchase when he testified at his deposition.

The pink slip for the Mercedes is dated November 3, 1984. The unsigned lease on the Mercedes showed that the outstanding balance was $15,000. At his deposition, Husband testified that he had paid $15,000 for the Mercedes.

2. Attorney's Fees

The court found that: "[Wife] has incurred the sum of $20,000.00 in attorney's fees in addition to such sums as have already been paid"; "it has been necessary for [Wife's] counsel to make 19 Court appearances"; "the trial in this matter has taken four days Court time"; and "[Wife's] counsel has been well-prepared during such time." Wife testified that prior to the commencement of trial, she had been advised that her legal fees were "just over $15,000."

The court ordered Husband to pay Wife's legal fees based on the finding that "[Wife] is unable to pay said sum and there are not sufficient liquid assets of the parties from which such legal fees could be paid."

3. Accountant's Fees

The court found that with respect to Wife's accountant's fees, the sum of $7,500 was a reasonable additional fee to be paid by Husband.

Krysler, Wife's accountant, testified that as of the end of May 1987, the amount that he was owed for accounting services was $9,601.25, with more work to be done. This amount was after applying the $2,500 already ordered to be paid. Wife testified that she had received a bill of approximately $10,000 for accounting services.

4. Valuation of Husband's Medical Practice

The court awarded the medical practice to Husband and valued it at $282,830.

Wife's accountant, Mr. Krysler testified that on the agreed date of valuation, the value of Husband's practice was $282,430, $282,830 and $282,000.

Husband's accountant Mr. Bigelson testified that the value of Husband's medical practice was $140,000.

5. Statement of Decision

Just prior to the court's rendering its tentative decision, Husband's counsel stated that: "What I want to say is if the court in its analysis were to make a finding as to this business valuation — accepting one of these practitioners and totally rejecting the other — then I have to request that we have a statement of decision showing calculations so that the record is clear as to what factors were used in arriving at whatever valuation." The court responded: "If you wish to have one, you may request that in writing."

A judgment on remaining issues was entered on March 11, 1988.

Husband filed a timely notice of appeal.

CONTENTIONS

1. The court's finding that the 1979 Mercedes Benz automobile was community property is reversible error.

2. The court's order for the payment of Wife's attorney's fees is not supported by the evidence.

3. The court's order for the payment of Wife's additional accountant's fees is not supported by the evidence.

4. The court's valuation of Husband's medical practice constitutes reversible error.

5. The court's refusal to issue a statement of decision constitutes reversible error.

DISCUSSION

* * *

> "'A judgment or order of the lower court is *presumed correct*. All intendments and presumptions are indulged to support it on matters as to which the record is silent, and error must be affirmatively shown. This is not only a general principle of appellate practice but an ingredient of the constitutional doctrine of reversible error.'" (Original italics.) (*Denham v. Superior Court* (1970) 2 Cal. 3d 557, 564 [86 Cal. Rptr. 65, 468 P.2d 193].)

"In resolving the issue of the sufficiency of the evidence, we are bound by the established rules of appellate review that all factual matters will be viewed most favorably to the prevailing party and in support of the judgment. All issues of credibility are likewise within the province of the trier of fact. 'In brief, the appellate court ordinarily looks only at the evidence supporting the successful party, and disregards the contrary showing.' [Citation.] All conflicts, therefore, must be resolved in favor of the respondent." (*Nestle v. City of Santa Monica* (1972) 6 Cal. 3d 920, 925–926 [101 Cal. Rptr. 568, 496 P.2d 480].)

1. *Sufficient Evidence Supports the Trial Court's Finding That the Mercedes Benz Was Community Property*

With respect to a finding by the trial court that an item is separate or community property, appellate review is limited to a determination of whether there is any substantial evidence, contradicted or uncontradicted, that supports the finding.

Husband contends that the Mercedes Benz was not community property because he testified at trial that he purchased the Mercedes in November of 1984 and the pink slip was dated November 3, 1984. However, there was sufficient contrary evidence to establish that the car had been purchased in 1983, prior to the separation of the parties in June of 1984.

The court noted that it had relied upon Husband's deposition testimony, which was introduced at trial. Husband testified at his deposition that the Mercedes had been purchased in 1983. At trial, Husband claimed to have mixed up the date of purchase with the extension of the lease. The trial court was entitled to disregard Husband's trial testimony and his claimed confusion regarding his deposition testimony.

First, the deposition took place in October 1984, prior to the claimed date of purchase. Second, Husband's credibility was further called into question by his conflicting statements regarding the amount paid for the car. At his deposition, Husband claimed to have paid $15,000 for the car, which corresponded to the payout listed on the unsigned lease. At trial, he claimed to have paid around $10,000 for the car.

2. *There Was No Abuse of Discretion in the Trial Court's Ordering Husband to Pay Wife's Attorney's Fees of $20,000*

Husband contends that the order for payment of attorney's fees is not supported by the evidence because the only evidence offered on the amount of the fees was Wife's testimony that prior to the commencement of trial, she had been advised that her legal fees were just over $15,000.

> "It is well settled that the award of attorney fees and costs in family law matters is within the broad discretion of the trial court and that court's decision in a particular case will not be disturbed on appeal absent a clear showing of abuse of discretion." (*In re Marriage of Bergman* (1985) 168 Cal. App. 3d 742, 763 [214 Cal. Rptr. 661].)

In the instant case, the court fixed the amount of fees based on its own experience as is evident from the court's finding that Wife's counsel had made 19 court appearances, participated in a 4 day trial and been well prepared.

"The California courts have repeatedly held that testimony or other direct evidence of the reasonable value of attorney's services need not be introduced because such evidence is necessarily before the trial court which hears the case." (*Frank v. Frank* (1963) 213 Cal. App. 2d 135, 137 [28 Cal. Rptr. 687].) "The knowledge and experience of the trial judge afford a sufficient basis for fixing the amount of a lawyer's fee, even though there was no specific evidence on the subject." (*Ibid.*)

We note that given the fundamental nature of time and unit value factors in determining an award of attorneys' fees, each factor presents a material issue upon which an explicit finding would be indispensable in any case where formal findings are mandatory, i.e., as when a statement of decision is requested by a party.

In this case, Husband did not request a statement of decision on the computation of attorney's fees, and thus he has waived any right to such a computation. (§632; *Homestead Supplies, Inc. v. Executive Life Ins. Co.* (1978) 81 Cal. App. 3d 978, 984 [147 Cal. Rptr. 22].)

Husband also asserts that the court's findings that Wife was unable to pay the fees and that there were not sufficient liquid assets of the parties from which such legal fees could be paid was inconsistent with the court's judgment ordering Husband to pay Wife certain sums. Husband cites no legal authority to support this assertion.

Civil Code section 4370 sets out a number of factors for the court to consider when ordering one spouse to pay the legal fees of the other spouse in a dissolution proceeding. Under the Family Law Act, awards of attorney fees must be based upon the need of the recipient and the payor's ability to pay.

In determining the issue as to who should pay the respective parties' attorney fees, it is necessary that the court consider the respective income and needs of the husband and wife. The wife is not required to impair her capital to finance marital dissolution litigation.

Husband does not discuss Wife's needs and expenses nor how the court's judgment would leave her with sufficient resources to pay her legal fees. In this case, Husband is a medical doctor and Wife is not employed and still attending college. Accordingly, in the absence of any showing to the contrary, we assume that the court's finding that Wife is unable to pay her legal fees is supported by sufficient evidence.

3. *There Was Substantial Evidence to Support the Trial Court's Order for Husband to Pay Wife's Accountant's Fees of an Additional $7,500*

Husband contends that there was insufficient evidence to support the court's ordering him to pay accountant's fees incurred by Wife since no billing statement was submitted by Wife's accountant and there was no testimony as to the actual services rendered, making the court's finding that $7,500 was a reasonable accountant's fee without any factual basis. Once again, Husband cites no legal authority for this contention nor does he contend that accountant's fees are not recoverable.

At the time Krysler, Wife's accountant, was examined about the bill, Krysler stated that he maintained time billing records. Husband's attorney did not object to this testimony or request that Krysler produce the bill even though he cross examined Krysler about Krysler's records. Furthermore, Husband did not request a statement of decision about the amount of accountant's fees owed. We conclude that Husband waived his right to attack the amount of accountant's fees by neither objecting at the time the amount was testified to nor requesting a statement of decision.

Moreover, there was sufficient evidence to support the court's finding that $7,500 was owed. Wife testified that she had received a bill for approximately $10,000, and Wife's accountant testified that as of the end of May 1987, he was owed $9,601.25 for accounting services, with more work to be done. This amount was after applying the $2,500 already ordered to be paid by the court.

4. *The Court's Failure to Prepare a Statement of Decision on the Issue of the Valuation of Husband's Medical Practice Is Reversible Error*

Husband contends that the trial court committed reversible error by not issuing a statement of decision as required by section 632.[2]

> "Where counsel makes a timely request for a statement of decision upon the trial of a question of fact by the court, that court's failure to prepare such a statement is reversible error." (*Social Service Union, Local 535 v. County of Monterey* (1989) 208 Cal. App. 3d 676, 681 [256 Cal. Rptr. 325].)

> "While a trial court issuing a statement of decision is required only to state ultimate rather than evidentiary facts it must, nevertheless, make such a statement. What is required is an explanation of the factual and legal basis for the court's decision as to the principal controverted issues at trial which are specified in the party's request for statement of decision. Where the court fails to make the required explanation reversible error results." (*McCurter v. Older* (1985) 173 Cal. App. 3d 582, 593 [219 Cal. Rptr. 104].) * * *

In the instant case, just prior to the court's rendering its tentative decision, Husband's counsel stated that: "What I want to say is if the court in its analysis were to make a finding as to this business valuation—accepting one of these practitioners and totally rejecting the other—then I have to request that we have a statement of decision showing calculations so that the record is clear as to what factors were used in arriving at whatever valuation."

Although not precisely identified as such, the crucial issue on this appeal is whether that statement is a request for a statement of decision pursuant to section 632. Wife argues that since Husband did not request a statement of decision until February 3, 1988, the request was untimely, having been made more than ten days after the oral announcement of decision on January 15, 1988. (§ 632; Cal. Rules of Court, rule 232(a).) The implication of Wife's reasoning is that a request for a statement of decision must be in writing. We note that the trial court informed Husband that: "If you wish to have one, you may request that in writing."

Former California Rules of Court, rule 232(b) provided that: "'A request for findings of fact and conclusions of law shall be *served and filed* within 10 days after oral announcement of intended decision in open court or, if mailing of the announcement of intended decision is required, within 10 days after such mailing, or, in the case of a subsequent modification or change in the announced intended decision, within 10 days after mailing of a copy thereof.'" (Italics added.) However, no such language appears in the current rule.

* * *

---

2. Section 632 provides that: "In superior, municipal, and justice courts, upon the trial of a question of fact by the court, written findings of fact and conclusions of law shall not be required. The *court shall issue* a statement of decision explaining the factual and legal basis for its decision as to each of the principal controverted issues at trial *upon the request* of any party appearing at the trial. The request must be made within 10 days after the court announces a tentative decision unless the trial is concluded within one calendar day or in less than eight hours over more than one day in which event the request must be made prior to the submission of the matter for decision. The request for a statement of decision shall specify those controverted issues as to which the party is requesting a statement of decision...." (Italics added.)

Therefore, we conclude that an oral request for a statement of decision is permissible under section 632. Even though in this case, Husband made the request just prior to the court's oral announcement of its tentative decision rather than after the announcement, we further conclude that under the circumstances of this case, we would be being overly technical not to honor his request, which was for only one item—the calculations used to determine the valuation of Husband's medical practice.

The *Hargrave* court concluded that the trial court had not met the mandate imposed by section 632 when, despite the wife's objection to the referee's terse statement of value of the community property business, she was provided with no explanation whatsoever of the factual or legal basis of the referee's determination that the goodwill had a value of $35,000. (*In re Marriage of Hargrave* [(1985)] 163 Cal. App. 3d 346, 354 [209 Cal. Rptr. 764].)

An appellate court concluded that a statement of decision was grossly inadequate because, among other things, it did not reveal what, if any, figures the court determined represented the parties' incomes and expenses. (*In re Marriage of Ramer* (1986) 187 Cal. App. 3d 263, 271 [231 Cal. Rptr. 647].)

The trial court here refused to issue a statement of decision and awarded the medical practice to Husband and valued it at $282,830. Under *Hargrave* and *Ramer*, such a statement is inadequate explanation of the factual and legal basis for the court's decision regarding the valuation of Husband's medical practice.

Since Husband's accountant testified to a different valuation for the medical practice, a finding in Husband's favor is possible. Therefore, we conclude that it was reversible error for the trial court to refuse to issue a statement of decision on the issue of the calculations used to determine the valuation of the medical practice.

The judgment is affirmed in part and reversed in part. Other than the valuation of Husband's medical practice, the judgment is affirmed in all respects. The matter is remanded for the sole purpose of rendering a statement of decision by the trial court on the issue of the valuation of the husband's medical practice under the existing evidence. Costs and attorney's fees on appeal are to be determined by the trial court.

[1] Scope of Appellate Review Determined by Record

[a] Adequate Record for Appellate Review

A judgment or order of a trial court is presumed to be correct on appeal, and all intendments and presumptions are indulged in favor of its correctness. *E.g., Marriage of Arceneaux*, 51 Cal. 3d 1130, 1133, 275 Cal. Rptr. 797, 800 P.2d 1227 (1990); *Denham v. Superior Court*, 2 Cal. 3d 557, 564, 86 Cal. Rptr. 65, 468 P.2d 193 (1970).

(1) A decision of the trial court must be affirmed if found to be correct by the appellate court, even if the reasons stated by the trial court for its decision are erroneous. *Davey v. Southern Pac. Co.,* 116 Cal. 325, 329, 48 P.117 (1897); *Sam Andrews' Sons v. A.L.R.B.,* 47 Cal. 3d 157, 176, 253 Cal. Rptr. 30, 763 P.2d 881 (1988). If correct upon any theory of the law applicable to the case, the decision must be sustained regardless of the considerations which may have moved the trial court to its conclusion. *D'Amico*

v. Bd. of Med. Examiners, 11 Cal. 3d 1, 19, 112 Cal. Rptr. 786, 520 P.2d 10 (1974) (affirming superior court ruling that the state statute violates constitution, even though trial court erroneously relied on "strict scrutiny" as opposed to "rational relationship" test in applying equal protection principles); *but see* CCP § 657; *Sanchez-Corea v. Bank of America,* 38 Cal. 3d 892, 905–906, 215 Cal. Rptr. 679, 701 P.2d 826 (1985) (observing that CCP § 657 requires an appellate court to affirm a new trial order if it should have been granted on any ground stated in the motion; however, an appellate court cannot affirm on grounds of insufficiency of the evidence or inadequate or excessive damages unless such ground is stated in the new trial order).

(2) The party appealing a judgment has the burden of showing reversible error by an adequate record. *E.g., Maria P. v. Riles,* 43 Cal. 3d 1281, 1295, 240 Cal. Rptr. 872, 743 P.2d 932 (1987); *Ballard v. Uribe,* 41 Cal. 3d 564, 574, 224 Cal. Rptr. 664, 715 P.2d 624 (1986). Appellant's responsibility to ensure a sufficient record on appeal has several components, discussed below.

[b] Statement of Decision

Upon timely request of any party in a nonjury trial, the trial court must issue a statement of decision explaining the factual and legal bases for its decision as to each principal controverted issue at trial. CCP §§ 632, 634. If the appellant fails to request a statement of decision as to specific issues to obtain an explanation of the trial court's tentative decision, the appellate court will imply findings to support the judgment. *Marriage of Arceneaux, supra,* 51 Cal. 3d at 1135.

(1) A judgment based on implied findings is difficult to reverse on appeal because the appellate court must assume the trial court made whatever findings were necessary to sustain the judgment. *See, e.g., Michael U. v. Jamie B.,* 39 Cal. 3d 787, 792–793, 218 Cal. Rptr. 39, 705 P.2d 362 (1985) (concluding, in a appeal by adoptive parents of award of custody of son to his natural teenage father; because no statement of decision requested, that the appellate court must assume that the trial court found an award of custody to natural father would not be detrimental to son and, consequently, the only issue before appellate court is whether substantial evidence supports this implied finding); *Marriage of Laube,* 204 Cal. App. 3d 1222, 1226, 251 Cal. Rptr. 745 (1988) (holding, on appeal from trial court's refusal to reinstate spousal support where wife argues error because husband now employed and consequently sole reason for temporary suspension of original indefinite spousal support order no longer applicable, that because wife requested no statement of decision the appellate court must assume that trial court determined wife no longer in need of spousal support despite husband's renewed ability to pay).

(2) A superior court, in a nonjury trial not completed within one day, must announce a tentative decision by written or oral statement. Rule 3.1590(a) & (c), Cal. Rules of Ct. This tentative decision does not constitute the judgment and is not binding on the court. Rule 3.1590(b). Any party may request a statement of decision within 10 days after the court announces its tentative decision. CCP § 632. If a party

does make such a request, the court then follows the procedures for preparation of the proposed statement, objections, and judgment detailed in Rule 3.1590(c)–(g). If a statement of decision is not requested, the court must merely prepare a proposed judgment following the procedures outlined in Rule 3.1590(h)–(m), and eventually files the judgment. The judgment so filed constitutes the decision upon which judgment is entered pursuant to CCP § 664. Rule 3.1590(l).

(3) May an appellant who has failed to request a statement of decision rely on the trial court's memorandum of tentative decision to demonstrate an erroneous basis for the trial court's judgment? In *Marriage of Ditto*, 206 Cal. App. 3d 643, 646–647, 253 Cal. Rptr. 770 (1988), the superior court's memorandum of intended decision employed the wrong legal standard in determining reimbursement for separate property contributions to community property, but neither party requested a statement of decision. The actual judgment merely confirmed separate property and divided community property, but was silent with respect to the court's reasoning. The Court of Appeal held that the appellant cannot rely on the superior court's memorandum of intended decision to demonstrate error in the judgment. The court noted that the trial court is not bound by its memorandum of intended decision, and such statements of intention cannot be resorted to for purposes of impeaching the trial court's actual judgment. *Marriage of Ditto*, 206 Cal. App. 3d at 647.

Do you understand why the Court of Appeal properly affirmed the judgment in *Marriage of Ditto* even though the appellate court acknowledged that the trial court announced an erroneous legal standard in its tentative decision? Would the result have been the same if the appellant had requested a statement of decision which, when issued by the trial court, utilized the erroneous legal standard? Why? A statement of decision may be crucial for review of a trial court's determination of questions of law, as well as of issue of fact, may it not?

(4) Is there any reason for an appealing party not to request a statement of decision? Why? The usual practice is for the trial court to ask the prevailing party to prepare and submit a proposed statement of decision. Rule 3.1590(f). This practice gives the prevailing party an opportunity to attempt to "sanitize" the tentative decision, does it not? What recourse does the losing party have? *See* Rule 3.1590(g) & (k); CCP § 634. Is this practice a good reason for the appealing party not to request a statement of decision? Why not?

(5) In *Marriage of Arceneaux, supra*, 51 Cal. 3d 1130, the appellant did request a statement of decision, but the trial court's statement contained significant errors and omissions. The appellant did not object to either the proposed or final statement in the trial court, but asserted on appeal that the defective statement constituted reversible error. The Supreme Court held that, by failing to bring defects in the statement to the attention of the trial court pursuant to CCP § 634, appellant waived his right to claim on appeal that the statement was deficient. And, with respect to the omissions and other deficiencies in the statement, the appellate court will imply findings to support the judgment. *Marriage of Arceneaux*, 51 Cal. 3d at 1135–1136. Is there any reason for an appealing party not to object to a defective statement of decision?

(6) For additional discussion of statements of decision generally, see § 13.03[C], Trial Without a Jury, *supra.*

[c] Complete Record of Proceedings

An appellate court is confined in its review to matters contained in the record of the trial court proceedings, or properly subject to judicial notice pursuant to Evidence Code § 459. *People v. Collie,* 30 Cal. 3d 43, 57, n. 10, 177 Cal. Rptr. 458, 634 P.2d 534 (1981) (giving no consideration to declaration of trial judge proffered during appeal); *Linda Vista Vill. v. Tecolote Investors,* 234 Cal. App. 4th 166, 184–86, 183 Cal. Rptr. 3d 521 (2015) (taking judicial notice of certain exhibits lodged with the trial court); *Tinsley v. Palo Alto Unified Sch. Dist.,* 91 Cal. App. 3d 871, 891, n. 11, 154 Cal. Rptr. 591 (1979) (taking judicial notice of official map indicating school districts).

The appellant is responsible not only for preserving matters in the record of the trial court proceedings, but also for assembling a trial court record which provides the appellate court with an adequate basis for determining whether reversal is appropriate. *See, e.g., Ballard v. Uribe,* 41 Cal. 3d 564, 574, 224 Cal. Rptr. 664, 715 P.2d 624 (1986) (ruling appellant's failure to include transcript of jury voir dire and of new trial hearing in record precludes the appellate court from ascertaining whether alleged juror misconduct of concealed bias and alleged error in denying motion for new trial occurred); *Maria P. v. Riles, supra,* 43 Cal. 3d at 1295 (holding appellate court cannot consider alleged error by trial court in method used to calculate attorney fee award because appellant failed to furnish adequate record of attorney fee proceedings).

[d] Preserving Error for Appeal

The appellant has the responsibility for making an adequate record for appeal in another sense — by making necessary objections during the trial court proceedings, or taking other appropriate actions, so as to preserve the error for appeal.

(1) Generally, an issue must be raised in the trial court to be argued on appeal. *See, e.g., North Coast Bus. Park v. Nielsen Constr. Co.,* 17 Cal. App. 4th 22, 28–32, 21 Cal. Rptr. 2d 104 (1993). Likewise, the theory upon which a case is tried must be adhered to on appeal. *See, e.g., Ernst v. Searle,* 218 Cal. 233, 240–241, 22 P.2d 715 (1933); *Frink v. Prod,* 31 Cal. 3d 166, 170, 181 Cal. Rptr. 893, 643 P.2d 476 (1982). One major but ill-defined exception is that issues of law, or new legal theories based on undisputed facts, may be raised for the first time on appeal. *E.g., Ward v. Taggart,* 51 Cal. 2d 736, 742, 336 P.2d 534 (1959) (holding that although facts pleaded and proved by plaintiff do not sustain the judgment on the theory of tort advanced in the trial court, they are sufficient under the quasi-contract unjust enrichment theory advanced on appeal); *Fisher v. City of Berkeley,* 37 Cal. 3d 644, 654, n. 3, 209 Cal. Rptr. 682, 693 P.2d 261 (1984) (considering anti-trust issues with respect to validity of rent control ordinance even though raised for first time on appeal because based on undisputed facts and involves question of great public importance).

(2) Not only must an issue be raised in the trial court, but error must be preserved for appellate review by an appropriate challenge during the trial proceedings. *Doers v. Golden Gate Bridge Dist.*, 23 Cal. 3d 180, 184–185, n. 3, 151 Cal. Rptr. 837, 588 P.2d 1261 (1979) (observing appellate courts will not consider procedural errors where an objection could have been, but was not, presented to the lower court, or where acquiescence constitutes waiver or estoppel).

(3) Failure to register a timely objection in the proper manner generally waives the issue for appeal. *Doers, supra*, 23 Cal. 3d at 184–85; Evid. Code § 353(a) (no appellate consideration of erroneous admission of evidence unless record contains objection with specific grounds); *but see, e.g.*, CCP § 647 (listing trial court orders to which exception is deemed to be made); *Myers Bldg. Indus., Ltd. v. Interface Tech., Inc.*, 13 Cal. App. 4th 949, 957, n. 3, 17 Cal. Rptr. 2d 242 (1993) (raising issue regarding special verdicts on own motion because of due process consideration, despite lack of objection); *Consolidated Theaters, Inc. v. Theatrical Stage Emp. Union*, 69 Cal. 2d 713, 721, 73 Cal. Rptr. 213, 447 P.2d 325 (1968) (ruling failure to object to subject matter jurisdiction in the trial court does not preclude raising it for first time on appeal).

(4) What are the reasons for this prerequisite to asserting error on appeal? For discussion of the proper manner of making trial objections, *see generally* CEB, *California Trial Objections* (2016).

(5) Some trial errors require additional procedural steps, such as a motion to strike, to preserve them for appeal. *E.g., Sabella v. Southern Pac. Co.*, 70 Cal. 2d 311, 74 Cal. Rptr. 534, 449 P.2d 750 (1969) (requiring party to both object and request that jury be admonished to preserve for appeal issues of attorney misconduct during closing argument); CCP § 657(5) (stating that claim of excessive or inadequate damages cannot be reviewed on appeal unless first urged as error in a timely motion for new trial); CCP § 437c(b) & (d) (objections to form and competency of declarations, and other evidentiary objections, deemed waived unless made at summary judgment hearing).

[e] Offer of Proof

One frequently encountered and very important prerequisite to preserving error is contained in Evidence Code § 354(a): A judgment shall not be reversed by reason of erroneous exclusion of evidence unless "the substance, purpose, and relevance of the excluded evidence" is made part of the record through an offer of proof. *See, e.g., In re Mark C.*, 7 Cal. App. 4th 433, 444–456, 8 Cal. Rptr. 856 2d (1992) (concluding, because of uncertainty in the record concerning the nature of proffered expert testimony, that alleged error by trial court in excluding this evidence cannot be determined on appeal).

(1) Failure to make an adequate offer of proof generally precludes consideration of the alleged error on appeal. *See Helfend v. Southern Cal. Rapid Transit Dist.*, 2 Cal. 3d 1, 17–18, 84 Cal. Rptr. 173, 465 P.2d 61 (1970); *Pugh v. See's Candies, Inc.*, 203 Cal. App. 3d 743, 758, 250 Cal. Rptr. 195 (1988) (noting that although appellant's

arguments for admissibility of excluded evidence appear correct, failure to make an offer of proof precludes consideration of this error on appeal); *Semsch v. Henry Mayo Newhall Mem. Hosp.*, 171 Cal. App. 3d 162, 167, 216 Cal. Rptr. 913 (1985) (concluding appellant's offer of proof setting forth substance of excluded facts is deficient because it lacked specificity).

(2) Why is an offer of proof a prerequisite to subsequent appellate review of a trial court's ruling excluding evidence? Why is an offer of proof necessary when the appellate court can rule on the correctness of the exclusion based on the arguments before the court, and without knowing the specific content of the proffered evidence? Does this prerequisite have anything to do with the prejudicial error/harmless error rule? How so?

[2] Standards of Appellate Review

The term "appellate standard of review" refers to the degree of deference an appellate court must grant a particular type of trial court ruling. CEB, *California Civil Appellate Practice*, §§ 1.50–1.53 (3d ed. 2015). Generally speaking, an appellate court must apply one of three available standards of review in assessing the correctness of a trial court determination.

[a] Substantial Evidence Rule

An appellate court must apply the "substantial evidence rule" when reviewing a trial court's determination of an issue of fact, whether in a jury or nonjury trial, based on whether there was sufficient evidence to support the determination. *E.g., Pope v. Barrick*, 229 Cal. App. 4th 1238, 1245–47, 178 Cal. Rptr. 3d 42 (2014); *Alderson v. Alderson*, 180 Cal. App. 3d 450, 465, 225 Cal. Rptr. 610 (1986); *Bowers v. Bernards*, 150 Cal. App. 3d 870, 197 Cal. Rptr. 925 (1984). This standard is usually stated as follows:

> In reviewing the evidence on ... appeal all conflicts must be resolved in favor of the respondent, and all legitimate and reasonable inferences indulged in to uphold the verdict if possible. It is an elementary, but often overlooked principle of law, that when a verdict is attacked as being unsupported, the power of the appellate court begins and ends with a determination as to whether there is any substantial evidence, contradicted or uncontradicted, which will support the conclusion reached by the jury. When two or more inferences can be reasonably deduced from the facts, the reviewing court is without power to substitute its deductions for those of the trial court.

Crawford v. Southern Pac. Co., 3 Cal. 2d 427, 429, 45 P.2d 183 (1935).

(1) What is the rationale for the substantial evidence rule? May an appellate court give less deference to a trial court's factual determinations where they are based on controverted testimony in writing, such as declarations and affidavits, as opposed to oral testimony? *See, e.g., Shamblin v. Brattain*, 44 Cal. 3d 474, 479, 243 Cal. Rptr.

902, 749 P.2d 339 (1988); *Lubetzky v. Friedman*, 228 Cal. App. 3d 35, 39, 278 Cal. Rptr. 706 (1991).

(2) What constitutes "substantial evidence"? *See, e.g., Bowers v. Bernards, supra,* 150 Cal. App. 3d at 873 (observing that "substantial evidence" not synonymous with "any" evidence; but must be evidence of ponderable legal significance, reasonable in nature, credible, and of solid value); *Toyota Motor Sales U.S.A., Inc. v. Superior Court,* 220 Cal. App. 3d 864, 871–872, 269 Cal. Rptr. 647 (1990) (noting the focus is on the quality, not the quantity, of the evidence; very little solid evidence may be "substantial," while a lot of extremely weak evidence might be "insubstantial"). Does this mean that the appellate court weighs the evidence to determine if it is substantial? *See, e.g., In re Stephen W.,* 221 Cal. App. 3d 629, 642, 271 Cal. Rptr. 319 (1990). Does the testimony of a single witness, even if a party to the action, constitute "substantial evidence"? *See, e.g., Marriage of Mix,* 14 Cal. 3d 604, 614, 122 Cal. Rptr. 79, 536 P.2d 479 (1975); *Pope v. Barrick, supra,* 229 Cal. App. 4th at 1246–47.

(3) Does uncontroverted testimony in appellant's favor necessarily mean that a decision contrary to that testimony lacks substantial evidence? *See, e.g., Ortzman v. Van Der Waal,* 114 Cal. App. 2d 167, 170–171, 249 P.2d 846 (1952) (noting trier of fact may reject testimony of witness even though uncontradicted, provided trier does not act arbitrarily). Even if the uncontradicted testimony is the opinion of an expert? Compare *Pacific Gas & Elec. Co. v. Zuckerman,* 189 Cal. App. 3d 1113, 1135, 234 Cal. Rptr. 630 (1987) (ruling opinion of uncontradicted expert not substantial evidence under circumstances of case) with *Huber, Hunt & Nichols, Inc. v. Moore,* 67 Cal. App. 3d 278, 313, 136 Cal. Rptr. 603 (1977) (concluding uncontroverted expert evidence is conclusive and cannot be disregarded).

(4) Where facts are not in dispute or are uncontradicted, but two or more inferences may be deduced from these facts, the appellate court cannot substitute its decision for that of the trial court. *See, e.g., Shamblin v. Brattain, supra,* 44 Cal. 3d at 478–79; *Bowers v. Bernhards, supra,* 150 Cal. App. 3d at 874; *Estate of Teel,* 25 Cal. 2d 520, 526–527, 154 P.2d 384 (1944). Why not? Doesn't an appeal in such a case only present an issue of law, not fact?

(5) In light of the substantial evidence rule, how likely is it that an appellant will be successful in reversing a factual determination based on insufficiency of the evidence where conflicting evidence was introduced at trial? Where the appellant argues that the determination was against the weight of the evidence? Where the argument for reversal is that the respondent's evidence was not credible?

[b] Independent (De Novo) Review

An appellate court gives no deference to a trial court's determination of a pure question of law, but must engage in an independent ("de novo") review of the issue. *See, e.g., Parsons v. Bristol Dev. Co.,* 62 Cal. 2d 861, 865–866, 44 Cal. Rptr. 767, 402 P.2d 839 (1965); *Stratton v. First Nat. Life Ins. Co.,* 210 Cal. App. 3d 1071, 1083, 258 Cal. Rptr. 721 (1989). What constitutes a pure question of law? How can an appellant persuade the reviewing court that an issue is one of law as opposed to one of fact? What factors will the court consider in making this distinction? Why is it important for an appellant to have the appellate court characterize an issue as one of law?

(1) The most obvious example of an issue of law is where the appellate court must determine the proper interpretation of a statute. In such situations, the appellate court gives no deference to the lower court's interpretation. *See, e.g., California Teachers Assn. v. San Diego Cmty. Coll. Dist.*, 28 Cal. 3d 692, 699, 170 Cal. Rptr. 817, 621 P.2d 856 (1981) (noting appellate court not bound by lower court's interpretation of legislative intent and language of Education Code section); *Los Angeles County Safety Police Assn. v. County of L. A.*, 192 Cal. App. 3d 1378, 1384, 237 Cal. Rptr. 920 (1987) (observing that the proper interpretation of statutory language is question of law which appellate court reviews de novo, independent of trial court's ruling or its rationales).

(2) Some courts define a question of law as one that can be answered without considering conflicting evidence. *E.g., Chan v. Tsang*, 1 Cal. App. 4th 1578, 1583, 3 Cal. Rptr. 2d 14 (1991) ("If facts are not in dispute, the issue is one of law"). Does this mean that independent review is the proper standard where, for example, the appellate court reviews a trial court determination of negligence based on undisputed facts? *See, e.g., Callahan v. Gray*, 44 Cal. 2d 107, 111, 279 P.2d 963 (1955) (ruling that whether or not a party is guilty of negligence is ordinarily a question of mixed fact and law, and may be determined as a matter of law only if reasonable men following the law can draw only one conclusion from the evidence presented).

(3) Under what circumstances might de novo review be improper for such cases of undisputed facts? Why? *See, e.g., Mah See v. North American Accident Ins. Co.*, 190 Cal. 421, 426, 213 P.2d 42 (1923) (ruling that appellate review of sufficiency of evidence to support trial court finding of accidental, as opposed to intentional, death is by substantial evidence test even though facts surrounding death are uncontradicted); *Board of Ed. v. Jack M.*, 19 Cal. 3d 691, 698, n. 3, 139 Cal. Rptr. 700, 566 P.2d 602 (1977) (observing that a determination is one of ultimate fact if it can be reached by logical reasoning from undisputed evidence, but is one of law if it can be reached only by application of legal principles).

(4) An appellate court is not bound by the trial court's interpretation of a written instrument, such as a contract, but can independently interpret it on appeal. *E.g., Parsons, supra*, 62 Cal. 2d at 865–68; *Fragomeno v. Ins. Co. of the West*, 207 Cal. App. 3d 822, 827, 255 Cal. Rptr. 111 (1989) (ruling the interpretation of an insurance policy is an issue of law). Why isn't the interpretation of a contract generally considered an issue of fact?

[c] Abuse of Discretion

A wide variety of decisions are, by law, committed to the discretion of the trial court. These include dismissal for delay in prosecution under CCP § 583.410–.430,

Ladd v. Dart Equip. Corp., 230 Cal. App. 3d 1088, 1100, 281 Cal. Rptr. 813 (1991); amendment of pleadings and relief from default under CCP § 473, *Carol v. Abbott Labs,* 32 Cal. 3d 892, 897–89, 187 Cal. Rptr. 592, 654 P.2d 775 (1981); the determination of whether to issue a preliminary injunction, *Cohen v. Bd. of Supervisors,* 40 Cal. 3d 277, 286, 219 Cal. Rptr. 467, 707 P.2d 840 (1985); the amount of court-awarded attorneys fees, *e.g., Baggett v. Gates,* 32 Cal. 3d 128, 142, 185 Cal. Rptr. 232, 649 P.2d 874 (1982) (statutory private attorney general award under CCP § 1021.5); *Bussey v. Affleck,* 225 Cal. App. 3d 1162, 1165–1166, 275 Cal. Rptr. 646 (1990) (contractual award pursuant to Civil Code § 1717); the imposition of certain sanctions, *e.g., On v. Cow Hollow Properties,* 222 Cal. App. 3d 1568, 1576, 272 Cal. Rptr. 535 (1990) (attorneys fees for bad faith action pursuant to CCP § 128.5); *McFarland v. City of Sausalito,* 218 Cal. App. 3d 909, 911, 267 Cal. Rptr. 412 (1990) (sanctions for frivolous conduct under CCP § 128.5); the awarding of spousal support pursuant to Family Code §§ 4320–4336; awarding of interest in a non-contract action pursuant to Civil Code § 3288; motions for new trial, *e.g., Mosesian v. Pennwalt Corp.,* 191 Cal. App. 3d 851, 236 Cal. Rptr. 778 (1987).

(1) The appropriate standard of appellate review of such decisions is "abuse of discretion." What, precisely, does this standard mean? A typical general definition was stated in *Shamblin v. Brattain,* 44 Cal. 3d 474, 478–79, 243 Cal. Rptr. 902, 749 P.2d 339 (1988): "The appropriate test for abuse of discretion is whether the trial court exceeded the bounds of reason. When two or more inferences can reasonably be deduced from the facts, the reviewing court has no authority to substitute its decision for that of the trial court." The abuse of discretion standard is often intertwined with the other appellate standards of review. Why?

(2) In making a discretionary decision, a trial court must apply the correct legal standards and follow the proper procedure. *See, e.g., Dockery v. Hyatt,* 169 Cal. App. 3d 830, 215 Cal. Rptr. 488 (1985); *Bartling v. Glendale Adventist Med. Ctr.,* 184 Cal. App. 3d 97, 228 Cal. Rptr.847 (1986). The factual bases for the trial court's exercise of discretion must be supported by substantial evidence. *See, e.g., Westside Cmty. for Indep. Living, Inc. v. Obledo,* 33 Cal. 3d 348, 188 Cal. Rptr. 87, 657 P.2d 365 (1983); *Marriage of Connolly,* 23 Cal. 3d 590, 598, 153 Cal. Rptr. 423, 591 P.2d 911 (1979). Likewise, for example, although the trial court's determination of the balance of harm for a preliminary injunction is reviewed on appeal for abuse of discretion, the trial court's interpretation of a statute is a matter of law reviewed de novo. *Department of Fish & Game v. Anderson-Cottonwood Irrigation Dist.,* 8 Cal. App. 4th 1554, 11 Cal. Rptr. 2d 222 (1992); *Thornton v. Carlson,* 4 Cal. App. 4th 1249, 6 Cal. Rptr. 2d 375 (1992).

(3) For an extensive and thoughtful analysis of the discretionary decision-making process, as well as of appellate review for abuse of discretion, see *Hurtado v. Statewide Home Loan Co.,* 167 Cal. App. 3d 1019, 213 Cal. Rptr. 712 (1985), *disapproved on another point, Shamblin v. Brattain, supra* 44 Cal. 3d at 479, n. 4.

[d]   Scope of Appellate Review in Federal Court

The federal appellate courts apply the *de novo* review standard when reviewing questions of law, and the substantial evidence test when reviewing factual determinations made by a jury. But unlike the California courts, the federal courts must apply a different standard when reviewing factual determinations made by a trial judge in a nonjury case. Rule 52(a)(6), F.R.C.P., provides:

> Findings of fact, whether based on oral or other evidence, must not be set aside unless clearly erroneous, and the reviewing court must give due regard to the trial court's opportunity to judge of the witnesses' credibility.

Rule 52(a) requires the district court to set forth findings of fact and conclusions of law which explain its decision; unlike California, no request by a party is necessary. The findings may be stated orally and recorded in open court following the close of evidence, or appear in an opinion or memorandum of decision filed by the court. Rule 52(a)(1).

The federal courts have had considerable difficulty in defining and applying the "clearly erroneous" test, and in distinguishing it from the substantial evidence test. In *Anderson v. City of Bessemer City,* 470 U.S. 564, 573–576, 105 S. Ct. 1504, 84 L. Ed. 2d 518 (1985), the U.S. Supreme Court offered the following explanation:

> "A finding is 'clearly erroneous' when although there is evidence to support it, the reviewing court on the entire evidence is left with the definite and firm conviction that a mistake has been committed." *United States v. United States Gypsum Co.,* 333 U.S. 364, 395 (1948). * * * If the district court's account of the evidence is plausible in light of the record viewed in its entirety, the court of appeals may not reverse it even though convinced that had it been sitting as the trier of fact, it would have weighed the evidence differently. Where there are two permissible views of the evidence, the factfinder's choice between them cannot be clearly erroneous....

(1) Is the "clearly erroneous" test really different from the "substantial evidence" test? How so? Which standard is more deferential to the factual determinations made at trial? Why?

(2) Why do the federal appellate courts apply a different standard of review to factual determinations in nonjury cases as opposed to jury cases? What policy considerations support this federal approach? Why do the California appellate courts apply the same "substantial evidence" standard to review of factual determinations in both jury and nonjury cases? What policy reasons support California's uniform approach? Which approach, federal or California, do you favor? Why?

[e]   Administrative Mandamus

The standard for judicial review of an administrative agency decision pursuant to CCP § 1094.5 depends on whether the decision is "adjudicatory" as opposed to "legislative," and on whether an adjudicatory administrative decision "substantially affects a fundamental vested right." *See, e.g., Anton v. San Antonio Cmty. Hosp.,* 19 Cal. 3d 802, 140 Cal. Rptr. 442, 567 P.2d 1162 (1977), reproduced and discussed *infra,* § 15.03 of this chapter. If so, the superior court must exercise its independent judgment upon the evidence in the administrative record with respect to issues both of law *and* of fact. *Anton, supra,* 19 Cal. 3d at 820–21.

(1) Where a party claims that the agency findings are not supported by the evidence, in cases in which the court is authorized to exercise its independent judgment on the evidence, the court determines whether the findings are supported by the weight of the evidence. CCP § 1094.5(c).

(2) In all other cases, the superior court's role is limited to a determination of whether the agency findings are supported by substantial evidence in light of the whole administrative record. CCP § 1094.5(c). Why are there different standards of appellate review for determinations of administrative agency as opposed to those of a trial court?

(3) Administrative mandamus is discussed in more detail in § 15.03, Administrative Mandamus, *infra.*

[E] The Prejudicial Error Rule

[1] Error Must Be Proved

A judgment or order is presumed to be correct; error must be affirmatively shown by the appellant. *Denham v. Superior Court,* 2 Cal. 3d 557, 564, 86 Cal. Rptr. 65, 468 P.2d 193 (1970). Even where error is proven on appeal a reversal is not automatic. The appellate court will reverse or modify only for "prejudicial" error (as opposed to "harmless" error). Consequently, an appellant not only has the burden to prove error, but must also demonstrate that the error is prejudicial. *E.g., Soule v. General Motors Corp.,* 8 Cal. 4th 548, 573–580, 882 P.2d 298, 34 Cal. Rptr. 2d 607 (1994); *Pool v. City of Oakland,* 42 Cal. 3d 1051, 1069, 232 Cal. Rptr. 528, 728 P.2d 1163 (1986). The "prejudicial error" rule is based on Article VI, § 13, of the California Constitution; as well as statutes such as CCP § 475 and Evidence Code §§ 353, 354.

[2] What Constitutes "Prejudicial" Error, as Opposed to "Harmless" Error?

Article VI, § 13, of the California Constitution, states:

> No judgment shall be set aside, or new trial granted, in any cause, on the ground of misdirection of the jury, or of the improper admission or rejection of evidence, or for any error as to any matter of pleading, or for any error as to any matter of procedure, unless, after an examination of the entire cause, including the evidence, the court shall be of the opinion that the error complained of has resulted in a miscarriage of justice.

The California Supreme Court has interpreted the "miscarriage of justice" phrase as prohibiting reversal unless there is "a reasonable possibility that in the absence of the error, a result more favorable to the appealing party would have been reached." *Soule v. General Motors Corp., supra,* 8 Cal. 4th at 574, *Pool v. City of Oakland, supra,*

42 Cal. 3d at 1069. The factors relevant to this determination vary with type of error and the circumstances of each case.

[a] Factors Relevant in Determining Whether Error Is Prejudicial

What factors should an appellate court consider in determining whether the erroneous admission or exclusion of evidence requires reversal? *See, e.g., Clifton v. Ulis,* 17 Cal. 3d 99, 130 Cal. Rptr. 155, 549 P.2d 1251 (1976) (finding erroneous exclusion of prior inconsistent statement was prejudicial where evidence was of utmost importance to plaintiff's case); *Hrnjak v. Graymar, Inc.,* 4 Cal. 3d 725, 94 Cal. Rptr. 623, 484 P.2d 599 (1971) (concluding erroneous admission of evidence that plaintiff received collateral source insurance payments was prejudicial because issue of damages sharply contested and damage award was small); *National Union Fire Ins. Co. v. Tokio Marine & Nichido Fire Ins. Co.,* 233 Cal. App. 4th 1248, 183 Cal. Rptr. 3d 472 (2015) (finding erroneous exclusion of relevant and material expert evidence was prejudicial because the expert was plaintiff's sole witness on tire defects); *Alef v. Alta Bates Hospital,* 5 Cal. App. 4th 208, 219–220, 6 Cal. Rptr. 2 900 (1992) (deeming erroneous exclusion of expert medical testimony on standard of care prejudicial because critical to a major issue in the case).

What factors are relevant in determining whether attorney misconduct during trial is prejudicial? *See, e.g., Garden Grove Sch. Dist. v. Hendler,* 63 Cal. 2d 141, 45 Cal. Rptr. 313, 403 P.2d 721 (1965) (holding attorney misconduct in referring to facts not in evidence, alluding to his personal knowledge, using derogatory characterizations, and talking to juror during recess constituted prejudicial error); *Cassim v. Allstate Ins. Co.,* 33 Cal. 4th 780, 800–805,16 Cal. Rptr. 3d 374, 94 P.3d 513 (2004) (ruling plaintiff's misconduct during closing argument was harmless because not reasonably probable that defendant would have obtained a more favorable verdict in the absence of the argument); *Pope v. Babick,* 229 Cal. App. 4th 1238, 178 Cal. Rptr. 3d 42 (2014) (finding attorney's misconduct which directly violated trial court order by eliciting excluded evidence from a witness was not prejudicial because only a single question and answer, the trial court gave the jury a curative instruction, and the jury's verdict supported by substantial evidence).

Should the appellate court consider the cumulative effect of numerous errors? *See, e.g., Johnson v. Tosco Corp.,* 1 Cal. App. 4th 123, 141, 1 Cal. Rptr. 2d 747 (1991) (finding cumulative effect of jury instructions and erroneous restriction of expert testimony constitutes prejudice); *Delzell v. Day,* 36 Cal. 2d 349, 223 P.2d 625 (1950) (ruling the cumulative effect of judge's and opposing counsel's improper comments constituted prejudicial error even though, taken separately, they would not justify reversal).

[b] Erroneous Jury Instructions

The California Supreme Court has, on several occasions, analyzed the prejudicial effect of erroneous jury instructions. Perhaps the most important of these cases is *Soule v. General Motors Corp.,* 8 Cal. 4th 548, 882 P.2d 298, 34 Cal. Rptr. 2d 607 (1994), where the Supreme Court considered whether two types of instructional errors—giving an improper instruction based on the record and refusing to give another although supported by the evidence—required reversal. First, the Supreme Court provided guidance for applying the constitutional requirement for "an examination of an entire cause" when assessing prejudice from instructional error:

> In assessing prejudice from an erroneous instruction, we consider, insofar as relevant, "(1) the degree of conflict in the evidence on critical issues [citations]; (2) whether respondent's argument to the jury may have contributed to the instruction's misleading effect [citation]; (3) whether the jury requested a rereading of the erroneous instruction [citation] or of related evidence [citation]; (4) the closeness of the jury's verdict [citation]; and (5) the effect of other instructions in remedying the error [citations]." (*Pool v. City of Oakland* (1986) 42 Cal. 3d 1051, 1069–1070 [232 Cal. Rptr. 528, 728 P.2d 1163], quoting *LeMons v. Regents of University of California* (1978) 21 Cal. 3d 869, 876 [148 Cal. Rptr. 355, 582 P.2d 946].)

Soule, supra, 8 Cal. 4th at 570–71. Next, the Supreme Court rejected the traditional view that certain forms of instructional error in civil cases are "inherently" prejudicial:

> We ... conclude that there is no rule of automatic reversal or "inherent" prejudice applicable to any category of civil instructional error, whether of commission or omission. A judgment may not be reversed for instructional error in a civil case "unless, after an examination of the entire cause, including the evidence, the court shall be of the opinion that the error complained of has resulted in a miscarriage of justice." (Cal. Const., art. VI, § 13.) Contrary implications in prior decisions ... are disapproved and overruled.
>
> Instructional error in a civil case is prejudicial "where it seems probable" that the error "prejudicially affected the verdict." (*See Pool v. City of Oakland, supra*, 42 Cal. 3d 1051, 1069; *LeMons v. Regents of University of California, supra*, 21 Cal. 3d 869, 875.) Of course, that determination depends heavily on the particular nature of the error, including its natural and probable effect on a party's ability to place his full case before the jury.
>
> But the analysis cannot stop there. Actual prejudice must be assessed in the context of the individual trial record. For this purpose, the multifactor test set forth in such cases as *LeMons* and *Pool*, both *supra*, is as pertinent in cases of instructional omission as in cases where instructions were erroneously given. Thus, when deciding whether an error of instructional omission was prejudicial, the court must also evaluate (1) the state of the evidence, (2) the effect of other instructions, (3) the effect of counsel's arguments, and (4) any indications by the jury itself that it was misled.

Soule, 8 Cal. 4th at 580–81. Finally, after applying this multifactor test, the *Soule* Court concluded the trial court's two instructional errors were harmless because it was not reasonably probable defendant would have obtained a more favorable result in their absence. *Id.* at 570 & 582–83. Because neither error caused actual prejudice, the jury verdict for the plaintiff was affirmed. *Id.* at 583.

As *Soule* demonstrates, not every erroneous instruction leads to reversal. In *Pool v. City of Oakland*, 42 Cal. 3d 1051, 1068–1073, 232 Cal. Rptr. 528, 728 P.2d 1163 (1986), for example, the court found that the trial court erred in improperly instructing the jury on a false arrest cause of action. However, the court affirmed the jury's verdict for plaintiff, finding no prejudice because the jury rendered a general verdict against defendant after being instructed on several causes of action, including false imprisonment, any one of which could have been relied upon by the jury.

However, in *Mitchell v. Gonzales*, 54 Cal. 3d 1041, 1054–1056, 1 Cal. Rptr. 2d 913, 819 P.2d 872 (1991), the Supreme Court held that a jury instruction approved by the Judicial Council, the proximate cause instruction which contains the "but for" test of cause in fact, is erroneous and should no longer be used in negligence cases. The court then determined, after applying the *LeMons* factors to the facts, that its use constituted prejudicial error. Likewise in *Seaman's Direct Buying Serv., Inc. v. Standard Oil Co.*, 36 Cal. 3d 752, 206 Cal. Rptr. 354, 686 P.2d 1158 (1984), the Supreme Court found the trial court's instructions erroneously permitted the jury to award punitive damages for tortious denial of the existence of a contract regardless of whether that denial was in good or bad faith. Applying the five *LeMons* factors and noting that only nine of the twelve jurors concurred in the verdict, the Supreme Court concluded the erroneous instruction constituted prejudicial error and reversed the tort damages judgment.

Other, more recent decisions have applied the *LeMons* multi-factor test with varying results depending on the circumstances of each case. *Compare Rutherford v. Owens-Illinois, Inc.*, 16 Cal. 4th 953, 67 Cal. Rptr. 2d 16, 941 P.2d 1203 (1997) (concluding the trial court erred in instructing the jury in an asbestos-exposure personal injury action that the burden of proof was on the defendants to prove that their products were not a legal cause of plaintiff's injuries, but that the error was not prejudicial in the context of that case); *Adams v. MHC Colony Park Ltd. Partnership*, 224 Cal. App. 4th 601, 169 Cal. Rptr. 3d 146 (2014) (ruling instructional error did not cause prejudice because the jury would not have awarded damages to the unsuccessful plaintiff if the jury had been properly instructed on public nuisance); *with Mendoza v. Western Med. Ctr. Santa Ana*, 222 Cal. App. 4th 1334, 166 Cal. Rptr. 3d 720 (2014) (concluding instructional error regarding causation was prejudicial because verdict was close, but a new trial was appropriate because the verdict was supported by substantial evidence); *Buzgheia v. Leasco Sierra Grove*, 60 Cal. App. 4th 374, 70 Cal. Rptr. 2d 427 (1997) (holding the trial court's instruction which incorrectly placed the burden of proof on the defendant with respect to a key issue was prejudicial and reversible error, where the evidence stood in relative equipoise as to this issue and the jury could reasonably have decided the issue either way).

[c] Juror Misconduct

One of the more interesting applications of the prejudicial error rule concerns juror misconduct during trial. In *Hasson v. Ford Motor Co.*, 32 Cal. 3d 388, 185 Cal. Rptr. 654, 650 P.2d 1171 (1982), appellant Ford sought reversal of a multi-million dollar products liability verdict because members of the jury were reading novels and working crossword puzzles during presentation of evidence. The Supreme Court found that certain jurors did engage in these activities, and that such misconduct raised a presumption of prejudice. Nevertheless the court affirmed the jury verdict, finding that this presumption had been rebutted (*id.* at 417–418):

> However, the presumption is not conclusive; it may be rebutted by an affirmative evidentiary showing that prejudice does not exist or by a reviewing court's examination of the entire record to determine whether there is a reasonable probability of actual harm to the complaining party resulting from the misconduct.... Some of the factors to be considered when determining whether the presumption is rebutted are the strength of the evidence that misconduct occurred, the nature and seriousness of the misconduct, and the probability that actual prejudice may have ensued.

> Here the jurors engaged in essentially neutral, albeit distracting, activities at unspecified times during the presentation of evidence. There was overwhelming proof of liability against Ford and no substantial likelihood that actual prejudice may have resulted from the jurors' activities. It was not clear what type of evidence was being presented while the misconduct occurred or even which side's case was being presented. In sum, the showing of misconduct is rebutted by an examination of the record which reveals no substantial likelihood that Ford was given anything less than a full and fair consideration of its case by an impartial jury. The instances of misconduct demonstrated here do not rise to the level of evidence "of such a character as is likely to have influenced the verdict improperly." (Evid. Code § 1150, subd. (a).)

See also Glage v. Hawes Firearms Co., 226 Cal. App. 3d 314, 276 Cal. Rptr. 430 (1990) (finding presumption of prejudice not rebutted where jurors consulted dictionary definitions to understand jury instructions). Juror misconduct as a basis for a new trial motion is discussed in detail in § 13.04, Judicial Supervision of Jury Decisions, *supra.*

[3] Prejudice Per Se?

The California courts have considered a few types of error "reversible per se" — prejudice is conclusively presumed and need not be proven. These include denial of the right to a jury trial, *e.g., Selby Constructors v. McCarthy,* 91 Cal. App. 3d 517, 527, 154 Cal. Rptr. 164 (1979) (ruling denial of right to jury trial is reversible error per se, without the need to demonstrate actual prejudice); *DiDonato v. Santini,* 232 Cal. App. 3d 721, 740, 283 Cal. Rptr. 751 (1991) (holding trial court's perfunctory denial of challenge to use of peremptory challenges to exclude women from jury was prejudicial error per se); undue restriction on right of cross-examination, *e.g., Fremont Indem. Co. v. Workers Comp. Appeals Bd.,* 153 Cal. App. 3d 965, 971, 200 Cal. Rptr. 762 (1984); erroneous sustaining of demurrer without leave to amend, *e.g., Deeter v. Angus,* 179 Cal. App. 3d 241, 251, 224 Cal. Rptr. 801 (1986); failure to render a statement of decision when timely requested and required by CCP § 632, *e.g., Wallis v. PHL Assoc., Inc.,* 220 Cal. App. 4th 814, 163 Cal. Rptr. 3d 482 (2013); *Social Serv.*

Union v. County of Monterey, 208 Cal. App. 3d 676, 681, 256 Cal. Rptr. 325 (1989); and an award of punitive damages entered without evidence of the defendant's financial condition, *see Adams v. Murakami,* 54 Cal. 3d 105, 284 Cal. Rptr. 318, 813 P.2d 1348 (1991). For more examples, see Eisenberg, Horvits & Weiner, *Civil Practice Guide, Civil Appeals and Writs,* ¶ 8:308–¶ 8:319 (Rutter Group 2015); CEB, *California Civil Appellate Practice* § 5.32 (3d ed. 2015).

In *Soule v. General Motors Corp., supra,* 8 Cal. 4th at 574–580, the California Supreme Court disapproved numerous prior decisions which had held that the erroneous denial of a correct specific jury instruction was per se prejudicial. The *Soule* court did not directly disapprove the various other prejudicial error per se decisions outside the civil jury instruction arena. Quoting from *People v. Cahill,* 5 Cal. 4th 478, 502, 20 Cal. Rptr. 2d 582, 853 P.2d 1037 (1993), the court suggested that a "fundamental denial of the orderly legal procedure" or a "structural defect in the trial mechanism" may be inherently prejudicial. *Soule,* 8 Cal. 4th at 577–78. What do these quoted standards mean? Do these standards call into question the various prejudice per se decisions identified in the preceding paragraph? Which ones, if any? Why?

[F]   Stays Pending Appeal

Code of Civil Procedure (2016)

Section 916(a). Stay on perfection of appeal.

Except as provided in Sections 917.1 to 917.9, inclusive, and in Section 116.810 [small claims court], the perfecting of an appeal stays proceedings in the trial court upon the judgment or order appealed from or upon the matters embraced therein or affected thereby, including enforcement of the judgment or order, but the trial court may proceed upon other matter embraced in the action and not affected by the judgment or order.

Section 917.1(a). Appeal from money judgment; undertaking to stay enforcement.

Unless an undertaking is given, the perfecting of an appeal shall not stay enforcement of the judgment or order in the trial court if the judgment or order is for any of the following:

> (1) Money or the payment of money, whether consisting of a special fund or not, and whether payable by the appellant or another party to the action.
>
> (2) Costs awarded pursuant to Section 998 which otherwise would not have been awarded as costs pursuant to Section 1033.5.
>
> (3) Costs awarded pursuant to Section 1141.21 which otherwise would not have been awarded as costs pursuant to Section 1033.5.

* * *

[1]   *General Rule and General Exceptions*

Code of Civil Procedure § 916(a) states that the perfecting of an appeal (*i.e.,* timely filing the notice of appeal) automatically stays enforcement of the trial court's judgment. However, the numerous exceptions contained in CCP §§ 917.1–917.9 swallow up this general rule.

[a] Undertaking Required

A judgment for money damages will not be stayed pending appeal "unless an undertaking is given." CCP § 917.1(a). An "undertaking" means the furnishing of some type of authorized security such as a bond by two or more sufficient personal sureties, or one sufficient admitted surety insurer, pursuant to CCP § 995.310, or depositing money or negotiable instruments into court pursuant to CCP § 995.710. *See generally* the Bond and Undertaking Law, CCP §§ 995.010–996.510. The amount of the required security is 1-1/2 to 2 times the amount of the money judgment, depending on the type of security furnished. CCP § 917.1(b).

Other judgments which require an undertaking to perfect a stay are designated in CCP § 917.2 (judgment and orders directing the assignment, delivery, or sale of personal property), § 917.4 (judgment and orders directing the sale, conveyance or delivery of real property), § 917.5 (appointment of receiver), § 917.65 (appeal of prejudgment attachment order). The trial court has discretion to waive the requirement for an undertaking if the appellant is indigent, CCP § 995.240; or is an executor, guardian, or other personal representative, CCP § 919.

[b] Discretionary Stays

Some judgments may be stayed pending appeal only by discretionary order of the trial or appellate court. *E.g.,* CCP § 917.7 (child custody); § 917.8 (usurpation of public office), § 1176 (unlawful detainer). The trial court has discretionary authority to require an undertaking in many other types of cases, as specified in CCP § 917.9. *See* CEB, *California Civil Appellate Practice*, § 6.20 (2011), for a chart of the procedures required to stay various judgments and orders.

[2] When General Rule Applicable

The filing of a notice of appeal does automatically stay enforcement of several common types of judgments. These include appeals from mandatory injunctions, *e.g., Agricultural Labor Relations Bd. v. Superior Court,* 149 Cal. App. 3d 709, 716–717, 196 Cal. Rptr. 920 (1983); writs of mandamus, *Hayworth v. City of Oakland,* 129 Cal. App. 3d 723, 727–728, 181 Cal. Rptr. 214 (1982); decrees of distribution and orders appointing personal representatives; and, pursuant to CCP § 995.220; denials of anti-SLAPP special motion to strike, *Varian Med. Sys., Inc. v. Delfino,* 35 Cal. 4th 180, 25 Cal. Rptr. 3d 298, 106 P.3d 958 (2005); and judgments against public entities and public officers. *See* CEB, *California Civil Appellate Practice,* § 6.19 (3d ed. 2015) (and cases cited therein).

[3] Procedure for Obtaining Stay

Where a judgment is automatically stayed, the filing of the notice of appeal is the only procedural prerequisite. But if a party wishes to prevent enforcement of an adverse judgment prior to perfecting an appeal, perhaps for the purpose of awaiting post-trial motions or analysis of whether to appeal, that party must obtain an immediate temporary stay. CCP § 918.

When an undertaking is required and the amount is fixed by statutory formula, the appellant need only post the proper security in the appropriate court to obtain a stay. CCP § 917.1(b). However, the amounts of some required undertakings are not fixed by statute but must be determined by order of the trial court. *E.g.*, CCP §§ 917.2–917.9. In such cases, the appellant must file a motion and obtain an order to fix the amount; and the respondent may object to the sufficiency of the security. *See, e.g.*, CCP §§ 922, 995.650–.660. The amount of the security may be modified during the appeal. CCP §§ 996.010, 996.030.

[4] *Purposes of Stays*

What are the purposes of stays pending appeal? Why is security a prerequisite to a stay pending appeal from certain judgments, such as money judgments, but not others? What purpose does such security serve? Is a stay pending appeal always necessary or desirable to the appellant? What factors should an appellant consider in deciding whether to obtain a stay pending appeal from a money judgment? Under what circumstances might a stay pending appeal be undesirable to such an appellant? CCP § 995.230 authorizes the respondent to waive a required security. What possible advantage is there for a respondent in doing this? *See* CCP § 995.250.

[5] *Writ of Supersedeas*

An appellant may petition the appellate court for a stay (writ of supersedeas) when the trial court has no authority to issue a stay, refuses to recognize a statutory stay, requires excessive security, or denies a discretionary stay. CCP § 923.

A writ of supersedeas may be the only possible recourse pending appeal to prevent the respondent from taking threatened action where the trial court has *denied* affirmative relief, such as temporary injunctive relief, *see San Francisco Bay Conservation & Dev. Com. v. Town of Emeryville*, 69 Cal. 2d 533, 538, 72 Cal. Rptr. 790, 446 P.2d 790 (1968); or where the trial has failed to apply the statutory provisions automatically staying a judgment while an appeal is pursued, *see Chapala Mgmt. Corp. v. Stanton*, 186 Cal. App. 4th 1532, 113 Cal. Rptr. 3d 617 (2010).

In order to obtain this discretionary extraordinary writ, the appellant must convince the appellate court that a stay is necessary to preserve the issues for appeal, that the appellant will suffer irreparable injury without a stay, and that the appeal is sound on the merits. *See, e.g., Mills v. County of Trinity*, 98 Cal. App. 3d 859, 159 Cal. Rptr. 679 (1979); *Black v. Coast Sav. & Loan Assn.*, 187 Cal. App. 3d 1494, 1499, 232 Cal. Rptr. 483 (1986). The procedure for petitioning for a writ of supersedeas is set forth in Rules 8.112 and 8.116, Cal. Rules of Ct. *See also* CEB, *California Civil Appellate Practice*, §§ 6.68–6.85 (3d ed. 2015).

[G] The Appellate Procedure

[1] Designating the Record on Appeal

As discussed above, error must be affirmatively demonstrated by an adequate record on appeal. If conduct alleged as error is not part of the record, the appellate court simply has no basis for reviewing the merits of the alleged error. *E.g., Ballard v. Uribe,* 41 Cal. 3d 564, 574, 224 Cal. Rptr. 664, 715 P.2d 624 (1986) (holding failure of appellant to include transcript of voir dire, hearing on new trial motion, and portion of trial dealing with damages precludes appellate court consideration of alleged error in those trial court proceedings); *Cosenza v. Kramer,* 152 Cal. App. 3d 1100, 1102, 200 Cal. Rptr. 18 (1984) (ruling appellant's failure to include complaint in clerk's transcript precludes appellate consideration of alleged pleading defect). The parties are responsible for designating the record on appeal, including a transcript of the relevant oral proceedings, documents filed with the trial court, and exhibits admitted or excluded by the trial court. How is this accomplished? The procedure for designating and assembling the record on appeal (clerk's transcripts, reporter's transcripts, appendixes, etc.) is governed largely by California Rules of Court. *E.g.,* Rules 8.120–8.160 (appeals from superior courts other than in limited civil cases); Rule 8.830–8.843 (appeals in limited civil cases).

[2] Applications and Motions

The California Rules of Court authorize a variety of applications and motions addressed to the reviewing court, such as extensions of time (Rule 8.60), voluntary dismissal (Rule 8.244), motions to dismiss the appeal (Rules 8.54, 8.57), and augmentation or correction of the record (Rule 8.155).

[3] Appellate Briefs

Written briefs are an essential component of the appellate process. Not only are they the primary vehicle for presenting arguments and persuading the court, but they frame the issues that will be considered by the appellate court. *See generally* Eisenberg, Horvitz, & Wiener, *California Practice Guide, Civil Appeals and Writs,* ¶ 9.1–¶ 9.294 (The Rutter Group 2015). Grounds for appeal not raised in the appellate briefs may be considered waived. *E.g., Mann v. Cracchiolo,* 38 Cal. 3d 18, 41, 210 Cal. Rptr. 762, 694 P.2d 1134 (1985) (ruling that although plaintiff appealed from certain orders, failure to attack them in opening brief waives appellate consideration); *Marriage of Laursen & Fogarty,* 197 Cal. App. 3d 1082, 1084, n. 1, 243 Cal. Rptr. 398 (1988) (noting that when appealing party fails to furnish court with either argument or authority upon a point urged as ground for reversal, the point will be deemed to have been abandoned); *In re Tiffany Y.,* 223 Cal. App. 3d 298, 302, 272 Cal. Rptr. 733 (1990) (applying general rule is that points raised for first time in reply brief will not be considered unless good cause shown for failure to present them in opening brief).

California Rules of Court 8.200–8.220 (and even more detailed local rules) specify the requirements for the form, style, format, and length of appellate briefs, as well as the time for service and filing. Close attention to these formal requirements is extremely important. Failure to file the appellant's opening brief within the prescribed time limits may result in dismissal of the appeal; failure to timely file the respondent's brief may result in submission based only on appellant's brief. Rule 8.220. And filing a brief which fails to comply with the requirements of the rules may result in public embarrassment, a stricken brief, or more drastic consequences. *See, e.g., Alicia T. v. County of L. A.,* 222 Cal. App. 3d 869, 884–886, 271 Cal. Rptr. 513 (1990) (imposing monetary sanctions on appellant's attorney for failure to comply with various court rules in opening and reply briefs, including failure to cite to the record, relying on unpublished opinions, and references to facts not in the record); *Berger v. Godden,* 163 Cal. App. 3d 1113, 210 Cal. Rptr. 109 (1985) (striking opening brief for failure to comply with format requirements, and dismissing appeal when second brief failed to advance any pertinent or intelligible legal argument); *Pierotti v. Torian,* 81 Cal. App. 4th 17, 96 Cal. Rptr. 2d 553 (2000) (ordering monetary sanctions in the amount of $26,000 in attorneys fees and costs on appeal, shared equally by the appellant and his attorneys, where the opening and reply briefs did not support all statements of fact with citations to the record and did not confine his statement to matters in the record on appeal).

There are many excellent practical guides on brief-writing for California civil appeals, such as CEB, *California Civil Appellate Practice,* §§ 12.1–14.67 (3d ed. 2015) (including forms and sample briefs); *California Appellate Practice Handbook* (7th ed. 2001). These resources really must be consulted before you draft your first appellate brief.

[4] Oral Argument

Article VI, sections 2 and 3, of the California Constitution is interpreted as guaranteeing a right of oral argument in both the Supreme Court and the Court of Appeal. *Moles v. Regents of Univ. of Cal.,* 32 Cal. 3d 867, 872, 187 Cal. Rptr. 557, 654 P.2d 740 (1982); *see* Rule 8.256, Cal. Rule of Ct. Counsel may waive the right to oral argument, but most appellate specialists recommend against such waiver. *See, e.g., California Civil Appellate Practice, supra,* § 16.15. What are the various reasons for requesting oral argument? *See In re Aguilar,* 34 Cal. 4th 386, 18 Cal. Rptr. 3d 874, 97 P.3d 815 (2004) ("As a general rule, this court does not permit parties to waive oral argument in cases before this court, and we, like all other courts, rely upon the presentation of oral argument by well-prepared attorneys to assist us in reaching an appropriate resolution of the often difficult questions presented in the cases before us"). In *Moles v. Regents of Univ. of Cal., supra,* 32 Cal. 3d at 872, the Supreme Court held that only justices who have heard the oral argument may participate in the decision, noting that "[o]ral argument provides the only opportunity for a dialogue between the litigant and the bench." Under what limited circumstances might a waiver be appropriate?

[5] Decision, Rehearing, Remittitur

[a] Submission and Decision

A cause pending in the court of appeal is considered "submitted" when the court has heard oral argument or approved a waiver, and the time has passed for filing all briefs and other papers. Rule 8.256(d), Cal. Rules of Ct. Unless the court vacates the submission pursuant to Rule 8.256(e) (or is willing to work without salary!), the court will decide the appeal within 90 days of its submission. Cal. Const., Art.VI, § 19; Govt. Code § 68210.

The court's determination typically includes both an opinion and a judgment. The opinion is, of course, the statement of the reasons for the court's decision. *See* Cal. Const., Art. VI, § 14 (Appellate court decisions on the merits must be in form of written opinion "with reasons stated"). The judgment, usually stated at the conclusion of the opinion, is the determination that the lower court's decision shall be affirmed, reversed, or modified. This distinction between the opinion and the judgment may be significant. Modification of the opinion does not postpone the date the decision becomes final for purposes of rehearing or review, but modification of the judgment begins that time anew. Rule 8.264(b) & (c), Cal. Rules of Ct.

(1) An appellate court "may affirm, reverse, or modify any order or judgment appealed from, and may direct the proper judgment or order to be entered, or direct a new trial or further proceedings." CCP § 43; *see* Art. VI, § 12, Cal. Const., *Morehart v. County of Santa Barbara, supra,* 7 Cal. 4th at 744. A reversal can be unqualified, partial, or with directions. Generally, an unqualified reversal vacates the trial court judgment and requires readjudication of all issues in the case. *See, e.g., Weisenburg v. Cragholm,* 5 Cal. 3d 892, 896, 97 Cal. Rptr. 862, 489 P.2d 1126 (1971) (observing that when a judgment is unqualifiedly reversed, the effect is the same as if it had never been entered, except that on retrial the opinion of the appellate court must be followed as far as applicable). An appellate court may order a judgment reversed and a new trial granted unless the appropriate party consents to a modification (*i.e.,* an addition or remission) of trial court's judgment. Rule 8.264(d) Cal. Rules of Ct.

(2) A decision of a reviewing court must be filed with the appellate court clerk to constitute a rendition of the judgment; the clerk must then immediately transmit a copy of the opinion to the lower court and the parties. Rule 8.264(a), Cal. Rules of Ct. This filing date determines when the decision will become final. Rule 8.264(a) & (b).

[b] Rehearing

Rule 8.268 permits an appellate court to grant a rehearing of its decision, upon petition filed within 15 days after the filing of the decision. The petition should neither reargue the appeal nor urge new points not raised during the appeal, but should direct the court to specific errors or contradictions in its opinion. *CAMSI IV v. Hunter Tech. Corp.,* 230 Cal. App. 3d 1525, 1542, 282 Cal. Rptr. 80 (1991); *but see Mounts v. Uyeda*, 227 Cal. App. 3d 111, 121, 277 Cal. Rptr. 730 (1991) (permitting respondent, who seeks to rely on new federal case declaring CCP § 351 unconstitutional, to raise constitutionality of this issue for first time on petition for rehearing).

(1) A petition for rehearing may be a prerequisite to review by the Supreme Court of alleged omissions or misstatements of material fact in a Court of Appeal opinion. Rule 8.500(c).

(2) A petition for rehearing pursuant to Rule 8.268 is addressed to the appellate court's discretion. However, pursuant to Government Code § 68081, if an appellate court renders a decision based on an issue not prepared or briefed by any party, it must give the parties an opportunity to file supplemental briefs on the issue. If not, any party's petition for rehearing must be granted. *Adoption of Alexander S.*, 44 Cal. 3d 857, 864, 245 Cal. Rptr. 1, 750 P.2d 778 (1988).

[c] Costs

Although the actual assessment of costs is made by the trial court after the issuance of the appellate court's remittitur, the judgment on appeal also determines which party is entitled to recovery of the costs of appeal. Rules 8.278, 8.891, Cal. Rules of Ct. Generally, the court will award costs to the "prevailing party," as defined by Rule 8.278 (a), but has discretion to otherwise apportion costs in the "interests of justice." Rule 8.278 (a)(5). Rule 8.278 (d) specifies the items recoverable as costs, which include certain costs of preparation of the record, reproduction of briefs, filing fees, and bond premium. *See, e.g., Rossa v. D.L Falk Constr.*, 53 Cal. 4th 387, 135 Cal. Rptr. 3d 329, 266 P.3d 1022 (2012) (discussing what costs are recoverable on appeal). Rule 8.278 (c) delineates the appellate court procedure for claiming costs. *See also* Rule 3.1700. The prevailing party may also be awarded attorney fees for the appeal, where authorized by statute or contract. *See, e.g.*, CCP § 1021.5; Civil Code § 1717; Rule 3.1702; *see generally* Eisenberg, Horvitz & Wiener, *California Practice Guide, Civil Appeals & Writs*, ¶ 14:112– ¶ 14:136 (The Rutter Group 2015).

[d] Sanctions

(1) *Monetary Sanctions*. An appellate court may impose monetary sanctions for pursuing a frivolous, dilatory, or bad faith appeal. CCP § 907; Family Code § 271; Rule 8.276(a), Cal. Rules of Ct. In *Marriage of Flaherty*, 31 Cal. 3d 637, 183 Cal. Rptr. 508, 646 P.2d 179 (1982), the Supreme Court defined a "frivolous appeal" as: (1) one prosecuted for an improper motive to harass or delay; *or* (2) one which indisputably has no merit, *i.e.*, "when any reasonable attorney would agree that the appeal is totally and completely without merit." *Marriage of Flaherty*, 31 Cal. 3d at 650. The court also noted that any definition must be read so as to avoid a serious chilling of litigants' rights of appeal, and that an "appeal that is simply without merit is *not* by definition frivolous and should not incur sanctions." *Id.* Finally, the court held that basic procedural due process protections must be observed before an appellate court imposes sanctions. *Id.* at 651–654.

Upon finding that an appeal is frivolous, the appellate court will award monetary sanctions, typically based on the amount of costs and fees incurred by the opposing party in defending against the frivolous appeal. *See, e.g., Kleveland v. Siegel & Wolensky, LLP*, 215 Cal. App. 4th 534, 155 Cal. Rptr. 3d 599 (2013) (ordering the attorney defendants to pay plaintiff the amount of $52,727.56 in attorney fees and costs related to the appeal, where defendants' briefs brazenly misrepresented the record and made arguments totally without merit); *Millennium Corporate Solutions v. Peckinpaugh*, 126 Cal. App. 4th 352, 23 Cal. Rptr. 3d 500 (2005) (imposing a sanction of $24,765 on appellant, representing attorney fees for time spent on the appeal by the respondent, for an appeal that indisputably had no merit). The California courts frequently impose additional sanctions, payable to the clerk of the appellate court, to compensate the state for the cost to the taxpayers of processing a frivolous appeal. *See, e.g., Bucor v. Ahmad*, 244 Cal. App. 4th 175, 191–96, 198 Cal. Rptr. 3d 127 (2016) (awarding sanctions jointly and severally against appellants and their attorneys in the amount of $31,311 payable to respondent, and $25,000 payable to the clerk); *Singh v. Lipworth*, 227 Cal. App. 4th 813, 830, 174 Cal. Rptr. 3d 131 (2014) (imposing $7,500 in sanctions payable directly to the clerk); *Kleveland, supra*, 215 Cal. App. 4th at 559–60 (assessing sanctions of $8,500 payable to the clerk).

(2) *Disentitlement Doctrine.* An appellate court has the inherent power, under the "disentitlement doctrine," to dismiss an appeal by a party that refuses to comply with a lower court order. *See Stoltenberg v. Ampton Inv. Inc.*, 215 Cal. App. 4th 1225, 159 Cal. Rptr. 3d 1 (2013) (discussing several cases). The disentitlement doctrine has been applied to a wide range of cases, including cases in which the appellant is a judgment debtor who has frustrated or obstructed legitimate efforts to enforce a judgment that was not stayed pending appeal. *E.g., Gwartz v. Weilert*, 231 Cal. App. 4th 750, 180 Cal. Rptr. 3d 809 (2014) (dismissing appeal under the disentitlement doctrine where appellate willfully disobeyed trial court's freeze order by transferring assets in an attempt to frustrate enforcement of money judgment during the appeal); *Stoltenberg, supra* (dismissing appeal where defendants repeatedly, and in contempt of sister-state orders, frustrated the enforcement of a California judgment that was the subject of their appeal).

For a thorough discussion of sanctions on appeal, see Eisenberg, Horvitz & Weiner, *California Practice Guide, Civil Appeals & Writs*, ¶ 11:95–¶ 11:158 (The Rutter Group 2015); *see also Coleman v. Gulf Ins. Grp.*, 41 Cal. 3d 782, 226 Cal. Rptr. 90, 718 P.2d 77 (1986); *Forthmann v. Boyer*, 97 Cal. App. 4th 977, 986–989, 118 Cal. Rptr. 2d 715 (2002); Jon B. Eisenberg, *Sanctions on Appeal: A Survey and a Proposal for Computation Guidelines*, 20 U.S.F. L. Rev. 13 (1985).

[e] Remittitur

The remittitur is the document issued by the reviewing court which communicates the final determination of the reviewing court to the lower court. CCP §§ 43; 912.

(1) The clerk of the reviewing court issues the remittitur (referred to as the "mandate" in federal court, Rule 41, F.R.A.P.), which consists of a certified copy of the

judgment or order of the reviewing court and its opinion. CCP §912. The clerk of the Court of Appeal normally issues the remittitur upon expiration of the period during which review in the Supreme Court may be determined. *See, e.g.,* Rule 8.272, Cal. Rules of Ct.; *Rare Coin Galleries, Inc. v. A-Mark Coin Co., Inc.,* 202 Cal. App. 3d 330, 335, 248 Cal. Rptr. 341 (1988). A remittitur issues from the Supreme Court when a judgment of that Court becomes final pursuant to Rule 8.540, Cal. Rules of Ct. For good cause shown, an appellate court may immediately issue, stay, or recall the remittitur. Rules 8.272(c), 8.540(c), Cal. Rules of Ct.

(2) When the remittitur issues, the reviewing court transfers jurisdiction to the lower court. *Riley v. Superior Court,* 49 Cal. 2d 305, 310, 316 P.2d 956 (1957). A reviewing court's remittitur defines the scope of the jurisdiction of the lower court to which the matter is returned. *See Griset v. Fair Political Practices Com.,* 25 Cal. 4th 688, 107 Cal. Rptr. 2d 149, 23 P.3d 43 (2001) (observing that an unqualified affirmance of the superior court's final judgment on the merits ordinarily sustains the judgment and ends the litigation, denying the superior court jurisdiction to reopen the case); *Hampton v. Superior Court,* 38 Cal. 2d 652, 656, 242 P.2d 1 (1952) (ruling a writ of prohibition is the proper remedy to restrain a trial court from proceeding in violation of the reviewing court's remittitur); *Butler v. Superior Court,* 104 Cal. App. 4th 979, 128 Cal. Rptr. 2d 403 (2002) (issuing a writ of mandate ordering the trial court to comply with remittitur instruction).

[f]   Appellate Review of "Limited Civil" Cases

An appeal in a "limited civil case" is to the Appellate Division of the Superior Court. CCP §904.2; see Rules 8.820–8.825, Cal. Rules of Ct. (setting forth time limits and procedures for appeals in limited civil cases). The Court of Appeal has authority to order transfer of such an appeal when the Superior Court certifies or the Court of Appeal on its own motion determines "that such transfer appears necessary to secure uniformity of decision or to settle important questions of law." CCP §911. The Court of Appeal's transfer authority to hear and decide a "limited civil case" does not include the discretion to select and review only an issue or issues not dispositive of the appeal, and then to direct the Appellate Division of the Superior Court to decide other issues necessary to the final disposition of the appeal. *Snukal v. Flightways Mfg., Inc.,* 23 Cal. 4th 754, 98 Cal. Rptr. 2d 1, 3 P.3d. 286 (2000) (holding that although the Court of Appeal has uncontrolled discretion in determining whether to transfer for decision a limited civil case, once it has embarked upon that course, it must decide those appellate issues necessary to resolution of the case on appeal).

Is a decision of the Appellate Division of the Superior Court in a "limited civil case" appealable to the Court of Appeal? *See Anchor Marine Repair Co. v. Magnan,* 93 Cal. App. 4th 525, 113 Cal. Rptr. 2d 284 (2001) (observing that there are only two procedures that permit the Court of Appeal to review decisions of the appellate division under certain circumstances—certification and extraordinary writ—but holding that no statute authorizes a party to appeal a decision of the appellate division to the Court of Appeal).

[6] Review by California Supreme Court

In 1984 the electorate passed Proposition 32, amending Article VI, § 12 of the California Constitution to permit the Supreme Court to review all or only part of a Court of Appeal decision. Rules implementing this amendment became effective in 1985. Prior to that time the Supreme Court reviewed decisions of the trial court after granting a hearing, as if the intermediate review by the court of appeal had never occurred. *See Morehart v. County of Santa Barbara, supra,* 7 Cal. 4th at 744 (contrasting prior and present practices). Now the Supreme Court has discretion to grant review of an entire Court of Appeal decision or only of selected issues, leaving undisturbed the court of appeals decision on the remaining issues. Rule 8.516, Cal. Rules of Ct. The current rules, including the depublication practice discussed below, provide the Supreme Court with more flexibility to accomplish its primary institutional functions: to decide important legal questions and to secure statewide uniformity of decision. Rule 8.500(b); *People v. Davis,* 147 Cal. 346, 348, 81 P. 718 (1905).

[a] General Procedure

The general procedure for Supreme Court review is set forth in California Rules of Court 8.500–8.552. A party seeking review must file and serve a petition for review within 10 days after the decision of the Court of Appeal becomes final. Rule 8.500(a) & (e).

[b] Discretionary Review

The jurisdiction of the Supreme Court in civil cases is, of course, discretionary. The grounds for review by the Supreme Court are set forth in Rule 8.500(b); by far the most important is where review "appears necessary to secure uniformity of decision or to settle an important question of law." Rule 8.500(b)(1). Over the past ten years, the Supreme Court has granted, on average, approximately four percent of the petitions for review. *See* Judicial Council of California, 2015 *Court Statistics Report, Supreme Court,* Fig. 19. Instead of granting review, the Supreme Court may supervise a Court of Appeal decision by use of the depublication process. Rules 8.1105–8.1125.

[c] Petition for Review

The petition for review is a self-contained document, whose form and format is generally prescribed by Rule 8.504. The respondent may file an answer within 20 days after the filing of the petition. Rule 8.500(e). For a thorough discussion of these documents, as well as sample forms, see CEB, *California Civil Appellate Practice,* §§ 27.12–27.28 (3d ed. 2015); Eisenberg, Horvitz & Weiner, *California Practice Guide, Civil Appeals & Writs,* ¶ 13:35–¶ 13:129 (The Rutter Group 2015).

[d]   Effect of Denial of Petition for Review

The Supreme Court must decide a petition for review within 60 days of its filing, extendable for good cause to 90 days. Rule 8.512(b). If the Supreme Court denies the petition, either by order or by failing to act on it within the time limitation, the clerk of the Court of Appeal immediately issues the remittitur. Rule 8.272 (a) & (b). What is the significance of the Supreme Court's denial of a petition for review with respect to the correctness of the Court of Appeal's decision? Should the denial be interpreted as Supreme Court approval of the Court of Appeal's judgment? Of its reasoning? *See People v. Davis, supra*, 147 Cal. at 350 (advising the denial of review should not be taken as an expression of any opinion by the Supreme Court, except that it did not consider that the interest of justice required review); *People v. Triggs*, 8 Cal. 3d 884, 890, 106 Cal. Rptr. 408, 506 P.2d 232 (1973). What significance attaches when the Supreme Court denies the petition for review but orders decertification of the published opinion of the Court of Appeal? *See* Rule 8.1125(d), and discussion of depublication, *infra*.

[e]   Options When Petition Granted

If the Supreme Court decides to grant a petition for review, it then has several options. It may review the entire Court of Appeal decision, or may review and decide only specific issues. Rule 8.516, Cal. Rules of Ct. With respect to issues not decided, the Supreme Court may order republication of those portions of the Court of Appeal's opinion resolving those issues, leave those portions unpublished, or may transfer the case back to the Court of Appeal to decide remaining issues. Rules 8.528, 8.1105. If after granting review the Supreme Court determines that the case involves issues already before the court in another case, it may "grant and hold" the new case until the lead case is decided. Rule 8.512(d).

The Supreme Court may even transfer the entire case back to the Court of Appeal with instructions for further proceedings pursuant to Rule 8.528(d), a routine practice where a petition for extraordinary writ has been summarily denied by the Court of Appeal. *See, e.g., Germann v. Workers' Comp. Appeals Bd.*, 123 Cal. App. 3d 776, 779, n. 1, 176 Cal. Rptr. 868 (1981); *Omaha Indem. Co. v. Superior Court*, 209 Cal. App. 3d 1266, 1270, 258 Cal. Rptr. 66 (1989). What is the immediate effect of a grant of a petition for review on the Court of Appeal's decision? Generally, an opinion superseded by a grant of review is not published, although the Supreme Court may order publication in whole or in part after its decision. Rule 8.1105(c).

The procedures for briefing, oral argument, disposition, and rehearing of a case accepted for review are governed by Rules 8.516–8.540. Generally, a decision of the Supreme Court becomes final 30 days after filing. Rule 8.532(b). The clerk issues the remittitur when the decision becomes final, unless the court directs an earlier issuance. Rule 8.532.

Review of a decision of the California Supreme Court involving a federal question may be sought by petition for writ of certiorari before the U.S. Supreme Court. 28 USC § 1257(a).

[7] Publication and Depublication of Appellate Court Opinions

[a] Supreme Court Opinions

Decisions on the merits by the Supreme Court and courts of appeal must be in writing with the court's reasons stated. Art. VI, § 14, Cal. Const. All such written opinions of the Supreme Court are published in the Official Reports. Rule 8.1105(a), Cal. Rules of Ct.

(1) An opinion of the Court of Appeal, however, cannot be published unless it meets one of the criteria set forth in Rule 8.1105(c) (*e.g.*, the opinion establishes a new rule of law, address or creates an apparent conflict in the law, involves a legal issue of continuing public interest, etc.). These criteria discourage publication; approximately 16% of the Courts of Appeal opinions in civil appeals are published. *See* Judicial Council of California, *2015 Court Statistics Report, Courts of Appeal*, Fig. 30 for 2013–2014.

(2) Partial publication is also authorized and is frequently utilized. If the Court of Appeal determines that only portions of its opinion meet the standards for publication, it can order publication of only those portions. Rule 8.1110(a), Cal. Rules of Ct. The unpublished parts are treated as an unpublished opinion. Rule 8.1110(c).

[b] Publication Procedures

The authority for establishing court rules for selective publication of court of appeal opinions is Article VI, Section 14, of the California Constitution, and Government Code § 68902. Under the current rules of court, opinions may be ordered published either by certification of the Court of Appeal rendering the opinion, by request of a party or non-party, or by independent order from the Supreme Court. Rules 8.1105–8.1120, Cal. Rules of Ct.

(1) Most commonly, publication decisions are made by the rendering Court of Appeal upon certification by a majority of the panel, prior to the decision's finality in that court, that the opinion meets the standards for publication. Rule 8.1105 (b) & (c). However, an opinion of the Court of Appeal is no longer considered published if the rendering court grants a rehearing. Rule 8.1105(e)(1)(A).

(2) If the rendering Court of Appeal does not certify its opinion for publication, any person (party or nonparty) may make a request for publication. Rule 8.1120(a) sets forth the procedure for such requests. Why might a party desire publication? A nonparty? Could there be a conflict of interest between a prevailing party and nonparties as to publication? How so? *See* Julie H. Biggs, *Censoring the Law in California: Decertification Revisited*, 30 Hastings L.J. 1577 (1979). The Supreme Court can order publication of a Court of Appeal opinion independent of any request or petition for review. Rule 8.1125(c). Rule 8.1120(d) specifies that such an order shall not be deemed an opinion by the Supreme Court of the correctness of the result or reasoning set forth in the opinion. Does Rule 8.1120(d) make any sense? Why else would the Supreme Court order publication of an otherwise unpublished court of appeal opinion?

(3) The practice and rule in effect before July 1, 2016, was that a grant of review by the Supreme Court automatically depublished the Court of Appeal decision that was under review. Amendments to the Rules of Court effective July 1, 2016, altered the effect of published Court of Appeal decisions after review is granted and while the review is pending. Under new Rule 8.1115(e), if the Supreme Court grants review of a published Court of Appeal decision, that decision now remains published and citable while review is pending and—similar to the result under the former rule—will not have binding or precedential effect on the superior courts, but will instead have a lesser status of "potentially persuasive value only." Advisory Committee Comment to Amended Rule 8.1115(e) (effective July 1, 2016). In other words, under the new Rule, a published Court of Appeal decision as to which review has been granted remains published and is citable, while review is pending, for any potentially persuasive value. *Id.* However, the new Rule also provides that the Supreme Court can order that a decision under review by that court have an effect other than the effect otherwise specified in the Rule, such as that while review is pending, specified parts of the published Court of Appeal opinion have binding or precedential effect rather that only potentially persuasive value. Rule 8.1115(e)(3); *see* Advisory Committee Comment, *supra*.

[c] Depublication by Supreme Court Order

The Supreme Court has the power to order depublication of a Court of Appeal opinion certified for publication, either on its own motion or pursuant to a request for depublication. Rules 8.1105(e), 8.1125(c). There are no specified standards for depublication, although one Supreme Court justice indicated that in most cases depublication is ordered "because a majority of the justices consider the opinion to be wrong in some significant way, such that it would mislead the bench and bar if it remained as citable precedent." Joseph R. Grodin, *The Depublication Practice of the California Supreme Court*, 72 Cal. L. Rev. 514, 515 (1984).

(1) Any person may request the Supreme Court to order depublication of a Court of Appeal opinion previously certified for publication. Rule 8.1125(a). The request procedure is set forth in Rule 8.1125(a)–(c). Why might a party request depublication? A nonparty? *See* Biggs, *Censoring the Law in California*, *supra* at 1582–84.

(2) The Supreme Court's depublication practice has been criticized on a variety of grounds, including that it is ordered without reasons stated and may leave attorneys and lower courts without guidance as to what the Supreme Court considers to be the law. *See* Stephen R. Barnett, *Making Decisions Disappear: Depublication and Stipulated Reversal in the California Supreme Court*, 26 Loy. L.A. L. Rev. 1033 (1993); Grodin, *The Depublication Practice*, *supra* at 520–523; Biggs, *Censoring the Law in California*, *supra*. Perhaps as a response to these various concerns, the Supreme Court's exercise of its depublication authority has declined dramatically over the past several years from over 100 opinions ordered depublished per year in the early 1990s to only 6 opinions in 2013–2014. *See* Judicial Council of California, *2015 Court Statistics Report, Supreme Court*, Fig. 23.

(3) Rule 8.1125(d) advises that a Supreme Court order directing depublication of a Court of Appeal opinion "is not an expression court's opinion of the correctness of the result of the decision or of any law stated in the opinion." This advice is sometimes questioned. *See People v. Dee,* 222 Cal. App. 3d 760, 765, 272 Cal. Rptr. 208 (1990) ("[T]o insist that those depublication orders are without significance would be to perpetuate a myth"); *but see People v. Saunders,* 5 Cal 4th 580, 592, n. 8, 20 Cal. Rpt. 2d 638 853 P.2d 1093 (1993) (disapproving of the *Dee* court's comment regarding the significance of depublication).

[d] Citation of Unpublished Opinions Prohibited

What difference does it make whether or not an opinion is published? Plenty.

(1) Generally, an unpublished opinion cannot be cited or relied on by a court or a party in any other action or proceeding. Rule 8.1115, Cal. Rules of Ct. This prohibition is subject to limited exceptions, most notably that such opinions may be cited or relied on "when the opinion is relevant under the doctrines of law of the case, res judicata, or collateral estoppel." Rule 8.1115(b)(1); *see, e.g., Hummel v. First Nat. Bank,* 191 Cal. App. 3d 489, 491, 236 Cal. Rptr. 449 (1987) (law of the case); *Los Angeles Police Protective League v. City of L. A.,* 102 Cal. App. 4th 85, 91, 124 Cal. Rptr. 2d 911 (2002) (collateral estoppel). Because an unpublished or depublished opinion cannot be cited, it has no precedential value. *See, e.g., Nelson v. Justice Court,* 86 Cal. App. 3d 64, 66, 150 Cal. Rptr. 39 (1978); *Heaton v. Marin Cnty. Emp. Retirement Bd.,* 63 Cal. App. 3d 421, 431, 133 Cal. Rptr. 809 (1976).

(2) Improper citation to an unpublished opinion in an appellate brief may result in the imposition of sanctions. *E.g., Alicia T. v. County of Los Angeles,* 222 Cal. App. 3d 869, 885–886, 271 Cal. Rptr. 513 (1990) (imposing monetary sanctions against appellant's counsel for repeatedly citing depublished cases). Attorneys should never be certain of a Court of Appeal opinion's publication status until actually published in the permanent volumes of the official reporters (*i.e.,* the California Appellate Reports). An opinion published in the advance sheets or retrieved through computer research may be depublished due to a later Supreme Court decertification order, granted rehearing, or petition for review.

[8] *Stipulated Reversals*

Prior to 2000, an appellate court's power to reverse or vacate a trial court's judgment when the parties reached a stipulation as a condition of a proposed settlement of a pending appeal was governed by the judicial rule set forth in *Neary v. Regents of the Univ. of Cal.,* 3 Cal. 4th 273, 10 Cal. Rptr. 2d 859, 834 P.2d 119 (1992). However, the judicial rule set forth in *Neary* was superseded by the Legislature. Effective January 1, 2000, CCP § 128(a)(8) was amended to read: "An appellate court shall not reverse or vacate a duly entered judgment upon an agreement or stipulation of the parties unless the court finds both of the following: (A) There is no reasonable possibility that the interests of nonparties or the public will be adversely affected by the reversal.

(B) the reasons of the parties for requesting reversal outweigh the erosion of public trust that may result from the nullification of a judgment and the risk that the availability of stipulated reversal will reduce the incentive for pretrial settlement."

The express purpose of amended CCP § 128(a)(8) was to overrule the *Neary* rule and to instead follow the federal court view of stipulated reversals set forth in *U.S. Bancorp Co. v. Bonner Mall Partnership*, 513 U.S. 18, 115 S. Ct. 386, 130 L. Ed. 2d 233 (1994). *See* Assembly Committee on Judiciary, Analysis of Assembly Bill 1676 (1999–2000 Reg. Sess.). In *Bancorp*, the U.S. Supreme Court held that, in the absence of exceptional circumstances, settlement during appeal does not justify vacatur of the judgment under review. The court specifically ruled that the requisite "exceptional circumstances do not include the mere fact that the settlement provides for a vacatur." *Bancorp*, 513 U.S. at 29. The court noted that judicial precedents are valuable to the legal community as a whole, and "are not merely the property of private litigants and should stand unless a court concludes that the public interest would be served by a vacatur." *Id*. at 26. The *Bancorp* court also rejected facilitation of settlement as a policy justification for stipulated vacatur. *Id*. at 27–29.

Lower court decisions have approved stipulated reversals only where all three of the requirements of CCP 128(a)(8) are satisfied. *Compare In re Rashad H.*, 78 Cal. App. 4th 376, 92 Cal. Rptr. 2d 723 (2000) (approving stipulated reversal of an order terminating parental rights) *with Muccianti v. Willow Creek Care Ctr.*, 108 Cal. App. 4th 13, 133 Cal. Rptr. 2d 1 (2003) (rejecting vacation of a wrongful death judgment against defendant health care facility that treated the elderly because it may deny the public the ability to discover defendant's bad acts).

§ 15.02 Extraordinary Writs

[A] Introductory Notes

[1] *Writs, Generally*

A writ is an order to an inferior court, administrative agency, board, corporation or individual which prevents, compels, or annuls certain acts. A California civil practitioner encounters many "ordinary" writs, such as attachment, execution, and injunction. An "extraordinary" writ, as discussed in this section, is something quite different. Generally speaking, an extraordinary writ allows a higher court to review actions of a lower tribunal when review by appeal is inadequate. *See, e.g.*, CCP §§ 1085, 1086, 1094.5. Extraordinary writs are therefore different from appeals, although both procedures involve review by an appellate court.

[2] *Appeals*

Appeals are heard as a matter of right. CCP §§ 904.1, 904.2, 906. Generally speaking, appeals are available only when authorized by statute. CCP §§ 901, 904. Many prejudgment orders are not immediately appealable — they can be appealed only as part of a final judgment at the conclusion of the case. *See* CCP §§ 904.1–.5. A few types of interlocutory orders are subject to immediate appeal prior to final judgment. These include preliminary injunctions, CCP § 904.1(a)(6); superior court orders imposing monetary sanctions which exceed $5,000, CCP § 904.1(a)(11)&(12); interlocutory judgments sustaining the defense that another action is pending, § 597; and various interlocutory orders qualifying for appeal under the collateral order rule. *See* discussion *supra*, § 15.01 of this Chapter. Is immediate appellate review unavailable for all other interlocutory orders and decisions? Of course not.

[3] Extraordinary Writs

Extraordinary writs provide a mechanism for potential immediate appellate review of non-appealable interlocutory decisions of trial tribunals. Writs are extraordinary remedies in the sense that they are speedy and discretionary and, unlike appeals, do not require appellate review as a matter of right. As will be discussed below, writs involve other foundational prerequisites not necessary for an appeal. This section focuses on the most typical use of extraordinary writs, *i.e.*, to review in the Court of Appeal or Supreme Court pretrial action taken by a Superior Court. Such writs are usually addressed to prejudgment orders that are not immediately appealable. *See* CEB, *California Civil Writ Practice* §§ 14.1–14.3, 16.86–16.145 (4th ed. 2016).

[4] Primer on Extraordinary Writ Practice

To most students and novice attorneys, California's extraordinary writ practice seems quite mysterious. This view is understandable. Due in part to the failure of most appellate opinions to clearly articulate specific standards for the issuance of writs, writ practice in California *is* somewhat mysterious! *See Omaha Indemnity Co. v. Superior Court*, reproduced *infra*. Also, the terminology employed to describe aspects of this practice is often arcane and misleading. A basic writ practice glossary may therefore be helpful:

[a] "Writ"

A "writ" is an order entered by a higher court directed at an inferior court, administrative agency, or individual. When a writ is sought from the Court of Appeal, for example, the process is referred to as "petitioning" for a writ. The "petition" is a set of documents which resembles a combination of a complaint and a brief. *See* CEB, *California Civil Writ Practice, Drafting the Writ Petition* §§ 18.5–18.60 (4th ed. 2016).

[b] Parties Involved

Usually there are three parties to a writ proceeding: the petitioner, the respondent, and the real party in interest. The "petitioner" is the party seeking relief from the appellate court, and the "respondent" is the inferior tribunal (usually a trial court) whose decision is being challenged by the petitioner. The "real party in interest" is the party who prevailed in the decision by the trial court. Generally the real party in interest, not the respondent, is expected to respond to the petition.

[c] Types of Writs

There are a number of different types of writs recognized in California. The two most frequently requested appellate writs are the "writ of mandate" (also referred to by the traditional name of "mandamus") authorized by CCP §§ 1084–1094, and the "writ of prohibition" authorized by CCP §§ 1102–1105, 1107–1108. Other appellate writs include the "writ of certiorari" (or "writ of review"), CCP §§ 1067–1077; "supersedeas," CCP §§ 923, Rule 8.112 & 8.116, Cal. Rules of Ct.; and "habeas corpus," Penal Code §§ 1473–1508. A "writ of mandate" is related to, but not the same device as, "administrative mandamus." Administrative mandamus, discussed separately in § 15.03 *infra*, is the process by which a court may review the validity of a final administrative hearing decision, pursuant to CCP § 1094.5.

[d] "Alternative" and "Peremptory" Writs

Writs of mandate and of prohibition may issue as either "alternative" or "peremptory" writs. CCP §§ 1087, 1104.

(1) An "alternative writ" is essentially an order to show cause. This writ, when issued, commands the respondent inferior court or agency to grant the requested relief or to show cause why such relief should not be granted. CCP §§ 1087 and 1104.

The issuance of an alternative writ usually constitutes a determination that the petitioner has satisfied the general procedural prerequisites to extraordinary writ review, but is not necessarily a decision for petitioner on the merits of petition. *E.g., Civil Serv. Employees Ins. Co. v. Superior Court*, 22 Cal. 3d 362, 149 Cal. Rptr. 360, 584 P.2d 497 (1978) (issuing an alternative writ of prohibition, but subsequently denying a peremptory writ); *Diamond v. Allison*, 8 Cal. 3d 736, 106 Cal. Rptr. 13, 305 P.2d 205 (1973) (granting, then later discharging, alternative writ and denying peremptory writ of mandate).

When an alternative writ is issued, the requested relief may be imposed on the respondent if no response is filed by the real party in interest. If the real party in interest wishes to contest the proposed relief, the real party should file a response (or "return") to the alternative writ by way of demurrer, verified answer, or both. CCP §§ 1089, 1105, Rule 8.487, Cal. Rules of Ct. This may be followed by a reply (or "replication") from the petitioner, and each party may be entitled to present oral argument. CCP §§ 1093–94, 1105, 1108. If the appellate court then grants the requested relief, a "peremptory writ" will issue and the alternative writ will be discharged. *E.g., Brandt v. Superior Court*, reproduced *infra*.

(2) A "peremptory writ" is the reviewing court's ultimate order that the respondent must grant the relief requested in the writ petition. CCP §§ 1087, 1097, 1104. As indicated above, a peremptory writ (of mandate or prohibition) may issue after the is-

suance of, and hearing on, an alternative writ. CCP §§ 1087, 1104. However, a peremptory writ may be "issued in the first instance"—without first requesting or granting an alternative writ—upon due notice. CCP §§ 1088, 1105; *see Palma v. U.S. Industrial Fasteners, Inc.,* reproduced *infra*.

[e] "Statutory" Writs

Certain extraordinary writs are referred to as "statutory" writs, as opposed to "common law" writs. Unlike the distinctions between "alternative" and "peremptory," or "mandate" and "prohibition," this classification carries little legal significance. A "statutory" writ is not a distinct type of writ, but is simply one where writ review is specifically authorized for a particular situation by a special statute. Such special statutory authorization for writ review usually contains specific time limitations for filing the writ petition, which may be jurisdictional and should be scrupulously followed. Writ review specifically authorized by statute applies to some very important interlocutory decisions, including the following:

(1) Denial of a motion to quash service of process, CCP §§ 418.10(a)(1) and (c) (Petition for writ of mandate within 10 days after notice to parties of the decision). Review by mandate is the exclusive remedy here, is it not? Why? *See McCorkle v. City of L. A.,* 70 Cal. 2d 252, 256–260, 74 Cal. Rptr. 389, 449 P.2d 453 (1969).

(2) Review of decisions on motions to change venue, CCP § 400 (Petition for writ of mandate within 20 days after service of notice of decision). Review by mandate is the exclusive appellate remedy here, is it not? Why? *See, e.g., Hennigan v. Boren,* 243 Cal. App. 2d 810, 814–815, 52 Cal. Rptr. 748 (1966).

(3) Review of a decision with respect to motion for summary judgment and summary adjudication of issues, except where summary judgment is granted in full, CCP § 437c(m) (petition for peremptory writ within 20 days of notice of entry of order). *See, e.g., Lilienthal & Fowler v. Superior Court,* 12 Cal. App. 4th 1848, 16 Cal. Rptr. 2d 458 (1993) (issuing writ directing trial court to vacate order denying summary adjudication and to reconsider motion). Why is this statutory authority for review by extraordinary writ inapplicable to orders which grant a full summary judgment? *See* CCP §§ 437c(m); 904.1(a)(1).

(4) Denial of a motion to stay or dismiss action on the ground of inconvenient forum, CCP §§ 418.10(a)(2) & (c) (authorizing petition for writ of mandate within 10 days after notice to parties of the decision). Why is writ review statutorily authorized only for *denial* of the motion? *See* CCP § 904.1(a)(3).

(5) Determinations with respect to good faith of a settlement, CCP § 877.6(e) (authorizing petition for writ of mandate within 20 days of notice of determination). *See, e.g., Everman v. Superior Court,* 8 Cal. App. 4th 466, 10 Cal. Rptr. 2d 176 (1992).

(6) Determination of disqualification of judge, CCP §§ 170.3, 170.6 (authorizing petition for writ of mandamus within 10 days of notice of decision). Review by man-

date is the exclusive means of appellate review of unsuccessful challenge, whether peremptory or for cause. *People v. Hull,* 1 Cal. 4th 266, 2 Cal. Rptr. 2d 526, 820 P.2d 1036 (1991).

(7) Other "statutory writ" authorizations are contained in CCP § 405.39 (review of motions to expunge lis pendens); § 404.6 (order coordinating, transferring, or consolidating actions); § 1176 (denial of stay of execution of unlawful detainer judgment); § 904.1(b) (review of monetary sanctions of $5,000 or less); and Government Code § 6259(c) (review of trial court order directing or refusing disclosure of public records). *See, e.g., Powers v. City of Richmond,* 10 Cal. 4th 85, 40 Cal. Rptr. 2d 839, 893 P.2d 1160 (1995) (holding superior court decisions in Public Records Act cases are not appealable but instead are immediately reviewable by extraordinary writ; such exclusive appellate review does not violate the California Constitution); *Times Mirror Co. v. Superior Court,* 53 Cal. 3d 1325, 1334, 283 Cal. Rptr. 893, 813 P.2d 240 (1991) (observing that the purpose of statutory writ review per Gov. Code § 6259(c) is to speed appellate review, not to limit its scope).

[f] "Common Law" Writs

All other extraordinary writs, not specifically authorized by a special statute, are sometimes referred to as "common law" writs. This is somewhat of a misnomer because although they have a common law ancestry, *see* Edward Jenks, *The Prerogative Writs in English Law,* 32 Yale L.J. 523 (1923), all of California's civil extraordinary writs are now authorized by statute. *See* CCP §§ 1067–1108, 923.

[g] "Extraordinary" Remedy

Writs are considered "extraordinary" remedies because they provide immediate and speedy appellate review of non-appealable trial court rulings, and are equitable and discretionary. *See Omaha Indemnity Co. v. Superior Court,* reproduced *infra.*

[B] Types of Extraordinary Writs

[1] *Writ of Mandate*

The most commonly sought writ is mandate (or traditional "mandamus"). The writ of mandate is referred to as a "nonjurisdictional" writ, simply meaning that it is available to correct error committed within the inferior tribunal's jurisdiction. *See* CCP §§ 1084–1085.

[a] Functions

Mandate has many varied uses. It is appropriate to enforce a trial court's mandatory duty to act. CCP § 1085. This includes: (a) the duty to perform a ministerial act when there is a statutory duty to perform it; (b) the duty to exercise discretion when there is a discretionary duty involved; and (c) the duty, in exercising discretion, not to abuse that discretion. *See* CEB, *California Civil Writ Practice* §§ 15.2–15.13 (4th ed. 2016), and cases cited therein.

[b] Ministerial Act

A ministerial act is defined as "an act that a public officer is required to perform in a prescribed manner in obedience to the mandate of legal authority and without regard to his own judgment or opinion concerning such act's propriety or impropriety, when a given state of facts exist." *Rodriguez v. Solis,* 1 Cal. App. 4th 495, 501, 2 Cal. Rptr. 2d 50 (1991). Discretion, on the other hand, "is the power conferred on public functionaries to act officially according to the dictates of their own judgment." *Id.* at 501–502; *see also Hutchinson v. City of Sacramento,* 17 Cal. App. 4th 791, 796, 21 Cal. Rptr. 2d 779 (1993) (Writ of mandate not proper to review city's enactment of a speed limit ordinance because not a ministerial act, but a legislative one involving exercise of discretion). Although mandamus does not generally lie to control the exercise of judicial discretion, the writ will issue where under the facts that discretion can only be exercised in one way. *Robbins v. Superior Court,* 38 Cal. 3d 199, 205, 211 Cal. Rptr. 398, 695 P.2d 695 (1985).

[c] Writ Issued Against Nonjudicial Entities

Although the discussion in this section focuses on use of mandamus to compel a trial court to perform an act, this writ is much broader in scope. Pursuant to CCP § 1085, a writ of mandate may be issued against a public officer, public body, corporation, board or person. *See, e.g., Sierra Club v. State Bd. of Forestry,* 7 Cal. 4th 1215, 1233–1234, 32 Cal. Rptr. 2d 19, 876 P.2d 505 (1994) (ruling environmental associations could use mandamus in superior court to compel state Board of Forestry to withdraw its approval of two timber harvesting plans); *Santa Clara Cnty. Counsel Attorneys Assn. v. Woodside,* 7 Cal. 4th 525, 28 Cal. Rptr. 2d 617, 869 P.2d 1142 (1994) (noting that the availability of writ relief to compel a public agency to perform an act prescribed by law has been long recognized, and affirming trial court's issuance of writ of mandate against county and county counsel for breach of duty to bargain in good faith).

A petitioner employing such traditional use of mandamus may file the writ petition in the Court of Appeal, *e.g., Andal v. Miller,* 28 Cal. App. 4th 358, 34 Cal. Rptr. 88 (1994); *State Bd. of Ed. v. Honig,* 13 Cal. App. 4th 720, 16 Cal. Rptr. 2d 727 (1993); but normally must initially file it in the Superior Court, *e.g., Driving School Assn. of Cal. v. San Mateo Union High Sch. Dist.,* 11 Cal. App. 4th 1513, 14 Cal. Rptr. 2d 908 (1992) (traditional mandamus in superior court against school district); *Salkin v. California Dental Assn.,* 176 Cal. App. 3d 1118, 224 Cal. Rptr. 352 (1986) (traditional mandamus against private professional association in superior court).

Traditional mandamus under § 1085 is related to, but different than, administrative mandamus to review an administrative adjudicatory decision under § 1094.5. *See, e.g., Western States Petroleum Assn. v. Superior Court,* 9 Cal. 4th 559, 38 Cal. Rptr. 2d 139, 888 P.2d 1268 (1995) (discussing similarities and differences); *Bright Dev. v. City of Tracy,* 20 Cal. App. 4th 783, 793–795, 24 Cal. Rptr. 2d 618 (1993) (explaining that administrative mandamus determines whether agency decision supported by administrative hearing record; traditional mandamus permits parties to present evidence outside the administrative record). Administrative mandamus is discussed in § 15.03 of this Chapter, *infra.*

[2]   Writ of Prohibition

Prohibition is the appropriate writ to restrain a threatened judicial act which is in excess of the inferior tribunal's jurisdiction. CCP § 1102. Prohibition has several prerequisites which distinguish it from mandamus and other writs. *See* CEB, *California Civil Writ Practice, supra,* §§ 15.14–15.26. Unlike mandamus, which orders the respondent to take some affirmative action, a writ of prohibition is preventative and requires the respondent not to take a particular action. CCP §§ 1085, 1102. Prohibition applies only to acts judicial in nature, whether by a trial court or an administrative agency. CCP § 1102. The challenged action must be actually threatened but not yet completed. CCP §§ 1102, 1104.

Prohibition is a jurisdictional writ, meaning that it is available only to remedy "jurisdictional" defects or errors. CCP § 1102; *see, e.g., Agricultural Labor Relations Bd. v. Superior Court,* 29 Cal. App. 4th 688, 34 Cal. Rptr. 2d 546 (1994) (finding writ of prohibition improper where agency acted within its jurisdiction). This notion of "jurisdiction" is defined broadly to include not only fundamental subject matter jurisdiction, but any act which exceeds the power or competency of the tribunal. *Kenneth Mebane Ranches v. Superior Court,* 10 Cal. App. 4th 276, 280, 12 Cal. Rptr. 2d 562 (1992) (granting writ of prohibition to review trial court's overruling of demurrer which raised jurisdictional challenge to condemning agency's power to maintain eminent domain action); *Inland Casino Corp. v. Superior Court,* 8 Cal. App. 4th 770, 10 Cal. Rptr. 2d 497 (1992) (issuing writ to review trial court's overruling of demurrer invoking jurisdictional issues of Indian lands). For a more thorough analysis of these, and the other niceties of prohibition and mandamus, see CEB, *California Civil Writ Practice, supra,* §§ 15.2–15.26; 8 Witkin, *California Procedure, Extraordinary Writs* §§ 18–26, 48–161 (5th ed. 2008).

[3]   Writ of Certiorari

Certiorari (or "writ of review") is the appropriate writ to review a completed judicial act of an inferior tribunal which is without or in excess of jurisdiction. CCP §§ 1067–1068. Certiorari is the counterpart to prohibition where the jurisdictional error under attack has already occurred. And as with prohibition, "jurisdiction" is broadly defined to encompass most unauthorized acts by a tribunal or officer exercising judicial functions. CCP § 1068; *see* CEB, *California Civil Writ Practice, supra,* §§ 15.27–15.38.

Some significant prerequisites make certiorari's usefulness very limited. First, although certiorari is available to review judicial acts which have been completed, this writ is inappropriate unless the completed act is also not appealable. CCP § 1068. Second, certiorari, when issued, simply commands the respondent to certify its record to the reviewing court in order to enable a decision on the merits of the petition. *See* CCP § 1071. And generally, administrative mandamus, *not* certiorari, must be used to review adjudicatory actions of state administrative agencies. CCP § 1094.5. However, certiorari is available to review the adjudicatory actions of state agencies of constitutional origin, such as the Workers' Compensation Board, the Agricultural Labor Relations Board, the Public Utilities Commission, and the Public Employment Relations Board. *See* Rules 8.495–8.498, Cal. Rules of Ct.

Other than this limited administrative review function, the most common use of certiorari is to review a contempt judgment. *See Moffat v. Moffat*, 27 Cal. 3d 645, 656, 165 Cal. Rptr. 877, 612 P.2d 967 (1980) (ruling superior court contempt order reviewable only by certiorari). Why contempt? *See* CCP §§ 904.1(a)(1), 1222.

[4] *Writ of Supersedeas*

Supersedeas is an auxiliary remedy which, when issued by an appellate court, stays enforcement of a judgment or enjoins parties during the pendency of an appeal. *See* CCP § 923; Rule 8.112, Cal. Rules of Ct. Many judgments are automatically stayed when appealed, or stayed upon the posting of a bond. CCP §§ 916–922. Other judgments may be stayed in the discretion of the trial courts. *E.g.*, CCP §§ 918.5, 919. When no stay is available from the trial court, the petitioner, after filing a notice of appeal, may seek a writ of supersedeas from an appellate court. CCP § 923. The appellate court, in its discretion, may issue a writ of supersedeas to preserve its jurisdiction and maintain the status quo during the appeal. *See, e.g., People ex rel. San Francisco Bay Conservation Com. v. Town of Emeryville*, 69 Cal. 2d 533, 536–539, 72 Cal. Rptr. 790, 446 P.2d 790 (1968).

[5] *Selecting the Appropriate Writ*

Selection of the appropriate writ can be difficult because they overlap in definition and function. For example, assume a trial court enters a discovery order compelling defendant to produce certain documents despite defendant's claim they are privileged. The order specifies that if the defendant does not comply within 10 days, he will be considered in contempt of court. Defendant wishes to petition for writ review of the order; but which writ is appropriate? Mandate? Prohibition? Or certiorari? And what are the consequences of choosing the wrong writ?

[a] Flexible Approach

Fortunately, the courts are fairly understanding and flexible when it comes to selecting the appropriate writ. Rarely will they refuse relief solely because the petitioner requested the wrong type of writ. *See, e.g., Anton v. San Antonio Cmty. Hosp.*, 19 Cal. 3d 802, 813–814, 140 Cal. Rptr. 442, 567 P.2d 1162 (1977) (treating petition brought as traditional mandamus pursuant to CCP § 1085 as one for administrative mandamus under § 1094.5); *Babb v. Superior Court*, 3 Cal. 3d 841, 850, 92 Cal. Rptr. 179, 479 P.2d 379 (1971) (issuing alternative writ of prohibition, subsequently finding mandate more appropriate and treating petition as one for mandate, and issuing peremptory writ). For numerous additional examples of courts issuing one type of writ relief although a different writ was requested, see 8 Witkin, *California Procedure, Extraordinary Writs* §§ 232–233 (5th ed. 2008).

[b] May an Improper Appeal Be Treated as a Writ?

Occasionally, two writs may be necessary to provide petitioner with full relief. And because Article VI, § 10, of the California Constitution authorizes proceedings for extraordinary relief "*in the nature* of mandamus, certiorari, and prohibition," some courts have actually issued hybrid writs. *See, e.g., Planned Parenthood Affiliates v. Van De Kamp*, 181 Cal. App. 3d 245, 226 Cal. Rptr. 361 (1986) (issuing writ known as "prohibitory mandate"); Witkin, *California Procedure, supra*, §§ 239–257 (citing cases). A reviewing court may even treat an appeal, when improper, as a petition for an extraordinary writ. *See, e.g., Morehart v. County of Santa Barbara*, 7 Cal. 4th 725, 744–747, 29 Cal. Rptr. 2d 804, 872 P.2d 143 (1994) (ruling that where circumstances were so unusual that postponement of an appeal from a nonappealable judgment would cause serious hardship and inconvenience, and directing court of appeal to treat premature appeal as a writ of mandate and to determine the merits); *Olson v. Cory*, 35 Cal. 3d 390, 400–401, 197 Cal. Rptr. 843, 673 P.2d 720 (1983) (same).

[c] Precision Unnecessary

Selecting the appropriate writ may greatly impress the reviewing court, and may even be expected when the choice is relatively clear. But life, not to mention the applicable time limitation for an extraordinary writ, is simply too short to worry about precision in unclear cases. The recommended approach may be to simply file a "Petition for Writ of Mandate, Prohibition, and/or Certiorari, or Other Appropriate Writ." *See* CEB, *California Civil Writ Practice, supra*, § 18.3.

[C] Writ Prerequisites and Procedures

Omaha Indemnity Company v. Superior Court

Court of Appeal of California, Second Appellate District
209 Cal. App. 3d 1266, 258 Cal. Rptr. 66 (1989)

GILBERT, JUSTICE.

An attorney files a writ petition with the Court of Appeal pointing out an apparent error of the trial court. The Court of Appeal summarily denies the petition. The bewildered attorney asks, "Why?"

If this case does not answer the question, we hope the following rule will at least assuage counsel's frustration: Error by the trial judge does not of itself ensure that a writ petition will be granted. A remedy will not be deemed inadequate merely because additional time and effort would be consumed by its being pursued through the ordinary course of the law.

In this action, plaintiffs are suing defendants for negligence. They are also suing defendants' insurance company in a cause of action for declaratory relief. Plaintiffs claim that they are third party beneficiaries of this insurance contract. The trial court has denied the motion of the insurance company to sever the declaratory relief cause of action, and the insurance company therefore seeks relief by way of extraordinary writ. We initially denied the writ, but after our Supreme Court directed us to issue an alternative writ, we shall now grant a writ of mandate.

BACKGROUND

Real parties Frank and Margaret Greinke owned rental property in the City of Santa Maria. In July of 1980, the Greinkes leased the premises to K. R. Trefts and Patricia M. Trefts. The lease agreement required the Trefts to purchase a general liability insurance policy for the mutual benefit of landlord and tenant. In July of 1982, Omaha Indemnity Company, an insurance company, issued a general liability policy to the Trefts.

The Greinkes claim that, on or about July 17, 1986, they became aware of damage to their property caused by an oil spill. They contend that the oil spill occurred during the Trefts' occupation of the property. The Greinkes demanded that Omaha compensate them, under the terms of the insurance policy, for the damage to the property. Omaha has purportedly denied coverage under the policy.

On March 14, 1988, the Greinkes sued the Trefts for damage resulting from the oil spill. They also sued Omaha for declaratory relief of their rights under the terms of the insurance contract.

Omaha demurred to the declaratory relief cause of action. In its demurrer it asserted that the Greinkes were not parties to the contract of insurance and, therefore, had no standing to pursue a claim for declaratory relief. It contended that the Greinkes had alleged neither interest in the insurance policy nor a denial of coverage. Thus, Omaha reasoned that there is no case or controversy pending against it.

The trial court was correct in overruling the demurrer. The Greinkes allege that they are the intended beneficiaries of the insurance policy and that Omaha had denied them coverage. In such instances, an action for declaratory relief is appropriate

In the alternative, Omaha moved to sever the declaratory relief action from the tort lawsuit. Omaha claimed that it would suffer prejudice should the lawsuit against both itself and the Trefts go forward. Further, it pointed out that severance would promote judicial economy in that there would be no need to try the declaratory relief action should the tenants be found not liable.

Although Omaha has requested our review of this ruling, it has neglected to supply us with a copy of the reporter's transcript. This did not simplify our task of review.

On August 2, 1988, we denied a petition for writ of mandate. On September 29, 1988, the Supreme Court granted a petition for review. It then ordered the case retransferred to us with the direction to issue an alternative writ in light of Evidence Code § 1155 and *Moradi-Shalal v. Fireman's Fund Ins. Companies* (1988) 46 Cal. 3d 287, 306 [250 Cal. Rptr. 116, 758 P.2d 58].

DISCUSSION

A. *Motion to Sever.*

Code of Civil Procedure section 1048, subdivision (b) states, in pertinent part: "The court, in furtherance of convenience or to avoid prejudice, or when separate trials will be conducive to expedition and economy, may order a separate trial of any cause of action...."

In a negligence action, Evidence Code section 1155 precludes the use of evidence that a tortfeasor has insurance for the injury that he has allegedly caused. "The evidence [of a party being insured] is regarded as both irrelevant and prejudicial to the defendant." (1 Witkin, Cal. Evidence (3d ed. 1986) § 417, p. 391.)

Our Supreme Court has stated that the suing of an insured for negligence and the insurer for bad faith in the same lawsuit "'... obviously [violates] both the letter and spirit of [Evid. Code, § 1155].' [*Royal Globe Ins. Co. v. Superior Court* (1979) 23 Cal. 3d 880, 891 (153 Cal. Rptr. 842, 592 P.2d 329).].... '[*Until*] *the liability of the insured is first determined*, the defense of the insured may be seriously hampered by discovery initiated by the injured claimant against the insurer.' [Citation.]" (*Moradi-Shalal v. Fireman's Fund Ins. Companies, supra,* 46 Cal. 3d at p. 306, italics in original.)

"It is within the discretion of the court to order a severance and separate trials of such actions [citations], and the exercise of such discretion will not be interfered with on appeal except when there has been a manifest abuse thereof. [Citation.]" (*McLellan v. McLellan* (1972) 23 Cal. App. 3d 343, 353 [100 Cal. Rptr. 258].) Although we find that the trial court abused its discretion when it denied Omaha's motion to sever, relief by way of extraordinary writ should not be considered a foregone conclusion.

B. *Relief by Way of Extraordinary Writ—Why It Is Hard to Get, and Why We Initially Denied the Petition.*

Approximately 90 percent of petitions seeking extraordinary relief are denied. (*See* Cal. Civil Writ Practice (Cont. Ed. Bar 1987) § 2.2, p. 50.) Only rarely does the court give detailed reasons for its rejection of a petition. Instead, counsel is usually notified in a terse minute order or postcard that the petition is denied. (*See* Cal. Civil Writ Practice, *supra,* at § 10.27, p. 408; 8 Witkin, Cal. Procedure (3d ed. 1985) Extraordinary Writs, § 165, p. 801.)

Although, as a rule, the court states no reason for its denial of a petition, it will on occasion refer to an authority in support of its order of denial. This oblique message, ostensibly designed to enlighten, often has the opposite effect and promotes anxiety among those attorneys unable to tolerate either uncertainty or ambiguity.

Case law has done little to explain why appellate courts deny writ petitions. The subject is most commonly broached in those cases in which relief has been granted. The appellate court in dicta will briefly explain why extraordinary relief is typically not available. The discussion primarily centers on the unique circumstances of the case at hand that were found to warrant extraordinary relief. (*See, e.g., Cianci v. Superior Court* (1985) 40 Cal. 3d 903, 908, fn. 2 [221 Cal. Rptr. 575, 710 P.2d 375].)

Just as case law has been disappointing as a source of information concerning the mysteries of the writ, so have attempts to impart information by hierophants of appellate practice. Those who have tried to extract a coherent set of rules from cases and treatises on writs have found it easier to comprehend a "washing bill in Babylonic cuneiform." (Gilbert & Sullivan, Pirates of Penzance (1879).)

The large number of rejections of writ petitions demonstrates that courts will not use their scarce resources to second-guess every ruling and order of the trial court, particularly when to do so would save neither time nor aid in the resolution of a lawsuit.

Writ relief, if it were granted at the drop of a hat, would interfere with an orderly administration of justice at the trial and appellate levels. Reviewing courts have been cautioned to guard against the tendency to take "'... too lax a view of the "extraordinary" nature of prerogative writs.... '" (8 Witkin, supra, at § 141, pp. 782–783) lest they run the risk of fostering the delay of trials, vexing litigants and trial courts with multiple proceedings, and adding to the delay of judgment appeals pending in the appellate court. (*Babb v. Superior Court* (1971) 3 Cal. 3d 841, 851 [92 Cal. Rptr. 179, 479 P.2d 379]; ...)

"If the rule were otherwise, in every ordinary action a defendant whenever he chose could halt the proceeding in the trial court by applying for a writ of prohibition to stop the ordinary progress of the action toward a judgment until a reviewing tribunal passed upon an intermediate question that had arisen. If such were the rule, reviewing courts would in innumerable cases be converted from appellate courts to nisi prius tribunals." (*Mitchell v. Superior Court* (1958) 50 Cal. 2d 827, 833–834 [330 P.2d 48] (conc. opn. of McComb, J.).)

Particularly today, "in an era of excessively crowded lower court dockets, it is in the interest of the fair and prompt administration of justice to discourage piecemeal litigation." (*Kerr v. United States District Court* (1976) 426 U.S. 394, 403 [48 L. Ed. 2d 725, 732, 96 S. Ct. 2119].)

Were reviewing courts to treat writs in the same manner as they do appeals, these courts would be trapped in an appellate gridlock. This in turn would cause ordinary appeals, waiting for review, to be shunted to the sidelines. One writer sees a writ petition as being a device used to "cut into line" ahead of those litigants awaiting determination of postjudgment appeals. (Davis, *Tips for Obtaining a Civil Writ* (Aug. 1985) Cal. Law. 55.)

The Court of Appeal is generally in a far better position to review a question when called upon to do so in an appeal instead of by way of a writ petition. When review takes place by way of appeal, the court has a more complete record, more time for deliberation and, therefore, more insight into the significance of the issues. "Unlike the ordinary appeal which moves in an orderly, predictable pattern onto and off the appellate court's calendar, writ proceedings follow no set procedural course." (Chernoff & Watson, *Writ Lore* (1981) 56 State Bar J.12.)

Further, some issues may diminish in importance as a case proceeds towards trial. Petitioners seeking extraordinary writs do not always consider that a purported error of a trial judge may (1) be cured prior to trial, (2) have little or no effect upon the outcome of trial, or (3) be properly considered on appeal. (*Hogya v. Superior Court* (1977) 75 Cal. App. 3d 122, 128 [142 Cal. Rptr. 325].)

An unrestrained exercise of the power to grant extraordinary writs carries the potential to undermine the relationship between trial and appellate courts. Writ petitions "'have the unfortunate consequence of making the judge a litigant, obliged to obtain personal counsel or to leave his defense to one of the litigants [appearing] before him' in the underlying case. [Citations.]" (*Kerr v. United States District Court, supra,* 426 U.S. at pp. 402–403. Judges should be umpires rather than players.

In order to confine the use of mandamus to its proper office, the Supreme Court, in various cases, has stated general criteria for determining the propriety of an extraordinary writ: (1) the issue tendered in the writ petition is of widespread interest (*Brandt v. Superior Court* (1985) 37 Cal. 3d 813, 816 [210 Cal. Rptr. 211, 693 P.2d 796]) or presents a significant and novel constitutional issue (*Britt v. Superior Court* (1978) 20 Cal. 3d 844, 851–852 [143 Cal. Rptr. 695, 574 P.2d 766]); (2) the trial court's order deprived petitioner of an opportunity to present a substantial portion of his cause of action (*Brandt, supra,* at p. 816; *Vasquez v. Superior Court* (1971) 4 Cal. 3d 800, 807 [94 Cal. Rptr. 796, 484 P.2d 964, 53 A.L.R.3d 513]); (3) conflicting trial court interpretations of the law require a resolution of the conflict (*Greyhound Corp. v. Superior Court* (1961) 56 Cal. 2d 355, 378 [15 Cal. Rptr. 90, 364 P.2d 266]); (4) the trial court's order is both clearly erroneous as a matter of law and substantially prejudices petitioner's case (*Babb v. Superior Court, supra,* 3 Cal. 3d at p. 851; *Schweiger v. Superior Court* (1970) 3 Cal. 3d 507, 517 [90 Cal. Rptr. 729, 476 P.2d 97]); (5) the party seeking the writ lacks an adequate means, such as a direct appeal, by which to attain relief (*Phelan v. Superior Court* (1950) 35 Cal. 2d 363, 370–372 [217 P.2d 951]); and (6) the petitioner will suffer harm or prejudice in a manner that cannot be corrected on appeal (*Valley Bank of Nevada v. Superior Court* (1975) 15 Cal. 3d 652 [125 Cal. Rptr. 553, 542 P.2d 977]; *Roberts v. Superior Court* (1973) 9 Cal. 3d 330 [107 Cal. Rptr. 309, 508 P.2d 309]). The extent to which these criteria apply depends on the facts and circumstances of the case. (*Hogya v. Superior Court, supra,* 75 Cal. App. 3d at pp. 127–130.)

To adequately and intelligently decide the issues in this case or any other case, the court must have a complete record. Here, we did not have a copy of the reporter's transcript, and consequently did not know whether the court had even denied the motion to sever. The minute order states only that the court did not grant the demurrer.

After the Supreme Court remanded the matter to this court, at oral argument the parties stipulated that respondent court had denied the motion to sever. This was helpful, but we still do not know upon what grounds the trial judge made his decision.

It is true that mandate, in certain instances, provides a more effective remedy than does appeal for the purpose of reviewing an order denying severance. If, however, the trial court here denied the motion for severance without prejudice to bring the motion at a later time, writ relief would be inappropriate.

Under such circumstances, the failure to order severance would not meet the definition of an "irreparable injury." It would constitute, at best, an "irreparable inconvenience." (*Ordway v. Superior Court* (1988) 198 Cal. App. 3d 98, 101, fn. 1 [243 Cal. Rptr. 536].) Upon proper application at a later time, Omaha may have succeeded in obtaining an order for severance. A trial court is entitled to change its mind before judgment and may vacate a prior order for consolidation and order severance.

Here, however, there is no indication that the motion was denied without prejudice. The Supreme Court's order directing that an alternative writ be issued constitutes a determination that, in the ordinary course of the law, the petitioner is without an adequate remedy. (*Payne v. Superior Court* (1976) 17 Cal. 3d 908, 925 [132 Cal. Rptr. 405, 553 P.2d 565].)

Let a writ of mandate issue ordering respondent superior court to grant the motion to sever. The stay of proceedings is dissolved.

Brandt v. Superior Court

Supreme Court of California
37 Cal. 3d 813, 210 Cal. Rptr. 211, 693 P.2d 796 (1985)

KAUS, JUSTICE.

When an insurer tortiously withholds benefits, are attorney's fees, reasonably incurred to compel payment of the policy benefits, recoverable as an element of the damages resulting from such tortious conduct? We hold that they are and accordingly issue a writ of mandate directing the trial court to reinstate the portion of the complaint seeking attorney's fees as damages.

According to the complaint real party in interest Standard Insurance Company (Standard) issued a group disability income insurance policy to Vicom Associates, petitioner's employer, under which petitioner was insured. Petitioner sustained a loss covered by the policy when he became totally disabled. He made a timely demand on Standard for benefits, which it unreasonably refused to pay. Petitioner therefore filed an action against Standard for (1) breach of contract, (2) breach of the covenant of good faith and fair dealing, and (3) for violation of the statutory prohibitions against unfair claims practices. (Ins. Code, §790.03.)

In his causes of action for breach of the duty of good faith and fair dealing and for the statutory violations, petitioner listed attorney's fees incurred in connection with the contract cause of action as part of the resulting damage. Standard successfully moved to strike the portions of the complaint seeking attorney's fees. Petitioner then filed the present mandate proceedings.

Although we are reluctant to exercise our discretion to review rulings at the pleading stage of a lawsuit, we do so here because of the compelling circumstances presented. (*See Babb v. Superior Court* (1971) 3 Cal. 3d 841, 851 [92 Cal. Rptr. 179, 479 P.2d 379].) The issue is of widespread interest, and the Courts of Appeal are in conflict.

Moreover, the trial court's ruling has effectively deprived petitioner of the opportunity to present a substantial portion of his cause of action. Under the circumstances, extraordinary relief is appropriate. (*Ibid.*; *Taylor v. Superior Court* (1979) 24 Cal. 3d 890, 894 [157 Cal. Rptr. 693, 598 P.2d 854].)

As noted, the Courts of Appeal are in conflict on the question of the recoverability of attorney's fees. The seminal cases on each side are *Mustachio v. Ohio Farmers Ins. Co.* (1975) 44 Cal. App. 3d 358 [118 Cal. Rptr. 581], which allowed recovery and *Austero v. Washington National Ins. Co.* (1982) 132 Cal. App. 3d 408 [182 Cal. Rptr. 919] (hereinafter *Austero*), which denied it. In *Mustachio*, attorney's fees incurred in connection with negotiations leading up to settlement of the insured's policy claim were held properly included as an element of damages in the insured's later tort action against the insurer for breach of its duty of good faith and fair dealing. In *Austero*, a divided court rejected the reasoning of *Mustachio* and reversed an award of attorney's fees, holding that in a bad faith tort action recovery of attorney's fees incurred to obtain benefits under the policy is precluded by Code of Civil Procedure section 1021. Presiding Justice Morris dissented, arguing that the majority's reliance on section 1021 misinterpreted the nature of the case. We agree and adopt much of Presiding Justice Morris' dissent. * * *

The alternative writ is discharged. Let a peremptory writ of mandate issue, commanding the trial court to vacate its order striking portions of petitioner's complaint.

Sav-On Drugs, Inc. v. Superior Court

Supreme Court of California
15 Cal. 3d 1, 123 Cal. Rptr. 283, 538 P.2d 739 (1975)

RICHARDSON, JUSTICE.

* * *

Preliminarily, it may be observed that the prerogative writ is not the favored method of reviewing discovery orders. Ordinarily the aggrieved party must raise the issue on direct appeal from a final judgment. (*Pacific Tel. & Tel. Co. v. Superior Court,* 2 Cal. 3d 161, 169 [84 Cal. Rptr. 718, 465 P.2d 854]; *Oceanside Union School Dist. v. Superior Court,* 58 Cal. 2d 180, 185–186, fn. 4 [23 Cal. Rptr. 375, 373 P.2d 439].) The premise upon which this general policy rests is that in the great majority of cases the delay due to interim review of discovery orders is likely to result in greater harm to the judicial process by reason of protracted delay than is the enforcement of a possibly improper discovery order. (2 Cal. 3d at p. 170.) Nonetheless, we have concluded that the instant case comes within an exception recognized in *Pacific Tel., supra,* 2 Cal. 3d at page 170, footnote 11 and more recently in *Roberts v. Superior Court,* 9 Cal. 3d 330, 335–336 [107 Cal. Rptr. 309, 508 P.2d 309], to the effect that we may properly entertain a petition for extraordinary relief when the petitioning party asserts, as here, that to compel an answer would violate a privilege.

* * *

Palma v. U.S. Industrial Fasteners, Inc.

Supreme Court of California
36 Cal. 3d 171, 203 Cal. Rptr. 626, 681 P.2d 893 (1984)

GRODIN, JUSTICE.

We are called upon to consider the circumstances and procedure appropriate to the issuance, by an appellate court, of a peremptory writ of mandate in the "first instance," i.e., without prior issuance of an alternative writ.

Plaintiff in this negligence action appeals from a summary judgment for defendants which the trial court entered in obedience to such a peremptory writ from the Court of Appeal. The petition which defendants filed in the Court of Appeal did not seek a peremptory writ in the first instance, and the court did not notify plaintiff that such relief was being considered. The record does not reflect an invitation by the court to respondent or real party in interest to file opposition, and none was filed. Finally, instead of an order for the writ, the appellate court issued a document purporting to constitute the writ itself.

Plaintiff questions the propriety of the summary judgment, contending that there are triable issues of material fact, but the preliminary question we must decide is whether he is precluded from raising that question now, by reason of his failure to seek review of the appellate court's prior action. Defendants argue that when plaintiff failed to petition this court for a hearing the "writ" became final, was res judicata, and constituted the law of the case.

For reasons we shall explain, a peremptory writ ought not be issued in the first instance by an appellate court unless the respondent, and real party in interest, have notice that such a procedure is being considered, or at least requested, and have either filed a response on the merits or been given the opportunity to do so. Moreover, the proper procedure is for the appellate court to issue an order or decision calling for issuance of the writ, rather than the writ itself, so as to provide opportunity for review before the writ becomes operative. * * * Reaching the merits of the appeal, we shall also conclude that because triable issues of fact are present the judgment must be reversed.

Procedural History.

On April 25, 1980, Richard Palma, appellant herein, filed a complaint for damages in the Los Angeles County Superior Court. Count one sought recovery for personal injuries naming as defendants U.S. Industrial Fasteners, Inc. (Fasteners), Maynard Greenberg, Victor R. Castro, David Valdez, and "Does 1 through 50 inclusive." That count alleged that on May 6, 1979, Fasteners owned a truck which Castro and Valdez drove negligently causing it to run over and injure Palma.

Count two alleged negligent hiring and supervision of, and entrustment to, Castro. Count three alleged negligent supervision by three "Doe" defendants of premises on which the conduct of certain Does constituted a threat to the safety of others and caused damage to Palma.

Fasteners moved for summary judgment pursuant to Code of Civil Procedure section 437c,[1] supporting the motion with affidavits showing that Castro, a former employee of Fasteners, had stolen the truck and had driven it to the home of Castro's former wife where the injury to Palma occurred. Fasteners asserted that Castro had not been negligent, that he was neither a permissive user of the truck nor an agent or employee of Fasteners, and that as the victim of a theft Fasteners was neither negligent nor liable for the injury caused by the stolen truck.

Castro also moved for summary judgment, but on April 26, 1982, the trial court denied both motions in an order reciting that triable issues of material fact were presented on the issue of negligence.

Fasteners and Greenberg thereupon filed in the Court of Appeal their petition for writ of mandate contending that the superior court had abused its discretion in denying their motion for summary judgment. They prayed for issuance of an alternative writ of mandate and, upon the return thereof, issuance of a peremptory writ of mandate commanding the superior court to set aside its order and enter a new order granting the motion. The petition was filed on July 14, 1982. No alternative writ issued, but on the following day the court issued a stay of the superior court proceedings as to the petitioners only. On an unspecified date the presiding justice wrote on the cover of the petition a directive that a "writ issue as per order," below which were entered his signature and those of two other justices of the division. On July 26, 1982, the clerk of the division issued a peremptory writ commanding the superior court to grant the motion for summary judgment. The initials of the three justices were entered below the attestation of the clerk. In the body of the writ there also appeared an order directing: "Pending the finality of this writ, the stay previously issued by this court shall remain in full force and effect."

The superior court complied with the writ on October 7, 1982, by entry of a minute order granting summary judgment. This appeal followed.

I.

The Court of Appeal has original jurisdiction over petitions for writs of mandate, jurisdiction which it shares with this court and the superior courts. (Cal. Const., art. VI, § 10.) In the exercise of that jurisdiction it may, upon ascertaining that the petition is in proper form and states a basis for relief, issue an alternative writ which commands the respondent to act in conformity with the prayer of the petition or, alternatively, show cause before the Court of Appeal why it should not be ordered to so act. (§ 1087.) The respondent may choose to act in conformity with the prayer, in which case the petition becomes moot; otherwise, the respondent and/or the real party in interest may file a written return setting forth the factual and legal bases which justify the respondent's refusal to do so. (§ 1089; Cal. Rules of Court, rule 56(c).) The matter is

---

1. All further references to code sections are to the Code of Civil Procedure unless otherwise indicated.

then a "cause" to be decided "in writing with reasons stated," as required by article VI, section 14 of the Constitution. The issues joined by the petition and return must therefore be decided by the Court of Appeal in a written opinion. (*People v. Medina* (1972) 6 Cal. 3d 484, 490 [99 Cal. Rptr. 630, 492 P.2d 686].) If the court concludes that a peremptory writ of mandate should be granted, the opinion will direct that it issue. If not, the petition will be denied.

In lieu of an alternative writ, the Court of Appeal is authorized by section 1088 to issue a peremptory writ in the first instance, thus dispensing with the need to await the filing of a return, oral argument, and the preparation of an appellate opinion.[6] Although this procedure was once considered appropriate only when unusual circumstances required immediate action, in recent years Courts of Appeal have increasingly resorted to issuance of a peremptory writ in the first instance when it appears that the petition and opposing papers on file adequately address the issues raised by the petition, that no factual dispute exists, and that the additional briefing that would follow issuance of an alternative writ is unnecessary to disposition of the petition.

A court's authority to issue a peremptory writ in the first instance is limited, however, to those cases in which the opposing parties have received "due notice" 10 days beforehand. (§ 1088.) That notice, like the alternative writ, must be served on each person against whom the writ is sought. (ibid.) An application for such a writ is required to be accompanied by proof of service upon both the respondent and the real party in interest, and both are given five days within which to file points and authorities in opposition. (§ 1107.)[7] * * * [I]t appears that the notice requirement in section 1088 was intended to place the respondent and real party in interest on notice, in the absence of an alternative writ, that a peremptory writ might issue.

Defendants contend that a formal request for issuance of a peremptory writ in the first instance is unnecessary because a party served with a petition for writ of mandate should be charged, as a matter of law, with knowledge of that possibility. Given the rarity of that procedure, however, there is a large gap between possibility and practical anticipation. Express notice at least serves to close the gap, particularly in the case of the litigant who may not be familiar with appellate practice.

---

6. Section 1088: "When the application to the court is made without notice to the adverse party, and the writ is allowed, the alternative must first be issued; but if the application is upon due notice and the writ is allowed, the peremptory may be issued in the first instance. With the alternative writ and also with any notice of an intention to apply for the writ, there must be served on each person against whom the writ is sought a copy of the petition. The notice of the application, when given, must be at least ten days. The writ cannot be granted by default. The case must be heard by the court, whether the adverse party appears or not."

Because the decision to grant a peremptory writ, unlike the summary denial of a petition seeking a writ, is determinative of a "cause" within the meaning of article VI, section 14, the order directing that it issue must, however, "be in writing with reasons stated." * * *

7. Sections 1088.5 and 1089.5, added in 1982, as amended in 1983, now provide that if a petition filed in a trial court does not pray for an alternative writ, the time within which the respondent, and by implication the real party in interest, may reply is 30 days.

We are mindful that a formal request for issuance of a peremptory writ in the first instance does not provide the same level of notice as the issuance of an alternative writ, since the latter conveys a tentative opinion of the court that a peremptory writ might be in the offing, while the former reflects merely the hopes of a litigant. When responding to a petition for an alternative writ in the Court of Appeal, the litigant often confronts a practical dilemma. Faced with the possibility of action ranging from outright denial of the petition to the issuance of a peremptory writ in the first instance, the real party may feel obliged to respond with a full scale barrage of legal armament under circumstances in which a narrowly targeted argument, or perhaps no argument at all, would suffice.

We therefore strongly approve the practice which, we are informed, exists in some districts and divisions of the Courts of Appeal, to routinely request informal opposition prior to the issuance of an alternative or peremptory writ. By eliminating the necessity for full scale response where such a response is unnecessary, such a practice helps to reduce the cost of litigation to the parties; and by encouraging opposition when the court is about to act affirmatively on a petition, it helps to conserve judicial resources as well. In the case of a peremptory writ in the first instance, such a practice helps also to assure that the respondent, or real party, has had full opportunity to oppose what may turn out to be the final, and to his interests adverse, resolution of a legal issue.

We conclude that "due notice" under section 1088 requires, at a minimum, that a peremptory writ of mandate or prohibition not issue in the first instance unless the parties adversely affected by the writ have received notice, from the petitioner or from the court, that the issuance of such a writ in the first instance is being sought or considered. In addition, an appellate court, absent exceptional circumstances, should not issue a peremptory writ in the first instance without having received, or solicited, opposition from the party or parties adversely affected.

In this case neither of those procedural safeguards is present. Their absence is not determinative of the question before us, however, since the trial court has already acted in accordance with the writ. We turn, therefore, to consideration of the asserted procedural defect in the writ itself, and to the impact on the instant appeal from the judgment entered pursuant to that writ.

II.

* * *

[W]e conclude that the doctrine of res judicata does not bar consideration of the merits of Fasteners' motion for summary judgment. * * * In any case in which the court issues an alternative writ and renders a written decision granting or denying relief, that decision has ordinary res judicata effect. Here, however, plaintiff had no notice that a peremptory writ was sought or might issue, there was no alternative writ, and the document issued by the Court of Appeal was not preceded by a decision or order subject to petition for hearing in this court. Consequently, the doctrine of res judicata need not be applied.

Similar considerations lead us to reject Fasteners' alternative argument that reconsideration of the merits is barred by the law of the case doctrine. Although that doctrine is generally applicable in writ proceedings as well as appeals, it has no application here where the plaintiff had no notice that the writ might issue and opportunity for review by this court on petition for hearing was foreclosed by the manner in which the writ issued.

III.

We turn now to plaintiff's argument that entry of summary judgment for Fasteners was error. * * *

Fasteners based its motion for summary judgment in part on the rule enunciated by this court in *Richards v. Stanley* (1954) 43 Cal. 2d 60 [271 P.2d 23]: ordinarily the duty of an owner of an automobile to use due care in the maintenance or operation of that automobile does not encompass a duty to protect others from the negligent operation of that vehicle by a thief, even when the owner has left the keys in the ignition. Plaintiff opposed the motion arguing that special circumstances present in this case established such a duty. * * *

The "special circumstance" to which we look in determining whether the owner operator of a vehicle owes a duty to third parties in the manner in which the vehicle is secured when not in use is nothing more than a test of foreseeability of harm. In negligence a defendant may be liable for injuries caused by his failure to use reasonable care in situations in which he owes a duty to the injured person. * * * Inasmuch as foreseeability of harm is in most cases, this one included, a question of fact, and triable issues of fact as to foreseeability were present here, the motions by defendants for summary judgment should not have been granted.

The motion to dismiss the appeal is denied. The judgment is reversed and the cause is remanded to the superior court with directions to vacate its order granting defendants' motions for summary judgment, to deny those motions, and to proceed in conformity with the views expressed in this opinion.

[1] *Basic Writ Prerequisites*

As *Omaha Indemnity*, reproduced *supra*, indicates, extraordinary writs are discretionary. The reviewing court is not required to decide the merits of a writ petition or even state a reason for denying an alternative writ. Under what circumstances will a court issue an alternative writ and entertain a peremptory writ petition on the merits? There are some basic statutory prerequisites common to all writs of mandate, prohibition, and certiorari.

[a] Inadequate Remedy at Law

First, the petitioner must have no "plain, speedy, and adequate remedy in the ordinary course of law." CCP §§ 1068, 1086, 1103. Generally, writ review is inappropriate if the challenged decision is immediately appealable. *Marriage of Skelley,* 18 Cal. 3d 365, 369, 134 Cal. Rptr. 197, 556 P.2d 297 (1976); *Phelan v. Superior Court,* 35 Cal.

2d 363, 370, 217 P.2d 951 (1950). An appeal is usually viewed as "adequate" even though it involves far greater expense and time than review by writ. *Rescue Army v. Municipal Ct.*, 28 Cal. 2d 460, 466, 171 P.2d 8 (1946); *Hogya v. Superior Court*, 75 Cal. App. 3d 122, 128–129, 142 Cal. Rptr. 325 (1977).

Is a writ ever appropriate to review an order which is immediately appealable? For example, when a trial court grants or denies a preliminary injunction, the order can be immediately appealed pursuant to CCP § 904.1(a)(6). Does this preclude appellate review by a writ of mandate? *See, e.g., Langford v. Superior Court*, 43 Cal. 3d 21, 233 Cal. Rptr. 387, 729 P.2d 822 (1987); *Robbins v. Superior Court*, 38 Cal. 3d 199, 205, 211 Cal. Rptr. 398, 695 P.2d 695 (1985).

(1) Exceptional circumstances may permit an appellate court to view relief by immediate appeal as "inadequate." *See, e.g., Phelan v. Superior Court*, 35 Cal. 2d 363, 370–372, 217 P.2d 951 (1950) (observing that where there is a right to an immediate appeal, that remedy should be considered adequate unless petitioner can show some special reason why it is rendered inadequate by the particular circumstances of his case); *Scharlin v. Superior Court*, 9 Cal. App. 4th 162, 167, 11 Cal. Rptr. 2d 448 (1992) (ruling that although superior court's determination regarding decedent's trust was appealable order, novel and significant trust issue merited extraordinary writ review); *Taylor v. Superior Court*, 218 Cal. App. 3d 1185, 1190, 267 Cal. Rptr. 519 (1990) (finding appeal from demurrer inadequate because estate will be dissipated before appeal resolved, and issuing peremptory writ of mandate); *Anderson v. Superior Court*, 213 Cal. App. 3d 1321, 1328, 262 Cal. Rptr. 405 (1980) (concluding writ of mandate appropriate to review immediately appealable order because petition presented issues of great public interest and of first impression which must be resolved promptly, and a writ will prevent multiplicity of appeals raising the identical issue). But the availability of an immediate appeal plus a stay pending appeal may be considered "adequate." *Arrow Sand & Gravel, Inc. v. Superior Court*, 38 Cal. 3d 884, 887, n. 3, 215 Cal. Rptr. 288, 700 P.2d 1290 (1985).

(2) Does review by appeal become "inadequate" because a party failed to file a timely notice of appeal? *See, e.g., Adoption of Alexander S.*, 44 Cal. 3d 857, 865, 245 Cal. Rptr. 1, 750 P.2d 778 (1988) (ruling writ of habeas corpus cannot serve as substitute for appeal in civil case, unless excuse shown for failure to file timely notice of appeal); *Andrews v. Police Court*, 21 Cal. 2d 479, 480, 133 P.2d 398 (1943) (holding mandamus may not be resorted to as substitute for appeal in absence of excuse for failure to timely pursue appeal); *Mauro B. v. Superior Court*, 230 Cal. App. 3d 949, 281 Cal. Rptr. 507 (1991) (reviewing numerous rules which hold that use of writ to review appealable order after time for appeal has passed is barred except where special circumstances constitute an excuse for failure to appeal). For a more thorough discussion of the factors which may influence a determination of the "adequacy" of appellate review, see CEB, *California Civil Writ Practice* §§ 15.56–15.60 (4th ed. 2016); 8 Witkin, *California Procedure, Extraordinary Writs* §§ 42–47, 53–73, 116–135 (5th ed. 2008); *Hogya v. Superior Court, supra*, 75 Cal. App. 3d at 128–132.

[b] Irreparable Injury

A second general prerequisite to writ review, similar to inadequacy of remedy at law, is that the petitioner will suffer "irreparable injury" if the writ is not granted. This prerequisite encompasses several related inquiries:

(1) One is whether the nature of the harm or prejudice is such that it cannot be corrected on appeal. *See, e.g., Roberts v. Superior Court,* 9 Cal. 3d 330, 336, 107 Cal. Rptr. 309, 508 P.2d 309 (1973) (holding use of extraordinary writ proper in discovery cases where trial court's order allegedly violated a privilege because the person seeking to exercise privilege must either succumb to court's order and disclose privileged information or subject himself to contempt for refusal to obey court's order pending appeal); *Roe v. Superior Court,* 229 Cal. App. 3d 832, 280 Cal. Rptr. 380 (1991) (directing court of appeal to issue alternative writ of mandate which seeks to prevent deposition of petitioner's psychotherapist based on privilege).

Although generally the courts will not find "irreparable injury" based on the fact that if the trial court's ruling is wrong the petitioner will unnecessarily incur the time and expense of going to trial, *see, e.g., Ordway v. Superior Court,* 198 Cal. App. 3d 98, 101, n. 1, 243 Cal. Rptr. 536 (1988), sometimes the courts will find writ review necessary to prevent an expensive trial and ultimate reversal, *see, e.g., Barret v. Superior Court,* 222 Cal. App. 3d 1176, 1183, 272 Cal. Rptr. 304 (1990) (ruling writ appropriate because if trial court's order is determined incorrect on an appeal, a second trial would be required); *Smith v. Superior Court,* 10 Cal. App. 4th 1033, 13 Cal. Rptr. 2d 133 (1992) (holding writ review of trial court's denial of motion to strike emotional distress and punitive damage allegations from complaint is proper because delay and expense of a trial made remedy of appeal inadequate and significant legal issue of importance involved).

(2) Another inquiry is whether the petitioner has requested the relief from the lower tribunal, and been denied, prior to seeking the relief by writ. Failure to raise the error in the lower court usually means that writ relief will be denied, unless it appears that the demand would have been futile. *See, e.g., Phelan v. Superior Court, supra,* 35 Cal. 2d at 372. Appellate courts may find an exception to this rule where a writ petition raises important constitutional issues, *e.g., Civil Serv. Emp. Ins. Co. v. Superior Court,* 22 Cal. 3d 362, 371, 374–375, 149 Cal. Rptr. 360, 584 P.2d 497 (1978); *California Labor Fed'n v. Cal. O.S.H.A. Standards Bd.,* 221 Cal. App. 3d 1547, 1555, 271 Cal. Rptr. 310 (1990) (entertaining writ petition although no relief sought in trial court because case involved issue of law of statewide importance affecting 11 million workers); where petitioner had no opportunity to raise the issue by objection in the lower court, *e.g., Morrisette v. Superior Court,* 236 Cal. App. 2d 597, 602, 46 Cal. Rptr. 153 (1965); *Monterey Club v. Superior Court,* 48 Cal. App. 2d 131, 143 (1941); or where the trial court failed or refused to rule on the issue, *see, e.g., Vannier v. Superior Court,* 32 Cal. 3d 163, 175, 185 Cal. Rptr. 427, 650 P.2d 302 (1982).

(3) A related inquiry, similar to inadequacy of legal remedy, is whether there are any alternative proceedings available which may remedy the petitioner's injury. An

appellate court is unlikely to entertain a writ where the petitioner has not yet attempted a post-trial motion, such as a motion for new trial or to vacate a judgment; or where the erroneous ruling does not preclude a challenge later during the trial process, such as a motion to sever denied or a dismissal, without prejudice; or where an order can be quickly remedied by the petitioner's own subsequent action, such as a partial demurrer sustained with leave to amend. As *Omaha Indemnity* notes, an irreparable inconvenience does not constitute an irreparable injury.

[c] Beneficial Interest

A final statutory prerequisite is that the petitioner must be "beneficially interested" in the outcome of the writ proceeding. CCP §§ 1069, 1086, 1103; *see also Municipal Court v. Superior Court (Gonzalez)*, 5 Cal. 4th 1126, 22 Cal. Rptr. 2d 504, 857 P.2d 325 (1993) (observing that if petitioner lacks standing, California courts have no power in mandamus or otherwise to render advisory opinions); *Save the Plastic Bag Coalition v. City of Manhattan Beach*, 52 Cal. 4th 155, 127 Cal. Rptr. 3d 710, 254 P.3d 1005 (2011) (ruling that when a petitioner seeks a writ of mandate to procure enforcement of a public duty, the concept of "public interest standing" applies and the writ petitioner need not show that he has any legal or special interest in the result since it is sufficient that he is interested as a citizen in having the laws executed and the duty performed).

[2] *Additional Writ Criteria*

[a] Nonstatutory Criteria

The criteria discussed above are the basic statutory prerequisites for writ review. As *Omaha Indemnity Co. v. Superior Court*, reproduced *supra*, indicates, the courts have stated additional general criteria for determining the propriety of review by extraordinary writ. What are they? Is it clear as to when and how they apply? How much weight should each criterion be given in a particular case? The *Omaha Indemnity* court commented that the "extent to which these apply depends on the facts and circumstances of the case." What does this mean? What does this statement tell practitioners about the writ review process? Is it obvious that the Court of Appeal in *Omaha Indemnity* misapplied these criteria when it initially denied the writ?

[b] Alternative Writ Issuance

The issuance of an alternative writ means that all the statutory prerequisites to writ review are satisfied. *See, e.g., Blue Chip Stamps v. Superior Court*, 18 Cal. 3d 381, 387, n. 4, 134 Cal. Rptr. 393, 556 P.2d 755 (1976); *Department of Public Admin. v. Superior Court*, 5 Cal. App. 4th 155, 166, 6 Cal. Rptr. 2d 714 (1992). Does it also mean all the other general criteria are satisfied? Can a court which has issued an alternative writ still deny a peremptory writ based on those foundational criteria, as opposed to the merits? If so, then what function is served by the prior issuance of an alternative writ?

[3] Proper Court for Writ

Article VI, § 10, of the California Constitution confers original concurrent juris-diction on the California Supreme Court, Court of Appeal, and Superior Courts "in proceedings for extraordinary relief in the nature of mandamus, certiorari, and pro-hibition." In which of these courts should a writ petition be filed? Generally, as a matter of judicial policy, a writ petition should be filed in the lowest court capable of granting the requested relief. *See* Rule 8.486(a)(1), Cal. Rule of Ct.; *Cohen v. Superior Court,* 267 Cal. App. 2d 268, 270–271, 72 Cal. Rptr. 814 (1968).

In exceptional circumstances, such as great public importance or urgency, a peti-tioner may file directly in the California Supreme Court. *E.g., California Redevelopment Assn. v. Matosantos,* 53 Cal. 4th 231, 253, 135 Cal. Rptr. 3d 683, 267 P.3d 580 (2011) (citing cases); *Legislature of Cal. v. Eu,* 54 Cal. 3d 492, 500, 286 Cal. Rptr. 283, 816 P.2d 1309 (1991) (exercising original jurisdiction over writ petition involving con-stitutional challenge to term limits initiative, Proposition 140, because of public im-portance of issues); *Raven v. Deukmejian,* 52 Cal. 3d 336, 340, 276 Cal. Rptr. 326, 801 P.2d 1077 (1990) (ruling constitutional challenge to Proposition 115, Criminal Victim's Justice Reform Act, involved important public issues justifying exercise of original jurisdiction); *see* 8 Witkin, *California Procedures, Extraordinary Writs* §§ 144–146 (4th ed. 2008) and cases discussed therein.

[4] Review of Writ Decisions

The summary denial of a writ petition by the Court of Appeal may be reviewed in the California Supreme Court by a petition for review; or, less favored, by filing a new writ petition in the Supreme Court. *See Hagan v. Superior Court, supra,* 57 Cal. 2d at 769–771.

A summary denial becomes final immediately upon filing of the order, and the petition for review must be filed within 10 calendar days. Rules 8.490(b)(1) & 8.500(e)(1), Cal. Rules of Ct. If the Court of Appeal issues an alternative writ, the matter then becomes a "cause" within the meaning of Article VI, Section 14, of the California Constitution and must be decided "in writing with reasons stated." *See Palma v. U.S. Industrial Fasteners, Inc., supra,* 36 Cal. 3d at 178. As *Palma* indicates, a decision on the merits of a peremptory writ by the Court of Appeal may be chal-lenged by filing a petition for review in the Supreme Court. A petition for review must be filed within 10 days after the Court of Appeal's decision becomes final. Rule 8.500(e)(1). When does an order granting a peremptory writ become final? *See* Rule 8.490(b). When can an appellate court actually issue the peremptory writ? *See Ng v. Superior Court,* 4 Cal. 4th 29, 33–34, 13 Cal. Rptr. 2d 856, 840 P.2d 961 (1992).

[5] Alternative vs. Peremptory Writ

[a] Choice of Writ Procedure

As *Palma v. U.S. Industrial Fasteners, Inc.,* reproduced *supra,* indicates, a petitioner has a choice between requesting issuance of an alternative writ (hopefully to be followed by respondent's compliance or by a peremptory writ), or requesting issuance of a peremptory writ in the first instance. What are the advantages of each choice? Disadvantages? Why is "due notice" required prior to the issuance of a peremptory writ in the first instance? This notice is sometimes referred to as "*Palma* notice." *See, e.g.,* CEB, *California Civil Writ Practice* §§ 22.18–22.22, 24.4 (4th ed. 2016). Precisely what manner of notice does *Palma* require when petitioner seeks a peremptory writ in the first instance? Why is such notice unnecessary when petitioner seeks an alternative writ?

[b]   Peremptory Writ in the First Instance

Recent Supreme Court decisions have cautioned that issuance of a peremptory writ in the first instance is the exception, and should not become routine. *Alexander v. Superior Court,* 5 Cal. 4th 1218, 1222–1223, 23 Cal. Rptr. 2d 397, 859 P.2d 96 (1993); *Ng v. Superior Court,* 4 Cal. 4th 29, 35, 13 Cal. Rptr. 2d 856, 840 P.2d 961 (1992). The court in *Ng, supra,* 4 Cal. 4th at 35, defined the circumstances under which the accelerated *Palma* procedure authorized by CCP § 1088 may be appropriate:

> Generally, that procedure should be adopted only when petitioner's entitlement to relief is so obvious that no purpose could reasonably be served by plenary consideration of the issue — for example, when such entitlement is conceded or when there has been clear error under well-settled principles of law and undisputed facts — or where there is an unusual urgency requiring acceleration of the normal process. If there is no compelling temporal urgency, and if the law and facts mandating the relief sought are not entirely clear, the normal writ procedure, including issuance of an alternative writ (*see Palma, supra*) should be followed.

Applying this *Ng* standard, the Supreme Court in *Alexander* concluded the Court of Appeal's use of the expedited writ procedure to resolve a discovery issue was inappropriate where the record suggested no "unusual urgency" and petitioner's entitlement to relief was unclear. *Alexander, supra,* 5 Cal. 4th at 1223. What circumstances constitute an "unusual urgency"? *See, e.g., Payless Drug Store v. Superior Court,* 20 Cal. App. 4th 277, 24 Cal. Rptr. 2d 506 (1993).

In *Brown, Winfield & Canzoneri, Inc. v. Superior Court,* 47 Cal. 4th 1233, 104 Cal. Rptr. 3d 145, 223 P.3d 15 (2010), the Supreme Court considered the propriety of so-called "suggestive" *Palma* notices. A "suggestive" *Palma* notice typically contains the following: Notice that the Court of Appeal intends to issue a peremptory writ in the first instance granting the relief requested by the petitioner; a discussion of the merits of the writ petition, with a suggestion that the trial court erred in the manner claimed by petitioner; a special grant to the trial court of power and jurisdiction to change the disputed interim order and enter in its place a new order consistent with the views of the appellate court, in which event the writ petition will be vacated as moot; and a solicitation of opposition to the issuance of a peremptory writ in the first instance, should the trial court elect not to follow the appellate court's recommendation. *Brown, Winfield & Canzoneri, supra,* 47 Cal. 4th at 1238.

The Supreme Court concluded that it is not improper for an appellate court to issue a suggestive *Palma* notice, and that it may do so without first having received or solicited opposition from the real party in interest. *Id.* at 1238, 1244–48. However, if a trial court decides on its own motion to revisit its interim ruling in response to a suggestive *Palma* notice, that court must inform the parties of its intent to do so and provide them with an opportunity to be heard. *Id.* at 1239, 1248–50.

[c] Practical Dilemma

Note the *Palma* court's discussion of the practical dilemma which confronts the litigant when responding to a petition for an alternative writ. If you represent the real party in interest in such a situation, what range of legal arguments are available to your client? Should you make them all in the response to the petition for an alternative writ? Should you not address the merits, but limit your response to a preliminary opposition designed to persuade the court that the writ should be summarily denied for foundational reasons? Simply remain silent, and hope the court summarily denies the petition? Which option is most appropriate? Most practical? Why? What scale of opposition would you make in responding to a *Palma* notice received by your client?

[d] Procedure After Issuance of Alternative Writ

When a Court of Appeal issues an alternative writ, what happens next procedurally? *See* CCP §§ 1089–1094. Does the issuance of an alternative writ suggest that the petitioner will win on the merits, *i.e.,* that the court will also issue a peremptory writ? Does the issuance of an alternative writ mean that the court has determined that all the statutory and foundational criteria for writ relief are satisfied? Or can the court, after considering the response to the alternative writ, still decline to issue a peremptory writ based solely on failure to satisfy foundational or procedural prerequisites, without reaching the merits? What does the *Omaha Indemnity* opinion indicate? *See also, e.g., Langford v. Superior Court,* 43 Cal. 3d 21, 27, 233 Cal. Rptr. 387, 729 P.2d 822 (1987) (observing that the granting of an alternative writ is considered a determination that there is no other adequate remedy); *but see MacPhail v. Court of Appeal,* 39 Cal. 3d 454, 458–463, 217 Cal. Rptr. 36, 703 P.2d 374 (1985) (criticizing, in a dissenting opinion, the inflexible rule that issuance of an alternative writ constitutes a determination of the inadequacy of available legal remedies).

[6] *Time Limitations for Filing Writ Petitions*

[a] Statutory Writs

As discussed previously, certain special statutes authorize review by extraordinary writ in specific circumstances. These statutes typically include very short time limitations for filing the writ petition in the appellate court. *E.g.,* CCP § 418.10(c) (within

10 days after service of written notice of entry of order denying motion to quash); § 437c(m) (within 20 days after service of written notice of entry of order denying summary judgment); Government Code § 6259(c) (within 20 days after receipt of trial court order determining disclosure under Public Records Act). Such limitations may be considered jurisdictional, and should be scrupulously observed. *See, e.g., Eldridge v. Superior Court*, 208 Cal. App. 3d 1350, 1354, 256 Cal. Rptr. 724 (1989); *Sturm, Ruger & Co. v. Superior Court*, 164 Cal. App. 3d 579, 210 Cal. Rptr. 573 (1985) (denying writ of mandate to review summary judgment denial because petition untimely under CCP § 437c); *but see Quattrone v. Superior Court*, 44 Cal. App. 3d 296, 300–301, 118 Cal. Rptr. 548 (1975) (ruling delay of one day in filing petition for mandate pursuant to CCP § 418.10(c) excused where that statute authorized an extension for good cause).

[b] Nonstatutory Writs

What time limitations apply for the filing of nonstatutory writ petitions? No absolute deadline applies, but the equitable doctrine of laches does. *E.g., Peterson v. Superior Court*, 31 Cal. 3d 147, 163–64, 181 Cal. Rptr. 784, 642 P.2d 1305 (1982); *Wagner v. Superior Court*, 12 Cal. App. 4th 1314, 1317, 16 Cal. Rptr. 2d 534 (1993). Laches requires an unreasonable delay in filing the petition plus prejudice to the real party in interest. *Peterson, supra*, 31 Cal. 3d at 163–64. Prejudice must be demonstrated, and will not be presumed from the length of the delay. *Conti v. Bd. of Civil Serv. Comm'rs*, 1 Cal. 3d 351, 359, 82 Cal. Rptr. 337, 461 P.2d 617 (1969). For a full discussion of the doctrine of laches, *see* § 4.07, The Doctrine of Laches, *supra*.

Because writ relief is extraordinary and discretionary, the petition should be filed as soon as possible. *See, e.g., In re Twighla T.*, 4 Cal. App. 4th 799, 802–803, 5 Cal. Rptr. 2d 752 (1992) (denying for unreasonable delay a writ petition filed 16 months after permanency planning order). Some appellate courts have even indicated that they are likely to summarily deny a writ petition filed later than 60 days after the challenged decision. *See, e.g., People v. Superior Court (Brent)*, 2 Cal. App. 4th 675, 682, 3 Cal. Rptr. 2d 375 (1992) (observing that where there is no statutory time limit for filing a writ, it must usually be filed within 60 days); *Popelka, Allard, McCowan & Jones v. Superior Court*, 107 Cal. App. 3d 496, 165 Cal. Rptr. 748 (1980) (noting as a general rule a writ petition should be filed within the 60-day period applicable to appeals). However, this "rule" is not jurisdictional; an appellate court may consider a writ petition at any time despite the 60-day rule if it considers the circumstances extraordinary. *See, e.g., Nixon Peabody LLP v. Superior Court*, 230 Cal. App. 4th 818, 821–22, 179 Cal. Rptr. 3d 96 (2014) (considering writ petition filed after 60-days of trial court's order where defendant diligently sought writ review after dismissal of its appeal from an unappealable order); *Volkswagen of America, Inc. v. Superior Court*, 94 Cal. App. 4th 695, 701–702, 114 Cal. Rptr. 2d 541 (2001) (exercising its discretion to review all orders of the trial court where petition untimely as to some but timely as to others because all the orders involved similar issues).

[7] Res Judicata and Law of the Case

A written decision on the merits of a writ petition, either granting or denying a peremptory writ, will ordinarily have a res judicata effect on subsequent proceedings between the parties involving the same issue determined by the writ. *See, e.g., Consumers Lobby Against Monopolies v. Public Util. Com.,* 25 Cal. 3d 891, 901, n. 3, 160 Cal. Rptr. 124, 603 P.2d 41 (1979).

Why did the Supreme Court in *Palma* not apply res judicata to the unappealed peremptory writ issued by the Court of Appeal? The law of the case doctrine also generally applies to writ proceedings to bar reconsideration of issues resolved by a peremptory writ at a later point in the same litigation. *Price v. Civil Service Com.,* 26 Cal. 3d 257, 267, n. 5, 161 Cal. Rptr. 475, 604 P.2d 1365 (1980). Why did this doctrine not apply to preclude reconsideration by a second writ petition of the plaintiff's summary judgment motion in *Palma*?

What is the res judicata effect of a summary denial of a writ petition? *See, e.g., Consumers Lobby Against Monopolies, supra,* 25 Cal. 3d at 901, n. 3; *Hagan v. Superior Court,* 57 Cal. 2d 767, 770, 22 Cal. Rptr. 201, 371 P.2d 977 (1962). An order refusing to issue an alternative writ but with reasons stated for the denial? *See Kowis v. Howard,* 3 Cal. 4th 888, 12 Cal. Rptr. 2d 728, 838 P.2d 250 (1992). What are the law of the case implications of a summary denial? *See Kowis, supra,* 3 Cal. 4th at 894–901 (ruling that regardless of whether summary denial is intended to be on the merits or is based on some other reason, such denial of a writ petition does not establish law of the case).

[8] Practical Considerations

[a] Practice Guides

There are many excellent practice guides for California extraordinary civil writ practice. *E.g.,* CEB, *California Civil Writ Practice* (4th ed. 2016); 8 Witkin, *California Procedure, Extraordinary Writs* (5th ed. 2008); *California Practice Guide, Civil Appeals and Writs,* Ch. 15, *Writs* (The Rutter Group 2015). These resources should be consulted for detailed instructions on how to prepare a petition or response, as well as for sample forms. What does a writ petition look like? California Rule of Court 8.486 specifies the form and content, service, points and authorities, and supporting documents required for a petition. For an excellent discussion of the form and content of writ petitions and accompanying documents, as well as checklists and sample forms, see CEB, *California Civil Writ Practice, supra,* §§ 18.5–18.60.

[b] Responsive Pleading

What does a responsive pleading look like? Rule 8.487(b) specifies that if an alternative writ is granted, the real party in interest may make a return by demurrer, verified answer, or both. Both should be filed at the same time because if the demurrer is overruled and no answer was filed, a peremptory writ may issue without leave to answer. Rule 8.487(b)(4). For a good discussion of the form and content of such responsive pleadings and accompanying points and authorities, as well as sample forms, see CEB, *California Writ Practice* §§ 23.1–23.55 (4th ed. 2016). What type of response is appropriate when no *Palma* notice has been given?

[9]   Most Writs Denied

The vast majority of writ petitions are denied, and most of these are summarily denied. *See, e.g.,* Judicial Council of California, *2015 Court Statistical Report, California Courts of Appeal,* Table 6 (1,751 civil writ petitions denied without opinion in fiscal year 2013–14, 141 disposed of by written opinion; 1,808 denied without written opinion in 2012–13, 103 disposed of with written opinion). What are the various reasons that courts disfavor writ petitions? Given the judicial attitude and high denial rate, why do parties continue to utilize the extraordinary writ process in great numbers? Do you think, on the whole, that California's current civil writ practice is good or bad for litigants? For the judicial system?

[10]   Discretion Revisited

[a]   Writ Use Widely Available

As the various authorities discussed above indicate, extraordinary writs in California are available to review a wide variety of pretrial orders. Few uses are completely off-limits, and new ones are limited only by the practitioner's imagination and creativity. *But see Manzetti v. Superior Court,* 21 Cal. App. 4th 373, 25 Cal. Rptr. 2d 857 (1993) (imposing sanctions on petitioner for filing second petition for writ of mandate following summary denial of prior identical petition regarding single discrete objection to discovery).

Some nonstatutory uses are almost routine, such as review of discovery orders which allegedly violate an asserted privilege or present issues of general concern. *See, e.g., Sav-On Drugs, Inc. v. Superior Court,* reproduced *supra; Hiott v. Superior Court,* 16 Cal. App. 4th 712, 20 Cal. Rptr. 2d 157 (1993) (finding writ proper to review motion to compel production of videotape where attorney-client privilege raised); *Bridgestone/Firestone, Inc. v. Superior Court,* 7 Cal. App. 4th 1384, 9 Cal. Rptr. 2d 709 (1992) (ruling extraordinary writ proper to review discovery order involving trade secrets); *Rancho Bernardo Dev. Co. v. Superior Court,* 2 Cal. App. 4th 358, 360, 2 Cal. Rptr. 2d 878 (1992) (reviewing trial court's ruling which limited expert witness fees during deposition).

Other uses are less frequent, such as writ review of rulings at the pleading stage of a lawsuit. *See, e.g., Brandt v. Superior Court,* reproduced *supra; Cianci v. Superior Court,* 40 Cal. 3d 903, 908, n.3, 221 Cal. Rptr. 575, 710 P.2d 375 (1985); *James W. v. Superior Court,* 17 Cal. App. 4th 246, 252, 21 Cal. Rptr. 2d 169 (1993) (granting writ to review demurrers sustained without leave to amend as to some but not all causes of action; trial court directed to vacate order sustaining demurrer on issue of defendants' immunity from suit); *California Physicians' Serv. v. Superior Court,* 9 Cal. App. 4th 1321, 12 Cal. Rptr. 2d 95 (1992) (granting writ to review overruled demurrer; trial court directed to sustain demurrer); *Cuadros v. Superior Court,* 6 Cal. App. 4th 671, 8 Cal. Rptr. 2d 18 (1992) (issuing writ directing trial court to set aside order denying petitioner's motion to amend complaint, and to enter new order granting motion to amend).

Even in the more routine uses, however, the courts may remind practitioners that extraordinary writ review is truly discretionary. *See, e.g., Oceanside Union Sch. Dist. v. Superior Court,* 58 Cal. 2d 180, 185, n.4, 23 Cal. Rptr. 375, 373 P.2d 439 (1962) (noting that although prerogative writs have been used frequently to review interim orders in discovery cases, these writs are discretionary and should only be used in discovery matters to review important questions of first impression); *Roberts v. Superior Court,* 9 Cal. 3d 330, 336, 107 Cal. Rptr. 309, 508 P.2d 309 (1973) (applying and clarifying *Oceanside* doctrine, and approving issuance of alternative writ where discovery was objected to based on violation of privilege).

[b] Discretionary?

Is it correct to say that all extraordinary writ review is discretionary? In what sense is prohibition discretionary when the petitioner seeks review of a discovery order which violates an important confidential privilege? Is mandamus discretionary when the petitioner seeks review of a denial of a motion to quash service of process pursuant to CCP § 418.10(a)(1)? Is certiorari discretionary when the petitioner seeks review of a contempt order?

The Supreme Court addressed the discretionary character of extraordinary writs in *Powers v. City of Richmond,* 10 Cal. 4th 85, 113–114, 40 Cal. Rptr. 2d 839, 893 P.2d 1160 (1995):

> Although appellate review by extraordinary writ petition is said to be discretionary, a court must exercise its discretion "within reasonable bounds and for a proper reason." (*Scott v. Municipal Court* (1974) 40 Cal. App. 3d 995, 997 [115 Cal. Rptr. 620].) The discretionary aspect of writ review comes into play primarily when the petitioner has another remedy by appeal and the issue is whether the alternative remedy is adequate. (*See, e.g., Consumers Lobby Against Monopolies v. Public Utilities Com.* (1979) 25 Cal. 3d 891, 901, fn. 3 [160 Cal. Rptr. 124, 603 P.2d 41] [stating that courts have discretion to deny extraordinary writ petitions "[b]ecause the law does provide other means of judicial review in such cases"].)
>
> When an extraordinary writ proceeding is the only avenue of appellate review, a reviewing court's discretion is quite restricted. Referring to the writ of mandate, this court has said: "'Its issuance is not necessarily a matter of right, but lies rather in the discretion of the court, but where one has a substantial right to protect or enforce, and this may be accomplished by such a writ, and there is no other plain, speedy and adequate remedy in the ordinary course of law, he [or she] is entitled as a matter of right to the writ, or perhaps more correctly, in other words, it would be an abuse of discretion to refuse it.'" (*Dowell v. Superior Court* (1956) 47 Cal. 2d 483, 486–487 [304 P.2d 1009], quoting *Potomac Oil Co. v. Dye* (1909) 10 Cal. App. 534, 537 [102 P.

677]; …) Accordingly, when writ review is the exclusive means of appellate review of a final order or judgment, an appellate court may not deny an apparently meritorious writ petition, timely presented in a formally and procedurally sufficient manner, merely because, for example, the petition presents no important issue of law or because the court considers the case less worthy of its attention than other matters.

May an appellate court summarily deny an extraordinary writ petition that when review by extraordinary writ is the exclusive means of appellate review of a judgment of the superior court? *See Leone v. Med. Bd. of Cal.*, 22 Cal. 4th 660, 94 Cal. Rptr. 2d 61, 995 P.2d 191 (2000) (observing that the appellate jurisdiction clause of the California Constitution does not require the Legislature to provide for direct appeals in all cases within the original jurisdiction of the superior courts, and does not preclude a court of appeal from summarily denying an extraordinary writ petition that lacks substantive merit or is procedurally defective).

[D]   Extraordinary Writs in Federal Courts

[1]   Statutory Authority

The federal All Writs Statute, 28 U.S.C. § 1651(a), authorizes the issuance of extraordinary writs by federal appellate courts. The primary writ employed by federal courts is mandamus, and that discretionary writ is subject to the same basic criteria as in the California courts. *See generally* Robert S. Berger, *The Mandamus Powers of the United States Courts of Appeals: A Complex and Confused Means of Appellate Control*, 31 BUFF. L. REV. 37-106 (1982).

[2]   Judicial Hostility

The U.S. Supreme Court decries the use of mandamus with much the same admonitory language as does the California Supreme Court, but, in contrast, actually discourages writ use by denying petitions. *E.g., Kerr v. U. S. Dist. Court,* 426 U.S. 394, 402, 96 S. Ct. 2119, 48 L. Ed. 2d 725 (1976) (observing that the remedy of mandamus is a drastic one, and not available to review discovery order despite serious claim of privilege because alternative remedy apparently available); *Allied Chem. Corp. v. Daiflon, Inc.,* 449 U.S. 33, 101 S. Ct. 188, 66 L. Ed. 2d 193 (1980) (per curiam) (ruling a writ will issue only in extraordinary circumstances); *Moses H. Cone Hosp. v. Mercury Constr. Corp.,* 460 U.S. 1, 8, fn.6, 103 S. Ct. 927, 74 L. Ed. 2d 765 (1985) (holding a court of appeals cannot engage in review by extraordinary writ when it can exercise the same review by a contemporaneous ordinary appeal).

[a]   Limited Mandamus Use Authorized by U.S. Supreme Court

Despite this genuinely chilly reception to extraordinary writs, even the U.S. Supreme Court authorizes mandamus in very special circumstances. *See, e.g., Mallard v. U.S.*

Dist. Court, 490 U.S. 296, 109 S. Ct. 1814, 104 L. Ed. 2d 318 (1989) (holding court of appeals erred in denying writ of mandamus to review trial court's order that unwilling attorney must represent an indigent client in a civil case); *Schlagenhauf v. Holder,* 379 U.S. 104, 109–111, 85 S. Ct. 234, 13 L. Ed. 2d 152 (1964) (ruling mandamus will lie to review discovery issue of first impression concerning discovery rules themselves, in order to settle new and important problems); *see also George V. Burke,* Annotation, *Mandamus As Appropriate Remedy to Control Action of Federal Court in Civil Cases—Supreme Court Cases,* 57 L. Ed. 2d 1203–1241 (2012). The federal courts of appeals occasionally permit review of pretrial orders by mandamus in limited categories of cases, such as review of recusal decisions and discovery decisions involving important privilege issues. *E.g., Colonial Times, Inc. v. Gasch,* 509 F.2d 517, 523–526 (D.C. Cir. 1975); *see* Berger, *The Mandamus Power of the United States Courts of Appeals, supra,* and cases discussed therein.

[b]   Mandamus Use by Ninth Circuit

The Court of Appeals for the Ninth Circuit reviewed numerous Supreme Court cases in *Bauman v. U.S. Dist. Court,* 557 F.2d 650 (9th Cir. 1977), and identified five specific guidelines for mandamus: (1) The party seeking the writ has no other adequate means, such as a direct appeal, to attain the relief he or she desires; (2) The petitioner will be damaged or prejudiced in a way not correctable on appeal; (3) The district court's order is clearly erroneous as a matter of law; (4) The district court's order is an oft-repeated error, or manifests a persistent disregard of the federal rules; and (5) the district court's order raises new and important problems, or issues of law of first impression. *Id.* at 654–55; *see United States v. U.S. Dist. Ct. (In re United States),* 791 F. 3d 945 (9th Cir. 2015) (assessing whether a writ of mandamus is warranted by weighing and applying the five *Bauman* factors).

§ 15.03   Administrative Mandamus

[A]   Introductory Note

"Administrative mandamus" refers to the procedure authorized by CCP § 1094.5 by which a petitioner may obtain judicial review of the validity of a final administrative hearing decision. This mandamus review process applies to most state-level agencies, boards, corporations, and officers. CCP § 1094.5. Section 1094.6 extends this process to local-level agencies, such as cities and counties, as well as to local commissions, boards and officials.

[B]   General Prerequisites

Code of Civil Procedure § 1094.5 (2016)

(a) Where the writ [of mandate] is issued for the purpose of inquiring into the validity of any final administrative order or decision made as the result of a proceeding in which by law a hearing is required to be given, evidence is required to be taken, and discretion in the determination of facts is vested in the inferior tribunal, corporation, board, or officer, the case shall be heard by the court sitting without a jury. All or part of the record of the proceedings before the inferior tribunal, corporation, board, or officer may be filed with the petition, may be filed with respondent's points and authorities, or may be ordered to be filed by the court. * * *

(b) The inquiry in such a case shall extend to the questions whether the respondent has proceeded without, or in excess of, jurisdiction; whether there was a fair trial; and whether there was any prejudicial abuse of discretion. Abuse of discretion is established if the respondent has not proceeded in the manner required by law, the order or decision is not supported by the findings, or the findings are not supported by the evidence.

(c) Where it is claimed that the findings are not supported by the evidence, in cases in which the court is authorized by law to exercise its independent judgment on the evidence, abuse of discretion is established if the court determines that the findings are not supported by the weight of the evidence. In all other cases, abuse of discretion is established if the court determines that the findings are not supported by substantial evidence in the light of the whole record. * * *

(e) Where the court finds that there is relevant evidence that, in the exercise of reasonable diligence, could not have been produced or which was improperly excluded at the hearing before respondent, it may enter judgment as provided in subdivision (f) remanding the case to be reconsidered in the light of that evidence; or, in cases in which the court is authorized by law to exercise its independent judgment on the evidence, the court may admit the evidence at the hearing on the writ without remanding the case.

(f) The court shall enter judgment either commanding respondent to set aside the order or decision, or denying the writ. Where the judgment commands that the order or decision be set aside, it may order the reconsideration of the case in the light of the court's opinion and judgment and may order respondent to take such further action as is specially enjoined upon it by law, but the judgment shall not limit or control in any way the discretion legally vested in the respondent. * * *

Anton v. San Antonio Community Hospital

Supreme Court of California
19 Cal. 3d 802, 140 Cal. Rptr. 442, 567 P.2d 1162 (1977)

SULLIVAN, JUSTICE.

Plaintiff Achilles P. Anton, a licensed physician and surgeon, appeals from a judgment denying his petition for a writ of mandate sought under Code of Civil Procedure section 1085 to compel defendant San Antonio Community Hospital, a private, nonprofit hospital corporation, to reinstate his hospital rights and privileges and reappoint him to the medical staff. * * *

For 13 years preceding the events here in question, plaintiff had been a member of defendant hospital's medical staff—an unincorporated association organized under the auspices of the hospital's board of directors as required by section 2392.5 of the Business and Professions Code. During that period, however, he had been the subject of several corrective and/or disciplinary actions taken by committees of the medical staff relative to his failure to complete hospital medical records.

In October 1973 the medical staff commenced an investigation of plaintiff's hospital medical practices. A committee report made in the same month indicated, inter alia, that "there is evidence of poor medical judgment and overutilization of the hospital. Many of these patients did not appear to need actual hospital care, multiple tests were performed without medical indication, and there were several questionable industrial cases." * * * It was recommended that appropriate action be taken in accordance with medical staff bylaws.

In December 1973 the hospital's board of directors, having been advised of the foregoing recommendation, met for the purpose of reappointing staff members for the year 1974. After some discussion it was determined that all staff members with the exception of plaintiff should be reappointed and that action on plaintiff's reappointment should be tabled until the January meeting of the board.

In January 1974, at a special joint meeting of the executive and credentials committees of the medical staff, it was resolved that plaintiff's hospital privileges should be summarily suspended "on the basis of his failure to document proper care of his patients by failure to complete the histories and physical examinations in accordance with the Rules and Regulations of the Medical Staff Bylaws. Dr. Anton to be notified by certified mail of his suspension and informed that he may request a preliminary hearing before this committee in accordance with Article III, section 8, of the Medical Staff Bylaws." The indicated notification was sent, and a preliminary hearing was requested and held, resulting in the upholding of the suspension of hospital privileges.

In February 1974 plaintiff requested a formal hearing on the matter of his suspension.... * * * On March 5, 1974, the formal hearing was commenced before the judicial review committee, which had been appointed by the executive committee and consisted of five members and two alternates, all of whom were members of the medical staff. A court reporter was present and transcribed all proceedings.... [N]either plaintiff nor the medical staff was represented by counsel; plaintiff was assisted in the proceedings by a member of the medical staff and the staff itself was represented by two other members. * * *

At its conclusion the judicial review committee, after deliberating in the presence of the hearing officer and the two alternates, recommended to the medical staff and board of directors that plaintiff's hospital privileges be suspended and that he not be reappointed to the medical staff. In its formal report and recommendation the committee cited as reasons for its decision the four charges which had been set forth in the letter of February 11, finding each of the charges to be true.

On March 25, 1974, plaintiff made a written request for an appellate review of the judicial review committee decision as authorized by the ... medical staff bylaws. He was thereupon notified by letter that on April 24 an appellate review hearing would take place before the board of directors, as authorized by the revised ... bylaws.

On the appointed date plaintiff appeared with his attorney at the hearing. Also present were the members of the board of directors and their attorney. No one appeared on behalf of the medical staff or any of its committees. After introducing himself plaintiff's counsel stated that plaintiff would answer any questions that the board would care to put to him, but the attorney for the board pointed out that under the revised bylaws it was incumbent upon plaintiff to show either that the procedures required by the bylaws had not been complied with or that the decision of the judicial review committee was not supported by substantial evidence. Thereupon plaintiff's attorney orally advanced five alleged errors and improprieties in the previous proceedings.... Counsel concluded by stating that the committee hearing had contained other flaws as well, but that he would not undertake to enumerate them at that time. To this the board's attorney responded that counsel should call the attention of the board to each alleged prejudicial impropriety in order that plaintiff might claim exhaustion of his intraorganizational remedies should he subsequently wish to do so. Counsel, however, again declined to further enumerate the claimed errors or to become more specific regarding alleged prejudice, stating that the hearing in progress was not the appropriate forum for so doing. Plaintiff and his counsel were thereupon excused from the hearing.

On May 13, 1974, the board of directors, after reconvening to continue their deliberations, resolved to "sustain the decision of the Judicial Review Committee in regard to the medical staff membership of Dr. Anton." Plaintiff was notified of the decision, and this action in mandate followed.

Following argument by the parties at the hearing on the order to show cause, the trial court issued a notice of intended decision in which it determined, inter alia: (1) that plaintiff was not entitled to a trial de novo before the court but only to a judicial review of the administrative record; (2) that the substantial evidence test rather than the independent judgment test was to be applied in evaluating the decision of the board; (3) that all charges found to be true by the judicial review committee were supported by substantial evidence in the record except the second charge, i.e., that dealing with the failure to complete "hospital records in general"; and (4) that plaintiff was accorded "minimal due process of law," as required by applicable decisions. Findings of fact and conclusions of law detailing these determinations were filed, and judgment was entered denying the writ.

I

We first confront the question of the proper rule of judicial review in this matter. The trial court, plaintiff contends, was in error when, in reviewing the administrative record, it refused to exercise its independent judgment on the evidence and instead limited itself to a determination of whether the decision of the board was supported by substantial evidence in light of the whole record. In so doing, it is urged, the trial court improperly ignored the principle announced by this court in *Bixby v. Pierno* (1971) 4 Cal. 3d 130 [93 Cal. Rptr. 234, 481 P.2d 242], and *Strumsky v. San Diego County Employees Retirement Assn.* (1974) 11 Cal. 3d 28 [112 Cal. Rptr. 805, 520 P.2d 29]. For reasons to appear below, we conclude that plaintiff is correct.

At the outset of our discussion of this issue we offer several observations relative to the procedural posture of this case.

As indicated above, the instant proceeding was brought, according to the express terms of the complaint, pursuant to the provisions of section 1085 of the Code of Civil Procedure, dealing with so-called "traditional mandate." The trial court, however, perceiving that the matter before it involved the review of an administrative decision based upon a full administrative record, chose to treat the proceeding essentially as though it had been brought pursuant to the provisions of section 1094.5 of the same code, dealing with so-called "administrative mandate." For reasons to appear below we have concluded that this was proper; in short, the matter could have and should have been brought as a section 1094.5 proceeding, and the trial court was correct in so treating it.

While the Legislature, in its 1945 enactment of section 1094.5 of the Code of Civil Procedure, did not thereby bring into being "a separate and distinctive legal personality ... removed from the general law of mandamus ..." (*Grant v. Board of Medical Examiners* (1965) 232 Cal. App. 2d 820, 826 [43 Cal. Rptr. 270]), it did establish a specialized procedure for the review by mandate of certain types of administrative decisions, whose characteristics it specifically delineated in the statute. That procedure, the Legislature provided, was to be used in all cases "[where] *the writ* [i.e., the writ of mandate] is issued for the purpose of inquiring into the validity of *any* final administrative order or decision made as the result of a proceeding in which *by law* [1] a hearing is required to be given, [2] evidence is required to be taken and [3] discretion in the determination of facts is vested in the inferior tribunal, corporation, board, or officer...." (Code Civ. Proc., § 1094.5, subd. (a); italics added.) Thus, by the very terms of the statute, the procedure there set forth is to be utilized in all cases in which review of a final adjudicatory order[9] is sought by mandate and the three indicated elements are present.[11]

It is manifest that all of the stated conditions for section 1094.5 review are present in the instant case. The decision in question is clearly final and is adjudicatory rather

9. Section 1094.5 review is available only with respect to adjudicatory, as opposed to legislative, administrative actions. "Generally speaking, a legislative action is the formulation of a rule to be applied to all future cases, while an adjudicatory act involves the actual application of such a rule to a specific set of existing facts." (*Strunsky, supra*, at p.35, fn, 2;....

11. There are, of course, many situations in which the subject elements are not necessary to a valid administrative order or decision. In such cases review of the order or decision by means of section 1094.5 is not available, and review is normally obtained by means of section 1085 mandate or an action for declaratory relief.

than legislative in character. Moreover, the elements of hearing, evidence, and discretion in the determination of facts are clearly required by law in cases such as that before us. Our decision in *Pinsker v. Pacific Coast Society of Orthodontists* (1974) 12 Cal. 3d 541 [116 Cal. Rptr. 245, 526 P.2d 253], referring to a long and well-established line of cases of similar purport, made it clear that a physician may neither be refused admission to, nor expelled from, the staff of a hospital, *whether public or private*, in the absence of a procedure comporting with the minimum common law requirements of procedural due process and including each of the elements which here concern us. These principles were made the subject of an explicit holding in *Ascherman v. Saint Francis Memorial Hosp.* (1975) 45 Cal. App. 3d 507 [119 Cal. Rptr. 507], dealing with admission to the staff of a *private* hospital. It is therefore clear that the case before us fulfills all of the statutory requirements for review under the procedure established by section 1094.5. * * *

It has been widely assumed that mandate review via section 1094.5 is available only with respect to administrative decisions by governmental agencies. However, we find nothing in the statutory language or supporting legislative materials which would lead us to accept that assumption as warranted. Section 1094.5, as we have pointed out above, is by its terms made applicable to "*any final administrative order or decision* made as the result of a proceeding in which by law a hearing is required to be given, evidence is required to be taken and discretion in the determination of facts is vested in the *inferior tribunal, corporation, board or officer....*" Clearly this language is not limited, on its face at least, to governmental as opposed to nongovernmental agencies. Moreover, the last-italicized language appears to have been drawn directly from the terms of section 1085, dealing with so-called "traditional mandate." It has long been clear, of course, that section 1085 mandate is available not only to compel official acts on the part of governmental agencies but also to compel nongovernmental bodies or officers to perform their legal duties. It would seem to follow, therefore, that section 1094.5, by using substantially identical language in describing the kind of administrative body whose decisions are subject to review under its provisions, was intended to apply to the same spectrum of agencies to which section 1085 has been held applicable in all cases in which the *subject decision is the product of a proceeding in which a hearing and related procedural protections are required by law*. This, as we have pointed out above, is just such a case. * * *

Finally, we point out a compelling practical consideration which renders the use of section 1094.5 procedures particularly appropriate in cases of this kind. Section 32000 et seq. of the Health and Safety Code, the so-called Local District Hospital Law, makes specific provision for a hearing in matters of this nature which arise in the context of a public hospital operated by a hospital district, and the clear applicability of our decision in *Pinsker v. Pacific Coast Society of Orthodontists, supra*, 12 Cal. 3d 541, insures that such a hearing will be accompanied by the related procedural protections requisite to section 1094.5 review. It would be incongruous, we believe, to hold that the decisions of *private* hospital boards, which are required by the same decision to be based upon a hearing of substantially identical scope and purport, were to be subject to some different form of review. * * *

For all of the foregoing reasons, then, we conclude that the trial court was correct in treating the instant proceeding as one for administrative review pursuant to the provisions of section 1094.5 of the Code of Civil Procedure.

II

As we have pointed out above, however, it is plaintiff's contention that the trial court, although it properly treated the proceeding as one seeking 1094.5 review of an administrative decision, erroneously refused to exercise its independent judgment on the evidence. In so doing, it is urged, the court acted contrary to the principles laid down by us in our *Bixby* and *Strumsky* decisions.

The rule governing the scope of review to be applied in section 1094.5 proceedings when it is claimed that there has been an abuse of discretion because the findings are not supported by the evidence is set forth in subdivision (c) of the section as follows: "[In] cases in which the court is authorized by law to exercise its independent judgment on the evidence, abuse of discretion is established if the court determines that the findings are not supported by the weight of the evidence; ... in all other cases abuse of discretion is established if the court determines that the findings are not supported by substantial evidence in light of the whole record." In our *Bixby* decision, applying this language in the context of a case involving a nonconstitutional state agency of statewide jurisdiction, we held that the independent judgment test was to apply in all cases in which the subject decision substantially affected a fundamental vested right. In the subsequent *Strumsky* case we extended this rule of review to the determinations of local governmental agencies and state agencies of local jurisdiction. The issue before us today, then, is whether the same rule of review[19] should be applied as well to the determinations of nongovernmental agencies which are subject to review under section 1094.5. We hold that it should. * * *

As we made clear in *Bixby*, the basic consideration in determining the scope of judicial review to be afforded administrative decisions of an adjudicatory nature is *the importance of the affected right to the individual who stands in jeopardy of losing it*. Thus, we explained, "[if] ... the right has been acquired by the individual, and if the right is fundamental, the courts have held the loss of it is sufficiently vital to the individual to compel a full and independent review. The abrogation of the right is too important to the individual to relegate it to exclusive administrative extinction." (*Bixby*, *supra*, at p. 144.) We continued this basic approach in *Strumsky*, where, after

---

19. Our full statement of the rule, as set forth in *Strumsky*, was as follows: "[If] the order or decision of the agency substantially affects a fundamental vested right, the court, in determining under section 1094.5 of the Code of Civil Procedure whether there has been an abuse of discretion because the findings are not supported by the evidence, must exercise its independent judgment on the evidence and find an abuse of discretion if the findings are not supported by the weight of the evidence. If, on the other hand, the order or decision does not substantially affect a fundamental vested right, the trial court's inquiry will be limited to a determination of whether or not the findings are supported by substantial evidence in light of the whole record." (11 Cal. 3d at pp. 44–45.)

reiterating the substance of *Bixby* in this respect, we said: "This reasoning, of course, applies with equal force to all administrative decisions of an adjudicatory nature-regardless of the administrative agency involved." (*Strumsky, supra,* at pp. 34–35, fn. omitted.) In *Bixby,* however, we had relied in our decision upon the separation-of-powers doctrine, holding in essence that that doctrine required careful *judicial* scrutiny of state administrative decisions affecting fundamental vested rights. (*Bixby, supra,* at pp. 141–144.) *Strumsky,* on the other hand, involved a local agency, to which the doctrine of separation of powers is not applicable. The question therefore arose whether this latter fact *prevented* the application of the rule developed in *Bixby.* We concluded that it did not. * * *

By the same token, the separation-of-powers doctrine, while equally inapplicable to *prevent* the exercise of judicial powers by nongovernmental agencies, is irrelevant to the determination whether such powers *are possessed* by such agencies. It is clear, of course, that the agency whose decision we here consider has not been invested with judicial powers by the Constitution. Accordingly its adjudicatory decisions are subject to review under the same rules which are applicable to all decisions by administrative agencies lacking judicial powers. Those rules, which as we have pointed out are grounded in the nature of the right affected by the decision, include the rule of review announced in the *Bixby* and *Strumsky* cases.

We proceed to apply the *Bixby-Strumsky* rule to the instant case. That rule, as stated by us in *Strumsky,* provides that if the subject order or decision "substantially affects a fundamental vested right, the court, in determining under section 1094.5 of the Code of Civil Procedure whether there has been an abuse of discretion because the findings are not supported by the evidence, must exercise its independent judgment on the evidence and find an abuse of discretion if the findings are not supported by the weight of the evidence. If, on the other hand, the order or decision does not substantially affect a fundamental vested right, the trial court's inquiry will be limited to a determination of whether or not the findings are supported by substantial evidence in light of the whole record." (11 Cal. 3d at pp. 44–45.) The issue before us, then, in determining whether the trial court erroneously refused to exercise its independent judgment on the evidence, is whether or not the administrative decision here in question "substantially affects a fundamental vested right."

We think it manifest-and indeed defendant has not contended otherwise-that the decision before us has a substantial effect on a right which is "fundamental." "In determining whether the right is fundamental the courts do not alone weigh the economic aspect of it, but the effect of it in human terms and the importance of it to the individual in the life situation." (*Bixby v Pierno, supra,* 4 Cal. 3d 130, 144.) As the court said in *Edwards v. Fresno Community Hosp.* (1974) 38 Cal. App. 3d 702, 705 [113 Cal. Rptr. 579], "Although the term 'hospital privileges' connotes personal activity and personal rights may be incidentally involved in the exercise of these privileges, the essential nature of a qualified physician's right to use the facilities of a hospital is a property interest which directly relates to the pursuit of his livelihood." This interest is clearly fundamental within the meaning of *Bixby* and *Strumsky.*

It is urged, however, that the right here affected, while fundamental in character, can by no means be considered vested. Reference is made to section 2392.5 of the Business and Professions Code..., which provides in subdivision (a) that it is unprofessional conduct for a physician to practice at a hospital such as defendant unless medical staff appointments are made on an *annual* or biennial basis. In view of this fact—and also presumably in view of the fact that staff appointments at defendant hospital are made on an annual basis—it is argued that the right to medical staff membership and associated privileges cannot be considered vested for more than the term of the appointment, and that upon expiration of the term the physician becomes comparable to an applicant for a license or franchise and wholly without a vested right to reappointment. (*See Bixby v. Pierno, supra*, 4 Cal. 3d 130, 146, and cases there cited.)

This contention, we believe, wholly ignores the realities of the situation confronting us. Aside from the fact that plaintiff had been consistently appointed to defendant's medical staff for each of the 12 years preceding the events here in question, it is clear to us that the admission of a physician to medical staff membership establishes a relationship between physician and hospital which, although formally limited in duration by force of law, gives rise to rights and obligations which find no parallel in the license and franchise cases to which defendant has reference. An obvious distinction, of course, lies in the fact that the previously admitted physician, unlike the normal applicant for a license or franchise, may not be denied reappointment to the medical staff absent a hearing and other procedural prerequisites consistent with minimal due process protections.[22] More significant for our present purposes, however, is the consideration that a hospital board, through its act of initially admitting a physician to medical staff membership, has thereby, in the exercise of its discretion, necessarily determined his fitness for such membership at the time of admission *and granted him the full rights of membership.*[23] The fact that review of this appointment is made mandatory on an annual or biennial basis (through a statutory requirement of reappointment at that interval, as determined by the hospital's bylaws) can by no means be said to render it probationary or tentative in effect. In short, the full rights of staff membership vest upon appointment, subject to divestment upon periodic review only after a showing of adequate cause for such divestment in a proceeding consistent with minimal due process requirements. * * *

On the basis of the foregoing, we think it manifest that the right affected by the decision here in question is both fundamental and vested within the meaning of *Bixby*

---

22. ... [T]his rule is equally applicable in the case of an initial application for medical staff membership and hospital privileges. We shall point out below, however, that certain other distinctions between the appointment and reappointment situations require a different result in the two cases on the question whether the interest affected by a decision is vested for purposes of the *Bixby-Strumsky* test.

23. Compare *Bixby v. Pierno, supra*, 4 Cal. 3d 130, 146: "Once the agency has initially exercised its expertise and determined that an individual fulfills the requirements to practice his profession, the agency's subsequent revocation of the license calls for an independent judgment review of the facts underlying such administrative decision."

and *Strumsky*. It therefore appears that the trial court was in error when it refused to exercise its independent judgment on the evidence presented before the administrative body in order to determine whether the findings offered in support of the decision were supported by the weight of the evidence. This error requires that we reverse the judgment and remand the cause to the trial court for further proceedings under the proper standard of review.[24]

III

Plaintiff's remaining contentions all relate to the requirement — foreshadowed in *Pinsker v. Pacific Coast Society of Orthodontists, supra*, 12 Cal. 3d 541, and explicitly articulated in *Ascherman v. Saint Francis Memorial Hosp., supra*, 45 Cal. App. 3d 507, 511 — that membership decisions of hospital staff associations, whether in public or private hospitals, "must be rendered pursuant to minimal requisites of fair procedure required by established common law principles." (*Ascherman, supra*.) For reasons which appear below, we conclude that none of the points advanced has merit. * * *

B

It is urged that "minimal due process" required some participation by plaintiff in the selection of the judicial review committee, and that three of the five members of the committee were prejudiced against him. It does not appear, however, that plaintiff raised the matter of prejudice before the committee; indeed, he did not even raise it when, represented by counsel, he appeared before the board of directors at the appellate review hearing. * * *

C

Plaintiff further contends that it was fundamentally unfair to require him to proceed with the hearing before the judicial review committee without the assistance of counsel. * * *

... [W]e find that the rule here in question — rendering representation by counsel a matter within the discretion of the judicial review committee — is not offensive to the standard of "minimal due process" which is applicable in proceedings of this kind.

D

Finally it is urged by plaintiff that a hospital bylaw placing the burden of going forward with the evidence and the burden of proof upon him is inconsistent with the requirement of minimal fair procedure set forth in *Pinsker* and *Ascherman*. * * *

We hold ... that the bylaw in question is not violative of the applicable standard. "The common law requirement of a fair procedure does not compel formal proceedings with all the embellishments of a court trial ... nor adherence to a single mode

---

24. Because significant portions of the administrative proceedings here subject to review took place before a panel of medical doctors exercising professional judgment on matters of proper medical technique and practice, the trial court may find the record of those proceedings inadequate for the purpose of informed judicial review. If so the trial court, prior to undertaking its deliberations, may wish to remand the matter to the administrative body for further proceedings directed to the preparation of an adequate record.

of process. It may be satisfied by any one of a variety of procedures which afford a fair opportunity for an [affected party] to present his position. As such, this court should not attempt to fix a rigid procedure that must invariably be observed. Instead, the associations themselves should retain the initial and primary responsibility for devising a method which provides an [affected party] adequate notice of the 'charges' against him and a reasonable opportunity to respond. In drafting such procedure ... the organization should consider the nature of the tendered issue and should fashion its procedure to insure a *fair* opportunity for an [affected party] to present his position. Although the association retains discretion in formalizing such procedures, the courts remain available to afford relief in the event of the abuse of such discretion." (*Pinsker v. Pacific Coast Society of Orthodontists, supra,* 12 Cal. 3d 541, 555–556, fn. omitted.)

We cannot conclude that the adoption and application of the bylaw here in question constitutes an abuse of the indicated discretion. * * *

The judgment is reversed and the cause is remanded to the trial court for further proceedings consistent with this opinion.

CLARK, JUSTICE, Dissenting.

The instant case demonstrates the need to rethink California's unique rule requiring trial de novo review of administrative determinations. The rule frequently defeats the beneficial purposes of administrative adjudication-appropriate expertise, economical and speedy determination, and recognition of institutional policy. Further, the constitutional theory advanced for the trial de novo rule is erroneous. Finally, having been rejected by other jurisdictions, the rule should be reconsidered, allowing the Legislature to establish a process with greater deference to administrative determination.

THE TRIAL DE NOVO RULE

If the decision of an administrative agency affects a "fundamental vested right," the trial de novo rule requires the trial court to exercise its independent judgment by *reweighing the evidence* to determine whether the administrative findings are unsupported by the evidence.[1] (*Strumsky v. San Diego County Employees Retirement Assn.* (1974) 11 Cal. 3d 28, 44 [112 Cal. Rptr. 805, 520 P.2d 29].) If the agency's decision has not affected a fundamental vested right, the trial court's inquiry is limited to the customary test of determining whether the findings are unsupported by *substantial evidence* in light of the whole record. (*Id.* at pp. 44–45.)

PURPOSES OF ADMINISTRATIVE TRIBUNALS

The beneficial purposes of administrative adjudication include special expertise, simplified procedure permitting economical and speedy determination, and the tribunal's superior ability — due to staffing, tradition, and procedure — to operate as a

---

1. Earlier cases appear to have created a presumption in favor of the correctness of the administrative agency's findings. (E.g., *Dare v. Bd. of Medical Examiners* (1943) 21 Cal. 2d 790, 800 [136 P.2d 304].) Such a presumption, while perhaps desirable, appears inconsistent with the concept of independent judgment. (*Bixby v. Pierno* (1971) 4 Cal. 3d 130, 154, fn. 12 [93 Cal. Rptr. 234, 481 P.2d 242] (Burke, J., conc. & dis.).)

policy-making body implementing legislative will. (Jaffe, Judicial Control of Administrative Action (1965) pp. 25–26.) However, as illustrated by the instant case, these purposes are substantially frustrated by the trial de novo rule.

Expertise

The charges present questions involving a high degree of medical expertise. Timely completion of patient histories and physical examinations are factual questions laymen and judges might be competent to determine. However, questions whether plaintiff visited hospitalized patients on a timely basis, or overutilized facilities, involve not only the issues of when patients were visited and what practices were used but also require application of appropriate medical standards.

Institutional competency requires that questions of medical judgment lie with the medical staff and the hospital administration. They—rather than judges—are trained to make these judgments. The statement of the majority (ante, fn. 24) that the trial judge might remand the matter for further proceedings to create a record more fully reflecting doctors' views of proper medical techniques and practices admits the problem. A judge's cram course in medicine is a poor substitute for the professional judgment of the highly educated practitioners in the field.

Economical and Speedy Determination

The inefficiency of the trial de novo process is illustrated by the possibility that repeated remands to the medical staff with attendant delays and expense may be necessary to educate the judge as to simple medical matters—matters obvious to all medical practitioners but not to untrained persons. * * *

In addition, the trial de novo rule is inherently inefficient. The proper approach to adjudicate conflicting claims is to first determine the facts, next the legal principles applicable to those facts, and finally the consequences flowing from the facts and the legal principles. While the agency initially determines the facts, the trial judge under the trial de novo rule must redetermine them, and in cases of variance between the determinations, the agency must then fix the consequences. * * *

Institutional Policy

The most glaring failure of the trial de novo rule is that it may result in trial judges rather than designated officials determining the institution's policy. The hospital administration and medical staff should run the hospital. Judges are not trained to do so. Yet when he decides what constitutes proper utilization or how often a doctor should visit his hospitalized patient, the trial judge determines questions of policy and undertakes operating the hospital in a real sense.

Substantial Evidence Rule

In contrast to the trial de novo rule, the traditional substantial evidence rule requires deference to administrative expertise, reduces expense and delay stemming from trial court processing, and permits administrators to exercise more fully the institutional discretion vested in them. The administrator's action is reviewable only for clear abuse of that discretion.

CONSTITUTIONAL BASIS

The constitutional basis asserted for the trial de novo rule is article VI, section 1 of our state Constitution, vesting judicial power in the courts.[2] It is claimed that in absence of constitutional provision vesting judicial power in an agency, it possesses none, and that administrative adjudication affecting vested and fundamental rights constitutes improper exercise of judicial power. (*Strumsky v. San Diego County Employees Retirement Assn., supra,* 11 Cal. 3d 28, 35–45.)

The fallacies in the argument have been well expressed by Chief Justice Gibson, Justice Traynor, and Justice Burke in their scholarly concurring or dissenting opinions in ... *Bixby v. Pierno* (1971) 4 Cal. 3d 130 [93 Cal. Rptr. 234, 481 P.2d 242], and *Strumsky v. San Diego County Employees Retirement Assn., supra,* 11 Cal. 3d 28. Additionally, numerous commentators have criticized the rule. (*See* authorities cited *Harlow v. Carleson* (1976) 16 Cal. 3d 731, 739–740 [129 Cal. Rptr. 298, 548 P.2d 698] (dis. opn.).) For example, Professor Davis refers to the *Strumsky* decision extending the trial de novo rule to local agencies as an erratic movement "back into medievalism." (Davis, Administrative Law of the Seventies, Supplementing Administrative Law Treatise (1976) pp. 8–9.) The fallacies in the asserted constitutional basis for the trial de novo rule need not be repeated here. Interestingly, while every state vests judicial power in the courts, none has felt compelled to adopt California's trial de novo rule.

Finally, attention must be called to an inherent inconsistency in today's majority opinion. We are told on the one hand that plaintiff's rights are of such importance that decisions affecting them necessarily involve an exercise of the judicial power and, on the other, that it is entirely proper to exclude attorneys from the presentation of evidence in this judicial proceeding. The majority in effect forces the physician to practice law. The majority may not have it both ways—either the proceeding is an exercise of judicial power or it is not.

[1] Administrative Mandamus, Generally

[a] Exclusive Means of Judicial Review

Administrative mandamus is the exclusive means of judicial review of adjudicatory decisions of most, but not all, state administrative agencies. For a few state agencies, usually ones of constitutional origin, a writ of review (or certiorari) is specified by statute as the appropriate method for such judicial review. These include the Agricultural Labor Relations Board, Labor Code § 1160.8, Rule 8.498, Cal. Rules of Ct.; the Alcoholic Beverage Control Appeals Board, Bus. & Prof. Code §§ 23090–23090.7; the

---

2. Article VI, section 1, of our Constitution provides: "The judicial power of this State is vested in the Supreme Court, courts of appeal, superior courts, municipal courts, and justice courts. All except justice courts are courts of record." Although *Strumsky v. San Diego County Employees Retirement Assn., supra,* 11 Cal. 3d 28, 35, also mentioned the separation of powers clause (Cal. Const., art. III, 3), the court recognized that the clause did not apply to local agencies. (11 Cal. 3d at p. 36.) Since *Strumsky* held that the trial de novo rule applied to local agencies, it is apparent that the rule is presently based on article VI, section 1.

Public Employment Relations Board, Gov. Code § 3542; the Public Utilities Commission, Pub. Util. Code §§ 1756–1759, Rule 8.496, Cal. Rules of Ct.; the Workers' Compensation Appeals Board, Labor Code §§ 5950–5955, Rule 8.495, Cal. Rules of Ct.; and the State Bar of California, Bus. & Prof. Code § 6082, Rule 9.13, Cal. Rules of Ct.

[b]   Review of Nongovernment Decisions

As *Anton v. San Antonio Community Hospital,* reproduced *supra*, illustrates, administrative mandamus is available not only to review adjudicatory decisions of governmental entities, but also of certain nongovernment entities. Nearly all such cases, like *Anton*, involve private hospitals. *See, e.g., Rhee v. El Camino Hosp. Dist.,* 201 Cal. App. 3d 477, 247 Cal. Rptr. 244 (1988). The extent of Section 1094.5's application to other private entities is unclear. *See, e.g., Wallin v. Vienna Sausage Mfg. Co.* 156 Cal. App 3d 1051, 203 Cal. Rptr. 375 (1984) (ruling § 1094.5 authorized judicial review of grievance hearing under collective bargaining agreement); *Bray v. Intl. Molders & Allied Workers Union,* 155 Cal. App. 3d 608, 202 Cal. Rptr. 269 (1984) (concluding labor union's hearing and decision to oust local union secretary proper subject of judicial review under § 1094.5). What other types of nongovernmental entities may arguably be subject to administrative mandamus?

[2]   Decisions Subject to Administrative Mandamus

Not all actions by administrative agencies are subject to review by administrative mandamus. This writ is applicable only to final administrative decisions made as a result of a proceeding in which by law: (a) a hearing is required to be given, (b) evidence is required to be taken, and (c) discretion in the determination of facts is vested in the agency. CCP § 1094.5(a).

[a]   What Constitutes Evidentiary Hearing?

The first two criteria present few problems. An evidentiary hearing required by the Administrative Procedure Act or some other statute, by local ordinance, agency rule or regulation, or by due process, is one "required by law." *See, e.g., Civil Serv. Comm'n v. Velez,* 14 Cal. App. 4th 115, 17 Cal. Rptr. 2d 490 (1993) (concluding the fact that no hearing was held did not preclude review by administrative mandate; if hearing is required by law, administrative mandamus may be appropriate to secure it). What law required the hearing in *Anton*? Occasionally administrative mandamus is deemed inappropriate because a hearing, although given to petitioner, was not *required* to be given by law, *see, e.g., Weary v. Civil Serv. Comm'n,* 140 Cal. App. 3d 189, 195, 189 Cal. Rptr. 442 (1983) (holding administrative mandamus under § 1094.5 improper review method where hearing granted at commission's discretion, but not required by law); *Taylor v. State Personnel Bd.,* 101 Cal. App. 3d 498, 161 Cal. Rptr. 677 (1980) (ruling judicial review of state board order inappropriate under § 1094.5 because hearing, although provided, not required by statute, rule, or due process); or because the administrative proceeding is informal and does not permit testimony, *see, e.g., Wasko v. Dept. of Corrections,* 211 Cal. App. 3d 996, 1001, 259 Cal. Rptr. 764 (1989). What procedure is appropriate to obtain judicial review of hearing decisions in such cases? *See, e.g., Scott B. v. Bd. of Tr. of Orange Cnty. High Sch. of the Arts,* 217 Cal. App. 4th 117, 158 Cal. Rptr. 3d 173 (2013) (applying CCP § 1085 because agency not required to hold hearing).

[b] What Constitutes Agency Discretion?

The third criterion generally means that, for administrative mandamus to apply, the agency's decision under review must be adjudicative (or "quasi-judicial") in nature; and not be legislative (or "quasi-legislative"). How did the court in *Anton* define these terms? Is the distinction a clear one? How should the courts further distinguish between "quasi-judicial" and "quasi-legislative" acts, for purposes of § 1094.5(a)? Is it based on whether the agency conducts a hearing? Engages in fact-finding as part of the decision-making process? Or is fact-finding a part of both administrative functions? *See, e.g., Shapell Indus. v. Governing Bd.,* 1 Cal. App. 4th 218, 231, 1 Cal. Rptr. 2d 818 (1991).

Many courts quote from Professor Davis's *Administrative Law Treatise* (1958), § 15.03, p. 353, that a legislative action is based upon "facts which help the tribunal determine the *content of law* and of policy and help the tribunal to exercise its judgment or discretion in determining what course of action to take," while an adjudicative decision generally rest on "facts concerning the immediate parties—who did what, where, when, how, and with what motive or intent...." *E.g., Joint Council of Interns & Residents v. Bd. of Supervisors,* 210 Cal. App. 3d 1202, 1209–1210, 258 Cal. Rptr. 762 (1989); *Dominey v. Dept. of Personnel Admin.,* 205 Cal. App. 3d 729, 737, 252 Cal. Rptr. 620 (1988). The distinction depends on the function performed by the agency, and not on the nature of the decision-making body or the procedural characteristics of the process. *20th Century Ins. Co. v. Garamendi,* 8 Cal. 4th 216, 275, 32 Cal. Rptr. 2d 807, 878 P.2d 566 (1994) (noting that the classification of administrative action contemplates "*only* the function performed"). *Pitts v. Perluss,* 58 Cal. 2d 824, 834, 27 Cal. Rptr. 19 (1962).

[c] Adjudicative vs. Legislative Decision?

With these additional explanations in mind, how would you classify the administrative actions in the following cases:

(1) A petition for writ of mandate which seeks to vacate respondent school district's resolution imposing a school facilities fee on new commercial construction within the district, and to refund fees imposed against petitioner? *See Garrick Dev. Co. v. Hayward Unified Sch. Dist.,* 3 Cal. App. 4th 320, 4 Cal. Rptr. 2d 897 (1992); *Shapell Indus. v. Governing Bd.,* 1 Cal. App. 4th 218, 1 Cal. Rptr. 2d 818 (1991).

(2) Mandate petition brought by state investigators to review a grievance hearing decision by respondent Department of Personnel Administration (DPA) and compel the DPA (1) to award them back pay for work performed out of class and (2) to reclassify their positions as that of special agents? *See Dominey v. Dept. of Personnel Admin.,* 205 Cal. App. 3d 729, 252 Cal. Rptr. 620 (1988).

(3) A petition for writ of mandate to compel respondent City to grant petitioner's application for a residential development allotment and to vacate award to rival developers? *See Harroman Co. v. Town of Tiburon*, 235 Cal. App. 3d 388, 1 Cal. Rptr. 2d 72 (1991); *Pacifica Corp. v. City of Camarillo*, 149 Cal. App. 3d 168, 196 Cal. Rptr. 670 (1983).

(4) Is a city's decision to rezone property a legislative or adjudicative act? Does it make a difference whether the zoning decision affects several large parcels and many owners as opposed to only a single lot owned by one person? What about a decision on a variance or a use permit? *See, e.g., Saad v. City of Berkeley*, 24 Cal. App. 4th 1206, 30 Cal. Rptr. 2d 95 (1994); *Consaul v. City of San Diego*, 6 Cal. App. 4th 1781, 8 Cal. Rptr. 2d 762 (1992). Approval of subdivisions? Are generic classifications possible, or must such land-use decisions be classified on a case-by-case basis? Are generic classifications desirable? *See Arnel Dev. Co. v. City of Costa Mesa*, 28 Cal. 3d 511, 169 Cal. Rptr. 904, 620 P.2d 565 (1980), and cases discussed therein.

(5) A petition filed by an environmental group challenging a city's certification of an Environmental Impact Report for a development project? *See A Local & Regional Monitor v. City of L. A.*, 12 Cal. App. 4th 1773, 1793, 16 Cal. Rptr. 2d 358 (1993); *Del Mar Terrace Conservancy, Inc. v. City Council*, 10 Cal. App. 4th 712, 12 Cal. Rptr. 2d 785 (1992).

(6) Is the State Insurance Commissioner's adoption of regulations implementing the rate rollback provisions of Proposition 103, promulgated after hearings, a legislative or adjudicative act? What about rate rollback order as to certain groups of insurers, made by the Commissioner after conducting consolidated evidentiary hearings? As to individual insurers? *See 20th Century Ins. Co. v. Garamendi*, 8 Cal. 4th 216, 275–279, 32 Cal. Rptr. 2d 807, 878 P.2d 556 (1994).

[3]   Administrative vs. Traditional Mandamus

[a]   When Is Traditional Mandamus Applicable?

If the challenged agency action is deemed "quasi-legislative" and § 1094.5 therefore inapplicable, what procedure is available for judicial review? *See, e.g., Pac. Legal Found. v. Cal. Coastal Comm'n*, 33 Cal. 3d 158, 188 Cal. Rptr. 104, 655 P.2d 306 (1982). What is the appropriate review procedure to challenge a quasi-legislative action where the administrative agency was required by law to conduct a hearing and receive evidence? *See, e.g., Western States Petroleum Assn. v. Superior Court*, 9 Cal. 4th 559, 38 Cal. Rptr. 2d 139, 888 P.2d 1268 (1995); *20th Century Ins. Co. v. Garamendi*, 8 Cal. 4th 216, 278–279, 32 Cal. Rptr. 807, 878 P.2d 566 (1994) (noting that the fact that regulations are formulated under quasi-adjudicative procedures does not undermine their quasi-legislative nature).

[b]   When Is Administrative Mandamus Applicable?

Is administrative mandamus the proper method of judicial review where a petitioner seeks to attack the validity of an administrative regulation? Does the answer depend on the circumstance of the attack? Why? Compare *20th Century Ins. Co. v. Garamendi,* *supra,* and *Pacific Legal Found. v. Cal. Coastal Comm'n, supra* (ruling administrative mandamus inappropriate for challenge to agency guidelines as facially invalid) with *Woods v. Superior Court,* 28 Cal. 3d 668, 676–681, 170 Cal. Rptr. 484, 620 P.2d 1032 (1981) (holding administrative mandamus appropriate method for rejected welfare applicant to contest validity of department regulation). What if the regulation attacked is one which grants discretion to the agency to hold a hearing, and the petitioner seeks to compel the agency to exercise that discretion and provide an individual hearing. *See Saleeby v. State Bar,* 39 Cal. 3d 547, 216 Cal. Rptr. 367, 702 P.2d 525 (1985).

[c] Which Type of Review Is More Advantageous?

From the petitioner's perspective, is it more advantageous to obtain judicial review pursuant to CCP § 1094.5 as opposed to some other method, such as traditional mandamus pursuant to CCP § 1085? *See Southern Cal. Gas v. South Coast Quality Mgmt. Dist.,* 200 Cal. App. 4th 251, 267–28, 133 Cal. Rptr. 3d 7 (2011) (discussing cases and concluding that of all administrative decisions, quasi-legislative acts receive the most deferential level of judicial scrutiny); *Balch Enter., Inc. v. New Haven Unified Sch. Dist.,* 219 Cal. App. 3d 783, 791–792, 268 Cal. Rptr. 543 (1990) (comparing scope and standards of review between administrative and traditional mandamus); *Joint Council of Interns & Residents v. Bd. of Supervisors,* 210 Cal. App. 3d 1202, 1209, 258 Cal. Rptr. 762 (1989) (same). Which method provides greater opportunity to introduce additional evidence in the Superior Court? *See No Oil, Inc. v. City of L. A.,* 13 Cal. 3d 68, 79, n.6, 118 Cal. Rptr. 34, 529 P.2d 66 (1974); CCP § 1094.5(e). Has a longer statute of limitations? Which method may permit a jury trial to resolve factual conflicts? Compare CCP § 1090 with § 1094.5(a). Which provides more options with respect to available remedies?

[4] *Other Prerequisites to Administrative Mandamus*

[a] Finality

Another prerequisite to issuance of a writ of administrative mandamus is that the administrative decision or order under review must be "final" within the meaning of CCP § 1094.5(a). *E.g., Bollengier v. Doctors Med. Ctr.,* 222 Cal. App. 3rd 1115, 1125–32, 272 Cal. Rptr. 273 (1990) (ruling a § 1094.5 writ will issue only to review a final administrative decision; requirement regarded as an aspect of exhaustion of administrative remedies); *Kumar v. Nat. Med. Enter., Inc.,* 218 Cal. App. 3d 1050, 1055–56, 267 Cal. Rptr. 452 (1990) (setting aside agency hearing decision and remanding because of unfair hearing procedures held to no longer constitute a final agency decision on merits of petitioner's reinstatement claim).

Generally, agency decisions are final when rendered. *See Sierra Club v. San Joaquin Local Agency Formation Comm'n,* 21 Cal. 4th 489, 87 Cal. Rptr. 2d 702, 981 P.2d 543 (1999). The right to petition for judicial review is not necessarily affected by a party's failure to request a reconsideration or rehearing before that agency. *Sierra Club,* 21

Cal. 4th at 509–510. A request for reconsideration of an agency decision may be necessary, however, where appropriate to raise matters not previously brought to the agency's attentions. *Id.* at 510. Individual statutory schemes governing agency adjudication may expressly make reconsideration unnecessary prior to judicial review. *E.g.*, Gov. Code § 19588 (petition for reconsideration not required prior to seeking judicial review of State Personnel Board proceedings). The most important such exception applies to proceedings governed by the Administrative Procedure Act (APA). Gov. Code §§ 11500–11529. Although reconsideration is available, the APA provides that the right to petition for administrative mandamus "shall not be affected by the failure to seek reconsideration before the agency." Gov. Code. § 11523.

[b]   Traditional Mandamus Prerequisites

As *Anton* indicates, administrative mandamus is not a separate and distinct type of extraordinary writ. When consistent with CCP § 1094.5, the statutory prerequisites governing traditional mandamus apply. *Woods v. Superior Court,* 28 Cal. 3d 668, 673–74, 170 Cal. Rptr. 484, 620 P.2d 1032 (1981); *Grant v. Bd. of Med. Examiners,* 232 Cal. App. 2d 820, 826, 43 Cal. Rptr. 270 (1965). Consequently, a petitioner must satisfy the two basic requirements of CCP § 1086 for the writ to issue — the petitioner must be "beneficially interested" and have no other adequate legal remedy. *See Woods, supra,* 28 Cal. 3d at 673–74.

This latter prerequisite generally requires the petitioner to raise and fully present all relevant issues during the administrative process, and to exhaust administrative remedies, prior to seeking judicial review. *E.g., Lopez v. Civil Serv. Com.,* 232 Cal. App. 3d 307, 315, 283 Cal. Rptr. 447 (1991); *see generally CEB California Administrative Mandamus,* §§ 3.1–3.76 (3d ed. 2016).

[C]   Nature of Judicial Review by Administrative Mandamus

[1]   Scope of Judicial Review under § 1094.5(b)

The scope of a reviewing court's inquiry on an administrative mandamus petition extends to the following questions: Whether the respondent agency has proceeded without or in excess of jurisdiction, whether there was a fair trial, and whether there was any prejudicial abuse of discretion. CCP § 1094.5(b). How is "abuse of discretion" defined by § 1094.5(b)? Is this statutory definition the same as that used in regular appellate review? How does § 1094.5(c) affect your answer to this question? For an exhaustive discussion of what constitutes prejudicial abuse of discretion within the meaning of § 1094.5(b), see CEB, *California Administrative Mandamus,* §§ 6.55–6.175 (3d ed. 2016).

[a]   Fair Trial

What principles guide the reviewing court in determining whether a governmental agency provided the petitioner with a "fair trial"? *See Doe v. Univ. of Southern Cal.,*

246 Cal. App. 4th 221, 239–248, 200 Cal. Rptr. 3d 851 (2016) (discussing constitutional and common law requirements for a fair hearing under § 1094.5); *Nightlife Partners, Ltd. v. City of Beverly Hills*, 108 Cal. App. 4th 81, 90–98, 133 Cal. Rptr. 2d 234 (2003) (discussing procedural due process in the context of administrative proceedings); CEB, *California Administrative Mandamus, supra*, §§ 6.36–6.54. What principle did the *Anton* court rely on in determining the fairness of a hearing before a non-governmental board? What is the proper relief when the reviewing court determines that the petitioner was not afforded a "fair trial"? *See, e.g., Pinheiro v. Civil Serv. Comm'n for Cnty. of Fresno*, 245 Cal. App. 4th 1458, 1471–72, 200 Cal. Rptr. 3d 525 (2016); *Rosenblit v. Superior Court*, 231 Cal. App. 3d 1434, 282 Cal. Rptr. 819 (1991). When the court determines there was a "prejudicial abuse of discretion"?

[b] Sufficiency of Agency Findings

A petitioner may establish prejudicial abuse of discretion under § 1094.5(b) by establishing that the respondent agency's "decision is not supported by the findings." What does this mean? Implicit here is the requirement that the agency must set forth findings of fact in support of its adjudicatory decision, is it not? *See Topanga Assn. for a Scenic Cmty. v. City of L.A.*, 11 Cal. 3d 506, 515, 113 Cal. Rptr. 836, 522 P.2d 12 (1971) (ruling § 1094.5 implicitly required an agency rendering an adjudicatory decision to "set forth findings that bridge the analytic gap between raw evidence and the decision or acts"); *see also* Gov. Code § 11425.50 (APA requires a decision to "include a statement of the factual and legal basis for the decision"). And these findings must not only be made but must be "sufficient" to support the agency decision. *See, e.g., Topanga Assn., supra*, 11 Cal. 3d at 514–18; *J.L. Thomas, Inc. v. Cnty. of L.A.*, 232 Cal. App. 3d 916, 283 Cal. Rptr. 815 (1991).

What factors determine the sufficiency of such factual findings? *See, e.g., Getz v. City of West Hollywood*, 233 Cal. App. 3d 625, 630, 284 Cal. Rptr. 631 (1991) (ruling four-page summary of evidence, three-page analysis of evidence explaining the reasoning of the decision, nine findings of fact and six conclusions of law, constitute sufficient findings); *Pacifica Corp. v. City of Camarillo*, 149 Cal. App. 3d 168, 179–180, 196 Cal. Rptr. 670 (1983) (Formal judicial-type findings not required, but transcript of oral remarks plus agency award may not constitute adequate findings). What functions do such agency findings serve? *See, Topanga Assn., supra*, 11 Cal. 3d at 516–517; *Bam, Inc. v. Bd. of Police Comm'rs*, 7 Cal. App. 4th 1343, 9 Cal. Rptr. 2d 738 (1992). What judicial relief is appropriate when the decision is not supported by the findings? *Ocheltree v. Gourley*, 102 Cal. App. 4th 1013, 126 Cal. Rptr. 2d 77 (2002) (holding trial court erred by deciding administrative mandamus case without reading the administrative record because it could not have independently weighed the evidence).

[2] *Nature of Judicial Review under § 1094.5(c)*

As *Anton v. San Antonio Community Hospital*, reproduced *supra*, discusses, a petitioner may also establish prejudicial abuse of discretion by showing that the agency's "findings are not supported by the evidence." In making this determination, the reviewing court has a choice of two standards for judicial review of the evidentiary basis of an administrative agency's adjudicatory decision: The independent judgment (or "weight of the evidence") standard or the "substantial evidence" standard. CCP § 1094.5(c). The administrative mandamus statute does not provide general guidance as to when each standard is appropriate, but instead leaves this task to the courts for determination on a case-by-case basis. *Unterthiner v. Desert Hosp. Dist.*, 33 Cal. 3d 285, 294, 188 Cal. Rptr. 590, 656 P.2d 554 (1983); *Bixby v. Pierno*, 4 Cal. 3d 130, 144, 93 Cal. Rptr. 234, 481 P.2d 242 (1971).

[a] The Independent Judgment Standard

What is the "weight of the evidence" (or "independent judgment") standard? How is it different from the "substantial evidence" standard? If the reviewing court applies the "weight of the evidence" standard, can it literally reweigh the evidence and second guess the agency? Resolve evidentiary conflicts in a manner different than the agency? Draw different inferences from the evidence? Can the reviewing court resolve credibility questions (contrary to the agency's findings) where testimony is in conflict? *See, e.g., Pittsburg Unified Sch. Dist. v. Com. on Prof'l Competence*, 146 Cal. App. 3d 964, 977, 194 Cal. Rptr. 672 (1983). Even when the testimony of a witness is uncontradicted? *See, e.g., Hosford v. Bd. of Admin.*, 77 Cal. App. 3d 854, 863–865, 143 Cal. Rptr. 760 (1978) (reviewing expert witness testimony at agency hearing). Because judicial review generally is limited to a transcript of the agency hearing record, is the court's independent judgment on credibility likely to be more accurate than the agency's?

In *Fukuda v. City of Angels*, 20 Cal 4th 805, 85 Cal. Rptr. 2d 696, 977 P.2d 693 (1999), the Supreme Court addressed several important questions of administrative law arising in instances in which a trial court is required, pursuant to CCP § 1094.5, to exercise "independent judgment" review of an agency determination. The court concluded first that "[i]n exercising its independent judgment, a trial court must afford a strong presumption of correctness concerning administrative findings;" and second that "the party challenging the administrative decision bears the burden of convincing the court that the administrative findings are contrary to the weight of the evidence." *Fukuda, supra*, 20 Cal. 4th at 817.

What do these two conclusions of the *Fukuda* court mean? How can the trial judge presume the correctness of administrative findings and still exercise independent review? The *Fukuda* court observed: "[T]he presumption provides the trial court with a starting point for review—but it is only a presumption, and may be overcome. Because the trial court ultimately must exercise its own judgment, that court is free to substitute its own findings after first giving due respect to the agency findings." *Id.* at 818. Does the court's observation clarify the nature of the "strong presumption of correctness?"

Finally, the Supreme Court in *Fukuda* held that in view of the long-standing duration of the judicial precedent establishing and reaffirming independent judgment review, and the legislative history of CCP § 1094.5, which impliedly recognizes the rule, it would be inappropriate to judicially abrogate the independent judgment rule, and that the policy arguments advanced in support of such a change properly should be directed at the Legislature. *Fukuda*, 20 Cal. 4th at 823. What policy arguments favor the discontinuation of the "independent judgment" standard of review in administrative mandamus cases?

[b]   Complete Record

The "in light of the whole record" language in § 1094.5(c) means that the reviewing court must consider all the evidence introduced at the administrative hearing, and not just isolate the evidence which supports the agency findings. *E.g., Bixby v. Pierno, supra*, 4 Cal. 3d 130, 149, fn.22; *Buckhart v. San Francisco Residential Rent Control Bd.*, 197 Cal. App. 3d 1032, 243 Cal. Rptr. 298 (1988) (ruling trial court cannot proceed with administrative mandamus without the complete administrative record, including the hearing evidence); *Ocheltree v. Gourley*, 102 Cal. App. 4th 1013, 126 Cal. Rptr. 2d 77 (2002) (holding trial court erred by deciding administrative mandamus case without reading the administrative record because it could not have independently weighed the evidence).

[c]   The Substantial Evidence Standard

Under the substantial evidence test, the court must resolve reasonable doubts in favor of the administrative decision and uphold that decision if there is any substantial evidence to support the findings. *See, e.g., Desmond v. Cnty. of Contra Costa*, 21 Cal. App. 4th 330, 334–36, 25 Cal. Rptr. 2d 842 (1993); *Security Envtl. Sys., Inc. v. South Coast Air Quality Mgmt. Dist.*, 229 Cal. App. 3d 110, 132, 280 Cal. Rptr. 108 (1991). In applying this test, the court may not consider evidence outside the administrative record, must consider the entire record, and must deny the writ if there is any substantial evidence in the record to support the agency findings. *E.g., Smith v. Cnty. of Los Angeles*, 211 Cal. App. 3d 188, 198, 259 Cal. Rptr. 231 (1989). Accordingly, the court must view the evidence in the light most favorable to the agency's decision, indulging in support thereof every reasonable deducible inference. *E.g., Donia v. Alcoholic Beverage Control Appeals Bd.*, 167 Cal. App. 3d 588, 595, 213 Cal. Rptr. 447 (1985), *disapproved on another point, Kowis v. Howard,* 3 Cal. 4th 888, 896, 899, 12 Cal. Rptr. 2d 728, 838 P.2d 250 (1992). In what ways is this standard different from the independent judgment ("weight of the evidence") standard? Under which standard is the agency's decision more likely to be upheld by the reviewing court?

[d]   Trial De Novo?

The dissent in *Anton* refers to the independent judgment standard as the "trial de novo" standard. Is the dissent's reference an accurate one? Does the reviewing court actually review the case *de novo* by conducting a wholly new evidentiary hearing? *See, e.g., Cerberonics, Inc. v. Unemployment Ins. Appeals Bd.*, 152 Cal. App. 3d 172, 175– 176, 199 Cal. Rptr. 292 (1984) ("Except where evidence has been improperly excluded at the administrative hearing or could not be produced by the exercise of reasonable diligence, the superior court's independent review focuses on the evidentiary record made at the administrative level (Code Civ. Proc., § 1094.5, subds. (a) and (e))"); *Hackethal v. Loma Linda Cmty. Hosp. Corp.*, 91 Cal. App. 3d 59, 63, 153 Cal. Rptr. 783 (1979) (A true trial de novo would usurp administrative adjudicatory power vested in agency). Does the reviewing court have more authority to consider new evidence than when applying the substantial evidence standard? *See, e.g., Cooper v. Kizer,* 230 Cal. App. 3d 1291, 1300, 282 Cal. Rptr. 492 (1991) (ruling § 1094.5 does not contemplate that there should be a trial *de novo* even under the independent review test; public policy requires a litigant to produce all existing evidence on his behalf at the administrative hearing, with limited exceptions for new evidence provided for by § 1094.5(e)); *Toyota of Visalia, Inc. v. New Motor Vehicle Co.,* 188 Cal. App. 3d 872, 881–882, 233 Cal. Rptr. 708 (1987) (holding trial court erred in admitting into evidence exhibits that were available but not offered at administrative hearing, even though trial court properly applied the independent judgment standard).

[e] New Evidence

Under limited circumstances, a trial court has the discretion to receive evidence which, in the exercise of reasonable diligence, could not have been produced or which was improperly excluded at the administrative hearing. CCP § 1094.5(e); *Sierra Club v. Cal. Coastal Comm'n,* 35 Cal. 4th 839, 863–65, 28 Cal. Rptr. 3d 316, 111 P.3d 294 (2005) (discussing the prerequisites that must be established in order for a reviewing court to consider evidence that is not part of the administrative record). Does this include evidence of events which transpired after the agency's decision? *See Curtis v. Bd. of Retirement,* 177 Cal. App. 3d 293, 299, 223 Cal. Rptr. 123 (1986). If the court determines that new evidence is admissible, should the court directly receive the evidence or remand the case back to the agency with instruction to admit the evidence and redetermine the case? *See Voices of the Wetlands v. State Water Resources Control Bd.,* 52 Cal. 4th 499, 128 Cal. Rptr. 3d 658, 257 P.3d 81 (2011) (concluding CCP § 1094.5(e) & (f) do not prohibit the use of prejudgment limited remand for new evidence and reconsideration of issues pertinent to the agency's decision). Does the court's ability to directly receive new evidence depend on whether the court must apply the independent judgment standard as opposed to the substantial evidence standard? *See* CCP § 1094.5(e). Why?

[3] *The Fundamental Vested Right Test*

As *Anton v. San Antonio Community Hospital*, reproduced *supra*, discusses, with respect to most agencies whose adjudicatory powers do not come directly from the state Constitution, the reviewing court must apply the independent judgment standard where the agency decision substantially affects a "fundamental vested right." How do *Anton, Bixby,* and *Strumsky* define this test? Does this definition give clear guidance to the lower courts?

A number of Supreme Court cases since *Anton* have further defined the twin concepts of "fundamental" and "vested" rights. *See, e.g., County of Alameda v. Bd. of Re-*

tirement, 46 Cal. 3d 902, 906–910, 251 Cal. Rptr. 267, 760 P.2d 464 (1988) (noting that there has been a steady expansion in the class of rights which fits this "fundamental vested" distinction); *Underthiner v. Desert Hosp. Dist.*, 33 Cal. 3d 285, 294–298, 188 Cal. Rptr. 590, 656 P.2d 554 (1983) (holding substantial evidence rule applicable to decisions denying initial applications by doctors for hospital privileges); *Interstate Brands v. Unemployment Ins. Appeals Bd.*, 26 Cal. 3d 770, 777–782, 163 Cal. Rptr. 619, 608 P.2d 707 (1980) (ruling a right may be deemed "fundamental" on either or both of two bases: (1) the character and quality of its economic aspect; (2) the character and quality of its human aspect).

[a] General Distinction Possible?

A general distinction made by the Supreme Court in *Bixby v. Pierno, supra*, 4 Cal. 3d at 146, is still followed in cases involving judicial review of administrative professional licensing decisions: The independent judgment standard applies to review of license revocations and suspensions, but the substantial evidence standard applies to review of initial application denials. *See, e.g., Underthiner, supra*, 33 Cal. 3d at 295–98; *County of Alameda, supra*, 46 Cal. 3d at 907–908.

However, this distinction has not always held up in nonlicensing cases. In *Frink v. Prod*, 31 Cal. 3d 166, 177–180, 181 Cal. Rptr. 893, 643 P.2d 476 (1982), the Supreme Court held that the independent judgment standard applies to judicial review of administrative decisions denying *applications* for welfare benefits, defining and linking the concepts of "fundamental" and "vested" in the following manner:

> *Bixby* and *Interstate Brands* establish that for purposes of determining applicability of independent judgment review the terms fundamental and vested are not used to establish absolutes but are used in a relative sense, and they show that it is the weighing of both the fundamental nature and the vested nature of the right which determines whether independent judgment review is required. Thus, both cases explaining the term fundamental refer to the effect of the right in economic and human terms and to the importance of it to the individual. Effect and importance of rights may vary greatly, and by defining fundamental in terms of effect and importance, the cases reflect that the fundamental character of rights may vary significantly. Similarly, *Bixby* speaks of rights being "possessed" by the individual in discussing the vested requirement (4 Cal. 3d at p. 144); *Interstate Brands* specifically recognizes independent judgment review may be applicable although the administrative decision does not involve "vested property rights in the traditional sense" (26 Cal. 3d at p. 779). And both cases refer to the "degree to which that right is 'vested.'" *Interstate Brands* points out that under the *Bixby* formulation the effect and importance of rights and the degree to which they are possessed are to be weighed together, stating that the "search for 'vestedness' and the search for 'fundamentalness' are one and the same. The ultimate question in each case is whether the affected right is deemed to be of sufficient

significance to preclude its extinction or abridgement by a body lacking *judicial* power." (26 Cal. 3d at p. 779, fn. 5.). * * *

The right of the needy applicant to welfare benefits is as fundamental as the right of a recipient to continued benefits. Because need is a condition of benefits, erroneous denial of aid in either case deprives the eligible person " 'of the very means for his survival and his situation becomes immediately desperate.' " [Citation omitted.]

The decisions subsequent to *Bixby* denying independent review to decisions on applications for welfare benefits were not based on the theory that there was no fundamental right but reasoned that the right of the applicant was not vested. [Citation omitted.] Although *Bixby* distinguished between possessed and vested rights and rights "merely sought," it immediately pointed out the reason for substantial evidence review in the latter situation: "[S]ince the administrative agency must engage in the delicate task of determining whether the individual qualifies for the sought right, the courts have deferred to the administrative expertise of the agency." When the court, discussing licensing cases, returned to the vested issue, it again pointed out that courts "are relatively ill-equipped to determine whether an individual would be qualified, for example, to practice a particular profession or trade. [Citation.].... Once the agency has initially exercised its expertise and determined that an individual fulfills the requirements to practice his profession, the agency's subsequent revocation of the license calls for an independent judgment review." (4 Cal. 3d at p. 146.)

In cases not involving licensing, independent judgment review has not been limited to decisions terminating or revoking benefits but has been applied to decisions on applications for benefits. (E.g., *Strumsky v. San Diego County Employees Retirement Assn.* (1974) 11 Cal. 3d 28, 45 [112 Cal. Rptr. 805, 520 P.2d 29] [widow's service-connected death allowance]; *Thomas v. California Empl. Stab. Com.* (1952) 39 Cal. 2d 501, 504 [247 P.2d 561] [unemployment insurance benefit]; *Kerrigan v. Fair Employment Practice Com.* (1979) 91 Cal. App. 3d 43, 48–52 [154 Cal. Rptr. 29] [age discrimination against applicant for employment]; *Quintana v. Board of Administration* (1976) 54 Cal. App. 3d 1018, 1021 et seq. [127 Cal. Rptr. 11] [disability pension application].) "[T]he meaning of vested, 'possessed by,' need not be limited to describing tangible wealth; constitutional and statutory rights can also be 'possessed' by a person; to that extent they are vested." (*Kerrigan v. Fair Employment Practice Com., supra,* 91 Cal. App. 3d 43, 51.)

Evaluating the degree to which the right is vested, it is apparent that the right to welfare benefits is not based on expertise, competence, learning, or purchase or ownership claim. Determination of qualification for public assistance does not involve the "delicate task" of evaluating competence to engage in a broad field of endeavor as is true in most licensing cases.

Rather, the qualification for public assistance primarily is based on need, the absence of income or other source of funds. The applicant for public assistance is seeking aid because of deterioration of his life situation in economic terms. Unlike the applicant for a license, he is not seeking advancement of his earlier life situation. The statutory public assistance programs provide protection to citizens who through economic adversity are in need and as such should be viewed as residual rights possessed by all of the citizenry to be exercised when circumstances require.

While the degree to which the right is vested may not be overwhelming, the degree of fundamentalness is. Weighing them together as required by *Bixby* and *Interstate Brands*, we conclude the independent judgment standard should be applied to decisions denying applications for welfare benefits. * * *

Do you understand the Supreme Court's reasoning in *Frink v. Prod* when it distinguishes between licensing and non-licensing cases with respect to review of application denials? Do you agree with its reasoning? Do you understand why the court applies the independent judgment standard to review of license revocations, but the substantial evidence test to review of license application denials? Do you agree with the court's reasoning? Doesn't an administrative agency exercise the same degree of expertise in revoking a license as it does in denying an initial application for a license? And, in light of the complexities of our welfare system, doesn't a welfare agency exercise considerable administrative expertise in determining whether an applicant is eligible for welfare benefits?

[b] Some Classification Problems

Which of the following administrative decisions "substantially affect fundamental vested rights":

(1) Denial of an application for a variance or a conditional use permit to operate a business establishment? *See, e.g., Goat Hill Tavern v. City of Costa Mesa*, 6 Cal. App. 4th 1519, 8 Cal. Rptr. 2d 385 (1992); *Smith v County of L.A.*, 211 Cal. App. 3d 188, 199, 259 Cal. Rptr. 231 (1989); *see also Amerco Real Estate Co. v. West Sacramento*, 224 Cal. App. 4th 778, 783–85, 169 Cal. Rptr. 3d 184 (2014) (discussing various land use cases). Revocation of a conditional use permit that had been previously granted to the permittee? *See Malibu Mountains Recreation, Inc. v. County of L. A.*, 67 Cal. App. 4th 359, 367–70, 79 Cal. Rptr. 2d 25 (1998); *HPT IHG-2 Prop. Trust v. City of Anaheim*, 243 Cal. App. 4th 188, 198–200, 196 Cal. Rptr. 3d 326 (2015).

(2) Refusal to extend a previously issued permit to build a hazardous waste incinerator, where petitioner received initial permit subject to later completion of satisfactory environmental impact report, where petitioner already expended two million dollars in preparation costs? *See Security Envtl. Sys., Inc. v. South Coast Air Quality Mgmt. Dist.*, 229 Cal. App. 3d 110, 280 Cal. Rptr. 108 (1991).

(3) Denial by school retirement board of a teacher's application for disability allowance? *See Abshear v. Teachers' Retirement Bd.*, 231 Cal. App. 3d 1629, 282 Cal.

Rptr. 833 (1991); *Alberda v. Bd. of Retirement of Fresno Cnty.*, 214 Cal. App. 4th 426, 433–36, 153 Cal. Rptr. 3d 823 (2013).

(4) Denial of an application for Medi-Cal (Medicaid) benefits for the disabled? *See Oldham v. Kizer,* 235 Cal. App. 3d 1046, 1057, Cal. Rptr. 2d 195 (1991); *Cooper v. Kizer,* 230 Cal. App. 3d 1291, 282 Cal. Rptr. 492 (1991).

(5) Denial by a city of an application for a rental increase for a 725-unit mobile home park pursuant to a mobile home rent control ordinance? *See MHC Operating Ltd. Partnership v. City of San Jose,* 106 Cal. App. 4th 204, 217–18, 130 Cal. Rptr. 2d 564 (2003).

(6) Denial of an application for a teaching position? Refusal to renew the teaching contract of a nontenured teacher? Refusal to retain a tenured teacher? *See Turner v. Bd. of Trustees,* 16 Cal. 3d 818, 824–25, 129 Cal. Rptr. 443, 548 P.2d 1115 (1976).

(7) Suspension of driver's license by the DMV? *See Berlinghieri v. Dept. of Motor Vehicles,* 33 Cal. 3d 392, 188 Cal. Rptr. 891, 657 P.2d 383 (1983). Where suspension is for excess blood alcohol level? *See Coombs v. Pierce,* 1 Cal. App. 4th 568, 2 Cal. Rptr. 2d 249 (1991).

(8) Denial by the Appeals Board of an employee's application for unemployment insurance benefits? The granting of unemployment insurance benefits to striking employees by Appeals Board, where the employer seeks review of the Appeal Board's order? *See Interstate Brands v. Unemployment Ins. Appeals Bd.,* 26 Cal. 3d 770, 163 Cal. Rptr. 619, 608 P.2d 707 (1980).

(9) Denial by agency of an application for pension benefits? Decision by agency to modify an individual employee's pension rights prior to retirement? *See Miller v. State of Cal.,* 18 Cal. 3d 808, 135 Cal. Rptr. 386, 557 P.2d 970 (1977).

(10) Does a decision of the Department of Industrial Relations upholding the issuance of a stop work order for failure to procure workers' compensation, thereby ordering the employer company to cease doing business until it procures workers' compensation insurance for its employees, substantially affect a fundamental vest right? *See JKH Enter., Inc. v. Dept. of Indus. Relations,* 142 Cal. App. 4th 1046, 48 Cal. Rptr. 3d 563 (2006) (observing that when a case involves purely economic interests, courts are far less likely to find a right to be of the fundamental vested character); *see also Ogundare v. Dept. of Indus. Relations,* 214 Cal. App. 4th 822, 827–29, 154 Cal. Rptr. 3d 369 (2015) (concluding contractor's one-year disbarment from working on public projects did not implicate a fundamental vested right and was purely economic).

(11) In *The Termo Co. v. Luther,* 169 Cal. App. 4th 394, 86 Cal. Rptr. 3d 687 (2008), the ruled that an order of the State Oil and Gas Supervisor directing the defendants to plug and abandon 28 oil wells substantially affects a fundamental vested right. The court viewed the defendants' right to extract oil as vested because they had been in the business of pumping oil from these wells for over 20 years, and as fundamental "considering its potentially massive economic aspect and its considerable effect in human terms." *Id.* at 408. Do you agree with this ruling? Doesn't this case involve purely economic interests?

[c] Exceptions

There are two exceptions to the general rule regarding application of the independent judgment standard. These exceptions result in a reviewing court applying the substantial evidence standard even though the agency's adjudicatory decision clearly and substantially affects a fundamental vested right.

(1) The first exception is where the California Constitution specifically confers adjudicative powers on a statewide agency. *See Bixby v. Pierno, supra,* 4 Cal. 3d at 141, n.7; *Strumsky v. San Diego Cnty. Emp. Retirement Assn., supra,* 11 Cal. 3d at 36 & 42. These constitutional agencies include the Appeals Board of the Department of Alcoholic Beverage Control, Art. XX, § 22, Cal. Const.; the Public Utilities Commission, Art. XII, § 5; the State Personnel Board, Art. VII, § 2; the Industrial Welfare Commission, Art. XIV, § 1; Regents of the University of California, Art. IX, § 9; and the Workers' Compensation Appeals Board, Art. XIV, § 4 and Labor Code §§ 5950–5952. In one instance the California Constitution confers adjudicative power on local agencies to equalize assessments, Art. XIII, § 16, making judicial review subject to the substantial evidence test. *See Hunt-Wesson Foods, Inc. v. Cnty. of Alameda,* 41 Cal. App. 3d 163, 116 Cal. Rptr. 160 (1974).

(2) The second exception is where the Legislature by statute specifies that an agency's findings of fact must be reviewed by the substantial evidence test, even though the agency is not of constitutional origin. One example of this exception is CCP § 1094.5(d), added by the legislature in 1978 to supersede the specific holding in *Anton v. San Antonio Community Hospital,* reproduced *supra,* which requires application of the substantial evidence standard in most cases arising from private or municipal hospital boards. Another is the Agricultural Labor Relations Act (ALRA), which requires the Court of Appeal to apply the substantial evidence test when reviewing findings of the Agricultural Labor Relations Board. Labor Code § 1160.8. The Supreme Court upheld the validity of this exception in *Tex-Cal Mgmt., Inc. v. Agricultural Labor Relations Bd.,* 24 Cal. 3d 335, 156 Cal. Rptr. 1, 595 P.2d 579 (1979), and ruled that "the legislature may accord finality to the findings of a statewide agency that are supported by substantial evidence on the record considered as a whole and are made under the safeguards equivalent to those provided by the ALRA for unfair labor practice proceedings, whether or not the California Constitution provides for that agency's exercising judicial power." *Tex-Cal,* 24 Cal. 3d at 346.

In light of the constitutional bases for the requirement that a court must apply the independent judgment standard in reviewing a nonconstitutional agency's findings affecting fundamental vested rights, can the holding in *Tex-Cal* be reconciled with the reasoning of *Bixby, Strumsky,* and *Anton?* What practical considerations support the *Tex-Cal* holding? What does *Tex-Cal* require, in addition to a statute specifically imposing the substantial evidence test, to make this exception valid?

Does *Tex-Cal* mean that the Legislature, if it chooses to, could statutorily require the substantial evidence standard for *all* administrative mandamus actions? *See* Ken Hahus, Comment, *A Proposal for a Single Uniform Substantial Evidence Rule in Review of Administrative Decision*, 12 Pacific L.J. 41–67 (1980); Jamin Hawks, Comment, *Tex-Cal Land Management, Inc. v. Agricultural Labor Relations Board: Administrative Adjudications and the Substantial Evidence Standard of Judicial Review*, 68 Cal. L. Rev. 618–640 (1980). If this is what *Tex-Cal* authorizes, why has the legislature not yet so amended CCP § 1094.5(c)?

[d]   Quasi-Legislative Decisions

Is a court required to apply the independent judgment standard when it reviews findings of an administrative agency made during a "quasi-legislative" decision which substantially affects a fundamental vested right? *See Strumsky v. San Diego County Emp. Retirement Assn., supra*, 11 Cal. 3d at 34, fn.2 (holding judicial review is limited to an examination of the agency proceeding to determine whether its legislative action has been arbitrary, capricious, or entirely lacking in evidentiary support, or whether the agency has failed to follow some procedure and give notices required by law). Why not? When it reviews an adjudicatory decision of a local government agency which substantially affects a fundamental vested right?

[e]   Constitutional Basis

What are the constitutional bases for the independent judgment review requirement? Do you understand why separation of powers is no longer the (sole) constitutional basis? Are the limitations on administrative agencies imposed by the Judicial Powers Clause of the California Constitution, Art. VI, § 1, analogous to those placed on federal adjudicatory agencies by Article III of the United States Constitution? *See, e.g., Commodity Futures Trading Comm'n v. Schor*, 478 U.S. 833, 106 S. Ct. 3245, 92 L. Ed. 2d 675 (1986).

[f]   Criticisms

As the *Anton* dissent indicates, the independent judgment standard has been sharply criticized by many scholars and dissenting justices. *See, e.g.,* Sam Walker, *Judicially Created Uncertainty: The Past, Present, and Future of California Writ of Administrative Mandamus*, 24 U.C. Davis L. Rev. 783–839 (1991); Mary Lu Christie, Comment, *Strumsky v. San Diego County Employees Retirement Association: Determining the Scope of Judicial Review of Administrative Decisions in California*, 26 Hastings L.J. 1465–1501 (1975); *County of Alameda v. Bd. of Retirement, supra*, 46 Cal. 3d 902, 910–917 (1988) (dissenting Opinion of Justice Broussard). The California position seems very much to be a minority view. What is the general nature of these criticisms? Are these criticisms based on pragmatic policy grounds, as opposed to constitutional construction grounds? Are there any pragmatic policies which support California's application of the independent judgment standard to certain agency decisions? What are they? *See Bixby v. Pierno, supra*, 4 Cal. 3d at 147. Are they convincing? Consider Professor Jaffe's observation:

> The California rule can be justified in so far as it gives additional procedural
> protection to an interest of great importance as where a professional license

has been revoked. The protection may be the more needed to overcome likely prejudices of a professional licensing body against mavericks and unconventional practitioners.

Jaffe, *Judicial Control of Administrative Action* (1965), pp. 191–192 (fn. omitted).

[g] Repudiation of Specific Holding in *Anton*

In 1978 the Legislature repudiated the specific holding in *Anton* by enacting subsection (d) of CCP § 1094.5, which now requires the substantial evidence test for judicial review of most *private* hospital board decisions. The constitutionality of § 1904.5(d) was upheld in *Anton v. San Antonio Cmty. Hosp.,* 132 Cal. App. 3d 638, 183 Cal. Rptr. 423 (1982). Section § 1094.5(d) does not apply to decisions of *public* hospital boards, *Underthiner v. Desert Hosp. Dist., supra,* 33 Cal. 3d at 297, n.6; and by its terms requires the independent review standard in cases where the petition alleges certain discriminatory practices by private hospitals.

[D] Administrative Mandamus Procedures

[1] *Statutes of Limitations for Administrative Mandamus*

Although administrative mandamus actions are subject to statutes of limitations, no one general statute governs. Determining the applicable statute of limitations period is quite complicated and merits considerable caution. A petitioner must follow a multi-step calculation process and, when the result is uncertain, should observe the shortest possible limitations period. CEB, *California Administrative Mandamus* §§ 9.1– 9.16 (3d ed. 2016) (suggesting four-step analytical approach for determining applicable statute of limitations). In addition to whatever statute of limitations may apply, an administrative mandamus action is also subject to the defense of laches. *See Johnson v. City of Loma Linda,* 24 Cal. 4th 61, 99 Cal. Rptr. 2d 316, 5 P.3d 874 (2000).

[2] *The Writ Petition*

A petition for a writ of administrative mandamus is essentially a complaint, which is accompanied by the administrative record. (*See* Govt. Code § 11523 and CCP § 1094.6(c) for what usually comprises the administrative record.) The general rules of pleading in Superior Court apply, except as otherwise provided in CCP § 1109. For an excellent practical guide to administrative mandamus proceedings, including sample forms of pleadings and motions, see generally CEB, *California Administrative Mandamus* §§ 10.17–13.27 (3d ed. 2016).

As *Anton* illustrates, a court will usually treat an incorrectly denominated petition for traditional mandamus as one for administrative mandamus. Of course, the time limitations and other prerequisites for administrative mandamus must be satisfied. *See, e.g., City of Santee v. Superior Court,* 228 Cal. App. 3d 713, 279 Cal. Rptr. 22 (1991) (ruling that where administrative mandamus is sole remedy, failure to file timely writ petition precludes action for declaratory and injunctive relief). In cases where the method of review is unclear, the recommended course is to file a "Petition for a Writ of Administrative Mandamus (CCP § 1094.5) or Mandate (CCP § 1085)." *See* CEB, *California Administrative Mandamus, supra,* §§ 5.35, 10.25. Can a court treat an untimely petition for writ of administrative mandamus as one for traditional mandamus? *See, e.g., Morton v. Bd. of Registered Nursing,* 235 Cal. App. 3d 1560, 1566, 1 Cal. Rptr. 2d 502 (1991) ("But simply calling a goose a duck will not make it quack").

[3]   *Remedies Available Through Administrative Mandamus*

[a]   Judgment, Generally

The Superior Court must enter a judgment either denying the writ, or commanding the respondent to set aside its decision and take action as specified by the court's judgment. CCP § 1094.5(f).

[b]   Money Damages

Can the Superior Court award money damages to a successful petitioner in an administrative mandamus action? Section 1095 authorizes the recovery of damages through peremptory writ of mandate, and this includes administrative mandamus actions. *E.g., Austin v. Bd. of Retirement,* 209 Cal. App. 3d 1528, 258 Cal. Rptr. 106 (1989); *Eureka Teachers' Assn. v. Bd. of Ed.,* 202 Cal. App. 3d 469, 247 Cal. Rptr. 790 (1988). When the respondent is a state or local agency, the petitioner must comply with the immunity limitations and claim-filing requirements of the Government Claims Act, Govt. Code § 810 *et seq.,* prior to seeking money damages in court. *State of Cal. v. Superior Court,* 12 Cal. 3d 237, 115 Cal. Rptr. 497, 524 P.2d 1281 (1974); *Loehr v. Ventura Cnty. Cmty. Coll. Dist.,* 147 Cal. App. 3d 1071, 195 Cal. Rptr. 576 (1983). *See* § 4.05 [D], *supra.* This causes some tricky statute of limitation problems because the agency may not approve or disapprove the filed claim prior to the expiration of the shorter limitation period for commencing an administrative mandamus action. *See* CEB, *California Administrative Mandamus, supra,* §§ 1.12 and 3.77–3.83 (suggested procedure is to file petition for administrative mandamus with limitations period, allege the pending claim, and then amend the petition. When the claim is rejected, allege that fact.)

[4]   *Appellate Review*

Review of a Superior Court judgment in an administrative mandamus action may be by appeal. *See* CCP § 1094.5(g); *but see Powers v. City of Richmond,* 10 Cal. 4th 85, 40 Cal. Rptr. 2d 839, 893 P.2d 1160 (1995) (upholding Gov. Code § 6259(c), which makes extraordinary writ the exclusive mode of appellate review in Public Record Act actions, as not violative of the appellate jurisdiction provision of the California Constitution, Art. VI, § 11); *Leone v. Med. Bd. of Cal.,* 22 Cal. 4th 660, 94 Cal. Rptr. 2d 61, 995 P.2d 191 (2000) (holding Bus. & Prof. Code § 2337, which requires appellate court review of a superior court decision reviewing the revocation, suspension, or restriction of a physician's medical license by the Medical Board of California by way of a petition for an extraordinary writ, does not violate the appellate jurisdiction clause). The ordinary rules for appeals in civil cases apply, except for any special rules relating to mandamus. CCP § 1110. Several special rules regarding stay orders pending appeal apply to administrative mandamus appeals. CCP § 1094.5(g)–(h).

Assume that the Superior Court properly applied the independent judgment standard in reviewing findings of an administrative agency, and the court enters new findings of fact as part of its administrative mandamus judgment. On appeal, what standard of review should the Court of Appeal apply in determining whether the trial court's findings are supported by the record? *See, e.g., County of Alameda v. Bd. of Retirement*, 46 Cal. 3d 902, 910; 37 Cal. 3d 205, 212, 207 Cal. Rptr. 823, 689 P.2d 453 (1984); *JKH Enter., Inc. v. Dept. of Indus. Relations*, 142 Cal. App. 4th 1046, 1058, 48 Cal. Rptr. 3d 563 (2006) (observing that if the trial court exercised independent judgment, it is the trial court's judgment that is the subject of appellate court review under the substantial evidence test; if the trial court properly applied the substantial evidence review, then the appellate court reviews the administrative record to determine whether the agency's findings were supported by substantial evidence).

Table of Cases

Index

[References are to sections]

A

S